CollegeBoard

D0517301

2009

Getting Financial Aid

2009

Getting Financial Aid

Third Edition

The College Board, New York

The College Board: Connecting Students to College Success

The College Board is a not-for-profit membership association whose mission is to connect students to college success and opportunity. Founded in 1900, the association is composed of more than 5,400 schools, colleges, universities, and other educational organizations. Each year, the College Board serves seven million students and their parents, 23,000 high schools, and 3,500 colleges through major programs and services in college admissions, guidance, assessment, financial aid, enrollment, and teaching and learning. Among its best-known programs are the SAT®, the PSAT/NMSQT®, and the Advanced Placement Program® (AP®). The College Board is committed to the principles of excellence and equity, and that commitment is embodied in all of its programs, services, activities, and concerns.

Visit the College Board on the Web: www.collegeboard.com.

Editorial inquiries concerning this book should be directed to College Planning Services, College Board, 45 Columbus Avenue, New York, NY 10023-6992; or telephone 212 713-8000.

Copies of this book are available from your local bookseller or may be ordered from College Board Publications, P.O. Box 869010, Plano, TX 75074-0998. The book may also be ordered online through the College Board Store at www.collegeboard.com. The price is $19.95.

ISBN-13: 978-0-87447-825-9

ISBN-10: 0-87447-825-1

Printed in the United States of America

Distributed by Macmillan

Contents

List of Figures

List of Tables

List of Worksheets

Preface

Financial aid is a great equalizer. In 2007, over $130.5 billion in aid was awarded from government and private sources. Coupled with the wide range of lower-cost college options available, financial aid should make a college education affordable for just about everyone.

Yet a recent study by the American Council on Education shows that each year almost *two million* students who are eligible for this boon don't even apply for it. We assume these students are either unaware of the possibility of aid, or mistakenly believe financial aid is not for them.

And many parents and students who apply for financial aid find the process to be confusing, even intimidating. Like the tax code, the forms and guidelines appear to be full of exceptions, convolutions, and incomprehensible terms.

But it doesn't have to be that way. A central aim of this book is to take the confusion and intimidation out of the process by giving clear and direct explanations of what financial aid is all about and simple, step-by-step directions for how to get it. By combining these explanations and directions with costs and financial aid facts for every accredited college that reports this data, we hope this book will achieve our ultimate goal of connecting students to colleges that match both their needs and their means.

Acknowledgments

We gratefully acknowledge the contributions of the many individuals who helped bring this book into being. George Ochoa, our writer for Part I of this book, "Financial Aid, Step by Step," transformed a complicated and intricate subject into clear and simple prose. Without his talent, the purpose of this guide could not have been achieved.

Renée Gernand provided leadership and editorial guidance throughout the project. Kathie Little and Jack Joyce, our resident experts on financial aid, reviewed the content and kept our course true, as did Sandy Baum, Cindy Bailey, Myra Baas Smith, and Linda Peckham. Kate Crane copyedited the manuscript, and Betty Keim proofread the finished book.

While we had the advantage of many "in house" resources, we also relied upon the knowledge and advice of seven financial aid officers who took time from their busy schedules to give us interviews: Vincent Amoroso of the University of North Carolina at Chapel Hill, Bonnie Lee Behm of Villanova University, Elizabeth Bickford of the University of Oregon, Joe Paul Case of Amherst College, Mary San Agustin of Palomar College, Mike Scott of Texas Christian University, and Forrest Stuart of Rhodes College. We hope you will find their insight and advice, quoted throughout Part I, as illuminating as we did.

The descriptions of colleges presented in Part III, "Financial Aid, College by College," were compiled from the College Board's Annual Survey of Colleges. A team of editors, led by Stan Bernstein, edited, verified, and double-checked the data with the colleges. A team of programmers and composers at Content Data Solutions, Inc., converted the database into readable pages.

Finally, we would like to thank the Marketing & Publication Services team who, under Kathryn Diminnie's direction, turned the manuscript into a finished book, especially John Ulicny, Kevin Iwano, Caitlin McClure, Alessandra Cirillo, and Kiki Black.

Tom Vanderberg, Senior Editor
College Planning Services

Michael Polizzi, Assistant Editor

How to Use This Book

Part I: Financial Aid, Step by Step

The first chapter, "Yes, You Can Afford College," establishes our central point: a college can be found to fit any budget. If you are skeptical about that, please start here—we think we make a strong case.

Steps 1 through 11 provide easy-to-follow directions on how to get financial aid, including what you need to know, what you need to do, and when you need to do it.

These "steps" are presented in a logical sequence. But depending upon your own circumstances—where you are in the college application process, your family's finances, what kinds of colleges you're applying to, and the policies of those individual colleges—you may need to take the steps in a slightly different order, skip some steps, or do some steps simultaneously. To keep track of what should be done when, consult the planning calendar on the inside front cover.

Financial aid officers and the forms you need to fill out often use jargon that can at times seem vague or confusing. Terms like "need" and "cost of attendance" have specific meanings that might not be the same as what you would assume. Throughout Part I, you'll find key terms defined in "Know the Lingo" sidebars (you'll also find a detailed, comprehensive glossary at the end of this book). Other sidebars emphasize or illustrate the main points of each step.

Throughout Part I, you'll find graphs and charts that also illustrate key points, and tables that summarize information and let you compare different financial aid options. You'll also find checklists and prefilled sample worksheets that will help you plan and keep track of your applications. Blank copies of those worksheets for you to fill in are in Part II.

Part II: Tables and Worksheets

One of the worksheets that you'll find in Part II will help you compare the financial aid award letters that you'll receive from colleges. To drive home the point that no two award letters are alike, we've included two samples in Part II, immediately after the comparison worksheet. These are actual award letters that were sent to the same aid applicant by two different universities, the names of which we've changed.

Part II also includes a series of worksheets that you can use to estimate how much the federal government will say you should pay for college out-of-pocket—that's your "expected family contribution" (EFC) used by colleges to award financial aid. (You'll learn more about the EFC and how it's calculated in Part I.) These worksheets are designed for dependent students and their parents. If you are an independent student, you can do the same thing with the online tools at the collegeboard.com Web site. In addition to worksheets, Part II includes a sample of the preapplication worksheet for the Free Application for Federal Student Aid (FAFSA). This worksheet shows all of the questions included on *last year's* FAFSA; it may be that some questions will change somewhat in the year you fill this out. Finally, in Part II you'll find lists of state aid programs, state-sponsored 529 college savings plans, and other useful places to find more information.

Part III: Financial Aid College by College

This is where we help you get the "financial aid picture" at specific colleges, including scholarships the colleges offer to entering students, and required forms and deadlines. To place this picture in context, we give you brief facts about the kind of college it is, and its basic costs. This information can help you compare the colleges you are considering and find colleges that look affordable. But keep in mind that the financial aid figures are mostly based on averages, meaning many students will be above or below these benchmarks.

The college descriptions in Part III are arranged alphabetically by state or territory. Running headers at the top of each page will help you orient yourself and find schools quickly. An alphabetical index of all the colleges in the book appears in Part IV.

Every college described in this book is accredited by an agency recognized by the U.S. Department of Education. Accreditation is a process in which an outside agency ensures that a college meets certain basic standards—it's a stamp of approval on the college's teaching, facilities, and administration. For financial aid purposes, accreditation by a federally recognized agency means that federal student aid dollars can be used to attend the institution.

The *College Board College Handbook* also includes full descriptions of the colleges in this book, going beyond the cost and financial aid details presented here to include information about admissions requirements, academics, housing, student life, athletics, and more.

Where the College Information Comes From

The information in the college descriptions comes from the College Board's most recent Annual Survey of Colleges, which was conducted in the spring of 2008. Every college reported its own cost and financial aid information to us. Where possible, our staff of editors verified the information by consulting third-party sources, including public university system or district offices, state education departments, and the federal government's Integrated Postsecondary Educational Database System (IPEDS). The information presented was current at the time this book went to press in May 2008—but be warned that it may have changed by the time you're reading this. Once you have narrowed down a list of colleges that you're interested in, you should confirm critical information, such as financial aid application deadlines and requirements, by visiting the colleges' Web sites or contacting their financial aid offices.

What's in the College Descriptions

Each college description begins with a shaded box that contains the name of the college, the city or town it's located in, and its Web site address. For every college, its six-digit "federal code"—the code you will need in order to have your FAFSA information sent to the college—appears in this box. If a college requires the College Board's CSS/Financial Aid PROFILE®, its four-digit CSS® code also appears in this box. (The CSS code is the same code you use to send SAT® and ACT scores and AP® Exam grades to a college; the federal code is only used for the FAFSA.)

Below the college name box you'll find a brief summary of what type of college it is—whether it's a four-year private university, a two-year community college, or a four-year culinary school run on a for-profit basis. (Definitions of all the different types of schools you might find here are in the glossary.) You'll also find information about the number of students who were enrolled in the 2007-08 school year, and the relative difficulty of obtaining admission to the college.

BASIC COSTS

"Basic Costs" lists the tuition, fees, room, and board charged by the college. The date indicates the school year for which these numbers apply—if the college was unable to report final or projected figures for the upcoming school year, last year's figures are given. If the college combines tuition, fees, and room and board expenses, that single figure is given as a comprehensive fee.

It's important to note that these figures do not include other out-of-pocket costs, such as books, supplies, transportation, and personal expenses. These costs can be substantial, depending upon where and how you live, and what you study. But since these costs vary widely from student to student, we felt it would be misleading to display average amounts.

FINANCIAL AID PICTURE

The core of each college's description is the information about the financial aid it offers. Again, the date indicates the school year for which the college reported numbers—either the current year or the prior year. Depending on the aid programs offered by the college and the figures they reported, you may see one or several of these elements of the financial aid picture:

- **Students with Need.** This shows how financial aid was given to students who could not afford the full cost of attending the college on their own (a full explanation of how "need" is determined is found in Part I, Step 1). The focus is on the entering freshman class but, if a college was unable to provide that breakdown, the numbers are for all undergraduates. Most colleges disclosed the average percentage of need met by financial aid packages, and the relative proportion of aid given as scholarships and grants as opposed to loans or work-study jobs. Use this data to get a sense of how likely a college is to meet your full need, and how much aid will probably come in the form of loans.

- **Students Without Need.** Even though a student does not need financial aid, it's still possible that a college will provide aid based on merit or other criteria, such as alumni affiliation or minority status. That's what is shown here. If a college has a policy of only awarding aid to students who have need, this is also stated here.

- **Scholarships Offered.** This gives details on merit scholarships offered by the college and their criteria for being awarded. Here you can get a sense of whether your GPA or SAT scores put you in the right ballpark for a merit-based grant. You'll also find information about the number of student-athletes who were given a scholarship by the college, and the average award.

- **Cumulative Student Debt.** This tells you how many students borrowed money to pay for college and how much they owed, on average, when they graduated. This is another way for you to measure how much of a college's aid will be loan based. The numbers here only include student loans taken out through the college—not PLUS loans, private education loans, or other borrowing done through a third-party lender.

FINANCIAL AID PROCEDURES

The financial aid application forms required by the college, and the priority date and/or deadlines that the financial aid office has set, appear here. This section also includes information about notification—that is, when you can expect to hear back from the financial aid office after applying, and by when they will need your final answer about whether you'll be attending. Unless otherwise noted, all dates given in this section are for applicants who intend to enroll in the fall of 2009. If you plan to apply for admission to the spring 2010 term, contact the college's financial aid office to find out about their policies and deadlines.

CONTACT

The final section of each college description lists the mailing address of the school's financial aid office.

Part IV: Scholarship Lists

If you want to zero in on colleges that offer scholarships for your particular talents and interests, the lists in Part IV will help you do that. Arranged alphabetically by state, these lists will point you to colleges that offer scholarships for a variety of achievements. Please note that, in many cases, merit is not the only criterion used by the college when awarding aid: it may require recipients to also demonstrate financial need by submitting the FAFSA or another financial aid form.

At some colleges, every applicant is automatically considered for merit scholarships. At others, you have to specifically apply for a given scholarship. And in some cases, a scholarship is only open to you if you've been recommended by your principal, school counselor, or teacher.

What's in the Scholarship Lists

Each list points to colleges that offer aid for a specific talent or area of interest.

Academics. This list names colleges that offer merit aid for academic achievement. Typical criteria include the classes you've taken, your GPA, and your standardized test scores.

Art. This list includes colleges that offer merit aid for artistic ability, as reflected by grades in art classes, teacher recommendations, and/or a portfolio you submit to the college.

Athletics. If a college offers scholarships for a certain sport, it will be listed here. The letters "M" and "W" indicate whether the scholarship is available to men, women, or both. Please note that, at most colleges, only a very few athletes receive significant scholarships. No one should rely on athletic achievements alone to get into college or to pay for it. Instead, make sure your academic record is solid, and be sure to apply for need-based financial aid by submitting the FAFSA and any other required forms.

Music/Drama. This list includes colleges and conservatories that offer merit aid for talent in the performing arts, as reflected by grades in music, dance, or drama classes; teacher recommendations; and/or an audition or a submitted tape.

ROTC. Three lists are included here, one each for the Air Force, Army, and Naval Reserve Officers Training Corps. (Marine Corps ROTC is included in Naval ROTC; the Coast Guard and Merchant Marine do not have ROTC programs.) The schools listed may not necessarily have all their ROTC programs on campus; they may have a sponsorship agreement with a neighboring college or university instead. If you enroll in ROTC, you will need to apply separately for the actual ROTC scholarship from the service branch you've chosen—the money doesn't come automatically. (For information on how much money is awarded and how to apply, consult *The College Board Scholarship Handbook*, or visit your local recruiting station.) Some colleges offer additional institutional scholarships for ROTC candidates from their own funds, beyond what's awarded by the Department of Defense.

Part I

Financial Aid Step by Step

Yes, You Can Afford College

Yes, you can afford college. How do we know? Because most colleges are not as expensive as you think. Because if a college wants you as a student, it will try to help you with financial aid. Because most students get financial aid. And because there are ways to reduce the amount you have to pay now, including working part-time and taking out loans.

This is not what everyone will tell you. You may hear discouraging words like, "Most colleges are expensive" and "You won't qualify for financial aid." People may hint that college is not worth all the trouble. The financial aid forms may look complicated and confusing.

We will show you how to get past these doubts. You *can* afford college, and we will show you how. College is worth the expense; you should apply for financial aid. With our step-by-step guide through the process, you'll sidestep confusion and be able to focus on the important decisions in front of you.

This book will help you if you have already saved some money for college—and also if you have not. It will help if you are a student, or a parent of a student. It will help if you have already decided what colleges to apply to, and also if you are not sure where you'd like to go. You may be the first in your family to consider college, or the latest in a family tradition. You might think your family doesn't make enough money to afford college, or that it makes too much to be awarded financial aid. You may have an expensive "dream college" you hope to attend, or you may be looking only for the best buy. You may plan to work or not to work, commute or live on campus, rely on your parents' money or pay your own way. No matter what your situation, you can afford college and we will help you do it.

Why You Can Afford College

Despite media hype about pricey colleges and the soaring cost of higher education, most colleges are not as expensive as you might think. In addition, the published prices of many colleges, though high, are not the whole story. If a college wants you as a student, and if you and your parents don't have enough money, the college will usually offer help so you can attend. That help is financial aid—and because of it, **a college's published tuition and fees are not what most people pay.**

Financial aid is a great equalizer, and most students benefit from it. Currently 62 percent of full-time college students receive grants or scholarships to help them foot the bill. Those grants come either from the government, the college, or both, and do not have to be paid back. Many students also receive other forms of help, including federal tax credits and deductions that allow their families to keep more of their money at tax time. Thanks to all this assistance, full-time college students pay, on average, much less than the advertised price of their education. In 2007-08, for example, students at four-year private colleges paid an average net price of $14,400 in tuition and fees instead of the published price of $23,712. Students at four-year public universities received a proportionally similar discount.

Even expensive colleges are less costly than you might think because they offer more financial aid. Since a high-priced college often awards more assistance than a low-priced one, a particular student might end up paying the same out-of-pocket cost at both, or even less at the college with a higher sticker price. **That's why you shouldn't rule out your "dream college" as too expensive until you find out if it wants you and what kind of financial aid package it will give you**.

That said, there are great deals to be found. At a public college—one supported by a state or local government—the average tuition and fees in 2007-08 were $6,185 a year. That's a 74 percent saving over the $23,712 a year charged by private colleges. Another way to save money is to spend your first two years at a community college, which is a public college that specializes in two-year education programs. Published tuition and fees at community colleges averaged just over $2,300 a year—a 60 percent saving over the average at a public four-year college.

Here's one last reason you can afford college: you don't have to pay every penny up front. You can borrow money at a low interest rate and pay it back after your studies are over. There are also ways to reduce the amount you have to pay right now. (*See Step 11 for more on these "out-of-pocket" options*).

MYTH/FACT

Myth: Most colleges are expensive.

Fact: The most expensive colleges get the most media attention, which creates the illusion that all colleges are expensive. The truth is that colleges vary greatly in price, and most are much more affordable than people think, especially once financial aid is factored in.

Figure 1:
Average Total Costs by Type of College

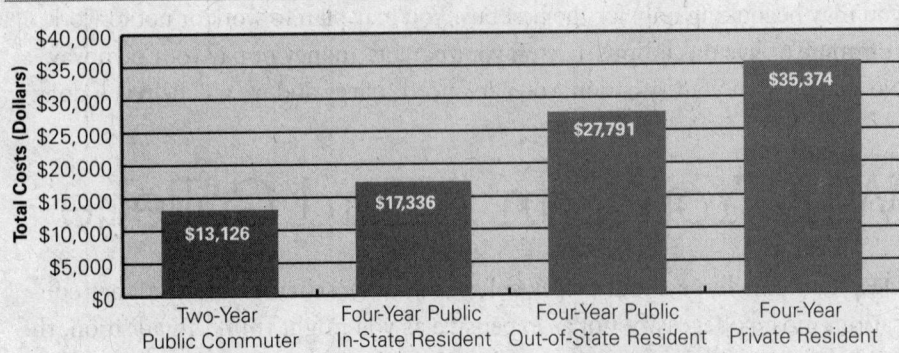

Prices given here are for the total cost of attendance: tuition, fees, room, board, books and supplies, transportation, and personal expenses. See Step 3 for more about the components of college costs.

Is College Worth It?

Even if you can afford college, is it a good idea? No matter how much financial aid you get, college will still require a sacrifice of money, time, and effort. Kids who go straight to work after high school have more spending money sooner. Does college give enough bang for the buck?

The answer is yes for many reasons including: money, job insurance, and personal growth.

In terms of money, college clearly pays. The difference in earnings between college graduates and high school graduates has increased sharply over the past three decades. The typical male college graduate now earns 65 percent more than the typical male high school graduate; for women, the difference is 60 percent. **College graduates earn an average of $1 million more over their careers than high school graduates**. Even if you borrow to pay for part of your education, it's still worth it. Provided you borrow intelligently, your increased earnings will help you pay back the loan. (*See Step 11 for more about loans.*)

You might think that the increased earnings from your college education won't make up for the total costs and the years that you won't be in the work force. But Figure 3 on the next page shows otherwise. The grey line shows the cumulative earnings at each age for the average high school graduate

Figure 2:
Average Annual Earnings by Education Level

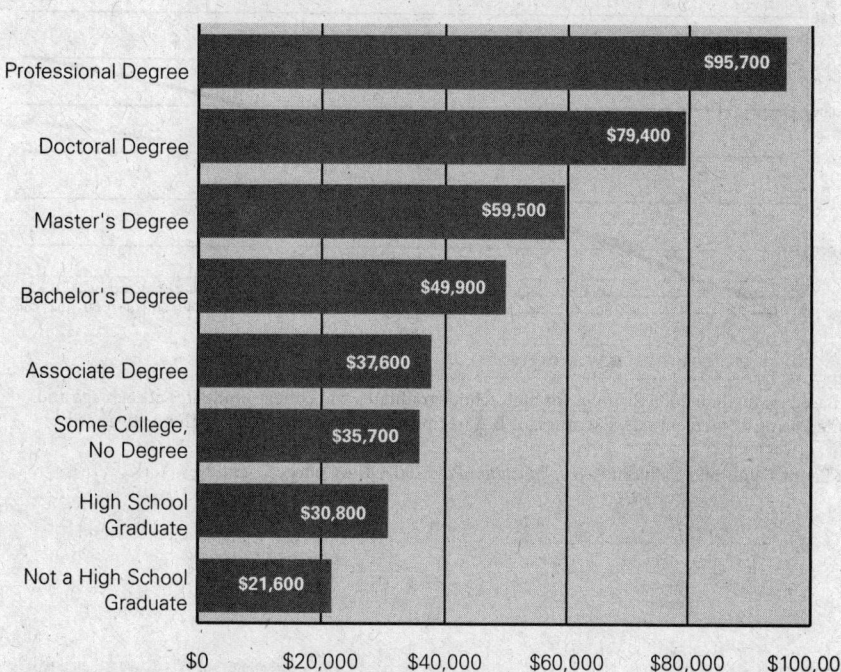

Note: Includes full-time, year-round workers age 25 and older.
Sources: U.S. Census Bureau, 2004a, PINC-03; Internal Revenue Service, 2004, Table 3; McIntyre, et al., 2003; calculations by the authors.

who enters the workforce full-time at the age of 18. The black line shows the cumulative earnings at each age for the average college graduate who enters the workforce at age 22, after subtracting average tuition and fees paid over four years at a public college or university. As you can see, by age 32 the lines intersect. From that point on, the investment in college pays off.

College also provides job insurance in a world whose economy is constantly changing. As new industries develop and many jobs are outsourced to foreign countries, you can compete better with a college degree. A college degree teaches you how to acquire knowledge and put it to use no matter what the circumstances. In fact, some higher-education credential—at least an associate degree—is a minimum to stay employed in the "knowledge economy" of the twenty-first century. **A mere high school diploma is obsolete; college helps to ensure employment**.

But the value of college can't be reduced to dollars alone. It involves intangibles, things you can't touch directly: how you value yourself, your dreams, and your ambitions. If you are an artist, a musician, a writer, a builder, a scientist, or a thinker, college will help you cultivate those talents. If you are hoping to find yourself, meet people who are more like you, and meet people who are different and interesting, college can contribute to that search too. College provides rich ground for personal growth.

On every front, as a matter of value for dollars, college is a good buy. You can afford college—and it is worth the price.

Figure 3:
Estimated Cumulative Earnings Minus College Costs

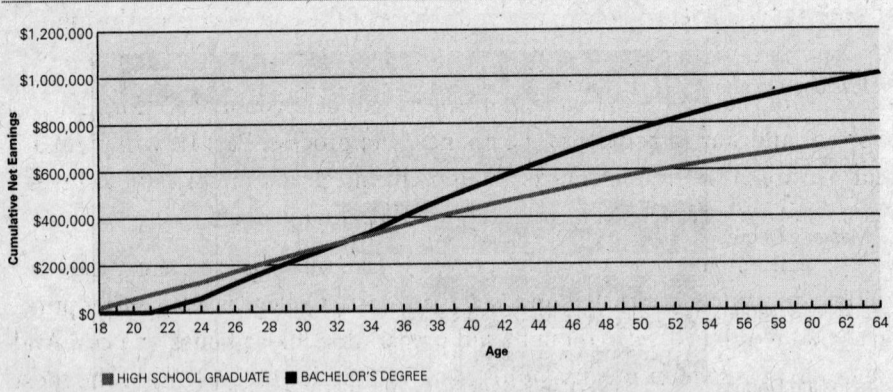

Notes: Based on median 2005 earnings for high school graduates and college graduates at each age and discounted using a 3 percent rate. Earnings for B.A. recipients include only those with no advanced degree.
Source: Baum, Sandy and Kathleen Payea, *Education Pays 2007*, The College Board, New York.

How This Book Will Help You

KEEP IN MIND

Don't approach the chronology of this book too rigidly—**not all steps have to come in this order.** For example, Step 9, "Look for Other Sources of Money," can be done at any time. Since outside scholarships aren't tied to a particular college, you can start researching and applying for them before you've even made a short list of schools. In fact, this is a good idea since the application deadline for these scholarships may be as early as November 1, before most college admissions applications are due.

Through this book, you will learn how to make college affordable for you. You'll find out exactly what you need to know so you can apply for financial aid, choose an affordable college, and control costs while at college. In Part I, we will walk you step-by-step through the process. There are 11 steps in all:

- **Step 1:** you'll find out the key facts about financial aid.

- **Step 2:** you'll get an idea of how much financial aid you can get.

- **Step 3:** you'll see how and why college costs vary.

- **Step 4:** you'll figure out which forms you need to fill out, and when.

- **Step 5:** you'll learn how to fill out the Free Application for Federal Student Aid (FAFSA).

- **Step 6:** you'll find out how to complete the CSS/Financial Aid PROFILE® form (called the PROFILE for short), if your colleges require it.

- **Step 7:** you'll learn how to fill out any other forms a particular college might require.

- **Step 8:** if your family has special circumstances, you'll find out the best way to explain them to colleges.

- **Step 9:** you'll learn about scholarships and other aid you can get from sources outside of a college.

- **Step 10:** you'll learn how to compare award letters from colleges and decide which offer is best for you.

- **Step 11:** you'll learn how to pay your share of the cost of college through work, loans, and other means.

In Part II of the book, tables and worksheets will help you make informed decisions and stay in control of the financial aid process. Part III will paint a clear picture of the financial facts about each college you might want to investigate. That includes its costs and its approach to financial aid.

No one will tell you that paying for college is fun. But what you're getting—a college education—is worth it and is within reach. College is a big-ticket purchase that requires careful thought and preparation, like a house or a car. And it shouldn't be done in the dark. This book will guide you into one of the most important purchases you'll ever make—with your eyes wide open.

Step 1: Let's Go Over the Basics

QUICK OVERVIEW

The first step to getting financial aid is to understand the basic facts about it. In this step we will explain what financial aid is (money to help you pay for college), what types there are (the kind that comes free and the kind that doesn't), who gets it, and where it comes from.

The most important point: almost everyone qualifies for at least one form of financial aid. As long as you apply, the chances are excellent that you will get some.

Just What Is Financial Aid?

KNOW THE LINGO

Grant—money that is given away for free, usually on the basis of who needs it

Merit scholarship—money that is given away for free on the basis of academic qualifications or special talents

Subsidized loan—money that you have to pay back with interest; however, the federal government pays the interest for you while you are in college

Work-study—a program in which you take a part-time job to earn money for your education; the federal government pays part of your salary

Financial aid package—What a college offers to an accepted student who has applied for aid. Usually a mix of grants, loans, and/or work-study.

Financial aid is money given or loaned to you to help you pay for college. Different forms have different rules. The vast majority of aid comes from the federal government, and most of it consists of loans that you must pay back. However, some aid does not require repayment—which makes it the best kind of aid to get.

If you qualify for financial aid, your college will put together an aid "package," usually with different types of aid bundled together. You and your parents will almost certainly still have to pay something, but the aid package will help. Most students qualify for some form of financial aid, so it makes sense to apply for it.

You'll apply for financial aid either at the same time or soon after you apply for admission. You may have to fill out more than one application. At the very least you will fill out the FAFSA, or federal government form. You may also fill out another form, the PROFILE, which many colleges require. And some colleges and state aid agencies require their own financial aid forms, too. The colleges to which you apply will use the forms to figure out what your family can afford to pay and what your "need" is—that is, the difference between what you can pay and what the college actually costs. If the school wants you as a student but sees that you can't handle the whole bill, it will make you a financial aid offer to help you meet your need. If you accept, that financial aid package is your award.

You will need to apply for financial aid every year that you are in college, mainly because your family's financial situation changes yearly. As a result, your financial aid package will probably be somewhat different from year to year.

Financial aid is a helping hand, not a free pass. In the United States, everyone has a right to a free public school education, but not to a free college education. The federal government and most colleges agree that students and their parents are the ones most responsible for paying for college. "The primary responsibility of paying for the student's education lies with the student and his or her parents," says Forrest M. Stuart, the director of financial aid at Rhodes College in Memphis, Tennessee. "Financial aid comes in to fill that gap, if you will, between what they can afford and what the college costs." Even so, financial aid can be the deciding factor in whether or not a student attends college.

Types of Aid

Financial aid may come in many forms. However, all forms can be grouped into two major categories: gift aid and self-help aid.

GIFT AID

Gift aid is free money, money that you don't have to pay back or work for. Naturally, this is the kind of aid most people want. It can take the form of grants or scholarships.

The terms "grant" and "scholarship" are often used interchangeably to mean free money. But here's the difference. A grant is usually given only on the basis of need, or your family's inability to pay the full cost of college. Scholarships are usually awarded only to those who have "merit," such as proven ability in academics, the arts, or athletics. Once you're in college, you may have to maintain a minimum GPA or take certain courses to continue receiving a scholarship.

SELF-HELP AID

Self-help aid is money that requires a contribution from you. That can mean paying back the money (if the aid is a loan) or working for the money (if the aid is a work-study job).

The most common form of self-help aid is also the most common of any form of financial aid: the loan. A loan is money that you have to pay back with interest. In light of that, you might not consider this aid at all. But it is—a loan means you don't have to pay the full price of college all at once: you can stretch the payments over time, as you would when buying a house or a car. Furthermore, some student loans are subsidized by the federal government. With these loans, you don't have to pay the interest that comes due while you're in college. The federal government subsidizes, or helps to pay, the loan by paying that interest while you're enrolled and for the first few months after you graduate.

EXPERT ADVICE

"One of the **most important things for students** to understand is what loans are about, and what indebtedness means, so that they don't stumble through four years of college having signed promissory notes blindly, and then come to the end of their senior year and say, I really owe that much money? They should know that they have to pay loans back, and they should **think about their total indebtedness** in relation to what their prospective income is and how it might affect some life choices."

—*Joe Paul Case, dean and director of financial aid, Amherst College, Amherst, Massachusetts*

Subsidized loans, which are awarded based on need and administered by the college, are the best kind. But you can also take out unsubsidized student loans and parent loans, which are not packaged by most colleges. However, be careful not to take on more debt than necessary. No matter what kind of loan you take out, you will have to pay it back.

Another form of self-help is work-study. This is financial aid in the form of a job. Since you earn the money through your work, this too may not seem like aid. But it is, because the federal work-study program pays most of your wages. And work-study jobs are usually available right on campus, with limits on your hours so that you won't be unduly distracted from studying.

Aid can also come in the form of tax cuts—income tax deductions and credits for education. But colleges don't award this variety, and you don't apply for it in the same way as you would loans or grants, so we will discuss it separately, in Step 11.

Who Gets Aid?

Grants and loans are not just for the poorest of the poor, nor are scholarships only for the smartest of the smart. The truth about who gets financial aid is somewhat different from what many people think.

Those Who Need It

Most financial aid is based on need, not merit. There is money for merit, but since the 1950s most colleges in the United States have focused their financial aid packages on meeting financial need.

However, there is a lot of confusion about what need means. Many people think it means a state of dire poverty, so that no working-class or middle-class student need apply. "A lot of people think that they either have to be on welfare or Social Security—really poor—to get financial aid, and that's not correct," says Mary San Agustin, director of financial aid and scholarships at Palomar College in San Marcos, California. On the other hand, some rich families mistakenly think they are needy because their high living expenses leave them little money for college. "It's this expectation of, I pay my taxes, so my kid should be entitled to some federal financial aid regardless of how much money I make," says Ms. San Agustin.

Need simply means that your family can't afford to pay the full cost of a particular college. The *amount* of your need will vary from college to college, because it depends on the cost of attending an individual college. Whether your family has need is determined not by whether you think you are rich or poor, but by the financial aid forms you fill out.

Just fill out the forms. If you do have need, you will be considered for financial aid.

Those Who Don't

Despite the overall emphasis on need, many colleges do give away money on the basis of merit. They do this to attract the students they want most, and they may award this money even if it is more than the student needs. However, in many cases, the student both needs the money and has earned it on the basis of merit.

Don't think that only geniuses get merit aid. At many colleges a "B"-average GPA can put you in the running for merit money. Sometimes a separate application for merit aid is required to put you into consideration; sometimes your application for admission is enough. In either case, don't count yourself out by not applying; apply and let the college decide.

Grants are sometimes awarded based on neither need nor merit. For example, you may get a grant if you are in a certain field of study, are a resident of the state, or are a student from the same town as the college. (*See Step 9 for more about grants and scholarships.*)

Part-Time Students

Some kinds of aid are only available to students enrolled in college full-time—usually 12 or more credit hours of courses per semester. But part-time students are eligible for some financial aid. For example, federal programs such as the Stafford loan require only that students be enrolled at least half-time, whereas others, like the Pell Grant, are available to students enrolled less than half-time. Also, some employers offer tuition reimbursement benefits to students who work full-time and go to college part-time.

Where the Money Comes From

Financial aid comes from three basic sources: governments (both federal and state), colleges, and outside benefactors.

From the Government

The lion's share of total financial aid awarded in this country comes from the federal government. Fully 66 percent of all student aid is sent from Washington. The largest chunk of that consists of federal loans, which total $60 billion a year and represent 53 percent of all student aid. The loans take multiple shapes. Perkins and Stafford loans are for students, while parents may take out a PLUS loan to help pay for their children's educations.

The federal government also funds several grants, including the Pell Grant, the Supplemental Educational Opportunity Grant (SEOG), the Academic Competitiveness Grant, and the SMART Grant. The Pell and SEOG are strictly need-based, while the last two are based on both need and academic criteria. The government also funds the federal work-study program.

KNOW THE LINGO

Merit aid—aid awarded on the basis of academics, character, or talent

Need-based aid—aid awarded on the basis of a family's inability to pay the cost of attending a particular college

Non-need-based aid—aid awarded on some basis other than need or merit, such as grants with eligibility requirements related to field of study or state residence

A much smaller piece of the financial aid pie (6 percent) comes from individual state governments. Most of this aid is for use only at colleges within the state, though a few states offer "portable" aid, which state residents can take with them to a college in another state.

From the College

A great deal of financial aid comes from individual colleges, using their own "institutional" funds. In fact, colleges award nearly half of all grants. Many, though not all, award merit scholarships as well as need-based grants. They may also offer on-campus job opportunities and loans.

Private colleges give more financial aid than public ones, but their tuition is usually higher as well. Public colleges award less aid, but taxpayer support keeps their tuition lower.

Outside Grants and Scholarships

Outside grants and scholarships come from sources other than the government or the college. These sources may include corporations like Coca-Cola or community groups like the Elks Club. Some are well known, such as the National Merit Scholarship, but altogether they are the smallest piece of the financial aid pie: **only 8 percent of all student aid comes from this source**. Pursue them, but don't expect them to outweigh the other aid you will get.

Bear in mind also that your outside scholarship is unlikely to expand the total aid you receive. Most colleges will use an outside scholarship to substitute for some other piece of aid rather than increase the total aid package. Think of your financial aid package as a barrel: when the barrel is full, no more can be added unless something is taken away. The last thing colleges will take away is whatever sum of money your family is expected to contribute. However, at many colleges, the first thing taken away is self-help aid such as loans. Since that could reduce the total amount you will have to pay back

Figure 4:
Undergraduate Student Aid (in billions) by Source, 2006-07

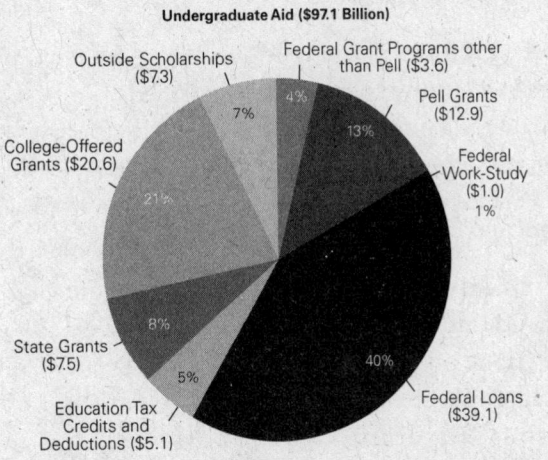

later, it is worth applying for outside scholarships. (See Step 9 for more on these sources of aid.)

There is a lot of financial aid out there, in many forms. Apply for it—there is a good chance you will get some. These are the main things to know about financial aid:

- It is money to help you pay for college.
- It may come in the form of a gift (grants and scholarships) or in the form of self-help (loans and work-study).
- Most people get it because they need it, though some get it solely because of merit.
- The federal government funds most of it, but states, colleges, and outside sources also help.

QUICK RECAP

Step 2: Estimate How Financial Aid Will Work for You

QUICK OVERVIEW

Only rarely does a student get a "free ride" scholarship. You and your parents will have to contribute some money to your education—the precise amount will be determined by the college's analysis of financial aid forms you'll fill out. But even before you fill out the forms, you can estimate your share of the cost and begin planning for how to pay it.

Don't Count Yourself Out

Most college students get some financial aid, but few receive exactly the same financial aid package. Financial aid packages are as individual as the financial circumstances of the students who apply. One family makes $50,000 a year and has two children, a house, and a savings account; another makes $50,000 a year but has only one child, a rented apartment, and no savings. What financial aid package will each family receive? The answer: it depends on several factors. Families must first submit their applications for consideration by the colleges.

"Probably the question I'm most often asked is, 'is there a cutoff?'" says Joe Paul Case, the dean and director of financial aid at Amherst College in Amherst, Massachusetts. Financial aid officers agree that there is no single salary cutoff for financial aid—no one income figure that will definitely exclude a student from receiving financial aid. Income is only one criterion for giving out aid: colleges also consider such factors as family size, number of children in college, and savings. Many students who would be eligible for financial aid fail to apply because they don't realize this.

"I always tell families, don't cut yourself off from the application process," says Bonnie Lee Behm, the director of financial assistance at Villanova University in Villanova, Pennsylvania. "Apply and let it work through the system."

Even if you feel absolutely sure that your family doesn't qualify for financial aid, fill out the forms. Your family circumstances might change suddenly—a lost job, health problems, a new child. Then you may need financial aid, and it will help to be in the system already. A college can assist you faster if your financial aid application is on file.

EXPERT ADVICE

"We always encourage students to **go ahead and apply** for financial aid even though you may not qualify for anything but a student loan. **At least get the paperwork in**, because if something happens in the middle of the year, we already have the financial aid data we need to make adjustments."

—*Forrest M. Stuart, director of financial aid, Rhodes College, Memphis, Tennessee*

What "Expected Family Contribution" Means

Even though you probably will qualify for some financial aid, it's very unlikely that you will get the fabled "full ride." Colleges do sometimes award full tuition—or even full room and board—to a student they greatly want to attract, but that is rare. Almost always, the family is expected to contribute some money. The exact dollar amount will be based on the family's ability to pay. That dollar amount is the expected family contribution, or EFC.

The EFC is carefully calculated to be your "fair share." It is what you can afford to pay based on your financial circumstances—no more and no less. The formulas that the federal government and colleges use to calculate EFC are ultimately intended to make sure that the EFC is fair.

In some ways, the concept of EFC works in your favor. No matter what a college costs, so long as it awards you the full financial aid you need you won't have to pay more than your EFC—the amount your family is able to pay. Say your EFC is $8,000. At a college with a total cost of attendance of $11,000, you could get up to $3,000 in financial aid. At a college where the total cost is $25,000, you could get up to $17,000 in aid. **Because of financial aid, any college is at least worth considering; no college should be ruled out in advance as too expensive.**

On the other hand, even though the expected family contribution is based on ability to pay, that does not simply mean how much the family would like to pay. For any purchase, most people would *like* to pay zero dollars. But what they are *able* to pay is how much money they have minus how much they need to keep for other things, such as food, rent, heat, and retirement. When colleges award financial aid, they calculate your ability to pay by looking at your income and financial assets as you lay them out in your financial aid application. Using what are called need-analysis formulas, they analyze your data to see how much of the college costs you are able to pay (your EFC) and how much you are unable to pay (your need). How much you would like to pay is not part of the calculation.

Costs − EFC = Need

Your expected family contribution is your family's share of college costs. Any cost greater than that is your need. Need varies from college to college because it depends on the cost of the individual college. **It's simple arithmetic: college costs minus your EFC equals the amount of aid you need**. At colleges that award enough financial aid to meet your need, the aid package will equal the amount of your need. Costs minus aid equals what you pay.

Unmet Need (a.k.a. "Gap")

Unfortunately, not all colleges will award enough aid to meet your full need. Some colleges may "gap" your package—that is, not meet your full need. Economics plays a part here. While some colleges may have enough aid dollars available to meet every student's full need, some colleges lack such funds. If your college cannot meet your full need, costs minus aid will still equal what you pay. But what you pay will be more than your EFC. (*See Step 11 for more information on loans* and other ways to help fill such a gap.)

If you do encounter a "gap" in your award, compare the package with the ones you've gotten from other schools, and consider your priorities. Do you want to go to that college, no matter the cost? Or does cost matter more? (*For more on this topic, see Step 10.*)

It Depends on the College

The amount of aid you get—along with the kind of aid you get, whether gift or self-help—ultimately depends on the college. Formulas and forms are important, but so is the professional judgment of the financial aid officer. And so is the desire of the college to attract you to its campus.

How Colleges Calculate Your Need

As you saw in Step 1, financial aid comes from two main sources: government money (usually in the form of loans and work-study), and the college's own "institutional" money—usually in the form of grants and scholarships. Your financial aid package will probably contain money from both sources.

Just as there are two main sources of aid, there are two main formulas that colleges use to figure out how much aid you should get. One is called the "Federal Methodology," used for aid coming from government money. Most colleges use it to award their own institutional funds as well. The Federal Methodology is based on the FAFSA, the federal financial aid form.

For aid coming out of their own money, some colleges and scholarship programs use a different formula called the "Institutional Methodology." This is based on the PROFILE (more formally known as the College Board's CSS/ Financial Aid PROFILE® application) and/or the college's own financial aid application form. (*For more about these forms, see Steps 6 and 7*). Colleges that require the Institutional Methodology do so because they think it presents a fuller picture of your family's financial situation. "I just think it does a much better job of measuring ability to pay," says Forrest M. Stuart, whose institution, Rhodes College, requires the PROFILE.

So what does all this mean to you? The differences between the two formulas make it possible that your expected family contribution will be lower under one

KEEP IN MIND

If a college offers you a financial aid award that doesn't meet your full need, you may be able to fill the "gap" in your package with an **outside scholarship**. For more on outside scholarships, see Step 9.

or the other; it all depends on your individual family circumstances, and the individual college(s) you are applying to. You don't have to know how these formulas work or remember what they are called. The thing to remember is, if you apply to several colleges, because of these different formulas you might end up with a different EFC for one college than you do for another.

Will College Savings Count Against You?

While some families save diligently for their children's college educations, others think this is a mistake. They worry that having a lot of savings will keep colleges from awarding financial aid. **But savings help you more than they hurt you**, and here is why.

When calculating your EFC, colleges subtract what they call an "asset protection allowance" from the amount you have saved. This "allowance" is the amount of money considered reasonable to set aside for educational savings and family emergencies. These "free" savings are not assessed at all. In Federal Methodology, the allowance varies based on the age of the oldest parent, and it can be several tens of thousands of dollars for a married couple in their 40s or 50s. These savings are clearly worth having, since they aren't included when calculating your EFC. (See Table 12 on page 138 to get an estimate of what your parents' asset protection allowance may be.)

Even if your family saves more than the asset protection allowance, those savings will be assessed at a maximum rate of only 5.6 percent. So even if 5.6 percent of your excess savings count "against" you when it comes to federal need determination, 94.4 percent count "for" you. You can use them to meet your expected contribution, whatever it turns out to be. That's good news, because your family will be expected to pay much more out of income than out of savings. Most colleges will expect your parents to contribute between 22 and 47 percent of their income toward your EFC.

Essentially, your family will be expected to pay some part of your college costs out of pocket, and if you have savings, you have a pot to draw from. The alternatives are to pay it out of your monthly income or to borrow it—both of which are less appealing choices than using savings. "If I were preparing to send a son or daughter off to school, I would want to have as much savings available to me as I realistically could," says Vincent Amoroso, deputy director of the Office of Scholarships and Student Aid at the University of North Carolina at Chapel Hill. "The reason is because, just like in other situations, having money on hand makes it easier for me to make choices that are good for myself and my child."

To be sure, there are other factors your family should consider before saving for college, such as whether they have enough money to save for retirement. But if they can put away any money for college, they should do so without hesitating. (*See Step 11 for information on tax-free college savings plans.*)

KNOW THE LINGO

EFC (Expected Family Contribution)—How much money a family is expected to pay for college.

Need—The difference between your EFC and the cost of attending a particular college you've chosen. Financial aid is designed to meet your need, not your EFC.

Unmet need—The difference (if any) between the your need and the financial aid offered by a particular college. Informally, unmet need is also called a **gap**.

Asset protection allowance— The amount of money considered reasonable to set aside for educational savings and emergencies, and is therefore not part of your EFC.

Responsibilities Within the Family

Who should pay for college? Is it entirely the parents' duty, or should the student be responsible? If both, which combination of both? There is no single right answer to questions like these. But families need to discuss the topic, and the sooner the better. Your college will expect someone in the family to make a contribution, and you and your parents should figure out who that is before the bill comes due.

"Families should discuss college costs, family budget, financial aid, and financing options at the beginning of the college application process, not at the end," says Carlene Riccelli, a college adviser at Amherst Regional High School in Amherst, Massachusetts. Try to reach decisions that are as specific as possible, so that you each know what's expected of you. Try to make the decisions fair, so that no one feels used. What portion of your summer job income should go toward college? If your family takes out loans, should they be in your name, your parents' name, or both? Don't forget to discuss ways of keeping costs down, such as living at home and taking community college courses.

If your family is nontraditional, the discussion should include all adults involved in your care. When considering the financial need of students with divorced parents, for example, some colleges that use the Institutional Methodology will assess the income and assets of both natural parents. It will be up to the family to decide how to pay the expected family contribution, but part of that contribution will be based on the income and assets of the parent without custody. (*See Step 8 for more about parental custody and financial aid.*)

While it's important to talk about money, your family also needs to talk about other aspects of choosing a college, such as its academic and social environment. Some of the discussion will have nothing to do with money, but others will have financial aspects: for example, going away to an expensive college versus staying home and commuting to a cheaper one. Step 3 will further explore how to think about these issues. But the important thing is to start having the discussions—financial and otherwise—as early as possible.

Crunch Some Numbers

If you want a sneak peek at what your expected family contribution will be, crunch some numbers. Part II contains worksheets and tables that you can use to calculate the EFC of a "typical" family under the Federal Methodology. Use the worksheets to add up your income, then subtract deductions and allowances. Total up your assets, too. Apply the formulas in the worksheets to calculate the contribution that is expected from you as a student. Then use the next set of worksheets and tables to calculate your parents' expected contribution. When you're finished, you will have your estimated EFC.

The figure you come up with will only be an estimate. Your actual EFC may be higher or lower, depending on the exact data you ultimately submit and the particular college's financial aid policies. But at least this exercise will give you a ballpark figure for what you can expect to pay.

Online Calculators

If you'd prefer to estimate your EFC online, there are several Web sites with special calculators. They include:

- **collegeboard.com**—Our Financial Aid EasyPlanner lets you "Do the Math" not only on EFC but on college costs, savings, and loans.
- **College and university Web sites**—These sites sometimes include calculators geared to their individual financial aid policies.

Figure 5:

Sample EFC Illustration

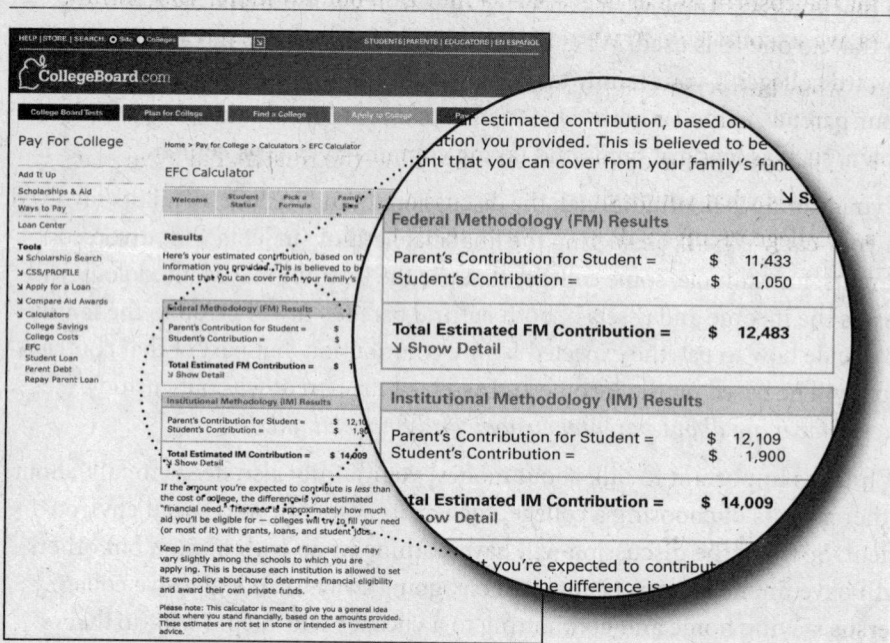

Online calculators like the one at www.collgeboard.com can help you estimate your expected family contribution.

Your Unique Situation Counts Too

Colleges expect families to contribute some money toward students' education, and the amount they expect is your EFC. But colleges are not just faceless buildings of stone, and your EFC is not fixed in cement. The financial aid officer in charge of distributing a college's financial aid is a human being, and he or she does have some room to adjust how the EFC calculations are made based on your individual circumstances.

Step 8 will go into greater detail on how to notify your college about changes in your family's financial situation, such as a lost job. And Step 10 will discuss how to appeal if you think the college hasn't taken all your circumstances into account. Generally, financial aid officers are sympathetic if you are struggling with problems such as caring for an elderly parent or a lost job. They will be less sympathetic if it seems that you've chosen your financial problems—such as buying a new motorcycle with money that could have gone to pay your college bill. Still, financial aid officers are not heartless, and they will try to help when there is genuine distress.

QUICK RECAP

The American education system expects families to bear as much responsibility for the costs of higher education as they can, but not more. Your family will have to contribute to your college costs, but will also receive help.

- Your family will be required to pay an expected family contribution, or EFC.
- The costs of the college you attend minus the financial aid you receive equals what you pay.
- College savings will not be held against you.

Step 3: Choosing Colleges, Thinking Costs

QUICK OVERVIEW

This step shows you how to think about cost when choosing a college. You'll see why you shouldn't exclude any college from consideration just because of its price. You'll learn what your different college expenses will be, from tuition to pizza money; how costs can vary from college to college; and how to factor in the financial aid package the college is likely to give.

KNOW THE LINGO

Total cost of attendance—Not just tuition, but also all fees, room and board, transportation, books and supplies, and personal expenses.

Public college—A college or university that is subsidized by taxes and other public revenues and governed by a county, state, or federal government agency.

Community college—A two-year public college subsidized by a local government, such as a county or city.

Out-of-state tuition—What public colleges charge students from other states; often more than double the rate for in-state residents.

Reciprocity agreement—A deal between neighboring states that allows residents to attend a public college in either state at the in-state tuition rate.

How to Think About College Costs

When you're thinking about where to apply for college, its "list price" should not be the main consideration. Because financial aid will probably be available to help meet your need, even a college that appears exorbitant may in fact be within reach. A college's published costs are only one part of the equation when it comes to what you'll actually pay. **Until you've applied for and received an offer of financial aid, you won't know the real cost to your family.**

Remember that financial aid works like this: Total cost of attendance *minus* your family's expected family contribution (EFC) *equals* your financial need. As long as the college meets your need, the amount you pay stays the same whatever the price of the college. "I don't think college cost really should be a factor to where students apply for admission," says Vincent Amoroso of the University of North Carolina. "I say that because your family contribution, in theory, is the same whether you apply to a school that costs $4,000 or to a school that costs $40,000."

In practice, your expected family contribution may actually vary somewhat from college to college. As noted in Step 2, a college using the Federal Methodology to assess your ability to pay might calculate a higher or lower EFC than a college that uses the Institutional Methodology. Even two institutions using the same methodology might calculate slightly different EFCs, depending on how they have treated any special circumstances that may apply to your family. (*See Step 8 for more on special circumstances.*) But, in general, the principle holds that your EFC will be constant from college to college, while your need will vary depending on the price of each college.

The main thing to consider when applying for college is whether you and that school will be a good fit. Look for the academic and social aspects that are likely to make you happy and successful there. Are you artistic? Are you mathematical? Do you love to learn for learning's sake? Do you have strong career ambitions in a particular field? Do you long to get away and see the world? Or does it matter more to stay near your family and the place where you grew up? "Students should not just look at a school because it's affordable," says Bonnie Lee Behm of Villanova University. "They should look at a school because it's the right fit for them academically, socially, spiritually, and physically. Is cost an important part? Yes. It's a consideration, but only one among many." **And remember—you can find a good fit at more than one college.**

To discover what specific colleges have to offer, research them. You can find a lot of information about majors offered, the composition of the student body, academic policies, and extracurricular and athletic offerings in the *College Board College Handbook.* You can also learn more on the College Search engine on collegeboard.com, and from college guidebooks and Web sites. If you know people who have gone to the colleges you're considering, talk to them and get their opinions.

So, when deciding which colleges to apply to, don't focus too much on cost. But do be aware of what the costs are; cost may become a factor depending on what financial aid packages you are ultimately offered. Even though your EFC should in principle be the same at all colleges, not all schools always meet full need. And even those that do may meet it with different packages—some with more loans, others with more grants. It makes sense to know what kinds of packages a particular school is likely to give.

By using Part III of this book as a guide, and also by contacting the admissions and financial aid offices of the colleges you're considering, gather as much information as you can about the costs of the school and the type of aid they offer. The rest of Step 3 suggests the kinds of information you should be seeking from each school.

Choosing Colleges

Both you and your parents should be involved in the discussion about where to apply for college. You will share the responsibility for paying for college, so you should all have a voice. Furthermore, your parents can give you good advice about what colleges to consider based on their life experiences, their knowledge of you, and their understanding of the family finances—even if they themselves have never been to college. The deciding vote, however, should be yours. You are the one who will have to start and finish college, and you are more likely to do so successfully if you have chosen the college yourself. "Only the student knows the fit that he or she will have at a particular institution academically, socially, and financially as well," says Forrest Stuart of Rhodes College.

When you begin choosing where to apply, don't exclude any college. Let every college be on the table, even if it seems too difficult academically or financially. Aim high. Shop around. The best colleges for you may not be the ones that occur to you first.

If a college is a good fit for you, there is probably a way to make it work financially. "Apply to those colleges that you think, okay, maybe we could afford these, but also apply above that level, because some schools may be much more manageable than you expect," says Bonnie Lee Behm of Villanova University.

Do Consider a "Financial Safety"

Even though all colleges should be on the drawing board, you should also consider applying to a financial "safety" school—one that is a good academic fit and that you feel fairly confident you can afford. Your financial safety school is one you would be happy attending and that has either low published costs or will almost certainly offer enough grant money to make attendance affordable. A public university in your state, a local community college, or a private university where you are highly likely to win a merit scholarship might all be financial safeties.

A financial safety is a good idea because your top choices may not give you as much financial aid as you want. "We know students who are really strong academically, but they're not at the top of their class, and they apply to the college of their dreams," says Elizabeth Bickford, director of the Office of Student Financial Aid and Scholarships at the University of Oregon in Eugene. Despite their hopes for a full merit scholarship, such students may find that they can enroll only if they are willing to take out a large amount in unsubsidized loans—something their family may not be willing to do.

In these and other situations, a financial safety is a good backup. For example, if you accept admission to a far-off university, but find that you can't get used to it and want to come back to the financial safety school near home, it will be easier to transfer if you've already applied and been admitted. Still, Elizabeth Bickford says she encourages students to "dream large, because it's your one opportunity. When you go from high school to that first year in college, that's where most of the scholarships are—for entering freshmen. It's your opportunity to make that big step away from home."

KNOW THE LINGO

Need-blind admissions—If a college has a "need-blind admissions" policy, this means that it will admit a student solely on the basis of his or her academic merit or other characteristics, regardless of their ability to pay. However, it does not mean the college guarantees to meet full need. You may be admitted, but the college may be unable to offer a financial aid package equal to your need.

Figure 6:
Distribution of Full-Time Undergraduates at Four-Year Institutions
by Tuition and Fee Charges

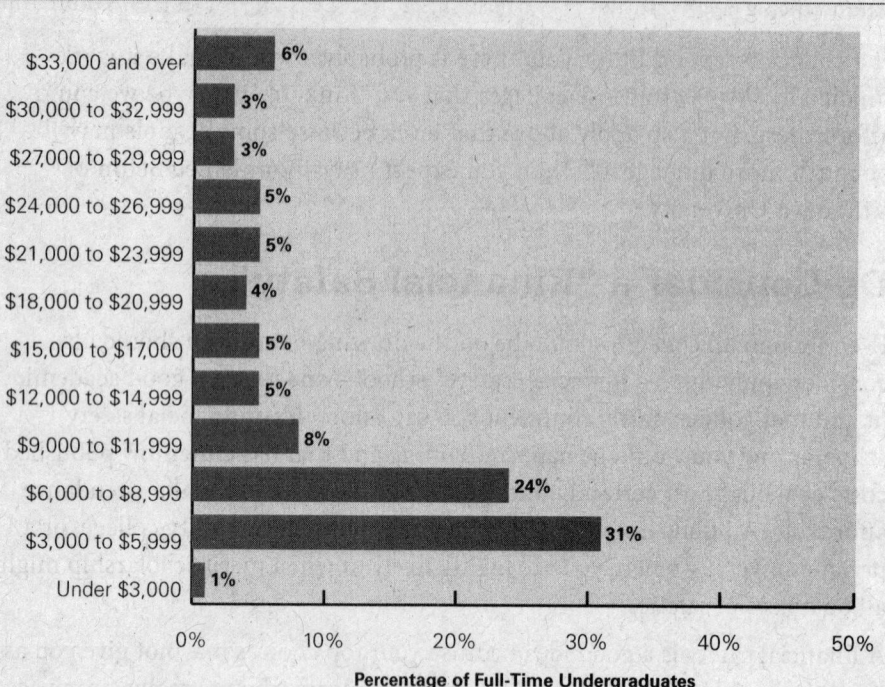

Fifty-six percent of full-time undergraduates attend colleges with published tuition and fee charges of less than $9,000. After financial aid, many of those students pay an even lower "net price" for tuition.

Source: *Annual Survey of Colleges 2007,* The College Board, New York, NY.

Components of College Costs

The price of a college education has several parts. The most obvious is tuition, the cost of taking courses. Tuition varies depending on how many courses you take, but full-time students pay a flat rate for a full schedule of courses. If you attend part-time, you will likely pay by credit hours, a measure of how long each class is. Most courses are three credit hours apiece, which usually translates to three one-hour classes each week. Most full-time students take an average of four or five courses per semester, for a total of 12 to 15 credit hours per semester for a full load.

Fees are another component of college costs. Fees are usually billed to all students as funding for the college's general expenses, such as the library or student activities. But there may be additional special fees for students enrolled in certain classes or activities. A chemistry student may pay lab fees, for example.

Tuition and fees are just one part of what you'll pay for college, and often not even half. Another large component is room and board. "Room" is the cost of housing you, and "board" is the cost of food. You may live in a dorm on campus, or off campus—in an apartment or a house with other students, or at home with your parents. You may be on a meal plan where all your meals are prepared for you for one price, or you may fend for yourself, buying groceries and cooking meals. Either way, these basic living expenses are your room and board.

Taken together, tuition, fees, room, and board are the largest chunk of college costs. On average, at four-year public colleges across the nation, these elements together make up 77 percent of what students pay for college—tuition and fees 34 percent, room and board 43 percent. Yet there is still another 23 percent of costs to be accounted for. These include:

- Books and supplies—class expenses that are not covered by tuition and will vary depending on the courses you take.

- Transportation expenses—for on-campus students, this is the cost of trips home during holidays; for commuters, this is the cost of either mass transit or a car. Car costs include parking, gas, insurance, and maintenance.

- Computer equipment costs—if required by the college. Some colleges may insist that you buy a certain model of computer, or bring your own computer but have special hardware and software installed to make it work on the campus network.

- Personal expenses—everything from snacks outside the meal plan to newspaper subscriptions to haircuts and toothpaste to membership fees for student groups.

How Costs Can Vary

Each college has different price tags for each of the cost components. For example, on average, books and supplies cost $950 for the first year at the University of Nebraska, but $1,500 at the Kansas City Art Institute. Table 1 on page 28 shows national averages for cost components.

To get specifics for a particular college that you're considering, check its Web site and look for the school's published estimate of what the average student spends on the different expense categories. The college will use these averages as part of the calculation of your "total cost of attendance," which will partly determine how much aid you're awarded. You can also consult Part III of this book for a school-by-school summary of costs.

However, remember that these average costs are only averages. You are an individual, and you may pay more or less than average, depending on your individual circumstances. For example, if you attend college in California but your family lives in New York, you will pay more for traveling to and from home than if your family is also in California.

Textbook and supply costs can also vary widely depending on your major. If you are an architecture or drafting student, you might have to buy an expensive computer-aided design program that your English major friends won't need. Science students might need to buy a statistical-modeling software package; studio artists a graphic-design suite. At least software like this only has to be bought once and is then used to do work for several classes; furthermore, educational discounts may be available for such purchases. In some programs, students might have to buy supplies that frequently get used up and must be replenished, such as brushes and paints for art students.

Rooming costs will vary a little between different dorm complexes on campus—for example, newer dorms may cost more, and a single room is always more expensive than one shared with a roommate. There will also be differences between various off-campus rooming locations.

Finally, your personal expenses may be higher or lower than average depending on lifestyle factors—but they will almost always be higher than you think. As James Schembari wrote in the *New York Times*, there is always a need for "pizza money"—money to buy pizza, go on a road trip, or hang out at the student union. Books, supplies, travel, and everyday expenses "can add $3,000 or more a year, depending on parents' generosity and where their child goes to college," wrote Mr. Schembari.

Table 1:
Average Estimated Undergraduate Budgets, 2007-08

SECTOR	TUITION AND FEES	BOOKS AND SUPPLIES	ROOM AND BOARD	TRANSPOR-TATION	OTHER EXPENSES	TOTAL EXPENSES*
Public Two-Year						
Resident	$2,361	$921	—	—	—	—
Commuter	$2,361	$921	$6,875	$1,270	$1,699	$13,126
Public Four-Year						
Resident	$6,185	$988	$7,404	$911	$1,848	$17,336
Commuter	$6,185	$988	$7,419	$1,284	$2,138	$18,014
Out-of-State	$16,640	$988	$7,404	$911	$1,848	$27,791
Private Four-Year						
Resident	$23,712	$988	$8,595	$768	$1,311	$35,374
Commuter	$23,712	$988	$7,499	$1,138	$1,664	$35,001

— Sample too small to provide meaningful information.
* Average total expenses include room and board costs for commuter students, which are average estimated living expenses for students living off campus but not with parents.
Note: Estimates of individual budget items are based on reporting by institutional financial aid offices.
Source: *Annual Survey of Colleges*, The College Board, New York, NY.

PART I: FINANCIAL AID STEP BY STEP

Ways to Reduce Costs

There are a few time-tested ways of saving money on some of the major cost components of college. To save money on tuition and fees, many students have attended public colleges and community colleges. To save money on room and board, many have commuted rather than roomed on campus. Here are the pros and cons for these money-saving techniques.

Public vs. Private, In-State vs. Out-of-State

Attending a public college in your own state is an excellent way to save money on tuition and fees. Public colleges are subsidized by state taxes, so their tuition and fees for state residents are usually much less than at private colleges—74 percent less, on average. Depending on the school, the quality of education may be as good or even better than what you would get at a private college.

On the other hand, the true cost picture is more complicated than it looks. Even though private colleges charge more for tuition and fees, most of them also give more scholarships and grants than public colleges do, which helps to even out the costs. "There's an adage that the more expensive the school, the more money they give away," says Mike Scott of Texas Christian University, a private institution.

Cost isn't everything. If a particular private school has some valuable characteristic that you want—smaller classes, professors you want to study with—it may be worth the extra tuition money. But cost is a factor to consider. If a certain state school can give you all that you want from college, why not go there and save some money?

If you would like to study at a public college or university in another state, be aware that most public schools charge higher tuition to students from out of state than they do to in-state students. Public colleges currently charge an average of $6,185 in tuition and fees to a state resident, but $16,640 to an out-of-state student. The in- and out-of-state rates for specific public colleges and universities are listed in Part III.

PAYING IN-STATE RATES IN ANOTHER STATE

It is sometimes possible to get the in-state tuition rate, or at least a lowered tuition rate, even if you are an out-of-state student. For example, some state universities have "reciprocity agreements" with neighboring states. South Dakota residents pay tuition rates comparable to state residents at the University of Minnesota and vice versa. There are also discipline-based "consortiums" of public colleges that let you get the in-state tuition rate at another state's public college if your desired major is not available at any public college in your own state.

Your school counselor and state board of education Web site can give you more information about programs for paying in-state rates in another state.

GOOD TO KNOW

This section discusses ways to **find inexpensive colleges** during your college search. For tips on how to cut costs once you've enrolled, see Step 11.

Community Colleges

Community colleges are another great way of saving money on tuition and fees. A community college is a two-year school subsidized by a state, county, or city. Its cost for tuition and fees is usually much lower than that of a four-year institution—62 percent lower, on average, than a public four-year college. Community colleges often charge tuition in three tiers—in district, in state, and out of state—with the lowest price for those who live in the local district. Though most community colleges do not offer a four-year bachelor's degree (though the number that do are on the rise), they do provide courses whose credits can be transferred toward a bachelor's degree at another college. Because those courses cost much less, this can be a way to save money in your first two years of college—money you can use to help pay for the last two years. Four out of 10 college-bound high school graduates start their college education this way.

There are other reasons to attend a community college besides saving money. If you aren't sure whether you want to go to a four-year college, a community college will give you a sense of what the college experience is like. If you don't know what kind of program you want to pursue—science, art, business, or something else—you can explore different subject areas at a community college before committing to a program. And if you need to be able to work, perhaps to support a family, you can work out a more flexible schedule at a community college, where many students work full-time and attend classes at night and on weekends.

A community college is also a golden opportunity for students who didn't do well enough in high school to win admission to the college of their choice. Community colleges are open to everyone, and some have agreements with four-year colleges that guarantee admission in the third year for students who have maintained good grades. This is the case in California, according to Mary San Agustin of Palomar College, a community college. If students, she says, "have their heart set in going, let's say, to Stanford or U.C. Berkeley, we have an excellent articulation program that allows them to take the two-year required courses and get guaranteed admissions in their junior year at those schools that they prefer to go to." In this way, **a community college can open the door to a four-year college for you**.

Of course, there are advantages to entering a four-year college as a freshman rather than two years later as a transfer from a community college. Socially and academically, you may enjoy a fuller college experience. "It's all the things that you can't quite name," says Elizabeth Bickford of the University of Oregon. "There is something that you do lose in that transition as an 18- or 19-year-old." But those factors have to be balanced against financial realities, as Ms. Bickford found when she was making her own college decisions. "I'm a community college transfer to a four-year myself. So is my husband. We wouldn't have financially been able to make it if we hadn't done it that way. I think it's a good way to make it if all the support isn't there."

Living at Home

A good way to save money on room and board is to commute. Instead of paying for campus housing and meals—an average cost of $8,595 a year for private colleges—you continue to live at home. There your housing and meal costs remain whatever they have been, and you commute to campus daily by train, bus, car, or other means. This will probably be more inconvenient than living on campus, where you would only have to walk a few steps from your dorm to the classroom. But you will almost certainly save a lot of money.

However, commuting has hidden costs. You will have transportation expenses that you wouldn't have if you lived on campus. If you can use mass transit, these costs will probably be low enough to make economic sense. But if you have to buy a car and pay for gas and insurance, your transportation costs might end up being close to the costs of on-campus room and board. And if you're thinking of relying on family and friends for rides to and from campus, remember that their schedules may not overlap with yours. Your own schedule may change day to day and semester to semester, depending on your classes and activities. You probably will need your own car if mass transit isn't available.

Also, don't forget that you cost money at home, too. You're still eating and using utilities at home, and you'll inevitably add pick-up meals on campus to those costs. Financial aid packages usually offer help in paying for room and board as well as tuition and fees, so your actual cost for living on campus would probably not be as high as the published price.

We're not saying that commuting isn't a bargain—it usually is. (There are other good reasons to live at home, too.) But if you are thinking of commuting just to save money, don't commit to it until you weigh all the costs and assess the financial aid offers from any "live away" colleges to which you may apply.

Living Off-Campus

If you don't want to commute but still want to save money on room and board, you might want to consider living off-campus. By residing near campus in an apartment that you share with classmates, you may be able to live more cheaply than you could in the dorms. **But be sure to check the college's policies**—many do not allow freshmen to live off campus if they're under 21 and not living with their parents.

How to Factor in Financial Aid

Every college publishes an average price for the various cost components, but that published price is probably not the price you will end up paying. Your financial aid package will reduce your actual costs. Yet financial aid packages vary from college to college as much as costs do. In thinking about where you will apply, you need to find out some financial aid basics about each college on your short list. How great a percentage of need does it usually meet? How much aid does it award in grants and how much in loans? Does the college offer any merit scholarships or other forms of aid not based on need?

Part III of this book, "Financial Aid College by College," gives you these financial aid basics, along with a number of other essential facts. These include:

- the school's Web address
- what type of school it is, such as public or private
- how many students are enrolled
- how selective the school is
- basic costs, including tuition, fees, room, and board
- financial aid application procedures, including deadlines and required forms
- contact information for the financial aid office

In addition, the "Financial Aid Picture" section of each college's profile tells you how much aid is being distributed to how many students and in what form. This information is useful, but note that it only shows averages. Since few families are "average," the numbers in the financial aid profile shouldn't be considered a guarantee of what you'll get or how much you'll have to pay. For example, in-state students at public colleges usually borrow much less than the average debt per student listed in the profiles, while out-of-state students usually borrow more. What you can use the profiles for is to compare colleges: This college meets a greater percentage of need than most; this college awards a relatively large portion of aid in grants.

Check with the Financial Aid Office Before You Apply

Before you apply for financial aid, check with the financial aid offices of the colleges to which you're planning to apply for admission—by simply visiting their Web site, or by talking to them on the phone or in person. Confirm which forms you need to complete and the deadlines. Better to get these details right before you get started than to find out after the fact that you filed too late or didn't file the proper form.

Bear in mind also that each college has its own financial aid policies, such as how outside scholarships are treated and whether or not aid awards can be appealed. When you contact the office, whether long distance or in a campus visit, find out as much as you can about these policies, along with facts about costs and the financial aid process. If possible, schedule an interview with a member of the financial aid staff. They'll give you a lot of information, but don't expect them to offer you aid until they've seen your forms.

KEEP IN MIND

The **college profiles in Part III** of this book give the "financial aid picture" for each college, based on averages. Use these profiles to **compare colleges only**; the aid you would get at any college is based on your own individual circumstances, so the amount might be higher or lower than the average for that college.

Questions to Ask Colleges

Here are some questions worth asking the aid office:

✔ What are your average costs for the first year for:
- tuition and fees
- room and board
- books and supplies
- transportation
- other personal expenses

✔ What is the range of costs for:
- rooms (single, double)
- board (different meal plans)
- tuition rates (flat rate, per credit, etc.)

✔ By how much will total costs increase each year?

✔ How much have tuition and fees and room and board increased over the past three to five years?

✔ Does financial need have an impact on admissions decisions?

✔ Does the school offer both need-based and merit-based financial aid?

✔ Do I need to file a separate application for merit-based scholarships?

✔ If the financial aid package isn't enough, under what conditions, if any, will the aid office reconsider the offer?

✔ How will the aid package change from year to year?

✔ What will happen if my family's financial situation changes?

✔ What are the terms and conditions of your aid programs? For example, what are the academic requirements or other conditions for renewing financial aid from year to year?

✔ When can we expect to receive bills from the college? Is there an option to spread the yearly payment over equal monthly installments?

QUICK RECAP

When deciding where to apply to college, cost is a factor, but not the most important factor. Don't exclude any college from consideration because of its "sticker price"—what you will actually pay might be much less. Remember:

- Each school has different costs and financial aid policies.
- When choosing colleges to apply to, consider a "financial safety."
- Your costs might vary from the published averages.
- You might be able to save money at a public college or community college or by commuting—but there are pros and cons to all those strategies.
- Research the colleges you're considering and contact their financial aid offices early.

Step 4: Get Ready for the Forms

Depending on where you'll apply, you may need to file up to three kinds of forms to get financial aid: the FAFSA, the CSS/Financial Aid PROFILE, and forms for individual colleges or states. Step 4 gets you ready for those forms. There are two main things to remember. First, file before the deadlines. The early bird—or at least the timely bird—gets the worm. Second, don't be intimidated. The forms are easier to fill out than they look.

Forms You'll Fill Out

Applying for financial aid is basically a matter of filling out a few financial aid forms on time. The forms may look complicated and be hard to face, but they are simpler than they look, and millions of people fill them out every year. We will guide you through them so they make sense.

The three steps that follow this one walk you through the forms you may need to complete: the FAFSA (Step 5), the PROFILE (Step 6), and whatever forms your individual colleges may require (Step 7). This step will help you create a timeline of which colleges require which forms when.

You may not need to fill out all the forms we describe. Most colleges require only one form, the FAFSA. If you do need to fill out more than one form, take heart. Most of the other forms ask for information similar to what the FAFSA requests. Repeating that information may be annoying, but it isn't hard.

FAFSA: The Federal Form

This is the big one. The FAFSA, or Free Application for Federal Student Aid, must be completed by everyone who wants federal government aid. Just about every college financial aid program requires it, even if they also require other forms. Most schools and states use nothing but the FAFSA to determine eligibility for aid.

There is no charge for completing the FAFSA, which you should fill out online if possible at www.fafsa.ed.gov.

KEEP IN MIND

Even though this book presents the financial aid forms in order of FAFSA, PROFILE, and institutional forms, **you may need to submit these forms in a different order** depending on the financial aid deadlines of your colleges. In some cases, you may have to file PROFILE a few weeks before FAFSA, or the institutional form on the same day as FAFSA.

FILING THE FAFSA

You cannot file the FAFSA before January 1 of the year for which you're seeking aid. For example, if you will start college in September 2009, you cannot file the FAFSA before January 1, 2009. If you want a head start, visit the FAFSA Web site earlier so you can familiarize yourself with the form and start working on your application as soon after January 1 as possible. If you don't have all your tax documents together before you need to file, you can estimate your tax information using your end-of-year pay stubs and last year's income tax return (see "Get Your Stuff Together" on page 41).

Once it's January 1, however, you should aim to file your FAFSA as soon as possible. Don't be fooled by the federal filing deadline (June 30). **Most college deadlines for financial aid are in February or March**, and they need your FAFSA information by then. The window of time between January 1 and the financial aid deadlines, some of which fall as early as February 1, isn't big. So, come January, the earlier that you start working on the FAFSA, the better. **Don't worry about filing your tax return first**: If you don't have all your tax documents together before you need to file your FAFSA, you can estimate your tax information using your end-of-year pay stubs and last year's income tax returns (see "Get Your Stuff Together" on page 41). You can correct your FAFSA with actual tax figures later.

The most important thing is to leave time for your FAFSA to be processed after it's filed. If you're filing on paper, leave at least four weeks before your earliest college or state deadline. If you're filing online, you can wait until only a week before the earliest deadline.

The FAFSA may seem complicated, but it's a lot easier than it looks. We'll walk you through it in Step 5.

On the FAFSA, you'll provide financial information about yourself and also about your parents, if you're a dependent student. The information will be based on your income tax returns plus your own reporting of your financial assets, such as bank accounts and savings bonds. The federal government will use that data to calculate your Expected Family Contribution, or EFC.

Soon after you've submitted the FAFSA, you'll receive the Student Aid Report (SAR). This lists the information you reported on your FAFSA and tells you what your EFC is. This report is important. Check it over as soon as possible and, if necessary, update it with your family's latest tax return information. **Don't sit on the SAR: keep the process moving quickly.**

WHERE TO GET A PAPER FAFSA

If you don't have Internet access or just prefer to work on paper, you can request the paper FAFSA by calling 800 433-3243. After you submit the paper FAFSA you'll have to allow at least four weeks for mailing and processing before your earliest deadline.

If you use the paper FAFSA, you can only list four colleges to receive your information. You can add up to six more later, but you'll have to wait until your FAFSA is processed and you've received your Student Aid Report (SAR).

GOOD TO KNOW

If you're filing both the PROFILE and the FAFSA, it might help to **do the PROFILE first**. One feature of the PROFILE Web site is that once you've completed your application, it will create a worksheet you can use to fill out the FAFSA.

PROFILE

In addition to the FAFSA, some colleges and scholarship programs also require that you fill out the CSS/Financial Aid PROFILE® to award their own nonfederal funds. They believe this form gives a more complete picture of students' financial circumstances, allowing them to allocate money as fairly as possible. The PROFILE service is administered by the College Board, though the College Board itself does not give out any need-based scholarships.

A few colleges require PROFILE only if you're applying for early decision or early action. Others require it for all applicants. If your college requires it and you're applying early, it is often the first form to fill out—ahead of even FAFSA. To find out if your colleges require PROFILE, look them up in Part III of this book or contact their financial aid offices.

PROFILE is online only; there are no paper forms. You can register for PROFILE at www.collegeboard.com beginning October 1 of the year before you intend to start college. Once you register, you can either complete your application then and there or return to it at a later time. It's best if you submit it at least one week before your earliest college financial aid deadline. You can use the same application for multiple colleges, and you'll receive an online acknowledgment confirming the schools to which you're sending the information.

There is a $25 fee to send your PROFILE to one college, plus a fee of $16 for each additional institution. However, depending on the information you submit, you may qualify for a fee waiver. Automatically awarded to low-income, first-time applicants, the fee waiver covers the costs of the PROFILE registration and up to six school reports.

College Forms

Some colleges—most of them private—require you to complete their own financial aid form as well as the FAFSA. Usually the forms are not complicated, and filling them out is not a big deal. Mike Scott of Texas Christian University says, "We have a very simple online form, where we just ask a couple of extra questions." Some of the questions are about projected enrollment: "Are they going to be full-time or part-time? When do they think they're going to graduate?" Others are aimed at matching students to outside sources of aid.

Find out if your colleges require you to file their own form, and if they do, file them on time.

State Forms

Most states offer need-based financial aid to their residents, and most colleges will require you to apply for it. Ask your school counselor for information on what form you need to complete to apply for state scholarship or grant programs. In many states, the FAFSA alone is enough to establish eligibility for state aid—but some states require their own form. If your state does, find out the deadline and add it to your master timeline for applying for aid. (*A table showing the deadlines for state aid, and which forms each state requires, appears on page 72 of this book.*)

Know the Deadlines!

Deadlines count. If you're on time, the colleges to which you've applied will have more money to give you; if you're late, they will have less money—or even none. **Late means less money, so be on time!** That means knowing and keeping track of all the financial aid deadlines you have to meet.

This can be tricky, because the deadlines are not all the same. Many schools and states may require you to fill out their own financial aid forms, and those forms may have deadlines that differ from those of the FAFSA or PROFILE. And **keep in mind that a college's due date for financial aid applications is typically different from its due date for admissions applications**.

Many colleges have no firm deadline or closing date for applying for financial aid; rather, they have a "priority" date. Often falling in February or March, the priority date is the date by which the school needs to receive your application to make its most attractive aid offer. After that date, funds may be limited or used up, and you may not get as much aid as you need. "I urge my students to apply for aid by the priority date," says Lauri Benton, a counselor at Columbia High School in Decatur, Georgia. "They are more likely to get the aid they need early in the process, when the colleges have ample money to award."

Some colleges accept financial aid applications on a "rolling" basis. This means that applications are reviewed as they come in on a first-come, first-reviewed basis. Applicants are notified—that is, sent a financial aid award letter—a few weeks after they submit their forms. Most colleges that have a priority date will review late applications on a rolling basis. If you're applying to a rolling-applications college that doesn't have any set deadlines or priority dates, you're best off applying by mid-February or early March, when they will probably still have enough money available to meet your need.

Part III of this book, "Financial Aid College by College," lists deadlines and priority dates for colleges, along with their required forms. But it is worth confirming this information with the schools to which you're applying—at least by visiting their Web sites in November or December. Remember: time is money. To get the most aid available, apply by the priority date. (*See also "Do You Get More Money If You Apply Early?" on page 40.*)

Creating a Timeline for Aid Applications

There are a lot of dates to remember as you apply for financial aid, but they don't have to be overwhelming. You can stay on top of them by making a timeline.

When you've found out the priority dates of the colleges and scholarship programs to which you're applying, as well as those of your state financial aid agency, list them in chronological order. Make that list part of a month-by-month timeline. Don't worry about the past; start the timeline with whatever month you're in now. The chart on the opposite page is an example of the sort of timeline you might construct. (*A blank copy of this chart for you to fill in appears in Part II on page 121.*)

EXPERT ADVICE

"If you **meet our priority date**, we're going to guarantee you a full package here. You'll get 100 percent of need if you meet that priority deadline. If you don't, then it's what's left over, if we have money left over. And we typically do—but we don't have enough to meet 100 percent of the need of every late applicant."

—*Vincent Amoroso, deputy director, Office of Scholarships and Student Aid, University of North Carolina at Chapel Hill*

SAMPLE WORKSHEET 1:
Meet Your Application Deadlines

		COLLEGE 1:	COLLEGE 2:	COLLEGE 3:
	College Name	*1st Choice Univ.*	*Private Univ.*	*Financial Safety*
FORMS REQUIRED	FAFSA	*Yes*	*Yes*	*Yes*
	PROFILE	*For ED (by 11/1)*	*Yes*	*No*
	State form	*Yes*	*No*	*Yes*
	Institutional form	*No*	*Laptop loaner*	*Yes*
	Tax returns	*Verification only*	*Verification only*	*Yes*
	Other			
SCHOOL CODES	Federal code	*999999*	*888888*	*777777*
	CSS code	*999Z*	*999X*	
PRIORITY DATE		*3/1 (FAFSA, State Form)*	*2/1*	*3/15*
CLOSING DATE		*None*	*2/15*	*None*
AFTER APPLYING	Need to send letter?			
	Documentation required?			
COMPARE AWARDS	Notification date	*12/15*	*4/1*	*2 weeks after applying*
	Reply-by date	*Immediately (if accepted ED)*	*5/1*	*4 weeks after notification*

For a blank version of this worksheet that you can photocopy for your own use, see page 121.

Throughout the period that you're applying for aid, keep your timeline where you can see it, check off what you've done, and remind yourself of what to do next. This will put the deadlines in your control. (*See the inside front cover of this book for a calendar of important dates and reminders.*)

Do You Get More Money If You Apply Early?

No. If you apply for financial aid Tuesday and another student applies Wednesday, you don't get more money than that student—so long as both of you apply by the deadline (or the priority date). However, when it comes to the college's own funds, and certain "campus-based" federal student aid programs (such as federal work-study), aid is distributed first-come, first-served once that date has passed. If you apply for aid after the college's deadline or priority date, the pool of funds may be used up. So always apply on time.

WHAT ABOUT EARLY DECISION?

Many schools allow students to apply for admission under early-decision or early-action programs. Whether early acceptance to a school affects the student's financial aid package varies from school to school. Depending on the college, the student accepted early may get more financial aid, less, or the same.

If you are considering early-decision programs, ask each school's financial aid officer: How is financial aid affected if I apply early decision? You may not know exactly what aid you'll get until after you accept. Don't panic: The rules of early decision allow you to turn down the college's acceptance offer if it doesn't offer you enough aid. Just don't put all your eggs into one basket—be sure to apply to a "financial safety school" as well.

The Benefits of Web-Based Applications

The FAFSA can be filled out and submitted online at www.fafsa.ed.gov. A limited number of paper FAFSAs are available for students who do not have access to a computer (see page 36 for information) but it is better to file online. Doing so cuts processing time by several weeks—essential if you're running late. It can also reduce delays due to errors because the site edits your information before you submit it, allowing you to correct it before submitting. Also, once you have submitted the form online, you will instantly get your EFC back from the Web site, which reduces some of the anxiety in the process. The FAFSA Web site gives lots of help in completing the form.

If you do file online, save and print out a hard copy of the confirmation you'll receive after submitting your application. If you file a paper form, make a photocopy for your records.

KEEP IN MIND

When you fill out the FAFSA, both you and one of your parents need a **Personal Identification Number**. This is important: the PIN will allow you to sign your FAFSA electronically, which will cut down your processing time. **You and one of your parents must each request a PIN** at **www.pin.ed.gov**. You should register for your PINs **before you fill out the FAFSA**. A good time to ask for your PINs is November of your senior year. **Remember your PIN and write it down in a safe place:** if you forget it, the government can't "remind" you of it later on.

PROFILE is only available online. If you don't have a computer at home, find out if one of your parents can use a computer at work, or use a computer at your school's guidance office or the library. After you register for the PROFILE, you can print a customized preapplication worksheet to help you gather the information you'll need, then complete the application online.

Figure 7:
FAFSA PIN Site

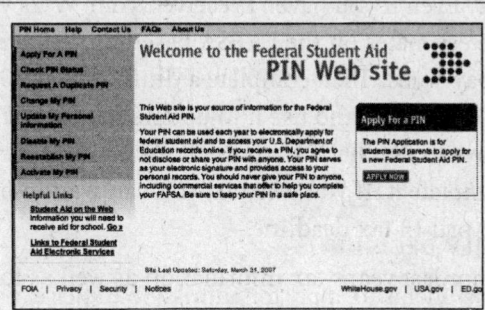

Get Your Stuff Together

For maximum efficiency, gather all the records you need to complete the forms before you sit down to work on them. That will save you a lot of time getting up, hunting around, and forgetting where you left off. For both you and your parents, you'll probably need tax returns and related documents (such as W-2 forms) for the year that just ended, as well as end-of-year pay stubs, bank statements, and other financial records. If you're filling out the PROFILE, you will also need tax documents from the previous year. If your parents own their home, you will need current mortgage information to fill out the PROFILE.

The FAFSA and PROFILE preapplication worksheets are basically a way to help you gather your information before filling out the actual application. Use them that way. Add a list of all the records you need to assemble. It should be comprehensive and indicate which records are for all forms and which are for PROFILE only.

Establish Eligibility

To be eligible for federal financial aid, among other requirements, you'll have to:

- be a U.S. citizen or eligible noncitizen
- have a valid Social Security Number
- not have been convicted of sale or possession of drugs
- if male and at least 18 years old, be registered with the Selective Service (in most cases)

Most of these requirements will not require extra work for most students. But two of them may. If you don't have a Social Security Number, get one as soon as possible (go to www.ssa.gov to learn how), and certainly before you file your

FAFSA. And if you are male, you can register for the Selective Service through the FAFSA application if you haven't already. If you do have a drug conviction, you may still be able to establish eligibility by completing a treatment program.

Tax Forms and Other Records

Income tax returns are due on April 15, but most colleges want your financial aid forms much sooner. **Don't wait until your taxes are done to file your financial aid forms**. Even if you haven't received your W-2s yet, you can still file the FAFSA. Use estimates on the FAFSA based on last year's return and your current-year pay stubs. Then complete a draft of your 1040 tax return as soon as possible afterward, and use it to update the SAR if necessary. You don't necessarily have to file the 1040 to use it for your financial aid forms; you just need to complete it. If you owe tax, you can wait to file the tax return until closer to the April 15 tax deadline.

PROFILE asks you for last year's tax information as well as for this year's. For this year, it asks you whether the figures are estimated or final. It also asks for estimated income for next year, which you can base on this year's information.

You'll have to file some forms to get financial aid, but they aren't as difficult as they might look. The main forms are FAFSA and PROFILE, plus whatever other forms your colleges or state may require.

- File on time—filing late can cost you money.

- File your FAFSA online. Get a PIN for yourself and for one of your parents early—and don't lose them.

- Make a timeline to keep track of your deadlines, including college priority dates.

- As early as possible, check with your colleges to be sure you know what forms they each require.

- Gather together the records you need to fill out the forms.

- If you don't have one already, get a Social Security Number.

**QUICK
RECAP**

Step 5: Fill Out the FAFSA

QUICK OVERVIEW

The FAFSA may look intimidating, but it's actually pretty easy to fill out. The questions mainly concern your income and assets and those of your parents, but they also touch on other matters, such as your citizenship status and the schools to which you want the FAFSA to be sent. We'll walk you through it, and give you tips about how to avoid delays. Above all: file on time!

General Advice

Nobody likes to fill out forms, with their cramped boxes and unfamiliar terms. And no one enjoys having to share information about family finances. But the potential result—money to help you pay for college—is well worth it. And you will see in this step that the FAFSA is really pretty simple. In fact, the form has only seven sections, one of which is, essentially, "sign here."

Again, remember that you don't have to do the steps in this book in exactly the order presented. If the colleges require you to submit the PROFILE before the FAFSA, then do the PROFILE first, even though we present the FAFSA first. In fact, one nice thing about the PROFILE is that, after you've submitted it, you'll receive a worksheet that you can use to fill out the FAFSA, making this step much easier.

Help is available by phone and online if you have questions about FAFSA (see the "Good to Know" sidebar on page 45). And don't be afraid to call the financial aid offices of the colleges to which you're applying. If you're confused about this or any other aspect of the financial aid process, these offices can help. "People look at the FAFSA and they find it a bit overwhelming initially," says Vincent Amoroso, of the University of North Carolina at Chapel Hill. "They come to us seeking guidance and reassurance on how to get through the application process. We show them that it's not as complicated as it looks."

Apply on Time

You can't file your FAFSA before January 1 of the year you're applying for aid. Most college deadlines for financial aid are in March, and some fall as early

EXPERT ADVICE

"Our job is to get students through this maze. You'd call a mechanic if your car is broken. Well, why not call us if you have a question about financial aid applications? That's our job—to get you through the process."

—Bonnie Lee Behm, director of financial assistance, Villanova University

as February, so the window for filing is narrow. You have to leave time for your FAFSA to be processed. Be sure to file your online form at least one week before the earliest deadline.

Don't wait until the April 15 tax deadline to file your FAFSA. Most priority dates will be long over by then. If your earliest deadline doesn't fall until March, you can wait for W-2s, 1099s, and other official tax documents to arrive from employers and banks and then complete draft income tax returns. You don't have to file those draft returns with the IRS, but you can use the information from them on your FAFSA. The advantage of using draft tax returns this way is that you probably won't have to correct your FAFSA after you've submitted it, and it will be easier to answer the questions on the form that refer directly to lines on the 1040.

If your earliest deadline falls in February, however, you should have a backup plan in case W-2s don't arrive in time. The best thing to do in this case is to use end-of-year pay stubs, quarterly bank statements, and similar records to estimate your and your parents' income. You can also use 1040 forms for the previous year as a frame of reference, but don't just plug in the information from last year's returns into the FAFSA—you really do need to estimate the current information, not duplicate old information. (Also, be warned that the numbers assigned to each line of the 1040 tend to change whenever the IRS adds new credits or deductions, so the references on the FAFSA you're filling out may not match old 1040s.)

No matter how you derive the numbers, remember this above all: get the FAFSA in on time.

Read Instructions Carefully; Fill Out the Form Accurately

With the FAFSA as with all financial aid forms, accuracy is vital. Read the directions. Understand the terms that are being used. Many terms, such as "date of birth," are straightforward, but others, such as "investments," require you to read the instructions carefully so you know what they mean in this context. Even the term "parent," as discussed below, has a special meaning on the FAFSA.

Be as complete and accurate as you can about your financial circumstances. If you submit incorrect data, you might create delays that could endanger your aid. By avoiding errors, you will increase your chances of getting all the aid for which you are eligible.

Keep Track of Your Pin and Password

You can submit a paper FAFSA, but it's easier and faster to submit your FAFSA online at www.fafsa.ed.gov. Filing the FAFSA on the Web can reduce processing time by a couple of weeks. It also reduces delays due to errors: the site edits your information before you submit it, so if you made errors or left out information, you can correct it before submitting it.

KNOW THE LINGO

If you've never filed an income tax return before—or if your parents file for you—you may not be familiar with these IRS forms:

1040—the main form of your tax return, this is a summary of all the taxable income you or your parents made last year, possible deductions from that income, the tax owed on that income, and credits that give some of that tax back.

W-2—a tax form prepared by the employer stating how much taxable income they paid you last year, as well as untaxed benefits you or your parents received from them. Information on this form is used on both the 1040 and the FAFSA.

1099—a form similar to the W-2 that shows income you received from anyone other than an employer. For example, if one of your parents is an independent contractor, he or she may receive a 1099-MISC showing the nonemployee compensation a client paid them.

1098—a tax form showing payments for which you can take a deduction or credit. For example, if you take out a student loan, once you begin repaying it you will receive a 1098-E from your lender every year showing how much interest you paid on the loan.

You don't have to complete the FAFSA on the Web in one sitting. At the start, you'll supply a password that will allow you to leave the application before completing it and to return later, so long as you come back within 45 days. But **make sure you write down the password and keep it in a safe place** where you can find it again. Unlike most Web sites, the FAFSA site provides no hint or reminder to aid your memory. If you forget the password, there will be no way to retrieve your data, and you'll have to start over.

Get PINs ahead of time for both yourself and for one of your parents so you can sign the form electronically. The PINs can be ordered at www.pin.ed.gov. You should do this in advance because it will take a week to get the PINs—a delay you may not be able to afford later in the process. Write down the PIN in a safe place; if you forget it, that could make you miss your deadline.

Figure 8:
FAFSA on the Web

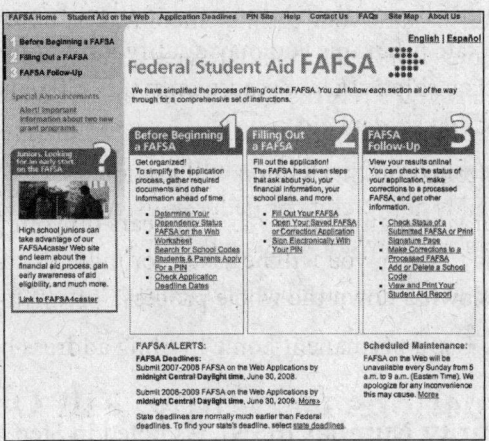

Let's Walk Through It

The FAFSA consists of seven sections, or "steps," each of which contains a number of questions with a common theme. The exact order or wording of these questions may change from year to year (last year's preapplication worksheet is in Part II), but the substance remains more or less the same. And the purpose never changes: to provide information about yourself and your family that colleges will use to figure out how much federal student aid you qualify for.

There are a few general tips to keep in mind while filling out the FAFSA:

- The word "you" always means you, the student.

- The word "college" means a college, university, community college, or any other school beyond high school.

- The phrase "net worth" means the current value of an asset (such as a business) minus the amount of debt owed on it.

- Questions about income are for the previous year; questions about assets ask for their value as of the day you fill out the form.

- When entering dollar figures, round to the nearest dollar and don't use commas or decimal points.

- If you have special financial circumstances that you need to explain, you can't do it on the FAFSA. Instead, write to your colleges directly (*see Step 8 of this book, "Make Your Special Circumstances Known."*)

Here is a step-by-step walk–through of the key questions on the FAFSA. Since the online form is interactive, it will automatically skip over some questions or sections depending on how you answer. For example, if you say that you're not married, you won't be asked questions about your spouse. Worksheets are available for download as PDFs from the Web site.

FAFSA Step One: About Yourself

These questions gather basic information used to identify you and determine which federal and state programs you may qualify for. For example, the question about your citizenship is there because only U.S. citizens (or eligible noncitizens) can get federal student aid.

Here's the main information this section will ask for:

Your name. Enter your name exactly as it appears on your Social Security card. If the two don't match, you will be asked for more documentation through the mail, slowing down the whole process.

Where you live. Use a permanent home mailing address here, not a school or office address.

Your Social Security Number (SSN). As noted in Step 4 of this book, you need to have an SSN to apply for federal aid.

Your date of birth.

Your permanent telephone number. Use a permanent home or cell phone number, not a school or office number.

Your driver's license number (if any).

Your e-mail address. This is optional, but if you provide it, the government can send you your Student Aid Report (SAR) by e-mail instead of snail mail, so it will reach you faster.

Whether you are a citizen or an eligible noncitizen. You are a citizen if you were born in this country or became a citizen through the naturalization process. An eligible noncitizen is someone such as a U.S. permanent resident holding a green card (Permanent Resident Card), or someone who has refugee status who is allowed to live permanently in the United States. It is not someone visiting on a student visa. If you're an eligible noncitizen, you'll have to fill in your Alien Registration Number. If you're neither a citizen nor an eligible noncitizen, you can't get federal aid, but you may be eligible for state or college aid—so you should still fill out the FAFSA, unless you don't have a social security number. In that case, call your colleges.

Whether you're single, married, divorced, widowed, or separated.

The state in which you legally reside. Your answer will determine whether you're eligible for scholarships and grants from your state. It's also used to estimate how much state income tax you pay. In some cases, your state of legal residence—where you officially live—might be different from the state where you're actually living at the time you fill out the FAFSA. This might be the case if you've recently moved or one of your parents is in the military.

Whether you're male. If you are and you haven't registered with the Selective Service yet, you'll have the option of registering now via the FAFSA. To get federal aid, male students 18 years or older must be registered with the Selective Service, the agency responsible for providing drafted men to the armed forces in an emergency.

What degree will you be working on in the next school year. Some aid programs are not available for graduate study, a second bachelor's degree, or nondegree study. If you are undecided about what type of degree you will be pursuing (for example, if you're applying to both two-year and four-year colleges), check "undecided," but be sure to follow up with each college you're applying to after you've submitted the FAFSA.

What year of college you'll be in next year. Your answer determines which aid programs you qualify for. For example, the SMART grant is only available to students in their junior or senior year of college.

Your enrollment status next school year. Most aid programs are not available to students who will be attending less than half-time (that is, taking fewer than six credits per semester). Some are only available for full-time students. If you're not sure how many credits you will take, check "undecided," but be sure to follow up with each college you're applying to after you've submitted the FAFSA.

Whether you're interested in loans and work-study. The best answer is "both." Preserve your options. It doesn't matter if you aren't sure. Answering no won't make colleges more likely to give you grants, but it might keep you from getting loan or work-study aid if you change your mind later. By the time you change your mind, all the funds might be gone.

The highest level of education completed by your father and mother. This won't affect your federal aid, but some states use this information to award scholarships to students who are the first in their family to attend college.

Whether you've ever been convicted of possessing or selling illegal drugs. Say "yes" only if the offense occurred while you were receiving federal student aid (unlikely if this is your first FAFSA), it's still on your record, and you were tried as an adult.

FAFSA Step Two: Are You Independent?

The questions in this step determine whether or not you're an independent student. To be considered independent for the purpose of federal student aid eligibility, it doesn't matter if you feel independent, have a job, or even live on your own. It also has nothing to do with whether your parents claim you as a dependent on their tax return. But if you can truthfully answer "yes" to at least one of the questions in this step, you will be considered independent.

The things that would classify you as independent are:

- You turn age 24 or older in the year you start college.

- You'll be enrolled in a graduate degree program in the year for which you're seeking aid.

- You're married.

- You have children who get more than half of their support from you.

- You have dependents other than your children or spouse who live with you and get more than half their support from you.

- You're an orphan, or you've been a ward/dependent of the court.

- You're currently serving in, or are a veteran of, the active-duty U.S. armed forces. (If you served only as a reservist and were never activated for reasons other than training, answer "no.")

If you are independent, then you can skip FAFSA Step Three, which asks about your parents' income and assets. But there are certain cases where a college financial aid office will want to know about your parents' finances even if you are an independent. If you do meet one of the criteria on the list above, it's a good idea to ask the colleges to which you're applying whether they'll consider you fully independent for the purpose of awarding their own institutional funds. If one or more of them won't, you should fill out FAFSA Step Three. The online application will ask you whether you want to fill it out or skip it.

FAFSA Step Three: Your Parents' Income and Assets

These questions are about your parents' income and assets. If you're a dependent student, you have to answer these questions even if you don't live with your parents. When you're ready to submit the application, you will also need one of your parents to sign it, either on the paper form or by using a PIN on the electronic version.

Modern family life can make the definition of "parent" complicated. But the FAFSA definitions are fairly clear:

- If both your parents are living and married to each other, answer the questions about both of them.

- If only one of your parents is living, answer the questions about him or her.

- If your widowed parent remarried, answer the questions about your stepparent too.

- If you were raised by a single parent, answer the questions about him or her.

- If your parents are divorced or separated, answer the questions about the parent you lived with the most during the past 12 months.

- If that parent remarried, answer the questions about your stepparent, too.

- Don't provide information about grandparents, legal guardians, or foster parents. FAFSA doesn't consider them your parents unless they have legally adopted you.

This step is the most work, but it's not hard. Here's a run-down of the important questions:

Their social security numbers: Unlike you, your parents are not required to have social security numbers in order for you to file the FAFSA (but in that case you have to enter zeroes). But if they do have social security numbers, they must provide them.

Their names: Again, if they have social security cards, their names must exactly match.

Whether they've completed a tax return for the past year. This means the return that is due the coming April 15.

Whether they're eligible to file the 1040A or 1040EZ tax form. It's to your advantage if they can answer yes, they're eligible to file this form. If they would normally file the 1040A but filed the full 1040 only to take advantage of an education tax benefit relating to a child already in college, they can still check this box.

The number of people in your parents' household: These include you and your parents. The number who will be in college during the next year is also asked for: that also includes you (but not your parents). These questions affect how much money your parents will be expected to contribute to your education.

Their income tax information: These questions are easy to answer if they've already completed a draft of their tax return. But if they haven't, ask them to give estimates, using W2's or pay stubs, bank statements, and last year's return. **Don't miss any college deadlines or priority dates because your parents haven't done their taxes yet.** After you submit your FAFSA, you'll be able to correct the estimated figures on your SAR.

What their untaxed income and benefits are. These include items like earned income credits, welfare benefits, Social Security benefits, child support, and other money that didn't get taxed. It also includes any contributions your parents made for the last tax year to deductible Individual Retirement Accounts (IRAs) or employer-sponsored retirement plans such as 401(k)s or 403(b)s. Add this up on worksheets and fill in the totals on the FAFSA. If you're filling out the worksheets online, the information will appear on the confirmation page you'll see after submitting, which you should print out and keep on file in case a financial aid administrator asks about them later.

Veterans' education benefits. Here your parents would report any education benefits they get as a result of military service, such as GI Bill funds. (They

GOOD TO KNOW

Most students are eligible to file IRS Form 1040EZ or 1040A as their tax return. Some parents can, too. (The rules determining whether you can are explained in the FAFSA instructions.) **If both you and your parents are eligible to file the 1040A or 1040EZ,** you may qualify for a "simplified needs analysis," wherein only your income (not your assets) will be assessed when calculating your expected family contribution.

should report the monthly benefit amount, not the annual amount.) These are not used in calculating your EFC, but colleges take them into account when putting together an aid package, as described in Step 9 of this book.

What their assets are. These include cash, savings, and the value of investments, such as stocks and bonds. The amounts to put down are "as of" the day you fill out the FAFSA. Often that is just a best guess, using the most recent bank statements. (Keep in mind that the amount of aid you are entitled to is based much more on family income than on assets.) They do *not* include the home where your parents primarily live (a summer cottage would be included), a family-owned business of less than 100 employees, or a family farm that they live on and operate. However, if your parents own more than one home—a summer cottage, for example, or an investment property—they also should report their equity in that home on the "investments" line. If they own a farm that they don't live on, they also should report the value of that farm as a business. Another thing your parents do not need to include here is any money they have in tax-advantaged retirement accounts, such as IRAs, 401(k)s, 403(b)s, and the like.

FAFSA Step Four: Your Own Income and Assets

These questions ask about *your* income and assets—the student's. Income is how much money you made last year; assets are what you own and the savings you have. If you are married, they also want to know about your spouse's income and assets. They won't ask about your parents' income and assets until later.

These are the main things that this section asks for:

Whether you've completed a tax return for the past year. This means the return that is due the coming April 15, not the one you filed a year ago. If you have filed a return or plan to file one, they will ask what form you're using, for example, the 1040 or 1040A. If you're not going to file any tax return, they will still ask how much you (and, if you have one, your spouse) earned from working.

The number of people in your household: This question refers to the number of people in *your* household, if you have one—not your parents'.

Whether you're eligible to file the 1040A or 1040EZ tax form. The instructions on the FAFSA explain who can file these forms. Most students can. If you can, say yes.

What income and tax information you and your spouse will report on your tax returns. Again, these questions are easy to answer if you've already completed a draft of your tax return. But if you haven't completed your tax return yet, you should estimate what the information on the completed return will be and update the information later. Use pay stubs and, if you have one, your prior-year tax return to make the income estimates. Just don't put off filing the FAFSA because you haven't done your taxes yet. **You're not required to file your tax return before completing the FAFSA.**

What your untaxed income and benefits are. Once again, th͏ include items like earned income credits, welfare benefits, Social Secu͏ efits, child support, and other money that came to you without being taxed. You will be asked about these in a series of questions on screen. (If you are filling out the paper FAFSA, you should use the worksheets that come with the form to add them all up, then fill in the totals on your FAFSA. Don't submit the worksheets, but keep copies of them on file. A financial aid office may want those details later.)

Veterans' noneducation benefits. If you are a veteran, the untaxed-income worksheets will ask you to list your noneducation benefits. But if you're receiving veteran's education benefits (for example, GI Bill funds) that are paid directly to a college, do not report those as income in this section (you'll report them a little later in a separate question). Do report any military pensions, health benefits, or the like.

What your assets are. This question is meant to provide a snapshot of your assets, the money or property you currently own. Using current banking statements and investment records, say how much cash and savings you have, as well the total value of any stocks, other investments, or investment properties that you might own. If you're still in high school, chances are that you only have a small savings or checking account, which you should report on the line asking for "cash, savings accounts, and checking accounts." You may also have some government savings bonds, certificates of deposit (CDs), or a few shares of stock; those should be reported on the line asking about "investments."

Don't include any college savings accounts in this step unless you are independent (you answered "yes" to any question in FAFSA Step 2) and they are owned by you in your own name.

FAFSA Step Five: College Codes

Now you're in the home stretch. There are no more questions about your family's finances or personal life. All this section of the FAFSA asks is which colleges should receive your FAFSA information. You list the colleges, and the government will send the processed information to them for free.

You can list up to ten colleges online; but if you are using the paper FAFSA, you can only list four. In either case you can add additional schools later, when you get your Student Aid Report (SAR). In choosing which colleges to list first, *pick the ones whose financial aid deadlines come first.*

Identify each college by its federal school code. You can find the federal school code in Part III of this book (see Figure 9 on page 52). You can also get it from www.fafsa.ed.gov or the colleges' financial aid Web sites.

For each college, you have to say whether you plan to live on campus, off campus, or with your parents. Your answer will affect the housing costs that the school will estimate for you, and therefore your financial need. If you haven't made a decision yet, assume you'll live on campus.

You don't need to request that your information be sent to a state agency; the government will automatically send your processed information to the agency of your state government that administers financial aid programs for state residents, whether scholarships, grants, or loans. Do be aware, however, that some states require an additional financial aid form, as discussed in Step 7 of this book.

Figure 9:
Finding a College's Federal Code

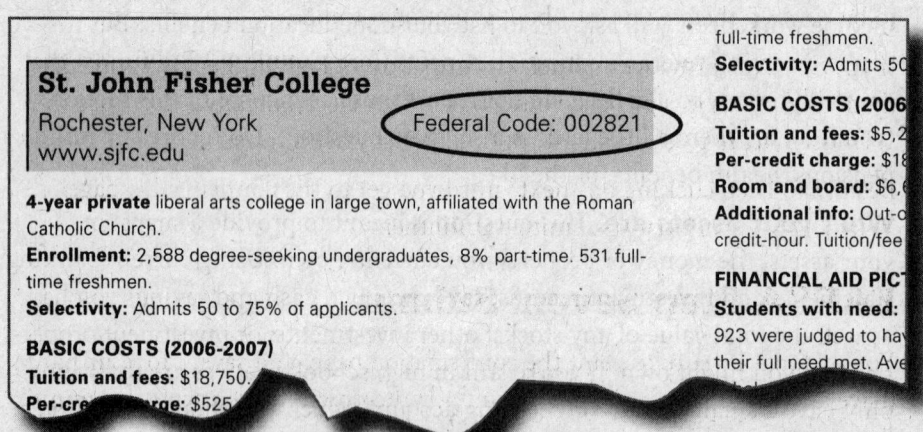

The Federal Code for each college in Part III of this book can be found in its college description.

FAFSA Step Six: Review Your Answers, Then Sign

This is easy, but it's still an important step. Take the time to carefully review all your answers for accuracy and spelling—even your name. When you're satisfied, it's time to sign.

You'll see a list of terms you must agree to by signing. There is nothing onerous here, but there is a scary-sounding penalty for giving "false or misleading information." This does *not* mean honest mistakes or estimates that turn out to be way off; they're talking about intentional fraud.

If your parents provided financial information in FAFSA Step Two, one of them also needs to sign. Use your PINs to sign electronically—don't use the "print signature page and mail" option. It just wastes time.

Be sure to keep clicking on "next" until you get to the confirmation page! Your FAFSA is not truly submitted until then.

FAFSA Step Seven: Submit

You're done! Be sure to print the confirmation page, and save it to your hard drive as well. If you don't have a printer, write down the confirmation number, date, and time. This is your proof that your FAFSA was received.

If you file using the paper form, make a photocopy of it before mailing it, and keep that photocopy together with the worksheets you filled out and all the records you used.

Check Your Student Aid Report!

After you submit your FAFSA, you'll receive your Student Aid Report, or SAR. How long it will take for you to receive it, and in what form, will depend on how you filed the FAFSA. If you filed FAFSA on the Web and signed it with your PIN, you should recieve it immediately, or at most within one to three days. If you filed a paper FAFSA and did not provide an e-mail address, you'll receive a paper SAR within about four weeks.

In whatever form the SAR reaches you, check it over carefully. It will include a summary detailing the information you supplied on the FAFSA. Make sure this information is correct. If not, then you must make corrections. It's easy to do—just go back to www.fafsa.ed.gov and follow the link under "FAFSA Follow Up."

Make corrections only if the data on the SAR doesn't accurately represent your family's financial situation at the time the FAFSA was originally filed. For example, if you estimated the previous year's income but have since filed a tax return with exact figures, substitute those figures now. Or if you mistyped a number, or if the federal data-entry clerk misread your handwriting, correct that. But **don't make changes that reflect changes to your income or assets since you filed the FAFSA**. If important changes of that sort have happened—such as a lost job—inform your colleges individually rather than through the FAFSA (*see Step 8 "Make Your Special Circumstances Known"*).

At the top of the SAR's front page, you should also see an estimate of your EFC: the amount of money your family is expected to contribute toward college costs. The only reason you won't see it is if your SAR has been rejected because you didn't provide required signatures, valid Social Security Numbers, or enough data to calculate the EFC. If that happens to you, submit the necessary corrections and you'll get your EFC estimate. **The actual EFC calculated by a given college may be different than what you'll see here**, especially if that college uses a different formula, or if its financial aid office has adjusted your EFC based on special circumstances that you brought to the college's attention.

The colleges you requested to receive your FAFSA information will automatically get your SAR. At the corrections stage, you'll have an opportunity to add more colleges to receive your FAFSA information. You can also give a school permission to add itself to the list. Just provide the college with the Data Release Number (DRN) at the bottom-left corner of the first page of the SAR. The school will use your DRN to access your application record.

The SAR gives you an estimate of how much money your family is expected to pay for college, but not how much financial aid you'll receive. You'll find that out when your individual colleges send you their award letters. Even so, by filing your FAFSA, you've taken a big step toward getting those letters.

If the expected family contribution (EFC) indicated on the SAR looks too high for your family to afford, you should talk to your parents and discuss other financing options with them (*see Step 11, "Consider Your Out-of-Pocket Options"*). It could also mean that you need to explain some special financial circumstances to the colleges to which you've applied to (see Step 8).

KEEP IN MIND

Eligibility for **federal student aid does not automatically continue** from one year to the next. You have to reapply every year that you're in college. Do that by filling out a **Renewal FAFSA**. This is a partially preformatted version of the FAFSA that you can use so long as you applied for federal aid the previous year.

QUICK RECAP

The FAFSA is easier than it looks. Most of it is about your income and assets, and that of your parents. It's organized in seven steps. Remember:

- File on time. Submit your FAFSA as soon as possible, beginning January 1 of the year you'll start college.
- It helps to have your tax return finished first, but don't let that delay you. You can estimate your figures and correct them later.
- Read instructions.
- Be accurate.
- Reapply every year.

Step 6: Fill out the PROFILE (If Required)

QUICK OVERVIEW

Whether you have to fill out the CSS/Financial Aid PROFILE depends on the colleges to which you're applying. If you do, you'll find it mainly asks for "more of the same"—information about your family's income, expenses, and assets—rather than something completely new. The online form is customized to your situation, so you won't be presented with too many questions that don't apply to you. However, the application does take time to fill out, so leave yourself plenty of time to submit it before your colleges' deadlines.

General Advice

Step 6 is to fill out the CSS/Financial Aid PROFILE—but only if you need to. If the schools to which you're applying don't require this financial aid form, you don't have to complete it. Find out if they require it by checking Part III of this book or the colleges' Web sites.

The PROFILE is administered by the College Board, a not-for-profit association of schools and colleges (and the publisher of this book). It is available online only: you can't file on paper. The upside of this is that PROFILE is available 24 hours a day, seven days a week. Furthermore, its system of online edits alerts you to missing or incorrect information before you submit the application, eliminating a potential source of delays. Firewall protection and data encryption protect the information you submit about your family and its finances. The downside is that if you don't have a computer with Internet access at home, you will have to use one at your school, a library, or a parent's workplace.

The PROFILE doesn't replace the FAFSA: you still need to complete that, too, because that's the form required for federal student aid, which any college will expect you to seek before they give away their own institutional funds. The schools that require the PROFILE do so because they believe it gives a more complete account of your financial situation to guide them in awarding their own funds. The College Board provides the colleges with your PROFILE information, and the colleges use it to calculate your expected family contribution and your need.

Since it's designed to give a more complete picture of your finances, it is not surprising that the PROFILE is longer than the FAFSA. It's the same general concept, but you'll need to gather more records to answer all the questions, and it will take more time to fill out.

Figure 10:

CSS/Financial Aid PROFILE Online

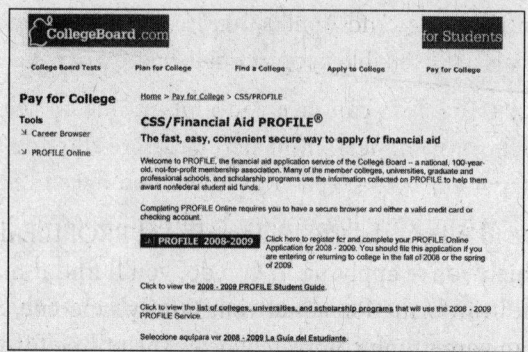

Register and File Early

Because the PROFILE form is more involved, and because colleges may ask for additional information even after the form is filed (such as data on a family-owned farm or store), register well before your colleges' deadlines and leave yourself lots of time to fill out the application. The College Board usually processes your PROFILE information and transmits it to colleges within two business days, but delays can happen—especially in late January and early February. Also, don't assume it can all be completed in one session; you may need to gather additional information to complete the form (especially if a college asks for additional information in section Q). Fortunately, you can go back and forth to your application online, rather than having to finish it in one sitting.

It's best to submit the PROFILE at least one week before your earliest financial aid priority date. Remember, colleges use PROFILE information to determine who gets their limited grant dollars. If you file late, you will have to make do with whatever funds, if any, are left over.

You may need to submit the PROFILE ahead of the FAFSA, depending on the deadlines your colleges set. In fact, some of the colleges that require the PROFILE will ask you to submit it before you submit your FAFSA. This is especially likely if you're applying early decision or early action for admission to the college. If a college requires the PROFILE before January 1, you can submit a PROFILE with estimated income figures for this year based on your year-to-date pay stubs and your previous year's tax return, then send corrections to the college later if necessary.

Even if college deadlines don't require the PROFILE first, it may save you time to complete it before the FAFSA. The PROFILE collects all the information asked for by the FAFSA, and when you complete the application, PROFILE

GOOD TO KNOW

Help is available to get you through the PROFILE application. If you're not sure about how to answer any question, **check the online Help Desk** that's built into the online application. If you can't find an answer to your question there, contact the PROFILE help line, either by e-mail (**help@cssprofile.org**) or by phone (**305 829-9793**; TTD 800 915-9990). From October to April, PROFILE customer service hours are Monday through Friday, 8 a.m. to 10 p.m. Eastern Time.

You can also contact the financial aid office at the college to which you're applying. In addition, your high school counselor may be able to answer your questions.

will generate a worksheet that you can print out and use to complete the FAFSA.

Preparing for the PROFILE

You can get ready to complete the PROFILE with the Preapplication Worksheet, available from the PROFILE site at collegeboard.com. (The worksheet is customized for you after you have registered.) You can also download and print out the PROFILE Registration Guide and Application Instructions from the same site. All of these materials are available in both English and Spanish.

The Preapplication Worksheet can save you a lot of time by helping you gather all your necessary family financial information before starting the application. Filling it out on paper can also speed your way if you have to file the application on a computer where your log-in time is limited, such as at school or a library.

Whether you're filling out the Preapplication Worksheet or the PROFILE itself, you'll need to gather more records to fill out the PROFILE than you will for the FAFSA. For example, in addition to asking about your parents' income for the year before you plan to enter college, the PROFILE asks about their income the year before that, as well as their projected income in the year to come. There are also questions about your projected summer and school-year earnings during your first year in college. The purpose of this is to give financial aid officers a better idea of whether last year's income was typical or unusually low or high. But it also means that you must collect more documents, such as tax returns for the prior year, and you'll need to estimate future income.

Documents You'll Need Before You Fill Out Your PROFILE

It's a good idea to gather the necessary records before you start and have them handy as you work on the PROFILE. You'll need records for both yourself and your parents.

- ✔ U.S. income tax return for the year before you start college, if completed, or pay stubs and other income-related records for estimates
- ✔ U.S. income tax return for the year before that
- ✔ W-2 forms and other records of money earned the year before you start college
- ✔ Records of untaxed income for those two years
- ✔ Current bank statements and mortgage information
- ✔ Records of stocks, bonds, trusts, and other investments

As with the FAFSA, it's easiest if you've already completed your tax return for the most recent tax year before you start filling out the PROFILE. But don't let that hold you up. Estimate your tax return information if you haven't completed your return by the time you need to file the PROFILE. (There are tools on the PROFILE site to help you and your parents estimate this information.) You can correct PROFILE information, if necessary, directly with the colleges after filing your return.

How to Register/File on the Web

Just like registering ahead of time for a FAFSA PIN, **it's best to register for the PROFILE well before the first college's deadline.** Since the PROFILE is entirely Web based, you do this online at www.collegeboard.com. You'll need to create a collegeboard.com account (with a username and password) before you can file; setting up the account is free. (If you previously registered online for the SAT, you already have this account: it's the same one you used then.) If you don't have Internet access at home, ask your school counselor or librarian if you can use one of the school's computers.

It's smart to register for PROFILE as soon as you're sure about where you'll be applying for aid, but in any case at least one week before the earliest financial aid filing date you need to meet. Registrations are accepted beginning October 1 of the year before you intend to start college. Once you register, you can either complete your application then and there or return to it at a later time. Your PROFILE application will be customized to your circumstances based on the information you give when you register.

Most families will have to pay a fee of $25 to have their PROFILE sent to one college, plus $16 for each additional college. The fee can be paid with most major credit cards, some bank debit cards, or by an electronic withdrawal from your checking account. Low-income families applying for the first time may qualify for a fee waiver (see sidebar).

Registration will involve providing some preliminary information such as your date of birth; mailing address; the year in school for which you're seeking aid; whether you are a U.S. citizen, a veteran, or an orphan; whether you have dependents or have separated or divorced parents; and whether your parents own a home, or all or part of a business or farm. The questions usually won't involve looking up documents; just answer them straightforwardly. Some of them (such as the questions about date of birth and being a veteran) are intended to clarify whether you're a dependent or independent student.

GOOD TO KNOW

If your family's income and assets are very low, and you are applying for financial aid for the first time, **you may be eligible for a fee waiver** covering registration costs and up to six school reports. Whether you qualify will be determined based on the information that you provide in the PROFILE form itself. **You will automatically get the fee waiver if you qualify**—you don't have to apply for it separately.

Figure 11:

Finding a College's CSS code

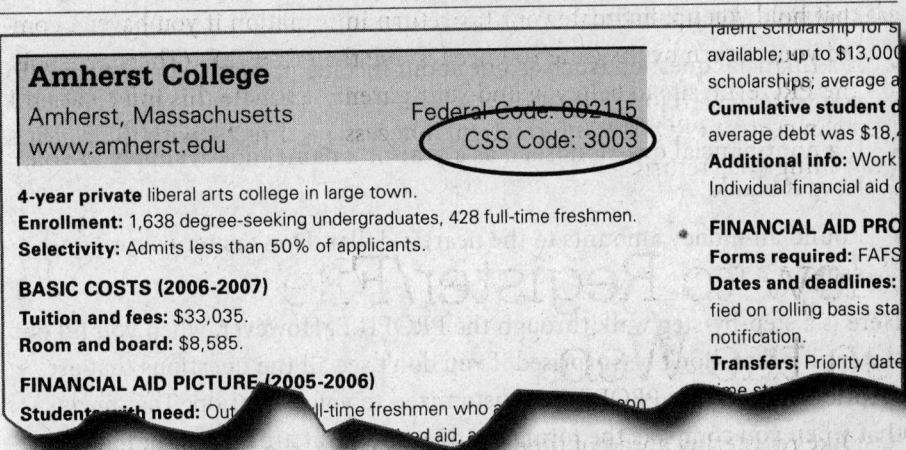

The College Scholarship Service® (CSS®) Code for each college in Part III of this book can be found in its college description.

During registration you will also be asked a few very basic questions about your family's finances; these determine whether you will be asked certain questions that usually don't apply to low-income families. For example, if your parents rent their house, they won't be asked about home equity in The Parents Assets section.

You will also have to select the colleges or scholarship programs to which you would like to have your PROFILE report sent. You'll need to give their CSS codes, which you can find in Part III of this book, the PROFILE Registration Guide, or on collegeboard.com. You can add more colleges to this list after you register, or even after filing your application (*see "After Submitting Your PROFILE" on page 66*).

Let's Walk Through It

The PROFILE application has 15 sections. The application includes questions about you and your finances and questions about your parents and their finances. There is a place for you to explain in writing any special financial circumstances (section ES) and a place for any additional questions that may be required by one or more of the schools to which you're applying (section SQ). In addition, if your parents are divorced or separated, your noncustodial parent might need to complete an online Noncustodial PROFILE. If your family owns a business or farm, they might need to fill out a Business/Farm Supplement. That supplement cannot be filed online; the form has to be downloaded, printed, and mailed in.

To help you fill out the PROFILE, there are instructions online that you can follow, along with other avenues for help (see sidebar on page 57). A few general points to keep in mind:

- If a financial question (such as one about income or assets) doesn't apply to you, enter a zero (0).

- If a nonfinancial question (such as a year or a name) doesn't apply to you, leave it blank.

- Round all money amounts to the nearest dollar. Don't enter commas or cents.

Here is a step-by-step walk through the PROFILE. However, when you fill out the application, don't be surprised if you don't see all the questions that are mentioned here. The PROFILE is customized to your situation. That means that when you complete the form, any questions that are known not to apply to you won't even be presented. For example, if your parents are married, you won't be shown any questions that assume you have a noncustodial parent.

Section SD: Student's Data

This is the beginning of the part of PROFILE that focuses on you, the student applying for aid. In Section A, you provide some basic information about yourself. Much like on the FAFSA, you'll be asked to name your current legal state of residence, which may not be the same as the state you're actually living in now (see page 47).

If you're an independent student, you'll be asked about your spouse, children, and any other dependents. These questions are asked because you may have greater financial need if other people depend on you for financial support.

Section SI: Student's Income and Benefits for the Previous Year

This section asks about your income and benefits in the year before you intend to start college.

If you have a completed tax return for that year, this section is mostly a matter of copying the amounts from the correct lines, such as the adjusted gross income and income tax paid. If you haven't filed a return but plan to do so later, you'll have to fill in estimates. If you don't plan to file a return but you did make some money last year, you'll have to report it. Untaxed income and benefits, such as Social Security benefits, also go in this section. A worksheet is available for you to tally it up.

Section SR: Student's Expected Summer/School-Year Resources for the Coming School Year

Here you're asked to state your expected resources for this coming summer and this coming school year. You're also asked about scholarships you expect to get from sources other than the colleges to which you're applying and how much money your parents think they'll be able to pay for your college expenses.

This may seem like a strange series of questions, especially if you don't know yet where you'll be going to college next year, or where (even if) you'll be working. But colleges that use the PROFILE want to have as clear a picture as possible of your future resources, not just your past ones. For example, if you currently have an after-school job but will leave that job when you graduate, the financial aid offices need to know that the income from that job won't be available to you anymore once you've started college.

Do the best you can to estimate these figures. If you're not sure how to answer in your particular case, check the PROFILE help online or contact the financial aid office at the college to which you're applying.

Section SA: Student's Assets

This section asks about your assets—the money or property you, the student, currently own. These too affect your ability to pay for college. You need to list any cash you have and any checking or savings accounts in your name. Give their value as of the day you're filling out the application. You should also include any investments, such as certificates of deposit, savings bonds, stocks, or real estate that you own. If you have any Individual Retirement Accounts (IRAs) or other tax-advantaged retirement accounts, you should also list them here.

If you're an independent student, then any money you have in 529 prepaid tuition or college savings plans or Coverdell savings accounts should be included here. If you're a dependent, those will be considered your parents' assets, and the information about them should go in Section PA.

This section will also ask you to answer questions about any trust accounts your parents or other relatives may have established for you. A trust account is money that is held for you by somebody else until you reach a certain age, at which point it becomes yours. Colleges want to know about this because if you have a trust, that money will eventually reach your hands, lowering your ultimate financial need. If you have any trust accounts, list their value here and answer the questions about them. But don't include money in Section 529 prepaid tuition plans; those aren't the same as trusts.

Section SE: Student's Expenses for the Previous Year

You only need to answer these questions if you're an independent student. If so, you'll be asked about any child support you or your spouse paid to a former spouse and any medical and dental expenses you had last year that weren't covered by insurance. Most colleges will consider these expenses in determining your financial need.

Section PD: Parents' Data

Now the PROFILE application switches its focus from you, the student, to your parents. The term "parents" as PROFILE understands it might need some defining. It basically means your custodial parents, the people with whom you live. If both your parents are living, married to each other, and have custody of you, answer the questions about both of them. But if that isn't the case, follow these rules:

- If your birth or adoptive parents are divorced, separated, or were never married, then you only need to provide information about the parent with whom you live. If you lived with both equally in the past 12 months, answer the questions about the parent who provided most of your financial support.

- If you have a widowed or single parent or a legal guardian, answer the questions only about that person.

- If your parent (as defined above) has married or remarried, include information about your stepparent too.

Your parents should use this section to provide information about themselves, including name, date of birth, employment status, and whether they themselves are in college or graduate school. Some of these questions have to do with clarifying financial strength—for example, the question about what kind of retirement plans your parents have. Some are just matters of housekeeping, such as their preferred daytime telephone number in case they need to be contacted.

Section PF: Parents' Household Information

Here your parents give basic information about their household, such as how many members are in their household and how many of them will be in college. The more dependents your parents have, and the more college educations they have to pay for, the less they will be expected to contribute to your own college education.

Section FM: Dependent Family Member Listing

This section asks questions about dependent members of your household other than your parents. If you're an independent student, the household in question here is the one you described in Section SD; if you're a dependent, it's your parents' household as described in Section PD.

The questions in Section FM ask for more information about these household members: their names, how they're related to you, their ages, and to what extent you or your parents are required to pay for their school or college education last year and next year. The reason for these questions is that if household members other than you are enrolled in college, and your family is paying heavily to fund those educations, the colleges will take this into account when they determine the expected family contribution (EFC) to your own education. If there are younger children in the family, the colleges will assume that a certain portion of the household's income and assets need to be saved for their college educations, which will also affect your EFC.

Section PI: Parents' Income and Benefits for the Previous Year

In this section, your parents report their income and benefits for the year before you intend to start college. Just as with the section about your income, this is important in establishing the resources they have available to pay for college.

If your parents have a completed tax return, filling in this section is mostly a matter of copying from the right lines. If they haven't filed a return but will do so later, they'll need to estimate the amounts. If they don't plan to file a return, they still have to report income. Again they have to list untaxed income and benefits, such as Social Security benefits, child support, or the earned income credit.

Section PP: Parents' Income and Benefits for the Year Before Last

Here your parents are asked to give information about income and benefits not for the year before you intend to start college, but the year before that year. Together with sections PI and PF, this is meant to give the PROFILE colleges a long-term view of your family's finances in order to clarify whether or not last year was typical. This section is fairly easy to fill out: for most of the questions—e.g., adjusted gross income, income taxes, and itemized deductions—your family has only to look up their tax return for that year. You also have to calculate any untaxed income and benefits, using a worksheet that's provided.

Section PF: Parents' Expected Income and Benefits for This Year

Here your parents have to estimate how much they expect to receive in income and benefits during the year in which you start college. Again, the idea is to establish as clear a picture as possible about your family's finances in the long term, and to show whether the year before you started college was typical or not. Your parents will have to estimate work income, other taxable income, and untaxed income and benefits. In Section ES, explain any unusual increases or decreases in income and benefits (10 percent or more) from last year.

Section PA: Parents' Assets

This section asks about your parents' assets because these are resources that can help them finance college. There are questions about cash and savings and checking accounts (with their value as of the day you fill out the form). If they own their home, there are questions about home equity, the difference between the current market value of their home and the outstanding mortgage debt.

There are also questions about the current market value of any other assets they own, including investments, businesses, farms, other real estate, and the value of any of their retirement accounts, such as IRAs, 401(k)s, or 403(b)s. They also need to include educational savings accounts, such as 529 prepaid tuition or college savings plans or Coverdell savings accounts that they've opened for you or one of your siblings.

Section PE: Parents' Expenses

This section asks about certain special expenses your parents might have. These are not just any expenses, such as grocery bills or vacation airfare, but specific costs that might legitimately affect their ability to pay for college. Included here are child support payments, certain educational costs, and medical and dental expenses not covered by insurance.

Section NP: Information About a Noncustodial Parent

If your parents are divorced or separated, this section asks for information about the parent who doesn't have custody of you. But it should be filled out by your custodial parent. If for any reason you can't get sufficient information about the noncustodial parent, explain why in Section ES. Many colleges want this information because they believe it is the responsibility of both your biological or adoptive parents to pay for your college costs, even if they no longer live together, and even if the parent who does have custody of you has remarried. That's why, after you've filled out this section and submitted your PROFILE, they may request that your noncustodial parent fill out a supplemental form, the Noncustodial PROFILE (*see "After Submitting Your PROFILE" on page 66*). The section you're filling out here is not that supplemental form; your noncustodial parent will fill out that form if it's required.

Section ES: Explanations/ Special Circumstances

This is the one free-form part of the PROFILE, where you write rather than fill in boxes. This section gives you a chance to explain anything unusual in your application or any special circumstances that affect your family's ability to pay for college. You can mention, for example, reasons for unusually high medical or dental expenses, steep rises or falls in income from year to year, or loss of employment. You should also give information about any outside scholarships you've been awarded. This allows the PROFILE colleges to better understand your financial picture.

In addition to telling the colleges about anything you think it's important that they know about, you should also use this section to expand on your answers to certain questions in previous sections, per the instructions that you'll find on the PROFILE Web site. For example, if there are more than six dependent members of your household, you won't be able to list them all in section FM. The instructions will tell you to list the additional members here.

You're limited to 27 lines of information in this section. If you need more space, send the information on paper directly to your colleges, including your name and Social Security number on all correspondence. (**See Step 8 for tips on how to let your college know about your special circumstances.**)

Section CF: College Financing

This section gives your parents the opportunity to have the College Board evaluate their credit record and let them know if they're preapproved for a College Board–sponsored PLUS loan, a type of federal loan that is not subsidized and is taken out in the parents' name. If your parents don't want to authorize the College Board to make this evaluation, just say no: this section is entirely optional. If they do authorize it, it doesn't commit your parents to taking out a PLUS loan from the College Board (or anyone else). All they'll get is information about their eligibility for such a loan. The fact that your parents have expressed interest in a PLUS loan—or any other information from this section of the PROFILE, for that matter—is not shared with the colleges to which you're applying, and will not affect your eligibility for need-based financial aid.

Section SQ: Supplemental Information

Section SQ may not be included in your application. You will only see it if one or more of the colleges to which you're applying requires more information. In that case, you'll see additional questions here. Your answers to these questions will be used only by the colleges that ask for them. Some of the questions colleges ask here are used to determine your eligibility for purely need-based financial aid; others are used to determine if you're eligible for scholarships that have non-need-based criteria.

Here are some examples of the types of questions you might see:

- What is the year, make, and model of the family's primary car?
- Do you or either of your parents receive free food or housing as a job benefit?
- What is your family's religious denomination? (This information will be used to determine scholarship eligibility.)
- What field of study do you plan to major in?

After Submitting Your PROFILE

After you complete your PROFILE, you'll receive an online PROFILE acknowledgment that confirms the colleges to which you're sending the information and gives you the opportunity to correct any data you submitted. You should print the acknowledgment, which includes the list of colleges and the data you entered on the form. Once you submit your PROFILE, you can't revise your information online. Use the printed acknowledgment to make changes, if necessary, to the PROFILE information, and send those corrections directly to your colleges.

The College Board analyzes your data and reports it to the colleges to which you're applying. The schools then apply their own institutional policies to figure out your expected family contribution (EFC). From this analysis, they determine how great your need is and how much institutional financial aid to give you.

SENDING YOUR PROFILE TO ADDITIONAL COLLEGES

You can delete colleges from your list of schools only before you submit the application. After that, all the listed colleges will get your information. But you can add colleges whenever you want, even after you submit the application. Just go to the PROFILE Web site and click on "Add Colleges to Submitted Application." The fee is $16 for each additional college or program to which you want your information sent.

When you add additional colleges, you will also be given the opportunity to update or correct any of the information on your original application. Please note, however, that this new information will only be sent to the colleges

GOOD TO KNOW

If only one of your birth parents has custody of you, your college may still require information from both parents. If that happens, the main PROFILE application collects information from one parent, and the **Noncustodial PROFILE** collects information from the other. After the information is processed, the college will complete the EFC calculation. How to divide up payment of the EFC among you and your parents is a family decision.

you're adding. You should directly contact the colleges to which you submitted your original application to update your information with them.

SUPPLEMENTAL PROFILE FORMS

Some colleges require supplemental information that's not on the main PROFILE application. For example, one college might require information about a farm or small business owned by your parents, while another might not. If that happens, the PROFILE Web site will instruct you during the registration process to download the Business/Farm Supplement form, print it, fill it out, and send it to the college that wants it. Or a college may require a Noncustodial PROFILE if you don't live with both of your birth parents. When you register for the PROFILE and indicate that your biological or adoptive parents are not married, you will receive an e-mail with instructions, a temporary password, and a link to forward to your noncustodial parent for him or her to complete. This form can be completed only by the noncustodial parent.

Don't be surprised, then, if after you submit the PROFILE you get a follow-up message instructing you to fill out a supplemental form. Don't panic, either: this is not an audit, but a normal part of the process that sometimes happens. However, be aware that these follow-ups take additional time. All the more reason to leave yourself plenty of time to file the PROFILE before your college financial aid deadlines.

QUICK RECAP

Since the PROFILE form is customized, the application may not necessarily be the same length as the FAFSA. In some cases the PROFILE will contain more questions than the FAFSA and in some cases it will contain fewer. The main difference is that it tries to get a more complete picture of your family's finances. A few points to keep in mind:

- File early.
- The PROFILE is online only, so you have to submit it on a computer.
- Prepare by using the Preapplication Worksheet.
- There are fees, but students from low-income families may qualify for a fee waiver.
- After you submit your PROFILE, you'll get an online acknowledgment confirming that you submitted it. To make corrections to your information, you should write your colleges directly.
- Depending on your circumstances, you or one of your parents may have to submit a supplemental form to one or more of your colleges.

Step 7: Fill Out Any Other Required Forms

QUICK OVERVIEW

The FAFSA and PROFILE are the big ones, but don't forget to file any other forms that may be required by your state or by the colleges to which you're applying. You don't want to have your application for financial aid marked "incomplete" because you didn't file a one-page form. These forms can vary widely from college to college, and from state to state.

Some Colleges Have Their Own Financial Aid Application

Some colleges have their own forms that you have to submit in addition to the FAFSA and the PROFILE. A purpose of the form may be to get more information about your finances, or to find out if you're a member of a particular group that is eligible for a special scholarship or grant. If a college requires such a form from all first-time applicants, its description in Part III of the book will say "institutional form required" under the "application procedures" section. Contact the financial aid office at your colleges to find out more.

The good news is that these forms are generally not long or complicated—they are usually just a page or two in length. They manage to stay short because they are intended not to duplicate the FAFSA or PROFILE forms but to supplement them and help the financial aid office keep track of applications. Such a "one pager" might, for example, ask for basic identifying information, some demographic facts, and whether you are interested in loans and work-study. This kind of form is typical at community colleges and most four-year public colleges. "It's almost like an update form," Mary San Agustin says of the institutional form currently in use at her institution, Palomar College. "It's basically just a supplemental form in case any changes occurred since the time the student applied for admission or completed the FAFSA."

Sometimes a college might require a longer form that asks questions about your finances that are about as broad and deep as the FAFSA or PROFILE. Usually this only happens with colleges that use their own formulas to calculate need, but choose not to use the PROFILE to help them with it.

Another reason a college might require its own financial aid form is if it requires every student to have a computer on campus. Such schools sometimes have a supplemental form that qualifies needy applicants for a stipend to buy a computer, or places them in a "loaner" program so they can borrow one. The University of Virginia has two forms that deal with computers. One form is for its "laptop loaner" program, and a different form is for a "one-time computer expense" that allows students who want to buy a laptop to add the purchase price to their cost of attendance; that way their aid package may cover the cost.

Still another kind of institutional form is one for early-decision applicants. Such a form works as a sort of "pre-read" meant to help students get an early estimate of their expected family contribution and the financial aid package they will receive if they accept an early-decision offer. (The rules of early decision require them to accept the offer if the college offers enough financial aid for them to attend.) Some schools offer a similar pre-read form for student athletes who are being recruited by a coach.

Scholarship and Grant Forms

Some colleges require a separate form for students applying for merit scholarships. This isn't always the case: at many schools, every student who applies for admission is automatically considered for merit scholarships. But at some schools, you must file a separate application for merit scholarships. The rules may even differ from department to department, depending on your major. "Theater majors may have to audition," says Bonnie Lee Behm of Villanova University. "Or a film major may need to send in a tape." Contact the financial aid office at your colleges for more details, and check with the department in which you're interested in majoring.

Some institutional forms ask questions to find out if you qualify for financial aid funds set aside for students with particular characteristics. For example, the college might offer grants that are only available to children of alumni or descendants of the town's founding families. At most colleges, these grants are part of the need-based aid program, so you have to demonstrate need through the FAFSA along with proving you have the right characteristics for the grant.

Verification of Your Tax Return

Some colleges require you to send copies of your family's federal or state tax returns. They may tell you to mail them with your initial application, or they may require them for only a few applicants who have been selected for verification.

"Verification" doesn't mean that you did something wrong. It's not like an IRS audit, where only suspicious tax returns are selected for special scrutiny. Since colleges disburse federal money—in the form of grants, work-study, and loans—they are required by law to check the information that a certain percentage of financial aid applicants has submitted. Some colleges exceed this minimum requirement and, for the sake of safety and fairness, verify all applications.

If you are selected for verification by one or more colleges, you'll have to submit tax documents: for example, the 1040 and any attached schedules, along with the W-2s or 1099s you received from employers and banks. Usually you'll also have to fill out a form that allows colleges to confirm details, like how many of your siblings are enrolled in college. The college may ask you to send your documents directly to the financial aid office, or it might ask you to send them to the College Board's Institutional Documentation (IDOC™) service.

Some colleges will request verification if the data you submitted on the FAFSA looks unusual. As an extreme example, people who reported that they had no income last year may be asked how they supported themselves.

State Forms

Most states rely on the FAFSA to award their need-based grants and loans to students. But a few states have their own financial aid forms. For example, New York State has an application for its Tuition Assistance Program (TAP) that is sent to eligible students who submit a FAFSA. See Table 2 on the next page for a list of states that require their own forms; the list gives the name of each form and the program's Web site and mailing address.

Even though the thought of filling out yet another form may seem burdensome, and you feel sure that you won't qualify for the state aid program, fill it out. If you don't, your application might be marked "incomplete" at your colleges. These state forms are usually short and don't take long to fill out, especially once you do the prep work of filling out the FAFSA. **When you file the FAFSA online, you'll be automatically directed to your state's form.** (If you file the FAFSA paper form, you'll usually have to send away for a paper copy of your state form.)

Table 2:
State Aid Deadlines

STATE	FORM(S) REQUIRED	DEADLINE	NOTES
Alaska	FAFSA	4/15	
Arizona	FAFSA	6/30	
Arkansas	FAFSA	6/1	Higher Education Opportunity Grant Academic Challenge awards
California	FAFSA, state form	3/2	Initial awards
		9/2	Additional community college awards
Delaware	FAFSA	4/15	
District of Columbia	FAFSA, DC form	6/30	
Florida	FAFSA	5/15	
Illinois	FAFSA	9/30	First-time applicants
		8/15	Continuing applicants
Indiana	FAFSA	3/10	
Iowa	FAFSA	7/1	
Kansas	FAFSA, state form	4/1	
Kentucky	FAFSA	3/15	
Louisiana	FAFSA	7/1	Closing date
Maine	FAFSA	5/1	
Maryland	FAFSA	3/1	
Massachusetts	FAFSA	5/1	
Michigan	FAFSA	3/1	
Minnesota	FAFSA	30 days after start of term	
Missouri	FAFSA	4/1	
Montana	FAFSA	3/1	
New Hampshire	FAFSA	5/1	
New Jersey	FAFSA	6/1	Tuition Aid Grant applicants
		10/1	All other applicants
		3/1	Spring-term applicants only
New York	FAFSA, state form	5/1	
North Carolina	FAFSA	3/15	
North Dakota	FAFSA	3/15	
Ohio	FAFSA	10/1	
Oklahoma	FAFSA	4/15	Priority date
Pennsylvania	FAFSA, state form	5/1	Degree program candidates
		8/1	Other applicants
Rhode Island	FAFSA	3/1	
South Carolina	FAFSA	6/30	
Tennessee	FAFSA	3/1	
West Virginia	FAFSA, state form	3/1	

Residents of states not listed in this table should contact their state aid office directly. See page 139 for a list of addresses, phone numbers, and Web sites for each state's aid office.

QUICK RECAP

In addition to the FAFSA and PROFILE, some states and colleges have financial aid forms of their own. Here's what to know about them:

- They're usually short.
- Their questions vary from school to school and from state to state.
- They may determine if you're eligible for special grants.
- They may help verify your financial information, perhaps through questions about your tax returns.
- If state aid is available, apply for it, or your colleges might consider your financial aid application incomplete.
- If one of your colleges requires an institutional application, fill it out, or you'll disqualify yourself from financial aid.

Step 8: Make Your Special Circumstances Known

QUICK OVERVIEW

If something in your family's financial life can't be explained on the financial aid forms, make sure your colleges know about it. These "special circumstances" may include a lost job, high medical expenses, or supporting an extended family. Colleges are willing to listen and, if you make your case, may be able to improve your financial aid package by taking those circumstances into account. This step is about how to prepare your case.

Be a Person, Not Just a Form

Sometimes the financial aid forms you fill out don't tell the whole story. They may not show that your family sends money every month to support relatives in another country. Since the forms are based on last year's tax forms, they may not reveal this year's events: how one of your parents just lost a job, or will be shifting from full-time to half-time work. When the forms don't adequately report a special circumstance that affects your family's ability to pay for college, let your college know—it may change how much financial aid you get!

Even if you're not sure your circumstance qualifies as special, speak up. The financial aid office will let you know whether it qualifies. Don't think you're limited to communicating with your college only through the financial aid forms. If there's any doubt in your mind about whether those forms give a true picture of your family's situation, feel free to go beyond the form and contact the financial aid office. **Be a person, not just a form**. There are two reasons to do this: it guarantees that the college knows how much you are able to pay, and it shows that you're interested in the college—which may affect the lengths to which they'll go to help you.

Using the Financial Aid Forms

In some cases, you can inform your colleges of special circumstances through the financial aid forms themselves—the FAFSA, PROFILE, and institutional forms (Steps 5, 6, and 7, respectively, of this book). If you're supporting children, if you've been in the military, or if your parents are divorced, your FAFSA form will make that clear. For colleges requiring PROFILE, you can use Section ES of that form to describe special financial circumstances. Elsewhere on the PROFILE form, you can list special family expenses, such as your family's medical and dental expenses, or any private school tuition that your parents might pay for your younger siblings. While forms may serve well enough, it may still be a good idea to write a letter or schedule a visit. If there's any doubt in your mind about whether forms convey your situation, definitely contact the college.

Going Beyond the Forms

You may have special circumstances that aren't covered by the forms. Or financially significant events may happen after you submit the forms—events that may be too complicated to explain in a simple correction. If that happens, communicate with the aid office as soon as possible after you realize you have special circumstances or after any financial hardships arise. The sooner you act, the sooner the college can adjust your award—and the more likely they are to still have the funds available to do so.

Even after you start college, if a financial emergency occurs, let the school know. The financial aid director can often help needy students with unusual expenses, such as medical costs, emergency trips home, or funding to allow them to take an unpaid internship in the summer instead of working for money.

How to Contact the College

A letter to the financial aid office explaining your circumstances is often the best way to state your case. Some schools have a form specifically for explaining special circumstances; it's worth asking your colleges what they prefer. The more closely you follow their procedures, the more likely you are to be heard.

No matter how you communicate with your college, be polite, clear, and specific. There's no need for a despairing or bullying tone. **Remember, you're trying to put a face to the form, so make it a friendly one**. You'll get further by calmly presenting your situation and giving as many relevant specifics as possible. A school will want to know not only that a parent got laid off, but what the prospects for reemployment might be, whether the parent has filed for unemployment benefits and, if so, the amount of the benefit payments awarded to the parent. Don't be surprised or offended if the college responds to you with a request for documentation, such as a copy of your tax return or a recent pay stub.

The Special Circumstances Form

Some colleges have a form through which you can let them know about special circumstances. At Rhodes College, it's called the Special Financial Circumstances Form, and it is available on the school's Web site. "The purpose of the form is not to make everybody jump through a hoop," says Forrest

Stuart, the director of financial aid at Rhodes. "It's to help the parents and the student put on paper all the information we need to help them out."

The form asks the student for the specific data—such as about changes in income and expenses—that the financial aid office will need to reach a decision about their case. It helps the school treat students equally, and it prevents the vagueness that might be found in a letter. "A lot of time we'll just get letters—I've lost my job, I need more aid," says Stuart. "Well, that doesn't tell me a whole lot. But if I can see some concrete information, then that gives me an idea of how I can help this student."

Communicating by Letter

With many schools, the best way to contact the aid office is in a letter. Often, it can strengthen your case to enclose photocopies of supporting documentation with the letter—for example, a paper showing your parent was laid off. The aid officer may also ask you for specific documentation.

After sending your letter, follow up with the financial aid office a week or two later to make sure they received it and to see if they have any questions. You can do this by e-mail or telephone. If you live close by, or have scheduled a campus visit, you should also visit the aid office, but call first to make an appointment.

E-Mail

Some colleges prefer to have you contact them by e-mail. At the University of Oregon, applicants can communicate their special financial circumstances through the school's Web site, where they can find an e-mail address for the financial aid office. "That way, they can do it whenever they think about it," says Elizabeth Bickford, the financial aid director.

Examples of Special Situations

Many circumstances can affect your family's ability to pay for college. They may include a change in your financial situation from what was reported in the financial aid forms, such as a lost job, emergency expenses, health problems, or even a windfall that misrepresents your usual level of income.

Family ties can also have financial implications, such as supporting an extended family or going through a divorce. And if you've served in the military, there are some special instructions you need to follow on the financial aid forms.

Change in Financial Situation

Financial aid officers want to know not only that your financial aid situation changed, but why it changed. Certain types of changes are more likely than others to persuade them to give you more financial aid. Generally, aid

---

EXPERT ADVICE

"**We must have documentation**, and what we really like too is a nice **letter explaining the situation**. But on top of that, we also like to have a phone call or, if the student's already on campus, to have them come in and talk to us. That way, we can have a **dialogue about the situation** and give them some direction on what to provide to us and how to provide it."

—*Vincent Amoroso, deputy director, Office of Scholarships and Student Aid, University of North Carolina, Chapel Hill* officers will look more kindly on circumstances that are beyond your control, rather than the result of poor planning. For example, if your father gets laid off because his company has fallen on hard times, that is more likely to get attention than if he retires early to spend more time golfing. And the college is more likely to turn a sympathetic eye to necessary roof repairs than a loan to install a backyard Jacuzzi.

LOST JOB OR LOST INCOME

If you or your parents had a job when you filled out the FAFSA, and now you don't, that will clearly affect your ability to pay. Even if you receive a severance package or collect unemployment benefits, your long-term ability to pay will still be reduced. This is information your financial aid office needs to know. For Palomar College, you would fill out a form that allows the financial aid office to override the FAFSA data with the new data. "You have to still report 2007," according to Palomar's Mary San Agustin, "but we override it with the current-year income."

Equally important are unusual changes in other sources of income besides wages and salaries. For example, suppose a student's mother becomes disabled in August and has to stop working, and her employer's disability insurance plan gives her a large percentage of her salary for the first six months (through February), but a much lower percentage afterward. The FAFSA will show a larger income than she will be receiving once the student arrives in college. This change in disability benefits, like a lost job, needs to be explained to the college.

EMERGENCY SAVINGS DRAWDOWN

An emergency may force your family to spend some of the savings that you reported on the financial aid forms. For example, suppose your house is damaged by a fire the day after you submit the FAFSA. Your family needs to spend a large amount of money to pay for the repairs. Depending on where the money comes from—regular savings, a retirement account, borrowing through a home-equity loan—this will have different effects on your need calculation. But no matter what the emergency or the source of the money you wind up spending is, you should tell the aid office.

Sometimes one crisis will have several different effects. Hurricane Katrina in 2005 might not only have destroyed an applicant's home in Louisiana, but put the family breadwinners temporarily out of work. In such a case, make sure the aid office knows about all the different effects on your financial situation.

HEALTH PROBLEMS

A serious health problem in your family can have financial as well as medical effects. It may involve both an emergency savings drawdown to pay for medical expenses, and loss of income if the patient is too sick to work. If someone in your family has recently become disabled, developed a chronic illness, or had major surgery, this has a clear impact on your family's ability to pay for college. Your college's financial aid office should be able to help.

GOOD TO KNOW

If you're explaining your special financial circumstances by letter, it's best to send it to the financial aid office via mail or fax, so that it can be **easily incorporated into your file**. Write and format it as a standard business letter. **Put your name and Social Security Number** in the first paragraph, so the financial aid office won't have trouble matching the letter to your file.

A letter, or the school's own "special circumstances" form (if they have one), is a good way to let a college know about your family's medical problem. But the financial aid forms provide some paths as well. The PROFILE form allows you to list medical expenses that weren't covered by insurance last year, and estimate the same for this year. You can also explain high medical expenses in the "Explanations/Special Circumstances" box (Section ES). The FAFSA, on the other hand doesn't ask specifically about medical expenses. If your college only uses the FAFSA, and you have unusually high medical expenses, a letter to the college makes sense.

WINDFALL

In financial terms, a windfall is a sum of money you didn't expect to get, which is normally a good thing—but even a windfall can have its downside. On your financial aid forms, if you received a windfall last year, that makes your annual income look higher than it normally is, which will tend to raise your expected family contribution (EFC).

Some windfalls are better than others. A windfall is usually understood as a genuine, one-time boost to your finances. It might be an inheritance from an aunt you never knew or an unusually high year-end bonus from your job. If you get such a windfall, inform the aid office that your income was higher than usual last year, and that they shouldn't expect a repeat performance next year.

But some windfalls not only make your annual income look bigger than it is, but represent an overall loss to your financial position. Examples include a severance package on losing your job, or an early withdrawal from a retirement plan, such as an IRA, to cover an emergency. In both situations, your records for that year show a boost in income, but that apparent good news conceals bad financial news—that you lost your job, in one case, and suffered a massive hit to your retirement savings in the other. If you experience this kind of windfall, explain the reality to your aid office.

Family Ties

Not every family has two parents married to each other. And some families have stronger ties to grandparents, uncles, aunts, and cousins than others. Different families live in different ways. The way your family lives may have financial implications that your financial aid office should recognize.

SUPPORTING EXTENDED FAMILY

The financial aid forms tell the colleges about how many people live in your household, including you, your parents, and your siblings. But many families give financial support to an extended family of relatives who live outside the household. Immigrant families, for example, often send money regularly to grandparents, aunts, or uncles in another country. Since that decreases the amount you have available to pay for college, make sure the financial aid office knows about it.

DIVORCED OR SEPARATED PARENTS

If your parents have divorced or separated, make sure the colleges know how that has affected your ability to pay. To do this, follow the rules on the financial aid forms. For the FAFSA, provide only the information on the parent you lived with more during the past 12 months (your custodial parent)—and, if that parent has remarried, your stepparent. For the PROFILE, provide not only that data but also information on your other parent, the one who does not have custody of you—your noncustodial parent. That information goes in Section NP of the PROFILE.

Some colleges that use PROFILE will also want your noncustodial parent to submit information separately on the Noncustodial PROFILE. That information will be confidential; you and your custodial parent won't be able to see the data the other parent provides, nor will that parent see yours. However, the information submitted by your noncustodial parent will affect the college's calculation of your total expected family contribution (EFC). If you don't think it will be possible to get your noncustodial parent to fill out the form, let the college know. However, the school isn't likely to waive its requirement for the form for anything less than a significant reason.

In the parent-income section of either the FAFSA or PROFILE, a custodial parent who is receiving alimony or child support payments should report only what he or she received, not what he or she was supposed to receive. In certain circumstances, documented evidence that your noncustodial parent is behind in payments could help support your case if you appeal your award.

Military Service

If you're currently serving in the active-duty military or the reserves, or if you are a veteran, don't assume that your military benefits alone will meet your full financial need. At most institutions, they no longer will. Benefits or not, you should apply for financial aid by submitting the FAFSA and any other required forms.

When filling out these forms, there are a few points to remember. Read the instructions carefully to make sure you qualify as a veteran for purposes of federal student aid. You should report housing allowances, subsistence allowances, and untaxed combat pay as income. But don't include veterans' education benefits or ROTC scholarships when answering the questions about your untaxed income. The colleges consider them outside resources to be reported separately. (*See Step 9 for more information on outside resources.*)

Veterans are as liable as anyone to the special situations discussed earlier, from lost jobs to medical crises. That includes windfalls. For example, if you received a lot of combat pay last year but have now been discharged and won't receive it again, you should explain that to the colleges.

For more information on the intricacies of how veterans' benefits affect the FAFSA, see the FinAid.org Web site at www.finaid.org/military.

If there are special circumstances that affect your ability to pay for college, let your college know.

QUICK RECAP

- Tell the college financial aid office as soon as you know about your special circumstances—either before you get your award or afterward.
- If you have to go beyond the forms, write a letter, e-mail, call, or visit.
- Explain your situation clearly, documenting it where appropriate.
- The situations that may affect your ability to pay range from a lost job or high medical bills to status as a veteran or an undocumented immigrant.

Step 9: Look for Scholarships

It's worth it to look for financial aid beyond what you'll get from colleges and federal student aid programs. This "outside money" probably won't amount to a "full ride," but it can help. Begin your search for outside scholarships around the time you start looking for a college because many scholarships have early deadlines.

Scholarships Colleges Give You vs. Scholarships You Get on Your Own

KNOW THE LINGO

Outside money—Grants and scholarships that come from sources other than colleges or the federal government, such as states and private organizations.

Portable money—Grants and scholarships that you can take with you to whichever college you attend.

College-offered money—Grants and scholarships that colleges award from their own funds.

Financial aid doesn't come only from the government and colleges. It also comes in the form of scholarships from outside sources, including states and private donors. This money doesn't come looking for you: you have to find the programs that fit you and apply. You will have to qualify for the scholarship in some way, whether through academic merit, artistic talent, or fitting some set of criteria, such as being a person of Japanese descent living in either Connecticut, New York, or New Jersey. **Very few outside scholarships offer anything close to full tuition, fees, room, and board**. But they're worth the search because every little bit helps.

The scholarships you can get from outside sources are not exactly like the scholarships you might get from your college. These are the basic facts to know about each type.

College-Offered Scholarships

In most cases, you don't have to apply separately for the scholarships that colleges award. You're automatically considered for them when you apply to the school. If you qualify, the college will include the scholarship in your financial aid package as they see fit. However, some colleges have merit-based scholarships for which you must apply separately.

To find out what the rules are for scholarship aid at your colleges, contact the schools or look at their Web sites, which usually describe the process for applying for scholarships under "admissions" and then under "financial aid." Be sure to do this research *before* you submit your application for admission. At some colleges, you have to indicate on your admissions application that you are applying for a special scholarship; for example, this is true of Boston University's Trustee Scholar Program. At others, you don't have to apply for special scholarships until after you've submitted your application for admission.

Many college merit scholarships have to be renewed from year to year. To make sure yours is renewed, know the school's criteria for keeping it—for example, maintaining a certain GPA. Different scholarships will have different criteria at each college.

Outside Scholarships: State Sources

Almost every state offers scholarships to their residents. These scholarships are usually available only for state residents attending colleges within the state, though a few states offer "portable" aid that a state resident can take to a college in another state.

Take the time to research scholarships and grants in your state. Almost every state has a department of education Web site that describes state scholarships and how to apply for them. These are usually separate from the state-sponsored, need-based financial aid programs that you apply for through the FAFSA or the state's own financial aid form, such as the Tuition Assistance Program (TAP) in New York State. An example of a state-sponsored, merit-based scholarship program with a separate application process is Florida's Merit Scholars Award, for which applicants must show high academic achievement.

Outside Scholarships: Private Sources

Private scholarships are offered by many sources, including foundations, corporations, civic groups, religious organizations, veterans' associations, and the military. The Society of Women Engineers offers the Bechtel Corporation Scholarship to high-achieving female students of engineering. United Methodist Scholarships are available to students who belong to that Christian denomination. The Senator George J. Mitchell Scholarship Research Institute offers awards to Maine residents studying in state.

Don't assume you have to be a genius to get a private scholarship. Although many scholarship programs consider academic merit, a range of conditions may qualify you for a scholarship, including interests, ethnic background, and community work. The Los Padres Foundation grants scholarships to low-income Latino students. California students pursuing a career in agriculture are eligible for a California Farm Bureau Scholarship.

Most scholarships come with limits. Though a few programs will pay full tuition, the amount of most awards is much smaller, as little as $500 or $1,000.

Many awards are limited to the freshman year of study. Fortunately, other scholarships are only for later years. The Bechtel Corporation Scholarship, for example, is just for women in their sophomore, junior, or senior year of study. And once you've declared a major you may find yourself eligible for a scholarship that is aimed only at students in your academic discipline.

Searching for Scholarships

Searching for private scholarships takes effort. But there are a number of Web-based scholarship search engines, like the ones on collegeboard.com and fastweb.com, that can help you zero in on scholarships for which you may qualify. If you like using this book, you might prefer to search for scholarships using the *College Board Scholarship Handbook*. It describes more than 2,100 outside scholarships, internships, and loan programs, and is indexed by eligibility requirements—such as minority status, religious affiliation, and state of residence—to help you match yourself to the programs.

Beware of commercial scholarship search companies that offer to help you find scholarships for a fee. Some do a responsible job, but many charge exorbitant fees and make fraudulent claims. For example, if they "guarantee" you a scholarship or promise to "do all the work for you," they are probably lying. Getting a scholarship is never guaranteed and, no matter what, you are going to have to do some work to apply.

Your school counselor may be of more help. Many private scholarships send application forms directly to school counselors. Tell your counselor in your junior year or early in your senior year that you are interested in applying for private scholarships.

Figure 12:

collegeboard.com's Scholarship Search

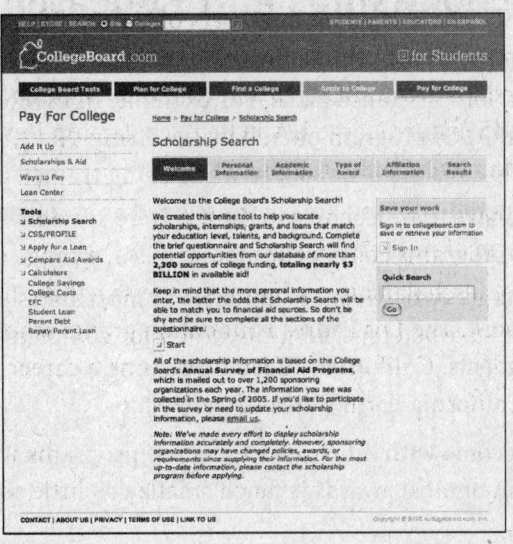

Start researching options as soon as possible. You'll need time to learn about scholarships, request information and application materials, and complete your application. Some programs, such as the Discover Card Tribute Award Scholarship Program (see sidebar on page 89), are looking only for students in their junior year of high school. Even if you're past that point, look as soon as you can—in the summer before your senior year, or by October or November of that year.

Look Locally

The national and state programs that you'll find on Web-based scholarship search engines and in print directories are good sources of scholarship aid. But don't forget to look even closer to home: your own county, city, town, employer, or church. When looking for scholarships, it pays to look locally.

The fact is, you are more likely to obtain a scholarship from a local organization than from a state or national one. On the local level, you will be competing with a smaller pool of applicants and are more likely to have characteristics that interest the donors. Again, your school counselor can help. The counseling office will have a file of local scholarships—from banks, the Kiwanis, the local garden club, and other groups. Let your counselor know you are looking for scholarships; stop by the counseling office regularly to read the scholarship files or check the scholarship bulletin board. The office may also use Internet announcements, e-mail postings, or newsletters to spread the word about scholarship programs to interested students.

Employers can also be a source of scholarship money. If you have a part-time job after school or a summer job, check to see if the company that employs you has a scholarship program or offers tuition assistance. For example, Chick-fil-A has a well-known scholarship program for its restaurant employees. Some companies provide their employees with a dependent tuition-assistance benefit. That means one of your parents might be able to get his or her employer to pay some of your tuition.

Military Scholarships and Education Benefits

In return for military service, the armed forces offer a variety of college scholarships and education-assistance plans. For example, in the Reserve Officer Training Corps (ROTC) program offered by the Army, Navy, and Air Force, you get scholarship assistance for college while being trained as a military officer. When you graduate, you are commissioned as an officer in the reserves and begin your term of military service.

Educational assistance for veterans is available in most states. If you're a veteran, contact your state veterans' administration for complete information and application forms.

Applying for Scholarships

Once you find the programs for which you qualify, you have to apply. This may mean not only another form to fill out, but compiling supporting documents, such as transcripts, recommendations, and an essay. Depending on the program, you may have to provide evidence of leadership, patriotism, depth of character, desire to serve, or financial need. Get to know the requirements of each scholarship as early as possible, so you can do any necessary extra work on time.

A few pointers to remember:

Apply early! Apply as early as possible to scholarship programs. If you can, do it in the fall of your senior year, even if the deadlines aren't until February or March. Very often, scholarship programs will have awarded all their funds for the year on a first-come, first-served basis before their stated deadline.

Follow directions. Read instructions carefully and do what they say. Scholarship programs receive hundreds and even thousands of applications. Don't lose out because of failure to submit a typewritten essay versus a handwritten one if required, or to provide appropriate recommendations. If you have a question about your eligibility for a particular scholarship or how to complete the application, contact the scholarship sponsors.

Be organized. It's a good idea to create a separate file for each scholarship and sort them by their due dates. Track application deadlines and requirements using Worksheet 2 (**a blank copy of this worksheet appears on page 122**). In one place, store the different supporting documents you may need, such as transcripts, standardized test scores, and letters of recommendation.

Check your work. Proofread your applications for spelling or grammatical errors, fill in all blanks, and make sure your handwriting is legible.

Keep copies of everything. If application materials get lost, having copies on file will make it easier to resend the application quickly.

Reapply. Some programs only offer money for the first year of college, but others can be renewed each subsequent year. If your program is one of them, it pays to reapply once you're in college.

SAMPLE WORKSHEET 2:
Scholarship Application Planner

	PROGRAM 1	PROGRAM 2	PROGRAM 3
PROGRAM/SPONSOR	National Merit Scholarship	Young Epidemiology Scholars	First Bank
ELIGIBILITY REQUIREMENTS	Academic merit	Academic merit	Need, local residency
TYPE OF AWARD	Scholarship	Scholarship	Internship
AMOUNT OF AWARD	$2,500	$1,000 or more	$2,500
CAN BE USED FOR	Tuition/fees	Any expense	Any expense
CAN BE USED AT	First-choice college	Any college	In-state colleges
DEADLINE	October 1 (give essay to English teacher for review)	February 1	April 1st
FORMS REQUIRED	NMSC application	Web form	Application (includes need analysis)
TEST SCORES REQUIRED	PSAT/NMSQT (already took), SAT (by December)	None	SAT
ESSAY OR ACADEMIC SAMPLE	Personal statement, academic transcript	Essay, research project	None required
RECOMMENDATIONS	Principal	None	One teacher (Mr. Filmer), Local branch manager
NOTIFICATION BEGINS	February	Not sure	May 15th
REQUIREMENTS TO KEEP AFTER FRESHMAN YEAR	One-time payment only	One-time payment only	Based on performance during internship

For a blank version of this worksheet that you can photocopy for your own use, see page 122.

How a Scholarship Can Affect Your Financial Aid Package

SCHOLARSHIP PROFILE

The **Discover Card Tribute Award Scholarship** is one example of the many sources of private scholarship aid. Run by Discover Financial Services, Inc., and the American Association of School Administrators, this national program issues up to 10 scholarships of $30,000 each. To be eligible, you must be a high school junior who demonstrates achievement in three of four areas: special talents, leadership, community service, and obstacles overcome. You also need a minimum cumulative GPA of 2.75 for the ninth and tenth grades.

If a college to which you're applying hasn't met your full need—that is, if there's a "gap" in your financial aid award—outside scholarships can be used to fill that gap. That will make the college much more affordable and give you more choices when it comes time to decide which college you want to attend.

If, on the other hand, a college is already meeting your full need, it works a little differently. It would be nice if your outside scholarship were added on top of all your other financial aid to make your total aid package even bigger. But it probably won't be. Following federal policy, your college will most likely count any outside scholarship or tuition assistance you receive as an "outside resource" that decreases your aid package dollar for dollar. So the total amount of your financial aid package will be exactly the same.

You might think this is unfair: this is money you found and, in the case of employer tuition assistance and veteran's benefits, money you earned. On the other hand, it is money that's available to pay for your education without your having to dip into your income and assets. The philosophy behind financial aid is that everyone should pay what they can out of income and assets (your expected family contribution, or EFC), and then financial aid, including any outside resources, makes up the difference. The only way you can pay less than your EFC is if you get so many outside scholarships that they exceed your financial need. This is highly unlikely.

However, **it is still worth getting outside scholarships**. For one thing, it increases your freedom to choose a college regardless of cost. "If I'm a student, the more money that I can bring to the table for myself, the better position I'm going to be in to exercise choices that I might want to make," says Vincent Amoroso of the University of North Carolina at Chapel Hill. For another thing, many colleges will use your outside scholarship money to reduce the self-help part of your aid package first—loans and work-study. This can significantly reduce the amount of money you'll owe after college or the time you'll need to spend working during college.

At some colleges, your outside scholarships will not be used to reduce your gift aid (grants and scholarships) unless the amount exceeds your self-help aid. Others use a formula in which at least a portion of your outside money will be used to decrease loans. For example, the first $500 in outside scholarships might be used to reduce your loans, then any funds remaining would be split 50/50 between reducing loans and cutting grants. Colleges that don't meet your full financial need may first apply outside scholarships toward filling the gap. Most colleges decide these issues on a case-by-case basis, but a few have stated policies that they publish on their financial aid Web page or will share with you if asked.

No matter what their policies, colleges welcome outside scholarships because they may reduce the amounts of college funds that have to be spent. Indeed, some schools encourage students to look for outside scholarships. According to Vincent Amoroso, the institutional financial aid form at his college asks students for data related to outside sources of financial aid, including global foundations, to "help us know [if] the student might match up to one of these other foundations that's awarding money."

In making admissions decisions, admissions offices are likely to look on outside scholarships favorably. Students who have searched for and found outside scholarships on their own will probably be seen as students with initiative and a sense of responsibility. That makes the student a stronger candidate for admission.

If you win a scholarship after you've already submitted your FAFSA and/or PROFILE, tell the colleges to which you've applied. Many schools have a special form specifically designed for you to submit this information. If you don't tell the colleges about a scholarship, it could jeopardize your eligibility for federal aid.

Tax Effects

Your outside scholarship may be taxed as income—this depends on the use for which it's designated by the program that awards the scholarship. Generally, scholarship dollars used for costs that are purely educational, such as tuition and fees, will be tax-free. But money used for living expenses, transportation, or books will be taxed as unearned income. The scholarship program will let you know how much (if any) of your award is taxable, and will send you a copy of the IRS's Form 1098 at the end of each tax year.

If your employer gives you tuition assistance, it's tax free up to $5,250 a year. After that amount, it's taxable. If you get tuition assistance from your parent's employer, the entire amount will be added to your parent's taxable income, but they might be able to deduct some of that amount (*see Table 7 on page 111 for more info*).

It takes work to hunt down and apply for outside scholarships, but it's worth it. Just remember:

- Outside scholarships will probably provide only a small part of the money you need for college, but every little bit helps.
- There are national and statewide scholarships programs, but look locally too.
- Web sites, books, and your school counselor can help you match outside scholarships to your qualifications.
- Search and apply early, and follow instructions.
- Your outside scholarship may affect the financial aid package awarded by your college, and it may be taxable as income.

QUICK RECAP

Step 10: Weigh the Offers

QUICK OVERVIEW

After you've submitted all the financial aid forms, you'll receive offers of financial aid from the colleges that have accepted you. This step will help you weigh these award letters and make an informed decision based on an "apples to apples" comparison of the packages. If an award leaves you with a larger out-of-pocket share than you think your family can handle, you can appeal.

Comparing Award Letters from Colleges

Sometime after a college accepts you for admission, it will send you a financial aid award letter. The letter will detail your award—the financial aid package the college is offering you. It will contain an outline of the expected costs you will incur during a year at the college, your expected family contribution (EFC) toward those costs, and the types and amounts of financial aid the college is offering to make up the difference between the costs and the EFC.

The letter will also contain instructions on how to accept the aid package and how to contact the aid office if you have any questions or want to appeal the award. Often, the award letter will come with a thick packet of supplementary documents, including promissory notes for any loans offered and information about work-study jobs, if you've been offered those.

It's best to wait until you have the award letters from all the different colleges that have accepted you before deciding which one to accept. If you have questions, wait until you've gotten answers from all the financial aid offices involved before you decide.

The offers in your award letters will differ. The amount and type of aid given will vary, and the letters may also differ in format, especially in how they itemize costs. In weighing the offers, the important thing is to compare apples to apples and not apples to oranges. For example, just because School A offers $10,000 in financial aid while School B only offers $8,000 doesn't necessarily

KNOW THE LINGO

Aid package—The total amount of all financial aid being offered to a student by a college.

Award letter—A document that a college sends to a student detailing the financial aid package. It indicates the type and amount of each scholarship, grant, loan, or work-study opportunity being offered.

Appeal—A request that a college reconsider its financial aid package.

PART I: FINANCIAL AID STEP BY STEP

Compare Your Awards

	COLLEGE 1	COLLEGE 2	COLLEGE 3
Step 1. List the name of each college you want to consider attending, the award deadline, and the total cost of attendance. This figure should be in your award letter. If not, refer to the college catalog or contact the college financial aid office.			
Name of college	*Private Univ.*	*Small College*	*Regional State*
Award deadline date	*5/1*	*5/1*	*4 weeks*
Total cost of attendance	*$31,825*	*$33,410*	*$15,566*
Step 2. List the financial aid awards each school is offering. Don't forget that grants, scholarships, and work-study do not have to be repaid, while all loans must be repaid.			
Grants and scholarships			
• Pell Grant (federal)			
• SEOG (federal)			
• State	*can't use*	*$2,000*	*$2,000*
• College	*$12,700*	*$13,785*	*$941*
• Other			
Total grants/scholarships	*$12,700*	*$15,785*	*$2,941*
Percentage of package that is grant/scholarship	*60%*	*74%*	*53%*
Work-study opportunities	*$2,000*	*$1,000*	
Loans			
• Stafford-Direct (federal)	*$2,625*	*$2,625*	*$2,625*
• Perkins (federal)	*$4,000*	*$2,000*	
• Other			
Total loans	*$6,625*	*$4,625*	*$2,625*
Percentage of package that is work or loans	*40%*	*26%*	*47%*
Total financial aid award	*$21,325*	*$21,410*	*$5,566*
Grants and scholarships + work-study + loans			
Step 3. Calculate what it will cost you to attend each college you are considering. For each college, enter the total cost of attendance. Then, subtract the total financial aid award from the total cost of attendance. That number is the net cost, or what it will cost you to attend that college.			
a) Total cost of attendance	*$31,825*	*$33,410*	*$15,566*
b) Total financial aid award	*$21,325*	*$21,410*	*$5,566*
c) Net cost to attend (a minus b)	*$10,500*	*$12,000*	*$10,000*

For a blank version of this worksheet that you can photocopy for your own use, see page 123.

EXPERT ADVICE

"It's **not simply the dollar amount of the grant or scholarship** that families should focus on. They need to **lay out, side by side, the full picture**. What's the cost of attendance, including out-of-pocket expenses? What's the family contribution? What are the elements of aid? What's going to happen with loans, with work?"

—Joe Paul Case, dean and director of financial aid, Amherst College, Amherst, Massachusetts

mean School A has the better deal. If School A's aid package has $3,000 in grants and $7,000 in loans, but School B has $6,000 in grants and $2,000 in loans, School B is offering you more free money (grants) than School A.

There is another reason why a financial aid package may not be as big as it seems: higher costs. If one school's costs are higher than another's, you may be left with a higher out-of-pocket expense even after subtracting a "bigger" aid package. **Don't be dazzled by a large award. Instead, look for the bottom line: your net cost to attend the school**.

Here's a true story to illustrate this further. **Two sample award letters appear in Part II** (see pages 124, 125). These were taken from actual letters received by a student. Only the names of the colleges involved have been changed, to "Blue University" and "Green University". The student's first-choice college was Blue U, which cost about $2,000 more than Green U. When she first compared the letters, she was very upset because it looked like Green U was giving her a much bigger scholarship, and much more total aid.

But her school counselor showed her that Blue U was actually offering the better deal. First of all, the grants and scholarship from Green U only looked bigger because they were presented as a total. Secondly, the student loans offered by Blue U (Stafford and Perkins) were subsidized, while the Stafford loan offered by Green U was not. That meant at Green U she would have to pay interest on the loan while she was in college. And third, the $14,810 Green U was "offering" as a parent PLUS loan wasn't really aid at all, but just an option for how her family could pay for their contribution. Bottom line, the true cost to her would be about the same at both colleges, even though Blue U is more expensive.

Collegeboard.com has an online "Compare Your Aid Awards" tool that lets you do this kind of side-by-side comparison of your awards. You can also use Worksheet 3 to break out the different components of costs and aid packages and compare them side by side (a blank copy of this worksheet appears on page 123). When doing this analysis, keep an eye out for both quantity and quality. On the quantity side, for example, the "Family Share of Costs" figure tells you the amount of money your family will be expected to contribute. Your family will need to decide whether this amount is affordable. Look especially for evidence of "gapping," the practice of leaving a gap between the cost of attendance and the money accounted for by aid and EFC. You will be expected to fill that gap—in effect increasing your EFC.

On the quality side, consider the figures for "% of Award That Is Gift Aid" and "% of Award That Is Loan." The higher the proportion of gift aid (grant or scholarships) to loans, the better the award.

Loans vs. Grants

All other things being equal, it's better to receive a grant or scholarship than a loan. For that reason, a financial aid package with a high percentage of gift aid is more attractive, on the face of it, than one with a high percentage of loans. But there are circumstances where you might take the award that offers more loans and less gift aid: for example, if that college is a better fit for you overall.

In any event, don't be surprised if your award includes loans. Most aid packages contain them. Loans are optional; you don't have to take them out. But if offered as part of a need-based aid package, they can be an excellent way to help finance your education. The alternative—taking only grant aid and trying to pay the costs that the loans would cover out-of-pocket—could put your family under much more financial stress than the loan would.

It's usually in your best interest to accept subsidized Stafford and Perkins loans that are part of the aid package: the repayment terms are good and the government pays the interest while you're in school. Unsubsidized loans—such as unsubsidized Stafford, PLUS loan, and private loans from a bank—should be studied more carefully to make sure the terms are acceptable. You should understand the specific terms of each loan, including its interest rate, the origination fee, the term of the loan, and the grace period before repayment begins. You should also realize that unsubsidized loans are not need based and are typically used to help your families pay their EFC. If a college offers them as part of your aid package, consider them as an option, but don't weigh them equally with subsidized loans in the package.

Work-study jobs are also optional, but if you're offered one and you can manage the time, take it. Having a job on campus brings in income, expands your social networks, allows you to make contacts with professors and administrators, and gives you experience that can improve your résumé.

Appealing Your Award

Even though your award letters are printed in black and white, they aren't necessarily the last word. It is possible to appeal the awards: to ask the colleges to reconsider their aid packages. There is no guarantee that they will grant your request, but there are circumstances where it's worth trying.

One reason you might appeal a package is if it has a lot of unsubsidized loans. However, bear in the mind that the college probably offered those loans because there wasn't enough gift aid to go around. Another reason to appeal is if you don't think you can afford the expected family contribution. You will need to have evidence to make that case. The college based its calculation of your EFC on the financial information you submitted. If you think this calculation was wrong, ask the financial aid office how it was made and see if you can find out if a mistake occurred. It will help if you have special circumstances that weren't communicated in your financial aid forms, such as a recent layoff; situations like this will clearly demonstrate why your family would have difficulty paying its EFC. (*See Step 8, "Make Your Special Circumstances Known."*)

"I've changed financial aid packages on appeal if somebody can demonstrate why they can't afford it," says Forrest Stuart of Rhodes College. "It may be the need analysis just didn't take some things into account. If they can show me where there's a real problem, even to the point where they show me their monthly

Questions to Ask About Your Award

These are some questions to ask your college financial aid office if you're awarded gift aid:

✔ What do I have to do to keep my scholarship—do I have to do anything more than maintain satisfactory academic progress?

✔ Is there a minimum GPA or other condition?

✔ Is the scholarship renewable in subsequent years?

✔ If I win an outside scholarship, what happens to my aid?

Questions to ask if you're awarded a loan:

✔ What are the terms of my loan?

✔ What is the interest rate, and when do I start repayment?

✔ How much will I owe by the time I graduate?

✔ What will my monthly repayment be?

✔ By how much will my loan increase after my first year?

Questions to ask if you're awarded work-study:

✔ Do I have a "guaranteed" job, or will I have to find one?

✔ How are jobs assigned?

✔ How many hours per week will I be expected to work?

✔ What is the hourly wage?

✔ How often will I be paid?

✔ Will I be paid directly, or will my student account get credited?

budget, I might say, 'Man, you are right. You've got these medical expenses or you've got this and that. Let me see if I can help you.' I am not perfect, and the need analysis is not perfect, and we'll sometimes overlook something."

Still another reason for appealing an award is if you have better offers from other colleges, and would like to see if this college can match them. Some aid offices will consider matching a better offer from another college. But most will only hear an appeal that's based on your family's financial circumstances. "We don't bargain," says Mike Scott of Texas Christian University. "We just don't want to play that game of, 'Well, we'll give you more money simply because another school gave you more money.'"

You might see the entire appeal process as essentially negotiation or bargaining—trying to get as much as possible from the school you'd like to attend. However, most financial aid officers loathe the term "negotiate." Your appeal will have a better chance of success if it appears not a matter of haggling but of providing information not previously available to the financial aid office.

It will also help your cause if you are obviously doing your part to fund your education. A student who accepts the self-help components of a school's financial aid package will be more likely to get extra help than one who declined them. "If the student is not willing to somehow contribute, either by working or taking out a student loan, then we are very unlikely to give them any extra money," says Mike Scott.

A phone call is a good way to start the appeal process, even though most colleges will want you to put your reasons for an appeal in writing. Some have a specific form for appeals; others would like for you to state your case in a letter. Find out the college's preferred procedure by calling or checking their Web site. No matter how you file your appeal, your case will be stronger if you can provide data to back it up. A few days after filing your appeal, follow up with a phone call or, if possible, by visiting the aid office. Within a short time, the college will let you know its decision.

If you receive a revised award, take the new award letter and compare it to your other aid packages. **It's best not to decide where to enroll until you've received the final offer from each college.** But keep in mind the deadline set by each college for acceptance of its award. If you miss the deadline, you could lose the package. If you do need more time, try asking the college for an extension.

Follow Up: Accepting an Award

Once you've compared all the awards and any appeals have been ruled upon, you and your family will have to decide on a college. Many factors, including costs and financial aid, will be in play. If your first-choice college has accepted you but not given as much aid as you'd hoped, the choice may be difficult. Do you go to your first-choice college even though it's a financial risk for your family, or to a second-choice college your family can safely afford? In the end, your own preferences should have the greatest weight. Most of the loan debt, payable after graduation, will be on your shoulders. And your personal happiness at the school will have a major influence on whether you graduate successfully. If your family can put together a sensible financial plan to pay the costs, the best choice is the one that fits you best academically and personally.

Once you've decided which offer to accept, it's polite to send a note declining the offers of the colleges you're rejecting. That way any funds they offered you can be made available to other students. As for the offer you're accepting, follow whatever instructions came in the award packet. If you're being asked for more information, send it. Complete any forms that came with the award letter. Sign the letter and return it by the due date.

EXPERT ADVICE

"I tell families **not to use the word 'negotiate.'** If an aid package is much lower than what's being offered by similar institutions, families should call and ask if there is additional information that may make a difference."

—*Carlene Riccelli, college adviser, Amherst Regional High School, Amherst, Massachusetts*

QUICK RECAP

When you receive your award letters from colleges, you'll have to decide which offer to accept.

- Compare apples to apples, analyzing the awards to see what the real costs and financial aid elements are.
- Just because loans are offered, you don't have to accept them. But they're worth considering, especially if they're subsidized loans.
- If you appeal an award, you'll be on stronger ground if you can demonstrate circumstances that weren't previously made clear to the school.
- Your decision about which offer to accept should be based not just on cost but on how well the college fits you academically, socially, and personally.

Step 11: Consider Your Out-of-Pocket Options

Financial aid is intended to cover the difference between your expected family contribution (EFC) and the total cost of college. However, you still have to pay your EFC and whatever gap there might be between the aid you received and your financial need. This step is about ways to meet those out-of-pocket costs.

Making Up the Difference

For almost every family, college is going to cost money. Even a generous financial aid package will usually leave you with some bills to pay. Some packages will meet less than your full need and leave you spending more than your EFC. You can afford to make up this difference between the total cost of attendance and the aid you're receiving if you take advantage of the various resources available to you. Most families use a combination of savings, current income, and loans to pay their out-of-pocket costs. You'll have to decide how to do that in a way that fits your own particular situation. But you'll have help, because there are a number of programs and strategies that can help you save, pay, or borrow for college.

KNOW THE LINGO

EFC (Expected Family Contribution)—How much money a family is expected to pay for college out-of-pocket, based on the family's ability to pay.

Need—The difference between your EFC and the cost of attending a particular college you've chosen. Financial aid is designed to meet your need, not your EFC.

Unmet need—The difference (if any) between your need and the financial aid offered by a particular college. Informally, unmet need is also called a **gap**.

Save for It

You shouldn't spend your entire family savings on college: you need to leave some for other uses, such as retirement and emergency medical costs. But it makes sense to use some of your savings for college.

Don't worry if your family doesn't already have a huge sum of money saved for college. **Every little bit helps, and it's never too late to start saving.** Even while you're applying to college, your family can start saving. Try to save as much as you can from summer and after-school jobs, and encourage your parents to set aside some money from every paycheck. Talk with your parents about how much money you and they already have saved for your college costs, and discuss how your family can afford the rest of the bill.

Don't believe anyone who says you shouldn't save for college because it will reduce your chances of getting financial aid. As noted in Step 2, savings are worth having so you can pay out-of-pocket costs without having to borrow. Very little, if any, of your parents' savings are counted against you when your financial need is determined. "Parents should not avoid saving because, frankly, a family that has saved has a resource to draw on, whereas a family that hasn't is totally dependent on current income and loans," says Joe Paul Case, dean and director of financial aid at Amherst College in Amherst, Massachusetts.

There are a number of places families can put their savings. The most traditional is a regular bank savings account, which pays a little interest and offers freedom to withdraw and deposit money at any time. A certificate of deposit (CD) has stricter rules about when you can withdraw money, but it usually pays higher interest than a savings account. Both of these options are good for short-term, flexible savings. But neither has any tax incentives—tax breaks that make them especially attractive for college savings.

The following savings vehicles do come with tax breaks. For more details, see Table 3 on page 100:

529 college savings plan. Also known as the QTP (Qualified Tuition Program), these are tax-advantaged accounts sponsored by the various states. Interest earned in these plans is not taxed as income, and some states also offer a state income-tax deduction for contributions their residents make to the state's plan. There are no income restrictions, and contribution limits are high. Grandparents, uncles, and aunts are also allowed to contribute to the plan, even if they don't live in the same state as you and your parents—in fact, you don't have to be a resident of a state to contribute to its plan, and you can withdraw funds from a state's plan to pay for expenses at a college in another state. Most plans offer a few different investment types, such as a fund that invests in stocks or one that invests in bonds.

Coverdell Education Savings Account. These tax-free trust or custodial accounts are similar to 529s, but they're sponsored by banks and brokerage houses instead of states, and therefore offer a greater range of investment choices. They can be used to pay private elementary and high school costs as well as college costs, unlike 529s, which can only be used for college costs. Total contributions for the student can't be more than $2,000 in a given year, and your family income has to be less than $110,000 (for single filers) or $220,000 (for joint filers). You can contribute to both a 529 and a Coverdell in the same year for the same student.

529 prepaid tuition plan. Like the 529 college savings plans, these are sponsored by the states, but they work differently. A 529 prepaid tuition plan lets a family make advance tuition payments years before their children will enter college. That allows them to "lock in" today's tuition rates instead of paying the higher rates likely to prevail years from now. Provided the student is admitted, the plans are guaranteed to be honored by public universities and some private colleges in the state that sponsors the plan. However, these plans have drawbacks. They can only be used for tuition and fees, not for room, board, or other supplemental costs. When that's combined with the fact that the tuition rates are only locked in for in-state colleges, most parents prefer the more flexible 529 savings plans.

Independent 529 prepaid tuition plan. This is a special 529 prepaid tuition plan sponsored by a group of private colleges and universities and administered by TIAA-CREF. For more information, visit www.independent529plan.org.

U.S. savings bonds. If your parents pay for some of your college costs by cashing in U.S. government savings bonds, the interest that has accumulated on the bond may be tax exempt. That means the interest won't be taxed as income and your tax bill will be smaller. There's a penalty if you cash in the bonds less than five years after the date of issue, and there are some restrictions on the tax exemption. The bond must be issued after 1989 and your parent must have been age 24 or older when the bond was issued. This deduction can't overlap with any other education tax break. You can't use two different tax breaks to pay for the same expense. The family income must be less than $78,100 (for single filers) or $124,700 (for joint filers).

Uniform Gifts to Minors Act (UGMA) or Uniform Transfers to Minors Act (UTMA) account. These accounts allow parents to put money in the child's name so it will receive preferential tax treatment. Much of the earnings are taxed at the child's rate rather than the parent's rate. Such accounts were popular in the 1980s, but the advent of tax-free 529s and Coverdells has made them nearly obsolete as a college-savings vehicle.

Individual Retirement Account (IRA). Generally, it's not a good idea to raid the family retirement funds, such as IRAs, to pay for college. "We tell parents all the time, you can borrow money to pay for your kid's education. You cannot borrow money to retire with," says Mike Scott of Texas Christian University. It's usually better to take out a PLUS loan than to diminish retirement assets. Still, if your family does need to go into an IRA to pay college expenses, the government doesn't charge the 10 percent additional tax you would ordinarily have to pay for breaking open an IRA before age 59½.

Table 3:
Comparison of Education Savings Options

	COVERDELL EDUCATION SAVINGS ACCOUNT	529 COLLEGE SAVINGS PLAN	529 PREPAID TUITION PLAN	U.S. GOVERNMENT SAVINGS BONDS	UNIFORM GIFTS TO MINORS ACT ACCOUNT	INDIVIDUAL RETIREMENT ACCOUNT
Tax advantages	Earnings in account not taxed as income	Earnings in account not taxed as income Some states allow residents to deduct contributions for state income tax purposes	Earnings in account not taxed as income Some states allow residents to deduct contributions for state income tax purposes	Interest earned is not taxed if used for qualified expenses	Interest earned is taxed at child's rate	Exception to the 10% early withdrawal penalty rule
Expenses that qualify	• Tuition & fees • Books & supplies • Room & board (if at least half-time) • Expenses for special needs services • K–12 education expenses	• Tuition & fees • Books & supplies • Room & board (if at least half-time)	Tuition & fees	• Tuition & fees • Contributions to a Coverdell or 529	Any expense (not limited to education)	• Tuition & fees • Books & supplies • Room & board (if at least half-time)
Contribution limits	$2,000 per year	None	None	None	None	$4,000 per year ($5,000 if over 50)
Income phaseout for benefits	$95,000–$110,000 (single filers) $190,000–$220,000 (joint filers)	None	None	$63,100–$78,100 (single filers) $94,700–$124,700 (joint filers)	None	Varies by type of account
Other limitations	Assets must be distributed by age 30 Must pay 10% penalty if distributions not used for qualified expenses	Must pay 10% penalty if distributions not used for qualified expenses	Benefits may only be used at colleges that participate in the plan Must pay 10% penalty if distributions not used for qualified expenses	Applies only to Series EE or Series I bonds issued after 1989 and purchased after owner turned 24	Counted as student asset for financial aid purposes	Interest earned will still be taxed at your regular rate

Work for It

Besides a summer job, you might also want to consider working during the school year to help meet expenses. There are two basic approaches. You can go to college full-time while working part-time, or you can hold a full-time job while attending college part-time.

Full-Time Student, Part-Time Job

If you're offered a work-study job as part of your financial aid package, the earnings from that job will go toward your college costs. Even if you're not offered work-study, you may still be able to find a part-time job on or near campus. You can also work during the summer to make money to put toward college.

Work has benefits beyond the extra income it generates. It can help you structure your time, which can make you a more disciplined student. Studies have shown that students who work part-time get better grades and are more likely to finish college than those who don't work at all. If the job is on campus, it enhances the college experience by connecting students more closely with the school and giving them a chance to meet people they wouldn't meet in classes.

On the other hand, don't work so many hours that you jeopardize your ability to get through college. **If you're going to college full-time, the recommended workload is about 10 to 15 hours a week**. If you work more than 20 hours a week, you're likely to get overloaded and put yourself at risk of dropping out. If you take fewer courses to make time for work, you may drop below full-time status, which could make you ineligible for many grants and scholarships. If your financial situation makes you feel that you have to work more hours, it might be better to borrow more money so you don't have to work so much.

Part-Time Student, Full-Time Job

A different (and much more difficult) way of approaching work is to be a full-time worker who goes to college part-time. This is possible as long as you don't take too many credits in one semester. If you try for more than six to eight credits (two courses) while working full-time, you'll probably have trouble getting everything done. On the other hand, if you take fewer than six credits a semester, you won't be eligible for need-based subsidized Stafford or Perkins loans or a Pell Grant.

Working full-time while going to school part-time is an especially attractive way to pay for an associate degree or a vocational certificate. Most community colleges cater to working students and offer classes at night to meet their needs. If you take six credits per semester, you can probably earn an associate degree in four or five years.

If you're planning on earning a bachelor's degree, however, you should strongly consider attending college full-time and borrowing money to replace the income that you won't be earning through a job. Why? If you take only six credits a semester, it will take ten years to earn a bachelor's! You will probably earn more money in the long run if you get that bachelor's in the usual four or five years, and concentrate on your career after you've earned that degree.

Some employers offer tuition assistance or scholarship money to employees who are attending college. Check to see if your employer is one of them. For a typical educational assistance program, up to $5,250 of those benefits will be tax free each year.

Co-op and Internship Programs

Many colleges sponsor internships or "co-op" (cooperative) programs with local employers. Some interns and almost all co-op participants receive payment from their employers along with academic credit. In co-op programs, you may be able to alternate periods of full-time work and full-time study. Often the business at which you intern end ups hiring you after graduation, or at least recommending you to others. Internship and co-op programs can help you make money, get academic credit, gain job experience, and make contacts with potential employers.

Promising to Work Later

Holding a job during college is not the only way of using work to pay your college costs. There are several programs that allow you to commit to work in public service after graduation in exchange for either a non-need-based scholarship while in college or a stipend that can be used to repay student loans after college. The ROTC program is an example of the former, and AmeriCorps is an example of the latter.

ROTC

In return for military service, the armed forces offer career training and a number of educational benefits to help pay for college, including full college scholarships and education assistance plans. If you're interested in training to be a military officer during college in return for educational benefits, check with the Reserve Officers Training Corps (ROTC) office at your high school or on your college campus. Each branch of the military offers ROTC training. Part IV of this book contains lists of colleges that offer ROTC programs for each service branch.

OTHER SERVICE PROGRAMS

AmeriCorps is a network of national service programs for which you can work as a volunteer, full- or part-time for up to a year. After completing a term of service with AmeriCorps, you're eligible for an education award, which can be used either to repay student loans or to pay for college tuition. The amount of the award depends on how long you worked for the program, and for how many hours each week. (Currently, completion of one year's full-time service earns an award of $4,725.) For more information, go to www.americorps.org.

Another type of program is one that hinges on your financial aid package and the profession you choose after college. If you received a Perkins loan as part of your package, the loan may be forgiven if you enter certain professions serving the public, such as teaching, nursing, or law enforcement.

Borrow It

To borrow money is to spend today what you'll earn in the future. You will have to pay the loan back, with interest, when you start earning money after college. A loan can be intimidating because it assumes you'll have the money for repayment, and you may not feel sure of that. But rest assured that college will increase your earning power, which will make it possible to repay your loans.

There are many forms of "bad debt" in our society, such as credit card debt, where you borrow money on unfavorable terms to buy consumer goods that will have little or no value in a year. By comparison, an education loan is a "good debt." You are borrowing money on favorable terms to achieve an outcome—higher lifetime earnings—that will more than pay back the loan.

Subsidized Stafford loans, Perkins loans, and need-based state loans all have excellent terms that make them worth considering. Some institutions also offer their own need-based loans to qualified students. However, these loans are intended as financial aid to cover your need. In general, you won't be able to use them towards your expected family contribution.

However, loans are available that are not based on need and that your family can use to borrow money to meet their EFC. The terms are not as favorable as the need-based loans, but the loans may be helpful just the same. The most common types are the unsubsidized Stafford and the PLUS loan, both of which are guaranteed by the federal government, but there are also state and private sources.

How Much Should You Borrow?

If your family decides to borrow money to pay for college, they should consider the total debt that you will carry after graduation. That total debt includes any subsidized, need-meeting loans that you accept as part of the college's aid package as well as any non-need-based loans your family takes out to meet the EFC. When you pay back that debt, you'll do so in the form of monthly payments, and those payments should be reasonable ones that you can afford to pay from the income you're likely to have. The total monthly payment will usually be similar to a car payment—$200 to $300 a month. But the amount will vary with the amount borrowed and interest rate offered. See Table 4 on the next page for help in determining what your monthly payment will be. It shows monthly repayment over 10 years for a loan of $10,000 at various interest rates. To calculate a monthly payment for a loan amount not listed on the table, multiply the amount borrowed by the repayment factor for your interest rate. For example, if you borrowed $12,500 at 7.5 percent, your monthly payment would be $148.46 ($12,500 × .0118770).

There are some ways to make your repayment burden lighter after college. Many lenders will offer to cut your interest rate a bit if you make your first 12 monthly payments on time. If you borrow from multiple federal loan programs, such as the Perkins, subsidized Stafford, and unsubsidized Stafford, you can consolidate these loans after graduation, which will simplify things by allowing you to make only one payment a month. Consolidation also gives you the option of "re-amortizing" your loans—that means stretching your payments over a longer period of time than you would normally have left to repay the debt. If you re-amortize when you consolidate, you will usually have a lower monthly payment, but will pay more interest over the total life of all the loans.

Table 4:

Calculating Your Monthly Loan Payment

AMOUNT OF LOAN	INTEREST RATE	REPAYMENT FACTOR	MONTHLY PAYMENT
$10,000	4.00%	.010125	$101.25
	4.50%	.010364	$103.64
	5.00%	.010607	$106.07
	5.50%	.010853	$108.53
	6.00%	.011102	$111.02
	6.50%	.011355	$113.55
	7.00%	.011611	$116.11
	7.50%	.011870	$118.70
	8.00%	.012133	$121.33
	8.50%	.012399	$123.99
	9.00%	.012668	$126.68

> **GOOD TO KNOW**
>
> When you start paying back your educational loan, remember that the **interest may be tax deductible**. To a maximum of $2,500 per year, you can deduct the interest you pay from your income, which will lower your tax bite. In effect, the government will be subsidizing your loan. This is true for every kind of education loan, including PLUS loans.

Types of Non-Need-Based Loans

There are three basic types of loans you can use to pay your out-of-pocket costs: federal, state, and private.

FEDERAL LOANS

Federal loans have relatively low interest rates and are guaranteed by the federal government. This means that if you don't pay your loan back to the lender (though, of course, you should), the federal government will. That encourages lenders to lend you money even if you're a student with no credit history and little employment record.

Two basic kinds of federal loans are used for paying an EFC, one for students, one for parents:

- **Student Loans (Unsubsidized Stafford).** With an unsubsidized Stafford loan, you borrow money through participating colleges or directly from a bank or other lender. You'll be charged only interest while you're in school, and can either pay it while you're in school or let it accrue (accumulate) for payment after school. If you let the interest accrue, the bank will "capitalize" it into the principal of the loan when you start sending them payments after graduation. Table 5 shows the effects of interest accrual. The calculations on the table are for example only—they assume that you borrow $3,500 at the beginning of your freshman year and don't borrow any more to fund subsequent years of education. With this amount and the interest rate shown, letting the interest accrue saves you a $20 monthly payment while you're in college, but it ends up costing you about $407 more over the life of the loan. Whether or not you let interest accrue, six months after leaving school (your grace period), you have to begin paying back both the principal and the interest. To apply for an unsubsidized Stafford loan, ask your college financial aid office; they will refer you to lenders.

Table 5:
Effects of Letting Interest Accrue While You're In College

	INTEREST RATE IN COLLEGE	MONTHLY PAYMENT IN COLLEGE	DEBT REMAINING AFTER COLLEGE	INTEREST RATE AFTER COLLEGE	MONTHLY PAYMENT AFTER COLLEGE	TOTAL INTEREST PAID OVER LIFE OF THE LOAN
Subsidized Stafford	0%	$0	$3,500.00	6.0%	$38.86	$1,162.86
Unsubsidized Stafford (no interest accrual)	6.8%	$19.83	$3,500.00	6.8%	$40.28	$2,404.60
Unsubsidized Stafford (interest accrual option)	6.8%	$0	$4,571.00	6.8%	$52.60	$2,812.00

- **Parent Loans (PLUS).** With a PLUS loan, your parents borrow money to pay for your education either through the school or a third-party lender. They can borrow any amount up to the student's total cost of attendance minus the financial aid you receive. To get a PLUS loan, your parents have to fill out an application and pass a credit review. They will have to start making payments on the entire debt—both the principal and the interest —as soon as the loan money is disbursed to the school.

If you take out a federal loan, you'll receive a loan repayment schedule that spells out when your first payment is due and the number, frequency, and amounts of the payments. You'll have to pay back the loan on schedule or go into default, an official state of failure to repay a loan. That would hurt your credit rating—your ability to borrow more money later.

Under certain circumstances, such as economic hardship, you can postpone repayment of a federal student loan by applying for a deferment (during which no interest accumulates) or forbearance (during which it does). Under exceptional circumstances, such as total disability or teaching in a designated low-income school, some borrowers get a loan discharge, or cancellation of the debt. These rules apply to all federal student loans, but not to PLUS loans.

STATE LOANS

Some states sponsor loan programs for students and parents in their state. These loans are usually neither subsidized nor based on need. Check with your state financial aid agency to find out more.

PRIVATE LOANS

Many banks, credit unions, and other organizations offer their own education loans. These usually have slightly higher interest rates than federal loans, but they have lower interest rates than other consumer borrowing options, and may have attractive features, such as deferred repayment while in school. The borrowers— usually parents—have to prove their creditworthiness to get these loans.

HOME-EQUITY LOANS

Many parents consider taking out a loan against their home equity to pay for their children's higher education. While this may be an attractive option for your family, you should keep in mind that, unlike PLUS loans and other education loans, home-equity loans do come with the condition that if you can't pay back the loan, the bank can foreclose on your house.

Table 6:
Comparison of Education Loan Options

	SUBSIDIZED STAFFORD	PERKINS	UNSUBSIDIZED STAFFORD	PLUS	PRIVATE/ ALTERNATIVE EDUCATION LOAN	HOME EQUITY LOAN OR LINE OF CREDIT
BORROWING LIMIT	$3,500 first year $4,500 second year $5,500 third and fourth years Higher limits for independent students and for graduate study	$4,000/year $20,000 undergraduate maximum	Same as for Subsidized Stafford Students whose parents have been turned down for a PLUS Loan may borrow more.	Maximum is difference between total cost of attendance and financial aid awarded	Depends on credit check Maximum is difference between total cost of attendance and financial aid awarded	Depends on credit check and home equity
INTEREST RATES FOR 2008-09	In school: 0% In repayment: 3.4% (fixed)	In school: 0% In repayment: 5% (fixed)	In school: 6.8% (fixed) In repayment: 6.8% (fixed)	8.5% (fixed)	Depends on lender and credit check; range from 7% to 12%; may be fixed or variable	Depends on lender and credit check; may be fixed or variable
PROS	Interest that accumulates while you're in college paid by federal government	No origination fee Interest that accumulates while you're in college paid by federal government Debt may be forgiven if you enter a career in the public service	Option of not making payments during college and "capitalizing" accrued interest into the loan upon graduation Same deferment, and forbearance rules as subsidized loans	No collateral required	Available for nondegree programs and adult continuing education Repayment term may be longer than for federal loans	Can use money for non-educational purposes Repayment term may be longer than for federal loans
CONS	Only available to students with financial need 4% origination fee (may be discounted by lender)	Only available to students with financial need Amount of loan you're offered subject to college financial aid office's discretion	4% origination fee (may be discounted by lender)	Parents must pass credit check to take out loan Parents must begin paying interest immediately 4% origination fee	Student must pass credit check Parents may have to co-sign promissory note May have high origination fees	Home used as collateral for loan Can take several months to secure loan; may need to have house appraised

Cut It

In addition to spending past, present, and future resources to pay your college bill, you can also take steps to make that bill smaller. This is an especially smart move if it looks like college won't be affordable otherwise, even when you contribute all you can from savings, current income, and loans. But some strategies to cut college costs are worth using even if your family is financially comfortable.

Tuition "On the Cheap"

Tuition, the cost of taking classes, is usually high at four-year colleges. But you can get a reduced rate on those classes by taking them ahead of time at your own high school or a community college. By doing this, you may also be able to reduce the number of semesters you have to spend in college, which will cut not only your tuition costs but all other costs, such as room and board. Some colleges offer accelerated programs that will help you do that.

AP®/CLEP® OUT

Several programs let you earn college-level credit or advanced placement. They include the Advanced Placement Program® (AP) and the College-Level Examination Program® (CLEP®) which are sponsored by the College Board; and the International Baccalaureate (IB) program. The programs differ in various ways. For example, students take AP and IB courses as part of their high school curriculum, but they can prepare to take the CLEP examinations by any number of means—in school, on the job, or just reading books in their spare time. These programs are similar, however, in that you earn credit by taking an examination and receiving a score that your college accepts.

Colleges differ as to which programs, courses, and scores they accept and how much credit they grant. But every credit you receive means a credit you don't have to pay for in college. Depending on your exam scores and your college's policies, you may be able to graduate a semester or even a year early if you've taken enough AP or IB exams.

CLEP exams can often be taken on campus or at a nearby campus, and can be used to bypass introductory-level courses. For more information see collegeboard.com/clep. To find out about your college's policy on AP credit, go to collegeboard.com and use the AP Credit Policy Info tool.

TAKE COMMUNITY COLLEGE CLASSES OVER THE SUMMER

Courses at a community college usually cost much less than at a four-year college. Find out if there are courses you can take at a local community college in the summers and transfer to your four-year college. For example, if you don't have the knowledge of a certain subject that you need to pass a CLEP exam, you may still be able to take that course at a community college over the summer and transfer the credit to your four-year college.

OTHER ACCELERATED PROGRAMS

Some colleges offer an "accelerated program" designed for students who want to graduate in three years. These programs require a lot of work and dedication, but they will cut your college costs substantially by eliminating an entire year of expenses. It's possible to get through these programs if you're determined.

Cutting Other Expenses

Tuition is not the only college cost you can cut. Room, board, books, supplies, transportation—all of these add substantially to your total college bill. (Most people are shocked at what college textbooks cost these days.) Here are some suggestions to reduce these expenses:

BOOKS

- ✔ Buy used textbooks instead of new ones.
- ✔ Comparison shop for textbooks online.
- ✔ Sell your textbooks at the end of the semester.

ROOM AND BOARD

- ✔ Live off campus in a house or apartment that you share with class-mates. That can be cheaper than a college dorm. (But check the policy at the college you want to attend—many require freshmen to live on campus.)
- ✔ If you plan to live in a dorm in your sophomore year and beyond, try to get a position as a resident adviser and the free room and board that comes with it.

TRANSPORTATION

- ✔ If you're commuting to school, carpool with a classmate from your area.

Education Tax Breaks

Federal student aid isn't the only way that Uncle Sam can help you pay for college. There are also tax breaks available for higher-education costs. By reducing the amount your family has to pay the government at tax time, these programs amount to federal subsidies for out-of-pocket costs. Some of them take the form of tax credits, which cut your taxes dollar for dollar: that is, a $1 tax credit would make your tax bill $1 smaller. Others take the form of tax deductions,

GOOD TO KNOW

The information about higher-education tax breaks printed here is current as of early 2007. **To make sure you qualify for a deduction or credit** before you file, download IRS Publication 970, "Tax Benefits for Higher Education," from www.irs.gov.

which lower the amount of your income that is subject to tax, indirectly lowering your tax bill.

There are two federal income tax credits for higher-education expenses: **the Hope tax credit and the Lifetime Learning tax credit**. Both of these benefits let your family reduce the tax they pay by a fraction of their out-of-pocket costs, but the criteria for eligibility are different. The Hope tax credit, which is worth up to $1,650 per student per year, is available to families that have a first- or second-year student enrolled at least half-time in an undergraduate degree program. To be eligible for the Lifetime Learning tax credit, you don't have to be enrolled half-time or even be in a degree program. It's available for almost any kind of postsecondary education and training. The Lifetime Learning tax credit is equal to 20 percent of your family's tuition expenses, up to a $2,000 credit for $10,000 in tuition. Unlike the Hope Scholarship Credit, the Lifetime Learning Credit is calculated on a per-family, not a per-student, basis, so the maximum credit has to be shared among all students in the family.

Your family can't use both of these credits for the same student in the same year, though they can use both credits if they're applied to separate students. For either tax credit, the amount depends in part on your family's income, as calculated according to a formula called modified adjusted gross income. The more your family makes, the less money they'll be eligible for. Past a certain level of income ($55,000 for single filers; $110,000 for joint filers), your family won't be eligible at all. Still, for many people, the tax credits are a big help in paying the tuition bills.

If your family's income is too high to qualify for either the Hope or Lifetime Learning credits, there's also a tax deduction that may help. With the tuition and fees deduction, you can deduct up to $4,000 of college tuition and fees as long as your family income isn't more than $80,000 (for single filers) or $160,000 (for joint filers). If you claim this deduction, you can't claim the Hope or Lifetime Learning credits for the same student that year.

Interest paid on student loans is tax deductible to a maximum of $2,500 per year. This benefit applies to all loans used to pay for college, including PLUS loans. To be eligible for this deduction, your income has to be lower than $65,000 (for single filers) or $135,000 (for joint filers). The tax break is only for interest—the amount you pay the lender as the price for borrowing a sum of money, rather than the starting sum itself (the principal). If you take out a student loan, the lender will send a 1098 form to you at the end of each tax year telling you how much of your payments went to interest that year.

Some states also allow you to take tax credits or deductions off your state income taxes. Find out about yours from your state government.

PART I: FINANCIAL AID STEP BY STEP

Table 7:

Federal Income Tax Benefits for Higher Education

	HOPE EDUCATION CREDIT	LIFETIME LEARNING CREDIT	TUITION AND FEES DEDUCTION	STUDENT LOAN INTEREST DEDUCTION
AVAILABLE FOR	Tuition and fees only 1st two years of undergraduate study only Associate and bachelor's degree programs only	Tuition and fees only All years of study Any degree program, also nondegree courses to acquire job skills	Tuition and fees only All years of study Attendance at any postsecondary institution participating in a federal student aid program	Any higher education cost All years of study Any degree program
MAXIMUM VALUE	$1,650 credit per student	$2,000 credit per family	$4,000 deduction taken as an adjustment to gross income	$2,500 deduction from taxable income
MAXIMUM INCOME FOR ELIGIBILITY	$47,000–$57,000 (single filers) $94,000–$114,000 (joint filers)		$80,000 (single filers) $160,000 (joint filers)	$55,000–$70,000 (single filers) $110,000–$140,000 (joint filers)
CONDITIONS	Student must be enrolled at least half-time Student may not have felony drug conviction(s) Can be claimed for only two tax years for each student	Cannot claim both Lifetime Learning and Hope credits for same student in same year	May not claim if married and filing singly Cannot claim a Lifetime Learning or Hope credit for same student in the same year	Student must have been enrolled at least half-time May not claim if married and filing singly

To deal with out-of-pocket college costs, you have several options. You can draw on savings or current income to pay, or you can borrow some portion of the total bill. And you can cut the costs.

- Several savings options, including U.S. savings bonds, 529s, and Coverdell accounts, have tax benefits that can also help.
- You can work during college or promise to work later through programs like ROTC or AmeriCorps.
- You can borrow through student or parent loans.
- You can reduce your costs by such means as taking college-level courses for credit before you enter college.
- Tax breaks can help you meet college costs.

QUICK RECAP

Once You're in College

Once you're in college, you shouldn't be preoccupied with paying for it. Academics, extracurricular activities, and making friends are more important. But there are some things you need to do to stay on target financially. This chapter will tell you what they are.

Reapply for Aid Each Year!

Don't forget to reapply to renew your aid package every year! Check at your financial aid office to make sure you have the right forms and know what the deadlines are. Most colleges have a renewal deadline for financial aid that's a week or two later than the deadline for new applicants.

When you renew, don't expect your aid package to stay exactly the same. It may become more loan heavy each year, with more money in subsidized loans. The borrowing limits on the subsidized Stafford loan are higher for sophomores than for freshmen, and even higher for juniors and seniors. Also, keep in mind that some scholarships and grants are for freshmen only.

While you're reapplying for the financial aid you already have, keep an eye out for new opportunities. As you move on to higher grades and declare a major, you may become eligible for outside scholarships that weren't open to you in the past. Follow the guidelines in Step 9 to look for outside sources of money.

Stay on Track

EXPERT ADVICE

"There are students who tell me that the reason they didn't pass their class was they're **too busy working**, because they need the money to support themselves. And I tell them, you need to determine your priorities. There's a limit of how much financial aid I can give you to help offset that."

—*Mary San Agustin, director of financial aid and scholarships, Palomar College, San Marcos, California*

The next thing to keep in mind is that you have to maintain eligibility for financial aid. For federal student aid, stay in school at least half-time, and avoid illegal drugs. A drug-related conviction can lead to suspension or revocation of your federal-aid eligibility.

You don't have to maintain a particular GPA to maintain federal eligibility (though you do have to meet your individual school's standards for "satisfactory academic progress"). But the financial aid your college gives you, such as scholarships, may have specific academic requirements. Do your best in all your classes and stay on track academically, not only because it will help you get the most out of college but because it will help you keep your financial aid. To maintain or establish eligibility for academic scholarships, an on-campus job as a teaching or research assistant, or a "co-op" program between your department and a local employer, you'll need to be in good academic standing.

Maintain Grades

To keep up your grades, you'll have to make decisions about how to spend your time. It's important to build social relationships, pursue extracurricular activities, and earn money through work, but balance those against the need to maintain a good academic record. If you have a job, don't work so hard at it that you jeopardize your aid eligibility (see "Expert Advice" sidebar).

Don't Stay Too Long (Pick a Major, Any Major)

Did you know that only about one-third of all students who enter a four-year college graduate in four years? Most take six or more years to earn a bachelor's degree. Obviously, the longer you stay in college, the more it's going to cost you—not only in tuition, fees, room, board, and other expenses, but also in lost earnings from a delayed career.

Make it a goal to graduate on time. Make sure you are on track to complete your college's core requirements, as well as the core requirements for your major.

Speaking of majors, don't feel that you need to rush into choosing one. Except for some very specialized career and technical institutes, most colleges and universities allow you to take time during your first two years to take classes in different fields and make sure you know enough to choose a major that fits your interests and abilities. On the other hand, don't wait so long that you neglect to take the courses that are requirements for a major. You don't want to have to pay for an extra semester to get your biology degree because you didn't take that required organic chemistry course your sophomore year.

Transferring from a Community College

If you're going to a community college, and plan to transfer to a four-year college, **make sure you know all the transfer requirements**—including whatever courses are needed for the major you intend to declare. It helps if your community college has an articulation agreement with the four-year college specifying exactly what courses are required for transfer. Almost all community colleges have a transfer adviser on staff who can help you make sure you're on track. Get to know your adviser and check in with him or her regularly.

MYTH/FACT

Myth: Only certain majors will lead to high earnings after graduation.

Fact: Don't be fooled. If you're not drawn to the major, you probably won't like the work and will leave that field before you ever reach the high earnings. Instead, **choose a major based on your interests and talents**, not on someone else's predictions of industrial trends. And remember that many of today's highest paying fields—such as marketing and software engineering—require critical thinking skills that you will acquire in courses like anthropology and philosophy. To learn more about specific academic fields and what it's like to major in them, read the College Board's *Book of Majors*.

Watch Your Personal Expenses

The purpose of financial aid is to give you the money you need to pay for college costs. But that aid can quickly become too little if you spend too much. To avoid overspending, live within your means and don't run up frivolous debt. That means sticking to a budget and avoiding credit cards.

Student Budgeting

To live within your means, all you have to do is not spend more than you receive in income. The best way to do that is to create a budget at the beginning of each semester and stick to it. Your budget should list the funds you will receive (such as money from parents, savings, work, grants, and loans), subtract how much money you plan to spend on given items (such as tuition, fees, room, board, books, clothes, and recreation), and calculate the difference—the bottom line. If the bottom line is a negative number—that is, if your expenses exceed your income—you're overspending. Once you have a budget where your income is equal to or greater than your expenses, follow it, and you'll be living within your means.

To create a budget, first examine what you have actually been spending, then **set priorities if you're spending too much**. That alone can help you to spend less, as you realize you can make do with one latte a day instead of two. "You start making conscious decisions about what it is that you want to do," says Elizabeth Bickford of the University of Oregon at Eugene. "You're actually just taking control over your financial spending."

By all means have fun, but don't spend too much money on nonessential items like DVDs, high-end clothes, or trips to the beach. Some of your friends at college may have more money than you, but don't let social pressure push you into trying to spend like they do. Learn to suggest ordering pizza from the local hangout instead of driving to an expensive restaurant.

Save money wherever you can—for example, limit your cell phone use to free times. Comparison shop for groceries and supplies. And don't visit the ATM too often: it's too easy to withdraw money and overspend. See collegeboard.com for more advice on budgeting and financial planning.

Credit Card Debt

Be especially careful with your credit cards. They can be convenient for paying for big-ticket items like textbooks and airplane tickets, if you use them sparingly and pay off the entire amount when you get the bill. But if you abuse them, they can land you in a world of trouble.

A credit card is essentially a high-interest loan. Pulling it out at a cash register to make an impulse purchase may give you a feeling of freedom, but you won't feel free once you get the bill—especially when you're still paying interest on that impulse purchase months or years later. If you let the debt accumulate, it may swell so much that you won't be able to pay down the debt. This can affect your future academic career. If you miss payments on your credit cards, or if your credit card debt is high, you can hurt your credit rating. A bad credit rating can harm your chances of getting student loans to pay for graduate school, or a car loan when you start working. It can even prevent you from getting a job with certain security-conscious employers, such as banks or government agencies.

Use credit cards only when you know you can repay the debt promptly. Save them for emergencies. (A spring-break vacation is not an emergency.) Think through each credit card purchase before you spend. If you do get in over your head with credit card use, cut your expenses and talk to your family and financial aid administrator for more guidance.

Saving for Future Needs

While you're trying to live within your means, it's also wise to save for the future. Savings will give you greater freedom to cope with college and personal costs to come. If at all possible, make sure your budget includes money set aside for future needs. Your parents, of course, should do the same.

Try to save what you can from the jobs you have during the school year and in the summer. Think about the following as goals for your savings:

Students Should Think About…

- ✔ Next year's college expenses
- ✔ Application fees and tuition for graduate school
- ✔ A vacation with friends after you graduate
- ✔ Moving to another city after you graduate
- ✔ The unexpected (such as traveling to a friend's wedding or a family funeral)

Parents Should Think About…

- ✔ Next year's college expenses
- ✔ College expenses for younger children (if any)
- ✔ Retirement
- ✔ The unexpected (such as making it through a layoff or paying for a child's wedding)

Final Thoughts

Once you're in college, you may sometimes wonder if it's worth it. Can your family afford the expense? Will you be able to repay your student loans? If you've made reasonable choices along the way, the answer is yes. If you ever have doubts, visit your school's career center and do some research into the fields of work you might enter. Find out how much money you're likely to be earning when you first graduate, and how much five years later. A light might go on for you, as Elizabeth Bickford has often observed with other students. "When they see that relationship, many students say, 'Oh, wait a second, I can do that.'"

You will be able to pay back your student loans. College is a sound investment. You can afford college!

QUICK RECAP

Once you're in college, make sure you stay on track financially.

- Reapply for aid every year.
- Maintain your federal eligibility by staying in school the right number of hours and avoiding illegal drugs.
- Keep up your grades. Don't let them get derailed by too much time spent on work or other nonacademic activities.
- Declare a major at a suitable time.
- Make a budget and stick to it.
- Be wary of credit cards.
- Save for future expenses.
- Keep an eye out for new sources of outside scholarships.
- Remember that college is worth it!

Part II

Tables and Worksheets

WORKSHEET 1:
Meet Your Application Deadlines

	College Name	COLLEGE 1: *1st Choice Univ.*	COLLEGE 2: *Private Univ.*	COLLEGE 3: *Financial Safety*
FORMS REQUIRED	FAFSA			
	PROFILE			
	State form			
	Institutional form			
	Tax returns			
	Other			
SCHOOL CODES	Federal code			
	CSS code			
PRIORITY DATE				
CLOSING DATE				
AFTER APPLYING	Need to send letter?			
	Documentation required?			
COMPARE AWARDS	Notification date			
	Reply-by date			

WORKSHEET 2:
Scholarship Application Planner

	PROGRAM 1	PROGRAM 2	PROGRAM 3
PROGRAM/SPONSOR			
ELIGIBILITY REQUIREMENTS			
TYPE OF AWARD			
AMOUNT OF AWARD			
CAN BE USED FOR			
CAN BE USED AT			
DEADLINE			
FORMS REQUIRED			
TEST SCORES REQUIRED			
ESSAY OR ACADEMIC SAMPLE			
RECOMMENDATIONS			
NOTIFICATION BEGINS			
REQUIREMENTS TO KEEP AFTER FRESHMAN YEAR			

WORKSHEET 3:
Compare Your Awards

	COLLEGE 1	COLLEGE 2	COLLEGE 3
Step 1. List the name of each college you want to consider attending, the award deadline, and the total cost of attendance. This figure should be in your award letter. If not, refer to the college catalog or contact the college financial aid office.			
Name of college			
Award deadline date			
Total cost of attendance			
Step 2. List the financial aid awards each school is offering. Don't forget that grants, scholarships, and work-study do not have to be repaid, while all loans must be repaid.			
Grants and scholarships			
• Pell Grant (federal)			
• SEOG (federal)			
• State			
• College			
• Other			
Total grants/scholarships			
Percentage of package that is grant/scholarship			
Work-study opportunities			
Loans			
• Stafford-Direct (federal)			
• Perkins (federal)			
• Other			
Total loans			
Percentage of package that is work or loans			
Total financial aid award			
Grants and scholarships + work-study + loans			
Step 3. Calculate what it will cost you to attend each college you are considering. For each college, enter the total cost of attendance. Then, subtract the total financial aid award from the total cost of attendance. That number is the net cost, or what it will cost you to attend that college.			
a) Total cost of attendance			
b) Total financial aid award			
c) Net cost to attend (a minus b)			

Figure 13:
Sample Financial Aid Award Letter 1

Blue University   Cost of Attendance: $ 28,706.00

CLASS: 01

March 22, 2008

TENTATIVE
FINANCIAL AWARD NOTIFICATION FOR 2008-2009

Based on the information that you submitted on your FAFSA and to our office,
Blue University can offer you the following TENTATIVE awards.

This package is based on an award period from 09/10/08 to 06/06/09.

AID AWARD	ACCEPT AWARD		OFFERED AMOUNT
	Yes	NO	
FEDERAL PERKINS LOAN	_____	_____	$1,143
STATE WORK-STUDY	_____	_____	$2,400
BLUE EDUCATIONAL GRANT	_____	_____	$3,538
UNIVERSITY SCHOLARSHIP	_____	_____	$2,000
RESIDENCE HALL GRANT	_____	_____	$2,000
FEDERAL STAFFORD LOAN – SUB.	_____	_____	$2,625

Finalize your financial aid award as soon as possible by forwarding to our office the forms listed on
the Missing Documents Form included with this letter.

Please read the important information pamphlet! Indicate your intent by checking whether or not you
accept each aid award, then sign and return this letter in order to reserve your award(s).

Please refer to the Cost Worksheet to help determine your expenses for the academic year.

If direct loan amounts desired are less than above, please indicate below:

    Requested Federal Stafford Loan (Sub.) $ _____
    Requested Federal Perkins Loan $ _____

I acknowledge that I have read and will comply with all the supporting information in the Important
Information Pamphlet. Furthermore, if I receive any financial assistance not included in this award
letter, including tuition waivers or employer reimbursement, I will notify your office immediately.

Signature _____   Date _____

Figure 14:
Sample Financial Aid Award Letter 2

Green University | Office of Student Financial Planning

Cost of Attendance: $ 26,005.00

March 1, 2008

Step 1. Circle A for Accept or D for Decline for each individual award where indicated below:

	Fall 2008	Spring 2009	Total	A / D
Presidential Freshman Scholarship	$3,250	$3,250	$6,500	A / D
Green University Grant	$705	$705	$1,410	A / D
Total Grants and Scholarships			**$7,910**	
Federal Unsubsidized Stafford Loan	$1,313	$1,312	$2,625	A / D
Total Student Loans			**$2,625**	
Federal College Work-Study	$330	$330	$660	A / D
Federal PLUS Loan and/or Green Partnership Loan	$7,405	$7,405	$14,810	

Step 2. Please note the following:

Your awards are based on full-time enrollment for the fall and spring terms and residence hall occupancy for the fall and spring terms (for financial aid purposes, full-time is defined as 12 credits or more per term).

You have been offered loan(s) that require separate loan materials.

The amount of your Green University Grant was based upon residence hall occupancy for the fall and spring terms. A change in housing status may result in a reduction of this award.

Step 3. Please list other financial assistance, scholarships, or loans you will receive not indicated above. List the scholarship/donor name and the expected amount (example: Elks Club $100).

Name	Amount

Step 4. Attention: Your awards are not final until you complete the items on the ACTION REQUESTED page.

2008 — 2009
FAFSA ON THE WEB WORKSHEET
www.fafsa.ed.gov

START HERE
GO FURTHER
FEDERAL STUDENT AID

DO NOT MAIL THIS WORKSHEET.

You must complete and submit a *Free Application for Federal Student Aid* (FAFSA) to apply for federal student aid and to apply for most state and college aid. Applying online with *FAFSA on the Web* at **www.fafsa.ed.gov** is faster and easier than using a paper FAFSA.

For state or college aid, the deadline may be as early as January 2008. See the table to the right for state deadlines. Check with your high school counselor or your college's financial aid administrator about other deadlines.

- **Complete this Worksheet only if you plan to use *FAFSA on the Web* to apply for federal student aid.**

- Sections in gray are for parent information.

- In parentheses after each question is the number that is used on *FAFSA on the Web* and the paper FAFSA.

- **Submit your FAFSA early, but not before January 1, 2008.**

Apply Faster—Sign your FAFSA with a Federal Student Aid PIN.
If you do not have a PIN, you can apply for one at **www.pin.ed.gov**. You will receive your PIN and then you can electronically sign when you submit your FAFSA. If you are providing parent information, one parent must also sign your FAFSA. To sign electronically, your parent should also apply for a PIN.

You will need the following information to complete this Worksheet:

❏ Your Social Security Number and your parents' Social Security Numbers if you are providing parent information;

❏ Your driver's license number if you have one;

❏ Your Alien Registration Number if you are not a U.S. citizen;

❏ 2007 federal tax information or tax returns (including IRS W-2 information) for yourself (and spouse if you are married) and for your parents if you are providing parent information. If you have not yet filed a 2007 income tax return, you can still submit your FAFSA but you must provide income and tax information.

❏ Records of untaxed income, such as Social Security benefits, welfare benefits (e.g., TANF), and veterans benefits, for yourself, and your parents if you are providing parent information; and

❏ Information on savings, investments, and business and farm assets for yourself, and your parents if you are providing parent information.

STATE AID DEADLINES
Check with your financial aid administrator for these states and territories: AL, *AS, CO, *FM, GA, *GU, *HI, *MH, *MP, NE, *NM, *NV, OR, PR, *PW, *SD, *TX, UT, *VA, *VI, *VT, WA, WI, and *WY

	AK	April 15, 2008 *(date received)*
	AR	Academic Challenge - June 1, 2008
		Workforce Grant - Contact your financial aid administrator.
		Higher Education Opportunity Grant
		- June 1, 2008 (fall term)
		- November 1, 2008 (spring term)
		(date received)
	AZ	June 30, 2009 *(date received)*
*	CA	Initial awards - March 2, 2008
		Additional community college awards - September 2, 2008 *(date postmarked)*
#*	CT	February 15, 2008 *(date received)*
*	DC	June 30, 2008 *(date received by state)*
	DE	April 15, 2008 *(date received)*
	FL	May 15, 2008 *(date processed)*
	IA	July 1, 2008 *(date received)*
#*	ID	March 1, 2008 *(date received)*
#	IL	First-time applicants - September 30, 2008
		Continuing applicants - August 15, 2008 *(date received)*
	IN	March 10, 2008 *(date received)*
# *	KS	April 1, 2008 *(date received)*
#	KY	March 15, 2008 *(date received)*
	LA	July 1, 2008 *(date received)*
#	MA	May 1, 2008 *(date received)*
	MD	March 1, 2008 *(date received)*
	ME	May 1, 2008 *(date received)*
	MI	March 1, 2008 *(date received)*
	MN	30 days after term starts *(date received)*
	MO	April 1, 2008 *(date received)*
#	MS	MTAG and MESG Grants - September 15, 2008
		HELP Scholarship - March 31, 2008
#	MT	March 1, 2008 *(date received)*
	NC	March 15, 2008 *(date received)*
	ND	March 15, 2008 *(date received)*
	NH	May 1, 2008 *(date received)*
	NJ	June 1, 2008, if you received a Tuition Aid Grant in 2007-2008
		All other applicants
		- October 1, 2008, fall and spring terms
		- March 1, 2009, spring term only *(date received)*
*	NY	May 1, 2009 *(date received)*
	OH	October 1, 2008 *(date received)*
#	OK	April 15, 2008 *(date received)* for best consideration
*	PA	All 2007-2008 State Grant recipients & all non-2007-2008 State Grant recipients in degree programs - May 1, 2008
		All other applicants - August 1, 2008 *(date received)*
#	RI	March 1, 2008 *(date received)*
	SC	Tuition Grants - June 30, 2008 *(date received)*
#	TN	State Grant - March 1, 2008
		State Lottery - September 1, 2008 *(date received)*
*	WV	March 1, 2008 *(date received)*

\# For priority consideration, submit application by date specified.

* Additional form may be required.

WARNING!	**NOTE:**
Be wary of organizations that charge a fee to submit your application or to find you money for college. In general, the help you pay for can be obtained for free from your college or from Federal Student Aid.	If you or your family have unusual circumstances (such as loss of employment), complete *FAFSA on the Web* to the extent you can, then submit the application and consult the financial aid office at the college you plan to attend.

PART II: TABLES AND WORKSHEETS

SECTION 1 – STUDENT INFORMATION

- **Use of this Worksheet is optional. It should not be submitted to Federal Student Aid or to your college.**
- Not all of the questions from *FAFSA on the Web* appear in this Worksheet, but questions are generally ordered as they appear online.
- Once you are online, you may be able to skip some questions based on your answers to earlier questions.

Your Social Security Number (Q8)

Your last name (Q1)

Your driver's license number (optional) (Q11)

Are you a U.S. citizen? (Q14)

If you are neither a citizen nor an eligible noncitizen, you are not eligible for federal student aid. However, you should still complete the application, because you may be eligible for state or college aid.

If you are in the U.S. on an F1 or F2 student visa, or a J1 or J2 exchange visitor visa, or a G series visa (pertaining to international organizations), you must answer "Neither citizen nor eligible noncitizen."

❑ U.S. citizen (U.S. national)
❑ Eligible noncitizen
   Generally you are an eligible noncitizen if you are:
   • A permanent U.S. resident with a Permanent Resident Card (I-551);
   • A conditional permanent resident (I-551C); or
   • The holder of an Arrival-Departure Record (I-94) from the Department of Homeland Security showing any of the following designations: "Refugee," "Asylum Granted," "Parolee" (I-94 confirms paroled for a minimum of one year and status has not expired), "Victim of human trafficking," T-Visa holder (T-1, T-2, T-3, etc.) or "Cuban-Haitian Entrant."
❑ Neither citizen nor eligible noncitizen

Your Alien Registration Number (Q15) If you are an eligible noncitizen, enter your eight- or nine-digit Alien Registration Number.

A

Your marital status as of today (Q16)
"As of today" refers to the day that you sign your FAFSA.

❑ Single, divorced, or widowed
❑ Married/remarried   ❑ Separated

Month and year you were married, separated, divorced or widowed (Q17) (Example: Month and year: 05/1997)

M M Y Y Y Y

Your state of legal residence (Q18)

Did you become a legal resident of your state before January 1, 2003? (Q19)

❑ Yes   ❑ No

If "No," when did you become a legal resident of your state? (Q20)
(Example: Month and year: 05/2004)

M M Y Y Y Y

Most male students must register with the Selective Service System to get federal aid. If you are a male between the ages of 18 and 25 and **NOT** already registered with Selective Service, answer "Yes" and Selective Service will register you. (Q22)

❑ Yes   ❑ No

What degree or certificate will you be working on during the 2008-2009 school year? (Q23)

❑ 1st bachelor's degree
❑ 2nd bachelor's degree
❑ Associate degree (occupational/technical program)
❑ Associate degree (general education or transfer program)
❑ Certificate or diploma for completing an occupational, technical, or educational program of less than two years

❑ Certificate or diploma for completing an occupational, technical, or educational program of at least two years
❑ Teaching credential (nondegree program)
❑ Graduate or professional degree
❑ Other/Undecided

What will be your grade level when you begin the 2008-2009 school year? (Q24)

❑ 1st year/never attended college before
❑ 1st year/attended college
❑ 2nd year/sophomore
❑ 3rd year/junior

❑ 4th year/senior
❑ 5th year/other undergraduate
❑ 1st year graduate/professional
❑ Continuing graduate/professional or beyond

At the start of the 2008-2009 school year, what do you expect your enrollment status to be? (Q25)
(Enrollment definitions refer to undergraduate study.)

❑ Full-time (at least 12 credit hours in a term or 24 clock hours per week)
❑ 3/4-time (at least 9 credit hours in a term or 18 clock hours per week)
❑ Half-time (at least 6 credit hours in a term or 12 clock hours per week)
❑ Less than half-time (fewer than 6 credit hours in a term or less than 12 clock hours per week)
❑ Not sure

SECTION 1 (CONTINUED) – STUDENT INFORMATION

What types of student aid interest you? (Q26) Indicate if you are interested in other types of student financial aid, in addition to grants.	❏ Work-study (aid earned through work) ❏ Student loans (which you must pay back) ❏ Both work-study and student loans ❏ Neither ❏ Don't know
Will you have your first bachelor's degree before July 1, 2008? (Q28)	❏ Yes　　　　　　　　❏ No
Highest school your father completed (Q29) Some states and colleges offer aid based upon the level of schooling your parents have completed.	❏ Middle school/Jr. High ❏ High school ❏ College or beyond ❏ Other/unknown
Highest school your mother completed (Q30) Some states and colleges offer aid based upon the level of schooling your parents have completed.	❏ Middle school/Jr. High ❏ High school ❏ College or beyond ❏ Other/unknown
Have you been convicted for the possession or sale of illegal drugs for an offense that occurred while you were receiving federal student aid (grants, loans, and/or work-study)? (Q31) A federal law suspends eligibility for some students with drug convictions. Count only federal or state convictions for the possession or sale of illegal drugs if the offense occurred during a period of enrollment for which you were receiving federal student aid (grants, loans, and/or work-study). Do not count convictions that have been removed from your record, or occurred before you turned age 18, unless you were tried as an adult. If you answer "Yes," you can use an interactive worksheet when completing the FAFSA online, or you can print a worksheet at **www.fafsa.ed.gov/q31wksht89.pdf.** Based on your answers to the worksheet questions, you can determine if the conviction affects your eligibility for federal student aid.	❏ Yes If you have a conviction for possessing or selling illegal drugs, you should submit your FAFSA anyway. You may be eligible for non-federal student aid from state or private sources. ❏ No

SECTION 2 – STUDENT DEPENDENCY STATUS

Were you born before January 1, 1985? (Q48)	❏ Yes　　　　　　　　❏ No
At the beginning of the 2008-2009 school year, will you be working on a master's or doctorate program (such as an MA, MBA, MD, JD, PhD, EdD, or graduate certificate, etc.)? (Q49)	❏ Yes　　　　　　　　❏ No
As of today, are you married? (Q50) (Answer "Yes" if you are separated but not divorced.) "As of today" refers to the day that you sign your FAFSA.	❏ Yes　　　　　　　　❏ No
Do you have children who receive more than half of their support from you? (Q51)	❏ Yes　　　　　　　　❏ No
Do you have dependents other than your children/spouse who live with you and who receive more than half of their support from you, now and through June 30, 2009? (Q52)	❏ Yes　　　　　　　　❏ No
Are (a) both of your parents deceased, or (b) are you (or were you until age 18) a ward/dependent of the court? (Q53)	❏ Yes　　　　　　　　❏ No
Are you currently serving on active duty in the U.S. Armed Forces for purposes other than training? (Q54)	❏ Yes　　　　　　　　❏ No
Are you a veteran of the U.S. Armed Forces? (Q55) Answer "Yes," you are a veteran, if you (1) have engaged in active duty in the U.S. Armed Forces (Army, Navy, Air Force, Marines, or Coast Guard) or are a National Guard or Reserves enlistee who was called to active duty for purposes other than training, or were a cadet or midshipman at one of the service academies, and (2) were released under a condition other than dishonorable. Also answer "Yes" if you are not a veteran now but will be by June 30, 2009. Answer "No," you are not a veteran, if you (1) have never engaged in active duty in the U.S. Armed Forces, (2) are currently an ROTC student or a cadet or midshipman at a service academy, or (3) are a National Guard or Reserves enlistee activated only for training. Also answer "No" if you are currently serving in the U.S. Armed Forces and will continue to serve through June 30, 2009.	❏ Yes　　　　　　　　❏ No

If you answered "YES" to ANY of the previous questions, you do not have to provide parental information. Skip to Section 4 on page 6.
If you answered "NO" to ALL of the previous questions, then you must provide parental information. Complete Section 3 on the next page.

SECTION 3 – PARENTAL INFORMATION

- **If you answered "NO" to all the questions in Section 2, you must complete this section even if you do not live with your parents. Refer to your parents' IRS tax return when necessary.**
  - **Answer the questions as of the date you will complete and sign your FAFSA.**
  - **Grandparents, foster parents and legal guardians are not considered parents on this form unless they have legally adopted you.**
  - **If both of your parents are living and married to each other, answer the questions about them.**
  - **If your parent is widowed or single, answer the questions about that parent. If your widowed parent is remarried as of today, answer the questions about that parent and the person to whom your parent is married (your stepparent).**
  - **If your parents are divorced or separated, answer the questions about the parent you lived with more during the past 12 months. If you did not live with one parent more than the other, give answers about the parent who provided more financial support during the past 12 months, or during the most recent year that you actually received support from a parent. If this parent is remarried as of today, answer the questions about that parent and the person to whom your parent is married (your stepparent).**

What is your parents' marital status as of today? (Q56)
"As of today" refers to the day that you sign your FAFSA.

❑ Married/remarried
❑ Single
❑ Divorced/separated
❑ Widowed

Month and year your parents were married, separated, divorced, or widowed (Q57) (Example: Month and year: 05/1997)

M	M	Y	Y	Y	Y

What is your parents' e-mail address? (optional)

What is your father's (or stepfather's) Social Security Number? (Q58)

| | | | - | | | - | | | | |

What is your father's (or stepfather's) last name? (Q59)

What is your father's (or stepfather's) date of birth? (Q61)
(Example: Month, day and year: 05/07/1961)

M	M	D	D	Y	Y	Y	Y

What is your mother's (or stepmother's) Social Security Number? (Q62)

| | | | - | | | - | | | | |

What is your mother's (or stepmother's) last name? (Q63)

What is your mother's (or stepmother's) date of birth? (Q65)
(Example: Month, day and year: 05/07/1961)

M	M	D	D	Y	Y	Y	Y

What is your parents' state of legal residence? (Q68)

Did your parents become legal residents of the state before January 1, 2003? (Q69)

❑ Yes   ❑ No

If "No," give month and year legal residency began for the parent who has lived in the state the longest. (Q70) (Example: Month and year: 05/2004)

M	M	Y	Y	Y	Y

Have your parents completed a 2007 IRS income tax return or other income tax return? (Q76)

❑ Already completed
❑ Will file
❑ Will not file

What income tax return did your parents file or will they file for 2007? (Q77)

❑ IRS 1040
❑ IRS 1040A, 1040EZ
❑ A foreign tax return
❑ A tax return with Puerto Rico, another U.S. territory or a freely associated state

If your parents have filed or will file a 1040, were they eligible to file a 1040A or 1040EZ? (Q78)

In general, a person is eligible to file a 1040A or 1040EZ if he or she makes less than $100,000, does not itemize deductions, does not receive income from his or her business or farm, and does not receive alimony. A person is not eligible to file a 1040A or 1040EZ if he or she makes $100,000 or more, itemizes deductions, receives income from his or her own business or farm, is self-employed, receives alimony, or is required to file Schedule D for capital gains. If you filed a 1040 only to claim Hope or Lifetime Learning tax credits, and would have otherwise been eligible for a 1040A or 1040EZ, you should answer "Yes."

❑ Yes
❑ No
❑ Don't know

SECTION 3 (CONTINUED) – PARENTAL INFORMATION

In 2007, did you, your parents, or anyone in your parents' household receive benefits from any of the federal benefit programs listed? (Q71-75) Mark all the programs that apply.

Report benefits received for all of your parents' household members. Include in your parents' household: (1) your parents and yourself, even if you don't live with your parents; (2) your parents' other children if (a) your parents will provide more than half of their support from July 1, 2008, through June 30, 2009, or (b) the children could answer "No" to every question in Section 2 of this worksheet; and (3) other people only if they live with your parents, your parents provide more than half of their support, and your parents will continue to provide more than half of their support from July 1, 2008, through June 30, 2009.

- ❏ Supplemental Security Income
- ❏ Food Stamps
- ❏ Free or Reduced Price School Lunch
- ❏ Temporary Assistance for Needy Families (TANF)
- ❏ Special Supplemental Nutrition Program for Women, Infants, and Children (WIC)

What was your parents' adjusted gross income for 2007? (Q79)
Adjusted gross income is on IRS form 1040—line 37; 1040A—line 21; or 1040EZ—line 4.

$

Questions 82 and 83 ask about earnings (wages, salaries, tips, combat pay, etc.) in 2007. Answer the questions whether or not a tax return was filed. This information may be on the W-2 forms, or on IRS Form 1040—lines 7 + 12 + 18 + Box 14 of IRS Schedule K-1 (Form 1065); 1040A—line 7; or 1040EZ—line 1.

How much did your father/stepfather earn from working in 2007? (Q82)

$

How much did your mother/stepmother earn from working in 2007? (Q83)

$

What was the amount your parents paid in income tax for 2007? (Q80)
Income tax amount is on IRS Form 1040—line 57; 1040A—line 35; or 1040EZ—line 10.

$

Enter your parents' exemptions for 2007. (Q81)
Exemptions are on IRS Form 1040—line 6d or 1040A—line 6d. On the 1040EZ, if a person checked either the "you" or "spouse" box on line 5, use EZ worksheet line F to determine the number of exemptions ($3,400 equals one exemption). If a person didn't check either box on line 5, enter 01 if he or she is single, or 02 if he or she is married.

How many people are in your parents' household? (Q66)
Include in your parents' household: (1) your parents and yourself, even if you don't live with your parents, (2) your parents' other children if (a) your parents will provide more than half of their support from July 1, 2008, through June 30, 2009, or (b) the children could answer "No" to every question in Section 2 of this worksheet, and (3) include other people only if they live with your parents, your parents provide more than half of their support, and your parents will continue to provide more than half of their support from July 1, 2008, through June 30, 2009.

How many people in the question above will be college students in 2008-2009? (Q67)
Always count yourself. **Do not include your parents.** Include others only if they will attend college at least half-time in 2008-2009 in a program that leads to a college degree or certificate.

Parent FAFSA Worksheets A, B and C. Complete the Worksheets on page 8 to answer the questions below.

Your parents' amount from FAFSA Worksheet A (Q84) $

Your parents' amount from FAFSA Worksheet B (Q85) $

Your parents' amount from FAFSA Worksheet C (Q86) $

Parent Asset Information

- Investments include real estate (do not include the family home), trust funds, UGMA and UTMA accounts, money market funds, mutual funds, certificates of deposit, stocks, stock options, bonds, other securities, Coverdell savings accounts, 529 college savings plans, the refund value of 529 prepaid tuition plans, installment and land sale contracts (including mortgages held), commodities, etc. For more information about reporting educational savings plans call 1-800-4-FED-AID. Investment value means the current balance or market value of these investments as of today. Investment debt means only those debts that are related to the investments.
- Do not include the value of life insurance, retirement plans (pension funds, annuities, noneducation IRAs, Keogh plans, etc.) or cash, savings, and checking accounts already reported in Q43 and Q87.
- Business and/or investment farm value includes the market value of land, buildings, machinery, equipment, inventory, etc. Business and/or investment farm debt means only those debts for which the business or investment farm was used as collateral.

As of today, what is your parents' total current balance in cash, savings, and checking accounts? (Q87)

$

As of today, what is the net worth of your parents' investments, including real estate (not their home)? (Q88) Net worth means current value minus debt.

$

As of today, what is the net worth of your parents' current business and/or investment farms? (Q89) **Do not include** the value of a family farm that you (your spouse and/or your parents) live on and operate. Do not include the value of a small business that you (your spouse and/or your parents) own and control and that has 100 or fewer full-time or full-time equivalent employees.

$

SECTION 4 – STUDENT FINANCES

- Answer the questions as of the date you will complete and sign your FAFSA.
- This section asks about your income. Refer to your IRS tax return when necessary.
- If you filed a foreign tax return, convert all figures to U.S. dollars, using the exchange rate. To view the daily exchange rates, go to **www.federalreserve.gov/releases/h10/update**.
- If you are married as of today, report your and your spouse's income, even if you were not married in 2007. Ignore references to spouse if you are single, divorced, separated or widowed.

Have you completed a 2007 IRS income tax return or other income tax return? (Q32)	❏ Already completed ❏ Will file ❏ Will not file
What income tax return did you file or will you file for 2007? (Q33)	❏ IRS 1040 ❏ IRS 1040A or 1040EZ ❏ A foreign tax return ❏ A tax return with Puerto Rico, another U.S. territory or a freely associated state
If you filed or will file a 1040, were you eligible to file a 1040A or 1040EZ? (Q34) In general, you are eligible to file a 1040A or 1040EZ if you make less than $100,000, do not itemize deductions, do not receive income from your business or farm, and do not receive alimony. A person is not eligible to file a 1040A or 1040EZ if he or she makes $100,000 or more, itemizes deductions, receives income from his or her own business or farm, is self-employed, receives alimony, or is required to file Schedule D for capital gains. If you filed a 1040 only to claim Hope or Lifetime Learning tax credits, and you would otherwise have been eligible for a 1040A or 1040EZ, you should answer "Yes."	❏ Yes ❏ No ❏ Don't know
What was your (and your spouse's) adjusted gross income for 2007? (Q35) Adjusted gross income is on IRS Form 1040—line 37; 1040A—line 21; or 1040EZ—line 4.	$
Questions 38 and 39 ask about earnings (wages, salaries, tips, combat pay, etc.) in 2007. Answer the questions whether or not a tax return was filed. This information may be on the W-2 forms, or on IRS Form 1040—lines 7 + 12 + 18 + Box 14 of IRS Schedule K-1 (Form 1065); 1040A—line 7; or 1040EZ—line 1.	
How much did you earn from working in 2007? (Q38)	$
How much did your spouse earn from working in 2007? (Q39)	$
If you receive veterans' education benefits, for how many months from July 1, 2008, through June 30, 2009, will you receive these benefits? Use 01 to 12. (Q46)	
What is the amount of your monthly veterans' education benefits? (Q47)	$
What was your (and your spouse's) income tax for 2007? (Q36) Income tax amount is on IRS Form 1040—line 57; 1040A—line 35; or 1040EZ—line 10.	$
Enter your (and your spouse's) exemptions for 2007. (Q37) Exemptions are on IRS Form 1040—line 6d or 1040A—line 6d. On the 1040EZ, if a person checked either the "you" or "spouse" box on line 5, use EZ worksheet line F to determine the number of exemptions ($3,400 equals one exemption). If a person didn't check either box on line 5, enter 01 if he or she is single, or 02 if he or she is married.	

- If you answered "YES" to ANY question in Section 2, answer the following questions.
- If you answer "NO" to all the questions in Section 2, skip these questions and go to "Student FAFSA Worksheets A, B and C."

How many people are in your household? (Q90) Include in your household: (1) yourself (and your spouse, if you are married), (2) your children, if you will provide more than half of their support from July 1, 2008, through June 30, 2009, and (3) other people if they now live with you, you provide more than half of their support, and you will continue to provide more than half of their support from July 1, 2008, through June 30, 2009.	
How many people in the question above will be college students in 2008-2009? (Q91) Always count yourself. Include others only if they will attend college at least half-time in 2008-2009 in a program that leads to a college degree or certificate.	

PART II: TABLES AND WORKSHEETS

SECTION 4 (CONTINUED) – STUDENT FINANCES

In 2007, did you (or your spouse) or anyone in your household (from Q90) receive benefits from any of the federal benefit programs listed? (Q92-96) Mark all the programs that apply.

The federal benefit programs are listed in the answer column. Report benefits received for all of your household members. Use the instructions in Q90 to identify who is included in your household. Answering these questions will not reduce your eligibility for student aid or these other federal benefits.

❑ Supplemental Security Income
❑ Food Stamps
❑ Free or Reduced Price School Lunch
❑ Temporary Assistance for Needy Families (TANF)
❑ Special Supplemental Nutrition Program for Women, Infants, and Children (WIC)

Student FAFSA Worksheets A, B and C. Complete the Worksheets on page 8 to answer the questions below.

Your amount from FAFSA Worksheet A (Q40) $ _____

Your amount from FAFSA Worksheet B (Q41) $ _____

Your amount from FAFSA Worksheet C (Q42) $ _____

Student Asset Information (See page 5 for instructions on reporting assets.)

As of today, what is your (and your spouse's) total current balance of cash, savings and checking accounts? (Q43) $ _____

As of today, what is the net worth of your (and your spouse's) investments, including real estate (not your home)? (Q44)
Net worth means current value minus debt. $ _____

As of today, what is the net worth of your (and your spouse's) current business and/or investment farms? (Q45)
Do not include the value of a family farm that you (your spouse and/or your parents) live on and operate. Do not include the value of a small business that you (your spouse and/or your parents) own and control and that has 100 or fewer full-time or full-time equivalent employees. $ _____

SECTION 5 – COLLEGES TO RECEIVE INFORMATION

- If you do not know the school code, write the college's name. You will have a chance online to search for the school code.
- For each school code, indicate the corresponding housing plan.

	1st college	2nd college	3rd college	4th college	5th college
Federal School Code	_____ (Q97.a)	_____ (Q97.c)	_____ (Q97.e)	_____ (Q97.g)	_____ (Q97.i)
Housing Plan	❑ on campus ❑ off campus ❑ with parent (Q97.b)	❑ on campus ❑ off campus ❑ with parent (Q97.d)	❑ on campus ❑ off campus ❑ with parent (Q97.f)	❑ on campus ❑ off campus ❑ with parent (Q97.h)	❑ on campus ❑ off campus ❑ with parent (Q97.j)

	6th college	7th college	8th college	9th college	10th college
Federal School Code	_____ (Q97.k)	_____ (Q97.m)	_____ (Q97.o)	_____ (Q97.q)	_____ (Q97.s)
Housing Plan	❑ on campus ❑ off campus ❑ with parent (Q97.l)	❑ on campus ❑ off campus ❑ with parent (Q97.n)	❑ on campus ❑ off campus ❑ with parent (Q97.p)	❑ on campus ❑ off campus ❑ with parent (Q97.r)	❑ on campus ❑ off campus ❑ with parent (Q97.t)

Go to www.fafsa.ed.gov and enter the information from this worksheet.

Additional help is available online, or you can call 1-800-4-FED-AID.
TTY users (hearing impaired) may call 1-800-730-8913.
For more information on federal student aid visit **www.FederalStudentAid.ed.gov**. You can also talk with your college's financial aid office about other types of student aid that may be available

DO NOT MAIL THIS WORKSHEET.

FAFSA WORKSHEETS – CALENDAR YEAR 2007

**These worksheets are solely for completing the FAFSA Worksheet questions,
on page 7 for the student and, on page 5 for the student's parents.**

FAFSA Worksheet A—Report Annual Amounts

Student/Spouse For Page 7		Parents For Page 5
$	Earned income credit from IRS Form 1040—line 66a; 1040A—line 40a; or 1040EZ—line 8a.	$
$	Additional child tax credit from IRS Form 1040—line 68 or 1040A—line 41.	$
$	Welfare benefits, including Temporary Assistance for Needy Families (TANF). Do not include food stamps or subsidized housing.	$
$	Social Security benefits received, that were not taxed (such as SSI), for all household members as reported in question 90 (or 66 for your parents). Report benefits paid to parents in the Parents' column, and benefits paid directly to student (or spouse) in the Student/Spouse column.	$
$	Enter in question 40 on Page 7.	Enter in question 84 on Page 5. $

FAFSA Worksheet B—Report Annual Amounts

Student/Spouse For Page 7		Parents For Page 5
$	Payments to tax-deferred pension and savings plans (paid directly or withheld from earnings), including, but not limited to, amounts reported on the W-2 Form in Boxes 12a through 12d, codes D, E, F, G, H, and S.	$
$	IRA deductions and payments to self-employed SEP, SIMPLE, and Keogh and other qualified plans from IRS Form 1040—line 28 + line 32 or 1040A—line 17.	$
$	Child support received for all children. Don't include foster care or adoption payments.	$
$	Tax exempt interest income from IRS Form 1040—line 8b or 1040A—line 8b.	$
$	Foreign income exclusion from IRS Form 2555—line 45 or 2555EZ—line 18.	$
$	Untaxed portions of IRA distributions from IRS Form 1040—lines (15a minus 15b) or 1040A—lines (11a minus 11b). Exclude rollovers. If negative, enter a zero here.	$
$	Untaxed portions of pensions from IRS Form 1040—lines (16a minus 16b) or 1040A—lines (12a minus 12b). Exclude rollovers. If negative, enter a zero here.	$
$	Credit for federal tax on special fuels from IRS Form 4136—line 17 (nonfarmers only).	$
$	Housing, food and other living allowances paid to members of the military, clergy and others (including cash payments and cash value of benefits).	$
$	Veterans' noneducation benefits such as Disability, Death Pension, or Dependency & Indemnity Compensation (DIC), and/or VA Educational Work-Study allowances.	$
$	Other untaxed income not reported elsewhere on Worksheets A and B, such as workers' compensation, untaxed portions of railroad retirement benefits, Black Lung Benefits, disability, etc. Tax filers only: report combat pay not included in adjusted gross income (Q35 and Q79). Don't include student aid, Workforce Investment Act educational benefits, combat pay if you are not a tax filer, or benefits from flexible spending arrangements (e.g., cafeteria plans).	$
$	Money received, or paid on your behalf (e.g., bills), not reported elsewhere on this form.	XXXXXXXXX
$	Enter in question 41 on Page 7.	Enter in question 85 on Page 5. $

FAFSA Worksheet C—Report Annual Amounts

Student/Spouse For Page 7		Parents For Page 5
$	Education credits (Hope and Lifetime Learning tax credits) from IRS Form 1040—line 49 or 1040A—line 31.	$
$	Child support paid because of divorce or separation or as a result of a legal requirement. Don't include support for children in your (or your parents') household, as reported in question 90 (or question 66 for your parents).	$
$	Taxable earnings from need-based employment programs, such as Federal Work-Study and need-based employment portions of fellowships and assistantships.	$
$	Student grant and scholarship aid reported to the IRS in your (or your parents') adjusted gross income. Includes AmeriCorps benefits (awards, living allowances, and interest accrual payments), as well as grant or scholarship portions of fellowships and assistantships.	$
$	Enter in question 42 on Page 7.	Enter in question 86 on Page 5. $

Estimate Your EFC Under Federal Methodology

WORKSHEET 4A:
Estimate a Dependent Student's Expected Contribution

STUDENT'S INCOME	
1. Taxable income ("adjusted gross income" from IRS Form 1040)	$
2. Untaxed income/benefits	+
3. Taxable student aid	-
4. Total student's income (sum of lines 1 and 2, minus line 3)	=
Allowances	
5. U.S. income tax paid (from IRS Form 1040)	
6. State taxes paid (% from Table 8 x line 4)	+
7. F.I.C.A. (Table 2)	+
8. Income protection allowance	$3,000
9. Parents' negative available income offset (line 11 of parents' worksheet, if negative)	+
10. Total allowances (sum of lines 5–9)	=
11. Available income (line 4 minus line 10)	=
12. Available income assessment rate	x 0.50
13. Contribution from income (line 11 x line 12; if negative, enter $0)	=
Student's Assets*	
14. Cash, savings, and checking accounts	
15. Other real estate/investment equity	+
16. Business/nonfamily farm equity	+
17. Net assets (sum of lines 14–16)	=
18. Asset assessment rate	x 0.20
19. Contribution from assets (line 17 x line 18; if simple needs test or negative, enter $0)	=
Contribution**	
20. Total Student Contribution (sum of lines 13 and 19)	=

* If you are eligible to file an IRS 1040A or 1040EZ form, or you are not required to file a tax return, and your parents' taxable income is less than $50,000, no assets are included in the methodology.

** If your parents' adjusted gross income is $15,000 or less, and they file or are eligible to file an IRS 1040A or 1040EZ form, no contribution is expected.

WORKSHEET 4B:
Estimate the Parents' Expected Contribution

Parents' Income	
1. Taxable income ("adjusted gross income" from IRS Form 1040)	$
2. Untaxed income/benefits	+
3. Income exclusions (child support paid + education tax credits)	-
4. Total parents' income (sum of lines 1 and 2, minus line 3)	=
Allowances	
5. U.S. income tax paid (from IRS Form 1040)	
6. State taxes paid (% from Table 8 x line 4)	+
7. F.I.C.A. paid (Table 9)	+
8. Employment allowance (Table 9)	+
9. Income protection allowance (Table 10)	+
10. Total allowances (sum of lines 5–9)	=
11. Available income (line 4 minus line 10)	=
Parents' Assets*	
12. Cash, savings, and checking accounts	
13. Other real estate/investment equity	+
14. Adjusted business/nonfamily farm equity (Table 11)	+
15. Net worth (sum of lines 12–14)	=
16. Education Savings and Asset protection allowance (Table 12)	-
17. Discretionary net worth (line 15 minus line 16)	=
18. Conversion percentage	x 12%
19. Contribution from assets (line 17 x line 18; if simple needs test or negative, enter $0)	=
20. Adjusted available income (sum of line 11 and line 19)	=
Contribution**	
21. Total contribution (calculate using line 20 and Table 13)	=
22. Number of dependent children in college at least half-time	÷
23. Parents' contribution for student (line 21 divided by line 22; if negative, enter $0)	=

* If your parents are eligible to file an IRS 1040A or 1040EZ form, or are not required to file a tax return and their taxable income is less than $50,000, no assets are included in the methodology.

** If your parents' adjusted gross income is $15,000 or less, and they are eligible to file an IRS 1040A or 1040EZ form, or are not required to file a tax return, no contribution is expected.

TABLE 8: Federal EFC Allowances for State Taxes

	Parents TOTAL INCOME		Student TOTAL INCOME		Parents TOTAL INCOME		Student TOTAL INCOME
	$ 0–14,999	$15,000 or more	Any amount		$ 0–14,999	$15,000 or more	Any amount
Alabama*(AL)	3%	2%	2%	North Dakota*(ND)	2%	1%	1%
Alaska*(AK)	2	1	0	Northern Mariana Islands*(MP)	3	2	2
American Samoa (AS)	3	2	2	Ohio*(OH)	6	5	4
Arizona*(AZ)	4	3	3	Oklahoma*(OK)	6	5	3
Arkansas*(AR)	4	3	3	Oregon*(OR)	7	6	5
California*(CA)	7	6	5	Palau*(PW)	3	2	2
Canada*(CN)	3	2	2	Pennsylvania*(PA)	5	4	3
Colorado*(CO)	4	3	3	Puerto Rico*(PR)	3	2	2
Connecticut*(CT)	7	6	4	Rhode Island*(RI)	7	6	4
Delaware*(DE)	4	3	3	South Carolina*(SC)	5	4	3
District of Columbia*(DC)	7	6	6	South Dakota*(SD)	2	1	1
Federated States of Micronesia*(FM)	3	2	2	Tennessee*(TN)	2	1	1
Florida*(FL)	3	2	1	Texas*(TX)	3	2	1
Georgia*(GA)	6	5	3	Utah*(UT)	5	4	3
Guam*(GU)	3	2	2	Vermont*(VT)	5	4	3
Hawaii*(HI)	4	3	4	Virgin Islands*(VI)	3	2	2
Idaho*(ID)	5	4	3	Virginia*(VA)	5	4	3
Illinois*(IL)	5	4	2	Washington*(WA)	4	3	2
Indiana*(IN)	4	3	3	West Virginia*(WV)	3	2	2
Iowa*(IA)	5	4	3	Wisconsin*(WI)	7	6	4
Kansas*(KS)	5	4	3	Wyoming*(WY)	2	1	1
Kentucky*(KY)	5	4	4	Not Reported*(NR)	3	2	2
Louisiana*(LA)	3	2	2				
Maine*(ME)	6	5	4				
Marshall Islands*(MH)	3	2	2				
Maryland*(MD)	7	6	5				
Massachusetts*(MA)	6	5	4				
Mexico*(MX)	3	2	2				
Michigan*(MI)	5	4	3				
Minnesota*(MN)	6	5	4				
Mississippi	4	3	2				
Missouri*(MO)	5	4	3				
Montana*(MT)	5	4	3				
Nebraska*(NE)	5	4	3				
Nevada*(NV)	3	2	1				
New Hampshire*(NH)	5	4	1				
New Jersey*(NJ)	8	7	4				
New Mexico*(NM)	4	3	3				
New York*(NY)	9	8	6				
North Carolina*(NC)	6	5	4				

TABLE 9. Federal EFC Allowances for FICA and Employment

FICA: WAGES

$1 to $97,500	7.65% of income earned by each wage earner (maximum $7,312.50 per person)
$97,501 or more	$7,312.50 + 1.45% of income earned above $97,500 by each wage earner

EMPLOYMENT ALLOWANCE   35% of lesser earned income to a maximum $3,300 (single parent: 35% of earned income to a maximum of $3,300)

TABLE 10. Federal EFC Income Protection Allowance for Parents

Family Size* (including student)	Number in College**				
	1	2	3	4	5
2	$ 15,380	$ 12,750			
3	19,150	16,540	$ 13,900		
4	23,660	21,020	18,410	$ 15,720	
5	27,910	25,280	22,660	20,030	$ 17,410
6	32,650	30,010	27,400	24,770	22,450

*For each additional family member, add $3,590.
**For each additional college student, subtract $2,550.

TABLE 11. Federal EFC Adjusted Net Worth of a Business or Farm

NET WORTH	ADJUSTED NET WORTH		
Less than $1	$	0	
$1 to 110,000	$	0	+ 40% of net worth
$110,001 to 330,000	$	44,000	+ 50% of net worth over $110,000
$330,001 to 550,000	$	154,000	+ 60% of net worth over $330,000
$550,001 or more	$	286,000	+ 100% of net worth over $550,000

TABLE 12. Federal EFC Education Savings and Asset Protection Allowance for Parents

AGE OF OLDER PARENT OR STUDENT	COUPLE/ MARRIED	UNMARRIED/ SINGLE
25 or under	$ 0	$ 0
26	2,500	1,000
27	5,100	2,100
28	7,600	3,100
29	10,200	4,200
30	12,700	5,200
31	15,200	6,300
32	17,800	7,300
33	20,300	8,400
34	22,900	9,400
35	25,400	10,500
36	27,900	11,500
37	30,500	12,600
38	33,000	13,600
39	35,600	14,700
40	38,100	15,700
41	39,100	16,100
42	40,100	16,400
43	41,100	16,800
44	42,100	17,200
45	43,100	17,500
46	44,200	17,900
47	45,300	18,300
48	46,400	18,800
49	47,600	19,200
50	48,700	19,700
51	50,200	20,100
52	51,500	20,500
53	53,000	21,000
54	54,300	21,600
55	55,900	22,100
56	57,300	22,700
57	59,000	23,200
58	60,700	23,900
59	62,500	24,400
60	64,300	25,100
61	66,200	25,700
62	68,100	26,400
63	70,400	27,200
64	72,400	27,900
65 or over	74,800	28,700

TABLE 13. Federal EFC Parents' Contribution from Adjusted Available Income (AAI)

ADJUSTED AVAILABLE INCOME (AAI)	TOTAL CONTRIBUTIONS FROM INCOME
Less than $ -3,409 (3,409)	$ -750
$(3,409) to 13,400	22% of AI
$ 13,401 to 16,800	$ 2,948 + 25% of AAI over $ 13,400
$ 16,801 to 20,200	$ 3,798 + 29% of AAI over $ 16,800
$ 20,201 to 23,700	$ 4,784 + 34% of AAI over $ 20,200
$ 23,701 to 27,100	$ 5,974 + 40% of AAI over $ 23,700
$ 27,101 or more	$ 7,334 + 47% of AAI over $ 27,100

Contact Information for State Aid Programs

ALABAMA
Alabama Commission on Higher Education
P.O. Box 302000
Montgomery, AL 36130-2000
334 242-1998
www.ache.state.al.us

ALASKA
Alaska Commission on Postsecondary Education
P.O. Box 110505
Juneau, AK 99811-0505
800 441-2962
www.state.ak.us/acpe

ARIZONA
Arizona Department of Education
1535 W. Jefferson Street
Phoenix, AZ 85007
800 352-4558
www.ade.state.az.us

ARKANSAS
Arkansas Department of Higher Education
114 East Capitol Avenue
Little Rock, AR 72201
501 371-2000
www.arkansashighered.com

CALIFORNIA
California Student Aid Commission
P.O. Box 419026
Rancho Cordova, CA 95741-9026
888 224-7268
www.csac.ca.gov

COLORADO
Colorado Department of Education
201 East Colfax Avenue
Denver, CO 80203-1799
303 866-6600
www.cde.state.co.us

CONNECTICUT
Connecticut Department of Higher Education
61 Woodland Street
Hartford, CT 06105-2326
860 947-1800
www.ctdhe.org

DELAWARE
Delaware Higher Education Commission
820 North French Street
Wilmington, DE 19801-3509
800 292-7935
www.doe.state.de.us/high-ed

DISTRICT OF COLUMBIA
State Education Office
441 4th St., N.W., Suite 350 North
Washington, DC 20001
202 727-6436
www.seo.dc.gov

FLORIDA
Florida Department of Education
Office of Student Financial Assistance
1940 N. Monroe Street, Suite 70
Tallahassee, FL 32303-4759
888 827-2004
www.firn.edu/doe

GEORGIA
Georgia Student Finance Commission
2082 East Exchange Place
Tucker, GA 30084
800 505-4732
www.gsfc.org

HAWAII
Hawaii State Department of Education
P.O. Box 2360
Honolulu, HI 96804
808 586-3230
www.doe.k12.hi.us

IDAHO
Idaho State Department of Education
P.O. Box 83720
650 West State Street
Boise, ID 83720-0027
800 432-4601
www.sde.state.id.us

ILLINOIS
Illinois Student Assistance Commission
1755 Lake Cook Road
Deerfield, IL 60015-5209
800 899-4722
www.collegezone.com

INDIANA
State Student Assistance Commission of Indiana
150 W. Market Street, Suite 500
Indianapolis, IN 46204
888 528-4719
www.in.gov/ssaci

IOWA
Iowa College Student Aid Commission
200 10th Street, Fourth Floor
Des Moines, IA 50309-3609
515 242-3344
www.iowacollegeaid.org

KANSAS
Kansas Board of Regents
1000 SW Jackson Street, Suite 520
Topeka, KS 66612-1368
785 296-3421
www.kansasregents.org

KENTUCKY
KHEAA Student Aid Branch
P.O. Box 798
Frankfort, KY 40602
800 928-8926
www.kheaa.com

LOUISIANA
Louisiana Office of Student Financial Assistance
P.O. Box 91202
Baton Rouge, LA 70821-9202
800 259-5626
www.osfa.state.la.us

MAINE
Finance Authority of Maine
Education Assistance Division
P.O. Box 949
5 Community Drive
Augusta, ME 04332
800 228-3734
www.famemaine.com

MARYLAND
Maryland Higher Education Commission
Office of Student Financial Assistance
839 Bestgate Road, Suite 400
Annapolis, MD 21401
800 974-0203
www.mhec.state.md.us

MASSACHUSETTS
Massachusetts Board of Higher Education
Office of Student Financial Assistance
454 Broadway, Suite 200
Revere, MA 02151-3034
617 727-9420
www.osfa.mass.edu

MICHIGAN
Michigan Higher Education Assistance Authority
Office of Scholarships and Grants
P.O. Box 30462
Lansing, MI 48909-7962
888 447-2687
www.michigan.gov/mistudentaid

MINNESOTA
Minnesota Office of Higher Education
1450 Energy Park Drive, Suite 350
St. Paul, MN 55108-5227
800 657-3866
www.ohe.state.mn.us

MISSISSIPPI
Mississippi Office of Student Financial Aid
3825 Ridgewood Road
Jackson, MS 39211-6453
800 327-2980
www.ihl.state.ms.us/financialaid

MISSOURI
Missouri Department of Higher Education
3515 Amazonas Drive
Jefferson City, MO 65109-5717
800 473-6757
www.dhe.mo.gov

MONTANA
Montana Board of Regents
P.O. Box 203201
46 North Last Chance Gulch
Helena, MT 59620-3201
406 444-6570
www.bor.montana.edu

NEBRASKA
Nebraska Coordination Commission for Postsecondary Education
P.O. Box 95005
Lincoln, NE 68509-5005
402 471-2847
www.ccpe.state.ne.us

NEVADA
Nevada Department of Education
700 East 5th Street
Carson City, NV 89701
775 687-9228
www.doe.nv.gov

NEW HAMPSHIRE
New Hampshire Postsecondary Education Commission
3 Barrell Court, Suite 300
Concord, NH 03301-8543
603 271-2555
www.nh.gov/postsecondary

NEW JERSEY
New Jersey Higher Education Student Assistance Authority
P.O. Box 540
Trenton, NJ 08625
800 792-8670
www.hesaa.org

NEW MEXICO
New Mexico Higher Education Department
1068 Cerillos Road
Santa Fe, NM 87505
800 279-9777
www.hed.state.nm.us

NEW YORK
New York State Higher Education Services Corporation
99 Washington Avenue
Albany, NY 12255
888 697-4372
www.hesc.state.ny.us

NORTH CAROLINA
North Carolina State Education Assistance Authority
P.O. Box 14103
Research Triangle Park, NC 27709
919 549-8614
www.ncseaa.edu

NORTH DAKOTA
North Dakota University System
600 East Boulevard, Dept. 215
Bismarck, ND 58505-0230
701 328-2960
www.ndus.nodak.edu

OHIO
Ohio Board of Regents
30 East Broad Street, 36th floor
Columbus, OH 43215-3414
614 466-6000
www.regents.ohio.gov

OKLAHOMA
Oklahoma State Regents for Higher Education
Tuition Aid Grant Program
655 Research Parkway, Suite 200
Oklahoma City, OK 73104
405 225-9100
www.okhighered.org

OREGON
Oregon Student Assistance Commission
1500 Valley River Drive, Suite 100
Eugene, OR 97401
800 452-8807
www.osac.state.or.us

PENNSYLVANIA
Pennsylvania Higher Education Assistance Agency
1200 N. Seventh Street
Harrisburg, PA 17102-1444
800 692-7392
www.pheaa.org

PUERTO RICO
Departmento de Educacion
P.O. Box 190759
San Juan, PR 00919-0759
787 759-2000
www.de.gobierno.pr

RHODE ISLAND
Rhode Island Higher Education Assistance Authority
560 Jefferson Boulevard, Suite 100
Warwick, RI 02886
401 736-1100
www.riheaa.org

SOUTH CAROLINA
South Carolina Commission on Higher Education
1333 Main Street, Suite 200
Columbia, SC 29201
803 737-2260
www.che.sc.gov

SOUTH DAKOTA
South Dakota Department of Education
Office of Finance and Management
700 Governors Drive
Pierre, SD 57501
605 773-3134
http://doe.sd.gov/stateaid

TENNESSEE
Tennessee Student Assistance Corporation
404 James Robertson Parkway
Suite 1510, Parkway Towers
Nashville, TN 37243-0820
800 342-1663
www.state.tn.us/tsac

TEXAS
Texas Higher Education Coordinating Board
Division of Student Services
P.O. Box 12788, Capital Station
Austin, TX 78711
800 242-3062
www.collegefortexans.com

UTAH
Utah Higher Education Assistance Authority
Board of Regents Building, The Gateway
60 South 400 West
Salt Lake City, UT 84101-1284
801 321-7200
www.uheaa.org

VERMONT
Vermont Student Assistance Corporation
P.O. Box 999
Winooski, VT 05404
800 798-8722
www.vsac.org

VIRGINIA
State Council of Higher Education for Virginia
101 North 14th Street
Richmond, VA 23219
804 225-2600
www.schev.edu

WASHINGTON
Washington Higher Education Coordination Board
917 Lakeridge Way
P.O. Box 43430
Olympia, WA 98504-3430
360 753-7800
www.hecb.wa.gov

WEST VIRGINIA
West Virginia Higher Education Policy Commission
Central Office, Higher Education Grant Program
1018 Kanawha Boulevard East, Suite 700
Charleston, WV 25301-2800
304 558-4614
www.hepc.wvnet.edu

WISCONSIN
Wisconsin Higher Educational Aids Board
131 West Wilson, Suite 902
Madison, WI 53707
608 267-2206
www.heab.state.wi.us

WYOMING
Wyoming Department of Education
2300 Capitol Avenue
Hathaway Building, Second Floor
Cheyenne, WY 82002-0050
307 777-7690
www.k12.wy.us

GUAM
University of Guam
Student Financial Aid Office
UOG Station
Mangilao, GU 96923
671 735-2287
www.uog.edu

VIRGIN ISLANDS
Financial Aid Office, Virgin Islands Board of Education
P.O. Box 11900
St. Thomas, VI 00801
340 774-4546

Contact Information for State 529 Plans

STATE	PROGRAM NAME	CONTACT INFORMATION	PLAN TYPE
AK	**University of Alaska College Savings Plan**	University of Alaska 866 277-1005 http://www.uacollegesavings.com	Savings
	T. Rowe Price	800 369-3641 http://www.price529.com	Savings
AL	**Prepaid Affordable Tuition Plan (PACT)**	State Treasurer 800 252-7228 www.treasury.state.al.us/content/pact_intro.htm	Prepaid
	Van Kampen Investments	866 529-2228 http://www.treasury.state.al.us/website/529_he/college_ savings.htm	Savings
AZ	**Arizona Family College Savings Programs (AFCSP)**	800 888-2723 http://arizona.collegesavings.com	Savings
	Arizona Family College Savings Programs	Securities Management and Research, Inc. http://www.smrinvest.com/College/default.asp	Savings
	Fidelity Arizona College Savings Plan	Fidelity Investments 800 544-1262 http://personal.fidelity.com/planning/college/content/ landing_az.shtml.cvsr	Savings
	Pacific Funds 529 College Savings Plan	Pacific Life 800 722-2333 http://www.collegesavings.pacificlife.com	Savings
AR	**GIFT College Investing Plan**	Franklin Templeton Investments/Mercury Advisors 800 587-7301 http://thegiftplan.uii.upromise.com	Savings
CA	**Golden State ScholarShare College Savings Trust**	Golden State ScholarShare 800 544-5248 http://www.scholarshare.com	Savings
CO	**CollegeInvest—Scholars Choice College Savings**	Scholars Choice 888 572-4652 http://www.scholars-choice.com or http://www.collegeinvest.org	Savings
CT	**Connecticut Higher Education Trust (CHET)**	Connecticut's 529 College Savings Program 888 799-2438 http://www.aboutchet.com	Savings
DC	**DC College Savings Plan**	800 987-4859 http://www.dccollegesavings.com	Savings
DE	**Delaware College Investment Plan**	800 544-1655 http://personal.fidelity.com/planning/investment	Savings
FL	**Florida Prepaid College Program**	Florida Prepaid College Program Board 800 552-4723 http://www.florida529plans.com	Prepaid
	Florida College Investment Plan	Florida Prepaid College Program Board 800 552-4723 http://www.florida529plans.com	Savings
GA	**Path2College 529 Plan**	877 424-4377 www.path2college529.com	Savings
HI	**Hawaii's College Savings Program**	866 529-3343 www.hi529.com	Savings
IA	**College Savings Iowa**	Iowa State Treasurer's Office 888 672-9116 http://collegesavingsiowa.uii.upromise.com	Savings
ID	**Idaho College Savings Program (IDeal)**	866 433-2533 http://www.idsaves.org	Savings
IL	**College Illinois!**	877 877-3724 http://www.collegeillinois.com	Prepaid
	Bright Start College Savings Program	877 432-7444 http://www.brightstartsavings.com	Savings
IN	**CollegeChoice 529 Investment Plan**	One Group Investments 866 400-7526 http://www.collegechoiceplan.com	Savings
KS	**Kansas Learning Quest Education Savings**	American Century 800 579-2203 https://www.learningquestsavings.com	Savings
	Schwab 529 College Savings Plan	888 903-3863 http://www.schwab.com	Savings

STATE	PROGRAM NAME	CONTACT INFORMATION	PLAN TYPE
KY	**Kentucky's Affordable Prepaid Tuition (KAPT)**	Kentucky Higher Education Assistance Authority 888 919-5278 http://www.getkapt.com	Prepaid
	Kentucky Education Savings Plan Trust	Kentucky Higher Education Assistance Authority 877 598-7878 http://www.kysaves.com	Savings
LA	**START Saving Program**	Louisiana Office of Student Financial Assistance 800 259-5626 http://www.startsaving.la.gov/savings	Savings
MA	**The U.Plan**	Massachusetts Educational Finance Authority 800 449-6332 http://www.mefa.org	Prepaid
	The U.Fund College Investing Plan	Massachusetts Educational Finance Authority and Fidelity Investments 800 544-2776 http://personal.fidelity.com/planning/investment	Savings
MD	**Prepaid College Trust**	College Savings Plans of Maryland 888 463-4723 http://www.collegesavingsmd.org	Prepaid
	College Investment Plan	College Savings Plans of Maryland 888 463-4723 http://www.collegesavingsmd.org	Savings
ME	**NextGen College Investing Plan**	Merrill Lynch 877 463-9843 http://www.nextgenplan.com	Savings
MI	**Michigan Education Trust (MET)**	Michigan Department of Treasury 800 638-4543 http://www.michigan.gov/treasury	Prepaid
	Michigan Education Savings Program (MESP)	Michigan Department of Treasury 877 861-6377 http://www.misaves.com	Savings
MN	**Minnesota College Savings Plan**	877 338-4646 http://www.mnsaves.org	Savings
MO	**Missouri 529 College Savings Plan (MOST)**	888 414-6678 https://missourimost.s.upromise.com	Savings
MS	**Mississippi Prepaid Affordable College Tuition Program (MPACT)**	Mississippi State Treasury Department 800 987-4450 www.collegesavingsmississippi.com	Prepaid
	or **Mississippi Affordable College Savings (MACS)**	800 486-3670 http://www.collegesavingsms.com	Savings
MT	**Montana Family Education Savings Program**	800 888-2723 http://montana.collegesavings.com	Savings
	CollegeSure 529	Montana Commission for Higher Education 800 888-2723 http://montana.collegesavings.com	Savings
NC	**North Carolina's National College Savings Program**	College Foundation of North Carolina 866 866-2362 http://www.cfnc.org/savings	Savings
ND	**Morgan Stanley**	866 728-3529 http://www.collegesave4U.com	Savings
NE	**College Savings Plan of Nebraska**	Nebraska State Treasurer 888 993-3746 http://www.planforcollegenow.com	Savings
	TD Ameritrade 529 College Savings Plan	877 408-4644 http://www.savingforcollege.com/529_plan_details/	Savings
NH	**UNIQUE College Investing Plan**	Fidelity Investments 800 544-1914 http://personal.fidelity.com/planning	Savings
NJ	**New Jersey Better Educational Savings Trust (NJBEST)**	Higher Education Student Assistance Authority 877 465-2378 http://www.njbest.com	Savings
NM	**The Education Plan**	The Education Plan of New Mexico 800 337-5268 http://www.theeducationplan.com	Savings
NV	**Prepaid Tuition Program**	Nevada State Treasurer 888 477-2667 http://nevadatreasurer.gov	Prepaid
	USAA College Savings Plan	800 292-8825 http://www.savingforcollege.com/529_plan_details/	Savings
	Vanguard 529 Savings Plan	866 734-4524 http://www.vanguard.com	Savings
	The Upromise College Fund	800 587-7305 http://uii.s.upromise.com	Savings

STATE	PROGRAM NAME	CONTACT INFORMATION	PLAN TYPE
NY	**New York's 529 College Savings Program**	Comptroller & Higher Ed. Services Corp. 877 697-2837 http://nysaves.uii.upromise.com	Savings
OH	**Ohio CollegeAdvantage Savings Plan**	Ohio Tuition Trust Authority 800 233-6734 http://www.collegeadvantage.com	Savings
OK	**Oklahoma College Savings Plan**	877 654-7284 http://www.ok4saving.org	Savings
OR	**Oregon College Savings Plan**	Oregon Qualified Tuition Savings Board 866 772-8464 http://www.oregoncollegesavings.com	Savings
PA	**PA 529 Guaranteed Savings Plan**	Pennsylvania State Treasury 800 440-4000 http://pa529gsp.uii.upromise.com	Guaranteed Savings
	PA 529 Investment Plan	Pennsylvania State Treasury 800 294-6195 https://pa529invest.s.upromise.com	Savings
RI	**College Bound Fund**	AllianceBernstein 888 324-5057 http://ri.collegeboundfund.com/ri	Savings
SC	**South Carolina Tuition Prepayment Program (SCTPP)**	South Carolina Office of State Treasurer 888 772-4723 http://www.scgrad.org	Prepaid
	FUTURE Scholar	Nations Funds 888 244-5674 http://www.futurescholar.com	Savings
SD	**College Access 529**	Pimco Funds 866 529-7462 http://www.collegeaccess529.com	Savings
TN	**BEST Prepaid College Tuition Plan**	888 486-2378 http://treasury.state.tn.us/best	Prepaid
	BEST Savings Plan	State of Tennessee Treasury Department 888 486-2378 http://www.tnbest.org	Savings
TX	**Texas College Savings Plan**	Texas Comptroller of Public Accounts 800 445-4723 www.texascollegesavings.com	Savings
UT	**Utah Educational Savings Plan Trust (UESP)**	Utah State Board of Regents 800 418-2551 http://www.uesp.org	Savings
VA	**Virginia Prepaid Education Program (VPEP)**	Virginia College Savings Plan 888 567-0540 http://www.virginia529.com	Prepaid
	Virginia Education Savings Trust (VEST)	Virginia College Savings Plan 888 567-0540 http://www.virginia529.com	Savings
VT	**Vermont Higher Education Investment Plan**	Vermont Student Assistance Corporation 800 642-3177 http://www.services.vsac.org/ilwwcm/connect/VSAC	Savings
WA	**Guaranteed Education Tuition (GET) Program**	Committee on Advanced Tuition Payment 800 955-2318 http://www.get.wa.gov	Prepaid
WI	**EdVest**	EdVest College Savings Program 888 338-3789 http://www.wellsfargoadvantagefunds.com/wfweb/wf/ev/index.jsp	Savings
WV	**SMART529—Direct College Savings Plan**	Hartford Life Insurance Co. 866 574-3542 http://www.smart529.com	Savings
	SMART529 Select	866 574-3542 www.smart529select.com	Savings
WY	**The College Achievement Plan**	Mercury Asset Management 877 529-2655	Savings

PART II: TABLES AND WORKSHEETS

Part III

Financial Aid
College by College

Alabama

Alabama Agricultural and Mechanical University
Huntsville, Alabama
www.aamu.edu   Federal Code: 001002

4-year public university and agricultural college in small city.
Enrollment: 4,716 undergrads, 7% part-time. 882 full-time freshmen.
Selectivity: Admits less than 50% of applicants.

BASIC COSTS (2007-2008)
Tuition and fees: $4,930; out-of-state residents $9,220.
Per-credit charge: $143; out-of-state residents $286.
Room and board: $3,592.
Additional info: Part-time student required fees are $440. Tuition/fee waivers available for minority students.

FINANCIAL AID PICTURE
Students with need: Need-based aid available for full-time and part-time students. Work study available weekends and for part-time students.
Students without need: No-need awards available for athletics, minority status.
Scholarships offered: Presidential scholarship for students with 4.0 GPA, pays tuition and fees.

FINANCIAL AID PROCEDURES
Forms required: FAFSA, institutional form.
Dates and Deadlines: Applicants notified on a rolling basis; must reply within 2 week(s) of notification.

CONTACT
Sybrenna Harris, Director of Financial Aid
Box 908, Normal, AL 35762
(256) 372-4862

Alabama State University
Montgomery, Alabama
www.alasu.edu   Federal Code: 001005

4-year public university in small city.
Enrollment: 4,589 undergrads, 9% part-time. 1,366 full-time freshmen.
Selectivity: Admits less than 50% of applicants.

BASIC COSTS (2007-2008)
Tuition and fees: $4,508; out-of-state residents $8,516.
Per-credit charge: $167; out-of-state residents $334.
Room and board: $4,150.

FINANCIAL AID PICTURE (2007-2008)
Students with need: Out of 1,327 full-time freshmen who applied for aid, 1,279 were judged to have need. Of these, 1,023 received aid, and 235 had their full need met. Average financial aid package met 73% of need; average scholarship/grant was $4,313; average loan was $3,477. For part-time students, average financial aid package was $7,720.
Students without need: 8 full-time freshmen who did not demonstrate need for aid received scholarships/grants; average award was $6,600. No-need awards available for academics, alumni affiliation, art, athletics, job skills, leadership, minority status, music/drama, ROTC, state/district residency.
Scholarships offered: 54 full-time freshmen received athletic scholarships; average amount $8,560.
Cumulative student debt: 94% of graduating class had student loans; average debt was $26,926.

FINANCIAL AID PROCEDURES
Forms required: FAFSA.
Dates and Deadlines: Priority date 4/1; no closing date. Applicants notified on a rolling basis starting 5/15.
Transfers: Applicants notified on a rolling basis starting 5/1.

CONTACT
Dorenda Adams, Director of Financial Aid
PO Box 271, Montgomery, AL 36101-0271
(334) 229-4323

Amridge University
Montgomery, Alabama
www.amridgeuniversity.edu   Federal Code: 016885

4-year private university and seminary college in small city, affiliated with Church of Christ.
Enrollment: 342 undergrads, 27% part-time.
Selectivity: Open admission; but selective for some programs.

BASIC COSTS (2007-2008)
Additional info: $260 per-credit-hour charge (including required fees) for undergraduates; some courses require additional lab and/or exam fees, which are the responsibility of the student.

FINANCIAL AID PICTURE
Students with need: Need-based aid available for full-time and part-time students.
Students without need: No-need awards available for academics, leadership.
Additional info: Scholarships based on need and grades. Half-tuition scholarship is available for full-time undergraduate students.

FINANCIAL AID PROCEDURES
Forms required: FAFSA, institutional form.
Dates and Deadlines: Priority date 5/1; closing date 6/30. Applicants notified by 6/30; must reply by 8/15 or within 2 week(s) of notification.
Transfers: No deadline.

CONTACT
Rosemary Kennington, Financial Aid Director
1200 Taylor Road, Montgomery, AL 36117-3553
(800) 351-4040 ext. 7527

Athens State University
Athens, Alabama
www.athens.edu   Federal Code: 001008

Upper-division public business and teachers college in large town.
Enrollment: 2,858 undergrads, 53% part-time.

BASIC COSTS (2007-2008)
Tuition and fees: $4,050; out-of-state residents $7,350.
Per-credit charge: $110; out-of-state residents $220.

FINANCIAL AID PICTURE (2006-2007)
Students with need: 21% of average financial aid package awarded as scholarships/grants, 79% awarded as loans/jobs. Need-based aid available for part-time students. Work study available nights, weekends, and for part-time students.
Students without need: No-need awards available for academics, alumni affiliation, art, athletics, leadership, minority status.

FINANCIAL AID PROCEDURES
Forms required: FAFSA.
Dates and Deadlines: No deadline. Applicants notified on a rolling basis starting 6/1; must reply within 3 week(s) of notification.

CONTACT

Sarah McAbee, Director, Student Financial Services
300 North Beaty Street, Athens, AL 35611
(256) 233-8122

Auburn University

Auburn, Alabama
www.auburn.edu   Federal Code: 001009

4-year public university in large town.

Enrollment: 19,794 undergrads, 8% part-time. 4,069 full-time freshmen.

Selectivity: Admits 50 to 75% of applicants.

BASIC COSTS (2007-2008)

Tuition and fees: $5,834; out-of-state residents $16,334.

Per-credit charge: $217; out-of-state residents $651.

Room and board: $7,466.

FINANCIAL AID PICTURE (2006-2007)

Students with need: Out of 1,928 full-time freshmen who applied for aid, 1,333 were judged to have need. Of these, 1,235 received aid, and 425 had their full need met. Average financial aid package met 43% of need; average scholarship/grant was $5,025; average loan was $2,897. For part-time students, average financial aid package was $5,828.

Students without need: 445 full-time freshmen who did not demonstrate need for aid received scholarships/grants; average award was $4,060.

Scholarships offered: *Merit:* Entering Freshmen and General Scholarships require minimum 28 ACT or 1240 SAT and 3.25 GPA; up to full tuition awarded. National Merit and National Achievement Finalists; full tuition plus additional benefits. 3.5 GPA for transfers, financial need considered. *Athletic:* 80 full-time freshmen received athletic scholarships; average amount $11,008.

Cumulative student debt: 65% of graduating class had student loans; average debt was $25,176.

Additional info: State of Alabama has pre-paid college tuition plan for residents.

FINANCIAL AID PROCEDURES

Forms required: FAFSA, institutional form.

Dates and Deadlines: No deadline. Applicants notified on a rolling basis.

Transfers: No deadline. Applicants notified on a rolling basis; must reply within 2 week(s) of notification.

CONTACT

Mike Reynolds, Director of Student Financial Services
Quad Center, Auburn, AL 36849-5111
(334) 844-4080

Auburn University at Montgomery

Montgomery, Alabama
www.aum.edu   Federal Code: 008310

4-year public university in small city.

Enrollment: 4,134 undergrads, 33% part-time. 539 full-time freshmen.

Selectivity: Admits over 75% of applicants.

BASIC COSTS (2007-2008)

Tuition and fees: $5,010; out-of-state residents $14,490.

Per-credit charge: $158; out-of-state residents $474.

Room and board: $4,890.

FINANCIAL AID PICTURE (2007-2008)

Students with need: Out of 348 full-time freshmen who applied for aid, 270 were judged to have need. Of these, 258 received aid. For part-time students, average financial aid package was $5,505.

Students without need: No-need awards available for academics, alumni affiliation, art, athletics, job skills, leadership, minority status, music/drama, religious affiliation, ROTC.

FINANCIAL AID PROCEDURES

Forms required: FAFSA.

Dates and Deadlines: Priority date 3/15; no closing date. Applicants notified on a rolling basis starting 5/1; must reply within 2 week(s) of notification.

Transfers: Aid awarded based on need and the availability of funds.

CONTACT

Anthony Richey, Director of Financial Aid
7400 East Drive, Room 139 Taylor Center, Montgomery, AL 36124-4023
(334) 244-3571

Bevill State Community College

Sumiton, Alabama
www.bscc.edu   Federal Code: 005733

2-year public community college in small town.

Enrollment: 3,805 undergrads, 45% part-time. 735 full-time freshmen.

Selectivity: Open admission; but selective for some programs.

BASIC COSTS (2007-2008)

Tuition and fees: $2,700; out-of-state residents $4,830.

Per-credit charge: $71; out-of-state residents $142.

Additional info: Room-only rates for Bevill campuses: $1,350.

FINANCIAL AID PICTURE

Students with need: Need-based aid available for full-time and part-time students.

Students without need: No-need awards available for academics, athletics, leadership, music/drama.

FINANCIAL AID PROCEDURES

Forms required: FAFSA.

Dates and Deadlines: Priority date 5/1; no closing date. Applicants notified on a rolling basis starting 7/1.

CONTACT

Susanne Bush, Assistant to the Dean of Student Services
Box 800, Sumiton, AL 35148
(205) 387-0517 ext. 5814

Birmingham-Southern College

Birmingham, Alabama
www.bsc.edu   Federal Code: 001012

4-year private liberal arts college in large city, affiliated with United Methodist Church.

Enrollment: 1,339 undergrads, 2% part-time. 450 full-time freshmen.

Selectivity: Admits 50 to 75% of applicants.

BASIC COSTS (2008-2009)

Tuition and fees: $25,586.

Per-credit charge: $1,033.

Room and board: $8,595.

FINANCIAL AID PICTURE (2007-2008)

Students with need: Out of 305 full-time freshmen who applied for aid, 243 were judged to have need. Of these, 243 received aid, and 84 had their full need met. Average financial aid package met 83% of need; average scholarship/grant was $6,618; average loan was $4,586. For part-time students, average financial aid package was $10,623.

Students without need: 187 full-time freshmen who did not demonstrate need for aid received scholarships/grants; average award was $11,985. No-need awards available for academics, alumni affiliation, art, job skills, leadership, minority status, music/drama, religious affiliation, state/district residency.

Scholarships offered: McWane Honors Award: full tuition plus $11,000 per year stipend; based on academic achievement; 1 awarded. Neal and Anne Berte Scholarship: full tuition; academic achievement; 1 awarded. Blount-Monaghan/Vulcan Materials Company Scholarship: full tuition; academic achievement; 1 awarded. William Jones and Elizabeth Perry Rushton Scholarship: full tuition; based on academic achievement; 1 awarded. Phi Beta Kappa: full tuition; based on academic achievement. United Methodist Scholarship: $1,000-$2,500; awarded to United Methodist with recommendation from senior United Methodist Minister.

Cumulative student debt: 79% of graduating class had student loans; average debt was $24,166.

Additional info: Auditions required for music, theater, dance applicants seeking scholarships. Portfolios required for art applicants seeking scholarships, and essays recommended for all applicants seeking scholarships.

FINANCIAL AID PROCEDURES

Forms required: FAFSA.

Dates and Deadlines: Priority date 3/1; no closing date. Applicants notified on a rolling basis starting 3/1; must reply by 8/21.

Transfers: No deadline. Applicants notified on a rolling basis starting 3/1; must reply within 2 week(s) of notification.

CONTACT

Fred Carter, Director of Financial Aid Services
900 Arkadelphia Road, Birmingham, AL 35254
(205) 226-4688

Chattahoochee Valley Community College

Phenix City, Alabama
www.cv.edu   Federal Code: 012182

2-year public community college in small city.

Enrollment: 1,929 undergrads.

Selectivity: Open admission; but selective for some programs.

BASIC COSTS (2007-2008)

Tuition and fees: $2,700; out-of-state residents $4,830.

Per-credit charge: $71; out-of-state residents $142.

FINANCIAL AID PICTURE (2006-2007)

Students with need: Need-based aid available for part-time students. Work study available nights, weekends, and for part-time students.

Students without need: No-need awards available for academics, art, athletics, leadership, music/drama.

FINANCIAL AID PROCEDURES

Forms required: FAFSA.

Dates and Deadlines: Priority date 7/1; no closing date. Applicants notified on a rolling basis; must reply within 1 week(s) of notification.

CONTACT

Joan Waters, Director of Financial Aid
2602 College Drive, Phenix City, AL 36869
(334) 291-4915

Concordia College

Selma, Alabama   Federal Code: 010554
www.concordiaselma.edu   CSS Code: 1989

4-year private liberal arts college in large town, affiliated with Lutheran Church - Missouri Synod.

Enrollment: 554 undergrads.

Selectivity: Admits over 75% of applicants.

BASIC COSTS (2007-2008)

Tuition and fees: $6,826.

Room and board: $3,200.

Additional info: Tuition/fee waivers available for adults.

FINANCIAL AID PICTURE (2006-2007)

Students with need: 98% of average financial aid package awarded as scholarships/grants, 2% awarded as loans/jobs. Need-based aid available for part-time students.

Students without need: This college awards aid only to students with need.

FINANCIAL AID PROCEDURES

Forms required: FAFSA, CSS PROFILE, state aid form, institutional form.

Dates and Deadlines: Priority date 4/1; closing date 4/15. Applicants notified on a rolling basis starting 6/15; must reply within 2 week(s) of notification.

CONTACT

Tharsteen Bridges, Director of Financial Aid
1804 Green Street, Selma, AL 36701
(334) 847-5700 ext. 160

Faulkner University

Montgomery, Alabama
www.faulkner.edu   Federal Code: 001003

4-year private university and liberal arts college in large city, affiliated with Church of Christ.

Enrollment: 2,565 undergrads. 279 full-time freshmen.

Selectivity: Admits 50 to 75% of applicants.

BASIC COSTS (2008-2009)

Tuition and fees: $12,770.

Per-credit charge: $445.

Room and board: $6,350.

Additional info: Tuition/fee waivers available for adults, minority students, unemployed or children of unemployed.

FINANCIAL AID PICTURE (2007-2008)

Students with need: 32% of average financial aid package awarded as scholarships/grants, 68% awarded as loans/jobs. Need-based aid available for part-time students. Work study available nights, weekends, and for part-time students.

Students without need: No-need awards available for academics, alumni affiliation, art, athletics, leadership, music/drama, religious affiliation, ROTC, state/district residency.

FINANCIAL AID PROCEDURES

Forms required: FAFSA, state aid form, institutional form.

Dates and Deadlines: Priority date 5/1; no closing date. Applicants notified on a rolling basis starting 6/1; must reply within 3 week(s) of notification.

CONTACT

William Jackson, Director of Financial Aid
5345 Atlanta Highway, Montgomery, AL 36109-3398
(334) 386-7195

Gadsden State Community College

Gadsden, Alabama
www.gadsdenstate.edu   Federal Code: 001017

2-year public community and technical college in large town.

Enrollment: 5,516 undergrads, 44% part-time. 1,160 full-time freshmen.

Selectivity: Open admission; but selective for some programs.

BASIC COSTS (2007-2008)

Tuition and fees: $2,700; out-of-state residents $4,830.

Per-credit charge: $71; out-of-state residents $142.

Room and board: $2,800.

Additional info: Tuition/fee waivers available for minority students, unemployed or children of unemployed.

FINANCIAL AID PICTURE (2006-2007)

Students with need: For part-time students, average financial aid package was $1,010.

Students without need: No-need awards available for academics, alumni affiliation, art, athletics, leadership, minority status, music/drama, state/district residency.

FINANCIAL AID PROCEDURES

Forms required: FAFSA, institutional form.

Dates and Deadlines: Priority date 4/15; no closing date. Applicants notified on a rolling basis starting 6/10; must reply within 2 week(s) of notification.

CONTACT

Kelly D'Eath, Director of Financial Aid

1001 George Wallace Drive, Gadsden, AL 35902-0227

(256) 549-8267

Heritage Christian University

Florence, Alabama

www.hcu.edu   Federal Code: 015370

4-year private Bible college in large town, affiliated with Church of Christ.

Enrollment: 53 full-time undergrads.

Selectivity: Admits 50 to 75% of applicants.

BASIC COSTS (2007-2008)

Tuition and fees: $9,810.

Per-credit charge: $307.

Room only: $3,000.

FINANCIAL AID PICTURE (2007-2008)

Students with need: Need-based aid available for part-time students.

FINANCIAL AID PROCEDURES

Forms required: FAFSA.

Dates and Deadlines: Priority date 6/1; no closing date. Applicants notified on a rolling basis starting 6/1; must reply by 7/28 or within 2 week(s) of notification.

Transfers: No deadline. Applicants notified on a rolling basis; must reply by 7/28 or within 3 week(s) of notification.

CONTACT

Mechelle Thompson, Financial Aid Counselor

3625 Helton Drive, Florence, AL 35630

(256) 766-6610 ext. 224

Huntingdon College

Montgomery, Alabama

www.huntingdon.edu   Federal Code: 001019

4-year private liberal arts college in small city, affiliated with United Methodist Church.

Enrollment: 943 undergrads, 17% part-time. 254 full-time freshmen.

Selectivity: Admits 50 to 75% of applicants.

BASIC COSTS (2008-2009)

Tuition and fees: $20,020.

Per-credit charge: $800.

Room and board: $6,950.

Additional info: Tuition at time of enrollment locked for 4 years.

FINANCIAL AID PICTURE (2007-2008)

Students with need: Average financial aid package met 80% of need; average scholarship/grant was $7,673; average loan was $3,782. For part-time students, average financial aid package was $2,750.

Students without need: No-need awards available for academics, alumni affiliation, art, leadership, music/drama, religious affiliation, ROTC, state/district residency.

Cumulative student debt: 71% of graduating class had student loans; average debt was $13,696.

FINANCIAL AID PROCEDURES

Forms required: FAFSA, state aid form, institutional form.

Dates and Deadlines: Priority date 4/17; no closing date. Applicants notified on a rolling basis starting 3/1; must reply by 5/1 or within 4 week(s) of notification.

CONTACT

Belinda Duett, Director of Student Financial Services

1500 East Fairview Avenue, Montgomery, AL 36106-2148

(334) 833-4519

J. F. Drake State Technical College

Huntsville, Alabama

www.drakestate.edu   Federal Code: 00526

2-year public technical college in small city.

Enrollment: 675 undergrads, 38% part-time. 139 full-time freshmen.

Selectivity: Open admission; but selective for some programs.

BASIC COSTS (2007-2008)

Tuition and fees: $2,700; out-of-state residents $4,830.

Per-credit charge: $71; out-of-state residents $142.

FINANCIAL AID PICTURE

Students with need: Need-based aid available for full-time and part-time students.

Students without need: No-need awards available for academics, state/district residency.

FINANCIAL AID PROCEDURES

Forms required: FAFSA.

Dates and Deadlines: Priority date 7/1; no closing date. Applicants notified on a rolling basis.

CONTACT

Joylyn Trotman, Financial Aid Officer

3421 Meridian Street North, Huntsville, AL 35811

(256) 551-3127

Jacksonville State University

Jacksonville, Alabama

www.jsu.edu   Federal Code: 001020

4-year public university in small town.

Enrollment: 7,391 undergrads, 22% part-time. 1,252 full-time freshmen.

Selectivity: Admits over 75% of applicants.

BASIC COSTS (2007-2008)

Tuition and fees: $5,070; out-of-state residents $10,140.

Per-credit charge: $169; out-of-state residents $338.

Room and board: $3,763.

FINANCIAL AID PICTURE

Students with need: Need-based aid available for full-time and part-time students. Work study available nights, weekends, and for part-time students.

Students without need: No-need awards available for academics, alumni affiliation, art, athletics, music/drama, ROTC.

Scholarships offered: Entering freshmen from Alabama with ACT 28 or SAT 1230 can apply for 4-year tuition scholarship.

FINANCIAL AID PROCEDURES

Forms required: FAFSA, institutional form.

Dates and Deadlines: Priority date 3/15; no closing date. Applicants notified on a rolling basis starting 5/15; must reply within 2 week(s) of notification.

CONTACT

Vickie Adams, Director of Financial Aid

700 Pelham Road North, Jacksonville, AL 36265-1602

(256) 782-5006

Jefferson Davis Community College

Brewton, Alabama

www.jdcc.edu   Federal Code: 001021

2-year public nursing and community college in small town.

Enrollment: 1,085 undergrads, 42% part-time. 270 full-time freshmen.

Selectivity: Open admission; but selective for some programs.

BASIC COSTS (2007-2008)

Tuition and fees: $2,700; out-of-state residents $4,830.

Per-credit charge: $71; out-of-state residents $142.

Room only: $2,800.

FINANCIAL AID PICTURE (2006-2007)

Students with need: Out of 105 full-time freshmen who applied for aid; 80 were judged to have need. Of these, 71 received aid. Average financial aid package met 53% of need; average scholarship/grant was $600. For part-time students, average financial aid package was $3,754.

Students without need: 6 full-time freshmen who did not demonstrate need for aid received scholarships/grants; average award was $1,704. No-need awards available for academics, athletics, leadership.

Scholarships offered: 17 full-time freshmen received athletic scholarships; average amount $3,500.

FINANCIAL AID PROCEDURES

Forms required: FAFSA.

Dates and Deadlines: Priority date 5/8; no closing date. Applicants notified on a rolling basis; must reply within 2 week(s) of notification.

Transfers: Must reply within 2 week(s) of notification.

CONTACT

Vanessa Kyles, Director of Financial Aid

PO Box 958, Brewton, AL 36427

(251) 809-1516

Jefferson State Community College

Birmingham, Alabama

www.jeffstateonline.com   Federal Code: 001022

2-year public community college in large city.

Enrollment: 6,070 undergrads, 53% part-time. 864 full-time freshmen.

Selectivity: Open admission; but selective for some programs.

BASIC COSTS (2007-2008)

Tuition and fees: $3,060; out-of-state residents $5,190.

Per-credit charge: $71; out-of-state residents $142.

FINANCIAL AID PICTURE

Students with need: Need-based aid available for full-time and part-time students. Work study available nights.

Students without need: No-need awards available for academics, art, athletics, leadership, music/drama.

Additional info: Any Alabama resident over age 60 may attend classes tuition free, on a space available basis.

FINANCIAL AID PROCEDURES

Forms required: FAFSA, institutional form.

Dates and Deadlines: Priority date 5/1; no closing date. Applicants notified on a rolling basis starting 6/1.

Transfers: Transfer students not eligible for academic scholarships until 12 hours have been completed on campus.

CONTACT

Tracy Adams, Director, Financial Aid

2601 Carson Road, Birmingham, AL 35215-3098

(205) 856-8509

Judson College

Marion, Alabama

www.judson.edu   Federal Code: 001023

4-year private liberal arts college for women in small town, affiliated with Baptist faith.

Enrollment: 311 undergrads, 23% part-time. 79 full-time freshmen.

Selectivity: Admits over 75% of applicants.

BASIC COSTS (2007-2008)

Tuition and fees: $11,120.

Per-credit charge: $360.

Room and board: $7,120.

FINANCIAL AID PICTURE (2007-2008)

Students with need: Average financial aid package met 86% of need; average scholarship/grant was $7,837; average loan was $3,982. For part-time students, average financial aid package was $150.

Students without need: 13 full-time freshmen who did not demonstrate need for aid received scholarships/grants; average award was $6,646. No-need awards available for academics, art, athletics, leadership, music/drama, religious affiliation, state/district residency.

Scholarships offered: *Merit:* Garner-Webb Honors Scholarship; full tuition; up to 5 given to applicants who are National Merit Finalists or have ACT of 30 or above. Lockhart Competitive Scholarships; 1 full tuition, 2 for $2,500, 3 for $2,000; awarded based on exam scores. Music scholarships; $1,500; awarded based on audition. *Athletic:* 2 full-time freshmen received athletic scholarships; average amount $3,500.

Cumulative student debt: 69% of graduating class had student loans; average debt was $18,747.

FINANCIAL AID PROCEDURES

Forms required: FAFSA, state aid form, institutional form.

Dates and Deadlines: Priority date 3/1; no closing date. Applicants notified on a rolling basis starting 3/1; must reply within 2 week(s) of notification.

Transfers: No deadline. Applicants notified on a rolling basis; must reply within 2 week(s) of notification.

CONTACT

Doris Wilson, Director of Financial Aid

302 Bibb Street, Marion, AL 36756

(334) 683-5157

Lawson State Community College

Birmingham, Alabama

www.lawsonstate.edu   Federal Code: 001059

2-year public community college in small city.

Enrollment: 3,173 undergrads, 46% part-time. 633 full-time freshmen.

Selectivity: Open admission; but selective for some programs.

BASIC COSTS (2007-2008)

Tuition and fees: $3,000; out-of-state residents $5,130.

Per-credit charge: $71; out-of-state residents $142.

FINANCIAL AID PICTURE (2007-2008)

Students with need: 94% of average financial aid package awarded as scholarships/grants, 6% awarded as loans/jobs. Need-based aid available for part-time students. Work study available nights.

Students without need: This college awards aid only to students with need.

FINANCIAL AID PROCEDURES

Forms required: FAFSA.

Dates and Deadlines: Priority date 6/1; no closing date. Applicants notified on a rolling basis starting 8/1; must reply within 2 week(s) of notification.

CONTACT

Cassandra Byrd, Director of Student Financial Services
3060 Wilson Road SW, Birmingham, AL 35221-1717
(205) 929-6380

Marion Military Institute
Marion, Alabama
www.marionmilitary.edu   Federal Code: 001026

2-year public junior and military college in small town.

Enrollment: 389 undergrads, 12% part-time. 224 full-time freshmen.

Selectivity: Admits less than 50% of applicants.

BASIC COSTS (2007-2008)

Tuition and fees: $6,796; out-of-state residents $12,796.

Room and board: $3,450.

Additional info: Tuition at time of enrollment locked for 2 years.

FINANCIAL AID PICTURE

Students with need: Need-based aid available for full-time and part-time students.

Students without need: No-need awards available for academics, alumni affiliation, athletics, leadership, music/drama, ROTC.

FINANCIAL AID PROCEDURES

Forms required: FAFSA.

Dates and Deadlines: No deadline. Applicants notified on a rolling basis starting 6/15; must reply within 6 week(s) of notification.

Transfers: Priority date 5/15.

CONTACT

Director of Financial Aid
1101 Washington Street, Marion, AL 36756-0420
(334) 683-2309

Miles College
Birmingham, Alabama
www.miles.edu   Federal Code: 001028

4-year private liberal arts college in very large city, affiliated with Christian Methodist Episcopal Church.

Enrollment: 1,804 undergrads. 353 full-time freshmen.

Selectivity: Open admission; but selective for some programs.

BASIC COSTS (2007-2008)

Tuition and fees: $7,051.

Per-credit charge: $275.

Room and board: $4,866.

FINANCIAL AID PICTURE (2006-2007)

Students with need: Out of 349 full-time freshmen who applied for aid, 325 were judged to have need. Of these, 325 received aid, and 34 had their full need met. Average financial aid package met 10% of need; average loan was $2,213. For part-time students, average financial aid package was $2,645.

Students without need: This college awards aid only to students with need.

FINANCIAL AID PROCEDURES

Forms required: FAFSA, state aid form.

Dates and Deadlines: Priority date 4/15; no closing date. Applicants notified on a rolling basis starting 7/15; must reply within 2 week(s) of notification.

CONTACT

Percy Lanier, Financial Aid Administrator
5500 Myron-Massey Boulevard, Fairfield, AL 35064
(205) 929-1665

Northeast Alabama Community College
Rainsville, Alabama
www.nacc.edu   Federal Code: 001031

2-year public community college in rural community.

Enrollment: 2,014 undergrads.

Selectivity: Open admission; but selective for some programs.

BASIC COSTS (2007-2008)

Tuition and fees: $2,850; out-of-state residents $4,980.

Per-credit charge: $71; out-of-state residents $142.

Additional info: In-state costs apply to on-campus or distance-learning courses. Out-of-state distance-learning students pay $5,400 for academic year (or $180 per-credit-hour).

FINANCIAL AID PICTURE

Students with need: Need-based aid available for full-time and part-time students.

Students without need: No-need awards available for academics, art, leadership, minority status, music/drama.

FINANCIAL AID PROCEDURES

Forms required: FAFSA.

Dates and Deadlines: No deadline. Applicants notified on a rolling basis.

CONTACT

Nixon Willmon, Director of Financial Aid
Admissions Office, NACC, Rainsville, AL 35986-0159
(256) 228-6001 ext. 327

Northwest-Shoals Community College
Muscle Shoals, Alabama
www.nwscc.edu   Federal Code: 005697

2-year public community and technical college in large town.

Enrollment: 3,108 undergrads, 37% part-time. 697 full-time freshmen.

Selectivity: Open admission; but selective for some programs.

BASIC COSTS (2007-2008)

Tuition and fees: $2,880; out-of-state residents $5,010.

Per-credit charge: $71; out-of-state residents $142.

Room only: $1,600.

Additional info: Tuition at time of enrollment locked for 2 years; tuition/fee waivers available for minority students, unemployed or children of unemployed.

FINANCIAL AID PICTURE (2006-2007)

Students with need: 49% of average financial aid package awarded as scholarships/grants, 51% awarded as loans/jobs. Need-based aid available for part-time students. Work study available nights, weekends, and for part-time students.

Students without need: No-need awards available for academics, art, athletics, leadership, minority status, music/drama.

FINANCIAL AID PROCEDURES

Forms required: FAFSA, institutional form.

Dates and Deadlines: Priority date 4/1; no closing date. Applicants notified on a rolling basis; must reply within 2 week(s) of notification.

Transfers: No deadline. Applicants notified on a rolling basis; must reply within 2 week(s) of notification. Students without 1-year Alabama residency before fall term ineligible for state grant.

CONTACT

Joel Parris, Director of Student Financial Aid Services
PO Box 2545, Muscle Shoals, AL 35662
(256) 331-5368

Oakwood University

Huntsville, Alabama
www.oakwood.edu   Federal Code: 001033

4-year private liberal arts college in small city, affiliated with Seventh-day Adventists.

Enrollment: 1,778 undergrads, 5% part-time. 451 full-time freshmen.

Selectivity: Admits 50 to 75% of applicants.

BASIC COSTS (2008-2009)

Tuition and fees: $13,174.

Room and board: $7,458.

FINANCIAL AID PICTURE

Students with need: Need-based aid available for full-time students.

Students without need: No-need awards available for academics, leadership, religious affiliation, state/district residency.

FINANCIAL AID PROCEDURES

Forms required: FAFSA, state aid form.

Dates and Deadlines: Priority date 3/31; no closing date. Applicants notified on a rolling basis starting 4/1.

CONTACT

Compton Brathwaite, Director of Financial Aid
7000 Adventist Boulevard, NW, Huntsville, AL 35896
(256) 726-7208

Remington College: Mobile

Mobile, Alabama
www.educationamerica.com   Federal Code: 026055

2-year private technical college in large city.

Enrollment: 147 undergrads.

Selectivity: Open admission.

BASIC COSTS (2007-2008)

Additional info: Bachelor programs $32,050. Associate programs $39,650. Diploma programs (Allied Health) $13,050. Cost includes tuition, fees and books.

FINANCIAL AID PICTURE

Students with need: Need-based aid available for full-time students. Work study available nights.

Students without need: This college awards aid only to students with need.

FINANCIAL AID PROCEDURES

Forms required: FAFSA.

CONTACT

Linda Calvanese, Financial Aid Director
828 Downtowner Loop West, Mobile, AL 36609-5404
(251) 343-8200

Samford University

Birmingham, Alabama
www.samford.edu   Federal Code: 001036

4-year private university in small city, affiliated with Southern Baptist Convention.

Enrollment: 2,841 undergrads, 6% part-time. 644 full-time freshmen.

Selectivity: Admits over 75% of applicants.

BASIC COSTS (2007-2008)

Tuition and fees: $17,920.

Room and board: $6,320.

FINANCIAL AID PICTURE (2006-2007)

Students with need: Out of 446 full-time freshmen who applied for aid, 279 were judged to have need. Of these, 276 received aid, and 84 had their full need met. Average financial aid package met 76% of need; average scholarship/grant was $10,682; average loan was $2,523. For part-time students, average financial aid package was $6,898.

Students without need: 174 full-time freshmen who did not demonstrate need for aid received scholarships/grants; average award was $5,150. No-need awards available for academics, athletics, leadership, music/drama, religious affiliation, ROTC, state/district residency.

Scholarships offered: 39 full-time freshmen received athletic scholarships; average amount $11,635.

Cumulative student debt: 46% of graduating class had student loans; average debt was $18,700.

Additional info: Consideration for merit scholarships automatically given to students with admission files completed by December 15.

FINANCIAL AID PROCEDURES

Forms required: FAFSA.

Dates and Deadlines: Priority date 3/1; no closing date. Applicants notified by 4/1.

CONTACT

Lane Smith, Director of Financial Aid
800 Lakeshore Drive, Birmingham, AL 35229
(205) 726-2905

Shelton State Community College

Tuscaloosa, Alabama
www.sheltonstate.edu   Federal Code: 005691

2-year public community and technical college in small city.

Enrollment: 5,328 undergrads.

Selectivity: Open admission.

BASIC COSTS (2007-2008)

Tuition and fees: $2,700; out-of-state residents $4,830.

FINANCIAL AID PICTURE

Students with need: Need-based aid available for full-time and part-time students. Work study available nights.

Students without need: This college awards aid only to students with need.

FINANCIAL AID PROCEDURES

Forms required: FAFSA.

Dates and Deadlines: Priority date 6/30; no closing date. Applicants notified on a rolling basis starting 7/30.

CONTACT

JoeAnn Cousette, Financial Aid Coordinator
9500 Old Greensboro Road, Tuscaloosa, AL 35405-8522
(205) 391-2376

Snead State Community College

Boaz, Alabama
www.snead.edu   Federal Code: 001038

2-year public community college in small town.
Enrollment: 2,158 undergrads.
Selectivity: Open admission; but selective for some programs.

BASIC COSTS (2007-2008)

Tuition and fees: $2,820; out-of-state residents $4,950.
Per-credit charge: $71; out-of-state residents $142.
Room and board: $2,400.

FINANCIAL AID PICTURE

Students with need: Need-based aid available for full-time and part-time students. Work study available nights.
Students without need: No-need awards available for academics, alumni affiliation, art, athletics, leadership, music/drama.

FINANCIAL AID PROCEDURES

Forms required: FAFSA.
Dates and Deadlines: Priority date 4/15; no closing date. Applicants notified on a rolling basis starting 4/15.

CONTACT

Amanda Harbison, Financial Aid Officer
PO Box 734, Boaz, AL 35957-0734
(256) 840-4127

South University

Montgomery, Alabama
www.southuniversity.edu   •   Federal Code: 004463

4-year for-profit business and health science college in small city.
Enrollment: 504 undergrads.

BASIC COSTS (2007-2008)

Tuition and fees: $12,570.

FINANCIAL AID PICTURE

Students with need: Need-based aid available for full-time and part-time students.
Students without need: This college awards aid only to students with need.

FINANCIAL AID PROCEDURES

Forms required: FAFSA.
Dates and Deadlines: No deadline. Applicants notified on a rolling basis starting 6/1.
Transfers: No deadline. Applicants notified on a rolling basis.

CONTACT

James Berry, Director of Financial Aid
5355 Vaughn Road, Montgomery, AL 36116-1120
(334) 395-8800

Southeastern Bible College

Birmingham, Alabama
www.sebc.edu   Federal Code: 013857

4-year private Bible college in very large city, affiliated with nondenominational tradition.
Enrollment: 213 undergrads, 26% part-time. 31 full-time freshmen.
Selectivity: Admits over 75% of applicants.

BASIC COSTS (2007-2008)

Tuition and fees: $10,035.
Per-credit charge: $330.
Room only: $2,300.
Additional info: Tuition/fee waivers available for adults.

FINANCIAL AID PICTURE (2007-2008)

Students with need: 23% of average financial aid package awarded as scholarships/grants, 77% awarded as loans/jobs. Need-based aid available for part-time students. Work study available nights.
Students without need: No-need awards available for academics, leadership, music/drama.

FINANCIAL AID PROCEDURES

Forms required: FAFSA, state aid form, institutional form.
Dates and Deadlines: Priority date 5/1; closing date 8/15. Applicants notified by 7/15; must reply within 2 week(s) of notification.
Transfers: No deadline. Applicants notified on a rolling basis; must reply within 2 week(s) of notification.

CONTACT

Curtis Carter, Director of Financial Aid
2545 Valleydale Road, Birmingham, AL 35244-2083
(205) 970-9215

Southern Union State Community College

Wadley, Alabama
www.suscc.edu   Federal Code: 001040

2-year public community and technical college in small city.
Enrollment: 4,796 undergrads.
Selectivity: Open admission; but selective for some programs.

BASIC COSTS (2007-2008)

Tuition and fees: $2,700; out-of-state residents $4,830.
Per-credit charge: $71; out-of-state residents $142.
Room and board: $2,400.

FINANCIAL AID PICTURE

Students with need: Need-based aid available for full-time and part-time students.

FINANCIAL AID PROCEDURES

Forms required: FAFSA.
Dates and Deadlines: Priority date 7/1; no closing date. Applicants notified on a rolling basis.

CONTACT

Ellen Canada, Director of Financial Aid
750 Roberts Street, Wadley, AL 36276
(256) 395-2215

Spring Hill College

Mobile, Alabama
www.shc.edu   Federal Code: 001041

4-year private liberal arts college in large city, affiliated with Roman Catholic Church.
Enrollment: 1,268 undergrads, 8% part-time. 379 full-time freshmen.
Selectivity: Admits 50 to 75% of applicants.

BASIC COSTS (2008-2009)

Tuition and fees: $24,240.
Per-credit charge: $850.
Room and board: $9,260.

FINANCIAL AID PICTURE (2007-2008)

Students with need: Out of 317 full-time freshmen who applied for aid, 265 were judged to have need. Of these, 265 received aid, and 61 had their full need met. Average financial aid package met 84% of need; average scholarship/grant was $17,253; average loan was $4,188. For part-time students, average financial aid package was $6,500.

Students without need: 108 full-time freshmen who did not demonstrate need for aid received scholarships/grants; average award was $13,130. No-need awards available for academics, alumni affiliation, athletics, job skills, leadership, minority status, state/district residency.

Scholarships offered: *Merit:* Spring Hill Scholars scholarships: full tuition and fees annually for 4 years; 10 awarded for academic excellence, leadership, and service; 3.5 high school GPA and 28 ACT or 1230 SAT. Trustee Honors Scholarship: $16,000-$18,000 annually; 3.5 high school GPA and 28 ACT or 1230 SAT. Presidential Honors Scholarship: $13,000-$15,000 annually; awarded on the basis of grades, test scores, and leadership potential. Portier Scholarship: $12,000-$14,000 annually; awarded on the basis of grades, test scores, and leadership potential. Ignatian Leadership Award: $11,000-$13,000 annually; awarded on the basis of grades, test scores, and leadership potential. Gautrelet Award: $5,000-$7,500 annually; awarded on the basis of leadership, service, and potential contributions to the college community. *Athletic:* 28 full-time freshmen received athletic scholarships; average amount $2,047.

Cumulative student debt: 71% of graduating class had student loans; average debt was $13,176.

FINANCIAL AID PROCEDURES

Forms required: FAFSA, state aid form.

Dates and Deadlines: Priority date 3/1; no closing date. Applicants notified on a rolling basis starting 2/15; must reply by 5/1 or within 2 week(s) of notification.

Transfers: No deadline. Applicants notified on a rolling basis starting 2/1; must reply within 2 week(s) of notification. Transfer scholarships are awarded to students transferring to Spring Hill from an accredited college or university with a minimum cumulative grade point average of 3.0. These scholarships range from $4,000 to $10,000 annually and are renewable with a 2.5 GPA. Transfer students who are members of Phi Theta Kappa and/or transfer students who plan to pursue a degree in nursing may receive additional scholarship funding.

CONTACT

Ellen Foster, Director of Financial Aid
4000 Dauphin Street, Mobile, AL 36608-1791
(251) 380-3460

Stillman College

Tuscaloosa, Alabama
www.stillman.edu   Federal Code: 001044

4-year private liberal arts college in small city, affiliated with Presbyterian Church (USA).

Enrollment: 915 full-time undergrads. 289 full-time freshmen.

Selectivity: Admits less than 50% of applicants.

BASIC COSTS (2007-2008)

Tuition and fees: $12,186.

Per-credit charge: $456.

Room and board: $5,572.

FINANCIAL AID PICTURE (2006-2007)

Students with need: Average financial aid package met 75% of need; average scholarship/grant was $5,000; average loan was $5,500. For part-time students, average financial aid package was $6,842.

Students without need: This college awards aid only to students with need.

Scholarships offered: 6 full-time freshmen received athletic scholarships; average amount $3,000.

Cumulative student debt: 88% of graduating class had student loans; average debt was $22,625.

FINANCIAL AID PROCEDURES

Forms required: FAFSA, institutional form.

Dates and Deadlines: No deadline. Applicants notified on a rolling basis; must reply within 4 week(s) of notification.

Transfers: Priority date 3/15; no deadline. Applicants notified by 11/15.

CONTACT

Jacqueline Morris, Director of Financial Aid
3600 Stillman Boulevard, Tuscaloosa, AL 35403
(205) 366-8950

Troy University

Troy, Alabama
www.troy.edu   Federal Code: 001047

4-year public university in large town.

Enrollment: 21,046 undergrads, 53% part-time. 1,783 full-time freshmen.

Selectivity: Admits 50 to 75% of applicants.

BASIC COSTS (2007-2008)

Tuition and fees: $4,264; out-of-state residents $8,428.

Per-credit charge: $174; out-of-state residents $348.

Room and board: $5,718.

FINANCIAL AID PICTURE (2007-2008)

Students with need: Out of 1,178 full-time freshmen who applied for aid, 1,178 were judged to have need. Of these, 1,178 received aid. For part-time students, average financial aid package was $4,047.

Students without need: 359 full-time freshmen who did not demonstrate need for aid received scholarships/grants; average award was $2,699. No-need awards available for academics, alumni affiliation, art, athletics, leadership, minority status, music/drama, ROTC.

Scholarships offered: 45 full-time freshmen received athletic scholarships; average amount $4,205.

FINANCIAL AID PROCEDURES

Forms required: FAFSA, institutional form.

Dates and Deadlines: Closing date 5/1. Applicants notified on a rolling basis starting 5/1; must reply within 2 week(s) of notification.

CONTACT

Carol Supri, Director, Financial Aid
University Avenue, Adams Administration 111, Troy, AL 36082
(334) 670-3186

Tuskegee University

Tuskegee, Alabama   Federal Code: 001050
www.tuskegee.edu   CSS Code: 1813

4-year private university and liberal arts college in small town.

Enrollment: 2,514 undergrads, 3% part-time. 793 full-time freshmen.

Selectivity: Admits 50 to 75% of applicants.

BASIC COSTS (2008-2009)

Tuition and fees: $15,450.

Per-credit charge: $420.

Room and board: $7,130.

FINANCIAL AID PICTURE (2007-2008)

Students with need: Out of 722 full-time freshmen who applied for aid, 613 were judged to have need. Of these, 520 received aid, and 305 had their full need met. Average financial aid package met 81% of need; average scholarship/grant was $8,009; average loan was $5,725. Need-based aid available for part-time students.

PART III: FINANCIAL AID COLLEGE BY COLLEGE

Students without need: 230 full-time freshmen who did not demonstrate need for aid received scholarships/grants; average award was $6,005. No-need awards available for academics, athletics, ROTC, state/district residency.

Scholarships offered: 63 full-time freshmen received athletic scholarships; average amount $10,645.

FINANCIAL AID PROCEDURES

Forms required: FAFSA, CSS PROFILE, institutional form.

Dates and Deadlines: Closing date 3/31. Applicants notified on a rolling basis starting 5/15; must reply within 2 week(s) of notification.

CONTACT

A. James, Director, Financial Aid Services
102 Old Administration Building, Tuskegee, AL 36088
(334) 724-4733

University of Alabama
Tuscaloosa, Alabama
www.ua.edu   Federal Code: 001051

4-year public university in small city.

Enrollment: 20,910 undergrads, 8% part-time. 4,359 full-time freshmen.

Selectivity: Admits 50 to 75% of applicants.

BASIC COSTS (2007-2008)

Tuition and fees: $5,700; out-of-state residents $16,518.
Room and board: $5,868.

FINANCIAL AID PICTURE (2006-2007)

Students with need: Out of 2,157 full-time freshmen who applied for aid, 1,388 were judged to have need. Of these, 1,357 received aid, and 277 had their full need met. Average financial aid package met 66% of need; average scholarship/grant was $3,891; average loan was $2,714. For part-time students, average financial aid package was $6,989.

Students without need: 1,592 full-time freshmen who did not demonstrate need for aid received scholarships/grants; average award was $5,775. No-need awards available for academics, alumni affiliation, art, athletics, leadership, minority status, music/drama, ROTC, state/district residency.

Scholarships offered: 98 full-time freshmen received athletic scholarships; average amount $18,283.

Cumulative student debt: 48% of graduating class had student loans; average debt was $17,146.

FINANCIAL AID PROCEDURES

Forms required: FAFSA.

Dates and Deadlines: Priority date 3/1; no closing date. Applicants notified on a rolling basis starting 4/1; must reply within 3 week(s) of notification.

Transfers: Scholarship opportunities for transfer students.

CONTACT

Jeanetta Allen, Director, Student Financial Aid
Box 870132, Tuscaloosa, AL 35487-0132
(205) 348-6756

University of Alabama at Birmingham
Birmingham, Alabama
www.uab.edu   Federal Code: 001052

4-year public university in very large city.

Enrollment: 10,228 undergrads, 25% part-time. 1,487 full-time freshmen.

Selectivity: Admits over 75% of applicants.

BASIC COSTS (2007-2008)

Tuition and fees: $5,186; out-of-state residents $11,546.
Per-credit charge: $141; out-of-state residents $353.

Room and board: $7,500.

FINANCIAL AID PICTURE (2006-2007)

Students with need: Out of 1,172 full-time freshmen who applied for aid, 642 were judged to have need. Of these, 629 received aid, and 95 had their full need met. Average financial aid package met 33% of need; average scholarship/grant was $3,232; average loan was $2,831. For part-time students, average financial aid package was $5,898.

Students without need: 456 full-time freshmen who did not demonstrate need for aid received scholarships/grants; average award was $7,526. No-need awards available for academics, alumni affiliation, art, athletics, leadership, minority status, music/drama, ROTC.

Scholarships offered: 46 full-time freshmen received athletic scholarships; average amount $10,685.

FINANCIAL AID PROCEDURES

Forms required: FAFSA, institutional form.

Dates and Deadlines: Priority date 4/1; no closing date. Applicants notified on a rolling basis starting 4/1; must reply within 4 week(s) of notification.

Transfers: Must reply within 4 week(s) of notification.

CONTACT

Jan May, Director of Financial Aid
HUC 260, 1530 Third Avenue South, Birmingham, AL 35294-1150
(205) 934-8223

University of Alabama in Huntsville
Huntsville, Alabama
www.uah.edu   Federal Code: 001055

4-year public university in small city.

Enrollment: 5,562 undergrads, 24% part-time. 759 full-time freshmen.

Selectivity: Admits over 75% of applicants.

BASIC COSTS (2007-2008)

Tuition and fees: $5,216; out-of-state residents $11,024.
Per-credit charge: $195; out-of-state residents $413.
Room and board: $5,810.
Additional info: Per-credit-hour rate decreases as number of hours registered increases.

FINANCIAL AID PICTURE (2007-2008)

Students with need: Out of 671 full-time freshmen who applied for aid, 315 were judged to have need. Of these, 313 received aid, and 67 had their full need met. Average financial aid package met 68% of need; average scholarship/grant was $4,879; average loan was $3,600. For part-time students, average financial aid package was $6,067.

Students without need: 265 full-time freshmen who did not demonstrate need for aid received scholarships/grants; average award was $3,216. No-need awards available for academics, art, athletics, leadership, minority status, music/drama, ROTC.

Scholarships offered: 42 full-time freshmen received athletic scholarships; average amount $4,997.

Cumulative student debt: 39% of graduating class had student loans; average debt was $21,544.

Additional info: Application deadline for institutional scholarships is February 1.

FINANCIAL AID PROCEDURES

Forms required: FAFSA.

Dates and Deadlines: Priority date 4/1; closing date 7/31. Applicants notified on a rolling basis starting 4/1; must reply within 2 week(s) of notification.

CONTACT

Andy Weaver, Director of Student Financial Services
UAH Office of Undergraduate Admissions, Huntsville, AL 35899
(256) 824-6241

University of Mobile

Mobile, Alabama
www.umobile.edu   Federal Code: 001029

4-year private university and liberal arts college in small city, affiliated with Baptist faith.
Enrollment: 1,346 undergrads, 15% part-time. 208 full-time freshmen.
Selectivity: Admits over 75% of applicants.

BASIC COSTS (2008-2009)
Tuition and fees: $13,970.
Per-credit charge: $480.
Room and board: $7,170.

FINANCIAL AID PICTURE (2007-2008)
Students with need: Average financial aid package met 87% of need; average scholarship/grant was $1,981; average loan was $1,553. For part-time students, average financial aid package was $5,809.
Students without need: No-need awards available for academics, alumni affiliation, art, athletics, job skills, leadership, minority status, music/drama, religious affiliation, ROTC, state/district residency.

FINANCIAL AID PROCEDURES
Forms required: FAFSA, state aid form, institutional form.
Dates and Deadlines: Priority date 3/31; no closing date. Applicants notified on a rolling basis; must reply within 2 week(s) of notification.

CONTACT
Marie Batson, Associate Vice President for Enrollment Management
5735 College Parkway, Mobile, AL 36613-2842
(251) 442-2252

University of Montevallo

Montevallo, Alabama
www.montevallo.edu   Federal Code: 001004

4-year public university and liberal arts college in small town.
Enrollment: 2,473 undergrads, 10% part-time. 482 full-time freshmen.
Selectivity: Admits over 75% of applicants.

BASIC COSTS (2007-2008)
Tuition and fees: $6,080; out-of-state residents $11,930.
Per-credit charge: $195; out-of-state residents $390.
Room and board: $4,214.

FINANCIAL AID PICTURE (2007-2008)
Students with need: Average financial aid package met 71% of need; average scholarship/grant was $3,936; average loan was $2,988. For part-time students, average financial aid package was $5,788.
Students without need: No-need awards available for academics, art, athletics, job skills, leadership, minority status, music/drama, religious affiliation, ROTC.
Cumulative student debt: 58% of graduating class had student loans; average debt was $19,580.

FINANCIAL AID PROCEDURES
Forms required: FAFSA.
Dates and Deadlines: Priority date 4/1; no closing date. Applicants notified by 5/10; must reply within 2 week(s) of notification.

CONTACT
Maria Parker, Director of Financial Aid
Station 6030, Montevallo, AL 35115-6030
(205) 665-6050

University of North Alabama

Florence, Alabama
www.una.edu   Federal Code: 001016

4-year public university in large town.
Enrollment: 5,299 undergrads, 13% part-time. 930 full-time freshmen.
Selectivity: Admits over 75% of applicants.

BASIC COSTS (2007-2008)
Tuition and fees: $5,093; out-of-state residents $9,203.
Per-credit charge: $137; out-of-state residents $274.
Room and board: $4,460.

FINANCIAL AID PICTURE
Students with need: Need-based aid available for full-time and part-time students. Work study available nights, weekends, and for part-time students.
Students without need: No-need awards available for academics, art, athletics, leadership, minority status, music/drama, ROTC, state/district residency.

FINANCIAL AID PROCEDURES
Forms required: FAFSA.
Dates and Deadlines: Priority date 4/1; no closing date. Applicants notified on a rolling basis starting 5/31; must reply within 2 week(s) of notification.

CONTACT
Ben Baker, Director of Student Financial Services
One Harrison Plaza, UNA Box 5011, Florence, AL 35632-0001
(256) 765-4590

University of South Alabama

Mobile, Alabama
www.southalabama.edu   Federal Code: 001057

4-year public university in small city.
Enrollment: 10,459 undergrads, 26% part-time. 1,457 full-time freshmen.
Selectivity: Admits over 75% of applicants.

BASIC COSTS (2007-2008)
Tuition and fees: $4,822; out-of-state residents $8,842.
Per-credit charge: $134; out-of-state residents $268.
Room and board: $4,698.
Additional info: Tuition/fee waivers available for minority students.

FINANCIAL AID PICTURE (2006-2007)
Students with need: 21% of average financial aid package awarded as scholarships/grants, 79% awarded as loans/jobs. Need-based aid available for part-time students.
Students without need: No-need awards available for academics, alumni affiliation, art, athletics, minority status, music/drama, ROTC, state/district residency.

FINANCIAL AID PROCEDURES
Forms required: FAFSA, institutional form.
Dates and Deadlines: Priority date 5/1; no closing date. Applicants notified on a rolling basis starting 5/15.

CONTACT
Emily Johnston, Director of Financial Aid
Meisler Hall, Suite 2500, Mobile, AL 36688-0002
(251) 460-6231

University of West Alabama

Livingston, Alabama
www.uwa.edu   Federal Code: 001024

4-year public university in small town.
Enrollment: 1,999 undergrads.
Selectivity: Admits over 75% of applicants.

BASIC COSTS (2007-2008)
Tuition and fees: $4,607; out-of-state residents $8,713.
Per-credit charge: $174; out-of-state residents $348.
Room and board: $3,624.

FINANCIAL AID PICTURE
Students with need: Need-based aid available for full-time and part-time students. Work study available nights, weekends, and for part-time students.
Students without need: No-need awards available for academics, alumni affiliation, athletics, leadership, music/drama, state/district residency.

FINANCIAL AID PROCEDURES
Forms required: FAFSA.
Dates and Deadlines: Priority date 4/1; no closing date. Applicants notified on a rolling basis starting 6/1; must reply within 2 week(s) of notification.

CONTACT
Don Rainer, Director of Financial Aid
Station 4, Livingston, AL 35470
(205) 652-3576

Virginia College at Huntsville

Huntsville, Alabama
www.vc.edu   Federal Code: 030106

4-year for-profit business and technical college in small city.
Enrollment: 860 undergrads.
Selectivity: Open admission.

BASIC COSTS (2007-2008)
Additional info: Tuition is based on a quarterly charge which varies by program.

FINANCIAL AID PICTURE
Students with need: Need-based aid available for full-time and part-time students.

FINANCIAL AID PROCEDURES
Forms required: FAFSA, institutional form.
Dates and Deadlines: No deadline. Applicants notified on a rolling basis.

CONTACT
Samantha Williams, Student Finance Director
2800 Bob Wallace Avenue, Huntsville, AL 35805
(256) 533-7387

Alaska

Alaska Bible College

Glennallen, Alaska
www.akbible.edu   Federal Code: 014325

4-year private Bible college in rural community, affiliated with nondenominational tradition.
Enrollment: 23 undergrads.
Selectivity: Open admission; but selective for some programs.

BASIC COSTS (2007-2008)
Tuition and fees: $6,500.
Per-credit charge: $285.
Room and board: $5,000.

FINANCIAL AID PICTURE
Students with need: Need-based aid available for full-time students.
Students without need: This college awards aid only to students with need.

FINANCIAL AID PROCEDURES
Forms required: institutional form.
Dates and Deadlines: Priority date 4/30; closing date 8/1. Applicants notified on a rolling basis; must reply within 2 week(s) of notification.

CONTACT
Kevin Newman, Financial Aid Officer
Box 289, Glennallen, AK 99588-0289
(907) 822-3201

Alaska Pacific University

Anchorage, Alaska
www.alaskapacific.edu   Federal Code: 001061

4-year private university and liberal arts college in large city.
Enrollment: 452 undergrads, 39% part-time. 45 full-time freshmen.
Selectivity: Admits over 75% of applicants.

BASIC COSTS (2007-2008)
Tuition and fees: $21,010.
Per-credit charge: $695.
Room and board: $7,700.
Additional info: Tuition at time of enrollment locked for 4 years.

FINANCIAL AID PICTURE (2007-2008)
Students with need: Out of 41 full-time freshmen who applied for aid, 34 were judged to have need. Of these, 34 received aid. Average financial aid package met 88% of need; average scholarship/grant was $7,495; average loan was $3,353. For part-time students, average financial aid package was $4,184.
Students without need: 11 full-time freshmen who did not demonstrate need for aid received scholarships/grants; average award was $5,164. No-need awards available for academics, alumni affiliation, leadership, religious affiliation, state/district residency.
Scholarships offered: 3 full-time freshmen received athletic scholarships; average amount $4,733.
Cumulative student debt: 93% of graduating class had student loans; average debt was $10,197.

FINANCIAL AID PROCEDURES
Forms required: FAFSA.
Dates and Deadlines: Priority date 4/15; no closing date. Applicants notified on a rolling basis starting 2/1; must reply within 4 week(s) of notification.

CONTACT
Louise Driver, Director, Student Financial Services
4101 University Drive, Anchorage, AK 99508
(907) 564-8341

Prince William Sound Community College

Valdez, Alaska
www.pwscc.edu   Federal Code: 011462

2-year public community college in small town.
Enrollment: 150 undergrads.

Selectivity: Open admission.

BASIC COSTS (2007-2008)
Tuition and fees: $3,660.
Per-credit charge: $110.

FINANCIAL AID PICTURE
Students with need: Need-based aid available for full-time and part-time students.
Students without need: No-need awards available for state/district residency.

FINANCIAL AID PROCEDURES
Forms required: FAFSA.
Dates and Deadlines: Priority date 6/30; no closing date. Applicants notified on a rolling basis.
Transfers: Priority date 4/1; closing date 5/1.

CONTACT
Douglas Desorcie, Registrar
Box 97, Valdez, AK 99686
(907) 834-1666

University of Alaska Anchorage
Anchorage, Alaska
www.uaa.alaska.edu   Federal Code: 011462

4-year public university in large city.
Enrollment: 10,471 undergrads, 40% part-time. 1,324 full-time freshmen.
Selectivity: Open admission; but selective for some programs.

BASIC COSTS (2007-2008)
Tuition and fees: $4,400; out-of-state residents $13,370.
Per-credit charge: $128; out-of-state residents $427.
Room and board: $7,730.
Additional info: WUE students per-credit-hour charge is $192 for lower-division courses.

FINANCIAL AID PICTURE
Students with need: Need-based aid available for full-time and part-time students. Work study available nights, weekends, and for part-time students.
Students without need: No-need awards available for academics, athletics.

FINANCIAL AID PROCEDURES
Forms required: FAFSA, institutional form.
Dates and Deadlines: Priority date 4/1; closing date 8/1. Applicants notified on a rolling basis starting 3/15; must reply within 4 week(s) of notification.
Transfers: Closing date 4/15.

CONTACT
Ted Malone, Director of Financial Aid
PO Box 141629, Anchorage, AK 99514-1629
(907) 786-1586

University of Alaska Fairbanks
Fairbanks, Alaska
www.uaf.edu   Federal Code: 001063

4-year public university in small city.
Enrollment: 4,744 undergrads, 33% part-time. 793 full-time freshmen.
Selectivity: Admits over 75% of applicants. GED not accepted.

BASIC COSTS (2007-2008)
Tuition and fees: $4,496; out-of-state residents $13,466.
Per-credit charge: $128; out-of-state residents $427.
Room and board: $6,640.
Additional info: Estimated course and lab fees: $450 per year.

FINANCIAL AID PICTURE (2007-2008)
Students with need: Out of 692 full-time freshmen who applied for aid, 317 were judged to have need. Of these, 303 received aid, and 135 had their full need met. Average financial aid package met 49% of need; average scholarship/grant was $5,072; average loan was $8,423. For part-time students, average financial aid package was $8,405.
Students without need: 257 full-time freshmen who did not demonstrate need for aid received scholarships/grants; average award was $6,695. No-need awards available for academics, art, athletics, leadership, music/drama, ROTC, state/district residency.
Scholarships offered: 25 full-time freshmen received athletic scholarships; average amount $5,621.
Cumulative student debt: 52% of graduating class had student loans; average debt was $28,204.

FINANCIAL AID PROCEDURES
Forms required: FAFSA.
Dates and Deadlines: Priority date 2/15; closing date 7/1. Applicants notified on a rolling basis starting 3/1; must reply within 2 week(s) of notification.
Transfers: Priority date 2/1; closing date 8/1.

CONTACT
Theodore Malone, Director of Financial Aid
PO Box 757480, Fairbanks, AK 99775-7480
(888) 474-7256

University of Alaska Southeast
Juneau, Alaska
www.uas.alaska.edu   Federal Code: 001065

4-year public university and liberal arts college in large town.
Enrollment: 1,108 undergrads, 47% part-time. 108 full-time freshmen.
Selectivity: Open admission; but selective for some programs.

BASIC COSTS (2007-2008)
Tuition and fees: $4,368; out-of-state residents $13,338.
Per-credit charge: $128; out-of-state residents $427.
Room and board: $6,090.
Additional info: Tuition reported is for lower division offerings; for upper division, $123 per credit.

FINANCIAL AID PICTURE (2007-2008)
Students with need: 38% of average financial aid package awarded as scholarships/grants, 62% awarded as loans/jobs. Need-based aid available for part-time students. Work study available nights, weekends, and for part-time students.
Students without need: No-need awards available for academics, leadership.
Cumulative student debt: 41% of graduating class had student loans; average debt was $20,815.
Additional info: Transfer, continuing, and freshman scholarship deadline March 1.

FINANCIAL AID PROCEDURES
Forms required: FAFSA.
Dates and Deadlines: Priority date 6/1; no closing date. Applicants notified on a rolling basis starting 2/15; must reply within 3 week(s) of notification.

CONTACT
Barbara Burnett, Manager of Financial Aid
11120 Glacier Highway, Juneau, AK 99801-8681
(907) 796-6255

PART III: FINANCIAL AID COLLEGE BY COLLEGE

Arizona

Arizona State University

Tempe, Arizona
www.asu.edu   Federal Code: 001081

4-year public university in small city.
Enrollment: 38,597 undergrads, 23% part-time. 7,076 full-time freshmen.
Selectivity: Admits over 75% of applicants.

BASIC COSTS (2007-2008)
Tuition and fees: $4,971; out-of-state residents $17,003.
Per-credit charge: $252; out-of-state residents $702.
Room and board: $7,320.

FINANCIAL AID PICTURE (2006-2007)
Students with need: Out of 3,771 full-time freshmen who applied for aid, 2,628 were judged to have need. Of these, 2,628 received aid, and 590 had their full need met. Average financial aid package met 61% of need; average scholarship/grant was $6,447; average loan was $2,665. For part-time students, average financial aid package was $6,848.
Students without need: 1,719 full-time freshmen who did not demonstrate need for aid received scholarships/grants; average award was $6,616. No-need awards available for academics, art, athletics, leadership, music/drama, ROTC.
Scholarships offered: 47 full-time freshmen received athletic scholarships; average amount $14,246.
Cumulative student debt: 43% of graduating class had student loans; average debt was $16,856.

FINANCIAL AID PROCEDURES
Forms required: FAFSA.
Dates and Deadlines: Priority date 3/1; no closing date. Applicants notified on a rolling basis.

CONTACT
Craig Fennell, Director of Student Financial Assistance
Box 870112, Tempe, AZ 85287-0112
(480) 965-3355

Arizona State University West

Phoenix, Arizona
www.west.asu.edu   Federal Code: 001081

4-year public university in small city.
Enrollment: 5,860 undergrads, 27% part-time. 507 full-time freshmen.
Selectivity: Admits over 75% of applicants.

BASIC COSTS (2007-2008)
Tuition and fees: $4,766; out-of-state residents $16,999.
Per-credit charge: $240; out-of-state residents $702.

FINANCIAL AID PICTURE (2006-2007)
Students with need: Out of 309 full-time freshmen who applied for aid, 251 were judged to have need. Of these, 251 received aid, and 50 had their full need met. Average financial aid package met 64% of need; average scholarship/grant was $6,307; average loan was $2,510. For part-time students, average financial aid package was $6,639.
Students without need: 114 full-time freshmen who did not demonstrate need for aid received scholarships/grants; average award was $5,025. No-need awards available for academics.
Cumulative student debt: 54% of graduating class had student loans; average debt was $15,586.

FINANCIAL AID PROCEDURES
Forms required: FAFSA.
Dates and Deadlines: Priority date 2/1; closing date 3/1. Applicants notified on a rolling basis starting 3/15; must reply within 4 week(s) of notification.

CONTACT
Leah Samudio, Financial Aid Manager
PO Box 37100 MC 0250, Phoenix, AZ 85069-7100
(602) 543-8178

Arizona Western College

Yuma, Arizona
www.azwestern.edu   Federal Code: 001071

2-year public community college in small city.
Enrollment: 6,056 undergrads, 58% part-time. 126 full-time freshmen.
Selectivity: Open admission; but selective for some programs.

BASIC COSTS (2007-2008)
Tuition and fees: $1,380; out-of-state residents $5,940.
Per-credit charge: $46; out-of-state residents $52.
Room and board: $4,630.

FINANCIAL AID PICTURE
Students with need: Need-based aid available for full-time and part-time students. Work study available nights, weekends, and for part-time students.
Students without need: No-need awards available for academics, athletics.

FINANCIAL AID PROCEDURES
Forms required: FAFSA, institutional form.
Dates and Deadlines: Priority date 4/1; no closing date. Applicants notified on a rolling basis starting 5/1.

CONTACT
Lisa Seale, Director of Financial Aid
PO Box 929, Yuma, AZ 85366-0929
(928) 344-7634

Art Center Design College

Tucson, Arizona
www.theartcenter.edu   Federal Code: 024915

4-year for-profit visual arts college in very large city.
Enrollment: 318 undergrads.

BASIC COSTS (2007-2008)
Tuition and fees: $15,360.
Per-credit charge: $640.
Additional info: Tuition at time of enrollment locked for 4 years.

FINANCIAL AID PICTURE
Students with need: Need-based aid available for full-time and part-time students.
Students without need: This college awards aid only to students with need.

FINANCIAL AID PROCEDURES
Forms required: FAFSA.
Dates and Deadlines: No deadline.
Transfers: No deadline. Applicants notified on a rolling basis.

CONTACT
Amy Woods, Education Finance Advisor
2525 North Country Club Road, Tucson, AZ 85716
(520) 325-0123

Art Institute of Phoenix

Phoenix, Arizona
www.artinstitutes.edu/phoenix   Federal Code: 040513

3-year for-profit culinary school and visual arts college in very large city.

Enrollment: 1,109 undergrads.

BASIC COSTS (2007-2008)

Tuition and fees: $12,240.

Per-credit charge: $403.

FINANCIAL AID PICTURE

Students with need: Need-based aid available for full-time and part-time students.

FINANCIAL AID PROCEDURES

Forms required: FAFSA.

Dates and Deadlines: No deadline.

CONTACT

Lori Ryan, Director of Administrative and Financial Services
2233 West Dunlap Avenue, Phoenix, AZ 85021-2859

Central Arizona College

Coolidge, Arizona
www.centralaz.edu   Federal Code: 007283

2-year public community college in rural community.

Enrollment: 4,951 undergrads.

Selectivity: Open admission; but selective for some programs.

BASIC COSTS (2008-2009)

Tuition and fees: $1,705; out-of-state residents $7,501.

Per-credit charge: $60; out-of-state residents $120.

Room and board: $4,645.

FINANCIAL AID PICTURE

Students with need: Need-based aid available for full-time and part-time students. Work study available nights, weekends, and for part-time students.

FINANCIAL AID PROCEDURES

Forms required: FAFSA.

Dates and Deadlines: Priority date 5/1; closing date 7/15. Applicants notified by 5/30; must reply within 3 week(s) of notification.

CONTACT

Russ Banta, Finance Office
8470 North Overfield Road, Coolidge, AZ 85228-9778
(520) 494-5425

Chandler-Gilbert Community College: Pecos

Chandler, Arizona
www.cgc.maricopa.edu   Federal Code: 030722

2-year public community college in small city.

Enrollment: 1,471 undergrads, 54% part-time. 272 full-time freshmen.

Selectivity: Open admission.

BASIC COSTS (2007-2008)

Tuition and fees: $1,965; out-of-state residents $8,415.

Per-credit charge: $65; out-of-state residents $280.

FINANCIAL AID PICTURE

Students with need: Work study available nights, weekends, and for part-time students.

CONTACT

Doug Bullock, Director of Financial Aid
2626 East Pecos Road, Chandler, AZ 85225

Cochise College

Douglas, Arizona
www.cochise.edu   Federal Code: 001072

2-year public community college in large town.

Enrollment: 3,113 undergrads, 71% part-time. 2,273 full-time freshmen.

Selectivity: Open admission; but selective for some programs.

BASIC COSTS (2008-2009)

Tuition and fees: $1,540; out-of-state residents $7,330.

Room and board: $4,380.

FINANCIAL AID PICTURE (2006-2007)

Students with need: Out of 359 full-time freshmen who applied for aid, 304 were judged to have need. Of these, 288 received aid. For part-time students, average financial aid package was $5,402.

Students without need: 24 full-time freshmen who did not demonstrate need for aid received scholarships/grants; average award was $878. No-need awards available for academics, athletics.

Scholarships offered: 41 full-time freshmen received athletic scholarships; average amount $2,613.

FINANCIAL AID PROCEDURES

Forms required: FAFSA, institutional form.

Dates and Deadlines: Closing date 4/15. Applicants notified on a rolling basis starting 6/15; must reply within 2 week(s) of notification.

Transfers: Priority date 4/15; no deadline. Applicants notified on a rolling basis.

CONTACT

Dartle Atherton, Director of Financial Aid
901 North Colombo Avenue, Sierra Vista, AZ 85635
(520) 515-5417

DeVry University: Phoenix

Phoenix, Arizona
www.devry.edu   Federal Code: 008322

4-year for-profit university in large city.

Enrollment: 1,017 undergrads, 28% part-time. 219 full-time freshmen.

BASIC COSTS (2007-2008)

Tuition and fees: $13,220.

Per-credit charge: $490.

FINANCIAL AID PICTURE (2006-2007)

Students with need: Out of 190 full-time freshmen who applied for aid, 172 were judged to have need. Of these, 171 received aid, and 10 had their full need met. Average financial aid package met 39% of need; average scholarship/grant was $6,168; average loan was $4,388. For part-time students, average financial aid package was $7,808.

Students without need: This college awards aid only to students with need.

Cumulative student debt: 71% of graduating class had student loans; average debt was $41,439.

FINANCIAL AID PROCEDURES

Forms required: FAFSA.

Dates and Deadlines: No deadline. Applicants notified on a rolling basis.

CONTACT
Kathy Wyse, Dean of Student Finances
2149 West Dunlap Avenue, Phoenix, AZ 85021-2995
(602) 870-9229

Dine College
Tsaile, Arizona
www.dinecollege.edu   Federal Code: 008246

2-year public community college in rural community.
Enrollment: 927 undergrads.
Selectivity: Open admission.

BASIC COSTS (2007-2008)
Tuition and fees: $850.
Per-credit charge: $30.
Room and board: $3,764.

FINANCIAL AID PICTURE
Students with need: Need-based aid available for full-time and part-time students.
Students without need: This college awards aid only to students with need.

FINANCIAL AID PROCEDURES
Forms required: FAFSA, institutional form.
Dates and Deadlines: Priority date 4/15; no closing date. Applicants notified on a rolling basis starting 5/1; must reply within 4 week(s) of notification.
Transfers: Priority date 3/1; no deadline. Applicants notified on a rolling basis starting 1/1; must reply within 6 week(s) of notification.

CONTACT
Gary Segay, Director of Financial Aid
Box 67, Tsaile, AZ 86556
(928) 724-6738

Eastern Arizona College
Thatcher, Arizona
www.eac.edu   Federal Code: 001073

2-year public community college in large town.
Enrollment: 3,058 undergrads, 55% part-time. 524 full-time freshmen.
Selectivity: Open admission; but selective for some programs.

BASIC COSTS (2007-2008)
Tuition and fees: $1,300; out-of-state residents $6,540.
Per-credit charge: $55; out-of-state residents $110.
Room and board: $4,320.

FINANCIAL AID PICTURE (2007-2008)
Students with need: For part-time students, average financial aid package was $2,131.
Students without need: No-need awards available for academics, art, athletics, leadership, music/drama, state/district residency.
Scholarships offered: Departmental Scholarships; in-state tuition, based on 2.5 minimum GPA. Academic Scholarships; in-state tuition, based on 3.0 minimum GPA. Performing Arts Scholarships; amounts vary, based on 2.5 minimum GPA, audition.
Additional info: Limited number of tuition waivers for New Mexico residents. Unlimited number of waivers for those meeting WUE requirements.

FINANCIAL AID PROCEDURES
Forms required: FAFSA, institutional form.
Dates and Deadlines: Priority date 3/1; no closing date. Applicants notified on a rolling basis starting 3/15.
Transfers: No deadline. Applicants notified on a rolling basis starting 3/15.

CONTACT
Geraldine Covert, Director of Financial Aid
615 North Stadium Avenue, Thatcher, AZ 85552-0769
(928) 428-8287

Embry-Riddle Aeronautical University: Prescott Campus
Prescott, Arizona
www.embryriddle.edu   Federal Code: 014797

4-year private university in large town.
Enrollment: 1,667 undergrads, 7% part-time. 399 full-time freshmen.
Selectivity: Admits over 75% of applicants.

BASIC COSTS (2008-2009)
Tuition and fees: $27,180.
Per-credit charge: $1,100.
Room and board: $7,700.

FINANCIAL AID PICTURE (2007-2008)
Students with need: Out of 340 full-time freshmen who applied for aid, 278 were judged to have need. Of these, 278 received aid. For part-time students, average financial aid package was $13,693.
Students without need: No-need awards available for academics, alumni affiliation, athletics, leadership, ROTC.
Scholarships offered: 16 full-time freshmen received athletic scholarships; average amount $8,563.
Cumulative student debt: 83% of graduating class had student loans; average debt was $54,159.

FINANCIAL AID PROCEDURES
Forms required: FAFSA.
Dates and Deadlines: No deadline. Applicants notified on a rolling basis starting 3/1; must reply within 4 week(s) of notification.

CONTACT
Barbara Dryden, Director of Financial Aid
3700 North Willow Creek Road, Prescott, AZ 86301-3720
(928) 777-3765

Estrella Mountain Community College
Avondale, Arizona
www.estrellamountain.edu   Federal Code: 031563

2-year public community college in small city.
Enrollment: 2,133 undergrads.
Selectivity: Open admission.

BASIC COSTS (2007-2008)
Tuition and fees: $1,965; out-of-state residents $8,415.
Per-credit charge: $65; out-of-state residents $280.

FINANCIAL AID PICTURE (2006-2007)
Students with need: 77% of average financial aid package awarded as scholarships/grants, 23% awarded as loans/jobs. Need-based aid available for part-time students. Work study available nights.
Students without need: No-need awards available for leadership.

FINANCIAL AID PROCEDURES
Dates and Deadlines: Priority date 4/1; no closing date. Applicants notified on a rolling basis starting 4/15.

CONTACT
Rosanna Short, Director, Financial Aid
3000 North Dysart Road, Avondale, AZ 85392
(623) 935-8930

Gateway Community College
Phoenix, Arizona
www.gatewaycc.edu — Federal Code: 008303

2-year public community and technical college in very large city.
Enrollment: 6,313 undergrads.
Selectivity: Open admission; but selective for some programs.

BASIC COSTS (2007-2008)
Tuition and fees: $1,965; out-of-state residents $7,905.
Per-credit charge: $65; out-of-state residents $263.

FINANCIAL AID PICTURE
Students with need: Need-based aid available for full-time and part-time students. Work study available nights, weekends, and for part-time students.
Students without need: No-need awards available for athletics.

FINANCIAL AID PROCEDURES
Forms required: FAFSA, institutional form.
Dates and Deadlines: Priority date 4/15; no closing date. Applicants notified on a rolling basis starting 7/1; must reply within 4 week(s) of notification.

CONTACT
Suzanne Ringle, Director of Financial Aid
108 North 40th Street, Phoenix, AZ 85034
(602) 286-8115

Glendale Community College
Glendale, Arizona
www.gccaz.edu — Federal Code: 001076

2-year public community college in small city.
Enrollment: 4,446 undergrads, 61% part-time.
Selectivity: Open admission; but selective for some programs.

BASIC COSTS (2007-2008)
Tuition and fees: $1,960; out-of-state residents $8,410.
Per-credit charge: $65; out-of-state residents $280.

FINANCIAL AID PICTURE
Students with need: Need-based aid available for full-time and part-time students. Work study available nights, weekends, and for part-time students.

FINANCIAL AID PROCEDURES
Forms required: FAFSA.
Dates and Deadlines: Priority date 4/30; closing date 8/1. Applicants notified on a rolling basis starting 6/1.

CONTACT
Ellen Neel, Director of Financial Aid
6000 West Olive Avenue, Glendale, AZ 85302
(623) 845-3366

Grand Canyon University
Phoenix, Arizona
www.gcu.edu/clgbrd — Federal Code: 001074

4-year for-profit university in very large city.
Enrollment: 4,803 undergrads, 64% part-time. 58 full-time freshmen.
Selectivity: Open admission; but selective for some programs.

BASIC COSTS (2008-2009)
Tuition and fees: $16,030.
Per-credit charge: $645.

FINANCIAL AID PICTURE
Students with need: Need-based aid available for full-time students.

Students without need: No-need awards available for academics, athletics, leadership, religious affiliation, ROTC.

FINANCIAL AID PROCEDURES
Forms required: FAFSA.
Dates and Deadlines: No deadline. Applicants notified on a rolling basis.

CONTACT
David Weems, Director of Financial Aid
3300 West Camelback Road, Phoenix, AZ 85017
(602) 639-6522

International Institute of the Americas: Mesa
Mesa, Arizona
www.iia.edu — Federal Code: 022188

4-year private branch campus college in very large city.
Enrollment: 133 undergrads.
Selectivity: Open admission; but selective for some programs.

BASIC COSTS (2008-2009)
Tuition and fees: $11,400.
Additional info: Tuition and fees may vary by program.

FINANCIAL AID PICTURE
Students with need: Need-based aid available for full-time students.
Students without need: This college awards aid only to students with need.

FINANCIAL AID PROCEDURES
Forms required: FAFSA, institutional form.

CONTACT
Melba Moore, Director of Financial Aid
925 South Gilbert Road, Suite 201, Mesa, AZ 85204
(480) 545-8755

International Institute of the Americas: Phoenix
Phoenix, Arizona
www.iia.edu — Federal Code: 022188

4-year private nursing and career college in very large city.
Enrollment: 568 undergrads.
Selectivity: Open admission; but selective for some programs.

BASIC COSTS (2008-2009)
Tuition and fees: $11,400.
Additional info: Tuition and fees may vary by program.

FINANCIAL AID PICTURE
Students with need: Need-based aid available for full-time students.
Students without need: This college awards aid only to students with need.

FINANCIAL AID PROCEDURES
Forms required: FAFSA, institutional form.
Dates and Deadlines: No deadline.

CONTACT
Melba Moore, Financial Aid Director
6049 North 43rd Avenue, Phoenix, AZ 85019
(602) 644-7090

International Institute of the Americas: Tucson

Tucson, Arizona
www.iia.edu   Federal Code: 022188

4-year private branch campus college in very large city.
Enrollment: 292 undergrads.
Selectivity: Open admission; but selective for some programs.

BASIC COSTS (2008-2009)
Tuition and fees: $11,400.
Additional info: Tuition and fees may vary by program.

FINANCIAL AID PICTURE
Students with need: Need-based aid available for full-time and part-time students.
Students without need: This college awards aid only to students with need.

FINANCIAL AID PROCEDURES
Forms required: FAFSA, institutional form.
Dates and Deadlines: No deadline.

CONTACT
Melba Moore, Financial Aid Director
5441 East 22nd Street, Suite 125, Tucson, AZ 85711
(602) 644-7090

Mohave Community College

Kingman, Arizona
www.mohave.edu   Federal Code: 011864

2-year public community college in small city.
Enrollment: 2,975 undergrads.
Selectivity: Open admission; but selective for some programs.

BASIC COSTS (2008-2009)
Tuition and fees: $1,850; out-of-state residents $5,390.
Per-credit charge: $59; out-of-state residents $177.

FINANCIAL AID PICTURE
Students with need: Need-based aid available for full-time and part-time students. Work study available nights.

FINANCIAL AID PROCEDURES
Forms required: FAFSA, institutional form.
Dates and Deadlines: Priority date 4/15; no closing date. Applicants notified on a rolling basis starting 5/1; must reply within 2 week(s) of notification.

CONTACT
Bill Osborn, Director of Financial Aid
1971 Jagerson Avenue, Kingman, AZ 86409
(866) 664-2832

Northern Arizona University

Flagstaff, Arizona
www.nau.edu   Federal Code: 001082

4-year public university in small city.
Enrollment: 15,362 undergrads, 16% part-time. 2,607 full-time freshmen.
Selectivity: Open admission; but selective for out-of-state students.

BASIC COSTS (2007-2008)
Tuition and fees: $4,844; out-of-state residents $14,498.
Per-credit charge: $240; out-of-state residents $594.
Room and board: $6,572.

FINANCIAL AID PICTURE (2006-2007)
Students with need: Out of 1,961 full-time freshmen who applied for aid, 1,162 were judged to have need. Of these, 1,102 received aid, and 220 had their full need met. Average financial aid package met 68% of need; average scholarship/grant was $5,101; average loan was $2,666. For part-time students, average financial aid package was $6,849.
Students without need: 663 full-time freshmen who did not demonstrate need for aid received scholarships/grants; average award was $3,139. No-need awards available for academics, alumni affiliation, art, athletics, leadership, minority status, music/drama, ROTC, state/district residency.
Scholarships offered: 42 full-time freshmen received athletic scholarships; average amount $10,955.
Cumulative student debt: 53% of graduating class had student loans; average debt was $11,248.

FINANCIAL AID PROCEDURES
Forms required: FAFSA.
Dates and Deadlines: Priority date 3/1; no closing date. Applicants notified on a rolling basis starting 3/15.

CONTACT
Jack Edwards, Director of Financial Aid
PO Box 4084, Flagstaff, AZ 86011-4084
(928) 523-4951

Northland Pioneer College

Holbrook, Arizona
www.npc.edu   Federal Code: 011862

2-year public community and technical college in small town.
Enrollment: 1,942 undergrads.
Selectivity: Open admission; but selective for some programs.

BASIC COSTS (2007-2008)
Tuition and fees: $1,056; out-of-state residents $6,900.
Per-credit charge: $44; out-of-state residents $76.

FINANCIAL AID PICTURE
Students with need: Need-based aid available for full-time and part-time students. Work study available nights, weekends, and for part-time students.
Students without need: No-need awards available for academics, art, job skills, leadership, minority status, music/drama, state/district residency.

FINANCIAL AID PROCEDURES
Forms required: FAFSA, institutional form.
Dates and Deadlines: Priority date 6/1; no closing date. Applicants notified on a rolling basis starting 5/15; must reply within 2 week(s) of notification.

CONTACT
Beaulah Bob-Pennypacker, Financial Aid Coordinator
PO Box 610, Holbrook, AZ 86025-0610
(928) 524-7472

Paradise Valley Community College

Phoenix, Arizona
www.pvc.maricopa.edu   Federal Code: 026236

2-year public community college in very large city.
Enrollment: 3,100 undergrads.
Selectivity: Open admission.

BASIC COSTS (2007-2008)
Tuition and fees: $1,980; out-of-state residents $8,430.
Per-credit charge: $65; out-of-state residents $280.

FINANCIAL AID PICTURE

Students with need: Need-based aid available for full-time and part-time students.

FINANCIAL AID PROCEDURES

Forms required: FAFSA.

Dates and Deadlines: No deadline. Applicants notified on a rolling basis starting 6/1.

CONTACT

JoAnn Caufield, Director, Financial Aid
18401 North 32nd Street, Phoenix, AZ 85032
(602) 787-7100

Phoenix College

Phoenix, Arizona
www.pc.maricopa.edu   Federal Code: 001078

2-year public community college in very large city.

Enrollment: 2,573 full-time undergrads.

Selectivity: Open admission; but selective for some programs.

BASIC COSTS (2007-2008)

Tuition and fees: $1,980; out-of-state residents $8,130.

Per-credit charge: $65; out-of-state residents $270.

FINANCIAL AID PICTURE

Students with need: Work study available weekends and for part-time students.

FINANCIAL AID PROCEDURES

Forms required: FAFSA.

Dates and Deadlines: Priority date 6/30; no closing date. Applicants notified on a rolling basis starting 5/1.

CONTACT

Genevieve Watson, Director of Financial Aid
1202 West Thomas Road, Phoenix, AZ 85013
(602) 285-7404

Pima Community College

Tucson, Arizona
www.pima.edu   Federal Code: 007266

2-year public community and technical college in very large city.

Enrollment: 27,191 undergrads.

Selectivity: Open admission; but selective for some programs.

BASIC COSTS (2007-2008)

Tuition and fees: $1,565; out-of-state residents $7,235.

Per-credit charge: $47; out-of-state residents $80.

FINANCIAL AID PICTURE

Students with need: Need-based aid available for full-time and part-time students.

Students without need: No-need awards available for academics, alumni affiliation, art, athletics, minority status, music/drama.

FINANCIAL AID PROCEDURES

Forms required: FAFSA.

Dates and Deadlines: Priority date 3/15; no closing date. Applicants notified on a rolling basis starting 7/1; must reply within 2 week(s) of notification.

CONTACT

Anna Reese, Executive Director of Financial Aid
4905B East Broadway, Tucson, AZ 85709-1120
(520) 206-4950

Prescott College

Prescott, Arizona
www.prescott.edu   Federal Code: 013659

4-year private liberal arts college in large town.

Enrollment: 689 undergrads, 13% part-time. 71 full-time freshmen.

Selectivity: Admits over 75% of applicants.

BASIC COSTS (2008-2009)

Tuition and fees: $21,792.

Per-credit charge: $597.

Room only: $3,400.

Additional info: Health insurance is required; cost of school's health insurance is $413 for fall term and $579 for spring term.

FINANCIAL AID PICTURE (2007-2008)

Students with need: Out of 34 full-time freshmen who applied for aid, 20 were judged to have need. Of these, 20 received aid, and 1 had their full need met. Average financial aid package met 41% of need; average scholarship/grant was $4,713; average loan was $2,520. For part-time students, average financial aid package was $7,946.

Students without need: 12 full-time freshmen who did not demonstrate need for aid received scholarships/grants; average award was $4,000. No-need awards available for academics, alumni affiliation, minority status, state/district residency.

Cumulative student debt: 71% of graduating class had student loans; average debt was $21,723.

FINANCIAL AID PROCEDURES

Forms required: FAFSA.

Dates and Deadlines: Priority date 4/1; no closing date. Applicants notified on a rolling basis starting 3/15; must reply within 12 week(s) of notification. **Transfers:** No deadline. Applicants notified on a rolling basis; must reply within 12 week(s) of notification.

CONTACT

Terri Eckel, Director of Financial Aid
220 Grove Avenue, Prescott, AZ 86301
(928) 776-5225

Rio Salado College

Tempe, Arizona
www.riosalado.edu   Federal Code: 014483

2-year public virtual community college in very large city.

Enrollment: 1,193 undergrads.

Selectivity: Open admission; but selective for some programs.

BASIC COSTS (2008-2009)

Tuition and fees: $2,160; out-of-state residents $8,610.

Per-credit charge: $71; out-of-state residents $286.

FINANCIAL AID PICTURE

Students with need: Need-based aid available for full-time and part-time students.

Students without need: This college awards aid only to students with need.

FINANCIAL AID PROCEDURES

Forms required: FAFSA, institutional form.

Dates and Deadlines: Priority date 6/30; no closing date. Applicants notified on a rolling basis starting 6/30.

CONTACT

Linda Ross, Director of Financial Aid
2323 West 14th Street, Tempe, AZ 85281
(480) 517-8310

South Mountain Community College

Phoenix, Arizona
www.smc.maricopa.edu   Federal Code: 015001

2-year public community college in very large city.
Enrollment: 210 full-time undergrads.
Selectivity: Open admission.

BASIC COSTS (2007-2008)
Tuition and fees: $1,980; out-of-state residents $8,430.
Per-credit charge: $65; out-of-state residents $280.

FINANCIAL AID PICTURE
Students with need: Need-based aid available for full-time and part-time students. Work study available nights, weekends, and for part-time students.
Students without need: No-need awards available for academics, athletics, minority status, music/drama.

FINANCIAL AID PROCEDURES
Forms required: FAFSA.
Dates and Deadlines: Priority date 5/1; no closing date. Applicants notified on a rolling basis starting 5/15; must reply within 3 week(s) of notification.

CONTACT
Inez Moreno-Weinert, Director of Financial Aid and Placement
7050 South 24th Street, Phoenix, AZ 85042
(602) 243-8300

Southwestern College

Phoenix, Arizona
www.swcaz.edu   Federal Code: 007113

4-year private Bible college in very large city, affiliated with Baptist faith.
Enrollment: 361 undergrads.
Selectivity: Admits less than 50% of applicants.

BASIC COSTS (2007-2008)
Tuition and fees: $13,344.
Per-credit charge: $530.
Room and board: $5,046.

FINANCIAL AID PICTURE
Students with need: Need-based aid available for full-time and part-time students.
Students without need: No-need awards available for academics, alumni affiliation, leadership, music/drama, religious affiliation.

FINANCIAL AID PROCEDURES
Forms required: FAFSA, state aid form, institutional form.
Dates and Deadlines: Priority date 3/15; closing date 8/31. Applicants notified on a rolling basis.

CONTACT
Cheryl Hansen, Director of Financial Aid
2625 East Cactus Road, Phoenix, AZ 85032-7042
(602) 489-5500 ext. 115

Tohono O'odham Community College

Sells, Arizona
www.tocc.cc.az.us   Federal Code: 037844

2-year public community college in rural community.
Enrollment: 96 undergrads, 72% part-time. 4 full-time freshmen.
Selectivity: Open admission.

BASIC COSTS (2008-2009)
Tuition and fees: $1,270; out-of-state residents $6,340.
Per-credit charge: $42; out-of-state residents $72.

FINANCIAL AID PICTURE (2006-2007)
Students with need: 96% of average financial aid package awarded as scholarships/grants, 4% awarded as loans/jobs. Need-based aid available for part-time students.
Students without need: This college awards aid only to students with need.

FINANCIAL AID PROCEDURES
Forms required: FAFSA, institutional form.
Dates and Deadlines: No deadline. Applicants notified on a rolling basis.

CONTACT
Alvaro Rivera, Financial Aid Director
PO Box 3129, Sells, AZ 85634-3129
(520) 383-8401 ext. 41

University of Advancing Technology

Tempe, Arizona
www.uat.edu   Federal Code: 017188

4-year for-profit university and technical college in very large city.
Enrollment: 1,195 undergrads. 596 full-time freshmen.

BASIC COSTS (2008-2009)
Tuition and fees: $16,900.
Room and board: $8,400.
Additional info: Tuition at time of enrollment locked for 4 years.

FINANCIAL AID PICTURE
Students with need: Need-based aid available for full-time and part-time students.

FINANCIAL AID PROCEDURES
Forms required: FAFSA.
Dates and Deadlines: Priority date 4/15; no closing date. Applicants notified on a rolling basis; must reply within 2 week(s) of notification.
Transfers: No deadline. Must reply within 2 week(s) of notification. Loan periods may not overlap.

CONTACT
Lisa Frankowski, Manager of Student Financial Aid
2625 West Baseline Road, Tempe, AZ 85283-1056
(602) 383-8217

University of Arizona

Tucson, Arizona
www.arizona.edu   Federal Code: 001083

4-year public university in very large city.
Enrollment: 28,670 undergrads, 13% part-time. 5,788 full-time freshmen.
Selectivity: Admits over 75% of applicants.

BASIC COSTS (2007-2008)
Tuition and fees: $5,037; out-of-state residents $16,271.
Per-credit charge: $252; out-of-state residents $669.
Room and board: $7,370.
Additional info: Tuition/fee waivers available for minority students.

FINANCIAL AID PICTURE (2006-2007)

Students with need: Out of 3,378 full-time freshmen who applied for aid, 2,119 were judged to have need. Of these, 2,021 received aid, and 334 had their full need met. Average financial aid package met 64% of need; average scholarship/grant was $6,774; average loan was $3,042. For part-time students, average financial aid package was $6,138.

Students without need: 2,076 full-time freshmen who did not demonstrate need for aid received scholarships/grants; average award was $4,382. No-need awards available for academics, art.

Scholarships offered: Over $3 million in merit scholarships available to freshmen. National Merit scholarship packages range from $6,000-$10,000 a year.

Cumulative student debt: 45% of graduating class had student loans; average debt was $18,241.

FINANCIAL AID PROCEDURES

Forms required: FAFSA.

Dates and Deadlines: Priority date 3/1; no closing date. Applicants notified on a rolling basis starting 4/1; must reply within 3 week(s) of notification.

Transfers: Some waivers available for Arizona Community College transfer students with 3.2 GPA who are Arizona residents.

CONTACT

John Nametz, Director of Student Financial Aid
Robert L. Nugent Building, Tucson, AZ 85721-0040
(520) 621-1858

University of Phoenix

Phoenix, Arizona
www.phoenix.edu   Federal Code: 014593

4-year for-profit virtual university in very large city.

Enrollment: 246,589 full-time undergrads.

Selectivity: Open admission; but selective for some programs.

BASIC COSTS (2007-2008)

Tuition and fees: $10,290.

Per-credit charge: $343.

FINANCIAL AID PICTURE

Students with need: Need-based aid available for full-time students.

FINANCIAL AID PROCEDURES

Forms required: FAFSA, institutional form.

Dates and Deadlines: No deadline. Applicants notified on a rolling basis.

CONTACT

Robert Collins, Vice President, Student Financial Aid
4615 East Elwood Street, Phoenix, AZ 85040-1958
(480) 804-7600

Western International University

Phoenix, Arizona
www.wintu.edu   Federal Code: 014970

4-year for-profit university and business college in very large city.

Enrollment: 2,050 undergrads.

Selectivity: Admits over 75% of applicants.

BASIC COSTS (2007-2008)

Additional info: Per-credit-hour charge $333.

FINANCIAL AID PICTURE (2006-2007)

Students with need: Average financial aid package for all full-time undergraduates was $10,500.

Students without need: This college awards aid only to students with need.

Cumulative student debt: 60% of graduating class had student loans; average debt was $22,346.

FINANCIAL AID PROCEDURES

Forms required: FAFSA, institutional form.

Dates and Deadlines: No deadline. Applicants notified on a rolling basis.

Transfers: No deadline. Applicants notified on a rolling basis.

CONTACT

Ella Owen, Associate Director of Financial Services
9215 North Black Canyon Highway, Phoenix, AZ 85021
(602) 943-2311

Yavapai College

Prescott, Arizona
www.yc.edu   Federal Code: 001079

2-year public community college in large town.

Enrollment: 4,718 undergrads, 71% part-time. 355 full-time freshmen.

Selectivity: Open admission; but selective for some programs.

BASIC COSTS (2007-2008)

Tuition and fees: $1,470; out-of-state residents $8,140.

Per-credit charge: $49; out-of-state residents $327.

Room and board: $4,350.

FINANCIAL AID PICTURE

Students with need: Need-based aid available for full-time and part-time students.

Students without need: No-need awards available for academics, athletics.

FINANCIAL AID PROCEDURES

Forms required: FAFSA.

Dates and Deadlines: Priority date 4/1; no closing date. Applicants notified on a rolling basis.

CONTACT

Vikki Gill, Director of Financial Aid
1100 East Sheldon Street, Prescott, AZ 86301
(928) 776-2152

Arkansas

Arkansas Baptist College

Little Rock, Arkansas
www.arkansasbaptist.edu   Federal Code: 001087

4-year private liberal arts college in large city, affiliated with American Baptist Churches in the USA.

Enrollment: 542 undergrads, 16% part-time. 301 full-time freshmen.

Selectivity: Open admission.

BASIC COSTS (2007-2008)

Tuition and fees: $5,390.

Per-credit charge: $207.

Room and board: $8,042.

FINANCIAL AID PICTURE

Students with need: Need-based aid available for full-time and part-time students.

Students without need: This college awards aid only to students with need.

FINANCIAL AID PROCEDURES

Forms required: FAFSA.

Dates and Deadlines: Closing date 5/1. Applicants notified on a rolling basis starting 6/15.

CONTACT

Shirley Washington, Director of Admissions and Financial Aid
1621 Dr. Martin Luther King Drive, Little Rock, AR 72202
(501) 374-6135

Arkansas Northeastern College

Blytheville, Arkansas
www.anc.edu   Federal Code: 012860

2-year public community college in large town.
Enrollment: 1,360 undergrads.
Selectivity: Open admission; but selective for some programs.

BASIC COSTS (2008-2009)

Tuition and fees: $1,828; out-of-district residents $2,108; out-of-state residents $3,508.
Per-credit charge: $50; out-of-district residents $60; out-of-state residents $110.

FINANCIAL AID PICTURE

Students with need: Need-based aid available for full-time and part-time students. Work study available nights.
Students without need: No-need awards available for academics, minority status, music/drama, state/district residency.

FINANCIAL AID PROCEDURES

Forms required: FAFSA, institutional form.
Dates and Deadlines: Priority date 4/15; no closing date. Applicants notified on a rolling basis starting 5/1; must reply within 2 week(s) of notification.

CONTACT

Laura Yarbrough, Director of Financial Aid
Box 1109, Blytheville, AR 72316-1109
(870) 762-1020 ext. 1160

Arkansas State University

State University, Arkansas
www.astate.edu   Federal Code: 001090

4-year public university in small city.
Enrollment: 8,791 undergrads, 17% part-time. 1,666 full-time freshmen.
Selectivity: Admits over 75% of applicants.

BASIC COSTS (2007-2008)

Tuition and fees: $6,010; out-of-state residents $13,390.
Per-credit charge: $154; out-of-state residents $400.
Room and board: $5,060.

FINANCIAL AID PICTURE (2007-2008)

Students with need: Out of 1,539 full-time freshmen who applied for aid, 1,450 were judged to have need. Of these, 1,414 received aid, and 325 had their full need met. Average financial aid package met 68% of need; average scholarship/grant was $6,200; average loan was $4,200. Need-based aid available for part-time students.
Students without need: 210 full-time freshmen who did not demonstrate need for aid received scholarships/grants; average award was $4,800. No-need awards available for academics, alumni affiliation, art, athletics, leadership, minority status, music/drama, ROTC, state/district residency.
Scholarships offered: 64 full-time freshmen received athletic scholarships; average amount $10,000.
Cumulative student debt: 67% of graduating class had student loans; average debt was $18,500.

FINANCIAL AID PROCEDURES

Forms required: FAFSA, institutional form.
Dates and Deadlines: Priority date 2/15; closing date 7/1. Applicants notified on a rolling basis starting 6/1; must reply within 2 week(s) of notification.

CONTACT

Gregory Thornburg, Director of Financial Aid/Dean of Enrollment Services
PO Box 1630, State University, AR 72467-1630
(870) 972-2310

Arkansas State University: Beebe

Beebe, Arkansas
www.asub.edu   Federal Code: 001090

2-year public branch campus and community college in small town.
Enrollment: 3,310 undergrads.
Selectivity: Open admission.

BASIC COSTS (2007-2008)

Tuition and fees: $2,715; out-of-state residents $4,400.
Per-credit charge: $75; out-of-state residents $122.
Room and board: $2,680.

FINANCIAL AID PICTURE (2007-2008)

Students with need: 21% of average financial aid package awarded as scholarships/grants, 79% awarded as loans/jobs. Need-based aid available for part-time students. Work study available nights, weekends, and for part-time students.
Students without need: No-need awards available for academics, leadership, minority status, music/drama.

FINANCIAL AID PROCEDURES

Forms required: FAFSA, institutional form.
Dates and Deadlines: Priority date 6/1; no closing date. Applicants notified on a rolling basis starting 6/1; must reply within 2 week(s) of notification.

CONTACT

Linda Yelder, Director of Student Aid
PO Box 1000, Beebe, AR 72012-1000
(501) 882-8245

Arkansas State University: Mountain Home

Mountain Home, Arkansas
www.asumh.edu   Federal Code: 001090

1-year public community and technical college in large town.
Enrollment: 1,055 undergrads, 48% part-time. 193 full-time freshmen.
Selectivity: Open admission; but selective for some programs.

BASIC COSTS (2007-2008)

Tuition and fees: $2,370; out-of-state residents $3,900.
Per-credit charge: $71; out-of-state residents $122.

FINANCIAL AID PICTURE

Students with need: Need-based aid available for full-time and part-time students.
Students without need: No-need awards available for academics, state/district residency.

FINANCIAL AID PROCEDURES

Forms required: FAFSA, institutional form.
Dates and Deadlines: Priority date 7/1; no closing date. Applicants notified on a rolling basis starting 5/1; must reply within 2 week(s) of notification.

CONTACT

Lyndle McCurley, Vice Chancellor Administrative Affairs
1600 South College Street, Mountain Home, AR 72653
(870) 508-6195

Arkansas Tech University
Russellville, Arkansas
www.atu.edu   Federal Code: 001089

4-year public university and liberal arts college in large town.
Enrollment: 6,558 undergrads, 13% part-time. 1,459 full-time freshmen.
Selectivity: Admits over 75% of applicants.

BASIC COSTS (2007-2008)
Tuition and fees: $5,120; out-of-state residents $9,710.
Per-credit charge: $153; out-of-state residents $306.
Room and board: $4,422.

FINANCIAL AID PICTURE (2006-2007)
Students with need: Out of 1,091 full-time freshmen who applied for aid, 887 were judged to have need. Of these, 873 received aid, and 246 had their full need met. Average financial aid package met 36% of need; average scholarship/grant was $2,566; average loan was $1,005. For part-time students, average financial aid package was $4,295.
Students without need: 308 full-time freshmen who did not demonstrate need for aid received scholarships/grants; average award was $5,928. No-need awards available for academics, art, athletics, leadership, minority status, music/drama, ROTC.
Scholarships offered: 50 full-time freshmen received athletic scholarships; average amount $2,900.
Cumulative student debt: 56% of graduating class had student loans; average debt was $19,396.

FINANCIAL AID PROCEDURES
Forms required: FAFSA.
Dates and Deadlines: Priority date 4/15; no closing date. Applicants notified on a rolling basis starting 5/1; must reply within 2 week(s) of notification.

CONTACT
Shirley Goines, Director of Student Financial Aid
Doc Bryan Student Services Building #141, Russellville, AR 72801-2222
(479) 968-0399

Central Baptist College
Conway, Arkansas
www.cbc.edu   Federal Code: 001093

4-year private Bible and junior college in large town, affiliated with Baptist faith.
Enrollment: 566 undergrads, 19% part-time. 112 full-time freshmen.
Selectivity: Admits 50 to 75% of applicants.

BASIC COSTS (2007-2008)
Tuition and fees: $9,040.
Room and board: $5,000.

FINANCIAL AID PICTURE
Students with need: Need-based aid available for full-time students.
Students without need: No-need awards available for academics, state/district residency.

FINANCIAL AID PROCEDURES
Forms required: FAFSA.
Dates and Deadlines: Priority date 7/1; closing date 8/1. Applicants notified on a rolling basis starting 4/1.
Transfers: No deadline.

CONTACT

Christi Bell, Director of Financial Aid
1501 College Avenue, Conway, AR 72034
(501) 329-6872 ext. 185

Crowley's Ridge College
Paragould, Arkansas
www.crowleysridgecollege.edu   Federal Code: 001095

2-year private junior college in large town, affiliated with Church of Christ.
Enrollment: 118 undergrads.
Selectivity: Open admission.

BASIC COSTS (2008-2009)
Tuition and fees: $8,410.
Per-credit charge: $245.
Room and board: $5,300.
Additional info: Tuition/fee waivers available for adults.

FINANCIAL AID PICTURE (2007-2008)
Students with need: 91% of average financial aid package awarded as scholarships/grants, 9% awarded as loans/jobs. Work study available nights, weekends, and for part-time students.
Students without need: No-need awards available for academics, leadership, music/drama.

FINANCIAL AID PROCEDURES
Forms required: FAFSA.
Dates and Deadlines: No deadline.

CONTACT
David Goff, Director of Financial Aid
100 College Drive, Paragould, AR 72450
(870) 236-6901

East Arkansas Community College
Forrest City, Arkansas
www.eacc.edu   Federal Code: 012260

2-year public community college in large town.
Enrollment: 1,121 undergrads, 32% part-time. 247 full-time freshmen.
Selectivity: Open admission.

BASIC COSTS (2007-2008)
Tuition and fees: $1,770; out-of-district residents $2,010; out-of-state residents $2,370.
Per-credit charge: $51; out-of-district residents $59; out-of-state residents $71.

FINANCIAL AID PICTURE
Students with need: Need-based aid available for full-time and part-time students.
Students without need: This college awards aid only to students with need.

FINANCIAL AID PROCEDURES
Forms required: FAFSA.
Dates and Deadlines: Priority date 3/1; closing date 7/1. Applicants notified on a rolling basis starting 5/15; must reply within 2 week(s) of notification.

CONTACT
Alvin Coleman, Director of Financial Aid
1700 Newcastle Road, Forrest City, AR 72335-9598
(870) 633-4480 ext. 225

Ecclesia College

Springdale, Arkansas
www.ecollege.edu   Federal Code: 038553

4-year private liberal arts college in large town, affiliated with interdenominational tradition.
Enrollment: 104 undergrads.
Selectivity: Open admission; but selective for some programs.

BASIC COSTS (2008-2009)
Tuition and fees: $15,090.
Per-credit charge: $475.
Room and board: $5,485.
Additional info: Full-time students not living on campus may be subject to additional $600 nonresidents fee. Tuition/fee waivers available for adults.

FINANCIAL AID PICTURE (2006-2007)
Students with need: 44% of average financial aid package awarded as scholarships/grants, 56% awarded as loans/jobs. Need-based aid available for part-time students. Work study available nights, weekends, and for part-time students.
Students without need: No-need awards available for academics, athletics, leadership, music/drama.

FINANCIAL AID PROCEDURES
Forms required: FAFSA.
Dates and Deadlines: No deadline. Applicants notified on a rolling basis starting 7/1.

CONTACT
Jesse Wadkins, Financial Aid Officer
9653 Nations Drive, Springdale, AR 72762
(479) 248-7236 ext. 208

Harding University

Searcy, Arkansas
www.harding.edu   Federal Code: 001097

4-year private university in large town, affiliated with Church of Christ.
Enrollment: 4,063 undergrads, 5% part-time. 903 full-time freshmen.
Selectivity: Admits over 75% of applicants.

BASIC COSTS (2008-2009)
Tuition and fees: $13,130.
Per-credit charge: $423.
Room and board: $5,700.

FINANCIAL AID PICTURE (2006-2007)
Students with need: Out of 670 full-time freshmen who applied for aid, 467 were judged to have need. Of these, 466 received aid, and 150 had their full need met. Average financial aid package met 75% of need; average scholarship/grant was $6,300; average loan was $3,864. For part-time students, average financial aid package was $7,119.
Students without need: 187 full-time freshmen who did not demonstrate need for aid received scholarships/grants; average award was $3,468. No-need awards available for academics, art, athletics, music/drama, religious affiliation, ROTC, state/district residency.
Scholarships offered: 31 full-time freshmen received athletic scholarships; average amount $6,490.
Cumulative student debt: 74% of graduating class had student loans; average debt was $28,386.
Additional info: Music scholarships available, audition required.

FINANCIAL AID PROCEDURES
Forms required: FAFSA, institutional form.
Dates and Deadlines: Priority date 4/1; no closing date. Applicants notified on a rolling basis starting 2/15; must reply within 2 week(s) of notification.

Transfers: No deadline.

CONTACT
Jon Roberts, Director of Student Financial Services
915 East Market Avenue, Searcy, AR 72149-2255
(501) 279-4257

Henderson State University

Arkadelphia, Arkansas
www.getreddie.com   Federal Code: 001098

4-year public university and liberal arts college in large town.
Enrollment: 3,092 undergrads, 11% part-time. 786 full-time freshmen.
Selectivity: Admits 50 to 75% of applicants.

BASIC COSTS (2007-2008)
Tuition and fees: $5,981; out-of-state residents $10,601.
Per-credit charge: $154; out-of-state residents $308.

FINANCIAL AID PICTURE
Students with need: Need-based aid available for full-time and part-time students.
Students without need: No-need awards available for academics, alumni affiliation, art, athletics, leadership, minority status, music/drama, state/district residency.

FINANCIAL AID PROCEDURES
Forms required: FAFSA.
Dates and Deadlines: Priority date 6/1; no closing date. Applicants notified on a rolling basis starting 4/1; must reply within 2 week(s) of notification.

CONTACT
Vicky Taylor, Director of Financial Aid
1100 Henderson Street, Arkadelphia, AR 71999-0001
(870) 230-5094

Hendrix College

Conway, Arkansas
www.hendrix.edu   Federal Code: 001099

4-year private liberal arts college in small city, affiliated with United Methodist Church.
Enrollment: 1,189 undergrads, 1% part-time. 371 full-time freshmen.
Selectivity: Admits over 75% of applicants.

BASIC COSTS (2008-2009)
Tuition and fees: $26,080.
Room and board: $7,950.

FINANCIAL AID PICTURE (2007-2008)
Students with need: Out of 312 full-time freshmen who applied for aid, 232 were judged to have need. Of these, 232 received aid, and 19 had their full need met. Average financial aid package met 88% of need; average scholarship/grant was $16,387; average loan was $4,166. For part-time students, average financial aid package was $7,213.
Students without need: 128 full-time freshmen who did not demonstrate need for aid received scholarships/grants; average award was $18,931. No-need awards available for academics, art, leadership, music/drama, religious affiliation.
Scholarships offered: Hays Memorial Scholarship; full tuition, room, board, mandatory fees; based on academic excellence. Visual and Performing Arts Scholarships (music, theatre, art); $1,000 to $5,000 per year; auditions/portfolios required. Leadership and United Methodist (UMYF) scholarships; $1,000 to $3,500.
Cumulative student debt: 81% of graduating class had student loans; average debt was $17,490.

FINANCIAL AID PROCEDURES

Forms required: FAFSA.

Dates and Deadlines: Priority date 2/15; no closing date. Applicants notified on a rolling basis starting 3/1; must reply by 5/1 or within 2 week(s) of notification.

CONTACT

Mark Bandre, Director of Financial Aid
1600 Washington Avenue, Conway, AR 72032-3080
(501) 450-1368

John Brown University

Siloam Springs, Arkansas
www.jbu.edu   Federal Code: 001100

4-year private liberal arts college in large town, affiliated with interdenominational tradition.

Enrollment: 1,666 undergrads, 3% part-time. 361 full-time freshmen.

BASIC COSTS (2008-2009)

Tuition and fees: $18,066.

Per-credit charge: $720.

Room and board: $6,580.

Additional info: Tuition/fee waivers available for adults.

FINANCIAL AID PICTURE

Students with need: Need-based aid available for full-time students.

Students without need: No-need awards available for academics, alumni affiliation, art, athletics, leadership, music/drama, ROTC.

FINANCIAL AID PROCEDURES

Forms required: FAFSA, institutional form.

Dates and Deadlines: Priority date 3/1; no closing date. Applicants notified on a rolling basis starting 3/1; must reply within 4 week(s) of notification.

CONTACT

Kim Eldridge, Director of Financial Aid
2000 West University Street, Siloam Springs, AR 72761-2121
(888) 528-4636

Lyon College

Batesville, Arkansas
www.lyon.edu   Federal Code: 001088

4-year private liberal arts college in small town, affiliated with Presbyterian Church (USA).

Enrollment: 483 undergrads, 4% part-time. 142 full-time freshmen.

Selectivity: Admits 50 to 75% of applicants.

BASIC COSTS (2008-2009)

Tuition and fees: $19,034.

Per-credit charge: $695.

Room and board: $6,990.

FINANCIAL AID PICTURE (2007-2008)

Students with need: Out of 118 full-time freshmen who applied for aid, 96 were judged to have need. Of these, 96 received aid, and 33 had their full need met. Average financial aid package met 85% of need; average scholarship/grant was $11,863; average loan was $3,748. For part-time students, average financial aid package was $7,286.

Students without need: 35 full-time freshmen who did not demonstrate need for aid received scholarships/grants; average award was $10,769. No-need awards available for academics, art, athletics, leadership, minority status, music/drama, religious affiliation, state/district residency.

Scholarships offered: *Merit:* Brown Scholarship; tuition, room, board, mandatory fees and books; based on high school record, standardized test

scores; 4 awarded. Anderson Scholarship; tuition, mandatory fees and books; based on high school record, test scores; 4 awarded. Lyon Fellowship; $10,000; based on high school record, test scores, with a preference for students with a career interest in business or public service or a strong academic interest in computer science or the fine arts; up to 8 awarded.

Athletic: 25 full-time freshmen received athletic scholarships; average amount $5,190.

Cumulative student debt: 89% of graduating class had student loans; average debt was $16,234.

FINANCIAL AID PROCEDURES

Forms required: FAFSA.

Dates and Deadlines: Priority date 3/15; no closing date. Applicants notified on a rolling basis starting 3/1; must reply by 8/15.

CONTACT

Louise Strauser, Assistant Director of Student Financial Assistance
PO Box 2317, Batesville, AR 72503-2317
(870) 307-7257

Mid-South Community College

West Memphis, Arkansas
www.midsouthcc.edu   Federal Code: 015862

2-year public community and junior college in large town.

Enrollment: 1,005 undergrads, 62% part-time. 150 full-time freshmen.

Selectivity: Open admission.

BASIC COSTS (2007-2008)

Tuition and fees: $1,800; out-of-district residents $2,100; out-of-state residents $3,600.

Per-credit charge: $50; out-of-district residents $60; out-of-state residents $110.

FINANCIAL AID PICTURE

Students with need: Need-based aid available for full-time and part-time students. Work study available nights.

Students without need: No-need awards available for academics, state/district residency.

FINANCIAL AID PROCEDURES

Forms required: FAFSA, institutional form.

Dates and Deadlines: No deadline. Applicants notified on a rolling basis starting 6/1; must reply within 2 week(s) of notification.

CONTACT

Jackie Brubaker, Director of Financial Aid
2000 West Broadway, West Memphis, AR 72301
(870) 733-6741

National Park Community College

Hot Springs, Arkansas
www.npcc.edu   Federal Code: 012105

2-year public liberal arts and technical college in large town.

Enrollment: 2,503 undergrads, 48% part-time. 307 full-time freshmen.

Selectivity: Open admission; but selective for some programs.

BASIC COSTS (2007-2008)

Tuition and fees: $1,740; out-of-district residents $2,040; out-of-state residents $3,960.

Per-credit charge: $56; out-of-district residents $66; out-of-state residents $130.

FINANCIAL AID PICTURE

Students with need: Need-based aid available for full-time and part-time students. Work study available nights, weekends, and for part-time students.

Students without need: No-need awards available for academics, minority status, music/drama, state/district residency.

FINANCIAL AID PROCEDURES

Forms required: FAFSA, institutional form.

Dates and Deadlines: Priority date 7/1; no closing date. Applicants notified on a rolling basis starting 3/1.

Transfers: Transfer applicants must furnish evidence of good standing at previous institution to qualify for financial aid.

CONTACT

Lisa Hopper, Counselor and Financial Aid Adviser
101 College Drive, Hot Springs, AR 71913
(501) 760-4235

North Arkansas College

Harrison, Arkansas
www.northark.edu   Federal Code: 012261

2-year public community and technical college in large town.

Enrollment: 1,664 undergrads.

Selectivity: Open admission; but selective for some programs.

BASIC COSTS (2008-2009)

Tuition and fees: $1,800; out-of-district residents $2,460; out-of-state residents $4,590.

Per-credit charge: $60; out-of-district residents $82; out-of-state residents $153.

FINANCIAL AID PICTURE

Students with need: Need-based aid available for full-time and part-time students. Work study available nights.

Students without need: No-need awards available for academics, athletics, state/district residency.

FINANCIAL AID PROCEDURES

Forms required: FAFSA, institutional form.

Dates and Deadlines: Priority date 5/1; no closing date. Applicants notified on a rolling basis starting 5/1.

Transfers: No deadline. Applicants notified on a rolling basis starting 5/1.

CONTACT

Nancy Fountain, Director of Financial Aid
1515 Pioneer Drive, Harrison, AR 72601
(870) 391-3266

Northwest Arkansas Community College

Bentonville, Arkansas
www.nwacc.edu   Federal Code: 030633

2-year public community college in small city.

Enrollment: 5,600 undergrads, 62% part-time. 656 full-time freshmen.

Selectivity: Open admission; but selective for some programs.

BASIC COSTS (2008-2009)

Tuition and fees: $2,410; out-of-district residents $3,460; out-of-state residents $4,652.

Per-credit charge: $63; out-of-district residents $98; out-of-state residents $138.

FINANCIAL AID PICTURE

Students with need: Need-based aid available for full-time and part-time students. Work study available nights, weekends, and for part-time students.

Students without need: No-need awards available for academics, leadership, music/drama, state/district residency.

FINANCIAL AID PROCEDURES

Forms required: FAFSA, institutional form.

Dates and Deadlines: Priority date 4/1; no closing date. Applicants notified on a rolling basis starting 4/1; must reply within 2 week(s) of notification.

CONTACT

Michelle Cordell, Director of Financial Aid
One College Drive, Bentonville, AR 72712
(479) 619-4129

Ouachita Baptist University

Arkadelphia, Arkansas
www.obu.edu   Federal Code: 001102

4-year private liberal arts college in large town, affiliated with Southern Baptist Convention.

Enrollment: 1,398 undergrads.

Selectivity: Admits 50 to 75% of applicants.

BASIC COSTS (2008-2009)

Tuition and fees: $18,400.

Per-credit charge: $515.

Room and board: $5,530.

FINANCIAL AID PICTURE (2007-2008)

Students with need: Average financial aid package met 86% of need; average scholarship/grant was $10,681; average loan was $3,349. For part-time students, average financial aid package was $10,072.

Students without need: No-need awards available for academics, alumni affiliation, athletics, job skills, leadership, minority status, music/drama, religious affiliation, ROTC, state/district residency.

Cumulative student debt: 67% of graduating class had student loans; average debt was $14,591.

FINANCIAL AID PROCEDURES

Forms required: FAFSA.

Dates and Deadlines: Priority date 1/15; closing date 6/1. Applicants notified on a rolling basis starting 11/1; must reply by 5/1.

CONTACT

Chris Kear, Director of Financial Aid
OBU Box 3776, Arkadelphia, AR 71998-0001
(870) 245-5570

Ouachita Technical College

Malvern, Arkansas
www.otcweb.edu   Federal Code: 009976

2-year public community and technical college in small town.

Enrollment: 851 undergrads.

Selectivity: Open admission; but selective for some programs.

BASIC COSTS (2008-2009)

Tuition and fees: $2,150; out-of-state residents $3,830.

Per-credit charge: $56; out-of-state residents $112.

FINANCIAL AID PICTURE

Students with need: Need-based aid available for full-time and part-time students. Work study available nights.

FINANCIAL AID PROCEDURES

Forms required: FAFSA.

Dates and Deadlines: Closing date 6/30. Applicants notified on a rolling basis starting 7/1; must reply within 6 week(s) of notification.

CONTACT

Teresa Avery, Director of Financial Aid

One College Circle, Malvern, AR 72104

(501) 337-5000 ext. 1122

Ozarka College

Melbourne, Arkansas

www.ozarka.edu   Federal Code: 013217

2-year public community and technical college in rural community.

Enrollment: 806 undergrads.

Selectivity: Open admission; but selective for some programs.

BASIC COSTS (2007-2008)

Tuition and fees: $2,285; out-of-state residents $5,375.

Per-credit charge: $65; out-of-state residents $168.

FINANCIAL AID PICTURE

Students with need: Need-based aid available for full-time and part-time students.

FINANCIAL AID PROCEDURES

Forms required: FAFSA.

Dates and Deadlines: No deadline. Applicants notified on a rolling basis; must reply within 2 week(s) of notification.

CONTACT

Joyce Goff, Financial Aid Officer

218 College Drive, Melbourne, AR 72556-0010

(870) 368-7371 ext. 2010

Philander Smith College

Little Rock, Arkansas

www.philander.edu   Federal Code: 001103

4-year private liberal arts college in small city, affiliated with United Methodist Church.

Enrollment: 561 undergrads.

Selectivity: Admits less than 50% of applicants.

BASIC COSTS (2007-2008)

Tuition and fees: $8,490.

Room and board: $6,356.

FINANCIAL AID PICTURE (2007-2008)

Students with need: 35% of average financial aid package awarded as scholarships/grants, 65% awarded as loans/jobs. Need-based aid available for part-time students.

Students without need: This college awards aid only to students with need.

FINANCIAL AID PROCEDURES

Forms required: FAFSA, institutional form.

Dates and Deadlines: Priority date 3/1; no closing date. Applicants notified on a rolling basis starting 5/1; must reply within 2 week(s) of notification.

Transfers: Closing date 6/30.

CONTACT

David Page, Director of Financial Aid

One Trudie Kibbe Reed Drive, Little Rock, AR 72202-3718

(501) 370-5350

Phillips Community College of the University of Arkansas

Helena, Arkansas

www.pccua.edu   Federal Code: 001104

2-year public community college in large town.

Enrollment: 1,507 undergrads.

Selectivity: Open admission; but selective for some programs.

BASIC COSTS (2007-2008)

Tuition and fees: $1,910; out-of-district residents $2,180; out-of-state residents $3,320.

Per-credit charge: $52; out-of-district residents $61; out-of-state residents $99.

FINANCIAL AID PICTURE

Students with need: Need-based aid available for full-time and part-time students. Work study available nights.

Students without need: This college awards aid only to students with need.

Additional info: Tuition waivers are given to firefighters and law enforcement officers.

FINANCIAL AID PROCEDURES

Forms required: FAFSA.

Dates and Deadlines: Priority date 4/1; closing date 6/30. Applicants notified on a rolling basis starting 4/1; must reply within 2 week(s) of notification.

CONTACT

Barbra Stevenson, Director of Financial Aid

1000 Campus Drive, Helena, AR 72342

(870) 338-6474 ext. 1160

Pulaski Technical College

North Little Rock, Arkansas

www.pulaskitech.edu   Federal Code: 014167

2-year public community and technical college in small city.

Enrollment: 7,606 undergrads, 48% part-time. 892 full-time freshmen.

Selectivity: Open admission; but selective for some programs.

BASIC COSTS (2008-2009)

Tuition and fees: $2,630; out-of-state residents $4,160.

Per-credit charge: $77; out-of-state residents $128.

FINANCIAL AID PICTURE

Students with need: Need-based aid available for full-time and part-time students.

FINANCIAL AID PROCEDURES

Forms required: FAFSA, institutional form.

Dates and Deadlines: Priority date 5/15; no closing date. Applicants notified on a rolling basis starting 5/1; must reply within 2 week(s) of notification.

CONTACT

Kris Burford, Director Financial Aid

3000 West Scenic Drive, North Little Rock, AR 72118-3347

(501) 812-2289

Rich Mountain Community College

Mena, Arkansas

www.rmcc.edu   Federal Code: 012435

2-year public community college in small town.

Enrollment: 565 undergrads.

Selectivity: Open admission; but selective for some programs.

BASIC COSTS (2007-2008)

Tuition and fees: $1,440; out-of-district residents $2,160; out-of-state residents $5,190.

Per-credit charge: $45; out-of-district residents $69; out-of-state residents $170.

FINANCIAL AID PICTURE

Students with need: Need-based aid available for full-time and part-time students.

Students without need: No-need awards available for academics.

FINANCIAL AID PROCEDURES

Forms required: FAFSA, institutional form.

Dates and Deadlines: Priority date 7/1; no closing date. Applicants notified on a rolling basis starting 6/1; must reply within 2 week(s) of notification.

CONTACT

Mary Stenderfer, Director of Financial Aid
1100 College Drive, Mena, AR 71953
(479) 394-7622 ext. 1420

South Arkansas Community College

El Dorado, Arkansas
www.southark.edu   Federal Code: 013858

2-year public community and junior college in large town.

Enrollment: 1,214 undergrads.

Selectivity: Open admission.

BASIC COSTS (2007-2008)

Tuition and fees: $1,990; out-of-district residents $2,230; out-of-state residents $3,880.

Per-credit charge: $60; out-of-district residents $68; out-of-state residents $123.

Additional info: $25 lab fee for most courses.

FINANCIAL AID PICTURE

Students with need: Need-based aid available for full-time and part-time students.

FINANCIAL AID PROCEDURES

Forms required: FAFSA, institutional form.

Dates and Deadlines: Priority date 7/1; no closing date. Applicants notified on a rolling basis starting 7/1; must reply within 2 week(s) of notification.

CONTACT

Veronda Tatum, Director of Financial Aid
Box 7010, El Dorado, AR 71731-7010
(870) 864-7133

Southeast Arkansas College

Pine Bluff, Arkansas
www.seark.edu   Federal Code: 005707

2-year public community and technical college in small city.

Enrollment: 1,710 undergrads, 43% part-time. 215 full-time freshmen.

Selectivity: Open admission; but selective for some programs.

BASIC COSTS (2007-2008)

Tuition and fees: $1,720; out-of-state residents $3,220.

Per-credit charge: $50; out-of-state residents $100.

Additional info: $5 per credit hour technology fee. $5 assessment fee. $2 per hour services fee.

FINANCIAL AID PICTURE

Students with need: Need-based aid available for full-time and part-time students. Work study available nights, weekends, and for part-time students.

Students without need: No-need awards available for academics, leadership, state/district residency.

FINANCIAL AID PROCEDURES

Forms required: FAFSA.

Dates and Deadlines: Priority date 6/1; no closing date. Applicants notified on a rolling basis starting 5/1; must reply within 2 week(s) of notification.

CONTACT

Donna Cox, Director of Financial Aid
1900 Hazel Street, Pine Bluff, AR 71603
(870) 543-5968

Southern Arkansas University

Magnolia, Arkansas
www.saumag.edu   Federal Code: 001107

4-year public university in large town.

Enrollment: 2,660 undergrads, 14% part-time. 528 full-time freshmen.

Selectivity: Admits 50 to 75% of applicants.

BASIC COSTS (2007-2008)

Tuition and fees: $5,224; out-of-state residents $7,534.

Per-credit charge: $150; out-of-state residents $227.

Room and board: $4,100.

FINANCIAL AID PICTURE (2006-2007)

Students with need: 42% of average financial aid package awarded as scholarships/grants, 58% awarded as loans/jobs. Need-based aid available for part-time students. Work study available nights, weekends, and for part-time students.

Students without need: No-need awards available for academics, alumni affiliation, art, athletics, leadership, minority status, music/drama, state/district residency.

FINANCIAL AID PROCEDURES

Forms required: FAFSA.

Dates and Deadlines: Priority date 7/1; no closing date. Applicants notified on a rolling basis starting 4/15; must reply within 2 week(s) of notification.

CONTACT

Bronwyn Sneed, Director of Financial Aid
Box 9382, Magnolia, AR 71754-9382
(870) 235-4023

Southern Arkansas University Tech

Camden, Arkansas
www.sautech.edu   Federal Code: 007738

2-year public community and technical college in large town.

Enrollment: 787 undergrads, 32% part-time. 196 full-time freshmen.

Selectivity: Open admission; but selective for some programs.

BASIC COSTS (2007-2008)

Tuition and fees: $2,419; out-of-state residents $3,049.

Per-credit charge: $63; out-of-state residents $84.

FINANCIAL AID PICTURE (2006-2007)

Students with need: Need-based aid available for part-time students.

Students without need: No-need awards available for academics, state/district residency.

FINANCIAL AID PROCEDURES

Forms required: FAFSA.

Dates and Deadlines: Priority date 6/1; no closing date. Applicants notified on a rolling basis starting 5/1.

Transfers: Priority date 4/15; closing date 6/1. Applicants notified on a rolling basis starting 5/1.

CONTACT

Vicki Taylor, Director of Financial Aid

PO Box 3499, Camden, AR 71711-1599

(870) 574-4511

University of Arkansas

Fayetteville, Arkansas

www.uark.edu   Federal Code: 001108

4-year public university in small city.

Enrollment: 14,442 undergrads, 14% part-time. 2,726 full-time freshmen.

Selectivity: Admits 50 to 75% of applicants.

BASIC COSTS (2007-2008)

Tuition and fees: $6,038; out-of-state residents $14,492.

Per-credit charge: $159; out-of-state residents $441.

Room and board: $7,016.

FINANCIAL AID PICTURE (2006-2007)

Students with need: Out of 1,560 full-time freshmen who applied for aid, 999 were judged to have need. Of these, 966 received aid, and 203 had their full need met. Average financial aid package met 73% of need; average scholarship/grant was $4,131; average loan was $3,016. For part-time students, average financial aid package was $5,581.

Students without need: 519 full-time freshmen who did not demonstrate need for aid received scholarships/grants; average award was $6,148. No-need awards available for academics, alumni affiliation, art, athletics, leadership, minority status, music/drama, ROTC, state/district residency.

Scholarships offered: *Merit:* Sturgis Fellowship: $11,500, based on exceptional academic performance, 10 awards available to arts and sciences majors. Bodenhamer Fellowship: $11,000, based on strong academic performance and leadership. Chancellor's Scholarships: tuition, fees, room and board. University Scholarships: $4,000, based on rank in top 5-10% of high school class. Non-resident Tuition Award: non-resident tuition, for entering freshmen from neighboring states, based on minimum ACT score of 24 or SAT of 1090 (exclusive of writing) and 3.0 high school GPA. *Athletic:* 101 full-time freshmen received athletic scholarships; average amount $8,786.

Cumulative student debt: 46% of graduating class had student loans; average debt was $18,172.

FINANCIAL AID PROCEDURES

Forms required: FAFSA.

Dates and Deadlines: Priority date 3/15; no closing date. Applicants notified on a rolling basis starting 4/1; must reply within 4 week(s) of notification.

CONTACT

Kattie Wing, Director of Student Financial Services

232 Silas Hunt Hall, Fayetteville, AR 72701

(479) 575-3806

University of Arkansas at Fort Smith

Fort Smith, Arkansas

www.uafortsmith.edu   Federal Code: 001110

4-year public university in small city.

Enrollment: 5,833 undergrads, 30% part-time. 1,059 full-time freshmen.

Selectivity: Open admission; but selective for some programs.

BASIC COSTS (2007-2008)

Tuition and fees: $4,060; out-of-state residents $8,950.

Per-credit charge: $104; out-of-state residents $267.

FINANCIAL AID PICTURE (2006-2007)

Students with need: Out of 766 full-time freshmen who applied for aid, 566 were judged to have need. Of these, 546 received aid, and 102 had their full need met. Average financial aid package met 71% of need; average scholarship/grant was $3,447; average loan was $2,334. For part-time students, average financial aid package was $4,955.

Students without need: 245 full-time freshmen who did not demonstrate need for aid received scholarships/grants; average award was $2,752. No-need awards available for academics, athletics, job skills, leadership, music/drama.

Scholarships offered: 48 full-time freshmen received athletic scholarships; average amount $8,279.

Cumulative student debt: 47% of graduating class had student loans; average debt was $13,810.

FINANCIAL AID PROCEDURES

Forms required: FAFSA.

Dates and Deadlines: Priority date 6/15; no closing date. Applicants notified on a rolling basis starting 3/1; must reply within 4 week(s) of notification.

Transfers: No deadline. Applicants notified on a rolling basis starting 3/1; must reply within 4 week(s) of notification.

CONTACT

Alan Pixley, Director of Financial Aid

PO Box 3649, Fort Smith, AR 72913-3649

(479) 788-7090

University of Arkansas at Little Rock

Little Rock, Arkansas

www.ualr.edu   Federal Code: 001161

4-year public university in small city.

Enrollment: 8,908 undergrads, 38% part-time. 814 full-time freshmen.

BASIC COSTS (2007-2008)

Tuition and fees: $5,707; out-of-state residents $13,199.

Per-credit charge: $154; out-of-state residents $404.

Room only: $3,100.

Additional info: Fees vary depending on student's field of study.

FINANCIAL AID PICTURE

Students with need: Need-based aid available for full-time and part-time students.

FINANCIAL AID PROCEDURES

Forms required: FAFSA.

Dates and Deadlines: Closing date 8/1. Applicants notified on a rolling basis starting 5/1.

CONTACT

Tammy Harrison, Director of Admissions and Financial Aid

2801 South University Avenue, Little Rock, AR 72204

(501) 569-3035

University of Arkansas at Monticello

Monticello, Arkansas

www.uamont.edu   Federal Code: 001085

4-year public university and technical college in large town.

Enrollment: 2,604 undergrads, 18% part-time. 572 full-time freshmen.

Selectivity: Open admission.

BASIC COSTS (2007-2008)

Tuition and fees: $4,300; out-of-state residents $8,230.

Per-credit charge: $108; out-of-state residents $239.

Room and board: $3,690.

PART III: FINANCIAL AID COLLEGE BY COLLEGE

FINANCIAL AID PICTURE (2006-2007)

Students with need: 61% of average financial aid package awarded as scholarships/grants, 39% awarded as loans/jobs. Need-based aid available for part-time students. Work study available nights, weekends, and for part-time students.
Students without need: No-need awards available for academics, athletics, job skills, leadership, music/drama, state/district residency.

FINANCIAL AID PROCEDURES

Forms required: FAFSA, institutional form.
Dates and Deadlines: Priority date 5/1; no closing date. Applicants notified on a rolling basis starting 4/1; must reply within 2 week(s) of notification.

CONTACT

Susan Brewer, Director of Financial Aid
Box 3600, Monticello, AR 71656
(870) 460-1050

University of Arkansas at Pine Bluff

Pine Bluff, Arkansas
www.uapb.edu   Federal Code: 001086

4-year public university in small city.
Enrollment: 3,048 undergrads, 12% part-time. 788 full-time freshmen.
Selectivity: Admits 50 to 75% of applicants.

BASIC COSTS (2007-2008)

Tuition and fees: $4,499; out-of-state residents $8,909.
Per-credit charge: $110; out-of-state residents $257.
Room and board: $5,972.
Additional info: Tuition/fee waivers available for minority students.

FINANCIAL AID PICTURE

Students with need: Need-based aid available for full-time and part-time students. Work study available weekends and for part-time students.
Students without need: No-need awards available for academics, alumni affiliation, art, athletics, leadership, minority status, music/drama, religious affiliation, ROTC, state/district residency.

FINANCIAL AID PROCEDURES

Forms required: FAFSA.
Dates and Deadlines: Priority date 4/15; no closing date. Applicants notified on a rolling basis starting 3/1.
Transfers: Must supply financial aid transcript from prior college or university.

CONTACT

Janice Kearney, Director of Financial Aid
1200 North University Drive, Mail Slot 4981, Pine Bluff, AR 71601-2799
(870) 575-8302

University of Arkansas Community College at Morrilton

Morrilton, Arkansas   Federal Code: 005245
www.uaccm.edu   CSS Code: 3881

2-year public community college in small town.
Enrollment: 1,726 undergrads, 29% part-time. 483 full-time freshmen.
Selectivity: Open admission.

BASIC COSTS (2007-2008)

Tuition and fees: $2,430; out-of-district residents $2,610; out-of-state residents $3,570.
Per-credit charge: $64; out-of-district residents $70; out-of-state residents $102.

FINANCIAL AID PICTURE (2007-2008)

Students with need: Average financial aid package met 47% of need; average scholarship/grant was $4,412; average loan was $1,210. For part-time students, average financial aid package was $4,212.
Students without need: 13 full-time freshmen who did not demonstrate need for aid received scholarships/grants; average award was $783. No-need awards available for academics, leadership, state/district residency.

FINANCIAL AID PROCEDURES

Forms required: FAFSA, CSS PROFILE, institutional form.
Dates and Deadlines: Priority date 7/1; no closing date. Applicants notified by 5/1.

CONTACT

Teresa Cash, Director of Financial Aid
1537 University Boulevard, Morrilton, AR 72110
(501) 977-2055

University of Arkansas: Community College at Hope

Hope, Arkansas
www.uacch.edu   Federal Code: 005732

2-year public community and technical college in small town.
Enrollment: 966 undergrads.
Selectivity: Open admission; but selective for some programs.

BASIC COSTS (2007-2008)

Tuition and fees: $1,790; out-of-district residents $1,940; out-of-state residents $3,620.
Per-credit charge: $54; out-of-district residents $59; out-of-state residents $115.

FINANCIAL AID PICTURE

Students with need: Need-based aid available for full-time and part-time students. Work study available nights.
Students without need: No-need awards available for academics.

FINANCIAL AID PROCEDURES

Forms required: FAFSA, institutional form.
Dates and Deadlines: Priority date 7/6; no closing date. Applicants notified on a rolling basis starting 1/1; must reply within 4 week(s) of notification.

CONTACT

Jerald Barber, Vice Chancellor for Finance
2500 South Main, Hope, AR 71802-0140
(870) 722-8264

University of Central Arkansas

Conway, Arkansas
www.uca.edu   Federal Code: 001092

4-year public university in small city.
Enrollment: 9,921 undergrads, 9% part-time. 2,352 full-time freshmen.
Selectivity: Admits less than 50% of applicants.

BASIC COSTS (2007-2008)

Tuition and fees: $6,062; out-of-state residents $10,892.
Per-credit charge: $161; out-of-state residents $322.
Room and board: $4,600.

FINANCIAL AID PICTURE (2006-2007)

Students with need: Out of 531 full-time freshmen who applied for aid, 520 were judged to have need. Of these, 520 received aid, and 37 had their full need met. Average financial aid package met 51% of need; average scholarship/grant was $1,070; average loan was $1,195. For part-time students, average financial aid package was $5,775.

Students without need: 353 full-time freshmen who did not demonstrate need for aid received scholarships/grants; average award was $1,984. No-need awards available for academics, art, athletics, leadership, minority status, music/drama, ROTC, state/district residency.

Scholarships offered: 29 full-time freshmen received athletic scholarships; average amount $2,225.

Additional info: Room and board may be paid monthly.

FINANCIAL AID PROCEDURES

Forms required: FAFSA.

Dates and Deadlines: Priority date 4/15; closing date 7/1. Applicants notified on a rolling basis starting 5/4.

CONTACT

Cheryl Lyons, Director of Financial Aid
201 Donaghey Avenue, Conway, AR 72035
(501) 450-3140

University of the Ozarks

Clarksville, Arkansas
www.ozarks.edu   Federal Code: 001094

4-year private university and liberal arts college in small town, affiliated with Presbyterian Church (USA).

Enrollment: 612 undergrads, 3% part-time. 178 full-time freshmen.

Selectivity: Admits over 75% of applicants.

BASIC COSTS (2007-2008)

Tuition and fees: $16,130.

Per-credit charge: $654.

Room and board: $5,475.

Additional info: Tuition/fee waivers available for minority students.

FINANCIAL AID PICTURE (2007-2008)

Students with need: Out of 133 full-time freshmen who applied for aid, 115 were judged to have need. Of these, 115 received aid, and 51 had their full need met. Average financial aid package met 87% of need; average scholarship/grant was $12,775; average loan was $5,506. For part-time students, average financial aid package was $8,866.

Students without need: 54 full-time freshmen who did not demonstrate need for aid received scholarships/grants; average award was $14,340. No-need awards available for academics, alumni affiliation, art, leadership, minority status, music/drama, religious affiliation.

Cumulative student debt: 45% of graduating class had student loans; average debt was $18,817.

Additional info: Walton International Scholarship Program provides full scholarships to selected Central American and Mexican residents.

FINANCIAL AID PROCEDURES

Forms required: FAFSA.

Dates and Deadlines: Priority date 2/15; no closing date. Applicants notified on a rolling basis starting 3/15; must reply within 2 week(s) of notification.

CONTACT

Jana Hart, Dean of Admissions and Financial Aid
415 College Avenue, Clarksville, AR 72830
(479) 979-1221

Williams Baptist College

Walnut Ridge, Arkansas
www.wbcoll.edu   Federal Code: 001106

4-year private liberal arts college in small town, affiliated with Southern Baptist Convention.

Enrollment: 502 undergrads, 2% part-time. 126 full-time freshmen.

Selectivity: Admits 50 to 75% of applicants.

BASIC COSTS (2008-2009)

Tuition and fees: $10,950.

Per-credit charge: $425.

Room and board: $5,000.

FINANCIAL AID PICTURE (2006-2007)

Students with need: Out of 120 full-time freshmen who applied for aid, 90 were judged to have need. Of these, 90 received aid. For part-time students, average financial aid package was $5,798.

Students without need: 35 full-time freshmen who did not demonstrate need for aid received scholarships/grants; average award was $3,650. No-need awards available for academics, art, athletics, leadership, minority status, music/drama, religious affiliation, state/district residency.

Scholarships offered: *Merit:* Trustee's Scholarship: up to full tuition and room and board; based on minimum ACT composite score of 30 and minimum 3.5 high school GPA; 1 awarded; deadline March 1, renewable for 4 years with 3.25 cumulative GPA on at least 15 credit hours per semester. *Athletic:* 34 full-time freshmen received athletic scholarships; average amount $2,468.

Additional info: Art scholarship applicants must submit portfolio.

FINANCIAL AID PROCEDURES

Forms required: FAFSA.

Dates and Deadlines: Priority date 5/1; no closing date. Applicants notified on a rolling basis starting 4/1; must reply within 2 week(s) of notification.

Transfers: Priority date 4/1; no deadline. Applicants notified on a rolling basis starting 4/1; must reply within 2 week(s) of notification.

CONTACT

Barbara Turner, Director of Financial Aid
PO Box 3665, Walnut Ridge, AR 72476
(870) 759-4112

California

Academy of Art University

San Francisco, California
www.academyart.edu   Federal Code: 007531

4-year for-profit university and visual arts college in very large city.

Enrollment: 8,210 undergrads, 34% part-time. 680 full-time freshmen.

Selectivity: Open admission.

BASIC COSTS (2008-2009)

Tuition and fees: $20,380.

Per-credit charge: $670.

Room and board: $13,500.

FINANCIAL AID PICTURE (2006-2007)

Students with need: Out of 379 full-time freshmen who applied for aid, 316 were judged to have need. Of these, 312 received aid, and 2 had their full need met. Average financial aid package met 20% of need; average scholarship/grant was $3,957; average loan was $2,056. For part-time students, average financial aid package was $4,125.

Students without need: No-need awards available for academics, art.

Additional info: Numerous summer grant programs available.

FINANCIAL AID PROCEDURES

Forms required: FAFSA, institutional form.

Dates and Deadlines: Priority date 7/10; no closing date. Applicants notified on a rolling basis.

Transfers: Priority date 3/1; no deadline. Applicants notified on a rolling basis.

CONTACT

Joe Vollaro, Executive Vice President for Financial Aid/Compliance
79 New Montgomery Street, San Francisco, CA 94105-3410
(415) 618-6273

Allan Hancock College

Santa Maria, California
www.hancockcollege.edu   Federal Code: 001111

2-year public community college in small city.

Enrollment: 6,095 undergrads.

Selectivity: Open admission; but selective for some programs.

BASIC COSTS (2007-2008)

Tuition and fees: $642; out-of-state residents $5,832.

Per-credit charge: $20; out-of-state residents $193.

FINANCIAL AID PICTURE

Students with need: Need-based aid available for full-time and part-time students.

Students without need: This college awards aid only to students with need.

FINANCIAL AID PROCEDURES

Forms required: FAFSA.

Dates and Deadlines: Priority date 5/1; no closing date. Applicants notified on a rolling basis starting 6/1.

CONTACT

Robert Parisi, Financial Aid Director
800 South College Drive, Santa Maria, CA 93454-6399
(805) 922-6966 ext. 3200

Alliant International University

San Diego, California
www.alliant.edu   Federal Code: 011117

Upper-division private university in very large city.

Enrollment: 179 undergrads, 22% part-time.

BASIC COSTS (2008-2009)

Tuition and fees: $15,210.

Per-credit charge: $550.

Additional info: Tuition/fee waivers available for minority students.

FINANCIAL AID PICTURE (2007-2008)

Students with need: 48% of average financial aid package awarded as scholarships/grants, 52% awarded as loans/jobs. Need-based aid available for part-time students. Work study available nights, weekends, and for part-time students.

Students without need: No-need awards available for academics, alumni affiliation, athletics, leadership.

Scholarships offered: Grants and scholarships available based on GPA and SAT/ACT scores.

FINANCIAL AID PROCEDURES

Forms required: FAFSA.

Dates and Deadlines: Priority date 3/2; no closing date. Applicants notified on a rolling basis starting 2/1; must reply within 3 week(s) of notification.

CONTACT

Deborah Spindler, Director of Financial Aid
10455 Pomerado Road, San Diego, CA 92131-1799
(858) 635-4559

American Jewish University

Los Angeles, California
www.ajula.edu   Federal Code: 002741

4-year private university and liberal arts college in very large city, affiliated with Jewish faith.

Enrollment: 107 undergrads. 23 full-time freshmen.

Selectivity: Admits 50 to 75% of applicants.

BASIC COSTS (2007-2008)

Tuition and fees: $21,340.

Room and board: $11,070.

FINANCIAL AID PICTURE (2006-2007)

Students with need: Out of 21 full-time freshmen who applied for aid, 21 were judged to have need. Of these, 21 received aid. Average financial aid package met 49% of need; average scholarship/grant was $9,328; average loan was $3,662. Need-based aid available for part-time students.

Students without need: 7 full-time freshmen who did not demonstrate need for aid received scholarships/grants; average award was $10,473. No-need awards available for academics, leadership.

Scholarships offered: President's Scholarship: offered to incoming students with a GPA of 3.5 or higher. Ambassador's Scholarship: offered to incoming students with a GPA of 3.0 or higher; renewable for 4 years based on good academic standing. Transfer Excellence Award: offered to transfer students with GPA of 3.3 or higher; renewable based on good academic standing. Additional merit-based scholarships: Dean's Scholarship, Leadership & Service, Israel Experience, IDF/Bagrut Scholarship.

FINANCIAL AID PROCEDURES

Forms required: FAFSA, state aid form, institutional form.

Dates and Deadlines: Priority date 3/2; no closing date. Applicants notified on a rolling basis starting 3/15; must reply within 3 week(s) of notification.

Transfers: Priority date 2/16; no deadline. Applicants notified on a rolling basis starting 5/18; must reply within 3 week(s) of notification.

CONTACT

Larisa Zadoyen, Director of Financial Aid
15600 Mulholland Drive, Los Angeles, CA 90077
(310) 476-9777 ext. 252

American River College

Sacramento, California
www.arc.losrios.edu   Federal Code: 001232

2-year public community college in large city.

Enrollment: 20,828 undergrads.

Selectivity: Open admission; but selective for some programs.

BASIC COSTS (2007-2008)

Tuition and fees: $632; out-of-state residents $5,822.

Per-credit charge: $20; out-of-state residents $193.

Additional info: Tuition/fee waivers available for minority students.

FINANCIAL AID PICTURE

Students with need: Need-based aid available for full-time and part-time students.

Students without need: This college awards aid only to students with need.

FINANCIAL AID PROCEDURES

Forms required: FAFSA.

Dates and Deadlines: Priority date 3/2; no closing date. Applicants notified on a rolling basis starting 7/1; must reply within 2 week(s) of notification.

CONTACT

Roy Beckhorn, Financial Aid Supervisor

4700 College Oak Drive, Sacramento, CA 95841

(916) 484-8437

Antelope Valley College

Lancaster, California

www.avc.edu   Federal Code: 001113

2-year public community college in large city.

Enrollment: 9,300 undergrads.

Selectivity: Open admission; but selective for some programs.

BASIC COSTS (2007-2008)

Tuition and fees: $602; out-of-state residents $5,792.

Per-credit charge: $20; out-of-state residents $193.

FINANCIAL AID PICTURE

Students with need: Need-based aid available for full-time and part-time students.

FINANCIAL AID PROCEDURES

Forms required: FAFSA, state aid form, institutional form.

Dates and Deadlines: Priority date 3/2; no closing date. Applicants notified on a rolling basis starting 7/15; must reply within 2 week(s) of notification.

CONTACT

Sherrie Padilla, Director of Financial Aid

3041 West Avenue K, Lancaster, CA 93536-5426

(661) 722-6336

Antioch University Santa Barbara

Santa Barbara, California

www.antiochsb.edu   Federal Code: 003010

Upper-division private university and liberal arts college in small city.

Enrollment: 96 undergrads.

BASIC COSTS (2007-2008)

Tuition and fees: $14,718.

Per-credit charge: $490.

FINANCIAL AID PICTURE (2007-2008)

Students with need: Average financial aid package for all full-time undergraduates was $10,500; for part-time $10,500. 18% awarded as scholarships/grants, 82% awarded as loans/jobs. Work study available nights, weekends, and for part-time students.

Cumulative student debt: 75% of graduating class had student loans; average debt was $25,000.

FINANCIAL AID PROCEDURES

Forms required: FAFSA, institutional form.

Dates and Deadlines: Priority date 4/15; no closing date. Applicants notified on a rolling basis; must reply within 4 week(s) of notification.

Transfers: Priority date 4/1; no deadline.

CONTACT

Cecilia Schneider, Financial Aid Director

801 Garden Street, Suite 101, Santa Barbara, CA 93101-1581

(805) 962-8179 ext. 108

Art Center College of Design

Pasadena, California

www.artcenter.edu   Federal Code: 001116

4-year private visual arts college in small city.

Enrollment: 1,500 undergrads.

BASIC COSTS (2008-2009)

Tuition and fees: $30,284.

FINANCIAL AID PICTURE

Students with need: Need-based aid available for full-time students.

Students without need: This college awards aid only to students with need.

Additional info: Students may apply for scholarships after they enroll while progressing through the program.

FINANCIAL AID PROCEDURES

Forms required: FAFSA.

Dates and Deadlines: Priority date 3/1; no closing date. Applicants notified on a rolling basis starting 5/15; must reply within 4 week(s) of notification.

Transfers: Applicants notified on a rolling basis starting 1/1.

CONTACT

Clema McKenzie, Director of Financial Aid

1700 Lida Street, Pasadena, CA 91103

(626) 396-2215

Art Institute of California: Los Angeles

Santa Monica, California

www.artinstitutes.edu/losangeles   Federal Code: 007470

2-year for-profit visual arts college in small city.

Enrollment: 2,149 undergrads, 35% part-time. 329 full-time freshmen.

Selectivity: Admits less than 50% of applicants.

BASIC COSTS (2007-2008)

Tuition and fees: $22,322.

Per-credit charge: $464.

Additional info: Apartment-style housing: $2,663/quarter for 2-bedroom, $3,227/quarter for 1-bedroom unit. Tuition at time of enrollment locked for 2 years.

FINANCIAL AID PICTURE (2007-2008)

Students with need: Need-based aid available for full-time and part-time students. Work study available nights, weekends, and for part-time students.

Students without need: No-need awards available for academics.

FINANCIAL AID PROCEDURES

Forms required: FAFSA.

Dates and Deadlines: No deadline. Applicants notified on a rolling basis.

CONTACT

Kathleen Harris, Director of Student Financial Services

2900 31st Street, Santa Monica, CA 90405-3035

(310) 752-4700

Art Institute of California: Orange County

Santa Ana, California

www.artinstitutes.edu/orangecounty Federal Code: 007236

3-year for-profit culinary school and visual arts college in very large city.

Enrollment: 1,761 undergrads, 21% part-time. 342 full-time freshmen.

Selectivity: Admits less than 50% of applicants.

BASIC COSTS (2007-2008)

Additional info: Typical full-time load 16 credit hours per quarter. Housing costs $2,450-$3,300 per quarter. Culinary lab fee $315 per quarter, online fee $100 per class per quarter.

FINANCIAL AID PICTURE

Students with need: Need-based aid available for full-time and part-time students. Work study available nights, weekends, and for part-time students.
Students without need: No-need awards available for academics, art, minority status.

FINANCIAL AID PROCEDURES

Forms required: FAFSA, state aid form.
Dates and Deadlines: No deadline. Applicants notified on a rolling basis; must reply within 2 week(s) of notification.

CONTACT

Jennifer Olevson, Director of Student Financial Services
3601 West Sunflower Avenue, Santa Ana, CA 92704-9888
(714) 830-0202

Art Institute of California: San Diego

San Diego, California
www.artinstitutes.edu/sandiego   Federal Code: 016471

3-year for-profit visual arts college in very large city.
Enrollment: 2,145 undergrads.

BASIC COSTS (2008-2009)

Tuition and fees: $22,272.
Per-credit charge: $464.

FINANCIAL AID PICTURE

Students with need: Need-based aid available for full-time students.

CONTACT

Leslie Berry, Director of Student Financial Services
7650 Mission Valley Road, San Diego, CA 92108-4423
(800) 591-2422

Art Institute of California: San Francisco

San Francisco, California
www.artinstitutes.edu/sanfrancisco

4-year for-profit visual arts college in very large city.
Enrollment: 1,568 undergrads.
Selectivity: Admits less than 50% of applicants.

BASIC COSTS (2008-2009)

Tuition and fees: $29,184.
Per-credit charge: $456.
Room and board: $10,680.
Additional info: Starter kits additional $750-$1,300 estimate for all programs. Standard enrollment generally 16 credits/quarter.

FINANCIAL AID PICTURE (2006-2007)

Students with need: 100% of average financial aid package awarded as scholarships/grants, 0% awarded as loans/jobs.
Scholarships offered: The Art Institutes and Americans for the Arts Poster Design Competition; $2,000-$3,000 locally, up to $25,000 nationally; 2 awarded per Art Institute location, 10 awarded nationally. Evelyn Keedy Memorial Scholarship; $30,000; 1 awarded nationally.

FINANCIAL AID PROCEDURES

Forms required: FAFSA.
Dates and Deadlines: No deadline. Applicants notified on a rolling basis.

CONTACT

Maria Juravic, Director of Student Financial Services
1170 Market Street, San Francisco, CA 94102
(415) 865-0198

Azusa Pacific University

Azusa, California
www.apu.edu   Federal Code: 001117

4-year private university in small city, affiliated with interdenominational tradition.
Enrollment: 4,615 undergrads, 15% part-time. 865 full-time freshmen.
Selectivity: Admits 50 to 75% of applicants.

BASIC COSTS (2008-2009)

Tuition and fees: $26,640.
Per-credit charge: $1,075.
Room and board: $7,566.
Additional info: Tuition/fee waivers available for minority students.

FINANCIAL AID PICTURE (2006-2007)

Students with need: Out of 816 full-time freshmen who applied for aid, 535 were judged to have need. Of these, 534 received aid, and 64 had their full need met. Average financial aid package met 72% of need; average scholarship/grant was $9,538; average loan was $2,492. For part-time students, average financial aid package was $3,001.
Students without need: 263 full-time freshmen who did not demonstrate need for aid received scholarships/grants; average award was $4,129. No-need awards available for academics, athletics, leadership, minority status, music/drama, religious affiliation, ROTC.
Scholarships offered: 8 full-time freshmen received athletic scholarships; average amount $11,319.

FINANCIAL AID PROCEDURES

Forms required: FAFSA, institutional form.
Dates and Deadlines: Priority date 3/2; closing date 7/1. Applicants notified on a rolling basis starting 3/1; must reply within 3 week(s) of notification.
Transfers: Cal Grants not available to first time applicants who are seniors.

CONTACT

Todd Ross, Director of Student Financial Services
901 East Alosta Avenue, Azusa, CA 91702-7000
(626) 812-3009

Barstow Community College

Barstow, California
www.barstow.edu   Federal Code: 001119

2-year public community college in large town.
Enrollment: 1,797 undergrads.
Selectivity: Open admission.

BASIC COSTS (2007-2008)

Tuition and fees: $600; out-of-state residents $5,790.
Per-credit charge: $20; out-of-state residents $193.
Additional info: Tuition/fee waivers available for adults, unemployed or children of unemployed.

FINANCIAL AID PICTURE (2007-2008)

Students with need: Need-based aid available for part-time students.
Students without need: This college awards aid only to students with need.

FINANCIAL AID PROCEDURES

Forms required: FAFSA.

Dates and Deadlines: Closing date 5/22. Applicants notified on a rolling basis starting 7/1.

CONTACT

Danielle Cordova, Financial Aid Officer

2700 Barstow Road, Barstow, CA 92311-9984

(760) 252-2411 ext. 7205

Berkeley City College

Berkeley, California

www.berkeleycitycollege.edu   Federal Code: 014311

2-year public community college in small city.

Enrollment: 5,420 undergrads.

Selectivity: Open admission.

BASIC COSTS (2007-2008)

Tuition and fees: $600; out-of-state residents $5,790.

Per-credit charge: $20; out-of-state residents $193.

FINANCIAL AID PICTURE

Students with need: Need-based aid available for full-time and part-time students.

Students without need: This college awards aid only to students with need.

FINANCIAL AID PROCEDURES

Dates and Deadlines: No deadline. Applicants notified on a rolling basis.

CONTACT

Robert Vergas, Financial Aid Program Supervisor

2050 Center Street, Berkeley, CA 94704

(510) 981-2878

Bethany University

Scotts Valley, California

www.bethany.edu   Federal Code: 001121

4-year private Bible and liberal arts college in small town, affiliated with Assemblies of God.

Enrollment: 456 undergrads, 17% part-time. 62 full-time freshmen.

Selectivity: Admits 50 to 75% of applicants.

BASIC COSTS (2007-2008)

Tuition and fees: $17,360.

Per-credit charge: $685.

Room and board: $6,960.

FINANCIAL AID PICTURE

Students with need: Need-based aid available for full-time and part-time students. Work study available nights, weekends, and for part-time students.

Students without need: No-need awards available for academics, alumni affiliation, athletics, leadership, minority status, music/drama, religious affiliation.

FINANCIAL AID PROCEDURES

Forms required: FAFSA, institutional form.

Dates and Deadlines: Priority date 3/2; no closing date. Applicants notified on a rolling basis starting 4/15; must reply within 2 week(s) of notification.

CONTACT

Sue Garrick, Director of Financial Services

800 Bethany Drive, Scotts Valley, CA 95066-2898

(831) 438-3800 ext. 3901

Bethesda Christian University

Anaheim, California

www.bcu.edu   Federal Code: 032663

4-year private university and Bible college in large city, affiliated with Christian Church.

Enrollment: 254 undergrads.

Selectivity: Open admission.

BASIC COSTS (2007-2008)

Tuition and fees: $6,420.

Per-credit charge: $210.

FINANCIAL AID PICTURE

Students with need: Need-based aid available for full-time and part-time students.

Students without need: This college awards aid only to students with need.

FINANCIAL AID PROCEDURES

Forms required: FAFSA, institutional form.

Dates and Deadlines: Closing date 3/14. Applicants notified on a rolling basis starting 6/30.

Transfers: No deadline.

CONTACT

Tony Chiang, Director of Financial Aid

730 North Euclid Street, Anaheim, CA 92801

(714) 517-1945

Biola University

La Mirada, California

www.biola.edu   Federal Code: 001122

4-year private university and Bible college in large town, affiliated with interdenominational tradition.

Enrollment: 3,550 undergrads, 3% part-time. 790 full-time freshmen.

Selectivity: Admits over 75% of applicants.

BASIC COSTS (2008-2009)

Tuition and fees: $26,424.

Per-credit charge: $1,101.

Room and board: $7,410.

Additional info: Tuition/fee waivers available for minority students.

FINANCIAL AID PICTURE (2006-2007)

Students with need: Average financial aid package met 68% of need; average scholarship/grant was $11,339; average loan was $1,796. Need-based aid available for part-time students.

Students without need: No-need awards available for academics, alumni affiliation, art, athletics, leadership, minority status, music/drama, state/district residency.

Scholarships offered: Scholarships for Underrepresented Groups of Ethnicity; up to $6,500; based on GPA and ethnicity. Community Service Scholarship; $2,700; based on demonstration of outstanding spiritual leadership. Alumni Dependent Scholarship; $500; given to students whose parents completed 30 units of coursework at Biola University.

FINANCIAL AID PROCEDURES

Forms required: FAFSA, state aid form.

Dates and Deadlines: Priority date 1/1; no closing date. Applicants notified on a rolling basis starting 3/1.

Transfers: No deadline. Applicants notified on a rolling basis starting 3/1.

CONTACT

Jonathan Choy, Director of Financial Aid
13800 Biola Avenue, La Mirada, CA 90639-0001
(562) 903-4742

Cabrillo College

Aptos, California
www.cabrillo.edu   Federal Code: 001124

2-year public community college in large town.
Enrollment: 7,010 undergrads.
Selectivity: Open admission; but selective for some programs.

BASIC COSTS (2007-2008)

Tuition and fees: $638; out-of-state residents $5,858.
Per-credit charge: $20; out-of-state residents $194.

FINANCIAL AID PICTURE

Students with need: Need-based aid available for full-time and part-time students.

FINANCIAL AID PROCEDURES

Forms required: FAFSA, institutional form.
Dates and Deadlines: No deadline. Applicants notified on a rolling basis starting 7/31; must reply within 3 week(s) of notification.
Transfers: Academic transcript required.

CONTACT

Debbie Soria, Director of Financial Aid and Scholarships
6500 Soquel Drive, Aptos, CA 95003
(831) 479-6100

California Baptist University

Riverside, California
www.calbaptist.edu   Federal Code: 001125

4-year private university and liberal arts college in large city, affiliated with Southern Baptist Convention.
Enrollment: 2,952 undergrads, 14% part-time. 491 full-time freshmen.
Selectivity: Admits 50 to 75% of applicants.

BASIC COSTS (2008-2009)

Tuition and fees: $22,620.
Per-credit charge: $805.
Room and board: $7,910.

FINANCIAL AID PICTURE

Students with need: Need-based aid available for full-time and part-time students. Work study available nights, weekends, and for part-time students.
Students without need: No-need awards available for academics, art, athletics, leadership, music/drama, religious affiliation, ROTC.

FINANCIAL AID PROCEDURES

Forms required: FAFSA, state aid form.
Dates and Deadlines: Priority date 3/2; no closing date. Applicants notified on a rolling basis starting 3/2; must reply by 5/1 or within 3 week(s) of notification.
Transfers: No deadline. Applicants notified on a rolling basis starting 12/15.

CONTACT

Eileen Terry, Director of Financial Aid
8432 Magnolia Avenue, Riverside, CA 92504-3297
(951) 343-4236

California College of the Arts

San Francisco, California
www.cca.edu   Federal Code: 001127

4-year private visual arts college in very large city.
Enrollment: 1,285 undergrads, 7% part-time. 186 full-time freshmen.
Selectivity: Admits over 75% of applicants.

BASIC COSTS (2008-2009)

Tuition and fees: $31,382.
Per-credit charge: $1,293.
Room only: $6,600.

FINANCIAL AID PICTURE

Students with need: Need-based aid available for full-time and part-time students. Work study available nights, weekends, and for part-time students.
Students without need: No-need awards available for academics, art.
Scholarships offered: Creative Achievement Scholarship; up to $15,000 annually; renewable; based on academic achievement and strength of admissions portfolios.
Additional info: Application deadline for merit scholarships February 1.

FINANCIAL AID PROCEDURES

Forms required: FAFSA.
Dates and Deadlines: Priority date 3/1; no closing date. Applicants notified on a rolling basis starting 3/15; must reply by 5/1 or within 3 week(s) of notification.
Transfers: No deadline. Applicants notified on a rolling basis starting 3/15; must reply by 5/1 or within 3 week(s) of notification. Scholarships available for community college transfer students.

CONTACT

Shawn Brick, Director of Financial Aid
1111 Eighth Street, San Francisco, CA 94107-2247
(415) 703-9528

California Culinary Academy

San Francisco, California
www.caculinary.edu   Federal Code: 015698

2-year for-profit culinary school and career college in very large city.
Enrollment: 150 undergrads.
Selectivity: Admits over 75% of applicants.

BASIC COSTS (2008-2009)

Tuition and fees: $28,000.
Room only: $600.

FINANCIAL AID PICTURE

Students with need: Need-based aid available for full-time students.

FINANCIAL AID PROCEDURES

Forms required: FAFSA, state aid form.
Dates and Deadlines: No deadline. Applicants notified on a rolling basis; must reply within 1 week(s) of notification.

CONTACT

Matt Wakeman, Director of Financial Aid
350 Rhode Island, San Francisco, CA 94103
(415) 771-3500

California Design College

Los Angeles, California
www.artinstitutes.edu/cdc   Federal Code: 031254

4-year for-profit visual arts and technical college in very large city.
Enrollment: 882 undergrads, 41% part-time. 188 full-time freshmen.

BASIC COSTS (2008-2009)
Tuition and fees: $20,980.
Per-credit charge: $464.
Room only: $8,685.
Additional info: Cost for 7-quarter continuous enrollment associate degree program $52,118; cost for 12-quarter continuous enrollment bachelor's degree program $88,938. Fees vary by program.

FINANCIAL AID PICTURE (2006-2007)
Students with need: Out of 155 full-time freshmen who applied for aid, 155 were judged to have need. Of these, 155 received aid. For part-time students, average financial aid package was $3,830.
Cumulative student debt: 100% of graduating class had student loans; average debt was $37,551.

CONTACT
Adis Ceballos, Director of Student Financial Services
3440 Wilshire Boulevard, 10th Floor, Los Angeles, CA 90010

California Institute of Technology

Pasadena, California   Federal Code: 001131
www.caltech.edu   CSS Code: 4034

4-year private university in small city.
Enrollment: 913 undergrads. 214 full-time freshmen.
Selectivity: Admits less than 50% of applicants.

BASIC COSTS (2008-2009)
Tuition and fees: $34,515.
Room and board: $10,146.

FINANCIAL AID PICTURE (2006-2007)
Students with need: Out of 173 full-time freshmen who applied for aid, 129 were judged to have need. Of these, 129 received aid, and 129 had their full need met. Average financial aid package met 100% of need; average scholarship/grant was $22,026; average loan was $3,106.
Students without need: 10 full-time freshmen who did not demonstrate need for aid received scholarships/grants; average award was $28,315. No-need awards available for academics.
Scholarships offered: Merit scholarships available up to full tuition and room and board. Special application not required.
Cumulative student debt: 34% of graduating class had student loans; average debt was $5,156.

FINANCIAL AID PROCEDURES
Forms required: FAFSA, CSS PROFILE, state aid form.
Dates and Deadlines: Closing date 1/15. Applicants notified by 4/1; must reply by 5/1.
Transfers: Priority date 3/2; no deadline.

CONTACT
Don Crewell, Director of Financial Aid
1200 East California Boulevard, MC 1-94, Pasadena, CA 91125
(626) 395-6280

California Institute of the Arts

Valencia, California
www.calarts.edu   Federal Code: 001132

4-year private visual arts and performing arts college in small city.
Enrollment: 820 undergrads.
Selectivity: Admits less than 50% of applicants.

BASIC COSTS (2008-2009)
Tuition and fees: $33,436.
Room and board: $8,819.

FINANCIAL AID PICTURE
Students with need: Need-based aid available for full-time and part-time students. Work study available nights, weekends, and for part-time students.
Students without need: No-need awards available for academics, art, minority status, music/drama.

FINANCIAL AID PROCEDURES
Forms required: FAFSA.
Dates and Deadlines: Closing date 3/2. Applicants notified on a rolling basis starting 4/15; must reply within 3 week(s) of notification.
Transfers: Priority date 3/1.

CONTACT
Bobbi Heuer, Financial Aid Director
24700 McBean Parkway, Valencia, CA 91355
(661) 255-1050

California Lutheran University

Thousand Oaks, California
www.callutheran.edu   Federal Code: 001133

4-year private university and liberal arts college in small city, affiliated with Evangelical Lutheran Church in America.
Enrollment: 2,126 undergrads, 11% part-time. 446 full-time freshmen.
Selectivity: Admits 50 to 75% of applicants.

BASIC COSTS (2008-2009)
Tuition and fees: $27,850.
Room and board: $9,650.

FINANCIAL AID PICTURE (2007-2008)
Students with need: Out of 346 full-time freshmen who applied for aid, 263 were judged to have need. Of these, 263 received aid, and 78 had their full need met. Average financial aid package met 80% of need; average scholarship/grant was $7,550; average loan was $3,466. For part-time students, average financial aid package was $8,183.
Students without need: 125 full-time freshmen who did not demonstrate need for aid received scholarships/grants; average award was $10,407. No-need awards available for academics, alumni affiliation, art, leadership, minority status, music/drama, religious affiliation, state/district residency.
Scholarships offered: Presidential Scholarship Program: $16,000 up to full tuition; additional application required; 2 full tuition scholarships; 6 $20,000 scholarships; rest of students receive $16,000. UC Guarantee: amount TBA (approx. $15,000); student must be admitted to CLU and UCLA or UCSB. Visual and Performing Arts Scholarships: $500-$6,000; audition with department.
Cumulative student debt: 57% of graduating class had student loans; average debt was $13,057.

FINANCIAL AID PROCEDURES
Forms required: FAFSA.
Dates and Deadlines: Priority date 3/1; no closing date. Applicants notified on a rolling basis starting 3/15; must reply within 2 week(s) of notification.
Transfers: No deadline. Applicants notified on a rolling basis starting 3/15; must reply within 2 week(s) of notification.

CONTACT
Meghan Flores, Director of Financial Aid
60 West Olsen Road #1350, Thousand Oaks, CA 91360-2787
(805) 493-3115

California Maritime Academy
Vallejo, California
www.csum.edu   Federal Code: 001134

4-year public university and maritime college in small city.
Enrollment: 836 undergrads.

BASIC COSTS (2007-2008)
Tuition and fees: $3,728; out-of-state residents $13,898.
Room and board: $8,450.
Additional info: Each student participates in at least one cruise and one internship prior to graduation. Some majors have additional cruise requirements. The cost for a cruise is $3,500. The cost for an internship/co-op is $225. Additionally, each incoming student must purchase a uniform. Prices range from $1,550-$1,680 depending on the major.

FINANCIAL AID PICTURE
Students with need: Need-based aid available for full-time and part-time students.
Students without need: This college awards aid only to students with need.
Additional info: US Maritime Administration provides annual incentive payment of $3,000 per student, with certain conditions. Tuition waiver for children of deceased or disabled California veterans.

FINANCIAL AID PROCEDURES
Forms required: FAFSA.
Dates and Deadlines: Priority date 3/2; no closing date. Applicants notified on a rolling basis starting 4/1.

CONTACT
Ken Walsh, Director of Financial Aid
200 Maritime Academy Drive, Vallejo, CA 94590
(707) 654-1275

California Polytechnic State University: San Luis Obispo
San Luis Obispo, California
www.calpoly.edu   Federal Code: 001143

4-year public university in large town.
Enrollment: 18,728 undergrads, 5% part-time. 3,610 full-time freshmen.
Selectivity: Admits less than 50% of applicants.

BASIC COSTS (2007-2008)
Tuition and fees: $4,689; out-of-state residents $14,859.
Room and board: $8,817.
Additional info: Required fees vary by program.

FINANCIAL AID PICTURE (2006-2007)
Students with need: Out of 2,447 full-time freshmen who applied for aid, 1,158 were judged to have need. Of these, 1,053 received aid, and 105 had their full need met. Average financial aid package met 58% of need; average scholarship/grant was $1,765; average loan was $2,402. For part-time students, average financial aid package was $5,773.
Students without need: 163 full-time freshmen who did not demonstrate need for aid received scholarships/grants; average award was $2,373. No-need awards available for academics, alumni affiliation, art, athletics, job skills, leadership, music/drama, ROTC, state/district residency.
Scholarships offered: 86 full-time freshmen received athletic scholarships; average amount $1,999.

FINANCIAL AID PROCEDURES
Forms required: FAFSA.
Dates and Deadlines: Priority date 3/1; no closing date. Applicants notified on a rolling basis starting 4/15; must reply within 8 week(s) of notification.

CONTACT
Lois Kelly, Director, Financial Aid
Admissions Office, Cal Poly, San Luis Obispo, CA 93407-0031
(805) 756-2927

California School of Culinary Arts
Pasadena, California
www.csca.edu   Federal Code: 032103

2-year for-profit culinary school in very large city.
Enrollment: 1,586 undergrads.
Selectivity: Open admission.

BASIC COSTS (2007-2008)
Additional info: Diploma programs vary in cost. Associate of occupational studies in culinary arts program tuition: $43,950, fees $3,000. Associate of occupational students in hospitality/restaurant management tuition: $31,000, fees $4,015.

FINANCIAL AID PICTURE
Students with need: Need-based aid available for full-time and part-time students. Work study available nights, weekends, and for part-time students.

FINANCIAL AID PROCEDURES
Forms required: FAFSA.
Dates and Deadlines: No deadline. Applicants notified on a rolling basis.
Transfers: No deadline.

CONTACT
Kristen Hanle, Director of Student Finance
530 East Colorado Boulevard, Pasadena, CA 91101
(626) 229-1300

California State Polytechnic University: Pomona
Pomona, California
www.csupomona.edu   Federal Code: 001144

4-year public university in small city.
Enrollment: 19,615 undergrads, 17% part-time. 3,423 full-time freshmen.
Selectivity: Admits 50 to 75% of applicants.

BASIC COSTS (2007-2008)
Tuition and fees: $3,278; out-of-state residents $13,448.
Room and board: $8,493.

FINANCIAL AID PICTURE (2007-2008)
Students with need: Out of 2,365 full-time freshmen who applied for aid, 1,706 were judged to have need. Of these, 1,631 received aid, and 464 had their full need met. Average financial aid package met 77.3% of need; average scholarship/grant was $7,028; average loan was $2,964. For part-time students, average financial aid package was $7,347.
Students without need: 10 full-time freshmen who did not demonstrate need for aid received scholarships/grants; average award was $3,604. No-need awards available for academics, alumni affiliation, athletics, leadership, state/district residency.
Scholarships offered: 28 full-time freshmen received athletic scholarships; average amount $2,831.
Cumulative student debt: 33% of graduating class had student loans; average debt was $10,487.

FINANCIAL AID PROCEDURES
Forms required: FAFSA.
Dates and Deadlines: Priority date 3/2; no closing date. Applicants notified on a rolling basis starting 4/1.

CONTACT
Diana Minor, Director of Financial Aid
3801 West Temple Avenue, Pomona, CA 91768-4019
(909) 869-3700

California State University: Bakersfield
Bakersfield, California
www.csub.edu   Federal Code: 007993

4-year public university and liberal arts college in small city.
Enrollment: 4,991 full-time undergrads. 854 full-time freshmen.
Selectivity: Admits 50 to 75% of applicants.

BASIC COSTS (2007-2008)
Tuition and fees: $3,708; out-of-state residents $13,878.
Room and board: $6,537.

FINANCIAL AID PICTURE
Students with need: Need-based aid available for full-time and part-time students.
Students without need: This college awards aid only to students with need.

FINANCIAL AID PROCEDURES
Forms required: FAFSA.
Dates and Deadlines: Priority date 3/2; closing date 4/1. Applicants notified on a rolling basis; must reply within 2 week(s) of notification.

CONTACT
Clifford Smith, Associate Dean of Financial Aid
9001 Stockdale Highway, Bakersfield, CA 93311-1099
(661) 664-2011

California State University: Channel Islands
Camarillo, California
www.csuci.edu   Federal Code: 039803

4-year public university in small city.
Enrollment: 3,289 undergrads, 19% part-time. 510 full-time freshmen.
Selectivity: Admits 50 to 75% of applicants.

BASIC COSTS (2007-2008)
Tuition and fees: $3,332; out-of-state residents $13,502.
Room and board: $10,630.

FINANCIAL AID PICTURE (2006-2007)
Students with need: 61% of average financial aid package awarded as scholarships/grants, 39% awarded as loans/jobs.

CONTACT
One University Drive, Camarillo, CA 93012
(805) 437-8530

California State University: Chico
Chico, California
www.csuchico.edu   Federal Code: 001146

4-year public university and liberal arts college in small city.
Enrollment: 15,645 undergrads, 9% part-time. 2,710 full-time freshmen.

Selectivity: Admits over 75% of applicants.

BASIC COSTS (2007-2008)
Tuition and fees: $3,690; out-of-state residents $13,860.
Room and board: $9,022.

FINANCIAL AID PICTURE (2007-2008)
Students with need: Out of 1,634 full-time freshmen who applied for aid, 1,135 were judged to have need. Of these, 1,103 received aid, and 314 had their full need met. Average financial aid package met 88% of need; average scholarship/grant was $7,387; average loan was $3,402. For part-time students, average financial aid package was $8,109.
Students without need: 554 full-time freshmen who did not demonstrate need for aid received scholarships/grants; average award was $5,711. No-need awards available for academics, art, athletics, leadership, minority status, music/drama, religious affiliation.
Scholarships offered: *Merit:* President's Scholar Award; 10 awards at $12,000 each and 12 awards at $1,000 each. *Athletic:* 21 full-time freshmen received athletic scholarships; average amount $2,710.

FINANCIAL AID PROCEDURES
Forms required: FAFSA.
Dates and Deadlines: Priority date 3/2; no closing date. Applicants notified on a rolling basis starting 3/2.

CONTACT
Dan Reed, Director of Financial Aid
400 West First Street, Chico, CA 95929-0722
(530) 898-6451

California State University: Dominguez Hills
Carson, California
www.csudh.edu   Federal Code: 001141

4-year public university in small city.
Enrollment: 8,409 undergrads, 36% part-time. 974 full-time freshmen.
Selectivity: Admits 50 to 75% of applicants.

BASIC COSTS (2007-2008)
Tuition and fees: $3,377; out-of-state residents $13,547.
Room and board: $8,690.
Additional info: Tuition/fee waivers available for adults.

FINANCIAL AID PICTURE (2006-2007)
Students with need: Out of 710 full-time freshmen who applied for aid, 426 were judged to have need. Of these, 425 received aid, and 13 had their full need met. Average financial aid package met 76% of need; average scholarship/grant was $5,671; average loan was $2,320. For part-time students, average financial aid package was $5,896.
Students without need: 24 full-time freshmen who did not demonstrate need for aid received scholarships/grants; average award was $2,107. No-need awards available for academics, alumni affiliation, art, athletics, leadership, music/drama.
Scholarships offered: 13 full-time freshmen received athletic scholarships; average amount $2,768.
Cumulative student debt: 30% of graduating class had student loans; average debt was $14,817.

FINANCIAL AID PROCEDURES
Forms required: FAFSA.
Dates and Deadlines: Priority date 3/2; closing date 4/15. Applicants notified on a rolling basis starting 2/28; must reply within 4 week(s) of notification.

CONTACT
Delores Lee, Director of Financial Aid
1000 East Victoria Street, Carson, CA 90747
(310) 243-3696

California State University: East Bay

Hayward, California
www.csueastbay.edu   Federal Code: 001138

4-year public university in small city.
Enrollment: 10,391 undergrads, 19% part-time. 874 full-time freshmen.
Selectivity: Admits 50 to 75% of applicants.

BASIC COSTS (2007-2008)

Tuition and fees: $3,264; out-of-state residents $13,434.
Room only: $5,832.
Additional info: Quoted freshman room-only charge is for suite shared by 6 to 8 students. Additional $3,200 advance purchase of flexible retail meal credits required. (Standard meal plans not available).

FINANCIAL AID PICTURE (2006-2007)

Students with need: Out of 453 full-time freshmen who applied for aid, 406 were judged to have need. Of these, 390 received aid, and 76 had their full need met. Average financial aid package met 73% of need; average scholarship/grant was $7,497. For part-time students, average financial aid package was $5,443.
Cumulative student debt: 37% of graduating class had student loans; average debt was $12,400.

FINANCIAL AID PROCEDURES

Forms required: FAFSA.
Dates and Deadlines: Priority date 3/2; no closing date. Applicants notified on a rolling basis; must reply within 3 week(s) of notification.

CONTACT

Rhonda Johnson, Financial Aid Department
25800 Carlos Bee Boulevard, Hayward, CA 94542-3095
(510) 885-4746

California State University: Fresno

Fresno, California
www.csufresno.edu   Federal Code: 001147

4-year public university in very large city.
Enrollment: 19,191 undergrads, 19% part-time. 2,546 full-time freshmen.
Selectivity: Admits 50 to 75% of applicants.

BASIC COSTS (2007-2008)

Tuition and fees: $3,299; out-of-state residents $13,469.
Room and board: $7,053.
Additional info: Tuition/fee waivers available for adults, minority students, unemployed or children of unemployed.

FINANCIAL AID PICTURE (2007-2008)

Students with need: Average financial aid package met 82% of need; average scholarship/grant was $7,811; average loan was $3,029. For part-time students, average financial aid package was $6,841.
Students without need: No-need awards available for academics, alumni affiliation, art, athletics, leadership, music/drama, state/district residency.
Cumulative student debt: 64% of graduating class had student loans; average debt was $11,141.

FINANCIAL AID PROCEDURES

Forms required: FAFSA.
Dates and Deadlines: Priority date 3/3; no closing date. Applicants notified on a rolling basis starting 4/1; must reply within 3 week(s) of notification.

CONTACT

Maria Hernandez, Director of Financial Aid
5150 North Maple Avenue, M/S JA 57, Fresno, CA 93740-8026
(559) 278-2182

California State University: Fullerton

Fullerton, California
www.fullerton.edu   Federal Code: 001137

4-year public university in small city.
Enrollment: 29,788 undergrads, 24% part-time. 3,737 full-time freshmen.
Selectivity: Admits 50 to 75% of applicants.

BASIC COSTS (2007-2008)

Tuition and fees: $3,342; out-of-state residents $13,512.
Room only: $5,167.

FINANCIAL AID PICTURE (2006-2007)

Students with need: Out of 2,684 full-time freshmen who applied for aid, 1,881 were judged to have need. Of these, 1,116 received aid, and 108 had their full need met. Average financial aid package met 62% of need; average scholarship/grant was $6,711; average loan was $2,596. For part-time students, average financial aid package was $5,821.
Students without need: 300 full-time freshmen who did not demonstrate need for aid received scholarships/grants; average award was $4,442. No-need awards available for academics.
Scholarships offered: 49 full-time freshmen received athletic scholarships; average amount $4,933.
Cumulative student debt: 38% of graduating class had student loans; average debt was $14,762.
Additional info: Fee waiver for children of veterans killed in action or with service-connected disability whose annual income is $5,000 or less.

FINANCIAL AID PROCEDURES

Forms required: FAFSA.
Dates and Deadlines: Priority date 3/2; closing date 5/23. Applicants notified by 4/2; must reply within 3 week(s) of notification.
Transfers: Applicants notified by 4/2; must reply within 3 week(s) of notification.

CONTACT

Deborah McCracken, Director of Financial Aid
800 North State College Boulevard, Langsdorf Hall-114, Fullerton, CA 92831-6900
(714) 278-3125

California State University: Long Beach

Long Beach, California
www.csulb.edu   Federal Code: 001139

4-year public university in large city.
Enrollment: 30,605 undergrads, 21% part-time. 4,132 full-time freshmen.
Selectivity: Admits less than 50% of applicants.

BASIC COSTS (2007-2008)

Tuition and fees: $3,116; out-of-state residents $13,286.
Room and board: $7,536.

FINANCIAL AID PICTURE (2007-2008)

Students with need: Average financial aid package met 81% of need; average scholarship/grant was $5,400; average loan was $2,862. For part-time students, average financial aid package was $8,900.
Students without need: No-need awards available for academics, art, athletics, music/drama.
Scholarships offered: President's Scholar Award; full tuition and fees, campus housing, books.
Cumulative student debt: 39% of graduating class had student loans; average debt was $10,183.

FINANCIAL AID PROCEDURES

Forms required: FAFSA.

Dates and Deadlines: Priority date 3/2; no closing date. Applicants notified on a rolling basis starting 4/1; must reply within 3 week(s) of notification.
Transfers: Community college EOPS students may apply as EOP students and thus be eligible for an EOP Grant.

CONTACT
Janice Miller, Director of Financial Aid
1250 Bellflower Boulevard, Long Beach, CA 90840-0106
(562) 985-4641

California State University: Los Angeles
Los Angeles, California
www.calstatela.edu   Federal Code: 001140

4-year public university in very large city.
Enrollment: 15,727 undergrads, 26% part-time. 1,764 full-time freshmen.
Selectivity: Admits 50 to 75% of applicants.

BASIC COSTS (2007-2008)
Tuition and fees: $3,332; out-of-state residents $13,502.
Room only: $3,474.

FINANCIAL AID PICTURE (2007-2008)
Students with need: Average financial aid package met 78% of need; average scholarship/grant was $6,994; average loan was $3,364. For part-time students, average financial aid package was $6,876.

FINANCIAL AID PROCEDURES
Forms required: FAFSA.
Dates and Deadlines: Priority date 3/1; no closing date. Applicants notified on a rolling basis starting 4/1; must reply within 3 week(s) of notification.

CONTACT
Lindy Fong, Director of Center for Student Financial Aid
5151 State University Drive SA101, Los Angeles, CA 90032
(323) 343-1784

California State University: Monterey Bay
Seaside, California
www.csumb.edu   Federal Code: 032603

4-year public liberal arts and teachers college in large town.
Enrollment: 3,604 undergrads, 10% part-time. 733 full-time freshmen.
Selectivity: Admits 50 to 75% of applicants.

BASIC COSTS (2007-2008)
Tuition and fees: $3,256; out-of-state residents $13,426.
Room and board: $9,152.
Additional info: Tuition/fee waivers available for unemployed or children of unemployed.

FINANCIAL AID PICTURE
Students with need: Need-based aid available for full-time and part-time students. Work study available nights, weekends, and for part-time students.
Students without need: No-need awards available for academics, alumni affiliation, athletics, leadership, state/district residency.

FINANCIAL AID PROCEDURES
Forms required: FAFSA, state aid form, institutional form.
Dates and Deadlines: Priority date 3/2; no closing date. Applicants notified on a rolling basis starting 2/28.

CONTACT
Angeles Fuentes, Director of Financial Aid
100 Campus Center, Building 47, Seaside, CA 93955-8001
(831) 582-5100

California State University: Northridge
Northridge, California
www.csun.edu   Federal Code: 001153

4-year public university in very large city.
Enrollment: 29,485 undergrads, 26% part-time. 3,695 full-time freshmen.
Selectivity: Admits 50 to 75% of applicants.

BASIC COSTS (2007-2008)
Tuition and fees: $3,300; out-of-state residents $13,470.
Room and board: $9,350.

FINANCIAL AID PICTURE (2006-2007)
Students with need: Out of 2,750 full-time freshmen who applied for aid, 2,299 were judged to have need. Of these, 2,299 received aid. For part-time students, average financial aid package was $5,262.
Students without need: 90 full-time freshmen who did not demonstrate need for aid received scholarships/grants; average award was $1,507. No-need awards available for academics, athletics, state/district residency.
Scholarships offered: 54 full-time freshmen received athletic scholarships; average amount $5,226.
Cumulative student debt: 40% of graduating class had student loans; average debt was $13,225.

FINANCIAL AID PROCEDURES
Forms required: FAFSA.
Dates and Deadlines: Priority date 3/1; no closing date. Applicants notified on a rolling basis starting 4/1.

CONTACT
Lili Vidal, Director of Financial Aid
18111 Nordhoff Street, Northridge, CA 91328-8207
(818) 677-4085

California State University: Sacramento
Sacramento, California
www.csus.edu   Federal Code: 001233

4-year public university in very large city.
Enrollment: 23,724 undergrads, 24% part-time. 1,972 full-time freshmen.
Selectivity: Admits 50 to 75% of applicants.

BASIC COSTS (2007-2008)
Tuition and fees: $3,558; out-of-state residents $13,728.
Room and board: $10,102.

FINANCIAL AID PICTURE (2006-2007)
Students with need: Out of 1,471 full-time freshmen who applied for aid, 1,139 were judged to have need. Of these, 1,014 received aid, and 18 had their full need met. Average financial aid package met 63% of need; average scholarship/grant was $2,123; average loan was $2,339. For part-time students, average financial aid package was $6,485.
Students without need: 96 full-time freshmen who did not demonstrate need for aid received scholarships/grants; average award was $5,824.
Scholarships offered: 3 full-time freshmen received athletic scholarships; average amount $6,105.
Cumulative student debt: 32% of graduating class had student loans; average debt was $12,237.

FINANCIAL AID PROCEDURES
Forms required: FAFSA.
Dates and Deadlines: Applicants notified on a rolling basis starting 4/1; must reply within 4 week(s) of notification.

CONTACT
Craig Yamamoto, Financial Aid Director
6000 J Street, Sacramento, CA 95819-6048
(916) 278-6554

California State University: San Bernardino
San Bernardino, California
www.csusb.edu   Federal Code: 001142

4-year public university and liberal arts college in small city.
Enrollment: 13,311 undergrads, 17% part-time. 1,656 full-time freshmen.
Selectivity: Admits 50 to 75% of applicants.

BASIC COSTS (2007-2008)
Tuition and fees: $3,440; out-of-state residents $13,610.
Room and board: $9,000.

FINANCIAL AID PICTURE
Students with need: Need-based aid available for full-time students. Work study available weekends and for part-time students.

FINANCIAL AID PROCEDURES
Forms required: FAFSA.
Dates and Deadlines: Priority date 3/2; no closing date. Applicants notified on a rolling basis starting 4/1.

CONTACT
Roseanna Ruiz, Director of Financial Aid
5500 University Parkway, San Bernardino, CA 92407-2397
(909) 537-7800

California State University: San Marcos
San Marcos, California
www.csusm.edu   Federal Code: 030113

4-year public university in large town.
Enrollment: 7,997 undergrads, 25% part-time. 1,075 full-time freshmen.

BASIC COSTS (2007-2008)
Tuition and fees: $3,374; out-of-state residents $13,544.
Room and board: $9,090.

FINANCIAL AID PICTURE (2006-2007)
Students with need: 99% of average financial aid package awarded as scholarships/grants, 1% awarded as loans/jobs.
Students without need: No-need awards available for academics, athletics, leadership, state/district residency.
Scholarships offered: Fenstermaker scholarships: up to $6,000 a year; awarded to outstanding chemistry, biology, or computer science majors; renewable.

CONTACT
Cecilia Schouwe, Director of Financial Aid
333 South Twin Oaks Valley Road, San Marcos, CA 92096-0001
(760) 750-4850

California State University: Stanislaus
Turlock, California
www.csustan.edu   Federal Code: 001157

4-year public business and liberal arts college in small city.
Enrollment: 6,883 undergrads.

BASIC COSTS (2007-2008)
Tuition and fees: $3,307; out-of-state residents $13,477.
Room and board: $8,757.
Additional info: Tuition/fee waivers available for adults.

FINANCIAL AID PICTURE
Students with need: Need-based aid available for full-time and part-time students. Work study available nights, weekends, and for part-time students.
Students without need: No-need awards available for academics, alumni affiliation, art, athletics, leadership, minority status, music/drama, state/district residency.
Scholarships offered: President's Scholarships: $12,500, renewable for up to 4 years, awards based on GPA minimum of 3.8 and SAT of at least 1350 or ACT of at least 30, 20 available; Provost's Scholarships: $3,500, renewable for up to 4 years, awards based on GPA minimum of 3.5 and SAT of at least 1250 or ACT of at least 28, 20 available; Provost's Achievement Award for community college transfers: $2,000, renewable for up to 2 years, awards based on GPA minimum of 3.5 and completion of at least 45 transferable credits at time of application, 10 available.

FINANCIAL AID PROCEDURES
Forms required: FAFSA.
Dates and Deadlines: Priority date 3/2; no closing date. Applicants notified on a rolling basis starting 3/15; must reply within 3 week(s) of notification.
Transfers: No deadline. Applicants notified on a rolling basis; must reply within 3 week(s) of notification.

CONTACT
Mathew Sanchez, Director
801 West Monte Vista Avenue, Turlock, CA 95382-0256
(209) 667-3336

Cerro Coso Community College
Ridgecrest, California
www.cerrocoso.edu   Federal Code: 010111

2-year public community college in large town.
Enrollment: 2,101 undergrads.
Selectivity: Open admission.

BASIC COSTS (2007-2008)
Tuition and fees: $600; out-of-state residents $6,300.
Per-credit charge: $20; out-of-state residents $210.

FINANCIAL AID PICTURE
Students with need: Need-based aid available for full-time and part-time students. Work study available nights.

FINANCIAL AID PROCEDURES
Forms required: FAFSA.
Dates and Deadlines: Priority date 5/15; no closing date. Applicants notified on a rolling basis starting 6/1; must reply within 2 week(s) of notification.

CONTACT
Joanne Spiller, Director of Financial Aid and Scholarships
3000 College Heights Boulevard, Ridgecrest, CA 93555-7777
(760) 384-6221

Chabot College
Hayward, California
www.chabotcollege.edu   Federal Code: 001162

2-year public community college in large city.
Enrollment: 8,830 undergrads.
Selectivity: Open admission; but selective for some programs.

PART III: FINANCIAL AID COLLEGE BY COLLEGE

BASIC COSTS (2007-2008)
Tuition and fees: $626; out-of-state residents $5,726.
Per-credit charge: $20; out-of-state residents $190.

FINANCIAL AID PICTURE
Students with need: Work study available nights, weekends, and for part-time students.
Additional info: Tuition and/or fee waivers for low-income students.

FINANCIAL AID PROCEDURES
Forms required: FAFSA, institutional form.
Dates and Deadlines: Priority date 8/1; no closing date. Applicants notified on a rolling basis.

CONTACT
Kathryn Linzmeyer, Director of Financial Aid
25555 Hesperian Boulevard, Hayward, CA 94545
(510) 723-6746

Chaffey College
Rancho Cucamonga, California
www.chaffey.edu   Federal Code: 001163

2-year public community college in small city.
Enrollment: 12,564 undergrads.
Selectivity: Open admission.

BASIC COSTS (2007-2008)
Tuition and fees: $630; out-of-state residents $5,820.
Per-credit charge: $20; out-of-state residents $193.
Additional info: Tuition/fee waivers available for adults.

FINANCIAL AID PICTURE
Students with need: Need-based aid available for full-time and part-time students.
Students without need: No-need awards available for academics.
Additional info: State of California Board of Governors fee waivers to qualified state residents. Criteria for eligibility: households which receive public assistance, meet state's low income guidelines, and demonstrate need as defined by Title IV programs.

FINANCIAL AID PROCEDURES
Forms required: FAFSA.
Dates and Deadlines: No deadline. Applicants notified on a rolling basis starting 7/15; must reply within 2 week(s) of notification.

CONTACT
Karen Sanders, Financial Aid Supervisor
5885 Haven Avenue, Rancho Cucamonga, CA 91701-3002
(909) 652-6006

Chapman University
Orange, California
www.chapman.edu   Federal Code: 001164

4-year private university and liberal arts college in very large city, affiliated with Christian Church (Disciples of Christ).
Enrollment: 4,169 undergrads, 5% part-time. 934 full-time freshmen.
Selectivity: Admits less than 50% of applicants.

BASIC COSTS (2008-2009)
Tuition and fees: $34,700.
Per-credit charge: $1,050.
Room and board: $11,315.

FINANCIAL AID PICTURE (2006-2007)
Students with need: Out of 859 full-time freshmen who applied for aid, 529 were judged to have need. Of these, 529 received aid, and 529 had their full need met. Average financial aid package met 100% of need; average scholarship/grant was $20,323; average loan was $3,522. For part-time students, average financial aid package was $13,813.
Students without need: 200 full-time freshmen who did not demonstrate need for aid received scholarships/grants; average award was $125. No-need awards available for academics, alumni affiliation, art, music/drama, religious affiliation, ROTC.
Cumulative student debt: 67% of graduating class had student loans; average debt was $22,956.

FINANCIAL AID PROCEDURES
Forms required: FAFSA, state aid form.
Dates and Deadlines: Priority date 3/2; no closing date. Applicants notified on a rolling basis starting 3/15; must reply within 3 week(s) of notification.
Transfers: No deadline. Applicants notified on a rolling basis starting 3/15; must reply within 3 week(s) of notification.

CONTACT
Gregory Ball, Director of Financial Aid
One University Drive, Orange, CA 92866
(714) 997-6815

Charles R. Drew University of Medicine and Science
Los Angeles, California
www.cdrewu.edu   Federal Code: 013653

4-year private university and health science college in very large city.
Enrollment: 294 undergrads.
Selectivity: Admits less than 50% of applicants.

BASIC COSTS (2008-2009)
Additional info: Tuition $200/unit for associate degree programs, $250/unit for bachelor's degree programs, $400/unit for graduate degree programs. Required fees vary by program and enrollment.

FINANCIAL AID PICTURE (2007-2008)
Students with need: 46% of average financial aid package awarded as scholarships/grants, 54% awarded as loans/jobs.

CONTACT
Samuel Graham, Director of Financial Aid
1731 East 120th Street, Los Angeles, CA 90059
(323) 563-4824

Citrus College
Glendora, California
www.citruscollege.edu   Federal Code: 001166

2-year public community college in large town.
Enrollment: 13,095 undergrads.
Selectivity: Open admission.

BASIC COSTS (2007-2008)
Tuition and fees: $631; out-of-state residents $5,911.
Per-credit charge: $20; out-of-state residents $196.

FINANCIAL AID PICTURE
Students with need: Need-based aid available for full-time and part-time students. Work study available nights, weekends, and for part-time students.

FINANCIAL AID PROCEDURES
Forms required: FAFSA.

Dates and Deadlines: Priority date 3/1; no closing date. Applicants notified on a rolling basis; must reply within 2 week(s) of notification.

CONTACT

Lilia Medina, Director of Financial Aid
1000 West Foothill Boulevard, Glendora, CA 91741-1899
(626) 914-8592

City College of San Francisco

San Francisco, California
www.ccsf.edu   Federal Code: 012874

2-year public community college in very large city.
Enrollment: 22,332 undergrads, 67% part-time. 1,234 full-time freshmen.
Selectivity: Open admission; but selective for some programs.

BASIC COSTS (2007-2008)

Tuition and fees: $632; out-of-state residents $5,732.
Per-credit charge: $20; out-of-state residents $190.
Additional info: Tuition/fee waivers available for unemployed or children of unemployed.

FINANCIAL AID PICTURE

Students with need: Work study available nights, weekends, and for part-time students.
Additional info: Board of Governor fee waiver for low income students.

FINANCIAL AID PROCEDURES

Forms required: FAFSA.
Dates and Deadlines: Priority date 3/1; no closing date. Applicants notified on a rolling basis starting 7/1.

CONTACT

Jorge Bell, Dean, Financial Aid
Office of Admissions and Records E-107, San Francisco, CA 94112
(415) 239-3576

Claremont McKenna College

Claremont, California   Federal Code: 001170
www.claremontmckenna.edu   CSS Code: 4054

4-year private liberal arts college in large town.
Enrollment: 1,135 undergrads. 268 full-time freshmen.
Selectivity: Admits less than 50% of applicants.

BASIC COSTS (2008-2009)

Tuition and fees: $37,060.
Room and board: $11,930.

FINANCIAL AID PICTURE (2007-2008)

Students with need: Out of 151 full-time freshmen who applied for aid, 129 were judged to have need. Of these, 129 received aid, and 129 had their full need met. Average financial aid package met 100% of need; average scholarship/grant was $32,126; average loan was $2,624. Need-based aid available for part-time students.
Students without need: 16 full-time freshmen who did not demonstrate need for aid received scholarships/grants; average award was $8,762. No-need awards available for academics.
Scholarships offered: McKenna Achievement Award: $10,000; based on strong academic record and outstanding leadership and involvement; 30 awarded, renewable for total of 4 years. The Frank Seaver Leadership Scholarship: full tuition; awarded to students who demonstrate exceptional promise to become leaders intent on making a positive impact in the world; renewable for 4 years.
Cumulative student debt: 51% of graduating class had student loans; average debt was $10,518.

FINANCIAL AID PROCEDURES

Forms required: FAFSA, CSS PROFILE.
Dates and Deadlines: Closing date 2/1. Applicants notified by 4/1; must reply by 5/1.
Transfers: Closing date 3/2. Applicants notified by 5/15.

CONTACT

Georgette DeVeres, Associate Vice President of Admission & Financial Aid
890 Columbia Avenue, Claremont, CA 91711-6425
(909) 621-8088

Coastline Community College

Fountain Valley, California
www.coastline.edu   Federal Code: 013536

2-year public community college in small city.
Enrollment: 5,874 undergrads.
Selectivity: Open admission.

BASIC COSTS (2007-2008)

Tuition and fees: $658; out-of-state residents $5,848.
Per-credit charge: $20; out-of-state residents $193.
Additional info: Tuition/fee waivers available for unemployed or children of unemployed.

FINANCIAL AID PICTURE

Students with need: Need-based aid available for full-time and part-time students.
Students without need: This college awards aid only to students with need.
Additional info: Board of Governor's Grant: statewide fee waiver program for students or dependents receiving HFOL/TANF, SSI, General Relief, or whose income meets set standards or who are considered eligible through Federal needs analysis.

FINANCIAL AID PROCEDURES

Forms required: FAFSA, institutional form.
Dates and Deadlines: Priority date 3/2; no closing date. Applicants notified on a rolling basis starting 8/1; must reply within 2 week(s) of notification.

CONTACT

Cynthia Pienkowski, Director of Financial Aid
11460 Warner Avenue, Fountain Valley, CA 92708
(714) 241-6239

Cogswell Polytechnical College

Sunnyvale, California
www.cogswell.edu   Federal Code: 001177

4-year private visual arts and engineering college in small city.
Enrollment: 230 undergrads, 52% part-time. 22 full-time freshmen.
Selectivity: Admits 50 to 75% of applicants.

BASIC COSTS (2007-2008)

Tuition and fees: $16,548.
Per-credit charge: $682.

FINANCIAL AID PICTURE (2006-2007)

Students with need: 35% of average financial aid package awarded as scholarships/grants; 65% awarded as loans/jobs. Need-based aid available for part-time students.
Students without need: No-need awards available for academics.

FINANCIAL AID PROCEDURES

Forms required: FAFSA.
Dates and Deadlines: Priority date 3/2; no closing date. Applicants notified on a rolling basis starting 4/30; must reply within 4 week(s) of notification.

Transfers: No deadline. Applicants notified by 4/1; must reply within 4 week(s) of notification.

CONTACT
Andrew Hagedorn, Director of Financial Aid
1175 Bordeaux Drive, Sunnyvale, CA 94089-1299
(408) 541-0100

College of Marin: Kentfield
Kentfield, California
www.marin.edu   Federal Code: 001178

2-year public community college in small town.
Enrollment: 2,768 undergrads.
Selectivity: Open admission.

BASIC COSTS (2007-2008)
Tuition and fees: $630; out-of-state residents $6,000.
Per-credit charge: $20; out-of-state residents $199.

FINANCIAL AID PICTURE
Students with need: Need-based aid available for full-time and part-time students.

FINANCIAL AID PROCEDURES
Forms required: FAFSA.
Dates and Deadlines: Priority date 3/1; no closing date. Applicants notified on a rolling basis starting 5/15.

CONTACT
David Cook, Director of Financial Aid
835 College Avenue, Kentfield, CA 94904
(415) 457-8811 ext. 7405

College of the Canyons
Santa Clarita, California
www.canyons.edu   Federal Code: 008903

2-year public community college in small city.
Enrollment: 7,860 undergrads.
Selectivity: Open admission; but selective for some programs.

BASIC COSTS (2007-2008)
Tuition and fees: $638; out-of-state residents $5,168.
Per-credit charge: $20; out-of-state residents $171.

FINANCIAL AID PICTURE (2006-2007)
Students with need: 75% of average financial aid package awarded as scholarships/grants, 25% awarded as loans/jobs. Need-based aid available for part-time students. Work study available nights.
Students without need: No-need awards available for academics, alumni affiliation, art, leadership, music/drama.
Additional info: Enrollment fees waived for students enrolled concurrently in high school and COC. School has own payment plan.

FINANCIAL AID PROCEDURES
Forms required: FAFSA, state aid form.
Dates and Deadlines: Closing date 3/2. Applicants notified on a rolling basis starting 6/1; must reply within 4 week(s) of notification.
Transfers: No deadline.

CONTACT
Thomas Bilbruck, Director, Financial Aid and Scholarships
26455 Rockwell Canyon Road, Santa Clarita, CA 91355
(661) 362-3242

College of the Desert
Palm Desert, California
www.collegeofthedesert.edu   Federal Code: 001182

2-year public community college in small city.
Enrollment: 5,333 undergrads.
Selectivity: Open admission; but selective for some programs.

BASIC COSTS (2007-2008)
Tuition and fees: $630; out-of-state residents $5,490.
Per-credit charge: $20; out-of-state residents $182.
Additional info: Tuition/fee waivers available for adults, minority students, unemployed or children of unemployed.

FINANCIAL AID PICTURE (2006-2007)
Students with need: 92% of average financial aid package awarded as scholarships/grants, 8% awarded as loans/jobs. Need-based aid available for part-time students. Work study available weekends and for part-time students.
Students without need: This college awards aid only to students with need.

FINANCIAL AID PROCEDURES
Forms required: FAFSA.
Dates and Deadlines: Priority date 3/2; no closing date. Applicants notified on a rolling basis starting 7/1.

CONTACT
Heidi Granger, Director of Financial Aid
43-500 Monterey Avenue, Palm Desert, CA 92260
(760) 773-2532

College of the Redwoods
Eureka, California
www.redwoods.edu   Federal Code: 001185

2-year public community college in large town.
Enrollment: 4,516 undergrads, 53% part-time. 611 full-time freshmen.
Selectivity: Open admission; but selective for some programs.

BASIC COSTS (2007-2008)
Tuition and fees: $624; out-of-state residents $7,104.
Per-credit charge: $20; out-of-state residents $236.
Room and board: $5,900.

FINANCIAL AID PICTURE (2007-2008)
Students with need: 75% of average financial aid package awarded as scholarships/grants, 25% awarded as loans/jobs. Need-based aid available for part-time students.

FINANCIAL AID PROCEDURES
Forms required: FAFSA, institutional form.
Dates and Deadlines: Priority date 4/15; no closing date. Applicants notified on a rolling basis starting 5/1; must reply within 6 week(s) of notification.

CONTACT
Lynn Thiesen, Director of Financial Aid
7351 Tompkins Hill Road, Eureka, CA 95501-9300
(707) 476-4182

College of the Siskiyous
Weed, California
www.siskiyous.edu   Federal Code: 001187

2-year public community and junior college in small town.
Enrollment: 1,336 undergrads, 36% part-time. 431 full-time freshmen.

Selectivity: Open admission; but selective for some programs.

BASIC COSTS (2007-2008)

Tuition and fees: $624; out-of-state residents $6,174.
Per-credit charge: $20; out-of-state residents $205.
Room and board: $7,550.
Additional info: Oregon residents with interstate exchange program: $42 per unit (no enrollment fee).

FINANCIAL AID PICTURE

Students with need: Need-based aid available for full-time and part-time students. Work study available nights, weekends, and for part-time students.
Students without need: This college awards aid only to students with need.

FINANCIAL AID PROCEDURES

Forms required: FAFSA.
Dates and Deadlines: Priority date 4/30; no closing date. Applicants notified on a rolling basis starting 6/1; must reply within 2 week(s) of notification.
Transfers: No deadline. Applicants notified on a rolling basis. Academic transcripts required.

CONTACT

Vicki Wrobel, Director of Financial Aid
800 College Avenue, Weed, CA 96094-2899
(530) 938-5209

Columbia College

Sonora, California
www.gocolumbia.org   Federal Code: 007707

2-year public community college in small town.
Enrollment: 3,368 undergrads.
Selectivity: Open admission.

BASIC COSTS (2007-2008)

Tuition and fees: $642; out-of-state residents $5,832.
Per-credit charge: $20; out-of-state residents $193.

FINANCIAL AID PICTURE

Students with need: Need-based aid available for full-time and part-time students.
Students without need: No-need awards available for academics.

FINANCIAL AID PROCEDURES

Forms required: FAFSA, state aid form, institutional form.
Dates and Deadlines: Priority date 3/2; no closing date. Applicants notified on a rolling basis starting 6/15; must reply within 2 week(s) of notification.

CONTACT

Cass Larkin, Financial Aid Officer
11600 Columbia College Drive, Sonora, CA 95370
(209) 588-5105

Columbia College: Hollywood

Tarzana, California
www.columbiacollege.edu   Federal Code: 014697

4-year private visual arts college in very large city.
Enrollment: 314 undergrads, 8% part-time. 56 full-time freshmen.
Selectivity: Open admission; but selective for some programs.

BASIC COSTS (2007-2008)

Tuition and fees: $13,983.
Per-credit charge: $367.

FINANCIAL AID PICTURE (2007-2008)

Students with need: Out of 47 full-time freshmen who applied for aid, 33 were judged to have need. Of these, 33 received aid. Average financial aid package met 43% of need; average scholarship/grant was $3,300; average loan was $3,700. For part-time students, average financial aid package was $7,000.
Cumulative student debt: 75% of graduating class had student loans; average debt was $40,000.
Additional info: All financial aid forms due by second week of classes.

FINANCIAL AID PROCEDURES

Forms required: FAFSA, institutional form.
Dates and Deadlines: Priority date 2/1; no closing date. Applicants notified on a rolling basis starting 7/15; must reply within 3 week(s) of notification.

CONTACT

Jan Hastings, Fianancial Aid Manager
18618 Oxnard Street, Tarzana, CA 91356
(818) 401-1030

Concordia University

Irvine, California
www.cui.edu   Federal Code: 013885

4-year private university and liberal arts college in small city, affiliated with Lutheran Church - Missouri Synod.
Enrollment: 1,203 undergrads, 3% part-time. 226 full-time freshmen.
Selectivity: Admits 50 to 75% of applicants.

BASIC COSTS (2008-2009)

Tuition and fees: $23,930.
Per-credit charge: $665.
Room and board: $7,650.
Additional info: Tuition/fee waivers available for minority students.

FINANCIAL AID PICTURE (2007-2008)

Students with need: Out of 220 full-time freshmen who applied for aid, 163 were judged to have need. Of these, 163 received aid, and 44 had their full need met. Average financial aid package met 76% of need; average scholarship/grant was $13,780; average loan was $3,325. For part-time students, average financial aid package was $10,945.
Students without need: 43 full-time freshmen who did not demonstrate need for aid received scholarships/grants; average award was $7,169. No-need awards available for academics, alumni affiliation, art, athletics, leadership, music/drama, religious affiliation.
Scholarships offered: *Merit:* President: full tuition. National Merit finalist is a requirement. Honors: up to $10,000; based on 3.9-4.0 GPA. Honors applicant must also score 1300 SAT or 29 ACT. Regent: up to $8,000; based on 3.8-4.0 GPA. Provost: up to $5,000; based on 3.5-3.79 GPA. Dean's: up to $3,000; based on 3.2-3.49 GPA. Various other academic, music, theater, athletic scholarships; amounts vary. Freshman students must score 1000 SAT or 21 ACT. Academic scholarships are based on cumulative GPA. *Athletic:* 22 full-time freshmen received athletic scholarships; average amount $11,968.
Cumulative student debt: 67% of graduating class had student loans; average debt was $20,254.

FINANCIAL AID PROCEDURES

Forms required: FAFSA, state aid form, institutional form.
Dates and Deadlines: Priority date 3/2; closing date 4/1. Applicants notified on a rolling basis starting 2/1; must reply within 4 week(s) of notification.
Transfers: Must reply within 4 week(s) of notification.

CONTACT

Lori McDonald, Executive Director, Enrollment Services
1530 Concordia West, Irvine, CA 92612-3299
(949) 854-8002 ext. 1136

Copper Mountain College

Joshua Tree, California
www.cmccd.edu   Federal Code: 035424

2-year public community college in small town.
Enrollment: 1,866 undergrads.
Selectivity: Open admission.

BASIC COSTS (2007-2008)
Tuition and fees: $602; out-of-state residents $5,792.
Per-credit charge: $20; out-of-state residents $193.

FINANCIAL AID PICTURE
Students with need: Need-based aid available for full-time and part-time students.

FINANCIAL AID PROCEDURES
Forms required: FAFSA.
Dates and Deadlines: Priority date 3/2; no closing date.

CONTACT
Kathryn Verseman, Director of Financial Aid
6162 Rotary Way, Joshua Tree, CA 92252
(760) 366-3791 ext. 4235

Crafton Hills College

Yucaipa, California
www.craftonhills.edu   Federal Code: 009272

2-year public community college in large town.
Enrollment: 3,470 undergrads.
Selectivity: Open admission.

BASIC COSTS (2007-2008)
Tuition and fees: $642; out-of-state residents $5,892.
Per-credit charge: $20; out-of-state residents $195.
Additional info: Tuition/fee waivers available for adults, minority students, unemployed or children of unemployed.

FINANCIAL AID PICTURE
Students with need: Need-based aid available for full-time and part-time students. Work study available nights.
Students without need: This college awards aid only to students with need.

FINANCIAL AID PROCEDURES
Forms required: FAFSA, institutional form.
Dates and Deadlines: Priority date 4/15; closing date 6/2. Applicants notified on a rolling basis starting 7/31; must reply within 2 week(s) of notification.
Transfers: Priority date 1/2; closing date 3/2.

CONTACT
John Muskavitch, Director of Financial Aid
11711 Sand Canyon Road, Yucaipa, CA 92399-1799
(909) 794-2161 ext. 3242

Cuyamaca College

El Cajon, California
www.cuyamaca.net   Federal Code: 014435

2-year public community college in small city.
Enrollment: 4,951 undergrads.
Selectivity: Open admission; but selective for some programs.

BASIC COSTS (2007-2008)
Tuition and fees: $638; out-of-state residents $5,528.
Per-credit charge: $20; out-of-state residents $183.

FINANCIAL AID PICTURE
Students with need: Work study available nights, weekends, and for part-time students.

FINANCIAL AID PROCEDURES
Forms required: FAFSA.
Dates and Deadlines: Priority date 3/2; no closing date. Applicants notified on a rolling basis; must reply within 2 week(s) of notification.

CONTACT
900 Rancho San Diego Parkway, El Cajon, CA 92019-4304
(619) 660-4201

De Anza College

Cupertino, California
www.deanza.edu   Federal Code: 004480

2-year public community college in large town.
Enrollment: 16,921 undergrads.
Selectivity: Open admission; but selective for some programs.

BASIC COSTS (2007-2008)
Tuition and fees: $621; out-of-state residents $5,346.
Per-credit charge: $13; out-of-state residents $118.

FINANCIAL AID PICTURE
Students with need: Need-based aid available for full-time and part-time students.
Students without need: This college awards aid only to students with need.

FINANCIAL AID PROCEDURES
Forms required: FAFSA.
Dates and Deadlines: No deadline. Applicants notified on a rolling basis starting 5/15; must reply within 2 week(s) of notification.

CONTACT
Cindy Castillo, Director of Financial Aid
21250 Stevens Creek Boulevard, Cupertino, CA 95014
(408) 864-8718

Deep Springs College

Dyer, Nevada
www.deepsprings.edu   Federal Code: 015483

2-year private liberal arts college for men in rural community.
Enrollment: 25 undergrads.
Selectivity: Admits less than 50% of applicants.

BASIC COSTS (2007-2008)
Additional info: All students receive full scholarship covering tuition, room, and board. Tuition at time of enrollment locked for 2 years.

FINANCIAL AID PICTURE
Students with need: Work study available nights, weekends, and for part-time students.
Students without need: No-need awards available for academics.

FINANCIAL AID PROCEDURES
Dates and Deadlines: No deadline.

CONTACT

David Neidorf, President
Applications Committee, Dyer, NV 89010-9803
(760) 872-2000.

DeVry University: Fremont

Fremont, California
www.devry.edu   Federal Code: 008322

4-year for-profit university in small city.
Enrollment: 1,411 undergrads, 35% part-time. 199 full-time freshmen.

BASIC COSTS (2007-2008)

Tuition and fees: $14,640.
Per-credit charge: $525.

FINANCIAL AID PICTURE (2006-2007)

Students with need: Out of 162 full-time freshmen who applied for aid, 150 were judged to have need. Of these, 143 received aid. Average financial aid package met 28% of need; average scholarship/grant was $5,643; average loan was $4,202. For part-time students, average financial aid package was $7,598.
Students without need: This college awards aid only to students with need.
Cumulative student debt: 71% of graduating class had student loans; average debt was $38,241.

FINANCIAL AID PROCEDURES

Forms required: FAFSA.
Dates and Deadlines: No deadline. Applicants notified on a rolling basis.

CONTACT

Kim Kane, Director of Financial Aid
6600 Dumbarton Circle, Fremont, CA 94555-3615
(510) 574-1120

DeVry University: Long Beach

Long Beach, California
www.devry.edu   Federal Code: 023329

4-year for-profit university in large town.
Enrollment: 826 undergrads, 51% part-time. 109 full-time freshmen.

BASIC COSTS (2007-2008)

Tuition and fees: $14,010.
Per-credit charge: $500.

FINANCIAL AID PICTURE (2006-2007)

Students with need: Out of 75 full-time freshmen who applied for aid, 70 were judged to have need. Of these, 66 received aid, and 1 had their full need met. Average financial aid package met 29% of need; average scholarship/grant was $5,923; average loan was $4,448. For part-time students, average financial aid package was $7,863.
Students without need: This college awards aid only to students with need.
Cumulative student debt: 75% of graduating class had student loans; average debt was $14,313.

FINANCIAL AID PROCEDURES

Forms required: FAFSA.
Dates and Deadlines: No deadline. Applicants notified on a rolling basis.

CONTACT

Brenda Woods, Associate Director of Student Finance
3880 Kilroy Airport Way, Long Beach, CA 90806
(562) 427-0861

DeVry University: Pomona

Pomona, California
www.devry.edu   Federal Code: 023329

4-year for-profit university in small city.
Enrollment: 1,543 undergrads, 51% part-time. 171 full-time freshmen.

BASIC COSTS (2007-2008)

Tuition and fees: $14,020.
Per-credit charge: $500.

FINANCIAL AID PICTURE (2006-2007)

Students with need: Out of 113 full-time freshmen who applied for aid, 104 were judged to have need. Of these, 100 received aid, and 1 had their full need met. Average financial aid package met 25% of need; average scholarship/grant was $5,053; average loan was $4,027. For part-time students, average financial aid package was $7,536.
Students without need: This college awards aid only to students with need.
Cumulative student debt: 88% of graduating class had student loans; average debt was $43,193.

FINANCIAL AID PROCEDURES

Forms required: FAFSA.
Dates and Deadlines: No deadline. Applicants notified on a rolling basis.

CONTACT

Kathy Odom, Director of Financial Aid
901 Corporate Center Drive, Pomona, CA 91768-2642

DeVry University: Sherman Oaks

Sherman Oaks, California
www.devry.edu   Federal Code: 016219

4-year for-profit university in large city.
Enrollment: 462 undergrads, 53% part-time. 43 full-time freshmen.

BASIC COSTS (2007-2008)

Tuition and fees: $14,020.
Per-credit charge: $500.

FINANCIAL AID PICTURE (2006-2007)

Students with need: Out of 27 full-time freshmen who applied for aid, 26 were judged to have need. Of these, 25 received aid. Average financial aid package met 31% of need; average scholarship/grant was $6,860; average loan was $4,270. For part-time students, average financial aid package was $7,495.
Students without need: This college awards aid only to students with need.
Cumulative student debt: 100% of graduating class had student loans; average debt was $43,575.

FINANCIAL AID PROCEDURES

Forms required: FAFSA.
Dates and Deadlines: No deadline. Applicants notified on a rolling basis.

CONTACT

Lou LaSota, Director of Financial Aid
15301 Ventura Boulevard, D-100, Sherman Oaks, CA 91403
(818) 932-3111

Diablo Valley College

Pleasant Hill, California
www.dvc.edu   Federal Code: 001191

2-year public community college in large town.
Enrollment: 11,363 undergrads.
Selectivity: Open admission.

BASIC COSTS (2007-2008)
Tuition and fees: $610; out-of-state residents $5,500.
Per-credit charge: $20; out-of-state residents $183.

FINANCIAL AID PICTURE
Students with need: Need-based aid available for full-time and part-time students.

FINANCIAL AID PROCEDURES
Forms required: FAFSA, state aid form, institutional form.
Dates and Deadlines: Priority date 3/2; closing date 5/1. Applicants notified on a rolling basis starting 6/1; must reply within 2 week(s) of notification.

CONTACT
Brenda Jerez, Financial Aid Director
321 Golf Club Road, Pleasant Hill, CA 94523
(925) 685-1230 ext. 2290

Dominican School of Philosophy and Theology

Berkeley, California
www.dspt.edu   Federal Code: 016673

Upper-division private seminary college in small city, affiliated with Roman Catholic Church.
Enrollment: 2 undergrads.

BASIC COSTS (2007-2008)
Tuition and fees: $14,720.
Per-credit charge: $495.
Additional info: Required medical insurance for otherwise uninsured students costs approximately $3.600 per year.

FINANCIAL AID PICTURE
Students with need: Need-based aid available for full-time and part-time students.
Students without need: No-need awards available for academics.

FINANCIAL AID PROCEDURES
Forms required: FAFSA, institutional form.
Dates and Deadlines: Priority date 3/15; no closing date. Applicants notified on a rolling basis starting 5/15.
Transfers: Closing date 4/1.

CONTACT
John Knutsen, Director of Admissions
2301 Vine Street, Berkeley, CA 94708
(510) 649-2459

Dominican University of California

San Rafael, California
www.dominican.edu   Federal Code: 001196

4-year private university and liberal arts college in small city, affiliated with Roman Catholic heritage.
Enrollment: 1,469 undergrads, 20% part-time. 227 full-time freshmen.
Selectivity: Admits 50 to 75% of applicants.

BASIC COSTS (2007-2008)
Tuition and fees: $30,570.
Per-credit charge: $1,270.
Room and board: $12,000.

FINANCIAL AID PICTURE (2006-2007)
Students with need: Out of 199 full-time freshmen who applied for aid, 170 were judged to have need. Of these, 169 received aid, and 20 had their full need met. Average financial aid package met 37% of need; average scholarship/grant was $17,567; average loan was $2,905. For part-time students, average financial aid package was $7,978.
Students without need: No-need awards available for academics, alumni affiliation, athletics, leadership, minority status, music/drama.
Scholarships offered: 14 full-time freshmen received athletic scholarships; average amount $6,530.
Cumulative student debt: 84% of graduating class had student loans; average debt was $24,728.
Additional info: 4-year guarantee program.

FINANCIAL AID PROCEDURES
Forms required: FAFSA, institutional form.
Dates and Deadlines: Priority date 3/2; no closing date. Applicants notified on a rolling basis starting 3/15; must reply within 2 week(s) of notification.

CONTACT
Mary-Frances Causey, Director of Financial Aid
50 Acacia Avenue, San Rafael, CA 94901-2298
(415) 257-1350

East Los Angeles College

Monterey Park, California
www.elac.edu   Federal Code: 001222

2-year public community college in very large city.
Enrollment: 10,030 undergrads.
Selectivity: Open admission; but selective for some programs.

BASIC COSTS (2007-2008)
Tuition and fees: $622; out-of-state residents $5,812.
Per-credit charge: $20; out-of-state residents $193.

FINANCIAL AID PICTURE
Students with need: Need-based aid available for full-time and part-time students.
Students without need: No-need awards available for academics.
Additional info: Need-based enrollment fee waivers available through a state aid program.

FINANCIAL AID PROCEDURES
Forms required: FAFSA.
Dates and Deadlines: Closing date 3/2. Applicants notified on a rolling basis; must reply within 2 week(s) of notification.
Transfers: No deadline.

CONTACT
Gavino Herrera, Director of Financial Aid
1301 Avenida Cesar Chavez, Monterey Park, CA 91754
(323) 265-8738

Empire College

Santa Rosa, California
www.empcol.edu   Federal Code: 009032

2-year for-profit business college in small city.
Enrollment: 87 undergrads. 87 full-time freshmen.
Selectivity: Open admission.

BASIC COSTS (2008-2009)

Tuition and fees: $8,625.

FINANCIAL AID PICTURE

Students with need: Need-based aid available for full-time students.
Students without need: This college awards aid only to students with need.
Scholarships offered: Dean's Scholarship for high school seniors; 10 awarded; range from $250-$1,500. Dean's Scholarships for Empire College students; 7 awarded; range from $250-$1,000. Based on academic achievement, letter of intent, extracurricular activities and letter of recommendation.

FINANCIAL AID PROCEDURES

Forms required: FAFSA.
Dates and Deadlines: No deadline. Applicants notified on a rolling basis.

CONTACT

Mary O'Brien, Financial Aid Officer
3035 Cleveland Avenue, Santa Rosa, CA 95403-2100
(707) 546-4000

Feather River College

Quincy, California
www.frc.edu   Federal Code: 008597

2-year public community and liberal arts college in small town.
Enrollment: 627 undergrads.
Selectivity: Open admission.

BASIC COSTS (2007-2008)

Tuition and fees: $654; out-of-state residents $6,054.
Per-credit charge: $20; out-of-state residents $200.
Room only: $4,208.
Additional info: Tuition/fee waivers available for adults, unemployed or children of unemployed.

FINANCIAL AID PICTURE

Students with need: Need-based aid available for full-time and part-time students. Work study available nights, weekends, and for part-time students.

FINANCIAL AID PROCEDURES

Forms required: FAFSA.
Dates and Deadlines: No deadline. Applicants notified on a rolling basis starting 7/30; must reply within 3 week(s) of notification.

CONTACT

Financial Aid Director
570 Golden Eagle Avenue, Quincy, CA 95971
(530) 283-0202 ext. 296

Foothill College

Los Altos Hills, California
www.foothill.edu   Federal Code: 001199

2-year public community college in large town.
Enrollment: 7,844 undergrads.
Selectivity: Open admission; but selective for some programs.

BASIC COSTS (2007-2008)

Tuition and fees: $625; out-of-state residents $5,350.
Per-credit charge: $13; out-of-state residents $118.

FINANCIAL AID PICTURE

Students with need: Need-based aid available for full-time and part-time students.
Students without need: This college awards aid only to students with need.

Scholarships offered: Chancellor's Scholarship for first-time freshmen who graduate in the top 20 percent of high school class as Chancellor's Scholar; $1,200 for two years.

FINANCIAL AID PROCEDURES

Forms required: FAFSA, institutional form.
Dates and Deadlines: Priority date 3/30; no closing date. Applicants notified on a rolling basis; must reply within 2 week(s) of notification.
Transfers: Application required for CDL grants, March 2 due date for CAL grant application.

CONTACT

Kevin Harral, Director, Financial Aid
12345 El Monte Road, Los Altos Hills, CA 94022
(650) 949-7245

Fremont College

Cerritos, California
www.fremont.edu   Federal Code: 030399

2-year for-profit health science and career college in very large city.
Enrollment: 93 undergrads.
Selectivity: Open admission; but selective for some programs.

BASIC COSTS (2008-2009)

Additional info: Paralegal: $24,811. Sports therapy: $22,411. Business administration: $25,375. Tuition at time of enrollment locked for 2 years; tuition/fee waivers available for unemployed or children of unemployed.

FINANCIAL AID PICTURE (2006-2007)

Students with need: 47% of average financial aid package awarded as scholarships/grants, 53% awarded as loans/jobs.
Students without need: This college awards aid only to students with need.

FINANCIAL AID PROCEDURES

Forms required: FAFSA, institutional form.

CONTACT

Neeyah Francois, Director of Financial Aid
18000 Studebaker Road, 900A, Cerritos, CA 90703-5342
(562) 809-5100

Fresno City College

Fresno, California
www.fresnocitycollege.edu   Federal Code: 001307

2-year public community and liberal arts college in large city.
Enrollment: 10,693 undergrads.
Selectivity: Open admission; but selective for some programs.

BASIC COSTS (2007-2008)

Tuition and fees: $630; out-of-state residents $5,820.
Per-credit charge: $20; out-of-state residents $193.
Additional info: Tuition/fee waivers available for adults, minority students, unemployed or children of unemployed.

FINANCIAL AID PICTURE

Students with need: Need-based aid available for full-time and part-time students.
Students without need: This college awards aid only to students with need.
Additional info: Board of Governors Grant Program to offset enrollment fees based on untaxed income, low income, or calculated need. Students qualifying for program also automatically exempt from health fees. March 2 application deadline for California grants.

FINANCIAL AID PROCEDURES
Forms required: FAFSA, state aid form.
Dates and Deadlines: Priority date 4/15; no closing date. Applicants notified on a rolling basis starting 4/1.

CONTACT
Joaquin Jimenez, Associate Dean of Students
1101 East University Avenue, Fresno, CA 93741
(559) 442-8279

Fresno Pacific University
Fresno, California
www.fresno.edu   Federal Code: 001253

4-year private university and liberal arts college in large city, affiliated with Mennonite Brethren Church.
Enrollment: 1,515 undergrads, 15% part-time. 166 full-time freshmen.
Selectivity: Admits 50 to 75% of applicants.

BASIC COSTS (2007-2008)
Tuition and fees: $21,796.
Per-credit charge: $770.
Room and board: $6,600.

FINANCIAL AID PICTURE (2007-2008)
Students with need: Out of 165 full-time freshmen who applied for aid, 150 were judged to have need. Of these, 149 received aid, and 32 had their full need met. Average financial aid package met 71% of need; average scholarship/grant was $12,578; average loan was $2,539. For part-time students, average financial aid package was $6,464.
Students without need: No-need awards available for academics, athletics, music/drama.
Scholarships offered: *Merit:* Paragon Scholarship; 2 awarded; full tuition; requires 3.65 GPA, demonstrated Christian leadership, SAT 1150 or higher. President's Scholarship; 40 awarded; $6,500-$9,500; requires 3.65 GPA, demonstrated Christian leadership, SAT 1150 or higher. Provost Scholarship; 20 awarded; $4,000-$8,000; for transfer students with 3.5 GPA and demonstrated Christian leadership. SAT scores exclusive of Writing. *Athletic:* 39 full-time freshmen received athletic scholarships; average amount $6,966.
Cumulative student debt: 75% of graduating class had student loans; average debt was $18,604.

FINANCIAL AID PROCEDURES
Forms required: FAFSA, institutional form.
Dates and Deadlines: Priority date 3/2; no closing date. Applicants notified on a rolling basis starting 3/2; must reply by 7/30 or within 3 week(s) of notification.
Transfers: No deadline.

CONTACT
Ken Isaak, Director of Student Financial Services
1717 South Chestnut Avenue, Fresno, CA 93702-4709
(559) 453-2041

Glendale Community College
Glendale, California
www.glendale.edu   Federal Code: 001203

2-year public community college in small city.
Enrollment: 11,651 undergrads.
Selectivity: Open admission; but selective for some programs.

BASIC COSTS (2007-2008)
Tuition and fees: $633; out-of-state residents $5,583.
Per-credit charge: $20; out-of-state residents $185.

FINANCIAL AID PICTURE
Students with need: Need-based aid available for full-time and part-time students. Work study available nights, weekends, and for part-time students.
Students without need: This college awards aid only to students with need.

FINANCIAL AID PROCEDURES
Forms required: FAFSA, institutional form.
Dates and Deadlines: Priority date 4/15; no closing date. Applicants notified on a rolling basis starting 6/15; must reply within 2 week(s) of notification.
Transfers: No deadline.

CONTACT
Patricia Hurley, Director of Financial Aid
1500 North Verdugo Road, Glendale, CA 91208-2809
(818) 240-1000 ext. 5916

Golden Gate University
San Francisco, California
www.ggu.edu   Federal Code: 001205

4-year private university in very large city.
Enrollment: 492 undergrads, 78% part-time.

BASIC COSTS (2008-2009)
Tuition and fees: $16,200.
Per-credit charge: $510.

FINANCIAL AID PICTURE
Students with need: Need-based aid available for full-time and part-time students. Work study available nights.
Students without need: This college awards aid only to students with need.

FINANCIAL AID PROCEDURES
Forms required: FAFSA, institutional form.
Dates and Deadlines: Priority date 1/2; no closing date. Applicants notified on a rolling basis starting 4/1; must reply within 3 week(s) of notification.
Transfers: Priority date 6/14; no deadline. Applicants notified on a rolling basis starting 1/2; must reply within 3 week(s) of notification.

CONTACT
Louis Riccardi
536 Mission Street, San Francisco, CA 94105-2968
(415) 442-7270

Grossmont College
El Cajon, California
www.grossmont.edu   Federal Code: 001208

2-year public community college in small city.
Enrollment: 12,592 undergrads.
Selectivity: Open admission; but selective for some programs.

BASIC COSTS (2007-2008)
Tuition and fees: $630; out-of-state residents $5,520.
Per-credit charge: $20; out-of-state residents $183.

FINANCIAL AID PICTURE (2006-2007)
Students with need: 89% of average financial aid package awarded as scholarships/grants, 11% awarded as loans/jobs. Need-based aid available for part-time students. Work study available nights, weekends, and for part-time students.
Students without need: This college awards aid only to students with need.

FINANCIAL AID PROCEDURES

Forms required: FAFSA.

Dates and Deadlines: Priority date 2/1; no closing date. Applicants notified on a rolling basis starting 7/15; must reply within 2 week(s) of notification.

CONTACT

Michael Copenhaver, Director of Financial Aid

8800 Grossmont College Drive, El Cajon, CA 92020

(619) 644-7129

Harvey Mudd College

Claremont, California
www.hmc.edu

Federal Code: 001171
CSS Code: 4341

4-year private engineering and liberal arts college in small city.

Enrollment: 737 undergrads. 195 full-time freshmen.

Selectivity: Admits less than 50% of applicants.

BASIC COSTS (2008-2009)

Tuition and fees: $36,635.

Room and board: $11,971.

Additional info: Room and board expense covers 16-meal plan.

FINANCIAL AID PICTURE (2007-2008)

Students with need: Out of 139 full-time freshmen who applied for aid, 115 were judged to have need. Of these, 115 received aid, and 115 had their full need met. Average financial aid package met 100% of need; average scholarship/grant was $26,273; average loan was $3,455. For part-time students, average financial aid package was $844.

Students without need: 50 full-time freshmen who did not demonstrate need for aid received scholarships/grants; average award was $9,512. No-need awards available for academics.

Scholarships offered: Harvey S. Mudd Scholarship: for first-time freshmen in science and technology programs; $10,000 annually for 4 years; must maintain minimum 2.75 GPA. Harvey Mudd College-sponsored National Merit Scholarships: from $750 to $2,000 based on need.

Cumulative student debt: 55% of graduating class had student loans; average debt was $16,078.

FINANCIAL AID PROCEDURES

Forms required: FAFSA, CSS PROFILE, state aid form.

Dates and Deadlines: Closing date 2/1. Applicants notified by 4/1; must reply by 5/1 or within 2 week(s) of notification.

Transfers: Closing date 3/2. Applicants notified by 5/15; must reply by 6/10 or within 2 week(s) of notification.

CONTACT

Gilma Lopez, Director of Financial Aid

Kingston Hall, 301 Platt Boulevard, Claremont, CA 91711-5901

(909) 621-8055

Heald College: Concord

Concord, California
www.heald.edu

Federal Code: 030693

2-year private business college in small city.

Enrollment: 682 undergrads.

BASIC COSTS (2008-2009)

Tuition and fees: $10,800.

FINANCIAL AID PICTURE

Students with need: Need-based aid available for full-time and part-time students. Work study available nights, weekends, and for part-time students.

Students without need: This college awards aid only to students with need.

FINANCIAL AID PROCEDURES

Forms required: FAFSA.

Dates and Deadlines: No deadline. Applicants notified on a rolling basis.

CONTACT

Zelda Vinson, Director of Financial Aid

5130 Commercial Circle, Concord, CA 94520

(925) 288-5800

Heald College: Hayward

Hayward, California
www.heald.edu

Federal Code: 008532

2-year private technical college in small city.

Enrollment: 1,017 undergrads.

BASIC COSTS (2008-2009)

Tuition and fees: $10,800.

FINANCIAL AID PICTURE

Students with need: Need-based aid available for full-time and part-time students. Work study available nights, weekends, and for part-time students.

Students without need: This college awards aid only to students with need.

FINANCIAL AID PROCEDURES

Forms required: FAFSA.

Dates and Deadlines: No deadline.

CONTACT

Esther Andrade, Director of Financial Aid

25500 Industrial Boulevard, Hayward, CA 94545

(510) 783-2100

Heald College: Rancho Cordova

Rancho Cordova, California
www.heald.edu

Federal Code: 025931

2-year private technical college in large city.

Enrollment: 507 undergrads.

BASIC COSTS (2008-2009)

Tuition and fees: $10,800.

FINANCIAL AID PICTURE

Students with need: Need-based aid available for full-time and part-time students. Work study available nights, weekends, and for part-time students.

Students without need: This college awards aid only to students with need.

FINANCIAL AID PROCEDURES

Forms required: FAFSA.

Dates and Deadlines: No deadline.

CONTACT

Veronica Nava, Director of Financial Aid

2910 Prospect Park Drive, Rancho Cordova, CA 95670

(916) 638-1616

Heald College: Roseville

Roseville, California
www.heald.edu

2-year private business and junior college in small city.

Enrollment: 520 undergrads.

BASIC COSTS (2008-2009)

Tuition and fees: $10,800.

FINANCIAL AID PICTURE

Students with need: Need-based aid available for full-time and part-time students. Work study available nights, weekends, and for part-time students.

Students without need: This college awards aid only to students with need.

FINANCIAL AID PROCEDURES

Forms required: FAFSA.

Dates and Deadlines: No deadline.

CONTACT

Rhonda Shaw, Director of Financial Aid

7 Sierra Gate Plaza, Roseville, CA 95678

(916) 789-8600

Heald College: Salinas

Salinas, California

www.heald.edu   Federal Code: 030340

2-year private business college in small city.

Enrollment: 479 undergrads.

BASIC COSTS (2008-2009)

Tuition and fees: $10,800.

FINANCIAL AID PICTURE

Students with need: Need-based aid available for full-time and part-time students. Work study available nights, weekends, and for part-time students.

Students without need: This college awards aid only to students with need.

FINANCIAL AID PROCEDURES

Forms required: FAFSA.

Dates and Deadlines: No deadline.

CONTACT

Heloise Mata, Director of Financial Aid

1450 North Main Street, Salinas, CA 93906

(831) 443-1700

Heald College: San Francisco

San Francisco, California

www.heald.edu   Federal Code: 007234

2-year private business college in very large city.

Enrollment: 447 undergrads.

BASIC COSTS (2008-2009)

Tuition and fees: $10,800.

FINANCIAL AID PICTURE

Students with need: Need-based aid available for full-time and part-time students. Work study available nights, weekends, and for part-time students.

Students without need: This college awards aid only to students with need.

FINANCIAL AID PROCEDURES

Forms required: FAFSA.

Dates and Deadlines: No deadline.

CONTACT

Judy Bacchus, Director of Financial Aid

350 Mission Street, San Francisco, CA 94103

(415) 808-3000

Heald College: San Jose

Milpitas, California

www.heald.edu   Federal Code: 025932

2-year private business college in very large city.

Enrollment: 673 undergrads.

BASIC COSTS (2008-2009)

Tuition and fees: $10,800.

FINANCIAL AID PICTURE

Students with need: Need-based aid available for full-time and part-time students. Work study available nights, weekends, and for part-time students.

Students without need: This college awards aid only to students with need.

FINANCIAL AID PROCEDURES

Forms required: FAFSA.

Dates and Deadlines: No deadline. Applicants notified on a rolling basis starting 6/15; must reply within 2 week(s) of notification.

CONTACT

Lydia Cervantes, Director of Financial Aid

341 Great Mall Parkway, Milpitas, CA 95035

(408) 934-4900

Heald College: Stockton

Stockton, California

www.heald.edu   Federal Code: 025933

2-year private business college in large city.

Enrollment: 755 undergrads.

Selectivity: Open admission.

BASIC COSTS (2008-2009)

Tuition and fees: $10,800.

FINANCIAL AID PICTURE

Students with need: Need-based aid available for full-time students.

FINANCIAL AID PROCEDURES

Forms required: FAFSA.

Dates and Deadlines: No deadline.

CONTACT

Valerie Edwards-Bendy, Director of Financial Aid

1605 East March Lane, Stockton, CA 95210

(209) 473-5200

High-Tech Institute

Sacramento, California

www.hightechinstitute.edu   Federal Code: 022631

2-year for-profit technical college in very large city.

Enrollment: 474 undergrads.

Selectivity: Open admission.

BASIC COSTS (2007-2008)

Additional info: $17,700 for medical assistant program, $21,110 for dental assistant program, $37,300 for surgical technologist program, $32,500 for computer networking and information technology program, $19,900 for medical billing and coding program, $18,500 for massage therapy, $20,700 for pharmacy technician. Includes tuition, fees, book, supplies, and uniform.

FINANCIAL AID PICTURE

Students with need: Need-based aid available for full-time students.

FINANCIAL AID PROCEDURES

Forms required: FAFSA.

Dates and Deadlines: No deadline. Applicants notified on a rolling basis.

CONTACT

Katherine Matthews

9738 Lincoln Village Drive, Sacramento, CA 95827

(916) 929-9700

Holy Names University
Oakland, California
www.hnu.edu
Federal Code: 001183

4-year private university in large city, affiliated with Roman Catholic Church.

Enrollment: 656 undergrads, 23% part-time. 136 full-time freshmen.

Selectivity: Admits less than 50% of applicants.

BASIC COSTS (2008-2009)

Tuition and fees: $26,300.

Per-credit charge: $870.

Room and board: $8,540.

FINANCIAL AID PICTURE

Students with need: Need-based aid available for full-time and part-time students.

Students without need: No-need awards available for academics, athletics, leadership, music/drama, religious affiliation.

Scholarships offered: Aspiring Leadership Grant; $5,500 annually, based on 2.70-2.99 GPA. Honors Scholarship; $8,500 annually, based on 3.00-3.29 GPA. Dean's Scholarship; $9,500 annually, based on 3.30-3.49 GPA. President's Scholarship; $11,000 annually, based on 3.50-3.74 GPA. Regent's Scholarship; $12,000 annually, based on 3.75+ GPA. Durocher Scholarship; full tuition, campus residency required; based on evidence of leadership, contributions to school and/or community and academic achievement, minimum GPA 3.75, minimum SAT 1100 (exclusive of writing); 1 awarded per year.

FINANCIAL AID PROCEDURES

Forms required: FAFSA, state aid form.

Dates and Deadlines: Priority date 3/2; closing date 6/30. Applicants notified on a rolling basis starting 9/1; must reply by 5/1 or within 2 week(s) of notification.

Transfers: Applicants notified on a rolling basis starting 9/1; must reply by 5/1 or within 2 week(s) of notification.

CONTACT

Christina Miller, Director of Financial Aid

3500 Mountain Boulevard, Oakland, CA 94619-1699

(510) 436-1327

Hope International University
Fullerton, California
www.hiu.edu
Federal Code: 001252

4-year private university and liberal arts college in small city, affiliated with Independent Christian Churches and Churches of Christ.

Enrollment: 674 undergrads, 17% part-time. 122 full-time freshmen.

Selectivity: Admits 50 to 75% of applicants.

BASIC COSTS (2008-2009)

Tuition and fees: $21,885.

Per-credit charge: $799.

Room and board: $8,230.

FINANCIAL AID PICTURE (2007-2008)

Students with need: Out of 113 full-time freshmen who applied for aid, 93 were judged to have need. Of these, 93 received aid, and 31 had their full need met. Average financial aid package met 83% of need; average scholarship/grant was $14,963; average loan was $3,605. For part-time students, average financial aid package was $12,135.

Students without need: 24 full-time freshmen who did not demonstrate need for aid received scholarships/grants; average award was $18,423. No-need awards available for academics, alumni affiliation, athletics, leadership, music/drama.

FINANCIAL AID PROCEDURES

Forms required: FAFSA, institutional form.

Dates and Deadlines: Closing date 3/2. Applicants notified on a rolling basis starting 3/15; must reply within 2 week(s) of notification.

CONTACT

Rhoda Posey, Director of Student Financial Aid

2500 East Nutwood Avenue, Fullerton, CA 92831-3199

(714) 879-3901 ext. 2232

Humboldt State University
Arcata, California
www.humboldt.edu
Federal Code: 001149

4-year public university and liberal arts college in large town.

Enrollment: 6,581 undergrads, 9% part-time. 966 full-time freshmen.

Selectivity: Admits over 75% of applicants.

BASIC COSTS (2007-2008)

Tuition and fees: $3,843; out-of-state residents $14,013.

Room and board: $8,522.

FINANCIAL AID PICTURE (2006-2007)

Students with need: Out of 732 full-time freshmen who applied for aid, 516 were judged to have need. Of these, 481 received aid, and 23 had their full need met. Average financial aid package met 69% of need; average scholarship/grant was $4,045; average loan was $300. For part-time students, average financial aid package was $6,970.

Students without need: 17 full-time freshmen who did not demonstrate need for aid received scholarships/grants; average award was $1,378. No-need awards available for academics.

Scholarships offered: 14 full-time freshmen received athletic scholarships; average amount $2,910.

FINANCIAL AID PROCEDURES

Forms required: FAFSA.

Dates and Deadlines: Priority date 3/2; no closing date. Applicants notified on a rolling basis starting 3/1; must reply within 6 week(s) of notification.

Transfers: Need is most salient factor for some programs.

CONTACT

Kim Coughlin-Lamphear, Director of Financial Aid Arcata, CA 95521-8299

(707) 826-4321

Humphreys College
Stockton, California
www.humphreys.edu
Federal Code: 001212

4-year private business and liberal arts college in large city.

Enrollment: 666 undergrads, 41% part-time. 41 full-time freshmen.

Selectivity: Open admission.

BASIC COSTS (2008-2009)

Tuition and fees: $12,240.

Per-credit charge: $255.

Room only: $3,150.
Additional info: School-controlled apartment housing cost quoted, not including utilities.

FINANCIAL AID PICTURE (2007-2008)

Students with need: Out of 39 full-time freshmen who applied for aid, 36 were judged to have need. Of these, 36 received aid, and 36 had their full need met. Average financial aid package met 93% of need; average scholarship/grant was $4,310; average loan was $3,500. For part-time students, average financial aid package was $4,500.
Students without need: No-need awards available for academics, state/district residency.

FINANCIAL AID PROCEDURES

Forms required: FAFSA.
Dates and Deadlines: Closing date 6/30. Applicants notified on a rolling basis; must reply within 2 week(s) of notification.

CONTACT

Judi Lafeber, Director of Financial Aid
6650 Inglewood Avenue, Stockton, CA 95207-3896
(209) 478-0800 ext. 3

Irvine Valley College

Irvine, California
www.ivc.edu
Federal Code: 025395

2-year public community college in small city.
Enrollment: 1,053 undergrads.
Selectivity: Open admission.

BASIC COSTS (2007-2008)

Tuition and fees: $632; out-of-state residents $5,822.
Per-credit charge: $20; out-of-state residents $193.
Additional info: Tuition/fee waivers available for minority students.

FINANCIAL AID PICTURE

Students with need: Need-based aid available for full-time and part-time students. Work study available nights.
Students without need: This college awards aid only to students with need.

FINANCIAL AID PROCEDURES

Forms required: FAFSA, state aid form, institutional form.
Dates and Deadlines: No deadline. Applicants notified on a rolling basis starting 4/30.

CONTACT

Darryl Cox, Director of Financial Aid
5500 Irvine Center Drive, Irvine, CA 92618-4399
(949) 451-5287

John F. Kennedy University

Pleasant Hill, California
www.jfku.edu
Federal Code: 004484

4-year private business and liberal arts college in large town.
Enrollment: 236 undergrads.

BASIC COSTS (2007-2008)

Tuition and fees: $15,468.
Per-credit charge: $340.

FINANCIAL AID PICTURE

Students with need: Need-based aid available for full-time and part-time students.

Students without need: This college awards aid only to students with need.

FINANCIAL AID PROCEDURES

Forms required: FAFSA, institutional form.
Dates and Deadlines: Priority date 3/2; no closing date. Applicants notified on a rolling basis; must reply within 4 week(s) of notification.
Transfers: Priority date 4/1.

CONTACT

Mindy Bergeron, Director of Financial Aid
100 Ellinwood Way, Pleasant Hill, CA 94523-4817
(925) 969-3385

The King's College and Seminary

Los Angeles, California
www.kingscollege.edu

4-year private Bible and seminary college in very large city, affiliated with nondenominational tradition.
Enrollment: 547 undergrads.

BASIC COSTS (2007-2008)

Tuition and fees: $7,935.
Per-credit charge: $170.
Additional info: Seminary students pay $185 per credit hour.

FINANCIAL AID PICTURE

Students with need: Need-based aid available for full-time and part-time students. Work study available nights, weekends, and for part-time students.
Students without need: No-need awards available for academics, leadership.
Additional info: Specific scholarships may require specific essays.

FINANCIAL AID PROCEDURES

Forms required: FAFSA.
Dates and Deadlines: No deadline. Applicants notified on a rolling basis.

CONTACT

Norm Stoppenbrink, Financial Aid Officer
14800 Sherman Way, Los Angeles, CA 91405-2233
(818) 779-8271

La Sierra University

Riverside, California
www.lasierra.edu
Federal Code: 001215

4-year private university in large city, affiliated with Seventh-day Adventists.
Enrollment: 1,422 undergrads, 10% part-time. 313 full-time freshmen.
Selectivity: Admits less than 50% of applicants.

BASIC COSTS (2008-2009)

Tuition and fees: $23,354.
Per-credit charge: $620.
Room and board: $6,711.

FINANCIAL AID PICTURE (2006-2007)

Students with need: Out of 255 full-time freshmen who applied for aid, 228 were judged to have need. Of these, 226 received aid, and 38 had their full need met. Average financial aid package met 67% of need; average scholarship/grant was $14,617; average loan was $2,439. For part-time students, average financial aid package was $7,378.
Students without need: 84 full-time freshmen who did not demonstrate need for aid received scholarships/grants; average award was $7,925. No-need awards available for academics, leadership, music/drama, religious affiliation.

Cumulative student debt: 79% of graduating class had student loans; average debt was $26,163.

FINANCIAL AID PROCEDURES

Forms required: FAFSA, state aid form.

Dates and Deadlines: Priority date 3/2; no closing date. Applicants notified on a rolling basis starting 4/15; must reply by 9/1.

Transfers: No deadline. Applicants notified on a rolling basis.

CONTACT

Jay Teele, Director of Student Financial Services
4500 Riverwalk Parkway, Riverside, CA 92515-8247
(951) 785-2175

Las Positas College
Livermore, California
www.laspositascollege.edu   Federal Code: 030357

2-year public community college in small city.

Enrollment: 5,411 undergrads.

Selectivity: Open admission.

BASIC COSTS (2007-2008)

Tuition and fees: $626; out-of-state residents $5,726.

Per-credit charge: $20; out-of-state residents $190.

Additional info: Tuition/fee waivers available for unemployed or children of unemployed.

FINANCIAL AID PICTURE

Students with need: Need-based aid available for full-time students.

FINANCIAL AID PROCEDURES

Forms required: institutional form.

Dates and Deadlines: Priority date 5/1; no closing date. Applicants notified on a rolling basis starting 7/1; must reply within 2 week(s) of notification.

CONTACT

Andi Schreibman, Financial Aid Officer
3033 Collier Canyon Road, Livermore, CA 94551
(925) 424-1580

Life Pacific College
San Dimas, California
www.lifepacific.edu   Federal Code: 016029

4-year private Bible college in large town, affiliated with International Church of the Foursquare Gospel.

Enrollment: 399 undergrads, 28% part-time. 45 full-time freshmen.

Selectivity: Admits over 75% of applicants.

BASIC COSTS (2008-2009)

Tuition and fees: $11,450.

Per-credit charge: $375.

Room and board: $5,600.

FINANCIAL AID PICTURE (2007-2008)

Students with need: 100% of average financial aid package awarded as scholarships/grants, 0% awarded as loans/jobs. Need-based aid available for part-time students.

Students without need: No-need awards available for academics, alumni affiliation.

FINANCIAL AID PROCEDURES

Forms required: FAFSA.

Dates and Deadlines: Closing date 7/1. Applicants notified on a rolling basis starting 6/1.

CONTACT

Becky Huyck, Director of Financial Aid
Attn: Admissions, San Dimas, CA 91773-3203
(909) 599-5433 ext. 325

Loma Linda University
Loma Linda, California
www.llu.edu   Federal Code: 001218

3-year private health science and nursing college in large town, affiliated with Seventh-day Adventists.

Enrollment: 1,126 undergrads, 21% part-time.

BASIC COSTS (2008-2009)

Tuition and fees: $24,879.

Per-credit charge: $520.

Room only: $2,445.

Additional info: Tuition quoted for nursing program. Full-time tuition for dental hygiene program: $22,964 plus $1,530 fees. For allied health program $429 per credit hour; for certificate programs, $322/credit. Application fee may vary by program; tuition may vary by grade level in program.

FINANCIAL AID PICTURE (2006-2007)

Students with need: 19% of average financial aid package awarded as scholarships/grants, 81% awarded as loans/jobs. Need-based aid available for part-time students.

FINANCIAL AID PROCEDURES

Forms required: FAFSA.

Dates and Deadlines: Applicants notified on a rolling basis.

Transfers: Priority date 3/2; no deadline. Applicants notified on a rolling basis starting 4/1; must reply within 4 week(s) of notification.

CONTACT

Verdell Schaefer, Director of Financial Aid
Admissions Processing, Loma Linda, CA 92350
(909) 558-4509

Long Beach City College
Long Beach, California
www.lbcc.edu   Federal Code: 001219

2-year public community college in large city.

Enrollment: 10,533 undergrads.

Selectivity: Open admission.

BASIC COSTS (2007-2008)

Tuition and fees: $628; out-of-state residents $5,848.

Per-credit charge: $20; out-of-state residents $194.

FINANCIAL AID PICTURE

Students with need: Need-based aid available for full-time and part-time students.

Students without need: This college awards aid only to students with need.

FINANCIAL AID PROCEDURES

Forms required: FAFSA, institutional form.

Dates and Deadlines: Priority date 5/6; no closing date. Applicants notified on a rolling basis starting 7/6; must reply within 2 week(s) of notification.

CONTACT

Toni Dubois, Director of Financial Aid and Veterans Affairs
4901 East Carson Street, Long Beach, CA 90808
(562) 938-4257

Los Angeles City College
Los Angeles, California
www.lacitycollege.edu Federal Code: 001223

2-year public community college in very large city.
Enrollment: 2,833 undergrads, 66% part-time.
Selectivity: Open admission.

BASIC COSTS (2007-2008)
Tuition and fees: $622; out-of-state residents $5,812.
Per-credit charge: $20; out-of-state residents $193.

FINANCIAL AID PICTURE (2006-2007)
Students with need: 88% of average financial aid package awarded as scholarships/grants, 12% awarded as loans/jobs. Need-based aid available for part-time students.
Students without need: This college awards aid only to students with need.
Additional info: Fee waivers available for public assistance and Social Security insurance recipients; fee credits available for low income families.

FINANCIAL AID PROCEDURES
Forms required: FAFSA.
Dates and Deadlines: Priority date 3/2; no closing date. Applicants notified on a rolling basis starting 7/6; must reply within 2 week(s) of notification.
Transfers: No deadline. Applicants notified by 7/1.

CONTACT
Jeremy Villar, Dean of Student Services
855 North Vermont Avenue, Los Angeles, CA 90029-3589
(323) 953-4441

Los Angeles Harbor College
Wilmington, California
www.lahc.edu Federal Code: 001224

2-year public community college in small city.
Enrollment: 4,973 undergrads.
Selectivity: Open admission.

BASIC COSTS (2007-2008)
Tuition and fees: $622; out-of-state residents $5,812.
Per-credit charge: $20; out-of-state residents $193.

FINANCIAL AID PICTURE
Students with need: Need-based aid available for full-time and part-time students. Work study available nights, weekends, and for part-time students.
Students without need: This college awards aid only to students with need.

FINANCIAL AID PROCEDURES
Forms required: FAFSA, institutional form.
Dates and Deadlines: Priority date 3/2; no closing date. Applicants notified on a rolling basis; must reply within 2 week(s) of notification.
Transfers: Closing date 5/15.

CONTACT
Sheila Millman, Financial Aid Manager
1111 Figueroa Place, Wilmington, CA 90744-2397
(310) 233-4320

Los Angeles Pierce College
Woodland Hills, California
www.piercecollege.edu Federal Code: 001226

2-year public community college in very large city.
Enrollment: 9,971 undergrads.
Selectivity: Open admission; but selective for some programs.

BASIC COSTS (2007-2008)
Tuition and fees: $626; out-of-state residents $5,816.
Per-credit charge: $20; out-of-state residents $193.

FINANCIAL AID PICTURE
Students with need: Need-based aid available for full-time and part-time students.
Students without need: This college awards aid only to students with need.

FINANCIAL AID PROCEDURES
Forms required: FAFSA, institutional form.
Dates and Deadlines: Priority date 5/1; no closing date. Applicants notified on a rolling basis starting 8/1.

CONTACT
Marco de la Garza, Director of Financial Aid
6201 Winnetka Avenue, Woodland Hills, CA 91371
(818) 719-6428

Los Angeles Southwest College
Los Angeles, California
www.lasc.edu Federal Code: 007047

2-year public community college in very large city.
Enrollment: 6,034 undergrads.
Selectivity: Open admission; but selective for some programs.

BASIC COSTS (2007-2008)
Tuition and fees: $622; out-of-state residents $5,812.
Per-credit charge: $20; out-of-state residents $193.

FINANCIAL AID PICTURE
Students with need: Need-based aid available for full-time and part-time students.
Additional info: Board of Governors Enrollment Fee Waiver available to students receiving AFDC, SSI/SSP, or General Assistance. May also qualify on basis of income.

FINANCIAL AID PROCEDURES
Forms required: FAFSA.
Dates and Deadlines: No deadline. Applicants notified on a rolling basis; must reply within 2 week(s) of notification.

CONTACT
Marilyn Moy, Associate Dean, Student Services
1600 West Imperial Highway, Los Angeles, CA 90047-4899
(323) 241-5225

Los Angeles Trade and Technical College
Los Angeles, California
www.lattc.edu Federal Code: 001227

2-year public community and technical college in very large city.
Enrollment: 12,973 undergrads.
Selectivity: Open admission.

BASIC COSTS (2007-2008)

Tuition and fees: $622; out-of-state residents $5,812.
Per-credit charge: $20; out-of-state residents $193.

FINANCIAL AID PICTURE

Students with need: Need-based aid available for full-time and part-time students. Work study available nights, weekends, and for part-time students.
Students without need: This college awards aid only to students with need.

FINANCIAL AID PROCEDURES

Forms required: FAFSA.
Dates and Deadlines: Priority date 5/1; no closing date. Applicants notified on a rolling basis.
Transfers: No deadline.

CONTACT

Leann Roque, Financial Aid Manager
400 West Washington Boulevard, Los Angeles, CA 90015-4181
(213) 744-9016

Los Angeles Valley College

Valley Glen, California
www.lavc.edu
Federal Code: 001228

2-year public community college in very large city.
Enrollment: 8,678 undergrads.
Selectivity: Open admission; but selective for some programs.

BASIC COSTS (2007-2008)

Tuition and fees: $624; out-of-state residents $5,814.
Per-credit charge: $60; out-of-state residents $193.

FINANCIAL AID PICTURE

Students with need: Need-based aid available for full-time and part-time students.
Students without need: This college awards aid only to students with need.

FINANCIAL AID PROCEDURES

Forms required: FAFSA.
Dates and Deadlines: Priority date 6/12; no closing date. Applicants notified on a rolling basis.

CONTACT

Barbara Ralston, Associate Dean of Financial Aid
5800 Fulton Avenue, Valley Glen, CA 91401-4096
(818) 947-2412

Loyola Marymount University

Los Angeles, California
www.lmu.edu
Federal Code: 001234
CSS Code: 4403

4-year private university in very large city, affiliated with Roman Catholic Church.
Enrollment: 5,585 undergrads, 3% part-time. 1,267 full-time freshmen.
Selectivity: Admits 50 to 75% of applicants.

BASIC COSTS (2008-2009)

Tuition and fees: $33,902.
Per-credit charge: $1,386.
Room and board: $11,808.

FINANCIAL AID PICTURE (2007-2008)

Students with need: Out of 939 full-time freshmen who applied for aid, 654 were judged to have need. Of these, 630 received aid, and 194 had their full need met. Average financial aid package met 96% of need; average scholarship/grant was $17,301; average loan was $4,363. Need-based aid available for part-time students.
Students without need: 118 full-time freshmen who did not demonstrate need for aid received scholarships/grants; average award was $13,009. No-need awards available for academics, alumni affiliation, athletics, leadership, music/drama.
Scholarships offered: 58 full-time freshmen received athletic scholarships; average amount $25,942.
Cumulative student debt: 66% of graduating class had student loans; average debt was $28,548.

FINANCIAL AID PROCEDURES

Forms required: FAFSA, CSS PROFILE, state aid form.
Dates and Deadlines: Closing date 3/2. Applicants notified on a rolling basis starting 3/15; must reply by 5/1 or within 4 week(s) of notification.

CONTACT

Catherine Graham, Director of Financial Aid
Admissions, 1 LMU Drive, Los Angeles, CA 90045-8350
(310) 338-2700

Maric College: Panorama City

Panorama City, California
www.mariccollege.edu
Federal Code: 030445

2-year for-profit junior and technical college in very large city.
Enrollment: 90 undergrads.
Selectivity: Open admission.

BASIC COSTS (2007-2008)

Tuition and fees: $11,845.

FINANCIAL AID PICTURE

Students with need: Need-based aid available for full-time students. Work study available nights.
Students without need: This college awards aid only to students with need.

FINANCIAL AID PROCEDURES

Forms required: FAFSA, institutional form.
Dates and Deadlines: No deadline.
Transfers: No deadline.

CONTACT

Cynthia Arevalo
14355 Roscoe Boulevard, Panorama City, CA 91402
(818) 672-8907

Marymount College

Rancho Palos Verdes, California
www.marymountpv.edu
Federal Code: 010474

2-year private junior and liberal arts college in large town, affiliated with Roman Catholic Church.
Enrollment: 674 undergrads, 3% part-time. 351 full-time freshmen.
Selectivity: Admits 50 to 75% of applicants.

BASIC COSTS (2008-2009)

Tuition and fees: $23,548.
Room and board: $10,290.

FINANCIAL AID PICTURE (2006-2007)

Students with need: Out of 137 full-time freshmen who applied for aid, 122 were judged to have need. Of these, 122 received aid, and 3 had their full need met. Average financial aid package met 60% of need; average scholarship/grant was $12,752; average loan was $2,475.

Students without need: 28 full-time freshmen who did not demonstrate need for aid received scholarships/grants; average award was $7,186. No-need awards available for academics.

Cumulative student debt: 61% of graduating class had student loans; average debt was $21,621.

FINANCIAL AID PROCEDURES

Forms required: FAFSA.

Dates and Deadlines: Priority date 3/1; no closing date. Applicants notified on a rolling basis starting 2/1; must reply by 5/1 or within 4 week(s) of notification.

CONTACT

David Carnevale, Director of Financial Aid

30800 Palos Verdes Drive East, Rancho Palos Verdes, CA 90275-6299

(310) 303-7217

The Master's College
Santa Clarita, California
www.masters.edu   Federal Code: 001220

4-year private liberal arts and seminary college in small city, affiliated with Christian Church.

Enrollment: 1,112 undergrads, 16% part-time. 208 full-time freshmen.

Selectivity: Admits over 75% of applicants.

BASIC COSTS (2008-2009)

Tuition and fees: $23,120.

Per-credit charge: $965.

Room and board: $7,620.

FINANCIAL AID PICTURE (2006-2007)

Students with need: Out of 139 full-time freshmen who applied for aid, 125 were judged to have need. Of these, 124 received aid, and 35 had their full need met. Average financial aid package met 72% of need; average scholarship/grant was $12,648; average loan was $3,261. For part-time students, average financial aid package was $12,271.

Students without need: 42 full-time freshmen who did not demonstrate need for aid received scholarships/grants; average award was $11,327. No-need awards available for academics, alumni affiliation, art, athletics, leadership, music/drama.

Scholarships offered: 15 full-time freshmen received athletic scholarships; average amount $10,394.

Cumulative student debt: 50% of graduating class had student loans; average debt was $17,630.

FINANCIAL AID PROCEDURES

Forms required: FAFSA, state aid form, institutional form.

Dates and Deadlines: Priority date 3/2; no closing date. Applicants notified on a rolling basis starting 2/18; must reply by 5/1 or within 2 week(s) of notification.

Transfers: Closing date 3/2.

CONTACT

Gary Edwards, Director of Financial Aid

21726 Placerita Canyon Road, Santa Clarita, CA 91321-1200

(661) 259-3540 ext. 3391

Mendocino College
Ukiah, California
www.mendocino.edu   Federal Code: 011672

2-year public community college in large town.

Enrollment: 1,405 undergrads, 74% part-time. 108 full-time freshmen.

Selectivity: Open admission.

BASIC COSTS (2007-2008)

Tuition and fees: $634; out-of-state residents $6,184.

Per-credit charge: $20; out-of-state residents $205.

FINANCIAL AID PICTURE (2006-2007)

Students with need: For part-time students, average financial aid package was $1,018.

Students without need: No-need awards available for academics, leadership, state/district residency.

FINANCIAL AID PROCEDURES

Forms required: FAFSA.

Dates and Deadlines: Priority date 5/31; no closing date. Applicants notified on a rolling basis starting 7/1; must reply within 2 week(s) of notification.

CONTACT

Jacqueline Bradley, Director of Financial Aid

1000 Hensley Creek/Box 3000, Ukiah, CA 95482

(707) 468-3110

Menlo College
Atherton, California
www.menlo.edu   Federal Code: 001236

4-year private business and liberal arts college in small city.

Enrollment: 680 undergrads, 8% part-time. 166 full-time freshmen.

Selectivity: Admits less than 50% of applicants.

BASIC COSTS (2008-2009)

Tuition and fees: $30,900.

Room and board: $11,000.

FINANCIAL AID PICTURE (2007-2008)

Students with need: Out of 94 full-time freshmen who applied for aid, 87 were judged to have need. Of these, 87 received aid, and 6 had their full need met. Average financial aid package met 70% of need; average scholarship/grant was $20,020; average loan was $2,432. For part-time students, average financial aid package was $5,864.

Students without need: 55 full-time freshmen who did not demonstrate need for aid received scholarships/grants; average award was $10,531. No-need awards available for academics.

Scholarships offered: President's Scholarship: $12,000 annually; students with 3.5 GPA or higher. Dean's Scholarship: $11,000 annually; students with 3.1-3.49 GPA. Leadership Scholarship: $8,500 annually; students with 2.8-3.09 GPA.

Cumulative student debt: 60% of graduating class had student loans; average debt was $17,625.

FINANCIAL AID PROCEDURES

Forms required: FAFSA, state aid form.

Dates and Deadlines: Priority date 3/2; closing date 8/1. Applicants notified on a rolling basis starting 12/15; must reply by 5/1 or within 2 week(s) of notification.

Transfers: No deadline. Must reply by 5/1 or within 2 week(s) of notification.

CONTACT

Anne Heaton-Dunlap, Director of Financial Aid

1000 El Camino Real, Atherton, CA 94027

(650) 543-3880

Merritt College
Oakland, California
www.merritt.edu
Federal Code: 001267

2-year public community college in large city.
Enrollment: 7,409 undergrads.
Selectivity: Open admission.

BASIC COSTS (2007-2008)
Tuition and fees: $604; out-of-state residents $5,794.
Per-credit charge: $20; out-of-state residents $193.
Additional info: Tuition/fee waivers available for unemployed or children of unemployed.

FINANCIAL AID PICTURE
Students with need: Need-based aid available for full-time and part-time students.

FINANCIAL AID PROCEDURES
Forms required: FAFSA, institutional form.
Dates and Deadlines: Priority date 4/1; closing date 6/30. Applicants notified on a rolling basis starting 6/1.

CONTACT
Alice Freeman, Financial Aid Coordinator
12500 Campus Drive, Oakland, CA 94619
(510) 436-2465

Mills College
Oakland, California
www.mills.edu
Federal Code: 001238

4-year private liberal arts college for women in large city.
Enrollment: 930 undergrads, 5% part-time. 195 full-time freshmen.
Selectivity: Admits 50 to 75% of applicants.

BASIC COSTS (2008-2009)
Tuition and fees: $35,190.
Room and board: $10,550.

FINANCIAL AID PICTURE (2007-2008)
Students with need: Out of 163 full-time freshmen who applied for aid, 140 were judged to have need. Of these, 140 received aid, and 59 had their full need met. Average financial aid package met 88% of need; average scholarship/grant was $24,196; average loan was $4,487. For part-time students, average financial aid package was $7,985.
Students without need: 19 full-time freshmen who did not demonstrate need for aid received scholarships/grants; average award was $25,650. No-need awards available for academics, leadership, minority status, music/drama.
Scholarships offered: Trustee Scholarship: full tuition; for entering freshmen with strong academic records. Presidential and Regional Scholarships: $5,000-$11,500 annually; for entering freshmen with strong academic records. Donner Scholarship in Music: $5,000 annually; for entering freshmen with strong talent in music. Barbara Hazelton Floyd Scholarship in Music: $5,000 annually; for entering freshmen with strong talent in piano music. Scheffler Premedical Science Scholarships: $2,500 annually; for entering freshmen and transfers with strong academic records and an interest in attending medical school; 5 awarded. Arthur Vining Davis Science Scholarship: $2,500 annually; for entering freshmen and transfers with strong academic records and an interest in science, math, or computer science. Dean's Scholarship: $4,000-$10,000 annually; for entering transfers with strong academic records. Osher Scholarships: $2,500-$10,000 annually; for entering transfer students 23 years old or older with demonstrated leadership ability; 4-8 awarded.

Cumulative student debt: 91% of graduating class had student loans; average debt was $25,163.

FINANCIAL AID PROCEDURES
Forms required: FAFSA, institutional form.
Dates and Deadlines: Closing date 2/15. Applicants notified on a rolling basis starting 3/1; must reply by 5/1 or within 2 week(s) of notification.
Transfers: Priority date 3/2. Applications by March 2 for California residents, April 1 for out-of-state students.

CONTACT
David Gin, Associate Vice President for Student Finance and Administration Services
5000 MacArthur Boulevard, Oakland, CA 94613
(510) 430-2000

MiraCosta College
Oceanside, California
www.miracosta.edu
Federal Code: 001239

2-year public community college in large city.
Enrollment: 7,834 undergrads.
Selectivity: Open admission; but selective for some programs.

BASIC COSTS (2007-2008)
Tuition and fees: $638; out-of-state residents $5,528.
Per-credit charge: $20; out-of-state residents $183.

FINANCIAL AID PICTURE (2006-2007)
Students with need: 12% of average financial aid package awarded as scholarships/grants, 88% awarded as loans/jobs. Need-based aid available for part-time students. Work study available nights.
Additional info: Waiver of in-state fees for eligible low-income students.

FINANCIAL AID PROCEDURES
Forms required: FAFSA, state aid form, institutional form.
Dates and Deadlines: Priority date 4/8; no closing date. Applicants notified on a rolling basis; must reply within 4 week(s) of notification.

CONTACT
JoAnn Bernard, Financial Aid Director
One Barnard Drive, Oceanside, CA 92056-3899
(760) 795-6711

Modesto Junior College
Modesto, California
www.mjc.edu
Federal Code: 001240

2-year public community college in small city.
Enrollment: 19,236 undergrads.
Selectivity: Open admission; but selective for some programs.

BASIC COSTS (2007-2008)
Tuition and fees: $640; out-of-state residents $5,830.
Per-credit charge: $20; out-of-state residents $193.

FINANCIAL AID PICTURE
Students with need: Need-based aid available for full-time and part-time students. Work study available nights, weekends, and for part-time students.
Students without need: This college awards aid only to students with need.
Additional info: Modesto Junior College scholarship priority deadline 12/15.

FINANCIAL AID PROCEDURES
Forms required: FAFSA, state aid form, institutional form.
Dates and Deadlines: Priority date 3/2; no closing date. Applicants notified on a rolling basis starting 5/1; must reply within 2 week(s) of notification.

CONTACT

Myra Rush, Director Financial Aid, Scholarships

435 College Avenue, Modesto, CA 95350-5800

(209) 575-6023

Monterey Peninsula College

Monterey, California

www.mpc.edu   Federal Code: 001242

2-year public community college in large town.

Enrollment: 3,596 undergrads.

Selectivity: Open admission; but selective for some programs.

BASIC COSTS (2007-2008)

Tuition and fees: $660; out-of-state residents $5,850.

Per-credit charge: $20; out-of-state residents $193.

Additional info: Tuition/fee waivers available for adults, minority students, unemployed or children of unemployed.

FINANCIAL AID PICTURE

Students with need: Need-based aid available for full-time and part-time students.

FINANCIAL AID PROCEDURES

Forms required: FAFSA, institutional form.

Dates and Deadlines: Priority date 3/2; no closing date. Applicants notified on a rolling basis starting 6/1.

CONTACT

Claudia Martin, Director of Financial Aid

980 Fremont Street, Monterey, CA 93940-4799

(831) 646-4000

Mount St. Mary's College

Los Angeles, California

www.msmc.la.edu   Federal Code: 001243

4-year private liberal arts college in very large city, affiliated with Roman Catholic Church.

Enrollment: 1,898 undergrads, 24% part-time. 348 full-time freshmen.

BASIC COSTS (2008-2009)

Tuition and fees: $27,100.

Per-credit charge: $1,012.

Room and board: $9,830.

FINANCIAL AID PICTURE (2007-2008)

Students with need: Out of 343 full-time freshmen who applied for aid, 323 were judged to have need. Of these, 323 received aid. Average financial aid package met 75% of need; average scholarship/grant was $7,555; average loan was $2,844. For part-time students, average financial aid package was $3,760.

Students without need: 20 full-time freshmen who did not demonstrate need for aid received scholarships/grants; average award was $7,900. No-need awards available for academics, alumni affiliation, art, leadership, music/drama.

Cumulative student debt: 94% of graduating class had student loans; average debt was $28,156.

FINANCIAL AID PROCEDURES

Forms required: FAFSA, institutional form.

Dates and Deadlines: Priority date 3/1; closing date 4/30. Applicants notified on a rolling basis starting 2/1.

Transfers: No deadline.

CONTACT

La Royce Dodd, Director of Student Financing

12001 Chalon Road, Los Angeles, CA 90049

(310) 954-4195

Mount San Antonio College

Walnut, California

www.mtsac.edu   Federal Code: 001245

2-year public community college in small city.

Enrollment: 21,160 undergrads, 64% part-time. 1,802 full-time freshmen.

Selectivity: Open admission.

BASIC COSTS (2007-2008)

Tuition and fees: $532; out-of-state residents $4,684.

Per-credit charge: $20; out-of-state residents $173.

FINANCIAL AID PICTURE

Students with need: Need-based aid available for full-time and part-time students.

Students without need: This college awards aid only to students with need.

FINANCIAL AID PROCEDURES

Forms required: FAFSA, institutional form.

Dates and Deadlines: No deadline. Applicants notified on a rolling basis starting 6/1; must reply within 4 week(s) of notification.

CONTACT

Susanna Jones, Director Financial Aid

1100 North Grand Avenue, Walnut, CA 91789

(909) 594-5611

Mount San Jacinto College

San Jacinto, California

www.msjc.edu   Federal Code: 001246

2-year public community college in small city.

Enrollment: 6,687 undergrads.

Selectivity: Open admission; but selective for some programs.

BASIC COSTS (2007-2008)

Tuition and fees: $600; out-of-state residents $5,790.

Per-credit charge: $20; out-of-state residents $193.

FINANCIAL AID PICTURE

Students with need: Need-based aid available for full-time and part-time students. Work study available nights.

Students without need: This college awards aid only to students with need.

Additional info: Board of Governors Grant Program for state residents to defray cost of enrollment fee.

FINANCIAL AID PROCEDURES

Forms required: FAFSA, institutional form.

Dates and Deadlines: Priority date 3/2; no closing date. Applicants notified on a rolling basis starting 5/1; must reply within 3 week(s) of notification.

Transfers: No deadline.

CONTACT

Lisa Navarro, Financial Aid Director

1499 North State Street, San Jacinto, CA 92583

(951) 487-6752

MTI College

Sacramento, California
www.mticollege.edu
Federal Code: 012912

2-year for-profit business and technical college in large city.
Enrollment: 297 undergrads.

BASIC COSTS (2008-2009)
Tuition and fees: $11,025.

FINANCIAL AID PICTURE
Students with need: Need-based aid available for full-time students. Work study available nights.

CONTACT
Paula Perez, Director of Financial Aid
5221 Madison Avenue, Sacramento, CA 95841
(916) 339-1500

National Hispanic University

San Jose, California
www.nhu.edu
Federal Code: 016968

4-year private university in very large city.
Enrollment: 399 undergrads, 35% part-time. 55 full-time freshmen.
Selectivity: Admits 50 to 75% of applicants.

BASIC COSTS (2008-2009)
Tuition and fees: $6,080.
Per-credit charge: $235.

FINANCIAL AID PICTURE (2006-2007)
Students with need: 73% of average financial aid package awarded as scholarships/grants, 27% awarded as loans/jobs.
Students without need: No-need awards available for academics.

FINANCIAL AID PROCEDURES
Forms required: FAFSA.
Dates and Deadlines: No deadline.

CONTACT
Takeo Kubo, Director, Office of Financial Aid and Scholarship
14271 Story Road, San Jose, CA 95127-3823
(408) 254-6900

National Polytechnic College of Science

Wilmington, California
www.natpoly.edu
Federal Code: 011696

2-year for-profit technical and maritime college in small city.
Enrollment: 500 undergrads.

BASIC COSTS (2007-2008)
Additional info: Associate degree program charge (covering 12 months), $17,360; per-credit-hour charge, $280. Academic year is comprised of 30 weeks (36 quarter credits), with courses offered in five-week sessions. Undergraduate courses are scheduled, typically, for eight to ten hours per day (two days each week, five-week period). Some courses require basic supplies (e.g., wet suit, fins, weights, work boots) that are not covered by tuition; additional cost of these supplies could amount to $500 or more.

FINANCIAL AID PICTURE
Students with need: Need-based aid available for full-time students.
Additional info: Work-study programs available.

FINANCIAL AID PROCEDURES
Forms required: FAFSA, institutional form.

Dates and Deadlines: No deadline. Applicants notified on a rolling basis; must reply within 3 week(s) of notification.

CONTACT
Lida Castillo, Financial Aid Officer
272 South Fries Avenue, Wilmington, CA 90744
(310) 834-2501

National University

La Jolla, California
www.nu.edu
Federal Code: 011460

4-year private university in very large city.
Enrollment: 6,675 undergrads, 67% part-time. 1,074 full-time freshmen.
Selectivity: Open admission; but selective for some programs.

BASIC COSTS (2007-2008)
Tuition and fees: $9,720.

FINANCIAL AID PICTURE (2006-2007)
Students with need: Out of 381 full-time freshmen who applied for aid, 374 were judged to have need. Of these, 179 received aid. Need-based aid available for part-time students.

FINANCIAL AID PROCEDURES
Forms required: FAFSA, state aid form, institutional form.
Dates and Deadlines: No deadline. Applicants notified on a rolling basis.
Transfers: No deadline.

CONTACT
Valerie Ryan, Director of Financial Aid
11255 North Torrey Pines Road, La Jolla, CA 92037-1011
(858) 642-8500

NewSchool of Architecture & Design

San Diego, California
www.newschoolarch.edu
Federal Code: 030439

5-year for-profit visual arts and liberal arts college in very large city.
Enrollment: 304 undergrads.
Selectivity: Admits over 75% of applicants.

BASIC COSTS (2008-2009)
Tuition and fees: $18,945.
Per-credit charge: $600.

FINANCIAL AID PICTURE (2006-2007)
Students with need: 19% of average financial aid package awarded as scholarships/grants, 81% awarded as loans/jobs. Work study available nights.
Students without need: No-need awards available for academics.
Scholarships offered: Presidential Scholarship; $5,000 annually for 2 years; for incoming freshmen based on GPA, activity, recommendations, portfolio; 15 recipients.

FINANCIAL AID PROCEDURES
Forms required: FAFSA.
Dates and Deadlines: Priority date 3/2; no closing date. Applicants notified on a rolling basis.
Transfers: Priority date 4/1; no deadline.

CONTACT
Michelle Chatelain, Director of Financial Aid
1249 F Street, San Diego, CA 92101
(619) 235-4100 ext. 206

Notre Dame de Namur University
Belmont, California
www.ndnu.edu   Federal Code: 001179

4-year private liberal arts college in large town, affiliated with Roman Catholic Church.
Enrollment: 747 undergrads, 30% part-time. 96 full-time freshmen.
Selectivity: Admits over 75% of applicants.

BASIC COSTS (2008-2009)
Tuition and fees: $25,570.
Per-credit charge: $545.
Room and board: $10,680.

FINANCIAL AID PICTURE
Students with need: Need-based aid available for full-time and part-time students. Work study available nights, weekends, and for part-time students.
Students without need: No-need awards available for academics, alumni affiliation, athletics, leadership, music/drama, religious affiliation.
Scholarships offered: Presidential Scholarships: up to $12,000 per semester; based on academic merit and leadership; variable number available. Leadership Scholarship: up to $9,000 annually; based on academic merit and leadership or service; variable number available. Emerging Artist Scholarship: up to $9,500 annually; based on demonstrated talent in the performing and fine arts; variable number available. Belmont Scholarships: up to $8,000 annually; based on merit; variable number available. Bay Area Catholic High School: up to $7,500 per year to one student from each of Bay Area Catholic high schools in their freshman year at NDNU.

FINANCIAL AID PROCEDURES
Forms required: FAFSA. CSS PROFILE accepted but not required.
Dates and Deadlines: Priority date 3/2; no closing date. Applicants notified on a rolling basis starting 1/15.

CONTACT
Susan Pace, Director of Financial Aid
1500 Ralston Avenue, Belmont, CA 94002-1908
(650) 508-3600

Occidental College
Los Angeles, California   Federal Code: 001249
www.oxy.edu   CSS Code: 4581

4-year private liberal arts college in very large city, affiliated with nondenominational tradition.
Enrollment: 1,855 undergrads, 1% part-time. 477 full-time freshmen.
Selectivity: Admits less than 50% of applicants.

BASIC COSTS (2008-2009)
Tuition and fees: $37,071.
Room and board: $10,270.

FINANCIAL AID PICTURE (2006-2007)
Students with need: Out of 306 full-time freshmen who applied for aid, 234 were judged to have need. Of these, 233 received aid, and 233 had their full need met. Average financial aid package met 100% of need; average scholarship/grant was $24,752; average loan was $4,591. For part-time students, average financial aid package was $7,992.
Students without need: 114 full-time freshmen who did not demonstrate need for aid received scholarships/grants; average award was $14,936. No-need awards available for academics, leadership.
Scholarships offered: Margaret Bundy Scott Scholarship: $20,000. President's Scholarship: $15,000; awarded to top 10-15% of incoming class based on academic achievement, leadership, and citizenship.
Cumulative student debt: 68% of graduating class had student loans; average debt was $19,756.

FINANCIAL AID PROCEDURES
Forms required: FAFSA, CSS PROFILE, state aid form.
Dates and Deadlines: Priority date 11/15; closing date 2/1. Applicants notified by 3/24; must reply by 5/1.
Transfers: Closing date 3/15. Must reply within 2 week(s) of notification. California residents must apply for Cal Grant by completing FAFSA and CSAC's GPA verification form by March 2.

CONTACT
Maureen McRae Levy, Director of Financial Aid
1600 Campus Road, Los Angeles, CA 90041
(323) 259-2548

Ohlone College
Fremont, California
www.ohlone.edu   Federal Code: 004481

2-year public community college in large city.
Enrollment: 4,526 undergrads.
Selectivity: Open admission; but selective for some programs.

BASIC COSTS (2007-2008)
Tuition and fees: $652; out-of-state residents $5,842.
Per-credit charge: $20; out-of-state residents $193.
Additional info: Tuition/fee waivers available for adults, minority students, unemployed or children of unemployed.

FINANCIAL AID PICTURE
Students with need: Need-based aid available for full-time and part-time students.
Students without need: No-need awards available for academics.

FINANCIAL AID PROCEDURES
Forms required: FAFSA, state aid form, institutional form.
Dates and Deadlines: Priority date 7/1; no closing date. Applicants notified on a rolling basis starting 7/30; must reply within 2 week(s) of notification.

CONTACT
Debra Griffin, Financial Aid Director
43600 Mission Boulevard, Fremont, CA 94539-0390
(510) 659-6150

Orange Coast College
Costa Mesa, California
www.orangecoastcollege.edu   Federal Code: 001250

2-year public community college in small city.
Enrollment: 19,025 undergrads. 909 full-time freshmen.
Selectivity: Open admission.

BASIC COSTS (2007-2008)
Tuition and fees: $658; out-of-state residents $5,848.
Per-credit charge: $20; out-of-state residents $193.
Additional info: Tuition/fee waivers available for adults, minority students, unemployed or children of unemployed.

FINANCIAL AID PICTURE (2006-2007)
Students with need: Out of 908 full-time freshmen who applied for aid, 890 were judged to have need. Of these, 882 received aid, and 16 had their full need met. Average financial aid package met 38% of need; average scholarship/grant was $3,473; average loan was $1,884. For part-time students, average financial aid package was $3,523.
Students without need: 13 full-time freshmen who did not demonstrate need for aid received scholarships/grants; average award was $4,108. No-need awards available for academics.

Cumulative student debt: 99% of graduating class had student loans; average debt was $7,160.

FINANCIAL AID PROCEDURES

Forms required: FAFSA, institutional form.
Dates and Deadlines: Priority date 3/2; closing date 5/31. Applicants notified on a rolling basis; must reply within 2 week(s) of notification.

CONTACT

Melissa Moser, Financial Aid Director
2701 Fairview Road, Costa Mesa, CA 92628-5005
(714) 432-5508

Otis College of Art and Design

Los Angeles, California
www.otis.edu   Federal Code: 001251

4-year private visual arts college in very large city.
Enrollment: 1,117 undergrads, 1% part-time. 172 full-time freshmen.
Selectivity: Admits less than 50% of applicants.

BASIC COSTS (2008-2009)

Tuition and fees: $30,464.
Per-credit charge: $993.

FINANCIAL AID PICTURE (2007-2008)

Students with need: Out of 145 full-time freshmen who applied for aid, 124 were judged to have need. Of these, 124 received aid, and 4 had their full need met. Average financial aid package met 51% of need; average scholarship/grant was $8,864; average loan was $3,300. Need-based aid available for part-time students.
Students without need: 31 full-time freshmen who did not demonstrate need for aid received scholarships/grants; average award was $5,223. No-need awards available for academics, art.
Cumulative student debt: 67% of graduating class had student loans; average debt was $37,089.

FINANCIAL AID PROCEDURES

Forms required: FAFSA, state aid form.
Dates and Deadlines: Priority date 2/15; no closing date. Applicants notified on a rolling basis starting 3/1; must reply within 2 week(s) of notification.

CONTACT

Ji Choi, Director of Financial Aid
9045 Lincoln Boulevard, Los Angeles, CA 90045-9785
(310) 665-6880

Pacific Oaks College

Pasadena, California
www.pacificoaks.edu   Federal Code: 001255

Upper-division private teachers college in small city.
Enrollment: 237 undergrads, 97% part-time.

BASIC COSTS (2007-2008)

Tuition and fees: $23,910.
Per-credit charge: $795.

FINANCIAL AID PICTURE (2007-2008)

Students with need: 17% of average financial aid package awarded as scholarships/grants, 83% awarded as loans/jobs. Need-based aid available for part-time students. Work study available nights, weekends, and for part-time students.
Students without need: This college awards aid only to students with need.

FINANCIAL AID PROCEDURES

Dates and Deadlines: Priority date 4/15; no closing date. Applicants notified on a rolling basis starting 5/1; must reply by 5/15 or within 4 week(s) of notification.

CONTACT

Deb Kuntz, Director of Financial Aid
5 Westmoreland Place, Pasadena, CA 91103
(626) 397-1350

Pacific States University

Los Angeles, California
www.psuca.edu   Federal Code: 031633

4-year private university in very large city.
Enrollment: 34 undergrads.
Selectivity: Open admission; but selective for some programs.

BASIC COSTS (2008-2009)

Tuition and fees: $13,400.
Per-credit charge: $210.

FINANCIAL AID PICTURE

Students with need: Need-based aid available for full-time and part-time students.
Students without need: No-need awards available for academics.

FINANCIAL AID PROCEDURES

Forms required: FAFSA, institutional form.
Dates and Deadlines: No deadline.

CONTACT

Min Kim, Financial Aid Officer
1516 South Western Avenue, Los Angeles, CA 90006
(323) 731-2383 ext. 14

Pacific Union College

Angwin, California
www.puc.edu   Federal Code: 001258

4-year private liberal arts college in small town, affiliated with Seventh-day Adventists.
Enrollment: 1,358 undergrads, 13% part-time. 259 full-time freshmen.
Selectivity: Admits over 75% of applicants.

BASIC COSTS (2008-2009)

Tuition and fees: $22,695.
Per-credit charge: $656.
Room and board: $6,315.

FINANCIAL AID PICTURE

Students with need: Need-based aid available for full-time and part-time students.
Students without need: No-need awards available for leadership, religious affiliation.

FINANCIAL AID PROCEDURES

Forms required: FAFSA, state aid form, institutional form.
Dates and Deadlines: No deadline. Applicants notified on a rolling basis; must reply within 3 week(s) of notification.

CONTACT

Laurie Wheeler, Director of Student Financial Services
One Angwin Avenue, Angwin, CA 94508
(707) 965-7200

Palo Verde College

Blythe, California
www.paloverde.edu   Federal Code: 001259

2-year public community college in large town.
Enrollment: 1,286 undergrads.
Selectivity: Open admission; but selective for some programs.

BASIC COSTS (2007-2008)
Tuition and fees: $600; out-of-state residents $5,790.
Per-credit charge: $20; out-of-state residents $193.

FINANCIAL AID PICTURE
Students with need: Need-based aid available for full-time and part-time students. Work study available nights.
Students without need: This college awards aid only to students with need.

FINANCIAL AID PROCEDURES
Forms required: FAFSA, institutional form.
Dates and Deadlines: No deadline. Applicants notified on a rolling basis starting 7/1; must reply within 4 week(s) of notification.

CONTACT
Linda Pratt, Director of Financial Aid
One College Drive, Blythe, CA 92225
(760) 921-5410

Palomar College

San Marcos, California
www.palomar.edu   Federal Code: 001260

2-year public community college in large town.
Enrollment: 15,362 undergrads.
Selectivity: Open admission; but selective for some programs.

BASIC COSTS (2007-2008)
Tuition and fees: $630; out-of-state residents $5,520.
Per-credit charge: $20; out-of-state residents $183.

FINANCIAL AID PICTURE
Students with need: Need-based aid available for full-time and part-time students. Work study available nights.
Students without need: This college awards aid only to students with need.

FINANCIAL AID PROCEDURES
Forms required: FAFSA, institutional form.
Dates and Deadlines: Priority date 4/1; no closing date. Applicants notified on a rolling basis starting 6/1.
Transfers: No deadline.

CONTACT
Mary San Agustin, Financial Aid Director
1140 West Mission Road, San Marcos, CA 92069-1487
(760) 744-1150

Patten University

Oakland, California
www.patten.edu   Federal Code: 004490

4-year private university and liberal arts college in very large city, affiliated with interdenominational tradition.
Enrollment: 660 undergrads.

BASIC COSTS (2007-2008)
Tuition and fees: $11,880.
Per-credit charge: $495.
Room and board: $6,250.

FINANCIAL AID PICTURE
Students with need: Need-based aid available for full-time and part-time students.
Students without need: No-need awards available for academics, athletics, state/district residency.

FINANCIAL AID PROCEDURES
Forms required: FAFSA, institutional form.
Dates and Deadlines: Priority date 3/31; no closing date. Applicants notified on a rolling basis starting 5/31.
Transfers: No deadline.

CONTACT
Dennis Clark, Financial Aid Director
2433 Coolidge Avenue, Oakland, CA 94601-2699
(510) 261-8500 ext. 7747

Pepperdine University

Malibu, California
www.pepperdine.edu   Federal Code: 001264

4-year private university and liberal arts college in small city, affiliated with Church of Christ.
Enrollment: 3,381 undergrads, 14% part-time. 751 full-time freshmen.
Selectivity: Admits less than 50% of applicants.

BASIC COSTS (2008-2009)
Tuition and fees: $36,770.
Per-credit charge: $1,135.
Room and board: $10,480.

FINANCIAL AID PICTURE (2007-2008)
Students with need: Out of 456 full-time freshmen who applied for aid, 270 were judged to have need. Of these, 262 received aid, and 47 had their full need met. Average financial aid package met 85% of need; average scholarship/grant was $24,654; average loan was $4,769. For part-time students, average financial aid package was $14,254.
Students without need: 155 full-time freshmen who did not demonstrate need for aid received scholarships/grants; average award was $19,673. No-need awards available for academics, art, athletics, minority status, music/drama, religious affiliation, ROTC.
Scholarships offered: 43 full-time freshmen received athletic scholarships; average amount $29,516.
Cumulative student debt: 62% of graduating class had student loans; average debt was $33,234.

FINANCIAL AID PROCEDURES
Forms required: FAFSA, institutional form.
Dates and Deadlines: Closing date 2/15. Applicants notified by 4/15; must reply within 2 week(s) of notification.

CONTACT
Janet Lockhart, Director of Financial Assistance
24255 Pacific Coast Highway, Malibu, CA 90263-4392
(310) 506-4301

Pitzer College

Claremont, California
www.pitzer.edu

Federal Code: 001172
CSS Code: 4619

4-year private liberal arts college in large town.
Enrollment: 999 undergrads, 4% part-time. 243 full-time freshmen.
Selectivity: Admits less than 50% of applicants.

BASIC COSTS (2008-2009)

Tuition and fees: $37,870.
Room and board: $10,930.
Additional info: Part-time tuition: $4,313 per course.

FINANCIAL AID PICTURE (2007-2008)

Students with need: Out of 110 full-time freshmen who applied for aid, 83 were judged to have need. Of these, 83 received aid, and 83 had their full need met. Average financial aid package met 100% of need; average scholarship/grant was $26,794; average loan was $3,092. For part-time students, average financial aid package was $19,404.
Students without need: 18 full-time freshmen who did not demonstrate need for aid received scholarships/grants; average award was $5,000. No-need awards available for academics, leadership.
Scholarships offered: Trustee Community Scholar Award; $10,000 per year; 20 awarded; based on extraordinary academic achievement, outstanding leadership or exceptional community service.
Cumulative student debt: 43% of graduating class had student loans; average debt was $24,790.

FINANCIAL AID PROCEDURES

Forms required: FAFSA, CSS PROFILE, state aid form.
Dates and Deadlines: Closing date 2/1. Applicants notified by 4/1; must reply by 5/1.
Transfers: Closing date 3/1. Applicants notified by 5/15; must reply by 6/15.

CONTACT

Margaret Carothers, Director of Financial Aid
1050 North Mills Avenue, Claremont, CA 91711-6101
(909) 621-8208

Platt College: Huntington Beach

Huntington Beach, California
www.plattcollege.edu

Federal Code: 026203

2-year for-profit visual arts and technical college in large city.
Enrollment: 95 undergrads.

BASIC COSTS (2007-2008)

Additional info: Full academic program tuition ranges from $28,000 to $59,820. Tuition at time of enrollment locked for 2 years.

FINANCIAL AID PICTURE

Students with need: Need-based aid available for full-time and part-time students. Work study available nights.

FINANCIAL AID PROCEDURES

Forms required: FAFSA, institutional form.
Dates and Deadlines: Priority date 3/2; no closing date. Applicants notified on a rolling basis starting 1/1.

CONTACT

Melinda Serban
7755 Center Avenue, Suite 400, Huntington Beach, CA 92647
(714) 373-3240

Platt College: Los Angeles

Alhambra, California
www.plattcollege.edu

Federal Code: 030627

2-year for-profit visual arts and technical college in very large city.
Enrollment: 135 undergrads.

BASIC COSTS (2007-2008)

Additional info: Varies by program: associate degree cost range $26,780 (paralegal) to $28,370 (information technology). Tuition at time of enrollment locked for 2 years.

FINANCIAL AID PICTURE

Students with need: Need-based aid available for full-time and part-time students. Work study available nights.

FINANCIAL AID PROCEDURES

Forms required: FAFSA, institutional form.
Dates and Deadlines: Priority date 3/2; no closing date. Applicants notified on a rolling basis starting 1/1.

CONTACT

Frank Cardoza, Financial Aid Coordinator
1000 South Fremont Avenue A9W, Alhambra, CA 91803
(626) 300-5444 ext. 230

Platt College: Ontario

Ontario, California
www.plattcollege.edu

Federal Code: 030627

4-year for-profit branch campus and technical college in small city.
Enrollment: 250 undergrads.

BASIC COSTS (2007-2008)

Additional info: Annual tuition varies by program: $10,300–$14,230. Tuition at time of enrollment locked for 4 years.

FINANCIAL AID PICTURE

Students with need: Need-based aid available for full-time and part-time students. Work study available nights.
Scholarships offered: Presidential Scholarship, CAPPS Scholarship, Imagine America Scholarship: $1,000 each; based on application and essay; approximately 100 plus available per calendar year.

FINANCIAL AID PROCEDURES

Forms required: FAFSA, institutional form.
Dates and Deadlines: Priority date 3/2; no closing date. Applicants notified on a rolling basis starting 1/1.
Transfers: No deadline.

CONTACT

Rosemarie Young, Regional Director of Compliance and Civil Rights
3700 Inland Empire Boulevard, Ontario, CA 91764
(909) 941-9410

Platt College: San Diego

San Diego, California
www.platt.edu

Federal Code: 023043

4-year for-profit visual arts and technical college in very large city.
Enrollment: 281 undergrads. 168 full-time freshmen.
Selectivity: Open admission; but selective for some programs and for out-of-state students.

BASIC COSTS (2007-2008)

Additional info: Total program costs range from $16,200 to $28,400, depending on the program chosen. Bachelor degree tuition varies Tuition at time of enrollment locked for 4 years.

FINANCIAL AID PICTURE (2006-2007)

Students with need: 35% of average financial aid package awarded as scholarships/grants, 65% awarded as loans/jobs. Need-based aid available for part-time students.

FINANCIAL AID PROCEDURES

Forms required: FAFSA, state aid form, institutional form.
Dates and Deadlines: Closing date 3/2. Applicants notified on a rolling basis; must reply within 1 week(s) of notification.

CONTACT

Opel Oliver, Director of Financial Aid
6250 El Cajon Boulevard, San Diego, CA 92115
(619) 265-0107

Point Loma Nazarene University

San Diego, California
www.pointloma.edu   Federal Code: 001262

4-year private university and liberal arts college in very large city, affiliated with Church of the Nazarene.
Enrollment: 2,337 undergrads, 3% part-time. 468 full-time freshmen.
Selectivity: Admits 50 to 75% of applicants.

BASIC COSTS (2008-2009)

Tuition and fees: $25,120.
Room and board: $8,170.

FINANCIAL AID PICTURE (2006-2007)

Students with need: Out of 388 full-time freshmen who applied for aid, 293 were judged to have need. Of these, 291 received aid, and 44 had their full need met. Average financial aid package met 55% of need; average scholarship/grant was $10,664; average loan was $2,256. For part-time students, average financial aid package was $14,113.
Students without need: 115 full-time freshmen who did not demonstrate need for aid received scholarships/grants; average award was $8,422.
Scholarships offered: 12 full-time freshmen received athletic scholarships; average amount $8,542.
Cumulative student debt: 86% of graduating class had student loans; average debt was $19,525.

FINANCIAL AID PROCEDURES

Forms required: FAFSA, institutional form.
Dates and Deadlines: Closing date 3/2. Applicants notified on a rolling basis starting 3/1.
Transfers: Must reply within 4 week(s) of notification.

CONTACT

Pam Macias, Associate Director, Financial Aid
3900 Lomaland Drive, San Diego, CA 92106-2899
(619) 849-2068

Pomona College

Claremont, California   Federal Code: 001173
www.pomona.edu   CSS Code: 4607

4-year private liberal arts college in large town.
Enrollment: 1,521 undergrads. 375 full-time freshmen.
Selectivity: Admits less than 50% of applicants.

BASIC COSTS (2008-2009)

Tuition and fees: $35,625.
Room and board: $12,220.

FINANCIAL AID PICTURE (2006-2007)

Students with need: Out of 249 full-time freshmen who applied for aid, 190 were judged to have need. Of these, 190 received aid, and 190 had their full need met. Average financial aid package met 100% of need; average scholarship/grant was $29,000; average loan was $2,000. Need-based aid available for part-time students.
Students without need: This college awards aid only to students with need.
Cumulative student debt: 54% of graduating class had student loans; average debt was $11,300.

FINANCIAL AID PROCEDURES

Forms required: FAFSA, CSS PROFILE, state aid form.
Dates and Deadlines: Closing date 2/1. Applicants notified by 4/10; must reply by 5/1.
Transfers: Closing date 3/1. Candidates required to submit finanical aid transcript from previous institution directly to the college.

CONTACT

Patricia Coye, Director of Financial Aid
333 North College Way, Claremont, CA 91711-6312
(909) 621-8205

Reedley College

Reedley, California
www.reedleycollege.edu   Federal Code: 001308

2-year public community college in large town.
Enrollment: 6,472 undergrads.
Selectivity: Open admission.

BASIC COSTS (2007-2008)

Tuition and fees: $628; out-of-state residents $5,818.
Per-credit charge: $20; out-of-state residents $193.
Room and board: $4,880.
Additional info: Tuition/fee waivers available for adults, minority students, unemployed or children of unemployed.

FINANCIAL AID PICTURE

Students with need: Need-based aid available for full-time and part-time students.
Students without need: This college awards aid only to students with need.
Additional info: Board of Governors fee waiver available for low-income students. Book voucher available for EOPS students.

FINANCIAL AID PROCEDURES

Forms required: FAFSA, state aid form.
Dates and Deadlines: Priority date 3/2; no closing date. Applicants notified on a rolling basis starting 3/2; must reply within 3 week(s) of notification.
Transfers: Priority date 4/15. March 2 deadline for California grants.

CONTACT

Christina Cortes, Director, Financial Aid
995 North Reed Avenue, Reedley, CA 93654
(559) 638-3641

PART III: FINANCIAL AID COLLEGE BY COLLEGE

Rio Hondo College
Whittier, California
www.riohondo.edu   Federal Code: 001269

2-year public community college in small city.
Enrollment: 8,862 undergrads.
Selectivity: Open admission; but selective for some programs.

BASIC COSTS (2007-2008)
Tuition and fees: $626; out-of-state residents $5,816.
Per-credit charge: $20; out-of-state residents $193.

FINANCIAL AID PICTURE (2006-2007)
Students with need: 91% of average financial aid package awarded as scholarships/grants, 9% awarded as loans/jobs. Need-based aid available for part-time students.

FINANCIAL AID PROCEDURES
Forms required: FAFSA.
Dates and Deadlines: Priority date 7/15; no closing date. Applicants notified on a rolling basis.

CONTACT
Maria Romero, Director Financial Aid
3600 Workman Mill Road, Whittier, CA 90601-1699
(562) 908-3411

Riverside Community College
Riverside, California
www.rcc.edu   Federal Code: 001270

2-year public community college in large city.
Enrollment: 14,882 undergrads.
Selectivity: Open admission; but selective for some programs.

BASIC COSTS (2007-2008)
Tuition and fees: $648; out-of-state residents $5,838.
Per-credit charge: $20; out-of-state residents $193.
Additional info: Tuition/fee waivers available for adults, unemployed or children of unemployed.

FINANCIAL AID PICTURE
Students with need: Need-based aid available for full-time and part-time students. Work study available nights, weekends, and for part-time students.
Students without need: No-need awards available for academics, alumni affiliation, art, leadership, minority status, music/drama, state/district residency.

FINANCIAL AID PROCEDURES
Forms required: FAFSA, institutional form.
Dates and Deadlines: Priority date 3/1; no closing date. Applicants notified on a rolling basis starting 7/1.
Transfers: Students who received financial aid at another institution and earned less than 2.0 GPA ineligible for aid during first semester. Students must complete 6 units and earn 2.0 GPA to be eligible.

CONTACT
Eugenia Vincent, District Dean of Student Financial Services
4800 Magnolia Avenue, Riverside, CA 92506
(951) 222-8709

Sacramento City College
Sacramento, California
www.scc.losrios.edu   Federal Code: 001233

2-year public community college in large city.
Enrollment: 15,574 undergrads.
Selectivity: Open admission.

BASIC COSTS (2007-2008)
Tuition and fees: $632; out-of-state residents $5,822.
Per-credit charge: $20; out-of-state residents $193.

FINANCIAL AID PICTURE
Students with need: Need-based aid available for full-time and part-time students. Work study available nights, weekends, and for part-time students.

FINANCIAL AID PROCEDURES
Forms required: FAFSA, state aid form.
Dates and Deadlines: Priority date 3/2; no closing date. Applicants notified on a rolling basis starting 7/1; must reply within 2 week(s) of notification.
Transfers: Priority date 5/30.

CONTACT
Pat Maga, Financial Aid Supervisor
3835 Freeport Boulevard, Sacramento, CA 95822
(916) 558-2546

Saddleback College
Mission Viejo, California
www.saddleback.edu   Federal Code: 008918

2-year public community college in small city.
Enrollment: 9,479 undergrads.
Selectivity: Open admission; but selective for some programs.

BASIC COSTS (2007-2008)
Tuition and fees: $628; out-of-state residents $5,818.
Per-credit charge: $20; out-of-state residents $193.

FINANCIAL AID PICTURE (2006-2007)
Students with need: 70% of average financial aid package awarded as scholarships/grants, 30% awarded as loans/jobs. Need-based aid available for part-time students.
Students without need: This college awards aid only to students with need.

FINANCIAL AID PROCEDURES
Forms required: FAFSA.
Dates and Deadlines: Closing date 6/30. Applicants notified on a rolling basis starting 4/1.

CONTACT
Mary Hall, Director, Financial Aid
28000 Marguerite Parkway, Mission Viejo, CA 92692
(949) 582-4860

St. Mary's College of California
Moraga, California
www.stmarys-ca.edu   Federal Code: 001302

4-year private liberal arts college in large town, affiliated with Roman Catholic Church.
Enrollment: 2,504 undergrads, 5% part-time. 611 full-time freshmen.
Selectivity: Admits over 75% of applicants.

BASIC COSTS (2008-2009)
Tuition and fees: $33,250.
Room and board: $11,680.

FINANCIAL AID PICTURE (2007-2008)
Students with need: Out of 456 full-time freshmen who applied for aid, 391 were judged to have need. Of these, 382 received aid, and 41 had their full need met. Average financial aid package met 64% of need; average scholarship/grant was $18,857; average loan was $3,787. For part-time students, average financial aid package was $3,690.
Students without need: 32 full-time freshmen who did not demonstrate need for aid received scholarships/grants; average award was $13,060. No-need awards available for academics, alumni affiliation, athletics, leadership.
Scholarships offered: *Merit:* Honors at Entrance Scholarship Awards: Freshman students admitted with 3.7 GPA or higher and combined SAT score of at least 1200, or transfers with 30 + transferable academic semester units and 3.5 GPA; for fall term applicants must be admitted by March 1; $8,000 annually. Presidential Scholars Scholarships: for freshmen with 3.8 GPA or higher and combined SAT score of at least 1350 (exclusive of writing) $12,000 annually. Students who receive Presidential Scholarship will also receive Honors at Entrance Scholarship for total of $20,000 annually. *Athletic:* 48 full-time freshmen received athletic scholarships; average amount $24,586.
Cumulative student debt: 51% of graduating class had student loans; average debt was $26,230.

FINANCIAL AID PROCEDURES
Forms required: FAFSA, state aid form.
Dates and Deadlines: Priority date 2/15; no closing date. Applicants notified on a rolling basis starting 3/15; must reply by 5/1 or within 2 week(s) of notification.
Transfers: To receive consideration for all types of financial aid, transfer students must be admitted by March 1 prior to enrolling in the following fall term.

CONTACT
Linda Judge, Director of Financial Aid
Box 4800, Moraga, CA 94575-4800
(925) 631-4370

Samuel Merritt College
Oakland, California
www.samuelmerritt.edu   Federal Code: 007012

Upper-division private health science and nursing college in large city.
Enrollment: 368 undergrads, 2% part-time.
Selectivity: GED not accepted.

BASIC COSTS (2008-2009)
Tuition and fees: $33,572.
Per-credit charge: $1,370.
Room only: $6,344.

FINANCIAL AID PICTURE (2006-2007)
Students with need: Average financial aid package for all full-time undergraduates was $33,000; for part-time $26,000. 44% awarded as scholarships/grants, 56% awarded as loans/jobs. Work study available nights, weekends, and for part-time students.
Students without need: No-need awards available for academics, leadership, minority status.
Cumulative student debt: 97% of graduating class had student loans; average debt was $48,615.
Additional info: Ongoing private scholarships available. Students eligible to work in Medical Center (associated with college).

FINANCIAL AID PROCEDURES
Dates and Deadlines: No deadline.

Transfers: Priority date 3/1; no deadline. Applicants notified on a rolling basis; must reply within 3 week(s) of notification.

CONTACT
Mary Robinson, Director of Financial Aid
370 Hawthorne Avenue, Oakland, CA 94609-9954
(510) 869-6511

San Diego Christian College
El Cajon, California
www.sdcc.edu   Federal Code: 012031

4-year private liberal arts college in small city, affiliated with nondenominational tradition.
Enrollment: 469 undergrads, 10% part-time. 80 full-time freshmen.
Selectivity: Admits less than 50% of applicants.

BASIC COSTS (2007-2008)
Tuition and fees: $19,070.
Per-credit charge: $607.
Room and board: $7,540.

FINANCIAL AID PICTURE (2007-2008)
Students with need: Out of 55 full-time freshmen who applied for aid, 48 were judged to have need. Of these, 48 received aid, and 34 had their full need met. Average financial aid package met 85% of need; average scholarship/grant was $6,000; average loan was $3,500. Need-based aid available for part-time students.
Students without need: 17 full-time freshmen who did not demonstrate need for aid received scholarships/grants; average award was $5,192. No-need awards available for academics, athletics, leadership, music/drama, religious affiliation.
Scholarships offered: 31 full-time freshmen received athletic scholarships; average amount $8,464.

FINANCIAL AID PROCEDURES
Forms required: FAFSA, state aid form, institutional form.
Dates and Deadlines: Priority date 3/2; closing date 7/15. Applicants notified on a rolling basis starting 4/1; must reply by 5/1 or within 4 week(s) of notification.

CONTACT
Nancy Demars, Financial Aid Director
2100 Greenfield Drive, El Cajon, CA 92019-1157
(619) 590-1786

San Diego City College
San Diego, California
www.sdccd.edu   Federal Code: 001273

2-year public community college in very large city.
Enrollment: 6,186 undergrads.
Selectivity: Open admission.

BASIC COSTS (2007-2008)
Tuition and fees: $626; out-of-state residents $5,516.
Per-credit charge: $20; out-of-state residents $180.
Additional info: Tuition/fee waivers available for unemployed or children of unemployed.

FINANCIAL AID PICTURE (2006-2007)
Students with need: 80% of average financial aid package awarded as scholarships/grants, 20% awarded as loans/jobs. Need-based aid available for part-time students.
Students without need: This college awards aid only to students with need.

FINANCIAL AID PROCEDURES

Forms required: FAFSA.

Dates and Deadlines: Priority date 4/15; no closing date. Applicants notified on a rolling basis starting 7/1; must reply within 4 week(s) of notification.

Transfers: No deadline. Aid is limited to remaining eligibility based on receipt of aid from previous college.

CONTACT

Greg Sanchez, Director of Financial Aid

1313 Park Boulevard, San Diego, CA 92101-4787

(619) 388-3501

San Diego Miramar College

San Diego, California

www.miramarcollege.net   Federal Code: 014172

2-year public community college in very large city.

Enrollment: 9,020 undergrads.

Selectivity: Open admission.

BASIC COSTS (2007-2008)

Tuition and fees: $626; out-of-state residents $5,516.

Per-credit charge: $20; out-of-state residents $183.

Additional info: Tuition/fee waivers available for unemployed or children of unemployed.

FINANCIAL AID PICTURE

Students with need: Need-based aid available for full-time and part-time students.

Additional info: Private scholarships available.

FINANCIAL AID PROCEDURES

Forms required: FAFSA.

Dates and Deadlines: Priority date 3/2; no closing date. Applicants notified on a rolling basis; must reply within 3 week(s) of notification.

Transfers: No deadline. Transfers advised to apply early.

CONTACT

Ruthy Ofina, Financial Aid Officer

10440 Black Mountain Road, San Diego, CA 92126-2999

(619) 388-7865

San Diego State University

San Diego, California

www.sdsu.edu   Federal Code: 001151

4-year public university in very large city.

Enrollment: 30,460 undergrads, 17% part-time. 4,506 full-time freshmen.

Selectivity: Admits less than 50% of applicants.

BASIC COSTS (2007-2008)

Tuition and fees: $3,428; out-of-state residents $13,598.

Room and board: $10,904.

FINANCIAL AID PICTURE (2007-2008)

Students with need: Out of 3,440 full-time freshmen who applied for aid, 2,100 were judged to have need. Of these, 2,010 received aid, and 85 had their full need met. Average financial aid package met 67% of need; average scholarship/grant was $6,540; average loan was $2,350. For part-time students, average financial aid package was $7,200.

Students without need: 180 full-time freshmen who did not demonstrate need for aid received scholarships/grants; average award was $1,940. No-need awards available for academics, alumni affiliation, art, athletics, leadership, music/drama, ROTC, state/district residency.

Scholarships offered: *Merit:* Various departmental scholarships are open to first time freshman with declared majors. Brian Schultz Memorial Scholar-

ship, amount varies (1 awarded); recipient must be a cancer survivor or have been affected by cancer. *Athletic:* 80 full-time freshmen received athletic scholarships; average amount $12,500.

Cumulative student debt: 44% of graduating class had student loans; average debt was $14,500.

FINANCIAL AID PROCEDURES

Forms required: FAFSA, state aid form.

Dates and Deadlines: Priority date 3/2; no closing date. Applicants notified on a rolling basis starting 2/14.

Transfers: No deadline. Applicants notified on a rolling basis.

CONTACT

Chrys Dutton, Director of Financial Aid

5500 Campanile Drive, San Diego, CA 92182-7455

(619) 594-6323

San Francisco Art Institute

San Francisco, California

www.sfai.edu   Federal Code: 003948

4-year private visual arts college in very large city.

Enrollment: 383 undergrads.

Selectivity: Admits less than 50% of applicants.

BASIC COSTS (2008-2009)

Tuition and fees: $30,215.

Per-credit charge: $1,378.

Room and board: $9,675.

Additional info: Room charges vary for 12-month contract.

FINANCIAL AID PICTURE (2007-2008)

Students with need: 58% of average financial aid package awarded as scholarships/grants, 42% awarded as loans/jobs. Need-based aid available for part-time students.

Students without need: No-need awards available for academics, art.

Scholarships offered: Several awards based on portfolio reviews during application for admissions process.

FINANCIAL AID PROCEDURES

Forms required: FAFSA.

Dates and Deadlines: Priority date 3/1; closing date 5/31. Applicants notified on a rolling basis starting 4/15; must reply within 3 week(s) of notification.

Transfers: Priority date 6/30; no deadline. Applicants notified on a rolling basis starting 4/1; must reply within 3 week(s) of notification.

CONTACT

Rose Gardner-Stadler, Director of Financial Aid

800 Chestnut Street, San Francisco, CA 94133-2299

(415) 749-4520

San Francisco Conservatory of Music

San Francisco, California

www.sfcm.edu   Federal Code: 001278

4-year private music college in very large city.

Enrollment: 230 undergrads.

BASIC COSTS (2007-2008)

Tuition and fees: $30,054.

Per-credit charge: $1,320.

FINANCIAL AID PICTURE

Students with need: Need-based aid available for full-time and part-time students.

Students without need: This college awards aid only to students with need.

FINANCIAL AID PROCEDURES

Forms required: FAFSA, institutional form.

Dates and Deadlines: Priority date 3/1; no closing date. Applicants notified on a rolling basis starting 3/15; must reply by 5/1 or within 2 week(s) of notification.

Transfers: Priority date 2/1; closing date 4/1.

CONTACT

Doris Howard, Financial Aid Officer
50 Oak Street, San Francisco, CA 94102
(415) 503-6214

San Francisco State University
San Francisco, California
www.sfsu.edu   Federal Code: 001154

4-year public university in very large city.

Enrollment: 24,376 undergrads, 20% part-time. 3,342 full-time freshmen.

Selectivity: Admits 50 to 75% of applicants.

BASIC COSTS (2007-2008)

Tuition and fees: $3,456; out-of-state residents $13,626.

Room and board: $11,500.

FINANCIAL AID PICTURE (2007-2008)

Students with need: Average financial aid package met 64% of need; average scholarship/grant was $7,098; average loan was $2,370. For part-time students, average financial aid package was $7,169.

Students without need: This college awards aid only to students with need.

Scholarships offered: Presidential Scholarship; 3.8 GPA and California residency required.

Cumulative student debt: 39% of graduating class had student loans; average debt was $15,337.

FINANCIAL AID PROCEDURES

Forms required: FAFSA.

Dates and Deadlines: Priority date 3/2; no closing date. Applicants notified on a rolling basis starting 2/1; must reply within 2 week(s) of notification.

CONTACT

Barbara Hubler, Director of Financial Aid
1600 Holloway Avenue, San Francisco, CA 94132
(415) 338-7000

San Joaquin Delta College
Stockton, California
www.deltacollege.edu   Federal Code: 001280

2-year public community college in large city.

Enrollment: 12,237 undergrads.

Selectivity: Open admission; but selective for some programs.

BASIC COSTS (2007-2008)

Tuition and fees: $600; out-of-state residents $5,790.

Per-credit charge: $20; out-of-state residents $193.

FINANCIAL AID PICTURE

Students with need: Need-based aid available for full-time and part-time students. Work study available nights, weekends, and for part-time students.

Students without need: No-need awards available for academics, athletics.

Additional info: Enrollment fee waivers available for low-income California residents.

FINANCIAL AID PROCEDURES

Forms required: FAFSA, institutional form.

Dates and Deadlines: Priority date 4/15; no closing date. Applicants notified on a rolling basis starting 5/1; must reply within 3 week(s) of notification.

Transfers: No deadline.

CONTACT

Denise Donn, Director of Financial Aid
5151 Pacific Avenue, Stockton, CA 95207-6370
(209) 954-5115

San Joaquin Valley College
Visalia, California
www.sjvc.edu   Federal Code: 021207

2-year for-profit junior college in small city.

Enrollment: 1,040 undergrads.

Selectivity: Open admission; but selective for some programs.

BASIC COSTS (2007-2008)

Additional info: Costs may vary with program, annual tuition includes textbooks and supplies.

FINANCIAL AID PICTURE

Students with need: Need-based aid available for full-time students.

FINANCIAL AID PROCEDURES

Forms required: FAFSA, state aid form, institutional form.

Dates and Deadlines: No deadline.

CONTACT

Kevin Robinson, Vice President of Student Financial Services
8400 West Mineral King Avenue, Visalia, CA 93291-9283
(559) 651-2500

San Jose State University
San Jose, California
www.sjsu.edu   Federal Code: 001155

4-year public university and liberal arts college in very large city.

Enrollment: 24,390 undergrads, 23% part-time. 3,085 full-time freshmen.

Selectivity: Admits 50 to 75% of applicants.

BASIC COSTS (2007-2008)

Tuition and fees: $3,632; out-of-state residents $13,802.

Room and board: $9,505.

FINANCIAL AID PICTURE

Students with need: Need-based aid available for full-time and part-time students. Work study available nights, weekends, and for part-time students.

Students without need: This college awards aid only to students with need.

FINANCIAL AID PROCEDURES

Forms required: FAFSA.

Dates and Deadlines: Priority date 3/2; closing date 6/22. Applicants notified on a rolling basis starting 4/1; must reply within 2 week(s) of notification.

CONTACT

Colleen Brown, Director of Financial Aid
One Washington Square, San Jose, CA 95192-0011
(408) 283-7500

Santa Barbara City College

Santa Barbara, California
www.sbcc.edu   Federal Code: 001285

2-year public community college in small city.
Enrollment: 7,771 undergrads, 43% part-time. 1,393 full-time freshmen.
Selectivity: Open admission; but selective for some programs.

BASIC COSTS (2007-2008)

Tuition and fees: $670; out-of-state residents $5,860.
Per-credit charge: $20; out-of-state residents $193.
Additional info: Tuition/fee waivers available for unemployed or children of unemployed.

FINANCIAL AID PICTURE

Students with need: Need-based aid available for full-time and part-time students.
Additional info: California residents may qualify for Board of Governor's Financial Assistance Program, which will allow institutions to waive enrollment fee.

FINANCIAL AID PROCEDURES

Forms required: FAFSA.
Dates and Deadlines: No deadline. Applicants notified on a rolling basis starting 5/1; must reply within 2 week(s) of notification.

CONTACT

Brad Hardison, Director, Financial Aid
721 Cliff Drive, Santa Barbara, CA 93109-2394
(805) 965-0581 ext. 2716

Santa Clara University

Santa Clara, California   Federal Code: 001326
www.scu.edu   CSS Code: 4851

4-year private university in small city, affiliated with Roman Catholic Church.
Enrollment: 4,799 undergrads, 2% part-time. 1,202 full-time freshmen.
Selectivity: Admits 50 to 75% of applicants. GED not accepted.

BASIC COSTS (2008-2009)

Tuition and fees: $34,950.
Per-credit charge: $1,165.
Room and board: $11,070.

FINANCIAL AID PICTURE (2007-2008)

Students with need: Average financial aid package met 72% of need; average scholarship/grant was $16,111; average loan was $4,398. Need-based aid available for part-time students.
Students without need: 331 full-time freshmen who did not demonstrate need for aid received scholarships/grants; average award was $8,363. No-need awards available for academics, alumni affiliation, athletics, music/drama, ROTC.
Scholarships offered: *Merit:* Presidential Scholar at Entry: full tuition; 10 students awarded; admitted with distinction. Provost Scholar: half tuition; 40 students awarded; admitted with distinction. National Merit Scholarship: $2,000; 4 students awarded. Dean's Scholarship: $3,000 to $12,000; admitted with distinction. Honors Program Scholarship: $2,000; by invitation and based on high academic achievement. Bannan Merit Scholarship: amount varies; based on high academic achievement. Jesuit Ignation Award: amount varies, to students of Jesuit high schools. *Athletic:* 49 full-time freshmen received athletic scholarships; average amount $17,697.
Cumulative student debt: 46% of graduating class had student loans; average debt was $23,773.

FINANCIAL AID PROCEDURES

Forms required: FAFSA, CSS PROFILE.

Dates and Deadlines: Priority date 2/1; no closing date. Applicants notified by 4/1; must reply by 5/1 or within 2 week(s) of notification.
Transfers: No deadline. Applicants notified on a rolling basis starting 4/1; must reply by 5/1 or within 2 week(s) of notification.

CONTACT

Richard Toomey, Dean of Financial Services
500 El Camino Real, Santa Clara, CA 95053
(408) 554-4505

Santa Monica College

Santa Monica, California
www.smc.edu   Federal Code: 001286

2-year public community college in small city.
Enrollment: 20,248 undergrads.
Selectivity: Open admission; but selective for some programs.

BASIC COSTS (2007-2008)

Tuition and fees: $632; out-of-state residents $5,372.
Per-credit charge: $20; out-of-state residents $178.

FINANCIAL AID PICTURE

Students with need: Need-based aid available for full-time and part-time students.

FINANCIAL AID PROCEDURES

Forms required: FAFSA, institutional form.
Dates and Deadlines: No deadline. Applicants notified on a rolling basis starting 7/1; must reply within 2 week(s) of notification.
Transfers: No deadline.

CONTACT

Steve Myrow, Director of Financial Aid
1900 Pico Boulevard, Santa Monica, CA 90405-1628
(310) 434-4871

Santa Rosa Junior College

Santa Rosa, California
www.santarosa.edu   Federal Code: 001287

2-year public community college in small city.
Enrollment: 25,734 undergrads.
Selectivity: Open admission.

BASIC COSTS (2007-2008)

Tuition and fees: $628; out-of-state residents $5,818.
Per-credit charge: $20; out-of-state residents $193.

FINANCIAL AID PICTURE (2006-2007)

Students with need: 82% of average financial aid package awarded as scholarships/grants, 18% awarded as loans/jobs. Need-based aid available for part-time students. Work study available nights, weekends, and for part-time students.
Students without need: No-need awards available for academics, art, leadership, music/drama.
Scholarships offered: Doyle Scholarships available (need-based and GPA based) for high school graduates or college applicants with 2.75 GPA or higher.
Additional info: California's Board of Governors Program (BOG) provides fee waivers for applicants with need, welfare recipients, and families with low income.

FINANCIAL AID PROCEDURES

Forms required: FAFSA.
Dates and Deadlines: Priority date 3/1; no closing date. Applicants notified on a rolling basis starting 4/5.

CONTACT
Kristin Shear, Director of Financial Services
1501 Mendocino Avenue, Santa Rosa, CA 95401
(707) 527-4471

Santiago Canyon College
Orange, California
www.sccollege.edu

2-year public community college in small city.
Enrollment: 8,685 undergrads.
Selectivity: Open admission.

BASIC COSTS (2007-2008)
Tuition and fees: $628; out-of-state residents $6,148.
Per-credit charge: $20; out-of-state residents $204.
Additional info: Tuition/fee waivers available for adults, minority students, unemployed or children of unemployed.

FINANCIAL AID PICTURE
Students with need: Need-based aid available for full-time and part-time students.
Students without need: This college awards aid only to students with need.

FINANCIAL AID PROCEDURES
Forms required: FAFSA, state aid form, institutional form.
Dates and Deadlines: Priority date 7/1; no closing date. Applicants notified on a rolling basis starting 6/1.
Transfers: No deadline. Applicants notified by 6/1.

CONTACT
Syed Rizvi, Financial Aid Coordinator
8045 East Chapman Avenue, Orange, CA 92869
(714) 628-4876

School of Urban Missions: Oakland
Oakland, California
www.sum.edu   Federal Code: 037524

4-year private Bible college in very large city, affiliated with Assemblies of God.
Enrollment: 62 undergrads, 6% part-time. 5 full-time freshmen.
Selectivity: Admits over 75% of applicants.

BASIC COSTS (2008-2009)
Tuition and fees: $7,180.
Per-credit charge: $235.
Room only: $2,400.

FINANCIAL AID PICTURE (2006-2007)
Students with need: 33% of average financial aid package awarded as scholarships/grants, 67% awarded as loans/jobs. Need-based aid available for part-time students.
Students without need: No-need awards available for academics, leadership, religious affiliation.

FINANCIAL AID PROCEDURES
Forms required: FAFSA, state aid form, institutional form.
Dates and Deadlines: No deadline.
Transfers: No deadline. Applicants notified on a rolling basis.

CONTACT
Julie Williams, Financial Aid Director
735 105th Avenue, Oakland, CA 94603
(510) 567-6174

Scripps College
Claremont, California   Federal Code: 001174
www.scrippscollege.edu   CSS Code: 4693

4-year private liberal arts college for women in large town.
Enrollment: 889 undergrads. 227 full-time freshmen.
Selectivity: Admits less than 50% of applicants.

BASIC COSTS (2008-2009)
Tuition and fees: $37,950.
Per-credit charge: $1,179.
Room and board: $11,500.

FINANCIAL AID PICTURE
Students with need: Need-based aid available for full-time and part-time students. Work study available nights, weekends, and for part-time students.
Students without need: No-need awards available for academics, leadership.
Scholarships offered: James E. Scripps Scholarship; variable amount up to half-tuition; renewable; for distinguished young women whose intellectual and personal promise can be developed with a Scripps education.

FINANCIAL AID PROCEDURES
Forms required: FAFSA, CSS PROFILE.
Dates and Deadlines: Priority date 2/1; no closing date. Applicants notified by 4/1; must reply by 5/1 or within 2 week(s) of notification.
Transfers: Priority date 4/1; no deadline. Applicants notified by 5/1; must reply by 6/1 or within 2 week(s) of notification. Students applying for admission as a transfer student should be aware that financial aid may be limited or unavailable.

CONTACT
David Levy, Director of Financial Aid
1030 Columbia Avenue, Claremont, CA 91711
(909) 621-8275

Shasta College
Redding, California
www.shastacollege.edu   Federal Code: 001289

2-year public community college in small city.
Enrollment: 5,021 undergrads.
Selectivity: Open admission; but selective for some programs.

BASIC COSTS (2007-2008)
Tuition and fees: $673; out-of-state residents $5,653.
Per-credit charge: $20; out-of-state residents $186.
Room only: $2,610.

FINANCIAL AID PICTURE
Students with need: Need-based aid available for full-time and part-time students.
Students without need: This college awards aid only to students with need.

FINANCIAL AID PROCEDURES
Forms required: FAFSA, institutional form.
Dates and Deadlines: Priority date 3/2; no closing date. Applicants notified on a rolling basis starting 7/1.

CONTACT
Benna Starrett, Director of Financial Aid
Box 496006, Redding, CA 96049-6006
(530) 225-4735

Sierra College
Rocklin, California
www.sierracollege.edu   Federal Code: 001290

2-year public community college in large town.
Enrollment: 12,281 undergrads.
Selectivity: Open admission.

BASIC COSTS (2007-2008)
Tuition and fees: $640; out-of-state residents $5,830.
Per-credit charge: $20; out-of-state residents $193.
Room and board: $7,090.
Additional info: Tuition/fee waivers available for unemployed or children of unemployed.

FINANCIAL AID PICTURE
Students with need: Need-based aid available for full-time and part-time students. Work study available nights, weekends, and for part-time students.

FINANCIAL AID PROCEDURES
Forms required: FAFSA.
Dates and Deadlines: Priority date 3/2; closing date 4/22. Applicants notified on a rolling basis starting 5/15.
Transfers: No deadline.

CONTACT
Patricia Efseaff, Dean of Student Services
5000 Rocklin Road, Rocklin, CA 95677
(916) 781-0568

Simpson University
Redding, California
www.simpsonuniversity.edu   Federal Code: 001291

4-year private liberal arts college in small city, affiliated with Christian and Missionary Alliance.
Enrollment: 891 undergrads, 1% part-time. 180 full-time freshmen.
Selectivity: Admits 50 to 75% of applicants.

BASIC COSTS (2008-2009)
Tuition and fees: $19,500.
Per-credit charge: $825.
Room and board: $6,700.
Additional info: Tuition/fee waivers available for minority students.

FINANCIAL AID PICTURE (2006-2007)
Students with need: Out of 177 full-time freshmen who applied for aid, 170 were judged to have need. Of these, 170 received aid, and 60 had their full need met. Average financial aid package met 59% of need; average scholarship/grant was $10,406; average loan was $3,500. Need-based aid available for part-time students.
Students without need: 32 full-time freshmen who did not demonstrate need for aid received scholarships/grants; average award was $4,177. No-need awards available for academics, alumni affiliation, athletics, leadership, minority status, music/drama, religious affiliation, state/district residency.
Scholarships offered: *Merit:* Academic awards; up to full tuition for 4.0 GPA and 1200 minimum SAT (exclusive of Writing). *Athletic:* 61 full-time freshmen received athletic scholarships; average amount $2,500.
Additional info: Work-study programs available.

FINANCIAL AID PROCEDURES
Forms required: FAFSA, institutional form.
Dates and Deadlines: Priority date 3/2; no closing date. Applicants notified on a rolling basis starting 3/1; must reply within 4 week(s) of notification.
Transfers: No deadline. Applicants notified on a rolling basis starting 3/1; must reply within 4 week(s) of notification.

CONTACT
James Herberger, Director of Enrollment Management
2211 College View Drive, Redding, CA 96003-8606
(530) 226-4111

Skyline College
San Bruno, California
www.skylinecollege.edu   Federal Code: 007713

2-year public community college in small city.
Enrollment: 4,924 undergrads.
Selectivity: Open admission; but selective for some programs.

BASIC COSTS (2007-2008)
Tuition and fees: $628; out-of-state residents $6,148.
Per-credit charge: $20; out-of-state residents $204.

FINANCIAL AID PICTURE
Students with need: Need-based aid available for full-time and part-time students.

FINANCIAL AID PROCEDURES
Forms required: FAFSA, institutional form.
Dates and Deadlines: Priority date 3/2; no closing date. Applicants notified on a rolling basis starting 5/1; must reply within 2 week(s) of notification.

CONTACT
Maria Escobar, Director of Financial Aid
3300 College Drive, San Bruno, CA 94066
(650) 738-4236

Soka University of America
Aliso Viejo, California
www.soka.edu   Federal Code: 038144

4-year private university and liberal arts college in large town.
Enrollment: 362 undergrads. 101 full-time freshmen.
Selectivity: Admits 50 to 75% of applicants.

BASIC COSTS (2008-2009)
Tuition and fees: $23,434.
Room and board: $9,000.

FINANCIAL AID PICTURE (2007-2008)
Students with need: Out of 101 full-time freshmen who applied for aid, 101 were judged to have need. Of these, 101 received aid, and 2 had their full need met. Average financial aid package met 82% of need; average scholarship/grant was $8,750; average loan was $3,500. Need-based aid available for part-time students.
Students without need: 4 full-time freshmen who did not demonstrate need for aid received scholarships/grants; average award was $10,000. No-need awards available for academics.

FINANCIAL AID PROCEDURES
Forms required: FAFSA.
Dates and Deadlines: Closing date 3/1. Applicants notified on a rolling basis starting 3/15; must reply within 4 week(s) of notification.

CONTACT
Christopher Brown, Director of Admission and Financial Aid
1 University Drive, Aliso Viejo, CA 92656-8081
(949) 480-4150

Sonoma State University

Rohnert Park, California
www.sonoma.edu   Federal Code: 001156

4-year public university and liberal arts college in large town.
Enrollment: 7,603 undergrads, 4% part-time. 1,657 full-time freshmen.
Selectivity: Admits 50 to 75% of applicants.

BASIC COSTS (2007-2008)
Tuition and fees: $3,946; out-of-state residents $14,116.
Room and board: $9,730.

FINANCIAL AID PICTURE (2006-2007)
Students with need: Average financial aid package met 73% of need; average scholarship/grant was $6,853; average loan was $2,419. For part-time students, average financial aid package was $10,861.
Students without need: No-need awards available for academics, alumni affiliation, art, athletics, leadership, minority status, music/drama.
Cumulative student debt: 20% of graduating class had student loans; average debt was $15,170.

FINANCIAL AID PROCEDURES
Forms required: FAFSA.
Dates and Deadlines: Priority date 1/31; no closing date. Applicants notified on a rolling basis starting 3/15; must reply within 2 week(s) of notification.

CONTACT
Susan Gutierrez, Director, Financial Aid
1801 East Cotati Avenue, Rohnert Park, CA 94928
(707) 664-2389

Southern California Institute of Architecture

Los Angeles, California
www.sciarc.edu   Federal Code: 014073

5-year private visual arts and technical college in very large city.
Enrollment: 256 undergrads. 73 full-time freshmen.
Selectivity: Admits 50 to 75% of applicants.

BASIC COSTS (2008-2009)
Tuition and fees: $21,544.
Additional info: International student fee (one-time only) $500. International student mandatory health insurance premium (per year) $822.

FINANCIAL AID PICTURE (2007-2008)
Students with need: For part-time students, average financial aid package was $11,000.
Students without need: No-need awards available for academics, state/district residency.

FINANCIAL AID PROCEDURES
Forms required: FAFSA, institutional form.
Dates and Deadlines: No deadline. Must reply within 2 week(s) of notification.
Transfers: Priority date 3/2; closing date 5/2. Applicants notified on a rolling basis starting 4/15.

CONTACT
Helen Lara, Financial Aid Director
960 East 3rd Street, Los Angeles, CA 90013
(213) 613-2200 ext. 326

Southwestern College

Chula Vista, California
www.swccd.edu   Federal Code: 001294

2-year public community college in small city.
Enrollment: 19,839 undergrads.
Selectivity: Open admission; but selective for some programs.

BASIC COSTS (2007-2008)
Tuition and fees: $624; out-of-state residents $5,514.
Per-credit charge: $20; out-of-state residents $183.

FINANCIAL AID PICTURE
Students with need: Need-based aid available for full-time and part-time students. Work study available nights, weekends, and for part-time students.

FINANCIAL AID PROCEDURES
Forms required: FAFSA, state aid form.
Dates and Deadlines: Closing date 3/2. Applicants notified on a rolling basis starting 7/1.

CONTACT
Arthur Lopez, Director of Financial Aid
900 Otay Lakes Road, Chula Vista, CA 91910-7297
(619) 482-6357

Stanford University

Stanford, California   Federal Code: 001305
www.stanford.edu   CSS Code: 4704

4-year private university in small city.
Enrollment: 6,520 undergrads. 1,648 full-time freshmen.
Selectivity: Admits less than 50% of applicants.

BASIC COSTS (2008-2009)
Tuition and fees: $36,030.
Room and board: $11,182.

FINANCIAL AID PICTURE (2006-2007)
Students with need: Out of 1,017 full-time freshmen who applied for aid, 758 were judged to have need. Of these, 750 received aid, and 600 had their full need met. Average financial aid package met 100% of need; average scholarship/grant was $28,829; average loan was $1,939. Need-based aid available for part-time students.
Students without need: This college awards aid only to students with need.
Scholarships offered: 114 full-time freshmen received athletic scholarships; average amount $30,406.
Cumulative student debt: 44% of graduating class had student loans; average debt was $16,728.
Additional info: Families with annual incomes of less than $45,000 not expected to contribute to cost of tuition.

FINANCIAL AID PROCEDURES
Forms required: FAFSA, CSS PROFILE.
Dates and Deadlines: Priority date 2/15; no closing date. Applicants notified on a rolling basis starting 4/3; must reply by 5/1.
Transfers: Priority date 3/15.

CONTACT
Karen Cooper, Director, Financial Aid
Montag Hall, Stanford, CA 94305-6106
(650) 723-3058

Taft College
Taft, California
www.taftcollege.edu   Federal Code: 001309

2-year public community college in small town.
Enrollment: 1,684 undergrads.
Selectivity: Open admission.

BASIC COSTS (2007-2008)
Tuition and fees: $600; out-of-state residents $5,790.
Per-credit charge: $20; out-of-state residents $193.
Room and board: $3,468.

FINANCIAL AID PICTURE
Students with need: Need-based aid available for full-time and part-time students. Work study available nights.
Students without need: No-need awards available for academics.
Scholarships offered: Taft College Merit Awards: $250; for students from local high schools; available for 2 years; based on GPA of 3.0 or higher. Taft College High School Merit Award: $600; for students from local high schools. Taft College Nonresident Awards: $4,230; applied to nonresident tuition; available for 1 year; based on GPA of 3.0 or higher.

FINANCIAL AID PROCEDURES
Forms required: FAFSA, institutional form.
Dates and Deadlines: No deadline. Applicants notified on a rolling basis; must reply within 4 week(s) of notification.
Transfers: No deadline.

CONTACT
Gayle Roberts, Director of Financial Aid
29 Emmons Park Drive, Taft, CA 93268
(661) 763-7762

Thomas Aquinas College
Santa Paula, California
www.thomasaquinas.edu   Federal Code: 023580

4-year private liberal arts college in rural community, affiliated with Roman Catholic Church.
Enrollment: 360 undergrads. 102 full-time freshmen.
Selectivity: Admits 50 to 75% of applicants.

BASIC COSTS (2008-2009)
Tuition and fees: $21,400.
Room and board: $6,950.

FINANCIAL AID PICTURE (2007-2008)
Students with need: Out of 82 full-time freshmen who applied for aid, 71 were judged to have need. Of these, 71 received aid, and 71 had their full need met. Average financial aid package met 100% of need; average scholarship/grant was $12,148; average loan was $2,719.
Students without need: This college awards aid only to students with need.
Cumulative student debt: 62% of graduating class had student loans; average debt was $14,000.

FINANCIAL AID PROCEDURES
Forms required: FAFSA, state aid form, institutional form.
Dates and Deadlines: Closing date 3/2. Applicants notified on a rolling basis starting 1/1; must reply by 5/1 or within 2 week(s) of notification.

CONTACT
Gregory Becher, Director of Financial Aid
10,000 North Ojai Road, Santa Paula, CA 93060-9621
(800) 634-9797

University of California: Berkeley
Berkeley, California
www.berkeley.edu   Federal Code: 001312

4-year public university in small city.
Enrollment: 24,636 undergrads.
Selectivity: Admits less than 50% of applicants.

BASIC COSTS (2007-2008)
Tuition and fees: $7,164; out-of-state residents $26,784.
Room and board: $13,848.

FINANCIAL AID PICTURE
Students with need: Need-based aid available for full-time and part-time students.
Students without need: No-need awards available for academics.
Scholarships offered: University Scholarship, President's Undergraduate Fellowships, Regents and Chancellor's Scholarships, Alumni Scholarships.

FINANCIAL AID PROCEDURES
Forms required: FAFSA, state aid form.
Dates and Deadlines: Closing date 3/2. Applicants notified by 4/15.
Transfers: Closing date 3/2. Applicants notified by 4/15.

CONTACT
Cheryl Resh, Director, Financial Aid
110 Sproul Hall, #5800, Berkeley, CA 94720-5800
(510) 642-6000

University of California: Davis
Davis, California
www.ucdavis.edu   Federal Code: 001313

4-year public university in small city.
Enrollment: 23,373 undergrads, 1% part-time. 4,279 full-time freshmen.
Selectivity: Admits 50 to 75% of applicants.

BASIC COSTS (2007-2008)
Tuition and fees: $8,109; out-of-state residents $27,729.
Room and board: $11,533.
Additional info: Students must purchase the Student Health Insurance Plan (SHIP) unless they are able to prove comparable coverage.

FINANCIAL AID PICTURE (2006-2007)
Students with need: Out of 3,289 full-time freshmen who applied for aid, 2,263 were judged to have need. Of these, 2,129 received aid, and 381 had their full need met. Average financial aid package met 76% of need; average scholarship/grant was $11,037; average loan was $4,532. For part-time students, average financial aid package was $13,871.
Students without need: This college awards aid only to students with need.
Scholarships offered: 40 full-time freshmen received athletic scholarships; average amount $8,634.
Cumulative student debt: 46% of graduating class had student loans; average debt was $13,835.

FINANCIAL AID PROCEDURES
Forms required: FAFSA, state aid form.
Dates and Deadlines: Priority date 3/2; no closing date. Applicants notified on a rolling basis starting 3/15.

CONTACT
Kathryn Maloney, Interim Director, Financial Aid
178 Mrak Hall, Davis, CA 95616
(530) 752-2390

University of California: Irvine

Irvine, California
www.uci.edu   Federal Code: 001314

4-year public university in small city.
Enrollment: 21,696 undergrads, 2% part-time. 4,818 full-time freshmen.
Selectivity: Admits 50 to 75% of applicants.

BASIC COSTS (2007-2008)
Tuition and fees: $7,555; out-of-state residents $27,175.
Room and board: $10,266.

FINANCIAL AID PICTURE (2006-2007)
Students with need: Out of 3,603 full-time freshmen who applied for aid, 2,308 were judged to have need. Of these, 2,114 received aid, and 1,003 had their full need met. Average financial aid package met 83% of need; average scholarship/grant was $10,038; average loan was $5,458. For part-time students, average financial aid package was $10,524.
Students without need: 144 full-time freshmen who did not demonstrate need for aid received scholarships/grants; average award was $8,614. No-need awards available for academics, alumni affiliation, art, athletics, music/drama, state/district residency.
Scholarships offered: 42 full-time freshmen received athletic scholarships; average amount $9,120.
Cumulative student debt: 52% of graduating class had student loans; average debt was $12,074.

FINANCIAL AID PROCEDURES
Forms required: FAFSA, state aid form.
Dates and Deadlines: Closing date 3/2. Applicants notified by 4/1; must reply by 5/1.

CONTACT
Chris Shultz, Director of Financial Aid
204 Aldrich Hall, Irvine, CA 92697-1075
(949) 824-8262

University of California: Los Angeles

Los Angeles, California
www.ucla.edu   Federal Code: 001315

4-year public university in very large city.
Enrollment: 25,928 undergrads, 4% part-time. 4,515 full-time freshmen.
Selectivity: Admits less than 50% of applicants.

BASIC COSTS (2007-2008)
Tuition and fees: $7,038; out-of-state residents $26,658.
Room and board: $12,420.

FINANCIAL AID PICTURE (2006-2007)
Students with need: Out of 2,722 full-time freshmen who applied for aid, 2,228 were judged to have need. Of these, 2,228 received aid, and 705 had their full need met. Average financial aid package met 81% of need; average scholarship/grant was $12,276; average loan was $5,222. For part-time students, average financial aid package was $11,696.
Students without need: 274 full-time freshmen who did not demonstrate need for aid received scholarships/grants; average award was $4,054. No-need awards available for academics, alumni affiliation, athletics, ROTC.
Scholarships offered: 81 full-time freshmen received athletic scholarships; average amount $11,850.
Cumulative student debt: 46% of graduating class had student loans; average debt was $15,996.

FINANCIAL AID PROCEDURES
Forms required: FAFSA.
Dates and Deadlines: Priority date 3/2; no closing date. Applicants notified on a rolling basis starting 3/15; must reply within 3 week(s) of notification.

CONTACT
Ronald Johnson, Director, Financial Aid Office
1147 Murphy Hall, Los Angeles, CA 90095-1436
(310) 206-0400

University of California: Merced

Merced, California
www.ucmerced.edu   Federal Code: 001313

4-year public university in small city.
Enrollment: 1,750 undergrads. 668 full-time freshmen.
Selectivity: Admits over 75% of applicants.

BASIC COSTS (2007-2008)
Tuition and fees: $7,148; out-of-state residents $26,768.
Room and board: $10,714.

FINANCIAL AID PICTURE
Students with need: Need-based aid available for full-time and part-time students. Work study available nights, weekends, and for part-time students.
Students without need: No-need awards available for academics.
Scholarships offered: Regents' Scholarships; based on strength and breadth of academic program, grades, personal statement, extracurricular activities, community activities, first-generation attendance, other indicators of academic excellence and promise.

FINANCIAL AID PROCEDURES
Forms required: FAFSA.
Dates and Deadlines: Priority date 3/2; no closing date. Applicants notified on a rolling basis starting 3/2.
Transfers: Priority date 3/2. Applicants notified on a rolling basis; must reply by 6/1.

CONTACT
Diana Ralls, Director of Financial Aid & Scholarships
5200 North Lake Road, Merced, CA 95343-5603
(209) 228-4243

University of California: Riverside

Riverside, California
www.ucr.edu   Federal Code: 001316

4-year public university in large city.
Enrollment: 14,973 undergrads, 3% part-time. 3,701 full-time freshmen.
Selectivity: Admits over 75% of applicants.

BASIC COSTS (2007-2008)
Tuition and fees: $7,355; out-of-state residents $26,975.
Room and board: $10,800.

FINANCIAL AID PICTURE (2007-2008)
Students with need: Out of 2,978 full-time freshmen who applied for aid, 2,395 were judged to have need. Of these, 2,321 received aid, and 1,338 had their full need met. Average financial aid package met 88% of need; average scholarship/grant was $11,857; average loan was $4,889. For part-time students, average financial aid package was $10,050.
Students without need: 56 full-time freshmen who did not demonstrate need for aid received scholarships/grants; average award was $6,443. No-need awards available for academics, alumni affiliation, art, athletics, job skills, leadership, music/drama, religious affiliation, state/district residency.
Scholarships offered: *Merit:* Regents and Chancellor's Scholarships: available to top-ranked incoming freshmen, including international and home-schooled admits. *Athletic:* 25 full-time freshmen received athletic scholarships; average amount $10,782.
Cumulative student debt: 64% of graduating class had student loans; average debt was $14,992.

FINANCIAL AID PROCEDURES

Forms required: FAFSA, state aid form.

Dates and Deadlines: Closing date 3/2. Applicants notified on a rolling basis starting 3/1; must reply by 5/1 or within 3 week(s) of notification.

Transfers: Deadlines may be extended for mid-year admissions.

CONTACT

Sheryl Hayes, Director of Financial Aid
Admissions Office, Riverside, CA 92521
(951) 827-3878

University of California: San Diego
La Jolla, California
www.ucsd.edu   Federal Code: 001317

4-year public university in large town.

Enrollment: 22,048 undergrads. 4,301 full-time freshmen.

Selectivity: Admits less than 50% of applicants.

BASIC COSTS (2007-2008)

Tuition and fees: $7,435; out-of-state residents $27,019.

Room and board: $10,237.

FINANCIAL AID PICTURE (2006-2007)

Students with need: Out of 3,264 full-time freshmen who applied for aid, 2,246 were judged to have need. Of these, 2,113 received aid, and 449 had their full need met. Average financial aid package met 82% of need; average scholarship/grant was $10,233; average loan was $4,273. For part-time students, average financial aid package was $13,311.

Students without need: 98 full-time freshmen who did not demonstrate need for aid received scholarships/grants; average award was $7,275. No-need awards available for academics, art, leadership, music/drama.

FINANCIAL AID PROCEDURES

Forms required: FAFSA, state aid form.

Dates and Deadlines: Priority date 3/2; no closing date. Applicants notified on a rolling basis starting 3/15; must reply within 3 week(s) of notification.

Transfers: Applicants notified on a rolling basis; must reply within 3 week(s) of notification.

CONTACT

Ann Klein, Director of Financial Aid
9500 Gilman Drive, 0021, La Jolla, CA 92093-0021
(858) 534-4480

University of California: Santa Barbara
Santa Barbara, California
www.ucsb.edu   Federal Code: 001320

4-year public university in small city.

Enrollment: 18,412 undergrads, 2% part-time. 4,089 full-time freshmen.

Selectivity: Admits 50 to 75% of applicants.

BASIC COSTS (2007-2008)

Tuition and fees: $7,896; out-of-state residents $27,516.

Room and board: $11,946.

FINANCIAL AID PICTURE (2006-2007)

Students with need: Out of 3,053 full-time freshmen who applied for aid, 2,061 were judged to have need. Of these, 1,872 received aid, and 534 had their full need met. Average financial aid package met 81% of need; average scholarship/grant was $12,584; average loan was $5,398. For part-time students, average financial aid package was $10,527.

Students without need: 83 full-time freshmen who did not demonstrate need for aid received scholarships/grants; average award was $6,491. No-need awards available for academics, athletics.

Scholarships offered: 17 full-time freshmen received athletic scholarships; average amount $8,660.

Cumulative student debt: 48% of graduating class had student loans; average debt was $15,808.

FINANCIAL AID PROCEDURES

Forms required: FAFSA.

Dates and Deadlines: Priority date 3/2; closing date 5/31. Applicants notified on a rolling basis starting 3/15; must reply within 2 week(s) of notification.

Transfers: California residents must apply for a CAL grant from the California Student Aid Commission; must complete and submit FAFSA by March 2.

CONTACT

Ron Andrade, Director of Financial Aid
1210 Cheadle Hall, Santa Barbara, CA 93106-2014
(805) 893-2432

University of California: Santa Cruz
Santa Cruz, California
www.ucsc.edu   Federal Code: 001321

4-year public university in small city.

Enrollment: 14,381 undergrads, 3% part-time. 3,313 full-time freshmen.

Selectivity: Admits over 75% of applicants.

BASIC COSTS (2007-2008)

Tuition and fees: $7,645; out-of-state residents $27,229.

Room and board: $12,482.

Additional info: Tuition/fee waivers available for unemployed or children of unemployed.

FINANCIAL AID PICTURE (2006-2007)

Students with need: Out of 2,464 full-time freshmen who applied for aid, 1,662 were judged to have need. Of these, 1,548 received aid, and 753 had their full need met. Average financial aid package met 86% of need; average scholarship/grant was $11,525; average loan was $4,746. For part-time students, average financial aid package was $11,234.

Students without need: 53 full-time freshmen who did not demonstrate need for aid received scholarships/grants; average award was $8,117. No-need awards available for academics, alumni affiliation, art, leadership, music/drama.

Cumulative student debt: 51% of graduating class had student loans; average debt was $14,381.

FINANCIAL AID PROCEDURES

Forms required: FAFSA, state aid form.

Dates and Deadlines: Closing date 3/2. Applicants notified on a rolling basis starting 4/1; must reply within 4 week(s) of notification.

CONTACT

Ann Draper, Director of Financial Aid
Cook House, 1156 High Street, Santa Cruz, CA 95064
(831) 459-2963

University of La Verne
La Verne, California
www.ulv.edu   Federal Code: 001216

4-year private university and liberal arts college in large town.

Enrollment: 1,671 undergrads, 5% part-time. 334 full-time freshmen.

Selectivity: Admits 50 to 75% of applicants.

BASIC COSTS (2008-2009)

Tuition and fees: $26,910.

Per-credit charge: $760.

Room and board: $10,460.

FINANCIAL AID PICTURE (2007-2008)

Students with need: Out of 305 full-time freshmen who applied for aid, 276 were judged to have need. Of these, 276 received aid, and 21 had their full need met. For part-time students, average financial aid package was $13,805.

Students without need: 40 full-time freshmen who did not demonstrate need for aid received scholarships/grants; average award was $9,400. No-need awards available for academics, alumni affiliation, art, leadership, minority status, music/drama, religious affiliation.

Scholarships offered: Trustee Award: $12,000. Founders Award: $10,000. 1891 Award: $9,000. Leo Award: $6,000.

FINANCIAL AID PROCEDURES

Forms required: FAFSA, state aid form.

Dates and Deadlines: Priority date 3/2; no closing date. Applicants notified on a rolling basis starting 3/2; must reply within 1 week(s) of notification.

Transfers: No deadline. Award amounts for transfer students are: Trustee Award-$7,000; Founders Award-$5,000; 1891 Award-$3,000.

CONTACT

Leatha Webster, Director of Financial Aid
1950 Third Street, La Verne, CA 91750
(800) 649-0160

University of Redlands

Redlands, California
www.redlands.edu   Federal Code: 001322

4-year private university and liberal arts college in small city.

Enrollment: 2,353 undergrads, 1% part-time. 604 full-time freshmen.

Selectivity: Admits 50 to 75% of applicants.

BASIC COSTS (2008-2009)

Tuition and fees: $32,294.

Per-credit charge: $1,000.

Room and board: $10,122.

FINANCIAL AID PICTURE (2007-2008)

Students with need: Out of 478 full-time freshmen who applied for aid, 382 were judged to have need. Of these, 382 received aid, and 358 had their full need met. Average financial aid package met 85% of need; average scholarship/grant was $23,666; average loan was $6,545. For part-time students, average financial aid package was $16,515.

Students without need: 92 full-time freshmen who did not demonstrate need for aid received scholarships/grants; average award was $12,406. No-need awards available for academics, art, music/drama.

FINANCIAL AID PROCEDURES

Forms required: FAFSA, state aid form.

Dates and Deadlines: Priority date 2/15; no closing date. Applicants notified on a rolling basis starting 2/28; must reply by 5/1.

Transfers: No deadline.

CONTACT

Craig Slaughter, Financial Aid Director
1200 East Colton Avenue, Redlands, CA 92373-0999
(909) 748-8047

University of San Diego

San Diego, California
www.sandiego.edu   Federal Code: 010395

4-year private university in very large city, affiliated with Roman Catholic Church.

Enrollment: 4,906 undergrads, 3% part-time. 1,106 full-time freshmen.

Selectivity: Admits less than 50% of applicants.

BASIC COSTS (2008-2009)

Tuition and fees: $34,264.

Room and board: $11,870.

FINANCIAL AID PICTURE (2006-2007)

Students with need: Out of 677 full-time freshmen who applied for aid, 495 were judged to have need. Of these, 488 received aid, and 73 had their full need met. Average financial aid package met 73% of need; average scholarship/grant was $17,710; average loan was $4,845. For part-time students, average financial aid package was $9,100.

Students without need: 235 full-time freshmen who did not demonstrate need for aid received scholarships/grants; average award was $11,594. No-need awards available for academics, athletics, leadership, music/drama, religious affiliation, ROTC.

Scholarships offered: 32 full-time freshmen received athletic scholarships; average amount $28,758.

Cumulative student debt: 38% of graduating class had student loans; average debt was $26,639.

FINANCIAL AID PROCEDURES

Forms required: FAFSA.

Dates and Deadlines: Closing date 3/2. Applicants notified on a rolling basis starting 3/1; must reply by 5/1 or within 3 week(s) of notification.

Transfers: No deadline. Entering transfer students not eligible for institutional merit-based scholarships.

CONTACT

Judith Lewis Logue, Director of Financial Aid Services
5998 Alcala Park, San Diego, CA 92110
(619) 260-4514

University of San Francisco

San Francisco, California
www.usfca.edu   Federal Code: 001325

4-year private university in very large city, affiliated with Roman Catholic Church.

Enrollment: 4,872 undergrads, 3% part-time. 1,053 full-time freshmen.

Selectivity: Admits 50 to 75% of applicants.

BASIC COSTS (2008-2009)

Tuition and fees: $33,500.

Per-credit charge: $1,180.

Room and board: $11,130.

Additional info: Nursing clinical lab fee, $150 per lab. Nursing clinical lab malpractice insurance, $25 per lab.

FINANCIAL AID PICTURE

Students with need: Need-based aid available for full-time and part-time students.

Students without need: No-need awards available for academics, athletics, ROTC.

Scholarships offered: University Scholars Program: $19,500 per year for 4 years; must have 3.8 weighted GPA and combined SAT of 1320 on Critical Reading and Math sections or ACT composite of 30. Applicants must apply for admission by November 15.

Additional info: Individualized installment plans available.

FINANCIAL AID PROCEDURES

Forms required: FAFSA.

Dates and Deadlines: Priority date 2/1; no closing date. Applicants notified on a rolling basis starting 4/1; must reply within 4 week(s) of notification.

CONTACT

Susan Murphy, Senior Associate Dean, Director, Enrollment and Financial Services
2130 Fulton Street, San Francisco, CA 94117-1046
(415) 422-6303

University of Southern California

Los Angeles, California
www.usc.edu

Federal Code: 001328
CSS Code: 4852

4-year private university in very large city.
Enrollment: 16,091 undergrads, 3% part-time. 2,962 full-time freshmen.
Selectivity: Admits less than 50% of applicants. GED not accepted.

BASIC COSTS (2008-2009)
Tuition and fees: $35,954.
Per-credit charge: $1,185.
Room and board: $10,858.

FINANCIAL AID PICTURE (2006-2007)
Students with need: Out of 1,608 full-time freshmen who applied for aid, 1,073 were judged to have need. Of these, 1,073 received aid, and 1,045 had their full need met. Average financial aid package met 100% of need; average scholarship/grant was $20,999; average loan was $3,816. For part-time students, average financial aid package was $15,007.
Students without need: 706 full-time freshmen who did not demonstrate need for aid received scholarships/grants; average award was $13,757. No-need awards available for academics, alumni affiliation, art, athletics, leadership, music/drama, ROTC.
Scholarships offered: 76 full-time freshmen received athletic scholarships; average amount $33,812.
Cumulative student debt: 53% of graduating class had student loans; average debt was $25,578.

FINANCIAL AID PROCEDURES
Forms required: FAFSA, CSS PROFILE.
Dates and Deadlines: Priority date 1/22; no closing date. Applicants notified on a rolling basis starting 3/15; must reply by 5/1.
Transfers: Priority date 1/20; closing date 2/1. Applicants notified by 5/1; must reply by 6/1.

CONTACT
Susan Ikerd, Associate Dean and Director
Office of Admission, Los Angeles, CA 90089-1158
(213) 740-1111

University of the Pacific

Stockton, California
www.pacific.edu

Federal Code: 001329

4-year private university in large city.
Enrollment: 3,456 undergrads, 3% part-time. 762 full-time freshmen.
Selectivity: Admits 50 to 75% of applicants.

BASIC COSTS (2008-2009)
Tuition and fees: $30,730.
Per-credit charge: $1,044.
Room and board: $10,185.

FINANCIAL AID PICTURE (2007-2008)
Students with need: Out of 593 full-time freshmen who applied for aid, 488 were judged to have need. Of these, 488 received aid, and 174 had their full need met. For part-time students, average financial aid package was $19,032.
Students without need: 143 full-time freshmen who did not demonstrate need for aid received scholarships/grants; average award was $8,580. No-need awards available for academics, athletics, leadership, music/drama, religious affiliation.
Scholarships offered: 24 full-time freshmen received athletic scholarships; average amount $19,578.

FINANCIAL AID PROCEDURES
Forms required: FAFSA.

Dates and Deadlines: Priority date 2/15; no closing date. Applicants notified on a rolling basis starting 3/15.

CONTACT
Lynn Fox, Director of Financial Aid
3601 Pacific Avenue, Stockton, CA 95211-0197
(209) 946-2011

Vanguard University of Southern California

Costa Mesa, California
www.vanguard.edu

Federal Code: 001293

4-year private university and liberal arts college in small city, affiliated with Assemblies of God.
Enrollment: 1,872 undergrads, 19% part-time. 370 full-time freshmen.
Selectivity: Admits over 75% of applicants.

BASIC COSTS (2008-2009)
Tuition and fees: $22,986.
Per-credit charge: $936.
Room and board: $7,532.

FINANCIAL AID PICTURE (2007-2008)
Students with need: 68% of average financial aid package awarded as scholarships/grants, 32% awarded as loans/jobs. Need-based aid available for part-time students.
Students without need: No-need awards available for academics, athletics, music/drama.

FINANCIAL AID PROCEDURES
Forms required: FAFSA, state aid form.
Dates and Deadlines: Priority date 3/2; no closing date. Applicants notified on a rolling basis starting 4/1; must reply within 3 week(s) of notification.
Transfers: Applicants notified on a rolling basis.

CONTACT
Robyn Fournier, Director of Financial Aid
55 Fair Drive, Costa Mesa, CA 92626-9601
(714) 556-3610 ext. 4250

Victor Valley College

Victorville, California
www.vvc.edu

Federal Code: 001335
CSS Code: 4932

2-year public community college in small city.
Enrollment: 4,472 undergrads.
Selectivity: Open admission; but selective for some programs.

BASIC COSTS (2007-2008)
Tuition and fees: $610; out-of-state residents $5,800.
Per-credit charge: $20; out-of-state residents $193.
Additional info: Nevada residents pay $71 per unit which includes enrollment fee as part of Good Neighbor policy.

FINANCIAL AID PICTURE
Students with need: Need-based aid available for full-time and part-time students.
Additional info: Board of Governors grant pays enrollment fee in full for low-income students.

FINANCIAL AID PROCEDURES
Forms required: FAFSA, CSS PROFILE, state aid form, institutional form.
Dates and Deadlines: Priority date 3/2; no closing date. Applicants notified on a rolling basis starting 8/1; must reply within 4 week(s) of notification.

CONTACT

Sharon Groom, Director, Office of Financial Aid
18422 Bear Valley Road, Victorville, CA 92392-5849
(760) 245-4271 ext. 2277

West Hills College: Coalinga

Coalinga, California
www.westhillscollege.com   Federal Code: 001176

2-year public community college in small town.
Enrollment: 1,371 undergrads, 43% part-time. 189 full-time freshmen.
Selectivity: Open admission.

BASIC COSTS (2007-2008)
Tuition and fees: $600; out-of-state residents $5,790.
Per-credit charge: $20; out-of-state residents $193.
Room and board: $5,171.
Additional info: Additional $250 refundable deposit for room and board plan. Tuition/fee waivers available for unemployed or children of unemployed.

FINANCIAL AID PICTURE
Students with need: Need-based aid available for full-time and part-time students.

FINANCIAL AID PROCEDURES
Forms required: FAFSA.
Dates and Deadlines: Priority date 3/2; no closing date. Applicants notified on a rolling basis starting 6/1.

CONTACT
Dolores Smith, District Director, Financial Aid
300 Cherry Lane, Coalinga, CA 93210
(559) 934-2310

West Los Angeles College

Culver City, California
www.wlac.edu   Federal Code: 008596

2-year public community college in large town.
Enrollment: 9,261 undergrads.
Selectivity: Open admission.

BASIC COSTS (2007-2008)
Tuition and fees: $624; out-of-state residents $5,814.
Per-credit charge: $20; out-of-state residents $193.
Additional info: Tuition/fee waivers available for unemployed or children of unemployed.

FINANCIAL AID PICTURE
Students with need: Need-based aid available for full-time and part-time students.
Students without need: This college awards aid only to students with need.
Additional info: California residents may qualify for Board of Governors Grant Program.

FINANCIAL AID PROCEDURES
Forms required: FAFSA.
Dates and Deadlines: No deadline. Applicants notified on a rolling basis; must reply within 4 week(s) of notification.
Transfers: No deadline.

CONTACT
Glenn Schenk, Financial Aid Manager
9000 Overland Avenue, Culver City, CA 90230
(310) 287-4533

West Valley College

Saratoga, California
www.westvalley.edu   Federal Code: 001338

2-year public community college in large town.
Enrollment: 14,615 undergrads.
Selectivity: Open admission.

BASIC COSTS (2007-2008)
Tuition and fees: $654; out-of-state residents $5,844.
Per-credit charge: $20; out-of-state residents $193.
Additional info: Tuition/fee waivers available for unemployed or children of unemployed.

FINANCIAL AID PICTURE
Students with need: Need-based aid available for full-time and part-time students.
Students without need: This college awards aid only to students with need.

FINANCIAL AID PROCEDURES
Forms required: FAFSA.
Dates and Deadlines: Priority date 5/31; no closing date. Applicants notified on a rolling basis starting 7/1.

CONTACT
Maritza Cantarero, Director of Financial Aid
14000 Fruitvale Avenue, Saratoga, CA 95070-5698
(408) 867-2200

Westmont College

Santa Barbara, California
www.westmont.edu   Federal Code: 001341

4-year private liberal arts college in small city, affiliated with nondenominational tradition.
Enrollment: 1,333 undergrads, 2% part-time. 388 full-time freshmen.
Selectivity: Admits 50 to 75% of applicants.

BASIC COSTS (2008-2009)
Tuition and fees: $33,170.
Room and board: $10,080.

FINANCIAL AID PICTURE (2007-2008)
Students with need: Out of 299 full-time freshmen who applied for aid, 248 were judged to have need. Of these, 248 received aid, and 30 had their full need met. Average financial aid package met 73% of need; average scholarship/grant was $17,696; average loan was $4,675.
Students without need: 101 full-time freshmen who did not demonstrate need for aid received scholarships/grants; average award was $11,544. No-need awards available for academics, art, athletics, leadership, minority status, music/drama.
Scholarships offered: *Merit:* Scholarships automatically awarded to entering students based on high school GPA and SAT or ACT scores (first-year students) or college academic GPA (transfers): renewable annually; unlimited number awarded until class is full. First-year scholarships: Presidential ($11,000), must maintain 3.25 GPA; Provost ($9,000), must maintain 3.0 GPA; Dean's ($7,000), must maintain 2.75 GPA. Transfer scholarships: Presidential ($5,000), must have 3.75 GPA and 24 or more transferable credits; Provost ($4,000), must have 3.35 GPA and 24 or more transferable credits. *Athletic:* 17 full-time freshmen received athletic scholarships; average amount $5,055.
Cumulative student debt: 53% of graduating class had student loans; average debt was $25,008.

FINANCIAL AID PROCEDURES
Forms required: FAFSA.

Dates and Deadlines: Priority date 3/1; no closing date. Applicants notified on a rolling basis starting 3/15; must reply by 5/1 or within 2 week(s) of notification.

Transfers: Applicants notified on a rolling basis starting 4/1; must reply by 5/1 or within 2 week(s) of notification. Transfer students may qualify for academic merit scholarships.

CONTACT
Diane Horvath, Director of Financial Aid
955 La Paz Road, Santa Barbara, CA 93108-1089
(888) 963-4624

Westwood College: Inland Empire
Upland, California
www.westwood.edu   Federal Code: 007548

3-year for-profit business and technical college in small city.
Enrollment: 1,000 undergrads.

BASIC COSTS (2008-2009)
Tuition and fees: $14,061.

FINANCIAL AID PICTURE
Students with need: Need-based aid available for full-time and part-time students. Work study available nights, weekends, and for part-time students.
Students without need: No-need awards available for academics.

FINANCIAL AID PROCEDURES
Forms required: FAFSA, institutional form.
Dates and Deadlines: No deadline. Must reply within 1 week(s) of notification.
Transfers: No deadline.

CONTACT
Erin Vargas, Director of Financial Aid
20 West Seventh Street, Upland, CA 91786
(909) 931-7599

Whittier College
Whittier, California   Federal Code: 001342
www.whittier.edu   CSS Code: 4952

4-year private liberal arts college in small city.
Enrollment: 1,257 undergrads, 2% part-time. 308 full-time freshmen.
Selectivity: Admits 50 to 75% of applicants.

BASIC COSTS (2007-2008)
Tuition and fees: $30,160.
Per-credit charge: $1,250.
Room and board: $8,750.

FINANCIAL AID PICTURE (2007-2008)
Students with need: Average financial aid package met 94% of need; average scholarship/grant was $15,995; average loan was $6,331. For part-time students, average financial aid package was $23,346.
Students without need: No-need awards available for academics, alumni affiliation, art, leadership, minority status.
Additional info: Auditions required for talent scholarship applicants in art, music, and theater.

FINANCIAL AID PROCEDURES
Forms required: FAFSA, CSS PROFILE.
Dates and Deadlines: Priority date 3/1; closing date 6/30. Applicants notified on a rolling basis starting 2/15; must reply within 2 week(s) of notification.
Transfers: Priority date 2/1. Applicants notified on a rolling basis starting 3/1; must reply by 6/1 or within 2 week(s) of notification.

CONTACT
Vernon Bridges, Director of Student Financing
13406 East Philadelphia Street, Whittier, CA 90608-0634
(562) 907-4285

William Jessup University
Rocklin, California
www.jessup.edu   Federal Code: 001281

4-year private Bible and liberal arts college in small city, affiliated with nondenominational tradition.
Enrollment: 504 undergrads, 15% part-time. 56 full-time freshmen.
Selectivity: Admits 50 to 75% of applicants.

BASIC COSTS (2008-2009)
Tuition and fees: $20,480.
Per-credit charge: $868.
Room and board: $7,470.

FINANCIAL AID PICTURE
Students with need: Need-based aid available for full-time and part-time students. Work study available nights, weekends, and for part-time students.
Students without need: No-need awards available for academics, athletics, music/drama.

FINANCIAL AID PROCEDURES
Forms required: FAFSA.
Dates and Deadlines: Priority date 3/2; closing date 8/15. Applicants notified on a rolling basis starting 3/2; must reply by 6/1 or within 2 week(s) of notification.

CONTACT
Korey Compaan, Director of Financial Aid
333 Sunset Boulevard, Rocklin, CA 95765
(916) 577-2233

Woodbury University
Burbank, California
www.woodbury.edu   Federal Code: 001343

4-year private university in very large city.
Enrollment: 1,277 undergrads, 18% part-time. 159 full-time freshmen.
Selectivity: Admits over 75% of applicants.

BASIC COSTS (2007-2008)
Tuition and fees: $25,198.
Per-credit charge: $811.
Room and board: $8,660.

FINANCIAL AID PICTURE (2007-2008)
Students with need: Out of 140 full-time freshmen who applied for aid, 129 were judged to have need. Of these, 127 received aid, and 17 had their full need met. Average financial aid package met 59% of need; average scholarship/grant was $13,923; average loan was $3,367. For part-time students, average financial aid package was $10,931.
Students without need: 9 full-time freshmen who did not demonstrate need for aid received scholarships/grants; average award was $20,276. No-need awards available for academics.
Cumulative student debt: 58% of graduating class had student loans; average debt was $33,241.

FINANCIAL AID PROCEDURES
Forms required: FAFSA, institutional form.
Dates and Deadlines: Priority date 3/2; no closing date. Applicants notified on a rolling basis starting 3/15; must reply by 5/1 or within 2 week(s) of notification.

Transfers: No deadline. Applicants notified on a rolling basis starting 3/15; must reply by 5/1 or within 2 week(s) of notification.

CONTACT
Celeastia Williams, Director of Enrollment Services
7500 Glenoaks Boulevard, Burbank, CA 91510-7846
(818) 767-0888 ext. 273

Yuba Community College District
Marysville, California
www.yccd.edu Federal Code: 001344

2-year public community college in small city.
Enrollment: 6,099 undergrads.
Selectivity: Open admission; but selective for some programs.

BASIC COSTS (2007-2008)
Tuition and fees: $612; out-of-state residents $5,952.
Per-credit charge: $20; out-of-state residents $198.
Additional info: Tuition/fee waivers available for adults.

FINANCIAL AID PICTURE
Students with need: Need-based aid available for full-time and part-time students.
Students without need: No-need awards available for academics, athletics, job skills, minority status, music/drama.
Additional info: Tuition fee waiver based on Board of Governors Grant.

FINANCIAL AID PROCEDURES
Forms required: FAFSA.
Dates and Deadlines: Closing date 3/1. Applicants notified on a rolling basis starting 4/1.

CONTACT
Marisela Arce, Associate Dean for EOP&S and Financial Aid
2088 North Beale Road, Marysville, CA 95901
(530) 741-6781

Colorado

Adams State College
Alamosa, Colorado
www.adams.edu Federal Code: 001345

4-year public liberal arts college in small town.
Enrollment: 2,104 undergrads, 18% part-time. 487 full-time freshmen.
Selectivity: Admits 50 to 75% of applicants.

BASIC COSTS (2007-2008)
Tuition and fees: $3,464; out-of-state residents $10,808.
Room and board: $6,560.

FINANCIAL AID PICTURE (2006-2007)
Students with need: Out of 452 full-time freshmen who applied for aid, 359 were judged to have need. Of these, 353 received aid, and 4 had their full need met. Average financial aid package met 50% of need; average scholarship/grant was $3,800; average loan was $2,512. For part-time students, average financial aid package was $4,571.
Students without need: 20 full-time freshmen who did not demonstrate need for aid received scholarships/grants; average award was $2,168. No-need awards available for academics, alumni affiliation, art, athletics, leadership, minority status, music/drama, state/district residency.
Scholarships offered: 25 full-time freshmen received athletic scholarships; average amount $2,017.

Cumulative student debt: 73% of graduating class had student loans; average debt was $17,990.

FINANCIAL AID PROCEDURES
Forms required: FAFSA.
Dates and Deadlines: Priority date 3/1; closing date 4/15. Applicants notified on a rolling basis starting 4/30; must reply within 4 week(s) of notification.
Transfers: No deadline. Applicants notified on a rolling basis starting 4/30.

CONTACT
Phil Schroeder, Director of Financial Aid
208 Edgemont Boulevard, Alamosa, CO 81102
(719) 587-7306

Aims Community College
Greeley, Colorado
www.aims.edu Federal Code: 007582

2-year public community college in small city.
Enrollment: 3,384 undergrads.
Selectivity: Open admission; but selective for some programs.

BASIC COSTS (2007-2008)
Tuition and fees: $2,165; out-of-district residents $2,945; out-of-state residents $10,685.
Per-credit charge: $52; out-of-district residents $78; out-of-state residents $336.
Additional info: Tuition/fee waivers available for adults.

FINANCIAL AID PICTURE
Students with need: Need-based aid available for full-time students.

FINANCIAL AID PROCEDURES
Forms required: FAFSA.
Dates and Deadlines: Priority date 4/15; no closing date. Applicants notified on a rolling basis starting 6/1.

CONTACT
Teri Dorchuck, Financial Aid Director
5401 West 20th Street, Greeley, CO 80632
(970) 330-8008 ext. 6304

Arapahoe Community College
Littleton, Colorado
www.arapahoe.edu Federal Code: 001346

2-year public community college in small city.
Enrollment: 5,318 undergrads, 66% part-time. 576 full-time freshmen.
Selectivity: Open admission; but selective for some programs.

BASIC COSTS (2007-2008)
Tuition and fees: $2,486; out-of-state residents $10,889.
Per-credit charge: $77; out-of-state residents $357.
Additional info: In-state tuition based upon assumption of Colorado Opportunity Fund waiver of $89 per-credit-hour.

FINANCIAL AID PICTURE
Students with need: Need-based aid available for full-time and part-time students. Work study available nights, weekends, and for part-time students.
Students without need: No-need awards available for academics, leadership, state/district residency.
Scholarships offered: President's Scholarship; based on minimum 3.0 GPA, references. College Bound Scholarship; based on high GED score. All awards $750 for full-time students, $375 for half-time, $563 for three-quarters time. Awards made on first-come first-served basis.

FINANCIAL AID PROCEDURES

Forms required: FAFSA, institutional form.
Dates and Deadlines: Priority date 5/1; no closing date. Applicants notified on a rolling basis starting 5/1; must reply within 3 week(s) of notification.
Transfers: No deadline. Applicants notified on a rolling basis starting 5/1.

CONTACT

Thad Spaulding, Associate Director of Financial Aid
PO Box 9002, Littleton, CO 80160-9002
(303) 797-5661

Art Institute of Colorado
Denver, Colorado
www.aic.artinstitutes.edu   Federal Code: 013961

4-year for-profit visual arts and technical college in very large city.
Enrollment: 2,245 undergrads, 32% part-time. 392 full-time freshmen.

BASIC COSTS (2008-2009)

Tuition and fees: $21,985.
Per-credit charge: $436.
Additional info: Supply kit $530-$2,155 depending on program. Tuition at time of enrollment locked for 4 years.

FINANCIAL AID PICTURE

Students with need: Need-based aid available for full-time and part-time students. Work study available nights, weekends, and for part-time students.
Additional info: Tuition at time of first enrollment guaranteed to students for 4 years providing student maintains continuous attendance and completes program within 150% of program length.

FINANCIAL AID PROCEDURES

Forms required: FAFSA, institutional form.
Dates and Deadlines: No deadline. Applicants notified on a rolling basis.
Transfers: No deadline.

CONTACT

Shannon May, Director of Student Financial Services
1200 Lincoln Street, Denver, CO 80203
(303) 824-4757

Bel-Rea Institute of Animal Technology
Denver, Colorado
www.bel-rea.com   Federal Code: 012670

2-year for-profit technical college in very large city.
Enrollment: 650 undergrads.

BASIC COSTS (2007-2008)

Additional info: Tuition for full associate program $20,750 including fees. Tuition at time of enrollment locked for 2 years.

FINANCIAL AID PICTURE

Students with need: Need-based aid available for full-time students.
Students without need: This college awards aid only to students with need.

FINANCIAL AID PROCEDURES

Forms required: FAFSA.
Dates and Deadlines: Priority date 8/31; no closing date. Applicants notified on a rolling basis starting 8/15.
Transfers: No deadline.

CONTACT

Stasi Botinelli, Financial Aid Director
1681 South Dayton Street, Denver, CO 80247
(303) 751-8700

Cambridge College
Aurora, Colorado
www.cambridgecollege.com   Federal Code: 021829

2-year for-profit technical college in small city.
Enrollment: 585 full-time undergrads.

BASIC COSTS (2007-2008)

Additional info: Tuition for full associate degree programs ranges from $16,550 to $24,500 depending on program; tuition for diploma programs ranges from $7,950 to $10,150. Books and supplies included. Housing provided by private company.

FINANCIAL AID PICTURE

Students with need: Need-based aid available for full-time students.
Students without need: This college awards aid only to students with need.

FINANCIAL AID PROCEDURES

Forms required: FAFSA, institutional form.
Dates and Deadlines: No deadline. Applicants notified on a rolling basis.

CONTACT

Gerry Major, Director of Financial Aid
350 Blackhawk Street, Aurora, CO 80011
(720) 859-7900

CollegeAmerica: Denver
Denver, Colorado
www.collegeamerica.com   Federal Code: 025943

2-year for-profit technical college in very large city.
Enrollment: 455 undergrads.
Selectivity: Open admission.

BASIC COSTS (2007-2008)

Additional info: Tuition, fees, books, and supplies: $29,950 for Associate degree programs; $54,900 for Bachelor's degree programs. Tuition at time of enrollment locked for 2 years.

FINANCIAL AID PICTURE

Students with need: Need-based aid available for full-time students.
Students without need: This college awards aid only to students with need.
Scholarships offered: High School Academic Scholarship.

FINANCIAL AID PROCEDURES

Forms required: FAFSA, institutional form.
Dates and Deadlines: No deadline. Applicants notified on a rolling basis; must reply within 4 week(s) of notification.
Transfers: No deadline. Applicants notified on a rolling basis.

CONTACT

Ruby Rowe, Corporate Director of Financial Aid
1385 South Colorado Boulevard, 5th Floor, Denver, CO 80222-1912
(303) 691-9756

Colorado Christian University
Lakewood, Colorado
www.ccu.edu   Federal Code: 009401

4-year private university and liberal arts college in large city, affiliated with non-denominational tradition.
Enrollment: 920 undergrads, 4% part-time. 250 full-time freshmen.
Selectivity: Admits 50 to 75% of applicants.

BASIC COSTS (2008-2009)

Tuition and fees: $20,130.

Per-credit charge: $850.

Room and board: $8,050.

FINANCIAL AID PICTURE (2006-2007)

Students with need: Out of 212 full-time freshmen who applied for aid, 193 were judged to have need. Of these, 187 received aid. Average financial aid package met 71% of need; average scholarship/grant was $4,000; average loan was $2,750. Need-based aid available for part-time students.

Students without need: 26 full-time freshmen who did not demonstrate need for aid received scholarships/grants; average award was $3,237. No-need awards available for academics, athletics, leadership, music/drama.

Scholarships offered: 34 full-time freshmen received athletic scholarships; average amount $5,100.

Cumulative student debt: 61% of graduating class had student loans; average debt was $16,650.

FINANCIAL AID PROCEDURES

Forms required: FAFSA.

Dates and Deadlines: Priority date 3/15; no closing date. Applicants notified on a rolling basis starting 4/1; must reply by 5/1 or within 4 week(s) of notification.

CONTACT

Steve Woodburn, Director of Student Financial Aid

8787 West Alameda Avenue, Lakewood, CO 80226

(303) 963-3230

Colorado College

Colorado Springs, Colorado

www.coloradocollege.edu

Federal Code: 001347

CSS Code: 4072

4-year private liberal arts college in large city.

Enrollment: 2,034 undergrads. 524 full-time freshmen.

Selectivity: Admits less than 50% of applicants.

BASIC COSTS (2008-2009)

Tuition and fees: $35,844.

Per-credit charge: $1,120.

Room and board: $9,096.

FINANCIAL AID PICTURE (2007-2008)

Students with need: Out of 236 full-time freshmen who applied for aid, 190 were judged to have need. Of these, 190 received aid, and 145 had their full need met. Average financial aid package met 98% of need; average scholarship/grant was $27,305; average loan was $3,653. Need-based aid available for part-time students.

Students without need: 26 full-time freshmen who did not demonstrate need for aid received scholarships/grants; average award was $10,961. No-need awards available for academics, athletics.

Scholarships offered: *Merit:* Barnes Scholarship; full tuition; available in all natural sciences; 4 or 5 awarded in chemistry, 4 available in remaining natural sciences. Trustee Scholarship; $7,000; based on highly rated entering students; 10 awarded. Merit Awards; up to $2,000; for National Merit finalists. Men's Ice Hockey and Women's Soccer merit awards. Colorado College Scholars; 10 merit awards for highly rated entering students from Colorado. *Athletic:* 5 full-time freshmen received athletic scholarships; average amount $33,426.

Cumulative student debt: 9% of graduating class had student loans; average debt was $16,503.

Additional info: Need-based financial aid available only to students enrolled half-time or more.

FINANCIAL AID PROCEDURES

Forms required: FAFSA, CSS PROFILE.

Dates and Deadlines: Closing date 2/15. Applicants notified by 3/20; must reply by 5/1.

Transfers: Closing date 4/1. Transfer students might not receive full-need package during first year.

CONTACT

James Swanson, Director of Financial Aid

14 East Cache La Poudre, Colorado Springs, CO 80903-9854

(719) 389-6651

Colorado Mountain College

Glenwood Springs, Colorado

www.coloradomtn.edu

Federal Code: 004506

2-year public community and liberal arts college in small town.

Enrollment: 4,940 undergrads.

Selectivity: Open admission; but selective for some programs.

BASIC COSTS (2007-2008)

Tuition and fees: $1,490; out-of-district residents $2,360; out-of-state residents $7,130.

Per-credit charge: $43; out-of-district residents $72; out-of-state residents $231.

Room and board: $6,866.

FINANCIAL AID PICTURE

Students with need: Need-based aid available for full-time and part-time students. Work study available nights, weekends, and for part-time students.

Students without need: This college awards aid only to students with need.

FINANCIAL AID PROCEDURES

Forms required: FAFSA.

Dates and Deadlines: Priority date 3/31; no closing date. Applicants notified on a rolling basis starting 5/15; must reply within 4 week(s) of notification.

Transfers: Transfer scholarships available for Colorado residents with 3.0 GPA and minimum 20 credit hours from previous schools.

CONTACT

Gary Lewis, Director of Student Financial Aid

831 Grand Avenue, Glenwood Springs, CO 81601

(970) 947-8277

Colorado Northwestern Community College

Rangely, Colorado

www.cncc.edu

Federal Code: 001359

2-year public community college in small town.

Enrollment: 1,003 undergrads.

Selectivity: Open admission; but selective for some programs.

BASIC COSTS (2007-2008)

Tuition and fees: $2,548; out-of-state residents $5,218.

Per-credit charge: $77; out-of-state residents $166.

Room and board: $5,650.

Additional info: In-state tuition based upon assumption of Colorado Opportunity Fund waiver of $86 per-credit-hour.

FINANCIAL AID PICTURE

Students with need: Need-based aid available for full-time and part-time students. Work study available nights, weekends, and for part-time students.

Students without need: No-need awards available for academics, athletics, state/district residency.

Scholarships offered: Academic Scholarships; $200-$1,000; for Colorado residents, based on grades, specific talent, area of study; requires application, essay, informal interview, 2.5 GPA.

FINANCIAL AID PROCEDURES

Forms required: FAFSA, institutional form.

Dates and Deadlines: Priority date 5/1; no closing date. Applicants notified on a rolling basis starting 5/15; must reply within 4 week(s) of notification.

Transfers: No deadline.

CONTACT

Merrie Byers, Financial Aid Technician
500 Kennedy Drive, Rangely, CO 81648
(970) 675-3204

Colorado School of Healing Arts

Lakewood, Colorado
www.csha.net   Federal Code: 035844

2-year for-profit health science college in small city.

Enrollment: 240 undergrads, 36% part-time. 58 full-time freshmen.

Selectivity: Open admission.

BASIC COSTS (2008-2009)

Tuition and fees: $10,959.

Per-credit charge: $150.

Additional info: Books, massage table package, materials fees, and insurance are included in required fees.

FINANCIAL AID PICTURE

Students with need: Need-based aid available for full-time and part-time students.

Students without need: This college awards aid only to students with need.

FINANCIAL AID PROCEDURES

Forms required: FAFSA.

Dates and Deadlines: No deadline.

CONTACT

Gina Simpson, Director of Financial Aid
7655 West Mississippi, Suite 100, Lakewood, CO 80226
(303) 986-2320

Colorado School of Mines

Golden, Colorado
www.mines.edu   Federal Code: 001348

4-year public university and engineering college in large town.

Enrollment: 3,300 undergrads, 18% part-time. 790 full-time freshmen.

Selectivity: Admits over 75% of applicants.

BASIC COSTS (2007-2008)

Tuition and fees: $10,258; out-of-state residents $23,244.

Per-credit charge: $335; out-of-state residents $806.

Room and board: $7,350.

FINANCIAL AID PICTURE (2007-2008)

Students with need: Out of 592 full-time freshmen who applied for aid, 533 were judged to have need. Of these, 533 received aid, and 432 had their full need met. Average financial aid package met 93% of need; average scholarship/grant was $8,350; average loan was $5,100. Need-based aid available for part-time students.

Students without need: 85 full-time freshmen who did not demonstrate need for aid received scholarships/grants; average award was $5,500. No-need awards available for academics, alumni affiliation, athletics, music/drama, ROTC, state/district residency.

Scholarships offered: 125 full-time freshmen received athletic scholarships; average amount $2,800.

Cumulative student debt: 70% of graduating class had student loans; average debt was $18,500.

FINANCIAL AID PROCEDURES

Forms required: FAFSA.

Dates and Deadlines: Priority date 3/1; no closing date. Applicants notified on a rolling basis starting 3/15; must reply by 5/1 or within 2 week(s) of notification.

Transfers: Applicants notified on a rolling basis starting 3/15; must reply by 5/1 or within 2 week(s) of notification. Federal aid only (Pell grant and Stafford loan) available for second undergraduate degree candidates.

CONTACT

Roger Koester, Director of Financial Aid
Undergraduate Admissions, Golden, CO 80401
(303) 273-3220

Colorado State University

Fort Collins, Colorado
www.colostate.edu   Federal Code: 001350

4-year public university in small city.

Enrollment: 20,765 undergrads, 8% part-time. 4,010 full-time freshmen.

Selectivity: Admits over 75% of applicants.

BASIC COSTS (2007-2008)

Tuition and fees: $5,419; out-of-state residents $18,859.

Per-credit charge: $202; out-of-state residents $874.

Room and board: $7,382.

FINANCIAL AID PICTURE (2006-2007)

Students with need: Out of 2,608 full-time freshmen who applied for aid, 1,366 were judged to have need. Of these, 1,366 received aid, and 458 had their full need met. Average financial aid package met 72% of need; average scholarship/grant was $7,099; average loan was $3,227. For part-time students, average financial aid package was $6,503.

Students without need: 337 full-time freshmen who did not demonstrate need for aid received scholarships/grants; average award was $2,630. No-need awards available for academics, art, athletics, leadership, music/drama, ROTC, state/district residency.

Scholarships offered: 60 full-time freshmen received athletic scholarships; average amount $14,677.

Cumulative student debt: 55% of graduating class had student loans; average debt was $18,912.

FINANCIAL AID PROCEDURES

Forms required: FAFSA.

Dates and Deadlines: Priority date 3/1; no closing date. Applicants notified on a rolling basis starting 3/1.

CONTACT

Sandra Calhoun, Director of Student Financial Services
Office of Admissions/Colorado State University, Fort Collins, CO 80523-1062
(970) 491-6321

Colorado State University: Pueblo

Pueblo, Colorado
www.colostate-pueblo.edu   Federal Code: 001365

4-year public university in small city.

Enrollment: 3,947 undergrads, 22% part-time. 588 full-time freshmen.

Selectivity: Admits over 75% of applicants.

BASIC COSTS (2008-2009)

Tuition and fees: $4,557; out-of-state residents $14,757.
Room and board: $6,300.
Additional info: WUE tuition is 44% less than out-of-state rate. Differential tuition charged for business, nursing, computer information systems, and engineering courses at $16 more per-credit-hour.

FINANCIAL AID PICTURE (2007-2008)

Students with need: Average financial aid package met 62% of need; average scholarship/grant was $5,678; average loan was $3,119. For part-time students, average financial aid package was $6,781.
Students without need: No-need awards available for academics, alumni affiliation, art, athletics, job skills, leadership, minority status, music/drama, ROTC, state/district residency.
Cumulative student debt: 54% of graduating class had student loans; average debt was $16,481.

FINANCIAL AID PROCEDURES

Forms required: FAFSA, institutional form.
Dates and Deadlines: Priority date 3/1; no closing date. Applicants notified on a rolling basis starting 3/15; must reply within 3 week(s) of notification.

CONTACT

Sean McGivney, Director of Financial Aid
2200 Bonforte Boulevard, Pueblo, CO 81001-4901
(719) 549-2753

Colorado Technical University

Colorado Springs, Colorado
www.coloradotech.edu   Federal Code: 010148

4-year for-profit university and technical college in large city.
Enrollment: 1,500 undergrads.

BASIC COSTS (2007-2008)

Tuition and fees: $12,540.
Per-credit charge: $275.
Additional info: Lab fees $30 per lab class.

FINANCIAL AID PICTURE

Students with need: Need-based aid available for full-time and part-time students. Work study available nights, weekends, and for part-time students.
Students without need: No-need awards available for academics, ROTC.

FINANCIAL AID PROCEDURES

Forms required: FAFSA.
Dates and Deadlines: No deadline. Applicants notified on a rolling basis starting 6/30.
Transfers: No deadline.

CONTACT

Jagger Harris, Director, Financial Aid
4435 North Chestnut Street, Colorado Springs, CO 80907
(719) 598-0200

Community College of Aurora

Aurora, Colorado
www.ccaurora.edu   Federal Code: 016058

2-year public community college in large city.
Enrollment: 1,294 full-time undergrads.
Selectivity: Open admission.

BASIC COSTS (2007-2008)

Tuition and fees: $2,429; out-of-state residents $10,832.
Per-credit charge: $77; out-of-state residents $357.

Additional info: In-state tuition based upon assumption of Colorado Opportunity Fund waiver of $89 per-credit-hour.

FINANCIAL AID PICTURE

Students with need: Need-based aid available for full-time and part-time students. Work study available nights.

FINANCIAL AID PROCEDURES

Forms required: FAFSA, institutional form.
Dates and Deadlines: Priority date 6/1; no closing date. Applicants notified on a rolling basis starting 7/15.

CONTACT

John Young, Executive Director, Financial Aid
16000 East CentreTech Parkway, Aurora, CO 80011-9036
(303) 360-4709

Community College of Denver

Denver, Colorado
www.ccd.edu   Federal Code: 009542

2-year public community college in very large city.
Enrollment: 5,566 undergrads, 65% part-time. 383 full-time freshmen.
Selectivity: Open admission; but selective for some programs.

BASIC COSTS (2007-2008)

Tuition and fees: $2,954; out-of-state residents $11,357.
Per-credit charge: $77; out-of-state residents $345.
Additional info: In-state tuition based upon assumption of Colorado Opportunity Fund waiver of $89 per-credit-hour.

FINANCIAL AID PICTURE (2006-2007)

Students with need: 69% of average financial aid package awarded as scholarships/grants, 31% awarded as loans/jobs. Need-based aid available for part-time students.
Students without need: No-need awards available for academics, leadership, state/district residency.

FINANCIAL AID PROCEDURES

Forms required: FAFSA, institutional form.
Dates and Deadlines: Priority date 3/1; no closing date.

CONTACT

Karla Nash, Director of Financial Aid
Campus Box 201, PO Box 173363, Denver, CO 80217-3363
(303) 556-2420

DeVry University: Westminster

Westminster, Colorado
www.devry.edu   Federal Code: 014831

4-year for-profit university in very large city.
Enrollment: 596 undergrads, 51% part-time. 64 full-time freshmen.

BASIC COSTS (2007-2008)

Tuition and fees: $14,020.
Per-credit charge: $500.

FINANCIAL AID PICTURE (2006-2007)

Students with need: Out of 41 full-time freshmen who applied for aid, 35 were judged to have need. Of these, 35 received aid, and 2 had their full need met. Average financial aid package met 30% of need; average scholarship/grant was $3,847; average loan was $4,362. For part-time students, average financial aid package was $8,169.
Students without need: This college awards aid only to students with need.

Cumulative student debt: 33% of graduating class had student loans; average debt was $55,459.

FINANCIAL AID PROCEDURES

Forms required: FAFSA.

Dates and Deadlines: No deadline. Applicants notified on a rolling basis.

CONTACT

Terry Bargas, Director of Financial Aid

1870 West 122 Avenue, Westminster, CO 80234-2010

(303) 329-3340

Everest College: Aurora

Aurora, Colorado

www.cci.edu   Federal Code: 004507

2-year for-profit branch campus and technical college in large city.

Enrollment: 61 undergrads, 15% part-time. 52 full-time freshmen.

Selectivity: Open admission.

BASIC COSTS (2007-2008)

Additional info: $287 per credit hour for all linear programs; $25 registration fee and tech fee per quarter.

FINANCIAL AID PICTURE

Students with need: Need-based aid available for full-time and part-time students. Work study available nights.

Students without need: This college awards aid only to students with need.

FINANCIAL AID PROCEDURES

Forms required: FAFSA, state aid form, institutional form.

Dates and Deadlines: No deadline. Applicants notified on a rolling basis; must reply within 4 week(s) of notification.

Transfers: $4,500 limitation on Colorado State Grant per award year.

CONTACT

Kim Martinez, Finance Director

14280 East Jewell Suite 100, Aurora, CO 80012

(303) 745-6244 ext. 104

Everest College: Colorado Springs

Colorado Springs, Colorado

www.cci.edu   Federal Code: 004503

2-year for-profit business and junior college in large city.

Enrollment: 400 undergrads.

Selectivity: Admits over 75% of applicants.

BASIC COSTS (2007-2008)

Additional info: $298 per credit hour for all linear programs; $150 in required fees. Tuition at time of enrollment locked for 2 years.

FINANCIAL AID PICTURE

Students with need: Need-based aid available for full-time and part-time students. Work study available nights.

FINANCIAL AID PROCEDURES

Forms required: FAFSA, institutional form.

Dates and Deadlines: No deadline. Applicants notified on a rolling basis starting 7/1.

Transfers: No deadline.

CONTACT

1815 Jet Wing Drive, Colorado Springs, CO 80916

(719) 638-6580

Fort Lewis College

Durango, Colorado

www.fortlewis.edu   Federal Code: 001353

4-year public liberal arts college in large town.

Enrollment: 3,788 undergrads, 9% part-time. 886 full-time freshmen.

Selectivity: Admits 50 to 75% of applicants.

BASIC COSTS (2007-2008)

Tuition and fees: $6,464; out-of-state residents $14,994.

Per-credit charge: $221; out-of-state residents $692.

Room and board: $6,876.

Additional info: Tuition/fee waivers available for minority students.

FINANCIAL AID PICTURE (2006-2007)

Students with need: Out of 595 full-time freshmen who applied for aid, 417 were judged to have need. Of these, 408 received aid, and 61 had their full need met. Average financial aid package met 61% of need; average scholarship/grant was $3,733; average loan was $2,448. For part-time students, average financial aid package was $4,591.

Students without need: 96 full-time freshmen who did not demonstrate need for aid received scholarships/grants; average award was $1,931. No-need awards available for academics, alumni affiliation, art, athletics, leadership, minority status, music/drama, state/district residency.

Scholarships offered: *Merit:* Fort Lewis Merit Scholarships; $500 resident, $1,000 non-resident (non-Western Undergraduate Exchange state); index of 92 or higher required. Western Undergraduate Exchange; tuition is 1.5 times in-state tuition; must be from WUE states with index of 92 or higher required. New Mexico Reciprocal; in-state tuition; must be New Mexico resident with index of 101 or higher. *Athletic:* 27 full-time freshmen received athletic scholarships; average amount $2,933.

Cumulative student debt: 57% of graduating class had student loans; average debt was $17,431.

Additional info: Tuition waived for Native Americans of federally recognized tribes; census number and Certificate of Indian Blood must accompany application.

FINANCIAL AID PROCEDURES

Forms required: FAFSA.

Dates and Deadlines: Priority date 2/15; no closing date. Applicants notified on a rolling basis starting 3/15; must reply within 2 week(s) of notification.

Transfers: Closing date 2/15. Applicants notified on a rolling basis starting 3/15; must reply within 2 week(s) of notification.

CONTACT

Elaine Redwine, Director of Financial Aid

1000 Rim Drive, Durango, CO 81301-3999

(970) 247-7142

Front Range Community College

Westminster, Colorado

www.frontrange.edu   Federal Code: 007933

2-year public community college in large city.

Enrollment: 12,537 undergrads, 63% part-time. 1,667 full-time freshmen.

Selectivity: Open admission.

BASIC COSTS (2007-2008)

Tuition and fees: $2,599; out-of-state residents $11,002.

Per-credit charge: $77; out-of-state residents $357.

Additional info: In-state tuition based upon assumption of Colorado Opportunity Fund waiver of $89 per-credit-hour.

FINANCIAL AID PICTURE (2006-2007)

Students with need: 40% of average financial aid package awarded as scholarships/grants, 60% awarded as loans/jobs. Need-based aid available for part-time students. Work study available nights, weekends, and for part-time students.

Students without need: No-need awards available for academics, job skills, leadership, state/district residency.

FINANCIAL AID PROCEDURES

Forms required: FAFSA, institutional form.

Dates and Deadlines: Priority date 5/1; no closing date. Applicants notified on a rolling basis starting 7/1; must reply within 3 week(s) of notification.

CONTACT

Director of Financial Aid
3645 West 112th Avenue, Westminster, CO 80031
(303) 439-9454

IntelliTec College

Colorado Springs, Colorado
www.intelliteccollege.com   Federal Code: 008635

2-year for-profit technical college in large city.

Enrollment: 500 undergrads.

Selectivity: Open admission.

BASIC COSTS (2007-2008)

Additional info: Tuition at time of enrollment locked for 2 years.

FINANCIAL AID PICTURE

Students with need: Need-based aid available for full-time and part-time students. Work study available nights.

Students without need: This college awards aid only to students with need.

FINANCIAL AID PROCEDURES

Forms required: FAFSA, state aid form, institutional form.

Dates and Deadlines: No deadline. Applicants notified on a rolling basis.

Transfers: No deadline.

CONTACT

Laurie Roth, Financial Services Representative
2315 East Pikes Peak Avenue, Colorado Springs, CO 80909
(719) 632-7626

IntelliTec College: Grand Junction

Grand Junction, Colorado
www.intelliteccollege.edu   Federal Code: 030669

2-year for-profit technical college in small city.

Enrollment: 250 undergrads.

Selectivity: Open admission.

BASIC COSTS (2007-2008)

Tuition and fees: $17,000.

Additional info: Tuition at time of enrollment locked for 2 years.

FINANCIAL AID PICTURE

Students with need: Need-based aid available for full-time students.

Students without need: This college awards aid only to students with need.

FINANCIAL AID PROCEDURES

Forms required: FAFSA.

Dates and Deadlines: No deadline. Applicants notified on a rolling basis.

Transfers: No deadline.

CONTACT

Lisa Watson, Director of Financial Sevices
772 Horizon Drive, Grand Junction, CO 81506
(970) 245-8101

Johnson & Wales University: Denver

Denver, Colorado
www.jwu.edu   Federal Code: 003404

4-year private university in large city.

Enrollment: 1,465 undergrads, 3% part-time. 359 full-time freshmen.

Selectivity: Admits over 75% of applicants.

BASIC COSTS (2007-2008)

Tuition and fees: $21,717.

Per-credit charge: $379.

Room and board: $8,550.

Additional info: Weekend meal plan available for $987.

FINANCIAL AID PICTURE (2007-2008)

Students with need: Out of 299 full-time freshmen who applied for aid, 247 were judged to have need. Of these, 247 received aid, and 32 had their full need met. Average financial aid package met 72% of need; average scholarship/grant was $7,294; average loan was $3,116. For part-time students, average financial aid package was $13,500.

Students without need: 71 full-time freshmen who did not demonstrate need for aid received scholarships/grants; average award was $5,391. No-need awards available for academics, leadership.

Cumulative student debt: 74% of graduating class had student loans; average debt was $24,664.

FINANCIAL AID PROCEDURES

Forms required: FAFSA.

Dates and Deadlines: No deadline. Applicants notified on a rolling basis starting 3/1; must reply within 2 week(s) of notification.

CONTACT

Lynn Robinson, Chief Financial Aid Officer
7150 Montview Boulevard, Denver, CO 80220
(800) 342-5598 ext. 4648

Lamar Community College

Lamar, Colorado
www.lamarcc.edu   Federal Code: 001355

2-year public community college in large town.

Enrollment: 500 undergrads.

Selectivity: Open admission; but selective for some programs.

BASIC COSTS (2007-2008)

Tuition and fees: $2,639; out-of-state residents $5,309.

Per-credit charge: $77; out-of-state residents $166.

Room and board: $4,757.

Additional info: In-state tuition based upon assumption of Colorado Opportunity Fund waiver of $89 per-credit-hour.

FINANCIAL AID PICTURE

Students with need: Need-based aid available for full-time and part-time students.

FINANCIAL AID PROCEDURES

Forms required: FAFSA, institutional form.

Dates and Deadlines: Priority date 4/1; no closing date. Applicants notified on a rolling basis starting 7/1.

Transfers: No deadline.

CONTACT

Teale Hemphill, Director of Financial Aid
2401 South Main Street, Lamar, CO 81052-3999

Mesa State College
Grand Junction, Colorado
www.mesastate.edu   Federal Code: 001358

4-year public community and liberal arts college in small city.
Enrollment: 5,585 undergrads, 22% part-time. 1,125 full-time freshmen.
Selectivity: Admits over 75% of applicants.

BASIC COSTS (2007-2008)

Tuition and fees: $4,342; out-of-state residents $12,245.
Per-credit charge: $150; out-of-state residents $441.
Room and board: $8,167.

FINANCIAL AID PICTURE (2006-2007)

Students with need: Out of 934 full-time freshmen who applied for aid, 841 were judged to have need. Of these, 841 received aid, and 128 had their full need met. Average financial aid package met 46% of need; average scholarship/grant was $3,903; average loan was $2,320. For part-time students, average financial aid package was $4,681.
Students without need: 43 full-time freshmen who did not demonstrate need for aid received scholarships/grants; average award was $2,354. No-need awards available for academics, art, athletics, leadership, minority status, music/drama.
Scholarships offered: 19 full-time freshmen received athletic scholarships; average amount $2,200.
Cumulative student debt: 53% of graduating class had student loans; average debt was $18,353.

FINANCIAL AID PROCEDURES

Forms required: FAFSA.
Dates and Deadlines: Priority date 3/1; no closing date. Applicants notified on a rolling basis starting 4/1; must reply within 5 week(s) of notification.

CONTACT

Curt Martin, Director of Financial Aid
1100 North Avenue, Grand Junction, CO 81501
(970) 248-1396

Metropolitan State College of Denver
Denver, Colorado
www.mscd.edu   Federal Code: 001360

4-year public liberal arts college in very large city.
Enrollment: 20,298 undergrads.

BASIC COSTS (2007-2008)

Tuition and fees: $3,033; out-of-state residents $11,134.
Per-credit charge: $101; out-of-state residents $439.

FINANCIAL AID PICTURE

Students with need: Need-based aid available for full-time and part-time students.
Students without need: No-need awards available for academics, art, athletics, job skills, music/drama, state/district residency.

FINANCIAL AID PROCEDURES

Forms required: FAFSA.
Dates and Deadlines: Priority date 2/15; no closing date. Applicants notified on a rolling basis starting 3/1.
Transfers: No deadline.

CONTACT

Cindy Hejl, Director of Financial Aid
Campus Box 16, Denver, CO 80217

Morgan Community College
Fort Morgan, Colorado
www.morgancc.edu   Federal Code: 009981

2-year public community college in large town.
Enrollment: 528 undergrads.
Selectivity: Open admission; but selective for some programs.

BASIC COSTS (2007-2008)

Tuition and fees: $2,479; out-of-state residents $10,882.
Per-credit charge: $77; out-of-state residents $357.
Additional info: In-state tuition based upon assumption of Colorado Opportunity Fund waiver of $89 per-credit-hour.

FINANCIAL AID PICTURE (2007-2008)

Students with need: 68% of average financial aid package awarded as scholarships/grants, 32% awarded as loans/jobs. Need-based aid available for part-time students. Work study available nights, weekends, and for part-time students.

FINANCIAL AID PROCEDURES

Forms required: FAFSA.
Dates and Deadlines: Priority date 6/1; no closing date. Applicants notified on a rolling basis.

CONTACT

Trina Gutierrez, Director of Financial Aid
920 Barlow Road, Fort Morgan, CO 80701
(970) 542-3100

Naropa University
Boulder, Colorado
www.naropa.edu   Federal Code: 014652

4-year private liberal arts college in small city.
Enrollment: 456 undergrads, 6% part-time. 66 full-time freshmen.
Selectivity: Admits over 75% of applicants.

BASIC COSTS (2008-2009)

Tuition and fees: $22,074.
Per-credit charge: $712.
Room and board: $7,036.

FINANCIAL AID PICTURE (2007-2008)

Students with need: Out of 48 full-time freshmen who applied for aid, 47 were judged to have need. Of these, 47 received aid, and 1 had their full need met. Average financial aid package met 88% of need; average scholarship/grant was $13,129; average loan was $4,176. For part-time students, average financial aid package was $7,864.
Students without need: This college awards aid only to students with need.
Cumulative student debt: 7% of graduating class had student loans; average debt was $26,582.

FINANCIAL AID PROCEDURES

Forms required: FAFSA.
Dates and Deadlines: Priority date 3/1; no closing date. Applicants notified on a rolling basis starting 3/1; must reply within 4 week(s) of notification.
Transfers: No deadline. Applicants notified on a rolling basis starting 3/1; must reply within 4 week(s) of notification.

PART III: FINANCIAL AID COLLEGE BY COLLEGE

CONTACT

Cheryl Barbour, Assistant Vice President of Student Administrative Services

2130 Arapahoe Avenue, Boulder, CO 80302-6697

(303) 546-3534

Nazarene Bible College

Colorado Springs, Colorado

www.nbc.edu   Federal Code: 013007

4-year private Bible college in very large city, affiliated with Church of the Nazarene.

Enrollment: 810 undergrads.

Selectivity: Open admission; but selective for some programs.

BASIC COSTS (2008-2009)

Tuition and fees: $8,550.

Per-credit charge: $275.

FINANCIAL AID PICTURE

Students with need: Need-based aid available for full-time and part-time students.

Students without need: No-need awards available for religious affiliation.

Additional info: Tuition waiver available to students serving as student body officers.

FINANCIAL AID PROCEDURES

Forms required: FAFSA.

Dates and Deadlines: Priority date 6/1; no closing date. Applicants notified on a rolling basis starting 6/15; must reply within 2 week(s) of notification.

CONTACT

Mal Britton, Director of Financial Aid

1111 Academy Park Loop, Colorado Springs, CO 80910-3717

(719) 884-5050 ext. 5050

Northeastern Junior College

Sterling, Colorado

www.njc.edu   Federal Code: 001361

2-year public junior college in large town.

Enrollment: 1,082 undergrads, 23% part-time. 383 full-time freshmen.

Selectivity: Open admission; but selective for some programs.

BASIC COSTS (2007-2008)

Tuition and fees: $2,909; out-of-state residents $5,579.

Per-credit charge: $77; out-of-state residents $166.

Room and board: $5,316.

Additional info: In-state tuition based upon assumption of Colorado Opportunity Fund waiver of $89 per-credit-hour. Tuition/fee waivers available for adults, minority students.

FINANCIAL AID PICTURE (2006-2007)

Students with need: 58% of average financial aid package awarded as scholarships/grants, 42% awarded as loans/jobs. Need-based aid available for part-time students.

Students without need: No-need awards available for academics, alumni affiliation, art, athletics, job skills, leadership, music/drama, state/district residency.

Additional info: Need-based financial aid available to part-time students taking 6 credits or more per semester.

FINANCIAL AID PROCEDURES

Forms required: FAFSA, institutional form.

Dates and Deadlines: Priority date 3/1; no closing date. Applicants notified on a rolling basis starting 4/15; must reply within 3 week(s) of notification.

Transfers: No deadline. Applicants notified on a rolling basis starting 4/15; must reply within 3 week(s) of notification.

CONTACT

Alice Weingardt, Financial Aid Director

100 College Avenue, Sterling, CO 80751

(970) 521-6800

Otero Junior College

La Junta, Colorado

www.ojc.edu   Federal Code: 001362

2-year public community and junior college in small town.

Enrollment: 1,250 undergrads.

Selectivity: Open admission; but selective for some programs.

BASIC COSTS (2007-2008)

Tuition and fees: $2,509; out-of-state residents $5,179.

Per-credit charge: $77; out-of-state residents $166.

Room and board: $4,692.

Additional info: In-state tuition based upon assumption of Colorado Opportunity Fund waiver of $89 per-credit-hour.

FINANCIAL AID PICTURE

Students with need: Need-based aid available for full-time and part-time students. Work study available nights, weekends, and for part-time students.

Students without need: No-need awards available for academics, athletics, state/district residency.

FINANCIAL AID PROCEDURES

Forms required: FAFSA.

Dates and Deadlines: Priority date 4/15; no closing date. Applicants notified on a rolling basis starting 4/15; must reply within 2 week(s) of notification.

Transfers: No deadline. Applicants notified on a rolling basis starting 4/15; must reply within 2 week(s) of notification.

CONTACT

Jennifer Carrica, Financial Aid Director

1802 Colorado Avenue, La Junta, CO 81050

(719) 384-6834

Pikes Peak Community College

Colorado Springs, Colorado

www.ppcc.edu   Federal Code: 008896

2-year public community college in large city.

Enrollment: 10,797 undergrads, 63% part-time. 1,113 full-time freshmen.

Selectivity: Open admission.

BASIC COSTS (2007-2008)

Tuition and fees: $2,578; out-of-state residents $10,981.

Per-credit charge: $77; out-of-state residents $357.

Additional info: In-state tuition eligible for Colorado Opportunity Fund (COF) waiver, currently $89 per credit hour.

FINANCIAL AID PICTURE

Students with need: Need-based aid available for full-time and part-time students. Work study available nights.

FINANCIAL AID PROCEDURES

Forms required: FAFSA.

Dates and Deadlines: Priority date 7/1; no closing date. Applicants notified on a rolling basis starting 8/1; must reply within 2 week(s) of notification.

CONTACT

Sherri McCullough, Assistant Director of Financial Aid

5675 South Academy Boulevard, Colorado Springs, CO 80906-5498

(719) 502-3000

Platt College: Aurora

Aurora, Colorado

www.plattcolorado.edu   Federal Code: 030149

4-year for-profit visual arts and technical college in large city.

Enrollment: 165 undergrads.

BASIC COSTS (2007-2008)

Additional info: Visual and Performing Arts: associate program: $34,000; Bachelor's program: $50,107. Nursing program (RN): $68,000. Costs include tuition, registration fee, lab fees, supplies. Cost of books, art kit vary with program.

FINANCIAL AID PICTURE

Students with need: Need-based aid available for full-time students.

Students without need: This college awards aid only to students with need.

FINANCIAL AID PROCEDURES

Forms required: FAFSA, institutional form.

Dates and Deadlines: No deadline. Applicants notified on a rolling basis.

CONTACT

Margie Rose, Director of Financial Aid

3100 South Parker Road, Aurora, CO 80014

(303) 369-5151

Pueblo Community College

Pueblo, Colorado

www.pueblocc.edu   Federal Code: 014829

2-year public community college in small city.

Enrollment: 4,150 undergrads.

Selectivity: Open admission; but selective for some programs.

BASIC COSTS (2007-2008)

Tuition and fees: $2,578; out-of-state residents $10,981.

Per-credit charge: $77; out-of-state residents $357.

Additional info: In-state tuition based upon assumption of Colorado Opportunity Fund waiver of $89 per-credit-hour.

FINANCIAL AID PICTURE

Students with need: Need-based aid available for full-time and part-time students.

Students without need: No-need awards available for academics, state/district residency.

FINANCIAL AID PROCEDURES

Forms required: FAFSA, institutional form.

Dates and Deadlines: Priority date 3/15; no closing date. Applicants notified on a rolling basis starting 4/15.

CONTACT

Ron Swartwood, Director of Financial Aid

900 West Orman Avenue, Pueblo, CO 81004-1499

(719) 549-3020

Red Rocks Community College

Lakewood, Colorado

www.rrcc.edu   Federal Code: 009543

2-year public community college in small city.

Enrollment: 5,065 undergrads, 65% part-time. 629 full-time freshmen.

Selectivity: Open admission.

BASIC COSTS (2007-2008)

Tuition and fees: $2,587; out-of-state residents $10,990.

Per-credit charge: $77; out-of-state residents $357.

Additional info: In-state tuition based upon assumption of Colorado Opportunity Fund waiver of $89 per-credit-hour.

FINANCIAL AID PICTURE

Students with need: Need-based aid available for full-time and part-time students. Work study available nights, weekends, and for part-time students.

FINANCIAL AID PROCEDURES

Forms required: FAFSA, institutional form.

Dates and Deadlines: Priority date 4/1; no closing date. Applicants notified on a rolling basis starting 6/1; must reply within 2 week(s) of notification.

CONTACT

Linda Crook, Director of Financial Aid

13300 West Sixth Avenue, Lakewood, CO 80228-1255

(303) 914-6256

Redstone College

Broomfield, Colorado

www.redstonecollege.com   Federal Code: 007297

2-year for-profit technical college in small city.

Enrollment: 535 undergrads.

Selectivity: Open admission.

BASIC COSTS (2007-2008)

Additional info: Tuition for entire associate degree ranges from $13,239 to $32,378 depending on program of study. Tuition at time of enrollment locked for 2 years.

FINANCIAL AID PICTURE

Students with need: Need-based aid available for full-time students.

Students without need: This college awards aid only to students with need.

FINANCIAL AID PROCEDURES

Forms required: FAFSA, state aid form.

Dates and Deadlines: No deadline. Applicants notified on a rolling basis; must reply within 2 week(s) of notification.

CONTACT

Alicia Harbin, Financial Aid Director

10851 West 120th Avenue, Broomfield, CO 80021-3401

Regis University

Denver, Colorado

www.regis.edu   Federal Code: 001363

4-year private university and liberal arts college in very large city, affiliated with Roman Catholic Church.

Enrollment: 1,623 undergrads, 3% part-time. 406 full-time freshmen.

Selectivity: Admits 50 to 75% of applicants.

BASIC COSTS (2008-2009)

Tuition and fees: $28,700.
Per-credit charge: $888.
Room and board: $8,982.

FINANCIAL AID PICTURE (2006-2007)

Students with need: Out of 401 full-time freshmen who applied for aid, 244 were judged to have need. Of these, 244 received aid, and 105 had their full need met. For part-time students, average financial aid package was $65.
Students without need: 56 full-time freshmen who did not demonstrate need for aid received scholarships/grants; average award was $7,099. No-need awards available for academics, athletics, leadership, minority status, religious affiliation, ROTC, state/district residency.
Scholarships offered: 25 full-time freshmen received athletic scholarships; average amount $3,856.
Additional info: Tuition free for any student maintaining the required amount of credit hours who does not graduate in four years.

FINANCIAL AID PROCEDURES

Forms required: FAFSA.
Dates and Deadlines: Priority date 3/1; no closing date. Applicants notified on a rolling basis starting 3/15.

CONTACT

Ellie Miller, Director of Financial Aid
3333 Regis Boulevard, Mail Code B20, Denver, CO 80221-1099
(800) 388-2366 ext. 4126

Remington College: Colorado Springs

Colorado Springs, Colorado
www.remingtoncollege.com   Federal Code: 030121

2-year for-profit technical college in very large city.
Enrollment: 175 undergrads.
Selectivity: Open admission; but selective for some programs.

BASIC COSTS (2007-2008)

Additional info: Tuition varies by program and ranges from $13,000 to $13,860. Tuition at time of enrollment locked for 2 years.

FINANCIAL AID PICTURE

Students with need: Need-based aid available for full-time and part-time students.
Students without need: This college awards aid only to students with need.

FINANCIAL AID PROCEDURES

Forms required: FAFSA.
Dates and Deadlines: No deadline. Applicants notified on a rolling basis; must reply within 3 week(s) of notification.
Transfers: No deadline. Applicants notified on a rolling basis.

CONTACT

Tara Miller, Director of Student Finance
6050 Erin Park Drive, Colorado Springs, CO 80918
(719) 532-1234 ext. 202

Rocky Mountain College of Art & Design

Denver, Colorado
www.rmcad.edu   Federal Code: 013991

4-year for-profit visual arts college in very large city.
Enrollment: 496 undergrads, 13% part-time. 121 full-time freshmen.
Selectivity: Admits over 75% of applicants.

BASIC COSTS (2007-2008)

Tuition and fees: $19,752.
Per-credit charge: $823.
Room and board: $8,440.

FINANCIAL AID PICTURE

Students with need: Need-based aid available for full-time and part-time students. Work study available nights, weekends, and for part-time students.
Students without need: No-need awards available for academics, art, state/district residency.

FINANCIAL AID PROCEDURES

Forms required: FAFSA, state aid form, institutional form.
Dates and Deadlines: Priority date 3/15; no closing date. Applicants notified on a rolling basis starting 4/15; must reply within 2 week(s) of notification.

CONTACT

Tammy Dybdahl, Director of Financial Aid
1600 Pierce Street, Denver, CO 80214
(303) 753-6046

Teikyo Loretto Heights University

Denver, Colorado
www.tlhu.edu   Federal Code: 032893

4-year private business and liberal arts college in very large city.
Enrollment: 372 undergrads.

BASIC COSTS (2007-2008)

Tuition and fees: $14,970.
Per-credit charge: $499.
Room and board: $7,300.

FINANCIAL AID PICTURE

Students with need: Need-based aid available for full-time and part-time students. Work study available nights.

FINANCIAL AID PROCEDURES

Forms required: FAFSA.
Dates and Deadlines: No deadline.

CONTACT

Agustina Giron
3001 South Federal Boulevard, Denver, CO 80236
(303) 937-4538

Trinidad State Junior College

Trinidad, Colorado
www.trinidadstate.edu   Federal Code: 001368

2-year public community and junior college in small town.
Enrollment: 1,276 undergrads.
Selectivity: Open admission; but selective for some programs.

BASIC COSTS (2007-2008)

Tuition and fees: $2,622; out-of-state residents $5,292.
Per-credit charge: $77; out-of-state residents $166.
Room and board: $4,555.
Additional info: In-state tuition based upon assumption of Colorado Opportunity Fund waiver of $86 per-credit-hour.

FINANCIAL AID PICTURE (2006-2007)

Students with need: 72% of average financial aid package awarded as scholarships/grants, 28% awarded as loans/jobs. Need-based aid available for part-time students. Work study available nights.
Students without need: No-need awards available for academics, athletics, state/district residency.

FINANCIAL AID PROCEDURES

Forms required: FAFSA, institutional form.

Dates and Deadlines: Priority date 5/1; no closing date. Applicants notified on a rolling basis starting 6/15.

CONTACT

Gary Fresquez, Financial Aid Director
600 Prospect Street, Trinidad, CO 81082
(719) 846-5553

United States Air Force Academy

USAF Academy, Colorado
www.usafa.edu   Federal Code: 001369

4-year public university and military college in large city.

Enrollment: 4,467 undergrads. 1,214 full-time freshmen.

Selectivity: Admits less than 50% of applicants.

BASIC COSTS (2007-2008)

Additional info: Tuition, room, board, medical and dental care paid by U.S. Government. Each cadet receives monthly salary to pay for uniforms, supplies and personal expenses. A government loan is advanced to each member of the freshman class.

CONTACT

HQ USAF/RRS, 2304 Cadet Drive, Suite 2300, USAF Academy, CO 80840

University of Colorado at Boulder

Boulder, Colorado
www.colorado.edu   Federal Code: 001370

4-year public university in small city.

Enrollment: 25,521 undergrads, 7% part-time. 5,550 full-time freshmen.

Selectivity: Admits over 75% of applicants.

BASIC COSTS (2007-2008)

Tuition and fees: $6,635; out-of-state residents $24,797.

Room and board: $9,088.

Additional info: One-time matriculation fee of $108.

FINANCIAL AID PICTURE (2007-2008)

Students with need: Out of 4,602 full-time freshmen who applied for aid, 2,378 were judged to have need. Of these, 2,352 received aid, and 1,872 had their full need met. Average financial aid package met 92% of need; average scholarship/grant was $5,158; average loan was $4,413. For part-time students, average financial aid package was $10,534.

Students without need: 2,067 full-time freshmen who did not demonstrate need for aid received scholarships/grants; average award was $3,047. No-need awards available for academics, alumni affiliation, art, athletics, leadership, music/drama, ROTC, state/district residency.

Scholarships offered: Merit: Presidential Scholars Program; $10,000 annual tuition reduction for four years; for entering non-resident freshmen in the top 3-5% of CU-Boulder's admitted non-resident freshman class; based on high school GPA, class rank, and test scores; must maintain 2.75 CU GPA for renewal. Chancellor's Achievement Scholarship; $15,000 over four years; for entering non-resident freshmen in the top 25% of CU-Boulder's admitted non-resident freshman class; based on high school GPA and test scores; must maintain 2.75 CU GPA for renewal. Chancellor's Citizenship Scholarship; $25,000 over four years; for top entering Colorado resident freshmen; 25 awards based on academic excellence, commitment to the principles of the Colorado Creed, and contribution to campus diversity; must maintain 2.75 CU GPA for renewal. CU Parents Association Freshmen Scholarship; $1,000; based on full-time entering freshman status with 3.5 GPA, academic excellence and extracurricular activities; 10-20 awarded annually; nonrenewable. Norlin Scholars Program; $2,000; based on excellent academic or cre-

ative ability; 25 awards; renewable for 2 or 4 years, contingent upon academic progress. **Athletic:** 58 full-time freshmen received athletic scholarships; average amount $13,303.

Cumulative student debt: 41% of graduating class had student loans; average debt was $18,037.

FINANCIAL AID PROCEDURES

Forms required: FAFSA.

Dates and Deadlines: Priority date 4/1; no closing date. Applicants notified on a rolling basis starting 2/1; must reply within 3 week(s) of notification.

Transfers: Some financial aid programs available exclusively to transfer students.

CONTACT

Gwen Pomper, Director of Financial Aid
552 UCB, Boulder, CO 80309-0552
(303) 492-5091

University of Colorado at Colorado Springs

Colorado Springs, Colorado
www.uccs.edu   Federal Code: 004509

4-year public university in large city.

Enrollment: 6,181 undergrads, 21% part-time. 667 full-time freshmen.

Selectivity: Admits 50 to 75% of applicants.

BASIC COSTS (2007-2008)

Tuition and fees: $5,431; out-of-state residents $16,381.

Room and board: $6,898.

FINANCIAL AID PICTURE (2006-2007)

Students with need: Out of 574 full-time freshmen who applied for aid, 306 were judged to have need. Of these, 287 received aid, and 59 had their full need met. Average financial aid package met 54% of need; average scholarship/grant was $5,537; average loan was $2,523. For part-time students, average financial aid package was $4,886.

Students without need: 126 full-time freshmen who did not demonstrate need for aid received scholarships/grants; average award was $1,546. No-need awards available for academics, alumni affiliation, athletics, state/district residency.

Scholarships offered: Merit: College Opportunity Fund for in-state undergraduates. **Athletic:** 8 full-time freshmen received athletic scholarships; average amount $2,138.

Cumulative student debt: 59% of graduating class had student loans; average debt was $20,860.

FINANCIAL AID PROCEDURES

Forms required: FAFSA.

Dates and Deadlines: Priority date 4/1; no closing date. Applicants notified on a rolling basis starting 4/15.

CONTACT

Lee Noble, Director of Financial Aid
PO Box 7150, Colorado Springs, CO 80933-7150
(719) 262-3460

University of Colorado at Denver

Denver, Colorado
www.ucdhsc.edu   Federal Code: 006740

4-year public university in very large city.

Enrollment: 8,327 undergrads, 27% part-time. 870 full-time freshmen.

Selectivity: Admits 50 to 75% of applicants.

BASIC COSTS (2007-2008)

Tuition and fees: $5,815; out-of-state residents $17,771.

Per-credit charge: $216; out-of-state residents $709.

Additional info: Tuition varies by program. One-time matriculation fee of $115 required.

FINANCIAL AID PICTURE (2006-2007)

Students with need: Out of 507 full-time freshmen who applied for aid, 379 were judged to have need. Of these, 372 received aid. Average financial aid package met 69% of need; average scholarship/grant was $4,715; average loan was $3,014. For part-time students, average financial aid package was $8,780.

Students without need: 100 full-time freshmen who did not demonstrate need for aid received scholarships/grants; average award was $902. No-need awards available for academics, art, leadership, music/drama.

Cumulative student debt: 44% of graduating class had student loans; average debt was $16,321.

FINANCIAL AID PROCEDURES

Forms required: FAFSA, institutional form.

Dates and Deadlines: Closing date 4/1. Applicants notified on a rolling basis starting 5/1.

CONTACT

Patrick McTee, Director of Financial Aid

Box 173364, Campus Box 167, Denver, CO 80217-3364

(303) 556-2886

University of Denver

Denver, Colorado

www.du.edu   Federal Code: 001371

4-year private university in very large city, affiliated with United Methodist Church.

Enrollment: 5,260 undergrads, 9% part-time. 1,135 full-time freshmen.

Selectivity: Admits 50 to 75% of applicants.

BASIC COSTS (2008-2009)

Tuition and fees: $33,810.

Per-credit charge: $916.

Room and board: $9,093.

FINANCIAL AID PICTURE (2006-2007)

Students with need: Out of 669 full-time freshmen who applied for aid, 449 were judged to have need. Of these, 449 received aid, and 79 had their full need met. Average financial aid package met 76% of need; average scholarship/grant was $18,283; average loan was $3,218. For part-time students, average financial aid package was $6,092.

Students without need: 492 full-time freshmen who did not demonstrate need for aid received scholarships/grants; average award was $9,642. No-need awards available for academics, art, athletics, leadership, minority status, music/drama, state/district residency.

Scholarships offered: 39 full-time freshmen received athletic scholarships; average amount $20,807.

Cumulative student debt: 45% of graduating class had student loans; average debt was $25,375.

FINANCIAL AID PROCEDURES

Forms required: FAFSA.

Dates and Deadlines: Priority date 3/1; no closing date.

CONTACT

Barbara McFall, Director of Financial Aid

2197 South University Boulevard, Denver, CO 80208

(303) 871-4020

University of Northern Colorado

Greeley, Colorado

www.unco.edu   Federal Code: 001349

4-year public university in small city.

Enrollment: 10,038 undergrads, 9% part-time. 2,235 full-time freshmen.

Selectivity: Admits over 75% of applicants.

BASIC COSTS (2007-2008)

Tuition and fees: $4,313; out-of-state residents $12,893.

Room and board: $7,292.

Additional info: Costs reflect student share of tuition after the Colorado College Opportunity Fund.

FINANCIAL AID PICTURE (2006-2007)

Students with need: 46% of average financial aid package awarded as scholarships/grants, 54% awarded as loans/jobs. Need-based aid available for part-time students. Work study available nights, weekends, and for part-time students.

Students without need: No-need awards available for academics, athletics, music/drama.

FINANCIAL AID PROCEDURES

Forms required: FAFSA.

Dates and Deadlines: Priority date 3/1; no closing date. Applicants notified on a rolling basis starting 4/15; must reply within 4 week(s) of notification.

CONTACT

Donni Clark, Director of Student Financial Resources

Campus Box 10, Greeley, CO 80639

(970) 351-2502

Western State College of Colorado

Gunnison, Colorado

www.western.edu   Federal Code: 001372

4-year public liberal arts college in small town.

Enrollment: 2,400 undergrads.

BASIC COSTS (2007-2008)

Tuition and fees: $3,573; out-of-state residents $12,405.

Per-credit charge: $112; out-of-state residents $480.

Room and board: $7,522.

Additional info: Tuition/fee waivers available for unemployed or children of unemployed.

FINANCIAL AID PICTURE (2007-2008)

Students with need: Average financial aid package met 60% of need; average scholarship/grant was $3,500; average loan was $2,625.

Students without need: No-need awards available for academics, alumni affiliation, art, athletics, leadership, music/drama.

Scholarships offered: Academic Excellence Award; $1,000; minimum 3.5 GPA and 22 ACT or 1010 SAT. Non-resident Leadership Award, $2,500; 3.2 GPA, 990 SAT, leadership activities. SAT scores exclusive of Writing.

Cumulative student debt: 67% of graduating class had student loans; average debt was $19,800.

FINANCIAL AID PROCEDURES

Forms required: FAFSA.

Dates and Deadlines: Priority date 4/1; no closing date. Applicants notified on a rolling basis starting 4/1; must reply within 4 week(s) of notification.

CONTACT

Marty Somero, Director of Financial Aid

600 North Adams Street, Gunnison, CO 81231

(970) 943-3085

Westwood College: Denver South

Denver, Colorado
www.westwood.edu   Federal Code: 007548

4-year for-profit technical college in very large city.
Enrollment: 325 undergrads.
Selectivity: Admits over 75% of applicants.

BASIC COSTS (2007-2008)
Tuition and fees: $22,275.
Additional info: Tuition and fees may vary by program.

FINANCIAL AID PICTURE
Students with need: Need-based aid available for full-time and part-time students. Work study available nights.

FINANCIAL AID PROCEDURES
Forms required: FAFSA, state aid form, institutional form.
Dates and Deadlines: No deadline. Applicants notified on a rolling basis; must reply within 2 week(s) of notification.

CONTACT
Alexandra Hoffman, Director of Student Affairs
3150 South Sheridan Boulevard, Denver, CO 80227-5507
(303) 934-1122

Connecticut

Albertus Magnus College

New Haven, Connecticut
www.albertus.edu   Federal Code: 001374

4-year private liberal arts college in small city, affiliated with Roman Catholic Church.
Enrollment: 1,682 undergrads, 5% part-time. 127 full-time freshmen.
Selectivity: Admits over 75% of applicants.

BASIC COSTS (2008-2009)
Tuition and fees: $22,724.
Per-credit charge: $907.
Room and board: $9,442.

FINANCIAL AID PICTURE (2007-2008)
Students with need: Average financial aid package met 47% of need; average scholarship/grant was $9,273; average loan was $3,186. For part-time students, average financial aid package was $5,563.
Students without need: No-need awards available for academics, art, job skills, leadership, music/drama, religious affiliation, state/district residency.
Cumulative student debt: 96% of graduating class had student loans; average debt was $15,252.

FINANCIAL AID PROCEDURES
Forms required: FAFSA, institutional form.
Dates and Deadlines: Closing date 2/28. Applicants notified on a rolling basis starting 3/1; must reply within 2 week(s) of notification.
Transfers: No deadline. Must reply within 2 week(s) of notification.

CONTACT
Andrew Foster, Director of Financial Aid
700 Prospect Street, New Haven, CT 06511-1189
(203) 773-8508

Asnuntuck Community College

Enfield, Connecticut
www.acc.commnet.edu   Federal Code: 011150

2-year public community and technical college in large town.
Enrollment: 1,042 undergrads.
Selectivity: Open admission.

BASIC COSTS (2007-2008)
Tuition and fees: $2,828; out-of-state residents $8,444.
Per-credit charge: $104; out-of-state residents $312.

FINANCIAL AID PICTURE
Students with need: Need-based aid available for full-time and part-time students. Work study available nights, weekends, and for part-time students.
Students without need: This college awards aid only to students with need.

FINANCIAL AID PROCEDURES
Forms required: FAFSA, institutional form.
Dates and Deadlines: Priority date 6/1; no closing date. Applicants notified on a rolling basis starting 7/1; must reply within 2 week(s) of notification.
Transfers: Financial aid transcript required.

CONTACT
Donna Jones-Searle, Director of Financial Aid
170 Elm Street, Enfield, CT 06082
(860) 253-3030

Briarwood College

Southington, Connecticut
www.briarwood.edu   Federal Code: 009407

4-year for-profit junior college in large town.
Enrollment: 663 undergrads, 36% part-time. 150 full-time freshmen.
Selectivity: Open admission; but selective for some programs.

BASIC COSTS (2007-2008)
Tuition and fees: $17,135.
Per-credit charge: $540.
Room only: $3,600.
Additional info: Tuition at time of enrollment locked for 4 years.

FINANCIAL AID PICTURE
Students with need: Need-based aid available for full-time and part-time students. Work study available nights, weekends, and for part-time students.
Students without need: No-need awards available for academics, alumni affiliation, leadership.

FINANCIAL AID PROCEDURES
Forms required: FAFSA.
Dates and Deadlines: Priority date 4/30; no closing date. Applicants notified on a rolling basis starting 3/15; must reply within 2 week(s) of notification.
Transfers: Priority date 4/15.

CONTACT
2279 Mount Vernon Road, Southington, CT 06489-1057
(860) 628-4751 ext. 213

Capital Community College

Hartford, Connecticut
www.ccc.commnet.edu   Federal Code: 007635

2-year public community and technical college in small city.
Enrollment: 3,177 undergrads, 69% part-time. 302 full-time freshmen.
Selectivity: Open admission; but selective for some programs.

BASIC COSTS (2007-2008)

Tuition and fees: $2,828; out-of-state residents $8,444.

Per-credit charge: $104; out-of-state residents $312.

Additional info: Tuition/fee waivers available for minority students.

FINANCIAL AID PICTURE

Students with need: Need-based aid available for full-time and part-time students. Work study available nights, weekends, and for part-time students.

Students without need: This college awards aid only to students with need.

FINANCIAL AID PROCEDURES

Forms required: FAFSA.

Dates and Deadlines: Closing date 7/15. Applicants notified on a rolling basis starting 7/15; must reply within 2 week(s) of notification.

Transfers: Closing date 7/1.

CONTACT

Margaret Wolf, Director of Financial Aid

950 Main Street, Hartford, CT 06103-1207

(860) 906-5090

Central Connecticut State University

New Britain, Connecticut

www.ccsu.edu   Federal Code: 001378

4-year public university in small city.

Enrollment: 9,161 undergrads, 17% part-time. 1,469 full-time freshmen.

Selectivity: Admits 50 to 75% of applicants.

BASIC COSTS (2007-2008)

Tuition and fees: $6,734; out-of-state residents $15,454.

Room and board: $8,350.

FINANCIAL AID PICTURE (2006-2007)

Students with need: Out of 923 full-time freshmen who applied for aid, 601 were judged to have need. Of these, 575 received aid, and 95 had their full need met. Average financial aid package met 71% of need; average scholarship/grant was $3,443; average loan was $2,834. For part-time students, average financial aid package was $6,176.

Students without need: 50 full-time freshmen who did not demonstrate need for aid received scholarships/grants; average award was $2,391. No-need awards available for academics, athletics, minority status.

Scholarships offered: 48 full-time freshmen received athletic scholarships; average amount $8,273.

Cumulative student debt: 28% of graduating class had student loans; average debt was $17,875.

FINANCIAL AID PROCEDURES

Forms required: FAFSA.

Dates and Deadlines: Priority date 3/1; closing date 9/15. Applicants notified on a rolling basis starting 3/30; must reply within 2 week(s) of notification.

CONTACT

Richard Bishop, Director of Financial Aid

1615 Stanley Street, New Britain, CT 06050

(860) 832-2200

Charter Oak State College

New Britain, Connecticut

www.charteroak.edu   Federal Code: 032343

4-year public virtual liberal arts college in small city.

Enrollment: 1,557 undergrads, 95% part-time.

BASIC COSTS (2007-2008)

Per-credit charge: $172; out-of-state residents $244.

Additional info: In-state matriculation fee: $995; out-of-state fees: $1,310. Cost of education varies due to students having the option to take courses at other institutions.

FINANCIAL AID PICTURE

Students with need: Need-based aid available for full-time and part-time students.

Students without need: This college awards aid only to students with need.

FINANCIAL AID PROCEDURES

Forms required: FAFSA, institutional form.

Dates and Deadlines: No deadline. Applicants notified on a rolling basis starting 8/23.

CONTACT

Deborah Flinn, Director of Financial Aid

55 Paul Manafort Drive, New Britain, CT 06053-2142

(860) 832-3872

Clemens College

Suffield, Connecticut

www.clemenscollege.edu

2-year for-profit culinary school and business college in small town.

Enrollment: 57 undergrads.

Selectivity: Admits 50 to 75% of applicants.

BASIC COSTS (2007-2008)

Tuition and fees: $19,770.

Room and board: $5,690.

Additional info: International students who have no health insurance are required to purchase it for $350 per 11-week term. Culinary students pay an extra $667.80 for cutlery and tools.

FINANCIAL AID PICTURE

Students with need: Need-based aid available for full-time and part-time students. Work study available nights, weekends, and for part-time students.

Students without need: No-need awards available for academics.

FINANCIAL AID PROCEDURES

Dates and Deadlines: No deadline. Applicants notified on a rolling basis starting 1/1.

CONTACT

Joanne Seymour, Director of Financial Aid

1760 Mapleton Avenue, Suffield, CT 06078

(860) 668-3515

Connecticut College

New London, Connecticut   Federal Code: 001379

www.conncoll.edu   CSS Code: 3284

4-year private liberal arts college in large town.

Enrollment: 1,746 undergrads, 1% part-time. 492 full-time freshmen.

Selectivity: Admits less than 50% of applicants.

BASIC COSTS (2008-2009)

Comprehensive fee: $49,385.

FINANCIAL AID PICTURE (2007-2008)

Students with need: Out of 252 full-time freshmen who applied for aid, 201 were judged to have need. Of these, 201 received aid, and 201 had their full need met. Average financial aid package met 100% of need; average scholarship/grant was $27,364; average loan was $3,649. Need-based aid available for part-time students.

Students without need: This college awards aid only to students with need.

Cumulative student debt: 35% of graduating class had student loans; average debt was $21,523.

FINANCIAL AID PROCEDURES

Forms required: FAFSA, CSS PROFILE.

Dates and Deadlines: Closing date 2/1. Applicants notified by 4/1; must reply by 5/1.

Transfers: Closing date 4/1.

CONTACT

Elaine Solinga, Director of Financial Aid

270 Mohegan Avenue, New London, CT 06320-4196

(860) 439-2058

Eastern Connecticut State University

Willimantic, Connecticut

www.easternct.edu   Federal Code: 001425

4-year public university and liberal arts college in large town.

Enrollment: 4,704 undergrads, 16% part-time. 954 full-time freshmen.

Selectivity: Admits 50 to 75% of applicants:

BASIC COSTS (2007-2008)

Tuition and fees: $6,961; out-of-state residents $14,446.

Room and board: $8,415.

FINANCIAL AID PICTURE (2006-2007)

Students with need: Out of 931 full-time freshmen who applied for aid, 624 were judged to have need. Of these, 485 received aid, and 49 had their full need met. Average financial aid package met 64% of need; average scholarship/grant was $6,079; average loan was $2,623. For part-time students, average financial aid package was $7,209.

Students without need: 65 full-time freshmen who did not demonstrate need for aid received scholarships/grants; average award was $2,644. No-need awards available for academics.

Cumulative student debt: 58% of graduating class had student loans; average debt was $15,380.

Additional info: Tuition waiver for Veterans and members of National Guard.

FINANCIAL AID PROCEDURES

Forms required: FAFSA.

Dates and Deadlines: Priority date 3/15; no closing date. Applicants notified on a rolling basis starting 2/15; must reply within 2 week(s) of notification.

Transfers: Must reply within 2 week(s) of notification.

CONTACT

Richard Savage, Director of Financial Aid

83 Windham Street, Willimantic, CT 06226-2295

(860) 465-5205

Fairfield University

Fairfield, Connecticut   Federal Code: 001385

www.fairfield.edu   CSS Code: 3390

4-year private university in small city, affiliated with Roman Catholic Church.

Enrollment: 3,893 undergrads, 11% part-time. 842 full-time freshmen.

Selectivity: Admits 50 to 75% of applicants. GED not accepted.

BASIC COSTS (2008-2009)

Tuition and fees: $36,075.

Per-credit charge: $475.

Room and board: $10,850.

FINANCIAL AID PICTURE (2007-2008)

Students with need: Out of 552 full-time freshmen who applied for aid, 441 were judged to have need. Of these, 438 received aid, and 92 had their full need met. Average financial aid package met 86% of need; average scholarship/grant was $20,313; average loan was $4,591. Need-based aid available for part-time students.

Students without need: 43 full-time freshmen who did not demonstrate need for aid received scholarships/grants; average award was $11,721. No-need awards available for academics, alumni affiliation, art, athletics, leadership, music/drama.

Scholarships offered: *Merit:* University Fellow Scholarship: $15,000 annual grant/computer/research stipend; awarded to students in top 5% of class with high SAT scores. Presidential Scholarship: $12,000 annual grant/research stipend; awarded to students in top 10% of class with high SAT scores. Dean's Scholarship: $10,000 annual grant; for students in top 20% of class. Approximately 100-160 total scholarships available. ***Athletic:*** 64 full-time freshmen received athletic scholarships; average amount $18,232.

Cumulative student debt: 60% of graduating class had student loans; average debt was $31,984.

FINANCIAL AID PROCEDURES

Forms required: FAFSA, CSS PROFILE.

Dates and Deadlines: Closing date 2/15. Applicants notified by 4/1; must reply by 5/1.

Transfers: Closing date 5/1. Applicants notified on a rolling basis starting 5/1; must reply within 3 week(s) of notification.

CONTACT

Erin Chiaro, Director of Financial Aid

1073 North Benson Road, Fairfield, CT 06824-5195

(203) 254-4125

Gateway Community College

New Haven, Connecticut

www.gwcc.commnet.edu   Federal Code: 008303

2-year public community college in small city.

Enrollment: 4,787 undergrads, 56% part-time. 803 full-time freshmen.

Selectivity: Open admission; but selective for some programs.

BASIC COSTS (2007-2008)

Tuition and fees: $2,828; out-of-state residents $8,444.

Per-credit charge: $104; out-of-state residents $312.

FINANCIAL AID PICTURE

Students with need: Need-based aid available for full-time and part-time students. Work study available nights, weekends, and for part-time students.

Students without need: This college awards aid only to students with need.

FINANCIAL AID PROCEDURES

Forms required: FAFSA, institutional form.

Dates and Deadlines: No deadline. Applicants notified on a rolling basis; must reply within 2 week(s) of notification.

CONTACT

Raymond Zeek, Director of Financial Aid

60 Sargent Drive, New Haven, CT 06511-5970

(203) 285-2032

Holy Apostles College and Seminary

Cromwell, Connecticut
www.holyapostles.edu   Federal Code: 001389

4-year private liberal arts and seminary college in large town, affiliated with Roman Catholic Church.
Enrollment: 32 undergrads, 47% part-time. 4 full-time freshmen.
Selectivity: Admits over 75% of applicants.

BASIC COSTS (2008-2009)
Tuition and fees: $7,800.
Per-credit charge: $325.

FINANCIAL AID PICTURE (2006-2007)
Students with need: Out of 2 full-time freshmen who applied for aid, 2 were judged to have need. Of these, 2 received aid. Need-based aid available for part-time students.
Students without need: This college awards aid only to students with need.

FINANCIAL AID PROCEDURES
Forms required: FAFSA, institutional form.
Dates and Deadlines: No deadline. Applicants notified on a rolling basis starting 9/15.
Transfers: No deadline.

CONTACT
Henry Miller, Financial Aid Director
33 Prospect Hill Road, Cromwell, CT 06416-2005
(860) 632-8120

Housatonic Community College

Bridgeport, Connecticut
www.hcc.commnet.edu   Federal Code: 004513

2-year public community college in small city.
Enrollment: 3,894 undergrads.
Selectivity: Open admission; but selective for some programs.

BASIC COSTS (2007-2008)
Tuition and fees: $2,828; out-of-state residents $8,444.
Per-credit charge: $104; out-of-state residents $312.

FINANCIAL AID PICTURE
Students with need: Need-based aid available for full-time and part-time students.
Students without need: This college awards aid only to students with need.

FINANCIAL AID PROCEDURES
Forms required: FAFSA.
Dates and Deadlines: Priority date 11/1; closing date 5/1. Applicants notified on a rolling basis starting 6/1.

CONTACT
Barbara Surowiec, Director of Financial Aid
900 Lafayette Boulevard, Bridgeport, CT 06604-4704
(203) 332-5047

Lyme Academy College of Fine Arts

Old Lyme, Connecticut   Federal Code: 030794
www.lymeacademy.edu   CSS Code: 1791

4-year private visual arts college in small town.
Enrollment: 100 undergrads, 9% part-time. 11 full-time freshmen.
Selectivity: Admits over 75% of applicants.

BASIC COSTS (2008-2009)
Tuition and fees: $21,480.
Per-credit charge: $845.

FINANCIAL AID PICTURE (2007-2008)
Students with need: Out of 11 full-time freshmen who applied for aid, 11 were judged to have need. Of these, 11 received aid. Need-based aid available for part-time students.
Students without need: No-need awards available for academics, art, leadership.

FINANCIAL AID PROCEDURES
Forms required: FAFSA, institutional form. CSS PROFILE required of all new first year students.
Dates and Deadlines: Priority date 2/15; closing date 4/15. Applicants notified on a rolling basis starting 3/1; must reply by 5/1 or within 2 week(s) of notification.
Transfers: Closing date 7/31. Applicants notified on a rolling basis starting 3/1; must reply by 5/1 or within 2 week(s) of notification.

CONTACT
Jim Falconer, Director of Financial Aid
84 Lyme Street, Old Lyme, CT 06371
(860) 434-3571 ext. 114

Manchester Community College

Manchester, Connecticut
www.mcc.commnet.edu   Federal Code: 001392

2-year public community college in small city.
Enrollment: 5,420 undergrads, 50% part-time. 1,099 full-time freshmen.
Selectivity: Open admission; but selective for some programs.

BASIC COSTS (2007-2008)
Tuition and fees: $2,828; out-of-state residents $8,444.
Per-credit charge: $104; out-of-state residents $312.

FINANCIAL AID PICTURE (2006-2007)
Students with need: 94% of average financial aid package awarded as scholarships/grants, 6% awarded as loans/jobs. Need-based aid available for part-time students.

FINANCIAL AID PROCEDURES
Forms required: FAFSA.
Dates and Deadlines: Priority date 5/15; no closing date. Applicants notified on a rolling basis starting 5/1; must reply within 2 week(s) of notification.

CONTACT
Ivette Rivera-Dreyer, Director of Financial Aid
Great Path PO Box 1046, MS 12, Manchester, CT 06040-1046
(860) 512-3380

Middlesex Community College

Middletown, Connecticut
www.mxcc.commnet.edu   Federal Code: 008038

2-year public community college in large town.
Enrollment: 1,849 undergrads, 50% part-time. 351 full-time freshmen.
Selectivity: Open admission; but selective for some programs.

BASIC COSTS (2007-2008)
Tuition and fees: $2,828; out-of-state residents $8,444.
Per-credit charge: $109; out-of-state residents $316.
Additional info: Out-of-state tuition includes fees.

FINANCIAL AID PICTURE

Students with need: Need-based aid available for full-time and part-time students.

Students without need: This college awards aid only to students with need.

Additional info: Tuition and/or fee waiver for veterans.

FINANCIAL AID PROCEDURES

Forms required: FAFSA, institutional form.

Dates and Deadlines: Priority date 6/1; no closing date. Applicants notified on a rolling basis starting 7/1; must reply within 2 week(s) of notification.

Transfers: Closing date 9/1.

CONTACT

Gennaro DeAngelis, Director of Financial Aid
100 Training Hill Road, Middletown, CT 06457
(860) 343-5741

Mitchell College

New London, Connecticut
www.mitchell.edu
Federal Code: 001393

4-year private liberal arts college in small city.

Enrollment: 868 undergrads, 13% part-time. 260 full-time freshmen.

BASIC COSTS (2007-2008)

Tuition and fees: $23,093.

Per-credit charge: $275.

Room and board: $10,406.

FINANCIAL AID PICTURE

Students with need: Need-based aid available for full-time and part-time students. Work study available nights, weekends, and for part-time students.

Students without need: No-need awards available for academics, alumni affiliation, leadership.

FINANCIAL AID PROCEDURES

Forms required: FAFSA.

Dates and Deadlines: Priority date 3/1; no closing date. Applicants notified on a rolling basis starting 2/15; must reply within 2 week(s) of notification.

CONTACT

Jacklyn Stoltz, Director of Financial Aid
437 Pequot Avenue, New London, CT 06320-4498
(860) 701-5040

Naugatuck Valley Community College

Waterbury, Connecticut
www.nvcc.commnet.edu
Federal Code: 006982

2-year public community and technical college in small city.

Enrollment: 4,964 undergrads, 52% part-time. 908 full-time freshmen.

Selectivity: Open admission; but selective for some programs.

BASIC COSTS (2007-2008)

Tuition and fees: $2,828; out-of-state residents $8,444.

Per-credit charge: $104; out-of-state residents $312.

FINANCIAL AID PICTURE

Students with need: Need-based aid available for full-time and part-time students.

Students without need: This college awards aid only to students with need.

FINANCIAL AID PROCEDURES

Forms required: FAFSA.

Dates and Deadlines: Priority date 4/1; no closing date. Applicants notified on a rolling basis starting 6/1.

Transfers: Financial aid transcripts from all previous schools attended.

CONTACT

Catherine Hardy, Director of Financial Aid Services
750 Chase Parkway, Waterbury, CT 06708-3089
(203) 575-8006

Norwalk Community College

Norwalk, Connecticut
www.ncc.commnet.edu
Federal Code: 001399

2-year public community and technical college in small city.

Enrollment: 2,000 full-time undergrads.

Selectivity: Open admission; but selective for some programs.

BASIC COSTS (2007-2008)

Tuition and fees: $2,828; out-of-state residents $8,444.

Per-credit charge: $162; out-of-state residents $448.

Additional info: New England Regional Student Program: $241.25 per credit-hour.

FINANCIAL AID PICTURE

Students with need: Need-based aid available for full-time and part-time students.

Students without need: No-need awards available for academics, alumni affiliation.

FINANCIAL AID PROCEDURES

Forms required: FAFSA, institutional form.

Dates and Deadlines: Priority date 7/1; no closing date. Applicants notified on a rolling basis starting 7/1; must reply within 2 week(s) of notification.

CONTACT

Norma McNerney, Director of Financial Aid
188 Richards Avenue, Norwalk, CT 06854-1655
(203) 857-7023

Paier College of Art

Hamden, Connecticut
www.paiercollegeofart.edu
Federal Code: 007459

4-year for-profit visual arts college in small city.

Enrollment: 207 undergrads, 32% part-time. 16 full-time freshmen.

Selectivity: Admits 50 to 75% of applicants.

BASIC COSTS (2008-2009)

Tuition and fees: $12,365.

Per-credit charge: $380.

FINANCIAL AID PICTURE (2006-2007)

Students with need: Out of 10 full-time freshmen who applied for aid, 7 were judged to have need. Of these, 7 received aid. Average financial aid package met 61% of need; average scholarship/grant was $5,557; average loan was $3,107. For part-time students, average financial aid package was $5,320.

Cumulative student debt: 94% of graduating class had student loans; average debt was $19,347.

FINANCIAL AID PROCEDURES

Forms required: FAFSA.

Dates and Deadlines: Priority date 4/15; no closing date. Applicants notified on a rolling basis starting 6/1; must reply within 3 week(s) of notification.

Transfers: No deadline. Applicants notified on a rolling basis starting 6/1; must reply within 3 week(s) of notification.

CONTACT

John DeRose, Director of Financial Aid

20 Gorham Avenue, Hamden, CT 06514-3902

(203) 287-3034

Post University

Waterbury, Connecticut

www.post.edu
Federal Code: 001401

4-year for-profit university and business college in small city.

Enrollment: 1,112 undergrads.

Selectivity: Admits 50 to 75% of applicants.

BASIC COSTS (2007-2008)

Tuition and fees: $22,550.

Per-credit charge: $725.

Room and board: $8,750.

FINANCIAL AID PICTURE

Students with need: Need-based aid available for full-time and part-time students. Work study available nights, weekends, and for part-time students.

Additional info: Academic merit scholarships available based on GPA and test scores. Renewable contingent upon maintaining specific GPA.

FINANCIAL AID PROCEDURES

Forms required: FAFSA.

Dates and Deadlines: Priority date 3/15; no closing date. Applicants notified on a rolling basis starting 4/15; must reply by 5/1 or within 3 week(s) of notification.

CONTACT

Edward Hastings, Director of Financial Aid

800 Country Club Road, Waterbury, CT 06723-2540

(203) 596-4527

Quinebaug Valley Community College

Danielson, Connecticut

www.qvcc.commnet.edu
Federal Code: 010530

2-year public community and technical college in large town.

Enrollment: 1,595 undergrads, 60% part-time. 240 full-time freshmen.

Selectivity: Open admission; but selective for some programs.

BASIC COSTS (2007-2008)

Tuition and fees: $2,828; out-of-state residents $8,444.

Per-credit charge: $104; out-of-state residents $312.

FINANCIAL AID PICTURE (2007-2008)

Students with need: 95% of average financial aid package awarded as scholarships/grants, 5% awarded as loans/jobs. Need-based aid available for part-time students. Work study available nights, weekends, and for part-time students.

Students without need: This college awards aid only to students with need.

FINANCIAL AID PROCEDURES

Forms required: FAFSA.

Dates and Deadlines: Closing date 10/1. Applicants notified on a rolling basis starting 5/1.

CONTACT

Alfred Williams, Director of Financial Aid

742 Upper Maple Street, Danielson, CT 06239-1440

(860) 412-7212

Quinnipiac University

Hamden, Connecticut

www.quinnipiac.edu
Federal Code: 001402

4-year private university in small city.

Enrollment: 5,650 undergrads, 3% part-time. 1,357 full-time freshmen.

Selectivity: Admits less than 50% of applicants.

BASIC COSTS (2008-2009)

Tuition and fees: $30,900.

Per-credit charge: $710.

Room and board: $11,800.

FINANCIAL AID PICTURE (2007-2008)

Students with need: Out of 1,036 full-time freshmen who applied for aid, 763 were judged to have need. Of these, 760 received aid, and 124 had their full need met. Average financial aid package met 71% of need; average scholarship/grant was $12,861; average loan was $3,648. For part-time students, average financial aid package was $7,562.

Students without need: 185 full-time freshmen who did not demonstrate need for aid received scholarships/grants; average award was $9,380. No-need awards available for academics, athletics.

Scholarships offered: *Merit:* Scholarships range from $4,000-$16,000 per year; based on high school class rank and SAT or ACT scores; renewable provided students maintain full-time status and a miminum 3.0 GPA. *Athletic:* 57 full-time freshmen received athletic scholarships; average amount $25,357.

Cumulative student debt: 71% of graduating class had student loans; average debt was $35,086.

FINANCIAL AID PROCEDURES

Forms required: FAFSA.

Dates and Deadlines: Priority date 3/1; no closing date. Applicants notified on a rolling basis starting 2/15; must reply by 5/1 or within 2 week(s) of notification.

Transfers: Priority date 6/1. Applicants notified on a rolling basis starting 3/1; must reply by 5/1 or within 2 week(s) of notification. Students transferring with two years of full time college work completed and a cumulative gpa of 3.5 may be eligible for a transfer scholarship.

CONTACT

Dominic Yoia, Director of Financial Aid

275 Mount Carmel Avenue, Hamden, CT 06518-1908

(800) 462-1944

Sacred Heart University

Fairfield, Connecticut

www.sacredheart.edu
Federal Code: 001403

CSS Code: 3780

4-year private university and liberal arts college in large town, affiliated with Roman Catholic Church.

Enrollment: 4,188 undergrads, 17% part-time. 956 full-time freshmen.

Selectivity: Admits 50 to 75% of applicants.

BASIC COSTS (2007-2008)

Tuition and fees: $27,150.

Per-credit charge: $425.

Room and board: $10,816.

Additional info: Tuition/fee waivers available for minority students.

FINANCIAL AID PICTURE (2007-2008)

Students with need: Out of 807 full-time freshmen who applied for aid, 635 were judged to have need. Of these, 632 received aid, and 190 had their full need met. Average financial aid package met 69% of need; average scholarship/grant was $10,886; average loan was $5,677. For part-time students, average financial aid package was $8,675.

PART III: FINANCIAL AID COLLEGE BY COLLEGE

Students without need: 197 full-time freshmen who did not demonstrate need for aid received scholarships/grants; average award was $9,683. No-need awards available for academics, alumni affiliation, art, athletics, leadership, minority status, music/drama, ROTC.

Scholarships offered: 50 full-time freshmen received athletic scholarships; average amount $16,500.

Cumulative student debt: 94% of graduating class had student loans; average debt was $25,505.

FINANCIAL AID PROCEDURES

Forms required: FAFSA, CSS PROFILE.

Dates and Deadlines: Priority date 2/15; no closing date. Applicants notified on a rolling basis starting 3/1; must reply within 2 week(s) of notification.

Transfers: Priority date 5/1; no deadline. Applicants notified on a rolling basis.

CONTACT

Julie Savino, Dean of University Financial Assistance
5151 Park Avenue, Fairfield, CT 06825
(203) 371-7980

St. Joseph College
West Hartford, Connecticut
www.sjc.edu

4-year private liberal arts college for women in small city, affiliated with Roman Catholic Church.

Enrollment: 945 undergrads, 22% part-time. 133 full-time freshmen.

Selectivity: Admits over 75% of applicants.

BASIC COSTS (2007-2008)

Tuition and fees: $24,690.

Per-credit charge: $530.

Room and board: $11,880.

FINANCIAL AID PICTURE (2006-2007)

Students with need: Out of 131 full-time freshmen who applied for aid, 121 were judged to have need. Of these, 121 received aid. Average financial aid package met 70% of need; average scholarship/grant was $12,781; average loan was $1,870. For part-time students, average financial aid package was $3,814.

Students without need: 13 full-time freshmen who did not demonstrate need for aid received scholarships/grants; average award was $9,885. No-need awards available for academics, state/district residency.

Cumulative student debt: 82% of graduating class had student loans; average debt was $23,550.

FINANCIAL AID PROCEDURES

Forms required: FAFSA.

Dates and Deadlines: Priority date 2/15; no closing date. Applicants notified on a rolling basis starting 3/1; must reply within 2 week(s) of notification.

CONTACT

1678 Asylum Avenue, West Hartford, CT 06117

Southern Connecticut State University
New Haven, Connecticut
www.southernct.edu   Federal Code: 001406

4-year public university in small city.

Enrollment: 8,515 undergrads, 16% part-time. 1,516 full-time freshmen.

Selectivity: Admits less than 50% of applicants.

BASIC COSTS (2007-2008)

Tuition and fees: $6,624; out-of-state residents $14,110.

Room and board: $8,502.

Additional info: Out-of-state students pay an additional $1,234 in fees.

FINANCIAL AID PICTURE (2006-2007)

Students with need: Out of 1,289 full-time freshmen who applied for aid, 794 were judged to have need. Of these, 742 received aid, and 223 had their full need met. Average financial aid package met 77% of need; average scholarship/grant was $5,179; average loan was $2,797. For part-time students, average financial aid package was $3,425.

Students without need: 268 full-time freshmen who did not demonstrate need for aid received scholarships/grants; average award was $2,577. No-need awards available for academics, alumni affiliation, athletics, ROTC.

Scholarships offered: *Merit:* General Academic Achievement Awards; 90 awarded. Presidential Scholarships, Trustees Scholarships available. *Athletic:* 43 full-time freshmen received athletic scholarships; average amount $6,388.

Cumulative student debt: 29% of graduating class had student loans; average debt was $15,016.

FINANCIAL AID PROCEDURES

Forms required: FAFSA.

Dates and Deadlines: Closing date 3/9. Applicants notified on a rolling basis starting 3/9; must reply within 2 week(s) of notification.

Transfers: Applicants notified on a rolling basis starting 6/15; must reply within 2 week(s) of notification.

CONTACT

Avon Dennis, Director, Financial Aid & Scholarships
131 Farnham Avenue, New Haven, CT 06515-1202
(203) 392-5222

Three Rivers Community College
Norwich, Connecticut
www.trcc.commnet.edu   Federal Code: 009765

2-year public community and technical college in large town.

Enrollment: 3,445 undergrads, 63% part-time. 489 full-time freshmen.

Selectivity: Open admission; but selective for some programs.

BASIC COSTS (2007-2008)

Tuition and fees: $2,828; out-of-state residents $8,444.

Per-credit charge: $104; out-of-state residents $312.

Additional info: Out-of-state required fees: $992.

FINANCIAL AID PICTURE (2006-2007)

Students with need: Out of 290 full-time freshmen who applied for aid, 285 were judged to have need. Of these, 204 received aid, and 46 had their full need met. Average financial aid package met 45% of need; average scholarship/grant was $3,465; average loan was $2,805. For part-time students, average financial aid package was $3,899.

Students without need: This college awards aid only to students with need.

Scholarships offered: Available for continuing students; ranging from $75 to $500.

FINANCIAL AID PROCEDURES

Forms required: FAFSA.

Dates and Deadlines: Priority date 7/15; no closing date. Applicants notified on a rolling basis; must reply within 2 week(s) of notification.

CONTACT

Dan Zaneski, Financial Aid Director
7 Mahan Drive, Norwich, CT 06360-2479
(860) 823-2870

Trinity College
Hartford, Connecticut
www.trincoll.edu
Federal Code: 001414
CSS Code: 3899

4-year private liberal arts college in large city.
Enrollment: 2,243 undergrads, 2% part-time. 576 full-time freshmen.
Selectivity: Admits less than 50% of applicants.

BASIC COSTS (2008-2009)
Tuition and fees: $38,733.
Room and board: $9,900.
Additional info: One-time $25 transcript fee for new students only. Tuition/fee waivers available for adults.

FINANCIAL AID PICTURE (2007-2008)
Students with need: Out of 262 full-time freshmen who applied for aid, 214 were judged to have need. Of these, 214 received aid, and 214 had their full need met. Average financial aid package met 100% of need; average scholarship/grant was $29,793; average loan was $3,632. Need-based aid available for part-time students.
Students without need: 8 full-time freshmen who did not demonstrate need for aid received scholarships/grants; average award was $32,596. No-need awards available for academics, leadership.
Cumulative student debt: 43% of graduating class had student loans; average debt was $19,835.

FINANCIAL AID PROCEDURES
Forms required: FAFSA, CSS PROFILE.
Dates and Deadlines: Priority date 2/1; closing date 3/1. Applicants notified by 4/1; must reply by 5/1 or within 2 week(s) of notification.
Transfers: Closing date 4/1. Applicants notified on a rolling basis starting 5/15; must reply within 2 week(s) of notification.

CONTACT
Kelly O'Brien, Director of Financial Aid
300 Summit Street, Hartford, CT 06106
(860) 297-2046

Tunxis Community College
Farmington, Connecticut
www.tunxis.commnet.edu
Federal Code: 009764

2-year public community college in large town.
Enrollment: 2,951 undergrads, 52% part-time. 427 full-time freshmen.
Selectivity: Open admission; but selective for some programs.

BASIC COSTS (2007-2008)
Tuition and fees: $2,828; out-of-state residents $8,444.
Per-credit charge: $104; out-of-state residents $312.

FINANCIAL AID PICTURE (2006-2007)
Students with need: 80% of average financial aid package awarded as scholarships/grants, 20% awarded as loans/jobs. Need-based aid available for part-time students. Work study available nights, weekends, and for part-time students.
Students without need: No-need awards available for academics, leadership.
Additional info: Financial aid available to all students showing need. Part-time students encouraged to apply.

FINANCIAL AID PROCEDURES
Forms required: FAFSA.
Dates and Deadlines: Priority date 6/1; no closing date. Applicants notified on a rolling basis starting 3/1.

CONTACT
David Welsh, Director of Financial Aid
271 Scott Swamp Road, Farmington, CT 06032-3187
(860) 255-3513

United States Coast Guard Academy
New London, Connecticut
www.uscga.edu
Federal Code: 001415

4-year public engineering and military and maritime college in small city.
Enrollment: 963 undergrads. 252 full-time freshmen.
Selectivity: Admits less than 50% of applicants.

BASIC COSTS (2008-2009)
Additional info: All tuition, room and board paid for by U.S. government. Students make one-time entrance deposit of $3,000 to help defray cost of uniforms, books, supplies and personal computer. All students paid monthly stipend of $734.

FINANCIAL AID PROCEDURES
Dates and Deadlines: No deadline.

CONTACT
31 Mohegan Avenue, New London, CT 06320
(860) 444-8309

University of Bridgeport
Bridgeport, Connecticut
www.bridgeport.edu
Federal Code: 001416

4-year private university in small city.
Enrollment: 1,791 undergrads, 32% part-time. 334 full-time freshmen.
Selectivity: Admits 50 to 75% of applicants.

BASIC COSTS (2007-2008)
Tuition and fees: $22,860.
Per-credit charge: $705.
Room and board: $10,000.

FINANCIAL AID PICTURE
Students with need: Need-based aid available for full-time and part-time students. Work study available nights, weekends, and for part-time students.
Students without need: No-need awards available for academics, athletics, state/district residency.
Scholarships offered: Academic Excellence and Leadership Scholarship; up to full tuition, room, and board; for students ranking in the top quarter of high school class with SAT score greater than 1200. Academic Scholarship; up to full tuition; for students in the top quarter of class and SAT score greater than 1100. Academic Grant; up to half of tuition costs; for students in top half of class and SAT greater than 1100. Challenge Grant; $3,000; for students in the top half of class and SAT greater than 1000. All SAT scores exclusive of writing.

FINANCIAL AID PROCEDURES
Forms required: FAFSA, institutional form.
Dates and Deadlines: Priority date 4/1; no closing date. Applicants notified on a rolling basis starting 4/1; must reply within 4 week(s) of notification.

CONTACT
Kathleen Gailor, Director of Financial Aid
126 Park Avenue, Bridgeport, CT 06604
(203) 576-4568

University of Connecticut
Storrs, Connecticut
www.uconn.edu   Federal Code: 007997

4-year public university in large town.

Enrollment: 16,036 undergrads, 3% part-time. 3,167 full-time freshmen.
Selectivity: Admits less than 50% of applicants.

BASIC COSTS (2008-2009)
Tuition and fees: $9,338; out-of-state residents $24,050.
Per-credit charge: $300; out-of-state residents $913.
Room and board: $9,300.
Additional info: Incoming out-of-state New England residents pay 175% of in-state tuition rate for programs of study not offered at their home state university.

FINANCIAL AID PICTURE (2007-2008)
Students with need: Out of 2,503 full-time freshmen who applied for aid, 1,604 were judged to have need. Of these, 1,583 received aid, and 274 had their full need met. Average financial aid package met 73% of need; average scholarship/grant was $6,719; average loan was $3,840. For part-time students, average financial aid package was $6,463.
Students without need: 263 full-time freshmen who did not demonstrate need for aid received scholarships/grants; average award was $6,471. No-need awards available for academics, art, athletics, leadership, minority status, music/drama.
Scholarships offered: 87 full-time freshmen received athletic scholarships; average amount $20,399.
Cumulative student debt: 61% of graduating class had student loans; average debt was $20,658.
Additional info: Institution offers variety of need-based financial aid programs. Financial assistance packages may include grants, loans and work-study awards.

FINANCIAL AID PROCEDURES
Forms required: FAFSA.
Dates and Deadlines: Priority date 3/1; no closing date. Applicants notified on a rolling basis starting 3/1; must reply within 4 week(s) of notification.

CONTACT
Jean Main, Director of Financial Aid
2131 Hillside Road, Unit 3088, Storrs, CT 06269-3088
(860) 486-2819

University of Hartford
West Hartford, Connecticut
www.hartford.edu   Federal Code: 001422

4-year private university in small city.

Enrollment: 5,364 undergrads, 11% part-time. 1,465 full-time freshmen.
Selectivity: Admits 50 to 75% of applicants.

BASIC COSTS (2008-2009)
Tuition and fees: $28,172.
Per-credit charge: $400.
Room and board: $10,876.
Additional info: Tuition/fee waivers available for minority students.

FINANCIAL AID PICTURE (2006-2007)
Students with need: Out of 1,178 full-time freshmen who applied for aid, 1,034 were judged to have need. Of these, 1,030 received aid, and 336 had their full need met. Average financial aid package met 73% of need; average scholarship/grant was $13,565; average loan was $2,862. For part-time students, average financial aid package was $5,820.

Students without need: 366 full-time freshmen who did not demonstrate need for aid received scholarships/grants; average award was $7,141. No-need awards available for academics, art, athletics, music/drama.
Scholarships offered: 20 full-time freshmen received athletic scholarships; average amount $28,197.
Cumulative student debt: 69% of graduating class had student loans; average debt was $27,018.

FINANCIAL AID PROCEDURES
Forms required: FAFSA, institutional form.
Dates and Deadlines: Priority date 2/1; no closing date. Applicants notified on a rolling basis starting 3/1; must reply by 5/1.

CONTACT
Suzanne Peters, Director of Student Financial Assistance
Bates House, West Hartford, CT 06117-1599
(860) 768-4296

University of New Haven
West Haven, Connecticut
www.newhaven.edu   Federal Code: 001397

4-year private university in small city.

Enrollment: 2,963 undergrads, 13% part-time. 700 full-time freshmen.
Selectivity: Admits 50 to 75% of applicants.

BASIC COSTS (2008-2009)
Tuition and fees: $26,868.
Per-credit charge: $846.
Room and board: $10,581.

FINANCIAL AID PICTURE (2007-2008)
Students with need: Out of 635 full-time freshmen who applied for aid, 568 were judged to have need. Of these, 564 received aid, and 91 had their full need met. Average financial aid package met 73% of need; average scholarship/grant was $15,438; average loan was $4,514. For part-time students, average financial aid package was $5,032.
Students without need: 96 full-time freshmen who did not demonstrate need for aid received scholarships/grants; average award was $13,880. No-need awards available for academics, athletics.
Scholarships offered: *Merit:* Presidential Scholarship; half-tuition; for applicants in top 15% of class with 1200 SAT (exclusive of Writing) or ACT equivalent. Academic Achievement Awards available. *Athletic:* 12 full-time freshmen received athletic scholarships; average amount $12,243.
Cumulative student debt: 53% of graduating class had student loans; average debt was $35,843.

FINANCIAL AID PROCEDURES
Forms required: FAFSA.
Dates and Deadlines: Priority date 3/1; closing date 3/1. Applicants notified on a rolling basis starting 3/15; must reply by 5/1 or within 2 week(s) of notification.

CONTACT
Karen Flynn, Director of Financial Aid
300 Boston Post Road, West Haven, CT 06516
(203) 932-7315

Wesleyan University
Middletown, Connecticut
www.wesleyan.edu   CSS Code: 3959

4-year private university and liberal arts college in large town.
Enrollment: 2,787 undergrads. 720 full-time freshmen.
Selectivity: Admits less than 50% of applicants.

BASIC COSTS (2008-2009)

Tuition and fees: $38,934.
Room and board: $10,636.

FINANCIAL AID PICTURE (2006-2007)

Students with need: Out of 397 full-time freshmen who applied for aid, 317 were judged to have need. Of these, 317 received aid, and 317 had their full need met. Average financial aid package met 100% of need; average scholarship/grant was $26,366; average loan was $2,968.
Students without need: This college awards aid only to students with need.
Scholarships offered: Freeman Asian Scholars, international first-year applicants from select East and Southeast Asian countries, 22 awarded.
Cumulative student debt: 45% of graduating class had student loans; average debt was $21,464.

FINANCIAL AID PROCEDURES

Forms required: FAFSA, CSS PROFILE.
Dates and Deadlines: Closing date 2/15. Applicants notified by 4/1; must reply by 5/1.
Transfers: Priority date 2/15; closing date 3/15. Applicants notified by 5/15; must reply by 6/1 or within 2 week(s) of notification. No financial aid available for international transfer candidates.

CONTACT

Jennifer Lawton, Director of Financial Aid
70 Wyllys Avenue, Middletown, CT 06459-0260
(860) 685-2800

Western Connecticut State University

Danbury, Connecticut
www.wcsu.edu   Federal Code: 001380

4-year public university in small city.
Enrollment: 5,092 undergrads, 14% part-time. 913 full-time freshmen.
Selectivity: Admits 50 to 75% of applicants.

BASIC COSTS (2007-2008)

Tuition and fees: $6,624; out-of-state residents $15,344.
Room and board: $8,400.

FINANCIAL AID PICTURE (2007-2008)

Students with need: Out of 671 full-time freshmen who applied for aid, 476 were judged to have need. Of these, 460 received aid, and 135 had their full need met. Average financial aid package met 63% of need; average scholarship/grant was $2,639; average loan was $2,009. For part-time students, average financial aid package was $5,827.
Students without need: 24 full-time freshmen who did not demonstrate need for aid received scholarships/grants; average award was $1,692. No-need awards available for academics.

FINANCIAL AID PROCEDURES

Forms required: FAFSA, institutional form.
Dates and Deadlines: Priority date 3/15; closing date 4/15. Applicants notified on a rolling basis starting 3/15; must reply by 5/1 or within 2 week(s) of notification.

CONTACT

Nancy Barton, Director, Financial Aid/Veterans Affairs
181 White Street, Danbury, CT 06810
(203) 837-8580

Yale University

New Haven, Connecticut   Federal Code: 001426
www.yale.edu   CSS Code: 3987

4-year private university in small city.
Enrollment: 5,291 undergrads. 1,318 full-time freshmen.
Selectivity: Admits less than 50% of applicants.

BASIC COSTS (2008-2009)

Tuition and fees: $35,300.
Room and board: $10,700.

FINANCIAL AID PICTURE

Students with need: Need-based aid available for full-time and part-time students. Work study available nights, weekends, and for part-time students.
Students without need: This college awards aid only to students with need.
Additional info: All scholarships based on demonstrated need.

FINANCIAL AID PROCEDURES

Forms required: FAFSA, CSS PROFILE.
Dates and Deadlines: Closing date 3/1. Applicants notified by 4/1; must reply by 5/1 or within 1 week(s) of notification.

CONTACT

Caesar Storlazzi, Director of University Financial Aid
Box 208234, New Haven, CT 06520-8234
(203) 432-2700

Delaware

Delaware State University

Dover, Delaware
www.desu.edu   Federal Code: 001428

4-year public university in large town.
Enrollment: 3,374 undergrads, 11% part-time. 788 full-time freshmen.
Selectivity: Admits less than 50% of applicants.

BASIC COSTS (2007-2008)

Tuition and fees: $6,146; out-of-state residents $13,100.
Per-credit charge: $224; out-of-state residents $513.
Room and board: $9,006.

FINANCIAL AID PICTURE (2006-2007)

Students with need: Out of 760 full-time freshmen who applied for aid, 682 were judged to have need. Of these, 659 received aid, and 209 had their full need met. Average financial aid package met 58% of need; average scholarship/grant was $2,445; average loan was $2,945. For part-time students, average financial aid package was $7,057.
Students without need: This college awards aid only to students with need.
Scholarships offered: 17 full-time freshmen received athletic scholarships; average amount $18,856.
Additional info: Students must file FAFSA by March 17 every year.

FINANCIAL AID PROCEDURES

Forms required: FAFSA.
Dates and Deadlines: Priority date 3/1; closing date 7/1. Applicants notified on a rolling basis starting 4/1; must reply by 8/20.
Transfers: Closing date 2/15.

CONTACT

Lynn Iocono, Executive Director of Student Financial Services
1200 North DuPont Highway, Dover, DE 19901
(302) 857-6250

Goldey-Beacom College

Wilmington, Delaware
www.gbc.edu
Federal Code: 001429

4-year private business college in small city.

Enrollment: 874 undergrads, 31% part-time. 167 full-time freshmen.

BASIC COSTS (2008-2009)

Tuition and fees: $16,980.
Per-credit charge: $556.
Room only: $4,982.

FINANCIAL AID PICTURE (2007-2008)

Students with need: Need-based aid available for part-time students. Work study available nights, weekends, and for part-time students.

Students without need: This college awards aid only to students with need.

Additional info: Essays required for scholarship applicants.

FINANCIAL AID PROCEDURES

Forms required: FAFSA.

Dates and Deadlines: Priority date 4/1; no closing date. Applicants notified on a rolling basis starting 2/15; must reply within 2 week(s) of notification.

Transfers: No deadline. Applicants notified on a rolling basis starting 2/15; must reply within 2 week(s) of notification.

CONTACT

Jane Lysle, Dean of Enrollment Management
4701 Limestone Road, Wilmington, DE 19808
(302) 225-6265

University of Delaware

Newark, Delaware
www.udel.edu
Federal Code: 001431

4-year public university in large town.

Enrollment: 15,318 undergrads, 5% part-time. 3,764 full-time freshmen.

Selectivity: Admits 50 to 75% of applicants.

BASIC COSTS (2007-2008)

Tuition and fees: $8,150; out-of-state residents $19,400.
Room and board: $7,948.

FINANCIAL AID PICTURE (2006-2007)

Students with need: Out of 2,888 full-time freshmen who applied for aid, 1,596 were judged to have need. Of these, 1,563 received aid, and 805 had their full need met. Average financial aid package met 79% of need; average scholarship/grant was $5,947; average loan was $5,117. For part-time students, average financial aid package was $7,878.

Students without need: This college awards aid only to students with need.

Scholarships offered: *Merit:* All freshman applicants evaluated for a wide range of merit scholarships ranging from $1,000 to full cost of education. *Athletic:* 150 full-time freshmen received athletic scholarships; average amount $9,067.

Cumulative student debt: 44% of graduating class had student loans; average debt was $17,200.

Additional info: December 15 application deadline to receive scholarship consideration. Sibling/parent tuition credit plan. Senior citizen tuition credit for state residents over 60.

FINANCIAL AID PROCEDURES

Forms required: FAFSA.

Dates and Deadlines: Priority date 2/1; closing date 3/15. Applicants notified on a rolling basis starting 3/15; must reply by 5/1 or within 3 week(s) of notification.

Transfers: No deadline. Aid usualy limited to federal and state programs.

CONTACT

Johnie Burton, Director of Financial Aid
116 Hullihen Hall, Newark, DE 19716
(302) 831-8761

Wesley College

Dover, Delaware
www.wesley.edu
Federal Code: 001433

4-year private liberal arts college in large town, affiliated with United Methodist Church.

Enrollment: 1,808 undergrads.

BASIC COSTS (2008-2009)

Tuition and fees: $18,530.
Per-credit charge: $740.
Room and board: $8,400.

FINANCIAL AID PICTURE

Students with need: Need-based aid available for full-time and part-time students. Work study available nights, weekends, and for part-time students.

Students without need: This college awards aid only to students with need.

FINANCIAL AID PROCEDURES

Forms required: FAFSA, institutional form.

Dates and Deadlines: Priority date 2/1; no closing date. Applicants notified on a rolling basis starting 1/1; must reply within 2 week(s) of notification.

Transfers: No deadline. Applicants notified on a rolling basis; must reply within 2 week(s) of notification.

CONTACT

James Marks, Director of Student Financial Planning
120 North State Street, Dover, DE 19901-3875
(302) 736-2334

Wilmington University

New Castle, Delaware
www.wilmu.edu
Federal Code: 007948

4-year private liberal arts college in large town.

Enrollment: 4,638 undergrads.

Selectivity: Open admission.

BASIC COSTS (2008-2009)

Tuition and fees: $8,760.
Per-credit charge: $292.

FINANCIAL AID PICTURE

Students with need: Need-based aid available for full-time and part-time students. Work study available nights, weekends, and for part-time students.

Students without need: No-need awards available for academics, athletics.

FINANCIAL AID PROCEDURES

Forms required: FAFSA.

Dates and Deadlines: Priority date 4/30; no closing date. Applicants notified on a rolling basis starting 8/5; must reply within 2 week(s) of notification.

CONTACT

Trudy Yingling, Director of Student Financial Services
320 Dupont Highway, New Castle, DE 19720
(302) 328-9401 ext. 107

District of Columbia

American University
Washington, District of Columbia
www.american.edu   Federal Code: 001434

4-year private university in very large city, affiliated with United Methodist Church.
Enrollment: 5,824 undergrads, 3% part-time. 1,286 full-time freshmen.
Selectivity: Admits 50 to 75% of applicants.

BASIC COSTS (2008-2009)
Tuition and fees: $33,283.
Per-credit charge: $1,093.
Room and board: $12,418.

FINANCIAL AID PICTURE (2007-2008)
Students with need: Out of 944 full-time freshmen who applied for aid, 577 were judged to have need. Of these, 577 received aid, and 285 had their full need met. Average financial aid package met 48% of need; average scholarship/grant was $13,571; average loan was $4,252. For part-time students, average financial aid package was $17,801.
Students without need: This college awards aid only to students with need.
Scholarships offered: *Merit:* United Methodist scholarship; supplemental application required. *Athletic:* 35 full-time freshmen received athletic scholarships; average amount $18,765.
Additional info: Early decision applicants must submit estimated AU institutional financial aid application by 11/15 and a FASFA as soon as possible after Jan 1.

FINANCIAL AID PROCEDURES
Forms required: FAFSA, institutional form.
Dates and Deadlines: Closing date 2/15. Applicants notified by 4/1; must reply by 5/1 or within 4 week(s) of notification.
Transfers: Priority date 3/1. Phi Theta Kappa scholarship available.

CONTACT
Brian Lee-Sang, Director of Financial Aid
4400 Massachusetts Avenue NW, Washington, DC 20016-8001
(202) 885-6100

Catholic University of America
Washington, District of Columbia
www.cua.edu   Federal Code: 001437

4-year private university in very large city, affiliated with Roman Catholic Church.
Enrollment: 3,245 undergrads, 7% part-time. 864 full-time freshmen.
Selectivity: Admits over 75% of applicants.

BASIC COSTS (2008-2009)
Tuition and fees: $30,670.
Per-credit charge: $1,125.
Room and board: $11,320.
Additional info: Full-time tuition for School of Engineering $30,770. Full-time tuition for School of Architecture $31,220. Part-time tuition for School of Architecture $1,135 per credit hour. Tuition/fee waivers available for adults.

FINANCIAL AID PICTURE (2007-2008)
Students with need: Out of 642 full-time freshmen who applied for aid, 500 were judged to have need. Of these, 500 received aid, and 218 had their full need met. Average financial aid package met 83% of need; average scholarship/grant was $15,520; average loan was $7,955. For part-time students, average financial aid package was $5,179.
Students without need: 325 full-time freshmen who did not demonstrate need for aid received scholarships/grants; average award was $8,947. No-need awards available for academics, alumni affiliation, leadership, music/drama, religious affiliation, state/district residency.

FINANCIAL AID PROCEDURES
Forms required: FAFSA.
Dates and Deadlines: Priority date 3/1; no closing date. Applicants notified on a rolling basis starting 4/1; must reply by 5/1 or within 2 week(s) of notification.
Transfers: No deadline. Applicants notified on a rolling basis starting 4/1; must reply by 5/1 or within 2 week(s) of notification.

CONTACT
Donald Bosse, Director of Financial Aid
620 Michigan Avenue, NE, Washington, DC 20064
(202) 319-5307

Corcoran College of Art and Design
Washington, District of Columbia
www.corcoran.edu   Federal Code: 011950

4-year private visual arts college in very large city.
Enrollment: 337 undergrads, 14% part-time. 57 full-time freshmen.
Selectivity: Admits 50 to 75% of applicants.

BASIC COSTS (2008-2009)
Tuition and fees: $27,380.
Room only: $9,694.

FINANCIAL AID PICTURE
Students with need: Need-based aid available for full-time and part-time students. Work study available nights, weekends, and for part-time students.
Students without need: No-need awards available for academics, art.
Scholarships offered: Dean's Merit Scholarship; $1,500-$5,000 for first year of study; based on art portfolio and academics. Academic Achievement and President's Awards; $1,000-$8,000 per year; four-year renewable. Faculty Chair Grants; full and half tuition awards.

FINANCIAL AID PROCEDURES
Forms required: FAFSA, institutional form.
Dates and Deadlines: Priority date 3/15; no closing date. Applicants notified on a rolling basis starting 4/15; must reply by 5/1 or within 2 week(s) of notification.
Transfers: Must reply within 2 week(s) of notification.

CONTACT
Diane Morris, Director of Financial Aid
500 17th Street, NW, Washington, DC 20006-4804
(202) 639-1818

Gallaudet University
Washington, District of Columbia
www.gallaudet.edu   Federal Code: 001443

4-year private university and liberal arts college in very large city.
Enrollment: 1,018 undergrads.
Selectivity: Admits 50 to 75% of applicants.

BASIC COSTS (2007-2008)

Tuition and fees: $10,906.

Per-credit charge: $527.

Room and board: $9,030.

Additional info: Students from developing countries may apply for reduction in percentage of tuition surcharge.

FINANCIAL AID PICTURE

Students with need: Need-based aid available for full-time and part-time students.

Students without need: No-need awards available for academics.

Additional info: Institution receives substantial aid from state vocational rehabilitation agencies, supplemented by institutional grants when needed.

FINANCIAL AID PROCEDURES

Forms required: FAFSA, institutional form.

Dates and Deadlines: Priority date 7/1; no closing date. Applicants notified on a rolling basis starting 4/1; must reply within 4 week(s) of notification.

CONTACT

Nancy Goodman, Director of Financial Aid

800 Florida Avenue, NE, Washington, DC 20002

(202) 651-5290

George Washington University

Washington, District of Columbia   Federal Code: 001444

www.gwu.edu   CSS Code: 5246

4-year private university in very large city.

Enrollment: 10,370 undergrads, 7% part-time. 2,440 full-time freshmen.

Selectivity: Admits less than 50% of applicants. GED not accepted.

BASIC COSTS (2008-2009)

Tuition and fees: $40,437.

Per-credit charge: $1,123.

Room and board: $9,920.

Additional info: Tuition stays fixed until student graduates, for a maximum of five years.

FINANCIAL AID PICTURE (2006-2007)

Students with need: Out of 1,282 full-time freshmen who applied for aid, 966 were judged to have need. Of these, 910 received aid, and 591 had their full need met. Average financial aid package met 91% of need; average scholarship/grant was $21,246; average loan was $5,679. For part-time students, average financial aid package was $14,000.

Students without need: 441 full-time freshmen who did not demonstrate need for aid received scholarships/grants; average award was $22,632. No-need awards available for academics, art, athletics, music/drama.

Scholarships offered: 29 full-time freshmen received athletic scholarships; average amount $20,414.

Cumulative student debt: 49% of graduating class had student loans; average debt was $30,817.

Additional info: Auditions required for performing arts scholarships.

FINANCIAL AID PROCEDURES

Forms required: FAFSA, CSS PROFILE.

Dates and Deadlines: Closing date 2/1. Applicants notified on a rolling basis starting 3/24; must reply by 5/1.

Transfers: Priority date 4/1; closing date 5/1.

CONTACT

Daniel Small, Director of Student Financial Assistance

2121 I Street NW, Suite 201, Washington, DC 20052

(202) 994-6620

Georgetown University

Washington, District of Columbia   Federal Code: 001445

www.georgetown.edu   CSS Code: 5244

4-year private university in very large city, affiliated with Roman Catholic Church.

Enrollment: 6,623 undergrads, 2% part-time. 1,579 full-time freshmen.

Selectivity: Admits less than 50% of applicants.

BASIC COSTS (2008-2009)

Tuition and fees: $37,947.

Per-credit charge: $1,564.

Room and board: $12,753.

FINANCIAL AID PICTURE (2007-2008)

Students with need: Out of 881 full-time freshmen who applied for aid, 638 were judged to have need. Of these, 632 received aid, and 632 had their full need met. Average financial aid package met 100% of need; average scholarship/grant was $24,371; average loan was $1,956. Need-based aid available for part-time students.

Students without need: No-need awards available for athletics.

Scholarships offered: 53 full-time freshmen received athletic scholarships; average amount $20,828.

Cumulative student debt: 46% of graduating class had student loans; average debt was $27,117.

FINANCIAL AID PROCEDURES

Forms required: FAFSA, CSS PROFILE.

Dates and Deadlines: Closing date 2/1. Applicants notified by 4/1; must reply by 5/1 or within 2 week(s) of notification.

Transfers: Priority date 3/1. Applicants notified by 5/15; must reply by 5/30 or within 2 week(s) of notification.

CONTACT

Patricia McWade, Dean of Student Financial Services

103 White-Gravenor, Washington, DC 20057-1002

(202) 687-4547

Howard University

Washington, District of Columbia

www.howard.edu   Federal Code: 001448

4-year private university in very large city.

Enrollment: 6,973 undergrads, 6% part-time. 1,443 full-time freshmen.

Selectivity: Admits 50 to 75% of applicants.

BASIC COSTS (2008-2009)

Tuition and fees: $15,010.

Per-credit charge: $592.

Room and board: $7,436.

FINANCIAL AID PICTURE (2007-2008)

Students with need: Out of 1,280 full-time freshmen who applied for aid, 1,109 were judged to have need. Of these, 767 received aid, and 259 had their full need met. Average financial aid package met 80% of need; average scholarship/grant was $9,431; average loan was $5,191. Need-based aid available for part-time students.

Students without need: This college awards aid only to students with need.

Scholarships offered: 583 full-time freshmen received athletic scholarships; average amount $882.

Cumulative student debt: 80% of graduating class had student loans; average debt was $16,473.

FINANCIAL AID PROCEDURES

Forms required: FAFSA, institutional form.

Dates and Deadlines: Priority date 2/15; closing date 8/15. Applicants notified on a rolling basis starting 4/1; must reply by 8/1 or within 4 week(s) of notification.

CONTACT
Marcus DeCosta, Associate Director, Office of Financial Aid, Scholarships, and Student Employment
2400 Sixth Street NW, Washington, DC 20059
(202) 806-2820

Potomac College
Washington, District of Columbia
www.potomac.edu   Federal Code: 032183

3-year for-profit business college in very large city.
Enrollment: 580 undergrads.
Selectivity: Open admission.

BASIC COSTS (2007-2008)
Tuition and fees: $13,480.
Per-credit charge: $445.

FINANCIAL AID PICTURE
Students with need: Need-based aid available for full-time and part-time students.

FINANCIAL AID PROCEDURES
Forms required: FAFSA, institutional form.
Dates and Deadlines: No deadline. Applicants notified on a rolling basis; must reply within 4 week(s) of notification.

CONTACT
Phyllis Crews, Director of Financial Aid
4000 Chesapeake Street NW, Washington, DC 20016
(202) 686-0876

Southeastern University
Washington, District of Columbia
www.seu.edu   Federal Code: 001456

4-year private business and liberal arts college in very large city.
Enrollment: 562 undergrads.
Selectivity: Open admission.

BASIC COSTS (2007-2008)
Tuition and fees: $12,525.
Per-credit charge: $255.
Additional info: Reduction in fees available for early registration. Online programs: $320 per credit hour.

FINANCIAL AID PICTURE
Students with need: Need-based aid available for full-time and part-time students.
Students without need: No-need awards available for academics, state/district residency.

FINANCIAL AID PROCEDURES
Forms required: FAFSA, institutional form.
Dates and Deadlines: Closing date 8/15. Applicants notified on a rolling basis; must reply within 2 week(s) of notification.

CONTACT
Peter Canine, CFO & Director of Financial Aid
501 I Street SW, Washington, DC 20024
(202) 478-8214 ext. 276

Trinity Washington University
Washington, District of Columbia
www.trinitydc.edu   Federal Code: 001460

4-year private liberal arts college for women in very large city, affiliated with Roman Catholic Church.
Enrollment: 1,032 undergrads.
Selectivity: Admits over 75% of applicants.

BASIC COSTS (2008-2009)
Tuition and fees: $18,960.
Per-credit charge: $650.
Room and board: $8,450.
Additional info: Mandatory health insurance.

FINANCIAL AID PICTURE (2007-2008)
Students with need: 57% of average financial aid package awarded as scholarships/grants, 43% awarded as loans/jobs. Need-based aid available for part-time students.
Students without need: No-need awards available for academics, alumni affiliation, leadership.

FINANCIAL AID PROCEDURES
Forms required: FAFSA.
Dates and Deadlines: Priority date 3/1; no closing date. Applicants notified on a rolling basis starting 2/1; must reply within 2 week(s) of notification.

CONTACT
Dana Baumgartner, Vice President
125 Michigan Avenue, NE, Washington, DC 20017
(202) 884-9530

University of the District of Columbia
Washington, District of Columbia
www.udc.edu   Federal Code: 007015

4-year public university and liberal arts college in very large city.
Enrollment: 5,137 undergrads.
Selectivity: Open admission.

BASIC COSTS (2008-2009)
Tuition and fees: $3,770; out-of-state residents $7,070.
Per-credit charge: $105; out-of-state residents $215.

FINANCIAL AID PICTURE
Students with need: Need-based aid available for full-time and part-time students. Work study available nights, weekends, and for part-time students.
Students without need: This college awards aid only to students with need.

FINANCIAL AID PROCEDURES
Forms required: FAFSA.
Dates and Deadlines: Priority date 3/15; no closing date. Applicants notified on a rolling basis starting 5/1; must reply within 2 week(s) of notification.

CONTACT
Willis Parker, Director of Financial Aid
4200 Connecticut Avenue NW, Washington, DC 20008
(202) 274-5060

Florida

Art Institute of Fort Lauderdale
Fort Lauderdale, Florida
www.aifl.edu   Federal Code: 010195

4-year for-profit visual arts and technical college in large city.
Enrollment: 2,821 undergrads, 44% part-time. 428 full-time freshmen.

BASIC COSTS (2007-2008)
Tuition and fees: $18,945.
Per-credit charge: $421.
Additional info: Tuition at time of enrollment locked for 4 years.

FINANCIAL AID PICTURE (2006-2007)
Students with need: 18% of average financial aid package awarded as scholarships/grants, 82% awarded as loans/jobs. Need-based aid available for part-time students. Work study available nights, weekends, and for part-time students.
Students without need: This college awards aid only to students with need.
Scholarships offered: Art Institute's International Excellence Award; $200-$300 per quarter; based on GPA.
Additional info: Internal scholarships available. Financial planning program allows personalized service to budget and meet college costs through individualized payment plans.

FINANCIAL AID PROCEDURES
Forms required: FAFSA.
Dates and Deadlines: No deadline.

CONTACT
Joy Cummings, Director of Student Financial Service
1799 Southeast 17th Street, Fort Lauderdale, FL 33316
(954) 308-2165

Ave Maria University
Ave Maria, Florida
www.avemaria.edu

4-year private university and liberal arts college in small town, affiliated with Roman Catholic Church.
Enrollment: 451 undergrads.
Selectivity: Admits 50 to 75% of applicants.

BASIC COSTS (2007-2008)
Tuition and fees: $16,255.
Room and board: $7,140.

FINANCIAL AID PICTURE (2007-2008)
Students with need: Average financial aid package met 80% of need; average scholarship/grant was $12,923; average loan was $3,254. For part-time students, average financial aid package was $10,982.

CONTACT
Anne Hart, Director of Financial Aid
5050 Ave Maria Boulevard, Ave Maria, FL 34142-9505

Baptist College of Florida
Graceville, Florida
www.baptistcollege.edu   Federal Code: 013001

4-year private Bible and teachers college in small town, affiliated with Southern Baptist Convention.
Enrollment: 539 undergrads, 29% part-time. 38 full-time freshmen.
Selectivity: Admits 50 to 75% of applicants.

BASIC COSTS (2008-2009)
Tuition and fees: $8,150.
Per-credit charge: $260.
Room and board: $3,886.

FINANCIAL AID PICTURE
Students with need: Need-based aid available for full-time and part-time students. Work study available nights, weekends, and for part-time students.
Students without need: No-need awards available for academics, minority status, music/drama, religious affiliation.

FINANCIAL AID PROCEDURES
Forms required: FAFSA, state aid form, institutional form.
Dates and Deadlines: Priority date 4/1; closing date 4/15. Applicants notified on a rolling basis starting 6/15; must reply within 4 week(s) of notification.
Transfers: No deadline.

CONTACT
Angela Rathel, Director of Financial Aid
5400 College Drive, Graceville, FL 32440-3306
(850) 263-3261 ext. 461

Barry University
Miami Shores, Florida
www.barry.edu   Federal Code: 001466

4-year private university in large town, affiliated with Roman Catholic Church.
Enrollment: 5,053 undergrads, 20% part-time. 472 full-time freshmen.
Selectivity: Admits 50 to 75% of applicants.

BASIC COSTS (2007-2008)
Tuition and fees: $24,500.
Per-credit charge: $720.
Room and board: $8,200.

FINANCIAL AID PICTURE (2007-2008)
Students with need: Out of 388 full-time freshmen who applied for aid, 350 were judged to have need. Of these, 348 received aid, and 38 had their full need met. Average financial aid package met 69% of need; average scholarship/grant was $4,602; average loan was $5,475. For part-time students, average financial aid package was $5,995.
Students without need: 93 full-time freshmen who did not demonstrate need for aid received scholarships/grants; average award was $8,836. No-need awards available for academics, art, athletics, music/drama.
Scholarships offered: 24 full-time freshmen received athletic scholarships; average amount $11,929.
Cumulative student debt: 76% of graduating class had student loans; average debt was $20,619.

FINANCIAL AID PROCEDURES
Forms required: FAFSA.
Dates and Deadlines: No deadline. Applicants notified on a rolling basis starting 1/25.

CONTACT
H. Dart Humeston, Director of Financial Aid
11300 Northeast Second Avenue, Miami Shores, FL 33161-6695
(305) 899-3673

Beacon College

Leesburg, Florida
www.beaconcollege.edu   Federal Code: 033733

4-year private liberal arts college in large town.
Enrollment: 117 undergrads. 19 full-time freshmen.
Selectivity: Admits 50 to 75% of applicants.

BASIC COSTS (2008-2009)

Tuition and fees: $26,150.
Per-credit charge: $510.
Room and board: $8,000.
Additional info: Tuition/fee waivers available for minority students, unemployed or children of unemployed.

FINANCIAL AID PICTURE (2006-2007)

Students with need: Out of 12 full-time freshmen who applied for aid, 12 were judged to have need. Of these, 12 received aid. Average financial aid package met 90% of need; average scholarship/grant was $15,000. Need-based aid available for part-time students.
Students without need: This college awards aid only to students with need.
Scholarships offered: Paul and Dorothy Heim Civic Award: $500; awarded annually. Ehil E. Brodbeck Book Scholarship: pays complete book costs for 1 semester; awarded annually based on merit or financial need.
Additional info: Work-study programs offered based on financial need.

FINANCIAL AID PROCEDURES

Forms required: FAFSA, state aid form, institutional form.
Dates and Deadlines: Priority date 4/1; no closing date. Applicants notified on a rolling basis starting 4/1; must reply within 2 week(s) of notification.
Transfers: No deadline. Applicants notified on a rolling basis starting 4/1; must reply within 2 week(s) of notification.

CONTACT

Kimberly Padget, Financial Aid Coordinator
105 East Main Street, Leesburg, FL 34748
(352) 787-7660

Bethune-Cookman University

Daytona Beach, Florida
www.cookman.edu   Federal Code: 001467

4-year private liberal arts college in small city, affiliated with United Methodist Church.
Enrollment: 3,312 undergrads, 6% part-time. 1,131 full-time freshmen.
Selectivity: Admits 50 to 75% of applicants.

BASIC COSTS (2008-2009)

Tuition and fees: $12,966.
Per-credit charge: $516.
Room and board: $7,672.

FINANCIAL AID PICTURE (2007-2008)

Students with need: 60% of average financial aid package awarded as scholarships/grants, 40% awarded as loans/jobs. Need-based aid available for part-time students. Work study available nights, weekends, and for part-time students.
Students without need: This college awards aid only to students with need.

FINANCIAL AID PROCEDURES

Forms required: FAFSA.
Dates and Deadlines: Priority date 4/1; no closing date. Applicants notified on a rolling basis starting 4/1; must reply within 3 week(s) of notification.

CONTACT

Joseph Coleman, Director of Financial Aid
Dr. Mary McLeod Bethune Boulevard, Daytona Beach, FL 32114-3099
(800) 553-9369

Brevard Community College

Cocoa, Florida
www.brevardcc.edu   Federal Code: 001470

2-year public community college in large town.
Enrollment: 13,024 undergrads, 57% part-time. 1,277 full-time freshmen.
Selectivity: Open admission; but selective for some programs.

BASIC COSTS (2007-2008)

Tuition and fees: $2,027; out-of-state residents $6,990.
Per-credit charge: $55; out-of-state residents $220.

FINANCIAL AID PICTURE

Students with need: Need-based aid available for full-time and part-time students.
Students without need: No-need awards available for academics, athletics.

FINANCIAL AID PROCEDURES

Forms required: FAFSA.
Dates and Deadlines: Priority date 4/15; closing date 6/30. Applicants notified on a rolling basis starting 6/1; must reply within 2 week(s) of notification.
Transfers: Transfer students must complete at least 15 credit hours with 3.5 GPA to be considered for merit scholarship.

CONTACT

Barry Paine, Dean of Financial Aid/Veteran Affairs
1519 Clearlake Road, Cocoa, FL 32922-9987
(321) 433-5530

Broward Community College

Fort Lauderdale, Florida
www.broward.edu   Federal Code: 001500

2-year public community college in small city.
Enrollment: 26,028 undergrads, 63% part-time. 2,882 full-time freshmen.
Selectivity: Open admission; but selective for some programs.

BASIC COSTS (2007-2008)

Tuition and fees: $2,004; out-of-state residents $7,172.
Additional info: Tuition/fee waivers available for adults, minority students.

FINANCIAL AID PICTURE (2006-2007)

Students with need: 75% of average financial aid package awarded as scholarships/grants, 25% awarded as loans/jobs. Need-based aid available for part-time students. Work study available nights, weekends, and for part-time students.
Students without need: No-need awards available for academics, athletics, leadership, state/district residency.

FINANCIAL AID PROCEDURES

Forms required: FAFSA, institutional form.
Dates and Deadlines: Priority date 4/15; closing date 7/1. Applicants notified on a rolling basis starting 7/15.
Transfers: No deadline.

CONTACT

Marcia Conliffe, Student Success and Enrollment Management Services
225 East Las Olas Boulevard, Fort Lauderdale, FL 33301
(954) 201-7635

Carlos Albizu University
Miami, Florida
www.albizu.edu
Federal Code: 010724

4-year private university and branch campus college in very large city.
Enrollment: 425 undergrads.
Selectivity: Open admission.

BASIC COSTS (2007-2008)
Tuition and fees: $12,468.
Additional info: Reported tuition, fees and per credit hour charge are for bachelor's degree program in business. Other programs individually priced.

FINANCIAL AID PICTURE
Students with need: Need-based aid available for full-time and part-time students. Work study available nights.
Students without need: This college awards aid only to students with need.

FINANCIAL AID PROCEDURES
Forms required: FAFSA, institutional form.
Dates and Deadlines: Priority date 6/1; no closing date. Applicants notified on a rolling basis starting 2/1.
Transfers: No deadline. Applicants notified on a rolling basis.

CONTACT
Ramona Morales, Financial Aid Director
2173 NW 99th Avenue, Miami, FL 33172
(305) 593-1223 ext. 153

Central Florida College
Winter Park, Florida
www.centralfloridacollege.edu
Federal Code: 022455

2-year for-profit technical college in very large city.
Enrollment: 450 undergrads.
Selectivity: Open admission.

BASIC COSTS (2007-2008)
Additional info: Certificate and diploma programs range fron $10,690 to $15,225. Associate of Science degrees range from $21,995 to $24,995; including books.

FINANCIAL AID PICTURE
Students with need: Need-based aid available for full-time students.
Students without need: This college awards aid only to students with need.

FINANCIAL AID PROCEDURES
Forms required: FAFSA.
Dates and Deadlines: No deadline.

CONTACT
Cathy Lane, Corporate Finance Director
1573 West Fairbanks Avenue, Winter Park, FL 32789
(407) 843-3984

Central Florida Community College
Ocala, Florida
www.cf.edu
Federal Code: 001471

2-year public community college in small city.
Enrollment: 5,615 undergrads, 55% part-time. 671 full-time freshmen.
Selectivity: Open admission; but selective for some programs.

BASIC COSTS (2007-2008)
Tuition and fees: $2,038; out-of-state residents $7,382.
Additional info: Tuition/fee waivers available for minority students.

FINANCIAL AID PICTURE
Students with need: Need-based aid available for full-time and part-time students.
Students without need: No-need awards available for academics, athletics, minority status, music/drama, state/district residency.

FINANCIAL AID PROCEDURES
Forms required: FAFSA.
Dates and Deadlines: No deadline.

CONTACT
Walter Fleming, Director, Financial Aid
3001 SW College Road, Ocala, FL 34474-4415
(352) 873-5803 ext. 1340

Chipola Junior College
Marianna, Florida
www.chipola.edu
Federal Code: 001472

4-year public community and junior college in small town.
Enrollment: 1,400 undergrads.
Selectivity: Open admission; but selective for some programs.

BASIC COSTS (2007-2008)
Tuition and fees: $2,037; out-of-state residents $6,001.

FINANCIAL AID PICTURE
Students with need: Need-based aid available for full-time and part-time students. Work study available nights.
Students without need: No-need awards available for academics, alumni affiliation, art, athletics, job skills, leadership, minority status, music/drama.

FINANCIAL AID PROCEDURES
Forms required: FAFSA, institutional form.
Dates and Deadlines: Priority date 5/1; no closing date. Applicants notified on a rolling basis starting 1/2; must reply within 2 week(s) of notification.

CONTACT
Sybil Cloud, Director of Financial Aid
3094 Indian Circle, Marianna, FL 32446
(850) 718-2223

City College: Miami
Miami, Florida
www.citycollege.edu
Federal Code: 025154

4-year for-profit business and health science college in large city.
Enrollment: 271 undergrads.

BASIC COSTS (2007-2008)
Tuition and fees: $9,900.
Per-credit charge: $195.

FINANCIAL AID PICTURE
Students with need: Need-based aid available for full-time and part-time students.
Students without need: This college awards aid only to students with need.

FINANCIAL AID PROCEDURES
Forms required: FAFSA, institutional form.
Dates and Deadlines: No deadline. Applicants notified on a rolling basis.

CONTACT
Esther Fike, President
9300 South Dadeland Boulevard, Miami, FL 33156
(305) 666-9242

Clearwater Christian College
Clearwater, Florida
www.clearwater.edu   Federal Code: 015025

4-year private liberal arts college in small city, affiliated with nondenominational tradition.
Enrollment: 575 undergrads, 2% part-time. 175 full-time freshmen.
Selectivity: Admits over 75% of applicants.

BASIC COSTS (2007-2008)
Tuition and fees: $13,160.
Per-credit charge: $485.
Room and board: $5,610.

FINANCIAL AID PICTURE (2007-2008)
Students with need: Out of 149 full-time freshmen who applied for aid, 120 were judged to have need. Of these, 120 received aid, and 17 had their full need met. Average financial aid package met 62% of need; average scholarship/grant was $3,477; average loan was $1,866. Need-based aid available for part-time students.
Students without need: 42 full-time freshmen who did not demonstrate need for aid received scholarships/grants; average award was $2,946. No-need awards available for academics, alumni affiliation, leadership, music/drama, religious affiliation, ROTC.
Scholarships offered: Scholarships up to $5,000 available to incoming freshmen who participate in the peer mentoring program; scholarships up to $4,000 available to international students.
Additional info: Special consideration given to children of Christian service workers; need-based scholarships available to first-generation students; scholarships up to $3,000 available to dual-enrolled students.

FINANCIAL AID PROCEDURES
Forms required: FAFSA, state aid form, institutional form.
Dates and Deadlines: Priority date 3/15; no closing date. Applicants notified on a rolling basis starting 4/15; must reply within 2 week(s) of notification.
Transfers: Transfer academic scholarship of $750 per semester awarded to sophomore or junior transfer with at least 3.25 cumulative GPA. After transferring, student must maintain 3.5 GPA.

CONTACT
Ruth Strum, Director of Financial Aid
3400 Gulf-to-Bay Boulevard, Clearwater, FL 33759-4595
(727) 726-1153 ext. 214

College of Business and Technology: Flagler
Miami, Florida
www.cbt.edu   Federal Code: 030716

2-year private junior and technical college in very large city.
Enrollment: 153 undergrads. 77 full-time freshmen.
Selectivity: Open admission.

BASIC COSTS (2007-2008)
Tuition and fees: $11,772.
Per-credit charge: $322.

FINANCIAL AID PICTURE
Students with need: Need-based aid available for full-time and part-time students. Work study available nights.

Students without need: This college awards aid only to students with need.

FINANCIAL AID PROCEDURES
Forms required: FAFSA.
Dates and Deadlines: No deadline.

CONTACT
Julio Espinal, Financial Aid Director
8230 West Flagler Street, Miami, FL 33144

Daytona Beach Community College
Daytona Beach, Florida
www.dbc.edu   Federal Code: 001475

2-year public community and technical college in large city.
Enrollment: 12,111 undergrads.
Selectivity: Open admission; but selective for some programs.

BASIC COSTS (2007-2008)
Tuition and fees: $2,083; out-of-state residents $8,225.

FINANCIAL AID PICTURE (2006-2007)
Students with need: 67% of average financial aid package awarded as scholarships/grants, 33% awarded as loans/jobs. Need-based aid available for part-time students.
Students without need: No-need awards available for athletics, leadership, music/drama.

FINANCIAL AID PROCEDURES
Forms required: FAFSA.
Dates and Deadlines: No deadline. Applicants notified on a rolling basis starting 2/15.

CONTACT
Aileen Morrissey, Director of Financial Aid
DBCC Admissions Office, Daytona Beach, FL 32114-2811
(386) 506-3000 ext. 3015

DeVry University: Miramar
Miramar, Florida
www.devry.edu

4-year for-profit university in large town.
Enrollment: 886 undergrads, 50% part-time. 81 full-time freshmen.

BASIC COSTS (2007-2008)
Tuition and fees: $14,020.
Per-credit charge: $500.

FINANCIAL AID PICTURE (2006-2007)
Students with need: Out of 35 full-time freshmen who applied for aid, 31 were judged to have need. Of these, 30 received aid. Average financial aid package met 42% of need; average scholarship/grant was $6,768. For part-time students, average financial aid package was $7,402.
Students without need: This college awards aid only to students with need.
Cumulative student debt: 86% of graduating class had student loans; average debt was $48,592.

FINANCIAL AID PROCEDURES
Forms required: FAFSA.
Dates and Deadlines: No deadline. Applicants notified on a rolling basis.

CONTACT
Scott Howard, Assistant Director of Student Finance
2300 Southwest 145th Avenue, Miramar, FL 33027
(954) 499-9700

DeVry University: Orlando

Orlando, Florida
www.devry.edu
Federal Code: 022966

4-year for-profit university in very large city.

Enrollment: 1,249 undergrads, 48% part-time. 114 full-time freshmen.

BASIC COSTS (2007-2008)

Tuition and fees: $14,020.

Per-credit charge: $500.

FINANCIAL AID PICTURE (2006-2007)

Students with need: Out of 80 full-time freshmen who applied for aid, 78 were judged to have need. Of these, 77 received aid, and 2 had their full need met. Average financial aid package met 31% of need; average scholarship/grant was $5,547; average loan was $4,272. For part-time students, average financial aid package was $7,025.

Students without need: This college awards aid only to students with need.

Cumulative student debt: 71% of graduating class had student loans; average debt was $41,439.

FINANCIAL AID PROCEDURES

Forms required: FAFSA.

Dates and Deadlines: No deadline. Applicants notified on a rolling basis.

CONTACT

Estrella Velasquez Domenech, Director of Student Finance

4000 Millennia Boulevard, Orlando, FL 32839-2426

(407) 345-2800

Eckerd College

St. Petersburg, Florida
www.eckerd.edu
Federal Code: 001487

4-year private liberal arts college in large city, affiliated with Presbyterian Church (USA).

Enrollment: 1,826 undergrads, 1% part-time. 536 full-time freshmen.

Selectivity: Admits 50 to 75% of applicants.

BASIC COSTS (2008-2009)

Tuition and fees: $30,590.

Per-credit charge: $1,043.

Room and board: $8,754.

FINANCIAL AID PICTURE

Students with need: Need-based aid available for full-time and part-time students.

Students without need: No-need awards available for academics, art, athletics, leadership, music/drama, religious affiliation.

Scholarships offered: Academic scholarships: ranging from $7,000 to $10,000 per year; available to entering freshmen regardless of financial need. Trustee, Presidential, and Dean's Scholarships: range from $13,000 to $25,000 awarded to outstanding freshmen with strong scholastic records and leadership potential. Limited number of Artistic Achievement Awards in music, theater, visual art and creative writing also available through separate application process.

FINANCIAL AID PROCEDURES

Forms required: FAFSA.

Dates and Deadlines: Priority date 3/1; no closing date. Applicants notified on a rolling basis starting 2/1.

CONTACT

Patricia Watkins, Director of Financial Aid

4200 54th Avenue South, St. Petersburg, FL 33711-4700

(727) 864-8334

Edward Waters College

Jacksonville, Florida
www.ewc.edu
Federal Code: 001478

4-year private liberal arts college in very large city, affiliated with African Methodist Episcopal Church.

Enrollment: 811 undergrads, 8% part-time. 199 full-time freshmen.

Selectivity: Open admission.

BASIC COSTS (2008-2009)

Tuition and fees: $10,618.

Per-credit charge: $382.

Room and board: $6,474.

FINANCIAL AID PICTURE

Students with need: Need-based aid available for full-time and part-time students. Work study available nights, weekends, and for part-time students.

FINANCIAL AID PROCEDURES

Forms required: FAFSA.

Dates and Deadlines: Closing date 4/15. Applicants notified on a rolling basis starting 5/1; must reply within 2 week(s) of notification.

CONTACT

Landi Myrick, Director of Financial Aid

1658 Kings Road, Jacksonville, FL 32209

(904) 470-8190

Embry-Riddle Aeronautical University

Daytona Beach, Florida
www.embryriddle.edu
Federal Code: 001479

4-year private university in small city.

Enrollment: 4,531 undergrads, 9% part-time. 935 full-time freshmen.

Selectivity: Admits over 75% of applicants.

BASIC COSTS (2008-2009)

Tuition and fees: $27,540.

Per-credit charge: $1,100.

Room and board: $9,580.

FINANCIAL AID PICTURE (2007-2008)

Students with need: Out of 781 full-time freshmen who applied for aid, 642 were judged to have need. Of these, 642 received aid. For part-time students, average financial aid package was $12,666.

Students without need: No-need awards available for academics, alumni affiliation, athletics, leadership, ROTC.

Scholarships offered: 19 full-time freshmen received athletic scholarships; average amount $10,736.

Cumulative student debt: 75% of graduating class had student loans; average debt was $57,502.

FINANCIAL AID PROCEDURES

Forms required: FAFSA.

Dates and Deadlines: No deadline. Applicants notified on a rolling basis starting 3/1; must reply within 4 week(s) of notification.

CONTACT

Barbara Dryden, Director of Financial Aid

600 South Clyde Morris Boulevard, Daytona Beach, FL 32114-3900

(386) 226-6300

Embry-Riddle Aeronautical University: Worldwide Campus

Daytona Beach, Florida
www.embryriddle.edu   Federal Code: 001479

4-year private university in small city.

Enrollment: 11,569 undergrads, 82% part-time. 32 full-time freshmen.

BASIC COSTS (2008-2009)

Additional info: Per credit hour charges range from $215 to $275.

FINANCIAL AID PICTURE (2007-2008)

Students with need: Out of 8 full-time freshmen who applied for aid, 4 were judged to have need. Of these, 4 received aid. For part-time students, average financial aid package was $4,781.

Students without need: No-need awards available for academics.

Cumulative student debt: 25% of graduating class had student loans; average debt was $29,305.

FINANCIAL AID PROCEDURES

Forms required: FAFSA.

Dates and Deadlines: Priority date 4/15; no closing date. Applicants notified on a rolling basis starting 3/1; must reply within 4 week(s) of notification.

CONTACT

Barbara Dryden, Director of Financial Aid
600 South Clyde Morris Boulevard, Daytona Beach, FL 32114-3900
(386) 226-6300

Everest University: Brandon

Tampa, Florida
www.everest.edu   Federal Code: 001534

4-year for-profit university and business college in very large city.

Enrollment: 800 undergrads.

Selectivity: Open admission; but selective for some programs.

BASIC COSTS (2007-2008)

Tuition and fees: $13,695.

Per-credit charge: $299.

FINANCIAL AID PICTURE

Students with need: Need-based aid available for full-time and part-time students.

Students without need: This college awards aid only to students with need.

FINANCIAL AID PROCEDURES

Forms required: FAFSA, institutional form.

Dates and Deadlines: No deadline. Applicants notified on a rolling basis; must reply within 2 week(s) of notification.

CONTACT

Jose Nieves, Director of Financial Aid
3924 Coconut Palm Drive, Tampa, FL 33619
(813) 621-0041 ext. 118

Everest University: Lakeland

Lakeland, Florida
www.everest.edu   Federal Code: 025998

4-year for-profit university and branch campus college in small city.

Enrollment: 700 undergrads.

BASIC COSTS (2007-2008)

Tuition and fees: $13,695.

Per-credit charge: $299.

FINANCIAL AID PICTURE

Students with need: Need-based aid available for full-time and part-time students.

Students without need: This college awards aid only to students with need.

FINANCIAL AID PROCEDURES

Dates and Deadlines: No deadline.

CONTACT

Andrew Feldberg
995 East Memorial Boulevard, Suite 110, Lakeland, FL 33801-1919
(863) 686-1449 ext. 101

Everest University: Pompano Beach

Pompano Beach, Florida
www.everest.edu   Federal Code: 008146

4-year for-profit business college in small city.

Enrollment: 1,500 undergrads.

BASIC COSTS (2007-2008)

Tuition and fees: $13,695.

Per-credit charge: $299.

Additional info: Tuition may vary by program.

FINANCIAL AID PICTURE

Students with need: Need-based aid available for full-time and part-time students.

FINANCIAL AID PROCEDURES

Forms required: FAFSA, institutional form.

Dates and Deadlines: No deadline. Applicants notified on a rolling basis starting 6/1.

CONTACT

Sharon Scheible, Director of Financial Aid
225 North Federal Highway, Pompano Beach, FL 33062
(954) 783-7339

Everest University: Tampa

Tampa, Florida
www.everest.edu   Federal Code: 001534

4-year for-profit university and business college in large city.

Enrollment: 1,300 undergrads.

Selectivity: Open admission.

BASIC COSTS (2007-2008)

Tuition and fees: $13,695.

Per-credit charge: $299.

Additional info: Cost of tuition may vary with program.

FINANCIAL AID PICTURE

Students with need: Need-based aid available for full-time and part-time students.

Students without need: This college awards aid only to students with need.

FINANCIAL AID PROCEDURES

Forms required: FAFSA.

Dates and Deadlines: No deadline. Applicants notified on a rolling basis.

CONTACT

Jennifer Hayne, Director of Financial Aid

3319 West Hillsborough Avenue, Tampa, FL 33614

(813) 879-6000 ext. 145

Flagler College

St. Augustine, Florida

www.flagler.edu   Federal Code: 007893

4-year private liberal arts college in large town.

Enrollment: 2,537 undergrads, 3% part-time. 579 full-time freshmen.

Selectivity: Admits less than 50% of applicants.

BASIC COSTS (2008-2009)

Tuition and fees: $13,600.

Per-credit charge: $455.

Room and board: $6,900.

FINANCIAL AID PICTURE (2007-2008)

Students with need: Average financial aid package met 76% of need; average scholarship/grant was $4,529; average loan was $3,549. For part-time students, average financial aid package was $3,853.

Students without need: No-need awards available for academics, art, athletics, job skills, leadership, minority status, music/drama, state/district residency.

Cumulative student debt: 54% of graduating class had student loans; average debt was $15,186.

FINANCIAL AID PROCEDURES

Forms required: FAFSA, state aid form, institutional form.

Dates and Deadlines: Priority date 4/1; no closing date. Applicants notified on a rolling basis starting 4/1; must reply within 2 week(s) of notification.

Transfers: No deadline. Applicants notified on a rolling basis starting 3/1; must reply within 2 week(s) of notification. Transfer students receiving Florida-sponsored aid must notify Florida Office of Student Financial Assistance of their transfer.

CONTACT

Christopher Haffner, Director of Financial Aid

74 King Street, St. Augustine, FL 32084

(800) 304-4208

Florida Agricultural and Mechanical University

Tallahassee, Florida

www.famu.edu   Federal Code: 001480

4-year public university in small city.

Enrollment: 9,566 undergrads, 12% part-time. 1,874 full-time freshmen.

Selectivity: Admits 50 to 75% of applicants.

BASIC COSTS (2007-2008)

Tuition and fees: $3,264; out-of-state residents $15,186.

Room and board: $5,844.

FINANCIAL AID PICTURE (2006-2007)

Students with need: Average financial aid package met 77% of need; average scholarship/grant was $6,034; average loan was $5,940. For part-time students, average financial aid package was $7,608.

Students without need: No-need awards available for academics, art, leadership.

Cumulative student debt: 83% of graduating class had student loans; average debt was $29,742.

FINANCIAL AID PROCEDURES

Forms required: FAFSA.

Dates and Deadlines: Priority date 3/1; closing date 6/30. Applicants notified on a rolling basis starting 3/1; must reply within 2 week(s) of notification.

Transfers: No deadline. Applicants notified on a rolling basis.

CONTACT

Marcia Boyd, Director of Financial Aid

FHAC, G-9, Tallahassee, FL 32307-3200

(850) 599-3730

Florida Atlantic University

Boca Raton, Florida

www.fau.edu   Federal Code: 001481

4-year public university in small city.

Enrollment: 20,525 undergrads, 40% part-time. 2,520 full-time freshmen.

Selectivity: Admits 50 to 75% of applicants.

BASIC COSTS (2007-2008)

Tuition and fees: $3,344; out-of-state residents $16,409.

Per-credit charge: $74; out-of-state residents $488.

Room and board: $8,360.

FINANCIAL AID PICTURE (2007-2008)

Students with need: Out of 2,113 full-time freshmen who applied for aid, 1,135 were judged to have need. Of these, 1,111 received aid, and 259 had their full need met. Average financial aid package met 97% of need; average scholarship/grant was $7,338; average loan was $3,165. For part-time students, average financial aid package was $5,604.

Students without need: 115 full-time freshmen who did not demonstrate need for aid received scholarships/grants; average award was $1,993. No-need awards available for academics, athletics, music/drama, state/district residency.

Scholarships offered: 41 full-time freshmen received athletic scholarships; average amount $7,925.

FINANCIAL AID PROCEDURES

Forms required: FAFSA.

Dates and Deadlines: Priority date 3/1; no closing date. Applicants notified on a rolling basis starting 4/1; must reply within 3 week(s) of notification.

CONTACT

Carol Pfeilsticker, Director of Financial Aid

777 Glades Road, Boca Raton, FL 33431

(561) 297-2738

Florida Christian College

Kissimmee, Florida

www.fcc.edu   Federal Code: 015192

4-year private Bible and teachers college in small city, affiliated with Christian Churches and Churches of Christ.

Enrollment: 226 undergrads, 28% part-time. 27 full-time freshmen.

BASIC COSTS (2007-2008)

Tuition and fees: $10,200.

Per-credit charge: $325.

Room only: $2,400.

Additional info: Tuition at time of enrollment locked for 4 years.

FINANCIAL AID PICTURE

Students with need: Need-based aid available for full-time and part-time students. Work study available nights, weekends, and for part-time students.

Students without need: No-need awards available for academics, alumni affiliation, leadership, music/drama, religious affiliation, state/district residency.

FINANCIAL AID PROCEDURES

Forms required: FAFSA, institutional form.

Dates and Deadlines: Priority date 5/1; closing date 7/15. Applicants notified on a rolling basis starting 3/1.

Transfers: Available only if funding remains.

CONTACT

Bruce Dusterhoft, Director of Student Financial Aid

1011 Bill Beck Boulevard, Kissimmee, FL 34744-4402

(407) 569-1365

Florida College

Temple Terrace, Florida

www.floridacollege.edu Federal Code: 001482

4-year private liberal arts college in large town.

Enrollment: 524 undergrads, 5% part-time. 216 full-time freshmen.

Selectivity: Admits over 75% of applicants.

BASIC COSTS (2008-2009)

Tuition and fees: $12,060.

Per-credit charge: $450.

Room and board: $6,300.

FINANCIAL AID PICTURE (2007-2008)

Students with need: Out of 129 full-time freshmen who applied for aid, 129 were judged to have need. Of these, 129 received aid, and 22 had their full need met. Average financial aid package met 86% of need; average scholarship/grant was $1,933; average loan was $1,686. For part-time students, average financial aid package was $2,653.

Students without need: 50 full-time freshmen who did not demonstrate need for aid received scholarships/grants; average award was $787. No-need awards available for academics, athletics, music/drama, state/district residency.

Scholarships offered: 31 full-time freshmen received athletic scholarships; average amount $1,290.

Additional info: Music and forensic scholarships available. Audition required for music scholarships.

FINANCIAL AID PROCEDURES

Forms required: FAFSA, state aid form, institutional form.

Dates and Deadlines: Priority date 4/1; closing date 6/1. Applicants notified on a rolling basis starting 3/1; must reply within 2 week(s) of notification.

Transfers: No deadline.

CONTACT

Lisa McClister, Financial Aid Director

119 North Glen Arven Avenue, Temple Terrace, FL 33617

(813) 899-6774

Florida College of Natural Health: Bradenton

Bradenton, Florida

www.fcnh.com

2-year for-profit health science and career college in small city.

Enrollment: 62 undergrads.

Selectivity: Open admission; but selective for some programs.

BASIC COSTS (2007-2008)

Additional info: 4 degree programs with $335 per credit hour charge. 2 diploma programs with flat rate: therapeutic massage 6-month training program, $9,720; skincare 4-to 5-month training program, $4,650.

FINANCIAL AID PICTURE

Students with need: Need-based aid available for full-time students.

Students without need: This college awards aid only to students with need.

FINANCIAL AID PROCEDURES

Forms required: FAFSA.

Dates and Deadlines: No deadline. Applicants notified on a rolling basis.

CONTACT

Jorge Villasante, Director of Financial Aid

616 67th Street Circle East, Bradenton, FL 34208

(954) 975-6400

Florida Community College at Jacksonville

Jacksonville, Florida

www.fccj.edu Federal Code: 001484

2-year public community college in very large city.

Enrollment: 19,016 undergrads, 66% part-time. 1,609 full-time freshmen.

Selectivity: Open admission; but selective for some programs.

BASIC COSTS (2007-2008)

Tuition and fees: $1,949; out-of-state residents $7,452.

FINANCIAL AID PICTURE (2007-2008)

Students with need: 58% of average financial aid package awarded as scholarships/grants, 42% awarded as loans/jobs. Need-based aid available for part-time students. Work study available nights, weekends, and for part-time students.

Students without need: No-need awards available for academics, alumni affiliation, art, athletics, job skills, leadership, minority status, music/drama.

FINANCIAL AID PROCEDURES

Forms required: FAFSA, institutional form.

Dates and Deadlines: Priority date 8/1; no closing date. Applicants notified by 7/1.

CONTACT

Joel Friedman, Director of Student Aid

501 West State Street, Jacksonville, FL 32202

(904) 632-3352

Florida Gulf Coast University

Ft. Myers, Florida

www.fgcu.edu Federal Code: 032553

4-year public university in small city.

Enrollment: 7,996 undergrads, 21% part-time. 1,516 full-time freshmen.

Selectivity: Admits over 75% of applicants.

BASIC COSTS (2007-2008)

Tuition and fees: $3,656; out-of-state residents $16,174.

Room and board: $6,860.

FINANCIAL AID PICTURE (2006-2007)

Students with need: Out of 1,260 full-time freshmen who applied for aid, 569 were judged to have need. Of these, 569 received aid, and 61 had their full need met. Average financial aid package met 64% of need; average scholarship/grant was $3,605; average loan was $2,688. For part-time students, average financial aid package was $5,399.

Students without need: 116 full-time freshmen who did not demonstrate need for aid received scholarships/grants; average award was $3,658. No-need awards available for academics, alumni affiliation, athletics, leadership, minority status, music/drama, religious affiliation, state/district residency.

Scholarships offered: 11 full-time freshmen received athletic scholarships; average amount $3,842.

Cumulative student debt: 35% of graduating class had student loans; average debt was $9,449.

FINANCIAL AID PROCEDURES

Forms required: FAFSA.

Dates and Deadlines: Priority date 3/1; closing date 6/30. Applicants notified on a rolling basis starting 2/15.

Transfers: Applicants notified on a rolling basis.

CONTACT

Jorge Lopez-Rosado, Director, Student Financial Aid
10501 FGCU Boulevard South, Ft. Myers, FL 33965-6565
(239) 590-7920

Florida Hospital College of Health Sciences

Orlando, Florida
www.FHCHS.edu   Federal Code: 031155

4-year private health science and nursing college in large city, affiliated with Seventh-day Adventists.

Enrollment: 2,149 undergrads, 68% part-time. 77 full-time freshmen.

BASIC COSTS (2008-2009)

Tuition and fees: $8,540.

Per-credit charge: $275.

Room only: $3,360.

Additional info: Fees vary according to program.

FINANCIAL AID PICTURE

Students with need: Need-based aid available for full-time and part-time students.

Students without need: No-need awards available for state/district residency.

FINANCIAL AID PROCEDURES

Forms required: FAFSA, institutional form.

Dates and Deadlines: Priority date 4/12; no closing date. Applicants notified on a rolling basis starting 3/1.

CONTACT

Starr Bender, Director of Financial Aid
671 Winyah Drive, Orlando, FL 32803
(407) 303-6963

Florida Institute of Technology

Melbourne, Florida
www.fit.edu   Federal Code: 001469

4-year private university in small city.

Enrollment: 2,508 undergrads, 4% part-time. 677 full-time freshmen.

Selectivity: Admits over 75% of applicants.

BASIC COSTS (2008-2009)

Tuition and fees: $30,190.

Per-credit charge: $898.

Room and board: $10,250.

Additional info: Tuition $27,280 for aeronautics, business, psychology, and humanities programs.

FINANCIAL AID PICTURE (2007-2008)

Students with need: Average financial aid package met 85% of need; average scholarship/grant was $18,517; average loan was $4,320. For part-time students, average financial aid package was $10,850.

Students without need: No-need awards available for academics, alumni affiliation, athletics, ROTC, state/district residency.

Cumulative student debt: 68% of graduating class had student loans; average debt was $28,740.

FINANCIAL AID PROCEDURES

Forms required: FAFSA, state aid form.

Dates and Deadlines: Priority date 3/1; no closing date. Applicants notified on a rolling basis starting 2/15; must reply by 5/1 or within 4 week(s) of notification.

Transfers: No deadline. Applicants notified on a rolling basis starting 2/15; must reply within 4 week(s) of notification.

CONTACT

Jay Lally, Director of Financial Aid
150 West University Boulevard, Melbourne, FL 32901-6975
(321) 674-8070

Florida International University

Miami, Florida
www.fiu.edu   Federal Code: 009635

4-year public university in very large city.

Enrollment: 29,584 undergrads, 37% part-time. 3,074 full-time freshmen.

Selectivity: Admits less than 50% of applicants.

BASIC COSTS (2007-2008)

Tuition and fees: $3,466; out-of-state residents $15,865.

Room and board: $10,608.

Additional info: Tuition/fee waivers available for minority students.

FINANCIAL AID PICTURE

Students with need: Need-based aid available for full-time and part-time students.

Students without need: No-need awards available for academics, art, minority status, music/drama, state/district residency.

FINANCIAL AID PROCEDURES

Forms required: FAFSA.

Dates and Deadlines: Priority date 3/1; closing date 5/15. Must reply within 4 week(s) of notification.

CONTACT

Francisco Valines, Director of Financial Aid
University Park Campus, PC 140, Miami, FL 33199
(305) 348-7272

Florida Keys Community College

Key West, Florida
www.fkcc.edu   Federal Code: 001485

2-year public community college in large town.

Enrollment: 898 undergrads.

Selectivity: Open admission; but selective for some programs.

BASIC COSTS (2007-2008)

Tuition and fees: $2,125; out-of-state residents $8,069.

FINANCIAL AID PICTURE

Students with need: Need-based aid available for full-time and part-time students.

Students without need: No-need awards available for academics, art, leadership, minority status.

FINANCIAL AID PROCEDURES

Forms required: FAFSA, institutional form.

Dates and Deadlines: Priority date 5/1; no closing date. Applicants notified on a rolling basis starting 6/15; must reply within 2 week(s) of notification.

Transfers: Closing date 5/1. Florida Student Assistance Grant available to students paying Florida resident tuition.

CONTACT
Lynn Burris, Financial Aid Director
5901 College Road, Key West, FL 33040
(305) 809-3523

Florida Memorial University
Miami Gardens, Florida
www.fmuniv.edu   Federal Code: 001486

4-year private liberal arts college in very large city, affiliated with American Baptist Churches in the USA.
Enrollment: 1,669 undergrads, 9% part-time. 510 full-time freshmen.

BASIC COSTS (2008-2009)
Tuition and fees: $12,254.
Per-credit charge: $438.
Room and board: $5,340.

FINANCIAL AID PICTURE
Students with need: Need-based aid available for full-time and part-time students.
Additional info: Need-based financial aid available to part-time students taking 6 credits or more per semester.

FINANCIAL AID PROCEDURES
Dates and Deadlines: No deadline. Applicants notified on a rolling basis; must reply within 2 week(s) of notification.
Transfers: Priority date 3/15; closing date 4/15.

CONTACT
Brian Phillip, Director of Financial Aid
15800 Northwest 42 Avenue, Miami Gardens, FL 33054
(305) 430-1168

Florida National College
Hialeah, Florida
www.fnc.edu   Federal Code: 017069

2-year for-profit community and junior college in very large city.
Enrollment: 2,058 undergrads.
Selectivity: Open admission; but selective for some programs.

BASIC COSTS (2008-2009)
Tuition and fees: $12,594.
Per-credit charge: $400.

FINANCIAL AID PICTURE (2006-2007)
Students with need: 0% of average financial aid package awarded as scholarships/grants, 100% awarded as loans/jobs. Need-based aid available for part-time students.
Students without need: This college awards aid only to students with need.

FINANCIAL AID PROCEDURES
Forms required: FAFSA, institutional form.
Dates and Deadlines: No deadline.

CONTACT
Omar Sanchez, Vice President for Planning and Research
4425 West 20th Avenue, Hialeah, FL 33012
(305) 821-3333 ext. 1003

Florida Southern College
Lakeland, Florida
www.flsouthern.edu   Federal Code: 001488

4-year private liberal arts college in small city, affiliated with United Methodist Church.
Enrollment: 1,687 undergrads, 3% part-time. 423 full-time freshmen.
Selectivity: Admits 50 to 75% of applicants.

BASIC COSTS (2008-2009)
Tuition and fees: $22,145.
Per-credit charge: $650.
Room and board: $7,850.

FINANCIAL AID PICTURE (2007-2008)
Students with need: Out of 323 full-time freshmen who applied for aid, 265 were judged to have need. Of these, 263 received aid, and 95 had their full need met. Average financial aid package met 78% of need; average scholarship/grant was $5,233; average loan was $1,885. For part-time students, average financial aid package was $4,708.
Students without need: 150 full-time freshmen who did not demonstrate need for aid received scholarships/grants; average award was $14,524. No-need awards available for academics, alumni affiliation, art, athletics, job skills, leadership, music/drama, religious affiliation, ROTC.
Scholarships offered: 53 full-time freshmen received athletic scholarships; average amount $10,136.
Cumulative student debt: 66% of graduating class had student loans; average debt was $8,914.

FINANCIAL AID PROCEDURES
Forms required: FAFSA, institutional form.
Dates and Deadlines: Priority date 3/1; closing date 7/1. Applicants notified on a rolling basis starting 3/1; must reply within 3 week(s) of notification.

CONTACT
William Healy, Director of Financial Aid
111 Lake Hollingsworth Drive, Lakeland, FL 33801-5698
(863) 680-4140

Florida State University
Tallahassee, Florida
www.fsu.edu   Federal Code: 001489

4-year public university in small city.
Enrollment: 31,231 undergrads, 11% part-time. 5,797 full-time freshmen.
Selectivity: Admits 50 to 75% of applicants.

BASIC COSTS (2007-2008)
Tuition and fees: $3,355; out-of-state residents $17,403.
Room and board: $8,000.

FINANCIAL AID PICTURE (2007-2008)
Students with need: Out of 3,771 full-time freshmen who applied for aid, 1,855 were judged to have need. Of these, 1,855 received aid, and 1,390 had their full need met. Average financial aid package met 68% of need; average scholarship/grant was $3,467; average loan was $2,885. For part-time students, average financial aid package was $8,429.
Students without need: 421 full-time freshmen who did not demonstrate need for aid received scholarships/grants; average award was $2,274. No-need awards available for academics, athletics, state/district residency.
Scholarships offered: 411 full-time freshmen received athletic scholarships; average amount $276.
Cumulative student debt: 32% of graduating class had student loans; average debt was $13,855.

FINANCIAL AID PROCEDURES
Forms required: FAFSA.

Dates and Deadlines: No deadline. Applicants notified on a rolling basis starting 3/15.

CONTACT

Darryl Marshall, Director of Financial Aid
PO Box 3062400, Tallahassee, FL 32306-2400
(850) 644-0539

Florida Technical College: Deland

Deland, Florida
www.flatech.edu

2-year for-profit junior and technical college in small city.
Enrollment: 230 undergrads.
Selectivity: Open admission.

BASIC COSTS (2007-2008)

Additional info: $4,347 tuition per quarter for paralegal, medical assistant, business, computer drafting & design, electronics/computer technology; $4,713 tuition per quarter for network hardware, network administration/programming, e-commerce, web-design and graphics design. $3650 per quarter for Criminal Justice and $3667 per quarter for Network Administration/Hardware with Wirelss technology. Required fees $100. Tuition includes cost of books and supplies.

FINANCIAL AID PICTURE

Students with need: Need-based aid available for full-time and part-time students. Work study available nights.
Students without need: This college awards aid only to students with need.

FINANCIAL AID PROCEDURES

Forms required: FAFSA.
Dates and Deadlines: No deadline. Applicants notified on a rolling basis.

CONTACT

Aida Shehu, Director of Financial Aid
1199 South Woodland Boulevard, Deland, FL 32720
(386) 734-3303

Florida Technical College: Orlando

Orlando, Florida
www.flatech.edu   Federal Code: 015670

2-year for-profit technical college in large city.
Enrollment: 163 undergrads.
Selectivity: Open admission.

BASIC COSTS (2008-2009)

Additional info: Network administration/hardware with wireless technology, $22,000 annually. Tuition includes cost of books and supplies.

FINANCIAL AID PICTURE

Students with need: Need-based aid available for full-time and part-time students.
Students without need: This college awards aid only to students with need.

FINANCIAL AID PROCEDURES

Forms required: FAFSA, institutional form.
Dates and Deadlines: No deadline. Applicants notified on a rolling basis.

CONTACT

Scott Berg, Financial Services
12689 Challenger Parkway, #130, Orlando, FL 32826-2707
(407) 447-7300

Full Sail University

Winter Park, Florida
www.fullsail.com   Federal Code: 016812

2-year for-profit visual arts and technical college in very large city.
Enrollment: 5,697 undergrads.
Selectivity: Open admission; but selective for some programs.

BASIC COSTS (2007-2008)

Additional info: Annual tuition for associate and bachelor degree programs range from $13,000 to $16,000. Includes books and supplies.

FINANCIAL AID PICTURE

Students with need: Need-based aid available for full-time students. Work study available nights, weekends, and for part-time students.

FINANCIAL AID PROCEDURES

Forms required: FAFSA.
Dates and Deadlines: No deadline. Applicants notified on a rolling basis; must reply within 2 week(s) of notification.

CONTACT

3300 University Boulevard, Winter Park, FL 32792-7429
(407) 679-0100 ext. 2300

Gulf Coast Community College

Panama City, Florida
www.gulfcoast.edu   Federal Code: 001490

2-year public community college in small city.
Enrollment: 7,251 undergrads, 68% part-time.
Selectivity: Open admission; but selective for some programs.

BASIC COSTS (2007-2008)

Tuition and fees: $1,968; out-of-state residents $7,109.

FINANCIAL AID PICTURE

Students with need: Need-based aid available for full-time and part-time students. Work study available nights, weekends, and for part-time students.
Students without need: No-need awards available for academics, athletics, job skills, leadership, minority status, music/drama, state/district residency.
Scholarships offered: GCCC Foundation scholarships: based on academic performance, financial need and other criteria; more than $350,000 total annually.

FINANCIAL AID PROCEDURES

Forms required: FAFSA.
Dates and Deadlines: Priority date 4/1; closing date 7/1. Applicants notified on a rolling basis starting 7/1.
Transfers: Priority date 11/1; no deadline.

CONTACT

Chris Westlake, Associate Director of Financial Aid
5230 West Highway 98, Panama City, FL 32401-1041
(850) 872-3845

Heritage Institute: Jacksonville

Jacksonville, Florida
www.heritage-education.com

2-year private health science and career college in very large city.
Enrollment: 260 undergrads.
Selectivity: Open admission.

BASIC COSTS (2007-2008)

Additional info: Total cost of occupational associate degree program: $16,550; includes tuition, fees, books and supplies.

FINANCIAL AID PICTURE

Students with need: Need-based aid available for full-time students.

FINANCIAL AID PROCEDURES

Forms required: FAFSA.

Dates and Deadlines: No deadline. Applicants notified on a rolling basis.

CONTACT

4130 Salisbury Road North, Suite 1100, Jacksonville, FL 32216

Hillsborough Community College
Tampa, Florida
www.hccfl.edu   Federal Code: 007870

2-year public community college in large city.

Enrollment: 17,487 undergrads, 62% part-time. 1,825 full-time freshmen.

Selectivity: Open admission; but selective for some programs.

BASIC COSTS (2007-2008)

Tuition and fees: $2,091; out-of-state residents $7,468.

Per-credit charge: $70; out-of-state residents $249.

FINANCIAL AID PICTURE

Students with need: Need-based aid available for full-time and part-time students. Work study available nights, weekends, and for part-time students.

FINANCIAL AID PROCEDURES

Forms required: FAFSA, institutional form.

Dates and Deadlines: Closing date 6/30. Applicants notified on a rolling basis.

Transfers: No deadline. Transfer students must submit academic transcripts prior to obtaining student loans at sophomore level.

CONTACT

Charlotte Johns, Director of Financial Aid
Box 31127, Tampa, FL 33631-3127
(813) 253-7235

Hobe Sound Bible College
Hobe Sound, Florida
www.hsbc.edu   Federal Code: 015463

4-year private Bible college in small town, affiliated with interdenominational tradition.

Enrollment: 160 undergrads.

BASIC COSTS (2007-2008)

Tuition and fees: $4,650.

Per-credit charge: $190.

Room and board: $4,000.

FINANCIAL AID PICTURE

Students with need: Need-based aid available for full-time and part-time students.

Students without need: No-need awards available for academics, leadership.

FINANCIAL AID PROCEDURES

Forms required: FAFSA.

Dates and Deadlines: Closing date 8/1.

CONTACT

John Churchill, Director of Financial Aid
Box 1065, Hobe Sound, FL 33475
(772) 546-5534 ext. 1003

Hodges University
Naples, Florida
www.hodges.edu   Federal Code: 030375

4-year private business college in small city.

Enrollment: 1,475 undergrads, 24% part-time. 140 full-time freshmen.

Selectivity: Admits over 75% of applicants.

BASIC COSTS (2007-2008)

Tuition and fees: $13,130.

Per-credit charge: $425.

FINANCIAL AID PICTURE (2007-2008)

Students with need: Out of 126 full-time freshmen who applied for aid, 112 were judged to have need. Of these, 112 received aid, and 23 had their full need met. Average financial aid package met 60% of need; average scholarship/grant was $2,300; average loan was $2,600. For part-time students, average financial aid package was $5,800.

Students without need: 22 full-time freshmen who did not demonstrate need for aid received scholarships/grants; average award was $340. No-need awards available for academics.

Cumulative student debt: 81% of graduating class had student loans; average debt was $18,100.

FINANCIAL AID PROCEDURES

Forms required: FAFSA.

Dates and Deadlines: Priority date 9/7; no closing date. Applicants notified on a rolling basis starting 7/7.

Transfers: No deadline. Applicants notified on a rolling basis.

CONTACT

Joe Gilchrist, Vice President of Student Financial Assistance
2655 Northbrooke Drive, Naples, FL 34119
(239) 513-1122

Indian River Community College
Fort Pierce, Florida
www.ircc.edu   Federal Code: 001493

2-year public community college in small city.

Enrollment: 7,885 undergrads.

Selectivity: Open admission; but selective for some programs.

BASIC COSTS (2007-2008)

Tuition and fees: $1,980; out-of-state residents $7,295.

FINANCIAL AID PICTURE (2006-2007)

Students with need: Need-based aid available for part-time students.

Students without need: No-need awards available for academics, athletics, minority status, music/drama, state/district residency.

FINANCIAL AID PROCEDURES

Forms required: FAFSA, institutional form.

Dates and Deadlines: Priority date 7/18; no closing date. Applicants notified on a rolling basis starting 5/15.

CONTACT

Mary Lewis, Director of Financial Aid
3209 Virginia Avenue, Fort Pierce, FL 34981-5596
(772) 462-7450

International Academy of Design and Technology: Tampa

Tampa, Florida
www.academy.edu   Federal Code: 030314

4-year for-profit visual arts and technical college in very large city.
Enrollment: 1,985 undergrads.
Selectivity: Open admission.

BASIC COSTS (2007-2008)

Tuition and fees: $18,780.
Per-credit charge: $385.

FINANCIAL AID PICTURE (2006-2007)

Students with need: 39% of average financial aid package awarded as scholarships/grants, 61% awarded as loans/jobs. Need-based aid available for part-time students. Work study available nights, weekends, and for part-time students.
Students without need: No-need awards available for academics.

FINANCIAL AID PROCEDURES

Forms required: FAFSA.
Dates and Deadlines: No deadline.

CONTACT

Tim Coppola, Vice President of Finance
5104 Eisenhower Boulevard, Tampa, FL 33634
(813) 880-8056

Jacksonville University

Jacksonville, Florida
www.ju.edu   Federal Code: 001495

4-year private university and liberal arts college in very large city.
Enrollment: 2,893 undergrads, 26% part-time. 578 full-time freshmen.
Selectivity: Admits less than 50% of applicants.

BASIC COSTS (2007-2008)

Tuition and fees: $22,500.
Per-credit charge: $750.
Room and board: $8,280.
Additional info: $540 mandatory health insurance fee charged unless proof of other coverage is provided.

FINANCIAL AID PICTURE

Students with need: Need-based aid available for full-time and part-time students. Work study available nights, weekends, and for part-time students.
Students without need: No-need awards available for academics, art, athletics, job skills, leadership, music/drama, ROTC, state/district residency.

FINANCIAL AID PROCEDURES

Forms required: FAFSA.
Dates and Deadlines: Priority date 2/1; closing date 3/15. Applicants notified on a rolling basis starting 2/1; must reply by 5/1 or within 3 week(s) of notification.
Transfers: No deadline. Applicants notified on a rolling basis.

CONTACT

Catherine Huntress, Financial Aid Director
2800 University Boulevard North, Jacksonville, FL 32211-3394
(904) 256-7060

Johnson & Wales University: North Miami

North Miami, Florida
www.jwu.edu   Federal Code: 003404

4-year private university in large city.
Enrollment: 1,955 undergrads, 6% part-time. 524 full-time freshmen.
Selectivity: Admits 50 to 75% of applicants.

BASIC COSTS (2007-2008)

Tuition and fees: $21,717.
Per-credit charge: $379.
Room and board: $9,600.

FINANCIAL AID PICTURE (2007-2008)

Students with need: Average financial aid package met 69% of need; average scholarship/grant was $10,656; average loan was $3,368. For part-time students, average financial aid package was $13,635.
Students without need: No-need awards available for academics, alumni affiliation, job skills, leadership, state/district residency.

FINANCIAL AID PROCEDURES

Forms required: FAFSA.
Dates and Deadlines: No deadline. Applicants notified on a rolling basis starting 3/1; must reply within 2 week(s) of notification.

CONTACT

Lynn Robinson, Director, Financial Aid
1701 Northeast 127th Street, North Miami, FL 33181
(800) 342-5598

Jones College

Jacksonville, Florida
www.jones.edu   Federal Code: 001497

4-year private business and teachers college in very large city.
Enrollment: 600 undergrads.
Selectivity: Open admission.

BASIC COSTS (2008-2009)

Tuition and fees: $8,340.
Per-credit charge: $275.

FINANCIAL AID PICTURE

Students with need: Need-based aid available for full-time and part-time students. Work study available nights, weekends, and for part-time students.
Students without need: This college awards aid only to students with need.

FINANCIAL AID PROCEDURES

Forms required: FAFSA.
Dates and Deadlines: No deadline. Applicants notified on a rolling basis.

CONTACT

Becky Davis, Financial Assistance Director
5353 Arlington Expressway, Jacksonville, FL 32211
(904) 743-1122 ext. 100

Jones College: Miami

Miami, Florida
www.jones.edu   Federal Code: 001497

4-year private business and career college in very large city.
Enrollment: 108 undergrads, 44% part-time. 5 full-time freshmen.
Selectivity: Open admission.

BASIC COSTS (2008-2009)
Tuition and fees: $8,340.
Per-credit charge: $275.

FINANCIAL AID PICTURE
Students with need: Need-based aid available for full-time and part-time students. Work study available nights.
Students without need: This college awards aid only to students with need.

FINANCIAL AID PROCEDURES
Forms required: FAFSA.
Dates and Deadlines: No deadline. Applicants notified on a rolling basis.

CONTACT
Caridad Cortes, Counselor
11430 North Kendall Drive, Suite 200, Miami, FL 33176
(305) 275-9996

Keiser University
Ft. Lauderdale, Florida
www.keiseruniversity.edu   Federal Code: 015159

4-year for-profit business and health science college in large city.
Enrollment: 1,524 undergrads.

BASIC COSTS (2007-2008)
Additional info: Students in business, health services administration, accounting, and computer technology programs pay additional $600 fee per year for lease of computer.

FINANCIAL AID PICTURE
Students with need: Need-based aid available for full-time and part-time students.

FINANCIAL AID PROCEDURES
Forms required: FAFSA.
Dates and Deadlines: No deadline.

CONTACT
Gloria Wright, Director of Financial Aid
1500 Northwest 49th Street, Fort Lauderdale, FL 33309
(954) 776-4456

Key College
Dania Beach, Florida
www.keycollege.edu   Federal Code: 015191

2-year for-profit business and technical college in very large city.
Enrollment: 181 undergrads.
Selectivity: Open admission; but selective for some programs.

BASIC COSTS (2008-2009)
Tuition and fees: $9,210.

FINANCIAL AID PICTURE
Students with need: Work study available nights.
Additional info: Federal Supplemental Educational Opportunities Grant (FSEOG), PELL grant, FFEL (federal loan program) available; direct loans offered.

FINANCIAL AID PROCEDURES
Dates and Deadlines: No deadline.

CONTACT
Jo McGrath, Director of Financial Services
225 Dania Beach Boulevard, Dania Beach, FL 33004
(954) 923-4440

Lake City Community College
Lake City, Florida
www.lakecitycc.edu   Federal Code: 001501

2-year public community college in large town.
Enrollment: 2,723 undergrads, 57% part-time. 294 full-time freshmen.
Selectivity: Open admission; but selective for some programs.

BASIC COSTS (2007-2008)
Tuition and fees: $1,986; out-of-state residents $7,638.
Room and board: $5,395.
Additional info: Tuition/fee waivers available for minority students.

FINANCIAL AID PICTURE
Students with need: Need-based aid available for full-time and part-time students.
Students without need: No-need awards available for academics, athletics.

FINANCIAL AID PROCEDURES
Forms required: FAFSA, institutional form.
Dates and Deadlines: Priority date 6/1; no closing date. Applicants notified on a rolling basis starting 6/1; must reply within 2 week(s) of notification.

CONTACT
Debberin Tunsil, Director of Financial Aid
149 SE College Place, Lake City, FL 32025-8703
(386) 754-4282

Lake-Sumter Community College
Leesburg, Florida
www.lscc.edu   Federal Code: 001502

2-year public community college in small city.
Enrollment: 3,337 undergrads, 63% part-time. 434 full-time freshmen.
Selectivity: Open admission; but selective for some programs.

BASIC COSTS (2007-2008)
Tuition and fees: $2,038; out-of-state residents $7,581.

FINANCIAL AID PICTURE
Students with need: Need-based aid available for full-time and part-time students. Work study available nights.
Students without need: No-need awards available for academics, art, athletics, leadership, minority status, music/drama, state/district residency.

FINANCIAL AID PROCEDURES
Forms required: FAFSA, institutional form.
Dates and Deadlines: Priority date 4/15; no closing date. Applicants notified on a rolling basis starting 7/1.

CONTACT
Audrey Maxwell, Financial Aid Director
9501 U.S. Highway 441, Leesburg, FL 34788-8751
(352) 365-3512

Lynn University
Boca Raton, Florida
www.lynn.edu   Federal Code: 001505

4-year private university in small city.
Enrollment: 2,144 undergrads, 10% part-time. 520 full-time freshmen.
Selectivity: Admits 50 to 75% of applicants.

BASIC COSTS (2007-2008)
Tuition and fees: $28,490.
Room and board: $10,100.

FINANCIAL AID PICTURE (2007-2008)

Students with need: Out of 338 full-time freshmen who applied for aid, 286 were judged to have need. Of these, 283 received aid, and 86 had their full need met. Average financial aid package met 90% of need; average scholarship/grant was $26,075; average loan was $3,899. For part-time students, average financial aid package was $5,476.

Students without need: 30 full-time freshmen who did not demonstrate need for aid received scholarships/grants; average award was $21,079. No-need awards available for academics, athletics, leadership, music/drama, religious affiliation, ROTC, state/district residency.

Scholarships offered: 29 full-time freshmen received athletic scholarships; average amount $20,983.

Cumulative student debt: 33% of graduating class had student loans; average debt was $18,620.

FINANCIAL AID PROCEDURES

Forms required: FAFSA, institutional form.

Dates and Deadlines: Priority date 3/1; no closing date. Applicants notified on a rolling basis starting 2/1; must reply within 2 week(s) of notification.

Transfers: Scholarships and grants available.

CONTACT

William Healy, Director of Financial Services
3601 North Military Trail, Boca Raton, FL 33431-5598
(561) 237-7185

Manatee Community College

Bradenton, Florida
www.mccfl.edu   Federal Code: 001504

2-year public community college in small city.

Enrollment: 8,814 undergrads, 52% part-time. 1,174 full-time freshmen.

Selectivity: Open admission; but selective for some programs.

BASIC COSTS (2007-2008)

Tuition and fees: $2,091; out-of-state residents $7,908.

FINANCIAL AID PICTURE (2007-2008)

Students with need: Out of 710 full-time freshmen who applied for aid, 510 were judged to have need. Of these, 510 received aid, and 449 had their full need met. Need-based aid available for part-time students.

Students without need: 254 full-time freshmen who did not demonstrate need for aid received scholarships/grants; average award was $3,477. No-need awards available for academics, art, athletics, music/drama, state/district residency.

FINANCIAL AID PROCEDURES

Forms required: FAFSA.

Dates and Deadlines: Priority date 6/1; closing date 7/28. Applicants notified on a rolling basis starting 3/15.

CONTACT

Anders Nilsen, Director of Financial Aid
Box 1849, Bradenton, FL 34206-1849
(941) 752-5037

Miami Dade College

Miami, Florida
www.mdc.edu   Federal Code: 001506

2-year public community college in very large city.

Enrollment: 46,674 undergrads, 61% part-time. 8,993 full-time freshmen.

Selectivity: Open admission; but selective for some programs.

BASIC COSTS (2007-2008)

Tuition and fees: $2,068; out-of-state residents $6,863.

FINANCIAL AID PICTURE (2006-2007)

Students with need: Out of 6,007 full-time freshmen who applied for aid, 5,342 were judged to have need. Of these, 4,983 received aid, and 3,531 had their full need met. Need-based aid available for part-time students.

Students without need: No-need awards available for academics, art, athletics, music/drama, state/district residency.

FINANCIAL AID PROCEDURES

Forms required: FAFSA.

Dates and Deadlines: Priority date 3/15; no closing date. Applicants notified on a rolling basis starting 5/15.

CONTACT

Ana Sarasti, Collegewide Director of Financial Aid
11011 SW 104th Street, Miami, FL 33176-3393
(305) 237-2122

New College of Florida

Sarasota, Florida
www.ncf.edu   Federal Code: 039574

4-year public liberal arts college in small city.

Enrollment: 767 undergrads. 202 full-time freshmen.

Selectivity: Admits 50 to 75% of applicants.

BASIC COSTS (2007-2008)

Tuition and fees: $3,143; out-of-state residents $16,682.

Room and board: $6,936.

FINANCIAL AID PICTURE (2007-2008)

Students with need: Out of 137 full-time freshmen who applied for aid, 79 were judged to have need. Of these, 79 received aid, and 58 had their full need met. Average financial aid package met 95% of need; average scholarship/grant was $8,113; average loan was $2,603.

Students without need: 118 full-time freshmen who did not demonstrate need for aid received scholarships/grants; average award was $3,015. No-need awards available for academics, state/district residency.

Cumulative student debt: 35% of graduating class had student loans; average debt was $11,720.

FINANCIAL AID PROCEDURES

Forms required: FAFSA.

Dates and Deadlines: Priority date 2/15; no closing date. Applicants notified on a rolling basis starting 10/1; must reply by 5/1 or within 4 week(s) of notification.

Transfers: No deadline. Applicants notified on a rolling basis starting 10/1; must reply by 5/1 or within 4 week(s) of notification.

CONTACT

Monica Baldwin, Director of Financial Aid
5800 Bay Shore Road, Sarasota, FL 34243-2109
(941) 487-5001

North Florida Community College

Madison, Florida
www.nfcc.edu   Federal Code: 001508

2-year public community college in rural community.

Enrollment: 820 undergrads.

Selectivity: Open admission; but selective for some programs.

BASIC COSTS (2007-2008)

Tuition and fees: $1,960; out-of-state residents $6,826.

FINANCIAL AID PICTURE (2006-2007)

Students with need: 99% of average financial aid package awarded as scholarships/grants, 1% awarded as loans/jobs. Need-based aid available for part-time students. Work study available nights, weekends, and for part-time students.

Students without need: This college awards aid only to students with need.

FINANCIAL AID PROCEDURES

Forms required: FAFSA.

Dates and Deadlines: Priority date 5/15; no closing date. Applicants notified on a rolling basis starting 6/20; must reply within 2 week(s) of notification. .

CONTACT

Amelia Mulkey, Director of Financial Aid
325 NW Turner Davis Drive, Madison, FL 32340
(850) 973-1621

Northwood University: Florida

West Palm Beach, Florida
www.northwood.edu   Federal Code: 013040

4-year private university and business college in small city.

Enrollment: 673 undergrads, 3% part-time. 141 full-time freshmen.

Selectivity: Admits 50 to 75% of applicants.

BASIC COSTS (2008-2009)

Tuition and fees: $17,544.

Per-credit charge: $346.

Room and board: $8,404.

FINANCIAL AID PICTURE (2007-2008)

Students with need: Out of 89 full-time freshmen who applied for aid, 75 were judged to have need. Of these, 75 received aid, and 9 had their full need met. Average financial aid package met 62% of need; average scholarship/grant was $7,375; average loan was $3,256. For part-time students, average financial aid package was $10,873.

Students without need: 62 full-time freshmen who did not demonstrate need for aid received scholarships/grants; average award was $5,278. No-need awards available for academics, alumni affiliation, athletics, leadership, minority status, state/district residency.

Scholarships offered: 18 full-time freshmen received athletic scholarships; average amount $9,752.

Cumulative student debt: 50% of graduating class had student loans; average debt was $24,535.

FINANCIAL AID PROCEDURES

Forms required: FAFSA, state aid form.

Dates and Deadlines: No deadline. Applicants notified on a rolling basis starting 3/1.

CONTACT

Teresa Palmer, Director of Financial Aid
2600 North Military Trail, West Palm Beach, FL 33409-2911
(561) 478-5590

Nova Southeastern University

Fort Lauderdale, Florida
www.nova.edu   Federal Code: 001509

4-year private university in small city.

Enrollment: 5,403 undergrads, 34% part-time. 489 full-time freshmen.

Selectivity: Admits 50 to 75% of applicants.

BASIC COSTS (2008-2009)

Tuition and fees: $20,350.

Per-credit charge: $660.

Room and board: $8,360.

FINANCIAL AID PICTURE (2006-2007)

Students with need: 52% of average financial aid package awarded as scholarships/grants, 48% awarded as loans/jobs. Need-based aid available for part-time students. Work study available nights, weekends, and for part-time students.

Students without need: No-need awards available for academics, athletics, leadership, music/drama.

FINANCIAL AID PROCEDURES

Forms required: FAFSA, state aid form.

Dates and Deadlines: Priority date 4/15; no closing date. Applicants notified on a rolling basis starting 3/15.

CONTACT

Stephanie Brown, Associate Vice President, Student Financial Services and Registration
3301 College Avenue, Fort Lauderdale, FL 33314
(954) 262-3380

Okaloosa-Walton College

Niceville, Florida
www.owc.edu   Federal Code: 001510

4-year public business and community college in large town.

Enrollment: 4,554 undergrads.

Selectivity: Open admission.

BASIC COSTS (2007-2008)

Tuition and fees: $1,763; out-of-state residents $6,730.

Additional info: Tuition/fee waivers available for minority students.

FINANCIAL AID PICTURE

Students with need: Need-based aid available for full-time and part-time students. Work study available nights.

Students without need: No-need awards available for academics, art, athletics, leadership, minority status, music/drama.

FINANCIAL AID PROCEDURES

Forms required: FAFSA, institutional form.

Dates and Deadlines: Priority date 4/1; no closing date. Applicants notified on a rolling basis starting 2/1; must reply within 2 week(s) of notification.

Transfers: Academic transcript evaluated to determine student eligibility for financial aid.

CONTACT

Pat Bennett, Director of Financial Aid
100 College Boulevard, Niceville, FL 32578-1295
(850) 678-5111

Palm Beach Atlantic University

West Palm Beach, Florida
www.pba.edu   Federal Code: 008849

4-year private university and liberal arts college in large city, affiliated with non-denominational tradition.

Enrollment: 2,471 undergrads, 8% part-time. 393 full-time freshmen.

Selectivity: Admits over 75% of applicants.

BASIC COSTS (2007-2008)

Tuition and fees: $20,210.

Room and board: $8,086.

Additional info: Per-credit-hour charge ranges from $395 to $760 depending on the number of credits.

FINANCIAL AID PICTURE (2006-2007)

Students with need: Out of 310 full-time freshmen who applied for aid, 254 were judged to have need. Of these, 254 received aid, and 55 had their full need met. Average financial aid package met 18% of need; average scholarship/grant was $1,590; average loan was $2,371. For part-time students, average financial aid package was $1,805.

Students without need: 56 full-time freshmen who did not demonstrate need for aid received scholarships/grants; average award was $4,721. No-need awards available for academics, alumni affiliation, athletics, minority status, music/drama, state/district residency.

Scholarships offered: 21 full-time freshmen received athletic scholarships; average amount $8,188.

Cumulative student debt: 70% of graduating class had student loans; average debt was $12,883.

FINANCIAL AID PROCEDURES

Forms required: FAFSA, state aid form.

Dates and Deadlines: Priority date 2/1; no closing date. Applicants notified on a rolling basis starting 3/1; must reply within 3 week(s) of notification.

Transfers: Applicants notified on a rolling basis starting 3/1; must reply within 3 week(s) of notification. Florida residential undergraduate students eligible for grant from state if enrolled on full-time basis.

CONTACT

Becky Moore, Director, Student Financial Planning
PO Box 24708, West Palm Beach, FL 33416-4708
(561) 803-2126

Palm Beach Community College

Lake Worth, Florida
www.pbcc.edu   Federal Code: 001512

2-year public community college in large town.

Enrollment: 14,588 undergrads, 57% part-time. 1,735 full-time freshmen.

Selectivity: Open admission; but selective for some programs.

BASIC COSTS (2007-2008)

Tuition and fees: $1,995; out-of-state residents $7,110.

FINANCIAL AID PICTURE (2007-2008)

Students with need: 78% of average financial aid package awarded as scholarships/grants, 22% awarded as loans/jobs. Work study available nights, weekends, and for part-time students.

Students without need: No-need awards available for academics, alumni affiliation, athletics, leadership, state/district residency.

FINANCIAL AID PROCEDURES

Forms required: FAFSA, institutional form.

Dates and Deadlines: Priority date 7/1; no closing date. Applicants notified on a rolling basis; must reply within 2 week(s) of notification.

CONTACT

David Bodwell, Director of Student Financial Aid
4200 Congress Avenue, Lake Worth, FL 33461
(561) 868-3330

Pasco-Hernando Community College

New Port Richey, Florida
www.phcc.edu   Federal Code: 010652

2-year public community college in large town.

Enrollment: 8,065 undergrads.

Selectivity: Open admission; but selective for some programs.

BASIC COSTS (2007-2008)

Tuition and fees: $1,970; out-of-state residents $7,371.

FINANCIAL AID PICTURE

Students with need: Need-based aid available for full-time and part-time students. Work study available nights, weekends, and for part-time students.

Students without need: No-need awards available for academics, athletics, minority status.

Additional info: Childcare assistance grants available to eligible students.

FINANCIAL AID PROCEDURES

Forms required: FAFSA.

Dates and Deadlines: Priority date 4/1; no closing date. Applicants notified on a rolling basis starting 3/1.

Transfers: Priority date 3/1.

CONTACT

Rebecca Shanafelt, Director of Financial Aid/Veterans Services
10230 Ridge Road, New Port Richey, FL 34654-5199
(727) 816-3463

Polk Community College

Winter Haven, Florida
www.polk.edu   Federal Code: 001514

2-year public community college in large town.

Enrollment: 6,063 undergrads, 64% part-time. 745 full-time freshmen.

Selectivity: Open admission; but selective for some programs.

BASIC COSTS (2007-2008)

Tuition and fees: $2,006; out-of-state residents $7,393.

FINANCIAL AID PICTURE

Students with need: Need-based aid available for full-time and part-time students. Work study available nights, weekends, and for part-time students.

Students without need: No-need awards available for academics, athletics, leadership, state/district residency.

FINANCIAL AID PROCEDURES

Forms required: FAFSA.

Dates and Deadlines: Priority date 5/15; no closing date. Applicants notified on a rolling basis.

CONTACT

Olivia Maultsby, Director of Financial Aid
999 Avenue H NE, Winter Haven, FL 33881-4299
(863) 297-1004

Rasmussen College: Ocala

Ocala, Florida
www.rasmussen.edu   Federal Code: 008501

4-year for-profit business and health science and nursing and technical college in small city.

Enrollment: 500 undergrads.

Selectivity: Open admission; but selective for some programs.

BASIC COSTS (2007-2008)

Tuition and fees: $10,185.

FINANCIAL AID PICTURE

Students with need: Need-based aid available for full-time and part-time students.

FINANCIAL AID PROCEDURES

Forms required: institutional form.

Dates and Deadlines: Applicants notified on a rolling basis; must reply within 1 week(s) of notification.

CONTACT

Peter Beasley, Campus Director

2221 Southwest 19th Avenue Road, Ocala, FL 34471-7051

(352) 629-1941 ext. 130

Remington College: Tampa

Tampa, Florida

www.remingtoncollege.edu   Federal Code: 007586

4-year for-profit technical college in very large city.

Enrollment: 261 undergrads.

Selectivity: Open admission.

BASIC COSTS (2007-2008)

Additional info: Costs of entire programs leading to certificate, associate degree, bachelor's degree range from $13,000 to $38,880; includes books and supplies.

FINANCIAL AID PICTURE

Students with need: Need-based aid available for full-time students.

Students without need: This college awards aid only to students with need.

FINANCIAL AID PROCEDURES

Forms required: FAFSA, institutional form.

Dates and Deadlines: No deadline.

CONTACT

Michael Wernon, Director of Student Financial Services

2410 East Busch Boulevard, Tampa, FL 33612

(813) 935-5700 ext. 217

Ringling College of Art and Design

Sarasota, Florida

www.ringling.edu   Federal Code: 012574

4-year private visual arts college in small city.

Enrollment: 1,199 undergrads, 4% part-time. 292 full-time freshmen.

Selectivity: Admits 50 to 75% of applicants.

BASIC COSTS (2007-2008)

Tuition and fees: $25,110.

Per-credit charge: $1,135.

Room and board: $10,000.

FINANCIAL AID PICTURE (2007-2008)

Students with need: Out of 212 full-time freshmen who applied for aid, 181 were judged to have need. Of these, 181 received aid, and 23 had their full need met. Average financial aid package met 43% of need; average scholarship/grant was $6,927; average loan was $8,039. For part-time students, average financial aid package was $10,135.

Students without need: This college awards aid only to students with need.

Scholarships offered: Presidential Scholarship: (amount determined annually;) up to 4 awards based on portfolio.

Cumulative student debt: 99% of graduating class had student loans; average debt was $46,060.

FINANCIAL AID PROCEDURES

Forms required: FAFSA.

Dates and Deadlines: Priority date 3/1; no closing date. Applicants notified on a rolling basis starting 4/1; must reply within 2 week(s) of notification.

Transfers: Must reply within 2 week(s) of notification.

CONTACT

Kurt Wolf, Director of Financial Aid

2700 North Tamiami Trail, Sarasota, FL 34234-5895

(941) 359-7534

Rollins College

Winter Park, Florida

www.rollins.edu   Federal Code: 001515

4-year private liberal arts college in large town.

Enrollment: 1,778 undergrads. 525 full-time freshmen.

Selectivity: Admits 50 to 75% of applicants.

BASIC COSTS (2008-2009)

Tuition and fees: $34,520.

Room and board: $10,780.

FINANCIAL AID PICTURE (2007-2008)

Students with need: Out of 253 full-time freshmen who applied for aid, 210 were judged to have need. Of these, 210 received aid, and 96 had their full need met. Average financial aid package met 92% of need; average scholarship/grant was $25,245; average loan was $4,241.

Students without need: 88 full-time freshmen who did not demonstrate need for aid received scholarships/grants; average award was $15,444. No-need awards available for academics, art, athletics, leadership, music/drama, state/district residency.

Scholarships offered: *Merit:* Presidential, Alonzo Rollins: $4,000-$15,000 per year; based on academic record; 130 available per year. Donald Cram: $3,000-$5,000 per year; based on academic record, science major; 10 available per year. *Athletic:* 24 full-time freshmen received athletic scholarships; average amount $16,307.

Cumulative student debt: 45% of graduating class had student loans; average debt was $23,298.

Additional info: Audition required for theater arts and music scholarship applicants. Portfolio required for art scholarships.

FINANCIAL AID PROCEDURES

Forms required: FAFSA, institutional form.

Dates and Deadlines: Closing date 3/1. Applicants notified on a rolling basis starting 3/1.

Transfers: Priority date 4/15; no deadline.

CONTACT

Phil Asbury, Director of Financial Aid

1000 Holt Avenue, Winter Park, FL 32789

(407) 646-2395

Saint Johns River Community College

Palatka, Florida

www.sjrcc.cc.fl.us   Federal Code: 001523

2-year public community college in large town.

Enrollment: 4,025 undergrads.

Selectivity: Open admission; but selective for some programs.

BASIC COSTS (2007-2008)

Tuition and fees: $2,091; out-of-state residents $7,565.

FINANCIAL AID PICTURE (2006-2007)

Students with need: 70% of average financial aid package awarded as scholarships/grants; 30% awarded as loans/jobs. Need-based aid available for part-time students.

FINANCIAL AID PROCEDURES

Forms required: FAFSA.

Dates and Deadlines: Priority date 5/15; no closing date. Applicants notified on a rolling basis.

CONTACT

Wayne Bodiford, Director of Financial Aid
5001 St. Johns Avenue, Palatka, FL 32177-3897
(386) 312-4040

St. Leo University

Saint Leo, Florida
www.saintleo.edu   Federal Code: 001526

4-year private university in rural community, affiliated with Roman Catholic Church.
Enrollment: 1,587 undergrads, 5% part-time. 456 full-time freshmen.
Selectivity: Admits 50 to 75% of applicants.

BASIC COSTS (2008-2009)

Tuition and fees: $17,150.
Room and board: $8,430.

FINANCIAL AID PICTURE (2007-2008)

Students with need: Out of 400 full-time freshmen who applied for aid, 305 were judged to have need. Of these, 305 received aid, and 152 had their full need met. Average financial aid package met 90% of need; average scholarship/grant was $11,296; average loan was $4,214. For part-time students, average financial aid package was $16,189.
Students without need: 3 full-time freshmen who did not demonstrate need for aid received scholarships/grants; average award was $18,400. No-need awards available for academics, alumni affiliation, athletics, leadership, minority status, music/drama, religious affiliation, state/district residency.
Scholarships offered: 18 full-time freshmen received athletic scholarships; average amount $6,175.
Cumulative student debt: 75% of graduating class had student loans; average debt was $20,638.

FINANCIAL AID PROCEDURES

Forms required: FAFSA.
Dates and Deadlines: Priority date 4/1; no closing date. Applicants notified on a rolling basis starting 1/31.

CONTACT

Brenda Wright, Assistant Vice President, Student Financial Services
Office of Admission, Saint Leo, FL 33574-6665
(800) 240-7658

St. Petersburg College

St. Petersburg, Florida
www.spcollege.edu   Federal Code: 001528

4-year public community college in large city.
Enrollment: 19,827 undergrads, 65% part-time. 1,831 full-time freshmen.
Selectivity: Open admission; but selective for some programs.

BASIC COSTS (2007-2008)

Tuition and fees: $2,091; out-of-state residents $7,558.

FINANCIAL AID PICTURE

Students with need: Need-based aid available for full-time and part-time students. Work study available nights.
Students without need: No-need awards available for academics, art, athletics, minority status, music/drama.

FINANCIAL AID PROCEDURES

Forms required: FAFSA, institutional form.
Dates and Deadlines: Priority date 4/15; no closing date. Applicants notified on a rolling basis starting 5/15; must reply within 2 week(s) of notification.

CONTACT

Marcia McConnell, Director of Financial Aid
Box 13489, St. Petersburg, FL 33733-3489
(727) 791-2443

Saint Thomas University

Miami Gardens, Florida
www.stu.edu   Federal Code: 001468

4-year private university in very large city, affiliated with Roman Catholic Church.
Enrollment: 1,150 undergrads, 5% part-time. 245 full-time freshmen.
Selectivity: Admits 50 to 75% of applicants.

BASIC COSTS (2007-2008)

Tuition and fees: $19,680.
Per-credit charge: $656.
Room and board: $6,206.

FINANCIAL AID PICTURE (2006-2007)

Students with need: Out of 215 full-time freshmen who applied for aid, 194 were judged to have need. Of these, 194 received aid, and 36 had their full need met.
Students without need: 40 full-time freshmen who did not demonstrate need for aid received scholarships/grants; average award was $6,410. No-need awards available for academics, athletics, leadership, music/drama, religious affiliation, state/district residency.
Scholarships offered: 12 full-time freshmen received athletic scholarships; average amount $12,223.

FINANCIAL AID PROCEDURES

Forms required: FAFSA, state aid form.
Dates and Deadlines: Priority date 4/2; no closing date. Applicants notified on a rolling basis starting 3/1.
Transfers: Priority date 4/15.

CONTACT

Ahn Do, Director of Financial Aid
16401 Northwest 37th Avenue, Miami Gardens, FL 33054-6459
(305) 628-6547

Santa Fe Community College

Gainesville, Florida
www.santafe.cc.fl.us   Federal Code: 001519

2-year public community college in small city.
Enrollment: 13,544 undergrads.
Selectivity: Open admission; but selective for some programs.

BASIC COSTS (2007-2008)

Tuition and fees: $2,006; out-of-state residents $7,577.
Additional info: Tuition/fee waivers available for minority students.

FINANCIAL AID PICTURE

Students with need: Need-based aid available for full-time and part-time students.
Students without need: No-need awards available for academics, art, athletics, leadership, minority status, music/drama, state/district residency.

FINANCIAL AID PROCEDURES

Forms required: FAFSA.
Dates and Deadlines: Priority date 3/15; closing date 6/30. Applicants notified by 8/1.
Transfers: Must have minimum 2.0 GPA to be eligible for financial aid.

CONTACT
Peggy Werts, Director of Financial Aid
3000 NW 83rd Street, Gainesville, FL 32606
(352) 395-5480

Schiller International University
Largo, Florida
www.schiller.edu   Federal Code: 023141

4-year for-profit university in large town.
Enrollment: 81 undergrads.
Selectivity: Open admission.

BASIC COSTS (2007-2008)
Tuition and fees: $17,465.
Per-credit charge: $490.
Room and board: $7,900.

FINANCIAL AID PICTURE
Students with need: Need-based aid available for full-time and part-time students. Work study available nights, weekends, and for part-time students.
Students without need: No-need awards available for academics, alumni affiliation, leadership, minority status, state/district residency.
Additional info: Special scholarship program for U.S. college students studying abroad at European campuses of Schiller. Work-study available to students taking 2 or more courses.

FINANCIAL AID PROCEDURES
Forms required: FAFSA, state aid form, institutional form.
Dates and Deadlines: Closing date 4/1. Applicants notified on a rolling basis starting 5/1; must reply within 3 week(s) of notification.

CONTACT
Jennifer Fraser, Director of Financial Aid
300 East Bay Drive, Largo, FL 33770-3716
(727) 736-5082 ext. 253

Seminole Community College
Sanford, Florida
www.scc-fl.edu   Federal Code: 001520

2-year public community college in large town.
Enrollment: 10,634 undergrads, 57% part-time. 1,473 full-time freshmen.
Selectivity: Open admission; but selective for some programs.

BASIC COSTS (2007-2008)
Tuition and fees: $2,081; out-of-state residents $7,571.

FINANCIAL AID PICTURE (2006-2007)
Students with need: 41% of average financial aid package awarded as scholarships/grants, 59% awarded as loans/jobs. Need-based aid available for part-time students.
Students without need: No-need awards available for academics, art, athletics, leadership, minority status, music/drama, state/district residency.

FINANCIAL AID PROCEDURES
Forms required: FAFSA.
Dates and Deadlines: No deadline. Applicants notified on a rolling basis starting 4/1.
Transfers: No deadline. Applicants notified on a rolling basis starting 4/1.

CONTACT
Robert Lynn, Director of Financial Aid
100 Weldon Boulevard, Sanford, FL 32773-6199
(407) 708-4722 ext. 3422

South Florida Community College
Avon Park, Florida
www.southflorida.edu   Federal Code: 001522

2-year public community and technical college in small town.
Enrollment: 1,822 undergrads, 63% part-time. 209 full-time freshmen.
Selectivity: Open admission; but selective for some programs.

BASIC COSTS (2007-2008)
Tuition and fees: $2,039; out-of-state residents $7,672.
Additional info: Tuition/fee waivers available for minority students.

FINANCIAL AID PICTURE (2006-2007)
Students with need: 89% of average financial aid package awarded as scholarships/grants, 11% awarded as loans/jobs. Need-based aid available for part-time students.
Students without need: No-need awards available for academics, athletics, leadership, minority status, music/drama, state/district residency.

FINANCIAL AID PROCEDURES
Forms required: FAFSA.
Dates and Deadlines: Priority date 3/15; no closing date. Applicants notified on a rolling basis starting 4/1.
Transfers: Students must maintain satisfactory academic progress.

CONTACT
Susie Johnson, Director of Financial Aid
600 West College Drive, Avon Park, FL 33825
(863) 453-6661 ext. 7254

South University: West Palm Beach Campus
West Palm Beach, Florida
www.southuniversity.edu

4-year for-profit business and health science and nursing college in large city.
Enrollment: 767 undergrads.

BASIC COSTS (2007-2008)
Tuition and fees: $12,570.

FINANCIAL AID PICTURE
Students with need: Need-based aid available for full-time and part-time students. Work study available nights.
Students without need: No-need awards available for academics.

FINANCIAL AID PROCEDURES
Forms required: FAFSA, institutional form.
Dates and Deadlines: No deadline. Applicants notified on a rolling basis; must reply within 2 week(s) of notification.

CONTACT
Marlene Hetzel, Assistant Director of Financial Aid
1760 North Congress Avenue, West Palm Beach, FL 33409-5178
(561) 697-9200

Southeastern University
Lakeland, Florida
www.seuniversity.edu   Federal Code: 001521

4-year private liberal arts and teachers college in small city, affiliated with Assemblies of God.
Enrollment: 2,646 undergrads, 5% part-time. 558 full-time freshmen.
Selectivity: Open admission; but selective for some programs.

BASIC COSTS (2008-2009)
Tuition and fees: $14,470.
Per-credit charge: $540.
Room and board: $7,000.

FINANCIAL AID PICTURE (2007-2008)
Students with need: Out of 484 full-time freshmen who applied for aid, 382 were judged to have need. Of these, 380 received aid, and 69 had their full need met. Average financial aid package met 22% of need; average scholarship/grant was $6,582; average loan was $3,369. Need-based aid available for part-time students.
Students without need: 143 full-time freshmen who did not demonstrate need for aid received scholarships/grants; average award was $12,641. No-need awards available for academics, leadership, music/drama, state/district residency.
Cumulative student debt: 95% of graduating class had student loans; average debt was $20,825.

FINANCIAL AID PROCEDURES
Forms required: FAFSA, state aid form, institutional form.
Dates and Deadlines: Priority date 4/15; no closing date. Applicants notified on a rolling basis starting 2/15; must reply within 3 week(s) of notification.

CONTACT
Carol Bradley, Financial Aid Director
1000 Longfellow Boulevard, Lakeland, FL 33801-6034
(863) 667-5024

Southwest Florida College
Ft. Myers, Florida
www.swfc.edu   Federal Code: 016068

2-year private junior college in small city.
Enrollment: 1,489 undergrads, 15% part-time. 196 full-time freshmen.
Selectivity: Open admission; but selective for some programs.

BASIC COSTS (2008-2009)
Tuition and fees: $9,710.
Per-credit charge: $255.
Additional info: Required fees do not include lab or online fees.

FINANCIAL AID PICTURE
Students with need: Need-based aid available for full-time and part-time students. Work study available nights.

FINANCIAL AID PROCEDURES
Forms required: FAFSA.
Dates and Deadlines: Priority date 4/15; no closing date. Applicants notified on a rolling basis.

CONTACT
Laura Selvey, Director of Financial Aid
1685 Medical Lane, Ft. Myers, FL 33907-1108
(813) 630-4401

Stetson University
DeLand, Florida
www.stetson.edu   Federal Code: 001531

4-year private university in large town.
Enrollment: 2,219 undergrads, 4% part-time. 557 full-time freshmen.
Selectivity: Admits 50 to 75% of applicants.

BASIC COSTS (2008-2009)
Tuition and fees: $30,216.
Per-credit charge: $870.
Room and board: $8,436.

FINANCIAL AID PICTURE (2007-2008)
Students with need: Out of 404 full-time freshmen who applied for aid, 331 were judged to have need. Of these, 331 received aid, and 127 had their full need met. Average financial aid package met 87% of need; average scholarship/grant was $18,180; average loan was $4,787. For part-time students, average financial aid package was $12,039.
Students without need: 198 full-time freshmen who did not demonstrate need for aid received scholarships/grants; average award was $11,456. No-need awards available for academics, alumni affiliation, art, athletics, leadership, minority status, music/drama, religious affiliation, ROTC, state/district residency.
Scholarships offered: 23 full-time freshmen received athletic scholarships; average amount $13,984.
Cumulative student debt: 73% of graduating class had student loans; average debt was $25,656.

FINANCIAL AID PROCEDURES
Forms required: FAFSA, institutional form.
Dates and Deadlines: Priority date 3/15; no closing date. Applicants notified on a rolling basis.

CONTACT
Deborah Thompson, Vice President for Enrollment Management and Campus Life
Campus Box 8378, DeLand, FL 32723
(386) 822-7120

Tallahassee Community College
Tallahassee, Florida
www.tcc.fl.edu   Federal Code: 001533

2-year public community college in small city.
Enrollment: 12,673 undergrads.
Selectivity: Open admission; but selective for some programs.

BASIC COSTS (2007-2008)
Tuition and fees: $1,875; out-of-state residents $6,705.

FINANCIAL AID PICTURE (2006-2007)
Students with need: 47% of average financial aid package awarded as scholarships/grants, 53% awarded as loans/jobs. Need-based aid available for part-time students.
Students without need: No-need awards available for academics, art, athletics, leadership, music/drama, state/district residency.

FINANCIAL AID PROCEDURES
Forms required: FAFSA, institutional form.
Dates and Deadlines: Priority date 5/1; no closing date. Applicants notified on a rolling basis starting 5/15.

CONTACT
William Spiers, Director of Financial Aid
444 Appleyard Drive, Tallahassee, FL 32304
(850) 201-8399

Trinity College of Florida
Trinity, Florida
www.trinitycollege.edu   Federal Code: 030282

4-year private Bible college in small city, affiliated with interdenominational tradition.
Enrollment: 174 undergrads, 32% part-time. 29 full-time freshmen.
Selectivity: Admits 50 to 75% of applicants.

BASIC COSTS (2008-2009)

Tuition and fees: $10,550.
Per-credit charge: $405.
Room and board: $5,940.

FINANCIAL AID PICTURE (2007-2008)

Students with need: Out of 29 full-time freshmen who applied for aid, 25 were judged to have need. Of these, 25 received aid, and 3 had their full need met. Average financial aid package met 82% of need; average scholarship/grant was $3,237; average loan was $2,035. For part-time students, average financial aid package was $2,470.
Students without need: This college awards aid only to students with need.
Cumulative student debt: 54% of graduating class had student loans; average debt was $24,197.

FINANCIAL AID PROCEDURES

Forms required: FAFSA, institutional form.
Dates and Deadlines: Priority date 3/15; closing date 8/2. Applicants notified on a rolling basis.
Transfers: No deadline. Applicants notified on a rolling basis.

CONTACT

Sue Wayne, Financial Aid Director
2430 Welbilt Boulevard, Trinity, FL 34655-4401
(727) 569-1413

University of Central Florida

Orlando, Florida
www.ucf.edu   Federal Code: 003954

4-year public university in very large city.
Enrollment: 41,051 undergrads, 24% part-time. 6,408 full-time freshmen.
Selectivity: Admits 50 to 75% of applicants.

BASIC COSTS (2007-2008)

Tuition and fees: $3,561; out-of-state residents $17,763.
Room and board: $8,164.

FINANCIAL AID PICTURE (2006-2007)

Students with need: Out of 4,305 full-time freshmen who applied for aid, 3,338 were judged to have need. Of these, 3,271 received aid, and 748 had their full need met. Average financial aid package met 58% of need; average scholarship/grant was $3,593; average loan was $2,670. For part-time students, average financial aid package was $4,728.
Students without need: 406 full-time freshmen who did not demonstrate need for aid received scholarships/grants; average award was $1,960. No-need awards available for academics, alumni affiliation, athletics, leadership, ROTC, state/district residency.
Scholarships offered: *Merit:* Academic scholarships: $2,000-$24,000 over 4-year period, freshmen automatically considered. ***Athletic:*** 62 full-time freshmen received athletic scholarships; average amount $7,879.
Cumulative student debt: 44% of graduating class had student loans; average debt was $13,373.

FINANCIAL AID PROCEDURES

Forms required: FAFSA.
Dates and Deadlines: Priority date 3/1; closing date 6/30. Applicants notified on a rolling basis starting 3/15; must reply within 3 week(s) of notification.

CONTACT

Mary McKinney, Executive Director of Financial Aid
Box 160111, Orlando, FL 32816-0111
(407) 823-2827

University of Florida

Gainesville, Florida
www.ufl.edu   Federal Code: 001535

4-year public university in small city.
Enrollment: 34,534 undergrads, 6% part-time. 6,702 full-time freshmen.
Selectivity: Admits less than 50% of applicants.

BASIC COSTS (2007-2008)

Tuition and fees: $3,370; out-of-state residents $17,150.
Per-credit charge: $74; out-of-state residents $537.
Room and board: $7,020.
Additional info: Tuition/fee waivers available for minority students.

FINANCIAL AID PICTURE (2006-2007)

Students with need: Out of 4,145 full-time freshmen who applied for aid, 2,621 were judged to have need. Of these, 2,613 received aid, and 973 had their full need met. Average financial aid package met 87% of need; average scholarship/grant was $6,197; average loan was $3,117. Need-based aid available for part-time students.
Students without need: 3,814 full-time freshmen who did not demonstrate need for aid received scholarships/grants; average award was $5,598. No-need awards available for academics, art, athletics, leadership, minority status, music/drama, ROTC, state/district residency.
Scholarships offered: 84 full-time freshmen received athletic scholarships; average amount $12,059.
Cumulative student debt: 41% of graduating class had student loans; average debt was $14,830.

FINANCIAL AID PROCEDURES

Forms required: FAFSA.
Dates and Deadlines: Priority date 3/15; no closing date. Applicants notified on a rolling basis starting 4/1.
Transfers: No deadline. Applicants notified on a rolling basis starting 4/1.

CONTACT

Karen Fooks, Director of Student Financial Aid
201 Criser Hall-PO Box 114000, Gainesville, FL 32611-4000
(352) 392-1275

University of Miami

Coral Gables, Florida
www.miami.edu   Federal Code: 001536

4-year private university in small city.
Enrollment: 9,997 undergrads, 5% part-time. 1,980 full-time freshmen.
Selectivity: Admits less than 50% of applicants.

BASIC COSTS (2008-2009)

Tuition and fees: $34,834.
Per-credit charge: $1,424.
Room and board: $10,254.

FINANCIAL AID PICTURE (2007-2008)

Students with need: Out of 1,219 full-time freshmen who applied for aid, 945 were judged to have need. Of these, 945 received aid, and 348 had their full need met. Average financial aid package met 84% of need; average scholarship/grant was $20,226; average loan was $4,412. For part-time students, average financial aid package was $17,084.
Students without need: 525 full-time freshmen who did not demonstrate need for aid received scholarships/grants; average award was $16,910. No-need awards available for academics, athletics, music/drama, ROTC.
Scholarships offered: *Merit:* Singer Scholarship: full tuition; minimum 1500 SAT or 34 ACT; A+ average; rank in top 1% of high school graduating class. University Scholarship: three-quarters tuition; minimum 1400 SAT or 32 ACT; A average; class rank in top 5%. Dean's Scholarship: half-tuition; renewable;

minimum 1350 SAT or 31 ACT; A average; class rank in top 7%. Trustee Scholarship: one-third tuition; 1300 SAT or 30 ACT; A average; class rank in top 10%. Collegiate Scholarship: one-quarter tuition; top 10% in high school class; A- average; 1280 SAT or 29 ACT. All SAT scores exclusive of Writing. Ronald M. Hammond Scholarships: full tuition; renewable; B+ average; 1150 SAT or 26 ACT; for exceptionally well-qualified graduating high school seniors of black/African-American descent who are Florida residents. Music scholarships: based on performance ability, academic achievement and financial need. National Merit Scholarships: $750-$2,000; for National Merit finalists. *Athletic:* 59 full-time freshmen received athletic scholarships; average amount $25,933.

Cumulative student debt: 56% of graduating class had student loans; average debt was $23,576.

FINANCIAL AID PROCEDURES

Forms required: FAFSA.

Dates and Deadlines: Priority date 2/1; no closing date. Applicants notified on a rolling basis starting 3/1.

Transfers: Priority date 3/1; no deadline. Applicants notified by 4/15.

CONTACT

James Bauer, Assisstant Dean of Enrollment Management and Director of Financial Assistance Services
132 Ashe Building, Coral Gables, FL 33124-4616
(305) 284-5212

University of North Florida
Jacksonville, Florida
www.unf.edu   Federal Code: 009841

4-year public university in very large city.
Enrollment: 14,250 undergrads, 27% part-time. 2,025 full-time freshmen.
Selectivity: Admits 50 to 75% of applicants.

BASIC COSTS (2007-2008)

Tuition and fees: $3,491; out-of-state residents $15,134.
Room and board: $7,011.

FINANCIAL AID PICTURE

Students with need: Need-based aid available for full-time and part-time students.

Students without need: No-need awards available for academics, athletics, leadership, minority status, music/drama, state/district residency.

FINANCIAL AID PROCEDURES

Forms required: FAFSA.

Dates and Deadlines: Priority date 4/1; no closing date. Applicants notified on a rolling basis starting 3/15; must reply within 2 week(s) of notification.

Transfers: Must reply within 2 week(s) of notification. Students must submit financial aid transcripts from previous institutions attended.

CONTACT

Anissa Cameron, Associate Director Processing - Financial Aid
1 UNF Drive, Jacksonville, FL 32224-7699
(904) 620-2604

University of South Florida
Tampa, Florida
www.usf.edu   Federal Code: 001537

4-year public university in very large city.
Enrollment: 33,998 undergrads, 28% part-time. 3,977 full-time freshmen.
Selectivity: Admits less than 50% of applicants.

BASIC COSTS (2007-2008)

Tuition and fees: $3,456; out-of-state residents $16,155.
Room and board: $7,590.
Additional info: Tuition/fee waivers available for unemployed or children of unemployed.

FINANCIAL AID PICTURE

Students with need: Need-based aid available for full-time and part-time students. Work study available nights, weekends, and for part-time students.
Students without need: No-need awards available for academics, alumni affiliation, art, athletics, job skills, leadership, minority status, music/drama, religious affiliation, ROTC, state/district residency.
Additional info: Deferred tuition payment plan available for late financial aid recipients.

FINANCIAL AID PROCEDURES

Forms required: FAFSA.

Dates and Deadlines: Priority date 3/1; no closing date. Applicants notified on a rolling basis starting 3/15; must reply within 4 week(s) of notification.

CONTACT

Student Financial Aid
4202 East Fowler Avenue, SVC 1036, Tampa, FL 33620-9951
(813) 974-4700

University of Tampa
Tampa, Florida
www.ut.edu   Federal Code: 001538

4-year private university and liberal arts college in large city.
Enrollment: 4,887 undergrads, 8% part-time. 1,167 full-time freshmen.
Selectivity: Admits less than 50% of applicants.

BASIC COSTS (2007-2008)

Tuition and fees: $20,682.
Room and board: $7,616.

FINANCIAL AID PICTURE (2007-2008)

Students with need: Out of 795 full-time freshmen who applied for aid, 592 were judged to have need. Of these, 592 received aid, and 148 had their full need met. Average financial aid package met 78% of need; average scholarship/grant was $7,221; average loan was $4,529. For part-time students, average financial aid package was $5,596.
Students without need: 184 full-time freshmen who did not demonstrate need for aid received scholarships/grants; average award was $5,869. No-need awards available for academics, alumni affiliation, art, athletics, leadership, music/drama, ROTC, state/district residency.
Scholarships offered: *Merit:* Presidential Scholarships: up to $8,500; 3.5 GPA. Dean's Scholarships: up to $8,000; 3.2 GPA. Departmental scholarships also awarded. *Athletic:* 4 full-time freshmen received athletic scholarships; average amount $6,000.
Cumulative student debt: 68% of graduating class had student loans; average debt was $22,901.
Additional info: Early aid estimator service.

FINANCIAL AID PROCEDURES

Forms required: FAFSA, state aid form.
Dates and Deadlines: No deadline. Applicants notified on a rolling basis starting 2/1; must reply within 3 week(s) of notification.
Transfers: No deadline. Must reply within 3 week(s) of notification. Transfer scholarships available; Phi Theta Kappa Scholarships.

CONTACT

John Marsh, Director of Financial Aid
401 West Kennedy Boulevard, Tampa, FL 33606-1490
(813) 253-6239

University of West Florida

Pensacola, Florida
www.uwf.edu   Federal Code: 003955

4-year public university in small city.
Enrollment: 8,334 undergrads, 29% part-time. 917 full-time freshmen.
Selectivity: Admits 50 to 75% of applicants.

BASIC COSTS (2007-2008)
Tuition and fees: $3,351; out-of-state residents $16,233.
Room and board: $7,255.
Additional info: There is a $10 per course, per semester fee for online courses.

FINANCIAL AID PICTURE (2006-2007)
Students with need: 49% of average financial aid package awarded as scholarships/grants, 51% awarded as loans/jobs. Need-based aid available for part-time students. Work study available nights, weekends, and for part-time students.
Students without need: No-need awards available for academics, alumni affiliation, art, athletics, minority status, music/drama, ROTC.
Scholarships offered: John C. Pace Scholars: $16,000; based on high school record and leadership; 8 awards. John C. Pace Honors and Presidential Scholarships: $4,000; based on high school record. Both available to Florida residents only. Non-Florida tuition reduction scholarships available to non-residents.

FINANCIAL AID PROCEDURES
Forms required: FAFSA, institutional form.
Dates and Deadlines: Priority date 3/1; no closing date. Applicants notified on a rolling basis starting 2/1.

CONTACT
Cathy Brown, Director of Student Financial Aid
11000 University Parkway, Pensacola, FL 32514-5750
(850) 474-2400

Valencia Community College

Orlando, Florida
www.valenciacc.edu   Federal Code: 006750

2-year public community college in very large city.
Enrollment: 26,707 undergrads, 51% part-time. 4,423 full-time freshmen.
Selectivity: Open admission; but selective for some programs.

BASIC COSTS (2007-2008)
Tuition and fees: $2,091; out-of-state residents $7,858.

FINANCIAL AID PICTURE
Students with need: Need-based aid available for full-time and part-time students. Work study available nights.

FINANCIAL AID PROCEDURES
Forms required: FAFSA.
Dates and Deadlines: Closing date 5/15. Applicants notified on a rolling basis starting 4/2; must reply within 2 week(s) of notification.
Transfers: No deadline.

CONTACT
Brad Honious, Director, Financial Aid
PO Box 3028, Orlando, FL 32802-3028
(407) 299-5000

Virginia College at Pensacola

Pensacola, Florida
www.vc.edu/pensacola

2-year for-profit business and health science college in small city.
Enrollment: 181 undergrads.
Selectivity: Open admission.

BASIC COSTS (2007-2008)
Tuition and fees: $11,625.
Per-credit charge: $230.

FINANCIAL AID PICTURE (2006-2007)
Students with need: 85% of average financial aid package awarded as scholarships/grants, 15% awarded as loans/jobs.

CONTACT
Tammie Nadeau, Director of Financial Planning
19 West Garden Street, Pensacola, FL 32502

Warner Southern College

Lake Wales, Florida
www.warner.edu   Federal Code: 008848

4-year private liberal arts college in large town, affiliated with Church of God.
Enrollment: 1,025 undergrads, 10% part-time. 143 full-time freshmen.
Selectivity: Admits 50 to 75% of applicants.

BASIC COSTS (2007-2008)
Tuition and fees: $13,860.
Room and board: $6,381.
Additional info: One-time $50 security deposit for incoming freshmen living on campus.

FINANCIAL AID PICTURE
Students with need: Need-based aid available for full-time and part-time students.
Students without need: No-need awards available for academics, alumni affiliation, art, athletics, leadership, music/drama, religious affiliation, state/district residency.

FINANCIAL AID PROCEDURES
Forms required: FAFSA, state aid form.
Dates and Deadlines: Priority date 5/1; no closing date. Applicants notified on a rolling basis starting 3/15; must reply within 2 week(s) of notification.
Transfers: Priority date 10/1; closing date 5/15. Applicants notified on a rolling basis; must reply within 2 week(s) of notification.

CONTACT
Lorrie Steedley, Financial Aid Director
13895 Highway 27, Lake Wales, FL 33859
(863) 638-7202

Webber International University

Babson Park, Florida
www.webber.edu   Federal Code: 001540

4-year private university and business college in rural community.
Enrollment: 535 undergrads, 11% part-time. 118 full-time freshmen.
Selectivity: Admits 50 to 75% of applicants.

BASIC COSTS (2008-2009)
Tuition and fees: $17,000.
Per-credit charge: $235.
Room and board: $6,354.
Additional info: Tuition/fee waivers available for adults.

FINANCIAL AID PICTURE (2007-2008)

Students with need: Out of 105 full-time freshmen who applied for aid, 71 were judged to have need. Of these, 71 received aid, and 24 had their full need met. Average financial aid package met 62% of need; average scholarship/grant was $12,702; average loan was $3,550. For part-time students, average financial aid package was $5,255.

Students without need: 23 full-time freshmen who did not demonstrate need for aid received scholarships/grants; average award was $6,237. No-need awards available for academics, alumni affiliation, athletics, leadership, state/district residency.

Scholarships offered: 34 full-time freshmen received athletic scholarships; average amount $5,985.

Cumulative student debt: 65% of graduating class had student loans; average debt was $2,062.

FINANCIAL AID PROCEDURES

Forms required: FAFSA, state aid form.

Dates and Deadlines: Priority date 5/1; closing date 8/1. Applicants notified on a rolling basis starting 4/1; must reply within 4 week(s) of notification.

Transfers: Eligibility for academic scholarships predicated on 12 hours of transferable credit.

CONTACT

Kathleen Wilson, Registrar

1201 North Scenic Highway, Babson Park, FL 33827-0096

(863) 638-2930

Georgia

Agnes Scott College
Decatur, Georgia
www.agnesscott.edu   Federal Code: 001542

4-year private liberal arts college for women in very large city, affiliated with Presbyterian Church (USA).

Enrollment: 827 undergrads, 1% part-time. 218 full-time freshmen.

Selectivity: Admits less than 50% of applicants.

BASIC COSTS (2008-2009)

Tuition and fees: $29,060.

Per-credit charge: $1,175.

Room and board: $9,850.

FINANCIAL AID PICTURE (2007-2008)

Students with need: Out of 179 full-time freshmen who applied for aid, 154 were judged to have need. Of these, 154 received aid, and 148 had their full need met. Average financial aid package met 99% of need; average scholarship/grant was $23,386; average loan was $3,262. For part-time students, average financial aid package was $18,187.

Students without need: 64 full-time freshmen who did not demonstrate need for aid received scholarships/grants; average award was $15,673. No-need awards available for academics, leadership, music/drama, religious affiliation, state/district residency.

Scholarships offered: Presidential and Honor Scholarships; $8,750 to full tuition, room and board. College will match HOPE Scholarship for HOPE-eligible Georgia residents who meet college admission criteria. Leadership and community service awards also available.

Cumulative student debt: 73% of graduating class had student loans; average debt was $24,070.

Additional info: Middle Income Assistance Grants available. Auditions required for music scholarship applicants.

FINANCIAL AID PROCEDURES

Forms required: FAFSA.

Dates and Deadlines: Priority date 2/15; closing date 5/1. Applicants notified on a rolling basis starting 3/1; must reply by 5/1 or within 2 week(s) of notification.

Transfers: Must reply by 5/1 or within 2 week(s) of notification. Merit scholarships available.

CONTACT

Lauren Cobb

Office of Admissions, Decatur, GA 30030-3797

(404) 471-6395

Albany State University
Albany, Georgia
www.asurams.edu   Federal Code: 001544

4-year public university and liberal arts college in small city.

Enrollment: 3,614 undergrads, 14% part-time. 586 full-time freshmen.

Selectivity: Admits less than 50% of applicants.

BASIC COSTS (2007-2008)

Tuition and fees: $3,470; out-of-state residents $12,074.

Room and board: $4,914.

Additional info: Tuition at time of enrollment locked for 4 years.

FINANCIAL AID PICTURE

Students with need: Need-based aid available for full-time and part-time students. Work study available nights, weekends, and for part-time students.

Students without need: No-need awards available for academics, alumni affiliation, art, athletics, music/drama, ROTC.

FINANCIAL AID PROCEDURES

Forms required: FAFSA, state aid form.

Dates and Deadlines: Priority date 4/15; closing date 4/30. Applicants notified on a rolling basis; must reply within 2 week(s) of notification.

Transfers: Must reply within 2 week(s) of notification.

CONTACT

Thomas Harris, Director of Financial Aid

504 College Drive, Albany, GA 31705-2796

(229) 430-4650

Albany Technical College
Albany, Georgia
www.albanytech.edu   Federal Code: 005601

2-year public technical college in small city.

Enrollment: 2,346 undergrads, 46% part-time. 262 full-time freshmen.

Selectivity: Open admission.

BASIC COSTS (2007-2008)

Tuition and fees: $1,359; out-of-state residents $2,475.

Per-credit charge: $31; out-of-state residents $62.

FINANCIAL AID PICTURE

Students with need: Need-based aid available for full-time and part-time students. Work study available nights.

Students without need: No-need awards available for academics, state/district residency.

FINANCIAL AID PROCEDURES

Forms required: FAFSA, state aid form.

Dates and Deadlines: No deadline. Applicants notified on a rolling basis starting 5/1.

CONTACT

Helen Catt, Financial Aid Director
1704 South Slappy Boulevard, Albany, GA 31701-3514
(229) 430-3506

Andrew College
Cuthbert, Georgia
www.andrewcollege.edu   Federal Code: 001545

2-year private junior and liberal arts college in small town, affiliated with United Methodist Church.

Enrollment: 271 undergrads.

BASIC COSTS (2008-2009)
Tuition and fees: $10,976.
Room and board: $6,894.

FINANCIAL AID PICTURE
Students with need: Need-based aid available for full-time and part-time students.

Students without need: No-need awards available for academics, art, athletics, leadership, music/drama, religious affiliation, state/district residency.

FINANCIAL AID PROCEDURES
Forms required: FAFSA, state aid form, institutional form.
Dates and Deadlines: Priority date 4/1; closing date 8/1. Applicants notified on a rolling basis starting 4/15.

CONTACT
Amy Thompson, Financial Aid Administrator
413 College Street, Cuthbert, GA 39840-1395
(229) 732-5938

Armstrong Atlantic State University
Savannah, Georgia
www.armstrong.edu   Federal Code: 001546

4-year public university in small city.

Enrollment: 5,997 undergrads, 34% part-time. 732 full-time freshmen.
Selectivity: Admits 50 to 75% of applicants.

BASIC COSTS (2007-2008)
Tuition and fees: $3,424; out-of-state residents $12,028.
Per-credit charge: $120; out-of-state residents $478.
Room only: $5,000.
Additional info: Room-only housing apartment style for all students. Tuition at time of enrollment locked for 4 years.

FINANCIAL AID PICTURE (2006-2007)
Students with need: Average financial aid package met 85% of need; average scholarship/grant was $2,706; average loan was $2,368. For part-time students, average financial aid package was $6,333.
Students without need: No-need awards available for academics, alumni affiliation, art, athletics, leadership, minority status, music/drama, state/district residency.
Cumulative student debt: 55% of graduating class had student loans; average debt was $11,000.

FINANCIAL AID PROCEDURES
Forms required: FAFSA.
Dates and Deadlines: Priority date 3/15; no closing date. Applicants notified on a rolling basis starting 2/1; must reply by 4/15 or within 2 week(s) of notification.

CONTACT

Lee Ann Kirkland, Financial Aid Director
11935 Abercorn Street, Savannah, GA 31419-1997
(912) 927-5272

Art Institute of Atlanta
Atlanta, Georgia
www.aia.artinstitutes.edu   Federal Code: 009270

4-year for-profit visual arts college in very large city.
Enrollment: 3,187 undergrads.
Selectivity: Admits less than 50% of applicants.

BASIC COSTS (2008-2009)
Tuition and fees: $19,575.
Per-credit charge: $435.
Room only: $9,075.
Additional info: Students purchase starting kits for programs; costs vary depending on programs. Some programs require lab fees. Tuition at time of enrollment locked for 4 years.

FINANCIAL AID PICTURE (2006-2007)
Students with need: 31% of average financial aid package awarded as scholarships/grants, 69% awarded as loans/jobs. Need-based aid available for part-time students. Work study available nights, weekends, and for part-time students.
Students without need: No-need awards available for academics, art, state/district residency.
Scholarships offered: Art Institutes Scholarship Competition awards $2,000 - $56,064 depending on program to winning high school seniors selected on merits of written essay, original artwork, resume, letter(s) of recommendation, and high school academic achievement; up to 1 full-tuition, 2 half-tuition, and 24 partial-tuition scholarships available. Art Institutes Culinary Scholarship Competition awards $2,000 - $32,704 to winning high school seniors selected through three-part elimination-style competition to prove academic ability, culinary expertise, and commitment to succeed; up to 1 full-tuition or 2 partial-tuition scholarships available. Various other scholarships and awards available.

FINANCIAL AID PROCEDURES
Forms required: FAFSA, state aid form.
Dates and Deadlines: No deadline. Applicants notified on a rolling basis starting 3/15.

CONTACT
Rachel Oliver, Director of Student Financial Services
6600 Peachtree Dunwoody Road, Atlanta, GA 30328
(770) 394-8300

Athens Technical College
Athens, Georgia
www.athenstech.edu   Federal Code: 005600

2-year public technical college in small city.
Enrollment: 3,436 undergrads, 58% part-time. 386 full-time freshmen.
Selectivity: Open admission; but selective for some programs.

BASIC COSTS (2007-2008)
Tuition and fees: $1,359; out-of-state residents $2,475.
Per-credit charge: $31; out-of-state residents $62.

FINANCIAL AID PICTURE
Students with need: Need-based aid available for full-time and part-time students.
Students without need: No-need awards available for academics, leadership.

FINANCIAL AID PROCEDURES

Forms required: FAFSA.

Dates and Deadlines: No deadline. Applicants notified on a rolling basis starting 6/15; must reply within 2 week(s) of notification.

CONTACT

Courtney Ray, Director of Financial Aid

800 US Highway 29 North, Athens, GA 30601-1500

(706) 355-5009

Atlanta Metropolitan College
Atlanta, Georgia

www.atlm.edu   Federal Code: 012165

2-year public junior college in very large city.

Enrollment: 1,814 undergrads, 46% part-time. 180 full-time freshmen.

Selectivity: Admits less than 50% of applicants.

BASIC COSTS (2007-2008)

Tuition and fees: $2,040; out-of-state residents $7,280.

Per-credit charge: $73; out-of-state residents $292.

FINANCIAL AID PICTURE (2006-2007)

Students with need: 76% of average financial aid package awarded as scholarships/grants, 24% awarded as loans/jobs. Need-based aid available for part-time students. Work study available nights, weekends, and for part-time students.

Students without need: This college awards aid only to students with need.

FINANCIAL AID PROCEDURES

Forms required: FAFSA, state aid form.

Dates and Deadlines: Closing date 6/1. Applicants notified on a rolling basis; must reply by 6/30.

Transfers: Priority date 6/1; closing date 6/30. Applicants notified on a rolling basis; must reply by 6/30.

CONTACT

Gwendolyn Peterson, Director

1630 Metropolitan Parkway, SW, Atlanta, GA 30310-4498

(404) 756-4002

Atlanta Technical College
Atlanta, Georgia

www.atlantatech.org

2-year public community and technical college in very large city.

Enrollment: 2,937 undergrads, 48% part-time. 404 full-time freshmen.

Selectivity: Open admission; but selective for some programs.

BASIC COSTS (2007-2008)

Tuition and fees: $1,362; out-of-state residents $2,478.

Per-credit charge: $31; out-of-state residents $62.

FINANCIAL AID PICTURE

Students with need: Need-based aid available for full-time and part-time students. Work study available nights.

FINANCIAL AID PROCEDURES

Forms required: state aid form.

Dates and Deadlines: Priority date 3/1; no closing date. Applicants notified on a rolling basis starting 4/15.

CONTACT

Deborah Clark, Director of Financial Aid

1560 Metropolitan Parkway, SW, Atlanta, GA 30310-4446

Augusta State University
Augusta, Georgia

www.aug.edu   Federal Code: 001552

4-year public liberal arts and teachers college in small city.

Enrollment: 5,479 undergrads, 29% part-time. 869 full-time freshmen.

Selectivity: Admits 50 to 75% of applicants.

BASIC COSTS (2007-2008)

Tuition and fees: $3,404; out-of-state residents $12,008.

Per-credit charge: $120; out-of-state residents $478.

FINANCIAL AID PICTURE (2006-2007)

Students with need: Out of 609 full-time freshmen who applied for aid, 502 were judged to have need. Of these, 467 received aid, and 5 had their full need met. For part-time students, average financial aid package was $2,373.

Students without need: 85 full-time freshmen who did not demonstrate need for aid received scholarships/grants; average award was $1,606. No-need awards available for academics, art, athletics, leadership, minority status, music/drama, ROTC, state/district residency.

Scholarships offered: 4 full-time freshmen received athletic scholarships; average amount $4,181.

Cumulative student debt: 32% of graduating class had student loans; average debt was $5,296.

FINANCIAL AID PROCEDURES

Forms required: FAFSA, institutional form.

Dates and Deadlines: Closing date 6/1. Applicants notified on a rolling basis starting 3/1; must reply within 4 week(s) of notification.

CONTACT

Willene Holmes, Director of Financial Aid

2500 Walton Way, Augusta, GA 30904-2200

(706) 737-1431

Bainbridge College
Bainbridge, Georgia

www.bainbridge.edu   Federal Code: 011074

2-year public community and technical college in large town.

Enrollment: 2,654 undergrads, 60% part-time. 440 full-time freshmen.

BASIC COSTS (2007-2008)

Tuition and fees: $1,950; out-of-state residents $7,190.

Per-credit charge: $73; out-of-state residents $292.

FINANCIAL AID PICTURE

Students with need: Need-based aid available for full-time and part-time students.

Students without need: This college awards aid only to students with need.

Scholarships offered: Small number of merit scholarships available.

Additional info: 30-day loans available for tuition and fees.

FINANCIAL AID PROCEDURES

Forms required: FAFSA, institutional form.

Dates and Deadlines: Priority date 6/1; closing date 8/1. Applicants notified on a rolling basis starting 6/1; must reply within 2 week(s) of notification.

Transfers: Priority date 6/11.

CONTACT

Judy Curry, Director of Financial Aid

2500 East Shotwell Street, Bainbridge, GA 39818-0990

(229) 248-2505

Bauder College

Atlanta, Georgia
www.bauder.edu
Federal Code: 011574

4-year for-profit career college in very large city.
Enrollment: 806 undergrads.
Selectivity: Open admission.

BASIC COSTS (2007-2008)

Additional info: Cost of tuition for design majors in 18-21 month associate degree program is $28,195; books $2,300; $100 administrative fee, $350 student activity fee; $400 technology fee; $250 graduation fee. Tuition only for the associate degree programs varies from $19,580 -$28,195. Tuition for newly instituted bachelor of science in business program is $47,263.

FINANCIAL AID PICTURE

Students with need: Need-based aid available for full-time and part-time students. Work study available nights, weekends, and for part-time students.
Students without need: This college awards aid only to students with need.

FINANCIAL AID PROCEDURES

Forms required: FAFSA, institutional form.
Dates and Deadlines: No deadline. Applicants notified on a rolling basis starting 7/15.

CONTACT

Bela Akbasheva, Director of Financial Aid
384 Northyards Boulevard NW, Ste 190, Atlanta, GA 30313
(404) 237-7573

Berry College

Mount Berry, Georgia
www.berry.edu
Federal Code: 001554

4-year private liberal arts college in large town.
Enrollment: 1,719 undergrads, 1% part-time. 524 full-time freshmen.
Selectivity: Admits 50 to 75% of applicants.

BASIC COSTS (2008-2009)

Tuition and fees: $22,370.
Per-credit charge: $739.
Room and board: $7,978.

FINANCIAL AID PICTURE (2007-2008)

Students with need: Out of 446 full-time freshmen who applied for aid, 322 were judged to have need. Of these, 322 received aid, and 94 had their full need met. Average financial aid package met 84% of need; average scholarship/grant was $13,083; average loan was $3,995. For part-time students, average financial aid package was $8,777.
Students without need: 201 full-time freshmen who did not demonstrate need for aid received scholarships/grants; average award was $21,268. No-need awards available for academics, art, athletics, minority status, music/drama.
Scholarships offered: *Merit:* HOPE Scholarship; $3,000 annually; for entering freshmen based on legal residence in Georgia and graduation from eligible high school with at least a B average in college preparatory coursework. *Athletic:* 34 full-time freshmen received athletic scholarships; average amount $10,624.
Cumulative student debt: 65% of graduating class had student loans; average debt was $14,349.
Additional info: Students are encouraged to work on-campus up to 20 hours per week.

FINANCIAL AID PROCEDURES

Dates and Deadlines: Priority date 4/1; no closing date. Applicants notified on a rolling basis starting 3/15; must reply by 5/1 or within 4 week(s) of notification.
Transfers: No deadline. Applicants notified on a rolling basis starting 4/1; must reply by 5/1 or within 4 week(s) of notification.

CONTACT

J. Elmore, Director of Student Financial Aid
PO Box 490159, Mount Berry, GA 30149-0159
(706) 236-1714

Brenau University

Gainesville, Georgia
www.brenau.edu
Federal Code: 001556

4-year private liberal arts college for women in small city.
Enrollment: 851 undergrads, 6% part-time. 216 full-time freshmen.
Selectivity: Admits less than 50% of applicants.

BASIC COSTS (2007-2008)

Tuition and fees: $17,700.
Per-credit charge: $583.
Room and board: $8,950.

FINANCIAL AID PICTURE (2007-2008)

Students with need: Out of 186 full-time freshmen who applied for aid, 168 were judged to have need. Of these, 168 received aid, and 49 had their full need met. Average financial aid package met 81% of need; average scholarship/grant was $14,631; average loan was $3,251. For part-time students, average financial aid package was $7,860.
Students without need: 34 full-time freshmen who did not demonstrate need for aid received scholarships/grants; average award was $898. No-need awards available for academics, art, athletics, leadership, minority status, music/drama.
Scholarships offered: 5 full-time freshmen received athletic scholarships; average amount $14,060.
Cumulative student debt: 53% of graduating class had student loans; average debt was $14,663.

FINANCIAL AID PROCEDURES

Forms required: FAFSA, state aid form.
Dates and Deadlines: Priority date 4/1; no closing date. Applicants notified on a rolling basis starting 3/1.

CONTACT

Pam Barrett, Director of Scholarships and Financial Assistance
500 Washington Street SE, Gainesville, GA 30501
(770) 534-6152

Brewton-Parker College

Mount Vernon, Georgia
www.bpc.edu
Federal Code: 001557

4-year private liberal arts college in small town, affiliated with Southern Baptist Convention.
Enrollment: 1,030 undergrads, 30% part-time. 237 full-time freshmen.
Selectivity: Admits over 75% of applicants.

BASIC COSTS (2008-2009)

Tuition and fees: $14,730.
Per-credit charge: $420.
Room and board: $6,240.
Additional info: $130 per-credit fee for applied music surcharge.

FINANCIAL AID PICTURE (2006-2007)

Students with need: Need-based aid available for part-time students.

Students without need: No-need awards available for academics, athletics, music/drama, religious affiliation, state/district residency.

Scholarships offered: Scholarships available for academic achievement and SAT scores for incoming freshman transfer students, ranging from $1,500-$3,000 per academic year, available for four years.

Cumulative student debt: 90% of graduating class had student loans; average debt was $25,912.

FINANCIAL AID PROCEDURES

Forms required: FAFSA, state aid form.

Dates and Deadlines: Priority date 5/1; no closing date. Applicants notified on a rolling basis starting 2/27; must reply within 2 week(s) of notification.

CONTACT

Jackie White, Assistant Director of Financial Aid
Brewton-Parker College # 2011, Mount Vernon, GA 30445
(912) 583-2241 ext. 209

Central Georgia Technical College
Macon, Georgia
www.cgtcollege.edu   Federal Code: 005763

2-year public community and technical college in small city.

Enrollment: 4,999 undergrads, 53% part-time. 436 full-time freshmen.

Selectivity: Open admission; but selective for some programs.

BASIC COSTS (2007-2008)

Tuition and fees: $1,359; out-of-state residents $2,475.

Per-credit charge: $31; out-of-state residents $62.

FINANCIAL AID PICTURE

Students with need: Need-based aid available for full-time and part-time students.

FINANCIAL AID PROCEDURES

Forms required: FAFSA, state aid form, institutional form.

Dates and Deadlines: Closing date 7/14.

CONTACT

Pennie Strong, Director, Financial Aid
3300 Macon Tech Drive, Macon, GA 31206
(478) 757-3422

Chattahoochee Technical College
Marietta, Georgia
www.chattcollege.com   Federal Code: 005620

2-year public technical college in large city.

Enrollment: 4,300 undergrads, 55% part-time. 598 full-time freshmen.

Selectivity: Open admission; but selective for some programs.

BASIC COSTS (2007-2008)

Tuition and fees: $1,380; out-of-state residents $2,496.

Per-credit charge: $31; out-of-state residents $62.

FINANCIAL AID PICTURE

Students with need: Need-based aid available for full-time and part-time students. Work study available nights, weekends, and for part-time students.

Students without need: No-need awards available for state/district residency.

FINANCIAL AID PROCEDURES

Forms required: FAFSA, institutional form.

Dates and Deadlines: Priority date 7/15; no closing date. Applicants notified on a rolling basis starting 6/15.

CONTACT

Lori Burnette, Director of Financial Aid
980 South Cobb Drive, Marietta, GA 30060-3300
(770) 528-4531

Clark Atlanta University
Atlanta, Georgia
www.cau.edu   Federal Code: 001559

4-year private university in very large city, affiliated with United Methodist Church.

Enrollment: 3,533 undergrads, 4% part-time. 1,055 full-time freshmen.

Selectivity: Admits 50 to 75% of applicants.

BASIC COSTS (2008-2009)

Tuition and fees: $17,038.

Per-credit charge: $680.

Room and board: $7,120.

Additional info: Tuition at time of enrollment locked for 4 years.

FINANCIAL AID PICTURE (2007-2008)

Students with need: Average financial aid package met 11% of need; average scholarship/grant was $5,546; average loan was $3,442. For part-time students, average financial aid package was $5,324.

Students without need: No-need awards available for academics, art, athletics, minority status, music/drama, religious affiliation, state/district residency.

Cumulative student debt: 96% of graduating class had student loans; average debt was $35,909.

FINANCIAL AID PROCEDURES

Forms required: FAFSA, state aid form.

Dates and Deadlines: Priority date 3/1; no closing date. Applicants notified on a rolling basis starting 4/1.

CONTACT

Michael Francois, Associate Director of Financial Aid
223 James P. Brawley Drive, SW, Atlanta, GA 30314-4391
(404) 880-6018

Clayton State University
Morrow, Georgia
www.clayton.edu   Federal Code: 008976

4-year public liberal arts and technical college in small city.

Enrollment: 5,985 undergrads.

Selectivity: Admits less than 50% of applicants.

BASIC COSTS (2007-2008)

Tuition and fees: $3,582; out-of-state residents $12,186.

Per-credit charge: $120; out-of-state residents $478.

FINANCIAL AID PICTURE

Students with need: Need-based aid available for full-time and part-time students.

Students without need: No-need awards available for academics.

FINANCIAL AID PROCEDURES

Forms required: FAFSA, state aid form.

Dates and Deadlines: Priority date 7/18; no closing date. Applicants notified on a rolling basis starting 3/12.

CONTACT

Patricia Barton, Director of Financial Aid
5900 North Lee Street, Morrow, GA 30260-0285
(770) 961-3551

Coastal Georgia Community College
Brunswick, Georgia
www.cgcc.edu   Federal Code: 001558

2-year public community college in large town.
Enrollment: 2,943 undergrads, 63% part-time. 438 full-time freshmen.
Selectivity: Open admission; but selective for some programs.

BASIC COSTS (2007-2008)
Tuition and fees: $1,962; out-of-state residents $7,202.
Per-credit charge: $73; out-of-state residents $292.
Additional info: Guaranteed tuition plan locks tuition rate for up to 3 years.
Cost will vary among students. Tuition at time of enrollment locked for 2 years.

FINANCIAL AID PICTURE
Students with need: Need-based aid available for full-time and part-time students. Work study available nights, weekends, and for part-time students.
Students without need: No-need awards available for academics, athletics, leadership, state/district residency.

FINANCIAL AID PROCEDURES
Forms required: FAFSA.
Dates and Deadlines: Priority date 5/1; no closing date. Applicants notified on a rolling basis starting 7/1.
Transfers: No deadline. Applicants notified on a rolling basis.

CONTACT
Rodney Clements, Financial Aid Director
3700 Altama Avenue, Brunswick, GA 31520
(912) 264-7262

Columbus State University
Columbus, Georgia
www.colstate.edu   Federal Code: 001561

4-year public university and liberal arts college in large city.
Enrollment: 6,462 undergrads, 30% part-time. 945 full-time freshmen.
Selectivity: Admits 50 to 75% of applicants. GED not accepted.

BASIC COSTS (2007-2008)
Tuition and fees: $3,514; out-of-state residents $12,118.
Per-credit charge: $120; out-of-state residents $478.
Room and board: $6,220.
Additional info: Tuition at time of enrollment locked for 4 years.

FINANCIAL AID PICTURE (2007-2008)
Students with need: Out of 735 full-time freshmen who applied for aid, 582 were judged to have need. Of these, 448 received aid, and 301 had their full need met. Average financial aid package met 63% of need; average scholarship/grant was $3,359; average loan was $2,816. For part-time students, average financial aid package was $3,158.
Students without need: 363 full-time freshmen who did not demonstrate need for aid received scholarships/grants; average award was $1,658. No-need awards available for academics, alumni affiliation, art, athletics, job skills, leadership, minority status, music/drama, ROTC.
Scholarships offered: 26 full-time freshmen received athletic scholarships; average amount $2,380.
Cumulative student debt: 73% of graduating class had student loans; average debt was $26,591.

FINANCIAL AID PROCEDURES
Forms required: FAFSA.
Dates and Deadlines: Priority date 5/1; no closing date. Applicants notified on a rolling basis starting 4/1; must reply within 4 week(s) of notification.

CONTACT
Janis Bowles, Director of Financial Aid
4225 University Avenue, Columbus, GA 31907-5645
(706) 568-2036

Columbus Technical College
Columbus, Georgia
www.columbustech.org   Federal Code: 005624

2-year public technical college in small city.
Enrollment: 3,467 undergrads, 58% part-time. 355 full-time freshmen.
Selectivity: Open admission; but selective for some programs.

BASIC COSTS (2007-2008)
Tuition and fees: $1,347; out-of-state residents $2,463.
Per-credit charge: $31; out-of-state residents $62.

FINANCIAL AID PICTURE
Students with need: Need-based aid available for full-time and part-time students.

FINANCIAL AID PROCEDURES
Forms required: FAFSA.
Dates and Deadlines: No deadline. Applicants notified on a rolling basis.

CONTACT
Debbie Henshaw, Director, Financial Aid
928 Manchester Expressway, Columbus, GA 31904
(706) 649-1859

Covenant College
Lookout Mountain, Georgia
www.covenant.edu   Federal Code: 003484

4-year private liberal arts college in small city, affiliated with Presbyterian Church in America.
Enrollment: 989 undergrads, 2% part-time. 297 full-time freshmen.
Selectivity: Admits 50 to 75% of applicants.

BASIC COSTS (2008-2009)
Tuition and fees: $24,320.
Per-credit charge: $985.
Room and board: $6,900.

FINANCIAL AID PICTURE (2006-2007)
Students with need: Out of 257 full-time freshmen who applied for aid, 214 were judged to have need. Of these, 214 received aid, and 54 had their full need met. Average financial aid package met 83% of need; average scholarship/grant was $12,617; average loan was $4,161. For part-time students, average financial aid package was $15,390.
Students without need: 68 full-time freshmen who did not demonstrate need for aid received scholarships/grants; average award was $6,680. No-need awards available for academics, alumni affiliation, art, athletics, job skills, leadership, minority status, music/drama, religious affiliation, state/district residency.
Scholarships offered: *Merit:* Maclellan Scholars Program; minimum SAT 1200 (exclusive of Writing) or ACT 27, high school GPA 3.3. Presidential Scholarship; based on GPA, leadership, Christian commitment, extracurricular activities, work experience, references. *Athletic:* 23 full-time freshmen received athletic scholarships; average amount $3,739.
Cumulative student debt: 58% of graduating class had student loans; average debt was $16,385.

FINANCIAL AID PROCEDURES
Forms required: FAFSA, state aid form.

Dates and Deadlines: No deadline. Applicants notified on a rolling basis starting 2/1; must reply within 3 week(s) of notification.
Transfers: Some scholarships may be depleted for mid-semester transfers, such as athletic, diversity or music.

CONTACT

Brenda Rapier, Director of Financial Aid
14049 Scenic Highway, Lookout Mountain, GA 30750
(706) 419-1126

Dalton State College

Dalton, Georgia
www.daltonstate.edu   Federal Code: 003956

4-year public liberal arts and teachers college in large town.
Enrollment: 4,532 undergrads, 48% part-time. 879 full-time freshmen.
Selectivity: Admits 50 to 75% of applicants.

BASIC COSTS (2007-2008)

Tuition and fees: $2,088; out-of-state residents $7,704.
Per-credit charge: $78; out-of-state residents $312.

FINANCIAL AID PICTURE (2006-2007)

Students with need: 72% of average financial aid package awarded as scholarships/grants, 28% awarded as loans/jobs. Need-based aid available for part-time students.
Students without need: No-need awards available for academics, leadership, minority status, state/district residency.

FINANCIAL AID PROCEDURES

Forms required: FAFSA, state aid form, institutional form.
Dates and Deadlines: Priority date 7/1; no closing date. Applicants notified on a rolling basis starting 7/1.
Transfers: No deadline. Applicants notified on a rolling basis.

CONTACT

Dianne Cox, Director of Student Financial Aid
650 College Drive, Dalton, GA 30720
(706) 272-4545

Darton College

Albany, Georgia
www.darton.edu   Federal Code: 001543

2-year public community college in small city.
Enrollment: 2,102 full-time undergrads.

BASIC COSTS (2007-2008)

Tuition and fees: $2,110; out-of-state residents $7,350.
Per-credit charge: $73; out-of-state residents $292.

FINANCIAL AID PICTURE

Students with need: Need-based aid available for full-time and part-time students. Work study available nights, weekends, and for part-time students.
Students without need: No-need awards available for academics, alumni affiliation, art, athletics, music/drama, state/district residency.
Additional info: Auditions, portfolios, essays, extracurricular activities impact scholarship decisions.

FINANCIAL AID PROCEDURES

Forms required: FAFSA, state aid form, institutional form.
Dates and Deadlines: No deadline. Applicants notified on a rolling basis; must reply within 3 week(s) of notification.

CONTACT

Martha Whittle, Director of Financial Aid
2400 Gillionville Road, Albany, GA 31707-3098
(229) 430-6746

DeKalb Technical College

Clarkston, Georgia
www.dekalbtech.edu   Federal Code: 016582

2-year public technical college in large city.
Enrollment: 3,691 undergrads, 62% part-time. 327 full-time freshmen.
Selectivity: Open admission; but selective for some programs.

BASIC COSTS (2007-2008)

Tuition and fees: $1,407; out-of-state residents $2,523.
Per-credit charge: $31; out-of-state residents $62.
Additional info: Truck driving and flight technology are higher cost programs.

FINANCIAL AID PICTURE

Students with need: Need-based aid available for full-time and part-time students. Work study available nights, weekends, and for part-time students.

FINANCIAL AID PROCEDURES

Forms required: FAFSA.
Dates and Deadlines: Priority date 7/15; closing date 8/20. Applicants notified on a rolling basis starting 6/1.
Transfers: No deadline.

CONTACT

John Gottardy, Director of Financial Aid
495 North Indian Creek Drive, Clarkston, GA 30021-2397
(404) 297-9522 ext. 1166

DeVry University: Alpharetta

Alpharetta, Georgia
www.devry.edu   Federal Code: 009224

4-year for-profit university in large town.
Enrollment: 672 undergrads, 56% part-time. 41 full-time freshmen.

BASIC COSTS (2007-2008)

Tuition and fees: $13,220.
Per-credit charge: $490.

FINANCIAL AID PICTURE (2006-2007)

Students with need: Out of 22 full-time freshmen who applied for aid, 18 were judged to have need. Of these, 18 received aid, and 1 had their full need met. Average financial aid package met 38% of need; average scholarship/grant was $5,669; average loan was $5,016. For part-time students, average financial aid package was $7,965.
Students without need: This college awards aid only to students with need.
Cumulative student debt: 83% of graduating class had student loans; average debt was $40,694.

FINANCIAL AID PROCEDURES

Forms required: FAFSA.
Dates and Deadlines: No deadline. Applicants notified on a rolling basis.

CONTACT

David Pickett, Assistant Director of Financial Aid
2555 Northwinds Parkway, Alpharetta, GA 30004
(770) 521-4900

DeVry University: Decatur

Decatur, Georgia
www.devry.edu   Federal Code: 009224

4-year for-profit university in large town.
Enrollment: 2,087 undergrads, 46% part-time. 130 full-time freshmen.

BASIC COSTS (2007-2008)

Tuition and fees: $13,220.
Per-credit charge: $490.

FINANCIAL AID PICTURE (2006-2007)

Students with need: Out of 95 full-time freshmen who applied for aid, 85 were judged to have need. Of these, 80 received aid, and 3 had their full need met. Average financial aid package met 36% of need; average scholarship/grant was $5,214; average loan was $4,569. For part-time students, average financial aid package was $8,298.
Students without need: This college awards aid only to students with need.
Cumulative student debt: 77% of graduating class had student loans; average debt was $39,171.

FINANCIAL AID PROCEDURES

Forms required: FAFSA.
Dates and Deadlines: No deadline. Applicants notified on a rolling basis.

CONTACT

Robin Winston, Director of Financial Aid
250 North Arcadia Avenue, Decatur, GA 30030-2198
(404) 292-7900

East Georgia College

Swainsboro, Georgia
www.ega.edu   Federal Code: 010997

2-year public community and junior college in small town.
Enrollment: 1,987 undergrads.

BASIC COSTS (2007-2008)

Tuition and fees: $1,922; out-of-state residents $7,162.
Per-credit charge: $73; out-of-state residents $292.

FINANCIAL AID PICTURE

Students with need: Need-based aid available for full-time and part-time students.
Students without need: No-need awards available for academics, leadership, state/district residency.

FINANCIAL AID PROCEDURES

Forms required: FAFSA, institutional form.
Dates and Deadlines: Priority date 6/15; no closing date. Applicants notified on a rolling basis starting 6/15; must reply within 2 week(s) of notification.

CONTACT

Barbara Green, Director of Financial Aid
131 College Circle, Swainsboro, GA 30401-2699
(478) 289-2009

Emmanuel College

Franklin Springs, Georgia
www.ec.edu   Federal Code: 001563

4-year private liberal arts college in rural community, affiliated with Pentecostal Holiness Church.
Enrollment: 600 undergrads, 3% part-time. 140 full-time freshmen.
Selectivity: Admits less than 50% of applicants.

BASIC COSTS (2008-2009)

Tuition and fees: $12,260.
Per-credit charge: $504.
Room and board: $5,584.
Additional info: Tuition/fee waivers available for adults.

FINANCIAL AID PICTURE (2007-2008)

Students with need: Out of 121 full-time freshmen who applied for aid, 111 were judged to have need. Of these, 111 received aid, and 20 had their full need met. Average financial aid package met 68% of need; average scholarship/grant was $6,867; average loan was $3,131. For part-time students, average financial aid package was $5,665.
Students without need: 17 full-time freshmen who did not demonstrate need for aid received scholarships/grants; average award was $3,185. No-need awards available for academics, art, athletics, leadership, music/drama, religious affiliation, state/district residency.
Scholarships offered: 11 full-time freshmen received athletic scholarships; average amount $4,482.
Cumulative student debt: 69% of graduating class had student loans; average debt was $20,238.

FINANCIAL AID PROCEDURES

Forms required: FAFSA, state aid form, institutional form.
Dates and Deadlines: Priority date 5/1; closing date 8/1. Applicants notified on a rolling basis starting 3/1; must reply within 2 week(s) of notification.
Transfers: Students on probation at previous institution may be accepted and funded for one semester. Continued funding dependent on satisfactory performance.

CONTACT

Gloria Hambrick, Financial Aid Director
181 Spring Street, Franklin Springs, GA 30639-0129
(706) 245-7226

Emory University

Atlanta, Georgia   Federal Code: 001564
www.emory.edu   CSS Code: 5187

4-year private university in very large city, affiliated with United Methodist Church.
Enrollment: 5,094 undergrads. 1,235 full-time freshmen.
Selectivity: Admits less than 50% of applicants. GED not accepted.

BASIC COSTS (2007-2008)

Tuition and fees: $34,336.
Per-credit charge: $1,413.
Room and board: $11,020.

FINANCIAL AID PICTURE

Students with need: Need-based aid available for full-time and part-time students. Work study available nights, weekends, and for part-time students.
Students without need: No-need awards available for academics, art, leadership, music/drama, religious affiliation, state/district residency.
Scholarships offered: Emory Scholars program; two-thirds tuition to full-cost; based on academic merit of incoming first-year students, requires nomination by appropriate high school official by November 1st of senior year; renewable for four years of undergraduate study.

FINANCIAL AID PROCEDURES

Forms required: FAFSA, CSS PROFILE.
Dates and Deadlines: Priority date 2/15; closing date 4/1. Applicants notified by 4/15; must reply by 5/1 or within 4 week(s) of notification.
Transfers: No deadline. Applicants notified on a rolling basis. Limitations on aid available to transfer students. Financial aid filing deadline for transfers is 30 days following transfer student admission date.

CONTACT

Dean Bentley, Director of Financial Aid
200 Boisfeuillet Jones Center, Atlanta, GA 30322
(800) 727-6039

Fort Valley State University

Fort Valley, Georgia
www.fvsu.edu   Federal Code: 001566

4-year public liberal arts and teachers college in small town.
Enrollment: 2,467 undergrads.
Selectivity: Admits less than 50% of applicants.

BASIC COSTS (2007-2008)
Tuition and fees: $3,558; out-of-state residents $12,162.
Per-credit charge: $120; out-of-state residents $478.
Room and board: $5,660.

FINANCIAL AID PICTURE
Students with need: Need-based aid available for full-time and part-time students.
Students without need: No-need awards available for academics, athletics, ROTC, state/district residency.

FINANCIAL AID PROCEDURES
Forms required: FAFSA, institutional form.
Dates and Deadlines: Priority date 4/1; no closing date. Must reply within 1 week(s) of notification.
Transfers: Financial aid transcripts must be received from former institutions before application for aid will be considered complete and reviewed for awards.

CONTACT

Eula Solomon, Director of Financial Aid
1005 State University Drive, Fort Valley, GA 31030-4313
(478) 825-6351

Gainesville State College

Gainesville, Georgia
www.gsc.edu   Federal Code: 001567

2-year public community and junior college in large town.
Enrollment: 7,247 undergrads.
Selectivity: Admits over 75% of applicants.

BASIC COSTS (2007-2008)
Tuition and fees: $2,112; out-of-state residents $7,728.
Per-credit charge: $78; out-of-state residents $312.
Additional info: Tuition at time of enrollment locked for 2 years.

FINANCIAL AID PICTURE (2006-2007)
Students with need: 71% of average financial aid package awarded as scholarships/grants, 29% awarded as loans/jobs. Need-based aid available for part-time students. Work study available nights, weekends, and for part-time students.
Students without need: No-need awards available for academics, art, leadership, music/drama.

FINANCIAL AID PROCEDURES
Forms required: FAFSA.
Dates and Deadlines: Priority date 6/1; no closing date. Applicants notified on a rolling basis starting 5/1; must reply within 2 week(s) of notification.
Transfers: No deadline. Applicants notified on a rolling basis starting 5/1; must reply within 2 week(s) of notification. Must have minimum 2.0 GPA to be eligible for financial aid.

CONTACT

Susan Smith, Financial Aid Director
PO Box 1358, Gainesville, GA 30503
(678) 717-3642

Georgia College and State University

Milledgeville, Georgia
www.gcsu.edu   Federal Code: 001602

4-year public university and liberal arts college in large town.
Enrollment: 5,292 undergrads, 9% part-time. 1,071 full-time freshmen.
Selectivity: Admits 50 to 75% of applicants.

BASIC COSTS (2007-2008)
Tuition and fees: $5,066; out-of-state residents $17,688.
Per-credit charge: $160; out-of-state residents $638.
Room and board: $7,380.
Additional info: Tuition at time of enrollment locked for 4 years.

FINANCIAL AID PICTURE (2006-2007)
Students with need: Out of 1,040 full-time freshmen who applied for aid, 354 were judged to have need. Of these, 352 received aid, and 12 had their full need met. Average financial aid package met 28% of need; average scholarship/grant was $2,751; average loan was $2,172. For part-time students, average financial aid package was $4,411.
Students without need: 36 full-time freshmen who did not demonstrate need for aid received scholarships/grants; average award was $1,983. No-need awards available for academics, alumni affiliation, art, athletics, job skills, leadership, minority status, music/drama, religious affiliation, ROTC, state/district residency.
Scholarships offered: *Merit:* Presidential Scholarship (renewable) $4,000 per year; 1300 SAT or equivalent ACT, 3.5 high school GPA. Exceptional Student (renewable) 1200 SAT or 26 ACT, 3.0 high school GPA. Academic Excellence and Academic Achievement Scholarship (one-time award) 1200 SAT or 26 ACT and 3.0 GPA. Distinguished Scholars Award (available to non-Georgia residents); valued between $5,000 - $10,000 and may be renewable. *Athletic:* 24 full-time freshmen received athletic scholarships; average amount $2,559.

FINANCIAL AID PROCEDURES
Forms required: FAFSA.
Dates and Deadlines: Priority date 3/1; no closing date. Applicants notified on a rolling basis starting 3/1; must reply within 2 week(s) of notification.
Transfers: No deadline. Applicants notified on a rolling basis starting 3/1; must reply within 2 week(s) of notification.

CONTACT

Suzanne Pittman, Assistant Vice President for Enrollment Management
Campus Box 23, Milledgeville, GA 31061-0490
(478) 445-5149

Georgia Highlands College

Rome, Georgia
www.highlands.edu   Federal Code: 009507

2-year public community and liberal arts college in small city.
Enrollment: 4,346 undergrads, 44% part-time. 988 full-time freshmen.
Selectivity: Admits over 75% of applicants.

BASIC COSTS (2007-2008)
Tuition and fees: $1,948; out-of-state residents $7,188.
Per-credit charge: $73; out-of-state residents $292.
Additional info: Tuition at time of enrollment locked for 2 years.

FINANCIAL AID PICTURE (2006-2007)

Students with need: 44% of average financial aid package awarded as scholarships/grants, 56% awarded as loans/jobs. Need-based aid available for part-time students. Work study available nights.

Students without need: No-need awards available for academics, art.

FINANCIAL AID PROCEDURES

Forms required: FAFSA.

Dates and Deadlines: Closing date 4/1. Applicants notified on a rolling basis starting 4/1; must reply within 2 week(s) of notification.

CONTACT

Donna Childres, Director of Financial Aid

3175 Cedartown Highway SE, Rome, GA 30161

(706) 295-6311

Georgia Institute of Technology

Atlanta, Georgia

www.gatech.edu   Federal Code: 001569

4-year public university in very large city.

Enrollment: 12,316 undergrads, 5% part-time. 2,628 full-time freshmen.

Selectivity: Admits 50 to 75% of applicants.

BASIC COSTS (2007-2008)

Tuition and fees: $5,642; out-of-state residents $23,366.

Per-credit charge: $188; out-of-state residents $926.

Room and board: $7,924.

Additional info: Tuition at time of enrollment locked for 4 years.

FINANCIAL AID PICTURE (2007-2008)

Students with need: Out of 1,979 full-time freshmen who applied for aid, 865 were judged to have need. Of these, 838 received aid, and 339 had their full need met. Average financial aid package met 55% of need; average scholarship/grant was $5,826; average loan was $3,546. For part-time students, average financial aid package was $7,891.

Students without need: 236 full-time freshmen who did not demonstrate need for aid received scholarships/grants; average award was $3,339. No-need awards available for academics, alumni affiliation, athletics, leadership, state/district residency.

Scholarships offered: *Merit:* President's Scholarship Program; 4-year awards range from half to full tuition; for freshmen with outstanding academic/leadership qualities. *Athletic:* 76 full-time freshmen received athletic scholarships; average amount $13,946.

Cumulative student debt: 47% of graduating class had student loans; average debt was $21,436.

FINANCIAL AID PROCEDURES

Forms required: FAFSA, institutional form.

Dates and Deadlines: Closing date 3/1. Applicants notified on a rolling basis starting 4/1; must reply by 5/1.

Transfers: Closing date 5/1. Applicants notified on a rolling basis starting 6/1. Student must be officially admitted, all final transcripts must be received, and transcripts must be articulated.

CONTACT

Marie Mons, Director of Student Financial Planning and Services

Georgia Institute of Technology, Atlanta, GA 30332-0320

(404) 894-4160

Georgia Military College

Milledgeville, Georgia

www.gmc.cc.ga.us   Federal Code: 001571

2-year public community and junior and military college in large town.

Enrollment: 3,186 undergrads, 35% part-time. 1,073 full-time freshmen.

Selectivity: Open admission; but selective for some programs.

BASIC COSTS (2007-2008)

Tuition and fees: $12,050.

Per-credit charge: $98; out-of-district residents $98.

Room and board: $4,890.

Additional info: Quoted full-time tuition and fees are for cadet students. Additional $1,150 for uniforms.

FINANCIAL AID PICTURE

Students with need: Need-based aid available for full-time and part-time students. Work study available nights.

Students without need: No-need awards available for athletics, leadership, ROTC, state/district residency.

Additional info: Institutional aid offered to those enrolled in Cadet Corps who reside on campus.

FINANCIAL AID PROCEDURES

Forms required: FAFSA, state aid form.

Dates and Deadlines: No deadline. Applicants notified on a rolling basis starting 3/1.

CONTACT

Alisa Stephens, Director of Financial Aid

201 East Greene Street, Milledgeville, GA 31061

(478) 445-0840

Georgia Perimeter College

Clarkston, Georgia

www.gpc.edu   Federal Code: 001562

2-year public junior and liberal arts college in very large city.

Enrollment: 19,847 undergrads, 54% part-time. 2,554 full-time freshmen.

Selectivity: Admits 50 to 75% of applicants.

BASIC COSTS (2007-2008)

Tuition and fees: $2,234; out-of-state residents $7,474.

Per-credit charge: $73; out-of-state residents $292.

FINANCIAL AID PICTURE (2006-2007)

Students with need: 64% of average financial aid package awarded as scholarships/grants, 36% awarded as loans/jobs. Need-based aid available for part-time students. Work study available nights, weekends, and for part-time students.

FINANCIAL AID PROCEDURES

Forms required: FAFSA.

Dates and Deadlines: Closing date 6/1. Applicants notified on a rolling basis; must reply within 3 week(s) of notification.

Transfers: Priority date 6/1; no deadline.

CONTACT

Sheletha Champion, Director, Student Financial Services

555 North Indian Creek Drive, Clarkston, GA 30021-2361

(678) 891-3400

Georgia Southern University

Statesboro, Georgia

www.georgiasouthern.edu   Federal Code: 001572

4-year public university in large town.

Enrollment: 14,157 undergrads, 7% part-time. 2,732 full-time freshmen.

Selectivity: Admits less than 50% of applicants. GED not accepted.

BASIC COSTS (2007-2008)

Tuition and fees: $4,082; out-of-state residents $12,954.

Per-credit charge: $124; out-of-state residents $493.

Room and board: $6,860.

Additional info: Tuition at time of enrollment locked for 4 years.

FINANCIAL AID PICTURE (2006-2007)

Students with need: Out of 2,534 full-time freshmen who applied for aid, 1,268 were judged to have need. Of these, 1,257 received aid, and 264 had their full need met. Average financial aid package met 65% of need; average scholarship/grant was $5,439; average loan was $2,487. For part-time students, average financial aid package was $5,313.

Students without need: 144 full-time freshmen who did not demonstrate need for aid received scholarships/grants; average award was $1,605. No-need awards available for academics, alumni affiliation, art, athletics, leadership, minority status, music/drama, ROTC, state/district residency.

Scholarships offered: 46 full-time freshmen received athletic scholarships; average amount $5,098.

Cumulative student debt: 67% of graduating class had student loans; average debt was $18,618.

Additional info: The majority of scholarships available are need-blind.

FINANCIAL AID PROCEDURES

Forms required: FAFSA.

Dates and Deadlines: Closing date 4/20. Applicants notified on a rolling basis starting 4/20.

Transfers: No deadline. Applicants notified on a rolling basis starting 4/20.

CONTACT

Connie Murphey, Director of Financial Aid

PO Box 8024, Statesboro, GA 30460

(912) 681-5413

Georgia Southwestern State University
Americus, Georgia
www.gsw.edu   Federal Code: 001573

4-year public university and liberal arts college in large town.

Enrollment: 2,209 undergrads, 24% part-time. 388 full-time freshmen.

Selectivity: Admits over 75% of applicants.

BASIC COSTS (2007-2008)

Tuition and fees: $3,526; out-of-state residents $12,130.

Per-credit charge: $120; out-of-state residents $478.

Room and board: $5,274.

Additional info: Tuition at time of enrollment locked for 4 years.

FINANCIAL AID PICTURE

Students with need: Need-based aid available for full-time and part-time students.

Students without need: No-need awards available for academics, athletics, leadership.

Scholarships offered: Wheatley Scholarship: $2,000-2,500; 3.0 in college preparatory course and either 1100 SAT (exclusive of Writing) or 24 ACT.

FINANCIAL AID PROCEDURES

Forms required: FAFSA, institutional form.

Dates and Deadlines: Priority date 4/1; closing date 6/1. Applicants notified on a rolling basis starting 3/1.

CONTACT

Freida Jones, Director of Financial Aid

800 Georgia Southwestern State University Drive, Americus, GA 31709-9957

(229) 928-1378

Georgia State University
Atlanta, Georgia
www.gsu.edu   Federal Code: 001574

4-year public university in very large city.

Enrollment: 19,282 undergrads, 25% part-time. 2,470 full-time freshmen.

Selectivity: Admits 50 to 75% of applicants. GED not accepted.

BASIC COSTS (2007-2008)

Tuition and fees: $5,484; out-of-state residents $18,972.

Per-credit charge: $188; out-of-state residents $750.

Room only: $5,950.

FINANCIAL AID PICTURE (2007-2008)

Students with need: Out of 2,048 full-time freshmen who applied for aid, 1,502 were judged to have need. Of these, 1,440 received aid, and 428 had their full need met. Average financial aid package met 28% of need; average scholarship/grant was $2,863; average loan was $3,249. For part-time students, average financial aid package was $9,367.

Students without need: This college awards aid only to students with need.

Scholarships offered: 21 full-time freshmen received athletic scholarships; average amount $9,848.

FINANCIAL AID PROCEDURES

Forms required: FAFSA.

Dates and Deadlines: Priority date 4/1; closing date 11/1. Applicants notified on a rolling basis starting 3/30; must reply within 2 week(s) of notification.

CONTACT

Louis Scott, Acting Director of Student Financial Aid

Box 4009, Atlanta, GA 30302-4009

(404) 413-2400

Gordon College
Barnesville, Georgia
www.gdn.edu   Federal Code: 001575

2-year public junior college in small town.

Enrollment: 3,629 undergrads, 33% part-time. 1,048 full-time freshmen.

Selectivity: Admits over 75% of applicants.

BASIC COSTS (2007-2008)

Tuition and fees: $2,152; out-of-state residents $7,768.

Per-credit charge: $78; out-of-state residents $312.

Room and board: $4,350.

FINANCIAL AID PICTURE

Students with need: Need-based aid available for full-time and part-time students. Work study available nights, weekends, and for part-time students.

Students without need: No-need awards available for academics, athletics, music/drama, state/district residency.

FINANCIAL AID PROCEDURES

Forms required: institutional form.

Dates and Deadlines: Priority date 5/1; no closing date. Applicants notified on a rolling basis starting 5/1.

CONTACT

Larry Mitcham, Director of Financial Aid

419 College Drive, Barnesville, GA 30204

(770) 358-5059

Gupton Jones College of Funeral Service

Decatur, Georgia
www.gupton-jones.edu   Federal Code: 010771

2-year private technical college in very large city.
Enrollment: 175 undergrads.
Selectivity: Open admission.

BASIC COSTS (2007-2008)
Tuition and fees: $8,400.

FINANCIAL AID PICTURE
Students with need: Need-based aid available for full-time and part-time students.
Students without need: This college awards aid only to students with need.

FINANCIAL AID PROCEDURES
Forms required: FAFSA.
Dates and Deadlines: No deadline. Applicants notified on a rolling basis.

CONTACT
James Hinz, Dean
5141 Snapfinger Woods Drive, Decatur, GA 30035
(770) 593-2257

Gwinnett College

Lilburn, Georgia
www.gwinnettcollege.edu   Federal Code: 025830

2-year for-profit junior and career college in large city.
Enrollment: 347 undergrads.
Selectivity: Open admission; but selective for some programs.

BASIC COSTS (2007-2008)
Additional info: 2007 tuition $550 per class. Required number of classes varies by program. Massage therapy program charges $179 per credit hour.

FINANCIAL AID PICTURE
Students with need: Need-based aid available for full-time and part-time students.

FINANCIAL AID PROCEDURES
Forms required: FAFSA.

CONTACT
James Davidson, Director of Financial Aid
4230 Highway 29, Lilburn, GA 30047
(770) 381-7200

Gwinnett Technical College

Lawrenceville, Georgia
www.gwinnetttech.edu   Federal Code: 016139

2-year public technical college in large town.
Enrollment: 4,579 undergrads, 53% part-time. 514 full-time freshmen.
Selectivity: Open admission; but selective for some programs.

BASIC COSTS (2007-2008)
Tuition and fees: $1,425; out-of-state residents $2,541.
Per-credit charge: $31; out-of-state residents $62.

FINANCIAL AID PICTURE (2007-2008)
Students with need: Need-based aid available for part-time students.

FINANCIAL AID PROCEDURES
Forms required: FAFSA.
Dates and Deadlines: Closing date 7/1.
Transfers: Priority date 7/1; no deadline.

CONTACT
Stephen Whitaker, Director of Financial Aid
5150 Sugarloaf Parkway, Lawrenceville, GA 30243
(770) 962-7580 ext. 6637

Herzing College

Atlanta, Georgia
www.herzing.edu   Federal Code: 014030

3-year for-profit business and technical college in very large city.
Enrollment: 441 undergrads.
Selectivity: Admits over 75% of applicants.

BASIC COSTS (2007-2008)
Tuition and fees: $11,100.
Per-credit charge: $370.
Additional info: Costs may vary by program. Tuition includes use of books. Additional charges for technology and engineering programs; surcharge for technology programs.

FINANCIAL AID PICTURE
Students with need: Need-based aid available for full-time and part-time students. Work study available nights.
Students without need: No-need awards available for academics.

FINANCIAL AID PROCEDURES
Forms required: FAFSA, institutional form.
Dates and Deadlines: No deadline. Applicants notified on a rolling basis.

CONTACT
Latasha Watkins, Financial Aid Director
3393 Peachtree Road NE, Suite 1003, Atlanta, GA 30326
(404) 816-4533

Kennesaw State University

Kennesaw, Georgia
www.kennesaw.edu   Federal Code: 001577

4-year public university in large town.
Enrollment: 18,213 undergrads, 27% part-time. 2,274 full-time freshmen.
Selectivity: Admits 50 to 75% of applicants. GED not accepted.

BASIC COSTS (2007-2008)
Tuition and fees: $3,806; out-of-state residents $12,678.
Per-credit charge: $124; out-of-state residents $493.
Room only: $4,990.

FINANCIAL AID PICTURE (2007-2008)
Students with need: Out of 1,602 full-time freshmen who applied for aid, 904 were judged to have need. Of these, 894 received aid, and 118 had their full need met. Average financial aid package met 20% of need; average scholarship/grant was $8,135; average loan was $2,374. For part-time students, average financial aid package was $10,117.
Students without need: 1,001 full-time freshmen who did not demonstrate need for aid received scholarships/grants; average award was $860. No-need awards available for academics, alumni affiliation, art, athletics, job skills, leadership, minority status, music/drama, ROTC, state/district residency.
Scholarships offered: 15 full-time freshmen received athletic scholarships; average amount $850.

FINANCIAL AID PROCEDURES
Forms required: FAFSA.

PART III: FINANCIAL AID COLLEGE BY COLLEGE

Dates and Deadlines: Priority date 4/1; closing date 7/1. Applicants notified on a rolling basis starting 5/15.

Transfers: No deadline. Applicants notified on a rolling basis starting 5/15.

CONTACT

Ron Day, Director of Financial Aid

1000 Chastain Road, Kennesaw, GA 30144-5591

(770) 423-6074

LaGrange College
LaGrange, Georgia
www.lagrange.edu   Federal Code: 001578

4-year private liberal arts college in large town, affiliated with United Methodist Church.

Enrollment: 989 undergrads, 8% part-time. 263 full-time freshmen.

Selectivity: Admits 50 to 75% of applicants.

BASIC COSTS (2008-2009)

Tuition and fees: $19,900.

Per-credit charge: $820.

Room and board: $8,168.

FINANCIAL AID PICTURE (2006-2007)

Students with need: Out of 241 full-time freshmen who applied for aid, 203 were judged to have need. Of these, 202 received aid, and 53 had their full need met. Average financial aid package met 86% of need; average scholarship/grant was $11,414; average loan was $2,631. For part-time students, average financial aid package was $8,875.

Students without need: 51 full-time freshmen who did not demonstrate need for aid received scholarships/grants; average award was $7,165. No-need awards available for academics, art, job skills, leadership, minority status, music/drama, religious affiliation, state/district residency.

Scholarships offered: Below are the scholarships admission is awarding to entering freshmen. Presidential cover tuition, room and board (Competitive Scholarship) Fellows $12,000 per year (Competitive Scholarship) Deans $10,000 per year (Competitive Scholarship) Founders $8,000 per year Lafayette $ 6,000 per year Quadrangle $ 4,500 per year.

Cumulative student debt: 63% of graduating class had student loans; average debt was $19,596.

FINANCIAL AID PROCEDURES

Forms required: FAFSA, state aid form.

Dates and Deadlines: Priority date 4/1; no closing date. Applicants notified on a rolling basis starting 3/15; must reply by 8/15 or within 2 week(s) of notification.

CONTACT

Sylvia Smith, Director of Financial Aid

601 Broad Street, LaGrange, GA 30240-2999

(706) 880-8241

Life University
Marietta, Georgia
www.life.edu   Federal Code: 014170

4-year private university in very large city.

Enrollment: 536 undergrads, 27% part-time. 27 full-time freshmen.

Selectivity: Admits less than 50% of applicants.

BASIC COSTS (2007-2008)

Tuition and fees: $7,605.

Per-credit charge: $158.

FINANCIAL AID PICTURE (2007-2008)

Students with need: 23% of average financial aid package awarded as scholarships/grants, 77% awarded as loans/jobs.

FINANCIAL AID PROCEDURES

Forms required: FAFSA, state aid form, institutional form.

Dates and Deadlines: Priority date 3/1; closing date 6/15. Applicants notified on a rolling basis starting 5/1.

CONTACT

Michelle Nixon, Director of Financial Aid

1269 Barclay Circle, Marietta, GA 30060

(770) 426-2901

Macon State College
Macon, Georgia
www.maconstate.edu   Federal Code: 007728

4-year public business and health science college in small city.

Enrollment: 6,234 undergrads.

Selectivity: Admits 50 to 75% of applicants.

BASIC COSTS (2007-2008)

Tuition and fees: $2,060; out-of-state residents $7,676.

Per-credit charge: $78; out-of-state residents $312.

Additional info: Tuition at time of enrollment locked for 4 years.

FINANCIAL AID PICTURE (2006-2007)

Students with need: 53% of average financial aid package awarded as scholarships/grants, 47% awarded as loans/jobs. Need-based aid available for part-time students. Work study available nights, weekends, and for part-time students.

Students without need: This college awards aid only to students with need.

FINANCIAL AID PROCEDURES

Forms required: FAFSA.

Dates and Deadlines: Priority date 4/1; no closing date. Applicants notified on a rolling basis starting 4/15; must reply within 2 week(s) of notification.

CONTACT

Pat Simmons, Director of Financial Aid

100 College Station Drive, Macon, GA 31206-5145

(478) 471-2717

Medical College of Georgia
Augusta, Georgia
www.mcg.edu   Federal Code: 001579

Upper-division public health science college in large city.

Enrollment: 591 undergrads, 14% part-time.

BASIC COSTS (2007-2008)

Tuition and fees: $5,184; out-of-state residents $18,672.

Per-credit charge: $188; out-of-state residents $750.

Room and board: $1,642.

Additional info: Tuition at time of enrollment locked for 2 years.

FINANCIAL AID PICTURE

Students with need: Need-based aid available for full-time and part-time students. Work study available nights, weekends, and for part-time students.

Students without need: No-need awards available for academics, state/district residency.

Additional info: State Hope scholarships only available to Georgia residents.

FINANCIAL AID PROCEDURES

Forms required: FAFSA, state aid form, institutional form.

Dates and Deadlines: No deadline. Applicants notified on a rolling basis; must reply within 2 week(s) of notification.
Transfers: Priority date 3/31; closing date 5/30. Applicants notified on a rolling basis; must reply within 2 week(s) of notification.

CONTACT

Beverly Boggs, Director of Financial Aid
Office of Academic Admissions, Room 170 Kelly Building, Augusta, GA 30912-7310
(706) 721-4901

Mercer University
Macon, Georgia
www.mercer.edu   Federal Code: 001580

4-year private university in small city, affiliated with Baptist faith.
Enrollment: 2,245 undergrads, 2% part-time. 582 full-time freshmen.
Selectivity: Admits 50 to 75% of applicants. GED not accepted.

BASIC COSTS (2007-2008)
Tuition and fees: $26,960.
Per-credit charge: $892.
Room and board: $8,015.

FINANCIAL AID PICTURE (2007-2008)
Students with need: Out of 519 full-time freshmen who applied for aid, 417 were judged to have need. Of these, 417 received aid, and 229 had their full need met. Average financial aid package met 91% of need; average scholarship/grant was $19,186; average loan was $5,653. For part-time students, average financial aid package was $11,435.
Students without need: 161 full-time freshmen who did not demonstrate need for aid received scholarships/grants; average award was $17,780. No-need awards available for academics, art, athletics, job skills, leadership, music/drama, religious affiliation, ROTC, state/district residency.
Scholarships offered: *Merit:* Various scholarships: primarily based on high school GPA, SAT/ACT scores, and personal interview (for some); early applications given highest consideration. National Merit finalists and semi-finalists guaranteed full-tuition scholarships. *Athletic:* 38 full-time freshmen received athletic scholarships; average amount $13,942.
Cumulative student debt: 67% of graduating class had student loans; average debt was $24,251.

FINANCIAL AID PROCEDURES
Forms required: FAFSA, state aid form, institutional form.
Dates and Deadlines: Priority date 4/1; no closing date. Applicants notified on a rolling basis starting 3/15; must reply within 2 week(s) of notification.
Transfers: Priority date 6/1; no deadline.

CONTACT
Carol Williams, Associate Vice President, Student Financial Planning
1400 Coleman Avenue, Macon, GA 31207-0001
(478) 301-2670

Middle Georgia College
Cochran, Georgia
www.mgc.edu   Federal Code: 001581

2-year public junior college in small town.
Enrollment: 3,086 undergrads.
Selectivity: Admits over 75% of applicants.

BASIC COSTS (2007-2008)
Tuition and fees: $2,246; out-of-state residents $7,862.
Per-credit charge: $78; out-of-state residents $312.
Room and board: $4,770.

FINANCIAL AID PICTURE
Students with need: Need-based aid available for full-time and part-time students. Work study available nights, weekends, and for part-time students.
Students without need: No-need awards available for academics, alumni affiliation, art, athletics, job skills, leadership, minority status, music/drama, state/district residency.

FINANCIAL AID PROCEDURES
Forms required: FAFSA.
Dates and Deadlines: Priority date 4/1; no closing date. Applicants notified on a rolling basis starting 5/1.

CONTACT
Jon Finkelstein, Director of Financial Aid
1100 Second Street SE, Cochran, GA 31014
(478) 934-3133

Morehouse College
Atlanta, Georgia   Federal Code: 001582
www.morehouse.edu   CSS Code: 5415

4-year private liberal arts college for men in very large city.
Enrollment: 2,810 undergrads, 5% part-time. 676 full-time freshmen.
Selectivity: Admits 50 to 75% of applicants.

BASIC COSTS (2007-2008)
Tuition and fees: $18,678.
Per-credit charge: $707.
Room and board: $9,928.

FINANCIAL AID PICTURE (2006-2007)
Students with need: Out of 676 full-time freshmen who applied for aid, 676 were judged to have need. Of these, 676 received aid, and 35 had their full need met. Average financial aid package met 28% of need; average scholarship/grant was $7,484; average loan was $2,625. Need-based aid available for part-time students.
Students without need: 220 full-time freshmen who did not demonstrate need for aid received scholarships/grants; average award was $10,000. No-need awards available for academics, alumni affiliation, art, athletics, leadership, music/drama, ROTC, state/district residency.
Scholarships offered: 105 full-time freshmen received athletic scholarships; average amount $4,000.
Cumulative student debt: 94% of graduating class had student loans; average debt was $35,000.

FINANCIAL AID PROCEDURES
Forms required: FAFSA, CSS PROFILE, state aid form, institutional form.
Dates and Deadlines: Priority date 2/15; closing date 4/1. Must reply by 5/1.
Transfers: Applicants notified by 4/1; must reply by 5/1.

CONTACT
James Stotts, Director of Financial Aid
830 Westview Drive SW, Atlanta, GA 30314
(404) 215-2638

North Georgia College & State University
Dahlonega, Georgia
www.ngcsu.edu   Federal Code: 001585

4-year public university and military college in small town.
Enrollment: 4,498 undergrads, 17% part-time. 780 full-time freshmen.
Selectivity: Admits 50 to 75% of applicants.

BASIC COSTS (2007-2008)
Tuition and fees: $3,810; out-of-state residents $12,414.
Per-credit charge: $120; out-of-state residents $478.

PART III: FINANCIAL AID COLLEGE BY COLLEGE

Room and board: $5,042.

FINANCIAL AID PICTURE

Students with need: Need-based aid available for full-time and part-time students.

Students without need: No-need awards available for academics, alumni affiliation, art, athletics, leadership, music/drama, ROTC, state/district residency.

Scholarships offered: ROTC grant; $1,500 a year; available to Georgia residents. Out-of-state tuition waiver; $5,628 per year.

FINANCIAL AID PROCEDURES

Forms required: FAFSA.

Dates and Deadlines: Priority date 5/1; no closing date. Applicants notified on a rolling basis starting 3/15; must reply within 3 week(s) of notification.

CONTACT

Jill Rayner, Director of Financial Aid
82 College Circle, Dahlonega, GA 30597
(706) 864-1412

North Georgia Technical College

Clarkesville, Georgia
www.northgatech.edu   Federal Code: 005619

2-year public community and technical college in large town.

Enrollment: 1,940 undergrads, 44% part-time. 389 full-time freshmen.

Selectivity: Open admission; but selective for some programs.

BASIC COSTS (2007-2008)

Additional info: Tuition varies from $31-$53 per credit hour (excluding Commercial Truck Driving) for Georgia residents, depending on program. Tuition for out-of-state students is twice the rate of Georgia students, and tuition for foreign students is four times the Georgia resident rate. Required fees are $380 a year. Room and board for double occupancy is $3600 annually. Tuition/fee waivers available for unemployed or children of unemployed.

FINANCIAL AID PICTURE

Students with need: Need-based aid available for full-time and part-time students. Work study available nights, weekends, and for part-time students.

CONTACT

Kim Kelley, Director of Financial Aid
1500 Highway 197, Clarkesville, GA 30523

Northwestern Technical College

Rock Spring, Georgia
www.northwesterntech.edu   Federal Code: 005257

2-year public technical college in small town.

Enrollment: 1,537 undergrads, 53% part-time. 235 full-time freshmen.

Selectivity: Open admission; but selective for some programs.

BASIC COSTS (2007-2008)

Tuition and fees: $1,359; out-of-state residents $2,475.

Per-credit charge: $31; out-of-state residents $62.

Additional info: Truck driving and flight technology are higher cost programs.

FINANCIAL AID PICTURE

Students with need: Need-based aid available for full-time and part-time students.

FINANCIAL AID PROCEDURES

Forms required: FAFSA, institutional form.

Dates and Deadlines: No deadline.

CONTACT

Sara Twiggs, Director of Financial Aid
265 Bicentennial Trail, Rock Spring, GA 30739
(706) 764-3575

Oglethorpe University

Atlanta, Georgia
www.oglethorpe.edu   Federal Code: 001586

4-year private liberal arts college in very large city.

Enrollment: 943 undergrads, 12% part-time. 179 full-time freshmen.

BASIC COSTS (2008-2009)

Tuition and fees: $25,580.

Room and board: $9,500.

FINANCIAL AID PICTURE (2007-2008)

Students with need: Out of 138 full-time freshmen who applied for aid, 113 were judged to have need. Of these, 113 received aid, and 32 had their full need met. Average financial aid package met 92% of need; average scholarship/grant was $20,245; average loan was $3,364. For part-time students, average financial aid package was $7,010.

Students without need: 60 full-time freshmen who did not demonstrate need for aid received scholarships/grants; average award was $8,949. No-need awards available for academics, leadership, music/drama.

Cumulative student debt: 58% of graduating class had student loans; average debt was $26,299.

FINANCIAL AID PROCEDURES

Forms required: FAFSA, state aid form, institutional form.

Dates and Deadlines: Priority date 2/1; no closing date. Applicants notified on a rolling basis starting 4/1; must reply by 5/1 or within 3 week(s) of notification.

Transfers: No deadline.

CONTACT

Patrick Bonones, Director of Financial Aid
4484 Peachtree Road NE, Atlanta, GA 30319-2797
(404) 364-8356

Oxford College of Emory University

Oxford, Georgia   Federal Code: 001565
www.emory.edu/oxford   CSS Code: 5186

2-year private branch campus and liberal arts college in large town, affiliated with United Methodist Church.

Enrollment: 715 undergrads. 382 full-time freshmen.

Selectivity: Admits 50 to 75% of applicants. GED not accepted.

BASIC COSTS (2008-2009)

Tuition and fees: $30,062.

Per-credit charge: $1,233.

Room and board: $8,496.

FINANCIAL AID PICTURE (2006-2007)

Students with need: 79% of average financial aid package awarded as scholarships/grants, 21% awarded as loans/jobs. Need-based aid available for part-time students. Work study available nights, weekends, and for part-time students.

Students without need: No-need awards available for academics, leadership, religious affiliation, state/district residency.

Scholarships offered: Woodruff Scholarships; full tuition, room and board for 4 years. Dean's Scholarship; full tuition for 4 years. Faculty Scholarships; half tuition for 4 years. 2-year scholarships; range from $6,500 to $8,000 a year.

Additional info: Deadline of November 1 to apply for Oxford College Scholars Program.

FINANCIAL AID PROCEDURES

Forms required: FAFSA, CSS PROFILE.

Dates and Deadlines: Priority date 2/1; closing date 3/1. Applicants notified by 4/1; must reply by 5/1 or within 2 week(s) of notification.

CONTACT

Jennifer Taylor, Dean of Enrollment Services
100 Hamill Street, Oxford, GA 30054-1418
(770) 784-8303

Paine College
Augusta, Georgia
www.paine.edu   Federal Code: 001587

4-year private liberal arts college in large city, affiliated with Christian Methodist Episcopal Church and United Methodist Church.

Enrollment: 908 undergrads, 6% part-time. 242 full-time freshmen.

Selectivity: Admits less than 50% of applicants.

BASIC COSTS (2007-2008)

Tuition and fees: $10,694.

Per-credit charge: $412.

Room and board: $5,216.

FINANCIAL AID PICTURE (2007-2008)

Students with need: Out of 242 full-time freshmen who applied for aid, 234 were judged to have need. Of these, 230 received aid, and 16 had their full need met. Average financial aid package met 56% of need; average scholarship/grant was $6,461; average loan was $3,248. For part-time students, average financial aid package was $6,043.

Students without need: 7 full-time freshmen who did not demonstrate need for aid received scholarships/grants; average award was $14,442. No-need awards available for academics, alumni affiliation, athletics, music/drama, religious affiliation, ROTC.

Scholarships offered: 3 full-time freshmen received athletic scholarships; average amount $10,155.

Cumulative student debt: 92% of graduating class had student loans; average debt was $27,327.

FINANCIAL AID PROCEDURES

Forms required: FAFSA, institutional form.

Dates and Deadlines: Priority date 3/1; no closing date. Applicants notified on a rolling basis starting 5/1; must reply within 2 week(s) of notification.

CONTACT

Gerri Bogan, Director of Financial Aid
1235 15th Street, Augusta, GA 30901-3182
(706) 821-8262

Piedmont College
Demorest, Georgia
www.piedmont.edu   Federal Code: 001588

4-year private liberal arts and teachers college in rural community, affiliated with United Church of Christ.

Enrollment: 1,056 undergrads, 15% part-time. 201 full-time freshmen.

Selectivity: Admits less than 50% of applicants.

BASIC COSTS (2007-2008)

Tuition and fees: $16,500.

Per-credit charge: $688.

Room and board: $6,000.

Additional info: Tuition/fee waivers available for adults.

FINANCIAL AID PICTURE (2007-2008)

Students with need: Average financial aid package met 77% of need; average scholarship/grant was $794; average loan was $2,841. For part-time students, average financial aid package was $7,992.

Students without need: No-need awards available for academics, art, leadership, music/drama, religious affiliation, state/district residency.

Scholarships offered: Each year high school seniors superior in academics, leadership, and extracurricular activities are invited to campus for an overnight scholarship competition.

Cumulative student debt: 74% of graduating class had student loans; average debt was $15,580.

Additional info: College meets 100% of unmet direct financial need for early applicants through grants, scholarships, and loan programs.

FINANCIAL AID PROCEDURES

Forms required: FAFSA, state aid form, institutional form.

Dates and Deadlines: Priority date 5/1; no closing date. Applicants notified on a rolling basis; must reply within 2 week(s) of notification.

Transfers: Priority date 5/5. Must reply within 2 week(s) of notification.

CONTACT

Kimberly Lovell, Director of Financial Aid
165 Central Avenue, Demorest, GA 30535-0010
(706) 776-0114 ext. 1191

Reinhardt College
Waleska, Georgia
www.reinhardt.edu   Federal Code: 001589

4-year private business and teachers college in rural community, affiliated with United Methodist Church.

Enrollment: 971 undergrads, 9% part-time. 273 full-time freshmen.

BASIC COSTS (2007-2008)

Tuition and fees: $14,970.

Per-credit charge: $495.

Room and board: $7,284.

FINANCIAL AID PICTURE

Students with need: Need-based aid available for full-time and part-time students.

Students without need: No-need awards available for academics, art, athletics.

FINANCIAL AID PROCEDURES

Forms required: state aid form.

Dates and Deadlines: Priority date 5/1; no closing date. Applicants notified on a rolling basis starting 3/15; must reply within 2 week(s) of notification.

CONTACT

Robert Gregory, Director of Financial Aid
7300 Reinhardt College Circle, Waleska, GA 30183
(770) 720-5667

Savannah College of Art and Design
Savannah, Georgia
www.scad.edu   Federal Code: 015022

4-year private visual arts and performing arts college in small city.

Enrollment: 7,423 undergrads, 9% part-time. 1,565 full-time freshmen.

Selectivity: Admits 50 to 75% of applicants.

BASIC COSTS (2008-2009)

Tuition and fees: $25,965.

Per-credit charge: $577.

Room and board: $10,585.

Additional info: A one-time matriculation fee of $500 is required of all students.

FINANCIAL AID PICTURE (2007-2008)

Students with need: Out of 1,122 full-time freshmen who applied for aid, 887 were judged to have need. Of these, 874 received aid, and 446 had their full need met. Average financial aid package met 11% of need; average scholarship/grant was $3,772; average loan was $3,409. For part-time students, average financial aid package was $10,202.

Students without need: 491 full-time freshmen who did not demonstrate need for aid received scholarships/grants; average award was $8,180. No-need awards available for academics, art, athletics, music/drama.

Scholarships offered: 38 full-time freshmen received athletic scholarships; average amount $5,332.

Additional info: Degree-seeking students may be awarded maximum of one scholarship from college, but may receive additional scholarships from other sources, as well as additional forms of financial aid. Scholarships based on academic achievement are awarded through admission office.

FINANCIAL AID PROCEDURES

Forms required: FAFSA, state aid form, institutional form.

Dates and Deadlines: Priority date 2/15; no closing date. Applicants notified on a rolling basis starting 6/1; must reply within 4 week(s) of notification.

Transfers: Priority date 4/1; no deadline. Applicants notified on a rolling basis. Transfer students eligible to apply for academic and portfolio scholarships.

CONTACT

Cindy Bradley, Director of Financial Aid
PO Box 2072, Savannah, GA 31402-2072
(912) 525-6109

Savannah River College
Augusta, Georgia
www.savannahrivercollege.edu   Federal Code: 013115

2-year for-profit junior and technical college in small city.

Enrollment: 268 undergrads, 4% part-time. 31 full-time freshmen.

BASIC COSTS (2007-2008)

Tuition and fees: $8,395.

FINANCIAL AID PICTURE (2007-2008)

Students with need: Out of 31 full-time freshmen who applied for aid, 26 were judged to have need. Of these, 26 received aid, and 26 had their full need met. Average financial aid package met 100% of need; average scholarship/grant was $4,050; average loan was $2,625. Need-based aid available for part-time students.

Students without need: This college awards aid only to students with need.

Cumulative student debt: 96% of graduating class had student loans; average debt was $3,631.

FINANCIAL AID PROCEDURES

Forms required: FAFSA, institutional form.

Dates and Deadlines: No deadline.

CONTACT

Amy Barnett, Financial Aid Officer
2528 Center West Parkway, Building A, Augusta, GA 30909

Savannah Technical College
Savannah, Georgia
www.savannahtech.edu   Federal Code: 005618

2-year public technical college in small city.

Enrollment: 3,748 undergrads, 53% part-time. 486 full-time freshmen.

Selectivity: Open admission; but selective for some programs.

BASIC COSTS (2007-2008)

Tuition and fees: $1,359; out-of-state residents $2,475.

Per-credit charge: $31; out-of-state residents $62.

FINANCIAL AID PICTURE (2006-2007)

Students with need: Need-based aid available for part-time students.

Students without need: No-need awards available for academics, leadership, minority status, state/district residency.

FINANCIAL AID PROCEDURES

Forms required: FAFSA.

Dates and Deadlines: No deadline. Applicants notified on a rolling basis.

CONTACT

Timothy Cranford, Financial Aid Director
5717 White Bluff Road, Savannah, GA 31405-5521
(912) 443-5705

Shorter College
Rome, Georgia
www.shorter.edu   Federal Code: 001591

4-year private liberal arts college in large town, affiliated with Southern Baptist Convention.

Enrollment: 1,019 undergrads, 2% part-time. 276 full-time freshmen.

Selectivity: Admits 50 to 75% of applicants.

BASIC COSTS (2008-2009)

Tuition and fees: $15,770.

Per-credit charge: $420.

Room and board: $7,400.

FINANCIAL AID PICTURE (2007-2008)

Students with need: Out of 225 full-time freshmen who applied for aid, 189 were judged to have need. Of these, 189 received aid, and 51 had their full need met. Average financial aid package met 71% of need; average scholarship/grant was $11,103; average loan was $3,637. For part-time students, average financial aid package was $7,698.

Students without need: 250 full-time freshmen who did not demonstrate need for aid received scholarships/grants; average award was $7,253. No-need awards available for academics, art, athletics, music/drama, religious affiliation.

Scholarships offered: 74 full-time freshmen received athletic scholarships; average amount $6,621.

Cumulative student debt: 70% of graduating class had student loans; average debt was $18,078.

Additional info: Cost is reduced for all in-state students by state tuition equalization grant program. College matches for out-of-state full-time students.

FINANCIAL AID PROCEDURES

Forms required: FAFSA, state aid form, institutional form.

Dates and Deadlines: Priority date 4/1; no closing date. Applicants notified on a rolling basis starting 4/1; must reply within 2 week(s) of notification.

Transfers: Priority date 4/15; no deadline. Applicants notified on a rolling basis starting 3/31; must reply within 2 week(s) of notification.

CONTACT

Tara Jones, Director of Financial Aid
315 Shorter Avenue, Rome, GA 30165
(706) 233-7227

South Georgia College

Douglas, Georgia
www.sgc.edu   Federal Code: 001592

2-year public community and junior college in large town.
Enrollment: 1,756 undergrads.
Selectivity: Open admission.

BASIC COSTS (2007-2008)
Tuition and fees: $2,076; out-of-state residents $7,316.
Per-credit charge: $73; out-of-state residents $292.
Room and board: $7,060.

FINANCIAL AID PICTURE
Students with need: Need-based aid available for full-time and part-time students.
Students without need: No-need awards available for academics.

FINANCIAL AID PROCEDURES
Forms required: FAFSA, institutional form.
Dates and Deadlines: Priority date 4/1; no closing date. Applicants notified on a rolling basis starting 7/6; must reply within 2 week(s) of notification.

CONTACT
Wes Brown, Director of Financial Aid
100 West College Park Drive, Douglas, GA 31533-5098
(912) 389-4285

Southeastern Technical College

Vidalia, Georgia
www.southeasterntech.org/

2-year public technical college in large town.
Enrollment: 911 undergrads.
Selectivity: Open admission.

BASIC COSTS (2007-2008)
Tuition and fees: $1,440; out-of-state residents $2,556.
Per-credit charge: $31; out-of-state residents $62.

FINANCIAL AID PICTURE
Students with need: Need-based aid available for full-time and part-time students. Work study available nights.
Students without need: No-need awards available for state/district residency.

FINANCIAL AID PROCEDURES
Forms required: FAFSA, state aid form, institutional form.
Dates and Deadlines: No deadline. Applicants notified on a rolling basis starting 4/6.

CONTACT
Rebecca Ethredge, Financial Aid Director
3001 East First Street, Vidalia, GA 30474

Southern Polytechnic State University

Marietta, Georgia
www.spsu.edu   Federal Code: 001570

4-year public university and engineering college in small city.
Enrollment: 3,827 undergrads, 30% part-time. 485 full-time freshmen.
Selectivity: Admits 50 to 75% of applicants. GED not accepted.

BASIC COSTS (2007-2008)
Tuition and fees: $3,872; out-of-state residents $13,590.
Per-credit charge: $136; out-of-state residents $540.

Room and board: $5,780.
Additional info: Tuition at time of enrollment locked for 4 years.

FINANCIAL AID PICTURE (2007-2008)
Students with need: Out of 394 full-time freshmen who applied for aid, 394 were judged to have need. Of these, 376 received aid, and 161 had their full need met. Average financial aid package met 80% of need; average scholarship/grant was $2,940; average loan was $3,206. For part-time students, average financial aid package was $3,205.
Students without need: 3 full-time freshmen who did not demonstrate need for aid received scholarships/grants; average award was $6,634. No-need awards available for academics, athletics.
Scholarships offered: 9 full-time freshmen received athletic scholarships; average amount $4,766.
Cumulative student debt: 37% of graduating class had student loans; average debt was $10,422.

FINANCIAL AID PROCEDURES
Forms required: FAFSA.
Dates and Deadlines: Priority date 4/1; no closing date. Applicants notified on a rolling basis starting 6/1.
Transfers: No deadline. Applicants notified on a rolling basis starting 5/1.

CONTACT
Gary Bush, Director of Financial Aid
1100 South Marietta Parkway, Marietta, GA 30060-2896
(678) 915-7290

Southwest Georgia Technical College

Thomasville, Georgia
www.southwestgatech.edu   Federal Code: 005615

2-year public technical college in large town.
Enrollment: 1,154 undergrads, 60% part-time. 90 full-time freshmen.
Selectivity: Open admission; but selective for some programs.

BASIC COSTS (2007-2008)
Tuition and fees: $1,359; out-of-state residents $2,475.
Per-credit charge: $31; out-of-state residents $62.
Additional info: Truck driving and flight technology are higher cost programs.

FINANCIAL AID PICTURE
Students with need: Need-based aid available for full-time and part-time students. Work study available nights.
Students without need: No-need awards available for state/district residency.
Scholarships offered: Hope Scholarship; full tuition; available to GA residents with 3.0 minimum GPA.

FINANCIAL AID PROCEDURES
Forms required: FAFSA, institutional form.
Dates and Deadlines: No deadline. Applicants notified on a rolling basis starting 7/1.

CONTACT
Michael Rayburn, Director of Financial Aid
15689 US Highway 19N, Thomasville, GA 31792
(229) 225-5221

Spelman College

Atlanta, Georgia
www.spelman.edu   Federal Code: 001594

4-year private liberal arts college for women in very large city.
Enrollment: 2,337 undergrads, 4% part-time. 569 full-time freshmen.

Selectivity: Admits less than 50% of applicants.

BASIC COSTS (2007-2008)

Tuition and fees: $18,615.

Room and board: $9,200.

FINANCIAL AID PICTURE (2006-2007)

Students with need: Out of 523 full-time freshmen who applied for aid, 471 were judged to have need. Of these, 455 received aid, and 10 had their full need met. Average financial aid package met 87% of need; average scholarship/grant was $3,500; average loan was $2,625. Need-based aid available for part-time students.

Students without need: 65 full-time freshmen who did not demonstrate need for aid received scholarships/grants. No-need awards available for academics, alumni affiliation, leadership, music/drama, state/district residency.

FINANCIAL AID PROCEDURES

Forms required: FAFSA, institutional form.

Dates and Deadlines: Priority date 3/1; no closing date. Applicants notified on a rolling basis starting 2/15; must reply within 2 week(s) of notification.

Transfers: Closing date 10/1. No special aid for transfer students for the first year.

CONTACT

Lenora Jackson, Director of Student Financial Services

350 Spelman Lane SW, Campus Box 277, Atlanta, GA 30314

(404) 270-5212

Thomas University

Thomasville, Georgia

www.thomasu.edu   Federal Code: 001555

4-year private university and liberal arts college in large town.

Enrollment: 456 undergrads, 34% part-time. 140 full-time freshmen.

Selectivity: Open admission; but selective for some programs.

BASIC COSTS (2007-2008)

Tuition and fees: $11,040.

Per-credit charge: $415.

Room only: $2,626.

FINANCIAL AID PICTURE

Students with need: Need-based aid available for full-time and part-time students.

Students without need: No-need awards available for academics, athletics, leadership, state/district residency.

FINANCIAL AID PROCEDURES

Forms required: FAFSA, state aid form.

Dates and Deadlines: Priority date 5/1; no closing date. Applicants notified on a rolling basis.

Transfers: Student must submit official academic transcripts from all colleges attended. Financial aid received during current academic year from previous school will be verified through the National Student Loan Data System (NSLDS).

CONTACT

Angela Keys, Director of Financial Aid

1501 Millpond Road, Thomasville, GA 31792-7499

(229) 227-6931

Toccoa Falls College

Toccoa Falls, Georgia

www.tfc.edu   Federal Code: 001596

4-year private Bible and liberal arts college in large town, affiliated with Christian and Missionary Alliance.

Enrollment: 969 undergrads, 7% part-time. 221 full-time freshmen.

Selectivity: Admits 50 to 75% of applicants.

BASIC COSTS (2008-2009)

Tuition and fees: $14,625.

Per-credit charge: $604.

Room and board: $5,350.

FINANCIAL AID PICTURE

Students with need: Need-based aid available for full-time and part-time students.

Students without need: No-need awards available for academics, alumni affiliation, leadership, music/drama, religious affiliation, state/district residency.

Scholarships offered: Trustee; $7,500; ACT score of 28 or SAT score of 1250 and high school GPA of 3.8; renewable with GPA of 3.5. President; $6,000; ACT score of 26 or SAT score 1200 and high school GPA of 3.5; renewable with GPA of 3.25. Dean; $4,500; ACT score of 25 or SAT score of 1150 and high school GPA of 3.2; renewable with GPA of 3.0. Director; $4,000; ACT score of 21 or SAT score of 1000 and high school GPA of 3.0; renewable with GPA of 2.75. Faculty; $5,000; have earned at least 24 college credits and college GPA of 3.5; renewable with GPA of 3.5. Home School; $5,500; ACT score of 26 or SAT score of 1200 and home school GPA of 3.0; renewable with a GPA of 3.0; Leadership; $6,000; ACT score of 22 or SAT score of 1050 and high school GPA of 3.00 and two letters of recommendation, personal essay, application by April 1; 10 available, renewable by maintaining leadership standards and a GPA of 2.75. Music; $5,000; ACT score of 22 or SAT score of 1050 and high school GPA of 3.0 and audition, May 1 deadline; 8 available, renewable by maintaining music standards and a GPA of 2.75.

FINANCIAL AID PROCEDURES

Forms required: FAFSA, institutional form.

Dates and Deadlines: Priority date 5/1; closing date 8/1. Applicants notified on a rolling basis starting 3/1; must reply within 2 week(s) of notification.

Transfers: Priority date 12/15; no deadline. Applicants notified on a rolling basis starting 10/1; must reply within 2 week(s) of notification. Need based aid awarded to students based on documented need reflected in information submitted to the federal government.

CONTACT

Kimberly Daniel, Director of Financial Aid

PO Box 800899, Toccoa Falls, GA 30598-0368

(706) 886-6831 ext. 5435

Truett-McConnell College

Cleveland, Georgia

www.truett.edu   Federal Code: 001597

4-year private liberal arts college in small town, affiliated with Southern Baptist Convention.

Enrollment: 395 undergrads.

Selectivity: Admits less than 50% of applicants.

BASIC COSTS (2008-2009)

Tuition and fees: $14,000.

Per-credit charge: $450.

Room and board: $5,100.

FINANCIAL AID PICTURE

Students with need: Need-based aid available for full-time and part-time students.

Students without need: No-need awards available for academics, athletics, music/drama, religious affiliation, state/district residency.

Additional info: Installment plan available.

FINANCIAL AID PROCEDURES

Forms required: FAFSA, state aid form, institutional form.

Dates and Deadlines: Priority date 6/1; no closing date. Applicants notified on a rolling basis starting 4/1; must reply within 2 week(s) of notification.

CONTACT

Becky Moore, Director of Financial Aid
100 Alumni Drive, Cleveland, GA 30528
(800) 226-8621

University of Georgia

Athens, Georgia
www.uga.edu   Federal Code: 001598

4-year public university in small city.

Enrollment: 24,971 undergrads, 7% part-time. 4,674 full-time freshmen.

Selectivity: Admits 50 to 75% of applicants.

BASIC COSTS (2007-2008)

Tuition and fees: $5,622; out-of-state residents $20,726.

Per-credit charge: $188; out-of-state residents $817.

Room and board: $7,292.

FINANCIAL AID PICTURE (2007-2008)

Students with need: Out of 2,960 full-time freshmen who applied for aid, 1,449 were judged to have need. Of these, 1,439 received aid, and 613 had their full need met. Average financial aid package met 80% of need; average scholarship/grant was $7,492; average loan was $2,917. For part-time students, average financial aid package was $5,673.

Students without need: 272 full-time freshmen who did not demonstrate need for aid received scholarships/grants; average award was $2,196. No-need awards available for academics, athletics, ROTC, state/district residency.

Scholarships offered: 98 full-time freshmen received athletic scholarships; average amount $10,640.

Cumulative student debt: 39% of graduating class had student loans; average debt was $14,420.

FINANCIAL AID PROCEDURES

Forms required: FAFSA.

Dates and Deadlines: Priority date 3/1; no closing date. Applicants notified on a rolling basis starting 5/15; must reply within 2 week(s) of notification.

CONTACT

Susan Little, Director, Student Financial Aid
Office of Undergraduate Admissions, Athens, GA 30602-1633
(706) 542-6147

University of West Georgia

Carrollton, Georgia
www.westga.edu   Federal Code: 001601

4-year public university in large town.

Enrollment: 8,842 undergrads, 16% part-time. 2,041 full-time freshmen.

Selectivity: Admits 50 to 75% of applicants. GED not accepted.

BASIC COSTS (2007-2008)

Tuition and fees: $3,918; out-of-state residents $12,790.

Per-credit charge: $124; out-of-state residents $493.

Room and board: $5,406.

Additional info: Tuition/fee waivers available for adults, minority students.

FINANCIAL AID PICTURE (2007-2008)

Students with need: Average financial aid package met 65% of need; average scholarship/grant was $4,997; average loan was $3,196. For part-time students, average financial aid package was $5,732.

Students without need: No-need awards available for academics, alumni affiliation, art, athletics, leadership, minority status, music/drama, religious affiliation, state/district residency.

Cumulative student debt: 29% of graduating class had student loans; average debt was $16,130.

FINANCIAL AID PROCEDURES

Forms required: FAFSA.

Dates and Deadlines: Priority date 4/1; closing date 7/7. Applicants notified on a rolling basis starting 3/1.

CONTACT

Kimberly Jordan, Director of Financial Aid
1601 Maple Street, Carrollton, GA 30118
(678) 839-6421

Valdosta State University

Valdosta, Georgia
www.valdosta.edu   Federal Code: 001599

4-year public university in small city.

Enrollment: 9,696 undergrads, 15% part-time. 1,986 full-time freshmen.

Selectivity: Admits 50 to 75% of applicants. GED not accepted.

BASIC COSTS (2007-2008)

Tuition and fees: $4,038; out-of-state residents $12,910.

Per-credit charge: $124; out-of-state residents $493.

Room and board: $5,990.

Additional info: Tuition at time of enrollment locked for 4 years.

FINANCIAL AID PICTURE (2006-2007)

Students with need: Out of 1,574 full-time freshmen who applied for aid, 1,126 were judged to have need. Of these, 1,121 received aid, and 161 had their full need met. Average financial aid package met 62% of need; average scholarship/grant was $5,584; average loan was $2,461. For part-time students, average financial aid package was $6,518.

Students without need: 27 full-time freshmen who did not demonstrate need for aid received scholarships/grants; average award was $1,290. No-need awards available for academics, art, athletics, music/drama, ROTC.

Scholarships offered: 7 full-time freshmen received athletic scholarships; average amount $1,792.

Cumulative student debt: 66% of graduating class had student loans; average debt was $17,250.

FINANCIAL AID PROCEDURES

Forms required: FAFSA.

Dates and Deadlines: Priority date 5/1; closing date 6/15. Applicants notified on a rolling basis starting 6/1.

CONTACT

Doug Tanner, Director of Financial Aid
1500 North Patterson Street, Valdosta, GA 31698
(229) 333-5935

Waycross College

Waycross, Georgia
www.waycross.edu   Federal Code: 013537

2-year public community and liberal arts college in large town.

Enrollment: 935 undergrads.

BASIC COSTS (2007-2008)

Tuition and fees: $1,904; out-of-state residents $7,144.

Per-credit charge: $73; out-of-state residents $292.

Additional info: Tuition/fee waivers available for adults.

FINANCIAL AID PICTURE

Students with need: Need-based aid available for full-time and part-time students. Work study available nights.

Students without need: No-need awards available for academics, alumni affiliation, leadership.

FINANCIAL AID PROCEDURES

Forms required: FAFSA, institutional form.

Dates and Deadlines: Priority date 6/1; no closing date. Applicants notified on a rolling basis; must reply within 2 week(s) of notification.

CONTACT

Debbie Howard, Assistant Director of Financial Aid
2001 South Georgia Parkway, Waycross, GA 31503
(912) 285-6035

Wesleyan College

Macon, Georgia
www.wesleyancollege.edu   Federal Code: 001600

4-year private liberal arts college for women in small city, affiliated with United Methodist Church.

Enrollment: 547 undergrads, 33% part-time. 108 full-time freshmen.

Selectivity: Admits less than 50% of applicants.

BASIC COSTS (2008-2009)

Tuition and fees: $17,000.

Per-credit charge: $405.

Room and board: $7,800.

Additional info: Tuition/fee waivers available for adults.

FINANCIAL AID PICTURE

Students with need: Need-based aid available for full-time and part-time students. Work study available nights, weekends, and for part-time students.

Students without need: No-need awards available for academics, alumni affiliation, art, job skills, leadership, minority status, music/drama, religious affiliation, state/district residency.

Scholarships offered: Academic Scholarships: range in value from $1,000 to $10,000; based on minimum 1100 SAT or 25 ACT and 3.75 GPA, or 1200 SAT/27 ACT and 3.5 GPA. SAT scores exclusive of Writing. Leadership Awards and scholarships for music, art and theater: range from $1,000-$3,000.

Additional info: Fellowships available based on number of hours and cumulative GPA transferred in, with minimum 30 semester or 45 quarter hours and 3.0 GPA required.

FINANCIAL AID PROCEDURES

Forms required: FAFSA, state aid form, institutional form.

Dates and Deadlines: Priority date 5/1; closing date 6/3. Applicants notified on a rolling basis starting 3/1; must reply by 5/1 or within 3 week(s) of notification.

CONTACT

Patricia Gibbs, Vice President for Enrollment Services and Student Affairs
4760 Forsyth Road, Macon, GA 31210-4462
(478) 757-5205

West Georgia Technical College

LaGrange, Georgia
www.westgatech.edu   Federal Code: 005614

2-year public technical college in small city.

Enrollment: 1,558 undergrads, 55% part-time. 239 full-time freshmen.

Selectivity: Open admission; but selective for some programs.

BASIC COSTS (2007-2008)

Tuition and fees: $1,359; out-of-state residents $2,475.

Per-credit charge: $31; out-of-state residents $62.

Additional info: Tuition reciprocity with bordering states. Commercial truck driving program is $2048 per quarter. Basic welding and EMT programs are $40 per-credit-hour.

FINANCIAL AID PICTURE

Students with need: Need-based aid available for full-time and part-time students. Work study available nights.

Students without need: No-need awards available for state/district residency.

FINANCIAL AID PROCEDURES

Forms required: FAFSA, state aid form, institutional form.

Dates and Deadlines: No deadline. Applicants notified on a rolling basis; must reply within 1 week(s) of notification.

Transfers: Aid must be in order or cash paid at registration for classes.

CONTACT

Dorothy Cantor, Financial Aid Coordinator
303 Fort Drive, LaGrange, GA 30240
(706) 845-4323

Young Harris College

Young Harris, Georgia
www.yhc.edu   Federal Code: 001604

2-year private liberal arts college in rural community, affiliated with United Methodist Church.

Enrollment: 639 undergrads; 4% part-time. 356 full-time freshmen.

Selectivity: Admits 50 to 75% of applicants.

BASIC COSTS (2008-2009)

Tuition and fees: $16,630.

Per-credit charge: $500.

Room and board: $5,220.

FINANCIAL AID PICTURE (2006-2007)

Students with need: Out of 252 full-time freshmen who applied for aid, 180 were judged to have need. Of these, 180 received aid, and 51 had their full need met. Average financial aid package met 78% of need; average scholarship/grant was $9,750; average loan was $2,276. For part-time students, average financial aid package was $11,724.

Students without need: 175 full-time freshmen who did not demonstrate need for aid received scholarships/grants; average award was $9,638. No-need awards available for academics, art, athletics, job skills, music/drama, state/district residency.

Scholarships offered: Academic Scholarships; $3,500-$8,500; based on index including GPA and SAT/ACT. Additional awards to a percentage of recipients range from additional $1,000 to full tuition, room and board.

FINANCIAL AID PROCEDURES

Forms required: FAFSA, state aid form, institutional form.
Dates and Deadlines: Priority date 4/1; no closing date. Applicants notified on a rolling basis starting 3/1; must reply within 2 week(s) of notification.

CONTACT

Clinton Hobbs, Vice President for Enrollment Management
PO Box 116, Young Harris, GA 30582-0116
(706) 379-3111 ext. 5117

Hawaii

Brigham Young University-Hawaii

Laie, Hawaii
www.byuh.edu   Federal Code: 001606

4-year private university and liberal arts college in small town, affiliated with Church of Jesus Christ of Latter-day Saints.
Enrollment: 2,312 undergrads, 7% part-time. 211 full-time freshmen.
Selectivity: Admits less than 50% of applicants. GED not accepted.

BASIC COSTS (2008-2009)

Tuition and fees: $3,600.
Room and board: $5,568.
Additional info: 100% higher tuition and per-credit-hour charges for students who are not members of The Church of Jesus Christ of Latter-day Saints.

FINANCIAL AID PICTURE (2006-2007)

Students with need: Out of 185 full-time freshmen who applied for aid, 171 were judged to have need. Of these, 164 received aid, and 90 had their full need met. Average financial aid package met 75% of need; average scholarship/grant was $3,500; average loan was $2,280. For part-time students, average financial aid package was $5,300.
Students without need: 70 full-time freshmen who did not demonstrate need for aid received scholarships/grants; average award was $1,500. No-need awards available for academics, art, athletics, leadership, music/drama, state/district residency.
Scholarships offered: 27 full-time freshmen received athletic scholarships; average amount $2,200.

FINANCIAL AID PROCEDURES

Forms required: FAFSA.
Dates and Deadlines: Closing date 3/15. Applicants notified by 5/1; must reply by 8/31.
Transfers: Closing date 3/15.

CONTACT

Wes Duke, Director of Financial Aid
55-220 Kulanui Street, #1973, Laie, HI 96762-1294
(808) 293-3530

Chaminade University of Honolulu

Honolulu, Hawaii
www.chaminade.edu   Federal Code: 001605

4-year private university in large city, affiliated with Roman Catholic Church.
Enrollment: 1,095 undergrads.
Selectivity: Admits over 75% of applicants.

BASIC COSTS (2008-2009)

Tuition and fees: $15,640.
Per-credit charge: $520.
Room and board: $9,800.

FINANCIAL AID PICTURE

Students with need: Need-based aid available for full-time and part-time students.
Students without need: No-need awards available for academics, art, athletics, leadership, religious affiliation, ROTC, state/district residency.
Additional info: For students whose eligibility for federal and institutional aid does not meet entire costs, alternative student loans may be secured for eligible applicants.

FINANCIAL AID PROCEDURES

Forms required: FAFSA.
Dates and Deadlines: Priority date 2/15; no closing date. Applicants notified on a rolling basis starting 2/15; must reply within 4 week(s) of notification.

CONTACT

Eric Nemoto, Associate Dean of Enrollment Management
3140 Waialae Avenue, Honolulu, HI 96816
(808) 735-4780

Hawaii Pacific University

Honolulu, Hawaii
www.hpu.edu   Federal Code: 007279

4-year private university and liberal arts college in large city.
Enrollment: 6,128 undergrads, 37% part-time. 596 full-time freshmen.
Selectivity: Admits over 75% of applicants.

BASIC COSTS (2008-2009)

Tuition and fees: $13,080.
Per-credit charge: $542.
Room and board: $10,560.

FINANCIAL AID PICTURE (2007-2008)

Students with need: Out of 485 full-time freshmen who applied for aid, 267 were judged to have need. Of these, 251 received aid, and 14 had their full need met. Average financial aid package met 79% of need; average scholarship/grant was $4,511; average loan was $5,487. For part-time students, average financial aid package was $9,012.
Students without need: 67 full-time freshmen who did not demonstrate need for aid received scholarships/grants; average award was $400. No-need awards available for academics, alumni affiliation, athletics, job skills, leadership, music/drama, religious affiliation, ROTC.
Scholarships offered: Makana Scholarship: $2,600; 3.5 GPA or higher. Phi Theta Kappa Scholarship: $6,500; for member of Phi Theta Kappa.

FINANCIAL AID PROCEDURES

Forms required: FAFSA.
Dates and Deadlines: Priority date 3/1; no closing date. Applicants notified on a rolling basis starting 4/1; must reply within 3 week(s) of notification.

CONTACT

Adam Hatch, Director of Financial Aid
1164 Bishop Street, Honolulu, HI 96813
(808) 544-0253

Heald College: Honolulu

Honolulu, Hawaii
www.heald.edu   Federal Code: E00886

2-year private business and technical college in very large city.
Enrollment: 995 undergrads.
Selectivity: Open admission.

BASIC COSTS (2008-2009)

Tuition and fees: $10,800.
Additional info: Fees vary by program.

FINANCIAL AID PICTURE

Students with need: Need-based aid available for full-time and part-time students. Work study available nights, weekends, and for part-time students.
Students without need: This college awards aid only to students with need.

FINANCIAL AID PROCEDURES

Forms required: FAFSA.
Dates and Deadlines: No deadline.

CONTACT

Candice Wong, Director of Financial Aid
1500 Kapiolani Boulevard, Honolulu, HI 96814-3715
(808) 955-1500

Remington College: Honolulu

Honolulu, Hawaii
www.remingtoncollege.edu   Federal Code: 030121

2-year for-profit branch campus college in very large city.
Enrollment: 455 undergrads.

BASIC COSTS (2007-2008)

Additional info: Costs of entire programs leading to certificate, associate degree, bachelor's degree range from $13,000 to $38,880; includes books and supplies. Tuition at time of enrollment locked for 2 years.

FINANCIAL AID PICTURE

Students with need: Need-based aid available for full-time students.
Students without need: This college awards aid only to students with need.

FINANCIAL AID PROCEDURES

Forms required: FAFSA.
Dates and Deadlines: No deadline. Applicants notified on a rolling basis.

CONTACT

Erwin Ramello, Director of Financial Services
1111 Bishop Street, Suite 400, Honolulu, HI 96813-2811

University of Hawaii at Hilo

Hilo, Hawaii
www.uhh.hawaii.edu   Federal Code: 001611

4-year public university in large town.
Enrollment: 3,144 undergrads.
Selectivity: Admits 50 to 75% of applicants.

BASIC COSTS (2007-2008)

Tuition and fees: $3,676; out-of-state residents $11,212.
Per-credit charge: $147; out-of-state residents $461.
Room and board: $6,792.
Additional info: Tuition at time of enrollment locked for 4 years.

FINANCIAL AID PICTURE

Students with need: Need-based aid available for full-time and part-time students. Work study available nights, weekends, and for part-time students.
Additional info: Hawaii student incentive grants and tuition waivers (merit and need-based) available to Hawaii residents at participating institutions.

FINANCIAL AID PROCEDURES

Forms required: FAFSA.
Dates and Deadlines: Priority date 3/1; no closing date. Applicants notified on a rolling basis starting 4/15; must reply within 2 week(s) of notification.

CONTACT

Jeff Schofield, Financial Aid Director
200 West Kawili Street, Hilo, HI 96720-4091
(808) 974-7324

University of Hawaii at Manoa

Honolulu, Hawaii
www.manoa.hawaii.edu   Federal Code: 001610

4-year public university in very large city.
Enrollment: 13,386 undergrads, 18% part-time. 1,609 full-time freshmen.
Selectivity: Admits 50 to 75% of applicants.

BASIC COSTS (2007-2008)

Tuition and fees: $5,390; out-of-state residents $14,654.
Per-credit charge: $214; out-of-state residents $600.
Room and board: $7,335.
Additional info: Tuition/fee waivers available for minority students.

FINANCIAL AID PICTURE (2006-2007)

Students with need: Out of 1,086 full-time freshmen who applied for aid, 545 were judged to have need. Of these, 510 received aid, and 154 had their full need met. Average financial aid package met 68% of need; average scholarship/grant was $4,898; average loan was $2,535. For part-time students, average financial aid package was $5,913.
Students without need: 373 full-time freshmen who did not demonstrate need for aid received scholarships/grants; average award was $4,805. No-need awards available for academics, alumni affiliation, art, athletics, job skills, leadership, minority status, music/drama, religious affiliation, ROTC, state/district residency.
Scholarships offered: 31 full-time freshmen received athletic scholarships; average amount $12,387.
Cumulative student debt: 28% of graduating class had student loans; average debt was $12,094.
Additional info: Hawaii student incentive grants and tuition waivers (merit and need-based) available to Hawaii residents at participating institutions.

FINANCIAL AID PROCEDURES

Forms required: FAFSA.
Dates and Deadlines: Priority date 3/1; no closing date. Applicants notified on a rolling basis starting 3/15; must reply within 4 week(s) of notification.
Transfers: No deadline. Applicants notified on a rolling basis starting 3/15; must reply within 4 week(s) of notification.

CONTACT

Linda Clemons, Director of Financial Aid
2600 Campus Road, QLC Rm 001, Honolulu, HI 96822
(808) 956-7251

University of Hawaii: Hawaii Community College

Hilo, Hawaii
www.hawcc.hawaii.edu   Federal Code: 005258

2-year public community college in small city.
Enrollment: 2,310 undergrads.
Selectivity: Open admission.

BASIC COSTS (2007-2008)

Tuition and fees: $2,024; out-of-state residents $7,814.
Per-credit charge: $63; out-of-state residents $256.

FINANCIAL AID PICTURE

Students with need: Need-based aid available for full-time and part-time students.

Students without need: This college awards aid only to students with need.
Additional info: Hawaii student incentive grants and tuition waivers (merit and need-based) available to Hawaii residents.

FINANCIAL AID PROCEDURES
Forms required: FAFSA.
Dates and Deadlines: Priority date 4/1; no closing date. Applicants notified on a rolling basis starting 5/1; must reply within 2 week(s) of notification.
Transfers: Residents of Guam, Federated States of Micronesia, Palau, Marianas Islands and certain other island nations considered residents for tuition purpose.

CONTACT
Sheryl Lundberg-Spregue, Financial Aid Officer
200 West Kawili Street, Hilo, HI 96720-4091
(808) 974-7663

University of Hawaii: Honolulu Community College
Honolulu, Hawaii
honolulu.hawaii.edu   Federal Code: 001612

2-year public community and technical college in very large city.
Enrollment: 3,326 undergrads.
Selectivity: Open admission; but selective for out-of-state students.

BASIC COSTS (2007-2008)
Tuition and fees: $1,920; out-of-state residents $7,710.
Per-credit charge: $63; out-of-state residents $256.

FINANCIAL AID PICTURE
Students with need: Need-based aid available for full-time and part-time students.
Students without need: No-need awards available for academics, state/district residency.
Additional info: Hawaii student incentive grants and tuition waivers (merit and need-based) available to Hawaii residents at participating institutions.

FINANCIAL AID PROCEDURES
Forms required: FAFSA.
Dates and Deadlines: Priority date 4/1; no closing date. Applicants notified on a rolling basis starting 7/1; must reply within 3 week(s) of notification.

CONTACT
Jannine Oyama, Financial Aid Officer
874 Dillingham Boulevard, Honolulu, HI 96817
(808) 845-9116

University of Hawaii: Kapiolani Community College
Honolulu, Hawaii
www.kcc.hawaii.edu   Federal Code: 001613

2-year public community college in very large city.
Enrollment: 4,909 undergrads.
Selectivity: Open admission; but selective for some programs.

BASIC COSTS (2007-2008)
Tuition and fees: $1,950; out-of-state residents $7,740.
Per-credit charge: $63; out-of-state residents $256.

FINANCIAL AID PICTURE
Students with need: Need-based aid available for full-time and part-time students.

Students without need: This college awards aid only to students with need.
Additional info: Hawaii student incentive grants and tuition waivers (merit and need-based) available to Hawaii residents.

FINANCIAL AID PROCEDURES
Forms required: FAFSA.
Dates and Deadlines: Priority date 4/1; no closing date. Applicants notified on a rolling basis; must reply within 2 week(s) of notification.

CONTACT
Coleen Oshiro, Financial Aid Officer
4303 Diamond Head Road, Honolulu, HI 96816-4421
(808) 734-9555

University of Hawaii: Kauai Community College
Lihue, Hawaii
www.kauai.hawaii.edu   Federal Code: 001614

2-year public community college in small city.
Enrollment: 201 undergrads, 29% part-time. 143 full-time freshmen.
Selectivity: Open admission; but selective for out-of-state students.

BASIC COSTS (2007-2008)
Tuition and fees: $1,930; out-of-state residents $7,720.
Per-credit charge: $63; out-of-state residents $256.

FINANCIAL AID PICTURE
Students with need: Work study available nights.
Additional info: Hawaii student incentive grants and tuition waivers (merit and need-based) available to Hawaii residents.

FINANCIAL AID PROCEDURES
Forms required: FAFSA, institutional form.
Dates and Deadlines: Priority date 4/1; closing date 5/1. Applicants notified on a rolling basis starting 5/1.
Transfers: Academic transcript evaluation by end of first semester is required.

CONTACT
Juana Santacruz, Financial Aid Officer
3-1901 Kaumualii Highway, Lihue, HI 96766-9500
(808) 245-8256

University of Hawaii: Maui Community College
Kahului, Hawaii
www.maui.hawaii.edu

2-year public community college in small city.
Enrollment: 2,303 undergrads, 56% part-time. 289 full-time freshmen.
Selectivity: Open admission; but selective for some programs.

BASIC COSTS (2007-2008)
Tuition and fees: $1,940; out-of-state residents $9,650.
Per-credit charge: $63; out-of-state residents $320.
Additional info: Tuition/fee waivers available for minority students.

FINANCIAL AID PICTURE (2006-2007)
Students with need: 43% of average financial aid package awarded as scholarships/grants, 57% awarded as loans/jobs. Need-based aid available for part-time students. Work study available nights.

FINANCIAL AID PROCEDURES
Forms required: FAFSA, institutional form.

Dates and Deadlines: Priority date 4/1; no closing date. Applicants notified on a rolling basis starting 6/1; must reply within 4 week(s) of notification.

CONTACT

Cathy Bio

310 West Kaahumanu Avenue, Kahului, HI 96732-1617

(808) 984-3277

University of Hawaii: West Oahu

Pearl City, Hawaii

www.westoahu.hawaii.edu   Federal Code: 014315

4-year public liberal arts and teachers college in large town.

Enrollment: 911 undergrads,.64% part-time. 22 full-time freshmen.

Selectivity: Admits 50 to 75% of applicants.

BASIC COSTS (2007-2008)

Tuition and fees: $3,226; out-of-state residents $10,186.

Per-credit charge: $134; out-of-state residents $424.

Additional info: Foreign students pay out-of-state tuition rates. However, citizens of an eligible Pacific island district, commonwealth, territory or insular jurisdiction, state or nation which does not provide public institutions that grant baccalaureate degrees may be allowed to pay 150% of the resident tuition.

FINANCIAL AID PICTURE (2006-2007)

Students with need: 49% of average financial aid package awarded as scholarships/grants, 51% awarded as loans/jobs. Need-based aid available for part-time students.

Students without need: No-need awards available for academics, alumni affiliation, leadership, state/district residency.

Additional info: Tuition waivers (merit and need-based) available to Hawaii residents.

FINANCIAL AID PROCEDURES

Forms required: FAFSA.

Dates and Deadlines: Priority date 4/1; no closing date.

Transfers: No deadline. Applicants notified by 7/1.

CONTACT

Jodie Kuba, Financial Aid Officer

96-129 Ala Ike, Pearl City, HI 96782

(808) 454-4700

University of Hawaii: Windward Community College

Kaneohe, Hawaii

www.wcc.hawaii.edu   Federal Code: 010390

2-year public community college in small city.

Enrollment: 1,761 undergrads.

Selectivity: Open admission.

BASIC COSTS (2007-2008)

Tuition and fees: $1,930; out-of-state residents $7,720.

Per-credit charge: $63; out-of-state residents $256.

Additional info: Tuition/fee waivers available for minority students.

FINANCIAL AID PICTURE

Students with need: Need-based aid available for full-time and part-time students.

Additional info: Hawaii student incentive grants and tuition waivers (merit and need-based) available to Hawaii residents.

FINANCIAL AID PROCEDURES

Forms required: FAFSA.

Dates and Deadlines: Priority date 4/1; no closing date. Applicants notified on a rolling basis starting 3/15; must reply within 2 week(s) of notification.

CONTACT

Steven Chigawa, Financial Aid Officer

45-720 Kea'ahala Road, Kaneohe, HI 96744

(808) 235-7449

Idaho

Boise Bible College

Boise, Idaho

www.boisebible.edu   Federal Code: 015783

4-year private Bible college in small city, affiliated with nondenominational tradition.

Enrollment: 167 undergrads, 10% part-time. 47 full-time freshmen.

Selectivity: Admits 50 to 75% of applicants.

BASIC COSTS (2007-2008)

Tuition and fees: $7,776.

Per-credit charge: $320.

Room and board: $4,740.

FINANCIAL AID PICTURE

Students with need: Need-based aid available for full-time and part-time students.

Students without need: No-need awards available for academics, leadership, music/drama, religious affiliation.

FINANCIAL AID PROCEDURES

Forms required: FAFSA, institutional form.

Dates and Deadlines: Priority date 5/1; no closing date. Applicants notified on a rolling basis starting 5/2; must reply by 8/1 or within 2 week(s) of notification.

Transfers: Financial aid and academic transcripts must be on file before federal aid is awarded.

CONTACT

Joyce Anderson, Financial Aid Officer

8695 West Marigold Street, Boise, ID 83714-1220

(800) 893-7755

Boise State University

Boise, Idaho

www.boisestate.edu   Federal Code: 001616

4-year public university and technical college in small city.

Enrollment: 16,571 undergrads, 32% part-time. 2,286 full-time freshmen.

Selectivity: Admits over 75% of applicants.

BASIC COSTS (2007-2008)

Tuition and fees: $4,410; out-of-state residents $12,578.

Per-credit charge: $227.

Room and board: $5,273.

Additional info: Out-of-state students (undergraduate and graduate) taking less than 8 credit hours pay in-state rate.

FINANCIAL AID PICTURE (2007-2008)

Students with need: Average financial aid package met 64% of need; average scholarship/grant was $3,640; average loan was $3,526. For part-time students, average financial aid package was $7,809.

Students without need: No-need awards available for academics, athletics, music/drama, ROTC, state/district residency.

Cumulative student debt: 66% of graduating class had student loans; average debt was $21,937.

FINANCIAL AID PROCEDURES

Forms required: FAFSA.

Dates and Deadlines: Priority date 4/1; no closing date. Applicants notified on a rolling basis starting 6/1; must reply within 2 week(s) of notification.

Transfers: Financial aid transcripts required from all postsecondary schools attended whether or not financial aid was received.

CONTACT

David Tolman, Director of Financial Aid
1910 University Drive, Boise, ID 83725
(208) 426-1664

Brigham Young University-Idaho

Rexburg, Idaho
www.byui.edu   Federal Code: 001625

4-year private university in large town, affiliated with Church of Jesus Christ of Latter-day Saints.

Enrollment: 13,155 undergrads.

BASIC COSTS (2007-2008)

Tuition and fees: $3,360.

Room and board: $6,300.

Additional info: Tuition for students who are not members of The Church of Jesus Christ of Latter-day Saints is $6,120 for academic year.

FINANCIAL AID PICTURE

Students with need: Need-based aid available for full-time and part-time students.

Students without need: No-need awards available for academics, athletics, leadership.

Additional info: Application deadline for merit scholarships 3/1.

FINANCIAL AID PROCEDURES

Forms required: FAFSA.

Dates and Deadlines: Priority date 5/1; no closing date. Applicants notified on a rolling basis starting 2/1.

CONTACT

Aaron Sans, Director of Financial Aid
120 Kimball Building, Rexburg, ID 83460-1615
(208) 496-1015

College of Idaho

Caldwell, Idaho
www.collegeofidaho.edu   Federal Code: 001617

4-year private liberal arts college in large town.

Enrollment: 813 undergrads, 4% part-time. 227 full-time freshmen.

Selectivity: Admits over 75% of applicants.

BASIC COSTS (2008-2009)

Tuition and fees: $18,990.

Per-credit charge: $760.

Room and board: $6,631.

Additional info: Tuition/fee waivers available for adults.

FINANCIAL AID PICTURE (2007-2008)

Students with need: Out of 153 full-time freshmen who applied for aid, 101 were judged to have need. Of these, 101 received aid, and 35 had their full need met. Average financial aid package met 78% of need; average scholarship/grant was $4,188; average loan was $4,615. For part-time students, average financial aid package was $8,994.

Students without need: 81 full-time freshmen who did not demonstrate need for aid received scholarships/grants; average award was $11,556. No-need awards available for academics, alumni affiliation, art, athletics, leadership, minority status, music/drama, religious affiliation, ROTC, state/district residency.

Scholarships offered: *Merit:* Albertson Heritage Scholarship: full tuition; minimum 3.85-4.0 GPA and 31-33 ACT or 1380-1470 SAT. Presidential Scholarship: $10,000/year; requirements range from 2.9 GPA and 36 ACT or 1590 SAT to 4.0 GPA and 29 ACT or 1280 SAT. Trustee Scholarship: $7,500/year; requirements range from 2.50 GPA and 36 ACT or 1590 SAT to 4.0 GPA and 25 ACT or 1125 SAT. Dean Grant: $5,000/year; requirements range from 2.5 GPA and 32 ACT or 1400 SAT to 4.0 GPA and 24 ACT or 1090 SAT. All SAT scores exclusive of writing. Alumni Scholarship: $2,500; 2.5 GPA and 27 ACT or 1200 SAT. ***Athletic:*** 81 full-time freshmen received athletic scholarships; average amount $10,824.

Cumulative student debt: 56% of graduating class had student loans; average debt was $26,170.

FINANCIAL AID PROCEDURES

Forms required: FAFSA, institutional form.

Dates and Deadlines: Priority date 2/15; no closing date. Applicants notified on a rolling basis starting 1/31; must reply within 3 week(s) of notification.

Transfers: No deadline. Applicants notified on a rolling basis starting 1/31; must reply within 3 week(s) of notification.

CONTACT

Juanitta Pearson, Director of Student Financial Services
2112 Cleveland Boulevard, Caldwell, ID 83605
(208) 459-5308

College of Southern Idaho

Twin Falls, Idaho
www.csi.edu   Federal Code: 001619

2-year public community and junior college in large town.

Enrollment: 5,227 undergrads.

Selectivity: Open admission; but selective for some programs.

BASIC COSTS (2007-2008)

Tuition and fees: $2,100; out-of-state residents $5,900.

Per-credit charge: $105; out-of-state residents $295.

Room and board: $4,630.

FINANCIAL AID PICTURE

Students with need: Need-based aid available for full-time and part-time students.

Additional info: Out-of-state tuition waivers based on GPA and activities.

FINANCIAL AID PROCEDURES

Forms required: FAFSA.

Dates and Deadlines: Priority date 3/1; no closing date. Applicants notified on a rolling basis starting 4/30; must reply within 3 week(s) of notification.

CONTACT

Colin Randolph, Director of Student Financial Aid
Box 1238, Twin Falls, ID 83303-1238
(208) 732-6273

Eastern Idaho Technical College

Idaho Falls, Idaho
www.eitc.edu   Federal Code: 011133

2-year public technical college in small city.

Enrollment: 647 undergrads, 68% part-time. 66 full-time freshmen.

Selectivity: Open admission; but selective for some programs.

PART III: FINANCIAL AID COLLEGE BY COLLEGE

BASIC COSTS (2007-2008)

Tuition and fees: $1,758; out-of-state residents $6,112.

Per-credit charge: $82; out-of-state residents $164.

Additional info: Fees may vary according to the program of study.

FINANCIAL AID PICTURE

Students with need: Need-based aid available for full-time and part-time students.

Students without need: No-need awards available for academics, job skills, state/district residency.

FINANCIAL AID PROCEDURES

Forms required: FAFSA, institutional form.

Dates and Deadlines: Priority date 6/1; no closing date. Applicants notified on a rolling basis starting 6/6; must reply within 4 week(s) of notification.

CONTACT

Shayna Sharp, Director of Financial Aid

1600 South 25th East, Idaho Falls, ID 83404-5788

(208) 524-3000 ext. 3389

Idaho State University

Pocatello, Idaho

www.isu.edu

Federal Code: 001620

4-year public university in small city.

Enrollment: 9,347 undergrads, 26% part-time. 950 full-time freshmen.

Selectivity: Admits over 75% of applicants.

BASIC COSTS (2007-2008)

Tuition and fees: $4,400; out-of-state residents $13,084.

Per-credit charge: $221; out-of-state residents $341.

Room and board: $5,346.

Additional info: $1,046 refundable health insurance.

FINANCIAL AID PICTURE (2006-2007)

Students with need: Out of 762 full-time freshmen who applied for aid, 549 were judged to have need. Of these, 535 received aid, and 57 had their full need met. Average financial aid package met 56% of need; average scholarship/grant was $2,908; average loan was $2,088. For part-time students, average financial aid package was $3,759.

Students without need: 319 full-time freshmen who did not demonstrate need for aid received scholarships/grants; average award was $2,226. No-need awards available for academics, alumni affiliation, art, athletics, leadership, minority status, music/drama, ROTC, state/district residency.

Scholarships offered: 52 full-time freshmen received athletic scholarships; average amount $8,968.

Cumulative student debt: 72% of graduating class had student loans; average debt was $21,862.

FINANCIAL AID PROCEDURES

Forms required: FAFSA.

Dates and Deadlines: Priority date 3/1; no closing date. Applicants notified on a rolling basis starting 4/1.

CONTACT

Doug Severs, Director of Financial Aid

921 South 8th Stop 8270, Pocatello, ID 83209-8270

(208) 282-2756

Lewis-Clark State College

Lewiston, Idaho

www.lcsc.edu

Federal Code: 001621

4-year public liberal arts and technical college in small city.

Enrollment: 2,944 undergrads, 23% part-time. 454 full-time freshmen.

Selectivity: Admits 50 to 75% of applicants.

BASIC COSTS (2007-2008)

Tuition and fees: $4,092; out-of-state residents $11,382.

Per-credit charge: $204.

Room and board: $4,800.

FINANCIAL AID PICTURE (2006-2007)

Students with need: Out of 358 full-time freshmen who applied for aid, 302 were judged to have need. Of these, 290 received aid, and 14 had their full need met. Average financial aid package met 5% of need; average scholarship/grant was $2,966; average loan was $2,246. For part-time students, average financial aid package was $5,243.

Students without need: 209 full-time freshmen who did not demonstrate need for aid received scholarships/grants; average award was $1,413. No-need awards available for academics, alumni affiliation, art, athletics, leadership, minority status, music/drama.

Scholarships offered: 24 full-time freshmen received athletic scholarships; average amount $5,764.

FINANCIAL AID PROCEDURES

Forms required: FAFSA.

Dates and Deadlines: Priority date 3/1; no closing date. Applicants notified on a rolling basis starting 4/15; must reply within 2 week(s) of notification.

CONTACT

Laura Hughes, Director of Financial Aid

500 Eighth Avenue, Lewiston, ID 83501-2698

(208) 792-2224

North Idaho College

Coeur d'Alene, Idaho

www.nic.edu

Federal Code: 001623

2-year public community college in large town.

Enrollment: 3,789 undergrads, 37% part-time. 816 full-time freshmen.

Selectivity: Open admission; but selective for some programs.

BASIC COSTS (2007-2008)

Tuition and fees: $2,110; out-of-district residents $3,110; out-of-state residents $7,478.

Per-credit charge: $141; out-of-district residents $204; out-of-state residents $426.

Room and board: $5,620.

Additional info: Tuition/fee waivers available for minority students.

FINANCIAL AID PICTURE (2006-2007)

Students with need: 59% of average financial aid package awarded as scholarships/grants, 41% awarded as loans/jobs. Need-based aid available for part-time students. Work study available weekends and for part-time students.

Students without need: No-need awards available for academics, art, athletics, leadership, minority status, music/drama, state/district residency.

FINANCIAL AID PROCEDURES

Forms required: FAFSA.

Dates and Deadlines: Priority date 3/15; no closing date. Applicants notified on a rolling basis starting 4/1; must reply within 2 week(s) of notification.

CONTACT

Jennifer Montgomery, Director of Financial Aid

1000 West Garden Avenue, Coeur d'Alene, ID 83814-2199

(208) 769-3368

Northwest Nazarene University
Nampa, Idaho
www.nnu.edu   Federal Code: 001624

4-year private university in small city, affiliated with Church of the Nazarene.
Enrollment: 1,189 undergrads, 5% part-time. 238 full-time freshmen.
Selectivity: Admits 50 to 75% of applicants.

BASIC COSTS (2008-2009)
Tuition and fees: $21,170.
Per-credit charge: $905.
Room and board: $5,520.

FINANCIAL AID PICTURE (2007-2008)
Students with need: Out of 204 full-time freshmen who applied for aid, 184 were judged to have need. Of these, 184 received aid, and 49 had their full need met. Average financial aid package met 84% of need; average scholarship/grant was $7,818; average loan was $3,503. For part-time students, average financial aid package was $10,971.
Students without need: 54 full-time freshmen who did not demonstrate need for aid received scholarships/grants; average award was $5,140. No-need awards available for academics, alumni affiliation, art, athletics, leadership, minority status, music/drama, religious affiliation, ROTC.
Scholarships offered: *Merit:* Merit scholarships for freshmen based primarily on cumulative high school GPA and ACT test scores. *Athletic:* 48 full-time freshmen received athletic scholarships; average amount $6,129.
Cumulative student debt: 76% of graduating class had student loans; average debt was $23,841.

FINANCIAL AID PROCEDURES
Forms required: FAFSA, institutional form.
Dates and Deadlines: Priority date 3/1; no closing date. Applicants notified on a rolling basis starting 3/1; must reply within 3 week(s) of notification.

CONTACT
Wes Maggard, Director of Financial Aid
623 Holly Street, Nampa, ID 83686-5897
(208) 467-8347

University of Idaho
Moscow, Idaho
www.uidaho.edu   Federal Code: 001626

4-year public university in large town.
Enrollment: 8,471 undergrads, 6% part-time. 1,613 full-time freshmen.
Selectivity: Admits over 75% of applicants.

BASIC COSTS (2007-2008)
Tuition and fees: $4,410; out-of-state residents $14,490.
Per-credit charge: $212; out-of-state residents $360.
Room and board: $6,424.
Additional info: Tuition/fee waivers available for minority students.

FINANCIAL AID PICTURE (2006-2007)
Students with need: Out of 1,238 full-time freshmen who applied for aid, 926 were judged to have need. Of these, 909 received aid, and 233 had their full need met. Average financial aid package met 75% of need; average scholarship/grant was $3,136; average loan was $3,410. For part-time students, average financial aid package was $6,685.
Students without need: 490 full-time freshmen who did not demonstrate need for aid received scholarships/grants; average award was $3,024. No-need awards available for academics, alumni affiliation, art, athletics, leadership, minority status, music/drama, religious affiliation, ROTC, state/district residency.
Scholarships offered: 50 full-time freshmen received athletic scholarships; average amount $13,300.

Cumulative student debt: 66% of graduating class had student loans; average debt was $21,609.

FINANCIAL AID PROCEDURES
Forms required: FAFSA.
Dates and Deadlines: Priority date 2/15; no closing date. Applicants notified on a rolling basis starting 3/30; must reply within 4 week(s) of notification.
Transfers: No deadline. Applicants notified on a rolling basis starting 3/30; must reply within 4 week(s) of notification.

CONTACT
Daniel Davenport, Director of Admissions and Student Financial Aid
PO Box 444264, Moscow, ID 83844-4264
(208) 885-6312

Illinois

Augustana College
Rock Island, Illinois
www.augustana.edu   Federal Code: 001633

4-year private liberal arts college in large city, affiliated with Evangelical Lutheran Church in America.
Enrollment: 2,518 undergrads, 1% part-time. 691 full-time freshmen.
Selectivity: Admits 50 to 75% of applicants.

BASIC COSTS (2008-2009)
Tuition and fees: $30,150.
Per-credit charge: $1,300.
Room and board: $7,650.
Additional info: Tuition at time of enrollment locked for 4 years.

FINANCIAL AID PICTURE (2006-2007)
Students with need: Out of 580 full-time freshmen who applied for aid, 467 were judged to have need. Of these, 466 received aid, and 136 had their full need met. Average financial aid package met 83% of need; average scholarship/grant was $12,891; average loan was $3,717.
Students without need: 111 full-time freshmen who did not demonstrate need for aid received scholarships/grants; average award was $10,210. No-need awards available for academics, alumni affiliation, art, leadership, music/drama, religious affiliation.
Scholarships offered: Presidential Scholarship; $10,000 to full tuition; 28 ACT composite score (1260 combined SAT score in critical reading and mathematics) and rank in the top ten percent of high school class. Dean's Scholarship; $7,750-$9,000; 25 ACT composite score or above (1140 combined SAT score in critical reading and mathematics) and rank in the top 20 percent of their high school class. Founders Scholarship; $5,000-$7,500; must plan to enroll full-time at Augustana College. Transfer Scholarship; $3,000-$6,000; demonstrated outstanding academic performance in previous college studies.
Cumulative student debt: 70% of graduating class had student loans; average debt was $16,716.

FINANCIAL AID PROCEDURES
Forms required: FAFSA, institutional form.
Dates and Deadlines: Priority date 4/1; no closing date. Applicants notified on a rolling basis.
Transfers: Priority date 5/1. Financial aid transcripts from previous institutions required.

CONTACT
Sue Standley, Director of Financial Assistance
639 38th Street, Rock Island, IL 61201-2296
(309) 794-7207

Aurora University

Aurora, Illinois
www.aurora.edu   Federal Code: 001634

4-year private university in small city.

Enrollment: 2,065 undergrads, 14% part-time. 342 full-time freshmen.

Selectivity: Admits 50 to 75% of applicants.

BASIC COSTS (2008-2009)

Tuition and fees: $17,500.

Per-credit charge: $530.

Room and board: $7,250.

Additional info: Course laboratory fees in sciences, photography, nursing, physical education and student teaching. Tuition will vary for several adult degree completion programs.

FINANCIAL AID PICTURE (2007-2008)

Students with need: Out of 306 full-time freshmen who applied for aid, 255 were judged to have need. Of these, 255 received aid, and 82 had their full need met. Average financial aid package met 88% of need; average scholarship/grant was $6,633; average loan was $3,287. For part-time students, average financial aid package was $10,032.

Students without need: 79 full-time freshmen who did not demonstrate need for aid received scholarships/grants; average award was $10,042. No-need awards available for academics, alumni affiliation, art, music/drama, religious affiliation, ROTC, state/district residency.

Scholarships offered: Board of Trustees scholarships; $8,000. James E. Crimi Presidential Scholarships; $6,500. Dean's scholarships; $6,000. Aurora University Opportunity Grants; $3,000-$5,000.

Cumulative student debt: 77% of graduating class had student loans; average debt was $18,078.

FINANCIAL AID PROCEDURES

Forms required: FAFSA.

Dates and Deadlines: Priority date 4/15; no closing date. Applicants notified on a rolling basis starting 3/1; must reply by 5/1 or within 3 week(s) of notification.

CONTACT

Heather McKane, Dean of Student Financial Services
347 South Gladstone Avenue, Aurora, IL 60506-4892
(630) 844-5533

Benedictine University

Lisle, Illinois
www.ben.edu   Federal Code: 001767

4-year private university and liberal arts college in large town, affiliated with Roman Catholic Church.

Enrollment: 2,883 undergrads, 32% part-time. 386 full-time freshmen.

Selectivity: Admits over 75% of applicants.

BASIC COSTS (2008-2009)

Tuition and fees: $21,310.

Per-credit charge: $695.

Room and board: $6,955.

Additional info: Tuition/fee waivers available for adults, minority students.

FINANCIAL AID PICTURE (2007-2008)

Students with need: For part-time students, average financial aid package was $4,706.

Students without need: No-need awards available for academics, alumni affiliation, minority status, music/drama, ROTC.

Additional info: Need-based financial aid available to part-time students who are enrolled at least half-time.

FINANCIAL AID PROCEDURES

Forms required: FAFSA, institutional form.

Dates and Deadlines: Priority date 4/15; no closing date. Applicants notified on a rolling basis starting 2/15; must reply within 2 week(s) of notification.

Transfers: No deadline.

CONTACT

Diane Battistella, Associate Dean
5700 College Road, Lisle, IL 60532
(630) 829-6100

Black Hawk College

Moline, Illinois
www.bhc.edu   Federal Code: 001638

2-year public community college in large town.

Enrollment: 4,801 undergrads, 44% part-time. 758 full-time freshmen.

Selectivity: Open admission; but selective for some programs.

BASIC COSTS (2007-2008)

Tuition and fees: $2,430; out-of-district residents $4,650; out-of-state residents $8,220.

Per-credit charge: $74; out-of-district residents $148; out-of-state residents $267.

Additional info: Agreement with 5 contiguous Iowa counties for special tuition rate of $108 per credit plus required fees of $210. $88 per-credit-hour charge for on-line classes.

FINANCIAL AID PICTURE (2006-2007)

Students with need: Out of 638 full-time freshmen who applied for aid, 425 were judged to have need. Of these, 374 received aid, and 61 had their full need met. Average financial aid package met 76% of need; average scholarship/grant was $2,032; average loan was $1,421. For part-time students, average financial aid package was $1,445.

Students without need: 50 full-time freshmen who did not demonstrate need for aid received scholarships/grants; average award was $1,001. No-need awards available for academics, art, athletics, leadership, music/drama, state/district residency.

Scholarships offered: *Merit:* Scholarship program; based on need and/or merit. Tuition awards; awarded to students who graduate in the top 10% of their class. *Athletic:* 54 full-time freshmen received athletic scholarships; average amount $2,094.

Cumulative student debt: 25% of graduating class had student loans; average debt was $4,377.

Additional info: 5/15 deadline for scholarships.

FINANCIAL AID PROCEDURES

Forms required: FAFSA.

Dates and Deadlines: Priority date 5/15; no closing date. Applicants notified on a rolling basis starting 5/1.

CONTACT

Joanna Dye, Director, Financial Aid
6600 34th Avenue, Moline, IL 61265-5899
(309) 796-5400

Blackburn College

Carlinville, Illinois
www.blackburn.edu   Federal Code: 001639

4-year private liberal arts college in small town, affiliated with Presbyterian Church (USA).

Enrollment: 613 undergrads, 2% part-time. 180 full-time freshmen.

Selectivity: Admits 50 to 75% of applicants.

BASIC COSTS (2008-2009)

Tuition and fees: $13,610.

Per-credit charge: $450.

Room and board: $4,363.

Additional info: All on-campus students participate in a work program which reduces net tuition costs.

FINANCIAL AID PICTURE (2007-2008)

Students with need: Out of 179 full-time freshmen who applied for aid, 159 were judged to have need. Of these, 159 received aid, and 73 had their full need met. Average financial aid package met 88% of need; average scholarship/grant was $9,955; average loan was $2,004. For part-time students, average financial aid package was $3,127.

Students without need: 21 full-time freshmen who did not demonstrate need for aid received scholarships/grants; average award was $7,099. No-need awards available for academics, state/district residency.

Cumulative student debt: 97% of graduating class had student loans; average debt was $19,500.

Additional info: Each resident student works 160 hours per semester.

FINANCIAL AID PROCEDURES

Forms required: FAFSA.

Dates and Deadlines: Priority date 4/1; no closing date. Applicants notified on a rolling basis starting 3/1; must reply within 4 week(s) of notification.

Transfers: No deadline. Applicants notified on a rolling basis; must reply within 4 week(s) of notification.

CONTACT

Jane Kelsey, Director of Financial Aid

700 College Avenue, Carlinville, IL 62626

(217) 854-3231 ext. 4283

Blessing-Rieman College of Nursing

Quincy, Illinois

www.brcn.edu   Federal Code: 006214

4-year private nursing college in large town.

Enrollment: 211 undergrads, 6% part-time. 20 full-time freshmen.

Selectivity: Admits over 75% of applicants.

BASIC COSTS (2007-2008)

Tuition and fees: $17,775.

Per-credit charge: $465.

Additional info: Tuition and fees are average costs charged to freshman. Partnered with Quincy University and Culver-Stockton College. Freshmen and sophomores pay partnering school's tuition rate.

FINANCIAL AID PICTURE

Students with need: Need-based aid available for full-time and part-time students.

Additional info: Financial aid for freshmen and sophomores administered by Culver-Stockton College and Quincy University.

FINANCIAL AID PROCEDURES

Forms required: FAFSA.

Dates and Deadlines: No deadline.

CONTACT

Sara Brehm, Financial Aid Officer

PO Box 7005, Quincy, IL 62305-7005

(217) 228-5520 ext. 6993

Bradley University

Peoria, Illinois

www.bradley.edu   Federal Code: 001641

4-year private university in large city.

Enrollment: 5,205 undergrads, 5% part-time. 1,076 full-time freshmen.

Selectivity: Admits over 75% of applicants.

BASIC COSTS (2007-2008)

Tuition and fees: $21,378.

Room and board: $7,050.

FINANCIAL AID PICTURE (2006-2007)

Students with need: Out of 905 full-time freshmen who applied for aid, 686 were judged to have need. Of these, 686 received aid, and 322 had their full need met. Average financial aid package met 79% of need; average scholarship/grant was $11,370; average loan was $3,713. Need-based aid available for part-time students.

Students without need: 251 full-time freshmen who did not demonstrate need for aid received scholarships/grants; average award was $11,067. No-need awards available for academics, alumni affiliation, art, athletics, leadership, music/drama.

Scholarships offered: 13 full-time freshmen received athletic scholarships; average amount $13,747.

FINANCIAL AID PROCEDURES

Forms required: FAFSA.

Dates and Deadlines: Priority date 3/1; no closing date. Applicants notified on a rolling basis starting 2/15.

CONTACT

Dave Pardieck, Financial Assistance Director

1501 West Bradley Avenue, Peoria, IL 61625

(309) 677-3089

Carl Sandburg College

Galesburg, Illinois

www.sandburg.edu   Federal Code: 007265

2-year public community college in large town.

Enrollment: 2,124 undergrads.

Selectivity: Open admission; but selective for some programs.

BASIC COSTS (2007-2008)

Tuition and fees: $3,285; out-of-district residents $4,635; out-of-state residents $5,010.

FINANCIAL AID PICTURE

Students with need: Need-based aid available for full-time students.

Students without need: No-need awards available for academics, art, athletics.

FINANCIAL AID PROCEDURES

Forms required: FAFSA, institutional form.

Dates and Deadlines: Priority date 5/1; no closing date. Applicants notified on a rolling basis starting 6/15; must reply within 2 week(s) of notification.

CONTACT

Lisa Hanson, Director of Financial Aid

2400 Tom L. Wilson Boulevard, Galesburg, IL 61401

(309) 341-5283

Chicago State University
Chicago, Illinois
www.csu.edu   Federal Code: 001694

4-year public university in very large city.

Enrollment: 5,157 undergrads.

Selectivity: Admits 50 to 75% of applicants.

BASIC COSTS (2007-2008)

Tuition and fees: $7,730; out-of-state residents $13,850.

Per-credit charge: $206; out-of-state residents $410.

Room and board: $6,752.

Additional info: Rates are guaranteed for all four years. Tuition quoted is for first-time freshmen. Tuition at time of enrollment locked for 4 years.

FINANCIAL AID PICTURE (2006-2007)

Students with need: 52% of average financial aid package awarded as scholarships/grants, 48% awarded as loans/jobs.

Students without need: No-need awards available for academics, athletics, ROTC, state/district residency.

Additional info: Freshmen of outstanding academic ability and talent eligible for Scholars Program full-tuition scholarship.

FINANCIAL AID PROCEDURES

Forms required: FAFSA, institutional form.

Dates and Deadlines: Priority date 3/1; no closing date.

Transfers: Priority date 3/31. Must have valid financial aid transcripts from previous institutions whether or not aid was received.

CONTACT

Brenda Hooker, Director

9501 South King Drive, Chicago, IL 60628

(773) 995-2304

City Colleges of Chicago: Harold Washington College
Chicago, Illinois
www.ccc.edu   Federal Code: 001652

2-year public community college in very large city.

Enrollment: 7,623 undergrads.

Selectivity: Open admission; but selective for some programs.

BASIC COSTS (2007-2008)

Tuition and fees: $2,410; out-of-district residents $5,949; out-of-state residents $9,543.

Per-credit charge: $72; out-of-district residents $190; out-of-state residents $310.

FINANCIAL AID PICTURE

Students with need: Need-based aid available for full-time and part-time students. Work study available nights.

Students without need: This college awards aid only to students with need.

FINANCIAL AID PROCEDURES

Forms required: FAFSA.

Dates and Deadlines: Priority date 5/1; closing date 6/30. Applicants notified on a rolling basis starting 7/1; must reply within 2 week(s) of notification.

CONTACT

Francois Hasouk, Director of Financial Aid

30 East Lake Street, Chicago, IL 60601

(312) 553-6041

City Colleges of Chicago: Harry S. Truman College
Chicago, Illinois
www.ccc.edu   Federal Code: 001648

2-year public community college in very large city.

Enrollment: 4,991 undergrads.

Selectivity: Open admission; but selective for some programs.

BASIC COSTS (2007-2008)

Tuition and fees: $2,410; out-of-district residents $5,949; out-of-state residents $9,543.

Per-credit charge: $72; out-of-district residents $190; out-of-state residents $310.

FINANCIAL AID PICTURE

Students with need: Need-based aid available for full-time and part-time students. Work study available nights, weekends, and for part-time students.

Students without need: This college awards aid only to students with need.

FINANCIAL AID PROCEDURES

Forms required: FAFSA.

Dates and Deadlines: No deadline. Applicants notified on a rolling basis starting 7/1; must reply within 3 week(s) of notification.

CONTACT

Shirley Howell, Director of Financial Aid

1145 West Wilson Avenue, Chicago, IL 60640

(773) 907-4810

City Colleges of Chicago: Kennedy-King College
Chicago, Illinois
www.ccc.edu   Federal Code: 001654

2-year public community college in very large city.

Enrollment: 4,245 undergrads.

Selectivity: Open admission.

BASIC COSTS (2007-2008)

Tuition and fees: $2,410; out-of-district residents $5,949; out-of-state residents $9,543.

Per-credit charge: $72; out-of-district residents $190; out-of-state residents $310.

Additional info: Lab fees for technical and vocational courses.

FINANCIAL AID PICTURE

Students with need: Need-based aid available for full-time and part-time students.

Students without need: This college awards aid only to students with need.

FINANCIAL AID PROCEDURES

Forms required: FAFSA.

Dates and Deadlines: Priority date 8/1; no closing date. Applicants notified on a rolling basis starting 8/15; must reply within 2 week(s) of notification.

CONTACT

Alicia Williams, Financial Aid Supervisor

6800 South Wentworth Avenue, Chicago, IL 60621

(773) 602-5133

City Colleges of Chicago: Malcolm X College

Chicago, Illinois
www.malcolmx.ccc.edu   Federal Code: 001650

2-year public community and junior college in very large city.
Enrollment: 3,554 undergrads.
Selectivity: Open admission; but selective for some programs.

BASIC COSTS (2007-2008)
Tuition and fees: $2,410; out-of-district residents $5,949; out-of-state residents $9,543.
Per-credit charge: $72; out-of-district residents $190; out-of-state residents $310.
Additional info: Some courses require a $20 lab fee.

FINANCIAL AID PICTURE
Students with need: Need-based aid available for full-time and part-time students. Work study available nights, weekends, and for part-time students.
Students without need: This college awards aid only to students with need.

FINANCIAL AID PROCEDURES
Forms required: FAFSA, institutional form.
Dates and Deadlines: Priority date 7/1; no closing date. Applicants notified on a rolling basis starting 7/1; must reply within 2 week(s) of notification.

CONTACT
Patricia Burke, Director, Financial Aid
1900 West Van Buren Street, Chicago, IL 60612
(312) 850-7146

City Colleges of Chicago: Olive-Harvey College

Chicago, Illinois
www.ccc.edu   Federal Code: 009767

2-year public community college in very large city.
Enrollment: 2,278 undergrads.
Selectivity: Open admission; but selective for some programs.

BASIC COSTS (2007-2008)
Tuition and fees: $2,410; out-of-district residents $5,949; out-of-state residents $9,543.
Per-credit charge: $72; out-of-district residents $190; out-of-state residents $310.

FINANCIAL AID PICTURE
Students with need: Need-based aid available for full-time and part-time students.

FINANCIAL AID PROCEDURES
Forms required: FAFSA.
Dates and Deadlines: Priority date 8/15; no closing date. Applicants notified on a rolling basis; must reply within 3 week(s) of notification.

CONTACT
Michael Shields, Director of Financial Aid
10001 South Woodlawn Avenue, Chicago, IL 60628
(773) 291-6391

City Colleges of Chicago: Richard J. Daley College

Chicago, Illinois
daley.ccc.edu   Federal Code: 001649

2-year public community college in very large city.
Enrollment: 4,015 undergrads.
Selectivity: Open admission; but selective for some programs.

BASIC COSTS (2007-2008)
Tuition and fees: $2,410; out-of-district residents $5,949; out-of-state residents $9,543.
Per-credit charge: $72; out-of-district residents $190; out-of-state residents $310.

FINANCIAL AID PICTURE
Students with need: Need-based aid available for full-time students.

FINANCIAL AID PROCEDURES
Forms required: FAFSA.
Dates and Deadlines: No deadline. Applicants notified on a rolling basis.
Transfers: College workstudy jobs and Federal Supplemental Educational Opportunity Grant (SEOG) may not be available to transfers.

CONTACT
Thelma Barnes, Dean of Student Services
7500 South Pulaski Road, Chicago, IL 60652
(773) 838-7579

City Colleges of Chicago: Wright College

Chicago, Illinois
www.ccc.edu   Federal Code: 001655

2-year public community college in very large city.
Enrollment: 7,013 undergrads.
Selectivity: Open admission.

BASIC COSTS (2007-2008)
Tuition and fees: $2,410; out-of-district residents $5,949; out-of-state residents $9,543.
Per-credit charge: $72; out-of-district residents $190; out-of-state residents $310.
Additional info: Tuition at time of enrollment locked for 2 years.

FINANCIAL AID PICTURE
Students with need: Need-based aid available for full-time and part-time students. Work study available nights, weekends, and for part-time students.

FINANCIAL AID PROCEDURES
Forms required: FAFSA, institutional form.
Dates and Deadlines: Priority date 6/1; no closing date. Applicants notified on a rolling basis starting 7/15.

CONTACT
Marco Sepulveda, Financial Aid Director
4300 North Narragansett Avenue, Chicago, IL 60634-4276
(773) 481-8100

College of DuPage

Glen Ellyn, Illinois
www.cod.edu   Federal Code: 006656

2-year public community college in large town.
Enrollment: 21,988 undergrads, 59% part-time. 1,913 full-time freshmen.
Selectivity: Open admission; but selective for some programs.

BASIC COSTS (2008-2009)

Tuition and fees: $3,240; out-of-district residents $8,880; out-of-state residents $10,770.

Per-credit charge: $88; out-of-district residents $276; out-of-state residents $339.

FINANCIAL AID PICTURE (2006-2007)

Students with need: Out of 713 full-time freshmen who applied for aid, 489 were judged to have need. Of these, 390 received aid, and 19 had their full need met. Average financial aid package met 66% of need; average scholarship/grant was $3,973; average loan was $2,112. For part-time students, average financial aid package was $4,065.

Students without need: 14 full-time freshmen who did not demonstrate need for aid received scholarships/grants; average award was $1,179. No-need awards available for academics, art, leadership, minority status, music/drama, state/district residency.

FINANCIAL AID PROCEDURES

Forms required: FAFSA.

Dates and Deadlines: Priority date 4/30; no closing date. Applicants notified on a rolling basis starting 6/1; must reply within 2 week(s) of notification.

Transfers: No deadline. Applicants notified on a rolling basis; must reply within 2 week(s) of notification. Must have financial aid application on file indicating previous institutions attended.

CONTACT

Mark Holysz, Director of Student Financial Aid
425 Fawell Boulevard, Glen Ellyn, IL 60137-6599
(630) 942-2251

College of Lake County

Grayslake, Illinois
www.clcillinois.edu   Federal Code: 007694

2-year public community college in large town.

Enrollment: 12,192 undergrads, 64% part-time. 1,243 full-time freshmen.

Selectivity: Open admission; but selective for some programs.

BASIC COSTS (2008-2009)

Tuition and fees: $2,700; out-of-district residents $6,450; out-of-state residents $8,580.

Per-credit charge: $76; out-of-district residents $201; out-of-state residents $272.

Additional info: Tuition/fee waivers available for minority students.

FINANCIAL AID PICTURE

Students with need: Need-based aid available for full-time and part-time students. Work study available nights.

Students without need: No-need awards available for academics, alumni affiliation, art, athletics, leadership, minority status, music/drama.

Scholarships offered: Academic Achievement Scholarship: based on GPA and student essay; tuition and fees.

FINANCIAL AID PROCEDURES

Forms required: FAFSA.

Dates and Deadlines: Priority date 6/5; no closing date. Applicants notified on a rolling basis starting 6/15; must reply within 2 week(s) of notification.

CONTACT

Karen Hlavin, Assistant Vice President, Student Development
19351 West Washington Street, Grayslake, IL 60030-1198
(847) 543-2062

College of Office Technology

Chicago, Illinois
www.cot.edu   Federal Code: 017378

2-year for-profit business college in very large city.

Enrollment: 368 undergrads.

Selectivity: Open admission.

BASIC COSTS (2008-2009)

Tuition and fees: $9,925.

FINANCIAL AID PICTURE

Students with need: Need-based aid available for full-time and part-time students.

Students without need: This college awards aid only to students with need.

FINANCIAL AID PROCEDURES

Forms required: FAFSA.

Dates and Deadlines: No deadline. Applicants notified on a rolling basis.

CONTACT

Paula Terronez, Educational Operations and Financial Aid Director
1520 West Division Street, Chicago, IL 60622-3312
(773) 278-0042

Columbia College Chicago

Chicago, Illinois
www.colum.edu   Federal Code: 001665

4-year private visual arts and liberal arts college in very large city.

Enrollment: 11,256 undergrads, 11% part-time. 2,166 full-time freshmen.

Selectivity: Open admission; but selective for some programs.

BASIC COSTS (2007-2008)

Tuition and fees: $17,564.

Per-credit charge: $592.

Room and board: $12,018.

FINANCIAL AID PICTURE

Students with need: Need-based aid available for full-time and part-time students.

Students without need: No-need awards available for academics, art, leadership, music/drama, state/district residency.

FINANCIAL AID PROCEDURES

Forms required: FAFSA, institutional form.

Dates and Deadlines: Priority date 5/1; no closing date. Applicants notified on a rolling basis.

CONTACT

Jennifer Waters, Executive Director of Student Financial Services
600 South Michigan Avenue, Chicago, IL 60605-1996
(866) 705-0200

Concordia University

River Forest, Illinois
www.cuchicago.edu   Federal Code: 001666

4-year private university and teachers college in large town, affiliated with Lutheran Church - Missouri Synod.

Enrollment: 1,026 undergrads, 5% part-time. 204 full-time freshmen.

Selectivity: Admits over 75% of applicants.

BASIC COSTS (2008-2009)

Tuition and fees: $22,390.
Per-credit charge: $685.
Room and board: $7,350.

FINANCIAL AID PICTURE (2006-2007)

Students with need: Out of 197 full-time freshmen who applied for aid, 174 were judged to have need. Of these, 174 received aid, and 63 had their full need met. Average financial aid package met 77% of need; average scholarship/grant was $10,486; average loan was $5,843. For part-time students, average financial aid package was $10,978.
Students without need: 30 full-time freshmen who did not demonstrate need for aid received scholarships/grants; average award was $6,125. No-need awards available for academics, alumni affiliation, music/drama, religious affiliation, state/district residency.
Scholarships offered: Presidential Honors; full tuition; selection by essay; 5 per year. Presidential Scholarships; up to $12,000; selection by ACT and GP. Community Awards; up to $7000; selection by ACT and GPA. Transfer Honors; up to $10,000; selection by GPA. Music Scholarships; amount varies; selection by audition.
Cumulative student debt: 78% of graduating class had student loans; average debt was $16,393.

FINANCIAL AID PROCEDURES

Forms required: FAFSA.
Dates and Deadlines: Priority date 4/1; closing date 8/15. Applicants notified on a rolling basis; must reply within 4 week(s) of notification.
Transfers: No deadline. Applicants notified on a rolling basis; must reply within 4 week(s) of notification.

CONTACT

Patricia Williamson, Director of Student Financial Planning
7400 Augusta Street, River Forest, IL 60305-1499
(708) 209-3113

Cooking & Hospitality Institute of Chicago

Chicago, Illinois
www.chic.edu   Federal Code: 016758

2-year for-profit culinary school in very large city.
Enrollment: 1,002 undergrads, 2% part-time. 177 full-time freshmen.
Selectivity: Open admission.

BASIC COSTS (2008-2009)

Additional info: Tuition for associate of applied science in Le Cordon Bleu Culinary Arts: $39,950; associate of applied science in Le Cordon Bleu Patisserie and Baking: $38,500; certificate in Le Cordon Bleu Culinary Arts: $12,200. Tuition at time of enrollment locked for 2 years.

FINANCIAL AID PICTURE

Students with need: Need-based aid available for full-time and part-time students. Work study available nights.

FINANCIAL AID PROCEDURES

Forms required: FAFSA, institutional form.
Dates and Deadlines: No deadline. Applicants notified on a rolling basis.
Transfers: No deadline. Applicants notified on a rolling basis.

CONTACT

Lauren Lewis, Director of Student Finance
361 West Chestnut, Chicago, IL 60610-3050
(312) 944-0882

Danville Area Community College

Danville, Illinois
www.dacc.edu   Federal Code: 001669

2-year public community college in large town.
Enrollment: 2,285 undergrads.
Selectivity: Open admission.

BASIC COSTS (2007-2008)

Tuition and fees: $2,340; out-of-state residents $4,800.
Per-credit charge: $68; out-of-state residents $150.

FINANCIAL AID PICTURE (2006-2007)

Students with need: Average financial aid package met 67% of need; average scholarship/grant was $1,620; average loan was $2,625. Need-based aid available for part-time students.
Students without need: No-need awards available for academics, athletics, minority status.
Cumulative student debt: 3% of graduating class had student loans; average debt was $6,125.

FINANCIAL AID PROCEDURES

Forms required: FAFSA, institutional form.
Dates and Deadlines: Priority date 7/1; no closing date. Applicants notified on a rolling basis starting 6/1.
Transfers: NSLDS reviewed before aid disbursed.

CONTACT

Janet Ingargiola, Director of Financial Aid
2000 East Main Street, Danville, IL 61832
(217) 443-8891

DePaul University

Chicago, Illinois
www.depaul.edu   Federal Code: 001671

4-year private university in very large city, affiliated with Roman Catholic Church.
Enrollment: 14,661 undergrads, 23% part-time. 2,522 full-time freshmen.
Selectivity: Admits 50 to 75% of applicants.

BASIC COSTS (2007-2008)

Tuition and fees: $24,110.
Per-credit charge: $422.
Room and board: $9,801.

FINANCIAL AID PICTURE (2006-2007)

Students with need: Out of 2,102 full-time freshmen who applied for aid, 1,572 were judged to have need. Of these, 1,520 received aid, and 183 had their full need met. Average financial aid package met 67% of need; average scholarship/grant was $13,038; average loan was $3,915. For part-time students, average financial aid package was $11,023.
Students without need: 156 full-time freshmen who did not demonstrate need for aid received scholarships/grants; average award was $8,870. No-need awards available for academics, art, athletics, leadership, music/drama, ROTC, state/district residency.
Scholarships offered: *Merit:* Various scholarships; based on top 10% of class, 1100 SAT (exclusive of writing) or 26 ACT, and active in student/community organizations. *Athletic:* 43 full-time freshmen received athletic scholarships; average amount $19,764.
Cumulative student debt: 65% of graduating class had student loans; average debt was $22,569.

FINANCIAL AID PROCEDURES

Forms required: FAFSA.
Dates and Deadlines: Priority date 2/1; closing date 5/1. Applicants notified on a rolling basis starting 3/15; must reply by 5/1 or within 4 week(s) of notification.

Transfers: Closing date 4/1. Applicants notified by 6/1. 5 different scholarships awarded to fall incoming transfer students who have been admitted and have submitted scholarship application by April 1. Scholarships range from $3,000-$7,000, and vary based on competitiveness of pool and student's qualifications.

CONTACT

Paula Luff, Director of Financial Aid
1 East Jackson Boulevard, Chicago, IL 60604-2287
(312) 362-8091

DeVry University: Addison

Addison, Illinois
www.devry.edu   Federal Code: 016219

4-year for-profit university in large town.
Enrollment: 1,312 undergrads, 40% part-time. 186 full-time freshmen.

BASIC COSTS (2007-2008)

Tuition and fees: $13,220.
Per-credit charge: $490.

FINANCIAL AID PICTURE (2006-2007)

Students with need: Out of 111 full-time freshmen who applied for aid, 95 were judged to have need. Of these, 93 received aid, and 2 had their full need met. Average financial aid package met 38% of need; average scholarship/grant was $6,161; average loan was $3,853. For part-time students, average financial aid package was $8,289.
Students without need: This college awards aid only to students with need.
Cumulative student debt: 75% of graduating class had student loans; average debt was $28,773.

FINANCIAL AID PROCEDURES

Forms required: FAFSA.
Dates and Deadlines: No deadline. Applicants notified on a rolling basis.

CONTACT

Sajel Anin, Director of Student Finance
1221 North Swift Road, Addison, IL 60101-6106
(630) 953-1300

DeVry University: Chicago

Chicago, Illinois
www.devry.edu   Federal Code: 010727

4-year for-profit university in very large city.
Enrollment: 1,791 undergrads, 45% part-time. 308 full-time freshmen.

BASIC COSTS (2007-2008)

Tuition and fees: $13,220.
Per-credit charge: $490.

FINANCIAL AID PICTURE (2006-2007)

Students with need: Out of 120 full-time freshmen who applied for aid, 112 were judged to have need. Of these, 107 received aid, and 1 had their full need met. Average financial aid package met 42% of need; average scholarship/grant was $8,433; average loan was $4,842. For part-time students, average financial aid package was $10,313.
Students without need: This college awards aid only to students with need.
Cumulative student debt: 84% of graduating class had student loans; average debt was $49,617.

FINANCIAL AID PROCEDURES

Forms required: FAFSA.
Dates and Deadlines: No deadline. Applicants notified on a rolling basis.

CONTACT

Milena Dobrina, Director of Financial Aid
3300 North Campbell Avenue, Chicago, IL 60618-5994
(773) 929-8509

DeVry University: Online

Oakbrook Terrace, Illinois
www.devry.edu

4-year for-profit virtual college in small city.
Enrollment: 8,596 undergrads, 68% part-time. 526 full-time freshmen.

FINANCIAL AID PICTURE (2006-2007)

Students with need: Out of 75 full-time freshmen who applied for aid, 73 were judged to have need. Of these, 70 received aid. Average financial aid package met 32% of need; average scholarship/grant was $6,163; average loan was $4,226. For part-time students, average financial aid package was $7,496.
Students without need: 65 full-time freshmen who did not demonstrate need for aid received scholarships/grants; average award was $7,768. No-need awards available for academics.
Cumulative student debt: 64% of graduating class had student loans; average debt was $35,423.

FINANCIAL AID PROCEDURES

Forms required: FAFSA.
Dates and Deadlines: No deadline. Applicants notified on a rolling basis.

CONTACT

One Tower Lane, Oakbrook Terrace, IL 60181

DeVry University: Tinley Park

Tinley Park, Illinois
www.devry.edu   Federal Code: 022966

4-year for-profit university in large town.
Enrollment: 1,059 undergrads, 40% part-time. 148 full-time freshmen.

BASIC COSTS (2007-2008)

Tuition and fees: $13,220.
Per-credit charge: $490.

FINANCIAL AID PICTURE (2006-2007)

Students with need: Out of 116 full-time freshmen who applied for aid, 106 were judged to have need. Of these, 105 received aid, and 2 had their full need met. Average financial aid package met 36% of need; average scholarship/grant was $5,631; average loan was $4,021. For part-time students, average financial aid package was $8,825.
Students without need: This college awards aid only to students with need.
Cumulative student debt: 86% of graduating class had student loans; average debt was $37,902.

FINANCIAL AID PROCEDURES

Forms required: FAFSA.
Dates and Deadlines: No deadline. Applicants notified on a rolling basis.

CONTACT

Sejal Amin, Director of Student Finance
18624 West Creek Drive, Tinley Park, IL 60477-6243
(708) 342-3219

Dominican University

River Forest, Illinois
www.dom.edu   Federal Code: 001750

4-year private university and liberal arts college in large town, affiliated with Roman Catholic Church.

Enrollment: 1,531 undergrads, 10% part-time. 366 full-time freshmen.

Selectivity: Admits over 75% of applicants.

BASIC COSTS (2008-2009)

Tuition and fees: $23,950.

Per-credit charge: $790.

Room and board: $7,350.

FINANCIAL AID PICTURE (2007-2008)

Students with need: Out of 311 full-time freshmen who applied for aid, 286 were judged to have need. Of these, 285 received aid, and 46 had their full need met. Average financial aid package met 85% of need; average scholarship/grant was $14,688; average loan was $3,249. For part-time students, average financial aid package was $8,352.

Students without need: 48 full-time freshmen who did not demonstrate need for aid received scholarships/grants; average award was $10,398. No-need awards available for academics, alumni affiliation, leadership.

Scholarships offered: Presidential Scholarships; $14,000. Dean's Scholarships; $12,000, University Honor Scholarships; $10.000. Achievement Scholarships; $8,000. All based on ACT/SAT scores and class rank. Ida Brechtel Scholarships; $7,500 up to full tuition; for students majoring in chemistry or biology/chemistry.

FINANCIAL AID PROCEDURES

Forms required: FAFSA.

Dates and Deadlines: Priority date 6/1; no closing date. Applicants notified on a rolling basis starting 2/15; must reply within 2 week(s) of notification.

Transfers: No deadline. Applicants notified on a rolling basis starting 3/15; must reply within 3 week(s) of notification. Merit scholarships available to full-time students with GPA of 3.3 from previous institution. Phi Theta Kappa scholarships available to PTK members.

CONTACT

Michael Shields, Director of Financial Aid

7900 West Division Street, River Forest, IL 60305-1099

(708) 524-6809

East-West University

Chicago, Illinois
www.eastwest.edu   Federal Code: 015310

4-year private university in very large city.

Enrollment: 1,150 undergrads, 2% part-time. 392 full-time freshmen.

Selectivity: Open admission.

BASIC COSTS (2007-2008)

Tuition and fees: $12,825.

Per-credit charge: $405.

FINANCIAL AID PICTURE

Students with need: Need-based aid available for full-time and part-time students.

Students without need: No-need awards available for academics.

Additional info: Foreign students eligible for institutional scholarship.

FINANCIAL AID PROCEDURES

Forms required: FAFSA.

Dates and Deadlines: No deadline. Applicants notified on a rolling basis starting 1/4; must reply within 4 week(s) of notification.

Transfers: Closing date 4/1.

CONTACT

Elizabeth Guzman, Director of Financial Aid

816 South Michigan Avenue, Chicago, IL 60605

(312) 939-0111

Eastern Illinois University

Charleston, Illinois
www.eiu.edu   Federal Code: 001674

4-year public university and teachers college in large town.

Enrollment: 10,152 undergrads, 9% part-time. 1,641 full-time freshmen.

Selectivity: Admits 50 to 75% of applicants.

BASIC COSTS (2007-2008)

Tuition and fees: $7,990; out-of-state residents $19,654.

Per-credit charge: $194; out-of-state residents $583.

Room and board: $7,124.

Additional info: New students have a guaranteed tuition rate for 4 years. Tuition at time of enrollment locked for 4 years.

FINANCIAL AID PICTURE (2007-2008)

Students with need: Out of 1,409 full-time freshmen who applied for aid, 864 were judged to have need. Of these, 829 received aid, and 94 had their full need met. Average financial aid package met 75% of need; average scholarship/grant was $2,651; average loan was $3,016. For part-time students, average financial aid package was $6,867.

Students without need: 90 full-time freshmen who did not demonstrate need for aid received scholarships/grants; average award was $3,239. No-need awards available for academics, art, athletics, leadership, music/drama, ROTC.

Scholarships offered: 49 full-time freshmen received athletic scholarships; average amount $9,158.

Cumulative student debt: 84% of graduating class had student loans; average debt was $15,555.

FINANCIAL AID PROCEDURES

Forms required: FAFSA.

Dates and Deadlines: Priority date 3/1; no closing date. Applicants notified on a rolling basis starting 3/1; must reply within 2 week(s) of notification.

CONTACT

Jone Zieren, Director of Financial Aid

600 Lincoln Avenue, Charleston, IL 61920-3011

(217) 581-3713

Elgin Community College

Elgin, Illinois
www.elgin.edu   Federal Code: 001675

2-year public community college in small city.

Enrollment: 6,589 undergrads, 57% part-time. 619 full-time freshmen.

Selectivity: Open admission; but selective for some programs.

BASIC COSTS (2007-2008)

Tuition and fees: $2,740; out-of-district residents $10,789; out-of-state residents $13,127.

Per-credit charge: $91; out-of-district residents $359; out-of-state residents $437.

FINANCIAL AID PICTURE

Students with need: Need-based aid available for full-time and part-time students. Work study available nights, weekends, and for part-time students.

Students without need: No-need awards available for academics, alumni affiliation, art, athletics, job skills, leadership, minority status, music/drama, religious affiliation, ROTC, state/district residency.

FINANCIAL AID PROCEDURES

Forms required: FAFSA, institutional form.

Dates and Deadlines: Priority date 5/15; no closing date. Applicants notified on a rolling basis starting 4/7; must reply within 3 week(s) of notification.

CONTACT

Carol Robertson, Vice President of Finance & Administration

1700 Spartan Drive, Elgin, IL 60123-7193

(847) 214-7520

Elmhurst College

Elmhurst, Illinois

www.elmhurst.edu   Federal Code: 001676

4-year private liberal arts college in large town, affiliated with United Church of Christ.

Enrollment: 2,808 undergrads, 9% part-time. 483 full-time freshmen.

BASIC COSTS (2007-2008)

Tuition and fees: $24,760.

Per-credit charge: $700.

Room and board: $8,064.

FINANCIAL AID PICTURE (2006-2007)

Students with need: Out of 413 full-time freshmen who applied for aid, 345 were judged to have need. Of these, 345 received aid, and 92 had their full need met. Average financial aid package met 90% of need; average scholarship/grant was $8,509; average loan was $3,007. For part-time students, average financial aid package was $10,578.

Students without need: 94 full-time freshmen who did not demonstrate need for aid received scholarships/grants; average award was $8,517. No-need awards available for academics, alumni affiliation, art, minority status, music/drama, religious affiliation, state/district residency.

Scholarships offered: Presidential Scholarship: $12,000-$17,000; 405 awarded. Dean's Scholarship: 8,000-$11,000; 389 awarded. Founder's Scholarship: $4,000-$7,000; 245 awarded. Combination of class rank, test scores, and GPA considered.

Additional info: Must be admitted to the college by 1/15 to be considered for scholarships.

FINANCIAL AID PROCEDURES

Forms required: FAFSA.

Dates and Deadlines: Priority date 4/15; no closing date. Applicants notified on a rolling basis starting 2/21; must reply within 3 week(s) of notification.

CONTACT

Ruth Pusich, Director of Financial Aid

190 South Prospect Avenue, Elmhurst, IL 60126-3296

(630) 617-3075

Eureka College

Eureka, Illinois

www.eureka.edu   Federal Code: 001678

4-year private liberal arts college in small town, affiliated with Christian Church (Disciples of Christ).

Enrollment: 685 undergrads. 129 full-time freshmen.

Selectivity: Admits 50 to 75% of applicants.

BASIC COSTS (2007-2008)

Tuition and fees: $15,270.

Per-credit charge: $395.

Room and board: $6,720.

FINANCIAL AID PICTURE

Students with need: Need-based aid available for full-time and part-time students. Work study available nights, weekends, and for part-time students.

Students without need: No-need awards available for academics, alumni affiliation, art, leadership, music/drama, religious affiliation.

Scholarships offered: Reagan Fellows Program: full tuition; 5 awarded. Sandifer Mentorships: fully paid mentorship anywhere in the world at end of sophomore year; all freshmen eligible. Eureka College Ministry Fellowship: full tuition scholarships; 2 available each year.

FINANCIAL AID PROCEDURES

Forms required: FAFSA.

Dates and Deadlines: Priority date 4/15; no closing date. Applicants notified on a rolling basis starting 2/15; must reply by 5/1 or within 3 week(s) of notification.

Transfers: No deadline. Applicants notified on a rolling basis; must reply within 2 week(s) of notification.

CONTACT

Ellen Rigsby, Director of Financial Aid

300 East College Avenue, Eureka, IL 61530-1500

(309) 467-6311

Governors State University

University Park, Illinois

www.govst.edu   Federal Code: 009145

Upper-division public university in large town.

Enrollment: 2,370 undergrads, 63% part-time.

Selectivity: Open admission; but selective for some programs.

BASIC COSTS (2007-2008)

Tuition and fees: $5,966; out-of-state residents $16,706.

Per-credit charge: $179; out-of-state residents $537.

Additional info: Tuition/fee waivers available for minority students.

FINANCIAL AID PICTURE

Students with need: Need-based aid available for full-time and part-time students. Work study available nights, weekends, and for part-time students.

Students without need: No-need awards available for academics, ROTC, state/district residency.

FINANCIAL AID PROCEDURES

Forms required: FAFSA.

Dates and Deadlines: Priority date 5/1; closing date 10/1. Applicants notified on a rolling basis.

Transfers: No aid for second bachelor's or second master's degree.

CONTACT

Freda Whisenton-Comer, Office of Financial Aid

One University Parkway, University Park, IL 60466

(708) 534-4480

Greenville College

Greenville, Illinois

www.greenville.edu   Federal Code: 001684

4-year private liberal arts college in small town, affiliated with Free Methodist Church of North America.

Enrollment: 1,353 undergrads, 2% part-time. 303 full-time freshmen.

Selectivity: Admits over 75% of applicants.

BASIC COSTS (2008-2009)

Tuition and fees: $19,428.

Per-credit charge: $406.

Room and board: $6,568.

FINANCIAL AID PICTURE (2006-2007)

Students with need: Out of 276 full-time freshmen who applied for aid, 244 were judged to have need. Of these, 244 received aid, and 28 had their full need met. Average financial aid package met 81% of need; average scholarship/grant was $11,664; average loan was $3,336. For part-time students, average financial aid package was $6,925.

Students without need: 51 full-time freshmen who did not demonstrate need for aid received scholarships/grants; average award was $9,635. No-need awards available for academics, alumni affiliation, art, leadership, minority status, music/drama, religious affiliation, state/district residency.

Scholarships offered: President's Scholarships; $8,000; requiring cumulative GPA of 3.0, ACT of 27 or SAT of 1210, and leadership qualities. Dean's Scholarship; $6,000; for GPA of 3.0, ACT of 22 or SAT of 1020, and leadership qualities. Leadership Scholarships; $500-$4,000; for GPA of 2.5, ACT of 18 or SAT 860, and leadership qualities. (All SAT scores are exclusive of Writing.).

Cumulative student debt: 85% of graduating class had student loans; average debt was $15,894.

FINANCIAL AID PROCEDURES

Forms required: FAFSA.

Dates and Deadlines: Priority date 5/1; no closing date. Applicants notified on a rolling basis starting 3/15; must reply within 3 week(s) of notification.

Transfers: No deadline. Applicants notified on a rolling basis; must reply within 3 week(s) of notification.

CONTACT

Marilae Latham, Director of Financial Aid
315 East College Avenue, Greenville, IL 62246-0159
(618) 664-7111

Harper College
Palatine, Illinois
www.harpercollege.edu   Federal Code: 003961

2-year public community college in small city.

Enrollment: 13,343 undergrads, 52% part-time. 2,049 full-time freshmen.

Selectivity: Open admission; but selective for some programs.

BASIC COSTS (2008-2009)

Tuition and fees: $3,234; out-of-district residents $10,194; out-of-state residents $12,504.

Per-credit charge: $90; out-of-district residents $322; out-of-state residents $399.

Additional info: In-district tuition rates available to employees of in-district companies who reside outside college district.

FINANCIAL AID PICTURE (2006-2007)

Students with need: 78% of average financial aid package awarded as scholarships/grants, 22% awarded as loans/jobs. Need-based aid available for part-time students. Work study available nights, weekends, and for part-time students.

Students without need: No-need awards available for academics, art, leadership, minority status, music/drama, state/district residency.

Scholarships offered: Distinguished Scholar Award; full tuition and fees; available to full-time students during regular academic year who graduate in top 10% of class from district high school; renewable for second year.

FINANCIAL AID PROCEDURES

Forms required: FAFSA, institutional form.

Dates and Deadlines: Priority date 3/1; no closing date. Applicants notified on a rolling basis starting 3/1; must reply within 2 week(s) of notification.

Transfers: No deadline. Applicants notified on a rolling basis starting 3/1; must reply within 2 week(s) of notification.

CONTACT

Earl Dowling, Director, Scholarships and Financial Assistance
1200 West Algonquin Road, Palatine, IL 60067-7398
(847) 925-6248

Heartland Community College
Normal, Illinois
www.heartland.edu   Federal Code: 030838

2-year public community college in small city.

Enrollment: 4,758 undergrads, 56% part-time. 596 full-time freshmen.

Selectivity: Open admission; but selective for some programs.

BASIC COSTS (2008-2009)

Tuition and fees: $2,310; out-of-district residents $4,470; out-of-state residents $6,630.

Per-credit charge: $72; out-of-district residents $144; out-of-state residents $216.

FINANCIAL AID PICTURE (2006-2007)

Students with need: 97% of average financial aid package awarded as scholarships/grants, 3% awarded as loans/jobs. Need-based aid available for part-time students. Work study available nights, weekends, and for part-time students.

Students without need: No-need awards available for academics, alumni affiliation, athletics, job skills, leadership, minority status, state/district residency.

FINANCIAL AID PROCEDURES

Forms required: FAFSA, institutional form.

Dates and Deadlines: Priority date 4/1; no closing date. Applicants notified on a rolling basis starting 5/15; must reply within 2 week(s) of notification.

CONTACT

Cheryl Schaffer, Director of Financial Aid
1500 West Raab Road, Normal, IL 61761
(309) 268-8020

Highland Community College
Freeport, Illinois
www.highland.edu   Federal Code: 001681

2-year public community college in large town.

Enrollment: 1,844 undergrads, 43% part-time. 289 full-time freshmen.

Selectivity: Open admission; but selective for some programs.

BASIC COSTS (2007-2008)

Tuition and fees: $2,340; out-of-district residents $3,870; out-of-state residents $3,870.

Per-credit charge: $72; out-of-district residents $123; out-of-state residents $123.

FINANCIAL AID PICTURE (2006-2007)

Students with need: 79% of average financial aid package awarded as scholarships/grants, 21% awarded as loans/jobs. Need-based aid available for part-time students. Work study available nights.

Students without need: No-need awards available for academics, athletics.

FINANCIAL AID PROCEDURES

Forms required: FAFSA, institutional form.

Dates and Deadlines: No deadline. Applicants notified on a rolling basis starting 8/1; must reply within 2 week(s) of notification.

Transfers: No deadline. Applicants notified on a rolling basis starting 4/1.

CONTACT
Kathy Bangasser, Director of Financial Aid
2998 West Pearl City Road, Freeport, IL 61032-9341
(815) 599-3500

Illinois College
Jacksonville, Illinois
www.ic.edu   Federal Code: 001688

4-year private liberal arts college in large town, affiliated with United Church of Christ and Presbyterian Church (USA).
Enrollment: 990 undergrads, 1% part-time. 260 full-time freshmen.
Selectivity: Admits over 75% of applicants.

BASIC COSTS (2008-2009)
Tuition and fees: $20,300.
Room and board: $7,230.

FINANCIAL AID PICTURE (2007-2008)
Students with need: Average financial aid package met 91% of need; average scholarship/grant was $8,174; average loan was $4,361. For part-time students, average financial aid package was $4,607.
Students without need: No-need awards available for academics, art, leadership, minority status, music/drama.
Scholarships offered: College transfer scholarship; available with 12 transferable credit hours and minimum 3.0 GPA.
Cumulative student debt: 95% of graduating class had student loans; average debt was $18,870.

FINANCIAL AID PROCEDURES
Forms required: FAFSA.
Dates and Deadlines: Priority date 3/1; no closing date. Applicants notified on a rolling basis starting 3/1; must reply within 2 week(s) of notification.
Transfers: No deadline. Applicants notified on a rolling basis starting 6/1; must reply within 2 week(s) of notification.

CONTACT
Katherine Taylor, Director of Financial Aid
1101 West College Avenue, Jacksonville, IL 62650
(217) 245-3035

Illinois Eastern Community Colleges: Frontier Community College
Fairfield, Illinois
www.iecc.edu/fcc   Federal Code: 014090

2-year public community college in small town.
Enrollment: 1,353 undergrads.
Selectivity: Open admission; but selective for some programs.

BASIC COSTS (2007-2008)
Tuition and fees: $1,810; out-of-district residents $5,583; out-of-state residents $6,905.
Per-credit charge: $57; out-of-district residents $183; out-of-state residents $227.
Additional info: Students in qualifying Indiana districts pay per-credit-hour rate of $96.

FINANCIAL AID PICTURE
Students with need: Need-based aid available for full-time and part-time students.
Students without need: No-need awards available for academics, state/district residency.

FINANCIAL AID PROCEDURES
Forms required: FAFSA, institutional form.

Dates and Deadlines: No deadline. Applicants notified on a rolling basis starting 8/1; must reply within 2 week(s) of notification.

CONTACT
Carroll Hilliard, Director of Financial Assistance and Community Services
2 Frontier Drive, Fairfield, IL 62837-9801
(618) 842-3711

Illinois Eastern Community Colleges: Lincoln Trail College
Robinson, Illinois
www.iecc.edu/ltc   Federal Code: 009786

2-year public community college in small town.
Enrollment: 902 undergrads, 43% part-time. 78 full-time freshmen.
Selectivity: Open admission.

BASIC COSTS (2007-2008)
Tuition and fees: $1,810; out-of-district residents $5,583; out-of-state residents $6,905.
Per-credit charge: $57; out-of-district residents $183; out-of-state residents $227.
Additional info: Students in qualifying Indiana districts pay per-credit-hour rate of $96.

FINANCIAL AID PICTURE
Students with need: Need-based aid available for full-time and part-time students.
Students without need: No-need awards available for academics, athletics, state/district residency.

FINANCIAL AID PROCEDURES
Forms required: FAFSA, institutional form.
Dates and Deadlines: No deadline. Applicants notified on a rolling basis starting 8/1; must reply within 2 week(s) of notification.

CONTACT
Jennifer Barthelemy, Coordinator of Financial Aid
11220 State Highway 1, Robinson, IL 62454-5707
(618) 544-8657

Illinois Eastern Community Colleges: Olney Central College
Olney, Illinois
www.iecc.edu/occ   Federal Code: 001742

2-year public community college in small town.
Enrollment: 890 undergrads, 21% part-time. 118 full-time freshmen.
Selectivity: Open admission; but selective for some programs.

BASIC COSTS (2007-2008)
Tuition and fees: $1,810; out-of-district residents $5,583; out-of-state residents $6,905.
Per-credit charge: $57; out-of-district residents $183; out-of-state residents $227.
Additional info: Students in qualifying Indiana districts pay per-credit-hour rate of $96.

FINANCIAL AID PICTURE
Students with need: Need-based aid available for full-time and part-time students.
Students without need: No-need awards available for academics, athletics, state/district residency.

FINANCIAL AID PROCEDURES
Forms required: FAFSA, institutional form.

Dates and Deadlines: No deadline. Applicants notified on a rolling basis starting 8/1; must reply within 2 week(s) of notification.

CONTACT

Vicki Stuckey, Financial Aid Coordinator
305 North West Street, Olney, IL 62450
(618) 395-7777

Illinois Eastern Community Colleges: Wabash Valley College

Mount Carmel, Illinois
www.iecc.edu/wvc   Federal Code: 001779

2-year public community college in small town.

Enrollment: 841 undergrads, 34% part-time. 106 full-time freshmen.

Selectivity: Open admission.

BASIC COSTS (2007-2008)

Tuition and fees: $1,810; out-of-district residents $5,583; out-of-state residents $6,905.

Per-credit charge: $57; out-of-district residents $183; out-of-state residents $227.

Additional info: Students in qualifying Indiana districts pay per-credit-hour rate of $96.

FINANCIAL AID PICTURE

Students with need: Need-based aid available for full-time and part-time students.

Students without need: No-need awards available for academics, athletics, state/district residency.

FINANCIAL AID PROCEDURES

Forms required: FAFSA, institutional form.

Dates and Deadlines: No deadline. Applicants notified on a rolling basis starting 8/1; must reply within 2 week(s) of notification.

CONTACT

Melinda Silvernale, Financial Aid Coordinator
2200 College Drive, Mount Carmel, IL 62863-2657
(618) 262-8641

Illinois Institute of Art: Chicago

Chicago, Illinois
www.ilic.artinstitutes.edu   Federal Code: 012584

4-year for-profit visual arts college in very large city.

Enrollment: 3,000 undergrads.

BASIC COSTS (2007-2008)

Tuition and fees: $20,784.

Per-credit charge: $433.

Room and board: $6,570.

FINANCIAL AID PICTURE

Students with need: Need-based aid available for full-time and part-time students.

FINANCIAL AID PROCEDURES

Forms required: FAFSA.

Dates and Deadlines: Priority date 5/1; no closing date. Applicants notified on a rolling basis.

CONTACT

Charles Munro, Financial Aid Officer
350 North Orleans Street, Chicago, IL 60654

Illinois Institute of Art: Schaumburg

Schaumburg, Illinois
www.ilis.aii.edu   Federal Code: 012584

3-year for-profit visual arts college in small city.

Enrollment: 1,268 undergrads.

Selectivity: Open admission; but selective for some programs.

BASIC COSTS (2007-2008)

Tuition and fees: $20,784.

Per-credit charge: $433.

Room and board: $6,570.

FINANCIAL AID PICTURE

Students with need: Need-based aid available for full-time and part-time students. Work study available nights, weekends, and for part-time students.

Students without need: No-need awards available for academics, art.

Additional info: Merit scholarships based on GPA; talent-based scholarships.

FINANCIAL AID PROCEDURES

Forms required: FAFSA.

Dates and Deadlines: Priority date 3/1; no closing date.

Transfers: No deadline. Applicants notified on a rolling basis.

CONTACT

Joe Payne, Director of Student Financial Services
1000 North Plaza Drive, Schaumburg, IL 60173
(800) 314-3450

Illinois Institute of Technology

Chicago, Illinois
www.iit.edu   Federal Code: 001691

4-year private university and engineering college in very large city.

Enrollment: 2,479 undergrads, 6% part-time. 484 full-time freshmen.

Selectivity: Admits 50 to 75% of applicants.

BASIC COSTS (2007-2008)

Tuition and fees: $25,746.

Per-credit charge: $778.

Room and board: $8,618.

Additional info: Tuition and fees cover unlimited number of courses during academic year and include library and computer usage fees.

FINANCIAL AID PICTURE (2006-2007)

Students with need: Out of 401 full-time freshmen who applied for aid, 341 were judged to have need. Of these, 341 received aid, and 103 had their full need met. Average financial aid package met 87% of need; average scholarship/grant was $14,593; average loan was $3,118. For part-time students, average financial aid package was $9,265.

Students without need: 141 full-time freshmen who did not demonstrate need for aid received scholarships/grants; average award was $12,064. No-need awards available for academics, alumni affiliation, athletics, leadership, minority status, ROTC.

Scholarships offered: *Merit:* Henry Heald Scholarship; up to $10,000; based on student application. University Scholarship; up to $10,000; based on student application. Crown Scholarship (College of Architecture); full-tuition; based on student application, on-campus interview and portfolio. Camras Scholarship; 3/4-tuition and full-tuition; based on student application, on-campus interview and essay. Leadership Edge Scholarship (Stuart School of Business); based on student application, on-campus interview and essay.

Athletic: 13 full-time freshmen received athletic scholarships; average amount $3,804.

Cumulative student debt: 61% of graduating class had student loans; average debt was $21,326.

FINANCIAL AID PROCEDURES

Forms required: FAFSA.

Dates and Deadlines: Priority date 4/15; no closing date. Applicants notified on a rolling basis starting 3/1; must reply by 5/1 or within 2 week(s) of notification.

Transfers: No deadline.

CONTACT

Virginia Foster, Director for Financial Aid
10 West 33rd Street, Chicago, IL 60616
(312) 567-7219

Illinois State University
Normal, Illinois
www.ilstu.edu   Federal Code: 001692

4-year public university in small city.

Enrollment: 17,637 undergrads, 6% part-time. 3,141 full-time freshmen.

Selectivity: Admits 50 to 75% of applicants.

BASIC COSTS (2007-2008)

Tuition and fees: $9,019; out-of-state residents $16,339.

Per-credit charge: $233; out-of-state residents $477.

Room and board: $6,848.

Additional info: Tuition at time of enrollment locked for 4 years.

FINANCIAL AID PICTURE (2007-2008)

Students with need: Out of 2,376 full-time freshmen who applied for aid, 1,637 were judged to have need. Of these, 1,432 received aid, and 593 had their full need met. Average financial aid package met 78% of need; average scholarship/grant was $8,318; average loan was $5,179. For part-time students, average financial aid package was $10,335.

Students without need: 43 full-time freshmen who did not demonstrate need for aid received scholarships/grants; average award was $1,689. No-need awards available for academics, art, athletics, music/drama.

Scholarships offered: *Merit:* Various non-need based merit scholarships available, including Presidential Scholars' Program, Provost's Scholarship, and Dean's Scholarship. ***Athletic:*** 38 full-time freshmen received athletic scholarships; average amount $10,977.

Cumulative student debt: 57% of graduating class had student loans; average debt was $18,053.

FINANCIAL AID PROCEDURES

Forms required: FAFSA.

Dates and Deadlines: Priority date 3/1; no closing date. Applicants notified on a rolling basis starting 4/1; must reply within 2 week(s) of notification.

CONTACT

Jana Albrecht, Director of Financial Aid
Campus Box 2200, Normal, IL 61790-2200
(309) 438-2231

Illinois Valley Community College
Oglesby, Illinois
www.ivcc.edu   Federal Code: 001705

2-year public community college in small town.

Enrollment: 2,804 undergrads.

Selectivity: Open admission; but selective for some programs.

BASIC COSTS (2007-2008)

Tuition and fees: $1,973; out-of-district residents $6,639; out-of-state residents $7,619.

Per-credit charge: $66; out-of-district residents $214; out-of-state residents $247.

FINANCIAL AID PICTURE

Students with need: Need-based aid available for full-time and part-time students.

FINANCIAL AID PROCEDURES

Forms required: FAFSA.

Dates and Deadlines: Priority date 5/1; no closing date. Applicants notified on a rolling basis starting 5/1.

CONTACT

Steve Crick, Director, Financial Aid
815 North Orlando Smith Avenue, Oglesby, IL 61348-9693
(815) 224-0438

Illinois Wesleyan University
Bloomington, Illinois   Federal Code: 001696
www.iwu.edu   CSS Code: 1320

4-year private university and liberal arts college in small city.

Enrollment: 2,088 undergrads. 538 full-time freshmen.

Selectivity: Admits 50 to 75% of applicants.

BASIC COSTS (2008-2009)

Tuition and fees: $32,434.

Per-credit charge: $1,008.

Room and board: $7,350.

FINANCIAL AID PICTURE (2007-2008)

Students with need: Out of 412 full-time freshmen who applied for aid, 305 were judged to have need. Of these, 305 received aid, and 116 had their full need met. Average financial aid package met 93% of need; average scholarship/grant was $16,880; average loan was $4,099.

Students without need: 194 full-time freshmen who did not demonstrate need for aid received scholarships/grants; average award was $8,415. No-need awards available for academics, art, music/drama.

Scholarships offered: Academic scholarships: $5,000-16,000; based on high school academic performance, recommendations, testing. Talent awards: $6,500-$11,000; available in music, art, theater, and musical theater. Limited number of full-tuition awards in music.

Cumulative student debt: 64% of graduating class had student loans; average debt was $24,234.

FINANCIAL AID PROCEDURES

Forms required: FAFSA, CSS PROFILE, institutional form.

Dates and Deadlines: Closing date 3/1. Applicants notified on a rolling basis starting 2/15; must reply by 5/1 or within 3 week(s) of notification.

Transfers: No deadline. Applicants notified on a rolling basis; must reply by 5/1 or within 3 week(s) of notification.

CONTACT

Scott Seibring, Director of Financial Aid
PO Box 2900, Bloomington, IL 61702-2900
(309) 556-3096

International Academy of Design and Technology: Chicago
Chicago, Illinois
www.iadtchicago.edu   Federal Code: 021603

4-year for-profit visual arts and technical college in very large city.

Enrollment: 2,091 undergrads.

Selectivity: Open admission.

BASIC COSTS (2007-2008)

Tuition and fees: $17,250.

FINANCIAL AID PICTURE (2006-2007)

Students with need: 36% of average financial aid package awarded as scholarships/grants, 64% awarded as loans/jobs. Need-based aid available for part-time students.

Students without need: This college awards aid only to students with need.

Additional info: College work study programs available to day and evening students.

FINANCIAL AID PROCEDURES

Forms required: FAFSA.

Dates and Deadlines: No deadline. Applicants notified on a rolling basis.

Transfers: No deadline. Applicants notified on a rolling basis; must reply within 2 week(s) of notification.

CONTACT

Andrea Watkins, Associate Director of Financial Aid
One North State Street, Suite 500, Chicago, IL 60602
(312) 980-9200 ext. 9251

International Academy of Design and Technology: Schaumburg

Schaumburg, Illinois
www.iadtschaumburg.com

4-year for-profit visual arts and technical college in small city.

Enrollment: 246 undergrads.

Selectivity: Open admission.

BASIC COSTS (2007-2008)

Tuition and fees: $15,000.

Additional info: Bachelor's degree program is $58,800 plus books and fees.

FINANCIAL AID PICTURE (2006-2007)

Students with need: 22% of average financial aid package awarded as scholarships/grants, 78% awarded as loans/jobs.

CONTACT

Chris Miller, Assistant Financial Aid Director
915 National Parkway, Schaumburg, IL 60173

John A. Logan College

Carterville, Illinois
www.jalc.edu
Federal Code: 008076

2-year public community college in small town.

Enrollment: 2,306 undergrads, 25% part-time. 432 full-time freshmen.

Selectivity: Open admission; but selective for some programs.

BASIC COSTS (2008-2009)

Tuition and fees: $2,130; out-of-district residents $5,030; out-of-state residents $6,984.

Per-credit charge: $71; out-of-district residents $168; out-of-state residents $233.

FINANCIAL AID PICTURE

Students with need: Need-based aid available for full-time and part-time students.

Students without need: This college awards aid only to students with need.

FINANCIAL AID PROCEDURES

Forms required: FAFSA, institutional form.

Dates and Deadlines: Priority date 5/1; no closing date. Applicants notified on a rolling basis starting 5/1.

CONTACT

Stacy Holloway, Director for Student Financial Assistance
700 Logan College Road, Carterville, IL 62918
(618) 985-3741 ext. 8308

John Wood Community College

Quincy, Illinois
www.jwcc.edu
Federal Code: 012813

2-year public community college in large town.

Enrollment: 1,873 undergrads, 45% part-time. 440 full-time freshmen.

Selectivity: Open admission; but selective for some programs.

BASIC COSTS (2007-2008)

Tuition and fees: $3,120; out-of-state residents $6,120.

Per-credit charge: $96; out-of-state residents $196.

FINANCIAL AID PICTURE

Students with need: Need-based aid available for full-time and part-time students. Work study available nights, weekends, and for part-time students.

FINANCIAL AID PROCEDURES

Forms required: FAFSA.

Dates and Deadlines: No deadline. Applicants notified on a rolling basis starting 3/1.

CONTACT

Melanie Lechtenberg, Director of Financial Aid
1301 South 48th Street, Quincy, IL 62305-8736
(217) 641-4336

Joliet Junior College

Joliet, Illinois
www.jjc.edu
Federal Code: 001699

2-year public community college in small city.

Enrollment: 10,722 undergrads.

Selectivity: Open admission; but selective for some programs and for out-of-state students.

BASIC COSTS (2007-2008)

Tuition and fees: $2,280; out-of-district residents $7,403; out-of-state residents $8,485.

Per-credit charge: $62; out-of-district residents $233; out-of-state residents $262.

Additional info: Additional course fees range from $3 to $90.

FINANCIAL AID PICTURE

Students with need: Need-based aid available for full-time and part-time students. Work study available nights, weekends, and for part-time students.

Students without need: No-need awards available for academics.

FINANCIAL AID PROCEDURES

Forms required: FAFSA, institutional form.

Dates and Deadlines: Priority date 5/1; closing date 6/30. Applicants notified on a rolling basis starting 5/15.

CONTACT

John Rdzak, Director of Financial Aid
1215 Houbolt Road, Joliet, IL 60431-8938
(815) 729-9020 ext. 2528

Judson University

Elgin, Illinois
www.judsonu.edu   Federal Code: 001700

4-year private university and liberal arts college in small city, affiliated with American Baptist Churches in the USA.
Enrollment: 1,165 undergrads.
Selectivity: Admits 50 to 75% of applicants.

BASIC COSTS (2007-2008)
Tuition and fees: $20,420.
Per-credit charge: $675.
Room and board: $7,200.

FINANCIAL AID PICTURE
Students with need: Need-based aid available for full-time students. Work study available nights, weekends, and for part-time students.
Students without need: No-need awards available for academics, alumni affiliation, art, athletics, music/drama.
Scholarships offered: Academic Merit Award (1): incoming freshmen with ACT score of 25 (1140 SAT) or higher with a 3.33 GPA or higher; $7000. Academic Merit Award (2): incoming freshmen with ACT score of 25 (1140 SAT) or higher with a 3.32 GPA or less; $5000. Academic Merit Award (3): incoming freshmen with ACT score from 19-24 (910-1110 SAT) with a 3.3 GPA or higher; $5000.

FINANCIAL AID PROCEDURES
Forms required: FAFSA.
Dates and Deadlines: Priority date 3/1; closing date 8/1. Applicants notified on a rolling basis starting 3/1; must reply within 4 week(s) of notification.
Transfers: Applicants notified on a rolling basis starting 3/1; must reply within 4 week(s) of notification.

CONTACT
Michael Davis, Director of Financial Aid
1151 North State Street, Elgin, IL 60123-1404
(800) 879-5376

Kankakee Community College

Kankakee, Illinois
www.kcc.edu   Federal Code: 007690

2-year public community college in large town.
Enrollment: 2,551 undergrads, 55% part-time. 183 full-time freshmen.
Selectivity: Open admission; but selective for some programs.

BASIC COSTS (2007-2008)
Tuition and fees: $2,070; out-of-district residents $5,143; out-of-state residents $9,275.
Per-credit charge: $69; out-of-district residents $171; out-of-state residents $309.

FINANCIAL AID PICTURE
Students with need: Need-based aid available for full-time and part-time students.
Students without need: No-need awards available for athletics.

FINANCIAL AID PROCEDURES
Forms required: FAFSA, institutional form.
Dates and Deadlines: Priority date 6/1; no closing date. Applicants notified on a rolling basis; must reply within 4 week(s) of notification.

CONTACT
John Perry, Director of Financial Aid
100 College Drive, Kankakee, IL 60901-6505
(815) 802-8550

Kaskaskia College

Centralia, Illinois
www.kaskaskia.edu   Federal Code: 001701

2-year public community college in large town.
Enrollment: 2,795 undergrads, 42% part-time. 337 full-time freshmen.
Selectivity: Open admission; but selective for some programs.

BASIC COSTS (2007-2008)
Tuition and fees: $2,040; out-of-district residents $3,720; out-of-state residents $8,416.
Per-credit charge: $61; out-of-district residents $117; out-of-state residents $274.

FINANCIAL AID PICTURE (2007-2008)
Students with need: Out of 220 full-time freshmen who applied for aid, 220 were judged to have need. Of these, 220 received aid. Average financial aid package met 65% of need; average scholarship/grant was $2,261; average loan was $1,713. For part-time students, average financial aid package was $3,735.
Students without need: 68 full-time freshmen who did not demonstrate need for aid received scholarships/grants; average award was $779. No-need awards available for academics, athletics, state/district residency.
Scholarships offered: 39 full-time freshmen received athletic scholarships; average amount $3,166.

FINANCIAL AID PROCEDURES
Forms required: FAFSA.
Dates and Deadlines: Priority date 5/15; no closing date. Applicants notified on a rolling basis starting 4/1; must reply within 2 week(s) of notification.
Transfers: No deadline. Applicants notified on a rolling basis.

CONTACT
Lisa Collier, Director of Financial Aid
27210 College Road, Centralia, IL 62801
(618) 545-3080

Kishwaukee College

Malta, Illinois
www.kishwaukeecollege.edu   Federal Code: 007684

2-year public community college in rural community.
Enrollment: 3,694 undergrads.
Selectivity: Open admission; but selective for some programs.

BASIC COSTS (2007-2008)
Tuition and fees: $2,310; out-of-district residents $8,055; out-of-state residents $8,706.
Per-credit charge: $68; out-of-district residents $260; out-of-state residents $281.

FINANCIAL AID PICTURE
Students with need: Need-based aid available for full-time and part-time students. Work study available nights, weekends, and for part-time students.
Students without need: No-need awards available for academics, athletics, leadership, music/drama, state/district residency.

FINANCIAL AID PROCEDURES
Forms required: FAFSA, institutional form.
Dates and Deadlines: Priority date 5/1; no closing date. Applicants notified on a rolling basis starting 5/1; must reply within 2 week(s) of notification.
Transfers: Must reply within 2 week(s) of notification. Some state programs not available to sophomore status students.

CONTACT

Pamela Wagener, Director, Financial Aid/Veterans Affairs

21193 Malta Road, Malta, IL 60150-9699

(815) 825-2086 ext. 224

Knox College

Galesburg, Illinois

www.knox.edu

Federal Code: 001704

4-year private liberal arts college in large town.

Enrollment: 1,353 undergrads. 307 full-time freshmen.

Selectivity: Admits 50 to 75% of applicants.

BASIC COSTS (2008-2009)

Tuition and fees: $30,507.

Room and board: $6,726.

FINANCIAL AID PICTURE (2007-2008)

Students with need: Out of 263 full-time freshmen who applied for aid, 221 were judged to have need. Of these, 221 received aid, and 96 had their full need met. Average financial aid package met 95% of need; average scholarship/grant was $17,969; average loan was $5,078. Need-based aid available for part-time students.

Students without need: 74 full-time freshmen who did not demonstrate need for aid received scholarships/grants; average award was $9,703. No-need awards available for academics, art, music/drama.

Scholarships offered: Academic scholarship; up to $15,000; based on high school academic performance and class rank. Visual and performing arts scholarships (in music, art, theater, dance, writing); up to $4,000; based on auditions or submission of portfolios. Social Concerns Scholarships; up to $4,000; based on community service activity.

FINANCIAL AID PROCEDURES

Forms required: FAFSA, institutional form.

Dates and Deadlines: Priority date 2/1; no closing date. Applicants notified on a rolling basis starting 3/15; must reply by 5/1 or within 2 week(s) of notification.

Transfers: Priority date 4/1. Applicants notified on a rolling basis starting 4/15; must reply by 6/1 or within 2 week(s) of notification. Students who are one-year internationals and who have no previous college work are considered to be first-year in aid computations, but not in enrollment, retention, and graduation.

CONTACT

Teresa Jackson, Director of Financial Aid

Knox College - Campus Box 148, Galesburg, IL 61401-4999

(309) 341-7149

Lake Forest College

Lake Forest, Illinois

www.lakeforest.edu

Federal Code: 001706

4-year private liberal arts college in large town, affiliated with Presbyterian Church (USA).

Enrollment: 1,408 undergrads, 1% part-time. 356 full-time freshmen.

Selectivity: Admits 50 to 75% of applicants.

BASIC COSTS (2008-2009)

Tuition and fees: $32,520.

Per-credit charge: $1,004.

Room and board: $7,724.

FINANCIAL AID PICTURE (2007-2008)

Students with need: Out of 235 full-time freshmen who applied for aid, 189 were judged to have need. Of these, 188 received aid, and 37 had their full need met. Average financial aid package met 88% of need; average scholarship/grant was $20,096; average loan was $4,444. For part-time students, average financial aid package was $14,173.

Students without need: 121 full-time freshmen who did not demonstrate need for aid received scholarships/grants; average award was $19,083. No-need awards available for academics, alumni affiliation, art, leadership, music/drama.

Scholarships offered: Academic Scholarships; up to $16,000; non-need based. Forester Scholarships; $1,000-$5,000; awarded in art, modern languages, leadership, music, math and computer science, science, theater, and writing; non-need based.

FINANCIAL AID PROCEDURES

Forms required: FAFSA.

Dates and Deadlines: Priority date 2/15; no closing date. Applicants notified on a rolling basis starting 2/15; must reply by 5/1 or within 3 week(s) of notification.

Transfers: Closing date 6/1. Applicants notified on a rolling basis starting 1/3; must reply within 3 week(s) of notification.

CONTACT

Gerard Cebrzynski, Financial Aid Director

555 North Sheridan Road, Lake Forest, IL 60045-2399

(847) 735-5015

Lake Land College

Mattoon, Illinois

www.lakelandcollege.edu

Federal Code: 007644

2-year public community college in large town.

Enrollment: 5,467 undergrads.

Selectivity: Open admission; but selective for some programs.

BASIC COSTS (2007-2008)

Tuition and fees: $2,214; out-of-district residents $4,779; out-of-state residents $8,769.

Per-credit charge: $74; out-of-district residents $144; out-of-state residents $277.

FINANCIAL AID PICTURE (2006-2007)

Students with need: 78% of average financial aid package awarded as scholarships/grants, 22% awarded as loans/jobs. Need-based aid available for part-time students. Work study available nights, weekends, and for part-time students.

Students without need: No-need awards available for academics, athletics.

FINANCIAL AID PROCEDURES

Forms required: FAFSA.

Dates and Deadlines: Priority date 5/1; no closing date. Applicants notified on a rolling basis starting 6/1.

Transfers: No deadline.

CONTACT

Paula Carpenter, Director of Financial Aid and Veteran Services

5001 Lake Land Boulevard, Mattoon, IL 61938-9366

(217) 234-5231

Lakeview College of Nursing

Danville, Illinois

www.lakeviewcol.edu

Federal Code: 010501

Upper-division private nursing college in large town.

Enrollment: 252 undergrads.

Selectivity: Open admission; but selective for some programs.

BASIC COSTS (2007-2008)
Tuition and fees: $10,950.
Per-credit charge: $365.

FINANCIAL AID PICTURE
Students with need: Need-based aid available for full-time and part-time students.
Students without need: This college awards aid only to students with need.

FINANCIAL AID PROCEDURES
Forms required: FAFSA, institutional form.
Dates and Deadlines: Closing date 4/15.
Transfers: Priority date 4/15; no deadline.

CONTACT
Janet Ingargiola, Director of Financial Aid
903 North Logan Avenue, Danville, IL 61832
(217) 554-6887

Lewis and Clark Community College
Godfrey, Illinois
www.lc.edu
Federal Code: 010020

2-year public community college in large town.
Enrollment: 4,393 undergrads.
Selectivity: Open admission; but selective for some programs.

BASIC COSTS (2007-2008)
Tuition and fees: $2,400; out-of-district residents $6,660; out-of-state residents $8,790.
Per-credit charge: $71; out-of-district residents $213; out-of-state residents $284.
Additional info: Out-of-state, out-of-district on-line tuition is $95 per credit including fees.

FINANCIAL AID PICTURE
Students with need: Need-based aid available for full-time and part-time students.

FINANCIAL AID PROCEDURES
Forms required: FAFSA.
Dates and Deadlines: Priority date 6/1; no closing date. Applicants notified on a rolling basis starting 8/1; must reply within 3 week(s) of notification.
Transfers: No deadline. Applicants notified on a rolling basis.

CONTACT
Angela Weaver, Director, Financial Aid
5800 Godfrey Road, Godfrey, IL 62035-2466
(618) 468-2223

Lewis University
Romeoville, Illinois
www.lewisu.edu
Federal Code: 001707

4-year private university in large town, affiliated with Roman Catholic Church.
Enrollment: 3,822 undergrads, 23% part-time. 635 full-time freshmen.
Selectivity: Admits 50 to 75% of applicants.

BASIC COSTS (2008-2009)
Tuition and fees: $21,990.
Per-credit charge: $705.
Room and board: $8,000.
Additional info: Tuition/fee waivers available for adults.

FINANCIAL AID PICTURE (2007-2008)
Students with need: Average financial aid package met 77% of need; average scholarship/grant was $7,694; average loan was $4,846. For part-time students, average financial aid package was $9,984.
Students without need: No-need awards available for academics, alumni affiliation, art, athletics, job skills, music/drama, religious affiliation, ROTC.

FINANCIAL AID PROCEDURES
Forms required: FAFSA.
Dates and Deadlines: Closing date 5/1. Applicants notified on a rolling basis starting 2/1; must reply by 5/1 or within 2 week(s) of notification.
Transfers: No deadline. Applicants notified on a rolling basis; must reply by 8/1 or within 2 week(s) of notification.

CONTACT
Janeen Decharinte, Director of Financial Aid
One University Parkway, Romeoville, IL 60446-2200
(815) 836-5262

Lexington College
Chicago, Illinois
www.lexingtoncollege.edu
Federal Code: 016942

4-year private hospitality management college for women in very large city, affiliated with Roman Catholic Church.
Enrollment: 57 undergrads.
Selectivity: Admits less than 50% of applicants.

BASIC COSTS (2007-2008)
Tuition and fees: $20,550.
Per-credit charge: $665.
Room and board: $8,000.

FINANCIAL AID PICTURE
Students with need: Need-based aid available for full-time and part-time students.
Students without need: This college awards aid only to students with need.
Additional info: Work-study is available.

FINANCIAL AID PROCEDURES
Forms required: FAFSA.
Dates and Deadlines: Priority date 5/15; no closing date. Applicants notified on a rolling basis starting 7/1; must reply within 2 week(s) of notification.
Transfers: Closing date 5/15. Students who enroll and then transfer to another college within a given term can only receive Illinois state aid at one institution per academic year.

CONTACT
Maria LeBron, Director of Financial Aid
310 South Peoria Street, Suite 512, Chicago, IL 60607-3534
(312) 226-6294 ext. 227

Lincoln Christian College and Seminary
Lincoln, Illinois
www.lccs.edu
Federal Code: 001708

4-year private Bible and seminary college in large town, affiliated with Church of Christ.
Enrollment: 636 undergrads.
Selectivity: Admits over 75% of applicants.

BASIC COSTS (2008-2009)
Tuition and fees: $11,790.
Per-credit charge: $393.
Room and board: $5,355.

FINANCIAL AID PICTURE

Students with need: Need-based aid available for full-time and part-time students. Work study available nights, weekends, and for part-time students.
Students without need: No-need awards available for academics.

FINANCIAL AID PROCEDURES

Forms required: FAFSA, institutional form.
Dates and Deadlines: Priority date 8/10; no closing date. Applicants notified on a rolling basis starting 3/1; must reply within 2 week(s) of notification.

CONTACT

Nancy Siddens, Co-Director of Student Financial Aid
100 Campus View Drive, Lincoln, IL 62656-2167
(217) 732-3168 ext. 2304

Lincoln College

Lincoln, Illinois
www.lincolncollege.edu
Federal Code: 001709

2-year private junior college in large town.
Enrollment: 800 undergrads.

BASIC COSTS (2007-2008)
Tuition and fees: $18,000.
Per-credit charge: $600.
Room and board: $6,000.
Additional info: Tuition at time of enrollment locked for 2 years.

FINANCIAL AID PICTURE

Students with need: Need-based aid available for full-time and part-time students. Work study available nights, weekends, and for part-time students.
Students without need: No-need awards available for academics, art, athletics, music/drama.
Additional info: Auditions recommended for music, speech, theater, broadcasting, and dance scholarship candidates, portfolios recommended for art and technical theater scholarship candidates.

FINANCIAL AID PROCEDURES

Forms required: FAFSA.
Dates and Deadlines: Priority date 6/1; closing date 7/1. Applicants notified on a rolling basis starting 6/1; must reply within 3 week(s) of notification.

CONTACT

Kevin Stephens, Director of Financial Aid
300 Keokuk Street, Lincoln, IL 62656
(217) 732-3155 ext. 230

Lincoln Land Community College

Springfield, Illinois
www.llcc.edu
Federal Code: 007170

2-year public community and junior college in small city.
Enrollment: 5,196 undergrads, 56% part-time. 511 full-time freshmen.
Selectivity: Open admission; but selective for some programs.

BASIC COSTS (2008-2009)
Tuition and fees: $2,505; out-of-district residents $4,710; out-of-state residents $6,915.
Per-credit charge: $74; out-of-district residents $147; out-of-state residents $221.
Additional info: Tuition/fee waivers available for minority students.

FINANCIAL AID PICTURE

Students with need: Need-based aid available for full-time and part-time students. Work study available nights.
Students without need: No-need awards available for academics, athletics, minority status, state/district residency.

FINANCIAL AID PROCEDURES

Forms required: FAFSA, institutional form.
Dates and Deadlines: Priority date 5/1; no closing date. Applicants notified on a rolling basis starting 4/15; must reply within 2 week(s) of notification.

CONTACT

Lee Bursi, Associate Vice President, Financial Aid
5250 Shepherd Road, Springfield, IL 62794-9256
(217) 786-2237

Loyola University Chicago

Chicago, Illinois
www.luc.edu
Federal Code: 001710

4-year private university in very large city, affiliated with Roman Catholic Church.
Enrollment: 9,365 undergrads, 5% part-time. 2,130 full-time freshmen.
Selectivity: Admits 50 to 75% of applicants.

BASIC COSTS (2008-2009)
Tuition and fees: $29,486.
Per-credit charge: $580.
Room and board: $10,490.

FINANCIAL AID PICTURE (2006-2007)
Students with need: Out of 1,825 full-time freshmen who applied for aid, 1,538 were judged to have need. Of these, 1,532 received aid, and 127 had their full need met. Average financial aid package met 78% of need; average scholarship/grant was $14,896; average loan was $3,041. For part-time students, average financial aid package was $10,715.
Students without need: 338 full-time freshmen who did not demonstrate need for aid received scholarships/grants; average award was $6,048. No-need awards available for academics, athletics, leadership, music/drama, religious affiliation.
Scholarships offered: 19 full-time freshmen received athletic scholarships; average amount $13,988.
Cumulative student debt: 67% of graduating class had student loans; average debt was $25,470.

FINANCIAL AID PROCEDURES

Forms required: FAFSA.
Dates and Deadlines: Priority date 3/1; no closing date. Applicants notified on a rolling basis starting 2/15; must reply within 3 week(s) of notification.
Transfers: FAFSA must be filed by July 1 to receive Illinois map grant.

CONTACT

Eric Weems, Director, Student Financial Assistance
820 North Michigan Avenue, Chicago, IL 60611-9810
(773) 508-3155

MacMurray College

Jacksonville, Illinois
www.mac.edu
Federal Code: 001717

4-year private liberal arts college in large town, affiliated with United Methodist Church.
Enrollment: 634 undergrads.
Selectivity: Admits 50 to 75% of applicants.

BASIC COSTS (2008-2009)
Tuition and fees: $17,450.
Per-credit charge: $565.
Room and board: $6,995.

FINANCIAL AID PICTURE

Students with need: Need-based aid available for full-time and part-time students. Work study available nights, weekends, and for part-time students.

Students without need: No-need awards available for academics, alumni affiliation, art, leadership, music/drama, religious affiliation.

Scholarships offered: Academic scholarships: $500-$1,4000; based on merit. Music performance and art competition scholarships available. Transfer scholarships: to $10,000; based on academic merit. Leadership scholarships: available based on committee selection.

Additional info: Merit scholarships for accepted, enrolled freshman based on academic record. Need-based program meets 100% of direct tuition charges after family contribution and financial aid.

FINANCIAL AID PROCEDURES

Forms required: FAFSA.

Dates and Deadlines: Priority date 5/1; no closing date. Applicants notified on a rolling basis starting 2/1; must reply within 2 week(s) of notification.

Transfers: No deadline.

CONTACT

Debbie Wellhausen, Director of Financial Aid
447 East College Avenue, Jacksonville, IL 62650-2590
(217) 479-7041

McHenry County College

Crystal Lake, Illinois
www.mchenry.edu   Federal Code: 007691

2-year public community college in large town.

Enrollment: 5,275 undergrads.

Selectivity: Open admission.

BASIC COSTS (2007-2008)

Tuition and fees: $2,474; out-of-district residents $8,414; out-of-state residents $9,674.

Per-credit charge: $73; out-of-district residents $271; out-of-state residents $313.

FINANCIAL AID PICTURE

Students with need: Need-based aid available for full-time and part-time students. Work study available nights, weekends, and for part-time students.

Students without need: No-need awards available for academics, athletics, leadership, music/drama, state/district residency.

Scholarships offered: President's Scholarship: full tuition for two years; based on talent in academic areas; students must complete portfolio and have 3.0 GPA. Founding Faculty Scholarship: full tuition for 2 years; based on GPA and essay.

Additional info: Students can apply throughout the award year for federal and state aid. Students with physical handicaps or learning disabilities may apply for special needs scholarship.

FINANCIAL AID PROCEDURES

Forms required: FAFSA, institutional form.

Dates and Deadlines: Priority date 6/1; no closing date. Applicants notified on a rolling basis starting 5/1.

CONTACT

Marianne Devenny, Director, Office of Financial Aid and Records
8900 U.S. Highway 14, Crystal Lake, IL 60012-2761
(815) 455-8761

McKendree University

Lebanon, Illinois
www.mckendree.edu   Federal Code: 001722

4-year private university and liberal arts college in small town, affiliated with United Methodist Church.

Enrollment: 2,363 undergrads, 29% part-time. 339 full-time freshmen.

Selectivity: Admits 50 to 75% of applicants.

BASIC COSTS (2008-2009)

Tuition and fees: $21,270.

Per-credit charge: $690.

Room and board: $8,220.

FINANCIAL AID PICTURE (2007-2008)

Students with need: Average financial aid package met 85% of need; average scholarship/grant was $14,548; average loan was $2,898. For part-time students, average financial aid package was $5,802.

Students without need: No-need awards available for academics, alumni affiliation, art, athletics, leadership, minority status, music/drama, religious affiliation.

Scholarships offered: Academic Scholarships; $4,000 to $17,000; 25 ACT or 3.4 GPA.

Cumulative student debt: 54% of graduating class had student loans; average debt was $17,648.

FINANCIAL AID PROCEDURES

Forms required: FAFSA.

Dates and Deadlines: Priority date 5/31; no closing date. Applicants notified on a rolling basis starting 3/1; must reply within 4 week(s) of notification.

Transfers: No deadline. Applicants notified on a rolling basis.

CONTACT

Chris Hall, Vice President for Admission and Financial Aid
701 College Road, Lebanon, IL 62254
(618) 537-6829

Midstate College

Peoria, Illinois
www.midstate.edu   Federal Code: 004568

4-year for-profit business college in small city.

Enrollment: 560 undergrads, 58% part-time. 10 full-time freshmen.

Selectivity: Open admission; but selective for some programs.

BASIC COSTS (2008-2009)

Tuition and fees: $11,985.

Per-credit charge: $283.

Additional info: Fees vary according to program.

FINANCIAL AID PICTURE

Students with need: Work study available nights, weekends, and for part-time students.

Additional info: Work-study program available.

FINANCIAL AID PROCEDURES

Forms required: FAFSA, institutional form.

Dates and Deadlines: No deadline. Applicants notified on a rolling basis; must reply within 4 week(s) of notification.

CONTACT

Janet Ozuna, Director of Finance
411 West Northmoor Road, Peoria, IL 61614-3558
(800) 251-4299

Millikin University

Decatur, Illinois
www.millikin.edu   Federal Code: 001724

4-year private university in small city, affiliated with Presbyterian Church (USA).

Enrollment: 2,295 undergrads, 5% part-time. 476 full-time freshmen.

Selectivity: Admits 50 to 75% of applicants.

BASIC COSTS (2008-2009)

Tuition and fees: $25,295.

Per-credit charge: $820.

Room and board: $7,485.

FINANCIAL AID PICTURE (2006-2007)

Students with need: Out of 446 full-time freshmen who applied for aid, 373 were judged to have need. Of these, 372 received aid, and 150 had their full need met. Average financial aid package met 87% of need; average scholarship/grant was $6,540; average loan was $3,486. For part-time students, average financial aid package was $6,914.

Students without need: 73 full-time freshmen who did not demonstrate need for aid received scholarships/grants; average award was $7,757. No-need awards available for academics, alumni affiliation, art, leadership, minority status, music/drama.

Scholarships offered: Freshman Honors Scholar Program; at least $10,000, may qualify for more based on financial aid.

Cumulative student debt: 79% of graduating class had student loans; average debt was $21,177.

FINANCIAL AID PROCEDURES

Forms required: FAFSA.

Dates and Deadlines: Priority date 3/15; no closing date. Applicants notified on a rolling basis starting 3/15; must reply by 5/1 or within 4 week(s) of notification.

Transfers: No deadline. Applicants notified on a rolling basis starting 3/15; must reply by 5/1 or within 4 week(s) of notification.

CONTACT

Cheryl Howerton, Director of Financial Aid
1184 West Main Street, Decatur, IL 62522-2084
(217) 424-6317

Monmouth College

Monmouth, Illinois
www.monm.edu   Federal Code: 001725

4-year private liberal arts college in large town, affiliated with Presbyterian Church (USA).

Enrollment: 1,331 undergrads, 1% part-time. 393 full-time freshmen.

Selectivity: Admits over 75% of applicants.

BASIC COSTS (2008-2009)

Tuition and fees: $24,000.

Per-credit charge: $800.

Room and board: $7,000.

FINANCIAL AID PICTURE (2007-2008)

Students with need: Out of 385 full-time freshmen who applied for aid, 331 were judged to have need. Of these, 331 received aid, and 93 had their full need met. Average financial aid package met 90% of need; average scholarship/grant was $15,150; average loan was $2,715. For part-time students, average financial aid package was $15,616.

Students without need: 61 full-time freshmen who did not demonstrate need for aid received scholarships/grants; average award was $9,282. No-need awards available for academics, art, music/drama, ROTC.

Cumulative student debt: 84% of graduating class had student loans; average debt was $22,781.

FINANCIAL AID PROCEDURES

Forms required: FAFSA.

Dates and Deadlines: Priority date 3/1; no closing date. Applicants notified on a rolling basis starting 3/1; must reply by 8/31.

CONTACT

Jayne Whiteside, Director of Financial Aid
700 East Broadway, Monmouth, IL 61462-9989
(309) 457-2129

Moody Bible Institute

Chicago, Illinois
www.moody.edu   Federal Code: 001727

4-year private Bible college in very large city, affiliated with interdenominational tradition.

Enrollment: 2,840 undergrads.

BASIC COSTS (2007-2008)

Additional info: Undergraduate students in the BA and BMus programs on main campus are not charged tuition. Undergraduate students taking courses through distance learning programs (ABS, BSBS) and in BSMAT (Bachelor of Science in Missionary Aviation) program pay tuition of $199 per credit hour. Tuition at time of enrollment locked for 4 years.

FINANCIAL AID PICTURE

Students with need: Need-based aid available for full-time students.

Students without need: This college awards aid only to students with need.

Additional info: Aid available to upperclassmen is based on private and not federal/state sources.

FINANCIAL AID PROCEDURES

Dates and Deadlines: No deadline.

Transfers: Students should complete two semesters of study in residence before applying for aid.

CONTACT

Esther Kim, Financial Aid Coordinator
820 North La Salle Boulevard, Chicago, IL 60610
(312) 329-4178

Moraine Valley Community College

Palos Hills, Illinois
www.morainevalley.edu   Federal Code: 007692

2-year public community college in large town.

Enrollment: 10,758 undergrads, 47% part-time. 1,435 full-time freshmen.

Selectivity: Open admission; but selective for some programs.

BASIC COSTS (2008-2009)

Tuition and fees: $2,222; out-of-district residents $6,422; out-of-state residents $7,712.

Per-credit charge: $69; out-of-district residents $209; out-of-state residents $252.

FINANCIAL AID PICTURE (2007-2008)

Students with need: 90% of average financial aid package awarded as scholarships/grants, 10% awarded as loans/jobs. Need-based aid available for part-time students. Work study available nights.

Students without need: No-need awards available for academics, athletics, leadership.

FINANCIAL AID PROCEDURES

Forms required: FAFSA, institutional form.

Dates and Deadlines: Priority date 5/1; no closing date. Applicants notified on a rolling basis starting 3/1; must reply within 4 week(s) of notification.

CONTACT

Laurie Anema, Director of Financial Aid
9000 West College Parkway, Palos Hills, IL 60465-0937
(708) 974-5726

Morrison Institute of Technology
Morrison, Illinois
www.morrison.tec.il.us
Federal Code: 008880

2-year private junior and technical college in small town.

Enrollment: 144 undergrads.

Selectivity: Open admission.

BASIC COSTS (2008-2009)
Tuition and fees: $13,360.
Per-credit charge: $545.
Room only: $2,700.

FINANCIAL AID PICTURE (2007-2008)
Students with need: Need-based aid available for part-time students. Work study available nights, weekends, and for part-time students.

Students without need: No-need awards available for academics.

FINANCIAL AID PROCEDURES
Forms required: FAFSA, institutional form.

Dates and Deadlines: No deadline. Applicants notified on a rolling basis; must reply within 2 week(s) of notification.

CONTACT
Julie Damhoff, Financial Aid Officer
701 Portland Avenue, Morrison, IL 61270-2959
(815) 772-7218

Morton College
Cicero, Illinois
www.morton.edu
Federal Code: 001728

2-year public community college in small city.

Enrollment: 2,183 undergrads, 59% part-time. 213 full-time freshmen.

Selectivity: Open admission; but selective for some programs and for out-of-state students.

BASIC COSTS (2007-2008)
Tuition and fees: $2,452; out-of-district residents $6,292; out-of-state residents $8,212.
Per-credit charge: $64; out-of-district residents $192; out-of-state residents $256.

FINANCIAL AID PICTURE
Students with need: Need-based aid available for full-time and part-time students. Work study available nights, weekends, and for part-time students.

FINANCIAL AID PROCEDURES
Forms required: FAFSA, institutional form.

Dates and Deadlines: Priority date 6/1; no closing date. Applicants notified on a rolling basis starting 8/1.

CONTACT
Nicole Smith-Peterson, Coordinator of Financial Aid
3801 South Central Avenue, Cicero, IL 60804-4398
(708) 656-8000 ext. 428

North Central College
Naperville, Illinois
www.northcentralcollege.edu
Federal Code: 001734

4-year private liberal arts college in small city, affiliated with United Methodist Church.

Enrollment: 2,142 undergrads, 6% part-time. 421 full-time freshmen.

Selectivity: Admits 50 to 75% of applicants.

BASIC COSTS (2008-2009)
Tuition and fees: $25,938.
Per-credit charge: $645.
Room and board: $8,217.

FINANCIAL AID PICTURE (2007-2008)
Students with need: Out of 362 full-time freshmen who applied for aid, 301 were judged to have need. Of these, 301 received aid, and 78 had their full need met. Average financial aid package met 84% of need; average scholarship/grant was $15,724; average loan was $2,799. For part-time students, average financial aid package was $10,807.

Students without need: 92 full-time freshmen who did not demonstrate need for aid received scholarships/grants; average award was $8,029. No-need awards available for academics, art, leadership, minority status, music/drama, religious affiliation, ROTC, state/district residency.

Scholarships offered: Numerous merit and talent scholarship opportunities available.

Cumulative student debt: 75% of graduating class had student loans; average debt was $23,575.

FINANCIAL AID PROCEDURES
Forms required: FAFSA, institutional form.

Dates and Deadlines: No deadline. Applicants notified on a rolling basis starting 3/1; must reply within 4 week(s) of notification.

CONTACT
Marty Rossman, Director of Financial Aid
PO Box 3063, Naperville, IL 60566-7063
(630) 637-5600

North Park University
Chicago, Illinois
www.northpark.edu
Federal Code: 001735

4-year private university and liberal arts college in very large city, affiliated with Evangelical Covenant Church.

Enrollment: 2,160 undergrads, 18% part-time. 368 full-time freshmen.

Selectivity: Admits 50 to 75% of applicants.

BASIC COSTS (2008-2009)
Tuition and fees: $17,600.
Per-credit charge: $650.
Room and board: $7,520.

FINANCIAL AID PICTURE (2006-2007)
Students with need: Out of 319 full-time freshmen who applied for aid, 249 were judged to have need. Of these, 249 received aid, and 38 had their full need met. Average financial aid package met 74% of need; average scholarship/grant was $7,186; average loan was $2,331.

Students without need: 75 full-time freshmen who did not demonstrate need for aid received scholarships/grants; average award was $3,070. No-need awards available for academics, art, music/drama, religious affiliation.

Cumulative student debt: 75% of graduating class had student loans; average debt was $19,300.

FINANCIAL AID PROCEDURES
Forms required: FAFSA.

Dates and Deadlines: Priority date 5/1; closing date 8/1. Applicants notified on a rolling basis starting 10/1; must reply by 5/1 or within 3 week(s) of notification.

CONTACT
Lucy Shaker, Director of Financial Aid
3225 West Foster Avenue, Chicago, IL 60625-4895
(773) 244-5506

Northeastern Illinois University

Chicago, Illinois
www.neiu.edu   Federal Code: 001693

4-year public university in very large city.

Enrollment: 8,891 undergrads, 44% part-time. 870 full-time freshmen.

Selectivity: Admits 50 to 75% of applicants.

BASIC COSTS (2008-2009)

Tuition and fees: $8,016; out-of-state residents $14,616.

Per-credit charge: $220; out-of-state residents $440.

FINANCIAL AID PICTURE (2007-2008)

Students with need: Out of 635 full-time freshmen who applied for aid, 467 were judged to have need. Of these, 455 received aid, and 22 had their full need met. Average financial aid package met 57% of need; average scholarship/grant was $6,631; average loan was $3,006. For part-time students, average financial aid package was $5,229.

Students without need: 17 full-time freshmen who did not demonstrate need for aid received scholarships/grants; average award was $1,408. No-need awards available for academics, art, leadership, music/drama.

FINANCIAL AID PROCEDURES

Forms required: FAFSA, institutional form.

Dates and Deadlines: Priority date 2/28; no closing date. Applicants notified on a rolling basis starting 4/1; must reply within 3 week(s) of notification.

CONTACT

J. Jennings, Director of Financial Aid
5500 North St. Louis Avenue, Chicago, IL 60625
(773) 442-5000

Northern Illinois University

DeKalb, Illinois
www.niu.edu   Federal Code: 001737

4-year public university in large town.

Enrollment: 18,915 undergrads, 10% part-time. 2,995 full-time freshmen.

Selectivity: Admits 50 to 75% of applicants.

BASIC COSTS (2007-2008)

Tuition and fees: $7,889; out-of-state residents $14,039.

Per-credit charge: $227; out-of-state residents $454.

Room and board: $8,200.

Additional info: Tuition/fee waivers available for minority students.

FINANCIAL AID PICTURE (2007-2008)

Students with need: For part-time students, average financial aid package was $7,700.

Students without need: No-need awards available for academics, athletics, ROTC.

FINANCIAL AID PROCEDURES

Forms required: FAFSA, institutional form.

Dates and Deadlines: Priority date 3/1; no closing date. Applicants notified on a rolling basis starting 4/15.

CONTACT

Kathleen Brunson, Director of Student Financial Aid DeKalb, IL 60115-2854
(815) 753-1395

Northwestern Business College

Chicago, Illinois
www.northwesternbc.edu   Federal Code: 012362

2-year for-profit technical college in very large city.

Enrollment: 1,987 undergrads.

Selectivity: Admits 50 to 75% of applicants.

BASIC COSTS (2008-2009)

Tuition and fees: $18,997.

Per-credit charge: $370.

Additional info: Tuition may be higher for some classes.

FINANCIAL AID PICTURE (2007-2008)

Students with need: 50% of average financial aid package awarded as scholarships/grants, 50% awarded as loans/jobs. Need-based aid available for part-time students. Work study available nights.

Students without need: No-need awards available for academics.

Scholarships offered: President's Scholarship: $400 per quarter, up to $2,400. Vice-Presidential Scholarship: $300 per quarter, up to $1,800. Early bird scholarships: $750 first year, $1,500 sophomore year; must enroll by May 31 for fall quarter, must be full time.

Additional info: State grant programs for Illinois residents and alternative loans offered.

FINANCIAL AID PROCEDURES

Forms required: FAFSA, institutional form.

Dates and Deadlines: Priority date 6/30; no closing date. Applicants notified on a rolling basis starting 8/15; must reply within 4 week(s) of notification.

CONTACT

Frank McClinton, Director of Financial Assistance
4839 North Milwaukee Avenue, Chicago, IL 60630
(708) 237-5050

Northwestern University

Evanston, Illinois   Federal Code: 001739
www.northwestern.edu   CSS Code: 1565

4-year private university in small city.

Enrollment: 8,176 undergrads, 1% part-time. 1,981 full-time freshmen.

Selectivity: Admits less than 50% of applicants.

BASIC COSTS (2007-2008)

Tuition and fees: $35,429.

Room and board: $10,776.

FINANCIAL AID PICTURE (2007-2008)

Students with need: Out of 1,031 full-time freshmen who applied for aid, 845 were judged to have need. Of these, 845 received aid, and 845 had their full need met. Average financial aid package met 100% of need; average scholarship/grant was $25,228; average loan was $3,633.

Students without need: This college awards aid only to students with need.

Scholarships offered: 101 full-time freshmen received athletic scholarships; average amount $25,317.

Cumulative student debt: 46% of graduating class had student loans; average debt was $18,393.

FINANCIAL AID PROCEDURES

Forms required: FAFSA, CSS PROFILE.

Dates and Deadlines: Closing date 2/15. Applicants notified by 4/15; must reply by 5/1 or within 2 week(s) of notification.

Transfers: Closing date 6/1. Transfer student aid limited for first year.

CONTACT

Carolyn Lindley, Director of University Financial Aid

1801 Hinman Avenue, Evanston, IL 60204-3060

(847) 491-7400

Oakton Community College
Des Plaines, Illinois

www.oakton.edu   Federal Code: 009896

2-year public community college in small city.

Enrollment: 5,066 undergrads.

Selectivity: Open admission; but selective for some programs.

BASIC COSTS (2007-2008)

Tuition and fees: $2,578; out-of-district residents $7,134; out-of-state residents $9,016.

Per-credit charge: $82; out-of-district residents $234; out-of-state residents $297.

FINANCIAL AID PICTURE

Students with need: Need-based aid available for full-time and part-time students. Work study available nights, weekends, and for part-time students.

Students without need: No-need awards available for academics, art, leadership, minority status, music/drama, state/district residency.

Additional info: Foundation Scholarships application available January through mid-March.

FINANCIAL AID PROCEDURES

Forms required: FAFSA, institutional form.

Dates and Deadlines: Priority date 5/1; no closing date. Applicants notified on a rolling basis starting 5/1; must reply within 2 week(s) of notification.

Transfers: Applicants notified on a rolling basis starting 5/1.

CONTACT

Cheryl Warmann, Director of Financial Aid

1600 East Golf Road, Des Plaines, IL 60016

(847) 635-1708

Olivet Nazarene University
Bourbonnais, Illinois

www.olivet.edu   Federal Code: 001741

4-year private university and liberal arts college in small city, affiliated with Church of the Nazarene.

Enrollment: 3,190 undergrads, 16% part-time. 704 full-time freshmen.

Selectivity: Admits over 75% of applicants.

BASIC COSTS (2008-2009)

Tuition and fees: $21,590.

Per-credit charge: $865.

Room and board: $6,400.

FINANCIAL AID PICTURE

Students with need: Need-based aid available for full-time and part-time students. Work study available nights, weekends, and for part-time students.

Students without need: No-need awards available for academics, art, athletics, leadership, music/drama, religious affiliation, ROTC, state/district residency.

FINANCIAL AID PROCEDURES

Forms required: FAFSA, institutional form.

Dates and Deadlines: Priority date 3/1; no closing date. Applicants notified on a rolling basis starting 1/15; must reply within 2 week(s) of notification.

CONTACT

Greg Bruner, Director of Financial Aid

One University Avenue, Bourbonnais, IL 60914

(815) 939-5249

Parkland College
Champaign, Illinois

www.parkland.edu   Federal Code: 007118

2-year public community college in small city.

Enrollment: 9,210 undergrads, 53% part-time. 804 full-time freshmen.

Selectivity: Open admission; but selective for some programs.

BASIC COSTS (2007-2008)

Tuition and fees: $2,550; out-of-district residents $6,660; out-of-state residents $10,230.

Per-credit charge: $82; out-of-district residents $219; out-of-state residents $338.

Additional info: For Internet classes, in-district students pay $82; all others pay $122 per credit hour.

FINANCIAL AID PICTURE (2006-2007)

Students with need: Out of 373 full-time freshmen who applied for aid, 313 were judged to have need. Of these, 228 received aid, and 47 had their full need met. Average financial aid package met 65% of need; average scholarship/grant was $4,239. For part-time students, average financial aid package was $4,243.

Students without need: No-need awards available for academics, art, athletics, leadership, minority status, music/drama, state/district residency.

Cumulative student debt: 41% of graduating class had student loans; average debt was $5,648.

FINANCIAL AID PROCEDURES

Forms required: FAFSA, institutional form.

Dates and Deadlines: Priority date 3/1; no closing date. Applicants notified on a rolling basis starting 6/1; must reply within 2 week(s) of notification.

CONTACT

Tom Wendt, Director of Financial Aid

2400 West Bradley Avenue, Champaign, IL 61821-1899

(217) 351-2276

Prairie State College
Chicago Heights, Illinois

www.prairiestate.edu   Federal Code: 001640

2-year public community college in large town.

Enrollment: 4,642 undergrads.

Selectivity: Open admission; but selective for some programs.

BASIC COSTS (2007-2008)

Tuition and fees: $2,620; out-of-district residents $7,340; out-of-state residents $9,980.

Per-credit charge: $87; out-of-district residents $244; out-of-state residents $332.

FINANCIAL AID PICTURE

Students with need: Need-based aid available for full-time and part-time students. Work study available nights, weekends, and for part-time students.

FINANCIAL AID PROCEDURES

Forms required: FAFSA, institutional form.

Dates and Deadlines: Priority date 7/1; no closing date. Applicants notified on a rolling basis; must reply within 2 week(s) of notification.

CONTACT

Alice Garcia, Director of Financial Aid
202 South Halsted Street, Chicago Heights, IL 60411
(708) 709-3523

Principia College

Elsah, Illinois
www.prin.edu

Federal Code: 001744
CSS Code: 1630

4-year private liberal arts college in rural community, affiliated with First Church of Christ, Scientist (Christian Science).

Enrollment: 500 undergrads.

Selectivity: Admits over 75% of applicants.

BASIC COSTS (2008-2009)

Tuition and fees: $22,950.

Room and board: $8,475.

FINANCIAL AID PICTURE

Students with need: Need-based aid available for full-time and part-time students.

Students without need: No-need awards available for academics, alumni affiliation.

Scholarships offered: Trustee Scholarship; full tuition; Chairman's Scholarship, 3/4 tuition; Presidential Scholarship; 1/2 tuition. Dean's Scholarship; 1/4 tuition; Arthur Schulz, Jr. Alumni Scholarship; $4,500. 4-year scholarships based on high school GPA and test scores. Dean's and Arthur Schulz Scholarships available for transfer students who meet the above criteria with a minimum 3.5 GPA. Children and grandchildren of alumni eligible for 4-year scholarships based on high school or transfer GPA.

Additional info: Need-based tuition reduction work plan combines job with grant.

FINANCIAL AID PROCEDURES

Forms required: CSS PROFILE, institutional form.

Dates and Deadlines: Closing date 3/1. Applicants notified by 4/1.

Transfers: Priority date 3/1.

CONTACT

Julia Conant, Director of Financial Aid
One Maybeck Place, Elsah, IL 62028-9799
(800) 277-4648 ext. 2812

Quincy University

Quincy, Illinois
www.quincy.edu

Federal Code: 001745

4-year private university and liberal arts college in large town, affiliated with Roman Catholic Church.

Enrollment: 982 undergrads, 7% part-time. 234 full-time freshmen.

Selectivity: Admits over 75% of applicants.

BASIC COSTS (2008-2009)

Tuition and fees: $20,790.

Per-credit charge: $480.

Room and board: $7,900.

FINANCIAL AID PICTURE (2007-2008)

Students with need: Out of 220 full-time freshmen who applied for aid, 186 were judged to have need. Of these, 186 received aid, and 21 had their full need met. Average financial aid package met 82% of need; average scholarship/grant was $16,971; average loan was $3,734. For part-time students, average financial aid package was $3,395.

Students without need: 10 full-time freshmen who did not demonstrate need for aid received scholarships/grants; average award was $10,828. No-need awards available for academics, alumni affiliation, art, athletics, music/drama.

Scholarships offered: *Merit:* Academic scholarships; $2,500-$10,000 per year; based on ACT and high school GPA; unlimited number awarded. *Athletic:* 23 full-time freshmen received athletic scholarships; average amount $9,591.

Cumulative student debt: 76% of graduating class had student loans; average debt was $19,612.

FINANCIAL AID PROCEDURES

Forms required: FAFSA.

Dates and Deadlines: Priority date 4/15; no closing date. Applicants notified on a rolling basis starting 2/15; must reply by 5/1 or within 2 week(s) of notification.

CONTACT

Keith Walker, Director of Financial Aid
1800 College Avenue, Quincy, IL 62301-2699
(217) 228-5260

Rend Lake College

Ina, Illinois
www.rlc.edu

Federal Code: 007119

2-year public community college in rural community.

Enrollment: 4,850 undergrads.

Selectivity: Open admission; but selective for some programs.

BASIC COSTS (2007-2008)

Tuition and fees: $2,070; out-of-district residents $3,060; out-of-state residents $4,500.

Per-credit charge: $69; out-of-district residents $102; out-of-state residents $150.

FINANCIAL AID PICTURE

Students with need: Need-based aid available for full-time and part-time students.

Students without need: No-need awards available for academics, art, athletics, leadership, music/drama, state/district residency.

FINANCIAL AID PROCEDURES

Forms required: FAFSA.

Dates and Deadlines: No deadline. Applicants notified on a rolling basis starting 3/15; must reply within 4 week(s) of notification.

CONTACT

Douglas Carlson, Director of Financial Aid
468 North Ken Gray Parkway, Ina, IL 62846
(618) 437-5321 ext. 1385

Richland Community College

Decatur, Illinois
www.richland.edu

Federal Code: 010879

2-year public community college in small city.

Enrollment: 2,502 undergrads, 61% part-time. 246 full-time freshmen.

Selectivity: Open admission; but selective for some programs.

BASIC COSTS (2007-2008)

Tuition and fees: $2,070; out-of-district residents $10,659; out-of-state residents $11,625.

Per-credit charge: $65; out-of-district residents $351; out-of-state residents $388.

FINANCIAL AID PICTURE (2006-2007)

Students with need: Out of 153 full-time freshmen who applied for aid, 94 were judged to have need. Of these, 79 received aid, and 1 had their full need met. Average financial aid package met 42% of need; average scholarship/grant was $3,723; average loan was $1,952. For part-time students, average financial aid package was $2,892.

Students without need: 11 full-time freshmen who did not demonstrate need for aid received scholarships/grants; average award was $53. No-need awards available for academics.

FINANCIAL AID PROCEDURES

Forms required: FAFSA.

Dates and Deadlines: Closing date 6/30. Applicants notified on a rolling basis starting 3/20.

Transfers: No deadline. Applicants notified on a rolling basis.

CONTACT

Deborah McGee, Director of Financial Aid
One College Park, Decatur, IL 62521
(217) 875-7200 ext. 271

Robert Morris College: Chicago

Chicago, Illinois
www.robertmorris.edu   Federal Code: 001746

4-year private university in very large city.
Enrollment: 4,535 undergrads, 5% part-time. 1,306 full-time freshmen.
Selectivity: Admits over 75% of applicants.

BASIC COSTS (2008-2009)

Tuition and fees: $18,000.
Per-credit charge: $442.
Additional info: Lab fees vary by program.

FINANCIAL AID PICTURE (2006-2007)

Students with need: Out of 1,306 full-time freshmen who applied for aid, 1,281 were judged to have need. Of these, 1,239 received aid, and 18 had their full need met. Average financial aid package met 39% of need; average scholarship/grant was $8,352; average loan was $4,171. For part-time students, average financial aid package was $9,347.

Students without need: 12 full-time freshmen who did not demonstrate need for aid received scholarships/grants; average award was $11,364. No-need awards available for academics, art, athletics, state/district residency.

Scholarships offered: 8 full-time freshmen received athletic scholarships; average amount $5,545.

Cumulative student debt: 96% of graduating class had student loans; average debt was $22,116.

FINANCIAL AID PROCEDURES

Forms required: FAFSA.

Dates and Deadlines: No deadline. Applicants notified on a rolling basis.

Transfers: No deadline. Applicants notified on a rolling basis.

CONTACT

Leigh Taylor, Vice President of Financial Aid
401South State Street, Chicago, IL 60605
(312) 935-4075

Rock Valley College

Rockford, Illinois
www.rockvalleycollege.edu

2-year public community college in small city.
Enrollment: 6,682 undergrads.
Selectivity: Open admission; but selective for some programs.

BASIC COSTS (2007-2008)

Tuition and fees: $2,084; out-of-district residents $7,604; out-of-state residents $12,284.

Per-credit charge: $61; out-of-district residents $245; out-of-state residents $401.

Additional info: Costs vary by program.

FINANCIAL AID PICTURE

Students with need: Need-based aid available for full-time and part-time students. Work study available nights.

Students without need: No-need awards available for academics, ROTC.

FINANCIAL AID PROCEDURES

Forms required: FAFSA.

Dates and Deadlines: No deadline. Applicants notified on a rolling basis starting 4/1; must reply within 2 week(s) of notification.

CONTACT

Cindi Stonesifer, Director of Financial Aid
3301 North Mulford Road, Rockford, IL 61114-5699
(815) 921-4150

Rockford Business College

Rockford, Illinois
www.rockfordbusinesscollege.edu Federal Code: 008545

2-year for-profit business and technical and career college in small city.
Enrollment: 560 undergrads, 56% part-time. 67 full-time freshmen.
Selectivity: Open admission.

BASIC COSTS (2008-2009)

Tuition and fees: $9,750.
Per-credit charge: $190.

FINANCIAL AID PICTURE

Students with need: Need-based aid available for full-time and part-time students. Work study available nights.

Students without need: This college awards aid only to students with need.

FINANCIAL AID PROCEDURES

Forms required: FAFSA.

Dates and Deadlines: No deadline. Applicants notified on a rolling basis.

CONTACT

Estella Sears, Director of Financial Aid
730 North Church Street, Rockford, IL 61103
(815) 967-7311

Rockford College

Rockford, Illinois
www.rockford.edu   Federal Code: 001748

4-year private liberal arts college in small city.
Enrollment: 862 undergrads, 13% part-time. 92 full-time freshmen.

BASIC COSTS (2008-2009)

Tuition and fees: $23,500.
Per-credit charge: $625.
Room and board: $6,750.

FINANCIAL AID PICTURE (2006-2007)

Students with need: Out of 86 full-time freshmen who applied for aid, 78 were judged to have need. Of these, 78 received aid, and 4 had their full need met. Average financial aid package met 69% of need; average scholarship/grant was $13,400; average loan was $2,356. For part-time students, average financial aid package was $6,130.

Students without need: 13 full-time freshmen who did not demonstrate need for aid received scholarships/grants; average award was $10,705. No-need awards available for academics, alumni affiliation, leadership, minority status, music/drama, state/district residency.

Cumulative student debt: 87% of graduating class had student loans; average debt was $34,500.

FINANCIAL AID PROCEDURES

Forms required: FAFSA.

Dates and Deadlines: Priority date 3/1; no closing date. Applicants notified on a rolling basis starting 3/15; must reply within 4 week(s) of notification.

Transfers: No deadline. Applicants notified on a rolling basis starting 3/15; must reply within 4 week(s) of notification.

CONTACT

Todd Free, Assistant Vice President for Business
5050 East State Street, Rockford, IL 61108-2393
(815) 226-3383

Roosevelt University
Chicago, Illinois
www.roosevelt.edu Federal Code: 001749

4-year private university in very large city.

Enrollment: 3,861 undergrads, 43% part-time. 263 full-time freshmen.

Selectivity: Admits less than 50% of applicants.

BASIC COSTS (2007-2008)

Tuition and fees: $16,930.

Per-credit charge: $600.

Room and board: $10,572.

Additional info: Tuition for Chicago College of the Performing Arts is $23,750 per year.

FINANCIAL AID PICTURE

Students with need: Need-based aid available for full-time students.

Students without need: No-need awards available for academics, alumni affiliation, leadership, minority status, music/drama, state/district residency.

Scholarships offered: Presidential Award: full tuition; based on GPA, SAT or ACT test scores, and community involvement; 5 awarded. Honors Program: $14,000-$42,000 over 4 years; 3.5 GPA, ACT of 23, and involvement; 20-30 awarded. Recognition Award: $1,500-$6,000 annually; for transfers and freshmen; 60 awarded. Music and Theater Scholarships: tuition and housing; for transfers and freshmen based on talent; approximately 90 awarded.

FINANCIAL AID PROCEDURES

Forms required: FAFSA, institutional form.

Dates and Deadlines: Priority date 4/1; no closing date. Applicants notified on a rolling basis starting 3/15; must reply within 2 week(s) of notification.

CONTACT

Walter O'Neill, Director of Financial Aid
430 South Michigan Avenue, Chicago, IL 60605-1394
(312) 341-3565

Rosalind Franklin University of Medicine and Science
North Chicago, Illinois
www.rosalindfranklin.edu Federal Code: 001659

Upper-division private university and health science college in large town.

Enrollment: 4 undergrads.

BASIC COSTS (2007-2008)

Tuition and fees: $14,803.

Additional info: Full-time tuition rate is for bachelor's degree program in Medical Technology.

FINANCIAL AID PICTURE

Students with need: Need-based aid available for full-time and part-time students.

Students without need: This college awards aid only to students with need.

Additional info: Financial aid application deadline 60 days prior to program start.

FINANCIAL AID PROCEDURES

Forms required: FAFSA, institutional form.

Dates and Deadlines: No deadline. Applicants notified on a rolling basis.

CONTACT

Maryann DeCaire, Executive Director Admissions, Records & Financial Aid
3333 Green Bay Road, North Chicago, IL 60064-3095
(847) 578-3217

Rush University
Chicago, Illinois
www.rushu.rush.edu Federal Code: 009800

Upper-division private health science and nursing college in very large city.

Enrollment: 244 undergrads, 6% part-time.

BASIC COSTS (2007-2008)

Tuition and fees: $20,058.

Per-credit charge: $579.

Room only: $8,406.

Additional info: Tuition costs vary by program.

FINANCIAL AID PICTURE (2006-2007)

Students with need: Average financial aid package for all full-time undergraduates was $20,012; for part-time $8,709. 36% awarded as scholarships/grants, 64% awarded as loans/jobs. Work study available nights, weekends, and for part-time students.

FINANCIAL AID PROCEDURES

Forms required: FAFSA, institutional form.

Dates and Deadlines: No deadline.

Transfers: Priority date 5/1; no deadline. Applicants notified on a rolling basis starting 4/1; must reply within 3 week(s) of notification.

CONTACT

David Nelson, Director of Student Financial Aid
College Admissions, Chicago, IL 60612
(312) 942-6256

St. Francis Medical Center College of Nursing
Peoria, Illinois
www.sfmccon.edu Federal Code: 006240

Upper-division private nursing college in small city, affiliated with Roman Catholic Church.

Enrollment: 329 undergrads, 16% part-time.

BASIC COSTS (2008-2009)

Tuition and fees: $13,910.

Per-credit charge: $455.

Room only: $2,000.

FINANCIAL AID PICTURE (2006-2007)

Students with need: Average financial aid package for all full-time undergraduates was $13,909; for part-time $12,516. 52% awarded as scholarships/grants, 48% awarded as loans/jobs.

Students without need: No-need awards available for academics, alumni affiliation.

Additional info: Modified Education Employment Program available to full-time students on a limited basis. Tuition waiver program for hospital employees available.

FINANCIAL AID PROCEDURES

Forms required: FAFSA, institutional form.

Dates and Deadlines: Priority date 6/1; no closing date. Applicants notified by 10/30; must reply within 4 week(s) of notification.

Transfers: No deadline. Applicants notified on a rolling basis starting 5/15; must reply within 2 week(s) of notification.

CONTACT

Nancy Perryman, Coordinator Student Finance, Financial Assistance
511 NE Greenleaf Street, Peoria, IL 61603-3783
(309) 655-4119

St. John's College

Springfield, Illinois
www.st-johns.org/education/schools/nursing
Federal Code: 030980

Upper-division private nursing college in small city, affiliated with Roman Catholic Church.

Enrollment: 69 undergrads.

BASIC COSTS (2008-2009)

Tuition and fees: $12,068.

Per-credit charge: $486.

FINANCIAL AID PICTURE (2007-2008)

Students with need: 59% of average financial aid package awarded as scholarships/grants, 41% awarded as loans/jobs.

CONTACT

Mary Deatherage, Financial Aid Officer
729 East Carpenter Street, Springfield, IL 62702
(217) 544-6464 ext. 44705

St. Xavier University

Chicago, Illinois
www.sxu.edu
Federal Code: 001768

4-year private university in very large city, affiliated with Roman Catholic Church.

Enrollment: 3,251 undergrads, 21% part-time. 510 full-time freshmen.

Selectivity: Admits over 75% of applicants.

BASIC COSTS (2007-2008)

Tuition and fees: $21,236.

Per-credit charge: $704.

Room and board: $7,626.

FINANCIAL AID PICTURE

Students with need: Need-based aid available for full-time and part-time students.

Students without need: No-need awards available for academics, athletics, music/drama.

FINANCIAL AID PROCEDURES

Forms required: FAFSA.

Dates and Deadlines: Priority date 3/1; no closing date. Applicants notified on a rolling basis starting 2/1; must reply by 5/1 or within 2 week(s) of notification.

CONTACT

Susan Swisher, Director of Financial Aid
3700 West 103rd Street, Chicago, IL 60655
(773) 298-3070

Sauk Valley Community College

Dixon, Illinois
www.svcc.edu
Federal Code: 001752

2-year public community college in large town.

Enrollment: 1,933 undergrads, 44% part-time. 248 full-time freshmen.

Selectivity: Open admission; but selective for some programs.

BASIC COSTS (2007-2008)

Tuition and fees: $2,460; out-of-district residents $7,320; out-of-state residents $8,340.

Per-credit charge: $82; out-of-district residents $244; out-of-state residents $276.

Room only: $4,131.

FINANCIAL AID PICTURE (2006-2007)

Students with need: Out of 180 full-time freshmen who applied for aid, 142 were judged to have need. Of these, 123 received aid, and 3 had their full need met. Average financial aid package met 43% of need; average scholarship/grant was $3,669; average loan was $1,749. For part-time students, average financial aid package was $2,948.

Students without need: No-need awards available for academics, art, athletics, leadership, minority status, ROTC, state/district residency.

FINANCIAL AID PROCEDURES

Forms required: FAFSA, state aid form, institutional form.

Dates and Deadlines: Priority date 3/1; no closing date. Applicants notified on a rolling basis starting 5/1; must reply within 4 week(s) of notification.

Transfers: Priority date 3/9; no deadline. Applicants notified on a rolling basis starting 3/1; must reply within 4 week(s) of notification.

CONTACT

Debra Stiefel, Coordinator of Financial Aid
173 Illinois Route 2, Dixon, IL 61021-9110
(815) 288-5511 ext. 339

School of the Art Institute of Chicago

Chicago, Illinois
www.saic.edu
Federal Code: 001753

4-year private visual arts college in very large city.

Enrollment: 2,330 undergrads, 6% part-time. 452 full-time freshmen.

Selectivity: Admits over 75% of applicants.

BASIC COSTS (2007-2008)

Tuition and fees: $31,040.

Per-credit charge: $1,025.

Room only: $8,900.

Additional info: Students will be required to purchase a laptop through SAIC. Costs range from $2,000 to $2,200.

FINANCIAL AID PICTURE

Students with need: Need-based aid available for full-time and part-time students. Work study available nights, weekends, and for part-time students.

Students without need: No-need awards available for academics, art.

Scholarships offered: Merit scholarships; $3,000, $6,000, $12,000 and full tuition; renewable annually.

FINANCIAL AID PROCEDURES

Forms required: FAFSA.

Dates and Deadlines: Priority date 3/15; no closing date. Applicants notified on a rolling basis starting 3/1.

CONTACT

Patrick James, Director of Financial Aid

36 South Wabash Avenue, Chicago, IL 60603

(312) 629-6600

Shawnee Community College

Ullin, Illinois

www.shawneecc.edu   Federal Code: 007693

2-year public community college in rural community.

Enrollment: 1,613 undergrads.

Selectivity: Open admission; but selective for some programs.

BASIC COSTS (2007-2008)

Tuition and fees: $1,950; out-of-state residents $3,000.

Per-credit charge: $65; out-of-state residents $100.

FINANCIAL AID PICTURE

Students with need: Need-based aid available for full-time and part-time students.*

Students without need: This college awards aid only to students with need.

FINANCIAL AID PROCEDURES

Forms required: FAFSA.

Dates and Deadlines: Priority date 9/1; no closing date. Applicants notified on a rolling basis; must reply within 2 week(s) of notification.

CONTACT

Tammy Capps, Director of Financial Aid

8364 Shawnee College Road, Ullin, IL 62992

(618) 634-3280 ext. 3280

Shimer College

Chicago, Illinois

www.shimer.edu   Federal Code: 001756

4-year private liberal arts college in very large city.

Enrollment: 76 undergrads. 7 full-time freshmen.

Selectivity: Admits 50 to 75% of applicants.

BASIC COSTS (2007-2008)

Tuition and fees: $24,890.

Room and board: $8,830.

Additional info: Required fee figure includes cost of books for core curriculum required of all undergraduates. Tuition/fee waivers available for adults.

FINANCIAL AID PICTURE (2006-2007)

Students with need: Out of 7 full-time freshmen who applied for aid, 7 were judged to have need. Of these, 7 received aid. Average financial aid package met 33% of need; average scholarship/grant was $7,361; average loan was $6,366. For part-time students, average financial aid package was $9,732.

Students without need: 1 full-time freshmen who did not demonstrate need for aid received scholarships/grants; average award was $4,000. No-need awards available for academics, alumni affiliation, music/drama.

Cumulative student debt: 50% of graduating class had student loans; average debt was $26,000.

FINANCIAL AID PROCEDURES

Forms required: FAFSA, institutional form.

Dates and Deadlines: No deadline. Applicants notified on a rolling basis starting 4/1; must reply by 5/1 or within 3 week(s) of notification.

Transfers: Closing date 8/1. Applicants notified on a rolling basis.

CONTACT

Janet Henthorn, Financial Aid Officer

3424 South State Street, Chicago, IL 60616

(312) 235-3507

South Suburban College of Cook County

South Holland, Illinois

www.southsuburbancollege.edu   Federal Code: 001769

2-year public community college in large town.

Enrollment: 5,702 undergrads.

Selectivity: Open admission; but selective for some programs.

BASIC COSTS (2007-2008)

Tuition and fees: $3,113; out-of-district residents $8,453; out-of-state residents $10,103.

Per-credit charge: $90; out-of-district residents $268; out-of-state residents $323.

Additional info: Some students may qualify for a tuition rate of $105 per credit hour for special programs in other in-state community college districts, in Lake County Illinois and in Chicago. Students need to inquire at the Registration area for additional information. Tuition/fee waivers available for adults.

FINANCIAL AID PICTURE

Students with need: Need-based aid available for full-time and part-time students. Work study available nights.

Students without need: No-need awards available for academics, art, athletics, music/drama, state/district residency.

FINANCIAL AID PROCEDURES

Forms required: FAFSA.

Dates and Deadlines: Priority date 6/1; no closing date. Applicants notified on a rolling basis starting 7/1.

Transfers: No deadline. Applicants notified on a rolling basis.

CONTACT

John Semple, Director of Financial Aid

15800 South State Street, South Holland, IL 60473

(708) 596-2000 ext. 2321

Southeastern Illinois College

Harrisburg, Illinois

www.sic.edu   Federal Code: 001757

2-year public community college in small town.

Enrollment: 1,420 undergrads.

Selectivity: Open admission; but selective for some programs.

BASIC COSTS (2007-2008)

Tuition and fees: $1,980; out-of-district residents $2,850; out-of-state residents $3,270.

Per-credit charge: $64; out-of-district residents $93; out-of-state residents $107.

FINANCIAL AID PICTURE

Students with need: Need-based aid available for full-time and part-time students.

Students without need: No-need awards available for academics, alumni affiliation, art, athletics, music/drama.

FINANCIAL AID PROCEDURES

Forms required: FAFSA.

Dates and Deadlines: No deadline. Applicants notified on a rolling basis starting 4/15; must reply within 2 week(s) of notification.

CONTACT

Joseph Schmitt, Director of Financial Aid
3575 College Road, Harrisburg, IL 62946
(618) 252-5400 ext. 2450

Southern Illinois University Carbondale
Carbondale, Illinois
www.siuc.edu　　　　　　　　　　Federal Code: 001758

4-year public university in large town.
Enrollment: 16,125 undergrads, 10% part-time. 2,609 full-time freshmen.
Selectivity: Admits 50 to 75% of applicants.

BASIC COSTS (2007-2008)

Tuition and fees: $8,899; out-of-state residents $18,421.
Per-credit charge: $212; out-of-state residents $529.
Room and board: $6,666.
Additional info: Tuition at time of enrollment locked for 4 years.

FINANCIAL AID PICTURE (2007-2008)

Students with need: Out of 2,136 full-time freshmen who applied for aid, 1,672 were judged to have need. Of these, 1,651 received aid, and 1,490 had their full need met. Average financial aid package met 97% of need; average scholarship/grant was $7,282; average loan was $3,869. For part-time students, average financial aid package was $8,977.
Students without need: 187 full-time freshmen who did not demonstrate need for aid received scholarships/grants; average award was $5,512. No-need awards available for academics, alumni affiliation, art, athletics, job skills, leadership, minority status, music/drama, ROTC, state/district residency.
Scholarships offered: 38 full-time freshmen received athletic scholarships; average amount $13,280.
Cumulative student debt: 44% of graduating class had student loans; average debt was $17,295.
Additional info: Need-based financial aid available to part-time students enrolled in minimum of 6 semester hours.

FINANCIAL AID PROCEDURES

Forms required: FAFSA.
Dates and Deadlines: Priority date 4/1; no closing date. Applicants notified on a rolling basis starting 3/23; must reply within 3 week(s) of notification.

CONTACT

Billie Hamilton, Director, Financial Aid
Mailcode 4701, Carbondale, IL 62901-4701
(618) 453-4334

Southern Illinois University Edwardsville
Edwardsville, Illinois
www.siue.edu　　　　　　　　　　Federal Code: 001759

4-year public university in very large city.
Enrollment: 10,843 undergrads, 15% part-time. 1,837 full-time freshmen.
Selectivity: Admits over 75% of applicants.

BASIC COSTS (2007-2008)

Tuition and fees: $7,033; out-of-state residents $14,874.
Per-credit charge: $174.
Room and board: $6,750.
Additional info: Required fees include book rental. Tuition at time of enrollment locked for 4 years.

FINANCIAL AID PICTURE

Students with need: Need-based aid available for full-time and part-time students. Work study available nights, weekends, and for part-time students.
Students without need: This college awards aid only to students with need.

FINANCIAL AID PROCEDURES

Forms required: FAFSA.
Dates and Deadlines: Priority date 3/1; closing date 6/1. Applicants notified on a rolling basis starting 3/15; must reply within 4 week(s) of notification.

CONTACT

Sharon Berry, Director of Student Financial Aid
Campus Box 1600, Rendleman Hall, Rm 2120, Edwardsville, IL 62026-1600
(618) 650-3880

Spoon River College
Canton, Illinois
www.src.edu　　　　　　　　　　Federal Code: 001643

2-year public community college in large town.
Enrollment: 1,435 undergrads.
Selectivity: Open admission; but selective for some programs.

BASIC COSTS (2008-2009)

Tuition and fees: $2,640; out-of-district residents $6,030; out-of-state residents $7,110.
Per-credit charge: $78; out-of-district residents $191; out-of-state residents $227.

FINANCIAL AID PICTURE (2006-2007)

Students with need: 81% of average financial aid package awarded as scholarships/grants, 19% awarded as loans/jobs. Need-based aid available for part-time students. Work study available nights.
Students without need: No-need awards available for academics, athletics.

FINANCIAL AID PROCEDURES

Forms required: FAFSA.
Dates and Deadlines: Closing date 7/2. Applicants notified on a rolling basis starting 3/15.

CONTACT

Jo Branson, Director of Financial Aid
23235 North County Road 22, Canton, IL 61520
(309) 649-7030

Springfield College in Illinois
Springfield, Illinois
www.sci.edu　　　　　　　　　　Federal Code: 001761

2-year private junior and liberal arts college in small city, affiliated with Roman Catholic Church.
Enrollment: 608 undergrads, 53% part-time. 130 full-time freshmen.
Selectivity: Admits 50 to 75% of applicants.

BASIC COSTS (2007-2008)

Tuition and fees: $7,744.
Per-credit charge: $312.
Room only: $2,750.

FINANCIAL AID PICTURE

Students with need: Need-based aid available for full-time and part-time students. Work study available nights, weekends, and for part-time students.
Students without need: No-need awards available for academics, art, athletics, leadership, religious affiliation.

FINANCIAL AID PROCEDURES

Forms required: FAFSA, institutional form.
Dates and Deadlines: Priority date 3/1; no closing date. Applicants notified on a rolling basis starting 3/15; must reply within 2 week(s) of notification.

CONTACT

Josephine Negro, Director of Financial Aid
1500 North Fifth Street, Springfield, IL 62702-2694
(217) 525-1420 ext. 244

Trinity Christian College

Palos Heights, Illinois
www.trnty.edu   Federal Code: 001771

4-year private liberal arts college in very large city, affiliated with Reformed (unaffiliated).
Enrollment: 1,217 undergrads, 16% part-time. 240 full-time freshmen.
Selectivity: Admits over 75% of applicants.

BASIC COSTS (2008-2009)

Tuition and fees: $20,256.
Per-credit charge: $664.
Room and board: $7,420.

FINANCIAL AID PICTURE (2007-2008)

Students with need: Out of 231 full-time freshmen who applied for aid, 223 were judged to have need. Of these, 223 received aid, and 14 had their full need met. Average financial aid package met 51% of need; average scholarship/grant was $7,053; average loan was $4,305. Need-based aid available for part-time students.
Students without need: 91 full-time freshmen who did not demonstrate need for aid received scholarships/grants; average award was $6,529. No-need awards available for academics, alumni affiliation, art, athletics, leadership, minority status, music/drama, religious affiliation.
Scholarships offered: 28 full-time freshmen received athletic scholarships; average amount $5,964.
Additional info: High school transcripts and ACT or SAT scores required for merit scholarships.

FINANCIAL AID PROCEDURES

Forms required: FAFSA, institutional form.
Dates and Deadlines: Priority date 2/15; closing date 4/15. Applicants notified on a rolling basis starting 4/1; must reply by 5/1 or within 2 week(s) of notification.
Transfers: Applicants notified by 2/28; must reply by 5/1 or within 2 week(s) of notification.

CONTACT

Denise Coleman, Director of Financial Aid
6601 West College Drive, Palos Heights, IL 60463
(708) 239-4706

Trinity International University

Deerfield, Illinois
www.tiu.edu   Federal Code: 001772

4-year private university and liberal arts college in large town, affiliated with Evangelical Free Church of America.
Enrollment: 1,048 undergrads, 15% part-time. 166 full-time freshmen.
Selectivity: Admits over 75% of applicants.

BASIC COSTS (2008-2009)

Tuition and fees: $21,930.
Per-credit charge: $900.
Room and board: $7,270.
Additional info: Tuition/fee waivers available for minority students.

FINANCIAL AID PICTURE (2007-2008)

Students with need: Out of 164 full-time freshmen who applied for aid, 149 were judged to have need. Of these, 149 received aid, and 51 had their full need met. Average financial aid package met 90% of need; average scholarship/grant was $8,442; average loan was $4,157. For part-time students, average financial aid package was $7,251.
Students without need: 10 full-time freshmen who did not demonstrate need for aid received scholarships/grants; average award was $5,150. No-need awards available for academics, alumni affiliation, athletics, minority status, music/drama, religious affiliation.
Scholarships offered: 55 full-time freshmen received athletic scholarships; average amount $9,389.
Cumulative student debt: 77% of graduating class had student loans; average debt was $20,621.

FINANCIAL AID PROCEDURES

Forms required: FAFSA.
Dates and Deadlines: Priority date 4/1; no closing date. Applicants notified on a rolling basis starting 2/15; must reply within 4 week(s) of notification.
Transfers: No deadline. Applicants notified on a rolling basis; must reply within 4 week(s) of notification.

CONTACT

Ron Campbell, Director of Financial Aid
2065 Half Day Road, Deerfield, IL 60015
(847) 317-8060

Triton College

River Grove, Illinois
www.triton.edu   Federal Code: 001773

2-year public community and junior college in large town.
Enrollment: 10,603 undergrads, 67% part-time. 1,127 full-time freshmen.
Selectivity: Open admission; but selective for some programs.

BASIC COSTS (2008-2009)

Tuition and fees: $2,170; out-of-district residents $5,740; out-of-state residents $7,150.
Per-credit charge: $64; out-of-district residents $183; out-of-state residents $230.

FINANCIAL AID PICTURE (2006-2007)

Students with need: Out of 620 full-time freshmen who applied for aid, 446 were judged to have need. Of these, 446 received aid. For part-time students, average financial aid package was $664.
Students without need: 36 full-time freshmen who did not demonstrate need for aid received scholarships/grants; average award was $953. No-need awards available for academics, athletics, leadership.
Scholarships offered: Board of Trustees Honor Scholarship; covers tuition and fees; for in-district high school students in top 10% of graduating class.

FINANCIAL AID PROCEDURES

Forms required: FAFSA, institutional form.
Dates and Deadlines: Priority date 4/15; no closing date. Applicants notified on a rolling basis starting 4/1; must reply within 2 week(s) of notification.

CONTACT

Pat Zinga, Director of Financial Aid
2000 North Fifth Avenue, River Grove, IL 60171
(708) 456-0300 ext. 3441

PART III: FINANCIAL AID COLLEGE BY COLLEGE

University of Chicago

Chicago, Illinois
www.uchicago.edu

Federal Code: 001774
CSS Code: 1832

4-year private university and liberal arts college in very large city.

Enrollment: 4,898 undergrads, 1% part-time. 1,301 full-time freshmen.

Selectivity: Admits less than 50% of applicants.

BASIC COSTS (2007-2008)

Tuition and fees: $35,868.

Room and board: $11,139.

FINANCIAL AID PICTURE (2007-2008)

Students with need: Out of 849 full-time freshmen who applied for aid, 620 were judged to have need. Of these, 620 received aid, and 620 had their full need met. Average financial aid package met 100% of need; average scholarship/grant was $28,485; average loan was $4,777.

Students without need: 169 full-time freshmen who did not demonstrate need for aid received scholarships/grants; average award was $12,258. No-need awards available for academics, leadership.

Cumulative student debt: 54% of graduating class had student loans; average debt was $25,971.

FINANCIAL AID PROCEDURES

Forms required: FAFSA, CSS PROFILE, institutional form.

Dates and Deadlines: Closing date 2/1. Applicants notified by 4/15; must reply by 5/1.

Transfers: Closing date 3/1. Applicants notified on a rolling basis starting 4/15; must reply by 6/1.

CONTACT

Alicia Reyes, Director of College Aid
1101 East 58th Street, Chicago, IL 60637
(773) 702-8666

University of Illinois at Chicago

Chicago, Illinois
www.uic.edu

Federal Code: 001776

4-year public university in very large city.

Enrollment: 15,565 undergrads, 8% part-time. 2,822 full-time freshmen.

Selectivity: Admits 50 to 75% of applicants.

BASIC COSTS (2007-2008)

Tuition and fees: $9,744; out-of-state residents $22,134.

Room and board: $8,118.

Additional info: Tuition at time of enrollment locked for 4 years; tuition/fee waivers available for minority students.

FINANCIAL AID PICTURE (2006-2007)

Students with need: Out of 2,249 full-time freshmen who applied for aid, 1,666 were judged to have need. Of these, 1,608 received aid, and 492 had their full need met. Average financial aid package met 85% of need; average scholarship/grant was $9,416; average loan was $3,360. For part-time students, average financial aid package was $7,269.

Students without need: 260 full-time freshmen who did not demonstrate need for aid received scholarships/grants; average award was $1,786. No-need awards available for academics, art, athletics, music/drama, ROTC.

Scholarships offered: 21 full-time freshmen received athletic scholarships; average amount $20,870.

Cumulative student debt: 54% of graduating class had student loans; average debt was $15,564.

FINANCIAL AID PROCEDURES

Forms required: FAFSA.

Dates and Deadlines: Priority date 3/1; no closing date. Applicants notified on a rolling basis starting 3/15; must reply by 5/1 or within 2 week(s) of notification.

CONTACT

Timothy Opgenorth, Director of the Office of Student Financial Aid
PO Box 5220, Chicago, IL 60680-5220
(312) 996-3126

University of Illinois at Urbana-Champaign

Champaign, Illinois
www.illinois.edu

Federal Code: 001775

4-year public university in small city.

Enrollment: 30,395 undergrads, 2% part-time. 7,225 full-time freshmen.

Selectivity: Admits 50 to 75% of applicants.

BASIC COSTS (2007-2008)

Tuition and fees: $11,130; out-of-state residents $25,216.

Room and board: $8,196.

Additional info: Freshman costs reflect guaranteed tuition plan figures; tuition rate is guaranteed for 4 years. Tuition at time of enrollment locked for 4 years.

FINANCIAL AID PICTURE (2006-2007)

Students with need: Out of 4,959 full-time freshmen who applied for aid, 3,204 were judged to have need. Of these, 3,036 received aid, and 1,431 had their full need met. Average financial aid package met 71% of need; average scholarship/grant was $8,821; average loan was $3,715. For part-time students, average financial aid package was $6,875.

Students without need: 1,337 full-time freshmen who did not demonstrate need for aid received scholarships/grants; average award was $2,796. No-need awards available for academics, alumni affiliation, art, athletics, leadership, music/drama, ROTC, state/district residency.

Scholarships offered: *Merit:* President's Award Program: $1,000 - $4,000 for 4 years; for members of historically underrepresented group, with ACT score of 22-23 and in the top quarter of their class, or who have an ACT score of 24 or higher and are in the top half of their class. University Achievement Scholarship: $8,000; criteria set by each college, must maintain a 3.0 GPA for renewal; 50 available. Matthews Scholars: $2,000 per year, renewable for 4 years if GPA of 3.3 is maintained; criteria includes academic achievement, leadership skills, commitment to campus and community efforts, good sponsor relations, diversity of college gender and ethnicity; approximately 150 available. FMC Award of Excellence: $1,000 a year, non-renewable; criteria set by individual colleges; 20 available. Provost Scholarship: full tuition, renewable if maintain GPA of 3.0; National Achievement, National Hispanic Scholar finalists, or National Merit finalists who have indicated the University of Illinois at Urbana-Champaign as their top choice. Campus Merit: $3,000; Students in historically under-represented groups who are in the top 10 percent of their graduating class. National Merit: $500; National Merit finalists who indicated the University of Illinois as their top choice, renewable if maintain GPA of 3.0. James Hunter Anthony and Gerald Blackshear Scholarship: 1 year of tuition and fees, renewable if maintaining a GPA of 3.0; incoming freshmen who are graduates of an Illinois high school, with superior academic and leadership qualities (Need may also be considered.). *Athletic:* 42 full-time freshmen received athletic scholarships; average amount $16,907.

Cumulative student debt: 51% of graduating class had student loans; average debt was $17,057.

FINANCIAL AID PROCEDURES

Forms required: FAFSA.

Dates and Deadlines: Priority date 3/15; no closing date.

CONTACT

Daniel Mann, Director of Student Financial Aid
901 West Illinois, Urbana, IL 61801-3028
(217) 333-0100

University of Illinois: Springfield

Springfield, Illinois
www.uis.edu   Federal Code: 009333

4-year public university and liberal arts college in small city.

Enrollment: 2,696 undergrads, 38% part-time. 235 full-time freshmen.

Selectivity: Admits 50 to 75% of applicants.

BASIC COSTS (2007-2008)

Tuition and fees: $7,826; out-of-state residents $16,976.

Per-credit charge: $212; out-of-state residents $517.

Room and board: $8,446.

Additional info: Freshman costs reflect guaranteed tuition plan figures; tuition rate is guaranteed for 4 years.

FINANCIAL AID PICTURE (2006-2007)

Students with need: Out of 222 full-time freshmen who applied for aid, 135 were judged to have need. Of these, 135 received aid, and 15 had their full need met. Average financial aid package met 75% of need; average scholarship/grant was $6,271; average loan was $2,407. For part-time students, average financial aid package was $5,518.

Students without need: 98 full-time freshmen who did not demonstrate need for aid received scholarships/grants; average award was $1,938. No-need awards available for academics, alumni affiliation, art, athletics, job skills, leadership, minority status, music/drama, state/district residency.

Scholarships offered: 5 full-time freshmen received athletic scholarships; average amount $4,273.

Cumulative student debt: 71% of graduating class had student loans; average debt was $12,309.

FINANCIAL AID PROCEDURES

Forms required: FAFSA.

Dates and Deadlines: Priority date 4/1; closing date 11/15. Applicants notified on a rolling basis starting 1/1; must reply within 3 week(s) of notification.

Transfers: No deadline. Applicants notified on a rolling basis.

CONTACT

Gerard Joseph, Director of Financial Aid
One University Plaza, MS UHB 1080, Springfield, IL 62703
(217) 206-6724

University of St. Francis

Joliet, Illinois
www.stfrancis.edu   Federal Code: 001664

4-year private university and liberal arts college in small city, affiliated with Roman Catholic Church.

Enrollment: 1,282 undergrads, 5% part-time. 198 full-time freshmen.

Selectivity: Admits 50 to 75% of applicants.

BASIC COSTS (2008-2009)

Tuition and fees: $21,860.

Per-credit charge: $715.

Room and board: $7,744.

FINANCIAL AID PICTURE (2007-2008)

Students with need: Out of 184 full-time freshmen who applied for aid, 151 were judged to have need. Of these, 151 received aid, and 102 had their full need met. Average financial aid package met 82% of need; average scholarship/grant was $7,988; average loan was $3,876. For part-time students, average financial aid package was $6,400.

Students without need: 31 full-time freshmen who did not demonstrate need for aid received scholarships/grants; average award was $7,755. No-need awards available for academics, alumni affiliation, art, athletics, leadership, music/drama, religious affiliation, state/district residency.

Scholarships offered: 14 full-time freshmen received athletic scholarships; average amount $7,500.

Cumulative student debt: 74% of graduating class had student loans; average debt was $20,319.

FINANCIAL AID PROCEDURES

Forms required: FAFSA, institutional form.

Dates and Deadlines: Priority date 3/15; no closing date. Applicants notified on a rolling basis starting 2/15.

Transfers: Applicants notified on a rolling basis starting 2/15.

CONTACT

Bruce Foote, Executive Director Financial Aid Services
500 Wilcox Street, Joliet, IL 60435
(866) 890-8331

Waubonsee Community College

Sugar Grove, Illinois
www.waubonsee.edu   Federal Code: 006931

2-year public community college in small town.

Enrollment: 6,240 undergrads, 53% part-time. 1,000 full-time freshmen.

Selectivity: Open admission; but selective for some programs.

BASIC COSTS (2008-2009)

Tuition and fees: $2,460; out-of-district residents $7,350; out-of-state residents $8,160.

Per-credit charge: $79; out-of-district residents $242; out-of-state residents $269.

FINANCIAL AID PICTURE (2006-2007)

Students with need: 64% of average financial aid package awarded as scholarships/grants, 36% awarded as loans/jobs. Need-based aid available for part-time students. Work study available nights.

Students without need: No-need awards available for academics, art, athletics, leadership, minority status, music/drama.

Scholarships offered: Gustafson Scholarship: cost of 64 semester hours; awarded to selected local high school graduates.

FINANCIAL AID PROCEDURES

Forms required: FAFSA.

Dates and Deadlines: Closing date 12/1. Applicants notified on a rolling basis.

CONTACT

Charles Boudreau, Director of Student Financial Aid Services
Route 47 at Waubonsee Drive, Sugar Grove, IL 60554-9454
(630) 466-7900 ext. 5774

West Suburban College of Nursing

Oak Park, Illinois
www.wscn.edu   Federal Code: 022141

Upper-division private nursing college in very large city, affiliated with Roman Catholic Church.

Enrollment: 212 undergrads, 25% part-time.

BASIC COSTS (2007-2008)

Tuition and fees: $20,270.

Per-credit charge: $670.

Additional info: 16 month fast track nursing program available for $28,185.

FINANCIAL AID PICTURE (2006-2007)

Students with need: 31% of average financial aid package awarded as scholarships/grants, 69% awarded as loans/jobs. Need-based aid available for part-time students. Work study available nights, weekends, and for part-time students.

Students without need: No-need awards available for academics, alumni affiliation.

FINANCIAL AID PROCEDURES

Forms required: FAFSA.

Dates and Deadlines: Applicants notified on a rolling basis.

Transfers: No deadline. Applicants notified on a rolling basis; must reply within 3 week(s) of notification.

CONTACT

Shirley Howell, Financial Aid Officer
Three Erie Court, Oak Park, IL 60302
(708) 763-1426

Western Illinois University
Macomb, Illinois
www.wiu.edu   Federal Code: 001780

4-year public university in large town.

Enrollment: 11,145 undergrads, 9% part-time. 1,952 full-time freshmen.

Selectivity: Admits 50 to 75% of applicants.

BASIC COSTS (2008-2009)

Tuition and fees: $8,828; out-of-state residents $12,056.

Per-credit charge: $215; out-of-state residents $323.

Room and board: $7,210.

Additional info: Residents of nearby counties in Iowa and Missouri pay in-state tuition during first year. Incoming freshmen guaranteed the first year tuition rate for their entire 4 years, provided they are continually enrolled. Tuition at time of enrollment locked for 4 years.

FINANCIAL AID PICTURE

Students with need: Need-based aid available for full-time and part-time students.

Students without need: No-need awards available for academics, alumni affiliation, art, athletics, leadership, minority status, music/drama, ROTC.

FINANCIAL AID PROCEDURES

Forms required: FAFSA.

Dates and Deadlines: Priority date 2/15; no closing date. Applicants notified on a rolling basis starting 1/15.

CONTACT

William Bushaw, Director of Financial Aid
One University Circle, Macomb, IL 61455-1390
(309) 298-2446

Westwood College: DuPage
Woodridge, Illinois
www.westwood.edu   Federal Code: 030792

4-year for-profit technical college in large city.

Enrollment: 634 undergrads, 13% part-time. 184 full-time freshmen.

BASIC COSTS (2008-2009)

Additional info: Expenses vary by program; however, average cost for academic year is $14,867, which includes tuition, fees and books.

FINANCIAL AID PICTURE (2006-2007)

Students with need: 38% of average financial aid package awarded as scholarships/grants, 62% awarded as loans/jobs.

CONTACT

Silvia Hurtado, Director of Financial Aid
7155 Janes Avenue, Woodridge, IL 60517
(630) 434-8250 ext. 330

Westwood College: O'Hare Airport
Chicago, Illinois
www.westwood.edu   Federal Code: 023139

4-year for-profit technical and career college in very large city.

Enrollment: 519 undergrads.

Selectivity: Admits 50 to 75% of applicants.

BASIC COSTS (2007-2008)

Tuition and fees: $13,902.

Per-credit charge: $484.

FINANCIAL AID PICTURE

Students with need: Need-based aid available for full-time and part-time students. Work study available nights, weekends, and for part-time students.

FINANCIAL AID PROCEDURES

Forms required: FAFSA, institutional form.

Dates and Deadlines: Priority date 3/1; closing date 6/30.

CONTACT

Denise Brown, Senior Financial Aid Officer
8501 West Higgins Road, Chicago, IL 60631
(773) 380-6800

Wheaton College
Wheaton, Illinois
www.wheaton.edu   Federal Code: 001781

4-year private liberal arts college in small city, affiliated with nondenominational tradition.

Enrollment: 2,357 undergrads, 3% part-time. 559 full-time freshmen.

Selectivity: Admits 50 to 75% of applicants.

BASIC COSTS (2008-2009)

Tuition and fees: $25,500.

Per-credit charge: $1,063.

Room and board: $7,618.

FINANCIAL AID PICTURE (2007-2008)

Students with need: Out of 435 full-time freshmen who applied for aid, 295 were judged to have need. Of these, 289 received aid, and 101 had their full need met. Average financial aid package met 84% of need; average scholarship/grant was $15,172; average loan was $4,740. For part-time students, average financial aid package was $12,265.

Students without need: 111 full-time freshmen who did not demonstrate need for aid received scholarships/grants; average award was $4,100. No-need awards available for academics, alumni affiliation, art, minority status, music/drama.

Scholarships offered: President's Award:, $1000 per year for 4 yrs; U.S. citizens with 3.6 GPA on 4.0 scale, plus minimum 1400 SAT or 32 ACT; unlimited number.

Cumulative student debt: 53% of graduating class had student loans; average debt was $20,087.

FINANCIAL AID PROCEDURES

Forms required: FAFSA, institutional form.

Dates and Deadlines: Priority date 2/15; no closing date. Applicants notified on a rolling basis starting 3/1.

Transfers: Priority date 3/1; no deadline. Applicants notified on a rolling basis.

CONTACT

Donna Peltz, Director of Financial Aid
501 College Avenue, Wheaton, IL 60187-5593
(630) 752-5021

Indiana

Ancilla College

Donaldson, Indiana
www.ancilla.edu   Federal Code: 001784

2-year private community and liberal arts college in rural community, affiliated with Roman Catholic Church.
Enrollment: 511 undergrads.
Selectivity: Open admission; but selective for some programs.

BASIC COSTS (2008-2009)

Tuition and fees: $12,080.
Per-credit charge: $395.

FINANCIAL AID PICTURE (2007-2008)

Students with need: Need-based aid available for part-time students.
Students without need: No-need awards available for academics, athletics, job skills, leadership.

FINANCIAL AID PROCEDURES

Forms required: FAFSA, institutional form.
Dates and Deadlines: Closing date 3/1. Applicants notified on a rolling basis starting 3/1; must reply within 2 week(s) of notification.

CONTACT

Katherine Mills, Director of Financial Aid
9001 Union Road, Donaldson, IN 46513
(574) 936-8898 ext. 307

Anderson University

Anderson, Indiana
www.anderson.edu   Federal Code: 001785

4-year private liberal arts college in small city, affiliated with Church of God.
Enrollment: 2,131 undergrads, 9% part-time. 479 full-time freshmen.
Selectivity: Admits 50 to 75% of applicants. GED not accepted.

BASIC COSTS (2008-2009)

Tuition and fees: $21,920.
Per-credit charge: $914.
Room and board: $7,600.
Additional info: Tuition/fee waivers available for adults.

FINANCIAL AID PICTURE

Students with need: Need-based aid available for full-time and part-time students. Work study available nights, weekends, and for part-time students.
Students without need: No-need awards available for academics, leadership, minority status, music/drama, state/district residency.

FINANCIAL AID PROCEDURES

Forms required: FAFSA.
Dates and Deadlines: Priority date 3/1; no closing date. Applicants notified on a rolling basis starting 3/1.

CONTACT

Kenneth Nieman, Director of Financial Aid
1100 East Fifth Street, Anderson, IN 46012-3495
(765) 641-4182

Ball State University

Muncie, Indiana
www.bsu.edu   Federal Code: 001786

4-year public university in small city.
Enrollment: 16,422 undergrads, 6% part-time. 3,755 full-time freshmen.
Selectivity: Admits 50 to 75% of applicants.

BASIC COSTS (2008-2009)

Tuition and fees: $7,500; out-of-state residents $19,304.
Room and board: $7,598.

FINANCIAL AID PICTURE (2007-2008)

Students with need: Out of 3,172 full-time freshmen who applied for aid, 2,271 were judged to have need. Of these, 2,252 received aid, and 708 had their full need met. Average financial aid package met 66% of need; average scholarship/grant was $5,646; average loan was $3,584. For part-time students, average financial aid package was $6,963.
Students without need: 337 full-time freshmen who did not demonstrate need for aid received scholarships/grants; average award was $6,811. No-need awards available for academics, athletics, leadership, minority status, music/drama, ROTC, state/district residency.
Scholarships offered: 73 full-time freshmen received athletic scholarships; average amount $14,180.
Cumulative student debt: 65% of graduating class had student loans; average debt was $19,827.

FINANCIAL AID PROCEDURES

Forms required: FAFSA.
Dates and Deadlines: Priority date 3/10; no closing date. Applicants notified on a rolling basis starting 4/1.
Transfers: No deadline.

CONTACT

Robert Zellers, Director of Scholarships/Financial Aid
2000 University Avenue, Muncie, IN 47306-1022
(765) 285-5600

Bethel College

Mishawaka, Indiana
www.bethelcollege.edu   Federal Code: 001787

4-year private liberal arts college in large town, affiliated with Missionary Church.
Enrollment: 2,099 undergrads, 45% part-time. 248 full-time freshmen.
Selectivity: Admits over 75% of applicants.

BASIC COSTS (2007-2008)

Tuition and fees: $18,006.
Room and board: $5,630.
Additional info: All first-time, full-time students must pay a one-time fee of $600. Tuition/fee waivers available for adults, minority students.

FINANCIAL AID PICTURE (2007-2008)

Students with need: Out of 200 full-time freshmen who applied for aid, 179 were judged to have need. Of these, 179 received aid, and 18 had their full need met. Average financial aid package met 41% of need; average scholarship/grant was $7,770; average loan was $3,360. For part-time students, average financial aid package was $7,459.
Students without need: 10 full-time freshmen who did not demonstrate need for aid received scholarships/grants; average award was $7,300. No-need awards available for academics, art, athletics, job skills, leadership, minority status, music/drama, religious affiliation, ROTC, state/district residency.
Scholarships offered: 65 full-time freshmen received athletic scholarships; average amount $6,115.
Cumulative student debt: 42% of graduating class had student loans; average debt was $3,723.

FINANCIAL AID PROCEDURES

Forms required: FAFSA.

Dates and Deadlines: Priority date 3/1; no closing date. Applicants notified by 4/15; must reply within 3 week(s) of notification.

CONTACT

Guy Fisher, Director of Financial Aid

1001 West McKinley Avenue, Mishawaka, IN 46545

(574) 257-3316

Brown Mackie College: South Bend

South Bend, Indiana

www.brownmackie.edu   Federal Code: 004583

2-year for-profit community and technical college in small city.

Enrollment: 743 undergrads.

Selectivity: Open admission.

BASIC COSTS (2007-2008)

Tuition and fees: $12,240.

Per-credit charge: $260.

Additional info: Tuition at time of enrollment locked for 2 years.

FINANCIAL AID PICTURE

Students with need: Need-based aid available for full-time and part-time students.

Students without need: This college awards aid only to students with need.

Scholarships offered: Scholarships for high school seniors graduating by spring semester (one per school in recruiting area) based on 2.0 GPA or equivalent, extracurricular activities, outstanding character, and community contributions; $500. Students must begin classes in June, July, August or September following their high school graduation.

FINANCIAL AID PROCEDURES

Forms required: FAFSA.

Dates and Deadlines: No deadline. Applicants notified on a rolling basis; must reply within 1 week(s) of notification.

CONTACT

Sue Golden, Senior Financial Aid Officer

1030 East Jefferson Boulevard, South Bend, IN 46617

Butler University

Indianapolis, Indiana

www.butler.edu   Federal Code: 001788

4-year private university in very large city.

Enrollment: 3,593 undergrads, 1% part-time. 987 full-time freshmen.

Selectivity: Admits over 75% of applicants.

BASIC COSTS (2008-2009)

Tuition and fees: $28,266.

Per-credit charge: $1,150.

Room and board: $9,410.

FINANCIAL AID PICTURE (2007-2008)

Students with need: Out of 919 full-time freshmen who applied for aid, 621 were judged to have need. Of these, 621 received aid, and 152 had their full need met. Need-based aid available for part-time students.

Students without need: 259 full-time freshmen who did not demonstrate need for aid received scholarships/grants; average award was $10,789. No-need awards available for academics, athletics, music/drama.

Scholarships offered: 16 full-time freshmen received athletic scholarships; average amount $18,158.

FINANCIAL AID PROCEDURES

Forms required: FAFSA.

Dates and Deadlines: Priority date 3/1; no closing date. Applicants notified on a rolling basis starting 3/15; must reply within 3 week(s) of notification.

Transfers: Priority date 3/15; no deadline.

CONTACT

Richard Bellows, Executive Director of Financial Aid

4600 Sunset Avenue, Indianapolis, IN 46208

(317) 940-8200

Calumet College of St. Joseph

Whiting, Indiana

www.ccsj.edu   Federal Code: 001834

4-year private liberal arts college in small city, affiliated with Roman Catholic Church.

Enrollment: 1,025 undergrads, 57% part-time. 87 full-time freshmen.

Selectivity: Admits less than 50% of applicants.

BASIC COSTS (2008-2009)

Tuition and fees: $12,610.

Per-credit charge: $385.

FINANCIAL AID PICTURE (2006-2007)

Students with need: Out of 87 full-time freshmen who applied for aid, 69 were judged to have need. Of these, 69 received aid, and 18 had their full need met. Average financial aid package met 76% of need; average scholarship/grant was $9,625; average loan was $2,334. For part-time students, average financial aid package was $7,283.

Students without need: 11 full-time freshmen who did not demonstrate need for aid received scholarships/grants; average award was $4,534. No-need awards available for academics, alumni affiliation, religious affiliation.

Scholarships offered: 56 full-time freshmen received athletic scholarships; average amount $4,224.

Cumulative student debt: 62% of graduating class had student loans; average debt was $18,447.

Additional info: Immediate computerized estimate of financial aid eligibility available to students applying in person.

FINANCIAL AID PROCEDURES

Forms required: FAFSA.

Dates and Deadlines: Priority date 3/1; no closing date. Applicants notified on a rolling basis; must reply within 2 week(s) of notification.

CONTACT

Chuck Walz, Director of Financial Aid

2400 New York Avenue, Whiting, IN 46394-2195

(219) 473-4296

DePauw University

Greencastle, Indiana

www.depauw.edu   Federal Code: 001792

4-year private music and liberal arts college in small town, affiliated with United Methodist Church.

Enrollment: 2,350 undergrads. 664 full-time freshmen.

Selectivity: Admits 50 to 75% of applicants.

BASIC COSTS (2008-2009)

Tuition and fees: $31,825.

Room and board: $8,400.

FINANCIAL AID PICTURE (2007-2008)

Students with need: Out of 453 full-time freshmen who applied for aid, 364 were judged to have need. Of these, 363 received aid, and 166 had their full need met. Average financial aid package met 92% of need; average scholarship/grant was $22,991; average loan was $2,786. Need-based aid available for part-time students.

Students without need: 269 full-time freshmen who did not demonstrate need for aid received scholarships/grants; average award was $16,310. No-need awards available for academics, alumni affiliation, leadership, minority status, music/drama, ROTC.

Scholarships offered: Holton Scholarships: ranging from $1,000 to full tuition, recognizing exceptional leadership and/or service, 50 awarded.

Cumulative student debt: 50% of graduating class had student loans; average debt was $3,500.

FINANCIAL AID PROCEDURES

Forms required: FAFSA, institutional form.

Dates and Deadlines: Priority date 2/15; no closing date. Applicants notified by 3/27; must reply by 5/1.

Transfers: Applicants notified by 3/27; must reply by 5/1.

CONTACT

Richard Nash, Director of Financial Aid
101 East Seminary Street, Greencastle, IN 46135-1611
(765) 658-4030

DeVry University: Indianapolis

Indianapolis, Indiana
www.devry.edu

4-year for-profit university in very large city.

Enrollment: 185 undergrads, 74% part-time. 9 full-time freshmen.

BASIC COSTS (2007-2008)

Tuition and fees: $13,020.
Per-credit charge: $490.

FINANCIAL AID PICTURE (2006-2007)

Students with need: Out of 3 full-time freshmen who applied for aid, 3 were judged to have need. Of these, 3 received aid. Average financial aid package met 27% of need; average scholarship/grant was $5,271; average loan was $3,625. For part-time students, average financial aid package was $7,071.

Students without need: 2 full-time freshmen who did not demonstrate need for aid received scholarships/grants; average award was $11,795. No-need awards available for academics.

FINANCIAL AID PROCEDURES

Forms required: FAFSA.

Dates and Deadlines: No deadline. Applicants notified on a rolling basis.

CONTACT

9100 Keystone Crossing, Suite 350, Indianapolis, IN 46240

Earlham College

Richmond, Indiana
www.earlham.edu   Federal Code: 001793

4-year private liberal arts and seminary college in large town, affiliated with Society of Friends (Quaker).

Enrollment: 1,156 undergrads, 1% part-time. 303 full-time freshmen.

Selectivity: Admits 50 to 75% of applicants.

BASIC COSTS (2008-2009)

Tuition and fees: $34,030.
Per-credit charge: $1,109.

Room and board: $6,814.

FINANCIAL AID PICTURE (2006-2007)

Students with need: Out of 214 full-time freshmen who applied for aid, 189 were judged to have need. Of these, 187 received aid, and 86 had their full need met. Average financial aid package met 95% of need; average scholarship/grant was $15,897; average loan was $3,733. Need-based aid available for part-time students.

Students without need: 65 full-time freshmen who did not demonstrate need for aid received scholarships/grants; average award was $7,657. No-need awards available for academics, minority status, religious affiliation.

Cumulative student debt: 69% of graduating class had student loans; average debt was $19,688.

FINANCIAL AID PROCEDURES

Forms required: FAFSA, institutional form.

Dates and Deadlines: Closing date 3/1. Applicants notified on a rolling basis starting 2/15; must reply by 5/1.

Transfers: Priority date 3/1; no deadline. Deadline for State of Indiana Grants, 3/1 (FAFSA date).

CONTACT

Robert Arnold, Director of Financial Aid
801 National Road West, Richmond, IN 47374-4095
(765) 983-1217

Franklin College

Franklin, Indiana
www.franklincollege.edu   Federal Code: 001798

4-year private liberal arts college in large town, affiliated with American Baptist Churches in the USA.

Enrollment: 1,130 undergrads, 10% part-time. 304 full-time freshmen.

Selectivity: Admits 50 to 75% of applicants.

BASIC COSTS (2008-2009)

Tuition and fees: $21,325.
Room and board: $6,390.

FINANCIAL AID PICTURE (2006-2007)

Students with need: Out of 271 full-time freshmen who applied for aid, 238 were judged to have need. Of these, 237 received aid, and 42 had their full need met. Average financial aid package met 84% of need; average scholarship/grant was $13,576; average loan was $3,519. For part-time students, average financial aid package was $11,512.

Students without need: This college awards aid only to students with need.

Cumulative student debt: 85% of graduating class had student loans; average debt was $19,858.

FINANCIAL AID PROCEDURES

Forms required: FAFSA, institutional form.

Dates and Deadlines: Closing date 3/1. Applicants notified by 4/1; must reply by 5/1 or within 4 week(s) of notification.

Transfers: Must reply by 5/1 or within 2 week(s) of notification.

CONTACT

Elizabeth Sappenfield, Director of Financial Aid
101 Branigin Boulevard, Franklin, IN 46131-2623
(317) 738-8075

Goshen College

Goshen, Indiana
www.goshen.edu   Federal Code: 001799

4-year private liberal arts college in large town, affiliated with Mennonite Church.

Enrollment: 955 undergrads, 8% part-time. 206 full-time freshmen.

Selectivity: Admits 50 to 75% of applicants.

BASIC COSTS (2008-2009)

Tuition and fees: $22,300.

Per-credit charge: $890.

Room and board: $7,400.

FINANCIAL AID PICTURE (2006-2007)

Students with need: Out of 206 full-time freshmen who applied for aid, 160 were judged to have need. Of these, 160 received aid, and 45 had their full need met. Average financial aid package met 84% of need; average scholarship/grant was $12,612; average loan was $3,832. For part-time students, average financial aid package was $5,000.

Students without need: 17 full-time freshmen who did not demonstrate need for aid received scholarships/grants; average award was $9,207. No-need awards available for academics, art, athletics, leadership, music/drama.

Scholarships offered: *Merit:* President's Leadership Award: $15,000; must meet 2 of the following criteria: 3.8/4.0 high school GPA, 1270/1600 SAT or 29 ACT, top 5% of class, National Merit semi-finalist; 15 awards offered each year, renews annually with a 3.20 GPA. Menno Simons Scholarships: $8,000 for 3.75 GPA and SAT of 1200/1600 or ACT of 26. Wens Honors Scholarship: $7,000 for 3.50 GPA and SAT of 1100/1600 or ACT of 25. Yoder Honors Scholarship: $6,000 for 3.30 GPA and SAT of 1050/1600 or ACT of 22. Kratz Honors Scholarship: $3,000 for 3.0 GPA. *Athletic:* 12 full-time freshmen received athletic scholarships; average amount $5,583.

Cumulative student debt: 67% of graduating class had student loans; average debt was $18,985.

FINANCIAL AID PROCEDURES

Forms required: FAFSA, institutional form.

Dates and Deadlines: Priority date 2/1; no closing date. Applicants notified by 3/1; must reply by 5/1 or within 2 week(s) of notification.

Transfers: Priority date 3/10; no deadline. Applicants notified by 3/1; must reply by 5/1 or within 2 week(s) of notification.

CONTACT

James Histand, Vice President for Finance
1700 South Main Street, Goshen, IN 46526
(574) 535-7522

Grace College

Winona Lake, Indiana
www.grace.edu   Federal Code: 001800

4-year private liberal arts college in large town, affiliated with Brethren Church.

Enrollment: 1,146 undergrads, 6% part-time. 247 full-time freshmen.

Selectivity: Admits 50 to 75% of applicants.

BASIC COSTS (2008-2009)

Tuition and fees: $20,376.

Per-credit charge: $450.

Room and board: $6,648.

Additional info: Tuition/fee waivers available for minority students.

FINANCIAL AID PICTURE (2007-2008)

Students with need: 78% of average financial aid package awarded as scholarships/grants, 22% awarded as loans/jobs. Need-based aid available for part-time students. Work study available nights, weekends, and for part-time students.

Students without need: No-need awards available for academics, art, athletics, leadership, music/drama.

FINANCIAL AID PROCEDURES

Forms required: FAFSA.

Dates and Deadlines: Closing date 3/10. Applicants notified on a rolling basis starting 3/1; must reply by 5/1.

Transfers: Applicants notified by 3/15; must reply by 5/1. Applicants who miss the dates for admission and financial aid are notified on a rolling basis until class is full.

CONTACT

Charlette Sauders, Director of Financial Aid Services
200 Seminary Drive, Winona Lake, IN 46590
(574) 372-5100 ext. 6162

Hanover College

Hanover, Indiana
www.hanover.edu   Federal Code: 001801

4-year private liberal arts college in rural community, affiliated with Presbyterian Church (USA).

Enrollment: 916 undergrads. 231 full-time freshmen.

Selectivity: Admits 50 to 75% of applicants. GED not accepted.

BASIC COSTS (2008-2009)

Tuition and fees: $25,220.

Per-credit charge: $686.

Room and board: $7,500.

FINANCIAL AID PICTURE (2007-2008)

Students with need: Out of 199 full-time freshmen who applied for aid, 165 were judged to have need. Of these, 165 received aid, and 75 had their full need met. Average financial aid package met 91% of need; average scholarship/grant was $17,868; average loan was $2,501. For part-time students, average financial aid package was $10,769.

Students without need: 65 full-time freshmen who did not demonstrate need for aid received scholarships/grants; average award was $16,305. No-need awards available for academics, alumni affiliation, music/drama, religious affiliation, state/district residency.

Cumulative student debt: 58% of graduating class had student loans; average debt was $21,597.

Additional info: Academic Honors Diploma Scholarship is a grant program committed to meeting 100% of Indiana student's demonstrated need. Available to Indiana students who graduate with an Academic Honors Diploma (AHD), have completed their application for admission by January 15, and file a complete and valid FAFSA by March 10.

FINANCIAL AID PROCEDURES

Forms required: FAFSA.

Dates and Deadlines: Priority date 3/10; no closing date. Applicants notified on a rolling basis starting 3/1; must reply by 5/1.

Transfers: No deadline. Applicants notified on a rolling basis starting 3/1; must reply by 5/1 or within 2 week(s) of notification.

CONTACT

Jon Riester, Associate Dean of Financial Assistance and Admission
PO Box 108, Hanover, IN 47243-0108
(812) 866-7030

Holy Cross College
Notre Dame, Indiana
www.hcc-nd.edu   Federal Code: 007263

4-year private liberal arts college in small city, affiliated with Roman Catholic Church.

Enrollment: 481 undergrads.

BASIC COSTS (2007-2008)
Tuition and fees: $15,660.
Per-credit charge: $520.
Room and board: $8,250.

FINANCIAL AID PICTURE
Students with need: Need-based aid available for full-time and part-time students. Work study available nights, weekends, and for part-time students.
Students without need: No-need awards available for academics, leadership.

FINANCIAL AID PROCEDURES
Forms required: FAFSA.
Dates and Deadlines: Priority date 3/1; no closing date. Applicants notified on a rolling basis starting 5/1; must reply within 2 week(s) of notification.

CONTACT
Robert Benjamin, Director of Financial Aid
54515 State Road 933N, Notre Dame, IN 46556-0308
(574) 239-8400

Huntington University
Huntington, Indiana
www.huntington.edu   Federal Code: 001803

4-year private university and liberal arts college in large town, affiliated with United Brethren in Christ.

Enrollment: 866 undergrads, 3% part-time. 242 full-time freshmen.
Selectivity: Admits over 75% of applicants.

BASIC COSTS (2008-2009)
Tuition and fees: $20,300.
Per-credit charge: $570.
Room and board: $6,940.

FINANCIAL AID PICTURE (2007-2008)
Students with need: Out of 218 full-time freshmen who applied for aid, 185 were judged to have need. Of these, 185 received aid, and 20 had their full need met. Average financial aid package met 79% of need; average scholarship/grant was $12,311; average loan was $4,086. For part-time students, average financial aid package was $5,217.
Students without need: 45 full-time freshmen who did not demonstrate need for aid received scholarships/grants; average award was $7,354. No-need awards available for academics, alumni affiliation, art, athletics, leadership, music/drama, religious affiliation.
Scholarships offered: 9 full-time freshmen received athletic scholarships; average amount $5,640.
Cumulative student debt: 66% of graduating class had student loans; average debt was $24,267.
Additional info: Students may lock in their tuition rate for all four years.

FINANCIAL AID PROCEDURES
Forms required: FAFSA.
Dates and Deadlines: Priority date 3/1; no closing date. Applicants notified on a rolling basis starting 3/1; must reply by 5/1 or within 2 week(s) of notification.
Transfers: No deadline. Applicants notified on a rolling basis; must reply by 5/1 or within 2 week(s) of notification.

CONTACT
Sharon Woods, Director of Financial Aid
2303 College Avenue, Huntington, IN 46750-1237
(260) 359-4015

Indiana Business College: Anderson
Anderson, Indiana
www.ibcschools.edu   Federal Code: 015227

2-year for-profit business and health science college in small city.

Enrollment: 206 undergrads.

BASIC COSTS (2007-2008)
Additional info: Tuition and fees vary by program: $194 to $268 per credit hour.

FINANCIAL AID PICTURE
Students with need: Need-based aid available for full-time and part-time students.
Additional info: Work-study programs available.

FINANCIAL AID PROCEDURES
Forms required: FAFSA.
Dates and Deadlines: Applicants notified on a rolling basis.

CONTACT
140 East 53rd Street, Anderson, IN 46013
(800) 422-4723

Indiana Business College: Columbus
Columbus, Indiana
www.ibcschools.edu   Federal Code: 015226

2-year for-profit business and health science college in large town.

Enrollment: 270 undergrads.

BASIC COSTS (2007-2008)
Additional info: Tuition and fees vary by program: $194 to $268 per credit hour.

FINANCIAL AID PICTURE
Students with need: Need-based aid available for full-time and part-time students.
Additional info: Work-study programs are available.

FINANCIAL AID PROCEDURES
Forms required: FAFSA.
Dates and Deadlines: Applicants notified on a rolling basis.

CONTACT
2222 Poshard Drive, Columbus, IN 47203
(800) 422-4723

Indiana Business College: Evansville
Evansville, Indiana
www.ibcschools.edu   Federal Code: E00778

2-year for-profit business and health science college in small city.

Enrollment: 321 undergrads.

BASIC COSTS (2007-2008)
Additional info: Tuition and fees vary by program: $194 to $268 per credit hour.

FINANCIAL AID PICTURE

Students with need: Need-based aid available for full-time and part-time students.

Additional info: Work-study programs are available.

FINANCIAL AID PROCEDURES

Forms required: FAFSA.

Dates and Deadlines: Applicants notified on a rolling basis.

CONTACT

4601 Theater Drive, Evansville, IN 47715

(800) 422-4723

Indiana Business College: Fort Wayne

Fort Wayne, Indiana

www.ibcschools.edu

2-year for-profit business and health science college in large city.

Enrollment: 474 undergrads.

BASIC COSTS (2007-2008)

Additional info: Tuition and fees vary by program: $194 to $268 per credit hour.

FINANCIAL AID PICTURE

Students with need: Need-based aid available for full-time and part-time students.

Additional info: Work-Study programs are available.

FINANCIAL AID PROCEDURES

Forms required: FAFSA.

Transfers: Applicants notified on a rolling basis.

CONTACT

6413 North Clinton Street, Fort Wayne, IN 46825

(800) 422-4723

Indiana Business College: Indianapolis

Indianapolis, Indiana

www.ibcschools.edu   Federal Code: 075218

2-year for-profit business and health science college in very large city.

Enrollment: 1,486 undergrads.

BASIC COSTS (2007-2008)

Additional info: Tuition and fees vary by program: $194 to $268 per credit hour.

FINANCIAL AID PICTURE

Students with need: Need-based aid available for full-time and part-time students.

Additional info: Work-study programs are available.

FINANCIAL AID PROCEDURES

Forms required: FAFSA.

Dates and Deadlines: Applicants notified on a rolling basis.

CONTACT

550 East Washington Street, Indianapolis, IN 46204

(800) 422-4723

Indiana Business College: Indianapolis Northwest

Indianapolis, Indiana

www.ibcschools.edu   Federal Code: E01209

2-year for-profit business and health science college in very large city.

Enrollment: 218 undergrads.

BASIC COSTS (2007-2008)

Additional info: Tuition and fees vary by program: $194 to $268 per credit hour.

FINANCIAL AID PICTURE

Students with need: Need-based aid available for full-time students.

FINANCIAL AID PROCEDURES

Forms required: FAFSA.

CONTACT

6300 Technology Center Drive, Indianapolis, IN 46278

Indiana Business College: Lafayette

Lafayette, Indiana

www.ibcschools.edu   Federal Code: 015224

2-year for-profit business and health science college in small city.

Enrollment: 325 undergrads.

BASIC COSTS (2007-2008)

Additional info: Tuition and fees vary by program: $194 to $268 per credit hour.

FINANCIAL AID PICTURE

Students with need: Need-based aid available for full-time and part-time students.

Additional info: Work-Study Programs are available.

FINANCIAL AID PROCEDURES

Forms required: FAFSA.

Dates and Deadlines: Applicants notified on a rolling basis.

Transfers: Applicants notified on a rolling basis.

CONTACT

4705 Meijer Court, Lafayette, IN 47905

(800) 422-4723

Indiana Business College: Marion

Marion, Indiana

www.ibcschools.edu   Federal Code: 015223

2-year for-profit business and health science college in large town.

Enrollment: 137 undergrads.

BASIC COSTS (2007-2008)

Additional info: Tuition and fees vary by program: $194 to $268 per credit hour.

FINANCIAL AID PICTURE

Students with need: Need-based aid available for full-time and part-time students.

Additional info: Work-Study Programs are available.

FINANCIAL AID PROCEDURES

Forms required: FAFSA.

Dates and Deadlines: Applicants notified on a rolling basis.

CONTACT

830 North Miller Avenue, Marion, IN 46952

(800) 422-4723

Indiana Business College: Medical

Indianapolis, Indiana

www.ibcschools.edu   Federal Code: E00777

2-year for-profit health science college in very large city.

Enrollment: 565 undergrads.

BASIC COSTS (2007-2008)

Additional info: Tuition and fees vary by program: $194 to $268 per credit hour.

FINANCIAL AID PICTURE

Students with need: Need-based aid available for full-time and part-time students.

Additional info: Work-study programs are available.

FINANCIAL AID PROCEDURES

Forms required: FAFSA.

Dates and Deadlines: Applicants notified on a rolling basis.

Transfers: Applicants notified on a rolling basis.

CONTACT

8150 Brookville Road, Indianapolis, IN 46239

(800) 422-4723

Indiana Business College: Muncie

Muncie, Indiana

www.ibcschools.edu   Federal Code: 015222

2-year for-profit business and health science college in small city.

Enrollment: 323 undergrads.

BASIC COSTS (2007-2008)

Additional info: Tuition and fees vary by program: $194 to $268 per credit hour.

FINANCIAL AID PICTURE

Students with need: Need-based aid available for full-time and part-time students.

Additional info: Work-Study Programs are available.

FINANCIAL AID PROCEDURES

Forms required: FAFSA.

Dates and Deadlines: Applicants notified on a rolling basis.

Transfers: Applicants notified on a rolling basis.

CONTACT

411 West Riggin Road, Muncie, IN 47303

(800) 422-4723

Indiana Business College: Terre Haute

Terre Haute, Indiana

www.ibcschools.edu   Federal Code: 015220

2-year for-profit business and health science college in small city.

Enrollment: 263 undergrads.

Selectivity: Open admission; but selective for some programs.

BASIC COSTS (2007-2008)

Additional info: Tuition and fees vary by program: $194 to $268 per credit hour.

FINANCIAL AID PICTURE

Students with need: Need-based aid available for full-time and part-time students.

Additional info: Work-study programs are available.

FINANCIAL AID PROCEDURES

Forms required: FAFSA.

Dates and Deadlines: Applicants notified on a rolling basis.

Transfers: Applicants notified on a rolling basis.

CONTACT

David Marshall, Director of Financial Aid

1378 South State Road 46, Terre Haute, IN 47803

(812) 877-2100

Indiana Institute of Technology

Fort Wayne, Indiana

www.indianatech.edu   Federal Code: 001805

4-year private business and engineering college in large city.

Enrollment: 3,026 undergrads, 40% part-time. 303 full-time freshmen.

Selectivity: Admits 50 to 75% of applicants.

BASIC COSTS (2008-2009)

Tuition and fees: $20,280.

Per-credit charge: $666.

Room and board: $7,650.

Additional info: Tuition/fee waivers available for adults.

FINANCIAL AID PICTURE

Students with need: Need-based aid available for full-time and part-time students. Work study available nights, weekends, and for part-time students.

Students without need: No-need awards available for academics, alumni affiliation, athletics, leadership, minority status, music/drama, state/district residency.

FINANCIAL AID PROCEDURES

Forms required: FAFSA, institutional form.

Dates and Deadlines: Closing date 3/10. Applicants notified on a rolling basis starting 2/2; must reply within 2 week(s) of notification.

Transfers: Priority date 3/10; no deadline. Applicants notified on a rolling basis starting 2/2; must reply within 2 week(s) of notification.

CONTACT

Judy Roy, Vice President of Finance and Administration

1600 East Washington Boulevard, Fort Wayne, IN 46803-1297

(260) 422-5561 ext. 2208

Indiana State University

Terre Haute, Indiana

www.indstate.edu   Federal Code: 001807

4-year public university in small city.

Enrollment: 8,303 undergrads, 13% part-time. 1,660 full-time freshmen.

Selectivity: Admits 50 to 75% of applicants.

BASIC COSTS (2008-2009)

Tuition and fees: $7,148; out-of-state residents $15,402.

Per-credit charge: $245.

FINANCIAL AID PICTURE (2006-2007)

Students with need: Out of 1,453 full-time freshmen who applied for aid, 1,166 were judged to have need. Of these, 1,131 received aid, and 145 had their full need met. Average financial aid package met 75% of need; average scholarship/grant was $5,398; average loan was $2,508. For part-time students, average financial aid package was $5,050.

Students without need: This college awards aid only to students with need.

Scholarships offered: 73 full-time freshmen received athletic scholarships; average amount $8,891.

Cumulative student debt: 64% of graduating class had student loans; average debt was $20,868.

Additional info: Financial aid application deadline March 1 for Indiana residents applying for state grant.

FINANCIAL AID PROCEDURES

Forms required: FAFSA.

Dates and Deadlines: Priority date 3/1; no closing date. Applicants notified on a rolling basis starting 4/15.

CONTACT

Charlene Shivers, Director of Student Financial Aid
Office of Admissions, Erickson 114, Terre Haute, IN 47809-9989
(800) 841-4744

Indiana University Bloomington

Bloomington, Indiana
www.iub.edu   Federal Code: 001809

4-year public university in small city.

Enrollment: 29,734 undergrads, 3% part-time. 7,253 full-time freshmen.

Selectivity: Admits 50 to 75% of applicants.

BASIC COSTS (2007-2008)

Tuition and fees: $7,837; out-of-state residents $22,316.

Per-credit charge: $219; out-of-state residents $671.

Room and board: $6,676.

FINANCIAL AID PICTURE (2006-2007)

Students with need: Out of 4,786 full-time freshmen who applied for aid, 3,010 were judged to have need. Of these, 2,907 received aid, and 573 had their full need met. Average financial aid package met 66% of need; average scholarship/grant was $7,213; average loan was $2,869. For part-time students, average financial aid package was $6,126.

Students without need: 1,785 full-time freshmen who did not demonstrate need for aid received scholarships/grants; average award was $4,978. No-need awards available for academics, art, athletics, leadership, minority status, music/drama, religious affiliation, ROTC.

Scholarships offered: *Merit:* Wells Scholarship: all costs for 4 years; individual schools nominate students; 25 students selected each year. Honors College Scholarship: $1,000-$6,000; 1300 SAT (30 ACT), top 10% class rank. Hudson & Holland: $4,000-$7,000; 1000 SAT (25 ACT), top 20% class rank, minimum 3.0 GPA, based on African, Hispanic, Native American ethnicity. Mathematics and Science Scholarship: $5,000-$6,000; 1000 SAT (25 ACT), top 20% class rank, minimum 3.0 GPA. E.W. Kelley Scholars Program: tuition, room and board, books (overseas study funding, if requested); business major, 1300 SAT (30 ACT), top 10% class rank. School of Music Dean's Award: competitive awards, varying in amount; exceptional talent displayed in audition. Residence Scholarship (via Honors College): $1,500; 1100 SAT (27 ACT), top 10% class rank. Faculty Scholarship: competitive awards, varying in amount; out-of-state residence; superior test scores and class rank. Valedictorian Award: $1,000; Indiana residence, highest ranking in high school class. 21st Century Scholars Award: in-state instructional fees; Indiana residence, fulfilled terms of pledged in eighth grade, filed FAFSA before March 1 of senior year. Army and Air Force ROTC Scholarships: tuition, fees, books, $200 monthly stipend. All SAT scores listed are exclusive of the writing portion. *Athletic:* 85 full-time freshmen received athletic scholarships; average amount $15,105.

Cumulative student debt: 56% of graduating class had student loans; average debt was $19,889.

Additional info: Majority of institutional gift aid merit-based. Some need-based grants go to merit winners with financial need.

FINANCIAL AID PROCEDURES

Forms required: FAFSA.

Dates and Deadlines: Priority date 3/1; no closing date. Applicants notified on a rolling basis starting 4/1.

Transfers: Except for school of music, no merit-based aid for transfer students.

CONTACT

Susan Pugh, Director of Student Financial Assistance
300 North Jordan Avenue, Bloomington, IN 47405
(812) 855-0321

Indiana University East

Richmond, Indiana
www.iue.edu   Federal Code: 001811

4-year public university and branch campus college in large town.

Enrollment: 1,974 undergrads, 37% part-time. 247 full-time freshmen.

Selectivity: Open admission; but selective for some programs.

BASIC COSTS (2007-2008)

Tuition and fees: $5,292; out-of-state residents $12,831.

Per-credit charge: $164; out-of-state residents $416.

FINANCIAL AID PICTURE (2006-2007)

Students with need: Out of 221 full-time freshmen who applied for aid, 178 were judged to have need. Of these, 170 received aid, and 14 had their full need met. Average financial aid package met 59% of need; average scholarship/grant was $4,700; average loan was $2,156. For part-time students, average financial aid package was $4,162.

Students without need: 13 full-time freshmen who did not demonstrate need for aid received scholarships/grants; average award was $1,030. No-need awards available for academics, alumni affiliation, leadership.

Cumulative student debt: 46% of graduating class had student loans; average debt was $24,830.

FINANCIAL AID PROCEDURES

Forms required: FAFSA, institutional form.

Dates and Deadlines: Priority date 3/1; no closing date. Applicants notified on a rolling basis starting 5/1; must reply within 2 week(s) of notification.

CONTACT

William Gill, Director of Financial Aid
2325 Chester Boulevard, Richmond, IN 47374-1289
(765) 973-8288

Indiana University Kokomo

Kokomo, Indiana
www.iuk.edu   Federal Code: 001814

4-year public university in large town.

Enrollment: 2,387 undergrads, 42% part-time. 354 full-time freshmen.

Selectivity: Admits over 75% of applicants.

BASIC COSTS (2007-2008)

Tuition and fees: $5,325; out-of-state residents $12,861.

Per-credit charge: $164; out-of-state residents $415.

FINANCIAL AID PICTURE (2006-2007)

Students with need: Out of 287 full-time freshmen who applied for aid, 206 were judged to have need. Of these, 185 received aid, and 25 had their full need met. Average financial aid package met 58% of need; average scholarship/grant was $4,658; average loan was $2,278. For part-time students, average financial aid package was $4,970.

Students without need: 33 full-time freshmen who did not demonstrate need for aid received scholarships/grants; average award was $1,523. No-need awards available for academics.

Cumulative student debt: 60% of graduating class had student loans; average debt was $19,319.

FINANCIAL AID PROCEDURES

Forms required: FAFSA, institutional form.

Dates and Deadlines: Closing date 3/1. Applicants notified on a rolling basis starting 5/1; must reply within 4 week(s) of notification.

CONTACT

Director of Financial Aid
Box 9003, KC 230A, Kokomo, IN 46904-9003
(765) 455-9216

Indiana University Northwest

Gary, Indiana
www.iun.edu   Federal Code: 001815

4-year public university in small city.

Enrollment: 3,965 undergrads, 39% part-time. 621 full-time freshmen.

Selectivity: Admits over 75% of applicants.

BASIC COSTS (2007-2008)

Tuition and fees: $5,398.

Per-credit charge: $165; out-of-state residents $416.

FINANCIAL AID PICTURE (2006-2007)

Students with need: Out of 486 full-time freshmen who applied for aid, 378 were judged to have need. Of these, 346 received aid, and 23 had their full need met. Average financial aid package met 50% of need; average scholarship/grant was $4,778; average loan was $2,306. For part-time students, average financial aid package was $4,682.

Students without need: 26 full-time freshmen who did not demonstrate need for aid received scholarships/grants; average award was $4,388. No-need awards available for academics, athletics.

Scholarships offered: 3 full-time freshmen received athletic scholarships; average amount $567.

Cumulative student debt: 68% of graduating class had student loans; average debt was $23,604.

FINANCIAL AID PROCEDURES

Forms required: FAFSA, institutional form.

Dates and Deadlines: Priority date 3/1; no closing date. Applicants notified on a rolling basis starting 5/1; must reply within 2 week(s) of notification.

CONTACT

R. Douglas Irvine, Financial Aid Director
3400 Broadway, Gary, IN 46408
(877) 280-4593

Indiana University South Bend

South Bend, Indiana
www.iusb.edu   Federal Code: 001816

4-year public university in small city.

Enrollment: 5,718 undergrads, 36% part-time. 824 full-time freshmen.

Selectivity: Admits over 75% of applicants.

BASIC COSTS (2007-2008)

Tuition and fees: $5,491; out-of-state residents $13,918.

Per-credit charge: $169; out-of-state residents $450.

FINANCIAL AID PICTURE (2006-2007)

Students with need: Out of 635 full-time freshmen who applied for aid, 479 were judged to have need. Of these, 442 received aid, and 24 had their full need met. Average financial aid package met 51% of need; average scholarship/grant was $4,450; average loan was $2,097. For part-time students, average financial aid package was $4,295.

Students without need: 19 full-time freshmen who did not demonstrate need for aid received scholarships/grants; average award was $3,179. No-need awards available for academics, athletics.

Scholarships offered: *Merit:* Honors Scholarship: $1,200 per academic year (full-time); entering freshman, 1200 or more SAT (exclusive of Writing) or 27 ACT; rank top 10 percent, 3.5 GPA; renewable up to 8 semesters. Alumni Scholarship: $3,500 freshman year; must be first-time freshman from Northern Indiana, meet Honors Scholarship criteria, submit essay and 3 letters of recommendation. *Athletic:* 2 full-time freshmen received athletic scholarships; average amount $2,750.

Cumulative student debt: 67% of graduating class had student loans; average debt was $20,848.

FINANCIAL AID PROCEDURES

Forms required: FAFSA, institutional form.

Dates and Deadlines: Closing date 3/1. Applicants notified on a rolling basis starting 5/1.

Transfers: No deadline.

CONTACT

Beverly Cooper, Director of Financial Aid
1700 Mishawaka Avenue, South Bend, IN 46634-7111
(574) 520-4357

Indiana University Southeast

New Albany, Indiana
www.ius.edu   Federal Code: 001817

4-year public university in large town.

Enrollment: 5,167 undergrads, 36% part-time. 761 full-time freshmen.

Selectivity: Admits over 75% of applicants.

BASIC COSTS (2007-2008)

Tuition and fees: $5,376; out-of-state residents $12,913.

Per-credit charge: $164; out-of-state residents $416.

FINANCIAL AID PICTURE (2006-2007)

Students with need: Out of 564 full-time freshmen who applied for aid, 414 were judged to have need. Of these, 381 received aid, and 47 had their full need met. Average financial aid package met 54% of need; average scholarship/grant was $4,474; average loan was $2,265. For part-time students, average financial aid package was $4,566.

Students without need: 49 full-time freshmen who did not demonstrate need for aid received scholarships/grants; average award was $1,474. No-need awards available for academics, art, athletics, leadership, minority status, music/drama.

Scholarships offered: 5 full-time freshmen received athletic scholarships; average amount $800.

Cumulative student debt: 57% of graduating class had student loans; average debt was $19,830.

FINANCIAL AID PROCEDURES

Forms required: FAFSA.

Dates and Deadlines: Priority date 3/1; no closing date. Applicants notified on a rolling basis starting 5/1; must reply within 3 week(s) of notification.

CONTACT

Brittany Hubbard, Director of Financial Aid
4201 Grant Line Road, New Albany, IN 47150-6405
(812) 941-2246 ext. 2260

Indiana University-Purdue University Fort Wayne

Fort Wayne, Indiana
www.ipfw.edu   Federal Code: 001828

4-year public university and branch campus college in large city.
Enrollment: 10,659 undergrads, 31% part-time. 1,651 full-time freshmen.
Selectivity: Admits over 75% of applicants.

BASIC COSTS (2007-2008)

Tuition and fees: $6,312; out-of-state residents $14,666.
Per-credit charge: $185; out-of-state residents $463.
Room only: $5,140.

FINANCIAL AID PICTURE (2006-2007)

Students with need: Out of 1,369 full-time freshmen who applied for aid, 1,063 were judged to have need. Of these, 985 received aid, and 27 had their full need met. Average financial aid package met 45% of need; average scholarship/grant was $4,428; average loan was $2,264. For part-time students, average financial aid package was $5,054.
Students without need: 19 full-time freshmen who did not demonstrate need for aid received scholarships/grants; average award was $870. No-need awards available for academics, athletics, state/district residency.
Scholarships offered: 19 full-time freshmen received athletic scholarships; average amount $5,700.
Cumulative student debt: 60% of graduating class had student loans; average debt was $19,209.

FINANCIAL AID PROCEDURES

Forms required: FAFSA.
Dates and Deadlines: Priority date 3/10; no closing date. Applicants notified on a rolling basis starting 5/15; must reply within 3 week(s) of notification.

CONTACT

Judith Cramer, Director of Financial Aid
2101 East Coliseum Boulevard, Fort Wayne, IN 46805-1499
(260) 481-6820

Indiana University-Purdue University Indianapolis

Indianapolis, Indiana
www.iupui.edu   Federal Code: 001813

4-year public university in very large city.
Enrollment: 20,136 undergrads, 29% part-time. 2,659 full-time freshmen.
Selectivity: Admits 50 to 75% of applicants.

BASIC COSTS (2007-2008)

Tuition and fees: $6,851; out-of-state residents $18,905.
Per-credit charge: $207; out-of-state residents $609.
Room and board: $5,100.

FINANCIAL AID PICTURE (2006-2007)

Students with need: Out of 2,128 full-time freshmen who applied for aid, 1,686 were judged to have need. Of these, 1,615 received aid, and 116 had their full need met. Average financial aid package met 52% of need; average scholarship/grant was $5,690; average loan was $2,371. For part-time students, average financial aid package was $4,837.
Students without need: 262 full-time freshmen who did not demonstrate need for aid received scholarships/grants; average award was $2,650. No-need awards available for academics, ROTC.
Scholarships offered: 18 full-time freshmen received athletic scholarships; average amount $5,208.
Cumulative student debt: 78% of graduating class had student loans; average debt was $20,036.

FINANCIAL AID PROCEDURES

Forms required: FAFSA.
Dates and Deadlines: Priority date 3/1; no closing date. Applicants notified on a rolling basis starting 4/1.

CONTACT

Kathy Purvis, Director of Scholarships and Financial Aid
425 North University Boulevard, Cavanaugh Hall R129, Indianapolis, IN 46202-5143
(317) 274-4162

Indiana Wesleyan University

Marion, Indiana
www.indwes.edu   Federal Code: 001822

4-year private university and liberal arts college in large town, affiliated with Wesleyan Church.
Enrollment: 2,881 undergrads, 3% part-time. 746 full-time freshmen.
Selectivity: Admits over 75% of applicants.

BASIC COSTS (2008-2009)

Tuition and fees: $19,376.
Per-credit charge: $692.
Room and board: $6,564.
Additional info: Required fees vary by program but are minimal.

FINANCIAL AID PICTURE (2007-2008)

Students with need: Out of 718 full-time freshmen who applied for aid, 639 were judged to have need. Of these, 639 received aid, and 61 had their full need met. Average financial aid package met 79% of need; average scholarship/grant was $12,667; average loan was $3,127. For part-time students, average financial aid package was $4,643.
Students without need: 67 full-time freshmen who did not demonstrate need for aid received scholarships/grants; average award was $6,429. No-need awards available for academics, alumni affiliation, art, athletics, music/drama, ROTC.
Scholarships offered: *Merit:* Academic Scholarships with awards ranging from $750 to $6,000, 3.2 GPA and 1050 SAT (exclusive of Writing) or 23 ACT. *Athletic:* 55 full-time freshmen received athletic scholarships; average amount $6,218.

FINANCIAL AID PROCEDURES

Forms required: FAFSA.
Dates and Deadlines: Closing date 3/1. Applicants notified by 4/1.

CONTACT

Thomas Ratliff, Associate Vice President for Financial Aid
4201 South Washington Street, Marion, IN 46953-4999
(765) 677-2116

Ivy Tech Community College: Bloomington

Bloomington, Indiana
www.ivytech.edu   Federal Code: 035213

2-year public community college in small city.
Enrollment: 4,435 undergrads, 50% part-time. 753 full-time freshmen.
Selectivity: Open admission; but selective for some programs.

BASIC COSTS (2007-2008)

Tuition and fees: $2,819; out-of-state residents $5,653.
Per-credit charge: $91; out-of-state residents $186.
Additional info: Out-of-state distance education tuition: $119 per credit hour ($3,584 for academic year).

FINANCIAL AID PICTURE

Students with need: Need-based aid available for full-time and part-time students. Work study available nights.

FINANCIAL AID PROCEDURES

Forms required: FAFSA.

Dates and Deadlines: Priority date 3/1; no closing date. Applicants notified on a rolling basis starting 7/1.

CONTACT

Lori Handy, Director of Financial Aid
200 Daniels Way, Bloomington, IN 47404-1511
(812) 332-1559

Ivy Tech Community College: Central Indiana

Indianapolis, Indiana
www.ivytech.edu   Federal Code: 009917

2-year public community college in very large city.

Enrollment: 12,639 undergrads, 65% part-time. 1,327 full-time freshmen.

Selectivity: Open admission; but selective for some programs.

BASIC COSTS (2007-2008)

Tuition and fees: $2,819; out-of-state residents $5,653.

Per-credit charge: $91; out-of-state residents $186.

Additional info: Out-of-state distance education tuition: $119 per credit hour ($3,584 for academic year).

FINANCIAL AID PICTURE

Students with need: Need-based aid available for full-time and part-time students. Work study available nights.

FINANCIAL AID PROCEDURES

Forms required: FAFSA.

Dates and Deadlines: Priority date 3/1; no closing date. Applicants notified on a rolling basis starting 7/1.

CONTACT

Daniel Adams, Director of Financial Aid
50 West Fall Creek Parkway North Drive, Indianapolis, IN 46208-5752
(317) 921-4882

Ivy Tech Community College: Columbus

Columbus, Indiana
www.ivytech.edu   Federal Code: 010038

2-year public community college in large town.

Enrollment: 2,407 undergrads, 61% part-time. 232 full-time freshmen.

Selectivity: Open admission; but selective for some programs.

BASIC COSTS (2007-2008)

Tuition and fees: $2,819; out-of-state residents $5,653.

Per-credit charge: $91; out-of-state residents $186.

Additional info: Out-of-state distance education tuition: $119 per credit hour ($3,584 for academic year).

FINANCIAL AID PICTURE

Students with need: Need-based aid available for full-time and part-time students. Work study available nights.

FINANCIAL AID PROCEDURES

Forms required: FAFSA.

Dates and Deadlines: Priority date 3/1; no closing date. Applicants notified on a rolling basis starting 7/1.

CONTACT

Donna Bentz, Director of Financial Aid
4475 Central Avenue, Columbus, IN 47203-1868
(812) 372-9925

Ivy Tech Community College: East Central

Muncie, Indiana
www.ivytech.edu   Federal Code: 009924

2-year public community college in small city.

Enrollment: 5,610 undergrads, 51% part-time. 746 full-time freshmen.

Selectivity: Open admission; but selective for some programs.

BASIC COSTS (2007-2008)

Tuition and fees: $2,819; out-of-state residents $5,653.

Per-credit charge: $91; out-of-state residents $186.

Additional info: Out-of-state distance education tuition: $119 per credit hour ($3,584 for academic year).

FINANCIAL AID PICTURE

Students with need: Need-based aid available for full-time and part-time students. Work study available nights.

Additional info: Higher Education Aid (HEA), Child of Disabled/Deceased Veterans (CDV), Ivy Tech Scholarships (IVTC) and grants, vocational rehabilitation and veteran's assistance available. None require repayment.

FINANCIAL AID PROCEDURES

Forms required: FAFSA.

Dates and Deadlines: Priority date 3/1; no closing date. Applicants notified on a rolling basis starting 7/1.

CONTACT

Sylvia Bogle, Director of Financial Aid
4301 South Cowan Road, Muncie, IN 47302-9448
(765) 289-2291 ext. 1222

Ivy Tech Community College: Kokomo

Kokomo, Indiana
www.ivytech.edu   Federal Code: 010041

2-year public community college in large town.

Enrollment: 3,194 undergrads, 67% part-time. 199 full-time freshmen.

Selectivity: Open admission; but selective for some programs.

BASIC COSTS (2007-2008)

Tuition and fees: $2,819; out-of-state residents $5,653.

Per-credit charge: $91; out-of-state residents $186.

Additional info: Out-of-state distance education tuition: $119 per credit hour ($3,584 for academic year).

FINANCIAL AID PICTURE

Students with need: Need-based aid available for full-time and part-time students. Work study available nights.

FINANCIAL AID PROCEDURES

Forms required: FAFSA.

Dates and Deadlines: Priority date 3/1; no closing date. Applicants notified on a rolling basis starting 7/1.

Transfers: Applicants notified on a rolling basis starting 7/1.

CONTACT

David Scheblo, Director of Financial Aid
1815 East Morgan Street, Kokomo, IN 46903-1373
(765) 459-0561

PART III: FINANCIAL AID COLLEGE BY COLLEGE

Ivy Tech Community College: Lafayette

Lafayette, Indiana
www.ivytech.edu   Federal Code: 010039

2-year public community college in large town.
Enrollment: 4,573 undergrads, 45% part-time. 694 full-time freshmen.
Selectivity: Open admission; but selective for some programs.

BASIC COSTS (2007-2008)
Tuition and fees: $2,819; out-of-state residents $5,653.
Per-credit charge: $91; out-of-state residents $186.
Additional info: Out-of-state distance education tuition: $119 per credit hour ($3,584 for academic year).

FINANCIAL AID PICTURE
Students with need: Need-based aid available for full-time and part-time students. Work study available nights.

FINANCIAL AID PROCEDURES
Forms required: FAFSA.
Dates and Deadlines: Priority date 3/1; no closing date. Applicants notified on a rolling basis starting 7/1.

CONTACT
Christina Coon, Director of Financial Aid
3101 South Creasy Lane, Lafayette, IN 47905-6299
(765) 772-9100

Ivy Tech Community College: North Central

South Bend, Indiana
www.ivytech.edu   Federal Code: 008423

2-year public community college in small city.
Enrollment: 4,625 undergrads, 68% part-time. 384 full-time freshmen.
Selectivity: Open admission; but selective for some programs.

BASIC COSTS (2007-2008)
Tuition and fees: $2,819; out-of-state residents $5,653.
Per-credit charge: $91; out-of-state residents $186.
Additional info: Out-of-state distance education tuition: $119 per credit hour ($3,584 for academic year).

FINANCIAL AID PICTURE
Students with need: Need-based aid available for full-time and part-time students. Work study available nights.

FINANCIAL AID PROCEDURES
Forms required: FAFSA.
Dates and Deadlines: Priority date 3/1; no closing date. Applicants notified on a rolling basis starting 7/1.

CONTACT
Jeff Fisher, Director of Financial Aid
220 Dean Johnson Boulevard, South Bend, IN 46601-3415
(219) 289-7001

Ivy Tech Community College: Northeast

Fort Wayne, Indiana
www.ivytech.edu   Federal Code: 009926

2-year public community college in small city.
Enrollment: 5,704 undergrads, 58% part-time. 545 full-time freshmen.
Selectivity: Open admission; but selective for some programs.

BASIC COSTS (2007-2008)
Tuition and fees: $2,819; out-of-state residents $5,653.
Per-credit charge: $91; out-of-state residents $186.
Additional info: Out-of-state distance education tuition: $119 per credit hour ($3,584 for academic year).

FINANCIAL AID PICTURE
Students with need: Need-based aid available for full-time and part-time students. Work study available nights.

FINANCIAL AID PROCEDURES
Forms required: FAFSA.
Dates and Deadlines: Priority date 3/1; no closing date. Applicants notified on a rolling basis starting 7/1.

CONTACT
Teresa Sweazey, Director of Financial Aid
3800 North Anthony Boulevard, Fort Wayne, IN 46805-1489
(260) 482-9171

Ivy Tech Community College: Northwest

Gary, Indiana
www.ivytech.edu   Federal Code: 010040

2-year public community college in small city.
Enrollment: 4,540 undergrads, 62% part-time. 434 full-time freshmen.
Selectivity: Open admission; but selective for some programs.

BASIC COSTS (2007-2008)
Tuition and fees: $2,819; out-of-state residents $5,653.
Per-credit charge: $91; out-of-state residents $186.
Additional info: Out-of-state distance education tuition: $119 per credit hour ($3,584 for academic year).

FINANCIAL AID PICTURE
Students with need: Need-based aid available for full-time and part-time students. Work study available nights.

FINANCIAL AID PROCEDURES
Forms required: FAFSA.
Dates and Deadlines: Priority date 3/1; no closing date. Applicants notified on a rolling basis starting 7/1.

CONTACT
Barb Jerzyk, Director of Financial Aid
1440 East 35th Avenue, Gary, IN 46409-1499
(219) 981-1111

Ivy Tech Community College: Richmond

Richmond, Indiana
www.ivytech.edu   Federal Code: 010037

2-year public community college in large town.
Enrollment: 1,976 undergrads, 64% part-time. 168 full-time freshmen.
Selectivity: Open admission; but selective for some programs.

BASIC COSTS (2007-2008)
Tuition and fees: $2,819; out-of-state residents $5,653.
Per-credit charge: $91; out-of-state residents $186.
Additional info: Out-of-state distance education tuition: $119 per credit hour ($3,584 for academic year).

FINANCIAL AID PICTURE
Students with need: Need-based aid available for full-time and part-time students. Work study available nights.

FINANCIAL AID PROCEDURES
Forms required: FAFSA.

Dates and Deadlines: Priority date 3/1; no closing date. Applicants notified on a rolling basis starting 7/1.

CONTACT

Ann Franzen-Roha, Director of Financial Aid

2357 Chester Boulevard, Richmond, IN 47374-1298

(765) 966-2656

Ivy Tech Community College: South Central

Sellersburg, Indiana

www.ivytech.edu   Federal Code: 010109

2-year public community college in small town.

Enrollment: 3,181 undergrads, 62% part-time. 295 full-time freshmen.

Selectivity: Open admission; but selective for some programs.

BASIC COSTS (2007-2008)

Tuition and fees: $2,819; out-of-state residents $5,653.

Per-credit charge: $91; out-of-state residents $186.

Additional info: Out-of-state distance education tuition: $119 per credit hour ($3,584 for academic year).

FINANCIAL AID PICTURE

Students with need: Need-based aid available for full-time and part-time students. Work study available nights.

FINANCIAL AID PROCEDURES

Forms required: FAFSA.

Dates and Deadlines: Priority date 3/1; no closing date. Applicants notified on a rolling basis starting 7/1.

CONTACT

Gary Cottrill, Director of Financial Aid

8204 Highway 311, Sellersburg, IN 47172-1897

(812) 246-3301

Ivy Tech Community College: Southeast

Madison, Indiana

www.ivytech.edu   Federal Code: 009923

2-year public community college in large town.

Enrollment: 1,792 undergrads, 58% part-time. 203 full-time freshmen.

Selectivity: Open admission; but selective for some programs.

BASIC COSTS (2007-2008)

Tuition and fees: $2,819; out-of-state residents $5,653.

Per-credit charge: $91; out-of-state residents $186.

Additional info: Out-of-state distance education tuition: $119 per credit hour ($3,584 for academic year).

FINANCIAL AID PICTURE

Students with need: Need-based aid available for full-time and part-time students. Work study available nights.

FINANCIAL AID PROCEDURES

Forms required: FAFSA.

Dates and Deadlines: Priority date 3/1; no closing date. Applicants notified on a rolling basis starting 7/1.

CONTACT

Richard Hill, Director of Financial Aid

590 Ivy Tech Drive, Madison, IN 47250-1881

(812) 265-2580 ext. 4148

Ivy Tech Community College: Southwest

Evansville, Indiana

www.ivytech.edu   Federal Code: 009925

2-year public community college in small city.

Enrollment: 4,393 undergrads, 58% part-time. 447 full-time freshmen.

Selectivity: Open admission; but selective for some programs.

BASIC COSTS (2007-2008)

Tuition and fees: $2,819; out-of-state residents $5,653.

Per-credit charge: $91; out-of-state residents $186.

Additional info: Out-of-state distance education tuition: $119 per credit hour ($3,584 for academic year).

FINANCIAL AID PICTURE

Students with need: Need-based aid available for full-time and part-time students. Work study available nights.

FINANCIAL AID PROCEDURES

Forms required: FAFSA.

Dates and Deadlines: Priority date 3/1; no closing date. Applicants notified on a rolling basis starting 7/1.

CONTACT

Kristi Eidson-Spahn, Director of Financial Aid

3501 First Avenue, Evansville, IN 47710-3398

(812) 426-2865

Ivy Tech Community College: Wabash Valley

Terre Haute, Indiana

www.ivytech.edu   Federal Code: 008547

2-year public community college in small city.

Enrollment: 4,647 undergrads, 54% part-time. 483 full-time freshmen.

Selectivity: Open admission; but selective for some programs.

BASIC COSTS (2007-2008)

Tuition and fees: $2,819; out-of-state residents $5,653.

Per-credit charge: $91; out-of-state residents $186.

Additional info: Out-of-state distance education tuition: $119 per credit hour ($3,584 for academic year).

FINANCIAL AID PICTURE

Students with need: Need-based aid available for full-time and part-time students. Work study available nights.

FINANCIAL AID PROCEDURES

Forms required: FAFSA.

Dates and Deadlines: Priority date 3/1; no closing date. Applicants notified on a rolling basis starting 7/1.

Transfers: Applicants notified on a rolling basis starting 7/1.

CONTACT

Julie Wonderlin, Director of Financial Aid

8000 South Education Drive, Terre Haute, IN 47802-4898

(812) 299-1121

Kaplan College: Indianapolis

Indianapolis, Indiana

www.kcindy.com   Federal Code: 009777

2-year for-profit business and health science college in very large city.

Enrollment: 10 full-time undergrads.

BASIC COSTS (2007-2008)
Tuition and fees: $11,001.
Additional info: Tuition and fees include uniform cost where applicable.

FINANCIAL AID PICTURE
Students with need: Need-based aid available for full-time students.
Students without need: This college awards aid only to students with need.

CONTACT
Phyllis Robbins, Financial Aid Administrator
7302 Woodland Drive, Indianapolis, IN 46278-1736
(317) 293-6503

Kaplan College: Merrillville
Merrillville, Indiana
www.sawyercollege.edu   Federal Code: 022018

2-year for-profit technical college in large town.
Enrollment: 347 undergrads, 18% part-time. 59 full-time freshmen.

BASIC COSTS (2007-2008)
Tuition and fees: $9,813.

FINANCIAL AID PICTURE
Students with need: Need-based aid available for full-time and part-time students.

FINANCIAL AID PROCEDURES
Forms required: FAFSA.
Dates and Deadlines: No deadline. Applicants notified on a rolling basis.

CONTACT
Lisa Coff, Director of Financial Aid
3803 East Lincoln Highway, Merrillville, IN 46410
(219) 947-8400 ext. 8409

Manchester College
North Manchester, Indiana
www.manchester.edu   Federal Code: 001820

4-year private liberal arts college in small town, affiliated with Church of the Brethren.
Enrollment: 1,011 undergrads, 1% part-time. 317 full-time freshmen.
Selectivity: Admits 50 to 75% of applicants.

BASIC COSTS (2008-2009)
Tuition and fees: $22,700.
Per-credit charge: $670.
Room and board: $8,100.
Additional info: Health insurance and other fees as required.

FINANCIAL AID PICTURE (2007-2008)
Students with need: Average financial aid package met 91% of need; average scholarship/grant was $15,776; average loan was $5,277. For part-time students, average financial aid package was $20,594.
Students without need: No-need awards available for academics, alumni affiliation, minority status, music/drama, religious affiliation.
Scholarships offered: Honors Fellowship; full tuition; based on academics; 2 awarded. Presidential Leadership Award; $2,500 travel grant; 3 awarded. Trustee Scholarships; $12,000; based on merit; 40 awarded to each incoming class. Presidential Scholarships; $9,000; based on merit. Arts, service, modern language scholarships; $9,000; based on merit/ability.
Additional info: Students are automatically considered for all scholarship programs.

FINANCIAL AID PROCEDURES
Forms required: FAFSA.
Dates and Deadlines: Priority date 3/1; no closing date. Applicants notified on a rolling basis starting 2/15; must reply within 2 week(s) of notification.
Transfers: Aid eligibility remaining determined by reviewing total credit hours transferred and financial aid transcripts.

CONTACT
Gina Voelz, Director of Financial Aid
604 East College Avenue, North Manchester, IN 46962-0365
(260) 982-5066

Marian College
Indianapolis, Indiana
www.marian.edu   Federal Code: 001821

4-year private liberal arts college in very large city, affiliated with Roman Catholic Church.
Enrollment: 1,906 undergrads, 26% part-time. 267 full-time freshmen.
Selectivity: Admits 50 to 75% of applicants.

BASIC COSTS (2007-2008)
Tuition and fees: $20,800.
Per-credit charge: $870.
Room and board: $7,400.

FINANCIAL AID PICTURE (2006-2007)
Students with need: Out of 251 full-time freshmen who applied for aid, 232 were judged to have need. Of these, 232 received aid, and 69 had their full need met. Average financial aid package met 88% of need; average scholarship/grant was $9,414; average loan was $3,486. For part-time students, average financial aid package was $13,869.
Students without need: 12 full-time freshmen who did not demonstrate need for aid received scholarships/grants; average award was $11,972. No-need awards available for academics, alumni affiliation, art, athletics, leadership, music/drama, religious affiliation.
Scholarships offered: 18 full-time freshmen received athletic scholarships; average amount $8,900.
Cumulative student debt: 81% of graduating class had student loans; average debt was $25,107.

FINANCIAL AID PROCEDURES
Forms required: FAFSA, institutional form.
Dates and Deadlines: Closing date 3/10. Applicants notified on a rolling basis starting 3/15; must reply within 3 week(s) of notification.
Transfers: No deadline. Applicants notified on a rolling basis starting 3/15; must reply within 3 week(s) of notification.

CONTACT
John Shelton, Dean for Financial Aid and Enrollment
3200 Cold Spring Road, Indianapolis, IN 46222-1997
(317) 955-6040

Oakland City University
Oakland City, Indiana
www.oak.edu   Federal Code: 001824

4-year private university and liberal arts college in small town, affiliated with Baptist General Conference.
Enrollment: 1,492 undergrads, 11% part-time. 337 full-time freshmen.
Selectivity: Open admission; but selective for some programs.

BASIC COSTS (2007-2008)
Tuition and fees: $14,820.
Per-credit charge: $482.
Room and board: $5,900.

Additional info: Tuition/fee waivers available for minority students, unemployed or children of unemployed.

FINANCIAL AID PICTURE (2007-2008)

Students with need: 70% of average financial aid package awarded as scholarships/grants, 30% awarded as loans/jobs. Need-based aid available for part-time students. Work study available nights, weekends, and for part-time students.

Students without need: No-need awards available for academics, alumni affiliation, art, athletics, minority status, music/drama, religious affiliation.

FINANCIAL AID PROCEDURES

Forms required: FAFSA.

Dates and Deadlines: Closing date 3/1. Applicants notified on a rolling basis starting 5/1.

CONTACT

Caren Richeson, Director of Financial Aid
138 North Lucretia Street, Oakland City, IN 47660
(812) 749-1224

Purdue University

West Lafayette, Indiana
www.purdue.edu   Federal Code: 001825

4-year public university in small city.

Enrollment: 30,952 undergrads, 4% part-time. 6,735 full-time freshmen.
Selectivity: Admits over 75% of applicants.

BASIC COSTS (2007-2008)

Tuition and fees: $7,416; out-of-state residents $22,224.
Per-credit charge: $250; out-of-state residents $723.
Room and board: $7,962.
Additional info: Engineering students pay additional $628 fee per year. Management students pay additional $978 fee per year.

FINANCIAL AID PICTURE (2007-2008)

Students with need: Out of 4,821 full-time freshmen who applied for aid, 2,994 were judged to have need. Of these, 2,984 received aid, and 1,090 had their full need met. Average financial aid package met 93% of need; average scholarship/grant was $10,988; average loan was $3,490. For part-time students, average financial aid package was $8,549.

Students without need: 1,187 full-time freshmen who did not demonstrate need for aid received scholarships/grants; average award was $15,083. No-need awards available for academics, athletics, leadership, music/drama, ROTC, state/district residency.

Scholarships offered: 78 full-time freshmen received athletic scholarships; average amount $20,304.

Cumulative student debt: 48% of graduating class had student loans; average debt was $21,636.

Additional info: Cooperative work for credit available in many programs.

FINANCIAL AID PROCEDURES

Forms required: FAFSA.

Dates and Deadlines: Priority date 3/1; no closing date. Applicants notified by 4/15.

CONTACT

Joyce Hall, Director of Financial Aid
475 Stadium Mall Drive, West Lafayette, IN 47907-2050
(765) 494-5050

Purdue University Calumet

Hammond, Indiana
www.calumet.purdue.edu   Federal Code: 001827

4-year public university and branch campus college in small city.

Enrollment: 8,097 undergrads, 34% part-time. 1,123 full-time freshmen.
Selectivity: Admits over 75% of applicants.

BASIC COSTS (2007-2008)

Tuition and fees: $5,807; out-of-state residents $12,797.
Per-credit charge: $176; out-of-state residents $409.

FINANCIAL AID PICTURE (2006-2007)

Students with need: Out of 834 full-time freshmen who applied for aid, 613 were judged to have need. Of these, 548 received aid, and 79 had their full need met. Average financial aid package met 19% of need; average scholarship/grant was $2,648; average loan was $1,405. For part-time students, average financial aid package was $3,058.

Students without need: 27 full-time freshmen who did not demonstrate need for aid received scholarships/grants; average award was $633. No-need awards available for academics, alumni affiliation, athletics, minority status, state/district residency.

Scholarships offered: 3 full-time freshmen received athletic scholarships; average amount $1,667.

Cumulative student debt: 56% of graduating class had student loans; average debt was $17,529.

FINANCIAL AID PROCEDURES

Forms required: FAFSA.

Dates and Deadlines: Priority date 3/10; closing date 6/30. Applicants notified on a rolling basis starting 5/1; must reply within 2 week(s) of notification.

CONTACT

Carol Zencka, Director of Financial Aid and Student Accounts
2200 169th Street, Hammond, IN 46323-2094
(219) 989-2301

Purdue University North Central

Westville, Indiana
www.pnc.edu   Federal Code: 001826

4-year public branch campus college in rural community.

Enrollment: 3,512 undergrads, 35% part-time. 691 full-time freshmen.
Selectivity: Admits over 75% of applicants.

BASIC COSTS (2007-2008)

Tuition and fees: $5,817; out-of-state residents $13,593.
Per-credit charge: $175; out-of-state residents $434.
Additional info: Tuition/fee waivers available for minority students.

FINANCIAL AID PICTURE (2007-2008)

Students with need: Average financial aid package met 60% of need; average scholarship/grant was $4,958; average loan was $2,970. For part-time students, average financial aid package was $1,805.

Students without need: This college awards aid only to students with need.

Scholarships offered: 6 full-time freshmen received athletic scholarships; average amount $625.

Cumulative student debt: 63% of graduating class had student loans; average debt was $18,937.

FINANCIAL AID PROCEDURES

Forms required: FAFSA.

Dates and Deadlines: Priority date 3/10; closing date 6/30. Applicants notified on a rolling basis starting 5/31; must reply within 2 week(s) of notification.

Transfers: No deadline. Transfer students not considered for campus-based financial aid.

CONTACT

Bryant Dabney, Director of Financial Aid
1401 South US Highway 421, Westville, IN 46391-9528
(219) 785-5278

Rose-Hulman Institute of Technology

Terre Haute, Indiana
www.rose-hulman.edu   Federal Code: 001830

4-year private engineering college in small city.

Enrollment: 1,821 undergrads. 474 full-time freshmen.

Selectivity: Admits 50 to 75% of applicants. GED not accepted.

BASIC COSTS (2008-2009)

Tuition and fees: $32,826.

Per-credit charge: $939.

Room and board: $8,868.

Additional info: Purchase of laptop computer (approximately $2,900) required of freshmen.

FINANCIAL AID PICTURE (2007-2008)

Students with need: Out of 417 full-time freshmen who applied for aid, 335 were judged to have need. Of these, 335 received aid, and 56 had their full need met. Average financial aid package met 88% of need; average scholarship/grant was $17,652; average loan was $14,434. For part-time students, average financial aid package was $11,750.

Students without need: 128 full-time freshmen who did not demonstrate need for aid received scholarships/grants; average award was $8,708. No-need awards available for academics, minority status, ROTC.

Cumulative student debt: 74% of graduating class had student loans; average debt was $32,612.

FINANCIAL AID PROCEDURES

Forms required: FAFSA.

Dates and Deadlines: Priority date 3/1; no closing date. Applicants notified on a rolling basis starting 3/10.

Transfers: No deadline. Applicants notified on a rolling basis; must reply by 6/1.

CONTACT

Melinda Middleton, Director of Financial Aid
Office of Admissions, Terre Haute, IN 47803-3999
(800) 248-7448

Saint Joseph's College

Rensselaer, Indiana
www.saintjoe.edu   Federal Code: 001833

4-year private liberal arts college in small town, affiliated with Roman Catholic Church.

Enrollment: 1,051 undergrads, 3% part-time. 237 full-time freshmen.

Selectivity: Admits over 75% of applicants.

BASIC COSTS (2008-2009)

Tuition and fees: $23,180.

Per-credit charge: $770.

Room and board: $7,170.

FINANCIAL AID PICTURE (2006-2007)

Students with need: Out of 231 full-time freshmen who applied for aid, 201 were judged to have need. Of these, 201 received aid, and 48 had their full need met. Average financial aid package met 76% of need; average scholarship/grant was $13,285; average loan was $3,157. For part-time students, average financial aid package was $5,510.

Students without need: 26 full-time freshmen who did not demonstrate need for aid received scholarships/grants; average award was $12,058. No-need awards available for academics, alumni affiliation, athletics, minority status, music/drama.

Scholarships offered: 13 full-time freshmen received athletic scholarships; average amount $7,685.

Cumulative student debt: 83% of graduating class had student loans; average debt was $26,406.

FINANCIAL AID PROCEDURES

Forms required: FAFSA.

Dates and Deadlines: Priority date 3/1; no closing date. Applicants notified on a rolling basis starting 3/1; must reply by 5/1 or within 2 week(s) of notification.

Transfers: No deadline. Applicants notified on a rolling basis; must reply by 5/1 or within 2 week(s) of notification. Limited institutional academic scholarship.

CONTACT

Debra Sizemore, Director of Student Financial Services
Box 890, Rensselaer, IN 47978
(219) 866-6163

St. Mary-of-the-Woods College

St. Mary-of-the-Woods, Indiana
www.smwc.edu   Federal Code: 001835

4-year private liberal arts college for women in rural community, affiliated with Roman Catholic Church.

Enrollment: 1,279 undergrads, 68% part-time. 76 full-time freshmen.

Selectivity: Admits over 75% of applicants.

BASIC COSTS (2008-2009)

Tuition and fees: $21,550.

Per-credit charge: $396.

Room and board: $7,890.

Additional info: Tuition/fee waivers available for minority students.

FINANCIAL AID PICTURE (2006-2007)

Students with need: Out of 72 full-time freshmen who applied for aid, 66 were judged to have need. Of these, 66 received aid, and 30 had their full need met. Average financial aid package met 85% of need; average scholarship/grant was $16,817; average loan was $3,145. Need-based aid available for part-time students.

Students without need: 9 full-time freshmen who did not demonstrate need for aid received scholarships/grants; average award was $20,597. No-need awards available for academics, alumni affiliation, art, athletics, leadership, minority status, music/drama, state/district residency.

Scholarships offered: 4 full-time freshmen received athletic scholarships; average amount $5,911.

Additional info: Portfolio or audition required of applicants who wish to be considered for Creative Arts Scholarship.

FINANCIAL AID PROCEDURES

Forms required: FAFSA.

Dates and Deadlines: Priority date 3/1; no closing date. Applicants notified on a rolling basis starting 12/1; must reply within 6 week(s) of notification.

Transfers: Priority date 7/1; no deadline. Applicants notified on a rolling basis; must reply within 8 week(s) of notification.

CONTACT

Ruby Robinson, Director of Financial Aid
Guerin Hall, SMWC, St. Mary of the Woods, IN 47876
(812) 535-5109

Saint Mary's College

Notre Dame, Indiana
www.saintmarys.edu

Federal Code: 001836
CSS Code: 1702

4-year private liberal arts college for women in small city, affiliated with Roman Catholic Church.

Enrollment: 1,591 undergrads, 2% part-time. 479 full-time freshmen.
Selectivity: Admits over 75% of applicants.

BASIC COSTS (2008-2009)

Tuition and fees: $28,212.
Per-credit charge: $1,091.
Room and board: $8,938.

FINANCIAL AID PICTURE (2007-2008)

Students with need: Out of 461 full-time freshmen who applied for aid, 317 were judged to have need. Of these, 314 received aid, and 44 had their full need met. Average financial aid package met 84% of need; average scholarship/grant was $14,699; average loan was $4,059. Need-based aid available for part-time students.
Students without need: 129 full-time freshmen who did not demonstrate need for aid received scholarships/grants; average award was $9,264. No-need awards available for academics, art.
Cumulative student debt: 71% of graduating class had student loans; average debt was $28,908.

FINANCIAL AID PROCEDURES

Forms required: FAFSA, CSS PROFILE.
Dates and Deadlines: Priority date 3/1; no closing date. Applicants notified on a rolling basis starting 12/15; must reply by 5/1.
Transfers: Priority date 5/15. To meet Indiana grant deadlines, Indiana residents must submit FAFSA by March 1.

CONTACT

Kathleen Brown, Director of Financial Aid Notre Dame, IN 46556-5001
(574) 284-4557

Taylor University

Upland, Indiana
www.taylor.edu

Federal Code: 001838

4-year private university and liberal arts college in small town, affiliated with interdenominational tradition.

Enrollment: 1,858 undergrads, 2% part-time. 472 full-time freshmen.
Selectivity: Admits over 75% of applicants.

BASIC COSTS (2008-2009)

Tuition and fees: $24,546.
Per-credit charge: $691.
Room and board: $6,352.

FINANCIAL AID PICTURE (2007-2008)

Students with need: Out of 373 full-time freshmen who applied for aid, 309 were judged to have need. Of these, 309 received aid, and 72 had their full need met. Average financial aid package met 77% of need; average scholarship/grant was $12,526; average loan was $4,514. For part-time students, average financial aid package was $6,882.
Students without need: 95 full-time freshmen who did not demonstrate need for aid received scholarships/grants; average award was $5,218. No-need awards available for academics, alumni affiliation, art, athletics, leader-

ship, minority status, music/drama, religious affiliation, state/district residency.
Scholarships offered: 10 full-time freshmen received athletic scholarships; average amount $7,523.
Cumulative student debt: 57% of graduating class had student loans; average debt was $18,681.

FINANCIAL AID PROCEDURES

Forms required: FAFSA.
Dates and Deadlines: Closing date 3/10. Applicants notified on a rolling basis starting 3/1; must reply by 5/1.

CONTACT

Tim Nace, Assist Dean, Enrollment Management
236 West Reade Avenue, Upland, IN 46989-1001
(765) 998-5358

Taylor University Fort Wayne

Fort Wayne, Indiana
www.fw.taylor.edu

Federal Code: 001838

4-year private university and liberal arts college in large city, affiliated with Christian Church.

Enrollment: 363 undergrads, 18% part-time. 77 full-time freshmen.
Selectivity: Admits 50 to 75% of applicants.

BASIC COSTS (2008-2009)

Tuition and fees: $21,164.
Room and board: $5,610.

FINANCIAL AID PICTURE (2007-2008)

Students with need: Out of 75 full-time freshmen who applied for aid, 67 were judged to have need. Of these, 67 received aid, and 15 had their full need met. Average financial aid package met 84% of need; average scholarship/grant was $14,119; average loan was $4,625. For part-time students, average financial aid package was $5,259.
Students without need: 10 full-time freshmen who did not demonstrate need for aid received scholarships/grants; average award was $4,594. No-need awards available for academics, alumni affiliation, athletics, leadership, music/drama.
Scholarships offered: Ramseyer Leadership Scholarship: $2,000; based on academics and school and community involvement; 10 awarded annually. Academic Scholarships: $1,000-$9,000: based on high school GPA, rank, and test score; awarded to all who meet requirements.
Cumulative student debt: 78% of graduating class had student loans; average debt was $20,707.

FINANCIAL AID PROCEDURES

Forms required: institutional form.
Dates and Deadlines: Priority date 3/1; no closing date. Applicants notified on a rolling basis starting 2/15; must reply by 5/1 or within 2 week(s) of notification.
Transfers: No deadline. Applicants notified on a rolling basis starting 3/1; must reply by 8/15.

CONTACT

Paul Johnston, Director of Financial Aid
1025 West Rudisill Boulevard, Fort Wayne, IN 46807
(800) 233-3922

Tri-State University

Angola, Indiana
www.tristate.edu

Federal Code: 001839

4-year private university and engineering college in small town.
Enrollment: 1,265 undergrads, 6% part-time. 416 full-time freshmen.

Selectivity: Admits 50 to 75% of applicants.

BASIC COSTS (2008-2009)
Tuition and fees: $23,450.
Per-credit charge: $730.
Room and board: $6,700.

FINANCIAL AID PICTURE (2007-2008)
Students with need: Out of 415 full-time freshmen who applied for aid, 290 were judged to have need. Of these, 290 received aid, and 290 had their full need met. For part-time students, average financial aid package was $4,012.
Students without need: 125 full-time freshmen who did not demonstrate need for aid received scholarships/grants; average award was $8,355. No-need awards available for academics, alumni affiliation, music/drama, ROTC.
Cumulative student debt: 76% of graduating class had student loans; average debt was $16,950.

FINANCIAL AID PROCEDURES
Forms required: FAFSA.
Dates and Deadlines: Priority date 3/10; closing date 3/10. Applicants notified on a rolling basis starting 2/1; must reply by 5/1 or within 2 week(s) of notification.
Transfers: No deadline. Applicants notified on a rolling basis starting 3/1; must reply by 5/1 or within 2 week(s) of notification.

CONTACT
Kim Bennett, Executive Director of Admission and Financial Aid
One University Avenue, Angola, IN 46703
(260) 665-4158

University of Evansville
Evansville, Indiana
www.evansville.edu   Federal Code: 001795

4-year private university and liberal arts college in small city, affiliated with United Methodist Church.
Enrollment: 2,539 undergrads, 5% part-time. 652 full-time freshmen.
Selectivity: Admits over 75% of applicants.

BASIC COSTS (2008-2009)
Tuition and fees: $25,845.
Per-credit charge: $690.
Room and board: $8,170.

FINANCIAL AID PICTURE (2007-2008)
Students with need: Out of 570 full-time freshmen who applied for aid, 487 were judged to have need. Of these, 487 received aid, and 152 had their full need met. Average financial aid package met 89% of need; average scholarship/grant was $18,368; average loan was $3,915. For part-time students, average financial aid package was $5,974.
Students without need: 140 full-time freshmen who did not demonstrate need for aid received scholarships/grants; average award was $12,379. No-need awards available for academics, alumni affiliation, art, athletics, leadership, minority status, music/drama, religious affiliation.
Scholarships offered: 22 full-time freshmen received athletic scholarships; average amount $19,856.
Cumulative student debt: 69% of graduating class had student loans; average debt was $22,960.
Additional info: Early financial planning service allows prospective students to get free estimate of available aid.

FINANCIAL AID PROCEDURES
Forms required: FAFSA.
Dates and Deadlines: Priority date 3/10; no closing date. Applicants notified on a rolling basis starting 3/24; must reply by 5/1.
Transfers: Must reply by 6/1. Indiana state aid is available for a total of 8 semesters.

CONTACT
JoAnn Laugel, Director of Financial Aid
1800 Lincoln Avenue, Evansville, IN 47722
(812) 488-2364

University of Indianapolis
Indianapolis, Indiana
www.uindy.edu   Federal Code: 001804

4-year private university and liberal arts college in very large city, affiliated with United Methodist Church.
Enrollment: 3,474 undergrads, 24% part-time. 743 full-time freshmen.
Selectivity: Admits over 75% of applicants.

BASIC COSTS (2008-2009)
Tuition and fees: $20,470.
Per-credit charge: $847.
Room and board: $7,790.

FINANCIAL AID PICTURE
Students with need: Need-based aid available for full-time and part-time students. Work study available nights, weekends, and for part-time students.
Students without need: No-need awards available for academics, alumni affiliation, art, athletics, job skills, leadership, music/drama, religious affiliation, state/district residency.
Scholarships offered: Presidential Scholarship: upper 5% of class, 1270 SAT/29 ACT, strong college prep; full tuition. Dean's Scholarship: upper 7% of class, 1270 SAT/29 ACT, demonstrated leadership, strong college prep; 50% tuition. Alumni Scholarship: upper 15% of class, 1100 SAT/24 ACT, alumnus connection to school; 30% tuition. Service Award: demonstrated commitment to community volunteerism; $2,500. United Methodist Award: demonstrated commitment to church, activities; $2,500. SAT scores listed are exclusive of the writing portion.

FINANCIAL AID PROCEDURES
Forms required: FAFSA, institutional form.
Dates and Deadlines: Priority date 3/10; no closing date. Applicants notified on a rolling basis starting 3/1; must reply within 3 week(s) of notification.
Transfers: No deadline. Applicants notified on a rolling basis starting 3/1.

CONTACT
Linda Handy, Director of Financial Aid
1400 East Hanna Avenue, Indianapolis, IN 46227-3697
(317) 788-3217

University of Notre Dame
Notre Dame, Indiana   Federal Code: 001840
www.nd.edu   CSS Code: 1841

4-year private university in small city, affiliated with Roman Catholic Church.
Enrollment: 8,369 undergrads. 1,989 full-time freshmen.
Selectivity: Admits less than 50% of applicants. GED not accepted.

BASIC COSTS (2008-2009)
Tuition and fees: $36,847.
Per-credit charge: $1,514.
Room and board: $9,828.

FINANCIAL AID PICTURE (2007-2008)
Students with need: Out of 1,386 full-time freshmen who applied for aid, 933 were judged to have need. Of these, 933 received aid, and 922 had their full need met. Average financial aid package met 100% of need; average scholarship/grant was $24,124; average loan was $3,291. Need-based aid available for part-time students.

Students without need: 35 full-time freshmen who did not demonstrate need for aid received scholarships/grants; average award was $6,316. No-need awards available for athletics, job skills, ROTC.

Scholarships offered: 115 full-time freshmen received athletic scholarships; average amount $24,599.

Cumulative student debt: 57% of graduating class had student loans; average debt was $27,569.

FINANCIAL AID PROCEDURES

Forms required: FAFSA, CSS PROFILE.

Dates and Deadlines: Priority date 2/15; closing date 2/15. Applicants notified by 4/1; must reply by 5/1.

Transfers: Priority date 3/31; closing date 3/31. Applicants notified on a rolling basis; must reply within 2 week(s) of notification. Require signed and completed federal tax returns, including all schedules and W-2 forms from both the applicant and the parents of the applicant.

CONTACT

Joseph Russo, Director, Student Finance Strategies
220 Main Building, Notre Dame, IN 46556
(574) 631-6436

University of St. Francis

Fort Wayne, Indiana
www.sf.edu   Federal Code: 001832

4-year private university and liberal arts college in small city, affiliated with Roman Catholic Church.

Enrollment: 1,789 undergrads, 18% part-time. 366 full-time freshmen.

BASIC COSTS (2007-2008)

Tuition and fees: $19,570.

Per-credit charge: $590.

Room and board: $6,006.

Additional info: Tuition/fee waivers available for adults.

FINANCIAL AID PICTURE (2006-2007)

Students with need: Out of 357 full-time freshmen who applied for aid, 304 were judged to have need. Of these, 302 received aid, and 91 had their full need met. Average financial aid package met 77% of need; average scholarship/grant was $11,396; average loan was $2,388. For part-time students, average financial aid package was $7,486.

Students without need: 54 full-time freshmen who did not demonstrate need for aid received scholarships/grants; average award was $9,472. No-need awards available for academics, alumni affiliation, art, athletics, music/drama.

Scholarships offered: 34 full-time freshmen received athletic scholarships; average amount $5,467.

Cumulative student debt: 97% of graduating class had student loans; average debt was $23,009.

FINANCIAL AID PROCEDURES

Forms required: FAFSA.

Dates and Deadlines: Priority date 3/10; no closing date. Applicants notified on a rolling basis starting 3/1.

CONTACT

Jamie McGrath, Director of Financial Aid
2701 Spring Street, Fort Wayne, IN 46808
(260) 434-3283

University of Southern Indiana

Evansville, Indiana
www.usi.edu   Federal Code: 001808

4-year public university and liberal arts college in small city.

Enrollment: 9,008 undergrads, 16% part-time. 2,074 full-time freshmen.

Selectivity: Admits over 75% of applicants.

BASIC COSTS (2008-2009)

Tuition and fees: $5,219; out-of-state residents $12,154.

Per-credit charge: $167; out-of-state residents $378.

Room and board: $6,542.

FINANCIAL AID PICTURE (2007-2008)

Students with need: Out of 1,809 full-time freshmen who applied for aid, 1,257 were judged to have need. Of these, 1,224 received aid, and 392 had their full need met. Average financial aid package met 73% of need; average scholarship/grant was $2,688; average loan was $3,155. For part-time students, average financial aid package was $8,613.

Students without need: 217 full-time freshmen who did not demonstrate need for aid received scholarships/grants; average award was $1,499. No-need awards available for academics, alumni affiliation, art, athletics, job skills, leadership, music/drama, state/district residency.

Scholarships offered: 21 full-time freshmen received athletic scholarships; average amount $1,934.

FINANCIAL AID PROCEDURES

Forms required: FAFSA, institutional form.

Dates and Deadlines: Closing date 3/1. Applicants notified on a rolling basis starting 4/15.

CONTACT

James Patton, Director of Student Financial Assistance
8600 University Boulevard, Evansville, IN 47712
(812) 464-1767

Valparaiso University

Valparaiso, Indiana
www.valpo.edu   Federal Code: 001842

4-year private university in large town, affiliated with Lutheran Church.

Enrollment: 2,834 undergrads, 4% part-time. 713 full-time freshmen.

Selectivity: Admits over 75% of applicants.

BASIC COSTS (2008-2009)

Tuition and fees: $26,950.

Per-credit charge: $620.

Room and board: $7,620.

Additional info: College of engineering sophomores, juniors, and seniors pay an additional fee of $700. Nursing lab and test fee is $525 at the beginning of sophomore year.

FINANCIAL AID PICTURE (2007-2008)

Students with need: Out of 656 full-time freshmen who applied for aid, 546 were judged to have need. Of these, 546 received aid, and 154 had their full need met. Average financial aid package met 84% of need; average scholarship/grant was $16,502; average loan was $5,441. For part-time students, average financial aid package was $7,069.

Students without need: 137 full-time freshmen who did not demonstrate need for aid received scholarships/grants; average award was $9,417. No-need awards available for academics, alumni affiliation, art, athletics, leadership, music/drama, religious affiliation, ROTC.

Scholarships offered: *Merit:* Academic Scholarships: $6,000 to full-tuition. Transfer, Departmental, Lutheran Scholarships also available: Amounts vary. *Athletic:* 15 full-time freshmen received athletic scholarships; average amount $16,103.

Cumulative student debt: 73% of graduating class had student loans; average debt was $26,259.

Additional info: Financial assistance based on need, academic record, talent, etc., available through university.

FINANCIAL AID PROCEDURES

Forms required: FAFSA.

Dates and Deadlines: Priority date 3/1; no closing date. Applicants notified on a rolling basis starting 3/1; must reply by 5/1.

Transfers: Transfer students are eligible for scholarships based on previous college work. Scholarship amounts vary depending on the cumulative grade point average at the previous institutions.

CONTACT

Robert Helgeson, Director of Financial Aid
Kretzmann Hall, 1700 Chapel Drive, Valparaiso, IN 46383-6493
(219) 464-5015

Vincennes University

Vincennes, Indiana
www.vinu.edu
Federal Code: 001843

2-year public junior and technical college in large town.

Enrollment: 8,203 undergrads, 39% part-time. 2,010 full-time freshmen.

Selectivity: Open admission; but selective for some programs.

BASIC COSTS (2008-2009)

Tuition and fees: $4,203; out-of-state residents $9,932.

Per-credit charge: $134; out-of-state residents $327.

Room and board: $7,036.

Additional info: Students from Crawford, Richland, Lawrence and Wabash counties in Illinois pay tuition of $197.40 per credit hour (including capital improvement and technology fees, not including student activity fee).

FINANCIAL AID PICTURE

Students with need: Need-based aid available for full-time and part-time students. Work study available nights, weekends, and for part-time students.

Students without need: No-need awards available for academics, art, athletics, leadership, music/drama, state/district residency.

Scholarships offered: Presidential Scholarship: $2,000 annually; 1100 SAT and rank in upper 10% of class; 10 awarded. Blue & Gold Scholarship: $1,100 annually; 1010 SAT and rank in upper half of class; 40 awarded. Indiana Academic Honors Diploma: $900 annually. Walters Scholarship: tuition and room and board; for candidates in good standing. Education Scholarship: for education majors, based on SAT scores and rank in upper 10% of class; 1 awarded. Validictorian/Salutatorian scholarships available.

FINANCIAL AID PROCEDURES

Forms required: FAFSA.

Dates and Deadlines: Priority date 3/1; closing date 5/1. Applicants notified on a rolling basis starting 5/1; must reply by 8/24.

Transfers: Transfer students must notify state student assistance commission within 30 days of start of term.

CONTACT

Stanley Werne, Director of Financial Aid
1002 North First Street, Vincennes, IN 47591
(812) 888-4361

Wabash College

Crawfordsville, Indiana
www.wabash.edu
Federal Code: 001844
CSS Code: 1895

4-year private liberal arts college for men in large town.

Enrollment: 910 undergrads. 252 full-time freshmen.

Selectivity: Admits less than 50% of applicants.

BASIC COSTS (2008-2009)

Tuition and fees: $27,950.

Room and board: $7,900.

FINANCIAL AID PICTURE (2007-2008)

Students with need: Out of 224 full-time freshmen who applied for aid, 186 were judged to have need. Of these, 186 received aid, and 186 had their full need met. Average financial aid package met 100% of need; average scholarship/grant was $18,094; average loan was $4,878. Need-based aid available for part-time students.

Students without need: 48 full-time freshmen who did not demonstrate need for aid received scholarships/grants; average award was $15,803. No-need awards available for academics, art, leadership, music/drama, state/district residency.

Scholarships offered: Lilly Awards Program; covers full tuition, room, board, fees, and travel stipend; recognizes outstanding personal achievement and potential for leadership. Fine Arts Fellows; awards ranging up to $12,000; based on creativity/ability; approximately 16 awarded each year. Honor Scholars; awards ranging up to $12,000; based on competitive exams; approximately 40 awarded each year. Unlimited President's Scholarships based on class rank, SAT scores.

Cumulative student debt: 77% of graduating class had student loans; average debt was $21,497.

FINANCIAL AID PROCEDURES

Forms required: FAFSA, CSS PROFILE.

Dates and Deadlines: Priority date 2/15; closing date 3/1. Applicants notified by 4/1; must reply by 5/1 or within 2 week(s) of notification.

Transfers: Applicants notified by 4/1; must reply by 5/1 or within 2 week(s) of notification.

CONTACT

Clint Gasaway, Director of Financial Aid
PO Box 352, Crawfordsville, IN 47933
(800) 718-9746

Iowa

AIB College of Business

Des Moines, Iowa
www.aib.edu
Federal Code: 003963

2-year private business college in large city.

Enrollment: 956 undergrads, 40% part-time. 190 full-time freshmen.

Selectivity: Admits over 75% of applicants.

BASIC COSTS (2008-2009)

Tuition and fees: $12,120.

Per-credit charge: $220.

Room only: $3,150.

Additional info: Tuition/fee waivers available for minority students.

FINANCIAL AID PICTURE (2006-2007)

Students with need: Out of 188 full-time freshmen who applied for aid, 171 were judged to have need. Of these, 171 received aid, and 13 had their full need met. Average financial aid package met 66% of need; average scholarship/grant was $4,553; average loan was $3,062. For part-time students, average financial aid package was $7,271.

Students without need: 17 full-time freshmen who did not demonstrate need for aid received scholarships/grants; average award was $3,991. No-need awards available for academics, alumni affiliation, leadership.

Scholarships offered: Founder's Scholarship; full tuition; minimum 3.75 cumulative high school GPA and upper 10% of high school graduating class or 3.75 cumulative GPA and 28 or higher ACT; up to four students per year.

FINANCIAL AID PROCEDURES

Forms required: FAFSA, institutional form.

Dates and Deadlines: Priority date 4/1; no closing date. Applicants notified on a rolling basis starting 3/1; must reply within 2 week(s) of notification.

Transfers: No deadline. Applicants notified on a rolling basis starting 3/1; must reply within 2 week(s) of notification. Prior aid from previous institutions taken into consideration.

CONTACT

Connie Loven, Financial Aid Director
2500 Fleur Drive, Des Moines, IA 50321-1799
(515) 244-4221

Allen College
Waterloo, Iowa
www.allencollege.edu   Federal Code: 030691

4-year private health science and nursing college in small city.

Enrollment: 377 undergrads, 12% part-time. 26 full-time freshmen.

Selectivity: Admits over 75% of applicants.

BASIC COSTS (2008-2009)

Tuition and fees: $14,895.

Per-credit charge: $458.

Room and board: $6,178.

FINANCIAL AID PICTURE (2006-2007)

Students with need: Out of 26 full-time freshmen who applied for aid, 24 were judged to have need. Of these, 24 received aid, and 1 had their full need met. Average financial aid package met 49% of need; average scholarship/grant was $5,348; average loan was $2,186. For part-time students, average financial aid package was $7,160.

Students without need: 2 full-time freshmen who did not demonstrate need for aid received scholarships/grants; average award was $438. No-need awards available for academics, leadership, minority status, ROTC.

Cumulative student debt: 93% of graduating class had student loans; average debt was $13,340.

FINANCIAL AID PROCEDURES

Forms required: FAFSA, institutional form.

Dates and Deadlines: Priority date 6/1; no closing date. Applicants notified on a rolling basis starting 4/1; must reply within 2 week(s) of notification.

Transfers: No deadline. Applicants notified on a rolling basis starting 4/1; must reply within 2 week(s) of notification.

CONTACT

Kathie Walters, Financial Aid Director
1825 Logan Avenue, Waterloo, IA 50703
(319) 226-2003

Ashford University
Clinton, Iowa
www.ashford.edu   Federal Code: 001881

4-year for-profit university in large town.

Enrollment: 9,805 undergrads, 1% part-time. 802 full-time freshmen.

BASIC COSTS (2007-2008)

Tuition and fees: $15,890.

Per-credit charge: $447.

Room and board: $5,800.

Additional info: Tuition/fee waivers available for minority students, unemployed or children of unemployed.

FINANCIAL AID PICTURE (2007-2008)

Students with need: 46% of average financial aid package awarded as scholarships/grants, 54% awarded as loans/jobs. Need-based aid available for part-time students. Work study available nights, weekends, and for part-time students.

Students without need: No-need awards available for academics, art, athletics, music/drama.

Scholarships offered: Divisional Award: up to full tuition; high school GPA of at least 3.2 and ACT score between 23 and 26. Presidential Scholarships: $1,500-$5,000; rank in top 20% of high school class, or ACT composite of 26 or higher, or have GPA of at least 3.2. Departmental Awards: maximum $1,500; competitive exams in various departments. Leadership Awards: maximum $1,000; extracurricular activities and GPA of at least 2.3. Counselor's Choice Awards: $500; recommendation from high school guidance counselor, GPA between 2.50 and 3.19, ACT composite between 19 and 25, and at least one extracurricular activity.

FINANCIAL AID PROCEDURES

Forms required: FAFSA, institutional form.

Dates and Deadlines: Priority date 3/1; no closing date. Applicants notified on a rolling basis starting 2/15; must reply within 2 week(s) of notification.

Transfers: Students with GPA of 3.0 or higher eligible for Presidential Scholarship.

CONTACT

Lisa Kramer, Director of Financial Aid
400 North Bluff Boulevard, Clinton, IA 52733-2967
(563) 242-4023 ext. 1242

Briar Cliff University
Sioux City, Iowa
www.briarcliff.edu   Federal Code: 001846

4-year private liberal arts college in small city, affiliated with Roman Catholic Church.

Enrollment: 1,074 undergrads, 11% part-time. 259 full-time freshmen.

Selectivity: Admits 50 to 75% of applicants.

BASIC COSTS (2008-2009)

Tuition and fees: $21,510.

Per-credit charge: $696.

Room and board: $6,411.

FINANCIAL AID PICTURE (2006-2007)

Students with need: Out of 250 full-time freshmen who applied for aid, 200 were judged to have need. Of these, 200 received aid, and 175 had their full need met. Average financial aid package met 92% of need; average scholarship/grant was $6,400; average loan was $3,800. For part-time students, average financial aid package was $7,800.

Students without need: 59 full-time freshmen who did not demonstrate need for aid received scholarships/grants; average award was $9,800. No-need awards available for academics, alumni affiliation, art, athletics, leadership, music/drama, religious affiliation, state/district residency.

Scholarships offered: *Merit:* 3-5 Presidential Scholarships awarded each year for achievement and demonstrated leadership, based on application and on-campus interview. Scholarships are also given for academic achievement, outstanding fine arts and athletic ability, and for leadership development. Special scholarships recognize transfer students, siblings, alumni children, and high school students from parishes in the Diocese of Sioux City.

Athletic: 38 full-time freshmen received athletic scholarships; average amount $4,400.

Cumulative student debt: 85% of graduating class had student loans; average debt was $26,002.

Additional info: 97% of Briar Cliff's student body receive some sort of aid.

FINANCIAL AID PROCEDURES

Forms required: FAFSA.

PART III: FINANCIAL AID COLLEGE BY COLLEGE

Dates and Deadlines: Priority date 3/15; no closing date. Applicants notified on a rolling basis starting 3/15; must reply by 5/1 or within 2 week(s) of notification.
Transfers: Closing date 3/15.

CONTACT

Robert Piechota, Director of Financial Aid
3303 Rebecca Street, Sioux City, IA 51104-0100
(712) 279-5200

Buena Vista University
Storm Lake, Iowa
www.bvu.edu   Federal Code: 001847

4-year private liberal arts college in large town, affiliated with Presbyterian Church (USA).
Enrollment: 1,022 undergrads. 228 full-time freshmen.
Selectivity: Admits 50 to 75% of applicants.

BASIC COSTS (2008-2009)

Tuition and fees: $24,796.
Per-credit charge: $833.
Room and board: $7,014.

FINANCIAL AID PICTURE (2007-2008)

Students with need: Average financial aid package met 93% of need; average scholarship/grant was $9,007; average loan was $4,884. For part-time students, average financial aid package was $13,819.
Students without need: No-need awards available for academics, art, minority status, music/drama, religious affiliation.
Cumulative student debt: 94% of graduating class had student loans; average debt was $31,771.
Additional info: Portfolio required of art scholarship applicants, audition required of music and drama scholarship applicants.

FINANCIAL AID PROCEDURES

Forms required: FAFSA.
Dates and Deadlines: Priority date 6/1; no closing date. Applicants notified on a rolling basis starting 2/20.

CONTACT

Leanne Valentine, Director of Financial Assistance
610 West Fourth Street, Storm Lake, IA 50588
(714) 749-2164

Central College
Pella, Iowa
www.central.edu   Federal Code: 001850

4-year private liberal arts college in large town, affiliated with Reformed Church in America.
Enrollment: 1,452 undergrads, 2% part-time. 424 full-time freshmen.
Selectivity: Admits over 75% of applicants.

BASIC COSTS (2007-2008)

Tuition and fees: $22,510.
Per-credit charge: $772.
Room and board: $7,624.
Additional info: Costs provided are for main campus only. International location costs may vary by program location.

FINANCIAL AID PICTURE (2007-2008)

Students with need: Out of 397 full-time freshmen who applied for aid, 344 were judged to have need. Of these, 344 received aid, and 61 had their full need met. Average financial aid package met 83% of need; average scholarship/grant was $15,042; average loan was $3,765. For part-time students, average financial aid package was $8,446.
Students without need: 79 full-time freshmen who did not demonstrate need for aid received scholarships/grants; average award was $9,763. No-need awards available for academics, alumni affiliation, art, leadership, minority status, music/drama, religious affiliation, state/district residency.
Additional info: Institutional parent loan program and interest-earning, tuition prepayment savings account available. Auditions required for music and theater scholarships, portfolios required for art scholarships. Monthly payment plan available.

FINANCIAL AID PROCEDURES

Forms required: FAFSA.
Dates and Deadlines: Priority date 3/15; no closing date. Applicants notified on a rolling basis starting 3/15; must reply by 5/1 or within 2 week(s) of notification.
Transfers: Applicants notified on a rolling basis starting 3/15; must reply by 5/1 or within 2 week(s) of notification. Transfers only eligible for total of 4 years of state funds.

CONTACT

Jean Vander Wert, Financial Aid Director
812 University Street, Pella, IA 50219-1999
(641) 628-5336

Clarke College
Dubuque, Iowa
www.clarke.edu   Federal Code: 001852

4-year private liberal arts college in small city, affiliated with Roman Catholic Church.
Enrollment: 1,008 undergrads, 12% part-time. 187 full-time freshmen.
Selectivity: Admits 50 to 75% of applicants.

BASIC COSTS (2008-2009)

Tuition and fees: $22,378.
Per-credit charge: $550.
Room and board: $6,574.

FINANCIAL AID PICTURE (2007-2008)

Students with need: 68% of average financial aid package awarded as scholarships/grants, 32% awarded as loans/jobs. Need-based aid available for part-time students. Work study available nights, weekends, and for part-time students.
Students without need: No-need awards available for academics, alumni affiliation, art, athletics, leadership, music/drama, religious affiliation, state/district residency.
Additional info: Reduced tuition for family members of BVMs.

FINANCIAL AID PROCEDURES

Forms required: FAFSA.
Dates and Deadlines: Priority date 4/15; no closing date. Applicants notified on a rolling basis starting 3/15; must reply by 5/1 or within 2 week(s) of notification.

CONTACT

Ann Heisler, Director of Financial Aid
1550 Clarke Drive, Dubuque, IA 52001-3198
(563) 588-6327

Coe College

Cedar Rapids, Iowa
www.coe.edu   Federal Code: 001854

4-year private liberal arts college in small city, affiliated with Presbyterian Church (USA).

Enrollment: 1,298 undergrads.
Selectivity: Admits 50 to 75% of applicants.

BASIC COSTS (2007-2008)
Tuition and fees: $26,390.
Room and board: $6,600.
Additional info: Cost per course for part-time students (fewer than 3.0 course credits) is $3,200. Tuition/fee waivers available for adults.

FINANCIAL AID PICTURE
Students with need: Need-based aid available for full-time and part-time students. Work study available nights, weekends, and for part-time students.
Students without need: No-need awards available for academics, alumni affiliation, art, leadership, music/drama, ROTC.
Scholarships offered: Scholarships for business/economics, music, art, theater, writing, foreign language, science: based on portfolio or audition: available for non-majors except in science and business/economics. Academic Awards: $6,000-$19,000; based on high school achievement.

FINANCIAL AID PROCEDURES
Forms required: FAFSA.
Dates and Deadlines: Priority date 3/1; no closing date. Applicants notified on a rolling basis starting 3/15; must reply by 5/1 or within 2 week(s) of notification.

CONTACT
Barb Hoffman, Director of Financial Aid
1220 First Avenue NE, Cedar Rapids, IA 52402
(319) 399-8540

Cornell College

Mount Vernon, Iowa
www.cornellcollege.edu   Federal Code: 001856

4-year private liberal arts college in small town, affiliated with United Methodist Church.

Enrollment: 1,075 undergrads, 1% part-time. 316 full-time freshmen.
Selectivity: Admits less than 50% of applicants.

BASIC COSTS (2008-2009)
Tuition and fees: $27,860.
Per-credit charge: $865.
Room and board: $7,220.
Additional info: Tuition/fee waivers available for adults, minority students.

FINANCIAL AID PICTURE (2007-2008)
Students with need: Out of 270 full-time freshmen who applied for aid, 214 were judged to have need. Of these, 214 received aid, and 166 had their full need met. Average financial aid package met 93% of need; average scholarship/grant was $10,815; average loan was $3,370. For part-time students, average financial aid package was $14,335.
Students without need: 84 full-time freshmen who did not demonstrate need for aid received scholarships/grants; average award was $10,350. No-need awards available for academics, art, leadership, minority status, music/drama, religious affiliation, state/district residency.
Cumulative student debt: 79% of graduating class had student loans; average debt was $26,115.
Additional info: Portfolio required for art scholarship applicants. Audition required for music scholarship applicants.

FINANCIAL AID PROCEDURES
Forms required: FAFSA, institutional form.
Dates and Deadlines: Closing date 3/1. Applicants notified on a rolling basis starting 3/1; must reply by 5/1 or within 2 week(s) of notification.
Transfers: Priority date 3/1; no deadline. Applicants notified on a rolling basis starting 3/1; must reply by 5/1 or within 2 week(s) of notification.

CONTACT
Cindi Reints, Director of Financial Assistance
600 First Street SW, Mount Vernon, IA 52314-1098
(319) 895-4216

Des Moines Area Community College

Ankeny, Iowa
www.dmacc.edu   Federal Code: 004589

2-year public community college in large town.
Enrollment: 18,320 undergrads, 62% part-time. 1,969 full-time freshmen.
Selectivity: Open admission; but selective for some programs.

BASIC COSTS (2007-2008)
Tuition and fees: $3,060; out-of-state residents $6,120.
Per-credit charge: $102; out-of-state residents $204.

FINANCIAL AID PICTURE
Students with need: Need-based aid available for full-time and part-time students. Work study available nights, weekends, and for part-time students.
Students without need: No-need awards available for academics, athletics, state/district residency.
Scholarships offered: DMACC Foundation Freshmen Scholar Award; full tuition, fees and books for maximum of 15 credit hours per semester; based on available funds, offered fall term; open to all high school seniors in top 10% of graduating class.

FINANCIAL AID PROCEDURES
Forms required: FAFSA.
Dates and Deadlines: Priority date 4/1; no closing date. Applicants notified on a rolling basis starting 4/1; must reply within 2 week(s) of notification.

CONTACT
DeLores Hawkins, Director of Financial Aid
2006 South Ankeny Boulevard, Ankeny, IA 50023-3993
(515) 964-6282

Dordt College

Sioux Center, Iowa
www.dordt.edu   Federal Code: 001859

4-year private liberal arts college in small town, affiliated with Christian Reformed Church.

Enrollment: 1,263 undergrads, 4% part-time. 391 full-time freshmen.
Selectivity: Admits over 75% of applicants.

BASIC COSTS (2008-2009)
Tuition and fees: $21,040.
Per-credit charge: $840.
Room and board: $5,720.
Additional info: Tuition/fee waivers available for adults.

FINANCIAL AID PICTURE (2006-2007)
Students with need: Out of 341 full-time freshmen who applied for aid, 296 were judged to have need. Of these, 296 received aid, and 45 had their full need met. Average financial aid package met 86% of need; average scholarship/grant was $10,287; average loan was $5,160. For part-time students, average financial aid package was $4,316.

Students without need: 70 full-time freshmen who did not demonstrate need for aid received scholarships/grants; average award was $9,702. No-need awards available for academics, alumni affiliation, art, athletics, job skills, leadership, minority status, music/drama, religious affiliation, state/district residency.

Scholarships offered: 20 full-time freshmen received athletic scholarships; average amount $4,269.

Cumulative student debt: 87% of graduating class had student loans; average debt was $18,120.

FINANCIAL AID PROCEDURES

Forms required: FAFSA, institutional form.

Dates and Deadlines: Priority date 4/1; no closing date. Applicants notified on a rolling basis starting 3/15; must reply within 3 week(s) of notification.

CONTACT

Michael Epema, Director of Financial Aid
498 Fourth Avenue, NE, Sioux Center, IA 51250
(712) 722-6087

Drake University
Des Moines, Iowa
www.drake.edu   Federal Code: 001860

4-year private university in large city.

Enrollment: 3,362 undergrads, 5% part-time. 924 full-time freshmen.

Selectivity: Admits over 75% of applicants.

BASIC COSTS (2008-2009)

Tuition and fees: $24,872.
Per-credit charge: $450.
Room and board: $7,410.

FINANCIAL AID PICTURE (2007-2008)

Students with need: Out of 744 full-time freshmen who applied for aid, 565 were judged to have need. Of these, 565 received aid, and 208 had their full need met. Average financial aid package met 89% of need; average scholarship/grant was $13,469; average loan was $5,462. For part-time students, average financial aid package was $8,426.

Students without need: 310 full-time freshmen who did not demonstrate need for aid received scholarships/grants; average award was $10,794. No-need awards available for academics, alumni affiliation, art, athletics, music/drama, ROTC, state/district residency.

Scholarships offered: *Merit:* Drake University Presidential Scholarship: $7,000-$12,000; based on academic merit and awards; unlimited available. National Alumni Scholarship Competition: 6 full-time tuition, room and board and 10 full-time tuition scholarships; available to top students. *Athletic:* 29 full-time freshmen received athletic scholarships; average amount $16,381.

Cumulative student debt: 62% of graduating class had student loans; average debt was $29,959.

FINANCIAL AID PROCEDURES

Forms required: FAFSA.

Dates and Deadlines: Priority date 3/1; no closing date. Applicants notified on a rolling basis starting 3/1.

Transfers: No deadline. Applicants notified on a rolling basis starting 3/1; must reply by 5/1 or within 2 week(s) of notification. FAFSA must be filed by July 1 for Iowa Tuition Grant deadline.

CONTACT

Susan Ladd, Director of Student Financial Planning
2507 University Avenue, Des Moines, IA 50311-4505
(515) 271-2905

Ellsworth Community College
Iowa Falls, Iowa
www.iavalley.cc.ia.us/ecc   Federal Code: 001862

2-year public community college in small town.

Enrollment: 1,025 undergrads.

Selectivity: Open admission; but selective for some programs.

BASIC COSTS (2007-2008)

Tuition and fees: $4,065; out-of-state residents $4,905.
Per-credit charge: $112; out-of-state residents $140.
Additional info: Tuition/fee waivers available for adults.

FINANCIAL AID PICTURE (2006-2007)

Students with need: 48% of average financial aid package awarded as scholarships/grants, 52% awarded as loans/jobs. Need-based aid available for part-time students. Work study available nights, weekends, and for part-time students.

Students without need: No-need awards available for academics, art, athletics, leadership, minority status, music/drama.

Scholarships offered: Academic scholarships based upon ACT score and GPA; unlimited number offered; $500-$1,800. Directors Scholarship: 1st or 2nd in class; $2,300; unlimited number offered. For freshman and sophomore years.

FINANCIAL AID PROCEDURES

Forms required: FAFSA, institutional form.

Dates and Deadlines: Priority date 4/1; no closing date. Applicants notified on a rolling basis starting 2/15; must reply within 4 week(s) of notification.

Transfers: Priority date 4/15.

CONTACT

Tara Miller, Financial Aid Administrator
1100 College Avenue, Iowa Falls, IA 50126
(641) 648-4611 ext. 432

Emmaus Bible College
Dubuque, Iowa
www.emmaus.edu   Federal Code: 016487

4-year private Bible college in small city, affiliated with Brethren Church.

Enrollment: 235 undergrads.

BASIC COSTS (2007-2008)

Tuition and fees: $10,118.
Room and board: $4,782.

FINANCIAL AID PICTURE

Students with need: Need-based aid available for full-time and part-time students.

Students without need: No-need awards available for academics, music/drama.

FINANCIAL AID PROCEDURES

Forms required: FAFSA, institutional form.

Dates and Deadlines: Priority date 5/15; closing date 7/1. Applicants notified on a rolling basis starting 3/1; must reply within 2 week(s) of notification.

CONTACT

Steve Seeman, Financial Aid Director
2570 Asbury Road, Dubuque, IA 52001
(563) 588-8000 ext. 1309

Faith Baptist Bible College and Theological Seminary
Ankeny, Iowa
www.faith.edu   Federal Code: 007121

4-year private Bible and seminary college in large town, affiliated with General Association of Regular Baptist Churches.

Enrollment: 320 undergrads, 11% part-time. 96 full-time freshmen.

Selectivity: Admits over 75% of applicants.

BASIC COSTS (2008-2009)
Tuition and fees: $12,706.

Per-credit charge: $450.

Room and board: $5,010.

FINANCIAL AID PICTURE
Students with need: Need-based aid available for full-time and part-time students.

Students without need: No-need awards available for academics, leadership, music/drama.

FINANCIAL AID PROCEDURES
Forms required: FAFSA.

Dates and Deadlines: Priority date 4/1; no closing date. Applicants notified on a rolling basis starting 3/15.

CONTACT
Breck Appell, Financial Assistance Director
1900 NW Fourth Street, Ankeny, IA 50023
(515) 964-0601 ext. 216

Graceland University
Lamoni, Iowa
www.graceland.edu   Federal Code: 001866

4-year private university and liberal arts college in rural community, affiliated with Community of Christ.

Enrollment: 1,480 undergrads.

Selectivity: Admits 50 to 75% of applicants.

BASIC COSTS (2007-2008)
Tuition and fees: $17,900.

Per-credit charge: $560.

Room and board: $6,000.

FINANCIAL AID PICTURE (2007-2008)
Students with need: Average financial aid package met 92% of need; average scholarship/grant was $14,957; average loan was $4,944. For part-time students, average financial aid package was $8,223.

Students without need: No-need awards available for academics, alumni affiliation, art, athletics, job skills, leadership, music/drama, religious affiliation.

Cumulative student debt: 80% of graduating class had student loans; average debt was $26,415.

FINANCIAL AID PROCEDURES
Forms required: FAFSA.

Dates and Deadlines: Priority date 3/1; no closing date. Applicants notified on a rolling basis starting 3/1; must reply within 2 week(s) of notification.

Transfers: Must reply within 2 week(s) of notification.

CONTACT
Sharon Mesle-Morain, Director of Student Finance
One University Place, Lamoni, IA 50140
(641) 784-5140

Grand View College
Des Moines, Iowa
www.gvc.edu   Federal Code: 001867

4-year private liberal arts college in large city, affiliated with Evangelical Lutheran Church in America.

Enrollment: 1,680 undergrads, 20% part-time. 171 full-time freshmen.

Selectivity: Admits over 75% of applicants.

BASIC COSTS (2008-2009)
Tuition and fees: $18,554.

Per-credit charge: $475.

Room and board: $6,164.

FINANCIAL AID PICTURE (2007-2008)
Students with need: Out of 157 full-time freshmen who applied for aid, 137 were judged to have need. Of these, 137 received aid, and 45 had their full need met. Average financial aid package met 92% of need; average scholarship/grant was $14,486; average loan was $3,688. For part-time students, average financial aid package was $9,152.

Students without need: 29 full-time freshmen who did not demonstrate need for aid received scholarships/grants; average award was $5,655. No-need awards available for academics, alumni affiliation, art, athletics, leadership, music/drama, religious affiliation.

Scholarships offered: *Merit:* Presidential Scholarship; $8,000. Honors Scholarship; $7,000. Viking Incentive Program; $6,500. All for first-time, full-time freshmen. *Athletic:* 8 full-time freshmen received athletic scholarships; average amount $5,575.

Cumulative student debt: 94% of graduating class had student loans; average debt was $23,624.

FINANCIAL AID PROCEDURES
Forms required: FAFSA.

Dates and Deadlines: Priority date 3/1; no closing date. Applicants notified on a rolling basis starting 3/1; must reply by 5/1 or within 4 week(s) of notification.

CONTACT
Michele Dunne, Director of Financial Aid
1200 Grandview Avenue, Des Moines, IA 50316-1599
(515) 263-2963

Grinnell College
Grinnell, Iowa
www.grinnell.edu   Federal Code: 001868

4-year private liberal arts college in small town.

Enrollment: 1,623 undergrads. 426 full-time freshmen.

Selectivity: Admits less than 50% of applicants.

BASIC COSTS (2008-2009)
Tuition and fees: $35,428.

Per-credit charge: $1,092.

Room and board: $8,272.

FINANCIAL AID PICTURE (2007-2008)
Students with need: Out of 330 full-time freshmen who applied for aid, 267 were judged to have need. Of these, 267 received aid, and 267 had their full need met. Average financial aid package met 100% of need; average scholarship/grant was $24,252; average loan was $4,842. For part-time students, average financial aid package was $3,000.

Students without need: 96 full-time freshmen who did not demonstrate need for aid received scholarships/grants; average award was $9,172. No-need awards available for academics.

Cumulative student debt: 58% of graduating class had student loans; average debt was $18,340.

Additional info: Students may apply financial aid to off-campus study programs.

FINANCIAL AID PROCEDURES

Forms required: FAFSA, institutional form.

Dates and Deadlines: Closing date 2/1. Applicants notified by 4/1; must reply by 5/1.

CONTACT

Arnold Woods, Director of Student Financial Aid
1103 Park Street, Grinnell, IA 50112-1690
(641) 269-3250

Hawkeye Community College

Waterloo, Iowa
www.hawkeyecollege.edu   Federal Code: 004595

2-year public community and technical college in small city.

Enrollment: 4,434 undergrads, 48% part-time. 1,239 full-time freshmen.

Selectivity: Open admission; but selective for some programs.

BASIC COSTS (2007-2008)

Tuition and fees: $3,570; out-of-state residents $6,810.

Per-credit charge: $108; out-of-state residents $216.

FINANCIAL AID PICTURE (2007-2008)

Students with need: 42% of average financial aid package awarded as scholarships/grants, 58% awarded as loans/jobs. Work study available nights, weekends, and for part-time students.

Students without need: No-need awards available for academics, state/district residency.

FINANCIAL AID PROCEDURES

Forms required: FAFSA, institutional form.

Dates and Deadlines: Priority date 3/15; no closing date. Applicants notified on a rolling basis starting 4/25; must reply within 2 week(s) of notification.

CONTACT

Lois Mulbrook, Director of Financial Aid
Box 8015, Waterloo, IA 50704-8015
(319) 296-4020

Indian Hills Community College

Ottumwa, Iowa
www.indianhills.edu   Federal Code: 008298

2-year public community college in large town.

Enrollment: 3,019 undergrads, 22% part-time. 931 full-time freshmen.

Selectivity: Open admission; but selective for some programs.

BASIC COSTS (2007-2008)

Tuition and fees: $3,405; out-of-state residents $5,085.

Per-credit charge: $111; out-of-state residents $167.

Room and board: $4,875.

FINANCIAL AID PICTURE

Students with need: Need-based aid available for full-time and part-time students.

Students without need: No-need awards available for athletics, state/district residency.

FINANCIAL AID PROCEDURES

Forms required: FAFSA, institutional form.

Dates and Deadlines: Priority date 4/1; no closing date. Applicants notified on a rolling basis starting 6/1; must reply within 2 week(s) of notification.

CONTACT

Jo Altheide, Financial Aid
623 Indian Hills Drive, Building 12, Ottumwa, IA 52501

Iowa Central Community College

Fort Dodge, Iowa
www.iowacentral.edu   Federal Code: 004597

2-year public community college in large town.

Enrollment: 5,731 undergrads.

Selectivity: Open admission; but selective for some programs.

BASIC COSTS (2007-2008)

Tuition and fees: $3,390; out-of-state residents $4,920.

Per-credit charge: $102; out-of-state residents $153.

Room and board: $4,625.

FINANCIAL AID PICTURE

Students with need: Need-based aid available for full-time and part-time students. Work study available nights, weekends, and for part-time students.

Students without need: No-need awards available for academics, art, athletics, leadership, music/drama.

FINANCIAL AID PROCEDURES

Forms required: FAFSA.

Dates and Deadlines: Priority date 3/8; no closing date. Applicants notified on a rolling basis starting 4/15; must reply within 2 week(s) of notification.

CONTACT

Angie Martin, Director of Financial Aid
330 Avenue M, Fort Dodge, IA 50501

Iowa Lakes Community College

Estherville, Iowa
www.iowalakes.edu   Federal Code: 001864

2-year public community college in small town.

Enrollment: 1,982 undergrads, 36% part-time. 517 full-time freshmen.

Selectivity: Open admission; but selective for some programs.

BASIC COSTS (2007-2008)

Tuition and fees: $3,822; out-of-state residents $3,942.

Per-credit charge: $113; out-of-state residents $117.

Room and board: $4,350.

FINANCIAL AID PICTURE

Students with need: Need-based aid available for full-time and part-time students.

Students without need: This college awards aid only to students with need.

FINANCIAL AID PROCEDURES

Forms required: FAFSA, institutional form.

Dates and Deadlines: Priority date 4/22; no closing date. Applicants notified on a rolling basis starting 4/15.

CONTACT

John Beneke, Director of Financial Aid
300 South 18th Street, Estherville, IA 51334-2725
(712) 362-7917

Iowa State University
Ames, Iowa
www.iastate.edu   Federal Code: 001869

4-year public university in small city.
Enrollment: 20,613 undergrads, 5% part-time. 4,335 full-time freshmen.
Selectivity: Admits over 75% of applicants.

BASIC COSTS (2007-2008)
Tuition and fees: $6,161; out-of-state residents $16,919.
Per-credit charge: $223; out-of-district residents $223; out-of-state residents $672.
Room and board: $6,645.
Additional info: Additional tuition of $1,558 for junior and senior engineering students; additional $211 in fees for engineering and for computer science programs; additional $40 in fees for business program.

FINANCIAL AID PICTURE (2007-2008)
Students with need: Out of 3,275 full-time freshmen who applied for aid, 2,084 were judged to have need. Of these, 2,050 received aid, and 979 had their full need met. Average financial aid package met 84% of need; average scholarship/grant was $5,728; average loan was $3,551. For part-time students, average financial aid package was $8,041.
Students without need: 1,407 full-time freshmen who did not demonstrate need for aid received scholarships/grants; average award was $2,321. No-need awards available for academics, art, athletics, leadership, minority status, music/drama, ROTC, state/district residency.
Scholarships offered: 76 full-time freshmen received athletic scholarships; average amount $15,158.
Additional info: Short-term loan program available to meet unplanned needs. Financial counseling clinic provides budget and credit education assistance.

FINANCIAL AID PROCEDURES
Forms required: FAFSA.
Dates and Deadlines: Priority date 3/1; no closing date. Applicants notified on a rolling basis starting 4/1.
Transfers: Priority date 2/15.

CONTACT
Roberta Johnson, Director of Student Financial Aid
100 Alumni Hall, Ames, IA 50011-2011
(515) 294-0066

Iowa Wesleyan College
Mount Pleasant, Iowa
www.iwc.edu   Federal Code: 001871

4-year private liberal arts college in small town, affiliated with United Methodist Church.
Enrollment: 833 undergrads, 24% part-time. 127 full-time freshmen.
Selectivity: Admits 50 to 75% of applicants.

BASIC COSTS (2008-2009)
Tuition and fees: $20,000.
Per-credit charge: $495.
Room and board: $6,240.

FINANCIAL AID PICTURE
Students with need: Need-based aid available for full-time and part-time students. Work study available nights, weekends, and for part-time students.
Students without need: No-need awards available for academics, art, athletics, music/drama.
Scholarships offered: Unlimited merit based scholarships to students who qualify based on ACT or SAT and cumulative GPA.

FINANCIAL AID PROCEDURES
Forms required: FAFSA.
Dates and Deadlines: Priority date 4/1; no closing date. Applicants notified on a rolling basis starting 3/1; must reply within 2 week(s) of notification.

CONTACT
Deb Morrissey, Director of Financial Aid
601 North Main Street, Mount Pleasant, IA 52641-1398
(319) 385-6242

Iowa Western Community College
Council Bluffs, Iowa
www.iwcc.edu   Federal Code: 004598

2-year public community and technical college in small city.
Enrollment: 5,052 undergrads.
Selectivity: Open admission; but selective for some programs.

BASIC COSTS (2007-2008)
Tuition and fees: $3,780; out-of-state residents $5,280.
Per-credit charge: $106; out-of-state residents $159.
Room and board: $5,300.

FINANCIAL AID PICTURE (2007-2008)
Students with need: 50% of average financial aid package awarded as scholarships/grants, 50% awarded as loans/jobs. Need-based aid available for part-time students.
Students without need: No-need awards available for athletics, music/drama.

FINANCIAL AID PROCEDURES
Forms required: FAFSA.
Dates and Deadlines: Priority date 7/1; no closing date. Applicants notified on a rolling basis starting 3/1; must reply within 3 week(s) of notification.

CONTACT
Blaine Duistermars, Director of Financial Aid
2700 College Road, Council Bluffs, IA 51502-3004
(800) 432-5852 ext. 292

Kaplan University: Cedar Falls
Cedar Falls, Iowa
www.kucampus.edu   Federal Code: 004220

4-year for-profit university and branch campus college in small city.
Enrollment: 478 undergrads.
Selectivity: Open admission; but selective for some programs.

BASIC COSTS (2007-2008)
Tuition and fees: $11,250.
Per-credit charge: $375.
Additional info: Costs may vary by program.

FINANCIAL AID PICTURE
Students with need: Need-based aid available for full-time and part-time students. Work study available nights, weekends, and for part-time students.
Students without need: This college awards aid only to students with need.

FINANCIAL AID PROCEDURES
Forms required: FAFSA, institutional form.
Dates and Deadlines: No deadline. Applicants notified on a rolling basis.
Transfers: No deadline. Applicants notified on a rolling basis.

CONTACT

Brenda Biersner, Director of Finance

7009 Nordic Drive, Cedar Falls, IA 50613

(319) 277-0220

Kaplan University: Cedar Rapids

Cedar Rapids, Iowa

www.kucampus.edu   Federal Code: 004220

4-year for-profit university and Bible college in small city.

Enrollment: 542 undergrads.

Selectivity: Open admission; but selective for some programs.

BASIC COSTS (2007-2008)

Tuition and fees: $13,532.

Per-credit charge: $375.

FINANCIAL AID PICTURE

Students with need: Need-based aid available for full-time and part-time students. Work study available nights, weekends, and for part-time students.

Students without need: No-need awards available for academics.

FINANCIAL AID PROCEDURES

Forms required: FAFSA, institutional form.

Dates and Deadlines: Priority date 6/30; no closing date. Applicants notified on a rolling basis.

Transfers: Priority date of 07/08 for filing Iowa Tuition Grant application.

CONTACT

Susan Spivey, President

3165 Edgewood Parkway, SW, Cedar Rapids, IA 52404

(319) 363-0481

Kaplan University: Davenport

Davenport, Iowa

www.kucampus.edu   Federal Code: 004586

4-year for-profit university in large city.

Enrollment: 32,669 undergrads.

Selectivity: Open admission.

BASIC COSTS (2007-2008)

Tuition and fees: $13,680.

Per-credit charge: $380.

Additional info: Tuition figure includes books.

FINANCIAL AID PICTURE

Students with need: Need-based aid available for full-time and part-time students. Work study available nights.

Students without need: No-need awards available for academics.

FINANCIAL AID PROCEDURES

Forms required: FAFSA, institutional form.

Dates and Deadlines: Priority date 5/15; no closing date. Applicants notified on a rolling basis starting 3/4; must reply by 6/15 or within 2 week(s) of notification.

Transfers: Priority date 6/15.

CONTACT

Connie Bishop, Assistant Director of Financial Aid

1801 East Kimberly Road, Suite 1, Davenport, IA 52807-2095

(563) 355-3500

Kaplan University: Des Moines

Urbandale, Iowa

www.kucampus.edu   Federal Code: 004220

4-year for-profit university in large city.

Enrollment: 710 undergrads.

Selectivity: Open admission; but selective for some programs.

BASIC COSTS (2007-2008)

Tuition and fees: $13,482.

Per-credit charge: $300.

Additional info: Tuition includes books and fees.

FINANCIAL AID PICTURE

Students with need: Need-based aid available for full-time and part-time students. Work study available nights, weekends, and for part-time students.

Students without need: This college awards aid only to students with need.

FINANCIAL AID PROCEDURES

Forms required: FAFSA, institutional form.

Dates and Deadlines: Priority date 6/30; no closing date.

CONTACT

Summer Vaselaar, Assistant Director of Student Finance

4655 121st Street, Urbandale, IA 50323

(515) 727-2100

Kirkwood Community College

Cedar Rapids, Iowa

www.kirkwood.edu   Federal Code: 004076

2-year public community college in small city.

Enrollment: 15,091 undergrads.

Selectivity: Open admission; but selective for some programs.

BASIC COSTS (2008-2009)

Tuition and fees: $3,210; out-of-state residents $3,960.

Per-credit charge: $107; out-of-state residents $132.

FINANCIAL AID PICTURE

Students with need: Need-based aid available for full-time and part-time students. Work study available nights, weekends, and for part-time students.

Students without need: No-need awards available for art, athletics, leadership, music/drama.

FINANCIAL AID PROCEDURES

Forms required: FAFSA.

Dates and Deadlines: Priority date 7/1; no closing date. Applicants notified on a rolling basis starting 4/1.

CONTACT

Peg Julius, Director of Financial Aid

6301 Kirkwood Boulevard SW, Cedar Rapids, IA 52406

(319) 398-1274

Loras College

Dubuque, Iowa

www.loras.edu   Federal Code: 001873

4-year private liberal arts college in small city, affiliated with Roman Catholic Church.

Enrollment: 1,500 undergrads, 3% part-time. 375 full-time freshmen.

Selectivity: Admits 50 to 75% of applicants.

BASIC COSTS (2008-2009)

Tuition and fees: $24,438.
Per-credit charge: $465.
Room and board: $6,727.
Additional info: Tuition/fee waivers available for minority students.

FINANCIAL AID PICTURE (2007-2008)

Students with need: Out of 353 full-time freshmen who applied for aid, 339 were judged to have need. Of these, 339 received aid, and 112 had their full need met. Need-based aid available for part-time students.

Students without need: 56 full-time freshmen who did not demonstrate need for aid received scholarships/grants; average award was $8,791. No-need awards available for academics, alumni affiliation, leadership, minority status, music/drama.

Cumulative student debt: 88% of graduating class had student loans; average debt was $23,528.

Additional info: Audition or portfolio recommended for music and art financial aid applicants.

FINANCIAL AID PROCEDURES

Forms required: FAFSA.
Dates and Deadlines: Priority date 4/15; no closing date. Applicants notified on a rolling basis starting 3/1; must reply within 3 week(s) of notification.

CONTACT

Julie Dunn, Director of Financial Planning
1450 Alta Vista Street, Dubuque, IA 52004-0178
(563) 588-7136

Luther College

Decorah, Iowa
www.luther.edu
Federal Code: 001874

4-year private liberal arts college in small town, affiliated with Evangelical Lutheran Church in America.
Enrollment: 2,405 undergrads. 659 full-time freshmen.
Selectivity: Admits over 75% of applicants.

BASIC COSTS (2008-2009)

Tuition and fees: $31,707.
Per-credit charge: $1,104.
Room and board: $5,040.

FINANCIAL AID PICTURE (2007-2008)

Students with need: Out of 550 full-time freshmen who applied for aid, 463 were judged to have need. Of these, 463 received aid, and 166 had their full need met. Average financial aid package met 93% of need; average scholarship/grant was $15,913; average loan was $5,224. For part-time students, average financial aid package was $12,306.

Students without need: 79 full-time freshmen who did not demonstrate need for aid received scholarships/grants; average award was $10,991. No-need awards available for academics, alumni affiliation, art, minority status, music/drama.

Scholarships offered: Academic scholarship; $4,000-$17,000; based on class rank and SAT/ACT. National Merit Scholarship; $1,000-$2,000; depending on qualification. Diversity Enrichment Scholarship; $3,000-$5,000 awarded to students with broadly diverse and distinctive backgrounds. Church Matching Scholarship; up to $750; for students from member churches. Music scholarship; $1,000-$4,000, plus one scholarship that covers one credit hour of private instruction. Legacy Award; $1,000 for children of Luther College alumni. Competitive Nursing scholarship; $1,000; determined by nursing faculty and strength of admission file. Art scholarship; $150-$500; determined by evaluation of portfolio.

Cumulative student debt: 76% of graduating class had student loans; average debt was $19,765.

FINANCIAL AID PROCEDURES

Forms required: FAFSA, institutional form.
Dates and Deadlines: Priority date 3/1; no closing date. Applicants notified on a rolling basis starting 3/1; must reply by 5/1 or within 4 week(s) of notification.

CONTACT

Janice Cordell, Director of Student Financial Planning
700 College Drive, Decorah, IA 52101-1042
(563) 387-1018

Maharishi University of Management

Fairfield, Iowa
www.mum.edu
Federal Code: 011113

4-year private university and liberal arts college in small town.
Enrollment: 199 undergrads, 5% part-time. 43 full-time freshmen.

BASIC COSTS (2008-2009)

Tuition and fees: $24,430.
Per-credit charge: $550.
Room and board: $6,000.

FINANCIAL AID PICTURE (2006-2007)

Students with need: Out of 42 full-time freshmen who applied for aid, 40 were judged to have need. Of these, 40 received aid, and 10 had their full need met. Average financial aid package met 89% of need; average scholarship/grant was $15,138; average loan was $6,625. Need-based aid available for part-time students.

Scholarships offered: Shelley Hoffman Scholarship: $500-$900; based on creative writing and/or cerebral palsy; 7 awarded. National Merit Scholarship: full tuition; for NMS finalists; 4 awarded. Ray Prat Scholarship: $500-$1,750; for musically-talented undergraduates; 4 awarded. Girl Scout Gold Award Scholarship: $1,500 renewable; for GS Gold Award recipients; 5 awarded. DeRoy D. Thomas Scholarship: $3,000 each; open to outstanding African American; 1 awarded.

Cumulative student debt: 83% of graduating class had student loans; average debt was $22,691.

Additional info: Students may earn scholarships through volunteer staff program.

FINANCIAL AID PROCEDURES

Forms required: FAFSA.
Dates and Deadlines: Priority date 7/15; closing date 7/30. Applicants notified on a rolling basis starting 3/1; must reply within 4 week(s) of notification.
Transfers: No deadline. Applicants notified on a rolling basis starting 3/15; must reply within 4 week(s) of notification.

CONTACT

Bill Christensen, Director of Financial Aid
1000 North Fourth Street, Fairfield, IA 52557
(641) 472-1156

Mercy College of Health Sciences

Des Moines, Iowa
www.mchs.edu
Federal Code: 006273

4-year private health science college in large city, affiliated with Roman Catholic Church.
Enrollment: 680 undergrads, 38% part-time. 59 full-time freshmen.
Selectivity: Admits over 75% of applicants.

BASIC COSTS (2007-2008)

Tuition and fees: $12,600.
Per-credit charge: $425.

FINANCIAL AID PICTURE (2006-2007)

Students with need: 15% of average financial aid package awarded as scholarships/grants, 85% awarded as loans/jobs. Need-based aid available for part-time students. Work study available nights, weekends, and for part-time students.

Students without need: No-need awards available for academics.

FINANCIAL AID PROCEDURES

Forms required: FAFSA.

Dates and Deadlines: Closing date 7/1. Applicants notified on a rolling basis; must reply by 1/1 or within 2 week(s) of notification.

Transfers: Students must submit information by 7/1 to be eligible for Iowa Tuition Grant.

CONTACT

Wayne Dille, Financial Aid Director
928 Sixth Avenue, Des Moines, IA 50309
(515) 643-6611

Morningside College
Sioux City, Iowa
www.morningside.edu   Federal Code: 001879

4-year private liberal arts college in small city, affiliated with United Methodist Church.

Enrollment: 1,181 undergrads, 3% part-time. 290 full-time freshmen.

Selectivity: Admits over 75% of applicants.

BASIC COSTS (2007-2008)

Tuition and fees: $20,010.

Room and board: $6,166.

Additional info: Tuition/fee waivers available for adults.

FINANCIAL AID PICTURE (2007-2008)

Students with need: Out of 287 full-time freshmen who applied for aid, 263 were judged to have need. Of these, 263 received aid, and 120 had their full need met. Average financial aid package met 85% of need; average scholarship/grant was $13,644; average loan was $3,806. For part-time students, average financial aid package was $6,827.

Students without need: 27 full-time freshmen who did not demonstrate need for aid received scholarships/grants; average award was $10,369. No-need awards available for academics, alumni affiliation, art, athletics, job skills, leadership, music/drama, religious affiliation, ROTC, state/district residency.

Scholarships offered: *Merit:* President's Scholarship; $6,000 to $10,000; ACT 27 and top 10% of class. Dean's Scholarship; $3,000 to $6,000; ACT 23 or top 20% of class. Mustang Co-Curricular Award; up to $3,000; based on leadership and involvement. National Merit; full tuition. Talent Awards; up to $4,000; based on talents in the areas of art, cheerleading, creative writing, computer technology, mass communications, music, and/or theater. *Athletic:* 152 full-time freshmen received athletic scholarships; average amount $2,361.

Cumulative student debt: 89% of graduating class had student loans; average debt was $36,937.

FINANCIAL AID PROCEDURES

Forms required: FAFSA.

Dates and Deadlines: Priority date 3/1; no closing date. Applicants notified on a rolling basis starting 3/31.

CONTACT

Karen Gagnon, Director Student Financial Planning
1501 Morningside Avenue, Sioux City, IA 51106
(712) 274-5159

Mount Mercy College
Cedar Rapids, Iowa
www.mtmercy.edu   Federal Code: 001880

4-year private liberal arts college in small city, affiliated with Roman Catholic Church.

Enrollment: 1,480 undergrads, 37% part-time. 140 full-time freshmen.

Selectivity: Admits 50 to 75% of applicants.

BASIC COSTS (2008-2009)

Tuition and fees: $21,125.

Per-credit charge: $585.

Room and board: $6,270.

FINANCIAL AID PICTURE (2007-2008)

Students with need: Out of 130 full-time freshmen who applied for aid, 106 were judged to have need. Of these, 106 received aid, and 49 had their full need met. Average financial aid package met 82% of need; average scholarship/grant was $16,233; average loan was $6,257. For part-time students, average financial aid package was $9,241.

Students without need: 18 full-time freshmen who did not demonstrate need for aid received scholarships/grants; average award was $7,118. No-need awards available for academics, art, leadership, music/drama.

Cumulative student debt: 89% of graduating class had student loans; average debt was $27,083.

FINANCIAL AID PROCEDURES

Forms required: FAFSA.

Dates and Deadlines: Priority date 3/1; no closing date. Applicants notified on a rolling basis starting 3/15; must reply by 5/1 or within 3 week(s) of notification.

Transfers: No deadline. Applicants notified on a rolling basis starting 3/1; must reply within 3 week(s) of notification.

CONTACT

Bethany Rinderknecht, Financial Aid Counselor
1330 Elmhurst Drive NE, Cedar Rapids, IA 52402-4797
(319) 368-6467

North Iowa Area Community College
Mason City, Iowa
www.niacc.edu   Federal Code: 001877

2-year public community college in large town.

Enrollment: 3,100 undergrads, 46% part-time. 646 full-time freshmen.

Selectivity: Open admission; but selective for some programs.

BASIC COSTS (2007-2008)

Tuition and fees: $3,363; out-of-state residents $4,861.

Per-credit charge: $99; out-of-state residents $149.

Room and board: $4,280.

FINANCIAL AID PICTURE (2006-2007)

Students with need: Out of 602 full-time freshmen who applied for aid, 505 were judged to have need. Of these, 502 received aid, and 65 had their full need met. Average financial aid package met 59% of need; average scholarship/grant was $2,928; average loan was $2,800. For part-time students, average financial aid package was $3,111.

Students without need: No-need awards available for academics, alumni affiliation, art, athletics, leadership, music/drama.

FINANCIAL AID PROCEDURES

Forms required: FAFSA, institutional form.

Dates and Deadlines: Priority date 3/1; no closing date. Applicants notified on a rolling basis starting 4/1; must reply within 2 week(s) of notification.

CONTACT
Mary Bloomingdale, Director of Financial Aid
500 College Drive, Mason City, IA 50401
(641) 422-4351

Northeast Iowa Community College
Calmar, Iowa
www.nicc.edu   Federal Code: 004587

2-year public community college in rural community.
Enrollment: 3,028 undergrads, 33% part-time. 649 full-time freshmen.
Selectivity: Open admission; but selective for some programs.

BASIC COSTS (2008-2009)
Tuition and fees: $4,050.
Per-credit charge: $121.

FINANCIAL AID PICTURE
Students with need: Need-based aid available for full-time and part-time students. Work study available nights.
Students without need: No-need awards available for academics, leadership.

FINANCIAL AID PROCEDURES
Forms required: FAFSA.
Dates and Deadlines: Priority date 7/1; no closing date. Applicants notified on a rolling basis starting 5/1.

CONTACT
Jeff Murphy, Director of Financial Aid
Box 400, Calmar, IA 52132
(563) 526-3263 ext. 447

Northwestern College
Orange City, Iowa
www.nwciowa.edu   Federal Code: 001883

4-year private liberal arts college in small town, affiliated with Reformed Church in America.
Enrollment: 1,269 undergrads, 1% part-time. 324 full-time freshmen.
Selectivity: Admits over 75% of applicants.

BASIC COSTS (2008-2009)
Tuition and fees: $22,950.
Room and board: $6,580.
Additional info: 1-4 credits, $445 per credit hour; 5-8 credits, $660 per credit hour; 9-11 credits, $870 per credit hour. Tuition/fee waivers available for adults.

FINANCIAL AID PICTURE
Students with need: Need-based aid available for full-time and part-time students.
Students without need: No-need awards available for academics, art, athletics, music/drama, religious affiliation, state/district residency.

FINANCIAL AID PROCEDURES
Forms required: FAFSA.
Dates and Deadlines: Priority date 4/1; closing date 6/30. Applicants notified on a rolling basis starting 3/15; must reply within 3 week(s) of notification.
Transfers: No deadline. College financial aid transcript required for aid.

CONTACT
Gerry Korver, Director of Financial Aid
101 Seventh Street, SW, Orange City, IA 51041
(712) 707-7131

St. Ambrose University
Davenport, Iowa
www.sau.edu   Federal Code: 001889

4-year private university and liberal arts college in small city, affiliated with Roman Catholic Church.
Enrollment: 2,779 undergrads, 16% part-time. 509 full-time freshmen.
Selectivity: Admits 50 to 75% of applicants.

BASIC COSTS (2008-2009)
Tuition and fees: $21,610.
Per-credit charge: $672.
Room and board: $7,825.
Additional info: Tuition/fee waivers available for adults.

FINANCIAL AID PICTURE (2007-2008)
Students with need: Out of 508 full-time freshmen who applied for aid, 370 were judged to have need. Of these, 369 received aid, and 115 had their full need met. Average financial aid package met 29% of need; average scholarship/grant was $10,522; average loan was $3,816. For part-time students, average financial aid package was $14,638.
Students without need: 138 full-time freshmen who did not demonstrate need for aid received scholarships/grants; average award was $7,017. No-need awards available for academics, alumni affiliation, art, athletics, job skills, music/drama.
Scholarships offered: *Merit:* Ambrose Scholarship; 4.0 GPA and 30 ACT or 1320 SAT score required. Presidential Scholarship; 3.8 GPA and ACT 26-29 or SAT 1170-1319 required. SAT scores listed are exclusive of Writing. *Athletic:* 51 full-time freshmen received athletic scholarships; average amount $3,691.
Cumulative student debt: 77% of graduating class had student loans; average debt was $32,444.
Additional info: Iowa applicants must apply for financial aid by July 1. Audition required for music, drama scholarship applicants.

FINANCIAL AID PROCEDURES
Forms required: FAFSA.
Dates and Deadlines: Priority date 3/15; no closing date. Applicants notified on a rolling basis starting 2/1; must reply within 2 week(s) of notification.
Transfers: No deadline. Must reply within 2 week(s) of notification.

CONTACT
Julie Haack, Director of Financial Aid
518 West Locust Street, Davenport, IA 52803-2898
(563) 333-6314

St. Luke's College
Sioux City, Iowa
www.stlukescollege.edu   Federal Code: 007291

2-year private health science college in small city, affiliated with Lutheran and Methodist churches.
Enrollment: 148 undergrads, 47% part-time. 1 full-time freshmen.
Selectivity: Admits less than 50% of applicants.

BASIC COSTS (2008-2009)
Tuition and fees: $13,725.
Per-credit charge: $375.
Additional info: Summer general fee: $125.

FINANCIAL AID PICTURE (2007-2008)
Students with need: Out of 1 full-time freshmen who applied for aid, 1 were judged to have need. Of these, 1 received aid, and 1 had their full need met. For part-time students, average financial aid package was $12,325.
Students without need: No-need awards available for academics, job skills, leadership.

FINANCIAL AID PROCEDURES

Forms required: FAFSA.

Dates and Deadlines: Priority date 3/1; no closing date. Applicants notified on a rolling basis starting 4/1; must reply within 2 week(s) of notification.

CONTACT

Danelle Johannsen, Director, Student and Administrative Services

2720 Stone Park Boulevard, Sioux City, IA 51104

(712) 279-3377

Simpson College

Indianola, Iowa

www.simpson.edu   Federal Code: 001887

4-year private liberal arts college in large town, affiliated with United Methodist Church.

Enrollment: 1,910 undergrads, 21% part-time. 385 full-time freshmen.

Selectivity: Admits over 75% of applicants.

BASIC COSTS (2008-2009)

Tuition and fees: $24,771.

Per-credit charge: $275.

Room and board: $6,988.

Additional info: Tuition/fee waivers available for adults, minority students.

FINANCIAL AID PICTURE (2007-2008)

Students with need: Out of 385 full-time freshmen who applied for aid, 339 were judged to have need. Of these, 339 received aid, and 111 had their full need met. Average financial aid package met 89% of need; average scholarship/grant was $16,149; average loan was $3,650. For part-time students, average financial aid package was $5,804.

Students without need: 42 full-time freshmen who did not demonstrate need for aid received scholarships/grants; average award was $9,783. No-need awards available for academics, alumni affiliation, art, leadership, minority status, music/drama, religious affiliation, state/district residency.

Cumulative student debt: 88% of graduating class had student loans; average debt was $29,255.

Additional info: Music and theater scholarships based on audition. Art scholarships based on portfolio.

FINANCIAL AID PROCEDURES

Forms required: FAFSA.

Dates and Deadlines: Priority date 4/1; no closing date. Applicants notified on a rolling basis starting 3/12; must reply by 5/1 or within 3 week(s) of notification.

CONTACT

Tracie Pavon, Director of Financial Assistance

701 North C Street, Indianola, IA 50125

(515) 961-1630

Southeastern Community College: North Campus

West Burlington, Iowa

www.scciowa.edu   Federal Code: 004603

2-year public community and junior college in large town.

Enrollment: 2,404 undergrads, 30% part-time. 385 full-time freshmen.

Selectivity: Open admission; but selective for some programs.

BASIC COSTS (2007-2008)

Tuition and fees: $3,210; out-of-state residents $3,570.

Per-credit charge: $107; out-of-state residents $119.

FINANCIAL AID PICTURE (2006-2007)

Students with need: Out of 332 full-time freshmen who applied for aid, 332 were judged to have need. Of these, 321 received aid. For part-time students, average financial aid package was $4,267.

Students without need: No-need awards available for academics, art, athletics, minority status.

Scholarships offered: 10 full-time freshmen received athletic scholarships; average amount $3,705.

FINANCIAL AID PROCEDURES

Forms required: FAFSA.

Dates and Deadlines: Priority date 7/1; no closing date. Applicants notified on a rolling basis starting 3/1; must reply within 4 week(s) of notification.

CONTACT

Gwen Scholer, Financial Aid Director

1500 West Agency Road, West Burlington, IA 52655-0605

(319) 752-2731 ext. 5014

Southwestern Community College

Creston, Iowa

www.swcciowa.edu   Federal Code: 001857

2-year public community college in small town.

Enrollment: 1,019 undergrads.

Selectivity: Open admission; but selective for some programs.

BASIC COSTS (2007-2008)

Tuition and fees: $3,920; out-of-state residents $4,934.

Per-credit charge: $123; out-of-state residents $155.

Room and board: $4,500.

FINANCIAL AID PICTURE

Students with need: Need-based aid available for full-time and part-time students. Work study available nights, weekends, and for part-time students.

Students without need: No-need awards available for academics, athletics, leadership, music/drama, state/district residency.

FINANCIAL AID PROCEDURES

Forms required: FAFSA.

Dates and Deadlines: Priority date 7/1; no closing date. Applicants notified on a rolling basis starting 6/1; must reply within 2 week(s) of notification.

CONTACT

Tracy Sleep, Financial Aid Officer

1501 West Townline Street, Creston, IA 50801

(641) 782-1333

University of Dubuque

Dubuque, Iowa

www.dbq.edu   Federal Code: 001891

4-year private university and seminary college in small city, affiliated with Presbyterian Church (USA).

Enrollment: 1,240 undergrads.

Selectivity: Admits 50 to 75% of applicants.

BASIC COSTS (2007-2008)

Tuition and fees: $19,180.

Per-credit charge: $425.

Room and board: $6,520.

FINANCIAL AID PICTURE

Students with need: Need-based aid available for full-time and part-time students. Work study available nights, weekends, and for part-time students.

Students without need: No-need awards available for academics, alumni affiliation, music/drama, ROTC.

Scholarships offered: Presidential Scholarship: $6,000 per annum for 4 years; top 20% of high school graduation class and top 20% of ACT. Honors Scholarship: top 20% of high school class, or top 20% of ACT/SAT, or 3.5 GPA or greater.

FINANCIAL AID PROCEDURES

Forms required: FAFSA.

Dates and Deadlines: Priority date 4/1; no closing date. Applicants notified on a rolling basis starting 3/1; must reply within 3 week(s) of notification.

Transfers: No deadline. Applicants notified on a rolling basis starting 3/1; must reply within 3 week(s) of notification. Iowa Tuition Grant available to Iowa residents.

CONTACT

Timothy Kremer, Dean of Student Financial Planning and Scholarships
2000 University Avenue, Dubuque, IA 52001-5099
(563) 589-3396

University of Iowa

Iowa City, Iowa
www.uiowa.edu   Federal Code: 001892

4-year public university in small city.

Enrollment: 20,207 undergrads, 8% part-time. 4,117 full-time freshmen.

Selectivity: Admits over 75% of applicants.

BASIC COSTS (2007-2008)

Tuition and fees: $6,293; out-of-state residents $19,465.

Per-credit charge: $224; out-of-state residents $816.

Room and board: $6,685.

FINANCIAL AID PICTURE (2006-2007)

Students with need: Out of 2,983 full-time freshmen who applied for aid, 1,983 were judged to have need. Of these, 1,884 received aid, and 1,875 had their full need met. Average financial aid package met 99% of need; average scholarship/grant was $4,529; average loan was $2,845. Need-based aid available for part-time students.

Students without need: 783 full-time freshmen who did not demonstrate need for aid received scholarships/grants; average award was $1,788. No-need awards available for academics, alumni affiliation, art, athletics, leadership, minority status, music/drama, ROTC, state/district residency.

Scholarships offered: *Merit:* Presidential Scholarship: $52,000; based on ACT/SAT, GPA, essay; 20 awarded. Old Gold Scholarship: $12,000; awarded to runners-up for Presidential Scholarship; 350 awarded. National Scholars Award: $12,080; for non-residents based on admission index. Iowa Heritage Award: $6,000; nonresident students who have a parent, step-parent, legal guardian, or grandparent who graduated from UI. Advantage Iowa Award: $2,000 to full tuition; merit based for U.S. citizens or permanent residents whose enrollment will contribute to a diverse learning environment; criteria includes race/ethnic background, socioeconomic factors, whether student is a first-generation college student, participant in federal TRIO program; automatic consideration given. *Athletic:* 73 full-time freshmen received athletic scholarships; average amount $12,625.

Cumulative student debt: 61% of graduating class had student loans; average debt was $22,181.

FINANCIAL AID PROCEDURES

Forms required: FAFSA, institutional form.

Dates and Deadlines: Priority date 1/1; no closing date. Applicants notified on a rolling basis starting 3/1.

Transfers: No deadline. Applicants notified on a rolling basis starting 3/15.

CONTACT

Mark Warner, Assistant Provost for Enrollment Services
107 Calvin Hall, Iowa City, IA 52242-1396
(319) 335-1450

University of Northern Iowa

Cedar Falls, Iowa
www.uni.edu   Federal Code: 001890

4-year public university in small city.

Enrollment: 10,756 undergrads, 9% part-time. 1,934 full-time freshmen.

Selectivity: Admits over 75% of applicants.

BASIC COSTS (2007-2008)

Tuition and fees: $6,190; out-of-state residents $14,282.

Per-credit charge: $223; out-of-district residents $223; out-of-state residents $561.

Room and board: $6,268.

FINANCIAL AID PICTURE (2007-2008)

Students with need: Out of 1,699 full-time freshmen who applied for aid, 1,156 were judged to have need. Of these, 1,114 received aid, and 280 had their full need met. Average financial aid package met 74% of need; average scholarship/grant was $3,727; average loan was $3,534. For part-time students, average financial aid package was $6,494.

Students without need: 452 full-time freshmen who did not demonstrate need for aid received scholarships/grants; average award was $2,519. No-need awards available for academics, alumni affiliation, art, athletics, leadership, minority status, music/drama, ROTC, state/district residency.

Scholarships offered: *Merit:* Presidential Scholarship: $7,000; for upper 10% of high school class or top 5 of class of 50 or less, ACT composite of 29 or above, academic excellence, extracurricular achievements, leadership and demonstrated potential for making a significant contribution to society; 20 awards available. Provost Scholarship: $2,000 per year for four years; same criteria as Presidential Scholarship; 30 available. Distinguished Scholars Award; $1,500; for rank in upper 25% of high school class; Iowa residents; renewable for a second year with a 3.0 GPA or above. *Athletic:* 59 full-time freshmen received athletic scholarships; average amount $10,195.

Cumulative student debt: 78% of graduating class had student loans; average debt was $22,541.

FINANCIAL AID PROCEDURES

Forms required: FAFSA.

Dates and Deadlines: No deadline. Applicants notified on a rolling basis starting 3/1.

CONTACT

Roland Carrillo, Director Financial Aid and Student Employment
Towers 130, Cedar Falls, IA 50614-0018
(319) 273-2700

Upper Iowa University

Fayette, Iowa
www.uiu.edu   Federal Code: 001893

4-year private university in rural community.

Enrollment: 745 undergrads.

Selectivity: Admits 50 to 75% of applicants.

BASIC COSTS (2007-2008)

Tuition and fees: $19,625.

Room and board: $6,075.

FINANCIAL AID PICTURE

Students with need: Need-based aid available for full-time and part-time students.

Students without need: No-need awards available for academics.

FINANCIAL AID PROCEDURES

Forms required: FAFSA.

Dates and Deadlines: Priority date 6/1; no closing date. Applicants notified on a rolling basis starting 4/1.

CONTACT

Jobyna Johnston, Director of Financial Aid
Parker Fox Hall, Fayette, IA 52142
(800) 553-4150 ext. 3

Vennard College

University Park, Iowa
www.vennard.edu   Federal Code: 001894

4-year private Bible college in large town, affiliated with interdenominational tradition.

Enrollment: 70 undergrads, 4% part-time. 11 full-time freshmen.
Selectivity: Admits 50 to 75% of applicants.

BASIC COSTS (2007-2008)
Tuition and fees: $9,750.
Room and board: $4,950.

FINANCIAL AID PICTURE (2006-2007)
Students with need: 46% of average financial aid package awarded as scholarships/grants, 54% awarded as loans/jobs. Need-based aid available for part-time students. Work study available nights, weekends, and for part-time students.
Students without need: No-need awards available for religious affiliation.
Additional info: Institutional aid award available (sum of financial need grant and academic scholarship); FAFSA required. New students must have ACT/SAT score and GPA from high school; transfer students must have a GPA based on transcript from at least 24 credit hours from previous college.

FINANCIAL AID PROCEDURES
Forms required: FAFSA.
Dates and Deadlines: Priority date 7/1; no closing date. Applicants notified on a rolling basis starting 8/29; must reply within 8 week(s) of notification.
Transfers: No deadline. Applicants notified on a rolling basis starting 8/29; must reply within 8 week(s) of notification. Academic scholarships available to full-time new transfer students. 2.2 college GPA for 2 consecutive semesters of credit work in degree granting program required.

CONTACT
Michelle Williams, Financial Aid Director
Box 29, University Park, IA 52595-0029
(641) 673-8391 ext. 218

Waldorf College

Forest City, Iowa
www.waldorf.edu   Federal Code: 001895

4-year private liberal arts college in small town, affiliated with Evangelical Lutheran Church in America.

Enrollment: 566 undergrads.
Selectivity: Admits 50 to 75% of applicants.

BASIC COSTS (2008-2009)
Tuition and fees: $19,504.
Per-credit charge: $435.
Room and board: $5,921.

FINANCIAL AID PICTURE
Students with need: Need-based aid available for full-time and part-time students. Work study available nights, weekends, and for part-time students.
Students without need: No-need awards available for academics, alumni affiliation, athletics, job skills, leadership, music/drama, religious affiliation, state/district residency.

FINANCIAL AID PROCEDURES
Forms required: FAFSA, institutional form.

Dates and Deadlines: Priority date 3/1; no closing date. Applicants notified on a rolling basis starting 3/1; must reply within 2 week(s) of notification.
Transfers: Applicants notified on a rolling basis starting 3/1; must reply within 2 week(s) of notification.

CONTACT
Duane Polsdofer, Director of Student Financial Aid
106 South Sixth Street, Forest City, IA 50436-1713
(641) 585-8120

Wartburg College

Waverly, Iowa
www.wartburg.edu   Federal Code: 001896

4-year private liberal arts college in small town, affiliated with Evangelical Lutheran Church in America.

Enrollment: 1,764 undergrads, 2% part-time. 504 full-time freshmen.
Selectivity: Admits over 75% of applicants.

BASIC COSTS (2008-2009)
Tuition and fees: $26,160.
Per-credit charge: $910.
Room and board: $7,255.

FINANCIAL AID PICTURE (2006-2007)
Students with need: Out of 463 full-time freshmen who applied for aid, 402 were judged to have need. Of these, 402 received aid, and 168 had their full need met. Average financial aid package met 90% of need; average scholarship/grant was $14,629; average loan was $4,680. For part-time students, average financial aid package was $7,233.
Students without need: 101 full-time freshmen who did not demonstrate need for aid received scholarships/grants; average award was $15,122. No-need awards available for academics, alumni affiliation, music/drama, religious affiliation.
Scholarships offered: Regents scholarship: up to full tuition, fees, room and board; minimum ACT score of 28, (1240 SAT, exclusive of writing) or rank in top 10% of class; renewable for 4 years; based on maintaining 3.0 cumulative GPA. Students who participate in Regents Scholarship competition not eligible for Presidential Scholarship. Presidential Scholarship: up to $6,000 per year, renewable for 4 years, based on maintaining 2.7 cumulative GPA; minimum ACT score of 25 (1140 SAT, exclusive of writing) or rank in top 20% of class or cumulative GPA of 3.5 or above.
Cumulative student debt: 84% of graduating class had student loans; average debt was $26,835.

FINANCIAL AID PROCEDURES
Forms required: FAFSA.
Dates and Deadlines: Priority date 3/1; no closing date. Applicants notified on a rolling basis starting 3/1; must reply within 2 week(s) of notification.

CONTACT
Jennifer Sassman, Director of Financial Aid
100 Wartburg Boulevard, PO Box 1003, Waverly, IA 50677-0903
(319) 352-8262

Western Iowa Tech Community College

Sioux City, Iowa
www.witcc.com   Federal Code: 004590

2-year public community college in small city.
Enrollment: 2,444 undergrads, 37% part-time. 290 full-time freshmen.
Selectivity: Open admission; but selective for some programs.

BASIC COSTS (2008-2009)
Tuition and fees: $3,675; out-of-state residents $4,455.
Per-credit charge: $107; out-of-state residents $133.

Room and board: $4,900.

FINANCIAL AID PICTURE (2006-2007)

Students with need: 39% of average financial aid package awarded as scholarships/grants, 61% awarded as loans/jobs. Need-based aid available for part-time students. Work study available nights, weekends, and for part-time students.

Students without need: No-need awards available for academics, leadership, music/drama.

FINANCIAL AID PROCEDURES

Forms required: FAFSA.

Dates and Deadlines: No deadline. Applicants notified on a rolling basis starting 4/1.

CONTACT

Donald Duzik, Director of Financial Aid
Box 5199, Sioux City, IA 51102-5199
(712) 274-6402

William Penn University
Oskaloosa, Iowa
www.wmpenn.edu   Federal Code: 001900

4-year private liberal arts college in large town, affiliated with Society of Friends (Quaker).

Enrollment: 1,833 undergrads.
Selectivity: Admits 50 to 75% of applicants.

BASIC COSTS (2008-2009)

Tuition and fees: $18,034.
Room and board: $5,132.
Additional info: Per-credit-hour charge of $215 for 1-7 credits, $425 for credits in excess of 18.

FINANCIAL AID PICTURE

Students with need: Need-based aid available for full-time and part-time students. Work study available nights, weekends, and for part-time students.

Students without need: No-need awards available for academics, alumni affiliation, athletics, leadership, music/drama, religious affiliation.

Scholarships offered: Participation awards: up to $3,000 per year for music, drama, media, cheerleading, dance, religious leadership. Academic scholarships: based on high school GPA, ACT or SAT, class rank.

FINANCIAL AID PROCEDURES

Forms required: FAFSA.

Dates and Deadlines: Priority date 7/1; no closing date. Applicants notified on a rolling basis starting 1/1; must reply within 2 week(s) of notification.

Transfers: Priority date 4/1; no deadline. Applicants notified on a rolling basis starting 1/1.

CONTACT

Cyndi Peiffer, Director of Financial Aid
201 Trueblood Avenue, Oskaloosa, IA 52577
(641) 673-1060

Kansas

Allen County Community College
Iola, Kansas
www.allencc.edu   Federal Code: 001901

2-year public community college in small town.

Enrollment: 2,800 undergrads.
Selectivity: Open admission.

BASIC COSTS (2007-2008)

Tuition and fees: $1,650; out-of-district residents $1,740; out-of-state residents $1,740.

Per-credit charge: $39; out-of-district residents $42; out-of-state residents $42.

Room and board: $3,800.

FINANCIAL AID PICTURE

Students with need: Need-based aid available for full-time and part-time students. Work study available nights, weekends, and for part-time students.

Students without need: No-need awards available for academics, art, athletics, music/drama, state/district residency.

Additional info: Scholarships for livestock judging, cheerleading, choir, dance, drama, art, academic challenge, and student ambassadors.

FINANCIAL AID PROCEDURES

Forms required: FAFSA.

Dates and Deadlines: Closing date 8/1. Applicants notified on a rolling basis starting 6/1; must reply within 2 week(s) of notification.

CONTACT

Vicki Curry, Director of Financial Aid/Registrar
1801 North Cottonwood, Iola, KS 66749
(620) 365-5116 ext. 221

Baker University
Baldwin City, Kansas
www.bakeru.edu   Federal Code: 001903

4-year private liberal arts and teachers college in small town, affiliated with United Methodist Church.

Enrollment: 911 undergrads, 1% part-time. 250 full-time freshmen.
Selectivity: Admits 50 to 75% of applicants.

BASIC COSTS (2007-2008)

Tuition and fees: $18,830.
Per-credit charge: $550.
Room and board: $6,150.

FINANCIAL AID PICTURE (2007-2008)

Students with need: Average financial aid package met 85% of need; average scholarship/grant was $6,358; average loan was $4,136. For part-time students, average financial aid package was $8,006.

Students without need: No-need awards available for academics, alumni affiliation, art, athletics, leadership, music/drama, religious affiliation, ROTC.

Scholarships offered: Presidential Scholarships, $8,000; 28 ACT or 1260 SAT, 3.70 GPA, top 10% class rank. Faculty Merit Scholarships, $7,000; 25 ACT or 1140 SAT, 3.40 GPA, top 25% class rank. University Scholarships, $6,000; 22 ACT or 1030 SAT, 3.10 GPA, top 50% class rank. Academic Leadership Scholarships, $1,000; 22 ACT or 1030 SAT, 3.10 GPA, top 50% class rank. SAT scores listed are exclusive of the writing portion.

FINANCIAL AID PROCEDURES

Forms required: FAFSA, institutional form.

Dates and Deadlines: Priority date 3/1; no closing date. Applicants notified on a rolling basis starting 3/1; must reply by 5/1 or within 6 week(s) of notification.

Transfers: No deadline. Applicants notified on a rolling basis starting 3/1; must reply within 6 week(s) of notification.

CONTACT

Jeanne Mott, Director of Financial Aid
618 Eighth Street, Baldwin City, KS 66006-0065
(785) 594-4595

Barclay College
Haviland, Kansas
www.barclaycollege.edu   Federal Code: 001917

4-year private Bible college in rural community, affiliated with Evangelical Friends Alliance and Friends United Meeting.

Enrollment: 114 undergrads, 10% part-time. 37 full-time freshmen.

Selectivity: Admits over 75% of applicants.

BASIC COSTS (2007-2008)
Tuition and fees: $12,300.
Per-credit charge: $350.
Room and board: $6,000.

FINANCIAL AID PICTURE (2007-2008)
Students with need: 72% of average financial aid package awarded as scholarships/grants, 28% awarded as loans/jobs. Need-based aid available for part-time students. Work study available nights, weekends, and for part-time students.

Students without need: No-need awards available for academics, alumni affiliation, leadership, music/drama, state/district residency.

Scholarships offered: President's Academic Award; $2,600 for 3.8 GPA or ACT score of 30. Dean's Academic Award; $2,000 for 3.6 GPA or ACT scores of 27-29. Trustees Academic Award; $1,600; for 3.4 GPA or ACT scores of 25-26.

FINANCIAL AID PROCEDURES
Forms required: FAFSA, institutional form.
Dates and Deadlines: Priority date 5/31; closing date 7/15. Applicants notified on a rolling basis starting 1/1; must reply within 4 week(s) of notification.

CONTACT
Ryan Haase, Director of Student Financial Services
607 North Kingman, Haviland, KS 67059
(620) 862-5252 ext. 41

Barton County Community College
Great Bend, Kansas
www.bartonccc.edu   Federal Code: 004608

2-year public community college in large town.

Enrollment: 3,057 undergrads, 69% part-time. 373 full-time freshmen.

Selectivity: Open admission; but selective for some programs.

BASIC COSTS (2007-2008)
Tuition and fees: $2,010; out-of-state residents $2,580.
Per-credit charge: $49; out-of-state residents $68.
Room and board: $3,854.

FINANCIAL AID PICTURE (2006-2007)
Students with need: 58% of average financial aid package awarded as scholarships/grants, 42% awarded as loans/jobs. Need-based aid available for part-time students.

Students without need: No-need awards available for academics, athletics.

FINANCIAL AID PROCEDURES
Forms required: FAFSA, state aid form.
Dates and Deadlines: Priority date 3/1; no closing date. Applicants notified on a rolling basis starting 6/1; must reply within 4 week(s) of notification.

CONTACT
Myrna Perkins, Assistant Dean of Student Services & Director of Financial Aid
245 North East 30th Road, Great Bend, KS 67530-9283
(620) 792-2701

Benedictine College
Atchison, Kansas
www.benedictine.edu   Federal Code: 010256

4-year private liberal arts college in large town, affiliated with Roman Catholic Church.

Enrollment: 1,306 undergrads, 1% part-time. 363 full-time freshmen.

Selectivity: Admits 50 to 75% of applicants.

BASIC COSTS (2008-2009)
Tuition and fees: $18,800.
Room and board: $6,400.

FINANCIAL AID PICTURE (2007-2008)
Students with need: 39% of average financial aid package awarded as scholarships/grants, 61% awarded as loans/jobs. Need-based aid available for part-time students. Work study available nights, weekends, and for part-time students.

Students without need: No-need awards available for academics, alumni affiliation, art, athletics, job skills, leadership, minority status, music/drama, religious affiliation, ROTC.

Scholarships offered: Presidential Scholarship; full tuition. Dean's Scholarship; partial tuition. Both renewable every year, 5 recipients each, must maintain 3.5 GPA. Students must be admitted by Jan. 31. Academic Scholarships; renewable every year; ranges from $2,500-$7,500 depending on ACT scores; unlimited number.

FINANCIAL AID PROCEDURES
Forms required: FAFSA.
Dates and Deadlines: Priority date 3/15; no closing date. Applicants notified on a rolling basis starting 2/1; must reply within 2 week(s) of notification.
Transfers: No deadline. Applicants notified on a rolling basis. Scholarship available for students transferring 2.0 cumulative GPA.

CONTACT
Tony Tanking, Director Financial Aid
1020 North Second Street, Atchison, KS 66002-1499
(913) 367-5340 ext. 2484

Bethany College
Lindsborg, Kansas
www.bethanylb.edu   Federal Code: 001904

4-year private liberal arts college in small town, affiliated with Evangelical Lutheran Church in America.

Enrollment: 520 undergrads, 2% part-time. 128 full-time freshmen.

Selectivity: Admits 50 to 75% of applicants.

BASIC COSTS (2008-2009)
Tuition and fees: $18,124.
Per-credit charge: $300.
Room and board: $5,650.

FINANCIAL AID PICTURE (2007-2008)
Students with need: Out of 126 full-time freshmen who applied for aid, 111 were judged to have need. Of these, 111 received aid, and 52 had their full need met. Average financial aid package met 100% of need; average scholarship/grant was $6,462; average loan was $5,265. For part-time students, average financial aid package was $4,609.

Students without need: 3 full-time freshmen who did not demonstrate need for aid received scholarships/grants; average award was $6,167. No-need awards available for academics, alumni affiliation, art, athletics, leadership, music/drama, religious affiliation.

Scholarships offered: 7 full-time freshmen received athletic scholarships; average amount $2,629.

Cumulative student debt: 83% of graduating class had student loans; average debt was $17,717.

Additional info: State financial aid deadline March 15.

FINANCIAL AID PROCEDURES

Forms required: FAFSA.

Dates and Deadlines: Priority date 3/15; no closing date. Applicants notified on a rolling basis starting 2/1; must reply within 3 week(s) of notification.

CONTACT

Brenda Meagher, Director of Financial Aid
335 East Swensson, Lindsborg, KS 67456-1897
(785) 227-3311 ext. 8114

Bethel College

North Newton, Kansas
www.bethelks.edu   Federal Code: 001905

4-year private liberal arts college in large town, affiliated with Mennonite Church.

Enrollment: 541 undergrads, 5% part-time. 104 full-time freshmen.

Selectivity: Admits over 75% of applicants.

BASIC COSTS (2008-2009)

Tuition and fees: $18,900.

Per-credit charge: $680.

Room and board: $6,650.

FINANCIAL AID PICTURE (2006-2007)

Students with need: Out of 97 full-time freshmen who applied for aid, 97 were judged to have need. Of these, 97 received aid, and 43 had their full need met. Average financial aid package met 97% of need; average scholarship/grant was $3,805; average loan was $3,717. For part-time students, average financial aid package was $9,584.

Students without need: 7 full-time freshmen who did not demonstrate need for aid received scholarships/grants; average award was $12,518. No-need awards available for academics, alumni affiliation, art, athletics, minority status, music/drama, religious affiliation, state/district residency.

Scholarships offered: *Merit:* Scholarships for academically talented students, ranging from 16% to 50% of tuition. ***Athletic:*** 66 full-time freshmen received athletic scholarships; average amount $3,259.

Cumulative student debt: 86% of graduating class had student loans; average debt was $20,724.

FINANCIAL AID PROCEDURES

Forms required: FAFSA.

Dates and Deadlines: No deadline. Applicants notified on a rolling basis starting 2/1; must reply within 2 week(s) of notification.

Transfers: Applicants notified on a rolling basis starting 2/1; must reply within 2 week(s) of notification.

CONTACT

Tony Graber, Director of Financial Aid
300 East 27th Street, North Newton, KS 67117-0531
(800) 522-1887 ext. 232

Butler County Community College

El Dorado, Kansas
www.butlercc.edu   Federal Code: 001906

2-year public community college in large town.

Enrollment: 5,290 undergrads, 48% part-time. 1,002 full-time freshmen.

Selectivity: Open admission; but selective for some programs.

BASIC COSTS (2007-2008)

Tuition and fees: $1,838; out-of-district residents $2,168; out-of-state residents $3,548.

Per-credit charge: $47; out-of-district residents $58; out-of-state residents $104.

Room and board: $4,600.

Additional info: Tuition/fee waivers available for unemployed or children of unemployed.

FINANCIAL AID PICTURE

Students with need: Need-based aid available for full-time and part-time students. Work study available nights, weekends, and for part-time students.

Students without need: No-need awards available for academics, art, athletics, music/drama.

FINANCIAL AID PROCEDURES

Forms required: FAFSA, institutional form.

Dates and Deadlines: Priority date 4/1; no closing date. Applicants notified on a rolling basis starting 5/1; must reply within 2 week(s) of notification.

Transfers: Students with 90 hours or more must have classes validated by degree-granting 4-year institution.

CONTACT

Susie Edwards, Director of Financial Aid
901 South Haverhill Road, El Dorado, KS 67042-3280
(316) 322-3121

Central Christian College of Kansas

McPherson, Kansas
www.centralchristian.edu   Federal Code: 001908

4-year private liberal arts college in large town, affiliated with Free Methodist Church of North America.

Enrollment: 307 undergrads. 85 full-time freshmen.

Selectivity: Admits less than 50% of applicants.

BASIC COSTS (2008-2009)

Tuition and fees: $16,000.

Per-credit charge: $450.

Room and board: $5,500.

FINANCIAL AID PICTURE (2007-2008)

Students with need: Out of 74 full-time freshmen who applied for aid, 66 were judged to have need. Of these, 66 received aid, and 12 had their full need met. Average financial aid package met 78% of need; average scholarship/grant was $4,354; average loan was $4,472. For part-time students, average financial aid package was $7,925.

Students without need: 17 full-time freshmen who did not demonstrate need for aid received scholarships/grants; average award was $5,039. No-need awards available for academics, alumni affiliation, athletics, leadership, music/drama, religious affiliation.

Scholarships offered: *Merit:* National Merit Scholarship: full tuition; National Merit semifinalists. Trustees Scholarship: 60% tuition; minimum score of 30 on ACT/1340 on SAT and minimum 3.5 high school GPA. Valedictorian Scholarship: half tuition; for students who are first in their class, with minimum 27 ACT/1220 SAT and 3.5 GPA. SAT scores listed are exclusive of the writing portion. ***Athletic:*** 57 full-time freshmen received athletic scholarships; average amount $1,625.

Cumulative student debt: 73% of graduating class had student loans; average debt was $20,000.

FINANCIAL AID PROCEDURES

Forms required: FAFSA.

Dates and Deadlines: Priority date 3/1; no closing date. Applicants notified on a rolling basis starting 3/1; must reply within 4 week(s) of notification.

Transfers: No deadline. Applicants notified on a rolling basis starting 3/1; must reply within 4 week(s) of notification.

CONTACT

Mike Reimer, Director of Financial Aid
1200 South Main, McPherson, KS 67460-5740
(620) 241-0723 ext. 333

Cloud County Community College
Concordia, Kansas
www.cloud.edu   Federal Code: 001909

2-year public community college in small town.
Enrollment: 1,009 undergrads.
Selectivity: Open admission.

BASIC COSTS (2007-2008)
Tuition and fees: $2,310; out-of-state residents $2,970.
Per-credit charge: $58; out-of-state residents $99.
Room and board: $4,440.

FINANCIAL AID PICTURE
Students with need: Need-based aid available for full-time and part-time students. Work study available nights, weekends, and for part-time students.

FINANCIAL AID PROCEDURES
Forms required: FAFSA.
Dates and Deadlines: Priority date 4/1; no closing date. Applicants notified on a rolling basis starting 5/1; must reply within 4 week(s) of notification.

CONTACT
Sherry Campbell, Director of Student Financial Aid
2221 Campus Drive, Concordia, KS 66901-1002
(785) 243-1435 ext. 280

Coffeyville Community College
Coffeyville, Kansas
www.coffeyville.edu   Federal Code: 001910

2-year public community college in large town.
Enrollment: 1,375 undergrads, 28% part-time. 416 full-time freshmen.
Selectivity: Open admission.

BASIC COSTS (2007-2008)
Tuition and fees: $1,725; out-of-state residents $2,925.
Per-credit charge: $25; out-of-state residents $65.
Room and board: $3,825.
Additional info: Oklahoma border county resident tuition: $32.50 per-credit-hour. International students pay $2,835 in required fees.

FINANCIAL AID PICTURE
Students with need: Need-based aid available for full-time and part-time students. Work study available nights, weekends, and for part-time students.
Students without need: No-need awards available for academics, alumni affiliation, art, athletics, leadership, music/drama.

FINANCIAL AID PROCEDURES
Forms required: FAFSA.
Dates and Deadlines: Priority date 8/1; no closing date. Applicants notified on a rolling basis starting 6/20.

CONTACT
Rhonda Baker, Director of Financial Aid
400 West 11th Street, Coffeyville, KS 67337-5064
(620) 252-7357

Colby Community College
Colby, Kansas
www.colbycc.edu   Federal Code: 001911

2-year public community college in small town.
Enrollment: 594 undergrads, 9% part-time. 188 full-time freshmen.
Selectivity: Open admission; but selective for some programs.

BASIC COSTS (2007-2008)
Tuition and fees: $2,304; out-of-state residents $3,474.
Per-credit charge: $48; out-of-state residents $87.
Room and board: $3,788.
Additional info: Nebraska and Colorado border county residents pay $58 per credit hour for tuition, and additional $30 per credit hour for required fees.

FINANCIAL AID PICTURE (2007-2008)
Students with need: For part-time students, average financial aid package was $5,144.
Students without need: No-need awards available for academics, athletics, music/drama.

FINANCIAL AID PROCEDURES
Forms required: FAFSA, state aid form.
Dates and Deadlines: Priority date 6/1; no closing date. Applicants notified on a rolling basis starting 5/1.

CONTACT
Paula Halvorson, Director of Financial Aid
1255 South Range Avenue, Colby, KS 67701
(785) 460-4695

Cowley County Community College
Arkansas City, Kansas
www.cowley.edu   Federal Code: 001902

2-year public community and technical college in large town.
Enrollment: 4,280 undergrads, 49% part-time. 690 full-time freshmen.
Selectivity: Open admission; but selective for some programs.

BASIC COSTS (2007-2008)
Tuition and fees: $1,990; out-of-district residents $2,140; out-of-state residents $3,700.
Per-credit charge: $45; out-of-district residents $50; out-of-state residents $102.
Room and board: $3,600.
Additional info: Oklahoma border county resident tuition: $50 per-credit-hour.

FINANCIAL AID PICTURE (2007-2008)
Students with need: For part-time students, average financial aid package was $2,053.
Students without need: No-need awards available for academics, art, athletics, leadership, music/drama, state/district residency.

FINANCIAL AID PROCEDURES
Forms required: FAFSA.
Dates and Deadlines: Priority date 4/15; no closing date. Applicants notified on a rolling basis starting 1/15; must reply within 2 week(s) of notification.

CONTACT
Sally Palmer, Director of Financial Aid
PO Box 1147, Arkansas City, KS 67005-1147
(620) 442-0430 ext. 5248

Dodge City Community College

Dodge City, Kansas
www.dccc.cc.ks.us   Federal Code: 001913

2-year public community and technical college in large town.
Enrollment: 1,812 undergrads.
Selectivity: Open admission; but selective for some programs.

BASIC COSTS (2007-2008)

Tuition and fees: $1,950; out-of-state residents $2,850.
Per-credit charge: $35; out-of-state residents $45.
Room and board: $4,210.

FINANCIAL AID PICTURE

Students with need: Need-based aid available for full-time and part-time students. Work study available nights, weekends, and for part-time students.
Students without need: No-need awards available for academics, athletics, music/drama, state/district residency.

FINANCIAL AID PROCEDURES

Forms required: FAFSA, institutional form.
Dates and Deadlines: Priority date 3/15; no closing date. Applicants notified on a rolling basis; must reply within 2 week(s) of notification.

CONTACT

Anthony Lyons, Dean of Students
2501 North 14th Avenue, Dodge City, KS 67801-2399
(620) 227-9336

Donnelly College

Kansas City, Kansas
www.donnelly.edu   Federal Code: 001914

2-year private junior and liberal arts college in large city, affiliated with Roman Catholic Church.
Enrollment: 565 undergrads. 34 full-time freshmen.
Selectivity: Open admission.

BASIC COSTS (2007-2008)

Tuition and fees: $4,900.
Per-credit charge: $175.

FINANCIAL AID PICTURE (2006-2007)

Students with need: Out of 23 full-time freshmen who applied for aid, 23 were judged to have need. Of these, 23 received aid. Average financial aid package met 99% of need; average scholarship/grant was $2,384; average loan was $1,209. For part-time students, average financial aid package was $1,150.
Students without need: No-need awards available for academics.

FINANCIAL AID PROCEDURES

Forms required: FAFSA, institutional form.
Dates and Deadlines: Priority date 4/1; no closing date. Applicants notified on a rolling basis starting 7/1.
Transfers: Applicants notified on a rolling basis.

CONTACT

Belinda Ogan, Director of Financial Aid
608 North 18th Street, Kansas City, KS 66102-4210
(913) 621-8740

Emporia State University

Emporia, Kansas
www.emporia.edu   Federal Code: 001927

4-year public university and teachers college in large town.
Enrollment: 4,240 undergrads, 10% part-time. 727 full-time freshmen.
Selectivity: Admits over 75% of applicants.

BASIC COSTS (2007-2008)

Tuition and fees: $3,926; out-of-state residents $11,976.
Per-credit charge: $105; out-of-state residents $373.
Room and board: $5,582.

FINANCIAL AID PICTURE (2006-2007)

Students with need: Out of 682 full-time freshmen who applied for aid, 423 were judged to have need. Of these, 423 received aid, and 87 had their full need met. Average financial aid package met 70% of need; average scholarship/grant was $2,068; average loan was $2,530. For part-time students, average financial aid package was $4,277.
Students without need: 136 full-time freshmen who did not demonstrate need for aid received scholarships/grants; average award was $953. No-need awards available for academics, alumni affiliation, art, athletics, job skills, leadership, minority status, music/drama, religious affiliation, state/district residency.
Scholarships offered: *Merit:* Presidential Academic Awards; $1,000 to $1,200 (unlimited number) based on ACT. Challenge Awards; $500 (unlimited number) based on ACT/GPA. Transfer President's Academic Award; $500 to $1,000; based on cumulative GPA or Phi Theta Kappa membership. Guaranteed GPA Scholarship; $500 to $1,200; based on GPA for continuing full-time undergraduates. *Athletic:* 56 full-time freshmen received athletic scholarships; average amount $2,699.
Cumulative student debt: 70% of graduating class had student loans; average debt was $16,500.
Additional info: Institution's own payment plan is available.

FINANCIAL AID PROCEDURES

Forms required: FAFSA, state aid form.
Dates and Deadlines: Priority date 3/15; no closing date. Applicants notified on a rolling basis starting 2/2; must reply within 2 week(s) of notification.

CONTACT

M Henrie, Director of Financial Aid
1200 Commercial, Campus Box 4034, Emporia, KS 66801-5087
(620) 341-5457

Fort Hays State University

Hays, Kansas
www.fhsu.edu   Federal Code: 001915

4-year public university in large town.
Enrollment: 7,926 undergrads, 48% part-time. 759 full-time freshmen.
Selectivity: Admits over 75% of applicants.

BASIC COSTS (2007-2008)

Tuition and fees: $3,355; out-of-state residents $10,543.
Per-credit charge: $112; out-of-state residents $351.
Room and board: $5,878.

FINANCIAL AID PICTURE (2006-2007)

Students with need: Out of 533 full-time freshmen who applied for aid, 416 were judged to have need. Of these, 412 received aid, and 77 had their full need met. Average financial aid package met 66% of need; average scholarship/grant was $3,882; average loan was $2,278. For part-time students, average financial aid package was $5,135.
Students without need: 302 full-time freshmen who did not demonstrate need for aid received scholarships/grants; average award was $2,481. No-

need awards available for academics, art, athletics, leadership, minority status, music/drama.

Scholarships offered: 51 full-time freshmen received athletic scholarships; average amount $3,043.

Cumulative student debt: 51% of graduating class had student loans; average debt was $15,601.

FINANCIAL AID PROCEDURES

Forms required: FAFSA.

Dates and Deadlines: Priority date 3/15; no closing date. Applicants notified on a rolling basis starting 3/15; must reply within 2 week(s) of notification.

Transfers: No deadline. Applicants notified on a rolling basis starting 3/15; must reply within 3 week(s) of notification.

CONTACT

Craig Karlin, Director of Student Financial Aid
600 Park Street, Hays, KS 67601
(785) 628-4408

Friends University
Wichita, Kansas
www.friends.edu   Federal Code: 001918

4-year private business and liberal arts college in large city, affiliated with non-denominational tradition.

Enrollment: 1,354 undergrads.

BASIC COSTS (2008-2009)

Tuition and fees: $18,320.
Per-credit charge: $607.
Room and board: $5,450.

FINANCIAL AID PICTURE

Students with need: Need-based aid available for full-time and part-time students.

Students without need: No-need awards available for academics, alumni affiliation, art, athletics, leadership, music/drama.

Additional info: Scholarships for clergy/family of clergy available.

FINANCIAL AID PROCEDURES

Forms required: FAFSA, institutional form.

Dates and Deadlines: Priority date 3/15; no closing date. Applicants notified on a rolling basis; must reply within 3 week(s) of notification.

CONTACT

Brandon Pierce, Director of Financial Aid
2100 University, Wichita, KS 67213
(316) 295-5200

Garden City Community College
Garden City, Kansas
www.gccks.edu   Federal Code: 001919

2-year public community college in large town.

Enrollment: 1,067 undergrads.

Selectivity: Open admission; but selective for some programs.

BASIC COSTS (2007-2008)

Tuition and fees: $1,860; out-of-state residents $2,580.
Per-credit charge: $41; out-of-state residents $65.
Room and board: $4,250.

FINANCIAL AID PICTURE

Students with need: Need-based aid available for full-time and part-time students. Work study available nights, weekends, and for part-time students.

Students without need: No-need awards available for academics, art, athletics, leadership, minority status, music/drama, state/district residency.

FINANCIAL AID PROCEDURES

Forms required: FAFSA, institutional form.

Dates and Deadlines: Priority date 3/1; no closing date. Applicants notified on a rolling basis starting 4/15; must reply within 2 week(s) of notification.

CONTACT

Kathleen Blau, Director of Financial Aid
801 Campus Drive, Garden City, KS 67846-6333
(620) 276-9519

Haskell Indian Nations University
Lawrence, Kansas
www.haskell.edu   Federal Code: 010438

4-year public university in small city.

Enrollment: 889 undergrads.

BASIC COSTS (2007-2008)

Additional info: Haskell does not charge tuition. On-campus students pay $440 (includes room/board and required fees) for academic year; off-campus students pay $248 (required fees) for academic year.

FINANCIAL AID PICTURE

Students with need: Need-based aid available for full-time and part-time students. Work study available nights, weekends, and for part-time students.

Additional info: Some personal expenses may be offset by Bureau of Indian Affairs grants. Most students qualify for only minimum Pell grant.

FINANCIAL AID PROCEDURES

Forms required: FAFSA.

Dates and Deadlines: Priority date 5/15; no closing date. Applicants notified on a rolling basis starting 3/15; must reply within 9 week(s) of notification.

Transfers: Priority date 11/8; closing date 4/15.

CONTACT

Reta Beaver, Financial Aid Officer
155 Indian Avenue #5031, Lawrence, KS 66046-4800
(785) 830-2718

Hesston College
Hesston, Kansas
www.hesston.edu   Federal Code: 001920

2-year private junior college in small town, affiliated with Mennonite Church.

Enrollment: 420 undergrads, 9% part-time. 174 full-time freshmen.

Selectivity: Open admission; but selective for some programs.

BASIC COSTS (2007-2008)

Tuition and fees: $17,416.
Room and board: $6,180.

FINANCIAL AID PICTURE (2006-2007)

Students with need: Out of 164 full-time freshmen who applied for aid, 148 were judged to have need. Of these, 148 received aid, and 19 had their full need met. Average financial aid package met 80% of need; average scholarship/grant was $10,075; average loan was $3,600. Need-based aid available for part-time students.

Students without need: 27 full-time freshmen who did not demonstrate need for aid received scholarships/grants; average award was $1,500. No-need awards available for academics, alumni affiliation, athletics, job skills, music/drama.

Scholarships offered: 5 full-time freshmen received athletic scholarships; average amount $1,000.

FINANCIAL AID PROCEDURES

Forms required: FAFSA.

Dates and Deadlines: Priority date 4/1; no closing date. Applicants notified on a rolling basis starting 2/1; must reply within 4 week(s) of notification.

CONTACT

Marcia Mendez, Financial Aid Director
Box 3000, Hesston, KS 67062-2093
(800) 995-2757

Highland Community College

Highland, Kansas
www.highlandcc.edu   Federal Code: 001921

2-year public community college in rural community.
Enrollment: 1,329 undergrads, 26% part-time. 435 full-time freshmen.
Selectivity: Open admission; but selective for out-of-state students.

BASIC COSTS (2007-2008)

Tuition and fees: $1,890; out-of-district residents $2,280; out-of-state residents $3,810.
Per-credit charge: $37; out-of-district residents $50; out-of-state residents $101.
Room and board: $4,550.
Additional info: Out-of-state within 150 miles: $63 per-credit-hour.

FINANCIAL AID PICTURE (2007-2008)

Students with need: 50% of average financial aid package awarded as scholarships/grants, 50% awarded as loans/jobs. Need-based aid available for part-time students. Work study available nights, weekends, and for part-time students.
Students without need: No-need awards available for academics, alumni affiliation, art, athletics, leadership, minority status, music/drama.
Additional info: Auditions and portfolios important for certain scholarship candidates.

FINANCIAL AID PROCEDURES

Forms required: FAFSA, institutional form.
Dates and Deadlines: Priority date 4/1; no closing date. Applicants notified on a rolling basis starting 4/15; must reply within 14 week(s) of notification.

CONTACT

Kelly Twombly, Director of Student Financial Aid
606 West Main Street, Highland, KS 66035-0068
(785) 442-6023

Hutchinson Community College

Hutchinson, Kansas
www.hutchcc.edu   Federal Code: 001923

2-year public community college in large town.
Enrollment: 3,447 undergrads, 40% part-time. 800 full-time freshmen.
Selectivity: Open admission; but selective for some programs.

BASIC COSTS (2007-2008)

Tuition and fees: $2,070; out-of-state residents $3,090.
Per-credit charge: $54; out-of-state residents $88.
Room and board: $4,640.

FINANCIAL AID PICTURE

Students with need: Need-based aid available for full-time and part-time students.
Students without need: No-need awards available for academics, athletics, minority status, state/district residency.

FINANCIAL AID PROCEDURES

Forms required: FAFSA, institutional form.
Dates and Deadlines: Priority date 2/1; no closing date. Applicants notified on a rolling basis starting 4/1; must reply within 2 week(s) of notification.

CONTACT

Ron Menefee, Financial Aid Director
1300 North Plum, Hutchinson, KS 67501
(620) 665-3400

Independence Community College

Independence, Kansas
www.indycc.edu   Federal Code: 001924

2-year public community and junior college in large town.
Enrollment: 676 undergrads.
Selectivity: Open admission.

BASIC COSTS (2007-2008)

Tuition and fees: $1,650; out-of-district residents $1,650; out-of-state residents $2,850.
Per-credit charge: $25; out-of-district residents $28; out-of-state residents $68.
Room and board: $4,200.

FINANCIAL AID PICTURE

Students with need: Need-based aid available for full-time and part-time students.
Students without need: No-need awards available for academics, athletics.

FINANCIAL AID PROCEDURES

Forms required: FAFSA.
Dates and Deadlines: Priority date 4/1; no closing date. Applicants notified on a rolling basis.

CONTACT

Sheila Smither, Director of Financial Aid
1057 West College Avenue, Independence, KS 67301

Johnson County Community College

Overland Park, Kansas
www.jccc.edu   Federal Code: 008244

2-year public community college in very large city.
Enrollment: 7,736 undergrads.
Selectivity: Open admission; but selective for some programs.

BASIC COSTS (2007-2008)

Tuition and fees: $1,890; out-of-district residents $2,340; out-of-state residents $4,320.
Per-credit charge: $63; out-of-district residents $78; out-of-state residents $144.

FINANCIAL AID PICTURE

Students with need: Need-based aid available for full-time and part-time students.
Students without need: No-need awards available for academics.

FINANCIAL AID PROCEDURES

Forms required: FAFSA, state aid form.
Dates and Deadlines: Priority date 4/1; no closing date. Applicants notified on a rolling basis starting 4/15; must reply within 2 week(s) of notification.

CONTACT

Chris Christensen, Program Director for Student Financial Aid
12345 College Boulevard, Overland Park, KS 66210-1299
(913) 469-3840

Kansas City Kansas Community College

Kansas City, Kansas
www.kckcc.edu   Federal Code: 001925

2-year public community and junior college in very large city.

Enrollment: 4,339 undergrads, 58% part-time. 528 full-time freshmen.

Selectivity: Open admission; but selective for some programs.

BASIC COSTS (2007-2008)

Tuition and fees: $1,770; out-of-state residents $4,710.

Per-credit charge: $49; out-of-state residents $147.

Additional info: Fees vary by program.

FINANCIAL AID PICTURE (2006-2007)

Students with need: 44% of average financial aid package awarded as scholarships/grants, 56% awarded as loans/jobs. Need-based aid available for part-time students. Work study available nights, weekends, and for part-time students.

Students without need: No-need awards available for academics, art, athletics, music/drama.

FINANCIAL AID PROCEDURES

Forms required: FAFSA.

Dates and Deadlines: Priority date 4/15; no closing date. Applicants notified on a rolling basis starting 5/1; must reply within 4 week(s) of notification.

CONTACT

Mary Dorr, Director of Financial Aid

7250 State Avenue, Kansas City, KS 66112

(913) 288-7697

Kansas State University

Manhattan, Kansas
www.ksu.edu   Federal Code: 001928

4-year public university and technical college in large town.

Enrollment: 18,235 undergrads, 11% part-time. 3,521 full-time freshmen.

Selectivity: Admits over 75% of applicants.

BASIC COSTS (2007-2008)

Tuition and fees: $6,235; out-of-state residents $15,970.

Per-credit charge: $188; out-of-state residents $512.

Room and board: $6,084.

FINANCIAL AID PICTURE (2006-2007)

Students with need: Out of 2,595 full-time freshmen who applied for aid, 1,789 were judged to have need. Of these, 1,720 received aid, and 293 had their full need met. Average financial aid package met 83% of need; average scholarship/grant was $4,152; average loan was $2,898. For part-time students, average financial aid package was $5,031.

Students without need: 521 full-time freshmen who did not demonstrate need for aid received scholarships/grants; average award was $3,449. No-need awards available for academics, alumni affiliation, art, athletics, leadership, music/drama, ROTC, state/district residency.

Scholarships offered: 88 full-time freshmen received athletic scholarships; average amount $8,315.

FINANCIAL AID PROCEDURES

Forms required: FAFSA.

Dates and Deadlines: Priority date 3/1; no closing date. Applicants notified on a rolling basis starting 4/1; must reply within 2 week(s) of notification.

CONTACT

Larry Moeder, Director of Student Financial Assistance

119 Anderson Hall, Manhattan, KS 66506

(785) 532-6420

Kansas Wesleyan University

Salina, Kansas
www.kwu.edu   Federal Code: 001929

4-year private liberal arts college in large town, affiliated with United Methodist Church.

Enrollment: 802 undergrads.

BASIC COSTS (2007-2008)

Tuition and fees: $17,400.

Room and board: $6,000.

Additional info: $200 per-credit-hour charge for 1-5 credit hours; $1,800 per semester for 6-8 credit hours; $3,600 per semester for 9-11 credit hours. Tuition/fee waivers available for adults.

FINANCIAL AID PICTURE

Students with need: Need-based aid available for full-time and part-time students.

Students without need: No-need awards available for academics, alumni affiliation, art, athletics, music/drama, state/district residency.

Additional info: Awards available for residence hall students: minimum $7,000 for 3.0 GPA plus ACT score of 22 or SAT of 950 (exclusive of Writing); minimum $8,000 for 3.5 GPA plus ACT score of 22 or SAT score of 1030 (exclusive of Writing); minimum $9,000 for 3.75 GPA plus ACT score of 25 or SAT score of 1140 (exclusive of Writing). Application deadline March 15.

FINANCIAL AID PROCEDURES

Forms required: FAFSA.

Dates and Deadlines: Closing date 3/15. Applicants notified on a rolling basis starting 1/1; must reply by 8/1 or within 3 week(s) of notification.

Transfers: Academic scholarships based upon cumulative GPA of transferring credit hours.

CONTACT

Glenna Alexander, Director of Financial Assistance

100 East Claflin Avenue, Salina, KS 67401-6196

(785) 827-5541 ext. 1130

Labette Community College

Parsons, Kansas
www.labette.edu   Federal Code: 001930

2-year public community college in large town.

Enrollment: 934 undergrads, 54% part-time. 108 full-time freshmen.

Selectivity: Open admission; but selective for some programs.

BASIC COSTS (2007-2008)

Tuition and fees: $2,130; out-of-state residents $2,880.

Per-credit charge: $42; out-of-state residents $67.

Additional info: Residents of neighboring states (AR, MO, OK) pay per-credit-hour tuition rate of $63. Tuition/fee waivers available for adults, minority students, unemployed or children of unemployed.

FINANCIAL AID PICTURE

Students with need: Need-based aid available for full-time and part-time students. Work study available nights.

Students without need: No-need awards available for academics, leadership.

Scholarships offered: Foundation Scholarships.

FINANCIAL AID PROCEDURES

Forms required: FAFSA.

Dates and Deadlines: No deadline. Applicants notified on a rolling basis starting 4/4; must reply within 2 week(s) of notification.

CONTACT

Kathy Johnston, Director of Financial Aid

200 South 14th Street, Parsons, KS 67357

(620) 820-1219

Manhattan Area Technical College

Manhattan, Kansas

www.matc.net   Federal Code: 005500

2-year public technical college in large town.

Enrollment: 400 undergrads.

Selectivity: Open admission; but selective for some programs.

BASIC COSTS (2007-2008)

Tuition and fees: $2,250.

Per-credit charge: $63.

FINANCIAL AID PICTURE

Students with need: Need-based aid available for full-time and part-time students.

Students without need: No-need awards available for academics, leadership.

FINANCIAL AID PROCEDURES

Forms required: FAFSA, institutional form.

Dates and Deadlines: No deadline. Applicants notified on a rolling basis.

CONTACT

Kelly Hoggatt, Director of Financial Aid/Registrar

3136 Dickens Avenue, Manhattan, KS 66503-2499

(785) 587-2800 ext. 105

Manhattan Christian College

Manhattan, Kansas

www.mccks.edu   Federal Code: 001931

4-year private Bible college in large town, affiliated with Christian Church.

Enrollment: 380 undergrads.

BASIC COSTS (2007-2008)

Tuition and fees: $10,412.

Per-credit charge: $428.

Room and board: $6,400.

Additional info: Additional $6 required fee per-credit-hour, up to $72; $140 per-credit-hour charge for part-time, non-degree-seeking students. Part time non-degree and/or audit at $170 per-credit-hour.

FINANCIAL AID PICTURE

Students with need: Need-based aid available for full-time and part-time students.

Students without need: No-need awards available for academics, leadership.

FINANCIAL AID PROCEDURES

Forms required: FAFSA.

Dates and Deadlines: Priority date 4/1; no closing date. Applicants notified on a rolling basis starting 5/1; must reply within 2 week(s) of notification.

CONTACT

Margaret Carlisle, Director of Financial Aid

1415 Anderson Avenue, Manhattan, KS 66502

(785) 539-3571

McPherson College

McPherson, Kansas

www.mcpherson.edu   Federal Code: 001933

4-year private liberal arts college in large town, affiliated with Church of the Brethren.

Enrollment: 531 undergrads, 6% part-time. 134 full-time freshmen.

Selectivity: Admits over 75% of applicants.

BASIC COSTS (2008-2009)

Tuition and fees: $17,200.

Room and board: $6,500.

FINANCIAL AID PICTURE (2007-2008)

Students with need: Out of 130 full-time freshmen who applied for aid, 109 were judged to have need. Of these, 109 received aid, and 20 had their full need met. Average financial aid package met 87% of need; average scholarship/grant was $5,016; average loan was $5,416. For part-time students, average financial aid package was $6,215.

Students without need: 24 full-time freshmen who did not demonstrate need for aid received scholarships/grants; average award was $8,696. No-need awards available for academics, alumni affiliation, art, athletics, music/drama, religious affiliation, state/district residency.

Scholarships offered: Presidential Scholarship; $10,000 each year of attendance for four years; competition in fall and spring; 10 awards given per year.

Cumulative student debt: 91% of graduating class had student loans; average debt was $24,690.

FINANCIAL AID PROCEDURES

Forms required: FAFSA.

Dates and Deadlines: Priority date 3/1; no closing date. Applicants notified on a rolling basis starting 3/1; must reply within 3 week(s) of notification.

Transfers: No deadline. Applicants notified on a rolling basis; must reply within 3 week(s) of notification.

CONTACT

Steve Frick, Director of Financial Aid

1600 East Euclid Street, McPherson, KS 67460-1402

(620) 241-0731

MidAmerica Nazarene University

Olathe, Kansas

www.mnu.edu   Federal Code: 007032

4-year private university and liberal arts college in small city, affiliated with Church of the Nazarene.

Enrollment: 1,283 undergrads, 11% part-time. 216 full-time freshmen.

Selectivity: Admits over 75% of applicants.

BASIC COSTS (2008-2009)

Tuition and fees: $18,216.

Per-credit charge: $576.

Room and board: $6,480.

FINANCIAL AID PICTURE (2007-2008)

Students with need: Out of 196 full-time freshmen who applied for aid, 176 were judged to have need. Of these, 176 received aid, and 32 had their full need met. Average financial aid package met 73% of need; average scholarship/grant was $3,911; average loan was $4,679. For part-time students, average financial aid package was $6,183.

Students without need: 40 full-time freshmen who did not demonstrate need for aid received scholarships/grants; average award was $8,426. No-need awards available for academics, art, athletics, leadership, minority status, music/drama, religious affiliation, ROTC, state/district residency.

Scholarships offered: 100 full-time freshmen received athletic scholarships; average amount $4,289.

Cumulative student debt: 77% of graduating class had student loans; average debt was $28,678.

FINANCIAL AID PROCEDURES

Forms required: FAFSA, institutional form.

Dates and Deadlines: Priority date 3/1; no closing date. Applicants notified on a rolling basis starting 2/1; must reply within 2 week(s) of notification.

CONTACT

Rhonda Cole, Director of Student Financial Services
2030 East College Way, Olathe, KS 66062-1899
(913) 791-3298

Neosho County Community College
Chanute, Kansas
www.neosho.edu   Federal Code: 001936

2-year public community college in small town.

Enrollment: 1,994 undergrads.

Selectivity: Open admission; but selective for some programs.

BASIC COSTS (2007-2008)

Tuition and fees: $1,860; out-of-district residents $2,460; out-of-state residents $2,910.

Per-credit charge: $40.

Room and board: $3,940.

FINANCIAL AID PICTURE

Students with need: Need-based aid available for full-time and part-time students. Work study available nights, weekends, and for part-time students.

Students without need: No-need awards available for academics, art, athletics, music/drama, state/district residency.

Scholarships offered: Visual and performing arts, Academic Challenge stipends, industrial engineering and business scholarship.

FINANCIAL AID PROCEDURES

Forms required: FAFSA.

Dates and Deadlines: Priority date 4/1; no closing date. Applicants notified on a rolling basis; must reply within 6 week(s) of notification.

Transfers: All academic transcripts and financial aid transcripts must be on file before aid will be awarded.

CONTACT

Kerrie Coomes, Director of Financial Aid
800 West 14th Street, Chanute, KS 66720
(620) 431-2820 ext. 278

Newman University
Wichita, Kansas
www.newmanu.edu   Federal Code: 001939

4-year private university and liberal arts college in large city, affiliated with Roman Catholic Church.

Enrollment: 1,116 undergrads, 15% part-time. 124 full-time freshmen.

Selectivity: Admits 50 to 75% of applicants.

BASIC COSTS (2007-2008)

Tuition and fees: $17,988.

Per-credit charge: $589.

Room and board: $5,442.

Additional info: Tuition/fee waivers available for adults.

FINANCIAL AID PICTURE (2007-2008)

Students with need: Average financial aid package met 67% of need; average scholarship/grant was $4,255; average loan was $2,250. For part-time students, average financial aid package was $5,162.

Students without need: No-need awards available for academics, alumni affiliation, art, athletics, leadership, music/drama, religious affiliation.

Scholarships offered: Full tuition to any National Merit Finalist.

Cumulative student debt: 72% of graduating class had student loans; average debt was $24,308.

FINANCIAL AID PROCEDURES

Forms required: FAFSA, institutional form.

Dates and Deadlines: Priority date 3/1; no closing date. Applicants notified on a rolling basis starting 2/1.

CONTACT

Brenda Krehbiel, Director of Financial Aid
3100 McCormick, Wichita, KS 67213-2097
(316) 942-4291

North Central Kansas Technical College
Beloit, Kansas
www.ncktc.edu   Federal Code: 005265

2-year public technical college in small town.

Enrollment: 260 undergrads.

Selectivity: Open admission.

BASIC COSTS (2007-2008)

Tuition and fees: $3,171.

Room and board: $3,950.

FINANCIAL AID PICTURE

Students with need: Need-based aid available for full-time and part-time students. Work study available nights.

Students without need: This college awards aid only to students with need.

FINANCIAL AID PROCEDURES

Forms required: FAFSA, state aid form.

Dates and Deadlines: No deadline.

CONTACT

Gary Odle, Financial Aid Director
P.O. Box 507, Beloit, KS 67420
(800) 658-4655

Ottawa University
Ottawa, Kansas
www.ottawa.edu   Federal Code: 001937

4-year private liberal arts college in large town, affiliated with American Baptist Churches in the USA.

Enrollment: 484 undergrads.

Selectivity: Admits 50 to 75% of applicants.

BASIC COSTS (2007-2008)

Tuition and fees: $17,350.

Per-credit charge: $565.

Room and board: $5,930.

FINANCIAL AID PICTURE

Students with need: Need-based aid available for full-time and part-time students. Work study available nights, weekends, and for part-time students.

Students without need: No-need awards available for academics, alumni affiliation, athletics, music/drama, religious affiliation.

FINANCIAL AID PROCEDURES

Forms required: FAFSA.

Dates and Deadlines: Priority date 3/15; no closing date. Applicants notified on a rolling basis starting 2/1; must reply within 4 week(s) of notification.

Transfers: No deadline.

CONTACT

Gary Bateman, Financial Aid Administrator

1001 South Cedar Street, #17, Ottawa, KS 66067-3399

(785) 242-5200 ext. 5571

Pittsburg State University

Pittsburg, Kansas

www.pittstate.edu   Federal Code: 001926

4-year public university in large town.

Enrollment: 5,824 undergrads, 8% part-time. 899 full-time freshmen.

Selectivity: Admits over 75% of applicants.

BASIC COSTS (2007-2008)

Tuition and fees: $4,060; out-of-state residents $11,866.

Per-credit charge: $108; out-of-state residents $368.

Room and board: $5,088.

FINANCIAL AID PICTURE (2007-2008)

Students with need: Out of 836 full-time freshmen who applied for aid, 596 were judged to have need. Of these, 563 received aid, and 67 had their full need met. Average financial aid package met 86% of need; average scholarship/grant was $4,046; average loan was $3,402. For part-time students, average financial aid package was $4,309.

Students without need: 214 full-time freshmen who did not demonstrate need for aid received scholarships/grants; average award was $1,581. No-need awards available for academics, alumni affiliation, art, athletics, leadership, music/drama, ROTC.

Scholarships offered: 29 full-time freshmen received athletic scholarships; average amount $2,686.

Cumulative student debt: 69% of graduating class had student loans; average debt was $15,776.

FINANCIAL AID PROCEDURES

Forms required: FAFSA, state aid form, institutional form.

Dates and Deadlines: Priority date 3/1; no closing date. Applicants notified on a rolling basis; must reply within 2 week(s) of notification.

Transfers: Transfer student scholarships available.

CONTACT

Marilyn Haverly, Director of Student Financial Assistance

1701 South Broadway, Pittsburg, KS 66762

(620) 235-4240

Pratt Community College

Pratt, Kansas

www.prattcc.edu   Federal Code: 001938

2-year public community and technical college in small town.

Enrollment: 778 undergrads, 16% part-time. 270 full-time freshmen.

Selectivity: Open admission; but selective for some programs.

BASIC COSTS (2007-2008)

Tuition and fees: $2,190; out-of-state residents $2,190.

Per-credit charge: $44; out-of-state residents $44.

Room and board: $4,421.

Additional info: Out-of-district Kansas residents have additional fee of $100; out-of-state $200, and international students $300 for the year. Technology fee applicable for auto, ag power, and electrical power areas.

FINANCIAL AID PICTURE (2006-2007)

Students with need: 56% of average financial aid package awarded as scholarships/grants, 44% awarded as loans/jobs. Need-based aid available for part-time students.

Students without need: No-need awards available for academics, art, athletics, leadership, minority status, music/drama, state/district residency.

FINANCIAL AID PROCEDURES

Forms required: FAFSA, institutional form.

Dates and Deadlines: Priority date 5/1; closing date 8/1. Applicants notified on a rolling basis starting 2/1; must reply within 2 week(s) of notification.

CONTACT

Debbie Boley, Director of Financial Aid

348 Northeast State Road 61, Pratt, KS 67124-8317

(620) 672-9800 ext. 248

Seward County Community College

Liberal, Kansas

www.sccc.edu   Federal Code: 008228

2-year public community college in large town.

Enrollment: 1,387 undergrads.

Selectivity: Open admission; but selective for some programs.

BASIC COSTS (2007-2008)

Tuition and fees: $1,860; out-of-state residents $2,550.

Per-credit charge: $40; out-of-state residents $63.

Room and board: $4,100.

Additional info: Residents of neighboring counties in OK, TX and CO pay per-credit-hour rate of $50.

FINANCIAL AID PICTURE (2006-2007)

Students with need: 42% of average financial aid package awarded as scholarships/grants, 58% awarded as loans/jobs. Need-based aid available for part-time students.

Students without need: No-need awards available for academics, athletics.

FINANCIAL AID PROCEDURES

Forms required: FAFSA, institutional form.

Dates and Deadlines: Priority date 4/1; no closing date. Applicants notified on a rolling basis starting 6/15; must reply within 4 week(s) of notification.

CONTACT

Donna Fisher, Financial Aid Director

1801 North Kansas Avenue, Liberal, KS 67905-1137

(620) 417-1110

Southwestern College

Winfield, Kansas

www.sckans.edu   Federal Code: 001940

4-year private liberal arts college in large town, affiliated with United Methodist Church.

Enrollment: 1,415 undergrads, 60% part-time. 138 full-time freshmen.

Selectivity: Admits over 75% of applicants.

BASIC COSTS (2008-2009)

Tuition and fees: $18,700.

Per-credit charge: $775.

Room and board: $5,622.

FINANCIAL AID PICTURE (2007-2008)

Students with need: Out of 124 full-time freshmen who applied for aid, 109 were judged to have need. Of these, 109 received aid, and 25 had their full need met. Average financial aid package met 84% of need; average scholarship/grant was $12,073; average loan was $4,782. For part-time students, average financial aid package was $5,570.

Students without need: 28 full-time freshmen who did not demonstrate need for aid received scholarships/grants; average award was $9,200. No-

need awards available for academics, alumni affiliation, athletics, leadership, minority status, music/drama, religious affiliation.

Scholarships offered: Merit: Presidential Scholarship based on GPA, SAT/ACT scores, essay, resume, leadership, community service. Scholarships for major based on GPA, SAT scores, essay, interview; 3 awarded. **Athletic:** 10 full-time freshmen received athletic scholarships; average amount $3,200.

Cumulative student debt: 82% of graduating class had student loans; average debt was $20,589.

Additional info: Academic and activity grants available.

FINANCIAL AID PROCEDURES

Forms required: FAFSA, institutional form.

Dates and Deadlines: Priority date 4/1; closing date 8/15. Applicants notified on a rolling basis starting 2/1; must reply within 2 week(s) of notification.

Transfers: Activity grants and scholarships, except for presidential scholarship and premier scholarships, available to transfer students. Phi Theta Kappa scholarship available for transfer students who are members.

CONTACT

Brenda Hicks, Director of Financial Aid
100 College Street, Winfield, KS 67156
(620) 229-6215

Sterling College

Sterling, Kansas
www.sterling.edu   Federal Code: 001945

4-year private liberal arts college in rural community, affiliated with Presbyterian Church (USA).

Enrollment: 569 undergrads, 4% part-time. 197 full-time freshmen.

Selectivity: Admits 50 to 75% of applicants.

BASIC COSTS (2008-2009)

Tuition and fees: $16,700.

Room and board: $6,230.

Additional info: $335 per credit hour charge for 1 to 6 credits.

FINANCIAL AID PICTURE (2006-2007)

Students with need: Out of 86 full-time freshmen who applied for aid, 68 were judged to have need. Of these, 68 received aid, and 13 had their full need met. Average financial aid package met 77% of need; average scholarship/grant was $8,551; average loan was $2,988. For part-time students, average financial aid package was $14,547.

Students without need: 15 full-time freshmen who did not demonstrate need for aid received scholarships/grants; average award was $7,507. No-need awards available for academics, alumni affiliation, art, athletics, leadership, minority status, music/drama, religious affiliation, state/district residency.

Scholarships offered: 9 full-time freshmen received athletic scholarships; average amount $6,267.

Cumulative student debt: 68% of graduating class had student loans; average debt was $16,200.

FINANCIAL AID PROCEDURES

Forms required: FAFSA.

Dates and Deadlines: Priority date 4/1; no closing date. Applicants notified on a rolling basis starting 1/1; must reply within 3 week(s) of notification.

Transfers: Applicants notified on a rolling basis; must reply within 2 week(s) of notification.

CONTACT

Tricia Brothers, Financial Aid Coordinator
125 West Cooper, Sterling, KS 67579
(620) 278-4207

Tabor College

Hillsboro, Kansas
www.tabor.edu   Federal Code: 001946

4-year private liberal arts college in small town, affiliated with Mennonite Brethren Church.

Enrollment: 561 undergrads, 17% part-time. 120 full-time freshmen.

BASIC COSTS (2007-2008)

Tuition and fees: $17,650.

Per-credit charge: $720.

Room and board: $6,250.

Additional info: Tuition/fee waivers available for adults.

FINANCIAL AID PICTURE (2007-2008)

Students with need: Out of 120 full-time freshmen who applied for aid, 99 were judged to have need. Of these, 99 received aid, and 21 had their full need met. Average financial aid package met 79% of need; average scholarship/grant was $4,103; average loan was $5,567. For part-time students, average financial aid package was $9,293.

Students without need: 21 full-time freshmen who did not demonstrate need for aid received scholarships/grants; average award was $5,247. No-need awards available for academics, alumni affiliation, athletics, music/drama, religious affiliation, state/district residency.

Scholarships offered: 71 full-time freshmen received athletic scholarships; average amount $3,908.

Cumulative student debt: 83% of graduating class had student loans; average debt was $24,111.

FINANCIAL AID PROCEDURES

Forms required: FAFSA, state aid form.

Dates and Deadlines: Priority date 3/1; closing date 8/30. Applicants notified on a rolling basis starting 3/15; must reply within 4 week(s) of notification.

Transfers: Transfer students not eligible for Presidential, National Merit or Dean's scholarships.

CONTACT

Scott Franz, Director of Student Financial Assistance
400 South Jefferson, Hillsboro, KS 67063-1799
(620) 947-3121 ext. 1726

University of Kansas

Lawrence, Kansas
www.ku.edu   Federal Code: 001948

4-year public university in small city.

Enrollment: 19,943 undergrads, 10% part-time. 4,094 full-time freshmen.

Selectivity: Admits over 75% of applicants.

BASIC COSTS (2007-2008)

Tuition and fees: $7,146; out-of-state residents $17,556.

Per-credit charge: $213; out-of-state residents $560.

Room and board: $6,144.

Additional info: Tuition at time of enrollment locked for 4 years.

FINANCIAL AID PICTURE (2006-2007)

Students with need: Out of 3,222 full-time freshmen who applied for aid, 1,547 were judged to have need. Of these, 1,468 received aid, and 383 had their full need met. Average financial aid package met 60% of need; average scholarship/grant was $3,974; average loan was $2,257. For part-time students, average financial aid package was $5,663.

Students without need: 876 full-time freshmen who did not demonstrate need for aid received scholarships/grants; average award was $3,087. No-need awards available for academics, alumni affiliation, art, athletics, leadership, minority status, music/drama, ROTC, state/district residency.

Scholarships offered: 88 full-time freshmen received athletic scholarships; average amount $13,166.

Cumulative student debt: 47% of graduating class had student loans; average debt was $20,325.

Additional info: Work study available weekdays.

FINANCIAL AID PROCEDURES

Forms required: FAFSA.

Dates and Deadlines: Priority date 3/1; no closing date. Applicants notified on a rolling basis starting 4/1; must reply within 2 week(s) of notification.

CONTACT

Brenda Maigaard, Director of Student Financial Aid

1502 Iowa Street, Lawrence, KS 66045-7576

(785) 864-4700

University of Kansas Medical Center

Kansas City, Kansas

www.kumc.edu   Federal Code: 004605

Upper-division public university and health science college in small city.

Enrollment: 512 undergrads, 22% part-time.

Selectivity: Open admission; but selective for some programs.

BASIC COSTS (2007-2008)

Tuition and fees: $6,194; out-of-state residents $15,701.

Per-credit charge: $195; out-of-state residents $512.

Additional info: Annual tuition for medical students: $22,486 (residents) and $39,877 (nonresidents); required fees are $332. Tuition at time of enrollment locked for 2 years.

FINANCIAL AID PICTURE (2006-2007)

Students with need: Average financial aid package for all full-time undergraduates was $8,588; for part-time $8,897. 45% awarded as scholarships/grants, 55% awarded as loans/jobs. Work study available nights, weekends, and for part-time students.

Students without need: No-need awards available for academics, leadership, minority status, state/district residency.

FINANCIAL AID PROCEDURES

Dates and Deadlines: No deadline.

Transfers: Priority date 2/14; no deadline. Applicants notified on a rolling basis starting 4/1.

CONTACT

Sara Honeck, Director of Student Financial Aid

3901 Rainbow Boulevard, Kansas City, KS 66160-7116

(913) 588-5170

University of St. Mary

Leavenworth, Kansas

www.stmary.edu   Federal Code: 001943

4-year private university in large town, affiliated with Roman Catholic Church.

Enrollment: 475 undergrads, 14% part-time. 66 full-time freshmen.

Selectivity: Admits 50 to 75% of applicants.

BASIC COSTS (2008-2009)

Tuition and fees: $18,120.

Per-credit charge: $580.

Room and board: $6,400.

FINANCIAL AID PICTURE (2007-2008)

Students with need: Out of 66 full-time freshmen who applied for aid, 51 were judged to have need. Of these, 51 received aid, and 14 had their full need met. Average financial aid package met 47% of need; average scholarship/grant was $7,434; average loan was $3,814. For part-time students, average financial aid package was $5,161.

Students without need: 9 full-time freshmen who did not demonstrate need for aid received scholarships/grants; average award was $10,282. No-need awards available for academics, art, athletics, leadership, music/drama.

Scholarships offered: 30 full-time freshmen received athletic scholarships; average amount $2,394.

Cumulative student debt: 88% of graduating class had student loans; average debt was $19,000.

Additional info: Essays may be required for scholarship applicants. Auditions recommended for music and drama scholarship applicants. Portfolio reviews for art award applicants.

FINANCIAL AID PROCEDURES

Forms required: FAFSA.

Dates and Deadlines: Priority date 4/1; no closing date. Applicants notified on a rolling basis starting 2/8; must reply within 2 week(s) of notification.

Transfers: No deadline. Applicants notified on a rolling basis; must reply within 2 week(s) of notification.

CONTACT

Judy Wiedower, Director of Financial Aid

4100 South Fourth Street Trafficway, Leavenworth, KS 66048

(913) 682-5151 ext. 6450

Washburn University

Topeka, Kansas

www.washburn.edu   Federal Code: 001949

4-year public university in small city.

Enrollment: 5,675 undergrads, 29% part-time. 665 full-time freshmen.

Selectivity: Open admission; but selective for some programs.

BASIC COSTS (2007-2008)

Tuition and fees: $5,636; out-of-state residents $12,686.

Per-credit charge: $185; out-of-state residents $420.

Room and board: $5,281.

FINANCIAL AID PICTURE (2007-2008)

Students with need: Out of 591 full-time freshmen who applied for aid, 405 were judged to have need. Of these, 405 received aid, and 52 had their full need met. Average financial aid package met 40% of need; average scholarship/grant was $3,464; average loan was $3,391. For part-time students, average financial aid package was $6,755.

Students without need: 102 full-time freshmen who did not demonstrate need for aid received scholarships/grants; average award was $2,078. No-need awards available for academics, alumni affiliation, art, athletics, job skills, leadership, minority status, music/drama, religious affiliation, ROTC, state/district residency.

Scholarships offered: 24 full-time freshmen received athletic scholarships; average amount $5,676.

Cumulative student debt: 66% of graduating class had student loans; average debt was $17,400.

FINANCIAL AID PROCEDURES

Forms required: FAFSA.

Dates and Deadlines: Priority date 2/15; no closing date. Applicants notified on a rolling basis starting 3/15; must reply within 4 week(s) of notification.

Transfers: No deadline. Applicants notified on a rolling basis starting 3/15; must reply within 4 week(s) of notification.

CONTACT

Annita Huff, Director of Financial Aid

1700 Southwest College, Morgan 114, Topeka, KS 66621

(785) 670-1151

Wichita State University

Wichita, Kansas

www.wichita.edu

Federal Code: 001950

4-year public university in large city.

Enrollment: 10,261 undergrads, 29% part-time. 1,259 full-time freshmen.

Selectivity: Admits over 75% of applicants.

BASIC COSTS (2007-2008)

Tuition and fees: $4,804; out-of-state residents $12,151.

Per-credit charge: $130; out-of-state residents $375.

Room and board: $5,580.

FINANCIAL AID PICTURE (2006-2007)

Students with need: Out of 1,069 full-time freshmen who applied for aid, 570 were judged to have need. Of these, 546 received aid. Average financial aid package met 47% of need; average scholarship/grant was $3,178; average loan was $2,268. For part-time students, average financial aid package was $6,882.

Students without need: 355 full-time freshmen who did not demonstrate need for aid received scholarships/grants; average award was $2,777. No-need awards available for academics, alumni affiliation, art, athletics, leadership, music/drama.

Scholarships offered: 17 full-time freshmen received athletic scholarships; average amount $8,865.

Cumulative student debt: 61% of graduating class had student loans; average debt was $20,875.

Additional info: Top freshman applicants admitted by October 1 invited to university scholarship competition.

FINANCIAL AID PROCEDURES

Forms required: FAFSA, state aid form.

Dates and Deadlines: Priority date 3/1; no closing date. Applicants notified on a rolling basis starting 3/15; must reply within 2 week(s) of notification.

CONTACT

Deborah Byers, Director of Financial Aid

1845 Fairmount Box 124, Wichita, KS 67260-0124

(316) 978-3430

Kentucky

Alice Lloyd College

Pippa Passes, Kentucky

www.alc.edu

Federal Code: 001951

4-year private liberal arts college in rural community.

Enrollment: 607 undergrads, 2% part-time. 201 full-time freshmen.

Selectivity: Admits less than 50% of applicants.

BASIC COSTS (2007-2008)

Tuition and fees: $8,250.

Per-credit charge: $212.

Room and board: $4,050.

Additional info: Guaranteed tuition for students from 108-county central Appalachian service area in Kentucky, West Virginia, Virginia, Tennessee, and Ohio. Tuition/fee waivers available for minority students.

FINANCIAL AID PICTURE (2006-2007)

Students with need: Out of 201 full-time freshmen who applied for aid, 173 were judged to have need. Of these, 173 received aid, and 46 had their full need met. Average financial aid package met 73% of need; average scholarship/grant was $6,331; average loan was $276. Need-based aid available for part-time students.

Students without need: 28 full-time freshmen who did not demonstrate need for aid received scholarships/grants; average award was $8,046. No-need awards available for athletics, minority status, state/district residency.

Scholarships offered: *Merit:* Students meeting admissions criteria from one of 108 counties in West Virginia, Virginia, Tennessee, Ohio and Kentucky guaranteed free tuition of up to $3,180 per semester; based on admission application; no limit on awards given. Minority scholarships; tuition, room, and board; offered to students from 108 service areas. Alice Lloyd Scholars Program; tuition, room, board, fees, and books; awarded to up to 3 freshmen a year. *Athletic:* 8 full-time freshmen received athletic scholarships; average amount $5,717.

Cumulative student debt: 23% of graduating class had student loans; average debt was $5,379.

Additional info: All students receive financial aid through student work program. No student denied admission because of inability to pay. All full-time students required to work minimum of 10 hours per week.

FINANCIAL AID PROCEDURES

Forms required: FAFSA.

Dates and Deadlines: Priority date 3/15; no closing date. Applicants notified on a rolling basis starting 4/1; must reply within 6 week(s) of notification.

Transfers: Closing date 3/15. Tuition guarantee only for total of 10 semesters of course work from all schools attended.

CONTACT

Barbara Begley, Director of Financial Aid

100 Purpose Road, Pippa Passes, KY 41844

(606) 368-6058

Asbury College

Wilmore, Kentucky

www.asbury.edu

Federal Code: 001952

4-year private liberal arts college in small town, affiliated with interdenominational tradition.

Enrollment: 1,252 undergrads, 2% part-time. 312 full-time freshmen.

Selectivity: Admits 50 to 75% of applicants.

BASIC COSTS (2008-2009)

Tuition and fees: $22,413.

Per-credit charge: $855.

Room and board: $5,414.

Additional info: Tuition/fee waivers available for minority students.

FINANCIAL AID PICTURE (2007-2008)

Students with need: Out of 283 full-time freshmen who applied for aid, 219 were judged to have need. Of these, 219 received aid, and 67 had their full need met. Average financial aid package met 84% of need; average scholarship/grant was $10,398; average loan was $3,088. For part-time students, average financial aid package was $8,569.

Students without need: No-need awards available for academics, alumni affiliation, athletics, leadership, minority status, music/drama, religious affiliation, ROTC.

Cumulative student debt: 70% of graduating class had student loans; average debt was $23,690.

FINANCIAL AID PROCEDURES

Forms required: institutional form.

Dates and Deadlines: Priority date 3/1; no closing date. Applicants notified on a rolling basis starting 1/31; must reply within 4 week(s) of notification.

CONTACT

Ronald Anderson, Director of Financial Aid
One Macklem Drive, Wilmore, KY 40390-1198
(859) 858-3511 ext. 2195

Beckfield College

Florence, Kentucky
www.beckfield.edu   Federal Code: 016726

4-year for-profit business and health science and nursing college in large town.
Enrollment: 575 undergrads.
Selectivity: Open admission; but selective for some programs.

BASIC COSTS (2007-2008)

Tuition and fees: $10,990.
Per-credit charge: $242.
Additional info: Fees vary by program.

FINANCIAL AID PICTURE (2006-2007)

Students with need: Need-based aid available for part-time students.
Students without need: This college awards aid only to students with need.
Scholarships offered: High School scholarship; tuition for one course per quarter for maximum of 8 quarters; must achieve and maintain 3.0 GPA, be enrolled full-time, and enter college in July or October following graduation from high school. Merit scholarship; $100 per quarter; must maintain 4.0 GPA, perfect attendance, and carry at least 8 quarter credit hours.
Additional info: Deadline for filing of financial aid forms is end of first week of classes.

FINANCIAL AID PROCEDURES

Forms required: FAFSA.
Dates and Deadlines: Applicants notified on a rolling basis.

CONTACT

Pat Nettleton, Corporate Director of Financial Aid
16 Spiral Drive, Florence, KY 41042
(859) 371-9393

Bellarmine University

Louisville, Kentucky
www.bellarmine.edu   Federal Code: 001954

4-year private university and liberal arts college in very large city, affiliated with Roman Catholic Church.
Enrollment: 2,032 undergrads, 7% part-time. 568 full-time freshmen.
Selectivity: Admits 50 to 75% of applicants.

BASIC COSTS (2008-2009)

Tuition and fees: $28,030.
Per-credit charge: $640.
Room and board: $8,406.

FINANCIAL AID PICTURE (2007-2008)

Students with need: Out of 499 full-time freshmen who applied for aid, 446 were judged to have need. Of these, 446 received aid, and 133 had their full need met. Average financial aid package met 77% of need; average scholarship/grant was $17,918; average loan was $3,490. For part-time students, average financial aid package was $9,616.
Students without need: 53 full-time freshmen who did not demonstrate need for aid received scholarships/grants; average award was $13,598. No-need awards available for academics, alumni affiliation, art, athletics, leadership, minority status, music/drama, religious affiliation, ROTC, state/district residency.

Scholarships offered: *Merit:* Merit awards range from $5,500 to full tuition.
Athletic: 8 full-time freshmen received athletic scholarships; average amount $3,338.
Cumulative student debt: 65% of graduating class had student loans; average debt was $18,112.

FINANCIAL AID PROCEDURES

Forms required: FAFSA.
Dates and Deadlines: Priority date 3/1; no closing date. Applicants notified on a rolling basis starting 3/15; must reply by 5/1 or within 3 week(s) of notification.
Transfers: Applicants notified on a rolling basis starting 4/15; must reply within 3 week(s) of notification.

CONTACT

Heather Boutell, Director of Financial Aid
2001 Newburg Road, Louisville, KY 40205
(502) 452-8124

Berea College

Berea, Kentucky
www.berea.edu   Federal Code: 001955

4-year private liberal arts college in small town.
Enrollment: 1,528 undergrads. 421 full-time freshmen.
Selectivity: Admits less than 50% of applicants.

BASIC COSTS (2008-2009)

Additional info: Only those with financial need admitted. All students receive 4-year full-tuition scholarship. Students and families expected to pay toward room/board and fees if possible. While room/board costs are $5,768 and fees are $866 for the academic year, most students receive aid and pay $1,500 per academic year on average. Students required to earn portion of expenses by working minimum of 10 hours per week on campus. Value of full-time tuition for 2008/2009: $24,500.

FINANCIAL AID PICTURE (2007-2008)

Students with need: Out of 421 full-time freshmen who applied for aid, 421 were judged to have need. Of these, 421 received aid. Average financial aid package met 94% of need; average scholarship/grant was $27,733; average loan was $138. Need-based aid available for part-time students.
Students without need: This college awards aid only to students with need.
Cumulative student debt: 79% of graduating class had student loans; average debt was $7,705.

FINANCIAL AID PROCEDURES

Forms required: FAFSA.
Dates and Deadlines: Priority date 4/1; no closing date. Applicants notified on a rolling basis starting 5/1.
Transfers: Financial aid transcript from previous school(s) must be received before awarding aid.

CONTACT

Bryan Erslan, Director of Student Financial Aid Services
CPO 2220, Berea, KY 40404
(859) 985-3310

Bluegrass Community and Technical College

Lexington, Kentucky
www.bluegrass.kctcs.edu   Federal Code: 009707

2-year public community and technical college in large city.
Enrollment: 9,577 undergrads.
Selectivity: Open admission; but selective for some programs.

BASIC COSTS (2007-2008)
Tuition and fees: $3,450; out-of-state residents $10,350.
Per-credit charge: $115; out-of-state residents $345.
Room and board: $5,794.

FINANCIAL AID PICTURE
Students with need: Need-based aid available for full-time and part-time students. Work study available nights.
Students without need: No-need awards available for academics, minority status, state/district residency.

FINANCIAL AID PROCEDURES
Forms required: FAFSA, institutional form.
Dates and Deadlines: No deadline. Applicants notified on a rolling basis starting 6/5; must reply within 3 week(s) of notification.

CONTACT
Runan Pendergrast, Director of Financial Aid
200 Oswald Building, Cooper Drive, Lexington, KY 40506-0235

Brescia University
Owensboro, Kentucky
www.brescia.edu
Federal Code: 001958

4-year private university and liberal arts college in small city, affiliated with Roman Catholic Church.
Enrollment: 426 undergrads.
Selectivity: Admits over 75% of applicants.

BASIC COSTS (2008-2009)
Tuition and fees: $15,440.
Per-credit charge: $475.
Room and board: $7,000.

FINANCIAL AID PICTURE (2006-2007)
Students with need: 59% of average financial aid package awarded as scholarships/grants, 41% awarded as loans/jobs. Need-based aid available for part-time students. Work study available nights, weekends, and for part-time students.
Students without need: No-need awards available for academics, alumni affiliation, art, athletics, minority status, music/drama, religious affiliation, state/district residency.

FINANCIAL AID PROCEDURES
Forms required: FAFSA.
Dates and Deadlines: Priority date 8/1; closing date 8/23. Applicants notified on a rolling basis starting 3/1; must reply within 3 week(s) of notification.

CONTACT
Marcie Tilleet, Director of Financial Aid
717 Frederica Street, Owensboro, KY 42301-3023
(270) 685-3131 ext. 4216

Campbellsville University
Campbellsville, Kentucky
www.campbellsville.edu
Federal Code: 001959

4-year private university in large town, affiliated with Baptist faith.
Enrollment: 1,549 undergrads, 7% part-time. 355 full-time freshmen.
Selectivity: Admits 50 to 75% of applicants.

BASIC COSTS (2007-2008)
Tuition and fees: $17,260.
Per-credit charge: $703.
Room and board: $6,230.
Additional info: Tuition/fee waivers available for adults, minority students, unemployed or children of unemployed.

FINANCIAL AID PICTURE (2006-2007)
Students with need: Out of 279 full-time freshmen who applied for aid, 250 were judged to have need. Of these, 250 received aid, and 45 had their full need met. Average financial aid package met 73% of need; average scholarship/grant was $11,616; average loan was $2,150. For part-time students, average financial aid package was $12,341.
Students without need: 50 full-time freshmen who did not demonstrate need for aid received scholarships/grants; average award was $9,306.
Scholarships offered: 19 full-time freshmen received athletic scholarships; average amount $8,414.
Cumulative student debt: 54% of graduating class had student loans; average debt was $14,524.
Additional info: Matching scholarships available for students whose church contributes $200 annually. Performance grants available to members of marching band.

FINANCIAL AID PROCEDURES
Forms required: FAFSA.
Dates and Deadlines: Priority date 4/1; no closing date. Applicants notified on a rolling basis starting 5/15.

CONTACT
Chris Tolson, Director of Financial Aid
1 University Drive, Campbellsville, KY 42718-2799
(270) 789-5013

Centre College
Danville, Kentucky
www.centre.edu
Federal Code: 001961

4-year private liberal arts college in large town, affiliated with Presbyterian Church (USA).
Enrollment: 1,184 undergrads. 316 full-time freshmen.
Selectivity: Admits 50 to 75% of applicants.

BASIC COSTS (2007-2008)
Per-credit charge: $950.
Comprehensive fee: $35,000.
Additional info: Reduced comprehensive fee may be available if student is approved to live off-campus by dean of students.

FINANCIAL AID PICTURE (2007-2008)
Students with need: Out of 247 full-time freshmen who applied for aid, 183 were judged to have need. Of these, 183 received aid, and 67 had their full need met. Average financial aid package met 89% of need; average scholarship/grant was $19,673; average loan was $3,585.
Students without need: 116 full-time freshmen who did not demonstrate need for aid received scholarships/grants; average award was $12,214. No-need awards available for academics, alumni affiliation, music/drama, ROTC.
Scholarships offered: Institutional Merit Award; $7,500 to full tuition; applications must be on file by February 1; renewable. Program of Music and Drama Scholarships; $5,000; minimum award available to Centre Fellows and Kentucky Governor's Scholars.
Cumulative student debt: 55% of graduating class had student loans; average debt was $17,600.

FINANCIAL AID PROCEDURES
Forms required: FAFSA, institutional form.
Dates and Deadlines: Closing date 3/1. Applicants notified by 3/25; must reply by 5/1 or within 2 week(s) of notification.
Transfers: No deadline. Applicants notified on a rolling basis starting 3/1; must reply within 2 week(s) of notification. Financial aid transcript required.

CONTACT
Elaine Larson, Director of Student Financial Planning
600 West Walnut Street, Danville, KY 40422-1394
(859) 238-5365

Clear Creek Baptist Bible College

Pineville, Kentucky
www.ccbbc.edu   Federal Code: 017044

4-year private Bible college in small town, affiliated with Southern Baptist Convention.

Enrollment: 169 undergrads, 20% part-time. 21 full-time freshmen.

Selectivity: Open admission.

BASIC COSTS (2008-2009)

Tuition and fees: $5,322.

Per-credit charge: $226.

Room and board: $3,750.

Additional info: Room and board fee given for single student. Married student housing fees vary from $160 to $325 per month.

FINANCIAL AID PICTURE (2006-2007)

Students with need: Out of 21 full-time freshmen who applied for aid, 17 were judged to have need. Of these, 17 received aid. Average financial aid package met 49% of need; average scholarship/grant was $3,411. For part-time students, average financial aid package was $1,902.

Students without need: 4 full-time freshmen who did not demonstrate need for aid received scholarships/grants; average award was $450. No-need awards available for academics.

FINANCIAL AID PROCEDURES

Forms required: FAFSA, institutional form.

Dates and Deadlines: Priority date 6/30; no closing date. Applicants notified on a rolling basis; must reply by 8/1.

Transfers: Priority date 5/5; no deadline. Applicants notified on a rolling basis starting 5/5; must reply by 8/1.

CONTACT

Sam Risner, Director of Financial Aid
300 Clear Creek Road, Pineville, KY 40977-9754
(606) 337-3196 ext. 142

Draughons Junior College

Bowling Green, Kentucky
www.draughons.edu   Federal Code: 004934

2-year for-profit branch campus and junior college in large town.

Enrollment: 475 undergrads.

Selectivity: Open admission.

BASIC COSTS (2007-2008)

Tuition and fees: $8,415.

Per-credit charge: $215.

FINANCIAL AID PICTURE

Students with need: Need-based aid available for full-time and part-time students. Work study available nights.

Students without need: This college awards aid only to students with need.

FINANCIAL AID PROCEDURES

Forms required: FAFSA.

Dates and Deadlines: No deadline.

CONTACT

Mary Hood, Senior Financial Aid Officer
2421 Fitzgerald Industrial Drive, Bowling Green, KY 42101
(270) 843-6750

Eastern Kentucky University

Richmond, Kentucky
www.eku.edu   Federal Code: 001963

4-year public university in large town.

Enrollment: 12,996 undergrads, 16% part-time. 2,431 full-time freshmen.

Selectivity: Admits 50 to 75% of applicants.

BASIC COSTS (2007-2008)

Tuition and fees: $5,682; out-of-state residents $15,382.

Per-credit charge: $237; out-of-state residents $641.

Room and board: $5,479.

Additional info: Targeted out-of-state tuition: $8,884.

FINANCIAL AID PICTURE

Students with need: Need-based aid available for full-time and part-time students. Work study available nights, weekends, and for part-time students.

Students without need: No-need awards available for academics, alumni affiliation, art, athletics, job skills, leadership, minority status, music/drama, ROTC.

FINANCIAL AID PROCEDURES

Forms required: FAFSA.

Dates and Deadlines: Priority date 3/15; no closing date. Applicants notified on a rolling basis starting 4/1.

CONTACT

Shelley Park, Director of Financial Aid
SSB CPO 54, 521 Lancaster Avenue, Richmond, KY 40475-3102

Georgetown College

Georgetown, Kentucky
www.georgetowncollege.edu   Federal Code: 001964

4-year private liberal arts college in large town, affiliated with Southern Baptist Convention.

Enrollment: 1,335 undergrads, 2% part-time. 366 full-time freshmen.

Selectivity: Admits over 75% of applicants.

BASIC COSTS (2007-2008)

Tuition and fees: $22,360.

Per-credit charge: $930.

Room and board: $6,380.

FINANCIAL AID PICTURE (2007-2008)

Students with need: Out of 326 full-time freshmen who applied for aid, 277 were judged to have need. Of these, 277 received aid, and 131 had their full need met. Average financial aid package met 90% of need; average scholarship/grant was $18,787; average loan was $3,823.

Students without need: 90 full-time freshmen who did not demonstrate need for aid received scholarships/grants; average award was $11,763. No-need awards available for academics, alumni affiliation, art, athletics, leadership, minority status, music/drama, religious affiliation, ROTC, state/district residency.

Scholarships offered: 5 full-time freshmen received athletic scholarships; average amount $11,958.

Cumulative student debt: 45% of graduating class had student loans; average debt was $21,969.

FINANCIAL AID PROCEDURES

Forms required: FAFSA, institutional form.

Dates and Deadlines: Priority date 2/15; closing date 8/1. Applicants notified on a rolling basis starting 3/1; must reply by 5/1.

CONTACT

Rhyan Conyers, Director of Student Financial Planning
400 East College Street, Georgetown, KY 40324
(502) 863-8027

Hazard Community College

Hazard, Kentucky
www.hazard.kctcs.edu   Federal Code: 006962

2-year public community and technical college in small town.
Enrollment: 4,070 undergrads.
Selectivity: Open admission; but selective for some programs.

BASIC COSTS (2007-2008)

Tuition and fees: $3,450; out-of-state residents $10,350.
Per-credit charge: $115; out-of-state residents $345.

FINANCIAL AID PICTURE

Students with need: Need-based aid available for full-time and part-time students.
Students without need: This college awards aid only to students with need.

FINANCIAL AID PROCEDURES

Forms required: FAFSA.
Dates and Deadlines: Priority date 4/1; no closing date. Applicants notified on a rolling basis starting 6/15; must reply within 2 week(s) of notification.

CONTACT

Chuck Anderson, Financial Aid Director
One Community College Drive, Hazard, KY 41701
(606) 487-3061

Hopkinsville Community College

Hopkinsville, Kentucky
www.hopkinsville.kctcs.edu   Federal Code: 001994

2-year public community college in small city.
Enrollment: 2,909 undergrads, 55% part-time. 308 full-time freshmen.
Selectivity: Open admission.

BASIC COSTS (2007-2008)

Tuition and fees: $3,450; out-of-state residents $10,350.
Per-credit charge: $115; out-of-state residents $345.

FINANCIAL AID PICTURE

Students with need: Need-based aid available for full-time and part-time students. Work study available nights.
Students without need: No-need awards available for academics, leadership, minority status, state/district residency.
Additional info: ACT required for academic scholarships.

FINANCIAL AID PROCEDURES

Forms required: FAFSA.
Dates and Deadlines: No deadline. Applicants notified on a rolling basis starting 7/1.
Transfers: No deadline. Applicants notified on a rolling basis.

CONTACT

Vincent Shykes, Director, Financial Aid
PO Box 2100, Hopkinsville, KY 42241-2100
(270) 707-3831

Jefferson Community and Technical College

Louisville, Kentucky
www.jefferson.kctcs.edu   Federal Code: 006961

2-year public community and technical college in large city.
Enrollment: 11,205 undergrads, 58% part-time. 954 full-time freshmen.
Selectivity: Open admission; but selective for some programs.

BASIC COSTS (2007-2008)

Tuition and fees: $3,450; out-of-state residents $10,350.
Per-credit charge: $115; out-of-state residents $345.

FINANCIAL AID PICTURE

Students with need: Need-based aid available for full-time and part-time students.
Students without need: No-need awards available for academics, art, minority status.

FINANCIAL AID PROCEDURES

Forms required: FAFSA, institutional form.
Dates and Deadlines: Priority date 3/15; no closing date. Applicants notified on a rolling basis starting 6/15; must reply within 3 week(s) of notification.

CONTACT

Lisa Schrenger, Financial Aid Officer
109 East Broadway, Louisville, KY 40202
(502) 213-2137

Kentucky Christian University

Grayson, Kentucky
www.kcu.edu   Federal Code: 001965

4-year private Bible and liberal arts college in small town, affiliated with Christian Church/Church of Christ.
Enrollment: 570 undergrads, 3% part-time. 176 full-time freshmen.
Selectivity: Admits 50 to 75% of applicants.

BASIC COSTS (2008-2009)

Tuition and fees: $12,120.
Per-credit charge: $399.
Room and board: $5,298.

FINANCIAL AID PICTURE (2007-2008)

Students with need: Out of 157 full-time freshmen who applied for aid, 141 were judged to have need. Of these, 141 received aid, and 21 had their full need met. Average financial aid package met 62% of need; average scholarship/grant was $5,051; average loan was $3,471. For part-time students, average financial aid package was $2,874.
Students without need: 35 full-time freshmen who did not demonstrate need for aid received scholarships/grants; average award was $6,600. No-need awards available for academics, alumni affiliation, leadership, minority status, music/drama, religious affiliation.
Cumulative student debt: 77% of graduating class had student loans; average debt was $27,358.

FINANCIAL AID PROCEDURES

Forms required: FAFSA.
Dates and Deadlines: Priority date 3/1; no closing date. Applicants notified on a rolling basis starting 3/15; must reply within 2 week(s) of notification.

CONTACT

Jennie Bender, Director of Financial Aid
100 Academic Parkway, Grayson, KY 41143-2205
(606) 474-3226

Kentucky Mountain Bible College

Vancleve, Kentucky
www.kmbc.edu   Federal Code: 030021

4-year private Bible college in small town, affiliated with Kentucky Mountain Holiness Association.

Enrollment: 59 undergrads, 17% part-time. 7 full-time freshmen.

Selectivity: Admits less than 50% of applicants.

BASIC COSTS (2008-2009)

Tuition and fees: $5,940.

Per-credit charge: $180.

Room and board: $3,700.

FINANCIAL AID PICTURE (2007-2008)

Students with need: Out of 7 full-time freshmen who applied for aid, 7 were judged to have need. Of these, 7 received aid. For part-time students, average financial aid package was $2,300.

Students without need: 2 full-time freshmen who did not demonstrate need for aid received scholarships/grants; average award was $450. No-need awards available for academics, job skills, leadership, music/drama.

Cumulative student debt: 3% of graduating class had student loans; average debt was $2,700.

FINANCIAL AID PROCEDURES

Forms required: FAFSA, institutional form.

Dates and Deadlines: Priority date 4/1; closing date 6/30. Applicants notified on a rolling basis starting 3/15; must reply by 7/1.

Transfers: No deadline. Applicants notified on a rolling basis starting 8/30; must reply within 6 week(s) of notification.

CONTACT

Carla Frazier, Director of Financial Aid
Box 10, Vancleve, KY 41385-0010
(606) 693-5000 ext. 175

Kentucky State University

Frankfort, Kentucky
www.kysu.edu   Federal Code: 001968

4-year public university and liberal arts college in large town.

Enrollment: 2,201 undergrads, 15% part-time. 662 full-time freshmen.

Selectivity: Admits less than 50% of applicants.

BASIC COSTS (2007-2008)

Tuition and fees: $5,320; out-of-state residents $12,490.

Per-credit charge: $190; out-of-state residents $450..

Room and board: $6,340.

FINANCIAL AID PICTURE (2007-2008)

Students with need: For part-time students, average financial aid package was $2,082.

Students without need: No-need awards available for academics, alumni affiliation, art, athletics, music/drama.

Scholarships offered: 41 full-time freshmen received athletic scholarships; average amount $4,026.

FINANCIAL AID PROCEDURES

Forms required: FAFSA.

Dates and Deadlines: Priority date 4/15; closing date 6/30.

Transfers: No deadline. Applicants notified on a rolling basis; must reply within 4 week(s) of notification.

CONTACT

Carmella Conner, Director of Financial Aid
400 East Main Street, ASB 312, Frankfort, KY 40601
(502) 597-5960

Kentucky Wesleyan College

Owensboro, Kentucky
www.kwc.edu   Federal Code: 001969

4-year private liberal arts college in small city, affiliated with United Methodist Church.

Enrollment: 919 undergrads, 2% part-time. 351 full-time freshmen.

Selectivity: Admits over 75% of applicants.

BASIC COSTS (2008-2009)

Tuition and fees: $15,625.

Per-credit charge: $450.

Room and board: $6,160.

FINANCIAL AID PICTURE (2006-2007)

Students with need: Out of 331 full-time freshmen who applied for aid, 295 were judged to have need. Of these, 289 received aid, and 54 had their full need met. Average financial aid package met 68% of need; average scholarship/grant was $10,283; average loan was $2,634. For part-time students, average financial aid package was $10,189.

Students without need: 56 full-time freshmen who did not demonstrate need for aid received scholarships/grants; average award was $9,663. No-need awards available for academics, alumni affiliation, art, athletics, leadership, music/drama, religious affiliation, state/district residency.

Scholarships offered: Scholarships range from $1,000 to full tuition. Students compete in on-campus scholarship competitions.

Cumulative student debt: 88% of graduating class had student loans; average debt was $15,100.

FINANCIAL AID PROCEDURES

Forms required: FAFSA.

Dates and Deadlines: Closing date 3/15. Applicants notified on a rolling basis starting 2/15; must reply within 2 week(s) of notification.

CONTACT

Samantha Hayes, Director of Financial Aid
3000 Frederica Street, Owensboro, KY 42301
(270) 852-3130

Lindsey Wilson College

Columbia, Kentucky
www.lindsey.edu   Federal Code: 001972

4-year private liberal arts college in small town, affiliated with United Methodist Church.

Enrollment: 1,562 undergrads, 5% part-time. 352 full-time freshmen.

Selectivity: Open admission; but selective for some programs.

BASIC COSTS (2008-2009)

Tuition and fees: $16,670.

Per-credit charge: $685.

Room and board: $6,925.

FINANCIAL AID PICTURE

Students with need: Need-based aid available for full-time and part-time students.

Students without need: This college awards aid only to students with need.

FINANCIAL AID PROCEDURES

Forms required: FAFSA, institutional form.

Dates and Deadlines: Priority date 4/15; no closing date. Applicants notified on a rolling basis starting 5/1; must reply within 2 week(s) of notification.

Transfers: Applicants notified on a rolling basis.

CONTACT
Roger Drake, Vice President for Admimistration and Finance
210 Lindsey Wilson Street, Columbia, KY 42728
(270) 384-8022

Louisville Technical Institute
Louisville, Kentucky
www.louisvilletech.edu   Federal Code: 012088

2-year for-profit technical college in very large city.
Enrollment: 573 undergrads.
Selectivity: Admits over 75% of applicants.

BASIC COSTS (2008-2009)
Additional info: For 2008-09, the cost of associate degree programs range from $29,820 to $34,790. The Computer Graphic Design and Dynamic Web tech fee is $610 per quarter; the tech fee for Computer Network Administration and information Systems Security is $525 per quarter. Tuition at time of enrollment locked for 2 years; tuition/fee waivers available for adults.

FINANCIAL AID PICTURE
Students with need: Need-based aid available for full-time and part-time students. Work study available nights.
Students without need: No-need awards available for academics, art, job skills.
Scholarships offered: Academic Scholarships; up to $3,000; based on class rank, GPA, essay. Scholarship Day Competition; up to $1,500 based upon testing scores. Scholarship Fair Competition; up to $3,000; based upon open competition in electronics, drafting, interior design, computer networking and art skills. Kentucky Skills USA Scholarships; up to $1,500; based upon state championship competitions in such fields as drafting, electronics, etc.

FINANCIAL AID PROCEDURES
Forms required: FAFSA.
Dates and Deadlines: No deadline. Applicants notified on a rolling basis; must reply within 2 week(s) of notification.
Transfers: No deadline. Applicants notified on a rolling basis.

CONTACT
Kelley Hornback, Financial Planning Director
3901 Atkinson Square Drive, Louisville, KY 40218-4524
(502) 456-6509

Madisonville Community College
Madisonville, Kentucky
www.madisonville.kctcs.edu   Federal Code: 009010

2-year public community college in large town.
Enrollment: 4,000 undergrads.
Selectivity: Open admission.

BASIC COSTS (2007-2008)
Tuition and fees: $3,450; out-of-state residents $10,350.
Per-credit charge: $115; out-of-state residents $345.
Additional info: Tuition/fee waivers available for minority students, unemployed or children of unemployed.

FINANCIAL AID PICTURE
Students with need: Need-based aid available for full-time and part-time students. Work study available nights, weekends, and for part-time students.
Students without need: No-need awards available for minority status.

FINANCIAL AID PROCEDURES
Forms required: FAFSA, institutional form.
Dates and Deadlines: Priority date 3/15; no closing date. Applicants notified on a rolling basis; must reply within 3 week(s) of notification.

CONTACT
Caroline Clayton, Director of Financial Aid
2000 College Drive, Madisonville, KY 42431
(270) 821-6514

Maysville Community and Technical College
Maysville, Kentucky
www.maysville.kctcs.edu   Federal Code: 006960

2-year public community and technical college in small town.
Enrollment: 1,852 undergrads.
Selectivity: Open admission; but selective for some programs.

BASIC COSTS (2007-2008)
Tuition and fees: $3,450; out-of-state residents $10,350.
Per-credit charge: $115; out-of-state residents $345.

FINANCIAL AID PICTURE (2006-2007)
Students with need: 57% of average financial aid package awarded as scholarships/grants, 43% awarded as loans/jobs. Need-based aid available for part-time students. Work study available nights.
Students without need: No-need awards available for academics.

FINANCIAL AID PROCEDURES
Forms required: FAFSA, institutional form.
Dates and Deadlines: Priority date 4/1; no closing date. Applicants notified on a rolling basis starting 3/1; must reply within 3 week(s) of notification.

CONTACT
Leslie McCord, Financial Aid Director
1755 US 68, Maysville, KY 41056
(606) 759-7141 ext. 66207

Mid-Continent University
Mayfield, Kentucky
www.midcontinent.edu   Federal Code: 025762

4-year private Bible and liberal arts college in large town, affiliated with Southern Baptist Convention.
Enrollment: 1,541 undergrads, 14% part-time. 140 full-time freshmen.
Selectivity: Admits over 75% of applicants.

BASIC COSTS (2008-2009)
Tuition and fees: $13,100.
Per-credit charge: $395.
Room and board: $6,300.

FINANCIAL AID PICTURE (2006-2007)
Students with need: Out of 124 full-time freshmen who applied for aid, 114 were judged to have need. Of these, 114 received aid, and 15 had their full need met. Average financial aid package met 61% of need; average scholarship/grant was $6,619; average loan was $2,022. Need-based aid available for part-time students.
Students without need: 13 full-time freshmen who did not demonstrate need for aid received scholarships/grants; average award was $6,738. No-need awards available for academics.

FINANCIAL AID PROCEDURES
Forms required: FAFSA, institutional form.
Dates and Deadlines: Priority date 3/15; closing date 5/30. Applicants notified on a rolling basis starting 4/1.
Transfers: No deadline.

PART III: FINANCIAL AID COLLEGE BY COLLEGE

CONTACT

Kent Youngblood, Director of Financial Aid

99 Powell Road East, Mayfield, KY 42066-0357

(270) 247-8521 ext. 260

Midway College

Midway, Kentucky

www.midway.edu   Federal Code: 001975

4-year private liberal arts college for women in small town, affiliated with Christian Church (Disciples of Christ).

Enrollment: 1,395 undergrads, 26% part-time. 152 full-time freshmen.

Selectivity: Open admission; but selective for some programs.

BASIC COSTS (2007-2008)

Tuition and fees: $15,750.

Per-credit charge: $525.

Room and board: $6,400.

FINANCIAL AID PICTURE (2007-2008)

Students with need: Average financial aid package met 74% of need; average scholarship/grant was $10,212; average loan was $3,912. For part-time students, average financial aid package was $6,023.

Students without need: No-need awards available for academics, alumni affiliation, art, athletics, leadership, minority status, religious affiliation.

Cumulative student debt: 86% of graduating class had student loans; average debt was $18,223.

Additional info: Audition required of applicants for music scholarships. Portfolio required for art scholarships.

FINANCIAL AID PROCEDURES

Forms required: FAFSA, institutional form.

Dates and Deadlines: Priority date 4/1; closing date 8/1. Applicants notified on a rolling basis; must reply within 4 week(s) of notification.

CONTACT

Katie Conrad, Director of Financial Aid

512 East Stephens Street, Midway, KY 40347-1120

(859) 846-5410

Morehead State University

Morehead, Kentucky

www.moreheadstate.edu   Federal Code: 001976

4-year public university in small town.

Enrollment: 6,863 undergrads, 16% part-time. 1,373 full-time freshmen.

Selectivity: Admits 50 to 75% of applicants.

BASIC COSTS (2007-2008)

Tuition and fees: $5,280; out-of-state residents $13,340.

Per-credit charge: $220; out-of-state residents $560.

Room and board: $5,470.

FINANCIAL AID PICTURE

Students with need: Need-based aid available for full-time students. Work study available nights, weekends, and for part-time students.

Students without need: No-need awards available for academics, alumni affiliation, art, athletics, leadership, minority status, music/drama, ROTC, state/district residency.

FINANCIAL AID PROCEDURES

Forms required: FAFSA, institutional form.

Dates and Deadlines: Priority date 3/15; no closing date. Applicants notified on a rolling basis.

Transfers: Transfer scholarships available.

CONTACT

Carol Becker, Director of Financial Aid

100 Admissions Center, Morehead, KY 40351

(606) 783-2011

Murray State University

Murray, Kentucky

www.murraystate.edu   Federal Code: 001977

4-year public university in large town.

Enrollment: 7,749 undergrads, 11% part-time. 1,399 full-time freshmen.

Selectivity: Admits over 75% of applicants.

BASIC COSTS (2007-2008)

Tuition and fees: $5,418; out-of-state residents $14,718.

Per-credit charge: $226; out-of-state residents $613.

Room and board: $5,818.

Additional info: Tuition/fee waivers available for minority students.

FINANCIAL AID PICTURE (2007-2008)

Students with need: Average financial aid package met 92% of need; average scholarship/grant was $2,590; average loan was $1,855. For part-time students, average financial aid package was $4,012.

Students without need: No-need awards available for academics, alumni affiliation, art, athletics, job skills, leadership, minority status, music/drama, ROTC, state/district residency.

Cumulative student debt: 55% of graduating class had student loans; average debt was $15,010.

Additional info: Tuition discount for children and grandchildren of out-of-state alumni. Regional tuition for students from certain counties in Illinois, Tennessee, Missouri, and Indiana.

FINANCIAL AID PROCEDURES

Forms required: FAFSA, institutional form.

Dates and Deadlines: Priority date 4/1; no closing date. Applicants notified on a rolling basis starting 4/15.

Transfers: No deadline. Applicants notified on a rolling basis starting 4/15.

CONTACT

Charles Vinson, Director of Financial Aid

113 Sparks Hall, Murray, KY 42071

(270) 809-2546

National College: Danville

Danville, Kentucky

www.ncbt.edu   Federal Code: 010489

2-year for-profit business college in large town.

Enrollment: 279 undergrads.

Selectivity: Open admission.

BASIC COSTS (2007-2008)

Tuition and fees: $9,090.

Per-credit charge: $202.

FINANCIAL AID PICTURE

Students with need: Need-based aid available for full-time and part-time students.

Students without need: This college awards aid only to students with need.

FINANCIAL AID PROCEDURES

Forms required: FAFSA.

Dates and Deadlines: No deadline. Applicants notified on a rolling basis.

CONTACT

Pamela Cotton, Director of Financial Aid and Compliance Officer

PO Box 6400, Roanoke, VA 24017

(540) 986-1800

National College: Florence

Florence, Kentucky

www.ncbt.edu   Federal Code: 010489

2-year for-profit business college in large town.

Enrollment: 156 undergrads.

Selectivity: Open admission.

BASIC COSTS (2007-2008)

Tuition and fees: $9,090.

Per-credit charge: $202.

FINANCIAL AID PICTURE

Students with need: Need-based aid available for full-time and part-time students.

Students without need: This college awards aid only to students with need.

FINANCIAL AID PROCEDURES

Forms required: FAFSA.

Dates and Deadlines: No deadline. Applicants notified on a rolling basis.

CONTACT

Pamela Cotton, Director of Financial Aid and Compliance Officer

PO Box 6400, Roanoke, VA 24017

(540) 986-1800

National College: Lexington

Lexington, Kentucky

www.ncbt.edu   Federal Code: 010489

2-year for-profit business and junior college in small city.

Enrollment: 503 undergrads.

Selectivity: Open admission.

BASIC COSTS (2007-2008)

Tuition and fees: $9,090.

Per-credit charge: $202.

FINANCIAL AID PICTURE

Students with need: Need-based aid available for full-time and part-time students.

Students without need: This college awards aid only to students with need.

FINANCIAL AID PROCEDURES

Forms required: FAFSA.

Dates and Deadlines: No deadline. Applicants notified on a rolling basis.

CONTACT

Pamela Cotton, Director of Financial Aid and Compliance Officer

PO Box 6400, Roanoke, VA 24017

(859) 255-0621

National College: Louisville

Louisville, Kentucky

www.ncbt.edu   Federal Code: 010489

2-year for-profit business college in large city.

Enrollment: 819 undergrads.

Selectivity: Open admission.

BASIC COSTS (2007-2008)

Tuition and fees: $9,090.

Per-credit charge: $202.

FINANCIAL AID PICTURE

Students with need: Need-based aid available for full-time and part-time students.

Students without need: This college awards aid only to students with need.

FINANCIAL AID PROCEDURES

Forms required: FAFSA.

Dates and Deadlines: No deadline. Applicants notified on a rolling basis.

CONTACT

Pamela Cotton, Director of Financial Aid and Compliance Officer

PO Box 6400, Roanoke, VA 24017

(540) 986-1800

National College: Pikeville

Pikeville, Kentucky

www.ncbt.edu   Federal Code: 010489

2-year for-profit business college in large town.

Enrollment: 154 undergrads.

Selectivity: Open admission.

BASIC COSTS (2007-2008)

Tuition and fees: $9,090.

Per-credit charge: $202.

FINANCIAL AID PICTURE

Students with need: Need-based aid available for full-time and part-time students.

Students without need: This college awards aid only to students with need.

FINANCIAL AID PROCEDURES

Forms required: FAFSA.

Dates and Deadlines: No deadline.

CONTACT

Pamela Cotton, Director of Financial Aid and Compliance Officer

PO Box 6400, Roanoke, VA 24017

(540) 986-1800

National College: Richmond

Richmond, Kentucky

www.ncbt.edu   Federal Code: 010489

2-year for-profit business college in large town.

Enrollment: 287 undergrads.

Selectivity: Open admission.

BASIC COSTS (2007-2008)

Tuition and fees: $9,090.

Per-credit charge: $202.

FINANCIAL AID PICTURE

Students with need: Need-based aid available for full-time and part-time students.

Students without need: This college awards aid only to students with need.

FINANCIAL AID PROCEDURES

Forms required: FAFSA.

Dates and Deadlines: No deadline. Applicants notified on a rolling basis.

CONTACT

Pamela Cotton, Director of Financial Aid and Compliance Officer

PO Box 6400, Roanoke, VA 24017

(540) 986-1800

Northern Kentucky University

Highland Heights, Kentucky

www.nku.edu　　　　Federal Code: 009275

4-year public university in large city.

Enrollment: 12,058 undergrads, 23% part-time. 1,884 full-time freshmen.

Selectivity: Admits over 75% of applicants.

BASIC COSTS (2007-2008)

Tuition and fees: $5,952; out-of-state residents $10,776.

Per-credit charge: $248; out-of-state residents $449.

Room and board: $6,000.

FINANCIAL AID PICTURE

Students with need: Need-based aid available for full-time and part-time students.

Students without need: No-need awards available for academics, alumni affiliation, art, athletics, job skills, leadership, minority status, music/drama, state/district residency.

FINANCIAL AID PROCEDURES

Forms required: FAFSA.

Dates and Deadlines: Priority date 3/1; no closing date. Applicants notified on a rolling basis starting 4/1; must reply within 3 week(s) of notification.

CONTACT

Leah Stewart, Director of Financial Assistance

Administrative Center 401, Northern Kentucky University, Highland Heights, KY 41099

(859) 572-5143

Owensboro Community and Technical College

Owensboro, Kentucky

www.octc.kctcs.edu　　　　Federal Code: 030345

2-year public community and technical college in small city.

Enrollment: 2,802 undergrads, 43% part-time. 449 full-time freshmen.

Selectivity: Open admission; but selective for some programs.

BASIC COSTS (2007-2008)

Tuition and fees: $3,450; out-of-state residents $10,350.

Per-credit charge: $115; out-of-state residents $345.

FINANCIAL AID PICTURE

Students with need: Need-based aid available for full-time and part-time students.

Students without need: No-need awards available for academics, state/district residency.

FINANCIAL AID PROCEDURES

Forms required: FAFSA.

Dates and Deadlines: Priority date 3/16; no closing date. Applicants notified by 6/1; must reply within 2 week(s) of notification.

Transfers: Must have financial aid transcripts from previous institutions.

CONTACT

Bernice Ayer, Financial Aid Officer

4800 New Hartford Road, Owensboro, KY 42303-1899

(270) 686-4520

Paducah Technical College

Paducah, Kentucky　　　　Federal Code: 013661

www.paducahtech.edu　　　　CSS Code: 0669

2-year for-profit technical college in small city.

Enrollment: 250 undergrads.

Selectivity: Open admission.

BASIC COSTS (2007-2008)

Additional info: Cost per academic year approximately $10,320 plus $1,000 in fees. Tuition at time of enrollment locked for 2 years.

FINANCIAL AID PICTURE

Students with need: Need-based aid available for full-time students.

FINANCIAL AID PROCEDURES

Forms required: FAFSA, CSS PROFILE.

Dates and Deadlines: No deadline. Applicants notified on a rolling basis; must reply within 3 week(s) of notification.

CONTACT

Trisha Dukes, Financial Aid Officer

509 South 30th Street, Paducah, KY 42001

(270) 444-9676

Pikeville College

Pikeville, Kentucky

www.pc.edu　　　　Federal Code: 001980

4-year private liberal arts college in small town, affiliated with Presbyterian Church (USA).

Enrollment: 791 undergrads, 9% part-time. 233 full-time freshmen.

Selectivity: Open admission; but selective for some programs.

BASIC COSTS (2007-2008)

Tuition and fees: $13,750.

Per-credit charge: $573.

Room and board: $5,250.

FINANCIAL AID PICTURE (2007-2008)

Students with need: Out of 230 full-time freshmen who applied for aid, 228 were judged to have need. Of these, 228 received aid, and 84 had their full need met. Average financial aid package met 84% of need; average scholarship/grant was $12,036; average loan was $2,482. For part-time students, average financial aid package was $9,216.

Students without need: This college awards aid only to students with need.

Cumulative student debt: 72% of graduating class had student loans; average debt was $14,612.

FINANCIAL AID PROCEDURES

Forms required: FAFSA, institutional form.

Dates and Deadlines: Priority date 3/15; no closing date. Applicants notified on a rolling basis starting 1/15; must reply by 5/1 or within 2 week(s) of notification.

Transfers: No deadline. Must reply by 5/1 or within 2 week(s) of notification.

CONTACT

Judy Bradley, Financial Aid Director

147 Sycamore Street, Pikeville, KY 41501-1194

(606) 218-5253

St. Catharine College

St. Catharine, Kentucky
www.sccky.edu   Federal Code: 001983

4-year private health science and liberal arts college in large town, affiliated with Roman Catholic Church.

Enrollment: 548 undergrads.

Selectivity: Open admission.

BASIC COSTS (2007-2008)

Tuition and fees: $12,008.

Per-credit charge: $450.

Room and board: $6,300.

Additional info: Higher tuition applies for health science program.

FINANCIAL AID PICTURE

Students with need: Need-based aid available for full-time and part-time students.

Students without need: This college awards aid only to students with need.

FINANCIAL AID PROCEDURES

Forms required: FAFSA, institutional form.

Dates and Deadlines: Priority date 3/15; no closing date. Applicants notified on a rolling basis; must reply by 8/15.

CONTACT

Laura Dean, Financial Aid Director
2735 Bardstown Road, St. Catharine, KY 40061
(502) 336-5082

Somerset Community College

Somerset, Kentucky
www.somerset.kctcs.edu   Federal Code: 001997

2-year public community and technical college in large town.

Enrollment: 4,848 undergrads.

Selectivity: Open admission; but selective for some programs.

BASIC COSTS (2007-2008)

Tuition and fees: $3,450; out-of-state residents $10,350.

Per-credit charge: $115; out-of-state residents $345.

FINANCIAL AID PICTURE (2006-2007)

Students with need: 56% of average financial aid package awarded as scholarships/grants, 44% awarded as loans/jobs. Need-based aid available for part-time students.

Students without need: This college awards aid only to students with need.

FINANCIAL AID PROCEDURES

Forms required: FAFSA.

Dates and Deadlines: Priority date 3/1; no closing date. Applicants notified on a rolling basis starting 5/1; must reply within 2 week(s) of notification.

Transfers: Priority date 3/15; closing date 8/15. Applicants notified on a rolling basis starting 5/1; must reply within 2 week(s) of notification.

CONTACT

Shawn Anderson, Chief Financial Aid Officer
808 Monticello Street, Somerset, KY 42501
(606) 679-8501 ext. 16640

Southeast Kentucky Community and Technical College

Cumberland, Kentucky
www.secc.kctcs.edu   Federal Code: 001998

2-year public community and technical college in small town.

Enrollment: 2,061 undergrads, 39% part-time. 590 full-time freshmen.

Selectivity: Open admission; but selective for some programs.

BASIC COSTS (2007-2008)

Tuition and fees: $3,450; out-of-state residents $10,350.

Per-credit charge: $115; out-of-state residents $345.

FINANCIAL AID PICTURE

Students with need: Need-based aid available for full-time and part-time students.

Students without need: This college awards aid only to students with need.

Additional info: March 15 deadline for state financial aid.

FINANCIAL AID PROCEDURES

Forms required: FAFSA.

Dates and Deadlines: Priority date 3/15; no closing date. Applicants notified by 6/15; must reply within 2 week(s) of notification.

CONTACT

Charles Sellars, Dean of Student Affairs/Director Financial Aid
700 College Road, Cumberland, KY 40823
(606) 589-2145

Spencerian College: Lexington

Lexington, Kentucky
www.spencerian.edu   Federal Code: 004618

2-year for-profit branch campus and technical college in small city.

Enrollment: 646 undergrads, 31% part-time. 450 full-time freshmen.

Selectivity: Open admission.

BASIC COSTS (2007-2008)

Additional info: Cost of programs ranges from $8,000 to $40,000; program-specific fees are additional. Cost of housing is $480 per month. Tuition at time of enrollment locked for 2 years.

FINANCIAL AID PICTURE (2007-2008)

Students with need: Out of 435 full-time freshmen who applied for aid, 430 were judged to have need. Of these, 430 received aid, and 300 had their full need met. Average financial aid package met 65% of need; average scholarship/grant was $1,500; average loan was $4,000. Need-based aid available for part-time students.

Students without need: This college awards aid only to students with need.

Cumulative student debt: 97% of graduating class had student loans; average debt was $28,900.

FINANCIAL AID PROCEDURES

Forms required: FAFSA, state aid form, institutional form.

Dates and Deadlines: No deadline. Applicants notified on a rolling basis starting 1/1.

Transfers: No deadline. Applicants notified on a rolling basis.

CONTACT

Brian Highley, Director of Financial Planning
1575 Winchester Road, Lexington, KY 40505
(859) 223-9608 ext. 5421

Sullivan University

Louisville, Kentucky
www.sullivan.edu

Federal Code: 004619

4-year for-profit university in large city.
Enrollment: 4,201 undergrads.

BASIC COSTS (2007-2008)
Room only: $4,320.
Additional info: Tuition, fees and per-credit-hour charges vary by program. Tuition costs range from $14,400 to $15,570 per academic year. Tuition at time of enrollment locked for 4 years.

FINANCIAL AID PICTURE
Students with need: Need-based aid available for full-time and part-time students. Work study available nights.
Students without need: This college awards aid only to students with need.

FINANCIAL AID PROCEDURES
Forms required: FAFSA.
Dates and Deadlines: No deadline. Applicants notified on a rolling basis starting 1/2.

CONTACT
Lisa Wright, Financial Planning Director
3101 Bardstown Road, Louisville, KY 40205
(502) 456-6504

Thomas More College

Crestview Hills, Kentucky
www.thomasmore.edu

Federal Code: 002001

4-year private liberal arts college in small town, affiliated with Roman Catholic Church.
Enrollment: 1,293 undergrads, 10% part-time. 170 full-time freshmen.
Selectivity: Admits over 75% of applicants.

BASIC COSTS (2008-2009)
Tuition and fees: $22,220.
Per-credit charge: $515.
Room and board: $5,870.
Additional info: Tuition/fee waivers available for minority students.

FINANCIAL AID PICTURE (2006-2007)
Students with need: Out of 134 full-time freshmen who applied for aid, 134 were judged to have need. Of these, 134 received aid, and 134 had their full need met. Average financial aid package met 72% of need; average scholarship/grant was $7,549. Need-based aid available for part-time students.
Students without need: 12 full-time freshmen who did not demonstrate need for aid received scholarships/grants; average award was $7,000. No-need awards available for academics, alumni affiliation, art, job skills, leadership, minority status, music/drama, religious affiliation, ROTC, state/district residency.
Cumulative student debt: 82% of graduating class had student loans; average debt was $22,165.

FINANCIAL AID PROCEDURES
Forms required: FAFSA, institutional form.
Dates and Deadlines: Priority date 3/15; no closing date. Applicants notified on a rolling basis; must reply by 5/1.
Transfers: No deadline. Applicants notified on a rolling basis; must reply by 5/1.

CONTACT
Mary Givhan, Director of Financial Aid
333 Thomas More Parkway, Crestview Hills, KY 41017-3495
(859) 344-4043

Transylvania University

Lexington, Kentucky
www.transy.edu

Federal Code: 001987

4-year private liberal arts college in large city, affiliated with Christian Church (Disciples of Christ).
Enrollment: 1,149 undergrads. 287 full-time freshmen.
Selectivity: Admits over 75% of applicants.

BASIC COSTS (2008-2009)
Tuition and fees: $23,810.
Room and board: $7,450.
Additional info: Tuition/fee waivers available for minority students.

FINANCIAL AID PICTURE (2007-2008)
Students with need: Out of 239 full-time freshmen who applied for aid, 205 were judged to have need. Of these, 204 received aid, and 68 had their full need met. Average financial aid package met 86% of need; average scholarship/grant was $14,935; average loan was $3,338. Need-based aid available for part-time students.
Students without need: 81 full-time freshmen who did not demonstrate need for aid received scholarships/grants; average award was $11,257. No-need awards available for academics, art, leadership, minority status, music/drama, religious affiliation, ROTC, state/district residency.
Scholarships offered: William T. Young Merit Scholarships: 25 awarded; tuition and fees.
Cumulative student debt: 58% of graduating class had student loans; average debt was $18,250.
Additional info: Auditions and portfolios required for music and art scholarships respectively. Essays required for other scholarship programs. Applications for William T. Young scholarships must be received by December 1.

FINANCIAL AID PROCEDURES
Forms required: FAFSA.
Dates and Deadlines: Priority date 3/1; no closing date. Applicants notified on a rolling basis starting 3/15; must reply by 5/1 or within 2 week(s) of notification.
Transfers: No deadline. Applicants notified on a rolling basis starting 3/15; must reply by 8/6.

CONTACT
David Cecil, Director of Financial Aid
300 North Broadway, Lexington, KY 40508-1797
(859) 233-8239

Union College

Barbourville, Kentucky
www.unionky.edu

Federal Code: 001988

4-year private liberal arts and teachers college in small town, affiliated with United Methodist Church.
Enrollment: 694 undergrads, 7% part-time. 159 full-time freshmen.
Selectivity: Admits 50 to 75% of applicants.

BASIC COSTS (2008-2009)
Tuition and fees: $16,820.
Per-credit charge: $280.
Room and board: $5,250.

FINANCIAL AID PICTURE (2007-2008)

Students with need: Out of 141 full-time freshmen who applied for aid, 134 were judged to have need. Of these, 134 received aid, and 33 had their full need met. Average financial aid package met 82% of need; average scholarship/grant was $12,165; average loan was $5,050. For part-time students, average financial aid package was $7,168.

Students without need: 7 full-time freshmen who did not demonstrate need for aid received scholarships/grants; average award was $11,189. No-need awards available for academics, athletics, leadership, minority status, music/drama, religious affiliation, state/district residency.

Cumulative student debt: 100% of graduating class had student loans; average debt was $24,344.

FINANCIAL AID PROCEDURES

Forms required: FAFSA.

Dates and Deadlines: Priority date 3/15; no closing date. Applicants notified on a rolling basis starting 3/1; must reply within 2 week(s) of notification.

CONTACT

Sue Buttery, Associate Dean for Financial Aid
310 College Street, Box 005, Barbourville, KY 40906
(606) 546-1618

University of Kentucky

Lexington, Kentucky
www.uky.edu   Federal Code: 001989

4-year public university in large city.
Enrollment: 18,424 undergrads.
Selectivity: Admits over 75% of applicants.

BASIC COSTS (2007-2008)

Tuition and fees: $7,096; out-of-state residents $14,896.
Per-credit charge: $282; out-of-state residents $607.
Room and board: $5,809.
Additional info: Tuition charges include fees. Upper division tuition $7,302, in-state; $15,094, out-of-state. Tuition/fee waivers available for adults, minority students.

FINANCIAL AID PICTURE

Students with need: Need-based aid available for full-time and part-time students. Work study available weekends and for part-time students.
Students without need: No-need awards available for academics, alumni affiliation, art, athletics, job skills, leadership, minority status, music/drama, ROTC, state/district residency.

FINANCIAL AID PROCEDURES

Forms required: FAFSA.

Dates and Deadlines: Priority date 2/15; no closing date. Applicants notified on a rolling basis starting 4/1; must reply within 3 week(s) of notification.
Transfers: Priority date 4/1.

CONTACT

Lynda George, Director of Student Financial Aid
100 W.D. Funkhouser Building, Lexington, KY 40506-0054
(859) 257-3172

University of Louisville

Louisville, Kentucky
www.louisville.edu   Federal Code: 001999

4-year public university in very large city.
Enrollment: 14,101 undergrads, 18% part-time. 2,473 full-time freshmen.
Selectivity: Admits 50 to 75% of applicants.

BASIC COSTS (2007-2008)

Tuition and fees: $6,940; out-of-state residents $17,734.
Per-credit charge: $289; out-of-state residents $739.
Room and board: $5,722.

FINANCIAL AID PICTURE (2007-2008)

Students with need: Out of 1,818 full-time freshmen who applied for aid, 1,469 were judged to have need. Of these, 1,462 received aid, and 285 had their full need met. Average financial aid package met 63% of need; average scholarship/grant was $7,352; average loan was $3,342. For part-time students, average financial aid package was $7,549.

Students without need: 502 full-time freshmen who did not demonstrate need for aid received scholarships/grants; average award was $6,875. No-need awards available for academics, art, athletics, leadership, minority status, music/drama, ROTC.

Scholarships offered: 92 full-time freshmen received athletic scholarships; average amount $11,617.

FINANCIAL AID PROCEDURES

Forms required: FAFSA.

Dates and Deadlines: Priority date 3/15; no closing date. Applicants notified on a rolling basis starting 4/1; must reply by 5/1.
Transfers: Priority date 3/1.

CONTACT

Patricia Arauz, Director of Student Financial Aid
2211 South Brook Street, Louisville, KY 40292
(502) 852-5511

University of the Cumberlands

Williamsburg, Kentucky
www.ucumberlands.edu   Federal Code: 001962

4-year private liberal arts college in small town, affiliated with Baptist faith.
Enrollment: 1,463 undergrads, 3% part-time. 481 full-time freshmen.
Selectivity: Admits less than 50% of applicants.

BASIC COSTS (2008-2009)

Tuition and fees: $14,658.
Per-credit charge: $460.
Room and board: $6,626.

FINANCIAL AID PICTURE (2007-2008)

Students with need: Out of 442 full-time freshmen who applied for aid, 405 were judged to have need. Of these, 405 received aid, and 154 had their full need met. Average financial aid package met 94% of need; average scholarship/grant was $8,958; average loan was $3,116. For part-time students, average financial aid package was $5,295.

Students without need: 71 full-time freshmen who did not demonstrate need for aid received scholarships/grants; average award was $5,881. No-need awards available for academics, alumni affiliation, art, athletics, leadership, music/drama, religious affiliation, ROTC, state/district residency.

Scholarships offered: 198 full-time freshmen received athletic scholarships; average amount $4,244.

Cumulative student debt: 77% of graduating class had student loans; average debt was $17,117.

FINANCIAL AID PROCEDURES

Forms required: FAFSA.

Dates and Deadlines: Priority date 3/1; no closing date. Applicants notified on a rolling basis starting 4/1; must reply within 2 week(s) of notification.

CONTACT

Steve Allen, Director of Financial Planning
6178 College Station Drive, Williamsburg, KY 40769
(800) 343-1609

West Kentucky Community and Technical College

Paducah, Kentucky

www.westkentucky.kctcs.edu   Federal Code: 001979

2-year public community and technical college in large town.

Enrollment: 3,122 undergrads.

Selectivity: Open admission; but selective for some programs.

BASIC COSTS (2007-2008)

Tuition and fees: $3,450; out-of-state residents $10,350.

Per-credit charge: $115; out-of-state residents $345.

FINANCIAL AID PICTURE

Students with need: Need-based aid available for full-time and part-time students.

FINANCIAL AID PROCEDURES

Forms required: FAFSA.

Dates and Deadlines: Priority date 4/1; no closing date. Applicants notified on a rolling basis starting 7/15; must reply within 4 week(s) of notification.

CONTACT

Sandy Barlow, Financial Aid Officer

4810 Alben Barkley Drive, Paducah, KY 42002

(270) 534-3462

Western Kentucky University

Bowling Green, Kentucky

www.wku.edu   Federal Code: 002002

4-year public university in small city.

Enrollment: 15,502 undergrads, 15% part-time. 3,128 full-time freshmen.

Selectivity: Open admission; but selective for some programs.

BASIC COSTS (2007-2008)

Tuition and fees: $6,416; out-of-state residents $15,470.

Per-credit charge: $267; out-of-state residents $645.

Room and board: $5,964.

FINANCIAL AID PICTURE (2006-2007)

Students with need: Out of 2,491 full-time freshmen who applied for aid, 1,827 were judged to have need. Of these, 1,799 received aid, and 544 had their full need met. Average financial aid package met 30% of need; average scholarship/grant was $4,321; average loan was $2,322. For part-time students, average financial aid package was $6,993.

Students without need: 319 full-time freshmen who did not demonstrate need for aid received scholarships/grants; average award was $3,643. No-need awards available for academics, alumni affiliation, art, athletics, job skills, leadership, minority status, music/drama, religious affiliation, ROTC, state/district residency.

Scholarships offered: *Merit:* Academic scholarships; $200 to full tuition; number awarded varies. *Athletic:* 93 full-time freshmen received athletic scholarships; average amount $8,807.

Cumulative student debt: 53% of graduating class had student loans; average debt was $14,704.

FINANCIAL AID PROCEDURES

Forms required: FAFSA.

Dates and Deadlines: Priority date 4/1; no closing date. Applicants notified on a rolling basis starting 3/1.

Transfers: Transfer students receiving CAP Grant must notify the state agency by December 1 of each year.

CONTACT

Cindy Burnette, Director of Financial Assistance

1906 College Heights Boulevard, Bowling Green, KY 42101

(270) 745-2755

Louisiana

Baton Rouge Community College

Baton Rouge, Louisiana

www.mybrcc.edu   Federal Code: 037303

2-year public community college in large city.

Enrollment: 5,889 undergrads, 38% part-time. 1,101 full-time freshmen.

Selectivity: Open admission; but selective for some programs.

BASIC COSTS (2007-2008)

Tuition and fees: $1,806; out-of-state residents $4,614.

FINANCIAL AID PICTURE (2006-2007)

Students with need: 95% of average financial aid package awarded as scholarships/grants, 5% awarded as loans/jobs.

FINANCIAL AID PROCEDURES

Dates and Deadlines: Priority date 4/15; no closing date.

CONTACT

Calaundra Brown, Director of Financial Aid

5310 Florida Boulevard, Baton Rouge, LA 70806

(225) 216-8005

Bossier Parish Community College

Bossier City, Louisiana

www.bpcc.edu   Federal Code: 012033

2-year public community college in small city.

Enrollment: 4,227 undergrads, 38% part-time. 945 full-time freshmen.

Selectivity: Open admission; but selective for out-of-state students.

BASIC COSTS (2007-2008)

Tuition and fees: $1,760; out-of-state residents $3,900.

FINANCIAL AID PICTURE (2006-2007)

Students with need: Out of 732 full-time freshmen who applied for aid, 594 were judged to have need. Of these, 520 received aid. Average financial aid package met 45% of need; average scholarship/grant was $3,799; average loan was $1,659. For part-time students, average financial aid package was $3,250.

Students without need: 99 full-time freshmen who did not demonstrate need for aid received scholarships/grants; average award was $1,397. No-need awards available for academics, alumni affiliation, athletics, minority status, music/drama.

FINANCIAL AID PROCEDURES

Forms required: FAFSA.

Dates and Deadlines: Closing date 7/1. Applicants notified on a rolling basis.

Transfers: Priority date 6/1; no deadline.

CONTACT

Vickie Temple, Financial Aid Director

6220 East Texas Street, Bossier City, LA 71111-6922

(318) 678-6026

Centenary College of Louisiana

Shreveport, Louisiana
www.centenary.edu   Federal Code: 002003

4-year private liberal arts college in small city, affiliated with United Methodist Church.

Enrollment: 845 undergrads.
Selectivity: Admits 50 to 75% of applicants.

BASIC COSTS (2008-2009)

Tuition and fees: $21,630.
Per-credit charge: $700.
Room and board: $7,360.

FINANCIAL AID PICTURE

Students with need: Need-based aid available for full-time and part-time students. Work study available nights, weekends, and for part-time students.
Students without need: No-need awards available for academics, art, athletics, leadership, music/drama, religious affiliation, state/district residency.

FINANCIAL AID PROCEDURES

Forms required: FAFSA, institutional form.
Dates and Deadlines: Priority date 2/15; no closing date. Applicants notified on a rolling basis starting 2/15; must reply by 5/1.

CONTACT

MarySue Rix, Director of Financial Aid
Box 41188, Shreveport, LA 71134-1188
(318) 869-5137

Delgado Community College

New Orleans, Louisiana
www.dcc.edu   Federal Code: 004626

2-year public community college in very large city.
Enrollment: 12,224 undergrads.
Selectivity: Open admission; but selective for some programs.

BASIC COSTS (2007-2008)

Tuition and fees: $1,928; out-of-state residents $4,908.

FINANCIAL AID PICTURE

Students with need: Need-based aid available for full-time and part-time students. Work study available nights, weekends, and for part-time students.
Students without need: No-need awards available for academics, athletics, leadership, music/drama, state/district residency.

FINANCIAL AID PROCEDURES

Forms required: FAFSA, institutional form.
Dates and Deadlines: Priority date 5/1; closing date 7/15. Applicants notified on a rolling basis starting 4/1; must reply within 2 week(s) of notification.

CONTACT

Germaine Edwards, Director of Student Financial Assistance
615 City Park Avenue, New Orleans, LA 70119

Dillard University

New Orleans, Louisiana
www.dillard.edu   Federal Code: 002004

4-year private university and liberal arts college in very large city, affiliated with United Church of Christ and United Methodist Church.
Enrollment: 956 undergrads.
Selectivity: Admits less than 50% of applicants.

BASIC COSTS (2007-2008)

Tuition and fees: $12,240.
Per-credit charge: $490.
Room and board: $7,900.

FINANCIAL AID PICTURE

Students with need: Need-based aid available for full-time and part-time students. Work study available nights, weekends, and for part-time students.
Students without need: This college awards aid only to students with need.

FINANCIAL AID PROCEDURES

Forms required: FAFSA, institutional form.
Dates and Deadlines: Priority date 12/1; closing date 5/1. Applicants notified on a rolling basis starting 3/1; must reply by 5/1 or within 2 week(s) of notification.

CONTACT

Michael White, Director of Financial Aid
2601 Gentilly Boulevard, New Orleans, LA 70122-3097
(800) 216-8094

Grambling State University

Grambling, Louisiana
www.gram.edu   Federal Code: 002006

4-year public university in small town.
Enrollment: 4,747 undergrads, 8% part-time. 1,318 full-time freshmen.
Selectivity: Open admission; but selective for out-of-state students. GED not accepted.

BASIC COSTS (2007-2008)

Tuition and fees: $3,622; out-of-state residents $8,972.
Room and board: $5,072.

FINANCIAL AID PICTURE (2006-2007)

Students with need: Out of 1,145 full-time freshmen who applied for aid, 1,058 were judged to have need. Of these, 1,053 received aid, and 49 had their full need met. Average financial aid package met 90% of need; average scholarship/grant was $3,077; average loan was $2,357. For part-time students, average financial aid package was $2,190.
Students without need: 6 full-time freshmen who did not demonstrate need for aid received scholarships/grants; average award was $3,280. No-need awards available for academics, alumni affiliation, art, athletics, job skills, leadership, minority status, music/drama, religious affiliation, ROTC, state/district residency.
Scholarships offered: 32 full-time freshmen received athletic scholarships; average amount $6,285.
Cumulative student debt: 85% of graduating class had student loans; average debt was $30,000.

FINANCIAL AID PROCEDURES

Forms required: FAFSA.
Dates and Deadlines: Priority date 4/1; closing date 6/1. Applicants notified on a rolling basis starting 3/1; must reply within 2 week(s) of notification.
Transfers: Applicants notified on a rolling basis starting 3/1; must reply within 2 week(s) of notification.

CONTACT

Betty Rucker, Director of Student Financial Aid
403 Main Street, GSU Box 4200, Grambling, LA 71245
(318) 274-6190

ITI Technical College

Baton Rouge, Louisiana
www.iticollege.edu   Federal Code: 015270

2-year for-profit technical college in large city.
Enrollment: 323 undergrads. 175 full-time freshmen.
Selectivity: Open admission.

BASIC COSTS (2007-2008)
Additional info: Full-time tuition varies by program from $11,400 to $22,900.

FINANCIAL AID PICTURE
Students with need: Need-based aid available for full-time and part-time students.
Students without need: This college awards aid only to students with need.

FINANCIAL AID PROCEDURES
Forms required: FAFSA.
Dates and Deadlines: No deadline.

CONTACT
Connie Roubique, Financial Aid Director
13944 Airline Highway, Baton Rouge, LA 70817
(225) 752-4233

Louisiana College

Pineville, Louisiana
www.lacollege.edu   Federal Code: 002007

4-year private liberal arts college in small city, affiliated with Southern Baptist Convention.
Enrollment: 1,056 undergrads. 246 full-time freshmen.
Selectivity: Admits over 75% of applicants.

BASIC COSTS (2007-2008)
Tuition and fees: $11,490.
Per-credit charge: $340.
Room and board: $4,256.
Additional info: Tuition at time of enrollment locked for 4 years.

FINANCIAL AID PICTURE
Students with need: Need-based aid available for full-time and part-time students. Work study available nights, weekends, and for part-time students.
Students without need: No-need awards available for academics, art, leadership, music/drama, ROTC.

FINANCIAL AID PROCEDURES
Forms required: FAFSA, institutional form.
Dates and Deadlines: Priority date 3/31; no closing date. Applicants notified on a rolling basis starting 3/1; must reply by 5/1 or within 2 week(s) of notification.
Transfers: Scholarships available.

CONTACT
Ronnie LaLande, Director of Financial Aid
LC Box 566, Pineville, LA 71359
(318) 487-7386

Louisiana State University and Agricultural and Mechanical College

Baton Rouge, Louisiana
www.lsu.edu   Federal Code: 002010

4-year public university and agricultural college in large city.
Enrollment: 23,063 undergrads, 6% part-time. 4,541 full-time freshmen.

Selectivity: Admits 50 to 75% of applicants.

BASIC COSTS (2007-2008)
Tuition and fees: $4,543; out-of-state residents $12,843.
Room and board: $6,852.

FINANCIAL AID PICTURE (2006-2007)
Students with need: Out of 2,645 full-time freshmen who applied for aid, 1,533 were judged to have need. Of these, 1,533 received aid, and 322 had their full need met. Average financial aid package met 68% of need; average scholarship/grant was $6,791; average loan was $2,723. For part-time students, average financial aid package was $5,372.
Students without need: 1,125 full-time freshmen who did not demonstrate need for aid received scholarships/grants; average award was $2,856. No-need awards available for academics, alumni affiliation, art, athletics, leadership, music/drama, ROTC, state/district residency.
Scholarships offered: 108 full-time freshmen received athletic scholarships; average amount $12,864.
Cumulative student debt: 46% of graduating class had student loans; average debt was $17,057.

FINANCIAL AID PROCEDURES
Forms required: FAFSA, institutional form.
Dates and Deadlines: No deadline. Applicants notified on a rolling basis starting 3/1; must reply within 3 week(s) of notification.
Transfers: No deadline. Applicants notified on a rolling basis.

CONTACT
Mary Parker, Executive Director of Undergraduate Admissions & Student Aid
1146 Pleasant Halll, Baton Rouge, LA 70803-2750
(225) 578-3103

Louisiana State University at Alexandria

Alexandria, Louisiana
www.lsua.edu   Federal Code: 002011

4-year public university in small city.
Enrollment: 2,405 undergrads.
Selectivity: Open admission.

BASIC COSTS (2007-2008)
Tuition and fees: $3,158; out-of-state residents $5,619.
Per-credit charge: $213; out-of-state residents $315.
Additional info: On-campus housing (double-occupancy) $510 per month; meal plan $529 per 160 meals.

FINANCIAL AID PICTURE
Students with need: Need-based aid available for full-time and part-time students. Work study available nights.
Students without need: No-need awards available for academics, state/district residency.

FINANCIAL AID PROCEDURES
Forms required: FAFSA, institutional form.
Dates and Deadlines: Priority date 4/1; no closing date. Applicants notified on a rolling basis starting 4/20; must reply within 3 week(s) of notification.

CONTACT
Kenn Posey, Director of Student Aid and Scholarships
8100 Highway 71 South, Alexandria, LA 71302-9121
(318) 473-6423

Louisiana State University at Eunice

Eunice, Louisiana
www.lsue.edu   Federal Code: 002012

2-year public branch campus and community college in large town.
Enrollment: 2,864 undergrads.
Selectivity: Open admission; but selective for some programs.

BASIC COSTS (2007-2008)
Tuition and fees: $2,192; out-of-state residents $5,192.
Per-credit charge: $92.

FINANCIAL AID PICTURE (2007-2008)
Students with need: 97% of average financial aid package awarded as scholarships/grants, 3% awarded as loans/jobs. Need-based aid available for part-time students.

FINANCIAL AID PROCEDURES
Forms required: FAFSA, institutional form.
Dates and Deadlines: Priority date 6/1; no closing date. Applicants notified on a rolling basis starting 4/1; must reply within 2 week(s) of notification.

CONTACT
Jacqueline Lachapelle, Director of Financial Aid
Box 1129, Eunice, LA 70535
(337) 550-1282

Louisiana State University Health Sciences Center

New Orleans, Louisiana
www.lsuhsc.edu   Federal Code: 002014

Upper-division public health science and nursing college in large city.
Enrollment: 572 undergrads.

BASIC COSTS (2007-2008)
Tuition and fees: $3,978; out-of-state residents $7,110.
Room only: $2,210.

FINANCIAL AID PICTURE
Students with need: Need-based aid available for full-time and part-time students. Work study available nights, weekends, and for part-time students.
Students without need: No-need awards available for academics.

FINANCIAL AID PROCEDURES
Forms required: FAFSA, institutional form.
Dates and Deadlines: Priority date 4/15; no closing date. Applicants notified on a rolling basis starting 7/1.

CONTACT
Patrick Gorman, Director of Financial Aid
433 Bolivar Street, New Orleans, LA 70112-2223
(504) 568-4820

Louisiana State University in Shreveport

Shreveport, Louisiana
www.lsus.edu   Federal Code: 002013

4-year public university in large city.
Enrollment: 3,211 undergrads.
Selectivity: Admits over 75% of applicants.

BASIC COSTS (2007-2008)
Tuition and fees: $3,521; out-of-state residents $7,847.

FINANCIAL AID PICTURE
Students with need: Need-based aid available for full-time and part-time students. Work study available nights, weekends, and for part-time students.

FINANCIAL AID PROCEDURES
Dates and Deadlines: No deadline. Applicants notified on a rolling basis.

CONTACT
Betty McCrary, Director of Student Financial Aid
One University Place, Shreveport, LA 71115-2399
(318) 797-5363

Louisiana Tech University

Ruston, Louisiana
www.latech.edu   Federal Code: 002008

4-year public university in large town.
Enrollment: 8,375 undergrads.

BASIC COSTS (2007-2008)
Tuition and fees: $4,428; out-of-state residents $10,893.
Room and board: $4,470.

FINANCIAL AID PICTURE
Students with need: Need-based aid available for full-time and part-time students.
Students without need: No-need awards available for academics, art, athletics, leadership, music/drama, ROTC.

FINANCIAL AID PROCEDURES
Forms required: FAFSA, institutional form.
Dates and Deadlines: Priority date 4/15; no closing date. Applicants notified on a rolling basis starting 3/18; must reply within 4 week(s) of notification.
Transfers: Priority date 8/1; no deadline. Applicants notified on a rolling basis starting 8/20; must reply within 2 week(s) of notification.

CONTACT
Roger Vick, Director of Student Financial Aid
Box 3178, Ruston, LA 71272
(318) 257-2641

Loyola University New Orleans

New Orleans, Louisiana
www.loyno.edu   Federal Code: 002016

4-year private university and liberal arts college in large city, affiliated with Roman Catholic Church.
Enrollment: 2,591 undergrads, 10% part-time. 503 full-time freshmen.
Selectivity: Admits 50 to 75% of applicants.

BASIC COSTS (2008-2009)
Tuition and fees: $28,044.
Per-credit charge: $775.
Room and board: $9,394.

FINANCIAL AID PICTURE (2007-2008)
Students with need: Out of 382 full-time freshmen who applied for aid, 325 were judged to have need. Of these, 325 received aid, and 94 had their full need met. Average financial aid package met 84% of need; average scholarship/grant was $20,127; average loan was $3,361. For part-time students, average financial aid package was $6,289.
Students without need: 157 full-time freshmen who did not demonstrate need for aid received scholarships/grants; average award was $13,784. No-need awards available for academics, alumni affiliation, art, minority status, ROTC.
Scholarships offered: 1 full-time freshmen received athletic scholarships; average amount $33,134.

Cumulative student debt: 62% of graduating class had student loans; average debt was $21,020.

FINANCIAL AID PROCEDURES

Forms required: FAFSA.

Dates and Deadlines: Priority date 2/15; closing date 6/1. Applicants notified on a rolling basis starting 3/1; must reply by 5/1 or within 2 week(s) of notification.

Transfers: Priority date 3/1; closing date 5/1. Transfer scholarship deadline June 1.

CONTACT

Catherine Simoneaux, Director of Scholarships and Financial Aid
6363 St. Charles Avenue, New Orleans, LA 70118-6195
(504) 865-3231

McNeese State University

Lake Charles, Louisiana
www.mcneese.edu   Federal Code: 002017

4-year public university in small city.

Enrollment: 7,041 undergrads, 17% part-time. 1,252 full-time freshmen.

BASIC COSTS (2007-2008)

Tuition and fees: $3,233; out-of-state residents $9,299.

Room and board: $5,840.

FINANCIAL AID PICTURE

Students with need: Need-based aid available for full-time and part-time students. Work study available nights, weekends, and for part-time students.

Students without need: No-need awards available for academics, alumni affiliation, art, athletics, leadership, minority status, music/drama, state/district residency.

Additional info: Books may be charged and paid in 2 installments during semester.

FINANCIAL AID PROCEDURES

Forms required: FAFSA, institutional form.

Dates and Deadlines: Priority date 5/1; no closing date. Applicants notified on a rolling basis starting 4/15; must reply within 2 week(s) of notification.

Transfers: Transfer students must exhibit satisfactory academic progress at school most recently attended to be eligible for financial aid.

CONTACT

Taina Savoit, Director of Financial Aid
Box 91740 MSU, Lake Charles, LA 70609-1740
(337) 475-5065

Nicholls State University

Thibodaux, Louisiana
www.nicholls.edu   Federal Code: 002005

4-year public university in large town.

Enrollment: 6,118 undergrads, 20% part-time. 1,072 full-time freshmen.

Selectivity: Admits over 75% of applicants.

BASIC COSTS (2007-2008)

Tuition and fees: $3,595; out-of-state residents $9,043.

Room and board: $4,556.

FINANCIAL AID PICTURE (2006-2007)

Students with need: Out of 965 full-time freshmen who applied for aid, 506 were judged to have need. Of these, 500 received aid, and 261 had their full need met. Average financial aid package met 78% of need; average scholarship/grant was $2,160; average loan was $2,149. For part-time students, average financial aid package was $4,419.

Students without need: 89 full-time freshmen who did not demonstrate need for aid received scholarships/grants; average award was $2,238. No-need awards available for academics, athletics, state/district residency.

Scholarships offered: 24 full-time freshmen received athletic scholarships; average amount $4,763.

Cumulative student debt: 56% of graduating class had student loans; average debt was $16,710.

FINANCIAL AID PROCEDURES

Forms required: FAFSA, state aid form, institutional form.

Dates and Deadlines: Priority date 4/17; no closing date. Applicants notified on a rolling basis; must reply within 2 week(s) of notification.

Transfers: Priority date 5/1; no deadline. Applicants notified on a rolling basis.

CONTACT

Colette Lagarde, Director of Financial Aid
PO Box 2004-NSU, Thibodaux, LA 70310
(985) 448-4048

Northwestern State University

Natchitoches, Louisiana
www.nsula.edu   Federal Code: 002021

4-year public university in large town.

Enrollment: 7,677 undergrads, 27% part-time. 1,323 full-time freshmen.

Selectivity: Admits over 75% of applicants.

BASIC COSTS (2007-2008)

Tuition and fees: $3,528; out-of-state residents $9,606.

Room and board: $5,850.

FINANCIAL AID PICTURE (2006-2007)

Students with need: Out of 1,082 full-time freshmen who applied for aid, 939 were judged to have need. Of these, 914 received aid, and 261 had their full need met. Average financial aid package met 50% of need; average scholarship/grant was $3,657; average loan was $3,970. For part-time students, average financial aid package was $4,450.

Students without need: 261 full-time freshmen who did not demonstrate need for aid received scholarships/grants; average award was $4,120. No-need awards available for academics, alumni affiliation, art, athletics, job skills, leadership, minority status, music/drama, religious affiliation, ROTC, state/district residency.

Scholarships offered: 58 full-time freshmen received athletic scholarships; average amount $7,472.

Cumulative student debt: 70% of graduating class had student loans; average debt was $19,222.

FINANCIAL AID PROCEDURES

Forms required: FAFSA, institutional form.

Dates and Deadlines: Priority date 5/1; no closing date. Applicants notified on a rolling basis starting 5/1; must reply within 4 week(s) of notification.

Transfers: No deadline. Applicants notified on a rolling basis starting 5/1; must reply within 4 week(s) of notification.

CONTACT

Misti Adams, Director of Financial Aid
Roy Hall, Room 209, Natchitoches, LA 71497
(800) 823-3008

Nunez Community College

Chalmette, Louisiana
www.nunez.edu   Federal Code: 015130

2-year public community and technical college in large town.

Enrollment: 847 undergrads, 35% part-time. 109 full-time freshmen.

Selectivity: Open admission; but selective for some programs.

BASIC COSTS (2007-2008)

Tuition and fees: $1,770; out-of-state residents $4,290.

FINANCIAL AID PICTURE

Students with need: Need-based aid available for full-time and part-time students.

Additional info: Pell Grants, Stafford Loans, campus workstudy, and tuition waiver scholarships available. Louisiana National Guard tuition exemption, teacher tuition exemption, dependents of injured fire-police tuition waivers.

FINANCIAL AID PROCEDURES

Forms required: FAFSA, institutional form.

Dates and Deadlines: Priority date 4/1; closing date 7/1. Applicants notified by 8/1; must reply by 8/15.

Transfers: Applicant must supply academic transcripts from every postsecondary school attended.

CONTACT

Brandi Weber, Financial Aid Officer
3710 Paris Road, Chalmette, LA 70043
(504) 278-7487

Our Lady of the Lake College

Baton Rouge, Louisiana
www.ololcollege.edu   Federal Code: 031062

4-year private health science and nursing college in large city, affiliated with Roman Catholic Church.

Enrollment: 1,936 undergrads, 67% part-time. 2 full-time freshmen.

Selectivity: Admits over 75% of applicants.

BASIC COSTS (2008-2009)

Tuition and fees: $9,217.
Per-credit charge: $280.

FINANCIAL AID PICTURE (2006-2007)

Students with need: Out of 2 full-time freshmen who applied for aid, 2 were judged to have need. Of these, 2 received aid. For part-time students, average financial aid package was $2,366.

FINANCIAL AID PROCEDURES

Forms required: FAFSA, institutional form.

Dates and Deadlines: Closing date 3/1.

CONTACT

Tiffany MaGee, Director of Financial Aid
7434 Perkins Road, Baton Rouge, LA 70808
(225) 768-1714

Remington College: Baton Rouge

Baton Rouge, Louisiana
www.remingtoncollege.edu/batonrouge   Federal Code: E00907

2-year for-profit technical college in large city.

Enrollment: 410 undergrads.

Selectivity: Open admission; but selective for some programs.

BASIC COSTS (2007-2008)

Additional info: Costs of entire programs leading to certificate, associate degree, bachelor's degree range from $13,000 to $38,880; includes books and supplies.

FINANCIAL AID PICTURE

Students with need: Need-based aid available for full-time students. Work study available nights.

Students without need: This college awards aid only to students with need.

FINANCIAL AID PROCEDURES

Forms required: FAFSA.

Dates and Deadlines: No deadline. Applicants notified on a rolling basis; must reply within 1 week(s) of notification.

CONTACT

Bill Moody, National Director of Financial Aid
10551 Coursey Boulevard, Baton Rouge, LA 70816

Remington College: Lafayette

Lafayette, Louisiana
www.remingtoncollege.edu   Federal Code: 005203

2-year for-profit junior college in small city.

Enrollment: 242 undergrads.

Selectivity: Open admission.

BASIC COSTS (2007-2008)

Additional info: Costs of entire programs leading to certificate, associate degree, bachelor's degree range from $13,000 to $38,880; includes books and supplies.

FINANCIAL AID PICTURE

Students with need: Need-based aid available for full-time students. Work study available nights.

Students without need: This college awards aid only to students with need.

FINANCIAL AID PROCEDURES

Forms required: FAFSA, institutional form.

Dates and Deadlines: No deadline.

CONTACT

JoAnn Boudreaux, Director of Financial Aid
303 Rue Louis XIV, Lafayette, LA 70508
(337) 981-4010

St. Joseph Seminary College

St. Benedict, Louisiana
www.sjasc.edu   Federal Code: 002027

4-year private liberal arts and seminary college for men in rural community, affiliated with Roman Catholic Church.

Enrollment: 77 undergrads. 8 full-time freshmen.

Selectivity: Admits over 75% of applicants.

BASIC COSTS (2008-2009)

Tuition and fees: $12,769.
Room and board: $10,784.

FINANCIAL AID PICTURE

Students with need: Need-based aid available for full-time and part-time students.

Students without need: No-need awards available for academics, leadership.

FINANCIAL AID PROCEDURES

Forms required: FAFSA.

Dates and Deadlines: Priority date 3/15; no closing date. Applicants notified on a rolling basis starting 7/1; must reply within 4 week(s) of notification.

Transfers: Closing date 5/1.

CONTACT

George Binder, Director of Student Financial Aid
75376 River Road, St. Benedict, LA 70457-9990
(985) 867-2248

School of Urban Missions: New Orleans

New Orleans, Louisiana
www.sum.edu   Federal Code: 037524

4-year private Bible college in very large city, affiliated with Assemblies of God, Church of God in Christ.
Enrollment: 20 undergrads, 100% part-time.
Selectivity: Admits 50 to 75% of applicants.

BASIC COSTS (2008-2009)

Tuition and fees: $7,105.
Per-credit charge: $220.
Room only: $2,400.

FINANCIAL AID PICTURE (2006-2007)

Students with need: 33% of average financial aid package awarded as scholarships/grants, 67% awarded as loans/jobs. Need-based aid available for part-time students.
Students without need: No-need awards available for academics, leadership, religious affiliation.

FINANCIAL AID PROCEDURES

Forms required: FAFSA, institutional form.
Dates and Deadlines: No deadline.
Transfers: No deadline. Applicants notified on a rolling basis.

CONTACT

Rodney Suzuki, Business Administrator
511 Westbank Expressway, Gretna, LA 70053-3677
(510) 567-6174

Southeastern Louisiana University

Hammond, Louisiana
www.selu.edu   Federal Code: 002024

4-year public university in large town.
Enrollment: 12,796 undergrads. 2,568 full-time freshmen.
Selectivity: Admits over 75% of applicants.

BASIC COSTS (2007-2008)

Tuition and fees: $3,561; out-of-state residents $9,561.
Per-credit charge: $92; out-of-state residents $342.
Room and board: $5,990.

FINANCIAL AID PICTURE (2006-2007)

Students with need: Out of 2,215 full-time freshmen who applied for aid, 1,434 were judged to have need. Of these, 1,350 received aid, and 296 had their full need met. For part-time students, average financial aid package was $5,430.
Students without need: 205 full-time freshmen who did not demonstrate need for aid received scholarships/grants; average award was $1,857. No-need awards available for academics, alumni affiliation, art, athletics, job skills, leadership, music/drama, state/district residency.
Scholarships offered: *Merit:* Any student admitted with 24 or higher ACT and minimum 3.0 GPA on a seven-semester transcript qualifies for a scholarship. All scholarships awarded for eight semesters; annual awards $1,000 to $3,500. On-campus housing scholarships: eight semesters ranging from a half room award to full room award; based on ACT score and GPA. Presidential Honors Scholarship: 30 or higher ACT, minimum 3.0 GPA; annual awards $2,500 to $3,500 in addition to covering on-campus housing and meals (full

shared housing award and pack meal plan). *Athletic:* 44 full-time freshmen received athletic scholarships; average amount $4,356.
Cumulative student debt: 62% of graduating class had student loans; average debt was $16,519.

FINANCIAL AID PROCEDURES

Forms required: FAFSA, institutional form.
Dates and Deadlines: Priority date 5/1; no closing date. Applicants notified on a rolling basis starting 3/1; must reply within 2 week(s) of notification.
Transfers: Applicants notified on a rolling basis starting 3/1; must reply within 2 week(s) of notification. Financial aid is available for transfer students, including those admitted on probation.

CONTACT

Rosie Toney, Director of Financial Aid
SLU 10752, Hammond, LA 70402
(985) 549-2244

Southern University and Agricultural and Mechanical College

Baton Rouge, Louisiana
www.subr.edu   Federal Code: 002025

4-year public university in large city.
Enrollment: 6,830 undergrads, 11% part-time. 1,136 full-time freshmen.
Selectivity: Admits 50 to 75% of applicants.

BASIC COSTS (2007-2008)

Tuition and fees: $3,666; out-of-state residents $9,458.
Room and board: $6,504.

FINANCIAL AID PICTURE (2006-2007)

Students with need: Out of 1,078 full-time freshmen who applied for aid, 1,018 were judged to have need. Of these, 1,008 received aid, and 40 had their full need met. Average financial aid package met 89% of need; average scholarship/grant was $3,436; average loan was $2,399. For part-time students, average financial aid package was $4,256.
Students without need: 244 full-time freshmen who did not demonstrate need for aid received scholarships/grants; average award was $2,980. No-need awards available for academics, athletics, ROTC, state/district residency.
Scholarships offered: 55 full-time freshmen received athletic scholarships; average amount $5,592.
Cumulative student debt: 96% of graduating class had student loans; average debt was $23,000.

FINANCIAL AID PROCEDURES

Forms required: FAFSA.
Dates and Deadlines: Priority date 1/31; closing date 3/30. Applicants notified on a rolling basis starting 5/1; must reply within 3 week(s) of notification.
Transfers: Closing date 5/31. Applicants notified on a rolling basis starting 5/31; must reply within 3 week(s) of notification.

CONTACT

Ursula Shorty, Director of Financial Aid
T.H. Harris Hall, Baton Rouge, LA 70813
(225) 771-2790

Southern University at New Orleans

New Orleans, Louisiana
www.suno.edu   Federal Code: 002026

4-year public university in large city.
Enrollment: 2,139 undergrads.
Selectivity: Open admission.

BASIC COSTS (2007-2008)

Tuition and fees: $3,002; out-of-state residents $6,742.

FINANCIAL AID PICTURE

Students with need: Need-based aid available for full-time and part-time students.

Students without need: This college awards aid only to students with need.

FINANCIAL AID PROCEDURES

Forms required: FAFSA.

Dates and Deadlines: Closing date 4/1. Applicants notified by 5/15; must reply within 1 week(s) of notification.

CONTACT

Kathy Woods, Director of Financial Aid

6801 Press Drive, New Orleans, LA 70126

(504) 286-5263

Tulane University

New Orleans, Louisiana   Federal Code: 002029

www.tulane.edu   CSS Code: 6832

4-year private university in very large city.

Enrollment: 6,408 undergrads, 21% part-time. 1,324 full-time freshmen.

Selectivity: Admits less than 50% of applicants.

BASIC COSTS (2007-2008)

Tuition and fees: $36,610.

Per-credit charge: $1,488.

Room and board: $8,649.

FINANCIAL AID PICTURE (2006-2007)

Students with need: Out of 593 full-time freshmen who applied for aid, 437 were judged to have need. Of these, 437 received aid, and 299 had their full need met. Average financial aid package met 95% of need; average scholarship/grant was $22,761; average loan was $4,027. For part-time students, average financial aid package was $8,257.

Students without need: 249 full-time freshmen who did not demonstrate need for aid received scholarships/grants; average award was $20,541. No-need awards available for academics, athletics, leadership, state/district residency.

Scholarships offered: *Merit:* Dean's Honor Scholarship: full tuition. Distinguished Scholars Award: up to $18,000. Founders Scholarship: up to $16,000. Urban Scholars Award: full tuition. *Athletic:* 21 full-time freshmen received athletic scholarships; average amount $34,334.

Cumulative student debt: 44% of graduating class had student loans; average debt was $22,378.

Additional info: Application deadline for merit scholarships December 1.

FINANCIAL AID PROCEDURES

Forms required: FAFSA, CSS PROFILE.

Dates and Deadlines: Priority date 1/15; closing date 2/1. Applicants notified on a rolling basis starting 2/1; must reply by 5/1 or within 2 week(s) of notification.

Transfers: Applicants notified on a rolling basis starting 2/1; must reply by 5/1 or within 2 week(s) of notification.

CONTACT

Michael Goodman, Associate Vice President for Financial Aid

6823 St. Charles Avenue, New Orleans, LA 70118-5680

(504) 865-5723

University of Louisiana at Lafayette

Lafayette, Louisiana

www.louisiana.edu   Federal Code: 002031

4-year public university in small city.

Enrollment: 14,449 undergrads, 13% part-time. 2,710 full-time freshmen.

Selectivity: Admits 50 to 75% of applicants.

BASIC COSTS (2007-2008)

Tuition and fees: $3,430; out-of-state residents $9,612.

Room and board: $3,820.

FINANCIAL AID PICTURE

Students with need: Need-based aid available for full-time and part-time students. Work study available nights, weekends, and for part-time students.

Students without need: This college awards aid only to students with need.

FINANCIAL AID PROCEDURES

Forms required: FAFSA, institutional form.

Dates and Deadlines: Priority date 5/1; no closing date. Applicants notified on a rolling basis starting 4/1; must reply within 2 week(s) of notification.

CONTACT

Cindy Perez, Director, Student Financial Aid

Box 41210, Lafayette, LA 70504-1210

(337) 482-6506

University of Louisiana at Monroe

Monroe, Louisiana

www.ulm.edu   Federal Code: 002020

4-year public university in small city.

Enrollment: 7,262 undergrads, 19% part-time. 1,400 full-time freshmen.

Selectivity: Admits over 75% of applicants.

BASIC COSTS (2007-2008)

Tuition and fees: $3,607; out-of-state residents $9,559.

Room and board: $5,500.

FINANCIAL AID PICTURE

Students with need: Need-based aid available for full-time and part-time students.

Students without need: No-need awards available for academics, alumni affiliation, art, athletics, job skills, leadership, minority status, music/drama, religious affiliation, ROTC, state/district residency.

FINANCIAL AID PROCEDURES

Forms required: FAFSA.

Dates and Deadlines: Priority date 4/1; no closing date. Applicants notified on a rolling basis starting 6/1; must reply within 2 week(s) of notification.

CONTACT

Teri Smith, Director of Financial Aid

700 University Avenue, Monroe, LA 71209-1160

(318) 342-5320

University of New Orleans

New Orleans, Louisiana

www.uno.edu   Federal Code: 002015

4-year public university in very large city.

Enrollment: 8,653 undergrads, 25% part-time. 1,031 full-time freshmen.

Selectivity: Admits over 75% of applicants.

BASIC COSTS (2007-2008)

Tuition and fees: $3,984; out-of-state residents $11,028.
Per-credit charge: $521; out-of-state residents $1,859.
Room and board: $5,240.

FINANCIAL AID PICTURE (2007-2008)

Students with need: Out of 914 full-time freshmen who applied for aid, 688 were judged to have need. Of these, 469 received aid, and 133 had their full need met. Average financial aid package met 68% of need; average scholarship/grant was $5,059; average loan was $3,066. For part-time students, average financial aid package was $4,886.
Students without need: 69 full-time freshmen who did not demonstrate need for aid received scholarships/grants; average award was $2,154. No-need awards available for academics, athletics.
Scholarships offered: 11 full-time freshmen received athletic scholarships; average amount $6,108.
Cumulative student debt: 31% of graduating class had student loans; average debt was $24,657.
Additional info: Students in good academic and financial standing eligible to participate in Extended Payment Plan option.

FINANCIAL AID PROCEDURES

Forms required: FAFSA, institutional form.
Dates and Deadlines: Priority date 6/30; no closing date. Applicants notified on a rolling basis starting 4/20; must reply within 4 week(s) of notification.
Transfers: Mid-year transfers must submit financial aid transcript from all post-secondary schools attended. Others submit NSLDS.

CONTACT

Emily London-Jones, Director of Student Financial Aid
Administration Building Room 103, New Orleans, LA 70148
(504) 280-6603

Xavier University of Louisiana

New Orleans, Louisiana
www.xula.edu   Federal Code: 002032

4-year private university in very large city, affiliated with Roman Catholic Church.
Enrollment: 2,316 undergrads, 3% part-time. 441 full-time freshmen.
Selectivity: Admits 50 to 75% of applicants.

BASIC COSTS (2007-2008)

Tuition and fees: $14,700.
Per-credit charge: $600.
Room and board: $6,600.

FINANCIAL AID PICTURE (2006-2007)

Students with need: Out of 423 full-time freshmen who applied for aid, 379 were judged to have need. Of these, 374 received aid, and 91 had their full need met. Average financial aid package met 52% of need; average scholarship/grant was $6,629; average loan was $2,852. For part-time students, average financial aid package was $12,022.
Students without need: 19 full-time freshmen who did not demonstrate need for aid received scholarships/grants; average award was $4,759.
Scholarships offered: 12 full-time freshmen received athletic scholarships; average amount $14,222.
Cumulative student debt: 73% of graduating class had student loans; average debt was $41,742.

FINANCIAL AID PROCEDURES

Forms required: FAFSA.
Dates and Deadlines: Priority date 1/1; no closing date. Applicants notified on a rolling basis starting 4/1; must reply within 2 week(s) of notification.

CONTACT

Mildred Higgins, Director of Financial Aid
1 Drexel Drive, New Orleans, LA 70125-1098
(504) 520-7517

Maine

Andover College

Portland, Maine
www.andovercollege.edu   Federal Code: 009292

2-year for-profit business and junior college in small city.
Enrollment: 501 undergrads.
Selectivity: Open admission.

BASIC COSTS (2007-2008)

Tuition and fees: $8,100.
Per-credit charge: $230.
Additional info: Tuition at time of enrollment locked for 2 years.

FINANCIAL AID PICTURE (2006-2007)

Students with need: 46% of average financial aid package awarded as scholarships/grants, 54% awarded as loans/jobs.
Students without need: This college awards aid only to students with need.
Scholarships offered: Promising Scholar Program: students must submit 3 references and 2 essays; not based on high school academic record; 10 awarded; $1,410-$5,640 annually.
Additional info: Work-study positions available.

FINANCIAL AID PROCEDURES

Forms required: FAFSA.
Dates and Deadlines: No deadline. Applicants notified on a rolling basis.

CONTACT

Kelly Knight, Financial Aid Director
901 Washington Avenue, Portland, ME 04103
(207) 774-6126 ext. 8718

Bates College

Lewiston, Maine   Federal Code: 002036
www.bates.edu   CSS Code: 3076

4-year private liberal arts college in large town.
Enrollment: 1,660 undergrads. 442 full-time freshmen.
Selectivity: Admits less than 50% of applicants. GED not accepted.

BASIC COSTS (2007-2008)

Comprehensive fee: $46,800.

FINANCIAL AID PICTURE (2007-2008)

Students with need: Out of 203 full-time freshmen who applied for aid, 203 were judged to have need. Of these, 191 received aid, and 179 had their full need met. Average financial aid package met 100% of need; average scholarship/grant was $30,057; average loan was $3,704.
Students without need: This college awards aid only to students with need.
Cumulative student debt: 48% of graduating class had student loans; average debt was $13,947.
Additional info: Priority date for filing required financial aid forms for early decision students is 11/15.

FINANCIAL AID PROCEDURES

Forms required: FAFSA, CSS PROFILE.
Dates and Deadlines: Closing date 2/1. Applicants notified by 4/1; must reply by 5/1.

CONTACT

Wendy Glass, Acting Director of Student Financial Services
23 Campus Avenue, Lindholm House, Lewiston, ME 04240-9917
(207) 786-6096

Bowdoin College

Brunswick, Maine — Federal Code: 002038
www.bowdoin.edu — CSS Code: 3089

4-year private liberal arts college in large town.
Enrollment: 1,710 undergrads. 474 full-time freshmen.
Selectivity: Admits less than 50% of applicants. GED not accepted.

BASIC COSTS (2007-2008)

Tuition and fees: $36,370.
Room and board: $9,890.

FINANCIAL AID PICTURE (2006-2007)

Students with need: Out of 251 full-time freshmen who applied for aid, 197 were judged to have need. Of these, 197 received aid, and 197 had their full need met. Average financial aid package met 100% of need; average scholarship/grant was $26,293; average loan was $3,326.
Students without need: 17 full-time freshmen who did not demonstrate need for aid received scholarships/grants; average award was $1,000. No-need awards available for academics, leadership.
Scholarships offered: National Merit Scholarships average $1,000 per year.
Cumulative student debt: 48% of graduating class had student loans; average debt was $18,300.
Additional info: Regardless of financial circumstances, students admitted will receive money they need to attend. International students for regular admission must submit their financial aid applications by January 1st.

FINANCIAL AID PROCEDURES

Forms required: FAFSA, CSS PROFILE.
Dates and Deadlines: Closing date 2/15. Applicants notified by 4/5; must reply by 5/1 or within 1 week(s) of notification.
Transfers: Closing date 3/1. Applicants notified by 5/1; must reply by 6/1 or within 1 week(s) of notification. Financial aid usually not available for transfer students. Early Decision applicants must submit financial aid applications by November 15 (ED I) and January 1 (ED II).

CONTACT

Stephen Joyce, Director of Student Aid
5000 College Station, Brunswick, ME 04011-8441
(207) 725-3273

Central Maine Community College

Auburn, Maine
www.cmcc.edu — Federal Code: 005276

2-year public community and technical college in small city.
Enrollment: 1,881 undergrads, 48% part-time. 552 full-time freshmen.
Selectivity: Open admission; but selective for some programs.

BASIC COSTS (2007-2008)

Tuition and fees: $3,060; out-of-state residents $5,490.
Per-credit charge: $80; out-of-state residents $161.
Room and board: $6,376.
Additional info: Tuition/fee waivers available for minority students.

FINANCIAL AID PICTURE (2007-2008)

Students with need: 48% of average financial aid package awarded as scholarships/grants, 52% awarded as loans/jobs. Need-based aid available for part-time students. Work study available nights, weekends, and for part-time students.

Students without need: This college awards aid only to students with need.
Cumulative student debt: 57% of graduating class had student loans; average debt was $6,366.
Additional info: Tuition and/or fee waivers may be available to orphans, Native Americans, fire fighters, police, disabled veterans, dependents or survivors of veterans killed in line of duty.

FINANCIAL AID PROCEDURES

Forms required: FAFSA, institutional form.
Dates and Deadlines: Priority date 5/8; no closing date. Applicants notified on a rolling basis starting 3/15; must reply within 2 week(s) of notification.
Transfers: Priority date 8/1; no deadline. Applicants notified on a rolling basis starting 1/15; must reply within 2 week(s) of notification.

CONTACT

Monique Schreiber, Financial Aid Director
1250 Turner Street, Auburn, ME 04210
(207) 755-5269

Central Maine Medical Center College of Nursing and Health Professions

Lewiston, Maine
www.cmmcson.edu — Federal Code: 006305

2-year private nursing college in large town.
Enrollment: 119 undergrads, 82% part-time. 2 full-time freshmen.
Selectivity: Admits less than 50% of applicants.

BASIC COSTS (2008-2009)

Tuition and fees: $7,188.
Per-credit charge: $170.
Room only: $1,500.

FINANCIAL AID PICTURE (2006-2007)

Students with need: Out of 2 full-time freshmen who applied for aid, 2 were judged to have need. Of these, 2 received aid, and 2 had their full need met. Average financial aid package met 26% of need; average scholarship/grant was $6,625; average loan was $6,625. For part-time students, average financial aid package was $8,380.
Students without need: This college awards aid only to students with need.

FINANCIAL AID PROCEDURES

Forms required: FAFSA, institutional form.
Dates and Deadlines: Priority date 5/1; closing date 7/1. Applicants notified on a rolling basis starting 4/1; must reply within 2 week(s) of notification.

CONTACT

Keith Bourgault, Financial Aid Director
70 Middle Street, Lewiston, ME 04240
(207) 795-2270

Colby College

Waterville, Maine — Federal Code: 002039
www.colby.edu — CSS Code: 3280

4-year private liberal arts college in large town.
Enrollment: 1,867 undergrads. 475 full-time freshmen.
Selectivity: Admits less than 50% of applicants.

BASIC COSTS (2008-2009)

Comprehensive fee: $48,520.

FINANCIAL AID PICTURE (2006-2007)

Students with need: Out of 219 full-time freshmen who applied for aid, 190 were judged to have need. Of these, 190 received aid, and 190 had their full need met. Average financial aid package met 100% of need; average scholarship/grant was $28,110; average loan was $3,555.

Students without need: This college awards aid only to students with need.

Cumulative student debt: 44% of graduating class had student loans; average debt was $19,222.

FINANCIAL AID PROCEDURES

Forms required: FAFSA, CSS PROFILE.

Dates and Deadlines: Closing date 2/1. Applicants notified by 4/1; must reply by 5/1.

Transfers: Priority date 2/1; closing date 3/1. Must reply within 2 week(s) of notification.

CONTACT

Lucia Whittelsey, Director of Financial Aid
4800 Mayflower Hill, Waterville, ME 04901-8848
(800) 723-3032

College of the Atlantic

Bar Harbor, Maine
www.coa.edu   Federal Code: 011385

4-year private liberal arts college in small town.

Enrollment: 327 undergrads, 3% part-time. 84 full-time freshmen.

Selectivity: Admits over 75% of applicants.

BASIC COSTS (2007-2008)

Tuition and fees: $29,970.

Room and board: $8,190.

FINANCIAL AID PICTURE (2007-2008)

Students with need: Out of 71 full-time freshmen who applied for aid, 68 were judged to have need. Of these, 68 received aid, and 49 had their full need met. Average financial aid package met 97% of need; average scholarship/grant was $22,654; average loan was $3,341. For part-time students, average financial aid package was $22,182.

Students without need: This college awards aid only to students with need.

Cumulative student debt: 63% of graduating class had student loans; average debt was $19,692.

FINANCIAL AID PROCEDURES

Forms required: FAFSA, institutional form.

Dates and Deadlines: Closing date 2/15. Applicants notified by 4/1; must reply by 5/1.

Transfers: Priority date 2/15. Applicants notified by 4/1; must reply by 5/1. FAFSA must be filed by 5/1 for Maine residents to be eligible for Maine state grant.

CONTACT

Bruce Hazam, Director of Financial Aid
105 Eden Street, Bar Harbor, ME 04609
(207) 288-5015

Eastern Maine Community College

Bangor, Maine
www.emcc.edu   Federal Code: 005277

2-year public community and technical college in large town.

Enrollment: 1,577 undergrads, 32% part-time. 387 full-time freshmen.

Selectivity: Open admission; but selective for some programs.

BASIC COSTS (2007-2008)

Tuition and fees: $3,315; out-of-state residents $5,745.

Per-credit charge: $80; out-of-state residents $161.

Room and board: $6,360.

Additional info: Laboratory and technology fees vary with program. Tuition/fee waivers available for minority students.

FINANCIAL AID PICTURE

Students with need: Need-based aid available for full-time and part-time students. Work study available nights, weekends, and for part-time students.

Students without need: This college awards aid only to students with need.

FINANCIAL AID PROCEDURES

Forms required: FAFSA, institutional form.

Dates and Deadlines: Priority date 5/1; no closing date. Applicants notified on a rolling basis starting 5/1; must reply within 3 week(s) of notification.

CONTACT

Candace Ward, Registrar/Financial Aid Director
354 Hogan Road, Bangor, ME 04401
(207) 974-4625

Husson College

Bangor, Maine
www.husson.edu   Federal Code: 002043

4-year private business and health science college in large town.

Enrollment: 1,855 undergrads, 18% part-time. 403 full-time freshmen.

Selectivity: Admits over 75% of applicants.

BASIC COSTS (2008-2009)

Tuition and fees: $12,750.

Per-credit charge: $415.

Room and board: $6,790.

FINANCIAL AID PICTURE (2007-2008)

Students with need: Average financial aid package met 70% of need; average scholarship/grant was $8,601; average loan was $3,069. For part-time students, average financial aid package was $5,766.

Students without need: No-need awards available for academics, leadership.

Scholarships offered: Scholarships awarded based on academics and leadership, ranging from $1,000 to $4,000 renewable up to four years.

Cumulative student debt: 80% of graduating class had student loans; average debt was $29,834.

FINANCIAL AID PROCEDURES

Forms required: FAFSA.

Dates and Deadlines: Priority date 4/15; no closing date. Applicants notified on a rolling basis starting 4/1; must reply by 5/1 or within 2 week(s) of notification.

Transfers: No deadline. Applicants notified on a rolling basis starting 2/20.

CONTACT

Linda Conant, Director of Financial Aid
One College Circle, Bangor, ME 04401
(207) 941-7156

Kennebec Valley Community College

Fairfield, Maine
www.kvcc.me.edu   Federal Code: 009826

2-year public community and technical college in small town.

Enrollment: 1,396 undergrads.

Selectivity: Open admission; but selective for some programs.

BASIC COSTS (2007-2008)

Tuition and fees: $2,940; out-of-state residents $5,370.

Per-credit charge: $80; out-of-state residents $161.

Additional info: Health insurance required if student does not have own insurance. Lab fees vary depending on course.

FINANCIAL AID PICTURE (2006-2007)

Students with need: 69% of average financial aid package awarded as scholarships/grants, 31% awarded as loans/jobs. Need-based aid available for part-time students.

FINANCIAL AID PROCEDURES

Forms required: FAFSA, institutional form.

Dates and Deadlines: Priority date 4/1; no closing date. Applicants notified on a rolling basis starting 5/1.

CONTACT

Anne Connors, Director of Financial Aid

92 Western Avenue, Fairfield, ME 04937-1367

(207) 453-5121

Maine College of Art

Portland, Maine

www.meca.edu   Federal Code: 011673

4-year private visual arts college in small city.

Enrollment: 343 undergrads. 80 full-time freshmen.

Selectivity: Admits over 75% of applicants.

BASIC COSTS (2007-2008)

Tuition and fees: $26,090.

Per-credit charge: $1,059.

Room and board: $9,090.

Additional info: Studio fees vary per class.

FINANCIAL AID PICTURE (2007-2008)

Students with need: Average financial aid package met 57% of need; average scholarship/grant was $9,807; average loan was $3,725. For part-time students, average financial aid package was $12,483.

Students without need: No-need awards available for academics, art.

Cumulative student debt: 85% of graduating class had student loans; average debt was $32,560.

FINANCIAL AID PROCEDURES

Forms required: FAFSA.

Dates and Deadlines: Priority date 3/1; no closing date. Applicants notified on a rolling basis starting 2/15; must reply within 2 week(s) of notification.

Transfers: Closing date 4/15. Applicants notified on a rolling basis starting 2/15; must reply within 2 week(s) of notification.

CONTACT

Michelle LeClerc, Director of Financial Aid

522 Congress Street, Portland, ME 04101

(207) 879-5742 ext. 373

Maine Maritime Academy

Castine, Maine

www.mainemaritime.edu   Federal Code: 002044

4-year public business and engineering and maritime college in rural community.

Enrollment: 883 undergrads, 2% part-time. 250 full-time freshmen.

Selectivity: Admits 50 to 75% of applicants.

BASIC COSTS (2007-2008)

Tuition and fees: $8,705; out-of-district residents $12,205; out-of-state residents $15,305.

Room and board: $7,400.

Additional info: Fee of $2,400 for U.S. Coast Guard licensing programs.

FINANCIAL AID PICTURE

Students with need: Need-based aid available for full-time and part-time students. Work study available nights, weekends, and for part-time students.

Students without need: No-need awards available for academics, leadership, ROTC, state/district residency.

FINANCIAL AID PROCEDURES

Forms required: FAFSA, institutional form.

Dates and Deadlines: Priority date 4/15; no closing date. Applicants notified on a rolling basis starting 3/1; must reply within 4 week(s) of notification.

Transfers: Priority date 6/1.

CONTACT

Kathy Heath, Financial Aid Officer

66 Pleasant Street, Castine, ME 04420

(207) 326-2339

New England School of Communications

Bangor, Maine

www.nescom.edu   Federal Code: 023471

4-year private college of communications in small city.

Enrollment: 393 undergrads, 5% part-time. 144 full-time freshmen.

Selectivity: Admits 50 to 75% of applicants.

BASIC COSTS (2008-2009)

Tuition and fees: $10,680.

Per-credit charge: $350.

Room and board: $6,725.

Additional info: Additional cost of $160 for FireWire hard drive.

FINANCIAL AID PICTURE

Students with need: Need-based aid available for full-time and part-time students.

Students without need: No-need awards available for academics, leadership.

Scholarships offered: Scholarships are merit based for second semester.

FINANCIAL AID PROCEDURES

Forms required: FAFSA, institutional form.

Dates and Deadlines: Priority date 4/15; no closing date. Applicants notified on a rolling basis starting 2/1; must reply by 8/15.

Transfers: No deadline. Applicants notified on a rolling basis starting 2/15; must reply within 4 week(s) of notification.

CONTACT

Nicole Rediker, Director of Financial Aid

One College Circle, Bangor, ME 04401

(207) 941-7176

Northern Maine Community College

Presque Isle, Maine

www.nmcc.edu   Federal Code: 005760

2-year public technical college in small town.

Enrollment: 840 undergrads.

BASIC COSTS (2007-2008)

Tuition and fees: $2,990; out-of-state residents $5,420.

Per-credit charge: $80; out-of-state residents $161.

Room and board: $5,240.

Additional info: Tuition/fee waivers available for minority students.

FINANCIAL AID PICTURE

Students with need: Need-based aid available for full-time and part-time students.

FINANCIAL AID PROCEDURES

Forms required: FAFSA, institutional form.

Dates and Deadlines: Priority date 5/1; no closing date. Applicants notified on a rolling basis starting 4/15; must reply within 2 week(s) of notification.

CONTACT

Norma Smith, Assistant Financial Aid Director
33 Edgemont Drive, Presque Isle, ME 04769
(207) 768-2790

St. Joseph's College
Standish, Maine
www.sjcme.edu   Federal Code: 002051

4-year private liberal arts college in small town, affiliated with Roman Catholic Church.

Enrollment: 1,071 undergrads, 1% part-time. 319 full-time freshmen.

Selectivity: Admits over 75% of applicants.

BASIC COSTS (2007-2008)

Tuition and fees: $23,300.

Per-credit charge: $750.

Room and board: $9,600.

FINANCIAL AID PICTURE (2007-2008)

Students with need: Out of 295 full-time freshmen who applied for aid, 257 were judged to have need. Of these, 257 received aid, and 102 had their full need met. Average financial aid package met 84% of need; average scholarship/grant was $13,038; average loan was $4,434. For part-time students, average financial aid package was $3,369.

Students without need: 60 full-time freshmen who did not demonstrate need for aid received scholarships/grants; average award was $10,958. No-need awards available for academics, leadership.

FINANCIAL AID PROCEDURES

Forms required: FAFSA, institutional form.

Dates and Deadlines: Priority date 3/1; no closing date. Applicants notified on a rolling basis starting 3/1; must reply within 3 week(s) of notification.

CONTACT

Andrea Cross, Associate Dean for Financial Aid
278 Whites Bridge Road, Standish, ME 04084-5263
(800) 752-1266

Southern Maine Community College
South Portland, Maine
www.smccme.edu   Federal Code: 005525

2-year public community and technical college in large town.

Enrollment: 4,947 undergrads, 63% part-time.

Selectivity: Open admission; but selective for some programs.

BASIC COSTS (2007-2008)

Tuition and fees: $3,335; out-of-state residents $5,765.

Per-credit charge: $80; out-of-state residents $161.

Room and board: $7,282.

Additional info: Room and Board charge includes cable, internet services.

FINANCIAL AID PICTURE

Students with need: Need-based aid available for full-time and part-time students. Work study available nights, weekends, and for part-time students.

Students without need: This college awards aid only to students with need.

FINANCIAL AID PROCEDURES

Forms required: FAFSA.

Dates and Deadlines: Priority date 3/30; no closing date. Applicants notified on a rolling basis; must reply by 5/1 or within 2 week(s) of notification.

CONTACT

Scott MacDonald, Director of Financial Aid, Transfer and Employment Services
2 Fort Road, South Portland, ME 04106
(207) 741-5518

Thomas College
Waterville, Maine
www.thomas.edu   Federal Code: 002052

4-year private business and liberal arts college in large town.

Enrollment: 739 undergrads, 14% part-time. 218 full-time freshmen.

Selectivity: Admits over 75% of applicants.

BASIC COSTS (2008-2009)

Tuition and fees: $19,750.

Per-credit charge: $801.

Room and board: $8,170.

FINANCIAL AID PICTURE (2007-2008)

Students with need: Out of 214 full-time freshmen who applied for aid, 209 were judged to have need. Of these, 209 received aid, and 32 had their full need met. Average financial aid package met 85% of need; average scholarship/grant was $12,369; average loan was $4,173. For part-time students, average financial aid package was $16,201.

Students without need: 5 full-time freshmen who did not demonstrate need for aid received scholarships/grants; average award was $4,600. No-need awards available for academics, leadership, state/district residency.

Cumulative student debt: 75% of graduating class had student loans; average debt was $38,734.

FINANCIAL AID PROCEDURES

Forms required: FAFSA.

Dates and Deadlines: Priority date 2/15; no closing date. Applicants notified on a rolling basis starting 3/15; must reply within 2 week(s) of notification.

CONTACT

Jennifer Montgomery, Director of Student Financial Services
180 West River Road, Waterville, ME 04901
(207) 859-1105

Unity College
Unity, Maine
www.unity.edu   Federal Code: 006858

4-year private liberal arts college in rural community.

Enrollment: 552 undergrads, 3% part-time. 202 full-time freshmen.

Selectivity: Admits over 75% of applicants.

BASIC COSTS (2007-2008)

Tuition and fees: $19,620.

Per-credit charge: $700.

Room and board: $7,310.

FINANCIAL AID PICTURE (2007-2008)

Students with need: Average financial aid package met 78% of need; average scholarship/grant was $11,541; average loan was $4,644. For part-time students, average financial aid package was $9,153.

Students without need: No-need awards available for academics, leadership, minority status.

FINANCIAL AID PROCEDURES

Forms required: FAFSA.

Dates and Deadlines: Priority date 3/1; no closing date. Applicants notified on a rolling basis starting 2/15.

CONTACT

Rand Newell, Director of Financial Aid
P.O. 532, Unity, ME 04988-0532
(207) 948-3131 ext. 201

University of Maine

Orono, Maine
www.umaine.edu   Federal Code: 002053

4-year public university in large town.

Enrollment: 8,777 undergrads, 11% part-time. 1,853 full-time freshmen.

Selectivity: Admits over 75% of applicants.

BASIC COSTS (2007-2008)

Tuition and fees: $8,330; out-of-state residents $20,540.

Per-credit charge: $218; out-of-state residents $625.

Room and board: $7,484.

Additional info: New England Regional Student Program tuition is 150% of public in-district tuition.

FINANCIAL AID PICTURE (2007-2008)

Students with need: Average financial aid package met 87% of need; average scholarship/grant was $6,288; average loan was $4,024. For part-time students, average financial aid package was $8,896.

Students without need: No-need awards available for academics, alumni affiliation, art, athletics, job skills, leadership, minority status, music/drama, religious affiliation, ROTC, state/district residency.

Scholarships offered: Academic merit scholarships range in value from $1,000 to full tuition. All awards are renewable for up to eight (8) consecutive semesters, based upon academic performance. Top Scholar Awards and Tuition Scholarships pay full resident tuition or full nonresident differential per semester each academic year.

Cumulative student debt: 76% of graduating class had student loans; average debt was $22,630.

Additional info: Financial aid is available for students entering in the spring.

FINANCIAL AID PROCEDURES

Forms required: FAFSA.

Dates and Deadlines: Priority date 3/1; no closing date. Applicants notified on a rolling basis starting 3/15; must reply by 5/1 or within 2 week(s) of notification.

CONTACT

Peggy Crawford, Director of Student Financial Aid
5713 Chadbourne Hall, Orono, ME 04469-5713
(207) 581-1324

University of Maine at Augusta

Augusta, Maine
www.uma.edu   Federal Code: 006760

4-year public university in large town.

Enrollment: 4,207 undergrads, 65% part-time. 303 full-time freshmen.

Selectivity: Open admission; but selective for some programs.

BASIC COSTS (2007-2008)

Tuition and fees: $5,985; out-of-state residents $13,395.

Per-credit charge: $174; out-of-state residents $421.

Additional info: New England Regional Student Program tuition is 150% of public in-district tuition.

FINANCIAL AID PICTURE (2007-2008)

Students with need: Out of 256 full-time freshmen who applied for aid, 220 were judged to have need. Of these, 212 received aid, and 34 had their full need met. Average financial aid package met 68% of need; average scholarship/grant was $4,698; average loan was $3,376. For part-time students, average financial aid package was $6,438.

Students without need: 21 full-time freshmen who did not demonstrate need for aid received scholarships/grants; average award was $4,008. No-need awards available for academics, athletics, leadership, music/drama, state/district residency.

Scholarships offered: 1 full-time freshmen received athletic scholarships; average amount $1,150.

Cumulative student debt: 66% of graduating class had student loans; average debt was $14,473.

FINANCIAL AID PROCEDURES

Forms required: FAFSA.

Dates and Deadlines: Priority date 3/1; no closing date. Applicants notified on a rolling basis starting 3/15; must reply within 2 week(s) of notification.

CONTACT

Sherry McCollett, Coordinator of Financial Aid
46 University Drive, Augusta, ME 04330
(207) 621-3455

University of Maine at Farmington

Farmington, Maine
www.farmington.edu   Federal Code: 002040

4-year public liberal arts and teachers college in small town.

Enrollment: 2,137 undergrads, 5% part-time. 479 full-time freshmen.

Selectivity: Admits 50 to 75% of applicants.

BASIC COSTS (2007-2008)

Tuition and fees: $7,157; out-of-state residents $14,837.

Per-credit charge: $204; out-of-state residents $444.

Room and board: $6,722.

Additional info: New England Regional Student Program tuition and fees: $10,677. Tuition/fee waivers available for minority students.

FINANCIAL AID PICTURE

Students with need: Need-based aid available for full-time and part-time students. Work study available nights, weekends, and for part-time students.

Students without need: No-need awards available for academics, leadership, minority status, state/district residency.

Scholarships offered: Presidential Scholarships; $2,000 renewable annually; for non-residents graduating in top half of high school class.

Additional info: FAFSA must arrive at Federal processor by 3/1.

FINANCIAL AID PROCEDURES

Forms required: FAFSA.

Dates and Deadlines: Priority date 3/1; no closing date. Applicants notified on a rolling basis starting 3/15; must reply within 2 week(s) of notification.

CONTACT

Ronald Milliken, Director of Financial Aid
246 Main Street, Farmington, ME 04938
(207) 778-7100

University of Maine at Fort Kent

Fort Kent, Maine
www.umfk.maine.edu   Federal Code: 002041

4-year public university in small town.

Enrollment: 917 undergrads, 20% part-time. 115 full-time freshmen.

Selectivity: Open admission; but selective for some programs.

BASIC COSTS (2007-2008)

Tuition and fees: $5,790; out-of-state residents $13,440.
Per-credit charge: $171; out-of-state residents $426.
Room and board: $6,285.
Additional info: New England Regional tuition is 150% of public in-district tuition.

FINANCIAL AID PICTURE

Students with need: Need-based aid available for full-time and part-time students. Work study available nights, weekends, and for part-time students.
Students without need: No-need awards available for academics.

FINANCIAL AID PROCEDURES

Forms required: FAFSA.
Dates and Deadlines: Priority date 3/1; no closing date. Applicants notified on a rolling basis starting 3/15; must reply within 2 week(s) of notification.

CONTACT

Ellen Cost, Director of Financial Aid
23 University Drive, Fort Kent, ME 04743
(207) 834-7607

University of Maine at Machias

Machias, Maine
www.umm.maine.edu   Federal Code: 002055

4-year public university and liberal arts college in rural community.
Enrollment: 554 undergrads, 22% part-time. 108 full-time freshmen.
Selectivity: Admits over 75% of applicants.

BASIC COSTS (2007-2008)

Tuition and fees: $5,770; out-of-state residents $14,800.
Per-credit charge: $170; out-of-state residents $471.
Room and board: $6,270.
Additional info: New England Regional Student Program tuition is 150% of public in-district tuition. Tuition/fee waivers available for minority students.

FINANCIAL AID PICTURE

Students with need: Need-based aid available for full-time and part-time students.
Students without need: No-need awards available for academics, alumni affiliation, art, job skills, leadership, minority status, music/drama, state/district residency.

FINANCIAL AID PROCEDURES

Forms required: FAFSA.
Dates and Deadlines: Priority date 3/1; no closing date. Applicants notified on a rolling basis starting 2/15; must reply within 2 week(s) of notification.

CONTACT

Stephanie Larrabee, Director of Financial Aid
9 O'Brien Avenue, Machias, ME 04654
(207) 255-1203

University of New England

Biddeford, Maine
www.une.edu   Federal Code: 002050

4-year private university in small city.
Enrollment: 1,985 undergrads, 5% part-time. 478 full-time freshmen.
Selectivity: Admits over 75% of applicants.

BASIC COSTS (2007-2008)

Tuition and fees: $25,290.
Per-credit charge: $880.
Room and board: $9,860.

FINANCIAL AID PICTURE (2006-2007)

Students with need: Out of 453 full-time freshmen who applied for aid, 407 were judged to have need. Of these, 407 received aid, and 202 had their full need met. Average financial aid package met 86% of need; average scholarship/grant was $12,817; average loan was $9,154. For part-time students, average financial aid package was $14,071.
Students without need: 71 full-time freshmen who did not demonstrate need for aid received scholarships/grants; average award was $8,271. No-need awards available for academics, alumni affiliation, leadership.
Scholarships offered: UNE Scholarships and UNE Departmental Award; award amounts range from $1,000 to $12,000; non-need, based on academic qualifications as determined from GPA and SAT/ACT scores, must be a full-time undergraduate student and maintain a 2.5 GPA.
Cumulative student debt: 87% of graduating class had student loans; average debt was $39,014.

FINANCIAL AID PROCEDURES

Forms required: FAFSA.
Dates and Deadlines: Priority date 5/1; no closing date. Applicants notified on a rolling basis starting 2/1.

CONTACT

John Bowie, Director of Financial Aid
Hills Beach Road, Biddeford, ME 04005
(207) 602-2342

University of Southern Maine

Gorham, Maine
www.usm.maine.edu   Federal Code: 009762

4-year public university and liberal arts college in small city.
Enrollment: 6,603 undergrads, 29% part-time. 890 full-time freshmen.
Selectivity: Admits over 75% of applicants.

BASIC COSTS (2007-2008)

Tuition and fees: $6,670; out-of-state residents $17,140.
Per-credit charge: $198; out-of-state residents $547.
Room and board: $7,724.
Additional info: New England Regional Student Program tuition is 150% of public in-district tuition.

FINANCIAL AID PICTURE (2007-2008)

Students with need: Average financial aid package met 61% of need; average scholarship/grant was $4,449; average loan was $3,857. For part-time students, average financial aid package was $6,410.
Students without need: No-need awards available for academics, music/drama.
Scholarships offered: Range from $1,000 to $5,500 based on academic record, school/community leadership, and potential for intellectual/social contribution.

FINANCIAL AID PROCEDURES

Forms required: FAFSA.
Dates and Deadlines: Priority date 2/15; no closing date. Applicants notified on a rolling basis starting 3/15; must reply by 5/1 or within 2 week(s) of notification.
Transfers: Applicants notified on a rolling basis; must reply by 5/1 or within 2 week(s) of notification.

CONTACT

Keith Dubois, Director of Financial Aid Office
37 College Avenue, Gorham, ME 04038
(207) 780-5250

PART III: FINANCIAL AID COLLEGE BY COLLEGE

Washington County Community College
Calais, Maine
www.wccc.me.edu   Federal Code: 009231

2-year public community and technical college in small town.
Enrollment: 370 undergrads, 28% part-time.
Selectivity: Open admission; but selective for some programs.

BASIC COSTS (2007-2008)
Tuition and fees: $2,990; out-of-state residents $5,420.
Per-credit charge: $80; out-of-state residents $161.
Room only: $2,482.

FINANCIAL AID PICTURE
Students with need: Need-based aid available for full-time and part-time students.
Students without need: No-need awards available for academics.

FINANCIAL AID PROCEDURES
Forms required: FAFSA, institutional form.
Dates and Deadlines: Priority date 5/1; no closing date. Applicants notified on a rolling basis starting 6/1; must reply within 2 week(s) of notification.

CONTACT
Joyce Maker, Financial Aid Coordinator
One College Drive, Calais, ME 04619
(207) 454-1033

York County Community College
Wells, Maine
www.yccc.edu   Federal Code: 031229

2-year public community and technical college in small town.
Enrollment: 889 undergrads, 64% part-time. 77 full-time freshmen.
Selectivity: Open admission.

BASIC COSTS (2007-2008)
Tuition and fees: $3,050; out-of-state residents $5,480.
Per-credit charge: $80; out-of-state residents $161.
Additional info: Lecture and lab fees may vary per class. Tuition/fee waivers available for minority students.

FINANCIAL AID PICTURE (2006-2007)
Students with need: Out of 77 full-time freshmen who applied for aid, 48 were judged to have need. Of these, 46 received aid, and 5 had their full need met. Average financial aid package met 56% of need; average scholarship/grant was $3,472; average loan was $1,999. For part-time students, average financial aid package was $3,402.
Students without need: 6 full-time freshmen who did not demonstrate need for aid received scholarships/grants; average award was $2,716. No-need awards available for academics, art, leadership.

FINANCIAL AID PROCEDURES
Forms required: FAFSA.
Dates and Deadlines: Priority date 5/1; no closing date. Applicants notified by 3/1; must reply within 2 week(s) of notification.

CONTACT
David Daigle, Director of Financial Aid
112 College Drive, Wells, ME 04090
(207) 646-9282 ext. 312

Maryland

Allegany College of Maryland
Cumberland, Maryland
www.allegany.edu   Federal Code: 002057

2-year public community college in large town.
Enrollment: 2,887 undergrads, 31% part-time. 709 full-time freshmen.
Selectivity: Open admission; but selective for some programs.

BASIC COSTS (2007-2008)
Tuition and fees: $3,130; out-of-district residents $5,590; out-of-state residents $6,490.
Per-credit charge: $96; out-of-district residents $178; out-of-state residents $208.

FINANCIAL AID PICTURE (2006-2007)
Students with need: 68% of average financial aid package awarded as scholarships/grants, 32% awarded as loans/jobs. Need-based aid available for part-time students. Work study available nights.
Students without need: No-need awards available for academics, athletics, leadership, state/district residency.

FINANCIAL AID PROCEDURES
Forms required: FAFSA, institutional form.
Dates and Deadlines: Priority date 3/1; no closing date. Applicants notified on a rolling basis starting 4/15; must reply within 2 week(s) of notification.

CONTACT
Vicki Smith, Director of Financial Aid
12401 Willowbrook Road, SE, Cumberland, MD 21502
(301) 784-5213

Anne Arundel Community College
Arnold, Maryland
www.aacc.edu   Federal Code: 002058

2-year public community college in large town.
Enrollment: 11,973 undergrads.
Selectivity: Open admission; but selective for some programs.

BASIC COSTS (2007-2008)
Tuition and fees: $2,860; out-of-district residents $5,230; out-of-state residents $9,040.
Per-credit charge: $86; out-of-district residents $165; out-of-state residents $292.

FINANCIAL AID PICTURE
Students with need: Need-based aid available for full-time and part-time students. Work study available nights, weekends, and for part-time students.

FINANCIAL AID PROCEDURES
Forms required: FAFSA, institutional form.
Dates and Deadlines: Priority date 5/15; no closing date. Applicants notified on a rolling basis starting 7/1; must reply within 2 week(s) of notification.

CONTACT
Rich Heath, Director of Student Financial Services
101 College Parkway, Arnold, MD 21012-1895
(410) 777-2203

Baltimore City Community College

Baltimore, Maryland
www.bccc.edu
Federal Code: 002061

2-year public community college in very large city.
Enrollment: 6,814 undergrads.
Selectivity: Open admission; but selective for some programs.

BASIC COSTS (2008-2009)
Tuition and fees: $2,722; out-of-state residents $5,422.

FINANCIAL AID PICTURE
Students with need: Need-based aid available for full-time and part-time students. Work study available nights, weekends, and for part-time students.
Students without need: This college awards aid only to students with need.

FINANCIAL AID PROCEDURES
Forms required: FAFSA, state aid form, institutional form.
Dates and Deadlines: Priority date 6/1; no closing date. Applicants notified on a rolling basis starting 7/1; must reply within 2 week(s) of notification.

CONTACT
Denise Burrell, Director of Financial Aid
2901 Liberty Heights Avenue, Baltimore, MD 21215-7893
(410) 462-8500

Baltimore Hebrew University

Baltimore, Maryland
www.bhu.edu
Federal Code: 002060

4-year private university and teachers college in very large city.
Enrollment: 4 undergrads.

BASIC COSTS (2008-2009)
Tuition and fees: $11,250.
Per-credit charge: $467.

FINANCIAL AID PICTURE (2006-2007)
Students with need: 34% of average financial aid package awarded as scholarships/grants, 66% awarded as loans/jobs. Need-based aid available for part-time students.
Students without need: No-need awards available for academics.
Scholarships offered: Tuition subsidy for teachers employed at any Jewish congregational day school, nursery or kindergarten; Tuition subsidy for teachers employed at a school affiliated with Center for Jewish Education; Tuition discount for full-time employees of the Associated Jewish Community Federation of Baltimore.

FINANCIAL AID PROCEDURES
Forms required: FAFSA.
Dates and Deadlines: Priority date 4/15; closing date 6/1. Applicants notified on a rolling basis starting 7/15; must reply by 9/9.
Transfers: No deadline.

CONTACT
Kerri Moseley-Hobbs, Financial Aid Counselor
5800 Park Heights Avenue, Baltimore, MD 21215
(410) 578-6913

Baltimore International College

Baltimore, Maryland
www.bic.edu
Federal Code: 016376

4-year private culinary school and business college in very large city.
Enrollment: 478 undergrads, 4% part-time. 597 full-time freshmen.

Selectivity: Admits 50 to 75% of applicants.

BASIC COSTS (2007-2008)
Additional info: Fees shown are for culinary school and include use of computer, culinary supplies, upgrading and maintenance of kitchen equipment and facilities. Day students provided one full meal daily. Business program students pay lower fees.

FINANCIAL AID PICTURE (2006-2007)
Students with need: Out of 597 full-time freshmen who applied for aid, 563 were judged to have need. Of these, 563 received aid. Average financial aid package met 66% of need; average scholarship/grant was $6,102; average loan was $7,500.
Students without need: No-need awards available for academics, alumni affiliation, job skills, leadership, state/district residency.

FINANCIAL AID PROCEDURES
Forms required: FAFSA, institutional form.
Dates and Deadlines: Priority date 3/1; no closing date. Applicants notified on a rolling basis; must reply within 2 week(s) of notification.
Transfers: No deadline. Applicants notified on a rolling basis; must reply within 2 week(s) of notification.

CONTACT
Kim Wittler, Director of Student Financial Planning
17 Commerce Street, Baltimore, MD 21202-3230
(410) 752-0490

Bowie State University

Bowie, Maryland
www.bowiestate.edu
Federal Code: 002062

4-year public university in small city.
Enrollment: 4,179 undergrads, 14% part-time. 595 full-time freshmen.
Selectivity: Admits less than 50% of applicants.

BASIC COSTS (2007-2008)
Tuition and fees: $5,939; out-of-state residents $15,629.
Per-credit charge: $189; out-of-state residents $589.
Room and board: $6,105.

FINANCIAL AID PICTURE (2007-2008)
Students with need: Out of 470 full-time freshmen who applied for aid, 462 were judged to have need. Of these, 450 received aid, and 42 had their full need met. Average financial aid package met 44% of need; average scholarship/grant was $5,537; average loan was $3,131. Need-based aid available for part-time students.
Students without need: 4 full-time freshmen who did not demonstrate need for aid received scholarships/grants; average award was $119. No-need awards available for academics, alumni affiliation, art, athletics, leadership, music/drama, ROTC, state/district residency.
Scholarships offered: 22 full-time freshmen received athletic scholarships; average amount $4,073.

FINANCIAL AID PROCEDURES
Forms required: FAFSA.
Dates and Deadlines: Closing date 3/1. Applicants notified on a rolling basis starting 4/1; must reply within 2 week(s) of notification.
Transfers: Applicants notified on a rolling basis starting 4/1; must reply within 2 week(s) of notification.

CONTACT
Deborah Stanley, Director of Financial Aid
14000 Jericho Park Road, Bowie, MD 20715
(301) 860-3540

Carroll Community College
Westminster, Maryland
www.carrollcc.edu   Federal Code: 031007

2-year public community college in large town.

Enrollment: 3,413 undergrads, 53% part-time. 650 full-time freshmen.

Selectivity: Open admission; but selective for some programs.

BASIC COSTS (2007-2008)

Tuition and fees: $3,234; out-of-district residents $4,476; out-of-state residents $6,788.

FINANCIAL AID PICTURE (2006-2007)

Students with need: 98% of average financial aid package awarded as scholarships/grants, 2% awarded as loans/jobs. Need-based aid available for part-time students. Work study available nights, weekends, and for part-time students.

Students without need: No-need awards available for academics, art, job skills, leadership, state/district residency.

FINANCIAL AID PROCEDURES

Forms required: FAFSA.

Dates and Deadlines: Priority date 3/1; no closing date. Applicants notified by 6/1; must reply within 2 week(s) of notification.

CONTACT

Lori Henry, Director of Financial Aid
1601 Washington Road, Westminster, MD 21157
(410) 386-8437

Cecil College
North East, Maryland
www.cecil.edu   Federal Code: 008308

2-year public community college in large town.

Enrollment: 1,922 undergrads, 66% part-time. 234 full-time freshmen.

Selectivity: Open admission; but selective for some programs.

BASIC COSTS (2008-2009)

Tuition and fees: $2,912; out-of-district residents $5,612; out-of-state residents $6,962.

Per-credit charge: $85; out-of-district residents $175; out-of-state residents $220.

Additional info: Tuition at time of enrollment locked for 2 years.

FINANCIAL AID PICTURE (2006-2007)

Students with need: 48% of average financial aid package awarded as scholarships/grants, 52% awarded as loans/jobs. Work study available nights, weekends, and for part-time students.

Students without need: No-need awards available for academics, alumni affiliation, athletics, job skills, state/district residency.

FINANCIAL AID PROCEDURES

Forms required: FAFSA.

Dates and Deadlines: Priority date 8/1; no closing date. Applicants notified on a rolling basis; must reply within 2 week(s) of notification.

CONTACT

Kate Lockhart, Director of Financial Aid
One Seahawk Drive, North East, MD 21901
(410) 287-1003

Chesapeake College
Wye Mills, Maryland
www.chesapeake.edu   Federal Code: 004650

2-year public community college in rural community.

Enrollment: 1,948 undergrads.

Selectivity: Open admission; but selective for some programs.

BASIC COSTS (2007-2008)

Tuition and fees: $3,094; out-of-district residents $5,154; out-of-state residents $7,494.

Per-credit charge: $89; out-of-district residents $157; out-of-state residents $234.

FINANCIAL AID PICTURE

Students with need: Need-based aid available for full-time and part-time students.

Students without need: No-need awards available for academics, art, athletics, state/district residency.

FINANCIAL AID PROCEDURES

Forms required: FAFSA, institutional form.

Dates and Deadlines: Priority date 5/1; no closing date. Applicants notified on a rolling basis starting 5/1; must reply within 2 week(s) of notification.

CONTACT

Mindy Schaffer, Director of Financial Aid
Box 8, Wye Mills, MD 21679-0008
(410) 822-5400 ext. 252

College of Notre Dame of Maryland
Baltimore, Maryland
www.ndm.edu   Federal Code: 002065

4-year private liberal arts college for women in very large city, affiliated with Roman Catholic Church.

Enrollment: 1,476 undergrads.

Selectivity: Admits 50 to 75% of applicants.

BASIC COSTS (2007-2008)

Tuition and fees: $24,500.

Per-credit charge: $375.

Room and board: $8,600.

FINANCIAL AID PICTURE

Students with need: Need-based aid available for full-time and part-time students.

Students without need: No-need awards available for academics, alumni affiliation, art, leadership, music/drama, ROTC.

Scholarships offered: Academic/achievement awards; $6,000 to full tuition. Endowed scholarships; $1,000 to $8,000; variable criteria; usually 20-35 awards.

Additional info: Maximum consideration for financial aid if application received by February 15. Auditions and portfolios in areas of art, music and writing considered for scholarships.

FINANCIAL AID PROCEDURES

Forms required: FAFSA.

Dates and Deadlines: Priority date 2/15; no closing date. Applicants notified on a rolling basis starting 3/15; must reply by 5/1 or within 2 week(s) of notification.

Transfers: Applicants notified by 3/15; must reply by 5/1 or within 2 week(s) of notification. Specific non-need based merit scholarships available for transfer students. Transfer scholarships; range from $7000 to full tuition.

CONTACT
Zhana Goltser, Director of Financial Aid
4701 North Charles Street, Baltimore, MD 21210
(410) 532-5369

College of Southern Maryland
La Plata, Maryland
www.csmd.edu   Federal Code: 002064

2-year public community college in large town.
Enrollment: 5,912 undergrads, 60% part-time. 800 full-time freshmen.
Selectivity: Open admission; but selective for some programs.

BASIC COSTS (2007-2008)
Tuition and fees: $3,384; out-of-district residents $5,904; out-of-state residents $7,524.
Per-credit charge: $94; out-of-district residents $164; out-of-state residents $209.
Additional info: Out-of-district fees are an additional $420; out-of-state fees are an additional $690.

FINANCIAL AID PICTURE (2006-2007)
Students with need: 86% of average financial aid package awarded as scholarships/grants, 14% awarded as loans/jobs. Need-based aid available for part-time students. Work study available nights, weekends, and for part-time students.
Students without need: No-need awards available for academics, athletics, state/district residency.

FINANCIAL AID PROCEDURES
Forms required: FAFSA.
Dates and Deadlines: Priority date 3/1; no closing date. Applicants notified on a rolling basis starting 5/15; must reply within 2 week(s) of notification.

CONTACT
George Bachman, Director of Financial Assistance
College of Southern Maryland-AOD, La Plata, MD 20646-0910
(301) 934-7531

Columbia Union College
Takoma Park, Maryland
www.cuc.edu   Federal Code: 002067

4-year private liberal arts college in large town, affiliated with Seventh-day Adventists.
Enrollment: 876 undergrads, 26% part-time. 124 full-time freshmen.
Selectivity: Admits less than 50% of applicants.

BASIC COSTS (2008-2009)
Tuition and fees: $19,350.
Room and board: $6,559.

FINANCIAL AID PICTURE
Students with need: Need-based aid available for full-time and part-time students.
Students without need: No-need awards available for academics, athletics, leadership, music/drama, state/district residency.

FINANCIAL AID PROCEDURES
Forms required: FAFSA.
Dates and Deadlines: Closing date 3/31. Applicants notified on a rolling basis starting 5/31; must reply within 4 week(s) of notification.

CONTACT
Elaine Oliver, Director of Financial Aid
7600 Flower Avenue, Takoma Park, MD 20912
(301) 891-4005

Community College of Baltimore County
Baltimore, Maryland
www.ccbcmd.edu   Federal Code: 002063

2-year public community college in very large city.
Enrollment: 16,097 undergrads, 62% part-time. 2,042 full-time freshmen.
Selectivity: Open admission; but selective for some programs.

BASIC COSTS (2007-2008)
Tuition and fees: $3,016; out-of-district residents $5,536; out-of-state residents $7,396.
Per-credit charge: $90; out-of-district residents $174; out-of-state residents $236.

FINANCIAL AID PICTURE
Students with need: Need-based aid available for full-time and part-time students. Work study available nights, weekends, and for part-time students.
Students without need: No-need awards available for academics, athletics.
Additional info: On-campus employment typically available.

FINANCIAL AID PROCEDURES
Forms required: FAFSA.
Dates and Deadlines: Closing date 3/1. Applicants notified on a rolling basis starting 5/1; must reply within 2 week(s) of notification.

CONTACT
Jerome Lovick, Director of Financial Aid
7201 Rossville Boulevard, Baltimore, MD 21237
(410) 455-4170

Coppin State University
Baltimore, Maryland
www.coppin.edu   Federal Code: 002068

4-year public nursing and liberal arts college in very large city.
Enrollment: 3,151 undergrads, 22% part-time. 555 full-time freshmen.
Selectivity: Admits less than 50% of applicants.

BASIC COSTS (2007-2008)
Tuition and fees: $4,980; out-of-state residents $12,753.
Per-credit charge: $151; out-of-state residents $388.
Room and board: $6,799.

FINANCIAL AID PICTURE (2007-2008)
Students with need: 51% of average financial aid package awarded as scholarships/grants, 49% awarded as loans/jobs. Need-based aid available for part-time students.
Students without need: No-need awards available for academics, alumni affiliation, athletics, ROTC, state/district residency.
Scholarships offered: Gold Freshman Merit Award; $1,200 per year; awarded to freshmen with 950 combined SAT and 2.5 high school GPA. Gold Transfer Merit Award; $1,200 per year; awarded to Maryland Community College transfer students with 2.8 GPA and successful completion of 56 credits. Blue Freshman Merit Award; $800 per year; awarded to freshman with 900 combined SAT and 2.5 GPA. Blue Transfer Merit Award; $600 per year; awarded to Maryland Community College transfer students with 2.5 GPA and successful completion of 25 credits. SAT scores exclusive of Writing.
Additional info: Funds allocated by State of Maryland for minority students enrolled for at least 6 credits who are Maryland residents and U.S. citizens (Other Race Grant).

FINANCIAL AID PROCEDURES
Forms required: FAFSA.
Dates and Deadlines: Priority date 3/1; no closing date. Applicants notified on a rolling basis starting 4/15; must reply within 2 week(s) of notification.

CONTACT

Lady Jenkins, Director of Financial Aid
2500 West North Avenue, Baltimore, MD 21216
(410) 951-3636

DeVry University: Bethesda

Bethesda, Maryland
www.devry.edu

4-year for-profit university in small city.
Enrollment: 45 undergrads, 71% part-time. 5 full-time freshmen.

BASIC COSTS (2007-2008)

Tuition and fees: $14,440.
Per-credit charge: $525.

FINANCIAL AID PICTURE (2006-2007)

Students with need: For part-time students, average financial aid package was $6,370.
Students without need: No-need awards available for academics.

FINANCIAL AID PROCEDURES

Forms required: FAFSA.
Dates and Deadlines: No deadline. Applicants notified on a rolling basis.

CONTACT

4550 Montgomery Avenue, Suite 100 N, Bethesda, MD 20814

Frederick Community College

Frederick, Maryland
www.frederick.edu   Federal Code: 002071

2-year public community college in small city.
Enrollment: 4,458 undergrads, 57% part-time. 715 full-time freshmen.
Selectivity: Open admission; but selective for some programs.

BASIC COSTS (2008-2009)

Tuition and fees: $3,128; out-of-district residents $6,368; out-of-state residents $8,528.
Per-credit charge: $92; out-of-district residents $200; out-of-state residents $272.

FINANCIAL AID PICTURE (2006-2007)

Students with need: 82% of average financial aid package awarded as scholarships/grants, 18% awarded as loans/jobs. Need-based aid available for part-time students.
Students without need: No-need awards available for academics, athletics, state/district residency.
Scholarships offered: Scholarships available for Frederick County Public Schools students with high gpas to participate in student ambassador program; other general scholarships available for prospective students.

FINANCIAL AID PROCEDURES

Forms required: FAFSA, institutional form.
Dates and Deadlines: Priority date 6/15; no closing date. Applicants notified on a rolling basis starting 5/15; must reply within 2 week(s) of notification.
Transfers: Priority date 6/1. Applicants notified on a rolling basis starting 6/1. Financial aid transcripts from prior institutions must be submitted before awards are made.

CONTACT

Brenda Dayhoff, Director, Financial Aid
7932 Opossumtown Pike, Frederick, MD 21702
(301) 846-2480

Frostburg State University

Frostburg, Maryland
www.frostburg.edu   Federal Code: 002072

4-year public university and teachers college in small town.
Enrollment: 4,268 undergrads, 5% part-time. 1,057 full-time freshmen.
Selectivity: Admits 50 to 75% of applicants.

BASIC COSTS (2007-2008)

Tuition and fees: $6,550; out-of-state residents $16,162.
Per-credit charge: $207; out-of-state residents $411.
Room and board: $6,746.

FINANCIAL AID PICTURE

Students with need: Need-based aid available for full-time and part-time students.
Students without need: No-need awards available for academics, leadership, minority status.

FINANCIAL AID PROCEDURES

Forms required: FAFSA.
Dates and Deadlines: Priority date 3/1; no closing date. Applicants notified on a rolling basis starting 3/15; must reply within 3 week(s) of notification.

CONTACT

Angela Hovatter, Director of Financial Aid
101 Braddock Road, Frostburg, MD 21532-1099
(301) 687-4301

Garrett College

McHenry, Maryland
www.garrettcollege.edu   Federal Code: 010014

2-year public community college in rural community.
Enrollment: 590 undergrads.
Selectivity: Open admission.

BASIC COSTS (2007-2008)

Tuition and fees: $2,970; out-of-district residents $6,510; out-of-state residents $7,590.
Per-credit charge: $78; out-of-district residents $196; out-of-state residents $232.
Room and board: $4,300.

FINANCIAL AID PICTURE (2007-2008)

Students with need: Need-based aid available for part-time students.
Students without need: No-need awards available for academics, athletics, leadership.
Additional info: Many local scholarships both merit and need based.

FINANCIAL AID PROCEDURES

Forms required: FAFSA.
Dates and Deadlines: Closing date 3/1. Applicants notified on a rolling basis starting 5/15; must reply within 2 week(s) of notification.

CONTACT

Mary Peoples, Director of Financial Aid
687 Mosser Road, McHenry, MD 21541
(301) 387-3012

Goucher College

Baltimore, Maryland   Federal Code: 002073
www.goucher.edu   CSS Code: 5257

4-year private liberal arts college in small city.
Enrollment: 1,462 undergrads, 2% part-time. 399 full-time freshmen.

Selectivity: Admits 50 to 75% of applicants.

BASIC COSTS (2008-2009)
Tuition and fees: $32,636.
Per-credit charge: $1,075.
Room and board: $10,104.

FINANCIAL AID PICTURE (2007-2008)
Students with need: Out of 291 full-time freshmen who applied for aid, 237 were judged to have need. Of these, 234 received aid, and 53 had their full need met. Average financial aid package met 79% of need; average scholarship/grant was $19,682; average loan was $3,751. For part-time students, average financial aid package was $5,324.
Students without need: 97 full-time freshmen who did not demonstrate need for aid received scholarships/grants; average award was $17,375. No-need awards available for academics, art, leadership, music/drama.
Cumulative student debt: 58% of graduating class had student loans; average debt was $14,221.

FINANCIAL AID PROCEDURES
Forms required: FAFSA, CSS PROFILE.
Dates and Deadlines: Closing date 2/15. Applicants notified on a rolling basis starting 4/1; must reply by 5/1 or within 2 week(s) of notification.

CONTACT
Sharon Hassan, Director of Financial Aid
1021 Dulaney Valley Road, Baltimore, MD 21204-2753
(410) 337-6500

Hagerstown Community College
Hagerstown, Maryland
www.hagerstowncc.edu   Federal Code: 002074

2-year public community college in small city.
Enrollment: 3,010 undergrads, 56% part-time. 512 full-time freshmen.
Selectivity: Open admission; but selective for some programs.

BASIC COSTS (2007-2008)
Tuition and fees: $3,150; out-of-district residents $4,800; out-of-state residents $6,210.
Per-credit charge: $94; out-of-district residents $149; out-of-state residents $196.

FINANCIAL AID PICTURE
Students with need: Need-based aid available for full-time and part-time students. Work study available nights, weekends, and for part-time students.
Students without need: This college awards aid only to students with need.

FINANCIAL AID PROCEDURES
Forms required: FAFSA. .
Dates and Deadlines: Priority date 3/1; no closing date. Applicants notified on a rolling basis starting 5/1.
Transfers: No deadline.

CONTACT
Carolyn Cox, Director of Financial Aid
11400 Robinwood Drive, Hagerstown, MD 21742
(301) 790-2800 ext. 473

Harford Community College
Bel Air, Maryland
www.harford.edu   Federal Code: 002075

2-year public community college in small city.
Enrollment: 4,732 undergrads.
Selectivity: Open admission; but selective for some programs.

BASIC COSTS (2008-2009)
Tuition and fees: $2,607; out-of-district residents $5,077; out-of-state residents $7,347.
Per-credit charge: $79; out-of-district residents $158; out-of-state residents $237.
Additional info: Required fees based on $79 per credit in-county fee.

FINANCIAL AID PICTURE (2006-2007)
Students with need: 93% of average financial aid package awarded as scholarships/grants, 7% awarded as loans/jobs.
Scholarships offered: Alfred C. O'Connell Homes Scholarship; full tuition & fees for 2 years, grade point average of 3.25 & above; 25 awards.

FINANCIAL AID PROCEDURES
Forms required: FAFSA, institutional form.
Dates and Deadlines: Priority date 3/15; no closing date. Applicants notified on a rolling basis starting 4/1; must reply within 2 week(s) of notification.

CONTACT
Lynn Lee, Director of Financial Aid
401 Thomas Run Road, Bel Air, MD 21015
(410) 836-4257

Hood College
Frederick, Maryland
www.hood.edu   Federal Code: 002076

4-year private liberal arts college in small city.
Enrollment: 1,380 undergrads, 9% part-time. 295 full-time freshmen.
Selectivity: Admits 50 to 75% of applicants.

BASIC COSTS (2008-2009)
Tuition and fees: $26,580.
Per-credit charge: $755.
Room and board: $8,980.
Additional info: Tuition/fee waivers available for adults.

FINANCIAL AID PICTURE (2007-2008)
Students with need: Out of 258 full-time freshmen who applied for aid, 201 were judged to have need. Of these, 201 received aid, and 74 had their full need met. Average financial aid package met 89% of need; average scholarship/grant was $17,225; average loan was $4,048. For part-time students, average financial aid package was $7,882.
Students without need: 86 full-time freshmen who did not demonstrate need for aid received scholarships/grants; average award was $17,907. No-need awards available for academics, alumni affiliation, music/drama, ROTC.
Scholarships offered: Hood Trust Academic Scholarship: amount varies. Hodson Scholarship: amount varies. Project Excellence Scholarship: up to full tuition. Presidential Scholarship: $10,000-$13,000. Trustee Scholarship: $8,000-$10,000.
Cumulative student debt: 76% of graduating class had student loans; average debt was $19,890.

FINANCIAL AID PROCEDURES
Forms required: FAFSA.
Dates and Deadlines: Priority date 2/15; no closing date. Applicants notified on a rolling basis starting 3/1; must reply by 5/1 or within 3 week(s) of notification.

CONTACT
Ronald Shunk, Director of Financial Aid
401 Rosemont Avenue, Frederick, MD 21701-8575
(301) 696-3411

Howard Community College

Columbia, Maryland
www.howardcc.edu   Federal Code: 008175

2-year public community college in small city.
Enrollment: 6,702 undergrads, 58% part-time. 962 full-time freshmen.
Selectivity: Open admission; but selective for some programs.

BASIC COSTS (2008-2009)

Tuition and fees: $3,993; out-of-district residents $6,483; out-of-state residents $8,193.

FINANCIAL AID PICTURE (2006-2007)

Students with need: 76% of average financial aid package awarded as scholarships/grants, 24% awarded as loans/jobs. Need-based aid available for part-time students. Work study available nights, weekends, and for part-time students.

FINANCIAL AID PROCEDURES

Forms required: FAFSA.
Dates and Deadlines: Priority date 3/1; no closing date. Applicants notified on a rolling basis starting 4/1.

CONTACT

Katherine Allen, Director of Financial Aid
10901 Little Patuxent Parkway, Columbia, MD 21044-3197
(410) 772-4604

Johns Hopkins University

Baltimore, Maryland   Federal Code: 002077
www.jhu.edu   CSS Code: 5332

4-year private university in very large city.
Enrollment: 4,578 undergrads, 1% part-time. 1,206 full-time freshmen.
Selectivity: Admits less than 50% of applicants.

BASIC COSTS (2008-2009)

Tuition and fees: $38,200.
Per-credit charge: $1,260.
Room and board: $11,578.

FINANCIAL AID PICTURE (2007-2008)

Students with need: Out of 783 full-time freshmen who applied for aid, 585 were judged to have need. Of these, 585 received aid, and 73 had their full need met. Average financial aid package met 89% of need; average scholarship/grant was $26,290; average loan was $3,481.
Students without need: 14 full-time freshmen who did not demonstrate need for aid received scholarships/grants; average award was $27,471. No-need awards available for academics, athletics, leadership, ROTC, state/district residency.
Scholarships offered: *Merit:* Hodson Trust Scholarship; $23,000 annually for 4 years; 20 awards. Westgate Scholarship for engineering freshmen; tuition plus $1,000 for 4 years: academic excellence, leadership, demonstrated research experience required, 2 offered per year per class. Wilson Research grants; $10,000. Baltimore Scholars Program; full tuition scholarship for US citizens or permanent residents who have attended a Baltimore City public school for at least 10th, 11th, and 12th grades and meet a residency requirement. *Athletic:* 3 full-time freshmen received athletic scholarships; average amount $20,942.
Cumulative student debt: 52% of graduating class had student loans; average debt was $18,447.
Additional info: Selected students receive aid packages without loan expectation, grants to full need. Private merit aid does not reduce Hopkins grant.

FINANCIAL AID PROCEDURES

Forms required: FAFSA, CSS PROFILE.

Dates and Deadlines: Closing date 3/1. Applicants notified by 4/1; must reply by 5/1 or within 2 week(s) of notification.
Transfers: Closing date 3/15. Aid on funds-available basis.

CONTACT

Vincent Amoroso, Director of Student Financial Services
3400 North Charles Street, Mason Hall, Baltimore, MD 21218
(410) 516-8028

Johns Hopkins University: Peabody Conservatory of Music

Baltimore, Maryland
www.peabody.jhu.edu   Federal Code: E00233

4-year private music college in very large city.
Enrollment: 318 undergrads, 2% part-time. 58 full-time freshmen.
Selectivity: Admits 50 to 75% of applicants.

BASIC COSTS (2008-2009)

Tuition and fees: $34,060.
Per-credit charge: $940.
Room and board: $10,200.

FINANCIAL AID PICTURE

Students with need: Need-based aid available for full-time and part-time students.
Students without need: No-need awards available for academics, music/drama.

FINANCIAL AID PROCEDURES

Forms required: FAFSA, institutional form.
Dates and Deadlines: Closing date 2/1. Applicants notified by 4/7; must reply by 5/1 or within 2 week(s) of notification.

CONTACT

Thomas McDermott, Director of Financial Aid
One East Mount Vernon Place, Baltimore, MD 21202
(410) 659-8100 ext. 3023

Kaplan College: Hagerstown

Hagerstown, Maryland
www.KC-Hagerstown.com   Federal Code: 007946

2-year for-profit business and junior college in large town.
Enrollment: 611 undergrads.
Selectivity: Open admission; but selective for some programs.

BASIC COSTS (2007-2008)

Additional info: Tuition and fees vary from $13,248-$31,229 for entire program. Registration fee $55.

FINANCIAL AID PICTURE

Students with need: Need-based aid available for full-time and part-time students.

FINANCIAL AID PROCEDURES

Forms required: FAFSA, institutional form.
Dates and Deadlines: No deadline. Applicants notified on a rolling basis starting 6/1; must reply within 2 week(s) of notification.

CONTACT

Kristen Brezler, Director of Financial Aid
18618 Crestwood Drive, Hagerstown, MD 21742
(301) 739-2670

Loyola College in Maryland

Baltimore, Maryland
www.loyola.edu

Federal Code: 002078
CSS Code: 5370

4-year private business and liberal arts college in very large city, affiliated with Roman Catholic Church.

Enrollment: 3,542 undergrads. 983 full-time freshmen.

Selectivity: Admits 50 to 75% of applicants.

BASIC COSTS (2008-2009)

Tuition and fees: $36,240.

Per-credit charge: $580.

Room only: $7,790.

Additional info: Meal services are "a la carte." Students use funds deposited in restricted meal service "debit card" account.

FINANCIAL AID PICTURE (2007-2008)

Students with need: Average financial aid package met 98% of need; average scholarship/grant was $16,470; average loan was $5,730. For part-time students, average financial aid package was $2,640.

Students without need: No-need awards available for academics, athletics, minority status, ROTC.

Cumulative student debt: 72% of graduating class had student loans; average debt was $19,730.

FINANCIAL AID PROCEDURES

Forms required: FAFSA, CSS PROFILE.

Dates and Deadlines: Closing date 2/15. Applicants notified by 4/1; must reply by 5/1.

Transfers: No deadline. Academic (merit-based) scholarships not available to transfer students.

CONTACT

Mark Lindenmeyer, Director of Financial Aid
4501 North Charles Street, Baltimore, MD 21210-2699
(410) 617-2576

Maryland Institute College of Art

Baltimore, Maryland
www.mica.edu

Federal Code: 002080

4-year private visual arts college in very large city.

Enrollment: 1,668 undergrads, 1% part-time. 400 full-time freshmen.

Selectivity: Admits less than 50% of applicants.

BASIC COSTS (2007-2008)

Tuition and fees: $30,680.

Per-credit charge: $1,238.

Room and board: $8,390.

FINANCIAL AID PICTURE

Students with need: Need-based aid available for full-time and part-time students. Work study available nights, weekends, and for part-time students.

Students without need: No-need awards available for academics, art.

FINANCIAL AID PROCEDURES

Forms required: FAFSA, institutional form.

Dates and Deadlines: Closing date 3/1. Applicants notified by 4/13; must reply by 5/1.

Transfers: Priority date 3/1. Applicants notified by 4/20; must reply by 5/10.

CONTACT

Diane Prengaman, Associate Vice President for Financial Aid
1300 Mount Royal Avenue, Baltimore, MD 21217-4134
(410) 225-2285

McDaniel College

Westminster, Maryland
www.mcdaniel.edu

Federal Code: 002109

4-year private liberal arts college in large town.

Enrollment: 1,687 undergrads, 1% part-time. 430 full-time freshmen.

Selectivity: Admits 50 to 75% of applicants.

BASIC COSTS (2008-2009)

Tuition and fees: $30,780.

Per-credit charge: $962.

Room and board: $6,150.

Additional info: Tuition/fee waivers available for adults.

FINANCIAL AID PICTURE (2007-2008)

Students with need: Out of 364 full-time freshmen who applied for aid, 310 were judged to have need. Of these, 310 received aid, and 102 had their full need met. Average financial aid package met 96% of need; average scholarship/grant was $11,286; average loan was $4,500. For part-time students, average financial aid package was $6,140.

Students without need: 94 full-time freshmen who did not demonstrate need for aid received scholarships/grants; average award was $11,831. No-need awards available for academics, ROTC, state/district residency.

Cumulative student debt: 61% of graduating class had student loans; average debt was $23,284.

FINANCIAL AID PROCEDURES

Forms required: FAFSA, institutional form.

Dates and Deadlines: Priority date 3/1; no closing date. Applicants notified on a rolling basis starting 2/15; must reply by 5/1 or within 2 week(s) of notification.

Transfers: No deadline. Applicants notified on a rolling basis starting 2/15; must reply by 8/1 or within 2 week(s) of notification. Academic transfer scholarships and nontraditional student reduced tuition grants available.

CONTACT

Patricia Williams, Director of Financial Aid
Two College Hill, Westminster, MD 21157-4390
(410) 857-2233

Montgomery College

Rockville, Maryland
www.montgomerycollege.edu

Federal Code: 006911

2-year public community college in very large city.

Enrollment: 16,835 undergrads, 57% part-time. 2,073 full-time freshmen.

Selectivity: Open admission; but selective for some programs.

BASIC COSTS (2007-2008)

Tuition and fees: $3,876; out-of-district residents $7,512; out-of-state residents $9,996.

Per-credit charge: $96; out-of-district residents $197; out-of-state residents $266.

FINANCIAL AID PICTURE (2006-2007)

Students with need: 78% of average financial aid package awarded as scholarships/grants, 22% awarded as loans/jobs. Need-based aid available for part-time students. Work study available nights, weekends, and for part-time students.

Students without need: No-need awards available for academics, alumni affiliation, art, music/drama, state/district residency.

Scholarships offered: Board of Trustees Academic Potential Scholarship; first year of tuition; based on GPA and high school nominations; 125 awards available.

FINANCIAL AID PROCEDURES

Forms required: FAFSA, institutional form.

Dates and Deadlines: Priority date 5/15; no closing date. Applicants notified on a rolling basis starting 5/30.

CONTACT

Melissa Gregory, Director of Financial Aid
51 Mannakee Street, Rockville, MD 20850
(240) 567-5100

Morgan State University

Baltimore, Maryland
www.morgan.edu   Federal Code: 002083

4-year public university and liberal arts college in large city.
Enrollment: 5,959 undergrads.
Selectivity: Admits less than 50% of applicants.

BASIC COSTS (2007-2008)

Tuition and fees: $6,318; out-of-state residents $14,438.
Per-credit charge: $194; out-of-state residents $481.
Room and board: $7,650.
Additional info: Tuition/fee waivers available for minority students.

FINANCIAL AID PICTURE

Students with need: Need-based aid available for full-time and part-time students.

FINANCIAL AID PROCEDURES

Forms required: FAFSA.
Dates and Deadlines: Priority date 4/1; no closing date. Applicants notified on a rolling basis starting 6/1; must reply within 2 week(s) of notification.

CONTACT

Lillian Mitchell, Assistant Director
1700 East Cold Spring Lane, Baltimore, MD 21251
(443) 885-3170

Mount St. Mary's University

Emmitsburg, Maryland
www.msmary.edu   Federal Code: 002086

4-year private university and liberal arts college in rural community, affiliated with Roman Catholic Church.
Enrollment: 1,681 undergrads, 8% part-time. 449 full-time freshmen.
Selectivity: Admits over 75% of applicants.

BASIC COSTS (2008-2009)

Tuition and fees: $27,560.
Per-credit charge: $900.
Room and board: $9,520.

FINANCIAL AID PICTURE (2007-2008)

Students with need: Out of 380 full-time freshmen who applied for aid, 311 were judged to have need. Of these, 310 received aid, and 90 had their full need met. Average financial aid package met 76% of need; average scholarship/grant was $13,800; average loan was $4,393. For part-time students, average financial aid package was $2,935.
Students without need: 128 full-time freshmen who did not demonstrate need for aid received scholarships/grants; average award was $12,891. No-need awards available for academics, art, athletics, minority status, music/drama, ROTC.
Scholarships offered: *Merit:* Kuderer Scholarship; full-tuition scholarship for 4 years; based on competitive examinations, strong academic records and SAT scores of 1200 or higher (exclusive of writing); 3 awards. *Athletic:* 44 full-time freshmen received athletic scholarships; average amount $10,379.
Cumulative student debt: 61% of graduating class had student loans; average debt was $22,041.

FINANCIAL AID PROCEDURES

Forms required: FAFSA, institutional form.
Dates and Deadlines: Closing date 3/1. Applicants notified on a rolling basis starting 2/1; must reply by 5/1.
Transfers: Scholarships available based on GPA at previous institution.

CONTACT

David Reeder, Director of Financial Aid
16300 Old Emmitsburg Road, Emmitsburg, MD 21727
(800) 448-4347

Prince George's Community College

Largo, Maryland
www.pgcc.edu   Federal Code: 002089

2-year public community college in very large city.
Enrollment: 10,512 undergrads, 73% part-time. 972 full-time freshmen.
Selectivity: Open admission; but selective for some programs.

BASIC COSTS (2007-2008)

Tuition and fees: $2,900; out-of-district residents $5,030; out-of-state residents $7,670.
Per-credit charge: $94; out-of-district residents $165; out-of-state residents $263.
Additional info: Instructional services fees range from $22 to $32 per credit depending on course.

FINANCIAL AID PICTURE (2007-2008)

Students with need: Need-based aid available for full-time and part-time students.
Students without need: This college awards aid only to students with need.

FINANCIAL AID PROCEDURES

Forms required: FAFSA, institutional form.
Dates and Deadlines: Priority date 6/1; no closing date. Applicants notified on a rolling basis starting 6/1; must reply within 2 week(s) of notification.

CONTACT

Director of Financial Aid
301 Largo Road, Largo, MD 20774
(301) 322-0822

St. John's College

Annapolis, Maryland   Federal Code: 002092
www.stjohnscollege.edu   CSS Code: 5598

4-year private liberal arts college in large town.
Enrollment: 481 undergrads. 143 full-time freshmen.
Selectivity: Admits over 75% of applicants.

BASIC COSTS (2008-2009)

Tuition and fees: $39,154.
Room and board: $9,284.

FINANCIAL AID PICTURE (2007-2008)

Students with need: Out of 111 full-time freshmen who applied for aid, 89 were judged to have need. Of these, 89 received aid. Average financial aid package met 71% of need; average scholarship/grant was $25,640; average loan was $4,270. Need-based aid available for part-time students.
Students without need: This college awards aid only to students with need.

FINANCIAL AID PROCEDURES

Forms required: FAFSA, CSS PROFILE.
Dates and Deadlines: Priority date 2/15; no closing date. Applicants notified on a rolling basis starting 1/15; must reply by 5/1.

CONTACT

Paula Abernethy, Director of Financial Aid
PO Box 2800, Annapolis, MD 21404
(410) 626-2502

St. Mary's College of Maryland

St. Mary's City, Maryland
www.smcm.edu   Federal Code: 002095

4-year public liberal arts college in rural community.

Enrollment: 1,922 undergrads, 2% part-time. 428 full-time freshmen.

Selectivity: Admits 50 to 75% of applicants.

BASIC COSTS (2008-2009)

Tuition and fees: $12,604; out-of-state residents $23,454.

Per-credit charge: $160.

Room and board: $9,225.

FINANCIAL AID PICTURE (2006-2007)

Students with need: Out of 302 full-time freshmen who applied for aid, 194 were judged to have need. Of these, 194 received aid. Average financial aid package met 59% of need; average scholarship/grant was $3,500; average loan was $2,625. For part-time students, average financial aid package was $3,500.

Students without need: 146 full-time freshmen who did not demonstrate need for aid received scholarships/grants; average award was $3,000. No-need awards available for academics, alumni affiliation.

FINANCIAL AID PROCEDURES

Forms required: FAFSA.

Dates and Deadlines: Closing date 3/1. Applicants notified by 4/1; must reply by 5/1.

Transfers: Priority date 3/1; closing date 6/1. Must reply by 8/1 or within 2 week(s) of notification. All financial aid recipients must have GED or high school diploma. Financial aid transcript required from previous colleges attended.

CONTACT

Timothy Wolfe, Director of Financial Aid
18952 East Fisher Road, St. Mary's City, MD 20686-3001
(240) 895-3000

Salisbury University

Salisbury, Maryland
www.salisbury.edu   Federal Code: 002091

4-year public university and liberal arts college in large town.

Enrollment: 6,726 undergrads, 6% part-time. 1,028 full-time freshmen.

Selectivity: Admits 50 to 75% of applicants.

BASIC COSTS (2007-2008)

Tuition and fees: $6,412; out-of-state residents $14,500.

Per-credit charge: $200; out-of-state residents $537.

Room and board: $7,604.

FINANCIAL AID PICTURE (2006-2007)

Students with need: Out of 808 full-time freshmen who applied for aid, 463 were judged to have need. Of these, 431 received aid, and 87 had their full need met. Average financial aid package met 63% of need; average scholarship/grant was $6,324; average loan was $2,463. For part-time students, average financial aid package was $3,365.

Students without need: 202 full-time freshmen who did not demonstrate need for aid received scholarships/grants; average award was $3,054. No-need awards available for academics, alumni affiliation, art, leadership, music/drama, state/district residency.

Scholarships offered: Scholarships based on outstanding scholastic achievement, extra-curricular activities, geographic residence, degree program and additional factors; over 20 awarded.

Cumulative student debt: 52% of graduating class had student loans; average debt was $17,669.

Additional info: Job opportunities provided for almost 30% of full-time undergraduate students. Students can expect to earn $1500 per academic year by working 10 to 15 hours per week.

FINANCIAL AID PROCEDURES

Forms required: FAFSA.

Dates and Deadlines: Priority date 3/1; closing date 12/31. Applicants notified on a rolling basis starting 3/15; must reply by 5/1 or within 2 week(s) of notification.

Transfers: No deadline. Financial aid transcripts from previous schools required.

CONTACT

Elizabeth Zimmerman, Director of Financial Aid
1200 Camden Avenue, Salisbury, MD 21801-6862
(410) 543-6165

Sojourner-Douglass College

Baltimore, Maryland
www.sdc.edu   Federal Code: 021279

4-year private liberal arts college in very large city.

Enrollment: 1,246 undergrads, 32% part-time. 102 full-time freshmen.

BASIC COSTS (2007-2008)

Tuition and fees: $7,478.

FINANCIAL AID PICTURE

Students with need: Need-based aid available for full-time and part-time students.

FINANCIAL AID PROCEDURES

Forms required: FAFSA, institutional form.

Dates and Deadlines: Priority date 3/1; no closing date. Applicants notified on a rolling basis; must reply within 2 week(s) of notification.

CONTACT

Rebecca Chalk, Financial Aid Administrator
500 North Caroline Street, Baltimore, MD 21205
(410) 276-0306 ext. 260

Towson University

Towson, Maryland
www.towson.edu   Federal Code: 002099

4-year public university in large city.

Enrollment: 15,488 undergrads, 10% part-time. 2,654 full-time freshmen.

Selectivity: Admits 50 to 75% of applicants.

BASIC COSTS (2007-2008)

Tuition and fees: $7,234; out-of-state residents $17,174.

Per-credit charge: $235; out-of-state residents $566.

Room and board: $8,169.

FINANCIAL AID PICTURE (2007-2008)

Students with need: Out of 1,942 full-time freshmen who applied for aid, 1,222 were judged to have need. Of these, 1,166 received aid, and 239 had their full need met. Average financial aid package met 69% of need; average scholarship/grant was $7,295; average loan was $3,346. For part-time students, average financial aid package was $5,497.

Students without need: 302 full-time freshmen who did not demonstrate need for aid received scholarships/grants; average award was $4,424. No-need awards available for academics, athletics, job skills, music/drama.
Scholarships offered: *Merit:* Towson Scholar Award: full tuition, fees, room and board. Presidential Scholarship: full tuition and fees. University Scholarship: full tuition. Provost Scholarship: $1,000-$6,000. Selection based on GPA and combined SAT score. *Athletic:* 16 full-time freshmen received athletic scholarships; average amount $9,710.
Cumulative student debt: 51% of graduating class had student loans; average debt was $11,844.

FINANCIAL AID PROCEDURES

Forms required: FAFSA.
Dates and Deadlines: Priority date 1/31; no closing date. Applicants notified on a rolling basis starting 3/21; must reply within 2 week(s) of notification.
Transfers: Priority date 3/1.

CONTACT

Vincent Pecora, Director of Financial Aid
8000 York Road, Towson, MD 21252-0001
(410) 704-4236

United States Naval Academy
Annapolis, Maryland
www.usna.edu   Federal Code: 002101

4-year public military college in large town.
Enrollment: 4,443 undergrads. 1,161 full-time freshmen.
Selectivity: Admits less than 50% of applicants.

BASIC COSTS (2008-2009)

Additional info: First-year students pay one-time fee of $2,500 upon entering the Naval Academy for initial outfitting of uniforms and other supplies. Tuition, room and board, and medical and dental care provided by United States government. Each midshipman receives monthly salary of about $895 to cover costs of books, supplies, uniforms, laundry, and equipment, including microcomputer.

FINANCIAL AID PICTURE

Additional info: The United States Naval Academy does not charge tuition, room, or board; therefore no financial aid is required by students.

CONTACT

117 Decatur Road, Annapolis, MD 21402-5018

University of Baltimore
Baltimore, Maryland
www.ubalt.edu   Federal Code: 002102

4-year public business and liberal arts college in very large city.
Enrollment: 2,364 undergrads.
Selectivity: Admits less than 50% of applicants.

BASIC COSTS (2007-2008)

Tuition and fees: $6,934; out-of-state residents $19,716.
Per-credit charge: $243; out-of-state residents $754.

FINANCIAL AID PICTURE

Students with need: Need-based aid available for full-time and part-time students.
Additional info: Full need met for dependent students only.

FINANCIAL AID PROCEDURES

Forms required: FAFSA, institutional form.
Dates and Deadlines: No deadline. Applicants notified on a rolling basis.
Transfers: Priority date 4/1. Scholarship application deadline, March 1.

CONTACT

Janet Whelan, Acting Director, Financial Aid
1420 North Charles Street, Baltimore, MD 21201-5779
(410) 837-4763

University of Maryland: Baltimore
Baltimore, Maryland
www.umaryland.edu   Federal Code: 002104

Upper-division public university and health science college in very large city.
Enrollment: 803 undergrads, 31% part-time.

BASIC COSTS (2007-2008)

Tuition and fees: $7,689; out-of-state residents $20,261.
Per-credit charge: $301; out-of-state residents $503.

FINANCIAL AID PICTURE (2006-2007)

Students with need: 33% of average financial aid package awarded as scholarships/grants, 67% awarded as loans/jobs. Need-based aid available for part-time students. Work study available nights, weekends, and for part-time students.
Additional info: Maryland state deadline 3/1.

FINANCIAL AID PROCEDURES

Forms required: FAFSA, state aid form.
Dates and Deadlines: Priority date 3/15; no closing date. Applicants notified on a rolling basis starting 4/15; must reply within 2 week(s) of notification.

CONTACT

660 West Redwood Street, Room 021, Baltimore, MD 21201
(410) 706-7347

University of Maryland: Baltimore County
Baltimore, Maryland
www.umbc.edu   Federal Code: 002105

4-year public university in large city.
Enrollment: 9,304 undergrads, 15% part-time. 1,420 full-time freshmen.
Selectivity: Admits 50 to 75% of applicants.

BASIC COSTS (2007-2008)

Tuition and fees: $8,717; out-of-state residents $17,449.
Per-credit charge: $270; out-of-state residents $633.
Room and board: $8,658.

FINANCIAL AID PICTURE (2006-2007)

Students with need: Out of 992 full-time freshmen who applied for aid, 647 were judged to have need. Of these, 647 received aid, and 237 had their full need met. Average financial aid package met 87% of need; average scholarship/grant was $8,642; average loan was $3,037. For part-time students, average financial aid package was $8,130.
Students without need: 311 full-time freshmen who did not demonstrate need for aid received scholarships/grants; average award was $4,233. No-need awards available for academics, alumni affiliation, art, athletics, music/drama.
Scholarships offered: *Merit:* UMBC General Merit Awards, range from $500-$22,000 per year. Scholars Programs, awards range from $5,000-$22,000 per year. These programs include Center for Women and Information Technology (CWIT) Scholars Program, Humanities Scholars Program, Linehan Artist Scholars Program, Meyerhoff Scholars Program (Sciences and Engineering), and Sondheim Public Affairs Scholars Program Scholars Programs; tuition, fees, room and board. *Athletic:* 88 full-time freshmen received athletic scholarships; average amount $4,039.
Cumulative student debt: 55% of graduating class had student loans; average debt was $20,572.

FINANCIAL AID PROCEDURES

Forms required: FAFSA.

Dates and Deadlines: Priority date 2/14; no closing date. Applicants notified on a rolling basis starting 4/1; must reply within 2 week(s) of notification.

Transfers: Two-year merit scholarships available for transfer students from community colleges.

CONTACT

Stephanie Johnson, Director, Financial Aid
1000 Hilltop Circle, Baltimore, MD 21250
(410) 455-2387

University of Maryland: College Park

College Park, Maryland
www.maryland.edu   Federal Code: 002103

4-year public university in large town.

Enrollment: 25,251 undergrads, 6% part-time. 4,224 full-time freshmen.

Selectivity: Admits less than 50% of applicants.

BASIC COSTS (2007-2008)

Tuition and fees: $7,969; out-of-state residents $22,208.

Per-credit charge: $273; out-of-state residents $867.

Room and board: $8,854.

FINANCIAL AID PICTURE

Students with need: Need-based aid available for full-time and part-time students. Work study available nights, weekends, and for part-time students.

Students without need: No-need awards available for academics, art, athletics, music/drama.

Additional info: Prepaid tuition plans available through state.

FINANCIAL AID PROCEDURES

Forms required: FAFSA.

Dates and Deadlines: Priority date 2/15; no closing date. Applicants notified on a rolling basis starting 4/1.

CONTACT

Sarah Bauder, Director of Student Financial Aid
Mitchell Building, College Park, MD 20742-5235
(301) 314-9000

University of Maryland: Eastern Shore

Princess Anne, Maryland
www.umes.edu   Federal Code: 002106

4-year public university in rural community.

Enrollment: 3,539 undergrads, 7% part-time. 875 full-time freshmen.

Selectivity: Admits 50 to 75% of applicants.

BASIC COSTS (2007-2008)

Tuition and fees: $5,988; out-of-state residents $12,555.

Per-credit charge: $171; out-of-state residents $386.

Room and board: $6,580.

FINANCIAL AID PICTURE

Students with need: Need-based aid available for full-time and part-time students.

Students without need: No-need awards available for academics, alumni affiliation, art, athletics, leadership, music/drama, ROTC, state/district residency.

FINANCIAL AID PROCEDURES

Forms required: FAFSA.

Dates and Deadlines: Priority date 3/1; closing date 4/1. Applicants notified on a rolling basis starting 4/15.

CONTACT

James Kellam, Director of Financial Aid
Bird Hall, Princess Anne, MD 21853
(410) 651-6172

University of Maryland: University College

Adelphi, Maryland
www.umuc.edu   Federal Code: 011644

4-year public university in large town.

Enrollment: 19,893 undergrads, 85% part-time. 189 full-time freshmen.

Selectivity: Open admission.

BASIC COSTS (2007-2008)

Tuition and fees: $5,670; out-of-state residents $11,334.

Per-credit charge: $230; out-of-state residents $466.

FINANCIAL AID PICTURE (2006-2007)

Students with need: Out of 131 full-time freshmen who applied for aid, 125 were judged to have need. Of these, 76 received aid, and 1 had their full need met. Average financial aid package met 15% of need; average scholarship/grant was $2,475; average loan was $2,562. For part-time students, average financial aid package was $4,075.

Students without need: No-need awards available for academics, leadership.

FINANCIAL AID PROCEDURES

Forms required: FAFSA, institutional form.

Dates and Deadlines: Priority date 6/1; no closing date. Applicants notified on a rolling basis starting 5/1; must reply within 2 week(s) of notification.

CONTACT

Cheryl Storie, Associate Vice President, Financial Aid
3501 University Boulevard East, Adelphi, MD 20783-8010
(301) 985-7000

Villa Julie College

Stevenson, Maryland
www.vjc.edu   Federal Code: 002107

4-year private liberal arts college in very large city.

Enrollment: 3,047 undergrads, 16% part-time. 604 full-time freshmen.

Selectivity: Admits over 75% of applicants.

BASIC COSTS (2008-2009)

Tuition and fees: $19,200.

Per-credit charge: $455.

Room and board: $9,506.

FINANCIAL AID PICTURE (2007-2008)

Students with need: Out of 523 full-time freshmen who applied for aid, 414 were judged to have need. Of these, 413 received aid, and 126 had their full need met. Average financial aid package met 75% of need; average scholarship/grant was $12,227; average loan was $2,513. For part-time students, average financial aid package was $4,995.

Students without need: 174 full-time freshmen who did not demonstrate need for aid received scholarships/grants; average award was $7,802. No-need awards available for academics, art, leadership, music/drama, ROTC.

Cumulative student debt: 68% of graduating class had student loans; average debt was $15,580.

Additional info: Cooperative Education Program allows students to work in their field of study with area corporations.

FINANCIAL AID PROCEDURES

Forms required: FAFSA.

Dates and Deadlines: Priority date 2/15; no closing date. Applicants notified on a rolling basis starting 3/15; must reply by 5/1 or within 2 week(s) of notification.

CONTACT

Debra Bottoms, Director of Student Financial Aid
1525 Greenspring Valley Road, Stevenson, MD 21153-0641
(443) 334-2559

Washington Bible College

Lanham, Maryland
www.bible.edu   Federal Code: 001462

4-year private Bible and seminary college in large town, affiliated with nonde-nominational tradition.

Enrollment: 242 undergrads.

BASIC COSTS (2007-2008)

Tuition and fees: $11,810.
Per-credit charge: $380.
Room and board: $6,450.

FINANCIAL AID PICTURE

Students with need: Need-based aid available for full-time and part-time students. Work study available nights, weekends, and for part-time students.
Students without need: No-need awards available for academics, leadership, music/drama, state/district residency.

FINANCIAL AID PROCEDURES

Forms required: FAFSA, institutional form.
Dates and Deadlines: Closing date 3/1. Applicants notified on a rolling basis starting 7/1; must reply within 2 week(s) of notification.
Transfers: Priority date 7/1; no deadline. Applicants notified on a rolling basis; must reply within 2 week(s) of notification.

CONTACT

Diane Marineau, Administrator of Financial Aid
6511 Princess Garden Parkway, Lanham, MD 20706-3599
(301) 552-1400

Washington College

Chestertown, Maryland
www.washcoll.edu   Federal Code: 002108

4-year private liberal arts college in small town.

Enrollment: 1,162 undergrads, 1% part-time. 324 full-time freshmen.
Selectivity: Admits 50 to 75% of applicants.

BASIC COSTS (2007-2008)

Tuition and fees: $32,160.
Per-credit charge: $1,754.
Room and board: $6,790.

FINANCIAL AID PICTURE (2006-2007)

Students with need: 77% of average financial aid package awarded as scholarships/grants, 23% awarded as loans/jobs. Need-based aid available for part-time students. Work study available nights, weekends, and for part-time students.
Students without need: No-need awards available for academics.
Scholarships offered: National Honor Society Scholarship; $40,000 over 4 years; applicant must be member of National Honor Society.

FINANCIAL AID PROCEDURES

Forms required: FAFSA, institutional form.
Dates and Deadlines: Priority date 2/15; no closing date. Applicants notified on a rolling basis starting 3/15; must reply by 5/1.

CONTACT

Jean Narcum, Director of Financial Aid
300 Washington Avenue, Chestertown, MD 21620-1197
(410) 778-7214

Wor-Wic Community College

Salisbury, Maryland
www.worwic.edu   Federal Code: 013842

2-year public community college in large town.

Enrollment: 3,054 undergrads, 65% part-time. 400 full-time freshmen.
Selectivity: Open admission; but selective for some programs.

BASIC COSTS (2007-2008)

Tuition and fees: $2,404; out-of-district residents $5,884; out-of-state residents $6,844.
Per-credit charge: $76; out-of-district residents $192; out-of-state residents $224.

FINANCIAL AID PICTURE

Students with need: Need-based aid available for full-time and part-time students. Work study available nights, weekends, and for part-time students.
Students without need: No-need awards available for academics, state/district residency.

FINANCIAL AID PROCEDURES

Forms required: FAFSA, institutional form.
Dates and Deadlines: Priority date 6/1; no closing date. Applicants notified on a rolling basis starting 4/1.

CONTACT

Deborah Jenkins, Director of Financial Aid
32000 Campus Drive, Salisbury, MD 21804
(410) 334-2905

Massachusetts

American International College

Springfield, Massachusetts
www.aic.edu   Federal Code: 002114

4-year private liberal arts college in small city.

Enrollment: 1,510 undergrads, 8% part-time. 357 full-time freshmen.
Selectivity: Admits over 75% of applicants.

BASIC COSTS (2008-2009)

Tuition and fees: $24,100.
Per-credit charge: $497.
Room and board: $10,150.

FINANCIAL AID PICTURE (2007-2008)

Students with need: Average financial aid package met 75% of need; average scholarship/grant was $16,347; average loan was $3,426. For part-time students, average financial aid package was $17,849.
Students without need: No-need awards available for academics, alumni affiliation, athletics, leadership, state/district residency.
Scholarships offered: Presidential, Provost, Opportunity Scholarships: $5,000 to $11,000; based on class rank, SAT scores, GPA.
Cumulative student debt: 96% of graduating class had student loans; average debt was $32,136.

FINANCIAL AID PROCEDURES

Forms required: FAFSA, state aid form.

Dates and Deadlines: Priority date 5/1; no closing date. Applicants notified on a rolling basis starting 3/15; must reply by 5/1 or within 2 week(s) of notification.

CONTACT
Douglas Fish, Director of Financial Aid
1000 State Street, Springfield, MA 01109
(413) 205-3259

Amherst College
Amherst, Massachusetts
www.amherst.edu

Federal Code: 002115
CSS Code: 3003

4-year private liberal arts college in large town.
Enrollment: 1,683 undergrads. 476 full-time freshmen.
Selectivity: Admits less than 50% of applicants.

BASIC COSTS (2007-2008)
Tuition and fees: $36,232.
Room and board: $9,420.
Additional info: Health Insurance (waivable): $950.

FINANCIAL AID PICTURE (2007-2008)
Students with need: Out of 300 full-time freshmen who applied for aid, 241 were judged to have need. Of these, 241 received aid, and 241 had their full need met. Average financial aid package met 100% of need; average scholarship/grant was $34,777; average loan was $2,756.
Students without need: This college awards aid only to students with need.
Cumulative student debt: 43% of graduating class had student loans; average debt was $11,655.

FINANCIAL AID PROCEDURES
Forms required: FAFSA, CSS PROFILE.
Dates and Deadlines: Priority date 2/15; no closing date. Applicants notified by 4/1; must reply by 5/1.

CONTACT
Joe Case, Dean of Financial Aid
PO Box 5000, Amherst, MA 01002-5000
(413) 542-2296

Anna Maria College
Paxton, Massachusetts
www.annamaria.edu

Federal Code: 002117

4-year private liberal arts college in small town, affiliated with Roman Catholic Church.
Enrollment: 882 undergrads, 20% part-time. 258 full-time freshmen.
Selectivity: Admits over 75% of applicants.

BASIC COSTS (2008-2009)
Tuition and fees: $25,850.
Per-credit charge: $783.
Room and board: $9,350.
Additional info: Annual tuition for music program: $26,500.

FINANCIAL AID PICTURE (2007-2008)
Students with need: Out of 238 full-time freshmen who applied for aid, 214 were judged to have need. Of these, 214 received aid, and 24 had their full need met. Average financial aid package met 67% of need; average scholarship/grant was $10,288; average loan was $4,210. For part-time students, average financial aid package was $7,924.
Students without need: 35 full-time freshmen who did not demonstrate need for aid received scholarships/grants; average award was $7,686. No-

need awards available for academics, alumni affiliation, music/drama, religious affiliation, state/district residency.
Cumulative student debt: 79% of graduating class had student loans; average debt was $24,247.

FINANCIAL AID PROCEDURES
Forms required: FAFSA, state aid form.
Dates and Deadlines: Priority date 3/1; no closing date. Applicants notified on a rolling basis starting 4/1; must reply within 4 week(s) of notification.
Transfers: No deadline. Applicants notified on a rolling basis starting 4/1; must reply within 4 week(s) of notification. Deadline May 1 for state aid.

CONTACT
Colleen King, Director of Financial Aid
50 Sunset Lane, Box O, Paxton, MA 01612-1198
(508) 849-3363

Assumption College
Worcester, Massachusetts
www.assumption.edu

Federal Code: 002118

4-year private liberal arts college in small city, affiliated with Roman Catholic Church.
Enrollment: 2,172 undergrads. 597 full-time freshmen.
Selectivity: Admits 50 to 75% of applicants.

BASIC COSTS (2007-2008)
Tuition and fees: $27,485.
Per-credit charge: $911.
Room and board: $9,492.

FINANCIAL AID PICTURE (2007-2008)
Students with need: Out of 509 full-time freshmen who applied for aid, 443 were judged to have need. Of these, 443 received aid, and 83 had their full need met. Average financial aid package met 74% of need; average scholarship/grant was $14,322; average loan was $3,957. For part-time students, average financial aid package was $12,894.
Students without need: 119 full-time freshmen who did not demonstrate need for aid received scholarships/grants; average award was $12,655. No-need awards available for academics, athletics.
Scholarships offered: *Merit:* Merit scholarships; $2,500 to $20,000 per year; based on academic achievement and leadership talents. *Athletic:* 5 full-time freshmen received athletic scholarships; average amount $21,486.
Cumulative student debt: 80% of graduating class had student loans; average debt was $32,900.

FINANCIAL AID PROCEDURES
Forms required: FAFSA.
Dates and Deadlines: Closing date 2/1. Applicants notified on a rolling basis starting 2/16; must reply by 5/1.
Transfers: Closing date 3/1. Applicants notified on a rolling basis starting 5/1.

CONTACT
Linda Mularczyk, Director of Financial Aid
500 Salisbury Street, Worcester, MA 01609-1296
(508) 767-7158

Atlantic Union College
South Lancaster, Massachusetts
www.auc.edu

Federal Code: 002119

4-year private liberal arts college in small town, affiliated with Seventh-day Adventists.
Enrollment: 469 undergrads, 13% part-time. 107 full-time freshmen.
Selectivity: Admits less than 50% of applicants.

BASIC COSTS (2008-2009)

Tuition and fees: $16,570.

Room and board: $5,000.

Additional info: Additional fees for nursing program. Tuition/fee waivers available for adults.

FINANCIAL AID PICTURE (2007-2008)

Students with need: Average financial aid package met 41% of need; average scholarship/grant was $4,226; average loan was $3,846. For part-time students, average financial aid package was $6,892.

Students without need: No-need awards available for academics, alumni affiliation, leadership, music/drama, religious affiliation.

Cumulative student debt: 80% of graduating class had student loans; average debt was $29,844.

FINANCIAL AID PROCEDURES

Forms required: FAFSA.

Dates and Deadlines: Priority date 4/1; no closing date. Applicants notified on a rolling basis starting 3/1; must reply by 9/12 or within 2 week(s) of notification.

Transfers: Applicants notified on a rolling basis starting 4/1; must reply within 2 week(s) of notification.

CONTACT

Sandra Boucher, Financial Aid Director

Main Street, South Lancaster, MA 01561

(978) 368-2275

Babson College

Babson Park, Massachusetts   Federal Code: 002121

www.babson.edu   CSS Code: 3075

4-year private business college in large town.

Enrollment: 1,799 undergrads. 453 full-time freshmen.

Selectivity: Admits less than 50% of applicants.

BASIC COSTS (2008-2009)

Tuition and fees: $36,096.

Room and board: $12,020.

FINANCIAL AID PICTURE (2007-2008)

Students with need: Out of 244 full-time freshmen who applied for aid, 200 were judged to have need. Of these, 200 received aid, and 171 had their full need met. Average financial aid package met 96% of need; average scholarship/grant was $24,774; average loan was $3,215.

Students without need: 29 full-time freshmen who did not demonstrate need for aid received scholarships/grants; average award was $15,000. No-need awards available for academics, leadership.

Scholarships offered: Presidential Scholarship; half tuition; based on high school record, cocurricular achievements, demonstrated leadership, writing skills, standardized test scores; approximately 40 awarded each year. Women's Leadership Award; one quarter tuition; based on demonstrated leadership experience, future leadership potential, and academic achievement. Diversity Leadership Award; either full or half tuition; awarded to students with the greatest potential for leadership in creating a diverse Babson community.

Cumulative student debt: 51% of graduating class had student loans; average debt was $28,902.

FINANCIAL AID PROCEDURES

Forms required: FAFSA, CSS PROFILE.

Dates and Deadlines: Closing date 2/15. Applicants notified by 4/1; must reply by 5/1.

Transfers: Closing date 4/15.

CONTACT

Melissa Shaak, Director, Student Financial Services

231 Forest Street, Babson Park, MA 02457-0310

(781) 239-4219

Bard College at Simon's Rock

Great Barrington, Massachusetts   Federal Code: 009645

www.simons-rock.edu   CSS Code: 3795

4-year private liberal arts college in small town.

Enrollment: 408 undergrads, 1% part-time. 182 full-time freshmen.

BASIC COSTS (2007-2008)

Tuition and fees: $36,550.

Per-credit charge: $1,430.

Room and board: $9,730.

Additional info: Annual health services fee of $580.

FINANCIAL AID PICTURE

Students with need: Need-based aid available for full-time and part-time students. Work study available nights, weekends, and for part-time students.

Students without need: No-need awards available for academics, alumni affiliation, leadership, state/district residency.

Scholarships offered: Acceleration to Excellence Program (AEP); 2 years full tuition; based on excellent grades, community service, maturity; 20-25 awarded. Special application process.

FINANCIAL AID PROCEDURES

Forms required: FAFSA, CSS PROFILE.

Dates and Deadlines: Priority date 4/15; no closing date. Applicants notified on a rolling basis starting 4/15; must reply within 2 week(s) of notification.

CONTACT

Ann Gitto, Director of Financial Aid

84 Alford Road, Great Barrington, MA 01230-1990

(413) 528-7297

Bay Path College

Longmeadow, Massachusetts

www.baypath.edu   Federal Code: 002122

4-year private business college for women in large town.

Enrollment: 1,322 undergrads, 22% part-time. 198 full-time freshmen.

Selectivity: Admits over 75% of applicants.

BASIC COSTS (2008-2009)

Tuition and fees: $23,840.

Per-credit charge: $450.

Room and board: $9,750.

FINANCIAL AID PICTURE (2007-2008)

Students with need: Out of 185 full-time freshmen who applied for aid, 172 were judged to have need. Of these, 170 received aid, and 28 had their full need met. Average financial aid package met 77% of need; average scholarship/grant was $11,301; average loan was $4,655. For part-time students, average financial aid package was $3,512.

Students without need: 25 full-time freshmen who did not demonstrate need for aid received scholarships/grants; average award was $9,709. No-need awards available for academics, state/district residency.

Cumulative student debt: 40% of graduating class had student loans; average debt was $31,993.

FINANCIAL AID PROCEDURES

Forms required: FAFSA, institutional form.

Dates and Deadlines: Priority date 3/15; no closing date. Applicants notified on a rolling basis starting 3/1; must reply within 2 week(s) of notification.

CONTACT

Stephanie King, Director of Student Financial Services

588 Longmeadow Street, Longmeadow, MA 01106

(413) 565-1000 ext. 1345

Bay State College
Boston, Massachusetts
www.baystate.edu   Federal Code: 003965

2-year private junior college in very large city.
Enrollment: 810 undergrads.

BASIC COSTS (2007-2008)
Tuition and fees: $16,850.
Per-credit charge: $550.
Room and board: $10,500.
Additional info: Program specific fees for allied health, $475 and fashion design, $300.

FINANCIAL AID PICTURE
Students with need: Need-based aid available for full-time and part-time students. Work study available nights, weekends, and for part-time students.
Scholarships offered: Scholarship Day award; $1,000-$5,000; based on examination held on last Saturday of January; amount of award determined by score.

FINANCIAL AID PROCEDURES
Forms required: FAFSA, institutional form.
Dates and Deadlines: Closing date 3/15. Applicants notified on a rolling basis starting 3/15; must reply within 3 week(s) of notification.

CONTACT
Sanjetta Singh, Director of Financial Aid
122 Commonwealth Avenue, Boston, MA 02116
(617) 236-8038

Becker College
Worcester, Massachusetts
www.becker.edu   Federal Code: 002123

4-year private liberal arts college in small city.
Enrollment: 1,694 undergrads, 23% part-time. 551 full-time freshmen.
Selectivity: Admits over 75% of applicants.

BASIC COSTS (2007-2008)
Tuition and fees: $23,600.
Per-credit charge: $990.
Room and board: $9,300.
Additional info: Additional one-time charge of $285 for nursing program.

FINANCIAL AID PICTURE (2006-2007)
Students with need: Out of 441 full-time freshmen who applied for aid, 410 were judged to have need. Of these, 406 received aid, and 50 had their full need met. Average financial aid package met 47% of need; average scholarship/grant was $8,575; average loan was $2,304. For part-time students, average financial aid package was $5,533.
Students without need: 113 full-time freshmen who did not demonstrate need for aid received scholarships/grants; average award was $9,309. No-need awards available for academics.

FINANCIAL AID PROCEDURES
Forms required: FAFSA.
Dates and Deadlines: Priority date 3/1; no closing date. Applicants notified on a rolling basis starting 2/1; must reply within 2 week(s) of notification.

CONTACT
Denise Brindle, Director of Student Financial Services
61 Sever Street, Worcester, MA 01609
(508) 791-9241 ext. 242

Benjamin Franklin Institute of Technology
Boston, Massachusetts
www.bfit.edu   Federal Code: 002151

2-year private technical college in very large city.
Enrollment: 513 undergrads.

BASIC COSTS (2007-2008)
Tuition and fees: $12,750.
Per-credit charge: $531.
Additional info: Cost shown is for certificate program. Tuition for associate degree programs is $13,900 per year.

FINANCIAL AID PICTURE
Students with need: Need-based aid available for full-time and part-time students.
Students without need: No-need awards available for academics.

FINANCIAL AID PROCEDURES
Forms required: FAFSA.
Dates and Deadlines: Priority date 4/1; no closing date. Applicants notified on a rolling basis starting 3/1; must reply within 4 week(s) of notification.

CONTACT
Chris Verleger, Director of Financial Aid
41 Berkeley Street, Boston, MA 02116
(617) 423-4630

Bentley College
Waltham, Massachusetts   Federal Code: 002124
www.bentley.edu   CSS Code: 3096

4-year private business college in small city.
Enrollment: 4,148 undergrads, 5% part-time. 888 full-time freshmen.
Selectivity: Admits less than 50% of applicants.

BASIC COSTS (2007-2008)
Tuition and fees: $32,896.
Room and board: $10,940.

FINANCIAL AID PICTURE (2006-2007)
Students with need: Out of 689 full-time freshmen who applied for aid, 485 were judged to have need. Of these, 485 received aid, and 184 had their full need met. Average financial aid package met 93% of need; average scholarship/grant was $18,824; average loan was $3,828. For part-time students, average financial aid package was $4,616.
Students without need: 125 full-time freshmen who did not demonstrate need for aid received scholarships/grants; average award was $11,992. No-need awards available for academics, athletics, leadership, minority status.
Scholarships offered: *Merit:* Trustee Scholarships; full tuition; based on superior record of academic accomplishment. President's Scholarships; half or one-third tuition; based on excellent academic record. Service Learning Scholarships; $7,500; for students with excellent academic records who have demonstrated commitment to community service. *Athletic:* 10 full-time freshmen received athletic scholarships; average amount $30,349.
Cumulative student debt: 63% of graduating class had student loans; average debt was $31,665.
Additional info: Deadlines for receipt of CSS PROFILE: early decision 12/15, early action and regular decision 2/1.

FINANCIAL AID PROCEDURES
Forms required: FAFSA. CSS profile required if student is applying for institutional grants.
Dates and Deadlines: Closing date 2/1. Applicants notified on a rolling basis starting 3/25.

Transfers: Closing date 3/1. Applicants notified on a rolling basis starting 5/1; must reply by 6/1.

CONTACT
Donna Kendall, Director of Financial Assistance
175 Forest Street, Waltham, MA 02452-4705
(781) 891-3441

Berklee College of Music
Boston, Massachusetts
www.berklee.edu   Federal Code: 002126

4-year private music college in very large city.
Enrollment: 4,090 full-time undergrads.
Selectivity: Admits less than 50% of applicants.

BASIC COSTS (2008-2009)
Tuition and fees: $31;298.
Per-credit charge: $917.
Room and board: $14,360.
Additional info: Required fees include one-time charge for purchase of laptop, which all freshmen must purchase.

FINANCIAL AID PICTURE (2007-2008)
Students with need: Average financial aid package met 24% of need; average scholarship/grant was $6,882; average loan was $3,726. For part-time students, average financial aid package was $9,631.
Students without need: No-need awards available for academics, music/drama.
Scholarships offered: Berklee Entering Student Talent (BEST) Awards: based on evaluation of audition tape/CD. World Scholarship Tour.

FINANCIAL AID PROCEDURES
Forms required: FAFSA.
Dates and Deadlines: Priority date 3/1; no closing date. Applicants notified on a rolling basis starting 3/1; must reply within 3 week(s) of notification.
Transfers: Applicants notified on a rolling basis starting 3/1; must reply within 3 week(s) of notification.

CONTACT
Julie Poorman, Director of Financial Aid
1140 Boylston Street, Boston, MA 02215
(800) 538-3844

Berkshire Community College
Pittsfield, Massachusetts
www.berkshirecc.edu   Federal Code: 002167

2-year public community college in large town.
Enrollment: 1,776 undergrads, 50% part-time. 340 full-time freshmen.
Selectivity: Open admission; but selective for some programs.

BASIC COSTS (2007-2008)
Tuition and fees: $3,826; out-of-state residents $10,846.
Per-credit charge: $26; out-of-state residents $260.
Additional info: $140.50 per credit hour (tuition/fees): New England Regional tuition, New York residents.

FINANCIAL AID PICTURE (2006-2007)
Students with need: Average financial aid package for all full-time undergraduates was $3,232. 69% awarded as scholarships/grants, 31% awarded as loans/jobs. Need-based aid available for part-time students. Work study available nights, weekends, and for part-time students.
Cumulative student debt: 27% of graduating class had student loans; average debt was $2,775.

Additional info: Tuition waivers available to Massachusetts residents who fall into one of the following categories: Department of Social Services adopted or foster children, Massachusetts Rehabilitation Commission clients, high-scoring MCAS students, National Guard members, Native Americans, state employees and their dependents, veterans.

FINANCIAL AID PROCEDURES
Forms required: FAFSA.
Dates and Deadlines: Priority date 5/1; no closing date. Applicants notified on a rolling basis starting 5/10; must reply within 2 week(s) of notification.

CONTACT
Anne Moore, Director of Financial Aid
1350 West Street, Pittsfield, MA 01201-5786
(413) 236-1644

Boston Architectural College
Boston, Massachusetts
www.the-bac.edu   Federal Code: 003966

6-year private architecture and design college in very large city.
Enrollment: 584 undergrads.
Selectivity: Open admission.

BASIC COSTS (2008-2009)
Tuition and fees: $9,940.
Per-credit charge: $826.
Additional info: "Academic Only" program tuition is $13,272 plus $20 required fees.

FINANCIAL AID PICTURE (2007-2008)
Students with need: Average financial aid package met 18% of need; average scholarship/grant was $2,792; average loan was $4,551. For part-time students, average financial aid package was $5,783.
Students without need: No-need awards available for academics, art, leadership.
Cumulative student debt: 70% of graduating class had student loans; average debt was $26,650.

FINANCIAL AID PROCEDURES
Forms required: FAFSA.
Dates and Deadlines: Priority date 4/15; no closing date. Applicants notified on a rolling basis starting 3/1; must reply within 2 week(s) of notification.
Transfers: Applicants notified on a rolling basis starting 3/1; must reply within 2 week(s) of notification.

CONTACT
Anne Downey, Director of Financial Aid
320 Newbury Street, Boston, MA 02115-2795
(617) 585-0125

Boston College
Chestnut Hill, Massachusetts   Federal Code: 002128
www.bc.edu   CSS Code: 3083

4-year private university in small city, affiliated with Roman Catholic Church.
Enrollment: 9,081 undergrads. 2,284 full-time freshmen.
Selectivity: Admits less than 50% of applicants.

BASIC COSTS (2007-2008)
Tuition and fees: $35,674.
Room and board: $11,060.

FINANCIAL AID PICTURE (2006-2007)

Students with need: Out of 1,219 full-time freshmen who applied for aid, 960 were judged to have need. Of these, 960 received aid, and 960 had their full need met. Average financial aid package met 100% of need; average scholarship/grant was $21,777; average loan was $3,617. Need-based aid available for part-time students.

Students without need: 26 full-time freshmen who did not demonstrate need for aid received scholarships/grants; average award was $17,224. No-need awards available for academics, athletics, leadership, ROTC.

Scholarships offered: 60 full-time freshmen received athletic scholarships; average amount $34,246.

Cumulative student debt: 53% of graduating class had student loans; average debt was $20,350.

FINANCIAL AID PROCEDURES

Forms required: FAFSA, CSS PROFILE.

Dates and Deadlines: Priority date 2/1; no closing date. Applicants notified by 4/15; must reply by 5/1.

Transfers: Priority date 3/15. Must reply within 2 week(s) of notification.

CONTACT

Mary McGranahan, Director of Financial Aid
140 Commonwealth Avenue, Devlin Hall 208, Chestnut Hill, MA 02467-3809
(617) 552-3300

Boston Conservatory

Boston, Massachusetts
www.bostonconservatory.edu   Federal Code: 002129

4-year private music and performing arts college in very large city.
Enrollment: 459 undergrads. 154 full-time freshmen.
Selectivity: Admits less than 50% of applicants.

BASIC COSTS (2007-2008)

Tuition and fees: $30,110.
Per-credit charge: $1,170.
Room and board: $15,230.

FINANCIAL AID PICTURE (2007-2008)

Students with need: 48% of average financial aid package awarded as scholarships/grants, 52% awarded as loans/jobs. Need-based aid available for part-time students.

Students without need: No-need awards available for music/drama.

FINANCIAL AID PROCEDURES

Forms required: FAFSA, institutional form.
Dates and Deadlines: Closing date 2/1. Applicants notified by 4/1; must reply by 5/1.

CONTACT

Charlie Petit, Chief Financial Officer
8 The Fenway, Boston, MA 02215

Boston University

Boston, Massachusetts   Federal Code: 002130
www.bu.edu   CSS Code: 3087

4-year private university in very large city.
Enrollment: 16,673 undergrads, 2% part-time. 4,163 full-time freshmen.
Selectivity: Admits 50 to 75% of applicants.

BASIC COSTS (2007-2008)

Tuition and fees: $35,418.
Per-credit charge: $1,092.
Room and board: $10,950.

FINANCIAL AID PICTURE (2007-2008)

Students with need: Out of 2,410 full-time freshmen who applied for aid, 1,933 were judged to have need. Of these, 1,928 received aid, and 987 had their full need met. Average financial aid package met 88% of need; average scholarship/grant was $19,069; average loan was $4,736. For part-time students, average financial aid package was $16,395.

Students without need: 482 full-time freshmen who did not demonstrate need for aid received scholarships/grants; average award was $13,379. No-need awards available for academics, alumni affiliation, art, athletics, leadership, music/drama, religious affiliation, ROTC, state/district residency.

Scholarships offered: *Merit:* Trustee Scholar Program; full tuition and fees (renewable); candidates nominated by high school principals, headmasters, or students. University Scholarships; half tuition (renewable); based on exceptionally strong high school academic record. Dean's Scholarships; $10,000 (renewable); based on strong academic credentials; for students who have applied for need-based financial aid but have financial resources which exceed cost of attendance. Dr. Martin Luther King, Jr. Scholarship; full tuition; for academically gifted students with proven leadership abilities and strong commitment to social justice and community involvement. *Athletic:* 67 full-time freshmen received athletic scholarships; average amount $31,271.

Cumulative student debt: 60% of graduating class had student loans; average debt was $24,939.

Additional info: Financial aid deadline for early decision applicants: 11/01; notification date: 2/15.

FINANCIAL AID PROCEDURES

Forms required: FAFSA, CSS PROFILE, state aid form.
Dates and Deadlines: Closing date 2/15. Applicants notified on a rolling basis starting 3/15; must reply by 5/1 or within 2 week(s) of notification.
Transfers: Priority date 4/1. Transfer students cannot receive duplicate disbursements simultaneously from different institutions.

CONTACT

Christine McGuire, Director of Financial Assistance
121 Bay State Road, Boston, MA 02215
(617) 353-2965

Brandeis University

Waltham, Massachusetts   Federal Code: 002133
www.brandeis.edu   CSS Code: 3092

4-year private university in small city.
Enrollment: 3,203 undergrads. 701 full-time freshmen.
Selectivity: Admits less than 50% of applicants.

BASIC COSTS (2007-2008)

Tuition and fees: $35,702.
Room and board: $9,908.

FINANCIAL AID PICTURE (2007-2008)

Students with need: Out of 523 full-time freshmen who applied for aid, 387 were judged to have need. Of these, 375 received aid, and 130 had their full need met. Average financial aid package met 83% of need; average scholarship/grant was $23,806; average loan was $4,540. Need-based aid available for part-time students.

Students without need: 128 full-time freshmen who did not demonstrate need for aid received scholarships/grants; average award was $17,940. No-need awards available for academics.

Scholarships offered: Justice Brandeis Scholarships; full tuition. Martin Luther King scholarships; tuition and room and board. SERP Scholarships; $20,000; based on musical ability. Presidential scholarships; $20,000. Dean's Awards; $15,000. Waltham High School scholarships; full tuition.

Cumulative student debt: 74% of graduating class had student loans; average debt was $22,381.

FINANCIAL AID PROCEDURES

Forms required: FAFSA, CSS PROFILE.

Dates and Deadlines: Priority date 2/1; no closing date. Applicants notified on a rolling basis starting 4/1.
Transfers: Priority date 4/1. International transfer students seeking scholarship or need-based financial assistance must apply by 2/1.

CONTACT
Peter Giumette, Director of Student Financial Services
Box 549110, Waltham, MA 02454-9110
(781) 736-3700

Bridgewater State College
Bridgewater, Massachusetts
www.bridgew.edu   Federal Code: 002183

4-year public liberal arts and teachers college in large town.
Enrollment: 7,931 undergrads, 15% part-time. 1,551 full-time freshmen.
Selectivity: Admits 50 to 75% of applicants.

BASIC COSTS (2007-2008)
Tuition and fees: $6,034; out-of-state residents $12,174.
Per-credit charge: $38; out-of-state residents $294.
Room and board: $7,670.
Additional info: Tuition/fee waivers available for unemployed or children of unemployed.

FINANCIAL AID PICTURE (2006-2007)
Students with need: Out of 1,084 full-time freshmen who applied for aid, 731 were judged to have need. Of these, 720 received aid. For part-time students, average financial aid package was $3,846.
Students without need: 18 full-time freshmen who did not demonstrate need for aid received scholarships/grants; average award was $5,866. No-need awards available for academics, leadership, minority status, state/district residency.
Cumulative student debt: 73% of graduating class had student loans; average debt was $19,760.

FINANCIAL AID PROCEDURES
Forms required: FAFSA.
Dates and Deadlines: Priority date 3/1; no closing date. Applicants notified on a rolling basis starting 4/1.

CONTACT
Janet Gumbris, Director of Financial Aid
Gates House, Bridgewater, MA 02325
(508) 531-1341

Bristol Community College
Fall River, Massachusetts
www.bristolcc.edu   Federal Code: 002176

2-year public community college in small city.
Enrollment: 5,892 undergrads.
Selectivity: Open admission; but selective for some programs.

BASIC COSTS (2007-2008)
Tuition and fees: $3,750; out-of-state residents $9,930.
Per-credit charge: $24; out-of-state residents $230.
Additional info: Tuition/fee waivers available for unemployed or children of unemployed.

FINANCIAL AID PICTURE (2006-2007)
Students with need: 82% of average financial aid package awarded as scholarships/grants, 18% awarded as loans/jobs. Need-based aid available for part-time students. Work study available nights, weekends, and for part-time students.

Students without need: No-need awards available for academics, art, leadership, minority status, music/drama.

FINANCIAL AID PROCEDURES
Forms required: FAFSA, institutional form.
Dates and Deadlines: Priority date 5/1; no closing date. Applicants notified on a rolling basis starting 5/1; must reply within 2 week(s) of notification.
Transfers: No deadline. Applicants notified on a rolling basis starting 3/1.

CONTACT
David Allen, Director of Financial Aid
777 Elsbree Street, Fall River, MA 02720-7395
(508) 678-2811 ext. 2513

Bunker Hill Community College
Boston, Massachusetts
www.bhcc.mass.edu   Federal Code: 011210

2-year public community college in very large city.
Enrollment: 6,528 undergrads.
Selectivity: Open admission; but selective for some programs.

BASIC COSTS (2007-2008)
Tuition and fees: $3,180; out-of-state residents $9,360.
Per-credit charge: $24; out-of-state residents $230.
Additional info: New England Regional Tuition: $112 per-credit-hour. Tuition/fee waivers available for minority students.

FINANCIAL AID PICTURE
Students with need: Need-based aid available for full-time and part-time students.
Students without need: No-need awards available for academics.

FINANCIAL AID PROCEDURES
Forms required: FAFSA.
Dates and Deadlines: Priority date 4/15; no closing date. Applicants notified on a rolling basis starting 6/1; must reply within 2 week(s) of notification.
Transfers: No deadline. Applicants notified on a rolling basis; must reply within 2 week(s) of notification.

CONTACT
Susan Sullivan, Director of Financial Aid
250 New Rutherford Avenue, Boston, MA 02129-2925
(617) 228-2275

Cambridge College
Cambridge, Massachusetts
www.cambridgecollege.edu   Federal Code: 021829

4-year private liberal arts and teachers college in very large city.
Enrollment: 1,199 undergrads, 70% part-time. 6 full-time freshmen.
Selectivity: Open admission.

BASIC COSTS (2007-2008)
Tuition and fees: $10,350.
Per-credit charge: $345.

FINANCIAL AID PICTURE (2006-2007)
Students with need: Out of 3 full-time freshmen who applied for aid, 3 were judged to have need. Of these, 3 received aid. Average financial aid package met 35% of need; average loan was $1,312. For part-time students, average financial aid package was $5,232.
Students without need: This college awards aid only to students with need.

FINANCIAL AID PROCEDURES
Forms required: FAFSA, institutional form.

Dates and Deadlines: No deadline. Applicants notified on a rolling basis starting 5/1.
Transfers: No deadline. Applicants notified on a rolling basis.

CONTACT
Pamela Walker, Director of Financial Aid
1000 Massachusetts Avenue, Cambridge, MA 02138-5304
(617) 868-1000

Cape Cod Community College
West Barnstable, Massachusetts
www.capecod.edu   Federal Code: 002168

2-year public community college in small town.
Enrollment: 3,339 undergrads.
Selectivity: Open admission; but selective for some programs.

BASIC COSTS (2007-2008)
Tuition and fees: $3,946; out-of-state residents $10,126.
Per-credit charge: $24; out-of-state residents $230.
Additional info: Tuition/fee waivers available for minority students.

FINANCIAL AID PICTURE
Students with need: Need-based aid available for full-time and part-time students.
Students without need: No-need awards available for academics, art, job skills, leadership, music/drama, state/district residency.

FINANCIAL AID PROCEDURES
Forms required: FAFSA.
Dates and Deadlines: Priority date 5/1; no closing date. Applicants notified on a rolling basis starting 5/1.

CONTACT
Sherry Andersen, Director of Financial Aid
2240 Iyanough Road, West Barnstable, MA 02668-1599
(508) 362-2131 ext. 4393

Caritas Laboure College
Boston, Massachusetts
www.laboure.edu   Federal Code: 006324

2-year private health science and junior college in very large city, affiliated with Roman Catholic Church.
Enrollment: 533 undergrads.

BASIC COSTS (2007-2008)
Per-credit charge: $495.
Additional info: Cost of 4-term year is $19,760, inclusive of fees. Professional study courses are $540 per credit.

FINANCIAL AID PICTURE (2007-2008)
Students with need: 23% of average financial aid package awarded as scholarships/grants, 77% awarded as loans/jobs. Need-based aid available for part-time students. Work study available nights.
Students without need: No-need awards available for academics, alumni affiliation, leadership, religious affiliation.
Additional info: Allied Health Scholarship: covers cost of general education courses for students enrolled in electroneurodiagnostic technology, health information technology, and nutrition and food management programs; constitutes significant reduction in tuition. Caritas Christi Scholarship: for students who work 16 hours per week at a Caritas Christi healthcare agency; covers 25% of tuition for nursing and radiation therapy courses; also covers 50% of cost of nursing courses for students with LPN credential. Evening LPN Scholarship: discounts tuition 75% for evening nursing majors with LPN credential.

FINANCIAL AID PROCEDURES
Forms required: FAFSA, institutional form.
Dates and Deadlines: Priority date 4/1; no closing date. Applicants notified on a rolling basis starting 5/15; must reply within 2 week(s) of notification.
Transfers: Priority date 12/1.

CONTACT
Erin Hanlon, Chief Financial Officer
2120 Dorchester Avenue, Boston, MA 02124-5698
(617) 296-8300 ext. 4066

Clark University
Worcester, Massachusetts   Federal Code: 002139
www.clarku.edu   CSS Code: 3279

4-year private university and liberal arts college in small city.
Enrollment: 2,217 undergrads, 2% part-time. 572 full-time freshmen.
Selectivity: Admits 50 to 75% of applicants.

BASIC COSTS (2007-2008)
Tuition and fees: $32,865.
Per-credit charge: $1,019.
Room and board: $6,300.
Additional info: New student contingency fee: $50. Fifth-year tuition waived for eligible undergraduates admitted to accelerated bachelor's/master's programs.

FINANCIAL AID PICTURE (2007-2008)
Students with need: Out of 401 full-time freshmen who applied for aid, 310 were judged to have need. Of these, 301 received aid, and 218 had their full need met. Average financial aid package met 94% of need; average scholarship/grant was $18,954; average loan was $4,531. Need-based aid available for part-time students.
Students without need: 133 full-time freshmen who did not demonstrate need for aid received scholarships/grants; average award was $13,451. No-need awards available for academics, leadership.
Scholarships offered: Scholarships; $10,000-$16,000; based on superior academic achievement or community service involvement.
Cumulative student debt: 90% of graduating class had student loans; average debt was $21,100.

FINANCIAL AID PROCEDURES
Forms required: FAFSA, CSS PROFILE.
Dates and Deadlines: Closing date 2/1. Applicants notified by 3/31; must reply by 5/1 or within 2 week(s) of notification.
Transfers: Priority date 4/1; no deadline. Financial aid transcript from previous institution(s) attended required.

CONTACT
Mary Ellen Severance, Director of Financial Aid and Student Employment
950 Main Street, Worcester, MA 01610-1477
(508) 793-7478

College of the Holy Cross
Worcester, Massachusetts   Federal Code: 002141
www.holycross.edu   CSS Code: 3282

4-year private liberal arts college in small city, affiliated with Roman Catholic Church.
Enrollment: 2,817 undergrads. 717 full-time freshmen.
Selectivity: Admits less than 50% of applicants.

BASIC COSTS (2008-2009)
Tuition and fees: $37,242.
Room and board: $10,260.

FINANCIAL AID PICTURE (2007-2008)

Students with need: Average financial aid package met 100% of need; average scholarship/grant was $25,270; average loan was $4,957.

Students without need: No-need awards available for academics, athletics, ROTC.

FINANCIAL AID PROCEDURES

Forms required: FAFSA. CSS PROFILE required of all students applying for institutional aid.

Dates and Deadlines: Closing date 2/1. Applicants notified by 3/30; must reply by 5/1.

CONTACT

Lynne Myers, Director of Financial Aid
One College Street, Worcester, MA 01610-2395
(508) 793-2265

Curry College

Milton, Massachusetts
www.curry.edu   Federal Code: 002143

4-year private nursing and liberal arts college in large town.

Enrollment: 2,641 undergrads, 22% part-time. 634 full-time freshmen.

Selectivity: Admits 50 to 75% of applicants.

BASIC COSTS (2007-2008)

Tuition and fees: $25,755.

Per-credit charge: $835.

Room and board: $10,290.

Additional info: PAL (Program for Advancement of Learning) students pay additional program participation fee.

FINANCIAL AID PICTURE (2007-2008)

Students with need: Out of 456 full-time freshmen who applied for aid, 449 were judged to have need. Of these, 446 received aid, and 24 had their full need met. Average financial aid package met 68.9% of need; average scholarship/grant was $11,903; average loan was $3,612. For part-time students, average financial aid package was $5,103.

Students without need: 20 full-time freshmen who did not demonstrate need for aid received scholarships/grants; average award was $5,450. No-need awards available for academics, leadership.

Cumulative student debt: 58% of graduating class had student loans; average debt was $27,145.

FINANCIAL AID PROCEDURES

Forms required: FAFSA.

Dates and Deadlines: Priority date 3/1; no closing date. Applicants notified on a rolling basis starting 3/10; must reply by 5/1 or within 2 week(s) of notification.

CONTACT

Stephanny Elias, Director, Student Financial Services
1071 Blue Hill Avenue, Milton, MA 02186-9984
(617) 333-2354

Dean College

Franklin, Massachusetts
www.dean.edu   Federal Code: 002144

2-year private junior and liberal arts college in large town.

Enrollment: 1,093 undergrads, 8% part-time. 545 full-time freshmen.

Selectivity: Admits 50 to 75% of applicants.

BASIC COSTS (2007-2008)

Tuition and fees: $25,420.

Room and board: $10,960.

FINANCIAL AID PICTURE (2006-2007)

Students with need: Out of 396 full-time freshmen who applied for aid, 357 were judged to have need. Of these, 357 received aid, and 40 had their full need met. For part-time students, average financial aid package was $2,746.

Students without need: 355 full-time freshmen who did not demonstrate need for aid received scholarships/grants; average award was $9,554. No-need awards available for academics, athletics, leadership, music/drama, state/district residency.

Scholarships offered: *Merit:* Trustee's Scholarship; $10,000 - $12,000 per year; decision based on outstanding academic accomplishments or potential. President's Leadership Scholarship; $8,000 - $12,000 per year; given to students with leadership positions during their high school careers. Performing Arts Scholarship; $5,000 - $11,000 per year; achievement in dance or theater. *Athletic:* 56 full-time freshmen received athletic scholarships; average amount $3,336.

Cumulative student debt: 58% of graduating class had student loans; average debt was $12,067.

FINANCIAL AID PROCEDURES

Forms required: FAFSA.

Dates and Deadlines: Priority date 3/1; no closing date. Applicants notified on a rolling basis starting 3/1; must reply by 5/1 or within 3 week(s) of notification.

Transfers: No deadline. Applicants notified on a rolling basis starting 3/1.

CONTACT

Jenny Aguiar, Director of Financial Aid
99 Main Street, Franklin, MA 02038-1994
(508) 541-1518

Eastern Nazarene College

Quincy, Massachusetts
www.enc.edu   Federal Code: 002145

4-year private liberal arts college in small city, affiliated with Church of the Nazarene.

Enrollment: 649 undergrads.

Selectivity: Admits 50 to 75% of applicants.

BASIC COSTS (2007-2008)

Tuition and fees: $20,574.

Room and board: $7,395.

Additional info: Tuition/fee waivers available for minority students.

FINANCIAL AID PICTURE

Students with need: Need-based aid available for full-time and part-time students. Work study available nights, weekends, and for part-time students.

Students without need: No-need awards available for academics, alumni affiliation, leadership, music/drama, religious affiliation, state/district residency.

Scholarships offered: Activities Scholarship: up to $1,500 per year; based on documented school, community, and church activities; up to 25 awarded.

Additional info: Participant in Massachusetts University pre-payment plan.

FINANCIAL AID PROCEDURES

Forms required: FAFSA, institutional form.

Dates and Deadlines: Priority date 2/28; no closing date. Applicants notified on a rolling basis starting 3/15; must reply within 2 week(s) of notification.

Transfers: Aid limited to amount eligible minus what students received at prior institution. Pell grant may also vary, depending on cost of attendance versus other school's cost and student's enrollment status.

CONTACT

Rodney Neighbors, Director of Financial Aid
23 East Elm Avenue, Quincy, MA 02170-2999
(617) 745-3712

Elms College

Chicopee, Massachusetts
www.elms.edu   Federal Code: 002140

4-year private liberal arts college in small city, affiliated with Roman Catholic Church.

Enrollment: 976 undergrads. 182 full-time freshmen.

Selectivity: Admits over 75% of applicants.

BASIC COSTS (2007-2008)

Tuition and fees: $23,755.

Per-credit charge: $460.

Room and board: $8,820.

FINANCIAL AID PICTURE

Students with need: Need-based aid available for full-time and part-time students. Work study available nights, weekends, and for part-time students.

Students without need: No-need awards available for academics, alumni affiliation, leadership, religious affiliation, state/district residency.

FINANCIAL AID PROCEDURES

Forms required: FAFSA, institutional form.

Dates and Deadlines: Priority date 3/1; no closing date. Applicants notified on a rolling basis starting 3/10; must reply by 5/1 or within 2 week(s) of notification.

Transfers: Priority date 7/1; no deadline. Applicants notified on a rolling basis starting 5/1; must reply by 9/6.

CONTACT

Troy Davis, Director of Student Financial Aid Services
291 Springfield Street, Chicopee, MA 01013
(413) 592-3189

Emerson College

Boston, Massachusetts   Federal Code: 002146
www.emerson.edu   CSS Code: 3367

4-year private college of communication and the arts in very large city.

Enrollment: 3,293 undergrads, 2% part-time. 843 full-time freshmen.

Selectivity: Admits less than 50% of applicants.

BASIC COSTS (2008-2009)

Tuition and fees: $28,969.

Per-credit charge: $886.

Room and board: $11,832.

FINANCIAL AID PICTURE (2007-2008)

Students with need: Out of 627 full-time freshmen who applied for aid, 454 were judged to have need. Of these, 454 received aid, and 407 had their full need met. Average financial aid package met 75% of need; average scholarship/grant was $12,900; average loan was $3,698. For part-time students, average financial aid package was $10,883.

Students without need: 164 full-time freshmen who did not demonstrate need for aid received scholarships/grants; average award was $12,800. No-need awards available for academics, music/drama.

Scholarships offered: Trustee's Scholarships (Honors Program); half tuition. Dean's Scholarships; $8,000. Emerson Stage Scholarships; vary, based on performing arts audition and academic merit.

Cumulative student debt: 56% of graduating class had student loans; average debt was $33,233.

Additional info: Massachusetts Loan Plan available for parents of dependent undergraduates.

FINANCIAL AID PROCEDURES

Forms required: FAFSA, CSS PROFILE.

Dates and Deadlines: Priority date 3/1; no closing date. Applicants notified by 4/1; must reply by 5/1 or within 3 week(s) of notification.

Transfers: Priority date 4/1.

CONTACT

Michelle Smith, Director of Student Financial Services
120 Boylston Street, Boston, MA 02116-4624
(617) 824-8655

Emmanuel College

Boston, Massachusetts
www.emmanuel.edu   Federal Code: 002147

4-year private liberal arts college in very large city, affiliated with Roman Catholic Church.

Enrollment: 2,139 undergrads, 23% part-time. 582 full-time freshmen.

Selectivity: Admits 50 to 75% of applicants.

BASIC COSTS (2007-2008)

Tuition and fees: $26,250.

Per-credit charge: $816.

Room and board: $11,200.

FINANCIAL AID PICTURE (2007-2008)

Students with need: Out of 516 full-time freshmen who applied for aid, 475 were judged to have need. Of these, 475 received aid, and 133 had their full need met. Average financial aid package met 76% of need; average scholarship/grant was $15,007; average loan was $4,055. For part-time students, average financial aid package was $12,167.

Students without need: 67 full-time freshmen who did not demonstrate need for aid received scholarships/grants; average award was $10,539. No-need awards available for academics, alumni affiliation, leadership.

FINANCIAL AID PROCEDURES

Forms required: FAFSA, institutional form.

Dates and Deadlines: Priority date 4/1; no closing date. Applicants notified on a rolling basis starting 3/15.

CONTACT

Jennifer Porter, Assistant Vice President for Student Financial Services
400 The Fenway, Boston, MA 02115
(617) 735-9938

Endicott College

Beverly, Massachusetts
www.endicott.edu   Federal Code: 002148

4-year private liberal arts college in large town.

Enrollment: 2,128 undergrads, 8% part-time. 520 full-time freshmen.

Selectivity: Admits less than 50% of applicants.

BASIC COSTS (2007-2008)

Tuition and fees: $22,950.

Per-credit charge: $690.

Room and board: $10,800.

FINANCIAL AID PICTURE (2007-2008)

Students with need: Out of 334 full-time freshmen who applied for aid, 276 were judged to have need. Of these, 275 received aid, and 29 had their full need met. Average financial aid package met 57% of need; average scholarship/grant was $7,267; average loan was $3,710. For part-time students, average financial aid package was $10,070.

Students without need: No-need awards available for academics, alumni affiliation, art, leadership, ROTC, state/district residency.

Cumulative student debt: 73% of graduating class had student loans; average debt was $29,382.

FINANCIAL AID PROCEDURES

Forms required: FAFSA, institutional form.

Dates and Deadlines: Priority date 3/15; no closing date. Applicants notified on a rolling basis starting 3/15; must reply within 2 week(s) of notification.

CONTACT

Marcia Toomey, Director of Financial Aid
376 Hale Street, Beverly, MA 01915-9985
(978) 232-2060

Fisher College

Boston, Massachusetts
www.fisher.edu   Federal Code: 002150

2-year private liberal arts college in very large city.
Enrollment: 589 undergrads.
Selectivity: Admits 50 to 75% of applicants.

BASIC COSTS (2008-2009)
Tuition and fees: $23,065.
Room and board: $12,125.

FINANCIAL AID PICTURE
Students with need: Need-based aid available for full-time and part-time students. Work study available nights, weekends, and for part-time students.
Students without need: No-need awards available for academics, alumni affiliation, state/district residency.
Scholarships offered: Fisher Honor Scholarship; $2,500 (renewable with 3.0 GPA); based on outstanding academic and personal achievement, contribution to school and community. Business Administration and Computer Technology Scholarship; $1,500 for 2.5-2.99 GPA, $3,000 for minimum 3.0 GPA; renewable; for students enrolling in associate programs in business administration or computer technology.

FINANCIAL AID PROCEDURES
Forms required: FAFSA.
Dates and Deadlines: Priority date 3/1; no closing date. Applicants notified on a rolling basis starting 3/1; must reply within 2 week(s) of notification.

CONTACT

Frank Lauder, Director of Financial Aid
118 Beacon Street, Boston, MA 02116
(617) 236-4418

Fitchburg State College

Fitchburg, Massachusetts
www.fsc.edu   Federal Code: 002184

4-year public liberal arts and teachers college in small city.
Enrollment: 3,605 undergrads, 12% part-time. 699 full-time freshmen.
Selectivity: Admits 50 to 75% of applicants.

BASIC COSTS (2007-2008)
Tuition and fees: $5,992; out-of-state residents $12,072.
Room and board: $6,632.

FINANCIAL AID PICTURE
Students with need: Need-based aid available for full-time and part-time students. Work study available nights, weekends, and for part-time students.
Students without need: No-need awards available for academics, alumni affiliation, leadership, state/district residency.
Scholarships offered: Renewable scholarships awarded on basis of high school record and test scores.

FINANCIAL AID PROCEDURES
Forms required: FAFSA.
Dates and Deadlines: Priority date 2/1; no closing date. Applicants notified on a rolling basis starting 3/15; must reply within 2 week(s) of notification.

CONTACT

Pamela McCafferty, Dean of Enrollment Management
160 Pearl Street, Fitchburg, MA 01420-2697
(978) 665-3156

Framingham State College

Framingham, Massachusetts
www.framingham.edu   Federal Code: 002185

4-year public liberal arts and teachers college in small city.
Enrollment: 3,503 undergrads, 12% part-time. 714 full-time freshmen.
Selectivity: Admits 50 to 75% of applicants.

BASIC COSTS (2007-2008)
Tuition and fees: $5,799; out-of-state residents $11,879.
Per-credit charge: $40; out-of-state residents $294.
Room and board: $7,017.
Additional info: Fees include mandatory laptop purchase by new students. New England Regional tuition rate $1455.

FINANCIAL AID PICTURE (2006-2007)
Students with need: Out of 579 full-time freshmen who applied for aid, 369 were judged to have need. Of these, 369 received aid, and 167 had their full need met. Average financial aid package met 79% of need; average scholarship/grant was $4,238; average loan was $3,401. For part-time students, average financial aid package was $6,002.
Students without need: 23 full-time freshmen who did not demonstrate need for aid received scholarships/grants; average award was $2,441. No-need awards available for academics.
Scholarships offered: Senator Paul E. Tsongas Scholarship; full tuition and fees; available to Massachusetts residents; based on 3.75 high school GPA and test scores; 5 awarded. Merit scholarships available to students majoring in education, natural or physical sciences; based on GPA and test scores.

FINANCIAL AID PROCEDURES
Forms required: FAFSA.
Dates and Deadlines: Priority date 3/1; no closing date. Applicants notified on a rolling basis starting 4/15; must reply by 5/1 or within 2 week(s) of notification.
Transfers: Priority date 11/1; no deadline. Applicants notified on a rolling basis; must reply within 2 week(s) of notification.

CONTACT

Susan Lanzillo, Director of Financial Aid
100 State Street, Framingham, MA 01701-9101
(508) 626-4534

Franklin W. Olin College of Engineering

Needham, Massachusetts
www.olin.edu   Federal Code: 039463

4-year private engineering college in large town.
Enrollment: 296 undergrads. 75 full-time freshmen.
Selectivity: Admits less than 50% of applicants.

BASIC COSTS (2007-2008)
Additional info: Every admitted student receives 4-year full-tuition scholarship; $11,400 room/board and $1,425 required fees for academic year.

FINANCIAL AID PICTURE (2007-2008)
Students with need: Out of 34 full-time freshmen who applied for aid, 8 were judged to have need. Of these, 8 received aid, and 8 had their full need met. Average financial aid package met 100% of need; average scholarship/grant was $8,583; average loan was $1,458.

Students without need: 72 full-time freshmen who did not demonstrate need for aid received scholarships/grants; average award was $33,600. No-need awards available for academics, leadership.

Scholarships offered: All students receive full tuition scholarships.

Additional info: No financial aid forms necessary.

FINANCIAL AID PROCEDURES

Forms required: FAFSA.

Dates and Deadlines: Priority date 2/15; no closing date. Applicants notified on a rolling basis starting 3/31; must reply by 5/1.

CONTACT

Jean Ricker, Manager, Financial Aid
Olin Way, Needham, MA 02492-1245
(781) 292-2343

Gordon College

Wenham, Massachusetts
www.gordon.edu

Federal Code: 002153
CSS Code: 3417

4-year private liberal arts college in small town, affiliated with nondenominational tradition.

Enrollment: 1,521 undergrads, 2% part-time. 587 full-time freshmen.

Selectivity: Admits 50 to 75% of applicants.

BASIC COSTS (2007-2008)

Tuition and fees: $25,748.

Room and board: $6,906.

FINANCIAL AID PICTURE (2006-2007)

Students with need: Out of 320 full-time freshmen who applied for aid, 260 were judged to have need. Of these, 259 received aid, and 53 had their full need met. Average financial aid package met 66% of need; average scholarship/grant was $10,967; average loan was $2,963. For part-time students, average financial aid package was $10,612.

Students without need: 251 full-time freshmen who did not demonstrate need for aid received scholarships/grants; average award was $12,259. No-need awards available for academics, alumni affiliation, leadership, minority status, music/drama, religious affiliation.

Scholarships offered: A.J. Gordon Scholarship; $12,000; renewable annually; based on academic achievement and leadership. Dean's Scholarships; $8,000; renewable; based on academic record. Challenge Scholarships; $6,000; renewable; based on academic record. Choral Scholars Program; $7,000; renewable; for students with excellent ability/academic performance seeking career in vocal music field.

Cumulative student debt: 86% of graduating class had student loans; average debt was $30,116.

FINANCIAL AID PROCEDURES

Forms required: FAFSA, CSS PROFILE, state aid form.

Dates and Deadlines: Closing date 3/1. Applicants notified on a rolling basis starting 4/15; must reply by 5/1 or within 2 week(s) of notification.

Transfers: Priority date 3/15. Applicants notified on a rolling basis starting 4/1.

CONTACT

Barbara Layne, Associate Vice President of Enrollment
255 Grapevine Road, Wenham, MA 01984
(800) 343-1379

Greenfield Community College

Greenfield, Massachusetts
www.gcc.mass.edu

Federal Code: 002169

2-year public community college in large town.

Enrollment: 1,870 undergrads.

Selectivity: Open admission; but selective for some programs.

BASIC COSTS (2007-2008)

Tuition and fees: $4,488; out-of-state residents $12,138.

Per-credit charge: $26; out-of-state residents $281.

Additional info: Tuition/fee waivers available for adults.

FINANCIAL AID PICTURE

Students with need: Need-based aid available for full-time and part-time students. Work study available nights, weekends, and for part-time students.

Students without need: This college awards aid only to students with need.

FINANCIAL AID PROCEDURES

Forms required: FAFSA, institutional form.

Dates and Deadlines: Priority date 4/15; no closing date. Applicants notified on a rolling basis starting 5/1; must reply within 2 week(s) of notification.

CONTACT

Linda Dejardins, Director of Financial Aid
One College Drive, Greenfield, MA 01301
(413) 775-1109

Hampshire College

Amherst, Massachusetts
www.hampshire.edu

Federal Code: 004661
CSS Code: 3447

4-year private liberal arts college in large town.

Enrollment: 1,412 undergrads. 397 full-time freshmen.

Selectivity: Admits 50 to 75% of applicants.

BASIC COSTS (2008-2009)

Tuition and fees: $38,649.

Room and board: $10,080.

FINANCIAL AID PICTURE (2007-2008)

Students with need: Out of 255 full-time freshmen who applied for aid, 227 were judged to have need. Of these, 226 received aid, and 184 had their full need met. Average financial aid package met 97% of need; average scholarship/grant was $23,880; average loan was $3,000.

Students without need: 83 full-time freshmen who did not demonstrate need for aid received scholarships/grants; average award was $6,000. No-need awards available for academics, leadership, minority status.

Cumulative student debt: 56% of graduating class had student loans; average debt was $20,300.

FINANCIAL AID PROCEDURES

Forms required: FAFSA, CSS PROFILE.

Dates and Deadlines: Priority date 2/1; no closing date. Applicants notified on a rolling basis starting 4/1; must reply by 5/1 or within 2 week(s) of notification.

CONTACT

Kathleen Methot, Director of Financial Aid
893 West Street, Amherst, MA 01002-9988
(413) 559-5484

Harvard College

Cambridge, Massachusetts
www.college.harvard.edu

Federal Code: 002155
CSS Code: 3434

4-year private university in small city.

Enrollment: 6,648 undergrads. 1,654 full-time freshmen.

Selectivity: Admits less than 50% of applicants.

BASIC COSTS (2008-2009)
Tuition and fees: $36,173.
Room and board: $11,042.

FINANCIAL AID PICTURE (2007-2008)
Students with need: Out of 1,072 full-time freshmen who applied for aid, 906 were judged to have need. Of these, 906 received aid, and 906 had their full need met. Average financial aid package met 100% of need; average scholarship/grant was $34,806; average loan was $3,631. Need-based aid available for part-time students.
Students without need: This college awards aid only to students with need.
Cumulative student debt: 46% of graduating class had student loans; average debt was $9,290.
Additional info: Institution meets full need of all admitted students.

FINANCIAL AID PROCEDURES
Forms required: FAFSA. CSS PROFILE required of all US citizens and US permanent residents plus all Canadians.
Dates and Deadlines: Closing date 2/1. Applicants notified by 4/1; must reply by 5/1 or within 2 week(s) of notification.
Transfers: Closing date 2/15. Applicants notified by 5/30; must reply within 2 week(s) of notification.

CONTACT
Janet Irons, Senior Associate Director of Financial Aid
86 Brattle Street, Cambridge, MA 02138
(617) 495-1581

Hellenic College/Holy Cross

Brookline, Massachusetts
www.hchc.edu   Federal Code: 002154

4-year private liberal arts and seminary college in large town, affiliated with Eastern Orthodox Church.
Enrollment: 72 undergrads. 10 full-time freshmen.
Selectivity: Admits over 75% of applicants.

BASIC COSTS (2007-2008)
Tuition and fees: $17,325.
Room and board: $10,890.

FINANCIAL AID PICTURE
Students with need: Need-based aid available for full-time students. Work study available nights, weekends, and for part-time students.
Students without need: This college awards aid only to students with need.

FINANCIAL AID PROCEDURES
Forms required: FAFSA, institutional form.
Dates and Deadlines: Closing date 4/1. Applicants notified on a rolling basis starting 10/1; must reply within 2 week(s) of notification.
Transfers: No deadline. Applicants notified on a rolling basis; must reply within 2 week(s) of notification.

CONTACT
Sonia Belcher, Director of Financial Aid
50 Goddard Avenue, Brookline, MA 02445
(617) 850-1297

Holyoke Community College

Holyoke, Massachusetts
www.hcc.mass.edu   Federal Code: 002170

2-year public community college in large town.
Enrollment: 5,956 undergrads, 43% part-time. 1,343 full-time freshmen.
Selectivity: Open admission; but selective for some programs.

BASIC COSTS (2007-2008)
Tuition and fees: $3,428; out-of-state residents $9,608.
Per-credit charge: $24; out-of-state residents $230.

FINANCIAL AID PICTURE (2006-2007)
Students with need: 79% of average financial aid package awarded as scholarships/grants, 21% awarded as loans/jobs. Need-based aid available for part-time students. Work study available nights.
Students without need: No-need awards available for academics, art, leadership, music/drama.

FINANCIAL AID PROCEDURES
Forms required: FAFSA.
Dates and Deadlines: Priority date 5/1; no closing date. Applicants notified on a rolling basis starting 5/1; must reply within 2 week(s) of notification.

CONTACT
Karen Derouin, Director of Financial Aid
303 Homestead Avenue, Holyoke, MA 01040
(413) 552-2248

Lasell College

Newton, Massachusetts
www.lasell.edu   Federal Code: 002158

4-year private business and liberal arts college in small city.
Enrollment: 1,304 undergrads, 2% part-time. 425 full-time freshmen.
Selectivity: Admits 50 to 75% of applicants.

BASIC COSTS (2007-2008)
Tuition and fees: $21,850.
Per-credit charge: $700.
Room and board: $9,550.

FINANCIAL AID PICTURE (2007-2008)
Students with need: Average financial aid package met 69% of need; average scholarship/grant was $12,006; average loan was $3,400. For part-time students, average financial aid package was $9,050.
Students without need: No-need awards available for academics, alumni affiliation.
Cumulative student debt: 95% of graduating class had student loans; average debt was $26,500.

FINANCIAL AID PROCEDURES
Forms required: FAFSA, institutional form.
Dates and Deadlines: Priority date 3/1; no closing date. Applicants notified on a rolling basis starting 2/15; must reply by 5/1 or within 2 week(s) of notification.

CONTACT
Michele Kosboth, Director of Student Financial Planning
1844 Commonwealth Avenue, Newton, MA 02466
(617) 243-2227

Lesley University

Cambridge, Massachusetts
www.lesley.edu/lc   Federal Code: 002160

4-year private liberal arts and teachers college in very large city.
Enrollment: 1,225 undergrads, 6% part-time. 350 full-time freshmen.
Selectivity: Admits over 75% of applicants.

BASIC COSTS (2008-2009)
Tuition and fees: $27,510.
Per-credit charge: $1,135.

Room and board: $12,000.

FINANCIAL AID PICTURE (2007-2008)

Students with need: Out of 327 full-time freshmen who applied for aid, 258 were judged to have need. Of these, 250 received aid, and 11 had their full need met. Average financial aid package met 70% of need; average scholarship/grant was $12,625; average loan was $4,029. For part-time students, average financial aid package was $10,718.

Students without need: 64 full-time freshmen who did not demonstrate need for aid received scholarships/grants; average award was $8,306. No-need awards available for academics, art, leadership, minority status, state/district residency.

Scholarships offered: Freshmen scholarships; $5,000 to full tuition; for students with strong academic backgrounds who have shown a commitment to community service and making a difference in the lives of others.

Cumulative student debt: 91% of graduating class had student loans; average debt was $15,000.

FINANCIAL AID PROCEDURES

Forms required: FAFSA.

Dates and Deadlines: Priority date 2/15; no closing date. Applicants notified on a rolling basis starting 2/15.

Transfers: Priority date 3/15.

CONTACT

Scott Jewell, Director of Financial Aid
29 Everett Street, Cambridge, MA 02138-2790
(617) 349-8667

Marian Court College

Swampscott, Massachusetts
www.mariancourt.edu

Federal Code: 006873

2-year private junior college in large town, affiliated with Roman Catholic Church.

Enrollment: 220 full-time undergrads.

BASIC COSTS (2007-2008)

Tuition and fees: $13,956.

Additional info: Evening program: $675 for 3 credit course. Tuition/fee waivers available for adults.

FINANCIAL AID PICTURE

Students with need: Need-based aid available for full-time and part-time students.

Students without need: No-need awards available for academics.

FINANCIAL AID PROCEDURES

Forms required: FAFSA, institutional form.

Dates and Deadlines: Priority date 4/1; no closing date. Applicants notified on a rolling basis starting 4/15.

CONTACT

Kathy Angle, Director of Financial Aid
35 Little's Point Road, Swampscott, MA 01907-2896
(781) 595-6768

Massachusetts Bay Community College

Wellesley Hills, Massachusetts
www.massbay.edu

Federal Code: 002171

2-year public community college in large town.

Enrollment: 4,473 undergrads, 57% part-time. 724 full-time freshmen.

Selectivity: Open admission; but selective for some programs.

BASIC COSTS (2007-2008)

Tuition and fees: $3,650; out-of-state residents $9,830.

Per-credit charge: $24; out-of-state residents $230.

Additional info: NEBHE tuition rate is 150% of in-state cost and fees are approximately the same. Tuition/fee waivers available for unemployed or children of unemployed.

FINANCIAL AID PICTURE (2006-2007)

Students with need: 64% of average financial aid package awarded as scholarships/grants, 36% awarded as loans/jobs. Need-based aid available for part-time students.

FINANCIAL AID PROCEDURES

Forms required: FAFSA, institutional form.

Dates and Deadlines: Priority date 8/30; no closing date. Applicants notified on a rolling basis starting 4/1.

CONTACT

Paula Ogden, Director of Financial Aid/Assistant Dean of Students
50 Oakland Street, Wellesley Hills, MA 02481
(781) 239-2600

Massachusetts College of Art

Boston, Massachusetts
www.massart.edu

Federal Code: 002180

4-year public visual arts college in very large city.

Enrollment: 1,687 undergrads, 11% part-time. 275 full-time freshmen.

Selectivity: Admits 50 to 75% of applicants.

BASIC COSTS (2007-2008)

Tuition and fees: $7,450; out-of-state residents $21,900.

Room and board: $10,360.

Additional info: Tuition for New England resident students $13,000. Tuition/fee waivers available for unemployed or children of unemployed.

FINANCIAL AID PICTURE (2007-2008)

Students with need: Out of 225 full-time freshmen who applied for aid, 162 were judged to have need. Of these, 162 received aid. For part-time students, average financial aid package was $7,495.

Students without need: 4 full-time freshmen who did not demonstrate need for aid received scholarships/grants; average award was $3,265. No-need awards available for academics, art, leadership, state/district residency.

Additional info: Tuition waiver available to Vietnam veterans.

FINANCIAL AID PROCEDURES

Forms required: FAFSA.

Dates and Deadlines: Priority date 3/1; no closing date. Applicants notified on a rolling basis starting 3/15; must reply within 3 week(s) of notification.

Transfers: Priority date 5/1. Financial aid transcripts required.

CONTACT

Aurelio Ramirez, Director of Financial Aid
621 Huntington Avenue, Boston, MA 02115-5882
(617) 879-7850

Massachusetts College of Liberal Arts

North Adams, Massachusetts
www.mcla.edu

Federal Code: 002187

4-year public liberal arts college in large town.

Enrollment: 1,491 undergrads, 11% part-time. 343 full-time freshmen.

Selectivity: Admits 50 to 75% of applicants.

BASIC COSTS (2007-2008)

Tuition and fees: $6,168; out-of-state residents $17,474.

Room and board: $7,309.

Additional info: Tuition/fee waivers available for unemployed or children of unemployed.

FINANCIAL AID PICTURE (2007-2008)

Students with need: Out of 304 full-time freshmen who applied for aid, 210 were judged to have need. Of these, 210 received aid. Need-based aid available for part-time students.

Students without need: 28 full-time freshmen who did not demonstrate need for aid received scholarships/grants; average award was $3,149. No-need awards available for academics, alumni affiliation, art, leadership, minority status, music/drama.

FINANCIAL AID PROCEDURES

Forms required: FAFSA, institutional form.

Dates and Deadlines: Priority date 3/1; no closing date. Applicants notified on a rolling basis starting 3/1; must reply by 5/1 or within 2 week(s) of notification.

CONTACT

Elizabeth Petri, Director of Financial Aid
375 Church Street, North Adams, MA 01247
(413) 662-5219

Massachusetts College of Pharmacy and Health Sciences

Boston, Massachusetts
www.mcphs.edu   Federal Code: 002165

4-year private health science and pharmacy college in very large city.
Enrollment: 2,411 undergrads, 4% part-time. 549 full-time freshmen.
Selectivity: Admits 50 to 75% of applicants.

BASIC COSTS (2007-2008)

Tuition and fees: $22,700.
Per-credit charge: $810.
Room and board: $11,720.

FINANCIAL AID PICTURE (2007-2008)

Students with need: Out of 507 full-time freshmen who applied for aid, 452 were judged to have need. Of these, 449 received aid, and 44 had their full need met. Average financial aid package met 48% of need; average scholarship/grant was $9,749; average loan was $5,119. For part-time students, average financial aid package was $7,172.

Students without need: 92 full-time freshmen who did not demonstrate need for aid received scholarships/grants; average award was $12,575. No-need awards available for academics.

Cumulative student debt: 90% of graduating class had student loans; average debt was $54,495.

FINANCIAL AID PROCEDURES

Forms required: FAFSA.

Dates and Deadlines: Priority date 3/15; no closing date. Applicants notified on a rolling basis.

Transfers: Massachusetts State Grant deadline May 1.

CONTACT

Carrie Glass, Executive Director of Enrollment Services
179 Longwood Avenue, Boston, MA 02115-5896
(617) 732-2864

Massachusetts Institute of Technology

Cambridge, Massachusetts   Federal Code: 002178
www.mit.edu   CSS Code: 3514

4-year private university in small city.
Enrollment: 4,163 undergrads, 1% part-time. 1,005 full-time freshmen.
Selectivity: Admits less than 50% of applicants.

BASIC COSTS (2008-2009)

Tuition and fees: $36,390.
Per-credit charge: $565.
Room and board: $10,860.

FINANCIAL AID PICTURE (2006-2007)

Students with need: Out of 790 full-time freshmen who applied for aid, 644 were judged to have need. Of these, 644 received aid. Average financial aid package met 100% of need; average scholarship/grant was $30,428; average loan was $1,817. For part-time students, average financial aid package was $24,403.

Students without need: This college awards aid only to students with need.

Cumulative student debt: 41% of graduating class had student loans; average debt was $15,051.

Additional info: Filing deadline 2/15 for CSS PROFILE.

FINANCIAL AID PROCEDURES

Forms required: FAFSA, CSS PROFILE.

Dates and Deadlines: Closing date 2/15. Applicants notified by 4/1; must reply by 5/1.

Transfers: Closing date 3/1. Applicants notified by 4/15; must reply by 5/1. Access to MIT funds may be limited to fewer than 8 terms.

CONTACT

Elizabeth Hicks, Executive Director of Student Financial Services
77 Massachusetts Avenue, Rm 3-108, Cambridge, MA 02139-4307
(617) 253-4971

Massachusetts Maritime Academy

Buzzards Bay, Massachusetts
www.maritime.edu   Federal Code: 002181

4-year public military and maritime college in large town.
Enrollment: 1,062 undergrads.
Selectivity: Admits less than 50% of applicants.

BASIC COSTS (2007-2008)

Tuition and fees: $5,900; out-of-state residents $15,114.
Room and board: $7,812.
Additional info: Semester at Sea cost: $3,218.

FINANCIAL AID PICTURE

Students with need: Need-based aid available for full-time and part-time students. Work study available nights, weekends, and for part-time students.

Students without need: No-need awards available for academics, leadership, music/drama.

FINANCIAL AID PROCEDURES

Forms required: FAFSA, institutional form.

Dates and Deadlines: Priority date 4/30; no closing date. Applicants notified on a rolling basis starting 3/1.

CONTACT

Elizabeth Benway, Financial Aid Director
101 Academy Drive, Buzzards Bay, MA 02532-1803
(508) 830-5086

Merrimack College

North Andover, Massachusetts
www.merrimack.edu   Federal Code: 002120

4-year private business and liberal arts college in large town, affiliated with Roman Catholic Church.

Enrollment: 2,062 undergrads, 11% part-time. 421 full-time freshmen.
Selectivity: Admits 50 to 75% of applicants.

BASIC COSTS (2008-2009)

Tuition and fees: $29,810.
Per-credit charge: $1,085.
Room and board: $10,190.

FINANCIAL AID PICTURE (2006-2007)

Students with need: Out of 371 full-time freshmen who applied for aid, 360 were judged to have need. Of these, 360 received aid, and 300 had their full need met. Average financial aid package met 70% of need; average scholarship/grant was $13,000; average loan was $3,500.

Students without need: 20 full-time freshmen who did not demonstrate need for aid received scholarships/grants; average award was $12,000. No-need awards available for academics, athletics, leadership, minority status, religious affiliation.

Scholarships offered: 25 full-time freshmen received athletic scholarships; average amount $31,000.

Cumulative student debt: 72% of graduating class had student loans; average debt was $25,000.

Additional info: Accept the Challenge program provides tuition for students from Lawrence who meet program criteria.

FINANCIAL AID PROCEDURES

Forms required: FAFSA.

Dates and Deadlines: Closing date 2/1. Applicants notified by 3/15; must reply by 5/1 or within 2 week(s) of notification.

Transfers: Priority date 3/1; closing date 4/30. Must reply within 2 week(s) of notification.

CONTACT

Christine Mordach, Director of Financial Aid
315 Turnpike Street, North Andover, MA 01845
(978) 837-5186

Middlesex Community College

Bedford, Massachusetts
www.middlesex.mass.edu   Federal Code: 009936

2-year public community college in small city.
Enrollment: 7,234 undergrads.
Selectivity: Open admission; but selective for some programs.

BASIC COSTS (2007-2008)

Tuition and fees: $3,860; out-of-state residents $13,010.
Additional info: New England resident tuition $135 per credit hour. Tuition/fee waivers available for adults.

FINANCIAL AID PICTURE

Students with need: Need-based aid available for full-time and part-time students. Work study available nights, weekends, and for part-time students.
Students without need: This college awards aid only to students with need.
Additional info: Application priority date 5/1 for Massachusetts state funds.

FINANCIAL AID PROCEDURES

Forms required: FAFSA, institutional form.
Dates and Deadlines: Priority date 5/1; no closing date. Applicants notified on a rolling basis starting 6/1; must reply within 2 week(s) of notification.

CONTACT

Robert Baumel, Financial Aid Director
33 Kearney Square, Lowell, MA 01852-1987
(978) 656-3242

Mount Holyoke College

South Hadley, Massachusetts   Federal Code: 002192
www.mtholyoke.edu   CSS Code: 3529

4-year private liberal arts college for women in large town.
Enrollment: 2,185 undergrads, 2% part-time. 512 full-time freshmen.
Selectivity: Admits 50 to 75% of applicants.

BASIC COSTS (2008-2009)

Tuition and fees: $37,646.
Per-credit charge: $1,175.
Room and board: $11,020.

FINANCIAL AID PICTURE (2007-2008)

Students with need: Out of 362 full-time freshmen who applied for aid, 307 were judged to have need. Of these, 307 received aid, and 307 had their full need met. Average financial aid package met 100% of need; average scholarship/grant was $27,269; average loan was $3,713. For part-time students, average financial aid package was $23,745.

Students without need: 38 full-time freshmen who did not demonstrate need for aid received scholarships/grants; average award was $16,184. No-need awards available for academics, leadership.

Scholarships offered: Mount Holyoke College Leadership Awards; limited number; based on high school scholarship and extracurricular achievement; conditional annual renewal.

Cumulative student debt: 67% of graduating class had student loans; average debt was $22,270.

Additional info: Parent loan plans include MASSPLAN, Achievers and PLUS. 10-month payment plan offered.

FINANCIAL AID PROCEDURES

Forms required: FAFSA, CSS PROFILE.
Dates and Deadlines: Priority date 2/15; closing date 3/1. Applicants notified by 4/1; must reply by 5/1.
Transfers: Priority date 2/1; closing date 5/31. Applicants notified on a rolling basis; must reply within 4 week(s) of notification. Financial aid transcripts from all schools previously attended required.

CONTACT

Kathy Blaisdell, Director of Student Financial Services
Newhall Center, South Hadley, MA 01075-1488
(413) 538-2291

Mount Ida College

Newton, Massachusetts
www.mountida.edu   Federal Code: 002193

4-year private business and liberal arts college in small city.
Enrollment: 1,431 undergrads.
Selectivity: Admits over 75% of applicants.

BASIC COSTS (2007-2008)

Tuition and fees: $21,330.
Room and board: $10,635.

FINANCIAL AID PICTURE

Students with need: Need-based aid available for full-time and part-time students.

FINANCIAL AID PROCEDURES

Forms required: FAFSA, institutional form.
Dates and Deadlines: Priority date 5/1; no closing date. Applicants notified on a rolling basis starting 3/1; must reply within 3 week(s) of notification.

CONTACT
Thomas King, Assistant Director of Financial Aid
777 Dedham Street, Newton, MA 02459
(617) 928-4785

Mount Wachusett Community College

Gardner, Massachusetts
www.mwcc.edu   Federal Code: 002172

2-year public community college in large town.
Enrollment: 3,604 undergrads, 53% part-time. 650 full-time freshmen.
Selectivity: Open admission; but selective for some programs.

BASIC COSTS (2007-2008)
Tuition and fees: $4,420; out-of-state residents $10,570.
Per-credit charge: $25; out-of-state residents $230.
Additional info: New England resident tuition is $1,312.

FINANCIAL AID PICTURE (2007-2008)
Students with need: Out of 418 full-time freshmen who applied for aid, 316 were judged to have need. Of these, 314 received aid, and 58 had their full need met. Average financial aid package met 67% of need; average scholarship/grant was $4,092; average loan was $1,423. For part-time students, average financial aid package was $3,372.
Students without need: This college awards aid only to students with need.
Cumulative student debt: 37% of graduating class had student loans; average debt was $5,436.

FINANCIAL AID PROCEDURES
Forms required: FAFSA, institutional form.
Dates and Deadlines: Priority date 4/15; no closing date. Applicants notified on a rolling basis starting 5/1.

CONTACT
JoEllen Soucier, Director of Financial Aid
444 Green Street, Gardner, MA 01440-1000
(978) 632-6600 ext. 524

New England Conservatory of Music

Boston, Massachusetts
www.newenglandconservatory.edu Federal Code: 002194

4-year private music college in very large city.
Enrollment: 384 undergrads, 8% part-time. 90 full-time freshmen.
Selectivity: Admits less than 50% of applicants.

BASIC COSTS (2007-2008)
Tuition and fees: $30,975.
Per-credit charge: $1,000.
Room and board: $11,300.
Additional info: On-campus residents pay $335 health fee.

FINANCIAL AID PICTURE (2007-2008)
Students with need: Out of 58 full-time freshmen who applied for aid, 52 were judged to have need. Of these, 52 received aid, and 14 had their full need met. Average financial aid package met 69% of need; average scholarship/grant was $13,723; average loan was $4,909. Need-based aid available for part-time students.
Students without need: 28 full-time freshmen who did not demonstrate need for aid received scholarships/grants; average award was $16,293. No-need awards available for academics, music/drama.
Cumulative student debt: 79% of graduating class had student loans; average debt was $34,269.

FINANCIAL AID PROCEDURES
Forms required: FAFSA, institutional form.
Dates and Deadlines: Closing date 12/1. Applicants notified by 4/1; must reply by 5/1 or within 2 week(s) of notification.

CONTACT
Lauren Urbanek, Director of Financial Aid
290 Huntington Avenue, Boston, MA 02115
(617) 585-1110

New England Institute of Art

Brookline, Massachusetts
www.artinstitutes.edu/boston   Federal Code: 007486

4-year for-profit visual arts and technical college in very large city.
Enrollment: 1,684 undergrads.
Selectivity: Admits less than 50% of applicants.

BASIC COSTS (2007-2008)
Tuition and fees: $20,900.
Per-credit charge: $675.
Room and board: $11,300.

FINANCIAL AID PICTURE
Students with need: Need-based aid available for full-time and part-time students. Work study available nights, weekends, and for part-time students.
Students without need: No-need awards available for academics.

FINANCIAL AID PROCEDURES
Forms required: FAFSA, institutional form.
Dates and Deadlines: Priority date 5/1; no closing date. Applicants notified on a rolling basis starting 3/1.

CONTACT
Anna Kelly, Director of Student Financial Services
10 Brookline Place West, Brookline, MA 02445-7295
(617) 739-1700

Newbury College

Brookline, Massachusetts
www.newbury.edu   Federal Code: 007484

4-year private business and liberal arts college in large city.
Enrollment: 1,200 undergrads.
Selectivity: Admits over 75% of applicants.

BASIC COSTS (2007-2008)
Tuition and fees: $20,000.
Room and board: $10,100.

FINANCIAL AID PICTURE
Students with need: Need-based aid available for full-time and part-time students. Work study available nights.
Students without need: This college awards aid only to students with need.

FINANCIAL AID PROCEDURES
Forms required: FAFSA.
Dates and Deadlines: Closing date 5/1. Applicants notified on a rolling basis starting 3/1; must reply within 2 week(s) of notification.
Transfers: No deadline.

CONTACT
Jeannie Gonzales, Director of Financial Assistance
129 Fisher Avenue, Brookline, MA 02445
(617) 730-7196

Nichols College

Dudley, Massachusetts
www.nichols.edu   Federal Code: 002197

4-year private business and liberal arts college in small town.

Enrollment: 1,271 undergrads. 440 full-time freshmen.

Selectivity: Admits over 75% of applicants.

BASIC COSTS (2008-2009)

Tuition and fees: $26,970.

Per-credit charge: $795.

Room and board: $9,100.

FINANCIAL AID PICTURE (2007-2008)

Students with need: Out of 391 full-time freshmen who applied for aid, 356 were judged to have need. Of these, 356 received aid, and 22 had their full need met. Average financial aid package met 74% of need; average scholarship/grant was $14,237; average loan was $3,778. For part-time students, average financial aid package was $5,225.

Students without need: 22 full-time freshmen who did not demonstrate need for aid received scholarships/grants; average award was $9,018. No-need awards available for academics, alumni affiliation, ROTC.

Cumulative student debt: 84% of graduating class had student loans; average debt was $27,764.

FINANCIAL AID PROCEDURES

Forms required: FAFSA.

Dates and Deadlines: Priority date 3/1; closing date 6/1. Applicants notified on a rolling basis starting 2/26; must reply within 4 week(s) of notification.

CONTACT

Kathleen Goozey, Director of Financial Aid
PO Box 5000, Dudley, MA 01571-5000
(508) 213-2378

North Shore Community College

Danvers, Massachusetts
www.northshore.edu   Federal Code: 002173

2-year public community college in small city.

Enrollment: 6,331 undergrads, 53% part-time. 1,072 full-time freshmen.

Selectivity: Open admission; but selective for some programs.

BASIC COSTS (2007-2008)

Tuition and fees: $3,630; out-of-state residents $10,590.

Per-credit charge: $25; out-of-state residents $257.

Additional info: New England regional tuition: $133.50 per credit hour.

FINANCIAL AID PICTURE (2006-2007)

Students with need: Average financial aid package met 29% of need; average scholarship/grant was $2,034; average loan was $1,559. For part-time students, average financial aid package was $1,418.

Students without need: This college awards aid only to students with need.

FINANCIAL AID PROCEDURES

Forms required: FAFSA.

Dates and Deadlines: Priority date 5/1; no closing date. Applicants notified on a rolling basis starting 6/1; must reply within 2 week(s) of notification.

CONTACT

Susan Sullivan, Director of Student Financial Services
One Ferncroft Road, Danvers, MA 01923-0840
(978) 762-4000

Northeastern University

Boston, Massachusetts   Federal Code: 002199
www.northeastern.edu   CSS Code: 3667

4-year private university in very large city.

Enrollment: 15,339 undergrads. 2,871 full-time freshmen.

Selectivity: Admits less than 50% of applicants.

BASIC COSTS (2007-2008)

Tuition and fees: $31,899.

Room and board: $11,420.

FINANCIAL AID PICTURE (2007-2008)

Students with need: Out of 2,115 full-time freshmen who applied for aid, 1,647 were judged to have need. Of these, 1,639 received aid, and 338 had their full need met. Average financial aid package met 67% of need; average scholarship/grant was $15,019; average loan was $4,540.

Students without need: 876 full-time freshmen who did not demonstrate need for aid received scholarships/grants; average award was $13,970. No-need awards available for academics, athletics, minority status.

Scholarships offered: 59 full-time freshmen received athletic scholarships; average amount $29,483.

FINANCIAL AID PROCEDURES

Forms required: FAFSA, CSS PROFILE.

Dates and Deadlines: Closing date 2/15. Applicants notified on a rolling basis starting 2/15; must reply by 5/1.

Transfers: Institutional application and financial aid transcript from all previously attended colleges required.

CONTACT

M. Seamus Harreys, Dean and Director of Student Financial Services
360 Huntington Avenue, 150 Richards Hall, Boston, MA 02115-9959
(617) 373-3190

Northern Essex Community College

Haverhill, Massachusetts
www.necc.mass.edu   Federal Code: 002174

2-year public community college in small city.

Enrollment: 5,618 undergrads, 59% part-time. 797 full-time freshmen.

Selectivity: Open admission; but selective for some programs.

BASIC COSTS (2007-2008)

Tuition and fees: $3,420; out-of-state residents $10,650.

Per-credit charge: $25; out-of-state residents $266.

Additional info: New England residents pay $122 per credit hour.

FINANCIAL AID PICTURE

Students with need: Need-based aid available for full-time and part-time students.

Students without need: No-need awards available for academics.

FINANCIAL AID PROCEDURES

Forms required: FAFSA.

Dates and Deadlines: Priority date 5/1; no closing date. Applicants notified on a rolling basis starting 3/1; must reply within 2 week(s) of notification.

CONTACT

Anne-Marie Caruso, Assistant Dean for Financial Aid
100 Elliott Street, Haverhill, MA 01830-2399
(978) 556-3656

Pine Manor College
Chestnut Hill, Massachusetts
www.pmc.edu   Federal Code: 002201

4-year private liberal arts college for women in very large city.

Enrollment: 491 undergrads, 1% part-time. 170 full-time freshmen.

Selectivity: Admits 50 to 75% of applicants.

BASIC COSTS (2007-2008)
Tuition and fees: $17,750.

Room and board: $10,570.

FINANCIAL AID PICTURE (2006-2007)
Students with need: Out of 159 full-time freshmen who applied for aid, 155 were judged to have need. Of these, 154 received aid, and 4 had their full need met. Average financial aid package met 67% of need; average scholarship/grant was $13,170; average loan was $2,478. For part-time students, average financial aid package was $10,103.

Students without need: 14 full-time freshmen who did not demonstrate need for aid received scholarships/grants; average award was $8,180. No-need awards available for academics, alumni affiliation, leadership.

Cumulative student debt: 67% of graduating class had student loans; average debt was $32,875.

FINANCIAL AID PROCEDURES
Forms required: FAFSA.

Dates and Deadlines: Priority date 5/1; no closing date. Applicants notified on a rolling basis starting 3/1; must reply by 5/1 or within 2 week(s) of notification.

Transfers: No deadline. Applicants notified on a rolling basis starting 3/1; must reply by 5/1 or within 2 week(s) of notification.

CONTACT
Robin Engel, Dean of Admissions and Financial Aid
400 Heath Street, Chestnut Hill, MA 02467
(617) 731-7104

Quinsigamond Community College
Worcester, Massachusetts
www.qcc.edu   Federal Code: 002175

2-year public community college in small city.

Enrollment: 5,262 undergrads, 46% part-time. 1,118 full-time freshmen.

Selectivity: Open admission; but selective for some programs.

BASIC COSTS (2007-2008)
Tuition and fees: $3,870; out-of-state residents $10,050.

Per-credit charge: $24; out-of-state residents $230.

FINANCIAL AID PICTURE
Students with need: Need-based aid available for full-time and part-time students. Work study available nights, weekends, and for part-time students.

Students without need: This college awards aid only to students with need.

FINANCIAL AID PROCEDURES
Forms required: FAFSA.

Dates and Deadlines: Priority date 4/1; no closing date. Applicants notified on a rolling basis starting 4/1.

CONTACT
Beverly Guerin, Director of Financial Aid
670 West Boylston Street, Worcester, MA 01606
(508) 854-4261

Regis College
Weston, Massachusetts
www.regiscollege.edu   Federal Code: 002206

4-year private nursing and liberal arts college in large town, affiliated with Roman Catholic Church.

Enrollment: 934 undergrads, 22% part-time. 263 full-time freshmen.

Selectivity: Admits over 75% of applicants.

BASIC COSTS (2008-2009)
Tuition and fees: $27,800.

Room and board: $11,950.

Additional info: Tuition/fee waivers available for adults.

FINANCIAL AID PICTURE (2007-2008)
Students with need: Out of 245 full-time freshmen who applied for aid, 222 were judged to have need. Of these, 221 received aid, and 26 had their full need met. Average financial aid package met 60% of need; average scholarship/grant was $12,058; average loan was $4,716. For part-time students, average financial aid package was $3,789.

Students without need: 17 full-time freshmen who did not demonstrate need for aid received scholarships/grants; average award was $8,529. No-need awards available for academics, alumni affiliation, leadership, ROTC.

Scholarships offered: Family tuition discount scholarship; offered during any semester in which 2 or more unmarried, dependent siblings attend on a full-time basis.

Cumulative student debt: 85% of graduating class had student loans; average debt was $29,794.

FINANCIAL AID PROCEDURES
Forms required: FAFSA, institutional form.

Dates and Deadlines: Priority date 2/15; no closing date. Applicants notified on a rolling basis starting 3/15.

Transfers: No deadline. Applicants notified on a rolling basis.

CONTACT
Dolores Ludwick, Director of Financial Aid
235 Wellesley Street, Weston, MA 02493-1571
(781) 768-7180

Roxbury Community College
Roxbury Crossing, Massachusetts
www.rcc.mass.edu   Federal Code: 011930

2-year public community college in very large city.

Enrollment: 2,167 undergrads, 58% part-time. 340 full-time freshmen.

Selectivity: Open admission; but selective for some programs.

BASIC COSTS (2007-2008)
Tuition and fees: $3,660; out-of-state residents $10,290.

Per-credit charge: $26; out-of-state residents $247.

Additional info: New England Regional per-credit-hour charge $105.

FINANCIAL AID PICTURE
Students with need: Need-based aid available for full-time and part-time students.

Students without need: This college awards aid only to students with need.

FINANCIAL AID PROCEDURES
Forms required: FAFSA, institutional form.

Dates and Deadlines: Priority date 5/1; no closing date. Applicants notified on a rolling basis starting 6/15; must reply within 2 week(s) of notification.

CONTACT

Ray O'Rourke, Director of Financial Aid
1234 Columbus Avenue, Roxbury Crossing, MA 02120-3400
(617) 541-5322

School of the Museum of Fine Arts

Boston, Massachusetts
www.smfa.edu   Federal Code: 004667

4-year private visual arts college in very large city.
Enrollment: 640 undergrads, 6% part-time. 134 full-time freshmen.
Selectivity: Admits over 75% of applicants.

BASIC COSTS (2007-2008)

Tuition and fees: $27,970.
Per-credit charge: $1,130.
Room only: $12,200.

FINANCIAL AID PICTURE (2007-2008)

Students with need: Out of 91 full-time freshmen who applied for aid, 77 were judged to have need. Of these, 77 received aid, and 36 had their full need met. Average financial aid package met 36% of need; average scholarship/grant was $15,002; average loan was $3,416. For part-time students, average financial aid package was $8,550.
Students without need: 6 full-time freshmen who did not demonstrate need for aid received scholarships/grants; average award was $11,724. No-need awards available for art.
Scholarships offered: Awarded on strength of portfolio and potential for growth as an artist; no separate application needed.
Cumulative student debt: 50% of graduating class had student loans; average debt was $31,753.

FINANCIAL AID PROCEDURES

Forms required: FAFSA, institutional form.
Dates and Deadlines: Priority date 3/15; no closing date. Applicants notified on a rolling basis starting 4/15; must reply by 5/1 or within 2 week(s) of notification.

CONTACT

Elizabeth Goreham, Director of Financial Aid
230 The Fenway, Boston, MA 02115
(800) 776-0135

Simmons College

Boston, Massachusetts
www.simmons.edu   Federal Code: 002208

4-year private liberal arts college for women in large city.
Enrollment: 2,064 undergrads, 9% part-time. 520 full-time freshmen.
Selectivity: Admits 50 to 75% of applicants.

BASIC COSTS (2007-2008)

Tuition and fees: $28,302.
Per-credit charge: $857.
Room and board: $11,138.

FINANCIAL AID PICTURE (2007-2008)

Students with need: Average financial aid package met 69% of need; average scholarship/grant was $13,088; average loan was $3,615. For part-time students, average financial aid package was $14,775.
Students without need: No-need awards available for academics, alumni affiliation, leadership, minority status.
Cumulative student debt: 82% of graduating class had student loans; average debt was $34,940.

FINANCIAL AID PROCEDURES

Forms required: FAFSA.
Dates and Deadlines: Priority date 2/15; closing date 3/1. Applicants notified on a rolling basis starting 3/15; must reply by 5/1 or within 4 week(s) of notification.
Transfers: Priority date 3/1; closing date 4/1. Applicants notified on a rolling basis starting 3/15; must reply by 5/1 or within 4 week(s) of notification. Combination of grants, loans, employment opportunities available.

CONTACT

Diane Hallisey, Director of Student Financial Services
300 The Fenway, Boston, MA 02115-5898
(617) 521-2004

Smith College

Northampton, Massachusetts   Federal Code: 002209
www.smith.edu   CSS Code: 3762

4-year private liberal arts college for women in large town.
Enrollment: 2,569 undergrads. 656 full-time freshmen.
Selectivity: Admits 50 to 75% of applicants.

BASIC COSTS (2007-2008)

Tuition and fees: $34,186.
Per-credit charge: $1,060.
Room and board: $11,420.

FINANCIAL AID PICTURE (2007-2008)

Students with need: Out of 496 full-time freshmen who applied for aid, 396 were judged to have need. Of these, 396 received aid, and 396 had their full need met. Average financial aid package met 100% of need; average scholarship/grant was $26,530; average loan was $3,538. For part-time students, average financial aid package was $26,874.
Students without need: 30 full-time freshmen who did not demonstrate need for aid received scholarships/grants; average award was $7,651. No-need awards available for academics, state/district residency.
Scholarships offered: Zollman Scholarships: half-tuition; for academic excellence; 5 to 10 awarded. STRIDE scholarship: $5,000; for academic excellence; about 50 awarded. Springfield Partnership: full tuition; for academic excellence in Springfield public high school; up to 3 awarded. Picker Engineering scholarships: $10,000 per year. Mary Maples Dunn scholarships: $3,000 per year.
Cumulative student debt: 71% of graduating class had student loans; average debt was $21,868.
Additional info: Financial aid policy guarantees to meet full financial need, as calculated by college, of all admitted students.

FINANCIAL AID PROCEDURES

Forms required: FAFSA, CSS PROFILE.
Dates and Deadlines: Closing date 2/15. Applicants notified by 4/1; must reply by 5/1.
Transfers: Priority date 2/15; closing date 5/15. Applicants who apply after admission decision is made cannot receive college aid until they complete at least 32 credits at Smith.

CONTACT

Deborah Luekens, Director of Student Financial Services
7 College Lane, Northampton, MA 01063
(413) 585-2530

Springfield College

Springfield, Massachusetts
www.spfldcol.edu

Federal Code: 002211
CSS Code: 3763

4-year private health science and liberal arts college in small city.

Enrollment: 2,150 undergrads.

Selectivity: Admits 50 to 75% of applicants.

BASIC COSTS (2007-2008)

Tuition and fees: $24,075.

Per-credit charge: $719.

Room and board: $9,270.

FINANCIAL AID PICTURE

Students with need: Need-based aid available for full-time students.

Additional info: Co-operative education program available to students after freshman year.

FINANCIAL AID PROCEDURES

Forms required: FAFSA, CSS PROFILE, institutional form.

Dates and Deadlines: Priority date 3/15; no closing date. Applicants notified on a rolling basis starting 3/15; must reply by 5/1 or within 2 week(s) of notification.

Transfers: Priority date 4/15.

CONTACT

Edward Ciosek, Director of Financial Aid

263 Alden Street, Springfield, MA 01109

(413) 748-3000

Springfield Technical Community College

Springfield, Massachusetts
www.stcc.edu

Federal Code: 005549

2-year public community and technical college in small city.

Enrollment: 5,145 undergrads, 52% part-time. 752 full-time freshmen.

Selectivity: Open admission; but selective for some programs.

BASIC COSTS (2007-2008)

Tuition and fees: $3,576; out-of-state residents $10,086.

Per-credit charge: $25; out-of-state residents $242.

Additional info: New England reciprocal rate $232 per credit hour, including fees.

FINANCIAL AID PICTURE (2006-2007)

Students with need: 79% of average financial aid package awarded as scholarships/grants, 21% awarded as loans/jobs. Need-based aid available for part-time students.

Students without need: This college awards aid only to students with need.

FINANCIAL AID PROCEDURES

Forms required: FAFSA, institutional form.

Dates and Deadlines: Priority date 5/1; no closing date. Applicants notified on a rolling basis starting 7/1.

CONTACT

Mary Forni; Coordinator of Financial Aid Services

One Armory Square, Springfield, MA 01102-9000

(413) 755-4214

Stonehill College

Easton, Massachusetts
www.stonehill.edu

Federal Code: 002217
CSS Code: 3770

4-year private business and liberal arts college in large town, affiliated with Roman Catholic Church.

Enrollment: 2,413 undergrads, 3% part-time. 659 full-time freshmen.

Selectivity: Admits 50 to 75% of applicants.

BASIC COSTS (2007-2008)

Tuition and fees: $28,440.

Room and board: $11,430.

Additional info: Tuition/fee waivers available for minority students.

FINANCIAL AID PICTURE (2007-2008)

Students with need: Average financial aid package met 77% of need; average scholarship/grant was $15,790; average loan was $3,864. For part-time students, average financial aid package was $14,939.

Students without need: No-need awards available for academics, athletics, ROTC.

Cumulative student debt: 77% of graduating class had student loans; average debt was $16,661.

FINANCIAL AID PROCEDURES

Forms required: FAFSA, CSS PROFILE.

Dates and Deadlines: Priority date 2/1; no closing date. Applicants notified by 4/1; must reply by 5/1.

Transfers: Closing date 4/1.

CONTACT

Eileen O'Leary, Director of Student Aid and Finance

320 Washington Street, Easton, MA 02357-0100

(508) 565-1088

Suffolk University

Boston, Massachusetts
www.suffolk.edu

Federal Code: 002218

4-year private university in very large city.

Enrollment: 5,289 undergrads, 9% part-time. 1,310 full-time freshmen.

Selectivity: Admits over 75% of applicants.

BASIC COSTS (2007-2008)

Tuition and fees: $24,250.

Room and board: $13,360.

FINANCIAL AID PICTURE (2007-2008)

Students with need: Out of 956 full-time freshmen who applied for aid, 754 were judged to have need. Of these, 741 received aid, and 103 had their full need met. Average financial aid package met 63% of need; average scholarship/grant was $8,209; average loan was $3,733. For part-time students, average financial aid package was $8,124.

Students without need: 103 full-time freshmen who did not demonstrate need for aid received scholarships/grants; average award was $8,625. No-need awards available for academics, alumni affiliation.

Scholarships offered: Amounts vary; based on academic achievement, talent, and contribution to applicant's school and community.

Additional info: Foreign students may apply for institutional employment awards.

FINANCIAL AID PROCEDURES

Forms required: FAFSA, institutional form.

Dates and Deadlines: Closing date 3/1. Applicants notified on a rolling basis starting 3/1.

CONTACT

Christine Perry, Director of Financial Aid
8 Ashburton Place, Boston, MA 02108
(617) 573-8470

Tufts University

Medford, Massachusetts
www.tufts.edu

Federal Code: 002219
CSS Code: 3901

4-year private university in small city.
Enrollment: 5,015 undergrads, 1% part-time. 1,400 full-time freshmen.
Selectivity: Admits less than 50% of applicants.

BASIC COSTS (2007-2008)

Tuition and fees: $36,700.
Room and board: $10,160.

FINANCIAL AID PICTURE (2007-2008)

Students with need: Out of 758 full-time freshmen who applied for aid, 596 were judged to have need. Of these, 587 received aid, and 587 had their full need met. Average financial aid package met 100% of need. Need-based aid available for part-time students.
Students without need: This college awards aid only to students with need.
Scholarships offered: National Merit Scholarships; $500 for non-need; $2,000 for need.

FINANCIAL AID PROCEDURES

Forms required: FAFSA, CSS PROFILE.
Dates and Deadlines: Closing date 2/15. Applicants notified by 4/1; must reply by 5/1.
Transfers: Closing date 3/1. Applicants notified by 5/1; must reply within 2 week(s) of notification.

CONTACT

Patricia Reilly, Director of Financial Aid
Bendetson Hall, Medford, MA 02155
(617) 627-2000

University of Massachusetts Amherst

Amherst, Massachusetts
www.umass.edu

Federal Code: 002221

4-year public university in large town.
Enrollment: 19,621 undergrads, 6% part-time. 4,230 full-time freshmen.
Selectivity: Admits 50 to 75% of applicants.

BASIC COSTS (2007-2008)

Tuition and fees: $9,924; out-of-state residents $20,499.
Room and board: $8,052.

FINANCIAL AID PICTURE (2006-2007)

Students with need: Out of 3,667 full-time freshmen who applied for aid, 2,324 were judged to have need. Of these, 2,255 received aid, and 433 had their full need met. Average financial aid package met 82% of need; average scholarship/grant was $7,350; average loan was $3,021. For part-time students, average financial aid package was $10,039.
Students without need: 319 full-time freshmen who did not demonstrate need for aid received scholarships/grants; average award was $3,661. No-need awards available for academics, art, athletics, music/drama, ROTC, state/district residency.
Scholarships offered: *Merit:* All applicants automatically reviewed for merit scholarships. *Athletic:* 40 full-time freshmen received athletic scholarships; average amount $13,946.
Cumulative student debt: 56% of graduating class had student loans; average debt was $12,062.

FINANCIAL AID PROCEDURES

Forms required: FAFSA.
Dates and Deadlines: Priority date 3/1; no closing date. Applicants notified on a rolling basis starting 4/1.
Transfers: Financial aid transcripts required.

CONTACT

Suzanne Peters, Director of Financial Aid
University Admissions Center, Amherst, MA 01003-9291
(413) 545-0801

University of Massachusetts Boston

Boston, Massachusetts
www.umb.edu

Federal Code: 002222

4-year public university in very large city.
Enrollment: 8,999 undergrads, 29% part-time. 846 full-time freshmen.
Selectivity: Admits 50 to 75% of applicants.

BASIC COSTS (2007-2008)

Tuition and fees: $8,840; out-of-state residents $20,658.

FINANCIAL AID PICTURE (2006-2007)

Students with need: Out of 642 full-time freshmen who applied for aid, 526 were judged to have need. Of these, 526 received aid, and 277 had their full need met. Average financial aid package met 84% of need; average scholarship/grant was $6,225; average loan was $3,267. For part-time students, average financial aid package was $8,958.
Students without need: 44 full-time freshmen who did not demonstrate need for aid received scholarships/grants; average award was $1,922. No-need awards available for academics, leadership.
Cumulative student debt: 47% of graduating class had student loans; average debt was $17,772.
Additional info: Some Massachusetts state employees and Massachusetts Vietnam veterans eligible for tuition waiver. Some waivers available based on talent and academic excellence.

FINANCIAL AID PROCEDURES

Forms required: FAFSA.
Dates and Deadlines: Priority date 3/1; no closing date. Applicants notified on a rolling basis starting 3/21.

CONTACT

Judy Keyes, Director of Financial Aid Services
100 Morrissey Boulevard, Boston, MA 02125-3393
(617) 287-6300

University of Massachusetts Dartmouth

North Dartmouth, Massachusetts
www.umassd.edu

Federal Code: 002210

4-year public university in large town.
Enrollment: 7,600 undergrads, 10% part-time. 1,925 full-time freshmen.
Selectivity: Admits 50 to 75% of applicants.

BASIC COSTS (2007-2008)

Tuition and fees: $8,595; out-of-state residents $18,178.
Room and board: $9,173.

FINANCIAL AID PICTURE (2007-2008)

Students with need: Out of 1,560 full-time freshmen who applied for aid, 1,155 were judged to have need. Of these, 1,155 received aid, and 703 had their full need met. Average financial aid package met 93% of need; average scholarship/grant was $6,433; average loan was $4,841. For part-time students, average financial aid package was $8,873.

Students without need: 191 full-time freshmen who did not demonstrate need for aid received scholarships/grants; average award was $2,310. No-need awards available for academics, minority status, ROTC, state/district residency.

Scholarships offered: Chancellor's Merit Scholarship; approximately $2,000; for Massachusetts high school seniors with SAT 1250 (exclusive of Writing) and in top 25% of class, 50 awarded. Solveig E.J. Balestracci Scholarship; $1,000; for academic achievement in marine-related area for residents of New Bedford, Dartmouth, Acushnet, Westport, Mattapoisett, Marion, Rochester or Lakeville; 1 awarded. Boivon Scholarship; $1,000; based on academic involvement in French language and culture. A.J. Carvalho Memorial Scholarship; approximately $5,000; for New Bedford graduates of Portuguese descent with 3.0 GPA. Cranston Foundation Scholarship; $500; for students in the Textile Science Department.

Cumulative student debt: 76% of graduating class had student loans; average debt was $18,500.

FINANCIAL AID PROCEDURES

Forms required: FAFSA.

Dates and Deadlines: Priority date 3/1; no closing date. Applicants notified on a rolling basis starting 3/25; must reply within 3 week(s) of notification.

CONTACT

Bruce Palmer, Director of Financial Aid

285 Old Westport Road, North Dartmouth, MA 02747-2300

(508) 999-8632

University of Massachusetts Lowell

Lowell, Massachusetts

www.uml.edu   Federal Code: 002161

4-year public university in small city.

Enrollment: 7,663 undergrads, 22% part-time. 1,243 full-time freshmen.

Selectivity: Admits 50 to 75% of applicants.

BASIC COSTS (2007-2008)

Tuition and fees: $8,732; out-of-state residents $20,386.

Per-credit charge: $61; out-of-state residents $357.

Room and board: $6,978.

FINANCIAL AID PICTURE (2007-2008)

Students with need: Out of 989 full-time freshmen who applied for aid, 644 were judged to have need. Of these, 644 received aid, and 502 had their full need met. Average financial aid package met 94% of need; average scholarship/grant was $5,939; average loan was $3,845. For part-time students, average financial aid package was $7,394.

Students without need: 197 full-time freshmen who did not demonstrate need for aid received scholarships/grants; average award was $2,878. No-need awards available for academics, art, athletics, ROTC.

Scholarships offered: 46 full-time freshmen received athletic scholarships; average amount $6,737.

Cumulative student debt: 66% of graduating class had student loans; average debt was $17,869.

FINANCIAL AID PROCEDURES

Forms required: FAFSA.

Dates and Deadlines: Priority date 3/1; no closing date. Applicants notified on a rolling basis starting 3/25.

CONTACT

Carole King, Director of Financial Aid

883 Broadway Street, Room 110, Lowell, MA 01854-5104

(978) 934-4220

Urban College of Boston

Boston, Massachusetts

www.urbancollege.edu   Federal Code: 031305

2-year private community college in very large city.

Enrollment: 389 undergrads.

Selectivity: Open admission.

BASIC COSTS (2007-2008)

Tuition and fees: $4,670.

Per-credit charge: $155.

FINANCIAL AID PICTURE

Students with need: Need-based aid available for full-time and part-time students.

Students without need: This college awards aid only to students with need.

FINANCIAL AID PROCEDURES

Forms required: FAFSA.

Dates and Deadlines: No deadline. Applicants notified on a rolling basis starting 4/15.

CONTACT

Sandra Coswatte, Director of Financial Aid

178 Tremont Street, Seventh Floor, Boston, MA 02111

(617) 348-6220

Wellesley College

Wellesley, Massachusetts   Federal Code: 002224

www.wellesley.edu   CSS Code: 3957

4-year private liberal arts college for women in large town.

Enrollment: 2,247 undergrads, 1% part-time. 590 full-time freshmen.

Selectivity: Admits less than 50% of applicants.

BASIC COSTS (2007-2008)

Tuition and fees: $34,994.

Room and board: $10,826.

FINANCIAL AID PICTURE (2007-2008)

Students with need: Out of 410 full-time freshmen who applied for aid, 322 were judged to have need. Of these, 322 received aid, and 322 had their full need met. Average financial aid package met 100% of need; average scholarship/grant was $29,627; average loan was $2,435. Need-based aid available for part-time students.

Students without need: This college awards aid only to students with need.

Cumulative student debt: 52% of graduating class had student loans; average debt was $11,902.

FINANCIAL AID PROCEDURES

Forms required: FAFSA, CSS PROFILE, institutional form.

Dates and Deadlines: Priority date 1/22; closing date 1/22. Applicants notified by 4/1; must reply by 5/1.

Transfers: Closing date 3/1.

CONTACT

Kathryn Osmond, Director of Student Financial Services

106 Central Street, Wellesley, MA 02481-8203

(781) 283-2360

Wentworth Institute of Technology

Boston, Massachusetts
www.wit.edu   Federal Code: 002225

4-year private engineering and technical college in very large city.
Enrollment: 3,688 undergrads, 10% part-time. 976 full-time freshmen.
Selectivity: Admits over 75% of applicants.

BASIC COSTS (2007-2008)
Tuition and fees: $20,150.
Per-credit charge: $630.
Room and board: $9,650.
Additional info: Tuition includes cost of laptop computer; students in architecture and design programs pay $2,000 in required fees for academic year.

FINANCIAL AID PICTURE (2006-2007)
Students with need: Out of 976 full-time freshmen who applied for aid, 584 were judged to have need. Of these, 584 received aid, and 24 had their full need met. Average financial aid package met 40% of need; average scholarship/grant was $1,484; average loan was $2,533. For part-time students, average financial aid package was $6,625.
Students without need: 67 full-time freshmen who did not demonstrate need for aid received scholarships/grants; average award was $5,500. No-need awards available for academics, leadership, state/district residency.
Scholarships offered: Applicants for admission automatically considered for merit scholarships.

FINANCIAL AID PROCEDURES
Forms required: FAFSA.
Dates and Deadlines: Priority date 3/1; no closing date. Applicants notified on a rolling basis starting 3/15; must reply within 2 week(s) of notification.
Transfers: Review of NSLDS history within 30 days of beginning of enrollment required.

CONTACT
Rachelle Shahan-Riehl, Director of Financial Aid
550 Huntington Avenue, Boston, MA 02115
(617) 989-4020

Western New England College

Springfield, Massachusetts
www.wnec.edu   Federal Code: 002226

4-year private university in small city.
Enrollment: 2,749 undergrads, 11% part-time. 712 full-time freshmen.
Selectivity: Admits 50 to 75% of applicants.

BASIC COSTS (2007-2008)
Tuition and fees: $25,942.
Per-credit charge: $481.
Room and board: $9,998.

FINANCIAL AID PICTURE
Students with need: Need-based aid available for full-time and part-time students. Work study available nights, weekends, and for part-time students.
Students without need: No-need awards available for academics, music/drama, ROTC.

FINANCIAL AID PROCEDURES
Forms required: FAFSA.
Dates and Deadlines: Priority date 4/1; no closing date. Applicants notified on a rolling basis starting 3/15; must reply by 5/1 or within 2 week(s) of notification.

CONTACT
Kathy Chambers, Associate Director of Financial Aid
1215 Wilbraham Road, Springfield, MA 01119-2684
(800) 325-1122 ext. 2080

Westfield State College

Westfield, Massachusetts
www.wsc.ma.edu   Federal Code: 002189

4-year public liberal arts and teachers college in large town.
Enrollment: 4,540 undergrads, 9% part-time. 888 full-time freshmen.
Selectivity: Admits 50 to 75% of applicants.

BASIC COSTS (2007-2008)
Tuition and fees: $6,210; out-of-state residents $12,290.
Room and board: $6,458.
Additional info: New England Regional tuition and fees per year: $6695.

FINANCIAL AID PICTURE
Students with need: Need-based aid available for full-time and part-time students.
Students without need: No-need awards available for academics.

FINANCIAL AID PROCEDURES
Forms required: FAFSA.
Dates and Deadlines: Priority date 3/1; no closing date. Applicants notified by 4/15.

CONTACT
Catherine Ryan, Director of Student Administrative Services/Financial Aid
577 Western Avenue, Westfield, MA 01086-1630
(413) 572-5218

Wheaton College

Norton, Massachusetts   Federal Code: 002227
www.wheatoncollege.edu   CSS Code: 3963

4-year private liberal arts college in large town.
Enrollment: 1,551 undergrads. 418 full-time freshmen.
Selectivity: Admits less than 50% of applicants.

BASIC COSTS (2007-2008)
Tuition and fees: $36,690.
Room and board: $8,640.
Additional info: Freshmen pay one-time $50 general fee (non-refundable); all residents pay annual $120 technology fee.

FINANCIAL AID PICTURE (2007-2008)
Students with need: Out of 285 full-time freshmen who applied for aid, 226 were judged to have need. Of these, 226 received aid, and 151 had their full need met. Average financial aid package met 97% of need; average scholarship/grant was $22,563; average loan was $4,224. Need-based aid available for part-time students.
Students without need: 70 full-time freshmen who did not demonstrate need for aid received scholarships/grants; average award was $11,609. No-need awards available for academics.
Scholarships offered: Balfour Scholarship; $12,500 annually plus $4,000 total in research/internship/community service stipends. Trustee Scholarship; $10,000 annually plus $4,000 total in research/internship/community service stipends. Community Scholarship; $7,500 annually plus $3,000 total in research/internship/community service stipends. All selected from top 15% of applicant pool.
Cumulative student debt: 58% of graduating class had student loans; average debt was $23,222.

FINANCIAL AID PROCEDURES

Forms required: FAFSA, CSS PROFILE.

Dates and Deadlines: Closing date 2/1. Applicants notified by 4/1; must reply by 5/1.

Transfers: Closing date 4/1. Applicants notified by 5/15; must reply by 6/1. Very limited institutional grant funds available for late transfer applicants.

CONTACT

Robin Randall, Assistant Vice President for Enrollment and Student Financial Services

26 East Main Street, Norton, MA 02766

(508) 286-8232

Wheelock College

Boston, Massachusetts
www.wheelock.edu

Federal Code: 002228

4-year private liberal arts and teachers college in very large city.

Enrollment: 787 undergrads, 7% part-time. 224 full-time freshmen.

Selectivity: Admits 50 to 75% of applicants.

BASIC COSTS (2007-2008)

Tuition and fees: $26,080.

Per-credit charge: $794.

Room and board: $10,400.

FINANCIAL AID PICTURE (2007-2008)

Students with need: Average financial aid package met 69% of need; average scholarship/grant was $11,699; average loan was $3,124. For part-time students, average financial aid package was $9,875.

Students without need: No-need awards available for academics, job skills, leadership.

Scholarships offered: Wheelock College Grants: awarded based on SAT score of 1050 (exclusive of writing) plus 3.0 GPA; renewable if 3.0 GPA maintained.

Cumulative student debt: 86% of graduating class had student loans; average debt was $19,232.

FINANCIAL AID PROCEDURES

Forms required: FAFSA.

Dates and Deadlines: Priority date 2/15; no closing date. Applicants notified on a rolling basis starting 3/1; must reply by 5/1.

Transfers: Priority date 4/15. Applicants notified by 5/1; must reply by 6/1.

CONTACT

Melissa Holster, Director of Financial Aid

200 The Riverway, Boston, MA 02215-4176

(617) 879-2206

Williams College

Williamstown, Massachusetts
www.williams.edu

Federal Code: 002229
CSS Code: 3965

4-year private liberal arts college in small town, affiliated with United Church of Christ.

Enrollment: 1,962 undergrads. 541 full-time freshmen.

Selectivity: Admits less than 50% of applicants.

BASIC COSTS (2008-2009)

Tuition and fees: $37,640.

Room and board: $9,890.

FINANCIAL AID PICTURE (2007-2008)

Students with need: Out of 342 full-time freshmen who applied for aid, 278 were judged to have need. Of these, 278 received aid, and 278 had their full need met. Average financial aid package met 100% of need; average scholarship/grant was $33,292; average loan was $2,330. Need-based aid available for part-time students.

Students without need: This college awards aid only to students with need.

Cumulative student debt: 45% of graduating class had student loans; average debt was $9,727.

FINANCIAL AID PROCEDURES

Forms required: FAFSA, CSS PROFILE.

Dates and Deadlines: Closing date 2/1. Applicants notified by 4/1; must reply by 5/1.

Transfers: Closing date 4/1. Applicants notified by 5/15; must reply within 2 week(s) of notification.

CONTACT

Paul Boyer, Director of Financial Aid

33 Stetson Court, Williamstown, MA 01267

(413) 597-3131

Worcester Polytechnic Institute

Worcester, Massachusetts
www.wpi.edu

Federal Code: 002233
CSS Code: 3969

4-year private university in small city.

Enrollment: 3,009 undergrads, 1% part-time. 777 full-time freshmen.

Selectivity: Admits 50 to 75% of applicants.

BASIC COSTS (2007-2008)

Tuition and fees: $34,830.

Room and board: $10,410.

FINANCIAL AID PICTURE (2006-2007)

Students with need: Out of 690 full-time freshmen who applied for aid, 596 were judged to have need. Of these, 592 received aid, and 235 had their full need met. Average financial aid package met 67% of need; average scholarship/grant was $16,660; average loan was $4,928. For part-time students, average financial aid package was $7,405.

Students without need: 158 full-time freshmen who did not demonstrate need for aid received scholarships/grants; average award was $12,288. No-need awards available for academics, leadership, minority status, ROTC.

Scholarships offered: Merit scholarships; vary in amounts, but typically range between $12,500 and $25,000; renewable for 4 years.

Cumulative student debt: 82% of graduating class had student loans; average debt was $34,409.

FINANCIAL AID PROCEDURES

Forms required: FAFSA, CSS PROFILE.

Dates and Deadlines: Closing date 2/1. Applicants notified by 4/1; must reply by 5/1.

Transfers: Priority date 2/1; closing date 3/1. Applicants notified by 4/15; must reply by 5/1.

CONTACT

Monica Blondin, Director, Financial Aid

100 Institute Road, Worcester, MA 01609-2280

(508) 831-5469

Worcester State College

Worcester, Massachusetts
www.worcester.edu   Federal Code: 002190

4-year public liberal arts and teachers college in small city.

Enrollment: 4,020 undergrads, 17% part-time. 668 full-time freshmen.

Selectivity: Open admission; but selective for some programs.

BASIC COSTS (2007-2008)

Tuition and fees: $5,864; out-of-state residents $11,944.

Per-credit charge: $40; out-of-state residents $294.

Room and board: $7,958.

FINANCIAL AID PICTURE (2006-2007)

Students with need: Out of 590 full-time freshmen who applied for aid, 371 were judged to have need. Of these, 359 received aid, and 160 had their full need met. Average financial aid package met 82% of need; average scholarship/grant was $4,223; average loan was $1,809. For part-time students, average financial aid package was $5,919.

Scholarships offered: Presidential Scholarships: full in-state tuition and fees; 3.5 GPA and 1150 SAT; 15 awarded. Tsongas Scholarships: full in-state tuition and fees to Massachusetts residents; 3.7 GPA and 1200 SAT; 5 awarded. Access Scholarships: $1,000 per year: opportunity for underserved groups; 2.5 GPA and 920 SAT; 15 awarded. Teacher Education Scholarship: full in-state tuition and fees; 3.5 GPA and 1150 SAT; for future teachers; 15 awarded. Honors Scholarship: $1,500 per year; 3.2 GPA and 1100 SAT; 25 awarded. All SAT scores exclusive of writing. Transfer Scholarship: $1,000; . requires associate degree and 3.2 GPA; 25 awarded to Massachusetts residents.

Cumulative student debt: 41% of graduating class had student loans; average debt was $17,985.

Additional info: Veterans, Native Americans and those certified by Massachusetts Rehabilitation Commission and Massachusetts Commission for the Blind considered for tuition waivers while funds available. Tuition also waived for needy Massachusetts residents and in-state National Guard members.

FINANCIAL AID PROCEDURES

Forms required: FAFSA, institutional form.

Dates and Deadlines: Priority date 3/1; no closing date. Applicants notified on a rolling basis starting 3/1; must reply within 2 week(s) of notification.

CONTACT

Jayne McGinn, Director of Financial Aid
486 Chandler Street, Worcester, MA 01602-2597
(508) 929-8056

Michigan

Adrian College

Adrian, Michigan
www.adrian.edu   Federal Code: 002234

4-year private liberal arts college in large town, affiliated with United Methodist Church.

Enrollment: 1,269 undergrads. 492 full-time freshmen.

Selectivity: Admits 50 to 75% of applicants.

BASIC COSTS (2007-2008)

Tuition and fees: $21,620.

Per-credit charge: $650.

Room and board: $7,150.

FINANCIAL AID PICTURE (2007-2008)

Students with need: Out of 418 full-time freshmen who applied for aid, 376 were judged to have need. Of these, 376 received aid, and 376 had their full need met. Average financial aid package met 100% of need; average scholarship/grant was $9,211; average loan was $4,485. For part-time students, average financial aid package was $8,012.

Students without need: 38 full-time freshmen who did not demonstrate need for aid received scholarships/grants; average award was $8,146. No-need awards available for academics, alumni affiliation, art, leadership, music/drama, religious affiliation.

Scholarships offered: Academic scholarships; based on ACT score of 20 and GPA of 3.0.

Cumulative student debt: 81% of graduating class had student loans; average debt was $20,000.

FINANCIAL AID PROCEDURES

Forms required: FAFSA.

Dates and Deadlines: Closing date 3/1. Applicants notified on a rolling basis starting 3/15; must reply by 5/1 or within 2 week(s) of notification.

CONTACT

Andrew Spohn, Director of Financial Services
110 South Madison Street, Adrian, MI 49221-2575
(517) 265-5161 ext. 4306

Albion College

Albion, Michigan
www.albion.edu   Federal Code: 002235

4-year private liberal arts college in small town, affiliated with United Methodist Church.

Enrollment: 1,922 undergrads. 506 full-time freshmen.

Selectivity: Admits over 75% of applicants.

BASIC COSTS (2008-2009)

Tuition and fees: $28,880.

Per-credit charge: $1,206.

Room and board: $8,190.

FINANCIAL AID PICTURE (2007-2008)

Students with need: Out of 388 full-time freshmen who applied for aid, 328 were judged to have need. Of these, 328 received aid, and 151 had their full need met. Average financial aid package met 93% of need; average scholarship/grant was $18,674; average loan was $3,916.

Students without need: 159 full-time freshmen who did not demonstrate need for aid received scholarships/grants; average award was $12,498. No-need awards available for academics, alumni affiliation, art, music/drama, state/district residency.

Scholarships offered: Distinguished Albion Scholarships: full tuition for 4 years; awarded to students who present original research during on-campus competition; up to 10 awarded. Trustee Scholarships: $15,500; based on GPA and SAT or ACT. Presidential Scholarships: $14,000; based on GPA and SAT or ACT. Performing and Fine Arts Scholarships: up to $3,000. Speech Communication Scholarships: up to $8,000. Diversity Awards: $4,000 renewable annually; awarded to students involved with promoting and enhancing multicultural on-campus relations.

Cumulative student debt: 65% of graduating class had student loans; average debt was $25,340.

FINANCIAL AID PROCEDURES

Forms required: FAFSA.

Dates and Deadlines: Priority date 3/1; no closing date. Applicants notified on a rolling basis starting 3/15; must reply by 5/1 or within 2 week(s) of notification.

Transfers: Applicants notified on a rolling basis.

CONTACT

Doug Kellar, Associate Vice President for Enrollment and Financial Aid
611 East Porter Street, Albion, MI 49224-1831
(517) 629-0440

Alma College
Alma, Michigan
www.alma.edu   Federal Code: 002236

4-year private liberal arts college in small town, affiliated with Presbyterian Church (USA).

Enrollment: 1,304 undergrads, 1% part-time. 423 full-time freshmen.

Selectivity: Admits over 75% of applicants.

BASIC COSTS (2008-2009)

Tuition and fees: $24,850.

Per-credit charge: $955.

Room and board: $8,120.

FINANCIAL AID PICTURE (2007-2008)

Students with need: Out of 419 full-time freshmen who applied for aid, 336 were judged to have need. Of these, 336 received aid, and 112 had their full need met. Average financial aid package met 88% of need; average scholarship/grant was $17,631; average loan was $4,936. For part-time students, average financial aid package was $23,583.

Students without need: 78 full-time freshmen who did not demonstrate need for aid received scholarships/grants; average award was $17,648. No-need awards available for academics, alumni affiliation, art, music/drama.

Scholarships offered: Distinguished Scholar Award; up to full tuition; awarded to designated National Merit Scholarship Finalist. Trustee Honors Scholarship; $13,000; awarded on basis of superior academic achievement, national test scores. Presidential Scholarships; $12,000; awarded on basis of outstanding scholarship and high national test scores. Dean's Scholarship; $11,000; awarded on basis on academic achievement and high national test scores. Tartan Scholars Award ($8,000) and Achievement Awards ($6,000); both awards based on academic achievement or high national test scores. Performance Scholarships; up to $1,000; awarded to students with a demonstrated high level of accomplishment in the fine or performing arts.

Cumulative student debt: 92% of graduating class had student loans; average debt was $23,736.

Additional info: Auditions required for music, drama, dance scholarship candidates. Portfolios required for art scholarship candidates.

FINANCIAL AID PROCEDURES

Forms required: FAFSA.

Dates and Deadlines: Priority date 3/1; no closing date. Applicants notified on a rolling basis starting 3/1; must reply within 3 week(s) of notification.

Transfers: No deadline. Applicants notified on a rolling basis starting 3/1; must reply within 3 week(s) of notification.

CONTACT

Christopher Brown, Director of Student Financial Assistance
614 West Superior Street, Alma, MI 48801-1599
(989) 463-7347

Alpena Community College
Alpena, Michigan
www.alpenacc.edu   Federal Code: 002237

2-year public community college in large town.

Enrollment: 2,056 undergrads.

Selectivity: Open admission; but selective for some programs.

BASIC COSTS (2008-2009)

Tuition and fees: $3,020; out-of-district residents $3,320; out-of-state residents $5,720.

Per-credit charge: $80; out-of-district residents $120; out-of-state residents $160.

FINANCIAL AID PICTURE (2007-2008)

Students with need: 66% of average financial aid package awarded as scholarships/grants, 34% awarded as loans/jobs. Need-based aid available for part-time students.

Students without need: No-need awards available for academics, art, athletics, job skills, leadership, music/drama.

FINANCIAL AID PROCEDURES

Forms required: FAFSA.

Dates and Deadlines: Priority date 8/1; no closing date. Applicants notified on a rolling basis starting 5/15; must reply within 3 week(s) of notification.

CONTACT

Max Lindsay, Dean of Students
665 Johnson Street, Alpena, MI 49707
(989) 358-7205

Andrews University
Berrien Springs, Michigan
www.andrews.edu   Federal Code: 002238

4-year private university in small town, affiliated with Seventh-day Adventists.

Enrollment: 1,622 undergrads, 7% part-time. 333 full-time freshmen.

Selectivity: Admits 50 to 75% of applicants.

BASIC COSTS (2008-2009)

Tuition and fees: $19,940.

Per-credit charge: $805.

Room and board: $6,330.

FINANCIAL AID PICTURE

Students with need: Need-based aid available for full-time and part-time students. Work study available nights, weekends, and for part-time students.

Students without need: No-need awards available for academics, alumni affiliation, leadership, music/drama, religious affiliation.

FINANCIAL AID PROCEDURES

Forms required: FAFSA, institutional form.

Dates and Deadlines: Priority date 3/31; no closing date. Applicants notified on a rolling basis starting 3/15.

CONTACT

Elynda Bedney, Director of Student Financial Services
100 US Highway 31, Berrien Springs, MI 49104

Aquinas College
Grand Rapids, Michigan
www.aquinas.edu   Federal Code: 002239

4-year private liberal arts college in small city, affiliated with Roman Catholic Church.

Enrollment: 1,779 undergrads, 15% part-time. 412 full-time freshmen.

Selectivity: Admits over 75% of applicants. GED not accepted.

BASIC COSTS (2008-2009)

Tuition and fees: $21,150.

Per-credit charge: $662.

Room and board: $6,678.

Additional info: Tuition/fee waivers available for adults.

FINANCIAL AID PICTURE (2007-2008)

Students with need: Out of 380 full-time freshmen who applied for aid, 333 were judged to have need. Of these, 333 received aid, and 158 had their full need met. Average financial aid package met 93% of need; average scholarship/grant was $15,120; average loan was $2,723. For part-time students, average financial aid package was $3,120.

Students without need: 72 full-time freshmen who did not demonstrate need for aid received scholarships/grants; average award was $8,400. No-need awards available for academics, alumni affiliation, art, athletics, leadership, music/drama.

Scholarships offered: *Merit:* Spectrum Scholarship; $3,000 to full tuition; awarded to students who have excelled in academics, leadership or community service; renewable. *Athletic:* 8 full-time freshmen received athletic scholarships; average amount $3,025.

FINANCIAL AID PROCEDURES

Forms required: FAFSA.

Dates and Deadlines: Priority date 3/1; no closing date. Applicants notified on a rolling basis starting 2/15; must reply within 2 week(s) of notification.

Transfers: Priority date 4/15; closing date 7/1. Must reply within 2 week(s) of notification.

CONTACT

David Steffee, Director of Financial Aid
1607 Robinson Road Southeast, Grand Rapids, MI 49506-1799
(616) 632-2893

Baker College of Auburn Hills

Auburn Hills, Michigan
www.baker.edu
Federal Code: E00466

4-year private business and technical college in small city.
Enrollment: 3,701 undergrads.
Selectivity: Open admission.

BASIC COSTS (2008-2009)
Tuition and fees: $8,550.
Per-credit charge: $190.

FINANCIAL AID PICTURE
Students with need: Work study available nights, weekends, and for part-time students.
Students without need: No-need awards available for academics, alumni affiliation.

FINANCIAL AID PROCEDURES
Forms required: FAFSA, institutional form.
Dates and Deadlines: Priority date 2/21; closing date 9/1. Applicants notified on a rolling basis starting 4/1.
Transfers: Must have been deemed financial aid-eligible at previous school.

CONTACT
Greg Little, Financial Aid Director
1500 University Drive, Auburn Hills, MI 48326
(248) 340-0600

Baker College of Cadillac

Cadillac, Michigan
www.baker.edu
Federal Code: E00461

4-year private business and health science college in large town.
Enrollment: 1,806 undergrads.
Selectivity: Open admission.

BASIC COSTS (2008-2009)
Tuition and fees: $8,550.
Per-credit charge: $190.

FINANCIAL AID PICTURE
Students with need: Need-based aid available for full-time and part-time students. Work study available nights, weekends, and for part-time students.
Students without need: No-need awards available for academics.
Scholarships offered: Baker College Career Scholarships; $400 per term for 4 years; based on 2.5 GPA after junior year of high school. Board of Regents Scholarships; half tuition for 4 years; based on 3.5 GPA through grade 11.

FINANCIAL AID PROCEDURES
Forms required: FAFSA, institutional form.
Dates and Deadlines: Priority date 2/21; no closing date. Applicants notified on a rolling basis starting 5/1.
Transfers: Priority date 3/20; closing date 9/1.

CONTACT
Kristin Bonney, Financial Aid Officer
9600 East 13th Street, Cadillac, MI 49601
(231) 876-3118

Baker College of Clinton Township

Clinton Township, Michigan
www.baker.edu
Federal Code: E00462

4-year private business and technical college in very large city.
Enrollment: 5,608 undergrads.
Selectivity: Open admission; but selective for some programs.

BASIC COSTS (2008-2009)
Tuition and fees: $8,550.
Per-credit charge: $190.

FINANCIAL AID PICTURE
Students with need: Need-based aid available for full-time and part-time students. Work study available nights, weekends, and for part-time students.
Students without need: No-need awards available for academics, minority status.

FINANCIAL AID PROCEDURES
Forms required: FAFSA, institutional form.
Dates and Deadlines: Priority date 2/21; closing date 9/1. Applicants notified on a rolling basis starting 4/1.

CONTACT
Lisa Harvener, Vice President of Student Services
34401 Gratiot Avenue, Clinton Township, MI 48035
(586) 790-9589

Baker College of Muskegon

Muskegon, Michigan
www.baker.edu
Federal Code: E00463

4-year private business and technical college in small city.
Enrollment: 5,010 undergrads.
Selectivity: Open admission; but selective for some programs.

BASIC COSTS (2008-2009)
Tuition and fees: $8,550.
Per-credit charge: $190.
Room only: $2,865.

FINANCIAL AID PICTURE
Students with need: Need-based aid available for full-time and part-time students. Work study available nights, weekends, and for part-time students.

Students without need: No-need awards available for academics, minority status.
Scholarships offered: Career Scholarship; $4,800 over 4 years; based on GPA over 3.0. Board Regents Scholarship; one-half tuition for 4 years; based on GPA over 3.5. Alternative Scholarship; one-half tuition for 2 years; based on academic success in alternative high school education program.

FINANCIAL AID PROCEDURES
Forms required: FAFSA, institutional form.
Dates and Deadlines: Priority date 2/21; no closing date. Applicants notified on a rolling basis starting 4/1.
Transfers: Priority date 3/21.

CONTACT
Jody Zerlant, Director of Financial Aid
1903 Marquette Avenue, Muskegon, MI 49442
(231) 777-5231

Baker College of Owosso
Owosso, Michigan
www.baker.edu
Federal Code: E00464

4-year private business and technical college in large town.
Enrollment: 2,911 undergrads.
Selectivity: Open admission.

BASIC COSTS (2008-2009)
Tuition and fees: $8,550.
Per-credit charge: $190.
Room only: $2,700.

FINANCIAL AID PICTURE
Students with need: Need-based aid available for full-time and part-time students. Work study available nights, weekends, and for part-time students.
Students without need: No-need awards available for academics, minority status.

FINANCIAL AID PROCEDURES
Forms required: FAFSA, institutional form.
Dates and Deadlines: Priority date 2/21; closing date 9/1. Applicants notified on a rolling basis starting 4/1.
Transfers: Priority date 3/21.

CONTACT
Nicole Patterson, Financial Aid Director
1020 South Washington Street, Owosso, MI 48867
(989) 720-3430

Baker College of Port Huron
Port Huron, Michigan
www.baker.edu
Federal Code: E00465

4-year private business and technical college in large town.
Enrollment: 1,642 undergrads.
Selectivity: Open admission; but selective for some programs.

BASIC COSTS (2008-2009)
Tuition and fees: $8,550.
Per-credit charge: $190.

FINANCIAL AID PICTURE
Students with need: Need-based aid available for full-time and part-time students. Work study available nights.
Students without need: This college awards aid only to students with need.

FINANCIAL AID PROCEDURES
Forms required: FAFSA, institutional form.
Dates and Deadlines: Priority date 2/21; no closing date. Applicants notified on a rolling basis starting 4/1.
Transfers: Priority date 3/21; closing date 9/1.

CONTACT
Barbara Fosgard, Financial Aid Director
3403 Lapeer Road, Port Huron, MI 48060-2597
(810) 985-7000

Bay de Noc Community College
Escanaba, Michigan
www.baycollege.edu
Federal Code: 002240

2-year public community college in large town.
Enrollment: 1,993 undergrads, 37% part-time. 481 full-time freshmen.
Selectivity: Open admission; but selective for some programs.

BASIC COSTS (2007-2008)
Tuition and fees: $2,505; out-of-district residents $3,795; out-of-state residents $4,785.
Per-credit charge: $77; out-of-district residents $120; out-of-state residents $153.
Room and board: $2,450.
Additional info: Tuition and instructional fees based on contact hours.

FINANCIAL AID PICTURE
Students with need: Need-based aid available for full-time and part-time students. Work study available nights, weekends, and for part-time students.
Students without need: No-need awards available for academics.

FINANCIAL AID PROCEDURES
Forms required: FAFSA.
Dates and Deadlines: Priority date 4/1; no closing date. Applicants notified on a rolling basis starting 2/1; must reply within 2 week(s) of notification.

CONTACT
Sue Hebert, Financial Aid Director
2001 North Lincoln Road, Escanaba, MI 49829-2511
(906) 786-5802 ext. 1215

Bay Mills Community College
Brimley, Michigan
www.bmcc.edu
Federal Code: 030666

2-year public community college in rural community.
Enrollment: 200 full-time undergrads.
Selectivity: Open admission.

BASIC COSTS (2007-2008)
Tuition and fees: $2,910.
Per-credit charge: $85.

FINANCIAL AID PICTURE
Students with need: Work study available nights.

FINANCIAL AID PROCEDURES
Forms required: FAFSA, institutional form.

CONTACT
Tina Miller, Financial Aid Director
12214 West Lakeshore Drive, Brimley, MI 49715
(906) 248-3354 ext. 4224

Calvin College
Grand Rapids, Michigan
www.calvin.edu
Federal Code: 002241

4-year private liberal arts college in large city, affiliated with Christian Reformed Church.
Enrollment: 4,078 undergrads, 2% part-time. 1,025 full-time freshmen.
Selectivity: Admits over 75% of applicants.

BASIC COSTS (2008-2009)
Tuition and fees: $23,165.
Per-credit charge: $550.
Room and board: $7,970.

FINANCIAL AID PICTURE (2006-2007)
Students with need: Out of 864 full-time freshmen who applied for aid, 671 were judged to have need. Of these, 671 received aid, and 229 had their full need met. Average financial aid package met 87% of need; average scholarship/grant was $10,200; average loan was $4,200. For part-time students, average financial aid package was $8,700.
Students without need: 312 full-time freshmen who did not demonstrate need for aid received scholarships/grants; average award was $4,500. No-need awards available for academics, alumni affiliation, art, leadership, minority status, music/drama, religious affiliation, state/district residency.
Cumulative student debt: 66% of graduating class had student loans; average debt was $21,600.

FINANCIAL AID PROCEDURES
Forms required: FAFSA.
Dates and Deadlines: Priority date 2/15; no closing date. Applicants notified on a rolling basis starting 3/15.
Transfers: Priority date 3/15; closing date 8/15. Applicants notified on a rolling basis starting 3/15.

CONTACT
Dale Kuiper, Director of Admissions and Financial Aid
3201 Burton Street Southeast, Grand Rapids, MI 49546
(616) 526-6134

Central Michigan University
Mount Pleasant, Michigan
www.cmich.edu
Federal Code: 002243

4-year public university in large town.
Enrollment: 19,632 undergrads, 11% part-time. 3,785 full-time freshmen.
Selectivity: Admits 50 to 75% of applicants.

BASIC COSTS (2007-2008)
Tuition and fees: $9,120; out-of-state residents $21,210.
Per-credit charge: $304; out-of-state residents $707.
Room and board: $7,236.
Additional info: Four years guaranteed tuition plan. Tuition at time of enrollment locked for 4 years.

FINANCIAL AID PICTURE (2006-2007)
Students with need: Out of 2,992 full-time freshmen who applied for aid, 2,000 were judged to have need. Of these, 1,950 received aid, and 1,200 had their full need met. Average financial aid package met 84% of need; average scholarship/grant was $5,020; average loan was $3,909. For part-time students, average financial aid package was $6,699.
Students without need: 396 full-time freshmen who did not demonstrate need for aid received scholarships/grants; average award was $3,381. No-need awards available for academics, alumni affiliation, art, athletics, leadership, minority status, music/drama, ROTC, state/district residency.
Scholarships offered: *Merit:* President's Award; for out-of-state students; based on high school GPA of 3.0 or higher; awarded differential between in

and out-of-state tuition. *Athletic:* 46 full-time freshmen received athletic scholarships; average amount $12,280.
Cumulative student debt: 69% of graduating class had student loans; average debt was $22,128.
Additional info: Tuition waiver for Native American students qualifying under state program criteria.

FINANCIAL AID PROCEDURES
Forms required: FAFSA.
Dates and Deadlines: Priority date 3/1; no closing date. Applicants notified on a rolling basis starting 4/1.

CONTACT
Michael Owens, Director, Scholarships and Financial Aid
Admissions Office, Mount Pleasant, MI 48859
(989) 774-3674

Cleary University
Howell, Michigan
www.cleary.edu
Federal Code: 002246

4-year private university and business college in small city.
Enrollment: 644 undergrads, 40% part-time. 70 full-time freshmen.
Selectivity: Admits over 75% of applicants.

BASIC COSTS (2008-2009)
Tuition and fees: $14,880.
Per-credit charge: $310.
Additional info: Tuition prices guaranteed if student enrolled continuously. Tuition includes all books and fees. Tuition at time of enrollment locked for 4 years.

FINANCIAL AID PICTURE (2006-2007)
Students with need: Out of 46 full-time freshmen who applied for aid, 46 were judged to have need. Of these, 46 received aid, and 2 had their full need met. Average financial aid package met 35% of need; average scholarship/grant was $915; average loan was $1,103. For part-time students, average financial aid package was $9,493.
Students without need: 6 full-time freshmen who did not demonstrate need for aid received scholarships/grants; average award was $1,710. No-need awards available for academics.
Scholarships offered: Oren Beutler Endowed Scholarship: $750; new or continuing full-time student maintaining 3.0 GPA, demonstrated leadership and service to community; one awarded annually, renewable for 4 years.
Additional info: Filing electronically preferred; paper applications available. Tuition guarantee based on continuous enrollment. Essay and recommendations required for scholarship consideration.

FINANCIAL AID PROCEDURES
Forms required: FAFSA.
Dates and Deadlines: Priority date 3/15; closing date 8/15. Applicants notified on a rolling basis; must reply within 2 week(s) of notification.

CONTACT
Vesta Smith-Campbell, Director of Financial Aid
3750 Cleary Drive, Howell, MI 48843
(517) 548-3670

College for Creative Studies
Detroit, Michigan
www.collegeforcreativestudies.edu Federal Code: 006771

4-year private visual arts college in very large city.
Enrollment: 1,307 undergrads, 15% part-time. 241 full-time freshmen.
Selectivity: Admits less than 50% of applicants.

BASIC COSTS (2008-2009)

Tuition and fees: $28,275.

Per-credit charge: $903.

FINANCIAL AID PICTURE (2006-2007)

Students with need: 52% of average financial aid package awarded as scholarships/grants, 48% awarded as loans/jobs. Need-based aid available for part-time students. Work study available nights, weekends, and for part-time students.

Students without need: No-need awards available for academics, art.

Cumulative student debt: 80% of graduating class had student loans; average debt was $57,980.

FINANCIAL AID PROCEDURES

Forms required: FAFSA.

Dates and Deadlines: Priority date 7/1; no closing date. Applicants notified on a rolling basis starting 3/15; must reply within 3 week(s) of notification.

Transfers: Priority date 3/21.

CONTACT

Kristin Moskovitz, Director of Financial Aid

201 East Kirby, Detroit, MI 48202-4034

(313) 664-7495

Concordia University

Ann Arbor, Michigan

www.cuaa.edu   Federal Code: 002247

4-year private liberal arts and teachers college in small city, affiliated with Lutheran Church - Missouri Synod.

Enrollment: 493 undergrads, 14% part-time. 94 full-time freshmen.

Selectivity: Admits 50 to 75% of applicants.

BASIC COSTS (2007-2008)

Tuition and fees: $19,770.

Per-credit charge: $650.

Room and board: $7,350.

Additional info: Additional one-time fees for all undergraduates include: $125 pre-enrollment deposit, $100 matriculation fee.

FINANCIAL AID PICTURE (2007-2008)

Students with need: Average financial aid package met 35% of need; average scholarship/grant was $11,796; average loan was $5,633. For part-time students, average financial aid package was $6,423.

Students without need: No-need awards available for academics, alumni affiliation, art, athletics, leadership, music/drama, religious affiliation.

Cumulative student debt: 97% of graduating class had student loans; average debt was $30,680.

FINANCIAL AID PROCEDURES

Forms required: FAFSA, institutional form.

Dates and Deadlines: Closing date 3/1. Applicants notified on a rolling basis starting 3/1; must reply within 3 week(s) of notification.

Transfers: Priority date 5/1. Applicants notified on a rolling basis; must reply within 3 week(s) of notification.

CONTACT

Angela Acosta, Director of Financial Aid

4090 Geddes Road, Ann Arbor, MI 48105

(734) 995-7408

Cornerstone University

Grand Rapids, Michigan

www.cornerstone.edu   Federal Code: 002266

4-year private university and liberal arts college in small city, affiliated with Baptist faith.

Enrollment: 1,798 undergrads, 20% part-time. 269 full-time freshmen.

Selectivity: Admits 50 to 75% of applicants.

BASIC COSTS (2008-2009)

Tuition and fees: $19,530.

Per-credit charge: $735.

Room and board: $6,500.

Additional info: Tuition includes laptop computer.

FINANCIAL AID PICTURE (2007-2008)

Students with need: Out of 252 full-time freshmen who applied for aid, 232 were judged to have need. Of these, 232 received aid, and 36 had their full need met. Average financial aid package met 88% of need; average scholarship/grant was $10,750; average loan was $195. For part-time students, average financial aid package was $10,495.

Students without need: 31 full-time freshmen who did not demonstrate need for aid received scholarships/grants; average award was $4,565. No-need awards available for academics, athletics, leadership, music/drama, state/district residency.

Scholarships offered: *Merit:* Academic scholarships; based on high school GPA and ACT scores. *Athletic:* 49 full-time freshmen received athletic scholarships; average amount $4,622.

Cumulative student debt: 85% of graduating class had student loans; average debt was $26,710.

Additional info: Audition required for music scholarship applicants.

FINANCIAL AID PROCEDURES

Forms required: FAFSA.

Dates and Deadlines: Priority date 3/1; no closing date. Applicants notified on a rolling basis starting 3/15; must reply within 2 week(s) of notification.

Transfers: No deadline.

CONTACT

Geoff Marsh, Director of Student Financial Services

1001 East Beltline NE, Grand Rapids, MI 49525-5897

(616) 222-1424

Davenport University

Grand Rapids, Michigan

www.davenport.edu   Federal Code: 015260

4-year private university and business college in small city.

Enrollment: 10,579 undergrads, 70% part-time. 495 full-time freshmen.

Selectivity: Admits over 75% of applicants.

BASIC COSTS (2007-2008)

Tuition and fees: $12,445.

Per-credit charge: $409.

FINANCIAL AID PICTURE (2006-2007)

Students with need: 29% of average financial aid package awarded as scholarships/grants, 71% awarded as loans/jobs. Need-based aid available for part-time students. Work study available nights, weekends, and for part-time students.

Students without need: No-need awards available for academics, alumni affiliation, athletics, leadership.

FINANCIAL AID PROCEDURES

Forms required: FAFSA.

Dates and Deadlines: Priority date 3/1; no closing date. Applicants notified on a rolling basis starting 3/1; must reply within 2 week(s) of notification.

Transfers: No deadline. Applicants notified on a rolling basis.

CONTACT
David De Boer, Executive Director of Financial Aid
6191 Kraft Avenue SE, Grand Rapids, MI 49512-5926
(866) 925-3884

Delta College
University Center, Michigan
www.delta.edu   Federal Code: 002251

2-year public community and junior college in small city.
Enrollment: 10,422 undergrads.
Selectivity: Open admission.

BASIC COSTS (2007-2008)
Tuition and fees: $2,700; out-of-district residents $3,810; out-of-state residents $5,310.
Per-credit charge: $78; out-of-district residents $115; out-of-state residents $165.

FINANCIAL AID PICTURE
Students with need: Need-based aid available for full-time and part-time students. Work study available nights.
Students without need: No-need awards available for academics, athletics.

FINANCIAL AID PROCEDURES
Forms required: FAFSA.
Dates and Deadlines: Priority date 8/1; no closing date. Applicants notified on a rolling basis; must reply within 2 week(s) of notification.
Transfers: No deadline. Applicants notified on a rolling basis.

CONTACT
Kim Donat, Financial Aid Director
1961 Delta Road, University Center, MI 48710
(989) 686-9080

Eastern Michigan University
Ypsilanti, Michigan
www.emich.edu   Federal Code: 002259

4-year public university in small city.
Enrollment: 17,609 undergrads, 30% part-time. 2,272 full-time freshmen.
Selectivity: Admits 50 to 75% of applicants.

BASIC COSTS (2007-2008)
Tuition and fees: $7,490; out-of-state residents $19,925.
Per-credit charge: $213; out-of-state residents $628.
Room and board: $6,942.

FINANCIAL AID PICTURE (2006-2007)
Students with need: Out of 1,791 full-time freshmen who applied for aid, 1,336 were judged to have need. Of these, 1,289 received aid, and 189 had their full need met. Average financial aid package met 59% of need; average scholarship/grant was $3,356; average loan was $3,113. For part-time students, average financial aid package was $4,997.
Students without need: 628 full-time freshmen who did not demonstrate need for aid received scholarships/grants; average award was $2,821. No-need awards available for academics, alumni affiliation, art, athletics, leadership, minority status, music/drama, ROTC, state/district residency.
Scholarships offered: 83 full-time freshmen received athletic scholarships; average amount $12,122.
Cumulative student debt: 61% of graduating class had student loans; average debt was $25,145.

FINANCIAL AID PROCEDURES
Forms required: FAFSA.

Dates and Deadlines: Priority date 3/15; no closing date. Applicants notified on a rolling basis starting 3/1.
Transfers: No deadline. Applicants notified on a rolling basis.

CONTACT
Bernice Lindke, Director of Financial Aid
400 Pierce Hall, Ypsilanti, MI 48197
(734) 487-0455

Ferris State University
Big Rapids, Michigan
www.ferris.edu   Federal Code: 002260

4-year public university in large town.
Enrollment: 11,421 undergrads, 22% part-time. 2,031 full-time freshmen.

BASIC COSTS (2007-2008)
Tuition and fees: $8,862; out-of-state residents $16,062.
Per-credit charge: $290; out-of-state residents $530.
Room and board: $7,646.
Additional info: Midwest Compact states of Illinois, Indiana, Kansas, Minnesota, Missouri, Nebraska, Ohio, and Wisconsin tuition is $13,050.

FINANCIAL AID PICTURE (2007-2008)
Students with need: Out of 1,734 full-time freshmen who applied for aid, 1,353 were judged to have need. Of these, 1,316 received aid, and 202 had their full need met. Average financial aid package met 89% of need; average scholarship/grant was $3,789; average loan was $3,185. For part-time students, average financial aid package was $9,972.
Students without need: 237 full-time freshmen who did not demonstrate need for aid received scholarships/grants; average award was $3,524. No-need awards available for academics, alumni affiliation, art, athletics, leadership, minority status, music/drama, religious affiliation, ROTC.
Scholarships offered: 28 full-time freshmen received athletic scholarships; average amount $11,211.
Cumulative student debt: 72% of graduating class had student loans; average debt was $28,483.

FINANCIAL AID PROCEDURES
Forms required: FAFSA.
Dates and Deadlines: Priority date 3/1; no closing date. Applicants notified on a rolling basis starting 3/1; must reply within 2 week(s) of notification.
Transfers: Applicants notified on a rolling basis.

CONTACT
Kathryn Lake, Director of Financial Aid
1201 South State Street, CSS 201, Big Rapids, MI 49307-2714
(231) 591-2110

Finlandia University
Hancock, Michigan
www.finlandia.edu   Federal Code: 002322

4-year private university and liberal arts college in small town, affiliated with Evangelical Lutheran Church in America.
Enrollment: 543 undergrads, 14% part-time. 79 full-time freshmen.
Selectivity: Admits 50 to 75% of applicants.

BASIC COSTS (2007-2008)
Tuition and fees: $17,514.
Per-credit charge: $540.
Room and board: $5,800.

FINANCIAL AID PICTURE (2007-2008)

Students with need: Out of 68 full-time freshmen who applied for aid, 61 were judged to have need. Of these, 61 received aid. Average financial aid package met 10% of need; average scholarship/grant was $5,000; average loan was $3,500. For part-time students, average financial aid package was $7,000.

Students without need: 18 full-time freshmen who did not demonstrate need for aid received scholarships/grants; average award was $5,000. No-need awards available for academics, leadership, religious affiliation, state/district residency.

Cumulative student debt: 87% of graduating class had student loans; average debt was $20,000.

Additional info: Work/study program; up to $2,800 per year.

FINANCIAL AID PROCEDURES

Forms required: FAFSA, institutional form.

Dates and Deadlines: Priority date 3/1; closing date 8/1. Applicants notified on a rolling basis starting 3/1; must reply within 2 week(s) of notification.

Transfers: Applicants notified on a rolling basis starting 2/1; must reply within 2 week(s) of notification.

CONTACT

Sandra Turnquist, Director of Financial Aid
601 Quincy Street, Hancock, MI 49930-1882
(906) 487-7261

Glen Oaks Community College
Centreville, Michigan
www.glenoaks.edu   Federal Code: 002263

2-year public community college in rural community.

Enrollment: 925 undergrads, 86% part-time. 34 full-time freshmen.

Selectivity: Open admission; but selective for some programs.

BASIC COSTS (2007-2008)

Tuition and fees: $2,610.

Per-credit charge: $70.

Additional info: In-county residents pay $70 per contact hour. Students from service area counties (Branch and Cass counties in Michigan and LaGrange, Elkheart, Steuben counties in Indiana) pay $109 per contact hour. All others pay $140 per contact hour. Required fees for all students: $510.

FINANCIAL AID PICTURE

Students with need: Need-based aid available for full-time and part-time students. Work study available nights.

Students without need: No-need awards available for academics, art, athletics, leadership, minority status, music/drama.

FINANCIAL AID PROCEDURES

Forms required: FAFSA, institutional form.

Dates and Deadlines: No deadline. Applicants notified on a rolling basis.

CONTACT

Matthew Soucy, Director of Financial Aid and Scholarship
62249 Shimmel Road, Centreville, MI 49032-9719
(269) 467-9945 ext. 250

Gogebic Community College
Ironwood, Michigan
www.gogebic.edu   Federal Code: 002264

2-year public community college in small town.

Enrollment: 847 undergrads, 30% part-time. 181 full-time freshmen.

Selectivity: Open admission; but selective for some programs.

BASIC COSTS (2007-2008)

Tuition and fees: $2,851; out-of-district residents $3,451; out-of-state residents $4,231.

Per-credit charge: $79; out-of-district residents $99; out-of-state residents $125.

Room only: $3,570.

FINANCIAL AID PICTURE

Students with need: Need-based aid available for full-time and part-time students. Work study available nights, weekends, and for part-time students.

Students without need: No-need awards available for academics, art, athletics, job skills, leadership, music/drama, state/district residency.

FINANCIAL AID PROCEDURES

Forms required: FAFSA.

Dates and Deadlines: Priority date 5/1; no closing date. Applicants notified on a rolling basis starting 3/15; must reply within 2 week(s) of notification.

CONTACT

Sue Forbes, Director of Financial Aid
E4946 Jackson Road, Ironwood, MI 49938
(906) 932-4231 ext. 206

Grace Bible College
Grand Rapids, Michigan
www.gbcol.edu   Federal Code: 002265

4-year private Bible and liberal arts college in small city, affiliated with Grace Gospel Fellowship.

Enrollment: 156 undergrads, 4% part-time. 53 full-time freshmen.

Selectivity: Admits 50 to 75% of applicants.

BASIC COSTS (2007-2008)

Tuition and fees: $12,140.

Per-credit charge: $450.

Room and board: $6,400.

FINANCIAL AID PICTURE (2006-2007)

Students with need: Out of 49 full-time freshmen who applied for aid, 43 were judged to have need. Of these, 43 received aid, and 9 had their full need met. Average financial aid package met 64% of need; average scholarship/grant was $3,294; average loan was $3,823. For part-time students, average financial aid package was $1,447.

Students without need: 8 full-time freshmen who did not demonstrate need for aid received scholarships/grants; average award was $3,759. No-need awards available for academics, music/drama, religious affiliation.

Scholarships offered: 42 full-time freshmen received athletic scholarships; average amount $3,073.

Cumulative student debt: 70% of graduating class had student loans; average debt was $22,293.

FINANCIAL AID PROCEDURES

Forms required: FAFSA.

Dates and Deadlines: Priority date 3/1; no closing date. Applicants notified on a rolling basis starting 5/15; must reply within 2 week(s) of notification.

CONTACT

Daniel Wait, Financial Aid Director
1011 Aldon Street SW, PO Box 910, Grand Rapids, MI 49509
(616) 261-8557

Grand Rapids Community College

Grand Rapids, Michigan
www.grcc.edu   Federal Code: 002267

2-year public community college in small city.

Enrollment: 13,998 undergrads, 53% part-time. 2,368 full-time freshmen.

Selectivity: Open admission; but selective for some programs.

BASIC COSTS (2008-2009)

Tuition and fees: $2,540; out-of-district residents $5,030; out-of-state residents $7,280.

Per-credit charge: $82; out-of-district residents $165; out-of-state residents $240.

FINANCIAL AID PICTURE

Students with need: Need-based aid available for full-time and part-time students. Work study available nights, weekends, and for part-time students.

Students without need: No-need awards available for academics, alumni affiliation, art, athletics, leadership, minority status, music/drama, state/district residency.

Scholarships offered: Michigan Merit Award; $2,500; based on Michigan Educational Assessment Program scores.

Additional info: Tuition reimbursement and/or child-care services for single parents and displaced homemakers who meet Perkins guidelines.

FINANCIAL AID PROCEDURES

Forms required: FAFSA.

Dates and Deadlines: Priority date 4/1; no closing date. Applicants notified on a rolling basis starting 5/1; must reply within 3 week(s) of notification.

CONTACT

Jill Nutt, Executive Director of Student Financial Services
143 Bostwick Avenue NE, Grand Rapids, MI 49503-3295
(616) 234-4030

Grand Valley State University

Allendale, Michigan
www.gvsu.edu   Federal Code: 002268

4-year public university in small town.

Enrollment: 19,643 undergrads, 12% part-time. 3,448 full-time freshmen.

Selectivity: Admits 50 to 75% of applicants.

BASIC COSTS (2007-2008)

Tuition and fees: $7,240; out-of-state residents $12,510.

Per-credit charge: $315; out-of-state residents $532.

Room and board: $7,048.

Additional info: Per-credit-hour charge applies only to part-time students. Tuition/fee waivers available for minority students.

FINANCIAL AID PICTURE (2007-2008)

Students with need: Out of 2,898 full-time freshmen who applied for aid, 1,811 were judged to have need. Of these, 1,806 received aid, and 677 had their full need met. Average financial aid package met 89% of need; average scholarship/grant was $6,178; average loan was $3,650. For part-time students, average financial aid package was $5,337.

Students without need: 654 full-time freshmen who did not demonstrate need for aid received scholarships/grants; average award was $3,249. No-need awards available for academics, alumni affiliation, art, athletics, minority status, music/drama.

Scholarships offered: 45 full-time freshmen received athletic scholarships; average amount $6,019.

FINANCIAL AID PROCEDURES

Forms required: FAFSA.

Dates and Deadlines: Priority date 3/1; no closing date. Applicants notified on a rolling basis starting 4/1; must reply within 3 week(s) of notification.

CONTACT

Ken Fridsma, Director of Financial Aid
One Campus Drive, Allendale, MI 49401-9403
(616) 331-3234

Great Lakes Christian College

Lansing, Michigan
www.glcc.edu   Federal Code: 002269

4-year private Bible college in small city, affiliated with Church of Christ / Christian Church.

Enrollment: 260 undergrads. 48 full-time freshmen.

BASIC COSTS (2007-2008)

Tuition and fees: $9,910.

Per-credit charge: $304.

Room and board: $6,200.

FINANCIAL AID PICTURE

Students with need: Need-based aid available for full-time and part-time students. Work study available nights, weekends, and for part-time students.

Students without need: No-need awards available for academics, alumni affiliation, music/drama.

FINANCIAL AID PROCEDURES

Forms required: FAFSA, state aid form, institutional form.

Dates and Deadlines: Priority date 8/1; no closing date. Applicants notified on a rolling basis starting 5/1; must reply within 3 week(s) of notification.

Transfers: Priority date 3/31; closing date 8/31. Applicants notified on a rolling basis; must reply within 3 week(s) of notification. FAFSA due by 6/30.

CONTACT

Tedd Kees, Director of Financial Aid
6211 West Willow Highway, Lansing, MI 48917-1299
(517) 321-0242 ext. 227

Henry Ford Community College

Dearborn, Michigan
www.hfcc.edu   Federal Code: 002270

2-year public community college in small city.

Enrollment: 12,546 undergrads.

Selectivity: Open admission; but selective for some programs.

BASIC COSTS (2007-2008)

Tuition and fees: $2,112; out-of-district residents $3,762; out-of-state residents $4,002.

Per-credit charge: $57; out-of-district residents $112; out-of-state residents $120.

FINANCIAL AID PICTURE

Students with need: Work study available nights, weekends, and for part-time students.

FINANCIAL AID PROCEDURES

Forms required: FAFSA.

Dates and Deadlines: Priority date 4/1; no closing date. Applicants notified on a rolling basis starting 3/1.

CONTACT

Kevin Culler, Director of Financial Aid
5101 Evergreen Road, Dearborn, MI 48128
(313) 845-9616

PART III: FINANCIAL AID COLLEGE BY COLLEGE

Hillsdale College

Hillsdale, Michigan
www.hillsdale.edu   Federal Code: 002272

4-year private liberal arts college in large town.

Enrollment: 1,326 undergrads, 3% part-time. 312 full-time freshmen.

Selectivity: Admits 50 to 75% of applicants.

BASIC COSTS (2008-2009)

Tuition and fees: $19,920.

Per-credit charge: $760.

Room and board: $7,570.

FINANCIAL AID PICTURE (2007-2008)

Students with need: Out of 225 full-time freshmen who applied for aid, 170 were judged to have need. Of these, 170 received aid, and 58 had their full need met. Average financial aid package met 65% of need; average scholarship/grant was $6,200; average loan was $4,000.

Students without need: 110 full-time freshmen who did not demonstrate need for aid received scholarships/grants; average award was $5,500. No-need awards available for academics, alumni affiliation, art, athletics, leadership, music/drama, state/district residency.

Scholarships offered: *Merit:* Distinct Honor Scholarship: full tuition; 5 awarded. Presidential Scholarship: half tuition; 35 awarded. Trustee Scholarship: up to $8,000; 40 awarded. *Athletic:* 60 full-time freshmen received athletic scholarships; average amount $10,100.

Cumulative student debt: 62% of graduating class had student loans; average debt was $14,500.

Additional info: Campus employment available.

FINANCIAL AID PROCEDURES

Forms required: institutional form. CSS PROFILE required for returning students only.

Dates and Deadlines: Priority date 3/1; closing date 3/15. Applicants notified on a rolling basis starting 2/1; must reply by 5/1 or within 4 week(s) of notification.

Transfers: Priority date 2/1. Applicants notified on a rolling basis starting 2/1; must reply by 5/1 or within 4 week(s) of notification.

CONTACT

Richard Moeggenberg, Director of Financial Aid
33 East College Street, Hillsdale, MI 49242
(517) 607-2350

Hope College

Holland, Michigan
www.hope.edu   Federal Code: 002273

4-year private liberal arts college in small city, affiliated with Reformed Church in America.

Enrollment: 3,135 undergrads, 2% part-time. 819 full-time freshmen.

Selectivity: Admits over 75% of applicants.

BASIC COSTS (2008-2009)

Tuition and fees: $24,920.

Room and board: $7,650.

Additional info: Tuition/fee waivers available for minority students.

FINANCIAL AID PICTURE (2007-2008)

Students with need: Out of 691 full-time freshmen who applied for aid, 526 were judged to have need. Of these, 525 received aid, and 140 had their full need met. Average financial aid package met 86% of need; average scholarship/grant was $15,276; average loan was $4,454. For part-time students, average financial aid package was $8,118.

Students without need: 236 full-time freshmen who did not demonstrate need for aid received scholarships/grants; average award was $6,605. No-

need awards available for academics, alumni affiliation, art, minority status, music/drama, religious affiliation.

Scholarships offered: Merit Scholarships: $3,000-$17,000 per year. Talent Awards: $2,500; for music, art, theater, creative writing.

Cumulative student debt: 66% of graduating class had student loans; average debt was $23,554.

FINANCIAL AID PROCEDURES

Forms required: FAFSA, institutional form.

Dates and Deadlines: Priority date 3/1; no closing date. Applicants notified on a rolling basis starting 3/25.

Transfers: No deadline. Applicants notified on a rolling basis starting 3/25.

CONTACT

Phyllis Hooyman, Director of Financial Aid
69 East 10th Street, Holland, MI 49422-9000
(888) 439-8907

International Academy of Design and Technology: Detroit

Troy, Michigan
www.iadtdetroit.com/

4-year for-profit visual arts and technical college in small city.

Enrollment: 948 undergrads.

Selectivity: Open admission.

BASIC COSTS (2007-2008)

Tuition and fees: $16,620.

FINANCIAL AID PICTURE (2006-2007)

Students with need: 36% of average financial aid package awarded as scholarships/grants, 64% awarded as loans/jobs.

FINANCIAL AID PROCEDURES

Dates and Deadlines: No deadline.

CONTACT

Maureen Malane
1850 Research Drive, Troy, MI 48083

Jackson Community College

Jackson, Michigan
www.jccmi.edu   Federal Code: 002274

2-year public community college in small city.

Enrollment: 6,173 undergrads.

Selectivity: Open admission; but selective for some programs.

BASIC COSTS (2007-2008)

Tuition and fees: $2,955; out-of-district residents $4,035; out-of-state residents $5,205.

Per-credit charge: $83; out-of-district residents $118; out-of-state residents $157.

FINANCIAL AID PICTURE (2007-2008)

Students with need: 85% of average financial aid package awarded as scholarships/grants, 15% awarded as loans/jobs. Need-based aid available for part-time students. Work study available nights, weekends, and for part-time students.

Students without need: No-need awards available for academics, art, leadership, music/drama, state/district residency.

FINANCIAL AID PROCEDURES

Forms required: FAFSA, institutional form.

Dates and Deadlines: Priority date 6/15; no closing date. Applicants notified on a rolling basis starting 3/1.

CONTACT
Anthony Rana
2111 Emmons Road, Jackson, MI 49201-8399
(517) 796-8436

Kalamazoo College
Kalamazoo, Michigan
www.kzoo.edu
Federal Code: 002275

4-year private liberal arts college in small city.
Enrollment: 1,340 undergrads. 363 full-time freshmen.
Selectivity: Admits 50 to 75% of applicants.

BASIC COSTS (2008-2009)
Tuition and fees: $30,823.
Room and board: $7,443.

FINANCIAL AID PICTURE
Students with need: Need-based aid available for full-time students. Work study available nights, weekends, and for part-time students.
Students without need: No-need awards available for academics, alumni affiliation.
Scholarships offered: Honors Scholarship; $5,000 - $14,000; based on academic and co-curricular record and accomplishments; varied number awarded. Competitive Scholarships; $2,000; based on written exam in a subject area or a fine arts audition.
Additional info: Paid career development internship and senior project experiences available on campus.

FINANCIAL AID PROCEDURES
Forms required: FAFSA, institutional form. CSS PROFILE required for Early Decision applicants requesting need-based financial aid.
Dates and Deadlines: Priority date 2/15; no closing date. Applicants notified on a rolling basis starting 3/21; must reply by 5/1.
Transfers: Closing date 3/1.

CONTACT
Marian Stowers, Director of Financial Aid
Kalamazoo College Office of Admission, Kalamazoo, MI 49006-3295
(269) 337-7192

Kalamazoo Valley Community College
Kalamazoo, Michigan
www.kvcc.edu
Federal Code: 006949

2-year public community college in small city.
Enrollment: 10,056 undergrads.
Selectivity: Open admission.

BASIC COSTS (2007-2008)
Tuition and fees: $1,980; out-of-district residents $3,150; out-of-state residents $4,230.
Per-credit charge: $66; out-of-district residents $105; out-of-state residents $141.

FINANCIAL AID PICTURE
Students with need: Need-based aid available for full-time and part-time students. Work study available nights, weekends, and for part-time students.
Students without need: No-need awards available for academics, athletics.

FINANCIAL AID PROCEDURES
Forms required: FAFSA, institutional form.
Dates and Deadlines: Priority date 6/1; no closing date. Applicants notified on a rolling basis starting 5/1; must reply within 2 week(s) of notification.

CONTACT
Roger Miller, Director of Financial Aid
6767 West O Avenue, Kalamazoo, MI 49003-4070
(269) 488-4340

Kellogg Community College
Battle Creek, Michigan
www.kellogg.edu
Federal Code: 002276

2-year public community college in small city.
Enrollment: 4,368 undergrads, 62% part-time. 547 full-time freshmen.
Selectivity: Open admission; but selective for some programs.

BASIC COSTS (2007-2008)
Tuition and fees: $2,265; out-of-district residents $3,540; out-of-state residents $4,980.

FINANCIAL AID PICTURE (2007-2008)
Students with need: 34% of average financial aid package awarded as scholarships/grants, 66% awarded as loans/jobs. Need-based aid available for part-time students. Work study available nights.
Students without need: No-need awards available for academics, alumni affiliation, athletics.

FINANCIAL AID PROCEDURES
Forms required: FAFSA, institutional form.
Dates and Deadlines: Priority date 4/1; no closing date. Applicants notified on a rolling basis starting 4/1.
Transfers: No deadline. Applicants notified on a rolling basis.

CONTACT
Bernice LaFleur, Director, Financial Aid
450 North Avenue, Battle Creek, MI 49017-3397
(269) 965-4123

Kendall College of Art and Design of Ferris State University
Grand Rapids, Michigan
www.kcad.edu
Federal Code: 002260

4-year public visual arts college in large city.
Enrollment: 1,043 undergrads.
Selectivity: Admits over 75% of applicants.

BASIC COSTS (2007-2008)
Tuition and fees: $13,094; out-of-state residents $19,640.
Additional info: Studio art courses: $540 per credit hour in-state and $809 out-of-state. General education courses: $282 per credit hour in-state and $423 out-of-state.

FINANCIAL AID PICTURE
Students with need: Need-based aid available for full-time and part-time students. Work study available nights, weekends, and for part-time students.
Students without need: This college awards aid only to students with need.

FINANCIAL AID PROCEDURES
Forms required: FAFSA.
Dates and Deadlines: Closing date 2/15. Applicants notified on a rolling basis starting 4/15; must reply within 4 week(s) of notification.

CONTACT
Lori Deforest, Financial Aid Officer
17 Fountain Street NW, Grand Rapids, MI 49503-3002
(616) 451-2787

Kettering University
Flint, Michigan
www.kettering.edu   Federal Code: 002262

4-year private university and engineering college in small city.
Enrollment: 2,178 undergrads. 397 full-time freshmen.
Selectivity: Admits 50 to 75% of applicants. GED not accepted.

BASIC COSTS (2007-2008)
Tuition and fees: $25,658.
Per-credit charge: $789.
Room and board: $5,798.

FINANCIAL AID PICTURE (2006-2007)
Students with need: Out of 365 full-time freshmen who applied for aid, 333 were judged to have need. Of these, 333 received aid, and 27 had their full need met. Average financial aid package met 71% of need; average scholarship/grant was $12,579; average loan was $2,513. Need-based aid available for part-time students.
Students without need: 58 full-time freshmen who did not demonstrate need for aid received scholarships/grants; average award was $8,172. No-need awards available for academics, leadership, state/district residency.
Scholarships offered: Various scholarships; $20,000-$40,000 for 4 years; based on merit. Renewable scholarships; $250-$5,000 per year.
Cumulative student debt: 80% of graduating class had student loans; average debt was $47,487.

FINANCIAL AID PROCEDURES
Forms required: FAFSA.
Dates and Deadlines: Priority date 2/14; no closing date. Applicants notified on a rolling basis starting 2/1; must reply within 2 week(s) of notification.
Transfers: No deadline. Applicants notified on a rolling basis starting 2/7; must reply within 2 week(s) of notification.

CONTACT
Diane Bice, Director of Financial Aid
1700 West Third Avenue, Flint, MI 48504-4898
(810) 762-7859

Kirtland Community College
Roscommon, Michigan
www.kirtland.edu   Federal Code: 007171

2-year public community college in rural community.
Enrollment: 1,488 undergrads, 57% part-time. 159 full-time freshmen.
Selectivity: Open admission; but selective for some programs.

BASIC COSTS (2007-2008)
Tuition and fees: $2,753; out-of-district residents $4,596; out-of-state residents $5,550.
Per-credit charge: $74; out-of-district residents $135; out-of-state residents $167.
Room and board: $4,400.
Additional info: Tuition/fee waivers available for minority students.

FINANCIAL AID PICTURE (2007-2008)
Students with need: Average financial aid package met 50% of need; average scholarship/grant was $3,675; average loan was $913. For part-time students, average financial aid package was $3,335.
Students without need: No-need awards available for academics, athletics, minority status.
Cumulative student debt: 61% of graduating class had student loans; average debt was $4,029.
Additional info: Federal, state, and institutional work-study programs available.

FINANCIAL AID PROCEDURES
Forms required: FAFSA.
Dates and Deadlines: Priority date 5/1; no closing date. Applicants notified on a rolling basis.
Transfers: No deadline.

CONTACT
Christin Horndt, Director of Financial Aid
10775 North Saint Helen Road, Roscommon, MI 48653
(989) 275-5121

Kuyper College
Grand Rapids, Michigan
www.kuyper.edu   Federal Code: 002311

4-year private Bible college in large city, affiliated with Reformed Church.
Enrollment: 291 undergrads, 14% part-time. 67 full-time freshmen.
Selectivity: Admits less than 50% of applicants.

BASIC COSTS (2007-2008)
Tuition and fees: $12,685.
Room and board: $6,100.

FINANCIAL AID PICTURE (2007-2008)
Students with need: Out of 62 full-time freshmen who applied for aid, 53 were judged to have need. Of these, 53 received aid, and 9 had their full need met. Average financial aid package met 71% of need; average scholarship/grant was $7,491; average loan was $2,607. For part-time students, average financial aid package was $9,219.
Students without need: 2 full-time freshmen who did not demonstrate need for aid received scholarships/grants; average award was $4,625. No-need awards available for academics, leadership, minority status.
Scholarships offered: Kuyper Achievement Awards: $1,000-$6,000; GPA of 3.0-4.0, ACT of 21 and above. Christian Leadership Scholarship: $1,500 renewable annually; based on Christian service activities, 3.2 cumulative GPA.
Cumulative student debt: 74% of graduating class had student loans; average debt was $19,738.

FINANCIAL AID PROCEDURES
Forms required: FAFSA, institutional form.
Dates and Deadlines: Priority date 3/1; no closing date. Applicants notified on a rolling basis starting 3/15; must reply within 2 week(s) of notification.

CONTACT
Agnes Russell, Director of Financial Aid
3333 East Beltline Avenue Northeast, Grand Rapids, MI 49525-9749
(616) 988-3656

Lake Michigan College
Benton Harbor, Michigan
www.lakemichigancollege.edu   Federal Code: 002277

2-year public community college in large town.
Enrollment: 2,916 undergrads, 60% part-time. 428 full-time freshmen.
Selectivity: Open admission; but selective for some programs.

BASIC COSTS (2007-2008)
Tuition and fees: $3,105; out-of-district residents $4,170; out-of-state residents $5,190.
Per-credit charge: $73; out-of-district residents $108; out-of-state residents $142.
Additional info: Tuition/fee waivers available for adults.

FINANCIAL AID PICTURE (2006-2007)
Students with need: 91% of average financial aid package awarded as scholarships/grants, 9% awarded as loans/jobs.

FINANCIAL AID PROCEDURES

Forms required: FAFSA.

Dates and Deadlines: Priority date 3/1; no closing date. Applicants notified on a rolling basis; must reply within 2 week(s) of notification.

CONTACT

Anne Tews, Director of Financial Aid
2755 East Napier Avenue, Benton Harbor, MI 49022-1899
(269) 927-8100 ext. 5200

Lake Superior State University
Sault Ste. Marie, Michigan
www.lssu.edu   Federal Code: 002293

4-year public university in small city.

Enrollment: 2,455 undergrads, 16% part-time. 466 full-time freshmen.

Selectivity: Admits over 75% of applicants.

BASIC COSTS (2007-2008)

Tuition and fees: $7,386; out-of-state residents $14,562.

Per-credit charge: $299; out-of-state residents $598.

Room and board: $7,172.

Additional info: Residents of Ontario pay in-state tuition. Residents of Kansas, Minnesota, Missouri, Nebraska, and North Dakota eligible for Midwest Consortium agreement rate of $449 per credit.

FINANCIAL AID PICTURE (2006-2007)

Students with need: Out of 439 full-time freshmen who applied for aid, 428 were judged to have need. Of these, 428 received aid. Average financial aid package met 70% of need; average scholarship/grant was $4,298; average loan was $3,111. For part-time students, average financial aid package was $5,542.

Students without need: 8 full-time freshmen who did not demonstrate need for aid received scholarships/grants; average award was $3,379. No-need awards available for academics, alumni affiliation, athletics, state/district residency.

Scholarships offered: *Merit:* Board of Trustees Michigan Valedictorian Scholarship; up to $1,200 per year. Board of Trustees Academic Achievement Scholarship; up to $1,500 per year; 3.0 GPA and 19 ACT score. Board of Trustees Academic Honors Scholarship; up to $2,000 per year; 3.5 GPA and 24 ACT score. Board of Trustees Academic Excellence Scholarship; up to $4,000 per year; 3.7 GPA and 25 ACT score. Board of Trustees Distinguished Scholarship; up to $6,000 per year; 3.8 GPA and 27 ACT score. *Athletic:* 42 full-time freshmen received athletic scholarships; average amount $5,226.

Cumulative student debt: 69% of graduating class had student loans; average debt was $21,147.

FINANCIAL AID PROCEDURES

Forms required: FAFSA.

Dates and Deadlines: Priority date 2/21; no closing date. Applicants notified on a rolling basis starting 11/1; must reply within 3 week(s) of notification.

Transfers: Closing date 3/1. Applicants notified on a rolling basis starting 3/1.

CONTACT

Deborah Faust, Director of Financial Aid
650 West Easterday Avenue, Sault Ste. Marie, MI 49783-1699
(906) 635-2678

Lansing Community College
Lansing, Michigan
www.lansing.cc.mi.us   Federal Code: 002278

2-year public community college in small city.

Enrollment: 13,453 undergrads, 65% part-time. 1,313 full-time freshmen.

Selectivity: Open admission; but selective for some programs.

BASIC COSTS (2007-2008)

Tuition and fees: $2,100; out-of-district residents $3,650; out-of-state residents $5,450.

Per-credit charge: $67; out-of-district residents $120; out-of-state residents $180.

FINANCIAL AID PICTURE

Students with need: Need-based aid available for full-time and part-time students. Work study available nights, weekends, and for part-time students.

Students without need: No-need awards available for academics, athletics.

FINANCIAL AID PROCEDURES

Forms required: FAFSA.

Dates and Deadlines: Priority date 7/5; no closing date. Applicants notified on a rolling basis starting 4/3.

Transfers: Priority date 7/15.

CONTACT

Stephanie Bogard, Director, Financial Aid
422 North Washington Square, Lansing, MI 48901
(517) 483-1790

Lawrence Technological University
Southfield, Michigan
www.ltu.edu   Federal Code: 002279

4-year private university in small city.

Enrollment: 2,361 undergrads, 30% part-time. 309 full-time freshmen.

Selectivity: Admits 50 to 75% of applicants.

BASIC COSTS (2008-2009)

Tuition and fees: $21,979.

Per-credit charge: $722.

Room and board: $8,071.

FINANCIAL AID PICTURE (2006-2007)

Students with need: Out of 289 full-time freshmen who applied for aid, 225 were judged to have need. Of these, 225 received aid, and 58 had their full need met. Average financial aid package met 72% of need; average scholarship/grant was $8,301; average loan was $2,662. For part-time students, average financial aid package was $11,073.

Students without need: 40 full-time freshmen who did not demonstrate need for aid received scholarships/grants; average award was $6,869. No-need awards available for academics, alumni affiliation, job skills, minority status, ROTC, state/district residency.

Cumulative student debt: 66% of graduating class had student loans; average debt was $32,367.

Additional info: March 1 state deadline for Michigan Competitive Scholarship and Michigan Tuition Grant.

FINANCIAL AID PROCEDURES

Forms required: FAFSA.

Dates and Deadlines: Priority date 4/1; no closing date. Applicants notified on a rolling basis starting 3/1; must reply within 2 week(s) of notification.

CONTACT

Mark Martin, Director of Student Financial Aid
21000 West Ten Mile Road, Southfield, MI 48075-1058
(248) 204-2121

Macomb Community College
Warren, Michigan
www.macomb.edu   Federal Code: 008906

2-year public community college in small city.

Enrollment: 12,902 undergrads, 63% part-time. 769 full-time freshmen.

Selectivity: Open admission; but selective for some programs.

BASIC COSTS (2007-2008)

Tuition and fees: $2,140; out-of-district residents $3,250; out-of-state residents $4,210.

Per-credit charge: $70; out-of-district residents $107; out-of-state residents $139.

FINANCIAL AID PICTURE (2006-2007)

Students with need: Need-based aid available for part-time students. Work study available nights, weekends, and for part-time students.

Students without need: No-need awards available for academics, athletics, leadership, music/drama, state/district residency.

FINANCIAL AID PROCEDURES

Forms required: FAFSA, institutional form.

Dates and Deadlines: Priority date 4/15; no closing date. Applicants notified on a rolling basis starting 5/15; must reply within 2 week(s) of notification.

Transfers: Must submit financial aid transcripts from all institutions attended.

CONTACT

Judy Florian, Director of Financial Aid
14500 East Twelve Mile Road, Warren, MI 48088-3896
(586) 445-7228

Madonna University

Livonia, Michigan
www.madonna.edu
Federal Code: 002282

4-year private university and liberal arts college in small city, affiliated with Roman Catholic Church.

Enrollment: 2,779 undergrads, 45% part-time. 157 full-time freshmen.

Selectivity: Admits over 75% of applicants.

BASIC COSTS (2007-2008)

Tuition and fees: $11,680.

Per-credit charge: $386.

Room and board: $6,092.

Additional info: Nursing students pay $437 per credit hour. Nonresident aliens pay $2,500 deposit.

FINANCIAL AID PICTURE (2006-2007)

Students with need: Out of 123 full-time freshmen who applied for aid, 89 were judged to have need. Of these, 89 received aid, and 20 had their full need met. Average financial aid package met 60% of need; average scholarship/grant was $5,283; average loan was $1,980. For part-time students, average financial aid package was $5,779.

Students without need: 42 full-time freshmen who did not demonstrate need for aid received scholarships/grants; average award was $3,308. No-need awards available for academics, alumni affiliation, art, athletics, minority status, music/drama, religious affiliation, state/district residency.

Scholarships offered: 23 full-time freshmen received athletic scholarships; average amount $1,970.

FINANCIAL AID PROCEDURES

Forms required: FAFSA.

Dates and Deadlines: Priority date 2/21; no closing date. Applicants notified on a rolling basis starting 4/1; must reply by 9/1 or within 2 week(s) of notification.

Transfers: Deadline for state aid is May 15.

CONTACT

Chris Ziegler, Director of Financial Aid
36600 Schoolcraft Road, Livonia, MI 48150-1176
(734) 432-5664

Marygrove College

Detroit, Michigan
www.marygrove.edu
Federal Code: 002284

4-year private liberal arts college in very large city, affiliated with Roman Catholic Church.

Enrollment: 700 undergrads.

BASIC COSTS (2007-2008)

Tuition and fees: $14,690.

Per-credit charge: $512.

Room and board: $6,600.

FINANCIAL AID PICTURE

Students with need: Need-based aid available for full-time and part-time students.

Students without need: This college awards aid only to students with need.

FINANCIAL AID PROCEDURES

Forms required: FAFSA, institutional form.

Dates and Deadlines: Priority date 3/15; no closing date. Applicants notified on a rolling basis starting 5/15; must reply within 2 week(s) of notification.

CONTACT

Patricia Chaplin, Director of Financial Aid
8425 West McNichols Road, Detroit, MI 48221
(313) 927-1245

Michigan Jewish Institute

Oak Park, Michigan
www.mji.edu
Federal Code: 032843

4-year private business and liberal arts college in very large city, affiliated with Jewish faith.

Enrollment: 75 undergrads.

BASIC COSTS (2007-2008)

Tuition and fees: $10,800.

Per-credit charge: $336.

FINANCIAL AID PICTURE

Students with need: Work study available nights, weekends, and for part-time students.

Students without need: No-need awards available for academics.

Scholarships offered: Cooperative Computing program scholarships. Partial scholarships available for some programs.

FINANCIAL AID PROCEDURES

Transfers: Priority date 3/1; no deadline. Applicants notified on a rolling basis; must reply within 5 week(s) of notification.

CONTACT

Fran Herman, Registrar/Financial Aid Administrator
25401 Coolidge Highway, Oak Park, MI 48237
(248) 414-6900 ext. 102

Michigan State University

East Lansing, Michigan
www.msu.edu
Federal Code: 002290

4-year public university in small city.

Enrollment: 35,772 undergrads, 8% part-time. 7,408 full-time freshmen.

Selectivity: Admits 50 to 75% of applicants.

BASIC COSTS (2007-2008)

Tuition and fees: $9,640; out-of-state residents $23,500.
Per-credit charge: $280; out-of-state residents $742.
Room and board: $6,676.

FINANCIAL AID PICTURE (2007-2008)

Students with need: Out of 5,151 full-time freshmen who applied for aid, 3,296 were judged to have need. Of these, 3,282 received aid, and 1,078 had their full need met. Average financial aid package met 79% of need; average scholarship/grant was $7,339; average loan was $3,385. For part-time students, average financial aid package was $8,282.
Students without need: This college awards aid only to students with need.
Scholarships offered: 85 full-time freshmen received athletic scholarships; average amount $16,428.
Cumulative student debt: 59% of graduating class had student loans; average debt was $21,175.

FINANCIAL AID PROCEDURES

Forms required: FAFSA.
Dates and Deadlines: Priority date 3/15; no closing date. Applicants notified on a rolling basis starting 3/15; must reply within 4 week(s) of notification.

CONTACT

Richard Shipman, Director of Financial Aid
250 Administration Building, East Lansing, MI 48824
(517) 353-5940

Michigan Technological University

Houghton, Michigan
www.mtu.edu   Federal Code: 002292

4-year public university in small town.
Enrollment: 5,722 undergrads, 8% part-time. 1,221 full-time freshmen.
Selectivity: Admits over 75% of applicants.

BASIC COSTS (2007-2008)

Tuition and fees: $9,829; out-of-state residents $21,589.
Per-credit charge: $306; out-of-state residents $698.
Room and board: $7,315.

FINANCIAL AID PICTURE (2007-2008)

Students with need: Out of 986 full-time freshmen who applied for aid, 714 were judged to have need. Of these, 714 received aid, and 252 had their full need met. Average financial aid package met 84% of need; average scholarship/grant was $7,523; average loan was $4,146. Need-based aid available for part-time students.
Students without need: 343 full-time freshmen who did not demonstrate need for aid received scholarships/grants; average award was $3,317. No-need awards available for academics, alumni affiliation, art, athletics, job skills, leadership, ROTC, state/district residency.
Scholarships offered: *Merit:* Leading Scholar Awards; full tuition, room and board, plus $1,000; based on merit, Michigan residency, recommendation by high school teacher by mid-October of senior year. Presidential Scholars Program; $1,000 to $8,000; based on merit, Michigan residency. Merit Scholarships; $1,000-$2,000; based on merit and need, U.S. citizenship, finalist status in National Merit Scholarship Qualifying Test. National Scholars Program; $6,000-$12,000; merit-based for non-Michigan resident of U.S. or Canada. Alumni Legacy Award; equal to difference between resident and nonresident tuition; for non-Michigan residents who are children or grandchildren of alumni. Michigan Tech Alumni Legacy Award; $250 per year for maximum of 4 years; for Michigan residents who are children or grandchildren of alumni.
Athletic: 39 full-time freshmen received athletic scholarships; average amount $8,826.
Cumulative student debt: 65% of graduating class had student loans; average debt was $14,223.

FINANCIAL AID PROCEDURES

Forms required: FAFSA.
Dates and Deadlines: Priority date 2/16; no closing date. Applicants notified on a rolling basis starting 3/1; must reply within 4 week(s) of notification.
Transfers: Students transferring to Michigan Tech after one year or more attendance at a Michigan community college will be considered for an award from the Michigan Community College Scholarship program.

CONTACT

Timothy Malette, Director of Financial Aid
1400 Townsend Drive, Houghton, MI 49931-1295
(906) 487-2622

Mid Michigan Community College

Harrison, Michigan
www.midmich.edu   Federal Code: 006768

2-year public community college in small town.
Enrollment: 1,741 full-time undergrads.
Selectivity: Open admission; but selective for some programs.

BASIC COSTS (2007-2008)

Tuition and fees: $2,298; out-of-district residents $3,698; out-of-state residents $7,170.
Per-credit charge: $73; out-of-district residents $119; out-of-state residents $235.
Additional info: Tuition/fee waivers available for adults.

FINANCIAL AID PICTURE

Students with need: Need-based aid available for full-time and part-time students.
Students without need: No-need awards available for academics.
Scholarships offered: Scholastic Incentive Scholarships; $350 per semester; for any student who completes full-time semester, is enrolled full-time for next regular semester, maintains 3.5-3.89 GPA. $500 per semester for students meeting above criteria, maintaining 3.9-4.0 GPA.

FINANCIAL AID PROCEDURES

Forms required: FAFSA, institutional form.
Dates and Deadlines: Priority date 5/1; no closing date. Applicants notified on a rolling basis starting 4/1; must reply within 2 week(s) of notification.

CONTACT

Gale Crandell, Financial Aid Director
1375 South Clare Avenue, Harrison, MI 48625
(989) 386-6622

Monroe County Community College

Monroe, Michigan
www.monroeccc.edu   Federal Code: 002294

2-year public community college in large town.
Enrollment: 4,433 undergrads.
Selectivity: Open admission; but selective for some programs.

BASIC COSTS (2007-2008)

Tuition and fees: $2,150; out-of-district residents $3,530; out-of-state residents $3,890.
Per-credit charge: $68; out-of-district residents $116; out-of-state residents $128.
Additional info: Tuition/fee waivers available for minority students.

FINANCIAL AID PICTURE

Students with need: Need-based aid available for full-time and part-time students. Work study available nights, weekends, and for part-time students.

Students without need: No-need awards available for academics, alumni affiliation, art, leadership, music/drama, state/district residency.

FINANCIAL AID PROCEDURES

Forms required: FAFSA, institutional form.

Dates and Deadlines: Priority date 4/1; no closing date. Applicants notified on a rolling basis starting 4/1; must reply within 2 week(s) of notification.

CONTACT

Tracy Vogt, Director of Financial Aid/Placement
1555 South Raisinville Road, Monroe, MI 48161-9746
(734) 384-4135

Montcalm Community College
Sidney, Michigan
www.montcalm.edu   Federal Code: 002295

2-year public community and liberal arts college in rural community.

Enrollment: 2,356 undergrads, 48% part-time. 202 full-time freshmen.

Selectivity: Open admission; but selective for some programs.

BASIC COSTS (2007-2008)

Tuition and fees: $2,265; out-of-district residents $3,465; out-of-state residents $4,425.

Per-credit charge: $70; out-of-district residents $111; out-of-state residents $149.

FINANCIAL AID PICTURE

Students with need: Need-based aid available for full-time and part-time students.

Students without need: No-need awards available for academics, state/district residency.

FINANCIAL AID PROCEDURES

Forms required: FAFSA, institutional form.

Dates and Deadlines: Priority date 2/15; no closing date. Applicants notified on a rolling basis starting 6/15; must reply within 2 week(s) of notification.

Transfers: Priority date 4/1.

CONTACT

Rebecca Powell, Director of Financial Aid
2800 College Drive, Sidney, MI 48885
(989) 328-1228

Mott Community College
Flint, Michigan
www.mcc.edu   Federal Code: 002261

2-year public community college in large city.

Enrollment: 7,255 undergrads, 65% part-time. 375 full-time freshmen.

Selectivity: Open admission; but selective for some programs.

BASIC COSTS (2007-2008)

Tuition and fees: $2,712; out-of-district residents $3,942; out-of-state residents $5,172.

Per-credit charge: $82; out-of-district residents $123; out-of-state residents $164.

FINANCIAL AID PICTURE (2006-2007)

Students with need: 56% of average financial aid package awarded as scholarships/grants, 44% awarded as loans/jobs. Need-based aid available for part-time students. Work study available nights.

Students without need: No-need awards available for academics, alumni affiliation, art, athletics, leadership, minority status, music/drama, state/district residency.

FINANCIAL AID PROCEDURES

Forms required: FAFSA.

Dates and Deadlines: No deadline. Applicants notified on a rolling basis starting 5/1.

Transfers: Pell Grants adjusted for amount used at another institution.

CONTACT

Troy Boquette, Executive Director of Student Financial Services
1401 East Court Street, Flint, MI 48503-2089
(810) 762-0144

Muskegon Community College
Muskegon, Michigan
www.muskegoncc.edu   Federal Code: 002297

2-year public community college in small city.

Enrollment: 4,707 undergrads.

Selectivity: Open admission; but selective for some programs.

BASIC COSTS (2007-2008)

Tuition and fees: $2,270; out-of-district residents $3,470; out-of-state residents $4,610.

Per-credit charge: $67; out-of-district residents $107; out-of-state residents $145.

Additional info: Students also assessed contact hour fees, which vary according to residency status, and course fees, which vary.

FINANCIAL AID PICTURE

Students with need: Work study available nights, weekends, and for part-time students.

FINANCIAL AID PROCEDURES

Forms required: FAFSA, institutional form.

Dates and Deadlines: Priority date 5/1; no closing date. Applicants notified on a rolling basis starting 6/1; must reply within 2 week(s) of notification.

CONTACT

Bruce Wierda, Director of Financial Aid
221 South Quarterline Road, Muskegon, MI 49442
(231) 777-0221

North Central Michigan College
Petoskey, Michigan
www.ncmich.edu   Federal Code: 002299

2-year public community college in small town.

Enrollment: 2,228 undergrads.

Selectivity: Open admission; but selective for some programs.

BASIC COSTS (2007-2008)

Tuition and fees: $2,286; out-of-district residents $3,549; out-of-state residents $4,444.

Per-credit charge: $68; out-of-district residents $110; out-of-state residents $140.

Room only: $2,520.

FINANCIAL AID PICTURE

Students with need: Need-based aid available for full-time and part-time students. Work study available nights, weekends, and for part-time students.

FINANCIAL AID PROCEDURES

Forms required: FAFSA, institutional form.

Dates and Deadlines: Closing date 4/1. Applicants notified on a rolling basis starting 4/30.

CONTACT

Virginia Panoff, Director of Financial Aid
1515 Howard Street, Petoskey, MI 49770
(231) 348-6627

Northern Michigan University

Marquette, Michigan
www.nmu.edu   Federal Code: 002301

4-year public university in large town.

Enrollment: 8,287 undergrads, 7% part-time. 1,754 full-time freshmen.

Selectivity: Admits over 75% of applicants.

BASIC COSTS (2007-2008)

Tuition and fees: $6,709; out-of-state residents $10,645.

Per-credit charge: $256; out-of-state residents $420.

Room and board: $7,220.

Additional info: Excludes one-time $200 athletic fee for first time freshmen. All full-time students provided with laptop computer as part of tuition and fees. Tuition/fee waivers available for minority students.

FINANCIAL AID PICTURE (2006-2007)

Students with need: Out of 1,605 full-time freshmen who applied for aid, 1,074 were judged to have need. Of these, 1,044 received aid, and 265 had their full need met. Average financial aid package met 67% of need; average scholarship/grant was $3,665; average loan was $3,025. For part-time students, average financial aid package was $6,537.

Students without need: 143 full-time freshmen who did not demonstrate need for aid received scholarships/grants; average award was $2,845. No-need awards available for academics, alumni affiliation; art, athletics, leadership, minority status, music/drama, religious affiliation, ROTC, state/district residency.

Scholarships offered: *Merit:* Talent recognition awards: available in art and design, music, theater. Freshman Fellowship: $1,000 in student employment; 3.5 GPA and ACT 24. Dr. Edgar L. Harden Scholarship: 3.5 GPA and ACT 24. National Academic Award: $3,300; minimum 3.0 GPA and ACT 19; awarded to non-Michigan residents. NMU Merit Excellence Award: $2,750-$3,500; based on 3.0 GPA and 33 ACT. NMU Merit Award: $2,250-$3,000; 3.0 GPA and 30-32 ACT. NMU Scholars Award: $1,250-$2,000; 3.0 GPA and ACT 27-29. NMU Outstanding Achievement: $750-$1,500; 3.0 GPA and 25-26 ACT. *Athletic:* 14 full-time freshmen received athletic scholarships; average amount $5,170.

Cumulative student debt: 62% of graduating class had student loans; average debt was $19,730.

Additional info: Audition or portfolio required for music, drama, and art scholarship applicants. Alumni Dependent Tuition Program gives resident tuition rates to nonresident dependents of NMU alumni who received master's, baccalaureate, or associate degree; renewable.

FINANCIAL AID PROCEDURES

Forms required: FAFSA.

Dates and Deadlines: Priority date 3/1; no closing date. Applicants notified on a rolling basis starting 4/1; must reply within 2 week(s) of notification. **Transfers:** No deadline. Applicants notified on a rolling basis starting 4/1; must reply within 2 week(s) of notification. Merit-based transfer scholarships available.

CONTACT

Michael Rotundo, Director of Financial Aid
1401 Presque Isle Avenue, Marquette, MI 49855
(906) 227-2327

Northwestern Michigan College

Traverse City, Michigan
www.nmc.edu   Federal Code: 002302

2-year public community and maritime college in small city.

Enrollment: 4,000 undergrads.

Selectivity: Open admission; but selective for some programs.

BASIC COSTS (2007-2008)

Tuition and fees: $2,722; out-of-district residents $4,597; out-of-state residents $5,621.

Per-credit charge: $73; out-of-district residents $132; out-of-state residents $164.

Room and board: $6,800.

Additional info: Tuition/fee waivers available for adults, minority students, unemployed or children of unemployed.

FINANCIAL AID PICTURE

Students with need: Need-based aid available for full-time and part-time students. Work study available nights, weekends, and for part-time students. **Students without need:** No-need awards available for academics, art, job skills, leadership, minority status, music/drama, ROTC, state/district residency.

FINANCIAL AID PROCEDURES

Forms required: FAFSA.

Dates and Deadlines: Priority date 4/1; no closing date. Applicants notified on a rolling basis starting 5/1; must reply within 2 week(s) of notification.

CONTACT

Deb Faas, Director for Financial Aid
1701 East Front Street, Traverse City, MI 49686
(231) 995-1035

Northwood University: Michigan

Midland, Michigan
www.northwood.edu   Federal Code: 004072

4-year private university and business college in large town.

Enrollment: 1,979 undergrads, 4% part-time. 450 full-time freshmen.

Selectivity: Admits over 75% of applicants.

BASIC COSTS (2008-2009)

Tuition and fees: $17,544.

Per-credit charge: $346.

Room and board: $7,548.

FINANCIAL AID PICTURE (2007-2008)

Students with need: Out of 367 full-time freshmen who applied for aid, 320 were judged to have need. Of these, 319 received aid, and 64 had their full need met. Average financial aid package met 54% of need; average scholarship/grant was $6,272; average loan was $3,194. For part-time students, average financial aid package was $6,252.

Students without need: 80 full-time freshmen who did not demonstrate need for aid received scholarships/grants; average award was $5,660. No-need awards available for academics, alumni affiliation, athletics, leadership, minority status, ROTC.

Scholarships offered: *Merit:* Academic scholarships; $4,000-$9,000; based on test scores and GPA; unlimited number awarded. *Athletic:* 19 full-time freshmen received athletic scholarships; average amount $7,053.

Cumulative student debt: 68% of graduating class had student loans; average debt was $23,980.

FINANCIAL AID PROCEDURES

Forms required: FAFSA.

Dates and Deadlines: No deadline. Applicants notified on a rolling basis starting 3/1.

CONTACT
Theresa Mieler, Financial Aid Director
4000 Whiting Drive, Midland, MI 48640
(989) 837-4230

Oakland Community College

Bloomfield Hills, Michigan
www.oaklandcc.edu   Federal Code: 002303

2-year public community college in very large city.
Enrollment: 13,598 undergrads, 68% part-time. 1,067 full-time freshmen.
Selectivity: Open admission.

BASIC COSTS (2007-2008)
Tuition and fees: $1,825; out-of-district residents $3,040; out-of-state residents $4,236.
Per-credit charge: $59; out-of-district residents $99; out-of-state residents $139.

FINANCIAL AID PICTURE (2007-2008)
Students with need: Average financial aid package met 67% of need; average scholarship/grant was $3,800; average loan was $2,500. For part-time students, average financial aid package was $5,400.
Students without need: No-need awards available for academics, athletics.
Cumulative student debt: 26% of graduating class had student loans; average debt was $4,561.

FINANCIAL AID PROCEDURES
Forms required: FAFSA.
Dates and Deadlines: Priority date 4/15; no closing date. Applicants notified on a rolling basis starting 4/15.
Transfers: Closing date 6/30. Michigan residency required for aid to transfer students.

CONTACT
Wilma Porter, Director of Financial Assistance and Scholarships
2480 Opdyke Road, Bloomfield Hills, MI 48304-2266
(248) 341-2000

Oakland University

Rochester, Michigan
www.oakland.edu   Federal Code: 002307

4-year public university in small city.
Enrollment: 13,605 undergrads, 26% part-time. 2,186 full-time freshmen.
Selectivity: Admits over 75% of applicants.

BASIC COSTS (2007-2008)
Tuition and fees: $7,575; out-of-state residents $17,625.
Room and board: $6,670.

FINANCIAL AID PICTURE (2006-2007)
Students with need: Out of 1,440 full-time freshmen who applied for aid, 946 were judged to have need. Of these, 898 received aid, and 188 had their full need met. Average financial aid package met 75% of need; average scholarship/grant was $4,188; average loan was $4,977. For part-time students, average financial aid package was $7,216.
Students without need: 495 full-time freshmen who did not demonstrate need for aid received scholarships/grants; average award was $2,403. No-need awards available for academics, art, athletics, leadership, music/drama, state/district residency.
Scholarships offered: *Merit:* Wide range of scholarships awarded on the basis of accomplishment. *Athletic:* 81 full-time freshmen received athletic scholarships; average amount $7,160.
Cumulative student debt: 49% of graduating class had student loans; average debt was $17,033.

FINANCIAL AID PROCEDURES
Forms required: FAFSA.
Dates and Deadlines: Priority date 2/15; no closing date. Applicants notified on a rolling basis starting 3/15.
Transfers: Closing date 4/1.

CONTACT
Cindy Hermsen, Director of Financial Aid
101 North Foundation Hall, Rochester, MI 48309-4401
(248) 370-2550

Olivet College

Olivet, Michigan
www.olivetcollege.edu   Federal Code: 002308

4-year private liberal arts college in rural community, affiliated with Congregational Christian Churches and United Church of Christ.
Enrollment: 920 undergrads; 6% part-time. 209 full-time freshmen.
Selectivity: Admits 50 to 75% of applicants.

BASIC COSTS (2007-2008)
Tuition and fees: $19,302.
Per-credit charge: $580.
Room and board: $6,346.

FINANCIAL AID PICTURE
Students with need: Need-based aid available for full-time and part-time students.
Students without need: This college awards aid only to students with need.
Scholarships offered: Scholarships: up to $2,000; for students who demonstrate history of community service and civic responsibility during high school or college. Academic merit scholarships: up to full tuition. All scholarships renewable for 4 years.

FINANCIAL AID PROCEDURES
Forms required: FAFSA.
Dates and Deadlines: No deadline. Applicants notified on a rolling basis starting 2/1; must reply within 3 week(s) of notification.

CONTACT
Mark DeRuiter, Vice President for Finance
Admissions Office, Olivet, MI 49076

Rochester College

Rochester Hills, Michigan
www.rc.edu   Federal Code: 002288

4-year private liberal arts college in small city, affiliated with Church of Christ.
Enrollment: 957 undergrads, 34% part-time. 100 full-time freshmen.
Selectivity: Admits over 75% of applicants.

BASIC COSTS (2007-2008)
Tuition and fees: $14,860.
Per-credit charge: $435.
Room and board: $6,920.
Additional info: Tuition at time of enrollment locked for 4 years; tuition/fee waivers available for minority students.

FINANCIAL AID PICTURE
Students with need: Need-based aid available for full-time and part-time students. Work study available nights, weekends, and for part-time students.
Students without need: No-need awards available for academics, alumni affiliation, athletics, leadership, music/drama, state/district residency.

FINANCIAL AID PROCEDURES
Forms required: FAFSA.

Dates and Deadlines: Priority date 8/1; no closing date. Applicants notified on a rolling basis starting 6/1; must reply within 2 week(s) of notification.

CONTACT
Larry Norman, Director of Financial Aid
800 West Avon Road, Rochester Hills, MI 48307
(248) 218-2029

Sacred Heart Major Seminary
Detroit, Michigan
www.shms.org   Federal Code: 002313

4-year private seminary college in very large city, affiliated with Roman Catholic Church.
Enrollment: 39 undergrads, 5% part-time. 2 full-time freshmen.
Selectivity: Admits over 75% of applicants.

BASIC COSTS (2007-2008)
Tuition and fees: $12,530.
Per-credit charge: $295.
Room and board: $7,000.
Additional info: Tuition/fee waivers available for adults.

FINANCIAL AID PICTURE (2006-2007)
Students with need: Average financial aid package met 75% of need.
Students without need: No-need awards available for academics, religious affiliation.

FINANCIAL AID PROCEDURES
Forms required: FAFSA, institutional form.
Dates and Deadlines: No deadline. Applicants notified on a rolling basis.
Transfers: No deadline. Applicants notified on a rolling basis. Must submit certified high school transcript, copy of high school diploma, copy of GED certificate showing passing score, or college transcript showing associate degree as certification of eligibility; must submit financial aid transcripts from all previous post-secondary institutions attended.

CONTACT
Jeannette Murrell, Financial Aid Officer
2701 Chicago Boulevard, Detroit, MI 48206-1799
(313) 883-8781

Saginaw Valley State University
University Center, Michigan
www.svsu.edu   Federal Code: 002314

4-year public university in small city.
Enrollment: 7,785 undergrads, 19% part-time. 1,435 full-time freshmen.
Selectivity: Admits over 75% of applicants.

BASIC COSTS (2007-2008)
Tuition and fees: $6,258; out-of-state residents $14,283.
Per-credit charge: $194; out-of-state residents $461.
Room and board: $6,630.

FINANCIAL AID PICTURE (2006-2007)
Students with need: Out of 1,385 full-time freshmen who applied for aid, 904 were judged to have need. Of these, 892 received aid, and 213 had their full need met. Average financial aid package met 67% of need; average scholarship/grant was $3,098; average loan was $2,218. For part-time students, average financial aid package was $4,615.
Students without need: 384 full-time freshmen who did not demonstrate need for aid received scholarships/grants; average award was $3,857. No-need awards available for academics, art, athletics, leadership, minority status, music/drama.

Scholarships offered: *Merit:* Presidential Scholarships; tuition and selective fees up to 136 credit hours; granted to students who are first or second in high school class with minimum 24 ACT or 3.7 GPA and 28 ACT. Dean's Scholarship; $3,000 per year for four years; 3.0 GPA and 24 ACT. University Foundation Scholarship; tuition and selective fees for four courses and $1,000 to apply toward study abroad or a research project; 3.5 GPA and 24 ACT. University Scholarship; $1,000 per year for four years; 3.5 GPA. Various private scholarships also available. *Athletic:* 83 full-time freshmen received athletic scholarships; average amount $3,007.
Cumulative student debt: 55% of graduating class had student loans; average debt was $22,535.

FINANCIAL AID PROCEDURES
Forms required: FAFSA.
Dates and Deadlines: Priority date 2/14; no closing date. Applicants notified on a rolling basis starting 3/20; must reply within 10 week(s) of notification.
Transfers: No deadline. Applicants notified on a rolling basis; must reply within 10 week(s) of notification. Community college scholarship, private scholarships, and Transfer Dean's scholarships available.

CONTACT
Robert Lemuel, Director of Scholarships and Financial Aid
7400 Bay Road, University Center, MI 48710
(989) 964-4103

Schoolcraft College
Livonia, Michigan
www.schoolcraft.edu   Federal Code: 002315

2-year public community college in small city.
Enrollment: 9,269 undergrads, 61% part-time. 1,172 full-time freshmen.
Selectivity: Open admission; but selective for some programs.

BASIC COSTS (2007-2008)
Tuition and fees: $2,290; out-of-district residents $3,280; out-of-state residents $4,810.
Per-credit charge: $70; out-of-district residents $103; out-of-state residents $154.

FINANCIAL AID PICTURE
Students with need: Need-based aid available for full-time and part-time students. Work study available nights, weekends, and for part-time students.
Students without need: No-need awards available for academics, athletics, leadership, music/drama, state/district residency.
Scholarships offered: Trustee Scholarships; $1,000-$1,200; renewable for 2nd year; based on essay, placement test, trustee application, graduation from local high school; 80 awarded.

FINANCIAL AID PROCEDURES
Forms required: FAFSA.
Dates and Deadlines: No deadline. Applicants notified on a rolling basis starting 6/1.

CONTACT
Regina Mosley, Director of Financial Aid
18600 Haggerty Road, Livonia, MI 48152-2696
(734) 462-4433

Southwestern Michigan College
Dowagiac, Michigan
www.swmich.edu   Federal Code: 002317

2-year public community college in small town.
Enrollment: 2,032 undergrads, 50% part-time. 363 full-time freshmen.
Selectivity: Open admission; but selective for some programs.

BASIC COSTS (2007-2008)

Tuition and fees: $2,978; out-of-district residents $3,623; out-of-state residents $3,863.

Per-credit charge: $78; out-of-district residents $100; out-of-state residents $108.

FINANCIAL AID PICTURE (2006-2007)

Students with need: 87% of average financial aid package awarded as scholarships/grants, 13% awarded as loans/jobs. Need-based aid available for part-time students. Work study available nights, weekends, and for part-time students.

Students without need: No-need awards available for academics, art, leadership, music/drama.

FINANCIAL AID PROCEDURES

Forms required: FAFSA, institutional form.

Dates and Deadlines: Priority date 8/1; no closing date. Applicants notified on a rolling basis starting 4/1; must reply within 2 week(s) of notification.

CONTACT

Rob Wirt, Director of Financial Aid

58900 Cherry Grove Road, Dowagiac, MI 49047-9793

(269) 782-1313

Spring Arbor University

Spring Arbor, Michigan

www.arbor.edu   Federal Code: 002318

4-year private university and liberal arts college in rural community, affiliated with Free Methodist Church of North America.

Enrollment: 2,611 undergrads, 24% part-time. 339 full-time freshmen.

Selectivity: Admits over 75% of applicants.

BASIC COSTS (2008-2009)

Tuition and fees: $19,240.

Per-credit charge: $470.

Room and board: $6,650.

FINANCIAL AID PICTURE (2007-2008)

Students with need: Out of 322 full-time freshmen who applied for aid, 279 were judged to have need. Of these, 279 received aid, and 209 had their full need met. Average financial aid package met 97% of need; average scholarship/grant was $9,643; average loan was $3,677. For part-time students, average financial aid package was $9,963.

Students without need: 9 full-time freshmen who did not demonstrate need for aid received scholarships/grants; average award was $1,586. No-need awards available for academics, art, athletics, minority status, music/drama, religious affiliation.

Scholarships offered: *Merit:* President Scholarship: $5,000. Provost Scholarship: $3,000. Faculty Scholarship: $2,000. All based on GPA, ACT, rank in class. National Merit Finalist: full tuition. National Merit Semifinalist: half-tuition. Trustee scholarship: $7,500; based on 29 ACT/1280 SAT. *Athletic:* 57 full-time freshmen received athletic scholarships; average amount $5,407.

Cumulative student debt: 86% of graduating class had student loans; average debt was $13,864.

FINANCIAL AID PROCEDURES

Forms required: FAFSA.

Dates and Deadlines: Priority date 3/1; no closing date. Applicants notified on a rolling basis starting 3/1; must reply within 2 week(s) of notification.

Transfers: No deadline. Applicants notified on a rolling basis starting 5/1; must reply within 2 week(s) of notification. Financial aid transcript required from each college previously attended.

CONTACT

Lois Hardy, Director of Financial Aid

106 East Main Street, Spring Arbor, MI 49283-9799

(517) 750-6468

University of Detroit Mercy

Detroit, Michigan

www.udmercy.edu   Federal Code: 002323

4-year private university in very large city, affiliated with Roman Catholic Church.

Enrollment: 2,989 undergrads, 28% part-time. 528 full-time freshmen.

Selectivity: Admits 50 to 75% of applicants.

BASIC COSTS (2008-2009)

Tuition and fees: $27,319.

Per-credit charge: $655.

Room and board: $8,250.

Additional info: Engineering and architecture students pay slightly higher tuition.

FINANCIAL AID PICTURE

Students with need: Need-based aid available for full-time and part-time students.

Students without need: No-need awards available for academics, alumni affiliation, athletics, leadership, minority status, music/drama, religious affiliation.

FINANCIAL AID PROCEDURES

Forms required: FAFSA.

Dates and Deadlines: Priority date 3/1; no closing date. Applicants notified on a rolling basis starting 3/1; must reply within 3 week(s) of notification.

CONTACT

Sandra Ross, Director of Scholarship and Financial Aid

4001 West McNichols Road, Detroit, MI 48221-3038

(313) 993-3350

University of Michigan

Ann Arbor, Michigan   Federal Code: 002325

www.umich.edu   CSS Code: 1839

4-year public university in small city.

Enrollment: 25,916 undergrads, 3% part-time. 5,033 full-time freshmen.

Selectivity: Admits 50 to 75% of applicants.

BASIC COSTS (2007-2008)

Tuition and fees: $10,447; out-of-state residents $31,301.

Per-credit charge: $399; out-of-state residents $1,268.

Room and board: $8,190.

FINANCIAL AID PICTURE (2006-2007)

Students with need: Out of 3,408 full-time freshmen who applied for aid, 2,428 were judged to have need. Of these, 2,428 received aid, and 2,185 had their full need met. Average financial aid package met 90% of need; average scholarship/grant was $8,825; average loan was $5,839. Need-based aid available for part-time students.

Students without need: 2,127 full-time freshmen who did not demonstrate need for aid received scholarships/grants; average award was $5,498. No-need awards available for academics, alumni affiliation, art, athletics, leadership, music/drama, religious affiliation, ROTC, state/district residency.

Scholarships offered: 125 full-time freshmen received athletic scholarships; average amount $28,069.

FINANCIAL AID PROCEDURES

Forms required: FAFSA, CSS PROFILE.

Dates and Deadlines: Priority date 2/15; closing date 4/30. Applicants notified on a rolling basis starting 3/15; must reply within 2 week(s) of notification.

Transfers: Community College Scholarship available for qualified students.

CONTACT

Pamela Fowler, Executive Financial Aid DIrector

1220 Student Activities Building, Ann Arbor, MI 48109-1316

(734) 763-6600

University of Michigan: Dearborn

Dearborn, Michigan

www.umd.umich.edu   Federal Code: 002326

4-year public university in small city.

Enrollment: 6,212 undergrads, 32% part-time. 777 full-time freshmen.

Selectivity: Admits 50 to 75% of applicants.

BASIC COSTS (2007-2008)

Tuition and fees: $8,009; out-of-state residents $17,499.

FINANCIAL AID PICTURE (2006-2007)

Students with need: Out of 570 full-time freshmen who applied for aid, 336 were judged to have need. Of these, 336 received aid, and 41 had their full need met. Average financial aid package met 47% of need; average scholarship/grant was $3,817; average loan was $2,732.

Students without need: 637 full-time freshmen who did not demonstrate need for aid received scholarships/grants; average award was $3,068. No-need awards available for academics, alumni affiliation, athletics, job skills, leadership, minority status, ROTC.

Scholarships offered: 9 full-time freshmen received athletic scholarships; average amount $1,656.

Cumulative student debt: 56% of graduating class had student loans; average debt was $22,908.

FINANCIAL AID PROCEDURES

Forms required: FAFSA.

Dates and Deadlines: Priority date 2/15; no closing date. Applicants notified on a rolling basis starting 3/1; must reply within 3 week(s) of notification.

CONTACT

Noel Hornbacher, Director of Financial Aid

4901 Evergreen Road, 1145 UC, Dearborn, MI 48128-1491

(313) 593-5000

University of Michigan: Flint

Flint, Michigan

www.umflint.edu   Federal Code: 002327

4-year public university and branch campus college in small city.

Enrollment: 5,655 undergrads, 37% part-time. 475 full-time freshmen.

Selectivity: Admits over 75% of applicants.

BASIC COSTS (2007-2008)

Tuition and fees: $7,343; out-of-state residents $13,998.

Per-credit charge: $276; out-of-state residents $552.

FINANCIAL AID PICTURE (2006-2007)

Students with need: Out of 377 full-time freshmen who applied for aid, 266 were judged to have need. Of these, 254 received aid, and 53 had their full need met. Average financial aid package met 63% of need; average scholarship/grant was $4,119; average loan was $3,034. For part-time students, average financial aid package was $5,271.

Students without need: 27 full-time freshmen who did not demonstrate need for aid received scholarships/grants; average award was $3,398. No-need awards available for academics, art, leadership, music/drama.

Cumulative student debt: 23% of graduating class had student loans; average debt was $21,201.

Additional info: SAT/ACT scores must be submitted for scholarship consideration.

FINANCIAL AID PROCEDURES

Forms required: FAFSA.

Dates and Deadlines: Priority date 3/1; no closing date. Applicants notified on a rolling basis starting 3/15.

Transfers: Must not be in default or owe refunds for Title IV aid.

CONTACT

Lori Vedder, Director of Financial Aid

303 East Kearsley Street, Flint, MI 48502-1950

(810) 762-3444

Walsh College of Accountancy and Business Administration

Troy, Michigan

www.walshcollege.edu   Federal Code: 004071

Upper-division private business college in large city.

Enrollment: 1,047 undergrads.

BASIC COSTS (2007-2008)

Tuition and fees: $8,280.

Per-credit charge: $268.

FINANCIAL AID PICTURE (2006-2007)

Students with need: Average financial aid package for all full-time undergraduates was $10,334; for part-time $10,334. 23% awarded as scholarships/grants, 77% awarded as loans/jobs.

Students without need: No-need awards available for academics.

Cumulative student debt: 40% of graduating class had student loans; average debt was $12,603.

FINANCIAL AID PROCEDURES

Forms required: FAFSA.

Dates and Deadlines: Priority date 3/23; no closing date.

Transfers: Priority date 3/1; no deadline. Applicants notified on a rolling basis.

CONTACT

Howard Thomas, Director, Financial Aid

PO Box 7006, Troy, MI 48007-7006

(248) 823-1285

Wayne County Community College

Detroit, Michigan

www.wcccd.edu   Federal Code: 009230

2-year public community and liberal arts college in very large city.

Enrollment: 17,877 undergrads, 75% part-time. 2,357 full-time freshmen.

Selectivity: Open admission.

BASIC COSTS (2007-2008)

Tuition and fees: $1,964; out-of-district residents $2,462; out-of-state residents $3,053.

Per-credit charge: $57; out-of-district residents $73; out-of-state residents $93.

FINANCIAL AID PICTURE (2006-2007)

Students with need: 73% of average financial aid package awarded as scholarships/grants, 27% awarded as loans/jobs. Need-based aid available for part-time students. Work study available nights, weekends, and for part-time students.

Additional info: High school diploma, GED, or passing grade on ABT required for financial aid.

FINANCIAL AID PROCEDURES

Forms required: FAFSA.

Dates and Deadlines: Priority date 5/1; no closing date. Applicants notified on a rolling basis starting 5/1.

CONTACT

Alma Barnett-Cleveland, Executive District Director of Financial Aid
801 West Fort Street, Detroit, MI 48226
(313) 496-2595

Wayne State University
Detroit, Michigan
www.wayne.edu   Federal Code: 002329

4-year public university in very large city.
Enrollment: 19,964 undergrads, 38% part-time. 2,505 full-time freshmen.
Selectivity: Admits over 75% of applicants.

BASIC COSTS (2007-2008)
Tuition and fees: $7,649; out-of-state residents $16,400.
Per-credit charge: $226; out-of-state residents $518.
Room and board: $6,702.

FINANCIAL AID PICTURE (2006-2007)
Students with need: Out of 1,996 full-time freshmen who applied for aid, 1,654 were judged to have need. Of these, 1,619 received aid, and 160 had their full need met. Average financial aid package met 62% of need; average scholarship/grant was $3,703; average loan was $2,646. For part-time students, average financial aid package was $9,603.
Students without need: 263 full-time freshmen who did not demonstrate need for aid received scholarships/grants; average award was $3,033. No-need awards available for academics, art, athletics, leadership, music/drama.
Scholarships offered: *Merit:* Scholars Day award; amounts vary; invitation-only for top applicants who are admitted by 1/15; requires group interview. Presidential Scholarship; full-tuition for four years; selected from Scholars Day participants. *Athletic:* 34 full-time freshmen received athletic scholarships; average amount $8,794.
Cumulative student debt: 49% of graduating class had student loans; average debt was $17,284.

FINANCIAL AID PROCEDURES
Forms required: FAFSA.
Dates and Deadlines: Priority date 3/1; no closing date. Applicants notified on a rolling basis starting 4/15; must reply within 2 week(s) of notification.
Transfers: No deadline. Applicants notified on a rolling basis starting 4/1; must reply within 2 week(s) of notification.

CONTACT
Catherine Kay, Director of Scholarships and Financial Aid
42 West Warren, Detroit, MI 48202
(313) 577-3378

West Shore Community College
Scottville, Michigan
www.westshore.edu   Federal Code: 007950

2-year public community college in rural community.
Enrollment: 517 full-time undergrads.
Selectivity: Open admission; but selective for some programs.

BASIC COSTS (2007-2008)
Tuition and fees: $2,234; out-of-district residents $3,584; out-of-state residents $4,694.
Per-credit charge: $69; out-of-district residents $114; out-of-state residents $151.

FINANCIAL AID PICTURE
Students with need: Need-based aid available for full-time and part-time students. Work study available nights, weekends, and for part-time students.

FINANCIAL AID PROCEDURES
Forms required: FAFSA.
Dates and Deadlines: Priority date 3/15; no closing date. Applicants notified on a rolling basis starting 5/15; must reply within 2 week(s) of notification.

CONTACT
Victoria Oddo, Director of Student Services
3000 North Stiles Road, Scottville, MI 49454-0277
(231) 845-6211

Western Michigan University
Kalamazoo, Michigan
www.wmich.edu   Federal Code: 002330

4-year public university in small city.
Enrollment: 19,572 undergrads, 12% part-time. 3,475 full-time freshmen.
Selectivity: Admits over 75% of applicants.

BASIC COSTS (2007-2008)
Tuition and fees: $7,260; out-of-state residents $16,806.
Per-credit charge: $219; out-of-state residents $537.
Room and board: $7,042.

FINANCIAL AID PICTURE (2007-2008)
Students with need: Average financial aid package met 69% of need; average scholarship/grant was $4,500; average loan was $2,800. Need-based aid available for part-time students.
Students without need: No-need awards available for academics, alumni affiliation, art, athletics, minority status, music/drama, ROTC, state/district residency.
Scholarships offered: Medallion Scholarship; $3,000-$10,000 annually; based on academic performance in high school (3.8 GPA, 25 ACT or 1130 SAT, exclusive of writing); renewable for students maintaining full-time enrollment and 3.25 GPA.
Cumulative student debt: 52% of graduating class had student loans; average debt was $18,400.

FINANCIAL AID PROCEDURES
Forms required: FAFSA.
Dates and Deadlines: Priority date 3/15; no closing date. Applicants notified on a rolling basis starting 3/15.
Transfers: No deadline. Applicants notified on a rolling basis starting 3/15.

CONTACT
Mark Delorey, Director of Financial Aid
1903 West Michigan Avenue, Kalamazoo, MI 49008-5211
(269) 387-6000

Minnesota

Academy College
Bloomington, Minnesota
www.academycollege.edu   Federal Code: 013505

4-year for-profit junior and career college in large city.
Enrollment: 150 undergrads, 6% part-time. 22 full-time freshmen.
Selectivity: Open admission.

BASIC COSTS (2007-2008)
Additional info: Tuition ranges from $305 to $400 per credit hour depending on program.

FINANCIAL AID PICTURE (2006-2007)

Students with need: Out of 19 full-time freshmen who applied for aid, 19 were judged to have need. Of these, 19 received aid. Average financial aid package met 33% of need; average scholarship/grant was $6,116; average loan was $2,625. For part-time students, average financial aid package was $2,625.

Cumulative student debt: 100% of graduating class had student loans; average debt was $57,513.

FINANCIAL AID PROCEDURES

Forms required: FAFSA; institutional form.

Dates and Deadlines: No deadline. Applicants notified on a rolling basis.

CONTACT

Mary Erickson, Director of Administration
1101 East 78th Street, Bloomington, MN 55420
(952) 851-0066

Alexandria Technical College

Alexandria, Minnesota
www.alextech.edu   Federal Code: 005544

2-year public technical college in large town.

Enrollment: 1,743 undergrads.

Selectivity: Open admission; but selective for some programs.

BASIC COSTS (2007-2008)

Tuition and fees: $4,329; out-of-state residents $4,329.

Per-credit charge: $132; out-of-state residents $132.

FINANCIAL AID PICTURE

Students with need: Need-based aid available for full-time and part-time students.

Students without need: This college awards aid only to students with need.

FINANCIAL AID PROCEDURES

Forms required: FAFSA, institutional form.

Dates and Deadlines: Priority date 5/1; no closing date. Applicants notified on a rolling basis starting 6/30; must reply within 2 week(s) of notification.

Transfers: No deadline. Applicants notified on a rolling basis; must reply within 2 week(s) of notification.

CONTACT

Gary McFarland, Financial Aid Coordinator
1601 Jefferson Street, Alexandria, MN 56308-3799
(320) 762-4540

Anoka Technical College

Anoka, Minnesota
www.anokatech.edu   Federal Code: 007350

2-year public technical college in large town.

Enrollment: 1,590 undergrads, 55% part-time.

Selectivity: Open admission.

BASIC COSTS (2007-2008)

Tuition and fees: $4,586; out-of-state residents $4,586.

Per-credit charge: $139; out-of-state residents $139.

FINANCIAL AID PICTURE

Students with need: Need-based aid available for full-time and part-time students. Work study available nights.

Students without need: This college awards aid only to students with need.

FINANCIAL AID PROCEDURES

Forms required: FAFSA, institutional form.

Dates and Deadlines: No deadline. Applicants notified on a rolling basis starting 5/1.

CONTACT

Susan Rumpca, Director of Financial Aid
1355 West Highway 10, Anoka, MN 55303
(763) 576-4760

Anoka-Ramsey Community College

Coon Rapids, Minnesota
www.anokaramsey.edu   Federal Code: 002332

2-year public community college in small city.

Enrollment: 2,966 full-time undergrads.

Selectivity: Open admission; but selective for some programs and for out-of-state students.

BASIC COSTS (2007-2008)

Tuition and fees: $4,015; out-of-state residents $7,540.

Per-credit charge: $118; out-of-state residents $235.

Additional info: Various reciprocity agreements with some neighboring states provide tuition reduction to out-of-state students.

FINANCIAL AID PICTURE

Students with need: Work study available nights, weekends, and for part-time students.

Students without need: This college awards aid only to students with need.

FINANCIAL AID PROCEDURES

Forms required: FAFSA, institutional form.

Dates and Deadlines: Priority date 4/1; no closing date. Applicants notified on a rolling basis; must reply within 2 week(s) of notification.

CONTACT

Karla Seymour, Financial Aid Officer
11200 Mississippi Boulevard NW, Coon Rapids, MN 55433
(763) 433-1100

Art Institutes International Minnesota

Minneapolis, Minnesota
www.artinstitutes.edu/minneapolis Federal Code: 010248

4-year for-profit culinary school and visual arts college in large city.

Enrollment: 1,722 undergrads.

Selectivity: Open admission.

BASIC COSTS (2007-2008)

Tuition and fees: $19,872.

Per-credit charge: $414.

Additional info: Typical full-time credit load 16 credits/quarter. Starter kits for most programs $550-850. Tuition at time of enrollment locked for 4 years.

FINANCIAL AID PICTURE

Students with need: Need-based aid available for full-time students.

FINANCIAL AID PROCEDURES

Forms required: FAFSA.

CONTACT

Jeff Swenson, Director of Administrative and Financial Services
15 South Ninth Street, Minneapolis, MN 55402
(612) 332-3361

PART III: FINANCIAL AID COLLEGE BY COLLEGE

Augsburg College

Minneapolis, Minnesota
www.augsburg.edu   Federal Code: 002334

4-year private liberal arts college in large city, affiliated with Evangelical Lutheran Church in America.

Enrollment: 2,829 undergrads, 17% part-time. 423 full-time freshmen.
Selectivity: Admits 50 to 75% of applicants.

BASIC COSTS (2008-2009)

Tuition and fees: $26,103.
Room and board: $7,161.

FINANCIAL AID PICTURE (2006-2007)

Students with need: 37% of average financial aid package awarded as scholarships/grants, 63% awarded as loans/jobs. Need-based aid available for part-time students.
Students without need: No-need awards available for academics, alumni affiliation, leadership, minority status, music/drama, religious affiliation.
Scholarships offered: President's Scholarships: up to full tuition annually; 3.7 GPA and ACT/SAT score 27 or higher, number awarded determined annually. Regents Scholarships: $4,000-$10,000, top 30% of class rank or test scores. Must apply before 5/1 for both scholarships.

FINANCIAL AID PROCEDURES

Forms required: FAFSA.
Dates and Deadlines: Priority date 4/15; closing date 8/1. Applicants notified on a rolling basis starting 3/1; must reply within 3 week(s) of notification.
Transfers: Priority date 7/1; closing date 8/15. Applicants notified on a rolling basis starting 3/1; must reply by 9/1.

CONTACT

Paul Terrio, Director of Enrollment Services
2211 Riverside Avenue, Minneapolis, MN 55454
(612) 330-1046

Bemidji State University

Bemidji, Minnesota
www.bemidjistate.edu   Federal Code: 002336

4-year public university in large town.

Enrollment: 4,274 undergrads, 23% part-time. 730 full-time freshmen.
Selectivity: Admits over 75% of applicants.

BASIC COSTS (2007-2008)

Tuition and fees: $6,740; out-of-state residents $6,740.
Per-credit charge: $208; out-of-state residents $208.
Room and board: $5,874.
Additional info: Tuition/fee waivers available for minority students.

FINANCIAL AID PICTURE (2007-2008)

Students with need: Out of 608 full-time freshmen who applied for aid, 450 were judged to have need. Of these, 436 received aid, and 185 had their full need met. Average financial aid package met 78% of need; average scholarship/grant was $5,189; average loan was $3,366. For part-time students, average financial aid package was $7,032.
Students without need: 143 full-time freshmen who did not demonstrate need for aid received scholarships/grants; average award was $7,728. No-need awards available for academics, alumni affiliation, art, athletics, minority status, music/drama.
Scholarships offered: 70 full-time freshmen received athletic scholarships; average amount $3,838.
Cumulative student debt: 69% of graduating class had student loans; average debt was $20,470.

FINANCIAL AID PROCEDURES

Forms required: FAFSA, institutional form.

Dates and Deadlines: Priority date 5/15; no closing date. Applicants notified on a rolling basis starting 5/15.

CONTACT

Paul Lindseth, Director of Financial Aid
1500 Birchmont Drive NE, D-102, Bemidji, MN 56601
(218) 755-2034

Bethany Lutheran College

Mankato, Minnesota
www.blc.edu   Federal Code: 002337

4-year private liberal arts college in large town, affiliated with Evangelical Lutheran Synod.

Enrollment: 586 undergrads. 182 full-time freshmen.
Selectivity: Admits over 75% of applicants.

BASIC COSTS (2008-2009)

Tuition and fees: $18,710.
Per-credit charge: $780.
Room and board: $5,800.

FINANCIAL AID PICTURE (2006-2007)

Students with need: Out of 166 full-time freshmen who applied for aid, 145 were judged to have need. Of these, 145 received aid, and 40 had their full need met. Average financial aid package met 86% of need; average scholarship/grant was $10,556; average loan was $2,911. For part-time students, average financial aid package was $9,675.
Students without need: 34 full-time freshmen who did not demonstrate need for aid received scholarships/grants; average award was $7,311. No-need awards available for academics, art, music/drama.
Cumulative student debt: 82% of graduating class had student loans; average debt was $22,214.

FINANCIAL AID PROCEDURES

Forms required: FAFSA, institutional form.
Dates and Deadlines: Priority date 4/15; no closing date. Applicants notified on a rolling basis starting 3/1; must reply within 2 week(s) of notification.
Transfers: No deadline. Applicants notified on a rolling basis starting 3/1; must reply within 2 week(s) of notification.

CONTACT

Jeffrey Younge, Financial Aid Director
700 Luther Drive, Mankato, MN 56001-4490
(507) 344-7328

Bethel University

Saint Paul, Minnesota
www.bethel.edu   Federal Code: 002338

4-year private university and liberal arts college in large city, affiliated with Baptist General Conference.

Enrollment: 3,250 undergrads, 18% part-time. 664 full-time freshmen.
Selectivity: Admits over 75% of applicants.

BASIC COSTS (2008-2009)

Tuition and fees: $25,860.
Per-credit charge: $1,035.
Room and board: $7,620.
Additional info: 2008-2009 housing for first-time students $4,540. Rate frozen as long as student continues to reside in campus housing.

FINANCIAL AID PICTURE (2006-2007)

Students with need: Out of 522 full-time freshmen who applied for aid, 437 were judged to have need. Of these, 437 received aid, and 76 had their full need met. Average financial aid package met 78% of need; average scholarship/grant was $11,590; average loan was $3,662. For part-time students, average financial aid package was $9,440.

Students without need: 149 full-time freshmen who did not demonstrate need for aid received scholarships/grants; average award was $4,799. No-need awards available for academics, alumni affiliation, art, job skills, leadership, music/drama, religious affiliation, state/district residency.

Cumulative student debt: 78% of graduating class had student loans; average debt was $28,303.

FINANCIAL AID PROCEDURES

Forms required: FAFSA, institutional form.

Dates and Deadlines: Priority date 4/15; no closing date. Applicants notified on a rolling basis starting 3/1; must reply by 5/1 or within 3 week(s) of notification.

Transfers: Phi Theta Kappa Scholarship: merit based scholarship awarded to qualifying transfer students.

CONTACT

Jeffrey Olson, Director of Financial Aid

3900 Bethel Drive, Saint Paul, MN 55112-6999

(651) 638-6241

Carleton College
Northfield, Minnesota   Federal Code: 002340
www.carleton.edu   CSS Code: 6081

4-year private liberal arts college in large town.

Enrollment: 1,986 undergrads. 509 full-time freshmen.

Selectivity: Admits less than 50% of applicants.

BASIC COSTS (2008-2009)

Tuition and fees: $38,046.

Room and board: $9,993.

FINANCIAL AID PICTURE (2006-2007)

Students with need: Out of 373 full-time freshmen who applied for aid, 252 were judged to have need. Of these, 252 received aid, and 252 had their full need met. Average financial aid package met 100% of need; average scholarship/grant was $25,686; average loan was $3,978.

Students without need: 33 full-time freshmen who did not demonstrate need for aid received scholarships/grants; average award was $2,990. No-need awards available for academics.

Scholarships offered: National Merit, National Achievement, National Hispanic Scholars Awards: $2,000 per year; based on outstanding academic achievement and promise.

Cumulative student debt: 55% of graduating class had student loans; average debt was $19,185.

Additional info: Full financial need of all admitted applicants met through combination of work, loans, grants.

FINANCIAL AID PROCEDURES

Forms required: FAFSA, CSS PROFILE.

Dates and Deadlines: Priority date 2/15; closing date 2/15. Applicants notified by 4/1; must reply by 5/1 or within 2 week(s) of notification.

Transfers: Closing date 3/15. Applicants notified by 5/15; must reply by 6/1 or within 2 week(s) of notification.

CONTACT

Rodney Oto, Director of Student Financial Services

100 South College Street, Northfield, MN 55057

(507) 646-4138

Central Lakes College
Brainerd, Minnesota
www.clcmn.edu   Federal Code: 002339

2-year public community and technical college in large town.

Enrollment: 3,228 undergrads.

Selectivity: Open admission; but selective for some programs.

BASIC COSTS (2007-2008)

Tuition and fees: $4,419.

Per-credit charge: $130.

Additional info: In-state and out-of-state tuition rates same.

FINANCIAL AID PICTURE (2006-2007)

Students with need: 44% of average financial aid package awarded as scholarships/grants, 56% awarded as loans/jobs. Need-based aid available for part-time students.

FINANCIAL AID PROCEDURES

Forms required: FAFSA, institutional form.

Dates and Deadlines: Priority date 6/1; no closing date. Applicants notified on a rolling basis starting 6/10; must reply within 2 week(s) of notification.

CONTACT

Mike Barnaby, Director of Financial Aid

501 West College Drive, Brainerd, MN 56401

(218) 855-8025

Century Community and Technical College
White Bear Lake, Minnesota
www.century.edu   Federal Code: 010546

2-year public community and technical college in large town.

Enrollment: 7,631 undergrads, 52% part-time. 1,026 full-time freshmen.

Selectivity: Open admission; but selective for some programs.

BASIC COSTS (2007-2008)

Tuition and fees: $4,409; out-of-state residents $4,409.

Per-credit charge: $132; out-of-state residents $132.

FINANCIAL AID PICTURE (2006-2007)

Students with need: 37% of average financial aid package awarded as scholarships/grants, 63% awarded as loans/jobs. Need-based aid available for part-time students.

Students without need: This college awards aid only to students with need.

Additional info: Minnesota resident out of high school or not enrolled in college for 7 years without bachelor's or other higher degree offered cost of tuition and books for 1 course in 1 semester up to maximum of 5 credits.

FINANCIAL AID PROCEDURES

Forms required: FAFSA.

Dates and Deadlines: No deadline. Applicants notified on a rolling basis starting 5/15.

CONTACT

Lois Larson, Financial Aid Director

3300 Century Avenue North, White Bear Lake, MN 55110

(651) 779-3305

College of St. Benedict

St. Joseph, Minnesota
www.csbsju.edu   Federal Code: 002341

4-year private liberal arts college for women in small town, affiliated with Roman Catholic Church.

Enrollment: 2,049 undergrads. 537 full-time freshmen.
Selectivity: Admits over 75% of applicants.

BASIC COSTS (2008-2009)
Tuition and fees: $28,668.
Per-credit charge: $1,171.
Room and board: $7,959.

FINANCIAL AID PICTURE (2007-2008)
Students with need: Out of 443 full-time freshmen who applied for aid, 361 were judged to have need. Of these, 361 received aid, and 176 had their full need met. Average financial aid package met 92% of need; average scholarship/grant was $16,350; average loan was $3,718. For part-time students, average financial aid package was $16,055.
Students without need: 165 full-time freshmen who did not demonstrate need for aid received scholarships/grants; average award was $10,907. No-need awards available for academics, art, leadership, music/drama, ROTC.
Scholarships offered: Regents/Trustees Scholarship; $13,500; minimum 3.6 GPA, 30 ACT, 1980 SAT, demonstrated leadership and service, faculty interview. President's Scholarship; $7,500-$11,500 and Dean's Scholarships; $3,000-$7,000; GPA, high school rank, ACT/SAT scores, leadership and service. Art, Music and Theater Scholarships; up to $4,000; excellence in these subjects in high school, portfolio, tape, audition. Diversity Leadership Scholarships; up to $5,000; demonstrated diversity leadership and service in the area of cultural and ethnic diversity, personal statement on topic. Army ROTC and ROTC Nursing Scholarships; $23,000; demonstrated leadership potential, high school GPA, class standing, ACT/SAT scores, high achievement with broad interests and willingness to take on challenges. Phi Theta Kappa Scholarship; $1,000; member of Phi Theta Kappa (transfer students only).

FINANCIAL AID PROCEDURES
Forms required: FAFSA, institutional form.
Dates and Deadlines: Priority date 3/15; no closing date. Applicants notified on a rolling basis starting 3/15; must reply by 5/1.

CONTACT
Jane Haugen, Executive Director of Financial Aid
PO Box 7155, Collegeville, MN 56321-7155
(320) 363-5388

College of St. Catherine

St. Paul, Minnesota
www.stkate.edu   Federal Code: 002342

4-year private health science and liberal arts college for women in large city, affiliated with Roman Catholic Church.

Enrollment: 3,731 undergrads, 34% part-time. 365 full-time freshmen.
Selectivity: Admits over 75% of applicants.

BASIC COSTS (2007-2008)
Tuition and fees: $24,423.
Per-credit charge: $802.
Room and board: $6,788.

FINANCIAL AID PICTURE (2006-2007)
Students with need: Out of 336 full-time freshmen who applied for aid, 287 were judged to have need. Of these, 282 received aid, and 32 had their full need met. Average financial aid package met 72% of need; average scholarship/grant was $7,952; average loan was $3,285. For part-time students, average financial aid package was $14,073.

Students without need: 58 full-time freshmen who did not demonstrate need for aid received scholarships/grants; average award was $21,254. No-need awards available for academics, alumni affiliation, leadership.
Scholarships offered: St. Catherine of Alexandria Merit Scholarships: $2,000-$6,000; high school seniors in top 15% of class, evidence of academic preparation, outstanding leadership abilities, involvement in extracurricular activities and community service; renewable for 3 years.
Cumulative student debt: 82% of graduating class had student loans; average debt was $29,832.
Additional info: Audition required for music scholarships.

FINANCIAL AID PROCEDURES
Forms required: FAFSA, institutional form.
Dates and Deadlines: Priority date 4/15; no closing date. Applicants notified on a rolling basis starting 3/30; must reply within 2 week(s) of notification.

CONTACT
Elizabeth Stevens, Director of Financial Aid
2004 Randolph Avenue #4-02, St. Paul, MN 55105
(651) 690-6540

College of St. Scholastica

Duluth, Minnesota
www.css.edu   Federal Code: 002343

4-year private liberal arts college in small city, affiliated with Roman Catholic Church.

Enrollment: 1,986 undergrads, 2% part-time. 488 full-time freshmen.
Selectivity: Admits over 75% of applicants.

BASIC COSTS (2008-2009)
Tuition and fees: $26,489.
Per-credit charge: $819.
Room and board: $6,972.
Additional info: Tuition/fee waivers available for minority students.

FINANCIAL AID PICTURE (2007-2008)
Students with need: Out of 436 full-time freshmen who applied for aid, 394 were judged to have need. Of these, 393 received aid, and 76 had their full need met. Average financial aid package met 83% of need; average scholarship/grant was $6,641; average loan was $3,938. For part-time students, average financial aid package was $10,985.
Students without need: 42 full-time freshmen who did not demonstrate need for aid received scholarships/grants; average award was $10,565. No-need awards available for academics, alumni affiliation, religious affiliation, ROTC.
Scholarships offered: Benedictine Scholarship; $4,000-$12,500 per year for up to 4 years. Opportunity Grants; $6,500. Both based on GPA, SAT/ACT score; unlimited number awarded. Divisional Merit Awards; $4,000; available to transfer students; based on major; unlimited number awarded.
Cumulative student debt: 77% of graduating class had student loans; average debt was $34,032.

FINANCIAL AID PROCEDURES
Forms required: FAFSA, institutional form.
Dates and Deadlines: Priority date 3/15; no closing date. Applicants notified on a rolling basis starting 3/1; must reply by 5/1 or within 2 week(s) of notification.

CONTACT
Jon Erickson, Director of Financial Aid
1200 Kenwood Avenue, Duluth, MN 55811-4199
(218) 723-6047

College of Visual Arts

Saint Paul, Minnesota
www.cva.edu   Federal Code: 007462

4-year private visual arts college in large city.
Enrollment: 170 undergrads, 1% part-time. 44 full-time freshmen.
Selectivity: Admits over 75% of applicants.

BASIC COSTS (2008-2009)
Tuition and fees: $22,426.

FINANCIAL AID PICTURE (2007-2008)
Students with need: Average financial aid package met 51% of need; average scholarship/grant was $8,261; average loan was $3,423. For part-time students, average financial aid package was $11,125.
Students without need: No-need awards available for academics, art.
Scholarships offered: Merit scholarship program; provides annual awards ranging from $2,000 to $8,000;stipends are based on artistic and academic merit, as well as on overall strength of scholarship and admissions application; designed for prospective full-time first-year and transfer students.
Cumulative student debt: 90% of graduating class had student loans; average debt was $46,210.

FINANCIAL AID PROCEDURES
Forms required: FAFSA, institutional form.
Dates and Deadlines: Priority date 3/1; no closing date. Applicants notified on a rolling basis starting 2/15; must reply within 2 week(s) of notification.

CONTACT
Susan Ant, Director of Financial Aid
344 Summit Avenue, Saint Paul, MN 55102-2199
(651) 224-3416

Concordia College: Moorhead

Moorhead, Minnesota
www.concordiacollege.edu   Federal Code: 002346

4-year private liberal arts college in small city, affiliated with Evangelical Lutheran Church in America.
Enrollment: 2,720 undergrads, 1% part-time. 722 full-time freshmen.
Selectivity: Admits over 75% of applicants.

BASIC COSTS (2008-2009)
Tuition and fees: $24,120.
Per-credit charge: $940.
Room and board: $6,160.

FINANCIAL AID PICTURE (2006-2007)
Students with need: Out of 586 full-time freshmen who applied for aid, 469 were judged to have need. Of these, 469 received aid, and 124 had their full need met. Average financial aid package met 90% of need; average scholarship/grant was $11,709; average loan was $3,718. For part-time students, average financial aid package was $9,861.
Students without need: This college awards aid only to students with need.
Scholarships offered: Concordia National Merit Scholarship; $10,000 per year for 4 years; for National Merit Scholarship finalists listing Concordia as their first choice. Soli Deo Gloria Scholarship; $12,000 per year for 4 years; based on test scores, class rank or GPA, essay and interview. Faculty Scholarships; $8,000 per year for 4 years; based on test scores, class rank or GPA, essay, and faculty interview. Excellence Scholarships; $5,000-$7,000 per year for 4 years; based on test scores, class rank or GPA, essay, and faculty interview. Performing Arts Scholarships; $1,500-$3,500 per year for 4 years; available in music drama, forensics.
Cumulative student debt: 81% of graduating class had student loans; average debt was $22,661.

Additional info: Students in ACCORD program (age 25 and older) may apply for tuition reductions for first 4 courses.

FINANCIAL AID PROCEDURES
Forms required: FAFSA, institutional form.
Dates and Deadlines: Priority date 4/15; no closing date. Applicants notified on a rolling basis starting 3/1.

CONTACT
Jane Williams, Director of Financial Aid
901 Eighth Street South, Moorhead, MN 56562-9981
(218) 299-3010

Concordia University: St. Paul

St. Paul, Minnesota
www.csp.edu   Federal Code: 002347

4-year private university in large city, affiliated with Lutheran Church - Missouri Synod.
Enrollment: 1,418 undergrads, 8% part-time. 201 full-time freshmen.
Selectivity: Admits 50 to 75% of applicants.

BASIC COSTS (2008-2009)
Tuition and fees: $24,900.
Per-credit charge: $520.
Room and board: $6,900.
Additional info: Adult learners in degree completion programs have discounted tuition rates based on cost per credit. Rates vary by program.

FINANCIAL AID PICTURE (2007-2008)
Students with need: Average financial aid package met 79% of need; average scholarship/grant was $14,525; average loan was $3,734. For part-time students, average financial aid package was $6,214.
Students without need: No-need awards available for academics, art, athletics, minority status, music/drama, religious affiliation.
Cumulative student debt: 84% of graduating class had student loans; average debt was $27,548.
Additional info: Church districts and local congregations are major sources of aid for church-vocation students.

FINANCIAL AID PROCEDURES
Forms required: FAFSA, institutional form.
Dates and Deadlines: Priority date 5/1; no closing date. Applicants notified on a rolling basis starting 3/1; must reply within 3 week(s) of notification.
Transfers: Adult learners in degree completion programs are typically not eligible for institutional scholarships/grants because of discounted tuition rates.

CONTACT
Brian Heinemann, Vice President for Enrollment Management
275 Syndicate Street North, St. Paul, MN 55104-5494
(651) 603-6300

Crossroads College

Rochester, Minnesota
www.crossroadscollege.edu   Federal Code: 002366

4-year private Bible college in small city, affiliated with Christian Church.
Enrollment: 184 undergrads.
Selectivity: Admits 50 to 75% of applicants.

BASIC COSTS (2008-2009)
Tuition and fees: $13,210.
Per-credit charge: $375.
Room only: $3,800.

FINANCIAL AID PICTURE (2007-2008)

Students with need: 48% of average financial aid package awarded as scholarships/grants, 52% awarded as loans/jobs. Need-based aid available for part-time students. Work study available nights.

Students without need: No-need awards available for academics, leadership, music/drama, religious affiliation.

Scholarships offered: Home-Educated Grant; $500 per semester if home-schooled for two years during high school. Travel Grant; $500 per semester for student who resides in states other than Minnesota, Iowa, Wisconsin. Crossroads Matching Grant; church funds matched up to $500 per semester; awarded to first year students.

FINANCIAL AID PROCEDURES

Forms required: FAFSA, institutional form.

Dates and Deadlines: Priority date 4/1; no closing date. Applicants notified on a rolling basis starting 2/1; must reply within 4 week(s) of notification.

Transfers: Mid-year transfer students will have financial aid calculated with the prior school term award in mind.

CONTACT

Polly Kellogg-Bradley, Director of Financial Aid
920 Mayowood Road, SW, Rochester, MN 55902
(507) 288-4563

Crown College
St. Bonifacius, Minnesota
www.crown.edu   Federal Code: 002383

4-year private Bible and liberal arts college in small town, affiliated with Christian and Missionary Alliance.

Enrollment: 1,025 undergrads, 36% part-time. 142 full-time freshmen.

BASIC COSTS (2008-2009)

Tuition and fees: $19,198.

Per-credit charge: $799.

Room and board: $6,986.

Additional info: Tuition/fee waivers available for minority students.

FINANCIAL AID PICTURE (2007-2008)

Students with need: 44% of average financial aid package awarded as scholarships/grants, 56% awarded as loans/jobs. Need-based aid available for part-time students. Work study available nights, weekends, and for part-time students.

Students without need: No-need awards available for academics, alumni affiliation, leadership, minority status, music/drama, religious affiliation.

FINANCIAL AID PROCEDURES

Forms required: FAFSA, institutional form.

Dates and Deadlines: Priority date 4/1; closing date 8/1. Applicants notified on a rolling basis starting 4/1; must reply within 3 week(s) of notification.

Transfers: No deadline. Applicants notified on a rolling basis; must reply within 3 week(s) of notification. Cannot have attended more than 4 years of college to receive state grant.

CONTACT

Cheryl Fernandez, Director of Financial Aid
8700 College View Drive, St. Bonifacius, MN 55375-9001
(952) 446-4177

Dakota County Technical College
Rosemount, Minnesota
www.dctc.edu   Federal Code: 010402

2-year public technical college in large town.

Enrollment: 2,335 undergrads.

Selectivity: Open admission; but selective for some programs.

BASIC COSTS (2007-2008)

Tuition and fees: $4,749; out-of-state residents $8,994.

Per-credit charge: $142; out-of-state residents $283.

FINANCIAL AID PICTURE

Students with need: Need-based aid available for full-time and part-time students. Work study available nights, weekends, and for part-time students.

Students without need: No-need awards available for academics, leadership.

Scholarships offered: Dakota County Techical College scholarship.

FINANCIAL AID PROCEDURES

Forms required: FAFSA.

Dates and Deadlines: No deadline. Applicants notified on a rolling basis starting 3/15.

Transfers: No deadline. FAFSA must be processed within 14 days of the first day of the semester to be considered for Minnesota State Grant for the semester.

CONTACT

Scott Roelke, Director of Scholarships and Financial Aid
1300 145th Street East, Rosemount, MN 55068
(651) 423-8299

DeVry University: Edina
Edina, Minnesota
www.devry.edu

4-year for-profit university in large town.

Enrollment: 161 undergrads, 60% part-time. 10 full-time freshmen.

BASIC COSTS (2007-2008)

Tuition and fees: $13,020.

Per-credit charge: $490.

FINANCIAL AID PICTURE (2006-2007)

Students with need: Out of 2 full-time freshmen who applied for aid, 2 were judged to have need. Of these, 2 received aid. Average financial aid package met 32% of need; average scholarship/grant was $5,194; average loan was $4,125. For part-time students, average financial aid package was $6,880.

Students without need: 1 full-time freshmen who did not demonstrate need for aid received scholarships/grants; average award was $9,949. No-need awards available for academics.

FINANCIAL AID PROCEDURES

Forms required: FAFSA.

Dates and Deadlines: No deadline. Applicants notified on a rolling basis.

CONTACT

7700 France Avenue South, Suite 575, Edina, MN 55435

Dunwoody College of Technology
Minneapolis, Minnesota
www.dunwoody.edu   Federal Code: 004641

2-year private technical college in very large city.

Enrollment: 1,476 undergrads, 11% part-time. 374 full-time freshmen.

Selectivity: Admits 50 to 75% of applicants.

BASIC COSTS (2007-2008)

Tuition and fees: $12,633.

Per-credit charge: $174.

FINANCIAL AID PICTURE (2006-2007)

Students with need: Out of 312 full-time freshmen who applied for aid, 213 were judged to have need. Of these, 190 received aid, and 24 had their full need met. Average financial aid package met 41% of need; average scholarship/grant was $4,521; average loan was $3,447. For part-time students, average financial aid package was $7,142.

Students without need: 79 full-time freshmen who did not demonstrate need for aid received scholarships/grants; average award was $7,255. No-need awards available for academics.

Cumulative student debt: 95% of graduating class had student loans; average debt was $8,000.

FINANCIAL AID PROCEDURES

Forms required: FAFSA, state aid form.

Dates and Deadlines: Priority date 6/1; no closing date. Applicants notified on a rolling basis starting 2/1; must reply within 4 week(s) of notification.

CONTACT

Barb Charboneau, Director of Financial Aid
818 Dunwoody Boulevard, Minneapolis, MN 55403-1192
(612) 374-5800 ext. 3346

Globe University
Woodbury, Minnesota
www.globeuniversity.edu   Federal Code: 004642

4-year for-profit business and health science college in small city.

Enrollment: 795 undergrads.

Selectivity: Open admission.

BASIC COSTS (2007-2008)

Tuition and fees: $17,760.

Per-credit charge: $370.

FINANCIAL AID PICTURE

Students with need: Need-based aid available for full-time and part-time students.

FINANCIAL AID PROCEDURES

Forms required: FAFSA, institutional form.

Dates and Deadlines: No deadline. Applicants notified on a rolling basis starting 5/1.

CONTACT

Tina Kukowski, Office of Financial Aid
8089 Globe Drive, Woodbury, MN 55125
(651) 730-5100

Gustavus Adolphus College
St. Peter, Minnesota   Federal Code: 002353
www.gustavus.edu   CSS Code: 6253

4-year private liberal arts college in small town, affiliated with Evangelical Lutheran Church in America.

Enrollment: 2,577 undergrads. 685 full-time freshmen.

Selectivity: Admits over 75% of applicants.

BASIC COSTS (2007-2008)

Tuition and fees: $28,535.

Room and board: $6,775.

FINANCIAL AID PICTURE (2007-2008)

Students with need: Out of 561 full-time freshmen who applied for aid, 455 were judged to have need. Of these, 455 received aid, and 142 had their full need met. Average financial aid package met 92% of need; average scholarship/grant was $10,731; average loan was $2,981.

Students without need: 220 full-time freshmen who did not demonstrate need for aid received scholarships/grants; average award was $7,461. No-need awards available for academics, alumni affiliation, art, music/drama, religious affiliation, ROTC.

Scholarships offered: Presidential Scholarship: $10,000-$13,000. National Merit finalist: $1,000; academic. Legacy Scholarship: $1,500; academic for children or siblings of alumni. Jussi Bjorling Scholarship: $1,000-$4,000; for music; 40 awarded. Anderson Theatre and Dance Scholarship: $2,000; 15 awarded. Dean's Scholarship: $1,000-$1,500.

Cumulative student debt: 70% of graduating class had student loans; average debt was $24,297.

FINANCIAL AID PROCEDURES

Forms required: FAFSA, institutional form. CSS PROFILE required of students applying for need-based assistance.

Dates and Deadlines: Priority date 2/15; closing date 4/15. Applicants notified on a rolling basis starting 1/20; must reply by 5/1 or within 2 week(s) of notification.

Transfers: Applicants notified on a rolling basis starting 1/20; must reply by 5/1 or within 2 week(s) of notification.

CONTACT

Mary Booker, Director of Student Financial Assistance
800 West College Avenue, St. Peter, MN 56082
(507) 933-7527

Hamline University
St. Paul, Minnesota
www.hamline.edu   Federal Code: 002354

4-year private university and liberal arts college in very large city, affiliated with United Methodist Church.

Enrollment: 1,986 undergrads, 3% part-time. 424 full-time freshmen.

Selectivity: Admits over 75% of applicants.

BASIC COSTS (2008-2009)

Tuition and fees: $28,143.

Per-credit charge: $863.

Room and board: $7,784.

FINANCIAL AID PICTURE (2006-2007)

Students with need: Out of 377 full-time freshmen who applied for aid, 312 were judged to have need. Of these, 312 received aid, and 60 had their full need met. Average financial aid package met 83% of need; average scholarship/grant was $14,179; average loan was $3,783. For part-time students, average financial aid package was $7,264.

Students without need: 96 full-time freshmen who did not demonstrate need for aid received scholarships/grants; average award was $7,862. No-need awards available for academics, alumni affiliation, art, job skills, leadership, minority status, music/drama, religious affiliation, state/district residency.

Scholarships offered: Presidential Scholarship: $12,000 to full tuition; for students with excellent academic ability, strong sense of motivation. Hamline Honors Scholarship: $12,000; for students with successful academic record, involvement in school and community activities. Hamline Trustee Scholarship: $5,500; for new first-year students who have excelled academically. Departmental scholarships in biology, chemistry, French, German, music, physics, theater, creative writing: $3,000-$4,000 depending on department. National Merit Scholarship: full tuition. Diversity scholarships: $3,000. Eagle Scout or Gold Award Scholarships: amount varies. All scholarships renewable for a total of four years.

Cumulative student debt: 79% of graduating class had student loans; average debt was $30,518.

FINANCIAL AID PROCEDURES

Forms required: FAFSA.

Dates and Deadlines: Priority date 3/1; no closing date. Applicants notified on a rolling basis starting 3/1; must reply within 2 week(s) of notification. **Transfers:** Priority date 4/1; no deadline. Applicants notified on a rolling basis; must reply within 2 week(s) of notification. Students who qualify for Minnesota State Grant must carry 15 semester credits to qualify for full grant each semester. If less credit is carried, grant prorated.

CONTACT
Lynette Wahl, Director of Financial Aid
1536 Hewitt Avenue, St. Paul, MN 55104-1284
(651) 523-3000

Inver Hills Community College
Inver Grove Heights, Minnesota
www.inverhills.edu   Federal Code: 006935

2-year public community college in large town.
Enrollment: 4,574 undergrads, 53% part-time. 672 full-time freshmen.
Selectivity: Open admission; but selective for some programs.

BASIC COSTS (2007-2008)
Tuition and fees: $4,534; out-of-state residents $4,534.
Per-credit charge: $137; out-of-state residents $137.

FINANCIAL AID PICTURE
Students with need: Need-based aid available for full-time and part-time students. Work study available nights, weekends, and for part-time students. **Students without need:** This college awards aid only to students with need.

FINANCIAL AID PROCEDURES
Forms required: FAFSA.
Dates and Deadlines: No deadline. Applicants notified on a rolling basis starting 6/1.
Transfers: No deadline. Applicants notified on a rolling basis.

CONTACT
John Pogue, Financial Aid Officer
2500 80th Street East, Inver Grove Heights, MN 55076-3224
(651) 450-8518

Itasca Community College
Grand Rapids, Minnesota
www.itascacc.edu   Federal Code: 002356

2-year public junior and liberal arts college in large town.
Enrollment: 984 undergrads, 22% part-time. 325 full-time freshmen.
Selectivity: Open admission.

BASIC COSTS (2007-2008)
Tuition and fees: $4,337; out-of-state residents $5,305.
Per-credit charge: $129; out-of-state residents $161.
Additional info: Different reciprocity agreements for Wisconsin, North Dakota, and South Dakota.

FINANCIAL AID PICTURE (2006-2007)
Students with need: 63% of average financial aid package awarded as scholarships/grants, 37% awarded as loans/jobs. Need-based aid available for part-time students. Work study available nights, weekends, and for part-time students.
Students without need: No-need awards available for academics, leadership, music/drama, state/district residency.

FINANCIAL AID PROCEDURES
Forms required: FAFSA.
Dates and Deadlines: Priority date 5/1; no closing date. Applicants notified on a rolling basis starting 4/1.

Transfers: Applicants notified on a rolling basis starting 4/1.

CONTACT
Nathan Wright, Director of Financial Aid
1851 Highway 169 East, Grand Rapids, MN 55744
(218) 327-4467

Lake Superior College
Duluth, Minnesota
www.lsc.edu   Federal Code: 005757

2-year public community and technical college in small city.
Enrollment: 3,406 undergrads.
Selectivity: Open admission; but selective for some programs.

BASIC COSTS (2007-2008)
Tuition and fees: $4,157; out-of-state residents $7,745.
Per-credit charge: $120; out-of-state residents $239.
Additional info: Various reciprocity plans for residents of neighboring states may reduce tuition for out-of-state students.

FINANCIAL AID PICTURE
Students with need: Need-based aid available for full-time and part-time students. Work study available nights, weekends, and for part-time students.
Students without need: No-need awards available for academics, leadership.

FINANCIAL AID PROCEDURES
Forms required: FAFSA.
Dates and Deadlines: Priority date 5/1; no closing date. Applicants notified on a rolling basis starting 5/1.
Transfers: No deadline.

CONTACT
Sandra Olin, Director of Financial Aid
2101 Trinity Road, Duluth, MN 55811
(218) 733-7601

Lakeland Academy Division of Herzing College
Crystal, Minnesota
www.herzing.edu   Federal Code: 007590

2-year for-profit health science college in large city.
Enrollment: 273 undergrads.
Selectivity: Open admission; but selective for some programs.

BASIC COSTS (2008-2009)
Additional info: Cost of full programs ranges from $11,272 to $48,407, including fees and books.

FINANCIAL AID PICTURE (2006-2007)
Students with need: 39% of average financial aid package awarded as scholarships/grants, 61% awarded as loans/jobs.

FINANCIAL AID PROCEDURES
Forms required: FAFSA.

CONTACT
Jill Riverso, Director of Financial Aid
5700 West Broadway, Crystal, MN 55428
(763) 535-3000

Leech Lake Tribal College

Cass Lake, Minnesota
www.lltc.edu   Federal Code: 030964

2-year public Tribal College grounded in Anishinaabe knowledge and culture. in small town.

Enrollment: 226 undergrads.
Selectivity: Open admission.

BASIC COSTS (2007-2008)

Tuition and fees: $3,980.
Per-credit charge: $125.

FINANCIAL AID PICTURE

Students with need: Need-based aid available for full-time and part-time students.
Students without need: This college awards aid only to students with need.

FINANCIAL AID PROCEDURES

Forms required: FAFSA.

CONTACT

Barbara Carlson, Director of Financial Aid
PO Box 180, Cass Lake, MN 56633
(218) 335-4224

Macalester College

St. Paul, Minnesota   Federal Code: 002358
www.macalester.edu   CSS Code: 6390

4-year private liberal arts college in large city, affiliated with Presbyterian Church (USA).

Enrollment: 1,912 undergrads, 2% part-time. 485 full-time freshmen.
Selectivity: Admits less than 50% of applicants.

BASIC COSTS (2008-2009)

Tuition and fees: $36,504.
Per-credit charge: $1,135.
Room and board: $8,472.

FINANCIAL AID PICTURE (2007-2008)

Students with need: Out of 366 full-time freshmen who applied for aid, 320 were judged to have need. Of these, 320 received aid, and 320 had their full need met. Average financial aid package met 100% of need; average scholarship/grant was $24,674; average loan was $2,811. For part-time students, average financial aid package was $19,627.
Students without need: 24 full-time freshmen who did not demonstrate need for aid received scholarships/grants; average award was $4,168. No-need awards available for academics, minority status.
Scholarships offered: National Merit Scholarships; $5,000; to National Merit Finalists whose first choice college is Macalester. DeWitt Wallace Distinguished Scholarships; minimum $3,000; open to National Merit semifinalists, commended students, and finalists not awarded National Merit Scholarship. DeWitt Wallace Scholarships; minimum $3,000; to selected middle-income students with need and academic records worthy of recognition. Catherine Lealtad Scholarships; minimum $3,000; to African American, Latino, and Native American students with strong high school records. Students who are National Achievement or National Hispanic Scholarship finalists with strong high school record will receive a minimum annual award of $5,000.
Cumulative student debt: 70% of graduating class had student loans; average debt was $18,849.
Additional info: College meets full need for all admitted students. Minnesota Self Loan available to qualified students.

FINANCIAL AID PROCEDURES

Forms required: FAFSA, CSS PROFILE.

Dates and Deadlines: Priority date 2/8; closing date 3/1. Applicants notified by 4/1; must reply by 5/1 or within 1 week(s) of notification.
Transfers: Applicants notified by 5/15; must reply within 2 week(s) of notification.

CONTACT

Brian Lindeman, Director of Financial Aid
1600 Grand Avenue, St. Paul, MN 55105-1899
(651) 696-6214

Martin Luther College

New Ulm, Minnesota
www.mlc-wels.edu   Federal Code: 002361

4-year private college of theology and education in large town, affiliated with Wisconsin Evangelical Lutheran Synod.

Enrollment: 746 undergrads, 7% part-time. 165 full-time freshmen.
Selectivity: Admits over 75% of applicants.

BASIC COSTS (2008-2009)

Tuition and fees: $10,350.
Per-credit charge: $220.

FINANCIAL AID PICTURE (2006-2007)

Students with need: Out of 157 full-time freshmen who applied for aid, 121 were judged to have need. Of these, 121 received aid, and 31 had their full need met. Average financial aid package met 82% of need; average scholarship/grant was $4,741; average loan was $2,039. Need-based aid available for part-time students.
Students without need: 16 full-time freshmen who did not demonstrate need for aid received scholarships/grants; average award was $820. No-need awards available for academics, music/drama, religious affiliation.
Scholarships offered: Academic Scholarship; $500; 3.75 GPA after 6 semesters of high school or 27 ACT. Presidential Scholarship; $1,000; to student selected as high school valedictorian or ranked first in class after 7 semesters.
Cumulative student debt: 60% of graduating class had student loans; average debt was $15,954.

FINANCIAL AID PROCEDURES

Forms required: FAFSA, institutional form.
Dates and Deadlines: Priority date 4/15; closing date 9/30. Applicants notified by 3/1.

CONTACT

Gene Slettedahl, Director of Financial Aid
1995 Luther Court, New Ulm, MN 56073-3965
(507) 354-8221

Mesabi Range Community and Technical College

Virginia, Minnesota
www.mr.mnscu.edu   Federal Code: 004009

2-year public community and technical college in large town.

Enrollment: 863 full-time undergrads.
Selectivity: Open admission.

BASIC COSTS (2007-2008)

Tuition and fees: $4,344; out-of-state residents $5,312.
Per-credit charge: $129; out-of-state residents $161.

FINANCIAL AID PICTURE

Students with need: Need-based aid available for full-time and part-time students. Work study available nights, weekends, and for part-time students.

Students without need: No-need awards available for state/district residency.

FINANCIAL AID PROCEDURES

Forms required: FAFSA, institutional form.

Dates and Deadlines: Priority date 4/22; no closing date. Applicants notified on a rolling basis starting 5/1; must reply within 2 week(s) of notification.

CONTACT

George Walters, Director of Financial Aid
1001 Chestnut Street West, Virginia, MN 55792-3448
(218) 741-3095

Metropolitan State University

St. Paul, Minnesota
www.metrostate.edu   Federal Code: 010374

4-year public university in very large city.

Enrollment: 5,722 undergrads, 63% part-time. 57 full-time freshmen.

Selectivity: Admits 50 to 75% of applicants.

BASIC COSTS (2007-2008)

Tuition and fees: $5,293; out-of-state residents $10,333.

Per-credit charge: $167; out-of-state residents $335.

FINANCIAL AID PICTURE

Students with need: Need-based aid available for full-time and part-time students. Work study available nights, weekends, and for part-time students.

Students without need: No-need awards available for academics, leadership, minority status, state/district residency.

FINANCIAL AID PROCEDURES

Forms required: FAFSA.

Dates and Deadlines: Priority date 5/1; no closing date. Applicants notified on a rolling basis starting 5/1; must reply within 2 week(s) of notification.

CONTACT

Robert Bode, Director of Financial Aid
700 East Seventh Street, St. Paul, MN 55106-5000
(651) 793-1414

Minneapolis College of Art and Design

Minneapolis, Minnesota
www.mcad.edu   Federal Code: 002365

4-year private visual arts college in very large city.

Enrollment: 731 undergrads, 5% part-time. 153 full-time freshmen.

Selectivity: Admits 50 to 75% of applicants.

BASIC COSTS (2008-2009)

Tuition and fees: $29,300.

Per-credit charge: $940.

Room only: $4,160.

Additional info: Housing costs vary; figure quoted is for double-occupancy (furnished) one-bedroom apartment. Required fees include $900 laptop computer that freshmen must purchase.

FINANCIAL AID PICTURE (2007-2008)

Students with need: Out of 132 full-time freshmen who applied for aid, 112 were judged to have need. Of these, 111 received aid, and 14 had their full need met. Average financial aid package met 57% of need; average scholarship/grant was $10,506; average loan was $3,866. For part-time students, average financial aid package was $10,684.

Students without need: 24 full-time freshmen who did not demonstrate need for aid received scholarships/grants; average award was $14,160. No-need awards available for academics, alumni affiliation, art.

Scholarships offered: Admissions Merit Scholarships; $6,000-$12,000; based on admissions file. Students admitted to the college by February 15 automatically entered into scholarship competition.

Cumulative student debt: 90% of graduating class had student loans; average debt was $45,476.

FINANCIAL AID PROCEDURES

Forms required: FAFSA.

Dates and Deadlines: Priority date 3/15; no closing date. Applicants notified on a rolling basis starting 4/1; must reply by 5/1 or within 2 week(s) of notification.

CONTACT

Laura Link, Director, Financial Aid Office
2501 Stevens Avenue, Minneapolis, MN 55404
(612) 874-8782

Minneapolis Community and Technical College

Minneapolis, Minnesota
www.minneapolis.edu   Federal Code: 002362

2-year public community and technical college in large city.

Enrollment: 9,179 undergrads.

Selectivity: Open admission; but selective for some programs.

BASIC COSTS (2007-2008)

Tuition and fees: $4,442; out-of-state residents $4,442.

Per-credit charge: $136.

FINANCIAL AID PICTURE (2006-2007)

Students with need: 37% of average financial aid package awarded as scholarships/grants, 63% awarded as loans/jobs. Need-based aid available for part-time students. Work study available nights, weekends, and for part-time students.

Students without need: This college awards aid only to students with need.

FINANCIAL AID PROCEDURES

Forms required: FAFSA.

Dates and Deadlines: Priority date 6/1; no closing date. Applicants notified on a rolling basis starting 7/15; must reply within 2 week(s) of notification.

CONTACT

Angela Christensen, Director of Financial Aid
1501 Hennepin Avenue, Minneapolis, MN 55403-1779
(612) 659-6240

Minnesota School of Business: St. Cloud

Waite Park, Minnesota
www.msbcollege.edu

4-year for-profit virtual university and business and health science and technical and career college in small city.

Enrollment: 805 undergrads.

BASIC COSTS (2007-2008)

Tuition and fees: $17,810.

Per-credit charge: $370.

FINANCIAL AID PICTURE

Students with need: Need-based aid available for full-time and part-time students.

CONTACT

Renee Cannon, Director of Financial Aid
1201 Second Street South, Waite Park, MN 55387

Minnesota School of Business: Shakopee

Shakopee, Minnesota
www.msbcollege.edu

4-year for-profit business and technical college in large town.
Enrollment: 445 undergrads, 40% part-time. 44 full-time freshmen.
Selectivity: Admits over 75% of applicants.

BASIC COSTS (2008-2009)
Tuition and fees: $18,770.
Per-credit charge: $390.

FINANCIAL AID PICTURE (2007-2008)
Students with need: Out of 41 full-time freshmen who applied for aid, 40 were judged to have need. Of these, 40 received aid, and 18 had their full need met. Average financial aid package met 45% of need; average scholarship/grant was $4,500; average loan was $3,500. For part-time students, average financial aid package was $6,400.
Students without need: 1 full-time freshmen who did not demonstrate need for aid received scholarships/grants; average award was $2,500. No-need awards available for academics.
Cumulative student debt: 95% of graduating class had student loans; average debt was $20,000.

FINANCIAL AID PROCEDURES
Forms required: FAFSA, institutional form.
Dates and Deadlines: No deadline. Applicants notified on a rolling basis.

CONTACT
Karen Samstad, Director of Financial Aid
1200 Shakopee Town Square, Shakopee, MN 55379

Minnesota State College - Southeast Technical

Winona, Minnesota
www.southeastmn.edu   Federal Code: 002393

2-year public nursing and technical college in large town.
Enrollment: 1,863 undergrads, 38% part-time. 524 full-time freshmen.
Selectivity: Open admission.

BASIC COSTS (2007-2008)
Tuition and fees: $4,501; out-of-state residents $8,645.
Per-credit charge: $138; out-of-state residents $276.
Additional info: Various reciprocity agreements with neighboring states provide tuition reduction to some out-of-state students.

FINANCIAL AID PICTURE
Students with need: Need-based aid available for full-time and part-time students.
Students without need: No-need awards available for academics, leadership.

FINANCIAL AID PROCEDURES
Forms required: FAFSA, state aid form, institutional form.
Dates and Deadlines: Priority date 5/15; closing date 6/30. Applicants notified on a rolling basis; must reply within 3 week(s) of notification.
Transfers: Applicants notified on a rolling basis. Mid-year transfer application forms must be accompanied by financial aid transcript.

CONTACT
Anne Dahlen, Director of Financial Aid
1250 Homer Road, Winona, MN 55987-0409
(507) 453-2710

Minnesota State Community and Technical College: Fergus Falls

Fergus Falls, Minnesota
www.minnesota.edu   Federal Code: 002352

2-year public community and technical college in large town.
Enrollment: 3,318 full-time undergrads.
Selectivity: Open admission.

BASIC COSTS (2007-2008)
Tuition and fees: $4,737; out-of-state residents $4,737.
Per-credit charge: $138; out-of-state residents $138.
Room only: $2,450.
Additional info: Tuition/fee waivers available for adults.

FINANCIAL AID PICTURE
Students with need: Need-based aid available for full-time and part-time students. Work study available nights, weekends, and for part-time students.
Students without need: No-need awards available for academics, art, leadership, minority status, music/drama, state/district residency.
Scholarships offered: Academic and leadership scholarships; $400-$1,000 each; available to 1st and 2nd year students; over 150 awarded annually.

FINANCIAL AID PROCEDURES
Forms required: FAFSA, institutional form.
Dates and Deadlines: Priority date 6/1; no closing date. Applicants notified on a rolling basis starting 7/1.
Transfers: No deadline. Applicants notified on a rolling basis.

CONTACT
Tom Whelihan, Director of Financial Aid
1414 College Way, Fergus Falls, MN 56537-1000
(218) 736-1534

Minnesota State University: Mankato

Mankato, Minnesota
www.mnsu.edu   Federal Code: 002360

4-year public university in large town.
Enrollment: 12,534 undergrads.
Selectivity: Admits over 75% of applicants.

BASIC COSTS (2007-2008)
Tuition and fees: $6,050; out-of-state residents $12,854.
Per-credit charge: $243; out-of-state residents $484.
Room and board: $5,354.

FINANCIAL AID PICTURE (2007-2008)
Students with need: Average financial aid package met 75% of need; average scholarship/grant was $4,138; average loan was $3,025. For part-time students, average financial aid package was $5,311.
Students without need: No-need awards available for academics, alumni affiliation, art, athletics, leadership, minority status, music/drama.
Cumulative student debt: 75% of graduating class had student loans; average debt was $16,500.

FINANCIAL AID PROCEDURES
Forms required: FAFSA.
Dates and Deadlines: Priority date 3/15; no closing date. Applicants notified on a rolling basis starting 3/30; must reply within 2 week(s) of notification.

CONTACT
Sandra Loerts, Director of Financial Aid
122 Taylor Center, Mankato, MN 56001
(507) 389-1185

Minnesota State University: Moorhead

Moorhead, Minnesota
www.mnstate.edu   Federal Code: 002367

4-year public university in small city.
Enrollment: 6,638 undergrads.
Selectivity: Admits over 75% of applicants.

BASIC COSTS (2007-2008)
Tuition and fees: $5,948.
Per-credit charge: $169.
Room and board: $5,690.
Additional info: Out-of-state students pay same rate as in-state.

FINANCIAL AID PICTURE
Students with need: Need-based aid available for full-time and part-time students.
Students without need: No-need awards available for academics, art, athletics, leadership, music/drama, state/district residency.

FINANCIAL AID PROCEDURES
Forms required: FAFSA.
Dates and Deadlines: Priority date 2/15; no closing date. Applicants notified on a rolling basis starting 6/1; must reply within 2 week(s) of notification.

CONTACT
Carolyn Zehren, Director of Financial Aid and Scholarships
Owens Hall, Moorhead, MN 56563
(218) 236-2251

Minnesota West Community and Technical College

Granite Falls, Minnesota
www.mnwest.edu   Federal Code: 005263

2-year public community and junior and technical and career college in large town.
Enrollment: 2,859 undergrads.
Selectivity: Open admission.

BASIC COSTS (2007-2008)
Tuition and fees: $4,692; out-of-state residents $4,692.
Per-credit charge: $142.

FINANCIAL AID PICTURE
Students with need: Need-based aid available for full-time and part-time students.

FINANCIAL AID PROCEDURES
Forms required: FAFSA.
Dates and Deadlines: Priority date 6/8; no closing date. Applicants notified on a rolling basis starting 7/8; must reply within 2 week(s) of notification.

CONTACT
Marcia Rose, Financial Aid Director
1593 11th Avenue, Granite Falls, MN 56241
(320) 564-4511

Normandale Community College

Bloomington, Minnesota
www.normandale.edu   Federal Code: 007954

2-year public community college in very large city.
Enrollment: 9,239 undergrads.
Selectivity: Open admission; but selective for some programs.

BASIC COSTS (2007-2008)
Tuition and fees: $4,512; out-of-state residents $4,512.
Per-credit charge: $134; out-of-state residents $134.
Additional info: Tuition rates vary in states having reciprocity agreements with Minnesota.

FINANCIAL AID PICTURE
Students with need: Need-based aid available for full-time and part-time students. Work study available nights, weekends, and for part-time students.
Students without need: No-need awards available for academics, leadership, music/drama, state/district residency.

FINANCIAL AID PROCEDURES
Forms required: FAFSA.
Dates and Deadlines: Priority date 4/1; no closing date. Applicants notified on a rolling basis starting 4/15.

CONTACT
Catherine Breuer, Associate Dean for Financial Aid and Scholarships
9700 France Avenue South, Bloomington, MN 55431
(952) 487-8202

North Central University

Minneapolis, Minnesota
www.northcentral.edu   Federal Code: 002369

4-year private university and Bible college in large city, affiliated with Assemblies of God.
Enrollment: 1,181 undergrads, 9% part-time. 231 full-time freshmen.
Selectivity: Admits over 75% of applicants.

BASIC COSTS (2008-2009)
Tuition and fees: $14,586.
Per-credit charge: $456.
Room and board: $5,330.

FINANCIAL AID PICTURE (2006-2007)
Students with need: 41% of average financial aid package awarded as scholarships/grants, 59% awarded as loans/jobs. Need-based aid available for part-time students. Work study available nights, weekends, and for part-time students.
Students without need: No-need awards available for academics, music/drama.
Scholarships offered: President's Scholarship; $2,500 per year; renewable; awarded to first-time entering freshmen and transfer students based on academic performance. Dean's Scholarship; $1,500 per year; renewable; awarded to first-time entering freshmen and transfer students; based on academic performance.
Cumulative student debt: 84% of graduating class had student loans; average debt was $29,496.

FINANCIAL AID PROCEDURES
Forms required: FAFSA.
Dates and Deadlines: No deadline. Applicants notified on a rolling basis starting 3/1; must reply within 2 week(s) of notification.
Transfers: Priority date 4/15; no deadline. Applicants notified on a rolling basis starting 3/1.

CONTACT
Donna Jager, Director of Financial Aid
910 Elliot Avenue, Minneapolis, MN 55404
(800) 289-4488 ext. 289

North Hennepin Community College

Brooklyn Park, Minnesota
www.nhcc.edu   Federal Code: 002370

2-year public community college in small city.
Enrollment: 6,255 undergrads, 60% part-time. 901 full-time freshmen.
Selectivity: Open admission; but selective for some programs.

BASIC COSTS (2007-2008)
Tuition and fees: $4,420; out-of-state residents $4,420.
Per-credit charge: $137; out-of-state residents $137.

FINANCIAL AID PICTURE (2006-2007)
Students with need: 39% of average financial aid package awarded as scholarships/grants, 61% awarded as loans/jobs. Need-based aid available for part-time students. Work study available nights, weekends, and for part-time students.
Students without need: No-need awards available for academics, art, leadership.
Additional info: Computerized financial aid application.

FINANCIAL AID PROCEDURES
Forms required: FAFSA.
Dates and Deadlines: Priority date 4/15; no closing date. Applicants notified on a rolling basis starting 6/1.
Transfers: No deadline. Applicants notified on a rolling basis.

CONTACT
Jackie Olsson, Director of Financial Aid
7411 85th Avenue North, Minneapolis, MN 55445
(763) 424-0702

Northland Community & Technical College

Thief River Falls, Minnesota
www.northlandcollege.edu   Federal Code: 002385

2-year public community and technical college in small town.
Enrollment: 1,957 undergrads.
Selectivity: Open admission.

BASIC COSTS (2007-2008)
Tuition and fees: $4,764.
Per-credit charge: $145.
Additional info: Tuition is the same for both in-state and out-of-state students.

FINANCIAL AID PICTURE (2006-2007)
Students with need: 33% of average financial aid package awarded as scholarships/grants, 67% awarded as loans/jobs. Need-based aid available for part-time students. Work study available nights.
Students without need: No-need awards available for academics.

FINANCIAL AID PROCEDURES
Forms required: FAFSA.
Dates and Deadlines: Priority date 5/1; no closing date. Applicants notified on a rolling basis starting 5/15.

CONTACT
Donna Quam, Financial Aid Director
1101 Highway One East; Thief River Falls, MN 56701
(218) 681-0946

Northwest Technical College

Bemidji, Minnesota
www.ntcmn.edu   Federal Code: 005759

2-year public technical college in large town.
Enrollment: 891 undergrads, 36% part-time. 163 full-time freshmen.
Selectivity: Open admission.

BASIC COSTS (2007-2008)
Tuition and fees: $4,704; out-of-state residents $4,704.
Per-credit charge: $147; out-of-state residents $147.

FINANCIAL AID PICTURE (2007-2008)
Students with need: 58% of average financial aid package awarded as scholarships/grants, 42% awarded as loans/jobs. Need-based aid available for part-time students. Work study available nights.
Students without need: This college awards aid only to students with need.

FINANCIAL AID PROCEDURES
Forms required: FAFSA, institutional form.
Dates and Deadlines: Priority date 7/1; no closing date. Applicants notified on a rolling basis.

CONTACT
Paul Lindseth, Director of Financial Aid
905 Grant Avenue Southeast, Bemidji, MN 56601-4907
(218) 333-6648

Northwest Technical Institute

Eagan, Minnesota
www.nti.edu   Federal Code: 008267

2-year for-profit technical college in small city.
Enrollment: 126 undergrads.
Selectivity: Open admission.

BASIC COSTS (2008-2009)
Tuition and fees: $14,845.
Per-credit charge: $463.
Additional info: Tuition at time of enrollment locked for 2 years.

FINANCIAL AID PICTURE
Students with need: Need-based aid available for full-time and part-time students.

FINANCIAL AID PROCEDURES
Forms required: FAFSA, institutional form.
Dates and Deadlines: No deadline. Applicants notified on a rolling basis; must reply within 2 week(s) of notification.

CONTACT
Katherine Spear, Director of Financial Aid
950 Blue Gentian Road, Eagan, MN 55121
(952) 944-0080 ext. 101

Northwestern College

Saint Paul, Minnesota
www.nwc.edu   Federal Code: 002371

4-year private Bible and liberal arts college in very large city, affiliated with nondenominational tradition.
Enrollment: 1,845 undergrads, 3% part-time. 486 full-time freshmen.
Selectivity: Admits over 75% of applicants.

BASIC COSTS (2008-2009)

Tuition and fees: $22,250.

Per-credit charge: $950.

Room and board: $7,050.

Additional info: Computer technology fee of $170. Tuition/fee waivers available for minority students.

FINANCIAL AID PICTURE (2006-2007)

Students with need: Out of 477 full-time freshmen who applied for aid, 388 were judged to have need. Of these, 387 received aid, and 47 had their full need met. Average financial aid package met 70% of need; average scholarship/grant was $12,098; average loan was $3,020. For part-time students, average financial aid package was $8,072.

Students without need: 89 full-time freshmen who did not demonstrate need for aid received scholarships/grants; average award was $6,117. No-need awards available for academics, alumni affiliation, leadership, music/drama.

Scholarships offered: Eagle Scholars Program; $12,745 per year; ACT score of 30 or SAT score of 1320; up to 15 awarded yearly to incoming freshmen; renewable annually with successful involvement in program, including a cumulative GPA of 3.65 or higher.

Cumulative student debt: 78% of graduating class had student loans; average debt was $22,650.

Additional info: Students enrolled at least half-time in the FOCUS or Distance Education degree programs may apply for financial aid from the same Federal and state sources as traditional undergraduates do. However, their expense budgets and aid are less due to lower tuition: FOCUS, $315/credit; Center for Distance Education, $235/credit. Master's degree students with appropriate academic loads may apply for assistance from Federal student loan programs.

FINANCIAL AID PROCEDURES

Forms required: FAFSA, institutional form.

Dates and Deadlines: Priority date 3/1; closing date 6/1. Applicants notified on a rolling basis starting 3/1; must reply within 2 week(s) of notification.

CONTACT

Richard Blatchley, Director of Financial Aid

3003 Snelling Avenue North, Saint Paul, MN 55113-1598

(651) 631-5212

Oak Hills Christian College

Bemidji, Minnesota

www.oakhills.edu   Federal Code: 016116

4-year private Bible college in large town, affiliated with interdenominational tradition.

Enrollment: 163 undergrads, 11% part-time. 21 full-time freshmen.

Selectivity: Admits over 75% of applicants.

BASIC COSTS (2008-2009)

Tuition and fees: $12,820.

Per-credit charge: $375.

Room and board: $4,720.

Additional info: Tuition at time of enrollment locked for 4 years.

FINANCIAL AID PICTURE (2006-2007)

Students with need: Out of 21 full-time freshmen who applied for aid, 18 were judged to have need. Of these, 18 received aid. Average financial aid package met 56% of need; average scholarship/grant was $5,786; average loan was $1,873. For part-time students, average financial aid package was $3,457.

Students without need: 3 full-time freshmen who did not demonstrate need for aid received scholarships/grants; average award was $4,101. No-need awards available for academics, alumni affiliation.

Cumulative student debt: 78% of graduating class had student loans; average debt was $35,996.

FINANCIAL AID PROCEDURES

Forms required: FAFSA, institutional form.

Dates and Deadlines: No deadline. Applicants notified on a rolling basis starting 3/1.

Transfers: No deadline. Applicants notified on a rolling basis starting 3/1.

CONTACT

Dan Hovestol, Financial Aid Director

1600 Oak Hills Road, SW, Bemidji, MN 56601-8826

(218) 751-8671 ext. 1220

Pillsbury Baptist Bible College

Owatonna, Minnesota

www.pillsbury.edu   Federal Code: 016117

4-year private Bible college in large town, affiliated with Baptist faith.

Enrollment: 153 undergrads, 7% part-time. 46 full-time freshmen.

BASIC COSTS (2008-2009)

Tuition and fees: $10,228.

Per-credit charge: $285.

Room and board: $4,996.

FINANCIAL AID PICTURE (2006-2007)

Students with need: 67% of average financial aid package awarded as scholarships/grants, 33% awarded as loans/jobs.

FINANCIAL AID PROCEDURES

Dates and Deadlines: Priority date 4/15; no closing date.

CONTACT

Thomas Lawson, Financial Aid Administrator

315 South Grove Avenue, Owatonna, MN 55060

(507) 451-2710 ext. 271

Pine Technical College

Pine City, Minnesota

www.pinetech.edu   Federal Code: 005535

2-year public technical college in small town.

Enrollment: 512 undergrads.

Selectivity: Open admission; but selective for some programs.

BASIC COSTS (2007-2008)

Tuition and fees: $4,206; out-of-state residents $7,986.

Per-credit charge: $126; out-of-state residents $252.

Additional info: Various reciprocity agreements with some neighboring states provide tuition reduction to out-of-state students.

FINANCIAL AID PICTURE

Students with need: Need-based aid available for full-time and part-time students.

Students without need: No-need awards available for academics, state/district residency.

FINANCIAL AID PROCEDURES

Forms required: FAFSA, institutional form.

Dates and Deadlines: Priority date 5/5; no closing date. Applicants notified on a rolling basis starting 6/5.

CONTACT

Susan Pixley, Financial Aid Director

900 Fourth Street, SE, Pine City, MN 55063

(320) 629-5100 ext. 161

Rainy River Community College

International Falls, Minnesota
www.rrcc.mnscu.edu   Federal Code: 006775

2-year public community and technical college in small town.
Enrollment: 421 undergrads.
Selectivity: Open admission.

BASIC COSTS (2007-2008)
Tuition and fees: $4,380; out-of-state residents $5,348.
Per-credit charge: $129; out-of-state residents $161.
Additional info: Tuition/fee waivers available for unemployed or children of unemployed.

FINANCIAL AID PICTURE
Students with need: Need-based aid available for full-time and part-time students. Work study available nights, weekends, and for part-time students.
Students without need: No-need awards available for academics, alumni affiliation, minority status, state/district residency.
Additional info: Many scholarship and employment opportunities for applicants showing little or no need.

FINANCIAL AID PROCEDURES
Forms required: FAFSA, institutional form.
Dates and Deadlines: Priority date 6/1; no closing date. Applicants notified on a rolling basis starting 5/1; must reply within 3 week(s) of notification.

CONTACT
Scott Riley, Director of Financial Aid
1501 Highway 71, International Falls, MN 56649
(218) 285-7722

Rasmussen College: Eagan

Eagan, Minnesota
www.rasmussen.edu   Federal Code: 004648

4-year for-profit business and career college in small city.
Enrollment: 505 undergrads, 70% part-time. 52 full-time freshmen.
Selectivity: Open admission.

BASIC COSTS (2007-2008)
Additional info: Regular courses: $345/credit; networking classes: $445/credit; child care classes: $255/credit.

FINANCIAL AID PICTURE
Students with need: Need-based aid available for full-time and part-time students.
Students without need: This college awards aid only to students with need.

FINANCIAL AID PROCEDURES
Forms required: FAFSA, institutional form.
Dates and Deadlines: No deadline. Applicants notified on a rolling basis.

CONTACT
Jamie Hauer, Director of Financial Services
3500 Federal Drive, Eagan, MN 55122
(651) 687-9000

Rasmussen College: Eden Prairie

Eden Prairie, Minnesota
www.rasmussen.edu   Federal Code: 011686

2-year for-profit business and junior college in very large city.
Enrollment: 506 undergrads.
Selectivity: Open admission.

BASIC COSTS (2007-2008)
Additional info: Regular courses: $345/credit; networking classes: $445/credit; child care classes: $255/credit. Tuition at time of enrollment locked for 2 years.

FINANCIAL AID PICTURE
Students with need: Need-based aid available for full-time and part-time students.

FINANCIAL AID PROCEDURES
Forms required: FAFSA, state aid form, institutional form.
Dates and Deadlines: No deadline. Applicants notified on a rolling basis.

CONTACT
Lindsay Adams, Financial Aid Director
7905 Golden Triangle Drive, Suite 100, Eden Prairie, MN 55344
(952) 545-2000

Ridgewater College

Willmar, Minnesota
www.ridgewater.edu   Federal Code: 005252

2-year public community and technical college in large town.
Enrollment: 3,676 undergrads. 1,190 full-time freshmen.
Selectivity: Open admission; but selective for some programs.

BASIC COSTS (2007-2008)
Tuition and fees: $4,517; out-of-state residents $4,517.
Per-credit charge: $134; out-of-state residents $134.
Additional info: Some courses may carry higher per credit hour charge. Reciprocity agreements for in-state tuition rates with some neighboring states. Tuition/fee waivers available for adults.

FINANCIAL AID PICTURE (2007-2008)
Students with need: 33% of average financial aid package awarded as scholarships/grants, 67% awarded as loans/jobs. Need-based aid available for part-time students. Work study available nights, weekends, and for part-time students.
Additional info: Special funds are available for adult transfer students returning or continuing education after a 7-year absence from academic training. ALLISS grants provide reimbursement for one class, up to five credits for one semester.

FINANCIAL AID PROCEDURES
Forms required: FAFSA, institutional form.
Dates and Deadlines: No deadline. Applicants notified on a rolling basis.

CONTACT
Jim Rice, Director of Financial Aid
2101 15th Avenue Northwest, Willmar, MN 56201
(320) 222-7474

Riverland Community College

Austin, Minnesota
www.riverland.edu   Federal Code: 002335

2-year public community and technical college in large town.
Enrollment: 3,477 undergrads, 60% part-time. 533 full-time freshmen.
Selectivity: Open admission; but selective for some programs.

BASIC COSTS (2007-2008)
Tuition and fees: $4,590; out-of-state residents $4,590.
Per-credit charge: $136.
Additional info: Some courses carry a higher per-credit-hour charge.

FINANCIAL AID PICTURE (2006-2007)
Students with need: Need-based aid available for part-time students.

Students without need: This college awards aid only to students with need.

Cumulative student debt: 37% of graduating class had student loans; average debt was $3,248.

Additional info: One class tuition-free for Minnesota residents over 25 who have not attended college for at least 7 years.

FINANCIAL AID PROCEDURES

Forms required: FAFSA.

Dates and Deadlines: Priority date 5/15; no closing date. Applicants notified on a rolling basis; must reply within 5 week(s) of notification.

Transfers: No deadline. Applicants notified on a rolling basis.

CONTACT

Judy Robeck, Financial Aid Director
1900 Eighth Avenue, NW, Austin, MN 55912-1407
(507) 433-0511

Saint Cloud State University
St. Cloud, Minnesota
www.stcloudstate.edu   Federal Code: 002377

4-year public university in small city.

Enrollment: 13,381 undergrads, 12% part-time. 2,325 full-time freshmen.

Selectivity: Admits over 75% of applicants.

BASIC COSTS (2007-2008)

Tuition and fees: $5,955; out-of-state residents $12,097.

Per-credit charge: $175; out-of-state residents $380.

Room and board: $5,592.

FINANCIAL AID PICTURE

Students with need: Need-based aid available for full-time and part-time students. Work study available nights, weekends, and for part-time students.

Students without need: No-need awards available for academics, art, athletics, leadership, music/drama.

FINANCIAL AID PROCEDURES

Forms required: FAFSA, institutional form.

Dates and Deadlines: No deadline. Applicants notified on a rolling basis starting 6/15.

Transfers: No deadline. Applicants notified on a rolling basis starting 6/15.

CONTACT

Michael Uran, Financial Aid Director
720 Fourth Avenue South, St. Cloud, MN 56301
(320) 308-2047

St. Cloud Technical College
St. Cloud, Minnesota
www.sctc.edu   Federal Code: 005534

2-year public technical college in small city.

Enrollment: 3,333 undergrads, 28% part-time. 822 full-time freshmen.

Selectivity: Open admission; but selective for some programs.

BASIC COSTS (2007-2008)

Tuition and fees: $4,424; out-of-state residents $4,424.

Per-credit charge: $134.

Additional info: Higher per-credit-hour charges may apply to some programs. Various reciprocity agreements with some neighboring states provide tuition reduction to out-of-state students. Tuition for online courses is $144 per credit.

FINANCIAL AID PICTURE (2006-2007)

Students with need: 67% of average financial aid package awarded as scholarships/grants, 33% awarded as loans/jobs. Need-based aid available for part-time students. Work study available nights, weekends, and for part-time students.

Students without need: No-need awards available for academics, leadership, state/district residency.

FINANCIAL AID PROCEDURES

Forms required: FAFSA, institutional form.

Dates and Deadlines: No deadline. Applicants notified on a rolling basis starting 6/1.

CONTACT

Anita Baugh, Financial Aid Director
1540 Northway Drive, St. Cloud, MN 56303
(320) 308-5961

St. John's University
Collegeville, Minnesota
www.csbsju.edu   Federal Code: 002379

4-year private university and liberal arts college for men in rural community, affiliated with Roman Catholic Church.

Enrollment: 1,917 undergrads. 518 full-time freshmen.

Selectivity: Admits 50 to 75% of applicants.

BASIC COSTS (2008-2009)

Tuition and fees: $28,668.

Per-credit charge: $1,171.

Room and board: $7,248.

FINANCIAL AID PICTURE (2007-2008)

Students with need: Out of 380 full-time freshmen who applied for aid, 287 were judged to have need. Of these, 287 received aid, and 136 had their full need met. Average financial aid package met 94% of need; average scholarship/grant was $16,109; average loan was $4,267. For part-time students, average financial aid package was $9,180.

Students without need: 214 full-time freshmen who did not demonstrate need for aid received scholarships/grants; average award was $10,465. No-need awards available for academics, art, leadership, music/drama, ROTC.

Scholarships offered: Regents/Trustees Scholarships: $13,500; minimum 3.6 GPA, 30 ACT, 1980 SAT, demonstrated leadership and service, faculty interview. President's Scholarships: $7,500-$11,500; and Dean's Scholarships: $3,000-$7,000; GPA, high school rank, ACT/SAT scores, leadership and service. Art, Music and Theater Scholarships: up to $4,000; excellence in these subjects in high school, portfolio, tape, audition. Diversity Leadership Scholarships: up to $5,000; demonstrated diversity leadership and service in the area of cultural and ethnic diversity, personal statement on topic. Army ROTC and ROTC Nursing Scholarships: $23,000; demonstrated leadership potential, high school GPA, class standing, ACT/SAT scores, high achievement with broad interests and willingness to take on challenges. Phi Theta Kappa Scholarship: $1,000; member of Phi Theta Kappa (transfer students only).

FINANCIAL AID PROCEDURES

Forms required: FAFSA, institutional form.

Dates and Deadlines: Priority date 3/15; no closing date. Applicants notified on a rolling basis starting 3/15; must reply by 5/1.

CONTACT

Stuart Perry, Director of Financial Aid
PO Box 7155, Collegeville, MN 56321-7155
(320) 363-3664

St. Mary's University of Minnesota
Winona, Minnesota
www.smumn.edu   Federal Code: 002380

4-year private university in large town, affiliated with Roman Catholic Church.
Enrollment: 1,979 undergrads, 29% part-time. 397 full-time freshmen.
Selectivity: Admits over 75% of applicants.

BASIC COSTS (2008-2009)
Tuition and fees: $24,150.
Per-credit charge: $790.
Room and board: $6,380.

FINANCIAL AID PICTURE (2007-2008)
Students with need: Out of 336 full-time freshmen who applied for aid, 273 were judged to have need. Of these, 273 received aid, and 73 had their full need met. Average financial aid package met 81% of need; average scholarship/grant was $10,348; average loan was $3,356. Need-based aid available for part-time students.
Students without need: 124 full-time freshmen who did not demonstrate need for aid received scholarships/grants; average award was $6,357. No-need awards available for academics, alumni affiliation, art, leadership, minority status, music/drama, religious affiliation.
Cumulative student debt: 80% of graduating class had student loans; average debt was $26,511.

FINANCIAL AID PROCEDURES
Forms required: FAFSA.
Dates and Deadlines: Priority date 3/15; no closing date. Applicants notified on a rolling basis starting 2/1; must reply within 3 week(s) of notification.

CONTACT
Jayne Wobig, Director of Financial Aid
700 Terrace Heights, #2, Winona, MN 55987-1399
(507) 457-1437

St. Olaf College
Northfield, Minnesota   Federal Code: 002382
www.stolaf.edu   CSS Code: 6638

4-year private liberal arts college in large town, affiliated with Evangelical Lutheran Church in America.
Enrollment: 2,988 undergrads. 751 full-time freshmen.
Selectivity: Admits 50 to 75% of applicants.

BASIC COSTS (2008-2009)
Tuition and fees: $34,300.
Per-credit charge: $1,075.
Room and board: $7,900.
Additional info: Tuition/fee waivers available for adults.

FINANCIAL AID PICTURE (2007-2008)
Students with need: Out of 596 full-time freshmen who applied for aid, 466 were judged to have need. Of these, 466 received aid, and 466 had their full need met. Average financial aid package met 100% of need; average scholarship/grant was $15,483; average loan was $4,053.
Students without need: 147 full-time freshmen who did not demonstrate need for aid received scholarships/grants; average award was $8,259. No-need awards available for academics, leadership, music/drama.
Scholarships offered: Buntrock Scholarship: $12,000. Presidential Scholarship: $7,500. National Hispanic Scholar/Nat Achievement: $7,500. National Merit Scholarship: $7,500; TRiO Scholarships: $6,000. Music Scholarships: $4,000 - $7,000. Service Leadership Awards: $4,000. All are 4-year renewable; number awarded varies yearly.
Cumulative student debt: 64% of graduating class had student loans; average debt was $25,501.

Additional info: Limited number of music lesson fee waivers available for music majors, awarded on audition basis only.

FINANCIAL AID PROCEDURES
Forms required: FAFSA, CSS PROFILE.
Dates and Deadlines: Priority date 1/15; closing date 4/15. Applicants notified on a rolling basis starting 3/1; must reply by 5/1 or within 2 week(s) of notification.
Transfers: Closing date 1/15. Applicants notified by 3/1; must reply by 5/1 or within 2 week(s) of notification.

CONTACT
Katharine Ruby, Director of Financial Aid
1520 St. Olaf Avenue, Northfield, MN 55057
(507) 786-3019

St. Paul College
Saint Paul, Minnesota
www.saintpaul.edu   Federal Code: 005533

2-year public community and technical college in large city.
Enrollment: 4,596 undergrads, 59% part-time. 489 full-time freshmen.
Selectivity: Open admission.

BASIC COSTS (2007-2008)
Tuition and fees: $4,314; out-of-state residents $8,304.
Per-credit charge: $133; out-of-state residents $266.
Additional info: Various reciprocity agreements with some neighboring states provide tuition reduction to out-of-state students.

FINANCIAL AID PICTURE
Students with need: Need-based aid available for full-time and part-time students. Work study available nights.
Students without need: No-need awards available for leadership.

FINANCIAL AID PROCEDURES
Forms required: FAFSA.
Dates and Deadlines: No deadline. Applicants notified on a rolling basis starting 6/1.

CONTACT
Susan Prater, Financial Aid Director
235 Marshall Avenue, Saint Paul, MN 55102-1800
(651) 846-1386

South Central College
North Mankato, Minnesota
www.southcentral.edu   Federal Code: 005537

2-year public community and technical college in large town.
Enrollment: 2,838 undergrads, 47% part-time. 783 full-time freshmen.
Selectivity: Open admission.

BASIC COSTS (2007-2008)
Tuition and fees: $4,436.
Per-credit charge: $133.

FINANCIAL AID PICTURE
Students with need: Need-based aid available for full-time and part-time students. Work study available nights.

FINANCIAL AID PROCEDURES
Forms required: FAFSA, institutional form.
Dates and Deadlines: Priority date 5/1; no closing date. Applicants notified on a rolling basis starting 6/1.
Transfers: No deadline. Applicants notified on a rolling basis starting 6/1.

CONTACT

Jayne Dinse, Financial Aid Director
1920 Lee Boulevard, North Mankato, MN 56003
(507) 389-7220

Southwest Minnesota State University

Marshall, Minnesota
www.southwestmsu.edu   Federal Code: 002375

4-year public liberal arts and technical college in large town.
Enrollment: 2,600 undergrads, 14% part-time. 405 full-time freshmen.

BASIC COSTS (2007-2008)

Tuition and fees: $6,517.
Per-credit charge: $181.
Room and board: $5,616.

FINANCIAL AID PICTURE (2007-2008)

Students with need: Average financial aid package met 38% of need; average scholarship/grant was $4,865; average loan was $3,218. For part-time students, average financial aid package was $4,976.
Students without need: No-need awards available for academics, alumni affiliation, art, athletics, leadership, minority status, music/drama, state/district residency.
Cumulative student debt: 89% of graduating class had student loans; average debt was $20,892.

FINANCIAL AID PROCEDURES

Forms required: FAFSA, institutional form.
Dates and Deadlines: Priority date 3/1; no closing date. Applicants notified on a rolling basis starting 5/15.

CONTACT

David Vikander, Director of Financial Aid
1501 State Street, Marshall, MN 56258-1598
(507) 537-6281

University of Minnesota: Crookston

Crookston, Minnesota
www.UMCrookston.edu   Federal Code: 004069

4-year public branch campus college in small town.
Enrollment: 1,142 undergrads, 15% part-time. 238 full-time freshmen.
Selectivity: Admits over 75% of applicants.

BASIC COSTS (2007-2008)

Tuition and fees: $8,821; out-of-state residents $8,821.
Per-credit charge: $248.
Room and board: $5,622.
Additional info: Tuition at time of enrollment locked for 4 years; tuition/fee waivers available for minority students.

FINANCIAL AID PICTURE (2007-2008)

Students with need: 46% of average financial aid package awarded as scholarships/grants, 54% awarded as loans/jobs. Need-based aid available for part-time students. Work study available nights, weekends, and for part-time students.
Students without need: No-need awards available for academics, athletics, leadership, minority status, ROTC.
Scholarships offered: Merit Scholarship: based on a minimum GPA of 3.25 and a minimum ACT score of 21. Presidential Scholarship: $20,000 total ($5,000 annually for four years); based on ACT score of 30 and GPA of 3.25. Chancellor Scholarship: $8,000 total ($4,000 annually for two years); based on ACT score of 27-29 and GPA of 3.25. Distinguished Scholarship: $6,000 total ($3,000 annually for two years); based on ACT score of 25-26 and 3.25 GPA. Merriam Legacy Scholarship: $4,000 total ($2,000 annually for two

years); based on ACT score of 23-24 and a 3.25 GPA. Achievement Scholarship: $2,000; based on ACT score of 21-22 and 3.25 GPA.
Additional info: Tuition guarantee plan available to all students who apply for it.

FINANCIAL AID PROCEDURES

Forms required: FAFSA.
Dates and Deadlines: Priority date 2/15; no closing date. Applicants notified on a rolling basis starting 3/15.

CONTACT

Melissa Dingmann, Director of Financial Aid
2900 University Avenue, Crookston, MN 56716-5001
(218) 281-8563

University of Minnesota: Duluth

Duluth, Minnesota
www.d.umn.edu   Federal Code: 002388

4-year public university in small city.
Enrollment: 9,184 undergrads, 5% part-time. 2,139 full-time freshmen.
Selectivity: Admits 50 to 75% of applicants.

BASIC COSTS (2007-2008)

Tuition and fees: $9,600; out-of-state residents $19,227.
Per-credit charge: $296; out-of-state residents $666.
Room and board: $5,904.

FINANCIAL AID PICTURE

Students with need: Need-based aid available for full-time and part-time students. Work study available nights, weekends, and for part-time students.
Students without need: No-need awards available for academics, athletics, ROTC.

FINANCIAL AID PROCEDURES

Forms required: FAFSA.
Dates and Deadlines: Priority date 3/31; no closing date. Applicants notified on a rolling basis starting 3/1; must reply within 2 week(s) of notification.

CONTACT

Brenda Herzig, Director of Financial Aid
25 Solon Campus Center, Duluth, MN 55812-3000
(218) 726-8000

University of Minnesota: Morris

Morris, Minnesota
www.morris.umn.edu   Federal Code: 002389

4-year public university and liberal arts college in small town.
Enrollment: 1,686 undergrads.
Selectivity: Admits over 75% of applicants.

BASIC COSTS (2007-2008)

Tuition and fees: $9,331; out-of-state residents $9,331.
Per-credit charge: $296.
Room and board: $6,370.
Additional info: Tuition same for both in-state and out-of-state students except for Wisconsin residents, who pay lower rate due to reciprocity agreement.

FINANCIAL AID PICTURE

Students with need: Need-based aid available for full-time and part-time students. Work study available nights, weekends, and for part-time students.
Students without need: No-need awards available for academics, alumni affiliation, leadership, minority status, music/drama.
Scholarships offered: Chancellor's Scholarship: $3,500/year for 4 years; top 5%. Dean's Scholarship: $2,500/year for 4 years; top 10%. Founder's Schol-

arship; $1,000/year for 4 years; top 20%. National Merit Scholarship: full tuition scholarship for 4 years. Prairie Scholars Award: full tuition/year for 4 years; Morris Scholars Award: $5,000/year for 4 years plus one-time $2,500 research or creative project stipend. President's Distinguished Scholar Award: $1,000 to $3,000/year for four years.

Additional info: Land-grant program waiving tuition for Native Americans.

FINANCIAL AID PROCEDURES

Forms required: FAFSA.

Dates and Deadlines: Priority date 3/1; no closing date. Applicants notified on a rolling basis starting 3/1; must reply within 3 week(s) of notification.

CONTACT

Jill Beauregard, Director of Financial Aid
600 East 4th Street, Morris, MN 56267
(800) 992-8863

University of Minnesota: Twin Cities

Minneapolis, Minnesota
www.umn.edu/tc   Federal Code: 003969

4-year public university in very large city.

Enrollment: 28,703 undergrads, 9% part-time. 5,266 full-time freshmen.

Selectivity: Admits 50 to 75% of applicants.

BASIC COSTS (2007-2008)

Tuition and fees: $9,885; out-of-state residents $21,515.

Per-credit charge: $306; out-of-state residents $753.

Room and board: $7,062.

Additional info: Reported costs represent College of Liberal Arts and include annual technology/collegiate fee of an average of $224. Mandatory technology/other fees may vary by program.

FINANCIAL AID PICTURE (2007-2008)

Students with need: Out of 4,056 full-time freshmen who applied for aid, 2,701 were judged to have need. Of these, 2,671 received aid, and 1,519 had their full need met. Average financial aid package met 87% of need; average scholarship/grant was $7,751; average loan was $7,036. For part-time students, average financial aid package was $7,831.

Students without need: This college awards aid only to students with need.

FINANCIAL AID PROCEDURES

Forms required: FAFSA, institutional form.

Dates and Deadlines: Priority date 3/1; no closing date. Applicants notified on a rolling basis starting 2/15.

CONTACT

Kris Wright, Director of Financial Aid
240 Williamson Hall, 231 Pillsbury Drive SE, Minneapolis, MN 55455-0115
(612) 624-1111

University of St. Thomas

Saint Paul, Minnesota
www.stthomas.edu   Federal Code: 002345

4-year private university and liberal arts college in very large city, affiliated with Roman Catholic Church.

Enrollment: 5,939 undergrads, 5% part-time. 1,315 full-time freshmen.

Selectivity: Admits over 75% of applicants.

BASIC COSTS (2008-2009)

Tuition and fees: $27,822.

Room and board: $7,612.

FINANCIAL AID PICTURE (2007-2008)

Students with need: Out of 960 full-time freshmen who applied for aid, 477 were judged to have need. Of these, 477 received aid, and 359 had their full need met. Average financial aid package met 82% of need; average scholarship/grant was $13,690; average loan was $3,766. For part-time students, average financial aid package was $13,471.

Students without need: 348 full-time freshmen who did not demonstrate need for aid received scholarships/grants; average award was $8,578. No-need awards available for academics, music/drama, ROTC.

Cumulative student debt: 62% of graduating class had student loans; average debt was $33,499.

FINANCIAL AID PROCEDURES

Forms required: FAFSA.

Dates and Deadlines: Priority date 4/1; no closing date. Applicants notified on a rolling basis starting 3/1; must reply within 3 week(s) of notification.

Transfers: Recognition scholarship available for Minnesota community college transfer students.

CONTACT

Kris Getting, Director of Admissions and Financial Aid
2115 Summit Avenue, 32F, St. Paul, MN 55105-1096
(651) 962-6550

Vermilion Community College

Ely, Minnesota
www.vcc.edu   Federal Code: 002350

2-year public community and technical college in small town.

Enrollment: 541 undergrads, 6% part-time. 180 full-time freshmen.

Selectivity: Open admission.

BASIC COSTS (2007-2008)

Tuition and fees: $4,374; out-of-state residents $5,342.

Per-credit charge: $129; out-of-state residents $161.

Room and board: $4,740.

Additional info: Various reciprocity agreements with some neighboring states provide tuition reduction to out-of-state students.

FINANCIAL AID PICTURE

Students with need: Need-based aid available for full-time and part-time students. Work study available nights, weekends, and for part-time students.

FINANCIAL AID PROCEDURES

Forms required: FAFSA, institutional form.

Dates and Deadlines: No deadline. Applicants notified on a rolling basis starting 4/1.

CONTACT

Kristi L'Allier, Financial Aid Director
1900 East Camp Street, Ely, MN 55731-9989
(218) 235-2153

Walden University

Minneapolis, Minnesota
www.waldenu.edu   Federal Code: 025402

Upper-division for-profit virtual university in large city.

Enrollment: 1,369 undergrads, 94% part-time.

BASIC COSTS (2008-2009)

Tuition and fees: $11,520.

Per-credit charge: $250.

FINANCIAL AID PICTURE

Students with need: Need-based aid available for full-time and part-time students.

Students without need: This college awards aid only to students with need.

FINANCIAL AID PROCEDURES

Dates and Deadlines: Priority date 8/1; no closing date.
Transfers: No deadline. Applicants notified on a rolling basis.

CONTACT

Ernestine Whiting-Settles, Director of Financial Aid
650 South Exeter Street 8th Floor, Baltimore, MD 21202
(800) 925-3368

Winona State University

Winona, Minnesota
www.winona.edu   Federal Code: 002394

4-year public university in large town.
Enrollment: 7,443 undergrads, 7% part-time. 1,714 full-time freshmen.
Selectivity: Admits over 75% of applicants.

BASIC COSTS (2007-2008)

Tuition and fees: $6,336; out-of-state residents $10,798.
Per-credit charge: $185; out-of-state residents $335.
Room and board: $6,110.
Additional info: Fees include mandatory laptop lease for full-time students.

FINANCIAL AID PICTURE (2006-2007)

Students with need: Out of 1,319 full-time freshmen who applied for aid, 853 were judged to have need. Of these, 830 received aid, and 82 had their full need met. Average financial aid package met 36% of need; average scholarship/grant was $3,856; average loan was $2,334. Need-based aid available for part-time students.
Students without need: 391 full-time freshmen who did not demonstrate need for aid received scholarships/grants; average award was $1,521. No-need awards available for academics, alumni affiliation, art, athletics, leadership, minority status, music/drama, ROTC, state/district residency.
Scholarships offered: Outstanding Academics Honors Award: $2,500, renewable, top 5% of class, ACT 32 or above. WSU Foundation Board Scholarship: $2,000 renewable, top 15% of class, ACT 28-31, essay/interview. Presidential Honor Scholarships: $1,500 renewable; top 15% of class, ACT 28-31; $1,000, renewable, top 10% of class, ACT 27; $750, renewable, top 15% of class, ACT 26. Resident Tuition Scholarships: $3,400, renewable, to out-of-state students, top 15% of class or ACT 25.

FINANCIAL AID PROCEDURES

Forms required: FAFSA.
Dates and Deadlines: Priority date 3/1; no closing date. Applicants notified on a rolling basis starting 5/1; must reply within 3 week(s) of notification.

CONTACT

Greg Peterson, Director of Financial Aid
Office of Admissions, Winona, MN 55987
(800) 342-5978

Mississippi

Alcorn State University

Alcorn State, Mississippi
www.alcorn.edu   Federal Code: 002396

4-year public university and agricultural college in rural community.
Enrollment: 3,004 undergrads, 10% part-time. 505 full-time freshmen.
Selectivity: Admits 50 to 75% of applicants.

BASIC COSTS (2007-2008)

Tuition and fees: $4,320; out-of-state residents $9,816.
Per-credit charge: $180; out-of-state residents $409.
Room and board: $4,880.

FINANCIAL AID PICTURE (2007-2008)

Students with need: Out of 505 full-time freshmen who applied for aid, 484 were judged to have need. Of these, 484 received aid, and 238 had their full need met. Average financial aid package met 86% of need; average scholarship/grant was $3,768; average loan was $2,640. For part-time students, average financial aid package was $12,403.
Students without need: 118 full-time freshmen who did not demonstrate need for aid received scholarships/grants; average award was $5,999. No-need awards available for academics, athletics, ROTC.
Scholarships offered: 60 full-time freshmen received athletic scholarships; average amount $8,229.

FINANCIAL AID PROCEDURES

Forms required: FAFSA, institutional form.
Dates and Deadlines: Priority date 4/1; no closing date. Applicants notified on a rolling basis starting 4/1; must reply within 4 week(s) of notification.

CONTACT

Juanita Russell, Director of Financial Aid
1000 ASU Drive #300, Alcorn State, MS 39096-7500
(601) 877-6190

Belhaven College

Jackson, Mississippi
www.belhaven.edu   Federal Code: 002397

4-year private liberal arts college in large city, affiliated with Presbyterian Church (USA).
Enrollment: 2,071 undergrads, 4% part-time. 241 full-time freshmen.
Selectivity: Admits 50 to 75% of applicants.

BASIC COSTS (2008-2009)

Tuition and fees: $16,360.
Per-credit charge: $350.
Room and board: $6,120.

FINANCIAL AID PICTURE (2007-2008)

Students with need: Average financial aid package met 60% of need; average scholarship/grant was $8,602; average loan was $3,714. For part-time students, average financial aid package was $6,300.
Students without need: No-need awards available for academics, alumni affiliation, art, athletics, music/drama.
Cumulative student debt: 72% of graduating class had student loans; average debt was $24,609.

FINANCIAL AID PROCEDURES

Forms required: FAFSA, state aid form.
Dates and Deadlines: Priority date 3/1; no closing date. Applicants notified on a rolling basis starting 2/1.

CONTACT

Linda Phillips, Director of Financial Aid
1500 Peachtree Street, Jackson, MS 39202
(601) 968-5933

Blue Cliff College: Gulfport

Gulfport, Mississippi
www.bluecliffcollege.com   Federal Code: 035253

2-year for-profit technical college in small city.
Enrollment: 113 undergrads.

Selectivity: Open admission.

BASIC COSTS (2007-2008)
Tuition and fees: $11,350.
Per-credit charge: $200.

FINANCIAL AID PICTURE
Students with need: Need-based aid available for full-time and part-time students.
Students without need: This college awards aid only to students with need.

FINANCIAL AID PROCEDURES
Forms required: FAFSA.

CONTACT
12251 Bernard Parkway, Gulfport, MS 39503

Blue Mountain College
Blue Mountain, Mississippi
www.bmc.edu   Federal Code: 002398

4-year private liberal arts college in rural community, affiliated with Southern Baptist Convention.
Enrollment: 406 undergrads, 18% part-time. 57 full-time freshmen.
Selectivity: Admits 50 to 75% of applicants.

BASIC COSTS (2007-2008)
Tuition and fees: $8,020.
Per-credit charge: $245.
Room and board: $3,800.

FINANCIAL AID PICTURE (2007-2008)
Students with need: 47% of average financial aid package awarded as scholarships/grants, 53% awarded as loans/jobs. Need-based aid available for part-time students.
Students without need: No-need awards available for academics, alumni affiliation, athletics, religious affiliation, state/district residency.
Scholarships offered: ACT/SAT Scholarships: varies from $1,000 to $7,000 per year; based on ACT/SAT score; number varies depending on number of applicants. Valedictorian/Salutatorian Scholarships: $1,000 to $5,000 first year; based on rank in class; unlimited number available. Child of Alumnae/Alumni: $500 first year; must be dependent of graduate; unlimited number available.

FINANCIAL AID PROCEDURES
Forms required: FAFSA, institutional form.
Dates and Deadlines: Priority date 6/1; closing date 8/1. Applicants notified on a rolling basis starting 5/1; must reply within 2 week(s) of notification.
Transfers: No deadline.

CONTACT
Michelle Wiesing, Director of Financial Aid
PO Box 160, Blue Mountain, MS 38610-0160
(662) 685-4771 ext. 141

Coahoma Community College
Clarksdale, Mississippi
www.coahomacc.edu   Federal Code: 002401

2-year public community college in rural community.
Enrollment: 2,216 undergrads.
Selectivity: Open admission; but selective for some programs.

BASIC COSTS (2007-2008)
Tuition and fees: $1,800; out-of-state residents $4,700.
Per-credit charge: $90.

Room and board: $3,514.

FINANCIAL AID PICTURE
Students with need: Need-based aid available for full-time and part-time students.
Students without need: This college awards aid only to students with need.

FINANCIAL AID PROCEDURES
Forms required: FAFSA, institutional form.
Dates and Deadlines: Priority date 4/1; no closing date. Applicants notified on a rolling basis starting 7/1.
Transfers: Priority date 3/1.

CONTACT
Patricia Brooks, Director of Financial Aid
3240 Friars Point Road, Clarksdale, MS 38614-9799
(662) 627-2571

Copiah-Lincoln Community College
Wesson, Mississippi
www.colin.edu   Federal Code: 002402

2-year public community college in small town.
Enrollment: 2,149 full-time undergrads.
Selectivity: Open admission; but selective for some programs.

BASIC COSTS (2007-2008)
Tuition and fees: $1,800; out-of-state residents $3,700.
Per-credit charge: $105; out-of-state residents $180.
Room and board: $3,100.
Additional info: Parking Fee: 20.00.

FINANCIAL AID PICTURE
Students with need: Need-based aid available for full-time and part-time students. Work study available nights, weekends, and for part-time students.
Students without need: No-need awards available for academics, art, athletics, job skills, leadership, music/drama, state/district residency.

FINANCIAL AID PROCEDURES
Forms required: FAFSA.
Dates and Deadlines: Priority date 4/1; no closing date. Applicants notified on a rolling basis starting 4/1; must reply within 2 week(s) of notification.

CONTACT
Leslie Smith, Director of Financial Aid
Box 649, Wesson, MS 39191
(601) 643-8340

Delta State University
Cleveland, Mississippi
www.deltastate.edu   Federal Code: 002403

4-year public university in large town.
Enrollment: 3,356 undergrads.
Selectivity: Admits less than 50% of applicants.

BASIC COSTS (2007-2008)
Tuition and fees: $4,248; out-of-state residents $10,258.
Per-credit charge: $177; out-of-state residents $427.
Room and board: $4,896.

FINANCIAL AID PICTURE (2006-2007)
Students with need: 35% of average financial aid package awarded as scholarships/grants, 65% awarded as loans/jobs. Need-based aid available for part-time students. Work study available nights, weekends, and for part-time students.

Students without need: No-need awards available for academics, alumni affiliation, art, athletics, leadership, music/drama, religious affiliation, ROTC, state/district residency.

FINANCIAL AID PROCEDURES

Forms required: FAFSA, state aid form, institutional form.
Dates and Deadlines: Priority date 3/1; no closing date. Applicants notified on a rolling basis starting 4/1; must reply within 2 week(s) of notification.

CONTACT

Ann Mullins, Director of Student Financial Assistance
Kent Wyatt Hall Rm 117, Cleveland, MS 38733
(662) 846-4670

East Mississippi Community College
Scooba, Mississippi
www.eastms.edu   Federal Code: 002405

2-year public community college in rural community.
Enrollment: 4,012 undergrads.
Selectivity: Open admission; but selective for some programs.

BASIC COSTS (2007-2008)

Tuition and fees: $1,820; out-of-state residents $3,570.
Room and board: $2,800.
Additional info: $50 health fee for on-campus residents.

FINANCIAL AID PICTURE

Students with need: Need-based aid available for full-time and part-time students.
Students without need: No-need awards available for academics, art, athletics, leadership, music/drama, state/district residency.

FINANCIAL AID PROCEDURES

Forms required: FAFSA, state aid form, institutional form.
Dates and Deadlines: Priority date 4/1; no closing date. Applicants notified on a rolling basis starting 4/1; must reply within 2 week(s) of notification.

CONTACT

Jim Gibson, Financial Aid Director
Admissions Office, Scooba, MS 39358
(662) 476-5079

Hinds Community College
Raymond, Mississippi
www.hindscc.edu   Federal Code: 002407

2-year public branch campus and community college in small town.
Enrollment: 10,013 undergrads.
Selectivity: Open admission; but selective for some programs.

BASIC COSTS (2007-2008)

Tuition and fees: $1,740; out-of-state residents $3,946.
Per-credit charge: $85; out-of-state residents $170.
Room and board: $2,530.

FINANCIAL AID PICTURE (2006-2007)

Students with need: 98% of average financial aid package awarded as scholarships/grants, 2% awarded as loans/jobs. Need-based aid available for part-time students.
Students without need: No-need awards available for academics, art, athletics, job skills, leadership, minority status, music/drama, state/district residency.

FINANCIAL AID PROCEDURES

Forms required: FAFSA.

Dates and Deadlines: Priority date 4/1; no closing date. Applicants notified on a rolling basis starting 5/15; must reply within 2 week(s) of notification.
Transfers: Financial aid transcripts from all previous colleges must be on file prior to award letter being released.

CONTACT

Thurman Mitchell, Director of Financial Aid, Raymond Campus
505 East Main Street, Raymond, MS 39154-1100
(601) 857-3223

Itawamba Community College
Fulton, Mississippi
www.iccms.edu   Federal Code: 002409

2-year public community and technical college in small town.
Enrollment: 5,293 undergrads.
Selectivity: Open admission; but selective for some programs.

BASIC COSTS (2007-2008)

Tuition and fees: $1,630; out-of-state residents $3,380.
Per-credit charge: $85.
Room and board: $2,654.

FINANCIAL AID PICTURE

Students with need: Need-based aid available for full-time and part-time students.
Students without need: No-need awards available for academics, art, athletics, leadership, music/drama, state/district residency.

FINANCIAL AID PROCEDURES

Forms required: FAFSA, institutional form.
Dates and Deadlines: Priority date 4/30; no closing date. Applicants notified on a rolling basis starting 4/15.

CONTACT

Robert Walker, Director of Financial Aid
602 West Hill Street, Fulton, MS 38843-1099
(662) 862-8222

Jackson State University
Jackson, Mississippi
www.jsums.edu   Federal Code: 002410

4-year public university in small city.
Enrollment: 6,823 undergrads.
Selectivity: Admits less than 50% of applicants.

BASIC COSTS (2007-2008)

Tuition and fees: $4,432; out-of-state residents $9,976.
Per-credit charge: $185; out-of-state residents $416.
Room and board: $5,534.
Additional info: Annual utility fee of $44 for residents and $96 for non-residents.

FINANCIAL AID PICTURE (2006-2007)

Students with need: 36% of average financial aid package awarded as scholarships/grants, 64% awarded as loans/jobs. Need-based aid available for part-time students.
Students without need: This college awards aid only to students with need.

FINANCIAL AID PROCEDURES

Forms required: FAFSA.
Dates and Deadlines: Priority date 4/1; closing date 5/1. Applicants notified on a rolling basis starting 5/1.

CONTACT

Betty Moncure, Director, Admissions and Financial Aid
1400 JR Lynch Street, Jackson, MS 39217
(601) 979-2227

Magnolia Bible College
Kosciusko, Mississippi
www.magnolia.edu   Federal Code: 016788

4-year private Bible college in small town, affiliated with Church of Christ.
Enrollment: 35 undergrads, 34% part-time. 2 full-time freshmen.
Selectivity: Open admission.

BASIC COSTS (2008-2009)
Tuition and fees: $6,540.
Per-credit charge: $215.
Room only: $1,610.
Additional info: Reduced tuition for Attala County residents: $1,950 full-time, $65 per credit hour, $90 required fees.

FINANCIAL AID PICTURE (2007-2008)
Students with need: 92% of average financial aid package awarded as scholarships/grants, 8% awarded as loans/jobs. Need-based aid available for part-time students.
Students without need: No-need awards available for academics, leadership, religious affiliation.

FINANCIAL AID PROCEDURES
Forms required: FAFSA, institutional form.
Dates and Deadlines: Priority date 8/1; no closing date. Applicants notified on a rolling basis starting 4/15; must reply within 4 week(s) of notification.

CONTACT
Allen Coker, Financial Aid Coordinator
PO Box 1109, Kosciusko, MS 39090
(662) 289-2896 ext. 106

Meridian Community College
Meridian, Mississippi
www.meridiancc.edu   Federal Code: 002413

2-year public community college in large town.
Enrollment: 2,582 full-time undergrads.
Selectivity: Open admission; but selective for some programs.

BASIC COSTS (2007-2008)
Tuition and fees: $1,660; out-of-state residents $2,950.
Per-credit charge: $80; out-of-state residents $137.
Room and board: $3,350.

FINANCIAL AID PICTURE
Students with need: Need-based aid available for full-time and part-time students.
Students without need: No-need awards available for academics, art, athletics, leadership, music/drama, state/district residency.

FINANCIAL AID PROCEDURES
Forms required: FAFSA, institutional form.
Dates and Deadlines: Priority date 6/1; no closing date. Applicants notified on a rolling basis starting 5/15; must reply within 2 week(s) of notification.

CONTACT
Soraya Bazyari-Welden, Director of Financial Aid
910 Highway 19 North, Meridian, MS 39307-5890
(601) 484-8628

Millsaps College
Jackson, Mississippi
www.millsaps.edu   Federal Code: 002414

4-year private business and liberal arts college in large city, affiliated with United Methodist Church.
Enrollment: 1,029 undergrads, 1% part-time. 232 full-time freshmen.
Selectivity: Admits over 75% of applicants.

BASIC COSTS (2008-2009)
Tuition and fees: $24,754.
Per-credit charge: $720.
Room and board: $8,800.

FINANCIAL AID PICTURE (2006-2007)
Students with need: Out of 180 full-time freshmen who applied for aid, 127 were judged to have need. Of these, 127 received aid, and 52 had their full need met. Average financial aid package met 90% of need; average scholarship/grant was $16,156; average loan was $2,686. For part-time students, average financial aid package was $6,557.
Students without need: 98 full-time freshmen who did not demonstrate need for aid received scholarships/grants; average award was $15,604. No-need awards available for academics, art, leadership, music/drama, religious affiliation.
Cumulative student debt: 59% of graduating class had student loans; average debt was $21,495.

FINANCIAL AID PROCEDURES
Forms required: FAFSA, institutional form.
Dates and Deadlines: Priority date 3/1; no closing date. Applicants notified on a rolling basis starting 3/15; must reply by 5/1 or within 2 week(s) of notification.
Transfers: No deadline. Applicants notified on a rolling basis starting 3/15; must reply by 5/1 or within 2 week(s) of notification.

CONTACT
Patrick James, Director of Financial Aid
1701 North State Street, Jackson, MS 39210-0001
(601) 974-1220

Mississippi College
Clinton, Mississippi
www.mc.edu   Federal Code: 002415

4-year private university in large city, affiliated with Southern Baptist Convention.
Enrollment: 2,911 undergrads, 14% part-time. 553 full-time freshmen.
Selectivity: Admits 50 to 75% of applicants.

BASIC COSTS (2008-2009)
Tuition and fees: $12,800.
Per-credit charge: $382.
Room and board: $5,800.

FINANCIAL AID PICTURE (2007-2008)
Students with need: Out of 527 full-time freshmen who applied for aid, 296 were judged to have need. Of these, 294 received aid, and 118 had their full need met. Average financial aid package met 81% of need; average scholarship/grant was $11,184; average loan was $4,069. For part-time students, average financial aid package was $10,587.
Students without need: 227 full-time freshmen who did not demonstrate need for aid received scholarships/grants; average award was $10,383. No-need awards available for academics, alumni affiliation, art, leadership, music/drama, religious affiliation.

Scholarships offered: Merit Scholarships; up to $10,000; based on various criteria including leadership, academics, church and community involvement; extensive number awarded including some specifically for transfers.

Cumulative student debt: 73% of graduating class had student loans; average debt was $22,146.

Additional info: Student reply date for institutional scholarships: May 1.

FINANCIAL AID PROCEDURES

Forms required: FAFSA, state aid form.

Dates and Deadlines: Priority date 3/1; no closing date. Applicants notified on a rolling basis starting 3/1; must reply by 5/1.

Transfers: No deadline. Applicants notified on a rolling basis.

CONTACT

Karon McMillan, Director of Financial Aid
PO Box 4026, Clinton, MS 39058
(601) 925-3212

Mississippi State University
Mississippi State, Mississippi
www.msstate.edu   Federal Code: 002423

4-year public university in large town.

Enrollment: 13,049 undergrads, 10% part-time. 1,904 full-time freshmen.

Selectivity: Admits 50 to 75% of applicants.

BASIC COSTS (2007-2008)

Tuition and fees: $4,978; out-of-state residents $11,469.

Room and board: $6,951.

FINANCIAL AID PICTURE (2006-2007)

Students with need: Out of 1,357 full-time freshmen who applied for aid, 1,050 were judged to have need. Of these, 1,033 received aid, and 232 had their full need met. Average financial aid package met 63% of need; average scholarship/grant was $5,069; average loan was $2,898. For part-time students, average financial aid package was $8,150.

Students without need: 560 full-time freshmen who did not demonstrate need for aid received scholarships/grants; average award was $2,651. No-need awards available for academics, alumni affiliation, art, athletics, job skills, leadership, minority status, music/drama, ROTC, state/district residency.

Scholarships offered: *Merit:* Entering Freshman Scholarships; starting at $1,000 per year; based on minimum 24 ACT and 3.0 core GPA. Competitive Freshman Scholarships: covers cost of tuition, fees, room and board, books; based on a minimum 29 ACT and 3.5 core GPA. *Athletic:* 65 full-time freshmen received athletic scholarships; average amount $12,460.

Cumulative student debt: 41% of graduating class had student loans; average debt was $20,828.

Additional info: No institutional closing date for FAFSA.

FINANCIAL AID PROCEDURES

Forms required: FAFSA.

Dates and Deadlines: Priority date 4/1; no closing date. Applicants notified on a rolling basis starting 12/1; must reply by 5/1.

Transfers: No deadline. Applicants notified on a rolling basis.

CONTACT

Bruce Crain, Director
Box 6334, Mississippi State, MS 39762
(662) 325-2450

Mississippi University for Women
Columbus, Mississippi
www.muw.edu   Federal Code: 002422

4-year public university and liberal arts college in large town.

Enrollment: 2,003 undergrads.

Selectivity: Admits less than 50% of applicants.

BASIC COSTS (2007-2008)

Tuition and fees: $4,204; out-of-state residents $10,723.

Per-credit charge: $175; out-of-state residents $447.

Room and board: $4,740.

Additional info: Tuition/fee waivers available for adults, minority students.

FINANCIAL AID PICTURE (2006-2007)

Students with need: 45% of average financial aid package awarded as scholarships/grants, 55% awarded as loans/jobs. Need-based aid available for part-time students. Work study available nights, weekends, and for part-time students.

Students without need: No-need awards available for academics, alumni affiliation, leadership, minority status, music/drama, ROTC, state/district residency.

FINANCIAL AID PROCEDURES

Forms required: FAFSA, state aid form.

Dates and Deadlines: Priority date 3/1; no closing date. Applicants notified on a rolling basis starting 3/15; must reply within 2 week(s) of notification.

Transfers: Closing date 4/1.

CONTACT

Dan Miller, Director of Financial Aid
Box W-1613, Columbus, MS 39701
(662) 329-7114

Northeast Mississippi Community College
Booneville, Mississippi
www.nemcc.edu   Federal Code: 002426

2-year public community college in small town.

Enrollment: 3,429 undergrads, 12% part-time. 1,036 full-time freshmen.

Selectivity: Open admission; but selective for some programs.

BASIC COSTS (2008-2009)

Tuition and fees: $1,920; out-of-state residents $3,850.

Per-credit charge: $105; out-of-state residents $212.

Room and board: $2,984.

FINANCIAL AID PICTURE (2007-2008)

Students with need: 71% of average financial aid package awarded as scholarships/grants, 29% awarded as loans/jobs.

FINANCIAL AID PROCEDURES

Forms required: FAFSA, institutional form.

Dates and Deadlines: Priority date 4/1; closing date 6/30. Applicants notified on a rolling basis.

Transfers: No deadline.

CONTACT

Janice Prather, Director of Financial Aid
101 Cunningham Boulevard, Booneville, MS 38829

Northwest Mississippi Community College

Senatobia, Mississippi
www.northwestms.edu   Federal Code: 002427

2-year public community college in small town.
Enrollment: 6,825 undergrads.
Selectivity: Open admission; but selective for some programs.

BASIC COSTS (2008-2009)
Tuition and fees: $1,700; out-of-state residents $3,700.
Per-credit charge: $80; out-of-state residents $125.
Room and board: $2,700.
Additional info: Lab fees range from $15 to $25 per course.

FINANCIAL AID PICTURE (2006-2007)
Students with need: 82% of average financial aid package awarded as scholarships/grants, 18% awarded as loans/jobs.

FINANCIAL AID PROCEDURES
Forms required: FAFSA.
Dates and Deadlines: Priority date 4/1; no closing date. Applicants notified by 8/16.

CONTACT
Joe Boyles, Director of Financial Aid
4975 Highway 51 North, Senatobia, MS 38668
(662) 562-3271

Pearl River Community College

Poplarville, Mississippi
www.prcc.edu   Federal Code: 002430

2-year public community college in small town.
Enrollment: 3,791 undergrads.
Selectivity: Open admission; but selective for some programs.

BASIC COSTS (2007-2008)
Tuition and fees: $1,726; out-of-state residents $5,511.
Per-credit charge: $86; out-of-state residents $244.
Room and board: $3,400.

FINANCIAL AID PICTURE
Students with need: Need-based aid available for full-time and part-time students.
Students without need: No-need awards available for academics, alumni affiliation, athletics, leadership, music/drama, state/district residency.

FINANCIAL AID PROCEDURES
Forms required: FAFSA, institutional form.
Dates and Deadlines: Priority date 4/17; no closing date. Applicants notified on a rolling basis.

CONTACT
Peggy Shoemake, Director of Financial Aid
101 Highway 11 North, Poplarville, MS 39470
(601) 403-1212

Rust College

Holly Springs, Mississippi
www.rustcollege.edu   Federal Code: 002433

4-year private liberal arts college in small town, affiliated with United Methodist Church.
Enrollment: 967 undergrads.

Selectivity: Admits less than 50% of applicants.

BASIC COSTS (2007-2008)
Tuition and fees: $6,600.
Per-credit charge: $283.
Room and board: $3,100.
Additional info: Tuition/fee waivers available for adults.

FINANCIAL AID PICTURE
Students with need: Need-based aid available for full-time and part-time students.
Students without need: No-need awards available for academics, leadership, music/drama, religious affiliation, state/district residency.
Scholarships offered: Honor Track; full tuition; based on top 10% of high school graduating class, GPA 3.5 and above, ACT 22 or above, SAT 1030 or above, 3 letters of recommendation, essay; 17 awarded. Presidential Scholarship; $2,000; for top 10% of high school graduating class, GPA 3.25 and above, ACT 19 and above, SAT 910 and above; 17 awarded. Academic Dean's Scholarship; for top 10% of high school graduating class, GPA 3.0 or above, ACT 17 and above, SAT 830 and above; 17 awarded. SAT scores exclusive of Writing.

FINANCIAL AID PROCEDURES
Forms required: FAFSA, state aid form, institutional form.
Dates and Deadlines: Closing date 5/1. Applicants notified on a rolling basis starting 5/1; must reply within 2 week(s) of notification.
Transfers: No deadline. Financial aid transcripts from previous schools required.

CONTACT
Helen Street, Director of Financial Aid
150 Rust Avenue, Holly Springs, MS 38635-2328
(662) 252-8000 ext. 4062

Southwest Mississippi Community College

Summit, Mississippi
www.smcc.edu   Federal Code: 002436

2-year public community college in rural community.
Enrollment: 1,793 undergrads, 13% part-time. 535 full-time freshmen.
Selectivity: Open admission.

BASIC COSTS (2007-2008)
Tuition and fees: $1,800; out-of-state residents $4,500.
Per-credit charge: $75; out-of-state residents $170.
Room and board: $2,180.

FINANCIAL AID PICTURE
Students with need: Need-based aid available for full-time and part-time students.

FINANCIAL AID PROCEDURES
Dates and Deadlines: No deadline. Applicants notified on a rolling basis.

CONTACT
Stacey Hodges, Director of Financial Aid
1156 College Drive, Summit, MS 39666
(601) 276-3707

Tougaloo College

Tougaloo, Mississippi
www.tougaloo.edu   Federal Code: 002439

4-year private liberal arts college in large city, affiliated with United Christian Mission Society and United Church of Christ.
Enrollment: 856 undergrads, 5% part-time. 199 full-time freshmen.

Selectivity: Admits over 75% of applicants.

BASIC COSTS (2007-2008)

Additional info: Tuition/fee waivers available for adults.

FINANCIAL AID PICTURE

Students with need: Need-based aid available for full-time and part-time students.

Students without need: No-need awards available for academics, athletics, ROTC.

FINANCIAL AID PROCEDURES

Forms required: FAFSA, state aid form, institutional form.

Dates and Deadlines: Priority date 4/15; no closing date. Applicants notified on a rolling basis starting 5/1; must reply within 2 week(s) of notification.

CONTACT

Inez Morris, Director of Financial Aid
500 West County Line Road, Tougaloo, MS 39174
(601) 977-7766

University of Mississippi

University, Mississippi
www.olemiss.edu   Federal Code: 002440

4-year public university in large town.
Enrollment: 12,597 undergrads, 9% part-time. 2,527 full-time freshmen.
Selectivity: Admits over 75% of applicants.

BASIC COSTS (2007-2008)

Tuition and fees: $4,932; out-of-state residents $11,436.
Room and board: $5,398.
Additional info: Tuition/fee waivers available for minority students.

FINANCIAL AID PICTURE (2006-2007)

Students with need: Out of 1,524 full-time freshmen who applied for aid, 933 were judged to have need. Of these, 911 received aid, and 197 had their full need met. Average financial aid package met 50% of need; average scholarship/grant was $5,491; average loan was $3,195. For part-time students, average financial aid package was $5,492.

Students without need: 833 full-time freshmen who did not demonstrate need for aid received scholarships/grants; average award was $4,000. No-need awards available for academics, alumni affiliation, art, athletics, leadership, minority status, music/drama, ROTC, state/district residency.

Scholarships offered: 87 full-time freshmen received athletic scholarships; average amount $10,414.

Cumulative student debt: 41% of graduating class had student loans; average debt was $19,183.

FINANCIAL AID PROCEDURES

Forms required: FAFSA.

Dates and Deadlines: Priority date 3/15; no closing date. Applicants notified on a rolling basis starting 4/1; must reply within 3 week(s) of notification.

Transfers: No deadline. Applicants notified on a rolling basis starting 4/1; must reply within 3 week(s) of notification.

CONTACT

Laura Diven-Brown, Director
145 Martindale, University, MS 38677-1848
(800) 891-4596

University of Mississippi Medical Center

Jackson, Mississippi
www.umc.edu   Federal Code: 004688

Upper-division public health science college in large city.
Enrollment: 514 undergrads, 20% part-time.

Selectivity: Open admission; but selective for some programs. GED not accepted.

BASIC COSTS (2007-2008)

Tuition and fees: $5,104; out-of-state residents $11,608.
Additional info: Tuition and fees quoted are for semester-based nursing program. Required fees vary by program.

FINANCIAL AID PICTURE

Students with need: Need-based aid available for full-time and part-time students.

Students without need: This college awards aid only to students with need.

FINANCIAL AID PROCEDURES

Forms required: FAFSA, state aid form, institutional form.

Dates and Deadlines: Closing date 4/1. Applicants notified by 7/15; must reply within 2 week(s) of notification.

CONTACT

Stacey Carter, Director of Student Financial Aid
2500 North State Street, Jackson, MS 39216
(601) 984-1117

University of Southern Mississippi

Hattiesburg, Mississippi
www.usm.edu   Federal Code: 002441

4-year public university in small city.
Enrollment: 11,924 undergrads, 14% part-time. 1,730 full-time freshmen.
Selectivity: Admits 50 to 75% of applicants.

BASIC COSTS (2007-2008)

Tuition and fees: $5,174; out-of-state residents $11,952.
Per-credit charge: $205; out-of-state residents $488.
Room and board: $5,218.

FINANCIAL AID PICTURE (2006-2007)

Students with need: Out of 1,410 full-time freshmen who applied for aid, 1,110 were judged to have need. Of these, 1,065 received aid, and 311 had their full need met. Average financial aid package met 82% of need; average scholarship/grant was $3,879; average loan was $2,783. For part-time students, average financial aid package was $4,307.

Students without need: 240 full-time freshmen who did not demonstrate need for aid received scholarships/grants; average award was $3,111.

Scholarships offered: 48 full-time freshmen received athletic scholarships; average amount $6,160.

Cumulative student debt: 66% of graduating class had student loans; average debt was $17,646.

FINANCIAL AID PROCEDURES

Forms required: FAFSA, institutional form.

Dates and Deadlines: Priority date 3/15; no closing date. Applicants notified on a rolling basis starting 4/1; must reply within 4 week(s) of notification.

Transfers: Merit scholarships available to community college transfer students based on college GPA.

CONTACT

Kristi Motter, Director of Financial Aid
118 College Drive #5166, Hattiesburg, MS 39406-0001
(601) 266-4111

Wesley College
Florence, Mississippi
www.wesleycollege.edu   Federal Code: 011461

4-year private Bible college in small town, affiliated with Congregational Methodist Church.

Enrollment: 95 undergrads.
Selectivity: Admits less than 50% of applicants.

BASIC COSTS (2007-2008)
Tuition and fees: $8,270.
Per-credit charge: $253.
Room and board: $3,900.

FINANCIAL AID PICTURE
Students with need: Need-based aid available for full-time and part-time students. Work study available nights, weekends, and for part-time students.
Students without need: No-need awards available for academics, alumni affiliation, leadership, religious affiliation.

FINANCIAL AID PROCEDURES
Forms required: FAFSA.
Dates and Deadlines: Closing date 5/14. Applicants notified on a rolling basis starting 7/1; must reply within 2 week(s) of notification.

CONTACT
William Devore, Director of Financial Aid
PO Box 1070, Florence, MS 39073-0070
(601) 845-2265

William Carey University
Hattiesburg, Mississippi
www.wmcarey.edu   Federal Code: 002447

4-year private university and liberal arts college in small city, affiliated with Baptist faith.

Enrollment: 1,679 undergrads, 13% part-time. 165 full-time freshmen.
Selectivity: Admits over 75% of applicants.

BASIC COSTS (2008-2009)
Tuition and fees: $9,750.
Per-credit charge: $310.
Room and board: $3,810.

FINANCIAL AID PICTURE (2007-2008)
Students with need: Average financial aid package for all full-time undergraduates was $14,000. 17% awarded as scholarships/grants, 83% awarded as loans/jobs. Need-based aid available for part-time students. Work study available nights, weekends, and for part-time students.
Students without need: No-need awards available for academics, alumni affiliation, art, athletics, music/drama, religious affiliation.
Cumulative student debt: 85% of graduating class had student loans; average debt was $16,000.

FINANCIAL AID PROCEDURES
Forms required: FAFSA.
Dates and Deadlines: Priority date 4/1; closing date 9/1. Applicants notified on a rolling basis starting 6/1; must reply within 2 week(s) of notification.

CONTACT
William Curry, Dean of Enrollment Management & Records
498 Tuscan Avenue, Hattiesburg, MS 39401
(601) 318-6153

Missouri

Avila University
Kansas City, Missouri
www.avila.edu   Federal Code: 002449

4-year private university and liberal arts college in very large city, affiliated with Roman Catholic Church.
Enrollment: 1,065 undergrads, 18% part-time. 154 full-time freshmen.
Selectivity: Admits 50 to 75% of applicants.

BASIC COSTS (2008-2009)
Tuition and fees: $20,150.
Per-credit charge: $495.
Room and board: $5,800.

FINANCIAL AID PICTURE (2006-2007)
Students with need: Out of 149 full-time freshmen who applied for aid, 143 were judged to have need. Of these, 139 received aid, and 40 had their full need met. Average financial aid package met 25.4% of need; average scholarship/grant was $7,035; average loan was $2,345. For part-time students, average financial aid package was $6,874.
Students without need: 70 full-time freshmen who did not demonstrate need for aid received scholarships/grants; average award was $5,348. No-need awards available for academics, alumni affiliation, art, athletics, music/drama, religious affiliation.
Scholarships offered: 3 full-time freshmen received athletic scholarships; average amount $6,208.
Cumulative student debt: 96% of graduating class had student loans; average debt was $20,418.
Additional info: Financial aid adjusted for increases in tuition based on need.

FINANCIAL AID PROCEDURES
Forms required: FAFSA, institutional form.
Dates and Deadlines: Priority date 3/1; closing date 4/1. Applicants notified on a rolling basis starting 2/1; must reply within 2 week(s) of notification.
Transfers: No deadline. Applicants notified on a rolling basis; must reply within 2 week(s) of notification. Non-need-based academic scholarship available for transfer students.

CONTACT
Kimberly Warren, Director of Financial Aid
11901 Wornall Road, Kansas City, MO 64145-1007
(816) 501-3600

Baptist Bible College
Springfield, Missouri
www.baptist.edu   Federal Code: 013208

4-year private Bible and seminary college in small city, affiliated with Baptist faith.

Enrollment: 544 undergrads, 18% part-time. 123 full-time freshmen.

BASIC COSTS (2008-2009)
Tuition and fees: $13,610.
Per-credit charge: $206.
Room and board: $5,400.

FINANCIAL AID PICTURE
Students with need: Need-based aid available for full-time and part-time students.
Scholarships offered: Founder's Scholarship; $5,500-$9,500. Bible Scholarships; $800 per year.

FINANCIAL AID PROCEDURES

Forms required: FAFSA, institutional form.

Dates and Deadlines: Closing date 5/1. Applicants notified on a rolling basis; must reply within 2 week(s) of notification.

CONTACT

Bob Kotulski, Financial Aid Director
628 East Kearney Street, Springfield, MO 65803
(417) 268-6036

Bolivar Technical College

Bolivar, Missouri
www.bolivarcollege.org   Federal Code: 035793

2-year private nursing and technical college in small town.

Enrollment: 98 undergrads.

Selectivity: Admits over 75% of applicants.

BASIC COSTS (2007-2008)

Tuition and fees: $11,620.

Per-credit charge: $325.

Additional info: Tuition varies by program, $145-$325 per credit-hour.

FINANCIAL AID PICTURE (2007-2008)

Students with need: 51% of average financial aid package awarded as scholarships/grants, 49% awarded as loans/jobs.

FINANCIAL AID PROCEDURES

Dates and Deadlines: Priority date 4/1; no closing date.

CONTACT

Deborah George, Director of Financial Aid
PO Box 592, Bolivar, MO 65613
(417) 777-50622

Calvary Bible College and Theological Seminary

Kansas City, Missouri
www.calvary.edu   Federal Code: 002450

4-year private Bible and seminary college in large city, affiliated with nonde-nominational tradition.

Enrollment: 254 undergrads, 25% part-time. 43 full-time freshmen.

Selectivity: Open admission.

BASIC COSTS (2007-2008)

Tuition and fees: $8,500.

Per-credit charge: $260.

Room and board: $4,000.

Additional info: Tuition/fee waivers available for minority students.

FINANCIAL AID PICTURE (2006-2007)

Students with need: Out of 32 full-time freshmen who applied for aid, 32 were judged to have need. Of these, 32 received aid, and 2 had their full need met. Average financial aid package met 37% of need; average scholar-ship/grant was $3,826. For part-time students, average financial aid package was $5,397.

Students without need: No-need awards available for academics, alumni affiliation, job skills, music/drama, religious affiliation, ROTC.

Cumulative student debt: 32% of graduating class had student loans; aver-age debt was $15,486.

FINANCIAL AID PROCEDURES

Forms required: FAFSA, institutional form.

Dates and Deadlines: Priority date 3/1; closing date 4/1. Applicants notified on a rolling basis starting 5/1.

Transfers: Applicants notified on a rolling basis.

CONTACT

Jenny Olsen, Financial Aid Counselor
15800 Calvary Road, Kansas City, MO 64147
(816) 322-5152 ext. 1323

Central Methodist University

Fayette, Missouri
www.centralmethodist.edu   Federal Code: E00605

4-year private university and liberal arts college in small town, affiliated with United Methodist Church.

Enrollment: 914 undergrads, 3% part-time. 270 full-time freshmen.

Selectivity: Admits 50 to 75% of applicants.

BASIC COSTS (2008-2009)

Tuition and fees: $17,980.

Per-credit charge: $170.

Room and board: $6,000.

FINANCIAL AID PICTURE (2007-2008)

Students with need: Out of 270 full-time freshmen who applied for aid, 270 were judged to have need. Of these, 270 received aid, and 9 had their full need met. Average financial aid package met 56% of need; average scholar-ship/grant was $5,186; average loan was $3,306. For part-time students, av-erage financial aid package was $3,792.

Students without need: 36 full-time freshmen who did not demonstrate need for aid received scholarships/grants; average award was $9,305. No-need awards available for academics, alumni affiliation, athletics, leadership, music/drama, religious affiliation, ROTC.

Scholarships offered: 172 full-time freshmen received athletic scholarships; average amount $2,828.

Cumulative student debt: 87% of graduating class had student loans; aver-age debt was $25,463.

FINANCIAL AID PROCEDURES

Forms required: FAFSA.

Dates and Deadlines: Priority date 3/15; no closing date. Applicants notified on a rolling basis starting 1/30; must reply within 2 week(s) of notification.

Transfers: Institutional financial assistance based on merit is determined by college transfer GPA.

CONTACT

Linda Mackey, Director of Financial Aid
411 Central Methodist Square, Fayette, MO 65248-1198
(660) 248-6245

College of the Ozarks

Point Lookout, Missouri
www.cofo.edu   Federal Code: 002500

4-year private liberal arts college in small town, affiliated with Presbyterian Church (USA).

Enrollment: 1,336 undergrads, 2% part-time. 281 full-time freshmen.

Selectivity: Admits less than 50% of applicants.

BASIC COSTS (2008-2009)

Room and board: $4,700.

Additional info: Cost of full-time tuition met through combination of institu-tional work program and federal, state, and institutional funding. Required fees: $390. Full-time students participating in work program work 15 hours per week for 16 weeks and one 40-hour work week per semester. Part-time students (commuters only) pay $295 per credit hour for tuition and additional $390 per year as required fees.

FINANCIAL AID PICTURE (2007-2008)

Students with need: Average financial aid package met 84% of need; average scholarship/grant was $10,379. For part-time students, average financial aid package was $5,574.

Students without need: No-need awards available for academics, art, athletics, leadership, music/drama, ROTC, state/district residency.

Cumulative student debt: 14% of graduating class had student loans; average debt was $6,770.

FINANCIAL AID PROCEDURES

Forms required: FAFSA.

Dates and Deadlines: Priority date 2/15; no closing date. Applicants notified by 7/1.

Transfers: No deadline. Applicants notified on a rolling basis starting 2/15.

CONTACT

Kyla McCarty, Financial Aid Director
PO Box 17, Point Lookout, MO 65726-0017
(417) 334-6411 ext. 4290

Columbia College

Columbia, Missouri
www.ccis.edu   Federal Code: 002456

4-year private liberal arts college in small city, affiliated with Christian Church (Disciples of Christ).

Enrollment: 1,034 undergrads, 18% part-time. 171 full-time freshmen.

Selectivity: Admits 50 to 75% of applicants.

BASIC COSTS (2007-2008)

Tuition and fees: $13,034.

Per-credit charge: $279.

Room and board: $5,320.

FINANCIAL AID PICTURE (2006-2007)

Students with need: Out of 170 full-time freshmen who applied for aid, 107 were judged to have need. Of these, 103 received aid, and 36 had their full need met. Average financial aid package met 72% of need; average scholarship/grant was $6,255; average loan was $2,988. For part-time students, average financial aid package was $9,598.

Students without need: 43 full-time freshmen who did not demonstrate need for aid received scholarships/grants; average award was $7,325. No-need awards available for academics, alumni affiliation, art, athletics, leadership, music/drama, religious affiliation, ROTC, state/district residency.

Scholarships offered: *Merit:* Columbia College Scholarships:full tuition and room; requires 3.5 GPA, campus visit, interview, essay; renewable with 3.5 GPA. Half-tuition scholarships: minimum 3.4 GPA and 24 ACT; renewable for 3 years with 3.4 GPA. *Athletic:* 9 full-time freshmen received athletic scholarships; average amount $12,530.

Cumulative student debt: 56% of graduating class had student loans; average debt was $10,856.

FINANCIAL AID PROCEDURES

Forms required: FAFSA, institutional form.

Dates and Deadlines: Priority date 3/15; no closing date. Applicants notified on a rolling basis starting 3/1; must reply within 2 week(s) of notification.

Transfers: No deadline. Applicants notified on a rolling basis starting 3/15; must reply within 2 week(s) of notification.

CONTACT

Sharon Abernathy, Director of Financial Aid
1001 Rogers Street, Columbia, MO 65216
(573) 875-7360

Conception Seminary College

Conception, Missouri
www.conception.edu   Federal Code: 002467

4-year private seminary college for men in rural community, affiliated with Roman Catholic Church.

Enrollment: 95 undergrads. 19 full-time freshmen.

Selectivity: Admits over 75% of applicants.

BASIC COSTS (2008-2009)

Tuition and fees: $14,904.

Per-credit charge: $180.

Room and board: $8,736.

FINANCIAL AID PICTURE

Students with need: Need-based aid available for full-time and part-time students. Work study available nights, weekends, and for part-time students.

Students without need: No-need awards available for academics.

FINANCIAL AID PROCEDURES

Forms required: FAFSA.

Dates and Deadlines: No deadline. Applicants notified on a rolling basis starting 8/1; must reply by 8/20.

CONTACT

Justin Hernandez, Financial Aid Officer
Box 502, Conception, MO 64433-0502
(660) 944-2851

Cottey College

Nevada, Missouri
www.cottey.edu   Federal Code: 002458

2-year private junior and liberal arts college for women in small town.

Enrollment: 321 undergrads.

Selectivity: Admits 50 to 75% of applicants.

BASIC COSTS (2007-2008)

Tuition and fees: $13,510.

Room and board: $5,200.

FINANCIAL AID PICTURE

Students with need: Need-based aid available for full-time and part-time students. Work study available nights, weekends, and for part-time students.

Students without need: No-need awards available for academics, alumni affiliation, art, athletics, leadership, music/drama.

FINANCIAL AID PROCEDURES

Forms required: FAFSA.

Dates and Deadlines: Priority date 3/1; no closing date. Applicants notified on a rolling basis starting 3/15; must reply by 5/1 or within 4 week(s) of notification.

Transfers: Applicants notified on a rolling basis starting 3/15; must reply within 4 week(s) of notification.

CONTACT

Sherry Pennington, Coordinator of Financial Aid
1000 West Austin Boulevard, Nevada, MO 64772
(417) 667-8181 ext. 2190

Crowder College

Neosho, Missouri
www.crowder.edu   Federal Code: 002459

2-year public community and liberal arts college in small town.

Enrollment: 2,604 undergrads, 41% part-time. 496 full-time freshmen.

Selectivity: Open admission; but selective for some programs.

BASIC COSTS (2007-2008)

Tuition and fees: $2,310; out-of-district residents $3,090; out-of-state residents $3,900.

Per-credit charge: $65; out-of-district residents $91; out-of-state residents $118.

Room and board: $3,870.

FINANCIAL AID PICTURE

Students with need: Need-based aid available for full-time and part-time students. Work study available nights, weekends, and for part-time students.

Students without need: This college awards aid only to students with need.

FINANCIAL AID PROCEDURES

Forms required: FAFSA, institutional form.

Dates and Deadlines: Priority date 7/1; no closing date. Applicants notified on a rolling basis starting 5/15.

CONTACT

Michelle Paul, Director of Financial Aid
601 LaClede Avenue, Neosho, MO 64850
(417) 451-3223 ext. 5434

Culver-Stockton College
Canton, Missouri
www.culver.edu   Federal Code: 002460

4-year private liberal arts college in small town, affiliated with Christian Church (Disciples of Christ).

Enrollment: 807 undergrads, 5% part-time. 203 full-time freshmen.

Selectivity: Admits over 75% of applicants.

BASIC COSTS (2007-2008)

Tuition and fees: $16,850.

Per-credit charge: $450.

Room and board: $6,850.

FINANCIAL AID PICTURE (2007-2008)

Students with need: Out of 199 full-time freshmen who applied for aid, 182 were judged to have need. Of these, 182 received aid, and 35 had their full need met. Average financial aid package met 76% of need; average scholarship/grant was $11,565; average loan was $3,436. For part-time students, average financial aid package was $5,019.

Students without need: 21 full-time freshmen who did not demonstrate need for aid received scholarships/grants; average award was $14,674. No-need awards available for academics, alumni affiliation, art, athletics, job skills, leadership, music/drama, religious affiliation, state/district residency.

Scholarships offered: 19 full-time freshmen received athletic scholarships; average amount $1,761.

Cumulative student debt: 93% of graduating class had student loans; average debt was $22,509.

Additional info: Interview required for scholarships, audition required for music students, portfolio required for art students.

FINANCIAL AID PROCEDURES

Forms required: FAFSA.

Dates and Deadlines: Priority date 3/1; closing date 6/1. Applicants notified on a rolling basis starting 2/15; must reply within 2 week(s) of notification.

Transfers: Must reply within 2 week(s) of notification.

CONTACT

Tina Wiseman, Director of Financial Aid
One College Hill, Canton, MO 63435-1299
(573) 288-6307

DeVry University: Kansas City
Kansas City, Missouri
www.devry.edu

4-year for-profit university in large city.

Enrollment: 950 undergrads, 46% part-time. 148 full-time freshmen.

BASIC COSTS (2007-2008)

Tuition and fees: $13,220.

Per-credit charge: $490.

FINANCIAL AID PICTURE (2006-2007)

Students with need: Out of 119 full-time freshmen who applied for aid, 110 were judged to have need. Of these, 110 received aid, and 2 had their full need met. Average financial aid package met 37% of need; average scholarship/grant was $5,658; average loan was $4,309. For part-time students, average financial aid package was $7,596.

Students without need: This college awards aid only to students with need.

Cumulative student debt: 100% of graduating class had student loans; average debt was $37,452.

FINANCIAL AID PROCEDURES

Forms required: FAFSA.

Dates and Deadlines: No deadline. Applicants notified on a rolling basis.

CONTACT

Maureen Kelly, Senior Associate Director of Financial Aid
11224 Holmes Street, Kansas City, MO 64131-3626
(816) 941-0439

Drury University
Springfield, Missouri
www.drury.edu   Federal Code: 002461

4-year private university and liberal arts college in large city, affiliated with United Church of Christ and Christian Church (Disciples of Christ).

Enrollment: 1,605 undergrads, 2% part-time. 398 full-time freshmen.

Selectivity: Admits over 75% of applicants.

BASIC COSTS (2008-2009)

Tuition and fees: $18,409.

Per-credit charge: $600.

Room and board: $6,384.

FINANCIAL AID PICTURE (2007-2008)

Students with need: Out of 366 full-time freshmen who applied for aid, 349 were judged to have need. Of these, 349 received aid, and 294 had their full need met. Average financial aid package met 83% of need; average scholarship/grant was $5,898; average loan was $4,315. Need-based aid available for part-time students.

Students without need: 68 full-time freshmen who did not demonstrate need for aid received scholarships/grants; average award was $3,580. No-need awards available for academics, alumni affiliation, art, athletics, job skills, leadership, minority status, music/drama, religious affiliation.

Scholarships offered: *Merit:* Trustee Scholarship; tuition, room and board; 10 awarded. Presidential Scholarship; up to $12,000 per year; 10 awarded. Dean-s Scholarship; up to $8,000 a year; top 2% of high school class awarded. Academic Honor Scholarship; up to $5,000 a year. Presidential Leadership Scholarship; $2,000 a year. State scholarship; $2,000 a year. International Baccalaureate Award; $1,000 a year. Departmental Awards; amounts and requirements vary by department. Alumni Children's; $500 yearly. Church Scholarship; $500 yearly. *Athletic:* 22 full-time freshmen received athletic scholarships; average amount $7,250.

Cumulative student debt: 58% of graduating class had student loans; average debt was $18,225.

FINANCIAL AID PROCEDURES

Forms required: FAFSA, institutional form.

Dates and Deadlines: Closing date 3/15. Applicants notified on a rolling basis starting 3/30; must reply within 2 week(s) of notification.

Transfers: No deadline. Phi Theta Kappa Scholarship of $1,000 available.

CONTACT

Annette Avery, Director of Financial Aid

900 North Benton Avenue, Springfield, MO 65802-3712

(417) 873-7312

East Central College

Union, Missouri

www.eastcentral.edu   Federal Code: 008862

2-year public community college in small town.

Enrollment: 2,305 undergrads, 38% part-time. 563 full-time freshmen.

Selectivity: Open admission; but selective for some programs.

BASIC COSTS (2008-2009)

Tuition and fees: $2,130; out-of-district residents $2,910; out-of-state residents $4,230.

Per-credit charge: $61; out-of-district residents $87; out-of-state residents $131.

FINANCIAL AID PICTURE (2006-2007)

Students with need: 64% of average financial aid package awarded as scholarships/grants, 36% awarded as loans/jobs. Need-based aid available for part-time students. Work study available nights, weekends, and for part-time students.

Students without need: No-need awards available for academics, alumni affiliation, art, athletics, music/drama, state/district residency.

Cumulative student debt: 12% of graduating class had student loans; average debt was $4,525.

FINANCIAL AID PROCEDURES

Forms required: FAFSA.

Dates and Deadlines: Priority date 3/1; no closing date. Applicants notified on a rolling basis starting 3/15.

Transfers: No deadline. Applicants notified on a rolling basis starting 3/15.

CONTACT

Karen Koenig-Griffin, Director of Financial Aid

1964 Prairie Dell Road, Union, MO 63084-0529

(636) 583-5195 ext. 2777

Evangel University

Springfield, Missouri

www.evangel.edu   Federal Code: 002463

4-year private liberal arts college in small city, affiliated with Assemblies of God.

Enrollment: 1,534 undergrads, 5% part-time. 367 full-time freshmen.

Selectivity: Admits over 75% of applicants.

BASIC COSTS (2007-2008)

Tuition and fees: $14,340.

Per-credit charge: $528.

Room and board: $5,120.

FINANCIAL AID PICTURE (2006-2007)

Students with need: Out of 330 full-time freshmen who applied for aid, 297 were judged to have need. Of these, 297 received aid, and 26 had their full need met. Average financial aid package met 25% of need; average scholarship/grant was $5,673; average loan was $2,942. For part-time students, average financial aid package was $9,368.

Students without need: This college awards aid only to students with need.

Scholarships offered: 19 full-time freshmen received athletic scholarships; average amount $2,576.

FINANCIAL AID PROCEDURES

Forms required: FAFSA.

Dates and Deadlines: Priority date 4/1; closing date 6/1. Applicants notified on a rolling basis starting 4/1; must reply within 3 week(s) of notification.

CONTACT

Director of Financial Aid

1111 North Glenstone, Springfield, MO 65802

(417) 865-2811

Fontbonne University

St. Louis, Missouri

www.fontbonne.edu   Federal Code: 002464

4-year private liberal arts college in large city, affiliated with Roman Catholic Church.

Enrollment: 1,993 undergrads, 23% part-time. 189 full-time freshmen.

Selectivity: Admits over 75% of applicants.

BASIC COSTS (2008-2009)

Tuition and fees: $19,320.

Per-credit charge: $508.

Room and board: $7,210.

FINANCIAL AID PICTURE (2006-2007)

Students with need: Out of 111 full-time freshmen who applied for aid, 104 were judged to have need. Of these, 104 received aid, and 4 had their full need met. Average financial aid package met 46% of need; average scholarship/grant was $5,200; average loan was $2,625. For part-time students, average financial aid package was $5,500.

Students without need: 78 full-time freshmen who did not demonstrate need for aid received scholarships/grants; average award was $5,000. No-need awards available for academics, alumni affiliation, art, leadership, minority status, music/drama, religious affiliation, state/district residency.

Scholarships offered: Dean's Scholarship; $6,000-$8,000; GPA, ACT, rank criteria. Alumni Scholarship; $1,000-$6,000; GPA, ACT and class rank criteria. Presidential Scholarship; up to full tuition. Campus Service Scholarship;$500-$3,000; activities, leadership. Art, theater, English, writing and computer science scholarships also available.

Cumulative student debt: 85% of graduating class had student loans; average debt was $17,500.

FINANCIAL AID PROCEDURES

Forms required: FAFSA, institutional form.

Dates and Deadlines: Priority date 4/1; no closing date. Applicants notified on a rolling basis starting 2/1; must reply within 2 week(s) of notification.

CONTACT

Nicole Moore, Director of Financial Aid

6800 Wydown Boulevard, St. Louis, MO 63105

(314) 889-1414

Hannibal-LaGrange College

Hannibal, Missouri

www.hlg.edu   Federal Code: 009089

4-year private liberal arts college in large town, affiliated with Southern Baptist Convention.

Enrollment: 895 undergrads.

Selectivity: Admits over 75% of applicants.

BASIC COSTS (2008-2009)

Tuition and fees: $14,506.

Per-credit charge: $466.

Room and board: $5,270.

FINANCIAL AID PICTURE

Students with need: Need-based aid available for full-time and part-time students.

Students without need: No-need awards available for academics, art, athletics, music/drama, religious affiliation.

Additional info: Work-study opportunities vary according to on- and off-campus needs.

FINANCIAL AID PROCEDURES

Forms required: FAFSA, institutional form.

Dates and Deadlines: Closing date 7/1. Applicants notified on a rolling basis; must reply by 8/31.

Transfers: No deadline.

CONTACT

Brice Baumgardner, Director of Financial Aid

2800 Palmyra Road, Hannibal, MO 63401

(573) 629-3267

Harris-Stowe State University

St. Louis, Missouri

www.hssu.edu   Federal Code: 002466

4-year public university in large city.

Enrollment: 1,800 undergrads, 32% part-time. 376 full-time freshmen.

Selectivity: Admits over 75% of applicants.

BASIC COSTS (2007-2008)

Tuition and fees: $5,090; out-of-state residents $9,680.

Per-credit charge: $158; out-of-state residents $311.

FINANCIAL AID PICTURE

Students with need: Need-based aid available for full-time and part-time students. Work study available nights, weekends, and for part-time students.

Students without need: No-need awards available for academics, athletics, music/drama, state/district residency.

FINANCIAL AID PROCEDURES

Forms required: FAFSA, institutional form.

Dates and Deadlines: Priority date 4/1; no closing date. Must reply within 3 week(s) of notification.

CONTACT

Regina Blackshear, Director of Financial Assistance

3026 Laclede Avenue, St. Louis, MO 63103-2199

(314) 340-3500

Jefferson College

Hillsboro, Missouri

www.jeffco.edu   Federal Code: 002468

2-year public community and technical college in rural community.

Enrollment: 4,418 undergrads, 45% part-time. 857 full-time freshmen.

Selectivity: Open admission; but selective for some programs.

BASIC COSTS (2008-2009)

Tuition and fees: $2,550; out-of-district residents $3,840; out-of-state residents $5,100.

Per-credit charge: $85; out-of-district residents $128; out-of-state residents $170.

Room only: $3,400.

FINANCIAL AID PICTURE (2006-2007)

Students with need: Out of 697 full-time freshmen who applied for aid, 450 were judged to have need. Of these, 418 received aid, and 8 had their full need met. Average financial aid package met 42% of need; average scholarship/grant was $1,846; average loan was $2,102. For part-time students, average financial aid package was $2,155.

Students without need: 24 full-time freshmen who did not demonstrate need for aid received scholarships/grants; average award was $1,012. No-need awards available for academics, art, athletics, leadership, music/drama, state/district residency.

Scholarships offered: 147 full-time freshmen received athletic scholarships; average amount $4,408.

Cumulative student debt: 31% of graduating class had student loans; average debt was $9,977.

FINANCIAL AID PROCEDURES

Forms required: FAFSA.

Dates and Deadlines: Priority date 4/1; no closing date. Applicants notified on a rolling basis starting 4/15.

CONTACT

Julie Fraser, Director of Admissions and Financial Aid

1000 Viking Drive, Hillsboro, MO 63050-2441

(636) 797-3000 ext. 212

Kansas City Art Institute

Kansas City, Missouri

www.kcai.edu   Federal Code: 002473

4-year private visual arts college in large city.

Enrollment: 671 undergrads. 152 full-time freshmen.

Selectivity: Admits 50 to 75% of applicants.

BASIC COSTS (2008-2009)

Tuition and fees: $27,220.

Per-credit charge: $1,134.

Room and board: $8,294.

FINANCIAL AID PICTURE (2007-2008)

Students with need: Out of 152 full-time freshmen who applied for aid, 108 were judged to have need. Of these, 108 received aid, and 19 had their full need met. Average financial aid package met 73% of need; average scholarship/grant was $15,724; average loan was $5,657. For part-time students, average financial aid package was $14,245.

Students without need: 27 full-time freshmen who did not demonstrate need for aid received scholarships/grants; average award was $17,514. No-need awards available for academics, art.

Cumulative student debt: 87% of graduating class had student loans; average debt was $35,350.

Additional info: February 15 and March 15 priority application dates for merit scholarships; deadline July 1.

FINANCIAL AID PROCEDURES

Forms required: FAFSA.

Dates and Deadlines: Priority date 3/15; no closing date. Applicants notified on a rolling basis starting 4/1; must reply within 2 week(s) of notification.

Transfers: Applicants notified on a rolling basis starting 4/1; must reply within 2 week(s) of notification.

CONTACT

Lynn Boyer, Director of Financial Aid

4415 Warwick Boulevard, Kansas City, MO 64111-1820

(816) 802-3337

Lincoln University
Jefferson City, Missouri
www.lincolnu.edu   Federal Code: 002479

4-year public university and liberal arts college in large town.
Enrollment: 2,483 undergrads, 20% part-time. 578 full-time freshmen.
Selectivity: Open admission; but selective for some programs and for out-of-state students.

BASIC COSTS (2008-2009)
Tuition and fees: $6,175; out-of-state residents $10,885.
Per-credit charge: $189; out-of-state residents $346.
Room and board: $4,660.
Additional info: Students enrolled full-time must pay $229 per fall/spring semester or $81 per summer semester for insurance if they do not provide proof of other coverage. Enrollment in the student health insurance program is required for international students.

FINANCIAL AID PICTURE (2007-2008)
Students with need: Out of 498 full-time freshmen who applied for aid, 457 were judged to have need. Of these, 455 received aid, and 306 had their full need met. Average financial aid package met 76% of need; average scholarship/grant was $3,895; average loan was $2,896. For part-time students, average financial aid package was $4,706.
Students without need: No-need awards available for academics, art, athletics, job skills, leadership, minority status, music/drama, ROTC, state/district residency.
Scholarships offered: 40 full-time freshmen received athletic scholarships; average amount $6,430.
Cumulative student debt: 63% of graduating class had student loans; average debt was $20,845.

FINANCIAL AID PROCEDURES
Forms required: FAFSA, institutional form.
Dates and Deadlines: Priority date 3/1; no closing date. Applicants notified on a rolling basis starting 3/15; must reply within 2 week(s) of notification.
Transfers: Applicants notified on a rolling basis starting 3/15; must reply within 2 week(s) of notification.

CONTACT
Alfred Robinson, Director of Financial Aid and Student Employment
820 Chestnut Street/B-7 Young Hall, Jefferson City, MO 65102-0029
(573) 681-5363

Lindenwood University
St. Charles, Missouri
www.lindenwood.edu   Federal Code: 002480

4-year private university and liberal arts college in very large city, affiliated with Presbyterian Church (USA).
Enrollment: 5,872 undergrads, 4% part-time. 881 full-time freshmen.
Selectivity: Admits 50 to 75% of applicants.

BASIC COSTS (2008-2009)
Tuition and fees: $13,000.
Per-credit charge: $360.
Room and board: $6,860.

FINANCIAL AID PICTURE (2007-2008)
Students with need: 55% of average financial aid package awarded as scholarships/grants, 45% awarded as loans/jobs. Need-based aid available for part-time students. Work study available nights, weekends, and for part-time students.
Students without need: No-need awards available for academics, alumni affiliation, art, job skills, leadership, music/drama, ROTC.

FINANCIAL AID PROCEDURES
Forms required: FAFSA.
Dates and Deadlines: Priority date 4/1; no closing date. Applicants notified on a rolling basis.

CONTACT
Lori Bode, Director of Financial Aid
209 South Kingshighway, St. Charles, MO 63301-1695
(636) 949-4923

Maryville University of Saint Louis
St. Louis, Missouri
www.maryville.edu   Federal Code: 002482

4-year private university in very large city.
Enrollment: 2,674 undergrads, 38% part-time. 294 full-time freshmen.
Selectivity: Admits 50 to 75% of applicants.

BASIC COSTS (2008-2009)
Tuition and fees: $20,275.
Per-credit charge: $590.
Room and board: $7,900.

FINANCIAL AID PICTURE (2007-2008)
Students with need: Out of 255 full-time freshmen who applied for aid, 212 were judged to have need. Of these, 212 received aid, and 36 had their full need met. Average financial aid package met 72% of need; average scholarship/grant was $10,481; average loan was $5,576. For part-time students, average financial aid package was $7,498.
Students without need: 64 full-time freshmen who did not demonstrate need for aid received scholarships/grants; average award was $6,940. No-need awards available for academics, art, leadership, minority status, religious affiliation, ROTC, state/district residency.
Scholarships offered: University Scholars Program: awarded to full-time freshmen with 28 ACT or 1170 SAT (exclusive of writing), high school GPA 3.5-4.0; interview required. M-PACT Award: awarded to full-time freshmen based on campus activity and impact on student life.
Cumulative student debt: 76% of graduating class had student loans; average debt was $21,363.

FINANCIAL AID PROCEDURES
Forms required: FAFSA.
Dates and Deadlines: Priority date 3/1; no closing date. Applicants notified on a rolling basis starting 2/1; must reply by 5/1 or within 2 week(s) of notification.
Transfers: No deadline. Applicants notified on a rolling basis starting 2/1. Outstanding Transfer Student Award, PTK Award, Art & Design Award scholarships available.

CONTACT
Martha Harbaugh, Director of Financial Aid
650 Maryville University Drive, St. Louis, MO 63141-7299
(314) 529-9360

Metro Business College: Jefferson City
Jefferson City, Missouri
www.metrobusinesscollege.edu   Federal Code: 014710

2-year for-profit business and health science college in large town.
Enrollment: 152 undergrads, 12% part-time. 31 full-time freshmen.
Selectivity: Open admission; but selective for some programs.

BASIC COSTS (2007-2008)
Tuition and fees: $8,810.

FINANCIAL AID PICTURE

Students with need: Need-based aid available for full-time and part-time students.

FINANCIAL AID PROCEDURES

Forms required: FAFSA, institutional form.

Dates and Deadlines: No deadline. Applicants notified on a rolling basis.

CONTACT

Debbie Jenkins, Financial Aid Coordinator
1407 Southwest Boulevard, Jefferson City, MO 65109
(573) 635-6600

Metropolitan Community College: Blue River

Independence, Missouri
www.mcckc.edu   Federal Code: 009140

2-year public community college in small city.

Enrollment: 2,030 undergrads, 50% part-time. 334 full-time freshmen.

Selectivity: Open admission.

BASIC COSTS (2007-2008)

Tuition and fees: $2,400; out-of-district residents $4,260; out-of-state residents $5,700.

Per-credit charge: $75; out-of-district residents $137; out-of-state residents $185.

FINANCIAL AID PICTURE (2006-2007)

Students with need: For part-time students, average financial aid package was $1,991.

Students without need: No-need awards available for academics, athletics, leadership.

FINANCIAL AID PROCEDURES

Forms required: FAFSA, institutional form.

Dates and Deadlines: Priority date 5/30; closing date 8/20. Applicants notified on a rolling basis starting 4/8.

Transfers: No deadline.

CONTACT

Cindy Butler, District Director, Student Financial Aid
3200 Broadway, Kansas City, MO 64111-2429
(816) 759-1527

Metropolitan Community College: Longview

Lee's Summit, Missouri
www.mcckc.edu   Federal Code: 009140

2-year public community college in small city.

Enrollment: 3,906 undergrads, 45% part-time. 837 full-time freshmen.

Selectivity: Open admission; but selective for some programs.

BASIC COSTS (2007-2008)

Tuition and fees: $2,400; out-of-district residents $4,260; out-of-state residents $5,700.

Per-credit charge: $75; out-of-district residents $137; out-of-state residents $185.

FINANCIAL AID PICTURE (2006-2007)

Students with need: For part-time students, average financial aid package was $1,835.

Students without need: No-need awards available for academics, athletics, leadership.

FINANCIAL AID PROCEDURES

Forms required: FAFSA, institutional form.

Dates and Deadlines: Priority date 5/30; closing date 8/20. Applicants notified on a rolling basis starting 4/8.

Transfers: No deadline.

CONTACT

Cindy Butler, District Director, Student Financial Aid
500 Longview Road, Lee's Summit, MO 64081-2105
(816) 759-1527

Metropolitan Community College: Maple Woods

Kansas City, Missouri
www.mcckc.edu   Federal Code: 004432

2-year public community college in large city.

Enrollment: 3,100 undergrads, 46% part-time. 663 full-time freshmen.

Selectivity: Open admission; but selective for some programs.

BASIC COSTS (2007-2008)

Tuition and fees: $2,400; out-of-district residents $4,260; out-of-state residents $5,700.

Per-credit charge: $75; out-of-district residents $137; out-of-state residents $185.

FINANCIAL AID PICTURE (2006-2007)

Students with need: For part-time students, average financial aid package was $1,890.

Students without need: No-need awards available for academics, athletics, leadership.

FINANCIAL AID PROCEDURES

Forms required: FAFSA, institutional form.

Dates and Deadlines: Priority date 5/30; no closing date. Applicants notified on a rolling basis.

CONTACT

Cindy Butler, District Director, Student Financial Aid
2601 NE Barry Road, Kansas City, MO 64156-1299
(816) 759-1527

Metropolitan Community College: Penn Valley

Kansas City, Missouri
www.mcckc.edu   Federal Code: 002484

2-year public community college in large city.

Enrollment: 3,509 undergrads, 64% part-time. 371 full-time freshmen.

Selectivity: Open admission; but selective for some programs.

BASIC COSTS (2007-2008)

Tuition and fees: $2,400; out-of-district residents $4,260; out-of-state residents $5,700.

Per-credit charge: $75; out-of-district residents $137; out-of-state residents $185.

FINANCIAL AID PICTURE (2006-2007)

Students with need: For part-time students, average financial aid package was $2,159.

Students without need: No-need awards available for academics, athletics, leadership.

FINANCIAL AID PROCEDURES

Forms required: FAFSA, institutional form.

Dates and Deadlines: Priority date 5/30; no closing date. Applicants notified on a rolling basis starting 4/8.

CONTACT

Cindy Butler, District Director, Student Financial Aid
3201 Southwest Trafficway, Kansas City, MO 64111-2429
(816) 759-1527

Missouri Baptist University

St. Louis, Missouri
www.mobap.edu   Federal Code: 007540

4-year private university and liberal arts college in very large city, affiliated with Baptist faith.

Enrollment: 1,414 undergrads, 21% part-time. 178 full-time freshmen.
Selectivity: Admits 50 to 75% of applicants.

BASIC COSTS (2007-2008)

Tuition and fees: $15,850.
Per-credit charge: $505.
Room and board: $6,350.

FINANCIAL AID PICTURE

Students with need: Need-based aid available for full-time and part-time students.

Students without need: No-need awards available for academics, alumni affiliation, athletics, leadership, music/drama, religious affiliation.

FINANCIAL AID PROCEDURES

Forms required: FAFSA, institutional form.
Dates and Deadlines: Priority date 4/1; no closing date. Applicants notified on a rolling basis starting 4/15; must reply within 2 week(s) of notification.
Transfers: Institutional academic scholarships available.

CONTACT

Laurie Wallace, Director of Financial Services
One College Park Drive, St. Louis, MO 63141-8698
(314) 392-2366

Missouri Southern State University

Joplin, Missouri
www.mssu.edu   Federal Code: 002488

4-year public university and liberal arts college in large town.
Enrollment: 5,593 undergrads.
Selectivity: Admits over 75% of applicants.

BASIC COSTS (2007-2008)

Tuition and fees: $4,276; out-of-state residents $8,326.
Per-credit charge: $135; out-of-state residents $270.
Room and board: $4,720.

FINANCIAL AID PICTURE

Students with need: Need-based aid available for full-time and part-time students.

Students without need: No-need awards available for academics, alumni affiliation, art, athletics, job skills, leadership, minority status, music/drama, state/district residency.

FINANCIAL AID PROCEDURES

Forms required: FAFSA.
Dates and Deadlines: Priority date 2/15; no closing date. Applicants notified on a rolling basis starting 2/15; must reply within 3 week(s) of notification.

CONTACT

James Gilbert, Director of Student Financial Aid
3950 East Newman Road, Joplin, MO 64801-1595
(417) 625-9325

Missouri State University

Springfield, Missouri
www.missouristate.edu   Federal Code: 002503

4-year public university in small city.
Enrollment: 14,491 undergrads, 12% part-time. 2,613 full-time freshmen.
Selectivity: Admits 50 to 75% of applicants.

BASIC COSTS (2007-2008)

Tuition and fees: $5,988; out-of-state residents $11,088.
Per-credit charge: $179; out-of-state residents $349.
Room and board: $5,312.

FINANCIAL AID PICTURE (2007-2008)

Students with need: Out of 2,060 full-time freshmen who applied for aid, 1,410 were judged to have need. Of these, 1,393 received aid, and 326 had their full need met. Average financial aid package met 69% of need; average scholarship/grant was $5,406; average loan was $3,003. For part-time students, average financial aid package was $5,147.

Students without need: 868 full-time freshmen who did not demonstrate need for aid received scholarships/grants; average award was $8,008. No-need awards available for academics, alumni affiliation, art, athletics, job skills, leadership, minority status, music/drama, ROTC, state/district residency.

Scholarships offered: *Merit:* Presidential Scholarships; full tuition, room, and board; based on 30 ACT and rank in top 10% of class; 40 awarded, application deadline January 15. Board of Governors Scholarships; cover basic fees for 32 credit hours per year (plus two thirds of out of state fees for non-residents); based on 28 ACT and either top 10% class rank or 3.85 GPA; unlimited number of awards. Freshman Academic Scholarships; $2,000 per year (plus two thirds of out of state fees for non-residents); based on 26 ACT and either top 20% class rank or 3.7 GPA; unlimited number of awards. Freshman Recognition Scholarships; $1,000 per year (plus two thirds of out of state fees for non-residents); based on 24 ACT and either top 10% class rank or 3.85 GPA; unlimited number of awards. Multicultural Leadership Scholarships; cover required student fees (in-state); for students in top half of class who have demonstrated leadership in the minority community; 50 awarded; February 1 deadline. Applications must be received by March 1 to be considered for scholarships, unless otherwise noted. *Athletic:* 65 full-time freshmen received athletic scholarships; average amount $8,023.

Cumulative student debt: 79% of graduating class had student loans; average debt was $16,921.

Additional info: Extensive scholarship program offered to freshmen and transfer students. Out-of-state fee stipends available. Student employment service available to assist students in securing employment on campus and in community.

FINANCIAL AID PROCEDURES

Forms required: institutional form.
Dates and Deadlines: Priority date 3/31; no closing date. Applicants notified on a rolling basis starting 4/1.
Transfers: No deadline. Applicants notified on a rolling basis.

CONTACT

Vicki Mattocks, Director of Financial Aid
901 South National Avenue, Springfield, MO 65897
(417) 836-5262

Missouri State University: West Plains
West Plains, Missouri
www.wp.missouristate.edu   Federal Code: 031060

2-year public branch campus college in large town.

Enrollment: 1,340 undergrads, 28% part-time. 384 full-time freshmen.

Selectivity: Open admission; but selective for some programs.

BASIC COSTS (2008-2009)
Tuition and fees: $3,304; out-of-state residents $6,364.

Per-credit charge: $102; out-of-state residents $204.

Room and board: $4,632.

FINANCIAL AID PICTURE (2006-2007)
Students with need: 65% of average financial aid package awarded as scholarships/grants, 35% awarded as loans/jobs. Need-based aid available for part-time students. Work study available nights, weekends, and for part-time students.

Students without need: No-need awards available for academics, athletics, state/district residency.

FINANCIAL AID PROCEDURES
Forms required: FAFSA, institutional form.

Dates and Deadlines: Priority date 3/31; no closing date. Applicants notified on a rolling basis; must reply by 4/15.

CONTACT
Matthew Morris, Director if Business and support Services
128 Garfield Avenue, West Plains, MO 65775-2715
(417) 255-7243

Missouri University of Science and Technology
Rolla, Missouri
www.mst.edu   Federal Code: 002517

4-year public university and engineering college in large town.

Enrollment: 4,705 undergrads, 7% part-time. 935 full-time freshmen.

Selectivity: Admits 50 to 75% of applicants.

BASIC COSTS (2007-2008)
Tuition and fees: $8,172; out-of-state residents $18,828.

Per-credit charge: $236; out-of-state residents $591.

Room and board: $6,660.

Additional info: Tuition/fee waivers available for minority students.

FINANCIAL AID PICTURE (2006-2007)
Students with need: Out of 756 full-time freshmen who applied for aid, 583 were judged to have need. Of these, 583 received aid, and 179 had their full need met. Average financial aid package met 46% of need; average scholarship/grant was $4,978; average loan was $3,708. For part-time students, average financial aid package was $6,542.

Students without need: 334 full-time freshmen who did not demonstrate need for aid received scholarships/grants. No-need awards available for academics, alumni affiliation, athletics, job skills, leadership, minority status, music/drama, religious affiliation, ROTC, state/district residency.

Scholarships offered: 23 full-time freshmen received athletic scholarships.

FINANCIAL AID PROCEDURES
Forms required: FAFSA.

Dates and Deadlines: Priority date 3/1; no closing date. Applicants notified on a rolling basis; must reply within 3 week(s) of notification.

Transfers: Special scholarships available to transfer students.

CONTACT
Robert Whites, Director of Financial Assistance
106 Parker Hall, Rolla, MO 65409
(573) 341-4282

Missouri Valley College
Marshall, Missouri
www.moval.edu   Federal Code: 002489

4-year private liberal arts college in large town, affiliated with Presbyterian Church (USA).

Enrollment: 1,419 undergrads.

Selectivity: Admits 50 to 75% of applicants.

BASIC COSTS (2008-2009)
Tuition and fees: $15,950.

Room and board: $6,050.

FINANCIAL AID PICTURE
Students with need: Need-based aid available for full-time and part-time students. Work study available nights, weekends, and for part-time students.

Students without need: No-need awards available for academics, state/district residency.

Scholarships offered: Talent scholarships; $1,000 to $13,000; 100 awarded for general achievement.

FINANCIAL AID PROCEDURES
Forms required: FAFSA, state aid form.

Dates and Deadlines: Priority date 3/1; no closing date. Applicants notified on a rolling basis starting 2/1; must reply within 6 week(s) of notification.

Transfers: Closing date 3/1.

CONTACT
Charles Mayfield, Director of Financial Aid
500 East College Street, Marshall, MO 65340
(660) 831-4176

Missouri Western State University
St. Joseph, Missouri
www.missouriwestern.edu   Federal Code: 002490

4-year public business and liberal arts college in small city.

Enrollment: 5,301 undergrads.

Selectivity: Open admission; but selective for some programs.

BASIC COSTS (2007-2008)
Tuition and fees: $5,330; out-of-state residents $9,290.

Per-credit charge: $160; out-of-state residents $292.

Room and board: $5,784.

FINANCIAL AID PICTURE (2006-2007)
Students with need: 41% of average financial aid package awarded as scholarships/grants, 59% awarded as loans/jobs. Need-based aid available for part-time students.

Students without need: No-need awards available for academics, alumni affiliation, art, athletics, job skills, leadership, minority status, music/drama, state/district residency.

Scholarships offered: Golden Griffon Scholarship; up to $10,000 per year for 4 years; 27 ACT, top 10% of class or 3.5 GPA, evidence of involvement in extracurricular activities and community service; 2 essays and personal interview required; application deadline 2/1. President's Academic Scholarship; up to $4,000 per year; 25 ACT and either rank in the top 15% of class or 3.25 GPA required; application deadline 3/1.

FINANCIAL AID PROCEDURES
Forms required: FAFSA, institutional form.

Dates and Deadlines: Closing date 3/1. Applicants notified on a rolling basis starting 4/5; must reply within 3 week(s) of notification.

Transfers: Priority date 3/1; no deadline. Applicants notified on a rolling basis starting 4/15; must reply within 2 week(s) of notification.

CONTACT

Lisa Siudym, Director of Student Financial Aid
4525 Downs Drive, St. Joseph, MO 64507
(816) 271-4361

Moberly Area Community College

Moberly, Missouri
www.macc.edu   Federal Code: 002491

2-year public community college in large town.

Enrollment: 2,984 undergrads, 36% part-time. 686 full-time freshmen.

Selectivity: Open admission; but selective for some programs.

BASIC COSTS (2007-2008)

Tuition and fees: $2,160; out-of-district residents $2,970; out-of-state residents $4,380.

Per-credit charge: $61; out-of-district residents $88; out-of-state residents $135.

Room only: $2,200.

FINANCIAL AID PICTURE (2007-2008)

Students with need: Out of 575 full-time freshmen who applied for aid, 322 were judged to have need. Of these, 322 received aid, and 76 had their full need met. Average financial aid package met 50% of need; average scholarship/grant was $2,363; average loan was $2,676. For part-time students, average financial aid package was $3,620.

Students without need: 21 full-time freshmen who did not demonstrate need for aid received scholarships/grants; average award was $684. No-need awards available for academics, alumni affiliation, art, athletics, leadership, music/drama.

Scholarships offered: 12 full-time freshmen received athletic scholarships; average amount $6,463.

Cumulative student debt: 40% of graduating class had student loans; average debt was $6,200.

FINANCIAL AID PROCEDURES

Forms required: FAFSA.

Dates and Deadlines: Priority date 4/1; no closing date. Applicants notified on a rolling basis starting 4/1; must reply by 7/15 or within 2 week(s) of notification.

CONTACT

Amy Hager, Director of Financial Aid
101 College Avenue, Moberly, MO 65270-1304
(660) 263-4110 ext. 301

North Central Missouri College

Trenton, Missouri
www.ncmissouri.edu   Federal Code: 002514

2-year public community college in small town.

Enrollment: 1,020 undergrads.

Selectivity: Open admission; but selective for some programs.

BASIC COSTS (2008-2009)

Tuition and fees: $2,550; out-of-district residents $3,510; out-of-state residents $4,650.

Per-credit charge: $65; out-of-district residents $97; out-of-state residents $135.

Room and board: $4,924.

Additional info: Tuition/fee waivers available for adults, minority students.

FINANCIAL AID PICTURE

Students with need: Need-based aid available for full-time and part-time students.

Students without need: No-need awards available for academics, athletics, minority status, music/drama.

FINANCIAL AID PROCEDURES

Forms required: FAFSA, institutional form.

Dates and Deadlines: Priority date 3/15; no closing date. Applicants notified on a rolling basis starting 3/15.

Transfers: No deadline. Applicants notified on a rolling basis starting 4/1. Transfer students may not receive same awards after transferring since some funds campus-based.

CONTACT

Heather Turner, Financial Aid Director
1301 Main Street, Trenton, MO 64683
(660) 359-3948 ext. 402

Northwest Missouri State University

Maryville, Missouri
www.nwmissouri.edu   Federal Code: 002496

4-year public university in large town.

Enrollment: 5,607 undergrads, 10% part-time. 1,519 full-time freshmen.

Selectivity: Admits 50 to 75% of applicants.

BASIC COSTS (2007-2008)

Tuition and fees: $6,438; out-of-state residents $10,896.

Per-credit charge: $208; out-of-state residents $356.

Room and board: $6,276.

Additional info: New student fee of $100. Primary textbooks included in tuition. Tuition/fee waivers available for minority students.

FINANCIAL AID PICTURE

Students with need: Need-based aid available for full-time and part-time students. Work study available nights, weekends, and for part-time students.

Students without need: No-need awards available for academics, alumni affiliation, art, athletics, job skills, leadership, minority status, music/drama, state/district residency.

FINANCIAL AID PROCEDURES

Forms required: FAFSA.

Dates and Deadlines: Priority date 4/1; no closing date. Applicants notified on a rolling basis starting 3/15; must reply within 2 week(s) of notification.

Transfers: No deadline. Applicants notified on a rolling basis starting 5/10. Transfer scholarship based on academic record.

CONTACT

Del Morley, Director of Financial Assistance
800 University Drive, Maryville, MO 64468-6001
(660) 562-1363

Ozark Christian College

Joplin, Missouri
www.occ.edu   Federal Code: 015569

4-year private Bible college in large town, affiliated with nondenominational tradition.

Enrollment: 655 undergrads, 16% part-time. 128 full-time freshmen.

Selectivity: Admits over 75% of applicants.

BASIC COSTS (2008-2009)

Tuition and fees: $8,188.

Per-credit charge: $255.

Room and board: $4,170.

FINANCIAL AID PICTURE (2007-2008)

Students with need: 38% of average financial aid package awarded as scholarships/grants, 62% awarded as loans/jobs. Need-based aid available for part-time students.

Students without need: No-need awards available for academics, leadership.

FINANCIAL AID PROCEDURES

Forms required: FAFSA.

Dates and Deadlines: Priority date 4/1; no closing date. Applicants notified on a rolling basis starting 6/1; must reply within 4 week(s) of notification.

Transfers: Academic transcripts required. ACT scores may qualify student for grants or scholarships.

CONTACT

Kim Balentine, Director of Financial Aid
1111 North Main Street, Joplin, MO 64801
(417) 624-2518

Ozarks Technical Community College

Springfield, Missouri
www.otc.edu   Federal Code: 030830

2-year public community and technical college in small city.

Enrollment: 8,934 undergrads, 44% part-time. 1,748 full-time freshmen.

Selectivity: Open admission; but selective for some programs.

BASIC COSTS (2007-2008)

Tuition and fees: $2,850; out-of-district residents $3,750; out-of-state residents $4,725.

Per-credit charge: $78; out-of-district residents $108; out-of-state residents $140.

FINANCIAL AID PICTURE

Students with need: Need-based aid available for full-time and part-time students.

Students without need: This college awards aid only to students with need.

FINANCIAL AID PROCEDURES

Forms required: FAFSA, institutional form.

Dates and Deadlines: Priority date 5/1; closing date 7/1. Applicants notified on a rolling basis starting 5/16.

CONTACT

Jeff Ford, Director of Financial Aid
1001 East Chestnut Expressway, Springfield, MO 65802
(417) 447-6930

Park University

Parkville, Missouri
www.park.edu   Federal Code: 002498

4-year private university in small town.

Enrollment: 11,824 undergrads, 90% part-time. 167 full-time freshmen.

Selectivity: Admits 50 to 75% of applicants.

BASIC COSTS (2007-2008)

Tuition and fees: $7,800.

Per-credit charge: $260.

Room and board: $5,460.

Additional info: Tuition varies by program and hours taken.

FINANCIAL AID PICTURE (2006-2007)

Students with need: Out of 120 full-time freshmen who applied for aid, 68 were judged to have need. Of these, 68 received aid, and 29 had their full need met. Average financial aid package met 56% of need; average scholarship/grant was $3,527; average loan was $1,079. For part-time students, average financial aid package was $3,160.

Students without need: 24 full-time freshmen who did not demonstrate need for aid received scholarships/grants; average award was $4,708. No-need awards available for academics, alumni affiliation, art, athletics, job skills, leadership, minority status, music/drama, religious affiliation, ROTC.

Scholarships offered: 19 full-time freshmen received athletic scholarships; average amount $3,713.

FINANCIAL AID PROCEDURES

Forms required: FAFSA, institutional form.

Dates and Deadlines: Priority date 4/1; closing date 8/1. Applicants notified on a rolling basis starting 4/1.

Transfers: No deadline. Applicants notified by 11/1.

CONTACT

Cathy Colapietro, Director of Admissions and Student Financial Services
8700 River Park Drive, Parkville, MO 64152
(816) 584-6290

Patricia Stevens College

St. Louis, Missouri
www.patriciastevenscollege.edu   Federal Code: 008552

2-year for-profit junior and liberal arts college in very large city.

Enrollment: 175 undergrads.

Selectivity: Open admission; but selective for some programs.

BASIC COSTS (2007-2008)

Tuition and fees: $10,050.

Per-credit charge: $195.

Additional info: Use of textbooks included in tuition. Tuition at time of enrollment locked for 2 years.

FINANCIAL AID PICTURE

Students with need: Need-based aid available for full-time and part-time students.

Students without need: This college awards aid only to students with need.

FINANCIAL AID PROCEDURES

Forms required: FAFSA.

Dates and Deadlines: No deadline. Applicants notified on a rolling basis.

CONTACT

Greg Elsenrath, Financial Aid Director
330 North Fourth Street, Suite 306, St. Louis, MO 63102
(314) 421-0949 ext. 17

Ranken Technical College

St. Louis, Missouri
www.ranken.edu   Federal Code: 012500

2-year private technical college in very large city.

Enrollment: 1,739 undergrads, 34% part-time. 434 full-time freshmen.

Selectivity: Open admission.

BASIC COSTS (2008-2009)

Tuition and fees: $11,900.

Per-credit charge: $490.

Additional info: Book and tool costs vary by program.

FINANCIAL AID PICTURE (2006-2007)

Students with need: 17% of average financial aid package awarded as scholarships/grants, 83% awarded as loans/jobs. Need-based aid available for part-time students. Work study available nights.

FINANCIAL AID PROCEDURES

Forms required: FAFSA.

Dates and Deadlines: No deadline. Applicants notified on a rolling basis starting 4/1.

CONTACT

Peter Murtaugh, Vice President for Finance and Admimistration

4431 Finney Avenue, St. Louis, MO 63113

(314) 286-4863

Research College of Nursing

Kansas City, Missouri

www.researchcollege.edu   Federal Code: 006392

4-year for-profit nursing college in very large city.

Enrollment: 280 undergrads, 1% part-time. 53 full-time freshmen.

Selectivity: Admits 50 to 75% of applicants.

BASIC COSTS (2008-2009)

Tuition and fees: $24,480.

Per-credit charge: $790.

Room and board: $6,800.

FINANCIAL AID PICTURE

Students with need: Need-based aid available for full-time and part-time students.

Students without need: No-need awards available for academics, alumni affiliation, leadership.

Additional info: Financial aid handled by Rockhurst University for freshmen and sophomores.

FINANCIAL AID PROCEDURES

Forms required: FAFSA, institutional form.

Dates and Deadlines: Priority date 3/15; no closing date. Applicants notified on a rolling basis starting 3/15.

Transfers: No deadline.

CONTACT

Angela Karlin, Director of Financial Aid

2525 East Meyer Boulevard, Kansas City, MO 64132-1199

(816) 995-2814

Rockhurst University

Kansas City, Missouri

www.rockhurst.edu   Federal Code: 002499

4-year private business and liberal arts college in very large city, affiliated with Roman Catholic Church.

Enrollment: 1,598 undergrads, 9% part-time. 367 full-time freshmen.

Selectivity: Admits over 75% of applicants.

BASIC COSTS (2008-2009)

Tuition and fees: $24,700.

Per-credit charge: $792.

Room and board: $6,600.

FINANCIAL AID PICTURE (2007-2008)

Students with need: Out of 366 full-time freshmen who applied for aid, 334 were judged to have need. Of these, 334 received aid, and 83 had their full need met. Average financial aid package met 100% of need; average scholarship/grant was $4,855; average loan was $3,581. For part-time students, average financial aid package was $7,837.

Students without need: 31 full-time freshmen who did not demonstrate need for aid received scholarships/grants; average award was $11,039. No-need awards available for academics, alumni affiliation, athletics, leadership, music/drama, state/district residency.

Scholarships offered: 19 full-time freshmen received athletic scholarships; average amount $9,338.

Cumulative student debt: 71% of graduating class had student loans; average debt was $16,579.

Additional info: Auditions, portfolios required for some scholarships.

FINANCIAL AID PROCEDURES

Forms required: FAFSA.

Dates and Deadlines: Priority date 3/1; closing date 6/30. Applicants notified on a rolling basis starting 1/30; must reply within 4 week(s) of notification.

Transfers: Must reply within 2 week(s) of notification. Scholarships awarded to qualified first-time transfers.

CONTACT

Angela Karlin, Director of Financial Aid

1100 Rockhurst Road, Kansas City, MO 64110-2561

(816) 405-4600

St. Charles Community College

Cottleville, Missouri

www.stchas.edu   Federal Code: 025306

2-year public community college in small city.

Enrollment: 6,097 undergrads, 45% part-time. 1,189 full-time freshmen.

Selectivity: Open admission; but selective for some programs.

BASIC COSTS (2008-2009)

Tuition and fees: $2,400; out-of-district residents $3,540; out-of-state residents $5,250.

Per-credit charge: $80; out-of-district residents $118; out-of-state residents $175.

FINANCIAL AID PICTURE (2006-2007)

Students with need: 60% of average financial aid package awarded as scholarships/grants, 40% awarded as loans/jobs. Need-based aid available for part-time students.

Students without need: No-need awards available for academics, art, athletics, leadership, music/drama.

FINANCIAL AID PROCEDURES

Forms required: FAFSA, institutional form.

Dates and Deadlines: Priority date 8/1; no closing date. Applicants notified on a rolling basis starting 3/1.

CONTACT

Kathy Brockgreitens-Gober, Director of Admissions/Registrar/Financial Assistance

4601 Mid Rivers Mall Drive, Cottleville, MO 63376

(636) 922-8270

St. Louis Christian College

Florissant, Missouri

www.slcconline.edu   Federal Code: 012580

4-year private Bible college in small city, affiliated with Christian Church.

Enrollment: 318 undergrads, 14% part-time. 33 full-time freshmen.

Selectivity: Admits less than 50% of applicants.

BASIC COSTS (2007-2008)

Per-credit charge: $275.

Room and board: $5,800.

Additional info: Full-time residential students maintaining an acceptable GPA receive full scholarships for tuition; required fees are $990 annually. Full-time commuter students pay $130 per-credit-hour; required fees, $990.

FINANCIAL AID PICTURE (2007-2008)

Students with need: Average financial aid package met 78% of need; average scholarship/grant was $8,880; average loan was $1,803. For part-time students, average financial aid package was $6,531.

Students without need: No-need awards available for academics, alumni affiliation, leadership, music/drama, religious affiliation.

Scholarships offered: President's Scholarship: full tuition; ACT score 30+; 1 available. Chancellor's Scholarships: two-thirds tuition; ACT 28+; 2 available. Dean's Scholarships: half tuition; ACT 28+; unlimited number available.

Cumulative student debt: 13% of graduating class had student loans; average debt was $8,901.

FINANCIAL AID PROCEDURES

Forms required: FAFSA, institutional form.

Dates and Deadlines: Closing date 8/1. Applicants notified on a rolling basis starting 7/20; must reply within 2 week(s) of notification.

CONTACT

Cathi Wilhoit, Financial Aid Director
1360 Grandview Drive, Florissant, MO 63033
(314) 837-6777 ext. 1101

St. Louis Community College at Meramec

St. Louis, Missouri
www.stlcc.edu   Federal Code: 002471

2-year public community college in large city.

Enrollment: 24,567 undergrads.

Selectivity: Open admission; but selective for some programs.

BASIC COSTS (2007-2008)

Tuition and fees: $2,430; out-of-district residents $3,540; out-of-state residents $4,440.

Per-credit charge: $81; out-of-district residents $118; out-of-state residents $148.

FINANCIAL AID PICTURE

Students with need: Need-based aid available for full-time and part-time students.

FINANCIAL AID PROCEDURES

Forms required: FAFSA, institutional form.

Dates and Deadlines: Closing date 6/30. Applicants notified on a rolling basis starting 2/1.

CONTACT

Manager of Student Aid
11333 Big Bend Boulevard, Kirkwood, MO 63122-5799
(314) 984-7500

Saint Louis University

St. Louis, Missouri
www.slu.edu   Federal Code: 002506

4-year private university in very large city, affiliated with Roman Catholic Church.

Enrollment: 7,365 undergrads, 7% part-time. 1,558 full-time freshmen.

Selectivity: Admits over 75% of applicants.

BASIC COSTS (2008-2009)

Tuition and fees: $30,728.

Per-credit charge: $1,060.

Room and board: $8,760.

FINANCIAL AID PICTURE (2006-2007)

Students with need: Out of 1,196 full-time freshmen who applied for aid, 939 were judged to have need. Of these, 939 received aid, and 137 had their full need met. Average financial aid package met 62% of need; average scholarship/grant was $14,006; average loan was $3,017. For part-time students, average financial aid package was $7,724.

Students without need: 531 full-time freshmen who did not demonstrate need for aid received scholarships/grants; average award was $8,452. No-need awards available for academics, art, athletics, leadership, music/drama, religious affiliation, ROTC.

Scholarships offered: *Merit:* A number of merit based scholarships are available ranging from $3,000 to $15,000. Selection based on applicants' high school academic achievement, test scores, leadership, and community service. *Athletic:* 45 full-time freshmen received athletic scholarships; average amount $13,035.

Cumulative student debt: 66% of graduating class had student loans; average debt was $27,013.

Additional info: Presidential scholarship applications are due by December 1. Martin Luther King Jr. scholarship applications have a priority date of February 1.

FINANCIAL AID PROCEDURES

Forms required: FAFSA.

Dates and Deadlines: Priority date 3/1; no closing date. Applicants notified on a rolling basis starting 3/1; must reply by 5/1 or within 4 week(s) of notification.

Transfers: No deadline. Applicants notified on a rolling basis starting 3/1; must reply by 5/1 or within 4 week(s) of notification. Students should file FAFSA by March 1 for Missouri state funds.

CONTACT

Cari Wickliffe, Financial Aid Director
221 North Grand Boulevard, St. Louis, MO 63103-2097
(314) 977-2350

St. Luke's College

Kansas City, Missouri
www.saintlukescollege.edu   Federal Code: 009782

Upper-division private nursing college in large city, affiliated with Episcopal Church.

Enrollment: 115 undergrads.

BASIC COSTS (2008-2009)

Tuition and fees: $9,520.

Per-credit charge: $295.

FINANCIAL AID PICTURE

Students with need: Need-based aid available for full-time and part-time students.

FINANCIAL AID PROCEDURES

Forms required: FAFSA, institutional form.

Dates and Deadlines: No deadline. Applicants notified by 5/1.

CONTACT

Marcia Shaw, Director of Financial Aid
8320 Ward Parkway, Suite 300, Kansas City, MO 64114
(816) 932-2194

Southeast Missouri State University

Cape Girardeau, Missouri
www.semo.edu   Federal Code: 002501

4-year public university in large town.

Enrollment: 8,485 undergrads, 20% part-time. 1,624 full-time freshmen.

Selectivity: Admits over 75% of applicants.

BASIC COSTS (2007-2008)

Tuition and fees: $5,925; out-of-state residents $10,320.

Per-credit charge: $177; out-of-state residents $323.

Room and board: $5,923.

Additional info: Tuition at time of enrollment locked for 4 years.

FINANCIAL AID PICTURE (2007-2008)

Students with need: Out of 1,315 full-time freshmen who applied for aid, 903 were judged to have need. Of these, 880 received aid, and 115 had their full need met. Average financial aid package met 60% of need; average scholarship/grant was $4,448; average loan was $3,163. For part-time students, average financial aid package was $4,434.

Students without need: 412 full-time freshmen who did not demonstrate need for aid received scholarships/grants; average award was $3,744. No-need awards available for academics, alumni affiliation, art, athletics, job skills, leadership, minority status, music/drama, ROTC, state/district residency.

Scholarships offered: 23 full-time freshmen received athletic scholarships; average amount $8,819.

Cumulative student debt: 60% of graduating class had student loans; average debt was $17,142.

FINANCIAL AID PROCEDURES

Forms required: FAFSA.

Dates and Deadlines: Priority date 3/1; no closing date. Applicants notified on a rolling basis starting 4/1; must reply within 3 week(s) of notification.

Transfers: Applicants notified on a rolling basis starting 4/1; must reply by 8/15 or within 3 week(s) of notification.

CONTACT

Karen Walker, Director of Financial Aid Services
One University Plaza, Cape Girardeau, MO 63701
(573) 651-2253

Southwest Baptist University

Bolivar, Missouri
www.sbuniv.edu   Federal Code: 002502

4-year private university in small town, affiliated with Southern Baptist Convention.

Enrollment: 2,443 undergrads, 26% part-time. 445 full-time freshmen.

Selectivity: Admits 50 to 75% of applicants.

BASIC COSTS (2008-2009)

Tuition and fees: $15,704.

Room and board: $5,166.

FINANCIAL AID PICTURE (2007-2008)

Students with need: Out of 399 full-time freshmen who applied for aid, 316 were judged to have need. Of these, 315 received aid, and 105 had their full need met. Average financial aid package met 85% of need; average scholarship/grant was $4,480; average loan was $3,991. For part-time students, average financial aid package was $4,527.

Students without need: 108 full-time freshmen who did not demonstrate need for aid received scholarships/grants; average award was $5,806. No-need awards available for academics, art, athletics, minority status, music/drama, state/district residency.

Scholarships offered: 54 full-time freshmen received athletic scholarships; average amount $5,905.

Cumulative student debt: 69% of graduating class had student loans; average debt was $22,231.

FINANCIAL AID PROCEDURES

Forms required: FAFSA, institutional form.

Dates and Deadlines: Priority date 3/15; no closing date. Applicants notified on a rolling basis starting 3/1; must reply within 2 week(s) of notification.

CONTACT

Brad Gamble, Director of Financial Aid
1600 University Avenue, Bolivar, MO 65613-2597
(417) 328-1822

State Fair Community College

Sedalia, Missouri
www.sfccmo.edu   Federal Code: 007628

2-year public community college in large town.

Enrollment: 2,941 undergrads, 36% part-time. 686 full-time freshmen.

Selectivity: Open admission; but selective for some programs.

BASIC COSTS (2008-2009)

Tuition and fees: $2,460; out-of-district residents $3,300; out-of-state residents $4,980.

Per-credit charge: $68; out-of-district residents $96; out-of-state residents $152.

FINANCIAL AID PICTURE (2006-2007)

Students with need: 40% of average financial aid package awarded as scholarships/grants, 60% awarded as loans/jobs. Need-based aid available for part-time students. Work study available nights, weekends, and for part-time students.

Students without need: This college awards aid only to students with need.

FINANCIAL AID PROCEDURES

Forms required: FAFSA.

Dates and Deadlines: Priority date 7/1; no closing date. Applicants notified on a rolling basis starting 7/15; must reply within 3 week(s) of notification.

CONTACT

John Matthews, Director of Financial Aid
3201 West 16th Street, Sedalia, MO 65301-2199
(660) 596-7295

Stephens College

Columbia, Missouri
www.stephens.edu   Federal Code: 002512

4-year private liberal arts college for women in small city.

Enrollment: 861 undergrads, 20% part-time. 225 full-time freshmen.

Selectivity: Admits 50 to 75% of applicants.

BASIC COSTS (2008-2009)

Tuition and fees: $23,000.

Per-credit charge: $265.

Room and board: $8,730.

FINANCIAL AID PICTURE (2007-2008)

Students with need: Out of 202 full-time freshmen who applied for aid, 181 were judged to have need. Of these, 181 received aid, and 37 had their full need met. Average financial aid package met 79% of need; average scholarship/grant was $6,576; average loan was $4,009. For part-time students, average financial aid package was $2,887.

Students without need: 41 full-time freshmen who did not demonstrate need for aid received scholarships/grants; average award was $8,825. No-need awards available for academics, alumni affiliation, athletics, leadership.

Scholarships offered: 2 full-time freshmen received athletic scholarships; average amount $4,750.

Cumulative student debt: 75% of graduating class had student loans; average debt was $21,178.

FINANCIAL AID PROCEDURES

Forms required: FAFSA.

Dates and Deadlines: Priority date 3/15; no closing date. Applicants notified on a rolling basis starting 3/1.

Transfers: Phi Theta Kappa students transferring from 2-year institutions eligible for Phi Theta Kappa scholarship.

CONTACT

Rachel Touchatt, Director of Financial Aid
1200 East Broadway, Columbia, MO 65215
(800) 876-7106

Three Rivers Community College

Poplar Bluff, Missouri
www.trcc.edu   Federal Code: 004713

2-year public community college in large town.

Enrollment: 2,641 undergrads, 33% part-time. 606 full-time freshmen.

Selectivity: Open admission; but selective for some programs.

BASIC COSTS (2007-2008)

Tuition and fees: $2,325; out-of-district residents $3,495; out-of-state residents $4,245.

Per-credit charge: $64; out-of-district residents $103; out-of-state residents $128.

Additional info: Book rental $17 per book. Refundable book deposit fee $25 per semester. Lab fees vary per course.

FINANCIAL AID PICTURE (2006-2007)

Students with need: 72% of average financial aid package awarded as scholarships/grants, 28% awarded as loans/jobs. Need-based aid available for part-time students.

Students without need: No-need awards available for academics, athletics, state/district residency.

FINANCIAL AID PROCEDURES

Forms required: FAFSA, institutional form.

Dates and Deadlines: Priority date 5/1; no closing date. Applicants notified on a rolling basis starting 6/1; must reply within 2 week(s) of notification.

CONTACT

Robert Myers, Vice President for Finance & Govt Affairs
2080 Three Rivers Boulevard, Poplar Bluff, MO 63901-1308
(573) 840-9607

Truman State University

Kirksville, Missouri
www.truman.edu   Federal Code: 002495

4-year public university and liberal arts college in large town.

Enrollment: 5,496 undergrads, 2% part-time. 1,367 full-time freshmen.

Selectivity: Admits over 75% of applicants.

BASIC COSTS (2007-2008)

Tuition and fees: $6,432; out-of-state residents $11,042.

Per-credit charge: $259; out-of-state residents $450.

Room and board: $5,815.

FINANCIAL AID PICTURE (2006-2007)

Students with need: Out of 1,063 full-time freshmen who applied for aid, 537 were judged to have need. Of these, 537 received aid, and 358 had their full need met. Average financial aid package met 83% of need; average scholarship/grant was $2,857; average loan was $2,074. Need-based aid available for part-time students.

Students without need: 824 full-time freshmen who did not demonstrate need for aid received scholarships/grants; average award was $4,874. No-need awards available for academics, alumni affiliation, art, athletics, leadership, minority status, music/drama, ROTC, state/district residency.

Scholarships offered: *Merit:* Pershing Scholarship: tuition, room and board; awarded to outstanding scholars and leaders; up to $4,000 for study-abroad; 12 awarded. Truman Leadership Award: up to full tuition, room and board for Missouri residents; awarded for demonstrated leadership and academic achievement. *Athletic:* 78 full-time freshmen received athletic scholarships; average amount $3,103.

Cumulative student debt: 41% of graduating class had student loans; average debt was $17,091.

Additional info: Out-of-state students whose parents work in Missouri may deduct $1 for every dollar paid in Missouri income taxes from out-of-state tuition.

FINANCIAL AID PROCEDURES

Forms required: FAFSA, institutional form.

Dates and Deadlines: Priority date 4/1; no closing date. Applicants notified on a rolling basis starting 3/1; must reply within 4 week(s) of notification.

Transfers: Applicants notified on a rolling basis starting 3/1; must reply within 4 week(s) of notification. Limited number of automatic and competitive awards offered to transfer students.

CONTACT

Susanne Neely, Financial Aid Director
McClain Hall 205, Kirksville, MO 63501-9980
(660) 785-4130

University of Central Missouri

Warrensburg, Missouri
www.ucmo.edu   Federal Code: 02454

4-year public university in large town.

Enrollment: 8,333 undergrads, 16% part-time. 1,427 full-time freshmen.

Selectivity: Admits over 75% of applicants.

BASIC COSTS (2007-2008)

Tuition and fees: $6,225; out-of-state residents $11,845.

Per-credit charge: $187; out-of-state residents $375.

Room and board: $5,846.

FINANCIAL AID PICTURE

Students with need: Need-based aid available for full-time and part-time students. Work study available nights, weekends, and for part-time students.

Students without need: No-need awards available for academics, alumni affiliation, art, athletics, leadership, minority status, music/drama, ROTC, state/district residency.

Cumulative student debt: 62% of graduating class had student loans; average debt was $10,707.

FINANCIAL AID PROCEDURES

Forms required: FAFSA.

Dates and Deadlines: Priority date 3/1; no closing date. Applicants notified on a rolling basis starting 3/1; must reply within 2 week(s) of notification.

Transfers: No deadline. Must reply within 2 week(s) of notification.

CONTACT

Phil Shreves, Director, Student Financial Assistance
WDE 1400, Warrensburg, MO 64093
(660) 543-8080

University of Missouri: Columbia

Columbia, Missouri
www.missouri.edu   Federal Code: 002516

4-year public university in small city.

Enrollment: 21,385 undergrads, 5% part-time. 4,902 full-time freshmen.

Selectivity: Admits over 75% of applicants.

BASIC COSTS (2007-2008)

Tuition and fees: $8,099; out-of-state residents $18,755.
Per-credit charge: $236; out-of-state residents $591.
Room and board: $7,002.

FINANCIAL AID PICTURE

Students with need: Need-based aid available for full-time and part-time students. Work study available nights, weekends, and for part-time students.
Students without need: No-need awards available for academics, alumni affiliation, art, athletics, leadership, minority status, music/drama, ROTC, state/district residency.
Additional info: Scholarship available for international students based on success during 1st semester.

FINANCIAL AID PROCEDURES

Forms required: FAFSA.
Dates and Deadlines: Priority date 3/1; no closing date. Applicants notified on a rolling basis starting 4/1; must reply within 4 week(s) of notification.
Transfers: No deadline. Applicants notified on a rolling basis starting 4/1; must reply within 4 week(s) of notification.

CONTACT

Joe Camille, Director of Student Financial Aid
230 Jesse Hall, Columbia, MO 65211
(573) 882-7506

University of Missouri: Kansas City

Kansas City, Missouri
www.umkc.edu   Federal Code: 002518

4-year public university in large city.
Enrollment: 6,953 undergrads, 21% part-time. 916 full-time freshmen.
Selectivity: Admits 50 to 75% of applicants.

BASIC COSTS (2007-2008)

Tuition and fees: $7,946; out-of-state residents $18,642.
Per-credit charge: $236; out-of-state residents $591.
Room and board: $7,046.

FINANCIAL AID PICTURE (2007-2008)

Students with need: Out of 744 full-time freshmen who applied for aid, 598 were judged to have need. Of these, 577 received aid, and 74 had their full need met. Average financial aid package met 61% of need; average scholarship/grant was $7,748; average loan was $6,298. For part-time students, average financial aid package was $5,498.
Students without need: 318 full-time freshmen who did not demonstrate need for aid received scholarships/grants; average award was $2,839. No-need awards available for academics, alumni affiliation, art, athletics, leadership, minority status, music/drama, state/district residency.
Scholarships offered: 19 full-time freshmen received athletic scholarships; average amount $10,799.
Cumulative student debt: 88% of graduating class had student loans; average debt was $19,137.

FINANCIAL AID PROCEDURES

Forms required: FAFSA.
Dates and Deadlines: Priority date 3/1; no closing date. Applicants notified on a rolling basis starting 4/15; must reply within 2 week(s) of notification.

CONTACT

Jan Brandow, Director of Student Financial Aid
5100 Rockhill Road, AC120, Kansas City, MO 64110-2499
(816) 235-1154

University of Missouri: St. Louis

St. Louis, Missouri
www.umsl.edu   Federal Code: 002519

4-year public university in very large city.
Enrollment: 8,947 undergrads, 35% part-time. 462 full-time freshmen.
Selectivity: Admits less than 50% of applicants.

BASIC COSTS (2007-2008)

Tuition and fees: $8,264; out-of-state residents $18,920.
Per-credit charge: $236; out-of-state residents $591.
Room and board: $7,394.

FINANCIAL AID PICTURE (2007-2008)

Students with need: Out of 332 full-time freshmen who applied for aid, 281 were judged to have need. Of these, 277 received aid, and 54 had their full need met. Average financial aid package met 67% of need; average scholarship/grant was $6,433; average loan was $3,463. For part-time students, average financial aid package was $9,318.
Students without need: 75 full-time freshmen who did not demonstrate need for aid received scholarships/grants; average award was $5,267. No-need awards available for academics, alumni affiliation, art, athletics, music/drama, ROTC, state/district residency.
Scholarships offered: *Merit:* Curator's Scholarships for Missouri freshmen with high test scores and class rank; unlimited awarded; $3,500 renewable annually. Chancellor's Scholarships for freshmen with strong test scores and class rank; unlimited awarded; $2,500 annually. Pierre Laclede Honors College Scholarships for freshmen and transfer students; varying amounts. Mark Twain Scholarships for freshmen with strong test scores and class rank; $1,000 annually. National Access Scholarships for freshmen and transfer students with strong test scores and grade point average; amount varies. Scholarship to be applied to nonresident fee. *Athletic:* 17 full-time freshmen received athletic scholarships; average amount $12,908.
Cumulative student debt: 70% of graduating class had student loans; average debt was $21,956.

FINANCIAL AID PROCEDURES

Forms required: FAFSA.
Dates and Deadlines: Priority date 4/1; no closing date. Applicants notified on a rolling basis starting 4/1; must reply within 2 week(s) of notification.
Transfers: Transfer scholarships awarded on merit basis to students entering in both Fall and Spring semesters. Priority consideration given to students admitted by March 15th for Fall semester and by October 15th for the Spring semester. Students must transfer at least 45 credit hours and have minimum GPA of 3.25 to be eligible. Amounts vary, and additional criteria apply.

CONTACT

Tony Georges, Director of Student Financial Aid
One University Boulevard, St. Louis, MO 63121-4400
(314) 516-5526

Vatterott College: St. Joseph

St. Joseph, Missouri
www.vatterott-college.edu   Federal Code: 026092

2-year for-profit branch campus and technical college in small city.
Enrollment: 196 undergrads.
Selectivity: Open admission.

BASIC COSTS (2007-2008)

Additional info: Program cost ranges: $10,483 to $20,966 (certificate/diploma); $24,460 to $30,302 (associate degree).

FINANCIAL AID PICTURE

Students with need: Need-based aid available for full-time and part-time students.

Scholarships offered: Make the Grade Scholarship; up to $1,000; based on high school grades.

FINANCIAL AID PROCEDURES

Forms required: FAFSA.

Dates and Deadlines: No deadline.

CONTACT

Marcia Hurley, Financial Aid Administrator
3131 Frederick Avenue, St. Joseph, MO 64506
(816) 364-5399

Washington University in St. Louis

St. Louis, Missouri   Federal Code: 002520
www.wustl.edu   CSS Code: 6929

4-year private university in large city.

Enrollment: 6,467 undergrads, 6% part-time. 1,328 full-time freshmen.

Selectivity: Admits less than 50% of applicants.

BASIC COSTS (2008-2009)

Tuition and fees: $37,248.

Room and board: $11,636.

FINANCIAL AID PICTURE (2007-2008)

Students with need: Out of 939 full-time freshmen who applied for aid, 525 were judged to have need. Of these, 515 received aid, and 515 had their full need met. Average financial aid package met 100% of need; average scholarship/grant was $25,706; average loan was $4,868. Need-based aid available for part-time students.

Students without need: 242 full-time freshmen who did not demonstrate need for aid received scholarships/grants; average award was $9,460. No-need awards available for academics, ROTC.

Scholarships offered: Numerous merit scholarships available ranging up to full tuition plus stipend, renewable for 4 years.

FINANCIAL AID PROCEDURES

Forms required: FAFSA, CSS PROFILE.

Dates and Deadlines: Closing date 2/15. Applicants notified by 4/1; must reply by 5/1.

CONTACT

William Witbrodt, Director of Student Financial Services
Campus Box 1089, One Brookings Drive, St. Louis, MO 63130-4899
(314) 935-5900

Webster University

St. Louis, Missouri
www.webster.edu   Federal Code: 002521

4-year private university in large city.

Enrollment: 3,523 undergrads, 25% part-time. 429 full-time freshmen.

Selectivity: Admits 50 to 75% of applicants.

BASIC COSTS (2008-2009)

Tuition and fees: $20,440.

Per-credit charge: $525.

Room and board: $9,000.

Additional info: Tuition $23,940 for theater conservatory students.

FINANCIAL AID PICTURE (2006-2007)

Students with need: Out of 401 full-time freshmen who applied for aid, 340 were judged to have need. Of these, 340 received aid. For part-time students, average financial aid package was $10,398.

Students without need: 104 full-time freshmen who did not demonstrate need for aid received scholarships/grants; average award was $8,301. No-need awards available for academics, art, music/drama.

Scholarships offered: Daniel Webster Scholarships for students with 3.8 GPA, top 10% class rank, 29 ACT and interview; 5 awarded; full tuition. Webster Academic Scholarships for students with minimum 3.0 GPA and 23 ACT; unlimited awarded; ranging from $2,000-$10,000. Leadership Scholarships based on minimum 3.3 GPA and 24 ACT, resume of activities; 15 awarded; $1,500.

Cumulative student debt: 58% of graduating class had student loans; average debt was $22,690.

FINANCIAL AID PROCEDURES

Forms required: FAFSA, institutional form.

Dates and Deadlines: Priority date 4/1; no closing date. Applicants notified on a rolling basis starting 2/9; must reply within 2 week(s) of notification.

CONTACT

David Garafola, Vice President, Financial
470 East Lockwood Avenue, St. Louis, MO 63119-3194
(314) 968-6992

Westminster College

Fulton, Missouri
www.westminster-mo.edu   Federal Code: 002523

4-year private liberal arts college in large town, affiliated with Presbyterian Church (USA).

Enrollment: 953 undergrads, 1% part-time. 224 full-time freshmen.

Selectivity: Admits over 75% of applicants.

BASIC COSTS (2008-2009)

Tuition and fees: $17,250.

Per-credit charge: $750.

Room and board: $6,720.

Additional info: Tuition/fee waivers available for minority students.

FINANCIAL AID PICTURE (2007-2008)

Students with need: Out of 193 full-time freshmen who applied for aid, 149 were judged to have need. Of these, 149 received aid, and 99 had their full need met. Average financial aid package met 94% of need; average scholarship/grant was $11,498; average loan was $2,556. For part-time students, average financial aid package was $13,087.

Students without need: 121 full-time freshmen who did not demonstrate need for aid received scholarships/grants; average award was $9,043. No-need awards available for academics, alumni affiliation, leadership, minority status, music/drama, state/district residency.

Scholarships offered: Churchill Scholarship, $10,000-$15,000, 29-36 ACT or 1920 SAT and 3.5 GPA. Trustee's Scholarship, $8,000-$9,000, 27-28 ACT or 1820-1910 SAT and 3.0 GPA. President's Scholarship, $6,500-$7,500, 25-26 ACT or 1700-1810 SAT and 3.0 GPA. Dean's Scholarship, $5,500-$6,500, 23-24 ACT or 1590-1690 SAT and 3.0 GPA. Founder's Award, $3,000-$4,000, 21-22 ACT or 1500-1580 SAT and 2.75 GPA.

Cumulative student debt: 50% of graduating class had student loans; average debt was $18,958.

FINANCIAL AID PROCEDURES

Forms required: FAFSA.

Dates and Deadlines: Priority date 2/15; no closing date. Applicants notified on a rolling basis starting 3/1; must reply within 3 week(s) of notification.

Transfers: Applicants notified on a rolling basis starting 3/1; must reply within 3 week(s) of notification.

CONTACT

Aimee Bristow, Director of Financial Aid
501 Westminster Avenue, Fulton, MO 65251-1299
(573) 592-5365

William Jewell College

Liberty, Missouri
www.jewell.edu   Federal Code: 002524

4-year private liberal arts college in large town, affiliated with Christian Church.
Enrollment: 1,329 undergrads, 17% part-time. 288 full-time freshmen.
Selectivity: Admits over 75% of applicants.

BASIC COSTS (2008-2009)
Tuition and fees: $23,000.
Per-credit charge: $725.
Room and board: $6,130.
Additional info: Base tuition now covers 12 to 18 credits per semester.

FINANCIAL AID PICTURE (2007-2008)
Students with need: Out of 253 full-time freshmen who applied for aid, 208 were judged to have need. Of these, 208 received aid. For part-time students, average financial aid package was $1,575.
Students without need: No-need awards available for academics, alumni affiliation, art, athletics, music/drama.
Scholarships offered: *Merit:* Jewell Scholarship: $11,500 to full tuition; competitive academic scholarship offered annually by invitation only to qualified high school seniors; 4 full-tuition scholarships awarded annually. Oxbridge Honors Scholarship: $11,500; for students accepted into Oxbridge Honors Program. *Athletic:* 33 full-time freshmen received athletic scholarships; average amount $5,807.
Cumulative student debt: 71% of graduating class had student loans; average debt was $24,240.

FINANCIAL AID PROCEDURES
Forms required: FAFSA.
Dates and Deadlines: Priority date 3/1; no closing date. Applicants notified on a rolling basis starting 2/15; must reply within 1.5 week(s) of notification.
Transfers: Must reply within 1. week(s) of notification.

CONTACT
Susan Armstrong, Director, Financial Aid and Scholarship Services
500 College Hill, Liberty, MO 64068
(816) 415-5977

William Woods University

Fulton, Missouri
www.williamwoods.edu   Federal Code: 002525

4-year private university and liberal arts college in large town, affiliated with Christian Church (Disciples of Christ).
Enrollment: 963 undergrads, 18% part-time. 186 full-time freshmen.
Selectivity: Admits over 75% of applicants.

BASIC COSTS (2008-2009)
Tuition and fees: $16,690.
Per-credit charge: $540.
Room and board: $6,750.
Additional info: Commuter students pay additional $50 fee per year.

FINANCIAL AID PICTURE (2007-2008)
Students with need: Out of 145 full-time freshmen who applied for aid, 141 were judged to have need. Of these, 139 received aid, and 54 had their full need met. Average financial aid package met 82% of need; average scholarship/grant was $11,738; average loan was $4,026. For part-time students, average financial aid package was $4,233.
Students without need: 47 full-time freshmen who did not demonstrate need for aid received scholarships/grants; average award was $8,899. No-need awards available for academics, alumni affiliation, art, athletics, leadership, music/drama, religious affiliation.

Scholarships offered: *Merit:* LEAD (Leading, Educating, Achieving and Developing) Award; $5,000 for campus residents, $2,500 for commuters; based on commitment to campus and community involvement; renewable each year if commitment has been met in previous year. *Athletic:* 6 full-time freshmen received athletic scholarships; average amount $4,303.
Cumulative student debt: 74% of graduating class had student loans; average debt was $17,220.

FINANCIAL AID PROCEDURES
Forms required: FAFSA, institutional form.
Dates and Deadlines: Priority date 3/1; no closing date. Applicants notified on a rolling basis starting 3/15; must reply within 2 week(s) of notification.
Transfers: No deadline. Applicants notified on a rolling basis; must reply within 2 week(s) of notification.

CONTACT
Deana Ready, Director of Financial Aid
One University Avenue, Fulton, MO 65251-2388
(573) 592-4232

Montana

Blackfeet Community College

Browning, Montana
www.bfcc.org   Federal Code: 014902

2-year public community college in small town.
Enrollment: 465 undergrads.
Selectivity: Open admission.

BASIC COSTS (2007-2008)
Tuition and fees: $2,000.
Per-credit charge: $69.

FINANCIAL AID PICTURE
Students with need: Need-based aid available for full-time and part-time students.

FINANCIAL AID PROCEDURES
Forms required: FAFSA, institutional form.
Dates and Deadlines: No deadline.

CONTACT
Margaret Bird, Director of Financial Aid
Highway 2 & 89, Browning, MT 59417
(406) 338-5421 ext. 245

Carroll College

Helena, Montana
www.carroll.edu   Federal Code: 002526

4-year private liberal arts college in large town, affiliated with Roman Catholic Church.
Enrollment: 1,272 undergrads, 6% part-time. 327 full-time freshmen.

BASIC COSTS (2007-2008)
Tuition and fees: $19,620.
Room and board: $6,608.

FINANCIAL AID PICTURE
Students with need: Need-based aid available for full-time and part-time students. Work study available nights, weekends, and for part-time students.
Students without need: No-need awards available for academics, athletics, leadership, music/drama, religious affiliation, ROTC.

FINANCIAL AID PROCEDURES

Forms required: FAFSA.

Dates and Deadlines: Priority date 3/1; no closing date. Applicants notified on a rolling basis starting 3/1; must reply within 4 week(s) of notification.

CONTACT

Janet Riis, Director of Financial Aid
1601 North Benton Avenue, Helena, MT 59625
(406) 447-5425

Chief Dull Knife College

Lame Deer, Montana
www.cdkc.edu   Federal Code: 014878

2-year public junior college in rural community.

Enrollment: 180 undergrads.

Selectivity: Open admission.

BASIC COSTS (2007-2008)

Tuition and fees: $300.

FINANCIAL AID PICTURE

Students with need: Need-based aid available for full-time and part-time students. Work study available nights.

FINANCIAL AID PROCEDURES

Forms required: FAFSA, institutional form.

Dates and Deadlines: Priority date 3/1; no closing date. Applicants notified on a rolling basis; must reply within 2 week(s) of notification.

CONTACT

Debra Reed, Financial Aid Director
Box 98, Lame Deer, MT 59043
(406) 477-6215

Dawson Community College

Glendive, Montana
www.dawson.edu   Federal Code: 002529

2-year public community college in small town.

Enrollment: 322 undergrads, 20% part-time. 107 full-time freshmen.

Selectivity: Open admission.

BASIC COSTS (2007-2008)

Tuition and fees: $2,736; out-of-district residents $3,843; out-of-state residents $8,499.

Per-credit charge: $52; out-of-district residents $89; out-of-state residents $244.

Additional info: Western Undergraduate Exchange tuition: $133.80 per credit hour, $3,211 full-time.

FINANCIAL AID PICTURE

Students with need: Work study available nights, weekends, and for part-time students.

Students without need: No-need awards available for academics, art, athletics, music/drama.

FINANCIAL AID PROCEDURES

Forms required: FAFSA.

Dates and Deadlines: Priority date 3/1; no closing date. Applicants notified on a rolling basis starting 5/15; must reply within 2 week(s) of notification.

CONTACT

Jolene Myers, Director of Admissions
300 College Drive, Glendive, MT 59330
(406) 377-9410

Flathead Valley Community College

Kalispell, Montana
www.fvcc.edu   Federal Code: 006777

2-year public community college in large town.

Enrollment: 1,291 undergrads, 28% part-time. 219 full-time freshmen.

BASIC COSTS (2007-2008)

Tuition and fees: $3,080; out-of-district residents $4,256; out-of-state residents $9,240.

Per-credit charge: $110; out-of-district residents $152; out-of-state residents $330.

FINANCIAL AID PICTURE

Students with need: Need-based aid available for full-time and part-time students.

Students without need: No-need awards available for academics, athletics.

FINANCIAL AID PROCEDURES

Forms required: FAFSA.

Dates and Deadlines: Priority date 3/1; no closing date. Applicants notified by 4/15; must reply within 2 week(s) of notification.

CONTACT

Cynthia Kiefer, Financial Aid Director
777 Grandview Drive, Kalispell, MT 59901
(406) 756-3849

Fort Peck Community College

Poplar, Montana
www.fpcc.edu   Federal Code: 016616

2-year public community college in small town.

Enrollment: 405 undergrads.

Selectivity: Open admission.

BASIC COSTS (2007-2008)

Tuition and fees: $1,840.

Per-credit charge: $60.

Additional info: Tuition/fee waivers available for adults, minority students.

FINANCIAL AID PICTURE

Students with need: Need-based aid available for full-time and part-time students. Work study available nights.

FINANCIAL AID PROCEDURES

Forms required: FAFSA, institutional form.

Dates and Deadlines: No deadline. Applicants notified on a rolling basis; must reply within 2 week(s) of notification.

CONTACT

Lanette Clark, Financial Aid Officer
Box 398 605 Indian, Poplar, MT 59255-0398
(406) 768-6328

Helena College of Technology of the University of Montana

Helena, Montana
www.umhelena.edu   Federal Code: 007570

2-year public community and technical college in large town.

Enrollment: 800 undergrads.

Selectivity: Open admission.

BASIC COSTS (2007-2008)

Tuition and fees: $2,978; out-of-state residents $7,922.
Additional info: Tuition/fee waivers available for minority students.

FINANCIAL AID PICTURE

Students with need: Need-based aid available for full-time and part-time students.

FINANCIAL AID PROCEDURES

Forms required: FAFSA, institutional form.
Dates and Deadlines: Priority date 3/1; no closing date. Applicants notified on a rolling basis starting 5/1.

CONTACT

Victoria Glass, Director of Financial Aid
1115 North Roberts Street, Helena, MT 59601-3098
(406) 444-6879

Miles Community College

Miles City, Montana
www.milescc.edu   Federal Code: 002528

2-year public community college in small town.
Enrollment: 420 undergrads, 15% part-time. 132 full-time freshmen.
Selectivity: Open admission; but selective for some programs.

BASIC COSTS (2008-2009)

Tuition and fees: $3,420; out-of-district residents $4,290; out-of-state residents $7,080.
Per-credit charge: $71; out-of-district residents $100; out-of-state residents $193.
Room and board: $4,250.

FINANCIAL AID PICTURE

Students with need: Need-based aid available for full-time and part-time students. Work study available nights, weekends, and for part-time students.
Students without need: No-need awards available for academics, athletics, leadership.
Scholarships offered: Montana residents may apply for tuition waivers and scholarships. Students must maintain 3.0 GPA and carry 15 credits. Deadline for application 03/15.

FINANCIAL AID PROCEDURES

Forms required: FAFSA.
Dates and Deadlines: Priority date 3/1; no closing date. Applicants notified on a rolling basis starting 4/15; must reply within 4 week(s) of notification.

CONTACT

Loren Lancaster, Financial Aid Officer
2715 Dickinson Street, Miles City, MT 59301
(406) 874-6208

Montana State University College of Technology: Great Falls

Great Falls, Montana
www.msugf.edu   Federal Code: 009314

2-year public community and technical college in small city.
Enrollment: 1,273 undergrads, 46% part-time. 187 full-time freshmen.
Selectivity: Open admission; but selective for some programs.

BASIC COSTS (2007-2008)

Tuition and fees: $2,982; out-of-state residents $8,648.
Additional info: Tuition/fee waivers available for minority students, unemployed or children of unemployed.

FINANCIAL AID PICTURE

Students with need: Need-based aid available for full-time and part-time students. Work study available nights, weekends, and for part-time students.

FINANCIAL AID PROCEDURES

Forms required: FAFSA, institutional form.
Dates and Deadlines: Priority date 3/1; no closing date. Applicants notified on a rolling basis starting 4/1; must reply within 3 week(s) of notification.

CONTACT

Leah Habel, Financial Aid Director
2100 16th Avenue South, Great Falls, MT 59405
(406) 771-4334

Montana State University: Billings

Billings, Montana
www.msubillings.edu   Federal Code: 002530

4-year public university and technical college in small city.
Enrollment: 4,283 undergrads, 24% part-time. 642 full-time freshmen.
Selectivity: Admits over 75% of applicants.

BASIC COSTS (2007-2008)

Tuition and fees: $5,132; out-of-state residents $13,707.
Room and board: $4,882.

FINANCIAL AID PICTURE (2006-2007)

Students with need: Out of 555 full-time freshmen who applied for aid, 419 were judged to have need. Of these, 409 received aid, and 48 had their full need met. Average financial aid package met 50% of need; average scholarship/grant was $3,780; average loan was $2,255. For part-time students, average financial aid package was $6,281.
Students without need: 44 full-time freshmen who did not demonstrate need for aid received scholarships/grants; average award was $4,386. No-need awards available for academics, alumni affiliation, art, athletics, job skills, leadership, minority status, music/drama, state/district residency.
Scholarships offered: 63 full-time freshmen received athletic scholarships; average amount $6,759.
Cumulative student debt: 74% of graduating class had student loans; average debt was $16,948.
Additional info: Veterans and honors fee waivers offered.

FINANCIAL AID PROCEDURES

Forms required: FAFSA.
Dates and Deadlines: Priority date 3/1; no closing date. Applicants notified on a rolling basis starting 4/1; must reply within 3 week(s) of notification.

CONTACT

Judy Chapman, Director of Financial Aid
1500 University Drive, Billings, MT 59101-0298
(406) 657-2188

Montana State University: Bozeman

Bozeman, Montana
www.montana.edu   Federal Code: 002532

4-year public university in large town.
Enrollment: 10,461 undergrads, 15% part-time. 1,902 full-time freshmen.
Selectivity: Admits 50 to 75% of applicants.

BASIC COSTS (2007-2008)

Tuition and fees: $5,749; out-of-state residents $16,274.
Room and board: $6,926.
Additional info: Tuition/fee waivers available for minority students.

FINANCIAL AID PICTURE (2006-2007)

Students with need: Out of 1,319 full-time freshmen who applied for aid, 952 were judged to have need. Of these, 923 received aid, and 65 had their full need met. Average financial aid package met 66% of need; average scholarship/grant was $3,982; average loan was $3,317. For part-time students, average financial aid package was $8,043.

Students without need: 88 full-time freshmen who did not demonstrate need for aid received scholarships/grants; average award was $1,594. No-need awards available for academics, alumni affiliation, art, athletics, job skills, leadership, minority status, music/drama, ROTC, state/district residency.

Scholarships offered: 23 full-time freshmen received athletic scholarships; average amount $5,711.

Cumulative student debt: 69% of graduating class had student loans; average debt was $19,683.

FINANCIAL AID PROCEDURES

Forms required: FAFSA.

Dates and Deadlines: Priority date 3/1; no closing date. Applicants notified on a rolling basis starting 4/1; must reply within 3 week(s) of notification.

Transfers: Priority date 7/1; no deadline.

CONTACT

Brandi Payne, Director of Financial Aid Services
PO Box 172190, Bozeman, MT 59717-2190
(406) 994-2845

Montana State University: Northern

Havre, Montana
www.msun.edu   Federal Code: 002533

4-year public university and liberal arts college in large town.

Enrollment: 1,388 undergrads.

BASIC COSTS (2007-2008)

Tuition and fees: $4,357; out-of-state residents $14,493.

Room and board: $5,627.

Additional info: Tuition/fee waivers available for adults, minority students.

FINANCIAL AID PICTURE

Students with need: Need-based aid available for full-time and part-time students.

Students without need: No-need awards available for academics, athletics.

FINANCIAL AID PROCEDURES

Forms required: FAFSA, institutional form.

Dates and Deadlines: No deadline. Applicants notified on a rolling basis; must reply within 2 week(s) of notification.

CONTACT

Cindy Small, Director of Financial Aid
Box 7751, Havre, MT 59501

Montana Tech of the University of Montana

Butte, Montana
www.mtech.edu   Federal Code: 002531

4-year public engineering and technical college in large town.

Enrollment: 2,137 undergrads. 422 full-time freshmen.

Selectivity: Admits over 75% of applicants.

BASIC COSTS (2007-2008)

Tuition and fees: $5,635; out-of-state residents $15,067.

Room and board: $5,860.

Additional info: Tuition/fee waivers available for adults, minority students.

FINANCIAL AID PICTURE

Students with need: Need-based aid available for full-time and part-time students. Work study available nights, weekends, and for part-time students.

Students without need: This college awards aid only to students with need.

FINANCIAL AID PROCEDURES

Forms required: FAFSA, institutional form.

Dates and Deadlines: Priority date 3/1; no closing date. Applicants notified on a rolling basis starting 4/1; must reply within 2 week(s) of notification.

CONTACT

Mike Richardson, Director of Financial Aid
1300 West Park Street, Butte, MT 59701-8997
(406) 496-4212

Rocky Mountain College

Billings, Montana
www.rocky.edu   Federal Code: 002534

4-year private liberal arts college in small city, affiliated with United Church of Christ, United Methodist Church, United Presbyterian Church.

Enrollment: 834 undergrads, 6% part-time. 170 full-time freshmen.

Selectivity: Admits 50 to 75% of applicants.

BASIC COSTS (2007-2008)

Tuition and fees: $17,679.

Room and board: $5,700.

FINANCIAL AID PICTURE

Students with need: Need-based aid available for full-time and part-time students. Work study available nights, weekends, and for part-time students.

Students without need: No-need awards available for academics, alumni affiliation, art, athletics, leadership, minority status, music/drama, religious affiliation, state/district residency.

FINANCIAL AID PROCEDURES

Forms required: FAFSA, institutional form.

Dates and Deadlines: Priority date 3/1; no closing date. Applicants notified on a rolling basis starting 2/1; must reply within 4 week(s) of notification.

Transfers: No deadline. Applicants notified on a rolling basis starting 2/1; must reply within 4 week(s) of notification.

CONTACT

Lisa Browning, Vice President of Enrollment Services
1511 Poly Drive, Billings, MT 59102-1796
(406) 657-1031

Stone Child College

Box Elder, Montana
www.stonechild.edu   Federal Code: 026109

2-year public community and junior college in rural community.

Enrollment: 196 undergrads.

Selectivity: Open admission.

BASIC COSTS (2007-2008)

Tuition and fees: $670.

Additional info: Students not members of Federally recognized Native American tribe pay additional $420 in fees/year.

FINANCIAL AID PICTURE

Students with need: Need-based aid available for full-time and part-time students.

Students without need: No-need awards available for academics.

Additional info: Scholarships available to high school and GED graduates who apply for college admission during the first term after graduation.

FINANCIAL AID PROCEDURES

Forms required: FAFSA, institutional form.
Dates and Deadlines: Priority date 3/1; closing date 6/30. Applicants notified on a rolling basis.

CONTACT

Tiffany Galbavy, Financial Aid Director
RR1 Box 1082, Box Elder, MT 59521-9796
(406) 395-4313

University of Great Falls

Great Falls, Montana
www.ugf.edu   Federal Code: 002527

4-year private university and liberal arts college in small city, affiliated with Roman Catholic Church.
Enrollment: 612 undergrads, 22% part-time. 129 full-time freshmen.
Selectivity: Admits 50 to 75% of applicants.

BASIC COSTS (2008-2009)

Tuition and fees: $16,400.
Per-credit charge: $495.
Room and board: $6,490.

FINANCIAL AID PICTURE (2007-2008)

Students with need: 34% of average financial aid package awarded as scholarships/grants, 66% awarded as loans/jobs. Need-based aid available for part-time students. Work study available nights, weekends, and for part-time students.
Students without need: No-need awards available for academics, alumni affiliation, art, athletics, job skills, leadership, minority status, music/drama, religious affiliation, state/district residency.
Scholarships offered: Freshmen scholarships; $1,000-$6,000; based on high school GPA; renewable.

FINANCIAL AID PROCEDURES

Forms required: FAFSA.
Dates and Deadlines: Priority date 4/1; no closing date. Applicants notified on a rolling basis starting 3/1; must reply within 2 week(s) of notification.
Transfers: Transfer student scholarships; $2,500-$4,000; based on college GPA; renewable.

CONTACT

Peggy Boord, Director of Financial Aid
1301 20th Street South, Great Falls, MT 59405
(406) 791-5235

University of Montana: Missoula

Missoula, Montana   Federal Code: 002536
www.umt.edu   CSS Code: 4489

4-year public university and liberal arts college in small city.
Enrollment: 11,586 undergrads.
Selectivity: Admits over 75% of applicants.

BASIC COSTS (2007-2008)

Tuition and fees: $5,141; out-of-state residents $15,504.
Per-credit charge: $156; out-of-state residents $588.
Room and board: $6,026.
Additional info: Tuition/fee waivers available for minority students.

FINANCIAL AID PICTURE

Students with need: Need-based aid available for full-time and part-time students. Work study available nights, weekends, and for part-time students.
Students without need: No-need awards available for academics, art, athletics, leadership, music/drama, ROTC, state/district residency.

FINANCIAL AID PROCEDURES

Forms required: FAFSA, CSS PROFILE, institutional form.
Dates and Deadlines: Priority date 3/1; no closing date. Applicants notified on a rolling basis starting 4/1; must reply by 8/1 or within 4 week(s) of notification.

CONTACT

Myron Hanson, Director of Financial Aid
Lommasson Center 103, Missoula, MT 59812
(406) 243-5373

University of Montana: Western

Dillon, Montana
www.umwestern.edu   Federal Code: 002537

4-year public liberal arts and teachers college in small town.
Enrollment: 1,148 undergrads, 16% part-time. 243 full-time freshmen.
Selectivity: Open admission; but selective for some programs.

BASIC COSTS (2007-2008)

Tuition and fees: $3,659; out-of-state residents $12,428.
Room and board: $5,120.
Additional info: Tuition/fee waivers available for minority students.

FINANCIAL AID PICTURE (2006-2007)

Students with need: 55% of average financial aid package awarded as scholarships/grants, 45% awarded as loans/jobs. Need-based aid available for part-time students. Work study available nights, weekends, and for part-time students.
Students without need: No-need awards available for academics, alumni affiliation, art, athletics, leadership, minority status, state/district residency.
Cumulative student debt: 68% of graduating class had student loans; average debt was $24,050.
Additional info: Tuition and/or fee waivers for veterans, Native Americans and other minorities.

FINANCIAL AID PROCEDURES

Forms required: FAFSA.
Dates and Deadlines: Priority date 3/1; no closing date. Applicants notified on a rolling basis starting 3/1; must reply within 2 week(s) of notification.

CONTACT

Erica Jones, Director of Financial Aid
710 South Atlantic Street, Dillon, MT 59725
(406) 683-7511

Nebraska

Bellevue University

Bellevue, Nebraska
www.bellevue.edu   Federal Code: 002538

4-year private university and business college in large city.
Enrollment: 5,515 undergrads, 32% part-time. 104 full-time freshmen.
Selectivity: Open admission; but selective for some programs.

BASIC COSTS (2008-2009)

Tuition and fees: $6,165.
Per-credit charge: $220.
Additional info: Prices vary depending on program.

FINANCIAL AID PICTURE (2006-2007)

Students with need: For part-time students, average financial aid package was $984.

Students without need: No-need awards available for academics, athletics, leadership.

FINANCIAL AID PROCEDURES

Forms required: FAFSA, institutional form.

Dates and Deadlines: Priority date 4/15; no closing date. Applicants notified on a rolling basis starting 4/15; must reply within 2 week(s) of notification.

Transfers: No deadline.

CONTACT

Jon Dotterer, Director of Financial Aid
1000 Galvin Road South, Bellevue, NE 68005-3098
(402) 557-7326

Central Community College

Grand Island, Nebraska
www.cccneb.edu   Federal Code: 014468

2-year public community and technical college in large town.

Enrollment: 3,921 undergrads, 48% part-time. 707 full-time freshmen.

Selectivity: Open admission; but selective for some programs and for out-of-state students.

BASIC COSTS (2007-2008)

Tuition and fees: $2,190; out-of-state residents $3,045.

Per-credit charge: $73; out-of-state residents $106.

Room and board: $4,080.

FINANCIAL AID PICTURE

Students with need: Need-based aid available for full-time and part-time students. Work study available nights.

Students without need: No-need awards available for academics, art, athletics, job skills, leadership, music/drama.

FINANCIAL AID PROCEDURES

Forms required: FAFSA, institutional form.

Dates and Deadlines: Priority date 6/1; no closing date. Applicants notified on a rolling basis starting 3/1; must reply within 1 week(s) of notification.

CONTACT

Steve Millnitz, Financial Aid Officer
3134 West Highway 34, Grand Island, NE 68802-4903
(308) 398-7407

Chadron State College

Chadron, Nebraska
www.csc.edu   Federal Code: 002539

4-year public business and liberal arts and teachers college in small town.

Enrollment: 2,017 undergrads.

Selectivity: Open admission; but selective for some programs.

BASIC COSTS (2007-2008)

Tuition and fees: $4,212; out-of-state residents $7,512.

Per-credit charge: $110; out-of-state residents $220.

Room and board: $4,430.

FINANCIAL AID PICTURE

Students with need: Need-based aid available for full-time and part-time students. Work study available nights, weekends, and for part-time students.

Students without need: No-need awards available for academics, alumni affiliation, art, athletics, leadership, minority status, music/drama, state/district residency.

FINANCIAL AID PROCEDURES

Forms required: FAFSA, institutional form.

Dates and Deadlines: Priority date 6/1; no closing date. Applicants notified on a rolling basis starting 4/1; must reply within 2 week(s) of notification.

CONTACT

Sherry Douglas, Director of Financial Aid
1000 Main Street, Chadron, NE 69337
(308) 432-6230

Clarkson College

Omaha, Nebraska
www.clarksoncollege.edu   Federal Code: 009862

4-year private health science college in large city, affiliated with Episcopal Church.

Enrollment: 697 undergrads.

Selectivity: Open admission; but selective for some programs.

BASIC COSTS (2007-2008)

Tuition and fees: $12,720.

Per-credit charge: $385.

Room only: $4,200.

Additional info: Distance learning fee: $40 per credit hour in 2007-08.

FINANCIAL AID PICTURE (2006-2007)

Students with need: 21% of average financial aid package awarded as scholarships/grants, 79% awarded as loans/jobs. Need-based aid available for part-time students. Work study available nights, weekends, and for part-time students.

Students without need: No-need awards available for academics, alumni affiliation, minority status, religious affiliation.

FINANCIAL AID PROCEDURES

Forms required: FAFSA, institutional form.

Dates and Deadlines: Priority date 4/1; no closing date. Applicants notified on a rolling basis starting 4/13; must reply within 3 week(s) of notification.

Transfers: Priority date 3/1; no deadline. Applicants notified on a rolling basis starting 3/30.

CONTACT

Margie Harris, Director of Student Financial Services
101 South 42nd Street, Omaha, NE 68131-2739
(402) 552-2749

College of Saint Mary

Omaha, Nebraska
www.csm.edu   Federal Code: 002540

4-year private university and nursing and liberal arts and teachers college for women in large city, affiliated with Roman Catholic Church.

Enrollment: 793 undergrads, 22% part-time. 93 full-time freshmen.

Selectivity: Admits less than 50% of applicants.

BASIC COSTS (2008-2009)

Tuition and fees: $21,260.

Per-credit charge: $685.

Room and board: $6,400.

FINANCIAL AID PICTURE (2007-2008)

Students with need: Average financial aid package met 69% of need; average scholarship/grant was $12,447; average loan was $4,861. For part-time students, average financial aid package was $5,327.

Students without need: No-need awards available for academics, athletics, music/drama.

Cumulative student debt: 100% of graduating class had student loans; average debt was $21,566.

FINANCIAL AID PROCEDURES

Forms required: FAFSA.

Dates and Deadlines: Priority date 3/1; no closing date. Applicants notified on a rolling basis starting 3/1; must reply within 2 week(s) of notification.
Transfers: Must reply within 2 week(s) of notification. Scholarships available for transfer students.

CONTACT
Danni Warrick, Director of Financial Aid
7000 Mercy Road, Omaha, NE 68106
(402) 399-2362

Concordia University
Seward, Nebraska
www.cune.edu   Federal Code: 002541

4-year private university in small town, affiliated with Lutheran Church - Missouri Synod.
Enrollment: 1,066 undergrads, 2% part-time. 264 full-time freshmen.
Selectivity: Admits over 75% of applicants.

BASIC COSTS (2008-2009)
Tuition and fees: $20,700.
Per-credit charge: $640.
Room and board: $5,280.

FINANCIAL AID PICTURE
Students with need: Need-based aid available for full-time and part-time students. Work study available nights, weekends, and for part-time students.
Students without need: No-need awards available for academics, alumni affiliation, art, athletics, leadership, music/drama, religious affiliation.
Scholarships offered: President's scholarship: $15,000 per year; based on academic achievement. Regent's scholarship: $8,000-$11,000 per year; based on high school GPA and SAT/ACT scores. Achievement award: $3,500-$6,500 per year; based on high school GPA and SAT/ACT scores.

FINANCIAL AID PROCEDURES
Forms required: FAFSA.
Dates and Deadlines: Priority date 3/1; no closing date. Applicants notified on a rolling basis starting 3/1; must reply within 4 week(s) of notification.
Transfers: Applicants notified on a rolling basis starting 3/1; must reply within 4 week(s) of notification.

CONTACT
Gloria Hennig, Director of Financial Aid
800 North Columbia Avenue, Seward, NE 68434-1556
(800) 535-5494 ext. 7270

Creative Center
Omaha, Nebraska
www.creativecenter.edu   Federal Code: 031643

4-year for-profit visual arts and career college in large city.
Enrollment: 105 undergrads, 4% part-time.

BASIC COSTS (2008-2009)
Tuition and fees: $18,800.
Additional info: Required fees vary by year and program.

FINANCIAL AID PICTURE
Students with need: Need-based aid available for full-time and part-time students.
Students without need: No-need awards available for academics, art.
Scholarships offered: President's Award: $500. Founder's Award: $1,000. Both awards based on portfolio and high school academics. Andy Arrants Memorial Scholarship: supply kit (approx. $500); based on submitted artwork and essay.

FINANCIAL AID PROCEDURES
Forms required: FAFSA.
Dates and Deadlines: No deadline. Applicants notified on a rolling basis starting 1/1.
Transfers: No deadline. Applicants notified on a rolling basis.

CONTACT
Sandy LaRocca, Director of Financial Aid
10850 Emmet Street, Omaha, NE 68164
(402) 898-1000 ext. 203

Creighton University
Omaha, Nebraska
www.creighton.edu   Federal Code: 002542

4-year private university in large city, affiliated with Roman Catholic Church.
Enrollment: 4,104 undergrads, 7% part-time. 965 full-time freshmen.
Selectivity: Admits over 75% of applicants.

BASIC COSTS (2008-2009)
Tuition and fees: $28,542.
Per-credit charge: $853.
Room and board: $8,516.

FINANCIAL AID PICTURE (2006-2007)
Students with need: Out of 759 full-time freshmen who applied for aid, 585 were judged to have need. Of these, 585 received aid, and 256 had their full need met. Average financial aid package met 92% of need; average scholarship/grant was $14,853; average loan was $5,640. Need-based aid available for part-time students.
Students without need: 312 full-time freshmen who did not demonstrate need for aid received scholarships/grants; average award was $9,311. No-need awards available for academics, alumni affiliation, art, athletics, leadership, minority status, music/drama, ROTC.
Scholarships offered: *Merit:* William Jennings Bryan Debate and Speech Scholarship: $4,000. Diversity Scholarship & Native American Merit Scholarship; three-quarter tuition scholarships; awarded to students who show commitment to diversity; 3.3 GPA or higher on a 4.0 scale required; applicants evaluated on academic merit, community service, school activities, leadership, and financial need. First-generation college bound students and families that earn under $60,000 encouraged to apply. Ron Hansen Scholarship in Creative Writing: $4,000. Grace Keenan Scholarship for Excellence in the Arts: $3,000; awarded to students who intend to major in visual or performing arts. Christina M. Hixson Scholarship in Business Administration: $4,500; awarded to freshman business students from high schools in CO, IA, IL, KA, MN, MO, NE, ND, SD, WI or WY with a minimum of 3.0 GPA. College of Business Administration Ethics and Social Responsibility Scholarship: $4,500; awarded to students with exceptional service accomplishments and leadership potential; 3.8 GPA and a minimum 26 ACT or 1200 SAT. Presidential Scholarship; three-quarter tuition scholarship awarded to selected applicants in the top 10% of applicant pool, based upon academics. Scott Scholarship; full tuition scholarship in the College of Business Administration awarded to selected students in the top 10% of applicant pool, based on academics. G. Robert Muchemore Foundation Undergraduate Scholarship; full tuition scholarship awarded to graduates of Nebraska high schools entering as freshmen; based upon academics. *Athletic:* 46 full-time freshmen received athletic scholarships; average amount $14,325.
Cumulative student debt: 64% of graduating class had student loans; average debt was $29,074.

FINANCIAL AID PROCEDURES
Forms required: FAFSA, institutional form.
Dates and Deadlines: Priority date 3/1; no closing date. Applicants notified on a rolling basis starting 3/15; must reply by 5/1 or within 4 week(s) of notification.

Transfers: If transferring 24 or more hours of credit, student not eligible for academic (non-need) scholarships.

CONTACT

Robert Walker, Director of Financial Aid
2500 California Plaza, Omaha, NE 68178-0001
(402) 280-2731

Dana College

Blair, Nebraska
www.dana.edu   Federal Code: 002543

4-year private liberal arts college in small town, affiliated with Evangelical Lutheran Church in America.
Enrollment: 613 undergrads, 1% part-time. 185 full-time freshmen.
Selectivity: Admits 50 to 75% of applicants.

BASIC COSTS (2007-2008)

Tuition and fees: $19,370.
Per-credit charge: $530.
Room and board: $5,560.

FINANCIAL AID PICTURE (2007-2008)

Students with need: Out of 183 full-time freshmen who applied for aid, 159 were judged to have need. Of these, 159 received aid, and 45 had their full need met. Average financial aid package met 96% of need; average loan was $4,900. For part-time students, average financial aid package was $459.
Students without need: 24 full-time freshmen who did not demonstrate need for aid received scholarships/grants; average award was $4,178. No-need awards available for academics, alumni affiliation, art, athletics, music/drama, religious affiliation, ROTC, state/district residency.
Scholarships offered: *Merit:* Departmental scholarships, Presidential scholarships, All-American Scholarship, athletic and performing arts scholarships available. *Athletic:* 132 full-time freshmen received athletic scholarships; average amount $6,667.
Cumulative student debt: 91% of graduating class had student loans; average debt was $24,141.
Additional info: Auditions recommended for music and drama scholarship applicants. Portfolios recommended for art, graphic design, and cheerleading/dance scholarship applicants.

FINANCIAL AID PROCEDURES

Forms required: FAFSA, institutional form.
Dates and Deadlines: Priority date 4/7; no closing date. Applicants notified on a rolling basis starting 3/7; must reply within 3 week(s) of notification.
Transfers: Must reply within 3 week(s) of notification. Academic scholarships awarded on basis of high school GPA, rank, and test scores for students with 1 year or less as full time college student. Awards for transfers with 27 credits or more will be based on college GPA.

CONTACT

Rita McManigal, Director of Financial Aid
2848 College Drive, Blair, NE 68008-1099
(402) 426-7226

Doane College

Crete, Nebraska
www.doane.edu   Federal Code: 002544

4-year private liberal arts college in small town, affiliated with United Church of Christ.
Enrollment: 921 undergrads, 1% part-time. 259 full-time freshmen.
Selectivity: Admits over 75% of applicants.

BASIC COSTS (2007-2008)

Tuition and fees: $19,150.
Per-credit charge: $630.
Room and board: $5,410.

FINANCIAL AID PICTURE (2007-2008)

Students with need: Out of 236 full-time freshmen who applied for aid, 209 were judged to have need. Of these, 209 received aid, and 156 had their full need met. Average financial aid package met 94% of need; average scholarship/grant was $12,666; average loan was $3,390. Need-based aid available for part-time students.
Students without need: 122 full-time freshmen who did not demonstrate need for aid received scholarships/grants; average award was $11,800. No-need awards available for academics, art, athletics, music/drama.
Cumulative student debt: 91% of graduating class had student loans; average debt was $14,171.

FINANCIAL AID PROCEDURES

Forms required: FAFSA.
Dates and Deadlines: Priority date 3/1; no closing date. Applicants notified on a rolling basis starting 3/1; must reply within 2 week(s) of notification.

CONTACT

Janet Dodson, Director of Financial Aid
1014 Boswell Avenue, Crete, NE 68333
(402) 826-8260

Grace University

Omaha, Nebraska
www.graceuniversity.edu   Federal Code: 002547

4-year private university and Bible college in very large city, affiliated with interdenominational tradition.
Enrollment: 358 undergrads.

BASIC COSTS (2008-2009)

Tuition and fees: $14,490.
Per-credit charge: $390.
Room and board: $5,590.
Additional info: Tuition/fee waivers available for minority students.

FINANCIAL AID PICTURE

Students with need: Need-based aid available for full-time and part-time students. Work study available weekends and for part-time students.
Students without need: No-need awards available for academics, alumni affiliation, music/drama.

FINANCIAL AID PROCEDURES

Forms required: FAFSA, institutional form.
Dates and Deadlines: Priority date 3/1; no closing date. Applicants notified on a rolling basis starting 3/1; must reply within 2 week(s) of notification.
Transfers: No deadline. Applicants notified on a rolling basis starting 3/1; must reply within 2 week(s) of notification.

CONTACT

Dale Brown, Director of Revenue
1311 South Ninth Street, Omaha, NE 68108-3629
(402) 449-2810

Hastings College

Hastings, Nebraska
www.hastings.edu   Federal Code: 002548

4-year private liberal arts college in large town, affiliated with Presbyterian Church (USA).
Enrollment: 1,067 undergrads, 1% part-time. 304 full-time freshmen.

Selectivity: Admits over 75% of applicants.

BASIC COSTS (2007-2008)
Tuition and fees: $19,604.
Per-credit charge: $779.
Room and board: $5,432.
Additional info: Tuition/fee waivers available for adults.

FINANCIAL AID PICTURE
Students with need: Need-based aid available for full-time and part-time students. Work study available nights, weekends, and for part-time students.
Students without need: No-need awards available for academics, alumni affiliation, art, athletics, leadership, music/drama.
Scholarships offered: Walter Scott Scholarship Competition: full-tuition, for freshman; 3 awarded. Trustees Scholarships: $14,000 per year. President's Scholarships: $13,000 per year. Dean Scholarships: $12,000 per year. Ambassador Scholarships: $10,000 per year. Ringland Scholarships: $8,000 per year. Pro Rege Scholarships: $7,000 per year. Kessler Scholarship: full tuition, for Christian Ministry students; 3 awarded. Christian Ministry scholarships: $5,000 per year; 3 awarded.

FINANCIAL AID PROCEDURES
Forms required: FAFSA, institutional form.
Dates and Deadlines: No deadline. Applicants notified on a rolling basis starting 2/15; must reply within 2 week(s) of notification.
Transfers: No deadline. Stafford loans based on number of transferable credits.

CONTACT
Ian Roberts, Associate Vice President for Administration
710 North Turner Avenue, Hastings, NE 68901-7621
(402) 461-7391

Kaplan University: Lincoln
Lincoln, Nebraska
www.kucampus.edu   Federal Code: 004721

2-year for-profit branch campus college in small city.
Enrollment: 522 undergrads. 163 full-time freshmen.

BASIC COSTS (2008-2009)
Tuition and fees: $23,420.
Per-credit charge: $389.58.
Additional info: Full cost of tuition and fees leading to a certificate/diploma: $17,300; associate degree: $34,600; Bachelor's degree: $64,875. Costs listed are inclusive of tuition, fees, books, and supplies.

FINANCIAL AID PICTURE (2006-2007)
Students with need: Out of 163 full-time freshmen who applied for aid, 163 were judged to have need. Of these, 163 received aid, and 10 had their full need met. Average financial aid package met 6% of need; average scholarship/grant was $4,000; average loan was $3,500. Need-based aid available for part-time students.
Students without need: This college awards aid only to students with need.
Scholarships offered: 24 full-time freshmen received athletic scholarships; average amount $6,500.
Cumulative student debt: 100% of graduating class had student loans; average debt was $40,680.

FINANCIAL AID PROCEDURES
Forms required: FAFSA, institutional form.
Dates and Deadlines: No deadline. Applicants notified on a rolling basis starting 2/1.
Transfers: No deadline.

CONTACT
Crystal Faxon, Associate Director of Financial Aid
1821 K Street, Lincoln, NE 68508
(402) 474-5315

Kaplan University: Omaha
Omaha, Nebraska
www.kucampus.edu   Federal Code: 008491

2-year for-profit university and career college in large city.
Enrollment: 631 undergrads.
Selectivity: Open admission.

BASIC COSTS (2008-2009)
Tuition and fees: $4,700.

FINANCIAL AID PICTURE
Students with need: Need-based aid available for full-time and part-time students.
Students without need: This college awards aid only to students with need.

FINANCIAL AID PROCEDURES
Forms required: FAFSA.
Dates and Deadlines: No deadline. Applicants notified on a rolling basis.

CONTACT
Sharon McDonald, Director Of Financial Aid
3350 North 90th Street, Omaha, NE 68134

Little Priest Tribal College
Winnebago, Nebraska
www.lptc.bia.edu   Federal Code: 033233

2-year private community college in rural community.
Enrollment: 108 undergrads, 31% part-time. 21 full-time freshmen.
Selectivity: Open admission.

BASIC COSTS (2007-2008)
Tuition and fees: $2,985.
Per-credit charge: $80.

FINANCIAL AID PICTURE
Students with need: Need-based aid available for full-time and part-time students.

FINANCIAL AID PROCEDURES
Forms required: FAFSA, institutional form.
Dates and Deadlines: No deadline.

CONTACT
Billie Kitcheyan, Director of Financial Aid
PO Box 270, Winnebago, NE 68071
(402) 878-2380 ext. 125

Metropolitan Community College
Omaha, Nebraska
www.mccneb.edu   Federal Code: 004432

2-year public community and technical college in large city.
Enrollment: 6,627 undergrads, 56% part-time. 925 full-time freshmen.
Selectivity: Open admission; but selective for some programs.

BASIC COSTS (2007-2008)
Tuition and fees: $2,070; out-of-state residents $2,993.
Per-credit charge: $41; out-of-state residents $62.

FINANCIAL AID PICTURE

Students with need: Need-based aid available for full-time and part-time students.
Students without need: No-need awards available for academics.

FINANCIAL AID PROCEDURES

Forms required: FAFSA, institutional form.
Dates and Deadlines: Priority date 3/15; no closing date. Applicants notified on a rolling basis starting 4/15.

CONTACT

Director of Financial Aid/Veterans Services
Box 3777, Omaha, NE 68103-0777
(402) 457-2330

Mid-Plains Community College Area

North Platte, Nebraska
www.mpcc.edu   Federal Code: 002557

2-year public community and technical college in large town.
Enrollment: 1,209 undergrads.
Selectivity: Open admission; but selective for some programs.

BASIC COSTS (2008-2009)

Tuition and fees: $2,370; out-of-state residents $2,970.
Per-credit charge: $65; out-of-state residents $85.
Room and board: $4,700.

FINANCIAL AID PICTURE (2006-2007)

Students with need: 62% of average financial aid package awarded as scholarships/grants, 38% awarded as loans/jobs. Need-based aid available for part-time students. Work study available nights.
Students without need: No-need awards available for academics, art, athletics, music/drama.

FINANCIAL AID PROCEDURES

Forms required: FAFSA, institutional form.
Dates and Deadlines: Priority date 5/1; no closing date. Applicants notified on a rolling basis starting 5/1; must reply within 3 week(s) of notification.

CONTACT

Ted Fellers, Director of Financial Aid
1101 Halligan Drive, North Platte, NE 69101
(800) 658-4348

Midland Lutheran College

Fremont, Nebraska
www.mlc.edu   Federal Code: 002553

4-year private liberal arts college in large town, affiliated with Evangelical Lutheran Church in America.
Enrollment: 827 undergrads.
Selectivity: Admits over 75% of applicants.

BASIC COSTS (2007-2008)

Tuition and fees: $20,925.
Room and board: $5,150.
Additional info: Tuition/fee waivers available for minority students.

FINANCIAL AID PICTURE

Students with need: Need-based aid available for full-time and part-time students. Work study available nights, weekends, and for part-time students.
Students without need: No-need awards available for academics, alumni affiliation, art, athletics, leadership, minority status, music/drama, religious affiliation.

FINANCIAL AID PROCEDURES

Forms required: FAFSA.
Dates and Deadlines: Priority date 5/1; no closing date. Applicants notified on a rolling basis starting 3/1; must reply within 4 week(s) of notification.

CONTACT

Penny James, Director of Financial Aid
900 North Clarkson, Fremont, NE 68025
(402) 721-5480

Nebraska Christian College

Papillion, Nebraska
www.nechristian.edu   Federal Code: 012976

4-year private Bible college in large town, affiliated with Christian Church/Churches of Christ.
Enrollment: 149 undergrads.

BASIC COSTS (2008-2009)

Tuition and fees: $10,400.
Per-credit charge: $300.
Room and board: $4,800.

FINANCIAL AID PICTURE

Students with need: Need-based aid available for full-time and part-time students.
Students without need: No-need awards available for academics, leadership.

FINANCIAL AID PROCEDURES

Forms required: FAFSA, institutional form.
Dates and Deadlines: Priority date 6/1; no closing date. Applicants notified on a rolling basis starting 5/5.

CONTACT

Tina Larsen, Financial Aid Officer
12550 South 114th Street, Papillion, NE 68046

Nebraska College of Technical Agriculture

Curtis, Nebraska
www.ncta.unl.edu   Federal Code: 007358

2-year public agricultural college in rural community.
Enrollment: 262 full-time undergrads.
Selectivity: Open admission.

BASIC COSTS (2007-2008)

Tuition and fees: $3,204; out-of-state residents $5,949.
Per-credit charge: $92; out-of-state residents $184.
Room and board: $4,309.

FINANCIAL AID PICTURE (2006-2007)

Students with need: 49% of average financial aid package awarded as scholarships/grants, 51% awarded as loans/jobs. Need-based aid available for part-time students.
Students without need: This college awards aid only to students with need.

FINANCIAL AID PROCEDURES

Forms required: FAFSA.
Dates and Deadlines: Priority date 4/1; no closing date. Applicants notified on a rolling basis starting 5/1; must reply within 2 week(s) of notification.

CONTACT

Mary Ann Mercer, Financial Aid Coordinator
404 East 7th Street, Curtis, NE 69025-0069
(308) 367-5207

Nebraska Indian Community College

Macy, Nebraska
www.thenicc.edu   Federal Code: 015339

2-year public community college in rural community.
Enrollment: 140 undergrads.
Selectivity: Open admission.

BASIC COSTS (2007-2008)
Tuition and fees: $3,200.
Per-credit charge: $80.

FINANCIAL AID PICTURE
Students with need: Need-based aid available for full-time and part-time students.
Students without need: This college awards aid only to students with need.

FINANCIAL AID PROCEDURES
Forms required: FAFSA, state aid form, institutional form.
Dates and Deadlines: Priority date 7/15; no closing date. Applicants notified on a rolling basis starting 8/30; must reply within 2 week(s) of notification.

CONTACT
Lisa Ruszczyk, Director of Financial Aid
2451 St. Mary's Avenue, Omaha, NE 68105
(402) 837-5078 ext. 120

Nebraska Methodist College of Nursing and Allied Health

Omaha, Nebraska
www.methodistcollege.edu   Federal Code: 009937

4-year private health science and nursing college in large city, affiliated with United Methodist Church.
Enrollment: 504 undergrads, 26% part-time. 54 full-time freshmen.
Selectivity: Admits over 75% of applicants.

BASIC COSTS (2008-2009)
Tuition and fees: $13,440.
Per-credit charge: $428.
Room only: $6,150.

FINANCIAL AID PICTURE (2006-2007)
Students with need: Out of 37 full-time freshmen who applied for aid, 32 were judged to have need. Of these, 12 received aid, and 2 had their full need met. Average financial aid package met 25% of need; average scholarship/grant was $4,229; average loan was $2,760. For part-time students, average financial aid package was $6,749.
Students without need: 9 full-time freshmen who did not demonstrate need for aid received scholarships/grants; average award was $4,374. No-need awards available for academics, leadership, religious affiliation, ROTC.
Scholarships offered: President's Leadership Scholarship: $8,000 per year for 4 years; 4 awarded. Dean's Scholarship: $5,000 for 4 years; 3 awarded. Excellence in Allied Health Scholarship: $5,000 per year for 2 years; 3 awarded. Horizon Scholarship: $3,000 per year; based on academic and personal merit; 45 awarded.
Cumulative student debt: 86% of graduating class had student loans; average debt was $28,492.

FINANCIAL AID PROCEDURES
Forms required: FAFSA, institutional form.
Dates and Deadlines: Priority date 5/1; no closing date. Applicants notified on a rolling basis starting 3/1; must reply by 5/1 or within 4 week(s) of notification.
Transfers: Priority date 4/1; no deadline. Applicants notified on a rolling basis.

CONTACT
Brenda Boyd, Director of Financial Aid
720 North 87th Street, Omaha, NE 68114
(402) 354-7225

Nebraska Wesleyan University

Lincoln, Nebraska
www.nebrwesleyan.edu   Federal Code: 002555

4-year private liberal arts college in small city, affiliated with United Methodist Church.
Enrollment: 1,854 undergrads, 11% part-time. 439 full-time freshmen.
Selectivity: Admits over 75% of applicants.

BASIC COSTS (2008-2009)
Tuition and fees: $21,274.
Per-credit charge: $788.
Room and board: $5,710.
Additional info: Tuition/fee waivers available for adults.

FINANCIAL AID PICTURE (2007-2008)
Students with need: Out of 375 full-time freshmen who applied for aid, 320 were judged to have need. Of these, 320 received aid, and 42 had their full need met. Average financial aid package met 74% of need; average scholarship/grant was $11,913; average loan was $4,388. For part-time students, average financial aid package was $2,742.
Students without need: 110 full-time freshmen who did not demonstrate need for aid received scholarships/grants; average award was $7,335. No-need awards available for academics, art, music/drama, religious affiliation.
Scholarships offered: Huge-NWU Scholarship; tuition, books, fees, and room and board up to $25,000; competitive; one award per year. Board of Governors Scholar Award; $10,500; ACT 32 or SAT 1410. Wesleyan Scholar Award; $9,000; ACT 29-31 or SAT 1280-1400. Fredstrom Scholarship; $7,500; ACT 27-28 or SAT 1200-1270, or Top 10% class rank. President's Scholarship; $6,000; ACT 24-26 or SAT 1090-1190 or Top 25% class rank. Recognition Scholarship; $4,500; ACT 22-23 or SAT 1010-1080 or top 33% class rank.
Cumulative student debt: 77% of graduating class had student loans; average debt was $19,534.

FINANCIAL AID PROCEDURES
Forms required: FAFSA.
Dates and Deadlines: No deadline. Applicants notified on a rolling basis starting 3/1; must reply within 4 week(s) of notification.
Transfers: No deadline. Applicants notified on a rolling basis starting 3/1; must reply within 4 week(s) of notification.

CONTACT
Thomas Ochsner, Director of Scholarships and Financial Aid
5000 St. Paul Avenue, Lincoln, NE 68504
(402) 465-2212

Northeast Community College

Norfolk, Nebraska
www.northeastcollege.com   Federal Code: 002556

2-year public community college in large town.
Enrollment: 2,573 undergrads, 22% part-time. 782 full-time freshmen.

Selectivity: Open admission; but selective for some programs.

BASIC COSTS (2007-2008)
Tuition and fees: $2,190; out-of-state residents $2,910.
Per-credit charge: $62; out-of-state residents $86.
Room and board: $4,136.

FINANCIAL AID PICTURE
Students with need: Need-based aid available for full-time and part-time students. Work study available nights, weekends, and for part-time students.
Students without need: No-need awards available for academics, athletics, music/drama.

FINANCIAL AID PROCEDURES
Forms required: FAFSA, institutional form.
Dates and Deadlines: No deadline. Applicants notified on a rolling basis; must reply within 2 week(s) of notification.

CONTACT
Stacy Dieckman, Director of Financial Aid
801 East Benjamin Avenue, Norfolk, NE 68702-0469
(402) 844-7288

Peru State College
Peru, Nebraska
www.peru.edu   Federal Code: 002559

4-year public liberal arts and teachers college in rural community.
Enrollment: 1,482 undergrads.
Selectivity: Open admission; but selective for out-of-state students.

BASIC COSTS (2007-2008)
Tuition and fees: $4,066; out-of-state residents $7,366.
Per-credit charge: $110; out-of-state residents $220.
Room and board: $4,816.

FINANCIAL AID PICTURE (2006-2007)
Students with need: 37% of average financial aid package awarded as scholarships/grants, 63% awarded as loans/jobs. Need-based aid available for part-time students.
Students without need: This college awards aid only to students with need.

FINANCIAL AID PROCEDURES
Forms required: FAFSA, institutional form.
Dates and Deadlines: Priority date 3/1; no closing date. Applicants notified on a rolling basis starting 3/1; must reply within 2 week(s) of notification.
Transfers: Must have financial aid transcripts from all previous schools sent to college.

CONTACT
Diana Lind, Director of Financial Aid
Box 10, Peru, NE 68421-0010
(402) 872-2228

Southeast Community College
Lincoln, Nebraska
www.southeast.edu   Federal Code: 007591

2-year public community college in small city.
Enrollment: 7,520 undergrads.
Selectivity: Open admission.

BASIC COSTS (2007-2008)
Tuition and fees: $2,070; out-of-state residents $2,520.
Per-credit charge: $45; out-of-state residents $55.

FINANCIAL AID PICTURE
Students with need: Need-based aid available for full-time and part-time students. Work study available nights, weekends, and for part-time students.
Students without need: No-need awards available for academics.

FINANCIAL AID PROCEDURES
Forms required: FAFSA, institutional form.
Dates and Deadlines: No deadline. Applicants notified on a rolling basis; must reply within 2 week(s) of notification.

CONTACT
Dave Sonenberg, Dean of Financial Aid
8800 O Street, Lincoln, NE 68520
(402) 437-2619

Union College
Lincoln, Nebraska
www.ucollege.edu   Federal Code: 002563

4-year private liberal arts college in small city, affiliated with Seventh-day Adventists.
Enrollment: 867 undergrads, 12% part-time. 164 full-time freshmen.
Selectivity: Admits less than 50% of applicants.

BASIC COSTS (2007-2008)
Tuition and fees: $16,110.
Per-credit charge: $660.
Room and board: $4,468.

FINANCIAL AID PICTURE
Students with need: Need-based aid available for full-time and part-time students.
Students without need: No-need awards available for academics.
Additional info: Special institutional grants offered to all freshmen and sophomores demonstrating exceptional financial need.

FINANCIAL AID PROCEDURES
Forms required: FAFSA.
Dates and Deadlines: Priority date 5/1; no closing date. Applicants notified on a rolling basis starting 4/15; must reply by 5/1 or within 3 week(s) of notification.

CONTACT
Elaina Camarena, Director of Financial Aid
3800 South 48th Street, Lincoln, NE 68506-4300
(402) 486-2505

University of Nebraska - Kearney
Kearney, Nebraska
www.unk.edu   Federal Code: 002551

4-year public university in large town.
Enrollment: 5,090 undergrads, 9% part-time. 948 full-time freshmen.
Selectivity: Admits over 75% of applicants.

BASIC COSTS (2007-2008)
Tuition and fees: $5,021; out-of-state residents $9,341.
Room and board: $6,000.

FINANCIAL AID PICTURE
Students with need: Need-based aid available for full-time and part-time students.
Students without need: No-need awards available for academics, alumni affiliation, art, athletics, leadership, minority status, music/drama, state/district residency.

FINANCIAL AID PROCEDURES

Forms required: FAFSA, institutional form.

Dates and Deadlines: Priority date 4/1; no closing date. Applicants notified on a rolling basis starting 3/15; must reply within 2 week(s) of notification.

CONTACT

Mary Sommers, Director of Financial Aid
905 West 25th, Kearney, NE 68849
(308) 865-8520

University of Nebraska - Lincoln

Lincoln, Nebraska
www.unl.edu   Federal Code: 002565

4-year public university in small city.

Enrollment: 18,053 undergrads, 7% part-time. 4,215 full-time freshmen.

Selectivity: Admits 50 to 75% of applicants.

BASIC COSTS (2007-2008)

Tuition and fees: $6,216; out-of-state residents $16,236.

Per-credit charge: $170; out-of-state residents $504.

Room and board: $6,523.

FINANCIAL AID PICTURE (2006-2007)

Students with need: Out of 2,703 full-time freshmen who applied for aid, 1,744 were judged to have need. Of these, 1,722 received aid, and 546 had their full need met. Average financial aid package met 88% of need; average scholarship/grant was $6,419; average loan was $2,908. For part-time students, average financial aid package was $6,337.

Students without need: 608 full-time freshmen who did not demonstrate need for aid received scholarships/grants; average award was $4,588. No-need awards available for academics, alumni affiliation, art, athletics, leadership, minority status, music/drama, state/district residency.

Scholarships offered: 102 full-time freshmen received athletic scholarships; average amount $12,287.

Cumulative student debt: 61% of graduating class had student loans; average debt was $19,075.

FINANCIAL AID PROCEDURES

Forms required: FAFSA.

Dates and Deadlines: Priority date 4/15; no closing date. Applicants notified on a rolling basis starting 4/1.

Transfers: Priority application date of April 1 for scholarship consideration.

CONTACT

Craig Munier, Director of Scholarships and Financial Aid
1410 Q Street, Lincoln, NE 68588-0417
(402) 472-2030

University of Nebraska - Omaha

Omaha, Nebraska
www.unomaha.edu   Federal Code: 002554

4-year public university in large city.

Enrollment: 11,080 undergrads, 22% part-time. 1,604 full-time freshmen.

Selectivity: Admits over 75% of applicants.

BASIC COSTS (2007-2008)

Tuition and fees: $5,485; out-of-state residents $14,522.

Room and board: $4,840.

FINANCIAL AID PICTURE (2007-2008)

Students with need: Out of 1,156 full-time freshmen who applied for aid, 743 were judged to have need. Of these, 712 received aid. For part-time students, average financial aid package was $2,049.

Students without need: No-need awards available for academics, alumni affiliation, art, athletics, leadership, minority status, music/drama, ROTC, state/district residency.

FINANCIAL AID PROCEDURES

Forms required: FAFSA.

Dates and Deadlines: Priority date 3/1; no closing date. Applicants notified on a rolling basis starting 4/15; must reply within 2 week(s) of notification.

CONTACT

Randall Sell, Director of Financial Aid
6001 Dodge Street, Omaha, NE 68182-0005
(402) 554-2327

University of Nebraska Medical Center

Omaha, Nebraska
www.unmc.edu   Federal Code: 006895

Upper-division public health science college in very large city.

Enrollment: 812 undergrads, 7% part-time.

BASIC COSTS (2007-2008)

Tuition and fees: $5,450; out-of-state residents $15,470.

Per-credit charge: $170; out-of-state residents $504.

Additional info: Tuition varies by program. Tuition/fee waivers available for minority students.

FINANCIAL AID PICTURE (2006-2007)

Students with need: Average financial aid package for all full-time undergraduates was $8,239; for part-time $4,945. 34% awarded as scholarships/grants, 66% awarded as loans/jobs. Work study available nights, weekends, and for part-time students.

FINANCIAL AID PROCEDURES

Forms required: FAFSA, institutional form.

Dates and Deadlines: No deadline.

Transfers: Priority date 4/1; no deadline. Applicants notified on a rolling basis starting 5/1; must reply within 2 week(s) of notification.

CONTACT

Judith Walker, Director of Financial Aid
984230 Nebraska Medical Center, Omaha, NE 68198-4230
(402) 559-4199

Wayne State College

Wayne, Nebraska
www.wsc.edu   Federal Code: 002566

4-year public liberal arts and teachers college in small town.

Enrollment: 2,802 undergrads, 8% part-time. 654 full-time freshmen.

Selectivity: Open admission.

BASIC COSTS (2007-2008)

Tuition and fees: $4,322; out-of-state residents $7,622.

Per-credit charge: $110; out-of-state residents $220.

Room and board: $4,800.

FINANCIAL AID PICTURE (2007-2008)

Students with need: Out of 551 full-time freshmen who applied for aid, 409 were judged to have need. Of these, 402 received aid, and 100 had their full need met. Average financial aid package met 32% of need; average scholarship/grant was $1,657; average loan was $1,574. For part-time students, average financial aid package was $3,271.

Students without need: 19 full-time freshmen who did not demonstrate need for aid received scholarships/grants; average award was $757. No-need awards available for academics, alumni affiliation, art, athletics, leadership, minority status, music/drama, religious affiliation, state/district residency.

Scholarships offered: 26 full-time freshmen received athletic scholarships; average amount $807.

FINANCIAL AID PROCEDURES

Forms required: FAFSA.

Dates and Deadlines: Priority date 4/1; no closing date. Applicants notified on a rolling basis starting 3/1; must reply within 3 week(s) of notification.

CONTACT

Kyle Rose, Director of Financial Aid
1111 Main Street, Wayne, NE 68787
(402) 375-7230

Western Nebraska Community College

Scottsbluff, Nebraska
www.wn.edu   Federal Code: 002560

2-year public community college in large town.

Enrollment: 1,541 undergrads, 39% part-time. 383 full-time freshmen.

Selectivity: Open admission; but selective for some programs.

BASIC COSTS (2007-2008)

Tuition and fees: $2,220; out-of-state residents $2,580.

Per-credit charge: $61; out-of-state residents $73.

Room and board: $4,100.

FINANCIAL AID PICTURE (2007-2008)

Students with need: Out of 297 full-time freshmen who applied for aid, 237 were judged to have need. Of these, 236 received aid. Average financial aid package met 87% of need; average scholarship/grant was $3,864; average loan was $2,542. For part-time students, average financial aid package was $5,367.

Students without need: 64 full-time freshmen who did not demonstrate need for aid received scholarships/grants; average award was $817. No-need awards available for academics, art, athletics, leadership, music/drama, state/district residency.

Scholarships offered: 63 full-time freshmen received athletic scholarships; average amount $6,989.

Cumulative student debt: 18% of graduating class had student loans; average debt was $3,419.

FINANCIAL AID PROCEDURES

Forms required: FAFSA.

Dates and Deadlines: Priority date 3/1; no closing date. Applicants notified on a rolling basis starting 4/1.

Transfers: State of Nebraska limits the amount of Nebraska State Grant funds a student receives in any one year.

CONTACT

Sheila Johns, Director of Financial Aid
1601 East 27th Street, Scottsbluff, NE 69361
(308) 635-6011

York College

York, Nebraska
www.york.edu   Federal Code: 002567

4-year private liberal arts and teachers college in small town, affiliated with Church of Christ.

Enrollment: 385 undergrads, 6% part-time. 87 full-time freshmen.

BASIC COSTS (2007-2008)

Tuition and fees: $14,000.

Per-credit charge: $390.

Room and board: $4,500.

FINANCIAL AID PICTURE (2006-2007)

Students with need: Out of 78 full-time freshmen who applied for aid, 66 were judged to have need. Of these, 66 received aid, and 15 had their full need met. Average financial aid package met 23% of need; average scholarship/grant was $7,000; average loan was $4,904. For part-time students, average financial aid package was $5,806.

Students without need: 20 full-time freshmen who did not demonstrate need for aid received scholarships/grants; average award was $7,657. No-need awards available for academics, alumni affiliation, athletics, job skills, leadership, music/drama.

Scholarships offered: 13 full-time freshmen received athletic scholarships; average amount $5,292.

FINANCIAL AID PROCEDURES

Forms required: FAFSA.

Dates and Deadlines: Priority date 4/30; no closing date. Applicants notified on a rolling basis starting 3/1; must reply within 4 week(s) of notification.

Transfers: No deadline. Applicants notified on a rolling basis starting 3/1; must reply within 4 week(s) of notification.

CONTACT

Stewart Sikes, Director of Financial Aid
1125 East 8th Street, York, NE 68467
(402) 363-5624

Nevada

Art Institute of Las Vegas

Henderson, Nevada
www.ailv.artinstitutes.edu   Federal Code: 030846

4-year for-profit culinary school and visual arts college in very large city.

Enrollment: 1,075 undergrads.

Selectivity: Open admission; but selective for some programs.

BASIC COSTS (2007-2008)

Additional info: Tuition for full associate program: $48,272. Tuition for full bachelor's program: $82,752. Supply kit cost averages $11,000. Additional lab fees for culinary programs. Tuition at time of enrollment locked for 4 years.

FINANCIAL AID PICTURE (2007-2008)

Students with need: 25% of average financial aid package awarded as scholarships/grants, 75% awarded as loans/jobs. Need-based aid available for part-time students. Work study available nights, weekends, and for part-time students.

Students without need: No-need awards available for academics, state/district residency.

FINANCIAL AID PROCEDURES

Dates and Deadlines: No deadline. Applicants notified on a rolling basis.

Transfers: No deadline. Applicants notified on a rolling basis.

CONTACT

Dana Sirolli, Director of Student Financial Services
2350 Corporate Circle, Henderson, NV 89074-7737
(702) 369-9944

Career College of Northern Nevada

Reno, Nevada
www.ccnn.edu   Federal Code: 026215

2-year for-profit business and health science and technical college in large city.

Enrollment: 241 undergrads.

Selectivity: Open admission.

BASIC COSTS (2007-2008)

Additional info: Tuition for associate programs ranges from $18,623 to $24,375; diploma programs, $10,822 to $14,820. Fees are $210 to $672; books range from $1,000 to $1,600.

FINANCIAL AID PICTURE

Students with need: Need-based aid available for full-time students.
Students without need: This college awards aid only to students with need.

FINANCIAL AID PROCEDURES

Forms required: FAFSA.
Dates and Deadlines: Closing date 5/30. Applicants notified on a rolling basis.

CONTACT

Andrea Wiggins
1195 A Corporate Boulevard, Reno, NV 89502-2331
(775) 856-2266

College of Southern Nevada

Las Vegas, Nevada
www.csn.edu   Federal Code: 010362

2-year public community college in very large city.
Enrollment: 28,880 undergrads.
Selectivity: Open admission; but selective for some programs.

BASIC COSTS (2007-2008)

Tuition and fees: $1,763; out-of-state residents $7,148.
Per-credit charge: $55.
Additional info: Reduced tuition for nonresidents within 50 miles of Nevada border. Nonresident additional per-credit-hour charge: $54.75 for 1-6 credits, flat rate assessment of $5,385 for 7 credits and above.

FINANCIAL AID PICTURE

Students with need: Work study available nights, weekends, and for part-time students.
Students without need: No-need awards available for state/district residency.

FINANCIAL AID PROCEDURES

Forms required: FAFSA.
Dates and Deadlines: Priority date 5/1; closing date 6/30. Applicants notified on a rolling basis starting 7/15; must reply within 2 week(s) of notification.

CONTACT

Bernadette Lopez-Garrett, Financial Aid Director
6375 West Charleston Boulevard, Las Vegas, NV 89146-1164
(702) 651-4047

DeVry University: Henderson

Henderson, Nevada
www.devry.edu

4-year for-profit university in large city.
Enrollment: 127 undergrads, 55% part-time. 1 full-time freshmen.

BASIC COSTS (2007-2008)

Tuition and fees: $13,020.
Per-credit charge: $490.

FINANCIAL AID PICTURE (2006-2007)

Students with need: Average financial aid package for all full-time undergraduates was $5,125; for part-time $4,294. 14% awarded as scholarships/grants, 86% awarded as loans/jobs.

Students without need: No-need awards available for academics.

FINANCIAL AID PROCEDURES

Forms required: FAFSA.
Dates and Deadlines: No deadline. Applicants notified on a rolling basis.

CONTACT

2490 Paseo Verde Parkway, Suite 150, Henderson, NV 89074

Heritage College: Las Vegas

Las Vegas, Nevada
www.heritagecollege.com   Federal Code: 030432

2-year for-profit career college in very large city.
Enrollment: 325 undergrads.

BASIC COSTS (2008-2009)

Additional info: Cost of full programs: associate degree programs $27,004, diploma programs $14,004, including fees and books.

FINANCIAL AID PICTURE

Students with need: Need-based aid available for full-time students.

FINANCIAL AID PROCEDURES

Forms required: FAFSA, institutional form.
Dates and Deadlines: No deadline.

CONTACT

Carmen Torres, Financial Aid Director
3315 Spring Mountain Road, Las Vegas, NV 89102
(702) 368-2338

Sierra Nevada College

Incline Village, Nevada
www.sierranevada.edu   Federal Code: 009192

4-year private liberal arts college in small town.
Enrollment: 315 undergrads.

BASIC COSTS (2007-2008)

Tuition and fees: $22,305.
Per-credit charge: $986.
Room and board: $8,410.

FINANCIAL AID PICTURE

Students with need: Need-based aid available for full-time and part-time students.
Students without need: No-need awards available for academics, art, athletics.
Scholarships offered: Academic scholarships; $2,000-$13,000 per year; renewable.

FINANCIAL AID PROCEDURES

Forms required: FAFSA, institutional form.
Dates and Deadlines: Priority date 4/1; no closing date. Applicants notified on a rolling basis; must reply by 5/1 or within 4 week(s) of notification.
Transfers: Priority date 3/15; no deadline.

CONTACT

Julie McMillin, Director of Financial Aid
999 Tahoe Boulevard, Incline Village, NV 89451-4269
(775) 831-1314 ext. 7440

Truckee Meadows Community College

Reno, Nevada
www.tmcc.edu   Federal Code: 010363

2-year public community and technical college in large city.
Enrollment: 9,845 undergrads.
Selectivity: Open admission; but selective for some programs.

BASIC COSTS (2007-2008)
Tuition and fees: $1,763; out-of-state residents $7,148.
Per-credit charge: $55.
Additional info: Good Neighbor tuition: $36.25 per credit hour in addition to registration costs. Nonresident additional per-credit-hour charge: $54.75 for 1-6 credits, flat rate assessment of $5385 per year for 7 credits and above.

FINANCIAL AID PICTURE (2006-2007)
Students with need: 62% of average financial aid package awarded as scholarships/grants, 38% awarded as loans/jobs. Work study available nights, weekends, and for part-time students.
Students without need: No-need awards available for academics, art, leadership, minority status, music/drama, state/district residency.
Additional info: Institutional grants to state residents, short-term emergency loans available. Work-study applications must reply within 10 days of notification.

FINANCIAL AID PROCEDURES
Forms required: FAFSA, institutional form.
Dates and Deadlines: Closing date 6/30. Applicants notified by 5/15.
Transfers: Must provide academic transcript from previous institution.

CONTACT
Mona Buckheart, Director of Student Financial Aid
7000 Dandini Boulevard, Reno, NV 89512
(775) 673-7072

University of Nevada: Las Vegas

Las Vegas, Nevada
www.unlv.edu   Federal Code: 002569

4-year public university in very large city.
Enrollment: 20,971 undergrads, 26% part-time. 2,510 full-time freshmen.
Selectivity: Admits 50 to 75% of applicants. GED not accepted.

BASIC COSTS (2007-2008)
Tuition and fees: $4,031; out-of-state residents $14,842.
Per-credit charge: $117.
Room and board: $9,288.
Additional info: Reduced tuition rate for out-of-state students who live within 50 miles of Nevada border and for those who reside in Western Undergraduate Exchange states.

FINANCIAL AID PICTURE (2006-2007)
Students with need: Out of 1,700 full-time freshmen who applied for aid, 1,014 were judged to have need. Of these, 980 received aid, and 65 had their full need met. Average financial aid package met 56% of need; average scholarship/grant was $3,791; average loan was $2,362. For part-time students, average financial aid package was $5,210.
Students without need: 284 full-time freshmen who did not demonstrate need for aid received scholarships/grants; average award was $1,902. No-need awards available for academics, alumni affiliation, art, athletics, job skills, leadership, minority status, music/drama, ROTC, state/district residency.
Scholarships offered: 50 full-time freshmen received athletic scholarships; average amount $15,446.
Cumulative student debt: 43% of graduating class had student loans; average debt was $17,944.

Additional info: Tuition reduction for state residents through consortium programs and for out-of-state students graduating from high schools in designated counties bordering Nevada, for military dependents residing in-state, and for dependents of children of alumni not residing in-state.

FINANCIAL AID PROCEDURES
Forms required: FAFSA, institutional form.
Dates and Deadlines: Priority date 2/1; no closing date. Applicants notified on a rolling basis starting 3/20; must reply within 2 week(s) of notification.

CONTACT
Norm Bedford, Director of Student Financial Services
4505 Maryland Parkway Box 451021, Las Vegas, NV 89154-1021
(702) 895-3424

University of Nevada: Reno

Reno, Nevada
www.unr.edu   Federal Code: 002568

4-year public university in small city.
Enrollment: 12,659 undergrads, 18% part-time. 2,800 full-time freshmen.
Selectivity: Admits over 75% of applicants. GED not accepted.

BASIC COSTS (2007-2008)
Tuition and fees: $4,029; out-of-state residents $14,839.
Per-credit charge: $117.
Room and board: $8,319.
Additional info: Reduced tuition rate for out-of-state students who live within 50 miles of Nevada border. Nonresident additional per-credit-hour charge: $128.50 for 1-6 credits, flat rate assessment of $5405 for 7 credits and above.

FINANCIAL AID PICTURE (2006-2007)
Students with need: Average financial aid package met 55% of need; average scholarship/grant was $5,064; average loan was $2,774. For part-time students, average financial aid package was $5,214.
Students without need: 1,288 full-time freshmen who did not demonstrate need for aid received scholarships/grants; average award was $2,328. No-need awards available for academics, alumni affiliation, art, athletics, music/drama.
Scholarships offered: *Merit:* Presidential scholarship awards: $5,000 per year; must have 3.5 unweighted GPA and 1380 SAT (exclusive of writing) or 31 ACT; must be admitted by 2/1 of year prior to enrollment and meet Nevada residency requirements. Additional scholarships: ranging from $2,500 to $5,000; based on combination of test scores and unweighted GPA. *Athletic:* 72 full-time freshmen received athletic scholarships; average amount $12,427.
Cumulative student debt: 35% of graduating class had student loans; average debt was $13,657.
Additional info: Reduced out-of-state tuition available for children of alumni and for non-residents from some neighboring counties in California and participants in WUE program.

FINANCIAL AID PROCEDURES
Forms required: FAFSA.
Dates and Deadlines: Priority date 2/15; no closing date. Applicants notified on a rolling basis starting 4/1; must reply within 2 week(s) of notification.
Transfers: No deadline. Applicants notified on a rolling basis; must reply within 2 week(s) of notification. Transfer GPA must be 2.0 or higher to be eligible for aid.

CONTACT
Nancee Langley, Director, Student Financial Services
Mail Stop 120, Reno, NV 89557
(775) 784-4666

University of Southern Nevada

Henderson, Nevada
www.usn.edu   Federal Code: 040653

Upper-division private university in very large city.
Enrollment: 139 undergrads.

BASIC COSTS (2008-2009)
Additional info: Tuition and fees vary by program from $26,200 to $36,200.

FINANCIAL AID PICTURE (2007-2008)
Students with need: Average financial aid package for all full-time undergraduates was $27,340. 5% awarded as scholarships/grants, 95% awarded as loans/jobs.
Students without need: No-need awards available for academics.

FINANCIAL AID PROCEDURES
Dates and Deadlines: No deadline.
Transfers: Priority date 1/1; closing date 4/1. Applicants notified on a rolling basis starting 4/1; must reply within 2 week(s) of notification.

CONTACT
Debra Gambill, Director of Financial Aid
11 Sunset Way, Henderson, NV 89014
(702) 968-2026

Western Nevada College

Carson City, Nevada
www.wnc.edu   Federal Code: 013896

2-year public community college in small city.
Enrollment: 3,218 undergrads, 72% part-time. 298 full-time freshmen.
Selectivity: Open admission; but selective for some programs.

BASIC COSTS (2007-2008)
Tuition and fees: $1,763; out-of-state residents $7,148.
Per-credit charge: $55.
Additional info: Good Neighbor tuition: $32.75 additional per-credit-hour charge for student living within 50 miles of Nevada border for 1 year or more, or graduates of specifically designated high schools/community colleges from neighboring states. Nonresident additional per-credit-hour charge: $60.25 for 1-6 credits, flat rate assessment of $5385/yr for 7 credits and above.

FINANCIAL AID PICTURE
Students with need: Need-based aid available for full-time and part-time students. Work study available nights, weekends, and for part-time students.
Students without need: No-need awards available for academics, state/district residency.

FINANCIAL AID PROCEDURES
Forms required: FAFSA.
Dates and Deadlines: Priority date 4/15; no closing date. Applicants notified on a rolling basis.
Transfers: Maximum loan debt of $14,125 allowed. Loans received at other schools counted toward limit.

CONTACT
Lori Tiede, Director of Financial Aid
2201 West College Parkway, Carson City, NV 89703-7399
(775) 445-3264

New Hampshire

Chester College of New England

Chester, New Hampshire
www.chestercollege.edu   Federal Code: 004733

4-year private visual arts and liberal arts college in rural community.
Enrollment: 222 undergrads, 9% part-time. 62 full-time freshmen.
Selectivity: Admits 50 to 75% of applicants.

BASIC COSTS (2007-2008)
Tuition and fees: $15,930.
Per-credit charge: $640.
Room and board: $7,850.
Additional info: Lab fees vary per student; average cost $600.

FINANCIAL AID PICTURE
Students with need: Need-based aid available for full-time and part-time students. Work study available nights, weekends, and for part-time students.
Students without need: No-need awards available for academics, art, state/district residency.

FINANCIAL AID PROCEDURES
Forms required: FAFSA, state aid form.
Dates and Deadlines: Priority date 3/15; no closing date. Applicants notified on a rolling basis starting 12/1; must reply within 2 week(s) of notification.

CONTACT
Jason Graves, Director of Financial Aid
40 Chester Street, Chester, NH 03036
(603) 887-7404

Colby-Sawyer College

New London, New Hampshire
www.colby-sawyer.edu   Federal Code: 002572

4-year private liberal arts college in small town.
Enrollment: 942 undergrads, 1% part-time. 352 full-time freshmen.
Selectivity: Admits over 75% of applicants.

BASIC COSTS (2008-2009)
Tuition and fees: $29,620.
Per-credit charge: $990.
Room and board: $10,340.

FINANCIAL AID PICTURE (2007-2008)
Students with need: Out of 321 full-time freshmen who applied for aid, 286 were judged to have need. Of these, 286 received aid, and 96 had their full need met. Average financial aid package met 87% of need; average scholarship/grant was $18,412; average loan was $4,850. Need-based aid available for part-time students.
Students without need: 70 full-time freshmen who did not demonstrate need for aid received scholarships/grants; average award was $12,138. No-need awards available for academics, alumni affiliation, art, leadership, minority status, music/drama.
Cumulative student debt: 67% of graduating class had student loans; average debt was $18,306.

FINANCIAL AID PROCEDURES
Forms required: FAFSA.
Dates and Deadlines: Priority date 2/15; closing date 3/1. Applicants notified on a rolling basis starting 1/1; must reply by 5/1 or within 2 week(s) of notification.
Transfers: Priority date 3/1; closing date 4/15. Applicants notified on a rolling basis starting 12/15; must reply within 2 week(s) of notification.

CONTACT
Ted Craigie, Director of Financial Aid
541 Main Street, New London, NH 03257-7835
(603) 526-3717

Daniel Webster College
Nashua, New Hampshire
www.dwc.edu   Federal Code: 004731

4-year private college in small city.
Enrollment: 703 undergrads.
Selectivity: Admits over 75% of applicants.

BASIC COSTS (2008-2009)
Tuition and fees: $27,032.
Per-credit charge: $1,038.
Room and board: $9,369.

FINANCIAL AID PICTURE (2006-2007)
Students with need: 56% of average financial aid package awarded as scholarships/grants, 44% awarded as loans/jobs. Need-based aid available for part-time students. Work study available nights, weekends, and for part-time students.
Students without need: No-need awards available for academics, leadership.
Scholarships offered: Scholarships based on GPA and test scores, leadership, guidance counselor recommendation, awarded in amounts ranging from $500 to $7,500. Alumni and other scholarships range from $500 to full tuition.
Cumulative student debt: 79% of graduating class had student loans; average debt was $36,236.

FINANCIAL AID PROCEDURES
Forms required: FAFSA, institutional form.
Dates and Deadlines: Priority date 3/1; no closing date. Applicants notified on a rolling basis starting 3/15; must reply within 2 week(s) of notification.

CONTACT
Anne Sylvain, Director of Financial Assistance
20 University Drive, Nashua, NH 03063
(603) 577-6590

Dartmouth College
Hanover, New Hampshire   Federal Code: 002573
www.dartmouth.edu   CSS Code: 3351

4-year private university and liberal arts college in large town.
Enrollment: 4,085 undergrads. 1,115 full-time freshmen.
Selectivity: Admits less than 50% of applicants.

BASIC COSTS (2008-2009)
Tuition and fees: $37,250.
Room and board: $10,930.

FINANCIAL AID PICTURE (2006-2007)
Students with need: Out of 669 full-time freshmen who applied for aid, 512 were judged to have need. Of these, 512 received aid, and 512 had their full need met. Average financial aid package met 100% of need; average scholarship/grant was $30,269; average loan was $3,212. Need-based aid available for part-time students.
Students without need: This college awards aid only to students with need.
Cumulative student debt: 51% of graduating class had student loans; average debt was $20,926.

FINANCIAL AID PROCEDURES
Forms required: FAFSA, CSS PROFILE.
Dates and Deadlines: Closing date 2/1. Applicants notified by 3/31; must reply by 5/1.
Transfers: Closing date 3/15. Grant budget for transfer students is limited. Some admitted transfer students may not have their full needs met.

CONTACT
Virginia Hazen, Director of Financial Aid
6016 McNutt Hall, Hanover, NH 03755
(603) 646-2451

Franklin Pierce University
Rindge, New Hampshire
www.franklinpierce.edu   Federal Code: 002575

4-year private liberal arts college in small town.
Enrollment: 1,721 undergrads, 1% part-time. 547 full-time freshmen.
Selectivity: Admits 50 to 75% of applicants.

BASIC COSTS (2008-2009)
Tuition and fees: $28,300.
Per-credit charge: $810.
Room and board: $9,200.

FINANCIAL AID PICTURE (2007-2008)
Students with need: Average financial aid package met 70% of need; average scholarship/grant was $14,645; average loan was $3,462. For part-time students, average financial aid package was $17,211.
Students without need: No-need awards available for academics, alumni affiliation, athletics, leadership, music/drama.
Scholarships offered: Marlin Fitzwater Mass Communication: $2,000; 6 awarded. Robert Alvin Performing Arts-Theater, Music, Dance; $2,000; 2 awarded in each category. Leadership Scholarship: $2,000; 10 awarded.
Cumulative student debt: 67% of graduating class had student loans; average debt was $28,750.

FINANCIAL AID PROCEDURES
Forms required: FAFSA.
Dates and Deadlines: Closing date 3/1. Applicants notified on a rolling basis starting 3/1; must reply within 2 week(s) of notification.
Transfers: No deadline. Applicants notified on a rolling basis starting 3/1; must reply within 2 week(s) of notification.

CONTACT
Ken Ferreria, Director of Student Financial Services
40 University Drive, Rindge, NH 03461-0060
(603) 899-4180

Granite State College
Concord, New Hampshire
www.granite.edu   Federal Code: 031013

4-year public liberal arts college in large town.
Enrollment: 1,065 undergrads, 57% part-time. 34 full-time freshmen.
Selectivity: Open admission.

BASIC COSTS (2007-2008)
Tuition and fees: $6,920; out-of-state residents $7,460.
Per-credit charge: $222; out-of-state residents $240.

FINANCIAL AID PICTURE (2006-2007)
Students with need: 33% of average financial aid package awarded as scholarships/grants, 67% awarded as loans/jobs. Need-based aid available for part-time students.

FINANCIAL AID PROCEDURES

Forms required: FAFSA, institutional form.

Dates and Deadlines: No deadline. Applicants notified on a rolling basis starting 4/15.

Transfers: No deadline. Applicants notified on a rolling basis starting 4/15.

CONTACT

Lisa Jo Moher, Director of Financial Aid
8 Old Suncook Road, Concord, NH 03301-7317
(603) 228-3000 ext. 322

Great Bay Community College

Stratham, New Hampshire
www.stratham.nhctc.edu   Federal Code: 002583

2-year public community and technical college in small town.

Enrollment: 1,889 undergrads. 83 full-time freshmen.

Selectivity: Open admission; but selective for some programs and for out-of-state students.

BASIC COSTS (2007-2008)

Tuition and fees: $5,400; out-of-state residents $12,150.

Per-credit charge: $175; out-of-state residents $400.

Additional info: New England Regional tuition: $262 per credit hour.

FINANCIAL AID PICTURE (2006-2007)

Students with need: Out of 83 full-time freshmen who applied for aid, 83 were judged to have need. Of these, 83 received aid, and 83 had their full need met. Average financial aid package met 100% of need; average scholarship/grant was $3,414; average loan was $1,461. For part-time students, average financial aid package was $4,524.

Students without need: This college awards aid only to students with need.

FINANCIAL AID PROCEDURES

Forms required: FAFSA, institutional form.

Dates and Deadlines: Priority date 3/9; no closing date. Applicants notified on a rolling basis starting 5/9; must reply within 2 week(s) of notification.

Transfers: No deadline. Applicants notified on a rolling basis starting 5/9; must reply within 2 week(s) of notification.

CONTACT

Lauren Hughes, Director of Financial Aid
277 Portsmouth Avenue, Stratham, NH 03885
(603) 772-1194

Hesser College

Manchester, New Hampshire
www.hesser.edu   Federal Code: 004729

4-year for-profit business and junior college in small city.

Enrollment: 3,800 undergrads.

FINANCIAL AID PICTURE

Students with need: Need-based aid available for full-time and part-time students. Work study available nights, weekends, and for part-time students.

Students without need: This college awards aid only to students with need.

Additional info: Two private loans available to assist students in paying their balance; Tree Loan, SLM Loan.

FINANCIAL AID PROCEDURES

Forms required: FAFSA, institutional form.

Dates and Deadlines: Priority date 5/1; no closing date. Applicants notified on a rolling basis starting 3/1; must reply within 3 week(s) of notification.

CONTACT

Debra Gravel, Director of Financial Aid
3 Sundial Avenue, Manchester, NH 03103
(603) 668-6660 ext. 2210

Keene State College

Keene, New Hampshire
www.keene.edu   Federal Code: 002590

4-year public liberal arts and teachers college in large town.

Enrollment: 4,658 undergrads, 4% part-time. 1,141 full-time freshmen.

Selectivity: Admits 50 to 75% of applicants.

BASIC COSTS (2007-2008)

Tuition and fees: $8,298; out-of-state residents $15,848.

Per-credit charge: $258; out-of-state residents $572.

Room and board: $7,460.

Additional info: New England Regional tuition is 150% of in-state public institution tuition.

FINANCIAL AID PICTURE (2006-2007)

Students with need: Out of 947 full-time freshmen who applied for aid, 661 were judged to have need. Of these, 652 received aid, and 106 had their full need met. Average financial aid package met 67% of need; average scholarship/grant was $5,061; average loan was $3,155. For part-time students, average financial aid package was $4,733.

Students without need: 83 full-time freshmen who did not demonstrate need for aid received scholarships/grants; average award was $2,411. No-need awards available for academics, alumni affiliation, art, music/drama.

Cumulative student debt: 79% of graduating class had student loans; average debt was $23,775.

FINANCIAL AID PROCEDURES

Forms required: FAFSA.

Dates and Deadlines: Closing date 3/1. Applicants notified on a rolling basis; must reply within 4 week(s) of notification.

Transfers: Applicants notified on a rolling basis; must reply within 4 week(s) of notification.

CONTACT

Patricia Blodgett, Director of Financial Aid
229 Main Street, Keene, NH 03435-2604
(603) 358-2280

Lakes Region Community College

Laconia, New Hampshire
www.laconia.ccsnh.edu

2-year public community and technical college in large town.

Enrollment: 850 undergrads.

Selectivity: Open admission; but selective for some programs.

BASIC COSTS (2007-2008)

Tuition and fees: $5,370; out-of-state residents $12,120.

Per-credit charge: $175; out-of-state residents $400.

Additional info: New England regional tuition per-credit-hour charge: $262.

FINANCIAL AID PICTURE (2006-2007)

Students with need: 23% of average financial aid package awarded as scholarships/grants, 77% awarded as loans/jobs.

FINANCIAL AID PROCEDURES

Dates and Deadlines: Priority date 5/1; no closing date.

CONTACT

Susan Jacobs, Financial Aid Officer
379 Belmont Road, Laconia, NH 03246-9204
(603) 524-3207

Magdalen College

Warner, New Hampshire
www.magdalen.edu

4-year private liberal arts college in small town, affiliated with Roman Catholic Church.

Enrollment: 69 undergrads. 23 full-time freshmen.
Selectivity: Admits over 75% of applicants.

BASIC COSTS (2007-2008)

Tuition and fees: $11,470.
Room and board: $6,500.

FINANCIAL AID PICTURE

Students with need: Need-based aid available for full-time and part-time students.
Students without need: This college awards aid only to students with need.

FINANCIAL AID PROCEDURES

Forms required: institutional form.
Dates and Deadlines: Closing date 6/30. Applicants notified by 7/1; must reply by 7/1 or within 4 week(s) of notification.

CONTACT

Donald Regan, Financial Aid Director
511 Kearsarge Mountain Road, Warner, NH 03278
(603) 456-2656

Manchester Community College

Manchester, New Hampshire
www.manchester.nhctc.edu   Federal Code: 002582

2-year public community and technical college in small city.
Enrollment: 2,170 undergrads.
Selectivity: Open admission; but selective for some programs.

BASIC COSTS (2007-2008)

Tuition and fees: $5,430; out-of-state residents $12,180.
Per-credit charge: $175; out-of-state residents $400.
Additional info: New England Regional tuition: $262 per credit hour.

FINANCIAL AID PICTURE

Students with need: Work study available nights, weekends, and for part-time students.
Students without need: This college awards aid only to students with need.
Additional info: 100% of direct educational expenses met for all financial aid applicants.

FINANCIAL AID PROCEDURES

Forms required: FAFSA, institutional form.
Dates and Deadlines: Priority date 5/1; no closing date. Applicants notified on a rolling basis starting 4/15; must reply within 2 week(s) of notification.

CONTACT

Stephanie Hewitt, Financial Aid Officer
1066 Front Street, Manchester, NH 03102-8518
(603) 668-6706 ext. 273

Nashua Community College

Nashua, New Hampshire
www.nashua.ccsnh.edu   Federal Code: 009236

2-year public community and technical college in small city.
Enrollment: 1,537 undergrads.
Selectivity: Open admission; but selective for some programs.

BASIC COSTS (2007-2008)

Tuition and fees: $5,730; out-of-state residents $12,480.
Per-credit charge: $175; out-of-state residents $400.
Additional info: New England regional tuition: $262 per credit hour.

FINANCIAL AID PICTURE

Students with need: Need-based aid available for full-time and part-time students. Work study available nights.
Students without need: This college awards aid only to students with need.

FINANCIAL AID PROCEDURES

Forms required: FAFSA.
Dates and Deadlines: Priority date 5/1; no closing date. Applicants notified on a rolling basis starting 3/1; must reply within 2 week(s) of notification.

CONTACT

Lisbeth Gonzalez, Director of Financial Aid
505 Amherst Street, Nashua, NH 03063-1026
(603) 882-6923 ext. 1528

New England College

Henniker, New Hampshire
www.nec.edu   Federal Code: 002579

4-year private business and liberal arts and teachers college in small town.
Enrollment: 1,052 undergrads, 2% part-time. 303 full-time freshmen.
Selectivity: Admits 50 to 75% of applicants.

BASIC COSTS (2008-2009)

Tuition and fees: $26,472.
Per-credit charge: $821.
Room and board: $9,288.
Additional info: Tuition/fee waivers available for adults.

FINANCIAL AID PICTURE (2007-2008)

Students with need: Out of 265 full-time freshmen who applied for aid, 199 were judged to have need. Of these, 199 received aid, and 97 had their full need met. Average financial aid package met 88% of need; average scholarship/grant was $13,249; average loan was $7,287. For part-time students, average financial aid package was $23,311.
Students without need: 86 full-time freshmen who did not demonstrate need for aid received scholarships/grants; average award was $9,588. No-need awards available for academics, alumni affiliation, art, job skills, leadership, music/drama.
Cumulative student debt: 78% of graduating class had student loans; average debt was $29,874.

FINANCIAL AID PROCEDURES

Forms required: FAFSA, institutional form.
Dates and Deadlines: Priority date 4/1; no closing date. Applicants notified on a rolling basis starting 1/12; must reply within 2 week(s) of notification.
Transfers: No deadline. Applicants notified on a rolling basis starting 1/1; must reply within 2 week(s) of notification. May 1 deadline for state grant consideration.

CONTACT

Russell Stein, Director of Admission and Financial Aid
102 Bridge Street, Henniker, NH 03242
(603) 428-2226

Plymouth State University

Plymouth, New Hampshire
www.plymouth.edu   Federal Code: 002591

4-year public university and teachers college in small town.
Enrollment: 4,221 undergrads. 1,012 full-time freshmen.
Selectivity: Admits 50 to 75% of applicants.

BASIC COSTS (2007-2008)

Tuition and fees: $7,944; out-of-state residents $15,494.
Per-credit charge: $258; out-of-state residents $572.
Room and board: $8,030.
Additional info: New England Regional tuition: 150% of in-state public institution tuition.

FINANCIAL AID PICTURE (2006-2007)

Students with need: Out of 858 full-time freshmen who applied for aid, 601 were judged to have need. Of these, 592 received aid, and 30 had their full need met. Average financial aid package met 59% of need; average scholarship/grant was $5,062; average loan was $2,602. For part-time students, average financial aid package was $5,282.
Students without need: 67 full-time freshmen who did not demonstrate need for aid received scholarships/grants; average award was $2,367. No-need awards available for academics, minority status, music/drama.
Scholarships offered: Presidential Scholars; $3,500; based on outstanding academic performance and overall achievement. PSU Scholars; $2,500; based on overall merit and past achievement. New Hampshire Top Scholars; $2,500; for New Hampshire residents in top 15%. Music/Theater Talent Grants; $2,500; based on talent and audition. ALANA; $2,000; for minority students based on student's admission application.
Cumulative student debt: 79% of graduating class had student loans; average debt was $25,119.

FINANCIAL AID PROCEDURES

Forms required: FAFSA.
Dates and Deadlines: Priority date 3/1; no closing date. Applicants notified on a rolling basis starting 2/15; must reply by 5/1.
Transfers: Applicants notified by 5/1.

CONTACT

June Schlabach, Director of Financial Aid
17 High Street MSC 52, Plymouth, NH 03264-1595
(603) 535-2338

River Valley Community College

Claremont, New Hampshire
www.rivervalley.edu   Federal Code: 007560

2-year public technical college in large town.
Enrollment: 682 undergrads.
Selectivity: Open admission; but selective for some programs.

BASIC COSTS (2007-2008)

Tuition and fees: $5,340; out-of-state residents $12,090.
Per-credit charge: $175; out-of-state residents $400.
Additional info: New England Regional tuition: $262 per credit hour.

FINANCIAL AID PICTURE

Students with need: Need-based aid available for full-time and part-time students.

Students without need: This college awards aid only to students with need.

FINANCIAL AID PROCEDURES

Forms required: FAFSA.
Dates and Deadlines: Priority date 4/1; closing date 4/1. Applicants notified on a rolling basis; must reply within 2 week(s) of notification.

CONTACT

Julia Dower, Director of Financial Aid
One College Drive, Claremont, NH 03743-9707
(603) 542-7744

Rivier College

Nashua, New Hampshire
www.rivier.edu   Federal Code: 002586

4-year private liberal arts and teachers college in small city, affiliated with Roman Catholic Church.
Enrollment: 1,432 undergrads.

BASIC COSTS (2008-2009)

Tuition and fees: $23,750.
Per-credit charge: $760.
Room and board: $8,673.

FINANCIAL AID PICTURE

Students with need: Need-based aid available for full-time and part-time students. Work study available nights, weekends, and for part-time students.
Students without need: No-need awards available for academics, alumni affiliation, minority status.
Scholarships offered: Dean's Scholarship, $6,000 for residents, $5,000 for commuters, high school seniors with minimum 1000 SAT (exclusive of writing) and 3.0 GPA; renewable annually with minimum 2.67 GPA. Presidential Scholarship, $7,000 for residents, $6,000 for commuters, high school seniors with minimum 1150 SAT (exclusive of writing) and 3.4 GPA; renewable annually with minimum 3.0 GPA. Catholic High School Grant, $4,000 for residents, $3,000 for commuters, for students graduating from Catholic high school, renewable annually with 2.5 GPA. Honors Scholarship for honors program participants; $10,000 for residents, $2,000 for commuters. Alumni Scholarship, $2,000, for children of Rivier alumni, renewable annually with minimum 2.0 GPA. Trustee Scholarship, $8,000 for residents, $7,000 for commuters, for high school seniors with minimum 1200 SAT (exclusive of writing) and 3.4 GPA, renewable annually with minimum 3.0 GPA. Founders Scholarship for National Merit Finalists; full tuition, renewable with minimum 3.0 GPA.

FINANCIAL AID PROCEDURES

Forms required: FAFSA.
Dates and Deadlines: Priority date 2/1; no closing date. Applicants notified on a rolling basis starting 3/1; must reply by 5/1 or within 2 week(s) of notification.
Transfers: Priority date 3/1. Scholarship for transfer students with minimum 3.0 GPA and 15 transferable credits.

CONTACT

Valerie Patnaude, Director of Financial Aid
420 Main Street, Nashua, NH 03060-5086
(603) 897-8510

St. Anselm College

Manchester, New Hampshire   Federal Code: 002587
www.anselm.edu   CSS Code: 3748

4-year private nursing and liberal arts college in small city, affiliated with Roman Catholic Church.
Enrollment: 1,936 undergrads, 1% part-time. 569 full-time freshmen.

Selectivity: Admits 50 to 75% of applicants.

BASIC COSTS (2008-2009)

Tuition and fees: $29,170.

Room and board: $10,760.

Additional info: Tuition/fee waivers available for minority students.

FINANCIAL AID PICTURE (2007-2008)

Students with need: Out of 488 full-time freshmen who applied for aid, 387 were judged to have need. Of these, 384 received aid, and 112 had their full need met. Average financial aid package met 82% of need; average scholarship/grant was $14,350; average loan was $4,683. For part-time students, average financial aid package was $17,066.

Students without need: 117 full-time freshmen who did not demonstrate need for aid received scholarships/grants; average award was $12,883. No-need awards available for academics, athletics, state/district residency.

Scholarships offered: *Merit:* Presidential Scholarships: $12,500 to $3,500; based on grades, class rank, SAT results and extracurricular experience. *Athletic:* 4 full-time freshmen received athletic scholarships; average amount $28,629.

Cumulative student debt: 82% of graduating class had student loans; average debt was $33,655.

FINANCIAL AID PROCEDURES

Forms required: FAFSA, CSS PROFILE.

Dates and Deadlines: Closing date 3/15. Applicants notified on a rolling basis starting 3/10; must reply by 5/1.

Transfers: Merit scholarships not available for transfer students.

CONTACT

Elizabeth Keuffel, Director of Financial Aid

100 Saint Anselm Drive, Manchester, NH 03102-1310

(603) 641-7110

Southern New Hampshire University

Manchester, New Hampshire

www.snhu.edu   Federal Code: 002580

4-year private university in small city.

Enrollment: 1,953 undergrads, 2% part-time. 544 full-time freshmen.

Selectivity: Admits 50 to 75% of applicants.

BASIC COSTS (2008-2009)

Tuition and fees: $24,954.

Room and board: $9,600.

FINANCIAL AID PICTURE (2007-2008)

Students with need: Out of 464 full-time freshmen who applied for aid, 411 were judged to have need. Of these, 411 received aid, and 47 had their full need met. Average financial aid package met 69% of need; average scholarship/grant was $12,160; average loan was $4,555. For part-time students, average financial aid package was $6,769.

Students without need: 75 full-time freshmen who did not demonstrate need for aid received scholarships/grants; average award was $4,084. No-need awards available for academics, alumni affiliation, athletics, leadership, state/district residency.

Scholarships offered: *Merit:* Academic scholarship: $3000-$8000; awarded to new students based on 3.0 GPA and 1000 SAT (exclusive of writing); unlimited number awarded. Presidential scholarship: 3.5 GPA and 1100 SAT (exclusive of writing). *Athletic:* 16 full-time freshmen received athletic scholarships; average amount $12,986.

FINANCIAL AID PROCEDURES

Forms required: FAFSA.

Dates and Deadlines: Priority date 3/15; no closing date. Applicants notified on a rolling basis starting 3/1; must reply within 3 week(s) of notification.

CONTACT

Louisa Martin, Director of Financial Aid

2500 North River Road, Manchester, NH 03106-1045

(603) 668-2211

Thomas More College of Liberal Arts

Merrimack, New Hampshire

www.thomasmorecollege.edu   Federal Code: 030431

4-year private liberal arts college in large town, affiliated with Roman Catholic Church.

Enrollment: 100 undergrads.

Selectivity: Admits less than 50% of applicants.

BASIC COSTS (2007-2008)

Tuition and fees: $12,250.

Per-credit charge: $500.

Room and board: $8,300.

FINANCIAL AID PICTURE

Students with need: Need-based aid available for full-time and part-time students.

Students without need: No-need awards available for academics.

Scholarships offered: Thomas More Scholarship; full or partial tuition; based on superior academic achievement, exceptional promise or potential; several awarded. Commuter Grants; offered to full-time students within commuting distance of the college. Faith and Reason Essay Contest; half tuition for 4 years; based on essay. Summer Program Scholarship; $1,000; for students who have attended the Thomas More College Summer Program for high school students.

FINANCIAL AID PROCEDURES

Forms required: FAFSA.

Dates and Deadlines: Priority date 5/1; no closing date. Applicants notified on a rolling basis starting 5/15; must reply within 2 week(s) of notification.

CONTACT

Clint Hanson, Director of Financial Aid

Six Manchester Street, Merrimack, NH 03054-4818

(603) 880-8308 ext. 23

University of New Hampshire

Durham, New Hampshire

www.unh.edu   Federal Code: 002589

4-year public university in small town.

Enrollment: 11,622 undergrads, 2% part-time. 2,901 full-time freshmen.

Selectivity: Admits 50 to 75% of applicants.

BASIC COSTS (2007-2008)

Tuition and fees: $11,070; out-of-state residents $24,030.

Per-credit charge: $367; out-of-state residents $907.

Room and board: $8,168.

Additional info: New England Regional Student Program tuition 175% of in-state public institution tuition. College of Earth and Physical Science charges an extra $705 per year. Whittemore School of Business charges an extra $691 per year. Tuition/fee waivers available for minority students.

FINANCIAL AID PICTURE (2006-2007)

Students with need: Out of 2,409 full-time freshmen who applied for aid, 1,740 were judged to have need. Of these, 1,722 received aid, and 407 had their full need met. Average financial aid package met 83% of need; average scholarship/grant was $3,097; average loan was $2,210. For part-time students, average financial aid package was $12,581.

Students without need: 635 full-time freshmen who did not demonstrate need for aid received scholarships/grants; average award was $5,554. No-

need awards available for academics, art, athletics, leadership, music/drama, ROTC.

Scholarships offered: *Merit:* Presidential Scholarship: half tuition. Various other awards recognizing outstanding high school achievement determined during freshmen candidate application review process; no additional application materials required. ***Athletic:*** 49 full-time freshmen received athletic scholarships; average amount $22,619.

Cumulative student debt: 75% of graduating class had student loans; average debt was $25,145.

FINANCIAL AID PROCEDURES

Forms required: FAFSA.

Dates and Deadlines: Priority date 3/1; no closing date. Applicants notified on a rolling basis starting 3/1.

Transfers: Closing date 5/1.

CONTACT

Susan Allen, Director of Financial Aid
Grant House, Durham, NH 03824
(603) 862-3600

University of New Hampshire at Manchester

Manchester, New Hampshire
www.unhm.unh.edu   Federal Code: 002589

4-year public university and liberal arts college in small city.

Enrollment: 773 undergrads, 30% part-time. 110 full-time freshmen.

Selectivity: Admits 50 to 75% of applicants.

BASIC COSTS (2007-2008)

Tuition and fees: $8,515; out-of-state residents $21,145.

Per-credit charge: $244; out-of-state residents $870.

Additional info: New England Regional Student tuition 150% of in-state public institution tuition.

FINANCIAL AID PICTURE

Students with need: Work study available nights, weekends, and for part-time students.

Students without need: No-need awards available for academics, state/district residency.

FINANCIAL AID PROCEDURES

Forms required: FAFSA.

Dates and Deadlines: Closing date 3/1. Applicants notified on a rolling basis starting 4/1; must reply within 2 week(s) of notification.

Transfers: Priority date 3/1.

CONTACT

Jodi Abad, Director of Financial Aid
400 Commercial Street, Manchester, NH 03101-1113
(603) 641-4189

White Mountains Community College

Berlin, New Hampshire
www.berlin.ccsnh.edu   Federal Code: 005291

2-year public community and technical college in large town.

Enrollment: 610 undergrads.

BASIC COSTS (2007-2008)

Tuition and fees: $5,370; out-of-state residents $12,120.

Per-credit charge: $175; out-of-state residents $400.

Additional info: New England Regional tuition: $262 per credit hour.

FINANCIAL AID PICTURE

Students with need: Need-based aid available for full-time and part-time students.

Students without need: This college awards aid only to students with need.

FINANCIAL AID PROCEDURES

Forms required: FAFSA, institutional form.

Dates and Deadlines: Priority date 5/1; no closing date. Applicants notified on a rolling basis starting 5/1; must reply within 2 week(s) of notification.

CONTACT

Jacqueline Catello, Director of Financial Aid
2020 Riverside Drive, Berlin, NH 03570
(603) 752-1113

New Jersey

Atlantic Cape Community College

Mays Landing, New Jersey
www.atlantic.edu   Federal Code: 002596

2-year public culinary school and community college in small town.

Enrollment: 6,419 undergrads.

Selectivity: Open admission; but selective for some programs.

BASIC COSTS (2007-2008)

Tuition and fees: $3,030; out-of-district residents $5,520; out-of-state residents $10,500.

Per-credit charge: $83; out-of-district residents $166; out-of-state residents $332.

Additional info: Tuition/fee waivers available for unemployed or children of unemployed.

FINANCIAL AID PICTURE

Students with need: Need-based aid available for full-time and part-time students.

Additional info: Installment plan available for culinary arts majors. Employees of Atlantic City casinos may attend ACCC at in-county rates regardless of where they live.

FINANCIAL AID PROCEDURES

Forms required: FAFSA, institutional form.

Dates and Deadlines: Priority date 5/1; no closing date. Applicants notified on a rolling basis starting 5/1.

CONTACT

Linda Desantis, Director of Financial Aid & Veterans' Affairs
5100 Black Horse Pike, Mays Landing, NJ 08330
(609) 343-5082

Bergen Community College

Paramus, New Jersey
www.bergen.edu   Federal Code: 004736

2-year public community college in large town.

Enrollment: 12,930 undergrads, 42% part-time. 2,446 full-time freshmen.

Selectivity: Open admission; but selective for some programs.

BASIC COSTS (2007-2008)

Tuition and fees: $3,702; out-of-district residents $6,840; out-of-state residents $7,140.

Per-credit charge: $98; out-of-district residents $203; out-of-state residents $213.

FINANCIAL AID PICTURE (2006-2007)
Students with need: 79% of average financial aid package awarded as scholarships/grants, 21% awarded as loans/jobs.

FINANCIAL AID PROCEDURES
Forms required: FAFSA.
Dates and Deadlines: No deadline. Applicants notified on a rolling basis starting 6/1.
Transfers: Priority date 7/1.

CONTACT
Caroline Ofodile, Director of Financial Operations & Student Assistance
400 Paramus Road, Paramus, NJ 07652-1595
(201) 447-7200

Berkeley College
West Paterson, New Jersey
www.berkeleycollege.edu   Federal Code: 007502

4-year for-profit business college in large town.
Enrollment: 3,041 undergrads, 14% part-time. 641 full-time freshmen.

BASIC COSTS (2008-2009)
Tuition and fees: $19,050.
Per-credit charge: $435.
Room and board: $9,000.
Additional info: Tuition at time of enrollment locked for 4 years.

FINANCIAL AID PICTURE
Students with need: Need-based aid available for full-time students.
Students without need: No-need awards available for academics, alumni affiliation.
Additional info: Alumni scholarship examination given in November and December. Full and partial scholarships awarded.

FINANCIAL AID PROCEDURES
Forms required: FAFSA.
Dates and Deadlines: No deadline. Applicants notified on a rolling basis starting 3/1; must reply within 6 week(s) of notification.

CONTACT
Joan Kinni, Director, Student Finance
44 Rifle Camp Road, West Paterson, NJ 07424-0440
(973) 278-5400 ext. 1350

Bloomfield College
Bloomfield, New Jersey
www.bloomfield.edu   Federal Code: 002597

4-year private liberal arts and teachers college in large town, affiliated with Presbyterian Church (USA).
Enrollment: 2,033 undergrads, 23% part-time. 330 full-time freshmen.
Selectivity: Admits less than 50% of applicants.

BASIC COSTS (2007-2008)
Tuition and fees: $18,000.
Room and board: $8,650.

FINANCIAL AID PICTURE (2007-2008)
Students with need: Out of 330 full-time freshmen who applied for aid, 292 were judged to have need. Of these, 290 received aid, and 145 had their full need met. Average financial aid package met 66% of need; average scholarship/grant was $13,449; average loan was $4,860. For part-time students, average financial aid package was $9,484.
Students without need: 21 full-time freshmen who did not demonstrate need for aid received scholarships/grants; average award was $8,973. No-need awards available for academics, alumni affiliation, athletics, religious affiliation.
Scholarships offered: *Merit:* Trustee Scholar Award: up to $10,000; high school GPA of 3.2 or higher; top 25% of graduating class; SAT 1100+. Presidential Scholarship: up to $8,000; high school GPA of 3.0 or higher; top 33% of graduating class; SAT 950+. Transfer Scholarship: up to $5,000; transfer students from 2-year colleges with GPA of 3.0 or higher. Community Service Scholarships: up to $5,000 for high school seniors with a commitment to community service. Phi Theta Kappa Transfer Scholarships: awards of $6,000 for day transfer students from 2-year colleges with GPA of 3.5 or higher who are members of Phi Theta Kappa. All required SAT scores exclusive of Writing. *Athletic:* 7 full-time freshmen received athletic scholarships; average amount $10,818.
Cumulative student debt: 94% of graduating class had student loans; average debt was $19,476.

FINANCIAL AID PROCEDURES
Forms required: FAFSA.
Dates and Deadlines: Priority date 3/15; closing date 6/1. Applicants notified on a rolling basis starting 3/1; must reply within 2 week(s) of notification.
Transfers: Applicants notified on a rolling basis starting 3/1; must reply within 2 week(s) of notification.

CONTACT
Luis Gonzales, Director of Financial Aid
One Park Place, Bloomfield, NJ 07003
(973) 748-9000 ext. 212

Brookdale Community College
Lincroft, New Jersey
www.brookdalecc.edu   Federal Code: 008404

2-year public community college in small city.
Enrollment: 12,225 undergrads.
Selectivity: Open admission; but selective for some programs.

BASIC COSTS (2007-2008)
Tuition and fees: $3,768; out-of-district residents $6,858; out-of-state residents $7,428.
Per-credit charge: $103; out-of-district residents $206; out-of-state residents $225.
Additional info: Tuition/fee waivers available for unemployed or children of unemployed.

FINANCIAL AID PICTURE
Students with need: Need-based aid available for full-time and part-time students.
Students without need: No-need awards available for athletics.

FINANCIAL AID PROCEDURES
Forms required: FAFSA, institutional form.
Dates and Deadlines: Priority date 5/1; no closing date. Applicants notified on a rolling basis starting 5/1; must reply within 2 week(s) of notification.

CONTACT
Michael Bennett, Director of Financial Aid
765 Newman Springs Road, Lincroft, NJ 07738
(732) 224-2361

Burlington County College
Pemberton, New Jersey
www.bcc.edu   Federal Code: 007730

2-year public community college in small town.
Enrollment: 7,147 undergrads, 43% part-time. 1,639 full-time freshmen.
Selectivity: Open admission; but selective for some programs.

BASIC COSTS (2007-2008)

Tuition and fees: $2,685; out-of-district residents $3,255; out-of-state residents $5,205.

Per-credit charge: $73; out-of-district residents $92; out-of-state residents $157.

Additional info: Tuition/fee waivers available for unemployed or children of unemployed.

FINANCIAL AID PICTURE

Students with need: Need-based aid available for full-time and part-time students. Work study available nights, weekends, and for part-time students.

Students without need: This college awards aid only to students with need.

FINANCIAL AID PROCEDURES

Forms required: FAFSA, institutional form.

Dates and Deadlines: No deadline. Applicants notified on a rolling basis starting 7/1; must reply within 3 week(s) of notification.

CONTACT

Augustine Dominguez, Director of Financial Aid

601 Pemberton-Browns Mills Road, Pemberton, NJ 08068-1599

(609) 894-9, 1 ext. 1575

Caldwell College

Caldwell, New Jersey

www.caldwell.edu   Federal Code: 002598

4-year private liberal arts college in large town, affiliated with Roman Catholic Church.

Enrollment: 1,604 undergrads, 28% part-time. 285 full-time freshmen.

Selectivity: Admits 50 to 75% of applicants.

BASIC COSTS (2008-2009)

Tuition and fees: $23,600.

Per-credit charge: $640.

Room and board: $9,650.

FINANCIAL AID PICTURE (2007-2008)

Students with need: Out of 219 full-time freshmen who applied for aid, 194 were judged to have need. Of these, 194 received aid, and 76 had their full need met. Average financial aid package met 39% of need; average scholarship/grant was $3,551; average loan was $1,686. For part-time students, average financial aid package was $3,067.

Students without need: 58 full-time freshmen who did not demonstrate need for aid received scholarships/grants; average award was $7,721. No-need awards available for academics, alumni affiliation, art, athletics, leadership, music/drama, religious affiliation.

Scholarships offered: 20 full-time freshmen received athletic scholarships; average amount $3,082.

Cumulative student debt: 64% of graduating class had student loans; average debt was $21,873.

FINANCIAL AID PROCEDURES

Forms required: FAFSA, state aid form, institutional form.

Dates and Deadlines: Priority date 4/1; no closing date. Applicants notified on a rolling basis starting 3/1; must reply within 4 week(s) of notification.

Transfers: No deadline. Applicants notified on a rolling basis; must reply within 4 week(s) of notification. Students who have filed for aid through the state previously must file FAFSA by June 1 for succeeding year.

CONTACT

Shawn O'Neil, Financial Aid Director

9 Ryerson Avenue, Caldwell, NJ 07006-6195

(973) 618-3221

Camden County College

Blackwood, New Jersey

www.camdencc.edu   Federal Code: 006865

2-year public community college in large town.

Enrollment: 7,449 undergrads.

Selectivity: Open admission; but selective for some programs.

BASIC COSTS (2007-2008)

Tuition and fees: $3,000; out-of-state residents $3,120.

Per-credit charge: $83; out-of-state residents $87.

Additional info: Tuition/fee waivers available for unemployed or children of unemployed.

FINANCIAL AID PICTURE

Students with need: Need-based aid available for full-time and part-time students.

FINANCIAL AID PROCEDURES

Forms required: FAFSA, institutional form.

Dates and Deadlines: Closing date 7/1. Applicants notified on a rolling basis starting 7/1.

Transfers: Must submit financial aid transcripts from all previously attended institutions.

CONTACT

Aquila Galgon, Director of Financial Aid

Box 200, Blackwood, NJ 08012

(856) 227-7200

Centenary College

Hackettstown, New Jersey

www.centenarycollege.edu   Federal Code: 002599

4-year private liberal arts college in large town, affiliated with United Methodist Church.

Enrollment: 2,238 undergrads, 12% part-time. 288 full-time freshmen.

Selectivity: Admits 50 to 75% of applicants.

BASIC COSTS (2007-2008)

Tuition and fees: $24,100.

Per-credit charge: $445.

Room and board: $8,900.

Additional info: Additional fees required for equine majors and for comprehensive learning support program.

FINANCIAL AID PICTURE (2006-2007)

Students with need: Out of 272 full-time freshmen who applied for aid, 228 were judged to have need. Of these, 227 received aid, and 50 had their full need met. Average financial aid package met 69% of need; average scholarship/grant was $13,208; average loan was $3,675. For part-time students, average financial aid package was $10,934.

Students without need: 42 full-time freshmen who did not demonstrate need for aid received scholarships/grants; average award was $16,397. No-need awards available for academics, alumni affiliation, art, leadership, state/district residency.

Scholarships offered: Academic awards based on minimum GPA of 2.5, SAT 800 (exclusive of Writing) or ACT 16. Leadership awards available based on demonstrated leadership ability and potential. Equine Award, Centenary Resident Grant, Out-of-State Centenary Grant, Skylands Centenary Grant, Centenary United Methodist Scholarship also available.

Cumulative student debt: 93% of graduating class had student loans; average debt was $27,362.

FINANCIAL AID PROCEDURES

Forms required: FAFSA.

Dates and Deadlines: Priority date 4/15; no closing date. Applicants notified on a rolling basis starting 3/1.

Transfers: Students from New Jersey colleges who have received tuition aid grants (TAG) must apply by state deadline. Students must submit financial aid transcripts from all previous institutions attended.

CONTACT

Mike Corso, Director of Financial Aid
400 Jefferson Street, Hackettstown, NJ 07840-9989
(908) 852-1400 ext. 2350

The College of New Jersey

Ewing, New Jersey
www.tcnj.edu   Federal Code: 002642

4-year public liberal arts college in large town.
Enrollment: 6,164 undergrads, 2% part-time. 1,284 full-time freshmen.
Selectivity: Admits less than 50% of applicants.

BASIC COSTS (2007-2008)

Tuition and fees: $11,307; out-of-state residents $18,530.
Per-credit charge: $286; out-of-state residents $542.
Room and board: $9,242.
Additional info: Tuition/fee waivers available for unemployed or children of unemployed.

FINANCIAL AID PICTURE (2007-2008)

Students with need: Out of 1,069 full-time freshmen who applied for aid, 619 were judged to have need. Of these, 573 received aid, and 157 had their full need met. Average financial aid package met 54% of need; average scholarship/grant was $13,878; average loan was $3,676. For part-time students, average financial aid package was $4,794.
Students without need: 181 full-time freshmen who did not demonstrate need for aid received scholarships/grants; average award was $5,644. No-need awards available for academics.
Cumulative student debt: 55% of graduating class had student loans; average debt was $20,056.
Additional info: Merit scholarships available to New Jersey high school graduates based on academic distinction. Limited number of scholarships available to out-of-state students who demonstrate exceptional academic achievement in high school and on SAT.

FINANCIAL AID PROCEDURES

Forms required: FAFSA.
Dates and Deadlines: Priority date 3/1; closing date 10/1. Applicants notified on a rolling basis starting 6/1; must reply within 2 week(s) of notification.
Transfers: No deadline.

CONTACT

Jamie Hightower, Director of Student Financial Services
Box 7718, Ewing, NJ 08628
(609) 771-2211

College of St. Elizabeth

Morristown, New Jersey
www.cse.edu   Federal Code: 002600

4-year private liberal arts college for women in large town, affiliated with Roman Catholic Church.
Enrollment: 1,112 undergrads, 38% part-time. 160 full-time freshmen.
Selectivity: Admits over 75% of applicants.

BASIC COSTS (2007-2008)

Tuition and fees: $22,547.
Per-credit charge: $623.
Room and board: $9,900.

Additional info: Tuition/fee waivers available for adults.

FINANCIAL AID PICTURE (2007-2008)

Students with need: Average financial aid package for all full-time undergraduates was $18,985; for part-time $8,343. 72% awarded as scholarships/grants, 28% awarded as loans/jobs. Work study available nights, weekends, and for part-time students.
Students without need: No-need awards available for academics, alumni affiliation, art, leadership, state/district residency.
Scholarships offered: Presidential Scholarship for campus residents: full tuition. Elizabethan Scholarship: $8,000-$10,000. Seton Scholarship: $3,000-$7,000. Awards guaranteed to eligible students who apply by March 1 and enroll by May 1 for fall semester. Spring semester awards dependent upon availability of funds. International scholarships: awarded annually for fall semester only to first year students enrolled in Women's College; covers tuition, room and board; very competitive, based on academic record, SAT scores (if submitted) and TOEFL score.
Cumulative student debt: 81% of graduating class had student loans; average debt was $25,535.

FINANCIAL AID PROCEDURES

Forms required: FAFSA.
Dates and Deadlines: Priority date 3/1; no closing date. Applicants notified on a rolling basis starting 11/15; must reply by 5/1 or within 2 week(s) of notification.
Transfers: Priority date 4/15; closing date 8/20. Scholarships available for full-time students who enroll immediately following full-time enrollment at another college. Applicants must have completed minimum 32 credits and have minimum 3.0 GPA. Awards range from $3,500 to half tuition. Minimum of 5 awarded annually. Preference given to applications received by June 1 for fall semester and by December 1 for spring semester. Limited number of partial scholarships awarded to international students.

CONTACT

Director of Financial Aid
2 Convent Road, Morristown, NJ 07960-6989
(973) 290-4445

County College of Morris

Randolph, New Jersey
www.ccm.edu   Federal Code: 007106

2-year public community college in large town.
Enrollment: 6,628 undergrads.
Selectivity: Open admission; but selective for some programs.

BASIC COSTS (2007-2008)

Tuition and fees: $3,315; out-of-district residents $6,195; out-of-state residents $8,505.
Per-credit charge: $96; out-of-district residents $192; out-of-state residents $269.
Additional info: Tuition reciprocity agreements with neighboring counties allow some out-of-county residents to pay in-county rates. Tuition/fee waivers available for unemployed or children of unemployed.

FINANCIAL AID PICTURE

Students with need: Need-based aid available for full-time and part-time students.
Students without need: No-need awards available for athletics.

FINANCIAL AID PROCEDURES

Forms required: FAFSA.
Dates and Deadlines: Priority date 3/1; no closing date. Applicants notified on a rolling basis starting 5/1.

CONTACT

Harvey Willis, Director, Financial Aid
214 Center Grove Road, Randolph, NJ 07869-2086
(973) 328-5230

Cumberland County College
Vineland, New Jersey
www.cccnj.edu   Federal Code: 002601

2-year public community college in small city.
Enrollment: 3,527 undergrads.
Selectivity: Open admission; but selective for some programs.

BASIC COSTS (2007-2008)

Tuition and fees: $3,330; out-of-district residents $5,850; out-of-state residents $10,890.
Per-credit charge: $84; out-of-district residents $168; out-of-state residents $336.
Additional info: Tuition/fee waivers available for unemployed or children of unemployed.

FINANCIAL AID PICTURE

Students with need: Need-based aid available for full-time and part-time students.
Students without need: No-need awards available for academics.

FINANCIAL AID PROCEDURES

Forms required: FAFSA.
Dates and Deadlines: No deadline. Applicants notified on a rolling basis; must reply within 3 week(s) of notification.

CONTACT

Kimberly Mitchell, Director, Financial Aid
PO Box 1500, Vineland, NJ 08362-9912
(609) 691-8600

DeVry University: North Brunswick
North Brunswick, New Jersey
www.devry.edu   Federal Code: 009228

4-year for-profit university in small city.
Enrollment: 1,370 undergrads, 36% part-time. 201 full-time freshmen.

BASIC COSTS (2007-2008)

Tuition and fees: $13,220.
Per-credit charge: $490.

FINANCIAL AID PICTURE (2006-2007)

Students with need: Out of 144 full-time freshmen who applied for aid, 132 were judged to have need. Of these, 130 received aid, and 2 had their full need met. Average financial aid package met 41% of need; average scholarship/grant was $7,599; average loan was $4,091. For part-time students, average financial aid package was $7,182.
Students without need: This college awards aid only to students with need.
Cumulative student debt: 88% of graduating class had student loans; average debt was $22,355.

FINANCIAL AID PROCEDURES

Forms required: FAFSA.
Dates and Deadlines: No deadline. Applicants notified on a rolling basis.

CONTACT

Albert Cama, Director of Financial Aid
630 US Highway One, North Brunswick, NJ 08902-3362
(800) 333-3879

Drew University
Madison, New Jersey   Federal Code: 002603
www.drew.edu   CSS Code: 2193

4-year private university and liberal arts college in large town, affiliated with United Methodist Church.
Enrollment: 1,620 undergrads, 2% part-time. 452 full-time freshmen.
Selectivity: Admits over 75% of applicants.

BASIC COSTS (2007-2008)

Tuition and fees: $34,790.
Per-credit charge: $1,426.
Room and board: $9,476.

FINANCIAL AID PICTURE (2006-2007)

Students with need: Average financial aid package for all full-time undergraduates was $25,488. 81% awarded as scholarships/grants, 19% awarded as loans/jobs.
Students without need: No-need awards available for academics, art, minority status, music/drama.
Cumulative student debt: 62% of graduating class had student loans; average debt was $16,777.

FINANCIAL AID PROCEDURES

Forms required: FAFSA, CSS PROFILE.
Dates and Deadlines: Closing date 2/15. Applicants notified by 3/31; must reply by 5/1.
Transfers: No deadline.

CONTACT

Mary Beth Carey, Dean of College Admissions and Financial Assistance
36 Madison Avenue, Madison, NJ 07940-1493
(973) 408-3112

Essex County College
Newark, New Jersey
www.essex.edu   Federal Code: 007107

2-year public community college in large city.
Enrollment: 10,094 undergrads, 41% part-time. 2,239 full-time freshmen.
Selectivity: Open admission; but selective for some programs.

BASIC COSTS (2008-2009)

Tuition and fees: $3,765; out-of-district residents $6,615; out-of-state residents $6,615.
Per-credit charge: $95; out-of-district residents $190; out-of-state residents $190.
Additional info: Tuition/fee waivers available for unemployed or children of unemployed.

FINANCIAL AID PICTURE

Students with need: Need-based aid available for full-time and part-time students.

FINANCIAL AID PROCEDURES

Forms required: FAFSA, institutional form.
Dates and Deadlines: Priority date 6/30; no closing date. Applicants notified on a rolling basis starting 6/15; must reply within 3 week(s) of notification.

CONTACT

Mildred Cofer, Director of Financial Aid
303 University Avenue, Newark, NJ 07102
(973) 877-3000

Felician College

Lodi, New Jersey
www.felician.edu   Federal Code: 002610

4-year private liberal arts college in large city, affiliated with Roman Catholic Church.

Enrollment: 1,615 undergrads, 22% part-time. 294 full-time freshmen.

Selectivity: Admits 50 to 75% of applicants.

BASIC COSTS (2007-2008)

Tuition and fees: $21,900.

Per-credit charge: $675.

Room and board: $8,900.

Additional info: Tuition/fee waivers available for adults.

FINANCIAL AID PICTURE (2006-2007)

Students with need: Out of 252 full-time freshmen who applied for aid, 226 were judged to have need. Of these, 226 received aid, and 29 had their full need met. Average financial aid package met 85% of need; average scholarship/grant was $7,000; average loan was $3,500. For part-time students, average financial aid package was $4,000.

Students without need: 99 full-time freshmen who did not demonstrate need for aid received scholarships/grants; average award was $4,700. No-need awards available for academics, alumni affiliation, athletics, religious affiliation.

Scholarships offered: 34 full-time freshmen received athletic scholarships; average amount $11,062.

Cumulative student debt: 62% of graduating class had student loans; average debt was $23,000.

FINANCIAL AID PROCEDURES

Forms required: FAFSA.

Dates and Deadlines: Priority date 6/1; no closing date. Applicants notified on a rolling basis starting 4/1; must reply within 2 week(s) of notification.

CONTACT

Marc Chalfin, Executive Vice President for Business and Finance
262 South Main Street, Lodi, NJ 07644-2198
(201) 559-6000 ext. 6010

Georgian Court University

Lakewood, New Jersey
www.georgian.edu   Federal Code: 002608

4-year private university and liberal arts college for women in large town, affiliated with Roman Catholic Church.

Enrollment: 1,718 undergrads, 19% part-time. 226 full-time freshmen.

Selectivity: Admits over 75% of applicants.

BASIC COSTS (2008-2009)

Tuition and fees: $23,360.

Room and board: $9,112.

FINANCIAL AID PICTURE (2007-2008)

Students with need: Out of 218 full-time freshmen who applied for aid, 196 were judged to have need. Of these, 196 received aid, and 39 had their full need met. Average financial aid package met 83% of need; average scholarship/grant was $17,663; average loan was $3,388. For part-time students, average financial aid package was $6,764.

Students without need: 28 full-time freshmen who did not demonstrate need for aid received scholarships/grants; average award was $12,764. No-need awards available for academics, alumni affiliation, art, athletics, leadership, minority status, music/drama, religious affiliation.

Scholarships offered: 7 full-time freshmen received athletic scholarships; average amount $2,725.

Cumulative student debt: 90% of graduating class had student loans; average debt was $25,988.

FINANCIAL AID PROCEDURES

Forms required: FAFSA, institutional form.

Dates and Deadlines: Priority date 3/1; no closing date. Applicants notified on a rolling basis starting 2/1; must reply within 2 week(s) of notification.

Transfers: Transfer students who have outstanding financial obligations to previous college or who are in default are not admitted before being cleared by previous college or following federal guidelines concerning defaults.

CONTACT

Carol Strauss, Director of Financial Aid
900 Lakewood Avenue, Lakewood, NJ 08701-2697
(732) 987-2258

Gloucester County College

Sewell, New Jersey
www.gccnj.edu   Federal Code: 006901

2-year public community college in large town.

Enrollment: 3,423 full-time undergrads.

Selectivity: Open admission; but selective for some programs.

BASIC COSTS (2007-2008)

Tuition and fees: $2,880; out-of-district residents $2,970; out-of-state residents $5,370.

Per-credit charge: $77; out-of-district residents $80; out-of-state residents $160.

FINANCIAL AID PICTURE

Students with need: Need-based aid available for full-time and part-time students. Work study available nights.

Students without need: This college awards aid only to students with need.

FINANCIAL AID PROCEDURES

Forms required: FAFSA, institutional form.

Dates and Deadlines: Priority date 5/1; no closing date. Applicants notified on a rolling basis starting 3/20.

CONTACT

Jeffrey Williams, Financial Aid Director
1400 Tanyard Road, Sewell, NJ 08080
(856) 415-2210

Hudson County Community College

Jersey City, New Jersey
www.hccc.edu   Federal Code: 012954

2-year public community college in large city.

Enrollment: 6,773 undergrads.

Selectivity: Open admission.

BASIC COSTS (2007-2008)

Tuition and fees: $3,543; out-of-district residents $6,123.

Per-credit charge: $86; out-of-district residents $172; out-of-state residents $258.

FINANCIAL AID PICTURE (2006-2007)

Students with need: 98% of average financial aid package awarded as scholarships/grants, 2% awarded as loans/jobs. Need-based aid available for part-time students.

Students without need: This college awards aid only to students with need.

FINANCIAL AID PROCEDURES

Forms required: FAFSA.

Dates and Deadlines: Priority date 7/15; no closing date. Applicants notified on a rolling basis starting 6/1; must reply within 1 week(s) of notification.

Transfers: No deadline.

CONTACT

Pamela Norris-Littles, Director of Financial Aid
70 Sip Avenue, 1st Floor, Jersey City, NJ 07306
(201) 714-2145

Kean University
Union, New Jersey
www.kean.edu   Federal Code: 002622

4-year public university and liberal arts college in small city.

Enrollment: 10,137 undergrads, 22% part-time. 1,446 full-time freshmen.

Selectivity: Admits 50 to 75% of applicants.

BASIC COSTS (2007-2008)

Tuition and fees: $8,505; out-of-state residents $12,645.

Per-credit charge: $185; out-of-state residents $323.

Room and board: $9,190.

Additional info: Tuition/fee waivers available for unemployed or children of unemployed.

FINANCIAL AID PICTURE (2007-2008)

Students with need: Out of 1,238 full-time freshmen who applied for aid, 935 were judged to have need. Of these, 912 received aid, and 73 had their full need met. Average financial aid package met 55% of need; average scholarship/grant was $6,925; average loan was $3,466. For part-time students, average financial aid package was $5,590.

Students without need: 51 full-time freshmen who did not demonstrate need for aid received scholarships/grants; average award was $2,273. No-need awards available for academics, alumni affiliation, art, leadership, music/drama.

Scholarships offered: Academic Merit Scholarship: $1,000 award given to incoming freshmen with minimum cumulative 3.0 GPA and minimum 1010 SAT. Kean Scholarship: $2,500 award given to incoming freshmen with minimum cumulative 3.0 GPA and minimum 1310 SAT. Presidential Scholarship: $1,500 award given to incoming freshmen with minimum cumulative 3.0 GPA and minimum 1140 SAT. Trustee Scholarship: $2,000 award given to incoming freshmen with minimum cumulative 3.0 GPA and minimum 1260 SAT. New Jersey Center for Science and Technology Education (NJCSTE) Scholarship: Full-tuition scholarship awarded to incoming freshmen with minimum 3.0 GPA and minimum 1100 SAT who are interested in pursuing B.S./M.S. or B.S./M.A. degree programs in science and technology; all applicants must be interviewed by the NJCSTE. Visual and Performing Arts Scholarship: full tuition awarded to incoming freshman with minimum 3.0 GPA; requires portfolio review or audition by the School of Visual and Performing Arts. Dr. James E. Dorsey Scholarship: awarded to African-American and Latino students with a minimum cumulative 3.0 GPA and minimum 1000 SAT.

Cumulative student debt: 72% of graduating class had student loans; average debt was $30,140.

FINANCIAL AID PROCEDURES

Forms required: FAFSA.

Dates and Deadlines: Priority date 3/15; no closing date. Applicants notified on a rolling basis starting 3/15; must reply by 5/1.

Transfers: No deadline. Applicants notified on a rolling basis; must reply by 5/1.

CONTACT

Charlie Xu, Director
1000 Morris Avenue, Union, NJ 07083-0411
(908) 737-3190

Mercer County Community College
Trenton, New Jersey
www.mccc.edu   Federal Code: 002641

2-year public community college in small city.

Enrollment: 7,817 undergrads, 57% part-time. 1,286 full-time freshmen.

Selectivity: Open admission.

BASIC COSTS (2007-2008)

Tuition and fees: $3,060; out-of-district residents $4,110; out-of-state residents $6,270.

Per-credit charge: $102; out-of-district residents $137; out-of-state residents $209.

Additional info: Tuition/fee waivers available for unemployed or children of unemployed.

FINANCIAL AID PICTURE

Students with need: Need-based aid available for full-time and part-time students. Work study available nights.

Students without need: No-need awards available for academics, athletics, state/district residency.

Scholarships offered: MCCC Foundation Scholarship: $2,500; top 25% of high school class; 15 total awards. NJ STARS program: for top 20% of HS class.

FINANCIAL AID PROCEDURES

Forms required: FAFSA.

Dates and Deadlines: No deadline. Applicants notified on a rolling basis.

CONTACT

Reginald Page, Director of Financial Aid
Box B, Trenton, NJ 08690-1099
(609) 570-3210

Monmouth University
West Long Branch, New Jersey
www.monmouth.edu   Federal Code: 002616

4-year private university in small town.

Enrollment: 4,694 undergrads, 8% part-time. 945 full-time freshmen.

Selectivity: Admits 50 to 75% of applicants.

BASIC COSTS (2008-2009)

Tuition and fees: $24,098.

Per-credit charge: $680.

Room and board: $9,221.

FINANCIAL AID PICTURE (2007-2008)

Students with need: Out of 782 full-time freshmen who applied for aid, 599 were judged to have need. Of these, 598 received aid, and 38 had their full need met. Average financial aid package met 71% of need; average scholarship/grant was $11,468; average loan was $4,197. For part-time students, average financial aid package was $7,007.

Students without need: 302 full-time freshmen who did not demonstrate need for aid received scholarships/grants; average award was $6,565. No-need awards available for academics, alumni affiliation, art, athletics, leadership.

Scholarships offered: *Merit:* Academic Excellence Awards: from $2,000-$15,000; based on SAT scores and high school GPA; renewable annually as long as required GPA is maintained. *Athletic:* 27 full-time freshmen received athletic scholarships; average amount $12,855.

Cumulative student debt: 76% of graduating class had student loans; average debt was $34,484.

FINANCIAL AID PROCEDURES

Forms required: FAFSA.

Dates and Deadlines: No deadline. Applicants notified on a rolling basis starting 2/15; must reply within 2 week(s) of notification.
Transfers: No deadline. Applicants notified on a rolling basis; must reply within 2 week(s) of notification.

CONTACT
Claire Alasio, Associate Vice President for Enrollment Management
400 Cedar Avenue, West Long Branch, NJ 07764-1898
(732) 571-3463

Montclair State University
Upper Montclair, New Jersey
www.montclair.edu   Federal Code: 002617

4-year public university in large town.
Enrollment: 12,559 undergrads, 16% part-time. 2,018 full-time freshmen.
Selectivity: Admits 50 to 75% of applicants.

BASIC COSTS (2007-2008)
Tuition and fees: $8,895; out-of-state residents $16,164.
Per-credit charge: $213; out-of-state residents $455.
Room and board: $9,500.
Additional info: Tuition/fee waivers available for unemployed or children of unemployed.

FINANCIAL AID PICTURE (2007-2008)
Students with need: Out of 1,371 full-time freshmen who applied for aid, 1,035 were judged to have need. Of these, 980 received aid, and 411 had their full need met. Average financial aid package met 64% of need; average scholarship/grant was $6,904; average loan was $3,531. For part-time students, average financial aid package was $5,610.
Students without need: 35 full-time freshmen who did not demonstrate need for aid received scholarships/grants; average award was $5,771. No-need awards available for academics, alumni affiliation, art, leadership, minority status, music/drama, ROTC, state/district residency.

FINANCIAL AID PROCEDURES
Forms required: FAFSA.
Dates and Deadlines: Priority date 3/1; no closing date. Applicants notified on a rolling basis starting 4/1; must reply within 2 week(s) of notification.
Transfers: Students will be eligible for financial aid beginning fall semester of the academic year for which they are admitted.

CONTACT
Frank Cuozzo, Director of Financial Aid
One Normal Avenue, Upper Montclair, NJ 07043-1624
(973) 655-4461

New Jersey City University
Jersey City, New Jersey
www.njcu.edu   Federal Code: 002613

4-year public university in small city.
Enrollment: 6,242 undergrads, 28% part-time. 646 full-time freshmen.
Selectivity: Admits less than 50% of applicants.

BASIC COSTS (2007-2008)
Tuition and fees: $8,155; out-of-state residents $14,759.
Per-credit charge: $198; out-of-state residents $418.
Room and board: $8,299.

FINANCIAL AID PICTURE (2006-2007)
Students with need: Out of 552 full-time freshmen who applied for aid, 507 were judged to have need. Of these, 482 received aid, and 30 had their full need met. Average financial aid package met 60% of need; average scholarship/grant was $7,143; average loan was $2,733. For part-time students, average financial aid package was $4,158.
Students without need: 16 full-time freshmen who did not demonstrate need for aid received scholarships/grants; average award was $4,372.
Cumulative student debt: 78% of graduating class had student loans; average debt was $28,833.

FINANCIAL AID PROCEDURES
Forms required: FAFSA.
Dates and Deadlines: Priority date 4/15; no closing date. Applicants notified by 5/4.

CONTACT
Carmen Panlilio, Assistant Vice President for Admissions and Financial Aid
2039 Kennedy Boulevard, Jersey City, NJ 07305-1597
(201) 200-3173

New Jersey Institute of Technology
Newark, New Jersey
www.njit.edu   Federal Code: 002621

4-year public university in very large city.
Enrollment: 4,967 undergrads, 17% part-time. 731 full-time freshmen.
Selectivity: Admits 50 to 75% of applicants.

BASIC COSTS (2008-2009)
Tuition and fees: $11,350; out-of-state residents $20,082.
Per-credit charge: $370; out-of-state residents $788.
Room and board: $9,108.

FINANCIAL AID PICTURE
Students with need: Need-based aid available for full-time and part-time students.
Students without need: No-need awards available for academics, alumni affiliation, art, leadership, minority status, music/drama, ROTC, state/district residency.
Additional info: Extensive co-op program for all majors.

FINANCIAL AID PROCEDURES
Forms required: FAFSA.
Dates and Deadlines: Priority date 3/15; closing date 5/15. Applicants notified on a rolling basis starting 3/1; must reply within 2 week(s) of notification.
Transfers: Priority date 5/15.

CONTACT
Ivon Nunez, Director of Financial Aid
University Heights, Newark, NJ 07102
(973) 596-3478

Ocean County College
Toms River, New Jersey
www.ocean.edu   Federal Code: 002624

2-year public community college in small city.
Enrollment: 7,908 undergrads, 38% part-time. 1,837 full-time freshmen.
Selectivity: Open admission; but selective for some programs.

BASIC COSTS (2007-2008)
Tuition and fees: $3,510; out-of-district residents $4,530; out-of-state residents $6,900.
Per-credit charge: $90; out-of-district residents $124; out-of-state residents $203.

Additional info: Tuition/fee waivers available for unemployed or children of unemployed.

FINANCIAL AID PICTURE

Students with need: Need-based aid available for full-time and part-time students.

Students without need: This college awards aid only to students with need.

FINANCIAL AID PROCEDURES

Forms required: FAFSA.

Dates and Deadlines: Priority date 5/31; no closing date. Applicants notified on a rolling basis starting 7/15; must reply within 1 week(s) of notification.

CONTACT

Norma Betz, Director of Financial Aid
College Drive, Toms River, NJ 08754-2001
(732) 255-0400 ext. 2020

Passaic County Community College

Paterson, New Jersey
www.pccc.edu

Federal Code: 009994
CSS Code: 2694

2-year public community college in small city.

Enrollment: 7,493 undergrads.

Selectivity: Open admission; but selective for some programs.

BASIC COSTS (2007-2008)

Tuition and fees: $3,126; out-of-state residents $5,601.

Per-credit charge: $83; out-of-state residents $165.

Additional info: Additional course fees up to maximum of $600 per year. Tuition/fee waivers available for unemployed or children of unemployed.

FINANCIAL AID PICTURE (2006-2007)

Students with need: 99% of average financial aid package awarded as scholarships/grants, 1% awarded as loans/jobs. Need-based aid available for part-time students.

Students without need: No-need awards available for academics.

Additional info: Limited scholarship funds available for low income students eligible for federal or state aid.

FINANCIAL AID PROCEDURES

Forms required: FAFSA, CSS PROFILE.

Dates and Deadlines: Priority date 8/1; no closing date. Applicants notified on a rolling basis starting 8/1; must reply within 2 week(s) of notification.

Transfers: Priority date 5/15; closing date 6/30.

CONTACT

Sharon Audet, Director of Financial Aid
One College Boulevard, Paterson, NJ 07505-1179
(973) 684-6800

Princeton University

Princeton, New Jersey
www.princeton.edu

Federal Code: 002627

4-year private university in large town.

Enrollment: 4,833 undergrads. 1,239 full-time freshmen.

Selectivity: Admits less than 50% of applicants. GED not accepted.

BASIC COSTS (2008-2009)

Tuition and fees: $34,290.

Room and board: $11,405.

FINANCIAL AID PICTURE (2006-2007)

Students with need: Out of 781 full-time freshmen who applied for aid, 682 were judged to have need. Of these, 682 received aid, and 682 had their full need met. Average financial aid package met 100% of need; average scholarship/grant was $29,786.

Students without need: This college awards aid only to students with need.

Cumulative student debt: 22% of graduating class had student loans; average debt was $5,592.

Additional info: All aid need-based; all aid grant money (no loans); institution meets full demonstrated need.

FINANCIAL AID PROCEDURES

Forms required: FAFSA, institutional form.

Dates and Deadlines: Priority date 2/1; no closing date. Applicants notified by 4/1; must reply by 5/1.

CONTACT

Robin Moscato, Director of Financial Aid
Box 430, Princeton, NJ 08544-0430
(609) 258-3330

Ramapo College of New Jersey

Mahwah, New Jersey
www.ramapo.edu

Federal Code: 009344

4-year public liberal arts college in large town.

Enrollment: 5,131 undergrads, 8% part-time. 814 full-time freshmen.

Selectivity: Admits less than 50% of applicants.

BASIC COSTS (2007-2008)

Tuition and fees: $9,965; out-of-state residents $15,536.

Per-credit charge: $216; out-of-state residents $390.

Room and board: $10,310.

Additional info: Tuition/fee waivers available for minority students, unemployed or children of unemployed.

FINANCIAL AID PICTURE (2006-2007)

Students with need: Out of 638 full-time freshmen who applied for aid, 436 were judged to have need. Of these, 419 received aid, and 73 had their full need met. Average financial aid package met 79% of need; average scholarship/grant was $19,348; average loan was $2,622. For part-time students, average financial aid package was $3,975.

Students without need: 117 full-time freshmen who did not demonstrate need for aid received scholarships/grants; average award was $10,866. No-need awards available for academics, job skills.

FINANCIAL AID PROCEDURES

Forms required: FAFSA.

Dates and Deadlines: Priority date 3/1; no closing date. Applicants notified on a rolling basis starting 4/1; must reply by 5/1 or within 2 week(s) of notification.

CONTACT

Mark Singer, Director of Financial Aid
505 Ramapo Valley Road, Mahwah, NJ 07430-1680
(201) 684-7549

Raritan Valley Community College

Somerville, New Jersey
www.raritanval.edu

Federal Code: 007731

2-year public community college in large town.

Enrollment: 5,462 undergrads, 46% part-time. 279 full-time freshmen.

Selectivity: Open admission; but selective for some programs.

BASIC COSTS (2007-2008)

Tuition and fees: $3,490.

Per-credit charge: $87.

Additional info: Tuition/fee waivers available for unemployed or children of unemployed.

FINANCIAL AID PICTURE (2006-2007)

Students with need: Out of 262 full-time freshmen who applied for aid, 189 were judged to have need. Of these, 189 received aid, and 8 had their full need met. Average financial aid package met 71% of need; average scholarship/grant was $1,765; average loan was $1,772. For part-time students, average financial aid package was $2,260.

Students without need: 24 full-time freshmen who did not demonstrate need for aid received scholarships/grants; average award was $898. No-need awards available for academics.

FINANCIAL AID PROCEDURES

Forms required: FAFSA.

Dates and Deadlines: No deadline. Applicants notified on a rolling basis starting 4/1.

CONTACT

John Trojan, Vice President of Finance and Facilities

PO Box 3300, Somerville, NJ 08876-1265

(908) 526-1200 ext. 8268

Richard Stockton College of New Jersey
Pomona, New Jersey
www.stockton.edu   Federal Code: 009345

4-year public liberal arts college in large town.

Enrollment: 6,600 undergrads, 11% part-time. 787 full-time freshmen.

Selectivity: Admits 50 to 75% of applicants.

BASIC COSTS (2007-2008)

Tuition and fees: $9,091; out-of-state residents $13,685.

Per-credit charge: $199; out-of-state residents $352.

Room and board: $9,077.

Additional info: Tuition/fee waivers available for unemployed or children of unemployed.

FINANCIAL AID PICTURE (2007-2008)

Students with need: Out of 659 full-time freshmen who applied for aid, 507 were judged to have need. Of these, 482 received aid, and 239 had their full need met. Average financial aid package met 74% of need; average scholarship/grant was $8,148; average loan was $3,557. For part-time students, average financial aid package was $8,598.

Students without need: 69 full-time freshmen who did not demonstrate need for aid received scholarships/grants; average award was $3,803. No-need awards available for academics, art, leadership, minority status, music/drama, state/district residency.

Scholarships offered: Freshman Scholarship Program: awarded to incoming freshmen with high school class rank in the top 15% or higher and 1150 SAT (exclusive of Writing) or better; awards range up to full tuition, fees, and housing for all four years.

FINANCIAL AID PROCEDURES

Forms required: FAFSA.

Dates and Deadlines: Priority date 3/1; no closing date. Applicants notified on a rolling basis starting 4/1; must reply within 2 week(s) of notification.

CONTACT

Jeanne Lewis, Director of Financial Aid

Jim Leeds Road, Pomona, NJ 08240-0195

(609) 652-4201

Rider University
Lawrenceville, New Jersey
www.rider.edu   Federal Code: 002628

4-year private university in large town.

Enrollment: 4,534 undergrads, 14% part-time. 990 full-time freshmen.

Selectivity: Admits over 75% of applicants.

BASIC COSTS (2008-2009)

Tuition and fees: $27,730.

Per-credit charge: $870.

Room and board: $10,280.

FINANCIAL AID PICTURE (2007-2008)

Students with need: Out of 823 full-time freshmen who applied for aid, 672 were judged to have need. Of these, 672 received aid, and 133 had their full need met. Average financial aid package met 72% of need; average scholarship/grant was $14,041; average loan was $3,735. For part-time students, average financial aid package was $6,471.

Students without need: 206 full-time freshmen who did not demonstrate need for aid received scholarships/grants; average award was $10,709. No-need awards available for academics, alumni affiliation, art, athletics, leadership, minority status, music/drama, state/district residency.

Scholarships offered: 79 full-time freshmen received athletic scholarships; average amount $9,465.

Cumulative student debt: 76% of graduating class had student loans; average debt was $32,132.

FINANCIAL AID PROCEDURES

Forms required: FAFSA.

Dates and Deadlines: Priority date 3/1; no closing date. Applicants notified on a rolling basis starting 3/15.

Transfers: No deadline.

CONTACT

Drew Aromando, Director of Student Financial Services

2083 Lawrenceville Road, Lawrenceville, NJ 08648-3099

(609) 896-5360

Rowan University
Glassboro, New Jersey
www.rowan.edu   Federal Code: 002609

4-year public university and liberal arts college in large town.

Enrollment: 8,499 undergrads, 10% part-time. 1,205 full-time freshmen.

Selectivity: Admits 50 to 75% of applicants.

BASIC COSTS (2007-2008)

Tuition and fees: $10,068; out-of-state residents $17,376.

Per-credit charge: $282; out-of-state residents $564.

Room and board: $9,242.

FINANCIAL AID PICTURE (2006-2007)

Students with need: Out of 1,027 full-time freshmen who applied for aid, 673 were judged to have need. Of these, 636 received aid, and 209 had their full need met. Average financial aid package met 93% of need; average scholarship/grant was $7,955; average loan was $2,490. For part-time students, average financial aid package was $6,149.

Students without need: 107 full-time freshmen who did not demonstrate need for aid received scholarships/grants; average award was $4,098. No-need awards available for academics, art, music/drama.

FINANCIAL AID PROCEDURES

Forms required: FAFSA, institutional form.

Dates and Deadlines: Closing date 3/15. Applicants notified on a rolling basis starting 5/1; must reply within 2 week(s) of notification.

CONTACT

Luis Tavarez, Director of Financial Aid

Savitz Hall, 201 Mullica Hill Road, Glassboro, NJ 08028

(856) 256-4250

Saint Peter's College

Jersey City, New Jersey

www.spc.edu   Federal Code: 002638

4-year private liberal arts college in small city, affiliated with Roman Catholic Church.

Enrollment: 2,259 undergrads, 13% part-time. 539 full-time freshmen.

Selectivity: Admits 50 to 75% of applicants.

BASIC COSTS (2007-2008)

Tuition and fees: $24,026.

Per-credit charge: $784.

Room and board: $9,750.

FINANCIAL AID PICTURE (2006-2007)

Students with need: Out of 536 full-time freshmen who applied for aid, 448 were judged to have need. Of these, 446 received aid, and 42 had their full need met. Average financial aid package met 75% of need; average scholarship/grant was $16,336; average loan was $2,416. For part-time students, average financial aid package was $6,588.

Students without need: 86 full-time freshmen who did not demonstrate need for aid received scholarships/grants; average award was $11,585. No-need awards available for academics, athletics.

Scholarships offered: *Merit:* Academic Awards based on minimum SAT of 1100 (exclusive of Writing), minimum GPA of 3.0, and in top 20% of class: 50 awarded; full tuition. Incentive Awards for selected applicants with some qualities necessary for academic awards but who are otherwise ineligible: ranging from $500-$4,000 annually. Residential Grants based on academics and extracurricular activities: $500-$2,500 toward housing. *Athletic:* 9 full-time freshmen received athletic scholarships; average amount $18,088.

Additional info: Cooperative education internships available in all majors, with average salaries exceeding $5,200.

FINANCIAL AID PROCEDURES

Forms required: FAFSA.

Dates and Deadlines: Priority date 3/15; no closing date. Applicants notified on a rolling basis starting 2/15; must reply by 5/1 or within 2 week(s) of notification.

Transfers: Student and parents (if dependent students) must be New Jersey residents for at least 1 year prior to start date. Students must complete renewal application before June 1.

CONTACT

Steve Smith, Financial Aid

2641 Kennedy Boulevard, Jersey City, NJ 07306

(201) 761-6060

Salem Community College

Carneys Point, New Jersey

www.salemcc.edu   Federal Code: 005461

2-year public community college in small town.

Enrollment: 980 undergrads.

Selectivity: Open admission; but selective for some programs.

BASIC COSTS (2007-2008)

Tuition and fees: $3,395; out-of-state residents $3,695.

Per-credit charge: $83; out-of-state residents $93.

Additional info: Tuition/fee waivers available for unemployed or children of unemployed.

FINANCIAL AID PICTURE

Students with need: Need-based aid available for full-time and part-time students.

Students without need: This college awards aid only to students with need.

FINANCIAL AID PROCEDURES

Forms required: FAFSA, institutional form.

Dates and Deadlines: Priority date 6/1; no closing date. Applicants notified on a rolling basis starting 4/1; must reply within 2 week(s) of notification.

CONTACT

Sharon Eastlack, Coordinator of Financial Aid

460 Hollywood Avenue, Carneys Point, NJ 08069-2799

(856) 351-2699

Seton Hall University

South Orange, New Jersey

www.shu.edu   Federal Code: 002632

4-year private university in large town, affiliated with Roman Catholic Church.

Enrollment: 4,896 undergrads, 7% part-time. 1,054 full-time freshmen.

Selectivity: Admits 50 to 75% of applicants.

BASIC COSTS (2007-2008)

Tuition and fees: $27,850.

Per-credit charge: $797.

Room and board: $10,828.

Additional info: Required fees include lease of laptop computer.

FINANCIAL AID PICTURE (2006-2007)

Students with need: Out of 989 full-time freshmen who applied for aid, 851 were judged to have need. Of these, 837 received aid, and 117 had their full need met. Average financial aid package met 69% of need; average scholarship/grant was $6,000; average loan was $2,674. For part-time students, average financial aid package was $6,914.

Students without need: 229 full-time freshmen who did not demonstrate need for aid received scholarships/grants; average award was $12,515. No-need awards available for academics, alumni affiliation, athletics, leadership, minority status, ROTC, state/district residency.

Scholarships offered: 48 full-time freshmen received athletic scholarships; average amount $22,219.

Cumulative student debt: 61% of graduating class had student loans; average debt was $37,724.

FINANCIAL AID PROCEDURES

Forms required: FAFSA.

Dates and Deadlines: Priority date 2/15; no closing date. Applicants notified on a rolling basis starting 3/1; must reply by 5/1 or within 4 week(s) of notification.

Transfers: Transfer academic scholarships available.

CONTACT

Lasaundra Floyd, Director of Financial Aid

400 South Orange Avenue, South Orange, NJ 07079-2680

(973) 761-9350

Somerset Christian College

Zarephath, New Jersey

www.somerset.edu   Federal Code: 036663

4-year private Bible college in small town, affiliated with Pillar of Fire International.

Enrollment: 124 undergrads.

BASIC COSTS (2007-2008)

Tuition and fees: $6,940.

Per-credit charge: $300.

FINANCIAL AID PICTURE

Students with need: Need-based aid available for full-time and part-time students. Work study available nights.

Students without need: This college awards aid only to students with need.

FINANCIAL AID PROCEDURES

Forms required: FAFSA, state aid form.

Dates and Deadlines: No deadline. Applicants notified on a rolling basis starting 1/31.

CONTACT

Marsha Griffin, Financial Aid Administrator

10 College Way, Zarephath, NJ 08890

(800) 234-9305 ext. 1101

Stevens Institute of Technology

Hoboken, New Jersey

www.stevens.edu   Federal Code: 002639

4-year private university and engineering college in small city.

Enrollment: 2,040 undergrads. 498 full-time freshmen.

Selectivity: Admits 50 to 75% of applicants. GED not accepted.

BASIC COSTS (2008-2009)

Tuition and fees: $36,800.

Per-credit charge: $1,164.

Room and board: $11,100.

FINANCIAL AID PICTURE (2007-2008)

Students with need: Out of 441 full-time freshmen who applied for aid, 380 were judged to have need. Of these, 378 received aid, and 70 had their full need met. Average financial aid package met 81% of need; average scholarship/grant was $14,888; average loan was $3,684. Need-based aid available for part-time students.

Students without need: 34 full-time freshmen who did not demonstrate need for aid received scholarships/grants; average award was $11,143. No-need awards available for academics, leadership, music/drama, ROTC.

Scholarships offered: Neupauer Scholarship; full tuition and Edwin A. Stevens Scholarship; $3,000-$20,000; for top candidates in freshman class. Becton Dickinson Scholarship; full tuition; for top student pursuing engineering degree. DeBaun Performing Arts Scholarship; $1,000-$5,000.

Cumulative student debt: 66% of graduating class had student loans; average debt was $35,319.

FINANCIAL AID PROCEDURES

Forms required: FAFSA.

Dates and Deadlines: Priority date 2/15; no closing date. Applicants notified on a rolling basis starting 3/30; must reply by 5/1 or within 2 week(s) of notification.

Transfers: Transfer merit scholarships, Phi Theta Kappa awards.

CONTACT

Maureen Weatherall, Vice President for University Enrollment and Academic Services

One Castle Point on Hudson, Hoboken, NJ 07030

(201) 216-5555

Sussex County Community College

Newton, New Jersey

www.sussex.edu   Federal Code: 025688

2-year public community college in small town.

Enrollment: 2,904 undergrads.

Selectivity: Open admission; but selective for some programs.

BASIC COSTS (2007-2008)

Tuition and fees: $3,030; out-of-state residents $5,490.

Per-credit charge: $82; out-of-district residents $164; out-of-state residents $164.

Additional info: Residents of Wayne, Monroe and Pike County (PA): $123 per credit hour. Tuition/fee waivers available for unemployed or children of unemployed.

FINANCIAL AID PICTURE

Students with need: Need-based aid available for full-time and part-time students.

Students without need: This college awards aid only to students with need.

FINANCIAL AID PROCEDURES

Forms required: FAFSA, institutional form.

Dates and Deadlines: Closing date 6/1. Applicants notified on a rolling basis; must reply within 2 week(s) of notification.

CONTACT

James Pegg, Director, Financial Aid

One College Hill Road, Newton, NJ 07860

(973) 300-2225

Thomas Edison State College

Trenton, New Jersey

www.tesc.edu   Federal Code: 011648

4-year public liberal arts college in small city.

Enrollment: 15,963 undergrads, 100% part-time.

Selectivity: Open admission; but selective for some programs.

BASIC COSTS (2007-2008)

Tuition and fees: $4,300; out-of-state residents $6,150.

Per-credit charge: $125; out-of-state residents $165.

Additional info: Two tuition plans available–either the Comprehensive Tuition Plan: $4,300 per year (state residents and military personnel), $6,150 (out-of-state), which covers up to 36 credits per year for all credit-earning options; or the Enrolled Options Plan: $1,275 per year (state residents and military personnel), $2,300 (out-of-state) and $3,140 (international) for annual enrollment tuition and a technology services fee ($97). Tests, portfolios, courses and other fees at additional cost.

FINANCIAL AID PICTURE (2006-2007)

Students with need: 16% of average financial aid package awarded as scholarships/grants, 84% awarded as loans/jobs.

Additional info: Financial aid applications should be received two months before each new term begins.

FINANCIAL AID PROCEDURES

Forms required: FAFSA, institutional form.

Dates and Deadlines: No deadline. Applicants notified on a rolling basis.

Transfers: No deadline. Applicants notified on a rolling basis; must reply within 4 week(s) of notification.

CONTACT

James Owens, Director of Financial Aid

101 West State Street, Trenton, NJ 08608-1176

(609) 633-6489

Union County College

Cranford, New Jersey
www.ucc.edu   Federal Code: 002643

2-year public community college in large town.
Enrollment: 9,776 undergrads; 48% part-time. 1,915 full-time freshmen.
Selectivity: Open admission; but selective for some programs.

BASIC COSTS (2007-2008)
Tuition and fees: $3,390; out-of-district residents $6,000; out-of-state residents $6,000.
Per-credit charge: $87; out-of-district residents $174; out-of-state residents $174.
Additional info: Tuition/fee waivers available for unemployed or children of unemployed.

FINANCIAL AID PICTURE (2006-2007)
Students with need: 78% of average financial aid package awarded as scholarships/grants, 22% awarded as loans/jobs. Need-based aid available for part-time students. Work study available nights, weekends, and for part-time students.
Students without need: This college awards aid only to students with need.

FINANCIAL AID PROCEDURES
Forms required: FAFSA, institutional form.
Dates and Deadlines: Priority date 5/1; no closing date. Must reply within 2 week(s) of notification.

CONTACT
Elizabeth Riquez, Director of Financial Aid
1033 Springfield Avenue, Cranford, NJ 07016-1599
(908) 709-7018

University of Medicine and Dentistry of New Jersey: School of Health Related Professions

Newark, New Jersey
www.shrp.umdnj.edu

Upper-division public health science college in large city.
Enrollment: 600 undergrads.

BASIC COSTS (2007-2008)
Tuition and fees: $8,160; out-of-state residents $11,926.
Per-credit charge: $254; out-of-state residents $380.

FINANCIAL AID PICTURE
Students with need: Need-based aid available for full-time and part-time students.

FINANCIAL AID PROCEDURES
Forms required: FAFSA, institutional form.
Transfers: Priority date 5/4. Notification of awards on rolling basis; students must reply within 3 weeks of notification.

CONTACT
Cheryl White, Senior Financial Aid Analyst
65 Bergen Street, Newark, NJ 07101-1709
(973) 972-4376

Warren County Community College

Washington, New Jersey
www.warren.edu   Federal Code: 016857

2-year public community college in small town.
Enrollment: 1,743 undergrads.
Selectivity: Open admission; but selective for some programs.

BASIC COSTS (2007-2008)
Tuition and fees: $3,263; out-of-district residents $3,563; out-of-state residents $4,163.
Per-credit charge: $86; out-of-district residents $96; out-of-state residents $116.
Additional info: Tuition/fee waivers available for unemployed or children of unemployed.

FINANCIAL AID PICTURE
Students with need: Need-based aid available for full-time and part-time students. Work study available nights, weekends, and for part-time students.
Students without need: This college awards aid only to students with need.

FINANCIAL AID PROCEDURES
Forms required: FAFSA, institutional form.
Dates and Deadlines: Closing date 7/8. Applicants notified on a rolling basis; must reply within 2 week(s) of notification.
Transfers: No deadline. Applicants notified on a rolling basis.

CONTACT
Rose Lynch, Director of Financial Aid
Route 57 West, Washington, NJ 07882-4343
(908) 835-2456

William Paterson University of New Jersey

Wayne, New Jersey
www.wpunj.edu   Federal Code: 002625

4-year public university and liberal arts college in large town.
Enrollment: 8,760 undergrads, 17% part-time. 1,299 full-time freshmen.
Selectivity: Admits 50 to 75% of applicants.

BASIC COSTS (2007-2008)
Tuition and fees: $9,996; out-of-state residents $16,242.
Per-credit charge: $195; out-of-state residents $399.
Room and board: $10,250.
Additional info: Tuition/fee waivers available for unemployed or children of unemployed.

FINANCIAL AID PICTURE (2007-2008)
Students with need: Out of 1,034 full-time freshmen who applied for aid, 752 were judged to have need. Of these, 722 received aid, and 364 had their full need met. For part-time students, average financial aid package was $8,270.
Students without need: 82 full-time freshmen who did not demonstrate need for aid received scholarships/grants; average award was $8,400. No-need awards available for academics, alumni affiliation, minority status, music/drama.
Scholarships offered: Trustee Scholarship; full tuition for freshmen. Residential Scholarships; full tuition for freshmen and transfer. Distinguished, Academic Excellence, African American and Hispanic Students scholarships; $1,000 annually for 4 years.
Cumulative student debt: 63% of graduating class had student loans; average debt was $19,600.

FINANCIAL AID PROCEDURES

Forms required: FAFSA.

Dates and Deadlines: Priority date 4/1; no closing date. Applicants notified on a rolling basis starting 3/1; must reply within 2 week(s) of notification.

CONTACT

Robert Baumel, Director of Financial Aid
300 Pompton Road, Wayne, NJ 07470
(973) 720-2202

New Mexico

Central New Mexico Community College

Albuquerque, New Mexico
www.cnm.edu   Federal Code: 004742

2-year public community and technical college in very large city.

Enrollment: 18,778 undergrads, 65% part-time. 1,786 full-time freshmen.

Selectivity: Open admission.

BASIC COSTS (2007-2008)

Tuition and fees: $1,074; out-of-district residents $1,314; out-of-state residents $5,377.

Per-credit charge: $41; out-of-district residents $51; out-of-state residents $221.

Additional info: In-district students do not pay tuition for technical courses, only arts and sciences courses.

FINANCIAL AID PICTURE

Students with need: Need-based aid available for full-time and part-time students.

Students without need: No-need awards available for academics, state/district residency.

FINANCIAL AID PROCEDURES

Forms required: FAFSA.

Dates and Deadlines: Priority date 3/1; no closing date. Applicants notified by 5/1.

CONTACT

Lee Carillo, Director of Financial Aid
525 Buena Vista SE, Albuquerque, NM 87106
(505) 224-3090

Clovis Community College

Clovis, New Mexico
www.clovis.edu   Federal Code: 004743

2-year public community and junior college in large town.

Enrollment: 1,724 undergrads, 52% part-time. 134 full-time freshmen.

Selectivity: Open admission; but selective for some programs.

BASIC COSTS (2007-2008)

Tuition and fees: $808; out-of-district residents $856; out-of-state residents $1,552.

Per-credit charge: $49; out-of-district residents $51; out-of-state residents $51.

FINANCIAL AID PICTURE (2006-2007)

Students with need: 67% of average financial aid package awarded as scholarships/grants, 33% awarded as loans/jobs. Need-based aid available for part-time students. Work study available nights, weekends, and for part-time students.

Students without need: No-need awards available for academics, state/district residency.

FINANCIAL AID PROCEDURES

Forms required: FAFSA.

Dates and Deadlines: Priority date 9/1; no closing date. Applicants notified on a rolling basis starting 4/15.

CONTACT

April Chavez, Director of Financial Aid
417 Schepps Boulevard, Clovis, NM 88101-8381
(575) 769-4060

College of Santa Fe

Santa Fe, New Mexico
www.csf.edu   Federal Code: 002649

4-year private liberal arts college in small city.

Enrollment: 657 undergrads, 8% part-time. 166 full-time freshmen.

Selectivity: Admits over 75% of applicants.

BASIC COSTS (2008-2009)

Tuition and fees: $28,558.

Room and board: $8,458.

FINANCIAL AID PICTURE

Students with need: Need-based aid available for full-time and part-time students. Work study available nights, weekends, and for part-time students.

Students without need: No-need awards available for academics, alumni affiliation, art, athletics, leadership, minority status, music/drama.

FINANCIAL AID PROCEDURES

Forms required: FAFSA.

Dates and Deadlines: Priority date 3/15; no closing date. Applicants notified on a rolling basis starting 3/1; must reply by 5/1 or within 2 week(s) of notification.

Transfers: No deadline. Applicants notified on a rolling basis starting 3/1; must reply by 5/1 or within 2 week(s) of notification. No financial aid credited to student accounts until all financial aid transcripts received.

CONTACT

Jill Robertson, Director, Student Financial Services
1600 Saint Michael's Drive, Santa Fe, NM 87505-7634
(505) 473-6454

College of the Southwest

Hobbs, New Mexico
www.csw.edu   Federal Code: 013935

4-year private liberal arts and teachers college in large town.

Enrollment: 386 undergrads, 15% part-time. 64 full-time freshmen.

Selectivity: Open admission; but selective for some programs.

BASIC COSTS (2007-2008)

Tuition and fees: $11,700.

Per-credit charge: $390.

Room and board: $5,400.

FINANCIAL AID PICTURE (2007-2008)

Students with need: Need-based aid available for part-time students.

Students without need: No-need awards available for academics, alumni affiliation, athletics, leadership, music/drama, religious affiliation, state/district residency.

FINANCIAL AID PROCEDURES

Forms required: FAFSA, institutional form.

Dates and Deadlines: Priority date 4/1; closing date 6/1. Applicants notified on a rolling basis starting 4/1; must reply within 2 week(s) of notification.

Transfers: Priority date 3/1; closing date 6/15.

CONTACT

Kerrie Mitchell, Financial Aid Officer
6610 Lovington Highway #506, Hobbs, NM 88240
(505) 392-6563

Dona Ana Branch Community College of New Mexico State University

Las Cruces, New Mexico
www.dacc.nmsu.edu   Federal Code: 002657

2-year public branch campus and community college in small city.
Enrollment: 7,801 undergrads, 67% part-time. 716 full-time freshmen.
Selectivity: Open admission; but selective for some programs.

BASIC COSTS (2008-2009)

Tuition and fees: $1,200; out-of-district residents $1,440; out-of-state residents $3,600.
Per-credit charge: $50; out-of-district residents $60; out-of-state residents $150.
Room and board: $6,824.

FINANCIAL AID PICTURE

Students with need: Need-based aid available for full-time and part-time students.

FINANCIAL AID PROCEDURES

Forms required: FAFSA.
Dates and Deadlines: Priority date 3/1; no closing date. Applicants notified on a rolling basis starting 5/1.

CONTACT

Becky Ordunez, Chief Financial Aid Officer
MSC-3DA, Las Cruces, NM 88003-8001
(505) 527-7510

Eastern New Mexico University

Portales, New Mexico
www.enmu.edu   Federal Code: 002651

4-year public university in large town.
Enrollment: 2,966 undergrads, 20% part-time. 542 full-time freshmen.
Selectivity: Admits 50 to 75% of applicants.

BASIC COSTS (2007-2008)

Tuition and fees: $3,156; out-of-state residents $8,700.
Room and board: $4,888.

FINANCIAL AID PICTURE (2007-2008)

Students with need: Out of 333 full-time freshmen who applied for aid, 333 were judged to have need. Of these, 333 received aid, and 333 had their full need met. Average financial aid package met 35% of need; average scholarship/grant was $3,452; average loan was $3,393. For part-time students, average financial aid package was $6,900.
Students without need: 9 full-time freshmen who did not demonstrate need for aid received scholarships/grants; average award was $2,812. No-need awards available for academics, alumni affiliation, art, athletics, leadership, music/drama, state/district residency.
Scholarships offered: 88 full-time freshmen received athletic scholarships; average amount $2,672.
Cumulative student debt: 1% of graduating class had student loans; average debt was $12,223.

FINANCIAL AID PROCEDURES

Forms required: FAFSA.
Dates and Deadlines: Priority date 3/1; no closing date. Applicants notified by 4/1; must reply within 3 week(s) of notification.

Transfers: Child care grants and non-need-based college work study limited to New Mexico residents.

CONTACT

Joyce Eldridge, Director of Financial Aid
Station Seven, Portales, NM 88130
(575) 562-2194

Eastern New Mexico University: Roswell Campus

Roswell, New Mexico
www.roswell.enmu.edu   Federal Code: 002651

2-year public branch campus and community college in large town.
Enrollment: 2,326 undergrads.
Selectivity: Open admission; but selective for some programs.

BASIC COSTS (2007-2008)

Tuition and fees: $1,124; out-of-district residents $1,164; out-of-state residents $4,540.
Per-credit charge: $41; out-of-district residents $43; out-of-state residents $184.
Room and board: $4,680.

FINANCIAL AID PICTURE (2006-2007)

Students with need: 42% of average financial aid package awarded as scholarships/grants, 58% awarded as loans/jobs. Need-based aid available for part-time students. Work study available nights, weekends, and for part-time students.
Scholarships offered: New Mexico Lottery Scholarship; tuition for New Mexico residents; must attend school full-time the semester following high school graduation or GED and maintain 12 credit hours and 2.5 GPA.

FINANCIAL AID PROCEDURES

Forms required: FAFSA.
Dates and Deadlines: Priority date 4/1; no closing date. Applicants notified on a rolling basis starting 7/1; must reply within 3 week(s) of notification.
Transfers: All students receiving state aid must be New Mexico residents and enrolled in at least 6 credit hours.

CONTACT

Jessie Sjue, Director of Financial Aid
Box 6000, Roswell, NM 88202-6000
(575) 624-7152

Institute of American Indian Arts

Santa Fe, New Mexico
www.iaia.edu   Federal Code: 014152

4-year public visual arts college in small city.
Enrollment: 184 undergrads.

BASIC COSTS (2007-2008)

Tuition and fees: $2,550.
Per-credit charge: $100.
Room and board: $4,536.

FINANCIAL AID PICTURE

Students with need: Need-based aid available for full-time and part-time students. Work study available nights.
Students without need: No-need awards available for academics, art.
Scholarships offered: IAIA merit scholarships; $1,000 for all students with 3.0 GPA, $1,500 for 3.5 GPA, $2,000 for 4.0 GPA.
Additional info: For American Indian and Alaskan natives, financial aid available through Tribe or Native Corporation in which student is enrolled.

FINANCIAL AID PROCEDURES

Forms required: FAFSA, institutional form.

Dates and Deadlines: Priority date 3/15; no closing date. Applicants notified on a rolling basis starting 5/1.

CONTACT

Anna Nolasco, Financial Aid Manager

83 Avan Nu Po Road, Santa Fe, NM 87508-1300

(505) 424-5714

International Institute of the Americas: Albuquerque

Albuquerque, New Mexico

www.iia.edu   Federal Code: 022188

4-year for-profit branch campus college in large city.

Enrollment: 200 undergrads.

Selectivity: Open admission.

BASIC COSTS (2008-2009)

Tuition and fees: $11,400.

Additional info: Tuition and fees may vary by program.

FINANCIAL AID PICTURE

Students with need: Need-based aid available for full-time students.

Students without need: This college awards aid only to students with need.

FINANCIAL AID PROCEDURES

Forms required: FAFSA, institutional form.

Dates and Deadlines: No deadline.

CONTACT

Melba Moore, Director of Financial Aid

4201 Central Avenue NW, Suite J, Albuquerque, NM 87105

(602) 644-7090

Mesalands Community College

Tucumcari, New Mexico

www.mesalands.edu   Federal Code: 032063

2-year public community and technical college in small town.

Enrollment: 313 undergrads, 28% part-time. 115 full-time freshmen.

Selectivity: Open admission.

BASIC COSTS (2007-2008)

Tuition and fees: $1,475; out-of-state residents $2,387.

Per-credit charge: $39; out-of-state residents $69.

FINANCIAL AID PICTURE

Students with need: Need-based aid available for full-time and part-time students. Work study available nights.

Students without need: No-need awards available for academics, athletics, leadership, minority status, music/drama, state/district residency.

FINANCIAL AID PROCEDURES

Forms required: FAFSA.

Dates and Deadlines: Priority date 4/1; no closing date. Applicants notified on a rolling basis starting 4/1; must reply within 3 week(s) of notification.

CONTACT

Amanda Hammer, Director of Financial Aid

911 South Tenth Street, Tucumcari, NM 88401

(575) 461-4413 ext. 136

New Mexico Highlands University

Las Vegas, New Mexico

www.nmhu.edu   Federal Code: 002653

4-year public university in large town.

Enrollment: 1,882 undergrads, 24% part-time. 354 full-time freshmen.

Selectivity: Open admission.

BASIC COSTS (2007-2008)

Tuition and fees: $2,564; out-of-state residents $3,656.

Room and board: $4,476.

FINANCIAL AID PICTURE

Students with need: Need-based aid available for full-time and part-time students. Work study available nights, weekends, and for part-time students.

Students without need: No-need awards available for academics, athletics, leadership, minority status, music/drama, state/district residency.

Additional info: Work study funds available on no-need basis to state residents.

FINANCIAL AID PROCEDURES

Forms required: FAFSA, institutional form.

Dates and Deadlines: Priority date 3/1; closing date 5/1. Applicants notified on a rolling basis starting 5/15; must reply within 2 week(s) of notification.

Transfers: Closing date 6/30.

CONTACT

Eileen Sedillo, Director of Financial Aid

Box 9000, Las Vegas, NM 87701

(505) 454-3318

New Mexico Institute of Mining and Technology

Socorro, New Mexico

www.nmt.edu   Federal Code: 002654

4-year public engineering and liberal arts college in small town.

Enrollment: 1,138 undergrads, 4% part-time. 240 full-time freshmen.

Selectivity: Admits 50 to 75% of applicants.

BASIC COSTS (2007-2008)

Tuition and fees: $4,105; out-of-state residents $11,761.

Per-credit charge: $148; out-of-state residents $467.

Room and board: $5,300.

FINANCIAL AID PICTURE

Students with need: Need-based aid available for full-time and part-time students.

Students without need: No-need awards available for academics, alumni affiliation, minority status, state/district residency.

Additional info: Campus research projects offer student employment based on merit.

FINANCIAL AID PROCEDURES

Forms required: FAFSA, institutional form.

Dates and Deadlines: Priority date 6/1; no closing date. Applicants notified on a rolling basis starting 4/1; must reply within 2 week(s) of notification.

Transfers: Priority date 3/1; no deadline. Applicants notified on a rolling basis starting 4/1; must reply within 2 week(s) of notification. Financial aid transcripts required from all colleges attended.

CONTACT

Annette Kaus, Director of Financial Aid

801 Leroy Place, Socorro, NM 87801

(575) 835-5333

New Mexico Junior College

Hobbs, New Mexico
www.nmjc.edu   Federal Code: 002655

2-year public community and technical college in large town.
Enrollment: 3,066 undergrads.
Selectivity: Open admission; but selective for some programs.

BASIC COSTS (2007-2008)
Tuition and fees: $1,122; out-of-district residents $1,554; out-of-state residents $1,674.
Per-credit charge: $28; out-of-district residents $46; out-of-state residents $51.
Room and board: $3,750.

FINANCIAL AID PICTURE
Students with need: Need-based aid available for full-time and part-time students. Work study available nights, weekends, and for part-time students.
Students without need: No-need awards available for academics, art, athletics, leadership, music/drama.

FINANCIAL AID PROCEDURES
Forms required: FAFSA.
Dates and Deadlines: Priority date 6/1; no closing date. Applicants notified on a rolling basis; must reply within 2 week(s) of notification.

CONTACT
Laura Marquez, Director of Financial Aid
5317 Lovington Highway, Hobbs, NM 88240
(575) 392-4510

New Mexico Military Institute

Roswell, New Mexico
www.nmmi.edu   Federal Code: 002656

2-year public junior and military college in large town.
Enrollment: 466 undergrads.
Selectivity: Admits 50 to 75% of applicants.

BASIC COSTS (2008-2009)
Tuition and fees: $4,871; out-of-state residents $8,421.
Room and board: $3,830.

FINANCIAL AID PICTURE
Students with need: Need-based aid available for full-time students.
Students without need: No-need awards available for academics, alumni affiliation, athletics, ROTC, state/district residency.

FINANCIAL AID PROCEDURES
Forms required: FAFSA.
Dates and Deadlines: Priority date 4/1; no closing date. Applicants notified on a rolling basis starting 5/1; must reply within 3 week(s) of notification.
Transfers: New Mexico Scholars Program, New Mexico Success Scholarship programs available.

CONTACT
Sonya Rodriguez, Financial Aid Director
101 West College Boulevard, Roswell, NM 88201-5173
(505) 624-8066

New Mexico State University

Las Cruces, New Mexico
www.nmsu.edu   Federal Code: 002657

4-year public university in small city.
Enrollment: 13,056 undergrads, 13% part-time. 2,162 full-time freshmen.

Selectivity: Admits over 75% of applicants.

BASIC COSTS (2007-2008)
Tuition and fees: $4,452; out-of-state residents $14,180.
Per-credit charge: $185; out-of-state residents $591.
Room and board: $5,766.

FINANCIAL AID PICTURE (2007-2008)
Students with need: Out of 1,651 full-time freshmen who applied for aid, 1,256 were judged to have need. Of these, 1,214 received aid, and 130 had their full need met. Average financial aid package met 64% of need; average scholarship/grant was $5,458; average loan was $3,518. For part-time students, average financial aid package was $6,091.
Students without need: 678 full-time freshmen who did not demonstrate need for aid received scholarships/grants; average award was $3,667. No-need awards available for academics, alumni affiliation, athletics, leadership, minority status, state/district residency.
Scholarships offered: 35 full-time freshmen received athletic scholarships; average amount $7,714.

FINANCIAL AID PROCEDURES
Forms required: FAFSA, institutional form.
Dates and Deadlines: No deadline. Applicants notified on a rolling basis starting 3/1.

CONTACT
Tyler Pruett, Director of Financial Aid
Box 30001, MSC 3A, Las Cruces, NM 88003-8001
(575) 646-4105

New Mexico State University at Alamogordo

Alamogordo, New Mexico
alamo.nmsu.edu/   Federal Code: 002658

2-year public branch campus college in large town.
Enrollment: 2,017 undergrads.
Selectivity: Open admission; but selective for some programs.

BASIC COSTS (2007-2008)
Tuition and fees: $1,344; out-of-district residents $1,512; out-of-state residents $4,008.
Per-credit charge: $54; out-of-district residents $61; out-of-state residents $165.

FINANCIAL AID PICTURE
Students with need: Need-based aid available for full-time and part-time students.
Students without need: No-need awards available for academics, state/district residency.

FINANCIAL AID PROCEDURES
Forms required: FAFSA, institutional form.
Dates and Deadlines: Priority date 3/1; no closing date. Applicants notified by 6/1.

CONTACT
Sharon Fischer, Financial Aid Coordinator
2400 North Scenic Drive, Alamogordo, NM 88310
(505) 439-3600

Northern New Mexico College

Espanola, New Mexico
www.nnmc.edu   Federal Code: 005286

2-year public community and teachers college in small town.
Enrollment: 692 undergrads.

Selectivity: Open admission; but selective for some programs and for out-of-state students.

BASIC COSTS (2007-2008)

Tuition and fees: $1,030; out-of-state residents $2,206.
Per-credit charge: $36; out-of-state residents $85.
Room and board: $3,028.
Additional info: Upper division courses $85 per credit hour for in-state students, $360 per credit hour for out-of-state students.

FINANCIAL AID PICTURE

Students with need: Need-based aid available for full-time students.
Students without need: This college awards aid only to students with need.

FINANCIAL AID PROCEDURES

Forms required: FAFSA.
Dates and Deadlines: Priority date 3/1; no closing date. Applicants notified on a rolling basis starting 6/1; must reply within 2 week(s) of notification.

CONTACT

Alfredo Montoya, Director of Financial Aid
921 Paseo de Onate, Espanola, NM 87532
(505) 747-2128 ext. 128

St. John's College

Santa Fe, New Mexico
www.stjohnscollege.edu

Federal Code: 002093
CSS Code: 4737

4-year private liberal arts college in small city.
Enrollment: 436 undergrads. 117 full-time freshmen.
Selectivity: Admits over 75% of applicants.

BASIC COSTS (2008-2009)

Tuition and fees: $39,154.
Room and board: $9,284.

FINANCIAL AID PICTURE (2006-2007)

Students with need: Out of 73 full-time freshmen who applied for aid, 66 were judged to have need. Of these, 66 received aid, and 62 had their full need met. Average financial aid package met 93% of need; average scholarship/grant was $18,888; average loan was $3,225. For part-time students, average financial aid package was $18,692.
Cumulative student debt: 68% of graduating class had student loans; average debt was $26,263.
Additional info: 100% of need met for most of those qualified to receive aid. Families receive individual attention in determining need fairly. Independent students must submit parental data. Financial aid information also required of noncustodial parent in cases of separation or divorce. Aid awarded first-come, first-served until institutional money exhausted. Apply early by February 15; after April 1 aid difficult to obtain.

FINANCIAL AID PROCEDURES

Forms required: FAFSA, CSS PROFILE.
Dates and Deadlines: Priority date 2/15; no closing date. Applicants notified on a rolling basis starting 12/1; must reply by 5/1.

CONTACT

Michael Rodriguez, Director of Financial Aid
1160 Camino Cruz Blanca, Santa Fe, NM 87505-4599
(505) 984-6058

San Juan College

Farmington, New Mexico
www.sanjuancollege.edu

Federal Code: 002660

2-year public community college in large town.
Enrollment: 4,773 undergrads, 57% part-time. 578 full-time freshmen.
Selectivity: Open admission.

BASIC COSTS (2007-2008)

Tuition and fees: $720; out-of-state residents $960.
Per-credit charge: $30; out-of-state residents $40.

FINANCIAL AID PICTURE (2006-2007)

Students with need: 55% of average financial aid package awarded as scholarships/grants, 45% awarded as loans/jobs. Need-based aid available for part-time students. Work study available nights, weekends, and for part-time students.
Students without need: No-need awards available for academics, state/district residency.

FINANCIAL AID PROCEDURES

Forms required: FAFSA.
Dates and Deadlines: No deadline. Applicants notified on a rolling basis starting 7/1; must reply within 2 week(s) of notification.

CONTACT

Jerry McKeen, Director for Financial Aid
4601 College Boulevard, Farmington, NM 87402-4699
(505) 566-3323

Santa Fe Community College

Santa Fe, New Mexico
www.sfccnm.edu

Federal Code: 016065

2-year public community college in small city.
Enrollment: 1,974 undergrads.
Selectivity: Open admission.

BASIC COSTS (2007-2008)

Tuition and fees: $1,083; out-of-district residents $1,404; out-of-state residents $2,439.
Per-credit charge: $32; out-of-district residents $43; out-of-state residents $78.

FINANCIAL AID PICTURE (2006-2007)

Students with need: 75% of average financial aid package awarded as scholarships/grants, 25% awarded as loans/jobs. Need-based aid available for part-time students. Work study available nights, weekends, and for part-time students.
Students without need: No-need awards available for academics, state/district residency.

FINANCIAL AID PROCEDURES

Forms required: FAFSA, institutional form.
Dates and Deadlines: Priority date 5/1; no closing date. Applicants notified on a rolling basis starting 7/15; must reply within 4 week(s) of notification.

CONTACT

Scott Whitaker, Financial Aid Director
6401 Richards Avenue, Santa Fe, NM 87508-4887
(505) 428-1268

Southwestern Indian Polytechnic Institute

Albuquerque, New Mexico
www.sipi.bia.edu   Federal Code: 011185

2-year public community and technical college in large city.
Enrollment: 574 undergrads, 18% part-time. 203 full-time freshmen.
Selectivity: Open admission.

BASIC COSTS (2007-2008)
Additional info: Required fees: full-time Lodge student $280, full-time commuter $225, part-time $150. Tuition/fee waivers available for minority students.

FINANCIAL AID PICTURE
Students with need: Need-based aid available for full-time and part-time students. Work study available nights, weekends, and for part-time students.
Students without need: No-need awards available for academics, leadership, minority status.
Additional info: Students with valid membership in recognized Indian tribe attend tuition-free.

FINANCIAL AID PROCEDURES
Forms required: FAFSA.
Dates and Deadlines: Closing date 3/1. Applicants notified on a rolling basis starting 9/30.
Transfers: No deadline.

CONTACT
Marilyn Pargas, Financial Aid Specialist
9169 Coors Road Northwest, Albuquerque, NM 87184
(505) 346-2344

University of New Mexico

Albuquerque, New Mexico
www.unm.edu   Federal Code: 002663

4-year public university in very large city.
Enrollment: 18,259 undergrads.

BASIC COSTS (2007-2008)
Tuition and fees: $4,571; out-of-state residents $14,942.
Per-credit charge: $190; out-of-state residents $623.
Room and board: $7,020.

FINANCIAL AID PICTURE
Students with need: Need-based aid available for full-time and part-time students. Work study available nights, weekends, and for part-time students.
Students without need: No-need awards available for academics, alumni affiliation, art, athletics, job skills, leadership, minority status, music/drama, religious affiliation, ROTC, state/district residency.
Scholarships offered: Bridge to Success Scholarship: for first semester only while awaiting other scholarship aid; requires New Mexico residency, full-time status in degree-granting program, and acceptable GED test score and/or requisite high school GPA per sponsor.
Additional info: Regent scholarship program has priority date of 12/1. UNM scholars program has deadline of 2/1.

FINANCIAL AID PROCEDURES
Forms required: FAFSA.
Dates and Deadlines: Priority date 3/1; no closing date. Applicants notified on a rolling basis starting 4/15.
Transfers: Closing date 5/30.

CONTACT
Ronald Martinez, Director of Financial Aid
Office of Admissions, Albuquerque, NM 87196-4895
(505) 277-2041

Western New Mexico University

Silver City, New Mexico
www.wnmu.edu   Federal Code: 002664

4-year public university in large town.
Enrollment: 1,747 undergrads, 22% part-time. 209 full-time freshmen.
Selectivity: Open admission.

BASIC COSTS (2007-2008)
Tuition and fees: $3,218; out-of-state residents $11,887.
Room and board: $5,145.

FINANCIAL AID PICTURE (2006-2007)
Students with need: Out of 155 full-time freshmen who applied for aid, 155 were judged to have need. Of these, 155 received aid, and 17 had their full need met. Average financial aid package met 61% of need; average scholarship/grant was $3,767; average loan was $2,307. For part-time students, average financial aid package was $7,890.
Students without need: 19 full-time freshmen who did not demonstrate need for aid received scholarships/grants; average award was $1,248. No-need awards available for academics, athletics, state/district residency.
Scholarships offered: 24 full-time freshmen received athletic scholarships; average amount $2,625.

FINANCIAL AID PROCEDURES
Forms required: FAFSA, institutional form.
Dates and Deadlines: Closing date 4/1. Applicants notified on a rolling basis starting 4/1; must reply within 2 week(s) of notification.

CONTACT
Charles Kelly, Director of Financial Aid
Castorena 106, Silver City, NM 88062
(505) 538-6173

New York

Adelphi University

Garden City, New York
www.adelphi.edu   Federal Code: 002666

4-year private university in large town.
Enrollment: 4,973 undergrads, 16% part-time. 826 full-time freshmen.
Selectivity: Admits 50 to 75% of applicants.

BASIC COSTS (2007-2008)
Tuition and fees: $23,000.
Room and board: $9,900.
Additional info: Tuition, fees, and per-credit-hour charges for upper-division nursing, social work, and education programs are slightly higher.

FINANCIAL AID PICTURE (2006-2007)
Students with need: Out of 713 full-time freshmen who applied for aid, 579 were judged to have need. Of these, 567 received aid, and 2 had their full need met. Average financial aid package met 33% of need; average scholarship/grant was $4,965; average loan was $3,449. Need-based aid available for part-time students.
Students without need: 38 full-time freshmen who did not demonstrate need for aid received scholarships/grants; average award was $8,505. No-

need awards available for academics, alumni affiliation, art, athletics, job skills, leadership, minority status, music/drama, religious affiliation.
Scholarships offered: Merit: Trustee Scholarship: up to full tuition; top 10% of high school class, 1350 SAT, 3.7 GPA required; 12 available. Presidential Scholarship: $12,500 to $14,500; top 10% of high school class, 1350 SAT, 3.5 GPA required; 25 available. Provost Scholarship: $10,000 to $12,000; top 15% of high school class, 1250 SAT, 3.3 GPA required; 55 available. Dean's Scholarship: $4,000 to $9,500; top 25% of high school class, 1000 SAT, 3.0 GPA required; 252 available. SAT scores listed exclusive of Writing. **Athletic:** 20 full-time freshmen received athletic scholarships; average amount $10,535.

FINANCIAL AID PROCEDURES
Forms required: FAFSA, state aid form.
Dates and Deadlines: Priority date 3/15; no closing date. Applicants notified on a rolling basis starting 2/15.
Transfers: No deadline.

CONTACT
Sheryl Mihopulos, Director of Financial Aid
One South Avenue, Levermore 110, Garden City, NY 11530-0701
(516) 877-3080

Adirondack Community College
Queensbury, New York
www.sunyacc.edu   Federal Code: 002860

2-year public community college in large town.
Enrollment: 2,884 undergrads.
Selectivity: Open admission; but selective for some programs.

BASIC COSTS (2007-2008)
Tuition and fees: $3,357; out-of-state residents $6,487.
Per-credit charge: $131; out-of-state residents $262.

FINANCIAL AID PICTURE
Students with need: Need-based aid available for full-time and part-time students.
Students without need: This college awards aid only to students with need.
Scholarships offered: Academic Excellence Scholarship: $750 per semester for up to 4 semesters; for local high school graduates who are 1st or 2nd in class, GPA 3.5. Hill Scholarship: $500 per semester for 4 semesters; for Fort Edward High School graduate.

FINANCIAL AID PROCEDURES
Forms required: FAFSA, state aid form, institutional form.
Dates and Deadlines: Priority date 4/15; no closing date. Applicants notified on a rolling basis starting 5/1.

CONTACT
Maureen Reilly, Director of Financial Aid
640 Bay Road, Queensbury, NY 12804
(518) 743-2223

Albany College of Pharmacy
Albany, New York
www.acp.edu   Federal Code: 002885

4-year private health science and pharmacy college in small city.
Enrollment: 1,015 undergrads. 257 full-time freshmen.
Selectivity: Admits 50 to 75% of applicants.

BASIC COSTS (2008-2009)
Tuition and fees: $24,450.
Per-credit charge: $735.

Room and board: $7,600.
Additional info: Fees include mandatory laptop purchase.

FINANCIAL AID PICTURE (2007-2008)
Students with need: Out of 232 full-time freshmen who applied for aid, 190 were judged to have need. Of these, 189 received aid, and 33 had their full need met. Average financial aid package met 51.25% of need; average scholarship/grant was $7,982; average loan was $3,345. Need-based aid available for part-time students.
Students without need: 48 full-time freshmen who did not demonstrate need for aid received scholarships/grants; average award was $13,581. No-need awards available for academics.
Cumulative student debt: 92% of graduating class had student loans; average debt was $20,010.

FINANCIAL AID PROCEDURES
Forms required: FAFSA.
Dates and Deadlines: Priority date 2/1; closing date 3/1. Applicants notified on a rolling basis starting 3/25; must reply within 2 week(s) of notification.

CONTACT
Tiffany Gutierrez, Vice President, Enrollment Management
106 New Scotland Avenue, Albany, NY 12208-3492
(518) 694-7256

Alfred University
Alfred, New York
www.alfred.edu   Federal Code: 002668

4-year private university in rural community.
Enrollment: 1,955 undergrads. 489 full-time freshmen.
Selectivity: Admits 50 to 75% of applicants.

BASIC COSTS (2008-2009)
Tuition and fees: $24,278.
Per-credit charge: $760.
Room and board: $10,796.
Additional info: Tuition info provided is for students enrolling in the College of Business or the College of Liberal Arts and Sciences. Costs for students enrolling in the School of Engineering vary by program and/or residency. Costs for students enrolling in the School of Art and Design vary by residency.

FINANCIAL AID PICTURE (2006-2007)
Students with need: Out of 428 full-time freshmen who applied for aid, 365 were judged to have need. Of these, 364 received aid, and 57 had their full need met. Average financial aid package met 89% of need; average scholarship/grant was $15,390; average loan was $4,243. For part-time students, average financial aid package was $1,895.
Students without need: 39 full-time freshmen who did not demonstrate need for aid received scholarships/grants; average award was $7,862. No-need awards available for academics, art, leadership, music/drama.
Cumulative student debt: 83% of graduating class had student loans; average debt was $23,292.

FINANCIAL AID PROCEDURES
Forms required: FAFSA, state aid form, institutional form.
Dates and Deadlines: Priority date 2/1; closing date 3/15. Applicants notified on a rolling basis starting 2/15; must reply by 5/1 or within 2 week(s) of notification.
Transfers: Closing date 5/15. Applicants notified on a rolling basis starting 2/15; must reply by 5/1 or within 2 week(s) of notification.

CONTACT
Earl Pierce, Director of Student Financial Aid
Alumni Hall, Alfred, NY 14802-1205
(607) 871-2159

American Academy McAllister Institute of Funeral Service
New York, New York
www.funeraleducation.org   Federal Code: 010813

2-year private school of mortuary science in very large city.
Enrollment: 178 undergrads.
Selectivity: Open admission.

BASIC COSTS (2007-2008)
Tuition and fees: $11,370.
Additional info: Tuition at time of enrollment locked for 2 years.

FINANCIAL AID PICTURE
Students with need: Need-based aid available for full-time students.
Students without need: This college awards aid only to students with need.

FINANCIAL AID PROCEDURES
Forms required: FAFSA, state aid form.
Dates and Deadlines: Applicants notified on a rolling basis starting 7/1; must reply by 9/1 or within 3 week(s) of notification.
Transfers: Priority date 6/1.

CONTACT
Jaway Tso, Financial Aid Administrator
619 West 54th Street, New York, NY 10019-3602
(212) 220-4275

American Academy of Dramatic Arts
New York, New York
www.aada.org   Federal Code: 007465

2-year private junior and performing arts college in very large city.
Enrollment: 228 undergrads. 59 full-time freshmen.
Selectivity: Admits less than 50% of applicants.

BASIC COSTS (2008-2009)
Tuition and fees: $20,000.

FINANCIAL AID PICTURE (2006-2007)
Students with need: Out of 38 full-time freshmen who applied for aid, 36 were judged to have need. Of these, 31 received aid. Average financial aid package met 62% of need; average scholarship/grant was $2,000; average loan was $2,675.
Students without need: This college awards aid only to students with need.
Additional info: Need-based incentive grants of $200-$500 for first-year students available. Merit awards of $500-$1,500. Scholarships of $500-$3,000 available for second year. Scholarships of $500-$5,000 available for post-degree third year.

FINANCIAL AID PROCEDURES
Forms required: FAFSA, institutional form.
Dates and Deadlines: No deadline. Applicants notified on a rolling basis.

CONTACT
Roberto Lopez, Financial Aid Director
120 Madison Avenue, New York, NY 10016
(212) 686-9244 ext. 342

ASA Institute of Business and Computer Technology
Brooklyn, New York
www.asa.edu   Federal Code: 030955

2-year for-profit career college in very large city.
Enrollment: 2,958 undergrads, 4% part-time. 890 full-time freshmen.
Selectivity: Admits over 75% of applicants.

BASIC COSTS (2008-2009)
Tuition and fees: $11,499.
Per-credit charge: $470.

FINANCIAL AID PICTURE (2006-2007)
Students with need: 59% of average financial aid package awarded as scholarships/grants, 41% awarded as loans/jobs. Need-based aid available for part-time students. Work study available nights, weekends, and for part-time students.
Students without need: No-need awards available for academics, alumni affiliation, leadership, state/district residency.

FINANCIAL AID PROCEDURES
Forms required: FAFSA, state aid form.
Dates and Deadlines: No deadline. Applicants notified on a rolling basis starting 7/6; must reply by 10/6.
Transfers: No deadline. Applicants notified on a rolling basis starting 7/6; must reply by 10/6.

CONTACT
Victoria Shtamler, Assistant Vice President of Financial Aid
151 Lawrence Street, Brooklyn, NY 11201
(718) 532-1431

Bard College
Annandale-on-Hudson, New York   Federal Code: 002671
www.bard.edu   CSS Code: 2037

4-year private liberal arts college in small town, affiliated with Episcopal Church.
Enrollment: 1,737 undergrads, 3% part-time. 491 full-time freshmen.
Selectivity: Admits less than 50% of applicants.

BASIC COSTS (2008-2009)
Tuition and fees: $38,374.
Per-credit charge: $1,176.
Room and board: $10,866.
Additional info: Fees for first-year students only: $230 security deposit and ID card; $650 for meals for Language and Thinking workshop.

FINANCIAL AID PICTURE (2007-2008)
Students with need: Out of 322 full-time freshmen who applied for aid, 290 were judged to have need. Of these, 290 received aid, and 174 had their full need met. Average financial aid package met 89% of need; average scholarship/grant was $25,971; average loan was $3,721. For part-time students, average financial aid package was $12,635.
Students without need: 6 full-time freshmen who did not demonstrate need for aid received scholarships/grants; average award was $15,797. No-need awards available for academics.
Scholarships offered: Distinguished Scientist Scholarship: full tuition; for students intending to major in math or sciences; 10-20 awarded annually.
Cumulative student debt: 65% of graduating class had student loans; average debt was $19,507.
Additional info: Excellence and Equal Cost Program for students who graduate in top 10 of public high school class lowers fees to levels equivalent to those at home state university or college.

FINANCIAL AID PROCEDURES

Forms required: FAFSA, CSS PROFILE, state aid form.
Dates and Deadlines: Priority date 2/1; closing date 2/15. Applicants notified by 4/1; must reply by 5/1.
Transfers: Applicants notified by 4/1; must reply by 5/1.

CONTACT

Denise Ackerman, Director of Financial Aid
30 Campus Road, Annandale-on-Hudson, NY 12504-5000
(845) 758-7526

Barnard College
New York, New York
www.barnard.edu
Federal Code: 002708
CSS Code: 2038

4-year private liberal arts college for women in very large city.
Enrollment: 2,346 undergrads, 2% part-time. 559 full-time freshmen.
Selectivity: Admits less than 50% of applicants.

BASIC COSTS (2008-2009)

Tuition and fees: $37,538.
Per-credit charge: $1,200.
Room and board: $11,926.

FINANCIAL AID PICTURE (2007-2008)

Students with need: Out of 312 full-time freshmen who applied for aid, 248 were judged to have need. Of these, 248 received aid, and 248 had their full need met. Average financial aid package met 100% of need; average scholarship/grant was $29,509; average loan was $3,052. Need-based aid available for part-time students.
Students without need: This college awards aid only to students with need.
Cumulative student debt: 44% of graduating class had student loans; average debt was $17,630.

FINANCIAL AID PROCEDURES

Forms required: FAFSA, CSS PROFILE, state aid form, institutional form.
Dates and Deadlines: Closing date 2/1. Applicants notified by 3/31; must reply by 5/1.
Transfers: Closing date 4/1. Transfers admitted in the spring are not eligible for institutional grant aid.

CONTACT

Gregory Brown, Vice President for Finance & Planning
3009 Broadway, New York, NY 10027-6598
(212) 854-2154

Berkeley College
White Plains, New York
www.berkeleycollege.edu
Federal Code: 007421

4-year for-profit business college in small city.
Enrollment: 704 undergrads, 7% part-time. 148 full-time freshmen.

BASIC COSTS (2008-2009)

Tuition and fees: $19,050.
Per-credit charge: $435.
Room and board: $9,000.
Additional info: Part-time students pay $75 administrative fee per quarter. Tuition at time of enrollment locked for 4 years.

FINANCIAL AID PICTURE

Students with need: Need-based aid available for full-time students.
Students without need: No-need awards available for academics, alumni affiliation.

Additional info: Alumni scholarship examination given in November and December. Full and partial scholarships awarded.

FINANCIAL AID PROCEDURES

Forms required: FAFSA, state aid form.
Dates and Deadlines: No deadline. Applicants notified on a rolling basis starting 3/1; must reply within 6 week(s) of notification.

CONTACT

David Seltzer, Director, Financial Aid
99 Church Street, White Plains, NY 10601
(914) 694-1122

Berkeley College of New York City
New York, New York
www.berkeleycollege.edu
Federal Code: 008556

4-year for-profit business college in very large city.
Enrollment: 2,595 undergrads, 10% part-time. 345 full-time freshmen.
Selectivity: Admits 50 to 75% of applicants.

BASIC COSTS (2008-2009)

Tuition and fees: $19,050.
Per-credit charge: $435.
Additional info: Part-time students pay $75 administrative fee per quarter. Tuition at time of enrollment locked for 4 years.

FINANCIAL AID PICTURE

Students with need: Need-based aid available for full-time students.
Students without need: No-need awards available for academics, alumni affiliation.
Additional info: Alumni scholarship examination given in November and December. Full and partial scholarships awarded.

FINANCIAL AID PROCEDURES

Forms required: FAFSA.
Dates and Deadlines: No deadline. Applicants notified on a rolling basis starting 3/1; must reply within 6 week(s) of notification.
Transfers: New York State TAP Grant eligibility may be affected.

CONTACT

Lori Farrior, Director, Financial Aid
3 East 43rd Street, New York, NY 10017
(212) 986-4343

Broome Community College
Binghamton, New York
www.sunybroome.edu
Federal Code: 002862

2-year public community college in small city.
Enrollment: 5,336 undergrads, 23% part-time. 1,338 full-time freshmen.
Selectivity: Open admission; but selective for some programs.

BASIC COSTS (2007-2008)

Tuition and fees: $3,363; out-of-state residents $6,421.
Per-credit charge: $128; out-of-state residents $256.

FINANCIAL AID PICTURE

Students with need: Need-based aid available for full-time and part-time students. Work study available nights.

FINANCIAL AID PROCEDURES

Forms required: FAFSA.
Dates and Deadlines: Priority date 3/1; no closing date. Applicants notified on a rolling basis starting 3/15; must reply within 2 week(s) of notification.

CONTACT

Doug Lukasik, Director of Financial Aid
Box 1017, Binghamton, NY 13902
(607) 778-5028

Bryant & Stratton College: Albany

Albany, New York
www.bryantstratton.edu   Federal Code: 004749

2-year for-profit business college in small city.
Enrollment: 617 undergrads, 32% part-time. 124 full-time freshmen.

BASIC COSTS (2008-2009)

Tuition and fees: $13,740.
Additional info: Tuition may vary depending on program.

FINANCIAL AID PICTURE (2006-2007)

Students with need: 45% of average financial aid package awarded as scholarships/grants, 55% awarded as loans/jobs. Need-based aid available for part-time students. Work study available nights, weekends, and for part-time students.
Students without need: This college awards aid only to students with need.

FINANCIAL AID PROCEDURES

Forms required: FAFSA, state aid form.
Dates and Deadlines: No deadline. Applicants notified on a rolling basis.

CONTACT

Judy Harris, Business Office Director
1259 Central Avenue, Albany, NY 12205
(518) 437-1802

Bryant & Stratton College: Buffalo

Buffalo, New York
www.bryantstratton.edu   Federal Code: 002678

2-year for-profit business and career college in large city.
Enrollment: 614 undergrads, 32% part-time. 166 full-time freshmen.
Selectivity: Open admission.

BASIC COSTS (2008-2009)

Tuition and fees: $13,740.
Per-credit charge: $458.
Additional info: IT, BBA, medical assisting, medical administrative assistant, paralegal program cost: $14,430 per year, $481 per credit hour. $100 graduation fee in final semester.

FINANCIAL AID PICTURE (2007-2008)

Students with need: 36% of average financial aid package awarded as scholarships/grants, 64% awarded as loans/jobs.

FINANCIAL AID PROCEDURES

Dates and Deadlines: No deadline. Applicants notified on a rolling basis.

CONTACT

Jim Ayers, Financial Aid Supervisor
465 Main Street, Suite 400, Buffalo, NY 14203
(716) 884-9120

Bryant & Stratton College: Syracuse

Syracuse, New York
www.bryantstratton.edu   Federal Code: 008276

2-year for-profit business college in small city.
Enrollment: 809 undergrads.

Selectivity: Open admission.

BASIC COSTS (2007-2008)

Tuition and fees: $13,080.
Per-credit charge: $436.

FINANCIAL AID PICTURE (2007-2008)

Students with need: Work study available nights, weekends, and for part-time students.
Students without need: This college awards aid only to students with need.

FINANCIAL AID PROCEDURES

Forms required: FAFSA.
Dates and Deadlines: No deadline. Applicants notified on a rolling basis starting 10/1.
Transfers: Priority date 5/1.

CONTACT

Tami Eiklor, Financial Aid Director
953 James Street, Syracuse, NY 13203
(315) 472-6603

Canisius College

Buffalo, New York
www.canisius.edu   Federal Code: 002681

4-year private liberal arts and teachers college in large city, affiliated with Roman Catholic Church.
Enrollment: 3,301 undergrads, 3% part-time. 846 full-time freshmen.
Selectivity: Admits over 75% of applicants.

BASIC COSTS (2007-2008)

Tuition and fees: $26,427.
Per-credit charge: $724.
Room and board: $9,770.
Additional info: Tuition/fee waivers available for minority students.

FINANCIAL AID PICTURE (2007-2008)

Students with need: Out of 771 full-time freshmen who applied for aid, 710 were judged to have need. Of these, 710 received aid, and 253 had their full need met. Average financial aid package met 89% of need; average scholarship/grant was $18,196; average loan was $3,501. Need-based aid available for part-time students.
Students without need: 126 full-time freshmen who did not demonstrate need for aid received scholarships/grants; average award was $12,624. No-need awards available for academics, alumni affiliation, art, athletics, job skills, music/drama, religious affiliation, ROTC.
Scholarships offered: *Merit:* Presidential Scholarships: $20,000 per year for four years. Ignatian Scholarships: $15,000 per year for four years; applicants who apply by Nov. 15 given priority consideration. Trustee's Scholarship: $12,000 per year for on-campus student, $10,000 per year for off-campus student; based on high school GPA, test scores. Dean's Scholarship: $10,000 per year for on-campus student, $8,000 per year for off-campus student; based on high school GPA, test scores. Benefactor's Scholarship: $7,000 per year for on-campus student, $5,000 per year for off-campus student; based on high school GPA, test scores. International Scholarships: international students, including Canadian students, may be eligible for academic scholarships based on academic records. *Athletic:* 18 full-time freshmen received athletic scholarships; average amount $23,114.
Cumulative student debt: 73% of graduating class had student loans; average debt was $29,512.

FINANCIAL AID PROCEDURES

Forms required: FAFSA, state aid form.
Dates and Deadlines: Priority date 2/15; no closing date. Applicants notified on a rolling basis starting 3/1; must reply within 2 week(s) of notification.

CONTACT

Curtis Gaume, Director of Student Financial Aid
2001 Main Street, Buffalo, NY 14208-1098
(800) 541-6348

Cayuga County Community College

Auburn, New York
www.cayuga-cc.edu   Federal Code: 002861

2-year public community college in large town.
Enrollment: 2,704 undergrads, 24% part-time. 487 full-time freshmen.
Selectivity: Open admission; but selective for some programs.

BASIC COSTS (2007-2008)

Tuition and fees: $3,716; out-of-state residents $6,970.
Per-credit charge: $120; out-of-state residents $240.

FINANCIAL AID PICTURE (2006-2007)

Students with need: Out of 438 full-time freshmen who applied for aid, 413 were judged to have need. Of these, 413 received aid. Need-based aid available for part-time students.
Students without need: This college awards aid only to students with need.

FINANCIAL AID PROCEDURES

Forms required: FAFSA, state aid form.
Dates and Deadlines: Closing date 5/1. Applicants notified on a rolling basis starting 3/15.

CONTACT

Judi Miladin, Director of Financial Aid
197 Franklin Street, Auburn, NY 13021-3099
(315) 255-1743 ext. 2470

Cazenovia College

Cazenovia, New York
www.cazenovia.edu   Federal Code: 002685

4-year private liberal arts college in small town.
Enrollment: 1,024 undergrads, 8% part-time. 330 full-time freshmen.
Selectivity: Admits over 75% of applicants.

BASIC COSTS (2008-2009)

Tuition and fees: $22,894.
Room and board: $9,502.

FINANCIAL AID PICTURE (2007-2008)

Students with need: Average financial aid package for all full-time undergraduates was $18,614. 65% awarded as scholarships/grants, 35% awarded as loans/jobs. Need-based aid available for part-time students. Work study available nights, weekends, and for part-time students.
Students without need: No-need awards available for academics.

FINANCIAL AID PROCEDURES

Forms required: FAFSA, state aid form.
Dates and Deadlines: Priority date 3/15; no closing date. Applicants notified on a rolling basis starting 11/1; must reply by 5/1 or within 2 week(s) of notification.
Transfers: No deadline. Applicants notified on a rolling basis starting 11/1; must reply by 5/1 or within 2 week(s) of notification.

CONTACT

Christine Mandel, Director of Financial Aid
3 Sullivan Street, Cazenovia, NY 13035
(315) 655-7887

City University of New York: Baruch College

New York, New York
www.baruch.cuny.edu   Federal Code: 007273

4-year public business and liberal arts college in very large city.
Enrollment: 12,626 undergrads, 24% part-time. 1,470 full-time freshmen.
Selectivity: Admits less than 50% of applicants.

BASIC COSTS (2007-2008)

Tuition and fees: $4,320; out-of-state residents $11,120.
Per-credit charge: $170; out-of-state residents $360.

FINANCIAL AID PICTURE (2007-2008)

Students with need: Out of 1,352 full-time freshmen who applied for aid, 1,081 were judged to have need. Of these, 1,069 received aid, and 256 had their full need met. Average financial aid package met 69% of need; average scholarship/grant was $4,967; average loan was $2,852. For part-time students, average financial aid package was $2,410.
Students without need: 23 full-time freshmen who did not demonstrate need for aid received scholarships/grants; average award was $4,250. No-need awards available for academics, state/district residency.
Scholarships offered: Honors college scholarships based on SAT scores and high school GPA.
Cumulative student debt: 19% of graduating class had student loans; average debt was $14,159.

FINANCIAL AID PROCEDURES

Forms required: FAFSA, state aid form.
Dates and Deadlines: Priority date 3/15; closing date 4/30. Applicants notified on a rolling basis starting 4/1; must reply by 6/1 or within 6 week(s) of notification.
Transfers: Priority date 4/1; no deadline. Applicants notified on a rolling basis; must reply within 4 week(s) of notification.

CONTACT

Nancy West, Director of Financial Aid
One Bernard Baruch Way, Box H-0720, New York, NY 10010-5585
(646) 312-1360

City University of New York: Borough of Manhattan Community College

New York, New York
www.bmcc.cuny.edu   Federal Code: 002691

2-year public community college in very large city.
Enrollment: 18,462 undergrads.
Selectivity: Open admission; but selective for some programs.

BASIC COSTS (2007-2008)

Tuition and fees: $3,068; out-of-state residents $5,968.
Per-credit charge: $120; out-of-state residents $190.

FINANCIAL AID PICTURE (2006-2007)

Students with need: 82% of average financial aid package awarded as scholarships/grants, 18% awarded as loans/jobs. Need-based aid available for part-time students.
Students without need: This college awards aid only to students with need.

FINANCIAL AID PROCEDURES

Forms required: FAFSA, institutional form.
Dates and Deadlines: Priority date 4/15; closing date 5/1. Applicants notified on a rolling basis starting 8/1; must reply within 2 week(s) of notification.

CONTACT

Howard Entin, Director of Financial Aid
199 Chambers Street, New York, NY 10007-1097
(212) 220-1430

City University of New York: Bronx Community College

Bronx, New York
www.bcc.cuny.edu   Federal Code: 002692

2-year public community college in very large city.
Enrollment: 8,420 undergrads.
Selectivity: Open admission.

BASIC COSTS (2007-2008)

Tuition and fees: $3,104; out-of-state residents $6,004.
Per-credit charge: $120; out-of-state residents $190.

FINANCIAL AID PICTURE

Students with need: Need-based aid available for full-time and part-time students. Work study available nights, weekends, and for part-time students.

FINANCIAL AID PROCEDURES

Forms required: FAFSA.
Dates and Deadlines: Closing date 7/15. Applicants notified on a rolling basis starting 8/1.

CONTACT

Orlando Lopez, Financial Aid Officer
West 181st Street and University Avenue, Bronx, NY 10453
(718) 289-5700

City University of New York: Brooklyn College

Brooklyn, New York
www.brooklyn.cuny.edu   Federal Code: 002687

4-year public liberal arts college in very large city.
Enrollment: 11,923 undergrads, 25% part-time. 1,300 full-time freshmen.
Selectivity: Admits less than 50% of applicants.

BASIC COSTS (2007-2008)

Tuition and fees: $4,377; out-of-state residents $11,177.
Per-credit charge: $170; out-of-state residents $360.

FINANCIAL AID PICTURE

Students with need: Need-based aid available for full-time and part-time students. Work study available nights, weekends, and for part-time students.
Students without need: No-need awards available for academics, art, leadership, music/drama, state/district residency.
Scholarships offered: Presidential Scholarship Program; for 25 freshman students for 8 tuition payments totalling $13,000. Brooklyn College Freshman Scholarships; $1,000 per year of study at Brooklyn College. Many scholarships for freshman students based on degree of study, academic merit, and community service.

FINANCIAL AID PROCEDURES

Forms required: FAFSA, state aid form.
Dates and Deadlines: Priority date 4/1; no closing date. Applicants notified on a rolling basis starting 5/1.

CONTACT

Sherwood Johnson, Director of Financial Aid
2900 Bedford Avenue, Brooklyn, NY 11210
(718) 951-5051

City University of New York: City College

New York, New York
www.ccny.cuny.edu   Federal Code: 002688

4-year public university in very large city.
Enrollment: 10,683 undergrads, 24% part-time. 1,528 full-time freshmen.
Selectivity: Admits less than 50% of applicants.

BASIC COSTS (2007-2008)

Tuition and fees: $4,279; out-of-state residents $11,079.
Per-credit charge: $170; out-of-state residents $360.
Additional info: Tuition/fee waivers available for minority students.

FINANCIAL AID PICTURE (2006-2007)

Students with need: Out of 1,329 full-time freshmen who applied for aid, 1,128 were judged to have need. Of these, 1,015 received aid, and 761 had their full need met. Average financial aid package met 79% of need; average scholarship/grant was $5,110; average loan was $1,500. Need-based aid available for part-time students.
Students without need: 365 full-time freshmen who did not demonstrate need for aid received scholarships/grants; average award was $1,830. No-need awards available for academics, alumni affiliation, leadership.
Cumulative student debt: 35% of graduating class had student loans; average debt was $16,800.

FINANCIAL AID PROCEDURES

Forms required: FAFSA.
Dates and Deadlines: Priority date 4/1; no closing date. Applicants notified on a rolling basis starting 4/15.
Transfers: Priority date 3/31; no deadline. Applicants notified on a rolling basis starting 3/31.

CONTACT

Thelma Mason, Director of Financial Aid
160 Convent Avenue, New York, NY 10031
(212) 650-7000

City University of New York: College of Staten Island

Staten Island, New York
www.csi.cuny.edu   Federal Code: 002698

4-year public liberal arts college in very large city.
Enrollment: 11,197 undergrads, 28% part-time. 2,272 full-time freshmen.
Selectivity: Admits over 75% of applicants.

BASIC COSTS (2007-2008)

Tuition and fees: $4,328; out-of-state residents $11,128.
Per-credit charge: $170; out-of-state residents $360.

FINANCIAL AID PICTURE (2007-2008)

Students with need: Out of 1,744 full-time freshmen who applied for aid, 1,263 were judged to have need. Of these, 1,219 received aid, and 53 had their full need met. Average financial aid package met 61% of need; average scholarship/grant was $5,319; average loan was $2,842. For part-time students, average financial aid package was $2,369.
Students without need: 235 full-time freshmen who did not demonstrate need for aid received scholarships/grants; average award was $1,699. No-need awards available for academics, art, athletics, job skills, leadership, minority status, music/drama, state/district residency.

FINANCIAL AID PROCEDURES

Forms required: FAFSA, state aid form.
Dates and Deadlines: Priority date 3/31; no closing date. Applicants notified on a rolling basis starting 4/30.
Transfers: No deadline.

CONTACT

Philippe Marius, Director of Financial Aid

2800 Victory Boulevard 2A-104, Staten Island, NY 10314

(718) 982-2030

City University of New York: Hostos Community College

Bronx, New York

www.hostos.cuny.edu   Federal Code: 008611

2-year public community college in very large city.

Enrollment: 4,416 undergrads, 35% part-time. 752 full-time freshmen.

Selectivity: Open admission; but selective for some programs.

BASIC COSTS (2007-2008)

Tuition and fees: $3,105; out-of-state residents $6,005.

Per-credit charge: $120; out-of-state residents $190.

FINANCIAL AID PICTURE

Students with need: Need-based aid available for full-time and part-time students.

FINANCIAL AID PROCEDURES

Forms required: FAFSA, state aid form, institutional form.

Dates and Deadlines: Priority date 7/1; no closing date. Applicants notified on a rolling basis; must reply within 3 week(s) of notification.

CONTACT

Joseph Alicea, Director of Financial Aid

500 Grand Concourse, Bronx, NY 10451

(718) 518-6555

City University of New York: Hunter College

New York, New York

www.hunter.cuny.edu   Federal Code: 002689

4-year public liberal arts college in very large city.

Enrollment: 14,573 undergrads, 27% part-time. 1,820 full-time freshmen.

Selectivity: Admits less than 50% of applicants.

BASIC COSTS (2007-2008)

Tuition and fees: $4,349; out-of-state residents $11,149.

Per-credit charge: $170; out-of-state residents $360.

Room only: $3,726.

Additional info: Dormitory availability very limited.

FINANCIAL AID PICTURE (2006-2007)

Students with need: Out of 1,489 full-time freshmen who applied for aid, 1,129 were judged to have need. Of these, 1,107 received aid, and 315 had their full need met. Average financial aid package met 76% of need; average scholarship/grant was $5,443; average loan was $2,952. For part-time students, average financial aid package was $4,146.

Students without need: 277 full-time freshmen who did not demonstrate need for aid received scholarships/grants; average award was $1,785. No-need awards available for academics.

Cumulative student debt: 38% of graduating class had student loans; average debt was $7,124.

FINANCIAL AID PROCEDURES

Forms required: FAFSA, state aid form.

Dates and Deadlines: Priority date 5/1; no closing date. Applicants notified on a rolling basis starting 5/15.

CONTACT

Aristalia Rodriguez, Director of Financial Aid

695 Park Avenue, New York, NY 10021

(212) 772-4820

City University of New York: John Jay College of Criminal Justice

New York, New York

www.jjay.cuny.edu/   Federal Code: 002693

4-year public College of criminal justice and public safety in very large city.

Enrollment: 12,634 undergrads, 24% part-time. 2,756 full-time freshmen.

Selectivity: Admits over 75% of applicants.

BASIC COSTS (2007-2008)

Tuition and fees: $4,279; out-of-state residents $11,079.

Per-credit charge: $170; out-of-state residents $360.

FINANCIAL AID PICTURE (2006-2007)

Students with need: Out of 2,488 full-time freshmen who applied for aid, 2,140 were judged to have need. Of these, 1,982 received aid. Average financial aid package met 85% of need; average scholarship/grant was $3,125. For part-time students, average financial aid package was $6,500.

Students without need: No-need awards available for academics, state/district residency.

Cumulative student debt: 46% of graduating class had student loans; average debt was $14,000.

FINANCIAL AID PROCEDURES

Forms required: FAFSA.

Dates and Deadlines: No deadline. Applicants notified on a rolling basis starting 7/15; must reply within 2 week(s) of notification.

CONTACT

Fay Williams, Director of Financial Aid

445 West 59th Street, New York, NY 10019

(212) 237-8151

City University of New York: Kingsborough Community College

Brooklyn, New York

www.kbcc.cuny.edu   Federal Code: 002694

2-year public community college in very large city.

Enrollment: 10,943 undergrads, 27% part-time. 2,018 full-time freshmen.

Selectivity: Open admission.

BASIC COSTS (2007-2008)

Tuition and fees: $3,100; out-of-state residents $6,000.

Per-credit charge: $120; out-of-state residents $190.

FINANCIAL AID PICTURE

Students with need: Need-based aid available for full-time and part-time students.

Students without need: This college awards aid only to students with need.

FINANCIAL AID PROCEDURES

Forms required: FAFSA.

Dates and Deadlines: Closing date 4/30. Applicants notified on a rolling basis; must reply within 2 week(s) of notification.

CONTACT

Wayne Harewood, Director of Financial Aid

2001 Oriental Boulevard, Brooklyn, NY 11235

(718) 368-4644

City University of New York: LaGuardia Community College

Long Island City, New York
www.lagcc.cuny.edu   Federal Code: 010051

2-year public community college in very large city.
Enrollment: 12,678 undergrads, 38% part-time. 3,283 full-time freshmen.
Selectivity: Open admission.

BASIC COSTS (2007-2008)
Tuition and fees: $3,092; out-of-state residents $5,992.
Per-credit charge: $120; out-of-state residents $190.

FINANCIAL AID PICTURE (2006-2007)
Students with need: Out of 2,319 full-time freshmen who applied for aid, 2,199 were judged to have need. Of these, 2,087 received aid. Average financial aid package met 54% of need; average scholarship/grant was $2,124. For part-time students, average financial aid package was $1,891.
Students without need: This college awards aid only to students with need.

FINANCIAL AID PROCEDURES
Forms required: FAFSA, state aid form, institutional form.
Dates and Deadlines: Priority date 4/15; no closing date. Applicants notified on a rolling basis starting 3/1; must reply within 4 week(s) of notification.

CONTACT
Gail Baksh-Jarrett, Director of Financial Aid
31-10 Thomson Avenue, Long Island City, NY 11101
(718) 482-7200

City University of New York: Lehman College

Bronx, New York
www.lehman.cuny.edu   Federal Code: 007022

4-year public liberal arts college in very large city.
Enrollment: 8,236 undergrads, 33% part-time. 875 full-time freshmen.
Selectivity: Admits less than 50% of applicants.

BASIC COSTS (2007-2008)
Tuition and fees: $4,290; out-of-state residents $11,090.
Per-credit charge: $170; out-of-state residents $360.

FINANCIAL AID PICTURE (2006-2007)
Students with need: Out of 860 full-time freshmen who applied for aid, 845 were judged to have need. Of these, 841 received aid, and 21 had their full need met. Average financial aid package met 92% of need; average scholarship/grant was $1,535; average loan was $1,380. For part-time students, average financial aid package was $1,714.
Students without need: This college awards aid only to students with need.
Cumulative student debt: 34% of graduating class had student loans; average debt was $11,500.

FINANCIAL AID PROCEDURES
Forms required: FAFSA, state aid form.
Dates and Deadlines: No deadline. Applicants notified on a rolling basis starting 3/1.
Transfers: Applicants notified on a rolling basis starting 3/1.

CONTACT
David Martinez, Director of Financial Aid
250 Bedford Park Boulevard West, Bronx, NY 10468
(718) 960-8545

City University of New York: Medgar Evers College

Brooklyn, New York
www.mec.cuny.edu   Federal Code: 010097

4-year public business and liberal arts college in very large city.
Enrollment: 5,245 undergrads, 34% part-time. 807 full-time freshmen.
Selectivity: Open admission; but selective for some programs.

BASIC COSTS (2007-2008)
Tuition and fees: $4,252; out-of-state residents $11,052.
Per-credit charge: $170; out-of-state residents $360.

FINANCIAL AID PICTURE
Students with need: Need-based aid available for full-time and part-time students. Work study available weekends and for part-time students.
Students without need: No-need awards available for academics, leadership.

FINANCIAL AID PROCEDURES
Forms required: FAFSA, state aid form.
Dates and Deadlines: Priority date 1/2; closing date 7/31. Applicants notified on a rolling basis; must reply within 3 week(s) of notification.
Transfers: Priority date 3/1. Must reply within 2 week(s) of notification.

CONTACT
Conley James, Director of Financial Aid
1665 Bedford Avenue, Brooklyn, NY 11225-2201
(718) 270-6194

City University of New York: New York City College of Technology

Brooklyn, New York
www.citytech.cuny.edu   Federal Code: 002696

4-year public technical college in very large city.
Enrollment: 12,630 undergrads, 39% part-time. 2,568 full-time freshmen.
Selectivity: Open admission; but selective for some programs.

BASIC COSTS (2007-2008)
Tuition and fees: $4,289; out-of-state residents $11,089.
Per-credit charge: $170; out-of-state residents $360.

FINANCIAL AID PICTURE (2007-2008)
Students with need: Out of 2,210 full-time freshmen who applied for aid, 1,942 were judged to have need. Of these, 1,884 received aid, and 94 had their full need met. Average financial aid package met 58% of need; average scholarship/grant was $913; average loan was $2,211. For part-time students, average financial aid package was $3,681.
Students without need: 42 full-time freshmen who did not demonstrate need for aid received scholarships/grants; average award was $1,250. No-need awards available for state/district residency.
Additional info: Foreign students applying for aid must have resided in New York for at least 1 year.

FINANCIAL AID PROCEDURES
Forms required: FAFSA.
Dates and Deadlines: Priority date 5/15; no closing date.

CONTACT
Sandra Higgins, Director of Financial Aid
300 Jay Street Namm G17, Brooklyn, NY 11201
(718) 260-5700

City University of New York: Queens College

Flushing, New York
www.qc.cuny.edu   Federal Code: 002690

4-year public liberal arts and teachers college in very large city.
Enrollment: 13,901 undergrads, 26% part-time. 1,754 full-time freshmen.
Selectivity: Admits less than 50% of applicants.

BASIC COSTS (2007-2008)

Tuition and fees: $4,377; out-of-state residents $11,177.
Per-credit charge: $170; out-of-state residents $360.

FINANCIAL AID PICTURE (2007-2008)

Students with need: Out of 1,333 full-time freshmen who applied for aid, 1,213 were judged to have need. Of these, 970 received aid, and 247 had their full need met. Average financial aid package met 77% of need; average scholarship/grant was $1,250; average loan was $2,625. For part-time students, average financial aid package was $5,400.
Students without need: 81 full-time freshmen who did not demonstrate need for aid received scholarships/grants; average award was $773. No-need awards available for academics, athletics, music/drama, state/district residency.
Scholarships offered: *Merit:* CUNY Honors College; full tuition. Regents Award for Deceased or Disabled Veterans; $450 per year. Vietnam Veteran Tuition Aid Program; cost of tuition per semester. Regents Award for children of deceased police officers, firefighters, or corrections officers; $450 per year. Paul Douglas Teacher Scholarship Program; up to $5,000 per year. State Aid to Native Americans; $1,100 per year. SEEK Presidential Scholarship; Beinstock Memorial Scholarship for students with disabilities; CMP Publications Scholarship in Journalism or English; Daly Scholarship in the Physical Sciences; Foster Scholarship for women and minorities; Kupferberg Memorial Scholarship; Linakis Scholarship; Mitsui USA Scholarships; Nagdimon Scholarship; Queens College Scholarships; Weprin Memorial Scholarship in the Public Interest. ***Athletic:*** 28 full-time freshmen received athletic scholarships; average amount $4,600.
Cumulative student debt: 41% of graduating class had student loans; average debt was $14,000.

FINANCIAL AID PROCEDURES

Forms required: FAFSA, state aid form, institutional form.
Dates and Deadlines: Priority date 2/1; no closing date. Applicants notified on a rolling basis starting 3/1; must reply within 3 week(s) of notification.
Transfers: Priority date 5/1; no deadline. Applicants notified on a rolling basis.

CONTACT

Rena Smith-Kiawu, Director of Financial Aid
6530 Kissena Boulevard, Jefferson 117, Flushing, NY 11367-1597
(718) 997-5123

City University of New York: Queensborough Community College

Bayside, New York
www.qcc.cuny.edu   Federal Code: 002697

2-year public community college in very large city.
Enrollment: 11,325 undergrads.
Selectivity: Open admission.

BASIC COSTS (2007-2008)

Tuition and fees: $3,086; out-of-state residents $5,986.
Per-credit charge: $120; out-of-state residents $190.

FINANCIAL AID PICTURE

Students with need: Need-based aid available for full-time students.

FINANCIAL AID PROCEDURES

Forms required: FAFSA, institutional form.
Dates and Deadlines: No deadline. Applicants notified on a rolling basis starting 7/15.

CONTACT

Veronica Lukas, Director of Financial Aid
Springfield Boulevard & 56th Avenue, Bayside, NY 11364-1497
(718) 631-6262

City University of New York: York College

Jamaica, New York
www.york.cuny.edu   Federal Code: 004759

4-year public liberal arts college in very large city.
Enrollment: 5,868 undergrads, 30% part-time. 1,017 full-time freshmen.

BASIC COSTS (2007-2008)

Tuition and fees: $4,262; out-of-state residents $11,062.
Per-credit charge: $170; out-of-state residents $360.

FINANCIAL AID PICTURE (2007-2008)

Students with need: Out of 814 full-time freshmen who applied for aid, 767 were judged to have need. Of these, 728 received aid, and 52 had their full need met. Average financial aid package met 36% of need; average scholarship/grant was $4,569; average loan was $2,357. For part-time students, average financial aid package was $3,663.
Students without need: 110 full-time freshmen who did not demonstrate need for aid received scholarships/grants; average award was $1,034. No-need awards available for academics.
Cumulative student debt: 20% of graduating class had student loans; average debt was $8,899.

FINANCIAL AID PROCEDURES

Forms required: FAFSA.
Dates and Deadlines: Priority date 5/1; no closing date. Applicants notified on a rolling basis starting 3/1.
Transfers: No deadline. Applicants notified on a rolling basis starting 3/1.

CONTACT

Cathy Tsiapanos, Director of Financial Aid
94-20 Guy R. Brewer Boulevard, Jamaica, NY 11451-9989
(718) 262-2000 ext. 2230

Clarkson University

Potsdam, New York
www.clarkson.edu   Federal Code: 002699

4-year private university in large town.
Enrollment: 2,521 undergrads. 682 full-time freshmen.
Selectivity: Admits over 75% of applicants.

BASIC COSTS (2008-2009)

Tuition and fees: $31,010.
Per-credit charge: $1,011.
Room and board: $10,612.
Additional info: Tuition/fee waivers available for minority students.

FINANCIAL AID PICTURE (2007-2008)

Students with need: Out of 574 full-time freshmen who applied for aid, 499 were judged to have need. Of these, 499 received aid, and 41 had their full need met. Average financial aid package met 86% of need; average scholarship/grant was $14,270; average loan was $5,100. Need-based aid available for part-time students.
Students without need: 75 full-time freshmen who did not demonstrate need for aid received scholarships/grants; average award was $14,529. No-

need awards available for academics, alumni affiliation, leadership, minority status, ROTC.

Scholarships offered: 11 full-time freshmen received athletic scholarships; average amount $39,990.

Cumulative student debt: 87% of graduating class had student loans; average debt was $33,774.

FINANCIAL AID PROCEDURES

Forms required: FAFSA, state aid form, institutional form.

Dates and Deadlines: Priority date 2/15; no closing date. Applicants notified on a rolling basis starting 3/19; must reply by 5/1 or within 2 week(s) of notification.

Transfers: Closing date 4/15. Applicants notified on a rolling basis. Presidential Scholarships, Phi Theta Kappa scholarships and Alpha Beta Gamma Awards available, in addition to state and federal programs.

CONTACT

April Grant, Associate Director of Financial Aid

Holcroft House, Potsdam, NY 13699-5605

(315) 268-6413

Clinton Community College

Plattsburgh, New York

www.clinton.edu   Federal Code: 006787

2-year public community college in large town.

Enrollment: 1,448 undergrads.

Selectivity: Open admission; but selective for some programs.

BASIC COSTS (2007-2008)

Tuition and fees: $3,466; out-of-state residents $8,296.

Per-credit charge: $134; out-of-state residents $335.

FINANCIAL AID PICTURE

Students with need: Need-based aid available for full-time and part-time students.

Students without need: This college awards aid only to students with need.

FINANCIAL AID PROCEDURES

Forms required: FAFSA, state aid form.

Dates and Deadlines: Priority date 6/2; no closing date. Applicants notified on a rolling basis starting 5/1; must reply within 2 week(s) of notification.

CONTACT

Karen Burnam, Director of Financial Aid

136 Clinton Point Drive, Plattsburgh, NY 12901-4297

(518) 562-4125

Cochran School of Nursing-St. John's Riverside Hospital

Yonkers, New York

www.cochranschoolofnursing.us   Federal Code: 006443

2-year private nursing college in small city.

Enrollment: 322 undergrads, 67% part-time.

BASIC COSTS (2008-2009)

Additional info: Tuition and fees for full 2-year AAS program $26,683.

FINANCIAL AID PICTURE

Students with need: Need-based aid available for full-time and part-time students.

Students without need: This college awards aid only to students with need.

FINANCIAL AID PROCEDURES

Forms required: FAFSA.

Dates and Deadlines: No deadline. Applicants notified on a rolling basis.

CONTACT

Geraldine Owens, Financial Aid Officer

967 North Broadway, Yonkers, NY 10701

(914) 964-4265

Colgate University

Hamilton, New York   Federal Code: 002701

www.colgate.edu   CSS Code: 2086

4-year private liberal arts college in small town.

Enrollment: 2,800 undergrads. 746 full-time freshmen.

Selectivity: Admits less than 50% of applicants.

BASIC COSTS (2008-2009)

Tuition and fees: $39,545.

Room and board: $9,625.

FINANCIAL AID PICTURE (2007-2008)

Students with need: Out of 276 full-time freshmen who applied for aid, 219 were judged to have need. Of these, 219 received aid, and 219 had their full need met. Average financial aid package met 100% of need; average scholarship/grant was $30,297; average loan was $1,877.

Students without need: No-need awards available for athletics.

Scholarships offered: 41 full-time freshmen received athletic scholarships; average amount $34,474.

Cumulative student debt: 36% of graduating class had student loans; average debt was $16,666.

FINANCIAL AID PROCEDURES

Forms required: FAFSA, CSS PROFILE.

Dates and Deadlines: Closing date 1/15. Applicants notified by 4/1; must reply by 5/1 or within 2 week(s) of notification.

Transfers: Closing date 3/15. Applicants notified by 4/30; must reply by 5/15 or within 2 week(s) of notification. Financial aid for transfer students extremely limited.

CONTACT

Marcelle Tyburski, Director of Financial Aid

13 Oak Drive, Hamilton, NY 13346-1383

(315) 228-7431

College of Mount St. Vincent

Riverdale, New York

www.mountsaintvincent.edu   Federal Code: 002703

4-year private liberal arts college in very large city, affiliated with Roman Catholic Church.

Enrollment: 1,417 undergrads, 8% part-time. 394 full-time freshmen.

Selectivity: Admits 50 to 75% of applicants.

BASIC COSTS (2008-2009)

Tuition and fees: $24,600.

Per-credit charge: $700.

Room and board: $9,370.

FINANCIAL AID PICTURE (2006-2007)

Students with need: Out of 360 full-time freshmen who applied for aid, 304 were judged to have need. Of these, 304 received aid. Average financial aid package met 78% of need; average scholarship/grant was $9,000; average loan was $2,200.

Students without need: 54 full-time freshmen who did not demonstrate need for aid received scholarships/grants; average award was $11,500. No-need awards available for academics, alumni affiliation, leadership.
Cumulative student debt: 80% of graduating class had student loans; average debt was $17,000.

FINANCIAL AID PROCEDURES

Forms required: FAFSA, state aid form.
Dates and Deadlines: Priority date 3/1; no closing date. Applicants notified on a rolling basis starting 3/1; must reply by 5/1 or within 3 week(s) of notification.
Transfers: Priority date 5/15. Applicants notified on a rolling basis starting 3/1; must reply by 5/1 or within 3 week(s) of notification.

CONTACT

Monica Simotas, Director of Financial Aid
6301 Riverdale Avenue, Riverdale, NY 10471-1093
(718) 405-3289

College of New Rochelle
New Rochelle, New York
www.cnr.edu
Federal Code: 002704

4-year private nursing and liberal arts college for women in small city, affiliated with Roman Catholic Church.
Enrollment: 933 undergrads, 33% part-time. 116 full-time freshmen.
Selectivity: Admits less than 50% of applicants.

BASIC COSTS (2007-2008)

Tuition and fees: $23,700.
Per-credit charge: $781.
Room and board: $8,700.
Additional info: All incoming freshmen given laptop at no additional cost.

FINANCIAL AID PICTURE

Students with need: Need-based aid available for full-time and part-time students. Work study available nights, weekends, and for part-time students.
Students without need: No-need awards available for academics, art, leadership.

FINANCIAL AID PROCEDURES

Forms required: FAFSA, institutional form.
Dates and Deadlines: Priority date 3/1; no closing date. Applicants notified on a rolling basis starting 1/1; must reply within 2 week(s) of notification.

CONTACT

Ann Pelak, Director of Financial Aid
29 Castle Place, New Rochelle, NY 10805-2339
(914) 654-5225

College of Saint Rose
Albany, New York
www.strose.edu
Federal Code: 002705

4-year private liberal arts and teachers college in small city, affiliated with Roman Catholic Church.
Enrollment: 3,116 undergrads, 6% part-time. 622 full-time freshmen.
Selectivity: Admits 50 to 75% of applicants.

BASIC COSTS (2008-2009)

Tuition and fees: $21,972.
Room and board: $9,086.

FINANCIAL AID PICTURE (2006-2007)

Students with need: Out of 602 full-time freshmen who applied for aid, 520 were judged to have need. Of these, 519 received aid, and 27 had their full need met. Average financial aid package met 49% of need; average scholarship/grant was $3,190; average loan was $1,805. For part-time students, average financial aid package was $4,228.
Students without need: 36 full-time freshmen who did not demonstrate need for aid received scholarships/grants; average award was $1,578. No-need awards available for academics, alumni affiliation, art, athletics, minority status, music/drama.
Scholarships offered: *Merit:* Rooney Gibbons Scholarship: award amounts range from $2,000 to full tuition; freshmen applicants admitted by February 1 automatically considered. *Athletic:* 10 full-time freshmen received athletic scholarships; average amount $7,308.
Cumulative student debt: 85% of graduating class had student loans; average debt was $24,920.

FINANCIAL AID PROCEDURES

Forms required: FAFSA.
Dates and Deadlines: Priority date 3/1; no closing date. Applicants notified on a rolling basis starting 3/15; must reply by 5/1 or within 2 week(s) of notification.

CONTACT

James Vallee, Director of Financial Aid
432 Western Avenue, Albany, NY 12203
(518) 458-5424

College of Westchester
White Plains, New York
www.cw.edu
Federal Code: 005208

2-year for-profit business and career college in large town.
Enrollment: 979 undergrads, 20% part-time. 210 full-time freshmen.
Selectivity: Admits over 75% of applicants.

BASIC COSTS (2008-2009)

Tuition and fees: $19,800.
Per-credit charge: $630.
Additional info: Tuition/fee waivers available for unemployed or children of unemployed.

FINANCIAL AID PICTURE

Students with need: Need-based aid available for full-time and part-time students. Work study available nights, weekends, and for part-time students.
Students without need: No-need awards available for academics, alumni affiliation.

FINANCIAL AID PROCEDURES

Forms required: FAFSA, state aid form, institutional form.
Dates and Deadlines: No deadline. Applicants notified on a rolling basis starting 1/7; must reply within 2 week(s) of notification.

CONTACT

Dianne Pepitone, Director, Student Financial Services
325 Central Park Avenue, White Plains, NY 10602
(914) 948-4442 ext. 473

Columbia University
New York, New York
www.columbia.edu
Federal Code: E00485
CSS Code: 2116

4-year private university and engineering and liberal arts college in very large city.
Enrollment: 5,602 undergrads. 1,333 full-time freshmen.
Selectivity: Admits less than 50% of applicants.

PART III: FINANCIAL AID COLLEGE BY COLLEGE

BASIC COSTS (2007-2008)

Tuition and fees: $37,223.

Room and board: $9,937.

FINANCIAL AID PICTURE (2007-2008)

Students with need: Out of 852 full-time freshmen who applied for aid, 691 were judged to have need. Of these, 691 received aid, and 691 had their full need met. Average financial aid package met 100% of need; average scholarship/grant was $32,035; average loan was $3,346.

Students without need: This college awards aid only to students with need.

FINANCIAL AID PROCEDURES

Forms required: FAFSA, CSS PROFILE.

Dates and Deadlines: Closing date 3/1. Applicants notified by 4/1.

Transfers: Closing date 4/20. Institutional financial aid for transfer candidates limited at this time.

CONTACT

Nanette DiLauro, Director of Financial Aid Operations

212 Hamilton Hall, MC 2807, New York, NY 10027

(212) 854-3711

Columbia University: School of General Studies

New York, New York

www.gs.columbia.edu

Federal Code: E00487

4-year private university and liberal arts college in very large city.

Enrollment: 1,190 undergrads, 41% part-time. 16 full-time freshmen.

Selectivity: Admits less than 50% of applicants.

BASIC COSTS (2007-2008)

Tuition and fees: $36,013.

Per-credit charge: $1,146.

Additional info: Institutionally managed double-occupancy apartments available averaging $900/month rent.

FINANCIAL AID PICTURE (2007-2008)

Students with need: 54% of average financial aid package awarded as scholarships/grants, 46% awarded as loans/jobs. Need-based aid available for part-time students.

Students without need: This college awards aid only to students with need.

Scholarships offered: All applicants should submit General Studies Application for Financial Aid.

FINANCIAL AID PROCEDURES

Forms required: FAFSA, institutional form.

Dates and Deadlines: Priority date 4/15; closing date 6/1. Applicants notified on a rolling basis; must reply within 3 week(s) of notification.

Transfers: Applicants notified on a rolling basis starting 4/1; must reply within 2 week(s) of notification.

CONTACT

William Bailey, Director of Educational Financing

408 Lewisohn Hall, Mail Code 4101, New York, NY 10027

(212) 854-5410

Columbia-Greene Community College

Hudson, New York

www.sunycgcc.edu

Federal Code: 006789

2-year public community college in small town.

Enrollment: 1,438 undergrads, 31% part-time. 379 full-time freshmen.

Selectivity: Open admission; but selective for some programs.

BASIC COSTS (2007-2008)

Tuition and fees: $3,352; out-of-state residents $6,394.

Per-credit charge: $128; out-of-state residents $256.

FINANCIAL AID PICTURE

Students with need: Need-based aid available for full-time and part-time students. Work study available nights, weekends, and for part-time students.

Students without need: No-need awards available for academics, state/district residency.

FINANCIAL AID PROCEDURES

Forms required: FAFSA, institutional form.

Dates and Deadlines: Priority date 5/1; no closing date. Applicants notified on a rolling basis starting 7/1; must reply within 2 week(s) of notification.

CONTACT

Earl Tretheway, Director of Financial Aid

4400 Route 23, Hudson, NY 12534

Concordia College

Bronxville, New York

www.concordia-ny.edu

Federal Code: 002709

4-year private liberal arts college in small town, affiliated with Lutheran Church - Missouri Synod.

Enrollment: 673 undergrads, 5% part-time. 128 full-time freshmen.

Selectivity: Admits 50 to 75% of applicants.

BASIC COSTS (2007-2008)

Tuition and fees: $21,950.

Room and board: $8,520.

FINANCIAL AID PICTURE

Students with need: Need-based aid available for full-time and part-time students. Work study available nights, weekends, and for part-time students.

Students without need: No-need awards available for academics, athletics, leadership, music/drama.

Scholarships offered: Fellows Scholarship: $15,000 a year; for 1800 SAT (exclusive of Writing) and 95 average. Merit Scholarships: $6,000-$9,000 for 80 average and above. Lutheran students grants available.

FINANCIAL AID PROCEDURES

Forms required: FAFSA, state aid form.

Dates and Deadlines: Priority date 4/1; no closing date. Applicants notified on a rolling basis starting 4/1; must reply by 5/1 or within 3 week(s) of notification.

CONTACT

Janice Spikereit, Director of Financial Aid

171 White Plains Road, Bronxville, NY 10708

(914) 337-9300 ext. 2146

Cooper Union for the Advancement of Science and Art

New York, New York

www.cooper.edu

Federal Code: 002710

CSS Code: 2097

4-year private visual arts and engineering college in very large city.

Enrollment: 889 undergrads. 219 full-time freshmen.

Selectivity: Admits less than 50% of applicants.

BASIC COSTS (2008-2009)

Tuition and fees: $34,600.

Room only: $9,700.

Additional info: Every student admitted receives full-tuition scholarship (covering tuition only) for duration of enrollment. International students assessed annual filing fee of $1,750.

FINANCIAL AID PICTURE (2006-2007)

Students with need: Out of 120 full-time freshmen who applied for aid, 76 were judged to have need. Of these, 76 received aid, and 45 had their full need met. Average financial aid package met 92% of need; average scholarship/grant was $3,156; average loan was $2,639.

Students without need: 143 full-time freshmen who did not demonstrate need for aid received scholarships/grants; average award was $30,000. No-need awards available for academics.

Additional info: All students receive full-tuition scholarships valued at approximately $30,000 per year. Students able to document need receive financial aid package that may include combination of grants, loans, work-study, internships.

FINANCIAL AID PROCEDURES

Forms required: FAFSA, CSS PROFILE.

Dates and Deadlines: Priority date 4/15; closing date 6/1. Applicants notified by 6/1; must reply by 6/30 or within 2 week(s) of notification.

Transfers: Applicants notified by 6/1; must reply by 6/30 or within 2 week(s) of notification. Late financial aid applications processed on rolling basis.

CONTACT

Mary Ruokonen, Director of Financial Aid
30 Cooper Square, Suite 300, New York, NY 10003-7183
(212) 353-4130

Cornell University
Ithaca, New York
www.cornell.edu
Federal Code: 002711
CSS Code: 2098

4-year private university in large town.

Enrollment: 13,455 undergrads. 3,010 full-time freshmen.

Selectivity: Admits less than 50% of applicants.

BASIC COSTS (2008-2009)

Tuition and fees: $36,504.

Room and board: $11,690.

Additional info: Tuition amounts listed are for Endowed/Private colleges only: Architecture, Art & Planning; Arts & Sciences; Engineering; Hotel Administration. Contract/State college amounts differ and vary by residency and program.

FINANCIAL AID PICTURE (2007-2008)

Students with need: Out of 1,407 full-time freshmen who applied for aid, 1,310 were judged to have need. Of these, 1,310 received aid, and 1,310 had their full need met. Average financial aid package met 100% of need; average scholarship/grant was $21,824; average loan was $5,180.

Students without need: This college awards aid only to students with need.

Cumulative student debt: 54% of graduating class had student loans; average debt was $23,936.

FINANCIAL AID PROCEDURES

Forms required: FAFSA, CSS PROFILE, institutional form.

Dates and Deadlines: Closing date 2/11. Applicants notified by 4/1; must reply by 5/1 or within 2 week(s) of notification.

Transfers: Submit Cornell aid application forms in addition to regular required forms.

CONTACT

Thomas Keane, Director, Financial Aid and Student Employment
410 Thurston Avenue, Ithaca, NY 14850-2488
(607) 255-2000

Corning Community College
Corning, New York
www.corning-cc.edu
Federal Code: 002863

2-year public community college in large town.

Enrollment: 3,203 undergrads.

Selectivity: Open admission; but selective for some programs.

BASIC COSTS (2007-2008)

Tuition and fees: $3,726; out-of-state residents $7,076.

Per-credit charge: $140; out-of-state residents $280.

FINANCIAL AID PICTURE

Students with need: Need-based aid available for full-time and part-time students. Work study available weekends and for part-time students.

Students without need: This college awards aid only to students with need.

FINANCIAL AID PROCEDURES

Forms required: FAFSA.

Dates and Deadlines: Priority date 4/1; no closing date. Applicants notified on a rolling basis starting 4/15; must reply within 2 week(s) of notification.

CONTACT

Barbara Snow, Director of Financial Aid
One Academic Drive, Corning, NY 14830
(607) 962-9011

Culinary Institute of America
Hyde Park, New York
www.ciachef.edu
Federal Code: 007304

4-year private culinary school in large town.

Enrollment: 2,738 undergrads. 572 full-time freshmen.

Selectivity: Admits 50 to 75% of applicants.

BASIC COSTS (2007-2008)

Tuition and fees: $22,370.

Room and board: $6,890.

Additional info: Room and board costs shown for typical undergraduate; costs may vary.

FINANCIAL AID PICTURE

Students with need: Need-based aid available for full-time students. Work study available nights, weekends, and for part-time students.

Students without need: No-need awards available for academics, alumni affiliation, job skills, leadership, minority status.

Scholarships offered: Cream of the Crop Scholarship: up to $20,000; 10 per year; for prospective students with outstanding academic and leadership skills.

FINANCIAL AID PROCEDURES

Forms required: FAFSA.

Dates and Deadlines: Priority date 12/15; no closing date. Applicants notified by 4/1; must reply by 5/1 or within 4 week(s) of notification.

CONTACT

Patricia Arcuri, Director of Financial Aid
1946 Campus Drive, Hyde Park, NY 12538-1499
(845) 451-1243

Daemen College

Amherst, New York
www.daemen.edu
Federal Code: 002808

4-year private liberal arts college in small city.
Enrollment: 1,571 undergrads, 14% part-time. 368 full-time freshmen.
Selectivity: Admits 50 to 75% of applicants.

BASIC COSTS (2007-2008)
Tuition and fees: $18,750.
Per-credit charge: $610.
Room and board: $8,610.

FINANCIAL AID PICTURE (2006-2007)
Students with need: Out of 323 full-time freshmen who applied for aid, 323 were judged to have need. Of these, 323 received aid, and 53 had their full need met. Average financial aid package met 71.3% of need; average scholarship/grant was $8,931; average loan was $3,149. For part-time students, average financial aid package was $7,575.
Students without need: 2 full-time freshmen who did not demonstrate need for aid received scholarships/grants; average award was $17,440. No-need awards available for academics, art, athletics, leadership.
Scholarships offered: *Merit:* President's Scholarship, Dean's Scholarship, and Alumni Grant: $2,500-$10,000; renewable awards to freshmen and transfers, based on high school GPA & SAT scores. Competitive and renewable Trustee Scholarship: $17,000 (2 awards) and $14,000 (4 awards). Renewable visual arts scholarships: $5,000; 2 awards.
Athletic: 3 full-time freshmen received athletic scholarships; average amount $6,833.
Cumulative student debt: 87% of graduating class had student loans; average debt was $20,465.

FINANCIAL AID PROCEDURES
Forms required: FAFSA, state aid form.
Dates and Deadlines: Priority date 2/15; no closing date. Applicants notified on a rolling basis starting 2/1; must reply within 2 week(s) of notification.

CONTACT
Jeffrey Pagano, Director of Financial Aid
4380 Main Street, Amherst, NY 14226-3592
(716) 839-8254

DeVry Institute of Technology: New York

Long Island City, New York
www.devry.edu
Federal Code: 003099

4-year for-profit business and technical college in very large city.
Enrollment: 880 undergrads, 29% part-time. 155 full-time freshmen.

BASIC COSTS (2007-2008)
Tuition and fees: $14,640.
Per-credit charge: $525.

FINANCIAL AID PICTURE (2006-2007)
Students with need: Need-based aid available for full-time and part-time students.
Students without need: This college awards aid only to students with need.

FINANCIAL AID PROCEDURES
Forms required: FAFSA.
Dates and Deadlines: No deadline. Applicants notified on a rolling basis.

CONTACT
Elvira Senese, Director, Student Finance
3020 Thomson Avenue, Long Island City, NY 11101-3051
(718) 472-2728

Dominican College of Blauvelt

Orangeburg, New York
www.dc.edu
Federal Code: 002713

4-year private health science and liberal arts college in small town.
Enrollment: 1,698 undergrads, 26% part-time. 331 full-time freshmen.
Selectivity: Admits over 75% of applicants.

BASIC COSTS (2008-2009)
Tuition and fees: $20,300.
Per-credit charge: $640.
Room and board: $9,730.

FINANCIAL AID PICTURE (2007-2008)
Students with need: Out of 320 full-time freshmen who applied for aid, 302 were judged to have need. Of these, 302 received aid, and 32 had their full need met. Average financial aid package met 62% of need; average scholarship/grant was $11,745; average loan was $3,466. For part-time students, average financial aid package was $6,340.
Students without need: 67 full-time freshmen who did not demonstrate need for aid received scholarships/grants; average award was $10,446. No-need awards available for academics, athletics.
Scholarships offered: *Merit:* All applicants considered for non-need based scholarships or grants based on high school GPA and SAT/ACT scores. *Athletic:* 19 full-time freshmen received athletic scholarships; average amount $9,101.
Cumulative student debt: 100% of graduating class had student loans; average debt was $24,313.
Additional info: Individual financial aid counseling available.

FINANCIAL AID PROCEDURES
Forms required: FAFSA, state aid form.
Dates and Deadlines: Priority date 2/15; no closing date. Applicants notified on a rolling basis starting 2/1.

CONTACT
Eileen Felske, Director of Financial Aid
470 Western Highway, Orangeburg, NY 10962-1210
(845) 848-7821

Dowling College

Oakdale, New York
www.dowling.edu
Federal Code: 002667

4-year private liberal arts college in large town.
Enrollment: 2,914 undergrads, 26% part-time. 466 full-time freshmen.
Selectivity: Admits over 75% of applicants.

BASIC COSTS (2007-2008)
Tuition and fees: $19,270.
Per-credit charge: $606.
Room and board: $8,907.

FINANCIAL AID PICTURE (2007-2008)
Students with need: Out of 308 full-time freshmen who applied for aid, 297 were judged to have need. Of these, 266 received aid, and 28 had their full need met. Average financial aid package met 28% of need; average scholarship/grant was $2,572; average loan was $3,589. For part-time students, average financial aid package was $1,590.
Students without need: 212 full-time freshmen who did not demonstrate need for aid received scholarships/grants; average award was $4,420. No-need awards available for academics, alumni affiliation, athletics.
Scholarships offered: 51 full-time freshmen received athletic scholarships; average amount $7,197.
Cumulative student debt: 73% of graduating class had student loans; average debt was $28,585.

FINANCIAL AID PROCEDURES

Forms required: FAFSA, state aid form.

Dates and Deadlines: Priority date 4/30; no closing date. Applicants notified on a rolling basis starting 3/1.

Transfers: No deadline. Applicants notified on a rolling basis. Academic scholarships available for transfers with associate degrees.

CONTACT

Patricia Noren, Director of Student Financial Services & Bursar

150 Idle Hour Boulevard, Oakdale, NY 11769-1999

(631) 244-3368

Dutchess Community College

Poughkeepsie, New York

www.sunydutchess.edu   Federal Code: 002864

2-year public community college in large town.

Enrollment: 6,686 undergrads. 1,547 full-time freshmen.

Selectivity: Open admission; but selective for some programs.

BASIC COSTS (2007-2008)

Tuition and fees: $3,217; out-of-state residents $6,017.

Per-credit charge: $115; out-of-state residents $230.

FINANCIAL AID PICTURE (2006-2007)

Students with need: 85% of average financial aid package awarded as scholarships/grants, 15% awarded as loans/jobs. Need-based aid available for part-time students.

FINANCIAL AID PROCEDURES

Forms required: FAFSA, state aid form, institutional form.

Dates and Deadlines: Priority date 5/1; no closing date. Applicants notified on a rolling basis starting 5/15; must reply within 2 week(s) of notification.

CONTACT

Susan Mead, Director of Financial Aid

53 Pendell Road, Poughkeepsie, NY 12601-1595

(845) 431-8030

D'Youville College

Buffalo, New York

www.dyc.edu   Federal Code: 002712

4-year private health science and liberal arts college in large city.

Enrollment: 1,532 undergrads, 12% part-time. 245 full-time freshmen.

Selectivity: Admits 50 to 75% of applicants.

BASIC COSTS (2008-2009)

Tuition and fees: $19,000.

Room and board: $9,300.

Additional info: Substantial tuition reduction depending on SAT scores.

FINANCIAL AID PICTURE (2006-2007)

Students with need: Out of 175 full-time freshmen who applied for aid, 159 were judged to have need. Of these, 157 received aid, and 42 had their full need met. Average financial aid package met 77% of need; average scholarship/grant was $9,335; average loan was $4,482. For part-time students, average financial aid package was $13,086.

Students without need: 31 full-time freshmen who did not demonstrate need for aid received scholarships/grants; average award was $8,545. No-need awards available for academics, leadership, religious affiliation, ROTC.

Cumulative student debt: 88% of graduating class had student loans; average debt was $24,580.

FINANCIAL AID PROCEDURES

Forms required: FAFSA, state aid form.

Dates and Deadlines: Priority date 3/1; no closing date. Applicants notified on a rolling basis starting 4/1; must reply within 2 week(s) of notification.

Transfers: Applicants notified on a rolling basis starting 4/1; must reply within 2 week(s) of notification. .

CONTACT

Lorraine Metz, Director of Financial Aid

320 Porter Avenue, Buffalo, NY 14201-1084

(716) 829-7500

Eastman School of Music of the University of Rochester

Rochester, New York

www.esm.rochester.edu   Federal Code: 008124

4-year private music and performing arts college in large city.

Enrollment: 504 undergrads.

BASIC COSTS (2007-2008)

Tuition and fees: $32,626.

Per-credit charge: $990.

Room and board: $10,600.

FINANCIAL AID PICTURE

Students with need: Need-based aid available for full-time and part-time students.

Students without need: No-need awards available for academics, alumni affiliation, job skills, leadership, minority status, music/drama, state/district residency.

Scholarships offered: All merit scholarships awarded based on admission criteria, and do not require separate application, audition, or interview.

FINANCIAL AID PROCEDURES

Forms required: FAFSA, state aid form, institutional form.

Dates and Deadlines: Closing date 2/28. Applicants notified on a rolling basis starting 3/15; must reply by 5/1 or within 2 week(s) of notification.

Transfers: No deadline. Applicants notified on a rolling basis starting 3/15; must reply by 5/1 or within 2 week(s) of notification.

CONTACT

Mary Ellen Nugent, Director of Financial Aid

26 Gibbs Street, Rochester, NY 14604-2599

(585) 274-1070

Elmira Business Institute

Elmira, New York

www.ebi-college.com   Federal Code: 009043

2-year for-profit business and technical college in large town.

Enrollment: 150 undergrads.

Selectivity: Open admission.

BASIC COSTS (2007-2008)

Tuition and fees: $8,450.

Per-credit charge: $275.

Additional info: Tuition at time of enrollment locked for 2 years.

FINANCIAL AID PICTURE

Students with need: Need-based aid available for full-time and part-time students.

Students without need: This college awards aid only to students with need.

FINANCIAL AID PROCEDURES

Forms required: FAFSA, state aid form, institutional form.

Dates and Deadlines: Closing date 5/1.

CONTACT

Lisa Roan

303 North Main Street, Elmira, NY 14901

(607) 733-7177

Elmira Business Institute: Vestal

Vestal, New York

www.ebi-college.com   Federal Code: 9043

2-year for-profit business and technical college in small city.

Enrollment: 74 undergrads, 31% part-time.

Selectivity: Open admission.

BASIC COSTS (2007-2008)

Tuition and fees: $8,450.

Per-credit charge: $275.

FINANCIAL AID PICTURE

Students with need: Need-based aid available for full-time and part-time students.

Students without need: This college awards aid only to students with need.

FINANCIAL AID PROCEDURES

Forms required: FAFSA, state aid form, institutional form.

Dates and Deadlines: No deadline. Applicants notified on a rolling basis.

CONTACT

Sue Reinbold, Administrator

4100 Vestal Road, Vestal, NY 13850

Elmira College

Elmira, New York

www.elmira.edu   Federal Code: 002718

4-year private liberal arts college in large town.

Enrollment: 1,176 undergrads.

Selectivity: Admits over 75% of applicants.

BASIC COSTS (2008-2009)

Tuition and fees: $33,200.

Room and board: $10,100.

FINANCIAL AID PICTURE (2007-2008)

Students with need: Average financial aid package met 83% of need; average scholarship/grant was $21,674; average loan was $4,738. Need-based aid available for part-time students.

Students without need: No-need awards available for academics, leadership, ROTC.

Scholarships offered: Scholarships for valedictorian and salutatorian: 20 anticipated awards; full and 75% tuition respectively, renewable. Scholarships based on GPA, test scores, class rank, leadership: $18,000, $15,000, $12,000, $10,000 or $6,000, renewable awards.

Cumulative student debt: 80% of graduating class had student loans; average debt was $26,212.

Additional info: Sibling Scholarship program provides 50% discounts on second family member's room and board, regardless of need.

FINANCIAL AID PROCEDURES

Forms required: FAFSA, state aid form.

Dates and Deadlines: Priority date 2/1; closing date 6/30. Applicants notified on a rolling basis starting 2/1; must reply by 5/1 or within 2 week(s) of notification.

Transfers: No deadline. Applicants notified on a rolling basis starting 2/1; must reply by 5/1 or within 2 week(s) of notification.

CONTACT

Kathleen Cohen, Dean of Financial Aid

One Park Place, Elmira, NY 14901

(607) 735-1728

Erie Community College: City Campus

Buffalo, New York

www.ecc.edu   Federal Code: 010684

2-year public community college in large city.

Enrollment: 2,656 undergrads, 20% part-time. 550 full-time freshmen.

Selectivity: Open admission; but selective for some programs.

BASIC COSTS (2007-2008)

Tuition and fees: $3,339; out-of-district residents $6,326; out-of-state residents $6,326.

Per-credit charge: $125; out-of-state residents $250.

FINANCIAL AID PICTURE

Students with need: Need-based aid available for full-time and part-time students. Work study available weekends and for part-time students.

Students without need: This college awards aid only to students with need.

FINANCIAL AID PROCEDURES

Forms required: FAFSA, state aid form.

Dates and Deadlines: Priority date 6/1; no closing date. Applicants notified on a rolling basis starting 4/1; must reply within 2 week(s) of notification.

CONTACT

Scott Weltjen, Director of Financial Aid

121 Ellicott Street, Buffalo, NY 14203-2698

(716) 851-1177

Erie Community College: North Campus

Williamsville, New York

www.ecc.edu   Federal Code: 010684

2-year public community college in small city.

Enrollment: 5,204 undergrads, 25% part-time. 1,124 full-time freshmen.

Selectivity: Open admission; but selective for some programs.

BASIC COSTS (2007-2008)

Tuition and fees: $3,339; out-of-district residents $6,326; out-of-state residents $6,326.

Per-credit charge: $125; out-of-state residents $250.

FINANCIAL AID PICTURE

Students with need: Need-based aid available for full-time and part-time students. Work study available weekends and for part-time students.

Students without need: This college awards aid only to students with need.

FINANCIAL AID PROCEDURES

Forms required: FAFSA, state aid form.

Dates and Deadlines: Priority date 6/1; no closing date. Applicants notified on a rolling basis starting 4/1; must reply within 2 week(s) of notification.

CONTACT

Scott Weltjen, Director of Financial Aid

6205 Main Street, Williamsville, NY 14221-7095

(716) 851-1477

Erie Community College: South Campus
Orchard Park, New York
www.ecc.edu
Federal Code: 010684

2-year public community college in large town.
Enrollment: 3,216 undergrads, 22% part-time. 768 full-time freshmen.
Selectivity: Open admission; but selective for some programs.

BASIC COSTS (2007-2008)
Tuition and fees: $3,339; out-of-district residents $6,326; out-of-state residents $6,326.
Per-credit charge: $125; out-of-state residents $250.

FINANCIAL AID PICTURE
Students with need: Need-based aid available for full-time and part-time students. Work study available weekends and for part-time students.
Students without need: This college awards aid only to students with need.

FINANCIAL AID PROCEDURES
Forms required: FAFSA, state aid form.
Dates and Deadlines: Priority date 6/1; no closing date. Applicants notified on a rolling basis starting 4/1; must reply within 2 week(s) of notification.

CONTACT
Scott Weltjen, Director of Financial Aid
4041 Southwestern Boulevard, Orchard Park, NY 14127-2199
(716) 851-1677

Eugene Lang College The New School for Liberal Arts
New York, New York
www.lang.edu
Federal Code: 002780

4-year private liberal arts college in very large city.
Enrollment: 1,281 undergrads, 4% part-time. 320 full-time freshmen.
Selectivity: Admits 50 to 75% of applicants.

BASIC COSTS (2008-2009)
Tuition and fees: $33,060.
Per-credit charge: $1,100.
Room and board: $12,390.

FINANCIAL AID PICTURE (2007-2008)
Students with need: Out of 227 full-time freshmen who applied for aid, 162 were judged to have need. Of these, 162 received aid, and 35 had their full need met. Average financial aid package met 79% of need; average scholarship/grant was $12,438; average loan was $3,247.
Students without need: 34 full-time freshmen who did not demonstrate need for aid received scholarships/grants; average award was $3,168. No-need awards available for academics, music/drama.
Cumulative student debt: 76% of graduating class had student loans; average debt was $16,414.

FINANCIAL AID PROCEDURES
Forms required: FAFSA, state aid form.
Dates and Deadlines: Priority date 3/1; no closing date. Applicants notified on a rolling basis starting 3/1; must reply within 4 week(s) of notification.
Transfers: Must reply within 4 week(s) of notification.

CONTACT
Eileen Doyle, Assistant Vice President for Financial Aid
65 West 11th Street (3rd floor), New York, NY 10011-8693
(212) 229-8930

Excelsior College
Albany, New York
www.excelsior.edu
Federal Code: 014251

4-year private virtual liberal arts college in small city.
Enrollment: 33,422 undergrads, 100% part-time.
Selectivity: Open admission; but selective for some programs.

BASIC COSTS (2007-2008)
Additional info: Students charged $995 enrollment fee and $275 per credit hour. Because of nontraditional pricing, school does not charge set tuition based on 15 credit hours per semester.

FINANCIAL AID PICTURE (2006-2007)
Students with need: Need-based aid available for part-time students.
Students without need: This college awards aid only to students with need.
Additional info: Excelsior College is Title IV eligible for certain degree programs. College approved for all veterans educational benefit programs.

FINANCIAL AID PROCEDURES
Forms required: FAFSA, institutional form.
Dates and Deadlines: Priority date 7/1; no closing date. Applicants notified on a rolling basis starting 8/1; must reply within 2 week(s) of notification.

CONTACT
Thomas Dalton, Assistant Vice President for Enrollment Management
7 Columbia Circle, Albany, NY 12203-5159
(518) 464-8500

Fashion Institute of Technology
New York, New York
www.fitnyc.edu
Federal Code: 002866

4-year public visual arts and business college in very large city.
Enrollment: 7,535 undergrads, 12% part-time. 1,073 full-time freshmen.
Selectivity: Admits less than 50% of applicants.

BASIC COSTS (2007-2008)
Tuition and fees: $3,732; out-of-state residents $10,316.
Per-credit charge: $137; out-of-state residents $412.
Room and board: $10,095.

FINANCIAL AID PICTURE
Students with need: Need-based aid available for full-time and part-time students.
Students without need: This college awards aid only to students with need.

FINANCIAL AID PROCEDURES
Forms required: FAFSA, state aid form, institutional form.
Dates and Deadlines: Priority date 2/1; no closing date. Applicants notified on a rolling basis starting 4/15; must reply within 2 week(s) of notification.

CONTACT
Mina Friedmann, Director of Financial Aid
Seventh Avenue at 27th Street, New York, NY 10001-5992
(212) 217-7999

Finger Lakes Community College
Canandaigua, New York
www.flcc.edu
Federal Code: 007532

2-year public community college in small town.
Enrollment: 3,644 undergrads, 22% part-time. 1,201 full-time freshmen.
Selectivity: Open admission; but selective for some programs.

BASIC COSTS (2007-2008)

Tuition and fees: $3,482; out-of-state residents $6,612.
Per-credit charge: $120; out-of-state residents $240.

FINANCIAL AID PICTURE (2006-2007)

Students with need: 68% of average financial aid package awarded as scholarships/grants, 32% awarded as loans/jobs. Need-based aid available for part-time students. Work study available nights, weekends, and for part-time students.
Students without need: This college awards aid only to students with need.

FINANCIAL AID PROCEDURES

Forms required: FAFSA, state aid form, institutional form.
Dates and Deadlines: Priority date 4/1; no closing date. Applicants notified on a rolling basis starting 3/1.

CONTACT

Susan Romano, Director, Financial Aid
4355 Lake Shore Drive, Canandaigua, NY 14424-8395
(585) 394-3500 ext. 7275

Five Towns College
Dix Hills, New York
www.fivetowns.edu   Federal Code: 012561

4-year for-profit music and liberal arts college in large town.
Enrollment: 1,093 undergrads.
Selectivity: Admits 50 to 75% of applicants.

BASIC COSTS (2008-2009)

Tuition and fees: $17,800.
Per-credit charge: $725.
Room and board: $11,750.

FINANCIAL AID PICTURE

Students with need: Need-based aid available for full-time and part-time students. Work study available nights, weekends, and for part-time students.
Students without need: No-need awards available for academics, music/drama.

FINANCIAL AID PROCEDURES

Forms required: FAFSA, state aid form, institutional form.
Dates and Deadlines: Priority date 3/31; no closing date. Applicants notified on a rolling basis; must reply within 4 week(s) of notification.

CONTACT

Mary Venezia, Financial Aid Administrator
305 North Service Road, Dix Hills, NY 11746-6055
(631) 424-7000 ext. 2113

Fordham University
Bronx, New York   Federal Code: 002722
www.fordham.edu   CSS Code: 2259

4-year private university in very large city, affiliated with Roman Catholic Church.
Enrollment: 7,541 undergrads, 6% part-time. 1,702 full-time freshmen.
Selectivity: Admits less than 50% of applicants.

BASIC COSTS (2007-2008)

Tuition and fees: $32,720.
Per-credit charge: $697.
Room and board: $12,300.

FINANCIAL AID PICTURE (2006-2007)

Students with need: Out of 1,466 full-time freshmen who applied for aid, 1,080 were judged to have need. Of these, 1,079 received aid, and 235 had their full need met. Average financial aid package met 75% of need; average scholarship/grant was $15,417; average loan was $2,896. For part-time students, average financial aid package was $10,347.
Students without need: 371 full-time freshmen who did not demonstrate need for aid received scholarships/grants; average award was $8,260. No-need awards available for academics, athletics, ROTC.
Scholarships offered: 36 full-time freshmen received athletic scholarships; average amount $16,033.
Cumulative student debt: 64% of graduating class had student loans; average debt was $26,879.

FINANCIAL AID PROCEDURES

Forms required: FAFSA, CSS PROFILE.
Dates and Deadlines: Closing date 2/1. Applicants notified by 3/31; must reply by 5/1 or within 2 week(s) of notification.
Transfers: Priority date 2/1; closing date 5/1.

CONTACT

East 441 Fordham Road, Bronx, NY 10458

Fulton-Montgomery Community College
Johnstown, New York
www.fmcc.suny.edu   Federal Code: 002867

2-year public community college in large town.
Enrollment: 1,722 undergrads, 21% part-time. 553 full-time freshmen.
Selectivity: Open admission; but selective for some programs.

BASIC COSTS (2007-2008)

Tuition and fees: $3,468; out-of-state residents $6,562.
Per-credit charge: $128; out-of-state residents $256.

FINANCIAL AID PICTURE

Students with need: Need-based aid available for full-time and part-time students. Work study available nights, weekends, and for part-time students.
Students without need: No-need awards available for academics.
Scholarships offered: Academic Excellence Scholarship: $1,000 a year with limit of 2 years for residents of Fulton, Montgomery, or Hamilton or Galway Central School District. Applicants must have 3.5 cumulative GPA, submit an essay and list of extracurricular activities, and be enrolled full-time at college. Must maintain 3.3 cumulative GPA. CTW Scholarship: $1,000 a year with limit of 2 years, for Montgomery residents or applicants who attend high school in Montgomery County. Applicants must have B average. Must maintain 3.3 cumulative GPA at end of first year.

FINANCIAL AID PROCEDURES

Forms required: FAFSA, state aid form.
Dates and Deadlines: Priority date 6/1; no closing date. Applicants notified on a rolling basis starting 6/15; must reply within 2 week(s) of notification.

CONTACT

Rebecca Cozzocrea, Coordinator of Financial Aid
2805 State Highway 67, Johnstown, NY 12095
(518) 762-4651 ext. 8201

Genesee Community College
Batavia, New York
www.genesee.edu   Federal Code: 006782

2-year public community college in large town.
Enrollment: 3,753 undergrads, 24% part-time. 1,046 full-time freshmen.
Selectivity: Open admission; but selective for some programs.

BASIC COSTS (2007-2008)

Tuition and fees: $3,590; out-of-state residents $4,190.
Per-credit charge: $136; out-of-state residents $154.

FINANCIAL AID PICTURE

Students with need: Need-based aid available for full-time and part-time students. Work study available nights, weekends, and for part-time students.

FINANCIAL AID PROCEDURES

Forms required: FAFSA, state aid form.
Dates and Deadlines: Priority date 3/1; closing date 5/1. Applicants notified on a rolling basis starting 4/15; must reply within 2 week(s) of notification.
Transfers: No deadline.

CONTACT

Joseph Bailey, Director of Financial Aid
One College Road, Batavia, NY 14020-9704
(585) 345-6900

Globe Institute of Technology
New York, New York
www.globe.edu
Federal Code: 025408

4-year for-profit university and business college in very large city.
Enrollment: 2,305 undergrads.
Selectivity: Open admission; but selective for some programs.

BASIC COSTS (2008-2009)

Tuition and fees: $11,040.
Per-credit charge: $450.
Room and board: $5,000.
Additional info: Tuition at time of enrollment locked for 4 years; tuition/fee waivers available for adults, minority students, unemployed or children of unemployed.

FINANCIAL AID PICTURE

Students with need: Need-based aid available for full-time and part-time students. Work study available nights, weekends, and for part-time students.
Students without need: No-need awards available for academics, athletics.

FINANCIAL AID PROCEDURES

Forms required: FAFSA, state aid form, institutional form.
Dates and Deadlines: No deadline. Applicants notified on a rolling basis.
Transfers: No deadline. Applicants notified on a rolling basis.

CONTACT

Marcus Browne, Director of Financial Aid
291 Broadway, New York, NY 10007
(212) 349-4330

Hamilton College
Clinton, New York
www.hamilton.edu
Federal Code: 002728
CSS Code: 2286

4-year private liberal arts college in small town.
Enrollment: 1,810 undergrads. 468 full-time freshmen.
Selectivity: Admits less than 50% of applicants.

BASIC COSTS (2007-2008)

Tuition and fees: $36,860.
Room and board: $9,350.

FINANCIAL AID PICTURE (2007-2008)

Students with need: Out of 256 full-time freshmen who applied for aid, 191 were judged to have need. Of these, 191 received aid, and 191 had their full need met. Average financial aid package met 100% of need; average scholarship/grant was $27,356; average loan was $3,157.

Students without need: 7 full-time freshmen who did not demonstrate need for aid received scholarships/grants; average award was $18,811. No-need awards available for academics, leadership.
Scholarships offered: Summer research grants: $10,000 and $3,000; 10 awards to top applicants in entering class.
Cumulative student debt: 48% of graduating class had student loans; average debt was $16,808.
Additional info: Will meet demonstrated need of all aided applicants.

FINANCIAL AID PROCEDURES

Forms required: FAFSA, CSS PROFILE, state aid form, institutional form.
Dates and Deadlines: Closing date 2/8. Applicants notified by 4/1; must reply by 5/1.

CONTACT

Matt Malatesta, Director of Financial Aid
198 College Hill Road, Clinton, NY 13323-1293
(315) 859-4434

Hartwick College
Oneonta, New York
www.hartwick.edu
Federal Code: 002729

4-year private liberal arts college in large town.
Enrollment: 1,513 undergrads, 3% part-time. 452 full-time freshmen.
Selectivity: Admits over 75% of applicants.

BASIC COSTS (2008-2009)

Tuition and fees: $31,900.
Per-credit charge: $952.
Room and board: $8,685.
Additional info: New students (freshmen and transfers) must purchase laptop from college; cost of computer included in tuition.

FINANCIAL AID PICTURE

Students with need: Need-based aid available for full-time and part-time students. Work study available nights, weekends, and for part-time students.
Students without need: No-need awards available for academics, alumni affiliation, athletics, leadership, state/district residency.

FINANCIAL AID PROCEDURES

Forms required: FAFSA, institutional form.
Dates and Deadlines: Priority date 2/15; no closing date. Applicants notified by 3/15; must reply within 2 week(s) of notification.
Transfers: Priority date 8/1; no deadline. Applicants notified on a rolling basis starting 3/15; must reply within 2 week(s) of notification.

CONTACT

Melissa Allen, Director of Financial Aid
Box 4022, Oneonta, NY 13820-4022
(607) 431-4130

Helene Fuld College of Nursing
New York, New York
www.helenefuld.edu
Federal Code: 015395

2-year private nursing and junior college in very large city.
Enrollment: 335 undergrads.

BASIC COSTS (2007-2008)

Tuition and fees: $14,118.
Per-credit charge: $252.

FINANCIAL AID PICTURE

Students with need: Need-based aid available for full-time and part-time students.

Students without need: This college awards aid only to students with need.

FINANCIAL AID PROCEDURES

Forms required: FAFSA, state aid form.
Dates and Deadlines: No deadline. Applicants notified on a rolling basis.

CONTACT

Andrine Thomas, Financial Aid Counselor and Loan Coordinator
24 East 120th Street, New York, NY 10035
(212) 616-7253

Herkimer County Community College
Herkimer, New York
www.herkimer.edu   Federal Code: 004788

2-year public community college in small town.
Enrollment: 2,107 full-time undergrads.
Selectivity: Open admission; but selective for some programs.

BASIC COSTS (2007-2008)

Tuition and fees: $3,430; out-of-state residents $5,430.
Per-credit charge: $117; out-of-state residents $208.
Additional info: Apartment-style dorms with a la carte meal service available. Tuition/fee waivers available for unemployed or children of unemployed.

FINANCIAL AID PICTURE

Students with need: Need-based aid available for full-time and part-time students. Work study available nights, weekends, and for part-time students.

FINANCIAL AID PROCEDURES

Forms required: FAFSA, state aid form.
Dates and Deadlines: Priority date 5/1; no closing date. Applicants notified on a rolling basis starting 4/1; must reply within 2 week(s) of notification.

CONTACT

Susan Tripp, Director of Financial Aid
100 Reservoir Road, Herkimer, NY 13350-1598
(315) 866-0300 ext. 8282

Hilbert College
Hamburg, New York
www.hilbert.edu   Federal Code: 002735

4-year private liberal arts college in large town, affiliated with Roman Catholic Church.
Enrollment: 999 undergrads, 20% part-time. 209 full-time freshmen.
Selectivity: Admits over 75% of applicants.

BASIC COSTS (2008-2009)

Tuition and fees: $17,350.
Per-credit charge: $390.
Room and board: $6,950.
Additional info: Tuition/fee waivers available for minority students.

FINANCIAL AID PICTURE (2007-2008)

Students with need: Out of 206 full-time freshmen who applied for aid, 189 were judged to have need. Of these, 189 received aid, and 23 had their full need met. Average financial aid package met 67% of need; average scholarship/grant was $8,380; average loan was $3,953. For part-time students, average financial aid package was $5,061.
Students without need: 19 full-time freshmen who did not demonstrate need for aid received scholarships/grants; average award was $8,600. No-need awards available for academics, job skills, leadership, minority status, state/district residency.
Cumulative student debt: 93% of graduating class had student loans; average debt was $27,318.

FINANCIAL AID PROCEDURES

Forms required: FAFSA, state aid form.
Dates and Deadlines: Priority date 3/1; no closing date. Applicants notified on a rolling basis starting 3/15; must reply within 2 week(s) of notification.

CONTACT

Beverly Chudy, Director of Student Financial Aid
5200 South Park Avenue, Hamburg, NY 14075-1597
(716) 649-7900

Hobart and William Smith Colleges
Geneva, New York   Federal Code: 002731
www.hws.edu   CSS Code: 2294

4-year private liberal arts college in large town.
Enrollment: 1,998 undergrads. 466 full-time freshmen.
Selectivity: Admits 50 to 75% of applicants.

BASIC COSTS (2008-2009)

Tuition and fees: $38,860.
Room and board: $9,686.

FINANCIAL AID PICTURE (2006-2007)

Students with need: Out of 423 full-time freshmen who applied for aid, 337 were judged to have need. Of these, 335 received aid, and 273 had their full need met. Average financial aid package met 81% of need; average scholarship/grant was $22,309; average loan was $2,500.
Students without need: 126 full-time freshmen who did not demonstrate need for aid received scholarships/grants; average award was $18,077. No-need awards available for academics, art, leadership, music/drama.
Scholarships offered: Cornelius and Muriel P. Wood Scholarship and Richard Hersh Scholarship: full tuition for 4 years. Trustee Scholarship for Academic Excellence: $20,000 annually, for 4 years; based on GPA, test scores, class standing; 50 awarded. Faculty Scholarships: from $3,000-$15,000; 25-50 awarded. Phi Theta Kappa Trustee Scholarship: $2,500-$20,000 annually; for academically qualified transfer students with 2-year degree from junior or community college. Presidential Leaders Scholarship: $3,000-$12,000; based on academic excellence, leadership, personal qualities; 25-50 awarded. Arts Scholarships: $3,000-$15,000; for special talent in visual and performing arts; 15 awarded. Blackwell Medical Scholarships: full tuition for four years; MCAT waived, guaranteed seat at Upstate Medical Center at Syracuse University.
Cumulative student debt: 67% of graduating class had student loans; average debt was $25,924.

FINANCIAL AID PROCEDURES

Forms required: FAFSA, CSS PROFILE, state aid form.
Dates and Deadlines: Closing date 2/15. Applicants notified by 4/1; must reply by 5/1 or within 2 week(s) of notification.
Transfers: No deadline. Applicants notified on a rolling basis; must reply within 2 week(s) of notification.

CONTACT

Beth Turner, Director of Financial Aid Services and Office of Student Employment
629 South Main Street, Geneva, NY 14456
(315) 781-3315

Hofstra University
Hempstead, New York
www.hofstra.edu   Federal Code: 002732

4-year private university in large city.
Enrollment: 8,298 undergrads, 8% part-time. 1,710 full-time freshmen.
Selectivity: Admits 50 to 75% of applicants.

BASIC COSTS (2007-2008)

Tuition and fees: $26,730.
Per-credit charge: $785.
Room and board: $10,300.

FINANCIAL AID PICTURE (2006-2007)

Students with need: Out of 1,378 full-time freshmen who applied for aid, 1,067 were judged to have need. Of these, 1,056 received aid, and 182 had their full need met. Average financial aid package met 69% of need; average scholarship/grant was $9,131; average loan was $2,563. For part-time students, average financial aid package was $6,365.

Students without need: 339 full-time freshmen who did not demonstrate need for aid received scholarships/grants; average award was $8,528. No-need awards available for academics, alumni affiliation, art, athletics, leadership, music/drama, ROTC, state/district residency.

Scholarships offered: *Merit:* Hofstra's Distinguished Academic Scholar Program: full tuition; number awarded varies; for students with outstanding academic achievement. Hofstra Honors College Scholarships: varying amounts; awarded to students in Honors College. *Athletic:* 23 full-time freshmen received athletic scholarships; average amount $21,358.

Additional info: Special financial aid funds may be available for applicants with special talents and those with superior academic ability.

FINANCIAL AID PROCEDURES

Forms required: FAFSA, state aid form.
Dates and Deadlines: Priority date 2/15; no closing date. Applicants notified on a rolling basis starting 3/1.
Transfers: Awarded on basis of state residency, full-time status, remaining semester eligibility, and income level.

CONTACT

Jessica Eads, Dean of Admissions and Financial Aid
Admissions Center, 100 Hofstra University, Hempstead, NY 11549
(516) 463-8000

Houghton College

Houghton, New York
www.houghton.edu
Federal Code: 002734

4-year private liberal arts college in rural community, affiliated with Wesleyan Church.

Enrollment: 1,324 undergrads, 3% part-time. 265 full-time freshmen.
Selectivity: Admits over 75% of applicants.

BASIC COSTS (2008-2009)

Tuition and fees: $22,990.
Per-credit charge: $960.
Room and board: $6,930.
Additional info: Tuition includes laptop computer, fees. Tuition/fee waivers available for minority students.

FINANCIAL AID PICTURE (2007-2008)

Students with need: Out of 242 full-time freshmen who applied for aid, 217 were judged to have need. Of these, 217 received aid, and 46 had their full need met. Average financial aid package met 79% of need; average scholarship/grant was $9,800; average loan was $4,080. For part-time students, average financial aid package was $6,011.

Students without need: 36 full-time freshmen who did not demonstrate need for aid received scholarships/grants; average award was $8,526. No-need awards available for academics, alumni affiliation, art, athletics, music/drama, religious affiliation, ROTC, state/district residency.

Scholarships offered: *Merit:* Excellence Scholarships: $1,250-$7,500. Chamberlain Scholarships: $10,000; 35 awarded each year. Heritage Scholarships: $15,000; 6 awarded each year. Wesley Full Tuition Grant Program: scholarship awarded in conjuction with federal and state aid to meet the entire cost of tuition; 25 awarded each year. Phi Theta Kappa Scholarship: $2,000 (awarded to transfers who are members of PTK). Art Scholarships: $1,000-

$5,000 (based on art portfolio). Music Scholarships: $1,000-$10,000 (based on audition). *Athletic:* 33 full-time freshmen received athletic scholarships; average amount $5,577.

Cumulative student debt: 75% of graduating class had student loans; average debt was $28,515.

FINANCIAL AID PROCEDURES

Forms required: FAFSA.
Dates and Deadlines: Priority date 3/1; no closing date. Applicants notified on a rolling basis starting 3/15; must reply by 5/1.

CONTACT

Troy Martin, Director of Student Financial Services
1 Willard Avenue/Box 128, Houghton, NY 14744-0128
(585) 567-9328

Iona College

New Rochelle, New York
www.iona.edu
Federal Code: 002737

4-year private business and liberal arts college in small city, affiliated with Roman Catholic Church.

Enrollment: 3,480 undergrads, 4% part-time. 907 full-time freshmen.
Selectivity: Admits 50 to 75% of applicants.

BASIC COSTS (2008-2009)

Tuition and fees: $26,206.
Per-credit charge: $810.
Room and board: $10,800.

FINANCIAL AID PICTURE (2007-2008)

Students with need: Out of 898 full-time freshmen who applied for aid, 688 were judged to have need. Of these, 684 received aid, and 165 had their full need met. Average financial aid package met 25% of need; average scholarship/grant was $3,841; average loan was $2,081. For part-time students, average financial aid package was $5,481.

Students without need: 207 full-time freshmen who did not demonstrate need for aid received scholarships/grants; average award was $9,979. No-need awards available for academics, alumni affiliation, athletics, ROTC.

Scholarships offered: 69 full-time freshmen received athletic scholarships; average amount $9,159.

Cumulative student debt: 67% of graduating class had student loans; average debt was $19,451.

FINANCIAL AID PROCEDURES

Forms required: FAFSA, state aid form, institutional form.
Dates and Deadlines: Closing date 4/15. Applicants notified on a rolling basis starting 12/20; must reply by 5/1 or within 2 week(s) of notification.
Transfers: No deadline. Applicants notified on a rolling basis; must reply within 2 week(s) of notification.

CONTACT

Mary Grant, Associate Director of Student Financial Services
715 North Avenue, New Rochelle, NY 10801-1890
(914) 633-2497

Island Drafting and Technical Institute

Amityville, New York
www.idti.edu
Federal Code: 007375

2-year for-profit technical and career college in large town.
Enrollment: 123 undergrads. 49 full-time freshmen.
Selectivity: Open admission.

BASIC COSTS (2007-2008)

Tuition and fees: $12,800.

Per-credit charge: $415.

Additional info: Tuition at time of enrollment locked for 2 years.

FINANCIAL AID PICTURE

Students with need: Need-based aid available for full-time students.

Students without need: This college awards aid only to students with need.

FINANCIAL AID PROCEDURES

Dates and Deadlines: No deadline. Applicants notified on a rolling basis.

CONTACT

Daniel Greener, Financial Aid Office

128 Broadway, Amityville, NY 11701-2704

(631) 691-8733

Ithaca College

Ithaca, New York

www.ithaca.edu

Federal Code: 002739

4-year private health science and liberal arts college in large town.

Enrollment: 6,185 undergrads, 1% part-time. 1,797 full-time freshmen.

Selectivity: Admits 50 to 75% of applicants.

BASIC COSTS (2008-2009)

Tuition and fees: $30,606.

Per-credit charge: $1,020.

Room and board: $11,126.

Additional info: Tuition/fee waivers available for minority students.

FINANCIAL AID PICTURE

Students with need: Need-based aid available for full-time and part-time students. Work study available nights, weekends, and for part-time students.

Students without need: No-need awards available for academics, alumni affiliation, leadership, minority status, music/drama, ROTC.

Scholarships offered: President's Scholarships: $12,000-$16,000; awarded for academic achievement to approximately top 10% of applicants. Dean's Scholarships: $6,000-$9,000; awarded for academic ability to approximately top 11% to 35% of applicants. ALANA Scholarships: $4,000-$7,000 in addition to President's or Dean's Scholarship; awarded for academic achievement to 25% of applicants who represent minority groups. Flora Brown Awards: $5,000; given to those who are not merit eligible, but deserve recognition. MLK Scholarships: $18,000 each; awarded to approximately 15 students annually for academic excellence and community service. Ithaca Leadership Scholarships: $7,000; awarded for demonstrated leadership and above average academic performance; approximately 30 per year. Ithaca Premier Talent Scholarships: maximum award of $16,000 for selected applicants majoring in music and theater; approximately 10 available. Ithaca Sibling Grants: $1,000; awarded to students with concurrently enrolled sibling. Park Scholar Achievement awards: for outstanding achievement in communications; covers full cost of attendance; approximately 20 available per year. Ithaca College Merit Scholarship and Ithaca College National Merit Recognition Award: $2,000 scholarship plus Ithaca College President's Scholarship of $16,000; for students who designated Ithaca their first choice.

FINANCIAL AID PROCEDURES

Forms required: FAFSA.

Dates and Deadlines: Priority date 2/1; no closing date. Applicants notified on a rolling basis starting 2/15.

Transfers: No deadline. Applicants notified on a rolling basis; must reply by 2/1. All need-based and merit awards available for freshmen also available for transfers.

CONTACT

Larry Chambers, Director of Financial Aid

100 Job Hall, Ithaca, NY 14850-7020

(607) 274-3131

Jamestown Business College

Jamestown, New York

www.jbcny.org

Federal Code: 008495

2-year for-profit business and junior college in large town.

Enrollment: 252 undergrads. 88 full-time freshmen.

Selectivity: Admits over 75% of applicants.

BASIC COSTS (2008-2009)

Tuition and fees: $10,050.

FINANCIAL AID PICTURE (2006-2007)

Students with need: 71% of average financial aid package awarded as scholarships/grants, 29% awarded as loans/jobs. Need-based aid available for part-time students.

Students without need: No-need awards available for academics.

FINANCIAL AID PROCEDURES

Forms required: FAFSA, state aid form.

Dates and Deadlines: No deadline. Applicants notified on a rolling basis starting 2/15.

CONTACT

Diane Sturzenbecker, Financial Aid Officer

7 Fairmount Avenue, Jamestown, NY 14702-0429

(716) 664-5100

Jamestown Community College

Jamestown, New York

www.sunyjcc.edu

Federal Code: 002869

2-year public community college in large town.

Enrollment: 2,983 undergrads, 23% part-time. 808 full-time freshmen.

Selectivity: Open admission; but selective for some programs.

BASIC COSTS (2007-2008)

Tuition and fees: $3,800; out-of-state residents $7,150.

Per-credit charge: $140; out-of-state residents $253.

FINANCIAL AID PICTURE

Students with need: Need-based aid available for full-time and part-time students. Work study available nights, weekends, and for part-time students.

Students without need: No-need awards available for academics, alumni affiliation, art, athletics, music/drama, state/district residency.

Additional info: 100% resident tuition scholarship (less federal and state grants) for students in top 20% of high school graduating class with Regents diploma if residents of Chautauqua, Cattaraugus, or Allegany counties. Guaranteed in-state tuition rate for students in Warren, Potter, McKean and Forest counties in Pennsylvania, in top 20% of graduating class with an academic diploma.

FINANCIAL AID PROCEDURES

Forms required: FAFSA, state aid form.

Dates and Deadlines: Priority date 3/1; no closing date. Applicants notified on a rolling basis starting 4/15.

CONTACT

Laurie Vorp, Director of Financial Aid

525 Falconer Street, Jamestown, NY 14702-0020

(716) 665-5220

Jefferson Community College

Watertown, New York
www.sunyjefferson.edu
Federal Code: 002870

2-year public community college in large town.

Enrollment: 2,439 undergrads, 29% part-time. 627 full-time freshmen.

Selectivity: Open admission; but selective for some programs.

BASIC COSTS (2007-2008)

Tuition and fees: $3,479; out-of-state residents $5,989.

Per-credit charge: $128; out-of-state residents $233.

FINANCIAL AID PICTURE

Students with need: Need-based aid available for full-time and part-time students.

Students without need: This college awards aid only to students with need.

FINANCIAL AID PROCEDURES

Forms required: FAFSA, state aid form, institutional form.

Dates and Deadlines: Priority date 4/1; closing date 8/15. Applicants notified on a rolling basis starting 4/15; must reply within 2 week(s) of notification.

Transfers: No deadline.

CONTACT

James Ambrose, Director of Financial Aid
1220 Coffeen Street, Watertown, NY 13601
(315) 786-2355

Jewish Theological Seminary of America

New York, New York
www.jtsa.edu
CSS Code: 2339

4-year private university and seminary college in very large city, affiliated with Jewish faith.

Enrollment: 180 undergrads, 5% part-time. 40 full-time freshmen.

Selectivity: Admits 50 to 75% of applicants. GED not accepted.

BASIC COSTS (2008-2009)

Tuition and fees: $15,000.

Per-credit charge: $750.

Room and board: $9,200.

Additional info: Costs quoted paid to school only; separate costs assessed for dual-degree enrollment at Columbia University/Barnard College.

FINANCIAL AID PICTURE (2007-2008)

Students with need: Out of 13 full-time freshmen who applied for aid, 12 were judged to have need. Of these, 12 received aid, and 4 had their full need met. Average financial aid package met 88% of need; average scholarship/grant was $17,706; average loan was $3,500.

Students without need: 14 full-time freshmen who did not demonstrate need for aid received scholarships/grants; average award was $1,500. No-need awards available for academics, alumni affiliation, leadership.

Cumulative student debt: 31% of graduating class had student loans; average debt was $18,444.

FINANCIAL AID PROCEDURES

Forms required: FAFSA, CSS PROFILE, state aid form, institutional form.

Dates and Deadlines: Priority date 2/1; closing date 3/1. Applicants notified on a rolling basis starting 4/1; must reply within 4 week(s) of notification.

CONTACT

Linda Levine, Registrar/Director of Financial Aid
3080 Broadway, New York, NY 10027
(212) 678-8007

Juilliard School

New York, New York
www.juilliard.edu
Federal Code: 002742

4-year private music and performing arts college in very large city.

Enrollment: 491 undergrads. 106 full-time freshmen.

Selectivity: Admits less than 50% of applicants.

BASIC COSTS (2008-2009)

Tuition and fees: $28,640.

Room and board: $11,250.

FINANCIAL AID PICTURE (2007-2008)

Students with need: Out of 102 full-time freshmen who applied for aid, 80 were judged to have need. Of these, 80 received aid, and 30 had their full need met. Average financial aid package met 89% of need; average scholarship/grant was $21,248; average loan was $4,487. Need-based aid available for part-time students.

Students without need: 8 full-time freshmen who did not demonstrate need for aid received scholarships/grants; average award was $13,413. No-need awards available for music/drama.

Cumulative student debt: 64% of graduating class had student loans; average debt was $23,304.

FINANCIAL AID PROCEDURES

Forms required: FAFSA, institutional form.

Dates and Deadlines: Closing date 3/1. Applicants notified by 4/1; must reply by 5/1.

Transfers: Applicants notified by 4/1; must reply by 5/1 or within 2 week(s) of notification.

CONTACT

Tina Gonzalez, Director of Financial Aid
60 Lincoln Center Plaza, New York, NY 10023-6588
(212) 799-5000 ext. 211

Keuka College

Keuka Park, New York
www.keuka.edu
Federal Code: 002744

4-year private liberal arts college in rural community, affiliated with American Baptist Churches in the USA.

Enrollment: 1,441 undergrads, 22% part-time. 285 full-time freshmen.

Selectivity: Admits 50 to 75% of applicants.

BASIC COSTS (2008-2009)

Tuition and fees: $21,760.

Per-credit charge: $705.

Room and board: $8,850.

FINANCIAL AID PICTURE (2007-2008)

Students with need: Out of 272 full-time freshmen who applied for aid, 254 were judged to have need. Of these, 254 received aid, and 62 had their full need met. Average financial aid package met 76% of need; average scholarship/grant was $12,970; average loan was $5,251. For part-time students, average financial aid package was $5,939.

Students without need: 20 full-time freshmen who did not demonstrate need for aid received scholarships/grants; average award was $13,862. No-need awards available for academics, alumni affiliation, leadership, minority status, religious affiliation.

Scholarships offered: Goals Scholarship: 1/2 tuition; 82 average and 1000 SAT or 22 ACT required. Dean's Scholarship: 1/2-full tuition; 82 average and 1000 SAT or 22 ACT required. Presidential Scholarship: full tuition; based on GPA, SAT scores, class rank. SAT scores listed are exclusive of Writing portion.

Cumulative student debt: 88% of graduating class had student loans; average debt was $17,740.

FINANCIAL AID PROCEDURES

Forms required: FAFSA.

Dates and Deadlines: Priority date 3/15; no closing date. Applicants notified on a rolling basis starting 3/1; must reply by 5/1 or within 2 week(s) of notification.

CONTACT

Jerry Hiller, Vice President of Finance and Administration
141 Cental Avenue, Keuka Park, NY 14478-0098
(315) 279-5232

King's College

New York, New York
www.tkc.edu

Federal Code: 040953
CSS Code: 2871

4-year private liberal arts college in very large city, affiliated with nondenominational tradition.

Enrollment: 215 undergrads. 44 full-time freshmen.

Selectivity: Admits over 75% of applicants.

BASIC COSTS (2008-2009)

Tuition and fees: $22,850.

Per-credit charge: $950.

Room only: $8,750.

FINANCIAL AID PICTURE (2006-2007)

Students with need: Out of 38 full-time freshmen who applied for aid, 32 were judged to have need. Of these, 32 received aid, and 25 had their full need met. Average financial aid package met 95% of need; average scholarship/grant was $11,563; average loan was $4,583.

Students without need: 12 full-time freshmen who did not demonstrate need for aid received scholarships/grants; average award was $2,833. No-need awards available for academics.

Scholarships offered: Presidential Scholarships: unlimited number; based on SAT/ACTs and National Merit; award ranges from $1,500 to $8,000. Founders Scholarships: 4 awards given; $10,000 each; based on essay and presentation. Competition held in February.

Additional info: School does not participate in Title IV federal financial aid; students must file PROFILE and/or TAP application for institutional aid consideration.

FINANCIAL AID PROCEDURES

Forms required: CSS PROFILE.

Dates and Deadlines: Priority date 3/1; no closing date. Applicants notified on a rolling basis starting 4/1; must reply by 7/31.

CONTACT

Anna Peters, Director of Financial Aid
350 Fifth Avenue, Lower Lobby, New York, NY 10118
(212) 659-7200 ext. 7281

Laboratory Institute of Merchandising

New York, New York
www.limcollege.edu

Federal Code: 007466

4-year for-profit College of Fashion Business in very large city.

Enrollment: 1,107 undergrads, 4% part-time. 299 full-time freshmen.

Selectivity: Admits 50 to 75% of applicants.

BASIC COSTS (2008-2009)

Tuition and fees: $19,825.

Per-credit charge: $600.

Room and board: $18,700.

FINANCIAL AID PICTURE (2006-2007)

Students with need: Out of 200 full-time freshmen who applied for aid, 156 were judged to have need. Of these, 156 received aid. Need-based aid available for part-time students.

Students without need: This college awards aid only to students with need.

Cumulative student debt: 91% of graduating class had student loans; average debt was $19,593.

FINANCIAL AID PROCEDURES

Forms required: FAFSA, state aid form, institutional form.

Dates and Deadlines: Priority date 4/1; no closing date. Applicants notified on a rolling basis starting 2/15; must reply within 2 week(s) of notification.

CONTACT

Christopher Barto, Dean of Student Financial Services
12 East 53rd Street, New York, NY 10022
(212) 752-1530

Le Moyne College

Syracuse, New York
www.lemoyne.edu

Federal Code: 002748

4-year private liberal arts college in small city, affiliated with Roman Catholic Church.

Enrollment: 2,490 undergrads, 8% part-time. 545 full-time freshmen.

Selectivity: Admits 50 to 75% of applicants.

BASIC COSTS (2008-2009)

Tuition and fees: $25,000.

Per-credit charge: $509.

Room and board: $9,490.

FINANCIAL AID PICTURE (2006-2007)

Students with need: Out of 502 full-time freshmen who applied for aid, 444 were judged to have need. Of these, 441 received aid, and 127 had their full need met. Average financial aid package met 82% of need; average scholarship/grant was $15,998; average loan was $3,291. For part-time students, average financial aid package was $5,128.

Students without need: 71 full-time freshmen who did not demonstrate need for aid received scholarships/grants; average award was $12,421. No-need awards available for academics, alumni affiliation, athletics, leadership, minority status, ROTC.

Scholarships offered: *Merit:* Presidential Scholarships: $19,500. Dean Scholarships: $14,500. Ignation Scholarships (Jesuit High Schools): $14,500. Leadership Scholarships: $6,500; all based on academic criteria (GPA, rank, test scores). Loyola Scholarships: $14,500; for students of color; based on academic criteria. *Athletic:* 42 full-time freshmen received athletic scholarships; average amount $7,445.

Cumulative student debt: 83% of graduating class had student loans; average debt was $19,392.

Additional info: Parent loan program at low interest, monthly payment plans and alternative loans for students.

FINANCIAL AID PROCEDURES

Forms required: FAFSA, state aid form, institutional form.

Dates and Deadlines: Priority date 2/1; no closing date. Applicants notified by 3/15; must reply by 5/1 or within 2 week(s) of notification.

Transfers: Priority date 6/1; no deadline. Must reply by 5/1 or within 2 week(s) of notification.

CONTACT

William Cheetham, Director of Financial Aid
1419 Salt Springs Road, Syracuse, NY 13214-1301
(315) 445-4400

Long Island Business Institute

Commack, New York
www.libi.edu
Federal Code: 014514

2-year for-profit business college in large town.

Enrollment: 610 undergrads, 37% part-time. 122 full-time freshmen.
Selectivity: Open admission; but selective for some programs.

BASIC COSTS (2008-2009)
Tuition and fees: $10,200.
Per-credit charge: $325.
Additional info: Tuition varies by program.

FINANCIAL AID PICTURE (2007-2008)
Students with need: Out of 98 full-time freshmen who applied for aid, 98 were judged to have need. Of these, 98 received aid. Average financial aid package met 84% of need; average scholarship/grant was $3,300; average loan was $2,800. For part-time students, average financial aid package was $1,500.
Students without need: No-need awards available for academics.
Cumulative student debt: 95% of graduating class had student loans; average debt was $14,000.

FINANCIAL AID PROCEDURES
Forms required: FAFSA, state aid form.
Dates and Deadlines: No deadline. Must reply within 2 week(s) of notification.
Transfers: No deadline.

CONTACT
Nazaret Kiregian, Director of Financial Aid
6500 Jericho Turnpike, Commack, NY 11725
(631) 499-7100 ext. 13

Long Island University: Brooklyn Campus

Brooklyn, New York
www.liu.edu
Federal Code: 004779

4-year private university and branch campus college in very large city.
Enrollment: 5,047 undergrads, 15% part-time. 1,077 full-time freshmen.
Selectivity: Admits over 75% of applicants.

BASIC COSTS (2007-2008)
Tuition and fees: $25,922.
Per-credit charge: $771.
Room and board: $9,410.

FINANCIAL AID PICTURE
Students with need: Need-based aid available for full-time and part-time students.

FINANCIAL AID PROCEDURES
Forms required: FAFSA.
Dates and Deadlines: Priority date 3/15; no closing date. Applicants notified on a rolling basis.

CONTACT
Rose Iannicelli, Dean of Student Financial Services
1 University Plaza, Brooklyn, NY 11201
(718) 488-1037

Long Island University: C. W. Post Campus

Brookville, New York
www.liu.edu
Federal Code: 002751
CSS Code: 2070

4-year private university and branch campus and liberal arts college in small town.

Enrollment: 5,139 undergrads, 11% part-time. 1,102 full-time freshmen.
Selectivity: Admits over 75% of applicants.

BASIC COSTS (2007-2008)
Tuition and fees: $25,950.
Per-credit charge: $771.
Room and board: $9,600.

FINANCIAL AID PICTURE
Students with need: Need-based aid available for full-time and part-time students. Work study available nights, weekends, and for part-time students.

FINANCIAL AID PROCEDURES
Forms required: FAFSA, CSS PROFILE, state aid form.
Dates and Deadlines: Priority date 3/1; no closing date. Applicants notified on a rolling basis starting 3/1; must reply by 5/1.
Transfers: Applicants notified on a rolling basis starting 3/1; must reply by 5/1.

CONTACT
James Newell, Director of Student Financial Services
720 Northern Boulevard, Brookville, NY 11548-1300
(516) 299-2338

Manhattan College

Riverdale, New York
www.manhattan.edu
Federal Code: 002758

4-year private engineering and liberal arts college in very large city, affiliated with Roman Catholic Church.

Enrollment: 2,986 undergrads. 712 full-time freshmen.
Selectivity: Admits 50 to 75% of applicants.

BASIC COSTS (2008-2009)
Tuition and fees: $23,240.
Room and board: $9,300.
Additional info: Program fees range from $1,000 to $1,900 depending on program.

FINANCIAL AID PICTURE (2007-2008)
Students with need: 58% of average financial aid package awarded as scholarships/grants, 42% awarded as loans/jobs. Work study available nights, weekends, and for part-time students.
Students without need: This college awards aid only to students with need.

FINANCIAL AID PROCEDURES
Forms required: FAFSA.
Dates and Deadlines: Priority date 2/15; closing date 4/15. Applicants notified on a rolling basis starting 1/1; must reply by 5/1.
Transfers: Priority date 4/15; no deadline.

CONTACT
Ed Keough, Director of Student Financial Services
4513 Manhattan College Parkway, Riverdale, NY 10471
(718) 862-7100

Manhattan School of Music

New York, New York
www.msmnyc.edu

Federal Code: 002759
CSS Code: 2396

4-year private music college in very large city.

Enrollment: 415 undergrads, 1% part-time. 121 full-time freshmen.

Selectivity: Admits less than 50% of applicants.

BASIC COSTS (2008-2009)

Tuition and fees: $30,475.

Per-credit charge: $1,300.

Room and board: $13,700.

Additional info: Health fee of $2,250 required unless already insured.

FINANCIAL AID PICTURE (2007-2008)

Students with need: Out of 69 full-time freshmen who applied for aid, 58 were judged to have need. Of these, 55 received aid, and 9 had their full need met. Average financial aid package met 42% of need; average scholarship/grant was $15,229; average loan was $3,833. For part-time students, average financial aid package was $12,885.

Students without need: 8 full-time freshmen who did not demonstrate need for aid received scholarships/grants; average award was $13,550. No-need awards available for academics, alumni affiliation, leadership, music/drama.

FINANCIAL AID PROCEDURES

Forms required: FAFSA, CSS PROFILE, institutional form.

Dates and Deadlines: Closing date 3/1. Applicants notified by 4/1; must reply by 5/1 or within 2 week(s) of notification.

Transfers: Applicants notified by 4/1; must reply by 5/1 or within 2 week(s) of notification. CSS PROFILE required for transfer students.

CONTACT

Amy Anderson, Director of Admissions and Financial Aid
120 Claremont Avenue, New York, NY 10027-4698
(212) 749-2802 ext. 4463

Manhattanville College

Purchase, New York
www.manhattanville.edu

Federal Code: 002760

4-year private liberal arts and teachers college in small town.

Enrollment: 1,752 undergrads, 3% part-time.

Selectivity: Admits less than 50% of applicants.

BASIC COSTS (2008-2009)

Tuition and fees: $31,620.

Per-credit charge: $700.

Room and board: $13,040.

FINANCIAL AID PICTURE

Students with need: Need-based aid available for full-time and part-time students. Work study available nights, weekends, and for part-time students.

Students without need: No-need awards available for academics, alumni affiliation, art, leadership, music/drama.

Additional info: Upper level students may earn additional money and academic credit through internship program.

FINANCIAL AID PROCEDURES

Forms required: FAFSA, state aid form.

Dates and Deadlines: Closing date 3/1. Applicants notified on a rolling basis starting 2/1; must reply by 5/1 or within 2 week(s) of notification.

Transfers: No deadline.

CONTACT

Maria Barlaam, Director of Financial Aid
2900 Purchase Street, Purchase, NY 10577
(914) 323-5357

Mannes College The New School for Music

New York, New York
www.mannes.edu

Federal Code: 002780

4-year private music college in very large city.

Enrollment: 189 undergrads, 13% part-time. 55 full-time freshmen.

Selectivity: Admits less than 50% of applicants.

BASIC COSTS (2008-2009)

Tuition and fees: $32,150.

Per-credit charge: $1,030.

Room and board: $12,390.

Additional info: Tuition/fee waivers available for unemployed or children of unemployed.

FINANCIAL AID PICTURE (2007-2008)

Students with need: Out of 20 full-time freshmen who applied for aid, 9 were judged to have need. Of these, 9 received aid, and 1 had their full need met. Average financial aid package met 46% of need; average scholarship/grant was $4,757; average loan was $3,183.

Students without need: 5 full-time freshmen who did not demonstrate need for aid received scholarships/grants; average award was $14,502. No-need awards available for academics, music/drama.

Cumulative student debt: 78% of graduating class had student loans; average debt was $22,580.

Additional info: Closing date for scholarship applications 2 weeks prior to audition date.

FINANCIAL AID PROCEDURES

Forms required: FAFSA, state aid form.

Dates and Deadlines: Priority date 3/1; no closing date. Applicants notified on a rolling basis starting 3/1; must reply within 4 week(s) of notification.

CONTACT

Eileen Doyle, Executive Director of Undergraduate Financial Aid
150 West 85th Street, New York, NY 10024
(212) 580-0210

Maria College

Albany, New York
www.mariacollege.edu

Federal Code: 002763

2-year private junior college in small city.

Enrollment: 719 undergrads, 73% part-time. 60 full-time freshmen.

Selectivity: Admits 50 to 75% of applicants.

BASIC COSTS (2007-2008)

Tuition and fees: $8,400.

Per-credit charge: $295.

FINANCIAL AID PICTURE (2007-2008)

Students with need: Out of 52 full-time freshmen who applied for aid, 49 were judged to have need. Of these, 49 received aid, and 42 had their full need met. Average financial aid package met 89% of need; average scholarship/grant was $4,864; average loan was $2,425. For part-time students, average financial aid package was $4,590.

Students without need: This college awards aid only to students with need.

Cumulative student debt: 83% of graduating class had student loans; average debt was $8,267.

FINANCIAL AID PROCEDURES

Forms required: FAFSA, state aid form.

Dates and Deadlines: No deadline. Applicants notified on a rolling basis starting 2/1; must reply within 2 week(s) of notification.

Transfers: No deadline. Applicants notified on a rolling basis; must reply within 2 week(s) of notification.

CONTACT

Melissa Crossen, Director of Financial Aid
700 New Scotland Avenue, Albany, NY 12208
(518) 438-3111 ext. 229

Marist College
Poughkeepsie, New York
www.marist.edu
Federal Code: 002765

4-year private liberal arts college in small city.

Enrollment: 4,769 undergrads, 6% part-time. 1,019 full-time freshmen.

Selectivity: Admits less than 50% of applicants.

BASIC COSTS (2007-2008)

Tuition and fees: $24,040.

Per-credit charge: $550.

Room and board: $10,250.

Additional info: Tuition/fee waivers available for minority students.

FINANCIAL AID PICTURE (2007-2008)

Students with need: Out of 848 full-time freshmen who applied for aid, 606 were judged to have need. Of these, 604 received aid, and 157 had their full need met. Average financial aid package met 71% of need; average scholarship/grant was $11,723; average loan was $3,818. For part-time students, average financial aid package was $4,815.

Students without need: 320 full-time freshmen who did not demonstrate need for aid received scholarships/grants; average award was $7,072. No-need awards available for academics, athletics, music/drama, ROTC, state/district residency.

Scholarships offered: *Merit:* Awards vary, as much as $12,000 per recipient. ***Athletic:*** 82 full-time freshmen received athletic scholarships; average amount $9,804.

Cumulative student debt: 68% of graduating class had student loans; average debt was $28,374.

FINANCIAL AID PROCEDURES

Forms required: FAFSA, institutional form.

Dates and Deadlines: Priority date 2/15; closing date 5/1. Applicants notified on a rolling basis starting 3/15; must reply by 5/1 or within 2 week(s) of notification.

Transfers: No deadline. FAFSA should be filed as soon as possible after January 1.

CONTACT

Joe Weglarz, Executive Director, Student Financial Services
3399 North Road, Poughkeepsie, NY 12601-1387
(845) 575-3230

Marymount Manhattan College
New York, New York
www.mmm.edu
Federal Code: 002769

4-year private liberal arts college in very large city.

Enrollment: 1,813 undergrads, 14% part-time. 470 full-time freshmen.

Selectivity: Admits 50 to 75% of applicants.

BASIC COSTS (2008-2009)

Tuition and fees: $21,792.

Per-credit charge: $663.

Room and board: $12,660.

FINANCIAL AID PICTURE (2007-2008)

Students with need: Out of 364 full-time freshmen who applied for aid, 296 were judged to have need. Of these, 295 received aid, and 11 had their full need met. Average financial aid package met 52% of need; average scholarship/grant was $9,382; average loan was $2,996. For part-time students, average financial aid package was $8,604.

Students without need: 91 full-time freshmen who did not demonstrate need for aid received scholarships/grants; average award was $5,263. No-need awards available for academics, art, leadership, music/drama.

Cumulative student debt: 43% of graduating class had student loans; average debt was $16,903.

Additional info: Limited international scholarships for top applicants.

FINANCIAL AID PROCEDURES

Forms required: FAFSA.

Dates and Deadlines: Priority date 3/15; no closing date. Applicants notified on a rolling basis starting 3/15; must reply by 5/1 or within 3 week(s) of notification.

Transfers: Applicants notified by 3/1. Must submit academic and financial transcripts from previous institutions.

CONTACT

Paul Ciraulo, Executive VP for Administration and Finance
221 East 71st Street, New York, NY 10021-4597
(212) 517-0500

Medaille College
Buffalo, New York
www.medaille.edu
Federal Code: 002777

4-year private liberal arts college in large city.

Enrollment: 1,640 undergrads, 3% part-time. 329 full-time freshmen.

Selectivity: Admits over 75% of applicants.

BASIC COSTS (2008-2009)

Tuition and fees: $18,230.

Per-credit charge: $645.

Room and board: $8,846.

Additional info: Continuing students tuition is $17,420. Tuition/fee waivers available for adults.

FINANCIAL AID PICTURE (2006-2007)

Students with need: Out of 310 full-time freshmen who applied for aid, 287 were judged to have need. Of these, 282 received aid, and 26 had their full need met. Average financial aid package met 70% of need; average scholarship/grant was $6,982; average loan was $2,522. Need-based aid available for part-time students.

Students without need: 253 full-time freshmen who did not demonstrate need for aid received scholarships/grants; average award was $3,000. No-need awards available for academics, leadership.

Scholarships offered: Available on merit basis from $1,000 to $10,000.

Cumulative student debt: 90% of graduating class had student loans; average debt was $22,000.

FINANCIAL AID PROCEDURES

Forms required: FAFSA, state aid form.

Dates and Deadlines: Priority date 3/1; no closing date. Applicants notified on a rolling basis starting 3/1; must reply within 2 week(s) of notification.

CONTACT

Catherine Buzanski, Director of Financial Aid
18 Agassiz Circle, Buffalo, NY 14214
(716) 880-2256

Mercy College
Dobbs Ferry, New York
www.mercy.edu
Federal Code: 002772

4-year private liberal arts college in large town.
Enrollment: 4,905 undergrads, 31% part-time. 532 full-time freshmen.
Selectivity: Admits less than 50% of applicants.

BASIC COSTS (2007-2008)
Tuition and fees: $14,170.
Per-credit charge: $575.
Room and board: $9,444.

FINANCIAL AID PICTURE (2006-2007)
Students with need: 54% of average financial aid package awarded as scholarships/grants, 46% awarded as loans/jobs. Need-based aid available for part-time students. Work study available nights, weekends, and for part-time students.
Students without need: No-need awards available for athletics.

FINANCIAL AID PROCEDURES
Forms required: FAFSA, state aid form.
Dates and Deadlines: Priority date 2/15; no closing date. Applicants notified on a rolling basis starting 3/1; must reply within 4 week(s) of notification.

CONTACT
Margaret McGrail, Executive Director of Financial Aid
555 Broadway, Dobbs Ferry, NY 10522
(888) 464-6737

Metropolitan College of New York
New York, New York
www.metropolitan.edu
Federal Code: 009769

4-year private business and liberal arts college in very large city.
Enrollment: 651 undergrads.
Selectivity: Admits less than 50% of applicants.

BASIC COSTS (2008-2009)
Tuition and fees: $16,750.
Additional info: Tuition reported is undergraduate business program; other programs may vary in cost. Tuition at time of enrollment locked for 4 years.

FINANCIAL AID PICTURE (2006-2007)
Students with need: 23% of average financial aid package awarded as scholarships/grants, 77% awarded as loans/jobs. Need-based aid available for part-time students.
Students without need: No-need awards available for academics.
Scholarships offered: Presidential scholarships: up to $1,300 per semester; based on academic merit; given to top 10% of accepted students each semester.
Additional info: Limited merit scholarships.

FINANCIAL AID PROCEDURES
Forms required: FAFSA, state aid form.
Dates and Deadlines: Priority date 8/15; no closing date. Applicants notified on a rolling basis.

CONTACT
Timothy James, Director of Financial Aid
75 Varick Street, New York, NY 10013-1919
(212) 343-1234 ext. 3500

Mildred Elley
Latham, New York
www.mildred-elley.edu
Federal Code: 022195

2-year for-profit business college in very large city.
Enrollment: 409 undergrads.
Selectivity: Open admission.

BASIC COSTS (2007-2008)
Tuition and fees: $9,900.
Per-credit charge: $338.
Additional info: Tuition at time of enrollment locked for 2 years.

FINANCIAL AID PICTURE
Students with need: Need-based aid available for full-time and part-time students. Work study available nights.
Students without need: This college awards aid only to students with need.

FINANCIAL AID PROCEDURES
Forms required: FAFSA, state aid form.
Dates and Deadlines: No deadline.

CONTACT
Vincent Spanburgh, Director of Financial Aid Compliance
800 New Loudon Road, Suite 5120, Latham, NY 12110
(518) 786-0855 ext. 228

Mohawk Valley Community College
Utica, New York
www.mvcc.edu
Federal Code: 002871

2-year public community college in small city.
Enrollment: 4,635 undergrads, 20% part-time. 1,374 full-time freshmen.
Selectivity: Open admission; but selective for some programs.

BASIC COSTS (2007-2008)
Tuition and fees: $3,554; out-of-state residents $6,704.
Per-credit charge: $120; out-of-state residents $240.
Room and board: $7,150.

FINANCIAL AID PICTURE
Students with need: Need-based aid available for full-time and part-time students. Work study available nights, weekends, and for part-time students.

FINANCIAL AID PROCEDURES
Forms required: FAFSA, institutional form.
Dates and Deadlines: Priority date 4/15; no closing date. Applicants notified on a rolling basis starting 3/1; must reply within 2 week(s) of notification.
Transfers: Applicants notified on a rolling basis.

CONTACT
Annette Broski, Director, Student Financial Aid
1101 Sherman Drive, Utica, NY 13501-5394
(315) 792-5415

Molloy College
Rockville Centre, New York
www.molloy.edu
Federal Code: 002775

4-year private liberal arts college in large town, affiliated with Roman Catholic Church.
Enrollment: 2,848 undergrads, 26% part-time. 370 full-time freshmen.
Selectivity: Admits 50 to 75% of applicants.

BASIC COSTS (2007-2008)

Tuition and fees: $18,570.

Per-credit charge: $585.

Additional info: Tuition/fee waivers available for unemployed or children of unemployed.

FINANCIAL AID PICTURE (2007-2008)

Students with need: 39% of average financial aid package awarded as scholarships/grants, 61% awarded as loans/jobs. Need-based aid available for part-time students. Work study available nights, weekends, and for part-time students.

Students without need: No-need awards available for academics, art, athletics, leadership, music/drama.

Scholarships offered: Molloy Scholar Scholarship: full tuition; minimum 95 high school average and minimum 1250 SAT (exclusive of Writing) or 28 ACT; 10 awarded annually; renewable for 3.5 GPA. Dominican Academic Scholarship: $1,000 to $8,500; minimum 88 high school average and minimum 1000 SAT (exclusive of Writing); 50 awarded annually, renewable with 3.0 GPA. Community Service Awards: $1,000 to $3,000; awarded to incoming freshmen demonstrating commitment to community and school; 10 awarded annually; renewable for 2.5 GPA.

FINANCIAL AID PROCEDURES

Forms required: FAFSA, state aid form.

Dates and Deadlines: Priority date 4/15; closing date 5/1. Applicants notified on a rolling basis starting 3/1.

Transfers: All transfer applicants with a minimum of 30 credits and 3.0 GPA automatically considered for transfer scholarships ranging from $1,500-$3,000.

CONTACT

Ana Lockward, Director of Financial Aid

PO Box 5002, Rockville Centre, NY 11570

(516) 678-5000 ext. 6249

Monroe College

Bronx, New York

www.monroecollege.edu

Federal Code: 004799

4-year for-profit business and health science college in very large city.

Enrollment: 6,232 undergrads, 13% part-time. 1,205 full-time freshmen.

Selectivity: Admits 50 to 75% of applicants.

BASIC COSTS (2008-2009)

Tuition and fees: $11,212.

Per-credit charge: $438.

Room and board: $7,100.

FINANCIAL AID PICTURE

Students with need: Need-based aid available for full-time and part-time students. Work study available nights, weekends, and for part-time students.

Students without need: This college awards aid only to students with need.

FINANCIAL AID PROCEDURES

Forms required: FAFSA.

Dates and Deadlines: Closing date 3/31. Applicants notified on a rolling basis starting 7/1.

Transfers: No deadline. Applicants notified on a rolling basis.

CONTACT

Alex Ephrem, Senior Vice President

Monroe College Way, Bronx, NY 10468

(718) 933-6700

Monroe Community College

Rochester, New York

www.monroecc.edu

Federal Code: 002872

2-year public community college in large city.

Enrollment: 15,663 undergrads.

Selectivity: Open admission; but selective for some programs.

BASIC COSTS (2007-2008)

Tuition and fees: $3,190; out-of-state residents $5,990.

Per-credit charge: $117; out-of-state residents $234.

Room only: $5,290.

FINANCIAL AID PICTURE

Students with need: Need-based aid available for full-time and part-time students. Work study available nights.

Students without need: This college awards aid only to students with need.

FINANCIAL AID PROCEDURES

Forms required: FAFSA.

Dates and Deadlines: No deadline. Applicants notified on a rolling basis; must reply within 2 week(s) of notification.

CONTACT

Jerome St. Croix, Director of Financial Aid

Office of Admissions-Monroe Community College, Rochester, NY 14692-8908

(585) 292-2050

Mount St. Mary College

Newburgh, New York

www.msmc.edu

Federal Code: 002778

4-year private liberal arts college in large town.

Enrollment: 2,035 undergrads, 17% part-time. 364 full-time freshmen.

Selectivity: Admits over 75% of applicants.

BASIC COSTS (2007-2008)

Tuition and fees: $19,520.

Per-credit charge: $630.

Room and board: $10,400.

FINANCIAL AID PICTURE (2007-2008)

Students with need: Out of 337 full-time freshmen who applied for aid, 272 were judged to have need. Of these, 271 received aid, and 71 had their full need met. Average financial aid package met 61% of need; average scholarship/grant was $8,102; average loan was $4,833. For part-time students, average financial aid package was $6,937.

Students without need: 80 full-time freshmen who did not demonstrate need for aid received scholarships/grants; average award was $12,491. No-need awards available for academics, ROTC.

Scholarships offered: Presidential Scholarship: approximately $12,900; renewable each year with a 3.0 GPA. Merit Grants: range from $3,000-$8,500; renewable each year with a 2.5 GPA. Both based upon acceptance into full-time, traditional program, SAT/ACT test scores, high school GPA, and high school class rank.

Cumulative student debt: 78% of graduating class had student loans; average debt was $36,625.

FINANCIAL AID PROCEDURES

Forms required: FAFSA.

Dates and Deadlines: Closing date 2/15. Applicants notified on a rolling basis starting 4/1; must reply within 2 week(s) of notification.

Transfers: Closing date 3/15. Must reply within 2 week(s) of notification.

CONTACT

Michelle Taylor, Director of Financial Aid
330 Powell Avenue, Newburgh, NY 12550
(845) 569-3194

Nassau Community College

Garden City, New York
www.ncc.edu   Federal Code: 002873

2-year public community college in large town.
Enrollment: 19,872 undergrads, 29% part-time. 4,936 full-time freshmen.
Selectivity: Open admission; but selective for some programs.

BASIC COSTS (2007-2008)

Tuition and fees: $3,574; out-of-state residents $6,864.
Per-credit charge: $138; out-of-state residents $276.

FINANCIAL AID PICTURE (2006-2007)

Students with need: Out of 3,683 full-time freshmen who applied for aid, 2,765 were judged to have need. Of these, 2,425 received aid, and 50 had their full need met. Average financial aid package met 80% of need; average scholarship/grant was $854; average loan was $2,294. For part-time students, average financial aid package was $5,618.
Students without need: 10 full-time freshmen who did not demonstrate need for aid received scholarships/grants; average award was $1,024. No-need awards available for academics, minority status.

FINANCIAL AID PROCEDURES

Forms required: FAFSA, state aid form.
Dates and Deadlines: Priority date 6/7; no closing date. Applicants notified on a rolling basis; must reply within 1 week(s) of notification.

CONTACT

Evangeline Manjares, Associate Dean for Financial Aid
One Education Drive, Garden City, NY 11530
(516) 572-7396

Nazareth College of Rochester

Rochester, New York
www.naz.edu   Federal Code: 002779

4-year private liberal arts college in large city.
Enrollment: 2,120 undergrads, 6% part-time. 481 full-time freshmen.
Selectivity: Admits 50 to 75% of applicants.

BASIC COSTS (2008-2009)

Tuition and fees: $24,226.
Per-credit charge: $549.
Room and board: $9,916.

FINANCIAL AID PICTURE (2006-2007)

Students with need: Out of 442 full-time freshmen who applied for aid, 368 were judged to have need. Of these, 366 received aid, and 56 had their full need met. Average financial aid package met 77% of need; average scholarship/grant was $11,753; average loan was $2,941. For part-time students, average financial aid package was $6,044.
Students without need: 107 full-time freshmen who did not demonstrate need for aid received scholarships/grants; average award was $9,781. No-need awards available for academics, alumni affiliation, art, minority status, music/drama, ROTC, state/district residency.
Scholarships offered: Presidential Scholarship: $12,500 to full tuition. Dean's Scholarship: $10,000-12,000. Founders Scholarship: $7,500-9,500. Trustee Scholarship: $5,000-7,000. All awarded based on grades, test scores, class rank, and course load. Campus diversity, regional, art, music, and theater scholarships also available.

Cumulative student debt: 77% of graduating class had student loans; average debt was $26,795.

FINANCIAL AID PROCEDURES

Forms required: FAFSA. CSS PROFILE required of early decision applicants only.
Dates and Deadlines: Priority date 12/15; closing date 5/1. Applicants notified on a rolling basis starting 2/20; must reply by 5/1 or within 2 week(s) of notification.
Transfers: No deadline.

CONTACT

Bruce Woolley, Director of Financial Aid
4245 East Avenue, Rochester, NY 14618-3790
(585) 389-2310

New York Career Institute

New York, New York
www.nyci.com   Federal Code: 014576

2-year for-profit junior college in very large city.
Enrollment: 509 undergrads.

BASIC COSTS (2007-2008)

Additional info: Full-time tuition and fees for court reporting night program $10,800. Tuition for paralegal program $350 per credit hour.

FINANCIAL AID PICTURE

Students with need: Need-based aid available for full-time students. Work study available nights.

FINANCIAL AID PROCEDURES

Dates and Deadlines: No deadline. Applicants notified on a rolling basis.

CONTACT

Dennis Byrnes, Financial Aid Advisor
11 Park Place, New York, NY 10007

New York Institute of Technology

Old Westbury, New York
www.nyit.edu   Federal Code: 002782

4-year private university and health science college in large town.
Enrollment: 6,267 undergrads, 21% part-time. 1,359 full-time freshmen.
Selectivity: Admits 50 to 75% of applicants.

BASIC COSTS (2008-2009)

Tuition and fees: $22,750.
Per-credit charge: $747.
Room only: $10,310.
Additional info: Room only charges apply to Manhattan campus; board charges vary on other campuses. Tuition/fee costs reported for nontechnology majors, vary for other programs. Tuition/fee waivers available for unemployed or children of unemployed.

FINANCIAL AID PICTURE (2006-2007)

Students with need: Out of 1,053 full-time freshmen who applied for aid, 901 were judged to have need. Of these, 894 received aid. For part-time students, average financial aid package was $3,674.
Students without need: 199 full-time freshmen who did not demonstrate need for aid received scholarships/grants; average award was $7,444. No-need awards available for academics, athletics.
Scholarships offered: 21 full-time freshmen received athletic scholarships; average amount $17,060.

FINANCIAL AID PROCEDURES

Forms required: FAFSA.

Dates and Deadlines: Priority date 3/1; no closing date. Applicants notified on a rolling basis starting 3/15; must reply by 5/1 or within 2 week(s) of notification.

CONTACT
Clair Jacobi, Director of Financial Aid
Box 8000, Old Westbury, NY 11568
(516) 686-3835

New York School of Interior Design
New York, New York
www.nysid.edu   Federal Code: 013606

4-year private visual arts college in very large city.
Enrollment: 685 undergrads, 75% part-time. 19 full-time freshmen.
Selectivity: Admits less than 50% of applicants.

BASIC COSTS (2008-2009)
Tuition and fees: $19,790.
Per-credit charge: $650.

FINANCIAL AID PICTURE (2007-2008)
Students with need: Average financial aid package for all full-time undergraduates was $6,900; for part-time $4,650. 43% awarded as scholarships/grants, 57% awarded as loans/jobs. Work study available nights, weekends, and for part-time students.
Students without need: This college awards aid only to students with need.

FINANCIAL AID PROCEDURES
Forms required: FAFSA, state aid form, institutional form.
Dates and Deadlines: Priority date 5/1; no closing date. Applicants notified on a rolling basis starting 2/1; must reply within 2 week(s) of notification.
Transfers: Applicants notified on a rolling basis.

CONTACT
Nedi Goga, Financial Aid Officer
170 East 70th Street, New York, NY 10021-5110
(212) 472-1500 ext. 212

New York University
New York, New York
www.nyu.edu   Federal Code: 002785

4-year private university in very large city.
Enrollment: 20,899 undergrads, 6% part-time. 4,890 full-time freshmen.
Selectivity: Admits less than 50% of applicants.

BASIC COSTS (2007-2008)
Tuition and fees: $35,290.
Per-credit charge: $980.
Room and board: $12,200.

FINANCIAL AID PICTURE (2007-2008)
Students with need: Out of 3,225 full-time freshmen who applied for aid, 2,612 were judged to have need. Of these, 2,605 received aid. Average financial aid package met 68% of need; average scholarship/grant was $16,236; average loan was $5,203. For part-time students, average financial aid package was $9,489.
Students without need: 327 full-time freshmen who did not demonstrate need for aid received scholarships/grants; average award was $7,250. No-need awards available for academics.
Cumulative student debt: 58% of graduating class had student loans; average debt was $33,637.
Additional info: Both need-based and merit scholarships available to first-time students. Range from $1,000 to $25,000.

FINANCIAL AID PROCEDURES
Forms required: FAFSA, state aid form.
Dates and Deadlines: Closing date 2/15. Applicants notified on a rolling basis starting 4/1; must reply by 5/1.
Transfers: Priority date 3/1; no deadline.

CONTACT
Barbara Hall, Associate Provost for Admissions and Financial Aid
22 Washington Square North, New York, NY 10011-9108
(212) 998-4444

Niagara County Community College
Sanborn, New York
www.niagaracc.suny.edu   Federal Code: 002874

2-year public community college in rural community.
Enrollment: 4,175 undergrads, 27% part-time. 985 full-time freshmen.
Selectivity: Open admission; but selective for some programs.

BASIC COSTS (2007-2008)
Tuition and fees: $3,506; out-of-state residents $5,102.
Per-credit charge: $133; out-of-state residents $199.

FINANCIAL AID PICTURE (2006-2007)
Students with need: 58% of average financial aid package awarded as scholarships/grants, 42% awarded as loans/jobs. Need-based aid available for part-time students. Work study available nights.
Students without need: This college awards aid only to students with need.
Additional info: Assistance offered placing students in part-time employment. Students can charge books, food coupons, or $100 advance against anticipated financial aid.

FINANCIAL AID PROCEDURES
Forms required: FAFSA, state aid form.
Dates and Deadlines: Priority date 4/1; no closing date. Applicants notified on a rolling basis starting 5/1; must reply within 2 week(s) of notification.
Transfers: Must file appropriate state and federal change forms at least 4 weeks before registration date.

CONTACT
James Trimboli, Director of Financial Aid
3111 Saunders Settlement Road, Sanborn, NY 14132-9460
(716) 614-6266

Niagara University
Niagara University, New York
www.niagara.edu   Federal Code: 002788

4-year private university in small city, affiliated with Roman Catholic Church.
Enrollment: 3,219 undergrads, 3% part-time. 739 full-time freshmen.
Selectivity: Admits over 75% of applicants.

BASIC COSTS (2008-2009)
Tuition and fees: $23,575.
Per-credit charge: $750.
Room and board: $9,750.
Additional info: Tuition at time of enrollment locked for 4 years.

FINANCIAL AID PICTURE (2007-2008)
Students with need: Out of 719 full-time freshmen who applied for aid, 605 were judged to have need. Of these, 604 received aid, and 306 had their full need met. Average financial aid package met 80% of need; average scholarship/grant was $13,279; average loan was $4,665. For part-time students, average financial aid package was $9,556.

Students without need: 114 full-time freshmen who did not demonstrate need for aid received scholarships/grants; average award was $8,715. No-need awards available for academics, athletics, music/drama, ROTC.

Scholarships offered: 65 full-time freshmen received athletic scholarships; average amount $14,943.

Cumulative student debt: 82% of graduating class had student loans; average debt was $23,267.

Additional info: Opportunity program available for academically and economically disadvantaged students.

FINANCIAL AID PROCEDURES

Forms required: FAFSA, state aid form.

Dates and Deadlines: Priority date 2/15; no closing date. Applicants notified on a rolling basis starting 3/1; must reply within 3 week(s) of notification.

Transfers: Must reply within 3 week(s) of notification. Academic scholarship available: $8,000 per year based on minimum 3.34 GPA from transfer institution; $7,000 per year for 3.0 to 3.33 GPA.

CONTACT

Maureen Salfi, Director of Financial Aid Niagara University, NY 14109

(716) 286-8686

North Country Community College

Saranac Lake, New York

www.nccc.edu   Federal Code: 007111

2-year public community college in small town.

Enrollment: 1,054 undergrads, 13% part-time. 311 full-time freshmen.

Selectivity: Open admission; but selective for some programs.

BASIC COSTS (2007-2008)

Tuition and fees: $4,190; out-of-state residents $9,250.

Per-credit charge: $160; out-of-state residents $390.

Room and board: $8,300.

FINANCIAL AID PICTURE

Students with need: Need-based aid available for full-time and part-time students. Work study available nights, weekends, and for part-time students.

Students without need: This college awards aid only to students with need.

FINANCIAL AID PROCEDURES

Forms required: FAFSA, state aid form.

Dates and Deadlines: Priority date 4/1; no closing date. Applicants notified on a rolling basis starting 4/1; must reply within 3 week(s) of notification.

CONTACT

Edwin Trathen, Vice President for Enrollment and Student Services

23 Santanoni Avenue, Saranac Lake, NY 12983

(518) 891-2915 ext. 229

Nyack College

Nyack, New York

www.nyack.edu   Federal Code: 002790

4-year private liberal arts college in large town, affiliated with Christian and Missionary Alliance.

Enrollment: 2,019 undergrads.

BASIC COSTS (2008-2009)

Tuition and fees: $18,300.

Room and board: $7,800.

FINANCIAL AID PICTURE (2007-2008)

Students with need: 54% of average financial aid package awarded as scholarships/grants, 46% awarded as loans/jobs.

Students without need: No-need awards available for academics, alumni affiliation, art, athletics, leadership, minority status, music/drama, religious affiliation, state/district residency.

FINANCIAL AID PROCEDURES

Forms required: FAFSA, state aid form.

Dates and Deadlines: Priority date 3/1; no closing date. Applicants notified on a rolling basis starting 3/1; must reply by 4/1 or within 4 week(s) of notification.

CONTACT

Dona Schepens, Financial Aid Director

1 South Boulevard, Nyack, NY 10960-3698

(845) 358-1710 ext. 791

Onondaga Community College

Syracuse, New York

www.sunyocc.edu   Federal Code: 002875

2-year public community college in small city.

Enrollment: 7,138 undergrads, 25% part-time. 1,525 full-time freshmen.

Selectivity: Open admission; but selective for some programs.

BASIC COSTS (2007-2008)

Tuition and fees: $3,641; out-of-state residents $6,921.

Per-credit charge: $129; out-of-state residents $258.

FINANCIAL AID PICTURE

Students with need: Need-based aid available for full-time and part-time students.

Students without need: This college awards aid only to students with need.

FINANCIAL AID PROCEDURES

Forms required: FAFSA, state aid form.

Dates and Deadlines: Priority date 2/15; no closing date. Applicants notified on a rolling basis starting 4/15; must reply within 4 week(s) of notification.

CONTACT

Lorna Roberts, Director of Financial Aid

4585 West Seneca Turnpike, Syracuse, NY 13215-4585

(315) 469-2291

Orange County Community College

Middletown, New York

orange.cc.ny.us   Federal Code: 002876

2-year public community college in large town.

Enrollment: 6,697 undergrads.

Selectivity: Open admission; but selective for some programs.

BASIC COSTS (2007-2008)

Tuition and fees: $3,438; out-of-state residents $6,538.

Per-credit charge: $130; out-of-state residents $260.

Additional info: Tuition/fee waivers available for unemployed or children of unemployed.

FINANCIAL AID PICTURE

Students with need: Need-based aid available for full-time and part-time students.

FINANCIAL AID PROCEDURES

Forms required: FAFSA, state aid form, institutional form.

Dates and Deadlines: Priority date 5/1; no closing date. Applicants notified on a rolling basis starting 5/1; must reply within 4 week(s) of notification.

CONTACT

Rosemary Barrett, Coordinator of Finacial Aid
115 South Street, Middletown, NY 10940-0115
(845) 341-4190

Pace University
New York, New York
www.pace.edu   Federal Code: 002791

4-year private university in very large city.
Enrollment: 7,178 undergrads, 16% part-time. 1,537 full-time freshmen.
Selectivity: Admits over 75% of applicants.

BASIC COSTS (2008-2009)
Tuition and fees: $31,357.
Per-credit charge: $879.
Room and board: $11,180.

FINANCIAL AID PICTURE (2007-2008)
Students with need: Out of 1,322 full-time freshmen who applied for aid, 1,190 were judged to have need. Of these, 1,150 received aid, and 568 had their full need met. Average financial aid package met 88% of need; average scholarship/grant was $14,247; average loan was $4,042. For part-time students, average financial aid package was $5,812.
Students without need: 260 full-time freshmen who did not demonstrate need for aid received scholarships/grants; average award was $10,080. No-need awards available for academics, athletics.
Scholarships offered: 4 full-time freshmen received athletic scholarships; average amount $13,132.
Cumulative student debt: 70% of graduating class had student loans; average debt was $27,016.

FINANCIAL AID PROCEDURES
Forms required: FAFSA, state aid form.
Dates and Deadlines: Priority date 2/15; no closing date. Applicants notified on a rolling basis starting 2/28; must reply by 5/1 or within 2 week(s) of notification.

CONTACT
Mark Stephens, University Director, Financial Aid
1 Pace Plaza, New York, NY 10038
(212) 346-1300

Parsons The New School for Design
New York, New York
www.parsons.edu   Federal Code: 002780

4-year private visual arts college in very large city.
Enrollment: 3,537 undergrads, 7% part-time. 594 full-time freshmen.
Selectivity: Admits 50 to 75% of applicants.

BASIC COSTS (2008-2009)
Tuition and fees: $34,460.
Per-credit charge: $1,150.
Room and board: $12,390.

FINANCIAL AID PICTURE (2007-2008)
Students with need: Out of 444 full-time freshmen who applied for aid, 444 were judged to have need. Of these, 442 received aid, and 12 had their full need met. Average financial aid package met 56% of need; average scholarship/grant was $8,458; average loan was $3,280. Need-based aid available for part-time students.
Students without need: 146 full-time freshmen who did not demonstrate need for aid received scholarships/grants; average award was $5,648. No-need awards available for academics, art.

Cumulative student debt: 81% of graduating class had student loans; average debt was $21,054.

FINANCIAL AID PROCEDURES
Forms required: FAFSA, state aid form.
Dates and Deadlines: Priority date 3/1; no closing date. Applicants notified on a rolling basis starting 3/1; must reply within 4 week(s) of notification.

CONTACT
Eileen Doyle, Assistant Provost for University Financial Aid and Enrollment Management
65 Fifth Avenue, New York, NY 10011
(212) 229-8930

Paul Smith's College
Paul Smiths, New York
www.paulsmiths.edu   Federal Code: 002795

4-year private liberal arts college in rural community.
Enrollment: 912 undergrads.
Selectivity: Admits over 75% of applicants.

BASIC COSTS (2008-2009)
Tuition and fees: $19,250.
Room and board: $8,350.
Additional info: Program fees range from $580 to $1,880 depending on program.

FINANCIAL AID PICTURE
Students with need: Need-based aid available for full-time students. Work study available nights, weekends, and for part-time students.
Students without need: No-need awards available for academics.
Additional info: Merit aid only for international students; no financial aid application required.

FINANCIAL AID PROCEDURES
Forms required: FAFSA.
Dates and Deadlines: Priority date 3/31; no closing date. Applicants notified on a rolling basis starting 3/5; must reply within 4 week(s) of notification.
Transfers: No deadline. Applicants notified by 2/5; must reply within 4 week(s) of notification.

CONTACT
Mary Ellen Chamberlain, Director of Financial Aid
PO Box 265, Routes 30 & 86, Paul Smiths, NY 12970-0265
(518) 327-6220

Phillips Beth Israel School of Nursing
New York, New York
www.futurenursebi.org   Federal Code: 006438

2-year private nursing college in very large city.
Enrollment: 225 undergrads, 81% part-time. 3 full-time freshmen.
Selectivity: Admits less than 50% of applicants.

BASIC COSTS (2008-2009)
Tuition and fees: $16,310.
Per-credit charge: $340.

FINANCIAL AID PICTURE (2006-2007)
Students with need: 84% of average financial aid package awarded as scholarships/grants, 16% awarded as loans/jobs. Need-based aid available for part-time students.
Scholarships offered: Hillman Scholarship Program: full tuition, books, and uniforms; variable number awarded each year; based on academic achievement. Karpas Scholarship Program: $3,000 a year; 15 awarded; based on academic achievement.

FINANCIAL AID PROCEDURES

Forms required: FAFSA, state aid form, institutional form.

Dates and Deadlines: Closing date 6/1. Applicants notified by 8/1; must reply within 3 week(s) of notification.

Transfers: Applicants notified by 7/1; must reply within 2 week(s) of notification.

CONTACT

Wendy Chan, Financial Aid Director

776 Sixth Avenue, Fourth Floor, New York, NY 10001

(212) 614-6104

Polytechnic University

Brooklyn, New York   Federal Code: 002796

www.poly.edu   CSS Code: 2668

4-year private university in very large city.

Enrollment: 1,467 undergrads, 4% part-time. 380 full-time freshmen.

Selectivity: Admits 50 to 75% of applicants.

BASIC COSTS (2007-2008)

Tuition and fees: $30,972.

Per-credit charge: $951.

Room and board: $8,500.

FINANCIAL AID PICTURE (2006-2007)

Students with need: Out of 379 full-time freshmen who applied for aid, 297 were judged to have need. Of these, 297 received aid, and 205 had their full need met. Average financial aid package met 93% of need; average scholarship/grant was $8,413; average loan was $2,917. For part-time students, average financial aid package was $12,452.

Students without need: 80 full-time freshmen who did not demonstrate need for aid received scholarships/grants; average award was $17,066. No-need awards available for academics.

Scholarships offered: Board of Trustees Scholarships: full tuition, less any outside aid for which students are eligible; awarded to academically superior freshmen. Geiger/Fialkov Scholarships: full tuition less any outside aid for which students are eligible; awarded to superior freshmen majoring in engineering or computer science. High School Principal's Scholarship: for students nominated by high school principals in New York metropolitan region; $10,000 per year; Scholarship Committee selects recipients. Students must file FAFSA to be eligible for merit scholarships.

Cumulative student debt: 76% of graduating class had student loans; average debt was $25,012.

FINANCIAL AID PROCEDURES

Forms required: FAFSA, CSS PROFILE, state aid form, institutional form.

Dates and Deadlines: Priority date 3/1; no closing date. Applicants notified on a rolling basis starting 3/15; must reply within 2 week(s) of notification.

Transfers: Priority date 5/5; no deadline. Applicants notified on a rolling basis; must reply within 2 week(s) of notification.

CONTACT

6 Metrotech Center, Brooklyn, NY 11201-2999

(718) 260-3600

Pratt Institute

Brooklyn, New York

www.pratt.edu   Federal Code: 002798

4-year private university and visual arts college in very large city.

Enrollment: 3,040 undergrads, 5% part-time. 577 full-time freshmen.

Selectivity: Admits less than 50% of applicants.

BASIC COSTS (2008-2009)

Tuition and fees: $32,990.

Per-credit charge: $1,026.

Room and board: $9,476.

Additional info: All architecture students required to purchase laptop and software (discounted) during summer. All sophomore interior design majors required to purchase laptop computer. Laptop costs approximately $3,600.

FINANCIAL AID PICTURE

Students with need: Need-based aid available for full-time and part-time students.

Students without need: No-need awards available for academics, art.

FINANCIAL AID PROCEDURES

Forms required: FAFSA, state aid form, institutional form.

Dates and Deadlines: Closing date 2/1. Applicants notified on a rolling basis starting 3/11; must reply within 2 week(s) of notification.

Transfers: Must reply by 5/1 or within 2 week(s) of notification.

CONTACT

Karen Price-Scott, Director of Financial Aid

200 Willoughby Avenue, Brooklyn, NY 11205-3817

(718) 636-3519

Rensselaer Polytechnic Institute

Troy, New York   Federal Code: 002803

www.rpi.edu   CSS Code: 2757

4-year private university in small city.

Enrollment: 5,119 undergrads. 1,288 full-time freshmen.

Selectivity: Admits less than 50% of applicants.

BASIC COSTS (2008-2009)

Tuition and fees: $37,990.

Per-credit charge: $1,155.

Room and board: $10,730.

FINANCIAL AID PICTURE (2007-2008)

Students with need: Out of 1,014 full-time freshmen who applied for aid, 815 were judged to have need. Of these, 815 received aid, and 491 had their full need met. Average financial aid package met 85% of need; average scholarship/grant was $21,734; average loan was $6,507.

Students without need: 397 full-time freshmen who did not demonstrate need for aid received scholarships/grants; average award was $12,214. No-need awards available for academics, alumni affiliation, art, athletics, leadership, minority status, music/drama, ROTC.

Scholarships offered: *Merit:* Rensselaer Medals: $15,000; awarded by participating high schools for excellence in science and mathematics. Emily Roebling Award: $7,500; to top-ranking female admitted students. *Athletic:* 7 full-time freshmen received athletic scholarships; average amount $44,114.

Cumulative student debt: 74% of graduating class had student loans; average debt was $27,125.

FINANCIAL AID PROCEDURES

Forms required: FAFSA, CSS PROFILE.

Dates and Deadlines: Closing date 2/15. Applicants notified by 3/25.

Transfers: No deadline. Applicants notified on a rolling basis starting 3/31.

CONTACT

James Stevenson, Director of Financial Aid

110 Eighth Street, Troy, NY 12180-3590

(518) 276-6813

Roberts Wesleyan College

Rochester, New York
www.roberts.edu
Federal Code: 002805

4-year private liberal arts college in large city, affiliated with Free Methodist Church of North America.

Enrollment: 1,312 undergrads, 10% part-time. 211 full-time freshmen.

Selectivity: Admits 50 to 75% of applicants.

BASIC COSTS (2007-2008)

Tuition and fees: $21,352.

Room and board: $7,774.

FINANCIAL AID PICTURE (2006-2007)

Students with need: Out of 194 full-time freshmen who applied for aid, 180 were judged to have need. Of these, 180 received aid, and 44 had their full need met. Average financial aid package met 81% of need; average scholarship/grant was $12,647; average loan was $5,037. For part-time students, average financial aid package was $8,501.

Students without need: 31 full-time freshmen who did not demonstrate need for aid received scholarships/grants; average award was $8,333. No-need awards available for academics, alumni affiliation, art, athletics, music/drama, religious affiliation, ROTC, state/district residency.

Scholarships offered: 11 full-time freshmen received athletic scholarships; average amount $6,493.

Cumulative student debt: 94% of graduating class had student loans; average debt was $22,574.

Additional info: Dollars for Scholars offer matching grants of up to $750.

FINANCIAL AID PROCEDURES

Forms required: FAFSA, state aid form.

Dates and Deadlines: Priority date 3/15; no closing date. Applicants notified on a rolling basis starting 3/15; must reply by 5/1 or within 2 week(s) of notification.

Transfers: Applicants notified on a rolling basis starting 3/15.

CONTACT

Stephen Field, Director of Student Financial Services
2301 Westside Drive, Rochester, NY 14624-1997
(585) 594-6150

Rochester Institute of Technology

Rochester, New York
www.rit.edu
Federal Code: 002806

4-year private university in large city.

Enrollment: 12,779 undergrads, 7% part-time. 2,382 full-time freshmen.

Selectivity: Admits 50 to 75% of applicants.

BASIC COSTS (2008-2009)

Tuition and fees: $28,035.

Per-credit charge: $597.

Room and board: $9,381.

Additional info: Tuition/fee waivers available for unemployed or children of unemployed.

FINANCIAL AID PICTURE (2006-2007)

Students with need: Out of 2,071 full-time freshmen who applied for aid, 1,736 were judged to have need. Of these, 1,733 received aid, and 1,440 had their full need met. Average financial aid package met 88% of need; average scholarship/grant was $12,700; average loan was $5,000. For part-time students, average financial aid package was $6,500.

Students without need: 295 full-time freshmen who did not demonstrate need for aid received scholarships/grants; average award was $6,700. No-need awards available for academics, art, leadership, ROTC.

Scholarships offered: Presidential Scholarships: $6,000 to $12,500 per year; top 10% of high school class with minimum SAT of 1220 (or ACT 27) or top 20% of high school class with SAT of 1270 (or ACT 28). SAT scores exclusive of Writing portion.

Additional info: Most juniors and seniors participate in cooperative education program, earning an average $4,500-$6,500 per 3-month employment period through paid employment in jobs related to major.

FINANCIAL AID PROCEDURES

Forms required: FAFSA, state aid form.

Dates and Deadlines: Priority date 3/1; no closing date. Applicants notified on a rolling basis starting 3/15; must reply by 5/1.

Transfers: Priority date 3/15. Applicants notified on a rolling basis starting 4/1; must reply by 5/1. Special merit scholarship programs available specifically for transfers with high GPA.

CONTACT

Verna Hazen, Assistant Vice President and Director of Financial Aid
60 Lomb Memorial Drive, Rochester, NY 14623-5604
(585) 475-2186

Rockland Community College

Suffern, New York
www.sunyrockland.edu
Federal Code: 002877

2-year public community college in large town.

Enrollment: 5,413 undergrads.

Selectivity: Open admission.

BASIC COSTS (2007-2008)

Tuition and fees: $3,465; out-of-state residents $6,665.

Per-credit charge: $133; out-of-state residents $266.

FINANCIAL AID PICTURE (2006-2007)

Students with need: 88% of average financial aid package awarded as scholarships/grants, 12% awarded as loans/jobs. Need-based aid available for part-time students. Work study available nights, weekends, and for part-time students.

Scholarships offered: SUNY Empire State Honors Minority Scholarships: available to African American, Latino, and Native American students; 8 awarded; $1,000 per semester for 4 semesters. Jack Watson Scholarships: minimum 3.5 high school GPA or 94 average in Regents; 5 awarded; $1,163 per semester, renewable for 2nd year. Alumni Scholarships for children of alumni with 75 average; varying amounts.

FINANCIAL AID PROCEDURES

Forms required: FAFSA, institutional form.

Dates and Deadlines: Priority date 5/31; no closing date. Applicants notified on a rolling basis starting 6/1; must reply within 3 week(s) of notification.

CONTACT

Debra Brouabidi, Director of Financial Aid
145 College Road, Suffern, NY 10901
(845) 574-4000

Russell Sage College

Troy, New York
www.sage.edu/rsc
Federal Code: 002810

4-year private liberal arts college for women in small city.

Enrollment: 655 undergrads, 4% part-time. 82 full-time freshmen.

Selectivity: Admits over 75% of applicants.

BASIC COSTS (2008-2009)

Tuition and fees: $26,740.

Per-credit charge: $860.

Room and board: $9,200.

FINANCIAL AID PICTURE (2007-2008)

Students with need: Out of 81 full-time freshmen who applied for aid, 76 were judged to have need. Of these, 76 received aid, and 2 had their full need met. For part-time students, average financial aid package was $15,274.

Students without need: 3 full-time freshmen who did not demonstrate need for aid received scholarships/grants; average award was $9,000. No-need awards available for academics, alumni affiliation, leadership, music/drama.

Scholarships offered: Multiple awards to qualified students: presidential and dean's scholarship, Girl Scout scholarship, first-generation scholarship, valedictorian-salutatorian scholarship, student Sage scholarship, endowed scholarships for minority students and specific majors.

Cumulative student debt: 95% of graduating class had student loans; average debt was $28,000.

FINANCIAL AID PROCEDURES

Forms required: FAFSA, state aid form.

Dates and Deadlines: Priority date 3/1; no closing date. Applicants notified on a rolling basis starting 3/1; must reply by 5/1 or within 2 week(s) of notification.

Transfers: Phi Theta Kappa Transfer Scholarship available.

CONTACT

James Dease, Associate Vice President for Student Services
45 Ferry Street, Troy, NY 12180-4115
(518) 244-4525

Sage College of Albany
Albany, New York
www.sage.edu   Federal Code: 002811

4-year private business and liberal arts college in small city.

Enrollment: 883 undergrads, 36% part-time. 80 full-time freshmen.

Selectivity: Admits 50 to 75% of applicants.

BASIC COSTS (2008-2009)

Tuition and fees: $19,490.

Per-credit charge: $610.

Room and board: $9,350.

FINANCIAL AID PICTURE (2007-2008)

Students with need: Out of 77 full-time freshmen who applied for aid, 76 were judged to have need. Of these, 76 received aid, and 3 had their full need met. For part-time students, average financial aid package was $9,975.

Students without need: 2 full-time freshmen who did not demonstrate need for aid received scholarships/grants; average award was $6,000. No-need awards available for academics, art, leadership.

Scholarships offered: Multiple awards to qualified students: presidential and dean's scholarships, first-generation scholarship, art scholarship, valedictorian-salutatorian scholarship, diversity leadership scholarship. Endowed scholarships available for minority students and specific majors.

Cumulative student debt: 96% of graduating class had student loans; average debt was $14,500.

FINANCIAL AID PROCEDURES

Forms required: FAFSA, state aid form.

Dates and Deadlines: Priority date 3/1; no closing date. Applicants notified on a rolling basis starting 3/1; must reply within 2 week(s) of notification.

Transfers: Phi Theta Kappa transfer scholarship available.

CONTACT

James Dease, Associate Vice President for Student Services
140 New Scotland Avenue, Albany, NY 12208
(518) 292-1783

Saint Bonaventure University
St. Bonaventure, New York
www.sbu.edu   Federal Code: 002817

4-year private university in large town, affiliated with Roman Catholic Church.

Enrollment: 1,905 undergrads.

Selectivity: Admits over 75% of applicants.

BASIC COSTS (2007-2008)

Tuition and fees: $23,605.

Per-credit charge: $680.

Room and board: $8,490.

Additional info: Tuition/fee waivers available for minority students.

FINANCIAL AID PICTURE

Students with need: Need-based aid available for full-time and part-time students. Work study available nights, weekends, and for part-time students.

Students without need: No-need awards available for academics, art, athletics, leadership, minority status, music/drama, religious affiliation, ROTC, state/district residency.

FINANCIAL AID PROCEDURES

Forms required: FAFSA, state aid form, institutional form.

Dates and Deadlines: Priority date 2/1; no closing date. Applicants notified on a rolling basis starting 4/1; must reply by 5/1 or within 3 week(s) of notification.

Transfers: Closing date 5/1.

CONTACT

Elisabeth Rankin, Director of Financial Aid
Route 417, St. Bonaventure, NY 14778-2284
(716) 375-2400

St. Elizabeth College of Nursing
Utica, New York
www.secon.edu   Federal Code: 006461

2-year private nursing college in small city, affiliated with Roman Catholic Church.

Enrollment: 184 undergrads.

Selectivity: Admits less than 50% of applicants.

BASIC COSTS (2007-2008)

Tuition and fees: $12,350.

Per-credit charge: $300.

FINANCIAL AID PICTURE

Students with need: Need-based aid available for full-time and part-time students.

FINANCIAL AID PROCEDURES

Forms required: FAFSA, state aid form.

Dates and Deadlines: No deadline. Applicants notified on a rolling basis starting 1/1; must reply within 2 week(s) of notification.

CONTACT

Sherry Wojnas, Director, Financial Aid
2215 Genesee Street, Utica, NY 13501
(315) 798-8206

St. Francis College
Brooklyn Heights, New York
www.stfranciscollege.edu   Federal Code: 002820

4-year private liberal arts college in very large city, affiliated with Roman Catholic Church.

Enrollment: 2,224 undergrads, 13% part-time. 480 full-time freshmen.

Selectivity: Admits over 75% of applicants.

BASIC COSTS (2007-2008)

Tuition and fees: $14,970.

Additional info: Tuition/fee waivers available for unemployed or children of unemployed.

FINANCIAL AID PICTURE

Students with need: Need-based aid available for full-time and part-time students.

Students without need: No-need awards available for academics, athletics.

Scholarships offered: Presidential Scholarship: full tuition; minimum high school GPA 90: minimum SAT 1150. St. Francis Scholarship: $7,500; minimum high school GPA 85; minimum 1100 SAT. St. Clare Scholarship: $6,500; minimum 1100 SAT. St. Clare Scholarship: $6,500: minimum 85 high school GPA; minimum 1000 SAT. Dean's Scholarship: $3,500; minimum 1000 SAT. All scholarships renewable annually for 4-year period, provided student maintains full-time status and cumulative GPA of at least 3.0. SAT scores listed exclusive of Writing.

FINANCIAL AID PROCEDURES

Forms required: FAFSA, state aid form.

Dates and Deadlines: Priority date 2/15; no closing date. Applicants notified on a rolling basis starting 3/15; must reply within 2 week(s) of notification.

CONTACT

Joseph Cummings, Director, Student Financial Services
180 Remsen Street, Brooklyn Heights, NY 11201-9902
(718) 489-5255

St. John Fisher College

Rochester, New York
www.sjfc.edu   Federal Code: 002821

4-year private liberal arts college in large town, affiliated with Roman Catholic Church.

Enrollment: 2,796 undergrads, 6% part-time. 563 full-time freshmen.

Selectivity: Admits 50 to 75% of applicants.

BASIC COSTS (2007-2008)

Tuition and fees: $22,230.

Per-credit charge: $588.

Room and board: $9,380.

FINANCIAL AID PICTURE (2006-2007)

Students with need: Out of 543 full-time freshmen who applied for aid, 450 were judged to have need. Of these, 450 received aid, and 49 had their full need met. Average financial aid package met 85% of need; average scholarship/grant was $12,846; average loan was $4,483.

Students without need: 102 full-time freshmen who did not demonstrate need for aid received scholarships/grants; average award was $7,308. No-need awards available for academics, leadership.

Scholarships offered: Founders Award: $8,500. Presidential Scholarship: $10,000. Trustees Scholarship: $11,000. Fisher Service Scholars Program: one-third of cost of education; must be nominated. First Generation Scholars Program: $5,000 to one-third of cost of education; must be nominated. Honors and Science Scholars: $2,500 per year ($2,000 in scholarship and $500 in the form of book voucher); Science Scholars also receive laptop computer to use throughout 4 years of enrollment.

Cumulative student debt: 87% of graduating class had student loans; average debt was $31,206.

FINANCIAL AID PROCEDURES

Forms required: FAFSA, state aid form.

Dates and Deadlines: Priority date 2/15; no closing date. Applicants notified on a rolling basis starting 3/22; must reply by 5/1 or within 3 week(s) of notification.

Transfers: Closing date 2/15. Applicants notified on a rolling basis starting 2/15; must reply within 3 week(s) of notification.

CONTACT

Angela Monnat, Director of Financial Aid
3690 East Avenue, Rochester, NY 14618-3597
(585) 385-8042

St. John's University

Queens, New York
www.stjohns.edu   Federal Code: 002823

4-year private university in very large city, affiliated with Roman Catholic Church.

Enrollment: 12,178 undergrads, 4% part-time. 3,260 full-time freshmen.

Selectivity: Admits 50 to 75% of applicants.

BASIC COSTS (2007-2008)

Tuition and fees: $26,840.

Room and board: $12,070.

Additional info: Tuition may vary by program and class year. Four-year fixed rate tuition plan available for incoming freshmen. Tuition at time of enrollment locked for 4 years.

FINANCIAL AID PICTURE (2006-2007)

Students with need: Out of 2,896 full-time freshmen who applied for aid, 2,632 were judged to have need. Of these, 2,617 received aid, and 308 had their full need met. Average financial aid package met 70% of need; average scholarship/grant was $9,701; average loan was $3,603. For part-time students, average financial aid package was $10,636.

Students without need: 203 full-time freshmen who did not demonstrate need for aid received scholarships/grants; average award was $9,174. No-need awards available for academics, alumni affiliation, art, athletics, leadership, music/drama, religious affiliation, ROTC.

Scholarships offered: 54 full-time freshmen received athletic scholarships; average amount $25,286.

Cumulative student debt: 74% of graduating class had student loans; average debt was $28,010.

FINANCIAL AID PROCEDURES

Forms required: FAFSA.

Dates and Deadlines: Priority date 2/1; no closing date. Applicants notified on a rolling basis starting 3/15; must reply within 2 week(s) of notification.

Transfers: No deadline. Applicants notified by 3/15; must reply within 2 week(s) of notification. Scholarships available if 24 credits college study completed with a minimum GPA of 3.0.

CONTACT

Jorge Rodriguez, Assistant Vice President and Executive Director, Financial Aid
8000 Utopia Parkway, Queens, NY 11439
(718) 990-2000

St. Joseph's College

Brooklyn, New York
www.sjcny.edu   Federal Code: 002825

4-year private liberal arts and teachers college in very large city.

Enrollment: 1,059 undergrads, 31% part-time. 163 full-time freshmen.

Selectivity: Admits over 75% of applicants.

BASIC COSTS (2008-2009)

Tuition and fees: $14,532.

Per-credit charge: $460.

FINANCIAL AID PICTURE

Students with need: Need-based aid available for full-time and part-time students. Work study available nights, weekends, and for part-time students.
Students without need: No-need awards available for academics, alumni affiliation, leadership.

FINANCIAL AID PROCEDURES

Forms required: FAFSA, state aid form, institutional form.
Dates and Deadlines: Priority date 2/25; no closing date. Applicants notified on a rolling basis starting 4/1; must reply by 5/1 or within 2 week(s) of notification.
Transfers: Priority date 3/15; no deadline.

CONTACT

Carol Sullivan, Director of Financial Aid
245 Clinton Avenue, Brooklyn, NY 11205-3688
(718) 636-6808

St. Joseph's College of Nursing

Syracuse, New York
www.sjhsyr.org/nursing   Federal Code: 006467

2-year private nursing college in small city, affiliated with Roman Catholic Church.
Enrollment: 235 undergrads, 47% part-time. 18 full-time freshmen.
Selectivity: Admits less than 50% of applicants.

BASIC COSTS (2008-2009)

Tuition and fees: $12,787.
Room only: $3,500.
Additional info: Tuition includes liberal arts component of degree taken at other institution.

FINANCIAL AID PICTURE (2006-2007)

Students with need: 26% of average financial aid package awarded as scholarships/grants, 74% awarded as loans/jobs. Need-based aid available for part-time students.
Students without need: This college awards aid only to students with need.

FINANCIAL AID PROCEDURES

Forms required: FAFSA, state aid form.
Dates and Deadlines: Priority date 3/1; no closing date. Applicants notified on a rolling basis starting 6/15.

CONTACT

Theresa Moser, Director of Financial Aid
206 Prospect Avenue, Syracuse, NY 13203
(315) 448-5040

St. Joseph's College: Suffolk Campus

Patchogue, New York
www.sjcny.edu   Federal Code: E00505

4-year private branch campus and liberal arts college in large town.
Enrollment: 3,400 undergrads, 20% part-time. 489 full-time freshmen.
Selectivity: Admits over 75% of applicants.

BASIC COSTS (2007-2008)

Tuition and fees: $14,532.
Per-credit charge: $460.

FINANCIAL AID PICTURE

Students with need: Need-based aid available for full-time and part-time students. Work study available nights, weekends, and for part-time students.
Students without need: No-need awards available for academics.
Scholarships offered: Board of Trustees Scholarship: full tuition less outside aid; entering freshmen with a 92 high school average and 1200 SAT. Alumni

Scholarship: variable award on yearly basis to children of alumni based on need and merit. Scholastic Achievement Award: up to $8,000 per year for entering freshmen. Academic Achievement Scholarship: automatically awards up to $4,500 for 3.6 GPA or better and $3,000 for 3.3 GPA or better; to entering transfer students with 3.3 GPA or better and associate degree. SAT scores listed exclusive of Writing.

FINANCIAL AID PROCEDURES

Forms required: FAFSA, state aid form, institutional form.
Dates and Deadlines: Priority date 2/25; no closing date. Applicants notified on a rolling basis starting 3/15; must reply within 2 week(s) of notification.
Transfers: Priority date 3/15; no deadline. Applicants notified on a rolling basis starting 3/15; must reply within 2 week(s) of notification.

CONTACT

Joan Farley, Director of Financial Aid
155 West Roe Boulevard, Patchogue, NY 11772-2603
(631) 447-3214

St. Lawrence University

Canton, New York
www.stlawu.edu   Federal Code: 002829

4-year private liberal arts college in small town.
Enrollment: 2,160 undergrads. 627 full-time freshmen.
Selectivity: Admits less than 50% of applicants.

BASIC COSTS (2008-2009)

Tuition and fees: $37,915.
Room and board: $9,645.

FINANCIAL AID PICTURE (2007-2008)

Students with need: Out of 454 full-time freshmen who applied for aid, 389 were judged to have need. Of these, 389 received aid, and 206 had their full need met. Average financial aid package met 94% of need; average scholarship/grant was $24,660; average loan was $3,303.
Students without need: 99 full-time freshmen who did not demonstrate need for aid received scholarships/grants; average award was $11,293. No-need awards available for academics, alumni affiliation, athletics, minority status, ROTC.
Scholarships offered: *Merit:* Merit scholarships from $7,500 to $20,000 annually. Augsbury/North Country Scholarship: for students in some schools in northern New York and southern Ontario; nomination by counselor required. Community Service Scholarship: based on past and current service. Presidential Diversity Scholarship: for students of African American, Asian American, Hispanic American and Native American heritage. Sesquicentennial and University Scholarship: based on academic excellence, character and leadership. Vilas Scholarship: for students interested in business. *Athletic:* 4 full-time freshmen received athletic scholarships; average amount $44,077.
Cumulative student debt: 74% of graduating class had student loans; average debt was $28,776.

FINANCIAL AID PROCEDURES

Forms required: FAFSA, institutional form.
Dates and Deadlines: Closing date 2/1. Applicants notified by 3/31; must reply by 5/1 or within 2 week(s) of notification.
Transfers: Closing date 5/1. Applicants notified on a rolling basis starting 6/1; must reply within 2 week(s) of notification.

CONTACT

Patricia Farmer, Director of Financial Aid
Payson Hall, Canton, NY 13617
(315) 229-5265

St. Thomas Aquinas College

Sparkill, New York
www.stac.edu   Federal Code: 002832

4-year private liberal arts college in large town.

Enrollment: 1,437 undergrads, 7% part-time. 323 full-time freshmen.

Selectivity: Admits over 75% of applicants.

BASIC COSTS (2008-2009)

Tuition and fees: $20,000.

Per-credit charge: $630.

Room and board: $9,730.

FINANCIAL AID PICTURE (2006-2007)

Students with need: Out of 294 full-time freshmen who applied for aid, 216 were judged to have need. Of these, 211 received aid, and 31 had their full need met. Average financial aid package met 56% of need; average scholarship/grant was $9,225; average loan was $3,278. For part-time students, average financial aid package was $5,061.

Students without need: 36 full-time freshmen who did not demonstrate need for aid received scholarships/grants; average award was $7,658. No-need awards available for academics, athletics.

Scholarships offered: 11 full-time freshmen received athletic scholarships; average amount $4,518.

FINANCIAL AID PROCEDURES

Forms required: FAFSA, state aid form.

Dates and Deadlines: Priority date 2/15; no closing date. Applicants notified on a rolling basis starting 3/1; must reply by 5/1 or within 4 week(s) of notification.

Transfers: Closing date 5/1. Applicants notified on a rolling basis; must reply within 4 week(s) of notification.

CONTACT

Anna Chrissotimos, Director of Financial Aid
125 Route 340, Sparkill, NY 10976
(845) 398-4097

Sarah Lawrence College

Bronxville, New York   Federal Code: 002813
www.sarahlawrence.edu   CSS Code: 2810

4-year private liberal arts college in small city.

Enrollment: 1,314 undergrads, 4% part-time. 363 full-time freshmen.

Selectivity: Admits less than 50% of applicants.

BASIC COSTS (2007-2008)

Tuition and fees: $38,090.

Room and board: $13,316.

FINANCIAL AID PICTURE (2007-2008)

Students with need: Out of 224 full-time freshmen who applied for aid, 184 were judged to have need. Of these, 184 received aid, and 125 had their full need met. Average financial aid package met 92% of need; average scholarship/grant was $28,313; average loan was $2,576. For part-time students, average financial aid package was $17,467.

Students without need: This college awards aid only to students with need.

Cumulative student debt: 61% of graduating class had student loans; average debt was $16,322.

FINANCIAL AID PROCEDURES

Forms required: FAFSA, CSS PROFILE, state aid form.

Dates and Deadlines: Closing date 2/1. Applicants notified by 4/1; must reply by 5/1.

Transfers: Closing date 3/15. Maximum institutional grant to transfer students is $27,000 a year. Loans and work study available above and beyond this grant.

CONTACT

Heather McDonnell, Director of Financial Aid
One Mead Way, Bronxville, NY 10708-5999
(914) 395-2570

Schenectady County Community College

Schenectady, New York
www.sunysccc.edu   Federal Code: 006785

2-year public community college in small city.

Enrollment: 2,933 undergrads.

Selectivity: Open admission; but selective for some programs.

BASIC COSTS (2007-2008)

Tuition and fees: $3,104; out-of-state residents $5,994.

Per-credit charge: $117; out-of-state residents $234.

FINANCIAL AID PICTURE

Students with need: Need-based aid available for full-time and part-time students.

Students without need: This college awards aid only to students with need.

FINANCIAL AID PROCEDURES

Forms required: FAFSA.

Dates and Deadlines: Priority date 5/1; no closing date. Applicants notified on a rolling basis starting 4/15; must reply by 8/31.

CONTACT

Brian McGarvey, Director of Financial Aid
78 Washington Avenue, Schenectady, NY 12305
(518) 381-1352

School of Visual Arts

New York, New York
www.sva.edu   Federal Code: 007468

4-year for-profit visual arts college in very large city.

Enrollment: 3,323 undergrads, 3% part-time. 664 full-time freshmen.

Selectivity: Admits 50 to 75% of applicants.

BASIC COSTS (2008-2009)

Tuition and fees: $25,500.

Per-credit charge: $850.

Room only: $11,350.

Additional info: Additional fees vary by department.

FINANCIAL AID PICTURE (2007-2008)

Students with need: Out of 472 full-time freshmen who applied for aid, 411 were judged to have need. Of these, 405 received aid, and 3 had their full need met. Average financial aid package met 44% of need; average scholarship/grant was $5,859; average loan was $3,701. Need-based aid available for part-time students.

Students without need: 37 full-time freshmen who did not demonstrate need for aid received scholarships/grants; average award was $6,164. No-need awards available for art.

Scholarships offered: SVA matching scholarship available to full- and part-time undergraduate and graduate students. SVA will match 25% of any outside scholarship, up to $2500, that a student obtains for enrollment at SVA.

Cumulative student debt: 57% of graduating class had student loans; average debt was $30,259.

FINANCIAL AID PROCEDURES

Forms required: FAFSA, state aid form.

Dates and Deadlines: Priority date 2/1; no closing date. Applicants notified on a rolling basis starting 2/15; must reply within 4 week(s) of notification.

Transfers: No deadline. Applicants notified on a rolling basis; must reply within 4 week(s) of notification.

CONTACT

William Berrios, Director of Financial Aid
209 East 23rd Street, New York, NY 10010-3994
(212) 592-2030

Siena College

Loudonville, New York
www.siena.edu   Federal Code: 002816

4-year private liberal arts college in large town, affiliated with Roman Catholic Church.

Enrollment: 3,151 undergrads, 4% part-time. 690 full-time freshmen.

Selectivity: Admits 50 to 75% of applicants.

BASIC COSTS (2007-2008)

Tuition and fees: $22,685.

Per-credit charge: $450.

Room and board: $8,875.

FINANCIAL AID PICTURE (2006-2007)

Students with need: Out of 629 full-time freshmen who applied for aid, 488 were judged to have need. Of these, 487 received aid, and 78 had their full need met. Average financial aid package met 76% of need; average scholarship/grant was $11,995; average loan was $2,943. For part-time students, average financial aid package was $10,757.

Students without need: 129 full-time freshmen who did not demonstrate need for aid received scholarships/grants; average award was $5,716. No-need awards available for academics, art, athletics, leadership, minority status, ROTC, state/district residency.

Scholarships offered: 59 full-time freshmen received athletic scholarships; average amount $13,229.

Cumulative student debt: 77% of graduating class had student loans; average debt was $21,800.

FINANCIAL AID PROCEDURES

Forms required: FAFSA, state aid form.

Dates and Deadlines: Closing date 2/15. Applicants notified by 4/1; must reply by 5/1.

Transfers: Priority date 3/1.

CONTACT

Mary Lawyer, Assistant Vice President for Financial Aid
515 Loudon Road, Loudonville, NY 12211-1462
(518) 783-4288

Skidmore College

Saratoga Springs, New York   Federal Code: 002814
www.skidmore.edu   CSS Code: 2815

4-year private liberal arts college in large town.

Enrollment: 2,771 undergrads, 6% part-time. 687 full-time freshmen.

Selectivity: Admits less than 50% of applicants.

BASIC COSTS (2008-2009)

Tuition and fees: $38,888.

Per-credit charge: $1,270.

Room and board: $10,377.

FINANCIAL AID PICTURE (2007-2008)

Students with need: Out of 355 full-time freshmen who applied for aid, 295 were judged to have need. Of these, 295 received aid, and 244 had their full need met. Average financial aid package met 88% of need; average scholarship/grant was $30,321; average loan was $3,016.

Students without need: 3 full-time freshmen who did not demonstrate need for aid received scholarships/grants; average award was $10,000. No-need awards available for music/drama.

Scholarships offered: Porter Presidential Scholarships in Science and Mathematics: $10,000 annually; based on outstanding ability and achievement in math, science, or computer science. Filene Undergraduate Music Scholarships: $10,000 annually; based on music ability. No drama scholarships.

FINANCIAL AID PROCEDURES

Forms required: FAFSA, CSS PROFILE.

Dates and Deadlines: Closing date 1/15. Applicants notified by 4/1; must reply by 5/1.

Transfers: Priority date 4/1. Applicants notified on a rolling basis starting 4/15; must reply within 3 week(s) of notification. Some transfer students eligible for need-based grant assistance. Other transfer students eligible for grant assistance after 1 full year of enrollment or at beginning of junior year, whichever comes first.

CONTACT

Robert Shorb, Associate Dean, Director of Student Aid and Family Finance
815 North Broadway, Saratoga Springs, NY 12866
(518) 580-5750

State University of New York at Albany

Albany, New York
www.albany.edu   Federal Code: 002835

4-year public university in small city.

Enrollment: 12,449 undergrads, 5% part-time. 2,414 full-time freshmen.

Selectivity: Admits 50 to 75% of applicants.

BASIC COSTS (2007-2008)

Tuition and fees: $6,018; out-of-state residents $12,278.

Per-credit charge: $181; out-of-state residents $442.

Room and board: $9,032.

FINANCIAL AID PICTURE (2006-2007)

Students with need: Out of 2,035 full-time freshmen who applied for aid, 1,354 were judged to have need. Of these, 1,337 received aid, and 172 had their full need met. Average financial aid package met 70% of need; average scholarship/grant was $5,510; average loan was $3,324. For part-time students, average financial aid package was $4,591.

Students without need: 135 full-time freshmen who did not demonstrate need for aid received scholarships/grants; average award was $3,126. No-need awards available for academics, athletics, state/district residency.

Scholarships offered: *Merit:* Presidential Scholarship Awards: NY residents can receive up to $3,500 per year and out-of-state students can qualify for up to $6,000 per year in renewable scholarship funding; requires high school average of at least 90 and combined SAT Critical Reading and Math scores in upper 1200s or higher. All Presidential Scholarship recipients are invited to apply to The Honors College at the University at Albany. *Athletic:* 32 full-time freshmen received athletic scholarships; average amount $11,618.

Cumulative student debt: 86% of graduating class had student loans; average debt was $13,842.

FINANCIAL AID PROCEDURES

Forms required: FAFSA, state aid form.

Dates and Deadlines: Priority date 3/15; no closing date. Applicants notified on a rolling basis starting 3/15; must reply by 5/1 or within 2 week(s) of notification.

CONTACT

Beth Post, Director of Financial Aid
Office of Undergraduate Admissions, University Hall 112, Albany, NY 12222
(518) 442-3202

State University of New York at Binghamton

Binghamton, New York
www.binghamton.edu   Federal Code: 002836

4-year public university in small city.
Enrollment: 11,435 undergrads, 4% part-time. 2,218 full-time freshmen.
Selectivity: Admits less than 50% of applicants.

BASIC COSTS (2007-2008)

Tuition and fees: $6,012; out-of-state residents $12,272.
Per-credit charge: $181; out-of-state residents $442.
Room and board: $9,188.

FINANCIAL AID PICTURE (2007-2008)

Students with need: Out of 1,736 full-time freshmen who applied for aid, 945 were judged to have need. Of these, 936 received aid, and 820 had their full need met. Average financial aid package met 80% of need; average scholarship/grant was $5,421; average loan was $3,439. For part-time students, average financial aid package was $9,209.
Students without need: 190 full-time freshmen who did not demonstrate need for aid received scholarships/grants; average award was $1,114. No-need awards available for academics, art, athletics, leadership, minority status, music/drama, state/district residency.
Scholarships offered: 83 full-time freshmen received athletic scholarships; average amount $8,371.
Cumulative student debt: 56% of graduating class had student loans; average debt was $15,229.

FINANCIAL AID PROCEDURES

Forms required: FAFSA, state aid form.
Dates and Deadlines: Priority date 2/1; no closing date. Applicants notified on a rolling basis starting 3/17; must reply within 2 week(s) of notification.
Transfers: Priority date 2/1. Applicants notified on a rolling basis starting 3/1; must reply within 2 week(s) of notification.

CONTACT

Dennis Chavez, Director of Financial Aid and Employment
Box 6001, Binghamton, NY 13902-6001
(607) 777-2428

State University of New York at Buffalo

Buffalo, New York
www.buffalo.edu   Federal Code: 002837

4-year public university in large city.
Enrollment: 18,470 undergrads, 6% part-time. 3,257 full-time freshmen.
Selectivity: Admits 50 to 75% of applicants.

BASIC COSTS (2007-2008)

Tuition and fees: $6,218; out-of-state residents $12,478.
Per-credit charge: $181; out-of-state residents $442.
Room and board: $9,480.
Additional info: Tuition/fee waivers available for minority students.

FINANCIAL AID PICTURE

Students with need: Need-based aid available for full-time and part-time students. Work study available nights, weekends, and for part-time students.
Students without need: No-need awards available for academics, athletics, minority status, music/drama, state/district residency.

Scholarships offered: Honors program includes scholarships for high academic achievement, high SAT scores.

FINANCIAL AID PROCEDURES

Forms required: FAFSA.
Dates and Deadlines: Priority date 3/1; no closing date. Applicants notified on a rolling basis starting 2/1; must reply by 5/1.

CONTACT

Cheryl Taplin, Director of Student Academic Records & Financial Services
12 Capen Hall, Buffalo, NY 14260-1660
(716) 645-2450

State University of New York at Farmingdale

Farmingdale, New York
www.farmingdale.edu   Federal Code: 002858

4-year public technical college in large town.
Enrollment: 5,569 undergrads, 24% part-time. 986 full-time freshmen.
Selectivity: Admits 50 to 75% of applicants.

BASIC COSTS (2007-2008)

Tuition and fees: $5,340; out-of-state residents $11,600.
Per-credit charge: $181; out-of-state residents $442.
Room and board: $11,210.

FINANCIAL AID PICTURE

Students with need: Need-based aid available for full-time and part-time students.
Students without need: No-need awards available for academics.

FINANCIAL AID PROCEDURES

Forms required: FAFSA, state aid form, institutional form.
Dates and Deadlines: Priority date 4/1; no closing date. Applicants notified on a rolling basis starting 4/1.

CONTACT

Catherine Malnichuck, Director of Financial Services
2350 Broadhollow Road, Farmingdale, NY 11735-1021
(631) 420-2578

State University of New York at New Paltz

New Paltz, New York
www.newpaltz.edu   Federal Code: 002846

4-year public liberal arts college in large town.
Enrollment: 5,803 undergrads, 9% part-time. 974 full-time freshmen.
Selectivity: Admits less than 50% of applicants.

BASIC COSTS (2007-2008)

Tuition and fees: $5,390; out-of-state residents $11,650.
Per-credit charge: $181; out-of-state residents $442.
Room and board: $8,070.

FINANCIAL AID PICTURE (2006-2007)

Students with need: Out of 836 full-time freshmen who applied for aid, 501 were judged to have need. Of these, 496 received aid, and 95 had their full need met. Average financial aid package met 63% of need; average scholarship/grant was $2,528; average loan was $2,210. For part-time students, average financial aid package was $2,935.
Students without need: This college awards aid only to students with need.
Cumulative student debt: 75% of graduating class had student loans; average debt was $19,000.

FINANCIAL AID PROCEDURES

Forms required: FAFSA.

Dates and Deadlines: Priority date 3/15; no closing date. Applicants notified on a rolling basis starting 4/1; must reply within 4 week(s) of notification.

Transfers: No deadline. Applicants notified on a rolling basis starting 4/1; must reply within 4 week(s) of notification.

CONTACT

Daniel Sistarenik, Director of Financial Aid

100 Hawk Drive, New Paltz, NY 12561-2499

(845) 257-3250

State University of New York at Oswego

Oswego, New York

www.oswego.edu   Federal Code: 002848

4-year public university in large town.

Enrollment: 6,962 undergrads, 6% part-time. 1,351 full-time freshmen.

Selectivity: Admits 50 to 75% of applicants.

BASIC COSTS (2007-2008)

Tuition and fees: $5,434; out-of-state residents $11,694.

Per-credit charge: $181; out-of-state residents $442.

Room and board: $9,470.

FINANCIAL AID PICTURE (2006-2007)

Students with need: Out of 1,187 full-time freshmen who applied for aid, 833 were judged to have need. Of these, 812 received aid, and 322 had their full need met. Average financial aid package met 71% of need; average scholarship/grant was $5,067; average loan was $2,769. For part-time students, average financial aid package was $6,969.

Students without need: 295 full-time freshmen who did not demonstrate need for aid received scholarships/grants; average award was $4,814. No-need awards available for academics, state/district residency.

Scholarships offered: Annual scholarships: $500 to $4,400 annually; based on class rank in top 15%. Additional residential scholarships for out-of-state students: $4,490 annually; requires on-campus housing.

Cumulative student debt: 84% of graduating class had student loans; average debt was $21,845.

FINANCIAL AID PROCEDURES

Forms required: FAFSA.

Dates and Deadlines: Priority date 3/1; no closing date. Applicants notified on a rolling basis starting 3/1; must reply by 5/1 or within 3 week(s) of notification.

Transfers: Transfer students entering in January need to supply financial aid transcipts from prior colleges.

CONTACT

Mark Humbert, Director of Financial Aid

229 Sheldon Hall, Oswego, NY 13126-3599

(315) 312-2248

State University of New York at Purchase

Purchase, New York

www.purchase.edu   Federal Code: 006791

4-year public visual arts and business and liberal arts college in large town.

Enrollment: 3,764 undergrads, 6% part-time. 785 full-time freshmen.

Selectivity: Admits less than 50% of applicants.

BASIC COSTS (2007-2008)

Tuition and fees: $5,771; out-of-state residents $12,031.

Per-credit charge: $181; out-of-state residents $442.

Room and board: $9,444.

FINANCIAL AID PICTURE (2007-2008)

Students with need: Average financial aid package met 76% of need; average scholarship/grant was $4,712; average loan was $4,399. For part-time students, average financial aid package was $10,728.

Students without need: No-need awards available for academics, art, minority status, music/drama.

Cumulative student debt: 74% of graduating class had student loans; average debt was $19,247.

Additional info: All applicants automatically considered for scholarship upon review of applications, essays, auditions, and/or portfolio.

FINANCIAL AID PROCEDURES

Forms required: FAFSA, state aid form.

Dates and Deadlines: Priority date 2/1; no closing date. Applicants notified on a rolling basis starting 3/1; must reply within 2 week(s) of notification.

Transfers: Financial aid transcripts required from all previously attended institutions.

CONTACT

Emilie Devine, Director of Financial Aid

735 Anderson Hill Road, Purchase, NY 10577-1400

(914) 251-6350

State University of New York at Stony Brook

Stony Brook, New York

www.stonybrook.edu   Federal Code: 002838

4-year public university in large town.

Enrollment: 15,222 undergrads, 7% part-time. 2,674 full-time freshmen.

Selectivity: Admits less than 50% of applicants.

BASIC COSTS (2007-2008)

Tuition and fees: $5,760; out-of-state residents $12,020.

Per-credit charge: $181; out-of-state residents $442.

Room and board: $8,734.

FINANCIAL AID PICTURE (2006-2007)

Students with need: Out of 2,131 full-time freshmen who applied for aid, 1,476 were judged to have need. Of these, 1,453 received aid, and 225 had their full need met. Average financial aid package met 66% of need; average scholarship/grant was $6,674; average loan was $2,841. For part-time students, average financial aid package was $4,503.

Students without need: 314 full-time freshmen who did not demonstrate need for aid received scholarships/grants; average award was $3,019. No-need awards available for academics, alumni affiliation, art, athletics, job skills, leadership, music/drama.

Scholarships offered: 76 full-time freshmen received athletic scholarships; average amount $12,172.

Cumulative student debt: 59% of graduating class had student loans; average debt was $14,799.

FINANCIAL AID PROCEDURES

Forms required: FAFSA.

Dates and Deadlines: Priority date 3/1; no closing date. Applicants notified on a rolling basis starting 3/1; must reply by 5/1 or within 2 week(s) of notification.

CONTACT

Jacqueline Pascariello, Director Financial Aid

118 Administration Building, Stony Brook, NY 11794-1901

(631) 689-6000

PART III: FINANCIAL AID COLLEGE BY COLLEGE

State University of New York College at Brockport

Brockport, New York
www.brockport.edu   Federal Code: 002841

4-year public liberal arts college in small town.
Enrollment: 6,841 undergrads, 9% part-time. 942 full-time freshmen.
Selectivity: Admits less than 50% of applicants.

BASIC COSTS (2007-2008)
Tuition and fees: $5,406; out-of-state residents $11,666.
Per-credit charge: $181; out-of-state residents $442.
Room and board: $8,830.

FINANCIAL AID PICTURE (2006-2007)
Students with need: Out of 863 full-time freshmen who applied for aid, 624 were judged to have need. Of these, 621 received aid, and 155 had their full need met. Average financial aid package met 83% of need; average scholarship/grant was $4,131; average loan was $4,132. For part-time students, average financial aid package was $4,260.
Students without need: 73 full-time freshmen who did not demonstrate need for aid received scholarships/grants; average award was $4,081. No-need awards available for academics, alumni affiliation, leadership, minority status, ROTC, state/district residency.
Scholarships offered: Extraordinary Academic Scholarships: range from $2,250 to $12,100 per year; minimum qualifications include SAT scores of 1100 (24 ACT), rank in top 25% of class, 90 average or higher. SAT score listed exclusive of Writing portion.
Cumulative student debt: 82% of graduating class had student loans; average debt was $22,575.

FINANCIAL AID PROCEDURES
Forms required: FAFSA, state aid form.
Dates and Deadlines: Priority date 2/15; no closing date. Applicants notified on a rolling basis starting 2/15; must reply within 4 week(s) of notification.

CONTACT
J. Atkinson, Assistant Vice President for Enrollment Management and Student Affairs
350 New Campus Drive, Brockport, NY 14420-2915
(585) 395-2501

State University of New York College at Buffalo

Buffalo, New York
www.buffalostate.edu   Federal Code: 002842

4-year public liberal arts and teachers college in large city.
Enrollment: 8,935 undergrads, 10% part-time. 1,390 full-time freshmen.
Selectivity: Admits less than 50% of applicants.

BASIC COSTS (2007-2008)
Tuition and fees: $5,375; out-of-state residents $11,635.
Per-credit charge: $181; out-of-state residents $442.
Room and board: $8,514.
Additional info: Tuition/fee waivers available for minority students.

FINANCIAL AID PICTURE (2007-2008)
Students with need: Out of 1,220 full-time freshmen who applied for aid, 1,199 were judged to have need. Of these, 1,199 received aid, and 723 had their full need met. Average financial aid package met 71% of need; average scholarship/grant was $4,944; average loan was $3,128. For part-time students, average financial aid package was $9,814.
Students without need: This college awards aid only to students with need.

Scholarships offered: Empire Minority Scholarships; $1,000 annually for 4 years. Honors Program; $2,000 for 2 years and $1,000 for remaining 2 years.
Cumulative student debt: 69% of graduating class had student loans; average debt was $17,657.

FINANCIAL AID PROCEDURES
Forms required: FAFSA.
Dates and Deadlines: Priority date 3/15; closing date 5/1. Applicants notified on a rolling basis starting 5/1; must reply within 4 week(s) of notification.
Transfers: No deadline.

CONTACT
Kent McGowan, Director of Financial Aid
1300 Elmwood Avenue, Moot Hall, Buffalo, NY 14222-1095
(716) 878-4902

State University of New York College at Cortland

Cortland, New York
www.cortland.edu   Federal Code: 002843

4-year public university and liberal arts and teachers college in large town.
Enrollment: 5,904 undergrads, 2% part-time. 1,196 full-time freshmen.
Selectivity: Admits less than 50% of applicants.

BASIC COSTS (2007-2008)
Tuition and fees: $5,439; out-of-state residents $11,699.
Per-credit charge: $181; out-of-state residents $442.
Room and board: $8,760.

FINANCIAL AID PICTURE (2007-2008)
Students with need: Out of 1,069 full-time freshmen who applied for aid, 673 were judged to have need. Of these, 659 received aid, and 112 had their full need met. Average financial aid package met 73% of need; average scholarship/grant was $1,589; average loan was $1,950. Need-based aid available for part-time students.
Students without need: 282 full-time freshmen who did not demonstrate need for aid received scholarships/grants; average award was $3,758. No-need awards available for academics, leadership.

FINANCIAL AID PROCEDURES
Forms required: FAFSA, state aid form.
Dates and Deadlines: Priority date 3/1; closing date 4/1. Applicants notified on a rolling basis starting 3/1; must reply by 5/1 or within 4 week(s) of notification.
Transfers: Federal regulations require financial aid transcript from each post-secondary school attended even if student did not receive aid.

CONTACT
David Canaski, Director of Financial Aid
PO Box 2000, Cortland, NY 13045-0900
(607) 753-4717

State University of New York College at Fredonia

Fredonia, New York
www.fredonia.edu   Federal Code: 002844

4-year public liberal arts college in large town.
Enrollment: 5,067 undergrads, 3% part-time. 1,024 full-time freshmen.
Selectivity: Admits 50 to 75% of applicants.

BASIC COSTS (2007-2008)
Tuition and fees: $5,544; out-of-state residents $11,802.
Per-credit charge: $181; out-of-state residents $442.
Room and board: $8,640.

FINANCIAL AID PICTURE (2006-2007)

Students with need: Out of 902 full-time freshmen who applied for aid, 627 were judged to have need. Of these, 614 received aid, and 155 had their full need met. Average financial aid package met 78% of need; average scholarship/grant was $3,063; average loan was $2,944. For part-time students, average financial aid package was $6,565.

Students without need: 76 full-time freshmen who did not demonstrate need for aid received scholarships/grants; average award was $1,343. No-need awards available for academics, alumni affiliation, art, athletics, leadership, minority status, music/drama.

Scholarships offered: Foundation Freshman Award: 30 awarded; minimum 91 high school average, 1250 SAT or 28 ACT; $3,000. Fredonia Achievement Award: 60 awarded; minimum 87 high school average, 1100 SAT or 25 ACT, minimum 3.0 GPA for transfer students; $1,000. Fredonia Award for Excellence: high school valedictorians and salutatorians; $2,500 renewable for 4 years. Out-of-State Student Scholarships: 90 high school average, 1250 SAT or 28 ACT, 3.25 GPA for transfer students. SAT scores listed are exclusive of Writing portion. Foundation Academic Scholarship: awarded to students in the natural and social sciences.

Cumulative student debt: 82% of graduating class had student loans; average debt was $19,341.

FINANCIAL AID PROCEDURES

Forms required: FAFSA, state aid form.

Dates and Deadlines: Priority date 2/1; closing date 5/15. Applicants notified on a rolling basis starting 3/10; must reply within 4 week(s) of notification.

Transfers: Applicants notified on a rolling basis starting 10/15. Financial aid transcripts required from prior institutions attended.

CONTACT

Daniel Tramuta, Director of Financial Aid
178 Central Avenue, Fredonia, NY 14063-1136
(716) 673-3253

State University of New York College at Geneseo

Geneseo, New York
www.geneseo.edu   Federal Code: 002845

4-year public liberal arts college in small town.

Enrollment: 5,376 undergrads, 2% part-time. 1,032 full-time freshmen.

Selectivity: Admits less than 50% of applicants.

BASIC COSTS (2007-2008)

Tuition and fees: $5,616; out-of-state residents $11,876.

Per-credit charge: $181; out-of-state residents $442.

Room and board: $8,550.

FINANCIAL AID PICTURE (2007-2008)

Students with need: Out of 842 full-time freshmen who applied for aid, 417 were judged to have need. Of these, 417 received aid, and 334 had their full need met. Average financial aid package met 80% of need; average scholarship/grant was $2,946; average loan was $4,275. Need-based aid available for part-time students.

Students without need: 3 full-time freshmen who did not demonstrate need for aid received scholarships/grants; average award was $1,900. No-need awards available for academics, art, leadership, minority status, music/drama, religious affiliation, ROTC, state/district residency.

Cumulative student debt: 65% of graduating class had student loans; average debt was $18,300.

FINANCIAL AID PROCEDURES

Forms required: FAFSA, state aid form.

Dates and Deadlines: Closing date 2/15. Applicants notified on a rolling basis starting 3/15; must reply by 5/1.

CONTACT

Archie Cureton, Director of Financial Aid
1 College Circle, Geneseo, NY 14454-1471
(585) 245-5731

State University of New York College at Old Westbury

Old Westbury, New York
www.oldwestbury.edu   Federal Code: 007109

4-year public business and liberal arts college in small city.

Enrollment: 3,405 undergrads, 15% part-time. 413 full-time freshmen.

Selectivity: Admits 50 to 75% of applicants.

BASIC COSTS (2007-2008)

Tuition and fees: $5,177; out-of-state residents $11,437.

Per-credit charge: $181; out-of-state residents $442.

Room and board: $8,800.

FINANCIAL AID PICTURE (2006-2007)

Students with need: Out of 351 full-time freshmen who applied for aid, 349 were judged to have need. Of these, 315 received aid, and 315 had their full need met. Average financial aid package met 47% of need; average scholarship/grant was $5,893; average loan was $1,595. For part-time students, average financial aid package was $2,547.

Students without need: No-need awards available for academics, alumni affiliation, state/district residency.

Cumulative student debt: 51% of graduating class had student loans; average debt was $14,817.

FINANCIAL AID PROCEDURES

Forms required: FAFSA, state aid form, institutional form.

Dates and Deadlines: Priority date 4/1; no closing date. Applicants notified on a rolling basis starting 4/15; must reply within 2 week(s) of notification.

Transfers: No deadline. Applicants notified on a rolling basis starting 4/15; must reply within 2 week(s) of notification. Financial aid transcript required.

CONTACT

Mildred O'Keefe, Director of Financial Aid
Box 307, Old Westbury, NY 11568-0307
(516) 876-3222

State University of New York College at Oneonta

Oneonta, New York
www.oneonta.edu   Federal Code: 002847

4-year public liberal arts college in large town.

Enrollment: 5,620 undergrads, 2% part-time. 1,147 full-time freshmen.

Selectivity: Admits less than 50% of applicants.

BASIC COSTS (2007-2008)

Tuition and fees: $5,470; out-of-state residents $11,730.

Per-credit charge: $181; out-of-state residents $442.

Room and board: $7,966.

FINANCIAL AID PICTURE (2007-2008)

Students with need: Out of 950 full-time freshmen who applied for aid, 599 were judged to have need. Of these, 584 received aid, and 108 had their full need met. Average financial aid package met 63% of need; average scholarship/grant was $4,258; average loan was $3,964. For part-time students, average financial aid package was $5,715.

Students without need: 285 full-time freshmen who did not demonstrate need for aid received scholarships/grants; average award was $3,400. No-need awards available for academics.

Scholarships offered: Presidential Scholarships: $3,500; awarded to more than 60 applicants for academics, service, and extracurricular activities. Organization of Ancillary Services: $1,000; awarded to 64 applicants for academics, service, and extracurricular activities. OAS Minority Student Merit Scholarships: $3,500; awarded to 6 applicants for academics, service, and extracurricular activities. Mildred Haight Memorial Scholarships: $500; awarded to 22 applicants for academics.

Cumulative student debt: 75% of graduating class had student loans; average debt was $13,500.

FINANCIAL AID PROCEDURES

Forms required: FAFSA, state aid form.

Dates and Deadlines: Priority date 3/15; no closing date. Applicants notified on a rolling basis starting 3/1; must reply within 4 week(s) of notification.

Transfers: No deadline. Applicants notified on a rolling basis starting 3/1.

CONTACT

C. Goodhue, Director of Student Financial Aid

Admissions Office, 116 Alumni Hall, Oneonta, NY 13820-4016

(607) 436-2532

State University of New York College at Plattsburgh

Plattsburgh, New York

www.plattsburgh.edu   Federal Code: 002849

4-year public liberal arts and teachers college in large town.

Enrollment: 5,516 undergrads, 4% part-time. 973 full-time freshmen.

Selectivity: Admits less than 50% of applicants.

BASIC COSTS (2007-2008)

Tuition and fees: $5,407; out-of-state residents $11,667.

Per-credit charge: $181; out-of-state residents $442.

Room and board: $7,970.

FINANCIAL AID PICTURE (2007-2008)

Students with need: Out of 804 full-time freshmen who applied for aid, 550 were judged to have need. Of these, 541 received aid, and 168 had their full need met. Average financial aid package met 86% of need; average scholarship/grant was $5,534; average loan was $4,877. For part-time students, average financial aid package was $6,835.

Students without need: 338 full-time freshmen who did not demonstrate need for aid received scholarships/grants; average award was $5,155. No-need awards available for academics, alumni affiliation, art, leadership, minority status, music/drama, ROTC, state/district residency.

Cumulative student debt: 75% of graduating class had student loans; average debt was $21,855.

FINANCIAL AID PROCEDURES

Forms required: FAFSA, state aid form.

Dates and Deadlines: Priority date 2/15; no closing date. Applicants notified on a rolling basis starting 3/15; must reply within 6 week(s) of notification.

Transfers: Closing date 3/1. Applicants notified by 3/31.

CONTACT

Todd Moravec, Director of Financial Aid

Kehoe Administration Building, Plattsburgh, NY 12901

(518) 564-4076

State University of New York College at Potsdam

Potsdam, New York

www.potsdam.edu   Federal Code: 002850

4-year public liberal arts and teachers college in large town.

Enrollment: 3,571 undergrads, 3% part-time. 837 full-time freshmen.

Selectivity: Admits 50 to 75% of applicants.

BASIC COSTS (2007-2008)

Tuition and fees: $5,406; out-of-state residents $11,666.

Per-credit charge: $181; out-of-state residents $442.

Room and board: $8,420.

FINANCIAL AID PICTURE (2007-2008)

Students with need: Out of 753 full-time freshmen who applied for aid, 585 were judged to have need. Of these, 532 received aid, and 450 had their full need met. Average financial aid package met 85% of need; average scholarship/grant was $6,460; average loan was $4,255. For part-time students, average financial aid package was $8,619.

Students without need: 117 full-time freshmen who did not demonstrate need for aid received scholarships/grants; average award was $3,159. No-need awards available for academics, art, leadership, minority status, music/drama, ROTC.

Scholarships offered: Adirondack Scholars Program: based on high school GPA and standardized test scores. Mt. Emmons Scholarship: covers balance of in-state tuition and mandatory fees after TAP awards, $500 book stipend, residence hall fee waiver and board; renewable with minimum 3.25 GPA; 5 awarded. Navigator Scholarship: ranges from $1,000-$2,000; awarded to students who show academic promise and the potential for leadership; must have 1100 or greater SAT (exclusive of Writing) or ACT composite of 23 or minimum 90 high school average and history of participation and leadership in extracurricular activities and community service.

Cumulative student debt: 84% of graduating class had student loans; average debt was $18,272.

Additional info: Apply early to access limited, need-based awards.

FINANCIAL AID PROCEDURES

Forms required: FAFSA, state aid form.

Dates and Deadlines: Priority date 3/1; no closing date. Applicants notified on a rolling basis starting 2/1; must reply within 4 week(s) of notification.

Transfers: Adirondack Scholars Program; for incoming transfer students based upon outstanding academic achievement as measured by previous college GPA. Pacesetter Scholarship; $1,000 residence hall waiver to students with minimum cumulative GPA of 3.25 and higher. Renewable for 1 additional year with a cumulative 3.25 GPA. Capstone Scholarship; 6 $2,000 awards for students with minimum cumulative GPA of 3.50 and 13 $1,000 awards for students with minimum cumulative GPA of 3.25-3.49. Renewable for 1 additional year with a cumulative 3.25 GPA. Applies to fall applicants only.

CONTACT

Susan Aldrich, Director of Financial Aid

44 Pierrepont Avenue, Potsdam, NY 13676

(315) 267-2162

State University of New York College of Agriculture and Technology at Cobleskill

Cobleskill, New York

www.cobleskill.edu   Federal Code: 002856

2-year public agricultural and technical college in small town.

Enrollment: 2,559 undergrads, 4% part-time. 884 full-time freshmen.

Selectivity: Admits over 75% of applicants.

BASIC COSTS (2007-2008)

Tuition and fees: $5,449; out-of-state residents $11,709.

Per-credit charge: $181; out-of-state residents $442.

Room and board: $8,650.

FINANCIAL AID PICTURE (2006-2007)

Students with need: Out of 745 full-time freshmen who applied for aid, 463 were judged to have need. Of these, 395 received aid, and 53 had their full need met. Average financial aid package met 52% of need; average scholarship/grant was $4,195; average loan was $2,994. For part-time students, average financial aid package was $3,243.

Students without need: 161 full-time freshmen who did not demonstrate need for aid received scholarships/grants; average award was $1,670. No-need awards available for academics, alumni affiliation, leadership, state/district residency.

Cumulative student debt: 80% of graduating class had student loans; average debt was $21,353.

Additional info: Application deadline for scholarships March 15. Separate application required, available through admissions office.

FINANCIAL AID PROCEDURES

Forms required: FAFSA, state aid form.

Dates and Deadlines: Closing date 2/15. Applicants notified by 4/15; must reply within 3 week(s) of notification.

Transfers: Priority date 2/15; no deadline. Applicants notified on a rolling basis; must reply within 3 week(s) of notification.

CONTACT

Brian Smith, Director of Financial Aid

Knapp Hall, Cobleskill, NY 12043

(800) 295-8998

State University of New York College of Agriculture and Technology at Morrisville

Morrisville, New York

www.morrisville.edu   Federal Code: 002859

2-year public agricultural and technical college in small town.

Enrollment: 3,030 undergrads.

Selectivity: Admits over 75% of applicants.

BASIC COSTS (2007-2008)

Tuition and fees: $5,345; out-of-state residents $11,605.

Per-credit charge: $181; out-of-state residents $442.

Room and board: $7,810.

Additional info: Out-of-state associate degree students pay $7,210 tuition. Tuition/fee waivers available for unemployed or children of unemployed.

FINANCIAL AID PICTURE

Students with need: Need-based aid available for full-time and part-time students. Work study available nights, weekends, and for part-time students.

Students without need: No-need awards available for academics.

FINANCIAL AID PROCEDURES

Forms required: FAFSA, state aid form.

Dates and Deadlines: Priority date 2/1; no closing date. Applicants notified on a rolling basis starting 3/1; must reply within 3 week(s) of notification.

Transfers: No deadline. Applicants notified on a rolling basis; must reply within 3 week(s) of notification.

CONTACT

Dacia Banks, Director of Financial Aid

PO Box 901, Morrisville, NY 13408-0901

(800) 626-5844

State University of New York College of Environmental Science and Forestry

Syracuse, New York

www.esf.edu   Federal Code: 002851

4-year public university and liberal arts college in small city.

Enrollment: 1,455 undergrads, 3% part-time. 250 full-time freshmen.

Selectivity: Admits 50 to 75% of applicants.

BASIC COSTS (2007-2008)

Tuition and fees: $5,100; out-of-state residents $11,360.

Per-credit charge: $181; out-of-state residents $442.

Additional info: Room and board available through Syracuse University. Tuition/fee waivers available for minority students.

FINANCIAL AID PICTURE (2007-2008)

Students with need: Out of 242 full-time freshmen who applied for aid, 184 were judged to have need. Of these, 184 received aid, and 184 had their full need met. Average financial aid package met 100% of need; average scholarship/grant was $5,000; average loan was $5,500. For part-time students, average financial aid package was $7,500.

Students without need: 48 full-time freshmen who did not demonstrate need for aid received scholarships/grants; average award was $2,500. No-need awards available for academics, alumni affiliation, leadership, minority status, ROTC, state/district residency.

Cumulative student debt: 80% of graduating class had student loans; average debt was $4,750.

FINANCIAL AID PROCEDURES

Forms required: FAFSA, state aid form.

Dates and Deadlines: Priority date 3/1; no closing date. Applicants notified on a rolling basis starting 3/15; must reply within 2 week(s) of notification.

Transfers: Applicants notified by 3/15; must reply within 2 week(s) of notification.

CONTACT

John View, Director of Financial Aid

106 Bray Hall, Syracuse, NY 13210

(315) 470-6670

State University of New York College of Technology at Alfred

Alfred, New York

www.alfredstate.edu   Federal Code: 002854

2-year public liberal arts and technical college in rural community.

Enrollment: 3,027 undergrads, 6% part-time. 1,298 full-time freshmen.

Selectivity: Admits 50 to 75% of applicants.

BASIC COSTS (2007-2008)

Tuition and fees: $5,406; out-of-state residents $8,266.

Per-credit charge: $181; out-of-state residents $300.

Room and board: $8,040.

Additional info: Tuition for bachelor's degree: full-time out-of-state tuition $10,610; per-credit-hour $442 out-of-state.

FINANCIAL AID PICTURE (2006-2007)

Students with need: Need-based aid available for full-time and part-time students. Work study available nights, weekends, and for part-time students.

Students without need: No-need awards available for academics, alumni affiliation, job skills, minority status.

FINANCIAL AID PROCEDURES

Forms required: FAFSA, state aid form.

Dates and Deadlines: Priority date 3/1; no closing date. Applicants notified on a rolling basis starting 3/1; must reply within 3 week(s) of notification.

Transfers: Priority date 2/1; no deadline. Applicants notified on a rolling basis starting 1/1; must reply within 4 week(s) of notification.

CONTACT
Laura Giglio, Director of Financial Aid
Huntington Administration Building, Alfred, NY 14802-1196
(607) 587-4253

State University of New York College of Technology at Canton
Canton, New York
www.canton.edu   Federal Code: 002855

4-year public technical college in small town.
Enrollment: 2,384 undergrads, 8% part-time. 731 full-time freshmen.
Selectivity: Admits over 75% of applicants.

BASIC COSTS (2007-2008)
Tuition and fees: $5,498; out-of-state residents $8,358.
Per-credit charge: $181; out-of-state residents $300.
Room and board: $8,440.
Additional info: Out-of-state tuition for bachelor's degree program: $10,610; $442 per credit hour. Tuition/fee waivers available for unemployed or children of unemployed.

FINANCIAL AID PICTURE (2006-2007)
Students with need: 66% of average financial aid package awarded as scholarships/grants, 34% awarded as loans/jobs. Need-based aid available for part-time students. Work study available nights, weekends, and for part-time students.

FINANCIAL AID PROCEDURES
Forms required: FAFSA, state aid form.
Dates and Deadlines: Priority date 3/15; no closing date. Applicants notified on a rolling basis starting 2/1; must reply within 4 week(s) of notification.
Transfers: Financial aid transcripts required from all previously attended schools for mid-year transfers.

CONTACT
Kerrie Cooper, Director of Financial Aid
34 Cornell Drive, Canton, NY 13617-1098
(315) 386-7616

State University of New York College of Technology at Delhi
Delhi, New York
www.delhi.edu   Federal Code: 002857

2-year public junior college in rural community.
Enrollment: 2,593 undergrads.
Selectivity: Open admission; but selective for some programs.

BASIC COSTS (2007-2008)
Tuition and fees: $5,648; out-of-state residents $8,508.
Room and board: $8,490.
Additional info: Out-of-state tuition for bachelor's program: $10,610; per-credit-hour $442.

FINANCIAL AID PICTURE (2006-2007)
Students with need: 62% of average financial aid package awarded as scholarships/grants, 38% awarded as loans/jobs. Need-based aid available for part-time students.

FINANCIAL AID PROCEDURES
Forms required: FAFSA, state aid form.

Dates and Deadlines: Priority date 2/15; no closing date. Applicants notified on a rolling basis starting 3/1; must reply within 2 week(s) of notification.

CONTACT
Nancy Hughes, Financial Aid Director
2 Main Street, Delhi, NY 13753-1190
(607) 746-4000

State University of New York Downstate Medical Center
Brooklyn, New York
www.downstate.edu   Federal Code: 002839

Upper-division public health science and nursing college in very large city.
Enrollment: 309 undergrads, 37% part-time.

BASIC COSTS (2007-2008)
Tuition and fees: $4,745; out-of-state residents $11,005.
Per-credit charge: $181; out-of-state residents $442.
Room only: $4,525.
Additional info: Reported room-only price is for double studio; other room-only prices vary by accommodation from $4,076 to $8,255.

FINANCIAL AID PICTURE
Students with need: Need-based aid available for full-time and part-time students.

FINANCIAL AID PROCEDURES
Forms required: FAFSA.
Dates and Deadlines: Priority date 3/1; no closing date. Applicants notified on a rolling basis.

CONTACT
450 Clarkson Avenue, Box 60, Brooklyn, NY 11203-2098
(718) 270-2488

State University of New York Empire State College
Saratoga Springs, New York
www.esc.edu   Federal Code: 010286

4-year public liberal arts college in large town.
Enrollment: 10,731 undergrads, 63% part-time. 287 full-time freshmen.
Selectivity: Admits over 75% of applicants.

BASIC COSTS (2007-2008)
Tuition and fees: $4,575; out-of-state residents $10,835.
Per-credit charge: $181; out-of-state residents $442.

FINANCIAL AID PICTURE (2006-2007)
Students with need: 28% of average financial aid package awarded as scholarships/grants, 72% awarded as loans/jobs. Need-based aid available for part-time students.
Students without need: This college awards aid only to students with need.

FINANCIAL AID PROCEDURES
Forms required: FAFSA, state aid form.
Dates and Deadlines: Priority date 4/1; no closing date. Applicants notified on a rolling basis; must reply within 3 week(s) of notification.
Transfers: No deadline. Applicants notified on a rolling basis.

CONTACT
Linda Ryan, Executive Director of Business Services
111 West Avenue, Saratoga Springs, NY 12866-4391
(518) 587-2100 ext. 2311

State University of New York Institute of Technology at Utica/Rome

Utica, New York
www.sunyit.edu   Federal Code: 011678

4-year public business and nursing college in small city.
Enrollment: 1,913 undergrads, 27% part-time. 203 full-time freshmen.
Selectivity: Admits less than 50% of applicants.

BASIC COSTS (2007-2008)

Tuition and fees: $5,405; out-of-state residents $11,665.
Per-credit charge: $181; out-of-state residents $442.
Room and board: $7,950.

FINANCIAL AID PICTURE (2006-2007)

Students with need: Out of 186 full-time freshmen who applied for aid, 143 were judged to have need. Of these, 136 received aid. Need-based aid available for part-time students.
Students without need: 11 full-time freshmen who did not demonstrate need for aid received scholarships/grants; average award was $1,143. No-need awards available for academics.

FINANCIAL AID PROCEDURES

Forms required: FAFSA, state aid form.
Dates and Deadlines: Priority date 3/15; no closing date. Applicants notified on a rolling basis starting 3/17; must reply within 2 week(s) of notification.
Transfers: No deadline. Applicants notified on a rolling basis starting 3/17; must reply within 2 week(s) of notification.

CONTACT

Lisa Hoskey, Director of Financial Aid
Box 3050, Utica, NY 13504-3050
(315) 792-7210

State University of New York Maritime College

Throggs Neck, New York
www.sunymaritime.edu   Federal Code: 002853

4-year public maritime college in very large city.
Enrollment: 1,327 undergrads, 6% part-time. 243 full-time freshmen.
Selectivity: Admits 50 to 75% of applicants.

BASIC COSTS (2007-2008)

Tuition and fees: $6,364; out-of-state residents $12,624.
Per-credit charge: $181; out-of-state residents $442.
Room and board: $8,920.
Additional info: Additional required uniform charges.

FINANCIAL AID PICTURE (2006-2007)

Students with need: Out of 211 full-time freshmen who applied for aid, 127 were judged to have need. Of these, 125 received aid, and 9 had their full need met. Average financial aid package met 50% of need; average scholarship/grant was $4,689; average loan was $3,171. For part-time students, average financial aid package was $5,349.
Students without need: 23 full-time freshmen who did not demonstrate need for aid received scholarships/grants; average award was $2,022. No-need awards available for academics, leadership, ROTC, state/district residency.
Scholarships offered: NROTC Scholarships: tuition and full room for 4 years.
Cumulative student debt: 43% of graduating class had student loans; average debt was $9,017.
Additional info: All cadets who are United States citizens, physically qualified for Merchant Marine license, and not yet 25 at time of enrollment eligible to apply for Student Incentive Payment (SIP) of $3,000 per year from Maritime Administration of the Department of Transportation. Out-of-state students who elect to participate in SIP pay in-state tuition fees.

FINANCIAL AID PROCEDURES

Forms required: FAFSA, institutional form.
Dates and Deadlines: Priority date 3/1; closing date 7/15. Applicants notified on a rolling basis starting 3/15; must reply within 2 week(s) of notification.
Transfers: No deadline. Applicants notified on a rolling basis starting 3/15. Must have minimum 2.0 cumulative GPA if degree has not yet been earned.

CONTACT

Paul Bamonte, Director of Financial Aid
6 Pennyfield Avenue, Throggs Neck, NY 10465-4198
(718) 409-7267

State University of New York Upstate Medical University

Syracuse, New York
www.upstate.edu   Federal Code: 002840

Upper-division public health science and nursing college in small city.
Enrollment: 247 undergrads, 34% part-time.

BASIC COSTS (2007-2008)

Tuition and fees: $4,876; out-of-state residents $11,136.
Per-credit charge: $181; out-of-state residents $442.
Room only: $5,600.

FINANCIAL AID PICTURE (2006-2007)

Students with need: Average financial aid package for all full-time undergraduates was $10,217; for part-time $8,173. 32% awarded as scholarships/grants, 68% awarded as loans/jobs. Work study available nights, weekends, and for part-time students.
Students without need: This college awards aid only to students with need.
Cumulative student debt: 76% of graduating class had student loans; average debt was $17,136.

FINANCIAL AID PROCEDURES

Forms required: FAFSA.
Dates and Deadlines: Priority date 3/1; no closing date. Applicants notified on a rolling basis starting 6/1; must reply within 2 week(s) of notification.
Transfers: Applicants notified on a rolling basis; must reply within 2 week(s) of notification.

CONTACT

Irvin Bodofsky, Director of Financial Aid
766 Irving Avenue, Syracuse, NY 13210
(315) 464-4329

Suffolk County Community College

Selden, New York
www.sunysuffolk.edu   Federal Code: 002878

2-year public community college in large town.
Enrollment: 22,664 undergrads.
Selectivity: Open admission; but selective for some programs.

BASIC COSTS (2007-2008)

Tuition and fees: $3,574; out-of-state residents $6,830.

FINANCIAL AID PICTURE

Students with need: Need-based aid available for full-time and part-time students. Work study available nights, weekends, and for part-time students.
Students without need: No-need awards available for academics, art, leadership, minority status, music/drama.

FINANCIAL AID PROCEDURES

Forms required: FAFSA, state aid form.
Dates and Deadlines: Priority date 4/15; closing date 6/1. Applicants notified on a rolling basis starting 4/15; must reply within 2 week(s) of notification.
Transfers: No deadline. Applicants notified on a rolling basis starting 4/15.

CONTACT

Nancy Dunnagan, Director of Financial Aid
533 College Road, Selden, NY 11784
(631) 451-4110

Sullivan County Community College

Loch Sheldrake, New York
www.sullivan.suny.edu   Federal Code: 002879

2-year public community college in small town.
Enrollment: 1,283 undergrads.
Selectivity: Open admission; but selective for some programs.

BASIC COSTS (2007-2008)
Tuition and fees: $3,736; out-of-state residents $7,096.
Per-credit charge: $131; out-of-state residents $168.

FINANCIAL AID PICTURE
Students with need: Need-based aid available for full-time and part-time students.
Additional info: 60% of students hold part-time jobs locally.

FINANCIAL AID PROCEDURES
Forms required: FAFSA.
Dates and Deadlines: Priority date 4/15; no closing date. Applicants notified on a rolling basis starting 5/15; must reply within 2 week(s) of notification.

CONTACT
James Winderl, Director of Financial Aid
112 College Road, Loch Sheldrake, NY 12759-5151
(845) 434-5750 ext. 4231

Swedish Institute

New York, New York
www.swedishinstitute.com   Federal Code: 021700

2-year for-profit health science college in very large city.
Enrollment: 511 undergrads.

BASIC COSTS (2007-2008)
Tuition and fees: $8,420.
Per-credit charge: $275.
Additional info: Students generally attend 3 semesters/year.

FINANCIAL AID PICTURE
Students with need: Need-based aid available for full-time and part-time students.
Students without need: This college awards aid only to students with need.

FINANCIAL AID PROCEDURES
Forms required: FAFSA, institutional form.
Dates and Deadlines: No deadline.

CONTACT
John Tonkinson, CFO
226 West 26th Street, 5th Floor, New York, NY 10001-6700
(212) 924-5900 ext. 124

Syracuse University

Syracuse, New York   Federal Code: 002882
www.syr.edu   CSS Code: 2823

4-year private university in small city.
Enrollment: 11,796 undergrads, 1% part-time. 3,098 full-time freshmen.
Selectivity: Admits 50 to 75% of applicants.

BASIC COSTS (2008-2009)
Tuition and fees: $32,339.
Per-credit charge: $1,401.
Room and board: $11,520.

FINANCIAL AID PICTURE (2007-2008)
Students with need: Out of 2,250 full-time freshmen who applied for aid, 1,871 were judged to have need. Of these, 1,871 received aid, and 1,220 had their full need met. Average financial aid package met 84% of need; average scholarship/grant was $19,000; average loan was $4,600. Need-based aid available for part-time students.
Students without need: 390 full-time freshmen who did not demonstrate need for aid received scholarships/grants; average award was $9,440. No-need awards available for academics, art, athletics, music/drama, ROTC.
Scholarships offered: 88 full-time freshmen received athletic scholarships; average amount $36,700.
Cumulative student debt: 63% of graduating class had student loans; average debt was $27,152.

FINANCIAL AID PROCEDURES
Forms required: FAFSA, CSS PROFILE.
Dates and Deadlines: Closing date 2/1. Applicants notified by 3/30; must reply by 5/1.
Transfers: Applicants notified on a rolling basis starting 3/15; must reply by 5/1.

CONTACT
Youlonda Copeland-Morgan, Director of Scholarships and Student Aid
100 Crouse-Hinds Hall, Syracuse, NY 13244-2130
(315) 443-1513

Tompkins-Cortland Community College

Dryden, New York
www.TC3.edu   Federal Code: 006788

2-year public community college in small town.
Enrollment: 2,842 undergrads, 19% part-time. 824 full-time freshmen.
Selectivity: Open admission; but selective for some programs.

BASIC COSTS (2007-2008)
Tuition and fees: $3,913; out-of-state residents $7,538.
Per-credit charge: $128; out-of-state residents $266.

FINANCIAL AID PICTURE (2006-2007)
Students with need: 49% of average financial aid package awarded as scholarships/grants, 51% awarded as loans/jobs. Need-based aid available for part-time students. Work study available nights, weekends, and for part-time students.
Students without need: No-need awards available for academics.

FINANCIAL AID PROCEDURES
Forms required: FAFSA, state aid form, institutional form.
Dates and Deadlines: Priority date 4/15; no closing date. Applicants notified on a rolling basis starting 3/15; must reply within 4 week(s) of notification.

CONTACT
Michael McGraw, Director of Financial Aid
170 North Street, Dryden, NY 13053-0139
(607) 844-6581

Trocaire College

Buffalo, New York
www.trocaire.edu   Federal Code: 002812

2-year private junior college in large city, affiliated with Roman Catholic Church.

Enrollment: 1,025 undergrads.

Selectivity: Open admission; but selective for some programs.

BASIC COSTS (2007-2008)

Tuition and fees: $11,054.

Per-credit charge: $431.

FINANCIAL AID PICTURE

Students with need: Need-based aid available for full-time and part-time students.

Students without need: No-need awards available for academics, alumni affiliation.

FINANCIAL AID PROCEDURES

Forms required: FAFSA, state aid form.

Dates and Deadlines: Priority date 3/31; no closing date. Applicants notified on a rolling basis starting 3/1; must reply within 2 week(s) of notification.

CONTACT

Janet McGrath, Director of Financial Aid
360 Choate Avenue, Buffalo, NY 14220
(716) 826-1200

Ulster County Community College

Stone Ridge, New York
www.sunyulster.edu   Federal Code: 002880

2-year public community college in small town.

Enrollment: 2,137 undergrads, 31% part-time. 540 full-time freshmen.

Selectivity: Open admission; but selective for some programs.

BASIC COSTS (2007-2008)

Tuition and fees: $3,831; out-of-state residents $7,131.

Per-credit charge: $120; out-of-state residents $240.

FINANCIAL AID PICTURE

Students with need: Need-based aid available for full-time and part-time students.

FINANCIAL AID PROCEDURES

Forms required: FAFSA.

Dates and Deadlines: Priority date 6/1; no closing date. Applicants notified on a rolling basis starting 6/1; must reply within 2 week(s) of notification.

CONTACT

Director of Financial Aid
Cottekill Road, Stone Ridge, NY 12484
(845) 687-5000

Union College

Schenectady, New York   Federal Code: 002889
www.union.edu   CSS Code: 2920

4-year private engineering and liberal arts college in small city.

Enrollment: 2,134 undergrads. 560 full-time freshmen.

Selectivity: Admits less than 50% of applicants. GED not accepted.

BASIC COSTS (2008-2009)

Comprehensive fee: $48,552.

Additional info: Rebates offered to students living off-campus and/or not using a meal plan.

FINANCIAL AID PICTURE (2006-2007)

Students with need: Out of 298 full-time freshmen who applied for aid, 236 were judged to have need. Of these, 223 received aid, and 223 had their full need met. Average financial aid package met 100% of need; average scholarship/grant was $26,200; average loan was $3,200. Need-based aid available for part-time students.

Students without need: 52 full-time freshmen who did not demonstrate need for aid received scholarships/grants; average award was $10,300. No-need awards available for academics, ROTC.

Cumulative student debt: 54% of graduating class had student loans; average debt was $24,100.

Additional info: Cancellable loans given to eligible students who engage in public service work after graduation. Loans cancellable at rate of 20% for each year of service.

FINANCIAL AID PROCEDURES

Forms required: FAFSA, CSS PROFILE, state aid form.

Dates and Deadlines: Closing date 2/1. Applicants notified by 4/1; must reply by 5/1.

Transfers: Closing date 3/1. Financial aid applicants must submit the CSS PROFILE form and FAFSA to their respective processing agencies at least two months prior to application deadline.

CONTACT

Linda Parker, Director of Financial Aid
Grant Hall, Schenectady, NY 12308-2311
(518) 388-6123

United States Merchant Marine Academy

Kings Point, New York
www.usmma.edu   Federal Code: 002892

4-year public engineering and military and maritime college in large town.

Enrollment: 995 undergrads. 279 full-time freshmen.

Selectivity: Admits less than 50% of applicants.

BASIC COSTS (2007-2008)

Additional info: All midshipmen receive full tuition, room, board, and medical and dental expenses from the federal government. Total required freshmen fees include purchase of laptop computer, color printer, and PDA. International students pay required fees plus additional international student fee.

FINANCIAL AID PICTURE (2006-2007)

Students with need: 47% of average financial aid package awarded as scholarships/grants, 53% awarded as loans/jobs.

Additional info: Students paid by steamship companies while at sea.

FINANCIAL AID PROCEDURES

Forms required: FAFSA, institutional form.

Dates and Deadlines: Closing date 5/1. Applicants notified on a rolling basis starting 1/31.

CONTACT

Robert Johnson, Director of Admissions and Financial Aid
300 Steamboat Road, Admissions Center, Kings Point, NY 11024-1699
(516) 773-5295

United States Military Academy

West Point, New York
www.usma.edu   Federal Code: 002893

4-year public engineering and military college in small town.

Enrollment: 4,487 undergrads. 1,272 full-time freshmen.

Selectivity: Admits less than 50% of applicants.

BASIC COSTS (2008-2009)

Additional info: All cadets active duty members of U.S. Army and receive annual salary of approximately $10,148. Tuition, room and board, medical, and dental care provided by Army. Deposit of $2,900 required for initial uniforms, books, supplies, equipment, and fees. If needed, loans for deposit available from $100 to $2,900.

FINANCIAL AID PICTURE

Additional info: Cadets permitted to receive scholarships, but since there are no tuition, room, or board charges, scholarships stipulated for tuition, room or board only based on need rather than merit cannot be accepted. Scholarships may be used for textbooks, uniforms, and other expenses or used dollar for dollar to offset initial $2,900 deposit.

CONTACT

Stephanie Martin, Treasurer
646 Swift Road, West Point, NY 10996-1905
(845) 938-5516

University of Rochester

Rochester, New York
www.rochester.edu

Federal Code: 002894
CSS Code: 2928

4-year private university in large city.
Enrollment: 4,964 undergrads, 3% part-time. 1,182 full-time freshmen.
Selectivity: Admits less than 50% of applicants.

BASIC COSTS (2008-2009)

Tuition and fees: $37,250.
Per-credit charge: $1,138.
Room and board: $10,810.

FINANCIAL AID PICTURE

Students with need: Need-based aid available for full-time students. Work study available nights, weekends, and for part-time students.
Students without need: No-need awards available for academics, alumni affiliation, leadership, music/drama, ROTC, state/district residency.
Cumulative student debt: 60% of graduating class had student loans; average debt was $29,800.
Additional info: Alternative loans and financing information available.

FINANCIAL AID PROCEDURES

Forms required: FAFSA, CSS PROFILE, state aid form.
Dates and Deadlines: Closing date 2/1. Applicants notified by 4/1; must reply by 5/1.
Transfers: Priority date 2/1; no deadline.

CONTACT

Charles Puls, Director of Financial Aid
300 Wilson Boulevard, Rochester, NY 14627-0251
(585) 275-3228

Utica College

Utica, New York
www.utica.edu

Federal Code: 002883

4-year private college in small city.
Enrollment: 2,336 undergrads, 16% part-time. 489 full-time freshmen.
Selectivity: Admits over 75% of applicants.

BASIC COSTS (2007-2008)

Tuition and fees: $24,584.
Per-credit charge: $818.
Room and board: $10,030.

FINANCIAL AID PICTURE (2007-2008)

Students with need: Out of 471 full-time freshmen who applied for aid, 437 were judged to have need. Of these, 437 received aid, and 49 had their full need met. Average financial aid package met 76% of need; average scholarship/grant was $9,307; average loan was $3,426. For part-time students, average financial aid package was $6,203.
Students without need: 33 full-time freshmen who did not demonstrate need for aid received scholarships/grants; average award was $9,843. No-need awards available for academics.
Cumulative student debt: 86% of graduating class had student loans; average debt was $32,010.

FINANCIAL AID PROCEDURES

Forms required: FAFSA, state aid form.
Dates and Deadlines: Priority date 2/15; no closing date. Applicants notified on a rolling basis starting 2/1; must reply by 5/1 or within 4 week(s) of notification.
Transfers: Applicants notified on a rolling basis.

CONTACT

Anita Elliot, Director of Financial Aid
1600 Burrstone Road, Utica, NY 13502-4892
(315) 792-3179

Vassar College

Poughkeepsie, New York
www.vassar.edu

Federal Code: 002895
CSS Code: 2956

4-year private liberal arts college in small city.
Enrollment: 2,409 undergrads, 1% part-time. 677 full-time freshmen.
Selectivity: Admits less than 50% of applicants.

BASIC COSTS (2008-2009)

Tuition and fees: $40,210.
Per-credit charge: $1,335.
Room and board: $9,040.

FINANCIAL AID PICTURE (2007-2008)

Students with need: Out of 447 full-time freshmen who applied for aid, 363 were judged to have need. Of these, 363 received aid, and 363 had their full need met. Average financial aid package met 100% of need; average scholarship/grant was $29,613; average loan was $2,081.
Students without need: This college awards aid only to students with need.
Cumulative student debt: 53% of graduating class had student loans; average debt was $20,589.

FINANCIAL AID PROCEDURES

Forms required: FAFSA, CSS PROFILE, state aid form.
Dates and Deadlines: Closing date 2/1. Applicants notified by 3/30; must reply by 5/1.
Transfers: Closing date 4/1. Limited number of need-based award packages offered to transfers.

CONTACT

Michael Fraher, Director of Financial Aid
Box 10, 124 Raymond Avenue, Poughkeepsie, NY 12604-0077
(845) 437-5320

Vaughn College of Aeronautics and Technology

Flushing, New York
www.vaughn.edu

Federal Code: 002665

4-year private engineering and technical college in very large city.
Enrollment: 1,063 undergrads, 26% part-time. 185 full-time freshmen.

Selectivity: Admits over 75% of applicants.

BASIC COSTS (2008-2009)

Tuition and fees: $15,100.

Per-credit charge: $500.

Room and board: $11,900.

FINANCIAL AID PICTURE (2007-2008)

Students with need: Out of 125 full-time freshmen who applied for aid, 125 were judged to have need. Of these, 125 received aid, and 121 had their full need met. Average financial aid package met 85% of need; average scholarship/grant was $2,200; average loan was $3,500. For part-time students, average financial aid package was $14,700.

Students without need: 59 full-time freshmen who did not demonstrate need for aid received scholarships/grants; average award was $3,000. No-need awards available for academics, alumni affiliation, job skills, ROTC.

Cumulative student debt: 87% of graduating class had student loans; average debt was $17,125.

FINANCIAL AID PROCEDURES

Forms required: FAFSA, state aid form.

Dates and Deadlines: Priority date 1/15; no closing date. Applicants notified by 4/15; must reply within 2 week(s) of notification.

Transfers: No deadline. Applicants notified on a rolling basis; must reply within 2 week(s) of notification.

CONTACT

Dorothy Martin, Director of Financial Aid

86-01 23rd Avenue, Flushing, NY 11369

(718) 429-6600

Villa Maria College of Buffalo

Buffalo, New York

www.villa.edu   Federal Code: 002896

2-year private visual arts and liberal arts college in large city, affiliated with Roman Catholic Church.

Enrollment: 436 undergrads, 20% part-time. 145 full-time freshmen.

Selectivity: Open admission; but selective for some programs.

BASIC COSTS (2008-2009)

Tuition and fees: $13,990.

Per-credit charge: $455.

Additional info: Tuition/fee waivers available for unemployed or children of unemployed.

FINANCIAL AID PICTURE (2006-2007)

Students with need: Out of 141 full-time freshmen who applied for aid, 122 were judged to have need. Of these, 121 received aid, and 15 had their full need met. Average financial aid package met 83% of need; average scholarship/grant was $5,589; average loan was $1,864. For part-time students, average financial aid package was $3,792.

Students without need: 24 full-time freshmen who did not demonstrate need for aid received scholarships/grants; average award was $5,629. No-need awards available for academics, alumni affiliation, art, leadership, minority status, music/drama.

Scholarships offered: 6 full-time freshmen received athletic scholarships; average amount $1,917.

Cumulative student debt: 68% of graduating class had student loans; average debt was $2,812.

FINANCIAL AID PROCEDURES

Forms required: FAFSA.

Dates and Deadlines: No deadline. Applicants notified on a rolling basis starting 2/15; must reply within 2 week(s) of notification.

CONTACT

Christina Horner, Director of Financial Aid and Veterans Affairs

240 Pine Ridge Road, Buffalo, NY 14225-3999

(716) 896-0700 ext. 1850

Wagner College

Staten Island, New York

www.wagner.edu   Federal Code: 002899

4-year private liberal arts college in very large city, affiliated with Lutheran Church in America.

Enrollment: 1,926 undergrads, 2% part-time. 524 full-time freshmen.

Selectivity: Admits 50 to 75% of applicants.

BASIC COSTS (2008-2009)

Tuition and fees: $31,000.

Room and board: $9,250.

Additional info: Tuition/fee waivers available for unemployed or children of unemployed.

FINANCIAL AID PICTURE (2007-2008)

Students with need: Out of 407 full-time freshmen who applied for aid, 329 were judged to have need. Of these, 329 received aid, and 81 had their full need met. Average financial aid package met 73% of need; average scholarship/grant was $11,031; average loan was $4,205.

Students without need: 142 full-time freshmen who did not demonstrate need for aid received scholarships/grants; average award was $10,195. No-need awards available for academics, athletics, leadership, music/drama.

Scholarships offered: 24 full-time freshmen received athletic scholarships; average amount $14,305.

Cumulative student debt: 44% of graduating class had student loans; average debt was $35,717.

FINANCIAL AID PROCEDURES

Forms required: FAFSA, state aid form, institutional form.

Dates and Deadlines: Priority date 2/15; no closing date. Applicants notified on a rolling basis starting 3/1; must reply within 3 week(s) of notification.

Transfers: No deadline. Applicants notified on a rolling basis starting 3/1; must reply within 3 week(s) of notification.

CONTACT

Theresa Weimer, Director of Financial Aid

One Campus Road, Staten Island, NY 10301-4495

(718) 390-3183

Webb Institute

Glen Cove, New York

www.webb-institute.edu   Federal Code: 002900

4-year private engineering and maritime college in large town.

Enrollment: 91 undergrads. 24 full-time freshmen.

Selectivity: Admits less than 50% of applicants. GED not accepted.

BASIC COSTS (2008-2009)

Room and board: $9,500.

Additional info: All students receive 4-year, full-tuition scholarships.

FINANCIAL AID PICTURE (2006-2007)

Students with need: Out of 6 full-time freshmen who applied for aid, 6 were judged to have need. Of these, 6 received aid, and 2 had their full need met. Average financial aid package met 80% of need; average scholarship/grant was $3,000; average loan was $2,625.

Students without need: This college awards aid only to students with need.

Cumulative student debt: 20% of graduating class had student loans; average debt was $7,303.

FINANCIAL AID PROCEDURES

Forms required: FAFSA.

Dates and Deadlines: Closing date 7/1. Applicants notified by 8/1; must reply within 2 week(s) of notification.

CONTACT

William Murray, Director of Financial Aid

298 Crescent Beach Road, Glen Cove, NY 11542-1398

(516) 671-2213 ext. 104

Wells College
Aurora, New York
www.wells.edu   Federal Code: 002901

4-year private liberal arts college in rural community.

Enrollment: 544 undergrads, 1% part-time. 174 full-time freshmen.

Selectivity: Admits 50 to 75% of applicants.

BASIC COSTS (2008-2009)

Tuition and fees: $19,480.

Per-credit charge: $730.

Room and board: $8,420.

FINANCIAL AID PICTURE (2007-2008)

Students with need: Out of 150 full-time freshmen who applied for aid, 126 were judged to have need. Of these, 124 received aid, and 42 had their full need met. Average financial aid package met 92% of need; average scholarship/grant was $13,645; average loan was $3,920. Need-based aid available for part-time students.

Students without need: 34 full-time freshmen who did not demonstrate need for aid received scholarships/grants; average award was $6,850. No-need awards available for academics, alumni affiliation, leadership.

Scholarships offered: Henry Wells Scholarship: guaranteed first-year internship or related experience and paid $3,000 internship or experiential learning program in student's upper-class years; tuition-based scholarship valued at $8,000 a year for four years. 21st Century Leadership Award: $20,000 over 4 years; must have minimum 3.5 GPA; required to submit leadership transcript.

Cumulative student debt: 77% of graduating class had student loans; average debt was $20,355.

FINANCIAL AID PROCEDURES

Forms required: FAFSA. CSS PROFILE required of early decision candidates only.

Dates and Deadlines: Priority date 2/15; no closing date. Applicants notified on a rolling basis starting 3/1; must reply by 5/1.

Transfers: Priority date 3/1; no deadline. Applicants notified on a rolling basis starting 3/1; must reply by 8/1.

CONTACT

Cathleen Patella, Director of Financial Aid

170 Main Street, Aurora, NY 13026

(315) 364-3289

Westchester Community College
Valhalla, New York
www.sunywcc.edu   Federal Code: 002881

2-year public community college in large town.

Enrollment: 10,476 undergrads, 43% part-time. 2,070 full-time freshmen.

Selectivity: Open admission; but selective for some programs.

BASIC COSTS (2007-2008)

Tuition and fees: $3,803; out-of-state residents $8,979.

Per-credit charge: $144; out-of-state residents $360.

FINANCIAL AID PICTURE (2006-2007)

Students with need: 90% of average financial aid package awarded as scholarships/grants, 10% awarded as loans/jobs. Need-based aid available for part-time students. Work study available nights, weekends, and for part-time students.

Students without need: No-need awards available for academics.

Cumulative student debt: 12% of graduating class had student loans; average debt was $6,787.

FINANCIAL AID PROCEDURES

Forms required: FAFSA, state aid form, institutional form.

Dates and Deadlines: No deadline. Applicants notified on a rolling basis; must reply within 4 week(s) of notification.

Transfers: No deadline.

CONTACT

Eleanor Hackett, Director of Financial Aid

75 Grasslands Road, Valhalla, NY 10595

(914) 606-6773

Yeshiva Mikdash Melech
Brooklyn, New York   Federal Code: 014615

4-year private rabbinical college for men in very large city, affiliated with Jewish faith.

Enrollment: 105 undergrads.

BASIC COSTS (2008-2009)

Tuition and fees: $6,500.

Room and board: $3,800.

Additional info: Tuition/fee waivers available for adults.

FINANCIAL AID PICTURE

Students with need: Need-based aid available for full-time and part-time students. Work study available nights.

Students without need: No-need awards available for academics, leadership, religious affiliation.

FINANCIAL AID PROCEDURES

Forms required: FAFSA.

Dates and Deadlines: No deadline. Applicants notified on a rolling basis starting 5/1.

Transfers: No deadline. Applicants notified on a rolling basis starting 5/1.

CONTACT

Samuel Ani, Financial Aid Administrator

1326 Ocean Parkway, Brooklyn, NY 11230

(718) 339-1090

North Carolina

Alamance Community College
Graham, North Carolina
www.alamance.cc.nc.us   Federal Code: 005463

2-year public community college in large town.

Enrollment: 3,569 undergrads, 55% part-time. 344 full-time freshmen.

Selectivity: Open admission; but selective for some programs.

BASIC COSTS (2007-2008)

Tuition and fees: $1,290; out-of-state residents $7,029.

Per-credit charge: $42; out-of-state residents $233.

FINANCIAL AID PICTURE (2006-2007)

Students with need: Out of 227 full-time freshmen who applied for aid, 200 were judged to have need. Of these, 185 received aid. Average financial aid package met 30% of need; average scholarship/grant was $3,000. For part-time students, average financial aid package was $1,500.

Students without need: 50 full-time freshmen who did not demonstrate need for aid received scholarships/grants; average award was $500. No-need awards available for academics, state/district residency.

Cumulative student debt: 2% of graduating class had student loans; average debt was $5,000.

FINANCIAL AID PROCEDURES

Forms required: FAFSA.

Dates and Deadlines: Priority date 5/15; no closing date. Applicants notified on a rolling basis starting 3/15; must reply within 2 week(s) of notification.

Transfers: Supplemental educational opportunity grants limited.

CONTACT

Liz Solazzo, Director of Financial Aid
Box 8000, Graham, NC 27253
(336) 506-4109

Appalachian State University
Boone, North Carolina
www.appstate.edu   Federal Code: 002906

4-year public university in large town.

Enrollment: 13,763 undergrads, 5% part-time. 2,732 full-time freshmen.

Selectivity: Admits 50 to 75% of applicants. GED not accepted.

BASIC COSTS (2007-2008)

Tuition and fees: $4,241; out-of-state residents $13,983.

Room and board: $5,990.

FINANCIAL AID PICTURE

Students with need: Need-based aid available for full-time and part-time students. Work study available nights, weekends, and for part-time students.

Students without need: No-need awards available for academics, alumni affiliation, art, athletics, job skills, leadership, minority status, music/drama, religious affiliation, ROTC, state/district residency.

FINANCIAL AID PROCEDURES

Forms required: FAFSA.

Dates and Deadlines: Priority date 3/15; no closing date. Applicants notified on a rolling basis starting 4/1; must reply within 3 week(s) of notification.

Transfers: No deadline. Applicants notified on a rolling basis starting 4/1; must reply within 3 week(s) of notification.

CONTACT

Esther Manogin, Director
ASU Box 32004, Boone, NC 28608
(828) 262-2190

Barton College
Wilson, North Carolina
www.barton.edu   Federal Code: 002908

4-year private liberal arts college in large town, affiliated with Christian Church (Disciples of Christ).

Enrollment: 1,103 undergrads, 20% part-time. 217 full-time freshmen.

Selectivity: Admits 50 to 75% of applicants.

BASIC COSTS (2008-2009)

Tuition and fees: $19,938.

Per-credit charge: $785.

Room and board: $6,782.

Additional info: Tuition/fee waivers available for adults.

FINANCIAL AID PICTURE (2007-2008)

Students with need: Out of 188 full-time freshmen who applied for aid, 169 were judged to have need. Of these, 168 received aid, and 24 had their full need met. Average financial aid package met 72% of need; average scholarship/grant was $4,614; average loan was $4,172. For part-time students, average financial aid package was $4,554.

Students without need: 36 full-time freshmen who did not demonstrate need for aid received scholarships/grants; average award was $3,753. No-need awards available for academics, alumni affiliation, art, athletics, leadership, minority status, music/drama, religious affiliation, state/district residency.

Scholarships offered: 17 full-time freshmen received athletic scholarships; average amount $5,388.

Cumulative student debt: 76% of graduating class had student loans; average debt was $28,702.

FINANCIAL AID PROCEDURES

Forms required: FAFSA.

Dates and Deadlines: Priority date 4/1; no closing date. Applicants notified on a rolling basis starting 5/1; must reply within 2 week(s) of notification.

CONTACT

Bettie Westbrook, Director of Financial Aid
Box 5000, Wilson, NC 27893-7000
(252) 399-6323

Beaufort County Community College
Washington, North Carolina
www.beaufortccc.edu   Federal Code: 008558

2-year public community college in small town.

Enrollment: 786 undergrads.

Selectivity: Open admission; but selective for some programs.

BASIC COSTS (2007-2008)

Tuition and fees: $1,324; out-of-state residents $7,063.

Per-credit charge: $42; out-of-state residents $233.

Additional info: Some programs require insurance and uniforms.

FINANCIAL AID PICTURE

Students with need: Need-based aid available for full-time and part-time students.

Students without need: No-need awards available for academics.

FINANCIAL AID PROCEDURES

Forms required: FAFSA.

Dates and Deadlines: Priority date 6/1; no closing date. Applicants notified on a rolling basis starting 5/1; must reply within 2 week(s) of notification.

CONTACT

Harold Smith, Director of Financial Aid
Box 1069, Washington, NC 27889
(252) 940-6222

Belmont Abbey College
Belmont, North Carolina
www.belmontabbeycollege.edu   Federal Code: 002910

4-year private liberal arts college in small town, affiliated with Roman Catholic Church.

Enrollment: 1,300 undergrads, 6% part-time. 210 full-time freshmen.

Selectivity: Admits 50 to 75% of applicants.

BASIC COSTS (2007-2008)
Tuition and fees: $19,680.
Per-credit charge: $596.
Room and board: $9,713.

FINANCIAL AID PICTURE (2007-2008)
Students with need: Average financial aid package met 60% of need; average scholarship/grant was $11,610; average loan was $3,310. For part-time students, average financial aid package was $6,279.
Students without need: No-need awards available for academics, athletics, leadership, religious affiliation, state/district residency.
Scholarships offered: Many merit scholarships offered; ranging from $500 to $20,000; based solely on academic achievement.
Cumulative student debt: 72% of graduating class had student loans; average debt was $18,000.

FINANCIAL AID PROCEDURES
Forms required: FAFSA, state aid form.
Dates and Deadlines: Priority date 4/1; no closing date. Applicants notified on a rolling basis starting 3/1; must reply within 2 week(s) of notification.

CONTACT
Anne Stevens, Director of Enrollment Management
100 Belmont - Mt. Holly Road, Belmont, NC 28012-2795
(704) 825-6718

Bennett College
Greensboro, North Carolina
www.bennett.edu   Federal Code: 002911

4-year private liberal arts college for women in small city, affiliated with United Methodist Church.
Enrollment: 662 undergrads, 1% part-time. 223 full-time freshmen.
Selectivity: Admits less than 50% of applicants.

BASIC COSTS (2007-2008)
Tuition and fees: $14,648.
Per-credit charge: $531.
Room and board: $6,478.

FINANCIAL AID PICTURE (2007-2008)
Students with need: Out of 220 full-time freshmen who applied for aid, 211 were judged to have need. Of these, 208 received aid, and 6 had their full need met. Average financial aid package met 43% of need; average scholarship/grant was $7,834; average loan was $3,252. For part-time students, average financial aid package was $6,205.
Students without need: 9 full-time freshmen who did not demonstrate need for aid received scholarships/grants; average award was $12,246. No-need awards available for state/district residency.

FINANCIAL AID PROCEDURES
Forms required: FAFSA, institutional form.
Dates and Deadlines: Closing date 4/15. Applicants notified by 7/15.

CONTACT
Keisha Ragsdale, Director of Financial Aid
900 East Washington Street, Greensboro, NC 27401-3239
(336) 517-2204

Bladen Community College
Dublin, North Carolina
www.bladencc.edu   Federal Code: 007987

2-year public community college in rural community.
Enrollment: 1,370 undergrads.
Selectivity: Open admission; but selective for some programs.

BASIC COSTS (2007-2008)
Tuition and fees: $1,326; out-of-state residents $7,065.
Per-credit charge: $42; out-of-state residents $233.

FINANCIAL AID PICTURE
Students with need: Need-based aid available for full-time and part-time students. Work study available nights.

FINANCIAL AID PROCEDURES
Forms required: FAFSA.
Dates and Deadlines: Priority date 6/1; no closing date. Applicants notified on a rolling basis starting 8/1; must reply within 2 week(s) of notification.

CONTACT
Marva Dinkins, Financial Aid Director
Box 266, Dublin, NC 28332-0266
(910) 879-5562

Blue Ridge Community College
Flat Rock, North Carolina
www.blueridge.edu   Federal Code: 009684

2-year public community college in small town.
Enrollment: 810 full-time undergrads.
Selectivity: Open admission; but selective for some programs.

BASIC COSTS (2007-2008)
Tuition and fees: $1,333; out-of-state residents $7,072.
Per-credit charge: $42; out-of-state residents $233.

FINANCIAL AID PICTURE
Students with need: Need-based aid available for full-time and part-time students. Work study available nights.
Students without need: No-need awards available for academics, athletics, leadership, minority status, state/district residency.

FINANCIAL AID PROCEDURES
Forms required: FAFSA, institutional form.
Dates and Deadlines: Priority date 6/30; no closing date. Applicants notified on a rolling basis starting 2/1; must reply within 4 week(s) of notification.

CONTACT
Rita Blythe, Financial Aid Officer
180 West Campus Drive, Flat Rock, NC 28731-9624
(828) 694-1815

Brevard College
Brevard, North Carolina
www.brevard.edu   Federal Code: 002912

4-year private liberal arts college in small town, affiliated with United Methodist Church.
Enrollment: 647 undergrads, 3% part-time. 168 full-time freshmen.
Selectivity: Admits 50 to 75% of applicants.

BASIC COSTS (2008-2009)
Tuition and fees: $20,050.
Room and board: $7,540.
Additional info: Telecommunications fee $600 for on-campus residents.

FINANCIAL AID PICTURE (2007-2008)
Students with need: Average financial aid package met 74% of need; average scholarship/grant was $11,700; average loan was $3,740. For part-time students, average financial aid package was $14,495.
Students without need: No-need awards available for academics, art, athletics, job skills, leadership, minority status, music/drama, religious affiliation, state/district residency.

Cumulative student debt: 62% of graduating class had student loans; average debt was $16,996.

FINANCIAL AID PROCEDURES

Forms required: FAFSA, state aid form.

Dates and Deadlines: Priority date 4/15; no closing date. Applicants notified on a rolling basis starting 2/1; must reply within 4 week(s) of notification.

CONTACT

Lisanne Masterson, Director of Financial Aid
One Brevard College Drive, Brevard, NC 28712
(828) 884-8287

Brunswick Community College
Supply, North Carolina
www.brunswickcc.edu   Federal Code: 015285

2-year public community college in small town.

Enrollment: 1,136 undergrads.

Selectivity: Open admission; but selective for some programs.

BASIC COSTS (2007-2008)

Tuition and fees: $1,333; out-of-state residents $7,072.

Per-credit charge: $42; out-of-state residents $233.

FINANCIAL AID PICTURE (2007-2008)

Students with need: Need-based aid available for part-time students. Work study available nights, weekends, and for part-time students.

Students without need: No-need awards available for academics, state/district residency.

Scholarships offered: La Dane Williamson Universal Scholarship: $1,200 per year for 2 years; must be a resident of Brunswick County for 5 years prior to application, must be a high school graduate of Brunswick County or complete GED or adult high school diploma program at Brunswick Community College, must not be eligible for Pell. Brunswick Family Scholarship: may cover total amount of tuition and fees; for Brunswick County residents of 3 years prior to application with GED or high school graduate, must not be eligible for Pell.

Additional info: Attendance required at financial aid orientation session for those receiving federal student aid.

FINANCIAL AID PROCEDURES

Forms required: FAFSA, institutional form.

Dates and Deadlines: Priority date 6/1; closing date 6/15. Applicants notified on a rolling basis starting 3/1; must reply by 6/15 or within 2 week(s) of notification.

Transfers: Priority date 6/30; no deadline.

CONTACT

Paula Almond, Coordinator of Financial Aid and Veterans Affairs
Box 30, Supply, NC 28462
(910) 755-7422

Caldwell Community College and Technical Institute
Hudson, North Carolina
www.cccti.edu   Federal Code: 004835

2-year public community and technical college in small town.

Enrollment: 3,138 undergrads.

Selectivity: Open admission; but selective for some programs.

BASIC COSTS (2007-2008)

Tuition and fees: $1,292; out-of-state residents $7,031.

Per-credit charge: $42; out-of-state residents $233.

FINANCIAL AID PICTURE

Students with need: Need-based aid available for full-time and part-time students.

Students without need: This college awards aid only to students with need.

FINANCIAL AID PROCEDURES

Forms required: FAFSA.

Dates and Deadlines: Priority date 6/1; no closing date. Applicants notified on a rolling basis starting 6/30.

CONTACT

Eva Rader-Harmon, Director of Financial Aid
2855 Hickory Boulevard, Hudson, NC 28638-2672
(828) 726-2714

Campbell University
Buies Creek, North Carolina
www.campbell.edu   Federal Code: 002913

4-year private university and liberal arts college in small town, affiliated with Baptist State Convention of North Carolina.

Enrollment: 2,806 undergrads, 3% part-time. 888 full-time freshmen.

Selectivity: Admits 50 to 75% of applicants.

BASIC COSTS (2008-2009)

Tuition and fees: $20,350.

Per-credit charge: $325.

Room and board: $6,830.

FINANCIAL AID PICTURE (2007-2008)

Students with need: Out of 716 full-time freshmen who applied for aid, 597 were judged to have need. Of these, 597 received aid, and 597 had their full need met. Average financial aid package met 100% of need; average scholarship/grant was $5,459; average loan was $2,918. For part-time students, average financial aid package was $11,559.

Students without need: 188 full-time freshmen who did not demonstrate need for aid received scholarships/grants; average award was $6,901. No-need awards available for academics, athletics, music/drama, religious affiliation, ROTC, state/district residency.

Scholarships offered: *Merit:* Presidential Scholarship: $10,000-$14,000; SAT 1725 or ACT 25 and GPA 3.4. Campbell Scholarship: $6,000-9,000; SAT 1500 or ACT 21 and GPA 3.0. *Athletic:* 58 full-time freshmen received athletic scholarships; average amount $10,849.

Cumulative student debt: 75% of graduating class had student loans; average debt was $21,703.

FINANCIAL AID PROCEDURES

Forms required: FAFSA.

Dates and Deadlines: Priority date 3/15; no closing date. Applicants notified on a rolling basis starting 4/15; must reply within 2 week(s) of notification.

Transfers: Priority date 3/9. Applicants notified on a rolling basis starting 4/9; must reply within 2 week(s) of notification.

CONTACT

Nancy Beasley, Director of Financial Aid
PO Box 546, Buies Creek, NC 27506
(800) 334-4111 ext. 1310

Carolinas College of Health Sciences
Charlotte, North Carolina
www.carolinascollege.edu   Federal Code: 031042

2-year public health science and junior college in very large city.

Enrollment: 467 undergrads.

Selectivity: Admits less than 50% of applicants.

BASIC COSTS (2007-2008)

Tuition and fees: $6,350.
Per-credit charge: $205.
Additional info: Tuition varies by program.

FINANCIAL AID PICTURE

Students with need: Need-based aid available for full-time and part-time students.
Students without need: No-need awards available for academics.

FINANCIAL AID PROCEDURES

Forms required: FAFSA, institutional form.
Dates and Deadlines: Priority date 5/1; no closing date. Applicants notified on a rolling basis starting 5/1.

CONTACT

Jill Powell, Financial Aid Officer
PO Box 32861, Charlotte, NC 28232
(704) 355-8894

Carteret Community College

Morehead City, North Carolina
www.carteret.edu   Federal Code: 008081

2-year public community and technical college in small town.
Enrollment: 1,175 undergrads, 38% part-time.
Selectivity: Open admission; but selective for some programs.

BASIC COSTS (2007-2008)

Tuition and fees: $1,311; out-of-state residents $7,050.
Per-credit charge: $42; out-of-state residents $233.

FINANCIAL AID PICTURE

Students with need: Need-based aid available for full-time and part-time students.
Students without need: No-need awards available for academics, leadership, minority status, state/district residency.
Additional info: Institutional student loan program administered by college. Student may charge up to $600 for books, supplies and tuition per quarter. Repayment due by 11th week of semester.

FINANCIAL AID PROCEDURES

Forms required: FAFSA, institutional form.
Dates and Deadlines: No deadline. Applicants notified on a rolling basis starting 7/1; must reply within 2 week(s) of notification.

CONTACT

Brenda Long, Financial Aid Officer
3505 Arendell Street, Morehead City, NC 28557-2989
(252) 222-6297

Catawba College

Salisbury, North Carolina
www.catawba.edu   Federal Code: 002914

4-year private liberal arts college in large town, affiliated with United Church of Christ.
Enrollment: 1,291 undergrads, 5% part-time. 266 full-time freshmen.
Selectivity: Admits over 75% of applicants.

BASIC COSTS (2008-2009)

Tuition and fees: $22,290.
Per-credit charge: $590.
Room and board: $7,700.

FINANCIAL AID PICTURE (2007-2008)

Students with need: Average financial aid package met 84% of need; average scholarship/grant was $5,053; average loan was $4,539. For part-time students, average financial aid package was $9,410.
Students without need: 37 full-time freshmen who did not demonstrate need for aid received scholarships/grants; average award was $11,399. No-need awards available for academics, athletics, music/drama, state/district residency.
Scholarships offered: 78 full-time freshmen received athletic scholarships; average amount $6,860.
Cumulative student debt: 70% of graduating class had student loans; average debt was $21,726.

FINANCIAL AID PROCEDURES

Forms required: FAFSA, state aid form.
Dates and Deadlines: Priority date 3/15; no closing date. Applicants notified on a rolling basis starting 11/1; must reply within 2 week(s) of notification.

CONTACT

Melanie McCulloh, Director of Scholarships and Financial Assistance
2300 West Innes Street, Salisbury, NC 28144
(704) 637-4416

Catawba Valley Community College

Hickory, North Carolina
www.cvcc.edu   Federal Code: 005318

2-year public community college in large town.
Enrollment: 3,861 undergrads, 60% part-time. 507 full-time freshmen.
Selectivity: Open admission; but selective for some programs.

BASIC COSTS (2007-2008)

Tuition and fees: $1,284; out-of-state residents $7,023.
Per-credit charge: $42; out-of-state residents $233.
Additional info: Tuition/fee waivers available for unemployed or children of unemployed.

FINANCIAL AID PICTURE (2006-2007)

Students with need: Out of 410 full-time freshmen who applied for aid, 321 were judged to have need. Of these, 252 received aid. Need-based aid available for part-time students.
Students without need: No-need awards available for academics, leadership, music/drama.

FINANCIAL AID PROCEDURES

Forms required: FAFSA.
Dates and Deadlines: Closing date 3/15. Applicants notified on a rolling basis starting 5/15.

CONTACT

Debbie Barger, Director of Scholarships and Financial Aid
2550 Highway 70 SE, Hickory, NC 28602
(828) 327-7000 ext. 4214

Central Carolina Community College

Sanford, North Carolina
www.cccc.edu   Federal Code: 005449

2-year public community college in large town.
Enrollment: 4,708 undergrads.
Selectivity: Open admission; but selective for some programs.

BASIC COSTS (2007-2008)

Tuition and fees: $1,328; out-of-state residents $7,067.
Per-credit charge: $42; out-of-state residents $233.

FINANCIAL AID PICTURE

Students with need: Need-based aid available for full-time and part-time students. Work study available nights.

Students without need: No-need awards available for academics.

FINANCIAL AID PROCEDURES

Forms required: FAFSA, institutional form.

Dates and Deadlines: Priority date 3/15; closing date 5/1. Applicants notified on a rolling basis starting 7/1; must reply within 2 week(s) of notification.

Transfers: No deadline.

CONTACT

Kay Jedlica, Director of Financial Aid
1105 Kelly Drive, Sanford, NC 27330
(919) 718-7229

Central Piedmont Community College

Charlotte, North Carolina
www.cpcc.edu   Federal Code: 002915

2-year public community college in very large city.

Enrollment: 15,569 undergrads, 63% part-time. 1,385 full-time freshmen.

Selectivity: Open admission; but selective for some programs.

BASIC COSTS (2007-2008)

Tuition and fees: $1,440; out-of-state residents $7,179.

Per-credit charge: $42; out-of-state residents $233.

FINANCIAL AID PICTURE

Students with need: Need-based aid available for full-time and part-time students.

Students without need: No-need awards available for academics, minority status.

FINANCIAL AID PROCEDURES

Forms required: FAFSA.

Dates and Deadlines: Priority date 4/1; closing date 6/1. Applicants notified on a rolling basis.

CONTACT

Debbie Brooks, Director, Student Financial Aid
Box 35009, Charlotte, NC 28235-5009
(704) 330-6942

Chowan University

Murfreesboro, North Carolina
www.chowan.edu   Federal Code: 002916

4-year private university and liberal arts college in rural community, affiliated with Southern Baptist Convention.

Enrollment: 893 undergrads, 9% part-time. 336 full-time freshmen.

Selectivity: Admits 50 to 75% of applicants.

BASIC COSTS (2007-2008)

Tuition and fees: $16,920.

Per-credit charge: $315.

Room and board: $7,000.

Additional info: $90 Communications fee for residents only.

FINANCIAL AID PICTURE

Students with need: Need-based aid available for full-time and part-time students. Work study available nights, weekends, and for part-time students.

Students without need: No-need awards available for academics, athletics, leadership, music/drama, religious affiliation, state/district residency.

Scholarships offered: Scholarship program for students serving as student body president who qualify for admission; full tuition.

FINANCIAL AID PROCEDURES

Forms required: FAFSA.

Dates and Deadlines: Priority date 3/1; no closing date. Applicants notified on a rolling basis starting 3/1; must reply within 2 week(s) of notification.

CONTACT

Stephanie Harrell, Director of Financial Aid
One University Place, Murfreesboro, NC 27855-9901
(252) 398-1229

Cleveland Community College

Shelby, North Carolina
www.clevelandcommunitycollege.edu Federal Code: 008082

2-year public community college in large town.

Enrollment: 3,104 undergrads.

Selectivity: Open admission; but selective for some programs.

BASIC COSTS (2007-2008)

Tuition and fees: $1,298; out-of-state residents $7,037.

Per-credit charge: $42; out-of-state residents $233.

FINANCIAL AID PICTURE

Students with need: Need-based aid available for full-time and part-time students. Work study available nights.

FINANCIAL AID PROCEDURES

Forms required: FAFSA.

Dates and Deadlines: Priority date 7/1; no closing date. Applicants notified on a rolling basis.

CONTACT

Andy Gardner, Director of Financial Aid
137 South Post Road, Shelby, NC 28152
(704) 484-4096

Coastal Carolina Community College

Jacksonville, North Carolina
www.coastal.cc.nc.us   Federal Code: 005316

2-year public community college in large town.

Enrollment: 4,055 undergrads, 53% part-time. 517 full-time freshmen.

Selectivity: Open admission; but selective for some programs.

BASIC COSTS (2007-2008)

Tuition and fees: $1,290; out-of-state residents $7,029.

Per-credit charge: $42; out-of-state residents $233.

FINANCIAL AID PICTURE (2006-2007)

Students with need: Out of 292 full-time freshmen who applied for aid, 265 were judged to have need. Of these, 260 received aid, and 68 had their full need met. Average financial aid package met 28% of need; average scholarship/grant was $2,640. Need-based aid available for part-time students.

Students without need: No-need awards available for academics, state/district residency.

FINANCIAL AID PROCEDURES

Forms required: FAFSA, institutional form.

Dates and Deadlines: Priority date 5/15; no closing date. Applicants notified on a rolling basis starting 5/15; must reply within 2 week(s) of notification.

CONTACT

Ken Doherty, Director of Financial Aid and Veterans Programs
444 Western Boulevard, Jacksonville, NC 28546-6877
(910) 938-6247

College of the Albemarle
Elizabeth City, North Carolina
www.albemarle.cc.nc.us   Federal Code: 002917

2-year public branch campus and community college in large town.
Enrollment: 1,653 undergrads, 57% part-time. 194 full-time freshmen.
Selectivity: Open admission; but selective for some programs.

BASIC COSTS (2007-2008)
Tuition and fees: $1,414; out-of-state residents $7,535.
Per-credit charge: $42; out-of-state residents $233.

FINANCIAL AID PICTURE
Students with need: Need-based aid available for full-time and part-time students.
Students without need: No-need awards available for academics, art, leadership, minority status, music/drama, state/district residency.
Additional info: Separate application must be submitted for COA Private Scholarships.

FINANCIAL AID PROCEDURES
Forms required: FAFSA.
Dates and Deadlines: Priority date 3/15; no closing date. Applicants notified on a rolling basis starting 5/1; must reply within 2 week(s) of notification.

CONTACT
Angie Dawson, Director of Scholarships and Student Aid
1208 North Road Street, Elizabeth City, NC 27906-2327
(252) 335-0821 ext. 2355

Craven Community College
New Bern, North Carolina
www.cravencc.edu   Federal Code: 008086

2-year public community college in large town.
Enrollment: 2,533 undergrads.
Selectivity: Open admission; but selective for some programs.

BASIC COSTS (2007-2008)
Tuition and fees: $1,330; out-of-state residents $7,069.
Per-credit charge: $42; out-of-state residents $233.

FINANCIAL AID PICTURE (2006-2007)
Students with need: 94% of average financial aid package awarded as scholarships/grants, 6% awarded as loans/jobs.
Students without need: This college awards aid only to students with need.

FINANCIAL AID PROCEDURES
Forms required: FAFSA.
Dates and Deadlines: Priority date 3/31; no closing date. Applicants notified on a rolling basis starting 6/1.

CONTACT
Kathy Banks, Director of Financial Aid
800 College Court, New Bern, NC 28562
(252) 638-7216

Davidson College
Davidson, North Carolina   Federal Code: 002918
www.davidson.edu   CSS Code: 5150

4-year private liberal arts college in small town, affiliated with Presbyterian Church (USA).
Enrollment: 1,667 undergrads. 461 full-time freshmen.
Selectivity: Admits less than 50% of applicants. GED not accepted.

BASIC COSTS (2008-2009)
Tuition and fees: $33,479.
Room and board: $9,471.

FINANCIAL AID PICTURE (2006-2007)
Students with need: Out of 231 full-time freshmen who applied for aid, 152 were judged to have need. Of these, 148 received aid, and 148 had their full need met. Average financial aid package met 100% of need; average scholarship/grant was $19,364; average loan was $2,974. Need-based aid available for part-time students.
Students without need: 92 full-time freshmen who did not demonstrate need for aid received scholarships/grants; average award was $15,900. No-need awards available for academics, art, athletics, leadership, minority status, music/drama, ROTC.
Scholarships offered: *Merit:* Thompson S./Sarah S. Baker Scholarships: comprehensive fees; for first-time students with highest achievements; 3 awarded. John Montgomery Belk Scholarship: comprehensive fees; for Southeast applicants with highest achievements; 6 awarded. Amos Norris Scholarship: full cost; for first-time student athlete; 1 awarded. William Holt Terry Scholarships: full tuition; for first-year students with leadership skills and personal qualities, 2 awarded. John I. Smith Scholars Programs: full tuition; for first-year students with leadership, academic excellence, and commitment to community service; 2 awarded. *Athletic:* 42 full-time freshmen received athletic scholarships; average amount $14,320.
Cumulative student debt: 30% of graduating class had student loans; average debt was $28,100.

FINANCIAL AID PROCEDURES
Forms required: FAFSA, CSS PROFILE.
Dates and Deadlines: Closing date 2/15. Applicants notified by 4/1; must reply by 5/1.
Transfers: Priority date 2/15; closing date 3/15.

CONTACT
Chad Spencer, Assistant Dean of Admission and Financial Aid
Box 7156, Davidson, NC 28035-7156
(704) 894-2232

Davidson County Community College
Lexington, North Carolina
www.davidson.cc.nc.us   Federal Code: 002919

2-year public community college in large town.
Enrollment: 2,931 undergrads.
Selectivity: Open admission; but selective for some programs.

BASIC COSTS (2007-2008)
Tuition and fees: $1,333; out-of-state residents $7,072.
Per-credit charge: $42; out-of-state residents $233.

FINANCIAL AID PICTURE (2006-2007)
Students with need: 98% of average financial aid package awarded as scholarships/grants, 2% awarded as loans/jobs. Need-based aid available for part-time students.
Students without need: No-need awards available for academics, leadership.

FINANCIAL AID PROCEDURES
Forms required: FAFSA, institutional form.
Dates and Deadlines: Priority date 3/31; closing date 6/1. Applicants notified on a rolling basis starting 7/1; must reply within 2 week(s) of notification.

CONTACT
Anita Pennix, Director, Financial Aid
PO Box 1287, Lexington, NC 27293-1287
(336) 249-8186 ext. 237

DeVry University: Charlotte

Charlotte, North Carolina
www.devry.edu

4-year for-profit university in very large city.
Enrollment: 107 undergrads, 51% part-time. 11 full-time freshmen.

BASIC COSTS (2007-2008)
Tuition and fees: $13,020.
Per-credit charge: $490.

FINANCIAL AID PICTURE (2006-2007)
Students with need: Out of 3 full-time freshmen who applied for aid, 1 were judged to have need. Of these, 1 received aid. Average financial aid package met 58% of need; average scholarship/grant was $4,965; average loan was $2,625. For part-time students, average financial aid package was $6,228.
Students without need: No-need awards available for academics.

FINANCIAL AID PROCEDURES
Forms required: FAFSA.
Dates and Deadlines: No deadline. Applicants notified on a rolling basis.

CONTACT
4521 Sharon Road, Charlotte, NC 28211

Duke University

Durham, North Carolina   Federal Code: 002920
www.duke.edu   CSS Code: 5156

4-year private university in small city, affiliated with United Methodist Church.
Enrollment: 6,260 undergrads. 1,700 full-time freshmen.
Selectivity: Admits less than 50% of applicants. GED not accepted.

BASIC COSTS (2007-2008)
Tuition and fees: $35,512.
Room and board: $9,940.

FINANCIAL AID PICTURE
Students with need: Need-based aid available for full-time students.
Students without need: No-need awards available for academics, alumni affiliation, art, athletics, leadership, minority status, religious affiliation, ROTC, state/district residency.

FINANCIAL AID PROCEDURES
Forms required: FAFSA, CSS PROFILE.
Dates and Deadlines: Closing date 3/1. Applicants notified by 4/1; must reply by 5/1 or within 4 week(s) of notification.

CONTACT
James Belvin, Director of Financial Aid
2138 Campus Drive, Durham, NC 27708
(919) 684-6225

Durham Technical Community College

Durham, North Carolina
www.durhamtech.edu   Federal Code: 005448

2-year public community and technical college in small city.
Enrollment: 3,000 undergrads.
Selectivity: Open admission; but selective for some programs.

BASIC COSTS (2007-2008)
Tuition and fees: $1,330; out-of-state residents $7,069.
Per-credit charge: $42; out-of-state residents $233.

FINANCIAL AID PICTURE
Students with need: Need-based aid available for full-time and part-time students. Work study available nights.
Students without need: No-need awards available for academics, minority status, state/district residency.
Additional info: Special funds available to single parents for tuition, fees, books, supplies and child care expenses.

FINANCIAL AID PROCEDURES
Forms required: FAFSA.
Dates and Deadlines: Applicants notified on a rolling basis starting 1/31; must reply within 3 week(s) of notification.

CONTACT
Cameron Murray, Director of Financial Aid
1637 Lawson Street, Durham, NC 27703
(919) 686-3661

East Carolina University

Greenville, North Carolina
www.ecu.edu   Federal Code: 002923

4-year public university in small city.
Enrollment: 19,651 undergrads, 12% part-time. 4,196 full-time freshmen.
Selectivity: Admits over 75% of applicants.

BASIC COSTS (2007-2008)
Tuition and fees: $4,218; out-of-state residents $14,732.
Room and board: $7,450.

FINANCIAL AID PICTURE
Students with need: Need-based aid available for full-time and part-time students.
Students without need: No-need awards available for academics, alumni affiliation, art, athletics, minority status, ROTC.

FINANCIAL AID PROCEDURES
Forms required: FAFSA.
Dates and Deadlines: Priority date 4/15; no closing date. Applicants notified on a rolling basis starting 3/15; must reply within 3 week(s) of notification.

CONTACT
Sheryl Spivey, Director of Student Financial Aid
Office of Undergraduate Admissions, Greenville, NC 27858-4353
(252) 328-6610

Edgecombe Community College

Tarboro, North Carolina
www.edgecombe.edu   Federal Code: 008855

2-year public community college in large town.
Enrollment: 2,510 undergrads.
Selectivity: Open admission; but selective for some programs.

BASIC COSTS (2007-2008)
Tuition and fees: $1,284; out-of-state residents $7,023.
Per-credit charge: $42; out-of-state residents $220.

FINANCIAL AID PICTURE
Students with need: Need-based aid available for full-time and part-time students.
Students without need: This college awards aid only to students with need.

FINANCIAL AID PROCEDURES
Forms required: FAFSA, institutional form.

Dates and Deadlines: Closing date 6/30. Applicants notified on a rolling basis starting 8/15; must reply within 3 week(s) of notification.
Transfers: No deadline.

CONTACT
Brenda Mercer, Director of Financial Aid
2009 West Wilson Street, Tarboro, NC 27886
(252) 823-5166 ext. 258

Elizabeth City State University
Elizabeth City, North Carolina
www.ecsu.edu   Federal Code: 002926

4-year public liberal arts college in large town.
Enrollment: 2,658 undergrads, 7% part-time. 587 full-time freshmen.
Selectivity: Admits 50 to 75% of applicants.

BASIC COSTS (2007-2008)
Tuition and fees: $2,898; out-of-state residents $11,779.
Room and board: $5,147.

FINANCIAL AID PICTURE
Students with need: Need-based aid available for full-time students. Work study available nights, weekends, and for part-time students.
Students without need: No-need awards available for academics, athletics, minority status, ROTC, state/district residency.

FINANCIAL AID PROCEDURES
Forms required: FAFSA.
Dates and Deadlines: Priority date 3/1; closing date 8/15. Applicants notified on a rolling basis starting 6/1; must reply within 3 week(s) of notification.
Transfers: Closing date 8/1. Applicants notified on a rolling basis starting 6/1; must reply within 3 week(s) of notification.

CONTACT
Kenneth Wilson, Associate Director of Financial Aid
1704 Weeksville Road, Campus Box 901, Elizabeth City, NC 27909
(252) 335-3283

Elon University
Elon, North Carolina   Federal Code: 002927
www.elon.edu   CSS Code: 5183

4-year private university and liberal arts college in large town, affiliated with United Church of Christ.
Enrollment: 4,939 undergrads, 2% part-time. 1,286 full-time freshmen.
Selectivity: Admits less than 50% of applicants.

BASIC COSTS (2008-2009)
Tuition and fees: $24,076.
Per-credit charge: $746.
Room and board: $7,770.

FINANCIAL AID PICTURE (2007-2008)
Students with need: Out of 686 full-time freshmen who applied for aid, 403 were judged to have need. Of these, 400 received aid. Average financial aid package met 73% of need; average scholarship/grant was $8,527; average loan was $3,666. Need-based aid available for part-time students.
Students without need: 282 full-time freshmen who did not demonstrate need for aid received scholarships/grants; average award was $4,218. No-need awards available for academics, art, athletics, leadership, music/drama, ROTC, state/district residency.
Scholarships offered: Merit: Presidential Scholarships: $1,000-$4,500 annually; based on academic credentials. Fellows Programs (Communications, Science, Jefferson-Pilot Business, Honors, Isabella Cannon Leadership): $2,500-$8,000 annually; based on merit. North Carolina Teaching Fellows:

$13,000 annually. Engineering Scholarships: $3,000 annually. **Athletic:** 86 full-time freshmen received athletic scholarships; average amount $16,912.
Cumulative student debt: 41% of graduating class had student loans; average debt was $21,268.

FINANCIAL AID PROCEDURES
Forms required: FAFSA, CSS PROFILE, institutional form.
Dates and Deadlines: Priority date 2/15; no closing date. Applicants notified on a rolling basis starting 3/30.

CONTACT
Pat Murphy, Director of Financial Planning
2700 Campus Box, Elon, NC 27244-2010
(336) 278-7640

Fayetteville State University
Fayetteville, North Carolina
www.uncfsu.edu   Federal Code: 002928

4-year public university in small city.
Enrollment: 5,678 undergrads, 22% part-time. 931 full-time freshmen.

BASIC COSTS (2007-2008)
Tuition and fees: $3,020; out-of-state residents $13,202.
Room and board: $4,870.

FINANCIAL AID PICTURE
Students with need: Need-based aid available for full-time and part-time students. Work study available nights, weekends, and for part-time students.
Students without need: No-need awards available for academics, alumni affiliation, athletics, music/drama, ROTC, state/district residency.

FINANCIAL AID PROCEDURES
Forms required: FAFSA.
Dates and Deadlines: Priority date 3/1; closing date 4/1. Applicants notified on a rolling basis starting 4/15; must reply within 2 week(s) of notification.

CONTACT
Kamesia Ewing, Director of Financial Aid
1200 Murchison Road, Fayetteville, NC 28301-4298
(910) 672-1325

Fayetteville Technical Community College
Fayetteville, North Carolina
www.faytechcc.edu   Federal Code: 007640

2-year public community and technical college in large city.
Enrollment: 8,471 undergrads, 67% part-time. 2,572 full-time freshmen.
Selectivity: Open admission; but selective for some programs.

BASIC COSTS (2007-2008)
Tuition and fees: $1,320; out-of-state residents $7,059.
Per-credit charge: $42; out-of-state residents $233.

FINANCIAL AID PICTURE (2006-2007)
Students with need: 54% of average financial aid package awarded as scholarships/grants, 46% awarded as loans/jobs. Need-based aid available for part-time students.

FINANCIAL AID PROCEDURES
Forms required: FAFSA.
Dates and Deadlines: Priority date 6/1; closing date 7/15. Applicants notified on a rolling basis starting 2/1.
Transfers: No deadline.

CONTACT

Patricia Stephenson, Student Financial Aid Services Director
PO Box 35236, Fayetteville, NC 28303-0236
(910) 678-8242

Forsyth Technical Community College

Winston-Salem, North Carolina
www.forsythtech.edu   Federal Code: 005317

2-year public community and technical college in small city.
Enrollment: 6,140 undergrads, 55% part-time. 800 full-time freshmen.
Selectivity: Open admission; but selective for some programs.

BASIC COSTS (2007-2008)

Tuition and fees: $1,322; out-of-state residents $7,061.
Per-credit charge: $42; out-of-state residents $233.

FINANCIAL AID PICTURE

Students with need: Need-based aid available for full-time and part-time students. Work study available nights.
Students without need: No-need awards available for academics, state/district residency.
Additional info: Apply for aid as close to January 1 as possible for best consideration.

FINANCIAL AID PROCEDURES

Forms required: FAFSA, institutional form.
Dates and Deadlines: Priority date 6/1; no closing date. Applicants notified on a rolling basis starting 7/1; must reply within 2 week(s) of notification.
Transfers: Priority date 6/1; no deadline. Mid-year transfer students must submit a financial aid transcript from previous college in order for financial aid office to award any Federal Pell Grant funds to eligible students.

CONTACT

Ricky Hodges, Director of Student Financial Services
2100 Silas Creek Parkway, Winston-Salem, NC 27103

Gardner-Webb University

Boiling Springs, North Carolina
www.gardner-webb.edu   Federal Code: 002929

4-year private university and liberal arts college in small town, affiliated with Southern Baptist Convention.
Enrollment: 2,638 undergrads, 15% part-time. 416 full-time freshmen.
Selectivity: Admits 50 to 75% of applicants.

BASIC COSTS (2008-2009)

Tuition and fees: $20,465.
Per-credit charge: $328.
Room and board: $6,500.

FINANCIAL AID PICTURE

Students with need: Need-based aid available for full-time and part-time students.
Students without need: No-need awards available for academics, athletics, leadership, music/drama, religious affiliation, ROTC, state/district residency.

FINANCIAL AID PROCEDURES

Forms required: FAFSA.
Dates and Deadlines: No deadline. Applicants notified on a rolling basis starting 3/1; must reply within 2 week(s) of notification.

CONTACT

Debra Hintz, Director of Financial Planning
Box 817, Boiling Springs, NC 28017
(704) 406-4243

Gaston College

Dallas, North Carolina
www.gaston.cc.nc.us   Federal Code: 002973

2-year public community college in small town.
Enrollment: 4,522 undergrads.
Selectivity: Open admission; but selective for some programs.

BASIC COSTS (2007-2008)

Tuition and fees: $1,300; out-of-state residents $7,039.
Per-credit charge: $42; out-of-state residents $233.

FINANCIAL AID PICTURE

Students with need: Need-based aid available for full-time students.
Students without need: No-need awards available for academics, state/district residency.
Scholarships offered: Academic Scholarship: over 30 available, $1,100, GPA of 3.0 or better. Careers Scholarship: 10 available, $1,100 each, must pursue career in specified engineering technologies or industrial technologies major and have GPA of 3.0 or better.
Additional info: Grants/scholarships available for women pursuing nontraditional roles.

FINANCIAL AID PROCEDURES

Forms required: FAFSA, institutional form.
Dates and Deadlines: Priority date 3/15; no closing date. Applicants notified on a rolling basis.

CONTACT

Peggy Oates, Director of Financial Aid and Veterans Affairs
201 Highway 321 South, Dallas, NC 28034-1499
(704) 922-6227

Greensboro College

Greensboro, North Carolina
www.gborocollege.edu   Federal Code: 002930

4-year private liberal arts college in large city, affiliated with United Methodist Church.
Enrollment: 901 undergrads, 6% part-time. 215 full-time freshmen.
Selectivity: Admits 50 to 75% of applicants.

BASIC COSTS (2007-2008)

Tuition and fees: $20,810.
Per-credit charge: $565.
Room and board: $7,930.

FINANCIAL AID PICTURE

Students with need: Need-based aid available for full-time and part-time students. Work study available nights, weekends, and for part-time students.
Students without need: No-need awards available for academics, alumni affiliation, art, leadership, music/drama, religious affiliation, state/district residency.
Scholarships offered: Presidential Scholarships: full tuition, fees, room, and board; number of awards vary.

FINANCIAL AID PROCEDURES

Forms required: FAFSA, state aid form, institutional form.
Dates and Deadlines: Priority date 4/15; no closing date. Applicants notified on a rolling basis starting 2/1; must reply within 2 week(s) of notification.
Transfers: Closing date 4/15. Must reply within 4 week(s) of notification.

CONTACT

Director of Financial Aid
815 West Market Street, Greensboro, NC 27401-1875
(336) 272-7102

Guilford College
Greensboro, North Carolina
www.guilford.edu   Federal Code: 002931

4-year private liberal arts college in small city, affiliated with Society of Friends (Quaker).

Enrollment: 2,688 undergrads, 16% part-time. 430 full-time freshmen.
Selectivity: Admits 50 to 75% of applicants.

BASIC COSTS (2008-2009)
Tuition and fees: $26,030.
Per-credit charge: $795.
Room and board: $7,140.
Additional info: Parking fee $70, required athletic insurance $183. Tuition/fee waivers available for adults.

FINANCIAL AID PICTURE (2006-2007)
Students with need: Out of 331 full-time freshmen who applied for aid, 306 were judged to have need. Of these, 303 received aid, and 134 had their full need met. Average financial aid package met 76% of need; average scholarship/grant was $17,188; average loan was $5,300. For part-time students, average financial aid package was $3,602.
Students without need: 159 full-time freshmen who did not demonstrate need for aid received scholarships/grants; average award was $8,000. No-need awards available for academics.
Scholarships offered: Honors Scholarship: $7,500 to full tuition. Presidential Scholarship: $5,000. Incentive grants: $3,000; based on participation or leadership in school or community activities. Quaker Leadership Scholarships: $3,000; candidates must be active members of the Religious Society of Friends.
Cumulative student debt: 68% of graduating class had student loans; average debt was $22,130.

FINANCIAL AID PROCEDURES
Forms required: FAFSA.
Dates and Deadlines: Priority date 3/1; no closing date. Applicants notified on a rolling basis starting 2/15; must reply within 2 week(s) of notification.

CONTACT
Dianne Harrison, Director of Financial Aid
Admissions, New Garden Hall, Greensboro, NC 27410-4108
(336) 316-2354

Guilford Technical Community College
Jamestown, North Carolina
www.gtcc.edu   Federal Code: 004838

2-year public community college in large city.
Enrollment: 9,730 undergrads.
Selectivity: Open admission; but selective for some programs.

BASIC COSTS (2007-2008)
Tuition and fees: $1,392; out-of-state residents $7,131.
Per-credit charge: $42; out-of-state residents $233.

FINANCIAL AID PICTURE
Students with need: Need-based aid available for full-time and part-time students.

FINANCIAL AID PROCEDURES
Forms required: FAFSA.
Dates and Deadlines: Priority date 3/15; no closing date. Applicants notified on a rolling basis starting 7/1; must reply within 2 week(s) of notification.

CONTACT
Lisa Koretoff, Director of Financial Aid
PO Box 309, Jamestown, NC 27282
(336) 334-4822 ext. 5352

Halifax Community College
Weldon, North Carolina
www.hcc.cc.nc.us   Federal Code: 007986

2-year public community college in small town.
Enrollment: 1,326 undergrads.
Selectivity: Open admission; but selective for some programs.

BASIC COSTS (2007-2008)
Tuition and fees: $1,356; out-of-state residents $7,095.
Per-credit charge: $42; out-of-state residents $233.

FINANCIAL AID PICTURE (2006-2007)
Students with need: 94% of average financial aid package awarded as scholarships/grants, 6% awarded as loans/jobs.

FINANCIAL AID PROCEDURES
Dates and Deadlines: Priority date 6/1; no closing date. Applicants notified on a rolling basis starting 8/1; must reply within 2 week(s) of notification.

CONTACT
Tara Keeter, Director, Financial Aid
Drawer 809, Weldon, NC 27890
(252) 536-7223

Haywood Community College
Clyde, North Carolina
www.haywood.edu   Federal Code: 008083

2-year public community and technical college in rural community.
Enrollment: 1,520 undergrads.
Selectivity: Open admission; but selective for some programs.

BASIC COSTS (2007-2008)
Tuition and fees: $1,332; out-of-state residents $7,071.
Per-credit charge: $42; out-of-state residents $233.

FINANCIAL AID PICTURE (2006-2007)
Students with need: 98% of average financial aid package awarded as scholarships/grants, 2% awarded as loans/jobs. Need-based aid available for part-time students.
Students without need: No-need awards available for academics.
Additional info: Complete FAFSA by priority filing date for consideration for institutional scholarships.

FINANCIAL AID PROCEDURES
Forms required: FAFSA, institutional form.
Dates and Deadlines: Priority date 4/1; no closing date. Applicants notified on a rolling basis starting 4/15; must reply within 2 week(s) of notification.

CONTACT
Kathy Lovedahl, Coordinator Financial Aid
185 Freelander Drive, Clyde, NC 28721-9454
(828) 627-4506

High Point University
High Point, North Carolina
www.highpoint.edu   Federal Code: 002933

4-year private university in small city, affiliated with United Methodist Church.
Enrollment: 2,736 undergrads, 9% part-time. 508 full-time freshmen.

Selectivity: Admits 50 to 75% of applicants.

BASIC COSTS (2008-2009)

Per-credit charge: $588.

Comprehensive fee: $31,000.

FINANCIAL AID PICTURE (2006-2007)

Students with need: Out of 481 full-time freshmen who applied for aid, 304 were judged to have need. Of these, 304 received aid. Average financial aid package met 58% of need; average scholarship/grant was $3,412; average loan was $2,625. For part-time students, average financial aid package was $6,058.

Students without need: 27 full-time freshmen who did not demonstrate need for aid received scholarships/grants; average award was $8,576. No-need awards available for academics, alumni affiliation, art, athletics, leadership, music/drama, religious affiliation, state/district residency.

Scholarships offered: *Merit:* Awarded annually to qualified freshmen: University Fellows, $20,000; Presidential Fellows, $12,000; Presidential Scholars, $7,000; Leadership Fellows, $5,000; Leadership Scholars: $3,000. All scholarships based on merit. Application and interview required. ***Athletic:*** 28 full-time freshmen received athletic scholarships; average amount $15,088.

Cumulative student debt: 58% of graduating class had student loans; average debt was $16,850.

FINANCIAL AID PROCEDURES

Forms required: FAFSA, state aid form.

Dates and Deadlines: Priority date 3/1; no closing date. Applicants notified on a rolling basis starting 4/1; must reply within 3 week(s) of notification.

Transfers: No deadline. Applicants notified on a rolling basis starting 5/1; must reply within 3 week(s) of notification.

CONTACT

Julie Setzer, Director of Student Financial Services

833 Montlieu Avenue, High Point, NC 27262-3598

(336) 841-9166

Isothermal Community College

Spindale, North Carolina

www.isothermal.edu

Federal Code: 002934

2-year public community college in small town.

Enrollment: 1,590 undergrads, 45% part-time. 183 full-time freshmen.

Selectivity: Open admission.

BASIC COSTS (2007-2008)

Tuition and fees: $1,298; out-of-state residents $7,037.

Per-credit charge: $42; out-of-state residents $233.

FINANCIAL AID PICTURE

Students with need: Need-based aid available for full-time and part-time students. Work study available nights.

Students without need: No-need awards available for academics, job skills, leadership, minority status, music/drama, state/district residency.

FINANCIAL AID PROCEDURES

Forms required: FAFSA, institutional form.

Dates and Deadlines: Priority date 5/31; no closing date. Applicants notified on a rolling basis starting 4/30; must reply within 4 week(s) of notification.

CONTACT

Jeffery Boyle, Director of Financial Aid

PO Box 804, Spindale, NC 28160

(828) 286-3636 ext. 242

James Sprunt Community College

Kenansville, North Carolina

www.jamessprunt.edu

Federal Code: 007687

2-year public community college in rural community.

Enrollment: 956 undergrads, 48% part-time. 99 full-time freshmen.

Selectivity: Open admission; but selective for some programs.

BASIC COSTS (2007-2008)

Tuition and fees: $1,330; out-of-state residents $7,069.

Per-credit charge: $42; out-of-state residents $233.

FINANCIAL AID PICTURE (2007-2008)

Students with need: Out of 75 full-time freshmen who applied for aid, 75 were judged to have need. Of these, 75 received aid. Average financial aid package met 60% of need; average scholarship/grant was $600; average loan was $3,000. Need-based aid available for part-time students.

Students without need: This college awards aid only to students with need.

Cumulative student debt: 15% of graduating class had student loans; average debt was $3,500.

FINANCIAL AID PROCEDURES

Forms required: FAFSA, state aid form, institutional form.

Dates and Deadlines: Priority date 6/1; no closing date. Applicants notified on a rolling basis starting 7/15; must reply within 2 week(s) of notification.

CONTACT

Connie Taylor, Financial Aid Officer

PO Box 398, Kenansville, NC 28349-0398

(910) 296-2503

John Wesley College

High Point, North Carolina

www.johnwesley.edu

Federal Code: 013819

4-year private Bible college in small city, affiliated with interdenominational tradition.

Enrollment: 107 undergrads, 30% part-time. 4 full-time freshmen.

Selectivity: Admits 50 to 75% of applicants.

BASIC COSTS (2007-2008)

Tuition and fees: $10,914.

Per-credit charge: $465.

Room only: $2,344.

FINANCIAL AID PICTURE

Students with need: Need-based aid available for full-time and part-time students. Work study available nights, weekends, and for part-time students.

Scholarships offered: Early Acceptance; $100. Academic Honor; 10% of tuition.

Additional info: Early Acceptance Scholarships, Academic Honor Scholarships, Married Student Credit and Minister/Missionary Dependent Scholarship available.

FINANCIAL AID PROCEDURES

Forms required: FAFSA.

Dates and Deadlines: Priority date 3/15; no closing date. Applicants notified on a rolling basis starting 6/1; must reply within 3 week(s) of notification.

Transfers: Closing date 3/15.

CONTACT

Shirley Carter, Director of Financial Aid

2314 North Centennial, High Point, NC 27265-3197

(336) 889-2262 ext. 129

Johnson & Wales University: Charlotte
Charlotte, North Carolina
www.jwu.edu

4-year private university in very large city.
Enrollment: 2,569 undergrads, 2% part-time. 719 full-time freshmen.
Selectivity: Admits 50 to 75% of applicants.

BASIC COSTS (2007-2008)
Tuition and fees: $21,717.
Per-credit charge: $379.
Room and board: $8,550.

FINANCIAL AID PICTURE (2007-2008)
Students with need: Out of 603 full-time freshmen who applied for aid, 533 were judged to have need. Of these, 533 received aid, and 52 had their full need met. Average financial aid package met 67% of need; average scholarship/grant was $7,728; average loan was $3,319. For part-time students, average financial aid package was $12,445.
Students without need: 113 full-time freshmen who did not demonstrate need for aid received scholarships/grants; average award was $5,023. No-need awards available for academics, alumni affiliation, job skills, leadership.
Cumulative student debt: 90% of graduating class had student loans; average debt was $25,104.

FINANCIAL AID PROCEDURES
Forms required: FAFSA.
Dates and Deadlines: No deadline. Applicants notified by 3/1.
Transfers: No deadline. Applicants notified on a rolling basis.

CONTACT
Director of Financial Aid
801 West Trade Street, Charlotte, NC 28202
(800) 342-5598

Johnson C. Smith University
Charlotte, North Carolina
www.jcsu.edu   Federal Code: 002936

4-year private university and liberal arts college in very large city.
Enrollment: 1,463 undergrads, 3% part-time. 501 full-time freshmen.
Selectivity: Admits less than 50% of applicants.

BASIC COSTS (2007-2008)
Tuition and fees: $15,754.
Per-credit charge: $361.
Room and board: $6,132.

FINANCIAL AID PICTURE (2007-2008)
Students with need: Out of 427 full-time freshmen who applied for aid, 391 were judged to have need. Of these, 391 received aid, and 3 had their full need met. Average financial aid package met 56% of need; average scholarship/grant was $3,573; average loan was $3,500. Need-based aid available for part-time students.
Students without need: 1 full-time freshmen who did not demonstrate need for aid received scholarships/grants; average award was $21,886. No-need awards available for academics, athletics, ROTC, state/district residency.
Scholarships offered: 2 full-time freshmen received athletic scholarships; average amount $21,886.
Cumulative student debt: 84% of graduating class had student loans; average debt was $35,125.

FINANCIAL AID PROCEDURES
Forms required: FAFSA.
Dates and Deadlines: Priority date 3/1; no closing date. Applicants notified on a rolling basis starting 3/1; must reply within 2 week(s) of notification.

Transfers: No deadline. Applicants notified on a rolling basis starting 4/1; must reply within 2 week(s) of notification.

CONTACT
Cynthia Anderson, Director of Financial Aid
100 Beatties Ford Road, Charlotte, NC 28216-5398
(704) 378-1035

Johnston Community College
Smithfield, North Carolina
www.johnstoncc.edu   Federal Code: 009336

2-year public community and technical college in large town.
Enrollment: 4,174 undergrads.
Selectivity: Open admission; but selective for some programs.

BASIC COSTS (2007-2008)
Tuition and fees: $1,330; out-of-state residents $7,069.
Per-credit charge: $42; out-of-state residents $233.

FINANCIAL AID PICTURE
Students with need: Need-based aid available for full-time and part-time students.
Students without need: This college awards aid only to students with need.

FINANCIAL AID PROCEDURES
Forms required: FAFSA, institutional form.
Dates and Deadlines: Priority date 5/31; no closing date. Applicants notified on a rolling basis starting 6/1; must reply within 2 week(s) of notification.

CONTACT
Betty Woodall, Financial Aid Officer
Box 2350, Smithfield, NC 27577
(919) 209-2028

Lees-McRae College
Banner Elk, North Carolina
www.lmc.edu   Federal Code: 002923

4-year private liberal arts college in rural community, affiliated with Presbyterian Church (USA).
Enrollment: 871 undergrads, 2% part-time. 202 full-time freshmen.
Selectivity: Admits 50 to 75% of applicants.

BASIC COSTS (2007-2008)
Tuition and fees: $19,500.
Per-credit charge: $542.
Room and board: $6,500.

FINANCIAL AID PICTURE
Students with need: Need-based aid available for full-time and part-time students. Work study available nights, weekends, and for part-time students.
Students without need: No-need awards available for academics, alumni affiliation, athletics, leadership, minority status, music/drama, religious affiliation, state/district residency.

FINANCIAL AID PROCEDURES
Forms required: FAFSA.
Dates and Deadlines: Priority date 3/15; no closing date. Applicants notified on a rolling basis starting 3/1; must reply within 2 week(s) of notification.

CONTACT
Cathy Shell, Director of Financial Aid
Box 128, Banner Elk, NC 28604
(828) 898-8740

Lenoir Community College

Kinston, North Carolina
www.lenoir.cc.nc.us   Federal Code: 002940

2-year public community college in large town.
Enrollment: 2,172 undergrads.
Selectivity: Open admission; but selective for some programs.

BASIC COSTS (2007-2008)
Tuition and fees: $1,336; out-of-state residents $7,075.
Per-credit charge: $42; out-of-state residents $233.

FINANCIAL AID PICTURE
Students with need: Need-based aid available for full-time and part-time students. Work study available nights.
Students without need: No-need awards available for academics, athletics, leadership, state/district residency.

FINANCIAL AID PROCEDURES
Forms required: institutional form.
Dates and Deadlines: Priority date 7/1; closing date 8/15. Applicants notified on a rolling basis starting 8/1; must reply within 2 week(s) of notification.

CONTACT
Mary Anne Dawson, Director of Student Financial Aid
Box 188, Kinston, NC 28502-0188
(252) 527-6223

Lenoir-Rhyne College

Hickory, North Carolina
www.lrc.edu   Federal Code: 002941

4-year private liberal arts college in large town, affiliated with Evangelical Lutheran Church in America.
Enrollment: 1,366 undergrads, 5% part-time. 359 full-time freshmen.
Selectivity: Admits over 75% of applicants.

BASIC COSTS (2008-2009)
Tuition and fees: $23,070.
Per-credit charge: $960.
Room and board: $8,150.
Additional info: Tuition/fee waivers available for minority students.

FINANCIAL AID PICTURE (2006-2007)
Students with need: Out of 340 full-time freshmen who applied for aid, 310 were judged to have need. Of these, 310 received aid, and 109 had their full need met. Average financial aid package met 33% of need; average scholarship/grant was $12,337; average loan was $2,513. For part-time students, average financial aid package was $12,776.
Students without need: 132 full-time freshmen who did not demonstrate need for aid received scholarships/grants; average award was $17,944. No-need awards available for academics, athletics, job skills, leadership, minority status, music/drama, ROTC, state/district residency.
Scholarships offered: 4 full-time freshmen received athletic scholarships; average amount $3,194.
Cumulative student debt: 96% of graduating class had student loans; average debt was $27,563.

FINANCIAL AID PROCEDURES
Forms required: FAFSA, state aid form.
Dates and Deadlines: Priority date 3/1; closing date 8/1. Applicants notified on a rolling basis starting 3/1; must reply within 2 week(s) of notification.

CONTACT
Eva Harmon, Director of Financial Aid
PO Box 7227, Hickory, NC 28603
(828) 328-7304

Livingstone College

Salisbury, North Carolina
www.livingstone.edu   Federal Code: 002942

4-year private liberal arts college in large town, affiliated with African Methodist Episcopal Zion Church.
Enrollment: 960 undergrads.
Selectivity: Admits over 75% of applicants.

BASIC COSTS (2007-2008)
Tuition and fees: $12,474.
Per-credit charge: $507.
Room and board: $5,641.

FINANCIAL AID PICTURE
Students with need: Need-based aid available for full-time and part-time students. Work study available nights, weekends, and for part-time students.
Students without need: No-need awards available for academics, alumni affiliation, athletics, leadership, music/drama, religious affiliation, ROTC, state/district residency.

FINANCIAL AID PROCEDURES
Forms required: FAFSA, state aid form.
Dates and Deadlines: Priority date 3/15; closing date 6/30. Applicants notified by 5/1; must reply within 4 week(s) of notification.

CONTACT
Raymond Robinson, Director of Financial Aid
701 West Monroe Street, Salisbury, NC 28144-5213
(704) 216-6273

Louisburg College

Louisburg, North Carolina
www.louisburg.edu   Federal Code: 002943

2-year private junior college in small town, affiliated with United Methodist Church.
Enrollment: 730 undergrads.
Selectivity: Admits 50 to 75% of applicants.

BASIC COSTS (2007-2008)
Tuition and fees: $12,425.
Room and board: $7,775.

FINANCIAL AID PICTURE
Students with need: Need-based aid available for full-time students. Work study available nights, weekends, and for part-time students.
Additional info: Job location and development program helps students obtain work in the community.

FINANCIAL AID PROCEDURES
Forms required: FAFSA, institutional form.
Dates and Deadlines: Priority date 3/1; no closing date. Applicants notified on a rolling basis starting 3/15.

CONTACT
Sean Van Pallandt, Director of Financial Aid
501 North Main Street, Louisburg, NC 27549
(919) 497-3203

Mars Hill College

Mars Hill, North Carolina
www.mhc.edu   Federal Code: 002944

4-year private liberal arts college in small town, affiliated with Baptist faith.
Enrollment: 1,212 undergrads.

Selectivity: Admits 50 to 75% of applicants.

BASIC COSTS (2007-2008)

Tuition and fees: $18,812.
Per-credit charge: $624.
Room and board: $6,462.

FINANCIAL AID PICTURE (2007-2008)

Students with need: 70% of average financial aid package awarded as scholarships/grants, 30% awarded as loans/jobs. Need-based aid available for part-time students. Work study available nights.
Students without need: No-need awards available for academics, art, athletics, religious affiliation, state/district residency.
Scholarships offered: Awards based on merit, SAT/ACT scores, and GPA. Money available for four years, requiring minimum GPA.

FINANCIAL AID PROCEDURES

Forms required: FAFSA, state aid form, institutional form.
Dates and Deadlines: No deadline. Applicants notified on a rolling basis; must reply within 2 week(s) of notification.

CONTACT

Donna Griffith, Director of Financial Aid
Blackwell Hall, Box 370, Mars Hill, NC 28754
(828) 689-1123

Martin Community College

Williamston, North Carolina
www.martincc.edu
Federal Code: 007988

2-year public community and technical college in small town.
Enrollment: 612 undergrads.
Selectivity: Open admission; but selective for some programs.

BASIC COSTS (2007-2008)

Tuition and fees: $1,298; out-of-state residents $7,037.
Per-credit charge: $42; out-of-state residents $233.

FINANCIAL AID PICTURE

Students with need: Need-based aid available for full-time and part-time students. Work study available nights.
Students without need: No-need awards available for academics.

FINANCIAL AID PROCEDURES

Forms required: FAFSA.
Dates and Deadlines: Priority date 5/1; no closing date. Applicants notified on a rolling basis starting 5/1.

CONTACT

Michelle Lane, Director of Financial Aid
1161 Kehukee Park Road, Williamston, NC 27892-9988
(252) 792-1521 ext. 244

Mayland Community College

Spruce Pine, North Carolina
www.mayland.edu
Federal Code: 011197

2-year public community college in rural community.
Enrollment: 1,800 undergrads.
Selectivity: Open admission; but selective for some programs.

BASIC COSTS (2007-2008)

Tuition and fees: $1,332; out-of-state residents $7,071.
Per-credit charge: $42; out-of-state residents $233.

FINANCIAL AID PICTURE

Students with need: Need-based aid available for full-time and part-time students.

FINANCIAL AID PROCEDURES

Forms required: FAFSA, institutional form.
Dates and Deadlines: Priority date 3/15; no closing date. Applicants notified on a rolling basis starting 6/15.

CONTACT

Pamela Ellis, Financial Aid Coordinator
Box 547, Spruce Pine, NC 28777
(828) 765-7351

McDowell Technical Community College

Marion, North Carolina
www.mcdowelltech.edu
Federal Code: 008085

2-year public community and technical college in small town.
Enrollment: 930 undergrads.
Selectivity: Open admission; but selective for some programs.

BASIC COSTS (2007-2008)

Tuition and fees: $1,316; out-of-state residents $7,055.
Per-credit charge: $42; out-of-state residents $233.

FINANCIAL AID PICTURE (2006-2007)

Students with need: 99% of average financial aid package awarded as scholarships/grants, 1% awarded as loans/jobs. Need-based aid available for part-time students. Work study available nights.
Students without need: This college awards aid only to students with need.

FINANCIAL AID PROCEDURES

Forms required: FAFSA, institutional form.
Dates and Deadlines: Priority date 3/15; no closing date. Applicants notified on a rolling basis starting 7/1.

CONTACT

Kim Shuford, Director of Financial Aid
54 College Drive, Marion, NC 28752
(828) 652-0602

Meredith College

Raleigh, North Carolina
www.meredith.edu
Federal Code: 002945

4-year private liberal arts college for women in large city.
Enrollment: 1,937 undergrads, 9% part-time. 463 full-time freshmen.
Selectivity: Admits over 75% of applicants. GED not accepted.

BASIC COSTS (2008-2009)

Tuition and fees: $23,550.
Per-credit charge: $615.
Room and board: $6,740.
Additional info: Tuition includes a new laptop computer for each full-time freshman, which will be replaced with a new laptop during her junior year. Upon graduation from Meredith, the laptop remains the property of the student.

FINANCIAL AID PICTURE (2007-2008)

Students with need: Out of 372 full-time freshmen who applied for aid, 297 were judged to have need. Of these, 297 received aid, and 67 had their full need met. Average financial aid package met 81% of need; average scholarship/grant was $13,598; average loan was $3,494. For part-time students, average financial aid package was $6,494.
Students without need: 75 full-time freshmen who did not demonstrate need for aid received scholarships/grants; average award was $5,354. No-need awards available for academics, art, leadership, minority status, music/drama, religious affiliation, state/district residency.

Scholarships offered: Presidential Scholarships, tuition plus a stipend for study abroad, based on superior academic ability and achievement, 3-5 awarded. Talent Scholarships, varying amounts, available for students planning to major in art, music, interior design and computer science/mathematics/pre-engineering and based on on-campus competition. Teaching Fellows Scholarship, $6,500 per year to match a similar stipend from the State, plus a study abroad opportunity, based on state-wide competition, approximately 25 awarded.

Cumulative student debt: 73% of graduating class had student loans; average debt was $29,193.

FINANCIAL AID PROCEDURES

Forms required: FAFSA.

Dates and Deadlines: Priority date 2/15; no closing date. Applicants notified on a rolling basis starting 3/15; must reply by 5/1 or within 2 week(s) of notification.

CONTACT

Kevin Michaelsen, Director of Financial Assistance
3800 Hillsborough Street, Raleigh, NC 27607-5298
(919) 760-8565

Methodist University

Fayetteville, North Carolina
www.methodist.edu   Federal Code: 002946

4-year private liberal arts college in small city, affiliated with United Methodist Church.

Enrollment: 1,940 undergrads, 13% part-time. 449 full-time freshmen.

Selectivity: Admits 50 to 75% of applicants.

BASIC COSTS (2008-2009)

Tuition and fees: $21,944.

Per-credit charge: $675.

Room and board: $8,046.

Additional info: Professional golf management, professional tennis management, and music students have additional fees.

FINANCIAL AID PICTURE (2006-2007)

Students with need: Out of 449 full-time freshmen who applied for aid, 350 were judged to have need. Of these, 350 received aid, and 45 had their full need met. Average financial aid package met 71% of need; average scholarship/grant was $8,746; average loan was $2,330. For part-time students, average financial aid package was $4,144.

Students without need: 43 full-time freshmen who did not demonstrate need for aid received scholarships/grants; average award was $3,263. No-need awards available for academics, alumni affiliation, leadership, music/drama, religious affiliation, ROTC, state/district residency.

Scholarships offered: Presidential Scholarship: $5,250-$17,000/yr; 3.1+ GPA, 1000+ SAT or 22+ ACT. Merit scholarship: $3,250-$4,250; residential freshmen; 2.9+ GPA, 900+ SAT or 19+ ACT; leadership. SAT scores exclusive of Writing.

Cumulative student debt: 81% of graduating class had student loans; average debt was $24,716.

FINANCIAL AID PROCEDURES

Forms required: FAFSA.

Dates and Deadlines: Priority date 5/1; closing date 7/1. Applicants notified on a rolling basis starting 3/1; must reply within 2 week(s) of notification.

Transfers: No deadline. Applicants notified on a rolling basis; must reply within 2 week(s) of notification.

CONTACT

Bonnie Adamson, Director of Financial Aid
5400 Ramsey Street, Fayetteville, NC 28311-1498
(910) 630-7192

Miller-Motte Technical College

Wilmington, North Carolina
www.miller-motte.com   Federal Code: E00896

4-year for-profit technical college in small city.

Enrollment: 760 undergrads.

Selectivity: Open admission; but selective for some programs.

BASIC COSTS (2007-2008)

Tuition and fees: $10,890.

Per-credit charge: $220.

Additional info: Tuition at time of enrollment locked for 4 years.

FINANCIAL AID PICTURE

Students with need: Need-based aid available for full-time and part-time students. Work study available nights, weekends, and for part-time students.

Students without need: This college awards aid only to students with need.

FINANCIAL AID PROCEDURES

Forms required: FAFSA, institutional form.

Dates and Deadlines: No deadline.

CONTACT

Michele Carroll, Financial Aid Officer
5000 Market Street, Wilmington, NC 28405
(910) 392-4660

Mitchell Community College

Statesville, North Carolina
www.mitchellcc.edu   Federal Code: 002947

2-year public community college in large town.

Enrollment: 2,687 undergrads.

Selectivity: Open admission; but selective for some programs.

BASIC COSTS (2007-2008)

Tuition and fees: $1,328; out-of-state residents $7,067.

Per-credit charge: $42; out-of-state residents $233.

FINANCIAL AID PICTURE

Students with need: Need-based aid available for full-time and part-time students.

FINANCIAL AID PROCEDURES

Forms required: FAFSA, institutional form.

Dates and Deadlines: No deadline. Applicants notified on a rolling basis starting 3/1; must reply within 2 week(s) of notification.

Transfers: Students are monitored through NSLDS's Transfer Monitoring List.

CONTACT

Candace Cooper, Financial Aid Officer
500 West Broad Street, Statesville, NC 28677
(704) 878-3256

Montgomery Community College

Troy, North Carolina
www.montgomery.edu   Federal Code: 008087

2-year public community college in small town.

Enrollment: 991 undergrads.

Selectivity: Open admission; but selective for some programs.

BASIC COSTS (2007-2008)

Tuition and fees: $1,320; out-of-state residents $7,059.
Per-credit charge: $42; out-of-state residents $233.

FINANCIAL AID PICTURE

Students with need: Need-based aid available for full-time and part-time students. Work study available nights.
Students without need: No-need awards available for academics, minority status, state/district residency.

FINANCIAL AID PROCEDURES

Forms required: FAFSA, institutional form.
Dates and Deadlines: Priority date 7/15; no closing date. Applicants notified on a rolling basis starting 6/1.

CONTACT

Doni Cody, Director of Financial Aid
1011 Page Street, Troy, NC 27371-0787
(910) 576-6222 ext. 519

Montreat College

Montreat, North Carolina
www.montreat.edu   Federal Code: 002948

4-year private liberal arts college in small town, affiliated with Presbyterian Church (USA).

Enrollment: 984 undergrads, 2% part-time. 178 full-time freshmen.
Selectivity: Admits 50 to 75% of applicants.

BASIC COSTS (2008-2009)

Tuition and fees: $18,700.
Per-credit charge: $480.
Room and board: $6,000.

FINANCIAL AID PICTURE (2006-2007)

Students with need: 64% of average financial aid package awarded as scholarships/grants, 36% awarded as loans/jobs. Need-based aid available for part-time students. Work study available nights, weekends, and for part-time students.
Students without need: No-need awards available for academics, alumni affiliation, athletics, leadership, music/drama, religious affiliation, state/district residency.

FINANCIAL AID PROCEDURES

Forms required: FAFSA, state aid form, institutional form.
Dates and Deadlines: Priority date 3/15; no closing date. Applicants notified on a rolling basis starting 1/15; must reply within 2 week(s) of notification.
Transfers: Priority date 4/1; no deadline. Applicants notified on a rolling basis starting 1/15; must reply within 2 week(s) of notification.

CONTACT

Tony Robinson, Director of Financial Aid
Box 1267, Montreat, NC 28757-1267
(800) 545-4656

Mount Olive College

Mount Olive, North Carolina
www.mountolivecollege.edu   Federal Code: 002949

4-year private liberal arts college in small town, affiliated with Free Will Baptists.

Enrollment: 3,116 undergrads, 21% part-time. 375 full-time freshmen.
Selectivity: Open admission.

BASIC COSTS (2008-2009)

Tuition and fees: $13,126.
Per-credit charge: $250.

Room and board: $5,300.

FINANCIAL AID PICTURE (2006-2007)

Students with need: Out of 375 full-time freshmen who applied for aid, 317 were judged to have need. Of these, 313 received aid, and 50 had their full need met. Average financial aid package met 65% of need; average scholarship/grant was $7,351; average loan was $2,030. For part-time students, average financial aid package was $6,413.
Students without need: 39 full-time freshmen who did not demonstrate need for aid received scholarships/grants; average award was $4,976. No-need awards available for academics, art, athletics, leadership, music/drama, religious affiliation.
Scholarships offered: 17 full-time freshmen received athletic scholarships; average amount $3,689.
Cumulative student debt: 88% of graduating class had student loans; average debt was $12,450.

FINANCIAL AID PROCEDURES

Forms required: FAFSA, state aid form.
Dates and Deadlines: Priority date 3/1; no closing date. Applicants notified on a rolling basis starting 2/14; must reply within 2 week(s) of notification.
Transfers: Special scholarship program available for transfers from North Carolina community colleges.

CONTACT

Karen Statler, Director of Financial Aid
634 Henderson Street, Mount Olive, NC 28365
(919) 658-7164

Nash Community College

Rocky Mount, North Carolina
www.nash.cc.nc.us   Federal Code: 008557

2-year public community college in small city.
Enrollment: 2,000 undergrads.
Selectivity: Open admission; but selective for some programs.

BASIC COSTS (2007-2008)

Tuition and fees: $1,350; out-of-state residents $7,089.
Per-credit charge: $42; out-of-state residents $233.

FINANCIAL AID PICTURE

Students with need: Need-based aid available for full-time and part-time students.
Students without need: No-need awards available for academics.

FINANCIAL AID PROCEDURES

Forms required: FAFSA, institutional form.
Dates and Deadlines: Priority date 6/30; no closing date. Applicants notified on a rolling basis starting 7/15.

CONTACT

Tammy Lester, Financial Aid Officer
Box 7488, Rocky Mount, NC 27804-0488
(252) 451-8371

North Carolina Agricultural and Technical State University

Greensboro, North Carolina
www.ncat.edu   Federal Code: 002905

4-year public Historically Black College/University (HBCU) in small city.
Enrollment: 8,873 undergrads, 9% part-time. 1,569 full-time freshmen.
Selectivity: Admits 50 to 75% of applicants.

BASIC COSTS (2007-2008)
Tuition and fees: $3,500; out-of-state residents $12,942.
Room and board: $5,379.

FINANCIAL AID PICTURE (2007-2008)
Students with need: Average financial aid package met 52% of need; average scholarship/grant was $4,803; average loan was $3,182. Need-based aid available for part-time students.
Students without need: No-need awards available for academics, athletics, music/drama, ROTC.
Cumulative student debt: 85% of graduating class had student loans; average debt was $17,620.

FINANCIAL AID PROCEDURES
Forms required: FAFSA.
Dates and Deadlines: Priority date 3/15; no closing date. Applicants notified on a rolling basis starting 4/1; must reply within 2 week(s) of notification.

CONTACT
Sherri Avent, Director of Student Financial Aid
Webb Hall, Greensboro, NC 27411-0002
(800) 443-0835

North Carolina Central University
Durham, North Carolina
www.nccu.edu   Federal Code: 002950

4-year public university in small city.
Enrollment: 5,764 undergrads.
Selectivity: Admits 50 to 75% of applicants.

BASIC COSTS (2007-2008)
Tuition and fees: $3,666; out-of-state residents $13,411.
Room and board: $5,226.

FINANCIAL AID PICTURE
Students with need: Need-based aid available for full-time and part-time students.
Students without need: No-need awards available for academics, alumni affiliation, athletics, minority status, music/drama, state/district residency.
Additional info: Departmental grants based on need plus other available criteria.

FINANCIAL AID PROCEDURES
Forms required: FAFSA.
Dates and Deadlines: Priority date 4/1; no closing date. Applicants notified by 5/1; must reply within 2 week(s) of notification.

CONTACT
Sharon Oliver, Director of Student Financial Aid
PO Box 19717, Durham, NC 27707
(919) 530-6180

North Carolina School of the Arts
Winston-Salem, North Carolina
www.ncarts.edu   Federal Code: 003981

4-year public visual arts and performing arts college in small city.
Enrollment: 743 undergrads, 1% part-time. 185 full-time freshmen.
Selectivity: Admits less than 50% of applicants.

BASIC COSTS (2007-2008)
Tuition and fees: $5,061; out-of-state residents $16,491.
Room and board: $6,431.
Additional info: Required fees may vary by program.

FINANCIAL AID PICTURE
Students with need: Need-based aid available for full-time and part-time students. Work study available nights, weekends, and for part-time students.
Students without need: No-need awards available for academics, art, leadership, music/drama, state/district residency.

FINANCIAL AID PROCEDURES
Forms required: FAFSA.
Dates and Deadlines: Priority date 3/1; no closing date. Applicants notified on a rolling basis starting 4/1; must reply within 2 week(s) of notification.

CONTACT
Jane Kamiab, Director of Financial Aid
1533 South Main Street, Winston-Salem, NC 27127-2188
(336) 770-3297

North Carolina State University
Raleigh, North Carolina
www.ncsu.edu   Federal Code: 002972

4-year public university in large city.
Enrollment: 22,070 undergrads, 7% part-time. 4,907 full-time freshmen.
Selectivity: Admits 50 to 75% of applicants. GED not accepted.

BASIC COSTS (2007-2008)
Tuition and fees: $5,117; out-of-state residents $17,315.
Room and board: $7,370.

FINANCIAL AID PICTURE (2007-2008)
Students with need: Out of 3,295 full-time freshmen who applied for aid, 1,978 were judged to have need. Of these, 1,950 received aid, and 994 had their full need met. Average financial aid package met 85% of need; average scholarship/grant was $7,852; average loan was $2,351. For part-time students, average financial aid package was $6,863.
Students without need: 1,145 full-time freshmen who did not demonstrate need for aid received scholarships/grants; average award was $7,063. No-need awards available for academics, alumni affiliation, athletics, leadership, ROTC, state/district residency.
Scholarships offered: *Merit:* Park Scholarships- 4 year scholarship that covers almost all expenses - approximately 50 awarded each year. Caldwell scholarships awarded at end of freshmen year for 3 years covering most expenses. *Athletic:* 59 full-time freshmen received athletic scholarships; average amount $10,036.
Cumulative student debt: 50% of graduating class had student loans; average debt was $14,930.
Additional info: Freshman Merit Scholarships; students submitting complete admissions application by the November 1 Early Action deadline automatically considered, additional information may be required after initial review.

FINANCIAL AID PROCEDURES
Forms required: FAFSA, institutional form. CSS PROFILE recommended for early scholarship consideration.
Dates and Deadlines: Priority date 3/1; no closing date. Applicants notified on a rolling basis starting 3/15.

CONTACT
Julia Mallette, Associate Vice Provost and Director of Scholarships and Financial Aid
203 Peele Hall, Box 7103, Raleigh, NC 27695-7103
(919) 515-2421

North Carolina Wesleyan College
Rocky Mount, North Carolina
www.ncwc.edu
Federal Code: 002951

4-year private liberal arts college in small city, affiliated with United Methodist Church.

Enrollment: 1,510 undergrads, 23% part-time. 213 full-time freshmen.
Selectivity: Admits 50 to 75% of applicants.

BASIC COSTS (2008-2009)
Tuition and fees: $18,900.
Per-credit charge: $285.
Room and board: $7,100.

FINANCIAL AID PICTURE (2006-2007)
Students with need: 78% of average financial aid package awarded as scholarships/grants, 22% awarded as loans/jobs. Need-based aid available for part-time students.
Students without need: This college awards aid only to students with need.
Additional info: Scholarships based on GPA. Various scholarship and leadership awards available.

FINANCIAL AID PROCEDURES
Forms required: FAFSA.
Dates and Deadlines: Priority date 3/1; no closing date. Applicants notified on a rolling basis starting 1/1; must reply within 2 week(s) of notification.
Transfers: No deadline. Applicants notified on a rolling basis; must reply within 2 week(s) of notification.

CONTACT
Deana Summerlin, Director of Financial Aid
3400 North Wesleyan Boulevard, Rocky Mount, NC 27804
(252) 985-5295

Peace College
Raleigh, North Carolina
www.peace.edu
Federal Code: 002953

4-year private liberal arts college for women in large city, affiliated with Presbyterian Church (USA).

Enrollment: 658 undergrads, 3% part-time. 185 full-time freshmen.
Selectivity: Admits 50 to 75% of applicants.

BASIC COSTS (2008-2009)
Tuition and fees: $22,993.
Per-credit charge: $600.
Room and board: $7,820.

FINANCIAL AID PICTURE (2006-2007)
Students with need: Out of 162 full-time freshmen who applied for aid, 151 were judged to have need. Of these, 151 received aid, and 14 had their full need met. Average financial aid package met 77% of need; average scholarship/grant was $6,383; average loan was $2,855. For part-time students, average financial aid package was $8,737.
Students without need: 11 full-time freshmen who did not demonstrate need for aid received scholarships/grants; average award was $7,739. No-need awards available for academics.
Cumulative student debt: 75% of graduating class had student loans; average debt was $22,415.

FINANCIAL AID PROCEDURES
Forms required: FAFSA.
Dates and Deadlines: Priority date 3/15; no closing date. Applicants notified on a rolling basis starting 3/1; must reply by 5/1 or within 2 week(s) of notification.
Transfers: Priority date 3/1. Transfer merit scholarships available.

CONTACT
Angela Kirkley, Director of Financial Aid
15 East Peace Street, Raleigh, NC 27604-1194
(919) 508-2249

Pfeiffer University
Misenheimer, North Carolina
www.pfeiffer.edu
Federal Code: 002955

4-year private university and liberal arts college in rural community, affiliated with United Methodist Church.

Enrollment: 1,069 undergrads, 10% part-time. 189 full-time freshmen.
Selectivity: Admits over 75% of applicants.

BASIC COSTS (2008-2009)
Tuition and fees: $18,570.
Per-credit charge: $425.
Room and board: $7,360.

FINANCIAL AID PICTURE
Students with need: Need-based aid available for full-time students. Work study available nights, weekends, and for part-time students.
Students without need: No-need awards available for academics, alumni affiliation, athletics, leadership, music/drama, religious affiliation, state/district residency.
Scholarships offered: Honor, Presidential, University, and Legacy Scholarships - from $3,500 to full tuition per year.

FINANCIAL AID PROCEDURES
Forms required: FAFSA, state aid form.
Dates and Deadlines: Priority date 5/1; no closing date. Applicants notified on a rolling basis starting 3/1; must reply within 2 week(s) of notification.
Transfers: Priority date 3/15.

CONTACT
Amy Brown, Director of Financial Aid
Box 960, Misenheimer, NC 28109
(704) 463-1360 ext. 2070

Piedmont Baptist College
Winston-Salem, North Carolina
www.pbc.edu
Federal Code: 002956

4-year private Bible and seminary college in small city, affiliated with Baptist faith.

Enrollment: 258 undergrads, 29% part-time. 41 full-time freshmen.
Selectivity: Admits over 75% of applicants.

BASIC COSTS (2008-2009)
Tuition and fees: $10,800.
Per-credit charge: $435.
Room and board: $5,560.

FINANCIAL AID PICTURE
Students with need: Need-based aid available for full-time and part-time students. Work study available nights, weekends, and for part-time students.

FINANCIAL AID PROCEDURES
Forms required: institutional form.
Dates and Deadlines: No deadline. Applicants notified on a rolling basis starting 3/1.

CONTACT
Polly Trachian, Financial Aid Officer
420 South Board Street, Winston-Salem, NC 27101-5133
(336) 714-7987

Pitt Community College

Greenville, North Carolina
www.pittcc.edu   Federal Code: 004062

2-year public community and technical college in small city.
Enrollment: 5,302 undergrads.
Selectivity: Open admission; but selective for some programs.

BASIC COSTS (2007-2008)
Tuition and fees: $1,330; out-of-state residents $7,069.
Per-credit charge: $42; out-of-state residents $233.

FINANCIAL AID PICTURE
Students with need: Need-based aid available for full-time and part-time students. Work study available nights.
Students without need: No-need awards available for academics, athletics, ROTC.

FINANCIAL AID PROCEDURES
Forms required: FAFSA.
Dates and Deadlines: Priority date 3/15; no closing date. Applicants notified on a rolling basis starting 2/1.

CONTACT
Lisa Reichstein, Financial Aid Director
PO Drawer 7007, Greenville, NC 27835-7007
(252) 321-4339

Queens University of Charlotte

Charlotte, North Carolina
www.queens.edu   Federal Code: 002957

4-year private university in very large city, affiliated with Presbyterian Church (USA).
Enrollment: 1,688 undergrads, 35% part-time. 293 full-time freshmen.
Selectivity: Admits over 75% of applicants.

BASIC COSTS (2008-2009)
Tuition and fees: $22,068.
Per-credit charge: $335.
Room and board: $7,882.

FINANCIAL AID PICTURE (2007-2008)
Students with need: Out of 242 full-time freshmen who applied for aid, 194 were judged to have need. Of these, 194 received aid, and 42 had their full need met. Average financial aid package met 79% of need; average scholarship/grant was $13,043; average loan was $3,173. For part-time students, average financial aid package was $5,375.
Students without need: 80 full-time freshmen who did not demonstrate need for aid received scholarships/grants; average award was $11,405. No-need awards available for academics, art, athletics, leadership, minority status, music/drama.
Scholarships offered: *Merit:* Presidential Scholarships; full tuition; based on special application/recommendations; deadline 12/15; 12 awarded. *Athletic:* 34 full-time freshmen received athletic scholarships; average amount $4,798.
Cumulative student debt: 87% of graduating class had student loans; average debt was $19,532.

FINANCIAL AID PROCEDURES
Forms required: FAFSA, state aid form.
Dates and Deadlines: Priority date 3/1; no closing date. Applicants notified on a rolling basis starting 3/15; must reply by 5/1 or within 3 week(s) of notification.
Transfers: No deadline. Applicants notified on a rolling basis starting 3/15; must reply by 5/1 or within 3 week(s) of notification.

CONTACT
Eileen Dills, Associate Vice President of Student Financial Services
1900 Selwyn Ave, Charlotte, NC 28274
(704) 337-2225

Randolph Community College

Asheboro, North Carolina
www.randolph.edu   Federal Code: 005447

2-year public community and technical college in large town.
Enrollment: 4,549 undergrads.
Selectivity: Open admission; but selective for some programs.

BASIC COSTS (2007-2008)
Tuition and fees: $1,320; out-of-state residents $7,059.
Per-credit charge: $42; out-of-state residents $233.

FINANCIAL AID PICTURE (2006-2007)
Students with need: 98% of average financial aid package awarded as scholarships/grants, 2% awarded as loans/jobs. Work study available nights.
Students without need: No-need awards available for academics, leadership, minority status, state/district residency.

FINANCIAL AID PROCEDURES
Forms required: FAFSA.
Dates and Deadlines: No deadline. Applicants notified on a rolling basis.
Transfers: No deadline.

CONTACT
Chad Williams, Director of Financial Aid
PO Box 1009, Asheboro, NC 27204-1009
(336) 633-0222

Richmond Community College

Hamlet, North Carolina
www.richmondcc.edu   Federal Code: 005464

2-year public community college in small town.
Enrollment: 1,800 undergrads.
Selectivity: Open admission; but selective for some programs.

BASIC COSTS (2007-2008)
Tuition and fees: $1,298; out-of-state residents $7,037.
Per-credit charge: $42; out-of-state residents $233.

FINANCIAL AID PICTURE
Students with need: Need-based aid available for full-time and part-time students. Work study available nights.
Students without need: No-need awards available for academics, leadership.

FINANCIAL AID PROCEDURES
Forms required: FAFSA, institutional form.
Dates and Deadlines: No deadline. Applicants notified on a rolling basis starting 7/8; must reply within 2 week(s) of notification.

CONTACT
Beth McQueen, Director of Financial Aid
Box 1189, Hamlet, NC 28345
(910) 410-1726

Roanoke Bible College
Elizabeth City, North Carolina
www.roanokebible.edu   Federal Code: 014101

4-year private Bible college in large town, affiliated with Church of Christ.
Enrollment: 141 undergrads, 21% part-time. 28 full-time freshmen.
Selectivity: Admits 50 to 75% of applicants.

BASIC COSTS (2008-2009)
Tuition and fees: $9,150.
Per-credit charge: $295.
Room and board: $5,890.

FINANCIAL AID PICTURE (2006-2007)
Students with need: Out of 25 full-time freshmen who applied for aid, 23 were judged to have need. Of these, 23 received aid, and 1 had their full need met. Average financial aid package met 63% of need; average scholarship/grant was $3,492; average loan was $2,340. Need-based aid available for part-time students.
Students without need: 5 full-time freshmen who did not demonstrate need for aid received scholarships/grants; average award was $2,783. No-need awards available for academics, alumni affiliation, leadership, music/drama, religious affiliation.
Scholarships offered: Full tuition and half tuition available, based on demonstration of exceptional academic ability.
Cumulative student debt: 63% of graduating class had student loans; average debt was $25,371.

FINANCIAL AID PROCEDURES
Forms required: FAFSA, institutional form.
Dates and Deadlines: Priority date 3/15; no closing date. Applicants notified on a rolling basis starting 4/1; must reply within 2 week(s) of notification.

CONTACT
Lisa Pipkin, Financial Aid Administrator
715 North Poindexter Street, Elizabeth City, NC 27909
(252) 334-2020

Roanoke-Chowan Community College
Ahoskie, North Carolina
www.roanokechowan.edu   Federal Code: 008613

2-year public community college in small town.
Enrollment: 955 undergrads.
Selectivity: Open admission; but selective for some programs.

BASIC COSTS (2007-2008)
Tuition and fees: $1,394; out-of-state residents $7,133.
Per-credit charge: $42; out-of-state residents $233.

FINANCIAL AID PICTURE
Students with need: Need-based aid available for full-time and part-time students.
Students without need: No-need awards available for academics.

FINANCIAL AID PROCEDURES
Forms required: FAFSA.
Dates and Deadlines: Priority date 3/15; no closing date. Applicants notified on a rolling basis starting 7/1.

CONTACT
Tricia Sawyer, Financial Aid Director
109 Community College Road, Ahoskie, NC 27910-9522
(252) 862-1320

Robeson Community College
Lumberton, North Carolina
www.robeson.edu   Federal Code: 008612

2-year public community and technical college in large town.
Enrollment: 2,099 undergrads.
Selectivity: Open admission; but selective for some programs.

BASIC COSTS (2007-2008)
Tuition and fees: $1,320; out-of-state residents $7,059.
Per-credit charge: $42; out-of-state residents $233.

FINANCIAL AID PICTURE
Students with need: Need-based aid available for full-time and part-time students.

FINANCIAL AID PROCEDURES
Forms required: FAFSA.
Dates and Deadlines: Priority date 5/15; no closing date. Applicants notified on a rolling basis starting 7/31.

CONTACT
Vanessa Cogdell, Director of Financial Aid
PO Box 1420, Lumberton, NC 28359
(910) 272-3352

Rockingham Community College
Wentworth, North Carolina
www.rockinghamcc.edu   Federal Code: 002958

2-year public community college in rural community.
Enrollment: 1,777 undergrads, 52% part-time. 282 full-time freshmen.
Selectivity: Open admission; but selective for some programs.

BASIC COSTS (2007-2008)
Tuition and fees: $1,413; out-of-state residents $7,534.
Per-credit charge: $42; out-of-state residents $233.

FINANCIAL AID PICTURE
Students with need: Need-based aid available for full-time and part-time students.
Students without need: No-need awards available for academics, art, job skills, leadership, minority status, state/district residency.

FINANCIAL AID PROCEDURES
Forms required: FAFSA, institutional form.
Dates and Deadlines: Priority date 3/15; no closing date. Applicants notified on a rolling basis starting 5/30; must reply within 2 week(s) of notification.

CONTACT
Martha Jackson, Director of Financial Aid
Box 38, Wentworth, NC 27375-0038
(336) 342-4261 ext. 2204

Rowan-Cabarrus Community College
Salisbury, North Carolina
www.rowancabarrus.edu   Federal Code: 005754

2-year public community and technical college in large town.
Enrollment: 5,275 undergrads.
Selectivity: Open admission; but selective for some programs.

BASIC COSTS (2007-2008)
Tuition and fees: $1,324; out-of-state residents $7,063.
Per-credit charge: $42; out-of-state residents $230.

FINANCIAL AID PICTURE

Students with need: Need-based aid available for full-time and part-time students. Work study available nights.

Students without need: No-need awards available for academics, job skills, state/district residency.

FINANCIAL AID PROCEDURES

Forms required: FAFSA.

Dates and Deadlines: Priority date 3/15; closing date 8/1. Applicants notified on a rolling basis starting 5/1; must reply within 3 week(s) of notification.

Transfers: No deadline.

CONTACT

Lisa Ledbetter, Director, Financial Aid
Box 1595, Salisbury, NC 28145
(704) 637-0760 ext. 273

St. Andrews Presbyterian College

Laurinburg, North Carolina
www.sapc.edu
Federal Code: 002967

4-year private liberal arts college in large town, affiliated with Presbyterian Church (USA).

Enrollment: 726 undergrads, 4% part-time. 220 full-time freshmen.

Selectivity: Admits 50 to 75% of applicants.

BASIC COSTS (2007-2008)

Tuition and fees: $18,192.

Per-credit charge: $420.

Room and board: $7,992.

Additional info: Private living, lab fees, and equestrian fees additional.

FINANCIAL AID PICTURE (2007-2008)

Students with need: Out of 187 full-time freshmen who applied for aid, 149 were judged to have need. Of these, 149 received aid, and 50 had their full need met. Average financial aid package met 80% of need; average scholarship/grant was $11,066; average loan was $3,347. For part-time students, average financial aid package was $4,908.

Students without need: 67 full-time freshmen who did not demonstrate need for aid received scholarships/grants; average award was $10,938. No-need awards available for academics, alumni affiliation, athletics, leadership, music/drama, religious affiliation.

Scholarships offered: 46 full-time freshmen received athletic scholarships; average amount $3,559.

Cumulative student debt: 82% of graduating class had student loans; average debt was $16,922.

FINANCIAL AID PROCEDURES

Forms required: FAFSA, state aid form.

Dates and Deadlines: Priority date 5/1; no closing date. Applicants notified on a rolling basis starting 10/1; must reply within 2 week(s) of notification.

Transfers: No deadline. Applicants notified on a rolling basis starting 10/1.

CONTACT

Kim Driggers, Director, Financial Aid
1700 Dogwood Mile, Laurinburg, NC 28352
(910) 277-5560

St. Augustine's College

Raleigh, North Carolina
www.st-aug.edu
Federal Code: 002968

4-year private liberal arts college in large city, affiliated with Episcopal Church.

Enrollment: 1,267 undergrads.

BASIC COSTS (2007-2008)

Tuition and fees: $13,206.

Per-credit charge: $440.

Room and board: $6,590.

FINANCIAL AID PICTURE

Students with need: Need-based aid available for full-time and part-time students.

Students without need: No-need awards available for academics, art, athletics, leadership, minority status, music/drama, religious affiliation, ROTC, state/district residency.

Scholarships offered: Institutional Merit Scholarships based on high school record, evidence of leadership, and SAT score.

FINANCIAL AID PROCEDURES

Forms required: FAFSA, institutional form.

Dates and Deadlines: Closing date 3/15. Applicants notified on a rolling basis starting 5/1; must reply within 2 week(s) of notification.

Transfers: All transfer students must submit a financial aid transcript.

CONTACT

Rochelle King, Director of Financial Aid
1315 Oakwood Avenue, Raleigh, NC 27610-2298
(919) 516-4131

Salem College

Winston-Salem, North Carolina
www.salem.edu
Federal Code: 002960

4-year private liberal arts college for women in small city, affiliated with Moravian Church in America.

Enrollment: 741 undergrads, 16% part-time. 145 full-time freshmen.

Selectivity: Admits 50 to 75% of applicants.

BASIC COSTS (2007-2008)

Tuition and fees: $19,190.

Per-credit charge: $965.

Room and board: $10,050.

Additional info: Tuition/fee waivers available for adults.

FINANCIAL AID PICTURE (2006-2007)

Students with need: Out of 86 full-time freshmen who applied for aid, 81 were judged to have need. Of these, 81 received aid, and 81 had their full need met. Average financial aid package met 100% of need; average scholarship/grant was $9,828; average loan was $2,359. For part-time students, average financial aid package was $3,380.

Students without need: 9 full-time freshmen who did not demonstrate need for aid received scholarships/grants; average award was $9,933. No-need awards available for academics, alumni affiliation, leadership, minority status, music/drama, state/district residency.

Cumulative student debt: 70% of graduating class had student loans; average debt was $17,125.

FINANCIAL AID PROCEDURES

Forms required: FAFSA.

Dates and Deadlines: Priority date 3/1; no closing date. Applicants notified on a rolling basis starting 3/1; must reply by 5/1 or within 2 week(s) of notification.

CONTACT

Jerry Donna, Director of Financial Aid
PO Box 10548, Winston-Salem, NC 27108
(336) 721-2808

Sampson Community College

Clinton, North Carolina
www.sampsoncc.edu   Federal Code: 007892

2-year public community college in small town.

Enrollment: 1,550 undergrads, 59% part-time. 419 full-time freshmen.

Selectivity: Open admission; but selective for some programs.

BASIC COSTS (2007-2008)

Tuition and fees: $1,316; out-of-state residents $7,055.

Per-credit charge: $42; out-of-state residents $233.

FINANCIAL AID PICTURE

Students with need: Need-based aid available for full-time and part-time students.

Students without need: No-need awards available for academics, state/district residency.

Additional info: Short-term loans available to students waiting for federal aid to be approved. Covers tuition, fees and books only.

FINANCIAL AID PROCEDURES

Forms required: FAFSA.

Dates and Deadlines: Priority date 7/1; no closing date. Applicants notified on a rolling basis starting 7/15; must reply within 2 week(s) of notification.

CONTACT

Judy Tart, Director of Financial Aid
PO Box 318, Clinton, NC 28329
(910) 592-8084 ext. 2024

Sandhills Community College

Pinehurst, North Carolina
www.sandhills.edu   Federal Code: 002961

2-year public community college in large town.

Enrollment: 3,580 undergrads.

Selectivity: Open admission; but selective for some programs.

BASIC COSTS (2007-2008)

Tuition and fees: $1,330; out-of-state residents $7,069.

Per-credit charge: $42; out-of-state residents $233.

FINANCIAL AID PICTURE

Students with need: Need-based aid available for full-time and part-time students.

Students without need: No-need awards available for academics.

Scholarships offered: Sandhills Scholars; upper 15% of graduating class; 11 awarded.

Additional info: Scholarships available, limited loan capability.

FINANCIAL AID PROCEDURES

Forms required: FAFSA.

Dates and Deadlines: Priority date 6/1; no closing date. Applicants notified on a rolling basis starting 2/1; must reply by 8/1 or within 4 week(s) of notification.

CONTACT

Chad Williams, Director of Financial Aid
3395 Airport Road, Pinehurst, NC 28374
(910) 695-3743

Shaw University

Raleigh, North Carolina
www.shawuniversity.edu   Federal Code: 002962

4-year private university and liberal arts college in large city, affiliated with Baptist faith.

Enrollment: 2,606 undergrads, 10% part-time. 565 full-time freshmen.

Selectivity: Admits less than 50% of applicants.

BASIC COSTS (2007-2008)

Tuition and fees: $10,840.

Per-credit charge: $367.

Room and board: $6,800.

FINANCIAL AID PICTURE

Students with need: Need-based aid available for full-time and part-time students. Work study available nights, weekends, and for part-time students.

Students without need: No-need awards available for academics, alumni affiliation, art, athletics, music/drama, religious affiliation.

Scholarships offered: Presidential Scholarship, based on GPA and SAT.

FINANCIAL AID PROCEDURES

Forms required: FAFSA.

Dates and Deadlines: Priority date 3/1; no closing date. Applicants notified on a rolling basis starting 3/15; must reply within 2 week(s) of notification.

CONTACT

Rochelle King, Director of Financial Aid
118 East South Street, Raleigh, NC 27601
(919) 546-8240

South College

Asheville, North Carolina
www.southcollegenc.com   Federal Code: 010264

2-year for-profit health science and technical college in small city.

Enrollment: 135 undergrads.

Selectivity: Open admission; but selective for some programs.

BASIC COSTS (2007-2008)

Tuition and fees: $12,000.

FINANCIAL AID PICTURE

Students with need: Need-based aid available for full-time and part-time students.

FINANCIAL AID PROCEDURES

Forms required: FAFSA.

Dates and Deadlines: No deadline. Applicants notified on a rolling basis.

CONTACT

Nancy Silverest, Financial Aid Director
29 Turtle Creek Drive, Asheville, NC 28803
(828) 277-5521

South Piedmont Community College

Polkton, North Carolina
www.spcc.edu   Federal Code: 007985

2-year public community college in small city.

Enrollment: 2,258 undergrads.

Selectivity: Open admission; but selective for some programs.

BASIC COSTS (2007-2008)

Tuition and fees: $1,332; out-of-state residents $7,071.

Per-credit charge: $42; out-of-state residents $233.

FINANCIAL AID PICTURE (2007-2008)

Students with need: 98% of average financial aid package awarded as scholarships/grants, 2% awarded as loans/jobs. Need-based aid available for part-time students. Work study available nights, weekends, and for part-time students.

Additional info: Small amount of nonfederal scholarship aid available.

FINANCIAL AID PROCEDURES

Forms required: FAFSA.

Dates and Deadlines: No deadline. Applicants notified on a rolling basis.

CONTACT

Vickie Cameron, Director of Financial Aid
PO Box 126, Polkton, NC 28135
(704) 272-5325

Southeastern Community College

Whiteville, North Carolina
www.sccnc.edu   Federal Code: 002964

2-year public community college in small town.

Enrollment: 1,750 undergrads.

Selectivity: Open admission; but selective for some programs.

BASIC COSTS (2007-2008)

Tuition and fees: $1,329; out-of-state residents $7,068.

Per-credit charge: $42; out-of-state residents $233.

FINANCIAL AID PICTURE (2006-2007)

Students with need: 89% of average financial aid package awarded as scholarships/grants, 11% awarded as loans/jobs. Need-based aid available for part-time students.

Students without need: No-need awards available for academics, athletics, leadership, music/drama, state/district residency.

FINANCIAL AID PROCEDURES

Forms required: FAFSA.

Dates and Deadlines: Priority date 4/1; no closing date. Applicants notified on a rolling basis starting 6/1; must reply within 2 week(s) of notification.

CONTACT

Glenn Hanson, Director of Financial Aid
4564 Chadbourn Highway, Whiteville, NC 28472-0151
(910) 642-7141 ext. 214

Southwestern Community College

Sylva, North Carolina
www.southwesterncc.edu   Federal Code: 008466

2-year public community college in rural community.

Enrollment: 809 full-time undergrads.

Selectivity: Open admission; but selective for some programs.

BASIC COSTS (2007-2008)

Tuition and fees: $1,321; out-of-state residents $7,060.

Per-credit charge: $42; out-of-state residents $233.

FINANCIAL AID PICTURE

Students with need: Need-based aid available for full-time and part-time students.

FINANCIAL AID PROCEDURES

Forms required: FAFSA.

Dates and Deadlines: Priority date 4/30; no closing date. Applicants notified on a rolling basis starting 5/1; must reply within 2 week(s) of notification.

CONTACT

Melody Lawrence, Director of Financial Aid
447 College Drive, Sylva, NC 28779
(828) 586-4091 ext. 224

Stanly Community College

Albemarle, North Carolina
www.stanly.edu   Federal Code: 011194

2-year public community college in large town.

Enrollment: 1,600 undergrads.

Selectivity: Open admission; but selective for some programs.

BASIC COSTS (2007-2008)

Tuition and fees: $1,354; out-of-state residents $7,093.

Per-credit charge: $42; out-of-state residents $233.

FINANCIAL AID PICTURE

Students with need: Need-based aid available for full-time and part-time students.

Students without need: This college awards aid only to students with need.

FINANCIAL AID PROCEDURES

Forms required: FAFSA, institutional form.

Dates and Deadlines: Closing date 4/15. Applicants notified on a rolling basis starting 6/1; must reply within 2 week(s) of notification.

Transfers: No deadline. Applicants notified on a rolling basis.

CONTACT

Petra Fields, Director of Financial Aid
141 College Drive, Albemarle, NC 28001
(704) 991-0231

Surry Community College

Dobson, North Carolina
www.surry.edu   Federal Code: 002970

2-year public community college in rural community.

Enrollment: 1,578 full-time undergrads.

Selectivity: Open admission; but selective for some programs.

BASIC COSTS (2007-2008)

Tuition and fees: $1,331; out-of-state residents $7,070.

Per-credit charge: $42; out-of-state residents $233.

FINANCIAL AID PICTURE

Students with need: Need-based aid available for full-time and part-time students. Work study available nights.

Students without need: No-need awards available for academics.

FINANCIAL AID PROCEDURES

Forms required: FAFSA, institutional form.

Dates and Deadlines: Priority date 5/1; no closing date. Applicants notified on a rolling basis starting 6/1; must reply within 2 week(s) of notification.

Transfers: Priority date 6/1.

CONTACT

Andrea Simpson, Financial Aid Officer
630 South Main Street, Dobson, NC 27017
(336) 386-3263

Tri-County Community College
Murphy, North Carolina
www.tricountycc.edu   Federal Code: 009430

2-year public community college in rural community.
Enrollment: 785 undergrads.
Selectivity: Open admission.

BASIC COSTS (2007-2008)
Tuition and fees: $1,319; out-of-state residents $7,058.
Per-credit charge: $42; out-of-state residents $233.

FINANCIAL AID PICTURE
Students with need: Need-based aid available for full-time and part-time students.
Students without need: This college awards aid only to students with need.

FINANCIAL AID PROCEDURES
Forms required: FAFSA.
Dates and Deadlines: Priority date 6/30; no closing date. Applicants notified on a rolling basis starting 6/1; must reply within 4 week(s) of notification.

CONTACT
Diane Owl, Financial Aid Officer
4600 Highway 64 East, Murphy, NC 28906
(828) 837-6810

University of North Carolina at Asheville
Asheville, North Carolina
www.unca.edu   Federal Code: 002907

4-year public university and liberal arts college in small city.
Enrollment: 3,251 undergrads, 12% part-time. 569 full-time freshmen.
Selectivity: Admits over 75% of applicants. GED not accepted.

BASIC COSTS (2007-2008)
Tuition and fees: $4,164; out-of-state residents $15,154.
Room and board: $6,230.

FINANCIAL AID PICTURE (2006-2007)
Students with need: Out of 392 full-time freshmen who applied for aid, 202 were judged to have need. Of these, 200 received aid, and 70 had their full need met. Average financial aid package met 81% of need; average scholarship/grant was $4,608; average loan was $2,440. For part-time students, average financial aid package was $7,615.
Students without need: 36 full-time freshmen who did not demonstrate need for aid received scholarships/grants; average award was $3,175. No-need awards available for academics, alumni affiliation, art, athletics, job skills, leadership, minority status, music/drama, state/district residency.
Scholarships offered: Merit: North Carolina Teaching Fellows program: $6,500 per year; for outstanding North Carolina high school students with desire and talent to become teachers. University Laurels Program: $500 to full in-state tuition and fees; essay, list of co-curricular activities and participation in Laurels Interview Day. Leadership Scholarship: $1,000, renewable; solid academic record and leadership ability. **Athletic:** 26 full-time freshmen received athletic scholarships; average amount $7,091.
Cumulative student debt: 48% of graduating class had student loans; average debt was $15,972.

FINANCIAL AID PROCEDURES
Forms required: FAFSA.
Dates and Deadlines: Priority date 3/1; no closing date. Applicants notified on a rolling basis starting 3/15.

CONTACT
Pat McClellan, Dean of Academic Administration
CPO#1320, UNCA, Asheville, NC 28804-8510
(828) 251-6535

University of North Carolina at Chapel Hill
Chapel Hill, North Carolina   Federal Code: 002974
www.unc.edu   CSS Code: 5816

4-year public university in large town.
Enrollment: 17,138 undergrads, 2% part-time. 3,800 full-time freshmen.
Selectivity: Admits less than 50% of applicants. GED not accepted.

BASIC COSTS (2007-2008)
Tuition and fees: $5,340; out-of-state residents $20,988.
Room and board: $7,960.
Additional info: Fees may be higher for dental programs.

FINANCIAL AID PICTURE (2006-2007)
Students with need: Out of 2,858 full-time freshmen who applied for aid, 1,229 were judged to have need. Of these, 1,214 received aid, and 1,165 had their full need met. Average financial aid package met 100% of need; average scholarship/grant was $9,445; average loan was $2,663. For part-time students, average financial aid package was $8,011.
Students without need: 754 full-time freshmen who did not demonstrate need for aid received scholarships/grants; average award was $4,119. No-need awards available for academics, alumni affiliation, art, athletics, leadership, music/drama, religious affiliation, state/district residency.
Scholarships offered: Merit: Morehead Scholarships: full tuition and expenses; based on academic merit, leadership, athletics, moral character; approximately 50 awarded, in-state and out-of-state. Robertson Scholarships: full tuition and expenses; based on academic merit, leadership, community service; 15 to 18 awarded to both in-state and out-of-state residents. Carolina Scholars: $7,500 for in-state residents; cost of tuition, fees, room and board for non-NC residents; based on academic merit, leadership, residency specifications; 30-40 awarded with majority going to in-state residents. Pogue Scholarships: $7,500 for NC residents; cost of tuition, fees, room and board for non-NC residents; based on academic merit, leadership, involvement and interest in issues of diversity; 22 in-state, 5 out-of-state scholarships awarded. College Fellows Awards: $2,500; based on academic merit, leadership; North Carolina residency; 15-200 awarded. Other academic scholarships: $2,500, full cost; based on academic merit, leadership, North Carolina residency; approximately 75 awarded. As a result of legislation passed in 2005, non-residents receiving "full" academic scholarships are eligible for North Carolina residency status for tuition purposes. **Athletic:** 94 full-time freshmen received athletic scholarships; average amount $11,708.
Additional info: Carolina meets 100% of all need documented for both resident and non-resident undergraduates who quality for need based aid, with a favorable mix of approximately 2/3 grants and scholarships and 1/3 loans and work study.

FINANCIAL AID PROCEDURES
Forms required: FAFSA, CSS PROFILE.
Dates and Deadlines: Priority date 3/1; no closing date. Applicants notified on a rolling basis starting 3/15; must reply by 5/1.

CONTACT
Shirley Ort, Director for Office of Student Aid/Associate Provost
Jackson Hall CB #2200, Chapel Hill, NC 27599-2200
(919) 962-8396

University of North Carolina at Charlotte

Charlotte, North Carolina
www.uncc.edu
Federal Code: 002975

4-year public university in very large city.
Enrollment: 17,481 undergrads, 15% part-time. 2,933 full-time freshmen.
Selectivity: Admits over 75% of applicants.

BASIC COSTS (2007-2008)

Tuition and fees: $4,153; out-of-state residents $14,565.
Room and board: $6,034.

FINANCIAL AID PICTURE

Students with need: Need-based aid available for full-time and part-time students.
Students without need: No-need awards available for academics, athletics, leadership, music/drama.

FINANCIAL AID PROCEDURES

Forms required: FAFSA.
Dates and Deadlines: Priority date 4/1; no closing date. Applicants notified on a rolling basis starting 4/1; must reply within 3 week(s) of notification.

CONTACT

Anthony Carter, Director of Student Financial Aid
9201 University City Boulevard, Charlotte, NC 28223-0001
(704) 687-2461

University of North Carolina at Greensboro

Greensboro, North Carolina
www.uncg.edu
Federal Code: 002976

4-year public university in small city.
Enrollment: 13,245 undergrads, 13% part-time. 2,433 full-time freshmen.
Selectivity: Admits 50 to 75% of applicants. GED not accepted.

BASIC COSTS (2007-2008)

Tuition and fees: $4,029; out-of-state residents $15,297.
Room and board: $6,051.

FINANCIAL AID PICTURE (2007-2008)

Students with need: Out of 1,901 full-time freshmen who applied for aid, 1,681 were judged to have need. Of these, 1,649 received aid, and 493 had their full need met. Average financial aid package met 57% of need; average scholarship/grant was $5,831; average loan was $3,247. For part-time students, average financial aid package was $5,910.
Students without need: 92 full-time freshmen who did not demonstrate need for aid received scholarships/grants; average award was $4,245. No-need awards available for academics, alumni affiliation, art, athletics, leadership, music/drama, state/district residency.
Scholarships offered: 35 full-time freshmen received athletic scholarships; average amount $7,715.
Cumulative student debt: 62% of graduating class had student loans; average debt was $16,708.

FINANCIAL AID PROCEDURES

Forms required: FAFSA.
Dates and Deadlines: Priority date 3/1; no closing date. Applicants notified on a rolling basis starting 3/15; must reply within 3 week(s) of notification.

CONTACT

Deborah Tollefson, Director of Financial Aid
1400 Spring Garden Street, Greensboro, NC 27402-6170
(336) 334-5702

University of North Carolina at Pembroke

Pembroke, North Carolina
www.uncp.edu
Federal Code: 002954

4-year public university and liberal arts college in small town.
Enrollment: 5,002 undergrads, 18% part-time. 1,101 full-time freshmen.
Selectivity: Admits over 75% of applicants.

BASIC COSTS (2007-2008)

Tuition and fees: $3,507; out-of-state residents $12,767.
Room and board: $6,200.

FINANCIAL AID PICTURE

Students with need: Need-based aid available for full-time and part-time students.
Students without need: No-need awards available for alumni affiliation.

FINANCIAL AID PROCEDURES

Forms required: FAFSA.
Dates and Deadlines: Closing date 3/15. Applicants notified on a rolling basis starting 4/15; must reply within 2 week(s) of notification.

CONTACT

Bruce Blackmon, Director of Financial Aid
Box 1510, Pembroke, NC 28372
(910) 521-6255

University of North Carolina at Wilmington

Wilmington, North Carolina
www.uncw.edu
Federal Code: 002984

4-year public university in small city.
Enrollment: 10,481 undergrads, 7% part-time. 1,936 full-time freshmen.
Selectivity: Admits 50 to 75% of applicants.

BASIC COSTS (2007-2008)

Tuition and fees: $4,398; out-of-state residents $14,361.
Room and board: $6,999.

FINANCIAL AID PICTURE (2006-2007)

Students with need: Out of 1,012 full-time freshmen who applied for aid, 545 were judged to have need. Of these, 545 received aid, and 367 had their full need met. Average financial aid package met 88% of need; average scholarship/grant was $3,763; average loan was $2,792. Need-based aid available for part-time students.
Students without need: 50 full-time freshmen who did not demonstrate need for aid received scholarships/grants; average award was $1,355. No-need awards available for academics, athletics, leadership, minority status, music/drama, state/district residency.
Scholarships offered: 37 full-time freshmen received athletic scholarships; average amount $5,575.
Cumulative student debt: 52% of graduating class had student loans; average debt was $15,620.

FINANCIAL AID PROCEDURES

Forms required: FAFSA, institutional form.
Dates and Deadlines: Priority date 3/15; no closing date. Applicants notified on a rolling basis starting 4/1; must reply within 3 week(s) of notification.

CONTACT

Emily Bliss, Director of Financial Aid and Veteran Services
601 South College Road, Wilmington, NC 28403-5904
(910) 962-3177

PART III: FINANCIAL AID COLLEGE BY COLLEGE

Vance-Granville Community College

Henderson, North Carolina
www.vgcc.edu

Federal Code: 009903

2-year public community college in large town.

Enrollment: 3,343 undergrads.

Selectivity: Open admission; but selective for some programs.

BASIC COSTS (2007-2008)

Tuition and fees: $1,298; out-of-state residents $7,037.

Per-credit charge: $42; out-of-state residents $233.

FINANCIAL AID PICTURE (2006-2007)

Students with need: Need-based aid available for part-time students.

Students without need: No-need awards available for academics.

FINANCIAL AID PROCEDURES

Forms required: FAFSA.

Dates and Deadlines: Closing date 3/15. Applicants notified on a rolling basis starting 5/1; must reply within 2 week(s) of notification.

CONTACT

Frank Clark, Financial Aid Officer
Box 917, Henderson, NC 27536
(252) 492-2061

Wake Forest University

Winston-Salem, North Carolina
www.wfu.edu

Federal Code: 002978
CSS Code: 5885

4-year private university in small city.

Enrollment: 4,405 undergrads, 1% part-time. 1,123 full-time freshmen.

Selectivity: Admits less than 50% of applicants.

BASIC COSTS (2008-2009)

Tuition and fees: $36,975.

Per-credit charge: $1,517.

Room and board: $9,945.

Additional info: Tuition covers cost of an IBM Thinkpad computer and inkjet printer for freshmen.

FINANCIAL AID PICTURE (2007-2008)

Students with need: Out of 448 full-time freshmen who applied for aid, 345 were judged to have need. Of these, 342 received aid, and 278 had their full need met. Average financial aid package met 99% of need; average scholarship/grant was $21,976; average loan was $7,222. For part-time students, average financial aid package was $22,476.

Students without need: 66 full-time freshmen who did not demonstrate need for aid received scholarships/grants; average award was $12,427. No-need awards available for academics, alumni affiliation, art, athletics, leadership, music/drama, religious affiliation, ROTC, state/district residency.

Scholarships offered: *Merit:* Reynolds Scholarship: full tuition, room and board, books, fees for 4 years, also provides for summer study; 6 awarded. Joseph G. Gordon Scholarship: full tuition for 4 years; for underrepresented students with exceptional promise and leadership; 7 awarded. Carswell Scholarship: based on intellect and leadership; between 3/4 and full tuition for 4 years, including summer grant for travel and study projects; 10-12 awarded. Presidential Scholarship: for students gifted in areas such as writing, studio art, music theater, debate, leadership, dance, entrepreneurship, and community service; 20 awarded. Poteat Scholarship: $12,100; for North Carolina residents who are active members of a Baptist Church in North Carolina, must make an active contribution to church and society; 18 awarded. *Athletic:* 60 full-time freshmen received athletic scholarships; average amount $33,640.

Cumulative student debt: 37% of graduating class had student loans; average debt was $23,397.

Additional info: In fall 2008, freshmen with an annual family income of less than $40,000 will have their student loans capped at $4,000 per year during their college years. Other financial aid to the students will come from grant and scholarship increases and work-study opportunities.

FINANCIAL AID PROCEDURES

Forms required: FAFSA, CSS PROFILE, state aid form.

Dates and Deadlines: Priority date 2/1; closing date 3/1. Applicants notified by 4/1; must reply by 5/1 or within 4 week(s) of notification.

CONTACT

William Wells, Director of Financial Aid
PO Box 7305, Winston-Salem, NC 27109-7305
(336) 758-5154

Wake Technical Community College

Raleigh, North Carolina
www.waketech.edu

Federal Code: 004844

2-year public community and technical college in small city.

Enrollment: 11,997 undergrads.

Selectivity: Open admission; but selective for some programs.

BASIC COSTS (2007-2008)

Tuition and fees: $1,320; out-of-state residents $7,059.

Per-credit charge: $42; out-of-state residents $233.

FINANCIAL AID PICTURE

Students with need: Need-based aid available for full-time and part-time students.

Students without need: No-need awards available for academics, job skills, leadership, state/district residency.

FINANCIAL AID PROCEDURES

Forms required: FAFSA, institutional form.

Dates and Deadlines: Priority date 3/15; no closing date. Applicants notified on a rolling basis starting 4/1; must reply within 2 week(s) of notification.

Transfers: Child care grant and NCCCS Grant and Loan Program available.

CONTACT

Regina Huggins, Financial Aid Director
9101 Fayetteville Road, Raleigh, NC 27603
(919) 662-3254

Warren Wilson College

Asheville, North Carolina
www.warren-wilson.edu

Federal Code: 002979

4-year private liberal arts college in small city, affiliated with Presbyterian Church (USA).

Enrollment: 869 undergrads, 1% part-time. 235 full-time freshmen.

Selectivity: Admits over 75% of applicants.

BASIC COSTS (2007-2008)

Tuition and fees: $21,384.

Room and board: $6,700.

Additional info: All resident students required to work 15 hours per week in college's work program. $2,472 earnings credited toward tuition costs.

FINANCIAL AID PICTURE

Students with need: Need-based aid available for full-time and part-time students.

Students without need: No-need awards available for academics, art, job skills, leadership, religious affiliation, state/district residency.

Scholarships offered: Wilson Honor; 1 awarded; $5,000 annually. Warner Honor; 2 awarded; $4,000 annually. Transfer Honor; 2 awarded; $2,000 annually. Sutton Honor; 20 awarded; $1,000 annually. Work Scholarship; 2

awarded; $1,500 annually. Service Scholarship; 2 awarded; $1,500 annually. National Merit; unlimited numbers awarded; $4,000 annually. Valedictorian/Salutatorian Scholarship; 10 awarded; $2,000 annually. North Carolina Presidential Scholarship; 30 awarded; $1,000 annually. All renewable with 3.0 cumulative GPA and successful completion of a minimum of 12 credit hours each semester.

FINANCIAL AID PROCEDURES

Forms required: FAFSA, state aid form, institutional form.
Dates and Deadlines: Priority date 4/1; no closing date. Applicants notified on a rolling basis starting 3/1; must reply within 3 week(s) of notification.
Transfers: No deadline. Applicants notified on a rolling basis starting 3/1; must reply within 3 week(s) of notification.

CONTACT

Kathy Pack, Director of Financial Aid
Office of Admission, Asheville, NC 28815-9000
(828) 771-2082

Wayne Community College

Goldsboro, North Carolina
www.waynecc.edu
Federal Code: 008216

2-year public community college in large town.
Enrollment: 2,950 undergrads.
Selectivity: Open admission; but selective for some programs.

BASIC COSTS (2007-2008)

Tuition and fees: $1,316; out-of-state residents $7,055.
Per-credit charge: $42; out-of-state residents $233.

FINANCIAL AID PICTURE (2006-2007)

Students with need: 89% of average financial aid package awarded as scholarships/grants, 11% awarded as loans/jobs. Need-based aid available for part-time students. Work study available nights.
Students without need: No-need awards available for academics, job skills.

FINANCIAL AID PROCEDURES

Forms required: FAFSA, institutional form.
Dates and Deadlines: Priority date 3/15; no closing date. Applicants notified on a rolling basis starting 6/1; must reply within 2 week(s) of notification.

CONTACT

Karen Statler, Financial Aid Director
PO Box 8002, Goldsboro, NC 27533-8002
(919) 735-5151

Western Carolina University

Cullowhee, North Carolina
www.wcu.edu
Federal Code: 002981

4-year public university in small town.
Enrollment: 7,006 undergrads, 14% part-time. 1,250 full-time freshmen.
Selectivity: Admits 50 to 75% of applicants.

BASIC COSTS (2007-2008)

Tuition and fees: $4,278; out-of-state residents $13,861.
Room and board: $5,305.

FINANCIAL AID PICTURE (2007-2008)

Students with need: Out of 962 full-time freshmen who applied for aid, 673 were judged to have need. Of these, 666 received aid, and 375 had their full need met. Average financial aid package met 87% of need; average scholarship/grant was $5,906; average loan was $2,776. For part-time students, average financial aid package was $5,147.
Students without need: 59 full-time freshmen who did not demonstrate need for aid received scholarships/grants; average award was $2,109. No-

need awards available for academics, art, athletics, leadership, music/drama, state/district residency.
Scholarships offered: 70 full-time freshmen received athletic scholarships; average amount $6,419.
Cumulative student debt: 32% of graduating class had student loans; average debt was $11,285.

FINANCIAL AID PROCEDURES

Forms required: FAFSA, institutional form.
Dates and Deadlines: Priority date 3/31; no closing date. Applicants notified on a rolling basis starting 4/1.

CONTACT

Nancy Dillard, Director of Student Financial Aid
102 Camp Building, Cullowhee, NC 28723
(828) 227-7290

Western Piedmont Community College

Morganton, North Carolina
www.wpcc.edu
Federal Code: 002982

2-year public community college in large town.
Enrollment: 2,026 undergrads, 45% part-time. 292 full-time freshmen.
Selectivity: Open admission; but selective for some programs.

BASIC COSTS (2007-2008)

Tuition and fees: $1,287; out-of-state residents $7,026.
Per-credit charge: $42; out-of-state residents $233.

FINANCIAL AID PICTURE (2006-2007)

Students with need: Out of 196 full-time freshmen who applied for aid, 163 were judged to have need. Of these, 143 received aid, and 7 had their full need met. Average financial aid package met 65% of need; average scholarship/grant was $2,401; average loan was $2,900. For part-time students, average financial aid package was $3,305.
Students without need: 3 full-time freshmen who did not demonstrate need for aid received scholarships/grants; average award was $1,500. No-need awards available for academics.

FINANCIAL AID PROCEDURES

Forms required: FAFSA.
Dates and Deadlines: Priority date 6/1; no closing date. Applicants notified on a rolling basis starting 6/15; must reply within 2 week(s) of notification.

CONTACT

Keith Conley, Director of Financial Aid
1001 Burkemont Avenue, Morganton, NC 28655-4504
(828) 438-6042

Wilkes Community College

Wilkesboro, North Carolina
www.wilkescc.edu
Federal Code: 002983

2-year public community college in small town.
Enrollment: 2,536 undergrads.
Selectivity: Open admission; but selective for some programs.

BASIC COSTS (2007-2008)

Tuition and fees: $1,340; out-of-state residents $7,079.
Per-credit charge: $42; out-of-state residents $233.

FINANCIAL AID PICTURE

Students with need: Need-based aid available for full-time and part-time students. Work study available nights.
Students without need: No-need awards available for academics, art, job skills, leadership, minority status, music/drama, state/district residency.

FINANCIAL AID PROCEDURES

Forms required: FAFSA.

Dates and Deadlines: Priority date 5/1; closing date 6/1. Applicants notified on a rolling basis starting 4/1; must reply by 8/1.

Transfers: No deadline.

CONTACT

Vickie Call, Director of Financial Aid

1328 South Collegiate Drive, Wilkesboro, NC 28697-0120

(336) 838-6146

Wilson Community College

Wilson, North Carolina

www.wilsoncc.edu

Federal Code: 004845

2-year public community college in large town.

Enrollment: 1,510 undergrads.

Selectivity: Open admission; but selective for some programs.

BASIC COSTS (2007-2008)

Tuition and fees: $1,301; out-of-state residents $7,040.

Per-credit charge: $42; out-of-state residents $233.

FINANCIAL AID PICTURE

Students with need: Need-based aid available for full-time and part-time students.

Students without need: No-need awards available for academics.

FINANCIAL AID PROCEDURES

Forms required: FAFSA, institutional form.

Dates and Deadlines: Priority date 3/15; no closing date. Applicants notified on a rolling basis.

CONTACT

S Bissette, Director of Financial Aid and Veterans Affairs

Box 4305, Wilson, NC 27893-0305

(252) 246-1274

Wingate University

Wingate, North Carolina

www.wingate.edu

Federal Code: 002985

4-year private university and liberal arts college in small town, affiliated with Baptist faith.

Enrollment: 1,462 undergrads, 4% part-time. 426 full-time freshmen.

Selectivity: Admits 50 to 75% of applicants.

BASIC COSTS (2008-2009)

Tuition and fees: $19,350.

Per-credit charge: $610.

Room and board: $7,700.

Additional info: Some music and art courses carry a fee.

FINANCIAL AID PICTURE (2007-2008)

Students with need: Out of 380 full-time freshmen who applied for aid, 300 were judged to have need. Of these, 300 received aid, and 30 had their full need met. Average financial aid package met 82% of need; average scholarship/grant was $6,282; average loan was $2,049. For part-time students, average financial aid package was $3,728.

Students without need: 40 full-time freshmen who did not demonstrate need for aid received scholarships/grants; average award was $3,327. No-need awards available for academics, alumni affiliation, art, athletics, music/drama, state/district residency.

Scholarships offered: 41 full-time freshmen received athletic scholarships; average amount $4,616.

Cumulative student debt: 76% of graduating class had student loans; average debt was $29,086.

Additional info: Institutional aid may not be available after June 1.

FINANCIAL AID PROCEDURES

Forms required: FAFSA.

Dates and Deadlines: Priority date 5/1; no closing date. Applicants notified on a rolling basis starting 3/1; must reply within 2 week(s) of notification.

Transfers: Priority date 3/1; no deadline. Applicants notified on a rolling basis; must reply within 2 week(s) of notification. Must submit financial aid transcripts from previous colleges attended.

CONTACT

Teresa Williams, Director of Financial Planning

Campus Box 3059, Wingate, NC 28174-0157

(704) 233-8209

Winston-Salem State University

Winston-Salem, North Carolina

www.wssu.edu

Federal Code: 002986

4-year public university and health science college in small city.

Enrollment: 5,423 undergrads, 11% part-time. 992 full-time freshmen.

Selectivity: Admits 50 to 75% of applicants.

BASIC COSTS (2007-2008)

Tuition and fees: $3,299; out-of-state residents $11,940.

Room and board: $5,670.

FINANCIAL AID PICTURE (2006-2007)

Students with need: Out of 958 full-time freshmen who applied for aid, 931 were judged to have need. Of these, 786 received aid, and 94 had their full need met. Average financial aid package met 51% of need; average scholarship/grant was $2,049; average loan was $2,164. For part-time students, average financial aid package was $2,772.

Students without need: 17 full-time freshmen who did not demonstrate need for aid received scholarships/grants; average award was $4,024. No-need awards available for academics, athletics, ROTC, state/district residency.

Scholarships offered: 32 full-time freshmen received athletic scholarships; average amount $2,239.

Cumulative student debt: 83% of graduating class had student loans; average debt was $10,300.

FINANCIAL AID PROCEDURES

Forms required: FAFSA.

Dates and Deadlines: Closing date 3/15. Applicants notified by 5/15; must reply within 2 week(s) of notification.

Transfers: Closing date 3/15. Applicants notified on a rolling basis.

CONTACT

Raymond Solomon, Director of Financial Aid

601 Martin Luther King Jr Drive, Winston-Salem, NC 27110

(336) 750-3280

North Dakota

Bismarck State College

Bismarck, North Dakota

www.bismarckstate.edu

Federal Code: 002988

2-year public community college in small city.

Enrollment: 3,591 undergrads, 35% part-time. 763 full-time freshmen.

Selectivity: Open admission; but selective for some programs.

BASIC COSTS (2007-2008)

Tuition and fees: $3,773; out-of-state residents $9,124.

Per-credit charge: $107; out-of-state residents $285.

Room and board: $4,004.

Additional info: Full-time annual tuition for residents of Minnesota: $4,063. Full-time annual tuition for residents of South Dakota, Montana, Manitoba, Saskatchewan: $4,005. Tuition/fee waivers available for minority students.

FINANCIAL AID PICTURE

Students with need: Need-based aid available for full-time and part-time students. Work study available nights, weekends, and for part-time students.

Students without need: This college awards aid only to students with need.

Scholarships offered: Academic Scholarship; $900; for students enrolled in 15 credit hours who maintain 3.0 GPA; 79 awarded.

FINANCIAL AID PROCEDURES

Forms required: FAFSA.

Dates and Deadlines: Priority date 3/15; no closing date. Applicants notified on a rolling basis starting 6/1; must reply within 3 week(s) of notification.

Transfers: Financial aid based on funds available.

CONTACT

Jeffrey Jacobs, Director of Financial Aid

PO Box 5587, Bismarck, ND 58506-5587

(701) 224-5494

Dickinson State University

Dickinson, North Dakota

www.dsu.nodak.edu   Federal Code: 002989

4-year public university in large town.

Enrollment: 2,669 undergrads, 33% part-time. 358 full-time freshmen.

Selectivity: Open admission; but selective for some programs.

BASIC COSTS (2007-2008)

Tuition and fees: $4,749; out-of-state residents $11,143.

Room and board: $4,076.

Additional info: Tuition for Minnesota residents: $3,976. Tuition for South Dakota, Montana, Manitoba, Saskatchewan residents: $4,558. Tuition/fee waivers available for minority students.

FINANCIAL AID PICTURE (2006-2007)

Students with need: 38% of average financial aid package awarded as scholarships/grants, 62% awarded as loans/jobs. Need-based aid available for part-time students. Work study available nights, weekends, and for part-time students.

Students without need: No-need awards available for academics, alumni affiliation, art, athletics, job skills, leadership, minority status, music/drama, religious affiliation, state/district residency.

Additional info: Scholarships available to new students, priority deadline December 1.

FINANCIAL AID PROCEDURES

Forms required: FAFSA.

Dates and Deadlines: Priority date 3/15; no closing date. Must reply within 2 week(s) of notification.

CONTACT

Sandy Klein, Director of Financial Aid

291 Campus Drive, Dickinson, ND 58601-4896

(701) 483-2371

Jamestown College

Jamestown, North Dakota

www.jc.edu   Federal Code: 002990

4-year private liberal arts college in large town, affiliated with Presbyterian Church (USA).

Enrollment: 981 undergrads, 4% part-time. 265 full-time freshmen.

Selectivity: Admits over 75% of applicants.

BASIC COSTS (2008-2009)

Tuition and fees: $15,035.

Room and board: $4,850.

FINANCIAL AID PICTURE (2007-2008)

Students with need: Out of 241 full-time freshmen who applied for aid, 190 were judged to have need. Of these, 190 received aid, and 49 had their full need met. Average financial aid package met 79% of need; average scholarship/grant was $6,979; average loan was $3,421. For part-time students, average financial aid package was $4,491.

Students without need: 76 full-time freshmen who did not demonstrate need for aid received scholarships/grants; average award was $8,126. No-need awards available for academics, alumni affiliation, art, athletics, leadership, music/drama, religious affiliation.

Scholarships offered: *Merit:* Wilson Scholarships; full tuition; for academic merit and leadership. Presidential Scholarships; $10,000 annually; for academic merit and leadership. Honor Scholarships; $7,500 annually; for academic merit and leadership. Arnold Chemistry Scholarships; $2,500 annually; for chemistry majors. Trustee scholarships; $6,500 annually. Dean-s Scholarship; $4,500. Heritage Scholarship; $3,500. *Athletic:* 62 full-time freshmen received athletic scholarships; average amount $1,896.

Cumulative student debt: 91% of graduating class had student loans; average debt was $22,653.

Additional info: FAFSA must be received by March 15th for North Dakota residents to be considered for North Dakota state grants.

FINANCIAL AID PROCEDURES

Forms required: FAFSA.

Dates and Deadlines: Priority date 3/1; no closing date. Applicants notified on a rolling basis starting 2/1.

Transfers: No deadline. Applicants notified on a rolling basis starting 2/1.

CONTACT

Margery Michael, Director of Financial Aid

6081 College Lane, Jamestown, ND 58405

(701) 252-3467 ext. 2556

Lake Region State College

Devils Lake, North Dakota

www.lrsc.nodak.edu   Federal Code: 002991

2-year public community and technical college in small town.

Enrollment: 645 undergrads.

Selectivity: Open admission; but selective for some programs.

BASIC COSTS (2007-2008)

Tuition and fees: $3,762; out-of-state residents $3,762.

Per-credit charge: $122; out-of-state residents $122.

Room and board: $4,537.

Additional info: Tuition/fee waivers available for minority students.

FINANCIAL AID PICTURE (2006-2007)

Students with need: 77% of average financial aid package awarded as scholarships/grants, 23% awarded as loans/jobs. Need-based aid available for part-time students. Work study available nights, weekends, and for part-time students.

Students without need: No-need awards available for academics, athletics, leadership, minority status, music/drama.

FINANCIAL AID PROCEDURES

Forms required: FAFSA.

Dates and Deadlines: Priority date 3/15; no closing date. Applicants notified on a rolling basis starting 5/15; must reply within 2 week(s) of notification.

Transfers: No deadline. Applicants notified on a rolling basis starting 5/1; must reply within 4 week(s) of notification.

CONTACT

Katie Nettell, Director of Financial Aid
1801 College Drive North, Devils Lake, ND 58301-1598
(701) 662-1516

Mayville State University
Mayville, North Dakota
www.mayvillestate.edu
Federal Code: 002993

4-year public business and teachers college in small town.

Enrollment: 769 undergrads, 38% part-time. 137 full-time freshmen.

Selectivity: Open admission; but selective for some programs.

BASIC COSTS (2007-2008)

Tuition and fees: $5,438; out-of-state residents $7,335.

Per-credit charge: $158; out-of-state residents $237.

Room and board: $4,072.

Additional info: Full-time tuition for South Dakota, Montana, Kansas, Michigan, Missouri, Nebraska, Manitoba, and Saskatchewan residents: $4,743. Full-time tuition for Minnesota residents: $4,082. All other states and Canadian provinces: $5,692. Tuition/fee waivers available for minority students.

FINANCIAL AID PICTURE (2006-2007)

Students with need: Out of 128 full-time freshmen who applied for aid, 99 were judged to have need. Of these, 98 received aid, and 25 had their full need met. Average financial aid package met 40% of need; average scholarship/grant was $2,726; average loan was $2,718. For part-time students, average financial aid package was $6,162.

Students without need: 75 full-time freshmen who did not demonstrate need for aid received scholarships/grants; average award was $710. No-need awards available for academics, athletics, leadership, minority status, music/drama, state/district residency.

Scholarships offered: *Merit:* Non-resident academic scholarship; $450-1,900 per year; based on academic criteria of students from select states. *Athletic:* 23 full-time freshmen received athletic scholarships; average amount $1,345.

Cumulative student debt: 93% of graduating class had student loans; average debt was $17,161.

FINANCIAL AID PROCEDURES

Forms required: FAFSA.

Dates and Deadlines: Priority date 2/15; no closing date. Applicants notified on a rolling basis starting 5/1; must reply within 2 week(s) of notification.

CONTACT

Shirley Hanson, Director of Financial Aid
330 Third Street, NE, Mayville, ND 58257-1299
(701) 788-4893

Medcenter One College of Nursing
Bismarck, North Dakota
www.medcenterone.com/collegeofnursing
Federal Code: 009354

Upper-division private nursing college in small city.

Enrollment: 89 undergrads, 2% part-time.

BASIC COSTS (2008-2009)

Tuition and fees: $10,017.

Per-credit charge: $386.

FINANCIAL AID PICTURE (2006-2007)

Students with need: Average financial aid package for all full-time undergraduates was $12,174; for part-time $3,304. 44% awarded as scholarships/grants, 56% awarded as loans/jobs. Work study available weekends and for part-time students.

FINANCIAL AID PROCEDURES

Dates and Deadlines: No deadline.

Transfers: Priority date 3/1; no deadline. Applicants notified on a rolling basis starting 6/1; must reply within 2 week(s) of notification.

CONTACT

Janell Thomas, Director/Registrar
512 North 7th Street, Bismarck, ND 58501-4425
(701) 323-6270

Minot State University
Minot, North Dakota
www.minotstateu.edu
Federal Code: 002994

4-year public university and liberal arts college in large town.

Enrollment: 3,140 undergrads, 29% part-time. 419 full-time freshmen.

Selectivity: Admits over 75% of applicants.

BASIC COSTS (2007-2008)

Tuition and fees: $4,773; out-of-state residents $11,415.

Per-credit charge: $166; out-of-state residents $443.

Room and board: $3,914.

Additional info: Tuition/fee waivers available for minority students.

FINANCIAL AID PICTURE (2007-2008)

Students with need: Out of 403 full-time freshmen who applied for aid, 259 were judged to have need. Of these, 257 received aid, and 32 had their full need met. Average financial aid package met 86% of need; average scholarship/grant was $3,545; average loan was $3,629. For part-time students, average financial aid package was $6,318.

Students without need: 102 full-time freshmen who did not demonstrate need for aid received scholarships/grants; average award was $989. No-need awards available for academics, alumni affiliation, art, athletics, minority status, music/drama, state/district residency.

Scholarships offered: 49 full-time freshmen received athletic scholarships; average amount $1,175.

Cumulative student debt: 91% of graduating class had student loans; average debt was $16,035.

Additional info: Scholarship application deadline is 2/15.

FINANCIAL AID PROCEDURES

Forms required: FAFSA.

Dates and Deadlines: Priority date 3/15; no closing date. Applicants notified on a rolling basis starting 5/1; must reply within 2 week(s) of notification.

Transfers: Must reply within 4 week(s) of notification.

CONTACT

Dale Gehring, Director of Financial Aid
500 University Avenue West, Minot, ND 58707-5002
(701) 858-3375

Minot State University: Bottineau Campus

Bottineau, North Dakota
www.misu-b.nodak.edu — Federal Code: 002995

2-year public branch campus and junior college in small town.
Enrollment: 637 undergrads, 52% part-time. 180 full-time freshmen.
Selectivity: Open admission.

BASIC COSTS (2007-2008)

Tuition and fees: $3,634; out-of-state residents $5,120.
Per-credit charge: $124; out-of-state residents $310.
Room and board: $3,980.
Additional info: Tuition/fee waivers available for minority students.

FINANCIAL AID PICTURE

Students with need: Need-based aid available for full-time and part-time students. Work study available nights, weekends, and for part-time students.
Students without need: No-need awards available for academics, alumni affiliation, athletics, music/drama.

FINANCIAL AID PROCEDURES

Forms required: FAFSA.
Dates and Deadlines: Priority date 4/15; no closing date. Applicants notified on a rolling basis starting 6/1; must reply within 2 week(s) of notification.

CONTACT

Diane Christenson, Financial Aid Officer
105 Simrall Boulevard, Bottineau, ND 58318-1198
(701) 228-5437

North Dakota State College of Science

Wahpeton, North Dakota
www.ndscs.nodak.edu — Federal Code: 002996

2-year public junior and technical college in small town.
Enrollment: 3,190 undergrads.
Selectivity: Open admission; but selective for some programs.

BASIC COSTS (2007-2008)

Tuition and fees: $3,695; out-of-state residents $9,051.
Per-credit charge: $107; out-of-state residents $285.
Room and board: $4,258.
Additional info: Full-time tuition for Minnesota residents: $4,932. Full-time tuition for South Dakota, Montana, Saskatchewan, Manitoba residents: $4,776. Tuition/fee waivers available for minority students.

FINANCIAL AID PICTURE

Students with need: Need-based aid available for full-time and part-time students. Work study available nights, weekends, and for part-time students.
Students without need: No-need awards available for academics, athletics, job skills, music/drama, state/district residency.

FINANCIAL AID PROCEDURES

Forms required: FAFSA, institutional form.
Dates and Deadlines: Priority date 4/15; no closing date. Applicants notified on a rolling basis starting 6/1; must reply within 2 week(s) of notification.
Transfers: Priority date 3/15; no deadline. Must reply within 2 week(s) of notification.

CONTACT

Shelly Blome, Director of Financial Aid
800 North 6th Street, Wahpeton, ND 58076
(701) 671-2207

North Dakota State University

Fargo, North Dakota
www.ndsu.edu — Federal Code: 002997

4-year public university in small city.
Enrollment: 10,403 undergrads, 10% part-time. 2,190 full-time freshmen.
Selectivity: Admits over 75% of applicants.

BASIC COSTS (2007-2008)

Tuition and fees: $5,975; out-of-state residents $14,346.
Per-credit charge: $209; out-of-state residents $558.
Room and board: $5,820.
Additional info: Tuition for South Dakota, Montana, Manitoba, Saskatchewan residents: $7,519. Tuition/fee waivers available for minority students.

FINANCIAL AID PICTURE (2006-2007)

Students with need: Out of 1,934 full-time freshmen who applied for aid, 1,345 were judged to have need. Of these, 1,317 received aid, and 338 had their full need met. Average financial aid package met 36% of need; average scholarship/grant was $3,275; average loan was $3,370. For part-time students, average financial aid package was $5,369.
Students without need: 531 full-time freshmen who did not demonstrate need for aid received scholarships/grants; average award was $1,467. No-need awards available for academics, alumni affiliation, art, athletics, leadership, minority status, music/drama, ROTC, state/district residency.
Scholarships offered: *Merit:* New Student Scholarships: vary in amount awarded; based on 25 ACT or 1200 SAT (exclusive of writing) and 3.5 GPA. *Athletic:* 64 full-time freshmen received athletic scholarships; average amount $8,227.
Cumulative student debt: 68% of graduating class had student loans; average debt was $24,001.

FINANCIAL AID PROCEDURES

Forms required: FAFSA.
Dates and Deadlines: Closing date 3/15. Applicants notified on a rolling basis starting 3/15.
Transfers: Priority date 3/15.

CONTACT

Jeanne Enebo, Director of Student Financial Services
Ceres Hall 124, Fargo, ND 58105-5454
(701) 231-7533

Rasmussen College: Fargo

Fargo, North Dakota
www.rasmussen.edu — Federal Code: 004846

4-year for-profit career college in small city.
Enrollment: 730 undergrads, 49% part-time. 53 full-time freshmen.
Selectivity: Open admission.

BASIC COSTS (2007-2008)

Tuition and fees: $11,700.
Additional info: Per course tuition ranges from $845 to $1025 depending on course level.

FINANCIAL AID PICTURE

Students with need: Need-based aid available for full-time and part-time students. Work study available nights.
Students without need: This college awards aid only to students with need.
Additional info: Discount for members of the military and their families.

FINANCIAL AID PROCEDURES

Forms required: FAFSA, institutional form.

Dates and Deadlines: No deadline. Applicants notified on a rolling basis starting 1/1.

CONTACT

Darwin Olson, Financial Aid Director

4012 19th Avenue SW, Fargo, ND 58103

(701) 277-3889

Sitting Bull College

Fort Yates, North Dakota

www.sittingbull.edu

Federal Code: 014993

2-year public community college in small town.

Enrollment: 310 undergrads.

Selectivity: Open admission.

BASIC COSTS (2008-2009)

Tuition and fees: $3,140.

Per-credit charge: $100.

FINANCIAL AID PICTURE

Students with need: Need-based aid available for full-time and part-time students.

FINANCIAL AID PROCEDURES

Forms required: FAFSA, institutional form.

Dates and Deadlines: Priority date 5/1; no closing date. Applicants notified on a rolling basis starting 7/15; must reply within 6 week(s) of notification.

CONTACT

Donna Seaboy, Financial Aid Director

1341 92nd Street, Fort Yates, ND 58538

(701) 854-8013

Trinity Bible College

Ellendale, North Dakota

www.trinitybiblecollege.edu

Federal Code: 012059

4-year private Bible college in rural community, affiliated with Assemblies of God.

Enrollment: 283 undergrads, 10% part-time. 60 full-time freshmen.

Selectivity: Admits over 75% of applicants.

BASIC COSTS (2007-2008)

Tuition and fees: $11,970.

Per-credit charge: $355.

Room and board: $4,660.

FINANCIAL AID PICTURE

Students with need: Need-based aid available for full-time and part-time students. Work study available nights, weekends, and for part-time students.

Students without need: No-need awards available for academics, alumni affiliation, art, leadership, music/drama, religious affiliation.

FINANCIAL AID PROCEDURES

Forms required: FAFSA.

Dates and Deadlines: Priority date 3/1; closing date 9/1. Applicants notified on a rolling basis starting 3/1; must reply within 3 week(s) of notification.

CONTACT

Don Flaherty, Financial Aid Director

50 6th Avenue South, Ellendale, ND 58436-7150

(888) 822-2329

United Tribes Technical College

Bismarck, North Dakota

www.uttc.edu

Federal Code: 014470

2-year private technical college in small city.

Enrollment: 588 undergrads.

Selectivity: Open admission; but selective for some programs.

BASIC COSTS (2007-2008)

Additional info: Tuition/fee waivers available for adults, minority students.

FINANCIAL AID PICTURE

Students with need: Need-based aid available for full-time and part-time students. Work study available nights, weekends, and for part-time students.

FINANCIAL AID PROCEDURES

Forms required: FAFSA.

Dates and Deadlines: Priority date 5/29; no closing date. Applicants notified on a rolling basis starting 5/29; must reply within 2 week(s) of notification.

CONTACT

Nathan Stratton, Financial Aid Director

3315 University Drive, Bismarck, ND 58504

(701) 255-3285 ext. 1211

University of Mary

Bismarck, North Dakota

www.umary.edu

Federal Code: 002992

4-year private university in small city, affiliated with Roman Catholic Church.

Enrollment: 2,010 undergrads, 20% part-time. 353 full-time freshmen.

Selectivity: Admits over 75% of applicants.

BASIC COSTS (2008-2009)

Tuition and fees: $12,164.

Per-credit charge: $375.

Room and board: $4,820.

FINANCIAL AID PICTURE (2006-2007)

Students with need: 50% of average financial aid package awarded as scholarships/grants, 50% awarded as loans/jobs. Need-based aid available for part-time students. Work study available nights, weekends, and for part-time students.

Students without need: No-need awards available for academics, athletics, leadership, music/drama, state/district residency.

Scholarships offered: Presidential Merit Awards; $1,000-$7,000; large number awarded; guaranteed for 4 years. Athletic and music scholarships: varying amounts; limited number awarded. Music scholarships: require audition. Drama/forensics: varying amounts; limited number.

FINANCIAL AID PROCEDURES

Forms required: FAFSA.

Dates and Deadlines: Priority date 3/15; no closing date. Applicants notified on a rolling basis starting 4/1; must reply within 2 week(s) of notification.

Transfers: Priority date 5/1; no deadline. Applicants notified on a rolling basis starting 5/1; must reply within 2 week(s) of notification.

CONTACT

Brenda Zastophil, Director of Student Financial Aid

7500 University Drive, Bismarck, ND 58504-9652

(701) 355-8244 ext. 283

University of North Dakota

Grand Forks, North Dakota
www.und.edu   Federal Code: 003005

4-year public university in small city.

Enrollment: 10,085 undergrads, 13% part-time. 1,828 full-time freshmen.

Selectivity: Admits 50 to 75% of applicants.

BASIC COSTS (2007-2008)

Tuition and fees: $6,130; out-of-state residents $14,523.

Per-credit charge: $209; out-of-state residents $559.

Room and board: $5,451.

Additional info: Tuition for South Dakota, Montana, Saskatchewan, Manitoba residents: $7,538. Tuition/fee waivers available for minority students.

FINANCIAL AID PICTURE (2006-2007)

Students with need: Out of 1,577 full-time freshmen who applied for aid, 1,105 were judged to have need. Of these, 1,085 received aid, and 649 had their full need met. Average financial aid package met 36% of need; average scholarship/grant was $3,267; average loan was $4,512. For part-time students, average financial aid package was $5,865.

Students without need: 492 full-time freshmen who did not demonstrate need for aid received scholarships/grants; average award was $1,035. No-need awards available for academics, alumni affiliation, art, athletics, job skills, leadership, music/drama, religious affiliation, ROTC.

Scholarships offered: *Merit:* 15 freshmen will receive $2,500 a year for 4 years; they are either National Merit Finalists listing UND as first choice and in top 10% of graduating class, or in top 10% and have minimum composite of 32 on the ACT. 55 scholarships of $2,000/yr for 4 years provided to students in top 10% of graduating class who are National Merit Semifinalists or have ACT composite of 29-31. 40 students with ACT of 27-28 and in upper 10% of graduating class will receive $1,000 for their freshman year. *Athletic:* 49 full-time freshmen received athletic scholarships; average amount $5,837.

Cumulative student debt: 66% of graduating class had student loans; average debt was $21,330.

FINANCIAL AID PROCEDURES

Forms required: FAFSA.

Dates and Deadlines: Priority date 3/15; no closing date. Applicants notified on a rolling basis starting 5/15; must reply within 4 week(s) of notification.

CONTACT

Robin Holden, Director of Student Financial Aid
Twamley Hall Room 205 264 Centennial Drive Stop 8357, Grand Forks, ND 58202-8357
(701) 777-3121

Valley City State University

Valley City, North Dakota
www.vcsu.edu   Federal Code: 003008

4-year public liberal arts and teachers college in small town.

Enrollment: 901 undergrads, 25% part-time. 193 full-time freshmen.

Selectivity: Admits over 75% of applicants.

BASIC COSTS (2007-2008)

Tuition and fees: $5,584; out-of-state residents $12,165.

Per-credit charge: $131; out-of-state residents $351.

Room and board: $3,870.

Additional info: Full-time tuition for South Dakota, Montana, Manitoba, Saskatchewan residents: $4,926. Full-time tuition for WUE students: $5,911. Tuition/fee waivers available for minority students.

FINANCIAL AID PICTURE (2006-2007)

Students with need: Out of 191 full-time freshmen who applied for aid, 130 were judged to have need. Of these, 128 received aid, and 52 had their full need met. Average financial aid package met 70% of need; average scholarship/grant was $4,644; average loan was $3,052. For part-time students, average financial aid package was $5,723.

Students without need: 102 full-time freshmen who did not demonstrate need for aid received scholarships/grants; average award was $2,150. No-need awards available for academics, alumni affiliation, athletics, leadership, minority status, music/drama.

Scholarships offered: *Merit:* Presidents Scholarship; $2,500 per year for 4 years. Meredith Scholarship; $3,000 per year for 4 years; science or math students only. McCready Scholarship; tuition and books for 4 years. Freshmen scholarships; $1,000 to $2,500; $2,500 renewable for sophomore year. *Athletic:* 6 full-time freshmen received athletic scholarships; average amount $1,517.

Cumulative student debt: 71% of graduating class had student loans; average debt was $19,693.

FINANCIAL AID PROCEDURES

Forms required: FAFSA.

Dates and Deadlines: Priority date 3/15; no closing date. Applicants notified on a rolling basis starting 2/1; must reply within 4 week(s) of notification.

CONTACT

Betty Schumacher, Director of Financial Aid
101 College Street SW, Valley City, ND 58072-4098
(701) 845-7412

Williston State College

Williston, North Dakota
www.wsc.nodak.edu   Federal Code: 003007

2-year public community college in large town.

Enrollment: 582 undergrads.

Selectivity: Open admission; but selective for some programs.

BASIC COSTS (2007-2008)

Tuition and fees: $3,219; out-of-state residents $4,466.

Per-credit charge: $96; out-of-state residents $144.

Room and board: $3,044.

Additional info: Tuition for Minnesota residents: $3,521. Tuition for South Dakota, Montana, and Canadian residents: $2,493. Tuition/fee waivers available for minority students.

FINANCIAL AID PICTURE

Students with need: Need-based aid available for full-time and part-time students. Work study available nights, weekends, and for part-time students.

Students without need: No-need awards available for academics, athletics.

FINANCIAL AID PROCEDURES

Forms required: FAFSA.

Dates and Deadlines: Priority date 3/15; no closing date. Applicants notified on a rolling basis starting 5/15.

CONTACT

Lynn Hagen-Aaberg, Financial Aid Director
1410 University Avenue, Williston, ND 58802-1326
(701) 774-4244

Ohio

Antioch University McGregor
Yellow Springs, Ohio
www.mcgregor.edu
Federal Code: E00553

4-year private branch campus and liberal arts college in small town.
Enrollment: 169 undergrads.

BASIC COSTS (2007-2008)
Tuition and fees: $13,185.
Per-credit charge: $283.

FINANCIAL AID PICTURE
Students with need: Need-based aid available for full-time and part-time students.

FINANCIAL AID PROCEDURES
Dates and Deadlines: No deadline. Applicants notified on a rolling basis.

CONTACT
Kathy John, Director of Financial Aid
900 Dayton Street, Yellow Springs, OH 45387
(937) 769-1840

Art Academy of Cincinnati
Cincinnati, Ohio
www.artacademy.edu
Federal Code: 003011

4-year private visual arts college in large city.
Enrollment: 137 undergrads, 7% part-time. 37 full-time freshmen.
Selectivity: Admits less than 50% of applicants.

BASIC COSTS (2008-2009)
Tuition and fees: $21,300.
Per-credit charge: $875.
Room and board: $6,800.

FINANCIAL AID PICTURE
Students with need: Need-based aid available for full-time and part-time students.
Students without need: No-need awards available for academics, art.
Scholarships offered: Annual scholarships awarded to entering and transfer students and to continuing students based on portfolio competition.

FINANCIAL AID PROCEDURES
Forms required: FAFSA.
Dates and Deadlines: Priority date 4/1; no closing date. Applicants notified on a rolling basis starting 3/1.

CONTACT
Karen Geiger, Financial Aid Director
1212 Jackson Street, Cincinnati, OH 45202
(513) 562-8751

Art Institute of Cincinnati
Cincinnati, Ohio
www.theartinstituteofcincinnati.com Federal Code: 014804

2-year for-profit visual arts college in large city.
Enrollment: 75 undergrads.
Selectivity: Admits over 75% of applicants.

BASIC COSTS (2007-2008)
Tuition and fees: $13,147.
Additional info: Tuition at time of enrollment locked for 2 years.

FINANCIAL AID PICTURE
Students with need: Need-based aid available for full-time students.
Students without need: No-need awards available for academics, art.

FINANCIAL AID PROCEDURES
Forms required: FAFSA.
Dates and Deadlines: No deadline. Applicants notified on a rolling basis starting 9/1; must reply within 1 week(s) of notification.
Transfers: No deadline. Applicants notified on a rolling basis; must reply within 4 week(s) of notification.

CONTACT
Gary Lay, Financial Aid Director
1171 East Kemper Road, Cincinnati, OH 45246
(513) 751-1206

Ashland University
Ashland, Ohio
www.ashland.edu
Federal Code: 003012

4-year private university and liberal arts college in large town, affiliated with Brethren Church.
Enrollment: 2,712 undergrads, 8% part-time. 636 full-time freshmen.
Selectivity: Admits over 75% of applicants.

BASIC COSTS (2007-2008)
Tuition and fees: $22,898.
Per-credit charge: $682.
Room and board: $8,374.
Additional info: Tuition/fee waivers available for minority students.

FINANCIAL AID PICTURE (2007-2008)
Students with need: Out of 634 full-time freshmen who applied for aid, 530 were judged to have need. Of these, 530 received aid. Average financial aid package met 90% of need; average scholarship/grant was $14,841; average loan was $4,163. For part-time students, average financial aid package was $13,182.
Students without need: 77 full-time freshmen who did not demonstrate need for aid received scholarships/grants; average award was $6,960. No-need awards available for academics, alumni affiliation, art, athletics, job skills, leadership, minority status, music/drama, religious affiliation.
Scholarships offered: *Merit:* Presidential Scholarships for applicants with GPA 3.75-4.0 and ACT 27-36 or SAT 1200-1600, $10,000; GPA 3.5-3.74 and ACT 25-26 or SAT 1130-1190, $9,000; GPA 3.25-3.49 and ACT 23-24 or SAT 1050-1120, $8,000. Director's Scholarships for applicants with a 3.0+ GPA, ACT 21+, SAT 970+, $6,000. SAT scores exclusive of Writing. *Athletic:* 22 full-time freshmen received athletic scholarships; average amount $12,201.

FINANCIAL AID PROCEDURES
Forms required: FAFSA, institutional form.
Dates and Deadlines: Priority date 3/15; no closing date. Applicants notified on a rolling basis starting 3/15; must reply within 3 week(s) of notification.
Transfers: Applicants notified on a rolling basis starting 3/1; must reply within 3 week(s) of notification. Awards for students transferring in 15 credits or more will be based on the student's college transfer GPA while awards for students transferring fewer than 15 credits will be based on the student's high school GPA and ACT/SAT score.

CONTACT
Stephen Howell, Director of Financial Aid
401 College Avenue, Ashland, OH 44805-9981
(419) 289-5002

Brown Mackie College: Findlay
Findlay, Ohio
www.brownmackie.edu   Federal Code: 026162

2-year for-profit business and junior college in small city.
Enrollment: 202 undergrads, 50% part-time. 74 full-time freshmen.
Selectivity: Open admission.

BASIC COSTS (2008-2009)
Tuition and fees: $12,880.
Per-credit charge: $260.

FINANCIAL AID PICTURE (2006-2007)
Students with need: Out of 73 full-time freshmen who applied for aid, 71 were judged to have need. Of these, 71 received aid, and 3 had their full need met. Average financial aid package met 50% of need; average loan was $1,167. For part-time students, average financial aid package was $460.
Students without need: No-need awards available for academics, state/district residency.
Cumulative student debt: 97% of graduating class had student loans; average debt was $18,124.

FINANCIAL AID PROCEDURES
Forms required: FAFSA.
Dates and Deadlines: No deadline.
Transfers: No deadline.

CONTACT
Georgeana Munsey, Director of Financial Aid
1700 Fostoria Avenue, Suite 100, Findlay, OH 45840
(419) 423-2211

Brown Mackie College: North Canton
Canton, Ohio
www.brownmackie.edu   Federal Code: 030778

2-year for-profit career college in small city.
Enrollment: 1,090 undergrads.
Selectivity: Open admission.

BASIC COSTS (2007-2008)
Additional info: Tuition $208 per credit hour; fees $15 per credit hour.

FINANCIAL AID PICTURE
Students with need: Work study available nights.

FINANCIAL AID PROCEDURES
Forms required: FAFSA.

CONTACT
Joyce Cox, Director of Financial Aid
4300 Munson Street Northwest, Canton, OH 44718-3674

Bryant & Stratton College: Cleveland
Cleveland, Ohio
www.bryantstratton.edu   Federal Code: 022744

2-year for-profit technical college in very large city.
Enrollment: 248 full-time undergrads.

BASIC COSTS (2007-2008)
Tuition and fees: $13,080.
Per-credit charge: $436.

FINANCIAL AID PICTURE
Students with need: Need-based aid available for full-time and part-time students. Work study available nights.

Students without need: No-need awards available for academics.

FINANCIAL AID PROCEDURES
Forms required: FAFSA, institutional form.
Dates and Deadlines: No deadline. Applicants notified on a rolling basis starting 5/1; must reply within 2 week(s) of notification.
Transfers: No deadline. By state regulation, Ohio Institutional Grant can be awarded only 3 times a fiscal year.

CONTACT
Donna McCullough, Director of Financial Services
1700 East 13th Street, Cleveland, OH 44114-3203
(216) 771-1700

Bryant & Stratton College: Parma
Parma, Ohio
www.bryantstratton.edu   Federal Code: 015298

4-year for-profit nursing and junior college in small city.
Enrollment: 696 undergrads, 35% part-time. 214 full-time freshmen.
Selectivity: Open admission; but selective for some programs.

BASIC COSTS (2008-2009)
Tuition and fees: $13,080.
Per-credit charge: $436.

FINANCIAL AID PICTURE
Students with need: Need-based aid available for full-time and part-time students. Work study available nights.
Students without need: This college awards aid only to students with need.
Additional info: Competitive and matching scholarships offered to high school seniors.

FINANCIAL AID PROCEDURES
Forms required: FAFSA.
Dates and Deadlines: No deadline. Applicants notified on a rolling basis starting 6/1.
Transfers: Transfer form must be completed for state grant.

CONTACT
Colleen Garibotti, Financial Services Manager
12955 Snow Road, Parma, OH 44130-1013
(216) 265-3151 ext. 239

Bryant & Stratton College: Willoughby Hills
Willoughby Hills, Ohio
www.bryantstratton.edu   Federal Code: 022744

4-year for-profit business college in small town.
Enrollment: 520 undergrads.
Selectivity: Open admission.

BASIC COSTS (2007-2008)
Tuition and fees: $14,540.

FINANCIAL AID PICTURE
Students with need: Need-based aid available for full-time and part-time students.
Students without need: No-need awards available for academics.

FINANCIAL AID PROCEDURES
Forms required: FAFSA.
Dates and Deadlines: No deadline. Applicants notified on a rolling basis.

CONTACT

Lisa Patterson, Financial Aid Manager
27557 Chardon Road, Willoughby Hills, OH 44092
(440) 944-6800

Capital University

Columbus, Ohio
www.capital.edu   Federal Code: 003023

4-year private university in very large city, affiliated with Evangelical Lutheran Church in America.

Enrollment: 2,634 undergrads, 12% part-time. 629 full-time freshmen.
Selectivity: Admits 50 to 75% of applicants.

BASIC COSTS (2008-2009)

Tuition and fees: $27,680.
Per-credit charge: $925.
Room and board: $7,150.

FINANCIAL AID PICTURE

Students with need: Need-based aid available for full-time and part-time students. Work study available nights, weekends, and for part-time students.
Students without need: No-need awards available for academics, alumni affiliation, art, minority status, music/drama, religious affiliation, ROTC, state/district residency.
Scholarships offered: Scholarships and grants from $1,000 to full tuition available.

FINANCIAL AID PROCEDURES

Forms required: FAFSA.
Dates and Deadlines: Priority date 2/28; no closing date. Applicants notified on a rolling basis starting 3/1; must reply by 5/1.
Transfers: Priority date 7/15.

CONTACT

Pam Varda, Director of Financial Aid
One College and Main, Columbus, OH 43209-2394
(614) 236-6511

Case Western Reserve University

Cleveland, Ohio
www.case.edu   Federal Code: E00077

4-year private university in very large city.
Enrollment: 4,120 undergrads, 3% part-time. 1,133 full-time freshmen.
Selectivity: Admits 50 to 75% of applicants.

BASIC COSTS (2008-2009)

Tuition and fees: $35,572.
Per-credit charge: $1,436.
Room and board: $10,450.

FINANCIAL AID PICTURE (2007-2008)

Students with need: Out of 956 full-time freshmen who applied for aid, 790 were judged to have need. Of these, 790 received aid, and 695 had their full need met. Average financial aid package met 91% of need; average scholarship/grant was $24,021; average loan was $6,206. Need-based aid available for part-time students.
Students without need: 237 full-time freshmen who did not demonstrate need for aid received scholarships/grants; average award was $19,497. No-need awards available for academics, art, leadership, music/drama.
Cumulative student debt: 59% of graduating class had student loans; average debt was $32,195.

FINANCIAL AID PROCEDURES

Forms required: FAFSA, institutional form.

Dates and Deadlines: Priority date 2/1; no closing date. Applicants notified on a rolling basis starting 2/15; must reply by 5/1 or within 2 week(s) of notification.
Transfers: Priority date 5/15.

CONTACT

Donald Chenelle, Director of University Financial Aid
Tomlinson Hall, Cleveland, OH 44106-7055
(216) 368-4530

Cedarville University

Cedarville, Ohio
www.cedarville.edu   Federal Code: 003025

4-year private university and liberal arts college in small town, affiliated with Baptist faith.

Enrollment: 2,951 undergrads, 3% part-time. 820 full-time freshmen.
Selectivity: Admits over 75% of applicants.

BASIC COSTS (2007-2008)

Tuition and fees: $19,680.
Per-credit charge: $615.
Room and board: $5,010.

FINANCIAL AID PICTURE (2006-2007)

Students with need: Out of 654 full-time freshmen who applied for aid, 499 were judged to have need. Of these, 498 received aid, and 312 had their full need met. Average financial aid package met 34% of need; average scholarship/grant was $2,905; average loan was $2,687. For part-time students, average financial aid package was $8,755.
Students without need: 244 full-time freshmen who did not demonstrate need for aid received scholarships/grants; average award was $9,046. No-need awards available for academics, alumni affiliation, athletics, leadership, minority status, music/drama, ROTC, state/district residency.
Scholarships offered: 46 full-time freshmen received athletic scholarships; average amount $3,738.
Cumulative student debt: 69% of graduating class had student loans; average debt was $24,890.

FINANCIAL AID PROCEDURES

Forms required: FAFSA.
Dates and Deadlines: Priority date 3/1; no closing date. Applicants notified on a rolling basis starting 3/1; must reply within 4 week(s) of notification.
Transfers: No deadline. Applicants notified on a rolling basis starting 2/1.

CONTACT

Fred Merritt, Director of Financial Aid
251 North Main Street, Cedarville, OH 45314
(937) 766-7866

Central Ohio Technical College

Newark, Ohio
www.cotc.edu   Federal Code: 011046

2-year public technical college in large town.
Enrollment: 3,105 undergrads.
Selectivity: Open admission; but selective for some programs.

BASIC COSTS (2007-2008)

Tuition and fees: $3,600; out-of-state residents $6,300.
Per-credit charge: $100; out-of-state residents $175.

FINANCIAL AID PICTURE

Students with need: Need-based aid available for full-time and part-time students. Work study available nights, weekends, and for part-time students.
Students without need: No-need awards available for academics.

Scholarships offered: Presidential Achievement Award based on minimum high school GPA of 3.0; 5 awarded; $1,800 annually. Minority Achievement Award based on minimum high school GPA of 2.5; 2 awarded; $850 annually.

FINANCIAL AID PROCEDURES

Forms required: FAFSA.

Dates and Deadlines: Priority date 3/1; no closing date. Applicants notified on a rolling basis starting 5/1; must reply within 3 week(s) of notification.

CONTACT

Faith Phillips, Director of Financial Aid
1179 University Drive, Newark, OH 43055
(740) 366-9435

Central State University

Wilberforce, Ohio
www.centralstate.edu   Federal Code: 003026

4-year public university and liberal arts college in rural community.

Enrollment: 1,955 undergrads, 7% part-time. 571 full-time freshmen.

Selectivity: Admits less than 50% of applicants.

BASIC COSTS (2007-2008)

Tuition and fees: $5,294; out-of-state residents $11,462.

Room and board: $7,402.

FINANCIAL AID PICTURE (2007-2008)

Students with need: Out of 561 full-time freshmen who applied for aid, 522 were judged to have need. Of these, 521 received aid. Need-based aid available for part-time students.

Students without need: 14 full-time freshmen who did not demonstrate need for aid received scholarships/grants; average award was $4,448. No-need awards available for academics, alumni affiliation, art, athletics, leadership, music/drama, religious affiliation, ROTC.

Scholarships offered: 6 full-time freshmen received athletic scholarships; average amount $4,216.

Cumulative student debt: 85% of graduating class had student loans; average debt was $23,880.

FINANCIAL AID PROCEDURES

Forms required: FAFSA, institutional form.

Dates and Deadlines: Priority date 2/15; no closing date. Applicants notified on a rolling basis starting 5/1.

Transfers: No deadline.

CONTACT

Veronica Leech, Director of Financial Aid
PO Box 1004, Wilberforce, OH 45384-1004
(937) 376-6579

Chatfield College

St. Martin, Ohio
www.chatfield.edu   Federal Code: 010880

2-year private community and liberal arts college in rural community, affiliated with Roman Catholic Church.

Enrollment: 218 undergrads.

Selectivity: Open admission.

BASIC COSTS (2007-2008)

Tuition and fees: $9,190.

Per-credit charge: $295.

FINANCIAL AID PICTURE

Students with need: Need-based aid available for full-time and part-time students.

Students without need: No-need awards available for academics, leadership.

Additional info: Institutional grants/scholarships given primarily to first-year students to reduce debt load during initial year.

FINANCIAL AID PROCEDURES

Forms required: FAFSA, institutional form.

Dates and Deadlines: Priority date 4/25; closing date 8/3. Applicants notified on a rolling basis starting 4/1; must reply within 2 week(s) of notification.

CONTACT

Zana Smith, Director of Financial Aid
20918 State Route 251, St. Martin, OH 45118
(513) 875-3344

Cincinnati Christian University

Cincinnati, Ohio
www.ccuniversity.edu   Federal Code: 003029

4-year private university in very large city, affiliated with Church of Christ/Christian Church.

Enrollment: 775 undergrads.

BASIC COSTS (2008-2009)

Tuition and fees: $11,840.

Per-credit charge: $368.

Room and board: $6,260.

FINANCIAL AID PICTURE (2006-2007)

Students with need: 38% of average financial aid package awarded as scholarships/grants, 62% awarded as loans/jobs. Need-based aid available for part-time students. Work study available nights, weekends, and for part-time students.

FINANCIAL AID PROCEDURES

Forms required: FAFSA.

Dates and Deadlines: Priority date 3/1; no closing date. Applicants notified by 4/5; must reply by 6/5 or within 2 week(s) of notification.

Transfers: No deadline.

CONTACT

Michael Gibboney, Financial Aid Director
2700 Glenway Avenue, Cincinnati, OH 45204-3200
(513) 244-8100 ext. 8450

Cincinnati College of Mortuary Science

Cincinnati, Ohio
www.ccms.edu   Federal Code: 010906

4-year private school of mortuary science in large city.

Enrollment: 125 undergrads.

Selectivity: Open admission.

BASIC COSTS (2007-2008)

Tuition and fees: $14,250.

FINANCIAL AID PICTURE

Students with need: Need-based aid available for full-time and part-time students.

Students without need: This college awards aid only to students with need.

FINANCIAL AID PROCEDURES

Forms required: FAFSA.

Dates and Deadlines: Priority date 7/1; no closing date. Applicants notified on a rolling basis starting 3/1; must reply within 2 week(s) of notification.

CONTACT

Peggy Harmon, Financial Aid/Admissions Officer

645 West North Bend Road, Cincinnati, OH 45224-1428

(513) 761-2020

Cincinnati State Technical and Community College

Cincinnati, Ohio

www.cincinnatistate.edu   Federal Code: 010345

2-year public community and technical college in large city.

Enrollment: 7,487 undergrads, 56% part-time. 1,412 full-time freshmen.

Selectivity: Open admission; but selective for some programs.

BASIC COSTS (2007-2008)

Tuition and fees: $3,867; out-of-state residents $7,476.

Per-credit charge: $80; out-of-state residents $160.

FINANCIAL AID PICTURE (2006-2007)

Students with need: 81% of average financial aid package awarded as scholarships/grants, 19% awarded as loans/jobs. Need-based aid available for part-time students. Work study available nights, weekends, and for part-time students.

Students without need: No-need awards available for academics, athletics, state/district residency.

FINANCIAL AID PROCEDURES

Forms required: FAFSA.

Dates and Deadlines: Priority date 2/15; no closing date. Applicants notified on a rolling basis starting 3/15; must reply within 4 week(s) of notification.

CONTACT

Dawn Smith, Director of Student Financial Aid/Scholarships

3520 Central Parkway, Cincinnati, OH 45223-2690

(513) 569-1530

Clark State Community College

Springfield, Ohio

www.clarkstate.edu   Federal Code: 004852

2-year public community college in small city.

Enrollment: 1,249 full-time undergrads.

Selectivity: Open admission; but selective for some programs.

BASIC COSTS (2007-2008)

Tuition and fees: $3,684; out-of-state residents $6,828.

Per-credit charge: $78; out-of-state residents $143.

FINANCIAL AID PICTURE

Students with need: Work study available nights, weekends, and for part-time students.

FINANCIAL AID PROCEDURES

Forms required: FAFSA.

Dates and Deadlines: Priority date 6/15; no closing date. Applicants notified on a rolling basis.

CONTACT

Kathy Klay, Director of Financial Aid

Box 570, Springfield, OH 45501-0570

(937) 328-6034

Cleveland Institute of Art

Cleveland, Ohio

www.cia.edu   Federal Code: 003982

4-year private visual arts college in very large city.

Enrollment: 478 undergrads, 3% part-time. 100 full-time freshmen.

Selectivity: Admits 50 to 75% of applicants.

BASIC COSTS (2008-2009)

Tuition and fees: $31,010.

Per-credit charge: $1,215.

Room and board: $9,148.

FINANCIAL AID PICTURE (2007-2008)

Students with need: Out of 83 full-time freshmen who applied for aid, 78 were judged to have need. Of these, 78 received aid, and 6 had their full need met. Average financial aid package met 63% of need; average scholarship/grant was $15,597; average loan was $4,607. For part-time students, average financial aid package was $3,588.

Students without need: 22 full-time freshmen who did not demonstrate need for aid received scholarships/grants; average award was $14,427. No-need awards available for academics, art.

Cumulative student debt: 81% of graduating class had student loans; average debt was $57,968.

FINANCIAL AID PROCEDURES

Forms required: FAFSA, institutional form.

Dates and Deadlines: Priority date 3/15; no closing date. Applicants notified on a rolling basis starting 3/16; must reply within 4 week(s) of notification.

CONTACT

Michael Warinner, Director Financial Aid

11141 East Boulevard, Cleveland, OH 44106-1710

(216) 421-7425

Cleveland Institute of Music

Cleveland, Ohio

www.cim.edu   Federal Code: 003031

4-year private music college in very large city.

Enrollment: 228 undergrads.

Selectivity: Admits less than 50% of applicants.

BASIC COSTS (2008-2009)

Tuition and fees: $34,482.

Per-credit charge: $1,329.

Room and board: $10,480.

FINANCIAL AID PICTURE

Students with need: Need-based aid available for full-time and part-time students.

Students without need: No-need awards available for academics, music/drama.

FINANCIAL AID PROCEDURES

Forms required: FAFSA, institutional form.

Dates and Deadlines: Priority date 2/15; no closing date. Applicants notified on a rolling basis starting 4/1; must reply by 5/1 or within 2 week(s) of notification.

Transfers: Applicants notified on a rolling basis starting 4/1; must reply by 5/1 or within 2 week(s) of notification.

CONTACT

Kristie Gripp, Director of Financial Aid

11021 East Boulevard, Cleveland, OH 44106

(216) 791-5002 ext. 262

Cleveland State University

Cleveland, Ohio
www.csuohio.edu   Federal Code: 003032

4-year public university in very large city.
Enrollment: 9,221 undergrads, 24% part-time. 1,166 full-time freshmen.
Selectivity: Open admission; but selective for some programs and for out-of-state students.

BASIC COSTS (2007-2008)
Tuition and fees: $7,920; out-of-state residents $10,664.
Per-credit charge: $330; out-of-state residents $444.
Room and board: $8,098.

FINANCIAL AID PICTURE (2007-2008)
Students with need: Average financial aid package met 34% of need; average scholarship/grant was $5,970; average loan was $3,922. For part-time students, average financial aid package was $5,988.
Students without need: No-need awards available for academics, alumni affiliation, art, athletics, leadership, minority status, music/drama, religious affiliation, ROTC.

FINANCIAL AID PROCEDURES
Forms required: FAFSA.
Dates and Deadlines: Priority date 2/15; no closing date. Applicants notified on a rolling basis starting 3/15; must reply within 4 week(s) of notification.

CONTACT
Rachel Schmidt, Director of Financial Aid
1806 East 22nd Street, Cleveland, OH 44115-2403
(888) 278-6446

College of Mount St. Joseph

Cincinnati, Ohio
www.msj.edu   Federal Code: 003033

4-year private liberal arts college in very large city, affiliated with Roman Catholic Church.
Enrollment: 1,916 undergrads, 30% part-time. 335 full-time freshmen.
Selectivity: Admits 50 to 75% of applicants.

BASIC COSTS (2007-2008)
Tuition and fees: $21,200.
Per-credit charge: $450.
Room and board: $6,500.

FINANCIAL AID PICTURE (2007-2008)
Students with need: Out of 308 full-time freshmen who applied for aid, 271 were judged to have need. Of these, 271 received aid, and 42 had their full need met. Average financial aid package met 85% of need; average scholarship/grant was $12,857; average loan was $4,055. For part-time students, average financial aid package was $6,827.
Students without need: 60 full-time freshmen who did not demonstrate need for aid received scholarships/grants; average award was $5,766. No-need awards available for academics, art, leadership, music/drama, ROTC, state/district residency.
Scholarships offered: Presidential Scholarship: $10,000; 26-36 ACT or 1170 SAT. Trustee Scholarship: $9,000; 24-25 ACT or 1090 SAT. Dean's Scholarship: $7,000; 22-23 ACT or 1020 SAT. Merit Award: $5,000; 20-21 ACT or 940 SAT. Challenge Award: $2,000 per semester; 18-19 ACT or 860 SAT. Director's Award: $2,000 per semester; at least 21 ACT or 990 SAT and at least 2.75 high school GPA. Transfer Scholarship: $5,000; 3.00 college GPA with at least 24 hours earned. SAT scores exclusive of Writing.
Cumulative student debt: 83% of graduating class had student loans; average debt was $27,513.

Additional info: College offers financial aid to full and part-time students. Unlimited, renewable merit-based scholarships offered.

FINANCIAL AID PROCEDURES
Forms required: FAFSA.
Dates and Deadlines: Priority date 3/1; no closing date. Applicants notified on a rolling basis starting 2/15; must reply by 5/1 or within 4 week(s) of notification.
Transfers: Applicants notified on a rolling basis starting 2/15; must reply within 4 week(s) of notification.

CONTACT
Kathryn Kelly, Director of Student Administrative Services
5701 Delhi Road, Cincinnati, OH 45233-1670
(513) 244-4418

College of Wooster

Wooster, Ohio   Federal Code: 003037
www.wooster.edu   CSS Code: 1134

4-year private liberal arts college in large town.
Enrollment: 1,754 undergrads. 543 full-time freshmen.
Selectivity: Admits 50 to 75% of applicants.

BASIC COSTS (2008-2009)
Tuition and fees: $33,770.
Room and board: $8,650.

FINANCIAL AID PICTURE (2007-2008)
Students with need: Out of 430 full-time freshmen who applied for aid, 324 were judged to have need. Of these, 324 received aid, and 208 had their full need met. Average financial aid package met 92% of need; average scholarship/grant was $21,630; average loan was $4,630. Need-based aid available for part-time students.
Students without need: 200 full-time freshmen who did not demonstrate need for aid received scholarships/grants; average award was $14,407. No-need awards available for academics, minority status, music/drama, religious affiliation, state/district residency.
Cumulative student debt: 59% of graduating class had student loans; average debt was $25,044.

FINANCIAL AID PROCEDURES
Forms required: FAFSA, institutional form. Either CSS PROFILE or institution application from prospectives.
Dates and Deadlines: Priority date 2/15; no closing date. Applicants notified by 4/1; must reply by 5/1.

CONTACT
David Miller, Director of Financial Aid
847 College Avenue, Wooster, OH 44691-2363
(330) 263-2317

Columbus College of Art and Design

Columbus, Ohio
www.ccad.edu   Federal Code: 003039

4-year private visual arts college in very large city.
Enrollment: 1,375 undergrads, 5% part-time. 330 full-time freshmen.
Selectivity: Admits over 75% of applicants.

BASIC COSTS (2008-2009)
Tuition and fees: $23,564.
Per-credit charge: $955.
Room and board: $6,750.

FINANCIAL AID PICTURE (2007-2008)

Students with need: Out of 302 full-time freshmen who applied for aid, 270 were judged to have need. Of these, 269 received aid, and 53 had their full need met. Average financial aid package met 66% of need; average scholarship/grant was $12,623; average loan was $5,286. For part-time students, average financial aid package was $14,254.

Students without need: 64 full-time freshmen who did not demonstrate need for aid received scholarships/grants; average award was $15,591. No-need awards available for academics, art, ROTC, state/district residency.

Cumulative student debt: 79% of graduating class had student loans; average debt was $26,941.

FINANCIAL AID PROCEDURES

Forms required: FAFSA.

Dates and Deadlines: Priority date 3/2; closing date 6/4. Applicants notified on a rolling basis starting 3/15; must reply within 2 week(s) of notification.

CONTACT

Anna Marie Schofield, Director of Financial Aid
107 North Ninth Street, Columbus, OH 43215-3875
(614) 222-3274

Columbus State Community College

Columbus, Ohio
www.cscc.edu   Federal Code: 006867

2-year public community and technical college in very large city.

Enrollment: 13,051 undergrads.

Selectivity: Open admission; but selective for some programs.

BASIC COSTS (2007-2008)

Tuition and fees: $3,555; out-of-state residents $7,875.

Per-credit charge: $79; out-of-state residents $175.

FINANCIAL AID PICTURE

Students with need: Need-based aid available for full-time and part-time students. Work study available nights, weekends, and for part-time students.

Students without need: No-need awards available for athletics, state/district residency.

FINANCIAL AID PROCEDURES

Forms required: FAFSA.

Dates and Deadlines: Priority date 7/24; no closing date. Applicants notified on a rolling basis starting 4/1.

CONTACT

David Metz, Director of Financial Aid
550 East Spring Street, Columbus, OH 43216-1609
(614) 287-2648

Cuyahoga Community College: Metropolitan Campus

Cleveland, Ohio
www.tri-c.edu   Federal Code: 003040

2-year public community college in very large city.

Enrollment: 11,073 undergrads, 54% part-time. 1,447 full-time freshmen.

Selectivity: Open admission; but selective for some programs.

BASIC COSTS (2007-2008)

Tuition and fees: $2,416; out-of-district residents $3,194; out-of-state residents $6,541.

Per-credit charge: $81; out-of-district residents $106; out-of-state residents $218.

FINANCIAL AID PICTURE (2007-2008)

Students with need: Average financial aid package met 100% of need; average scholarship/grant was $5,517; average loan was $1,943. For part-time students, average financial aid package was $3,991.

Students without need: No-need awards available for academics, art, athletics, leadership, minority status, music/drama.

Cumulative student debt: 28% of graduating class had student loans; average debt was $8,238.

FINANCIAL AID PROCEDURES

Forms required: FAFSA, institutional form.

Dates and Deadlines: No deadline. Applicants notified on a rolling basis starting 5/8.

Transfers: Priority date 5/8.

CONTACT

Angela Johnson, Campus Director
2900 Community College Avenue, Cleveland, OH 44115-2878
(216) 987-4100

Davis College

Toledo, Ohio
www.daviscollege.edu   Federal Code: 004855

2-year for-profit junior college in large city.

Enrollment: 479 undergrads, 56% part-time. 23 full-time freshmen.

Selectivity: Admits over 75% of applicants.

BASIC COSTS (2007-2008)

Tuition and fees: $10,965.

Per-credit charge: $233.

FINANCIAL AID PICTURE

Students with need: Need-based aid available for full-time and part-time students. Work study available nights, weekends, and for part-time students.

Students without need: This college awards aid only to students with need.

FINANCIAL AID PROCEDURES

Forms required: FAFSA.

Dates and Deadlines: No deadline. Applicants notified on a rolling basis.

CONTACT

Carole Lulfs, Director of Financial Aid
4747 Monroe Street, Toledo, OH 43623
(419) 473-2700

Defiance College

Defiance, Ohio
www.defiance.edu   Federal Code: 003041

4-year private liberal arts college in large town, affiliated with United Church of Christ.

Enrollment: 869 undergrads, 17% part-time. 226 full-time freshmen.

Selectivity: Admits over 75% of applicants.

BASIC COSTS (2008-2009)

Tuition and fees: $21,830.

Per-credit charge: $345.

Room and board: $7,150.

Additional info: Tuition/fee waivers available for adults.

FINANCIAL AID PICTURE

Students with need: Need-based aid available for full-time and part-time students. Work study available nights, weekends, and for part-time students.

Students without need: No-need awards available for academics, leadership.

Scholarships offered: Presidential Scholar Program: $11,000 to full tuition; based on GPA of 3.5/4.0 and ACT composite of 27 or SAT combined score of 1210, interview required. Pilgrim Scholar Program: $10,000-$15,000; based on GPA of 3.2/4.0 and ACT composite of 24 or SAT combined score of 1090, interview required. Achievement Scholar Program: $9,000-$12,000; based on GPA of 2.8/4.0 and ACT composite of 21 or SAT combined score of 980, interview required. Defiance College Scholarship: $4,000-$10,000; based on GPA range from 2.5 to 4.0/4.0 and ACT composite range of 18 to 36 or SAT combined range from 850 to 1600. Citizen Leader Award: $2,000; awarded to students with a demonstrated record of service in their communities, application and interview required. Lillian Rae Dunlap Award: $1,000 awarded annually to recognize and reward the achievements of today's under-represented student population; minimum 2.25 GPA.

FINANCIAL AID PROCEDURES

Forms required: FAFSA.

Dates and Deadlines: Priority date 3/1; no closing date. Applicants notified on a rolling basis starting 3/15; must reply within 3 week(s) of notification.

CONTACT

Mary Cannon, Director of Financial Aid
701 North Clinton Street, Defiance, OH 43512-1695
(419) 784-2364

Denison University

Granville, Ohio
www.denison.edu   Federal Code: 003042

4-year private liberal arts college in small town.
Enrollment: 2,212 undergrads. 586 full-time freshmen.
Selectivity: Admits less than 50% of applicants.

BASIC COSTS (2007-2008)

Tuition and fees: $33,010.
Per-credit charge: $1,000.
Room and board: $8,570.
Additional info: Tuition/fee waivers available for adults.

FINANCIAL AID PICTURE (2007-2008)

Students with need: Out of 358 full-time freshmen who applied for aid, 271 were judged to have need. Of these, 271 received aid, and 168 had their full need met. Average financial aid package met 99% of need; average scholarship/grant was $21,848; average loan was $3,931. Need-based aid available for part-time students.

Students without need: 270 full-time freshmen who did not demonstrate need for aid received scholarships/grants; average award was $13,331. No-need awards available for academics, art, leadership, music/drama, state/district residency.

FINANCIAL AID PROCEDURES

Forms required: FAFSA.
Dates and Deadlines: Priority date 2/15; no closing date. Applicants notified by 3/30; must reply by 5/1 or within 2 week(s) of notification.

CONTACT

Nancy Hoover, Director of Financial Aid and Student Employment
Box H, Granville, OH 43023
(740) 587-6279

DeVry University: Columbus

Columbus, Ohio
www.devry.edu   Federal Code: 003099

4-year for-profit university in very large city.
Enrollment: 2,379 undergrads, 39% part-time. 332 full-time freshmen.

BASIC COSTS (2007-2008)

Tuition and fees: $13,220.
Per-credit charge: $490.

FINANCIAL AID PICTURE (2006-2007)

Students with need: Out of 258 full-time freshmen who applied for aid, 240 were judged to have need. Of these, 238 received aid, and 6 had their full need met. Average financial aid package met 41% of need; average scholarship/grant was $6,035; average loan was $4,381. For part-time students, average financial aid package was $8,175.

Students without need: This college awards aid only to students with need.

Cumulative student debt: 69% of graduating class had student loans; average debt was $39,090.

FINANCIAL AID PROCEDURES

Forms required: FAFSA.

Dates and Deadlines: No deadline. Applicants notified on a rolling basis.

CONTACT

Cynthia Price, Director of Financial Aid
1350 Alum Creek Drive, Columbus, OH 43209-2705
(614) 253-7291

Edison State Community College

Piqua, Ohio
www.edisonohio.edu   Federal Code: 012750

2-year public community college in large town.
Enrollment: 866 full-time undergrads.
Selectivity: Open admission; but selective for some programs.

BASIC COSTS (2007-2008)

Tuition and fees: $3,450; out-of-state residents $6,420.
Per-credit charge: $99; out-of-state residents $198.

FINANCIAL AID PICTURE

Students with need: Need-based aid available for full-time and part-time students. Work study available nights, weekends, and for part-time students.
Students without need: No-need awards available for academics, athletics.

FINANCIAL AID PROCEDURES

Forms required: FAFSA, institutional form.
Dates and Deadlines: Priority date 5/2; no closing date. Applicants notified on a rolling basis starting 5/15.

CONTACT

Kathi Richards, Director of Student Financial Aid
1973 Edison Drive, Piqua, OH 45356-9253
(937) 778-7910

Franciscan University of Steubenville

Steubenville, Ohio
www.franciscan.edu   Federal Code: 003036

4-year private university in large town, affiliated with Roman Catholic Church.
Enrollment: 1,976 undergrads, 5% part-time. 439 full-time freshmen.
Selectivity: Admits over 75% of applicants.

BASIC COSTS (2007-2008)

Tuition and fees: $18,180.
Per-credit charge: $595.
Room and board: $6,300.

FINANCIAL AID PICTURE

Students with need: Need-based aid available for full-time and part-time students. Work study available nights, weekends, and for part-time students.

Students without need: No-need awards available for academics, leadership, religious affiliation.

FINANCIAL AID PROCEDURES
Forms required: FAFSA.
Dates and Deadlines: No deadline. Applicants notified on a rolling basis starting 3/15; must reply within 3 week(s) of notification.
Transfers: Closing date 8/1.

CONTACT
John Herrmann, Director of Student Financial Services
1235 University Boulevard, Steubenville, OH 43952-1763
(740) 283-6211

Gallipolis Career College
Gallipolis, Ohio
www.gallipoliscareercollege.com   Federal Code: 030079

2-year for-profit business and technical college in small town.
Enrollment: 138 undergrads, 7% part-time. 37 full-time freshmen.
Selectivity: Open admission.

BASIC COSTS (2007-2008)
Tuition and fees: $9,170.
Per-credit charge: $190.

FINANCIAL AID PICTURE
Students with need: Need-based aid available for full-time and part-time students.
Students without need: This college awards aid only to students with need.

FINANCIAL AID PROCEDURES
Forms required: FAFSA, institutional form.
Dates and Deadlines: No deadline.

CONTACT
Jeanette Shirey, Financial Aid Administrator
1176 Jackson Pike, Suite 312, Gallipolis, OH 45631
(740) 446-4367

Heidelberg College
Tiffin, Ohio
www.heidelberg.edu   Federal Code: 003048

4-year private liberal arts college in large town, affiliated with United Church of Christ.
Enrollment: 1,255 undergrads, 7% part-time. 370 full-time freshmen.
Selectivity: Admits 50 to 75% of applicants.

BASIC COSTS (2008-2009)
Tuition and fees: $19,922.
Room and board: $8,138.

FINANCIAL AID PICTURE (2007-2008)
Students with need: Out of 356 full-time freshmen who applied for aid, 299 were judged to have need. Of these, 299 received aid, and 55 had their full need met. Average financial aid package met 88% of need; average scholarship/grant was $11,519; average loan was $4,514. Need-based aid available for part-time students.
Students without need: 44 full-time freshmen who did not demonstrate need for aid received scholarships/grants; average award was $7,506. No-need awards available for academics, music/drama, religious affiliation, state/district residency.
Cumulative student debt: 89% of graduating class had student loans; average debt was $30,589.

FINANCIAL AID PROCEDURES
Forms required: FAFSA.
Dates and Deadlines: Priority date 3/1; no closing date. Applicants notified on a rolling basis starting 3/15; must reply by 5/1 or within 2 week(s) of notification.

CONTACT
Juli Weininger, Director of Financial Aid
310 East Market Street, Tiffin, OH 44883-2462
(419) 448-2293

Hiram College
Hiram, Ohio
www.hiram.edu   Federal Code: 003049

4-year private liberal arts college in rural community, affiliated with Christian Church (Disciples of Christ).
Enrollment: 1,256 undergrads.
Selectivity: Admits over 75% of applicants.

BASIC COSTS (2007-2008)
Tuition and fees: $24,895.
Per-credit charge: $808.
Room and board: $7,980.
Additional info: Tuition at time of enrollment locked for 4 years.

FINANCIAL AID PICTURE
Students with need: Need-based aid available for full-time and part-time students. Work study available nights, weekends, and for part-time students.
Students without need: No-need awards available for academics, alumni affiliation, art, leadership, minority status, music/drama, religious affiliation, state/district residency.

FINANCIAL AID PROCEDURES
Forms required: FAFSA.
Dates and Deadlines: Priority date 2/15; no closing date. Applicants notified on a rolling basis starting 2/15; must reply by 5/1 or within 2 week(s) of notification.
Transfers: Transfer merit scholarships available. Phi Theta Kappa scholarships available.

CONTACT
Andrea Caputo, Director of Student Financial Aid
Teachout Price Hall, Hiram, OH 44234
(330) 569-5107

Hocking College
Nelsonville, Ohio
www.hocking.edu   Federal Code: 007598

2-year public technical college in small town.
Enrollment: 3,792 undergrads, 29% part-time. 2,914 full-time freshmen.
Selectivity: Open admission; but selective for some programs.

BASIC COSTS (2007-2008)
Tuition and fees: $3,546; out-of-state residents $7,092.
Per-credit charge: $99; out-of-state residents $197.

FINANCIAL AID PICTURE (2006-2007)
Students with need: Out of 2,232 full-time freshmen who applied for aid, 1,786 were judged to have need. Of these, 1,786 received aid. Need-based aid available for part-time students.
Students without need: 170 full-time freshmen who did not demonstrate need for aid received scholarships/grants; average award was $500. No-need awards available for academics, minority status, state/district residency.

FINANCIAL AID PROCEDURES

Forms required: FAFSA, institutional form.

Dates and Deadlines: Priority date 2/28; no closing date. Applicants notified on a rolling basis starting 4/15.

Transfers: Non-entitlement aid awarded on first-come, first-serve basis.

CONTACT

Roger Springer, Financial Services Director

3301 Hocking Parkway, Nelsonville, OH 45764-9704

(740) 753-7080

International College of Broadcasting

Dayton, Ohio

www.icbcollege.com   Federal Code: 013132

2-year for-profit technical college in small city.

Enrollment: 104 undergrads.

Selectivity: Open admission.

BASIC COSTS (2007-2008)

Tuition and fees: $8,715.

FINANCIAL AID PICTURE

Students with need: Need-based aid available for full-time and part-time students.

FINANCIAL AID PROCEDURES

Forms required: FAFSA.

Dates and Deadlines: No deadline. Applicants notified on a rolling basis starting 11/1.

CONTACT

Zena Williams, Financial Aid Director

6 South Smithville Road, Dayton, OH 45431

(937) 258-8251 ext. 203

James A. Rhodes State College

Lima, Ohio

www.rhodesstate.edu   Federal Code: 010027

2-year public technical college in large town.

Enrollment: 3,386 undergrads.

Selectivity: Open admission; but selective for some programs.

BASIC COSTS (2007-2008)

Tuition and fees: $4,229; out-of-state residents $8,382.

Per-credit charge: $92; out-of-state residents $185.

FINANCIAL AID PICTURE

Students with need: Need-based aid available for full-time and part-time students. Work study available nights, weekends, and for part-time students.

Students without need: No-need awards available for academics.

FINANCIAL AID PROCEDURES

Forms required: FAFSA.

Dates and Deadlines: Priority date 2/15; no closing date. Applicants notified on a rolling basis starting 5/1; must reply within 2 week(s) of notification.

CONTACT

Cathy Kohli, Director of Financial Aid

4240 Campus Drive, PS 148, Lima, OH 45804-3597

(419) 995-8800

Jefferson Community College

Steubenville, Ohio

www.jcc.edu   Federal Code: 007275

2-year public community and technical college in large town.

Enrollment: 1,727 undergrads, 47% part-time. 360 full-time freshmen.

Selectivity: Open admission; but selective for some programs.

BASIC COSTS (2007-2008)

Tuition and fees: $2,700; out-of-district residents $2,880; out-of-state residents $3,690.

Per-credit charge: $90; out-of-district residents $96; out-of-state residents $123.

Additional info: Residents of 5 neighboring West Virginia counties eligible for in-state, out-of-district tuition rates.

FINANCIAL AID PICTURE

Students with need: Need-based aid available for full-time and part-time students. Work study available nights, weekends, and for part-time students.

Students without need: This college awards aid only to students with need.

Scholarships offered: Horizon Grant; two-year tuition scholarship; awarded to all students graduating from a Jefferson County high school with a 2.5 or above grade point average; student must enroll full-time for the fall semester immediately following high school graduation.

FINANCIAL AID PROCEDURES

Forms required: FAFSA, institutional form.

Dates and Deadlines: Priority date 7/1; no closing date. Applicants notified on a rolling basis starting 6/15.

CONTACT

Kelly Wilson, Director of Student Information and Financial Aid

4000 Sunset Boulevard, Steubenville, OH 43952

(740) 264-5591 ext. 135

John Carroll University

University Heights, Ohio

www.jcu.edu   Federal Code: 003050

4-year private university and liberal arts college in large town, affiliated with Roman Catholic Church.

Enrollment: 3,022 undergrads, 3% part-time. 720 full-time freshmen.

Selectivity: Admits over 75% of applicants.

BASIC COSTS (2007-2008)

Tuition and fees: $26,434.

Per-credit charge: $791.

Room and board: $7,790.

FINANCIAL AID PICTURE

Students with need: Need-based aid available for full-time and part-time students.

Students without need: No-need awards available for academics, minority status, ROTC, state/district residency.

Scholarships offered: Presidential Leadership awards, Arrupe Scholarships and Magis Scholarships are based upon academic background, leadership and service and range from 1/4 to full tuition. The full tuition Castellano Scholarship is awarded each year to a student who will study Latin or Greek; the Mastin Scholarship is offered to 3 students each year who will study natural sciences or math; the Ignatian Mission Scholarship is offered each year to graduates of Jesuit high schools.

Additional info: Institutional form for need analysis required from upperclassmen and transfer students only.

FINANCIAL AID PROCEDURES

Forms required: FAFSA.

Dates and Deadlines: Priority date 2/1; no closing date. Applicants notified on a rolling basis starting 2/1; must reply by 5/1 or within 4 week(s) of notification.

Transfers: Renewable scholarships for students transferring from local community colleges.

CONTACT

Patrick Prosser, Director of Financial Aid
20700 North Park Boulevard, University Heights, OH 44118-4581
(216) 397-4248

Kent State University
Kent, Ohio
www.kent.edu   Federal Code: 003051

4-year public university in large town.

Enrollment: 17,674 undergrads, 14% part-time. 3,751 full-time freshmen.
Selectivity: Admits over 75% of applicants.

BASIC COSTS (2007-2008)

Tuition and fees: $8,430; out-of-state residents $15,862.
Per-credit charge: $384; out-of-state residents $722.
Room and board: $7,200.

FINANCIAL AID PICTURE (2007-2008)

Students with need: Out of 2,972 full-time freshmen who applied for aid, 2,421 were judged to have need. Of these, 2,421 received aid, and 370 had their full need met. Average financial aid package met 63% of need; average scholarship/grant was $5,762; average loan was $4,234. For part-time students, average financial aid package was $6,177.

Students without need: 562 full-time freshmen who did not demonstrate need for aid received scholarships/grants; average award was $3,678. No-need awards available for academics, alumni affiliation, art, athletics, leadership, minority status, music/drama, ROTC, state/district residency.

Scholarships offered: *Merit:* Trustee Scholarship; $1,000-$2,500 annually; based on minimum GPA 3.25, ACT scores, leadership activities; 500 available. *Athletic:* 42 full-time freshmen received athletic scholarships; average amount $16,096.

Cumulative student debt: 72% of graduating class had student loans; average debt was $23,456.

Additional info: Participant in US Department of Education's Quality Assurance Program and Experimental Sites Program.

FINANCIAL AID PROCEDURES

Forms required: FAFSA.

Dates and Deadlines: Priority date 3/1; no closing date. Applicants notified on a rolling basis starting 3/15; must reply within 2 week(s) of notification.

CONTACT

Mark Evans, Director of Student Financial Aid
PO Box 5190, Kent, OH 44242-0001
(330) 672-2972

Kent State University: Ashtabula
Ashtabula, Ohio
www.ashtabula.kent.edu   Federal Code: 003051

2-year public branch campus college in large town.

Enrollment: 1,376 undergrads, 54% part-time. 203 full-time freshmen.
Selectivity: Open admission; but selective for some programs.

BASIC COSTS (2007-2008)

Tuition and fees: $4,770; out-of-state residents $12,202.
Per-credit charge: $217; out-of-state residents $555.

FINANCIAL AID PICTURE (2007-2008)

Students with need: Out of 175 full-time freshmen who applied for aid, 159 were judged to have need. Of these, 159 received aid, and 9 had their full need met. Average financial aid package met 58% of need; average scholarship/grant was $5,487; average loan was $3,362. For part-time students, average financial aid package was $5,937.

Students without need: 6 full-time freshmen who did not demonstrate need for aid received scholarships/grants; average award was $1,567. No-need awards available for academics, alumni affiliation, art, athletics, job skills, leadership, minority status, music/drama, ROTC, state/district residency.

Cumulative student debt: 76% of graduating class had student loans; average debt was $17,142.

FINANCIAL AID PROCEDURES

Forms required: FAFSA.

Dates and Deadlines: Priority date 3/1; no closing date. Applicants notified on a rolling basis starting 3/15; must reply within 2 week(s) of notification.

CONTACT

Kelly Sanford, Admissions Counselor
3325 West l3th Street, Ashtabula, OH 44004
(440) 964-3322

Kent State University: East Liverpool
East Liverpool, Ohio
www.kenteliv.kent.edu   Federal Code: 003051

2-year public branch campus college in large town.

Enrollment: 803 undergrads, 59% part-time. 116 full-time freshmen.
Selectivity: Open admission; but selective for some programs.

BASIC COSTS (2007-2008)

Tuition and fees: $4,770; out-of-state residents $12,202.
Per-credit charge: $217; out-of-state residents $555.

FINANCIAL AID PICTURE (2007-2008)

Students with need: Out of 109 full-time freshmen who applied for aid, 99 were judged to have need. Of these, 99 received aid, and 4 had their full need met. Average financial aid package met 52% of need; average scholarship/grant was $5,189; average loan was $3,468. For part-time students, average financial aid package was $8,611.

Students without need: 4 full-time freshmen who did not demonstrate need for aid received scholarships/grants; average award was $563. No-need awards available for academics, alumni affiliation, art, athletics, leadership, minority status, music/drama, ROTC, state/district residency.

Cumulative student debt: 84% of graduating class had student loans; average debt was $19,410.

FINANCIAL AID PROCEDURES

Forms required: FAFSA.

Dates and Deadlines: Priority date 3/1; no closing date. Applicants notified on a rolling basis starting 3/15; must reply within 2 week(s) of notification.

CONTACT

Judy Olabisi, Fianacial Aid Coordinator
400 East Fourth Street, East Liverpool, OH 43920
(330) 385-3805

Kent State University: Geauga
Burton, Ohio
www.geauga.kent.edu   Federal Code: 003059

2-year public branch campus college in rural community.

Enrollment: 1,191 undergrads, 68% part-time. 111 full-time freshmen.
Selectivity: Open admission.

BASIC COSTS (2007-2008)

Tuition and fees: $4,770; out-of-state residents $12,202.
Per-credit charge: $217; out-of-state residents $555.

FINANCIAL AID PICTURE (2007-2008)

Students with need: Average financial aid package met 53% of need; average scholarship/grant was $4,139; average loan was $3,408. For part-time students, average financial aid package was $5,417.
Students without need: No-need awards available for academics, alumni affiliation, art, athletics, leadership, minority status, music/drama, ROTC, state/district residency.
Cumulative student debt: 63% of graduating class had student loans; average debt was $25,400.

FINANCIAL AID PROCEDURES

Forms required: FAFSA.
Dates and Deadlines: Priority date 3/1; no closing date. Applicants notified by 3/15; must reply within 2 week(s) of notification.

CONTACT

Donna Holcomb, Financial Aid Advisor
Office of Admissions, Burton, OH 44021
(440) 834-8846

Kent State University: Salem

Salem, Ohio
www.salem.kent.edu   Federal Code: 003061

2-year public branch campus college in large town.
Enrollment: 1,203 undergrads, 49% part-time. 166 full-time freshmen.
Selectivity: Open admission; but selective for some programs.

BASIC COSTS (2007-2008)

Tuition and fees: $4,770; out-of-state residents $12,202.
Per-credit charge: $217; out-of-state residents $555.

FINANCIAL AID PICTURE (2007-2008)

Students with need: Out of 136 full-time freshmen who applied for aid, 123 were judged to have need. Of these, 123 received aid, and 10 had their full need met. Average financial aid package met 60% of need; average scholarship/grant was $4,810; average loan was $3,482. For part-time students, average financial aid package was $5,720.
Students without need: 4 full-time freshmen who did not demonstrate need for aid received scholarships/grants; average award was $2,983. No-need awards available for academics, alumni affiliation, art, athletics, leadership, minority status, music/drama, ROTC.
Cumulative student debt: 75% of graduating class had student loans; average debt was $16,734.

FINANCIAL AID PROCEDURES

Forms required: FAFSA.
Dates and Deadlines: Priority date 3/1; no closing date. Applicants notified on a rolling basis starting 3/15; must reply within 2 week(s) of notification.
Transfers: Priority date 2/15.

CONTACT

Donna Holcomb, Financial Aid Advisor
2491 State Route 45 South, Salem, OH 44460
(440) 834-3737

Kent State University: Stark

Canton, Ohio
www.stark.kent.edu   Federal Code: 003054

2-year public branch campus college in small city.
Enrollment: 3,499 undergrads, 42% part-time. 593 full-time freshmen.

Selectivity: Open admission; but selective for some programs.

BASIC COSTS (2007-2008)

Tuition and fees: $4,770; out-of-state residents $12,202.
Per-credit charge: $217; out-of-state residents $555.

FINANCIAL AID PICTURE (2007-2008)

Students with need: Out of 445 full-time freshmen who applied for aid, 378 were judged to have need. Of these, 378 received aid, and 43 had their full need met. Average financial aid package met 62% of need; average scholarship/grant was $4,281; average loan was $3,359. For part-time students, average financial aid package was $5,451.
Students without need: 20 full-time freshmen who did not demonstrate need for aid received scholarships/grants; average award was $1,976. No-need awards available for academics, alumni affiliation, art, athletics, leadership, minority status, music/drama, ROTC, state/district residency.
Cumulative student debt: 69% of graduating class had student loans; average debt was $21,278.

FINANCIAL AID PROCEDURES

Forms required: FAFSA.
Dates and Deadlines: Priority date 3/1; no closing date. Applicants notified on a rolling basis starting 3/15; must reply within 2 week(s) of notification.

CONTACT

Nina Antram, Financial Aid Officer
6000 Frank Avenue NW, Canton, OH 44720-7599
(330) 499-9600

Kent State University: Trumbull

Warren, Ohio
www.trumbull.kent.edu   Federal Code: 003051

2-year public branch campus college in small city.
Enrollment: 1,972 undergrads, 50% part-time. 288 full-time freshmen.
Selectivity: Open admission.

BASIC COSTS (2007-2008)

Tuition and fees: $4,770; out-of-state residents $12,202.
Per-credit charge: $217; out-of-state residents $555.

FINANCIAL AID PICTURE (2007-2008)

Students with need: Out of 232 full-time freshmen who applied for aid, 206 were judged to have need. Of these, 206 received aid, and 18 had their full need met. Average financial aid package met 61% of need; average scholarship/grant was $4,782; average loan was $3,351. For part-time students, average financial aid package was $5,441.
Students without need: 3 full-time freshmen who did not demonstrate need for aid received scholarships/grants; average award was $1,433. No-need awards available for academics, alumni affiliation, art, athletics, leadership, minority status, music/drama, ROTC, state/district residency.
Cumulative student debt: 68% of graduating class had student loans; average debt was $20,334.

FINANCIAL AID PROCEDURES

Forms required: FAFSA.
Dates and Deadlines: Priority date 3/1; no closing date. Applicants notified on a rolling basis starting 3/15; must reply within 2 week(s) of notification.

CONTACT

Nina Antram, Financial Aid Coordinator
4314 Mahoning Avenue, NW, Warren, OH 44483-1998
(330) 847-0571

Kent State University: Tuscarawas
New Philadelphia, Ohio
www.tusc.kent.edu   Federal Code: 003051

2-year public branch campus college in large town.
Enrollment: 1,757 undergrads, 46% part-time. 308 full-time freshmen.
Selectivity: Open admission; but selective for some programs and for out-of-state students.

BASIC COSTS (2007-2008)
Tuition and fees: $4,770; out-of-state residents $12,202.
Per-credit charge: $217; out-of-state residents $555.

FINANCIAL AID PICTURE (2007-2008)
Students with need: Out of 257 full-time freshmen who applied for aid, 227 were judged to have need. Of these, 227 received aid, and 20 had their full need met. Average financial aid package met 61% of need; average scholarship/grant was $4,904; average loan was $3,480. For part-time students, average financial aid package was $5,582.
Students without need: 8 full-time freshmen who did not demonstrate need for aid received scholarships/grants; average award was $844. No-need awards available for academics, alumni affiliation, art, athletics, leadership, minority status, music/drama, ROTC.
Cumulative student debt: 75% of graduating class had student loans; average debt was $16,751.

FINANCIAL AID PROCEDURES
Forms required: FAFSA.
Dates and Deadlines: Closing date 3/1. Applicants notified on a rolling basis starting 3/15; must reply within 2 week(s) of notification.
Transfers: Financial aid transcripts from all previous institutions required.

CONTACT
Mark Evans, Financial Aid Director
330 University Drive Northeast, New Philadelphia, OH 44663-9403
(330) 339-3391

Kenyon College
Gambier, Ohio   Federal Code: 003065
www.kenyon.edu   CSS Code: 1370

4-year private liberal arts college in rural community.
Enrollment: 1,653 undergrads. 458 full-time freshmen.
Selectivity: Admits less than 50% of applicants.

BASIC COSTS (2008-2009)
Tuition and fees: $40,240.
Room and board: $6,590.

FINANCIAL AID PICTURE (2007-2008)
Students with need: Out of 253 full-time freshmen who applied for aid, 191 were judged to have need. Of these, 190 received aid, and 101 had their full need met. Average financial aid package met 98% of need; average scholarship/grant was $25,265; average loan was $3,318.
Students without need: 97 full-time freshmen who did not demonstrate need for aid received scholarships/grants; average award was $10,782. No-need awards available for academics, leadership, minority status.
Scholarships offered: Honor Scholarships, Science Scholarships, African-American Scholarships, Latino Scholarships, and Asian-American Scholarships competitively based on excellence in academic achievement, extracurricular leadership, and community involvement, and range from $11,000-$26,000 annually. Distinguished Academic Scholarships based on academic accomplishment, standardized test results, and extracurricular achievement; $4,000-$12,000. Scholarships for National Merit finalists available.
Cumulative student debt: 62% of graduating class had student loans; average debt was $19,489.

FINANCIAL AID PROCEDURES
Forms required: FAFSA, CSS PROFILE.
Dates and Deadlines: Closing date 2/15. Applicants notified by 4/1; must reply by 5/1.
Transfers: Closing date 4/15. Applicants notified by 5/15; must reply by 6/1.

CONTACT
Craig Daugherty, Director of Financial Aid
Ransom Hall, Gambier, OH 43022
(740) 427-5430

Kettering College of Medical Arts
Kettering, Ohio
www.kcma.edu   Federal Code: 007035

4-year private health science and nursing college in large city, affiliated with Seventh-day Adventists.
Enrollment: 738 undergrads, 45% part-time. 58 full-time freshmen.
Selectivity: Admits less than 50% of applicants.

BASIC COSTS (2008-2009)
Tuition and fees: $9,690.
Per-credit charge: $315.
Room only: $2,900.
Additional info: Tuition and fees may vary by program.

FINANCIAL AID PICTURE
Students with need: Need-based aid available for full-time and part-time students.
Students without need: No-need awards available for academics.

FINANCIAL AID PROCEDURES
Forms required: FAFSA, institutional form.
Dates and Deadlines: Priority date 3/31; no closing date. Applicants notified on a rolling basis starting 5/15; must reply within 3 week(s) of notification.

CONTACT
Kim Snell, Director of Student Finance
3737 Southern Boulevard, Kettering, OH 45429-1299
(937) 296-7210

Lake Erie College
Painesville, Ohio
www.lec.edu   Federal Code: 003066

4-year private liberal arts college in large town.
Enrollment: 795 undergrads, 4% part-time. 237 full-time freshmen.
Selectivity: Admits 50 to 75% of applicants.

BASIC COSTS (2008-2009)
Tuition and fees: $25,220.
Per-credit charge: $560.
Room and board: $7,650.
Additional info: Equestrian fee $880 per course.

FINANCIAL AID PICTURE (2006-2007)
Students with need: 72% of average financial aid package awarded as scholarships/grants, 28% awarded as loans/jobs. Need-based aid available for part-time students. Work study available nights, weekends, and for part-time students.
Students without need: No-need awards available for academics, art, leadership, music/drama, state/district residency.
Additional info: Twins' scholarship, sibling discount.

FINANCIAL AID PROCEDURES
Forms required: FAFSA.

Dates and Deadlines: No deadline. Applicants notified on a rolling basis; must reply within 2 week(s) of notification.
Transfers: No deadline.

CONTACT
Tricia Canfield, Director of Financial Aid
391 West Washington Street, Painesville, OH 44077-3389
(440) 375-7100

Lakeland Community College
Kirtland, Ohio
www.lakelandcc.edu   Federal Code: 006804

2-year public community college in large town.
Enrollment: 8,780 undergrads.
Selectivity: Open admission; but selective for some programs.

BASIC COSTS (2007-2008)
Tuition and fees: $2,698; out-of-district residents $3,306; out-of-state residents $7,067.
Per-credit charge: $79; out-of-district residents $99; out-of-state residents $225.

FINANCIAL AID PICTURE
Students with need: Need-based aid available for full-time and part-time students. Work study available nights, weekends, and for part-time students.
Students without need: No-need awards available for academics, art, athletics, job skills, leadership, minority status, music/drama, state/district residency.
Additional info: Loans available for tuition and books.

FINANCIAL AID PROCEDURES
Forms required: FAFSA, institutional form.
Dates and Deadlines: Priority date 3/1; no closing date. Applicants notified on a rolling basis starting 5/1.
Transfers: Ohio Instructional Grant Transfer Form.

CONTACT
Melissa Amspaugh, Director of Financial Aid
7700 Clocktower Drive, Kirtland, OH 44094
(440) 953-7070

Laura and Alvin Siegal College of Judaic Studies
Cleveland, Ohio
www.siegalcollege.edu   Federal Code: 012838

4-year private liberal arts and teachers college in large town, affiliated with Jewish faith.
Enrollment: 13 undergrads, 100% part-time.

BASIC COSTS (2007-2008)
Tuition and fees: $15,775.
Per-credit charge: $525.
Additional info: Tuition/fee waivers available for adults.

FINANCIAL AID PICTURE (2007-2008)
Students with need: 69% of average financial aid package awarded as scholarships/grants, 31% awarded as loans/jobs. Need-based aid available for part-time students.

FINANCIAL AID PROCEDURES
Forms required: institutional form.
Dates and Deadlines: No deadline. Applicants notified on a rolling basis.

CONTACT
Ruth Kronick, Director of Student Services
26500 Shaker Boulevard, Cleveland, OH 44122
(216) 464-4050 ext. 101

Lorain County Community College
Elyria, Ohio
www.lorainccc.edu   Federal Code: 003068

2-year public community college in small city.
Enrollment: 10,894 undergrads.
Selectivity: Open admission.

BASIC COSTS (2007-2008)
Tuition and fees: $2,400; out-of-district residents $2,890; out-of-state residents $5,838.
Per-credit charge: $88; out-of-district residents $106; out-of-state residents $220.

FINANCIAL AID PICTURE
Students with need: Need-based aid available for full-time and part-time students. Work study available nights, weekends, and for part-time students.
Students without need: No-need awards available for academics.
Scholarships offered: Presidential Scholarships and Trustee Scholarships available.

FINANCIAL AID PROCEDURES
Forms required: FAFSA.
Dates and Deadlines: Priority date 8/15; no closing date. Applicants notified on a rolling basis starting 7/1; must reply within 3 week(s) of notification.

CONTACT
Stephanie Sutton, Manager of Financial Aid
1005 Abbe Road North, Elyria, OH 44035-1691
(490) 366-4034

Lourdes College
Sylvania, Ohio
www.lourdes.edu   Federal Code: 003069

4-year private liberal arts college in large town, affiliated with Roman Catholic Church.
Enrollment: 1,700 undergrads, 44% part-time. 108 full-time freshmen.
Selectivity: Admits over 75% of applicants.

BASIC COSTS (2008-2009)
Tuition and fees: $14,730.
Per-credit charge: $431.

FINANCIAL AID PICTURE (2006-2007)
Students with need: Out of 92 full-time freshmen who applied for aid, 71 were judged to have need. Of these, 71 received aid. For part-time students, average financial aid package was $5,514.
Students without need: No-need awards available for academics, art, minority status, state/district residency.

FINANCIAL AID PROCEDURES
Forms required: FAFSA.
Dates and Deadlines: Priority date 3/1; no closing date. Applicants notified on a rolling basis starting 3/1; must reply within 4 week(s) of notification.

CONTACT
Denise McCluskey, Director of Financial Aid
6832 Convent Boulevard, Sylvania, OH 43560-2898
(419) 824-3732

Malone College
Canton, Ohio
www.malone.edu   Federal Code: 003072

4-year private liberal arts college in small city, affiliated with Evangelical Friends Church-Eastern Region.

Enrollment: 1,964 undergrads, 10% part-time. 388 full-time freshmen.

Selectivity: Admits over 75% of applicants.

BASIC COSTS (2008-2009)
Tuition and fees: $20,020.

Per-credit charge: $340.

Room and board: $6,830.

FINANCIAL AID PICTURE (2007-2008)
Students with need: Out of 356 full-time freshmen who applied for aid, 325 were judged to have need. Of these, 325 received aid, and 55 had their full need met. Average financial aid package met 74% of need; average scholarship/grant was $11,306; average loan was $4,282. For part-time students, average financial aid package was $5,802.

Students without need: 38 full-time freshmen who did not demonstrate need for aid received scholarships/grants; average award was $6,370. No-need awards available for academics, alumni affiliation, athletics, leadership, music/drama, religious affiliation.

Scholarships offered: 23 full-time freshmen received athletic scholarships; average amount $4,558.

Cumulative student debt: 85% of graduating class had student loans; average debt was $23,342.

Additional info: Prepayment discounts and employer deferred payments available for students in adult degree-completion programs. Employer deferred payment plan is available for traditional undergraduate students.

FINANCIAL AID PROCEDURES
Forms required: FAFSA.

Dates and Deadlines: Priority date 3/1; closing date 7/31. Applicants notified on a rolling basis starting 3/1; must reply within 2 week(s) of notification.

CONTACT
Pamela Pustay, Director of Financial Aid

515 25th Street Northwest, Canton, OH 44709-3897

(330) 471-8100 ext. 8159

Marietta College
Marietta, Ohio
www.marietta.edu   Federal Code: 003073

4-year private liberal arts college in large town.

Enrollment: 1,466 undergrads, 2% part-time. 415 full-time freshmen.

Selectivity: Admits over 75% of applicants.

BASIC COSTS (2008-2009)
Tuition and fees: $26,080.

Room and board: $7,764.

FINANCIAL AID PICTURE (2007-2008)
Students with need: Out of 394 full-time freshmen who applied for aid, 333 were judged to have need. Of these, 333 received aid, and 162 had their full need met. Average financial aid package met 94% of need; average scholarship/grant was $17,984; average loan was $4,125. For part-time students, average financial aid package was $13,281.

Students without need: 61 full-time freshmen who did not demonstrate need for aid received scholarships/grants; average award was $8,800. No-need awards available for academics, alumni affiliation, art, leadership, minority status, music/drama, state/district residency.

Scholarships offered: Marietta College Pioneer Scholars program recognizes high school seniors with outstanding academic achievements and potential with demonstrated extracurricular involvement, leadership, and service. The strongest students in our applicant pool (approximately the top third) each year are named as Pioneers Scholars, guaranteed a $6,000 Dean's Scholarship and an opportunity to interview for the higher awards during the Pioneer Scholars Competitions. McCoy Scholarship (full tuition, room/board), Trustees' Scholarships (up to 10 awarded full tuition), President's Scholarship (up to 20 awarded half tuition) and Dean's Awards (from $6,000-$10,000) are awarded through the Pioneer Scholar Competition. Other scholarships: Rickey Physics Scholarships, $18,000; Charles Sumner Harrison Awards for multicultural students and leaders, $5,000; Fine Arts Awards, $1,000-$3,000 by audition/portfolio. All scholarships renewable for four years.

Additional info: Auditions/portfolios for art, creative writing, music and theater required for competitive fine art scholarships.

FINANCIAL AID PROCEDURES
Forms required: FAFSA, institutional form.

Dates and Deadlines: Priority date 3/1; closing date 4/15. Applicants notified on a rolling basis starting 3/15; must reply by 5/1 or within 2 week(s) of notification.

Transfers: Priority date 4/15; closing date 6/15. Applicants notified on a rolling basis starting 4/1; must reply by 6/30 or within 2 week(s) of notification.

CONTACT
Kevin Lamb, Director of Student Financial Services

215 Fifth Street, Marietta, OH 45750-4005

(740) 376-4712

Marion Technical College
Marion, Ohio
www.mtc.edu   Federal Code: 010736

2-year public technical college in large town.

Enrollment: 1,410 undergrads.

Selectivity: Open admission; but selective for some programs.

BASIC COSTS (2007-2008)
Tuition and fees: $3,860; out-of-state residents $5,768.

Per-credit charge: $101; out-of-state residents $154.

FINANCIAL AID PICTURE (2007-2008)
Students with need: 68% of average financial aid package awarded as scholarships/grants, 32% awarded as loans/jobs. Need-based aid available for part-time students.

Students without need: No-need awards available for academics, leadership, minority status.

Scholarships offered: Foundation Scholarship: first year full tuition; for applicants in top 5% of class. President's Scholarship: $1,200; for applicants in top 50% of class. Tech Prep Scholarship: $1,200; for graduates of Tech Prep program. All scholarships require 2.5 GPA and successful completion of proficiency exams.

FINANCIAL AID PROCEDURES
Forms required: FAFSA, institutional form.

Dates and Deadlines: Closing date 6/1. Applicants notified on a rolling basis.

Transfers: No deadline. Applicants notified on a rolling basis.

CONTACT
R Andrew Harper, Vice President of Student Services

1467 Mount Vernon Avenue, Marion, OH 43302-5694

(740) 389-4636 ext. 221

MedCentral College of Nursing

Mansfield, Ohio
www.medcentral.edu   Federal Code: 035864

4-year private nursing college in small city.
Enrollment: 365 undergrads.
Selectivity: Admits 50 to 75% of applicants.

BASIC COSTS (2007-2008)

Tuition and fees: $10,545.
Per-credit charge: $325.
Room only: $4,890.

FINANCIAL AID PICTURE

Students with need: Need-based aid available for full-time and part-time students. Work study available nights, weekends, and for part-time students.
Students without need: No-need awards available for academics, leadership.
Cumulative student debt: 98% of graduating class had student loans; average debt was $17,125.

FINANCIAL AID PROCEDURES

Forms required: FAFSA, institutional form.
Dates and Deadlines: Priority date 4/2; closing date 9/15. Applicants notified on a rolling basis starting 4/1; must reply by 5/1 or within 2 week(s) of notification.
Transfers: Closing date 4/1. Applicants notified on a rolling basis starting 3/15; must reply by 5/1 or within 2 week(s) of notification.

CONTACT

Allen Wright, Director of Financial Aid
335 Glessner Avenue, Mansfield, OH 44903-2265
(419) 520-2600

Mercy College of Northwest Ohio

Toledo, Ohio
www.mercycollege.edu   Federal Code: 030970

4-year private health science and nursing college in large city, affiliated with Roman Catholic Church.
Enrollment: 797 undergrads, 49% part-time. 57 full-time freshmen.
Selectivity: Admits over 75% of applicants.

BASIC COSTS (2008-2009)

Tuition and fees: $9,546.

FINANCIAL AID PICTURE (2006-2007)

Students with need: Out of 46 full-time freshmen who applied for aid, 43 were judged to have need. Of these, 43 received aid, and 2 had their full need met. Average financial aid package met 45% of need; average scholarship/grant was $6,485; average loan was $2,920. For part-time students, average financial aid package was $4,750.
Students without need: 1 full-time freshmen who did not demonstrate need for aid received scholarships/grants; average award was $10,000. No-need awards available for academics, alumni affiliation, religious affiliation, state/district residency.
Cumulative student debt: 82% of graduating class had student loans; average debt was $15,069.

FINANCIAL AID PROCEDURES

Forms required: FAFSA.
Dates and Deadlines: Priority date 4/1; no closing date. Applicants notified on a rolling basis starting 3/1; must reply within 2 week(s) of notification.

CONTACT

Julie Leslie, Financial Aid Director
2221 Madison Avenue, Toledo, OH 43604
(419) 251-1598

Miami University: Hamilton Campus

Hamilton, Ohio
www.ham.muohio.edu   Federal Code: 003077

2-year public branch campus college in small city.
Enrollment: 3,247 undergrads, 24% part-time. 568 full-time freshmen.
Selectivity: Open admission; but selective for some programs.

BASIC COSTS (2007-2008)

Tuition and fees: $4,320; out-of-state residents $16,452.
Per-credit charge: $180; out-of-state residents $708.

FINANCIAL AID PICTURE

Students with need: Need-based aid available for full-time and part-time students. Work study available nights, weekends, and for part-time students.
Students without need: No-need awards available for academics, athletics, leadership, minority status, state/district residency.
Additional info: Special gift funds for needy, multicultural students who enter with appropriate academic record. Separate application required for scholarships; closing date January 31.

FINANCIAL AID PROCEDURES

Forms required: FAFSA.
Dates and Deadlines: Priority date 2/15; no closing date. Applicants notified on a rolling basis starting 4/1.
Transfers: Transfer students must complete one semester at Miami University to be considered for scholarships.

CONTACT

Ann Alfers, Financial Aid Coordinator
1601 University Boulevard, Hamilton, OH 45011-3399
(513) 785-3123

Miami University: Middletown Campus

Middletown, Ohio
www.mid.muohio.edu   Federal Code: 003077

2-year public branch campus and community college in large town.
Enrollment: 2,398 undergrads.
Selectivity: Open admission; but selective for some programs.

BASIC COSTS (2007-2008)

Tuition and fees: $4,350; out-of-state residents $17,210.
Per-credit charge: $180; out-of-state residents $716.
Additional info: Students paying by the credit hour pay $15 general fee per credit hour.

FINANCIAL AID PICTURE

Students with need: Need-based aid available for full-time and part-time students.
Students without need: This college awards aid only to students with need.

FINANCIAL AID PROCEDURES

Forms required: FAFSA.
Dates and Deadlines: Priority date 2/15; no closing date. Applicants notified on a rolling basis.
Transfers: Applicants must file by February 15 to be considered for campus-based aid or alumni scholarships.

CONTACT
Stacey Adams
4200 East University Boulevard, Middletown, OH 45042
(513) 727-3346

Miami University: Oxford Campus
Oxford, Ohio
www.muohio.edu   Federal Code: 003077

4-year public university in small town.
Enrollment: 14,479 undergrads, 2% part-time. 3,398 full-time freshmen.
Selectivity: Admits over 75% of applicants.

BASIC COSTS (2007-2008)
Tuition and fees: $11,925; out-of-state residents $24,377.
Per-credit charge: $875; out-of-state residents $875.
Room and board: $8,600.
Additional info: Tuition ranges from $7,161 to $9,911 depending on amount of built-in scholarship aid which varies by income.

FINANCIAL AID PICTURE
Students with need: Need-based aid available for full-time and part-time students. Work study available nights, weekends, and for part-time students.
Students without need: No-need awards available for academics, art, athletics, leadership, minority status, music/drama, ROTC, state/district residency.
Scholarships offered: Ohio Resident Scholarship and Ohio Leader Scholarship; added together, amounts range from $10,000 to $11,250 depending on need; all full-time students who are Ohio residents are eligible.

FINANCIAL AID PROCEDURES
Forms required: FAFSA.
Dates and Deadlines: Priority date 2/15; no closing date. Applicants notified on a rolling basis starting 3/20; must reply by 5/1 or within 3 week(s) of notification.
Transfers: Institutional merit scholarships not available to transfer students during first year of enrollment.

CONTACT
Chuck Knepfle, Director of Student Financial Aid
301 South Campus Avenue, Oxford, OH 45056-3434
(513) 529-8734

Mount Carmel College of Nursing
Columbus, Ohio
www.mccn.edu   Federal Code: 030719

4-year private nursing college in very large city, affiliated with Roman Catholic.
Enrollment: 641 undergrads.
Selectivity: Admits 50 to 75% of applicants.

BASIC COSTS (2007-2008)
Tuition and fees: $7,596.

FINANCIAL AID PICTURE (2007-2008)
Students with need: 52% of average financial aid package awarded as scholarships/grants, 48% awarded as loans/jobs.

FINANCIAL AID PROCEDURES
Forms required: FAFSA, institutional form.
Dates and Deadlines: Priority date 3/1; no closing date. Applicants notified on a rolling basis.

CONTACT
Alyncia Bowen, Financial Aid Director
127 South Davis Avenue, Columbus, OH 43222-1589
(614) 234-5800

Mount Union College
Alliance, Ohio
www.muc.edu   Federal Code: 003083

4-year private liberal arts college in large town, affiliated with United Methodist Church.
Enrollment: 2,128 undergrads, 3% part-time. 637 full-time freshmen.
Selectivity: Admits over 75% of applicants.

BASIC COSTS (2007-2008)
Tuition and fees: $22,050.
Per-credit charge: $920.
Room and board: $6,700.
Additional info: Tuition/fee waivers available for minority students.

FINANCIAL AID PICTURE (2006-2007)
Students with need: Out of 575 full-time freshmen who applied for aid, 502 were judged to have need. Of these, 502 received aid, and 102 had their full need met. Average financial aid package met 82% of need; average scholarship/grant was $13,334; average loan was $4,321. For part-time students, average financial aid package was $16,427.
Students without need: 114 full-time freshmen who did not demonstrate need for aid received scholarships/grants; average award was $12,200. No-need awards available for academics, alumni affiliation, art, job skills, leadership, music/drama, religious affiliation, ROTC, state/district residency.
Cumulative student debt: 94% of graduating class had student loans; average debt was $20,153.

FINANCIAL AID PROCEDURES
Forms required: FAFSA.
Dates and Deadlines: Priority date 4/1; no closing date. Applicants notified on a rolling basis starting 3/15; must reply within 4 week(s) of notification.
Transfers: No deadline. Applicants notified on a rolling basis; must reply within 4 week(s) of notification.

CONTACT
Sandra Pittenger, Director of Student Financial Services
1972 Clark Avenue, Alliance, OH 44601-3993
(330) 823-2674

Mount Vernon Nazarene University
Mount Vernon, Ohio
www.mvnu.edu   Federal Code: 007085

4-year private university in large town, affiliated with Church of the Nazarene.
Enrollment: 2,033 undergrads, 6% part-time. 351 full-time freshmen.
Selectivity: Admits over 75% of applicants.

BASIC COSTS (2007-2008)
Tuition and fees: $18,064.
Per-credit charge: $626.
Room and board: $5,286.

FINANCIAL AID PICTURE (2007-2008)
Students with need: Out of 351 full-time freshmen who applied for aid, 307 were judged to have need. Of these, 307 received aid, and 49 had their full need met. Average financial aid package met 76% of need; average scholarship/grant was $9,315; average loan was $3,889. For part-time students, average financial aid package was $6,178.
Students without need: 37 full-time freshmen who did not demonstrate need for aid received scholarships/grants; average award was $3,734. No-

need awards available for academics, athletics, leadership, minority status, music/drama, religious affiliation, state/district residency.

Scholarships offered: *Merit:* Hugh C. Benner Excellence Scholarship; $4,000 per year. Hugh C. Benner Memorial Scholarship; $3,250 per year. Hugh C. Benner Scholarship; $2,500 per year. Distinction Scholarship; $2,000 per year. Honor Scholarship; $1,500 per year. All based on ACT or SAT scores and require a minimum GPA to be maintained. Rank Scholarship; $1,250 per year; based on ACT or SAT scores and high school GPA or class rank, require maintenance of minimum GPA. Valedictorian/Salutatorian Scholarship; $500 per year; require maintenance of minimum GPA. Top Ten Scholarship; $1,000 per year; must rank in top ten of class at MVNU. ***Athletic:*** 11 full-time freshmen received athletic scholarships; average amount $2,430.

Cumulative student debt: 78% of graduating class had student loans; average debt was $21,855.

FINANCIAL AID PROCEDURES

Forms required: FAFSA, institutional form.

Dates and Deadlines: Priority date 3/15; no closing date. Applicants notified on a rolling basis starting 2/15; must reply within 2 week(s) of notification.

Transfers: No deadline. Applicants notified on a rolling basis starting 9/1; must reply within 2 week(s) of notification. Filing deadline for Ohio financial aid is October 1st.

CONTACT

Michelle Saigh, Director of Student Financial Planning
800 Martinsburg Road, Mount Vernon, OH 43050
(740) 397-9000 ext. 4520

Muskingum College
New Concord, Ohio
www.muskingum.edu   Federal Code: 003084

4-year private liberal arts college in small town, affiliated with Presbyterian Church (USA).

Enrollment: 1,648 undergrads, 6% part-time. 430 full-time freshmen.

Selectivity: Admits over 75% of applicants.

BASIC COSTS (2008-2009)

Tuition and fees: $19,125.

Per-credit charge: $385.

Room and board: $7,350.

Additional info: Tuition/fee waivers available for minority students.

FINANCIAL AID PICTURE (2007-2008)

Students with need: Out of 390 full-time freshmen who applied for aid, 345 were judged to have need. Of these, 345 received aid, and 80 had their full need met. Average financial aid package met 60% of need; average scholarship/grant was $12,590; average loan was $3,610. For part-time students, average financial aid package was $3,818.

Students without need: 66 full-time freshmen who did not demonstrate need for aid received scholarships/grants; average award was $6,510. No-need awards available for academics, alumni affiliation, art, leadership, minority status, music/drama, religious affiliation, state/district residency.

Cumulative student debt: 80% of graduating class had student loans; average debt was $23,619.

Additional info: Scholarship priority date February 1.

FINANCIAL AID PROCEDURES

Forms required: FAFSA.

Dates and Deadlines: Priority date 3/15; closing date 8/1. Applicants notified on a rolling basis starting 3/1; must reply by 5/1 or within 2 week(s) of notification.

CONTACT

Jeff Zellers, Vice President of Enrollment
163 Stormont Street, New Concord, OH 43762-1199
(740) 826-8139

North Central State College
Mansfield, Ohio
www.ncstatecollege.edu   Federal Code: 005313

2-year public technical college in small city.

Enrollment: 2,681 undergrads.

Selectivity: Open admission; but selective for some programs.

BASIC COSTS (2007-2008)

Tuition and fees: $2,907; out-of-state residents $5,804.

Per-credit charge: $81; out-of-state residents $162.

FINANCIAL AID PICTURE

Students with need: Need-based aid available for full-time and part-time students.

Students without need: This college awards aid only to students with need.

FINANCIAL AID PROCEDURES

Forms required: FAFSA.

Dates and Deadlines: Priority date 4/1; no closing date. Applicants notified on a rolling basis starting 5/30; must reply within 1 week(s) of notification.

CONTACT

Doris Smith, Assistant Dean of Financial Aid
Box 698, Mansfield, OH 44901
(419) 755-4899

Northwest State Community College
Archbold, Ohio
www.northweststate.edu   Federal Code: 008677

2-year public community and technical college in small town.

Enrollment: 1,830 undergrads.

Selectivity: Open admission; but selective for some programs.

BASIC COSTS (2007-2008)

Tuition and fees: $4,080; out-of-state residents $8,160.

Per-credit charge: $136; out-of-state residents $272.

FINANCIAL AID PICTURE

Students with need: Need-based aid available for full-time and part-time students.

Students without need: No-need awards available for academics.

FINANCIAL AID PROCEDURES

Forms required: FAFSA, institutional form.

Dates and Deadlines: Priority date 6/1; no closing date. Applicants notified on a rolling basis starting 4/1.

CONTACT

Amy Francis, Financial Aid Officer
22600 State Route 34, Archbold, OH 43502
(419) 267-5511 ext. 326

Notre Dame College
Cleveland, Ohio
www.notredamecollege.edu   Federal Code: 003085

4-year private liberal arts college in very large city, affiliated with Roman Catholic Church.

Enrollment: 1,639 undergrads.

Selectivity: Admits 50 to 75% of applicants.

BASIC COSTS (2007-2008)

Tuition and fees: $21,090.

Per-credit charge: $425.

Room and board: $7,156.

FINANCIAL AID PICTURE

Students with need: Need-based aid available for full-time students.

Students without need: No-need awards available for academics, state/district residency.

Scholarships offered: Merit Scholarships: based on cumulative high school and ACT or SAT scores; $2,500-$7,500. Presidential Scholarships: awarded to students with cumulative high school GPA of at least 3.9 and ACT composite of at least 27 or SAT total of at least 1210 (exclusive of writing); $3,000 awarded in addition to Merit Scholarships.

FINANCIAL AID PROCEDURES

Forms required: FAFSA.

Dates and Deadlines: Closing date 5/1. Applicants notified on a rolling basis starting 1/1; must reply within 2 week(s) of notification.

CONTACT

Mary McCrystal, Director of Student Financial Assistance

4545 College Road, Cleveland, OH 44121-4293

(216) 373-5263

Oberlin College

Oberlin, Ohio   Federal Code: 003086

www.oberlin.edu   CSS Code: 1587

4-year private music and liberal arts college in small town.

Enrollment: 2,762 undergrads, 2% part-time. 736 full-time freshmen.

Selectivity: Admits less than 50% of applicants.

BASIC COSTS (2007-2008)

Tuition and fees: $36,500.

Per-credit charge: $1,500.

Room and board: $9,280.

FINANCIAL AID PICTURE (2007-2008)

Students with need: 79% of average financial aid package awarded as scholarships/grants, 21% awarded as loans/jobs. Need-based aid available for part-time students.

Students without need: No-need awards available for academics, leadership, music/drama, state/district residency.

Scholarships offered: Bonner Scholarship; based on community service. John Frederick Oberlin Scholarship; based on academic merit. Stern Scholarship; based on excellence in sciences. Mary Elizabeth Johnston Scholarship; based on academic merit; available to Ohio residents only. Dean's Scholarship; available to Conservatory of Music students.

FINANCIAL AID PROCEDURES

Forms required: FAFSA, CSS PROFILE, institutional form.

Dates and Deadlines: Closing date 1/15. Applicants notified by 4/1; must reply by 5/1 or within 2 week(s) of notification.

Transfers: Closing date 3/1. Limited scholarship funding available for transfer students.

CONTACT

Robert Reddy, Director of Financial Aid

Carnegie Building, 101 North Professor Street, Oberlin, OH 44074

(440) 775-8142

Ohio Business College

Lorain, Ohio

www.ohiobusinesscollege.edu   Federal Code: 021585

2-year for-profit branch campus and business college in small city.

Enrollment: 177 undergrads.

Selectivity: Open admission.

BASIC COSTS (2008-2009)

Tuition and fees: $9,705.

Per-credit charge: $205.

FINANCIAL AID PICTURE

Students with need: Need-based aid available for full-time and part-time students.

FINANCIAL AID PROCEDURES

Forms required: FAFSA.

Dates and Deadlines: No deadline. Applicants notified on a rolling basis.

CONTACT

Becky Booher, Director of Financial Aid

1907 North Ridge Road, Lorain, OH 44055

Ohio Business College: Sandusky

Sandusky, Ohio

www.ohiobusinesscollege.edu   Federal Code: 021585

2-year for-profit business college in small city.

Enrollment: 270 undergrads.

Selectivity: Open admission.

BASIC COSTS (2008-2009)

Tuition and fees: $9,585.

Per-credit charge: $205.

FINANCIAL AID PICTURE

Students with need: Need-based aid available for full-time and part-time students.

FINANCIAL AID PROCEDURES

Forms required: FAFSA.

Dates and Deadlines: No deadline.

CONTACT

Gerilyn Wilson, Financial Aid Administrator

5202 Timber Commons Drive, Sandusky, OH 44870

(419) 627-8345 ext. 14

Ohio Christian University

Circleville, Ohio   Federal Code: 003030

www.ohiochristian.edu   CSS Code: 1088

4-year private Bible college in large town, affiliated with Churches of Christ in Christian Union.

Enrollment: 616 undergrads, 14% part-time. 151 full-time freshmen.

Selectivity: Open admission; but selective for some programs.

BASIC COSTS (2008-2009)

Tuition and fees: $13,635.

Per-credit charge: $431.

Room and board: $5,990.

FINANCIAL AID PICTURE (2006-2007)

Students with need: For part-time students, average financial aid package was $1,500.

Students without need: This college awards aid only to students with need.

Additional info: Religious affiliation tuition discount.

FINANCIAL AID PROCEDURES

Forms required: FAFSA, CSS PROFILE, institutional form.

Dates and Deadlines: Priority date 5/7; no closing date. Applicants notified on a rolling basis starting 5/1; must reply within 2 week(s) of notification.

CONTACT

Mike Fracassa, Director of Financial Aid

1476 Lancaster Pike, Circleville, OH 43113

(800) 701-0222

Ohio Dominican University

Columbus, Ohio

www.ohiodominican.edu   Federal Code: 003035

4-year private university and liberal arts college in very large city, affiliated with Roman Catholic Church.

Enrollment: 2,250 undergrads, 24% part-time. 392 full-time freshmen.

Selectivity: Admits 50 to 75% of applicants.

BASIC COSTS (2007-2008)

Tuition and fees: $21,794.

Per-credit charge: $425.

Room and board: $7,200.

FINANCIAL AID PICTURE

Students with need: Need-based aid available for full-time and part-time students. Work study available nights, weekends, and for part-time students.

Students without need: No-need awards available for academics, athletics, state/district residency.

FINANCIAL AID PROCEDURES

Forms required: FAFSA.

Dates and Deadlines: Priority date 4/1; no closing date. Applicants notified on a rolling basis starting 3/1; must reply within 2 week(s) of notification.

CONTACT

Cindy Hahn, Director of Financial Aid

1216 Sunbury Road, Columbus, OH 43219

(614) 251-4778

Ohio Institute of Photography and Technology

Dayton, Ohio

www.oipt.com   Federal Code: 020520

2-year for-profit technical college in very large city.

Enrollment: 566 undergrads.

Selectivity: Open admission; but selective for some programs.

BASIC COSTS (2007-2008)

Tuition and fees: $19,833.

Per-credit charge: $333.

Additional info: Tuition listed reflects the Photographic Technology program. Tuition varies by program.

FINANCIAL AID PICTURE

Students with need: Need-based aid available for full-time and part-time students.

FINANCIAL AID PROCEDURES

Forms required: FAFSA, institutional form.

Dates and Deadlines: No deadline. Applicants notified on a rolling basis starting 3/1.

CONTACT

Lynda Craft, Director of Financial Aid

2029 Edgefield Road, Dayton, OH 45439

(937) 294-6155

Ohio Northern University

Ada, Ohio

www.onu.edu   Federal Code: 003089

4-year private university in small town, affiliated with United Methodist Church.

Enrollment: 2,534 undergrads, 1% part-time. 722 full-time freshmen.

Selectivity: Admits over 75% of applicants.

BASIC COSTS (2008-2009)

Tuition and fees: $31,020.

Room and board: $7,890.

Additional info: Tuition/fee waivers available for minority students.

FINANCIAL AID PICTURE

Students with need: Need-based aid available for full-time and part-time students. Work study available nights, weekends, and for part-time students.

Students without need: No-need awards available for academics, alumni affiliation, art, leadership, music/drama, ROTC, state/district residency.

Scholarships offered: Presidential Scholarship; up to $25,000; minimum 3.5 GPA, 30 ACT or 1320 SAT, and on-campus competition. Trustees Scholarship; up to $22,000; minimum 3.5 GPA, 28 ACT or 1240 SAT, and on-campus competition. Academic Honors Scholarship; up to $20,000; minimum 3.3 GPA, 26 ACT or 1170 SAT, and on-campus competition. Distinguished Achievement Scholarship; up to $16,000; minimum 3.2 GPA, 24 ACT or 1090 SAT, on-campus competition, and leadership activities. Deans Scholarship; $6,000 to $12,000; minimum 3.3 GPA and 25 ACT or 1130 SAT. Criteria listed is for the Colleges of Arts & Sciences, Business Administration and Engineering. The College of Pharmacy has slightly higher credentials. SAT scores exclusive of Writing.

FINANCIAL AID PROCEDURES

Forms required: FAFSA, institutional form.

Dates and Deadlines: Priority date 4/15; closing date 6/1. Applicants notified on a rolling basis starting 2/15; must reply within 2 week(s) of notification.

CONTACT

Craig Sneider, Director of Financial Aid

525 South Main Street, Ada, OH 45810

(419) 772-2272

Ohio State University Agricultural Technical Institute

Wooster, Ohio

www.ati.osu.edu   Federal Code: 003090

2-year public agricultural college in large town.

Enrollment: 723 undergrads, 12% part-time. 299 full-time freshmen.

Selectivity: Open admission; but selective for out-of-state students.

BASIC COSTS (2007-2008)

Tuition and fees: $5,859; out-of-state residents $18,468.

FINANCIAL AID PICTURE (2007-2008)

Students with need: Out of 253 full-time freshmen who applied for aid, 207 were judged to have need. Of these, 204 received aid, and 18 had their full need met. Average financial aid package met 60% of need; average scholarship/grant was $4,496; average loan was $4,081. For part-time students, average financial aid package was $8,329.

Students without need: This college awards aid only to students with need.

FINANCIAL AID PROCEDURES

Forms required: FAFSA.

Dates and Deadlines: Priority date 3/1; no closing date. Applicants notified on a rolling basis starting 5/1; must reply within 4 week(s) of notification.

Transfers: Priority date 1/1; closing date 3/1.

CONTACT

Barbara LaMoreaux, Coordinator, Financial Aid
1328 Dover Road, Wooster, OH 44691

Ohio State University: Columbus Campus

Columbus, Ohio
www.osu.edu   Federal Code: 003090

4-year public university in very large city.

Enrollment: 37,848 undergrads, 6% part-time. 6,102 full-time freshmen.

Selectivity: Admits 50 to 75% of applicants.

BASIC COSTS (2007-2008)

Tuition and fees: $8,676; out-of-state residents $21,285.

Room and board: $7,365.

FINANCIAL AID PICTURE (2007-2008)

Students with need: Out of 4,934 full-time freshmen who applied for aid, 3,297 were judged to have need. Of these, 3,292 received aid, and 715 had their full need met. Average financial aid package met 72% of need; average scholarship/grant was $7,123; average loan was $3,938. For part-time students, average financial aid package was $8,415.

Students without need: 2,131 full-time freshmen who did not demonstrate need for aid received scholarships/grants; average award was $4,090. No-need awards available for academics, alumni affiliation, art, athletics, job skills, leadership, minority status, music/drama, ROTC, state/district residency.

Scholarships offered: 97 full-time freshmen received athletic scholarships; average amount $17,087.

Cumulative student debt: 55% of graduating class had student loans; average debt was $19,975.

FINANCIAL AID PROCEDURES

Forms required: FAFSA.

Dates and Deadlines: Priority date 2/15; no closing date. Applicants notified by 4/5; must reply by 5/1 or within 4 week(s) of notification.

Transfers: Priority date 6/25. Applicants notified by 5/29; must reply within 4 week(s) of notification.

CONTACT

Julia Benz, Director, Student Financial Aid
110 Enarson Hall, Columbus, OH 43210
(614) 292-0300

Ohio State University: Lima Campus

Lima, Ohio
www.lima.ohio-state.edu   Federal Code: 003090

4-year public branch campus college in large town.

Enrollment: 1,194 undergrads, 13% part-time. 477 full-time freshmen.

Selectivity: Open admission; but selective for out-of-state students.

BASIC COSTS (2007-2008)

Tuition and fees: $5,664; out-of-state residents $17,559.

FINANCIAL AID PICTURE (2007-2008)

Students with need: Average financial aid package met 63% of need; average scholarship/grant was $3,477; average loan was $3,814. For part-time students, average financial aid package was $7,908.

Students without need: No-need awards available for academics, alumni affiliation, art, athletics, job skills, leadership, minority status, music/drama, religious affiliation, ROTC, state/district residency.

FINANCIAL AID PROCEDURES

Forms required: FAFSA.

Dates and Deadlines: Priority date 3/1; no closing date. Applicants notified on a rolling basis starting 4/1; must reply within 4 week(s) of notification.

Transfers: Priority date 6/25. Applicants notified on a rolling basis starting 5/29; must reply within 4 week(s) of notification.

CONTACT

Bryan Albright, Coordinator, Financial Aid
4240 Campus Drive, Lima, OH 45804-3596
(419) 995-8147

Ohio State University: Mansfield Campus

Mansfield, Ohio
www.mansfield.ohio-state.edu   Federal Code: 003090

4-year public branch campus college in small city.

Enrollment: 1,180 undergrads, 14% part-time. 488 full-time freshmen.

Selectivity: Open admission; but selective for out-of-state students.

BASIC COSTS (2007-2008)

Tuition and fees: $5,664; out-of-state residents $18,273.

Room and board: $4,275.

FINANCIAL AID PICTURE (2007-2008)

Students with need: Out of 391 full-time freshmen who applied for aid, 312 were judged to have need. Of these, 308 received aid, and 31 had their full need met. Average financial aid package met 64% of need; average scholarship/grant was $4,720; average loan was $4,028. For part-time students, average financial aid package was $9,342.

Students without need: 49 full-time freshmen who did not demonstrate need for aid received scholarships/grants; average award was $1,612. No-need awards available for academics, alumni affiliation, art, athletics, job skills, leadership, minority status, music/drama, ROTC, state/district residency.

FINANCIAL AID PROCEDURES

Forms required: FAFSA.

Dates and Deadlines: Priority date 3/1; no closing date. Applicants notified on a rolling basis starting 4/5; must reply within 4 week(s) of notification.

Transfers: Priority date 6/25. Applicants notified on a rolling basis starting 5/29; must reply within 4 week(s) of notification.

CONTACT

Julia Benz, Director, Student Financial Aid
1680 University Drive, Mansfield, OH 44906
(419) 755-4011

Ohio State University: Marion Campus

Marion, Ohio
www.marion.ohio-state.edu   Federal Code: 003090

4-year public branch campus college in large town.

Enrollment: 1,437 undergrads, 14% part-time. 503 full-time freshmen.

Selectivity: Open admission; but selective for out-of-state students.

BASIC COSTS (2007-2008)

Tuition and fees: $5,664; out-of-state residents $18,273.

FINANCIAL AID PICTURE (2007-2008)

Students with need: Average financial aid package met 66% of need; average scholarship/grant was $4,177; average loan was $3,779. For part-time students, average financial aid package was $7,919.

Students without need: No-need awards available for academics, alumni affiliation, art, athletics, job skills, leadership, minority status, music/drama, ROTC, state/district residency.

FINANCIAL AID PROCEDURES

Forms required: FAFSA.

Dates and Deadlines: Priority date 3/1; no closing date. Applicants notified on a rolling basis starting 5/1; must reply within 4 week(s) of notification.

Transfers: Priority date 6/25. Applicants notified by 5/29; must reply within 4 week(s) of notification.

CONTACT

Matt Moreau, Direction, Financial Aid

1465 Mount Vernon Avenue, Marion, OH 43302

(740) 389-6786 ext. 6273

Ohio State University: Newark Campus
Newark, Ohio
www.newark.osu.edu   Federal Code: 003095

4-year public branch campus college in large town.

Enrollment: 2,325 undergrads, 11% part-time. 1,141 full-time freshmen.

Selectivity: Open admission; but selective for out-of-state students.

BASIC COSTS (2007-2008)

Tuition and fees: $5,664; out-of-state residents $18,273.

FINANCIAL AID PICTURE (2007-2008)

Students with need: Average financial aid package met 62% of need; average scholarship/grant was $4,739; average loan was $3,850. For part-time students, average financial aid package was $7,646.

Students without need: No-need awards available for academics, alumni affiliation, art, athletics, job skills, leadership, minority status, music/drama, ROTC, state/district residency.

FINANCIAL AID PROCEDURES

Forms required: FAFSA.

Dates and Deadlines: Priority date 3/1; no closing date. Applicants notified on a rolling basis starting 5/1; must reply within 4 week(s) of notification.

Transfers: Priority date 6/25. Applicants notified by 5/29; must reply within 4 week(s) of notification.

CONTACT

1179 University Drive, Newark, OH 43055

(740) 366-9435

Ohio University
Athens, Ohio
www.ohio.edu   Federal Code: 003100

4-year public university in large town.

Enrollment: 16,920 undergrads, 5% part-time. 3,994 full-time freshmen.

Selectivity: Admits over 75% of applicants.

BASIC COSTS (2007-2008)

Tuition and fees: $8,907; out-of-state residents $17,871.

Per-credit charge: $283; out-of-state residents $578.

Room and board: $8,427.

FINANCIAL AID PICTURE (2007-2008)

Students with need: Out of 3,520 full-time freshmen who applied for aid, 2,293 were judged to have need. Of these, 2,255 received aid, and 390 had their full need met. Average financial aid package met 60% of need; average scholarship/grant was $5,597; average loan was $3,434. For part-time students, average financial aid package was $6,712.

Students without need: 677 full-time freshmen who did not demonstrate need for aid received scholarships/grants; average award was $3,472. No-

need awards available for academics, art, athletics, minority status, music/drama, religious affiliation, ROTC.

Scholarships offered: 74 full-time freshmen received athletic scholarships; average amount $17,136.

Cumulative student debt: 65% of graduating class had student loans; average debt was $20,880.

FINANCIAL AID PROCEDURES

Forms required: FAFSA.

Dates and Deadlines: Priority date 3/15; closing date 4/1. Applicants notified on a rolling basis starting 4/1; must reply within 3 week(s) of notification.

CONTACT

Sondra Williams, Director, Student Financial Aid and Scholarships

120 Chubb Hall, Athens, OH 45701-2979

(740) 593-4141

Ohio University: Chillicothe Campus
Chillicothe, Ohio
www.chillicothe.ohiou.edu   Federal Code: 003102

4-year public branch campus college in large town.

Enrollment: 1,695 undergrads.

Selectivity: Open admission; but selective for some programs.

BASIC COSTS (2007-2008)

Tuition and fees: $4,581; out-of-state residents $8,904.

Per-credit charge: $139; out-of-state residents $270.

FINANCIAL AID PICTURE

Students with need: Need-based aid available for full-time and part-time students.

FINANCIAL AID PROCEDURES

Forms required: FAFSA.

Dates and Deadlines: No deadline. Applicants notified on a rolling basis.

CONTACT

Dennis Bothel, Coordinator of Academic Advising

101 University Drive, Chillicothe, OH 45601

(740) 774-7228

Ohio University: Lancaster Campus
Lancaster, Ohio
www.lancaster.ohiou.edu   Federal Code: 003104

4-year public branch campus college in large town.

Enrollment: 1,531 undergrads.

Selectivity: Open admission; but selective for some programs.

BASIC COSTS (2007-2008)

Tuition and fees: $4,581; out-of-state residents $8,904.

Per-credit charge: $139; out-of-state residents $270.

FINANCIAL AID PICTURE

Students with need: Need-based aid available for full-time and part-time students.

Additional info: Scholarship application deadline April 1.

FINANCIAL AID PROCEDURES

Forms required: FAFSA.

Dates and Deadlines: Priority date 2/15; no closing date. Applicants notified on a rolling basis; must reply within 2 week(s) of notification.

CONTACT

Pat Fox, Coordinator, Financial Aid

1570 Granville Pike, Lancaster, OH 43130

(740) 654-6711 ext. 209

Ohio University: Southern Campus at Ironton

Ironton, Ohio
www.southern.ohiou.edu   Federal Code: 003100

4-year public branch campus college in large town.
Enrollment: 1,354 full-time undergrads.
Selectivity: Open admission

BASIC COSTS (2007-2008)
Tuition and fees: $4,395; out-of-state residents $5,715.
Per-credit charge: $134; out-of-state residents $174.

FINANCIAL AID PICTURE
Students with need: Need-based aid available for full-time and part-time students.
Students without need: No-need awards available for academics, state/district residency.

FINANCIAL AID PROCEDURES
Forms required: FAFSA.
Dates and Deadlines: Priority date 3/15; no closing date. Applicants notified on a rolling basis.

CONTACT
Jacki Adkins, Director of Financial Aid
1804 Liberty Avenue, Ironton, OH 45638
(740) 533-4600

Ohio Valley College of Technology

East Liverpool, Ohio
www.ovct.edu   Federal Code: 016261

2-year for-profit business and technical college in large town.
Enrollment: 128 undergrads.
Selectivity: Admits over 75% of applicants.

BASIC COSTS (2007-2008)
Tuition and fees: $8,180.

FINANCIAL AID PICTURE
Students with need: Need-based aid available for full-time and part-time students.
Students without need: This college awards aid only to students with need.

FINANCIAL AID PROCEDURES
Forms required: FAFSA.
Dates and Deadlines: Priority date 10/1; no closing date. Applicants notified on a rolling basis; must reply within 6 week(s) of notification.

CONTACT
Mary Galeno, Financial Aid Officer
16808 St. Clair Avenue, PO Box 7000, East Liverpool, OH 43920

Ohio Wesleyan University

Delaware, Ohio
www.owu.edu   Federal Code: 003109

4-year private liberal arts college in large town, affiliated with United Methodist Church.
Enrollment: 1,960 undergrads, 1% part-time. 576 full-time freshmen.
Selectivity: Admits 50 to 75% of applicants.

BASIC COSTS (2007-2008)
Tuition and fees: $31,930.
Room and board: $8,030.

FINANCIAL AID PICTURE (2007-2008)
Students with need: Out of 391 full-time freshmen who applied for aid, 344 were judged to have need. Of these, 343 received aid, and 105 had their full need met. Average financial aid package met 90% of need; average scholarship/grant was $21,057; average loan was $5,168. For part-time students, average financial aid package was $23,665.
Students without need: 220 full-time freshmen who did not demonstrate need for aid received scholarships/grants; average award was $14,587. No-need awards available for academics, alumni affiliation, art, leadership, minority status, music/drama, religious affiliation, state/district residency.
Scholarships offered: Presidential scholarships; full tuition; 25 awarded. Trustee scholarships; 75% of tuition; 40 awarded. Faculty scholarships; 50% of tuition; 140 awarded.
Cumulative student debt: 76% of graduating class had student loans; average debt was $25,627.

FINANCIAL AID PROCEDURES
Forms required: FAFSA, institutional form.
Dates and Deadlines: Priority date 3/1; closing date 5/1. Applicants notified on a rolling basis starting 2/15; must reply by 5/1 or within 2 week(s) of notification.
Transfers: Must reply within 2 week(s) of notification.

CONTACT
Lee Harrell, Assistant Vice President of Admission and Financial Aid
75 South Sandusky Street, Delaware, OH 43015-2398
(740) 368-3050

Otterbein College

Westerville, Ohio
www.otterbein.edu   Federal Code: 003110

4-year private liberal arts college in large town, affiliated with United Methodist Church.
Enrollment: 2,715 undergrads, 16% part-time. 647 full-time freshmen.
Selectivity: Admits over 75% of applicants.

BASIC COSTS (2007-2008)
Tuition and fees: $25,065.
Room and board: $7,149.
Additional info: Tuition/fee waivers available for adults, minority students.

FINANCIAL AID PICTURE
Students with need: Work study available nights, weekends, and for part-time students.
Students without need: No-need awards available for academics, alumni affiliation, art, leadership, minority status, music/drama, state/district residency.

FINANCIAL AID PROCEDURES
Forms required: FAFSA.
Dates and Deadlines: Priority date 4/1; no closing date. Applicants notified on a rolling basis starting 2/15.
Transfers: Transfer students must complete appropriate state grant transfer paperwork.

CONTACT
Thomas Yarnell, Director of Financial Aid
One Otterbein College, Westerville, OH 43081
(614) 823-1502

Owens Community College: Toledo

Toledo, Ohio
www.owens.edu   Federal Code: 005753

2-year public community college in large city.
Enrollment: 9,191 undergrads, 54% part-time. 1,285 full-time freshmen.
Selectivity: Open admission; but selective for some programs.

BASIC COSTS (2007-2008)
Tuition and fees: $3,352; out-of-state residents $5,932.
Per-credit charge: $123; out-of-state residents $231.

FINANCIAL AID PICTURE (2007-2008)
Students with need: Average financial aid package met 2% of need; average scholarship/grant was $5,064; average loan was $3,201. For part-time students, average financial aid package was $5,385.
Students without need: No-need awards available for academics, alumni affiliation, athletics, leadership, state/district residency.
Additional info: Other types of financial aid available: federal family education loan program, private foundation loan (SCHELL).

FINANCIAL AID PROCEDURES
Forms required: FAFSA.
Dates and Deadlines: Priority date 3/31; no closing date. Applicants notified by 2/7.

CONTACT
Betsy Johnson, Director of Financial Aid
PO Box 10000, Toledo, OH 43699-1947
(567) 661-7343

Pontifical College Josephinum

Columbus, Ohio
www.pcj.edu   Federal Code: 003113

4-year private liberal arts and seminary college for men in very large city, affiliated with Roman Catholic Church.
Enrollment: 119 undergrads. 22 full-time freshmen.
Selectivity: Admits over 75% of applicants.

BASIC COSTS (2007-2008)
Tuition and fees: $15,677.
Per-credit charge: $606.
Room and board: $7,494.

FINANCIAL AID PICTURE (2006-2007)
Students with need: 71% of average financial aid package awarded as scholarships/grants, 29% awarded as loans/jobs. Need-based aid available for part-time students. Work study available nights, weekends, and for part-time students.
Students without need: This college awards aid only to students with need.

FINANCIAL AID PROCEDURES
Forms required: FAFSA, institutional form.
Dates and Deadlines: Priority date 9/2; no closing date. Applicants notified on a rolling basis starting 8/15; must reply within 2 week(s) of notification.

CONTACT
Marky Leichtnam, Director of Financial Aid
7625 North High Street, Columbus, OH 43235-1499
(614) 985-2212

Samuel Stephen College

Chillicothe, Ohio
www.samuelstephencollege.edu   Federal Code: 020568

2-year for-profit business college in large town.
Enrollment: 62 undergrads.
Selectivity: Open admission.

BASIC COSTS (2007-2008)
Tuition and fees: $7,035.
Per-credit charge: $185.

FINANCIAL AID PICTURE
Students with need: Need-based aid available for full-time and part-time students.
Students without need: This college awards aid only to students with need.
Scholarships offered: Ohio Legislative Scholarship: administered by the Ohio Council of Private Colleges and Schools, for Ohio-resident high school seniors nominated by their state representative who reviews applications; 2-year tuition for associate degree valued at $11,500.

FINANCIAL AID PROCEDURES
Forms required: FAFSA, institutional form.
Dates and Deadlines: No deadline.
Transfers: No deadline.

CONTACT
Connie Pruitt, Financial Aid Coordinator
1410 Industrial Drive, Chillicothe, OH 45601
(740) 774-2063

School of Advertising Art

Kettering, Ohio
www.saacollege.com   Federal Code: 017160

2-year for-profit visual arts and technical college in small city.
Enrollment: 150 undergrads.

BASIC COSTS (2007-2008)
Tuition and fees: $20,540.
Additional info: First year tuition for diploma program $16,200, required fees $2,150.

FINANCIAL AID PICTURE
Students with need: Need-based aid available for full-time students.
Students without need: This college awards aid only to students with need.

FINANCIAL AID PROCEDURES
Forms required: FAFSA, institutional form.
Dates and Deadlines: No deadline. Applicants notified by 7/1; must reply by 7/1 or within 1 week(s) of notification.
Transfers: Closing date 7/1. Must reply by 7/1 or within 1 week(s) of notification.

CONTACT
Tamara Arment, Financial Aid Director
1725 East David Road, Kettering, OH 45440-1612
(937) 294-0592 ext. 104

Shawnee State University
Portsmouth, Ohio
www.shawnee.edu   Federal Code: 009942

4-year public university in large town.
Enrollment: 2,798 undergrads, 18% part-time. 399 full-time freshmen.
Selectivity: Open admission; but selective for some programs.

BASIC COSTS (2007-2008)
Tuition and fees: $5,832; out-of-state residents $9,972.
Per-credit charge: $216; out-of-state residents $389.
Room and board: $7,410.

FINANCIAL AID PICTURE
Students with need: Need-based aid available for full-time and part-time students.
Students without need: No-need awards available for academics.
Additional info: ACT recommended for scholarship applicants.

FINANCIAL AID PROCEDURES
Forms required: FAFSA, institutional form.
Dates and Deadlines: Priority date 6/15; no closing date. Applicants notified on a rolling basis starting 5/1; must reply within 4 week(s) of notification.

CONTACT
Barbara Bradbury, Financial Aid Director
940 Second Street, Portsmouth, OH 45662
(740) 351-4243

Sinclair Community College
Dayton, Ohio
www.sinclair.edu   Federal Code: 003119

2-year public community college in small city.
Enrollment: 6,920 full-time undergrads.
Selectivity: Open admission; but selective for some programs.

BASIC COSTS (2007-2008)
Tuition and fees: $2,025; out-of-district residents $3,307; out-of-state residents $6,525.
Per-credit charge: $45; out-of-district residents $74; out-of-state residents $145.

FINANCIAL AID PICTURE
Students with need: Need-based aid available for full-time and part-time students. Work study available nights, weekends, and for part-time students.
Students without need: No-need awards available for academics, athletics, state/district residency.

FINANCIAL AID PROCEDURES
Forms required: FAFSA, institutional form.
Dates and Deadlines: Priority date 5/1; closing date 8/1. Applicants notified on a rolling basis.
Transfers: No deadline.

CONTACT
Carlyn Bozeman, Director of Financial Aid and Scholarships
444 West Third Street, Dayton, OH 45402-1460
(937) 512-3000

Southeastern Business College: New Boston
New Boston, Ohio
www.southeasternbusinesscollege.com

2-year for-profit branch campus and business college in rural community.
Enrollment: 50 undergrads.
Selectivity: Open admission.

FINANCIAL AID PICTURE
Students with need: Need-based aid available for full-time and part-time students.

FINANCIAL AID PROCEDURES
Forms required: FAFSA.
Dates and Deadlines: No deadline.

CONTACT
Angie Gammon, Financial Aid Officer
3879 Rhodes Avenue, New Boston, OH 45662
(740) 456-4124

Southern State Community College
Hillsboro, Ohio
www.sscc.edu   Federal Code: 012870

2-year public community college in small town.
Enrollment: 2,419 undergrads, 45% part-time. 489 full-time freshmen.
Selectivity: Open admission; but selective for some programs.

BASIC COSTS (2007-2008)
Tuition and fees: $3,390; out-of-state residents $6,528.
Per-credit charge: $87; out-of-state residents $168.

FINANCIAL AID PICTURE (2006-2007)
Students with need: 54% of average financial aid package awarded as scholarships/grants, 46% awarded as loans/jobs. Need-based aid available for part-time students.
Students without need: No-need awards available for academics, art, athletics, music/drama.

FINANCIAL AID PROCEDURES
Forms required: FAFSA, institutional form.
Dates and Deadlines: Priority date 7/1; closing date 9/1. Applicants notified by 4/15; must reply within 2 week(s) of notification.
Transfers: No deadline.

CONTACT
Janeen Deatley, Financial Aid Director
100 Hobart Drive, Hillsboro, OH 45133
(937) 393-3431 ext. 2610

Southwestern College: Tri-County
Cincinnati, Ohio
www.swcollege.net   Federal Code: 012128

2-year for-profit career college in small city.
Enrollment: 725 undergrads.
Selectivity: Open admission.

BASIC COSTS (2007-2008)
Tuition and fees: $10,050.

FINANCIAL AID PICTURE
Students with need: Need-based aid available for full-time students.

Students without need: This college awards aid only to students with need.

FINANCIAL AID PROCEDURES

Forms required: FAFSA, state aid form.

Dates and Deadlines: No deadline.

CONTACT

Jill Matosky, Financial Aid Director

149 Northland Boulevard, Cincinnati, OH 45246

(513) 874-0432

Southwestern College: Vine Street Campus

Cincinnati, Ohio

www.swcollege.net   Federal Code: 012128

2-year for-profit business and health science college in large city.

Enrollment: 416 undergrads.

Selectivity: Open admission.

FINANCIAL AID PICTURE

Students with need: Need-based aid available for full-time and part-time students.

Students without need: This college awards aid only to students with need.

FINANCIAL AID PROCEDURES

Forms required: FAFSA.

CONTACT

Charlene Williams, Financial Aid Director

632 Vine Street, Cincinnati, OH 45202

(513) 421-3212

Stark State College of Technology

North Canton, Ohio

www.starkstate.edu   Federal Code: 011141

2-year public technical college in small city.

Enrollment: 7,165 undergrads.

Selectivity: Open admission; but selective for some programs.

BASIC COSTS (2007-2008)

Tuition and fees: $3,810; out-of-state residents $5,610.

Per-credit charge: $103; out-of-state residents $163.

FINANCIAL AID PICTURE

Students with need: Need-based aid available for full-time and part-time students. Work study available nights, weekends, and for part-time students.

Students without need: This college awards aid only to students with need.

FINANCIAL AID PROCEDURES

Forms required: FAFSA, institutional form.

Dates and Deadlines: Priority date 5/1; no closing date. Applicants notified on a rolling basis starting 4/1; must reply within 4 week(s) of notification.

CONTACT

Amy Baker, Director of Financial Aid

6200 Frank Avenue NW, North Canton, OH 44720

(330) 494-6170

Stautzenberger College

Maumee, Ohio

www.sctoday.edu   Federal Code: 004866

2-year for-profit business and technical college in large city.

Enrollment: 759 undergrads.

Selectivity: Open admission.

BASIC COSTS (2008-2009)

Additional info: Tuition ranges from $195 to $360 per credit hour; required fees, $270.

FINANCIAL AID PICTURE

Students with need: Need-based aid available for full-time and part-time students.

Students without need: This college awards aid only to students with need.

FINANCIAL AID PROCEDURES

Forms required: FAFSA.

Dates and Deadlines: No deadline. Applicants notified on a rolling basis.

CONTACT

Mari Huffman, Financial Aid Officer

1796 Indian Wood Circle, Maumee, OH 43537

(419) 866-0261

Stautzenberger College: Strongsville

Strongsville, Ohio

www.sctoday.edu/strongsville

2-year for-profit career college in large town.

Enrollment: 299 undergrads, 66% part-time. 51 full-time freshmen.

Selectivity: Open admission.

BASIC COSTS (2007-2008)

Tuition and fees: $9,045.

Per-credit charge: $195.

FINANCIAL AID PICTURE

Students with need: Need-based aid available for full-time and part-time students.

Students without need: This college awards aid only to students with need.

FINANCIAL AID PROCEDURES

Forms required: FAFSA.

Dates and Deadlines: No deadline. Applicants notified on a rolling basis.

Transfers: No deadline. Applicants notified on a rolling basis.

CONTACT

Mari Huffman, Director of Financial Aid

12925 Pearl Road, Strongsville, OH 44136

Technology Education College

Columbus, Ohio

www.teccollege.com   Federal Code: 011005

2-year for-profit business and health science and technical and career college in very large city.

Enrollment: 244 undergrads.

Selectivity: Open admission.

BASIC COSTS (2007-2008)

Additional info: Tuition varies per program, but averages $11,300 per academic year.

FINANCIAL AID PICTURE

Students with need: Need-based aid available for full-time and part-time students. Work study available nights.

Students without need: This college awards aid only to students with need.

FINANCIAL AID PROCEDURES

Forms required: FAFSA.

Dates and Deadlines: No deadline. Applicants notified on a rolling basis.

CONTACT

Nicole Morgan, Director of Financial Aid

2745 Winchester Pike, Columbus, OH 43232

(614) 456-4600

Terra State Community College

Fremont, Ohio

www.terra.edu   Federal Code: 008278

2-year public community and technical college in large town.

Enrollment: 2,260 undergrads.

Selectivity: Open admission.

BASIC COSTS (2007-2008)

Tuition and fees: $3,406; out-of-state residents $5,656.

Per-credit charge: $108; out-of-state residents $176.

FINANCIAL AID PICTURE

Students with need: Need-based aid available for full-time and part-time students.

Students without need: No-need awards available for academics.

FINANCIAL AID PROCEDURES

Forms required: FAFSA, institutional form.

Dates and Deadlines: Priority date 5/1; no closing date. Applicants notified on a rolling basis starting 5/15.

CONTACT

Dale Stearns, Director of Financial Aid

2830 Napoleon Road, Fremont, OH 43420-9600

(419) 559-2344

Tiffin University

Tiffin, Ohio

www.tiffin.edu   Federal Code: 003121

4-year private university and business college in large town.

Enrollment: 1,565 undergrads, 6% part-time. 308 full-time freshmen.

Selectivity: Admits 50 to 75% of applicants.

BASIC COSTS (2007-2008)

Tuition and fees: $16,800.

Room and board: $7,080.

FINANCIAL AID PICTURE (2007-2008)

Students with need: Out of 292 full-time freshmen who applied for aid, 261 were judged to have need. Of these, 261 received aid, and 46 had their full need met. Average financial aid package met 18% of need; average scholarship/grant was $6,555; average loan was $3,281. For part-time students, average financial aid package was $6,476.

Students without need: 29 full-time freshmen who did not demonstrate need for aid received scholarships/grants; average award was $4,862. No-need awards available for academics, alumni affiliation, athletics, leadership, music/drama, state/district residency.

Scholarships offered: 12 full-time freshmen received athletic scholarships; average amount $4,417.

Cumulative student debt: 87% of graduating class had student loans; average debt was $21,400.

FINANCIAL AID PROCEDURES

Forms required: FAFSA.

Dates and Deadlines: No deadline. Applicants notified on a rolling basis starting 1/15; must reply within 2 week(s) of notification.

CONTACT

Tera Van Doran, Director of Financial Aid

155 Miami Street, Tiffin, OH 44883

(800) 968-6446 ext. 3279

Trumbull Business College

Warren, Ohio

www.tbc-trumbullbusiness.com   Federal Code: 013585

2-year for-profit business college in large town.

Enrollment: 325 undergrads.

Selectivity: Open admission.

BASIC COSTS (2007-2008)

Tuition and fees: $11,055.

Per-credit charge: $244.

FINANCIAL AID PICTURE

Students with need: Need-based aid available for full-time and part-time students.

FINANCIAL AID PROCEDURES

Forms required: FAFSA.

CONTACT

Florence Henning, Financial Assistance Director

3200 Ridge Road, Warren, OH 44484

(330) 369-3200 ext. 12

Union Institute & University

Cincinnati, Ohio

www.tui.edu   Federal Code: 010923

4-year private university and liberal arts college in very large city.

Enrollment: 929 undergrads, 33% part-time. 15 full-time freshmen.

BASIC COSTS (2007-2008)

Tuition and fees: $13,224.

Per-credit charge: $406.

FINANCIAL AID PICTURE

Students with need: Need-based aid available for full-time and part-time students.

Students without need: No-need awards available for academics, state/district residency.

FINANCIAL AID PROCEDURES

Forms required: FAFSA, institutional form.

Dates and Deadlines: No deadline. Must reply within 4 week(s) of notification.

CONTACT

Victoria Walker, Director of Financial Aid

440 East McMillan Street, Cincinnati, OH 45206

(800) 486-3116

University of Akron

Akron, Ohio
www.uakron.edu   Federal Code: 003123

4-year public university in small city.

Enrollment: 17,988 undergrads, 20% part-time. 3,562 full-time freshmen.

Selectivity: Open admission; but selective for some programs.

BASIC COSTS (2007-2008)

Tuition and fees: $8,384; out-of-state residents $17,632.

Room and board: $8,003.

FINANCIAL AID PICTURE (2006-2007)

Students with need: Out of 2,903 full-time freshmen who applied for aid, 2,356 were judged to have need. Of these, 2,356 received aid, and 120 had their full need met. Average financial aid package met 44% of need; average scholarship/grant was $4,889; average loan was $2,508. For part-time students, average financial aid package was $4,601.

Students without need: 256 full-time freshmen who did not demonstrate need for aid received scholarships/grants; average award was $2,923. No-need awards available for academics, alumni affiliation, art, athletics, leadership, music/drama, ROTC, state/district residency.

Scholarships offered: *Merit:* Scholarships for Excellence: $6,000 per year; 3.8 GPA, 30 ACT, 1320 SAT (exclusive of Writing); deadline February 1. Presidential Scholarships: $3,000 per year; criteria 3.8 GPA, 27 ACT, 1200 SAT. Honors Scholarships: $1,500-$3,000 per year; top 10% of class, GPA 3.5, deadline December 31. Jim and Vanita Oeschlager Leadership Award: $1,000-$17,000 per year; based on leadership and service. Academic Scholarship: $500-$1,500 per year; upper 30% of high school class, 21 ACT, 3.0 GPA. Akron Advantage Award: non-resident surcharge reduction of 60% or 100% for students who meet academic criteria from 49 states outside of Ohio plus U.S. territories. *Athletic:* 75 full-time freshmen received athletic scholarships; average amount $3,729.

Cumulative student debt: 60% of graduating class had student loans; average debt was $16,105.

FINANCIAL AID PROCEDURES

Forms required: FAFSA, institutional form.

Dates and Deadlines: Priority date 2/1; no closing date. Applicants notified on a rolling basis starting 4/1; must reply within 2 week(s) of notification.

Transfers: Priority date 3/1; no deadline. Applicants notified on a rolling basis starting 6/15; must reply within 2 week(s) of notification.

CONTACT

Douglas McNutt, Director, Student Financial Aid
The University of Akron, Akron, OH 44325-2001
(330) 972-7032

University of Akron: Wayne College

Orrville, Ohio
www.wayne.uakron.edu   Federal Code: 003123

2-year public branch campus and junior college in small town.

Enrollment: 1,559 undergrads.

Selectivity: Open admission.

BASIC COSTS (2007-2008)

Tuition and fees: $5,485; out-of-state residents $12,854.

FINANCIAL AID PICTURE

Students with need: Need-based aid available for full-time and part-time students. Work study available nights, weekends, and for part-time students.

Students without need: No-need awards available for academics, art, athletics, leadership, minority status, music/drama, state/district residency.

Additional info: All financial aid processed through University of Akron.

FINANCIAL AID PROCEDURES

Forms required: FAFSA, institutional form.

Dates and Deadlines: Closing date 3/15. Applicants notified on a rolling basis starting 4/15.

CONTACT

Theresa Mountel, Financial Aid Counselor
1901 Smucker Road, Orrville, OH 44667-9758
(330) 684-8900

University of Cincinnati

Cincinnati, Ohio
www.uc.edu   Federal Code: 003125

4-year public university in large city.

Enrollment: 19,796 undergrads, 15% part-time. 4,098 full-time freshmen.

Selectivity: Admits 50 to 75% of applicants.

BASIC COSTS (2007-2008)

Tuition and fees: $9,399; out-of-state residents $23,922.

Per-credit charge: $262; out-of-state residents $665.

Room and board: $8,799.

FINANCIAL AID PICTURE (2007-2008)

Students with need: Out of 3,174 full-time freshmen who applied for aid, 2,486 were judged to have need. Of these, 2,460 received aid, and 174 had their full need met. Average financial aid package met 59% of need; average scholarship/grant was $6,633; average loan was $3,990. For part-time students, average financial aid package was $6,323.

Students without need: 762 full-time freshmen who did not demonstrate need for aid received scholarships/grants; average award was $4,583. No-need awards available for academics, alumni affiliation, art, athletics, leadership, minority status, music/drama, ROTC, state/district residency.

Scholarships offered: 44 full-time freshmen received athletic scholarships; average amount $18,100.

Cumulative student debt: 65% of graduating class had student loans; average debt was $21,302.

FINANCIAL AID PROCEDURES

Forms required: FAFSA.

Dates and Deadlines: No deadline. Applicants notified on a rolling basis starting 3/10; must reply within 2 week(s) of notification.

CONTACT

Connie Williams, Director, Financial Aid
PO Box 210091, Cincinnati, OH 45221-0091
(513) 556-6982

University of Cincinnati: Clermont College

Batavia, Ohio
www.ucclermont.edu   Federal Code: 003125

2-year public branch campus college in small town.

Enrollment: 2,506 undergrads, 33% part-time. 539 full-time freshmen.

Selectivity: Open admission; but selective for some programs.

BASIC COSTS (2007-2008)

Tuition and fees: $4,542; out-of-state residents $11,394.

Per-credit charge: $127; out-of-state residents $317.

FINANCIAL AID PICTURE

Students with need: Need-based aid available for full-time and part-time students. Work study available nights, weekends, and for part-time students.

Students without need: No-need awards available for academics, state/district residency.

PART III: FINANCIAL AID COLLEGE BY COLLEGE

Additional info: All financial aid applications and awards administered through Uptown campus except in-house loans and scholarships.

FINANCIAL AID PROCEDURES

Forms required: FAFSA.

Dates and Deadlines: No deadline. Applicants notified on a rolling basis.

CONTACT

Jessica Max, University Services Associate
4200 Clermont College Drive, Batavia, OH 45103

University of Dayton

Dayton, Ohio
www.udayton.edu   Federal Code: 003127

4-year private university in small city, affiliated with Roman Catholic Church.

Enrollment: 7,154 undergrads, 4% part-time. 1,749 full-time freshmen.

Selectivity: Admits over 75% of applicants.

BASIC COSTS (2008-2009)

Tuition and fees: $27,330.

Per-credit charge: $873.

Room and board: $7,980.

Additional info: $1,299 additional cost to all new incoming students for purchase of computer from university. International students pay additional $75 per month for health and accident insurance. Engineering majors required to pay additional $750 per semester in fees. Tuition/fee waivers available for adults.

FINANCIAL AID PICTURE (2006-2007)

Students with need: Out of 1,339 full-time freshmen who applied for aid, 972 were judged to have need. Of these, 969 received aid, and 387 had their full need met. Average financial aid package met 99% of need; average scholarship/grant was $11,071; average loan was $6,210. For part-time students, average financial aid package was $4,372.

Students without need: 767 full-time freshmen who did not demonstrate need for aid received scholarships/grants; average award was $6,852. No-need awards available for academics, alumni affiliation, art, athletics, leadership, music/drama, ROTC, state/district residency.

Scholarships offered: *Merit:* Berry Scholarships: up to full tuition; based on GPA, ACT/SAT scores, service and leadership. Marianist Heritage Awards: $1,000 to full tuition; available to all graduates of Marianist high schools who meet academic criteria. Music talent awards: $1,000 to $5,000; based on auditions. President's Scholarship: $1,000 to $10,000; based on GPA, ACT/SAT scores, service and leadership. Visual arts awards; amounts vary; based on student portfolios. Chaminade Scholarships: $2,500; for students accepted to the Chaminade Scholars Program. National Merit Scholarships: $1,000 to $2,000; available to all students who are selected by the National Merit Scholarship Corporation and select UD as their first choice. Army ROTC awards: supplements U.S. Army ROTC awards with scholarship incentives. ***Athletic:*** 22 full-time freshmen received athletic scholarships; average amount $18,116.

Cumulative student debt: 59% of graduating class had student loans; average debt was $20,438.

FINANCIAL AID PROCEDURES

Forms required: FAFSA.

Dates and Deadlines: Priority date 3/31; no closing date. Applicants notified on a rolling basis starting 2/20; must reply by 5/1 or within 3 week(s) of notification.

Transfers: Priority date 6/1; no deadline. Applicants notified on a rolling basis starting 2/25. Students must submit FAFSA prior to October 1 each year for consideration for state funds.

CONTACT

Kathy Harmon, Director of Financial Aid
300 College Park, Dayton, OH 45469-1300
(937) 229-4311

University of Findlay

Findlay, Ohio
www.findlay.edu   Federal Code: 003045

4-year private university and health science college in large town, affiliated with Church of God.

Enrollment: 3,187 undergrads, 11% part-time. 708 full-time freshmen.

Selectivity: Admits 50 to 75% of applicants.

BASIC COSTS (2008-2009)

Tuition and fees: $24,670.

Per-credit charge: $528.

Room and board: $8,306.

Additional info: Pre-veterinary and equestrian students pay higher tuition in years one and two; pharmacy students pay higher tuition throughout the program.

FINANCIAL AID PICTURE (2006-2007)

Students with need: Out of 637 full-time freshmen who applied for aid, 488 were judged to have need. Of these, 488 received aid, and 43 had their full need met. Average financial aid package met 71% of need; average scholarship/grant was $11,972; average loan was $3,029.

Students without need: 110 full-time freshmen who did not demonstrate need for aid received scholarships/grants; average award was $9,909. No-need awards available for academics, alumni affiliation, athletics, music/drama, state/district residency.

Scholarships offered: *Merit:* Full tuition available to select valedictorian/salutatorians. Automatic academic awards available based on GPA, test scores. ***Athletic:*** 77 full-time freshmen received athletic scholarships; average amount $8,525.

FINANCIAL AID PROCEDURES

Forms required: FAFSA.

Dates and Deadlines: Priority date 8/1; closing date 9/1. Applicants notified on a rolling basis starting 3/1; must reply within 2 week(s) of notification.

CONTACT

Arman Habegger, Director of Financial Aid
1000 North Main Street, Findlay, OH 45840-3653
(419) 434-4791

University of Northwestern Ohio

Lima, Ohio
www.unoh.edu   Federal Code: 004861

2-year private business and technical college in large town.

Enrollment: 2,935 undergrads.

BASIC COSTS (2007-2008)

Tuition and fees: $8,820.

Per-credit charge: $190.

Room only: $2,640.

Additional info: $245 per credit hour charge for virtual classes. Tuition/fee waivers available for minority students.

FINANCIAL AID PICTURE (2006-2007)

Students with need: 37% of average financial aid package awarded as scholarships/grants, 63% awarded as loans/jobs. Need-based aid available for part-time students. Work study available nights.

Students without need: No-need awards available for academics, job skills, minority status.

FINANCIAL AID PROCEDURES

Forms required: FAFSA.

Dates and Deadlines: Priority date 4/1; no closing date. Applicants notified on a rolling basis starting 4/30; must reply within 2 week(s) of notification.

Transfers: No deadline. Applicants notified on a rolling basis.

CONTACT

Wendell Shick, Director of Financial Aid
1441 North Cable Road, Lima, OH 45805
(419) 227-3141

University of Rio Grande

Rio Grande, Ohio
www.rio.edu
Federal Code: 003116

4-year private community and liberal arts college in rural community.

Enrollment: 1,861 undergrads, 15% part-time. 531 full-time freshmen.

Selectivity: Open admission; but selective for some programs.

BASIC COSTS (2007-2008)

Tuition and fees: $16,600.

Room and board: $6,840.

Additional info: Tuition reported is for private university sector of institution. Public community college in-state in-district tuition: $2,880 ($96 per credit hour); in-state out-of-district, $3,450 ($115 per credit hour). All public community college undergraduates pay $632 in required fees. Out-of-state community college students charged private tuition rate.

FINANCIAL AID PICTURE (2006-2007)

Students with need: Out of 531 full-time freshmen who applied for aid, 440 were judged to have need. Of these, 440 received aid, and 339 had their full need met. Average financial aid package met 47% of need; average scholarship/grant was $1,218. For part-time students, average financial aid package was $7,565.

Students without need: 9 full-time freshmen who did not demonstrate need for aid received scholarships/grants; average award was $1,521. No-need awards available for academics, alumni affiliation, athletics, leadership, music/drama, state/district residency.

FINANCIAL AID PROCEDURES

Forms required: FAFSA, institutional form.

Dates and Deadlines: Priority date 3/15; no closing date. Applicants notified on a rolling basis starting 1/15; must reply within 3 week(s) of notification.

CONTACT

Michelle Alderman, Associate Director
218 North College Avenue, Rio Grande, OH 45674
(740) 245-7218

University of Toledo

Toledo, Ohio
www.utoledo.edu
Federal Code: 003131

4-year public university in large city.

Enrollment: 15,476 undergrads.

Selectivity: Open admission; but selective for some programs and for out-of-state students.

BASIC COSTS (2007-2008)

Tuition and fees: $7,926; out-of-state residents $16,738.

Per-credit charge: $284; out-of-state residents $651.

Room and board: $8,374.

FINANCIAL AID PICTURE

Students with need: Need-based aid available for full-time and part-time students.

Students without need: No-need awards available for academics, art, athletics, leadership, minority status, music/drama, ROTC, state/district residency.

Scholarships offered: Freshman merit scholarships: $100 to $4,500; 400 awarded.

Additional info: March priority date for federal aid. Students encouraged to apply as early as December for priority consideration for institutional aid.

FINANCIAL AID PROCEDURES

Forms required: FAFSA.

Dates and Deadlines: Priority date 4/1; no closing date. Applicants notified on a rolling basis starting 3/31; must reply within 4 week(s) of notification.

CONTACT

Carolyn Baumgartner, Director of Financial Aid
2801 West Bancroft Street, Toledo, OH 43606-3398
(419) 530-2800

Urbana University

Urbana, Ohio
www.urbana.edu
Federal Code: 003133

4-year private liberal arts college in large town.

Enrollment: 1,500 full-time undergrads.

BASIC COSTS (2007-2008)

Tuition and fees: $17,809.

Per-credit charge: $364.

Room and board: $7,378.

FINANCIAL AID PICTURE

Students with need: Need-based aid available for full-time and part-time students. Work study available nights, weekends, and for part-time students.

Students without need: No-need awards available for academics, alumni affiliation, athletics, music/drama.

Scholarships offered: All regularly accepted students receive cash scholarship for academics, music, or athletics.

FINANCIAL AID PROCEDURES

Forms required: FAFSA.

Dates and Deadlines: Closing date 4/1. Applicants notified on a rolling basis starting 3/1; must reply within 4 week(s) of notification.

Transfers: No deadline.

CONTACT

Amy Barnhart, Director of Financial Aid
579 College Way, Urbana, OH 43078
(937) 484-1355

Ursuline College

Pepper Pike, Ohio
www.ursuline.edu
Federal Code: 003134

4-year private liberal arts college for women in small town, affiliated with Roman Catholic Church.

Enrollment: 1,158 undergrads, 31% part-time. 124 full-time freshmen.

Selectivity: Admits 50 to 75% of applicants.

BASIC COSTS (2008-2009)

Tuition and fees: $22,060.

Per-credit charge: $728.

Room and board: $7,352.

FINANCIAL AID PICTURE (2006-2007)

Students with need: Out of 121 full-time freshmen who applied for aid, 112 were judged to have need. Of these, 112 received aid, and 29 had their full need met. Average financial aid package met 86% of need; average scholarship/grant was $14,903; average loan was $3,208. For part-time students, average financial aid package was $8,204.

Students without need: 12 full-time freshmen who did not demonstrate need for aid received scholarships/grants; average award was $9,431. No-need awards available for academics, art, athletics, leadership, religious affiliation, ROTC.

Scholarships offered: *Merit:* Ursuline Scholarship; $5,000 to $7,000 renewable. Ursuline Award; $1,500 to $3,500 renewable. Presidential Scholarship; $11,000 renewable. Dean's Scholarship; $9,000 renewable. Unlimited number available for each. *Athletic:* 5 full-time freshmen received athletic scholarships; average amount $1,937.

Cumulative student debt: 42% of graduating class had student loans; average debt was $24,150.

FINANCIAL AID PROCEDURES

Forms required: FAFSA, institutional form.

Dates and Deadlines: Priority date 3/15; no closing date. Applicants notified on a rolling basis starting 3/1; must reply within 2 week(s) of notification.

CONTACT

Mary Lynn Perri, Director of Financial Aid
2550 Lander Road, Pepper Pike, OH 44124-4398
(440) 646-8309

Virginia Marti College of Art and Design
Lakewood, Ohio
www.vmcad.edu   Federal Code: 012896

2-year for-profit visual arts and business college in small city.

Enrollment: 178 undergrads.

Selectivity: Admits over 75% of applicants.

BASIC COSTS (2007-2008)

Tuition and fees: $15,075.

Per-credit charge: $325.

Additional info: Tuition at time of enrollment locked for 2 years.

FINANCIAL AID PICTURE

Students with need: Need-based aid available for full-time students.

Students without need: This college awards aid only to students with need.

FINANCIAL AID PROCEDURES

Forms required: FAFSA.

Dates and Deadlines: No deadline. Applicants notified on a rolling basis.

CONTACT

Jennifer Minkiewicz, Financial Aid Officer
11724 Detroit Avenue, Lakewood, OH 44107

Walsh University
North Canton, Ohio
www.walsh.edu   Federal Code: 003135

4-year private university and liberal arts college in small city, affiliated with Roman Catholic Church.

Enrollment: 2,146 undergrads, 20% part-time. 453 full-time freshmen.

Selectivity: Admits over 75% of applicants.

BASIC COSTS (2008-2009)

Tuition and fees: $20,050.

Per-credit charge: $640.

Room and board: $7,760.

Additional info: Tuition/fee waivers available for minority students.

FINANCIAL AID PICTURE (2007-2008)

Students with need: Out of 427 full-time freshmen who applied for aid, 371 were judged to have need. Of these, 371 received aid, and 194 had their full need met. Average financial aid package met 72% of need; average scholarship/grant was $3,854; average loan was $2,420. For part-time students, average financial aid package was $6,254.

Students without need: 80 full-time freshmen who did not demonstrate need for aid received scholarships/grants; average award was $5,800. No-need awards available for academics, alumni affiliation, athletics, music/drama, religious affiliation, state/district residency.

Scholarships offered: *Merit:* $1,000 for incoming freshmen who have graduated from Catholic high school. *Athletic:* 83 full-time freshmen received athletic scholarships; average amount $3,452.

Cumulative student debt: 84% of graduating class had student loans; average debt was $18,882.

FINANCIAL AID PROCEDURES

Forms required: FAFSA, institutional form.

Dates and Deadlines: Priority date 3/15; no closing date. Applicants notified on a rolling basis starting 2/15.

Transfers: No deadline. Applicants notified on a rolling basis starting 3/15.

CONTACT

Holly Van Gilder, Financial Aid Director
2020 East Maple Street, North Canton, OH 44720-3396
(330) 490-7146

Wilberforce University
Wilberforce, Ohio
www.wilberforce.edu   Federal Code: 003141

4-year private liberal arts college in rural community, affiliated with African Methodist Episcopal Church.

Enrollment: 826 undergrads.

Selectivity: Admits 50 to 75% of applicants.

BASIC COSTS (2007-2008)

Tuition and fees: $11,560.

Per-credit charge: $438.

Room and board: $5,320.

FINANCIAL AID PICTURE

Students with need: Need-based aid available for full-time and part-time students.

FINANCIAL AID PROCEDURES

Forms required: FAFSA, institutional form.

Dates and Deadlines: Priority date 3/15; closing date 6/1. Applicants notified on a rolling basis starting 3/15; must reply within 2 week(s) of notification.

CONTACT

Shelline Perry, Director for Financial Aid
1055 North Bickett Road, Wilberforce, OH 45384-1001
(937) 708-5727

Wilmington College
Wilmington, Ohio
www.wilmington.edu   Federal Code: 003142

4-year private liberal arts college in large town, affiliated with Society of Friends (Quaker).

Enrollment: 1,428 undergrads, 16% part-time. 370 full-time freshmen.

Selectivity: Admits over 75% of applicants.

BASIC COSTS (2007-2008)

Tuition and fees: $22,078.

Per-credit charge: $395.

Room and board: $7,500.

FINANCIAL AID PICTURE

Students with need: Need-based aid available for full-time and part-time students.

Students without need: No-need awards available for academics, alumni affiliation, religious affiliation, state/district residency.

FINANCIAL AID PROCEDURES

Forms required: FAFSA.

Dates and Deadlines: Priority date 3/31; closing date 6/1. Applicants notified on a rolling basis starting 3/1; must reply by 5/1 or within 2 week(s) of notification.

CONTACT

Cheryl Louallen, Director of Financial Aid

Box 1325 Pyle Center, Wilmington, OH 45177

(937) 382-6661 ext. 249

Wittenberg University

Springfield, Ohio

www.wittenberg.edu   Federal Code: 003143

4-year private liberal arts college in small city, affiliated with Evangelical Lutheran Church in America.

Enrollment: 1,897 undergrads, 1% part-time. 551 full-time freshmen.

Selectivity: Admits 50 to 75% of applicants. GED not accepted.

BASIC COSTS (2007-2008)

Tuition and fees: $31,400.

Per-credit charge: $1,037.

Room and board: $7,880.

FINANCIAL AID PICTURE (2006-2007)

Students with need: Out of 493 full-time freshmen who applied for aid, 427 were judged to have need. Of these, 427 received aid. Average financial aid package met 90% of need; average scholarship/grant was $20,408; average loan was $3,035. For part-time students, average financial aid package was $7,724.

Students without need: This college awards aid only to students with need.

Scholarships offered: Smith Family Scholar Award; full tuition; renewable; based on academic achievement and other qualities. University Scholar Award; half tuition; renewable; based on academic achievement and other qualities. Broadwell Chinn Scholarship; half tuition; renewable; based on minority status, academic achievement, and other qualities.

Cumulative student debt: 88% of graduating class had student loans; average debt was $25,568.

Additional info: Auditions required from applicants for music, theater, and dance scholarships. Portfolio required of applicants for art scholarships.

FINANCIAL AID PROCEDURES

Forms required: FAFSA.

Dates and Deadlines: Priority date 3/15; no closing date. Applicants notified on a rolling basis starting 3/1; must reply by 5/1 or within 2 week(s) of notification.

Transfers: Priority date 5/15.

CONTACT

Jonathan Green, Director of Financial Aid

Ward Street and North Wittenberg, Springfield, OH 45501-0720

(937) 327-7321

Wright State University

Dayton, Ohio

www.wright.edu   Federal Code: 003078

4-year public university in small city.

Enrollment: 11,912 undergrads, 12% part-time. 2,352 full-time freshmen.

Selectivity: Open admission; but selective for some programs.

BASIC COSTS (2007-2008)

Tuition and fees: $7,278; out-of-state residents $14,004.

Per-credit charge: $219; out-of-state residents $425.

Room and board: $7,180.

FINANCIAL AID PICTURE

Students with need: Need-based aid available for full-time and part-time students.

Students without need: No-need awards available for academics, alumni affiliation, art, athletics, job skills, leadership, minority status, music/drama, ROTC.

Additional info: Academic scholarship applications must be submitted by February 1.

FINANCIAL AID PROCEDURES

Forms required: FAFSA.

Dates and Deadlines: Priority date 3/1; no closing date. Applicants notified on a rolling basis starting 2/15; must reply within 2 week(s) of notification.

CONTACT

David Darr, Director of Financial Aid

3640 Colonel Glenn Highway, Dayton, OH 45435

(937) 775-5727

Wright State University: Lake Campus

Celina, Ohio

www.wright.edu/lake   Federal Code: 003078

2-year public branch campus college in small town.

Enrollment: 588 undergrads, 22% part-time. 125 full-time freshmen.

Selectivity: Open admission; but selective for some programs.

BASIC COSTS (2007-2008)

Tuition and fees: $4,893; out-of-state residents $11,619.

Per-credit charge: $148; out-of-state residents $354.

Additional info: Tuition at time of enrollment locked for 2 years.

FINANCIAL AID PICTURE

Students with need: Need-based aid available for full-time and part-time students.

Students without need: No-need awards available for academics, athletics, state/district residency.

Additional info: Academic scholarship application deadline February 1. All financial aid applications and awards administered by Dayton campus.

FINANCIAL AID PROCEDURES

Forms required: FAFSA, institutional form.

Dates and Deadlines: Priority date 2/15; no closing date. Applicants notified on a rolling basis; must reply within 2 week(s) of notification.

CONTACT

B.J. Hobler, Registrar

7600 State Route 703, Celina, OH 45822-2952

(419) 586-0336

Xavier University
Cincinnati, Ohio
www.xavier.edu   Federal Code: 003144

4-year private university in large city, affiliated with Roman Catholic Church.
Enrollment: 3,814 undergrads, 9% part-time. 858 full-time freshmen.
Selectivity: Admits 50 to 75% of applicants.

BASIC COSTS (2008-2009)
Tuition and fees: $26,860.
Per-credit charge: $483.
Room and board: $9,270.
Additional info: Tuition/fee waivers available for adults, minority students.

FINANCIAL AID PICTURE (2007-2008)
Students with need: Out of 675 full-time freshmen who applied for aid, 500 were judged to have need. Of these, 499 received aid, and 134 had their full need met. Average financial aid package met 78% of need; average scholarship/grant was $10,815; average loan was $4,616. For part-time students, average financial aid package was $6,356.
Students without need: 232 full-time freshmen who did not demonstrate need for aid received scholarships/grants; average award was $10,368. No-need awards available for academics, alumni affiliation, art, athletics, job skills, music/drama, ROTC.
Scholarships offered: *Merit:* Xavier Service Fellowships; full room and board; four year scholarships to students demonstrating high academic achievement, outstanding service and leadership; 5 awarded annually. St. Francis Xavier Scholarships; full tuition; based on leadership, talent and highest academic achievement; renewable for 8 semesters; number awarded varies. Pedro Arrupe Scholarship; full tuition; awarded to African-American student in recognition of high academic achievement and community involvement; 1 awarded every four years. Weninger Scholarship; partial to full tuition; awarded to African-Americans for high academic achievement; renewable for 8 semesters; number awarded varies. Miguel Pro Scholarship, partial to full tuition, awarded to Hispanic/Latino students for high academic achievement, renewable for 8 semesters, number awarded varies. Chancellor Scholarship, valued at minimally $12,000, based on leadership, talent & highest academic achievement, 15 awarded annually. Trustee, Schawe, Presidential & Honor Scholarships, values range from $5000 to $11000; based on academic achievement; number awarded varies. *Athletic:* 41 full-time freshmen received athletic scholarships; average amount $15,921.
Cumulative student debt: 63% of graduating class had student loans; average debt was $24,769.

FINANCIAL AID PROCEDURES
Forms required: FAFSA.
Dates and Deadlines: Priority date 2/15; no closing date. Applicants notified on a rolling basis starting 2/15; must reply by 5/1.
Transfers: No deadline. Applicants notified on a rolling basis starting 2/15; must reply by 5/1.

CONTACT
Paul Calme, Director of Financial Aid
3800 Victory Parkway, Cincinnati, OH 45207-5311
(513) 745-3142

Youngstown State University
Youngstown, Ohio
www.ysu.edu   Federal Code: 003145

4-year public university in small city.
Enrollment: 11,912 undergrads, 19% part-time. 2,227 full-time freshmen.
Selectivity: Open admission; but selective for some programs and for out-of-state students.

BASIC COSTS (2007-2008)
Tuition and fees: $6,721; out-of-state residents $12,394.
Per-credit charge: $280; out-of-state residents $516.
Room and board: $6,740.
Additional info: Residents of any out-of-state area within 100 miles of campus are charged $9,414 yearly tuition. Per credit hour charge is $392.

FINANCIAL AID PICTURE (2006-2007)
Students with need: 33% of average financial aid package awarded as scholarships/grants, 67% awarded as loans/jobs. Need-based aid available for part-time students.
Students without need: No-need awards available for academics, alumni affiliation, athletics, ROTC, state/district residency.

FINANCIAL AID PROCEDURES
Forms required: FAFSA, institutional form.
Dates and Deadlines: Priority date 2/15; no closing date. Applicants notified on a rolling basis starting 5/30; must reply within 2 week(s) of notification.

CONTACT
Elaine Ruse, Director of Scholarships and Financial Aid
One University Plaza, Youngstown, OH 44555-0001
(330) 941-3505

Zane State College
Zanesville, Ohio
www.zanestate.edu   Federal Code: 008133

2-year public technical college in large town.
Enrollment: 1,751 undergrads, 43% part-time. 170 full-time freshmen.
Selectivity: Open admission; but selective for some programs.

BASIC COSTS (2007-2008)
Tuition and fees: $3,825; out-of-state residents $7,650.
Per-credit charge: $85; out-of-state residents $170.

FINANCIAL AID PICTURE
Students with need: Need-based aid available for full-time and part-time students.

FINANCIAL AID PROCEDURES
Forms required: FAFSA.
Dates and Deadlines: Priority date 5/1; closing date 7/15. Must reply by 9/1.

CONTACT
Amanda McPherson, Financial Aid Director
1555 Newark Road, Zanesville, OH 43701-2626
(740) 454-2501 ext. 1275

Oklahoma

Bacone College
Muskogee, Oklahoma
www.bacone.edu   Federal Code: 003147

4-year private liberal arts college in large town, affiliated with American Baptist Churches in the USA.
Enrollment: 880 undergrads, 18% part-time. 220 full-time freshmen.
Selectivity: Admits 50 to 75% of applicants.

BASIC COSTS (2007-2008)
Tuition and fees: $10,056.
Room and board: $6,300.

FINANCIAL AID PICTURE

Students with need: Need-based aid available for full-time and part-time students. Work study available nights, weekends, and for part-time students.
Students without need: This college awards aid only to students with need.

FINANCIAL AID PROCEDURES

Forms required: FAFSA.
Dates and Deadlines: Priority date 3/31; no closing date. Applicants notified on a rolling basis starting 4/1; must reply within 2 week(s) of notification.
Transfers: No deadline. Applicants notified on a rolling basis.

CONTACT

Cassie Doupe, Director of Financial Aid
2299 Old Bacone Road, Muskogee, OK 74403

Cameron University

Lawton, Oklahoma
www.cameron.edu   Federal Code: 003150

4-year public university and liberal arts college in small city.
Enrollment: 4,686 undergrads, 31% part-time. 701 full-time freshmen.
Selectivity: Open admission; but selective for some programs.

BASIC COSTS (2007-2008)

Tuition and fees: $3,756; out-of-state residents $9,105.
Per-credit charge: $86; out-of-state residents $264.
Room and board: $3,492.

FINANCIAL AID PICTURE (2006-2007)

Students with need: Out of 498 full-time freshmen who applied for aid, 443 were judged to have need. Of these, 385 received aid, and 315 had their full need met. Average financial aid package met 85% of need; average scholarship/grant was $3,500; average loan was $1,000. For part-time students, average financial aid package was $7,458.
Students without need: 105 full-time freshmen who did not demonstrate need for aid received scholarships/grants; average award was $500. No-need awards available for academics, alumni affiliation, art, athletics, leadership, music/drama, ROTC.
Scholarships offered: 17 full-time freshmen received athletic scholarships; average amount $1,500.
Cumulative student debt: 30% of graduating class had student loans; average debt was $6,300.

FINANCIAL AID PROCEDURES

Forms required: FAFSA.
Dates and Deadlines: Priority date 6/15; no closing date. Applicants notified on a rolling basis starting 4/1; must reply within 2 week(s) of notification.
Transfers: Priority date 6/1; no deadline. Applicants notified on a rolling basis starting 6/1. Academic transcripts required.

CONTACT

Carol Claiborne, Director of Financial Assistance
2800 West Gore Boulevard, Lawton, OK 73505-6377
(580) 581-2293

Carl Albert State College

Poteau, Oklahoma
www.carlalbert.edu   Federal Code: 003176

2-year public community and junior college in large town.
Enrollment: 2,575 undergrads.
Selectivity: Open admission; but selective for some programs.

BASIC COSTS (2007-2008)

Tuition and fees: $2,145; out-of-state residents $5,115.
Per-credit charge: $48; out-of-state residents $147.
Room and board: $3,124.
Additional info: Tuition/fee waivers available for minority students.

FINANCIAL AID PICTURE

Students with need: Need-based aid available for full-time and part-time students. Work study available nights.
Students without need: This college awards aid only to students with need.

FINANCIAL AID PROCEDURES

Forms required: FAFSA, institutional form.
Dates and Deadlines: No deadline. Applicants notified on a rolling basis.

CONTACT

Robin Benson, Director of Financial Aid
1507 South McKenna, Poteau, OK 74953-5208
(918) 647-1343

Connors State College

Warner, Oklahoma
www.connorsstate.edu   Federal Code: 003153

2-year public community and junior college in rural community.
Enrollment: 1,690 undergrads, 30% part-time. 515 full-time freshmen.
Selectivity: Open admission; but selective for some programs.

BASIC COSTS (2007-2008)

Tuition and fees: $2,379; out-of-state residents $5,694.
Per-credit charge: $60; out-of-state residents $171.
Room and board: $6,161.

FINANCIAL AID PICTURE

Students with need: Need-based aid available for full-time and part-time students.
Students without need: No-need awards available for academics, alumni affiliation, athletics, leadership, state/district residency.

FINANCIAL AID PROCEDURES

Forms required: FAFSA, institutional form.
Dates and Deadlines: Priority date 2/28; closing date 5/1. Applicants notified on a rolling basis starting 4/1; must reply within 2 week(s) of notification.

CONTACT

Wanda Fuller, Director of Financial Aid
RR 1, Box 1000, Warner, OK 74469-9700
(918) 463-6220

DeVry University: Oklahoma City Center

Oklahoma City, Oklahoma
www.devry.edu

4-year for-profit college in very large city.
Enrollment: 44 undergrads, 48% part-time. 3 full-time freshmen.

FINANCIAL AID PICTURE (2006-2007)

Students with need: Out of 2 full-time freshmen who applied for aid, 2 were judged to have need. Of these, 2 received aid. Average financial aid package met 8% of need; average scholarship/grant was $4,050. For part-time students, average financial aid package was $7,841.
Students without need: No-need awards available for academics.

FINANCIAL AID PROCEDURES

Forms required: FAFSA.
Dates and Deadlines: No deadline. Applicants notified on a rolling basis.

CONTACT
Lakepointe Towers, 4013 NW Expressway Street, Oklahoma City, OK 73116

East Central University
Ada, Oklahoma
www.ecok.edu   Federal Code: 003154

4-year public university in large town.
Enrollment: 3,657 undergrads, 19% part-time. 516 full-time freshmen.
Selectivity: Admits over 75% of applicants.

BASIC COSTS (2007-2008)
Tuition and fees: $3,841; out-of-state residents $9,314.
Per-credit charge: $89; out-of-state residents $271.
Room and board: $3,860.

FINANCIAL AID PICTURE (2007-2008)
Students with need: 46% of average financial aid package awarded as scholarships/grants, 54% awarded as loans/jobs. Need-based aid available for part-time students. Work study available nights, weekends, and for part-time students.
Students without need: No-need awards available for academics, athletics.

FINANCIAL AID PROCEDURES
Forms required: FAFSA.
Dates and Deadlines: Closing date 3/1. Applicants notified on a rolling basis starting 4/15; must reply within 2 week(s) of notification.

CONTACT
Marcia Carter, Director of Student Financial Aid
PMBJ8, 1100 East 14th Street, Ada, OK 74820
(580) 559-5243

Langston University
Langston, Oklahoma   Federal Code: 003157
www.lunet.edu   CSS Code: 6361

4-year public university and liberal arts college in rural community.
Enrollment: 2,461 undergrads, 14% part-time. 606 full-time freshmen.
Selectivity: Open admission; but selective for some programs.

BASIC COSTS (2007-2008)
Tuition and fees: $3,596; out-of-state residents $8,711.
Per-credit charge: $80; out-of-state residents $251.
Room and board: $5,740.
Additional info: Tuition at time of enrollment locked for 4 years.

FINANCIAL AID PICTURE (2006-2007)
Students with need: Out of 559 full-time freshmen who applied for aid, 477 were judged to have need. Of these, 472 received aid, and 182 had their full need met. Average financial aid package met 61% of need; average scholarship/grant was $854; average loan was $2,499. Need-based aid available for part-time students.
Students without need: This college awards aid only to students with need.
Cumulative student debt: 72% of graduating class had student loans; average debt was $14,789.

FINANCIAL AID PROCEDURES
Forms required: CSS PROFILE, state aid form.
Dates and Deadlines: Priority date 3/1; closing date 5/1. Applicants notified on a rolling basis starting 7/15; must reply within 2 week(s) of notification.

CONTACT
Yvonne Maxwell, Financial Aid Director
Box 728, Langston, OK 73050

Mid-America Christian University
Oklahoma City, Oklahoma
www.macu.edu   Federal Code: 006942

4-year private university and liberal arts college in very large city, affiliated with Church of God.
Enrollment: 744 undergrads.

BASIC COSTS (2008-2009)
Tuition and fees: $12,800.
Per-credit charge: $533.
Room and board: $5,176.

FINANCIAL AID PICTURE
Students with need: Need-based aid available for full-time and part-time students.
Students without need: No-need awards available for academics, leadership, minority status, music/drama.

FINANCIAL AID PROCEDURES
Forms required: FAFSA.
Dates and Deadlines: Priority date 5/1; no closing date. Applicants notified on a rolling basis starting 5/1.

CONTACT
James Menefee, Director of Student Financial Services
3500 SW 119th Street, Oklahoma City, OK 73170
(405) 692-3182

Northeastern Oklahoma Agricultural and Mechanical College
Miami, Oklahoma
www.neo.edu   Federal Code: 316000

2-year public community and junior college in large town.
Enrollment: 1,767 undergrads, 21% part-time. 655 full-time freshmen.
Selectivity: Open admission.

BASIC COSTS (2007-2008)
Tuition and fees: $2,286; out-of-state residents $5,761.
Per-credit charge: $53; out-of-state residents $169.
Room and board: $3,664.

FINANCIAL AID PICTURE (2006-2007)
Students with need: Out of 609 full-time freshmen who applied for aid, 440 were judged to have need. Of these, 439 received aid, and 95 had their full need met. Average financial aid package met 70% of need; average scholarship/grant was $4,548; average loan was $2,241. For part-time students, average financial aid package was $3,436.
Students without need: 100 full-time freshmen who did not demonstrate need for aid received scholarships/grants; average award was $2,518. No-need awards available for academics, art, athletics, leadership, music/drama, state/district residency.
Scholarships offered: 111 full-time freshmen received athletic scholarships; average amount $2,184.
Cumulative student debt: 22% of graduating class had student loans; average debt was $3,673.

FINANCIAL AID PROCEDURES
Forms required: FAFSA.
Dates and Deadlines: Priority date 4/1; no closing date. Applicants notified on a rolling basis starting 4/1; must reply by 8/30 or within 2 week(s) of notification.
Transfers: No deadline. Applicants notified on a rolling basis starting 4/1; must reply within 2 week(s) of notification.

CONTACT

Tammy Higgins, Director of Financial Aid

200 I Street Northeast, Miami, OK 74354-6497

(918) 540-6235

Northeastern State University

Tahlequah, Oklahoma

www.nsuok.edu   Federal Code: 003161

4-year public university in large town.

Enrollment: 8,181 undergrads, 25% part-time. 925 full-time freshmen.

Selectivity: Admits 50 to 75% of applicants.

BASIC COSTS (2007-2008)

Tuition and fees: $3,798; out-of-state residents $9,318.

Per-credit charge: $97; out-of-state residents $281.

Room and board: $5,592.

Additional info: Tuition/fee waivers available for adults, minority students.

FINANCIAL AID PICTURE (2007-2008)

Students with need: Out of 765 full-time freshmen who applied for aid, 603 were judged to have need. Of these, 574 received aid, and 358 had their full need met. Average financial aid package met 69% of need; average scholarship/grant was $4,121; average loan was $2,291. For part-time students, average financial aid package was $5,665.

Students without need: 110 full-time freshmen who did not demonstrate need for aid received scholarships/grants; average award was $1,107. No-need awards available for academics, alumni affiliation, art, athletics, job skills, leadership, minority status, music/drama, religious affiliation, ROTC, state/district residency.

Scholarships offered: *Merit:* Honors Program: $2,600 per year (minimum 28 ACT required), or up to $6,850 per year (minimum 30 ACT required); determined primarily by ACT and 3.8 high school GPA. *Athletic:* 46 full-time freshmen received athletic scholarships; average amount $5,123.

Cumulative student debt: 68% of graduating class had student loans; average debt was $19,971.

Additional info: Participates in off-campus job location & development program to assist students with off-campus employers to earn money for college expenses.

FINANCIAL AID PROCEDURES

Forms required: FAFSA, institutional form.

Dates and Deadlines: Priority date 4/1; no closing date. Applicants notified on a rolling basis starting 2/15.

Transfers: Priority date 12/15; no deadline. State grant deadline is April 15.

CONTACT

Teri Cochran, Director of Student Financial Services

600 North Grand Avenue, Tahlequah, OK 74464-2399

(918) 444-3456

Northwestern Oklahoma State University

Alva, Oklahoma

www.nwosu.edu   Federal Code: 003163

4-year public university and teachers college in small town.

Enrollment: 1,698 undergrads, 22% part-time. 235 full-time freshmen.

Selectivity: Admits over 75% of applicants.

BASIC COSTS (2007-2008)

Tuition and fees: $3,750; out-of-state residents $9,300.

Per-credit charge: $104; out-of-state residents $289.

Room and board: $3,400.

FINANCIAL AID PICTURE (2006-2007)

Students with need: Out of 181 full-time freshmen who applied for aid, 127 were judged to have need. Of these, 119 received aid, and 53 had their full need met. Average financial aid package met 66% of need; average scholarship/grant was $4,735; average loan was $2,222. For part-time students, average financial aid package was $4,801.

Students without need: 71 full-time freshmen who did not demonstrate need for aid received scholarships/grants; average award was $1,451. No-need awards available for academics, alumni affiliation, art, athletics, leadership, music/drama.

Scholarships offered: 7 full-time freshmen received athletic scholarships; average amount $1,458.

Cumulative student debt: 45% of graduating class had student loans; average debt was $13,808.

FINANCIAL AID PROCEDURES

Forms required: FAFSA.

Dates and Deadlines: No deadline. Applicants notified on a rolling basis starting 5/1.

CONTACT

Irala Magee, Director of Financial Aid

709 Oklahoma Boulevard, Alva, OK 73717-2799

(580) 327-8542

Oklahoma Baptist University

Shawnee, Oklahoma

www.okbu.edu   Federal Code: 003164

4-year private university and liberal arts college in large town, affiliated with Southern Baptist Convention.

Enrollment: 1,424 undergrads. 323 full-time freshmen.

Selectivity: Admits over 75% of applicants.

BASIC COSTS (2007-2008)

Tuition and fees: $15,994.

Room and board: $5,000.

FINANCIAL AID PICTURE (2006-2007)

Students with need: Out of 274 full-time freshmen who applied for aid, 221 were judged to have need. Of these, 221 received aid, and 128 had their full need met. Average financial aid package met 67% of need; average scholarship/grant was $3,980; average loan was $2,508. For part-time students, average financial aid package was $4,552.

Students without need: 102 full-time freshmen who did not demonstrate need for aid received scholarships/grants; average award was $1,417. No-need awards available for academics, alumni affiliation, art, athletics, job skills, leadership, music/drama, religious affiliation, ROTC, state/district residency.

Scholarships offered: *Merit:* Prichard Church Vocation Scholarship: $1,800; offered to all students preparing for vocational ministry associated with Southern Baptist Convention. Missionary Kid (MK) Scholarship: for children of Southern Baptist missionaries, guarantees student minimum $5,000 per year. OBU Bison Grants; based on award package and need: amount varies. *Athletic:* 84 full-time freshmen received athletic scholarships; average amount $6,351.

Cumulative student debt: 58% of graduating class had student loans; average debt was $17,008.

FINANCIAL AID PROCEDURES

Forms required: FAFSA, institutional form.

Dates and Deadlines: Priority date 3/1; no closing date. Applicants notified on a rolling basis starting 3/1; must reply by 5/1 or within 2 week(s) of notification.

Transfers: Priority date 4/1; no deadline. Applicants notified on a rolling basis starting 3/1; must reply within 2 week(s) of notification. Transfers receive 1 semester of financial aid on probationary basis. During probation semester, must complete 12 hours with at least 2.0 GPA in order to receive financial aid in subsequent semesters.

CONTACT
Jonna Raney, Director of Student Financial Services
500 West University, Shawnee, OK 74804
(405) 878-2016

Oklahoma Christian University
Oklahoma City, Oklahoma
www.oc.edu   Federal Code: 003165

4-year private liberal arts college in very large city, affiliated with Church of Christ.

Enrollment: 1,998 undergrads. 519 full-time freshmen.

Selectivity: Open admission; but selective for some programs.

BASIC COSTS (2008-2009)
Tuition and fees: $16,566.
Per-credit charge: $612.
Room and board: $6,390.

FINANCIAL AID PICTURE (2006-2007)
Students with need: Out of 435 full-time freshmen who applied for aid, 375 were judged to have need. Of these, 375 received aid, and 92 had their full need met. Average financial aid package met 40% of need; average scholarship/grant was $1,280; average loan was $2,521. For part-time students, average financial aid package was $8,550.

Students without need: 133 full-time freshmen who did not demonstrate need for aid received scholarships/grants; average award was $3,316. No-need awards available for academics, art, athletics, leadership, music/drama, religious affiliation, ROTC.

Scholarships offered: Merit: Awards to all students based on need and merit. Generous academic merit scholarships available. **Athletic:** 103 full-time freshmen received athletic scholarships; average amount $4,384.

Cumulative student debt: 77% of graduating class had student loans; average debt was $22,820.

FINANCIAL AID PROCEDURES
Forms required: FAFSA.
Dates and Deadlines: Priority date 3/15; closing date 8/31. Applicants notified on a rolling basis starting 1/15; must reply within 4 week(s) of notification.
Transfers: Applicants notified on a rolling basis starting 1/15; must reply within 4 week(s) of notification. Will award based on unofficial transcript. Must have all official transcripts before awards will be disbursed.

CONTACT
Clint LaRue, Director, Student Financial Services
Box 11000, Oklahoma City, OK 73136-1100
(405) 425-5190

Oklahoma City Community College
Oklahoma City, Oklahoma
www.occc.edu   Federal Code: 010391

2-year public community college in large city.

Enrollment: 10,151 undergrads, 61% part-time. 895 full-time freshmen.

Selectivity: Open admission; but selective for some programs.

BASIC COSTS (2007-2008)
Tuition and fees: $2,340; out-of-state residents $6,240.
Per-credit charge: $55; out-of-state residents $185.
Additional info: Tuition/fee waivers available for adults.

FINANCIAL AID PICTURE (2006-2007)
Students with need: 53% of average financial aid package awarded as scholarships/grants, 47% awarded as loans/jobs. Need-based aid available for part-time students. Work study available nights, weekends, and for part-time students.

Students without need: No-need awards available for academics, state/district residency.

FINANCIAL AID PROCEDURES
Forms required: FAFSA.
Dates and Deadlines: Priority date 7/1; no closing date. Applicants notified on a rolling basis starting 2/1.

CONTACT
Harold Case, Director of Financial Aid
7777 South May Avenue, Oklahoma City, OK 73159
(405) 682-7525

Oklahoma City University
Oklahoma City, Oklahoma
www.okcu.edu   Federal Code: 003166

4-year private university and liberal arts college in very large city, affiliated with United Methodist Church.

Enrollment: 2,129 undergrads, 16% part-time. 396 full-time freshmen.

Selectivity: Admits over 75% of applicants.

BASIC COSTS (2007-2008)
Tuition and fees: $20,800.
Per-credit charge: $670.
Room and board: $6,550.

FINANCIAL AID PICTURE (2006-2007)
Students with need: 83% of average financial aid package awarded as scholarships/grants, 17% awarded as loans/jobs. Need-based aid available for part-time students. Work study available nights, weekends, and for part-time students.

Students without need: No-need awards available for academics, art, athletics, job skills, leadership, music/drama, religious affiliation.

FINANCIAL AID PROCEDURES
Forms required: FAFSA, institutional form.
Dates and Deadlines: Priority date 3/1; closing date 6/30. Applicants notified on a rolling basis starting 2/24; must reply within 2 week(s) of notification.
Transfers: Applicants notified on a rolling basis starting 2/24; must reply within 2 week(s) of notification. Financial aid transcripts required from all previously attended institutions whether having received financial aid or not.

CONTACT
Denise Flis, Director of Financial Aid
2501 North Blackwelder Avenue, Oklahoma City, OK 73106
(405) 208-5211

Oklahoma Panhandle State University
Goodwell, Oklahoma
www.opsu.edu   Federal Code: 003174

4-year public agricultural and liberal arts college in rural community.

Enrollment: 1,078 undergrads, 12% part-time. 266 full-time freshmen.

Selectivity: Admits over 75% of applicants.

BASIC COSTS (2007-2008)
Tuition and fees: $3,249; out-of-state residents $8,139.
Per-credit charge: $83; out-of-state residents $246.
Room and board: $3,300.

FINANCIAL AID PICTURE

Students with need: Need-based aid available for full-time and part-time students.

Students without need: This college awards aid only to students with need.

FINANCIAL AID PROCEDURES

Forms required: FAFSA, institutional form.

Dates and Deadlines: Priority date 3/15; no closing date. Applicants notified by 5/1.

Transfers: No deadline. Applicants notified on a rolling basis.

CONTACT

Mel Riley, Director of Financial Aid
OPSU Admissions, Goodwell, OK 73939-0430
(580) 349-1582

Oklahoma State University

Stillwater, Oklahoma
osu.okstate.edu
Federal Code: 003170

4-year public university in small city.

Enrollment: 18,205 undergrads, 12% part-time. 3,123 full-time freshmen.

Selectivity: Admits over 75% of applicants.

BASIC COSTS (2007-2008)

Tuition and fees: $5,491; out-of-state residents $14,916.

Per-credit charge: $120; out-of-state residents $434.

Room and board: $6,267.

FINANCIAL AID PICTURE (2006-2007)

Students with need: Out of 2,016 full-time freshmen who applied for aid, 1,454 were judged to have need. Of these, 1,403 received aid, and 283 had their full need met. Average financial aid package met 76% of need; average scholarship/grant was $4,229; average loan was $2,673. For part-time students, average financial aid package was $5,489.

Students without need: 1,047 full-time freshmen who did not demonstrate need for aid received scholarships/grants; average award was $3,361. No-need awards available for academics, alumni affiliation, art, athletics, leadership, music/drama, ROTC, state/district residency.

Scholarships offered: 34 full-time freshmen received athletic scholarships; average amount $9,133.

Cumulative student debt: 55% of graduating class had student loans; average debt was $18,044.

FINANCIAL AID PROCEDURES

Forms required: FAFSA.

Dates and Deadlines: No deadline. Applicants notified on a rolling basis; must reply within 2 week(s) of notification.

CONTACT

Charles Bruce, Senior Director of Scholarships & Financial Aid
219 Student Union, Stillwater, OK 74078-7042
(405) 744-6604

Oklahoma State University: Oklahoma City

Oklahoma City, Oklahoma
www.osuokc.edu
Federal Code: 009647

2-year public branch campus and technical college in very large city.

Enrollment: 5,474 undergrads.

Selectivity: Open admission; but selective for some programs.

BASIC COSTS (2007-2008)

Tuition and fees: $2,705; out-of-state residents $7,175.

Per-credit charge: $71; out-of-state residents $220.

Additional info: Tuition/fee waivers available for adults, minority students.

FINANCIAL AID PICTURE

Students with need: Need-based aid available for full-time and part-time students.

Students without need: This college awards aid only to students with need.

FINANCIAL AID PROCEDURES

Forms required: FAFSA.

Dates and Deadlines: Priority date 7/15; no closing date. Applicants notified on a rolling basis starting 8/1; must reply within 2 week(s) of notification.

CONTACT

Bessie Carter, Director of Financial Aid
900 North Portland, Oklahoma City, OK 73107-6195
(405) 945-8646

Oklahoma State University: Okmulgee

Okmulgee, Oklahoma
www.osu-okmulgee.edu
Federal Code: 003172

2-year public branch campus and technical college in large town.

Enrollment: 2,034 undergrads.

Selectivity: Open admission; but selective for some programs.

BASIC COSTS (2007-2008)

Tuition and fees: $3,480; out-of-state residents $8,370.

Per-credit charge: $85; out-of-state residents $248.

Room and board: $5,652.

FINANCIAL AID PICTURE (2006-2007)

Students with need: 38% of average financial aid package awarded as scholarships/grants, 62% awarded as loans/jobs. Need-based aid available for part-time students. Work study available nights, weekends, and for part-time students.

FINANCIAL AID PROCEDURES

Forms required: FAFSA, institutional form.

Dates and Deadlines: Priority date 4/1; no closing date. Applicants notified on a rolling basis.

Transfers: Requirement of financial aid transcript from any institution(s) attended during transferring academic year.

CONTACT

Mary Bledsoe, Director of Student Financial Services
1801 East Fourth Street, Okmulgee, OK 74447-3901
(918) 293-5290

Oklahoma Wesleyan University

Bartlesville, Oklahoma
www.okwu.edu
Federal Code: 003151

4-year private university and liberal arts college in large town, affiliated with Wesleyan Church.

Enrollment: 989 undergrads.

Selectivity: Admits less than 50% of applicants.

BASIC COSTS (2008-2009)

Tuition and fees: $16,585.

Per-credit charge: $650.

Room and board: $6,050.

FINANCIAL AID PICTURE (2007-2008)

Students with need: 25% of average financial aid package awarded as scholarships/grants, 75% awarded as loans/jobs. Need-based aid available for part-time students. Work study available nights.

Students without need: No-need awards available for academics, alumni affiliation, athletics, leadership, music/drama, religious affiliation, state/district residency.

FINANCIAL AID PROCEDURES

Forms required: FAFSA, institutional form.

Dates and Deadlines: Priority date 4/1; no closing date. Applicants notified on a rolling basis starting 4/1; must reply by 5/1 or within 2 week(s) of notification.

Transfers: Priority date 3/1; closing date 8/1. Applicants notified on a rolling basis; must reply within 2 week(s) of notification.

CONTACT

Lee Kanakis, Director of Student Financial Services
2201 Silver Lake Road, Bartlesville, OK 74006
(918) 335-6282

Oral Roberts University

Tulsa, Oklahoma
www.oru.edu
Federal Code: 003985

4-year private university and liberal arts college in large city, affiliated with non-denominational tradition.

Enrollment: 2,714 undergrads, 9% part-time. 461 full-time freshmen.

Selectivity: Admits over 75% of applicants.

BASIC COSTS (2008-2009)

Tuition and fees: $18,386.

Per-credit charge: $742.

Room and board: $7,610.

FINANCIAL AID PICTURE (2007-2008)

Students with need: Out of 394 full-time freshmen who applied for aid, 344 were judged to have need. Of these, 344 received aid, and 122 had their full need met. Average financial aid package met 93% of need; average scholarship/grant was $9,086; average loan was $9,682. Need-based aid available for part-time students.

Students without need: 96 full-time freshmen who did not demonstrate need for aid received scholarships/grants; average award was $5,854. No-need awards available for academics, art, athletics, job skills, leadership, music/drama.

Scholarships offered: 7 full-time freshmen received athletic scholarships; average amount $18,134.

Cumulative student debt: 83% of graduating class had student loans; average debt was $35,200.

FINANCIAL AID PROCEDURES

Forms required: FAFSA.

Dates and Deadlines: Priority date 3/15; no closing date. Applicants notified on a rolling basis starting 2/15; must reply by 7/15.

Transfers: Priority date 3/30. Applicants notified on a rolling basis starting 4/1. Transfer applicants eligible for some scholarships.

CONTACT

Shannon Panthin, Director of Financial Aid
7777 South Lewis Avenue, Tulsa, OK 74171
(918) 495-6510

Platt College: Oklahoma City Central

Oklahoma City, Oklahoma
www.plattcollege.org
Federal Code: 023068

1-year for-profit branch campus and health science college in small city.

Enrollment: 325 undergrads.

Selectivity: Open admission; but selective for some programs.

BASIC COSTS (2007-2008)

Additional info: Tuition varies by program. Full-time tuition ranges from $8,945 to $19,945. Required fees $150.

FINANCIAL AID PICTURE

Students with need: Need-based aid available for full-time students.

FINANCIAL AID PROCEDURES

Forms required: FAFSA.

CONTACT

Amy Hocker, Financial Aid Director (OK City campus)
309 South Ann Arbor, Oklahoma City, OK 73128
(405) 946-7799

Platt College: Tulsa

Tulsa, Oklahoma
www.plattcollege.org
Federal Code: 016312

2-year for-profit health science college in large city.

Enrollment: 74 undergrads.

Selectivity: Open admission; but selective for some programs.

BASIC COSTS (2007-2008)

Additional info: Tuition varies by program.

FINANCIAL AID PICTURE

Students with need: Need-based aid available for full-time and part-time students.

Students without need: This college awards aid only to students with need.

FINANCIAL AID PROCEDURES

Forms required: FAFSA.

Dates and Deadlines: No deadline.

CONTACT

Linda Bates, Director of Compliance-Financial Services
3801 South Sheridan, Tulsa, OK 74145-1132
(918) 663-9000

Redlands Community College

El Reno, Oklahoma
www.redlandscc.edu
Federal Code: 003156

2-year public community college in large town.

Enrollment: 2,215 undergrads, 60% part-time. 266 full-time freshmen.

Selectivity: Open admission; but selective for some programs.

BASIC COSTS (2007-2008)

Tuition and fees: $2,640; out-of-state residents $4,890.

Per-credit charge: $88; out-of-state residents $163.

Additional info: Tuition/fee waivers available for adults.

FINANCIAL AID PICTURE

Students with need: Need-based aid available for full-time and part-time students. Work study available nights, weekends, and for part-time students.

Students without need: No-need awards available for academics, athletics, leadership.

FINANCIAL AID PROCEDURES

Forms required: FAFSA.

Dates and Deadlines: Priority date 3/30; no closing date. Applicants notified on a rolling basis starting 6/1; must reply within 2 week(s) of notification.

CONTACT

Karen Jeffers, Director of Financial Aid

1300 South Country Club Road, El Reno, OK 73036

(866) 415-6367 ext. 1442

Rogers State University

Claremore, Oklahoma

www.rsu.edu   Federal Code: 003168

4-year public university in large town.

Enrollment: 3,806 undergrads, 42% part-time. 671 full-time freshmen.

Selectivity: Open admission; but selective for some programs.

BASIC COSTS (2007-2008)

Tuition and fees: $3,893; out-of-state residents $8,858.

Per-credit charge: $83; out-of-state residents $248.

FINANCIAL AID PICTURE

Students with need: Need-based aid available for full-time and part-time students. Work study available nights, weekends, and for part-time students.

Students without need: No-need awards available for academics, athletics, leadership, music/drama.

FINANCIAL AID PROCEDURES

Forms required: FAFSA, institutional form.

Dates and Deadlines: Priority date 3/1; no closing date. Applicants notified on a rolling basis starting 4/1; must reply within 3 week(s) of notification.

Transfers: No deadline. Applicants notified on a rolling basis starting 4/7; must reply within 3 week(s) of notification.

CONTACT

Chris Steckmann, Director, Financial Aid

1701 West Will Rogers Boulevard, Claremore, OK 74017

(918) 343-7555

Rose State College

Midwest City, Oklahoma

www.rose.edu   Federal Code: 009185

2-year public community college in small city.

Enrollment: 7,107 undergrads, 61% part-time. 671 full-time freshmen.

Selectivity: Admits over 75% of applicants.

BASIC COSTS (2007-2008)

Tuition and fees: $2,340; out-of-state residents $6,798.

Per-credit charge: $60; out-of-state residents $209.

FINANCIAL AID PICTURE (2006-2007)

Students with need: 50% of average financial aid package awarded as scholarships/grants, 50% awarded as loans/jobs. Need-based aid available for part-time students. Work study available nights, weekends, and for part-time students.

Students without need: No-need awards available for academics, athletics.

FINANCIAL AID PROCEDURES

Forms required: FAFSA.

Dates and Deadlines: Priority date 6/1; no closing date. Applicants notified on a rolling basis starting 3/1; must reply within 4 week(s) of notification.

CONTACT

Steven Daffer, Director of Financial Aid

6420 SE 15th Street, Midwest City, OK 73110

(405) 733-7424

St. Gregory's University

Shawnee, Oklahoma

www.stgregorys.edu   Federal Code: 003183

4-year private university and liberal arts college in large town, affiliated with Roman Catholic Church.

Enrollment: 750 undergrads, 47% part-time. 84 full-time freshmen.

Selectivity: Admits 50 to 75% of applicants.

BASIC COSTS (2007-2008)

Tuition and fees: $14,710.

Per-credit charge: $460.

Room and board: $6,150.

Additional info: Tuition/fee waivers available for adults.

FINANCIAL AID PICTURE (2006-2007)

Students with need: Out of 71 full-time freshmen who applied for aid, 71 were judged to have need. Of these, 70 received aid, and 10 had their full need met. Average financial aid package met 66% of need; average scholarship/grant was $6,380; average loan was $3,264. Need-based aid available for part-time students.

Students without need: 11 full-time freshmen who did not demonstrate need for aid received scholarships/grants; average award was $1,750. No-need awards available for academics, alumni affiliation, art, athletics, job skills, leadership, music/drama, religious affiliation.

Scholarships offered: *Merit:* Leadership Scholarship: $500-$2,000. Academic Scholarship: $500-$5,100. Need-based scholarship: $500-$1,500.

Athletic: 36 full-time freshmen received athletic scholarships; average amount $7,581.

Cumulative student debt: 59% of graduating class had student loans; average debt was $16,957.

FINANCIAL AID PROCEDURES

Forms required: FAFSA, institutional form.

Dates and Deadlines: Priority date 4/1; no closing date. Applicants notified on a rolling basis starting 2/15; must reply within 3 week(s) of notification.

Transfers: No deadline. Applicants notified on a rolling basis.

CONTACT

Matt McCoin, Director of Financial Aid

1900 West MacArthur Drive, Shawnee, OK 74804

(405) 878-5412

Seminole State College

Seminole, Oklahoma

www.ssc.cc.ok.us   Federal Code: 003178

2-year public community and junior college in small town.

Enrollment: 1,820 undergrads.

Selectivity: Open admission; but selective for some programs.

BASIC COSTS (2007-2008)

Tuition and fees: $2,594; out-of-state residents $6,078.

Per-credit charge: $53; out-of-state residents $169.

Room and board: $5,420.

FINANCIAL AID PICTURE

Students with need: Need-based aid available for full-time students.

Students without need: No-need awards available for academics, athletics, state/district residency.

FINANCIAL AID PROCEDURES

Forms required: FAFSA, institutional form.
Dates and Deadlines: Priority date 4/1; no closing date. Applicants notified on a rolling basis starting 3/1; must reply within 4 week(s) of notification.

CONTACT

Chris Lindley, Director of Enrollment Management
2701 Boren Boulevard, Seminole, OK 74868
(405) 382-9247

Southeastern Oklahoma State University
Durant, Oklahoma
www.sosu.edu   Federal Code: 003179

4-year public liberal arts and teachers college in large town.
Enrollment: 3,585 undergrads, 21% part-time. 521 full-time freshmen.
Selectivity: Admits 50 to 75% of applicants.

BASIC COSTS (2007-2008)

Tuition and fees: $3,926; out-of-state residents $9,720.
Per-credit charge: $108; out-of-state residents $301.
Room and board: $4,530.
Additional info: Tuition/fee waivers available for minority students.

FINANCIAL AID PICTURE (2006-2007)

Students with need: Out of 434 full-time freshmen who applied for aid, 407 were judged to have need. Of these, 398 received aid, and 173 had their full need met. Average financial aid package met 64% of need; average scholarship/grant was $1,055; average loan was $1,199. For part-time students, average financial aid package was $981.
Students without need: 2 full-time freshmen who did not demonstrate need for aid received scholarships/grants; average award was $1,156. No-need awards available for academics, alumni affiliation, art, athletics, leadership, minority status, music/drama.
Scholarships offered: 52 full-time freshmen received athletic scholarships; average amount $1,467.
Cumulative student debt: 37% of graduating class had student loans; average debt was $6,852.

FINANCIAL AID PROCEDURES

Forms required: FAFSA, institutional form.
Dates and Deadlines: Priority date 3/1; no closing date. Applicants notified on a rolling basis starting 4/15; must reply within 2 week(s) of notification.

CONTACT

Sherry Hudson, Director of Student Financial Aid
1405 North Fourth Avenue, PMB 4225, Durant, OK 74701-0607
(580) 745-2186

Southwestern Christian University
Bethany, Oklahoma
www.swcu.edu   Federal Code: 003180

4-year private Bible college in large town, affiliated with Pentecostal Holiness Church.
Enrollment: 178 undergrads, 6% part-time. 37 full-time freshmen.

BASIC COSTS (2007-2008)

Tuition and fees: $9,020.
Per-credit charge: $299.
Room and board: $4,400.
Additional info: Adult education program $320 per credit hour.

FINANCIAL AID PICTURE

Students with need: Need-based aid available for full-time and part-time students. Work study available nights, weekends, and for part-time students.

Students without need: No-need awards available for academics, alumni affiliation, leadership, music/drama, religious affiliation.

FINANCIAL AID PROCEDURES

Forms required: FAFSA.
Dates and Deadlines: Priority date 8/1; no closing date. Applicants notified on a rolling basis starting 5/1; must reply within 2 week(s) of notification.

CONTACT

Daniel Watkins, Director of Financial Aid
Box 340, Bethany, OK 73008
(405) 789-7661 ext. 3456

Southwestern Oklahoma State University
Weatherford, Oklahoma
www.swosu.edu   Federal Code: 003181

4-year public university in large town.
Enrollment: 4,146 undergrads, 12% part-time. 877 full-time freshmen.
Selectivity: Admits over 75% of applicants.

BASIC COSTS (2007-2008)

Tuition and fees: $3,750; out-of-state residents $8,550.
Per-credit charge: $100; out-of-state residents $260.
Room and board: $4,700.

FINANCIAL AID PICTURE (2007-2008)

Students with need: Out of 665 full-time freshmen who applied for aid, 500 were judged to have need. Of these, 494 received aid, and 138 had their full need met. Average financial aid package met 92% of need; average scholarship/grant was $1,172; average loan was $1,422. For part-time students, average financial aid package was $3,019.
Students without need: 90 full-time freshmen who did not demonstrate need for aid received scholarships/grants; average award was $408. No-need awards available for academics, alumni affiliation, art, athletics, job skills, leadership, music/drama, state/district residency.
Scholarships offered: 30 full-time freshmen received athletic scholarships; average amount $682.

FINANCIAL AID PROCEDURES

Forms required: FAFSA, institutional form.
Dates and Deadlines: Priority date 3/1; no closing date. Applicants notified on a rolling basis starting 1/1.

CONTACT

Jerome Wichert, Director of Student Financial Services
100 Campus Drive, Weatherford, OK 73096
(508) 774-3786

Spartan College of Aeronautics and Technology
Tulsa, Oklahoma
www.spartan.edu   Federal Code: 007678

4-year for-profit technical college in large city.
Enrollment: 953 undergrads.

BASIC COSTS (2007-2008)

Additional info: Tech program tuition $13,200 per academic year; flight program tuition approximately $17,000 per academic year; bachelor's program tuition $10,359 per academic year. Books/tools and supplies vary by program. Tuition at time of enrollment locked for 4 years.

FINANCIAL AID PICTURE

Students with need: Need-based aid available for full-time and part-time students. Work study available nights, weekends, and for part-time students.

FINANCIAL AID PROCEDURES

Forms required: FAFSA, institutional form.

Dates and Deadlines: No deadline. Applicants notified on a rolling basis starting 2/1; must reply within 2 week(s) of notification.

Transfers: No deadline. Applicants notified on a rolling basis; must reply within 2 week(s) of notification.

CONTACT

Christina Foster, Director of Financial Aid

Box 582833, Tulsa, OK 74158-2833

(918) 836-6886

Tulsa Community College

Tulsa, Oklahoma

www.tulsacc.edu   Federal Code: 009763

2-year public community college in large city.

Enrollment: 11,512 undergrads, 59% part-time. 1,776 full-time freshmen.

Selectivity: Open admission; but selective for some programs.

BASIC COSTS (2007-2008)

Tuition and fees: $2,568; out-of-state residents $6,880.

Per-credit charge: $58; out-of-state residents $201.

Additional info: Tuition/fee waivers available for minority students.

FINANCIAL AID PICTURE

Students with need: Out of 1,258 full-time freshmen who applied for aid, 830 were judged to have need. Of these, 830 received aid. Need-based aid available for part-time students.

Students without need: No-need awards available for academics, art, leadership, music/drama, state/district residency.

FINANCIAL AID PROCEDURES

Forms required: FAFSA, institutional form.

Dates and Deadlines: Priority date 8/1; no closing date. Applicants notified on a rolling basis starting 4/1; must reply within 2 week(s) of notification.

CONTACT

Matt Short, Director of Student Financial Services

6111 East Skelly Drive, Tulsa, OK 74135

(918) 595-7155

Tulsa Welding School

Tulsa, Oklahoma

www.weldingschool.com   Federal Code: 015733

2-year for-profit technical college in very large city.

Enrollment: 736 undergrads.

Selectivity: Open admission.

BASIC COSTS (2007-2008)

Additional info: Tuition and fees vary by program from $7,910 to $13,900.

FINANCIAL AID PICTURE

Students with need: Need-based aid available for full-time students.

Students without need: This college awards aid only to students with need.

FINANCIAL AID PROCEDURES

Forms required: FAFSA.

CONTACT

Ava Edens, Financial Aid Director

2545 East 11th Street, Tulsa, OK 74104-3909

(918) 587-6789

University of Central Oklahoma

Edmond, Oklahoma

www.ucok.edu   Federal Code: 003152

4-year public university in small city.

Enrollment: 14,181 undergrads, 30% part-time. 1,815 full-time freshmen.

Selectivity: Admits 50 to 75% of applicants.

BASIC COSTS (2007-2008)

Tuition and fees: $3,857; out-of-state residents $9,729.

Per-credit charge: $111; out-of-state residents $306.

Room and board: $6,915.

Additional info: Tuition/fee waivers available for minority students.

FINANCIAL AID PICTURE (2006-2007)

Students with need: Out of 1,198 full-time freshmen who applied for aid, 886 were judged to have need. Of these, 815 received aid, and 66 had their full need met. Average financial aid package met 63% of need; average scholarship/grant was $5,651; average loan was $2,300. For part-time students, average financial aid package was $4,692.

Students without need: 158 full-time freshmen who did not demonstrate need for aid received scholarships/grants; average award was $2,338. No-need awards available for academics, alumni affiliation, art, athletics, leadership, minority status, music/drama, ROTC, state/district residency.

Scholarships offered: 37 full-time freshmen received athletic scholarships; average amount $3,463.

Cumulative student debt: 45% of graduating class had student loans; average debt was $15,785.

FINANCIAL AID PROCEDURES

Forms required: FAFSA, institutional form.

Dates and Deadlines: Priority date 5/31; no closing date. Applicants notified on a rolling basis starting 5/1; must reply by 6/30 or within 4 week(s) of notification.

Transfers: No deadline. Applicants notified on a rolling basis starting 5/1; must reply by 6/30 or within 4 week(s) of notification.

CONTACT

Sheila McGill, Director of Financial Aid

100 North University Drive, Edmond, OK 73034-0151

(405) 974-3334

University of Oklahoma

Norman, Oklahoma

www.ou.edu   Federal Code: 003184

4-year public university in small city.

Enrollment: 20,400 undergrads, 13% part-time. 3,303 full-time freshmen.

Selectivity: Admits over 75% of applicants.

BASIC COSTS (2007-2008)

Tuition and fees: $6,507; out-of-state residents $15,621.

Per-credit charge: $109; out-of-state residents $413.

Room and board: $7,058.

Additional info: Computer course fees and other college level fees vary by college. Tuition/fee waivers available for minority students.

FINANCIAL AID PICTURE (2006-2007)

Students with need: Out of 2,006 full-time freshmen who applied for aid, 1,626 were judged to have need. Of these, 1,626 received aid, and 764 had their full need met. Average financial aid package met 85% of need; average scholarship/grant was $4,359; average loan was $3,041. For part-time students, average financial aid package was $7,758.

Students without need: 494 full-time freshmen who did not demonstrate need for aid received scholarships/grants; average award was $1,048. No-

need awards available for academics, alumni affiliation, art, athletics, leadership, music/drama, religious affiliation, ROTC.

Scholarships offered: *Merit:* Presidents Leadership Class: $1,000 in state, $4,700 out-of-state;100 awarded. Scholar's Program: $1,500-$2,500 in-state and $2,500-$5,000 out-of-state; for academic merit. *Athletic:* 43 full-time freshmen received athletic scholarships; average amount $12,021.

Cumulative student debt: 47% of graduating class had student loans; average debt was $19,454.

Additional info: Institutional loans are available for early applicants who do not qualify for federal or state need-based aid.

FINANCIAL AID PROCEDURES

Forms required: FAFSA.

Dates and Deadlines: Priority date 3/1; no closing date. Applicants notified on a rolling basis starting 3/15; must reply within 6 week(s) of notification.

Transfers: Applicants notified on a rolling basis starting 3/1; must reply within 6 week(s) of notification. Transfer leadership resident tuition waiver and transfer academic excellence tuition waiver available.

CONTACT

Caryn Pacheco, Director of Financial Aid
1000 Asp Avenue, Norman, OK 73019-4076
(405) 325-5505

University of Science and Arts of Oklahoma

Chickasha, Oklahoma
www.usao.edu   Federal Code: 003167

4-year public university and liberal arts college in large town.

Enrollment: 1,096 undergrads, 12% part-time. 214 full-time freshmen.

Selectivity: Admits over 75% of applicants.

BASIC COSTS (2007-2008)

Tuition and fees: $4,050; out-of-state residents $9,630.

Per-credit charge: $96; out-of-state residents $282.

Room and board: $4,690.

FINANCIAL AID PICTURE (2007-2008)

Students with need: Out of 172 full-time freshmen who applied for aid, 138 were judged to have need. Of these, 135 received aid, and 40 had their full need met. Average financial aid package met 71% of need; average scholarship/grant was $5,692; average loan was $2,557. For part-time students, average financial aid package was $5,015.

Students without need: 41 full-time freshmen who did not demonstrate need for aid received scholarships/grants; average award was $4,504. No-need awards available for academics, art, athletics, leadership, music/drama, state/district residency.

Scholarships offered: 15 full-time freshmen received athletic scholarships; average amount $7,850.

Cumulative student debt: 51% of graduating class had student loans; average debt was $16,623.

FINANCIAL AID PROCEDURES

Forms required: FAFSA, institutional form.

Dates and Deadlines: Priority date 3/15; no closing date. Applicants notified on a rolling basis starting 3/15; must reply within 4 week(s) of notification.

Transfers: No deadline. Applicants notified on a rolling basis; must reply within 6 week(s) of notification.

CONTACT

Nancy Moats, Director of Financial Aid
1727 West Alabama, Chickasha, OK 73018-5322
(405) 574-1240

University of Tulsa

Tulsa, Oklahoma
www.utulsa.edu   Federal Code: 003185

4-year private university in large city, affiliated with Presbyterian Church (USA).

Enrollment: 2,920 undergrads, 4% part-time. 656 full-time freshmen.

Selectivity: Admits 50 to 75% of applicants.

BASIC COSTS (2008-2009)

Tuition and fees: $23,940.

Per-credit charge: $856.

Room and board: $7,776.

Additional info: A one-time $425 fee is charged first-time students for orientation, lifetime transcripts, course drop/add transactions, and graduation/commencement.

FINANCIAL AID PICTURE (2006-2007)

Students with need: Out of 594 full-time freshmen who applied for aid, 324 were judged to have need. Of these, 324 received aid, and 155 had their full need met. Average financial aid package met 87% of need; average scholarship/grant was $5,056; average loan was $5,136. For part-time students, average financial aid package was $11,414.

Students without need: 216 full-time freshmen who did not demonstrate need for aid received scholarships/grants; average award was $10,464. No-need awards available for academics, alumni affiliation, art, athletics, leadership, minority status, music/drama, religious affiliation.

Scholarships offered: 69 full-time freshmen received athletic scholarships; average amount $19,476.

Cumulative student debt: 54% of graduating class had student loans; average debt was $20,563.

FINANCIAL AID PROCEDURES

Forms required: FAFSA, institutional form.

Dates and Deadlines: Priority date 4/1; no closing date. Applicants notified on a rolling basis starting 3/1; must reply by 5/1 or within 2 week(s) of notification.

Transfers: Priority date 5/1. Applicants notified on a rolling basis starting 3/1; must reply by 5/1 or within 2 week(s) of notification.

CONTACT

Vicki Hendrickson, Director of Student Financial Services
800 South Tucker Drive, Tulsa, OK 74104-3189
(918) 631-2526

Vatterott College

Oklahoma City, Oklahoma
www.vatterott-college.com   Federal Code: 020693

4-year for-profit branch campus and career college in very large city.

Enrollment: 275 undergrads.

Selectivity: Open admission.

BASIC COSTS (2007-2008)

Additional info: Program cost ranges: $15,891 to $20,901 (certificate/diploma); $22,920 to $31,981 (associate degree); $57,458 (bachelor's degree).

FINANCIAL AID PICTURE

Students with need: Need-based aid available for full-time students.

Students without need: This college awards aid only to students with need.

FINANCIAL AID PROCEDURES

Forms required: FAFSA.

Dates and Deadlines: No deadline.

CONTACT

Janice Stepp, Financial Aid Director

4621 NW 23rd Street, Oklahoma City, OK 73127

(405) 945-0088

Western Oklahoma State College

Altus, Oklahoma

www.wosc.edu

Federal Code: 003146

2-year public community college in large town.

Enrollment: 580 full-time undergrads.

Selectivity: Open admission.

BASIC COSTS (2007-2008)

Tuition and fees: $2,471; out-of-state residents $5,771.

Per-credit charge: $52; out-of-state residents $162.

Room and board: $3,750.

FINANCIAL AID PICTURE (2006-2007)

Students with need: 65% of average financial aid package awarded as scholarships/grants, 35% awarded as loans/jobs. Need-based aid available for part-time students. Work study available nights, weekends, and for part-time students.

Students without need: No-need awards available for academics, alumni affiliation, art, athletics, leadership, music/drama, state/district residency.

FINANCIAL AID PROCEDURES

Forms required: FAFSA, institutional form.

Dates and Deadlines: Priority date 3/1; no closing date. Applicants notified on a rolling basis; must reply within 3 week(s) of notification.

CONTACT

Myrna Cross, Director of Financial Aid / Veterans' Affairs

2801 North Main Street, Altus, OK 73521

(580) 477-7709

Oregon

Art Institute of Portland

Portland, Oregon

www.aipd.artinstitutes.edu

Federal Code: 007819

4-year for-profit visual arts and liberal arts college in large city.

Enrollment: 1,722 undergrads, 42% part-time. 202 full-time freshmen.

Selectivity: Admits 50 to 75% of applicants.

BASIC COSTS (2007-2008)

Tuition and fees: $19,395.

Per-credit charge: $431.

Room only: $8,250.

Additional info: Tuition at time of enrollment locked for 4 years.

FINANCIAL AID PICTURE

Students with need: Need-based aid available for full-time and part-time students. Work study available nights, weekends, and for part-time students.

Students without need: No-need awards available for art.

Additional info: Applicants encouraged to apply early for financial aid. Scholarship deadlines range from January 1 to March 1.

FINANCIAL AID PROCEDURES

Forms required: FAFSA.

Dates and Deadlines: Priority date 3/1; no closing date. Applicants notified on a rolling basis starting 1/1; must reply within 5 week(s) of notification.

Transfers: No deadline. Applicants notified on a rolling basis starting 1/1.

CONTACT

Mickey Jacobson, Director of Student Financial Services

1122 Northwest Davis Street, Portland, OR 97209-2911

(503) 382-4784

Blue Mountain Community College

Pendleton, Oregon

www.bluecc.edu

Federal Code: 003186

2-year public community college in large town.

Enrollment: 1,400 undergrads.

Selectivity: Open admission; but selective for some programs.

BASIC COSTS (2007-2008)

Tuition and fees: $2,989; out-of-state residents $8,704.

Per-credit charge: $64; out-of-state residents $191.

Additional info: Washington, Idaho, Nevada, Montana, and California state residents pay in-state tuition.

FINANCIAL AID PICTURE

Students with need: Need-based aid available for full-time and part-time students. Work study available nights, weekends, and for part-time students.

Students without need: No-need awards available for athletics, music/drama.

FINANCIAL AID PROCEDURES

Forms required: FAFSA.

Dates and Deadlines: Priority date 3/30; no closing date. Applicants notified on a rolling basis starting 4/1; must reply within 2 week(s) of notification.

CONTACT

Karen Graybeal, Director of Financial Aid

2411 Northwest Carden Avenue, Pendleton, OR 97801

(541) 278-5790

Cascade College

Portland, Oregon

www.cascade.edu

4-year private branch campus and liberal arts college in very large city, affiliated with Church of Christ.

Enrollment: 262 undergrads, 1% part-time. 56 full-time freshmen.

Selectivity: Open admission.

BASIC COSTS (2008-2009)

Tuition and fees: $14,250.

Per-credit charge: $550.

Room and board: $6,700.

FINANCIAL AID PICTURE

Students with need: Need-based aid available for full-time and part-time students. Work study available nights, weekends, and for part-time students.

Students without need: No-need awards available for academics, alumni affiliation, athletics, leadership, music/drama, religious affiliation.

FINANCIAL AID PROCEDURES

Forms required: FAFSA.

Dates and Deadlines: No deadline.

Transfers: No deadline. Applicants notified on a rolling basis.

CONTACT

Mark Beekman, Director of Financial Aid

9101 East Burnside Street, Portland, OR 97216

(503) 257-1241

Central Oregon Community College
Bend, Oregon
www.cocc.edu   Federal Code: 003188

2-year public community college in small city.

Enrollment: 3,643 undergrads, 56% part-time. 427 full-time freshmen.

Selectivity: Open admission; but selective for some programs.

BASIC COSTS (2007-2008)

Tuition and fees: $2,958; out-of-district residents $3,993; out-of-state residents $8,088.

Per-credit charge: $63; out-of-district residents $86; out-of-state residents $176.

Room and board: $7,084.

Additional info: Residents of WA, ID, NV and CA pay the in-state, out-of-district tuition. Emergency Medical Services, Aviation, Nursing, Culinary and Massage Therapy programs carry additional fees.

FINANCIAL AID PICTURE (2007-2008)

Students with need: Out of 269 full-time freshmen who applied for aid, 202 were judged to have need. Of these, 188 received aid, and 59 had their full need met. Average financial aid package met 78% of need; average scholarship/grant was $4,770; average loan was $3,197. For part-time students, average financial aid package was $6,275.

Students without need: 14 full-time freshmen who did not demonstrate need for aid received scholarships/grants; average award was $2,700. No-need awards available for academics, state/district residency.

Additional info: Institution-sponsored short-term loans. Extensive part-time student employment.

FINANCIAL AID PROCEDURES

Forms required: FAFSA.

Dates and Deadlines: No deadline. Applicants notified on a rolling basis starting 3/30; must reply within 4 week(s) of notification.

CONTACT

Kevin Multop, Director of Financial Aid
2600 Northwest College Way, Bend, OR 97701-5998
(541) 383-7260

Chemeketa Community College
Salem, Oregon
www.chemeketa.edu   Federal Code: 003218

2-year public community and junior college in small city.

Enrollment: 6,350 undergrads, 57% part-time. 373 full-time freshmen.

Selectivity: Open admission; but selective for some programs.

BASIC COSTS (2007-2008)

Tuition and fees: $2,790; out-of-state residents $9,135.

Per-credit charge: $58; out-of-state residents $199.

Additional info: International students have additional required fees. Individual courses may have extra fees.

FINANCIAL AID PICTURE

Students with need: Need-based aid available for full-time and part-time students. Work study available nights, weekends, and for part-time students.

Students without need: This college awards aid only to students with need.

FINANCIAL AID PROCEDURES

Forms required: FAFSA.

Dates and Deadlines: Priority date 4/1; no closing date. Applicants notified on a rolling basis starting 6/30; must reply within 2 week(s) of notification.

Transfers: Priority date 6/30; no deadline. Applicants notified on a rolling basis; must reply within 4 week(s) of notification.

CONTACT

Kathy Campbell, Financial Aid Director
Admissions Office, Salem, OR 97305-1453
(503) 399-5018

Clackamas Community College
Oregon City, Oregon
www.clackamas.edu   Federal Code: 004878

2-year public community college in small city.

Enrollment: 1,960 full-time undergrads.

Selectivity: Open admission; but selective for some programs.

BASIC COSTS (2007-2008)

Tuition and fees: $2,790; out-of-state residents $9,135.

Per-credit charge: $57; out-of-state residents $198.

Additional info: In-state tuition applies to residents of Oregon, Washington, Idaho, Nevada and California. Tuition at time of enrollment locked for 2 years.

FINANCIAL AID PICTURE

Students with need: Need-based aid available for full-time and part-time students. Work study available nights, weekends, and for part-time students.

Students without need: No-need awards available for academics, art, athletics, leadership, music/drama.

Additional info: Institutional tuition rebate guarantee. Frozen tuition rates for new fall students who graduate within 3 years. Any tuition increase levied by college during those 3 years will be refunded to student upon graduation.

FINANCIAL AID PROCEDURES

Forms required: FAFSA, institutional form.

Dates and Deadlines: Priority date 4/10; no closing date. Applicants notified on a rolling basis starting 3/15; must reply within 3 week(s) of notification.

Transfers: No deadline. Applicants notified on a rolling basis.

CONTACT

Fayne Griffiths, Director, Student Financial Services
19600 Molalla Avenue, Oregon City, OR 97045
(503) 657-6958 ext. 2745

Clatsop Community College
Astoria, Oregon
www.clatsopcollege.com   Federal Code: 003189

2-year public community college in large town.

Enrollment: 567 undergrads.

Selectivity: Open admission; but selective for some programs.

BASIC COSTS (2007-2008)

Tuition and fees: $3,105; out-of-state residents $5,940.

Per-credit charge: $63; out-of-state residents $126.

FINANCIAL AID PICTURE (2006-2007)

Students with need: 66% of average financial aid package awarded as scholarships/grants, 34% awarded as loans/jobs. Need-based aid available for part-time students.

Students without need: No-need awards available for academics.

Scholarships offered: Rochester scholarships; $3,000-$5,000; awarded to math or science majors with 3.0 GPA; 3 reference letters required; number awarded varies yearly.

FINANCIAL AID PROCEDURES

Forms required: FAFSA, institutional form.

Dates and Deadlines: Priority date 5/1; no closing date. Applicants notified on a rolling basis starting 2/1.

Transfers: Students who apply after July 1 may only be eligible for Pell Grants and loans depending on availability of funds. Reply deadline 1 week before start of classes.

CONTACT

Sharon Boring, Director of Financial Aid
1653 Jerome Avenue, Astoria, OR 97103
(503) 338-2322

Concordia University
Portland, Oregon
www.cu-portland.edu   Federal Code: 003191

4-year private university and liberal arts college in very large city, affiliated with Lutheran Church - Missouri Synod.
Enrollment: 1,036 undergrads, 11% part-time. 182 full-time freshmen.
Selectivity: Admits 50 to 75% of applicants.

BASIC COSTS (2008-2009)

Tuition and fees: $22,100.
Per-credit charge: $680.
Room and board: $6,400.
Additional info: Tuition/fee waivers available for adults.

FINANCIAL AID PICTURE

Students with need: Need-based aid available for full-time and part-time students. Work study available nights, weekends, and for part-time students.
Students without need: No-need awards available for academics, athletics, leadership, music/drama, religious affiliation.
Scholarships offered: President's Scholarship: $8,000; based on academic index. Regent's Scholarship: $6,000; calculated from high school GPA and ACT/SAT score. University Award: $4,500; calculated from high school GPA and ACT/SAT score. Dean's Award: $5,000; based on academic index. Honors Scholarship: 50% tuition.

FINANCIAL AID PROCEDURES

Forms required: FAFSA.
Dates and Deadlines: No deadline. Applicants notified on a rolling basis starting 3/15; must reply by 5/1 or within 3 week(s) of notification.
Transfers: No deadline. Applicants notified on a rolling basis.

CONTACT

Rhoda Reseburg, Financial Aid Director
2811 Northeast Holman Street, Portland, OR 97211-6099
(503) 280-8514

Corban College
Salem, Oregon
www.corban.edu   Federal Code: 001339

4-year private liberal arts college in small city, affiliated with Baptist faith.
Enrollment: 861 undergrads, 11% part-time. 207 full-time freshmen.
Selectivity: Admits over 75% of applicants.

BASIC COSTS (2008-2009)

Tuition and fees: $22,320.
Per-credit charge: $918.
Room and board: $8,068.

FINANCIAL AID PICTURE

Students with need: Need-based aid available for full-time and part-time students.
Students without need: No-need awards available for academics, alumni affiliation, athletics, leadership, music/drama.

FINANCIAL AID PROCEDURES

Forms required: FAFSA.

Dates and Deadlines: Priority date 2/15; no closing date. Applicants notified by 3/1; must reply within 4 week(s) of notification.

CONTACT

Nathan Warthan, Director of Financial Aid
5000 Deer Park Drive SE, Salem, OR 97317-9392
(503) 375-7006

DeVry University: Portland
Portland, Oregon
www.devry.edu

4-year for-profit university in very large city.
Enrollment: 66 undergrads, 41% part-time. 12 full-time freshmen.

BASIC COSTS (2007-2008)

Tuition and fees: $13,020.
Per-credit charge: $490.

FINANCIAL AID PICTURE (2006-2007)

Students with need: Out of 7 full-time freshmen who applied for aid, 7 were judged to have need. Of these, 7 received aid. Average financial aid package met 23% of need; average scholarship/grant was $3,887; average loan was $3,573. For part-time students, average financial aid package was $6,469.
Students without need: No-need awards available for academics.
Cumulative student debt: 100% of graduating class had student loans; average debt was $44,210.

FINANCIAL AID PROCEDURES

Forms required: FAFSA.
Dates and Deadlines: No deadline. Applicants notified on a rolling basis.

CONTACT

Director of Financial Aid
Peterkort Center II, Portland, OR 97225
(503) 296-7468

Eastern Oregon University
LaGrande, Oregon
www.eou.edu   Federal Code: 003193

4-year public university and liberal arts college in large town.
Enrollment: 2,793 undergrads, 36% part-time. 309 full-time freshmen.
Selectivity: Admits 50 to 75% of applicants.

BASIC COSTS (2007-2008)

Tuition and fees: $6,072.
Per-credit charge: $103.
Room and board: $8,100.

FINANCIAL AID PICTURE (2007-2008)

Students with need: Out of 280 full-time freshmen who applied for aid, 215 were judged to have need. Of these, 214 received aid, and 69 had their full need met. Average financial aid package met 48% of need; average scholarship/grant was $3,944; average loan was $2,643. For part-time students, average financial aid package was $7,075.
Students without need: 2 full-time freshmen who did not demonstrate need for aid received scholarships/grants; average award was $690. No-need awards available for academics, art, leadership, minority status, music/drama, state/district residency.
Scholarships offered: *Merit:* University Scholars Scholarships; full-tuition; based on personal essay, recommendations, GPA, activities and awards; 65 awarded. *Athletic:* 34 full-time freshmen received athletic scholarships; average amount $1,245.

Cumulative student debt: 76% of graduating class had student loans; average debt was $20,745.

FINANCIAL AID PROCEDURES

Forms required: FAFSA.

Dates and Deadlines: Priority date 3/1; no closing date. Applicants notified on a rolling basis starting 4/1; must reply within 4 week(s) of notification.

Transfers: No deadline. Applicants notified on a rolling basis.

CONTACT

Eric Bucks, Director of Financial Aid

One University Boulevard, LaGrande, OR 97850

(541) 962-3550

Eugene Bible College

Eugene, Oregon

www.ebc.edu   Federal Code: 015167

4-year private Bible college in small city, affiliated with Open Bible Standard Churches.

Enrollment: 137 undergrads. 32 full-time freshmen.

Selectivity: Admits less than 50% of applicants.

BASIC COSTS (2007-2008)

Tuition and fees: $9,895.

Room and board: $5,095.

FINANCIAL AID PICTURE

Students with need: Need-based aid available for full-time and part-time students. Work study available nights, weekends, and for part-time students.

Students without need: No-need awards available for academics, athletics, leadership, music/drama.

Scholarships offered: Honors award: $300; must have 3.7 GPA or higher.

Additional info: Some early acceptance awards possible for those admitted by May 15. Distance awards to those coming from over 1,000 miles away. Some awards for husbands and wives enrolled at same time.

FINANCIAL AID PROCEDURES

Forms required: FAFSA.

Dates and Deadlines: Priority date 5/1; closing date 9/1. Applicants notified on a rolling basis starting 7/15; must reply within 4 week(s) of notification.

Transfers: No deadline.

CONTACT

Aaron Denbo, Director of Financial Aid

2155 Bailey Hill Road, Eugene, OR 97405

(800) 322-2638

George Fox University

Newberg, Oregon

www.georgefox.edu   Federal Code: 003194

4-year private university and seminary college in large town, affiliated with Society of Friends (Quaker).

Enrollment: 1,907 undergrads, 12% part-time. 435 full-time freshmen.

Selectivity: Admits over 75% of applicants.

BASIC COSTS (2008-2009)

Tuition and fees: $25,190.

Per-credit charge: $750.

Room and board: $8,000.

Additional info: Tuition/fee waivers available for minority students.

FINANCIAL AID PICTURE (2007-2008)

Students with need: Out of 398 full-time freshmen who applied for aid, 345 were judged to have need. Of these, 345 received aid, and 126 had their full need met. Average financial aid package met 88% of need; average scholarship/grant was $8,266; average loan was $3,668. For part-time students, average financial aid package was $9,753.

Students without need: 73 full-time freshmen who did not demonstrate need for aid received scholarships/grants; average award was $693. No-need awards available for academics, alumni affiliation, art, job skills, leadership, minority status, music/drama, religious affiliation.

Scholarships offered: Academic merit awards; $2,500-$10,000 per year; based on GPA, SAT/ACT scores and rigor of high school curriculum; renewable based on academic performance.

Additional info: Audition required for music and drama scholarships.

FINANCIAL AID PROCEDURES

Forms required: FAFSA, state aid form.

Dates and Deadlines: Priority date 2/1; no closing date. Applicants notified on a rolling basis starting 3/1; must reply within 6 week(s) of notification.

CONTACT

Rob Clarke, Executive Director of Student Financial Services

414 North Meridian Street, Newberg, OR 97132-2697

(503) 554-2290

Lane Community College

Eugene, Oregon

www.lanecc.edu   Federal Code: 003196

2-year public community college in small city.

Enrollment: 5,500 undergrads.

Selectivity: Open admission; but selective for some programs.

BASIC COSTS (2007-2008)

Tuition and fees: $3,615; out-of-state residents $11,625.

Per-credit charge: $73; out-of-state residents $251.

FINANCIAL AID PICTURE

Students with need: Need-based aid available for full-time and part-time students. Work study available nights, weekends, and for part-time students.

Students without need: No-need awards available for art, athletics, minority status, music/drama.

FINANCIAL AID PROCEDURES

Forms required: FAFSA.

Dates and Deadlines: Priority date 2/15; no closing date. Applicants notified on a rolling basis starting 6/1; must reply within 2 week(s) of notification.

CONTACT

Burt Logan, Director of Financial Aid

4000 East 30th Avenue, Eugene, OR 97405

(541) 463-3100

Lewis & Clark College

Portland, Oregon

www.lclark.edu   Federal Code: 003197
                                  CSS Code: 4384

4-year private liberal arts college in very large city.

Enrollment: 1,926 undergrads. 507 full-time freshmen.

Selectivity: Admits 50 to 75% of applicants.

BASIC COSTS (2007-2008)

Tuition and fees: $31,840.

Per-credit charge: $1,592.

Room and board: $8,450.

FINANCIAL AID PICTURE (2007-2008)

Students with need: Out of 373 full-time freshmen who applied for aid, 275 were judged to have need. Of these, 275 received aid, and 80 had their full need met. Average financial aid package met 86% of need; average scholarship/grant was $22,425; average loan was $4,205. Need-based aid available for part-time students.

Students without need: 65 full-time freshmen who did not demonstrate need for aid received scholarships/grants; average award was $6,885. No-need awards available for academics, leadership, music/drama.

Scholarships offered: Neely Scholarship: full tuition; up to 10 awards. Trustee Scholarship: half tuition; up to 15 awards. Deans Scholarships: $4,000-$8,000. Music scholarships: $1,000-$6,000; by audition. Forensic scholarships: $1,000-$5,000; separate application required. Leadership and service awards: $5,000.

Cumulative student debt: 58% of graduating class had student loans; average debt was $20,127.

FINANCIAL AID PROCEDURES

Forms required: FAFSA, CSS PROFILE.

Dates and Deadlines: Priority date 3/1; no closing date. Applicants notified on a rolling basis starting 3/1.

Transfers: Transfers eligible for merit-based Dean's scholarships of up to $10,000, not eligible for Neely or Trustee scholarships. Financial aid transcript form from previous institutions required.

CONTACT

Glenda Gaddis, Director of Student Financial Services
0615 SW Palatine Hill Road, Portland, OR 97219-7899
(503) 768-7090

Linfield College

McMinnville, Oregon
www.linfield.edu
Federal Code: 003198

4-year private business and liberal arts college in large town, affiliated with American Baptist Churches in the USA.

Enrollment: 1,646 undergrads, 1% part-time. 476 full-time freshmen.

Selectivity: Admits over 75% of applicants.

BASIC COSTS (2008-2009)

Tuition and fees: $27,414.

Per-credit charge: $845.

Room and board: $7,860.

FINANCIAL AID PICTURE (2007-2008)

Students with need: Out of 309 full-time freshmen who applied for aid, 309 were judged to have need. Of these, 309 received aid, and 109 had their full need met. Average financial aid package met 84% of need; average scholarship/grant was $8,921; average loan was $4,215. For part-time students, average financial aid package was $5,988.

Students without need: 123 full-time freshmen who did not demonstrate need for aid received scholarships/grants; average award was $10,200. No-need awards available for academics, music/drama.

Scholarships offered: National Merit: half- to full-tuition; for National Merit Scholarship Finalists who list Linfield as first choice. Trustee Scholarships: $11,000 to $116,200; based on academic record; must have 3.75 GPA. Faculty Scholarships: $7,500 to $10,800; based on academic record; must have 3.4 GPA. Linfield Competitive Scholarships: range from $10,000-$16,000. Separate application required; competitions held on McMinnville Campus by invitation only. Music Achievement Awards: $1,500-$2,500; audition or recorded performance required, must intend to major or minor in music. Leadership/ Service Scholarship: up to $3,000; up to 5 awards each year to students who have demonstrated high levels of leadership, initiative, and service to others through student government, school activities, community organizations, and church or social service agencies; invitations to apply extended by April 1 each year; candidates must complete separate application.

Academic All-Star Scholarships: supplement other academic scholarships with $2,500 for first place and $1,500 for 2nd or 3rd place.

Cumulative student debt: 70% of graduating class had student loans; average debt was $25,940.

FINANCIAL AID PROCEDURES

Forms required: FAFSA.

Dates and Deadlines: Priority date 2/1; no closing date. Applicants notified by 4/1; must reply by 5/1.

Transfers: Priority date 2/15. Most scholarships available to both freshman and transfer students. Transfer Scholarships: $5,000 to $10,000; for students who have attended 2- or 4-year accredited colleges full-time and have earned at least 3.25 GPA. Phi Theta Kappa Scholarships: $2,000; up to 10 awarded each year to members of Phi Theta Kappa; must have a 3.25 GPA in transferable courses.

CONTACT

Crisanne Werner, Director of Financial Aid
900 SE Baker Street, McMinnville, OR 97218-6894
(503) 883-2225

Linn-Benton Community College

Albany, Oregon
www.linnbenton.edu
Federal Code: 006938

2-year public community college in large town.

Enrollment: 4,986 undergrads, 48% part-time. 749 full-time freshmen.

Selectivity: Open admission; but selective for some programs.

BASIC COSTS (2007-2008)

Tuition and fees: $3,112; out-of-state residents $7,657.

Per-credit charge: $65; out-of-state residents $166.

Additional info: Tuition/fee waivers available for unemployed or children of unemployed.

FINANCIAL AID PICTURE (2006-2007)

Students with need: 62% of average financial aid package awarded as scholarships/grants, 38% awarded as loans/jobs. Need-based aid available for part-time students. Work study available nights, weekends, and for part-time students.

Students without need: No-need awards available for academics, art, job skills, leadership, music/drama, state/district residency.

FINANCIAL AID PROCEDURES

Forms required: FAFSA.

Dates and Deadlines: Priority date 4/1; no closing date. Applicants notified on a rolling basis starting 4/15; must reply within 2 week(s) of notification.

CONTACT

6500 SW Pacific Boulevard, Albany, OR 97321-3779
(541) 917-4850

Marylhurst University

Marylhurst, Oregon
www.marylhurst.edu
Federal Code: 003199

4-year private university and liberal arts college in large town, affiliated with Roman Catholic Church.

Enrollment: 194 full-time undergrads.

Selectivity: Open admission; but selective for some programs.

BASIC COSTS (2007-2008)

Tuition and fees: $15,570.

Per-credit charge: $336.

FINANCIAL AID PICTURE

Students with need: Need-based aid available for full-time and part-time students. Work study available weekends and for part-time students.

Students without need: No-need awards available for academics.

FINANCIAL AID PROCEDURES

Forms required: FAFSA, institutional form.

Dates and Deadlines: Priority date 6/1; no closing date. Applicants notified on a rolling basis starting 5/1.

CONTACT

Tracy Reisinger, Director of Financial Aid
PO Box 261, Marylhurst, OR 97036-0261
(503) 699-6253

Mt. Hood Community College
Gresham, Oregon
www.mhcc.cc.or.us   Federal Code: 003204

2-year public community college in small city.

Enrollment: 6,964 undergrads, 58% part-time. 949 full-time freshmen.

Selectivity: Open admission; but selective for some programs.

BASIC COSTS (2007-2008)

Tuition and fees: $3,240; out-of-state residents $9,675.

Per-credit charge: $66; out-of-state residents $209.

FINANCIAL AID PICTURE (2006-2007)

Students with need: Out of 585 full-time freshmen who applied for aid, 386 were judged to have need. Of these, 369 received aid, and 7 had their full need met. Average financial aid package met 69% of need; average scholarship/grant was $3,452; average loan was $1,848. For part-time students, average financial aid package was $4,321.

Students without need: 26 full-time freshmen who did not demonstrate need for aid received scholarships/grants; average award was $2,035. No-need awards available for academics.

Scholarships offered: 55 full-time freshmen received athletic scholarships; average amount $1,452.

Cumulative student debt: 39% of graduating class had student loans; average debt was $10,447.

FINANCIAL AID PROCEDURES

Forms required: FAFSA, institutional form.

Dates and Deadlines: No deadline. Applicants notified on a rolling basis starting 2/15; must reply within 4 week(s) of notification.

CONTACT

Patricia Martin, Associate Dean, Enrollment Services
26000 Southeast Stark Street, Gresham, OR 97030
(503) 491-7265

Multnomah Bible College
Portland, Oregon
www.multnomah.edu   Federal Code: 003206

4-year private Bible and seminary college in large city, affiliated with interdenominational tradition.

Enrollment: 567 undergrads, 8% part-time. 253 full-time freshmen.

Selectivity: Admits over 75% of applicants.

BASIC COSTS (2007-2008)

Tuition and fees: $13,480.

Per-credit charge: $558.

Room and board: $5,750.

FINANCIAL AID PICTURE (2006-2007)

Students with need: Out of 212 full-time freshmen who applied for aid, 176 were judged to have need. Of these, 124 received aid, and 2 had their full need met. Average financial aid package met 20% of need; average scholarship/grant was $3,496; average loan was $2,257. For part-time students, average financial aid package was $4,006.

Students without need: 33 full-time freshmen who did not demonstrate need for aid received scholarships/grants; average award was $7,032. No-need awards available for academics.

Cumulative student debt: 93% of graduating class had student loans; average debt was $20,738.

FINANCIAL AID PROCEDURES

Forms required: FAFSA, institutional form.

Dates and Deadlines: Priority date 3/1; closing date 8/1. Applicants notified on a rolling basis starting 4/1; must reply within 3 week(s) of notification.

CONTACT

Mary McGlothlan, Financial Aid Officer
8435 Northeast Glisan Street, Portland, OR 97220-5898
(503) 251-5337

Northwest Christian College
Eugene, Oregon
www.nwcc.edu   Federal Code: 003208

4-year private liberal arts college in small city, affiliated with Christian Church (Disciples of Christ).

Enrollment: 395 undergrads, 23% part-time. 53 full-time freshmen.

Selectivity: Admits less than 50% of applicants.

BASIC COSTS (2007-2008)

Tuition and fees: $21,481.

Per-credit charge: $716.

Room and board: $6,770.

FINANCIAL AID PICTURE (2007-2008)

Students with need: Average financial aid package met 75% of need; average scholarship/grant was $13,411; average loan was $1,919. For part-time students, average financial aid package was $17,690.

Students without need: No-need awards available for academics, athletics, leadership, music/drama, religious affiliation.

Scholarships offered: Presidential Scholarship: $5,000 per year; based on superior leadership and achievement and 2 of the following: 3.75 GPA, 1200 SAT, top 15% class rank. Dean's Scholarship: $4,000 per year; based on superior leadership and achievement and 2 of the following: 3.5 GPA, 1100 SAT, top 33% class rank. Achievement/Leadership Award: $3,000 per year; based on record of leadership/achievement and 2 of the following: 3.0 GPA, 1000 SAT, top 60% class rank. Valedictorian/Salutatorian Scholarship: $6,000 per year; must meet criteria for Presidential Scholarship and graduate as valedictorian or salutatorian. SAT scores exclusive of writing portion.

Cumulative student debt: 91% of graduating class had student loans; average debt was $25,085.

FINANCIAL AID PROCEDURES

Forms required: FAFSA.

Dates and Deadlines: Priority date 3/1; no closing date. Applicants notified on a rolling basis starting 4/1.

Transfers: No deadline. Applicants notified on a rolling basis.

CONTACT

Jocelyn Hubbs, Director of Financial Aid
828 East 11th Avenue, Eugene, OR 97401-3745
(541) 684-7291

Oregon Health & Science University

Portland, Oregon
www.ohsu.edu   Federal Code: 004883

3-year public university and health science college in very large city.

Enrollment: 591 undergrads.

BASIC COSTS (2007-2008)

Tuition and fees: $11,860; out-of-state residents $20,176.
Per-credit charge: $213; out-of-state residents $444.
Additional info: Tuition shown is for undergraduate nursing program; costs for other programs vary.

FINANCIAL AID PICTURE (2006-2007)

Students with need: Average financial aid package for all full-time undergraduates was $10,616; for part-time $9,914. 19% awarded as scholarships/grants, 81% awarded as loans/jobs. Work study available nights, weekends, and for part-time students.
Students without need: No-need awards available for academics, minority status, state/district residency.

FINANCIAL AID PROCEDURES

Forms required: FAFSA.
Dates and Deadlines: Priority date 3/1; no closing date. Applicants notified on a rolling basis starting 5/31.
Transfers: Applicants notified on a rolling basis starting 5/10; must reply within 4 week(s) of notification.

CONTACT

Cherie Honnell, Director of Financial Aid/Registrar
3181 SW Sam Jackson Park Road, Portland, OR 97239
(503) 494-7800

Oregon Institute of Technology

Klamath Falls, Oregon
www.oit.edu   Federal Code: 003211

4-year public engineering and health science and technical college in small city.

Enrollment: 2,534 undergrads. 186 full-time freshmen.

BASIC COSTS (2007-2008)

Tuition and fees: $6,144; out-of-state residents $16,179.
Per-credit charge: $105; out-of-district residents $328.
Room and board: $6,347.
Additional info: Tuition/fee waivers available for minority students.

FINANCIAL AID PICTURE (2006-2007)

Students with need: Out of 186 full-time freshmen who applied for aid, 168 were judged to have need. Of these, 164 received aid, and 82 had their full need met. Average financial aid package met 20% of need; average scholarship/grant was $3,943; average loan was $2,627. For part-time students, average financial aid package was $4,555.
Students without need: No-need awards available for academics, athletics, leadership, minority status.
Scholarships offered: 1 full-time freshmen received athletic scholarships; average amount $100.
Cumulative student debt: 70% of graduating class had student loans; average debt was $22,351.

FINANCIAL AID PROCEDURES

Forms required: FAFSA.
Dates and Deadlines: Priority date 3/1; no closing date. Applicants notified on a rolling basis starting 4/1; must reply within 3 week(s) of notification.
Transfers: Closing date 2/1.

CONTACT

Tracey Lehmann, Director of Financial Aid
3201 Campus Drive, Klamath Falls, OR 97601
(541) 885-1280

Oregon State University

Corvallis, Oregon
www.oregonstate.edu   Federal Code: 003210

4-year public university in small city.

Enrollment: 15,515 undergrads, 11% part-time. 2,953 full-time freshmen.
Selectivity: Admits over 75% of applicants.

BASIC COSTS (2007-2008)

Tuition and fees: $5,911; out-of-state residents $18,187.
Per-credit charge: $124; out-of-state residents $465.
Room and board: $7,251.

FINANCIAL AID PICTURE

Students with need: Need-based aid available for full-time students.
Students without need: No-need awards available for academics, athletics, job skills, leadership, minority status, ROTC, state/district residency.

FINANCIAL AID PROCEDURES

Forms required: FAFSA.
Dates and Deadlines: Priority date 2/1; closing date 5/1. Applicants notified on a rolling basis starting 4/1; must reply within 4 week(s) of notification.
Transfers: Priority date 3/1; no deadline.

CONTACT

Emilio Vejil, Director of Financial Aid
104 Kerr Administration Building, Corvallis, OR 97331-2130
(541) 731-2241

Pacific Northwest College of Art

Portland, Oregon
www.pnca.edu   Federal Code: 003207

4-year private visual arts college in large city.

Enrollment: 417 undergrads, 10% part-time. 90 full-time freshmen.
Selectivity: Admits 50 to 75% of applicants.

BASIC COSTS (2007-2008)

Tuition and fees: $19,359.

FINANCIAL AID PICTURE

Students with need: Need-based aid available for full-time and part-time students. Work study available nights, weekends, and for part-time students.
Students without need: No-need awards available for academics, art.
Scholarships offered: Leta Kennedy Student Scholarships; $10,000; based on artistic merit. Dorothy Lemelson Scholarship; cost of attendance; based on artistic and academic merit; renewable up to 4 years; 1 awarded. Other renewable scholarships available.

FINANCIAL AID PROCEDURES

Forms required: FAFSA.
Dates and Deadlines: Priority date 3/1; closing date 8/1. Applicants notified on a rolling basis starting 4/1; must reply by 5/1 or within 4 week(s) of notification.
Transfers: No deadline.

CONTACT

Peggy Burgus, Director of Financial Aid
1241 NW Johnson Street, Portland, OR 97209
(503) 821-8972

Pacific University
Forest Grove, Oregon
www.pacificu.edu
Federal Code: 003212

4-year private university in large town, affiliated with United Church of Christ.
Enrollment: 1,427 undergrads, 3% part-time. 369 full-time freshmen.
Selectivity: Admits over 75% of applicants.

BASIC COSTS (2007-2008)
Tuition and fees: $26,470.
Per-credit charge: $1,076.
Room and board: $7,170.

FINANCIAL AID PICTURE (2007-2008)
Students with need: Out of 338 full-time freshmen who applied for aid, 284 were judged to have need. Of these, 284 received aid, and 121 had their full need met. Average financial aid package met 82% of need; average scholarship/grant was $12,791; average loan was $6,873. For part-time students, average financial aid package was $24,252.
Students without need: 74 full-time freshmen who did not demonstrate need for aid received scholarships/grants; average award was $11,142. No-need awards available for academics, alumni affiliation, art, music/drama.
Scholarships offered: Honors Scholarship; $9,000. Presidential Scholarship; $8,000. Trustee Scholarship; $7,500. University Scholarship; $6,500. Pacesetters Scholarship; $1,000 to $3,000. Music and Forensics Talent Awards; $1,000 to $3,000. Number of awards varies.
Cumulative student debt: 80% of graduating class had student loans; average debt was $24,757.

FINANCIAL AID PROCEDURES
Forms required: FAFSA.
Dates and Deadlines: Priority date 3/1; no closing date. Applicants notified on a rolling basis starting 3/1; must reply within 2 week(s) of notification.

CONTACT
Michael Johnson, Director of Financial Aid
2043 College Way, Forest Grove, OR 97116-1797
(503) 352-2222

Pioneer Pacific College
Wilsonville, Oregon
www.pioneerpacific.edu
Federal Code: 016520

4-year for-profit technical college in large town.
Enrollment: 333 undergrads, 22% part-time. 65 full-time freshmen.
Selectivity: Open admission; but selective for some programs.

BASIC COSTS (2008-2009)
Tuition and fees: $10,677.
Per-credit charge: $411.
Additional info: Costs vary by program from $7,250 to $22,053. Certain programs have additional lab fees. Tuition at time of enrollment locked for 4 years.

FINANCIAL AID PICTURE
Students with need: Need-based aid available for full-time and part-time students.
Students without need: This college awards aid only to students with need.
Scholarships offered: High school scholarship program and community scholarship program available.

FINANCIAL AID PROCEDURES
Forms required: FAFSA.
Dates and Deadlines: No deadline. Applicants notified on a rolling basis starting 2/27.

CONTACT
Michael Hargrave, Executive Director of Financial Aid
27501 Southwest Parkway Avenue, Wilsonville, OR 97070
(503) 654-8000

Portland Community College
Portland, Oregon
www.pcc.edu
Federal Code: 003213

2-year public community college in very large city.
Enrollment: 24,363 undergrads.
Selectivity: Open admission; but selective for some programs.

BASIC COSTS (2007-2008)
Tuition and fees: $3,330; out-of-state residents $9,045.
Per-credit charge: $68; out-of-state residents $195.

FINANCIAL AID PICTURE (2007-2008)
Students with need: 38% of average financial aid package awarded as scholarships/grants, 62% awarded as loans/jobs. Need-based aid available for part-time students. Work study available nights, weekends, and for part-time students.
Students without need: This college awards aid only to students with need.

FINANCIAL AID PROCEDURES
Forms required: FAFSA.
Dates and Deadlines: Priority date 3/1; no closing date. Applicants notified on a rolling basis starting 6/1; must reply within 3 week(s) of notification.

CONTACT
Corbett Gottfried, Director of Financial Aid
Box 19000, Portland, OR 97280-0990
(503) 977-4934

Portland State University
Portland, Oregon
www.pdx.edu
Federal Code: 003216

4-year public university in very large city.
Enrollment: 16,524 undergrads, 31% part-time. 1,427 full-time freshmen.
Selectivity: Admits over 75% of applicants.

BASIC COSTS (2007-2008)
Tuition and fees: $5,765; out-of-state residents $17,831.

FINANCIAL AID PICTURE (2007-2008)
Students with need: Out of 1,002 full-time freshmen who applied for aid, 752 were judged to have need. Of these, 740 received aid, and 129 had their full need met. Average financial aid package met 57% of need; average scholarship/grant was $5,275; average loan was $3,375. For part-time students, average financial aid package was $6,543.
Students without need: 80 full-time freshmen who did not demonstrate need for aid received scholarships/grants; average award was $3,958. No-need awards available for academics, art, athletics, music/drama, state/district residency.
Scholarships offered: 49 full-time freshmen received athletic scholarships; average amount $8,965.
Cumulative student debt: 77% of graduating class had student loans; average debt was $16,445.

FINANCIAL AID PROCEDURES
Forms required: FAFSA.
Dates and Deadlines: Priority date 2/28; no closing date. Applicants notified on a rolling basis; must reply within 4 week(s) of notification.

CONTACT

Phillip Rodgers, Director of Financial Aid
PO Box 751-ADM, Portland, OR 97207-0751
(800) 547-8887

Reed College

Portland, Oregon
www.reed.edu

Federal Code: 003217
CSS Code: 4654

4-year private liberal arts college in very large city.
Enrollment: 1,426 undergrads, 1% part-time. 346 full-time freshmen.
Selectivity: Admits less than 50% of applicants.

BASIC COSTS (2008-2009)

Tuition and fees: $38,190.
Per-credit charge: $1,625.
Room and board: $9,920.

FINANCIAL AID PICTURE (2007-2008)

Students with need: Average financial aid package met 100% of need; average scholarship/grant was $29,915; average loan was $2,322.
Students without need: This college awards aid only to students with need.
Cumulative student debt: 59% of graduating class had student loans; average debt was $17,098.
Additional info: College meets demonstrated need of continuing students who have attended Reed minimum of 2 semesters, who file financial aid applications on time, and who maintain satisfactory academic progress. Institutional aid consideration is for total of 8 semesters.

FINANCIAL AID PROCEDURES

Forms required: FAFSA, CSS PROFILE, institutional form.
Dates and Deadlines: Closing date 1/15. Applicants notified by 4/1; must reply by 5/1 or within 2 week(s) of notification.
Transfers: Must reply by 6/1.

CONTACT

Leslie Limper, Director of Financial Aid
3203 SE Woodstock Boulevard, Portland, OR 97202-8199
(800) 547-4750

Rogue Community College

Grants Pass, Oregon
www.roguecc.edu

Federal Code: 010071

2-year public community college in large town.
Enrollment: 2,731 undergrads, 60% part-time. 170 full-time freshmen.
Selectivity: Open admission; but selective for some programs.

BASIC COSTS (2007-2008)

Tuition and fees: $3,300; out-of-state residents $3,930.
Per-credit charge: $66; out-of-state residents $80.
Additional info: Washington, Idaho, Nevada, and California residents pay in-state tuition. Tuition/fee waivers available for unemployed or children of unemployed.

FINANCIAL AID PICTURE (2006-2007)

Students with need: Out of 119 full-time freshmen who applied for aid, 96 were judged to have need. Of these, 89 received aid, and 21 had their full need met. Average financial aid package met 59% of need; average scholarship/grant was $833; average loan was $835. For part-time students, average financial aid package was $4,289.
Students without need: 12 full-time freshmen who did not demonstrate need for aid received scholarships/grants; average award was $493.
Cumulative student debt: 10% of graduating class had student loans; average debt was $4,624.

FINANCIAL AID PROCEDURES

Forms required: FAFSA, institutional form.
Dates and Deadlines: Priority date 5/1; no closing date. Applicants notified on a rolling basis; must reply within 2 week(s) of notification.

CONTACT

Anna Manley, Director of Financial Aid
3345 Redwood Highway, Grants Pass, OR 97527
(541) 956-7501

Southern Oregon University

Ashland, Oregon
www.sou.edu

Federal Code: 003219

4-year public university and liberal arts college in large town.
Enrollment: 4,058 undergrads, 21% part-time. 684 full-time freshmen.
Selectivity: Admits over 75% of applicants.

BASIC COSTS (2007-2008)

Tuition and fees: $5,502; out-of-state residents $17,580.
Room and board: $7,482.
Additional info: Tuition/fee waivers available for minority students.

FINANCIAL AID PICTURE

Students with need: Need-based aid available for full-time and part-time students. Work study available nights, weekends, and for part-time students.
Students without need: No-need awards available for academics, alumni affiliation, art, athletics, leadership, minority status, music/drama, religious affiliation, state/district residency.

FINANCIAL AID PROCEDURES

Forms required: FAFSA.
Dates and Deadlines: No deadline. Applicants notified on a rolling basis starting 3/1; must reply within 2 week(s) of notification.

CONTACT

Diana Watson-Paul, Associate Director of Financial Aid
1250 Siskiyou Boulevard, Ashland, OR 97520-5032
(541) 552-6600

Southwestern Oregon Community College

Coos Bay, Oregon
www.socc.edu

Federal Code: 003220

2-year public culinary school and community college in large town.
Enrollment: 1,573 undergrads.
Selectivity: Open admission; but selective for some programs.

BASIC COSTS (2007-2008)

Tuition and fees: $3,660.
Per-credit charge: $62.
Room and board: $6,160.
Additional info: Tuition/fee waivers available for adults, unemployed or children of unemployed.

FINANCIAL AID PICTURE

Students with need: Need-based aid available for full-time and part-time students.

FINANCIAL AID PROCEDURES

Forms required: FAFSA.
Dates and Deadlines: Priority date 2/28; closing date 6/30. Applicants notified on a rolling basis starting 5/1; must reply within 3 week(s) of notification.

CONTACT

Avena Singh, Director of Financial Aid

1988 Newmark Avenue, Coos Bay, OR 97420-2956

(541) 888-7337

Treasure Valley Community College
Ontario, Oregon
www.tvcc.cc   Federal Code: 003221

2-year public community college in small town.

Enrollment: 1,820 undergrads, 46% part-time. 386 full-time freshmen.

Selectivity: Open admission; but selective for some programs.

BASIC COSTS (2008-2009)

Tuition and fees: $3,420; out-of-state residents $3,870.

Per-credit charge: $66; out-of-state residents $76.

Room and board: $6,390.

FINANCIAL AID PICTURE (2007-2008)

Students with need: Average financial aid package met 37% of need; average scholarship/grant was $3,757; average loan was $2,856. For part-time students, average financial aid package was $5,108.

Students without need: No-need awards available for academics, athletics, leadership, music/drama, state/district residency.

FINANCIAL AID PROCEDURES

Forms required: FAFSA.

Dates and Deadlines: Priority date 4/1; no closing date. Applicants notified on a rolling basis starting 5/1.

CONTACT

Kevin Jensen, Director of Financial Aid

650 College Boulevard, Ontario, OR 97914

(541) 881-8822 ext. 286

Umpqua Community College
Roseburg, Oregon
www.umpqua.edu   Federal Code: 003222

2-year public community college in large town.

Enrollment: 994 undergrads, 40% part-time. 170 full-time freshmen.

Selectivity: Open admission; but selective for some programs.

BASIC COSTS (2007-2008)

Tuition and fees: $3,195; out-of-state residents $8,775.

Per-credit charge: $62; out-of-state residents $186.

FINANCIAL AID PICTURE (2006-2007)

Students with need: Out of 129 full-time freshmen who applied for aid, 120 were judged to have need. Of these, 117 received aid. Need-based aid available for part-time students.

Students without need: This college awards aid only to students with need.

FINANCIAL AID PROCEDURES

Forms required: FAFSA.

Dates and Deadlines: Priority date 3/1; no closing date. Applicants notified on a rolling basis starting 5/1; must reply within 2 week(s) of notification.

CONTACT

Laurie Spangenberg, Director of Financial Aid

1140 College Road, Roseburg, OR 97470-0226

(541) 440-4602

University of Oregon
Eugene, Oregon
www.uoregon.edu   Federal Code: 003223

4-year public university in small city.

Enrollment: 16,422 undergrads, 8% part-time. 3,508 full-time freshmen.

Selectivity: Admits over 75% of applicants.

BASIC COSTS (2007-2008)

Tuition and fees: $6,168; out-of-state residents $19,332.

Room and board: $8,166.

Additional info: Additional program-specific fees may apply.

FINANCIAL AID PICTURE (2007-2008)

Students with need: Out of 2,097 full-time freshmen who applied for aid, 1,251 were judged to have need. Of these, 1,165 received aid, and 314 had their full need met. Average financial aid package met 60% of need; average scholarship/grant was $4,776; average loan was $4,351. For part-time students, average financial aid package was $7,681.

Students without need: 376 full-time freshmen who did not demonstrate need for aid received scholarships/grants; average award was $2,279. No-need awards available for academics, athletics, leadership, minority status, music/drama, ROTC, state/district residency.

Scholarships offered: Presidential Scholarship: up to $6,000 per year for up to four years; merit-based for Oregon residents. National Merit Scholarship: $2,000 for up to 4 years. Staton Scholarship: $5,000 for up to 4 years; based on extraordinary financial need. Laurel Award: amounts vary; competitive merit award. General University Scholarship: up to $2,700; merit-based. Dean's Scholarship: up to $6,000 per year for up to 12 terms; merit-based. Diversity-Building Scholarship: amounts determined by DBS committee; for ethnic minority, first generation, or non-traditional students.

Cumulative student debt: 57% of graduating class had student loans; average debt was $18,728.

FINANCIAL AID PROCEDURES

Forms required: FAFSA.

Dates and Deadlines: Priority date 3/1; closing date 6/30. Applicants notified on a rolling basis starting 4/15; must reply within 4 week(s) of notification.

CONTACT

Elizabeth Bickford, Director, Financial Aid and Scholarships

1217 University of Oregon, Eugene, OR 97403-1217

(541) 346-3221

University of Portland
Portland, Oregon
www.up.edu   Federal Code: 003224

4-year private university in large city, affiliated with Roman Catholic Church.

Enrollment: 2,967 undergrads, 1% part-time. 722 full-time freshmen.

Selectivity: Admits 50 to 75% of applicants.

BASIC COSTS (2008-2009)

Tuition and fees: $30,450.

Per-credit charge: $925.

Room and board: $8,756.

FINANCIAL AID PICTURE (2006-2007)

Students with need: Out of 597 full-time freshmen who applied for aid, 388 were judged to have need. Of these, 387 received aid, and 97 had their full need met. Average financial aid package met 89% of need; average scholarship/grant was $13,838; average loan was $2,912. Need-based aid available for part-time students.

Students without need: 294 full-time freshmen who did not demonstrate need for aid received scholarships/grants; average award was $12,245. No-need awards available for academics, music/drama, ROTC.

Scholarships offered: President's Scholarship: up to $10,000. Holy Cross Scholarship: up to $6,000. Both based on academic excellence, other factors including school and community involvement. Arthur A. Schulte Scholarship: up to $6,000.

Cumulative student debt: 64% of graduating class had student loans; average debt was $22,253.

FINANCIAL AID PROCEDURES

Forms required: FAFSA, institutional form.

Dates and Deadlines: Priority date 3/1; no closing date. Applicants notified on a rolling basis starting 3/15; must reply within 3 week(s) of notification.

CONTACT

Paul Krull, Director of Financial Aid
5000 North Willamette Boulevard, Portland, OR 97203-5798
(503) 943-7311

Warner Pacific College
Portland, Oregon
www.warnerpacific.edu   Federal Code: 003225

4-year private liberal arts college in very large city, affiliated with Church of God.

Enrollment: 722 undergrads. 81 full-time freshmen.

Selectivity: Open admission; but selective for some programs.

BASIC COSTS (2007-2008)

Tuition and fees: $21,500.

Per-credit charge: $900.

Room and board: $6,028.

FINANCIAL AID PICTURE (2006-2007)

Students with need: Out of 78 full-time freshmen who applied for aid, 72 were judged to have need. Of these, 72 received aid, and 10 had their full need met. Average financial aid package met 75% of need; average scholarship/grant was $6,472; average loan was $4,182. For part-time students, average financial aid package was $11,068.

Students without need: 5 full-time freshmen who did not demonstrate need for aid received scholarships/grants; average award was $5,200. No-need awards available for academics, alumni affiliation, athletics, leadership, minority status, music/drama, religious affiliation.

Scholarships offered: 28 full-time freshmen received athletic scholarships; average amount $4,013.

FINANCIAL AID PROCEDURES

Forms required: FAFSA.

Dates and Deadlines: Priority date 3/1; closing date 8/30. Applicants notified on a rolling basis starting 3/1; must reply within 4 week(s) of notification.

Transfers: No deadline. Applicants notified on a rolling basis starting 3/1; must reply within 2 week(s) of notification.

CONTACT

Cindy Pollard, Director of Student Financial Assistance
2219 SE 68th Avenue, Portland, OR 97215-4026
(503) 517-1020

Western Oregon University
Monmouth, Oregon
www.wou.edu   Federal Code: 003209

4-year public liberal arts and teachers college in small town.

Enrollment: 4,390 undergrads, 12% part-time. 916 full-time freshmen.

Selectivity: Admits over 75% of applicants.

BASIC COSTS (2007-2008)

Tuition and fees: $5,982; out-of-state residents $16,332.

Per-credit charge: $105; out-of-state residents $355.

Room and board: $7,055.

Additional info: Tuition at time of enrollment locked for 4 years; tuition/fee waivers available for minority students.

FINANCIAL AID PICTURE (2006-2007)

Students with need: 38% of average financial aid package awarded as scholarships/grants, 62% awarded as loans/jobs. Need-based aid available for part-time students. Work study available nights, weekends, and for part-time students.

Students without need: No-need awards available for academics, art, athletics, leadership, minority status, music/drama, ROTC, state/district residency.

FINANCIAL AID PROCEDURES

Forms required: FAFSA.

Dates and Deadlines: Priority date 3/1; no closing date. Applicants notified on a rolling basis starting 3/20; must reply within 2 week(s) of notification.

CONTACT

Donna Fossum, Director of Financial Aid
345 North Monmouth Avenue, Monmouth, OR 97361
(503) 838-8475

Willamette University
Salem, Oregon
www.willamette.edu   Federal Code: 003227

4-year private university and liberal arts college in small city, affiliated with United Methodist Church.

Enrollment: 1,821 undergrads, 1% part-time. 444 full-time freshmen.

Selectivity: Admits over 75% of applicants.

BASIC COSTS (2007-2008)

Tuition and fees: $31,968.

Room and board: $7,570.

Additional info: Optional health insurance: $405.

FINANCIAL AID PICTURE (2007-2008)

Students with need: Out of 347 full-time freshmen who applied for aid, 275 were judged to have need. Of these, 275 received aid, and 59 had their full need met. Average financial aid package met 92% of need; average scholarship/grant was $19,469; average loan was $4,199. For part-time students, average financial aid package was $12,735.

Students without need: 146 full-time freshmen who did not demonstrate need for aid received scholarships/grants; average award was $10,519. No-need awards available for academics, music/drama.

Scholarships offered: Academic merit awards: $5,000-$15,000; based on superior academic achievement and promise. Music, forensics, theater scholarships: average $3,000-$5,000; based on talent. Mark O. Hatfield Scholarship: full tuition; based on excellent academic record and demonstrated commitment to service leadership.

Cumulative student debt: 64% of graduating class had student loans; average debt was $23,188.

FINANCIAL AID PROCEDURES

Forms required: FAFSA. CSS PROFILE recommended of early action applicants.

Dates and Deadlines: Closing date 2/1. Applicants notified by 4/1; must reply by 5/1 or within 2 week(s) of notification.

Transfers: Applicants notified by 4/15.

CONTACT

Patricia Hoban, Director of Financial Aid
900 State Street, Salem, OR 97301-3922
(503) 370-6273

Pennsylvania

Albright College

Reading, Pennsylvania
www.albright.edu
Federal Code: 003229

4-year private liberal arts college in small city, affiliated with United Methodist Church.

Enrollment: 2,153 undergrads, 1% part-time. 512 full-time freshmen.
Selectivity: Admits over 75% of applicants.

BASIC COSTS (2008-2009)

Tuition and fees: $30,570.
Room and board: $8,670.
Additional info: $3,721 per course (worth 4 credits). Tuition/fee waivers available for minority students.

FINANCIAL AID PICTURE (2007-2008)

Students with need: Out of 467 full-time freshmen who applied for aid, 437 were judged to have need. Of these, 430 received aid, and 101 had their full need met. Average financial aid package met 79% of need; average scholarship/grant was $16,975; average loan was $4,698. For part-time students, average financial aid package was $4,017.
Students without need: 45 full-time freshmen who did not demonstrate need for aid received scholarships/grants; average award was $18,359. No-need awards available for academics, alumni affiliation, art, leadership, minority status, music/drama, religious affiliation.
Cumulative student debt: 74% of graduating class had student loans; average debt was $31,253.

FINANCIAL AID PROCEDURES

Forms required: FAFSA.
Dates and Deadlines: Priority date 3/1; no closing date. Applicants notified on a rolling basis starting 2/15; must reply by 5/1 or within 2 week(s) of notification.
Transfers: Priority date 6/1; no deadline. Applicants notified on a rolling basis starting 2/15; must reply within 2 week(s) of notification.

CONTACT

Mary Duffy, Director of Financial Aid
13th & Bern Streets, Reading, PA 19612-5234
(610) 921-7515

Allegheny College

Meadville, Pennsylvania
www.allegheny.edu
Federal Code: 003230

4-year private liberal arts college in large town, affiliated with United Methodist Church.

Enrollment: 2,163 undergrads, 1% part-time. 582 full-time freshmen.
Selectivity: Admits 50 to 75% of applicants.

BASIC COSTS (2008-2009)

Tuition and fees: $32,000.
Per-credit charge: $1,320.
Room and board: $8,000.

FINANCIAL AID PICTURE (2007-2008)

Students with need: Out of 491 full-time freshmen who applied for aid, 403 were judged to have need. Of these, 403 received aid, and 201 had their full need met. Average financial aid package met 95% of need; average scholarship/grant was $18,078; average loan was $5,420. For part-time students, average financial aid package was $7,175.

Students without need: 156 full-time freshmen who did not demonstrate need for aid received scholarships/grants; average award was $10,567. No-need awards available for academics, leadership, minority status, state/district residency.
Scholarships offered: Trustee Scholarships; up to $15,000 per year.

FINANCIAL AID PROCEDURES

Forms required: FAFSA.
Dates and Deadlines: Priority date 2/15; no closing date. Applicants notified on a rolling basis starting 3/1; must reply by 5/1 or within 4 week(s) of notification.
Transfers: Priority date 6/1; no deadline. Applicants notified on a rolling basis; must reply within 3 week(s) of notification. Trustee Scholarships; up to $12,500; available for entering transfer students.

CONTACT

Sheryle Proper, Director of Financial Aid
520 North Main Street, Meadville, PA 16335
(800) 835-7780

Alvernia College

Reading, Pennsylvania
www.alvernia.edu
Federal Code: 003233

4-year private liberal arts college in small city, affiliated with Roman Catholic Church.

Enrollment: 1,922 undergrads, 19% part-time. 303 full-time freshmen.
Selectivity: Admits over 75% of applicants.

BASIC COSTS (2007-2008)

Tuition and fees: $21,614.
Per-credit charge: $600.
Room and board: $8,250.

FINANCIAL AID PICTURE (2006-2007)

Students with need: Out of 296 full-time freshmen who applied for aid, 269 were judged to have need. Of these, 269 received aid, and 55 had their full need met. Average financial aid package met 66% of need; average scholarship/grant was $10,369; average loan was $3,876. For part-time students, average financial aid package was $10,794.
Students without need: 30 full-time freshmen who did not demonstrate need for aid received scholarships/grants; average award was $13,100. No-need awards available for academics, alumni affiliation, ROTC.
Cumulative student debt: 98% of graduating class had student loans; average debt was $28,134.

FINANCIAL AID PROCEDURES

Forms required: FAFSA, state aid form.
Dates and Deadlines: No deadline. Applicants notified on a rolling basis starting 2/1; must reply within 2 week(s) of notification.
Transfers: Priority date 5/8; no deadline. Applicants notified on a rolling basis starting 2/8.

CONTACT

Rachel Gordon, Director of Financial Aid
400 St. Bernardine Street, Reading, PA 19607-1799
(610) 796-8356

Antonelli Institute of Art and Photography

Erdenheim, Pennsylvania
www.antonelli.edu
Federal Code: 007430

2-year for-profit visual arts and junior college in large town.
Enrollment: 235 undergrads, 1% part-time. 136 full-time freshmen.
Selectivity: Admits over 75% of applicants.

BASIC COSTS (2008-2009)

Tuition and fees: $19,325.

Per-credit charge: $640.

Room only: $7,400.

Additional info: Annual tuition for graphic design/commercial art students is $17,200; for photography students $19,200.

FINANCIAL AID PICTURE (2006-2007)

Students with need: Out of 104 full-time freshmen who applied for aid, 97 were judged to have need. Of these, 97 received aid. Average financial aid package met 22% of need; average scholarship/grant was $5,800; average loan was $2,625. For part-time students, average financial aid package was $6,137.

Students without need: This college awards aid only to students with need.

FINANCIAL AID PROCEDURES

Forms required: FAFSA.

Dates and Deadlines: No deadline. Applicants notified on a rolling basis; must reply within 2 week(s) of notification.

Transfers: Priority date 3/15; closing date 8/1.

CONTACT

Eugene Awot, Director of Financial Aid

300 Montgomery Avenue, Erdenheim, PA 19038-8242

(215) 836-2222

Arcadia University

Glenside, Pennsylvania

www.arcadia.edu　　　　　　Federal Code: 003235

4-year private university in large town, affiliated with Presbyterian Church (USA).

Enrollment: 1,889 full-time undergrads.

Selectivity: Admits over 75% of applicants.

BASIC COSTS (2008-2009)

Tuition and fees: $29,700.

Per-credit charge: $490.

Room and board: $10,280.

FINANCIAL AID PICTURE (2007-2008)

Students with need: Average financial aid package met 80% of need; average scholarship/grant was $14,470; average loan was $5,065. For part-time students, average financial aid package was $5,670.

Students without need: No-need awards available for academics, alumni affiliation, art, leadership, music/drama.

Scholarships offered: Distinguished Scholarships: $13,500 to $18,000; granted to full-time students based on grades, test scores, coursework taken, high school rank and involvement. Arcadia University Achievement Awards: $1,000-$13,000; granted to full-time students who have demonstrated outstanding leadership, exceptional community and/or volunteer service or special talents. Landman Scholarship: full tuition; based on academic excellence, outstanding leadership, and community and volunteer service. Writing Achievement Awards: offered to those who score among the highest in the applicant pool annually on SAT or ACT Writing Sections.

Cumulative student debt: 83% of graduating class had student loans; average debt was $33,597.

FINANCIAL AID PROCEDURES

Forms required: FAFSA, institutional form.

Dates and Deadlines: Priority date 3/1; no closing date. Applicants notified on a rolling basis starting 2/15; must reply by 5/1.

Transfers: Applicants notified on a rolling basis starting 2/15; must reply by 5/1.

CONTACT

Holly Kirkpatrick, Director of Enrollment Management and Director of Financial Aid

450 South Easton Road, Glenside, PA 19038-3295

(215) 572-2980

Art Institute of Philadelphia

Philadelphia, Pennsylvania

www.artinstitutes.edu/Philadelphia　Federal Code: 008350

4-year for-profit visual arts college in very large city.

Enrollment: 2,515 full-time undergrads.

Selectivity: Open admission.

BASIC COSTS (2007-2008)

Additional info: Costs vary by program and course of study. Diploma program, $14, 436; associate degree program, $31,383 - $48,120; bachelor's degree program, $72, 180. Additional fees may apply. Tuition at time of enrollment locked for 4 years.

FINANCIAL AID PICTURE

Students with need: Need-based aid available for full-time and part-time students. Work study available nights, weekends, and for part-time students.

Additional info: Institute-sponsored scholarships available.

FINANCIAL AID PROCEDURES

Forms required: FAFSA, institutional form.

Dates and Deadlines: Closing date 5/1. Applicants notified on a rolling basis starting 3/1; must reply within 2 week(s) of notification.

Transfers: No deadline. Transfer students applying for financial aid must meet standards for satisfactory academic progress as defined by State Grant Program.

CONTACT

Felicia Bryant, Director of Student Financial Services

1622 Chestnut Street, Philadelphia, PA 19103-5198

(215) 567-7080 ext. 6392

Baptist Bible College of Pennsylvania

Clarks Summit, Pennsylvania

www.bbc.edu　　　　　　Federal Code: 002670

4-year private Bible and seminary college in small city, affiliated with Baptist faith.

Enrollment: 668 undergrads, 5% part-time. 164 full-time freshmen.

Selectivity: Admits over 75% of applicants.

BASIC COSTS (2007-2008)

Tuition and fees: $15,060.

Per-credit charge: $490.

Room and board: $5,600.

FINANCIAL AID PICTURE (2006-2007)

Students with need: Need-based aid available for part-time students. Work study available nights, weekends, and for part-time students.

Students without need: No-need awards available for academics, leadership, music/drama, religious affiliation.

FINANCIAL AID PROCEDURES

Forms required: FAFSA, institutional form.

Dates and Deadlines: Closing date 5/1. Applicants notified on a rolling basis starting 4/1.

CONTACT

David Weinerth, Director of Student Financial Services

538 Venard Road, Clarks Summit, PA 18411-1297

(570) 585-9215

Bloomsburg University of Pennsylvania
Bloomsburg, Pennsylvania
www.bloomu.edu   Federal Code: 003315

4-year public university and liberal arts college in large town.
Enrollment: 7,667 undergrads, 5% part-time. 1,680 full-time freshmen.
Selectivity: Admits 50 to 75% of applicants.

BASIC COSTS (2007-2008)
Tuition and fees: $6,623; out-of-state residents $14,390.
Per-credit charge: $216; out-of-state residents $539.
Room and board: $6,030.
Additional info: Tuition/fee waivers available for minority students.

FINANCIAL AID PICTURE (2007-2008)
Students with need: Out of 1,493 full-time freshmen who applied for aid, 1,418 were judged to have need. Of these, 1,297 received aid, and 1,167 had their full need met. Average financial aid package met 69% of need; average scholarship/grant was $5,489; average loan was $3,223. For part-time students, average financial aid package was $6,948.
Students without need: 46 full-time freshmen who did not demonstrate need for aid received scholarships/grants; average award was $2,057. No-need awards available for academics, art, athletics, job skills, leadership, minority status, music/drama, ROTC, state/district residency.
Scholarships offered: 68 full-time freshmen received athletic scholarships; average amount $2,066.
Cumulative student debt: 71% of graduating class had student loans; average debt was $17,730.

FINANCIAL AID PROCEDURES
Forms required: FAFSA.
Dates and Deadlines: Priority date 3/15; no closing date. Applicants notified on a rolling basis starting 4/1.
Transfers: Evaluation of transfer credits must be completed before financial aid can be finalized.

CONTACT
Thomas Lyons, Director of Financial Aid
104 Student Service Center, Bloomsburg, PA 17815
(570) 389-4297

Bradford School: Pittsburgh
Pittsburgh, Pennsylvania
www.bradfordpittsburgh.edu   Federal Code: 009721

2-year for-profit junior college in very large city.
Enrollment: 425 full-time undergrads.

FINANCIAL AID PICTURE
Students with need: Need-based aid available for full-time students.

FINANCIAL AID PROCEDURES
Forms required: FAFSA.

CONTACT
Jane Storm, Director of Financial Aid
125 West Station Square Drive, Pittsburgh, PA 15219
(412) 391-6710

Bryn Athyn College of the New Church
Bryn Athyn, Pennsylvania
www.brynathyn.edu   Federal Code: 003228

4-year private liberal arts college in small town, affiliated with General Church of the New Jerusalem (Swedenborgian).
Enrollment: 118 undergrads, 3% part-time. 47 full-time freshmen.
Selectivity: Admits over 75% of applicants.

BASIC COSTS (2007-2008)
Tuition and fees: $10,114.
Per-credit charge: $319.
Room and board: $5,574.

FINANCIAL AID PICTURE (2007-2008)
Students with need: 84% of average financial aid package awarded as scholarships/grants, 16% awarded as loans/jobs. Need-based aid available for part-time students.
Students without need: No-need awards available for academics, leadership, religious affiliation.

FINANCIAL AID PROCEDURES
Forms required: FAFSA, institutional form.
Dates and Deadlines: Closing date 6/1. Applicants notified on a rolling basis starting 4/30; must reply by 9/30.
Transfers: No deadline. Applicants notified on a rolling basis starting 7/1; must reply within 6 week(s) of notification.

CONTACT
Wendy Cooper, Associate Director of Financial Aid
PO Box 717, Bryn Athyn, PA 19009-0717
(267) 502-2630

Bryn Mawr College
Bryn Mawr, Pennsylvania   Federal Code: 003237
www.brynmawr.edu   CSS Code: 2049

4-year private liberal arts college for women in very large city.
Enrollment: 1,275 undergrads, 1% part-time. 352 full-time freshmen.
Selectivity: Admits less than 50% of applicants.

BASIC COSTS (2007-2008)
Tuition and fees: $34,650.
Room and board: $11,024.

FINANCIAL AID PICTURE (2007-2008)
Students with need: Out of 240 full-time freshmen who applied for aid, 177 were judged to have need. Of these, 177 received aid, and 177 had their full need met. Average financial aid package met 100% of need; average scholarship/grant was $26,061; average loan was $3,397. For part-time students, average financial aid package was $7,285.
Students without need: This college awards aid only to students with need.
Cumulative student debt: 61% of graduating class had student loans; average debt was $19,049.

FINANCIAL AID PROCEDURES
Forms required: FAFSA, CSS PROFILE.
Dates and Deadlines: Priority date 2/5; closing date 3/1. Applicants notified by 3/23; must reply by 5/1.
Transfers: Closing date 3/15. Must reply by 5/1.

CONTACT
Ethel Desmarais, Director of Financial Aid
101 North Merion Avenue, Bryn Mawr, PA 19010-2899
(610) 526-5245

Bucknell University

Lewisburg, Pennsylvania
www.bucknell.edu

Federal Code: 003238
CSS Code: 2050

4-year private university in small town.
Enrollment: 3,495 undergrads. 887 full-time freshmen.
Selectivity: Admits less than 50% of applicants.

BASIC COSTS (2008-2009)
Tuition and fees: $39,652.
Room and board: $8,728.

FINANCIAL AID PICTURE (2007-2008)
Students with need: Out of 535 full-time freshmen who applied for aid, 422 were judged to have need. Of these, 422 received aid, and 422 had their full need met. Average financial aid package met 100% of need; average scholarship/grant was $21,300; average loan was $4,500.
Students without need: 30 full-time freshmen who did not demonstrate need for aid received scholarships/grants; average award was $11,126. No-need awards available for academics, art, athletics, leadership, music/drama, ROTC.
Scholarships offered: *Merit:* Scholarships available to a limited number of students who have demonstrated exceptional achievements in academics, art and performing arts, music, and athletics (limited to basketball). *Athletic:* 6 full-time freshmen received athletic scholarships; average amount $10,000.
Cumulative student debt: 64% of graduating class had student loans; average debt was $17,700.

FINANCIAL AID PROCEDURES
Forms required: FAFSA, CSS PROFILE.
Dates and Deadlines: Closing date 1/1. Applicants notified by 4/1; must reply by 5/1.
Transfers: Closing date 3/15. Applicants notified by 5/1; must reply by 6/1. Aid restricted to 2-year college graduates.

CONTACT
Andrea Leithner, Director of Financial Aid
Freas Hall, Lewisburg, PA 17837-9988
(570) 577-1331

Bucks County Community College

Newtown, Pennsylvania
www.bucks.edu

Federal Code: 003239

2-year public community college in large town.
Enrollment: 9,649 undergrads, 57% part-time. 1,801 full-time freshmen.
Selectivity: Open admission; but selective for some programs.

BASIC COSTS (2007-2008)
Tuition and fees: $3,434; out-of-district residents $6,524; out-of-state residents $9,614.
Per-credit charge: $93; out-of-district residents $186; out-of-state residents $279.

FINANCIAL AID PICTURE (2006-2007)
Students with need: 70% of average financial aid package awarded as scholarships/grants, 30% awarded as loans/jobs. Need-based aid available for part-time students. Work study available nights, weekends, and for part-time students.
Students without need: No-need awards available for academics.

FINANCIAL AID PROCEDURES
Forms required: FAFSA.
Dates and Deadlines: Closing date 5/1. Applicants notified on a rolling basis starting 6/1; must reply within 2 week(s) of notification.
Transfers: Applicants notified by 6/1; must reply within 2 week(s) of notification.

CONTACT
Donna Wilkoski, Director of Financial Aid
275 Swamp Road, Newtown, PA 18940
(215) 968-8200

Butler County Community College

Butler, Pennsylvania
www.bc3.edu

Federal Code: 003240

2-year public community college in large town.
Enrollment: 3,656 undergrads, 46% part-time.
Selectivity: Open admission; but selective for some programs.

BASIC COSTS (2007-2008)
Tuition and fees: $2,790; out-of-district residents $4,980; out-of-state residents $7,170.
Per-credit charge: $73; out-of-district residents $146; out-of-state residents $219.

FINANCIAL AID PICTURE (2006-2007)
Students with need: 50% of average financial aid package awarded as scholarships/grants, 50% awarded as loans/jobs. Need-based aid available for part-time students.
Students without need: No-need awards available for academics, state/district residency.

FINANCIAL AID PROCEDURES
Forms required: FAFSA.
Dates and Deadlines: Priority date 4/15; no closing date. Applicants notified on a rolling basis starting 5/1; must reply within 2 week(s) of notification.

CONTACT
Julianne Louttit, Director of Financial Aid
PO Box 1203, Butler, PA 16003-1203
(724) 287-8711 ext. 8329

Cabrini College

Radnor, Pennsylvania
www.cabrini.edu

Federal Code: 003241

4-year private liberal arts college in large town, affiliated with Roman Catholic Church.
Enrollment: 1,820 undergrads, 7% part-time. 513 full-time freshmen.
Selectivity: Admits over 75% of applicants.

BASIC COSTS (2007-2008)
Tuition and fees: $28,030.
Per-credit charge: $425.
Room and board: $10,290.

FINANCIAL AID PICTURE (2007-2008)
Students with need: Out of 457 full-time freshmen who applied for aid, 395 were judged to have need. Of these, 395 received aid, and 78 had their full need met. Average financial aid package met 69% of need; average scholarship/grant was $7,022; average loan was $3,811. For part-time students, average financial aid package was $5,155.
Students without need: 128 full-time freshmen who did not demonstrate need for aid received scholarships/grants; average award was $10,113. No-need awards available for academics, alumni affiliation.
Cumulative student debt: 77% of graduating class had student loans; average debt was $22,700.

FINANCIAL AID PROCEDURES
Forms required: FAFSA.
Dates and Deadlines: Closing date 4/1. Applicants notified on a rolling basis starting 3/1.

Transfers: Achievement scholarships available.

CONTACT

Michael Colahan, Financial Aid Director
610 King of Prussia Road, Radnor, PA 19087-3698
(610) 902-8420

California University of Pennsylvania

California, Pennsylvania
www.cup.edu   Federal Code: 003316

4-year public university in small town.

Enrollment: 6,606 undergrads, 10% part-time. 1,260 full-time freshmen.

Selectivity: Admits 50 to 75% of applicants.

BASIC COSTS (2007-2008)

Tuition and fees: $6,851; out-of-state residents $10,046.

Per-credit charge: $216; out-of-state residents $345.

Room and board: $8,548.

Additional info: Tuition/fee waivers available for adults, minority students.

FINANCIAL AID PICTURE (2006-2007)

Students with need: Out of 1,066 full-time freshmen who applied for aid, 841 were judged to have need. Of these, 836 received aid, and 41 had their full need met. Average financial aid package met 89% of need; average scholarship/grant was $4,642; average loan was $2,792. For part-time students, average financial aid package was $3,422.

Students without need: 279 full-time freshmen who did not demonstrate need for aid received scholarships/grants; average award was $2,282. No-need awards available for academics, alumni affiliation, art, athletics, leadership, minority status, music/drama, religious affiliation, ROTC, state/district residency.

Scholarships offered: 30 full-time freshmen received athletic scholarships; average amount $5,670.

FINANCIAL AID PROCEDURES

Forms required: FAFSA, state aid form.

Dates and Deadlines: Priority date 5/1; no closing date. Applicants notified on a rolling basis starting 4/1; must reply within 3 week(s) of notification.

CONTACT

Robert Thorn, Director of Financial Aid
250 University Avenue, California, PA 15419-1394
(724) 938-4415

Cambria-Rowe Business College

Johnstown, Pennsylvania
www.crbc.net   Federal Code: 004889

2-year for-profit business college in small city.

Enrollment: 185 undergrads.

BASIC COSTS (2007-2008)

Tuition and fees: $9,075.

Additional info: Depending on choice of laptop, fees could be as much as $1,140.

FINANCIAL AID PICTURE

Students with need: Need-based aid available for full-time and part-time students.

Students without need: No-need awards available for academics, leadership.

Scholarships offered: Presidential Grant (3 awarded) 50% tuition; FBLA Scholarship (2 awarded) $3,000.

FINANCIAL AID PROCEDURES

Forms required: FAFSA, state aid form.

Dates and Deadlines: Closing date 8/1. Applicants notified on a rolling basis.

Transfers: Closing date 5/1.

CONTACT

Judy Miller, Financial Aid Adviser
221 Central Avenue, Johnstown, PA 15902
(814) 536-5168

Cambria-Rowe Business College: Indiana

Indiana, Pennsylvania
www.crbc.net   Federal Code: 004889

2-year for-profit business and technical college in small town.

Enrollment: 195 undergrads, 7% part-time. 54 full-time freshmen.

Selectivity: Open admission.

BASIC COSTS (2008-2009)

Tuition and fees: $9,440.

Per-credit charge: $250.

Additional info: Depending on choice of laptop, fees could be as much as $1125.

FINANCIAL AID PICTURE

Students with need: Need-based aid available for full-time and part-time students.

FINANCIAL AID PROCEDURES

Forms required: FAFSA.

Dates and Deadlines: No deadline. Applicants notified on a rolling basis.

CONTACT

Judy Miller
422 South 13th Street, Indiana, PA 15701
(814) 536-5168

Career Training Academy

New Kensington, Pennsylvania
www.careerta.com   Federal Code: 026095

2-year for-profit career college in small town.

Enrollment: 85 undergrads.

Selectivity: Open admission; but selective for some programs.

BASIC COSTS (2007-2008)

Additional info: Total cost of 15-month associate degree program in massage therapy: $22,378 (includes tuition, books, portable massage table, uniforms, lab fees, insurance, graduation fees). Total cost of 15-month associate degree program in medical assistance: $18,812 (includes tuition, books, uniforms, lab fees, insurance, graduation fees). Other diploma programs will vary in cost and required length of study. Tuition at time of enrollment locked for 2 years.

FINANCIAL AID PICTURE

Students with need: Need-based aid available for full-time students.

Students without need: This college awards aid only to students with need.

Additional info: Work study available after class day.

FINANCIAL AID PROCEDURES

Forms required: FAFSA, institutional form.

Dates and Deadlines: No deadline.

CONTACT

Karen Schonbachler, Financial Services Coordinator
950 Fifth Avenue, New Kensington, PA 15068

Career Training Academy: Monroeville

Monroeville, Pennsylvania
www.careerta.edu   Federal Code: 026095

2-year for-profit branch campus college in small city.
Enrollment: 45 undergrads.
Selectivity: Open admission; but selective for some programs.

BASIC COSTS (2007-2008)
Additional info: Tuition ranges from $3,700 to $17,900 depending on program; required fees range from $210 to $3,100 depending on program.

FINANCIAL AID PICTURE
Students with need: Need-based aid available for full-time and part-time students.
Students without need: This college awards aid only to students with need.

FINANCIAL AID PROCEDURES
Forms required: FAFSA, state aid form, institutional form.

CONTACT
Karen Schonbachler, Financial Aid Supervisor
4314 Old William Penn Highway #103, Monroeville, PA 15146
(724) 337-1000

Carlow University

Pittsburgh, Pennsylvania
www.carlow.edu   Federal Code: 003303

4-year private university and liberal arts college for women in large city, affiliated with Roman Catholic Church.
Enrollment: 1,555 undergrads, 25% part-time. 265 full-time freshmen.
Selectivity: Admits 50 to 75% of applicants.

BASIC COSTS (2007-2008)
Tuition and fees: $19,514.
Per-credit charge: $612.
Room and board: $7,684.
Additional info: Nursing supplemental tuition is $150 per credit; student teaching fee is $222 for 3 to 6 credits. Tuition/fee waivers available for unemployed or children of unemployed.

FINANCIAL AID PICTURE (2006-2007)
Students with need: Average financial aid package met 70% of need. Need-based aid available for part-time students.
Students without need: No-need awards available for academics, athletics, leadership.
Scholarships offered: Full tuition scholarship: 3.75 GPA, 1300 SAT required. Half tuition scholarship; 3.5 GPA, 1200 SAT required. Presidential scholarship: $5,000 to $10,000; 3.25 GPA, 1000 SAT required. Valedictorian scholarship: $10,000. McAuley scholarship: $2,500; 3.25 GPA, 930 SAT required; one per Catholic high school in diocese of Pittsburgh, Johnston/Altoona and Greensburg. Legacy scholarship: $2,500; to children or grandchildren of alumnae. Dean's Recognition scholarship: $4,000; 3.00 GPA and 930 SAT required. Sister Maurice Whalen scholarship: to those who submit projects to Pittsburgh Regional Science and Engineering Fair, also requires 3.25 GPA and 1000 SAT. Rose Marie Beard Women of Spirit Honors Scholarship: $4,000 for first year; 3.5 GPA, 1100 SAT, rank in top 15% of high school class, evidence of significant leadership required. All SAT scores exclusive of Writing.
Cumulative student debt: 85% of graduating class had student loans; average debt was $25,224.

FINANCIAL AID PROCEDURES
Forms required: FAFSA.
Dates and Deadlines: Priority date 4/1; no closing date. Applicants notified on a rolling basis starting 2/15; must reply within 4 week(s) of notification.

CONTACT
Natalie Wilson, Director of Financial Aid
3333 Fifth Avenue, Pittsburgh, PA 15213-3165
(412) 578-6058

Carnegie Mellon University

Pittsburgh, Pennsylvania
www.cmu.edu   Federal Code: 003242

4-year private university in large city.
Enrollment: 5,758 undergrads, 2% part-time. 1,416 full-time freshmen.
Selectivity: Admits less than 50% of applicants.

BASIC COSTS (2007-2008)
Tuition and fees: $37,354.
Per-credit charge: $514.
Room and board: $9,660.

FINANCIAL AID PICTURE (2007-2008)
Students with need: Out of 942 full-time freshmen who applied for aid, 730 were judged to have need. Of these, 727 received aid, and 269 had their full need met. Average financial aid package met 82% of need; average scholarship/grant was $20,072; average loan was $4,442. For part-time students, average financial aid package was $18,091.
Students without need: 112 full-time freshmen who did not demonstrate need for aid received scholarships/grants; average award was $9,687. No-need awards available for academics, art, leadership, minority status, music/drama, state/district residency.
Cumulative student debt: 50% of graduating class had student loans; average debt was $39,346.
Additional info: Early need analysis offered; merit awards available. Students notified within week to 10 days of receipt of financial aid application.

FINANCIAL AID PROCEDURES
Forms required: FAFSA, institutional form.
Dates and Deadlines: Priority date 2/15; closing date 5/1.
Transfers: Students applying for spring transfer must file FAFSA by 11/1 and are notified of award 12/15 or soon after. College of Fine Arts applicants applying for fall transfer must file FAFSA by 2/15 and are notified of award by 4/15. All other applicants for fall transfer must submit FAFSA by 5/1 and are notified of award during the month of June.

CONTACT
Linda Anderson, Director of Enrollment Services
5000 Forbes Avenue, Pittsburgh, PA 15213-3890
(412) 268-8186

Cedar Crest College

Allentown, Pennsylvania
www.cedarcrest.edu   Federal Code: 003243

4-year private liberal arts college for women in small city.
Enrollment: 1,709 undergrads, 43% part-time. 219 full-time freshmen.
Selectivity: Admits 50 to 75% of applicants.

BASIC COSTS (2008-2009)
Tuition and fees: $26,542.
Room and board: $9,008.
Additional info: Average per-credit-hour cost is $568.

FINANCIAL AID PICTURE (2007-2008)
Students with need: Out of 216 full-time freshmen who applied for aid, 190 were judged to have need. Of these, 190 received aid, and 39 had their full need met. Average financial aid package met 80% of need; average scholarship/grant was $15,001; average loan was $3,816. For part-time students, average financial aid package was $5,782.

Students without need: 29 full-time freshmen who did not demonstrate need for aid received scholarships/grants; average award was $13,054. No-need awards available for academics, alumni affiliation, art, leadership, music/drama.

Scholarships offered: Presidential Scholarship; up to half tuition; for freshmen with SAT scores over 1150 and in top 10% of class; renewable for four years with GPA of 3.0. 1867 Award; one-third of tuition; renewable for four years with GPA of 3.0; for freshmen with SAT of 1100 and in top 25% of class. Girl Scout Gold Awards; $1,000 per year; for recipients of the Girl Scout Gold Award. Art, Dance, and Performing Arts Scholarships; $1,500 per year; based on portfolio review, audition, and commitment to the creative process. Governor's School of Excellence Award; $1,000 per year; for graduates of Governor's Schools of Excellence. Hugh O'Brian Youth (HOBY) Awards; $1,000 per year; for freshmen who are HOBY alumnae. SAT scores exclusive of Writing portion.

Cumulative student debt: 98% of graduating class had student loans; average debt was $29,879.

FINANCIAL AID PROCEDURES

Forms required: FAFSA, institutional form.

Dates and Deadlines: No deadline. Applicants notified on a rolling basis starting 11/1; must reply by 5/1 or within 3 week(s) of notification.

Transfers: Certain academic scholarships are available for transfers only, such as the Phi Theta Kappa Scholarship, Lifelong Learning Transfer Scholarship and Traditional Transfer Scholarship.

CONTACT

Lori Williams, Director of Financial Aid
100 College Drive, Allentown, PA 18104-6196
(610) 740-3785

Central Pennsylvania College
Summerdale, Pennsylvania
www.centralpenn.edu   Federal Code: 004890

4-year for-profit business and technical college in rural community.

Enrollment: 1,102 undergrads, 34% part-time. 110 full-time freshmen.

Selectivity: Open admission; but selective for some programs.

BASIC COSTS (2007-2008)

Tuition and fees: $12,648.

Per-credit charge: $333.

Room and board: $6,360.

FINANCIAL AID PICTURE

Students with need: Need-based aid available for full-time and part-time students.

Students without need: No-need awards available for academics, alumni affiliation, job skills, leadership, minority status, state/district residency.

FINANCIAL AID PROCEDURES

Forms required: FAFSA, state aid form, institutional form.

Dates and Deadlines: Priority date 3/15; no closing date. Applicants notified on a rolling basis starting 2/1; must reply within 2 week(s) of notification.

CONTACT

Kathy Shepard, Financial Aid Director
College Hill & Valley Roads, Summerdale, PA 17093-0309
(717) 728-2261

Chatham University
Pittsburgh, Pennsylvania
www.chatham.edu   Federal Code: 003244

4-year private university and liberal arts college for women in large city.

Enrollment: 651 undergrads, 10% part-time. 175 full-time freshmen.

Selectivity: Admits over 75% of applicants.

BASIC COSTS (2007-2008)

Tuition and fees: $25,816.

Room and board: $7,892.

FINANCIAL AID PICTURE (2007-2008)

Students with need: Out of 145 full-time freshmen who applied for aid, 135 were judged to have need. Of these, 135 received aid. Average financial aid package met 88% of need; average scholarship/grant was $4,937; average loan was $5,546. For part-time students, average financial aid package was $5,840.

Students without need: 40 full-time freshmen who did not demonstrate need for aid received scholarships/grants; average award was $13,048. No-need awards available for academics, alumni affiliation, leadership, music/drama, state/district residency.

Scholarships offered: Presidential Scholarship; up to $12,000. Trustee Scholarship; up to $9,000. Founders' Scholarship; up to $7,000. All based on academic excellence and renewable annually based on GPA of 2.8 or higher.

FINANCIAL AID PROCEDURES

Forms required: FAFSA.

Dates and Deadlines: Priority date 5/1; no closing date. Applicants notified on a rolling basis starting 2/15; must reply by 5/1 or within 2 week(s) of notification.

Transfers: Special scholarships are available for transfer students.

CONTACT

Jennifer Burns, Director of Financial Aid
Woodland Road, Pittsburgh, PA 15232
(412) 365-1777

Chestnut Hill College
Philadelphia, Pennsylvania
www.chc.edu   Federal Code: 003245

4-year private liberal arts college in very large city, affiliated with Roman Catholic Church.

Enrollment: 1,248 undergrads, 21% part-time. 234 full-time freshmen.

Selectivity: Admits 50 to 75% of applicants.

BASIC COSTS (2008-2009)

Tuition and fees: $26,000.

Per-credit charge: $550.

Room and board: $8,550.

FINANCIAL AID PICTURE (2007-2008)

Students with need: Average financial aid package met 79% of need; average scholarship/grant was $14,403; average loan was $5,827. For part-time students, average financial aid package was $7,278.

Students without need: No-need awards available for academics, alumni affiliation, leadership, religious affiliation.

Scholarships offered: Full-tuition and partial-tuition awards; based on academics.

Additional info: Application priority date 1/15 for merit-based scholarships.

FINANCIAL AID PROCEDURES

Forms required: FAFSA.

Dates and Deadlines: Closing date 4/15. Applicants notified on a rolling basis starting 1/31; must reply by 5/1 or within 3 week(s) of notification.

CONTACT

Nicholas Flocco, Director of Financial Aid
9601 Germantown Avenue, Philadelphia, PA 19118-2693
(215) 248-7182

Cheyney University of Pennsylvania
Cheyney, Pennsylvania
www.cheyney.edu   Federal Code: 003317

4-year public university in small town.
Enrollment: 1,318 undergrads.
Selectivity: Admits less than 50% of applicants.

BASIC COSTS (2007-2008)
Tuition and fees: $6,412; out-of-state residents $14,179.
Per-credit charge: $216; out-of-state residents $539.
Room and board: $6,856.
Additional info: Tuition for MD, NY, NJ and DE is $10,354. Tuition/fee waivers available for minority students.

FINANCIAL AID PICTURE
Students with need: Need-based aid available for full-time and part-time students.
Students without need: No-need awards available for academics, athletics.

FINANCIAL AID PROCEDURES
Forms required: FAFSA.
Dates and Deadlines: Priority date 3/15; no closing date. Applicants notified on a rolling basis starting 4/1; must reply within 2 week(s) of notification.

CONTACT
James Brown, Director of Financial Aid
1837 University Circle, Cheyney, PA 19319-0019
(610) 399-2302

CHI Institute: Broomall
Broomall, Pennsylvania
www.chitraining.com   Federal Code: 007781

2-year for-profit technical and career college in large town.
Enrollment: 1,015 undergrads.
Selectivity: Open admission.

BASIC COSTS (2007-2008)
Additional info: Tuition ranges from $13,251- $20,154 per 18-month program associate degree program, inclusive of books and fees.

FINANCIAL AID PICTURE
Students with need: Need-based aid available for full-time and part-time students.

FINANCIAL AID PROCEDURES
Forms required: FAFSA.
Dates and Deadlines: No deadline. Applicants notified on a rolling basis.

CONTACT
Chrissy Kapusniak, Director of Financial Aid
1991 Sproul Road, Suite 42, Broomall, PA 19008
(610) 355-3300

Clarion University of Pennsylvania
Clarion, Pennsylvania
www.clarion.edu   Federal Code: 003318

4-year public business and teachers college in small town.
Enrollment: 5,691 undergrads, 10% part-time. 1,305 full-time freshmen.
Selectivity: Admits 50 to 75% of applicants.

BASIC COSTS (2007-2008)
Tuition and fees: $6,867; out-of-state residents $12,044.
Per-credit charge: $216; out-of-state residents $431.

Room and board: $5,808.
Additional info: Tuition for incoming out of state residents with SAT of 1100 or higher and at least a 3.5 GPA or the top 20% of their graduating class is $7,766.

FINANCIAL AID PICTURE (2006-2007)
Students with need: Out of 1,192 full-time freshmen who applied for aid, 968 were judged to have need. Of these, 929 received aid, and 132 had their full need met. Average financial aid package met 61% of need; average scholarship/grant was $5,316; average loan was $2,505. For part-time students, average financial aid package was $3,830.
Students without need: 78 full-time freshmen who did not demonstrate need for aid received scholarships/grants; average award was $1,995. No-need awards available for academics, art, athletics, leadership, minority status, music/drama, state/district residency.
Scholarships offered: 66 full-time freshmen received athletic scholarships; average amount $1,852.

FINANCIAL AID PROCEDURES
Forms required: FAFSA.
Dates and Deadlines: Closing date 4/15. Applicants notified on a rolling basis starting 3/1.

CONTACT
Kenneth Grugel, Director of Financial Aid
840 Wood Street, Clarion, PA 16214
(814) 226-2315

Commonwealth Technical Institute
Johnstown, Pennsylvania
www.hgac.org

2-year private technical college in small city.
Enrollment: 94 undergrads. 94 full-time freshmen.
Selectivity: Open admission.

BASIC COSTS (2007-2008)
Tuition and fees: $11,224.
Room and board: $9,516.

FINANCIAL AID PICTURE
Students with need: Need-based aid available for full-time and part-time students. Work study available nights, weekends, and for part-time students.
Students without need: This college awards aid only to students with need.

FINANCIAL AID PROCEDURES
Forms required: FAFSA.
Dates and Deadlines: Closing date 5/1. Applicants notified on a rolling basis.

CONTACT
Sylvia Sabo, Administrative Assistant
727 Goucher Street, Johnstown, PA 15905-3902
(814) 255-8351

Community College of Allegheny County
Pittsburgh, Pennsylvania
www.ccac.edu

2-year public community college in very large city.
Enrollment: 16,907 undergrads, 57% part-time. 2,609 full-time freshmen.
Selectivity: Open admission; but selective for some programs.

BASIC COSTS (2007-2008)
Tuition and fees: $2,669; out-of-district residents $5,069; out-of-state residents $7,469.

Per-credit charge: $80; out-of-district residents $160; out-of-state residents $240.

Additional info: If county does not have community college, tuition is $2,820 per year. Nursing and allied health courses subject to additional fees.

FINANCIAL AID PICTURE

Students with need: Need-based aid available for full-time and part-time students. Work study available nights, weekends, and for part-time students.
Students without need: No-need awards available for academics, minority status.

FINANCIAL AID PROCEDURES

Forms required: FAFSA.
Dates and Deadlines: Priority date 5/1; no closing date. Applicants notified on a rolling basis starting 5/1.

CONTACT

Director of Financial Aid
800 Allegheny Avenue, Pittsburgh, PA 15233
(412) 323-2323

Community College of Beaver County

Monaca, Pennsylvania
www.ccbc.edu
Federal Code: 006807

2-year public community college in small town.
Enrollment: 1,865 undergrads, 39% part-time. 365 full-time freshmen.
Selectivity: Open admission; but selective for some programs.

BASIC COSTS (2007-2008)

Tuition and fees: $3,180; out-of-district residents $5,880; out-of-state residents $8,880.
Per-credit charge: $85; out-of-district residents $170; out-of-state residents $255.

FINANCIAL AID PICTURE (2006-2007)

Students with need: For part-time students, average financial aid package was $1,675.
Students without need: No-need awards available for academics, athletics, state/district residency.
Scholarships offered: Academic Excellence Scholarship; full tuition.

FINANCIAL AID PROCEDURES

Forms required: FAFSA, state aid form, institutional form.
Dates and Deadlines: Priority date 5/1; closing date 7/1. Applicants notified on a rolling basis starting 8/5; must reply within 2 week(s) of notification.
Transfers: Priority date 5/6.

CONTACT

Doug Mahler, Director of Financial Aid
One Campus Drive, Monaca, PA 15061-2588
(724) 775-8561 ext. 260

Community College of Philadelphia

Philadelphia, Pennsylvania
www.ccp.edu
Federal Code: 003249

2-year public community college in very large city.
Enrollment: 17,339 undergrads, 67% part-time. 1,754 full-time freshmen.
Selectivity: Open admission; but selective for some programs.

BASIC COSTS (2007-2008)

Tuition and fees: $4,410; out-of-district residents $8,160; out-of-state residents $11,910.
Per-credit charge: $115; out-of-district residents $230; out-of-state residents $345.

FINANCIAL AID PICTURE (2007-2008)

Students with need: 57% of average financial aid package awarded as scholarships/grants, 43% awarded as loans/jobs. Need-based aid available for part-time students. Work study available nights, weekends, and for part-time students.
Students without need: This college awards aid only to students with need.

FINANCIAL AID PROCEDURES

Forms required: FAFSA, institutional form.
Dates and Deadlines: Closing date 5/1. Applicants notified on a rolling basis.
Transfers: No deadline.

CONTACT

Gim Lim, Director of Financial Aid
1700 Spring Garden Street, Philadelphia, PA 19130-3991
(215) 751-8270

Consolidated School of Business: Lancaster

Lancaster, Pennsylvania
www.csb.edu
Federal Code: 030299

2-year for-profit business college in small city.
Enrollment: 166 undergrads.
Selectivity: Open admission.

BASIC COSTS (2007-2008)

Tuition and fees: $11,500.
Additional info: Tuition at time of enrollment locked for 2 years.

FINANCIAL AID PICTURE

Students with need: Need-based aid available for full-time and part-time students.

FINANCIAL AID PROCEDURES

Forms required: FAFSA, state aid form.
Dates and Deadlines: No deadline. Applicants notified on a rolling basis.

CONTACT

William Hoyt, Director of Financial Aid
2124 Ambassador Circle, Lancaster, PA 17603
(717) 394-6211

Consolidated School of Business: York

York, Pennsylvania
www.csb.edu
Federal Code: 022896

2-year for-profit business college in small city.
Enrollment: 140 undergrads.
Selectivity: Open admission.

BASIC COSTS (2007-2008)

Tuition and fees: $11,850.
Additional info: Pre-evaluation/placement testing fee $50. Tuition at time of enrollment locked for 2 years.

FINANCIAL AID PICTURE

Students with need: Need-based aid available for full-time and part-time students.

FINANCIAL AID PROCEDURES

Forms required: FAFSA, state aid form.
Dates and Deadlines: No deadline. Applicants notified on a rolling basis.

CONTACT
William Hoyt, Director of Financial Aid
York City Business and Industry Park, York, PA 17404
(717) 764-9550

Curtis Institute of Music
Philadelphia, Pennsylvania
www.curtis.edu   Federal Code: 003251

4-year private music college in very large city.
Enrollment: 137 undergrads. 14 full-time freshmen.
Selectivity: Admits less than 50% of applicants.

BASIC COSTS (2008-2009)
Additional info: Required fees $2,115; for bachelor of music students $2,215; additional expenses per year $15,850 (includes books, supplies, living expenses and miscellaneous).

FINANCIAL AID PICTURE (2007-2008)
Students with need: Average financial aid package met 80% of need; average scholarship/grant was $6,559; average loan was $3,857.
Students without need: This college awards aid only to students with need.
Cumulative student debt: 70% of graduating class had student loans; average debt was $17,000.

FINANCIAL AID PROCEDURES
Forms required: FAFSA, institutional form.
Dates and Deadlines: Closing date 3/1. Applicants notified by 4/1; must reply by 5/1.

CONTACT
Richard Woodland, Director, Student Financial Assistance
1726 Locust Street, Philadelphia, PA 19103-6187
(215) 717-3188

Dean Institute of Technology
Pittsburgh, Pennsylvania
www.deantech.edu   Federal Code: 009186

2-year for-profit technical college in large city.
Enrollment: 207 undergrads, 33% part-time. 34 full-time freshmen.
Selectivity: Open admission.

BASIC COSTS (2008-2009)
Tuition and fees: $18,550.
Per-credit charge: $215.

FINANCIAL AID PICTURE
Students with need: Need-based aid available for full-time and part-time students.

FINANCIAL AID PROCEDURES
Forms required: FAFSA.
Dates and Deadlines: Closing date 8/1. Applicants notified on a rolling basis; must reply within 8 week(s) of notification.

CONTACT
Nancy Grom, Director of Financial Aid
1501 West Liberty Avenue, Pittsburgh, PA 15226
(412) 531-4433 ext. 121

Delaware Valley College
Doylestown, Pennsylvania
www.delval.edu   Federal Code: 003252

4-year private agricultural and liberal arts college in large town.
Enrollment: 1,851 undergrads, 11% part-time. 476 full-time freshmen.
Selectivity: Admits 50 to 75% of applicants.

BASIC COSTS (2008-2009)
Tuition and fees: $27,078.
Per-credit charge: $681.
Room and board: $9,502.
Additional info: Tuition/fee waivers available for adults.

FINANCIAL AID PICTURE (2006-2007)
Students with need: Out of 433 full-time freshmen who applied for aid, 373 were judged to have need. Of these, 373 received aid, and 68 had their full need met. Average financial aid package met 75% of need; average scholarship/grant was $14,370; average loan was $3,233. For part-time students, average financial aid package was $3,649.
Students without need: 94 full-time freshmen who did not demonstrate need for aid received scholarships/grants; average award was $10,564. No-need awards available for academics, alumni affiliation, music/drama.
Cumulative student debt: 60% of graduating class had student loans; average debt was $21,461.

FINANCIAL AID PROCEDURES
Forms required: FAFSA.
Dates and Deadlines: Priority date 4/1; no closing date. Applicants notified on a rolling basis starting 2/1; must reply by 5/1.
Transfers: No deadline. Applicants notified on a rolling basis; must reply by 4/1.

CONTACT
Robert Sauer, Director of Financial Aid
700 East Butler Avenue, Doylestown, PA 18901-2697
(215) 489-2272

DeSales University
Center Valley, Pennsylvania
www.desales.edu   Federal Code: 003986

4-year private university in small town, affiliated with Roman Catholic Church.
Enrollment: 2,207 undergrads, 25% part-time. 391 full-time freshmen.
Selectivity: Admits over 75% of applicants.

BASIC COSTS (2008-2009)
Tuition and fees: $25,800.
Room and board: $9,330.

FINANCIAL AID PICTURE (2007-2008)
Students with need: Out of 335 full-time freshmen who applied for aid, 276 were judged to have need. Of these, 276 received aid, and 154 had their full need met. Average financial aid package met 74% of need; average scholarship/grant was $7,108; average loan was $3,275. For part-time students, average financial aid package was $7,599.
Students without need: 98 full-time freshmen who did not demonstrate need for aid received scholarships/grants; average award was $6,839. No-need awards available for academics, leadership, music/drama.
Scholarships offered: Presidential Scholarships; full tuition; top 5% of class and 1300 SAT. Trustee Scholarships; from $6,000; top 15% of class, minimum 1200 SAT. DeSales Scholarships; $4,000; top 25% of class, minimum 1100 SAT. All SAT scores exclusive of writing.
Cumulative student debt: 89% of graduating class had student loans; average debt was $7,217.

FINANCIAL AID PROCEDURES

Forms required: FAFSA, state aid form.

Dates and Deadlines: Priority date 2/1; closing date 5/1. Applicants notified on a rolling basis starting 2/15; must reply by 5/1 or within 2 week(s) of notification.

Transfers: No deadline. Transfer scholarships require 3.0 GPA, 8 completed courses. Transfer Opportunity Program (TOP), a grant equal to tuition at participating community college, requires associate degree to qualify.

CONTACT

Chanel Greene, Director of Financial Aid

2755 Station Avenue, Center Valley, PA 18034-9568

(610) 282-1100 ext. 1287

DeVry University: Fort Washington

Fort Washington, Pennsylvania

www.devry.edu

4-year for-profit university in large town.

Enrollment: 812 undergrads, 45% part-time. 134 full-time freshmen.

BASIC COSTS (2007-2008)

Tuition and fees: $14,640.

Per-credit charge: $525.

FINANCIAL AID PICTURE (2006-2007)

Students with need: Out of 108 full-time freshmen who applied for aid, 102 were judged to have need. Of these, 98 received aid, and 1 had their full need met. Average financial aid package met 30% of need; average scholarship/grant was $5,975; average loan was $4,399. For part-time students, average financial aid package was $7,825.

Students without need: This college awards aid only to students with need.

Cumulative student debt: 100% of graduating class had student loans; average debt was $54,209.

FINANCIAL AID PROCEDURES

Forms required: FAFSA.

Dates and Deadlines: No deadline. Applicants notified on a rolling basis.

CONTACT

Citristal Claiborne, Director of Financial Aid

1140 Virginia Drive, Fort Washington, PA 19034-3204

(215) 591-5724

Dickinson College

Carlisle, Pennsylvania

www.dickinson.edu

Federal Code: 003253

CSS Code: 2186

4-year private liberal arts college in large town.

Enrollment: 2,349 undergrads. 621 full-time freshmen.

Selectivity: Admits less than 50% of applicants.

BASIC COSTS (2008-2009)

Tuition and fees: $38,259.

Per-credit charge: $1,185.

Room and board: $9,600.

FINANCIAL AID PICTURE (2007-2008)

Students with need: Out of 386 full-time freshmen who applied for aid, 300 were judged to have need. Of these, 297 received aid, and 230 had their full need met. Average financial aid package met 96% of need; average scholarship/grant was $24,542; average loan was $4,175.

Students without need: 31 full-time freshmen who did not demonstrate need for aid received scholarships/grants; average award was $10,571. No-need awards available for academics, alumni affiliation, leadership, ROTC.

Scholarships offered: John Dickinson and Benjamin Rush Scholarships; awarded to most academically competitive students. Additional Engage the World Fellowship for selected John Dickinson Scholarship winners. John Montgomery Scholarship; awarded to first-year students who possess strong credentials, talent in the arts, or competency in 2 foreign languages in addition to English. Scholars must also demonstrate strong leadership in high school and community.

Cumulative student debt: 54% of graduating class had student loans; average debt was $22,853.

FINANCIAL AID PROCEDURES

Forms required: FAFSA, CSS PROFILE, state aid form.

Dates and Deadlines: Closing date 2/1. Applicants notified by 3/31; must reply by 5/1 or within 2 week(s) of notification.

Transfers: Closing date 4/1. Applicants notified on a rolling basis starting 5/1; must reply within 2 week(s) of notification.

CONTACT

Judith Carter, Director of Financial Aid

PO Box 1773, Carlisle, PA 17013-2896

(717) 245-1308

Douglas Education Center

Monessen, Pennsylvania

www.douglas-school.com

Federal Code: 013957

2-year for-profit visual arts and business college in small town.

Enrollment: 140 undergrads.

Selectivity: Open admission.

BASIC COSTS (2007-2008)

Additional info: All-inclusive associate, certificate and diploma programs in art, business, cosmetology and medical fields available from $3,235 to $35,750.

FINANCIAL AID PICTURE

Students with need: Need-based aid available for full-time and part-time students. Work study available nights, weekends, and for part-time students.

Students without need: This college awards aid only to students with need.

FINANCIAL AID PROCEDURES

Dates and Deadlines: No deadline. Applicants notified on a rolling basis.

CONTACT

Alison Pfender, Director of Financial Aid

130 Seventh Street, Monessen, PA 15062

(724) 684-3684 ext. 101

Drexel University

Philadelphia, Pennsylvania

www.drexel.edu

Federal Code: 003256

5-year private university in very large city.

Enrollment: 12,722 undergrads, 17% part-time. 2,290 full-time freshmen.

Selectivity: Admits 50 to 75% of applicants.

BASIC COSTS (2008-2009)

Tuition and fees: $30,440.

Per-credit charge: $785.

Room and board: $12,135.

Additional info: Tuition listed is for 5-year program with co-op quarter terms.

FINANCIAL AID PICTURE

Students with need: Need-based aid available for full-time students.

Students without need: No-need awards available for academics, alumni affiliation, art, athletics, leadership, music/drama, ROTC.

FINANCIAL AID PROCEDURES

Forms required: FAFSA.

Dates and Deadlines: Closing date 3/1. Applicants notified on a rolling basis starting 3/15.

Transfers: Priority date 3/2. Scholarships available in amounts up to $8,000. 3.2 GPA and 30 credit hours at time of application required for eligibility.

CONTACT

Helen Gourousis, Director of Financial Aid

3141 Chestnut Street, Philadelphia, PA 19104-2875

(215) 895-2537

DuBois Business College

DuBois, Pennsylvania

www.dbcollege.com   Federal Code: 004893

2-year for-profit business and technical college in large town.

Enrollment: 265 undergrads.

Selectivity: Open admission.

BASIC COSTS (2007-2008)

Tuition and fees: $9,000.

Per-credit charge: $190.

FINANCIAL AID PICTURE

Students with need: Need-based aid available for full-time students.

FINANCIAL AID PROCEDURES

Forms required: FAFSA.

Dates and Deadlines: Closing date 8/1. Applicants notified on a rolling basis.

CONTACT

Karen Alderton, Financial Aid Director

One Beaver Drive, DuBois, PA 15801

(814) 371-6920

Duquesne University

Pittsburgh, Pennsylvania

www.duq.edu   Federal Code: 003258

4-year private university in large city, affiliated with Roman Catholic Church.

Enrollment: 5,562 undergrads, 6% part-time. 1,323 full-time freshmen.

Selectivity: Admits 50 to 75% of applicants.

BASIC COSTS (2007-2008)

Tuition and fees: $23,950.

Room and board: $8,546.

FINANCIAL AID PICTURE (2006-2007)

Students with need: Out of 1,154 full-time freshmen who applied for aid, 924 were judged to have need. Of these, 924 received aid, and 550 had their full need met. Average financial aid package met 90% of need; average scholarship/grant was $11,279; average loan was $3,355. For part-time students, average financial aid package was $6,737.

Students without need: 555 full-time freshmen who did not demonstrate need for aid received scholarships/grants; average award was $6,592. No-need awards available for academics, athletics, music/drama, ROTC.

Scholarships offered: *Merit:* Competitive scholarships available for academically and/or artistically talented students. *Athletic:* 66 full-time freshmen received athletic scholarships; average amount $14,209.

Cumulative student debt: 80% of graduating class had student loans; average debt was $27,080.

FINANCIAL AID PROCEDURES

Forms required: FAFSA, institutional form.

Dates and Deadlines: Closing date 5/1. Applicants notified on a rolling basis starting 3/1; must reply by 5/1 or within 3 week(s) of notification.

Transfers: No deadline. Must reply within 3 week(s) of notification.

CONTACT

Richard Esposito, Director of Financial Aid

600 Forbes Avenue, Administration Building, Pittsburgh, PA 15282-0201

(412) 396-6607

East Stroudsburg University of Pennsylvania

East Stroudsburg, Pennsylvania

www4.esu.edu   Federal Code: 003320

4-year public university in large town.

Enrollment: 5,841 undergrads, 7% part-time. 1,240 full-time freshmen.

Selectivity: Admits 50 to 75% of applicants.

BASIC COSTS (2007-2008)

Tuition and fees: $6,809; out-of-state residents $14,575.

Per-credit charge: $216; out-of-state residents $539.

Room and board: $5,686.

Additional info: Tuition for incoming out of state residents who are high achieving science and technology majors (biology, chemistry, computer science, mathematics, and physics) is $7,766.

FINANCIAL AID PICTURE (2006-2007)

Students with need: Out of 1,040 full-time freshmen who applied for aid, 695 were judged to have need. Of these, 654 received aid, and 418 had their full need met. Average financial aid package met 75% of need; average scholarship/grant was $4,170; average loan was $2,519. For part-time students, average financial aid package was $3,227.

Students without need: 264 full-time freshmen who did not demonstrate need for aid received scholarships/grants; average award was $6,787. No-need awards available for academics, alumni affiliation, art, athletics, job skills, leadership, minority status, music/drama, religious affiliation, state/district residency.

Scholarships offered: 62 full-time freshmen received athletic scholarships; average amount $1,890.

FINANCIAL AID PROCEDURES

Forms required: FAFSA.

Dates and Deadlines: Closing date 3/1. Applicants notified by 4/1; must reply by 5/1.

CONTACT

Phyllis Swinson, Associate Director of Financial Aid

200 Prospect Street, East Stroudsburg, PA 18301-2999

(570) 422-2800

Edinboro University of Pennsylvania

Edinboro, Pennsylvania

www.edinboro.edu   Federal Code: 003321

4-year public liberal arts and teachers college in small town.

Enrollment: 6,127 undergrads, 10% part-time. 1,243 full-time freshmen.

Selectivity: Admits over 75% of applicants.

BASIC COSTS (2007-2008)

Tuition and fees: $6,767; out-of-state residents $9,356.

Per-credit charge: $216; out-of-state residents $324.

Room and board: $5,976.

FINANCIAL AID PICTURE (2006-2007)

Students with need: Out of 1,210 full-time freshmen who applied for aid, 1,025 were judged to have need. Of these, 987 received aid, and 52 had their full need met. Average financial aid package met 57% of need; average scholarship/grant was $2,194; average loan was $2,107. For part-time students, average financial aid package was $3,669.

Students without need: 100 full-time freshmen who did not demonstrate need for aid received scholarships/grants; average award was $2,499. No-need awards available for academics, alumni affiliation, art, athletics, job skills, leadership, minority status, music/drama, religious affiliation, ROTC, state/district residency.

Cumulative student debt: 45% of graduating class had student loans; average debt was $7,211.

FINANCIAL AID PROCEDURES

Forms required: FAFSA.

Dates and Deadlines: Priority date 3/15; closing date 5/1. Applicants notified on a rolling basis starting 3/20; must reply within 2 week(s) of notification.

CONTACT

Dorothy Body, Assistant Vice President for Student Financial Support and Services

200 East Normal Street, Edinboro, PA 16444

(888) 611-2680

Elizabethtown College

Elizabethtown, Pennsylvania

www.etown.edu

Federal Code: 003262

4-year private liberal arts college in large town, affiliated with Church of the Brethren.

Enrollment: 2,233 undergrads, 15% part-time. 509 full-time freshmen.

Selectivity: Admits 50 to 75% of applicants.

BASIC COSTS (2008-2009)

Tuition and fees: $30,650.

Per-credit charge: $740.

Room and board: $7,950.

FINANCIAL AID PICTURE (2007-2008)

Students with need: Out of 421 full-time freshmen who applied for aid, 362 were judged to have need. Of these, 362 received aid, and 84 had their full need met. Average financial aid package met 84% of need; average scholarship/grant was $16,581; average loan was $3,638. For part-time students, average financial aid package was $6,451.

Students without need: 126 full-time freshmen who did not demonstrate need for aid received scholarships/grants; average award was $14,469. No-need awards available for academics, art, music/drama, religious affiliation.

Scholarships offered: Presidential Scholarships; up to $15,000 annually; top 2% of class and minimum 1300 SAT score. Provost Scholarships; up to $12,500 annually; top 10% of class with minimum 1150 SAT; unlimited number awarded. Dean's Scholarships; up to $10,000 annually; for students with very strong academic achievement who do not qualify for other merit awards; unlimited number awarded. Music scholarships; $1,000-4,000; based on audition. SAT scores exclusive of writing portion.

FINANCIAL AID PROCEDURES

Forms required: FAFSA, institutional form.

Dates and Deadlines: Priority date 3/15; no closing date. Applicants notified on a rolling basis starting 3/1; must reply by 5/1 or within 2 week(s) of notification.

CONTACT

Elizabeth McCloud, Director of Financial Aid

One Alpha Drive, Elizabethtown, PA 17022-2298

(717) 361-1404

Erie Business Center

Erie, Pennsylvania

www.eriebc.edu

Federal Code: 004894

2-year for-profit business college in small city.

Enrollment: 325 undergrads.

Selectivity: Open admission.

BASIC COSTS (2007-2008)

Tuition and fees: $10,800.

Per-credit charge: $328.

FINANCIAL AID PICTURE

Students with need: Need-based aid available for full-time and part-time students.

FINANCIAL AID PROCEDURES

Forms required: FAFSA.

Dates and Deadlines: No deadline.

Transfers: Applicants notified on a rolling basis.

CONTACT

Barbara Heller, Financial Aid Administrator

246 West Ninth Street, Erie, PA 16501

(814) 456-7504 ext. 115

Franklin & Marshall College

Lancaster, Pennsylvania

www.fandm.edu

Federal Code: 003265
CSS Code: 2261

4-year private liberal arts college in small city.

Enrollment: 2,063 undergrads. 569 full-time freshmen.

Selectivity: Admits less than 50% of applicants.

BASIC COSTS (2008-2009)

Tuition and fees: $38,630.

Room and board: $9,870.

FINANCIAL AID PICTURE (2007-2008)

Students with need: Average financial aid package met 100% of need; average scholarship/grant was $23,468; average loan was $4,012.

Students without need: No-need awards available for academics, art, leadership, music/drama.

Scholarships offered: John Marshall Scholarships; $12,500 awarded annually; independent initiative in intellectual or service areas considered. National Merit Recognition; $18,000 renewable annually. Presidential Scholarships; $7,500 annually. All based on academic performance, class rank. Klein Scholarship; $5,000; awarded based on academic and community achievement. Gray Scholarship; awarded to outstanding applicants of African-, Latino-, and Asian-American descent; minimizes loans.

Cumulative student debt: 58% of graduating class had student loans; average debt was $24,752.

FINANCIAL AID PROCEDURES

Forms required: FAFSA, CSS PROFILE, institutional form.

Dates and Deadlines: Priority date 2/1; closing date 3/1. Applicants notified by 3/15; must reply by 5/1.

Transfers: Closing date 2/1.

CONTACT

Christopher Hanlon, Director of Student Aid

PO Box 3003, Lancaster, PA 17604-3003

(717) 291-3991

Gannon University

Erie, Pennsylvania
www.gannon.edu   Federal Code: 003266

4-year private university in small city, affiliated with Roman Catholic Church.
Enrollment: 2,460 undergrads, 7% part-time. 613 full-time freshmen.
Selectivity: Admits over 75% of applicants.

BASIC COSTS (2008-2009)

Tuition and fees: $22,662.
Per-credit charge: $685.
Room and board: $8,710.
Additional info: Tuition/fee waivers available for adults, unemployed or children of unemployed.

FINANCIAL AID PICTURE (2007-2008)

Students with need: Out of 598 full-time freshmen who applied for aid, 542 were judged to have need. Of these, 541 received aid, and 203 had their full need met. Average financial aid package met 83% of need; average scholarship/grant was $14,749; average loan was $3,384. For part-time students, average financial aid package was $5,108.
Students without need: 68 full-time freshmen who did not demonstrate need for aid received scholarships/grants; average award was $6,617. No-need awards available for academics, athletics, leadership, music/drama, religious affiliation, ROTC.
Scholarships offered: *Merit:* Academic Awards; $1,000 to full tuition; based on high school rank, GPA, and test scores. Leadership Awards; $1,000-$1,500; based on leadership and activities. Diocesan Scholarship; $1,000 Parish Grant; for students that belong to a parish within the Diocese of Erie. Diocesan High School Grant; $1,500; for students who attended a Catholic high school within the Diocese of Erie. Catholic High School Grant; $1,000; for any student who attended a Catholic high school outside of the Diocese of Erie. Athletic scholarships; $1,000 to full tuition, room and board. *Athletic:* 14 full-time freshmen received athletic scholarships; average amount $6,918.
Cumulative student debt: 87% of graduating class had student loans; average debt was $26,014.

FINANCIAL AID PROCEDURES

Forms required: FAFSA, institutional form.
Dates and Deadlines: Priority date 3/15; no closing date. Applicants notified on a rolling basis starting 11/1; must reply by 5/1 or within 4 week(s) of notification.

CONTACT

Sharon Krahe, Director of Financial Aid
109 University Square, Erie, PA 16541-0001
(814) 871-7337

Geneva College

Beaver Falls, Pennsylvania
www.geneva.edu   Federal Code: 003267

4-year private liberal arts college in large town, affiliated with Reformed Presbyterian Church of North America.
Enrollment: 1,639 undergrads, 8% part-time. 339 full-time freshmen.
Selectivity: Admits over 75% of applicants.

BASIC COSTS (2008-2009)

Tuition and fees: $20,400.
Per-credit charge: $680.
Room and board: $7,450.
Additional info: Tuition/fee waivers available for minority students.

FINANCIAL AID PICTURE (2007-2008)

Students with need: Out of 324 full-time freshmen who applied for aid, 278 were judged to have need. Of these, 278 received aid, and 74 had their full need met. Average financial aid package met 85% of need; average scholarship/grant was $13,139; average loan was $3,704. For part-time students, average financial aid package was $14,772.
Students without need: 57 full-time freshmen who did not demonstrate need for aid received scholarships/grants; average award was $10,554. No-need awards available for academics, music/drama, religious affiliation.
Scholarships offered: Academic scholarships, scholarships for National Merit finalists and semifinalists, grants for members of controlling church and other denominations identified by the college.
Cumulative student debt: 94% of graduating class had student loans; average debt was $25,197.

FINANCIAL AID PROCEDURES

Forms required: FAFSA.
Dates and Deadlines: Priority date 3/15; no closing date. Applicants notified on a rolling basis starting 3/1; must reply by 5/1 or within 4 week(s) of notification.
Transfers: Applicants notified on a rolling basis starting 3/1.

CONTACT

Steven Bell, Director of Financial Aid
3200 College Avenue, Beaver Falls, PA 15010
(724) 847-6530

Gettysburg College

Gettysburg, Pennsylvania   Federal Code: 003268
www.gettysburg.edu   CSS Code: 2275

4-year private liberal arts college in large town.
Enrollment: 2,485 undergrads, 1% part-time. 695 full-time freshmen.
Selectivity: Admits less than 50% of applicants.

BASIC COSTS (2008-2009)

Tuition and fees: $37,950.
Room and board: $9,100.

FINANCIAL AID PICTURE (2007-2008)

Students with need: Out of 460 full-time freshmen who applied for aid, 362 were judged to have need. Of these, 362 received aid, and 359 had their full need met. Average financial aid package met 100% of need; average scholarship/grant was $24,157; average loan was $3,848.
Students without need: 103 full-time freshmen who did not demonstrate need for aid received scholarships/grants; average award was $10,665. No-need awards available for academics, music/drama.
Scholarships offered: Presidential and Dean's Scholarships; based on high school class rank and standardized test scores; number awarded varies. Wagnild Scholarship and Sunderman Scholarships for music talent; audition required.
Cumulative student debt: 63% of graduating class had student loans; average debt was $27,440.

FINANCIAL AID PROCEDURES

Forms required: FAFSA, CSS PROFILE.
Dates and Deadlines: Closing date 2/15. Applicants notified by 3/26; must reply by 5/1.
Transfers: Priority date 4/15. Must reply within 2 week(s) of notification.

CONTACT

Christina Gormley, Director of Financial Aid
300 North Washington Street, Gettysburg, PA 17325-1484
(717) 337-6611

Grove City College
Grove City, Pennsylvania
www.gcc.edu   Federal Code: G03269

4-year private liberal arts college in small town, affiliated with Presbyterian Church (USA).
Enrollment: 2,490 undergrads, 1% part-time. 655 full-time freshmen.
Selectivity: Admits 50 to 75% of applicants.

BASIC COSTS (2008-2009)
Tuition and fees: $12,074.
Room and board: $6,440.
Additional info: Tuition includes cost of tablet PC and printer. Tuition/fee waivers available for minority students.

FINANCIAL AID PICTURE (2007-2008)
Students with need: Out of 421 full-time freshmen who applied for aid, 280 were judged to have need. Of these, 267 received aid, and 46 had their full need met. Average financial aid package met 62% of need; average scholarship/grant was $6,284.
Students without need: 187 full-time freshmen who did not demonstrate need for aid received scholarships/grants; average award was $5,965. No-need awards available for academics, leadership, minority status.
Scholarships offered: Trustee Scholarships; $5,000; issued to a select group of accepted students who meet academic requirements; 24 awarded. Presidential Scholarships; $500; for all valedictorians in class of 30 or more, salutatorians in class of 100 or more, and National Merit Finalists. Engineering Scholarships; $2,500; 4 awarded.
Cumulative student debt: 62% of graduating class had student loans; average debt was $24,721.
Additional info: Institutional aid applications required for institutional scholarships, loans, and student employment.

FINANCIAL AID PROCEDURES
Forms required: institutional form.
Dates and Deadlines: Closing date 4/15. Applicants notified on a rolling basis starting 3/15; must reply by 5/1.
Transfers: Closing date 12/15. Applicants notified on a rolling basis; must reply within 2 week(s) of notification. Financial aid form must be submitted with transfer enrollment application.

CONTACT
Thomas Ball, Director of Financial Aid
100 Campus Drive, Grove City, PA 16127-2104
(724) 458-3300

Gwynedd-Mercy College
Gwynedd Valley, Pennsylvania
www.gmc.edu   Federal Code: 003270

4-year private health science and liberal arts college in large town, affiliated with Roman Catholic Church.
Enrollment: 1,933 undergrads, 31% part-time. 281 full-time freshmen.
Selectivity: Admits less than 50% of applicants.

BASIC COSTS (2008-2009)
Tuition and fees: $22,790.
Per-credit charge: $495.
Room and board: $8,990.
Additional info: Tuition and fees for nursing and allied health programs $23,840 for full-time, and $570 per credit hour for part-time.

FINANCIAL AID PICTURE (2006-2007)
Students with need: Out of 261 full-time freshmen who applied for aid, 222 were judged to have need. Of these, 220 received aid, and 45 had their full need met. Average financial aid package met 74% of need; average scholarship/grant was $11,613; average loan was $2,339. Need-based aid available for part-time students.
Students without need: 63 full-time freshmen who did not demonstrate need for aid received scholarships/grants; average award was $12,477. No-need awards available for academics, leadership.
Scholarships offered: Presidential scholarship; $10,000; must have 1200 SAT and be in top 30% of class, essay required; 2/15 deadline. Connelly Scholarship; $6,000-$7,000; must have 1100 SAT and be in top 50% of class. Mother Mary Bernard Scholarship; $4,500 - $5,000; must have 1000 SAT, be in top 50% of class, and have documented leadership experience. Yearly scholarship for Catholic school graduates; $2,000 (tuition incentive grant). All SAT scores exclusive of Writing.
Cumulative student debt: 85% of graduating class had student loans; average debt was $18,972.

FINANCIAL AID PROCEDURES
Forms required: FAFSA, institutional form.
Dates and Deadlines: Priority date 3/1; closing date 7/15. Applicants notified on a rolling basis starting 3/1; must reply by 5/1 or within 2 week(s) of notification.
Transfers: Priority date 3/15.

CONTACT
Barbara Kaufmann, Director of Student Financial Aid
1325 Sumneytown Pike, Gwynedd Valley, PA 19437-0901
(215) 646-7300 ext. 483

Harcum College
Bryn Mawr, Pennsylvania
www.harcum.edu   Federal Code: 003272

2-year private junior college in large town.
Enrollment: 832 undergrads.
Selectivity: Admits 50 to 75% of applicants.

BASIC COSTS (2007-2008)
Tuition and fees: $16,200.
Per-credit charge: $533.
Room and board: $7,480.

FINANCIAL AID PICTURE (2007-2008)
Students with need: 97% of average financial aid package awarded as scholarships/grants, 3% awarded as loans/jobs. Need-based aid available for part-time students. Work study available nights, weekends, and for part-time students.
Students without need: No-need awards available for academics, leadership.
Scholarships offered: Scholarships available based on academic achievement.

FINANCIAL AID PROCEDURES
Forms required: FAFSA, institutional form.
Dates and Deadlines: Priority date 4/15; no closing date. Applicants notified on a rolling basis starting 3/1; must reply within 3 week(s) of notification.
Transfers: Priority date 3/15.

CONTACT
Eli Moinester, Director of Financial Aid
750 Montgomery Avenue, Bryn Mawr, PA 19010-3476
(610) 526-6098

Harrisburg Area Community College

Harrisburg, Pennsylvania
www.hacc.edu   Federal Code: 003273

2-year public community college in small city.
Enrollment: 11,180 undergrads, 67% part-time. 1,989 full-time freshmen.
Selectivity: Open admission; but selective for some programs.

BASIC COSTS (2007-2008)

Tuition and fees: $3,000; out-of-district residents $5,640; out-of-state residents $8,280.
Per-credit charge: $83; out-of-district residents $166; out-of-state residents $249.

FINANCIAL AID PICTURE (2006-2007)

Students with need: Out of 1,438 full-time freshmen who applied for aid, 960 were judged to have need. Of these, 863 received aid, and 47 had their full need met. Average financial aid package met 89% of need; average scholarship/grant was $1,621; average loan was $2,588. For part-time students, average financial aid package was $3,782.
Students without need: 3 full-time freshmen who did not demonstrate need for aid received scholarships/grants; average award was $833. No-need awards available for academics.
Additional info: Federal work study community service positions available.

FINANCIAL AID PROCEDURES

Forms required: FAFSA, institutional form.
Dates and Deadlines: Priority date 3/15; no closing date. Applicants notified on a rolling basis starting 6/1.
Transfers: PHEAA state grants require separate academic progress review by financial aid staff.

CONTACT

Robert Fryer, Director of Financial Aid
One HACC Drive, Cooper 206, Harrisburg, PA 17110-2999
(717) 780-2330

Haverford College

Haverford, Pennsylvania   Federal Code: 003274
www.haverford.edu   CSS Code: 2289

4-year private liberal arts college in large town.
Enrollment: 1,169 undergrads. 315 full-time freshmen.
Selectivity: Admits less than 50% of applicants.

BASIC COSTS (2008-2009)

Tuition and fees: $37,525.
Room and board: $11,450.

FINANCIAL AID PICTURE (2007-2008)

Students with need: Out of 182 full-time freshmen who applied for aid, 142 were judged to have need. Of these, 142 received aid, and 142 had their full need met. Average financial aid package met 100% of need; average scholarship/grant was $29,084; average loan was $2,905.
Students without need: This college awards aid only to students with need.
Cumulative student debt: 36% of graduating class had student loans; average debt was $17,125.

FINANCIAL AID PROCEDURES

Forms required: FAFSA, CSS PROFILE, state aid form.
Dates and Deadlines: Closing date 1/31. Applicants notified by 4/8; must reply by 5/1.
Transfers: Closing date 3/1.

CONTACT

David Hoy, Director of Financial Aid
370 Lancaster Avenue, Haverford, PA 19041-1392
(610) 896-1350

Holy Family University

Philadelphia, Pennsylvania
www.holyfamily.edu   Federal Code: 003275

4-year private university and liberal arts college in very large city, affiliated with Roman Catholic Church.
Enrollment: 2,122 undergrads, 32% part-time. 293 full-time freshmen.
Selectivity: Admits 50 to 75% of applicants.

BASIC COSTS (2008-2009)

Tuition and fees: $21,590.
Per-credit charge: $455.
Room and board: $9,400.

FINANCIAL AID PICTURE (2006-2007)

Students with need: Average financial aid package met 89% of need. Need-based aid available for part-time students.
Students without need: 42 full-time freshmen who did not demonstrate need for aid received scholarships/grants; average award was $7,700. No-need awards available for academics, alumni affiliation, athletics.
Scholarships offered: 72 full-time freshmen received athletic scholarships; average amount $5,700.
Cumulative student debt: 85% of graduating class had student loans; average debt was $18,000.

FINANCIAL AID PROCEDURES

Forms required: FAFSA, institutional form.
Dates and Deadlines: Priority date 3/1; no closing date. Applicants notified on a rolling basis starting 3/15; must reply within 2 week(s) of notification.
Transfers: Priority date 4/1; closing date 5/1. Applicants notified on a rolling basis starting 5/1; must reply within 3 week(s) of notification.

CONTACT

Janice Hetrick, Director of Financial Aid
9801 Frankford Avenue, Philadelphia, PA 19114-2009
(215) 637-5538

Hussian School of Art

Philadelphia, Pennsylvania
www.hussianart.edu   Federal Code: 007469

2-year for-profit visual arts and technical college in very large city.
Enrollment: 142 undergrads. 48 full-time freshmen.
Selectivity: Admits over 75% of applicants.

BASIC COSTS (2008-2009)

Tuition and fees: $11,550.
Additional info: Supply costs for freshmen are additional; estimated at $375.

FINANCIAL AID PICTURE

Students with need: Need-based aid available for full-time students.

FINANCIAL AID PROCEDURES

Forms required: FAFSA, state aid form, institutional form.
Dates and Deadlines: No deadline. Applicants notified on a rolling basis starting 2/15; must reply within 3 week(s) of notification.
Transfers: Priority date 3/15; no deadline. Applicants notified on a rolling basis starting 4/1.

CONTACT

Susan Cohen, Financial Aid Director
1118 Market Street, Philadelphia, PA 19107
(215) 981-0900

Immaculata University

Immaculata, Pennsylvania
www.immaculata.edu   Federal Code: 003276

4-year private university and liberal arts college in large town, affiliated with Roman Catholic Church.

Enrollment: 2,647 undergrads, 61% part-time. 277 full-time freshmen.

Selectivity: Admits over 75% of applicants.

BASIC COSTS (2008-2009)

Tuition and fees: $24,575.

Per-credit charge: $400.

Room and board: $10,400.

Additional info: Tuition and fees for entering freshmen guaranteed to not increase for the 4 years of enrollment. Tuition at time of enrollment locked for 4 years.

FINANCIAL AID PICTURE (2007-2008)

Students with need: Out of 254 full-time freshmen who applied for aid, 225 were judged to have need. Of these, 225 received aid, and 66 had their full need met. Average financial aid package met 26% of need; average scholarship/grant was $5,907; average loan was $3,507. For part-time students, average financial aid package was $5,115.

Students without need: 58 full-time freshmen who did not demonstrate need for aid received scholarships/grants; average award was $6,475. No-need awards available for academics, alumni affiliation, art, job skills, leadership, minority status, music/drama, religious affiliation, state/district residency.

FINANCIAL AID PROCEDURES

Forms required: FAFSA.

Dates and Deadlines: Priority date 2/15; closing date 4/15. Applicants notified on a rolling basis starting 2/1; must reply within 2 week(s) of notification.

Transfers: No deadline. Applicants notified on a rolling basis starting 1/1; must reply within 2 week(s) of notification.

CONTACT

Robert Forest, Director of Financial Aid
PO Box 642, Immaculata, PA 19345-0642
(610) 647-4400 ext. 3026

Indiana University of Pennsylvania

Indiana, Pennsylvania
www.iup.edu   Federal Code: 003277

4-year public university in large town.

Enrollment: 11,338 undergrads, 6% part-time. 2,543 full-time freshmen.

Selectivity: Admits 50 to 75% of applicants.

BASIC COSTS (2007-2008)

Tuition and fees: $6,695; out-of-state residents $14,461.

Per-credit charge: $216; out-of-state residents $539.

Room and board: $5,442.

Additional info: Additional fees for out-of-state students: $89. Tuition for OH, VA, WV, IN and MI residents; branch campus students from any state; out of state students with a high school GPA of at least 3.0, or any transfer student with GPA of at least 3.0 is $7,766.

FINANCIAL AID PICTURE (2006-2007)

Students with need: Out of 2,221 full-time freshmen who applied for aid, 1,706 were judged to have need. Of these, 1,695 received aid, and 177 had their full need met. Average financial aid package met 78% of need; average scholarship/grant was $5,512; average loan was $2,973. For part-time students, average financial aid package was $5,899.

Students without need: 103 full-time freshmen who did not demonstrate need for aid received scholarships/grants; average award was $1,765. No-need awards available for academics, alumni affiliation, art, athletics, job skills, leadership, music/drama, ROTC, state/district residency.

Scholarships offered: 65 full-time freshmen received athletic scholarships; average amount $3,080.

Cumulative student debt: 81% of graduating class had student loans; average debt was $22,431.

FINANCIAL AID PROCEDURES

Forms required: FAFSA.

Dates and Deadlines: Priority date 4/15; no closing date. Applicants notified on a rolling basis starting 3/15.

Transfers: Must reply within 2 week(s) of notification.

CONTACT

Patricia McCarthy, Director of Financial Aid
117 John Sutton Hall, 1011 South Drive, Indiana, PA 15705-1088
(724) 357-2218

JNA Institute of Culinary Arts

Philadelphia, Pennsylvania
www.culinaryarts.com   Federal Code: 031033

2-year for-profit technical college in very large city.

Enrollment: 75 undergrads.

Selectivity: Open admission.

BASIC COSTS (2008-2009)

Additional info: Tuition for 15-month associate program, $17,000; 6-month professional cooking diploma program, $8,500. Required fees $75 for both programs. Books and supplies are $225 for the diploma program and $1,050 for the associate program. Tuition at time of enrollment locked for 2 years.

FINANCIAL AID PICTURE

Students with need: Need-based aid available for full-time students.

FINANCIAL AID PROCEDURES

Forms required: FAFSA.

CONTACT

Gerald Connor, Financial Aid Director
1212 South Broad Street, Philadelphia, PA 19146
(215) 468-8800

Johnson College

Scranton, Pennsylvania
www.johnson.edu   Federal Code: 014734

2-year private technical college in small city.

Enrollment: 376 undergrads, 3% part-time. 156 full-time freshmen.

Selectivity: Open admission; but selective for some programs.

BASIC COSTS (2007-2008)

Tuition and fees: $13,858.

Per-credit charge: $350.

Room only: $3,400.

FINANCIAL AID PICTURE

Students with need: Need-based aid available for full-time and part-time students. Work study available nights, weekends, and for part-time students.

Students without need: No-need awards available for academics.

FINANCIAL AID PROCEDURES

Forms required: FAFSA, institutional form.

Dates and Deadlines: Priority date 4/28; no closing date. Applicants notified on a rolling basis starting 4/15; must reply within 2 week(s) of notification.

Transfers: Priority date 5/1.

CONTACT

Jo-Ann Orcutt, Director of Financial Aid

3427 North Main Avenue, Scranton, PA 18508

(570) 342-6404 ext. 126

Juniata College

Huntingdon, Pennsylvania

www.juniata.edu   Federal Code: 003279

4-year private liberal arts college in small town.

Enrollment: 1,410 undergrads, 1% part-time. 375 full-time freshmen.

Selectivity: Admits 50 to 75% of applicants.

BASIC COSTS (2008-2009)

Tuition and fees: $30,280.

Per-credit charge: $1,230.

Room and board: $8,420.

Additional info: Tuition/fee waivers available for adults.

FINANCIAL AID PICTURE (2007-2008)

Students with need: Out of 315 full-time freshmen who applied for aid, 271 were judged to have need. Of these, 271 received aid, and 94 had their full need met. Average financial aid package met 85% of need; average scholarship/grant was $17,666; average loan was $4,315. Need-based aid available for part-time students.

Students without need: 112 full-time freshmen who did not demonstrate need for aid received scholarships/grants; average award was $15,414. No-need awards available for academics, art.

Scholarships offered: Ron & Ann Wertz Arts Scholarship, Environmental Responsibility Scholarship, Richard M. Simpson Leadership Scholarship, J. Omar Good Service & Peacemaking Scholarship; full tuition; nominated by alumni, 1 awarded for each. Burkholder Scholarship; full tuition, room and board; 1 awarded. Friendship Scholarships; $2,000; awarded to international student. Calvert Ellis Scholarships; $15,000; based on high school GPA or SAT scores. Juniata Program for Area Residents Scholarships; half tuition; for area residents. Native American Indian Scholarship; up to $10,000. Ray Day Scholarship; up to $5,000; for a minority student. John & Irene Dale Scholarship; $3,000; for information technology student. Robert Steele Memorial Scholarship; up to $4,000; for medical/science student showing need. Metz Scholarship; up to $5,000; for intended major in business/economics. Anna Groninger Smith Memorial Scholarship; up to $4,000; for woman in business studies showing need. W & M Donham Scholarships; up to $2,000; for New England residents majoring in business/economics. Alumni Scholarships; up to $5,000; for children of alumni. Church of the Brethren Scholarships; up to $5,000; for Church of the Brethren members in various majors. Dorothy Baker Johnson Memorial Scholarship; up to $4,000; for women aiming for careers that require advanced degrees. Charles & Floretta Gibson scholarships; up to $4,000; for excellent character; based on need. Sam Hayes Jr. Scholarship; up to $1,500; for Pennsylvania FFA or 4H members; based on need. Frederick & Mary F. Beckley Scholarship; up to $5,000; for left-handed scholar. Heritage Scholarships; up to $8,000; for minority students with demonstrated commitment to leadership, community service and diversity.

Cumulative student debt: 84% of graduating class had student loans; average debt was $21,426.

FINANCIAL AID PROCEDURES

Forms required: FAFSA.

Dates and Deadlines: Closing date 3/1. Applicants notified on a rolling basis starting 2/21; must reply by 5/1.

CONTACT

Vincent Frank, Director of Student Financial Planning

1800 Moore Street, Huntingdon, PA 16652-2196

(814) 641-3142

Kaplan Career Institute: Pittsburgh

Pittsburgh, Pennsylvania

www.icmschool.com   Federal Code: 007436

2-year for-profit business and health science college in large city.

Enrollment: 827 undergrads.

BASIC COSTS (2008-2009)

Tuition and fees: $17,080.

Additional info: Tuition costs include books and supplies.

FINANCIAL AID PICTURE

Students with need: Need-based aid available for full-time and part-time students. Work study available nights.

Students without need: This college awards aid only to students with need.

FINANCIAL AID PROCEDURES

Forms required: FAFSA, state aid form, institutional form.

Dates and Deadlines: Closing date 4/30. Applicants notified on a rolling basis.

CONTACT

Christopher Fox, Director of Financial Aid

10 Wood Street, Pittsburgh, PA 15222

(412) 261-2647 ext. 265

Keystone College

La Plume, Pennsylvania

www.keystone.edu   Federal Code: 003280

4-year private junior and liberal arts college in small town.

Enrollment: 1,757 undergrads, 24% part-time. 339 full-time freshmen.

Selectivity: Admits over 75% of applicants.

BASIC COSTS (2007-2008)

Tuition and fees: $17,265.

Per-credit charge: $375.

Room and board: $8,400.

Additional info: Tuition/fee waivers available for adults.

FINANCIAL AID PICTURE (2006-2007)

Students with need: Average financial aid package met 70% of need; average scholarship/grant was $12,312; average loan was $2,625. For part-time students, average financial aid package was $2,325.

Students without need: 13 full-time freshmen who did not demonstrate need for aid received scholarships/grants; average award was $8,000. No-need awards available for academics, art, job skills, leadership, ROTC.

Scholarships offered: Academic Excellence Scholarship; one-half tuition up to full tuition; for all full-time, first-time students in the top 5% of their class with SAT scores of 1100 or above (exclusive of Writing). Presidential Scholarship; up to $6,500 each year; based on class rank and SAT/ACT scores. Trustee Scholarship; up to $6,000 each year; based on class rank and SAT/ACT scores. Leadership Award; up to $5,000 each year; students demonstrating non-athletic leadership skills in high school.

Cumulative student debt: 82% of graduating class had student loans; average debt was $21,125.

FINANCIAL AID PROCEDURES

Forms required: FAFSA, state aid form.

720 Pennsylvania Keystone College

Dates and Deadlines: Priority date 5/1; no closing date. Applicants notified on a rolling basis starting 2/2; must reply by 5/1 or within 2 week(s) of notification.

Transfers: Priority date 8/1; no deadline. Applicants notified on a rolling basis starting 11/1; must reply by 8/1 or within 3 week(s) of notification.

CONTACT
Ginger Kline, Director of Financial Aid
One College Green, La Plume, PA 18440-1099
(570) 945-8967

Keystone Technical Institute
Harrisburg, Pennsylvania
www.kti.edu   Federal Code: 022342

2-year for-profit health science and technical college in small city.
Enrollment: 282 undergrads.
Selectivity: Admits over 75% of applicants.

BASIC COSTS (2007-2008)
Tuition and fees: $13,006.

FINANCIAL AID PICTURE
Students with need: Need-based aid available for full-time and part-time students. Work study available nights.
Students without need: This college awards aid only to students with need.
Scholarships offered: Half-tuition scholarships; 13 available to degree-seeking students.

FINANCIAL AID PROCEDURES
Forms required: FAFSA, state aid form.
Dates and Deadlines: No deadline. Applicants notified on a rolling basis.
Transfers: State grant deadline for first-time recipients August 1. Renewal application deadline May 1.

CONTACT
Tracy Stewart, Financial Aid Coordinator
2301 Academy Drive, Harrisburg, PA 17112-1012
(717) 545-4747

King's College
Wilkes-Barre, Pennsylvania
www.kings.edu   Federal Code: 003282

4-year private business and liberal arts college in small city, affiliated with Roman Catholic Church.
Enrollment: 2,031 undergrads, 5% part-time. 557 full-time freshmen.
Selectivity: Admits over 75% of applicants.

BASIC COSTS (2008-2009)
Tuition and fees: $24,680.
Per-credit charge: $480.
Room and board: $9,370.

FINANCIAL AID PICTURE (2007-2008)
Students with need: Out of 523 full-time freshmen who applied for aid, 459 were judged to have need. Of these, 459 received aid, and 418 had their full need met. Average financial aid package met 78% of need; average scholarship/grant was $12,479; average loan was $4,140. For part-time students, average financial aid package was $5,680.
Students without need: 94 full-time freshmen who did not demonstrate need for aid received scholarships/grants; average award was $9,950. No-need awards available for academics, leadership, ROTC.
Cumulative student debt: 86% of graduating class had student loans; average debt was $28,139.

Additional info: Most minority students receive some aid in the form of a diversity scholarship.

FINANCIAL AID PROCEDURES
Forms required: FAFSA, institutional form.
Dates and Deadlines: Priority date 2/15; no closing date. Applicants notified on a rolling basis starting 3/1; must reply within 2 week(s) of notification.
Transfers: Priority date 2/1; no deadline. Applicants notified on a rolling basis; must reply by 5/1 or within 2 week(s) of notification.

CONTACT
Ellen McGuire, Director of Financial Aid
133 North River Street, Wilkes-Barre, PA 18711
(570) 208-5868

Kutztown University of Pennsylvania
Kutztown, Pennsylvania
www.kutztown.edu   Federal Code: 003322

4-year public university in small town.
Enrollment: 8,768 undergrads, 6% part-time. 1,967 full-time freshmen.
Selectivity: Admits 50 to 75% of applicants.

BASIC COSTS (2007-2008)
Tuition and fees: $6,873; out-of-state residents $14,640.
Per-credit charge: $216; out-of-state residents $539.
Room and board: $6,960.

FINANCIAL AID PICTURE (2006-2007)
Students with need: Out of 1,739 full-time freshmen who applied for aid, 1,212 were judged to have need. Of these, 1,212 received aid, and 611 had their full need met. Average financial aid package met 52% of need; average scholarship/grant was $4,917; average loan was $2,496. For part-time students, average financial aid package was $4,727.
Students without need: 87 full-time freshmen who did not demonstrate need for aid received scholarships/grants; average award was $1,829. No-need awards available for academics, art, athletics, leadership, minority status, music/drama, state/district residency.
Scholarships offered: 30 full-time freshmen received athletic scholarships; average amount $1,762.
Cumulative student debt: 82% of graduating class had student loans; average debt was $16,954.

FINANCIAL AID PROCEDURES
Forms required: FAFSA.
Dates and Deadlines: Priority date 2/15; no closing date. Applicants notified on a rolling basis starting 3/30; must reply by 5/1 or within 4 week(s) of notification.

CONTACT
Catherine McIntyre, Director of Financial Aid
Admissions Office, Kutztown, PA 19530-0730
(610) 683-4077

La Roche College
Pittsburgh, Pennsylvania
www.laroche.edu   Federal Code: 003987

4-year private liberal arts college in large city, affiliated with Roman Catholic Church.
Enrollment: 1,306 undergrads, 13% part-time. 295 full-time freshmen.
Selectivity: Admits 50 to 75% of applicants.

BASIC COSTS (2007-2008)
Tuition and fees: $19,270.
Per-credit charge: $557.

PART III: FINANCIAL AID COLLEGE BY COLLEGE

Room and board: $7,942.

FINANCIAL AID PICTURE (2007-2008)

Students with need: Out of 283 full-time freshmen who applied for aid, 283 were judged to have need. Of these, 281 received aid. Average financial aid package met 90% of need; average scholarship/grant was $3,090; average loan was $2,304. For part-time students, average financial aid package was $1,116.

Students without need: 12 full-time freshmen who did not demonstrate need for aid received scholarships/grants; average award was $6,468. No-need awards available for academics.

Cumulative student debt: 84% of graduating class had student loans; average debt was $18,750.

FINANCIAL AID PROCEDURES

Forms required: FAFSA.

Dates and Deadlines: Priority date 2/15; closing date 5/1. Applicants notified on a rolling basis starting 2/15; must reply within 2 week(s) of notification.

CONTACT

Sharon Platt, Director of Financial Aid
9000 Babcock Boulevard, Pittsburgh, PA 15237
(412) 536-1120

La Salle University

Philadelphia, Pennsylvania
www.lasalle.edu   Federal Code: 003287

4-year private university and liberal arts college in very large city, affiliated with Roman Catholic Church.

Enrollment: 4,024 undergrads, 22% part-time. 770 full-time freshmen.

Selectivity: Admits 50 to 75% of applicants.

BASIC COSTS (2008-2009)

Tuition and fees: $31,320.

Room and board: $10,690.

FINANCIAL AID PICTURE (2007-2008)

Students with need: Out of 690 full-time freshmen who applied for aid, 598 were judged to have need. Of these, 598 received aid, and 114 had their full need met. Average financial aid package met 73% of need; average scholarship/grant was $15,998; average loan was $3,762. For part-time students, average financial aid package was $6,915.

Students without need: 132 full-time freshmen who did not demonstrate need for aid received scholarships/grants; average award was $9,695. No-need awards available for academics, athletics, ROTC.

Scholarships offered: Merit: Christian Brothers Scholarship; full tuition; based on academics and extracurricular leadership. Community Service Scholarship; half tuition; based on involvement in community service and academics. Mission Grant; $4,000; for graduate of Catholic high school, 2.75 GPA or ranked in top 50% of class. **Athletic:** 41 full-time freshmen received athletic scholarships; average amount $10,276.

Cumulative student debt: 76% of graduating class had student loans; average debt was $32,794.

FINANCIAL AID PROCEDURES

Forms required: FAFSA.

Dates and Deadlines: Priority date 2/15; no closing date. Applicants notified on a rolling basis starting 3/15; must reply by 5/1 or within 2 week(s) of notification.

Transfers: Applicants notified on a rolling basis starting 3/15; must reply by 5/1 or within 2 week(s) of notification.

CONTACT

Michael Wisnieski, Director of Financial Aid
1900 West Olney Avenue, Philadelphia, PA 19141-1199
(215) 951-1070

Lackawanna College

Scranton, Pennsylvania
www.lackawanna.edu   Federal Code: 003283

2-year private junior college in small city.

Enrollment: 1,274 undergrads, 27% part-time. 266 full-time freshmen.

Selectivity: Open admission.

BASIC COSTS (2007-2008)

Tuition and fees: $10,150.

Per-credit charge: $335.

Room and board: $6,600.

FINANCIAL AID PICTURE (2007-2008)

Students with need: Average financial aid package met 61% of need; average scholarship/grant was $6,050; average loan was $3,376. For part-time students, average financial aid package was $5,847.

Students without need: No-need awards available for academics, athletics, leadership.

Cumulative student debt: 96% of graduating class had student loans; average debt was $13,128.

FINANCIAL AID PROCEDURES

Forms required: FAFSA, state aid form, institutional form.

Dates and Deadlines: Priority date 5/1; no closing date. Applicants notified on a rolling basis starting 5/1.

CONTACT

Babara Hapeman, Director of Financial Aid
501 Vine Street, Scranton, PA 18509
(570) 961-7859

Lafayette College

Easton, Pennsylvania   Federal Code: 003284
www.lafayette.edu   CSS Code: 2361

4-year private engineering and liberal arts college in large town, affiliated with Presbyterian Church (USA).

Enrollment: 2,366 undergrads, 1% part-time. 630 full-time freshmen.

Selectivity: Admits less than 50% of applicants.

BASIC COSTS (2008-2009)

Tuition and fees: $36,090.

Per-credit charge: $403.

Room and board: $11,248.

FINANCIAL AID PICTURE (2006-2007)

Students with need: Out of 442 full-time freshmen who applied for aid, 368 were judged to have need. Of these, 348 received aid, and 348 had their full need met. Average financial aid package met 100% of need; average scholarship/grant was $24,355; average loan was $3,606. For part-time students, average financial aid package was $5,080.

Students without need: 41 full-time freshmen who did not demonstrate need for aid received scholarships/grants; average award was $13,463. No-need awards available for academics, leadership, ROTC.

Scholarships offered: Merit: Marquis Scholarships; $16,000; based on academic merit. Trustee Scholarship; $8,000; based on academic merit; awarded to 15% of each entering class. **Athletic:** 6 full-time freshmen received athletic scholarships; average amount $42,412.

Cumulative student debt: 53% of graduating class had student loans; average debt was $18,452.

Additional info: Parent loans, up to $7,500 annually, available with college absorbing interest while student is enrolled. Family has 8 years after graduation to repay. Not limited to those demonstrating need.

FINANCIAL AID PROCEDURES

Forms required: FAFSA, CSS PROFILE.

Dates and Deadlines: Closing date 2/15. Applicants notified on a rolling basis starting 3/15; must reply by 5/1.
Transfers: Closing date 5/1.

CONTACT

Arlina DeNardo, Director of Student Financial Aid
118 Markle Hall, Easton, PA 18042-1770
(610) 330-5055

Lancaster Bible College

Lancaster, Pennsylvania
www.lbc.edu   Federal Code: 003285

4-year private Bible college in small city, affiliated with nondenominational tradition.
Enrollment: 655 undergrads, 14% part-time. 105 full-time freshmen.

BASIC COSTS (2007-2008)

Tuition and fees: $14,520.
Per-credit charge: $460.
Room and board: $6,170.

FINANCIAL AID PICTURE

Students with need: Need-based aid available for full-time and part-time students. Work study available nights, weekends, and for part-time students.
Students without need: No-need awards available for academics, alumni affiliation, leadership, music/drama, state/district residency.
Scholarships offered: Child of Full-time Christian Worker Scholarship; 50% reduction in tuition, room and board; available to dependent students where major wage earner or head of household is in full-time Christian work.

FINANCIAL AID PROCEDURES

Forms required: FAFSA, state aid form.
Dates and Deadlines: Priority date 5/1; no closing date. Applicants notified on a rolling basis starting 3/15; must reply within 3 week(s) of notification.

CONTACT

Karen Fox, Director of Financial Aid
901 Eden Road, Lancaster, PA 17608-3403
(717) 560-8254

Laurel Business Institute

Uniontown, Pennsylvania
www.laurel.edu   Federal Code: 017118

2-year for-profit technical college in large town.
Enrollment: 310 undergrads. 182 full-time freshmen.
Selectivity: Admits over 75% of applicants.

BASIC COSTS (2007-2008)

Additional info: Cost of 18-month associate program ranges from $17,005 to $25,000. Fees vary by program.

FINANCIAL AID PICTURE

Students with need: Need-based aid available for full-time and part-time students.
Students without need: This college awards aid only to students with need.
Scholarships offered: One full tuition, several half tuition (including GED scholarships); based on high school transcripts or GED scores, letters of reference, and personal interview.

FINANCIAL AID PROCEDURES

Forms required: FAFSA, institutional form.
Dates and Deadlines: Closing date 8/1. Applicants notified on a rolling basis; must reply within 4 week(s) of notification.
Transfers: No deadline. Must reply within 4 week(s) of notification.

CONTACT

Stephanie Migyanko, Director of Financial Aid
11 East Penn Street, Uniontown, PA 15401
(724) 439-4900

Lebanon Valley College

Annville, Pennsylvania
www.lvc.edu   Federal Code: 003288

4-year private liberal arts college in small town, affiliated with United Methodist Church.
Enrollment: 1,705 undergrads, 5% part-time. 451 full-time freshmen.
Selectivity: Admits 50 to 75% of applicants.

BASIC COSTS (2007-2008)

Tuition and fees: $27,800.
Per-credit charge: $475.
Room and board: $7,430.
Additional info: Tuition/fee waivers available for minority students.

FINANCIAL AID PICTURE (2007-2008)

Students with need: Out of 426 full-time freshmen who applied for aid, 375 were judged to have need. Of these, 374 received aid, and 130 had their full need met. Average financial aid package met 88% of need; average scholarship/grant was $17,087; average loan was $4,427. For part-time students, average financial aid package was $3,650.
Students without need: 62 full-time freshmen who did not demonstrate need for aid received scholarships/grants; average award was $11,932. No-need awards available for academics, alumni affiliation, music/drama.
Scholarships offered: Vickroy Scholarship; half tuition; automatic for admitted applicants in top 10% of graduating class. Leadership scholarship; one-third tuition; automatic for admitted applicants in top 20% of graduating class. Achievement Scholarship; one-quarter tuition; automatic for admitted applicants in top 30% of graduating class.
Cumulative student debt: 81% of graduating class had student loans; average debt was $27,566.

FINANCIAL AID PROCEDURES

Forms required: FAFSA, institutional form.
Dates and Deadlines: Priority date 3/1; no closing date. Applicants notified on a rolling basis starting 3/1; must reply by 5/1 or within 2 week(s) of notification.
Transfers: Must reply by 5/1 or within 2 week(s) of notification. Students transferring 15 or fewer credits are considered for scholarships on the same basis as high school seniors. Students transferring 16 or more credits are considered for scholarships based on their college academic performance and program.

CONTACT

Kendra Feigert, Director of Financial Aid
101 North College Avenue, Annville, PA 17003-1400
(717) 867-6181

Lehigh Carbon Community College

Schnecksville, Pennsylvania
www.lccc.edu   Federal Code: 006810

2-year public community college in small town.
Enrollment: 6,116 undergrads, 56% part-time. 1,110 full-time freshmen.
Selectivity: Open admission; but selective for some programs.

BASIC COSTS (2007-2008)

Tuition and fees: $2,850; out-of-district residents $5,520; out-of-state residents $8,190.

Per-credit charge: $80; out-of-district residents $169; out-of-state residents $243.

FINANCIAL AID PICTURE (2006-2007)

Students with need: Out of 720 full-time freshmen who applied for aid, 380 were judged to have need. Of these, 352 received aid. For part-time students, average financial aid package was $1,642.

Students without need: 257 full-time freshmen who did not demonstrate need for aid received scholarships/grants; average award was $589. No-need awards available for academics, state/district residency.

FINANCIAL AID PROCEDURES

Forms required: FAFSA.

Dates and Deadlines: No deadline. Applicants notified on a rolling basis starting 5/5; must reply within 2 week(s) of notification.

Transfers: No deadline. Applicants notified on a rolling basis.

CONTACT

Marian Snyder, Director of Financial Aid

4525 Education Park Drive, Schnecksville, PA 18078

(610) 799-1133

Lehigh University
Bethlehem, Pennsylvania
www.lehigh.edu
Federal Code: 003289
CSS Code: 2365

4-year private university in small city.

Enrollment: 4,732 undergrads, 2% part-time. 1,166 full-time freshmen.

Selectivity: Admits less than 50% of applicants.

BASIC COSTS (2008-2009)

Tuition and fees: $37,550.

Per-credit charge: $1,555.

Room and board: $9,770.

FINANCIAL AID PICTURE (2007-2008)

Students with need: Out of 709 full-time freshmen who applied for aid, 474 were judged to have need. Of these, 474 received aid, and 230 had their full need met. Average financial aid package met 97% of need; average scholarship/grant was $24,722; average loan was $3,375. For part-time students, average financial aid package was $28,074.

Students without need: 95 full-time freshmen who did not demonstrate need for aid received scholarships/grants; average award was $10,799. No-need awards available for academics, art, athletics, leadership, music/drama, ROTC.

Scholarships offered: *Merit:* Asa Packer Scholarships; $15,000; for exceptional academic and leadership skills. Dean's Scholarships; $10,000; for academic excellence and leadership skills. Baker Scholarship; $2,500; for excellence in music or theater and superior academic record. Choral Arts Scholarships; $2,500; for singing talent. *Athletic:* 7 full-time freshmen received athletic scholarships; average amount $43,690.

Cumulative student debt: 53% of graduating class had student loans; average debt was $26,768.

FINANCIAL AID PROCEDURES

Forms required: FAFSA, CSS PROFILE.

Dates and Deadlines: Closing date 2/1. Applicants notified by 3/30; must reply by 5/1 or within 3 week(s) of notification.

Transfers: Closing date 4/15. Applicants notified on a rolling basis; must reply within 3 week(s) of notification.

CONTACT

Linda Bell, Director of Financial Aid

27 Memorial Drive West, Bethlehem, PA 18015-3094

(610) 758-3181

Lincoln University
Lincoln University, Pennsylvania
www.lincoln.edu
Federal Code: 003290

4-year public university and liberal arts college in rural community.

Enrollment: 1,898 undergrads, 2% part-time. 630 full-time freshmen.

Selectivity: Admits less than 50% of applicants.

BASIC COSTS (2007-2008)

Tuition and fees: $7,762; out-of-state residents $12,190.

Per-credit charge: $228; out-of-state residents $388.

Room and board: $7,278.

Additional info: Out-of-state students pay additional $588 in fees.

FINANCIAL AID PICTURE (2007-2008)

Students with need: Out of 609 full-time freshmen who applied for aid, 564 were judged to have need. Of these, 556 received aid, and 37 had their full need met. Average financial aid package met 46% of need; average scholarship/grant was $5,863; average loan was $3,707. For part-time students, average financial aid package was $6,766.

Students without need: 29 full-time freshmen who did not demonstrate need for aid received scholarships/grants; average award was $5,518. No-need awards available for academics, alumni affiliation, leadership, music/drama.

Cumulative student debt: 84% of graduating class had student loans; average debt was $28,582.

FINANCIAL AID PROCEDURES

Forms required: FAFSA.

Dates and Deadlines: Closing date 5/1. Applicants notified on a rolling basis starting 4/1; must reply within 3 week(s) of notification.

CONTACT

Thelma Ross, Director of Financial Aid

PO Box 179, Lincoln University, PA 19352-0999

(800) 561-2606

Lock Haven University of Pennsylvania
Lock Haven, Pennsylvania
www.lhup.edu
Federal Code: 003323

4-year public university and liberal arts college in small town.

Enrollment: 4,779 undergrads, 6% part-time. 1,220 full-time freshmen.

Selectivity: Admits 50 to 75% of applicants.

BASIC COSTS (2007-2008)

Tuition and fees: $6,679; out-of-state residents $12,445.

Per-credit charge: $216; out-of-state residents $456.

Room and board: $6,188.

Additional info: Beginning Fall 2007, all freshmen are required to have a laptop computer for use in the classroom. Computers can be purchased through the university; cost of computer is not included in mandatory fees. The university has a small number of laptops available to students who cannot afford to make such a purchase. Tuition/fee waivers available for minority students.

FINANCIAL AID PICTURE (2007-2008)

Students with need: Out of 1,195 full-time freshmen who applied for aid, 932 were judged to have need. Of these, 932 received aid, and 419 had their full need met. Average financial aid package met 73% of need; average scholarship/grant was $5,182; average loan was $3,500. For part-time students, average financial aid package was $2,200.

Students without need: 45 full-time freshmen who did not demonstrate need for aid received scholarships/grants; average award was $932. No-need awards available for academics, art, athletics, leadership, minority status, music/drama, ROTC, state/district residency.

Scholarships offered: 54 full-time freshmen received athletic scholarships; average amount $3,158.

Cumulative student debt: 85% of graduating class had student loans; average debt was $22,407.

FINANCIAL AID PROCEDURES

Forms required: FAFSA.

Dates and Deadlines: Closing date 3/15. Applicants notified on a rolling basis starting 4/1; must reply within 2 week(s) of notification.

Transfers: Priority date 4/1.

CONTACT

James Theeuwes, Director of Student Financial Services
Akeley Hall, Lock Haven, PA 17745
(877) 405-3057

Luzerne County Community College
Nanticoke, Pennsylvania
www.luzerne.edu   Federal Code: 006811

2-year public community college in large town.

Enrollment: 6,007 undergrads, 47% part-time. 1,127 full-time freshmen.

Selectivity: Open admission; but selective for some programs.

BASIC COSTS (2007-2008)

Tuition and fees: $2,880; out-of-district residents $5,580; out-of-state residents $8,280.

Per-credit charge: $80; out-of-district residents $160; out-of-state residents $240.

FINANCIAL AID PICTURE

Students with need: Need-based aid available for full-time and part-time students.

FINANCIAL AID PROCEDURES

Forms required: FAFSA, institutional form.

Dates and Deadlines: Priority date 4/15; no closing date. Applicants notified on a rolling basis starting 7/1.

CONTACT

Mary Kosin, Director of Financial Aid
1333 South Prospect Street, Nanticoke, PA 18634-9804
(570) 740-0395

Lycoming College
Williamsport, Pennsylvania
www.lycoming.edu   Federal Code: 003293

4-year private liberal arts college in small city, affiliated with United Methodist Church.

Enrollment: 1,402 undergrads, 1% part-time. 400 full-time freshmen.

Selectivity: Admits over 75% of applicants.

BASIC COSTS (2007-2008)

Tuition and fees: $27,129.

Per-credit charge: $832.

Room and board: $7,238.

Additional info: Tuition/fee waivers available for minority students.

FINANCIAL AID PICTURE (2007-2008)

Students with need: Out of 366 full-time freshmen who applied for aid, 318 were judged to have need. Of these, 318 received aid, and 67 had their full need met. Average financial aid package met 83% of need; average scholarship/grant was $16,572; average loan was $4,399. For part-time students, average financial aid package was $11,860.

Students without need: 73 full-time freshmen who did not demonstrate need for aid received scholarships/grants; average award was $10,058. No-need awards available for academics, art, leadership, minority status, music/drama.

Cumulative student debt: 85% of graduating class had student loans; average debt was $26,538.

FINANCIAL AID PROCEDURES

Forms required: FAFSA, institutional form.

Dates and Deadlines: Priority date 3/1; no closing date. Applicants notified on a rolling basis starting 3/1; must reply by 5/1.

Transfers: No deadline.

CONTACT

Jamie Lowthert, Director of Financial Aid
700 College Place, Williamsport, PA 17701
(570) 321-4041

Manor College
Jenkintown, Pennsylvania
www.manor.edu   Federal Code: 003294

2-year private junior college in small town, affiliated with Ukrainian Catholic Church.

Enrollment: 768 undergrads, 41% part-time. 165 full-time freshmen.

Selectivity: Admits less than 50% of applicants.

BASIC COSTS (2007-2008)

Tuition and fees: $11,754.

Per-credit charge: $245.

Room and board: $5,510.

Additional info: Tuition for allied health program: $11,854; $335 per credit hour.

FINANCIAL AID PICTURE (2007-2008)

Students with need: Out of 151 full-time freshmen who applied for aid, 147 were judged to have need. Of these, 147 received aid, and 9 had their full need met. Average financial aid package met 32% of need; average scholarship/grant was $4,850; average loan was $3,025. For part-time students, average financial aid package was $4,680.

Students without need: 7 full-time freshmen who did not demonstrate need for aid received scholarships/grants; average award was $4,480. No-need awards available for academics, alumni affiliation, art.

Scholarships offered: *Merit:* Basilian Scholarship; for every freshman with A or B high school average and minimum 900 SAT (exclusive of writing). *Athletic:* 27 full-time freshmen received athletic scholarships; average amount $1,618.

Cumulative student debt: 97% of graduating class had student loans; average debt was $8,000.

FINANCIAL AID PROCEDURES

Forms required: FAFSA.

Dates and Deadlines: Priority date 4/1; no closing date. Applicants notified on a rolling basis starting 3/1; must reply within 2 week(s) of notification.

Transfers: No deadline. Applicants notified on a rolling basis starting 12/1; must reply within 2 week(s) of notification. Require academic transcript prior to packaging financial aid.

CONTACT

Peter Lysionek, Director of Financial Aid
700 Fox Chase Road, Jenkintown, PA 19046-3319
(215) 884-6051

Mansfield University of Pennsylvania

Mansfield, Pennsylvania
www.mansfield.edu   Federal Code: 003324

4-year public university and liberal arts college in small town.

Enrollment: 2,849 undergrads, 7% part-time. 669 full-time freshmen.

Selectivity: Admits 50 to 75% of applicants.

BASIC COSTS (2007-2008)

Tuition and fees: $6,979; out-of-state residents $14,746.

Per-credit charge: $216; out-of-state residents $539.

Room and board: $6,236.

Additional info: Tuition for NY residents is $8,544.

FINANCIAL AID PICTURE (2006-2007)

Students with need: Average financial aid package met 68% of need; average scholarship/grant was $4,065; average loan was $2,733. For part-time students, average financial aid package was $2,364.

Students without need: 54 full-time freshmen who did not demonstrate need for aid received scholarships/grants; average award was $1,858. No-need awards available for academics, art, athletics, leadership, music/drama, state/district residency.

Scholarships offered: 11 full-time freshmen received athletic scholarships; average amount $2,529.

Cumulative student debt: 74% of graduating class had student loans; average debt was $19,262.

FINANCIAL AID PROCEDURES

Forms required: FAFSA, institutional form.

Dates and Deadlines: Priority date 3/15; no closing date. Applicants notified on a rolling basis starting 3/15; must reply within 2 week(s) of notification.

CONTACT

Barbara Schmitt, Director of Financial Aid
Alumni Hall, Mansfield, PA 16933
(570) 662-4129

Marywood University

Scranton, Pennsylvania
www.marywood.edu   Federal Code: 003296

4-year private university in small city, affiliated with Roman Catholic Church.

Enrollment: 1,950 undergrads, 6% part-time. 408 full-time freshmen.

Selectivity: Admits 50 to 75% of applicants.

BASIC COSTS (2008-2009)

Tuition and fees: $25,390.

Room and board: $11,108.

FINANCIAL AID PICTURE (2007-2008)

Students with need: Out of 381 full-time freshmen who applied for aid, 330 were judged to have need. Of these, 329 received aid, and 87 had their full need met. Average financial aid package met 84% of need; average scholarship/grant was $14,835; average loan was $3,657. For part-time students, average financial aid package was $7,326.

Students without need: 72 full-time freshmen who did not demonstrate need for aid received scholarships/grants; average award was $10,255. No-need awards available for academics, alumni affiliation, art, leadership, minority status, music/drama.

Scholarships offered: Presidential Scholarships; full tuition; 1300 SAT and rank in upper 10% of graduating class. IHM Scholarships; 1150 SAT and rank in the upper 5% of high school class. Marywood Grants; for students with demonstrated academic ability. Talent Awards; for students who demonstrate proficiency and major in music, art, or theater. Other non-need-based merit scholarships available. SAT scores exclusive of Writing.

Cumulative student debt: 94% of graduating class had student loans; average debt was $31,346.

FINANCIAL AID PROCEDURES

Forms required: FAFSA.

Dates and Deadlines: Priority date 2/15; no closing date. Applicants notified on a rolling basis starting 2/15; must reply by 5/1 or within 3 week(s) of notification.

CONTACT

Stanley Skrutski, Director of Financial Aid
2300 Adams Avenue, Scranton, PA 18509-1598
(570) 348-6225

Mercyhurst College

Erie, Pennsylvania
www.mercyhurst.edu   Federal Code: 003297

4-year private liberal arts college in small city, affiliated with Roman Catholic Church.

Enrollment: 3,921 undergrads, 10% part-time. 670 full-time freshmen.

Selectivity: Admits 50 to 75% of applicants.

BASIC COSTS (2007-2008)

Tuition and fees: $21,876.

Per-credit charge: $679.

Room and board: $7,800.

Additional info: Tuition/fee waivers available for adults, minority students, unemployed or children of unemployed.

FINANCIAL AID PICTURE

Students with need: Need-based aid available for full-time and part-time students. Work study available nights, weekends, and for part-time students.

Students without need: No-need awards available for academics, alumni affiliation, art, athletics, leadership, minority status, music/drama, religious affiliation, ROTC.

FINANCIAL AID PROCEDURES

Forms required: FAFSA.

Dates and Deadlines: Priority date 3/1; no closing date. Applicants notified on a rolling basis starting 2/15; must reply by 5/1 or within 2 week(s) of notification.

Transfers: No deadline. Applicants notified on a rolling basis; must reply within 2 week(s) of notification.

CONTACT

Kathy Bialk, Director of Student Financial Services
501 East 38th Street, Erie, PA 16546-0001
(814) 824-2288

Messiah College

Grantham, Pennsylvania
www.messiah.edu   Federal Code: 003298

4-year private liberal arts college in small town, affiliated with interdenominational tradition.

Enrollment: 2,798 undergrads, 1% part-time. 723 full-time freshmen.

Selectivity: Admits over 75% of applicants.

BASIC COSTS (2008-2009)

Tuition and fees: $25,670.

Per-credit charge: $1,040.

Room and board: $7,610.

Additional info: Tuition/fee waivers available for adults.

FINANCIAL AID PICTURE (2007-2008)

Students with need: Out of 606 full-time freshmen who applied for aid, 516 were judged to have need. Of these, 516 received aid, and 112 had their full need met. Average financial aid package met 75% of need; average scholarship/grant was $12,374; average loan was $3,758. For part-time students, average financial aid package was $7,195.

Students without need: 199 full-time freshmen who did not demonstrate need for aid received scholarships/grants; average award was $8,329. No-need awards available for academics, art, leadership, music/drama, religious affiliation.

Cumulative student debt: 73% of graduating class had student loans; average debt was $33,283.

FINANCIAL AID PROCEDURES

Forms required: FAFSA.

Dates and Deadlines: Priority date 4/1; no closing date. Applicants notified on a rolling basis starting 3/15; must reply by 5/1 or within 4 week(s) of notification.

CONTACT

Greg Gearhart, Director of Financial Aid
PO Box 3005, Grantham, PA 17027-0800
(717) 691-6007

Millersville University of Pennsylvania
Millersville, Pennsylvania
www.millersville.edu   Federal Code: 003325

4-year public university and liberal arts college in small town.

Enrollment: 7,164 undergrads, 8% part-time. 1,341 full-time freshmen.

Selectivity: Admits 50 to 75% of applicants.

BASIC COSTS (2007-2008)

Tuition and fees: $6,624; out-of-state residents $14,391.

Per-credit charge: $216; out-of-state residents $539.

Room and board: $6,876.

FINANCIAL AID PICTURE (2006-2007)

Students with need: Out of 1,158 full-time freshmen who applied for aid, 758 were judged to have need. Of these, 734 received aid, and 100 had their full need met. Average financial aid package met 69% of need; average scholarship/grant was $4,868; average loan was $2,505. For part-time students, average financial aid package was $5,499.

Students without need: 38 full-time freshmen who did not demonstrate need for aid received scholarships/grants; average award was $3,326. No-need awards available for academics, athletics, minority status.

Scholarships offered: 16 full-time freshmen received athletic scholarships; average amount $1,600.

Cumulative student debt: 64% of graduating class had student loans; average debt was $19,555.

FINANCIAL AID PROCEDURES

Forms required: FAFSA.

Dates and Deadlines: Closing date 3/15. Applicants notified on a rolling basis starting 3/19; must reply within 2 week(s) of notification.

Transfers: No deadline. Applicants notified on a rolling basis.

CONTACT

Dwight Horsey, Director of Financial Aid
PO Box 1002, Millersville, PA 17551-0302
(717) 872-3026

Misericordia University
Dallas, Pennsylvania
www.misericordia.edu   Federal Code: 003247

4-year private health science and liberal arts college in large town, affiliated with Roman Catholic Church.

Enrollment: 2,003 undergrads, 26% part-time. 364 full-time freshmen.

Selectivity: Admits 50 to 75% of applicants.

BASIC COSTS (2008-2009)

Tuition and fees: $23,150.

Per-credit charge: $450.

Room and board: $9,650.

Additional info: Tuition/fee waivers available for adults.

FINANCIAL AID PICTURE (2007-2008)

Students with need: Out of 352 full-time freshmen who applied for aid, 308 were judged to have need. Of these, 308 received aid, and 47 had their full need met. Average financial aid package met 73% of need; average scholarship/grant was $11,435; average loan was $4,753. For part-time students, average financial aid package was $3,866.

Students without need: 43 full-time freshmen who did not demonstrate need for aid received scholarships/grants; average award was $6,613. No-need awards available for academics, alumni affiliation, leadership, minority status, state/district residency.

Scholarships offered: McAuley Award; $1,000-$5,000 per year; based on out-of-classroom activities. Partnership Scholarship; $2,500 per year; for students interested in specific careers. Academic Scholarship; $2,000-$15,000 per year; based on academic abilities.

Cumulative student debt: 77% of graduating class had student loans; average debt was $20,006.

FINANCIAL AID PROCEDURES

Forms required: FAFSA, institutional form.

Dates and Deadlines: Priority date 3/1; closing date 5/1. Applicants notified on a rolling basis starting 3/15; must reply by 5/1.

Transfers: No deadline. Applicants notified on a rolling basis starting 3/15.

CONTACT

Jane Dessoye, Executive Director of Enrollment Management
301 Lake Street, Dallas, PA 18612-1098
(570) 674-6280

Montgomery County Community College
Blue Bell, Pennsylvania
www.mc3.edu   Federal Code: 004452

2-year public community college in large town.

Enrollment: 11,592 undergrads, 56% part-time. 2,240 full-time freshmen.

Selectivity: Open admission; but selective for some programs.

BASIC COSTS (2008-2009)

Tuition and fees: $3,090; out-of-district residents $6,030; out-of-state residents $8,970.

Per-credit charge: $88; out-of-district residents $176; out-of-state residents $264.

Additional info: In-state, out-of-district tuition and out-of-state tuition both include additional fees per credit hour.

FINANCIAL AID PICTURE (2006-2007)

Students with need: Out of 879 full-time freshmen who applied for aid, 685 were judged to have need. Of these, 612 received aid, and 47 had their full need met. Average financial aid package met 15% of need; average scholarship/grant was $1,941; average loan was $1,656. For part-time students, average financial aid package was $2,788.

Students without need: 137 full-time freshmen who did not demonstrate need for aid received scholarships/grants; average award was $1,798. No-need awards available for academics.

FINANCIAL AID PROCEDURES

Forms required: FAFSA.
Dates and Deadlines: Priority date 5/1; no closing date. Applicants notified on a rolling basis starting 2/1.
Transfers: No deadline.

CONTACT

Cindy Haney, Director of Financial Aid
340 DeKalb Pike, Blue Bell, PA 19422
(215) 641-6566

Moore College of Art and Design

Philadelphia, Pennsylvania
www.moore.edu   Federal Code: 003300

4-year private visual arts college for women in very large city.
Enrollment: 557 undergrads.
Selectivity: Admits 50 to 75% of applicants.

BASIC COSTS (2008-2009)

Tuition and fees: $27,724.
Room and board: $10,500.

FINANCIAL AID PICTURE

Students with need: Need-based aid available for full-time and part-time students.
Students without need: No-need awards available for academics, art, leadership.

FINANCIAL AID PROCEDURES

Forms required: FAFSA.
Dates and Deadlines: Priority date 3/1; closing date 5/1. Applicants notified on a rolling basis starting 2/15; must reply within 2 week(s) of notification.
Transfers: Priority date 5/1; no deadline.

CONTACT

Kathleen Ellis-Foultz, Director of Financial Aid
The Parkway at 20th Street, Philadelphia, PA 19103-1179
(215) 568-4515

Moravian College

Bethlehem, Pennsylvania   Federal Code: 003301
www.moravian.edu   CSS Code: 2418

4-year private liberal arts college in small city, affiliated with Moravian Church in America.
Enrollment: 1,661 undergrads, 5% part-time. 401 full-time freshmen.
Selectivity: Admits 50 to 75% of applicants.

BASIC COSTS (2008-2009)

Tuition and fees: $30,062.
Per-credit charge: $821.
Room and board: $8,312.

FINANCIAL AID PICTURE (2007-2008)

Students with need: Out of 351 full-time freshmen who applied for aid, 303 were judged to have need. Of these, 303 received aid, and 41 had their full need met. Average financial aid package met 83% of need; average scholarship/grant was $16,505; average loan was $4,271. For part-time students, average financial aid package was $13,933.
Students without need: 78 full-time freshmen who did not demonstrate need for aid received scholarships/grants; average award was $13,064. No-

need awards available for academics, alumni affiliation, leadership, music/drama, religious affiliation, ROTC.
Scholarships offered: Comenius Scholarship; $10,000 to full tuition; top 10% of high school class and minimum 1850 SAT required. Founders Scholarship; $4,000-$8,000; for top 25% or 1700 SAT. Trustee Scholarship; $6,000-$10,000; must be National Honor Society member, in top 20% of class. All scholarships require at least 500 on each section of SAT. Other scholarships available based on interest in the sciences, leadership and interest in promoting diversity and/or challenging circumstances in attending college.

FINANCIAL AID PROCEDURES

Forms required: FAFSA, CSS PROFILE.
Dates and Deadlines: Priority date 2/14; closing date 3/15. Applicants notified on a rolling basis starting 4/1; must reply by 5/1 or within 2 week(s) of notification.
Transfers: Priority date 3/15; closing date 5/1. Applicants notified on a rolling basis starting 4/1.

CONTACT

Stephen Cassel, Director of Financial Aid
1200 Main Street, Bethlehem, PA 18018
(610) 861-1330

Mount Aloysius College

Cresson, Pennsylvania
www.mtaloy.edu   Federal Code: 003302

4-year private liberal arts college in small town, affiliated with Roman Catholic Church.
Enrollment: 1,483 undergrads, 22% part-time. 309 full-time freshmen.
Selectivity: Admits over 75% of applicants.

BASIC COSTS (2007-2008)

Tuition and fees: $15,990.
Per-credit charge: $450.
Room and board: $7,700.
Additional info: Tuition/fee waivers available for unemployed or children of unemployed.

FINANCIAL AID PICTURE (2006-2007)

Students with need: Out of 309 full-time freshmen who applied for aid, 274 were judged to have need. Of these, 274 received aid. Average financial aid package met 23% of need; average scholarship/grant was $2,120; average loan was $2,394. For part-time students, average financial aid package was $4,505.
Students without need: 35 full-time freshmen who did not demonstrate need for aid received scholarships/grants; average award was $2,350. No-need awards available for academics, art, leadership, music/drama, religious affiliation.
Cumulative student debt: 80% of graduating class had student loans; average debt was $23,672.

FINANCIAL AID PROCEDURES

Forms required: FAFSA.
Dates and Deadlines: Priority date 2/15; no closing date. Applicants notified on a rolling basis starting 3/15; must reply within 4 week(s) of notification.
Transfers: No deadline.

CONTACT

Stacy Schenk, Financial Aid Director
7373 Admiral Peary Highway, Cresson, PA 16630
(814) 886-6357

Muhlenberg College

Allentown, Pennsylvania   Federal Code: 003304
www.muhlenberg.edu   CSS Code: 2424

4-year private liberal arts college in small city, affiliated with Evangelical Lutheran Church in America.

Enrollment: 2,324 undergrads, 4% part-time. 551 full-time freshmen.
Selectivity: Admits less than 50% of applicants.

BASIC COSTS (2008-2009)
Tuition and fees: $35,375.
Room and board: $8,060.

FINANCIAL AID PICTURE (2007-2008)
Students with need: Out of 339 full-time freshmen who applied for aid, 234 were judged to have need. Of these, 234 received aid, and 216 had their full need met. Average financial aid package met 91% of need; average scholarship/grant was $19,116; average loan was $3,398. For part-time students, average financial aid package was $6,409.
Students without need: 171 full-time freshmen who did not demonstrate need for aid received scholarships/grants; average award was $10,585. No-need awards available for academics, art, leadership, music/drama.
Cumulative student debt: 81% of graduating class had student loans; average debt was $18,052.

FINANCIAL AID PROCEDURES
Forms required: FAFSA, CSS PROFILE, institutional form.
Dates and Deadlines: Closing date 2/15. Applicants notified by 4/1; must reply by 5/1.
Transfers: Closing date 4/15. Transfers awarded aid on a funds-available basis after returning students and freshmen have been served.

CONTACT
Gregory Mitton, Director of Financial Aid
2400 Chew Street, Allentown, PA 18104
(484) 664-3175

Neumann College

Aston, Pennsylvania
www.neumann.edu   Federal Code: 003988

4-year private liberal arts college in large town, affiliated with Roman Catholic Church.

Enrollment: 2,499 undergrads, 21% part-time. 544 full-time freshmen.
Selectivity: Admits over 75% of applicants.

BASIC COSTS (2007-2008)
Tuition and fees: $19,486.
Per-credit charge: $431.
Room and board: $8,838.

FINANCIAL AID PICTURE (2006-2007)
Students with need: Out of 490 full-time freshmen who applied for aid, 490 were judged to have need. Of these, 490 received aid, and 320 had their full need met.
Students without need: This college awards aid only to students with need.
Cumulative student debt: 70% of graduating class had student loans; average debt was $20,000.

FINANCIAL AID PROCEDURES
Forms required: FAFSA.
Dates and Deadlines: No deadline. Applicants notified on a rolling basis; must reply within 2 week(s) of notification.
Transfers: Priority date 3/7; closing date 6/1. Must reply within 2 week(s) of notification.

CONTACT
Katharine Markert, Director of Financial Aid
One Neumann Drive, Aston, PA 19014-1298
(610) 558-5520

New Castle School of Trades

Pulaski, Pennsylvania
www.ncstrades.com   Federal Code: 007780

2-year for-profit technical college in rural community.
Enrollment: 380 undergrads.
Selectivity: Admits over 75% of applicants.

BASIC COSTS (2007-2008)
Additional info: Tuition varies by program from $4,838 to $16,950. Costs include fees. Books and tool expenses additional, up to $2,672.

FINANCIAL AID PICTURE
Students with need: Need-based aid available for full-time and part-time students.

CONTACT
Trudy Sotter, Financial Aid
4164 US 422, Pulaski, PA 16143-9721
(724) 964-8811

Newport Business Institute: Lower Burrell

Lower Burrell, Pennsylvania
www.newportbusiness.com   Federal Code: 004901

2-year for-profit business college in small town.
Enrollment: 85 undergrads.
Selectivity: Open admission.

BASIC COSTS (2007-2008)
Tuition and fees: $9,525.

FINANCIAL AID PICTURE
Students with need: Need-based aid available for full-time and part-time students.
Students without need: No-need awards available for academics, leadership.

FINANCIAL AID PROCEDURES
Forms required: FAFSA, state aid form.
Dates and Deadlines: Closing date 5/1. Applicants notified on a rolling basis starting 5/1.

CONTACT
Rosemary Leipertz, Director of Financial Aid
945 Greensburg Road, Lower Burrell, PA 15068
(724) 339-7542

Northampton Community College

Bethlehem, Pennsylvania
www.northampton.edu   Federal Code: 007191

2-year public community college in small city.
Enrollment: 9,319 undergrads, 55% part-time. 1,578 full-time freshmen.
Selectivity: Open admission; but selective for some programs.

BASIC COSTS (2007-2008)
Tuition and fees: $3,000; out-of-district residents $5,190; out-of-state residents $7,380.

Per-credit charge: $73; out-of-district residents $146; out-of-state residents $219.
Room and board: $6,352.

FINANCIAL AID PICTURE (2007-2008)
Students with need: Average financial aid package for all full-time undergraduates was $2,780; for part-time $1,390. 72% awarded as scholarships/grants, 28% awarded as loans/jobs. Work study available nights, weekends, and for part-time students.
Students without need: No-need awards available for academics, alumni affiliation, art, leadership, minority status, music/drama.

FINANCIAL AID PROCEDURES
Forms required: FAFSA, institutional form.
Dates and Deadlines: Priority date 3/31; no closing date. Applicants notified on a rolling basis starting 6/1; must reply within 2 week(s) of notification.

CONTACT
Cindy King, Director of Financial Aid
3835 Green Pond Road, Bethlehem, PA 18020
(610) 861-5510

Oakbridge Academy of Arts
Lower Burrell, Pennsylvania
www.oaa.edu   Federal Code: 015063

2-year for-profit visual arts college in large town.
Enrollment: 55 undergrads.
Selectivity: Admits over 75% of applicants.

BASIC COSTS (2008-2009)
Tuition and fees: $9,750.

FINANCIAL AID PICTURE
Students with need: Need-based aid available for full-time and part-time students.
Students without need: This college awards aid only to students with need.
Scholarships offered: Jeanne H. Mullen art scholarship; half tuition; based on portfolio; 2 awarded per year.

FINANCIAL AID PROCEDURES
Forms required: FAFSA, state aid form.
Dates and Deadlines: Closing date 5/1. Applicants notified on a rolling basis.

CONTACT
Rosemary Leipertz, Financial Aid Director
1250 Greensburg Road, Lower Burrell, PA 15068
(724) 335-5336

Orleans Technical Institute - Center City Campus
Philadelphia, Pennsylvania
www.orleanstech.edu

2-year private technical college in very large city.
Enrollment: 365 full-time undergrads.
Selectivity: Open admission.

BASIC COSTS (2007-2008)
Additional info: Tuition for full associate program (3 years, including internship) is $32,000.

FINANCIAL AID PICTURE
Students with need: Need-based aid available for full-time and part-time students.

FINANCIAL AID PROCEDURES
Forms required: FAFSA, institutional form.
Dates and Deadlines: No deadline. Applicants notified on a rolling basis.

CONTACT
Latanya Byrd, Financial Aid Director
2770 Red Lion Road, Philadelphia, PA 19114
(215) 854-1822

Peirce College
Philadelphia, Pennsylvania
www.peirce.edu   Federal Code: 003309

4-year private business and technical college in very large city.
Enrollment: 2,172 undergrads, 59% part-time. 20 full-time freshmen.
Selectivity: Open admission.

BASIC COSTS (2007-2008)
Tuition and fees: $13,750.
Per-credit charge: $425.

FINANCIAL AID PICTURE (2006-2007)
Students with need: Out of 18 full-time freshmen who applied for aid, 18 were judged to have need. Of these, 18 received aid, and 16 had their full need met. Average financial aid package met 90% of need; average scholarship/grant was $5,252; average loan was $2,236. For part-time students, average financial aid package was $3,153.
Students without need: No-need awards available for academics, leadership.
Cumulative student debt: 82% of graduating class had student loans; average debt was $17,689.
Additional info: Tuition discounts available for US students serving in US military and in protect-and-serve fields.

FINANCIAL AID PROCEDURES
Forms required: FAFSA.
Dates and Deadlines: Priority date 6/1; no closing date. Applicants notified on a rolling basis; must reply within 3 week(s) of notification.

CONTACT
Lisa Gargiulo, Manager, Student Financial Services
1420 Pine Street, Philadelphia, PA 19102-4699
(888) 467-3472 ext. 9370

Penn State Abington
Abington, Pennsylvania
www.abington.psu.edu   Federal Code: 003329

4-year public branch campus college in small city.
Enrollment: 2,902 undergrads, 13% part-time. 863 full-time freshmen.
Selectivity: Admits over 75% of applicants.

BASIC COSTS (2007-2008)
Tuition and fees: $11,006; out-of-state residents $16,506.
Per-credit charge: $423; out-of-state residents $665.

FINANCIAL AID PICTURE (2006-2007)
Students with need: Out of 725 full-time freshmen who applied for aid, 559 were judged to have need. Of these, 548 received aid, and 27 had their full need met. Average financial aid package met 68% of need; average scholarship/grant was $6,317; average loan was $2,557. For part-time students, average financial aid package was $5,426.
Students without need: 40 full-time freshmen who did not demonstrate need for aid received scholarships/grants; average award was $1,800. No-need awards available for academics, alumni affiliation, athletics, ROTC.

Cumulative student debt: 67% of graduating class had student loans; average debt was $26,300.

FINANCIAL AID PROCEDURES

Forms required: FAFSA.

Dates and Deadlines: Priority date 2/15; no closing date. Applicants notified on a rolling basis starting 3/1.

Transfers: Closing date 5/1. Schools required to obtain student aid information through National Student Loan Data System (NSLDS).

CONTACT

Anna Griswold, Assistant Vice Provost for Student Aid
201 Shields Building, University Park, PA 16802-1294
(814) 865-6301

Penn State Altoona
Altoona, Pennsylvania
www.aa.psu.edu   Federal Code: 003329

4-year public branch campus college in small city.

Enrollment: 3,854 undergrads, 5% part-time. 1,477 full-time freshmen.

Selectivity: Admits 50 to 75% of applicants.

BASIC COSTS (2007-2008)

Tuition and fees: $11,464; out-of-state residents $17,246.

Per-credit charge: $455; out-of-state residents $696.

Room and board: $7,750.

FINANCIAL AID PICTURE (2006-2007)

Students with need: Out of 1,203 full-time freshmen who applied for aid, 924 were judged to have need. Of these, 886 received aid, and 52 had their full need met. Average financial aid package met 63% of need; average scholarship/grant was $5,387; average loan was $2,751. For part-time students, average financial aid package was $6,840.

Students without need: 30 full-time freshmen who did not demonstrate need for aid received scholarships/grants; average award was $687. No-need awards available for academics, alumni affiliation, athletics, ROTC.

Cumulative student debt: 67% of graduating class had student loans; average debt was $26,300.

FINANCIAL AID PROCEDURES

Forms required: FAFSA.

Dates and Deadlines: Priority date 2/15; no closing date. Applicants notified on a rolling basis starting 3/1.

Transfers: Closing date 5/1. Schools required to obtain student aid information through National Student Loan Data System (NSLDS).

CONTACT

Anna Griswold, Assistant Vice Provost for Student Aid
201 Shields Building, University Park, PA 16802-1294
(814) 865-6301

Penn State Beaver
Monaca, Pennsylvania
www.br.psu.edu   Federal Code: 003329

4-year public branch campus college in small town.

Enrollment: 697 undergrads, 6% part-time. 240 full-time freshmen.

Selectivity: Admits over 75% of applicants.

BASIC COSTS (2007-2008)

Tuition and fees: $11,006; out-of-state residents $16,506.

Per-credit charge: $423; out-of-state residents $665.

Room and board: $7,750.

FINANCIAL AID PICTURE (2006-2007)

Students with need: Out of 218 full-time freshmen who applied for aid, 174 were judged to have need. Of these, 172 received aid, and 6 had their full need met. Average financial aid package met 71% of need; average scholarship/grant was $5,555; average loan was $2,669. For part-time students, average financial aid package was $5,338.

Students without need: 28 full-time freshmen who did not demonstrate need for aid received scholarships/grants; average award was $1,732. No-need awards available for academics, alumni affiliation, athletics, ROTC.

Cumulative student debt: 67% of graduating class had student loans; average debt was $26,300.

FINANCIAL AID PROCEDURES

Forms required: FAFSA.

Dates and Deadlines: Priority date 2/15; no closing date. Applicants notified on a rolling basis starting 3/1.

Transfers: Closing date 5/1. Schools required to obtain student aid information through National Student Loan Data System (NSLDS).

CONTACT

Anna Griswold, Assistant Vice Provost for Student Aid
201 Shields Building, University Park, PA 16802-1294
(814) 865-6301

Penn State Berks
Reading, Pennsylvania
www.bk.psu.edu   Federal Code: 003329

4-year public branch campus college in small city.

Enrollment: 2,557 undergrads, 8% part-time. 952 full-time freshmen.

Selectivity: Admits over 75% of applicants.

BASIC COSTS (2007-2008)

Tuition and fees: $11,464; out-of-state residents $17,246.

Per-credit charge: $455; out-of-state residents $696.

Room and board: $8,420.

FINANCIAL AID PICTURE (2006-2007)

Students with need: Out of 776 full-time freshmen who applied for aid, 544 were judged to have need. Of these, 530 received aid, and 14 had their full need met. Average financial aid package met 61% of need; average scholarship/grant was $5,447; average loan was $2,668. For part-time students, average financial aid package was $5,918.

Students without need: 9 full-time freshmen who did not demonstrate need for aid received scholarships/grants; average award was $590. No-need awards available for academics, alumni affiliation, athletics, ROTC.

Cumulative student debt: 67% of graduating class had student loans; average debt was $26,300.

FINANCIAL AID PROCEDURES

Forms required: FAFSA.

Dates and Deadlines: Priority date 2/15; no closing date. Applicants notified on a rolling basis starting 3/1.

Transfers: Closing date 5/1. Schools required to obtain student aid information through National Student Loan Data System (NSLDS).

CONTACT

Anna Griswold, Assistant Vice Provost for Student Aid
201 Shields Building, University Park, PA 16802-1294
(814) 865-6301

PART III: FINANCIAL AID COLLEGE BY COLLEGE

Penn State Brandywine
Media, Pennsylvania
www.de.psu.edu Federal Code: 006922

4-year public branch campus college in small town.
Enrollment: 1,455 undergrads, 10% part-time. 459 full-time freshmen.
Selectivity: Admits over 75% of applicants.

BASIC COSTS (2007-2008)
Tuition and fees: $11,006; out-of-state residents $16,506.
Per-credit charge: $423; out-of-state residents $665.

FINANCIAL AID PICTURE (2006-2007)
Students with need: Out of 386 full-time freshmen who applied for aid, 272 were judged to have need. Of these, 263 received aid, and 20 had their full need met. Average financial aid package met 69% of need; average scholarship/grant was $5,922; average loan was $2,351. For part-time students, average financial aid package was $5,097.
Students without need: 41 full-time freshmen who did not demonstrate need for aid received scholarships/grants; average award was $2,500. No-need awards available for academics, alumni affiliation, athletics, ROTC.
Cumulative student debt: 67% of graduating class had student loans; average debt was $26,300.

FINANCIAL AID PROCEDURES
Forms required: FAFSA.
Dates and Deadlines: Priority date 2/15; no closing date. Applicants notified on a rolling basis starting 3/1.
Transfers: Closing date 5/1. Schools required to obtain student aid information through National Student Loan Data System (NSLDS).

CONTACT
Anna Griswold, Assistant Vice Provost for Student Aid
201 Shields Building, University Park, PA 16802-1294
(814) 865-6301

Penn State Dubois
DuBois, Pennsylvania
www.ds.psu.edu Federal Code: 003335

4-year public branch campus college in small town.
Enrollment: 724 undergrads, 15% part-time. 185 full-time freshmen.
Selectivity: Admits over 75% of applicants.

BASIC COSTS (2007-2008)
Tuition and fees: $10,996; out-of-state residents $16,496.
Per-credit charge: $423; out-of-state residents $665.

FINANCIAL AID PICTURE (2006-2007)
Students with need: Out of 176 full-time freshmen who applied for aid, 151 were judged to have need. Of these, 148 received aid, and 10 had their full need met. Average financial aid package met 65% of need; average scholarship/grant was $5,363; average loan was $2,555. For part-time students, average financial aid package was $6,421.
Students without need: 7 full-time freshmen who did not demonstrate need for aid received scholarships/grants; average award was $2,107. No-need awards available for academics, alumni affiliation, athletics, ROTC.
Cumulative student debt: 67% of graduating class had student loans; average debt was $26,300.

FINANCIAL AID PROCEDURES
Forms required: FAFSA.
Dates and Deadlines: Priority date 2/15; no closing date. Applicants notified on a rolling basis starting 3/1.
Transfers: Closing date 5/1. Schools required to obtain student aid information through National Student Loan Data System (NSLDS).

CONTACT
Anna Griswold, Assistant Vice Provost for Student Aid
201 Shields Building, University Park, PA 16802-1294
(814) 865-6301

Penn State Erie, The Behrend College
Erie, Pennsylvania
www.pserie.psu.edu Federal Code: 003329

4-year public branch campus college in small city.
Enrollment: 3,843 undergrads, 5% part-time. 1,018 full-time freshmen.
Selectivity: Admits over 75% of applicants.

BASIC COSTS (2007-2008)
Tuition and fees: $11,464; out-of-state residents $17,246.
Per-credit charge: $455; out-of-state residents $696.
Room and board: $7,750.

FINANCIAL AID PICTURE (2006-2007)
Students with need: Out of 892 full-time freshmen who applied for aid, 684 were judged to have need. Of these, 656 received aid, and 38 had their full need met. Average financial aid package met 67% of need; average scholarship/grant was $5,352; average loan was $2,897. For part-time students, average financial aid package was $5,662.
Students without need: 24 full-time freshmen who did not demonstrate need for aid received scholarships/grants; average award was $2,067. No-need awards available for academics, alumni affiliation, athletics, ROTC.
Cumulative student debt: 67% of graduating class had student loans; average debt was $26,300.

FINANCIAL AID PROCEDURES
Forms required: FAFSA.
Dates and Deadlines: Priority date 2/15; no closing date. Applicants notified on a rolling basis starting 3/1.
Transfers: Closing date 5/1. Schools required to obtain student aid information through National Student Loan Data System (NSLDS).

CONTACT
Anna Griswold, Assistant Vice Provost for Student Aid
201 Shields Building, University Park, PA 16801-1294
(814) 865-6301

Penn State Fayette, The Eberly Campus
Uniontown, Pennsylvania
www.fe.psu.edu Federal Code: 003329

4-year public branch campus college in large town.
Enrollment: 942 undergrads, 21% part-time. 204 full-time freshmen.
Selectivity: Admits over 75% of applicants.

BASIC COSTS (2007-2008)
Tuition and fees: $10,996; out-of-state residents $16,496.
Per-credit charge: $423; out-of-state residents $665.

FINANCIAL AID PICTURE (2006-2007)
Students with need: Out of 187 full-time freshmen who applied for aid, 160 were judged to have need. Of these, 159 received aid, and 17 had their full need met. Average financial aid package met 72% of need; average scholarship/grant was $5,551; average loan was $2,538. For part-time students, average financial aid package was $6,808.
Students without need: 19 full-time freshmen who did not demonstrate need for aid received scholarships/grants; average award was $1,664. No-need awards available for academics, alumni affiliation, athletics, ROTC.
Cumulative student debt: 67% of graduating class had student loans; average debt was $26,300.

CONTACT
Anna Griswold, Assistant Vice Provost for Student Aid
201 Shields Building, University Park, PA 16802-1294
(814) 865-6301

FINANCIAL AID PROCEDURES

Forms required: FAFSA.

Dates and Deadlines: Priority date 2/15; no closing date. Applicants notified on a rolling basis starting 3/1.

Transfers: Closing date 5/1. Schools required to obtain student aid information through National Student Loan Data System (NSLDS).

CONTACT

Anna Griswold, Assistant Vice Provost for Student Aid
201 Shields Building, University Park, PA 16802-1294
(814) 865-6301

Penn State Greater Allegheny

McKeesport, Pennsylvania
www.mk.psu.edu   Federal Code: 003329

4-year public branch campus college in large town.

Enrollment: 681 undergrads, 6% part-time. 230 full-time freshmen.

Selectivity: Admits over 75% of applicants.

BASIC COSTS (2007-2008)

Tuition and fees: $11,006; out-of-state residents $16,506.

Per-credit charge: $423; out-of-state residents $665.

Room and board: $7,750.

FINANCIAL AID PICTURE (2006-2007)

Students with need: Out of 205 full-time freshmen who applied for aid, 179 were judged to have need. Of these, 178 received aid, and 10 had their full need met. Average financial aid package met 73% of need; average scholarship/grant was $6,430; average loan was $2,555. For part-time students, average financial aid package was $7,483.

Students without need: 25 full-time freshmen who did not demonstrate need for aid received scholarships/grants; average award was $2,498. No-need awards available for academics, alumni affiliation, athletics, ROTC.

Cumulative student debt: 67% of graduating class had student loans; average debt was $26,300.

FINANCIAL AID PROCEDURES

Forms required: FAFSA.

Dates and Deadlines: Priority date 2/15; no closing date. Applicants notified on a rolling basis starting 3/1.

Transfers: Closing date 5/1. Schools required to obtain student aid information through National Student Loan Data System (NSLDS).

CONTACT

Anna Griswold, Assistant Vice Provost for Student Aid
201 Shields Building, University Park, PA 16802-1294
(814) 865-6301

Penn State Harrisburg

Middletown, Pennsylvania
www.hbg.psu.edu   Federal Code: 003329

4-year public branch campus college in small town.

Enrollment: 2,294 undergrads, 16% part-time. 337 full-time freshmen.

Selectivity: Admits 50 to 75% of applicants.

BASIC COSTS (2007-2008)

Tuition and fees: $11,454; out-of-state residents $17,236.

Per-credit charge: $455; out-of-state residents $696.

Room and board: $8,610.

FINANCIAL AID PICTURE (2006-2007)

Students with need: Out of 301 full-time freshmen who applied for aid, 226 were judged to have need. Of these, 217 received aid, and 13 had their full need met. Average financial aid package met 62% of need; average scholarship/grant was $5,857; average loan was $2,855. For part-time students, average financial aid package was $6,750.

Students without need: 4 full-time freshmen who did not demonstrate need for aid received scholarships/grants; average award was $1,362. No-need awards available for academics, alumni affiliation, athletics, ROTC.

Cumulative student debt: 67% of graduating class had student loans; average debt was $26,300.

FINANCIAL AID PROCEDURES

Forms required: FAFSA.

Dates and Deadlines: Priority date 2/15; no closing date. Applicants notified on a rolling basis starting 3/1.

Transfers: Closing date 5/1. Schools required to obtain student aid information through National Student Loan Data System (NSLDS).

CONTACT

Anna Griswold, Assistant Vice Provost for Student Aid
201 Shields Building, University Park, PA 16802-1294
(814) 865-6301

Penn State Hazleton

Hazleton, Pennsylvania
www.hn.psu.edu   Federal Code: 003338

4-year public branch campus college in large town.

Enrollment: 1,192 undergrads, 3% part-time. 539 full-time freshmen.

Selectivity: Admits over 75% of applicants.

BASIC COSTS (2007-2008)

Tuition and fees: $11,006; out-of-state residents $16,506.

Per-credit charge: $423; out-of-state residents $665.

Room and board: $7,750.

FINANCIAL AID PICTURE (2006-2007)

Students with need: Out of 477 full-time freshmen who applied for aid, 374 were judged to have need. Of these, 363 received aid, and 22 had their full need met. Average financial aid package met 63% of need; average scholarship/grant was $5,391; average loan was $2,673. For part-time students, average financial aid package was $5,250.

Students without need: 22 full-time freshmen who did not demonstrate need for aid received scholarships/grants; average award was $2,505. No-need awards available for academics, alumni affiliation, athletics, ROTC.

Cumulative student debt: 67% of graduating class had student loans; average debt was $26,300.

FINANCIAL AID PROCEDURES

Forms required: FAFSA.

Dates and Deadlines: Priority date 2/15; no closing date. Applicants notified on a rolling basis starting 3/1.

Transfers: Closing date 5/1. Schools required to obtain student aid information through National Student Loan Data System (NSLDS).

CONTACT

Anna Griswold, Assistant Vice Provost for Student Aid
201 Shields Building, University Park, PA 16802-1294
(814) 865-6301

Penn State Lehigh Valley

Fogelsville, Pennsylvania
www.lv.psu.edu   Federal Code: 003329

4-year public branch campus college in rural community.
Enrollment: 685 undergrads, 15% part-time. 199 full-time freshmen.
Selectivity: Admits over 75% of applicants.

BASIC COSTS (2007-2008)
Tuition and fees: $11,006; out-of-state residents $16,506.
Per-credit charge: $423; out-of-state residents $665.

FINANCIAL AID PICTURE (2006-2007)
Students with need: Out of 167 full-time freshmen who applied for aid, 115 were judged to have need. Of these, 113 received aid, and 6 had their full need met. Average financial aid package met 65% of need; average scholarship/grant was $5,623; average loan was $2,865. For part-time students, average financial aid package was $5,213.
Students without need: 17 full-time freshmen who did not demonstrate need for aid received scholarships/grants; average award was $1,888. No-need awards available for academics, alumni affiliation, athletics, ROTC.
Cumulative student debt: 67% of graduating class had student loans; average debt was $26,300.

FINANCIAL AID PROCEDURES
Forms required: FAFSA.
Dates and Deadlines: Priority date 2/15; no closing date. Applicants notified on a rolling basis starting 3/1.
Transfers: Closing date 5/1. Schools required to obtain student aid information through National Student Loan Data System (NSLDS).

CONTACT
Anna Griswold, Assistant Vice Provost for Student Aid
201 Shields Building, University Park, PA 16802-1294
(814) 865-6301

Penn State Mont Alto

Mont Alto, Pennsylvania
www.ma.psu.edu   Federal Code: 003340

4-year public branch campus college in rural community.
Enrollment: 1,025 undergrads, 19% part-time. 388 full-time freshmen.
Selectivity: Admits over 75% of applicants.

BASIC COSTS (2007-2008)
Tuition and fees: $11,006; out-of-state residents $16,506.
Per-credit charge: $423; out-of-state residents $665.
Room and board: $7,750.

FINANCIAL AID PICTURE (2006-2007)
Students with need: Out of 341 full-time freshmen who applied for aid, 281 were judged to have need. Of these, 275 received aid, and 29 had their full need met. Average financial aid package met 70% of need; average scholarship/grant was $5,881; average loan was $2,828. For part-time students, average financial aid package was $6,447.
Students without need: 27 full-time freshmen who did not demonstrate need for aid received scholarships/grants; average award was $2,395. No-need awards available for academics, alumni affiliation, athletics, ROTC.
Cumulative student debt: 67% of graduating class had student loans; average debt was $26,300.

FINANCIAL AID PROCEDURES
Forms required: FAFSA.
Dates and Deadlines: Priority date 2/15; no closing date. Applicants notified on a rolling basis starting 3/1.
Transfers: Closing date 5/1. Schools required to obtain student aid information through National Student Loan Data System (NSLDS).

CONTACT
Anna Griswold, Assistant Vice Provost for Student Aid
201 Shields Building, University Park, PA 16802-1294
(814) 865-6301

Penn State New Kensington

New Kensington, Pennsylvania
www.nk.psu.edu   Federal Code: 003329

4-year public branch campus college in large town.
Enrollment: 734 undergrads, 19% part-time. 200 full-time freshmen.
Selectivity: Admits over 75% of applicants.

BASIC COSTS (2007-2008)
Tuition and fees: $11,006; out-of-state residents $16,506.
Per-credit charge: $423; out-of-state residents $665.

FINANCIAL AID PICTURE (2006-2007)
Students with need: Out of 180 full-time freshmen who applied for aid, 139 were judged to have need. Of these, 136 received aid, and 21 had their full need met. Average financial aid package met 71% of need; average scholarship/grant was $4,768; average loan was $2,501. For part-time students, average financial aid package was $5,625.
Students without need: 27 full-time freshmen who did not demonstrate need for aid received scholarships/grants; average award was $2,315. No-need awards available for academics, alumni affiliation, athletics, ROTC.
Cumulative student debt: 67% of graduating class had student loans; average debt was $26,300.

FINANCIAL AID PROCEDURES
Forms required: FAFSA.
Dates and Deadlines: Priority date 2/15; no closing date. Applicants notified on a rolling basis starting 3/1.
Transfers: Closing date 5/1. Schools required to obtain student aid information through National Student Loan Data System (NSLDS).

CONTACT
Anna Griswold, Assistant Vice Provost for Student Aid
201 Shields Building, University Park, PA 16802-1294
(814) 865-6301

Penn State Schuylkill

Schuylkill Haven, Pennsylvania
www.sl.psu.edu   Federal Code: 003343

4-year public branch campus college in small town.
Enrollment: 827 undergrads, 10% part-time. 298 full-time freshmen.
Selectivity: Admits over 75% of applicants.

BASIC COSTS (2007-2008)
Tuition and fees: $10,996; out-of-state residents $16,496.
Per-credit charge: $423; out-of-state residents $665.

FINANCIAL AID PICTURE (2006-2007)
Students with need: Out of 287 full-time freshmen who applied for aid, 256 were judged to have need. Of these, 252 received aid, and 14 had their full need met. Average financial aid package met 70% of need; average scholarship/grant was $6,296; average loan was $2,687. For part-time students, average financial aid package was $6,593.
Students without need: 7 full-time freshmen who did not demonstrate need for aid received scholarships/grants; average award was $2,429. No-need awards available for academics, alumni affiliation, athletics, ROTC.
Cumulative student debt: 67% of graduating class had student loans; average debt was $26,300.

FINANCIAL AID PROCEDURES

Forms required: FAFSA.

Dates and Deadlines: Priority date 2/15; no closing date. Applicants notified on a rolling basis starting 3/1.

Transfers: Closing date 5/1. Schools required to obtain student aid information through National Student Loan Data System (NSLDS).

CONTACT

Anna Griswold, Assistant Vice Provost for Student Aid
201 Shields Building, University Park, PA 16802-1294
(814) 865-6301

Penn State Shenango
Sharon, Pennsylvania
www.shenango.psu.edu   Federal Code: 003329

Upper-division public branch campus college in large town.

Enrollment: 677 undergrads, 30% part-time. 120 full-time freshmen.

Selectivity: Admits over 75% of applicants.

BASIC COSTS (2007-2008)

Tuition and fees: $11,006; out-of-state residents $16,506.

Per-credit charge: $423; out-of-state residents $665.

FINANCIAL AID PICTURE (2006-2007)

Students with need: Out of 119 full-time freshmen who applied for aid, 109 were judged to have need. Of these, 108 received aid, and 5 had their full need met. Average financial aid package met 67% of need; average scholarship/grant was $5,960; average loan was $2,602. For part-time students, average financial aid package was $6,318.

Students without need: 8 full-time freshmen who did not demonstrate need for aid received scholarships/grants; average award was $2,548. No-need awards available for academics, alumni affiliation, athletics, ROTC.

Cumulative student debt: 67% of graduating class had student loans; average debt was $26,300.

FINANCIAL AID PROCEDURES

Forms required: FAFSA.

Dates and Deadlines: Priority date 2/15; no closing date. Applicants notified on a rolling basis starting 3/1.

Transfers: Closing date 5/1. Schools required to obtain student aid information through National Student Loan Data System (NSLDS).

CONTACT

Anna Griswold, Assistant Vice Provost for Student Aid
201 Shields Building, University Park, PA 16802-1294
(814) 865-6301

Penn State University Park
University Park, Pennsylvania
www.psu.edu   Federal Code: 003329

4-year public university in large town.

Enrollment: 35,876 undergrads, 2% part-time. 8,027 full-time freshmen.

Selectivity: Admits 50 to 75% of applicants.

BASIC COSTS (2007-2008)

Tuition and fees: $12,844; out-of-state residents $23,712.

Per-credit charge: $512; out-of-state residents $965.

Room and board: $7,750.

FINANCIAL AID PICTURE (2006-2007)

Students with need: Out of 6,038 full-time freshmen who applied for aid, 3,915 were judged to have need. Of these, 3,672 received aid, and 338 had their full need met. Average financial aid package met 65% of need; average scholarship/grant was $5,815; average loan was $2,737. For part-time students, average financial aid package was $7,272.

Students without need: 452 full-time freshmen who did not demonstrate need for aid received scholarships/grants; average award was $3,311. No-need awards available for academics, alumni affiliation, athletics, ROTC.

Scholarships offered: 149 full-time freshmen received athletic scholarships; average amount $16,500.

Cumulative student debt: 67% of graduating class had student loans; average debt was $26,300.

FINANCIAL AID PROCEDURES

Forms required: FAFSA.

Dates and Deadlines: Priority date 2/15; no closing date. Applicants notified on a rolling basis starting 3/1.

Transfers: Closing date 5/1. Schools required to obtain student aid information through National Student Loan Data System (NSLDS).

CONTACT

Anna Griswold, Assistant Vice Provost for Student Aid
201 Shields Building, University Park, PA 16802-1294
(814) 865-6301

Penn State Wilkes-Barre
Lehman, Pennsylvania
www.wb.psu.edu   Federal Code: 003329

4-year public branch campus college in small city.

Enrollment: 563 undergrads, 9% part-time. 183 full-time freshmen.

Selectivity: Admits over 75% of applicants.

BASIC COSTS (2007-2008)

Tuition and fees: $11,006; out-of-state residents $16,506.

Per-credit charge: $423; out-of-state residents $665.

FINANCIAL AID PICTURE (2006-2007)

Students with need: Out of 165 full-time freshmen who applied for aid, 131 were judged to have need. Of these, 130 received aid, and 6 had their full need met. Average financial aid package met 65% of need; average scholarship/grant was $5,475; average loan was $2,454. For part-time students, average financial aid package was $5,439.

Students without need: 18 full-time freshmen who did not demonstrate need for aid received scholarships/grants; average award was $2,933. No-need awards available for academics, alumni affiliation, athletics, ROTC.

Cumulative student debt: 67% of graduating class had student loans; average debt was $26,300.

FINANCIAL AID PROCEDURES

Forms required: FAFSA.

Dates and Deadlines: Priority date 2/15; no closing date. Applicants notified on a rolling basis starting 3/1.

Transfers: Closing date 5/1. Schools required to obtain student aid information through National Student Loan Data System (NSLDS).

CONTACT

Anna Griswold, Assistant Vice Provost for Student Aid
201 Shields Building, University Park, PA 16802-1294
(814) 865-6301

Penn State Worthington Scranton
Dunmore, Pennsylvania
www.sn.psu.edu   Federal Code: 003344

4-year public branch campus college in large town.
Enrollment: 1,185 undergrads, 17% part-time. 308 full-time freshmen.
Selectivity: Admits over 75% of applicants.

BASIC COSTS (2007-2008)
Tuition and fees: $10,986; out-of-state residents $16,486.
Per-credit charge: $423; out-of-state residents $665.

FINANCIAL AID PICTURE (2006-2007)
Students with need: Out of 269 full-time freshmen who applied for aid, 220 were judged to have need. Of these, 217 received aid, and 11 had their full need met. Average financial aid package met 60% of need; average scholarship/grant was $5,195; average loan was $2,613. For part-time students, average financial aid package was $5,897.
Students without need: 20 full-time freshmen who did not demonstrate need for aid received scholarships/grants; average award was $2,394. No-need awards available for academics, alumni affiliation, athletics, ROTC.
Cumulative student debt: 67% of graduating class had student loans; average debt was $26,300.

FINANCIAL AID PROCEDURES
Forms required: FAFSA.
Dates and Deadlines: Priority date 2/15; no closing date. Applicants notified on a rolling basis starting 3/1.
Transfers: Closing date 5/1. Schools required to obtain student aid information through National Student Loan Data System (NSLDS).

CONTACT
Anna Griswold, Assistant Vice Provost for Student Aid
201 Shields Building, University Park, PA 16802-1294
(814) 865-6301

Penn State York
York, Pennsylvania
www.yk.psu.edu   Federal Code: 003347

4-year public branch campus college in large town.
Enrollment: 1,070 undergrads, 24% part-time. 276 full-time freshmen.
Selectivity: Admits over 75% of applicants.

BASIC COSTS (2007-2008)
Tuition and fees: $10,986; out-of-state residents $16,486.
Per-credit charge: $423; out-of-state residents $665.

FINANCIAL AID PICTURE (2006-2007)
Students with need: Out of 241 full-time freshmen who applied for aid, 185 were judged to have need. Of these, 182 received aid, and 28 had their full need met. Average financial aid package met 66% of need; average scholarship/grant was $4,869; average loan was $2,506. For part-time students, average financial aid package was $6,194.
Students without need: 27 full-time freshmen who did not demonstrate need for aid received scholarships/grants; average award was $2,379. No-need awards available for academics, alumni affiliation, athletics, ROTC.
Cumulative student debt: 67% of graduating class had student loans; average debt was $26,300.

FINANCIAL AID PROCEDURES
Forms required: FAFSA.
Dates and Deadlines: Priority date 2/15; no closing date. Applicants notified on a rolling basis starting 3/1.
Transfers: Closing date 5/1. Schools required to obtain student aid information through National Student Loan Data System (NSLDS).

CONTACT
Anna Griswold, Assistant Vice Provost for Student Aid
201 Shields Building, University Park, PA 16802-1294
(814) 865-6301

Pennsylvania College of Technology
Williamsport, Pennsylvania
www.pct.edu   Federal Code: 003395

4-year public technical college in small city.
Enrollment: 6,565 undergrads, 13% part-time. 1,575 full-time freshmen.
Selectivity: Open admission; but selective for some programs.

BASIC COSTS (2007-2008)
Tuition and fees: $11,250; out-of-state residents $14,130.
Per-credit charge: $319; out-of-state residents $415.
Room and board: $7,770.

FINANCIAL AID PICTURE
Students with need: Need-based aid available for full-time and part-time students. Work study available nights, weekends, and for part-time students.
Students without need: No-need awards available for academics, alumni affiliation.

FINANCIAL AID PROCEDURES
Forms required: FAFSA, institutional form.
Dates and Deadlines: Priority date 4/1; no closing date. Applicants notified on a rolling basis starting 6/1; must reply by 7/1 or within 4 week(s) of notification.

CONTACT
Dennis Correll, Director of Financial Aid
One College Avenue, Williamsport, PA 17701
(570) 327-4766

Pennsylvania Culinary Institute
Pittsburgh, Pennsylvania
www.paculinary.com   Federal Code: 030068

2-year for-profit culinary school and technical college in large city.
Enrollment: 1,100 full-time undergrads.

BASIC COSTS (2007-2008)
Additional info: Total costs vary by program: Culinary Arts $41,870; Patisserie & Baking $36,470; Hospitality & Restaurant Management $35,503. Tuition at time of enrollment locked for 2 years.

FINANCIAL AID PICTURE
Students with need: Need-based aid available for full-time students.
Students without need: This college awards aid only to students with need.

FINANCIAL AID PROCEDURES
Forms required: FAFSA, institutional form.
Dates and Deadlines: No deadline. Applicants notified on a rolling basis.

CONTACT
Paul Steele, Director of Student Finance
717 Liberty Avenue, Pittsburgh, PA 15222
(412) 566-2433

Pennsylvania Highlands Community College

Johnstown, Pennsylvania
www.pennhighlands.edu   Federal Code: 031804

2-year public community college in large town.

Enrollment: 1,064 undergrads, 46% part-time. 195 full-time freshmen.

Selectivity: Open admission.

BASIC COSTS (2007-2008)

Tuition and fees: $3,180; out-of-district residents $5,730; out-of-state residents $8,280.

Per-credit charge: $85; out-of-district residents $170; out-of-state residents $255.

Additional info: Students in Windber and Conemaugh Twp pay rate of $110 per credit hour. Students outside Cambria County pay additional fee of $5 per credit.

FINANCIAL AID PICTURE

Students with need: Need-based aid available for full-time and part-time students. Work study available nights.

Students without need: No-need awards available for academics, state/district residency.

FINANCIAL AID PROCEDURES

Forms required: FAFSA.

Dates and Deadlines: Closing date 4/1. Applicants notified on a rolling basis; must reply by 8/1.

CONTACT

Brenda Coughenour, Director of Financial Aid
PO Box 68, Johnstown, PA 15907-0068
(814) 262-6454

Pennsylvania Institute of Technology

Media, Pennsylvania
www.pit.edu   Federal Code: 010998

2-year private technical college in small town.

Enrollment: 668 undergrads, 19% part-time. 357 full-time freshmen.

Selectivity: Open admission.

BASIC COSTS (2007-2008)

Tuition and fees: $9,330.

FINANCIAL AID PICTURE

Students with need: Need-based aid available for full-time and part-time students. Work study available nights, weekends, and for part-time students.

Students without need: No-need awards available for academics, leadership.

Scholarships offered: Presidential Scholarship; half tuition; for current high school graduates; SAT scores required.

FINANCIAL AID PROCEDURES

Forms required: FAFSA, institutional form.

Dates and Deadlines: Closing date 8/1. Applicants notified on a rolling basis starting 7/1.

Transfers: No deadline.

CONTACT

Crystal Donnelly, Director of Financial Aid
800 Manchester Avenue, Media, PA 19063-4098
(610) 892-1536

Philadelphia Biblical University

Langhorne, Pennsylvania
www.pbu.edu   Federal Code: 003351

4-year private university and Bible college in small town, affiliated with Protestant Evangelical tradition.

Enrollment: 1,060 undergrads, 6% part-time. 201 full-time freshmen.

Selectivity: Admits over 75% of applicants.

BASIC COSTS (2008-2009)

Tuition and fees: $17,785.

Per-credit charge: $526.

Room and board: $7,150.

FINANCIAL AID PICTURE (2007-2008)

Students with need: Out of 168 full-time freshmen who applied for aid, 147 were judged to have need. Of these, 147 received aid, and 37 had their full need met. Average financial aid package met 77% of need; average scholarship/grant was $10,569; average loan was $4,416. For part-time students, average financial aid package was $6,370.

Students without need: 52 full-time freshmen who did not demonstrate need for aid received scholarships/grants; average award was $7,547. No-need awards available for academics, leadership, minority status.

FINANCIAL AID PROCEDURES

Forms required: FAFSA.

Dates and Deadlines: Priority date 5/1; no closing date. Applicants notified on a rolling basis starting 3/15.

CONTACT

William Kellaris, Director of Financial Aid
200 Manor Avenue, Langhorne, PA 19047-2990
(215) 702-4246

Philadelphia University

Philadelphia, Pennsylvania
www.philau.edu   Federal Code: 003354

4-year private university in very large city.

Enrollment: 2,796 undergrads, 8% part-time. 738 full-time freshmen.

Selectivity: Admits 50 to 75% of applicants.

BASIC COSTS (2008-2009)

Tuition and fees: $26,700.

Per-credit charge: $472.

Room and board: $8,692.

FINANCIAL AID PICTURE (2007-2008)

Students with need: Out of 632 full-time freshmen who applied for aid, 523 were judged to have need. Of these, 523 received aid, and 56 had their full need met. Average financial aid package met 72% of need; average scholarship/grant was $13,651; average loan was $3,373. For part-time students, average financial aid package was $6,501.

Students without need: 215 full-time freshmen who did not demonstrate need for aid received scholarships/grants; average award was $6,274. No-need awards available for academics, athletics.

Scholarships offered: 17 full-time freshmen received athletic scholarships; average amount $8,780.

Cumulative student debt: 76% of graduating class had student loans; average debt was $28,345.

FINANCIAL AID PROCEDURES

Forms required: FAFSA.

Dates and Deadlines: Closing date 4/15. Applicants notified on a rolling basis starting 2/10; must reply by 5/1.

CONTACT
Lisa Cooper, Director of Financial Aid
School House Lane and Henry Avenue, Philadelphia, PA 19144-5497
(215) 951-2940

Pittsburgh Institute of Aeronautics
Pittsburgh, Pennsylvania
www.pia.edu   Federal Code: 005310

2-year private technical college in large city.
Enrollment: 400 undergrads.
Selectivity: Open admission.

BASIC COSTS (2007-2008)
Tuition and fees: $11,352.

FINANCIAL AID PICTURE
Students with need: Need-based aid available for full-time students.

FINANCIAL AID PROCEDURES
Forms required: FAFSA.
Dates and Deadlines: Priority date 5/1; no closing date. Applicants notified on a rolling basis.

CONTACT
Darla Mroski, Director of Finance
Box 10897, Pittsburgh, PA 15236-0897
(412) 346-2100

Pittsburgh Institute of Mortuary Science
Pittsburgh, Pennsylvania
www.pims.edu   Federal Code: 010814

2-year private technical college in large city.
Enrollment: 85 full-time undergrads.
Selectivity: Open admission.

BASIC COSTS (2007-2008)
Tuition and fees: $14,587.

FINANCIAL AID PICTURE
Students with need: Need-based aid available for full-time and part-time students.

FINANCIAL AID PROCEDURES
Forms required: FAFSA.
Dates and Deadlines: No deadline. Applicants notified on a rolling basis.

CONTACT
Karen Rocco, Financial Aid Officer
5808 Baum Boulevard, Pittsburgh, PA 15206-3706
(412) 362-8500

Pittsburgh Technical Institute
Oakdale, Pennsylvania
www.pti.edu   Federal Code: 007437

2-year for-profit technical and career college in large town.
Enrollment: 2,065 undergrads. 1,035 full-time freshmen.
Selectivity: Open admission; but selective for some programs.

BASIC COSTS (2007-2008)
Additional info: Tuition and supply costs vary by program and student use. Tuition does not increase if student maintains continuous and consistent enrollment. Tuition at time of enrollment locked for 2 years.

FINANCIAL AID PICTURE (2006-2007)
Students with need: 56% of average financial aid package awarded as scholarships/grants, 44% awarded as loans/jobs. Need-based aid available for part-time students.

FINANCIAL AID PROCEDURES
Forms required: FAFSA, state aid form, institutional form.
Dates and Deadlines: No deadline. Applicants notified on a rolling basis.
Transfers: Applicants notified on a rolling basis.

CONTACT
Mark Scott, Senior Vice President of Academic Affairs
1111 McKee Road, Oakdale, PA 15071-3205
(412) 809-5250

PJA School
Upper Darby, Pennsylvania
www.pjaschool.com   Federal Code: 023013

2-year for-profit business and career college in very large city.
Enrollment: 160 undergrads.

BASIC COSTS (2007-2008)
Tuition and fees: $10,630.
Additional info: Books and materials included in cost of tuition. Tuition at time of enrollment locked for 2 years.

FINANCIAL AID PICTURE
Students with need: Need-based aid available for full-time and part-time students.
Students without need: This college awards aid only to students with need.
Additional info: Interest-free payment plan available.

FINANCIAL AID PROCEDURES
Forms required: FAFSA, institutional form.
Dates and Deadlines: No deadline. Applicants notified on a rolling basis.

CONTACT
Gwen Dean, Director of Financial Aid
7900 West Chester Pike, Upper Darby, PA 19082
(610) 789-6700

Point Park University
Pittsburgh, Pennsylvania
www.pointpark.edu   Federal Code: 003357

4-year private university in large city.
Enrollment: 3,089 undergrads, 21% part-time. 448 full-time freshmen.
Selectivity: Admits over 75% of applicants.

BASIC COSTS (2008-2009)
Tuition and fees: $20,570.
Per-credit charge: $552.
Room and board: $8,940.
Additional info: Cost of tuition in bachelor of arts and bachelor of fine arts programs within Conservatory of Performing Arts: $23,980 or $681 per credit hour. Tuition/fee waivers available for adults, minority students, unemployed or children of unemployed.

FINANCIAL AID PICTURE (2007-2008)
Students with need: Average financial aid package met 73% of need; average scholarship/grant was $9,121; average loan was $5,491. For part-time students, average financial aid package was $8,824.
Students without need: No-need awards available for academics, alumni affiliation, art, athletics, job skills, leadership, music/drama.

Cumulative student debt: 65% of graduating class had student loans; average debt was $29,989.

FINANCIAL AID PROCEDURES

Forms required: FAFSA.

Dates and Deadlines: Priority date 5/1; no closing date. Applicants notified on a rolling basis starting 2/15; must reply within 2 week(s) of notification.

CONTACT

Sandra Cronin, Director of Financial Aid
201 Wood Street, Pittsburgh, PA 15222-1984
(412) 392-3935

Robert Morris University
Moon Township, Pennsylvania
www.rmu.edu   Federal Code: 001746

4-year private university in large town.

Enrollment: 3,878 undergrads, 17% part-time. 664 full-time freshmen.

Selectivity: Admits over 75% of applicants.

BASIC COSTS (2008-2009)

Tuition and fees: $19,740.

Per-credit charge: $640.

Room and board: $9,880.

FINANCIAL AID PICTURE (2007-2008)

Students with need: Out of 588 full-time freshmen who applied for aid, 500 were judged to have need. Of these, 500 received aid, and 164 had their full need met. Average financial aid package met 78% of need; average scholarship/grant was $10,151; average loan was $5,420. For part-time students, average financial aid package was $6,996.

Students without need: 147 full-time freshmen who did not demonstrate need for aid received scholarships/grants; average award was $10,882. No-need awards available for academics, athletics.

Scholarships offered: 31 full-time freshmen received athletic scholarships; average amount $12,118.

Cumulative student debt: 84% of graduating class had student loans; average debt was $25,960.

FINANCIAL AID PROCEDURES

Forms required: FAFSA.

Dates and Deadlines: No deadline. Applicants notified on a rolling basis starting 3/15.

CONTACT

Stephanie Thompson, Director of Financial Aid
6001 University Boulevard, Moon Township, PA 15108-1189
(412) 262-8677

Rosemont College
Rosemont, Pennsylvania
www.rosemont.edu   Federal Code: 003360

4-year private liberal arts college for women in small town, affiliated with Roman Catholic Church.

Enrollment: 551 undergrads, 28% part-time. 71 full-time freshmen.

Selectivity: Admits 50 to 75% of applicants.

BASIC COSTS (2007-2008)

Tuition and fees: $22,835.

Per-credit charge: $830.

Room and board: $9,200.

Additional info: Tuition/fee waivers available for adults.

FINANCIAL AID PICTURE (2007-2008)

Students with need: Out of 64 full-time freshmen who applied for aid, 58 were judged to have need. Of these, 58 received aid, and 12 had their full need met. Average financial aid package met 80% of need; average scholarship/grant was $18,109; average loan was $3,504. For part-time students, average financial aid package was $2,775.

Students without need: 13 full-time freshmen who did not demonstrate need for aid received scholarships/grants; average award was $6,119. No-need awards available for academics, alumni affiliation, art, job skills, religious affiliation.

Cumulative student debt: 86% of graduating class had student loans; average debt was $26,532.

FINANCIAL AID PROCEDURES

Forms required: FAFSA.

Dates and Deadlines: Priority date 2/15; no closing date. Applicants notified on a rolling basis starting 2/15; must reply by 5/1 or within 4 week(s) of notification.

Transfers: No deadline. Applicants notified on a rolling basis starting 2/15; must reply within 4 week(s) of notification.

CONTACT

Melissa Walsh, Director of Financial Aid
1400 Montgomery Avenue, Rosemont, PA 19010-1699
(610) 527-0200 ext. 2220

St. Francis University
Loretto, Pennsylvania
www.francis.edu   Federal Code: 003366

4-year private university and liberal arts college in rural community, affiliated with Roman Catholic Church.

Enrollment: 1,513 undergrads, 7% part-time. 395 full-time freshmen.

Selectivity: Admits over 75% of applicants.

BASIC COSTS (2007-2008)

Tuition and fees: $23,494.

Per-credit charge: $701.

Room and board: $7,984.

Additional info: Tuition/fee waivers available for adults.

FINANCIAL AID PICTURE (2006-2007)

Students with need: Out of 379 full-time freshmen who applied for aid, 350 were judged to have need. Of these, 349 received aid, and 78 had their full need met. Average financial aid package met 73% of need; average scholarship/grant was $13,688; average loan was $2,785. For part-time students, average financial aid package was $10,115.

Students without need: 41 full-time freshmen who did not demonstrate need for aid received scholarships/grants; average award was $10,587. No-need awards available for academics, alumni affiliation, athletics, music/drama, religious affiliation.

Scholarships offered: 58 full-time freshmen received athletic scholarships; average amount $8,367.

Cumulative student debt: 93% of graduating class had student loans; average debt was $15,600.

FINANCIAL AID PROCEDURES

Forms required: FAFSA.

Dates and Deadlines: Priority date 5/1; no closing date. Applicants notified on a rolling basis starting 3/1.

Transfers: No deadline. Applicants notified on a rolling basis. Associate degree transfer scholarship based on academic achievement. Returning adult student scholarships available to qualifying transfers after one semester.

CONTACT

Jamie Kosh, Director of Financial Aid
Box 600, Loretto, PA 15940

Saint Joseph's University

Philadelphia, Pennsylvania
www.sju.edu   Federal Code: 003367

4-year private university in very large city, affiliated with Roman Catholic Church.
Enrollment: 4,825 undergrads, 14% part-time. 1,086 full-time freshmen.
Selectivity: Admits 50 to 75% of applicants. GED not accepted.

BASIC COSTS (2008-2009)
Tuition and fees: $32,860.
Room and board: $11,230.

FINANCIAL AID PICTURE (2007-2008)
Students with need: Out of 769 full-time freshmen who applied for aid, 566 were judged to have need. Of these, 566 received aid, and 118 had their full need met. Average financial aid package met 85% of need; average scholarship/grant was $14,383; average loan was $3,047. Need-based aid available for part-time students.
Students without need: 468 full-time freshmen who did not demonstrate need for aid received scholarships/grants; average award was $10,756. No-need awards available for academics, art, athletics, minority status, music/drama, ROTC.
Scholarships offered: 30 full-time freshmen received athletic scholarships; average amount $16,178.

FINANCIAL AID PROCEDURES
Forms required: FAFSA.
Dates and Deadlines: Priority date 2/15; closing date 5/1. Applicants notified on a rolling basis starting 3/15.
Transfers: Financial aid for transfers subject to availability of funds.

CONTACT
Eileen Tucker, Director of Financial Aid
5600 City Avenue, Philadelphia, PA 19131
(610) 660-1556

St. Vincent College

Latrobe, Pennsylvania
www.stvincent.edu   Federal Code: 003368

4-year private liberal arts college in large town, affiliated with Roman Catholic Church.
Enrollment: 1,617 undergrads, 2% part-time. 421 full-time freshmen.
Selectivity: Admits 50 to 75% of applicants.

BASIC COSTS (2007-2008)
Tuition and fees: $24,106.
Per-credit charge: $734.
Room and board: $7,380.

FINANCIAL AID PICTURE (2007-2008)
Students with need: Out of 419 full-time freshmen who applied for aid, 333 were judged to have need. Of these, 333 received aid, and 111 had their full need met. Average financial aid package met 91% of need; average scholarship/grant was $15,854; average loan was $3,580. For part-time students, average financial aid package was $6,064.
Students without need: 85 full-time freshmen who did not demonstrate need for aid received scholarships/grants; average award was $11,576. No-need awards available for academics, alumni affiliation, leadership, minority status, music/drama, religious affiliation.
Scholarships offered: Academic Merit Scholarship; $1,000 to $11,000; based on high school GPA, class rank, and SAT scores. Wimmer Scholarship; open to students in top 10 percent of their high school class; based on exam, top scorer awarded full tuition, next 4 scorers awarded between $12,000 and full scholarship. Leadership Merit Grant; $500 to $3,000, based on extracurricular activities and recommendations.

FINANCIAL AID PROCEDURES
Forms required: FAFSA, state aid form.
Dates and Deadlines: Priority date 3/1; closing date 5/1. Applicants notified on a rolling basis starting 3/1; must reply within 2 week(s) of notification.
Transfers: Applicants notified on a rolling basis starting 3/1; must reply within 2 week(s) of notification.

CONTACT
Kimberly Woodley, Director of Financial Aid
300 Fraser Purchase Road, Latrobe, PA 15650-2690
(800) 782-5549

Seton Hill University

Greensburg, Pennsylvania
www.setonhill.edu   Federal Code: 003362

4-year private university and liberal arts college in large town, affiliated with Roman Catholic Church.
Enrollment: 1,535 undergrads, 18% part-time. 322 full-time freshmen.
Selectivity: Admits 50 to 75% of applicants.

BASIC COSTS (2007-2008)
Tuition and fees: $25,006.
Per-credit charge: $660.
Room and board: $7,740.
Additional info: Tuition/fee waivers available for adults.

FINANCIAL AID PICTURE (2007-2008)
Students with need: Out of 293 full-time freshmen who applied for aid, 274 were judged to have need. Of these, 272 received aid, and 71 had their full need met. Average financial aid package met 81% of need; average scholarship/grant was $17,293; average loan was $4,815. For part-time students, average financial aid package was $7,419.
Students without need: 36 full-time freshmen who did not demonstrate need for aid received scholarships/grants; average award was $17,680. No-need awards available for academics, alumni affiliation, art, athletics, job skills, music/drama.
Scholarships offered: *Merit:* Presidential Scholarships; up to one-half of tuition per academic year; given to top 10%, 20%, and 30% of high school class. Other scholarships include those for valedictorians, academic performance, special talents. *Athletic:* 31 full-time freshmen received athletic scholarships; average amount $9,177.
Cumulative student debt: 84% of graduating class had student loans; average debt was $26,872.

FINANCIAL AID PROCEDURES
Forms required: FAFSA, state aid form, institutional form.
Dates and Deadlines: Priority date 5/1; no closing date. Applicants notified on a rolling basis starting 11/15; must reply by 5/1 or within 2 week(s) of notification.
Transfers: Priority date 8/1; closing date 8/15. Applicants notified on a rolling basis starting 1/1; must reply within 2 week(s) of notification. Scholarship available for full-time transfer students with 3.5 GPA.

CONTACT
Maryann Dudas, Director of Financial Aid
1 Seton Hill Drive, Greensburg, PA 15601
(724) 838-4293

Shippensburg University of Pennsylvania

Shippensburg, Pennsylvania
www.ship.edu   Federal Code: 003326

4-year public university in small town.
Enrollment: 6,560 undergrads, 4% part-time. 1,722 full-time freshmen.

Selectivity: Admits over 75% of applicants.

BASIC COSTS (2007-2008)

Tuition and fees: $6,849; out-of-state residents $14,615.
Per-credit charge: $216; out-of-state residents $539.
Room and board: $6,272.
Additional info: Tuition for transfer students from five neighboring MD community colleges with dual admission agreements is $7,766.

FINANCIAL AID PICTURE (2007-2008)

Students with need: Out of 1,378 full-time freshmen who applied for aid, 885 were judged to have need. Of these, 875 received aid, and 151 had their full need met. Average financial aid package met 69% of need; average scholarship/grant was $4,916; average loan was $3,294. For part-time students, average financial aid package was $5,845.
Students without need: 162 full-time freshmen who did not demonstrate need for aid received scholarships/grants; average award was $2,800. No-need awards available for academics, athletics.
Scholarships offered: 43 full-time freshmen received athletic scholarships; average amount $1,850.
Cumulative student debt: 73% of graduating class had student loans; average debt was $20,256.

FINANCIAL AID PROCEDURES

Forms required: FAFSA.
Dates and Deadlines: Priority date 3/15; no closing date. Applicants notified on a rolling basis; must reply within 2 week(s) of notification.
Transfers: No deadline. Applicants notified on a rolling basis.

CONTACT

Peter D'Annibale, Director of Financial Aid
1871 Old Main Drive, Shippensburg, PA 17257-2299
(717) 477-1131

Slippery Rock University of Pennsylvania

Slippery Rock, Pennsylvania
www.sru.edu   Federal Code: 003327

4-year public university in rural community.
Enrollment: 7,521 undergrads, 7% part-time. 1,506 full-time freshmen.
Selectivity: Admits 50 to 75% of applicants.

BASIC COSTS (2007-2008)

Tuition and fees: $6,671; out-of-state residents $9,260.
Per-credit charge: $216; out-of-state residents $539.
Room and board: $7,862.
Additional info: Tuition for out-of-state residents with at least 3.0 GPA is $7,766.

FINANCIAL AID PICTURE (2007-2008)

Students with need: Out of 1,394 full-time freshmen who applied for aid, 1,036 were judged to have need. Of these, 1,018 received aid, and 473 had their full need met. Average financial aid package met 68% of need; average scholarship/grant was $3,524; average loan was $3,379. For part-time students, average financial aid package was $5,080.
Students without need: 322 full-time freshmen who did not demonstrate need for aid received scholarships/grants; average award was $4,685. No-need awards available for academics, alumni affiliation, art, athletics, job skills, leadership, minority status, music/drama, ROTC, state/district residency.
Scholarships offered: 74 full-time freshmen received athletic scholarships; average amount $2,130.
Cumulative student debt: 80% of graduating class had student loans; average debt was $21,680.
Additional info: May 1 closing date for Pennsylvania state grants.

FINANCIAL AID PROCEDURES

Forms required: FAFSA.

Dates and Deadlines: Priority date 5/1; no closing date. Applicants notified on a rolling basis starting 3/15; must reply within 4 week(s) of notification.

CONTACT

Patricia Hladio, Director of Financial Aid
1 Morrow Way, Slippery Rock, PA 16057-1383
(724) 738-2044

South Hills School of Business & Technology

State College, Pennsylvania
www.southhills.edu   Federal Code: 013263

2-year for-profit business and technical college in large town.
Enrollment: 637 undergrads, 10% part-time. 298 full-time freshmen.
Selectivity: Open admission; but selective for some programs.

BASIC COSTS (2007-2008)

Tuition and fees: $12,319.
Per-credit charge: $339.

FINANCIAL AID PICTURE (2007-2008)

Students with need: Average financial aid package met 10% of need; average scholarship/grant was $1,896; average loan was $3,500. For part-time students, average financial aid package was $2,272.
Students without need: This college awards aid only to students with need.

FINANCIAL AID PROCEDURES

Forms required: FAFSA.
Dates and Deadlines: Closing date 6/30. Applicants notified on a rolling basis starting 7/5.
Transfers: No deadline.

CONTACT

Harriet Arndt, Financial Aid Director
480 Waupelani Drive, State College, PA 16801-4516
(814) 234-7755

South Hills School of Business & Technology: Altoona

Altoona, Pennsylvania
www.southhills.edu   Federal Code: 010281

2-year for-profit business and technical college in small city.
Enrollment: 150 undergrads.
Selectivity: Open admission; but selective for some programs.

BASIC COSTS (2008-2009)

Tuition and fees: $12,981.
Per-credit charge: $356,

FINANCIAL AID PICTURE

Students with need: Need-based aid available for full-time and part-time students.
Students without need: This college awards aid only to students with need.

FINANCIAL AID PROCEDURES

Forms required: FAFSA.
Dates and Deadlines: Closing date 6/30. Applicants notified on a rolling basis starting 7/1.
Transfers: No deadline.

CONTACT

Joan Grassi, Financial Aid Counselor
508 58th Street, Altoona, PA 16602
(814) 944-6134 ext. 3052

Susquehanna University

Selinsgrove, Pennsylvania   Federal Code: 003369
www.susqu.edu   CSS Code: 2820

4-year private university and liberal arts college in small town, affiliated with Evangelical Lutheran Church in America.

Enrollment: 1,976 undergrads, 1% part-time. 591 full-time freshmen.
Selectivity: Admits over 75% of applicants.

BASIC COSTS (2008-2009)

Tuition and fees: $31,080.
Per-credit charge: $975.
Room and board: $8,800.

FINANCIAL AID PICTURE (2007-2008)

Students with need: Out of 476 full-time freshmen who applied for aid, 386 were judged to have need. Of these, 386 received aid, and 191 had their full need met. Average financial aid package met 84% of need; average scholarship/grant was $18,973; average loan was $3,745. For part-time students, average financial aid package was $16,815.
Students without need: 182 full-time freshmen who did not demonstrate need for aid received scholarships/grants; average award was $14,438. No-need awards available for academics, alumni affiliation, leadership, minority status, music/drama, ROTC.
Scholarships offered: Scholarships; $1,000 to $16,000; renewable annually; based on outstanding academic achievement, personal accomplishment, and/or musical talent. Alumni scholarships; $2,500; for 5 new legacy students with best academic records. Annual scholarships; $2,000; to dependent children of ordained Lutheran clergy.
Additional info: Graduated pay scale for federal work-study program.

FINANCIAL AID PROCEDURES

Forms required: FAFSA, CSS PROFILE.
Dates and Deadlines: Priority date 3/1; closing date 5/1. Applicants notified on a rolling basis starting 2/15; must reply by 5/1.
Transfers: Priority date 5/1; closing date 7/1. Transfer students eligible for financial aid and scholarship consideration.

CONTACT

Helen Nunn, Director of Financial Aid
514 University Avenue, Selinsgrove, PA 17870-1164
(570) 372-4450

Swarthmore College

Swarthmore, Pennsylvania   Federal Code: 003370
www.swarthmore.edu   CSS Code: 2821

4-year private liberal arts college in small town.

Enrollment: 1,480 undergrads. 365 full-time freshmen.
Selectivity: Admits less than 50% of applicants.

BASIC COSTS (2008-2009)

Tuition and fees: $36,490.
Room and board: $11,314.

FINANCIAL AID PICTURE (2007-2008)

Students with need: Out of 239 full-time freshmen who applied for aid, 176 were judged to have need. Of these, 176 received aid, and 176 had their full need met. Average financial aid package met 100% of need; average scholarship/grant was $30,073; average loan was $2,163.

Students without need: 1 full-time freshmen who did not demonstrate need for aid received scholarships/grants; average award was $34,564. No-need awards available for academics, leadership, state/district residency.
Additional info: 100% of demonstrated financial need met for all admitted students.

FINANCIAL AID PROCEDURES

Forms required: FAFSA, CSS PROFILE, state aid form, institutional form.
Dates and Deadlines: Closing date 2/15. Applicants notified by 4/1; must reply by 5/1.
Transfers: Closing date 4/1. Applicants notified by 5/15. No aid consideration possible for foreign national transfer applicants.

CONTACT

Laura Talbot, Director of Financial Aid
500 College Avenue, Swarthmore, PA 19081
(610) 328-8358

Talmudical Yeshiva of Philadelphia

Philadelphia, Pennsylvania   Federal Code: 012523

4-year private rabbinical college for men in very large city, affiliated with Jewish faith.

Enrollment: 112 undergrads. 111 full-time freshmen.
Selectivity: Admits over 75% of applicants.

BASIC COSTS (2007-2008)

Tuition and fees: $7,300.
Room and board: $6,000.

FINANCIAL AID PICTURE (2006-2007)

Students with need: Out of 27 full-time freshmen who applied for aid, 25 were judged to have need. Of these, 25 received aid.
Students without need: This college awards aid only to students with need.

FINANCIAL AID PROCEDURES

Forms required: FAFSA, institutional form.
Dates and Deadlines: Priority date 8/1; closing date 5/1. Applicants notified on a rolling basis starting 3/15; must reply within 2 week(s) of notification.

CONTACT

Chaya Hoberman, Financial Aid Officer
6063 Drexel Road, Philadelphia, PA 19131
(215) 477-1000

Temple University

Philadelphia, Pennsylvania
www.temple.edu   Federal Code: 003371

4-year public university in very large city.
Enrollment: 24,861 undergrads, 11% part-time. 3,851 full-time freshmen.
Selectivity: Admits 50 to 75% of applicants.

BASIC COSTS (2007-2008)

Tuition and fees: $10,802; out-of-state residents $19,320.
Per-credit charge: $397; out-of-state residents $668.
Room and board: $8,518.

FINANCIAL AID PICTURE (2006-2007)

Students with need: Out of 3,639 full-time freshmen who applied for aid, 2,660 were judged to have need. Of these, 2,608 received aid, and 868 had their full need met. Average financial aid package met 86% of need; average scholarship/grant was $5,511; average loan was $2,618. For part-time students, average financial aid package was $8,576.

Students without need: 979 full-time freshmen who did not demonstrate need for aid received scholarships/grants; average award was $4,870. No-need awards available for academics, art, athletics, music/drama, ROTC.

Scholarships offered: 32 full-time freshmen received athletic scholarships; average amount $12,277.

Cumulative student debt: 75% of graduating class had student loans; average debt was $29,046.

FINANCIAL AID PROCEDURES

Forms required: FAFSA.

Dates and Deadlines: Closing date 3/1. Applicants notified on a rolling basis starting 2/15; must reply by 5/1 or within 3 week(s) of notification.

Transfers: Priority date 3/1; no deadline. Must reply within 2 week(s) of notification.

CONTACT

John Morris, Director, Student Financial Services
103 Conwell Hall, Philadelphia, PA 19122-6096
(215) 204-2244

Thiel College

Greenville, Pennsylvania
www.thiel.edu   Federal Code: 003376

4-year private liberal arts college in small town, affiliated with Evangelical Lutheran Church in America.

Enrollment: 1,179 undergrads, 4% part-time. 347 full-time freshmen.

Selectivity: Admits over 75% of applicants.

BASIC COSTS (2007-2008)

Tuition and fees: $20,214.
Room and board: $7,840.

FINANCIAL AID PICTURE (2007-2008)

Students with need: Out of 321 full-time freshmen who applied for aid, 298 were judged to have need. Of these, 298 received aid, and 46 had their full need met. Average financial aid package met 74% of need; average scholarship/grant was $13,794; average loan was $4,466. For part-time students, average financial aid package was $8,440.

Students without need: 41 full-time freshmen who did not demonstrate need for aid received scholarships/grants; average award was $11,296. No-need awards available for academics, alumni affiliation, leadership, music/drama, religious affiliation, state/district residency.

FINANCIAL AID PROCEDURES

Forms required: FAFSA, state aid form.

Dates and Deadlines: Priority date 3/15; no closing date. Applicants notified on a rolling basis starting 2/15; must reply within 2 week(s) of notification.

Transfers: Priority date 6/1. Applicants notified on a rolling basis starting 2/1; must reply within 2 week(s) of notification.

CONTACT

Scott Hartle, Vice President Financial Services
75 College Avenue, Greenville, PA 16125-2181
(724) 589-2250

Thomas Jefferson University: College of Health Professions

Philadelphia, Pennsylvania
www.jefferson.edu/jchp   Federal Code: 012393

Upper-division private health science and nursing college in very large city.

Enrollment: 827 undergrads, 18% part-time.

BASIC COSTS (2007-2008)

Tuition and fees: $23,685.
Per-credit charge: $770.

FINANCIAL AID PICTURE (2006-2007)

Students with need: 40% of average financial aid package awarded as scholarships/grants, 60% awarded as loans/jobs.

Students without need: No-need awards available for academics, leadership, state/district residency.

Scholarships offered: Range of merit-based scholarships available for selected applicants.

FINANCIAL AID PROCEDURES

Forms required: FAFSA, institutional form.

Dates and Deadlines: Priority date 5/1; no closing date. Applicants notified on a rolling basis starting 4/1; must reply within 2 week(s) of notification.

Transfers: Applicants notified on a rolling basis starting 11/15; must reply within 2 week(s) of notification.

CONTACT

Susan McFadden, University Director of Financial Aid
130 South Ninth Street, Edison Building, Suite 100, Philadelphia, PA 19107
(215) 955-2867

Triangle Tech: Bethlehem

Bethlehem, Pennsylvania
www.triangle-tech.edu   Federal Code: 014895

2-year for-profit branch campus and technical college in small city.

Enrollment: 114 undergrads. 120 full-time freshmen.

Selectivity: Admits over 75% of applicants.

BASIC COSTS (2007-2008)

Tuition and fees: $12,919.
Per-credit charge: $349.

FINANCIAL AID PICTURE (2007-2008)

Students with need: Out of 117 full-time freshmen who applied for aid, 117 were judged to have need. Of these, 117 received aid. Average financial aid package met 31% of need; average scholarship/grant was $4,000; average loan was $3,721. Need-based aid available for part-time students.

Cumulative student debt: 53% of graduating class had student loans; average debt was $7,442.

FINANCIAL AID PROCEDURES

Forms required: FAFSA.

Dates and Deadlines: No deadline. Applicants notified on a rolling basis.

CONTACT

Catherine Waxter, Director of Financial Aid
31 South Commerce Way, LVIP IV, Bethlehem, PA 18017
(610) 691-1300

Triangle Tech: DuBois

DuBois, Pennsylvania
www.triangle-tech.edu   Federal Code: 021744

2-year for-profit technical college in large town.

Enrollment: 271 undergrads. 183 full-time freshmen.

Selectivity: Open admission.

BASIC COSTS (2008-2009)

Tuition and fees: $12,977.
Per-credit charge: $349.

FINANCIAL AID PICTURE (2006-2007)

Students with need: Out of 180 full-time freshmen who applied for aid, 180 were judged to have need. Of these, 180 received aid. Average financial aid package met 100% of need; average scholarship/grant was $3,375; average loan was $2,825. Need-based aid available for part-time students.

Students without need: This college awards aid only to students with need.

Cumulative student debt: 86% of graduating class had student loans; average debt was $14,500.

FINANCIAL AID PROCEDURES

Forms required: FAFSA, state aid form, institutional form.

Dates and Deadlines: No deadline. Applicants notified on a rolling basis.

CONTACT

Catherine Waxter, Corporate Director of Financial Aid
PO Box 551, DuBois, PA 15801-0551
(724) 832-1050

Triangle Tech: Erie

Erie, Pennsylvania
www.triangle-tech.edu   Federal Code: 014417

2-year for-profit technical college in small city.

Enrollment: 176 undergrads, 3% part-time. 66 full-time freshmen.

Selectivity: Open admission.

BASIC COSTS (2007-2008)

Tuition and fees: $12,869.

Per-credit charge: $349.

FINANCIAL AID PICTURE (2006-2007)

Students with need: Average financial aid package for all full-time undergraduates was $11,312. 49% awarded as scholarships/grants, 51% awarded as loans/jobs. Need-based aid available for part-time students.

Cumulative student debt: 66% of graduating class had student loans; average debt was $7,227.

FINANCIAL AID PROCEDURES

Forms required: FAFSA.

Dates and Deadlines: Applicants notified on a rolling basis.

CONTACT

Cathy Waxter, Corporate Director of Financial Aid
2000 Liberty Street, Erie, PA 16502-2594
(724) 832-1050

Triangle Tech: Greensburg

Greensburg, Pennsylvania
www.triangle-tech.edu   Federal Code: 014895

2-year for-profit technical college in large town.

Enrollment: 266 undergrads. 401 full-time freshmen.

Selectivity: Open admission.

BASIC COSTS (2007-2008)

Tuition and fees: $12,850.

Per-credit charge: $349.

Additional info: Tuition at time of enrollment locked for 2 years.

FINANCIAL AID PICTURE (2006-2007)

Students with need: Out of 229 full-time freshmen who applied for aid, 229 were judged to have need. Of these, 229 received aid, and 49 had their full need met. Average financial aid package met 80% of need; average scholarship/grant was $8,962; average loan was $2,625. Need-based aid available for part-time students.

Cumulative student debt: 57% of graduating class had student loans; average debt was $6,184.

FINANCIAL AID PROCEDURES

Forms required: FAFSA.

Dates and Deadlines: No deadline. Applicants notified on a rolling basis.

CONTACT

Catherine Waxter, Director of Financial Aid
222 East Pittsburgh Street, Suite A, Greensburg, PA 15601-3304
(724) 832-1050

Triangle Tech: Pittsburgh

Pittsburgh, Pennsylvania
www.triangle-tech.edu   Federal Code: 007839

2-year for-profit technical college in large city.

Enrollment: 277 undergrads. 422 full-time freshmen.

Selectivity: Open admission.

BASIC COSTS (2007-2008)

Tuition and fees: $12,930.

Per-credit charge: $349.

FINANCIAL AID PICTURE (2006-2007)

Students with need: Out of 286 full-time freshmen who applied for aid, 286 were judged to have need. Of these, 286 received aid, and 162 had their full need met. Average financial aid package met 57% of need; average scholarship/grant was $2,267; average loan was $5,868.

Students without need: This college awards aid only to students with need.

Cumulative student debt: 67% of graduating class had student loans; average debt was $5,930.

FINANCIAL AID PROCEDURES

Forms required: institutional form.

Dates and Deadlines: No deadline. Applicants notified on a rolling basis.

CONTACT

Cathy Waxter, Corporate Director of Financial Aid
1940 Perrysville Avenue, Pittsburgh, PA 15214-3897
(412) 359-1000

Triangle Tech: Sunbury

Sunbury, Pennsylvania
www.triangle-tech.edu

2-year for-profit technical college in large town.

Enrollment: 76 undergrads. 46 full-time freshmen.

Selectivity: Admits over 75% of applicants.

BASIC COSTS (2007-2008)

Tuition and fees: $13,042.

Per-credit charge: $349.

FINANCIAL AID PICTURE (2007-2008)

Students with need: Average financial aid package met 94% of need; average scholarship/grant was $3,561; average loan was $4,786.

FINANCIAL AID PROCEDURES

Forms required: FAFSA, institutional form.

Dates and Deadlines: No deadline.

CONTACT

Cathy Waxter, Director of Financial Aid
RR 1 Box 51, Sunbury, PA 17801

University of Pennsylvania

Philadelphia, Pennsylvania   Federal Code: 003378
www.upenn.edu   CSS Code: 2926

4-year private university in very large city.
Enrollment: 9,687 undergrads, 3% part-time. 2,385 full-time freshmen.
Selectivity: Admits less than 50% of applicants.

BASIC COSTS (2007-2008)

Tuition and fees: $35,916.
Room and board: $10,208.

FINANCIAL AID PICTURE (2006-2007)

Students with need: Out of 1,254 full-time freshmen who applied for aid,
951 were judged to have need. Of these, 951 received aid, and 951 had their
full need met. Average financial aid package met 100% of need; average
scholarship/grant was $26,102; average loan was $2,381. Need-based aid
available for part-time students.
Students without need: This college awards aid only to students with
need.
Cumulative student debt: 41% of graduating class had student loans; average debt was $18,800.

FINANCIAL AID PROCEDURES

Forms required: FAFSA, CSS PROFILE, institutional form.
Dates and Deadlines: Priority date 2/15; no closing date. Applicants notified
by 4/1; must reply by 5/1.
Transfers: Closing date 3/15. Applicants notified on a rolling basis starting
5/15; must reply within 4 week(s) of notification.

CONTACT

William Schilling, Director of Financial Aid
1 College Hall, Philadelphia, PA 19104
(215) 898-1988

University of Pittsburgh

Pittsburgh, Pennsylvania
www.pitt.edu   Federal Code: 008815

4-year public university in large city.
Enrollment: 16,798 undergrads, 7% part-time. 3,427 full-time freshmen.
Selectivity: Admits 50 to 75% of applicants. GED not accepted.

BASIC COSTS (2007-2008)

Tuition and fees: $12,876; out-of-state residents $22,386.
Per-credit charge: $504; out-of-state residents $900.
Room and board: $8,300.

FINANCIAL AID PICTURE (2007-2008)

Students with need: Out of 2,707 full-time freshmen who applied for aid,
1,903 were judged to have need. Of these, 1,861 received aid, and 707 had
their full need met. Average financial aid package met 78% of need; average
scholarship/grant was $8,577; average loan was $4,674. Need-based aid
available for part-time students.
Students without need: 303 full-time freshmen who did not demonstrate
need for aid received scholarships/grants; average award was $13,187. No-
need awards available for academics, athletics.
Scholarships offered: *Merit:* Academic Scholarships; $1,000 to full tuition,
room and board; renewable up to 4 years with 3.0 GPA. *Athletic:* 89 full-time
freshmen received athletic scholarships; average amount $18,229.

FINANCIAL AID PROCEDURES

Forms required: FAFSA, institutional form.
Dates and Deadlines: Priority date 3/1; no closing date. Applicants notified
on a rolling basis starting 3/15; must reply by 5/1 or within 3 week(s) of notification.

Transfers: Priority date 5/1; no deadline. Applicants notified on a rolling basis.
Transfer students not eligible for freshman scholarships.

CONTACT

Betsy Porter, Director, Office of Admissions and Financial Aid
4227 Fifth Avenue, 1st Floor, Alumni Hall, Pittsburgh, PA 15260
(412) 624-7488

University of Pittsburgh at Bradford

Bradford, Pennsylvania
www.upb.pitt.edu   Federal Code: 003380

4-year public university in large town.
Enrollment: 1,354 undergrads, 12% part-time. 320 full-time freshmen.
Selectivity: Admits over 75% of applicants.

BASIC COSTS (2007-2008)

Tuition and fees: $11,300; out-of-state residents $20,880.
Per-credit charge: $441; out-of-state residents $840.
Room and board: $6,850.

FINANCIAL AID PICTURE (2007-2008)

Students with need: Average financial aid package met 78% of need; average
scholarship/grant was $5,277; average loan was $3,407. For part-time
students, average financial aid package was $6,880.
Students without need: 54 full-time freshmen who did not demonstrate
need for aid received scholarships/grants; average award was $5,412. No-
need awards available for academics, alumni affiliation, ROTC, state/district
residency.
Scholarships offered: Panther Scholarship: for full-time on campus residents
or students who commute from Cameron, Elk, Forest, McKean, Potter, or
Warren counties. Valedictorian/Salutatorian Scholarship; for Pennsylvania students. International Student Scholarship; for international students who plan
to enroll full-time and reside on campus.
Cumulative student debt: 90% of graduating class had student loans; average debt was $24,910.

FINANCIAL AID PROCEDURES

Forms required: FAFSA.
Dates and Deadlines: Priority date 3/1; no closing date. Applicants notified
on a rolling basis starting 4/1; must reply within 2 week(s) of notification.
Transfers: No deadline. Applicants notified on a rolling basis starting 4/1;
must reply within 2 week(s) of notification. Transfers must meet academic
policy guidelines.

CONTACT

Melissa Ibanez, Director of Financial Aid
300 Campus Drive, Bradford, PA 16701
(814) 362-7550

University of Pittsburgh at Greensburg

Greensburg, Pennsylvania
www.upg.pitt.edu   Federal Code: 003381

4-year public branch campus and liberal arts college in large town.
Enrollment: 1,771 undergrads, 7% part-time. 488 full-time freshmen.
Selectivity: Admits over 75% of applicants.

BASIC COSTS (2007-2008)

Tuition and fees: $11,320; out-of-state residents $20,900.
Per-credit charge: $441; out-of-state residents $840.
Room and board: $7,000.

FINANCIAL AID PICTURE (2007-2008)

Students with need: Out of 407 full-time freshmen who applied for aid, 324 were judged to have need. Of these, 317 received aid, and 42 had their full need met. Average financial aid package met 66% of need; average scholarship/grant was $5,651; average loan was $4,270. For part-time students, average financial aid package was $6,067.

Students without need: 38 full-time freshmen who did not demonstrate need for aid received scholarships/grants; average award was $3,079. No-need awards available for academics, leadership, minority status.

Cumulative student debt: 78% of graduating class had student loans; average debt was $24,080.

FINANCIAL AID PROCEDURES

Forms required: FAFSA, state aid form.

Dates and Deadlines: Priority date 2/15; no closing date. Applicants notified on a rolling basis starting 3/15; must reply within 3 week(s) of notification.

Transfers: No deadline.

CONTACT

Brandi Darr, Director of Financial Aid
150 Finoli Drive, Greensburg, PA 15601
(724) 836-9881

University of Pittsburgh at Johnstown

Johnstown, Pennsylvania
www.upj.pitt.edu   Federal Code: 008815

4-year public engineering and liberal arts college in small city.

Enrollment: 3,116 undergrads, 6% part-time. 839 full-time freshmen.

Selectivity: Admits over 75% of applicants.

BASIC COSTS (2007-2008)

Tuition and fees: $11,332; out-of-state residents $20,912.

Per-credit charge: $441; out-of-state residents $840.

Room and board: $6,400.

FINANCIAL AID PICTURE (2007-2008)

Students with need: Out of 769 full-time freshmen who applied for aid, 648 were judged to have need. Of these, 632 received aid, and 20 had their full need met. Average financial aid package met 52% of need; average scholarship/grant was $5,357; average loan was $3,801. For part-time students, average financial aid package was $3,141.

Students without need: 34 full-time freshmen who did not demonstrate need for aid received scholarships/grants; average award was $3,694. No-need awards available for academics, athletics, leadership, minority status, state/district residency.

Scholarships offered: *Merit:* President's Scholarships and Leadership Scholarships; $1,500 to full tuition yearly; renewable; 1220 SAT (exclusive of Writing), 3.8 GPA, and top 10% of graduating class required; priority given to those who apply by 12/01. *Athletic:* 18 full-time freshmen received athletic scholarships; average amount $5,805.

Cumulative student debt: 86% of graduating class had student loans; average debt was $23,412.

FINANCIAL AID PROCEDURES

Forms required: FAFSA.

Dates and Deadlines: Priority date 4/1; no closing date. Applicants notified on a rolling basis starting 3/15; must reply within 2 week(s) of notification.

CONTACT

Jeanine Lawn, Director of Financial Aid
450 Schoolhouse Road, 157 Blackington Hall, Johnstown, PA 15904-1200
(800) 881-5544

University of Pittsburgh at Titusville

Titusville, Pennsylvania
www.upt.pitt.edu   Federal Code: 008815

2-year public branch campus and liberal arts college in small town.

Enrollment: 557 undergrads, 19% part-time. 221 full-time freshmen.

Selectivity: Admits over 75% of applicants.

BASIC COSTS (2007-2008)

Tuition and fees: $10,058; out-of-state residents $18,692.

Per-credit charge: $388; out-of-state residents $748.

Room and board: $7,594.

Additional info: Tuition/fee waivers available for adults.

FINANCIAL AID PICTURE (2007-2008)

Students with need: Average financial aid package met 85% of need; average scholarship/grant was $7,235; average loan was $3,224. For part-time students, average financial aid package was $5,206.

Students without need: No-need awards available for academics, athletics, state/district residency.

Scholarships offered: Science scholarships; $2,000; awarded to top 5 students with science as a major; renewable with 3.0 GPA and continued science major. Presidential scholarships; $2,500; awarded based on high school academic record; 6 awarded.

FINANCIAL AID PROCEDURES

Forms required: FAFSA.

Dates and Deadlines: Priority date 3/1; no closing date. Applicants notified on a rolling basis; must reply within 2 week(s) of notification.

Transfers: No deadline. Must reply within 2 week(s) of notification. Pennsylvania residents must apply by 5/1 for PHEAA. Transfer students must have completed 24 credits to renew. Information retrieved from NSLOS is utilized to determine transfer student eligibility for financial aid.

CONTACT

Sue Bloom, Director of Financial Aid
UPT Admissions Office, Titusville, PA 16354-0287
(814) 827-4495

University of Scranton

Scranton, Pennsylvania
www.scranton.edu   Federal Code: 003384

4-year private university and liberal arts college in small city, affiliated with Roman Catholic Church.

Enrollment: 3,994 undergrads, 4% part-time. 1,027 full-time freshmen.

Selectivity: Admits 50 to 75% of applicants.

BASIC COSTS (2008-2009)

Tuition and fees: $31,576.

Per-credit charge: $807.

Room and board: $10,990.

FINANCIAL AID PICTURE (2007-2008)

Students with need: Out of 853 full-time freshmen who applied for aid, 717 were judged to have need. Of these, 710 received aid, and 80 had their full need met. Average financial aid package met 75% of need; average scholarship/grant was $14,767; average loan was $3,345. For part-time students, average financial aid package was $11,641.

Students without need: 159 full-time freshmen who did not demonstrate need for aid received scholarships/grants; average award was $10,009. No-need awards available for academics, minority status, ROTC.

Cumulative student debt: 76% of graduating class had student loans; average debt was $26,169.

FINANCIAL AID PROCEDURES

Forms required: FAFSA.

Dates and Deadlines: Priority date 2/15; no closing date. Applicants notified on a rolling basis starting 3/1; must reply by 5/1 or within 2 week(s) of notification.

Transfers: Institutional grants available based on financial need.

CONTACT

William Burke, Director of Financial Aid
800 Linden Street, Scranton, PA 18510-4699
(570) 941-7700

University of the Arts

Philadelphia, Pennsylvania
www.uarts.edu   Federal Code: 003350

4-year private visual arts and performing arts college in very large city.

Enrollment: 2,181 undergrads.

Selectivity: Admits less than 50% of applicants.

BASIC COSTS (2008-2009)

Tuition and fees: $30,600.

Per-credit charge: $1,230.

Room only: $8,712.

FINANCIAL AID PICTURE

Students with need: Need-based aid available for full-time and part-time students. Work study available nights, weekends, and for part-time students.

Students without need: No-need awards available for academics, art, music/drama.

Scholarships offered: Merit awards; available to students who demonstrate exceptional talent and academic abilities.

FINANCIAL AID PROCEDURES

Forms required: FAFSA.

Dates and Deadlines: Priority date 3/1; no closing date. Applicants notified on a rolling basis starting 3/15; must reply within 2 week(s) of notification.

Transfers: Undergraduate transfers not eligible for federal, state, or university aid if 4-year degree previously conferred.

CONTACT

Chris Pesotski, Director, Financial Aid
320 South Broad Street, Philadelphia, PA 19102
(215) 717-6170

University of the Sciences in Philadelphia

Philadelphia, Pennsylvania
www.usp.edu   Federal Code: 003353

4-year private health science and pharmacy college in very large city.

Enrollment: 2,116 undergrads, 1% part-time. 501 full-time freshmen.

Selectivity: Admits 50 to 75% of applicants.

BASIC COSTS (2007-2008)

Tuition and fees: $26,930.

Per-credit charge: $1,067.

Room and board: $10,524.

Additional info: Tiered cost structure applies to students enrolled in 5- and 6-year programs that lead to professional degrees.

FINANCIAL AID PICTURE (2006-2007)

Students with need: Out of 455 full-time freshmen who applied for aid, 396 were judged to have need. Of these, 396 received aid, and 192 had their full need met. Average financial aid package met 98% of need; average scholarship/grant was $7,815; average loan was $2,792. For part-time students, average financial aid package was $10,934.

Students without need: 105 full-time freshmen who did not demonstrate need for aid received scholarships/grants; average award was $6,952. No-need awards available for academics, athletics.

Scholarships offered: 4 full-time freshmen received athletic scholarships; average amount $19,025.

Cumulative student debt: 24% of graduating class had student loans; average debt was $24,048.

FINANCIAL AID PROCEDURES

Forms required: FAFSA.

Dates and Deadlines: Closing date 3/15. Applicants notified on a rolling basis starting 1/15; must reply by 5/1 or within 2 week(s) of notification.

CONTACT

Paula Lehrberger, Director of Financial Aid
600 South 43rd Street, Philadelphia, PA 19104-4495
(215) 596-8894

Ursinus College

Collegeville, Pennsylvania   Federal Code: 003385
www.ursinus.edu   CSS Code: 2931

4-year private liberal arts college in small town.

Enrollment: 1,563 undergrads. 468 full-time freshmen.

Selectivity: Admits 50 to 75% of applicants. GED not accepted.

BASIC COSTS (2007-2008)

Tuition and fees: $35,160.

Per-credit charge: $1,094.

Room and board: $8,000.

FINANCIAL AID PICTURE (2007-2008)

Students with need: Out of 393 full-time freshmen who applied for aid, 306 were judged to have need. Of these, 306 received aid, and 86 had their full need met. Average financial aid package met 85% of need; average scholarship/grant was $19,726; average loan was $3,203.

Students without need: 130 full-time freshmen who did not demonstrate need for aid received scholarships/grants; average award was $12,481. No-need awards available for academics, alumni affiliation, art, leadership, music/drama.

Cumulative student debt: 75% of graduating class had student loans; average debt was $18,509.

FINANCIAL AID PROCEDURES

Forms required: FAFSA, CSS PROFILE.

Dates and Deadlines: Closing date 2/15. Applicants notified by 3/15; must reply by 5/1.

Transfers: Closing date 8/1.

CONTACT

Suzanne Sparrow, Director of Student Financial Services
PO Box 1000, Collegeville, PA 19426-1000
(610) 409-3600

Valley Forge Christian College

Phoenixville, Pennsylvania
www.vfcc.edu   Federal Code: 003306

4-year private liberal arts college in large town, affiliated with Assemblies of God.

Enrollment: 946 undergrads, 17% part-time. 157 full-time freshmen.

Selectivity: Admits 50 to 75% of applicants.

BASIC COSTS (2008-2009)

Tuition and fees: $12,990.

Room and board: $6,570.

FINANCIAL AID PICTURE (2007-2008)

Students with need: Average financial aid package met 49% of need; average scholarship/grant was $5,894; average loan was $3,288. For part-time students, average financial aid package was $6,746.

Students without need: No-need awards available for academics, leadership, music/drama, religious affiliation, state/district residency.

Scholarships offered: Trustee's Scholarship, President's Scholarship, Dean's Scholarship, Professor's Scholarship; ranging from full tuition (minimum 3.56 GPA, 1300 SAT or 29 ACT, and upper 10% class rank) to $1,000-$2,000 (minimum 3.5 GPA and 1030 SAT or 22 ACT); application required for awards; renewable with 3.5 GPA. SAT scores exclusive of Writing.

Cumulative student debt: 98% of graduating class had student loans; average debt was $33,319.

FINANCIAL AID PROCEDURES

Forms required: FAFSA.

Dates and Deadlines: Priority date 5/1; no closing date. Applicants notified on a rolling basis starting 3/15; must reply within 3 week(s) of notification.

CONTACT

Evie Meyer, Director of Financial Aid
1401 Charlestown Road, Phoenixville, PA 19460
(610) 917-1475

Valley Forge Military College
Wayne, Pennsylvania
www.vfmac.edu   Federal Code: 003386

2-year private junior and military college in small city.
Enrollment: 216 undergrads.

BASIC COSTS (2007-2008)
Tuition and fees: $25,766.
Room and board: $8,035.

FINANCIAL AID PICTURE
Students with need: Need-based aid available for full-time students. Work study available nights, weekends, and for part-time students.

Students without need: No-need awards available for academics, alumni affiliation, athletics, music/drama, ROTC, state/district residency.

Additional info: Students enrolled in advanced military science program can receive up to $5,000 from the Army. In addition, competitively awarded ROTC scholarships pay average of another $14,100 per school year for direct educational expenses.

FINANCIAL AID PROCEDURES
Forms required: FAFSA, institutional form.
Dates and Deadlines: Closing date 5/1. Applicants notified on a rolling basis starting 5/15; must reply within 2 week(s) of notification.
Transfers: Must submit financial aid transcripts from all previously attended colleges, even if aid was not received.

CONTACT
Donna Speranza, Financial Aid Director
1001 Eagle Road, Wayne, PA 19087
(610) 989-1300 ext. 1306

Vet Tech Institute
Pittsburgh, Pennsylvania
www.vettechinstitute.com   Federal Code: 008568

2-year for-profit health science and technical college in large city.
Enrollment: 325 undergrads.

BASIC COSTS (2008-2009)
Tuition and fees: $28,620.
Additional info: Tuition at time of enrollment locked for 2 years.

FINANCIAL AID PICTURE
Students with need: Work study available nights.
Students without need: No-need awards available for academics.
Scholarships offered: $1,000 scholarships; 5 offered to commuters. $2,000 scholarships; 2 offered to students not living at home. Awarded based on results of examination given at school in November and March.

FINANCIAL AID PROCEDURES
Forms required: FAFSA, state aid form.
Dates and Deadlines: No deadline. Applicants notified on a rolling basis.

CONTACT
Donna Durr, Financial Aid Coordinator
125 Seventh Street, Pittsburgh, PA 15222-3400
(800) 570-0693

Villanova University
Villanova, Pennsylvania
www.villanova.edu   Federal Code: 003388

4-year private university in small town, affiliated with Roman Catholic Church.
Enrollment: 6,949 undergrads, 4% part-time. 1,604 full-time freshmen.
Selectivity: Admits less than 50% of applicants.

BASIC COSTS (2007-2008)
Tuition and fees: $34,620.
Room and board: $9,810.
Additional info: Full-time tuition includes laptop for all freshmen.

FINANCIAL AID PICTURE (2007-2008)
Students with need: Out of 1,043 full-time freshmen who applied for aid, 767 were judged to have need. Of these, 763 received aid, and 160 had their full need met. Average financial aid package met 84% of need; average scholarship/grant was $20,714; average loan was $4,283. For part-time students, average financial aid package was $6,668.

Students without need: 96 full-time freshmen who did not demonstrate need for aid received scholarships/grants; average award was $8,972. No-need awards available for academics, alumni affiliation, athletics, leadership, minority status, religious affiliation, ROTC.

Scholarships offered: 34 full-time freshmen received athletic scholarships; average amount $33,093.

Cumulative student debt: 56% of graduating class had student loans; average debt was $28,107.

FINANCIAL AID PROCEDURES
Forms required: FAFSA, institutional form.
Dates and Deadlines: Closing date 2/7. Applicants notified by 4/1; must reply by 5/1 or within 2 week(s) of notification.
Transfers: Closing date 7/15. Applicants notified on a rolling basis starting 5/1; must reply within 2 week(s) of notification.

CONTACT
Bonnie Lee Behm, Director of Financial Assistance
800 Lancaster Avenue, Villanova, PA 19085-1672
(610) 519-4010

Washington & Jefferson College
Washington, Pennsylvania
www.washjeff.edu   Federal Code: 003389

4-year private liberal arts college in large town.
Enrollment: 1,514 undergrads, 1% part-time. 407 full-time freshmen.

Selectivity: Admits less than 50% of applicants.

BASIC COSTS (2008-2009)

Tuition and fees: $31,496.
Per-credit charge: $780.
Room and board: $8,488.

FINANCIAL AID PICTURE (2007-2008)

Students with need: Out of 366 full-time freshmen who applied for aid, 313 were judged to have need. Of these, 313 received aid, and 48 had their full need met. Average financial aid package met 82% of need; average scholarship/grant was $7,557; average loan was $3,864. For part-time students, average financial aid package was $20,185.

Students without need: 94 full-time freshmen who did not demonstrate need for aid received scholarships/grants; average award was $9,984. No-need awards available for academics, alumni affiliation.

Scholarships offered: Presidential Scholarship; based on distinguished academic performance. Scholars Award; based on distinguished academic performance. Joseph Hardy Sr. Scholarship; for students in entrepreneurial studies program. Dean's Award; based on academic performance in high school, distinguished achievement outside the classroom, and good citizenship. Challenge Grant; for students who show academic promise. Alumni Scholarship; for students whose father and/or mother are alumni.

Cumulative student debt: 75% of graduating class had student loans; average debt was $20,000.

FINANCIAL AID PROCEDURES

Forms required: FAFSA.
Dates and Deadlines: Priority date 3/1; no closing date. Applicants notified on a rolling basis starting 3/1.
Transfers: Must reply within 2 week(s) of notification. Students should complete the FAFSA as soon as possible. Financial aid awards will be made when FAFSA has been received and the student has been accepted for admission. For students selected for verification, these awards are estimated until the required tax documentation has been received and reviewed.

CONTACT

Michelle Vettorel, Director of Financial Aid
60 South Lincoln Street, Washington, PA 15301
(724) 223-6019

Waynesburg University

Waynesburg, Pennsylvania
www.waynesburg.edu   Federal Code: 003391

4-year private liberal arts college in small town, affiliated with Presbyterian Church (USA).
Enrollment: 1,614 undergrads, 5% part-time. 405 full-time freshmen.
Selectivity: Admits 50 to 75% of applicants.

BASIC COSTS (2007-2008)

Tuition and fees: $16,420.
Per-credit charge: $680.
Room and board: $6,700.

FINANCIAL AID PICTURE (2007-2008)

Students with need: Average financial aid package met 89% of need; average scholarship/grant was $11,145; average loan was $3,785. For part-time students, average financial aid package was $5,296.

Students without need: No-need awards available for academics, alumni affiliation, job skills, leadership, religious affiliation, state/district residency.

Scholarships offered: A.B. Miller Scholarship; $8,000. Presidential Honor Scholarship; $6,000. Honor Scholarship; $4,000. College Leadership Program; $1,000-$1,900.

Cumulative student debt: 82% of graduating class had student loans; average debt was $17,500.

FINANCIAL AID PROCEDURES

Forms required: FAFSA, state aid form.
Dates and Deadlines: Priority date 3/15; no closing date. Applicants notified on a rolling basis starting 2/15; must reply within 2 week(s) of notification.
Transfers: No deadline. Applicants notified on a rolling basis; must reply within 2 week(s) of notification.

CONTACT

Matthew Stokan, Director of Financial Aid
51 West College Street, Waynesburg, PA 15370-1222
(724) 852-3208

West Chester University of Pennsylvania

West Chester, Pennsylvania
www.wcupa.edu   Federal Code: 003328

4-year public university in large town.
Enrollment: 10,716 undergrads, 8% part-time. 1,885 full-time freshmen.
Selectivity: Admits less than 50% of applicants.

BASIC COSTS (2007-2008)

Tuition and fees: $6,676; out-of-state residents $14,443.
Per-credit charge: $216; out-of-state residents $539.
Room and board: $6,590.

FINANCIAL AID PICTURE (2006-2007)

Students with need: Out of 1,511 full-time freshmen who applied for aid, 1,044 were judged to have need. Of these, 994 received aid, and 115 had their full need met. Average financial aid package met 54% of need; average scholarship/grant was $4,795; average loan was $2,691. For part-time students, average financial aid package was $4,937.

Students without need: 96 full-time freshmen who did not demonstrate need for aid received scholarships/grants; average award was $3,968.

Scholarships offered: 28 full-time freshmen received athletic scholarships; average amount $2,800.

FINANCIAL AID PROCEDURES

Forms required: FAFSA.
Dates and Deadlines: Priority date 3/1; no closing date. Must reply within 4 week(s) of notification.

CONTACT

Dana Parker, Director of Financial Aid
Messikomer Hall, West Chester, PA 19383
(610) 436-2627

Westminster College

New Wilmington, Pennsylvania
www.westminster.edu   Federal Code: 003392

4-year private liberal arts college in small town, affiliated with Presbyterian Church (USA).
Enrollment: 1,308 undergrads.
Selectivity: Admits 50 to 75% of applicants.

BASIC COSTS (2008-2009)

Tuition and fees: $28,100.
Per-credit charge: $820.
Room and board: $8,100.
Additional info: Tuition/fee waivers available for adults.

FINANCIAL AID PICTURE (2007-2008)

Students with need: 69% of average financial aid package awarded as scholarships/grants, 31% awarded as loans/jobs. Need-based aid available for part-time students.

Students without need: No-need awards available for academics, athletics.

FINANCIAL AID PROCEDURES

Forms required: FAFSA, institutional form.

Dates and Deadlines: Closing date 5/1. Applicants notified on a rolling basis starting 11/1; must reply by 5/1 or within 3 week(s) of notification.

CONTACT

Cheryl Gerber, Director of Financial Aid

Admissions, Westminster College, New Wilmington, PA 16172-0001

(724) 946-7102

Westmoreland County Community College

Youngwood, Pennsylvania
www.wccc.edu   Federal Code: 010176

2-year public community college in small town.

Enrollment: 5,381 undergrads, 48% part-time. 1,150 full-time freshmen.

Selectivity: Open admission; but selective for some programs.

BASIC COSTS (2008-2009)

Tuition and fees: $2,820; out-of-district residents $5,340; out-of-state residents $7,680.

Per-credit charge: $78; out-of-district residents $156; out-of-state residents $234.

FINANCIAL AID PICTURE

Students with need: Need-based aid available for full-time and part-time students. Work study available nights.

Students without need: No-need awards available for academics.

FINANCIAL AID PROCEDURES

Forms required: FAFSA, institutional form.

Dates and Deadlines: No deadline. Applicants notified on a rolling basis starting 5/1.

CONTACT

Gary Means, Director of Financial Aid

145 Pavilion Lane, Youngwood, PA 15697-1895

(724) 925-4063

Widener University

Chester, Pennsylvania
www.widener.edu   Federal Code: 003313

4-year private university in large town.

Enrollment: 3,213 undergrads, 18% part-time. 782 full-time freshmen.

Selectivity: Admits 50 to 75% of applicants.

BASIC COSTS (2008-2009)

Tuition and fees: $30,450.

Per-credit charge: $1,000.

Room and board: $10,840.

Additional info: $950 additional fee for engineering students; $200 additional fee for junior/senior nursing students.

FINANCIAL AID PICTURE (2007-2008)

Students with need: Out of 692 full-time freshmen who applied for aid, 630 were judged to have need. Of these, 630 received aid, and 120 had their full need met. Average financial aid package met 84% of need; average scholarship/grant was $8,873; average loan was $4,267. For part-time students, average financial aid package was $7,615.

Students without need: 140 full-time freshmen who did not demonstrate need for aid received scholarships/grants; average award was $10,765. No-need awards available for academics, leadership, music/drama, ROTC.

Scholarships offered: Academic Scholarships; $4,000 to full tuition; based on SAT and GPA; renewable. Music, leadership, and community service scholarships; based on performance evaluations.

Cumulative student debt: 89% of graduating class had student loans; average debt was $34,215.

FINANCIAL AID PROCEDURES

Forms required: FAFSA.

Dates and Deadlines: Priority date 2/15; no closing date. Applicants notified on a rolling basis starting 3/15; must reply within 4 week(s) of notification.

Transfers: Transfer scholarships; $2,500 to $10,000; based on GPA and minimum of 24 transferable credits.

CONTACT

Thomas Malloy, Director of Financial Aid

One University Place, Chester, PA 19013

(610) 499-4174

Wilkes University

Wilkes-Barre, Pennsylvania
www.wilkes.edu   Federal Code: 003394

4-year private university in small city.

Enrollment: 2,257 undergrads, 7% part-time. 620 full-time freshmen.

Selectivity: Admits over 75% of applicants.

BASIC COSTS (2008-2009)

Tuition and fees: $25,170.

Per-credit charge: $660.

Room and board: $10,780.

FINANCIAL AID PICTURE (2007-2008)

Students with need: Out of 580 full-time freshmen who applied for aid, 529 were judged to have need. Of these, 529 received aid, and 23 had their full need met. Average financial aid package met 81% of need; average scholarship/grant was $15,215; average loan was $2,891. For part-time students, average financial aid package was $7,126.

Students without need: 40 full-time freshmen who did not demonstrate need for aid received scholarships/grants; average award was $9,225. No-need awards available for academics, leadership, minority status, music/drama.

Cumulative student debt: 88% of graduating class had student loans; average debt was $29,478.

FINANCIAL AID PROCEDURES

Forms required: FAFSA.

Dates and Deadlines: Priority date 3/1; no closing date. Applicants notified on a rolling basis starting 3/1.

CONTACT

Michael Frantz, Vice President of Enrollment Services

84 West South Street, Wilkes-Barre, PA 18766

(570) 408-2000

Wilson College

Chambersburg, Pennsylvania
www.wilson.edu   Federal Code: 003396

4-year private liberal arts college for women in large town, affiliated with Presbyterian Church (USA).

Enrollment: 521 undergrads, 35% part-time. 85 full-time freshmen.

Selectivity: Admits less than 50% of applicants.

BASIC COSTS (2008-2009)

Tuition and fees: $25,900.

Room and board: $8,630.

FINANCIAL AID PICTURE (2007-2008)

Students with need: Out of 73 full-time freshmen who applied for aid, 57 were judged to have need. Of these, 57 received aid, and 6 had their full need met. Average financial aid package met 78% of need; average scholarship/grant was $15,190; average loan was $4,346. For part-time students, average financial aid package was $5,446.

Students without need: 27 full-time freshmen who did not demonstrate need for aid received scholarships/grants; average award was $18,858. No-need awards available for academics, alumni affiliation, religious affiliation, state/district residency.

Scholarships offered: Scholarships; for full-time students who are members of Presbyterian Church, USA. Curran Scholarships; awarded to incoming students with significant community service.

Cumulative student debt: 81% of graduating class had student loans; average debt was $24,443.

FINANCIAL AID PROCEDURES

Forms required: FAFSA, state aid form, institutional form.

Dates and Deadlines: Priority date 4/30; no closing date. Applicants notified on a rolling basis starting 2/15.

Transfers: Tuition scholarships available to transfer articulation students who hold associate degrees from Harrisburg Area Community College, Hagerstown Community College, Central Penn College, Luzerne County Community College, Lehigh Carbon Community College, Harcum College, Frederick Community College, Howard Community College, Cottey College; transfer merit scholarships for students with 3.0 GPA; Phi Theta Kappa scholarship.

CONTACT

Linda Brittain, Associate Dean of Enrollment and Director of Financial Aid
1015 Philadelphia Avenue, Chambersburg, PA 17201-1285
(717) 262-2016

York College of Pennsylvania

York, Pennsylvania
www.ycp.edu   Federal Code: 003399

4-year private liberal arts college in small city.

Enrollment: 5,219 undergrads, 11% part-time. 1,178 full-time freshmen.

Selectivity: Admits 50 to 75% of applicants.

BASIC COSTS (2008-2009)

Tuition and fees: $13,680.

Per-credit charge: $385.

Room and board: $7,800.

FINANCIAL AID PICTURE (2007-2008)

Students with need: Out of 1,008 full-time freshmen who applied for aid, 644 were judged to have need. Of these, 641 received aid, and 181 had their full need met. Average financial aid package met 77% of need; average scholarship/grant was $4,826; average loan was $5,444. For part-time students, average financial aid package was $6,243.

Students without need: 224 full-time freshmen who did not demonstrate need for aid received scholarships/grants; average award was $2,695. No-need awards available for academics, alumni affiliation, art, music/drama.

Scholarships offered: Trustee Scholarships; full tuition; for students with top 20% class rank and 1210 SAT or 29 ACT; 10 awarded. Valedictorian and Salutatorian Scholarships; half tuition; for students who are valedictorians or salutatorians and have 1150 SAT or 26 ACT; unlimited number awarded. Dean's Academic Scholarships; one-third tuition; for students with top 40% class rank and 1150 SAT or 26 ACT; 175 awarded. SAT scores exclusive of Writing portion.

Cumulative student debt: 69% of graduating class had student loans; average debt was $20,625.

FINANCIAL AID PROCEDURES

Forms required: FAFSA.

Dates and Deadlines: Priority date 3/1; no closing date. Applicants notified on a rolling basis starting 2/15; must reply within 4 week(s) of notification.

CONTACT

Calvin Williams, Director of Financial Aid
441 Country Club Road, York, PA 17403-3651
(717) 849-1682

Puerto Rico

Atlantic College

Guaynabo, Puerto Rico
www.atlanticcollege-pr.com   Federal Code: 016871

4-year private visual arts and business and liberal arts college in small city.

Enrollment: 996 undergrads.

Selectivity: Open admission.

BASIC COSTS (2007-2008)

Additional info: Tuition at time of enrollment locked for 4 years.

FINANCIAL AID PICTURE

Students with need: Need-based aid available for full-time and part-time students. Work study available nights.

Students without need: This college awards aid only to students with need.

FINANCIAL AID PROCEDURES

Forms required: FAFSA, institutional form.

Dates and Deadlines: Closing date 6/30. Applicants notified on a rolling basis starting 4/1; must reply within 2 week(s) of notification.

Transfers: Priority date 1/7; closing date 6/7.

CONTACT

Janice Rivera, Director of Financial Aid
PO Box 3918, Guaynabo, PR 00970
(787) 789-4251

Bayamon Central University

Bayamon, Puerto Rico
www.ucb.edu.pr   Federal Code: 010015

4-year private university in large city, affiliated with Roman Catholic Church.

Enrollment: 2,133 undergrads.

Selectivity: Open admission; but selective for some programs and for out-of-state students.

BASIC COSTS (2007-2008)

Tuition and fees: $4,850.

Per-credit charge: $145.

FINANCIAL AID PICTURE

Students with need: Need-based aid available for full-time and part-time students. Work study available nights.

Students without need: This college awards aid only to students with need.

FINANCIAL AID PROCEDURES

Forms required: FAFSA, institutional form.

Dates and Deadlines: Priority date 5/31; closing date 7/2.

Transfers: Closing date 5/30.

CONTACT

Velma Aponte, Director of Financial Aid Office
PO Box 1725, Bayamon, PR 00960-1725
(787) 786-3030 ext. 2116

Carlos Albizu University: San Juan
San Juan, Puerto Rico
www.albizu.edu   Federal Code: 010724

Upper-division private university in large town.
Enrollment: 192 undergrads.

FINANCIAL AID PICTURE (2006-2007)
Students with need: 16% of average financial aid package awarded as scholarships/grants, 84% awarded as loans/jobs.

CONTACT
Doris Quero-Mendez, Financial Aid Director
151 Tanca Street, San Juan, PR 00902-3711
(787) 725-6500 ext. 1515

Colegio Pentecostal Mizpa
San Juan, Puerto Rico
www.colmizpa.edu   Federal Code: 035313

4-year private Bible college in very large city.
Enrollment: 250 undergrads, 64% part-time. 7 full-time freshmen.
Selectivity: Admits 50 to 75% of applicants.

BASIC COSTS (2007-2008)
Tuition and fees: $2,550.
Per-credit charge: $80.
Room and board: $1,250.

FINANCIAL AID PICTURE (2006-2007)
Students with need: Out of 7 full-time freshmen who applied for aid, 7 were judged to have need. Of these, 7 received aid. Need-based aid available for part-time students.
Students without need: This college awards aid only to students with need.

FINANCIAL AID PROCEDURES
Forms required: FAFSA.
Dates and Deadlines: No deadline.
Transfers: Applicants notified by 8/30.

CONTACT
Elisamuel Rodriguez, Administrative Dean
PO Box 20966, San Juan, PR 00928-0966

Columbia Centro Universitario: Caguas
Caguas, Puerto Rico
www.columbiaco.edu   Federal Code: 013517

4-year for-profit business and technical college in small city.
Enrollment: 791 undergrads. 205 full-time freshmen.
Selectivity: Open admission; but selective for some programs.

BASIC COSTS (2007-2008)
Tuition and fees: $3,850.
Per-credit charge: $145.

FINANCIAL AID PICTURE (2006-2007)
Students with need: Out of 185 full-time freshmen who applied for aid, 185 were judged to have need. Of these, 185 received aid. Need-based aid available for part-time students.
Students without need: This college awards aid only to students with need.

CONTACT
Virginia Guang, Financial Aid Administrator
PO Box 8517, Caguas, PR 00726
(787) 743-4041 ext. 223

Columbia Centro Universitario: Yauco
Yauco, Puerto Rico
www.columbiaco.edu   Federal Code: 008902

2-year for-profit business and nursing college in large town.
Enrollment: 440 undergrads.
Selectivity: Open admission; but selective for some programs.

BASIC COSTS (2007-2008)
Tuition and fees: $3,850.
Per-credit charge: $145.

FINANCIAL AID PICTURE
Students with need: Need-based aid available for full-time and part-time students. Work study available nights.
Students without need: This college awards aid only to students with need.

FINANCIAL AID PROCEDURES
Forms required: FAFSA, institutional form.

CONTACT
Edwin Vargas, Director of Financial Aid
Box 3062, Yauco, PR 00698-3062

Conservatory of Music of Puerto Rico
San Juan, Puerto Rico
www.cmpr.edu   Federal Code: 010819

4-year public music college in large city.
Enrollment: 361 undergrads, 30% part-time. 20 full-time freshmen.
Selectivity: Admits 50 to 75% of applicants.

BASIC COSTS (2007-2008)
Tuition and fees: $2,292.
Per-credit charge: $65.

FINANCIAL AID PICTURE
Students with need: Need-based aid available for full-time and part-time students. Work study available nights.
Students without need: This college awards aid only to students with need.

FINANCIAL AID PROCEDURES
Forms required: FAFSA, institutional form.
Dates and Deadlines: Priority date 6/30; no closing date. Applicants notified on a rolling basis starting 8/30.
Transfers: Closing date 4/15.

CONTACT
Jorge Medina, Financial Aid Officer
Rafael Lamar #350 Esq. Roosevelt, San Juan, PR 00918-2199
(787) 751-0160 ext. 231

Escuela de Artes Plasticas de Puerto Rico
San Juan, Puerto Rico
www.eap.edu   Federal Code: 017345

4-year public visual arts college in large city.
Enrollment: 494 undergrads.

Selectivity: Admits 50 to 75% of applicants.

BASIC COSTS (2008-2009)

Tuition and fees: $2,923.
Per-credit charge: $80.

FINANCIAL AID PICTURE (2006-2007)

Students with need: 99% of average financial aid package awarded as scholarships/grants, 1% awarded as loans/jobs. Need-based aid available for part-time students.
Students without need: This college awards aid only to students with need.

FINANCIAL AID PROCEDURES

Forms required: FAFSA, institutional form.
Dates and Deadlines: Priority date 4/25; closing date 5/23. Applicants notified by 7/11.

CONTACT

Alfred Melendez, Director of Financial Aid
PO Box 9021112, San Juan, PR 00902-1112

Huertas Junior College

Caguas, Puerto Rico
www.huertas.edu   Federal Code: 014105

2-year for-profit junior and technical college in small city.
Enrollment: 1,665 undergrads, 16% part-time. 424 full-time freshmen.
Selectivity: Open admission; but selective for some programs.

BASIC COSTS (2007-2008)

Tuition and fees: $4,960.
Additional info: Tuition at time of enrollment locked for 2 years.

FINANCIAL AID PICTURE (2007-2008)

Students with need: Need-based aid available for full-time and part-time students.
Students without need: This college awards aid only to students with need.

FINANCIAL AID PROCEDURES

Forms required: FAFSA, institutional form.
Dates and Deadlines: No deadline. Applicants notified on a rolling basis.

CONTACT

Celestino Cruz, Finance Director
P.O. Box 8429, Caguas, PR 00726
(787) 743-2156

Humacao Community College

Humacao, Puerto Rico   Federal Code: 014952

2-year private business and community college in small city.
Enrollment: 750 undergrads, 19% part-time. 241 full-time freshmen.
Selectivity: Open admission.

FINANCIAL AID PICTURE (2006-2007)

Students with need: Out of 235 full-time freshmen who applied for aid, 235 were judged to have need. Of these, 235 received aid. Need-based aid available for part-time students.
Students without need: This college awards aid only to students with need.

FINANCIAL AID PROCEDURES

Forms required: FAFSA, state aid form, institutional form.
Dates and Deadlines: Priority date 1/1; closing date 6/30. Applicants notified on a rolling basis starting 3/4.
Transfers: No deadline.

CONTACT

Marilis Feliciano, Financial Aid Director
PO Box 9139, Humacao, PR 00792-9139
(787) 852-1430 ext. 28

Inter American University of Puerto Rico: Aguadilla Campus

Aguadilla, Puerto Rico
www.aguadilla.inter.edu   Federal Code: 003939

4-year private university and liberal arts college in small city.
Enrollment: 3,953 undergrads, 15% part-time. 736 full-time freshmen.
Selectivity: Admits over 75% of applicants.

BASIC COSTS (2007-2008)

Tuition and fees: $4,874.
Per-credit charge: $147.
Additional info: Tuition at time of enrollment locked for 4 years.

FINANCIAL AID PICTURE

Students with need: Need-based aid available for full-time and part-time students. Work study available nights, weekends, and for part-time students.
Students without need: No-need awards available for academics.

FINANCIAL AID PROCEDURES

Forms required: FAFSA.
Dates and Deadlines: Closing date 4/30. Applicants notified by 6/15; must reply by 8/8.
Transfers: No deadline.

CONTACT

Gloria Cortes, Director of Financial Aid
Box 20000, Aguadilla, PR 00605
(787) 891-0925 ext. 2110

Inter American University of Puerto Rico: Arecibo Campus

Arecibo, Puerto Rico
www.arecibo.inter.edu   Federal Code: 005026

4-year private liberal arts college in small city.
Enrollment: 4,241 undergrads.

BASIC COSTS (2007-2008)

Tuition and fees: $4,886.
Per-credit charge: $147.

FINANCIAL AID PICTURE

Students with need: Need-based aid available for full-time and part-time students. Work study available nights, weekends, and for part-time students.
Students without need: No-need awards available for academics, athletics.

FINANCIAL AID PROCEDURES

Forms required: FAFSA, institutional form.
Dates and Deadlines: Priority date 4/28; no closing date. Applicants notified on a rolling basis.

CONTACT

Ramon de Jesus, Director of Financial Aid
PO Box 4050, Arecibo, PR 00614-4050
(787) 878-5475 ext. 2275

Inter American University of Puerto Rico: Barranquitas Campus

Barranquitas, Puerto Rico
www.br.inter.edu   Federal Code: 005027

4-year private university and branch campus college in large town.
Enrollment: 2,068 undergrads, 23% part-time. 267 full-time freshmen.

BASIC COSTS (2007-2008)

Tuition and fees: $4,874.
Per-credit charge: $147.
Additional info: Tuition at time of enrollment locked for 4 years; tuition/fee waivers available for adults, minority students.

FINANCIAL AID PICTURE

Students with need: Need-based aid available for full-time and part-time students.
Students without need: This college awards aid only to students with need.

FINANCIAL AID PROCEDURES

Forms required: FAFSA.
Dates and Deadlines: Closing date 4/30. Applicants notified on a rolling basis; must reply within 2 week(s) of notification.

CONTACT

Eduardo Fontanez, Financial Aid Director
PO Box 517, Barranquitas, PR 00794
(787) 857-3600 ext. 2050

Inter American University of Puerto Rico: Bayamon Campus

Bayamon, Puerto Rico
bc.inter.edu   Federal Code: 003938

4-year private university and engineering college in small city.
Enrollment: 4,983 undergrads, 16% part-time. 970 full-time freshmen.
Selectivity: Admits less than 50% of applicants.

BASIC COSTS (2007-2008)

Tuition and fees: $4,912.
Per-credit charge: $147.

FINANCIAL AID PICTURE (2007-2008)

Students with need: Average financial aid package met 3% of need; average scholarship/grant was $284; average loan was $303. For part-time students, average financial aid package was $169.
Students without need: This college awards aid only to students with need.

FINANCIAL AID PROCEDURES

Forms required: FAFSA.
Dates and Deadlines: Priority date 6/30; no closing date. Applicants notified on a rolling basis starting 5/10.

CONTACT

Hector Vargas, Interim Director of Financial Aid
500 Dr. John Will Harris Road, Bayamon, PR 00957
(787) 279-1912 ext. 2025

Inter American University of Puerto Rico: Guayama Campus

Guayama, Puerto Rico
www.guayama.inter.edu   Federal Code: 010764

4-year private university in large town.
Enrollment: 2,151 undergrads, 22% part-time. 370 full-time freshmen.
Selectivity: Admits over 75% of applicants.

BASIC COSTS (2007-2008)

Tuition and fees: $4,874.
Per-credit charge: $147.
Additional info: All undergraduates not already insured pay $240 for health insurance coverage.

FINANCIAL AID PICTURE (2007-2008)

Students with need: Average financial aid package met 3% of need; average scholarship/grant was $159; average loan was $489. For part-time students, average financial aid package was $241.
Students without need: This college awards aid only to students with need.

FINANCIAL AID PROCEDURES

Forms required: FAFSA, institutional form.
Dates and Deadlines: Closing date 4/29. Applicants notified by 6/15; must reply by 7/30.
Transfers: No deadline.

CONTACT

Jose Vechini-Rodriguez, Director of Financial Aid
PO Box 10004, Guayama, PR 00785
(787) 864-2222 ext. 2206

Inter American University of Puerto Rico: Metropolitan Campus

San Juan, Puerto Rico
metro.inter.edu   Federal Code: 003938

4-year private branch campus college in large city.
Enrollment: 6,780 undergrads, 30% part-time. 1,007 full-time freshmen.
Selectivity: Admits less than 50% of applicants.

BASIC COSTS (2007-2008)

Tuition and fees: $4,926.
Per-credit charge: $147.

FINANCIAL AID PICTURE (2007-2008)

Students with need: Out of 29 full-time freshmen who applied for aid, 14 were judged to have need. Of these, 11 received aid. For part-time students, average financial aid package was $654.
Scholarships offered: 1 full-time freshmen received athletic scholarships; average amount $271.

FINANCIAL AID PROCEDURES

Forms required: FAFSA.
Dates and Deadlines: Closing date 4/30. Applicants notified on a rolling basis.

CONTACT

Glenda Diaz, Director of Financial Aid
Box 191293, San Juan, PR 00919-1293
(787) 250-1912 ext. 2185

Inter American University of Puerto Rico: Ponce Campus

Mercedita, Puerto Rico
ponce.inter.edu   Federal Code: 005029

4-year private university in large town.

Enrollment: 5,163 undergrads, 17% part-time. 1,248 full-time freshmen.

Selectivity: Admits 50 to 75% of applicants.

BASIC COSTS (2007-2008)

Tuition and fees: $4,886.

Per-credit charge: $147.

FINANCIAL AID PICTURE (2007-2008)

Students with need: Out of 1,238 full-time freshmen who applied for aid, 1,229 were judged to have need. Of these, 984 received aid. Average financial aid package met 2% of need; average scholarship/grant was $208; average loan was $205. For part-time students, average financial aid package was $163.

Students without need: This college awards aid only to students with need.

Scholarships offered: *Merit:* Scholarship program for first-time freshmen with a high school academic index of 3.0 or higher. *Athletic:* 25 full-time freshmen received athletic scholarships; average amount $191.

FINANCIAL AID PROCEDURES

Forms required: FAFSA.

Dates and Deadlines: No deadline.

CONTACT

Juan Portalatin, Director of Financial Aid
104 Turpo Industrial Park Road #1, Mercedita, PR 00715-1602
(787) 841-0102

Inter American University of Puerto Rico: San German Campus

San German, Puerto Rico
www.sg.inter.edu   Federal Code: 00714

4-year private university in large town.

Enrollment: 4,645 undergrads, 15% part-time. 1,129 full-time freshmen.

Selectivity: Admits over 75% of applicants.

BASIC COSTS (2007-2008)

Tuition and fees: $4,939.

Per-credit charge: $147.

Room and board: $2,400.

Additional info: Tuition at time of enrollment locked for 4 years.

FINANCIAL AID PICTURE (2006-2007)

Students with need: Out of 1,095 full-time freshmen who applied for aid, 1,072 were judged to have need. Of these, 884 received aid. Average financial aid package met 4% of need; average scholarship/grant was $299; average loan was $461. For part-time students, average financial aid package was $227.

Students without need: No-need awards available for academics, athletics.

Scholarships offered: 26 full-time freshmen received athletic scholarships; average amount $444.

FINANCIAL AID PROCEDURES

Forms required: FAFSA, institutional form.

Dates and Deadlines: Closing date 5/14. Applicants notified on a rolling basis; must reply by 8/1.

CONTACT

Maria Lugo, Director of Financial Aid
Box 5100, San German, PR 00683-9801
(787) 264-1912

National College of Business and Technology: Arecibo

Arecibo, Puerto Rico
www.nationalcollegepr.edu   Federal Code: 015953

2-year for-profit business and technical college in small city.

Enrollment: 1,617 undergrads.

Selectivity: Open admission; but selective for some programs.

BASIC COSTS (2007-2008)

Tuition and fees: $6,295.

Per-credit charge: $135.

FINANCIAL AID PICTURE

Students with need: Need-based aid available for full-time and part-time students. Work study available nights, weekends, and for part-time students.

FINANCIAL AID PROCEDURES

Dates and Deadlines: Priority date 12/31; closing date 4/29. Applicants notified on a rolling basis starting 5/2; must reply by 5/15 or within 2 week(s) of notification.

CONTACT

Desi Lopez-Padilla, Vice President of Financial Aid and Compliance
PO Box 4035, MSC 452, Arecibo, PR 00614
(787) 780-5134 ext. 4110

National College of Business and Technology: Bayamon

Bayamón, Puerto Rico
www.nationalcollegepr.edu   Federal Code: 015953

2-year for-profit business and technical college in small city.

Enrollment: 2,408 undergrads.

Selectivity: Open admission; but selective for some programs.

BASIC COSTS (2007-2008)

Tuition and fees: $6,295.

Per-credit charge: $135.

FINANCIAL AID PICTURE

Students with need: Need-based aid available for full-time and part-time students. Work study available nights, weekends, and for part-time students.

Students without need: This college awards aid only to students with need.

FINANCIAL AID PROCEDURES

Forms required: FAFSA.

Dates and Deadlines: Priority date 12/31; closing date 4/29. Applicants notified on a rolling basis starting 5/2; must reply by 5/15 or within 2 week(s) of notification.

Transfers: No deadline.

CONTACT

Desi Lopez, Vice President of Financial Aid and Compliance
PO Box 2036, Bayamón, PR 00960
(787) 780-5134 ext. 4403

National College of Business and Technology: Rio Grande

Rio Grande, Puerto Rico
www.nationalcollegepr.edu   Federal Code: E01213

2-year for-profit business and technical college in small town.
Enrollment: 1,221 undergrads.
Selectivity: Open admission; but selective for some programs.

BASIC COSTS (2007-2008)
Tuition and fees: $6,295.
Per-credit charge: $135.

FINANCIAL AID PICTURE
Students with need: Need-based aid available for full-time and part-time students. Work study available nights, weekends, and for part-time students.
Students without need: This college awards aid only to students with need.

FINANCIAL AID PROCEDURES
Forms required: FAFSA.
Dates and Deadlines: Applicants notified on a rolling basis starting 4/29; must reply by 5/15 or within 2 week(s) of notification.
Transfers: No deadline.

CONTACT
Desi López, Vice President of Financial Aid and Compliance
PO Box 3064, Rio Grande, PR 00745
(787) 780-5134 ext. 4403

Pontifical Catholic University of Puerto Rico

Ponce, Puerto Rico
www.pucpr.edu   Federal Code: 003936

4-year private university in small city, affiliated with Roman Catholic Church.
Enrollment: 5,203 undergrads.
Selectivity: Admits over 75% of applicants.

BASIC COSTS (2007-2008)
Tuition and fees: $5,018.
Per-credit charge: $150.
Room only: $1,275.

FINANCIAL AID PICTURE
Students with need: Need-based aid available for full-time and part-time students. Work study available nights, weekends, and for part-time students.
Students without need: No-need awards available for academics, athletics.

FINANCIAL AID PROCEDURES
Forms required: FAFSA, institutional form.
Dates and Deadlines: Priority date 5/1; no closing date. Applicants notified by 6/15; must reply within 4 week(s) of notification.
Transfers: Priority date 5/8. Distribution of awards based on availability of funds when application received.

CONTACT
Rosalia Martinez, Director of Financial Aid
2250 Las Americas Avenue, Suite 284, Ponce, PR 00717-9777
(787) 651-2000 ext. 1054

Ramirez College of Business and Technology

San Juan, Puerto Rico
www.ramirezcollege.com   Federal Code: 001314

2-year for-profit business and technical college in large city.
Enrollment: 512 undergrads.

FINANCIAL AID PICTURE
Students with need: Need-based aid available for full-time and part-time students.
Students without need: This college awards aid only to students with need.

FINANCIAL AID PROCEDURES
Dates and Deadlines: Priority date 5/1; closing date 6/30. Applicants notified on a rolling basis starting 9/30; must reply within 2 week(s) of notification.

CONTACT
Domingo Maldonado, Director of Financial Aid
PO Box 21360, San Juan, PR 00928-1360
(787) 763-3120 ext. 012

Turabo University

Gurabo, Puerto Rico
www.suagm.edu/ut   Federal Code: 011719

4-year private university and liberal arts college in small city.
Enrollment: 12,677 undergrads, 20% part-time. 2,096 full-time freshmen.
Selectivity: Open admission; but selective for some programs.

BASIC COSTS (2007-2008)
Tuition and fees: $4,340.
Room and board: $4,993.

FINANCIAL AID PICTURE (2007-2008)
Students with need: Need-based aid available for part-time students.
Students without need: This college awards aid only to students with need.

FINANCIAL AID PROCEDURES
Forms required: FAFSA.
Dates and Deadlines: Priority date 5/30; no closing date. Applicants notified by 7/30.

CONTACT
Carmen Rivera-Lopez, Admissions and Financial Aid Director
PO Box 3030, Gurabo, PR 00778
(787) 743-797 ext. 4350

Universal Technology College of Puerto Rico

Aguadilla, Puerto Rico
www.unitecpr.edu/   Federal Code: 030297

2-year private health science and career college in small city.
Enrollment: 1,206 undergrads, 1% part-time. 594 full-time freshmen.
Selectivity: Open admission.

FINANCIAL AID PICTURE (2006-2007)
Students with need: Out of 594 full-time freshmen who applied for aid, 582 were judged to have need. Of these, 580 received aid, and 580 had their full need met. Average financial aid package met 98% of need; average scholarship/grant was $115. For part-time students, average financial aid package was $3,200.

Students without need: This college awards aid only to students with need.

FINANCIAL AID PROCEDURES

Forms required: FAFSA, state aid form, institutional form.
Dates and Deadlines: Priority date 4/30; closing date 6/30. Applicants notified on a rolling basis starting 2/1; must reply by 6/30.
Transfers: No deadline.

CONTACT

Samuel Hernandez, Financial Aid Administrator
Apartado 1955, Victoria Station, Aguadilla, PR 00605
(787) 882-2065 ext. 313

Universidad Adventista de las Antillas

Mayaguez, Puerto Rico
www.uaa.edu
Federal Code: 005019

4-year private university and liberal arts college in small city, affiliated with Seventh-day Adventists.
Enrollment: 581 undergrads, 7% part-time.
Selectivity: Open admission; but selective for some programs.

BASIC COSTS (2008-2009)

Tuition and fees: $6,892.
Per-credit charge: $140.
Room and board: $1,650.
Additional info: Tuition for nonresident aliens is the sum of private tuition ($4,500) and the Form I-20 deposit ($5,000); after the first year, these students receive credit refund at registration ($500 per semester). An average of $150 per semester is included in tuition for lab expenses.

FINANCIAL AID PICTURE

Students with need: Need-based aid available for full-time and part-time students.

FINANCIAL AID PROCEDURES

Forms required: FAFSA, institutional form.
Dates and Deadlines: No deadline. Applicants notified on a rolling basis starting 8/15; must reply within 3 week(s) of notification.

CONTACT

Heriberto Juarbe, Director of Financial Aid
PO Box 118, Mayaguez, PR 00681-0118
(787) 834-9595 ext. 2200

Universidad del Este

Carolina, Puerto Rico
www.suagm.edu/une
Federal Code: 011718

4-year private university and liberal arts college in small city.
Enrollment: 10,471 undergrads, 28% part-time. 1,804 full-time freshmen.
Selectivity: Open admission; but selective for some programs.

BASIC COSTS (2007-2008)

Tuition and fees: $4,340.
Room and board: $4,993.

FINANCIAL AID PICTURE (2007-2008)

Students with need: Need-based aid available for part-time students.
Students without need: No-need awards available for academics, athletics.

FINANCIAL AID PROCEDURES

Forms required: FAFSA, state aid form, institutional form.
Dates and Deadlines: Priority date 5/30; no closing date. Applicants notified by 7/30.

CONTACT

Clotilde Santiago, Admissions and Financial Aid Director
PO Box 2010, Carolina, PR 00984-2010
(787) 257-7373 ext. 3401

Universidad Metropolitana

Rio Piedras, Puerto Rico
www.suagm.edu/umet
Federal Code: 025875

4-year private university and liberal arts college in large city.
Enrollment: 9,314 undergrads, 19% part-time. 1,403 full-time freshmen.
Selectivity: Admits less than 50% of applicants.

BASIC COSTS (2007-2008)

Tuition and fees: $4,340.
Room and board: $4,993.

FINANCIAL AID PICTURE

Students with need: Need-based aid available for full-time and part-time students. Work study available nights.
Students without need: This college awards aid only to students with need.

FINANCIAL AID PROCEDURES

Forms required: FAFSA.
Dates and Deadlines: Priority date 5/30; no closing date. Applicants notified by 7/30.

CONTACT

Julio Rodriguez, Admissions and Financial Aid Director
Apartado 21150, Rio Piedras, PR 00928
(787) 766-1717 ext. 6587

Universidad Politecnica de Puerto Rico

Hato Rey, Puerto Rico
www.pupr.edu
Federal Code: 014055

5-year private university and engineering college in large city.
Enrollment: 5,185 undergrads. 687 full-time freshmen.
Selectivity: Admits over 75% of applicants.

BASIC COSTS (2007-2008)

Tuition and fees: $6,033.
Room and board: $5,355.

FINANCIAL AID PICTURE

Students with need: Need-based aid available for full-time and part-time students.
Students without need: No-need awards available for academics, music/drama.

FINANCIAL AID PROCEDURES

Forms required: FAFSA.
Dates and Deadlines: Priority date 5/15; closing date 6/30. Applicants notified by 7/15.

CONTACT

Lidia Cruz, Director of Financial Aid
PO Box 192017, San Juan, PR 00919-2017
(787) 622-8000 ext. 249

University College of San Juan

San Juan, Puerto Rico
www.cunisanjuan.edu   Federal Code: 010567

4-year public community and technical college in very large city.
Enrollment: 1,004 undergrads, 16% part-time. 1,004 full-time freshmen.
Selectivity: Admits over 75% of applicants.

BASIC COSTS (2007-2008)
Tuition and fees: $2,715.
Per-credit charge: $85.
Room and board: $6,350.
Additional info: Tuition at time of enrollment locked for 4 years.

FINANCIAL AID PICTURE (2006-2007)
Students with need: Need-based aid available for part-time students.
Students without need: This college awards aid only to students with need.

FINANCIAL AID PROCEDURES
Forms required: FAFSA, institutional form.
Dates and Deadlines: Closing date 9/30. Applicants notified by 10/30.
Transfers: Financial aid transcripts.

CONTACT
Haydee Zayas, Director of Financial Aid
180 Jose R. Oliver Avenue, San Juan, PR 00918
(787) 250-7111 ext. 2287

University of Puerto Rico: Aguadilla

Aguadilla, Puerto Rico
www.uprag.edu   Federal Code: 012123

4-year public liberal arts and technical college in small city.
Enrollment: 2,969 undergrads, 10% part-time. 811 full-time freshmen.
Selectivity: Admits over 75% of applicants.

BASIC COSTS (2007-2008)
Tuition and fees: $1,692; out-of-state residents $3,938.
Per-credit charge: $45.

FINANCIAL AID PICTURE (2006-2007)
Students with need: 84% of average financial aid package awarded as scholarships/grants, 16% awarded as loans/jobs. Need-based aid available for part-time students.
Students without need: This college awards aid only to students with need.

FINANCIAL AID PROCEDURES
Forms required: FAFSA, institutional form.
Dates and Deadlines: Closing date 5/6. Applicants notified on a rolling basis starting 4/1; must reply within 1 week(s) of notification.
Transfers: No deadline..

CONTACT
Doris Roman, Financial Aid Director
Box 250160, Aguadilla, PR 00604
(787) 890-0109

University of Puerto Rico: Arecibo

Arecibo, Puerto Rico
www.upra.edu   Federal Code: 007228

4-year public university in small city.
Enrollment: 3,868 undergrads, 10% part-time. 1,014 full-time freshmen.
Selectivity: Admits less than 50% of applicants.

BASIC COSTS (2007-2008)
Tuition and fees: $1,692; out-of-state residents $3,938.
Per-credit charge: $45.

FINANCIAL AID PICTURE
Students with need: Need-based aid available for full-time and part-time students.
Students without need: This college awards aid only to students with need.

FINANCIAL AID PROCEDURES
Forms required: FAFSA, institutional form.
Dates and Deadlines: Closing date 4/27.
Transfers: Closing date 5/25.

CONTACT
Myrta Ortiz, Financial Aid Officer
PO Box 4010, Arecibo, PR 00614-4010
(787) 815-0000 ext. 4501

University of Puerto Rico: Carolina Regional College

Carolina, Puerto Rico
www.uprc.edu   Federal Code: 003942

4-year public university in small city.
Enrollment: 4,236 undergrads, 28% part-time. 687 full-time freshmen.
Selectivity: Admits less than 50% of applicants.

BASIC COSTS (2007-2008)
Tuition and fees: $2,808; out-of-state residents $4,109.
Per-credit charge: $45.

FINANCIAL AID PICTURE (2006-2007)
Students with need: Out of 687 full-time freshmen who applied for aid, 687 were judged to have need. Of these, 687 received aid, and 2 had their full need met. Average financial aid package met 36% of need; average scholarship/grant was $381. For part-time students, average financial aid package was $2,804.
Students without need: This college awards aid only to students with need.

FINANCIAL AID PROCEDURES
Forms required: FAFSA, state aid form, institutional form.
Dates and Deadlines: Closing date 6/30. Applicants notified on a rolling basis starting 6/10.

CONTACT
Santa Castro, Financial Aid Officer/Director
PO Box 4800, Carolina, PR 00984-4800
(787) 769-0188

University of Puerto Rico: Cayey University College

Cayey, Puerto Rico
www.cayey.upr.edu   Federal Code: 007206

4-year public liberal arts college in large town.
Enrollment: 3,562 undergrads, 11% part-time. 796 full-time freshmen.
Selectivity: Admits less than 50% of applicants.

BASIC COSTS (2007-2008)
Tuition and fees: $1,692; out-of-state residents $3,938.
Per-credit charge: $45.
Additional info: Tuition at time of enrollment locked for 4 years.

FINANCIAL AID PICTURE

Students with need: Need-based aid available for full-time and part-time students. Work study available nights, weekends, and for part-time students.
Students without need: This college awards aid only to students with need.

FINANCIAL AID PROCEDURES

Forms required: FAFSA.
Dates and Deadlines: Closing date 6/30. Applicants notified by 7/30.
Transfers: Priority date 1/30; closing date 2/28.

CONTACT

James Rivera, Director of Financial Aid
Oficina de Admisiones UPR- Cayey, Cayey, PR 00736
(787) 738-2161 ext. 2061

University of Puerto Rico: Humacao

Humacao, Puerto Rico
www.uprh.edu
Federal Code: 003942

4-year public university and liberal arts college in small city.
Enrollment: 4,336 undergrads, 10% part-time. 1,105 full-time freshmen.
Selectivity: Admits less than 50% of applicants.

BASIC COSTS (2007-2008)

Tuition and fees: $1,692; out-of-state residents $3,938.
Per-credit charge: $45.

FINANCIAL AID PICTURE

Students with need: Need-based aid available for full-time and part-time students.
Students without need: No-need awards available for academics, athletics, music/drama.

FINANCIAL AID PROCEDURES

Forms required: FAFSA, institutional form.
Dates and Deadlines: Closing date 7/31. Applicants notified by 9/30.

CONTACT

Mariolga Rotger, Director of Financial Aid
100 Road 908 CUH Station, Humacao, PR 00791
(787) 850-0000 ext. 9342

University of Puerto Rico: Mayaguez

Mayaguez, Puerto Rico
www.uprm.edu
Federal Code: 003944

5-year public university in small city.
Enrollment: 11,534 undergrads, 7% part-time. 2,380 full-time freshmen.
Selectivity: Admits over 75% of applicants.

BASIC COSTS (2007-2008)

Tuition and fees: $1,692; out-of-state residents $3,938.
Per-credit charge: $45.

FINANCIAL AID PICTURE (2006-2007)

Students with need: 97% of average financial aid package awarded as scholarships/grants, 3% awarded as loans/jobs. Need-based aid available for part-time students. Work study available nights, weekends, and for part-time students.
Students without need: This college awards aid only to students with need.

FINANCIAL AID PROCEDURES

Forms required: FAFSA, institutional form.
Dates and Deadlines: Priority date 1/30; closing date 6/30. Applicants notified on a rolling basis starting 5/30.

Transfers: Deadline according to admission date.

CONTACT

Ana Rodriguez, Director of Financial Aid
Admissions Office, Mayaguez, PR 00681-9021
(787) 265-1920

University of Puerto Rico: Medical Sciences

San Juan, Puerto Rico
www.rcm.upr.edu
Federal Code: 003945

4-year public university in large city.
Enrollment: 414 undergrads, 17% part-time.

BASIC COSTS (2007-2008)

Tuition and fees: $1,692; out-of-state residents $3,938.
Per-credit charge: $45.

FINANCIAL AID PICTURE

Students with need: Need-based aid available for full-time and part-time students. Work study available nights, weekends, and for part-time students.
Students without need: This college awards aid only to students with need.

FINANCIAL AID PROCEDURES

Forms required: FAFSA, institutional form.
Dates and Deadlines: Priority date 4/30; closing date 6/15. Applicants notified on a rolling basis starting 8/1; must reply within 2 week(s) of notification.

CONTACT

Cruz Figueroa, Director, Financial Aid
P.O. Box 365067, San Juan, PR 00936-5067
(787) 758-2525 ext. 3205

University of Puerto Rico: Rio Piedras

San Juan, Puerto Rico
www.rrp.upr.edu
Federal Code: 007108

4-year public university in large city.
Enrollment: 15,094 undergrads, 15% part-time. 2,681 full-time freshmen.
Selectivity: Admits less than 50% of applicants.

BASIC COSTS (2007-2008)

Tuition and fees: $1,692; out-of-state residents $3,938.
Per-credit charge: $45.
Room and board: $7,580.

FINANCIAL AID PICTURE

Students with need: Need-based aid available for full-time and part-time students.
Students without need: This college awards aid only to students with need.
Additional info: Tuition waived for honor students, athletes, members of chorus, and others with special talents.

FINANCIAL AID PROCEDURES

Forms required: FAFSA.

CONTACT

Luz Santiago, Director of Financial Aid
Box 23344, San Juan, PR 00931-3344

University of Puerto Rico: Utuado
Utuado, Puerto Rico
www.uprutuado.edu   Federal Code: 010922

4-year public agricultural college in large town.
Enrollment: 1,527 undergrads, 7% part-time. 599 full-time freshmen.
Selectivity: Admits 50 to 75% of applicants. GED not accepted.

BASIC COSTS (2007-2008)
Tuition and fees: $1,692; out-of-state residents $3,938.
Per-credit charge: $45.

FINANCIAL AID PICTURE
Students with need: Need-based aid available for full-time and part-time students. Work study available nights.
Students without need: This college awards aid only to students with need.

FINANCIAL AID PROCEDURES
Forms required: FAFSA.
Dates and Deadlines: Priority date 5/31; no closing date. Applicants notified on a rolling basis starting 9/30; must reply within 4 week(s) of notification.
Transfers: Priority date 5/30; closing date 6/15. Closing date for Pell Grant applicants March 31.

CONTACT
Edgar Salva, Financial Assistance Officer
PO Box 2500, Utuado, PR 00641
(787) 894-2828 ext. 2603

University of the Sacred Heart
Santurce, Puerto Rico
www.sagrado.edu   Federal Code: 003937

4-year private university and liberal arts college in large city, affiliated with Roman Catholic Church.
Enrollment: 4,362 undergrads, 18% part-time. 690 full-time freshmen.

BASIC COSTS (2007-2008)
Tuition and fees: $5,670.
Per-credit charge: $160.
Room only: $2,300.

FINANCIAL AID PICTURE
Students with need: Need-based aid available for full-time and part-time students.
Students without need: No-need awards available for academics, athletics.

FINANCIAL AID PROCEDURES
Forms required: FAFSA, institutional form.
Dates and Deadlines: Priority date 4/30; closing date 5/30. Applicants notified on a rolling basis starting 6/15; must reply by 8/30.
Transfers: No deadline.

CONTACT
Luis Diaz, Director of Financial Aid
Universidad del Sagrado Corazon Oficina de Nuevo Ingreso, San Juan, PR 00914-0383

Rhode Island

Brown University
Providence, Rhode Island   Federal Code: 003401
www.brown.edu   CSS Code: 3094

4-year private university and liberal arts college in small city.
Enrollment: 5,813 undergrads, 1% part-time. 1,479 full-time freshmen.
Selectivity: Admits less than 50% of applicants. GED not accepted.

BASIC COSTS (2008-2009)
Tuition and fees: $37,718.
Room and board: $10,022.

FINANCIAL AID PICTURE
Students with need: Need-based aid available for full-time and part-time students.
Students without need: This college awards aid only to students with need.

FINANCIAL AID PROCEDURES
Forms required: FAFSA, CSS PROFILE.
Dates and Deadlines: Closing date 2/1. Applicants notified by 4/1; must reply by 5/1.
Transfers: Closing date 4/15.

CONTACT
James Tilton, Director of Financial Aid
45 Prospect Street, Providence, RI 02912
(401) 863-2721

Bryant University
Smithfield, Rhode Island
www.bryant.edu   Federal Code: 003402

4-year private business and liberal arts college in large town.
Enrollment: 3,328 undergrads, 4% part-time. 849 full-time freshmen.
Selectivity: Admits less than 50% of applicants.

BASIC COSTS (2008-2009)
Tuition and fees: $30,871.
Per-credit charge: $345.
Room and board: $11,251.
Additional info: Tuition includes cost of laptop computer. $800 non-refundable enrollment commitment deposit is required of both residents and commuters.

FINANCIAL AID PICTURE
Students with need: Need-based aid available for full-time and part-time students. Work study available nights, weekends, and for part-time students.
Students without need: No-need awards available for academics, athletics, minority status, ROTC.

FINANCIAL AID PROCEDURES
Forms required: FAFSA.
Dates and Deadlines: Priority date 2/15; closing date 2/15. Applicants notified by 3/24; must reply by 5/1.
Transfers: Closing date 4/1.

CONTACT
John Canning, Director of Financial Aid
1150 Douglas Pike, Smithfield, RI 02917
(401) 232-6020

Community College of Rhode Island
Warwick, Rhode Island
www.ccri.edu   Federal Code: 004916

2-year public community college in small city.
Enrollment: 15,081 undergrads, 59% part-time. 2,354 full-time freshmen.
Selectivity: Open admission; but selective for some programs.

BASIC COSTS (2007-2008)
Tuition and fees: $2,846; out-of-state residents $7,766.
Per-credit charge: $117; out-of-state residents $356.
Additional info: Tuition/fee waivers available for unemployed or children of unemployed.

FINANCIAL AID PICTURE
Students with need: Need-based aid available for full-time and part-time students. Work study available nights, weekends, and for part-time students.
Students without need: No-need awards available for athletics.

FINANCIAL AID PROCEDURES
Forms required: FAFSA, institutional form.
Dates and Deadlines: Priority date 3/1; no closing date. Applicants notified on a rolling basis starting 5/1; must reply within 2 week(s) of notification.

CONTACT
Christine Jenkins, Associate Dean of Enrollment Services
400 East Avenue, Warwick, RI 02886-1807
(401) 455-6006

Johnson & Wales University: Providence
Providence, Rhode Island
www.jwu.edu   Federal Code: 003404

4-year private university in small city.
Enrollment: 9,053 undergrads, 10% part-time. 2,283 full-time freshmen.
Selectivity: Admits 50 to 75% of applicants.

BASIC COSTS (2007-2008)
Tuition and fees: $21,717.
Per-credit charge: $379.
Room and board: $8,550.
Additional info: Freshman required fees also include $255 orientation fee. Weekend meal plan is also available for $987. Tuition at time of enrollment locked for 4 years.

FINANCIAL AID PICTURE (2007-2008)
Students with need: Out of 1,729 full-time freshmen who applied for aid, 1,517 were judged to have need. Of these, 1,512 received aid, and 131 had their full need met. Average financial aid package met 67% of need; average scholarship/grant was $8,460; average loan was $3,265. For part-time students, average financial aid package was $9,596.
Students without need: 370 full-time freshmen who did not demonstrate need for aid received scholarships/grants; average award was $3,554. No-need awards available for academics, alumni affiliation, job skills, leadership, state/district residency.
Cumulative student debt: 77% of graduating class had student loans; average debt was $26,193.

FINANCIAL AID PROCEDURES
Forms required: FAFSA.
Dates and Deadlines: No deadline. Applicants notified on a rolling basis starting 3/1; must reply within 2 week(s) of notification.
Transfers: Transfer scholarships available.

CONTACT
Lynn Robinson, Director of Financial Aid
8 Abbott Park Place, Providence, RI 02903-3703
(800) 342-5598 ext. 4648

New England Institute of Technology
Warwick, Rhode Island
www.neit.edu   Federal Code: 007845

4-year private technical college in small city.
Enrollment: 2,993 undergrads.
Selectivity: Open admission.

BASIC COSTS (2008-2009)
Tuition and fees: $17,165.
Per-credit charge: $390.
Additional info: Fees vary from $1,265 to $2,165 according to program. Tuition at time of enrollment locked for 4 years.

FINANCIAL AID PICTURE
Students with need: Need-based aid available for full-time and part-time students. Work study available nights, weekends, and for part-time students.
Students without need: No-need awards available for academics.
Additional info: Tuition at time of first enrollment guaranteed all students for 2 years.

FINANCIAL AID PROCEDURES
Forms required: FAFSA, institutional form.
Dates and Deadlines: Priority date 6/1; no closing date. Applicants notified on a rolling basis starting 6/15.

CONTACT
Larry Blair, Director of Financial Aid
2500 Post Road, Warwick, RI 02886-2286
(401) 467-7744

Providence College
Providence, Rhode Island   Federal Code: 003406
www.providence.edu   CSS Code: 3693

4-year private liberal arts college in small city, affiliated with Roman Catholic Church.
Enrollment: 3,959 undergrads. 988 full-time freshmen.
Selectivity: Admits less than 50% of applicants. GED not accepted.

BASIC COSTS (2008-2009)
Tuition and fees: $31,379.
Per-credit charge: $1,027.
Room and board: $10,810.
Additional info: Tuition/fee waivers available for minority students.

FINANCIAL AID PICTURE (2007-2008)
Students with need: Out of 716 full-time freshmen who applied for aid, 597 were judged to have need. Of these, 597 received aid, and 356 had their full need met. Average financial aid package met 66% of need; average scholarship/grant was $15,361; average loan was $4,431. For part-time students, average financial aid package was $5,155.
Students without need: 48 full-time freshmen who did not demonstrate need for aid received scholarships/grants; average award was $19,823. No-need awards available for academics, athletics, minority status, ROTC.
Scholarships offered: 42 full-time freshmen received athletic scholarships; average amount $20,102.
Cumulative student debt: 72% of graduating class had student loans; average debt was $35,216.

FINANCIAL AID PROCEDURES

Forms required: FAFSA, CSS PROFILE.

Dates and Deadlines: Closing date 2/1. Applicants notified by 4/1; must reply by 5/1.

Transfers: Closing date 4/15. Applicants notified by 6/30.

CONTACT

Sandra Oliveira, Director of Financial Aid

Harkins Hall 222, 549 River Avenue, Providence, RI 02918-0001

(401) 865-2286

Rhode Island College

Providence, Rhode Island

www.ric.edu — Federal Code: 003407

4-year public liberal arts college in small city.

Enrollment: 7,197 undergrads, 27% part-time. 1,090 full-time freshmen.

Selectivity: Admits 50 to 75% of applicants.

BASIC COSTS (2007-2008)

Tuition and fees: $5,256; out-of-state residents $13,664.

Per-credit charge: $190; out-of-state residents $532.

Room and board: $7,820.

Additional info: Permanent residents of Massachusetts communities within a 20-mile radius of Providence are eligible for Rhode Island's in-state tuition plus 50% of the in-state rate. Tuition/fee waivers available for unemployed or children of unemployed.

FINANCIAL AID PICTURE (2007-2008)

Students with need: Out of 921 full-time freshmen who applied for aid, 647 were judged to have need. Of these, 624 received aid, and 208 had their full need met. Average financial aid package met 42% of need; average scholarship/grant was $6,278; average loan was $2,997. For part-time students, average financial aid package was $5,288.

Students without need: 50 full-time freshmen who did not demonstrate need for aid received scholarships/grants; average award was $1,709. No-need awards available for academics, alumni affiliation, art, music/drama.

Scholarships offered: Presidential Scholarships; $2,000 per year; for entering freshmen in the top 30% of class with minimum combined SAT score of 1100 (exclusive of Writing) who apply for admission by Dec 15; approximately 100 awards available to each entering class.

Cumulative student debt: 70% of graduating class had student loans; average debt was $15,519.

FINANCIAL AID PROCEDURES

Forms required: FAFSA, institutional form.

Dates and Deadlines: Priority date 3/1; no closing date. Applicants notified on a rolling basis starting 3/15; must reply within 3 week(s) of notification.

Transfers: Priority date 5/15.

CONTACT

James Hanbury, Director of Financial Aid

600 Mount Pleasant Avenue, Providence, RI 02908

(401) 456-8033

Rhode Island School of Design

Providence, Rhode Island — Federal Code: 003409

www.risd.edu — CSS Code: 3726

4-year private visual arts college in small city.

Enrollment: 1,927 undergrads. 432 full-time freshmen.

Selectivity: Admits less than 50% of applicants.

BASIC COSTS (2008-2009)

Tuition and fees: $34,925.

Per-credit charge: $1,150.

Room and board: $10,260.

FINANCIAL AID PICTURE

Students with need: Need-based aid available for full-time students. Work study available nights, weekends, and for part-time students.

FINANCIAL AID PROCEDURES

Forms required: FAFSA, CSS PROFILE.

Dates and Deadlines: Closing date 2/15. Applicants notified by 4/1; must reply by 5/1.

Transfers: Closing date 3/15. Applicants notified by 4/25; must reply by 5/22. Transfer students with previous undergraduate degree not eligible for scholarship aid.

CONTACT

Peter Riefler, Director of Financial Aid

Two College Street, Providence, RI 02903-2791

(401) 454-6661

Roger Williams University

Bristol, Rhode Island — Federal Code: 003410

www.rwu.edu — CSS Code: 3729

4-year private university and liberal arts college in large town.

Enrollment: 4,353 undergrads, 12% part-time. 1,045 full-time freshmen.

Selectivity: Admits 50 to 75% of applicants.

BASIC COSTS (2007-2008)

Tuition and fees: $25,942.

Per-credit charge: $1,013.

Room and board: $11,240.

Additional info: Tuition differential for architecture program.

FINANCIAL AID PICTURE (2007-2008)

Students with need: Out of 742 full-time freshmen who applied for aid, 646 were judged to have need. Of these, 643 received aid, and 110 had their full need met. Average financial aid package met 88% of need; average scholarship/grant was $7,608; average loan was $4,539. For part-time students, average financial aid package was $5,986.

Students without need: 154 full-time freshmen who did not demonstrate need for aid received scholarships/grants; average award was $6,912. No-need awards available for academics, ROTC.

Cumulative student debt: 69% of graduating class had student loans; average debt was $31,400.

FINANCIAL AID PROCEDURES

Forms required: FAFSA, CSS PROFILE.

Dates and Deadlines: Priority date 1/1; closing date 2/1. Applicants notified on a rolling basis starting 3/20; must reply by 5/1.

Transfers: Must reply by 5/1.

CONTACT

Tracy DaCosta, Associate Dean of Enrollment Management

One Old Ferry Road, Bristol, RI 02809

(401) 254-3100

Salve Regina University

Newport, Rhode Island — Federal Code: 003411

www.salve.edu — CSS Code: 3759

4-year private university and liberal arts college in large town, affiliated with Roman Catholic Church.

Enrollment: 2,109 undergrads, 3% part-time. 566 full-time freshmen.

Selectivity: Admits 50 to 75% of applicants.

BASIC COSTS (2008-2009)

Tuition and fees: $31,500.
Per-credit charge: $965.
Room and board: $10,700.
Additional info: Required fees include a one-time laptop fee of $2,350 for all first-year students.

FINANCIAL AID PICTURE (2007-2008)

Students with need: Out of 445 full-time freshmen who applied for aid, 369 were judged to have need. Of these, 361 received aid, and 58 had their full need met. Average financial aid package met 74% of need; average scholarship/grant was $16,410; average loan was $4,870. For part-time students, average financial aid package was $8,111.

Students without need: 97 full-time freshmen who did not demonstrate need for aid received scholarships/grants. No-need awards available for academics, ROTC.

Cumulative student debt: 77% of graduating class had student loans; average debt was $30,752.

FINANCIAL AID PROCEDURES

Forms required: FAFSA, CSS PROFILE.
Dates and Deadlines: Priority date 3/1; no closing date. Applicants notified by 4/1; must reply by 4/15 or within 2 week(s) of notification.
Transfers: Closing date 2/1. Applicants notified by 3/1; must reply by 5/1 or within 2 week(s) of notification. Must provide financial aid transcripts from previous institutions attended.

CONTACT

Aida Mirante, Director of Financial Aid
100 Ochre Point Avenue, Newport, RI 02840-4192
(401) 341-2901

University of Rhode Island

Kingston, Rhode Island
www.uri.edu   Federal Code: 003414

4-year public university in small town.
Enrollment: 12,268 undergrads, 12% part-time. 2,993 full-time freshmen.
Selectivity: Admits over 75% of applicants.

BASIC COSTS (2007-2008)

Tuition and fees: $8,184; out-of-state residents $23,038.
Per-credit charge: $268; out-of-state residents $887.
Room and board: $8,732.
Additional info: Tuition/fee waivers available for unemployed or children of unemployed.

FINANCIAL AID PICTURE (2007-2008)

Students with need: Out of 2,484 full-time freshmen who applied for aid, 1,931 were judged to have need. Of these, 1,559 received aid, and 1,279 had their full need met. Average financial aid package met 72% of need; average scholarship/grant was $7,371; average loan was $7,290. For part-time students, average financial aid package was $7,993.

Students without need: 187 full-time freshmen who did not demonstrate need for aid received scholarships/grants; average award was $5,924. No-need awards available for academics, alumni affiliation, art, athletics, music/drama, ROTC.

Scholarships offered: *Merit:* Centennial Scholarship: up to full tuition for full-time students; based on a 3.0 GPA or better; minimum SAT score of 1150 (Math and Critical Reading ONLY); or minimum ACT score of 25; and rank in the top third of the class. *Athletic:* 5 full-time freshmen received athletic scholarships; average amount $4,668.

Cumulative student debt: 64% of graduating class had student loans; average debt was $21,125.

FINANCIAL AID PROCEDURES

Forms required: FAFSA.

Dates and Deadlines: Priority date 3/1; no closing date. Applicants notified on a rolling basis starting 3/31; must reply by 5/1.
Transfers: No deadline. Applicants notified on a rolling basis.

CONTACT

Horace Saccucci, Senior Associate Director of Enrollment Services
14 Upper College Road, Kingston, RI 02881-1322
(401) 874-9500

South Carolina

Aiken Technical College

Aiken, South Carolina
www.atc.edu   Federal Code: 010056

2-year public community and technical college in small city.
Enrollment: 2,529 undergrads.
Selectivity: Open admission; but selective for some programs.

BASIC COSTS (2007-2008)

Tuition and fees: $3,298; out-of-district residents $3,658; out-of-state residents $8,982.

FINANCIAL AID PICTURE

Students with need: Need-based aid available for full-time and part-time students. Work study available nights, weekends, and for part-time students.
Students without need: No-need awards available for academics, athletics, leadership, minority status, state/district residency.
Scholarships offered: Vernon Ford Scholarships: $1,000 annually; for candidates with minimum GPA of 3.0; 8 awarded annually. N. Augusta 2000: $2,000 annually; 2 awarded. Wachenhut Criminal Justice Scholarship: $1,000; 1 awarded. Presidential: $10,000 annually; 10 awarded.

FINANCIAL AID PROCEDURES

Forms required: FAFSA.
Dates and Deadlines: Priority date 5/1; closing date 6/30. Applicants notified on a rolling basis starting 4/1; must reply within 2 week(s) of notification.
Transfers: Applicants notified on a rolling basis; must reply within 2 week(s) of notification.

CONTACT

Amanda Chittum, Director of Financial Aid
PO Drawer 696, Aiken, SC 29802
(803) 593-9954 ext. 1261

Allen University

Columbia, South Carolina
www.allenuniversity.edu   Federal Code: 003417

4-year private university and liberal arts college in large city, affiliated with African Methodist Episcopal Church.
Enrollment: 651 undergrads, 2% part-time. 245 full-time freshmen.
Selectivity: Open admission.

BASIC COSTS (2008-2009)

Tuition and fees: $9,884.
Room and board: $5,240.

FINANCIAL AID PICTURE

Students with need: Need-based aid available for full-time and part-time students.
Students without need: No-need awards available for academics, athletics, music/drama, ROTC.

FINANCIAL AID PROCEDURES

Forms required: FAFSA.

Dates and Deadlines: Priority date 4/15; closing date 7/20. Applicants notified on a rolling basis starting 4/1; must reply within 2 week(s) of notification.
Transfers: No deadline.

CONTACT

Marilyn Polk, Director of Financial Aid
1530 Harden Street, Columbia, SC 29204
(803) 376-5736

Anderson University

Anderson, South Carolina
www.andersonuniversity.edu   Federal Code: 003418

4-year private liberal arts and teachers college in large town, affiliated with Southern Baptist Convention.
Enrollment: 1,597 undergrads, 12% part-time. 417 full-time freshmen.
Selectivity: Admits over 75% of applicants.

BASIC COSTS (2007-2008)

Tuition and fees: $17,850.
Per-credit charge: $500.
Room and board: $6,750.
Additional info: Tuition/fee waivers available for adults.

FINANCIAL AID PICTURE (2006-2007)

Students with need: Out of 347 full-time freshmen who applied for aid, 267 were judged to have need. Of these, 267 received aid, and 222 had their full need met. Average financial aid package met 90% of need; average scholarship/grant was $9,000; average loan was $3,100. For part-time students, average financial aid package was $14,600.
Students without need: 386 full-time freshmen who did not demonstrate need for aid received scholarships/grants; average award was $8,200. No-need awards available for academics, alumni affiliation, art, athletics, leadership, minority status, music/drama, religious affiliation, state/district residency.
Scholarships offered: 68 full-time freshmen received athletic scholarships; average amount $4,530.
Cumulative student debt: 76% of graduating class had student loans; average debt was $15,150.

FINANCIAL AID PROCEDURES

Forms required: FAFSA.
Dates and Deadlines: Priority date 3/1; closing date 6/30. Applicants notified on a rolling basis starting 3/15; must reply within 2 week(s) of notification.

CONTACT

Becky Pressley, Director of Financial Aid
316 Boulevard, Anderson, SC 29621-4002
(864) 231-2070

Benedict College

Columbia, South Carolina
www.benedict.edu   Federal Code: 003420

4-year private liberal arts college in very large city, affiliated with American Baptist Churches in the USA.
Enrollment: 2,641 undergrads, 2% part-time. 890 full-time freshmen.
Selectivity: Admits over 75% of applicants.

BASIC COSTS (2007-2008)

Tuition and fees: $14,010.
Per-credit charge: $419.
Room and board: $6,444.

FINANCIAL AID PICTURE

Students with need: Need-based aid available for full-time and part-time students.

FINANCIAL AID PROCEDURES

Forms required: FAFSA.
Dates and Deadlines: Priority date 4/15; no closing date. Applicants notified on a rolling basis starting 4/15.

CONTACT

Sul Black, Director of Financial Aid
1600 Harden Street, Columbia, SC 29204
(803) 253-5105

Central Carolina Technical College

Sumter, South Carolina
www.cctech.edu   Federal Code: 003995

2-year public community and technical college in large town.
Enrollment: 3,283 undergrads.
Selectivity: Open admission; but selective for some programs.

BASIC COSTS (2007-2008)

Tuition and fees: $2,925; out-of-district residents $3,425; out-of-state residents $5,181.

FINANCIAL AID PICTURE (2006-2007)

Students with need: 84% of average financial aid package awarded as scholarships/grants, 16% awarded as loans/jobs. Need-based aid available for part-time students. Work study available nights.
Students without need: This college awards aid only to students with need.

FINANCIAL AID PROCEDURES

Forms required: FAFSA, state aid form.
Dates and Deadlines: Priority date 6/15; no closing date. Applicants notified on a rolling basis; must reply within 2 week(s) of notification.

CONTACT

Sarah Dowd, Director of Financial Aid
506 North Guignard Drive, Sumter, SC 29150-2499
(803) 778-7831

Charleston Southern University

Charleston, South Carolina
www.csuniv.edu   Federal Code: 003419

4-year private university and liberal arts college in large city, affiliated with Southern Baptist Convention.
Enrollment: 2,831 undergrads, 14% part-time. 678 full-time freshmen.
Selectivity: Admits 50 to 75% of applicants.

BASIC COSTS (2008-2009)

Tuition and fees: $18,678.
Per-credit charge: $360.
Room and board: $7,178.

FINANCIAL AID PICTURE

Students with need: Need-based aid available for full-time and part-time students. Work study available nights, weekends, and for part-time students.
Students without need: No-need awards available for academics, athletics, religious affiliation, ROTC.

FINANCIAL AID PROCEDURES

Forms required: FAFSA, state aid form.
Dates and Deadlines: Priority date 4/15; no closing date. Applicants notified on a rolling basis starting 3/1; must reply within 2 week(s) of notification.

CONTACT

Pam Hester, Director of Financial Aid

9200 University Boulevard, Charleston, SC 29423-8087

(843) 863-7050

The Citadel
Charleston, South Carolina
www.citadel.edu   Federal Code: 003423

4-year public military college in large city.

Enrollment: 2,209 undergrads, 4% part-time. 621 full-time freshmen.

Selectivity: Admits over 75% of applicants.

BASIC COSTS (2007-2008)

Tuition and fees: $7,735; out-of-state residents $19,291.

Room and board: $5,390.

Additional info: Students in Corps of Cadets required to pay $1,000 in fees which include laundry and dry cleaning charges and infirmary fees. Freshmen also pay $5,470 deposit and upperclassmen pay $1,630 deposit for uniforms, books, and supplies.

FINANCIAL AID PICTURE (2007-2008)

Students with need: Out of 481 full-time freshmen who applied for aid, 362 were judged to have need. Of these, 342 received aid, and 113 had their full need met. Average financial aid package met 62% of need; average scholarship/grant was $12,135; average loan was $3,384. Need-based aid available for part-time students.

Students without need: 57 full-time freshmen who did not demonstrate need for aid received scholarships/grants; average award was $7,161. No-need awards available for academics, alumni affiliation, athletics, leadership, music/drama, religious affiliation, ROTC, state/district residency.

Scholarships offered: 33 full-time freshmen received athletic scholarships; average amount $22,111.

Cumulative student debt: 36% of graduating class had student loans; average debt was $20,089.

FINANCIAL AID PROCEDURES

Forms required: FAFSA.

Dates and Deadlines: Priority date 2/28; no closing date. Applicants notified on a rolling basis starting 4/1; must reply within 2 week(s) of notification.

Transfers: No deadline.

CONTACT

Henry Fuller, Director of Financial Aid

171 Moultrie Street, Charleston, SC 29409

(843) 953-5187

Claflin University
Orangeburg, South Carolina
www.claflin.edu   Federal Code: 003424

4-year private liberal arts college in large town, affiliated with United Methodist Church.

Enrollment: 1,627 undergrads, 3% part-time. 390 full-time freshmen.

Selectivity: Admits less than 50% of applicants.

BASIC COSTS (2007-2008)

Tuition and fees: $12,358.

Room and board: $6,640.

FINANCIAL AID PICTURE

Students with need: Need-based aid available for full-time students. Work study available nights.

FINANCIAL AID PROCEDURES

Forms required: FAFSA, institutional form.

Dates and Deadlines: Priority date 4/15; no closing date. Applicants notified on a rolling basis starting 5/15; must reply within 2 week(s) of notification.

CONTACT

Yolanda Frazier, Director of Financial Aid

400 Magnolia Street, Orangeburg, SC 29115

(803) 535-5334

Clemson University
Clemson, South Carolina
www.clemson.edu   Federal Code: 003425

4-year public university in large town.

Enrollment: 14,173 undergrads, 6% part-time. 2,707 full-time freshmen.

Selectivity: Admits 50 to 75% of applicants.

BASIC COSTS (2007-2008)

Tuition and fees: $9,870; out-of-state residents $21,800.

Room and board: $5,992.

Additional info: Laptop computer required of all entering new students. This cost has been estimated at $1600.

FINANCIAL AID PICTURE

Students with need: Need-based aid available for full-time and part-time students. Work study available nights, weekends, and for part-time students.

Students without need: No-need awards available for academics, art, athletics, leadership, minority status, music/drama, ROTC, state/district residency.

FINANCIAL AID PROCEDURES

Forms required: FAFSA.

Dates and Deadlines: Priority date 4/1; no closing date. Applicants notified on a rolling basis starting 4/1; must reply within 3 week(s) of notification.

Transfers: Transfer students must earn 12 semester hours before being considered for institutional scholarship.

CONTACT

Marvin Carmichael, Director of Student Financial Aid

105 Sikes Hall, Clemson, SC 29634-5124

(864) 656-2280

Coastal Carolina University
Conway, South Carolina
www.coastal.edu   Federal Code: 003451

4-year public university in small city.

Enrollment: 6,851 undergrads, 6% part-time. 1,468 full-time freshmen.

Selectivity: Admits 50 to 75% of applicants.

BASIC COSTS (2007-2008)

Tuition and fees: $7,600; out-of-state residents $16,590.

Per-credit charge: $317; out-of-state residents $691.

Room and board: $6,680.

FINANCIAL AID PICTURE (2006-2007)

Students with need: Out of 1,211 full-time freshmen who applied for aid, 858 were judged to have need. Of these, 827 received aid, and 108 had their full need met. Average financial aid package met 51% of need; average scholarship/grant was $3,165; average loan was $5,928. For part-time students, average financial aid package was $4,917.

Students without need: 336 full-time freshmen who did not demonstrate need for aid received scholarships/grants; average award was $9,354. No-need awards available for academics, art, athletics, leadership, music/drama, state/district residency.

Scholarships offered: 81 full-time freshmen received athletic scholarships; average amount $7,146.

Cumulative student debt: 66% of graduating class had student loans; average debt was $22,470.

FINANCIAL AID PROCEDURES

Forms required: FAFSA.

Dates and Deadlines: Priority date 4/1; no closing date. Applicants notified on a rolling basis starting 3/1.

CONTACT

Rondall Day, Director of Financial Aid
PO Box 261954, Conway, SC 29528-6054
(843) 349-2313

Coker College
Hartsville, South Carolina
www.coker.edu   Federal Code: 003427

4-year private liberal arts college in large town.

Enrollment: 635 undergrads.

Selectivity: Admits 50 to 75% of applicants.

BASIC COSTS (2007-2008)

Tuition and fees: $18,552.

Room and board: $5,920.

Additional info: Tuition/fee waivers available for adults.

FINANCIAL AID PICTURE

Students with need: Need-based aid available for full-time and part-time students. Work study available nights, weekends, and for part-time students.

Students without need: No-need awards available for academics, art, athletics, music/drama.

Scholarships offered: Scholarships for Excellence: awarded on a competitive basis to students showing potential for continued high performance and leadership; up to $17,000 per year; candidates may be invited to campus for interviews. President's Scholarships: based on SAT or ACT score and GPA; up to $7,500 per year. Dean's Scholarships: based on SAT or ACT score and GPA; up to $7,000 per year. Departmental Scholarships: art, dance, music, theater, biology, and chemistry scholarships to talented students; language and literature/ creative writing scholarship; range from $500 to $4,000 per year; art, dance, music, and theater scholarships require an audition or portfolio; some departments require an interview. Valedictorian Scholarships: $500 per year to students ranked number one in their class at the end of their junior year or first semester of their senior year.

Additional info: Endowed scholarship program for qualified applicants. June 1 deadline for filing South Carolina Tuition Grant forms.

FINANCIAL AID PROCEDURES

Forms required: FAFSA.

Dates and Deadlines: Priority date 4/1; closing date 6/1. Applicants notified on a rolling basis starting 12/1; must reply by 5/1 or within 3 week(s) of notification.

Transfers: No deadline.

CONTACT

Betty Williams, Director of Financial Aid
300 East College Avenue, Hartsville, SC 29550
(843) 383-8055

College of Charleston
Charleston, South Carolina
www.cofc.edu   Federal Code: 003428

4-year public liberal arts college in large city.

Enrollment: 9,499 undergrads, 6% part-time. 1,968 full-time freshmen.

Selectivity: Admits 50 to 75% of applicants.

BASIC COSTS (2007-2008)

Tuition and fees: $7,778; out-of-state residents $18,732.

Per-credit charge: $324; out-of-state residents $781.

Room and board: $8,495.

FINANCIAL AID PICTURE (2006-2007)

Students with need: Out of 1,150 full-time freshmen who applied for aid, 678 were judged to have need. Of these, 645 received aid, and 231 had their full need met. Average financial aid package met 66% of need; average scholarship/grant was $2,944; average loan was $2,737. For part-time students, average financial aid package was $7,836.

Students without need: 260 full-time freshmen who did not demonstrate need for aid received scholarships/grants; average award was $10,995. No-need awards available for academics, alumni affiliation, art, athletics, music/drama.

Scholarships offered: *Merit:* Foundation Scholarships: from $1,000-$4,000 annually for up to 4 years; based on high school performance, test scores, and leadership qualities, no additional application required. *Athletic:* 39 full-time freshmen received athletic scholarships; average amount $15,315.

FINANCIAL AID PROCEDURES

Forms required: FAFSA.

Dates and Deadlines: Priority date 3/15; no closing date. Applicants notified on a rolling basis starting 4/10; must reply within 8 week(s) of notification.

Transfers: No aid available to transfer students who enroll for first time in summer school.

CONTACT

Donald Griggs, Director of Financial Assistance and Veterans Affairs
Office of Admissions and Adult Student Services, Charleston, SC 29424-0001
(843) 953-5540

Columbia College
Columbia, South Carolina
www.columbiacollegesc.edu   Federal Code: 003430

4-year private liberal arts college for women in large city, affiliated with United Methodist Church.

Enrollment: 1,224 undergrads, 20% part-time. 258 full-time freshmen.

Selectivity: Admits 50 to 75% of applicants.

BASIC COSTS (2007-2008)

Tuition and fees: $21,650.

Per-credit charge: $570.

Room and board: $6,232.

FINANCIAL AID PICTURE (2006-2007)

Students with need: Out of 250 full-time freshmen who applied for aid, 216 were judged to have need. Of these, 216 received aid, and 119 had their full need met. Average financial aid package met 81% of need; average scholarship/grant was $8,601; average loan was $2,593. For part-time students, average financial aid package was $4,965.

Students without need: 33 full-time freshmen who did not demonstrate need for aid received scholarships/grants; average award was $886. No-need awards available for academics, alumni affiliation, art, athletics, leadership, music/drama.

Scholarships offered: *Merit:* Founders Scholarship: full tuition. Presidential Scholarships: $10,000 annually. Trustees Scholarships: $8,000 annually. *Athletic:* 6 full-time freshmen received athletic scholarships; average amount $2,833.

Cumulative student debt: 94% of graduating class had student loans; average debt was $16,976.

FINANCIAL AID PROCEDURES

Forms required: FAFSA.

Dates and Deadlines: Priority date 4/1; no closing date. Applicants notified on a rolling basis starting 3/15; must reply within 2 week(s) of notification.

Transfers: Priority date 4/15. Must meet institutional standards of satisfactory academic progress.

CONTACT

Donna Quick, Director of Financial Aid
1301 Columbia College Drive, Columbia, SC 29203
(803) 786-3612

Columbia International University
Columbia, South Carolina
www.ciu.edu   Federal Code: 003429

4-year private university and Bible college in small city, affiliated with multidenominational/evangelical churches.

Enrollment: 462 undergrads, 7% part-time. 92 full-time freshmen.
Selectivity: Admits 50 to 75% of applicants.

BASIC COSTS (2008-2009)

Tuition and fees: $15,665.
Per-credit charge: $640.
Room and board: $5,750.
Additional info: Tuition/fee waivers available for minority students.

FINANCIAL AID PICTURE (2007-2008)

Students with need: Out of 89 full-time freshmen who applied for aid, 69 were judged to have need. Of these, 69 received aid, and 32 had their full need met. Average financial aid package met 89% of need; average scholarship/grant was $9,090; average loan was $3,321. For part-time students, average financial aid package was $3,954.
Students without need: 81 full-time freshmen who did not demonstrate need for aid received scholarships/grants; average award was $7,298. No-need awards available for academics, leadership, state/district residency.
Additional info: Spouse scholarship program; special short quarter scholarships for missionaries on furlough.

FINANCIAL AID PROCEDURES

Forms required: FAFSA, institutional form.
Dates and Deadlines: Priority date 1/31; no closing date. Applicants notified on a rolling basis starting 12/18; must reply within 4 week(s) of notification.
Transfers: FAFSA must be processed by June 30 for state need-based aid. State aid requires 1-year residency prior to award in most cases. Non-need-based state aid requires graduation from state high school.

CONTACT

Bob Patton, Director of Financial Aid
PO Box 3122, Columbia, SC 29230-3122
(803) 777-2227 ext. 5036

Converse College
Spartanburg, South Carolina
www.converse.edu   Federal Code: 003431

4-year private music and liberal arts college for women in small city.
Enrollment: 730 undergrads, 13% part-time. 150 full-time freshmen.
Selectivity: Admits 50 to 75% of applicants.

BASIC COSTS (2008-2009)

Tuition and fees: $24,500.
Per-credit charge: $775.
Room and board: $7,550.
Additional info: Special fees for laboratory, studio art, computer programming, and other courses requiring special materials.

FINANCIAL AID PICTURE (2007-2008)

Students with need: Out of 137 full-time freshmen who applied for aid, 122 were judged to have need. Of these, 122 received aid, and 52 had their full need met. Average financial aid package met 93% of need; average scholarship/grant was $19,361; average loan was $4,597. For part-time students, average financial aid package was $7,418.
Students without need: 39 full-time freshmen who did not demonstrate need for aid received scholarships/grants; average award was $21,121. No-need awards available for academics, alumni affiliation, art, athletics, leadership, music/drama, ROTC, state/district residency.
Scholarships offered: 10 full-time freshmen received athletic scholarships; average amount $8,217.
Cumulative student debt: 64% of graduating class had student loans; average debt was $20,078.

FINANCIAL AID PROCEDURES

Forms required: FAFSA.
Dates and Deadlines: Closing date 3/1. Applicants notified on a rolling basis starting 3/1; must reply by 5/1 or within 2 week(s) of notification.

CONTACT

Margaret Collins, Director of Scholarships and Financial Assistance
580 East Main Street, Spartanburg, SC 29302-0006
(864) 596-9019

Denmark Technical College
Denmark, South Carolina
www.denmarktech.edu   Federal Code: 005363

2-year public technical college in small town.
Enrollment: 1,348 undergrads, 32% part-time. 414 full-time freshmen.
Selectivity: Open admission.

BASIC COSTS (2007-2008)

Tuition and fees: $2,378; out-of-state residents $4,466.
Room and board: $3,310.

FINANCIAL AID PICTURE

Students with need: Need-based aid available for full-time and part-time students.

FINANCIAL AID PROCEDURES

Forms required: FAFSA.
Dates and Deadlines: No deadline. Applicants notified on a rolling basis starting 6/1; must reply within 2 week(s) of notification.

CONTACT

Kelvin Bonnett, Assistant Director of Financial Aid
Solomon Blatt Boulevard, Denmark, SC 29042
(803) 793-5161

Erskine College
Due West, South Carolina
www.erskine.edu   Federal Code: 003432

4-year private liberal arts and seminary college in rural community, affiliated with Associate Reformed Presbyterian Church.
Enrollment: 567 undergrads, 2% part-time. 164 full-time freshmen.
Selectivity: Admits 50 to 75% of applicants.

BASIC COSTS (2008-2009)

Tuition and fees: $23,165.
Per-credit charge: $800.
Room and board: $7,961.

FINANCIAL AID PICTURE

Students with need: Need-based aid available for full-time and part-time students. Work study available nights, weekends, and for part-time students.
Students without need: No-need awards available for academics, alumni affiliation, art, athletics, leadership, minority status, music/drama, religious affiliation, state/district residency.
Additional info: Filing deadline 5/1 for institutional form, 6/30 for state form.

FINANCIAL AID PROCEDURES

Forms required: FAFSA, institutional form.
Dates and Deadlines: Priority date 4/1; no closing date. Applicants notified on a rolling basis starting 12/15; must reply within 2 week(s) of notification.
Transfers: Closing date 5/1. South Carolina residents must have earned 24 hours in previous year to receive SC tuition grant and 30 hours plus 3.0 GPA to receive the Life Scholarship.

CONTACT

Allison Sullivan, Director of Financial Aid
PO Box 338, Due West, SC 29639-0176
(864) 379-8832

Florence-Darlington Technical College

Florence, South Carolina
www.fdtc.edu   Federal Code: 003990

2-year public community and technical college in small city.
Enrollment: 2,192 full-time undergrads.
Selectivity: Open admission; but selective for some programs.

BASIC COSTS (2007-2008)

Tuition and fees: $3,190; out-of-district residents $3,452; out-of-state residents $5,286.

FINANCIAL AID PICTURE

Students with need: Need-based aid available for full-time and part-time students.
Students without need: No-need awards available for academics.

FINANCIAL AID PROCEDURES

Forms required: FAFSA.
Dates and Deadlines: Priority date 5/1; no closing date. Applicants notified on a rolling basis starting 7/1; must reply within 2 week(s) of notification.

CONTACT

Joseph Durant, Director of Financial Assistance
PO Box 100548, Florence, SC 29501-0548
(843) 661-8085

Forrest Junior College

Anderson, South Carolina
www.forrestcollege.edu   Federal Code: 004924

2-year for-profit community and junior college in large town.
Enrollment: 106 undergrads, 6% part-time. 82 full-time freshmen.
Selectivity: Open admission; but selective for some programs.

BASIC COSTS (2007-2008)

Tuition and fees: $7,160.
Per-credit charge: $148.

FINANCIAL AID PICTURE

Students with need: Need-based aid available for full-time and part-time students. Work study available nights, weekends, and for part-time students.
Students without need: This college awards aid only to students with need.

FINANCIAL AID PROCEDURES

Forms required: FAFSA.
Dates and Deadlines: No deadline. Applicants notified on a rolling basis starting 4/30; must reply by 5/31 or within 4 week(s) of notification.

CONTACT

Kathy Montgomery, Director of Financial Aid
601 East River Street, Anderson, SC 29624
(864) 225-7653

Francis Marion University

Florence, South Carolina
www.fmarion.edu   Federal Code: 009226

4-year public university and liberal arts college in small city.
Enrollment: 3,231 undergrads, 6% part-time. 778 full-time freshmen.
Selectivity: Admits 50 to 75% of applicants.

BASIC COSTS (2007-2008)

Tuition and fees: $7,038; out-of-state residents $13,841.
Per-credit charge: $340; out-of-state residents $680.
Room and board: $5,860.

FINANCIAL AID PICTURE (2007-2008)

Students with need: Out of 684 full-time freshmen who applied for aid, 613 were judged to have need. Of these, 599 received aid. Need-based aid available for part-time students.
Students without need: No-need awards available for academics, music/drama.
Cumulative student debt: 71% of graduating class had student loans; average debt was $22,027.

FINANCIAL AID PROCEDURES

Forms required: FAFSA, institutional form.
Dates and Deadlines: Priority date 3/1; no closing date. Applicants notified on a rolling basis starting 4/15.
Transfers: Institutional scholarships available after 1 semester completed in residence.

CONTACT

Kim Ellisor, Director of Financial Assistance
PO Box 100547, Florence, SC 29501-0547
(843) 661-1190

Furman University

Greenville, South Carolina
www.furman.edu   Federal Code: 003434

4-year private liberal arts college in small city.
Enrollment: 2,737 undergrads, 4% part-time. 699 full-time freshmen.
Selectivity: Admits 50 to 75% of applicants.

BASIC COSTS (2008-2009)

Tuition and fees: $34,568.
Per-credit charge: $1,064.
Room and board: $8,966.

FINANCIAL AID PICTURE (2007-2008)

Students with need: Out of 366 full-time freshmen who applied for aid, 290 were judged to have need. Of these, 290 received aid, and 137 had their full need met. Average financial aid package met 90% of need; average scholarship/grant was $21,673; average loan was $3,600. For part-time students, average financial aid package was $8,132.
Students without need: 183 full-time freshmen who did not demonstrate need for aid received scholarships/grants; average award was $14,047. No-

need awards available for academics, alumni affiliation, art, athletics, leadership, music/drama, religious affiliation, ROTC, state/district residency.

Scholarships offered: 59 full-time freshmen received athletic scholarships; average amount $24,654.

Cumulative student debt: 42% of graduating class had student loans; average debt was $24,512.

Additional info: 5-point comprehensive education financing plan includes financial aid packaging, money management counseling, debt management counseling, outside scholarship coordination, summer job-match program.

FINANCIAL AID PROCEDURES

Forms required: FAFSA, state aid form, institutional form.

Dates and Deadlines: Closing date 1/15. Applicants notified by 3/15; must reply by 5/1.

Transfers: Closing date 6/1. For South Carolina Tuition Grant, must have earned 24 credits in previous year. For Life Scholarship, must have 3.0 cumulative GPA and 30 credits earned.

CONTACT

Martin Carney, Director of Financial Aid
3300 Poinsett Highway, Greenville, SC 29613
(864) 294-2204

Greenville Technical College

Greenville, South Carolina
www.gvltec.edu   Federal Code: 003991

2-year public community and technical college in large city.

Enrollment: 12,899 undergrads, 54% part-time. 1,979 full-time freshmen.

Selectivity: Open admission; but selective for some programs.

BASIC COSTS (2007-2008)

Tuition and fees: $3,290; out-of-district residents $3,566; out-of-state residents $6,698.

FINANCIAL AID PICTURE

Students with need: Need-based aid available for full-time and part-time students. Work study available nights.

Students without need: No-need awards available for academics, state/district residency.

FINANCIAL AID PROCEDURES

Forms required: FAFSA.

Dates and Deadlines: Priority date 5/1; no closing date. Applicants notified on a rolling basis starting 6/15; must reply within 2 week(s) of notification.

CONTACT

Janie Reid, Financial Aid Director
PO Box 5616, Greenville, SC 29606-5616
(864) 250-8128

Horry-Georgetown Technical College

Conway, South Carolina
www.hgtc.edu   Federal Code: 004925

2-year public community and technical college in large town.

Enrollment: 5,249 undergrads, 56% part-time. 750 full-time freshmen.

Selectivity: Open admission; but selective for some programs.

BASIC COSTS (2007-2008)

Tuition and fees: $3,114; out-of-district residents $3,882; out-of-state residents $4,914.

FINANCIAL AID PICTURE

Students with need: Need-based aid available for full-time and part-time students.

Students without need: No-need awards available for academics, state/district residency.

Additional info: Participates in South Carolina lottery tuition assistance program. Full-time technical college students who are state residents receive assistance for tuition not covered by federal or need-based grants.

FINANCIAL AID PROCEDURES

Forms required: FAFSA.

Dates and Deadlines: Priority date 4/1; closing date 6/30. Applicants notified on a rolling basis starting 4/1.

CONTACT

Susan Thompson, Director of Financial Aid and Veterans Affairs
PO Box 261966, Conway, SC 29528
(843) 349-5251

Lander University

Greenwood, South Carolina
www.lander.edu   Federal Code: 003435

4-year public liberal arts and teachers college in large town.

Enrollment: 2,325 undergrads, 10% part-time. 433 full-time freshmen.

BASIC COSTS (2007-2008)

Tuition and fees: $7,888; out-of-state residents $14,776.

Per-credit charge: $322; out-of-state residents $609.

Room and board: $5,782.

FINANCIAL AID PICTURE

Students with need: Need-based aid available for full-time and part-time students. Work study available weekends and for part-time students.

Students without need: No-need awards available for academics, art, athletics, leadership, music/drama.

FINANCIAL AID PROCEDURES

Forms required: FAFSA.

Dates and Deadlines: Priority date 4/15; no closing date. Applicants notified on a rolling basis starting 4/15; must reply within 4 week(s) of notification.

CONTACT

Fred Hardin, Director of Financial Aid
Stanley Avenue, Greenwood, SC 29649-2099
(864) 388-8340

Limestone College

Gaffney, South Carolina
www.limestone.edu   Federal Code: 003436

4-year private liberal arts college in large town.

Enrollment: 780 undergrads, 2% part-time. 174 full-time freshmen.

Selectivity: Admits 50 to 75% of applicants.

BASIC COSTS (2008-2009)

Tuition and fees: $17,300.

Per-credit charge: $720.

Room and board: $6,400.

FINANCIAL AID PICTURE (2006-2007)

Students with need: Out of 134 full-time freshmen who applied for aid, 113 were judged to have need. Of these, 113 received aid, and 21 had their full need met. Average financial aid package met 60% of need; average scholarship/grant was $9,532; average loan was $2,338. For part-time students, average financial aid package was $9,167.

Students without need: 10 full-time freshmen who did not demonstrate need for aid received scholarships/grants; average award was $4,006. No-need awards available for academics, alumni affiliation, art, athletics, job skills, leadership, music/drama, religious affiliation, ROTC, state/district residency.

Scholarships offered: *Merit:* Presidential Scholarship: full tuition; SAT above 1300, GPA 3.5 or above; 1 available. Academic Dean Scholarships: partial tuition; based on academic achievement (GPA 3.0 or above). Founders Scholarships: partial tuition; GPA 2.75 or above. R.S. Campbell Scholarship: SAT above 1100, GPA 3.25 or above; 1 available. Leadership Scholarship: partial tuition; based on evidence of student leadership. Drada Hoover Scholarship: SAT 1200 or higher; GPA 3.5; top 10% of graduating class. SAT scores exclusive of Writing. *Athletic:* 3 full-time freshmen received athletic scholarships; average amount $5,333.

Cumulative student debt: 80% of graduating class had student loans; average debt was $21,349.

FINANCIAL AID PROCEDURES

Forms required: FAFSA.

Dates and Deadlines: Priority date 2/1; no closing date. Applicants notified on a rolling basis starting 1/15; must reply within 3 week(s) of notification.

Transfers: Priority date 5/1; no deadline. Applicants notified on a rolling basis; must reply within 3 week(s) of notification.

CONTACT

Lauren Mack, Director of Financial Aid
1115 College Drive, Gaffney, SC 29340-3799
(800) 795-7151 ext. 4577

Midlands Technical College
Columbia, South Carolina
www.midlandstech.edu   Federal Code: 003993

2-year public technical college in large city.
Enrollment: 10,406 undergrads, 53% part-time. 1,533 full-time freshmen.
Selectivity: Open admission; but selective for some programs.

BASIC COSTS (2007-2008)

Tuition and fees: $3,244; out-of-district residents $4,036; out-of-state residents $9,532.

FINANCIAL AID PICTURE (2006-2007)

Students with need: Average financial aid package met 66% of need; average scholarship/grant was $3,516; average loan was $2,957. For part-time students, average financial aid package was $3,626.

FINANCIAL AID PROCEDURES

Forms required: FAFSA.

Dates and Deadlines: Priority date 4/15; no closing date. Applicants notified on a rolling basis; must reply within 2 week(s) of notification.

CONTACT

Michele Bowles, Director of Student Financial Services
PO Box 2408, Columbia, SC 29202
(803) 738-7792

Morris College
Sumter, South Carolina
www.morris.edu   Federal Code: 218399

4-year private liberal arts college in large town, affiliated with Baptist faith.
Enrollment: 868 undergrads, 3% part-time. 295 full-time freshmen.
Selectivity: Admits over 75% of applicants.

BASIC COSTS (2008-2009)

Tuition and fees: $9,621.
Per-credit charge: $389.
Room and board: $4,258.

FINANCIAL AID PICTURE (2007-2008)

Students with need: Out of 295 full-time freshmen who applied for aid, 290 were judged to have need. Of these, 290 received aid, and 40 had their full need met. Average financial aid package met 78% of need; average scholarship/grant was $8,000; average loan was $3,500. For part-time students, average financial aid package was $6,400.

Students without need: This college awards aid only to students with need.

Scholarships offered: Presidential Scholarship: $750-$2,500; must have been admitted and rank in the first quarter of high school graduating class; larger awards available to salutatorians ($2,000) and valedictorians ($2,500); awards renewable up to 4 years if student maintains B average and excellent citizenship record. Luns C. Richardson Endowed Scholarship: $4,500; first-time freshman student who has been admitted, completed academic (college prep) curriculum with GPA of 3.5 or better, has exceptional letters of recommendation from at least 2 classroom teachers and one guidance counselor, principal, or assistant principal, and plans to enroll as full-time student for 4 consecutive years.

Additional info: Students are encouraged to complete FAFSA on the web.

FINANCIAL AID PROCEDURES

Forms required: FAFSA, institutional form.

Dates and Deadlines: Priority date 3/30; no closing date. Applicants notified on a rolling basis starting 6/1; must reply within 2 week(s) of notification.

Transfers: Must reply within 2 week(s) of notification.

CONTACT

Sandra Gibson, Financial Aid Officer
100 West College Street, Sumter, SC 29150-3599
(803) 934-3238

Newberry College
Newberry, South Carolina
www.newberry.edu   Federal Code: 003440

4-year private liberal arts college in small city, affiliated with Evangelical Lutheran Church in America.
Enrollment: 911 undergrads, 2% part-time. 326 full-time freshmen.

BASIC COSTS (2008-2009)

Tuition and fees: $21,560.
Per-credit charge: $500.
Room and board: $7,400.

FINANCIAL AID PICTURE (2006-2007)

Students with need: 70% of average financial aid package awarded as scholarships/grants, 30% awarded as loans/jobs. Need-based aid available for part-time students. Work study available nights, weekends, and for part-time students.

Students without need: No-need awards available for academics, alumni affiliation, athletics, music/drama, religious affiliation, ROTC, state/district residency.

FINANCIAL AID PROCEDURES

Forms required: FAFSA, institutional form.

Dates and Deadlines: Priority date 3/15; no closing date. Applicants notified on a rolling basis starting 3/1; must reply by 5/1 or within 2 week(s) of notification.

Transfers: Available for scholarship excellence.

CONTACT

Michael Ryan, Director of Financial Aid
2100 College Street, Newberry, SC 29108
(803) 321-5128

North Greenville University

Tigerville, South Carolina
www.ngu.edu
Federal Code: 003441

4-year private liberal arts college in rural community, affiliated with Southern Baptist Convention.

Enrollment: 1,868 undergrads, 5% part-time. 512 full-time freshmen.

Selectivity: Admits over 75% of applicants.

BASIC COSTS (2008-2009)

Tuition and fees: $11,680.

Per-credit charge: $200.

Room and board: $6,720.

FINANCIAL AID PICTURE

Students with need: Need-based aid available for full-time and part-time students.

Students without need: This college awards aid only to students with need.

FINANCIAL AID PROCEDURES

Forms required: FAFSA.

Dates and Deadlines: Priority date 6/1; closing date 6/30. Applicants notified on a rolling basis starting 8/1; must reply within 2 week(s) of notification.

Transfers: No deadline.

CONTACT

Mike Jordan, Director of Financial Aid
PO Box 1892, Tigerville, SC 29688-1892
(864) 977-7050

Orangeburg-Calhoun Technical College

Orangeburg, South Carolina
www.octech.edu
Federal Code: 006815

2-year public community and technical college in large town.

Enrollment: 2,188 undergrads, 45% part-time. 365 full-time freshmen.

Selectivity: Open admission; but selective for some programs.

BASIC COSTS (2007-2008)

Tuition and fees: $2,832; out-of-district residents $3,528; out-of-state residents $4,464.

FINANCIAL AID PICTURE

Students with need: Need-based aid available for full-time and part-time students.

Students without need: This college awards aid only to students with need.

Scholarships offered: College Foundation Scholarship: full academic tuition; for high school valedictorians and salutatorians.

FINANCIAL AID PROCEDURES

Forms required: FAFSA, institutional form.

Dates and Deadlines: Priority date 6/4; no closing date. Applicants notified on a rolling basis starting 5/1; must reply within 2 week(s) of notification.

Transfers: Priority date 6/1. Financial aid transcripts required of mid-year transfers prior to disbursement of aid.

CONTACT

Caroline Thornton, Director of Institutional Research
3250 St. Matthews Road, Orangeburg, SC 29118-8222
(803) 535-1249

Piedmont Technical College

Greenwood, South Carolina
www.ptc.edu
Federal Code: 003992

2-year public community and technical college in small city.

Enrollment: 3,948 undergrads.

Selectivity: Open admission; but selective for some programs.

BASIC COSTS (2007-2008)

Tuition and fees: $3,126; out-of-district residents $3,534; out-of-state residents $4,734.

Additional info: In Service Area, not fully supporting tuition, $3,288.

FINANCIAL AID PICTURE

Students with need: Need-based aid available for full-time and part-time students. Work study available nights, weekends, and for part-time students.

Students without need: This college awards aid only to students with need.

FINANCIAL AID PROCEDURES

Forms required: FAFSA.

Dates and Deadlines: Priority date 5/1; no closing date. Applicants notified on a rolling basis starting 6/1; must reply within 2 week(s) of notification.

CONTACT

Deborah Williams, Director of Financial Aid
PO Box 1467, Greenwood, SC 29648
(864) 941-8365

Presbyterian College

Clinton, South Carolina
www.presby.edu
Federal Code: 003445

4-year private liberal arts college in small town, affiliated with Presbyterian Church (USA).

Enrollment: 1,139 undergrads, 2% part-time. 290 full-time freshmen.

Selectivity: Admits 50 to 75% of applicants.

BASIC COSTS (2008-2009)

Tuition and fees: $27,902.

Per-credit charge: $1,060.

Room and board: $8,064.

FINANCIAL AID PICTURE

Students with need: Need-based aid available for full-time and part-time students.

Students without need: No-need awards available for academics, alumni affiliation, athletics, job skills, leadership, minority status, music/drama, religious affiliation, ROTC.

Scholarships offered: Academic and leadership scholarships, applications by December 5; number and amounts awarded vary; music awards based on audition.

FINANCIAL AID PROCEDURES

Forms required: FAFSA, institutional form.

Dates and Deadlines: Priority date 3/1; no closing date. Applicants notified on a rolling basis starting 4/1; must reply by 5/1.

CONTACT

Jeffrey Holliday, Director of Financial Aid
503 South Broad Street, Clinton, SC 29325-9989
(864) 833-8290

South Carolina State University

Orangeburg, South Carolina
www.scsu.edu   Federal Code: 003446

4-year public university in large town.
Enrollment: 4,289 undergrads, 6% part-time. 1,292 full-time freshmen.
Selectivity: Admits over 75% of applicants.

BASIC COSTS (2007-2008)
Tuition and fees: $7,161; out-of-state residents $14,322.
Per-credit charge: $303; out-of-state residents $597.
Room and board: $5,118.

FINANCIAL AID PICTURE
Students with need: Need-based aid available for full-time students.
Students without need: No-need awards available for academics, athletics, ROTC.

FINANCIAL AID PROCEDURES
Forms required: FAFSA.
Dates and Deadlines: Closing date 5/1. Applicants notified on a rolling basis starting 6/15; must reply by 8/1 or within 4 week(s) of notification.
Transfers: Must provide documentation on amount of state aid received, and which semesters it was received, prior to transfer.

CONTACT
Sandra Davis, Director of Financial Aid
300 College Street NE, Orangeburg, SC 29117
(803) 536-7185

South University

Columbia, South Carolina
www.southuniversity.edu   Federal Code: 004922

4-year for-profit university in small city.
Enrollment: 593 undergrads, 36% part-time. 33 full-time freshmen.
Selectivity: Open admission; but selective for some programs.

BASIC COSTS (2007-2008)
Tuition and fees: $12,390.
Per-credit charge: $270.

FINANCIAL AID PICTURE
Students with need: Need-based aid available for full-time and part-time students.
Students without need: This college awards aid only to students with need.

FINANCIAL AID PROCEDURES
Forms required: FAFSA.
Dates and Deadlines: Priority date 5/30; no closing date. Applicants notified on a rolling basis starting 5/30.

CONTACT
Walter Haversat, Financial Aid Director
9 Science Court, Columbia, SC 29203
(803) 799-9082

Southern Wesleyan University

Central, South Carolina
www.swu.edu   Federal Code: 003422

4-year private university and liberal arts college in small town, affiliated with Wesleyan Church.
Enrollment: 1,730 undergrads, 1% part-time. 151 full-time freshmen.
Selectivity: Admits over 75% of applicants.

BASIC COSTS (2007-2008)
Tuition and fees: $17,150.
Per-credit charge: $695.
Room and board: $6,200.

FINANCIAL AID PICTURE (2007-2008)
Students with need: Out of 150 full-time freshmen who applied for aid, 140 were judged to have need. Of these, 139 received aid, and 39 had their full need met. Average financial aid package met 80% of need; average scholarship/grant was $12,286; average loan was $4,037. For part-time students, average financial aid package was $5,906.
Students without need: 11 full-time freshmen who did not demonstrate need for aid received scholarships/grants; average award was $16,406. No-need awards available for academics, athletics, music/drama.
Scholarships offered: 12 full-time freshmen received athletic scholarships; average amount $2,637.
Cumulative student debt: 99% of graduating class had student loans; average debt was $27,812.

FINANCIAL AID PROCEDURES
Forms required: FAFSA, institutional form.
Dates and Deadlines: Priority date 3/31; closing date 6/30. Applicants notified on a rolling basis starting 2/1; must reply within 2 week(s) of notification.
Transfers: Priority date 4/1. Applicants notified on a rolling basis starting 2/1; must reply within 2 week(s) of notification.

CONTACT
Jeff Dennis, Financial Aid Director
PO Box 1020, Central, SC 29630-1020
(800) 289-1292

Spartanburg Community College

Spartanburg, South Carolina
www.sccsc.edu   Federal Code: 003994

2-year public community and technical college in small city.
Enrollment: 2,419 full-time undergrads.
Selectivity: Open admission; but selective for some programs.

BASIC COSTS (2007-2008)
Tuition and fees: $3,194; out-of-district residents $3,980; out-of-state residents $6,088.

FINANCIAL AID PICTURE (2006-2007)
Students with need: 98% of average financial aid package awarded as scholarships/grants, 2% awarded as loans/jobs. Need-based aid available for part-time students.
Additional info: Participates in South Carolina lottery tuition assistance program. Full-time technical college students who are state residents receive assistance for tuition not covered by federal or need-based grants.

FINANCIAL AID PROCEDURES
Forms required: FAFSA.
Dates and Deadlines: Priority date 2/28; closing date 5/1. Applicants notified on a rolling basis starting 5/1.
Transfers: No deadline.

CONTACT
Nancy Garmroth, Director of Financial Aid
Box 4386, Spartanburg, SC 29305-4386
(864) 592-4810

Spartanburg Methodist College

Spartanburg, South Carolina
www.smcsc.edu   Federal Code: 003447

2-year private junior and liberal arts college in small city, affiliated with United Methodist Church.

Enrollment: 770 undergrads, 2% part-time. 441 full-time freshmen.
Selectivity: Admits over 75% of applicants.

BASIC COSTS (2008-2009)

Tuition and fees: $11,731.
Per-credit charge: $312.
Room and board: $6,741.
Additional info: $150 enrollment fee for first-time enrollees. Tuition/fee waivers available for adults, unemployed or children of unemployed.

FINANCIAL AID PICTURE

Students with need: Need-based aid available for full-time and part-time students. Work study available nights, weekends, and for part-time students.
Students without need: No-need awards available for academics, athletics, job skills, leadership, music/drama, religious affiliation, state/district residency.
Scholarships offered: Milliken Scholars: $4,100. Camak Scholars: $3,500. Trustee Scholars: $3,000. Presidential Scholars: $2,400.

FINANCIAL AID PROCEDURES

Forms required: FAFSA.
Dates and Deadlines: Priority date 6/30; closing date 8/22. Applicants notified on a rolling basis starting 3/1; must reply within 2 week(s) of notification.
Transfers: No deadline. Applicants notified on a rolling basis starting 3/1; must reply within 2 week(s) of notification. To be eligible for financial aid, full time students must pass the equivalent of 12 hours.

CONTACT

Carolyn Sparks, Associate Dean of Admissions and Financial Aid
1000 Powell Mill Road, Spartanburg, SC 29301-5899
(864) 587-4298

Technical College of the Lowcountry

Beaufort, South Carolina
www.tcl.edu   Federal Code: 009910

2-year public community and technical college in small town.
Enrollment: 1,893 undergrads.
Selectivity: Open admission; but selective for some programs.

BASIC COSTS (2007-2008)

Tuition and fees: $3,150; out-of-state residents $6,912.

FINANCIAL AID PICTURE

Students with need: Need-based aid available for full-time and part-time students.
Students without need: This college awards aid only to students with need.
Additional info: State lottery aid may be available to South Carolina residents who take 6 credit hours or more.

FINANCIAL AID PROCEDURES

Forms required: FAFSA.
Dates and Deadlines: No deadline. Applicants notified on a rolling basis starting 7/1.

CONTACT

Cleo Martin, Coordinator of Financial Aid
921 South Ribaut Road, Beaufort, SC 29901-1288
(843) 525-8337

Tri-County Technical College

Pendleton, South Carolina
www.tctc.edu   Federal Code: 004926

2-year public community and technical college in small town.
Enrollment: 4,100 undergrads.
Selectivity: Open admission; but selective for some programs.

BASIC COSTS (2007-2008)

Tuition and fees: $2,976; out-of-district residents $3,294; out-of-state residents $6,594.

FINANCIAL AID PICTURE

Students with need: Need-based aid available for full-time and part-time students. Work study available nights.
Students without need: No-need awards available for academics, state/district residency.
Scholarships offered: General and departmental scholarships: more than 125 awarded; some with special qualification criteria, such as student's career field or place of residency.
Additional info: Deadline for application to institutional scholarships April 2.

FINANCIAL AID PROCEDURES

Forms required: FAFSA.
Dates and Deadlines: Priority date 6/30; no closing date. Applicants notified on a rolling basis starting 6/15; must reply within 2 week(s) of notification.
Transfers: Priority date 5/1; no deadline. Applicants notified on a rolling basis starting 6/1.

CONTACT

Bill Whitlock, Director of Financial Aid
Box 587, Pendleton, SC 29670
(864) 646-8361

Trident Technical College

Charleston, South Carolina
www.tridenttech.edu   Federal Code: 004920

2-year public community and technical college in large city.
Enrollment: 10,700 undergrads, 52% part-time. 1,558 full-time freshmen.
Selectivity: Open admission; but selective for some programs.

BASIC COSTS (2007-2008)

Tuition and fees: $3,220; out-of-district residents $3,574; out-of-state residents $6,200.

FINANCIAL AID PICTURE

Students with need: Need-based aid available for full-time and part-time students. Work study available nights, weekends, and for part-time students.

FINANCIAL AID PROCEDURES

Forms required: FAFSA.
Dates and Deadlines: No deadline. Applicants notified on a rolling basis; must reply within 6 week(s) of notification.
Transfers: No deadline. Applicants notified on a rolling basis; must reply within 6 week(s) of notification.

CONTACT

Ellen Green, Director of Financial Aid
Box 118067, AM-M, Charleston, SC 29423-8067
(843) 574-6147

University of South Carolina

Columbia, South Carolina
www.sc.edu   Federal Code: 003448

4-year public university in small city.
Enrollment: 18,497 undergrads, 7% part-time. 3,637 full-time freshmen.
Selectivity: Admits 50 to 75% of applicants.

BASIC COSTS (2007-2008)

Tuition and fees: $8,346; out-of-state residents $21,632.
Per-credit charge: $372; out-of-state residents $970.
Room and board: $6,550.
Additional info: Health professions (pharmacy, health, nursing), law and medical professions have higher undergraduate and graduate fees.

FINANCIAL AID PICTURE (2007-2008)

Students with need: Out of 2,546 full-time freshmen who applied for aid, 1,510 were judged to have need. Of these, 1,506 received aid, and 498 had their full need met. Average financial aid package met 76% of need; average scholarship/grant was $4,290; average loan was $1,961. For part-time students, average financial aid package was $7,232.
Students without need: 1,705 full-time freshmen who did not demonstrate need for aid received scholarships/grants; average award was $5,861. No-need awards available for academics, alumni affiliation, art, athletics, job skills, leadership, minority status, music/drama, religious affiliation, ROTC; state/district residency.
Scholarships offered: 115 full-time freshmen received athletic scholarships; average amount $10,743.
Cumulative student debt: 45% of graduating class had student loans; average debt was $21,129.

FINANCIAL AID PROCEDURES

Forms required: FAFSA.
Dates and Deadlines: Priority date 4/1; no closing date. Applicants notified on a rolling basis starting 4/1.

CONTACT

Edgar Miller, Director of Financial Aid and Scholarships
Office of Undergraduate Admissions, Columbia, SC 29208
(803) 777-8134

University of South Carolina at Aiken

Aiken, South Carolina
www.usca.edu   Federal Code: 003449

4-year public university and liberal arts college in large town.
Enrollment: 2,867 undergrads, 19% part-time. 584 full-time freshmen.
Selectivity: Admits 50 to 75% of applicants.

BASIC COSTS (2007-2008)

Tuition and fees: $7,036; out-of-state residents $13,952.
Per-credit charge: $295; out-of-state residents $590.
Room and board: $5,870.

FINANCIAL AID PICTURE (2006-2007)

Students with need: Out of 520 full-time freshmen who applied for aid, 281 were judged to have need. Of these, 237 received aid, and 72 had their full need met. Average financial aid package met 61% of need; average scholarship/grant was $1,310; average loan was $3,330. For part-time students, average financial aid package was $6,713.
Students without need: 23 full-time freshmen who did not demonstrate need for aid received scholarships/grants; average award was $1,550.
Scholarships offered: 46 full-time freshmen received athletic scholarships; average amount $46.
Cumulative student debt: 48% of graduating class had student loans; average debt was $23,642.

FINANCIAL AID PROCEDURES

Forms required: FAFSA.
Dates and Deadlines: Priority date 3/15; no closing date. Applicants notified on a rolling basis starting 4/20; must reply within 2 week(s) of notification.
Transfers: Financial aid transcripts from previous institutions required.

CONTACT

Glenn Shumpert, Director of Financial Aid
471 University Parkway, Aiken, SC 29801
(803) 641-3476

University of South Carolina at Beaufort

Bluffton, South Carolina
www.uscb.edu   Federal Code: 003450

4-year public university and liberal arts college in large town.
Enrollment: 1,192 undergrads, 27% part-time. 265 full-time freshmen.
Selectivity: Admits 50 to 75% of applicants.

BASIC COSTS (2007-2008)

Tuition and fees: $6,310; out-of-state residents $13,992.
Per-credit charge: $247; out-of-state residents $567.

FINANCIAL AID PICTURE

Students with need: Need-based aid available for full-time and part-time students. Work study available nights, weekends, and for part-time students.
Students without need: No-need awards available for academics, state/district residency.

FINANCIAL AID PROCEDURES

Forms required: FAFSA.
Dates and Deadlines: Priority date 4/15; no closing date. Applicants notified on a rolling basis starting 5/31; must reply within 2 week(s) of notification.

CONTACT

Patricia Greene, Director and VA Coordinator of Financial Aid
One University Boulevard, Bluffton, SC 29909
(843) 521-3104

University of South Carolina at Sumter

Sumter, South Carolina
www.uscsumter.edu   Federal Code: 003426

2-year public branch campus college in small city.
Enrollment: 949 undergrads.
Selectivity: Admits 50 to 75% of applicants.

BASIC COSTS (2007-2008)

Tuition and fees: $4,888; out-of-state residents $11,800.
Per-credit charge: $192; out-of-state residents $480.

FINANCIAL AID PICTURE

Students with need: Need-based aid available for full-time and part-time students. Work study available nights, weekends, and for part-time students.
Students without need: This college awards aid only to students with need.

FINANCIAL AID PROCEDURES

Forms required: FAFSA.
Dates and Deadlines: Priority date 4/15; no closing date. Applicants notified on a rolling basis starting 4/16; must reply within 2 week(s) of notification.

CONTACT

Sue Sims, Financial Aid Director
200 Miller Road, Sumter, SC 29150-2498
(803) 938-3766

University of South Carolina at Union

Union, South Carolina
uscunion.sc.edu   Federal Code: 004927

2-year public branch campus college in small town.
Enrollment: 277 undergrads.

BASIC COSTS (2007-2008)
Tuition and fees: $4,888; out-of-state residents $11,800.
Per-credit charge: $192; out-of-state residents $480.

FINANCIAL AID PICTURE
Students with need: Work study available nights, weekends, and for part-time students.
Students without need: This college awards aid only to students with need.

FINANCIAL AID PROCEDURES
Forms required: FAFSA.
Dates and Deadlines: Priority date 4/15; no closing date. Applicants notified on a rolling basis starting 7/15; must reply within 2 week(s) of notification.

CONTACT
Bobby Holcombe, Financial Aid Director
PO Drawer 729, Union, SC 29379
(864) 429-8728

University of South Carolina Upstate

Spartanburg, South Carolina
www.uscupstate.edu   Federal Code: 006951

4-year public university in small city.
Enrollment: 4,752 undergrads, 16% part-time. 781 full-time freshmen.
Selectivity: Admits 50 to 75% of applicants.

BASIC COSTS (2007-2008)
Tuition and fees: $7,920; out-of-state residents $15,912.
Per-credit charge: $322; out-of-state residents $665.
Room and board: $6,350.

FINANCIAL AID PICTURE (2006-2007)
Students with need: Out of 635 full-time freshmen who applied for aid, 480 were judged to have need. Of these, 478 received aid, and 94 had their full need met. Average financial aid package met 34% of need; average scholarship/grant was $4,160; average loan was $2,456. For part-time students, average financial aid package was $4,996.
Students without need: 18 full-time freshmen who did not demonstrate need for aid received scholarships/grants; average award was $2,014. No-need awards available for academics, athletics, minority status, ROTC, state/district residency.
Scholarships offered: 42 full-time freshmen received athletic scholarships; average amount $7,321.
Cumulative student debt: 65% of graduating class had student loans; average debt was $19,328.
Additional info: Out-of-state students who are recipients of financial aid may qualify for out-of-state fee waiver. Educational benefits available to veterans and children of deceased/disabled veterans.

FINANCIAL AID PROCEDURES
Forms required: FAFSA, institutional form.
Dates and Deadlines: Priority date 3/1; closing date 7/15. Applicants notified on a rolling basis starting 5/1; must reply within 2 week(s) of notification.
Transfers: Students eligible for financial assistance for total of 5 years or 10 full-time semesters at all post-secondary institutions attended for the bachelor's degree, and 5 full-time semesters of enrollment for associate's degree in nursing.

CONTACT
Kim Jenerette, Director of Financial Aid and Scholarships
800 University Way, Spartanburg, SC 29303
(864) 503-5340

University of South Carolina: Salkehatchie Regional Campus

Allendale, South Carolina
uscsalkehatchie.sc.edu   Federal Code: 003454

2-year public branch campus college in small town.
Enrollment: 702 undergrads.

BASIC COSTS (2007-2008)
Tuition and fees: $4,888; out-of-state residents $11,800.
Per-credit charge: $192; out-of-state residents $480.

FINANCIAL AID PICTURE
Students with need: Need-based aid available for full-time and part-time students. Work study available nights, weekends, and for part-time students.
Students without need: No-need awards available for academics.

FINANCIAL AID PROCEDURES
Forms required: FAFSA.
Dates and Deadlines: Priority date 4/30; no closing date. Applicants notified on a rolling basis starting 6/1.

CONTACT
Julie Hadwin, Director of Financial Aid
PO Box 617, Allendale, SC 29810
(803) 584-3446

Voorhees College

Denmark, South Carolina
www.voorhees.edu   Federal Code: 003455

4-year private liberal arts college in small town, affiliated with Episcopal Church.
Enrollment: 603 undergrads.

BASIC COSTS (2007-2008)
Tuition and fees: $8,984.
Per-credit charge: $273.
Room and board: $5,342.

FINANCIAL AID PICTURE
Students with need: Need-based aid available for full-time and part-time students. Work study available nights, weekends, and for part-time students.

FINANCIAL AID PROCEDURES
Forms required: FAFSA, institutional form.
Dates and Deadlines: Priority date 4/15; no closing date. Applicants notified on a rolling basis starting 3/1; must reply within 2 week(s) of notification.

CONTACT
Augusta Kitchen, Director of Student Financial Aid
213 Wiggins Road, Denmark, SC 29042
(803) 780-1159

Williamsburg Technical College

Kingstree, South Carolina
www.wiltech.edu   Federal Code: 009322

2-year public community and technical college in small town.
Enrollment: 563 undergrads, 65% part-time. 82 full-time freshmen.
Selectivity: Open admission.

BASIC COSTS (2007-2008)

Tuition and fees: $2,830; out-of-district residents $2,950; out-of-state residents $5,292.

FINANCIAL AID PICTURE

Students with need: Need-based aid available for full-time and part-time students. Work study available nights, weekends, and for part-time students.

Students without need: No-need awards available for academics, leadership, minority status, state/district residency.

Additional info: Tuition waivers for children of war veterans.

FINANCIAL AID PROCEDURES

Forms required: FAFSA.

Dates and Deadlines: Priority date 4/15; no closing date. Applicants notified on a rolling basis starting 7/1; must reply within 4 week(s) of notification.

CONTACT

Jean Boos, Director of Financial Aid
601 Martin Luther King Jr. Avenue, Kingstree, SC 29556-4197
(843) 355-4166

Winthrop University

Rock Hill, South Carolina
www.winthrop.edu   Federal Code: 003456

4-year public university in small city.

Enrollment: 4,757 undergrads, 6% part-time. 1,180 full-time freshmen.

Selectivity: Admits 50 to 75% of applicants.

BASIC COSTS (2007-2008)

Tuition and fees: $10,210; out-of-state residents $19,034.

Per-credit charge: $426; out-of-state residents $796.

Room and board: $5,800.

FINANCIAL AID PICTURE (2006-2007)

Students with need: Out of 981 full-time freshmen who applied for aid, 720 were judged to have need. Of these, 716 received aid, and 157 had their full need met. Average financial aid package met 70% of need; average scholarship/grant was $7,828; average loan was $2,763. For part-time students, average financial aid package was $4,575.

Students without need: 60 full-time freshmen who did not demonstrate need for aid received scholarships/grants; average award was $5,288. No-need awards available for academics, art, athletics, music/drama, state/district residency.

Scholarships offered: 41 full-time freshmen received athletic scholarships; average amount $7,458.

Additional info: Academic scholarships from $1,500 to full tuition and board awarded to approximately one-third of entering freshman class each year.

FINANCIAL AID PROCEDURES

Forms required: FAFSA.

Dates and Deadlines: Priority date 3/1; no closing date. Applicants notified on a rolling basis starting 4/1; must reply within 2 week(s) of notification.

Transfers: Transfer students are not eligible for academic scholarship their first year.

CONTACT

Betty Whalen, Director, Financial Resource Center
701 Oakland Avenue, Rock Hill, SC 29733
(803) 323-2189

Wofford College

Spartanburg, South Carolina
www.wofford.edu   Federal Code: 003457

4-year private liberal arts college in small city, affiliated with United Methodist Church.

Enrollment: 1,316 undergrads, 1% part-time. 385 full-time freshmen.

Selectivity: Admits 50 to 75% of applicants.

BASIC COSTS (2008-2009)

Tuition and fees: $29,465.

Per-credit charge: $1,085.

Room and board: $8,190.

FINANCIAL AID PICTURE

Students with need: Need-based aid available for full-time and part-time students.

Students without need: No-need awards available for academics, athletics, leadership, music/drama, religious affiliation, ROTC, state/district residency.

FINANCIAL AID PROCEDURES

Forms required: FAFSA.

Dates and Deadlines: Priority date 3/15; no closing date. Applicants notified on a rolling basis starting 3/31; must reply by 5/1.

CONTACT

Donna Hawkins, Director of Financial Aid
429 North Church Street, Spartanburg, SC 29303-3663
(864) 597-4149

York Technical College

Rock Hill, South Carolina
www.yorktech.com   Federal Code: 003996

2-year public technical college in large town.

Enrollment: 4,011 undergrads, 44% part-time. 792 full-time freshmen.

Selectivity: Open admission; but selective for some programs.

BASIC COSTS (2007-2008)

Tuition and fees: $3,124; out-of-district residents $3,448; out-of-state residents $7,000.

FINANCIAL AID PICTURE (2006-2007)

Students with need: Average financial aid package for all full-time undergraduates was $7,500; for part-time $3,800. 96% awarded as scholarships/grants, 4% awarded as loans/jobs. Work study available nights.

Students without need: No-need awards available for academics, leadership, state/district residency.

Cumulative student debt: 1% of graduating class had student loans; average debt was $4,200.

FINANCIAL AID PROCEDURES

Forms required: FAFSA.

Dates and Deadlines: Priority date 6/1; no closing date. Applicants notified on a rolling basis starting 3/1.

Transfers: No deadline. Applicants notified on a rolling basis starting 3/1.

CONTACT

Angela Fowler, Financial Aid Department Manager
452 South Anderson Road, Rock Hill, SC 29730
(803) 327-8005

South Dakota

Augustana College
Sioux Falls, South Dakota
www.augie.edu   Federal Code: 003458

4-year private liberal arts college in small city, affiliated with Evangelical Lutheran Church in America.

Enrollment: 1,718 undergrads, 6% part-time. 427 full-time freshmen.

Selectivity: Admits over 75% of applicants.

BASIC COSTS (2008-2009)

Tuition and fees: $22,452.

Per-credit charge: $336.

Room and board: $5,920.

Additional info: Tuition/fee waivers available for minority students.

FINANCIAL AID PICTURE (2007-2008)

Students with need: Out of 360 full-time freshmen who applied for aid, 290 were judged to have need. Of these, 290 received aid, and 67 had their full need met. Average financial aid package met 97% of need; average scholarship/grant was $14,219; average loan was $5,374. For part-time students, average financial aid package was $8,870.

Students without need: 130 full-time freshmen who did not demonstrate need for aid received scholarships/grants; average award was $9,460. No-need awards available for academics, alumni affiliation, art, athletics, leadership, minority status, music/drama, religious affiliation, state/district residency.

Scholarships offered: 48 full-time freshmen received athletic scholarships; average amount $8,420.

Cumulative student debt: 80% of graduating class had student loans; average debt was $28,000.

FINANCIAL AID PROCEDURES

Forms required: FAFSA.

Dates and Deadlines: Priority date 3/1; no closing date. Applicants notified on a rolling basis starting 3/15; must reply within 3 week(s) of notification.

Transfers: No deadline. Applicants notified on a rolling basis starting 4/1; must reply within 3 week(s) of notification.

CONTACT

Brenda Murtha, Director of Financial Aid
2001 South Summit Avenue, Sioux Falls, SD 57197-9990
(605) 274-5216

Black Hills State University
Spearfish, South Dakota
www.bhsu.edu   Federal Code: 003459

4-year public liberal arts and teachers college in small town.

Enrollment: 3,041 undergrads.

Selectivity: Admits over 75% of applicants.

BASIC COSTS (2007-2008)

Tuition and fees: $5,441; out-of-state residents $6,679.

Per-credit charge: $83; out-of-state residents $124.

Room and board: $5,226.

Additional info: Reciprocity agreements reduce tuition for some out-of-state students .

FINANCIAL AID PICTURE

Students with need: Need-based aid available for full-time and part-time students.

Students without need: This college awards aid only to students with need.

FINANCIAL AID PROCEDURES

Forms required: FAFSA.

Dates and Deadlines: Closing date 2/15. Applicants notified on a rolling basis starting 5/15; must reply within 3 week(s) of notification.

CONTACT

Deb Henriksen, Director of Financial Aid
University Street Box 9502, Spearfish, SD 57799-9502
(605) 642-6581

Dakota State University
Madison, South Dakota
www.dsu.edu   Federal Code: 003463

4-year public university in small town.

Enrollment: 1,403 undergrads, 21% part-time. 242 full-time freshmen.

Selectivity: Admits over 75% of applicants.

BASIC COSTS (2007-2008)

Tuition and fees: $6,045; out-of-state residents $7,283.

Per-credit charge: $83; out-of-state residents $124.

Room and board: $4,374.

Additional info: Reciprocity agreements reduce tuition for some out-of-state students.

FINANCIAL AID PICTURE (2006-2007)

Students with need: Average financial aid package met 85% of need; average scholarship/grant was $3,184; average loan was $3,322. For part-time students, average financial aid package was $4,690.

Students without need: No-need awards available for academics, alumni affiliation, art, athletics, leadership, minority status, music/drama, state/district residency.

Cumulative student debt: 86% of graduating class had student loans; average debt was $20,890.

Additional info: Application deadline for grants and scholarships March 1. No deadline for loan and job applications.

FINANCIAL AID PROCEDURES

Forms required: FAFSA.

Dates and Deadlines: Priority date 3/1; no closing date. Applicants notified on a rolling basis starting 4/1; must reply within 2 week(s) of notification.

Transfers: No deadline. Applicants notified on a rolling basis starting 4/1; must reply within 2 week(s) of notification.

CONTACT

Denise Grayson, Financial Aid Director
820 North Washington Avenue, Madison, SD 57042
(605) 256-5152

Dakota Wesleyan University
Mitchell, South Dakota
www.dwu.edu   Federal Code: 003461

4-year private university and liberal arts college in large town, affiliated with United Methodist Church.

Enrollment: 756 undergrads, 4% part-time. 155 full-time freshmen.

Selectivity: Admits 50 to 75% of applicants.

BASIC COSTS (2007-2008)

Tuition and fees: $17,500.

Per-credit charge: $375.

Room and board: $5,180.

FINANCIAL AID PICTURE (2007-2008)

Students with need: 55% of average financial aid package awarded as scholarships/grants, 45% awarded as loans/jobs. Need-based aid available for part-time students. Work study available nights, weekends, and for part-time students.

Students without need: No-need awards available for academics, alumni affiliation, art, athletics, leadership, minority status, music/drama, religious affiliation.

FINANCIAL AID PROCEDURES

Forms required: FAFSA.

Dates and Deadlines: Priority date 4/15; no closing date. Applicants notified on a rolling basis starting 3/1; must reply within 2 week(s) of notification.

Transfers: No deadline. Applicants notified on a rolling basis; must reply within 2 week(s) of notification.

CONTACT

Kristy O'Kief, Director of Financial Aid
1200 West University Avenue, Mitchell, SD 57301-4398
(605) 995-2650

Kilian Community College

Sioux Falls, South Dakota
www.kilian.edu   Federal Code: 015000

2-year private community college in small city.

Enrollment: 391 undergrads, 80% part-time. 38 full-time freshmen.

Selectivity: Open admission.

BASIC COSTS (2007-2008)

Tuition and fees: $6,675.

Per-credit charge: $215.

FINANCIAL AID PICTURE (2006-2007)

Students with need: Out of 32 full-time freshmen who applied for aid, 32 were judged to have need. Of these, 32 received aid, and 2 had their full need met. For part-time students, average financial aid package was $2,963.

Students without need: No-need awards available for academics, leadership, minority status.

Cumulative student debt: 90% of graduating class had student loans; average debt was $19,914.

FINANCIAL AID PROCEDURES

Forms required: FAFSA, institutional form.

Dates and Deadlines: No deadline. Applicants notified on a rolling basis starting 7/1; must reply within 2 week(s) of notification.

Transfers: No deadline. Applicants notified on a rolling basis starting 7/1; must reply within 2 week(s) of notification.

CONTACT

Patti Klinkhammer, Director of Financial Aid
300 East 6th Street, Sioux Falls, SD 57103-7020
(605) 221-3100

Lake Area Technical Institute

Watertown, South Dakota
www.lakeareatech.edu   Federal Code: 005309

2-year public technical college in large town.

Enrollment: 1,250 undergrads.

BASIC COSTS (2007-2008)

Tuition and fees: $4,000.

Per-credit charge: $74.

Additional info: Fees vary by program.

FINANCIAL AID PICTURE

Students with need: Need-based aid available for full-time and part-time students.

Students without need: This college awards aid only to students with need.

FINANCIAL AID PROCEDURES

Forms required: FAFSA.

Dates and Deadlines: Priority date 4/15; no closing date. Applicants notified on a rolling basis starting 5/1.

CONTACT

Richard Coplan, Financial Aid Director
PO Box 730, Watertown, SD 57201
(605) 882-5284

Mitchell Technical Institute

Mitchell, South Dakota
www.mitchelltech.com   Federal Code: 008284

2-year public culinary school and technical college in large town.

Enrollment: 568 undergrads, 10% part-time. 328 full-time freshmen.

Selectivity: Open admission; but selective for some programs.

BASIC COSTS (2008-2009)

Tuition and fees: $4,370.

FINANCIAL AID PICTURE (2006-2007)

Students with need: 31% of average financial aid package awarded as scholarships/grants, 69% awarded as loans/jobs. Need-based aid available for part-time students.

Cumulative student debt: 83% of graduating class had student loans; average debt was $9,850.

FINANCIAL AID PROCEDURES

Forms required: FAFSA.

Dates and Deadlines: No deadline. Applicants notified on a rolling basis; must reply within 3 week(s) of notification.

CONTACT

Grant Uecker, Financial Aid Coordinator
821 North Capital Street, Mitchell, SD 57301
(605) 995-3052 ext. 2315

Mount Marty College

Yankton, South Dakota
www.mtmc.edu   Federal Code: 003465

4-year private liberal arts college in large town, affiliated with Roman Catholic Church.

Enrollment: 829 undergrads, 26% part-time. 106 full-time freshmen.

Selectivity: Admits 50 to 75% of applicants.

BASIC COSTS (2007-2008)

Tuition and fees: $17,468.

Per-credit charge: $596.

Room and board: $5,058.

FINANCIAL AID PICTURE

Students with need: Need-based aid available for full-time and part-time students. Work study available nights, weekends, and for part-time students.

Students without need: No-need awards available for academics, art, athletics, leadership, music/drama, religious affiliation.

Additional info: Prestige scholarships application deadline 2/1.

FINANCIAL AID PROCEDURES

Forms required: FAFSA, institutional form.

Dates and Deadlines: Priority date 3/1; no closing date. Applicants notified on a rolling basis starting 3/15; must reply within 2 week(s) of notification. **Transfers:** No deadline. Applicants notified on a rolling basis; must reply within 2 week(s) of notification.

CONTACT

Kenneth Kocer, Director of Financial Assistance
1105 West Eighth Street, Yankton, SD 57078
(605) 668-1589

National American University: Rapid City

Rapid City, South Dakota
www.national.edu/rc
Federal Code: 004057

4-year for-profit business and technical college in small city.
Enrollment: 475 undergrads.
Selectivity: Open admission; but selective for some programs.

BASIC COSTS (2007-2008)
Tuition and fees: $11,835.
Room and board: $4,443.
Additional info: Tuition/fee waivers available for unemployed or children of unemployed.

FINANCIAL AID PICTURE
Students with need: Need-based aid available for full-time and part-time students. Work study available nights, weekends, and for part-time students.
Students without need: This college awards aid only to students with need.

FINANCIAL AID PROCEDURES
Forms required: FAFSA, institutional form.
Dates and Deadlines: No deadline. Applicants notified on a rolling basis; must reply within 4 week(s) of notification.

CONTACT
Cheryl Bullinger, Director of Financial Aid
321 Kansas City Street, Rapid City, SD 57701

Northern State University

Aberdeen, South Dakota
www.northern.edu
Federal Code: 003466

4-year public university and liberal arts college in large town.
Enrollment: 1,725 undergrads, 14% part-time. 340 full-time freshmen.
Selectivity: Admits over 75% of applicants.

BASIC COSTS (2007-2008)
Tuition and fees: $5,280; out-of-state residents $6,518.
Per-credit charge: $83; out-of-state residents $124.
Room and board: $4,155.
Additional info: Reciprocity agreements reduce tuition for some out-of-state students .

FINANCIAL AID PICTURE
Students with need: Need-based aid available for full-time and part-time students. Work study available nights, weekends, and for part-time students.
Students without need: No-need awards available for academics, art, athletics, leadership, minority status, music/drama, state/district residency.

FINANCIAL AID PROCEDURES
Forms required: FAFSA.
Dates and Deadlines: Priority date 3/1; no closing date. Applicants notified on a rolling basis starting 5/1; must reply within 2 week(s) of notification.
Transfers: Applicants notified by 4/15; must reply within 2 week(s) of notification. Financial aid transcript(s) required from all schools previously attended.

CONTACT
Sharon Kienow, Director of Student Financial Assistance
1200 South Jay Street, Aberdeen, SD 57401-7198
(605) 626-2640

Presentation College

Aberdeen, South Dakota
www.presentation.edu
Federal Code: 003467

4-year private business and health science college in large town, affiliated with Roman Catholic Church.
Enrollment: 700 undergrads.

BASIC COSTS (2007-2008)
Tuition and fees: $13,150.
Per-credit charge: $475.
Room and board: $4,875.

FINANCIAL AID PICTURE
Students with need: Need-based aid available for full-time and part-time students. Work study available nights, weekends, and for part-time students.

FINANCIAL AID PROCEDURES
Forms required: FAFSA.
Dates and Deadlines: Priority date 4/1; no closing date. Applicants notified on a rolling basis starting 5/1; must reply within 2 week(s) of notification.

CONTACT
Val Weisser, Financial Aid Director
1500 North Main Street, Aberdeen, SD 57401
(605) 229-8429

South Dakota School of Mines and Technology

Rapid City, South Dakota
www.sdsmt.edu
Federal Code: 003470

4-year public university and engineering college in small city.
Enrollment: 1,578 undergrads, 12% part-time. 274 full-time freshmen.
Selectivity: Admits over 75% of applicants.

BASIC COSTS (2007-2008)
Tuition and fees: $5,670; out-of-state residents $6,910.
Per-credit charge: $83; out-of-state residents $124.
Room and board: $4,600.
Additional info: Reciprocity agreements reduce tuition for some out-of-state students.

FINANCIAL AID PICTURE (2006-2007)
Students with need: Out of 263 full-time freshmen who applied for aid, 132 were judged to have need. Of these, 132 received aid, and 55 had their full need met. Average financial aid package met 80% of need; average scholarship/grant was $3,675; average loan was $2,432. For part-time students, average financial aid package was $5,693.
Students without need: 80 full-time freshmen who did not demonstrate need for aid received scholarships/grants; average award was $3,287. No-need awards available for academics, athletics, leadership, ROTC.
Scholarships offered: *Merit:* Presidential Scholarship: $100 to $5,000; 5 awarded. Surbeck Scholars: $7,000; 2 awarded. All based on ACT/SAT scores, high school GPA, and class rank. Number of awards may vary from year to year depending on availability of funding. *Athletic:* 18 full-time freshmen received athletic scholarships; average amount $2,592.
Additional info: Closing date for scholarship applications February 1.

FINANCIAL AID PROCEDURES
Forms required: FAFSA.

Dates and Deadlines: Priority date 3/15; no closing date. Applicants notified on a rolling basis starting 5/1; must reply within 3 week(s) of notification.

CONTACT

David Martin, Director of Financial Aid
501 East St. Joseph Street, Rapid City, SD 57701
(605) 394-2274

South Dakota State University

Brookings, South Dakota
www.sdstate.edu   Federal Code: 003471

4-year public university in large town.
Enrollment: 9,353 undergrads, 13% part-time. 1,937 full-time freshmen.
Selectivity: Admits over 75% of applicants.

BASIC COSTS (2007-2008)

Tuition and fees: $5,373; out-of-state residents $6,611.
Per-credit charge: $83; out-of-state residents $124.
Room and board: $5,240.
Additional info: Reduced out-of-state tuition for Minnesota students.

FINANCIAL AID PICTURE (2007-2008)

Students with need: Out of 1,661 full-time freshmen who applied for aid, 1,486 were judged to have need. Of these, 1,486 received aid, and 1,104 had their full need met. Average financial aid package met 87% of need; average scholarship/grant was $3,814; average loan was $4,534. Need-based aid available for part-time students.
Students without need: 442 full-time freshmen who did not demonstrate need for aid received scholarships/grants; average award was $1,553. No-need awards available for academics, art, athletics, job skills, leadership, minority status, music/drama, ROTC, state/district residency.
Scholarships offered: *Merit:* Academic scholarships for first-year freshmen: $500-$6,500; based on academic performance in high school; 1,420 awarded. Minimum academic scholarship for new first-year students: $1,000; based on ACT 24+; renewable. *Athletic:* 131 full-time freshmen received athletic scholarships; average amount $5,180.
Cumulative student debt: 82% of graduating class had student loans; average debt was $21,061.

FINANCIAL AID PROCEDURES

Forms required: FAFSA.
Dates and Deadlines: Priority date 3/11; no closing date. Applicants notified on a rolling basis starting 4/1; must reply within 3 week(s) of notification.
Transfers: No deadline. Applicants notified on a rolling basis starting 4/1; must reply within 3 week(s) of notification.

CONTACT

Jay Larsen, Director of Financial Aid
Box 2201 SAD 200, Brookings, SD 57007-0649
(605) 688-4695

Southeast Technical Institute

Sioux Falls, South Dakota
www.southeasttech.edu   Federal Code: 008285

2-year public technical college in small city.
Enrollment: 2,151 undergrads, 20% part-time. 578 full-time freshmen.
Selectivity: Open admission; but selective for some programs.

BASIC COSTS (2007-2008)

Tuition and fees: $3,577.
Per-credit charge: $74.
Additional info: $450 per semester laptop fee required for some students. Students able to keep laptop after paying for 4 semesters of the lease.

FINANCIAL AID PICTURE

Students with need: Need-based aid available for full-time and part-time students.
Students without need: This college awards aid only to students with need.

FINANCIAL AID PROCEDURES

Forms required: FAFSA.
Dates and Deadlines: Priority date 5/1; no closing date. Applicants notified on a rolling basis starting 5/1; must reply within 3 week(s) of notification.

CONTACT

Lynette Grabowska, Financial Aid Officer
2320 North Career Avenue, Sioux Falls, SD 57107
(605) 367-7867

University of Sioux Falls

Sioux Falls, South Dakota
www.usiouxfalls.edu   Federal Code: 003469

4-year private liberal arts college in small city, affiliated with American Baptist Churches in the USA.
Enrollment: 1,490 undergrads.
Selectivity: Admits over 75% of applicants.

BASIC COSTS (2007-2008)

Tuition and fees: $17,940.
Per-credit charge: $280.
Room and board: $5,400.

FINANCIAL AID PICTURE

Students with need: Need-based aid available for full-time and part-time students.
Students without need: No-need awards available for academics, alumni affiliation, art, athletics, job skills, leadership, minority status, music/drama, religious affiliation, state/district residency.

FINANCIAL AID PROCEDURES

Forms required: FAFSA.
Dates and Deadlines: Priority date 3/1; no closing date. Applicants notified on a rolling basis starting 3/1; must reply within 2 week(s) of notification.

CONTACT

Laura Olson, Director of Financial Aid
1101 West 22nd Street, Sioux Falls, SD 57105-1699
(605) 331-6623

University of South Dakota

Vermillion, South Dakota
www.usd.edu   Federal Code: 003474

4-year public university in small town.
Enrollment: 6,046 undergrads, 27% part-time. 1,020 full-time freshmen.
Selectivity: Admits over 75% of applicants.

BASIC COSTS (2007-2008)

Tuition and fees: $5,393; out-of-state residents $6,631.
Per-credit charge: $83; out-of-state residents $124.
Room and board: $5,174.
Additional info: Reciprocity agreement in place for Minnesota residents. Reduced tuition for Iowa residents.

FINANCIAL AID PICTURE (2006-2007)

Students with need: Out of 886 full-time freshmen who applied for aid, 602 were judged to have need. Of these, 543 received aid, and 436 had their full need met. Average financial aid package met 72% of need; average scholarship/grant was $3,700; average loan was $2,785. For part-time students, average financial aid package was $4,805.

Students without need: 263 full-time freshmen who did not demonstrate need for aid received scholarships/grants; average award was $3,224. No-need awards available for academics, art, athletics, leadership, minority status, music/drama, ROTC.

Scholarships offered: 84 full-time freshmen received athletic scholarships; average amount $3,879.

Cumulative student debt: 88% of graduating class had student loans; average debt was $22,781.

FINANCIAL AID PROCEDURES

Forms required: FAFSA.

Dates and Deadlines: Priority date 3/15; no closing date. Applicants notified on a rolling basis starting 5/5.

CONTACT

Julie Pier, Director of Student Financial Aid
414 East Clark Street, Vermillion, SD 57069-2390
(605) 677-5446

Western Dakota Technical Institute

Rapid City, South Dakota
www.wdt.edu   Federal Code: 010170

2-year public technical college in small city.
Enrollment: 1,026 undergrads.
Selectivity: Open admission; but selective for some programs.

BASIC COSTS (2007-2008)

Tuition and fees: $3,720.
Per-credit charge: $74.
Additional info: Total program cost ranges from $4,850- $13,150 depending on course of study.

FINANCIAL AID PICTURE

Students with need: Need-based aid available for full-time and part-time students. Work study available nights, weekends, and for part-time students.

FINANCIAL AID PROCEDURES

Forms required: FAFSA.

Dates and Deadlines: Priority date 4/20; no closing date. Applicants notified on a rolling basis starting 6/30; must reply within 2 week(s) of notification.

CONTACT

Starla Russell, Manager of Financial Aid
800 Mickelson Drive, Rapid City, SD 57703
(605) 394-4034

Tennessee

American Baptist College of ABT Seminary

Nashville, Tennessee
www.abcnash.edu   Federal Code: 010460

4-year private Bible college in very large city, affiliated with Baptist faith.
Enrollment: 108 undergrads, 28% part-time. 15 full-time freshmen.
Selectivity: Open admission.

BASIC COSTS (2007-2008)

Tuition and fees: $5,820.
Per-credit charge: $190.
Room only: $1,800.

FINANCIAL AID PICTURE

Students with need: Need-based aid available for full-time students.

FINANCIAL AID PROCEDURES

Forms required: FAFSA.

Dates and Deadlines: No deadline. Applicants notified on a rolling basis; must reply within 2 week(s) of notification.

CONTACT

Marcella Lockhart, Director of Enrollment Management
1800 Baptist World Center Drive, Nashville, TN 37207
(615) 687-6896 ext. 2227

Aquinas College

Nashville, Tennessee
www.aquinas-tn.edu   Federal Code: 003477

4-year private nursing and liberal arts college in very large city, affiliated with Roman Catholic Church.
Enrollment: 846 undergrads.
Selectivity: Admits 50 to 75% of applicants.

BASIC COSTS (2007-2008)

Tuition and fees: $15,005.
Per-credit charge: $486.
Additional info: Additional $40 per-credit hour for nursing classes. Additional required fees for nursing and teacher education programs.

FINANCIAL AID PICTURE

Students with need: Need-based aid available for full-time and part-time students. Work study available nights.

Students without need: No-need awards available for academics, alumni affiliation, leadership, religious affiliation.

FINANCIAL AID PROCEDURES

Forms required: FAFSA.

Dates and Deadlines: Priority date 3/1; no closing date. Applicants notified on a rolling basis starting 3/1; must reply within 2 week(s) of notification.

Transfers: No deadline. Applicants notified on a rolling basis; must reply within 2 week(s) of notification.

CONTACT

Zelena O'Sullivan, Director of Financial Aid
4210 Harding Road, Nashville, TN 37205-2086
(615) 297-7545 ext. 442

Austin Peay State University

Clarksville, Tennessee
www.apsu.edu   Federal Code: 003478

4-year public university and liberal arts college in small city.
Enrollment: 8,282 undergrads, 27% part-time. 1,167 full-time freshmen.
Selectivity: Admits over 75% of applicants.

BASIC COSTS (2007-2008)

Tuition and fees: $5,238; out-of-state residents $15,514.
Per-credit charge: $178; out-of-state residents $624.
Room and board: $5,510.

FINANCIAL AID PICTURE (2006-2007)

Students with need: Out of 1,131 full-time freshmen who applied for aid, 921 were judged to have need. Of these, 913 received aid. For part-time students, average financial aid package was $4,152.

Students without need: 190 full-time freshmen who did not demonstrate need for aid received scholarships/grants; average award was $4,870. No-need awards available for academics, art, athletics, leadership, music/drama, ROTC, state/district residency.

Scholarships offered: 65 full-time freshmen received athletic scholarships; average amount $5,968.

FINANCIAL AID PROCEDURES

Forms required: FAFSA.

Dates and Deadlines: Priority date 3/1; no closing date. Applicants notified on a rolling basis starting 5/1.

CONTACT

Donna Price, Director of Financial Aid
PO Box 4548, Clarksville, TN 37044
(931) 221-7907

Baptist College of Health Sciences
Memphis, Tennessee
www.bchs.edu   Federal Code: 034403

4-year private health science and nursing college in very large city, affiliated with Baptist faith.

Enrollment: 910 undergrads, 31% part-time. 49 full-time freshmen.

Selectivity: Admits less than 50% of applicants. GED not accepted.

BASIC COSTS (2008-2009)

Tuition and fees: $9,070.
Per-credit charge: $274.

FINANCIAL AID PICTURE (2006-2007)

Students with need: 39% of average financial aid package awarded as scholarships/grants, 61% awarded as loans/jobs.

CONTACT

Rex Thompson, Vice President, Business and Financial Services
1003 Monroe Avenue, Memphis, TN 38104
(901) 572-2446

Belmont University
Nashville, Tennessee
www.belmont.edu   Federal Code: 003479

4-year private university in very large city.

Enrollment: 3,979 undergrads, 8% part-time. 764 full-time freshmen.

Selectivity: Admits 50 to 75% of applicants.

BASIC COSTS (2008-2009)

Tuition and fees: $21,110.
Per-credit charge: $770.
Room and board: $8,200.

FINANCIAL AID PICTURE (2006-2007)

Students with need: Out of 695 full-time freshmen who applied for aid, 389 were judged to have need. Of these, 389 received aid, and 110 had their full need met. Average financial aid package met 84% of need; average scholarship/grant was $5,295; average loan was $2,739. For part-time students, average financial aid package was $5,337.

Students without need: 330 full-time freshmen who did not demonstrate need for aid received scholarships/grants; average award was $6,579. No-need awards available for academics, art, athletics, leadership, music/drama, religious affiliation, state/district residency.

Scholarships offered: 25 full-time freshmen received athletic scholarships; average amount $15,043.

Cumulative student debt: 56% of graduating class had student loans; average debt was $18,851.

FINANCIAL AID PROCEDURES

Forms required: FAFSA.

Dates and Deadlines: Priority date 3/1; no closing date. Applicants notified on a rolling basis starting 3/15; must reply by 5/1 or within 2 week(s) of notification.

Transfers: Applicants notified on a rolling basis starting 3/1; must reply by 5/1 or within 2 week(s) of notification. Scholarships available.

CONTACT

Paula Gill, Director of Student Financial Services
1900 Belmont Boulevard, Nashville, TN 37212-3757
(615) 460-6403

Bethel College
McKenzie, Tennessee
www.bethel-college.edu   Federal Code: 003480

4-year private liberal arts college in small town, affiliated with Presbyterian Church (USA).

Enrollment: 1,996 undergrads.

Selectivity: Admits 50 to 75% of applicants.

BASIC COSTS (2007-2008)

Tuition and fees: $11,690.
Per-credit charge: $341.
Room and board: $6,472.

FINANCIAL AID PICTURE

Students with need: Need-based aid available for full-time and part-time students. Work study available nights, weekends, and for part-time students.

Students without need: No-need awards available for academics, athletics, music/drama, religious affiliation, state/district residency.

FINANCIAL AID PROCEDURES

Forms required: FAFSA, institutional form.

Dates and Deadlines: Priority date 3/3; closing date 6/30. Applicants notified on a rolling basis starting 3/1.

Transfers: Financial aid transcripts from previously attended institutions required.

CONTACT

Laura Bateman, Director of Financial Aid
325 Cherry Avenue, McKenzie, TN 38201
(731) 352-4021

Bryan College
Dayton, Tennessee
www.bryan.edu   Federal Code: 003536

4-year private liberal arts college in small town, affiliated with interdenominational tradition.

Enrollment: 981 undergrads. 199 full-time freshmen.

Selectivity: Admits 50 to 75% of applicants.

BASIC COSTS (2007-2008)

Tuition and fees: $16,320.
Per-credit charge: $690.
Room and board: $4,770.

Additional info: Tuition/fee waivers available for adults, minority students, unemployed or children of unemployed.

FINANCIAL AID PICTURE (2006-2007)

Students with need: Out of 172 full-time freshmen who applied for aid, 150 were judged to have need. Of these, 147 received aid, and 43 had their full need met. Average financial aid package met 70% of need; average scholarship/grant was $5,611; average loan was $4,220. For part-time students, average financial aid package was $7,602.

Students without need: 23 full-time freshmen who did not demonstrate need for aid received scholarships/grants; average award was $3,506. No-need awards available for academics, alumni affiliation, art, athletics, job skills, leadership, music/drama.

Scholarships offered: 21 full-time freshmen received athletic scholarships; average amount $5,879.

Cumulative student debt: 67% of graduating class had student loans; average debt was $12,533.

FINANCIAL AID PROCEDURES

Forms required: FAFSA, institutional form.

Dates and Deadlines: Priority date 2/15; no closing date. Applicants notified on a rolling basis starting 1/1; must reply within 2 week(s) of notification.

CONTACT

Rick Taphorn, Director of Financial Aid
PO Box 7000, Dayton, TN 37321-7000
(423) 775-7339

Carson-Newman College

Jefferson City, Tennessee
www.cn.edu   Federal Code: 003481

4-year private liberal arts college in small town, affiliated with Southern Baptist Convention.

Enrollment: 1,815 undergrads, 5% part-time. 434 full-time freshmen.

Selectivity: Admits 50 to 75% of applicants.

BASIC COSTS (2007-2008)

Tuition and fees: $16,980.

Per-credit charge: $675.

Room and board: $5,360.

Additional info: Tuition/fee waivers available for adults, minority students.

FINANCIAL AID PICTURE (2007-2008)

Students with need: Out of 414 full-time freshmen who applied for aid, 325 were judged to have need. Of these, 325 received aid, and 110 had their full need met. Average financial aid package met 85% of need; average scholarship/grant was $12,231; average loan was $2,366. For part-time students, average financial aid package was $6,035.

Students without need: 105 full-time freshmen who did not demonstrate need for aid received scholarships/grants; average award was $6,077. No-need awards available for academics, art, athletics, leadership, minority status, music/drama, religious affiliation, ROTC.

Scholarships offered: 105 full-time freshmen received athletic scholarships; average amount $985.

Cumulative student debt: 67% of graduating class had student loans; average debt was $15,838.

FINANCIAL AID PROCEDURES

Forms required: FAFSA, institutional form.

Dates and Deadlines: Priority date 4/1; no closing date. Applicants notified on a rolling basis starting 2/1; must reply within 2 week(s) of notification.

CONTACT

Danette Seale, Director of Financial Aid
1646 Russell Avenue, Jefferson City, TN 37760
(865) 471-3247

Chattanooga State Technical Community College

Chattanooga, Tennessee
www.chattanoogastate.edu   Federal Code: 003998

2-year public community and technical college in small city.

Enrollment: 6,437 undergrads.

Selectivity: Open admission; but selective for some programs.

BASIC COSTS (2007-2008)

Tuition and fees: $2,641; out-of-state residents $9,717.

Per-credit charge: $101; out-of-state residents $407.

FINANCIAL AID PICTURE

Students with need: Need-based aid available for full-time and part-time students. Work study available nights, weekends, and for part-time students.

Students without need: No-need awards available for state/district residency.

FINANCIAL AID PROCEDURES

Forms required: FAFSA.

Dates and Deadlines: Priority date 4/1; no closing date. Applicants notified on a rolling basis starting 4/1; must reply within 2 week(s) of notification.

CONTACT

Jeanne Hinchee, Director of Financial Aid
4501 Amnicola Highway, Chattanooga, TN 37406
(423) 697-4402

Christian Brothers University

Memphis, Tennessee
www.cbu.edu   Federal Code: 003482

4-year private university in very large city, affiliated with Roman Catholic Church.

Enrollment: 1,430 undergrads, 16% part-time. 321 full-time freshmen.

Selectivity: Admits 50 to 75% of applicants.

BASIC COSTS (2008-2009)

Tuition and fees: $22,600.

Per-credit charge: $690.

Room and board: $6,050.

Additional info: Tuition/fee waivers available for adults.

FINANCIAL AID PICTURE (2007-2008)

Students with need: Out of 296 full-time freshmen who applied for aid, 229 were judged to have need. Of these, 229 received aid, and 64 had their full need met. Average financial aid package met 93% of need; average scholarship/grant was $6,626; average loan was $3,271. For part-time students, average financial aid package was $6,487.

Students without need: 76 full-time freshmen who did not demonstrate need for aid received scholarships/grants; average award was $8,032. No-need awards available for academics, alumni affiliation, athletics, music/drama, state/district residency.

Scholarships offered: 36 full-time freshmen received athletic scholarships; average amount $6,757.

Additional info: ROTC scholarships available to qualified applicants.

FINANCIAL AID PROCEDURES

Forms required: FAFSA.

Dates and Deadlines: Priority date 2/15; no closing date. Applicants notified on a rolling basis starting 3/1; must reply within 2 week(s) of notification.

CONTACT

Jim Shannon, Director of Student Financial Resources
650 East Parkway South, Memphis, TN 38104-5519
(901) 321-3305

Cleveland State Community College
Cleveland, Tennessee
www.clevelandstatecc.edu   Federal Code: 003999

2-year public community college in small city.
Enrollment: 2,295 undergrads, 39% part-time. 478 full-time freshmen.
Selectivity: Open admission; but selective for some programs.

BASIC COSTS (2007-2008)
Tuition and fees: $2,627; out-of-state residents $9,703.
Per-credit charge: $101; out-of-state residents $407.

FINANCIAL AID PICTURE (2007-2008)
Students with need: Out of 448 full-time freshmen who applied for aid, 280 were judged to have need. Of these, 269 received aid, and 54 had their full need met. Average financial aid package met 77% of need; average scholarship/grant was $4,247; average loan was $2,679. For part-time students, average financial aid package was $3,640.
Students without need: 115 full-time freshmen who did not demonstrate need for aid received scholarships/grants; average award was $3,169. No-need awards available for athletics, minority status.
Scholarships offered: 9 full-time freshmen received athletic scholarships; average amount $2,283.

FINANCIAL AID PROCEDURES
Forms required: FAFSA, institutional form.
Dates and Deadlines: Priority date 6/15; no closing date. Applicants notified on a rolling basis starting 7/1; must reply within 2 week(s) of notification.

CONTACT
Geraldine Parks, Director of Financial Aid
3535 Adkisson Drive, Cleveland, TN 37320-3570
(423) 478-6215

Columbia State Community College
Columbia, Tennessee
www.columbiastate.edu   Federal Code: 003483

2-year public community college in large town.
Enrollment: 4,633 undergrads.
Selectivity: Open admission; but selective for some programs.

BASIC COSTS (2007-2008)
Tuition and fees: $2,605; out-of-state residents $9,681.
Per-credit charge: $101; out-of-state residents $407.

FINANCIAL AID PICTURE
Students with need: Need-based aid available for full-time and part-time students.
Students without need: No-need awards available for academics, athletics, state/district residency.

FINANCIAL AID PROCEDURES
Forms required: FAFSA, institutional form.
Dates and Deadlines: Closing date 3/15. Applicants notified on a rolling basis starting 5/15; must reply within 2 week(s) of notification.

CONTACT
Pauletta Burns, Director, Financial Assistance
1665 Hampshire Pike, Columbia, TN 38401
(931) 540-2583

Crichton College
Memphis, Tennessee
www.crichton.edu   Federal Code: 009982

4-year private liberal arts college in very large city, affiliated with nondenominational tradition.
Enrollment: 906 undergrads, 36% part-time. 111 full-time freshmen.

BASIC COSTS (2007-2008)
Tuition and fees: $11,256.
Per-credit charge: $445.
Room and board: $7,982.

FINANCIAL AID PICTURE (2007-2008)
Students with need: Average financial aid package met 34% of need; average scholarship/grant was $3,044; average loan was $3,442. For part-time students, average financial aid package was $2,808.
Students without need: No-need awards available for academics, alumni affiliation, athletics, leadership, music/drama, religious affiliation.
Scholarships offered: Academic scholarships awarded based on student's academic information, including applicant's cumulative unweighted high school GPA and ACT or SAT test scores. Presidential Award - Potential Award Amount: $6,000 per year for four years Excellence Award - Potential Award Amount: $4,000 per year for four years Meritorious Award - Potential Award Amount: $2,000 per year for four years.

FINANCIAL AID PROCEDURES
Forms required: FAFSA, institutional form.
Dates and Deadlines: Priority date 3/15; no closing date. Applicants notified on a rolling basis starting 3/1; must reply within 2 week(s) of notification.
Transfers: No deadline. Applicants notified on a rolling basis; must reply within 2 week(s) of notification.

CONTACT
Melanie Johnson, Director of Student Finance
255 North Highland, Memphis, TN 38111-1375
(901) 320-9787

Cumberland University
Lebanon, Tennessee
www.cumberland.edu   Federal Code: 003485

4-year private university and liberal arts college in large town.
Enrollment: 994 undergrads, 9% part-time. 210 full-time freshmen.
Selectivity: Admits 50 to 75% of applicants.

BASIC COSTS (2008-2009)
Tuition and fees: $16,720.
Per-credit charge: $660.
Room and board: $6,070.

FINANCIAL AID PICTURE (2007-2008)
Students with need: Out of 203 full-time freshmen who applied for aid, 167 were judged to have need. Of these, 167 received aid, and 42 had their full need met. Average financial aid package met 70% of need; average scholarship/grant was $4,034; average loan was $2,806. For part-time students, average financial aid package was $6,927.
Students without need: 32 full-time freshmen who did not demonstrate need for aid received scholarships/grants; average award was $3,212. No-need awards available for academics, art, athletics, music/drama.
Scholarships offered: 33 full-time freshmen received athletic scholarships; average amount $7,899.

FINANCIAL AID PROCEDURES
Forms required: FAFSA, institutional form.
Dates and Deadlines: Priority date 2/1; no closing date. Applicants notified on a rolling basis starting 5/1; must reply within 2 week(s) of notification.

Transfers: Priority date 2/15. Applicants notified on a rolling basis starting 5/1.

CONTACT
Judy Jordan, VP of Fiscal Affairs
One Cumberland Square, Lebanon, TN 37087
(615) 444-2562 ext. 1222

Draughons Junior College: Nashville
Nashville, Tennessee
www.draughons.edu   Federal Code: 004934

2-year for-profit business and junior and career college in very large city.
Enrollment: 332 undergrads, 35% part-time. 121 full-time freshmen.
Selectivity: Open admission.

FINANCIAL AID PICTURE
Students with need: Need-based aid available for full-time and part-time students. Work study available nights.
Students without need: This college awards aid only to students with need.
Additional info: Financial aid form for in-state applicants must be filed before 5/1.

FINANCIAL AID PROCEDURES
Forms required: FAFSA.
Dates and Deadlines: No deadline. Applicants notified on a rolling basis.
Transfers: Students must notify Tennessee Student Assistance Corporation of institutional change before appropriate deadlines.

CONTACT
Chris Armstrong, Director of Financial Services
340 Plus Park at Pavilion Boulevard, Nashville, TN 37217
(615) 361-7555

Dyersburg State Community College
Dyersburg, Tennessee
www.dscc.edu   Federal Code: 006835

2-year public community college in large town.
Enrollment: 2,078 undergrads, 39% part-time. 503 full-time freshmen.
Selectivity: Open admission; but selective for some programs.

BASIC COSTS (2007-2008)
Tuition and fees: $2,635; out-of-state residents $9,711.
Per-credit charge: $101; out-of-state residents $407.

FINANCIAL AID PICTURE
Students with need: Need-based aid available for full-time and part-time students. Work study available nights.
Students without need: No-need awards available for academics, alumni affiliation, athletics, job skills, leadership, minority status, music/drama, state/district residency.

FINANCIAL AID PROCEDURES
Forms required: FAFSA.
Dates and Deadlines: Priority date 3/1; no closing date. Applicants notified on a rolling basis starting 3/1; must reply within 2 week(s) of notification.

CONTACT
Sandra Rockett, Director of Financial Aid
1510 Lake Road, Dyersburg, TN 38024
(731) 286-3238

East Tennessee State University
Johnson City, Tennessee
www.etsu.edu   Federal Code: 003487

4-year public university in small city.
Enrollment: 10,270 undergrads, 14% part-time. 1,921 full-time freshmen.
Selectivity: Admits over 75% of applicants.

BASIC COSTS (2007-2008)
Tuition and fees: $4,887; out-of-state residents $15,163.
Per-credit charge: $178; out-of-state residents $624.
Room and board: $5,166.

FINANCIAL AID PICTURE (2007-2008)
Students with need: Out of 1,655 full-time freshmen who applied for aid, 1,241 were judged to have need. Of these, 1,211 received aid, and 462 had their full need met. Average financial aid package met 81% of need; average scholarship/grant was $5,022; average loan was $1,235. For part-time students, average financial aid package was $4,659.
Students without need: 176 full-time freshmen who did not demonstrate need for aid received scholarships/grants; average award was $3,436. No-need awards available for academics, alumni affiliation, art, athletics, job skills, leadership, minority status, music/drama, religious affiliation, ROTC, state/district residency.
Scholarships offered: 28 full-time freshmen received athletic scholarships; average amount $14,998.
Cumulative student debt: 52% of graduating class had student loans; average debt was $20,437.
Additional info: Housing costs payable by installment.

FINANCIAL AID PROCEDURES
Forms required: FAFSA.
Dates and Deadlines: Priority date 4/15; no closing date. Applicants notified on a rolling basis starting 4/15; must reply within 2 week(s) of notification.

CONTACT
Margaret Miller, Director of Financial Aid
ETSU Box 70731, Johnson City, TN 37614
(423) 439-4300

Free Will Baptist Bible College
Nashville, Tennessee
www.fwbbc.edu   Federal Code: 030018

4-year private Bible and teachers college in very large city, affiliated with Free Will Baptists.
Enrollment: 291 undergrads, 18% part-time. 59 full-time freshmen.
Selectivity: Open admission.

BASIC COSTS (2008-2009)
Tuition and fees: $13,086.
Per-credit charge: $409.
Room and board: $53,582.

FINANCIAL AID PICTURE (2006-2007)
Students with need: 37% of average financial aid package awarded as scholarships/grants; 63% awarded as loans/jobs. Need-based aid available for part-time students. Work study available nights, weekends, and for part-time students.
Students without need: No-need awards available for academics, art, music/drama.
Scholarships offered: Presidential Honors Scholarship: $1,000 per semester, renewable for 8 semesters; high school GPA 3.5+, and ACT 29+, must maintain college GPA 3.25; awarded to four students yearly.

FINANCIAL AID PROCEDURES
Forms required: FAFSA, institutional form.

Dates and Deadlines: Priority date 4/15; no closing date. Applicants notified on a rolling basis starting 7/1; must reply within 2 week(s) of notification.
Transfers: No deadline.

CONTACT
Jeff Caudill, Director of Enrollment Services
3606 West End Avenue, Nashville, TN 37205-2403
(615) 844-5250

Freed-Hardeman University
Henderson, Tennessee
www.fhu.edu   Federal Code: 003492

4-year private university and liberal arts college in small town, affiliated with Church of Christ.
Enrollment: 1,428 undergrads, 4% part-time. 385 full-time freshmen.

BASIC COSTS (2007-2008)
Tuition and fees: $13,192.
Per-credit charge: $370.
Room and board: $6,560.
Additional info: Tuition/fee waivers available for minority students.

FINANCIAL AID PICTURE (2007-2008)
Students with need: Out of 329 full-time freshmen who applied for aid, 273 were judged to have need. Of these, 272 received aid, and 74 had their full need met. Average financial aid package met 76% of need; average scholarship/grant was $10,290; average loan was $3,438. For part-time students, average financial aid package was $11,530.
Students without need: 76 full-time freshmen who did not demonstrate need for aid received scholarships/grants; average award was $12,481. No-need awards available for academics, art, athletics, leadership, minority status, music/drama, state/district residency.
Scholarships offered: 15 full-time freshmen received athletic scholarships; average amount $7,949.
Cumulative student debt: 76% of graduating class had student loans; average debt was $34,216.

FINANCIAL AID PROCEDURES
Forms required: FAFSA.
Dates and Deadlines: Priority date 3/1; no closing date. Applicants notified on a rolling basis starting 3/1; must reply within 4 week(s) of notification.

CONTACT
Larry Cyr, Director of Financial Aid
158 East Main Street, Henderson, TN 38340
(731) 989-6662

Hiwassee College
Madisonville, Tennessee
www.hiwassee.edu   Federal Code: 003494

2-year private junior and liberal arts college in small town, affiliated with United Methodist Church.
Enrollment: 341 undergrads, 12% part-time. 179 full-time freshmen.
Selectivity: Admits 50 to 75% of applicants.

BASIC COSTS (2007-2008)
Tuition and fees: $11,130.
Per-credit charge: $445.
Room and board: $6,370.
Additional info: Tuition/fee waivers available for adults.

FINANCIAL AID PICTURE
Students with need: Need-based aid available for full-time and part-time students. Work study available nights, weekends, and for part-time students.

Students without need: No-need awards available for academics, alumni affiliation, athletics, job skills, leadership, music/drama, religious affiliation, state/district residency.

FINANCIAL AID PROCEDURES
Forms required: FAFSA, institutional form.
Dates and Deadlines: Priority date 5/1; no closing date. Applicants notified on a rolling basis starting 4/1; must reply within 2 week(s) of notification.
Transfers: No deadline. Applicants notified on a rolling basis starting 5/1; must reply within 2 week(s) of notification.

CONTACT
James Hemphill, Associate Vice President for Financial Aid
225 Hiwassee College Drive, Madisonville, TN 37354-6099
(423) 420-1221

International Academy of Design and Technology: Nashville
Nashville, Tennessee
www.iadtnashville.com

4-year for-profit branch campus and visual arts college in very large city.
Enrollment: 501 undergrads.
Selectivity: Open admission.

BASIC COSTS (2007-2008)
Tuition and fees: $15,875.

FINANCIAL AID PICTURE (2006-2007)
Students with need: 33% of average financial aid package awarded as scholarships/grants, 67% awarded as loans/jobs.

FINANCIAL AID PROCEDURES
Dates and Deadlines: No deadline.

CONTACT
Lisa Kennicott, Director of Financial Aid
1 Bridgestone Park, Nashville, TN 37214

Jackson State Community College
Jackson, Tennessee
www.jscc.edu   Federal Code: 004937

2-year public community college in small city.
Enrollment: 4,387 undergrads, 45% part-time. 759 full-time freshmen.
Selectivity: Open admission; but selective for some programs.

BASIC COSTS (2007-2008)
Tuition and fees: $2,617; out-of-state residents $9,693.
Per-credit charge: $101; out-of-state residents $407.
Additional info: Tuition/fee waivers available for adults, minority students.

FINANCIAL AID PICTURE (2006-2007)
Students with need: Out of 578 full-time freshmen who applied for aid, 465 were judged to have need. Of these, 452 received aid, and 31 had their full need met. Average financial aid package met 84% of need; average scholarship/grant was $3,294; average loan was $3,150. For part-time students, average financial aid package was $2,011.
Students without need: 73 full-time freshmen who did not demonstrate need for aid received scholarships/grants; average award was $1,747. No-need awards available for academics, art, athletics, job skills, leadership, minority status, music/drama.
Scholarships offered: 18 full-time freshmen received athletic scholarships; average amount $2,370.
Cumulative student debt: 2% of graduating class had student loans; average debt was $3,400.

FINANCIAL AID PROCEDURES

Forms required: FAFSA, institutional form.

Dates and Deadlines: Priority date 3/15; no closing date. Applicants notified on a rolling basis starting 6/1; must reply within 2 week(s) of notification.

CONTACT

Dewana Latimer, Director of Financial Aid

2046 North Parkway, Jackson, TN 38301-3797

(731) 425-2605

John A. Gupton College
Nashville, Tennessee
www.guptoncollege.com   Federal Code: 008859

2-year private school of mortuary science in large city.

Enrollment: 111 undergrads, 6% part-time. 44 full-time freshmen.

BASIC COSTS (2007-2008)

Tuition and fees: $6,960.

Per-credit charge: $232.

Room only: $3,600.

FINANCIAL AID PICTURE

Students with need: Need-based aid available for full-time and part-time students.

Students without need: This college awards aid only to students with need.

FINANCIAL AID PROCEDURES

Forms required: FAFSA.

Dates and Deadlines: No deadline. Applicants notified on a rolling basis.

CONTACT

B. Steven Spann, President/CFO

1616 Church Street, Nashville, TN 37203-2920

(615) 327-3927

Johnson Bible College
Knoxville, Tennessee
www.jbc.edu   Federal Code: 003495

4-year private Bible college in small city, affiliated with Christian Church.

Enrollment: 768 undergrads.

Selectivity: Admits over 75% of applicants.

BASIC COSTS (2007-2008)

Tuition and fees: $7,180.

Room and board: $4,890.

Additional info: Part-time students pay mandatory fee of $30.42 per credit hour. Tuition/fee waivers available for minority students.

FINANCIAL AID PICTURE

Students with need: Need-based aid available for full-time and part-time students. Work study available nights, weekends, and for part-time students.

Students without need: No-need awards available for academics, leadership, minority status, music/drama, religious affiliation, state/district residency.

FINANCIAL AID PROCEDURES

Forms required: FAFSA, institutional form.

Dates and Deadlines: Priority date 5/1; closing date 8/1. Applicants notified on a rolling basis starting 4/30; must reply within 2 week(s) of notification.

Transfers: No deadline.

CONTACT

Janette Overton, Financial Aid Director

7900 Johnson Drive, Knoxville, TN 37998-0001

(865) 251-2303

King College
Bristol, Tennessee
www.king.edu   Federal Code: 003496

4-year private nursing and liberal arts college in large town, affiliated with Presbyterian Church (USA).

Enrollment: 1,192 undergrads, 2% part-time. 183 full-time freshmen.

Selectivity: Admits less than 50% of applicants.

BASIC COSTS (2008-2009)

Tuition and fees: $20,582.

Per-credit charge: $600.

Room and board: $6,900.

FINANCIAL AID PICTURE (2007-2008)

Students with need: Out of 163 full-time freshmen who applied for aid, 151 were judged to have need. Of these, 151 received aid, and 46 had their full need met. Average financial aid package met 80% of need; average scholarship/grant was $14,147; average loan was $4,010. For part-time students, average financial aid package was $7,122.

Students without need: 19 full-time freshmen who did not demonstrate need for aid received scholarships/grants; average award was $12,206. No-need awards available for academics, athletics, music/drama.

Scholarships offered: 34 full-time freshmen received athletic scholarships; average amount $5,961.

Cumulative student debt: 77% of graduating class had student loans; average debt was $10,591.

FINANCIAL AID PROCEDURES

Forms required: FAFSA.

Dates and Deadlines: Priority date 3/1; no closing date. Applicants notified on a rolling basis starting 4/1; must reply within 2 week(s) of notification.

CONTACT

Brenda Clark, Financial Aid Director

1350 King College Road, Bristol, TN 37620-2699

(423) 652-4725

Lambuth University
Jackson, Tennessee
www.lambuth.edu   Federal Code: 003498

4-year private university and liberal arts college in small city, affiliated with United Methodist Church.

Enrollment: 721 undergrads, 2% part-time. 172 full-time freshmen.

Selectivity: Admits less than 50% of applicants.

BASIC COSTS (2008-2009)

Tuition and fees: $17,400.

Per-credit charge: $710.

Room and board: $7,570.

Additional info: Tuition/fee waivers available for adults.

FINANCIAL AID PICTURE (2007-2008)

Students with need: Out of 159 full-time freshmen who applied for aid, 137 were judged to have need. Of these, 135 received aid, and 65 had their full need met. Average financial aid package met 92% of need; average scholarship/grant was $14,484; average loan was $5,160. For part-time students, average financial aid package was $8,849.

Students without need: 24 full-time freshmen who did not demonstrate need for aid received scholarships/grants; average award was $9,223. No-

need awards available for academics, alumni affiliation, art, athletics, job skills, leadership, music/drama, religious affiliation, state/district residency.
Scholarships offered: *Merit:* Hyde Scholarships; full tuition, require admission acceptance deadline of February 1, ACT of 30 or higher, GPA, of 3.5 or higher, 2 awarded. Tennessee Hope Lottery Scholarships matched by Lambuth; up to $3,800. *Athletic:* 19 full-time freshmen received athletic scholarships; average amount $9,006.
Cumulative student debt: 64% of graduating class had student loans; average debt was $19,947.
Additional info: Part-time students eligible for federal and state aid, but not institutional aid.

FINANCIAL AID PROCEDURES

Forms required: FAFSA.
Dates and Deadlines: Priority date 2/15; no closing date. Applicants notified on a rolling basis starting 3/1; must reply by 5/1 or within 2 week(s) of notification.
Transfers: Applicants notified by 3/1; must reply by 5/1 or within 2 week(s) of notification.

CONTACT

Melissa Boyd, Director of Financial Aid
705 Lambuth Boulevard, Jackson, TN 38301-5296
(731) 425-3332

Lane College

Jackson, Tennessee
www.lanecollege.edu   Federal Code: 003499

4-year private liberal arts college in small city, affiliated with Christian Methodist Episcopal Church.
Enrollment: 1,766 undergrads, 1% part-time. 584 full-time freshmen.
Selectivity: Admits less than 50% of applicants.

BASIC COSTS (2007-2008)

Tuition and fees: $7,620.
Room and board: $5,000.

FINANCIAL AID PICTURE (2006-2007)

Students with need: Need-based aid available for part-time students.
Students without need: This college awards aid only to students with need.
Cumulative student debt: 84% of graduating class had student loans; average debt was $7,254.

FINANCIAL AID PROCEDURES

Forms required: FAFSA, institutional form.
Dates and Deadlines: Priority date 3/1; no closing date. Applicants notified on a rolling basis starting 3/31; must reply within 2 week(s) of notification.
Transfers: No deadline. Applicants notified on a rolling basis; must reply within 2 week(s) of notification.

CONTACT

Tony Calhoun, Director of Financial Aid
545 Lane Avenue, Jackson, TN 38301-4598
(731) 426-7537

Lee University

Cleveland, Tennessee
www.leeuniversity.edu   Federal Code: 003500

4-year private university and liberal arts college in large town, affiliated with Church of God.
Enrollment: 3,586 undergrads, 8% part-time. 785 full-time freshmen.
Selectivity: Open admission; but selective for some programs.

BASIC COSTS (2008-2009)

Tuition and fees: $11,094.
Per-credit charge: $451.
Room and board: $5,470.

FINANCIAL AID PICTURE (2007-2008)

Students with need: Average financial aid package met 66% of need; average scholarship/grant was $7,625; average loan was $3,478. For part-time students, average financial aid package was $7,116.
Students without need: No-need awards available for academics, alumni affiliation, athletics, leadership, minority status, music/drama, religious affiliation, state/district residency.
Cumulative student debt: 63% of graduating class had student loans; average debt was $25,991.

FINANCIAL AID PROCEDURES

Forms required: FAFSA.
Dates and Deadlines: Priority date 3/15; no closing date. Applicants notified on a rolling basis starting 2/1; must reply within 3 week(s) of notification.

CONTACT

Michael Ellis, Director of Student Financial Aid
1120 North Ocoee Street, Cleveland, TN 37320-3450
(423) 614-8304

LeMoyne-Owen College

Memphis, Tennessee
www.loc.edu   Federal Code: 003501

4-year private liberal arts college in very large city, affiliated with United Church of Christ and Tennessee Baptist Convention.
Enrollment: 569 undergrads, 15% part-time. 84 full-time freshmen.
Selectivity: Admits 50 to 75% of applicants.

BASIC COSTS (2007-2008)

Tuition and fees: $10,098.
Room and board: $4,852.

FINANCIAL AID PICTURE (2006-2007)

Students with need: Out of 83 full-time freshmen who applied for aid, 78 were judged to have need. Of these, 76 received aid, and 3 had their full need met. Average financial aid package met 47% of need; average scholarship/grant was $6,274; average loan was $2,226. For part-time students, average financial aid package was $8,613.
Students without need: 6 full-time freshmen who did not demonstrate need for aid received scholarships/grants; average award was $11,750. No-need awards available for academics, athletics, music/drama.
Cumulative student debt: 100% of graduating class had student loans; average debt was $22402.29.

FINANCIAL AID PROCEDURES

Forms required: FAFSA.
Dates and Deadlines: Priority date 4/15; no closing date. Applicants notified on a rolling basis starting 4/1.
Transfers: No deadline. Applicants notified on a rolling basis starting 4/1.

CONTACT

Phyllis Wilson-Torry, Director of Student Financial Services
807 Walker Avenue, Memphis, TN 38126
(901) 435-1555

Lincoln Memorial University
Harrogate, Tennessee
www.lmunet.edu   Federal Code: 003502

4-year private university and liberal arts college in small town.
Enrollment: 1,481 undergrads.
Selectivity: Admits 50 to 75% of applicants.

BASIC COSTS (2007-2008)
Tuition and fees: $14,400.
Per-credit charge: $600.
Room and board: $5,380.

FINANCIAL AID PICTURE
Students with need: Need-based aid available for full-time and part-time students.
Students without need: No-need awards available for academics, athletics, music/drama, state/district residency.

FINANCIAL AID PROCEDURES
Forms required: FAFSA.
Dates and Deadlines: Priority date 4/1; no closing date. Applicants notified on a rolling basis starting 4/15; must reply within 3 week(s) of notification.

CONTACT
Celena Rader-Lambdin, Director of Financial Aid
6965 Cumberland Gap Parkway, Harrogate, TN 37752-1901
(423) 869-6336

Lipscomb University
Nashville, Tennessee
www.lipscomb.edu   Federal Code: 003486

4-year private Bible and liberal arts college in very large city, affiliated with Church of Christ.
Enrollment: 2,319 undergrads, 8% part-time. 576 full-time freshmen.
Selectivity: Admits 50 to 75% of applicants.

BASIC COSTS (2008-2009)
Tuition and fees: $18,580.
Room and board: $7,400.

FINANCIAL AID PICTURE (2007-2008)
Students with need: Out of 564 full-time freshmen who applied for aid, 347 were judged to have need. Of these, 347 received aid, and 246 had their full need met. Average financial aid package met 69% of need; average scholarship/grant was $5,999; average loan was $4,138. For part-time students, average financial aid package was $10,310.
Students without need: 144 full-time freshmen who did not demonstrate need for aid received scholarships/grants; average award was $5,753. No-need awards available for academics, alumni affiliation, art, athletics, leadership, minority status, music/drama, religious affiliation, state/district residency.
Scholarships offered: 25 full-time freshmen received athletic scholarships; average amount $14,267.
Cumulative student debt: 65% of graduating class had student loans; average debt was $15,939.

FINANCIAL AID PROCEDURES
Forms required: FAFSA.
Dates and Deadlines: Priority date 3/1; no closing date. Applicants notified on a rolling basis starting 2/15.

CONTACT
Karita Waters, Director of Financial Aid
One University Park Drive, Nashville, TN 37204-3951
(615) 966-1791

Martin Methodist College
Pulaski, Tennessee
www.martinmethodist.edu   Federal Code: 003504

4-year private liberal arts college in small town, affiliated with United Methodist Church.
Enrollment: 286 undergrads. 224 full-time freshmen.
Selectivity: Open admission; but selective for some programs.

BASIC COSTS (2007-2008)
Tuition and fees: $16,554.
Per-credit charge: $675.
Room and board: $5,800.

FINANCIAL AID PICTURE
Students with need: Need-based aid available for full-time and part-time students. Work study available nights, weekends, and for part-time students.
Students without need: No-need awards available for academics, art, athletics, leadership, music/drama, religious affiliation, state/district residency.
Scholarships offered: Two full academic scholarships per year awarded through interview and essay competition.

FINANCIAL AID PROCEDURES
Forms required: FAFSA, institutional form.
Dates and Deadlines: No deadline. Applicants notified on a rolling basis starting 3/1; must reply within 2 week(s) of notification.
Transfers: Closing date 9/13.

CONTACT
Robby Shelton, Director of Financial Aid
433 West Madison, Pulaski, TN 38478-2799
(931) 363-9804

Maryville College
Maryville, Tennessee
www.maryvillecollege.edu   Federal Code: 003505

4-year private liberal arts college in small city, affiliated with Presbyterian Church (USA).
Enrollment: 1,176 undergrads, 1% part-time. 317 full-time freshmen.
Selectivity: Admits over 75% of applicants.

BASIC COSTS (2008-2009)
Tuition and fees: $26,947.
Per-credit charge: $1,095.
Room and board: $8,240.

FINANCIAL AID PICTURE (2007-2008)
Students with need: Out of 262 full-time freshmen who applied for aid, 262 were judged to have need. Of these, 262 received aid, and 107 had their full need met. Average financial aid package met 95% of need; average scholarship/grant was $14,783; average loan was $4,345. For part-time students, average financial aid package was $3,885.
Students without need: 55 full-time freshmen who did not demonstrate need for aid received scholarships/grants; average award was $12,661. No-need awards available for academics, art, leadership, minority status, music/drama, religious affiliation, state/district residency.
Scholarships offered: Presidential Scholarship; full tuition; awarded for leadership and academic ability. Dean's Scholarship; consisting of a large portion of tuition awarded to selected entering freshman with 3.5 GPA.
Cumulative student debt: 92% of graduating class had student loans; average debt was $15,140.

FINANCIAL AID PROCEDURES
Forms required: FAFSA.
Dates and Deadlines: Priority date 3/1; no closing date. Applicants notified on a rolling basis starting 3/15; must reply within 4 week(s) of notification.

CONTACT
Richard Brand, Director of Financial Aid

502 East Lamar Alexander Parkway, Maryville, TN 37804-5907

(865) 981-8100

Memphis College of Art
Memphis, Tennessee

www.mca.edu   Federal Code: 003507

4-year private visual arts college in very large city.

Enrollment: 284 undergrads, 10% part-time. 72 full-time freshmen.

Selectivity: Admits less than 50% of applicants.

BASIC COSTS (2007-2008)
Tuition and fees: $20,660.

Per-credit charge: $875.

Room and board: $7,860.

FINANCIAL AID PICTURE (2007-2008)
Students with need: Out of 66 full-time freshmen who applied for aid, 52 were judged to have need. Of these, 52 received aid, and 12 had their full need met. Average financial aid package met 75% of need; average scholarship/grant was $3,567; average loan was $3,500. For part-time students, average financial aid package was $6,709.

Students without need: 20 full-time freshmen who did not demonstrate need for aid received scholarships/grants; average award was $7,600. No-need awards available for academics, art.

Scholarships offered: Tuition scholarships ranging from $2,500 up to full tuition based on merit.

Cumulative student debt: 90% of graduating class had student loans; average debt was $25,183.

Additional info: Students considered for institutional resources through admissions application process.

FINANCIAL AID PROCEDURES
Forms required: FAFSA.

Dates and Deadlines: Priority date 3/1; no closing date. Applicants notified on a rolling basis starting 3/15; must reply within 3 week(s) of notification.

Transfers: Priority date 8/1. Applicants notified on a rolling basis; must reply within 3 week(s) of notification. Grants of $1,000 awarded to students who attended accredited junior or community college earning at least 60 credit hours.

CONTACT
Kara Ziegemeier, Director of Financial Aid

1930 Poplar Avenue, Memphis, TN 38104-2764

(901) 272-5136

Middle Tennessee State University
Murfreesboro, Tennessee

www.mtsu.edu   Federal Code: 003510

4-year public university in small city.

Enrollment: 19,883 undergrads, 11% part-time. 3,509 full-time freshmen.

Selectivity: Admits less than 50% of applicants.

BASIC COSTS (2007-2008)
Tuition and fees: $5,278; out-of-state residents $15,554.

Per-credit charge: $178; out-of-state residents $624.

Room and board: $6,204.

FINANCIAL AID PICTURE
Students with need: Need-based aid available for full-time and part-time students. Work study available nights, weekends, and for part-time students.

Students without need: No-need awards available for academics, alumni affiliation, art, athletics, job skills, leadership, minority status, music/drama, religious affiliation, ROTC, state/district residency.

Additional info: Application filing deadline for scholarships February 15.

FINANCIAL AID PROCEDURES
Forms required: FAFSA.

Dates and Deadlines: Priority date 5/1; no closing date. Applicants notified on a rolling basis starting 4/15; must reply within 2 week(s) of notification.

CONTACT
David Hutton, Director of Student Financial Aid

1301 East Main Street, Murfreesboro, TN 37132

(615) 898-2830

Miller-Motte Technical College: Clarksville
Clarksville, Tennessee

www.miller-motte.com   Federal Code: 026142

2-year for-profit business and health science college in small city.

Enrollment: 550 undergrads.

Selectivity: Open admission; but selective for some programs.

BASIC COSTS (2007-2008)
Tuition and fees: $9,900.

Per-credit charge: $220.

Additional info: Required fees vary by program. Tuition at time of enrollment locked for 2 years.

FINANCIAL AID PICTURE
Students with need: Need-based aid available for full-time and part-time students. Work study available nights, weekends, and for part-time students.

Students without need: This college awards aid only to students with need.

FINANCIAL AID PROCEDURES
Forms required: FAFSA, institutional form.

Dates and Deadlines: No deadline. Applicants notified on a rolling basis.

Transfers: No deadline.

CONTACT
Donna Green, Financial Aid Director

1820 Business Park Drive, Clarksville, TN 37040

(931) 553-0071

Milligan College
Milligan College, Tennessee

www.milligan.edu   Federal Code: 003511

4-year private liberal arts college in small city, affiliated with Christian Churches/Churches of Christ.

Enrollment: 761 undergrads, 3% part-time. 197 full-time freshmen.

Selectivity: Admits over 75% of applicants.

BASIC COSTS (2007-2008)
Tuition and fees: $19,510.

Per-credit charge: $520.

Room and board: $5,390.

FINANCIAL AID PICTURE
Students with need: Need-based aid available for full-time and part-time students. Work study available nights, weekends, and for part-time students.

Students without need: No-need awards available for academics, alumni affiliation, art, athletics, job skills, minority status, music/drama, religious affiliation, state/district residency.

FINANCIAL AID PROCEDURES

Forms required: FAFSA.

Dates and Deadlines: Priority date 3/1; no closing date. Applicants notified on a rolling basis starting 3/15; must reply within 2 week(s) of notification.

CONTACT

Diane Keasling, Coordinator of Financial Aid
Box 210, Milligan College, TN 37682
(423) 461-8967

Motlow State Community College

Lynchburg, Tennessee
www.mscc.cc.tn.us   Federal Code: 006836

2-year public community college in rural community.

Enrollment: 3,436 undergrads, 36% part-time. 913 full-time freshmen.

Selectivity: Open admission; but selective for some programs.

BASIC COSTS (2007-2008)

Tuition and fees: $2,623; out-of-state residents $9,699.

Per-credit charge: $101; out-of-state residents $407.

FINANCIAL AID PICTURE (2006-2007)

Students with need: 73% of average financial aid package awarded as scholarships/grants, 27% awarded as loans/jobs. Need-based aid available for part-time students.

Students without need: No-need awards available for academics, alumni affiliation, art, athletics, leadership, state/district residency.

FINANCIAL AID PROCEDURES

Forms required: FAFSA.

Dates and Deadlines: No deadline. Applicants notified on a rolling basis starting 3/15.

CONTACT

Joe Myers, Director of Financial Aid and Scholarships
Box 8500, Lynchburg, TN 37352-8500
(931) 393-1553

Nashville Auto-Diesel College

Nashville, Tennessee
www.nadcedu.com   Federal Code: 007440

1-year for-profit technical college in large city.

Enrollment: 2,700 undergrads.

BASIC COSTS (2007-2008)

Tuition and fees: $14,195.

Room and board: $5,502.

Additional info: Full program costs range from $21,400 to $32,600 for diploma programs; $27,400 to $34,900 for associate programs.

FINANCIAL AID PICTURE

Students with need: Need-based aid available for full-time students. Work study available nights, weekends, and for part-time students.

Students without need: This college awards aid only to students with need.

FINANCIAL AID PROCEDURES

Forms required: FAFSA, state aid form.

Dates and Deadlines: No deadline. Applicants notified on a rolling basis.

CONTACT

Jamie Cortinas, Director of Financial Aid
1524 Gallatin Road, Nashville, TN 37206
(615) 650-8202

Nashville State Community College

Nashville, Tennessee
www.nscc.edu   Federal Code: 007534

2-year public community and technical college in large city.

Enrollment: 7,077 undergrads.

Selectivity: Open admission; but selective for some programs.

BASIC COSTS (2007-2008)

Tuition and fees: $2,589; out-of-state residents $9,665.

Per-credit charge: $101; out-of-state residents $407.

FINANCIAL AID PICTURE (2007-2008)

Students with need: 63% of average financial aid package awarded as scholarships/grants, 37% awarded as loans/jobs. Need-based aid available for part-time students. Work study available nights, weekends, and for part-time students.

Students without need: No-need awards available for academics, minority status.

FINANCIAL AID PROCEDURES

Forms required: FAFSA, institutional form.

Dates and Deadlines: Priority date 3/1; no closing date. Applicants notified on a rolling basis starting 6/1; must reply within 2 week(s) of notification.

CONTACT

Stephen White, Director of Financial Aid
120 White Bridge Road, Nashville, TN 37209-4515
(615) 353-3250

National College: Bristol

Bristol, Tennessee
www.ncbt.edu   Federal Code: 003726

2-year for-profit business college in large town.

Enrollment: 277 undergrads.

Selectivity: Open admission.

BASIC COSTS (2007-2008)

Tuition and fees: $9,135.

Per-credit charge: $202.

FINANCIAL AID PICTURE

Students with need: Need-based aid available for full-time and part-time students.

Students without need: This college awards aid only to students with need.

FINANCIAL AID PROCEDURES

Forms required: FAFSA.

Dates and Deadlines: No deadline. Applicants notified on a rolling basis starting 9/1.

CONTACT

Pamela Cotton, Director of Financial Aid and Compliance Officer
1328 Highway 11W, Bristol, TN 37620

National College: Nashville

Nashville, Tennessee
www.ncbt.edu   Federal Code: 003726

2-year for-profit business and technical college in large city.

Enrollment: 327 undergrads.

Selectivity: Open admission.

BASIC COSTS (2007-2008)

Tuition and fees: $9,090.

Per-credit charge: $202.

FINANCIAL AID PICTURE

Students with need: Need-based aid available for full-time and part-time students.

Students without need: This college awards aid only to students with need.

FINANCIAL AID PROCEDURES

Forms required: FAFSA.

Dates and Deadlines: No deadline.

CONTACT

Pamela Cotton, Director of Financial Aid and Compliance Officer

PO Box 6400, Roanoke, VA 24017

(615) 333-3344

Northeast State Technical Community College

Blountville, Tennessee

www.NortheastState.edu   Federal Code: 005378

2-year public community and technical college in small city.

Enrollment: 5,237 undergrads.

Selectivity: Open admission; but selective for some programs.

BASIC COSTS (2007-2008)

Tuition and fees: $2,625; out-of-state residents $9,701.

Per-credit charge: $101; out-of-state residents $407.

FINANCIAL AID PICTURE

Students with need: Need-based aid available for full-time and part-time students. Work study available nights.

Students without need: No-need awards available for academics, alumni affiliation, art, job skills, leadership, minority status, music/drama, religious affiliation.

FINANCIAL AID PROCEDURES

Forms required: FAFSA.

Dates and Deadlines: Priority date 3/31; no closing date. Applicants notified on a rolling basis starting 3/1; must reply within 3 week(s) of notification.

CONTACT

Cruzita Lucero, Director of Financial Aid

Box 246, Blountville, TN 37617-0246

(423) 323-0252

Nossi College of Art

Goodlettsville, Tennessee

www.nossi.com   Federal Code: 017347

2-year private visual arts and technical college in large town.

Enrollment: 400 undergrads.

Selectivity: Admits 50 to 75% of applicants.

BASIC COSTS (2007-2008)

Additional info: Tuition for first year (3 semesters) $10,500; required fees $240.

FINANCIAL AID PICTURE

Students with need: Need-based aid available for full-time and part-time students.

CONTACT

Mary Kidd, Financial Aid Director

907 Rivergate Parkway, Building E-6, Goodlettsville, TN 37072

(615) 851-1088

O'More College of Design

Franklin, Tennessee

www.omorecollege.edu   Federal Code: 014663

4-year private visual arts college in large town.

Enrollment: 195 undergrads.

Selectivity: Admits less than 50% of applicants.

BASIC COSTS (2007-2008)

Tuition and fees: $15,514.

FINANCIAL AID PICTURE

Students with need: Need-based aid available for full-time and part-time students.

Students without need: This college awards aid only to students with need.

Scholarships offered: Academic scholarships available.

FINANCIAL AID PROCEDURES

Forms required: FAFSA.

Dates and Deadlines: Priority date 4/1; closing date 7/30. Applicants notified on a rolling basis starting 8/1.

Transfers: Priority date 5/5; no deadline.

CONTACT

Jane Pennington, Financial Aid Director

423 South Margin Street, Franklin, TN 37064-0908

(615) 794-4254 ext. 238

Pellissippi State Technical Community College

Knoxville, Tennessee

www.pstcc.edu   Federal Code: 012693

2-year public community and technical college in small city.

Enrollment: 8,608 undergrads.

Selectivity: Open admission.

BASIC COSTS (2007-2008)

Tuition and fees: $2,657; out-of-state residents $9,733.

Per-credit charge: $101; out-of-state residents $407.

FINANCIAL AID PICTURE

Students with need: Need-based aid available for full-time and part-time students. Work study available nights, weekends, and for part-time students.

Students without need: No-need awards available for academics, art, minority status, music/drama.

FINANCIAL AID PROCEDURES

Forms required: FAFSA.

Dates and Deadlines: Priority date 5/1; no closing date. Applicants notified on a rolling basis starting 7/15; must reply within 2 week(s) of notification.

CONTACT

Paul McKinney, Director of Financial Aid

Box 22990, Knoxville, TN 37933-0990

(423) 694-6565

PART III: FINANCIAL AID COLLEGE BY COLLEGE

Remington College: Memphis
Memphis, Tennessee
www.remingtoncollege.edu

2-year for-profit business and technical college in very large city.
Enrollment: 400 undergrads.

BASIC COSTS (2007-2008)
Additional info: Costs of entire programs leading to certificate, associate degree, bachelor's degree range from $13,000 to $36,960; includes books and supplies.

FINANCIAL AID PICTURE
Students with need: Need-based aid available for full-time and part-time students.
Students without need: This college awards aid only to students with need.

FINANCIAL AID PROCEDURES
Forms required: FAFSA, institutional form.
Dates and Deadlines: No deadline. Applicants notified on a rolling basis; must reply within 2 week(s) of notification.

CONTACT
Jimmy Bessinger, Director of Financial Services
2710 Nonconnah Boulevard, Memphis, TN 38132

Rhodes College
Memphis, Tennessee   Federal Code: 003519
www.rhodes.edu   CSS Code: 1730

4-year private liberal arts college in very large city, affiliated with Presbyterian Church (USA).
Enrollment: 1,670 undergrads, 1% part-time. 454 full-time freshmen.
Selectivity: Admits 50 to 75% of applicants.

BASIC COSTS (2007-2008)
Tuition and fees: $30,652.
Per-credit charge: $1,275.
Room and board: $7,468.

FINANCIAL AID PICTURE (2007-2008)
Students with need: Out of 289 full-time freshmen who applied for aid, 197 were judged to have need. Of these, 197 received aid, and 93 had their full need met. Average financial aid package met 88% of need; average scholarship/grant was $20,159; average loan was $4,151. For part-time students, average financial aid package was $9,600.
Students without need: 180 full-time freshmen who did not demonstrate need for aid received scholarships/grants; average award was $11,891. No-need awards available for academics, art, minority status, music/drama, religious affiliation.
Cumulative student debt: 45% of graduating class had student loans; average debt was $21,035.
Additional info: Auditions required for theater and music achievement awards and art achievement awards. Interviews recommended for merit scholarships.

FINANCIAL AID PROCEDURES
Forms required: FAFSA, CSS PROFILE.
Dates and Deadlines: Closing date 3/1. Must reply by 5/1.

CONTACT
Forrest Stuart, Director of Financial Aid
2000 North Parkway, Memphis, TN 38112
(901) 843-3810

Roane State Community College
Harriman, Tennessee
www.roanestate.edu   Federal Code: 009914

2-year public community and junior college in small town.
Enrollment: 4,427 undergrads, 34% part-time. 949 full-time freshmen.
Selectivity: Open admission; but selective for some programs.

BASIC COSTS (2007-2008)
Tuition and fees: $2,645; out-of-state residents $9,721.
Per-credit charge: $101; out-of-state residents $407.

FINANCIAL AID PICTURE
Students with need: Need-based aid available for full-time and part-time students. Work study available nights, weekends, and for part-time students.
Students without need: No-need awards available for academics, art, athletics, leadership, music/drama, state/district residency.

FINANCIAL AID PROCEDURES
Forms required: FAFSA, institutional form.
Dates and Deadlines: Priority date 4/1; no closing date. Applicants notified on a rolling basis starting 5/1.

CONTACT
Joy Goldberg, Assistant Vice President of Financial Aid
276 Patton Lane, Harriman, TN 37748
(865) 882-4545

South College
Knoxville, Tennessee
www.southcollegetn.edu   Federal Code: 004938

4-year for-profit liberal arts college in small city.
Enrollment: 715 undergrads.

BASIC COSTS (2007-2008)
Tuition and fees: $14,100.
Additional info: Reported annual costs are for programs in physical therapy assistance, radiography, health science. Costs of other programs vary by program.

FINANCIAL AID PICTURE
Students with need: Need-based aid available for full-time and part-time students.
Students without need: This college awards aid only to students with need.

FINANCIAL AID PROCEDURES
Forms required: FAFSA, institutional form.
Dates and Deadlines: No deadline. Applicants notified on a rolling basis.

CONTACT
Larry Broadwater, Financial Aid Director
3904 Lonas Drive, Knoxville, TN 37909
(865) 251-1800

Southern Adventist University
Collegedale, Tennessee
www.southern.edu   Federal Code: 003518

4-year private university and liberal arts college in small town, affiliated with Seventh-day Adventists.
Enrollment: 2,353 undergrads, 10% part-time. 522 full-time freshmen.
Selectivity: Admits 50 to 75% of applicants.

BASIC COSTS (2008-2009)

Tuition and fees: $16,560.

Per-credit charge: $669.

Room and board: $4,750.

FINANCIAL AID PICTURE

Students with need: Need-based aid available for full-time and part-time students.

Students without need: No-need awards available for academics, alumni affiliation, art, leadership, music/drama.

Scholarships offered: Freshman scholarship based on combination of high school GPA, ACT/SAT scores, leadership positions held.

FINANCIAL AID PROCEDURES

Forms required: FAFSA, state aid form.

Dates and Deadlines: Priority date 3/1; no closing date. Applicants notified on a rolling basis starting 2/15; must reply within 2 week(s) of notification.

CONTACT

Marc Grundy, Director of Student Finance

Box 370, Collegedale, TN 37315-0370

(423) 236-2844

Southwest Tennessee Community College

Memphis, Tennessee

www.southwest.tn.edu   Federal Code: 010439

2-year public community and technical college in very large city.

Enrollment: 9,486 undergrads.

Selectivity: Open admission; but selective for some programs.

BASIC COSTS (2007-2008)

Tuition and fees: $2,649; out-of-state residents $9,725.

Per-credit charge: $101; out-of-state residents $407.

Additional info: Tuition/fee waivers available for minority students.

FINANCIAL AID PICTURE

Students with need: Need-based aid available for full-time and part-time students. Work study available nights, weekends, and for part-time students.

Students without need: This college awards aid only to students with need.

Scholarships offered: President's Academic Scholarship for excellence; $1,200 annually; for students in top 20% of graduating class with an 18 or better ACT, must work 150 hours, recipients usually recruited from Shelby and Fayette counties; 15 awarded.

Additional info: State grants available to eligible students who apply by 4/1.

FINANCIAL AID PROCEDURES

Forms required: FAFSA.

Dates and Deadlines: Priority date 3/15; no closing date. Applicants notified on a rolling basis starting 6/1; must reply within 4 week(s) of notification.

Transfers: Priority date 4/15.

CONTACT

Tina Studaway, Executive Director Enrollment Services

PO Box 780, Memphis, TN 38101-0780

(901) 333-5960

Tennessee State University

Nashville, Tennessee

www.tnstate.edu   Federal Code: 003522

4-year public university in very large city.

Enrollment: 6,966 undergrads, 18% part-time. 1,209 full-time freshmen.

Selectivity: Admits 50 to 75% of applicants.

BASIC COSTS (2007-2008)

Tuition and fees: $4,856; out-of-state residents $15,132.

Per-credit charge: $178; out-of-state residents $624.

Room and board: $4,872.

Additional info: Tuition/fee waivers available for minority students.

FINANCIAL AID PICTURE (2006-2007)

Students with need: Out of 705 full-time freshmen who applied for aid, 625 were judged to have need. Of these, 615 received aid, and 293 had their full need met. Average financial aid package met 86% of need; average scholarship/grant was $856; average loan was $383. For part-time students, average financial aid package was $3,523.

Students without need: 65 full-time freshmen who did not demonstrate need for aid received scholarships/grants; average award was $7,340. No-need awards available for academics.

Scholarships offered: 15 full-time freshmen received athletic scholarships; average amount $9,305.

Cumulative student debt: 77% of graduating class had student loans; average debt was $21,910.

FINANCIAL AID PROCEDURES

Forms required: FAFSA.

Dates and Deadlines: Priority date 4/1; no closing date. Applicants notified on a rolling basis starting 4/15; must reply within 3 week(s) of notification.

CONTACT

Mary Chambliss, Director of Financial Aid

3500 John A. Merritt Boulevard, Nashville, TN 37209-1561

(615) 963-5701

Tennessee Technological University

Cookeville, Tennessee

www.tntech.edu   Federal Code: 003523

4-year public university in large town.

Enrollment: 7,875 undergrads, 9% part-time. 1,649 full-time freshmen.

Selectivity: Admits over 75% of applicants.

BASIC COSTS (2007-2008)

Tuition and fees: $4,980; out-of-state residents $15,256.

Per-credit charge: $178; out-of-state residents $624.

Room and board: $6,530.

Additional info: Tuition/fee waivers available for minority students.

FINANCIAL AID PICTURE (2006-2007)

Students with need: Out of 805 full-time freshmen who applied for aid, 523 were judged to have need. Of these, 519 received aid, and 149 had their full need met. Average financial aid package met 87% of need; average scholarship/grant was $3,922; average loan was $927. For part-time students, average financial aid package was $3,709.

Students without need: 245 full-time freshmen who did not demonstrate need for aid received scholarships/grants; average award was $5,271. No-need awards available for academics, alumni affiliation, art, athletics, leadership, minority status, music/drama, ROTC, state/district residency.

Scholarships offered: *Merit:* Presidential Scholarship; $4,000 renewable annually. Awarded to National Merit Finalists. *Athletic:* 23 full-time freshmen received athletic scholarships; average amount $13,681.

Cumulative student debt: 61% of graduating class had student loans; average debt was $3,599.

Additional info: Tuition and/or fee waivers available for children of Tennessee public school teachers.

FINANCIAL AID PROCEDURES

Forms required: FAFSA.

Dates and Deadlines: Priority date 3/15; no closing date. Applicants notified on a rolling basis starting 3/15; must reply within 2 week(s) of notification.

Transfers: No deadline. Applicants notified on a rolling basis starting 6/1; must reply within 2 week(s) of notification.

CONTACT
Lester McKenzie, Director of Student Financial Aid
Office of Admissions, Cookeville, TN 38505-0001
(931) 372-3073

Tennessee Temple University
Chattanooga, Tennessee
www.tntemple.edu   Federal Code: 003524

4-year private university and Bible college in small city, affiliated with Baptist faith.
Enrollment: 503 undergrads.
Selectivity: Admits less than 50% of applicants.

BASIC COSTS (2007-2008)
Tuition and fees: $9,520.
Room and board: $5,930.

FINANCIAL AID PICTURE
Students with need: Need-based aid available for full-time and part-time students. Work study available nights, weekends, and for part-time students.
Students without need: No-need awards available for academics, alumni affiliation, athletics, leadership, music/drama, state/district residency.

FINANCIAL AID PROCEDURES
Forms required: FAFSA.
Dates and Deadlines: Priority date 3/31; no closing date. Applicants notified on a rolling basis starting 2/15; must reply within 2 week(s) of notification.

CONTACT
Ricky Taphorn, Director of Financial Aid
1815 Union Avenue, Chattanooga, TN 37404
(423) 493-4207

Tennessee Wesleyan College
Athens, Tennessee
www.twcnet.edu   Federal Code: 003525

4-year private liberal arts and teachers college in large town, affiliated with United Methodist Church.
Enrollment: 846 undergrads, 13% part-time. 153 full-time freshmen.
Selectivity: Admits over 75% of applicants.

BASIC COSTS (2008-2009)
Tuition and fees: $17,050.
Per-credit charge: $435.
Room and board: $5,830.
Additional info: Tuition/fee waivers available for minority students.

FINANCIAL AID PICTURE
Students with need: Need-based aid available for full-time and part-time students. Work study available nights, weekends, and for part-time students.
Students without need: No-need awards available for academics, alumni affiliation, athletics, job skills, minority status, music/drama, religious affiliation.

FINANCIAL AID PROCEDURES
Forms required: FAFSA, institutional form.
Dates and Deadlines: No deadline. Applicants notified on a rolling basis starting 2/15; must reply within 2 week(s) of notification.

CONTACT
Bob Perry, Director of Financial Aid
204 East College Street, Athens, TN 37371-0040
(423) 746-5215

Trevecca Nazarene University
Nashville, Tennessee
www.trevecca.edu   Federal Code: 003526

4-year private university and liberal arts college in very large city, affiliated with Church of the Nazarene.
Enrollment: 1,200 undergrads, 11% part-time. 238 full-time freshmen.
Selectivity: Admits 50 to 75% of applicants.

BASIC COSTS (2008-2009)
Tuition and fees: $16,288.
Room and board: $7,134.

FINANCIAL AID PICTURE (2006-2007)
Students with need: 41% of average financial aid package awarded as scholarships/grants, 59% awarded as loans/jobs.
Students without need: No-need awards available for academics, alumni affiliation, athletics, leadership, minority status, music/drama, religious affiliation.

FINANCIAL AID PROCEDURES
Forms required: FAFSA.
Dates and Deadlines: Priority date 3/1; no closing date. Applicants notified on a rolling basis starting 3/1; must reply by 9/1 or within 2 week(s) of notification.

CONTACT
Eddie White, Assistant Director of Financial Aid
333 Murfreesboro Road, Nashville, TN 37210
(615) 248-1242

Tusculum College
Greeneville, Tennessee
www.tusculum.edu   Federal Code: 003527

4-year private liberal arts college in large town, affiliated with Presbyterian Church (USA).
Enrollment: 2,446 undergrads, 3% part-time. 360 full-time freshmen.
Selectivity: Admits 50 to 75% of applicants.

BASIC COSTS (2007-2008)
Tuition and fees: $17,385.
Room and board: $6,910.

FINANCIAL AID PICTURE
Students with need: Need-based aid available for full-time and part-time students. Work study available nights, weekends, and for part-time students.
Students without need: No-need awards available for academics, athletics, leadership, religious affiliation, state/district residency.

FINANCIAL AID PROCEDURES
Forms required: FAFSA.
Dates and Deadlines: Closing date 2/15. Applicants notified on a rolling basis starting 3/1; must reply within 3 week(s) of notification.

CONTACT
Steve Gehret, Director of Financial Aid
60 Shiloh Road, Greeneville, TN 37743
(423) 636-7377

Union University

Jackson, Tennessee
www.uu.edu   Federal Code: 003528

4-year private university and liberal arts college in small city, affiliated with Southern Baptist Convention.

Enrollment: 2,100 undergrads, 13% part-time. 399 full-time freshmen.

Selectivity: Admits over 75% of applicants.

BASIC COSTS (2007-2008)

Tuition and fees: $18,620.

Per-credit charge: $620.

Room and board: $6,500.

Additional info: Tuition/fee waivers available for minority students.

FINANCIAL AID PICTURE (2006-2007)

Students with need: Out of 367 full-time freshmen who applied for aid, 288 were judged to have need. Of these, 288 received aid, and 77 had their full need met. Average financial aid package met 77% of need; average scholarship/grant was $4,810; average loan was $2,693. For part-time students, average financial aid package was $6,778.

Students without need: 106 full-time freshmen who did not demonstrate need for aid received scholarships/grants; average award was $6,088. No-need awards available for academics, alumni affiliation, art, athletics, leadership, minority status, music/drama, religious affiliation, state/district residency.

Scholarships offered: 47 full-time freshmen received athletic scholarships; average amount $6,548.

Cumulative student debt: 56% of graduating class had student loans; average debt was $21,196.

FINANCIAL AID PROCEDURES

Forms required: FAFSA, institutional form.

Dates and Deadlines: Priority date 2/15; closing date 3/1. Applicants notified on a rolling basis starting 2/15; must reply by 5/1 or within 2 week(s) of notification.

CONTACT

John Brandt, Director of Financial Aid
1050 Union University Drive, Jackson, TN 38305-3697
(731) 661-5015

University of Memphis

Memphis, Tennessee
www.memphis.edu   Federal Code: 003509

4-year public university in very large city.

Enrollment: 15,228 undergrads, 24% part-time. 1,978 full-time freshmen.

Selectivity: Admits 50 to 75% of applicants.

BASIC COSTS (2007-2008)

Tuition and fees: $5,802; out-of-state residents $16,630.

Per-credit charge: $196; out-of-state residents $649.

Room and board: $5,360.

Additional info: Tuition/fee waivers available for adults, minority students.

FINANCIAL AID PICTURE (2007-2008)

Students with need: Out of 1,805 full-time freshmen who applied for aid, 1,263 were judged to have need. Of these, 1,187 received aid, and 153 had their full need met. Average financial aid package met 81% of need; average scholarship/grant was $5,472; average loan was $1,605. For part-time students, average financial aid package was $4,927.

Students without need: 911 full-time freshmen who did not demonstrate need for aid received scholarships/grants; average award was $7,649. No-need awards available for academics, alumni affiliation, art, athletics, leadership, minority status, music/drama, ROTC, state/district residency.

Scholarships offered: 54 full-time freshmen received athletic scholarships; average amount $11,340.

Cumulative student debt: 22% of graduating class had student loans; average debt was $21,487.

FINANCIAL AID PROCEDURES

Forms required: FAFSA.

Dates and Deadlines: Priority date 3/1; closing date 6/30. Applicants notified on a rolling basis starting 3/1; must reply within 2 week(s) of notification.

CONTACT

Richard Ritzman, Director of Student Financial Aid
101 Wilder Tower, Memphis, TN 38152
(901) 678-4825

University of Tennessee Health Science Center

Memphis, Tennessee
www.utmem.edu   Federal Code: 353006

Upper-division public university and health science college in very large city.

Enrollment: 294 undergrads, 2% part-time.

BASIC COSTS (2007-2008)

Tuition and fees: $5,194; out-of-state residents $11,784.

Additional info: Above cost are for bachelor's program in nursing. Other programs vary by cost. Tuition/fee waivers available for minority students.

FINANCIAL AID PICTURE (2007-2008)

Students with need: Average financial aid package for all full-time undergraduates was $8,460; for part-time $9,768. 25% awarded as scholarships/grants, 75% awarded as loans/jobs. Work study available nights, weekends, and for part-time students.

Students without need: No-need awards available for academics, leadership, minority status, state/district residency.

Additional info: Scholarships available to defray out-of-state portion of fees charged to out-of-state minority students.

FINANCIAL AID PROCEDURES

Forms required: FAFSA.

Dates and Deadlines: Priority date 2/28; no closing date. Applicants notified on a rolling basis starting 5/1; must reply within 2 week(s) of notification.

Transfers: No deadline. Applicants notified on a rolling basis starting 5/1; must reply within 2 week(s) of notification.

CONTACT

Felicia Christian, Director of Financial Aid
800 Madison Avenue, Memphis, TN 38163
(901) 448-5568

University of Tennessee: Chattanooga

Chattanooga, Tennessee
www.utc.edu   Federal Code: 003529

4-year public university in large city.

Enrollment: 7,987 undergrads, 11% part-time. 1,927 full-time freshmen.

Selectivity: Admits over 75% of applicants.

BASIC COSTS (2007-2008)

Tuition and fees: $5,062; out-of-state residents $15,024.

Per-credit charge: $166; out-of-state residents $709.

Room and board: $6,750.

FINANCIAL AID PICTURE (2007-2008)

Students with need: Out of 1,802 full-time freshmen who applied for aid, 1,114 were judged to have need. Of these, 1,091 received aid, and 706 had their full need met. Average financial aid package met 85% of need; average scholarship/grant was $4,199; average loan was $3,941. For part-time students, average financial aid package was $4,016.

Students without need: 317 full-time freshmen who did not demonstrate need for aid received scholarships/grants; average award was $2,963. No-need awards available for academics, alumni affiliation, art, athletics, job skills, leadership, minority status, music/drama, religious affiliation, ROTC, state/district residency.

Scholarships offered: 65 full-time freshmen received athletic scholarships; average amount $9,346.

Cumulative student debt: 61% of graduating class had student loans; average debt was $18,512.

FINANCIAL AID PROCEDURES

Forms required: FAFSA, institutional form.

Dates and Deadlines: Priority date 4/1; no closing date. Applicants notified on a rolling basis starting 3/1; must reply within 6 week(s) of notification.

Transfers: Applicants notified on a rolling basis starting 3/1; must reply within 6 week(s) of notification.

CONTACT

Rexann Bumpus, Director of Financial Aid
615 McCallie Avenue, Chattanooga, TN 37403
(423) 425-4677

University of Tennessee: Knoxville
Knoxville, Tennessee
www.tennessee.edu   Federal Code: 003530

4-year public university in large city.

Enrollment: 21,001 undergrads, 6% part-time. 4,331 full-time freshmen.

Selectivity: Admits 50 to 75% of applicants.

BASIC COSTS (2007-2008)

Tuition and fees: $5,932; out-of-state residents $17,874.

Per-credit charge: $214; out-of-state residents $712.

Room and board: $6,358.

Additional info: Out-of-state students pay additional required fees of $300.

FINANCIAL AID PICTURE (2007-2008)

Students with need: Out of 4,061 full-time freshmen who applied for aid, 2,044 were judged to have need. Of these, 2,006 received aid, and 810 had their full need met. Average financial aid package met 79% of need; average scholarship/grant was $2,627; average loan was $3,511. For part-time students, average financial aid package was $7,796.

Students without need: This college awards aid only to students with need.

Scholarships offered: *Merit:* Academic College Scholarship Application part of financial aid forms, must be completed by all students. *Athletic:* 81 full-time freshmen received athletic scholarships; average amount $16,531.

Cumulative student debt: 49% of graduating class had student loans; average debt was $19,341.

Additional info: Application priority date for scholarships 2/1.

FINANCIAL AID PROCEDURES

Forms required: FAFSA.

Dates and Deadlines: Priority date 3/1; no closing date. Applicants notified on a rolling basis starting 3/15; must reply within 3 week(s) of notification.

Transfers: Transfer students must provide financial aid transcripts from all colleges previously attended regardless of whether any aid was received.

CONTACT

Jeff Gerkin, Director of Financial Aid
320 Student Services Building, Knoxville, TN 37996-0230
(865) 974-3131

University of Tennessee: Martin
Martin, Tennessee
www.utm.edu   Federal Code: 003531

4-year public university in small town.

Enrollment: 5,827 undergrads, 10% part-time. 1,283 full-time freshmen.

Selectivity: Admits over 75% of applicants.

BASIC COSTS (2007-2008)

Tuition and fees: $5,005; out-of-state residents $15,045.

Per-credit charge: $173; out-of-state residents $592.

Room and board: $4,446.

FINANCIAL AID PICTURE (2007-2008)

Students with need: Out of 1,237 full-time freshmen who applied for aid, 858 were judged to have need. Of these, 848 received aid, and 410 had their full need met. Average financial aid package met 82% of need; average scholarship/grant was $5,402; average loan was $3,026. For part-time students, average financial aid package was $8,223.

Students without need: This college awards aid only to students with need.

Scholarships offered: 30 full-time freshmen received athletic scholarships; average amount $10,397.

Cumulative student debt: 45% of graduating class had student loans; average debt was $22,528.

FINANCIAL AID PROCEDURES

Forms required: FAFSA.

Dates and Deadlines: Priority date 3/1; no closing date. Applicants notified on a rolling basis starting 4/1.

CONTACT

Sandy Neel, Director of Student Financial Assistance
200 Hall Moody Administration Building, Martin, TN 38238
(731) 881-7040

University of the South
Sewanee, Tennessee
www.sewanee.edu   Federal Code: 003534

4-year private university in rural community, affiliated with Episcopal Church.

Enrollment: 1,455 undergrads. 402 full-time freshmen.

Selectivity: Admits 50 to 75% of applicants. GED not accepted.

BASIC COSTS (2007-2008)

Tuition and fees: $30,660.

Per-credit charge: $1,105.

Room and board: $8,780.

FINANCIAL AID PICTURE (2007-2008)

Students with need: Out of 243 full-time freshmen who applied for aid, 167 were judged to have need. Of these, 166 received aid, and 129 had their full need met. Average financial aid package met 93% of need; average scholarship/grant was $22,333; average loan was $3,272.

Students without need: 67 full-time freshmen who did not demonstrate need for aid received scholarships/grants; average award was $14,776. No-need awards available for academics, minority status, religious affiliation.

Scholarships offered: Benedict Scholars Program for exceptional freshmen; 3 full cost scholarships. Wilkins Scholarships for outstanding incoming freshmen; half tuition, 25 awarded.

Cumulative student debt: 44% of graduating class had student loans; average debt was $17,958.

FINANCIAL AID PROCEDURES
Forms required: FAFSA, institutional form.
Dates and Deadlines: Priority date 3/1; no closing date. Applicants notified by 4/1; must reply within 4 week(s) of notification.

CONTACT
David Gelinas, Director of Financial Aid
Office of Admission, Sewanee, TN 37383-1000
(931) 598-1312

Vanderbilt University
Nashville, Tennessee   Federal Code: 003535
www.vanderbilt.edu   CSS Code: 1871

4-year private university in very large city.
Enrollment: 6,496 undergrads, 1% part-time. 1,673 full-time freshmen.
Selectivity: Admits less than 50% of applicants.

BASIC COSTS (2007-2008)
Tuition and fees: $35,278.
Room and board: $11,446.

FINANCIAL AID PICTURE (2007-2008)
Students with need: Out of 885 full-time freshmen who applied for aid, 763 were judged to have need. Of these, 761 received aid, and 740 had their full need met. Average financial aid package met 100% of need; average scholarship/grant was $28,838; average loan was $3,413.
Students without need: 223 full-time freshmen who did not demonstrate need for aid received scholarships/grants; average award was $12,879. No-need awards available for academics, minority status, music/drama, state/district residency.
Scholarships offered: 37 full-time freshmen received athletic scholarships; average amount $30,446.
Cumulative student debt: 39% of graduating class had student loans; average debt was $20,755.

FINANCIAL AID PROCEDURES
Forms required: FAFSA, CSS PROFILE.
Dates and Deadlines: Priority date 2/1; no closing date. Applicants notified on a rolling basis starting 4/1.
Transfers: Priority date 4/15.

CONTACT
David Mohning, Director, Student Financial Aid
2305 West End Avenue, Nashville, TN 37203-1727
(615) 322-3591

Volunteer State Community College
Gallatin, Tennessee
www.volstate.edu   Federal Code: 009912

2-year public community and junior college in small city.
Enrollment: 5,446 undergrads, 41% part-time. 1,050 full-time freshmen.
Selectivity: Open admission; but selective for some programs.

BASIC COSTS (2007-2008)
Tuition and fees: $2,625; out-of-state residents $9,701.
Per-credit charge: $101; out-of-state residents $407.
Additional info: Tuition/fee waivers available for minority students.

FINANCIAL AID PICTURE
Students with need: Need-based aid available for full-time and part-time students.

Students without need: No-need awards available for academics, art, athletics, leadership, minority status, music/drama, religious affiliation, state/district residency.

FINANCIAL AID PROCEDURES
Forms required: FAFSA, institutional form.
Dates and Deadlines: Priority date 4/15; no closing date. Applicants notified on a rolling basis; must reply within 2 week(s) of notification.
Transfers: No deadline. Applicants notified on a rolling basis; must reply within 2 week(s) of notification.

CONTACT
Sue Pedigo, Director of Financial Aid
1480 Nashville Pike, Gallatin, TN 37066
(615) 452-8600 ext. 3456

Walters State Community College
Morristown, Tennessee
www.ws.edu   Federal Code: 008863

2-year public culinary school and community college in small city.
Enrollment: 4,607 undergrads, 36% part-time. 1,062 full-time freshmen.
Selectivity: Open admission; but selective for some programs.

BASIC COSTS (2007-2008)
Tuition and fees: $2,637; out-of-state residents $10,043.
Per-credit charge: $101; out-of-state residents $407.
Additional info: Tuition/fee waivers available for minority students.

FINANCIAL AID PICTURE (2006-2007)
Students with need: Out of 818 full-time freshmen who applied for aid, 570 were judged to have need. Of these, 540 received aid, and 126 had their full need met. Average financial aid package met 75% of need; average scholarship/grant was $3,618; average loan was $1,916. For part-time students, average financial aid package was $2,786.
Students without need: 175 full-time freshmen who did not demonstrate need for aid received scholarships/grants; average award was $2,601. No-need awards available for academics, athletics, music/drama, state/district residency.
Scholarships offered: 16 full-time freshmen received athletic scholarships; average amount $1,075.

FINANCIAL AID PROCEDURES
Forms required: FAFSA.
Dates and Deadlines: No deadline. Applicants notified on a rolling basis.

CONTACT
Linda Mason, Director of Financial Aid
500 South Davy Crockett Parkway, Morristown, TN 37813-6899
(423) 585-6811

Texas

Abilene Christian University
Abilene, Texas
www.acu.edu   Federal Code: 003537

4-year private university in small city, affiliated with Church of Christ.
Enrollment: 3,954 undergrads, 7% part-time. 962 full-time freshmen.
Selectivity: Admits less than 50% of applicants.

BASIC COSTS (2008-2009)
Tuition and fees: $18,855.
Per-credit charge: $596.
Room and board: $7,236.

FINANCIAL AID PICTURE (2006-2007)

Students with need: Out of 914 full-time freshmen who applied for aid, 587 were judged to have need. Of these, 587 received aid, and 133 had their full need met. Average financial aid package met 68% of need; average scholarship/grant was $9,604; average loan was $2,648. For part-time students, average financial aid package was $5,559.

Students without need: 295 full-time freshmen who did not demonstrate need for aid received scholarships/grants; average award was $6,117. No-need awards available for academics, art, athletics, leadership, minority status, music/drama, religious affiliation, state/district residency.

Scholarships offered: *Merit:* Presidential Scholarship: half or full tuition; based on interview, ACT or SAT scores. Heritage Award: $1,000 per year; based on Church of Christ, ACT or SAT scores. Transfer Scholarship: $1,000-$2,000; based on GPA. *Athletic:* 46 full-time freshmen received athletic scholarships; average amount $8,687.

Cumulative student debt: 71% of graduating class had student loans; average debt was $31,401.

Additional info: Early estimate service available.

FINANCIAL AID PROCEDURES

Forms required: FAFSA, institutional form.

Dates and Deadlines: Priority date 3/1; no closing date. Applicants notified on a rolling basis starting 4/1.

CONTACT

Michael Lewis, Director of Student Financial Services
ACU Box 29000, Abilene, TX 79699
(325) 674-6850

Alvin Community College

Alvin, Texas
www.alvincollege.edu   Federal Code: 003539

2-year public community and liberal arts college in large town.

Enrollment: 2,604 undergrads.

Selectivity: Open admission; but selective for some programs.

BASIC COSTS (2007-2008)

Tuition and fees: $1,250; out-of-district residents $2,090; out-of-state residents $3,650.

Per-credit charge: $30; out-of-district residents $58; out-of-state residents $110.

FINANCIAL AID PICTURE

Students with need: Need-based aid available for full-time and part-time students. Work study available nights, weekends, and for part-time students.

Students without need: This college awards aid only to students with need.

FINANCIAL AID PROCEDURES

Forms required: FAFSA.

Dates and Deadlines: Priority date 6/30; no closing date. Applicants notified on a rolling basis; must reply within 2 week(s) of notification.

CONTACT

Dora Sims, Director of Student Financial Aid and Placement
3110 Mustang Road, Alvin, TX 77511-4898
(281) 756-3524

Angelina College

Lufkin, Texas
www.angelina.edu   Federal Code: 006661

2-year public community college in large town.

Enrollment: 4,680 undergrads, 65% part-time. 452 full-time freshmen.

Selectivity: Open admission; but selective for some programs.

BASIC COSTS (2008-2009)

Tuition and fees: $1,200; out-of-district residents $1,800; out-of-state residents $2,550.

Per-credit charge: $33; out-of-district residents $53; out-of-state residents $78.

Room and board: $5,550.

Additional info: Students taking 1-3 credits pay higher per-credit-hour charge.

FINANCIAL AID PICTURE (2006-2007)

Students with need: 99% of average financial aid package awarded as scholarships/grants, 1% awarded as loans/jobs. Need-based aid available for part-time students. Work study available nights.

Students without need: This college awards aid only to students with need.

FINANCIAL AID PROCEDURES

Forms required: FAFSA, institutional form.

Dates and Deadlines: Priority date 7/15; no closing date. Applicants notified on a rolling basis starting 7/15.

CONTACT

Susan Jones, Director of Financial Aid
PO Box 1768, Lufkin, TX 75902-1768
(936) 633-5291

Angelo State University

San Angelo, Texas
www.angelo.edu   Federal Code: 003541

4-year public university in small city.

Enrollment: 5,720 undergrads, 15% part-time. 1,434 full-time freshmen.

Selectivity: Admits over 75% of applicants.

BASIC COSTS (2007-2008)

Tuition and fees: $5,111; out-of-state residents $13,451.

Per-credit charge: $125; out-of-state residents $378.

Room and board: $5,621.

FINANCIAL AID PICTURE

Students with need: Need-based aid available for full-time and part-time students. Work study available nights, weekends, and for part-time students.

Students without need: No-need awards available for academics, athletics, leadership, music/drama, ROTC.

Scholarships offered: Carr Academic Scholarship program: average award $2,200 per semester; 1 of every 6 students receives award. Special Academic Scholarships available for undergraduates planning on majoring in chemistry/biochemistry, math, physics, French, or German.

FINANCIAL AID PROCEDURES

Forms required: FAFSA, institutional form.

Dates and Deadlines: Priority date 5/1; no closing date. Applicants notified on a rolling basis starting 4/1.

Transfers: No deadline. Applicants notified on a rolling basis.

CONTACT

Lyn Wheeler, Director of Financial Aid
ASU Station #11014, San Angelo, TX 76909-1014
(800) 946-8627

Arlington Baptist College
Arlington, Texas
www.abconline.edu   Federal Code: 014305

4-year private Bible and teachers college in very large city, affiliated with Baptist faith.
Enrollment: 142 undergrads, 25% part-time. 80 full-time freshmen.
Selectivity: Open admission.

BASIC COSTS (2008-2009)
Tuition and fees: $6,090.
Per-credit charge: $185.
Room and board: $4,100.

FINANCIAL AID PICTURE (2006-2007)
Students with need: Out of 62 full-time freshmen who applied for aid, 28 were judged to have need. Of these, 28 received aid, and 28 had their full need met. Average financial aid package met 65% of need; average scholarship/grant was $2,809; average loan was $5,970. For part-time students, average financial aid package was $6,073.
Students without need: This college awards aid only to students with need.
Cumulative student debt: 75% of graduating class had student loans; average debt was $15,700.

FINANCIAL AID PROCEDURES
Forms required: FAFSA.
Dates and Deadlines: Closing date 8/15. Applicants notified on a rolling basis.

CONTACT
David Clogston, Business Manager
3001 West Division, Arlington, TX 76012
(817) 431-8741 ext. 114

Art Institute of Dallas
Dallas, Texas
www.aid.edu   Federal Code: 017360

4-year for-profit visual arts college in very large city.
Enrollment: 1,739 undergrads.
Selectivity: Open admission; but selective for some programs.

BASIC COSTS (2007-2008)
Additional info: Total program costs vary by program: bachelor's programs $80,952-$83,795; associate's programs $47,650-$49,921.

FINANCIAL AID PICTURE
Students with need: Need-based aid available for full-time students.

FINANCIAL AID PROCEDURES
Forms required: FAFSA.
Dates and Deadlines: Applicants notified on a rolling basis.

CONTACT
Two North Park, 8080 Park Lane, Dallas, TX 75231
(214) 692-8080

Austin College
Sherman, Texas
www.austincollege.edu   Federal Code: 003543

4-year private liberal arts and teachers college in small city, affiliated with Presbyterian Church (USA).
Enrollment: 1,312 undergrads. 334 full-time freshmen.
Selectivity: Admits 50 to 75% of applicants.

BASIC COSTS (2008-2009)
Tuition and fees: $26,555.
Per-credit charge: $956.
Room and board: $8,657.

FINANCIAL AID PICTURE (2007-2008)
Students with need: Out of 252 full-time freshmen who applied for aid, 201 were judged to have need. Of these, 201 received aid, and 201 had their full need met. Average financial aid package met 99% of need; average scholarship/grant was $16,988; average loan was $6,044. Need-based aid available for part-time students.
Students without need: 122 full-time freshmen who did not demonstrate need for aid received scholarships/grants; average award was $8,965. No-need awards available for academics, alumni affiliation, art, leadership, music/drama, religious affiliation, state/district residency.

FINANCIAL AID PROCEDURES
Forms required: FAFSA, institutional form.
Dates and Deadlines: Priority date 4/1; no closing date. Applicants notified on a rolling basis starting 3/1; must reply by 5/1.
Transfers: Applicants notified on a rolling basis starting 3/1; must reply by 5/1.

CONTACT
Laurie Coulter, Executive Director of Financial Aid
900 North Grand Avenue, Suite 6N, Sherman, TX 75090-4400
(903) 813-2900

Austin Community College
Austin, Texas
www.austincc.edu   Federal Code: 012015

2-year public community college in very large city.
Enrollment: 33,508 undergrads, 72% part-time. 751 full-time freshmen.
Selectivity: Open admission; but selective for some programs.

BASIC COSTS (2007-2008)
Tuition and fees: $1,608; out-of-district residents $3,978; out-of-state residents $8,208.
Per-credit charge: $39; out-of-district residents $118; out-of-state residents $259.

FINANCIAL AID PICTURE (2006-2007)
Students with need: Out of 684 full-time freshmen who applied for aid, 679 were judged to have need. Of these, 679 received aid. Need-based aid available for part-time students.

FINANCIAL AID PROCEDURES
Forms required: FAFSA, institutional form.
Dates and Deadlines: Closing date 4/1. Applicants notified on a rolling basis starting 6/1; must reply within 2 week(s) of notification.

CONTACT
Terry Bazan, Director, Financial Assistance
5930 Middle Fiskville Road, Austin, TX 78752-4390
(512) 223-7550

Baylor University
Waco, Texas
www.baylor.edu   Federal Code: 003545

4-year private university in small city, affiliated with Baptist faith.
Enrollment: 11,851 undergrads, 2% part-time. 2,729 full-time freshmen.
Selectivity: Admits 50 to 75% of applicants.

BASIC COSTS (2008-2009)

Tuition and fees: $26,234.
Per-credit charge: $986.
Room and board: $7,608.

FINANCIAL AID PICTURE (2007-2008)

Students with need: Out of 1,879 full-time freshmen who applied for aid, 1,469 were judged to have need. Of these, 1,468 received aid, and 210 had their full need met. Average financial aid package met 71% of need; average scholarship/grant was $13,967; average loan was $2,213. For part-time students, average financial aid package was $10,704.

Students without need: 1,022 full-time freshmen who did not demonstrate need for aid received scholarships/grants; average award was $7,615. No-need awards available for academics, art, athletics, job skills, leadership, music/drama, ROTC.

Scholarships offered: *Merit:* Regent's Scholarship: full tuition; limited to National Merit finalists who list Baylor as first choice; unlimited number. President's Scholarship: $36,000 to $56,000 divided over 4 years. Provost's Baylor Scholarship: $28,000 to $36,000 divided over 4 years. Dean's Scholarship: $8,000 to $20,000 divided over 4 years. There are a limited number of all awarded based on admission date, high school rank and SAT/ACT scores. *Athletic:* 81 full-time freshmen received athletic scholarships; average amount $19,585.

Cumulative student debt: 55% of graduating class had student loans; average debt was $32,763.

FINANCIAL AID PROCEDURES

Forms required: FAFSA.
Dates and Deadlines: Priority date 3/1; no closing date. Applicants notified on a rolling basis starting 3/10; must reply by 5/1 or within 2 week(s) of notification.
Transfers: Closing date 3/1. Must reply by 5/1 or within 2 week(s) of notification.

CONTACT

Jackie Diaz, Assistant Vice President
One Bear Place #97056, Waco, TX 76798-7056
(800) 229-5678

Blinn College

Brenham, Texas
www.blinn.edu   Federal Code: 003549

2-year public junior college in large town.
Enrollment: 14,710 undergrads.
Selectivity: Open admission; but selective for some programs.

BASIC COSTS (2008-2009)

Tuition and fees: $1,890; out-of-district residents $2,760; out-of-state residents $5,040.
Per-credit charge: $35; out-of-district residents $64; out-of-state residents $140.
Room and board: $4,940.

FINANCIAL AID PICTURE (2007-2008)

Students with need: 47% of average financial aid package awarded as scholarships/grants, 53% awarded as loans/jobs. Need-based aid available for part-time students.

FINANCIAL AID PROCEDURES

Forms required: FAFSA, institutional form.
Dates and Deadlines: Priority date 6/1; no closing date. Applicants notified on a rolling basis starting 7/1.

CONTACT

Tracy Lutkenhaus, Director of Financial Aid
902 College Avenue, Brenham, TX 77833
(979) 830-4144

Bradford School of Business

Houston, Texas
www.bradfordschoolhouston.edu

2-year for-profit technical college in very large city.
Enrollment: 53 undergrads.

BASIC COSTS (2008-2009)

Tuition and fees: $12,760.
Additional info: Lab fees vary depending upon program selected.

FINANCIAL AID PICTURE

Students with need: Need-based aid available for full-time students.

CONTACT

4669 Southwest Freeway, Houston, TX 77027

Cedar Valley College

Lancaster, Texas
www.cedarvalleycollege.edu   Federal Code: 014035

2-year public community college in large town.
Enrollment: 4,200 undergrads.
Selectivity: Open admission.

BASIC COSTS (2007-2008)

Tuition and fees: $1,170; out-of-district residents $2,160; out-of-state residents $3,450.
Per-credit charge: $39; out-of-district residents $72; out-of-state residents $115.

FINANCIAL AID PICTURE

Students with need: Need-based aid available for full-time students.

FINANCIAL AID PROCEDURES

Forms required: FAFSA.
Dates and Deadlines: Priority date 5/1; no closing date. Applicants notified on a rolling basis.

CONTACT

Huan Luong, Vice President, Business Services
3030 North Dallas Avenue, Lancaster, TX 75134
(972) 860-8280

Central Texas College

Killeen, Texas
www.ctcd.edu   Federal Code: 004003

2-year public community and technical college in small city.
Enrollment: 17,996 undergrads, 85% part-time. 855 full-time freshmen.
Selectivity: Open admission; but selective for some programs.

BASIC COSTS (2007-2008)

Tuition and fees: $1,470; out-of-district residents $1,770; out-of-state residents $4,290.
Per-credit charge: $36; out-of-district residents $46; out-of-state residents $130.
Room and board: $3,300.

FINANCIAL AID PICTURE

Students with need: Need-based aid available for full-time and part-time students. Work study available nights, weekends, and for part-time students.
Students without need: This college awards aid only to students with need.

FINANCIAL AID PROCEDURES

Forms required: FAFSA, institutional form.

Dates and Deadlines: Closing date 7/1. Applicants notified on a rolling basis starting 3/1; must reply within 4 week(s) of notification.

CONTACT

Annabelle Smith, Director of Student Financial Aid
Box 1800, Killeen, TX 76540
(254) 526-1508

Clarendon College

Clarendon, Texas
www.clarendoncollege.edu   Federal Code: 003554

2-year public community college in rural community.
Enrollment: 1,029 undergrads, 52% part-time. 244 full-time freshmen.
Selectivity: Open admission; but selective for some programs.

BASIC COSTS (2007-2008)
Tuition and fees: $2,280; out-of-district residents $2,850; out-of-state residents $3,420.
Room and board: $3,350.

FINANCIAL AID PICTURE
Students with need: Need-based aid available for full-time and part-time students. Work study available nights, weekends, and for part-time students.
Students without need: No-need awards available for academics, art, athletics, leadership, music/drama, state/district residency.

FINANCIAL AID PROCEDURES
Forms required: FAFSA, institutional form.
Dates and Deadlines: Priority date 7/1; closing date 9/1. Applicants notified on a rolling basis starting 8/1; must reply by 8/15 or within 2 week(s) of notification.
Transfers: No deadline.

CONTACT

Brandi Havens, Director of Financial Aid
PO Box 968, Clarendon, TX 79226
(806) 874-3571 ext. 112

Coastal Bend College

Beeville, Texas
www.coastalbend.edu   Federal Code: 003546

2-year public community and junior college in large town.
Enrollment: 3,142 undergrads.
Selectivity: Open admission; but selective for some programs.

BASIC COSTS (2007-2008)
Tuition and fees: $1,730; out-of-district residents $3,500; out-of-state residents $3,950.
Room only: $1,560.
Additional info: Meal ticket (a la carte) food service available.

FINANCIAL AID PICTURE (2006-2007)
Students with need: 67% of average financial aid package awarded as scholarships/grants, 33% awarded as loans/jobs. Need-based aid available for part-time students.
Students without need: No-need awards available for academics, leadership.

FINANCIAL AID PROCEDURES
Forms required: FAFSA, institutional form.
Dates and Deadlines: Priority date 4/1; no closing date. Applicants notified on a rolling basis starting 5/1; must reply within 2 week(s) of notification.
Transfers: No deadline. Applicants notified on a rolling basis.

CONTACT

Nora Morales, Director of Financial Aid
3800 Charco Road, Beeville, TX 78102
(361) 354-2238

College of Saint Thomas More

Fort Worth, Texas
www.cstm.edu   Federal Code: 031894

4-year private liberal arts college in very large city, affiliated with Roman Catholic Church.
Enrollment: 47 undergrads.

BASIC COSTS (2008-2009)
Tuition and fees: $12,150.
Per-credit charge: $400.
Room only: $4,050.
Additional info: Student housing includes use of private kitchen.

FINANCIAL AID PICTURE
Students with need: Need-based aid available for full-time and part-time students. Work study available nights.

CONTACT

Corky Swanson, Financial Aid Department
3020 Lubbock Avenue, Fort Worth, TX 76109
(817) 673-1934

College of the Mainland

Texas City, Texas
www.com.edu   Federal Code: 007096

2-year public community and technical college in large town.
Enrollment: 1,059 full-time undergrads.
Selectivity: Open admission; but selective for some programs.

BASIC COSTS (2007-2008)
Tuition and fees: $1,282; out-of-district residents $2,302; out-of-state residents $3,262.

FINANCIAL AID PICTURE
Students with need: Need-based aid available for full-time and part-time students. Work study available nights, weekends, and for part-time students.
Students without need: This college awards aid only to students with need.

FINANCIAL AID PROCEDURES
Forms required: FAFSA, institutional form.
Dates and Deadlines: No deadline. Applicants notified on a rolling basis.
Transfers: Priority date 8/1.

CONTACT

Lisa Templer, Assistant Director of Financial Aid
1200 Amburn Road, Texas City, TX 77591
(409) 938-1211 ext. 274

Collin County Community College District

Plano, Texas
www.ccccd.edu   Federal Code: 016792

2-year public community college in large city.
Enrollment: 19,754 undergrads, 59% part-time. 2,188 full-time freshmen.
Selectivity: Open admission; but selective for some programs.

FINANCIAL AID PICTURE (2006-2007)

Students with need: Out of 846 full-time freshmen who applied for aid, 641 were judged to have need. Of these, 537 received aid, and 120 had their full need met. Average financial aid package met 29% of need; average scholarship/grant was $3,283; average loan was $1,983. For part-time students, average financial aid package was $2,768.

Students without need: 25 full-time freshmen who did not demonstrate need for aid received scholarships/grants; average award was $1,149. No-need awards available for academics, art, athletics, music/drama.

Scholarships offered: 22 full-time freshmen received athletic scholarships; average amount $3,715.

Cumulative student debt: 30% of graduating class had student loans; average debt was $7,530.

FINANCIAL AID PROCEDURES

Forms required: FAFSA, institutional form.

Dates and Deadlines: Priority date 6/1; closing date 6/30. Applicants notified on a rolling basis starting 5/1; must reply within 2 week(s) of notification.

Transfers: Applicants must have cumulative GPA of 2.0 and less than 90 transferable credit hours.

CONTACT

Debra Wilkison, Director of Financial Aid
2800 East Spring Creek Parkway, Plano, TX 75074
(972) 881-5760

Commonwealth Institute of Funeral Service
Houston, Texas
www.commonwealthinst.org   Federal Code: 003556

2-year private school of mortuary science in very large city.

Enrollment: 115 undergrads.

Selectivity: Admits over 75% of applicants.

BASIC COSTS (2008-2009)

Tuition and fees: $6,290.

Per-credit charge: $143.

FINANCIAL AID PICTURE

Students with need: Need-based aid available for full-time and part-time students.

Students without need: This college awards aid only to students with need.

Scholarships offered: Scholarship awards: $250-$500 based on funds available; recipients selected on academic achievement, leadership and professional promise, as well as any stipulations by the donor, by a committee of Commonwealth Institute graduate employers, alumni, and benefactors.

FINANCIAL AID PROCEDURES

Forms required: FAFSA.

Dates and Deadlines: Priority date 7/20; no closing date. Applicants notified on a rolling basis starting 7/12.

CONTACT

Dennis Christie, Director of Financial Aid
415 Barren Springs Drive, Houston, TX 77090-5913
(281) 873-0262

Concordia University at Austin
Austin, Texas
www.concordia.edu   Federal Code: 003557

4-year private university and liberal arts college in very large city, affiliated with Lutheran Church - Missouri Synod.

Enrollment: 1,090 undergrads, 25% part-time. 160 full-time freshmen.

Selectivity: Admits 50 to 75% of applicants.

BASIC COSTS (2007-2008)

Tuition and fees: $18,910.

Per-credit charge: $620.

Room and board: $7,300.

Additional info: Tuition/fee waivers available for adults.

FINANCIAL AID PICTURE

Students with need: Need-based aid available for full-time and part-time students.

Students without need: No-need awards available for academics, leadership, music/drama, religious affiliation.

FINANCIAL AID PROCEDURES

Forms required: FAFSA, institutional form.

Dates and Deadlines: No deadline. Applicants notified on a rolling basis starting 2/15; must reply within 2 week(s) of notification.

Transfers: Financial aid transcripts from all previously attended trade/technical schools and colleges/universities required.

CONTACT

Cathy Schryer, Director of Financial Assistance
3400 Interstate 35 North, Austin, TX 78705-2799
(512) 486-2000

Dallas Baptist University
Dallas, Texas
www.dbu.edu   Federal Code: 003560

4-year private university in very large city, affiliated with Baptist faith.

Enrollment: 3,581 undergrads, 39% part-time. 328 full-time freshmen.

Selectivity: Admits 50 to 75% of applicants.

BASIC COSTS (2008-2009)

Tuition and fees: $16,440.

Per-credit charge: $548.

Room and board: $5,382.

FINANCIAL AID PICTURE (2007-2008)

Students with need: Out of 294 full-time freshmen who applied for aid, 198 were judged to have need. Of these, 196 received aid, and 108 had their full need met. Average financial aid package met 80% of need; average scholarship/grant was $2,957; average loan was $3,090. For part-time students, average financial aid package was $4,564.

Students without need: 98 full-time freshmen who did not demonstrate need for aid received scholarships/grants; average award was $10,658. No-need awards available for academics, athletics, job skills, leadership, music/drama, religious affiliation.

Scholarships offered: 27 full-time freshmen received athletic scholarships; average amount $9,622.

Cumulative student debt: 42% of graduating class had student loans; average debt was $18,570.

FINANCIAL AID PROCEDURES

Forms required: FAFSA, institutional form.

Dates and Deadlines: Priority date 3/15; closing date 5/1. Applicants notified on a rolling basis.

Transfers: Priority date 3/17; no deadline. Applicants notified on a rolling basis.

CONTACT

Donald Zackary, Director of Financial Aid
3000 Mountain Creek Parkway, Dallas, TX 75211-9299
(214) 333-5363

Dallas Christian College

Dallas, Texas
www.dallas.edu   Federal Code: 006941

4-year private Bible college in very large city, affiliated with nondenominational tradition.
Enrollment: 327 undergrads, 31% part-time. 43 full-time freshmen.
Selectivity: Admits less than 50% of applicants.

BASIC COSTS (2007-2008)
Tuition and fees: $9,720.
Per-credit charge: $299.
Room and board: $6,000.

FINANCIAL AID PICTURE
Students with need: Need-based aid available for full-time and part-time students.

FINANCIAL AID PROCEDURES
Forms required: FAFSA, institutional form.
Dates and Deadlines: Closing date 4/15. Applicants notified on a rolling basis; must reply within 2 week(s) of notification.

CONTACT
Mark Stanley, Chief Finance Officer
2700 Christian Parkway, Dallas, TX 75234-7299
(972) 241-3371 ext. 158

Del Mar College

Corpus Christi, Texas
www.delmar.edu   Federal Code: 003563

2-year public community college in large city.
Enrollment: 11,168 undergrads, 72% part-time. 588 full-time freshmen.
Selectivity: Open admission; but selective for some programs.

BASIC COSTS (2007-2008)
Tuition and fees: $1,914; out-of-district residents $4,914; out-of-state residents $6,024.
Per-credit charge: $35; out-of-district residents $135; out-of-state residents $172.

FINANCIAL AID PICTURE (2006-2007)
Students with need: 75% of average financial aid package awarded as scholarships/grants, 25% awarded as loans/jobs. Need-based aid available for part-time students. Work study available nights, weekends, and for part-time students.
Students without need: This college awards aid only to students with need.

FINANCIAL AID PROCEDURES
Forms required: FAFSA.
Dates and Deadlines: Priority date 5/1; no closing date. Applicants notified on a rolling basis starting 7/1; must reply within 2 week(s) of notification.

CONTACT
Enrique Garcia, Assistant Dean of Financial Aid and Retention Services
101 Baldwin Boulevard, Corpus Christi, TX 78404-3897
(361) 698-1293

DeVry University: Houston

Houston, Texas
www.devry.edu

4-year for-profit university in very large city.
Enrollment: 926 undergrads, 36% part-time. 100 full-time freshmen.

BASIC COSTS (2007-2008)
Tuition and fees: $13,220.
Per-credit charge: $490.

FINANCIAL AID PICTURE (2006-2007)
Students with need: Out of 78 full-time freshmen who applied for aid, 75 were judged to have need. Of these, 73 received aid. Average financial aid package met 37% of need; average scholarship/grant was $5,086; average loan was $4,607. For part-time students, average financial aid package was $7,927.
Students without need: 3 full-time freshmen who did not demonstrate need for aid received scholarships/grants; average award was $17,119. No-need awards available for academics.
Cumulative student debt: 100% of graduating class had student loans; average debt was $31,449.

FINANCIAL AID PROCEDURES
Forms required: FAFSA.
Dates and Deadlines: No deadline. Applicants notified on a rolling basis.

CONTACT
11125 Equity Drive, Houston, TX 77041-8217
(713) 973-3000

DeVry University: Irving

Dallas, Texas
www.devry.edu   Federal Code: 010139

4-year for-profit university in small city.
Enrollment: 1,453 undergrads, 52% part-time. 162 full-time freshmen.

BASIC COSTS (2007-2008)
Tuition and fees: $13,220.
Per-credit charge: $490.

FINANCIAL AID PICTURE (2006-2007)
Students with need: Out of 118 full-time freshmen who applied for aid, 112 were judged to have need. Of these, 112 received aid, and 1 had their full need met. Average financial aid package met 33% of need; average scholarship/grant was $4,718; average loan was $4,199. For part-time students, average financial aid package was $7,414.
Students without need: This college awards aid only to students with need.
Cumulative student debt: 82% of graduating class had student loans; average debt was $42,273.

FINANCIAL AID PROCEDURES
Forms required: FAFSA.
Dates and Deadlines: No deadline. Applicants notified on a rolling basis.

CONTACT
Nga Phan, Director, Financial Aid
4800 Regent Boulevard, Dallas, TX 75063-2439
(972) 929-9740

East Texas Baptist University

Marshall, Texas
www.etbu.edu   Federal Code: 003564

4-year private university and liberal arts college in large town, affiliated with Baptist faith.
Enrollment: 1,215 undergrads, 5% part-time. 312 full-time freshmen.
Selectivity: Admits 50 to 75% of applicants.

BASIC COSTS (2008-2009)
Tuition and fees: $16,140.
Per-credit charge: $560.

Room and board: $4,913.

Additional info: Tuition at time of enrollment locked for 4 years.

FINANCIAL AID PICTURE (2007-2008)

Students with need: Out of 294 full-time freshmen who applied for aid, 250 were judged to have need. Of these, 250 received aid, and 44 had their full need met. Average financial aid package met 63% of need; average scholarship/grant was $7,926; average loan was $3,518. For part-time students, average financial aid package was $5,674.

Students without need: 53 full-time freshmen who did not demonstrate need for aid received scholarships/grants; average award was $6,065. No-need awards available for academics, alumni affiliation, leadership, music/drama, religious affiliation.

Cumulative student debt: 83% of graduating class had student loans; average debt was $16,415.

FINANCIAL AID PROCEDURES

Forms required: FAFSA, institutional form.

Dates and Deadlines: Priority date 6/1; no closing date. Applicants notified on a rolling basis starting 1/15; must reply within 3 week(s) of notification.

Transfers: Applicants notified on a rolling basis starting 1/15; must reply within 3 week(s) of notification. Transfers may be ineligible for scholarships based on ACT/SAT tests.

CONTACT

Tommy Young, Director of Financial Aid

1209 North Grove, Marshall, TX 75670-1498

(903) 923-2138

Eastfield College

Mesquite, Texas

www.efc.dcccd.edu   Federal Code: 008510

2-year public community and liberal arts college in small city.

Enrollment: 5,427 undergrads, 77% part-time. 218 full-time freshmen.

Selectivity: Open admission.

BASIC COSTS (2007-2008)

Tuition and fees: $1,170; out-of-district residents $2,160; out-of-state residents $3,450.

Per-credit charge: $39; out-of-district residents $72; out-of-state residents $115.

FINANCIAL AID PICTURE

Students with need: Need-based aid available for full-time and part-time students. Work study available nights, weekends, and for part-time students.

Scholarships offered: Lecroy Scholars Program: $600 per semester; based on demonstrated church, community, or academic leadership and 3.0 GPA; requires enrollment in at least 12 credit hours; 5-10 awarded. Erin Tierney Kramp Encouragement Program: $600 per semester; based on demonstrated courage in the face of adversity, moral character, leadership, and high academic standards; requires enrollment in 8 hours for awarding semester, and maintenance of high academic standards; 2 awarded.

FINANCIAL AID PROCEDURES

Forms required: FAFSA, institutional form.

Dates and Deadlines: Priority date 5/1; no closing date. Applicants notified on a rolling basis starting 4/15.

CONTACT

Dana Mingo, Dean of Financial Aid

3737 Motley Drive, Mesquite, TX 75150

(972) 860-8385

El Centro College

Dallas, Texas

www.elcentrocollege.edu   Federal Code: 004453

2-year public community college in very large city.

Enrollment: 5,527 undergrads, 77% part-time. 252 full-time freshmen.

Selectivity: Open admission; but selective for some programs.

BASIC COSTS (2007-2008)

Tuition and fees: $1,170; out-of-district residents $2,160; out-of-state residents $3,450.

Per-credit charge: $39; out-of-district residents $72; out-of-state residents $115.

Additional info: Tuition/fee waivers available for minority students, unemployed or children of unemployed.

FINANCIAL AID PICTURE

Students with need: Need-based aid available for full-time and part-time students.

Additional info: Interview required for financial aid applicants.

FINANCIAL AID PROCEDURES

Forms required: FAFSA.

Dates and Deadlines: Priority date 5/1; no closing date. Applicants notified on a rolling basis; must reply within 2 week(s) of notification.

Transfers: Financial aid transcript may be required from previous institutions attended.

CONTACT

John Wells, Director of Financial Aid

801 Main Street, Dallas, TX 75202

(214) 860-2099

El Paso Community College

El Paso, Texas

www.epcc.edu   Federal Code: 010387

2-year public community college in very large city.

Enrollment: 23,509 undergrads. 2,579 full-time freshmen.

Selectivity: Open admission; but selective for some programs.

BASIC COSTS (2007-2008)

Tuition and fees: $1,700; out-of-state residents $2,442.

Per-credit charge: $47; out-of-state residents $71.

Additional info: Per-credit-hour costs listed are for each additional credit-hour beyond one credit-hour for in-state students, and beyond six credit-hours for out-of-state students.

FINANCIAL AID PICTURE

Students with need: Work study available nights, weekends, and for part-time students.

Students without need: No-need awards available for academics, athletics.

FINANCIAL AID PROCEDURES

Forms required: FAFSA, institutional form.

Dates and Deadlines: Priority date 5/1; no closing date. Applicants notified on a rolling basis starting 7/1; must reply within 2 week(s) of notification.

CONTACT

Linda Gonzalez-Hensgen, Director of Student Financial Services

Box 20500, El Paso, TX 79998

(915) 831-2566

Frank Phillips College
Borger, Texas
www.fpctx.edu   Federal Code: 003568

2-year public community and junior college in large town.
Enrollment: 721 undergrads, 46% part-time. 175 full-time freshmen.
Selectivity: Open admission.

BASIC COSTS (2007-2008)
Tuition and fees: $2,296; out-of-district residents $2,926; out-of-state residents $3,136.
Per-credit charge: $64; out-of-district residents $106; out-of-state residents $120.
Room and board: $3,820.

FINANCIAL AID PICTURE
Students with need: Need-based aid available for full-time and part-time students. Work study available nights, weekends, and for part-time students.
Students without need: No-need awards available for academics, athletics, music/drama, state/district residency.
Scholarships offered: Various scholarships available including BEDC, Presidential, Dean's, Access, Opportunity, and Re-entering Adult Learner.
Additional info: Some Texas fire department and police department personnel, active duty military personnel, children of military missing in action may qualify for reduced or waived tuition. Out-of-state tuition waived for students living in Oklahoma counties adjacent to Texas.

FINANCIAL AID PROCEDURES
Forms required: FAFSA, institutional form.
Dates and Deadlines: Applicants notified on a rolling basis; must reply within 2 week(s) of notification.

CONTACT
Beverly Fields, Director of Financial Services
Box 5118, Borger, TX 79008-5118
(806) 457-4200 ext. 718

Galveston College
Galveston, Texas
www.gc.edu   Federal Code: 004972

2-year public community college in small city.
Enrollment: 2,044 undergrads, 70% part-time. 170 full-time freshmen.
Selectivity: Open admission; but selective for some programs.

BASIC COSTS (2008-2009)
Tuition and fees: $1,414; out-of-state residents $2,314.
Per-credit charge: $30; out-of-state residents $60.

FINANCIAL AID PICTURE (2006-2007)
Students with need: 77% of average financial aid package awarded as scholarships/grants, 23% awarded as loans/jobs. Need-based aid available for part-time students.
Students without need: This college awards aid only to students with need.

FINANCIAL AID PROCEDURES
Forms required: FAFSA.
Dates and Deadlines: Priority date 6/9; no closing date. Applicants notified on a rolling basis starting 6/1.

CONTACT
Ron Crumedy, Financial Aid Manager
4015 Avenue Q, Galveston, TX 77550-7447
(409) 944-1235

Grayson County College
Denison, Texas
www.grayson.edu   Federal Code: 003570

2-year public community and technical college in large town.
Enrollment: 3,786 undergrads.
Selectivity: Open admission; but selective for some programs.

BASIC COSTS (2008-2009)
Tuition and fees: $1,344.
Per-credit charge: $43.
Room and board: $3,556.

FINANCIAL AID PICTURE
Students with need: Need-based aid available for full-time and part-time students.
Additional info: Short term loans available.

FINANCIAL AID PROCEDURES
Forms required: FAFSA.
Dates and Deadlines: Priority date 6/1; no closing date. Applicants notified on a rolling basis; must reply within 5 week(s) of notification.

CONTACT
Director of Financial Aid
6101 Grayson Drive, Denison, TX 75020
(903) 463-8642

Hallmark College of Aeronautics
San Antonio, Texas
www.hallmarkcollege.edu   Federal Code: 010509

2-year for-profit technical college in very large city.
Enrollment: 196 undergrads.

BASIC COSTS (2007-2008)
Additional info: Tuition for combined associate program in airframe technology or powerplant technology: $21,915. Tuition for diploma programs ranges from $12,181 to $17,384. Costs include books, equipment and supplies. Required fees: $200. Registration fee: $100. Course fees vary. International students pay additional 8%. Tuition at time of enrollment locked for 2 years.

FINANCIAL AID PICTURE
Students with need: Need-based aid available for full-time students.

FINANCIAL AID PROCEDURES
Forms required: FAFSA.
Dates and Deadlines: No deadline. Applicants notified on a rolling basis.

CONTACT
Grace Calixto, Director of Financial Planning
8901 Wetmore Road, San Antonio, TX 78230
(210) 690-9000

Hallmark College of Technology
San Antonio, Texas
www.hallmarkcollege.com   Federal Code: 010509

2-year for-profit business and technical college in very large city.
Enrollment: 484 undergrads.

BASIC COSTS (2008-2009)
Additional info: Costs for associate programs range from $17,500 to $26,985; additional registration fee $110 for all programs. Tuition at time of enrollment locked for 2 years.

FINANCIAL AID PICTURE

Students with need: Need-based aid available for full-time students.

FINANCIAL AID PROCEDURES

Forms required: FAFSA.

Dates and Deadlines: No deadline. Applicants notified on a rolling basis.

CONTACT

Grace Calixto, Director of Financial Planning
10401 IH 10 West, San Antonio, TX 78230-1737
(210) 690-9000

Hardin-Simmons University
Abilene, Texas
www.hsutx.edu   Federal Code: 003571

4-year private university in small city, affiliated with Baptist faith.

Enrollment: 1,991 undergrads, 12% part-time. 465 full-time freshmen.

Selectivity: Admits less than 50% of applicants.

BASIC COSTS (2008-2009)

Tuition and fees: $18,380.

Per-credit charge: $580.

Room and board: $5,180.

Additional info: Tuition at time of enrollment locked for 4 years.

FINANCIAL AID PICTURE (2007-2008)

Students with need: Out of 459 full-time freshmen who applied for aid, 334 were judged to have need. Of these, 334 received aid, and 128 had their full need met. Average financial aid package met 87% of need; average scholarship/grant was $7,429; average loan was $2,930. For part-time students, average financial aid package was $9,578.

Students without need: 115 full-time freshmen who did not demonstrate need for aid received scholarships/grants; average award was $3,778. No-need awards available for academics, art, job skills, leadership, music/drama, religious affiliation.

Cumulative student debt: 77% of graduating class had student loans; average debt was $31,934.

FINANCIAL AID PROCEDURES

Forms required: FAFSA.

Dates and Deadlines: Priority date 3/15; no closing date. Applicants notified on a rolling basis starting 1/1; must reply within 2 week(s) of notification.

CONTACT

Jim Jones, Director of Financial Aid and Scholarships
PO Box 16050, Abilene, TX 79698-0001
(325) 670-1206

Hill College
Hillsboro, Texas
www.hillcollege.edu   Federal Code: 003573

2-year public community and junior college in small town.

Enrollment: 3,544 undergrads.

Selectivity: Open admission; but selective for some programs.

BASIC COSTS (2007-2008)

Tuition and fees: $1,560; out-of-district residents $1,950; out-of-state residents $2,350.

Room and board: $2,800.

FINANCIAL AID PICTURE (2007-2008)

Students with need: 98% of average financial aid package awarded as scholarships/grants, 2% awarded as loans/jobs. Need-based aid available for part-time students.

Students without need: No-need awards available for academics, athletics, music/drama.

FINANCIAL AID PROCEDURES

Forms required: FAFSA, institutional form.

Dates and Deadlines: Priority date 7/1; no closing date. Applicants notified on a rolling basis.

CONTACT

Susan Russell, Director of Student Financial Aid
Box 619, Hillsboro, TX 76645
(254) 582-2555 ext. 285

Houston Baptist University
Houston, Texas
www.hbu.edu   Federal Code: 003576

4-year private university and liberal arts college in very large city, affiliated with Baptist faith.

Enrollment: 1,992 undergrads, 10% part-time. 449 full-time freshmen.

Selectivity: Admits less than 50% of applicants.

BASIC COSTS (2008-2009)

Tuition and fees: $18,820.

Per-credit charge: $700.

Room and board: $4,995.

Additional info: Tuition at time of enrollment locked for 4 years.

FINANCIAL AID PICTURE (2007-2008)

Students with need: Out of 322 full-time freshmen who applied for aid, 123 were judged to have need. Of these, 123 received aid, and 25 had their full need met. Average financial aid package met 69% of need; average scholarship/grant was $9,941; average loan was $3,294. For part-time students, average financial aid package was $12,314.

Students without need: 271 full-time freshmen who did not demonstrate need for aid received scholarships/grants; average award was $7,613. No-need awards available for academics, alumni affiliation, art, athletics, leadership, music/drama, religious affiliation.

Scholarships offered: *Merit:* Endowed Academic Scholarship: full or three-quarters tuition for four years; limited number available; for new freshmen with 1300 SAT or 30 ACT. Founders Academic Scholarship: minimum 1250 SAT or 28 ACT required for freshmen, 3.75 GPA on 30 or more semester hours required for transfers. Presidential Academic Scholarship: $4,300 per year, renewable; 1175 SAT or 26 ACT required for freshmen, 3.5 GPA required for transfers. Legacy Grant: $2,700 per year; renewable; 1100 SAT or 24 ACT required for freshman, 3.25 GPA required for transfers. All SAT scores are exclusive of Writing. Valedictorian Scholarship: $1,500 per year; renewable; for valedictorians from Texas high schools. Ministerial Dependents Grant: $4,300 per year; for dependent children of ordained/licensed Southern Baptist ministers and missionaries. Grants-In-Aid: awards vary; for students who contribute special abilities or services to the University; awarded in music, art, athletics and nursing. Church Matching Award: awards vary. *Athletic:* 45 full-time freshmen received athletic scholarships; average amount $13,994.

FINANCIAL AID PROCEDURES

Forms required: FAFSA.

Dates and Deadlines: Priority date 3/1; closing date 4/15. Applicants notified on a rolling basis starting 3/10.

CONTACT

Debora Burnett, Director of Financial Services
7502 Fondren Road, Houston, TX 77074-3298
(281) 649-3471

Houston Community College System

Houston, Texas
www.hccs.edu   Federal Code: 010422

2-year public community college in very large city.
Enrollment: 29,537 undergrads.
Selectivity: Open admission; but selective for some programs.

BASIC COSTS (2007-2008)

Tuition and fees: $1,636; out-of-district residents $3,256; out-of-state residents $3,856.

FINANCIAL AID PICTURE (2006-2007)

Students with need: Need-based aid available for full-time and part-time students. Work study available nights, weekends, and for part-time students.

FINANCIAL AID PROCEDURES

Dates and Deadlines: No deadline. Applicants notified on a rolling basis starting 6/1; must reply within 2 week(s) of notification.

CONTACT

Avis Horde, Director of Financial Aid
3100 Main, Houston, TX 77266-7517
(713) 718-8550

Howard College

Big Spring, Texas
www.howardcollege.edu   Federal Code: 003574

2-year public community college in large town.
Enrollment: 3,192 undergrads, 65% part-time. 254 full-time freshmen.
Selectivity: Open admission; but selective for some programs.

BASIC COSTS (2008-2009)

Tuition and fees: $1,712; out-of-district residents $2,132; out-of-state residents $2,832.
Room and board: $3,600.

FINANCIAL AID PICTURE

Students with need: Need-based aid available for full-time and part-time students.
Students without need: No-need awards available for academics, art, athletics, leadership, music/drama.

FINANCIAL AID PROCEDURES

Forms required: FAFSA, institutional form.
Dates and Deadlines: Priority date 4/1; no closing date. Applicants notified on a rolling basis starting 7/15; must reply within 2 week(s) of notification.

CONTACT

Rebecca Villanueva, Director of Financial Aid
1001 Birdwell Lane, Big Spring, TX 79720
(432) 264-5083

Howard Payne University

Brownwood, Texas
www.hputx.edu   Federal Code: 003575

4-year private liberal arts and teachers college in large town, affiliated with Baptist faith.
Enrollment: 1,173 undergrads, 11% part-time. 257 full-time freshmen.
Selectivity: Admits 50 to 75% of applicants.

BASIC COSTS (2008-2009)

Tuition and fees: $17,400.
Per-credit charge: $510.

Room and board: $5,051.
Additional info: First-year student tuition is guaranteed not to increase as long as the student is full-time and making satisfactory progress toward their degree.

FINANCIAL AID PICTURE

Students with need: Need-based aid available for full-time and part-time students.
Students without need: No-need awards available for academics, alumni affiliation, art, job skills, music/drama.

FINANCIAL AID PROCEDURES

Forms required: FAFSA, institutional form.
Dates and Deadlines: Priority date 3/1; no closing date. Applicants notified on a rolling basis starting 3/30; must reply within 3 week(s) of notification.

CONTACT

Glenda Huff, Director of Student Financial Aid
1000 Fisk Avenue, Brownwood, TX 76801
(325) 649-8015

Huston-Tillotson University

Austin, Texas
www.htu.edu   Federal Code: 003577

4-year private business and liberal arts college in very large city, affiliated with United Church of Christ and United Methodist Church.
Enrollment: 724 undergrads, 6% part-time. 188 full-time freshmen.
Selectivity: Admits less than 50% of applicants.

BASIC COSTS (2007-2008)

Tuition and fees: $10,038.
Room and board: $5,892.

FINANCIAL AID PICTURE (2006-2007)

Students with need: Out of 182 full-time freshmen who applied for aid, 179 were judged to have need. Of these, 179 received aid, and 12 had their full need met. Average financial aid package met 48% of need; average scholarship/grant was $6,689; average loan was $2,703. For part-time students, average financial aid package was $8,545.
Students without need: 26 full-time freshmen who did not demonstrate need for aid received scholarships/grants; average award was $8,155. No-need awards available for academics, alumni affiliation, art, athletics, job skills, leadership, minority status, music/drama, religious affiliation, ROTC, state/district residency.
Scholarships offered: 2 full-time freshmen received athletic scholarships; average amount $4,236.
Cumulative student debt: 87% of graduating class had student loans; average debt was $12,200.

FINANCIAL AID PROCEDURES

Forms required: FAFSA, institutional form.
Dates and Deadlines: Priority date 3/15; closing date 4/1. Applicants notified on a rolling basis starting 4/1; must reply within 4 week(s) of notification.
Transfers: No deadline.

CONTACT

Antonio Holloway, Director of Financial Aid
900 Chicon Street, Austin, TX 78702-2795
(512) 505-3031

Jacksonville College

Jacksonville, Texas
www.jacksonville-college.edu   Federal Code: 003579

2-year private junior and liberal arts college in large town, affiliated with Baptist faith.

Enrollment: 230 undergrads.

Selectivity: Open admission.

BASIC COSTS (2007-2008)

Tuition and fees: $6,146.

Per-credit charge: $185.

Room and board: $2,746.

FINANCIAL AID PICTURE

Students with need: Need-based aid available for full-time and part-time students.

Students without need: No-need awards available for academics, athletics, leadership, music/drama, religious affiliation, state/district residency.

FINANCIAL AID PROCEDURES

Forms required: FAFSA, state aid form, institutional form.

Dates and Deadlines: Priority date 8/1; no closing date. Applicants notified on a rolling basis.

Transfers: No deadline. Applicants notified on a rolling basis.

CONTACT

Don Compton, Financial Aid Officer
105 B.J. Albritton Drive, Jacksonville, TX 75766-4759
(903) 586-2518 ext. 7135

Jarvis Christian College

Hawkins, Texas
www.jarvis.edu   Federal Code: 003637

4-year private liberal arts and teachers college in rural community, affiliated with Christian Church (Disciples of Christ).

Enrollment: 712 undergrads, 12% part-time. 113 full-time freshmen.

Selectivity: Open admission.

BASIC COSTS (2008-2009)

Tuition and fees: $8,208.

Room and board: $4,954.

FINANCIAL AID PICTURE (2006-2007)

Students with need: Out of 113 full-time freshmen who applied for aid, 96 were judged to have need. Of these, 96 received aid, and 91 had their full need met. Average financial aid package met 97% of need; average scholarship/grant was $3,900; average loan was $3,100. For part-time students, average financial aid package was $8,400.

Students without need: 7 full-time freshmen who did not demonstrate need for aid received scholarships/grants; average award was $11,500. No-need awards available for academics, athletics, religious affiliation.

Scholarships offered: 6 full-time freshmen received athletic scholarships; average amount $5,600.

Cumulative student debt: 90% of graduating class had student loans; average debt was $15,200.

Additional info: High school transcript required for scholarship consideration.

FINANCIAL AID PROCEDURES

Forms required: FAFSA.

Dates and Deadlines: Priority date 5/31; no closing date. Applicants notified on a rolling basis starting 5/1; must reply within 2 week(s) of notification.

Transfers: Priority date 4/15; no deadline. Applicants notified on a rolling basis starting 7/1; must reply within 2 week(s) of notification.

CONTACT

Eric King, Director of Admission and Financial Aid
PO Box 1470, Hawkins, TX 75765-1470
(903) 769-5741

Kilgore College

Kilgore, Texas
www.kilgore.edu   Federal Code: 003580

2-year public community college in large town.

Enrollment: 5,150 undergrads, 48% part-time. 950 full-time freshmen.

Selectivity: Open admission; but selective for some programs.

BASIC COSTS (2007-2008)

Tuition and fees: $1,290; out-of-district residents $2,700; out-of-state residents $3,660.

Per-credit charge: $21; out-of-district residents $68; out-of-state residents $100.

Room and board: $3,630.

Additional info: Tuition/fee waivers available for unemployed or children of unemployed.

FINANCIAL AID PICTURE

Students with need: Need-based aid available for full-time and part-time students.

Students without need: No-need awards available for academics, alumni affiliation, art, athletics, job skills, leadership, music/drama, state/district residency.

Scholarships offered: Presidential Scholarships: tuition, fees and books for 4 semesters; ACT 25 or top 10% of senior class; 20 available; renewable at 2.5 GPA.

Additional info: State of Texas grants and loans available for honor graduates with unmet needs and for non-traditional students.

FINANCIAL AID PROCEDURES

Forms required: FAFSA, state aid form, institutional form.

Dates and Deadlines: Priority date 6/1; closing date 7/15. Applicants notified on a rolling basis starting 3/1; must reply within 2 week(s) of notification.

Transfers: No deadline. Transfer students must submit financial aid transcript from previous school plus all appropriate internal aid forms and show proof of high school graduation or GED.

CONTACT

Annette Morgan, Director of Financial Aid
1100 Broadway, Kilgore, TX 75662-3299
(903) 983-8183

Lamar State College at Orange

Orange, Texas
www.lsco.edu   Federal Code: 016748

2-year public junior and liberal arts college in small city.

Enrollment: 1,756 undergrads, 47% part-time. 316 full-time freshmen.

Selectivity: Open admission; but selective for some programs.

BASIC COSTS (2007-2008)

Tuition and fees: $3,340; out-of-state residents $11,680.

Per-credit charge: $82; out-of-state residents $360.

FINANCIAL AID PICTURE

Students with need: Need-based aid available for full-time and part-time students.

Students without need: This college awards aid only to students with need.

FINANCIAL AID PROCEDURES

Forms required: FAFSA, institutional form.
Dates and Deadlines: Priority date 4/1; no closing date. Applicants notified on a rolling basis starting 5/15; must reply within 2 week(s) of notification.

CONTACT

Kerry Olson, Director of Financial Aid
410 Front Street, Orange, TX 77630
(409) 882-3317

Lamar State College at Port Arthur

Port Arthur, Texas
www.lamarpa.edu   Federal Code: 016666

2-year public community and technical college in small city.
Enrollment: 2,279 undergrads.
Selectivity: Open admission; but selective for some programs.

BASIC COSTS (2007-2008)

Tuition and fees: $3,448; out-of-state residents $11,788.

FINANCIAL AID PICTURE

Students with need: Need-based aid available for full-time and part-time students. Work study available nights, weekends, and for part-time students.
Students without need: This college awards aid only to students with need.

FINANCIAL AID PROCEDURES

Forms required: FAFSA, institutional form.
Dates and Deadlines: Priority date 4/1; no closing date. Applicants notified on a rolling basis starting 4/15; must reply within 2 week(s) of notification.

CONTACT

Diane Hargett, Director of Financial Aid
Box 310, Port Arthur, TX 77641-0310
(409) 984-6203

Lamar University

Beaumont, Texas
www.lamar.edu   Federal Code: 003581

4-year public university in small city.
Enrollment: 8,428 undergrads, 13% part-time. 1,424 full-time freshmen.
Selectivity: Admits 50 to 75% of applicants.

BASIC COSTS (2008-2009)

Tuition and fees: $6,014; out-of-state residents $14,444.
Per-credit charge: $145; out-of-state residents $426.
Room and board: $6,290.

FINANCIAL AID PICTURE (2007-2008)

Students with need: Out of 1,039 full-time freshmen who applied for aid, 655 were judged to have need. Of these, 608 received aid, and 98 had their full need met. Average financial aid package met 51% of need. For part-time students, average financial aid package was $824.
Students without need: This college awards aid only to students with need.

FINANCIAL AID PROCEDURES

Forms required: FAFSA, institutional form.
Dates and Deadlines: Priority date 4/1; no closing date. Applicants notified on a rolling basis starting 4/1; must reply within 2 week(s) of notification.

CONTACT

Jill Rowley, Director of Financial Aid
Box 10009, Beaumont, TX 77705
(409) 880-8450

Laredo Community College

Laredo, Texas
www.laredo.edu   Federal Code: 003582

2-year public community college in large city.
Enrollment: 6,914 undergrads, 61% part-time. 658 full-time freshmen.
Selectivity: Open admission; but selective for some programs.

BASIC COSTS (2007-2008)

Tuition and fees: $1,716; out-of-district residents $2,766; out-of-state residents $3,816.
Per-credit charge: $35; out-of-district residents $70; out-of-state residents $105.
Room and board: $4,374.

FINANCIAL AID PICTURE (2006-2007)

Students with need: 90% of average financial aid package awarded as scholarships/grants, 10% awarded as loans/jobs.

FINANCIAL AID PROCEDURES

Forms required: FAFSA, state aid form, institutional form.
Dates and Deadlines: Priority date 5/1; no closing date. Applicants notified on a rolling basis.

CONTACT

Ricardo Moreno, Director of Financial Aid
West End Washington Street, Laredo, TX 78040-4395
(956) 721-5360

Lee College

Baytown, Texas
www.lee.edu   Federal Code: 003583

2-year public community college in small city.
Enrollment: 5,754 undergrads.
Selectivity: Open admission; but selective for some programs.

BASIC COSTS (2007-2008)

Tuition and fees: $1,302; out-of-district residents $2,052; out-of-state residents $3,102.
Per-credit charge: $25; out-of-district residents $50; out-of-state residents $85.

FINANCIAL AID PICTURE

Students with need: Need-based aid available for full-time and part-time students.
Students without need: No-need awards available for academics, art, athletics, job skills, music/drama.

FINANCIAL AID PROCEDURES

Forms required: FAFSA.
Dates and Deadlines: Priority date 4/1; no closing date. Applicants notified on a rolling basis starting 6/1.

CONTACT

Sharon Mullins, Financial Aid Officer
Box 818, Baytown, TX 77522
(281) 425-6362

LeTourneau University

Longview, Texas
www.letu.edu   Federal Code: 003584

4-year private university in small city, affiliated with nondenominational tradition.
Enrollment: 3,552 undergrads, 12% part-time. 323 full-time freshmen.

Selectivity: Admits 50 to 75% of applicants.

BASIC COSTS (2007-2008)

Tuition and fees: $17,910.

Room and board: $6,950.

Additional info: Tuition for 1-6 hours is $322 per credit, for 7-11 hours is $707 per credit.

FINANCIAL AID PICTURE

Students with need: Need-based aid available for full-time and part-time students. Work study available nights, weekends, and for part-time students.

Students without need: No-need awards available for academics, leadership.

Scholarships offered: Honor scholarship: up to $3,000 per year; GPA 3.0-3.29, ACT 25+ or SAT 1150+. Dean's Scholarship: up to $4,500 per year; GPA 3.3-3.59, ACT 27+ or SAT 1200+. Presidential Scholarship: up to $6,000 per year; GPA 3.60+, ACT 29+ or SAT 1300+. All SAT scores exclusive of Writing.

FINANCIAL AID PROCEDURES

Forms required: FAFSA.

Dates and Deadlines: Priority date 2/15; no closing date. Applicants notified on a rolling basis starting 3/1; must reply within 3 week(s) of notification.

CONTACT

Denise Welch, Director of Financial Aid

PO Box 7001, Longview, TX 75607-7001

(903) 233-4350

Lon Morris College

Jacksonville, Texas

www.lonmorris.edu   Federal Code: 003585

2-year private junior and liberal arts college in large town, affiliated with United Methodist Church.

Enrollment: 395 undergrads, 14% part-time. 177 full-time freshmen.

BASIC COSTS (2007-2008)

Tuition and fees: $10,950.

Room and board: $6,000.

FINANCIAL AID PICTURE

Students with need: Need-based aid available for full-time and part-time students. Work study available nights, weekends, and for part-time students.

Students without need: This college awards aid only to students with need.

FINANCIAL AID PROCEDURES

Forms required: FAFSA, state aid form, institutional form.

Dates and Deadlines: Priority date 5/1; no closing date. Applicants notified on a rolling basis starting 2/15; must reply within 2 week(s) of notification.

CONTACT

Kris Marquis, Financial Aid Director

800 College Avenue, Jacksonville, TX 75766

(903) 589-4061

Lone Star College System

The Woodlands, Texas

www.nhmccd.edu   Federal Code: 011145

2-year public community college in very large city.

Enrollment: 35,850 undergrads, 74% part-time. 1,881 full-time freshmen.

Selectivity: Open admission; but selective for some programs.

BASIC COSTS (2008-2009)

Tuition and fees: $1,360; out-of-district residents $2,860; out-of-state residents $3,310.

Per-credit charge: $36; out-of-district residents $86; out-of-state residents $101.

FINANCIAL AID PICTURE (2006-2007)

Students with need: 81% of average financial aid package awarded as scholarships/grants, 19% awarded as loans/jobs. Need-based aid available for part-time students. Work study available nights, weekends, and for part-time students.

Students without need: No-need awards available for academics.

FINANCIAL AID PROCEDURES

Forms required: FAFSA, institutional form.

Dates and Deadlines: Priority date 4/1; no closing date. Applicants notified on a rolling basis starting 4/1.

CONTACT

Jason Kot, District Director of Financial Aid

5000 Research Forest Drive, The Woodlands, TX 77381-4356

(832) 813-6607

Lubbock Christian University

Lubbock, Texas

www.lcu.edu   Federal Code: 003586

4-year private university and liberal arts college in small city, affiliated with Church of Christ.

Enrollment: 1,718 undergrads, 19% part-time. 256 full-time freshmen.

Selectivity: Admits 50 to 75% of applicants.

BASIC COSTS (2007-2008)

Tuition and fees: $14,290.

Room and board: $4,750.

FINANCIAL AID PICTURE (2006-2007)

Students with need: Out of 234 full-time freshmen who applied for aid, 200 were judged to have need. Of these, 200 received aid, and 30 had their full need met. Average financial aid package met 74% of need; average scholarship/grant was $8,234; average loan was $2,941. For part-time students, average financial aid package was $5,751.

Students without need: 52 full-time freshmen who did not demonstrate need for aid received scholarships/grants; average award was $10,373. No-need awards available for academics, athletics, job skills, leadership, music/drama.

Scholarships offered: 12 full-time freshmen received athletic scholarships; average amount $5,654.

Cumulative student debt: 81% of graduating class had student loans; average debt was $22,814.

FINANCIAL AID PROCEDURES

Forms required: FAFSA, institutional form.

Dates and Deadlines: Priority date 6/1; no closing date. Applicants notified on a rolling basis starting 3/1.

Transfers: No deadline. Applicants notified on a rolling basis.

CONTACT

Amy Hardesty, Director of Financial Aid

5601 19th Street, Lubbock, TX 79407

(806) 720-7178

McLennan Community College

Waco, Texas

www.mclennan.edu   Federal Code: 003590

2-year public community and junior college in small city.

Enrollment: 8,079 undergrads.

Selectivity: Open admission; but selective for some programs.

BASIC COSTS (2007-2008)

Tuition and fees: $1,950; out-of-district residents $2,310; out-of-state residents $3,750.

Per-credit charge: $56; out-of-district residents $68; out-of-state residents $116.

FINANCIAL AID PICTURE (2006-2007)

Students with need: 61% of average financial aid package awarded as scholarships/grants, 39% awarded as loans/jobs.

Students without need: No-need awards available for athletics.

Scholarships offered: Academic scholarship: awarded to individuals selected for Tartan scholar's program.

FINANCIAL AID PROCEDURES

Forms required: FAFSA.

Dates and Deadlines: Priority date 6/1; no closing date. Applicants notified on a rolling basis starting 5/1.

CONTACT

James Kubacak, Director of Financial Aid

1400 College Drive, Waco, TX 76708

(254) 299-8698

McMurry University

Abilene, Texas

www.mcm.edu   Federal Code: 003591

4-year private university and liberal arts college in small city, affiliated with United Methodist Church.

Enrollment: 1,365 undergrads, 13% part-time. 311 full-time freshmen.

Selectivity: Admits 50 to 75% of applicants.

BASIC COSTS (2008-2009)

Tuition and fees: $18,135.

Per-credit charge: $535.

Room and board: $6,657.

FINANCIAL AID PICTURE (2007-2008)

Students with need: Out of 291 full-time freshmen who applied for aid, 258 were judged to have need. Of these, 258 received aid, and 48 had their full need met. Average financial aid package met 93% of need; average scholarship/grant was $10,788; average loan was $3,723. For part-time students, average financial aid package was $6,303.

Students without need: 30 full-time freshmen who did not demonstrate need for aid received scholarships/grants; average award was $4,183. No-need awards available for academics, alumni affiliation, art, music/drama, religious affiliation, ROTC.

Scholarships offered: McMurry Technology Scholarship: $3,000-$8,500; minimum 3.0 GPA and 950 ACT; major in Computer Science or Computer Information Systems.

Cumulative student debt: 73% of graduating class had student loans; average debt was $23,050.

FINANCIAL AID PROCEDURES

Forms required: FAFSA.

Dates and Deadlines: Priority date 3/15; no closing date. Applicants notified on a rolling basis starting 2/1; must reply within 3 week(s) of notification.

Transfers: No deadline. Applicants notified on a rolling basis starting 2/1; must reply by 7/31.

CONTACT

Rachel Atkins, Director of Financial Aid

South 14th and Sayles Boulevard, Abilene, TX 79697-0001

(325) 793-4713

Midland College

Midland, Texas

www.midland.edu   Federal Code: 009797

2-year public community college in small city.

Enrollment: 3,485 undergrads, 68% part-time. 253 full-time freshmen.

Selectivity: Open admission; but selective for some programs.

BASIC COSTS (2007-2008)

Tuition and fees: $1,590; out-of-district residents $1,950; out-of-state residents $2,820.

Per-credit charge: $43; out-of-district residents $55; out-of-state residents $94.

Room and board: $3,420.

Additional info: Additional $48 charge per credit hour for baccalaureate program.

FINANCIAL AID PICTURE

Students with need: Need-based aid available for full-time and part-time students.

Students without need: No-need awards available for academics, athletics, minority status, music/drama, state/district residency.

Scholarships offered: Abell-Hangar Foundations Scholarships: varying amounts; renewable; available for full-time or part-time study to any Midland High, Midland Lee, or Greenwood High School graduate.

FINANCIAL AID PROCEDURES

Forms required: FAFSA.

Dates and Deadlines: Priority date 4/2; closing date 6/1. Applicants notified on a rolling basis starting 5/15; must reply within 2 week(s) of notification.

Transfers: No deadline.

CONTACT

Latisha Williams, Director of Financial Aid

3600 North Garfield, Midland, TX 79705

(432) 685-4733

Midwestern State University

Wichita Falls, Texas

www.mwsu.edu   Federal Code: 003592

4-year public university and liberal arts college in small city.

Enrollment: 5,348 undergrads, 27% part-time. 736 full-time freshmen.

Selectivity: Admits 50 to 75% of applicants.

BASIC COSTS (2007-2008)

Tuition and fees: $5,376; out-of-state residents $6,276.

Per-credit charge: $50; out-of-state residents $328.

Room and board: $5,350.

FINANCIAL AID PICTURE (2007-2008)

Students with need: Average financial aid package met 73% of need; average scholarship/grant was $5,058; average loan was $3,349. For part-time students, average financial aid package was $5,547.

Students without need: No-need awards available for academics, alumni affiliation, art, athletics, leadership, music/drama.

Cumulative student debt: 58% of graduating class had student loans; average debt was $16,627.

Additional info: Employees offered educational incentive plan in which tuition reimbursed provided employee meets stated criteria. Additionally, dependents and children of faculty and staff may receive scholarship to defer local tuition and fees.

FINANCIAL AID PROCEDURES

Forms required: FAFSA, institutional form.
Dates and Deadlines: Priority date 5/1; no closing date. Applicants notified on a rolling basis starting 4/1; must reply within 4 week(s) of notification.
Transfers: No deadline. Applicants notified on a rolling basis starting 3/15.

CONTACT

Kathy Pennartz, Director of Financial Aid
3410 Taft Boulevard, Wichita Falls, TX 76308-2099
(940) 397-4214

Mountain View College

Dallas, Texas
www.mvc.dcccd.edu   Federal Code: 008503

2-year public community college in very large city.
Enrollment: 6,827 undergrads.
Selectivity: Open admission.

BASIC COSTS (2007-2008)

Tuition and fees: $1,170; out-of-district residents $2,160; out-of-state residents $3,450.
Per-credit charge: $39; out-of-district residents $72; out-of-state residents $115.
Additional info: Tuition/fee waivers available for adults.

FINANCIAL AID PICTURE

Students with need: Need-based aid available for full-time and part-time students. Work study available nights, weekends, and for part-time students.
Students without need: No-need awards available for academics.

FINANCIAL AID PROCEDURES

Forms required: FAFSA, institutional form.
Dates and Deadlines: Priority date 5/1; no closing date. Applicants notified on a rolling basis starting 6/1.

CONTACT

Joseph Sanchez, Director of Financial Aid
4849 West Illinois Avenue, Dallas, TX 75211-6599
(214) 860-8688

North Central Texas College

Gainesville, Texas
www.nctc.edu   Federal Code: 003558

2-year public community college in large town.
Enrollment: 7,444 undergrads.
Selectivity: Open admission; but selective for some programs.

BASIC COSTS (2007-2008)

Tuition and fees: $1,290; out-of-district residents $2,160; out-of-state residents $3,210.
Per-credit charge: $34; out-of-district residents $63; out-of-state residents $98.
Room and board: $3,390.

FINANCIAL AID PICTURE

Students with need: Need-based aid available for full-time and part-time students. Work study available nights.
Students without need: This college awards aid only to students with need.

FINANCIAL AID PROCEDURES

Forms required: FAFSA.

Dates and Deadlines: Priority date 5/1; no closing date. Applicants notified on a rolling basis starting 6/1; must reply within 4 week(s) of notification.

CONTACT

Ashley Tatum, Director of Financial Aid
1525 West California Street, Gainesville, TX 76240

North Lake College

Irving, Texas
www.northlakecollege.edu   Federal Code: 014036

2-year public community and liberal arts college in small city.
Enrollment: 8,067 undergrads.
Selectivity: Open admission.

BASIC COSTS (2007-2008)

Tuition and fees: $1,170; out-of-district residents $2,160; out-of-state residents $3,450.
Per-credit charge: $39; out-of-district residents $72; out-of-state residents $115.

FINANCIAL AID PICTURE

Students with need: Need-based aid available for full-time and part-time students.
Students without need: No-need awards available for academics, minority status, state/district residency.

FINANCIAL AID PROCEDURES

Forms required: FAFSA, state aid form.
Dates and Deadlines: Priority date 3/1; closing date 5/1. Applicants notified on a rolling basis starting 7/1.
Transfers: Applicants notified on a rolling basis starting 8/1.

CONTACT

Paul Felix, Director of Financial Aid
5001 North MacArthur Boulevard, Irving, TX 75038-3899
(972) 273-3321

Northeast Texas Community College

Mount Pleasant, Texas
www.ntcc.edu   Federal Code: 016396

2-year public community college in large town.
Enrollment: 2,458 undergrads.
Selectivity: Open admission; but selective for some programs.

BASIC COSTS (2007-2008)

Tuition and fees: $1,800; out-of-district residents $2;640; out-of-state residents $3,956.
Per-credit charge: $28; out-of-district residents $56; out-of-state residents $96.
Room and board: $3,660.

FINANCIAL AID PICTURE (2006-2007)

Students with need: 97% of average financial aid package awarded as scholarships/grants, 3% awarded as loans/jobs. Need-based aid available for part-time students.
Students without need: No-need awards available for academics, art, athletics, job skills, music/drama, state/district residency.

FINANCIAL AID PROCEDURES

Forms required: FAFSA, institutional form.
Dates and Deadlines: Priority date 6/1; no closing date. Applicants notified on a rolling basis starting 6/1.

CONTACT

Patricia Durst, Director of Financial Aid
Box 1307, Mount Pleasant, TX 75456-1307
(903) 434-8145

Northwest Vista College

San Antonio, Texas
www.accd.edu/nvc   Federal Code: 033723

2-year public community college in very large city.
Enrollment: 10,672 undergrads.
Selectivity: Open admission.

BASIC COSTS (2007-2008)

Tuition and fees: $1,790; out-of-district residents $3,110; out-of-state residents $5,750.

FINANCIAL AID PICTURE

Students with need: Need-based aid available for full-time and part-time students. Work study available nights, weekends, and for part-time students.
Students without need: No-need awards available for academics, leadership.

FINANCIAL AID PROCEDURES

Forms required: FAFSA.
Dates and Deadlines: Priority date 4/1; no closing date. Applicants notified on a rolling basis starting 5/15; must reply within 2 week(s) of notification.

CONTACT

Noe Ortiz, Financial Aid Director
3535 North Ellison Drive, San Antonio, TX 78251-4217
(210) 348-2100

Northwood University: Texas

Cedar Hill, Texas
www.northwood.edu   Federal Code: 013040

4-year private university and business college in large town.
Enrollment: 526 undergrads, 5% part-time. 123 full-time freshmen.
Selectivity: Admits 50 to 75% of applicants.

BASIC COSTS (2007-2008)

Tuition and fees: $16,455.
Per-credit charge: $330.
Room and board: $6,888.

FINANCIAL AID PICTURE (2007-2008)

Students with need: Out of 104 full-time freshmen who applied for aid, 88 were judged to have need. Of these, 88 received aid, and 21 had their full need met. Average financial aid package met 59% of need; average scholarship/grant was $5,345; average loan was $3,259. For part-time students, average financial aid package was $7,165.
Students without need: 21 full-time freshmen who did not demonstrate need for aid received scholarships/grants; average award was $6,980. No-need awards available for academics, alumni affiliation, athletics, leadership, minority status, state/district residency.
Scholarships offered: *Merit:* Academic Scholarships: $4,000-$9,000; based on test scores and GPA; unlimited number awarded. *Athletic:* 11 full-time freshmen received athletic scholarships; average amount $8,021.
Cumulative student debt: 79% of graduating class had student loans; average debt was $20,170.

FINANCIAL AID PROCEDURES

Forms required: FAFSA.
Dates and Deadlines: No deadline. Applicants notified on a rolling basis starting 3/1.

CONTACT

Michael Rhodes, Director of Financial Aid
1114 West FM 1382, Cedar Hill, TX 75104
(972) 293-5430

Odessa College

Odessa, Texas
www.odessa.edu   Federal Code: 003596

2-year public community college in small city.
Enrollment: 3,806 undergrads, 64% part-time. 393 full-time freshmen.
Selectivity: Open admission; but selective for some programs.

BASIC COSTS (2008-2009)

Tuition and fees: $1,590; out-of-district residents $2,040; out-of-state residents $2,790.
Room and board: $4,200.

FINANCIAL AID PICTURE

Students with need: Need-based aid available for full-time and part-time students. Work study available nights.
Students without need: No-need awards available for academics, athletics, music/drama.

FINANCIAL AID PROCEDURES

Forms required: FAFSA.
Dates and Deadlines: Priority date 5/1; no closing date. Applicants notified on a rolling basis starting 6/15.

CONTACT

Dee Nesmith, Director of Student Financial Aid
201 West University, Odessa, TX 79764-7127
(432) 335-6429

Our Lady of the Lake University of San Antonio

San Antonio, Texas
www.ollusa.edu   Federal Code: 003598

4-year private university in very large city, affiliated with Roman Catholic Church.
Enrollment: 1,528 undergrads, 28% part-time. 284 full-time freshmen.
Selectivity: Admits less than 50% of applicants.

BASIC COSTS (2007-2008)

Tuition and fees: $19,116.
Per-credit charge: $604.
Room and board: $5,838.

FINANCIAL AID PICTURE

Students with need: Need-based aid available for full-time and part-time students. Work study available nights, weekends, and for part-time students.
Students without need: No-need awards available for academics, alumni affiliation, art, music/drama.
Scholarships offered: General academic scholarship: $1,205 awarded yearly, renewable. Art/fine arts and music: 4 awarded yearly, renewable. Children of faculty/staff: 60 awarded yearly, renewable. All based on GPA scores and high school record.

FINANCIAL AID PROCEDURES

Forms required: FAFSA.
Dates and Deadlines: Priority date 2/28; no closing date. Applicants notified on a rolling basis starting 4/1; must reply within 2 week(s) of notification.

CONTACT

Michael Sitka, Director of Financial Aid
411 Southwest 24th Street, San Antonio, TX 78207-4689
(210) 434-6711 ext. 2558

Palo Alto College

San Antonio, Texas
www.accd.edu   Federal Code: 016615

2-year public community college in very large city.
Enrollment: 8,021 undergrads.
Selectivity: Open admission.

BASIC COSTS (2007-2008)
Tuition and fees: $1,652; out-of-district residents $2,972; out-of-state residents $5,384.

FINANCIAL AID PICTURE (2006-2007)
Students with need: 86% of average financial aid package awarded as scholarships/grants, 14% awarded as loans/jobs. Need-based aid available for part-time students.
Students without need: This college awards aid only to students with need.
Scholarships offered: Alamo Community College District Scholarship: $1,000; 50 awarded.

FINANCIAL AID PROCEDURES
Forms required: FAFSA, state aid form.
Dates and Deadlines: Priority date 4/1; closing date 6/1. Applicants notified on a rolling basis starting 5/31.

CONTACT
Lamar Duarte, Director of Financial Aid
1400 West Villaret Boulevard, San Antonio, TX 78224-2499
(210) 921-5316

Panola College

Carthage, Texas
www.panola.edu   Federal Code: 003600

2-year public community and junior college in small town.
Enrollment: 1,879 undergrads, 54% part-time. 310 full-time freshmen.
Selectivity: Open admission; but selective for some programs.

BASIC COSTS (2007-2008)
Tuition and fees: $1,560; out-of-district residents $2,670; out-of-state residents $3,330.
Room and board: $4,042.

FINANCIAL AID PICTURE
Students with need: Need-based aid available for full-time and part-time students. Work study available nights, weekends, and for part-time students.
Students without need: No-need awards available for academics, alumni affiliation, art, athletics, leadership, music/drama.
Scholarships offered: Several departmental and organization-sponsored scholarships, Presidential scholarship, Dean's scholarship.

FINANCIAL AID PROCEDURES
Forms required: FAFSA, institutional form.
Dates and Deadlines: Priority date 6/1; no closing date. Applicants notified on a rolling basis starting 6/1.
Transfers: No deadline. Applicants notified on a rolling basis.

CONTACT
Mary Chance, Director of Financial Aid
1109 West Panola Street, Carthage, TX 75633
(903) 693-2039

Paris Junior College

Paris, Texas
www.parisjc.edu   Federal Code: 003601

2-year public community and junior college in large town.
Enrollment: 1,819 full-time undergrads.
Selectivity: Open admission; but selective for some programs.

BASIC COSTS (2008-2009)
Tuition and fees: $1,350; out-of-district residents $2,250; out-of-state residents $3,450.
Room and board: $4,132.

FINANCIAL AID PICTURE (2006-2007)
Students with need: Need-based aid available for part-time students.
Students without need: No-need awards available for athletics, music/drama.

FINANCIAL AID PROCEDURES
Forms required: FAFSA.
Dates and Deadlines: No deadline. Applicants notified on a rolling basis starting 6/1.

CONTACT
Linda Slawson, Director of Financial Aid
2400 Clarksville Street, Paris, TX 75460
(903) 782-0256

Prairie View A&M University

Prairie View, Texas
www.pvamu.edu   Federal Code: 003630

4-year public university in small town.
Enrollment: 6,118 undergrads.
Selectivity: Admits less than 50% of applicants.

BASIC COSTS (2008-2009)
Tuition and fees: $6,298; out-of-state residents $14,728.
Room and board: $6,652.

FINANCIAL AID PICTURE
Students with need: Need-based aid available for full-time and part-time students. Work study available nights, weekends, and for part-time students.
Students without need: No-need awards available for academics, athletics, ROTC.

FINANCIAL AID PROCEDURES
Forms required: FAFSA, institutional form.
Dates and Deadlines: Closing date 3/1. Applicants notified by 6/1; must reply by 8/1.
Transfers: Minimum 2.0 GPA from all colleges attended required to be considered for financial aid.

CONTACT
Carlos Clark, Director of Financial Aid
PO Box 519, MS 1009, Prairie View, TX 77446-0519

Ranger College

Ranger, Texas
www.rangercollege.edu   Federal Code: 003603

2-year public junior college in rural community.
Enrollment: 788 undergrads.
Selectivity: Open admission; but selective for some programs.

BASIC COSTS (2007-2008)

Tuition and fees: $2,194; out-of-state residents $2,294.

Per-credit charge: $43; out-of-state residents $49.

Room and board: $3,372.

FINANCIAL AID PICTURE

Students with need: Need-based aid available for full-time and part-time students.

Students without need: This college awards aid only to students with need.

FINANCIAL AID PROCEDURES

Forms required: FAFSA.

Dates and Deadlines: Priority date 6/1; closing date 7/24. Applicants notified on a rolling basis; must reply within 2 week(s) of notification.

Transfers: Applicants notified on a rolling basis; must reply within 2 week(s) of notification.

CONTACT

Pam Simon, Financial Aid Director

1100 College Circle, Ranger, TX 76470

(254) 647-3234 ext. 117

Remington College: Houston

Houston, Texas

www.remingtoncollege.edu   Federal Code: E00672

2-year for-profit technical college in very large city.

Enrollment: 213 undergrads.

Selectivity: Open admission.

BASIC COSTS (2007-2008)

Additional info: Costs of entire programs leading to certificate, associate degree, bachelor's degree range from $13,000 to $38,880; includes books and supplies. Tuition at time of enrollment locked for 2 years.

FINANCIAL AID PICTURE

Students with need: Need-based aid available for full-time and part-time students. Work study available nights.

Students without need: No-need awards available for state/district residency.

FINANCIAL AID PROCEDURES

Forms required: FAFSA, institutional form.

Dates and Deadlines: No deadline. Applicants notified on a rolling basis.

CONTACT

Jill Brown, Director, Financial Services

3110 Hayes Road, Suite 380, Houston, TX 77082

(281) 899-1240

Rice University

Houston, Texas   Federal Code: 003604

www.rice.edu   CSS Code: 6609

4-year private university in very large city.

Enrollment: 3,001 undergrads, 1% part-time. 742 full-time freshmen.

Selectivity: Admits less than 50% of applicants.

BASIC COSTS (2008-2009)

Tuition and fees: $30,479.

Per-credit charge: $1,249.

Room and board: $10,750.

FINANCIAL AID PICTURE (2007-2008)

Students with need: Out of 631 full-time freshmen who applied for aid, 291 were judged to have need. Of these, 291 received aid, and 291 had their full need met. Average financial aid package met 100% of need; average scholarship/grant was $24,776; average loan was $1,184. Need-based aid available for part-time students.

Students without need: 176 full-time freshmen who did not demonstrate need for aid received scholarships/grants; average award was $15,912. No-need awards available for academics, art, athletics, leadership, minority status, music/drama, ROTC, state/district residency.

Scholarships offered: 69 full-time freshmen received athletic scholarships; average amount $30,392.

Cumulative student debt: 57% of graduating class had student loans; average debt was $12,249.

FINANCIAL AID PROCEDURES

Forms required: FAFSA, CSS PROFILE.

Dates and Deadlines: Priority date 3/1; no closing date. Applicants notified by 4/15; must reply by 5/1 or within 1 week(s) of notification.

Transfers: Priority date 4/1.

CONTACT

Anne Walker, Director of Student Financial Services

6100 Main Street, Houston, TX 77251-1892

(713) 348-4958

Richland College

Dallas, Texas

www.rlc.dcccd.edu   Federal Code: 008504

2-year public community college in very large city.

Enrollment: 11,702 undergrads.

Selectivity: Open admission.

BASIC COSTS (2007-2008)

Tuition and fees: $1,170; out-of-district residents $2,160; out-of-state residents $3,450.

Per-credit charge: $39; out-of-district residents $72; out-of-state residents $115.

FINANCIAL AID PICTURE (2006-2007)

Students with need: 31% of average financial aid package awarded as scholarships/grants, 69% awarded as loans/jobs. Need-based aid available for part-time students. Work study available nights.

Students without need: No-need awards available for art, leadership, music/drama.

FINANCIAL AID PROCEDURES

Forms required: FAFSA.

Dates and Deadlines: Priority date 5/2; closing date 7/30. Applicants notified on a rolling basis starting 6/1; must reply within 2 week(s) of notification.

CONTACT

Bill McMullen, Director of Financial Aid

12800 Abrams Road, Dallas, TX 75243-2199

(972) 238-6188

St. Edward's University

Austin, Texas

www.stedwards.edu   Federal Code: 003621

4-year private university and liberal arts college in very large city, affiliated with Roman Catholic Church.

Enrollment: 4,312 undergrads, 23% part-time. 725 full-time freshmen.

Selectivity: Admits 50 to 75% of applicants.

BASIC COSTS (2008-2009)

Tuition and fees: $22,150.

Per-credit charge: $738.

Room and board: $8,158.

FINANCIAL AID PICTURE (2007-2008)

Students with need: Out of 579 full-time freshmen who applied for aid, 470 were judged to have need. Of these, 470 received aid, and 90 had their full need met. Average financial aid package met 78% of need; average scholarship/grant was $10,982; average loan was $3,433. For part-time students, average financial aid package was $6,376.

Students without need: 73 full-time freshmen who did not demonstrate need for aid received scholarships/grants; average award was $8,485. No-need awards available for academics, art, athletics, leadership, music/drama, state/district residency.

Scholarships offered: *Merit:* Trustees' Scholar Award: $9,000 per year; must have 1200 SAT (exclusive of Writing) and be in top 20% of class. Holy Cross Scholar Award: full tuition; must have 1250 SAT (exclusive of Writing), be in top 10% of class, and show superior leadership and service. Academic Scholar Award: $5,000 per year; must have 1100 SAT (exclusive of Writing) and be in top 25% of class. *Athletic:* 29 full-time freshmen received athletic scholarships; average amount $8,448.

Cumulative student debt: 72% of graduating class had student loans; average debt was $24,600.

FINANCIAL AID PROCEDURES

Forms required: FAFSA.

Dates and Deadlines: Priority date 3/1; closing date 4/15. Applicants notified on a rolling basis starting 1/15; must reply by 5/1 or within 2 week(s) of notification.

Transfers: Must reply by 5/1 or within 2 week(s) of notification.

CONTACT

Doris Constantine, Director of Student Financial Services

3001 South Congress Avenue, Austin, TX 78704-6425

(512) 448-8520

St. Mary's University

San Antonio, Texas

www.stmarytx.edu   Federal Code: 003623

4-year private university in very large city, affiliated with Roman Catholic Church.

Enrollment: 2,412 undergrads, 8% part-time. 565 full-time freshmen.

Selectivity: Admits 50 to 75% of applicants.

BASIC COSTS (2008-2009)

Tuition and fees: $21,156.

Per-credit charge: $640.

Room and board: $6,892.

Additional info: Notebook computer $1,000.

FINANCIAL AID PICTURE

Students with need: Need-based aid available for full-time and part-time students. Work study available nights, weekends, and for part-time students.

Students without need: No-need awards available for academics, alumni affiliation, athletics, leadership, music/drama, ROTC.

FINANCIAL AID PROCEDURES

Forms required: FAFSA.

Dates and Deadlines: Priority date 2/15; no closing date. Applicants notified on a rolling basis starting 5/1; must reply within 2 week(s) of notification.

CONTACT

David Krause, Director of Financial Assistance

One Camino Santa Maria, San Antonio, TX 78228

(210) 436-3141

St. Philip's College

San Antonio, Texas

www.accd.edu/spc   Federal Code: 003608

2-year public community college in very large city.

Enrollment: 9,256 undergrads, 58% part-time. 816 full-time freshmen.

Selectivity: Open admission.

BASIC COSTS (2007-2008)

Tuition and fees: $1,652; out-of-district residents $2,972; out-of-state residents $5,612.

Per-credit charge: $44; out-of-district residents $88; out-of-state residents $176.

FINANCIAL AID PICTURE (2006-2007)

Students with need: 69% of average financial aid package awarded as scholarships/grants, 31% awarded as loans/jobs. Need-based aid available for part-time students. Work study available nights, weekends, and for part-time students.

Students without need: This college awards aid only to students with need.

FINANCIAL AID PROCEDURES

Forms required: FAFSA.

Dates and Deadlines: Priority date 3/1; no closing date. Applicants notified on a rolling basis starting 7/15.

CONTACT

Diego Bernal, Director of Financial Aid

1801 Martin Luther King Drive, San Antonio, TX 78203

(210) 531-3272

Sam Houston State University

Huntsville, Texas

www.shsu.edu   Federal Code: 003606

4-year public university in large town.

Enrollment: 14,149 undergrads, 16% part-time. 2,166 full-time freshmen.

Selectivity: Admits over 75% of applicants.

BASIC COSTS (2008-2009)

Tuition and fees: $5,910; out-of-state residents $14,250.

Per-credit charge: $148; out-of-state residents $429.

Room and board: $6,046.

FINANCIAL AID PICTURE (2006-2007)

Students with need: Out of 1,535 full-time freshmen who applied for aid, 1,080 were judged to have need. Of these, 1,054 received aid, and 57 had their full need met. Average financial aid package met 38% of need; average scholarship/grant was $2,882; average loan was $2,184. For part-time students, average financial aid package was $4,283.

Students without need: 273 full-time freshmen who did not demonstrate need for aid received scholarships/grants; average award was $2,563. No-need awards available for academics, athletics, ROTC.

Scholarships offered: 57 full-time freshmen received athletic scholarships; average amount $6,493.

Cumulative student debt: 64% of graduating class had student loans; average debt was $19,112.

FINANCIAL AID PROCEDURES

Forms required: FAFSA, institutional form.

Dates and Deadlines: Priority date 3/31; closing date 5/31. Applicants notified on a rolling basis starting 5/1; must reply within 4 week(s) of notification.

CONTACT

Jack Parker, Vice President for Finance & Operations
Box 2418, Huntsville, TX 77341-2418
(936) 294-1774

San Antonio College

San Antonio, Texas
www.accd.edu/sac   Federal Code: 009163

2-year public community college in very large city.

Enrollment: 21,479 undergrads.

Selectivity: Open admission; but selective for some programs.

BASIC COSTS (2007-2008)

Tuition and fees: $1,576; out-of-district residents $2,836; out-of-state residents $5,356.

Per-credit charge: $42; out-of-district residents $84; out-of-state residents $168.

FINANCIAL AID PICTURE

Students with need: Need-based aid available for full-time and part-time students. Work study available nights, weekends, and for part-time students.

Students without need: This college awards aid only to students with need.

Additional info: Leveraging Educational Assistance Partnership (LEAP), public student incentive grant, towards excellence access and success grants (Texas and Texas II grants) available.

FINANCIAL AID PROCEDURES

Forms required: FAFSA.

Dates and Deadlines: Priority date 3/1; no closing date. Applicants notified by 7/1.

CONTACT

Tom Campos, Director of Student Financial Services
1300 San Pedro Avenue, San Antonio, TX 78212-4299
(210) 733-2150

San Jacinto College

Pasadena, Texas
www.sanjac.edu

2-year public community and technical college in very large city.

Enrollment: 23,805 undergrads, 60% part-time. 3,290 full-time freshmen.

Selectivity: Open admission; but selective for some programs.

BASIC COSTS (2008-2009)

Tuition and fees: $1,250; out-of-district residents $2,000; out-of-state residents $3,500.

Per-credit charge: $33; out-of-district residents $58; out-of-state residents $108.

FINANCIAL AID PICTURE (2006-2007)

Students with need: 68% of average financial aid package awarded as scholarships/grants, 32% awarded as loans/jobs. Need-based aid available for part-time students. Work study available nights, weekends, and for part-time students.

Students without need: This college awards aid only to students with need.

FINANCIAL AID PROCEDURES

Forms required: FAFSA, institutional form.

Dates and Deadlines: Priority date 7/1; no closing date. Applicants notified on a rolling basis starting 4/1; must reply within 4 week(s) of notification.

Transfers: Applicants notified on a rolling basis starting 4/1; must reply within 4 week(s) of notification.

CONTACT

Robert Merino, Director of Financial Aid
8060 Spencer Highway, Pasadena, TX 77505-5999
(281) 998-6150

Schreiner University

Kerrville, Texas
www.schreiner.edu   Federal Code: 003610

4-year private liberal arts college in large town, affiliated with Presbyterian Church (USA).

Enrollment: 926 undergrads, 5% part-time. 264 full-time freshmen.

Selectivity: Admits 50 to 75% of applicants.

BASIC COSTS (2007-2008)

Tuition and fees: $16,908.

Per-credit charge: $700.

Room and board: $8,822.

FINANCIAL AID PICTURE (2007-2008)

Students with need: Out of 231 full-time freshmen who applied for aid, 190 were judged to have need. Of these, 190 received aid, and 35 had their full need met. Average financial aid package met 73% of need; average scholarship/grant was $10,965; average loan was $2,980. For part-time students, average financial aid package was $7,954.

Students without need: 74 full-time freshmen who did not demonstrate need for aid received scholarships/grants; average award was $12,211. No-need awards available for academics, art, job skills, leadership, music/drama, religious affiliation.

Scholarships offered: Awards for students with exceptional academic achievement and leadership abilities; partial and full tuition; 3.5 GPA and 1100 SAT (exclusive of Writing) or 24 ACT; 66 awarded after participation in the Schreiner Scholars program.

Cumulative student debt: 81% of graduating class had student loans; average debt was $19,528.

FINANCIAL AID PROCEDURES

Forms required: FAFSA.

Dates and Deadlines: Priority date 4/1; no closing date. Applicants notified on a rolling basis starting 2/20; must reply within 2 week(s) of notification.

Transfers: Priority date 4/15; no deadline.

CONTACT

Toni Bryant, Director of Financial Aid
2100 Memorial Boulevard, Kerrville, TX 78028-5697
(800) 343-4919

South Plains College

Levelland, Texas
www.southplainscollege.edu   Federal Code: 003611

2-year public community and junior college in large town.

Enrollment: 9,197 undergrads, 56% part-time. 1,507 full-time freshmen.

Selectivity: Open admission; but selective for some programs.

BASIC COSTS (2008-2009)

Tuition and fees: $1,892; out-of-district residents $2,552; out-of-state residents $3,032.

Room and board: $3,200.

FINANCIAL AID PICTURE

Students with need: Need-based aid available for full-time and part-time students.

Students without need: No-need awards available for academics, athletics.

FINANCIAL AID PROCEDURES

Forms required: FAFSA.

Dates and Deadlines: Priority date 6/1; no closing date. Applicants notified on a rolling basis starting 6/30; must reply within 2 week(s) of notification.

CONTACT

Jim Ann Batenhorst, Director of Financial Aid
1401 South College Avenue, Levelland, TX 79336
(806) 894-9611

South Texas College
McAllen, Texas
www.southtexascollege.edu   Federal Code: 031034

2-year public community and technical college in small city.

Enrollment: 19,973 undergrads.

Selectivity: Open admission; but selective for some programs.

BASIC COSTS (2007-2008)

Tuition and fees: $2,207; out-of-district residents $2,720; out-of-state residents $6,497.

FINANCIAL AID PICTURE (2007-2008)

Students with need: 99% of average financial aid package awarded as scholarships/grants, 1% awarded as loans/jobs. Need-based aid available for part-time students. Work study available nights, weekends, and for part-time students.

Students without need: This college awards aid only to students with need.

FINANCIAL AID PROCEDURES

Forms required: FAFSA.

Dates and Deadlines: Priority date 3/1; no closing date. Applicants notified on a rolling basis starting 4/15.

CONTACT

Miguel Carranza, Director
3201 West Pecan Boulevard, McAllen, TX 78502
(956) 872-8375

Southern Methodist University
Dallas, Texas   Federal Code: 003613
www.smu.edu   CSS Code: 6660

4-year private university in large town, affiliated with United Methodist Church.

Enrollment: 6,081 undergrads, 4% part-time. 1,309 full-time freshmen.

Selectivity: Admits 50 to 75% of applicants. GED not accepted.

BASIC COSTS (2008-2009)

Tuition and fees: $33,170.

Per-credit charge: $1,230.

Room and board: $11,875.

FINANCIAL AID PICTURE (2007-2008)

Students with need: Out of 584 full-time freshmen who applied for aid, 408 were judged to have need. Of these, 408 received aid, and 180 had their full need met. Average financial aid package met 90% of need; average scholarship/grant was $16,282; average loan was $2,609. For part-time students, average financial aid package was $11,770.

Students without need: 580 full-time freshmen who did not demonstrate need for aid received scholarships/grants; average award was $11,140. No-need awards available for academics, art, athletics, leadership, music/drama, religious affiliation, ROTC, state/district residency.

Scholarships offered: 63 full-time freshmen received athletic scholarships; average amount $37,404.

Cumulative student debt: 33% of graduating class had student loans; average debt was $16,756.

FINANCIAL AID PROCEDURES

Forms required: FAFSA, CSS PROFILE.

Dates and Deadlines: Priority date 2/15; no closing date. Applicants notified on a rolling basis starting 3/15.

Transfers: Priority date 4/1. Merit scholarships available for community college and senior institution honor transfers. Students entering without scholarship aid will receive need-based aid up to cost of tuition.

CONTACT

Marc Peterson, Executive Director of Enrollment Services
PO Box 750181, Dallas, TX 75275-0181
(214) 768-2068

Southwest Institute of Technology
Austin, Texas
www.switaustin.com   Federal Code: 020936

2-year for-profit technical college in large city.

Enrollment: 35 undergrads.

Selectivity: Open admission.

BASIC COSTS (2008-2009)

Tuition and fees: $19,419.

Per-credit charge: $325.

FINANCIAL AID PICTURE (2007-2008)

Students with need: 55% of average financial aid package awarded as scholarships/grants, 45% awarded as loans/jobs. Work study available nights, weekends, and for part-time students.

Students without need: This college awards aid only to students with need.

FINANCIAL AID PROCEDURES

Forms required: FAFSA, institutional form.

Dates and Deadlines: No deadline.

CONTACT

Lisa Ruszczyk, Corporate Financial Aid Director
5424 Highway 290 West, Suite 200, Austin, TX 78735
(512) 892-2640

Southwestern Adventist University
Keene, Texas
www.swau.edu   Federal Code: 003619

4-year private university and liberal arts college in small town, affiliated with Seventh-day Adventists.

Enrollment: 820 undergrads, 15% part-time. 208 full-time freshmen.

Selectivity: Admits less than 50% of applicants.

BASIC COSTS (2008-2009)

Tuition and fees: $15,236.

Per-credit charge: $619.

Room and board: $6,742.

FINANCIAL AID PICTURE

Students with need: Need-based aid available for full-time and part-time students.

Students without need: No-need awards available for academics, leadership, music/drama.

FINANCIAL AID PROCEDURES

Forms required: FAFSA, institutional form.

Dates and Deadlines: Priority date 3/15; no closing date. Applicants notified on a rolling basis starting 4/15.

CONTACT

Patricia Norwood, Assistant Vice President for Financial Administration, Student Finance
Box 567, Keene, TX 76059
(817) 202-6262

Southwestern Assemblies of God University

Waxahachie, Texas
www.sagu.edu   Federal Code: 003616

4-year private university and Bible college in large town, affiliated with Assemblies of God.

Enrollment: 1,543 undergrads, 17% part-time. 197 full-time freshmen.

Selectivity: Admits over 75% of applicants.

BASIC COSTS (2007-2008)

Tuition and fees: $11,530.

Per-credit charge: $355.

Room and board: $5,282.

FINANCIAL AID PICTURE (2006-2007)

Students with need: Out of 168 full-time freshmen who applied for aid, 143 were judged to have need. Of these, 143 received aid, and 20 had their full need met. Average financial aid package met 68% of need; average scholarship/grant was $6,938; average loan was $2,973. For part-time students, average financial aid package was $8,386.

Students without need: 43 full-time freshmen who did not demonstrate need for aid received scholarships/grants; average award was $7,010.

Scholarships offered: 5 full-time freshmen received athletic scholarships; average amount $3,220.

Cumulative student debt: 86% of graduating class had student loans; average debt was $19,990.

FINANCIAL AID PROCEDURES

Forms required: FAFSA.

Dates and Deadlines: Priority date 3/1; closing date 6/1. Applicants notified on a rolling basis starting 6/1; must reply within 2 week(s) of notification.

CONTACT

Trevor Summers, Director of Financial Aid
1200 Sycamore Street, Waxahachie, TX 75165
(972) 825-4730

Southwestern University

Georgetown, Texas
www.southwestern.edu   Federal Code: 003620

4-year private liberal arts college in large town, affiliated with United Methodist Church.

Enrollment: 1,283 undergrads, 2% part-time. 371 full-time freshmen.

Selectivity: Admits 50 to 75% of applicants.

BASIC COSTS (2008-2009)

Tuition and fees: $27,940.

Per-credit charge: $1,165.

Room and board: $8,380.

FINANCIAL AID PICTURE (2007-2008)

Students with need: Out of 264 full-time freshmen who applied for aid, 197 were judged to have need. Of these, 197 received aid, and 112 had their full need met. Average financial aid package met 88% of need; average scholarship/grant was $17,465; average loan was $4,617. For part-time students, average financial aid package was $10,725.

Students without need: 120 full-time freshmen who did not demonstrate need for aid received scholarships/grants; average award was $10,510. No-need awards available for academics, art, minority status, music/drama, religious affiliation.

Scholarships offered: Academic Merit Scholarships: $2,000 to $19,000 per year. Brown Scholarships: full tuition, room and board. National Merit Finalist Awards: $2,000 per year. Fine Arts Scholarships: $3,500 to $10,000 per year; for students majoring in art, music or theater; based on talent, auditions or portfolio review. Music Performance Awards: up to $2,500; based on talent and awarded to non-fine arts majors who wish to participate in university ensemble. Dixon Scholarship: $5,000 per year or full tuition; awarded to high-achieving African-American, Hispanic, and Native American students. Beneficiary Grants: $6,000 per year; awarded to dependents of United Methodist clergy. Preministerial Scholarships: $3,000 per year; to students interested in full-time ministry careers.

Cumulative student debt: 57% of graduating class had student loans; average debt was $24,057.

FINANCIAL AID PROCEDURES

Forms required: FAFSA.

Dates and Deadlines: Closing date 3/1. Applicants notified on a rolling basis starting 3/1; must reply by 5/1 or within 2 week(s) of notification.

Transfers: Priority date 3/1; closing date 5/15.

CONTACT

James Gaeta, Director of Financial Aid
1001 East University Avenue, Georgetown, TX 78626
(512) 863-1259

Stephen F. Austin State University

Nacogdoches, Texas
www.sfasu.edu   Federal Code: 003624

4-year public university in large town.

Enrollment: 10,106 undergrads, 13% part-time. 2,080 full-time freshmen.

Selectivity: Admits 50 to 75% of applicants.

BASIC COSTS (2007-2008)

Tuition and fees: $6,162; out-of-state residents $14,502.

Per-credit charge: $147; out-of-state residents $425.

Room and board: $6,885.

FINANCIAL AID PICTURE (2006-2007)

Students with need: Out of 1,623 full-time freshmen who applied for aid, 1,175 were judged to have need. Of these, 1,155 received aid, and 647 had their full need met. Average financial aid package met 98% of need; average scholarship/grant was $4,212; average loan was $2,323. For part-time students, average financial aid package was $7,810.

Students without need: 180 full-time freshmen who did not demonstrate need for aid received scholarships/grants; average award was $3,727. No-need awards available for academics, alumni affiliation, athletics, leadership, music/drama, state/district residency.

Scholarships offered: *Merit:* Academic Excellence Scholarship Program: $2,000 per year; rank in top 10% of high school class or top quartile class with 1100 SAT (exclusive of Writing) or 24 ACT; renewable with 3.5 GPA. Dugas Full Support Scholarships: $4,000 per semester; active member of School of Honors; 3 awarded. University Scholars Program awards: $1,000 per semester; minimum 1220 SAT, 27 ACT, 3.0 GPA maintenance; up to 11 awarded. Student Foundation Association Leadership Scholarship: amounts vary; demonstrated leadership capabilities and academic achievement throughout high school career; 1 awarded. **Athletic:** 80 full-time freshmen received athletic scholarships; average amount $7,062.

Cumulative student debt: 67% of graduating class had student loans; average debt was $19,772.

FINANCIAL AID PROCEDURES
Forms required: FAFSA, institutional form.
Dates and Deadlines: Priority date 4/1; no closing date. Applicants notified on a rolling basis starting 4/10; must reply within 3 week(s) of notification.

CONTACT
Mike O'Rear, Director of Financial Aid
Box 13051, SFA Station, Nacogdoches, TX 75962-3051
(936) 468-2403

Sul Ross State University
Alpine, Texas
www.sulross.edu   Federal Code: 003625

4-year public university in small town.
Enrollment: 1,935 undergrads.
Selectivity: Admits over 75% of applicants.

BASIC COSTS (2008-2009)
Tuition and fees: $5,058; out-of-state residents $13,398.
Per-credit charge: $116; out-of-state residents $394.
Room and board: $6,190.

FINANCIAL AID PICTURE
Students with need: Need-based aid available for full-time and part-time students.
Students without need: No-need awards available for academics, alumni affiliation, leadership.

FINANCIAL AID PROCEDURES
Forms required: FAFSA, institutional form.
Dates and Deadlines: Priority date 5/1; no closing date. Applicants notified on a rolling basis starting 5/1; must reply within 2 week(s) of notification.

CONTACT
Rowena Gallego, Director Student Financial Assistance
Box C-2, Alpine, TX 79832
(432) 837-8055

Tarleton State University
Stephenville, Texas
www.tarleton.edu   Federal Code: 003631

4-year public university in large town.
Enrollment: 7,781 undergrads, 23% part-time. 1,190 full-time freshmen.
Selectivity: Admits 50 to 75% of applicants.

BASIC COSTS (2007-2008)
Tuition and fees: $4,864; out-of-state residents $13,204.
Per-credit charge: $120; out-of-state residents $398.
Room and board: $6,788.
Additional info: Distance learning fee additional $40 per credit hour.

FINANCIAL AID PICTURE (2006-2007)
Students with need: Out of 1,026 full-time freshmen who applied for aid, 942 were judged to have need. Of these, 680 received aid, and 600 had their full need met. Average financial aid package met 73% of need; average scholarship/grant was $4,158; average loan was $2,494. For part-time students, average financial aid package was $6,791.
Students without need: 352 full-time freshmen who did not demonstrate need for aid received scholarships/grants; average award was $4,844. No-

need awards available for academics, alumni affiliation, art, athletics, leadership, music/drama, ROTC.

Scholarships offered: 57 full-time freshmen received athletic scholarships; average amount $3,404.

Cumulative student debt: 55% of graduating class had student loans; average debt was $16,645.

FINANCIAL AID PROCEDURES
Forms required: FAFSA.
Dates and Deadlines: Priority date 4/1; closing date 10/15. Applicants notified on a rolling basis starting 2/1; must reply within 2 week(s) of notification.
Transfers: No deadline.

CONTACT
Betty Murray, Director, Student Financial Aid
Box T-0030, Stephenville, TX 76402
(254) 968-9070

Tarrant County College
Fort Worth, Texas
www.tccd.edu   Federal Code: 003626

2-year public community and liberal arts college in very large city.
Enrollment: 37,951 undergrads.
Selectivity: Open admission; but selective for some programs.

BASIC COSTS (2007-2008)
Tuition and fees: $1,500; out-of-district residents $1,890; out-of-state residents $4,500.
Per-credit charge: $50; out-of-district residents $63; out-of-state residents $150.

FINANCIAL AID PICTURE (2006-2007)
Students with need: 74% of average financial aid package awarded as scholarships/grants, 26% awarded as loans/jobs. Need-based aid available for part-time students.
Students without need: No-need awards available for academics.

FINANCIAL AID PROCEDURES
Forms required: FAFSA, institutional form.
Dates and Deadlines: Priority date 5/1; no closing date. Applicants notified on a rolling basis starting 5/1; must reply within 2 week(s) of notification.

CONTACT
David Ximenez, Director of Financial Aid
1500 Houston Street, Fort Worth, TX 76102-6599
(817) 515-5353

Temple College
Temple, Texas
www.templejc.edu   Federal Code: 003627

2-year public community college in small city.
Enrollment: 4,624 undergrads, 61% part-time. 495 full-time freshmen.
Selectivity: Open admission; but selective for some programs.

BASIC COSTS (2007-2008)
Tuition and fees: $2,100; out-of-district residents $3,300; out-of-state residents $5,280.
Per-credit charge: $70; out-of-district residents $110; out-of-state residents $176.

FINANCIAL AID PICTURE
Students with need: Need-based aid available for full-time and part-time students. Work study available nights.
Students without need: This college awards aid only to students with need.

FINANCIAL AID PROCEDURES

Forms required: FAFSA.

Dates and Deadlines: Priority date 6/1; no closing date. Applicants notified on a rolling basis starting 5/1; must reply within 4 week(s) of notification.

CONTACT

Fred Pena, Director of Financial Aid

2600 South First Street, Temple, TX 76504-7435

(254) 298-8321

Texarkana College

Texarkana, Texas

www.texarkanacollege.edu   Federal Code: 003628

2-year public community college in small city.

Enrollment: 4,299 undergrads.

Selectivity: Open admission.

BASIC COSTS (2008-2009)

Tuition and fees: $1,110; out-of-district residents $1,770; out-of-state residents $2,270.

Per-credit charge: $34; out-of-district residents $56; out-of-state residents $73.

Additional info: Arkansas and Oklahoma residents pay out-of-district rates.

FINANCIAL AID PICTURE

Students with need: Need-based aid available for full-time and part-time students. Work study available nights, weekends, and for part-time students.

Students without need: No-need awards available for academics, athletics.

FINANCIAL AID PROCEDURES

Forms required: FAFSA, institutional form.

Dates and Deadlines: Priority date 6/1; no closing date. Applicants notified on a rolling basis starting 3/1.

CONTACT

Robin Thomas, Director of Financial Aid

2500 North Robison Road, Texarkana, TX 75599

(903) 832-5565 ext. 3214

Texas A&M International University

Laredo, Texas

www.tamiu.edu   Federal Code: 009651

4-year public university in small city.

Enrollment: 4,065 undergrads, 34% part-time. 606 full-time freshmen.

Selectivity: Admits 50 to 75% of applicants.

BASIC COSTS (2007-2008)

Tuition and fees: $5,038; out-of-state residents $13,378.

Per-credit charge: $118; out-of-state residents $396.

Room and board: $6,630.

FINANCIAL AID PICTURE

Students with need: Need-based aid available for full-time and part-time students. Work study available nights.

Students without need: No-need awards available for academics.

FINANCIAL AID PROCEDURES

Forms required: FAFSA, institutional form.

Dates and Deadlines: Priority date 3/15; no closing date. Applicants notified on a rolling basis starting 7/15; must reply within 2 week(s) of notification.

CONTACT

Laura Elizondo, Director of Financial Aid

5201 University Boulevard, Laredo, TX 78041-1900

(956) 326-2225

Texas A&M University

College Station, Texas

www.tamu.edu   Federal Code: 003632

4-year public university in small city.

Enrollment: 37,341 undergrads, 9% part-time. 7,575 full-time freshmen.

Selectivity: Admits over 75% of applicants.

BASIC COSTS (2007-2008)

Tuition and fees: $7,335; out-of-state residents $15,675.

Per-credit charge: $156; out-of-state residents $434.

Room and board: $7,660.

FINANCIAL AID PICTURE (2007-2008)

Students with need: Out of 4,781 full-time freshmen who applied for aid, 2,841 were judged to have need. Of these, 2,772 received aid, and 1,543 had their full need met. Average financial aid package met 89.1% of need; average scholarship/grant was $9,752; average loan was $4,014. For part-time students, average financial aid package was $8,698.

Students without need: 989 full-time freshmen who did not demonstrate need for aid received scholarships/grants; average award was $4,004. No-need awards available for academics, alumni affiliation, art, athletics, job skills, leadership, music/drama, ROTC, state/district residency.

Scholarships offered: 55 full-time freshmen received athletic scholarships; average amount $7,197.

Cumulative student debt: 54% of graduating class had student loans; average debt was $19,940.

Additional info: Short-term loans available. Out-of-state students awarded academic scholarships of $1,000 or more are eligible for waiver of out-of-state tuition.

FINANCIAL AID PROCEDURES

Forms required: FAFSA, institutional form.

Dates and Deadlines: Priority date 3/31; no closing date. Applicants notified on a rolling basis starting 4/1; must reply within 4 week(s) of notification.

Transfers: Must provide previous financial aid transcript.

CONTACT

Joseph Pettibon, Assistant Provost - Student Financial Aid

PO Box 30014, College Station, TX 77842-3014

(979) 845-3236

Texas A&M University-Baylor College of Dentistry

Dallas, Texas

www.bcd.tamhsc.edu   Federal Code: 004948

Upper-division public health science college in very large city.

Enrollment: 60 undergrads.

BASIC COSTS (2007-2008)

Tuition and fees: $5,401; out-of-state residents $15,131.

Per-credit charge: $108; out-of-state residents $386.

FINANCIAL AID PICTURE (2006-2007)

Students with need: Average financial aid package for all full-time undergraduates was $10,016. 18% awarded as scholarships/grants, 82% awarded as loans/jobs. Need-based aid available for part-time students.

Students without need: No-need awards available for academics.

FINANCIAL AID PROCEDURES

Forms required: FAFSA, institutional form.

Dates and Deadlines: Priority date 3/15; no closing date. Applicants notified on a rolling basis starting 6/1; must reply within 2 week(s) of notification.

CONTACT

Kay Egbert, Director of Student Aid
PO Box 660677, Dallas, TX 75266-0677

Texas A&M University-Commerce

Commerce, Texas
www.tamu-commerce.edu   Federal Code: 003565

4-year public university in small town.
Enrollment: 5,166 undergrads, 60% part-time. 364 full-time freshmen.
Selectivity: Admits 50 to 75% of applicants.

BASIC COSTS (2007-2008)

Tuition and fees: $5,190; out-of-state residents $13,440.
Room and board: $6,340.

FINANCIAL AID PICTURE

Students with need: Need-based aid available for full-time and part-time students.
Students without need: No-need awards available for academics, art, athletics, leadership, music/drama.
Additional info: Work-study also available for full-time students.

FINANCIAL AID PROCEDURES

Forms required: FAFSA.
Dates and Deadlines: Priority date 4/1; no closing date. Applicants notified on a rolling basis starting 4/1; must reply within 2 week(s) of notification.

CONTACT

Dolly Lasater, Director of Financial Aid
Box 3011, Commerce, TX 75429-3011
(903) 886-5091

Texas A&M University-Galveston

Galveston, Texas
www.tamug.edu   Federal Code: 003632

4-year public university and branch campus college in small city.
Enrollment: 1,565 undergrads, 7% part-time. 413 full-time freshmen.
Selectivity: Admits over 75% of applicants.

BASIC COSTS (2007-2008)

Tuition and fees: $6,055; out-of-state residents $14,395.
Per-credit charge: $156; out-of-state residents $434.
Room and board: $6,105.

FINANCIAL AID PICTURE (2006-2007)

Students with need: Out of 245 full-time freshmen who applied for aid, 202 were judged to have need. Of these, 191 received aid, and 46 had their full need met. Average financial aid package met 15% of need; average scholarship/grant was $4,190; average loan was $2,550. For part-time students, average financial aid package was $8,094.
Students without need: 7 full-time freshmen who did not demonstrate need for aid received scholarships/grants; average award was $7,824. No-need awards available for academics, state/district residency.
Cumulative student debt: 86% of graduating class had student loans; average debt was $11,055.

FINANCIAL AID PROCEDURES

Forms required: FAFSA.
Dates and Deadlines: Priority date 4/1; no closing date. Applicants notified on a rolling basis starting 3/15; must reply within 3 week(s) of notification.

CONTACT

Dennis Carlton, Director of Financial Aid
PO Box 1675, Galveston, TX 77553-1675
(409) 740-4500

Texas A&M University-Kingsville

Kingsville, Texas
www.tamuk.edu   Federal Code: 003639

4-year public university in large town.
Enrollment: 5,009 undergrads.
Selectivity: Open admission; but selective for some programs.

BASIC COSTS (2007-2008)

Tuition and fees: $4,878; out-of-state residents $13,218.
Room and board: $4,654.

FINANCIAL AID PICTURE

Students with need: Need-based aid available for full-time students.
Students without need: No-need awards available for academics, leadership.

FINANCIAL AID PROCEDURES

Forms required: FAFSA.
Dates and Deadlines: Applicants notified on a rolling basis.

CONTACT

Filipe Leal, Director of Financial Aid Programs
MSC 105, Kingsville, TX 78363-8201
(361) 593-3911

Texas A&M University-Texarkana

Texarkana, Texas
www.tamut.edu   Federal Code: 031703

Upper-division public university in small city.
Enrollment: 1,003 undergrads, 57% part-time.

BASIC COSTS (2007-2008)

Tuition and fees: $3,721; out-of-state residents $12,061.

FINANCIAL AID PICTURE

Students with need: Need-based aid available for full-time and part-time students. Work study available nights, weekends, and for part-time students.
Students without need: No-need awards available for academics, leadership, state/district residency.

FINANCIAL AID PROCEDURES

Dates and Deadlines: Priority date 5/1; closing date 11/1.
Transfers: Applicants notified on a rolling basis; must reply within 10 week(s) of notification. Must have completed minimum of 54 semester hours of transferable college credit to apply for financial aid. Notified applicants must reply within 45 days from date of award letter. Exceptions made on individual basis. April 1 financial aid deadline for scholarships.

CONTACT

Marilyn Raney, Director of Financial Aid
2600 North Robinson Road, Texarkana, TX 75505-5518
(903) 233-3060

Texas Christian University

Fort Worth, Texas
www.tcu.edu   Federal Code: 003636

4-year private university in large city, affiliated with Christian Church (Disciples of Christ).
Enrollment: 7,264 undergrads, 4% part-time. 1,644 full-time freshmen.
Selectivity: Admits less than 50% of applicants. GED not accepted.

BASIC COSTS (2008-2009)

Tuition and fees: $26,948.

Per-credit charge: $1,135.

Room and board: $9,600.

Additional info: Tuition/fee waivers available for adults, minority students.

FINANCIAL AID PICTURE (2007-2008)

Students with need: Out of 799 full-time freshmen who applied for aid, 611 were judged to have need. Of these, 607 received aid, and 445 had their full need met. Average financial aid package met 78% of need; average scholarship/grant was $12,529; average loan was $8,667. For part-time students, average financial aid package was $15,690.

Students without need: 455 full-time freshmen who did not demonstrate need for aid received scholarships/grants; average award was $8,891. No-need awards available for academics, alumni affiliation, art, leadership, minority status, music/drama, religious affiliation, ROTC, state/district residency.

Scholarships offered: 72 full-time freshmen received athletic scholarships; average amount $18,638.

Cumulative student debt: 50% of graduating class had student loans; average debt was $23,651.

FINANCIAL AID PROCEDURES

Forms required: FAFSA.

Dates and Deadlines: Closing date 5/1. Applicants notified on a rolling basis starting 3/15; must reply by 5/1 or within 2 week(s) of notification.

Transfers: Priority date 6/1. Must reply by 5/1.

CONTACT

Michael Scott, Director of Scholarships and Student Financial Aid

TCU Box 297013, Fort Worth, TX 76129

(817) 257-7858

Texas College

Tyler, Texas

www.texascollege.edu   Federal Code: 003638

4-year private liberal arts college in small city, affiliated with Christian Methodist Episcopal Church.

Enrollment: 741 undergrads, 3% part-time. 193 full-time freshmen.

Selectivity: Open admission.

BASIC COSTS (2007-2008)

Tuition and fees: $8,746.

Per-credit charge: $330.

Room and board: $5,600.

FINANCIAL AID PICTURE (2006-2007)

Students with need: Out of 185 full-time freshmen who applied for aid, 181 were judged to have need. Of these, 177 received aid, and 11 had their full need met. Average financial aid package met 61% of need; average scholarship/grant was $6,268; average loan was $2,053. For part-time students, average financial aid package was $7,025.

Students without need: 32 full-time freshmen who did not demonstrate need for aid received scholarships/grants; average award was $2,284.

Scholarships offered: 22 full-time freshmen received athletic scholarships; average amount $3,313.

Cumulative student debt: 100% of graduating class had student loans; average debt was $12,939.

FINANCIAL AID PROCEDURES

Forms required: FAFSA, institutional form.

Dates and Deadlines: Priority date 6/1; no closing date. Applicants notified on a rolling basis starting 4/15; must reply within 2 week(s) of notification.

Transfers: Applicants notified on a rolling basis starting 4/15; must reply within 2 week(s) of notification.

CONTACT

Cecelia Jones, Director of Financial Aid

2404 North Grand Avenue, Tyler, TX 75712-4500

(903) 593-8311 ext. 2278

Texas Lutheran University

Seguin, Texas

www.tlu.edu   Federal Code: 003641

4-year private university and liberal arts college in large town, affiliated with Evangelical Lutheran Church in America.

Enrollment: 1,334 undergrads, 2% part-time. 387 full-time freshmen.

Selectivity: Admits 50 to 75% of applicants.

BASIC COSTS (2008-2009)

Tuition and fees: $20,970.

Per-credit charge: $700.

Room and board: $6,600.

FINANCIAL AID PICTURE (2006-2007)

Students with need: Out of 378 full-time freshmen who applied for aid, 281 were judged to have need. Of these, 281 received aid, and 115 had their full need met. Average financial aid package met 41% of need; average scholarship/grant was $11,431; average loan was $3,174. For part-time students, average financial aid package was $8,389.

Students without need: 96 full-time freshmen who did not demonstrate need for aid received scholarships/grants; average award was $7,438. No-need awards available for academics, alumni affiliation, art, job skills, leadership, music/drama, religious affiliation.

Scholarships offered: Pacesetter Award for College Excellence: up to $14,000 per year; 3.5 GPA and SAT/ACT 1250/28 or rank in top 10% of class with minimum 1100/24 SAT/ACT score, must be accepted by specific date and be invited to participate in on-campus Pacesetter event. Academic Excellence Award: up to $7,000 per year; minimum articulated high school GPA of 3.25 and either SAT/ACT 1150/25 or rank in top 15% of class; awarded automatically upon acceptance to TLU. All SAT scores exclusive of Writing.

Cumulative student debt: 72% of graduating class had student loans; average debt was $26,462.

FINANCIAL AID PROCEDURES

Forms required: FAFSA.

Dates and Deadlines: Priority date 4/1; no closing date. Applicants notified on a rolling basis starting 3/1; must reply within 2 week(s) of notification.

Transfers: No deadline. Applicants notified on a rolling basis; must reply within 2 week(s) of notification.

CONTACT

Cathleen Wright, Director Financial Aid

1000 West Court Street, Seguin, TX 78155-5999

(830) 372-8075

Texas Southern University

Houston, Texas

www.tsu.edu   Federal Code: 003642

4-year public university in very large city.

Enrollment: 7,572 undergrads, 20% part-time. 1,139 full-time freshmen.

Selectivity: Open admission; but selective for some programs.

BASIC COSTS (2007-2008)

Tuition and fees: $5,878; out-of-state residents $14,128.

Per-credit charge: $100; out-of-state residents $325.

Room and board: $6,664.

Additional info: Tuition/fee waivers available for minority students.

FINANCIAL AID PICTURE

Students with need: Need-based aid available for full-time and part-time students. Work study available nights, weekends, and for part-time students.
Students without need: This college awards aid only to students with need.

FINANCIAL AID PROCEDURES

Forms required: FAFSA.
Dates and Deadlines: Priority date 5/1; no closing date. Applicants notified on a rolling basis starting 6/1.
Transfers: Priority date 4/1; closing date 8/30.

CONTACT

Albert Tezeno, Director of Financial Aid
3100 Cleburne Street, Houston, TX 77004
(713) 313-7802

Texas State Technical College: Harlingen

Harlingen, Texas
www.harlingen.tstc.edu   Federal Code: 009225

2-year public technical college in small city.
Enrollment: 1,703 undergrads.
Selectivity: Open admission; but selective for some programs.

BASIC COSTS (2007-2008)

Tuition and fees: $2,690; out-of-state residents $6,200.
Per-credit charge: $65; out-of-state residents $182.
Room and board: $3,650.

FINANCIAL AID PICTURE (2007-2008)

Students with need: 72% of average financial aid package awarded as scholarships/grants, 28% awarded as loans/jobs. Need-based aid available for part-time students.

FINANCIAL AID PROCEDURES

Forms required: FAFSA, institutional form.
Dates and Deadlines: Closing date 4/30. Applicants notified on a rolling basis starting 6/30; must reply within 2 week(s) of notification.

CONTACT

Robert Gomez, Vice President of Financial Services
1902 North Loop 499, Harlingen, TX 78550-3697
(956) 364-4337

Texas State Technical College: Sweetwater

Sweetwater, Texas
www.westtexas.tstc.edu   Federal Code: 009932

2-year public technical college in large town.
Enrollment: 1,498 undergrads, 84% part-time. 99 full-time freshmen.
Selectivity: Open admission; but selective for some programs.

BASIC COSTS (2007-2008)

Tuition and fees: $2,710; out-of-state residents $6,220.
Per-credit charge: $65; out-of-state residents $182.
Room and board: $3,850.

FINANCIAL AID PICTURE (2006-2007)

Students with need: 20% of average financial aid package awarded as scholarships/grants, 80% awarded as loans/jobs. Need-based aid available for part-time students. Work study available nights, weekends, and for part-time students.
Students without need: No-need awards available for academics, leadership.

FINANCIAL AID PROCEDURES

Forms required: FAFSA, institutional form.
Dates and Deadlines: Priority date 5/1; no closing date. Applicants notified on a rolling basis starting 7/1.
Transfers: No deadline. Applicants notified on a rolling basis starting 7/1; must reply by 8/20.

CONTACT

Kevin Shipp, Associate Vice President of Student Accounting
300 Homer K Taylor Drive, Sweetwater, TX 79556
(325) 235-7378

Texas State Technical College: Waco

Waco, Texas
www.waco.tstc.edu   Federal Code: 003634

2-year public technical college in small city.
Enrollment: 4,210 undergrads.
Selectivity: Open admission.

BASIC COSTS (2007-2008)

Tuition and fees: $2,714; out-of-state residents $6,224.
Per-credit charge: $85; out-of-state residents $182.
Room and board: $4,050.

FINANCIAL AID PICTURE (2006-2007)

Students with need: 54% of average financial aid package awarded as scholarships/grants, 46% awarded as loans/jobs. Need-based aid available for part-time students.
Students without need: This college awards aid only to students with need.

FINANCIAL AID PROCEDURES

Forms required: FAFSA.
Dates and Deadlines: Priority date 6/1; no closing date. Applicants notified on a rolling basis starting 5/15.
Transfers: No deadline. Applicants notified on a rolling basis.

CONTACT

Jackie Adler, Director, Financial Aid
3801 Campus Drive, Waco, TX 76705
(254) 867-4814

Texas State University: San Marcos

San Marcos, Texas
www.txstate.edu   Federal Code: 003615

4-year public university in large town.
Enrollment: 24,038 undergrads, 18% part-time. 3,007 full-time freshmen.
Selectivity: Admits 50 to 75% of applicants.

BASIC COSTS (2008-2009)

Tuition and fees: $6,994; out-of-state residents $15,424.
Per-credit charge: $170; out-of-state residents $451.
Room and board: $6,012.

FINANCIAL AID PICTURE (2007-2008)

Students with need: Out of 1,991 full-time freshmen who applied for aid, 1,353 were judged to have need. Of these, 1,294 received aid, and 153 had their full need met. Average financial aid package met 66% of need; average scholarship/grant was $4,534; average loan was $3,085. For part-time students, average financial aid package was $8,522.
Students without need: 173 full-time freshmen who did not demonstrate need for aid received scholarships/grants; average award was $3,004. No-need awards available for academics, art, athletics, leadership, music/drama, ROTC, state/district residency.

Scholarships offered: *Merit:* Roy and Joan C. Mitte Foundation Scholarships: $5,050; 25 awarded; based on National Merit Competition finalist/semi-finalist status or valedictorian/salutatorian of high school class, or in top 5% of graduating class. President's Endowed Scholarships: $1,000; 9 awarded; based on minimum ACT score of 24 or SAT score of 1000 (exclusive of Writing), rank in upper 25% of high school class. Freshmen Program Scholarships: $200-$700; 10 awarded; based on ACT/SAT scores, high school grades, high school leadership activities. *Athletic:* 52 full-time freshmen received athletic scholarships; average amount $6,723.

Cumulative student debt: 55% of graduating class had student loans; average debt was $17,104.

FINANCIAL AID PROCEDURES

Forms required: FAFSA.

Dates and Deadlines: Priority date 4/1; no closing date. Applicants notified on a rolling basis starting 5/1; must reply within 3 week(s) of notification.

CONTACT

Mariko Gomez, Director of Financial Aid & Scholarship Office
429 North Guadalupe Street, San Marcos, TX 78666-5709
(512) 245-2315

Texas Tech University

Lubbock, Texas
www.ttu.edu   Federal Code: 003644

4-year public university in small city.

Enrollment: 22,996 undergrads, 8% part-time. 3,862 full-time freshmen.

Selectivity: Admits over 75% of applicants.

BASIC COSTS (2007-2008)

Tuition and fees: $6,783; out-of-state residents $15,123.

Per-credit charge: $144; out-of-state residents $422.

Room and board: $7,460.

Additional info: Students from adjacent counties in New Mexico and Oklahoma pay in-state tuition rates; students from all other counties in New Mexico and Oklahoma pay reduced out-of-state tuition rates.

FINANCIAL AID PICTURE (2006-2007)

Students with need: Out of 2,731 full-time freshmen who applied for aid, 1,462 were judged to have need. Of these, 1,434 received aid, and 115 had their full need met. Average financial aid package met 52% of need; average scholarship/grant was $5,794; average loan was $3,048. For part-time students, average financial aid package was $5,481.

Students without need: 248 full-time freshmen who did not demonstrate need for aid received scholarships/grants; average award was $2,007. No-need awards available for academics, art, athletics, job skills, leadership, music/drama, ROTC.

Scholarships offered: *Merit:* Presidential Plus Scholarship: $12,700 per year for up to 5 years; awarded to National Merit Finalists who select Texas Tech as school of choice. Presidential Endowed Scholarship: $4,000 per year for up to 5 years; top 10% of high school graduating class and SAT 1400 or ACT 31. Honors Endowed Scholarship: $2,500 per year up to 5 years; top 10% of high school graduating class and SAT 1300 or ACT 29. University Scholars Scholarship: $1,500 per year up to 4 years; top 10% of high school graduating class and SAT 1250 or ACT 28. Superior Scholastic Achievement Scholarship: $1,000 per year up to four years; top 10% of high school graduating class and SAT 1200 or ACT 26. All SAT scores exclusive of Writing. *Athletic:* 91 full-time freshmen received athletic scholarships; average amount $9,100.

Cumulative student debt: 58% of graduating class had student loans; average debt was $20,916.

FINANCIAL AID PROCEDURES

Forms required: FAFSA.

Dates and Deadlines: Priority date 4/15; no closing date. Applicants notified on a rolling basis; must reply within 2 week(s) of notification.

CONTACT

Becky Wilson, Director of Financial Aid
Box 45005, Lubbock, TX 79409-5005
(806) 742-3681

Texas Wesleyan University

Fort Worth, Texas
www.txwes.edu   Federal Code: 003645

4-year private university in large city, affiliated with United Methodist Church.

Enrollment: 1,422 undergrads, 23% part-time. 191 full-time freshmen.

Selectivity: Admits 50 to 75% of applicants.

BASIC COSTS (2008-2009)

Tuition and fees: $16,730.

Per-credit charge: $525.

Room and board: $6,100.

FINANCIAL AID PICTURE (2007-2008)

Students with need: Out of 169 full-time freshmen who applied for aid, 147 were judged to have need. Of these, 147 received aid, and 30 had their full need met. Average financial aid package met 59% of need; average scholarship/grant was $9,011; average loan was $2,500. For part-time students, average financial aid package was $6,201.

Students without need: This college awards aid only to students with need.

Scholarships offered: 11 full-time freshmen received athletic scholarships; average amount $8,787.

Cumulative student debt: 63% of graduating class had student loans; average debt was $19,000.

FINANCIAL AID PROCEDURES

Forms required: FAFSA.

Dates and Deadlines: Priority date 3/15; no closing date. Applicants notified on a rolling basis starting 3/15.

CONTACT

Shanna Hollis, Financial Aid Director
1201 Wesleyan Street, Fort Worth, TX 76105-1536
(817) 531-4420

Texas Woman's University

Denton, Texas
www.twu.edu   Federal Code: 003646

4-year public university in small city.

Enrollment: 6,986 undergrads, 28% part-time. 769 full-time freshmen.

Selectivity: Admits over 75% of applicants.

BASIC COSTS (2008-2009)

Tuition and fees: $6,540; out-of-state residents $14,880.

Per-credit charge: $143; out-of-state residents $421.

Room and board: $5,846.

FINANCIAL AID PICTURE

Students with need: Need-based aid available for full-time and part-time students. Work study available nights, weekends, and for part-time students.

Scholarships offered: Chancellor's Endowed Scholarship: full tuition and fees, room and board; based on high school valedictorian status, extracurricular activities, SAT score; 2 awarded. Presidential Scholarship: full tuition and fees; awarded to valedictorian or salutatorian. Honors Scholarship: $1,500 annually up to 4 years; based on admission to honors program and SAT score. New Freshman Scholarship: $1,500 annually up to 4 years; based on SAT/ACT score, class rank and GPA. Transfer Student Scholarship: $1,500 annually up to 4 years; based on GPA, must have completed at least 12 credit hours. New Student Scholarship: $1,800 annually up to four years; based on high school rank, ACT/SAT score; 150 awarded.

FINANCIAL AID PROCEDURES

Forms required: FAFSA, institutional form.

Dates and Deadlines: Priority date 4/1; no closing date. Applicants notified on a rolling basis starting 3/1; must reply within 2 week(s) of notification.

CONTACT

Governor Jackson, Director of Financial Aid

Box 425589, Denton, TX 76204-5589

(940) 898-3064

Trinity University

San Antonio, Texas

www.trinity.edu   Federal Code: 003647

4-year private liberal arts college in very large city, affiliated with Presbyterian Church (USA).

Enrollment: 2,464 undergrads, 1% part-time. 631 full-time freshmen.

Selectivity: Admits 50 to 75% of applicants.

BASIC COSTS (2008-2009)

Tuition and fees: $27,699.

Per-credit charge: $1,111.

Room and board: $8,822.

FINANCIAL AID PICTURE (2007-2008)

Students with need: Out of 371 full-time freshmen who applied for aid, 259 were judged to have need. Of these, 259 received aid, and 96 had their full need met. Average financial aid package met 92% of need; average scholarship/grant was $14,832; average loan was $5,189. For part-time students, average financial aid package was $4,634.

Students without need: 272 full-time freshmen who did not demonstrate need for aid received scholarships/grants; average award was $11,167. No-need awards available for academics, leadership, music/drama.

FINANCIAL AID PROCEDURES

Forms required: FAFSA.

Dates and Deadlines: Priority date 2/1; closing date 4/1. Must reply by 5/1 or within 4 week(s) of notification.

Transfers: Priority date 5/1; no deadline.

CONTACT

Sean Smith, Director of Financial Aid

One Trinity Place, San Antonio, TX 78212-7200

(210) 999-8315

Trinity Valley Community College

Athens, Texas

www.tvcc.edu   Federal Code: 003572

2-year public community college in large town.

Enrollment: 5,615 undergrads.

Selectivity: Open admission; but selective for some programs.

BASIC COSTS (2007-2008)

Tuition and fees: $1,050; out-of-district residents $1,650; out-of-state residents $2,400.

Per-credit charge: $20; out-of-district residents $40; out-of-state residents $65.

Room and board: $3,400.

Additional info: Tuition/fee waivers available for adults.

FINANCIAL AID PICTURE

Students with need: Need-based aid available for full-time and part-time students. Work study available nights, weekends, and for part-time students.

Students without need: No-need awards available for academics, athletics.

FINANCIAL AID PROCEDURES

Forms required: FAFSA, institutional form.

Dates and Deadlines: Priority date 7/1; no closing date. Applicants notified on a rolling basis starting 7/1; must reply within 2 week(s) of notification.

Transfers: Students on suspension at previous institution ineligible to receive aid.

CONTACT

Julie Lively, Director of Financial Aid

100 Cardinal Drive, Athens, TX 75751

(903) 675-6233

Tyler Junior College

Tyler, Texas

www.tjc.edu   Federal Code: 003648

2-year public junior college in small city.

Enrollment: 8,217 undergrads, 40% part-time. 1,770 full-time freshmen.

Selectivity: Open admission; but selective for some programs.

BASIC COSTS (2007-2008)

Tuition and fees: $1,592; out-of-district residents $2,552; out-of-state residents $3,392.

Per-credit charge: $48; out-of-district residents $80; out-of-state residents $108.

Room and board: $4,000.

FINANCIAL AID PICTURE

Students with need: Need-based aid available for full-time and part-time students.

Students without need: No-need awards available for academics, alumni affiliation, art, athletics, leadership, music/drama.

FINANCIAL AID PROCEDURES

Forms required: FAFSA, institutional form.

Dates and Deadlines: Priority date 6/1; no closing date. Applicants notified on a rolling basis starting 3/1; must reply within 2 week(s) of notification.

Transfers: Financial aid transcript required if student enrolled same year elsewhere.

CONTACT

Devon Wiggins, Director of Student Financial Aid and Scholarship

Box 9020, Tyler, TX 75711-9020

(903) 510-2385

University of Dallas

Irving, Texas

www.udallas.edu   Federal Code: 003651

4-year private university and liberal arts college in small city, affiliated with Roman Catholic Church.

Enrollment: 1,222 undergrads, 2% part-time. 315 full-time freshmen.

Selectivity: Admits 50 to 75% of applicants.

BASIC COSTS (2008-2009)

Tuition and fees: $24,770.

Per-credit charge: $975.

Room and board: $7,885.

FINANCIAL AID PICTURE (2006-2007)

Students with need: Out of 263 full-time freshmen who applied for aid, 202 were judged to have need. Of these, 202 received aid, and 79 had their full need met. Average financial aid package met 85% of need; average scholarship/grant was $14,886; average loan was $6,297. For part-time students, average financial aid package was $18,314.

Students without need: 112 full-time freshmen who did not demonstrate need for aid received scholarships/grants; average award was $11,060. No-need awards available for academics, alumni affiliation, art, leadership, music/drama.

Cumulative student debt: 70% of graduating class had student loans; average debt was $21,772.

FINANCIAL AID PROCEDURES

Forms required: FAFSA.

Dates and Deadlines: Priority date 3/1; closing date 7/1. Applicants notified on a rolling basis starting 3/1; must reply by 5/1 or within 2 week(s) of notification.

Transfers: Priority date 4/1; closing date 7/15. Must reply by 5/1 or within 2 week(s) of notification.

CONTACT

Laurie Rosenkrantz, Assistant Dean of Financial Aid and Enrollment
1845 East Northgate Drive, Irving, TX 75062-4736
(972) 721-5266

University of Houston
Houston, Texas
www.uh.edu   Federal Code: 003652

4-year public university in very large city.

Enrollment: 26,495 undergrads, 27% part-time. 3,223 full-time freshmen.

Selectivity: Admits over 75% of applicants.

BASIC COSTS (2007-2008)

Tuition and fees: $7,450; out-of-state residents $15,790.

Per-credit charge: $161; out-of-state residents $439.

Room and board: $6,651.

FINANCIAL AID PICTURE (2007-2008)

Students with need: Out of 2,279 full-time freshmen who applied for aid, 1,932 were judged to have need. Of these, 1,811 received aid, and 369 had their full need met. Average financial aid package met 68% of need; average scholarship/grant was $6,875; average loan was $3,739. For part-time students, average financial aid package was $8,209.

Students without need: 120 full-time freshmen who did not demonstrate need for aid received scholarships/grants; average award was $4,418. No-need awards available for academics, alumni affiliation, art, athletics, job skills, leadership, music/drama, ROTC, state/district residency.

Scholarships offered: 19 full-time freshmen received athletic scholarships; average amount $5,758.

FINANCIAL AID PROCEDURES

Forms required: FAFSA.

Dates and Deadlines: Priority date 4/1; no closing date. Applicants notified on a rolling basis starting 5/1; must reply within 4 week(s) of notification.

CONTACT

122 East Cullen Building, Houston, TX 77204-2023
(713) 743-1010

University of Houston: Clear Lake
Houston, Texas
www.uhcl.edu   Federal Code: 011711

Upper-division public university in very large city.

Enrollment: 4,280 undergrads.

BASIC COSTS (2007-2008)

Tuition and fees: $5,194; out-of-state residents $13,954.

Room only: $6,912.

FINANCIAL AID PICTURE

Students with need: Need-based aid available for full-time and part-time students. Work study available nights, weekends, and for part-time students.

Students without need: No-need awards available for state/district residency.

FINANCIAL AID PROCEDURES

Forms required: FAFSA, institutional form.

Dates and Deadlines: No deadline. Applicants notified on a rolling basis starting 6/4; must reply within 4 week(s) of notification.

Transfers: Priority date 4/1; no deadline. Applicants notified on a rolling basis starting 5/15; must reply within 4 week(s) of notification.

CONTACT

Lynda McKendree, Director, Financial Aid/Veterans Affairs
2700 Bay Area Boulevard, Houston, TX 77058-1098
(281) 283-2481

University of Houston: Downtown
Houston, Texas
www.uhd.edu   Federal Code: 003612

4-year public university in very large city.

Enrollment: 11,670 undergrads, 48% part-time. 831 full-time freshmen.

Selectivity: Open admission.

BASIC COSTS (2007-2008)

Tuition and fees: $4,832; out-of-state residents $13,172.

Per-credit charge: $135; out-of-state residents $413.

FINANCIAL AID PICTURE (2007-2008)

Students with need: Out of 664 full-time freshmen who applied for aid, 629 were judged to have need. Of these, 614 received aid, and 14 had their full need met. Average financial aid package met 51% of need; average scholarship/grant was $5,693; average loan was $3,264. For part-time students, average financial aid package was $6,616.

Students without need: 126 full-time freshmen who did not demonstrate need for aid received scholarships/grants; average award was $2,799. No-need awards available for academics, leadership, state/district residency.

Cumulative student debt: 77% of graduating class had student loans; average debt was $13,161.

FINANCIAL AID PROCEDURES

Forms required: FAFSA.

Dates and Deadlines: Priority date 4/1; no closing date. Applicants notified on a rolling basis starting 1/2; must reply within 8 week(s) of notification.

Transfers: No deadline. Applicants notified on a rolling basis starting 1/2; must reply within 8 week(s) of notification.

CONTACT

LaTasha Goudeau, Director of Scholarships and Financial Aid
One Main Street, Suite 350-S, Houston, TX 77002
(713) 221-8041

University of Houston: Victoria
Victoria, Texas
www.uhv.edu   Federal Code: 013231

Upper-division public university in small city.

Enrollment: 1,386 undergrads, 63% part-time.

BASIC COSTS (2007-2008)

Tuition and fees: $5,055; out-of-state residents $13,395.

Per-credit charge: $132; out-of-state residents $410.

FINANCIAL AID PICTURE (2006-2007)

Students with need: Average financial aid package for all full-time under-graduates was $6,795; for part-time $5,737. 43% awarded as scholarships/grants, 57% awarded as loans/jobs. Work study available weekends and for part-time students.

Students without need: No-need awards available for academics, athletics, leadership, state/district residency.

Additional info: Short-term loans available at registration.

FINANCIAL AID PROCEDURES

Forms required: FAFSA.

Dates and Deadlines: No deadline. Applicants notified on a rolling basis; must reply within 3 week(s) of notification.

Transfers: No deadline. Applicants notified on a rolling basis; must reply within 3 week(s) of notification.

CONTACT

Carolyn Mallory, Financial Aid Director
3007 North Ben Wilson, Victoria, TX 77901-4450
(361) 570-4131

University of Mary Hardin-Baylor

Belton, Texas
www.umhb.edu   Federal Code: 003588

4-year private university in large town, affiliated with Baptist faith.

Enrollment: 2,481 undergrads, 10% part-time. 479 full-time freshmen.

Selectivity: Admits over 75% of applicants.

BASIC COSTS (2008-2009)

Tuition and fees: $19,750.

Per-credit charge: $580.

Room and board: $5,350.

Additional info: Tuition/fee waivers available for minority students.

FINANCIAL AID PICTURE (2007-2008)

Students with need: Out of 395 full-time freshmen who applied for aid, 337 were judged to have need. Of these, 337 received aid, and 46 had their full need met. Average financial aid package met 64% of need; average scholarship/grant was $8,888; average loan was $3,911. For part-time students, average financial aid package was $7,528.

Students without need: 85 full-time freshmen who did not demonstrate need for aid received scholarships/grants; average award was $8,183. No-need awards available for academics, art, leadership, music/drama, religious affiliation.

FINANCIAL AID PROCEDURES

Forms required: FAFSA, institutional form.

Dates and Deadlines: Priority date 3/1; no closing date. Applicants notified on a rolling basis starting 2/1; must reply within 2 week(s) of notification.

CONTACT

Ron Brown, Associate VP for Enrollment Management/Director of Financial Aid
900 College Street, Belton, TX 76513
(254) 295-4517

University of North Texas

Denton, Texas
www.unt.edu   Federal Code: 003594

4-year public university and liberal arts college in small city.

Enrollment: 27,242 undergrads, 21% part-time. 3,648 full-time freshmen.

Selectivity: Admits 50 to 75% of applicants.

BASIC COSTS (2008-2009)

Tuition and fees: $6,767; out-of-state residents $15,107.

Per-credit charge: $161; out-of-state residents $439.

Room and board: $6,026.

FINANCIAL AID PICTURE (2007-2008)

Students with need: Out of 2,358 full-time freshmen who applied for aid, 1,571 were judged to have need. Of these, 1,539 received aid, and 397 had their full need met. Average financial aid package met 71% of need; average scholarship/grant was $4,788; average loan was $2,890. For part-time students, average financial aid package was $6,690.

Students without need: 377 full-time freshmen who did not demonstrate need for aid received scholarships/grants; average award was $3,448. No-need awards available for academics.

Scholarships offered: 35 full-time freshmen received athletic scholarships; average amount $9,704.

FINANCIAL AID PROCEDURES

Forms required: FAFSA.

Dates and Deadlines: Priority date 6/1; no closing date. Applicants notified on a rolling basis starting 4/1.

CONTACT

Carolyn Cunningham, Director of Financial Aid
1401 West Prairie, Suite 309, Denton, TX 76203
(940) 565-2016

University of St. Thomas

Houston, Texas
www.stthom.edu   Federal Code: 003654

4-year private university and liberal arts college in very large city, affiliated with Roman Catholic Church.

Enrollment: 1,609 undergrads, 20% part-time. 288 full-time freshmen.

Selectivity: Admits over 75% of applicants.

BASIC COSTS (2007-2008)

Tuition and fees: $19,070.

Per-credit charge: $630.

Room and board: $7,300.

FINANCIAL AID PICTURE (2007-2008)

Students with need: Out of 192 full-time freshmen who applied for aid, 163 were judged to have need. Of these, 163 received aid, and 24 had their full need met. Average financial aid package met 77% of need; average scholarship/grant was $12,446; average loan was $3,470. For part-time students, average financial aid package was $7,672.

Students without need: 63 full-time freshmen who did not demonstrate need for aid received scholarships/grants; average award was $8,097. No-need awards available for academics, athletics.

Scholarships offered: 6 full-time freshmen received athletic scholarships; average amount $6,767.

Cumulative student debt: 64% of graduating class had student loans; average debt was $21,780.

FINANCIAL AID PROCEDURES

Forms required: FAFSA.

Dates and Deadlines: No deadline. Applicants notified on a rolling basis starting 3/22; must reply within 2 week(s) of notification.

CONTACT

Scott Moore, Dean of Scholarships and Financial Aid
3800 Montrose Boulevard, Houston, TX 77006-4626
(713) 942-3465

University of Texas at Arlington

Arlington, Texas
www.uta.edu   Federal Code: 003656

4-year public university in large city.
Enrollment: 18,489 undergrads, 31% part-time. 2,094 full-time freshmen.
Selectivity: Admits over 75% of applicants. GED not accepted.

BASIC COSTS (2007-2008)
Tuition and fees: $7,194; out-of-state residents $15,534.
Room and board: $6,170.

FINANCIAL AID PICTURE (2007-2008)
Students with need: Average financial aid package met 71% of need; average scholarship/grant was $4,969; average loan was $2,873. For part-time students, average financial aid package was $5,438.
Scholarships offered: Academic Scholarships: $1,000-$4,000 per year, renewable; based on minimum SAT 1050 (exclusive of Writing) or ACT 22, top 25% of high school class.

FINANCIAL AID PROCEDURES
Forms required: FAFSA.
Dates and Deadlines: Priority date 5/15; no closing date. Applicants notified on a rolling basis starting 4/1; must reply within 3 week(s) of notification.
Transfers: Must reply within 3 week(s) of notification. To receive Texas grant or Texas B on Time loan, student must have either received Texas grant at prior school or completed associates degree at prior school.

CONTACT
Karen Krause, Director of Financial Aid
Box 19111, Arlington, TX 76019
(817) 272-3561

University of Texas at Austin

Austin, Texas
www.utexas.edu   Federal Code: 003658

4-year public university in very large city.
Enrollment: 36,881 undergrads, 7% part-time. 7,419 full-time freshmen.
Selectivity: Admits 50 to 75% of applicants.

BASIC COSTS (2007-2008)
Tuition and fees: $7,670; out-of-state residents $24,544.
Room and board: $8,576.

FINANCIAL AID PICTURE (2007-2008)
Students with need: Out of 5,100 full-time freshmen who applied for aid, 4,200 were judged to have need. Of these, 4,200 received aid, and 3,600 had their full need met. Average financial aid package met 89% of need; average scholarship/grant was $6,800; average loan was $3,800. Need-based aid available for part-time students.
Students without need: 1,250 full-time freshmen who did not demonstrate need for aid received scholarships/grants. No-need awards available for academics, art, athletics, leadership, music/drama, ROTC, state/district residency.
Cumulative student debt: 40% of graduating class had student loans; average debt was $17,000.

FINANCIAL AID PROCEDURES
Forms required: FAFSA.
Dates and Deadlines: Priority date 4/1; no closing date. Applicants notified on a rolling basis starting 3/15; must reply within 4 week(s) of notification.

CONTACT
Don Davis, Associate Director of Student Financial Services
PO Box 8058, Austin, TX 78713-8058
(512) 475-6282

University of Texas at Brownsville

Brownsville, Texas
www.utb.edu   Federal Code: 030646

4-year public university and community college in small city.
Enrollment: 9,724 undergrads.
Selectivity: Open admission; but selective for some programs.

BASIC COSTS (2007-2008)
Tuition and fees: $4,665; out-of-state residents $13,005.
Per-credit charge: $116; out-of-state residents $394.

FINANCIAL AID PICTURE
Students with need: Need-based aid available for full-time and part-time students.

FINANCIAL AID PROCEDURES
Forms required: FAFSA.
Dates and Deadlines: Priority date 4/1; closing date 8/15. Applicants notified on a rolling basis; must reply within 4 week(s) of notification.

CONTACT
Mari Chapa, Director of Financial Aid
80 Fort Brown, Brownsville, TX 78520
(956) 882-8277

University of Texas at Dallas

Richardson, Texas
www.utdallas.edu   Federal Code: 009741

4-year public university in very large city.
Enrollment: 9,096 undergrads, 27% part-time. 1,030 full-time freshmen.
Selectivity: Admits 50 to 75% of applicants.

BASIC COSTS (2007-2008)
Tuition and fees: $8,554; out-of-state residents $17,854.
Per-credit charge: $285; out-of-state residents $595.
Room and board: $6,671.

FINANCIAL AID PICTURE (2007-2008)
Students with need: Out of 629 full-time freshmen who applied for aid, 442 were judged to have need. Of these, 440 received aid, and 222 had their full need met. Average financial aid package met 84% of need; average scholarship/grant was $6,288; average loan was $2,648. For part-time students, average financial aid package was $7,094.
Students without need: 357 full-time freshmen who did not demonstrate need for aid received scholarships/grants; average award was $8,837. No-need awards available for academics.
Scholarships offered: Eugene McDermott Scholars Program Awards: full tuition and fees plus domestic and international travel costs for enhancement of scholar's education; based on being in top 10% of high school class, high scores on entrance exams, evidence of leadership abilities; 20 awarded.

FINANCIAL AID PROCEDURES
Forms required: FAFSA.
Dates and Deadlines: Priority date 3/31; closing date 4/12. Applicants notified on a rolling basis starting 3/1; must reply within 2 week(s) of notification.
Transfers: Priority date 4/1.

CONTACT
Cathy Coursey, Director of Financial Aid
Office of Admissions, Richardson, TX 75083-0688
(972) 883-2941

University of Texas at El Paso

El Paso, Texas
www.utep.edu   Federal Code: 003661

4-year public university in very large city.
Enrollment: 16,658 undergrads, 34% part-time. 2,231 full-time freshmen.
Selectivity: Admits over 75% of applicants.

BASIC COSTS (2007-2008)

Tuition and fees: $5,610; out-of-state residents $13,950.
Per-credit charge: $146; out-of-state residents $424.
Room and board: $7,696.
Additional info: Mexican citizens who show need may qualify for in-state tuition.

FINANCIAL AID PICTURE (2006-2007)

Students with need: Out of 1,723 full-time freshmen who applied for aid, 1,356 were judged to have need. Of these, 1,344 received aid, and 492 had their full need met. Average financial aid package met 80% of need; average scholarship/grant was $6,494; average loan was $2,827. For part-time students, average financial aid package was $10,237.
Students without need: 230 full-time freshmen who did not demonstrate need for aid received scholarships/grants; average award was $1,655. No-need awards available for academics, alumni affiliation, art, athletics, job skills, leadership, minority status, music/drama, religious affiliation, ROTC, state/district residency.
Scholarships offered: 19 full-time freshmen received athletic scholarships; average amount $7,223.
Cumulative student debt: 51% of graduating class had student loans; average debt was $7,230.
Additional info: Emergency loans available.

FINANCIAL AID PROCEDURES

Forms required: FAFSA, institutional form.
Dates and Deadlines: Closing date 3/15. Applicants notified by 6/30; must reply within 2 week(s) of notification.
Transfers: No deadline.

CONTACT

Raul Lerma, Director of Financial Aid
500 West University Avenue, El Paso, TX 79968-0510
(915) 747-5204

University of Texas at San Antonio

San Antonio, Texas
www.utsa.edu   Federal Code: 010115

4-year public university in very large city.
Enrollment: 24,280 undergrads, 23% part-time. 4,693 full-time freshmen.
Selectivity: Admits over 75% of applicants.

BASIC COSTS (2008-2009)

Tuition and fees: $7,100; out-of-state residents $15,530.
Per-credit charge: $160; out-of-state residents $441.
Room and board: $7,821.

FINANCIAL AID PICTURE (2006-2007)

Students with need: Out of 3,488 full-time freshmen who applied for aid, 2,317 were judged to have need. Of these, 2,198 received aid, and 561 had their full need met. Average financial aid package met 50% of need; average scholarship/grant was $4,636; average loan was $2,431. For part-time students, average financial aid package was $5,122.
Students without need: 322 full-time freshmen who did not demonstrate need for aid received scholarships/grants; average award was $1,570. No-need awards available for academics, alumni affiliation, art, athletics, job skills, leadership, music/drama, ROTC, state/district residency.

Scholarships offered: 75 full-time freshmen received athletic scholarships; average amount $6,318.
Cumulative student debt: 66% of graduating class had student loans; average debt was $18,687.

FINANCIAL AID PROCEDURES

Forms required: FAFSA, institutional form.
Dates and Deadlines: Priority date 3/31; no closing date. Applicants notified on a rolling basis starting 4/1; must reply within 4 week(s) of notification.
Transfers: No deadline. Applicants notified on a rolling basis starting 4/1; must reply within 4 week(s) of notification.

CONTACT

Lisa Blazer, Assistant Vice President of Financial Aid
One UTSA Circle, San Antonio, TX 78249-0617
(210) 458-7828

University of Texas at Tyler

Tyler, Texas
www.uttyler.edu   Federal Code: 011163

4-year public university in small city.
Enrollment: 4,938 undergrads, 22% part-time. 585 full-time freshmen.
Selectivity: Admits over 75% of applicants.

BASIC COSTS (2008-2009)

Tuition and fees: $5,742; out-of-state residents $14,172.
Per-credit charge: $50; out-of-state residents $331.
Room and board: $7,510.

FINANCIAL AID PICTURE (2006-2007)

Students with need: Out of 389 full-time freshmen who applied for aid, 245 were judged to have need. Of these, 245 received aid, and 39 had their full need met. Average financial aid package met 51% of need; average scholarship/grant was $5,050; average loan was $2,164. For part-time students, average financial aid package was $6,632.
Students without need: 56 full-time freshmen who did not demonstrate need for aid received scholarships/grants; average award was $2,829. No-need awards available for academics, art, music/drama.
Cumulative student debt: 55% of graduating class had student loans; average debt was $13,204.
Additional info: Apply early for all programs.

FINANCIAL AID PROCEDURES

Forms required: FAFSA, institutional form.
Dates and Deadlines: Priority date 4/1; no closing date. Applicants notified on a rolling basis starting 4/15; must reply within 2 week(s) of notification.

CONTACT

Candice Lindsey, Associate Dean of Enrollment Management, Financial Aid & Registrar
3900 University Boulevard, Tyler, TX 75799
(903) 566-7180

University of Texas Medical Branch at Galveston

Galveston, Texas
www.utmb.edu   Federal Code: 013976

Upper-division public health science and nursing college in small city.
Enrollment: 562 undergrads, 46% part-time.

BASIC COSTS (2007-2008)

Tuition and fees: $5,278; out-of-state residents $13,618.
Per-credit charge: $150; out-of-state residents $428.
Additional info: Tuition and fees vary by program.

FINANCIAL AID PICTURE

Students with need: Need-based aid available for full-time and part-time students. Work study available nights, weekends, and for part-time students.
Students without need: No-need awards available for academics, minority status, state/district residency.

FINANCIAL AID PROCEDURES

Forms required: FAFSA.
Dates and Deadlines: No deadline. Applicants notified on a rolling basis; must reply within 4 week(s) of notification.

CONTACT

Carl Gordon, Associate Director of Enrollment Services and University Financial Aid Officer
301 University Boulevard, Galveston, TX 77555-1305
(409) 772-1215

University of Texas of the Permian Basin

Odessa, Texas
www.utpb.edu   Federal Code: 009930

4-year public university in small city.
Enrollment: 2,634 undergrads, 26% part-time. 306 full-time freshmen.
Selectivity: Admits less than 50% of applicants.

BASIC COSTS (2007-2008)

Tuition and fees: $4,849; out-of-state residents $13,189.
Additional info: New Mexico residents living in areas contiguous to Texas border pay in-district rate; other New Mexico residents pay $5,749 for tuition plus fees.

FINANCIAL AID PICTURE (2006-2007)

Students with need: Out of 65 full-time freshmen who applied for aid, 48 were judged to have need. Of these, 48 received aid. Average financial aid package met 65% of need; average scholarship/grant was $5,394; average loan was $1,977. For part-time students, average financial aid package was $6,820.
Students without need: 12 full-time freshmen who did not demonstrate need for aid received scholarships/grants; average award was $2,292. No-need awards available for academics.
Scholarships offered: 5 full-time freshmen received athletic scholarships; average amount $2,280.
Cumulative student debt: 33% of graduating class had student loans; average debt was $2,078.

FINANCIAL AID PROCEDURES

Forms required: FAFSA.
Dates and Deadlines: Priority date 5/1; no closing date. Applicants notified on a rolling basis starting 6/1; must reply within 2 week(s) of notification.

CONTACT

Robert Vasquez, Director of Financial Aid and Placement
4901 East University Boulevard, Odessa, TX 79762
(432) 552-2620

University of Texas Southwestern Medical Center at Dallas

Dallas, Texas
www.utsouthwestern.edu   Federal Code: 010019

Upper-division public university and health science college in very large city.
Enrollment: 118 undergrads, 12% part-time.

BASIC COSTS (2007-2008)

Tuition and fees: $4,140; out-of-state residents $12,380.
Additional info: Tuition and fees are based on Allied Health program.

FINANCIAL AID PICTURE (2007-2008)

Students with need: Average financial aid package for all full-time undergraduates was $15,021. 19% awarded as scholarships/grants, 81% awarded as loans/jobs. Need-based aid available for part-time students. Work study available nights, weekends, and for part-time students.

FINANCIAL AID PROCEDURES

Dates and Deadlines: No deadline. Must reply within 2 week(s) of notification.
Transfers: Priority date 3/1. Applicants notified on a rolling basis starting 4/1; must reply within 3 week(s) of notification.

CONTACT

Charles Kettlewell, Registrar and Director of Financial Aid
5323 Harry Hines Boulevard, Dallas, TX 75390-9162
(214) 648-3611

University of Texas: Pan American

Edinburg, Texas
www.utpa.edu   Federal Code: 003599

4-year public university in small city.
Enrollment: 14,995 undergrads, 25% part-time. 2,695 full-time freshmen.
Selectivity: Admits 50 to 75% of applicants.

BASIC COSTS (2008-2009)

Tuition and fees: $5,125; out-of-state residents $13,555.
Per-credit charge: $138; out-of-state residents $419.
Room and board: $4,900.
Additional info: Mexican citizens may be eligible for in-state tuition rates.

FINANCIAL AID PICTURE (2006-2007)

Students with need: Out of 2,036 full-time freshmen who applied for aid, 1,910 were judged to have need. Of these, 1,879 received aid, and 165 had their full need met. Average financial aid package met 68% of need; average scholarship/grant was $7,753; average loan was $2,292. For part-time students, average financial aid package was $6,212.
Students without need: 119 full-time freshmen who did not demonstrate need for aid received scholarships/grants; average award was $6,020. No-need awards available for academics, alumni affiliation, art, athletics, leadership, music/drama, ROTC, state/district residency.
Scholarships offered: 22 full-time freshmen received athletic scholarships; average amount $4,455.
Cumulative student debt: 64% of graduating class had student loans; average debt was $11,995.

FINANCIAL AID PROCEDURES

Forms required: FAFSA.
Dates and Deadlines: Closing date 3/1. Applicants notified on a rolling basis starting 3/15; must reply within 2 week(s) of notification.
Transfers: Priority date 3/1; no deadline. Applicants notified on a rolling basis; must reply within 2 week(s) of notification.

CONTACT

Elaine Rivera, Executive Director of Student Financial Services
1201 West University Drive, Edinburg, TX 78541-2999
(956) 381-2501

University of the Incarnate Word

San Antonio, Texas
www.uiw.edu   Federal Code: 003578

4-year private university and liberal arts college in very large city, affiliated with Roman Catholic Church.
Enrollment: 4,666 undergrads, 38% part-time. 716 full-time freshmen.
Selectivity: Admits over 75% of applicants.

BASIC COSTS (2008-2009)

Tuition and fees: $20,260.

Per-credit charge: $640.

Room and board: $7,380.

FINANCIAL AID PICTURE (2007-2008)

Students with need: Out of 699 full-time freshmen who applied for aid, 550 were judged to have need. Of these, 550 received aid, and 157 had their full need met. Average financial aid package met 63% of need; average scholarship/grant was $6,970; average loan was $3,558. For part-time students, average financial aid package was $8,109.

Students without need: 146 full-time freshmen who did not demonstrate need for aid received scholarships/grants; average award was $5,199. No-need awards available for academics, alumni affiliation, art, athletics, leadership, music/drama, religious affiliation, ROTC, state/district residency.

Scholarships offered: 20 full-time freshmen received athletic scholarships; average amount $12,224.

Cumulative student debt: 83% of graduating class had student loans; average debt was $30,613.

Additional info: Students encouraged to pursue outside scholarship programs.

FINANCIAL AID PROCEDURES

Forms required: FAFSA.

Dates and Deadlines: Priority date 4/1; no closing date. Applicants notified on a rolling basis starting 2/15; must reply within 2 week(s) of notification.

CONTACT

Amy Carcanagues, Director of Financial Assistance

4301 Broadway, San Antonio, TX 78209-6397

(210) 829-6008

Vernon College
Vernon, Texas
www.vernoncollege.edu   Federal Code: 010060

2-year public community and junior college in large town.

Enrollment: 2,813 undergrads.

Selectivity: Open admission; but selective for some programs.

BASIC COSTS (2008-2009)

Tuition and fees: $1,875.

Per-credit charge: $55.

Room and board: $3,125.

FINANCIAL AID PICTURE (2007-2008)

Students with need: 82% of average financial aid package awarded as scholarships/grants, 18% awarded as loans/jobs. Need-based aid available for part-time students. Work study available nights, weekends, and for part-time students.

Students without need: This college awards aid only to students with need.

FINANCIAL AID PROCEDURES

Forms required: FAFSA.

Dates and Deadlines: Priority date 7/1; no closing date. Applicants notified on a rolling basis starting 4/1.

Transfers: No deadline. Applicants notified on a rolling basis.

CONTACT

Melissa Elliott, Director of Financial Aid

4400 College Drive, Vernon, TX 76384-4092

(940) 552-6291

Wayland Baptist University
Plainview, Texas
www.wbu.edu   Federal Code: 003663

4-year private university and liberal arts college in large town, affiliated with Southern Baptist Convention.

Enrollment: 934 undergrads, 11% part-time. 247 full-time freshmen.

Selectivity: Admits over 75% of applicants.

BASIC COSTS (2008-2009)

Tuition and fees: $12,000.

Per-credit charge: $380.

Room and board: $3,584.

FINANCIAL AID PICTURE (2007-2008)

Students with need: Out of 204 full-time freshmen who applied for aid, 162 were judged to have need. Of these, 161 received aid, and 33 had their full need met. Average financial aid package met 72% of need; average scholarship/grant was $7,685; average loan was $2,886. For part-time students, average financial aid package was $5,740.

Students without need: 52 full-time freshmen who did not demonstrate need for aid received scholarships/grants; average award was $9,919. No-need awards available for academics, alumni affiliation, art, athletics, job skills, leadership, minority status, music/drama, religious affiliation, state/district residency.

Scholarships offered: 18 full-time freshmen received athletic scholarships; average amount $5,586.

Cumulative student debt: 95% of graduating class had student loans; average debt was $18,288.

FINANCIAL AID PROCEDURES

Forms required: FAFSA, institutional form.

Dates and Deadlines: Priority date 5/1; no closing date. Applicants notified on a rolling basis starting 2/15; must reply within 3 week(s) of notification.

CONTACT

Karen LaQuey, Director of Financial Aid

1900 West Seventh Street, CMB #712, Plainview, TX 79072

(806) 291-3520

Weatherford College
Weatherford, Texas
www.wc.edu   Federal Code: 003664

2-year public community college in large town.

Enrollment: 4,092 undergrads, 49% part-time. 702 full-time freshmen.

Selectivity: Open admission; but selective for some programs.

BASIC COSTS (2007-2008)

Tuition and fees: $1,680; out-of-district residents $2,430; out-of-state residents $3,750.

Per-credit charge: $56; out-of-district residents $81; out-of-state residents $125.

Room and board: $7,080.

FINANCIAL AID PICTURE

Students with need: Work study available nights, weekends, and for part-time students.

Students without need: This college awards aid only to students with need.

FINANCIAL AID PROCEDURES

Forms required: FAFSA.

Dates and Deadlines: Priority date 7/3; no closing date. Applicants notified on a rolling basis; must reply within 2 week(s) of notification.

CONTACT

Kathy Bassham, Director of Student Financial Aid
225 College Park Drive, Weatherford, TX 76086
(817) 598-6295

West Texas A&M University

Canyon, Texas
www.wtamu.edu   Federal Code: 003665

4-year public university in large town.
Enrollment: 5,849 undergrads, 24% part-time. 923 full-time freshmen.
Selectivity: Admits 50 to 75% of applicants.

BASIC COSTS (2007-2008)
Tuition and fees: $4,920; out-of-state residents $13,260.
Per-credit charge: $120; out-of-state residents $328.
Room and board: $5,627.
Additional info: Out-of-district students from border counties pay in-state tuition. Tuition reduction plan available to students from border states.

FINANCIAL AID PICTURE
Students with need: Need-based aid available for full-time and part-time students. Work study available nights, weekends, and for part-time students.
Students without need: No-need awards available for academics, art, athletics, leadership, music/drama, state/district residency.
Additional info: Scholarship deadline February 1.

FINANCIAL AID PROCEDURES
Forms required: FAFSA.
Dates and Deadlines: Priority date 4/15; no closing date. Applicants notified on a rolling basis starting 3/1; must reply within 2 week(s) of notification.
Transfers: No deadline. Applicants notified on a rolling basis; must reply within 2 week(s) of notification. Must provide financial aid transcripts through last semester of attendance. All academic transcripts must be on file.

CONTACT
Jim Reed, Director of Financial Aid
2501 Fourth Avenue, WTAMU Box 60907, Canyon, TX 79016-0001
(806) 651-2055

Western Technical College

El Paso, Texas
www.wtc-ep.edu   Federal Code: 014535

2-year for-profit technical college in very large city.
Enrollment: 500 undergrads, 20% part-time.
Selectivity: Open admission; but selective for some programs.

BASIC COSTS (2007-2008)
Additional info: Tuition varies by program. Automotive: $20,595; refrigeration: $20,595; welding: $14,040; computer: $24,714; medical assisting: $9,828; massage therapy: $6,300; health information: $14,150. Registration fee $100.

FINANCIAL AID PICTURE
Students with need: Need-based aid available for full-time and part-time students.
Students without need: This college awards aid only to students with need.

FINANCIAL AID PROCEDURES
Forms required: FAFSA.
Dates and Deadlines: No deadline. Applicants notified on a rolling basis.

CONTACT

Jennifer Phillips, Financial Aid Director
9624 Plaza Circle, El Paso, TX 79927
(915) 532-3737 ext. 105

Western Texas College

Snyder, Texas
www.wtc.edu   Federal Code: 009549

2-year public community and junior college in large town.
Enrollment: 1,977 undergrads, 66% part-time. 203 full-time freshmen.
Selectivity: Open admission; but selective for some programs.

BASIC COSTS (2007-2008)
Tuition and fees: $1,740; out-of-district residents $1,950; out-of-state residents $2,340.
Per-credit charge: $39; out-of-district residents $46; out-of-state residents $59.
Room and board: $4,100.

FINANCIAL AID PICTURE (2007-2008)
Students with need: Out of 191 full-time freshmen who applied for aid, 140 were judged to have need. Of these, 90 received aid. Average financial aid package met 50% of need; average scholarship/grant was $1,000; average loan was $3,000. Need-based aid available for part-time students.
Students without need: 24 full-time freshmen who did not demonstrate need for aid received scholarships/grants; average award was $7,131. No-need awards available for academics, art, athletics, leadership, music/drama, state/district residency.
Scholarships offered: 45 full-time freshmen received athletic scholarships; average amount $44,232.

FINANCIAL AID PROCEDURES
Forms required: FAFSA, institutional form.
Dates and Deadlines: Priority date 7/1; no closing date. Applicants notified on a rolling basis starting 5/1; must reply within 2 week(s) of notification.

CONTACT
Kathy Hall, Director of Student Financial Aid
6200 College Avenue, Snyder, TX 79549
(325) 573-8511 ext. 309

Westwood College: Houston South

Houston, Texas
www.westwood.edu/   Federal Code: 007548

2-year for-profit technical college in very large city.
Enrollment: 300 undergrads.

BASIC COSTS (2007-2008)
Additional info: Tool Kits Range; $198 - $617 (one time charge).

FINANCIAL AID PICTURE
Students with need: Need-based aid available for full-time and part-time students.

FINANCIAL AID PROCEDURES
Forms required: FAFSA, institutional form.
Dates and Deadlines: No deadline.

CONTACT
Angela Cormier, Assistant Director of Student Finance
7322 Southwest Freeway, Houston, TX 77074
(713) 777-4779 ext. 13131

Wharton County Junior College
Wharton, Texas
www.wcjc.edu
Federal Code: 003668

2-year public junior college in small town.

Enrollment: 5,892 undergrads, 56% part-time. 953 full-time freshmen.

Selectivity: Open admission; but selective for some programs.

BASIC COSTS (2008-2009)
Tuition and fees: $1,620; out-of-state residents $2,580.
Per-credit charge: $32; out-of-state residents $64.
Room and board: $2,700.
Additional info: Annual out-of-district fees $1,380.

FINANCIAL AID PICTURE
Students with need: Need-based aid available for full-time and part-time students.

Students without need: No-need awards available for academics, athletics, music/drama.

FINANCIAL AID PROCEDURES
Forms required: FAFSA.
Dates and Deadlines: Closing date 6/1. Applicants notified on a rolling basis starting 8/1; must reply by 8/15.

CONTACT
Richard Hyde, Director of Financial Aid
911 Boling Highway, Wharton, TX 77488-0080
(979) 532-4560 ext. 6345

Wiley College
Marshall, Texas
www.wileyc.edu
Federal Code: 003669

4-year private liberal arts college in large town, affiliated with United Methodist Church.

Enrollment: 922 undergrads.

Selectivity: Open admission; but selective for some programs.

BASIC COSTS (2007-2008)
Tuition and fees: $9,150.
Per-credit charge: $253.
Room and board: $5,300.
Additional info: Reported tuition includes cost of books.

FINANCIAL AID PICTURE
Students with need: Need-based aid available for full-time and part-time students.

Students without need: This college awards aid only to students with need.

FINANCIAL AID PROCEDURES
Forms required: FAFSA, institutional form.
Dates and Deadlines: No deadline. Applicants notified on a rolling basis.

CONTACT
Lete Carreira, Assistant Director of Financial Aid
711 Wiley Avenue, Marshall, TX 75670
(903) 927-3217

Utah

Brigham Young University
Provo, Utah
www.byu.edu
Federal Code: 003670

4-year private university in small city, affiliated with Church of Jesus Christ of Latter-day Saints.

Enrollment: 30,873 undergrads, 10% part-time. 5,737 full-time freshmen.

Selectivity: Admits 50 to 75% of applicants.

BASIC COSTS (2007-2008)
Tuition and fees: $3,840.
Per-credit charge: $197.
Room and board: $6,460.
Additional info: Undergraduate 2-semester tuition $7,680 for nonmembers of The Church of Jesus Christ of Latter-day Saints. Undergraduate per-credit-hour charge $394 for nonmembers.

FINANCIAL AID PICTURE (2006-2007)
Students with need: Out of 2,083 full-time freshmen who applied for aid, 1,312 were judged to have need. Of these, 1,125 received aid. Average financial aid package met 21% of need; average scholarship/grant was $1,579; average loan was $733. For part-time students, average financial aid package was $3,842.

Students without need: 2,202 full-time freshmen who did not demonstrate need for aid received scholarships/grants; average award was $2,871. No-need awards available for academics, art, athletics, leadership, minority status, music/drama, religious affiliation, ROTC, state/district residency.

Scholarships offered: 145 full-time freshmen received athletic scholarships; average amount $3,473.

Cumulative student debt: 34% of graduating class had student loans; average debt was $13,245.

Additional info: Students notified of scholarships on or about April 20th.

FINANCIAL AID PROCEDURES
Forms required: FAFSA.
Dates and Deadlines: Priority date 4/15; no closing date. Applicants notified on a rolling basis starting 4/1.
Transfers: Must provide financial aid transcript.

CONTACT
Paul Conrad, Director of Financial Aid
A-153 ASB, BYU, Provo, UT 84602
(801) 422-4104

College of Eastern Utah
Price, Utah
www.ceu.edu
Federal Code: 003676

2-year public community college in small town.

Enrollment: 1,414 undergrads.

Selectivity: Open admission; but selective for some programs.

BASIC COSTS (2007-2008)
Tuition and fees: $2,161; out-of-state residents $7,964.
Room and board: $4,118.

FINANCIAL AID PICTURE
Students with need: Need-based aid available for full-ti students. Work study available nights, weekends, and

Students without need: No-need awards available letics, leadership, minority status, music/drama, re trict residency.

FINANCIAL AID PROCEDURES

Forms required: FAFSA, institutional form.

Dates and Deadlines: Priority date 2/1; no closing date. Applicants notified on a rolling basis starting 3/15; must reply within 2 week(s) of notification.

CONTACT

Kim Booth, Financial Aid Director

451 East 400 North, Price, UT 84501

(435) 613-5207

DeVry University: Sandy

Sandy, Utah

4-year for-profit college in small city.

Enrollment: 39 undergrads, 77% part-time. 3 full-time freshmen.

FINANCIAL AID PICTURE (2006-2007)

Students with need: Out of 1 full-time freshmen who applied for aid, 1 were judged to have need. Of these, 1 received aid. Average financial aid package met 22% of need; average loan was $2,625. For part-time students, average financial aid package was $6,464.

Students without need: No-need awards available for academics.

FINANCIAL AID PROCEDURES

Forms required: FAFSA.

Dates and Deadlines: No deadline. Applicants notified on a rolling basis.

CONTACT

9350 South 150 East, Suite 420, Sandy, UT 84070

Dixie State College of Utah

St. George, Utah

www.dixie.edu

Federal Code: 003671

4-year public technical college in small city.

Enrollment: 4,607 undergrads, 34% part-time. 991 full-time freshmen.

Selectivity: Open admission; but selective for some programs.

BASIC COSTS (2007-2008)

Tuition and fees: $2,728; out-of-state residents $9,460.

Room and board: $3,098.

FINANCIAL AID PICTURE

Students with need: Need-based aid available for full-time students. Work study available nights, weekends, and for part-time students.

Students without need: No-need awards available for academics, alumni affiliation, art, athletics, leadership, minority status, music/drama.

FINANCIAL AID PROCEDURES

Forms required: FAFSA.

Dates and Deadlines: Priority date 4/1; no closing date. Applicants notified on a rolling basis starting 5/1; must reply within 2 week(s) of notification.

CONTACT

York Butler, Director of Financial Aid

225 South 700 East, St. George, UT 84770-3876

(435) 652-7575

LDS Business College

Salt Lake City, Utah

www.ldsbc.edu

Federal Code: 003672

2-year private business and junior college in small city, affiliated with Church of Jesus Christ of Latter-day Saints.

Enrollment: 1,350 undergrads.

Selectivity: Open admission.

BASIC COSTS (2007-2008)

Tuition and fees: $2,600.

Per-credit charge: $108.

Room and board: $4,580.

Additional info: Students who are not members of The Church of Jesus Christ of Latter-day Saints pay tuition of $5,200 per academic year, $1216 per-credit-hour.

FINANCIAL AID PICTURE

Students with need: Need-based aid available for full-time and part-time students.

Students without need: No-need awards available for academics, leadership.

Scholarships offered: Service scholarships for The Church of Jesus Christ of Latter-day Saints missionaries who have returned from mission within past year. Covers half tuition for one semester.

FINANCIAL AID PROCEDURES

Forms required: FAFSA.

Dates and Deadlines: Priority date 7/1; no closing date. Applicants notified on a rolling basis starting 3/1; must reply within 3 week(s) of notification.

CONTACT

Doug Horne, Financial Aid Administrator

95 North 300 West, Salt Lake City, UT 84101-3500

(801) 524-8110

Salt Lake Community College

Salt Lake City, Utah

www.slcc.edu

Federal Code: 005220

2-year public community and technical college in very large city.

Enrollment: 23,375 undergrads, 68% part-time. 1,577 full-time freshmen.

Selectivity: Open admission; but selective for some programs.

BASIC COSTS (2007-2008)

Tuition and fees: $2,536; out-of-state residents $7,958.

Additional info: Tuition/fee waivers available for adults, minority students.

FINANCIAL AID PICTURE

Students with need: Need-based aid available for full-time and part-time students. Work study available nights, weekends, and for part-time students.

Students without need: No-need awards available for academics, alumni affiliation, art, athletics, leadership, minority status, music/drama.

FINANCIAL AID PROCEDURES

Forms required: FAFSA, institutional form.

Dates and Deadlines: Priority date 5/1; no closing date. Applicants notified on a rolling basis starting 5/1; must reply within 4 week(s) of notification.

CONTACT

Cristi Easton, Director of Financial Aid

4600 South Redwood Road, Salt Lake City, UT 84130-0808

(801) 957-4410

Snow College

Ephraim, Utah

www.snow.edu

Federal Code: 003679

2-year public community and junior college in small town.

Enrollment: 3,745 undergrads, 44% part-time. 1,044 full-time freshmen.

Selectivity: Open admission.

BASIC COSTS (2007-2008)

Tuition and fees: $2,262; out-of-state residents $7,889.

Room and board: $2,750.

FINANCIAL AID PICTURE

Students with need: Need-based aid available for full-time students.
Students without need: No-need awards available for academics, alumni affiliation, athletics, leadership, music/drama, state/district residency.

FINANCIAL AID PROCEDURES

Forms required: FAFSA, institutional form.
Dates and Deadlines: Priority date 3/1; closing date 7/15. Applicants notified on a rolling basis starting 8/1; must reply within 1 week(s) of notification.
Transfers: Priority date 3/15; closing date 6/15. Applicants notified on a rolling basis. F.A.T. required for midyear transfers.

CONTACT

Jack Dalene, Director of Financial Aid
150 East College Avenue, Ephraim, UT 84627
(435) 283-7132

Southern Utah University

Cedar City, Utah
www.suu.edu
Federal Code: 003678

4-year public university in large town.
Enrollment: 5,329 undergrads, 14% part-time; 1,163 full-time freshmen.
Selectivity: Admits over 75% of applicants.

BASIC COSTS (2007-2008)

Tuition and fees: $3,796; out-of-state residents $11,327.
Room and board: $4,922.

FINANCIAL AID PICTURE (2006-2007)

Students with need: Average financial aid package met 76% of need; average scholarship/grant was $3,952; average loan was $2,560. For part-time students, average financial aid package was $3,487.
Students without need: No-need awards available for academics, alumni affiliation, art, athletics, job skills, leadership, minority status, music/drama, state/district residency.
Cumulative student debt: 34% of graduating class had student loans; average debt was $8,311.

FINANCIAL AID PROCEDURES

Forms required: FAFSA, institutional form.
Dates and Deadlines: No deadline. Applicants notified by 11/6.

CONTACT

Paul Morris, Director of Financial Aid
351 West Center Street, Cedar City, UT 84720
(435) 586-7735

University of Utah

Salt Lake City, Utah
www.utah.edu
Federal Code: 003675

4-year public university in large city.
Enrollment: 20,560 undergrads, 30% part-time. 2,374 full-time freshmen.
Selectivity: Admits over 75% of applicants.

BASIC COSTS (2007-2008)

Tuition and fees: $4,987; out-of-state residents $15,662.
Room and board: $5,778.

FINANCIAL AID PICTURE (2007-2008)

Students with need: Out of 968 full-time freshmen who applied for aid, 666 were judged to have need. Of these, 658 received aid, and 139 had their full need met. Average financial aid package met 60% of need; average scholarship/grant was $5,530; average loan was $3,344. For part-time students, average financial aid package was $6,645.

Students without need: 180 full-time freshmen who did not demonstrate need for aid received scholarships/grants; average award was $5,143. No-need awards available for academics, alumni affiliation, art, athletics, leadership, minority status, music/drama, ROTC, state/district residency.
Scholarships offered: 7 full-time freshmen received athletic scholarships; average amount $19,005.
Cumulative student debt: 41% of graduating class had student loans; average debt was $13,994.

FINANCIAL AID PROCEDURES

Forms required: FAFSA, institutional form.
Dates and Deadlines: Closing date 3/15. Applicants notified on a rolling basis starting 4/15; must reply within 6 week(s) of notification.
Transfers: Priority date 2/15; no deadline. Applicants notified on a rolling basis starting 4/15; must reply within 6 week(s) of notification.

CONTACT

John Curl, Director of Financial Aid and Scholarship
201 South 1460 East, Room 250 S, Salt Lake City, UT 84112-9057
(801) 581-6211

Utah Career College

West Jordan, Utah
www.utahcollege.edu
Federal Code: 011166

4-year for-profit technical college in small city.
Enrollment: 689 undergrads.
Selectivity: Open admission; but selective for some programs.

BASIC COSTS (2007-2008)

Tuition and fees: $15,075.
Per-credit charge: $335.
Additional info: Nursing program courses $450 per credit hour.

FINANCIAL AID PICTURE

Students with need: Need-based aid available for full-time and part-time students.
Students without need: This college awards aid only to students with need.

FINANCIAL AID PROCEDURES

Forms required: FAFSA, institutional form.
Dates and Deadlines: No deadline. Applicants notified on a rolling basis starting 7/1; must reply within 2 week(s) of notification.

CONTACT

Nicole Whitesides, Director of Financial Aid
1902 West 7800 South, West Jordan, UT 84088
(801) 304-4224

Utah State University

Logan, Utah
www.usu.edu
Federal Code: 003677

4-year public university in small city.
Enrollment: 12,995 undergrads, 16% part-time. 2,375 full-time freshmen.
Selectivity: Admits over 75% of applicants.

BASIC COSTS (2007-2008)

Tuition and fees: $4,199; out-of-state residents $12,224.
Room and board: $4,580.

FINANCIAL AID PICTURE (2006-2007)

Students with need: Out of 1,002 full-time freshmen who applied for aid, 751 were judged to have need. Of these, 744 received aid, and 183 had their full need met. Average financial aid package met 61% of need; average scholarship/grant was $3,153; average loan was $2,749. For part-time students, average financial aid package was $3,862.

Students without need: 148 full-time freshmen who did not demonstrate need for aid received scholarships/grants; average award was $1,932. No-need awards available for academics, alumni affiliation, art, athletics, leadership, minority status, music/drama, religious affiliation, ROTC.

Scholarships offered: 60 full-time freshmen received athletic scholarships; average amount $7,668.

FINANCIAL AID PROCEDURES

Forms required: FAFSA.

Dates and Deadlines: No deadline. Applicants notified on a rolling basis starting 4/1; must reply within 4 week(s) of notification.

CONTACT

Steve Sharp, Director of Financial Aid
0160 Old Main Hill, Logan, UT 84322-0160
(435) 797-0173

Utah Valley State College

Orem, Utah
www.uvsc.edu   Federal Code: 004027

4-year public university and technical college in small city.

Enrollment: 20,159 undergrads, 45% part-time. 2,217 full-time freshmen.

Selectivity: Open admission.

BASIC COSTS (2007-2008)

Tuition and fees: $3,528; out-of-state residents $11,028.

FINANCIAL AID PICTURE (2007-2008)

Students with need: Out of 1,358 full-time freshmen who applied for aid, 1,165 were judged to have need. Of these, 764 received aid, and 48 had their full need met. Average financial aid package met 51% of need; average scholarship/grant was $3,670; average loan was $3,277. For part-time students, average financial aid package was $8,197.

Students without need: 444 full-time freshmen who did not demonstrate need for aid received scholarships/grants; average award was $2,725. No-need awards available for academics, alumni affiliation, art, athletics, leadership, minority status, music/drama.

Scholarships offered: 39 full-time freshmen received athletic scholarships; average amount $4,150.

FINANCIAL AID PROCEDURES

Forms required: FAFSA, institutional form.

Dates and Deadlines: Priority date 5/1; no closing date. Applicants notified on a rolling basis starting 1/1; must reply within 2 week(s) of notification.

Transfers: No deadline.

CONTACT

Michael Francis, Assistant Vice President for Finance and Controller
800 West University Parkway, Orem, UT 84058-5999
(801) 863-8442

Weber State University

Ogden, Utah
www.weber.edu   Federal Code: 003680

4-year public university in small city.

Enrollment: 17,617 undergrads, 46% part-time. 1,468 full-time freshmen.

Selectivity: Open admission; but selective for some programs.

BASIC COSTS (2007-2008)

Tuition and fees: $3,664; out-of-state residents $11,135.

Room and board: $6,634.

FINANCIAL AID PICTURE (2006-2007)

Students with need: 44% of average financial aid package awarded as scholarships/grants, 56% awarded as loans/jobs. Need-based aid available for part-time students. Work study available nights, weekends, and for part-time students.

Students without need: This college awards aid only to students with need.

FINANCIAL AID PROCEDURES

Forms required: FAFSA, institutional form.

Dates and Deadlines: Priority date 3/1; no closing date. Applicants notified on a rolling basis starting 3/15; must reply within 2 week(s) of notification.

CONTACT

Jeb Spencer, Director of Financial Aid
1137 University Circle, Ogden, UT 84408-1137
(801) 626-7569

Westminster College

Salt Lake City, Utah
www.westminstercollege.edu   Federal Code: 003681

4-year private liberal arts college in very large city.

Enrollment: 2,020 undergrads, 10% part-time. 443 full-time freshmen.

Selectivity: Admits over 75% of applicants.

BASIC COSTS (2008-2009)

Tuition and fees: $23,790.

Per-credit charge: $975.

Room and board: $6,672.

FINANCIAL AID PICTURE (2007-2008)

Students with need: Out of 307 full-time freshmen who applied for aid, 248 were judged to have need. Of these, 247 received aid, and 134 had their full need met. Average financial aid package met 90% of need; average scholarship/grant was $11,350; average loan was $3,590. For part-time students, average financial aid package was $11,856.

Students without need: 190 full-time freshmen who did not demonstrate need for aid received scholarships/grants; average award was $9,220. No-need awards available for academics, alumni affiliation, art, athletics, leadership, minority status, music/drama, religious affiliation, ROTC.

Scholarships offered: 13 full-time freshmen received athletic scholarships; average amount $5,280.

Cumulative student debt: 59% of graduating class had student loans; average debt was $16,800.

FINANCIAL AID PROCEDURES

Forms required: FAFSA.

Dates and Deadlines: Priority date 4/15; no closing date. Applicants notified on a rolling basis starting 3/15; must reply by 5/1 or within 3 week(s) of notification.

Transfers: Transfer students eligible for work study, loans, scholarships and grants which range in amounts from $3,000 to $8,000 per year, with full-time attendance and 3.0 GPA.

CONTACT

Craig Green, Director of Financial Aid
1840 South 1300 East, Salt Lake City, UT 84105
(801) 832-2500

838 **Vermont** Bennington College

Vermont

Bennington College
Bennington, Vermont
www.bennington.edu

Federal Code: 003682
CSS Code: 3080

4-year private liberal arts college in large town.
Enrollment: 583 undergrads. 204 full-time freshmen.
Selectivity: Admits 50 to 75% of applicants.

BASIC COSTS (2008-2009)
Tuition and fees: $38,270.
Per-credit charge: $1,165.
Room and board: $10,680.

FINANCIAL AID PICTURE (2007-2008)
Students with need: Out of 159 full-time freshmen who applied for aid, 145 were judged to have need. Of these, 145 received aid, and 16 had their full need met. Average financial aid package met 83% of need; average scholarship/grant was $25,065; average loan was $2,930. Need-based aid available for part-time students.
Students without need: 20 full-time freshmen who did not demonstrate need for aid received scholarships/grants; average award was $22,833. No-need awards available for academics, art, leadership, music/drama.
Cumulative student debt: 72% of graduating class had student loans; average debt was $20,936.
Additional info: All applicants for undergraduate admission considered for scholarships based on quality of overall application.

FINANCIAL AID PROCEDURES
Forms required: FAFSA, institutional form. CSS PROFILE required of early decision applicants only.
Dates and Deadlines: Priority date 3/1; no closing date. Applicants notified by 4/1; must reply by 5/1 or within 2 week(s) of notification.
Transfers: Priority date 3/15; closing date 8/1. Applicants notified on a rolling basis starting 5/1; must reply by 6/1 or within 2 week(s) of notification.

CONTACT
Meg Woolmington, Director of Financial Aid
One College Drive, Bennington, VT 05201-6003
(802) 440-4325

Burlington College
Burlington, Vermont
www.burlington.edu

Federal Code: 012183

4-year private liberal arts college in small city.
Enrollment: 172 undergrads, 30% part-time. 23 full-time freshmen.
Selectivity: Admits 50 to 75% of applicants.

BASIC COSTS (2008-2009)
Tuition and fees: $19,640.
Per-credit charge: $650.
Room only: $6,095.

FINANCIAL AID PICTURE (2007-2008)
Students with need: Out of 19 full-time freshmen who applied for aid, 17 were judged to have need. Of these, 16 received aid. Average financial aid package met 49% of need; average scholarship/grant was $5,394; average loan was $4,967. For part-time students, average financial aid package was $6,961.
Cumulative student debt: 43% of graduating class had student loans; average debt was $32,302.

FINANCIAL AID PROCEDURES
Forms required: FAFSA, state aid form.
Dates and Deadlines: No deadline. Applicants notified on a rolling basis.
Transfers: No deadline. Applicants notified on a rolling basis.

CONTACT
Betsy Barnett, Financial Aid Coordinator
95 North Avenue, Burlington, VT 05401
(802) 654-3759

Castleton State College
Castleton, Vermont
www.castleton.edu

Federal Code: 003683

4-year public liberal arts college in small town.
Enrollment: 1,873 undergrads, 10% part-time. 406 full-time freshmen.
Selectivity: Admits 50 to 75% of applicants.

BASIC COSTS (2007-2008)
Tuition and fees: $7,244; out-of-state residents $15,428.
Per-credit charge: $294; out-of-state residents $635.
Room and board: $7,220.
Additional info: New England Board of Higher Education rate for students from other New England states: 150% of Vermont resident tuition. Available to degree candidates in academic areas not offered by educational institutions in their home states.

FINANCIAL AID PICTURE (2006-2007)
Students with need: 30% of average financial aid package awarded as scholarships/grants, 70% awarded as loans/jobs. Need-based aid available for part-time students.
Students without need: No-need awards available for academics, alumni affiliation, art, leadership, music/drama, state/district residency.

FINANCIAL AID PROCEDURES
Forms required: FAFSA.
Dates and Deadlines: Priority date 2/15; no closing date. Applicants notified on a rolling basis starting 1/1; must reply by 5/1 or within 2 week(s) of notification.

CONTACT
Kathy O'Meara, Financial Aid Director
Seminary Street, Castleton, VT 05735
(802) 468-1286

Champlain College
Burlington, Vermont
www.champlain.edu

Federal Code: 003684

4-year private business and liberal arts college in small city.
Enrollment: 2,493 undergrads, 20% part-time. 465 full-time freshmen.
Selectivity: Admits 50 to 75% of applicants.

BASIC COSTS (2007-2008)
Tuition and fees: $22,550.
Per-credit charge: $940.
Room and board: $10,910.

FINANCIAL AID PICTURE (2007-2008)
Students with need: Out of 419 full-time freshmen who applied for aid, 349 were judged to have need. Of these, 349 received aid, and 24 had their full need met. Average financial aid package met 60% of need; average scholarship/grant was $6,000; average loan was $4,290. For part-time students, average financial aid package was $6,867.

PART III: FINANCIAL AID COLLEGE BY COLLEGE

Students without need: 85 full-time freshmen who did not demonstrate need for aid received scholarships/grants; average award was $1,988. No-need awards available for academics, leadership.

FINANCIAL AID PROCEDURES

Forms required: FAFSA.

Dates and Deadlines: Closing date 3/1. Applicants notified by 3/19; must reply by 5/1.

Transfers: Closing date 5/1. Applicants notified on a rolling basis starting 5/1; must reply within 2 week(s) of notification.

CONTACT

David Myette, Director of Financial Aid
163 South Willard Street, Burlington, VT 05402-0670
(802) 860-2730

College of St. Joseph in Vermont
Rutland, Vermont
www.csj.edu   Federal Code: 003685

4-year private liberal arts and teachers college in large town, affiliated with Roman Catholic Church.

Enrollment: 209 undergrads, 23% part-time. 31 full-time freshmen.

Selectivity: Admits over 75% of applicants.

BASIC COSTS (2008-2009)

Tuition and fees: $15,760.

Per-credit charge: $250.

Room and board: $7,600.

FINANCIAL AID PICTURE (2007-2008)

Students with need: Out of 30 full-time freshmen who applied for aid, 28 were judged to have need. Of these, 28 received aid, and 6 had their full need met. Average financial aid package met 76% of need; average scholarship/grant was $11,224; average loan was $3,306. For part-time students, average financial aid package was $5,143.

Students without need: 2 full-time freshmen who did not demonstrate need for aid received scholarships/grants; average award was $2,000. No-need awards available for academics, athletics.

Cumulative student debt: 100% of graduating class had student loans; average debt was $24,402.

Additional info: Instructors at local Catholic schools are granted a tuition reduction.

FINANCIAL AID PROCEDURES

Forms required: FAFSA, institutional form.

Dates and Deadlines: Priority date 3/1; no closing date. Applicants notified on a rolling basis starting 3/15.

CONTACT

Yvonne Payrits, Financial Aid Director
71 Clement Road, Rutland, VT 05701-3899
(802) 773-5900 ext. 3218

Community College of Vermont
Waterbury, Vermont
www.ccv.edu   Federal Code: 011167

2-year public community college in small town.

Enrollment: 3,869 undergrads.

Selectivity: Open admission.

BASIC COSTS (2007-2008)

Tuition and fees: $5,500; out-of-state residents $10,900.

Per-credit charge: $180; out-of-state residents $360.

Additional info: New England Board of Higher Education rate for students from other New England states: 150% of Vermont resident tuition. Available to degree candidates in academic areas not offered by educational institutions in their home states.

FINANCIAL AID PICTURE

Students with need: Need-based aid available for full-time and part-time students. Work study available nights.

Students without need: This college awards aid only to students with need.

FINANCIAL AID PROCEDURES

Forms required: FAFSA, state aid form, institutional form.

Dates and Deadlines: No deadline. Applicants notified on a rolling basis starting 9/1; must reply within 3 week(s) of notification.

CONTACT

Pam Chisholm, Director for Financial Aid
PO BOX 120, Waterbury, VT 05676-0120
(802) 241-3535

Goddard College
Plainfield, Vermont
www.goddard.edu   Federal Code: 003686

4-year private liberal arts college in rural community.

Enrollment: 242 undergrads. 8 full-time freshmen.

Selectivity: Open admission; but selective for some programs.

BASIC COSTS (2007-2008)

Additional info: Annual tuition for distance learning Bachelor of Arts is $12,130.

FINANCIAL AID PICTURE (2007-2008)

Students with need: Average financial aid package met 40% of need; average scholarship/grant was $4,630; average loan was $4,591.

Students without need: No-need awards available for academics, art, job skills, leadership, music/drama, state/district residency.

FINANCIAL AID PROCEDURES

Forms required: FAFSA.

Dates and Deadlines: Applicants notified on a rolling basis starting 4/15; must reply within 4 week(s) of notification.

CONTACT

Beverly Jene, Director of Financial Aid
123 Pitkin Road, Plainfield, VT 05667
(802) 454-8311

Green Mountain College
Poultney, Vermont
www.greenmtn.edu   Federal Code: 003687

4-year private liberal arts college in small town, affiliated with United Methodist Church.

Enrollment: 759 undergrads, 1% part-time. 255 full-time freshmen.

Selectivity: Admits over 75% of applicants.

BASIC COSTS (2007-2008)

Tuition and fees: $24,565.

Per-credit charge: $792.

Room and board: $8,982.

FINANCIAL AID PICTURE (2007-2008)

Students with need: Average financial aid package met 71% of need; average scholarship/grant was $16,071; average loan was $4,380. For part-time students, average financial aid package was $9,886.

Students without need: No-need awards available for academics, alumni affiliation, art, leadership, music/drama, religious affiliation.

Scholarships offered: Scholarships for art, performing arts, environmental service, leadership, service: range from $500-$5,000; renewable annually. Make A Difference Scholarship: full tuition; room and board; based on merit.

Cumulative student debt: 70% of graduating class had student loans; average debt was $37,014.

Additional info: Service/recognition awards available to all students.

FINANCIAL AID PROCEDURES

Forms required: FAFSA. CSS PROFILE is recommended to receive an earlier financial aid package.

Dates and Deadlines: Priority date 3/1; no closing date. Applicants notified on a rolling basis starting 1/1; must reply by 5/1 or within 4 week(s) of notification.

Transfers: No deadline. Applicants notified on a rolling basis; must reply by 5/1 or within 4 week(s) of notification.

CONTACT

Wendy Ellis, Director of Financial Aid
One College Circle, Poultney, VT 05764
(802) 287-8210

Johnson State College
Johnson, Vermont
www.jsc.vsc.edu   Federal Code: 003688

4-year public liberal arts college in rural community.
Enrollment: 1,470 undergrads.

BASIC COSTS (2007-2008)

Tuition and fees: $7,244; out-of-state residents $15,428.
Per-credit charge: $294; out-of-state residents $635.
Room and board: $7,220.
Additional info: New England Board of Higher Education rate for students from other New England states: 150% of Vermont resident tuition. Available to degree candidates in academic areas not offered by educational institutions in their home states.

FINANCIAL AID PICTURE

Students with need: Need-based aid available for full-time and part-time students.
Students without need: No-need awards available for academics.

FINANCIAL AID PROCEDURES

Forms required: FAFSA, state aid form.
Dates and Deadlines: Priority date 3/1; no closing date. Applicants notified on a rolling basis starting 4/1; must reply within 3 week(s) of notification.
Transfers: Financial aid transcripts from previously attended colleges required.

CONTACT

Penny Howrigan, Associate Dean of Enrollment Services
337 College Hill, Johnson, VT 05656
(800) 635-2356

Landmark College
Putney, Vermont
www.landmark.edu   Federal Code: 017157

2-year private liberal arts college in small town.
Enrollment: 462 undergrads, 38% part-time. 46 full-time freshmen.
Selectivity: Admits 50 to 75% of applicants.

BASIC COSTS (2008-2009)

Tuition and fees: $43,575.
Room and board: $7,800.
Additional info: Notebook computer and software required. Approximate cost through school $2,500.

FINANCIAL AID PICTURE (2007-2008)

Students with need: Average financial aid package for all full-time undergraduates was $22,100. 71% awarded as scholarships/grants, 29% awarded as loans/jobs. Need-based aid available for part-time students. Work study available nights, weekends, and for part-time students.

Students without need: No-need awards available for academics, art, athletics, leadership, minority status, music/drama.

Cumulative student debt: 49% of graduating class had student loans; average debt was $12,552.

Additional info: Students encouraged to apply to their state departments of vocational rehabilitation for additional financial assistance.

FINANCIAL AID PROCEDURES

Forms required: FAFSA.

Dates and Deadlines: Priority date 3/15; no closing date. Applicants notified on a rolling basis starting 4/15; must reply within 2 week(s) of notification.

Transfers: No deadline. Applicants notified on a rolling basis; must reply within 2 week(s) of notification.

CONTACT

Cathy Mullins, Director of Financial Aid
River Road South, Putney, VT 05346
(802) 387-6736

Lyndon State College
Lyndonville, Vermont
www.lyndonstate.edu   Federal Code: 003689

4-year public liberal arts and teachers college in small town.
Enrollment: 1,371 undergrads, 12% part-time.
Selectivity: Admits over 75% of applicants.

BASIC COSTS (2007-2008)

Tuition and fees: $7,244; out-of-state residents $15,428.
Per-credit charge: $294; out-of-state residents $635.
Room and board: $7,220.
Additional info: New England Board of Higher Education rate for students from other New England states: 150% of Vermont resident tuition. Available to degree candidates in academic areas not offered by educational institutions in their home states.

FINANCIAL AID PICTURE

Students with need: Need-based aid available for full-time and part-time students. Work study available nights, weekends, and for part-time students.
Students without need: No-need awards available for academics, leadership.

FINANCIAL AID PROCEDURES

Forms required: FAFSA.
Dates and Deadlines: Priority date 2/1; no closing date. Applicants notified on a rolling basis starting 4/1; must reply within 2 week(s) of notification.

CONTACT

Tanya Bradley, Director of Financial Aid
1001 College Road, Lyndonville, VT 05851
(802) 626-6218

Marlboro College

Marlboro, Vermont
www.marlboro.edu
Federal Code: 003690

4-year private liberal arts college in rural community.

Enrollment: 330 undergrads, 4% part-time. 67 full-time freshmen.

Selectivity: Admits 50 to 75% of applicants.

BASIC COSTS (2007-2008)

Tuition and fees: $30,680.

Per-credit charge: $990.

Room and board: $8,860.

FINANCIAL AID PICTURE (2007-2008)

Students with need: 67% of average financial aid package awarded as scholarships/grants, 33% awarded as loans/jobs. Need-based aid available for part-time students.

Students without need: No-need awards available for academics, leadership.

FINANCIAL AID PROCEDURES

Forms required: FAFSA.

Dates and Deadlines: Closing date 3/1. Applicants notified on a rolling basis starting 2/15; must reply by 5/1 or within 2 week(s) of notification.

CONTACT

Alan Young, Dean of Enrollment and Financial Aid
PO Box A, Marlboro, VT 05344-0300
(802) 258-9237

Middlebury College

Middlebury, Vermont
www.middlebury.edu
Federal Code: 003691
CSS Code: 3526

4-year private liberal arts college in small town.

Enrollment: 2,475 undergrads, 1% part-time. 563 full-time freshmen.

Selectivity: Admits less than 50% of applicants.

BASIC COSTS (2008-2009)

Comprehensive fee: $49,210.

FINANCIAL AID PICTURE (2006-2007)

Students with need: Out of 333 full-time freshmen who applied for aid, 255 were judged to have need. Of these, 255 received aid, and 255 had their full need met. Average financial aid package met 100% of need; average scholarship/grant was $29,097; average loan was $3,386. Need-based aid available for part-time students.

Students without need: This college awards aid only to students with need.

Cumulative student debt: 39% of graduating class had student loans; average debt was $20,808.

Additional info: College maintains need-blind admissions policy and meets full demonstrated financial need of students who qualify for admission, to degree resources permit.

FINANCIAL AID PROCEDURES

Forms required: FAFSA, CSS PROFILE, institutional form.

Dates and Deadlines: Priority date 11/15; closing date 1/1. Applicants notified by 4/1; must reply by 5/1.

Transfers: Closing date 3/1. Applicants notified by 4/15.

CONTACT

Kim Downs, Director of Student Financial Services
The Emma Willard House, Middlebury, VT 05753-6002
(802) 443-5158

New England Culinary Institute

Montpelier, Vermont
www.neci.edu
Federal Code: 022540

2-year for-profit culinary school in small town.

Enrollment: 637 undergrads. 127 full-time freshmen.

Selectivity: Admits 50 to 75% of applicants.

BASIC COSTS (2007-2008)

Tuition and fees: $25,652.

Room and board: $6,828.

Additional info: Costs vary with program. Required fees include books, knife kit, and library and room deposit.

FINANCIAL AID PICTURE

Students with need: Need-based aid available for full-time students. Work study available nights, weekends, and for part-time students.

Students without need: No-need awards available for academics, alumni affiliation, job skills.

Scholarships offered: Next Generation Scholarship: $1,000 awarded to students recommended by alumni. James Beard Foundation: $1,000-$2,000 awarded. Massachusetts Restaurant Association: up to $2,500 awarded. National Restaurant Association: up to $2,000 awarded.

FINANCIAL AID PROCEDURES

Forms required: FAFSA, state aid form.

Dates and Deadlines: No deadline. Applicants notified on a rolling basis.

Transfers: No deadline. Applicants notified on a rolling basis.

CONTACT

Jim Hutton, Financial Planner
56 College Street, Montpelier, VT 05602
(877) 223-6324

Norwich University

Northfield, Vermont
www.norwich.edu
Federal Code: 003692
CSS Code: 3669

4-year private university and military college in small town.

Enrollment: 1,995 undergrads.

Selectivity: Admits 50 to 75% of applicants.

BASIC COSTS (2007-2008)

Tuition and fees: $24,430.

Per-credit charge: $578.

Room and board: $8,522.

Additional info: Military students pay an additional $1,500 per year for cadet uniform for first and second years.

FINANCIAL AID PICTURE

Students with need: Need-based aid available for full-time and part-time students.

Students without need: No-need awards available for academics, leadership, music/drama, ROTC.

Additional info: Winners of ROTC scholarships receive full room and board; must maintain 2.75 GPA. Renewable up to 4 years.

FINANCIAL AID PROCEDURES

Forms required: FAFSA, CSS PROFILE, institutional form.

Dates and Deadlines: Priority date 3/1; no closing date. Applicants notified on a rolling basis starting 12/15.

CONTACT

Karen McGrath, Dean of Enrollment Management
158 Harmon Drive, Northfield, VT 05663
(802) 485-2015

St. Michael's College

Colchester, Vermont
www.smcvt.edu

Federal Code: 003694

4-year private liberal arts college in large town, affiliated with Roman Catholic Church.

Enrollment: 1,980 undergrads, 1% part-time. 524 full-time freshmen.
Selectivity: Admits 50 to 75% of applicants.

BASIC COSTS (2008-2009)

Tuition and fees: $31,940.
Per-credit charge: $1,055.
Room and board: $7,960.

FINANCIAL AID PICTURE (2007-2008)

Students with need: Out of 390 full-time freshmen who applied for aid, 296 were judged to have need. Of these, 296 received aid, and 86 had their full need met. Average financial aid package met 75% of need; average scholarship/grant was $13,095; average loan was $4,652. Need-based aid available for part-time students.
Students without need: 150 full-time freshmen who did not demonstrate need for aid received scholarships/grants; average award was $7,882. No-need awards available for academics, athletics, ROTC.
Scholarships offered: 3 full-time freshmen received athletic scholarships; average amount $37,405.
Cumulative student debt: 75% of graduating class had student loans; average debt was $24,451.

FINANCIAL AID PROCEDURES

Forms required: FAFSA. CSS PROFILE should be submitted by students who apply for early action and want early estimate on aid.
Dates and Deadlines: Priority date 3/15; no closing date. Applicants notified on a rolling basis starting 2/1; must reply by 5/1 or within 2 week(s) of notification.

CONTACT

Daniel Couture, Director of Student Financial Services
One Winooski Park, Colchester, VT 05439
(802) 654-3244

Southern Vermont College

Bennington, Vermont
www.svc.edu

Federal Code: 003693

4-year private liberal arts college in large town.

Enrollment: 406 undergrads, 17% part-time. 92 full-time freshmen.
Selectivity: Admits 50 to 75% of applicants.

BASIC COSTS (2008-2009)

Tuition and fees: $18,160.
Per-credit charge: $575.
Room and board: $8,500.
Additional info: Health insurance, if applicable, $650 per year.

FINANCIAL AID PICTURE

Students with need: Need-based aid available for full-time and part-time students. Work study available nights, weekends, and for part-time students.
Students without need: No-need awards available for academics, leadership.
Scholarships offered: Everett Scholarship: based on academic merit; $1,000-$5,000; deadline March 1; renewable. Leadership Scholarships and Presidential Scholarships: awarded to 5 first-time freshmen; $2,000; renewable annually.

FINANCIAL AID PROCEDURES

Forms required: FAFSA, state aid form, institutional form.
Dates and Deadlines: No deadline. Applicants notified on a rolling basis.

Transfers: $1,000 need-based transfer scholarship available for each transfer.

CONTACT

Joel Phelps, Director of Financial Aid Services
982 Mansion Drive, Bennington, VT 05201
(802) 447-6306

Sterling College

Craftsbury Common, Vermont
www.sterlingcollege.edu

Federal Code: 014991

4-year private agricultural and liberal arts college in rural community.

Enrollment: 104 undergrads, 2% part-time. 30 full-time freshmen.
Selectivity: Admits over 75% of applicants.

BASIC COSTS (2008-2009)

Tuition and fees: $21,655.
Per-credit charge: $650.
Room and board: $7,192.
Additional info: Students receive $1,550 tuition and book credit in exchange for work done on campus.

FINANCIAL AID PICTURE

Students with need: Need-based aid available for full-time and part-time students. Work study available nights, weekends, and for part-time students.
Students without need: No-need awards available for academics, leadership, state/district residency.
Scholarships offered: Achievement Scholarships: $700-$1,200; demonstration of a significant life achievement. Vermont Scholarship: $1,000-$2,000; for Vermont residents. Bounder Scholarship: $500; applicants who live west of the Mississippi or in the Deep South. Presidential Scholarship: $500-$5,000; applicants who have performed well academically, pursued some degree of activity in environmental, outdoor leadership, or resource management. SCA Award: $1,000; alumni of Student Conservation Association. Transfer Award: $1,000; transfer students for transfer costs. Environmental Steward Scholarship: full-tuition; awarded to student who has displayed exceptional commitment to environment. Vermont Youth Conservation Corps Award: $1,000; awarded to alumni of VYCC.

FINANCIAL AID PROCEDURES

Forms required: FAFSA, state aid form, institutional form.
Dates and Deadlines: Priority date 3/15; no closing date. Applicants notified on a rolling basis starting 2/1; must reply by 5/1 or within 2 week(s) of notification.

CONTACT

Edward Houston, Director of Financial Aid
PO Box 72, Craftsbury Common, VT 05827-0072
(800) 648-3591 ext. 103

University of Vermont

Burlington, Vermont
www.uvm.edu

Federal Code: 003696

4-year public university in large town.

Enrollment: 9,454 undergrads, 3% part-time. 2,178 full-time freshmen.
Selectivity: Admits 50 to 75% of applicants.

BASIC COSTS (2007-2008)

Tuition and fees: $12,054; out-of-state residents $27,938.
Per-credit charge: $434; out-of-state residents $1,096.
Room and board: $8,024.
Additional info: Additional $24 fee for on-campus students.

FINANCIAL AID PICTURE (2006-2007)

Students with need: Out of 1,574 full-time freshmen who applied for aid, 1,199 were judged to have need. Of these, 1,195 received aid, and 328 had their full need met. Average financial aid package met 80% of need; average scholarship/grant was $11,313; average loan was $5,764. For part-time students, average financial aid package was $8,866.

Students without need: 639 full-time freshmen who did not demonstrate need for aid received scholarships/grants; average award was $1,961. No-need awards available for academics, art, athletics, ROTC.

Scholarships offered: 38 full-time freshmen received athletic scholarships; average amount $18,677.

Cumulative student debt: 61% of graduating class had student loans; average debt was $23,567.

FINANCIAL AID PROCEDURES

Forms required: FAFSA.

Dates and Deadlines: Priority date 2/10; no closing date. Applicants notified on a rolling basis starting 3/15; must reply within 4 week(s) of notification.

Transfers: No deadline. Applicants notified on a rolling basis starting 3/15; must reply within 4 week(s) of notification. Merit-based scholarships not available to transfer students.

CONTACT

Cecilia Dry, Assistant Controller and Director Student Financial Services
194 South Prospect Street, Burlington, VT 05401-3596
(802) 656-5700

Vermont Technical College
Randolph Center, Vermont
www.vtc.edu   Federal Code: 003698

4-year public technical college in small town.

Enrollment: 1,378 undergrads, 16% part-time. 280 full-time freshmen.

Selectivity: Admits 50 to 75% of applicants.

BASIC COSTS (2007-2008)

Tuition and fees: $9,148; out-of-state residents $17,092.

Per-credit charge: $365; out-of-state residents $696.

Room and board: $7,220.

Additional info: New England Board of Higher Education rate for students from other New England states: 150% of Vermont resident tuition. Available to degree candidates in academic areas not offered by educational institutions in their home states.

FINANCIAL AID PICTURE

Students with need: Need-based aid available for full-time and part-time students. Work study available nights, weekends, and for part-time students.

Students without need: No-need awards available for academics.

Scholarships offered: Presidential Scholarship: $5,000; awarded to 5 non-residents. Scholars program: full tuition for 2 years (excluding room and board); awarded to 4 Vermont students.

FINANCIAL AID PROCEDURES

Forms required: FAFSA.

Dates and Deadlines: Priority date 3/1; no closing date. Applicants notified on a rolling basis starting 3/15; must reply within 2 week(s) of notification.

CONTACT

Cathy McCullough, Director of Financial Aid
PO Box 500, Randolph Center, VT 05061-0500
(800) 965-8790

Woodbury College
Montpelier, Vermont
www.woodbury-college.edu   Federal Code: 014348

4-year private technical and career college in small town.

Enrollment: 70 undergrads, 24% part-time. 2 full-time freshmen.

Selectivity: Open admission; but selective for some programs.

BASIC COSTS (2007-2008)

Tuition and fees: $16,050.

Per-credit charge: $663.

FINANCIAL AID PICTURE (2006-2007)

Students with need: Out of 2 full-time freshmen who applied for aid, 2 were judged to have need. Of these, 2 received aid. Average financial aid package met 48% of need; average scholarship/grant was $8,330; average loan was $3,500. For part-time students, average financial aid package was $7,131.

FINANCIAL AID PROCEDURES

Forms required: FAFSA, state aid form.

Dates and Deadlines: No deadline.

Transfers: No deadline. Applicants notified on a rolling basis.

CONTACT

Suzanne Rexford-Winston, Director of Financial Aid
660 Elm Street, Montpelier, VT 05602
(802) 229-0516 ext. 275

Virginia

Art Institute of Washington
Arlington, Virginia
www.aiw.artinstitutes.edu   Federal Code: 009270

4-year for-profit culinary school and visual arts college in small city.

Enrollment: 1,700 undergrads.

BASIC COSTS (2008-2009)

Tuition and fees: $20,880.

Room only: $8,370.

FINANCIAL AID PICTURE

Students with need: Need-based aid available for part-time students.

FINANCIAL AID PROCEDURES

Forms required: FAFSA, institutional form.

CONTACT

Sam Mill, Director of Student Financial Services
1820 North Fort Myer Drive, Arlington, VA 22209-1802
(703) 358-9550

Averett University
Danville, Virginia
www.averett.edu   Federal Code: 003702

4-year private university and liberal arts college in small city.

Enrollment: 790 undergrads, 4% part-time. 160 full-time freshmen.

Selectivity: Admits over 75% of applicants.

BASIC COSTS (2008-2009)

Tuition and fees: $21,300.

Room and board: $7,390.

FINANCIAL AID PICTURE (2006-2007)

Students with need: Out of 151 full-time freshmen who applied for aid, 124 were judged to have need. Of these, 124 received aid, and 25 had their full need met. Average financial aid package met 74% of need; average scholarship/grant was $9,211; average loan was $4,367. For part-time students, average financial aid package was $11,080.

Students without need: 52 full-time freshmen who did not demonstrate need for aid received scholarships/grants; average award was $11,994. No-need awards available for academics, alumni affiliation, art, leadership, minority status, music/drama, state/district residency.

Cumulative student debt: 70% of graduating class had student loans; average debt was $24,918.

FINANCIAL AID PROCEDURES

Forms required: FAFSA, state aid form.

Dates and Deadlines: Priority date 4/1; no closing date. Applicants notified on a rolling basis starting 2/15; must reply within 2 week(s) of notification.

Transfers: No deadline. Applicants notified on a rolling basis starting 2/15; must reply within 2 week(s) of notification.

CONTACT

Carl Bradsher, Dean of Financial Assistance
420 West Main Street, Danville, VA 24541
(434) 791-5890

Blue Ridge Community College

Weyers Cave, Virginia
www.brcc.edu
Federal Code: 006819

2-year public community college in rural community.

Enrollment: 4,084 undergrads, 59% part-time.

Selectivity: Open admission; but selective for some programs.

BASIC COSTS (2007-2008)

Tuition and fees: $2,470; out-of-state residents $7,634.

Per-credit charge: $77; out-of-state residents $249.

Additional info: Out of state students pay an additional $90 capital outlay fee.

FINANCIAL AID PICTURE (2006-2007)

Students with need: Need-based aid available for part-time students.

Students without need: No-need awards available for academics, job skills, leadership, minority status.

FINANCIAL AID PROCEDURES

Forms required: FAFSA, institutional form.

Dates and Deadlines: Priority date 5/1; no closing date. Applicants notified on a rolling basis starting 5/30; must reply within 2 week(s) of notification.

CONTACT

Robert Clemmer, Financial Aid Officer
Box 80, Weyers Cave, VA 24486-9989
(540) 234-9261 ext. 2223

Bluefield College

Bluefield, Virginia
www.bluefield.edu
Federal Code: 003703

4-year private liberal arts college in small town, affiliated with Baptist faith.

Enrollment: 761 undergrads, 16% part-time. 89 full-time freshmen.

Selectivity: Admits 50 to 75% of applicants.

BASIC COSTS (2008-2009)

Tuition and fees: $15,640.

Per-credit charge: $490.

Room and board: $6,560.

Additional info: Tuition/fee waivers available for adults.

FINANCIAL AID PICTURE (2007-2008)

Students with need: Average financial aid package met 81% of need; average scholarship/grant was $10,055; average loan was $3,162. For part-time students, average financial aid package was $8,808.

Students without need: No-need awards available for academics, art, athletics, leadership, music/drama, religious affiliation, state/district residency.

Cumulative student debt: 94% of graduating class had student loans; average debt was $15,417.

FINANCIAL AID PROCEDURES

Forms required: FAFSA, state aid form.

Dates and Deadlines: Priority date 3/15; no closing date. Applicants notified on a rolling basis starting 3/1; must reply within 3 week(s) of notification.

Transfers: No deadline. Applicants notified on a rolling basis starting 3/1; must reply within 3 week(s) of notification.

CONTACT

Sheila Nelson-Hensley, Director of Financial Aid
3000 College Drive, Bluefield, VA 24605
(276) 326-4215

Bridgewater College

Bridgewater, Virginia
www.bridgewater.edu
Federal Code: 003704

4-year private liberal arts college in small town, affiliated with Church of the Brethren.

Enrollment: 1,527 undergrads. 445 full-time freshmen.

Selectivity: Admits over 75% of applicants.

BASIC COSTS (2008-2009)

Tuition and fees: $23,090.

Per-credit charge: $775.

Room and board: $9,900.

Additional info: Tuition/fee waivers available for minority students.

FINANCIAL AID PICTURE (2007-2008)

Students with need: Out of 389 full-time freshmen who applied for aid, 328 were judged to have need. Of these, 328 received aid, and 93 had their full need met. Average financial aid package met 85% of need; average scholarship/grant was $4,669; average loan was $4,867. For part-time students, average financial aid package was $3,820.

Students without need: 115 full-time freshmen who did not demonstrate need for aid received scholarships/grants; average award was $10,080. No-need awards available for academics, music/drama, religious affiliation.

Cumulative student debt: 77% of graduating class had student loans; average debt was $29,050.

FINANCIAL AID PROCEDURES

Forms required: FAFSA, state aid form.

Dates and Deadlines: Priority date 3/1; no closing date. Applicants notified on a rolling basis starting 3/15; must reply within 2 week(s) of notification.

CONTACT

J. Fairchilds, Director of Financial Aid
402 East College Street, Bridgewater, VA 22812-1599
(540) 828-5377

Bryant & Stratton College: Richmond

Richmond, Virginia
www.bryantstratton.edu
Federal Code: 010061

2-year for-profit career college in small city.

Enrollment: 516 undergrads, 51% part-time. 127 full-time freshmen.

Selectivity: Open admission; but selective for some programs.

BASIC COSTS (2007-2008)

Tuition and fees: $13,185.

Per-credit charge: $415.

Additional info: Annual tuition for bachelor's degree may vary by program.

FINANCIAL AID PICTURE (2006-2007)

Students with need: 31% of average financial aid package awarded as scholarships/grants, 69% awarded as loans/jobs. Need-based aid available for part-time students.

Students without need: This college awards aid only to students with need.

Cumulative student debt: 90% of graduating class had student loans; average debt was $30,000.

FINANCIAL AID PROCEDURES

Forms required: FAFSA.

Dates and Deadlines: No deadline.

Transfers: No deadline.

CONTACT

Eric Blackwell, Business Office Director

8141 Hull Street Road, Richmond, VA 23235

(804) 745-2444

Bryant & Stratton College: Virginia Beach

Virginia Beach, Virginia

www.bryantstratton.edu   Federal Code: 002678

2-year for-profit business and junior college in large city.

Enrollment: 477 undergrads, 57% part-time. 119 full-time freshmen.

Selectivity: Open admission.

BASIC COSTS (2008-2009)

Tuition and fees: $13,205.

Per-credit charge: $436.

FINANCIAL AID PICTURE

Students with need: Need-based aid available for full-time and part-time students. Work study available nights.

FINANCIAL AID PROCEDURES

Forms required: FAFSA.

Dates and Deadlines: No deadline. Applicants notified on a rolling basis.

CONTACT

Bethann Verbal, Director of Financial Aid

301 Centre Pointe Drive, Virginia Beach, VA 23462-4417

(757) 499-7900

Christendom College

Front Royal, Virginia

www.christendom.edu

4-year private liberal arts college in large town, affiliated with Roman Catholic Church.

Enrollment: 397 undergrads, 2% part-time. 93 full-time freshmen.

Selectivity: Admits over 75% of applicants.

BASIC COSTS (2008-2009)

Tuition and fees: $18,806.

Room and board: $6,688.

FINANCIAL AID PICTURE (2007-2008)

Students with need: Out of 65 full-time freshmen who applied for aid, 43 were judged to have need. Of these, 43 received aid, and 43 had their full need met. Average financial aid package met 90% of need; average scholarship/grant was $6,130; average loan was $4,825.

Students without need: 24 full-time freshmen who did not demonstrate need for aid received scholarships/grants; average award was $6,940. No-need awards available for academics, alumni affiliation.

Cumulative student debt: 54% of graduating class had student loans; average debt was $13,570.

Additional info: Christendom accepts no direct federal aid, nor does it participate in indirect programs of federal aid.

FINANCIAL AID PROCEDURES

Forms required: institutional form.

Dates and Deadlines: Priority date 4/1; closing date 6/1. Applicants notified on a rolling basis starting 2/1; must reply within 4 week(s) of notification.

CONTACT

Alisa Polk, Financial Aid Officer

134 Christendom Drive, Front Royal, VA 22630

(800) 877-5456

Christopher Newport University

Newport News, Virginia

www.cnu.edu   Federal Code: 003706

4-year public university and liberal arts college in small city.

Enrollment: 4,663 undergrads, 4% part-time. 1,242 full-time freshmen.

Selectivity: Admits 50 to 75% of applicants.

BASIC COSTS (2008-2009)

Tuition and fees: $7,050; out-of-state residents $14,150.

Room and board: $8,500.

FINANCIAL AID PICTURE (2007-2008)

Students with need: Average financial aid package met 79% of need; average scholarship/grant was $4,890; average loan was $3,060. For part-time students, average financial aid package was $4,375.

Students without need: No-need awards available for academics, art, leadership, music/drama, ROTC, state/district residency.

Cumulative student debt: 57% of graduating class had student loans; average debt was $15,872.

FINANCIAL AID PROCEDURES

Forms required: FAFSA.

Dates and Deadlines: Priority date 3/1; no closing date. Applicants notified on a rolling basis starting 2/21; must reply within 2 week(s) of notification.

Transfers: No deadline. Applicants notified on a rolling basis starting 3/1; must reply within 2 week(s) of notification.

CONTACT

Mary Wigginton, Director of Financial Aid

1 University Place, Newport News, VA 23606

(757) 594-7170

College of William and Mary

Williamsburg, Virginia

www.wm.edu   Federal Code: 003705

4-year public university in large town.

Enrollment: 5,706 undergrads, 1% part-time. 1,345 full-time freshmen.

Selectivity: Admits less than 50% of applicants. GED not accepted.

BASIC COSTS (2007-2008)

Tuition and fees: $9,164; out-of-state residents $26,725.

Per-credit charge: $208; out-of-state residents $790.

Room and board: $7,385.

FINANCIAL AID PICTURE (2007-2008)

Students with need: Out of 883 full-time freshmen who applied for aid, 397 were judged to have need. Of these, 397 received aid, and 191 had their full need met. Average financial aid package met 85% of need; average scholarship/grant was $12,376; average loan was $2,330.

Students without need: 22 full-time freshmen who did not demonstrate need for aid received scholarships/grants; average award was $5,854. No-need awards available for academics, athletics, leadership, ROTC.

Scholarships offered: 72 full-time freshmen received athletic scholarships; average amount $14,521.

Cumulative student debt: 32% of graduating class had student loans; average debt was $15,602.

FINANCIAL AID PROCEDURES

Forms required: FAFSA. CSS PROFILE required of early decision applicants only.

Dates and Deadlines: Priority date 2/15; closing date 3/15. Applicants notified on a rolling basis starting 3/15; must reply by 5/1 or within 2 week(s) of notification.

CONTACT

Edward Irish, Director of Student Financial Aid

PO Box 8795, Williamsburg, VA 23187-8795

(757) 221-2420

Dabney S. Lancaster Community College

Clifton Forge, Virginia

www.dslcc.edu

Federal Code: 004996

2-year public community college in small town.

Enrollment: 527 undergrads.

Selectivity: Open admission; but selective for some programs.

BASIC COSTS (2007-2008)

Tuition and fees: $2,441; out-of-state residents $7,605.

Per-credit charge: $77; out-of-state residents $249.

Additional info: Out of state students pay an additional $90 capital outlay fee.

FINANCIAL AID PICTURE

Students with need: Need-based aid available for full-time and part-time students.

Students without need: This college awards aid only to students with need.

FINANCIAL AID PROCEDURES

Forms required: FAFSA, institutional form.

Dates and Deadlines: Priority date 3/15; no closing date. Applicants notified on a rolling basis starting 4/15; must reply within 2 week(s) of notification.

CONTACT

Sandra Haverlack, Financial Aid Officer

Box 1000, Clifton Forge, VA 24422

(540) 863-2822

Danville Community College

Danville, Virginia

www.dcc.vccs.edu

Federal Code: 003758

2-year public community college in small city.

Enrollment: 2,168 undergrads.

Selectivity: Open admission; but selective for some programs.

BASIC COSTS (2007-2008)

Tuition and fees: $2,437; out-of-state residents $7,601.

Per-credit charge: $77; out-of-state residents $249.

Additional info: Out of state students pay an additional $90 capital outlay fee.

FINANCIAL AID PICTURE

Students with need: Need-based aid available for full-time and part-time students.

Students without need: This college awards aid only to students with need.

Scholarships offered: Educational Foundation Scholarship: $250 to $1,500; based on separate application; deadline mid-March prior to award year.

FINANCIAL AID PROCEDURES

Forms required: FAFSA.

Dates and Deadlines: Priority date 6/1; no closing date. Applicants notified on a rolling basis starting 5/1; must reply within 2 week(s) of notification.

Transfers: Limited aid available to transfer students admitted in spring semester.

CONTACT

Mary Gore, Assistant Coordinator of Financial Aid

1008 South Main Street, Danville, VA 24541

(434) 797-8439

DeVry University: Arlington

Arlington, Virginia

www.devry.edu

4-year for-profit university in very large city.

Enrollment: 550 undergrads, 40% part-time. 989 full-time freshmen.

BASIC COSTS (2007-2008)

Tuition and fees: $14,640.

Per-credit charge: $525.

FINANCIAL AID PICTURE (2006-2007)

Students with need: Out of 54 full-time freshmen who applied for aid, 48 were judged to have need. Of these, 47 received aid, and 1 had their full need met. Average financial aid package met 35% of need; average scholarship/grant was $4,662; average loan was $4,328. For part-time students, average financial aid package was $6,812.

Students without need: This college awards aid only to students with need.

Cumulative student debt: 50% of graduating class had student loans; average debt was $31,875.

FINANCIAL AID PROCEDURES

Forms required: FAFSA.

Dates and Deadlines: No deadline. Applicants notified on a rolling basis.

CONTACT

Roberta McDevitt, Director of Student Finance

2450 Crystal Drive, Arlington, VA 22202

(703) 414-4000

Eastern Mennonite University

Harrisonburg, Virginia

www.emu.edu

Federal Code: 003708

4-year private university and liberal arts college in large town, affiliated with Mennonite Church.

Enrollment: 953 undergrads, 1% part-time. 203 full-time freshmen.

Selectivity: Admits 50 to 75% of applicants.

BASIC COSTS (2007-2008)

Tuition and fees: $21,960.
Room and board: $6,900.

FINANCIAL AID PICTURE

Students with need: Need-based aid available for full-time and part-time students. Work study available nights, weekends, and for part-time students.
Students without need: No-need awards available for academics, alumni affiliation, art, leadership, religious affiliation, state/district residency.
Scholarships offered: President's Scholarship: GPA of 3.9 or higher. Academic Achievement Scholarship: minimum 3.2 GPA. University Grant: minimum 2.5 GPA; minimum SAT score of 920 (exclusive of Writing) or ACT score of 20 required for all scholarships. Amounts based on GPA and test scores; no limit on number of awards. Full-tuition scholarships available for 2 honors program applicants with highest test scores and GPA; half tuition scholarships available for next 10 candidates.

FINANCIAL AID PROCEDURES

Forms required: FAFSA, state aid form.
Dates and Deadlines: Priority date 3/1; no closing date. Applicants notified on a rolling basis starting 3/1; must reply within 4 week(s) of notification.
Transfers: No deadline. Applicants notified on a rolling basis starting 3/1; must reply within 4 week(s) of notification.

CONTACT

Michele Hensley, Director of Financial Assistance
1200 Park Road, Harrisonburg, VA 22802-2462
(540) 432-4137

Eastern Shore Community College

Melfa, Virginia
www.es.vccs.edu   Federal Code: 003748

2-year public community college in rural community.
Enrollment: 571 undergrads.
Selectivity: Open admission.

BASIC COSTS (2007-2008)

Tuition and fees: $2,465; out-of-state residents $7,629.
Per-credit charge: $77; out-of-state residents $249.
Additional info: Out of state students pay an additional $90 capital outlay fee.

FINANCIAL AID PICTURE

Students with need: Need-based aid available for full-time and part-time students.
Students without need: This college awards aid only to students with need.
Additional info: ESCC is a member of the Servicemembers Opportunity Colleges (SOC) program. This is a world-wide network of colleges and universities working with the Armed Forces dedicated to helping service people and their families get college degrees.

FINANCIAL AID PROCEDURES

Forms required: FAFSA.
Dates and Deadlines: Priority date 5/1; no closing date. Applicants notified on a rolling basis starting 6/1; must reply within 2 week(s) of notification.

CONTACT

P. Smith, Chief Financial Aid Officer
29300 Lankford Highway, Melfa, VA 23410-9755
(757) 789-1732

ECPI College of Technology: Virginia Beach

Virginia Beach, Virginia
www.ecpi.edu   Federal Code: 010198

4-year for-profit health science and technical college in very large city.
Enrollment: 6,100 undergrads.

BASIC COSTS (2008-2009)

Tuition and fees: $10,300.
Per-credit charge: $272.

FINANCIAL AID PICTURE

Students with need: Need-based aid available for full-time and part-time students. Work study available nights.
Students without need: No-need awards available for academics.

FINANCIAL AID PROCEDURES

Forms required: institutional form.
Dates and Deadlines: No deadline. Applicants notified on a rolling basis.

CONTACT

Kathi Turner, Director of Financial Aid
5555 Greenwich Road, Suite 300, Virginia Beach, VA 23462-6542
(757) 671-7171 ext. 311

ECPI Technical College: Roanoke

Roanoke, Virginia
www.ecpitech.edu   Federal Code: 017205

2-year for-profit technical college in small city.
Enrollment: 295 undergrads.

BASIC COSTS (2007-2008)

Tuition and fees: $10,150.

FINANCIAL AID PICTURE

Students with need: Need-based aid available for full-time and part-time students.

FINANCIAL AID PROCEDURES

Forms required: FAFSA.
Dates and Deadlines: No deadline. Applicants notified on a rolling basis.

CONTACT

Carol Rouch, Director of Financial Aid
5234 Airport Road, Roanoke, VA 24012
(540) 563-8080

Emory & Henry College

Emory, Virginia
www.ehc.edu   Federal Code: 003709

4-year private liberal arts college in rural community, affiliated with United Methodist Church.
Enrollment: 977 undergrads. 257 full-time freshmen.
Selectivity: Admits 50 to 75% of applicants.

BASIC COSTS (2007-2008)

Tuition and fees: $22,320.
Per-credit charge: $930.
Room and board: $7,670.

FINANCIAL AID PICTURE (2007-2008)

Students with need: 73% of average financial aid package awarded as scholarships/grants, 27% awarded as loans/jobs. Need-based aid available for part-time students. Work study available nights, weekends, and for part-time students.

Students without need: No-need awards available for academics, art, leadership, minority status, music/drama, religious affiliation, state/district residency.

Additional info: Virginia residents eligible for additional in-state tuition grants.

FINANCIAL AID PROCEDURES

Forms required: FAFSA, state aid form.

Dates and Deadlines: Priority date 4/1; closing date 8/1. Applicants notified on a rolling basis starting 2/1; must reply within 4 week(s) of notification.

CONTACT

Scarlett Blevins, Coordinator, Financial Aid
Box 10, Emory, VA 24327
(276) 944-6115

Ferrum College

Ferrum, Virginia
www.ferrum.edu   Federal Code: 003711

4-year private liberal arts college in rural community, affiliated with United Methodist Church.

Enrollment: 1,240 undergrads, 2% part-time. 524 full-time freshmen.

Selectivity: Admits over 75% of applicants.

BASIC COSTS (2007-2008)

Tuition and fees: $20,885.

Room and board: $6,700.

FINANCIAL AID PICTURE (2007-2008)

Students with need: 66% of average financial aid package awarded as scholarships/grants, 34% awarded as loans/jobs. Need-based aid available for part-time students. Work study available nights, weekends, and for part-time students.

Students without need: No-need awards available for academics, job skills, leadership, religious affiliation, state/district residency.

Scholarships offered: Ferrum Scholarship: $5,000-10,000; high school GPA must be 3.0 or higher and SAT score must be 1500 or higher. Ferrum Merit Grant: $1,000-7,000; high school GPA must be 2.0 or higher and SAT score must be in the range of 1050.

FINANCIAL AID PROCEDURES

Forms required: FAFSA, state aid form.

Dates and Deadlines: Priority date 4/1; no closing date. Applicants notified on a rolling basis starting 3/1.

CONTACT

Doug Clark, Vice President for Enrollment
Spilman-Daniel House, Ferrum, VA 24088
(540) 365-4282

George Mason University

Fairfax, Virginia
www.gmu.edu   Federal Code: 003749

4-year public university in large town.

Enrollment: 17,983 undergrads, 23% part-time. 2,430 full-time freshmen.

Selectivity: Admits 50 to 75% of applicants.

BASIC COSTS (2007-2008)

Tuition and fees: $6,840; out-of-state residents $19,728.

Per-credit charge: $285; out-of-state residents $822.

Room and board: $7,020.

FINANCIAL AID PICTURE (2006-2007)

Students with need: Out of 1,522 full-time freshmen who applied for aid, 894 were judged to have need. Of these, 834 received aid, and 115 had their full need met. Average financial aid package met 68% of need; average scholarship/grant was $5,141; average loan was $2,763. For part-time students, average financial aid package was $5,748.

Students without need: 83 full-time freshmen who did not demonstrate need for aid received scholarships/grants; average award was $6,430. No-need awards available for academics, athletics, minority status, music/drama, ROTC, state/district residency.

Scholarships offered: 57 full-time freshmen received athletic scholarships; average amount $12,151.

Cumulative student debt: 49% of graduating class had student loans; average debt was $16,705.

FINANCIAL AID PROCEDURES

Forms required: FAFSA.

Dates and Deadlines: Priority date 3/1; no closing date. Applicants notified on a rolling basis starting 4/1; must reply within 3 week(s) of notification.

CONTACT

Jevita de Freitas, Director, Student Financial Aid
4400 University Drive, MSN 3A4, Fairfax, VA 22030-4444

Germanna Community College

Locust Grove, Virginia
www.germanna.edu   Federal Code: 008660

2-year public community college in rural community.

Enrollment: 3,092 undergrads, 68% part-time.

Selectivity: Open admission; but selective for some programs.

BASIC COSTS (2007-2008)

Tuition and fees: $2,458; out-of-state residents $7,622.

Per-credit charge: $77; out-of-state residents $249.

Additional info: An indirect cost fee of $31 per credit hour is charged to all out-of-state distance learning students.

FINANCIAL AID PICTURE (2006-2007)

Students with need: 98% of average financial aid package awarded as scholarships/grants, 2% awarded as loans/jobs. Need-based aid available for part-time students.

Students without need: No-need awards available for academics.

FINANCIAL AID PROCEDURES

Forms required: FAFSA.

Dates and Deadlines: Priority date 4/1; no closing date. Applicants notified on a rolling basis starting 5/15; must reply within 2 week(s) of notification.

CONTACT

Jim Brunner, Financial Aid Coordinator
2130 Germanna Highway, Locust Grove, VA 22508-2102
(540) 423-9124

Hampden-Sydney College

Hampden-Sydney, Virginia   Federal Code: 003713
www.hsc.edu   CSS Code: 5291

4-year private liberal arts college for men in rural community, affiliated with Presbyterian Church (USA).

Enrollment: 1,122 undergrads.

Selectivity: Admits 50 to 75% of applicants.

BASIC COSTS (2007-2008)

Tuition and fees: $27,732.

Per-credit charge: $854.

Room and board: $8,712.

Additional info: Fees are same for in-state and out-of-state students.

FINANCIAL AID PICTURE (2007-2008)

Students with need: Average financial aid package met 86% of need; average scholarship/grant was $17,219; average loan was $4,099. For part-time students, average financial aid package was $3,062.

Students without need: No-need awards available for academics, leadership, religious affiliation, ROTC, state/district residency.

Scholarships offered: Allan Scholarship: $20,000 annually. Venable Scholarship: $16,000 annually. Patrick Henry Scholarship: $12,000 annually. Achievement Awards: range from $2,000-$10,000 annually. All based on academic ability.

Cumulative student debt: 64% of graduating class had student loans; average debt was $16,472.

FINANCIAL AID PROCEDURES

Forms required: FAFSA, CSS PROFILE, state aid form.

Dates and Deadlines: Priority date 3/1; no closing date. Applicants notified on a rolling basis starting 2/1; must reply by 5/1 or within 2 week(s) of notification.

Transfers: No deadline. Applicants notified on a rolling basis; must reply within 2 week(s) of notification.

CONTACT

Keith Wellings, Director of Financial Aid

Box 667, Hampden-Sydney, VA 23943

(434) 223-6119

Hampton University

Hampton, Virginia

www.hamptonu.edu   Federal Code: 003714

4-year private university in small city.

Enrollment: 4,874 undergrads, 6% part-time. 1,179 full-time freshmen.

Selectivity: Admits less than 50% of applicants.

BASIC COSTS (2007-2008)

Tuition and fees: $15,610.

Per-credit charge: $350.

Room and board: $7,086.

FINANCIAL AID PICTURE

Students with need: Need-based aid available for full-time and part-time students. Work study available nights, weekends, and for part-time students.

Students without need: No-need awards available for academics, athletics, leadership, music/drama, ROTC.

FINANCIAL AID PROCEDURES

Forms required: FAFSA.

Dates and Deadlines: Priority date 3/1; no closing date. Applicants notified on a rolling basis starting 4/15; must reply within 2 week(s) of notification.

CONTACT

Marcia Boyd, Financial Aid Director

Office of Admissions, Hampton, VA 23668

(757) 727-5332

Hollins University

Roanoke, Virginia

www.hollins.edu   Federal Code: 003715

4-year private university and liberal arts college for women in small city.

Enrollment: 772 undergrads, 3% part-time. 205 full-time freshmen.

Selectivity: Admits over 75% of applicants.

BASIC COSTS (2007-2008)

Tuition and fees: $25,645.

Room and board: $9,140.

FINANCIAL AID PICTURE (2007-2008)

Students with need: Need-based aid available for part-time students.

Students without need: No-need awards available for academics, alumni affiliation, art, leadership, music/drama, state/district residency.

Scholarships offered: Scholar Awards: $5,000 full tuition; academic merit. Founder's Awards: $1,500-$7,000; organizational involvement. Creative Talent Awards: $1,500-$7,000; distinguished achievement or outstanding involvement in art, photography/film, creative writing, music, dance or theater.

FINANCIAL AID PROCEDURES

Forms required: FAFSA, state aid form.

Dates and Deadlines: Priority date 2/15; no closing date. Applicants notified on a rolling basis starting 3/1; must reply by 5/1.

Transfers: Priority date 7/1; closing date 7/15.

CONTACT

Karen Kendall, Director of Scholarships and Financial Assistance

PO Box 9707, Roanoke, VA 24020-1707

(540) 362-6332

J. Sargeant Reynolds Community College

Richmond, Virginia

www.reynolds.edu   Federal Code: 003759

2-year public community college in very large city.

Enrollment: 8,048 undergrads.

Selectivity: Open admission; but selective for some programs.

BASIC COSTS (2007-2008)

Tuition and fees: $2,597; out-of-state residents $7,761.

Per-credit charge: $77; out-of-state residents $249.

Additional info: Out of state students pay an additional $90 capital outlay fee.

FINANCIAL AID PICTURE

Students with need: Need-based aid available for full-time and part-time students. Work study available nights, weekends, and for part-time students.

Students without need: No-need awards available for academics.

Scholarships offered: Local Board Scholarship: full tuition; high school students with minimum 3.0 GPA; 23 awarded. Eric and Jeanette Lipman Endowed Scholarship: based on academic excellence; number and amount awarded varies. Central Fidelity Bank Scholarship: $1,500; first-year students; minimum 2.5 cumulative GPA; 2 awarded.

FINANCIAL AID PROCEDURES

Forms required: FAFSA.

Dates and Deadlines: Priority date 6/30; no closing date. Applicants notified on a rolling basis starting 7/15; must reply within 2 week(s) of notification.

CONTACT

Keisha Pope, Director of Financial Aid

Box 85622, Richmond, VA 23285-5622

(804) 523-5137

James Madison University

Harrisonburg, Virginia
www.jmu.edu   Federal Code: 003721

4-year public university in large town.

Enrollment: 16,108 undergrads, 3% part-time. 3,864 full-time freshmen.

Selectivity: Admits 50 to 75% of applicants.

BASIC COSTS (2007-2008)

Tuition and fees: $6,666; out-of-state residents $17,386.

Per-credit charge: $114; out-of-state residents $471.

Room and board: $7,108.

FINANCIAL AID PICTURE (2007-2008)

Students with need: Out of 2,719 full-time freshmen who applied for aid, 1,439 were judged to have need. Of these, 1,218 received aid, and 961 had their full need met. Average financial aid package met 45% of need; average scholarship/grant was $6,497; average loan was $3,615. For part-time students, average financial aid package was $6,299.

Students without need: 176 full-time freshmen who did not demonstrate need for aid received scholarships/grants; average award was $1,884. No-need awards available for academics, alumni affiliation, art, athletics, leadership, minority status, music/drama, state/district residency.

Scholarships offered: 77 full-time freshmen received athletic scholarships; average amount $12,946.

Cumulative student debt: 48% of graduating class had student loans; average debt was $16,546.

FINANCIAL AID PROCEDURES

Forms required: FAFSA.

Dates and Deadlines: Priority date 3/1; no closing date. Applicants notified on a rolling basis starting 4/1; must reply within 4 week(s) of notification.

Transfers: Closing date 3/1. Applicants notified on a rolling basis starting 4/1; must reply within 4 week(s) of notification.

CONTACT

Lisa Tumer, Director of Financial Aid and Scholarships
Sonner Hall, MSC 0101, Harrisonburg, VA 22807
(540) 568-7820

Jefferson College of Health Sciences

Roanoke, Virginia
www.jchs.edu   Federal Code: 009893

4-year private health science and nursing college in small city.

Enrollment: 927 undergrads, 29% part-time. 145 full-time freshmen.

Selectivity: Admits less than 50% of applicants.

BASIC COSTS (2007-2008)

Tuition and fees: $15,500.

Per-credit charge: $445.

Room and board: $6,310.

Additional info: Tuition for physician assistant program: $48,860 for full 2-year program.

FINANCIAL AID PICTURE (2006-2007)

Students with need: Out of 136 full-time freshmen who applied for aid, 122 were judged to have need. Of these, 122 received aid, and 85 had their full need met. Average financial aid package met 52% of need; average scholarship/grant was $3,121; average loan was $4,479. For part-time students, average financial aid package was $4,525.

Students without need: 4 full-time freshmen who did not demonstrate need for aid received scholarships/grants; average award was $958. No-need awards available for academics.

Cumulative student debt: 65% of graduating class had student loans; average debt was $12,358.

FINANCIAL AID PROCEDURES

Forms required: FAFSA, institutional form.

Dates and Deadlines: No deadline. Applicants notified on a rolling basis; must reply within 2 week(s) of notification.

CONTACT

Deborah Johnson, Financial Aid Officer
Box 13186, Roanoke, VA 24031-3186
(540) 985-8483

John Tyler Community College

Chester, Virginia
www.jtcc.edu   Federal Code: 004004

2-year public community college in small city.

Enrollment: 4,578 undergrads, 60% part-time. 410 full-time freshmen.

Selectivity: Open admission; but selective for some programs.

BASIC COSTS (2007-2008)

Tuition and fees: $2,455; out-of-state residents $7,619.

Per-credit charge: $77; out-of-state residents $249.

Additional info: Out of state students pay an additional $90 capital outlay fee.

FINANCIAL AID PICTURE

Students with need: Need-based aid available for full-time and part-time students. Work study available nights, weekends, and for part-time students.

Students without need: No-need awards available for academics, state/district residency.

FINANCIAL AID PROCEDURES

Forms required: FAFSA.

Dates and Deadlines: Priority date 5/15; closing date 7/15. Applicants notified on a rolling basis starting 6/15.

CONTACT

Fred Taylor, Vice President for Finance and Administration
13101 Jefferson Davis Highway, Chester, VA 23831-5316
(804) 706-5016

Liberty University

Lynchburg, Virginia
www.liberty.edu   Federal Code: 010392

4-year private university and seminary college in small city, affiliated with Baptist faith.

Enrollment: 18,475 undergrads, 30% part-time. 2,847 full-time freshmen.

Selectivity: Admits over 75% of applicants.

BASIC COSTS (2008-2009)

Tuition and fees: $16,434.

Per-credit charge: $515.

Room and board: $5,800.

FINANCIAL AID PICTURE

Students with need: Need-based aid available for full-time and part-time students.

Students without need: No-need awards available for academics, alumni affiliation, athletics, leadership, music/drama, religious affiliation, ROTC, state/district residency.

Scholarships offered: Liberty Academic Achievement Scholarship: based on combination of high school grades and standardized test scores. Students may qualify for up to $6,000. Additional $3,500 could be applied if student is also accepted into the Honors Program.

FINANCIAL AID PROCEDURES

Forms required: FAFSA, state aid form.

Dates and Deadlines: Closing date 3/1. Applicants notified on a rolling basis starting 3/15; must reply within 3 week(s) of notification.

Transfers: Applicants notified on a rolling basis starting 3/15; must reply within 3 week(s) of notification.

CONTACT

Robert Ritz, Director of Student Financial Aid

1971 University Boulevard, Lynchburg, VA 24502

(434) 582-2270

Longwood University

Farmville, Virginia

www.longwood.edu   Federal Code: 003719

4-year public university in small town.

Enrollment: 3,932 undergrads, 3% part-time. 988 full-time freshmen.

Selectivity: Admits 50 to 75% of applicants.

BASIC COSTS (2007-2008)

Tuition and fees: $8,058; out-of-state residents $16,259.

Room and board: $6,740.

Additional info: Required laptop computer for first year students $1,200.

FINANCIAL AID PICTURE (2007-2008)

Students with need: Out of 686 full-time freshmen who applied for aid, 427 were judged to have need. Of these, 427 received aid, and 114 had their full need met. Average financial aid package met 74% of need; average scholarship/grant was $5,053; average loan was $3,184. Need-based aid available for part-time students.

Students without need: 315 full-time freshmen who did not demonstrate need for aid received scholarships/grants; average award was $4,279. No-need awards available for academics, alumni affiliation, art, athletics, leadership, music/drama, ROTC, state/district residency.

Scholarships offered: Longwood Scholars: $2,200. Hull Scholarship: $5,000. Citizen Scholars: $5,500. All awards based on high school GPA and test scores.

Cumulative student debt: 58% of graduating class had student loans; average debt was $17,781.

FINANCIAL AID PROCEDURES

Forms required: FAFSA.

Dates and Deadlines: Priority date 3/1; no closing date. Applicants notified on a rolling basis starting 4/10.

Transfers: Applicants notified by 4/1; must reply by 5/1.

CONTACT

Karen Schinabeck, Director of Financial Aid

201 High Street, Farmville, VA 23909-1898

(434) 395-2077

Lord Fairfax Community College

Middletown, Virginia

www.lfcc.edu   Federal Code: 008659

2-year public community college in rural community.

Enrollment: 3,425 undergrads.

Selectivity: Open admission.

BASIC COSTS (2007-2008)

Tuition and fees: $2,467; out-of-state residents $7,631.

Per-credit charge: $77; out-of-state residents $249.

Additional info: Out-of-state students pay an additional $90 capital outlay fee.

FINANCIAL AID PICTURE

Students with need: Need-based aid available for full-time and part-time students.

Students without need: This college awards aid only to students with need.

FINANCIAL AID PROCEDURES

Forms required: FAFSA.

Dates and Deadlines: Priority date 5/1; no closing date. Applicants notified on a rolling basis starting 6/1.

CONTACT

Karen Bucher, Coordinator of Financial Aid

173 Skirmisher Lane, Middletown, VA 22645

(540) 868-7130

Lynchburg College

Lynchburg, Virginia

www.lynchburg.edu   Federal Code: 003720

4-year private liberal arts college in small city, affiliated with Christian Church (Disciples of Christ).

Enrollment: 2,046 undergrads, 3% part-time. 601 full-time freshmen.

Selectivity: Admits 50 to 75% of applicants.

BASIC COSTS (2008-2009)

Tuition and fees: $27,565.

Per-credit charge: $375.

Room and board: $7,000.

Additional info: Tuition/fee waivers available for adults.

FINANCIAL AID PICTURE (2007-2008)

Students with need: Out of 473 full-time freshmen who applied for aid, 396 were judged to have need. Of these, 396 received aid, and 119 had their full need met. Average financial aid package met 93% of need; average scholarship/grant was $17,717; average loan was $3,579. For part-time students, average financial aid package was $5,624.

Students without need: 206 full-time freshmen who did not demonstrate need for aid received scholarships/grants; average award was $9,020. No-need awards available for academics, art, leadership, music/drama, state/district residency.

Cumulative student debt: 68% of graduating class had student loans; average debt was $22,825.

FINANCIAL AID PROCEDURES

Forms required: FAFSA, state aid form.

Dates and Deadlines: Priority date 3/1; no closing date. Applicants notified on a rolling basis starting 3/5; must reply by 5/1 or within 2 week(s) of notification.

Transfers: Priority date 7/1; no deadline. Applicants notified on a rolling basis starting 3/5; must reply within 2 week(s) of notification.

CONTACT

Michelle Davis, Director of Financial Aid

1501 Lakeside Drive, Lynchburg, VA 24501-3199

(434) 544-8228

Mary Baldwin College

Staunton, Virginia

www.mbc.edu   Federal Code: 003723

4-year private liberal arts college for women in large town, affiliated with Presbyterian Church (USA).

Enrollment: 1,369 undergrads, 27% part-time. 258 full-time freshmen.

Selectivity: Admits 50 to 75% of applicants.

BASIC COSTS (2008-2009)

Tuition and fees: $23,645.

Per-credit charge: $400.

Room and board: $6,730.

FINANCIAL AID PICTURE (2006-2007)

Students with need: Average financial aid package met 93% of need; average scholarship/grant was $10,502; average loan was $1,886. For part-time students, average financial aid package was $7,851.

Students without need: No-need awards available for academics, leadership, state/district residency.

Cumulative student debt: 80% of graduating class had student loans; average debt was $23,646.

FINANCIAL AID PROCEDURES

Forms required: FAFSA, state aid form.

Dates and Deadlines: Priority date 5/15; no closing date. Applicants notified on a rolling basis starting 2/1.

CONTACT

Lisa Branson, Associate Vice President for Enrollment Management

Office of Admissions, Staunton, VA 24401

(540) 887-7022

Marymount University

Arlington, Virginia

www.marymount.edu   Federal Code: 003724

4-year private university in small city, affiliated with Roman Catholic Church.

Enrollment: 2,199 undergrads, 13% part-time. 365 full-time freshmen.

Selectivity: Admits over 75% of applicants.

BASIC COSTS (2008-2009)

Tuition and fees: $21,528.

Per-credit charge: $690.

Room and board: $9,190.

FINANCIAL AID PICTURE (2006-2007)

Students with need: Out of 287 full-time freshmen who applied for aid, 234 were judged to have need. Of these, 230 received aid, and 47 had their full need met. Average financial aid package met 81% of need; average scholarship/grant was $7,929; average loan was $2,590. For part-time students, average financial aid package was $5,872.

Students without need: 90 full-time freshmen who did not demonstrate need for aid received scholarships/grants; average award was $7,591. No-need awards available for academics, alumni affiliation, leadership, ROTC, state/district residency.

Scholarships offered: Freshman Academic Scholarship: requires GPA of 3.0 or better and combined SAT (exclusive of Writing) score of 1100 or higher.

Cumulative student debt: 70% of graduating class had student loans; average debt was $20,686.

FINANCIAL AID PROCEDURES

Forms required: FAFSA.

Dates and Deadlines: Priority date 3/1; no closing date. Applicants notified on a rolling basis starting 3/15; must reply within 2 week(s) of notification.

Transfers: No deadline. Applicants notified on a rolling basis; must reply within 2 week(s) of notification. Academic scholarships available; apply by May 1.

CONTACT

Debbie Raines, Director of Financial Aid

2807 North Glebe Road, Arlington, VA 22207-4299

(703) 284-1530

Miller-Motte Technical College: Lynchburg

Lynchburg, Virginia

www.miller-motte.com   Federal Code: 004992

2-year for-profit technical college in small city.

Enrollment: 295 undergrads.

Selectivity: Open admission.

BASIC COSTS (2007-2008)

Tuition and fees: $6,450.

Per-credit charge: $215.

FINANCIAL AID PICTURE

Students with need: Need-based aid available for full-time and part-time students. Work study available nights.

Students without need: This college awards aid only to students with need.

FINANCIAL AID PROCEDURES

Forms required: FAFSA.

Dates and Deadlines: No deadline. Applicants notified on a rolling basis.

CONTACT

Allison Connors, Director of Financial Aid

1011 Creekside Lane, Lynchburg, VA 24502

(434) 239-5222

Mountain Empire Community College

Big Stone Gap, Virginia

www.mecc.edu   Federal Code: 009629

2-year public community college in small town.

Enrollment: 1,930 undergrads.

Selectivity: Open admission; but selective for some programs.

BASIC COSTS (2007-2008)

Tuition and fees: $2,495; out-of-state residents $7,659.

Per-credit charge: $77; out-of-state residents $249.

Additional info: Out of state students pay an additional $90 capital outlay fee.

FINANCIAL AID PICTURE (2006-2007)

Students with need: Need-based aid available for part-time students.

Students without need: No-need awards available for academics, state/district residency.

Scholarships offered: Presidential Honor Scholarship: full tuition; for valedictorian or salutatorian. Dean's Academic Honor Award: $500-$1,000; for top 10 in graduating class.

Additional info: The college does not participate in loan programs. All financial aid is in form of grants, scholarships, or work study.

FINANCIAL AID PROCEDURES

Forms required: FAFSA.

Dates and Deadlines: Priority date 5/1; no closing date. Applicants notified on a rolling basis starting 1/1.

CONTACT

Director of Enrollment Services

3441 Mountain Empire Road, Big Stone Gap, VA 24219

(276) 523-2400 ext. 470

National College: Bluefield

Bluefield, Virginia
www.ncbt.edu   Federal Code: 003726

2-year for-profit business college in small city.
Enrollment: 190 undergrads.
Selectivity: Open admission.

BASIC COSTS (2008-2009)
Tuition and fees: $9,585.
Per-credit charge: $212.

FINANCIAL AID PICTURE
Students with need: Need-based aid available for full-time and part-time students.
Students without need: This college awards aid only to students with need.

FINANCIAL AID PROCEDURES
Forms required: FAFSA.
Dates and Deadlines: No deadline. Applicants notified on a rolling basis starting 9/1.

CONTACT
Pamela Cotton, Director of Financial Aid and Compliance Officer
PO Box 6400, Roanoke, VA 24017
(540) 986-1800

National College: Charlottesville

Charlottesville, Virginia
www.ncbt.edu   Federal Code: 003726

2-year for-profit business college in small city.
Enrollment: 174 undergrads.
Selectivity: Open admission.

BASIC COSTS (2008-2009)
Tuition and fees: $9,585.
Per-credit charge: $212.

FINANCIAL AID PICTURE
Students with need: Need-based aid available for full-time and part-time students.
Students without need: This college awards aid only to students with need.

FINANCIAL AID PROCEDURES
Forms required: FAFSA.
Dates and Deadlines: No deadline. Applicants notified on a rolling basis.

CONTACT
Pamela Cotton, Director of Financial Aid and Compliance Officer
PO Box 6400, Roanoke, VA 24017
(540) 986-1800

National College: Danville

Danville, Virginia
www.ncbt.edu   Federal Code: 003726

2-year for-profit branch campus and business college in small city.
Enrollment: 312 undergrads.
Selectivity: Open admission.

BASIC COSTS (2008-2009)
Tuition and fees: $9,585.
Per-credit charge: $212.

FINANCIAL AID PICTURE
Students with need: Need-based aid available for full-time and part-time students.
Students without need: This college awards aid only to students with need.

FINANCIAL AID PROCEDURES
Forms required: FAFSA.
Dates and Deadlines: No deadline. Applicants notified on a rolling basis starting 9/1.

CONTACT
Pamela Cotton, Director of Financial Aid and Compliance Officer
PO Box 6400, Roanoke, VA 24017
(540) 986-1800

National College: Harrisonburg

Harrisonburg, Virginia
www.national-college.edu   Federal Code: 003726

2-year for-profit business college in large town.
Enrollment: 282 undergrads.
Selectivity: Open admission.

BASIC COSTS (2008-2009)
Tuition and fees: $9,585.
Per-credit charge: $212.

FINANCIAL AID PICTURE
Students with need: Need-based aid available for full-time and part-time students.
Students without need: This college awards aid only to students with need.

FINANCIAL AID PROCEDURES
Forms required: FAFSA.
Dates and Deadlines: No deadline. Applicants notified on a rolling basis starting 9/1.

CONTACT
Pamela Cotton, Director of Financial Aid and Compliance Officer
PO Box 6400, Roanoke, VA 24017
(540) 986-1800

National College: Lynchburg

Lynchburg, Virginia
www.national-college.edu   Federal Code: 010489

2-year for-profit business college in small city.
Enrollment: 260 undergrads.
Selectivity: Open admission.

BASIC COSTS (2008-2009)
Tuition and fees: $9,585.
Per-credit charge: $212.

FINANCIAL AID PICTURE
Students with need: Need-based aid available for full-time and part-time students.
Students without need: This college awards aid only to students with need.

FINANCIAL AID PROCEDURES
Forms required: FAFSA.
Dates and Deadlines: No deadline. Applicants notified on a rolling basis starting 9/1.

CONTACT

Pamela Cotton, Director of Financial Aid and Compliance Officer
PO Box 6400, Roanoke, VA 24017
(540) 986-1000

National College: Martinsville

Martinsville, Virginia
www.national-college.edu   Federal Code: 003726

2-year private business and junior college in small city.
Enrollment: 267 undergrads.
Selectivity: Open admission.

BASIC COSTS (2008-2009)

Tuition and fees: $9,585.
Per-credit charge: $212.

FINANCIAL AID PICTURE

Students with need: Need-based aid available for full-time and part-time students.
Students without need: This college awards aid only to students with need.

FINANCIAL AID PROCEDURES

Forms required: FAFSA.
Dates and Deadlines: No deadline. Applicants notified on a rolling basis.

CONTACT

Pamela Cotton, Director of Financial Aid and Compliance Officer
PO Box 6400, Roanoke, VA 24017
(540) 986-1800

National College: Roanoke Valley

Roanoke, Virginia
www.national-college.edu   Federal Code: 003726

4-year for-profit business college in large city.
Enrollment: 599 undergrads.
Selectivity: Open admission.

BASIC COSTS (2008-2009)

Tuition and fees: $9,585.
Per-credit charge: $212.

FINANCIAL AID PICTURE

Students with need: Need-based aid available for full-time and part-time students.
Students without need: This college awards aid only to students with need.

FINANCIAL AID PROCEDURES

Forms required: FAFSA.
Dates and Deadlines: No deadline. Applicants notified on a rolling basis.

CONTACT

Pamela Cotton, Director of Financial Aid and Compliance Officer
PO Box 6400, Roanoke, VA 24017-0400
(540) 986-1800

New River Community College

Dublin, Virginia
www.nr.edu   Federal Code: 005223

2-year public community college in rural community.
Enrollment: 2,865 undergrads.

Selectivity: Open admission.

BASIC COSTS (2007-2008)

Tuition and fees: $2,467; out-of-state residents $7,631.
Per-credit charge: $77; out-of-state residents $249.
Additional info: Out of state students pay an additional $90 capital outlay fee.

FINANCIAL AID PICTURE

Students with need: Need-based aid available for full-time and part-time students.

FINANCIAL AID PROCEDURES

Forms required: FAFSA, institutional form.
Dates and Deadlines: Priority date 4/15; no closing date. Applicants notified on a rolling basis starting 6/1.

CONTACT

Joseph Sheffey, Coordinator of Financial Aid
Drawer 1127, Dublin, VA 24084
(540) 674-3615

Norfolk State University

Norfolk, Virginia
www.nsu.edu   Federal Code: 003765

4-year public university in small city.
Enrollment: 5,259 undergrads, 18% part-time. 938 full-time freshmen.
Selectivity: Admits 50 to 75% of applicants.

BASIC COSTS (2007-2008)

Tuition and fees: $5,322; out-of-state residents $16,242.
Per-credit charge: $235; out-of-state residents $599.
Room and board: $6,996.

FINANCIAL AID PICTURE

Students with need: Need-based aid available for full-time and part-time students.
Students without need: No-need awards available for academics, alumni affiliation, athletics, leadership, music/drama, ROTC, state/district residency.

FINANCIAL AID PROCEDURES

Forms required: FAFSA.
Dates and Deadlines: Priority date 5/31; no closing date. Applicants notified on a rolling basis starting 4/1; must reply within 2 week(s) of notification.

CONTACT

Kevin Burns, Director of Student Financial Services
700 Park Avenue, Norfolk, VA 23504
(757) 823-8381

Old Dominion University

Norfolk, Virginia
www.odu.edu   Federal Code: 003728

4-year public university in small city.
Enrollment: 15,655 undergrads, 26% part-time. 2,513 full-time freshmen.
Selectivity: Admits 50 to 75% of applicants.

BASIC COSTS (2008-2009)

Tuition and fees: $6,918; out-of-state residents $18,588.
Per-credit charge: $224; out-of-state residents $613.
Room and board: $7,100.

FINANCIAL AID PICTURE (2007-2008)

Students with need: Out of 1,861 full-time freshmen who applied for aid, 1,669 were judged to have need. Of these, 1,485 received aid, and 817 had their full need met. Average financial aid package met 85% of need; average scholarship/grant was $4,557; average loan was $3,393. For part-time students, average financial aid package was $5,308.

Students without need: 96 full-time freshmen who did not demonstrate need for aid received scholarships/grants; average award was $2,999. No-need awards available for academics, alumni affiliation, art, athletics, leadership, music/drama, ROTC, state/district residency.

Cumulative student debt: 81% of graduating class had student loans; average debt was $16,850.

FINANCIAL AID PROCEDURES

Forms required: FAFSA.

Dates and Deadlines: Priority date 2/15; closing date 3/15. Applicants notified on a rolling basis starting 2/1; must reply within 2 week(s) of notification.

Transfers: Applicants notified on a rolling basis starting 2/1; must reply within 2 week(s) of notification.

CONTACT

Veronica Finch, Director of Financial Aid

108 Rollins Hall, 5115 Hampton Boulevard, Norfolk, VA 23529

(757) 683-3683

Patrick Henry Community College

Martinsville, Virginia

www.ph.vccs.edu   Federal Code: 003751

2-year public community college in large town.

Enrollment: 2,888 undergrads.

Selectivity: Open admission.

BASIC COSTS (2007-2008)

Tuition and fees: $2,445; out-of-state residents $7,605.

Per-credit charge: $77; out-of-state residents $249.

Additional info: Out of state students pay an additional $90 capital outlay fee.

FINANCIAL AID PICTURE

Students with need: Need-based aid available for full-time and part-time students.

FINANCIAL AID PROCEDURES

Forms required: FAFSA.

Dates and Deadlines: Priority date 6/1; no closing date. Applicants notified on a rolling basis starting 6/15.

CONTACT

Joe Philpott, Financial Aid

Box 5311, Martinsville, VA 24115-5311

(276) 656-0317

Paul D. Camp Community College

Franklin, Virginia

www.pc.vccs.edu   Federal Code: 009159

2-year public community college in small town.

Enrollment: 756 undergrads.

Selectivity: Open admission; but selective for some programs.

BASIC COSTS (2007-2008)

Tuition and fees: $2,405; out-of-state residents $7,569.

Per-credit charge: $77; out-of-state residents $249.

Additional info: Out of state students pay an additional $90 capital outlay fee.

FINANCIAL AID PICTURE

Students with need: Need-based aid available for full-time and part-time students. Work study available nights.

FINANCIAL AID PROCEDURES

Forms required: FAFSA.

Dates and Deadlines: Priority date 6/1; no closing date. Applicants notified on a rolling basis starting 8/1; must reply within 2 week(s) of notification.

CONTACT

Teresa King, Financial Aid Coordinator

100 North College Drive, Franklin, VA 23851-0737

(757) 925-6307

Piedmont Virginia Community College

Charlottesville, Virginia

www.pvcc.edu   Federal Code: 009928

2-year public community college in large town.

Enrollment: 2,953 undergrads, 68% part-time. 238 full-time freshmen.

Selectivity: Open admission; but selective for some programs.

BASIC COSTS (2007-2008)

Tuition and fees: $2,470; out-of-state residents $7,634.

Per-credit charge: $77; out-of-state residents $249.

Additional info: Out of state students pay an additional $90 capital outlay fee.

FINANCIAL AID PICTURE (2006-2007)

Students with need: 66% of average financial aid package awarded as scholarships/grants, 34% awarded as loans/jobs. Need-based aid available for part-time students. Work study available nights, weekends, and for part-time students.

Students without need: No-need awards available for academics.

FINANCIAL AID PROCEDURES

Forms required: FAFSA.

Dates and Deadlines: No deadline. Applicants notified on a rolling basis starting 4/1.

Transfers: Must meet Satisfactory Academic Progress standards.

CONTACT

Carol Larson, Director of Financial Aid

501 College Drive, Charlottesville, VA 22902-7589

(434) 961-6545

Radford University

Radford, Virginia

www.radford.edu   Federal Code: 003732

4-year public university in large town.

Enrollment: 7,982 undergrads, 4% part-time. 1,731 full-time freshmen.

Selectivity: Admits over 75% of applicants.

BASIC COSTS (2007-2008)

Tuition and fees: $6,176; out-of-state residents $14,510.

Room and board: $6,490.

FINANCIAL AID PICTURE (2006-2007)

Students with need: Out of 1,108 full-time freshmen who applied for aid, 608 were judged to have need. Of these, 578 received aid, and 186 had their full need met. Average financial aid package met 76% of need; average scholarship/grant was $5,656; average loan was $2,581. For part-time students, average financial aid package was $6,361.

Students without need: 79 full-time freshmen who did not demonstrate need for aid received scholarships/grants; average award was $3,893. No-

need awards available for academics, alumni affiliation, art, athletics, leadership, music/drama, ROTC, state/district residency.

Scholarships offered: 45 full-time freshmen received athletic scholarships; average amount $6,312.

Cumulative student debt: 93% of graduating class had student loans; average debt was $16,554.

Additional info: Student's need and grades considered. Top consideration given to those with greatest need and who apply by deadline.

FINANCIAL AID PROCEDURES

Forms required: FAFSA.

Dates and Deadlines: Priority date 3/1; no closing date. Applicants notified on a rolling basis starting 4/15; must reply within 2 week(s) of notification.

CONTACT

Barbara Porter, Director of Financial Aid
209 Martin Hall, Radford, VA 24142
(540) 831-5408

Randolph College

Lynchburg, Virginia
www.randolphcollege.edu   Federal Code: 003734

4-year private liberal arts college in small city, affiliated with United Methodist Church.

Enrollment: 618 undergrads, 1% part-time. 178 full-time freshmen.
Selectivity: Admits over 75% of applicants.

BASIC COSTS (2008-2009)

Tuition and fees: $27,890.
Per-credit charge: $1,120.
Room and board: $9,310.
Additional info: Room and board charges include free use of laundry facilities. Tuition/fee waivers available for adults.

FINANCIAL AID PICTURE (2007-2008)

Students with need: Out of 143 full-time freshmen who applied for aid, 118 were judged to have need. Of these, 118 received aid, and 41 had their full need met. Average financial aid package met 84% of need; average scholarship/grant was $16,467; average loan was $4,947. For part-time students, average financial aid package was $10,987.

Students without need: 60 full-time freshmen who did not demonstrate need for aid received scholarships/grants; average award was $14,497. No-need awards available for academics, alumni affiliation, art, leadership, minority status, music/drama, religious affiliation, state/district residency.

Scholarships offered: Gottwald Scholarship: full tuition plus travel stipend; based on academic profile; 12 awarded.

Cumulative student debt: 75% of graduating class had student loans; average debt was $28,218.

Additional info: College offers approximately $2 million annually to incoming first-year students. Grants range up to full tuition. Students must reapply each year.

FINANCIAL AID PROCEDURES

Forms required: FAFSA, state aid form.
Dates and Deadlines: Priority date 3/1; no closing date. Applicants notified on a rolling basis starting 3/1; must reply by 5/1 or within 2 week(s) of notification.
Transfers: Priority date 2/1. Applicants notified on a rolling basis starting 3/1; must reply by 5/1 or within 2 week(s) of notification.

CONTACT

Katherine Cooper, Director of Student Financial Services
2500 Rivermont Avenue, Lynchburg, VA 24503-1555
(434) 947-8128

Randolph-Macon College

Ashland, Virginia
www.rmc.edu   Federal Code: 003733

4-year private liberal arts college in small town, affiliated with United Methodist Church.

Enrollment: 1,166 undergrads, 1% part-time. 392 full-time freshmen.
Selectivity: Admits 50 to 75% of applicants.

BASIC COSTS (2008-2009)

Tuition and fees: $28,355.
Per-credit charge: $1,020.
Room and board: $8,610.

FINANCIAL AID PICTURE (2007-2008)

Students with need: Out of 301 full-time freshmen who applied for aid, 242 were judged to have need. Of these, 242 received aid, and 57 had their full need met. Average financial aid package met 86% of need; average scholarship/grant was $16,112; average loan was $5,217. For part-time students, average financial aid package was $13,476.

Students without need: 150 full-time freshmen who did not demonstrate need for aid received scholarships/grants; average award was $15,437. No-need awards available for academics, alumni affiliation, minority status, religious affiliation, state/district residency.

Scholarships offered: Randolph-Macon's Presidential Scholars Program: $7,500 up to $20,000 per year; academic awards.

Cumulative student debt: 66% of graduating class had student loans; average debt was $22,725.

FINANCIAL AID PROCEDURES

Forms required: FAFSA, state aid form.
Dates and Deadlines: Priority date 2/1; closing date 3/1. Applicants notified by 3/15; must reply by 5/1 or within 2 week(s) of notification.
Transfers: Applicants notified by 3/15; must reply by 5/1 or within 2 week(s) of notification.

CONTACT

Mary Neal, Director of Financial Aid
PO Box 5005, Ashland, VA 23005-5505
(804) 752-7529

Rappahannock Community College

Glenns, Virginia
www.rappahannock.edu   Federal Code: 009160

2-year public community college in rural community.
Enrollment: 1,448 undergrads.
Selectivity: Open admission.

BASIC COSTS (2007-2008)

Tuition and fees: $2,534; out-of-state residents $7,599.
Per-credit charge: $77; out-of-state residents $249.
Additional info: Out of state students pay an additional $90 capital outlay fee.

FINANCIAL AID PICTURE

Students with need: Need-based aid available for full-time and part-time students.

FINANCIAL AID PROCEDURES

Forms required: FAFSA, institutional form.
Dates and Deadlines: Priority date 5/15; no closing date. Applicants notified on a rolling basis starting 6/30.

PART III: FINANCIAL AID COLLEGE BY COLLEGE

CONTACT

Carolyn Ward, Director of Financial Aid
12745 College Drive, Glenns, VA 23149-2616
(804) 758-6737

Regent University
Virginia Beach, Virginia
www.regent.edu   Federal Code: 030913

4-year private university in large city, affiliated with interdenominational tradition.

Enrollment: 1,177 undergrads, 51% part-time. 121 full-time freshmen.
Selectivity: Admits 50 to 75% of applicants.

BASIC COSTS (2008-2009)
Tuition and fees: $12,750.
Per-credit charge: $420.

FINANCIAL AID PICTURE (2006-2007)
Students with need: Out of 92 full-time freshmen who applied for aid, 92 were judged to have need. Of these, 92 received aid, and 6 had their full need met. Average financial aid package met 36% of need; average scholarship/grant was $4,203; average loan was $3,564. For part-time students, average financial aid package was $5,619.
Students without need: 5 full-time freshmen who did not demonstrate need for aid received scholarships/grants; average award was $1,481. No-need awards available for academics, leadership.
Cumulative student debt: 65% of graduating class had student loans; average debt was $21,224.

FINANCIAL AID PROCEDURES
Forms required: FAFSA, state aid form, institutional form.
Dates and Deadlines: Priority date 3/15; no closing date. Applicants notified on a rolling basis starting 3/1; must reply within 2 week(s) of notification.
Transfers: Closing date 8/1. Applicants notified on a rolling basis starting 3/15; must reply within 2 week(s) of notification. Must be able to determine number of transfer credits before full award package is offered. Student should submit all academic transcripts in a timely manner to ensure transfer articulation occurs in a timely manner.

CONTACT
Joe Dobrota, Director of Central Financial Aid
1000 Regent University Drive, SC 218, Virginia Beach, VA 23464-9800
(757) 226-4125

Richard Bland College
Petersburg, Virginia
www.rbc.edu   Federal Code: 003707

2-year public junior and liberal arts college in small city.
Enrollment: 1,060 undergrads, 26% part-time. 375 full-time freshmen.
Selectivity: Admits over 75% of applicants.

BASIC COSTS (2007-2008)
Tuition and fees: $2,644; out-of-state residents $10,802.
Per-credit charge: $103; out-of-state residents $451.

FINANCIAL AID PICTURE
Students with need: Need-based aid available for full-time and part-time students.
Students without need: No-need awards available for academics.
Scholarships offered: Presidential Scholarships: average $1,000; for full-time first-time Virginia residents; based on minimum 3.5 high school GPA.

FINANCIAL AID PROCEDURES
Forms required: FAFSA, institutional form.

Dates and Deadlines: Priority date 5/1; no closing date. Applicants notified by 6/1; must reply within 2 week(s) of notification.

CONTACT
Beverly Morris, Director of Financial Aid
11301 Johnson Road, Petersburg, VA 23805
(804) 862-6223

Roanoke College
Salem, Virginia
www.roanoke.edu   Federal Code: 003736

4-year private liberal arts college in large town, affiliated with Evangelical Lutheran Church in America.
Enrollment: 1,945 undergrads, 3% part-time. 566 full-time freshmen.
Selectivity: Admits 50 to 75% of applicants.

BASIC COSTS (2008-2009)
Tuition and fees: $27,935.
Room and board: $9,285.
Additional info: Tuition/fee waivers available for adults.

FINANCIAL AID PICTURE (2007-2008)
Students with need: Out of 436 full-time freshmen who applied for aid, 432 were judged to have need. Of these, 432 received aid, and 139 had their full need met. Average financial aid package met 92% of need; average scholarship/grant was $18,963; average loan was $3,912. For part-time students, average financial aid package was $6,393.
Students without need: 195 full-time freshmen who did not demonstrate need for aid received scholarships/grants; average award was $9,988. No-need awards available for academics, minority status, music/drama, religious affiliation.
Scholarships offered: William Beard Scholarship: 2 awarded; full tuition, room and board. Bittle Scholarship: full tuition; 6 awarded. Baughman Scholarship: half tuition; 25 awarded. Roanoke College Scholarship: $3,000-$6,000; variable number awarded. All based on superior academics and leadership ability.

FINANCIAL AID PROCEDURES
Forms required: FAFSA, state aid form.
Dates and Deadlines: Priority date 3/1; no closing date. Applicants notified on a rolling basis starting 11/1; must reply within 2 week(s) of notification.

CONTACT
Thomas Blair, Director of Financial Aid
221 College Lane, Salem, VA 24153-3794
(540) 375-2235

St. Paul's College
Lawrenceville, Virginia
www.saintpauls.edu   Federal Code: 003739

4-year private liberal arts college in small town, affiliated with Episcopal Church.
Enrollment: 687 undergrads, 3% part-time. 252 full-time freshmen.
Selectivity: Admits over 75% of applicants.

BASIC COSTS (2007-2008)
Tuition and fees: $12,020.
Per-credit charge: $470.
Room and board: $6,190.
Additional info: Tuition/fee waivers available for minority students.

FINANCIAL AID PICTURE (2006-2007)

Students with need: Out of 246 full-time freshmen who applied for aid, 246 were judged to have need. Of these, 246 received aid. Average financial aid package met 90% of need; average scholarship/grant was $10,900. For part-time students, average financial aid package was $1,998.

Students without need: No-need awards available for academics, athletics, leadership, ROTC.

Cumulative student debt: 88% of graduating class had student loans; average debt was $12,996.

FINANCIAL AID PROCEDURES

Forms required: FAFSA, state aid form.

Dates and Deadlines: No deadline. Applicants notified on a rolling basis starting 1/15; must reply by 7/1 or within 4 week(s) of notification.

Transfers: No deadline. Applicants notified on a rolling basis; must reply within 2 week(s) of notification.

CONTACT

Hester Austin-Walker, Director of Financial Aid
115 College Drive, Lawrenceville, VA 23868
(434) 848-6497

Shenandoah University

Winchester, Virginia
www.su.edu   Federal Code: 003737

4-year private university in small city, affiliated with United Methodist Church.

Enrollment: 1,587 undergrads, 5% part-time. 392 full-time freshmen.

Selectivity: Admits over 75% of applicants.

BASIC COSTS (2008-2009)

Tuition and fees: $23,340.
Per-credit charge: $670.
Room and board: $8,350.

FINANCIAL AID PICTURE (2006-2007)

Students with need: Out of 325 full-time freshmen who applied for aid, 325 were judged to have need. Of these, 325 received aid, and 62 had their full need met. Average financial aid package met 86% of need; average scholarship/grant was $15,022; average loan was $4,229. Need-based aid available for part-time students.

Students without need: 50 full-time freshmen who did not demonstrate need for aid received scholarships/grants; average award was $4,500. No-need awards available for academics, job skills, music/drama, religious affiliation, state/district residency.

Cumulative student debt: 85% of graduating class had student loans; average debt was $21,000.

FINANCIAL AID PROCEDURES

Forms required: FAFSA, state aid form.

Dates and Deadlines: Closing date 3/2. Applicants notified on a rolling basis starting 3/15; must reply within 2 week(s) of notification.

Transfers: Priority date 2/15; closing date 4/15. Applicants notified on a rolling basis starting 3/15.

CONTACT

Nancy Bragg, Director of Financial Aid
1460 University Drive, Winchester, VA 22601-5195
(540) 665-4538

Southern Virginia University

Buena Vista, Virginia
www.svu.edu   Federal Code: 003738

4-year private liberal arts college in small town, affiliated with Church of Jesus Christ of Latter-day Saints.

Enrollment: 698 undergrads, 4% part-time. 316 full-time freshmen.

Selectivity: Admits over 75% of applicants.

BASIC COSTS (2007-2008)

Tuition and fees: $16,500.
Per-credit charge: $595.
Room and board: $4,900.

FINANCIAL AID PICTURE (2006-2007)

Students with need: Out of 307 full-time freshmen who applied for aid, 275 were judged to have need. Of these, 275 received aid, and 19 had their full need met. Average financial aid package met 41% of need; average scholarship/grant was $6,475; average loan was $2,075. For part-time students, average financial aid package was $9,656.

Students without need: 40 full-time freshmen who did not demonstrate need for aid received scholarships/grants; average award was $4,729. No-need awards available for academics, art, athletics, leadership, music/drama.

Scholarships offered: 70 full-time freshmen received athletic scholarships.

FINANCIAL AID PROCEDURES

Forms required: FAFSA, state aid form.

Dates and Deadlines: Applicants notified on a rolling basis starting 2/1; must reply by 5/1 or within 3 week(s) of notification.

CONTACT

Margaret Murphy, Director of Financial Aid
One University Hill Drive, Buena Vista, VA 24416
(540) 261-4351

Southside Virginia Community College

Alberta, Virginia
www.sv.vccs.edu   Federal Code: 008661

2-year public community college in rural community.

Enrollment: 2,484 undergrads.

Selectivity: Open admission; but selective for some programs.

BASIC COSTS (2007-2008)

Tuition and fees: $2,465; out-of-state residents $7,629.
Per-credit charge: $77; out-of-state residents $249.
Additional info: Out of state students pay an additional $90 capital outlay fee.

FINANCIAL AID PICTURE (2007-2008)

Students with need: 97% of average financial aid package awarded as scholarships/grants, 3% awarded as loans/jobs. Need-based aid available for part-time students. Work study available nights.

Students without need: No-need awards available for academics.

Scholarships offered: Guaranteed Academic Merit Award: $1,500, for high school graduates within college's service area with 3.0 GPA who do not receive at least $1,500 in need-based aid.

FINANCIAL AID PROCEDURES

Forms required: FAFSA.

Dates and Deadlines: Priority date 6/1; closing date 8/1. Applicants notified on a rolling basis starting 6/15.

Transfers: State aid limited to in-state residents.

CONTACT
Sally Tharrington, Director of Financial Aid
109 Campus Drive, Alberta, VA 23821
(434) 736-2026

Southwest Virginia Community College
Richlands, Virginia
www.sw.edu   Federal Code: 007260

2-year public community college in small town.
Enrollment: 2,481 undergrads, 48% part-time. 372 full-time freshmen.
Selectivity: Open admission; but selective for some programs.

BASIC COSTS (2007-2008)
Tuition and fees: $2,450; out-of-state residents $7,614.
Per-credit charge: $77; out-of-state residents $249.
Additional info: Out of state students pay an additional $90 capital outlay fee.

FINANCIAL AID PICTURE
Students with need: Need-based aid available for full-time and part-time students.
Students without need: This college awards aid only to students with need.

FINANCIAL AID PROCEDURES
Forms required: FAFSA, institutional form.
Dates and Deadlines: Priority date 5/30; no closing date. Applicants notified on a rolling basis starting 7/1.

CONTACT
Rod Moore, Associate Vice President of Student Development Services
PO Box SVCC, Richlands, VA 24641
(276) 964-7290

Sweet Briar College
Sweet Briar, Virginia
www.sbc.edu   Federal Code: 003742

4-year private liberal arts college for women in rural community.
Enrollment: 636 undergrads, 1% part-time. 202 full-time freshmen.
Selectivity: Admits over 75% of applicants.

BASIC COSTS (2008-2009)
Tuition and fees: $26,995.
Per-credit charge: $890.
Room and board: $10,160.
Additional info: Tuition/fee waivers available for adults.

FINANCIAL AID PICTURE (2007-2008)
Students with need: Out of 140 full-time freshmen who applied for aid, 107 were judged to have need. Of these, 105 received aid, and 17 had their full need met. Average financial aid package met 73% of need; average scholarship/grant was $16,470; average loan was $7,667. For part-time students, average financial aid package was $12,879.
Students without need: 78 full-time freshmen who did not demonstrate need for aid received scholarships/grants; average award was $14,462. No-need awards available for academics, art, leadership, music/drama, state/district residency.
Scholarships offered: Founders and Prothro Scholarships: up to $15,000. Commonwealth Scholarships: up to $13,000. International Scholarships: up to $12,500; for international students of traditional college age who intend to study at Sweet Briar for 4 years and live in residence halls. Betty Bean Black Scholarships: up to $12,000. Sweet Briar Scholarships: up to $9,000; for students with special talents in specific area. All awards based on academic qualifications; renewable annually with specified GPA.

FINANCIAL AID PROCEDURES
Forms required: FAFSA.
Dates and Deadlines: Priority date 3/1; no closing date. Applicants notified on a rolling basis starting 3/1; must reply by 5/1 or within 2 week(s) of notification.
Transfers: Closing date 7/15.

CONTACT
Bobbi Carpenter, Director of Financial Aid
PO Box B, Sweet Briar, VA 24595

Thomas Nelson Community College
Hampton, Virginia
www.tncc.edu   Federal Code: 006871

2-year public community college in small city.
Enrollment: 7,001 undergrads.
Selectivity: Open admission; but selective for some programs.

BASIC COSTS (2007-2008)
Tuition and fees: $2,446; out-of-state residents $7,610.
Per-credit charge: $77; out-of-state residents $249.
Additional info: Out of state students pay an additional $90 capital outlay fee.

FINANCIAL AID PICTURE (2007-2008)
Students with need: 78% of average financial aid package awarded as scholarships/grants, 22% awarded as loans/jobs. Need-based aid available for part-time students. Work study available nights.

FINANCIAL AID PROCEDURES
Forms required: FAFSA, institutional form.
Dates and Deadlines: Priority date 5/1; no closing date. Applicants notified on a rolling basis starting 6/1; must reply within 2 week(s) of notification.
Transfers: Priority date 5/8; no deadline. Applicants notified on a rolling basis; must reply within 2 week(s) of notification.

CONTACT
Lisa Smith, Director of Financial Aid, Veterans Affairs, and Scholarships
Box 9407, Hampton, VA 23670
(757) 825-2848

Tidewater Community College
Norfolk, Virginia
www.tcc.vccs.edu   Federal Code: 003712

2-year public community college in large city.
Enrollment: 21,649 undergrads.
Selectivity: Open admission; but selective for some programs.

BASIC COSTS (2007-2008)
Tuition and fees: $2,566; out-of-state residents $7,730.
Per-credit charge: $77; out-of-state residents $249.
Additional info: Out of state students pay an additional $90 capital outlay fee.

FINANCIAL AID PICTURE (2006-2007)
Students with need: Need-based aid available for full-time and part-time students.
Students without need: This college awards aid only to students with need.

FINANCIAL AID PROCEDURES
Forms required: FAFSA.
Dates and Deadlines: Priority date 4/1; no closing date. Applicants notified on a rolling basis starting 4/1.

CONTACT

Norma Ferki, Director of Financial Aid

7000 College Drive/Portsmouth Campus, Portsmouth, VA 23703

(757) 822-1360

University of Mary Washington

Fredericksburg, Virginia

www.umw.edu   Federal Code: 003746

4-year public university and liberal arts college in small city.

Enrollment: 4,117 undergrads, 12% part-time. 909 full-time freshmen.

Selectivity: Admits over 75% of applicants.

BASIC COSTS (2008-2009)

Tuition and fees: $7,200; out-of-state residents $18,600.

Per-credit charge: $275; out-of-state residents $725.

Room and board: $7,500.

FINANCIAL AID PICTURE (2006-2007)

Students with need: Out of 591 full-time freshmen who applied for aid, 252 were judged to have need. Of these, 219 received aid, and 30 had their full need met. Average financial aid package met 50% of need; average scholarship/grant was $5,590; average loan was $2,640. For part-time students, average financial aid package was $8,170.

Students without need: 75 full-time freshmen who did not demonstrate need for aid received scholarships/grants; average award was $1,450. No-need awards available for academics, art, leadership, music/drama, state/district residency.

Scholarships offered: Scholastic Excellence Award: from $500 to $6,000; honors admissions automatically considered. Two Virginia residents will receive tuition, fees, room and board up to $10,000. One non-Virginia award for tuition, fees, room and board. All scholarships renewable.

Cumulative student debt: 57% of graduating class had student loans; average debt was $15,000.

FINANCIAL AID PROCEDURES

Forms required: FAFSA, institutional form.

Dates and Deadlines: Closing date 3/1. Applicants notified by 4/15; must reply by 5/1 or within 2 week(s) of notification.

CONTACT

Deborah Harber, Senior Associate Dean for Financial Aid

1301 College Avenue, Fredericksburg, VA 22401-5358

(540) 654-2468

University of Richmond

University of Richmond, Virginia

www.richmond.edu   Federal Code: 003744

4-year private university and liberal arts college in very large city.

Enrollment: 2,719 undergrads, 1% part-time. 793 full-time freshmen.

Selectivity: Admits less than 50% of applicants.

BASIC COSTS (2007-2008)

Tuition and fees: $37,610.

Per-credit charge: $1,500.

Room and board: $7,200.

FINANCIAL AID PICTURE (2007-2008)

Students with need: Out of 440 full-time freshmen who applied for aid, 344 were judged to have need. Of these, 344 received aid, and 331 had their full need met. Average financial aid package met 100% of need; average scholarship/grant was $29,533; average loan was $3,127. For part-time students, average financial aid package was $9,501.

Students without need: 61 full-time freshmen who did not demonstrate need for aid received scholarships/grants; average award was $29,539. No-

need awards available for academics, art, athletics, leadership, minority status, music/drama, ROTC, state/district residency.

Scholarships offered: *Merit:* Richmond Scholars program: full tuition scholarships; up to 50 entering freshmen. Presidential Scholarships: up to $15,000. *Athletic:* 45 full-time freshmen received athletic scholarships; average amount $28,513.

Cumulative student debt: 41% of graduating class had student loans; average debt was $19,214.

Additional info: Early decision: Financial aid package estimated using historical data; applicant still required to submit all financial aid forms.

FINANCIAL AID PROCEDURES

Forms required: FAFSA, institutional form.

Dates and Deadlines: Closing date 2/15. Applicants notified by 4/1; must reply by 5/1 or within 4 week(s) of notification.

CONTACT

Cindy Deffenbaugh, Director of Student Financial Aid

28 Westhampton Way, University of Richmond, VA 23173

(804) 289-8438

University of Virginia

Charlottesville, Virginia

www.virginia.edu   Federal Code: 003745

4-year public university in small city.

Enrollment: 13,726 undergrads, 2% part-time. 3,246 full-time freshmen.

Selectivity: Admits less than 50% of applicants.

BASIC COSTS (2007-2008)

Tuition and fees: $8,500; out-of-state residents $27,515.

Room and board: $7,435.

FINANCIAL AID PICTURE (2007-2008)

Students with need: Out of 1,787 full-time freshmen who applied for aid, 839 were judged to have need. Of these, 806 received aid, and 621 had their full need met. Average financial aid package met 94% of need; average scholarship/grant was $13,433; average loan was $4,065. For part-time students, average financial aid package was $14,689.

Students without need: No-need awards available for academics, athletics, leadership, minority status, music/drama, state/district residency.

Cumulative student debt: 33% of graduating class had student loans; average debt was $16,847.

Additional info: Access UVA program offers loan-free packages for low-income students, caps on need-based loans for all other students, and commitment to meet 100 percent of need for every student.

FINANCIAL AID PROCEDURES

Forms required: FAFSA, institutional form.

Dates and Deadlines: Priority date 3/1; no closing date. Applicants notified by 4/5.

CONTACT

Yvonne Hubbard, Director Student Financial Services

Box 400160, Charlottesville, VA 22904-4160

(434) 982-6000

University of Virginia's College at Wise

Wise, Virginia

www.uvawise.edu   Federal Code: 003747

4-year public liberal arts college in small town.

Enrollment: 1,657 undergrads, 10% part-time. 400 full-time freshmen.

Selectivity: Admits over 75% of applicants.

BASIC COSTS (2007-2008)

Tuition and fees: $6,151; out-of-state residents $17,715.

Per-credit charge: $141; out-of-state residents $618.

Room and board: $6,984.

FINANCIAL AID PICTURE (2007-2008)

Students with need: Out of 328 full-time freshmen who applied for aid, 256 were judged to have need. Of these, 256 received aid, and 243 had their full need met. Average financial aid package met 94% of need; average scholarship/grant was $5,041; average loan was $2,301. For part-time students, average financial aid package was $4,765.

Students without need: 127 full-time freshmen who did not demonstrate need for aid received scholarships/grants; average award was $2,312. No-need awards available for academics, alumni affiliation, art, athletics, job skills, leadership, music/drama, religious affiliation, state/district residency.

Scholarships offered: 48 full-time freshmen received athletic scholarships; average amount $1,664.

Cumulative student debt: 56% of graduating class had student loans; average debt was $9,206.

FINANCIAL AID PROCEDURES

Forms required: FAFSA.

Dates and Deadlines: Priority date 4/1; no closing date. Applicants notified on a rolling basis starting 2/15; must reply within 4 week(s) of notification.

CONTACT

Bill Wendle, Director of Financial Aid
1 College Avenue, Wise, VA 24293-4412
(276) 328-0139

Virginia Commonwealth University

Richmond, Virginia

www.vcu.edu   Federal Code: 003735

4-year public university in small city.

Enrollment: 20,232 undergrads, 14% part-time. 3,855 full-time freshmen.

Selectivity: Admits 50 to 75% of applicants.

BASIC COSTS (2007-2008)

Tuition and fees: $6,196; out-of-state residents $18,572.

Per-credit charge: $187; out-of-state residents $703.

Room and board: $7,567.

FINANCIAL AID PICTURE (2007-2008)

Students with need: Out of 2,521 full-time freshmen who applied for aid, 1,866 were judged to have need. Of these, 1,866 received aid, and 306 had their full need met. Average financial aid package met 69% of need; average scholarship/grant was $5,061; average loan was $4,116. For part-time students, average financial aid package was $8,755.

Students without need: 178 full-time freshmen who did not demonstrate need for aid received scholarships/grants; average award was $6,319. No-need awards available for academics, art, athletics, leadership, music/drama.

Scholarships offered: 20 full-time freshmen received athletic scholarships; average amount $12,066.

Cumulative student debt: 64% of graduating class had student loans; average debt was $20,468.

FINANCIAL AID PROCEDURES

Forms required: FAFSA.

Dates and Deadlines: Priority date 3/1; no closing date. Applicants notified on a rolling basis starting 3/15; must reply by 5/1 or within 3 week(s) of notification.

Transfers: Applicants notified by 6/15; must reply by 5/1 or within 4 week(s) of notification.

CONTACT

Susan Kadir, Director of Financial Aid
Box 842526, Richmond, VA 23284-2526
(804) 828-6669

Virginia Intermont College

Bristol, Virginia

www.vic.edu   Federal Code: 003752

4-year private liberal arts college in small city, affiliated with Baptist faith.

Enrollment: 627 undergrads, 16% part-time. 125 full-time freshmen.

Selectivity: Admits 50 to 75% of applicants.

BASIC COSTS (2007-2008)

Tuition and fees: $19,366.

Per-credit charge: $220.

Room and board: $6,495.

FINANCIAL AID PICTURE (2006-2007)

Students with need: Out of 83 full-time freshmen who applied for aid, 69 were judged to have need. Of these, 68 received aid, and 10 had their full need met. Average financial aid package met 53% of need; average scholarship/grant was $8,962; average loan was $2,795. For part-time students, average financial aid package was $6,213.

Students without need: 44 full-time freshmen who did not demonstrate need for aid received scholarships/grants; average award was $6,160. No-need awards available for art, athletics, music/drama, religious affiliation, state/district residency.

Scholarships offered: 27 full-time freshmen received athletic scholarships; average amount $11,392.

Cumulative student debt: 71% of graduating class had student loans; average debt was $19,217.

FINANCIAL AID PROCEDURES

Forms required: FAFSA, state aid form.

Dates and Deadlines: Priority date 3/1; closing date 6/1. Applicants notified on a rolling basis starting 2/15; must reply within 3 week(s) of notification.

Transfers: Applicants notified on a rolling basis; must reply within 3 week(s) of notification. Limited to certain number of units of state aid.

CONTACT

Denise Posey, Financial Aid Director
1013 Moore Street, Bristol, VA 24201
(276) 466-7871

Virginia Military Institute

Lexington, Virginia

www.vmi.edu   Federal Code: 003753

4-year public liberal arts and military college in small town.

Enrollment: 1,378 undergrads. 415 full-time freshmen.

Selectivity: Admits 50 to 75% of applicants. GED not accepted.

BASIC COSTS (2007-2008)

Tuition and fees: $10,048; out-of-state residents $25,892.

Room and board: $6,108.

FINANCIAL AID PICTURE (2006-2007)

Students with need: Out of 295 full-time freshmen who applied for aid, 216 were judged to have need. Of these, 215 received aid, and 96 had their full need met. Average financial aid package met 85% of need; average scholarship/grant was $9,397; average loan was $2,972.

Students without need: 63 full-time freshmen who did not demonstrate need for aid received scholarships/grants; average award was $4,521. No-need awards available for academics, athletics, leadership, music/drama, ROTC.

Scholarships offered: *Merit:* Institute Scholarship: up to $19,830; 10-12 awarded; for superior academic performance, demonstrated character and leadership, extracurricular activities, 3.7 high school GPA, minimum 1250 SAT (exclusive of Writing) or 27 ACT, rank in top 5% of class. *Athletic:* 29 full-time freshmen received athletic scholarships; average amount $11,398.

FINANCIAL AID PROCEDURES

Forms required: FAFSA, institutional form.

Dates and Deadlines: Priority date 3/1; no closing date. Applicants notified on a rolling basis starting 3/15; must reply by 5/1.

CONTACT

Timothy Golden, Director of Financial Aid

319 Letcher Avenue, Lexington, VA 24450-9967

(540) 464-7208

Virginia Polytechnic Institute and State University

Blacksburg, Virginia

www.vt.edu   Federal Code: 003754

4-year public university in large town.

Enrollment: 22,940 undergrads, 2% part-time. 5,085 full-time freshmen.

Selectivity: Admits 50 to 75% of applicants.

BASIC COSTS (2007-2008)

Tuition and fees: $7,397; out-of-state residents $19,605.

Room and board: $5,106.

FINANCIAL AID PICTURE (2006-2007)

Students with need: Out of 3,541 full-time freshmen who applied for aid, 2,083 were judged to have need. Of these, 1,762 received aid, and 286 had their full need met. Average financial aid package met 61% of need; average scholarship/grant was $5,569; average loan was $3,500. Need-based aid available for part-time students.

Students without need: 632 full-time freshmen who did not demonstrate need for aid received scholarships/grants; average award was $2,557. No-need awards available for art, athletics, ROTC.

Scholarships offered: 94 full-time freshmen received athletic scholarships; average amount $10,865.

Cumulative student debt: 53% of graduating class had student loans; average debt was $20,209.

FINANCIAL AID PROCEDURES

Forms required: FAFSA.

Dates and Deadlines: Priority date 3/11; no closing date. Applicants notified on a rolling basis starting 3/30; must reply by 5/1 or within 4 week(s) of notification.

Transfers: Priority date 2/1; closing date 3/11. Based on family EFC per FAFSA and available resources.

CONTACT

Barry Simmons, Director of Financial Aid

201 Burruss Hall, Blacksburg, VA 24061-0202

(540) 231-9555

Virginia State University

Petersburg, Virginia

www.vsu.edu   Federal Code: 003764

4-year public university in large town.

Enrollment: 4,195 undergrads, 6% part-time. 1,040 full-time freshmen.

Selectivity: Admits 50 to 75% of applicants.

BASIC COSTS (2007-2008)

Tuition and fees: $5,655; out-of-state residents $13,185.

Per-credit charge: $186; out-of-state residents $444.

Room and board: $7,340.

Additional info: Out of state students pay an additional fee.

FINANCIAL AID PICTURE

Students with need: Need-based aid available for full-time and part-time students. Work study available nights, weekends, and for part-time students.

Students without need: No-need awards available for academics, alumni affiliation, art, athletics, job skills, leadership, music/drama, religious affiliation, ROTC.

Scholarships offered: Presidential Scholarships: 3.2 GPA, SAT 1100 or ACT 24; $7,000. Provost's Scholarships: 3.0 GPA, SAT 1000 or ACT 21; $3,500. SAT exclusive of Writing. Fine and Performing Arts Scholarships: outstanding talent in music or fine arts, audition or portfolio may be required, recommendation required; $1,500. Math, Science, and Technology Scholarships: 3.0 GPA, above average ability in math, science, or technology, recommendation and essay required; $1,500.

Additional info: Strongly recommend that students apply for scholarship assistance through federal, state, local and private agencies.

FINANCIAL AID PROCEDURES

Forms required: FAFSA, institutional form.

Dates and Deadlines: Priority date 3/31; closing date 5/1. Applicants notified on a rolling basis starting 5/1; must reply within 2 week(s) of notification.

Transfers: Priority date 3/1.

CONTACT

Henry Debose, Director of Financial Aid

One Hayden Street, Petersburg, VA 23806

(804) 524-5990

Virginia Union University

Richmond, Virginia

www.vuu.edu   Federal Code: 003766

4-year private university and liberal arts college in small city, affiliated with Baptist faith.

Enrollment: 1,194 undergrads.

BASIC COSTS (2008-2009)

Tuition and fees: $13,662.

Room and board: $6,328.

FINANCIAL AID PICTURE

Students with need: Need-based aid available for full-time and part-time students. Work study available nights, weekends, and for part-time students.

Students without need: No-need awards available for academics, athletics, ROTC, state/district residency.

FINANCIAL AID PROCEDURES

Forms required: FAFSA.

Dates and Deadlines: Priority date 4/27; no closing date. Applicants notified on a rolling basis starting 5/1; must reply within 2 week(s) of notification.

Transfers: No deadline. Student must submit a financial aid transcript from all prior schools attended before receiving aid.

CONTACT

Mack-Tatum Donna, Director of Financial Aid

1500 North Lombardy Street, Richmond, VA 23220

(804) 257-5882

Virginia Wesleyan College

Norfolk, Virginia
www.vwc.edu   Federal Code: 003767

4-year private liberal arts college in large city, affiliated with United Methodist Church.

Enrollment: 1,379 undergrads, 13% part-time. 416 full-time freshmen.

Selectivity: Admits over 75% of applicants.

BASIC COSTS (2008-2009)

Tuition and fees: $26,438.

Per-credit charge: $1,081.

Room and board: $7,100.

Additional info: Damage deposit of $150 for residents. Tuition/fee waivers available for adults.

FINANCIAL AID PICTURE (2006-2007)

Students with need: Out of 409 full-time freshmen who applied for aid, 306 were judged to have need. Of these, 304 received aid, and 41 had their full need met. Average financial aid package met 68% of need; average scholarship/grant was $3,322; average loan was $2,958. For part-time students, average financial aid package was $4,449.

Students without need: 101 full-time freshmen who did not demonstrate need for aid received scholarships/grants; average award was $8,062. No-need awards available for academics, art, leadership, music/drama, religious affiliation, state/district residency.

FINANCIAL AID PROCEDURES

Forms required: FAFSA, state aid form.

Dates and Deadlines: Priority date 3/1; no closing date. Applicants notified on a rolling basis starting 2/15; must reply by 5/1 or within 2 week(s) of notification.

Transfers: 4-semester maximum of special aid available for students who graduated with 3.0 GPA and earned an associate degree from local community college. Must enroll full time and maintain 2.5 GPA minimum.

CONTACT

Angie Hawkins, Director of Financial Aid

1584 Wesleyan Drive, Norfolk, VA 23502-5599

(757) 455-3345

Virginia Western Community College

Roanoke, Virginia
www.virginiawestern.edu   Federal Code: 003760

2-year public community college in small city.

Enrollment: 4,665 undergrads.

Selectivity: Open admission; but selective for some programs.

BASIC COSTS (2007-2008)

Tuition and fees: $2,453; out-of-state residents $7,617.

Per-credit charge: $77; out-of-state residents $249.

Additional info: Out of state students pay an additional $90 capital outlay fee.

FINANCIAL AID PICTURE

Students with need: Need-based aid available for full-time and part-time students.

Students without need: No-need awards available for academics, state/district residency.

FINANCIAL AID PROCEDURES

Forms required: FAFSA.

Dates and Deadlines: No deadline. Applicants notified on a rolling basis starting 4/1.

Transfers: No deadline. Applicants notified on a rolling basis.

CONTACT

Carol Sliver, Financial Aid Officer

Box 14007, Roanoke, VA 24038

(540) 857-7331

Washington and Lee University

Lexington, Virginia   Federal Code: 003768
www.wlu.edu   CSS Code: 5887

4-year private university and liberal arts college in small town.

Enrollment: 1,774 undergrads. 463 full-time freshmen.

Selectivity: Admits less than 50% of applicants.

BASIC COSTS (2007-2008)

Tuition and fees: $35,445.

Room and board: $8,725.

FINANCIAL AID PICTURE (2006-2007)

Students with need: Out of 251 full-time freshmen who applied for aid, 171 were judged to have need. Of these, 171 received aid, and 152 had their full need met. Average financial aid package met 99% of need; average scholarship/grant was $27,360; average loan was $3,088. Need-based aid available for part-time students.

Students without need: 38 full-time freshmen who did not demonstrate need for aid received scholarships/grants; average award was $29,288. No-need awards available for academics.

Scholarships offered: Various memorial and endowed scholarships available.

Cumulative student debt: 31% of graduating class had student loans; average debt was $16,784.

FINANCIAL AID PROCEDURES

Forms required: FAFSA, CSS PROFILE.

Dates and Deadlines: Closing date 2/1. Applicants notified by 4/1; must reply by 5/1.

Transfers: Transfer students are awarded institutional funds only after commitments to enrolled students are met. Notification usually in late summer.

CONTACT

John DeCourcy, Director of Student Financial Aid

204 West Washington Street, Lexington, VA 24450-2116

(540) 458-8715

Wytheville Community College

Wytheville, Virginia
www.wcc.vccs.edu   Federal Code: 003761

2-year public community college in small town.

Enrollment: 1,668 undergrads.

Selectivity: Open admission; but selective for some programs.

BASIC COSTS (2007-2008)

Tuition and fees: $2,435; out-of-state residents $7,599.

Per-credit charge: $77; out-of-state residents $249.

Additional info: Out of state students pay an additional $90 capital outlay fee.

FINANCIAL AID PICTURE (2006-2007)

Students with need: 94% of average financial aid package awarded as scholarships/grants, 6% awarded as loans/jobs. Need-based aid available for part-time students.

Students without need: This college awards aid only to students with need.

FINANCIAL AID PROCEDURES

Forms required: FAFSA, institutional form.

Dates and Deadlines: Priority date 4/1; no closing date. Applicants notified on a rolling basis starting 5/1; must reply within 4 week(s) of notification.

CONTACT

Mary Gallagher, Financial Aid Coordinator
1000 East Main Street, Wytheville, VA 24382
(540) 223-4703

Washington

Antioch University Seattle
Seattle, Washington
www.antiochsea.edu   Federal Code: 003010

Upper-division private university and liberal arts college in very large city.
Enrollment: 250 undergrads.

BASIC COSTS (2007-2008)
Tuition and fees: $20,310.
Per-credit charge: $445.
Additional info: For BA with Teacher Prep program, $18,900 per year, $420 per credit hour.

FINANCIAL AID PICTURE
Students with need: Need-based aid available for full-time and part-time students. Work study available nights, weekends, and for part-time students.

FINANCIAL AID PROCEDURES
Forms required: FAFSA, institutional form.
Dates and Deadlines: Priority date 4/15; no closing date. Applicants notified on a rolling basis starting 5/1; must reply within 2 week(s) of notification.

CONTACT
Katy Stahl, Financial Aid Officer
2326 Sixth Avenue, Seattle, WA 98121-1814
(206) 441-5352 ext. 5010

Art Institute of Seattle
Seattle, Washington
www.ais.edu   Federal Code: 016210

4-year for-profit visual arts and technical college in very large city.
Enrollment: 2,261 undergrads, 32% part-time. 438 full-time freshmen.
Selectivity: Admits over 75% of applicants.

BASIC COSTS (2008-2009)
Tuition and fees: $20,565.
Per-credit charge: $435.
Room and board: $10,684.
Additional info: Tuition at time of enrollment locked for 4 years.

FINANCIAL AID PICTURE (2007-2008)
Students with need: 26% of average financial aid package awarded as scholarships/grants, 74% awarded as loans/jobs. Need-based aid available for part-time students. Work study available nights, weekends, and for part-time students.
Students without need: No-need awards available for academics, art.

FINANCIAL AID PROCEDURES
Forms required: FAFSA, state aid form.
Dates and Deadlines: Priority date 4/15; no closing date. Applicants notified on a rolling basis; must reply within 4 week(s) of notification.

CONTACT

Angela Hedwall, Director of Student Financial Services
2323 Elliott Avenue, Seattle, WA 98121-1622
(206) 239-2261

Bastyr University
Kenmore, Washington
www.bastyr.edu   Federal Code: 016059

Upper-division private university and health science college in small city.
Enrollment: 213 undergrads, 8% part-time.

BASIC COSTS (2007-2008)
Tuition and fees: $17,040.
Per-credit charge: $340.
Room and board: $3,650.

FINANCIAL AID PICTURE (2007-2008)
Students with need: Average financial aid package for all full-time under-graduates was $18,600. 77% awarded as scholarships/grants, 23% awarded as loans/jobs. Need-based aid available for part-time students. Work study available nights, weekends, and for part-time students.
Students without need: No-need awards available for academics.

FINANCIAL AID PROCEDURES
Forms required: FAFSA, institutional form.
Dates and Deadlines: Priority date 6/1; no closing date. Applicants notified on a rolling basis starting 5/15; must reply within 2 week(s) of notification.
Transfers: Priority date 5/1; no deadline. Applicants notified on a rolling basis; must reply within 3 week(s) of notification.

CONTACT
Carol Duke, Director of Financial Aid
14500 Juanita Drive, NE, Kenmore, WA 98028
(425) 602-3080

Bates Technical College
Tacoma, Washington
www.bates.ctc.edu   Federal Code: 012259

2-year public technical college in small city.
Enrollment: 1,210 undergrads.
Selectivity: Open admission.

BASIC COSTS (2007-2008)
Additional info: Programs range in costs from $3,841 to $5,055; cost includes tuition and some fees.

FINANCIAL AID PICTURE
Students with need: Need-based aid available for full-time and part-time students. Work study available nights.
Students without need: This college awards aid only to students with need.

FINANCIAL AID PROCEDURES
Forms required: FAFSA, institutional form.
Dates and Deadlines: No deadline. Applicants notified on a rolling basis starting 9/7.
Transfers: No deadline. Applicants notified on a rolling basis.

CONTACT
Susan Neese, Financial Aid Officer
1101 South Yakima Avenue, Tacoma, WA 98405
(253) 680-7025

Bellevue Community College

Bellevue, Washington
www.bcc.ctc.edu   Federal Code: 003769

2-year public community college in small city.
Enrollment: 5,000 undergrads.
Selectivity: Open admission; but selective for some programs.

BASIC COSTS (2007-2008)
Tuition and fees: $3,096; out-of-state residents $8,304.
Per-credit charge: $81; out-of-state residents $253.

FINANCIAL AID PICTURE (2006-2007)
Students with need: 77% of average financial aid package awarded as scholarships/grants, 23% awarded as loans/jobs. Need-based aid available for part-time students. Work study available nights, weekends, and for part-time students.
Students without need: No-need awards available for academics, athletics.

FINANCIAL AID PROCEDURES
Forms required: FAFSA, institutional form.
Dates and Deadlines: Priority date 4/16; no closing date. Applicants notified on a rolling basis starting 8/1.

CONTACT
Sherri Ballantyne, Director of Financial Aid
3000 Landerholm Circle SE, Bellevue, WA 98007-6484
(425) 564-2227

Bellingham Technical College

Bellingham, Washington
www.btc.ctc.edu   Federal Code: 016227

2-year public technical college in small city.
Enrollment: 2,084 undergrads.
Selectivity: Open admission.

BASIC COSTS (2007-2008)
Tuition and fees: $3,345.

FINANCIAL AID PICTURE
Students with need: Need-based aid available for full-time and part-time students.
Students without need: This college awards aid only to students with need.

FINANCIAL AID PROCEDURES
Forms required: FAFSA.
Dates and Deadlines: Priority date 4/30; no closing date. Applicants notified on a rolling basis starting 7/1; must reply within 2 week(s) of notification.

CONTACT
Jack Wollens, Director of Financial Aid
3028 Lindbergh Avenue, Bellingham, WA 98225
(360) 752-8351

Big Bend Community College

Moses Lake, Washington
www.bigbend.edu   Federal Code: 003770

2-year public community college in large town.
Enrollment: 1,154 undergrads, 25% part-time. 245 full-time freshmen.
Selectivity: Open admission; but selective for some programs.

BASIC COSTS (2007-2008)
Tuition and fees: $2,766; out-of-state residents $3,156.
Per-credit charge: $74; out-of-state residents $88.
Room only: $2,790.
Additional info: Tuition/fee waivers available for unemployed or children of unemployed.

FINANCIAL AID PICTURE (2006-2007)
Students with need: 79% of average financial aid package awarded as scholarships/grants, 21% awarded as loans/jobs. Need-based aid available for part-time students. Work study available nights, weekends, and for part-time students.
Students without need: This college awards aid only to students with need.

FINANCIAL AID PROCEDURES
Forms required: FAFSA, institutional form.
Dates and Deadlines: Priority date 4/15; no closing date. Applicants notified on a rolling basis starting 5/15; must reply within 2 week(s) of notification.

CONTACT
Charlene Rios, Director of Financial Aid
7662 Chanute Street, Moses Lake, WA 98837-3299
(509) 793-2034

Cascadia Community College

Bothell, Washington
www.cascadia.edu   Federal Code: 034835

2-year public community college in large town.
Enrollment: 1,367 undergrads.
Selectivity: Open admission.

BASIC COSTS (2007-2008)
Tuition and fees: $2,796; out-of-state residents $8,004.

FINANCIAL AID PICTURE
Students with need: Work study available nights, weekends, and for part-time students.

FINANCIAL AID PROCEDURES
Forms required: FAFSA, institutional form.
Dates and Deadlines: Priority date 4/16; no closing date.

CONTACT
Sybil Smith, Director of Student Financial Services
18345 Campus Way, NE, Bothell, WA 98011

Central Washington University

Ellensburg, Washington
www.cwu.edu   Federal Code: 003771

4-year public university in large town.
Enrollment: 9,463 undergrads, 10% part-time. 1,471 full-time freshmen.
Selectivity: Admits over 75% of applicants.

BASIC COSTS (2007-2008)
Tuition and fees: $5,493; out-of-state residents $14,894.
Room and board: $7,418.

FINANCIAL AID PICTURE
Students with need: Need-based aid available for full-time and part-time students.
Students without need: No-need awards available for academics, alumni affiliation, art, athletics, job skills, leadership, minority status, music/drama, religious affiliation, ROTC, state/district residency.

FINANCIAL AID PROCEDURES

Forms required: FAFSA.

Dates and Deadlines: Priority date 3/1; no closing date. Applicants notified on a rolling basis starting 4/15; must reply within 4 week(s) of notification.

Transfers: Equal Opportunity Grant available for junior-level transfers from selected Washington counties. May receive up to $2,500/year for three years.

CONTACT

Agnes Canedo, Director of Financial Aid
400 East University Way, Ellensburg, WA 98926-7463
(509) 963-1611

Centralia College
Centralia, Washington
www.centralia.edu   Federal Code: 003772

2-year public community college in large town.

Enrollment: 3,566 undergrads.

Selectivity: Open admission; but selective for some programs.

BASIC COSTS (2007-2008)

Tuition and fees: $2,946; out-of-state residents $3,335.

Per-credit charge: $74; out-of-state residents $88.

Additional info: Tuition/fee waivers available for unemployed or children of unemployed.

FINANCIAL AID PICTURE

Students with need: Need-based aid available for full-time and part-time students.

Students without need: No-need awards available for academics, alumni affiliation, art, athletics, leadership, minority status, music/drama.

FINANCIAL AID PROCEDURES

Forms required: FAFSA, institutional form.

Dates and Deadlines: Priority date 5/1; closing date 9/1. Applicants notified on a rolling basis starting 7/10; must reply within 2 week(s) of notification.

CONTACT

Tracy Dahl, Director of Financial Aid
600 Centralia College Boulevard, Centralia, WA 98531
(360) 736-9391 ext. 234

City University of Seattle
Bellevue, Washington
www.cityu.edu   Federal Code: 013022

Upper-division private university in very large city.

Enrollment: 1,443 undergrads, 44% part-time.

Selectivity: Open admission.

BASIC COSTS (2008-2009)

Tuition and fees: $14,580.

Per-credit charge: $324.

FINANCIAL AID PICTURE

Students with need: Need-based aid available for full-time and part-time students.

Students without need: No-need awards available for academics.

Additional info: All degree programs approved for veteran's administration educational benefits.

FINANCIAL AID PROCEDURES

Forms required: FAFSA, institutional form.

Dates and Deadlines: No deadline. Applicants notified on a rolling basis.

CONTACT

Jean Roberts, Director of Financial Aid
11900 NE First Street, Bellevue, WA 98005
(800) 426-5596

Clark College
Vancouver, Washington
www.clark.edu   Federal Code: 003773

2-year public community college in small city.

Enrollment: 5,237 undergrads.

Selectivity: Open admission; but selective for some programs.

BASIC COSTS (2007-2008)

Tuition and fees: $2,912; out-of-state residents $8,048.

Per-credit charge: $80; out-of-state residents $252.

Additional info: Tuition/fee waivers available for unemployed or children of unemployed.

FINANCIAL AID PICTURE (2006-2007)

Students with need: 71% of average financial aid package awarded as scholarships/grants, 29% awarded as loans/jobs. Need-based aid available for part-time students. Work study available nights, weekends, and for part-time students.

Students without need: No-need awards available for academics, alumni affiliation, art, athletics, job skills, leadership, minority status, music/drama, religious affiliation, ROTC, state/district residency.

Scholarships offered: Clark College Foundation Scholarships; range from $500 to full tuition; recipients selected from those completing Clark's Foundation Standard Scholarship application form.

FINANCIAL AID PROCEDURES

Forms required: FAFSA, institutional form.

Dates and Deadlines: Priority date 5/1; no closing date. Applicants notified on a rolling basis starting 5/1; must reply within 2 week(s) of notification.

CONTACT

Karen Driscoll, Director of Financial Aid
1933 Fort Vancouver Way, Vancouver, WA 98663
(360) 992-2153

Clover Park Technical College
Lakewood, Washington
www.cptc.edu   Federal Code: 015984

2-year public technical college in small city.

Enrollment: 2,290 undergrads.

Selectivity: Open admission; but selective for some programs.

BASIC COSTS (2007-2008)

Tuition and fees: $3,070.

FINANCIAL AID PICTURE

Students with need: Need-based aid available for full-time and part-time students. Work study available nights, weekends, and for part-time students.

Students without need: This college awards aid only to students with need.

FINANCIAL AID PROCEDURES

Forms required: FAFSA, institutional form.

Dates and Deadlines: Priority date 6/15; closing date 8/25. Applicants notified on a rolling basis.

CONTACT

Karen Specht, Financial Aid Director
4500 Steilacoom Boulevard, SW, Lakewood, WA 98499-4098
(253) 589-5660

Columbia Basin College
Pasco, Washington
www.columbiabasin.edu   Federal Code: 003774

2-year public community college in small city.
Enrollment: 7,140 undergrads.
Selectivity: Open admission; but selective for some programs.

BASIC COSTS (2007-2008)
Tuition and fees: $2,866; out-of-state residents $3,864.
Additional info: Tuition/fee waivers available for unemployed or children of unemployed.

FINANCIAL AID PICTURE
Students with need: Need-based aid available for full-time and part-time students. Work study available nights, weekends, and for part-time students.
Students without need: No-need awards available for academics, athletics, state/district residency.

FINANCIAL AID PROCEDURES
Forms required: FAFSA, institutional form.
Dates and Deadlines: Priority date 4/10; no closing date. Applicants notified on a rolling basis starting 6/15; must reply within 2 week(s) of notification.

CONTACT
Ceci Ratliff, Director of Student Financial Services
2600 North 20th Avenue, Pasco, WA 99301
(509) 542-4715

Cornish College of the Arts
Seattle, Washington
www.cornish.edu   Federal Code: 012315

4-year private visual arts and performing arts college in very large city.
Enrollment: 800 undergrads.

BASIC COSTS (2007-2008)
Tuition and fees: $24,100.
Per-credit charge: $1,000.
Additional info: Design majors required to have laptop computer and Adobe software, estimated cost $3,000.

FINANCIAL AID PICTURE (2007-2008)
Students with need: Average financial aid package met 59% of need; average scholarship/grant was $7,664; average loan was $3,653. For part-time students, average financial aid package was $12,395.
Students without need: No-need awards available for academics.

FINANCIAL AID PROCEDURES
Forms required: FAFSA, institutional form.
Dates and Deadlines: Priority date 2/15; no closing date. Applicants notified on a rolling basis starting 4/15; must reply by 5/1 or within 2 week(s) of notification.
Transfers: No deadline. Applicants notified on a rolling basis; must reply by 2/15.

CONTACT
Monique Theriault, Director for Financial Aid
1000 Lenora Street, Seattle, WA 98121
(206) 726-5014

DeVry University: Federal Way
Federal Way, Washington
www.devry.edu

4-year for-profit university in large city.
Enrollment: 661 undergrads, 32% part-time. 103 full-time freshmen.

BASIC COSTS (2007-2008)
Tuition and fees: $14,640.
Per-credit charge: $525.

FINANCIAL AID PICTURE (2006-2007)
Students with need: Out of 91 full-time freshmen who applied for aid, 85 were judged to have need. Of these, 85 received aid. Average financial aid package met 26% of need; average scholarship/grant was $4,325; average loan was $4,137. For part-time students, average financial aid package was $8,250.
Students without need: This college awards aid only to students with need.
Cumulative student debt: 50% of graduating class had student loans; average debt was $57,734.

FINANCIAL AID PROCEDURES
Forms required: FAFSA.
Dates and Deadlines: No deadline. Applicants notified on a rolling basis.

CONTACT
Scott Sand, Director of Financial Aid
3600 South 344th Way, Federal Way, WA 98001-9558
(253) 943-3060

DigiPen Institute of Technology
Redmond, Washington
www.digipen.edu   Federal Code: 037243

4-year for-profit visual arts and engineering college in large town.
Enrollment: 812 undergrads.

BASIC COSTS (2008-2009)
Additional info: Full-time tuition for academic year (based on 20 hours per term), $19,040; required fees, $160; per-credit-hour charge, $476. Full-time tuition for non-resident aliens for academic year (based on 20 hours per term), $24,840; per-credit-hour charge, $621.

FINANCIAL AID PICTURE
Students with need: Need-based aid available for full-time and part-time students.
Students without need: No-need awards available for job skills, leadership, minority status.
Scholarships offered: Institutional Need-Based Scholarship: $1,000; based on financial need and academic performance; 5 awarded annually. Imagine America Scholarship Program: $1,000; based on financial need, grade point average of 2.5 or greater, voluntary community service during the senior year; 3 awarded annually. First Scholarship: $2,500; based on essay and academic record; 2 awarded annually. First Scholarship: $1,000; based on essay and academic record; 5 awarded annually.
Additional info: Many aid programs are on a first-come, first-serve basis.

FINANCIAL AID PROCEDURES
Forms required: FAFSA, institutional form.
Dates and Deadlines: Priority date 4/15; no closing date. Applicants notified on a rolling basis starting 1/1; must reply within 4 week(s) of notification.
Transfers: No deadline. Applicants notified on a rolling basis starting 1/1; must reply within 4 week(s) of notification. Transfer student should meet with a financial aid administrator as soon as they are accepted. We will need prior financial aid history to determine eligibility.

CONTACT

Kim King, Director of Financial Aid

5001-150th Avenue Northeast, Redmond, WA 98052

(425) 895-4446

Edmonds Community College

Lynnwood, Washington

www.edcc.edu   Federal Code: 005001

2-year public community college in small city.

Enrollment: 7,761 undergrads.

Selectivity: Open admission.

BASIC COSTS (2007-2008)

Tuition and fees: $3,167; out-of-state residents $8,375.

FINANCIAL AID PICTURE

Students with need: Need-based aid available for full-time and part-time students. Work study available nights.

Students without need: No-need awards available for athletics.

FINANCIAL AID PROCEDURES

Forms required: FAFSA, institutional form.

Dates and Deadlines: Priority date 5/1; no closing date. Applicants notified on a rolling basis starting 6/1; must reply within 4 week(s) of notification.

CONTACT

Rae-Ellen Reas, Senior Associate Dean of Enrollment and Financial Services

20000 68th Avenue West, Lynnwood, WA 98036-5912

(425) 640-1457

Everett Community College

Everett, Washington

www.everettcc.edu   Federal Code: 003776

2-year public community college in small city.

Enrollment: 3,435 undergrads, 44% part-time. 199 full-time freshmen.

Selectivity: Open admission; but selective for some programs.

BASIC COSTS (2007-2008)

Tuition and fees: $2,781; out-of-state residents $7,989.

Per-credit charge: $74; out-of-state residents $246.

Additional info: Tuition at time of enrollment locked for 2 years.

FINANCIAL AID PICTURE (2006-2007)

Students with need: Out of 186 full-time freshmen who applied for aid, 148 were judged to have need. Of these, 130 received aid. Average financial aid package met 27% of need; average scholarship/grant was $4,980; average loan was $2,146. For part-time students, average financial aid package was $4,860.

Students without need: This college awards aid only to students with need.

Scholarships offered: 10 full-time freshmen received athletic scholarships; average amount $600.

Cumulative student debt: 13% of graduating class had student loans; average debt was $2,109.

FINANCIAL AID PROCEDURES

Forms required: FAFSA, institutional form.

Dates and Deadlines: Priority date 5/5; no closing date. Applicants notified on a rolling basis starting 4/15; must reply within 4 week(s) of notification.

Transfers: No deadline. Applicants notified on a rolling basis starting 6/15; must reply within 4 week(s) of notification.

CONTACT

Laurie Franklin, Director of Student Financial Services

2000 Tower Street, Everett, WA 98201-1352

(425) 388-9280

Evergreen State College

Olympia, Washington

www.evergreen.edu   Federal Code: 008155

4-year public college in small city.

Enrollment: 4,135 undergrads, 8% part-time. 578 full-time freshmen.

Selectivity: Admits over 75% of applicants.

BASIC COSTS (2007-2008)

Tuition and fees: $5,145; out-of-state residents $15,489.

Room and board: $6,541.

FINANCIAL AID PICTURE (2006-2007)

Students with need: Out of 384 full-time freshmen who applied for aid, 255 were judged to have need. Of these, 241 received aid, and 34 had their full need met. Average financial aid package met 55% of need; average scholarship/grant was $5,716; average loan was $2,845. For part-time students, average financial aid package was $3,133.

Students without need: 10 full-time freshmen who did not demonstrate need for aid received scholarships/grants; average award was $4,456. No-need awards available for academics, art, athletics.

Scholarships offered: 10 full-time freshmen received athletic scholarships; average amount $1,053.

Cumulative student debt: 61% of graduating class had student loans; average debt was $16,000.

Additional info: Application deadline for merit and cultural diversity scholarships February 1. Minority students may apply for tuition and fee waiver scholarships; amount of award equal to in-state tuition and fees. Discount waiver for employees. To meet priority deadline for required financial aid forms, official results of FAFSA must be received by March 15.

FINANCIAL AID PROCEDURES

Forms required: FAFSA, institutional form.

Dates and Deadlines: Priority date 3/15; no closing date. Applicants notified on a rolling basis starting 4/15; must reply within 4 week(s) of notification.

CONTACT

Lorraine Odom, Director of Financial Aid

2700 Evergreen Parkway NW, Olympia, WA 98505

(360) 867-6205

Gonzaga University

Spokane, Washington

www.gonzaga.edu   Federal Code: 003778

4-year private university and liberal arts college in large city, affiliated with Roman Catholic Church.

Enrollment: 4,318 undergrads, 2% part-time. 1,080 full-time freshmen.

Selectivity: Admits 50 to 75% of applicants. GED not accepted.

BASIC COSTS (2007-2008)

Tuition and fees: $26,538.

Per-credit charge: $760.

Room and board: $7,270.

Additional info: Tuition/fee waivers available for adults.

FINANCIAL AID PICTURE (2006-2007)

Students with need: Out of 807 full-time freshmen who applied for aid, 567 were judged to have need. Of these, 566 received aid, and 155 had their full need met. Average financial aid package met 88% of need; average scholarship/grant was $14,902; average loan was $4,135. For part-time students, average financial aid package was $6,358.

Students without need: 383 full-time freshmen who did not demonstrate need for aid received scholarships/grants; average award was $8,695. No-need awards available for academics, alumni affiliation, athletics, leadership, minority status, music/drama, ROTC.

Scholarships offered: *Merit:* All freshmen are considered for Academic Merit Scholarships: awards range from 3,000 to 10,000. *Athletic:* 40 full-time freshmen received athletic scholarships; average amount $17,640.

Cumulative student debt: 68% of graduating class had student loans; average debt was $23,971.

FINANCIAL AID PROCEDURES

Forms required: FAFSA.

Dates and Deadlines: Priority date 2/1; closing date 6/30. Applicants notified on a rolling basis starting 3/1; must reply by 5/1 or within 3 week(s) of notification.

Transfers: No deadline. Applicants notified on a rolling basis; must reply by 4/15 or within 3 week(s) of notification.

CONTACT

Thayne McCulloh, VP for Administration and Planning; Dean of Student Financial Services
502 East Boone Avenue, Spokane, WA 99258-0001
(509) 323-6582

Grays Harbor College

Aberdeen, Washington
www.ghc.ctc.edu   Federal Code: 003779

2-year public community college in large town.

Enrollment: 578 undergrads, 63% part-time. 50 full-time freshmen.

Selectivity: Open admission; but selective for some programs.

BASIC COSTS (2007-2008)

Tuition and fees: $3,113; out-of-state residents $8,321.

Additional info: Tuition/fee waivers available for adults, unemployed or children of unemployed.

FINANCIAL AID PICTURE (2006-2007)

Students with need: 82% of average financial aid package awarded as scholarships/grants, 18% awarded as loans/jobs. Need-based aid available for part-time students. Work study available nights.

Students without need: No-need awards available for academics, art, athletics, music/drama.

FINANCIAL AID PROCEDURES

Forms required: FAFSA, institutional form.

Dates and Deadlines: Priority date 5/1; no closing date. Applicants notified on a rolling basis starting 5/15.

CONTACT

Nadine Hibbs, Director of Financial Aid
1620 Edward P Smith Drive, Aberdeen, WA 98520
(360) 538-4081

Green River Community College

Auburn, Washington
www.greenriver.edu   Federal Code: 003780

2-year public community college in large town.

Enrollment: 819 undergrads.

Selectivity: Open admission; but selective for some programs.

BASIC COSTS (2007-2008)

Tuition and fees: $3,045; out-of-state residents $3,468.

Per-credit charge: $74; out-of-state residents $246.

FINANCIAL AID PICTURE

Students with need: Need-based aid available for full-time and part-time students.

Students without need: This college awards aid only to students with need.

FINANCIAL AID PROCEDURES

Forms required: FAFSA, institutional form.

Dates and Deadlines: Priority date 4/15; no closing date. Applicants notified on a rolling basis starting 6/30; must reply within 2 week(s) of notification.

CONTACT

Mary Edington, Director of Financial Aid
12401 SE 320th Street, Auburn, WA 98092
(253) 833-9111 ext. 2440

Heritage University

Toppenish, Washington
www.heritage.edu   Federal Code: 003777

4-year private liberal arts and teachers college in small town, affiliated with interdenominational tradition.

Enrollment: 788 undergrads, 31% part-time. 76 full-time freshmen.

Selectivity: Open admission.

BASIC COSTS (2008-2009)

Tuition and fees: $12,205.

Per-credit charge: $405.

FINANCIAL AID PICTURE (2007-2008)

Students with need: Average financial aid package met 75% of need; average scholarship/grant was $9,914; average loan was $2,697. For part-time students, average financial aid package was $8,608.

Students without need: No-need awards available for academics, leadership, minority status.

Cumulative student debt: 89% of graduating class had student loans; average debt was $18,986.

FINANCIAL AID PROCEDURES

Forms required: FAFSA, institutional form.

Dates and Deadlines: Priority date 2/10; no closing date. Applicants notified on a rolling basis; must reply within 2 week(s) of notification.

CONTACT

Dianne Fernandez, Director of Financial Aid
3240 Fort Road, Toppenish, WA 98948-9599
(509) 865-8502

Highline Community College

Des Moines, Washington
www.highline.edu   Federal Code: 003781

2-year public community college in small city.

Enrollment: 2,828 full-time undergrads.

Selectivity: Open admission; but selective for some programs.

BASIC COSTS (2007-2008)

Tuition and fees: $2,751; out-of-state residents $3,140.

Per-credit charge: $74; out-of-state residents $88.

FINANCIAL AID PICTURE

Students with need: Need-based aid available for full-time and part-time students.

FINANCIAL AID PROCEDURES

Forms required: FAFSA.

Dates and Deadlines: Priority date 5/31; no closing date. Applicants notified on a rolling basis starting 6/1.

CONTACT

Anna Nguyen, Associate Director of Financial Aid
2400 South 240th Street, Des Moines, WA 98198-9800
(206) 878-3710

International Academy of Design and Technology: Seattle

Seattle, Washington
www.iadtseattle.com   Federal Code: E01257

4-year for-profit university in very large city.
Enrollment: 562 undergrads.
Selectivity: Admits over 75% of applicants.

BASIC COSTS (2007-2008)

Tuition and fees: $15,300.
Per-credit charge: $340.

FINANCIAL AID PICTURE (2006-2007)

Students with need: 0% of average financial aid package awarded as scholarships/grants, 100% awarded as loans/jobs.

FINANCIAL AID PROCEDURES

Dates and Deadlines: No deadline.

CONTACT

Miki Sueoka, Director of Student Finance
645 Andover Park West, Seattle, WA 98188

Lake Washington Technical College

Kirkland, Washington
www.lwtc.ctc.edu   Federal Code: 005373

2-year public technical college in large town.
Enrollment: 4,811 undergrads.
Selectivity: Open admission; but selective for some programs.

BASIC COSTS (2007-2008)

Additional info: $75 per credit hour (1-5 credits); $37 per credit hour (more than 5 credits).

FINANCIAL AID PICTURE (2006-2007)

Students with need: 64% of average financial aid package awarded as scholarships/grants, 36% awarded as loans/jobs. Need-based aid available for part-time students.

FINANCIAL AID PROCEDURES

Forms required: FAFSA, institutional form.

Dates and Deadlines: Priority date 4/15; no closing date. Applicants notified on a rolling basis.

CONTACT

Bill Chaney, Director of Financial Aid
11605 132nd Avenue, NE, Kirkland, WA 98034

Lower Columbia College

Longview, Washington   Federal Code: 003782
www.lowercolumbia.edu   CSS Code: 4402

2-year public community college in small city.
Enrollment: 1,408 undergrads, 33% part-time. 230 full-time freshmen.
Selectivity: Open admission; but selective for some programs.

BASIC COSTS (2007-2008)

Tuition and fees: $2,874; out-of-state residents $3,586.
Per-credit charge: $74; out-of-state residents $96.
Additional info: Full-time "border county" tuition for students in Oregon's Clatsop, Multnomah, Washington, and Columbia counties: $2,881. Tuition/fee waivers available for adults, unemployed or children of unemployed.

FINANCIAL AID PICTURE (2006-2007)

Students with need: 59% of average financial aid package awarded as scholarships/grants, 41% awarded as loans/jobs. Need-based aid available for part-time students.

FINANCIAL AID PROCEDURES

Forms required: CSS PROFILE, institutional form.

Dates and Deadlines: Priority date 5/1; no closing date. Applicants notified on a rolling basis starting 4/21; must reply within 2 week(s) of notification.

Transfers: State-need grant awards transfer with students if previously awarded at another WA institution; SEOG usually not available to transfer students. Student employment, loans, Pell Grant available.

CONTACT

James Gorman, Director of Financial Aid
1600 Maple Street, Longview, WA 98632-0310
(360) 442-2311

North Seattle Community College

Seattle, Washington
www.northseattle.edu   Federal Code: 009704

2-year public community college in very large city.
Enrollment: 2,056 undergrads, 54% part-time. 371 full-time freshmen.
Selectivity: Open admission.

BASIC COSTS (2007-2008)

Tuition and fees: $2,935; out-of-state residents $8,143.
Per-credit charge: $74; out-of-state residents $246.
Additional info: Tuition/fee waivers available for unemployed or children of unemployed.

FINANCIAL AID PICTURE

Students with need: Need-based aid available for full-time and part-time students. Work study available nights, weekends, and for part-time students.

FINANCIAL AID PROCEDURES

Forms required: FAFSA, institutional form.

Dates and Deadlines: Priority date 4/30; closing date 8/31. Applicants notified on a rolling basis starting 8/1; must reply within 2 week(s) of notification.

CONTACT

Suzanne Scheldt, Director of Financial Aid
9600 College Way North, Seattle, WA 98103
(206) 528-4700

Northwest College of Art

Poulsbo, Washington
www.nca.edu   Federal Code: 026021

4-year for-profit visual arts college in small town.

Enrollment: 97 full-time undergrads.

BASIC COSTS (2008-2009)

Tuition and fees: $15,300.

Per-credit charge: $665.

FINANCIAL AID PICTURE

Students with need: Need-based aid available for full-time and part-time students.

Students without need: No-need awards available for academics, art, state/district residency.

FINANCIAL AID PROCEDURES

Forms required: FAFSA.

Dates and Deadlines: Priority date 3/1; closing date 6/1. Applicants notified on a rolling basis.

CONTACT

Heidi Townsend, Financial Aid Officer
16301 Creative Drive NE, Poulsbo, WA 98370
(360) 779-9993

Northwest University

Kirkland, Washington
www.northwestu.edu   Federal Code: 003783

4-year private university and liberal arts college in small city, affiliated with Assemblies of God.

Enrollment: 1,053 undergrads, 5% part-time. 169 full-time freshmen.

Selectivity: Admits over 75% of applicants.

BASIC COSTS (2008-2009)

Tuition and fees: $20,790.

Per-credit charge: $855.

Room and board: $6,578.

FINANCIAL AID PICTURE (2007-2008)

Students with need: Out of 134 full-time freshmen who applied for aid, 120 were judged to have need. Of these, 120 received aid, and 23 had their full need met. Average financial aid package met 75% of need; average scholarship/grant was $11,168; average loan was $3,682. For part-time students, average financial aid package was $10,221.

Students without need: 13 full-time freshmen who did not demonstrate need for aid received scholarships/grants; average award was $8,573. No-need awards available for academics, art, athletics, leadership, music/drama, religious affiliation.

Scholarships offered: 7 full-time freshmen received athletic scholarships; average amount $10,045.

Cumulative student debt: 88% of graduating class had student loans; average debt was $21,216.

FINANCIAL AID PROCEDURES

Forms required: FAFSA, institutional form.

Dates and Deadlines: Priority date 3/1; closing date 8/1. Applicants notified on a rolling basis starting 3/3; must reply within 4 week(s) of notification.

CONTACT

Lana Walter, Director of Financial Aid
5520 108th Avenue, NE, Kirkland, WA 98083-0579
(425) 889-5210

Olympic College

Bremerton, Washington
www.olympic.edu   Federal Code: 003784

2-year public community and liberal arts college in large town.

Enrollment: 6,675 undergrads.

Selectivity: Open admission; but selective for some programs.

BASIC COSTS (2007-2008)

Tuition and fees: $2,881; out-of-state residents $4,168.

Per-credit charge: $74; out-of-state residents $117.

FINANCIAL AID PICTURE (2007-2008)

Students with need: 76% of average financial aid package awarded as scholarships/grants, 24% awarded as loans/jobs. Need-based aid available for part-time students. Work study available nights.

Students without need: No-need awards available for academics, state/district residency.

FINANCIAL AID PROCEDURES

Forms required: FAFSA, institutional form.

Dates and Deadlines: Priority date 3/1; no closing date. Applicants notified on a rolling basis starting 6/1; must reply within 2 week(s) of notification.

CONTACT

Joseph Koroma, Associate Dean, Student Financial Services
1600 Chester Avenue, Bremerton, WA 98337-1699
(360) 475-7160

Pacific Lutheran University

Tacoma, Washington
www.plu.edu   Federal Code: 003785

4-year private university in large city, affiliated with Evangelical Lutheran Church in America.

Enrollment: 3,271 undergrads, 5% part-time. 715 full-time freshmen.

Selectivity: Admits over 75% of applicants.

BASIC COSTS (2008-2009)

Tuition and fees: $26,800.

Per-credit charge: $838.

Room and board: $8,200.

FINANCIAL AID PICTURE (2007-2008)

Students with need: Out of 636 full-time freshmen who applied for aid, 512 were judged to have need. Of these, 510 received aid, and 220 had their full need met. Average financial aid package met 92% of need; average scholarship/grant was $16,116; average loan was $5,715. For part-time students, average financial aid package was $12,642.

Students without need: 186 full-time freshmen who did not demonstrate need for aid received scholarships/grants; average award was $12,143. No-need awards available for academics, alumni affiliation, art, leadership, music/drama, religious affiliation, ROTC.

Cumulative student debt: 74% of graduating class had student loans; average debt was $23,348.

FINANCIAL AID PROCEDURES

Forms required: FAFSA.

Dates and Deadlines: Priority date 1/31; no closing date. Applicants notified on a rolling basis starting 3/15; must reply by 5/1 or within 4 week(s) of notification.

CONTACT

Kay Soltis, Director of Financial Aid
Office of Admissions, Tacoma, WA 98447-0003
(253) 535-7134

Peninsula College

Port Angeles, Washington
www.pc.ctc.edu
Federal Code: 003786

2-year public community college in large town.

Enrollment: 980 undergrads, 38% part-time. 197 full-time freshmen.

Selectivity: Open admission; but selective for some programs.

BASIC COSTS (2007-2008)

Tuition and fees: $2,763; out-of-state residents $3,152.

Per-credit charge: $77; out-of-state residents $90.

Additional info: Tuition/fee waivers available for unemployed or children of unemployed.

FINANCIAL AID PICTURE

Students with need: Need-based aid available for full-time and part-time students.

Students without need: No-need awards available for academics, athletics, job skills.

FINANCIAL AID PROCEDURES

Forms required: FAFSA, institutional form.

Dates and Deadlines: Priority date 4/1; no closing date. Applicants notified on a rolling basis starting 6/1; must reply within 2 week(s) of notification.

CONTACT

Krista Francis, Director of Financial Aid
1502 East Lauridsen Boulevard, Port Angeles, WA 98362
(360) 417-6390

Renton Technical College

Renton, Washington
www.RTC.edu
Federal Code: 014001

2-year public technical college in large town.

Enrollment: 1,047 undergrads.

Selectivity: Open admission.

BASIC COSTS (2007-2008)

Tuition and fees: $3,618.

FINANCIAL AID PICTURE (2006-2007)

Students with need: 84% of average financial aid package awarded as scholarships/grants, 16% awarded as loans/jobs. Need-based aid available for part-time students.

Students without need: This college awards aid only to students with need.

FINANCIAL AID PROCEDURES

Forms required: FAFSA, institutional form.

Dates and Deadlines: Priority date 5/1; no closing date. Applicants notified on a rolling basis.

CONTACT

Debbie Solomon, Director of Financial Aid
3000 NE Fourth Street, Renton, WA 98056-4195
(425) 235-5841

Saint Martin's University

Lacey, Washington
www.stmartin.edu
Federal Code: 003794

4-year private liberal arts college in large town, affiliated with Roman Catholic Church.

Enrollment: 1,245 undergrads, 15% part-time. 210 full-time freshmen.

Selectivity: Admits over 75% of applicants.

BASIC COSTS (2008-2009)

Tuition and fees: $24,110.

Per-credit charge: $794.

Room and board: $8,040.

FINANCIAL AID PICTURE (2006-2007)

Students with need: Out of 198 full-time freshmen who applied for aid, 174 were judged to have need. Of these, 172 received aid, and 48 had their full need met. Average financial aid package met 81% of need; average scholarship/grant was $14,580; average loan was $2,690. For part-time students, average financial aid package was $13,129.

Students without need: 36 full-time freshmen who did not demonstrate need for aid received scholarships/grants; average award was $11,715. No-need awards available for academics, alumni affiliation, athletics, leadership, music/drama, religious affiliation, ROTC, state/district residency.

Scholarships offered: 15 full-time freshmen received athletic scholarships; average amount $4,958.

Cumulative student debt: 83% of graduating class had student loans; average debt was $25,689.

FINANCIAL AID PROCEDURES

Forms required: FAFSA.

Dates and Deadlines: Priority date 3/1; no closing date. Applicants notified on a rolling basis starting 2/15.

CONTACT

Laura Miller, Director of Financial Aid
5300 Pacific Avenue SE, Lacey, WA 98503-7500
(360) 438-4397

Seattle Pacific University

Seattle, Washington
www.spu.edu
Federal Code: 003788

4-year private university in very large city, affiliated with Free Methodist Church of North America.

Enrollment: 3,015 undergrads, 4% part-time. 716 full-time freshmen.

Selectivity: Admits over 75% of applicants.

BASIC COSTS (2008-2009)

Tuition and fees: $26,817.

Per-credit charge: $736.

Room and board: $8,454.

FINANCIAL AID PICTURE (2007-2008)

Students with need: Out of 586 full-time freshmen who applied for aid, 463 were judged to have need. Of these, 462 received aid, and 87 had their full need met. Average financial aid package met 83% of need; average scholarship/grant was $18,303; average loan was $5,757. For part-time students, average financial aid package was $14,607.

Students without need: 202 full-time freshmen who did not demonstrate need for aid received scholarships/grants; average award was $12,304. No-need awards available for academics, alumni affiliation, art, athletics, leadership, minority status, music/drama, religious affiliation, ROTC.

Scholarships offered: 12 full-time freshmen received athletic scholarships; average amount $7,409.

Cumulative student debt: 70% of graduating class had student loans; average debt was $23,738.

FINANCIAL AID PROCEDURES

Forms required: FAFSA.

Dates and Deadlines: Priority date 4/1; no closing date. Applicants notified on a rolling basis starting 3/15; must reply by 5/1 or within 4 week(s) of notification.

Transfers: Priority date 2/1; no deadline. Applicants notified on a rolling basis starting 3/13; must reply by 5/1 or within 4 week(s) of notification.

CONTACT

Jordan Grant, Director of Financial Aid

3307 Third Avenue West, Seattle, WA 98119-1997

(206) 281-2061

Seattle University
Seattle, Washington

www.seattleu.edu   Federal Code: 003790

4-year private university in very large city, affiliated with Roman Catholic Church.

Enrollment: 4,234 undergrads, 7% part-time. 764 full-time freshmen.

Selectivity: Admits 50 to 75% of applicants.

BASIC COSTS (2007-2008)

Tuition and fees: $26,325.

Per-credit charge: $585.

Room and board: $7,860.

Additional info: $200 enrollment deposit, $95 matriculation fee required. $95 per-credit-hour charge for credit by examination. $95 per-credit-hour charge for validation of field experience.

FINANCIAL AID PICTURE (2007-2008)

Students with need: Out of 662 full-time freshmen who applied for aid, 472 were judged to have need. Of these, 468 received aid, and 66 had their full need met. Average financial aid package met 80% of need; average scholarship/grant was $6,420; average loan was $4,452. For part-time students, average financial aid package was $17,517.

Students without need: 18 full-time freshmen who did not demonstrate need for aid received scholarships/grants; average award was $6,712. No-need awards available for academics, alumni affiliation, athletics, leadership, minority status, music/drama, ROTC, state/district residency.

Scholarships offered: *Merit:* Sullivan Leadership Award: full tuition, room and board for 4 years, for entering freshmen of Oregon, Washington, or Idaho residency; service, leadership, strong academics (3.5 GPA) important, 6 awarded. Presidential Scholarship: $11,000 annually for 4 years. Trustee Scholarship: $8,000 annually for 4 years. Campion Scholarship: $5,000 annually for 4 years; for first-time freshmen of U.S. citizenship or permanent resident status, strong academic and extracurricular records important. *Athletic:* 27 full-time freshmen received athletic scholarships; average amount $7,851.

Cumulative student debt: 80% of graduating class had student loans; average debt was $20,067.

FINANCIAL AID PROCEDURES

Forms required: FAFSA.

Dates and Deadlines: Priority date 2/1; no closing date. Applicants notified on a rolling basis starting 3/21; must reply by 5/1 or within 2 week(s) of notification.

Transfers: Closing date 3/1.

CONTACT

Janet Cantelon, Director of Financial Aid

901 12th Avenue, Seattle, WA 98122-4340

(206) 296-2000

South Puget Sound Community College
Olympia, Washington

www.spscc.ctc.edu   Federal Code: 005372

2-year public community college in small city.

Enrollment: 2,749 undergrads, 44% part-time. 267 full-time freshmen.

Selectivity: Open admission; but selective for some programs.

BASIC COSTS (2007-2008)

Tuition and fees: $2,774; out-of-state residents $3,164.

Per-credit charge: $74; out-of-state residents $87.

FINANCIAL AID PICTURE

Students with need: Need-based aid available for full-time and part-time students.

Students without need: No-need awards available for academics, athletics.

FINANCIAL AID PROCEDURES

Forms required: FAFSA, institutional form.

Dates and Deadlines: Priority date 5/1; no closing date. Applicants notified on a rolling basis starting 7/10; must reply within 2 week(s) of notification.

CONTACT

Carla Idohl-Corwin, Dean of Student Financial Services

2011 Mottman Road, SW, Olympia, WA 98512-6218

(360) 596-5232

South Seattle Community College
Seattle, Washington

www.southseattle.edu   Federal Code: 009706

4-year public community college in very large city.

Enrollment: 3,230 undergrads.

Selectivity: Open admission; but selective for some programs.

BASIC COSTS (2007-2008)

Tuition and fees: $2,897; out-of-state residents $8,105.

Additional info: Tuition/fee waivers available for unemployed or children of unemployed.

FINANCIAL AID PICTURE (2006-2007)

Students with need: 94% of average financial aid package awarded as scholarships/grants, 6% awarded as loans/jobs. Need-based aid available for part-time students.

Students without need: No-need awards available for academics, state/district residency.

FINANCIAL AID PROCEDURES

Forms required: FAFSA, institutional form.

Dates and Deadlines: Priority date 4/16; no closing date. Applicants notified on a rolling basis starting 7/1.

CONTACT

Patricia Billings, Financial Aid Director

6000 16th Avenue, SW, Seattle, WA 98106-1499

(206) 764-5317

Spokane Falls Community College
Spokane, Washington

www.spokanefalls.edu   Federal Code: 009544

2-year public community college in small city.

Enrollment: 5,392 undergrads, 28% part-time. 1,406 full-time freshmen.

Selectivity: Open admission; but selective for some programs.

BASIC COSTS (2007-2008)

Tuition and fees: $2,807; out-of-state residents $3,331.

Per-credit charge: $74; out-of-state residents $100.

Additional info: Tuition/fee waivers available for unemployed or children of unemployed.

FINANCIAL AID PICTURE

Students with need: Need-based aid available for full-time and part-time students.

Students without need: This college awards aid only to students with need.

FINANCIAL AID PROCEDURES

Forms required: FAFSA, institutional form.

Dates and Deadlines: Priority date 4/1; no closing date. Applicants notified on a rolling basis starting 5/15; must reply within 2 week(s) of notification.

CONTACT

Assistant Dean of Student Services for Financial Aid
3410 West Fort George Wright Drive, Spokane, WA 99224
(509) 533-3550

Tacoma Community College

Tacoma, Washington
www.tacomacc.edu   Federal Code: 003796

2-year public community college in small city.
Enrollment: 5,142 undergrads, 40% part-time.
Selectivity: Open admission.

BASIC COSTS (2007-2008)

Tuition and fees: $2,909; out-of-state residents $3,298.
Additional info: Tuition/fee waivers available for unemployed or children of unemployed.

FINANCIAL AID PICTURE

Students with need: Need-based aid available for full-time and part-time students. Work study available nights, weekends, and for part-time students.
Students without need: This college awards aid only to students with need.

FINANCIAL AID PROCEDURES

Forms required: FAFSA, institutional form.
Dates and Deadlines: Priority date 3/26; no closing date. Applicants notified on a rolling basis starting 7/20; must reply within 4 week(s) of notification.

CONTACT

Kim Matison, Director, Financial Aid Services
6501 South 19th Street, Tacoma, WA 98466-9971
(253) 566-5080

Trinity Lutheran College

Issaquah, Washington
www.tlc.edu   Federal Code: 013525

4-year private Bible and liberal arts college in small city, affiliated with Lutheran Church.
Enrollment: 103 undergrads.
Selectivity: Admits over 75% of applicants.

BASIC COSTS (2007-2008)

Tuition and fees: $14,170.
Per-credit charge: $490.
Room and board: $6,078.

FINANCIAL AID PICTURE

Students with need: Need-based aid available for full-time and part-time students. Work study available nights, weekends, and for part-time students.
Students without need: No-need awards available for academics, alumni affiliation, art, leadership, music/drama.

FINANCIAL AID PROCEDURES

Forms required: FAFSA, institutional form.
Dates and Deadlines: Priority date 3/1; no closing date. Applicants notified on a rolling basis starting 3/15; must reply within 2 week(s) of notification.
Transfers: No deadline. Applicants notified on a rolling basis starting 3/15; must reply within 2 week(s) of notification.

CONTACT

Susan Dalgleish, Director of Financial Aid
4221 228th Avenue Southeast, Issaquah, WA 98029
(425) 961-5514

University of Puget Sound

Tacoma, Washington
www.ups.edu   Federal Code: 003797

4-year private university and liberal arts college in small city.
Enrollment: 2,527 undergrads, 1% part-time. 644 full-time freshmen.
Selectivity: Admits 50 to 75% of applicants.

BASIC COSTS (2008-2009)

Tuition and fees: $33,975.
Per-credit charge: $1,065.
Room and board: $8,760.

FINANCIAL AID PICTURE (2007-2008)

Students with need: Out of 466 full-time freshmen who applied for aid, 393 were judged to have need. Of these, 393 received aid, and 136 had their full need met. Average financial aid package met 86% of need; average scholarship/grant was $20,462; average loan was $4,655. Need-based aid available for part-time students.
Students without need: 143 full-time freshmen who did not demonstrate need for aid received scholarships/grants; average award was $6,335. No-need awards available for academics, alumni affiliation, art, leadership, music/drama, religious affiliation.
Scholarships offered: Wyatt Trustee Scholarship: $9,000 annually; Trustee Scholarships: $12,000 annually; President's Scholarships: $9,000 annually; Dean's Scholarships: $3,000 annually. All admitted freshmen eligible; renewable for 3 additional years.
Cumulative student debt: 60% of graduating class had student loans; average debt was $27,648.
Additional info: Cooperative education allows qualified upperclassmen to alternate semesters of full-time study and full-time work.

FINANCIAL AID PROCEDURES

Forms required: FAFSA. Students applying for Early Decision must complete the CSS PROFILE for notification of need-based financial aid eligibility.
Dates and Deadlines: Priority date 2/1; no closing date. Applicants notified on a rolling basis starting 3/15; must reply by 5/1 or within 2 week(s) of notification.
Transfers: Priority date 3/1; no deadline. Applicants notified on a rolling basis starting 3/15.

CONTACT

Maggie Mittuch, Associate Vice President of Student Financial Services
1500 North Warner Street, Tacoma, WA 98416-1062
(253) 879-3214

University of Washington

Seattle, Washington
www.washington.edu   Federal Code: 003798

4-year public university in very large city.
Enrollment: 26,509 undergrads, 9% part-time. 5,263 full-time freshmen.
Selectivity: Admits 50 to 75% of applicants.

BASIC COSTS (2007-2008)

Tuition and fees: $6,385; out-of-state residents $22,131.
Room and board: $9,198.

FINANCIAL AID PICTURE (2007-2008)

Students with need: Average financial aid package met 88% of need; average scholarship/grant was $5,300; average loan was $3,650. For part-time students, average financial aid package was $5,200.

Students without need: No-need awards available for academics, alumni affiliation, art, athletics, leadership, music/drama, ROTC.

Cumulative student debt: 49% of graduating class had student loans; average debt was $16,100.

Additional info: Tuition not due until third week of term.

FINANCIAL AID PROCEDURES

Forms required: FAFSA.

Dates and Deadlines: Priority date 2/28; no closing date. Applicants notified by 3/31; must reply within 3 week(s) of notification.

CONTACT

Kay Lewis, Director of Student Financial Aid
1410 Northeast Campus Parkway, Box 355852, Seattle, WA 98195-5852
(206) 543-6101

Walla Walla Community College

Walla Walla, Washington
www.wwcc.edu   Federal Code: 005006

2-year public community and technical college in large town.
Enrollment: 2,183 undergrads, 30% part-time. 412 full-time freshmen.
Selectivity: Open admission; but selective for some programs.

BASIC COSTS (2007-2008)

Tuition and fees: $2,916; out-of-state residents $4,009.
Per-credit charge: $82; out-of-state residents $96.
Additional info: Tuition/fee waivers available for unemployed or children of unemployed.

FINANCIAL AID PICTURE (2006-2007)

Students with need: 62% of average financial aid package awarded as scholarships/grants, 38% awarded as loans/jobs. Need-based aid available for part-time students. Work study available nights.

Students without need: No-need awards available for academics, athletics, leadership, music/drama.

FINANCIAL AID PROCEDURES

Forms required: FAFSA, institutional form.
Dates and Deadlines: Priority date 3/1; no closing date. Applicants notified on a rolling basis starting 6/1; must reply within 2 week(s) of notification.

CONTACT

Terri Johnson, Director of Financial Aid
500 Tausick Way, Walla Walla, WA 99362-9972
(509) 527-4303

Walla Walla University

College Place, Washington
www.wallawalla.edu   Federal Code: 003799

4-year private university and liberal arts college in large town, affiliated with Seventh-day Adventists.
Enrollment: 1,586 undergrads, 5% part-time. 307 full-time freshmen.
Selectivity: Admits over 75% of applicants.

BASIC COSTS (2008-2009)

Tuition and fees: $21,945.
Per-credit charge: $569.
Room and board: $5,055.

FINANCIAL AID PICTURE (2006-2007)

Students with need: Out of 302 full-time freshmen who applied for aid, 216 were judged to have need. Of these, 216 received aid, and 54 had their full need met. Average financial aid package met 90% of need; average scholarship/grant was $6,429; average loan was $6,374. For part-time students, average financial aid package was $17,568.

Students without need: 83 full-time freshmen who did not demonstrate need for aid received scholarships/grants; average award was $5,618. No-need awards available for academics, leadership, music/drama.

Cumulative student debt: 78% of graduating class had student loans; average debt was $28,482.

FINANCIAL AID PROCEDURES

Forms required: FAFSA, institutional form.
Dates and Deadlines: No deadline. Applicants notified on a rolling basis starting 3/15.

CONTACT

Cassie Ragenovich, Director of Student Financial Services
204 South College Avenue, College Place, WA 99324-3000
(509) 527-2815

Washington State University

Pullman, Washington
www.wsu.edu   Federal Code: 003800

4-year public university in large town.
Enrollment: 19,822 undergrads, 13% part-time. 2,825 full-time freshmen.
Selectivity: Admits over 75% of applicants.

BASIC COSTS (2007-2008)

Tuition and fees: $6,866; out-of-state residents $17,180.
Room and board: $7,316.

FINANCIAL AID PICTURE (2006-2007)

Students with need: Out of 2,281 full-time freshmen who applied for aid, 1,218 were judged to have need. Of these, 1,212 received aid, and 361 had their full need met. Average financial aid package met 75% of need; average scholarship/grant was $5,747; average loan was $3,005. For part-time students, average financial aid package was $8,891.

Students without need: 224 full-time freshmen who did not demonstrate need for aid received scholarships/grants; average award was $2,299. No-need awards available for academics, alumni affiliation, art, athletics, job skills, leadership, minority status, music/drama, religious affiliation, ROTC, state/district residency.

Scholarships offered: 82 full-time freshmen received athletic scholarships; average amount $12,911.

FINANCIAL AID PROCEDURES

Forms required: FAFSA.
Dates and Deadlines: Priority date 3/1; no closing date. Applicants notified on a rolling basis starting 4/15.
Transfers: No deadline. Applicants notified on a rolling basis starting 4/15. President's Scholarship available for transfer students with minimum 3.9 GPA.

CONTACT

Wayne Sparks, Director of Student Financial Aid
370 Lighty Student Services Bldg, Pullman, WA 99164-1067
(509) 335-9711

Wenatchee Valley College

Wenatchee, Washington
www.wvc.edu Federal Code: 003801

2-year public community college in small city.

Enrollment: 2,878 undergrads, 19% part-time. 470 full-time freshmen.

Selectivity: Open admission; but selective for some programs.

BASIC COSTS (2007-2008)

Tuition and fees: $2,772; out-of-state residents $3,161.

Per-credit charge: $74; out-of-state residents $88.

Additional info: Tuition/fee waivers available for adults, unemployed or children of unemployed.

FINANCIAL AID PICTURE

Students with need: Need-based aid available for full-time and part-time students.

Students without need: No-need awards available for academics, athletics, leadership.

FINANCIAL AID PROCEDURES

Forms required: FAFSA.

Dates and Deadlines: Closing date 3/1. Applicants notified by 7/2; must reply within 3 week(s) of notification.

CONTACT

Kevin Berg, Financial Aid Director

1300 Fifth Street, Wenatchee, WA 98801-1799

(509) 682-6845

Western Washington University

Bellingham, Washington
www.wwu.edu Federal Code: 003802

4-year public university in small city.

Enrollment: 12,967 undergrads, 8% part-time. 2,572 full-time freshmen.

Selectivity: Admits 50 to 75% of applicants.

BASIC COSTS (2007-2008)

Tuition and fees: $5,301; out-of-state residents $16,375.

Room and board: $7,090.

Additional info: Tuition/fee waivers available for adults, minority students.

FINANCIAL AID PICTURE (2007-2008)

Students with need: Out of 1,783 full-time freshmen who applied for aid, 943 were judged to have need. Of these, 912 received aid, and 291 had their full need met. Average financial aid package met 90% of need; average scholarship/grant was $6,816; average loan was $3,255. For part-time students, average financial aid package was $8,888.

Students without need: 39 full-time freshmen who did not demonstrate need for aid received scholarships/grants; average award was $1,298. No-need awards available for academics, alumni affiliation, art, athletics, job skills, leadership, minority status, music/drama, state/district residency.

Scholarships offered: 21 full-time freshmen received athletic scholarships; average amount $2,838.

Cumulative student debt: 50% of graduating class had student loans; average debt was $15,280.

Additional info: Short-term student loans ranging from $100 to $1,000 available on a quarterly basis.

FINANCIAL AID PROCEDURES

Forms required: FAFSA.

Dates and Deadlines: Priority date 2/15; no closing date. Applicants notified on a rolling basis starting 3/20; must reply within 3 week(s) of notification.

Transfers: No deadline. Applicants notified on a rolling basis starting 3/20; must reply within 3 week(s) of notification. Some state aid not available for out-of-state transfer students.

CONTACT

Clara Capron, Director of Financial Aid

516 High Street, Bellingham, WA 98225-9009

(360) 650-3470

Whatcom Community College

Bellingham, Washington
www.whatcom.ctc.edu Federal Code: 010364

2-year public community college in small city.

Enrollment: 2,796 undergrads.

Selectivity: Open admission.

BASIC COSTS (2007-2008)

Tuition and fees: $2,745; out-of-state residents $7,953.

Per-credit charge: $77; out-of-state residents $248.

FINANCIAL AID PICTURE

Students with need: Need-based aid available for full-time and part-time students. Work study available nights.

Students without need: No-need awards available for academics, athletics, state/district residency.

FINANCIAL AID PROCEDURES

Forms required: FAFSA, institutional form.

Dates and Deadlines: No deadline. Applicants notified on a rolling basis starting 7/1; must reply within 3 week(s) of notification.

CONTACT

Laura Pendleton, Director of Financial Aid

237 West Kellogg Road, Bellingham, WA 98226

(360) 647-3260

Whitman College

Walla Walla, Washington
www.whitman.edu Federal Code: 003803
CSS Code: 4951

4-year private liberal arts college in large town.

Enrollment: 1,455 undergrads, 1% part-time. 400 full-time freshmen.

Selectivity: Admits less than 50% of applicants.

BASIC COSTS (2008-2009)

Tuition and fees: $35,192.

Per-credit charge: $1,462.

Room and board: $8,820.

FINANCIAL AID PICTURE (2007-2008)

Students with need: Out of 248 full-time freshmen who applied for aid, 191 were judged to have need. Of these, 191 received aid, and 155 had their full need met. Average financial aid package met 95% of need; average scholarship/grant was $22,650; average loan was $4,013. For part-time students, average financial aid package was $28,600.

Students without need: 89 full-time freshmen who did not demonstrate need for aid received scholarships/grants; average award was $7,589. No-need awards available for academics, art, leadership, minority status, music/drama, religious affiliation, state/district residency.

Cumulative student debt: 53% of graduating class had student loans; average debt was $15,811.

FINANCIAL AID PROCEDURES

Forms required: FAFSA, CSS PROFILE.

Dates and Deadlines: Priority date 11/15; closing date 2/1. Applicants notified on a rolling basis starting 12/20; must reply within 2 week(s) of notification.

CONTACT

Tony Cabasco, Dean of Admission and Financial Aid
345 Boyer Avenue, Walla Walla, WA 99362-2046
(509) 527-5178

Whitworth University

Spokane, Washington
www.whitworth.edu   Federal Code: 003804

4-year private liberal arts college in large city, affiliated with Presbyterian Church (USA).

Enrollment: 2,310 undergrads, 12% part-time. 533 full-time freshmen.
Selectivity: Admits less than 50% of applicants.

BASIC COSTS (2008-2009)

Tuition and fees: $27,420.
Per-credit charge: $1,130.
Room and board: $7,700.
Additional info: Tuition/fee waivers available for minority students.

FINANCIAL AID PICTURE (2007-2008)

Students with need: Out of 438 full-time freshmen who applied for aid, 353 were judged to have need. Of these, 353 received aid, and 74 had their full need met. Average financial aid package met 86% of need; average scholarship/grant was $14,871; average loan was $4,755. For part-time students, average financial aid package was $9,577.
Students without need: 154 full-time freshmen who did not demonstrate need for aid received scholarships/grants; average award was $10,470. No-need awards available for academics, art, music/drama, ROTC.
Scholarships offered: Merit scholarships: $4,000 to 8,500; based on GPA, SAT/ACT scores and class rank.
Cumulative student debt: 69% of graduating class had student loans; average debt was $18,543.

FINANCIAL AID PROCEDURES

Forms required: FAFSA.
Dates and Deadlines: Priority date 3/1; no closing date. Applicants notified on a rolling basis starting 3/1; must reply by 5/1 or within 4 week(s) of notification.
Transfers: Priority date 4/1; no deadline. Applicants notified on a rolling basis starting 3/1; must reply by 5/1.

CONTACT

Wendy Olson, Director of Financial Aid
300 West Hawthorne Road, Spokane, WA 99251-0002
(509) 777-3215

Yakima Valley Community College

Yakima, Washington
www.yvcc.edu   Federal Code: 003805

2-year public community college in small city.
Enrollment: 2,829 undergrads, 28% part-time. 415 full-time freshmen.
Selectivity: Open admission; but selective for some programs.

BASIC COSTS (2007-2008)

Tuition and fees: $2,766; out-of-state residents $3,162.
Per-credit charge: $74; out-of-state residents $88.
Additional info: Tuition/fee waivers available for unemployed or children of unemployed.

FINANCIAL AID PICTURE (2006-2007)

Students with need: 68% of average financial aid package awarded as scholarships/grants, 32% awarded as loans/jobs. Need-based aid available for part-time students. Work study available nights, weekends, and for part-time students.

Students without need: No-need awards available for academics, athletics.

FINANCIAL AID PROCEDURES

Forms required: FAFSA.
Dates and Deadlines: Priority date 5/1; no closing date. Applicants notified on a rolling basis starting 8/1; must reply within 2 week(s) of notification.
Transfers: No deadline. Applicants notified on a rolling basis starting 8/1; must reply within 2 week(s) of notification.

CONTACT

Tom Alex, Director of Financial Aid
PO Box 22520, Yakima, WA 98907-2520
(509) 574-6855

West Virginia

Alderson-Broaddus College

Philippi, West Virginia
www.ab.edu   Federal Code: 003806

4-year private liberal arts college in small town, affiliated with American Baptist Churches in the USA.

Enrollment: 616 undergrads, 7% part-time. 140 full-time freshmen.
Selectivity: Admits 50 to 75% of applicants.

BASIC COSTS (2008-2009)

Tuition and fees: $21,020.
Per-credit charge: $694.
Room and board: $6,798.

FINANCIAL AID PICTURE (2006-2007)

Students with need: Out of 138 full-time freshmen who applied for aid, 133 were judged to have need. Of these, 133 received aid, and 42 had their full need met. Average financial aid package met 82% of need; average scholarship/grant was $14,793; average loan was $3,464. For part-time students, average financial aid package was $6,151.
Students without need: 5 full-time freshmen who did not demonstrate need for aid received scholarships/grants; average award was $6,300. No-need awards available for academics, athletics, music/drama.
Scholarships offered: 2 full-time freshmen received athletic scholarships; average amount $6,750.
Cumulative student debt: 94% of graduating class had student loans; average debt was $29,248.

FINANCIAL AID PROCEDURES

Forms required: FAFSA, state aid form.
Dates and Deadlines: Priority date 3/1; no closing date. Applicants notified on a rolling basis starting 2/15; must reply within 2 week(s) of notification.

CONTACT

Brian Weingart, Director of Financial Aid
101 College Hill Drive, Philippi, WV 26416
(304) 457-6354

American Public University System

Charles Town, West Virginia
www.apus.edu   Federal Code: 038193

4-year for-profit virtual university and liberal arts college in small town.
Enrollment: 20,201 undergrads.
Selectivity: Open admission.

BASIC COSTS (2008-2009)

Tuition and fees: $7,500.
Per-credit charge: $250.

Additional info: Distance learning only.

FINANCIAL AID PICTURE

Students with need: Need-based aid available for full-time and part-time students.

Additional info: Students should complete a Federal Student Aid Intent Form and register for classes at least 37 days prior to start to allow sufficient time for financial aid process.

FINANCIAL AID PROCEDURES

Forms required: FAFSA, institutional form.

Dates and Deadlines: No deadline. Applicants notified on a rolling basis; must reply within 14 week(s) of notification.

Transfers: Must reply within 14 week(s) of notification. All students including transfer students should ensure that their financial aid is processed and confirmed at least 10-14 days prior to beginning a semester.

CONTACT

Chip Woodward, Director of Financial Aid
111 West Congress Street, Charles Town, WV 25414
(877) 468-6268

Appalachian Bible College
Bradley, West Virginia
www.abc.edu   Federal Code: 007544

4-year private Bible college in rural community, affiliated with nondenominational tradition.

Enrollment: 223 undergrads, 6% part-time. 58 full-time freshmen.

Selectivity: Admits 50 to 75% of applicants.

BASIC COSTS (2008-2009)

Tuition and fees: $9,880.

Per-credit charge: $351.

Room and board: $5,160.

FINANCIAL AID PICTURE (2007-2008)

Students with need: 76% of average financial aid package awarded as scholarships/grants, 24% awarded as loans/jobs. Need-based aid available for part-time students.

Students without need: This college awards aid only to students with need.

Scholarships offered: Scholastic Achievement Scholarship: $1,500 per year; minimum 26 ACT or 1180 SAT (exclusive of Writing).

FINANCIAL AID PROCEDURES

Forms required: FAFSA, state aid form, institutional form.

Dates and Deadlines: Closing date 6/15. Applicants notified on a rolling basis starting 6/15; must reply by 8/1 or within 4 week(s) of notification.

CONTACT

Cindi Turner, Director of Financial Aid
PO Box ABC, Bradley, WV 25818-1353
(304) 877-6428 ext. 3247

Bethany College
Bethany, West Virginia
www.bethanywv.edu   Federal Code: 003808

4-year private liberal arts college in rural community, affiliated with Christian Church (Disciples of Christ).

Enrollment: 815 undergrads. 249 full-time freshmen.

Selectivity: Admits 50 to 75% of applicants.

BASIC COSTS (2007-2008)

Tuition and fees: $18,205.

Room and board: $7,777.

FINANCIAL AID PICTURE

Students with need: Need-based aid available for full-time students. Work study available nights, weekends, and for part-time students.

Students without need: No-need awards available for academics, alumni affiliation, art, leadership, music/drama, religious affiliation.

Additional info: Scholarships available for travel program.

FINANCIAL AID PROCEDURES

Forms required: FAFSA.

Dates and Deadlines: Priority date 3/1; closing date 5/1. Applicants notified on a rolling basis starting 2/1; must reply within 3 week(s) of notification.

Transfers: No deadline.

CONTACT

Sandra Neel, Associate Vice President Student Services
Office of Admission, Bethany, WV 26032-0428
(304) 829-7141

Bluefield State College
Bluefield, West Virginia
www.bluefieldstate.edu   Federal Code: 003809

4-year public liberal arts and technical college in large town.

Enrollment: 1,693 undergrads, 16% part-time. 225 full-time freshmen.

Selectivity: Admits over 75% of applicants.

BASIC COSTS (2007-2008)

Tuition and fees: $3,984; out-of-state residents $8,160.

Additional info: Tuition for students residing in border counties will pay $5,720.

FINANCIAL AID PICTURE (2007-2008)

Students with need: Average financial aid package met 70% of need; average scholarship/grant was $3,000; average loan was $3,300. For part-time students, average financial aid package was $3,000.

Students without need: No-need awards available for academics, alumni affiliation, art, athletics, job skills, leadership, minority status, music/drama, state/district residency.

FINANCIAL AID PROCEDURES

Forms required: FAFSA, state aid form, institutional form.

Dates and Deadlines: Closing date 3/1. Applicants notified by 5/1.

Transfers: No deadline.

CONTACT

Tom Ilse, Director of Financial Aid
219 Rock Street, Bluefield, WV 24701
(304) 327-4020

Concord University
Athens, West Virginia
www.concord.edu   Federal Code: 003810

4-year public university in small town.

Enrollment: 2,671 undergrads, 17% part-time. 618 full-time freshmen.

Selectivity: Admits 50 to 75% of applicants.

BASIC COSTS (2007-2008)

Tuition and fees: $4,414; out-of-state residents $9,806.

Per-credit charge: $184; out-of-state residents $409.

Room and board: $6,280.

FINANCIAL AID PICTURE (2006-2007)

Students with need: 41% of average financial aid package awarded as scholarships/grants, 59% awarded as loans/jobs. Need-based aid available for part-time students.

Students without need: No-need awards available for academics, alumni affiliation, art, athletics, job skills, leadership, minority status, music/drama, state/district residency.

Additional info: Room and board may be paid in 2 installments each semester: 60% at registration, 40% six weeks later. March 1 is priority deadline for state forms. April 15 is priority deadline for FAFSA.

FINANCIAL AID PROCEDURES

Forms required: FAFSA, state aid form, institutional form.

Dates and Deadlines: Applicants notified on a rolling basis starting 3/1; must reply within 2 week(s) of notification.

CONTACT

Patricia Harmon, Director of Financial Aid
PO Box 1000, Athens, WV 24712-1000
(304) 384-6069

Davis and Elkins College

Elkins, West Virginia
www.davisandelkins.edu   Federal Code: 003811

4-year private liberal arts college in small town, affiliated with Presbyterian Church (USA).

Enrollment: 599 undergrads, 5% part-time. 119 full-time freshmen.

Selectivity: Admits over 75% of applicants.

BASIC COSTS (2008-2009)

Tuition and fees: $20,060.

Per-credit charge: $630.

Room and board: $6,700.

FINANCIAL AID PICTURE (2006-2007)

Students with need: Out of 100 full-time freshmen who applied for aid, 83 were judged to have need. Of these, 83 received aid, and 23 had their full need met. Average financial aid package met 76% of need; average scholarship/grant was $4,220; average loan was $4,435. For part-time students, average financial aid package was $6,207.

Students without need: 35 full-time freshmen who did not demonstrate need for aid received scholarships/grants; average award was $4,723. No-need awards available for academics, alumni affiliation, art, athletics, leadership, minority status, music/drama, religious affiliation.

Scholarships offered: 39 full-time freshmen received athletic scholarships; average amount $5,071.

Cumulative student debt: 79% of graduating class had student loans; average debt was $23,973.

FINANCIAL AID PROCEDURES

Forms required: FAFSA.

Dates and Deadlines: Priority date 3/1; no closing date. Applicants notified on a rolling basis starting 5/1; must reply within 2 week(s) of notification.

Transfers: No deadline. Applicants notified on a rolling basis starting 5/1; must reply within 2 week(s) of notification.

CONTACT

Susan George, Director of Financial Aid
100 Campus Drive, Elkins, WV 26241
(304) 637-1373

Eastern West Virginia Community and Technical College

Moorefield, West Virginia
www.eastern.wvnet.edu

2-year public community and technical college in rural community.

Enrollment: 199 undergrads, 71% part-time. 18 full-time freshmen.

Selectivity: Open admission.

BASIC COSTS (2007-2008)

Tuition and fees: $1,776; out-of-state residents $6,822.

Per-credit charge: $74; out-of-state residents $284.

FINANCIAL AID PICTURE

Students with need: Need-based aid available for full-time and part-time students.

FINANCIAL AID PROCEDURES

Forms required: FAFSA, institutional form.

Dates and Deadlines: Priority date 6/1; no closing date. Applicants notified on a rolling basis; must reply within 2 week(s) of notification.

CONTACT

Robert Eagle, Director of Financial Aid
1929 State Road 55, Moorefield, WV 26836
(304) 434-8000

Fairmont State University

Fairmont, West Virginia
www.fairmontstate.edu   Federal Code: 003812

4-year public university and technical college in large town.

Enrollment: 6,227 undergrads, 18% part-time. 1,153 full-time freshmen.

Selectivity: Open admission; but selective for some programs.

BASIC COSTS (2007-2008)

Tuition and fees: $4,614; out-of-state residents $9,960.

Per-credit charge: $193; out-of-state residents $415.

Room and board: $6,684.

Additional info: Tuition/fee waivers available for adults, minority students.

FINANCIAL AID PICTURE

Students with need: Need-based aid available for full-time and part-time students. Work study available nights, weekends, and for part-time students.

Students without need: This college awards aid only to students with need.

FINANCIAL AID PROCEDURES

Forms required: FAFSA, state aid form.

Dates and Deadlines: Closing date 2/1. Applicants notified on a rolling basis starting 4/15; must reply within 2 week(s) of notification.

Transfers: Academic transcripts required.

CONTACT

George Yanchak, Director of Financial Aid and Scholarships
1201 Locust Avenue, Fairmont, WV 26554-2470
(304) 367-4213

Glenville State College

Glenville, West Virginia
www.glenville.edu   Federal Code: 003813

4-year public liberal arts and teachers college in rural community.

Enrollment: 1,155 undergrads, 7% part-time. 267 full-time freshmen.

Selectivity: Open admission; but selective for some programs.

BASIC COSTS (2007-2008)

Tuition and fees: $4,147; out-of-state residents $9,990.

Per-credit charge: $174; out-of-state residents $416.

Room and board: $5,800.

FINANCIAL AID PICTURE (2006-2007)

Students with need: Out of 250 full-time freshmen who applied for aid, 222 were judged to have need. Of these, 220 received aid, and 37 had their full need met. Average financial aid package met 70% of need; average scholarship/grant was $4,463; average loan was $2,334. Need-based aid available for part-time students.

Students without need: 19 full-time freshmen who did not demonstrate need for aid received scholarships/grants; average award was $1,722. No-need awards available for academics, athletics, music/drama, state/district residency.

Scholarships offered: 14 full-time freshmen received athletic scholarships; average amount $3,380.

Cumulative student debt: 71% of graduating class had student loans; average debt was $17,057.

FINANCIAL AID PROCEDURES

Dates and Deadlines: Priority date 2/1; no closing date. Applicants notified on a rolling basis starting 4/1; must reply within 2 week(s) of notification.

CONTACT

Karen Lay, Director of Financial Aid
200 High Street, Glenville, WV 26351-1292
(304) 462-4103

Marshall University
Huntington, West Virginia
www.marshall.edu
Federal Code: 003815

4-year public university in small city.

Enrollment: 8,904 undergrads, 12% part-time. 1,659 full-time freshmen.

Selectivity: Open admission; but selective for some programs and for out-of-state students.

BASIC COSTS (2007-2008)

Tuition and fees: $4,360; out-of-state residents $11,264.

Per-credit charge: $170; out-of-state residents $457.

Room and board: $6,818.

FINANCIAL AID PICTURE (2007-2008)

Students with need: Out of 1,075 full-time freshmen who applied for aid, 738 were judged to have need. Of these, 727 received aid, and 278 had their full need met. Average financial aid package met 57% of need; average scholarship/grant was $5,291; average loan was $4,345. For part-time students, average financial aid package was $6,150.

Students without need: 314 full-time freshmen who did not demonstrate need for aid received scholarships/grants; average award was $5,435. No-need awards available for academics, art, athletics, minority status, music/drama, ROTC, state/district residency.

Scholarships offered: *Merit:* Michael Perry Scholarship: $500 to incoming freshman with 3.2 GPA and 20 ACT score; $750 to incoming freshman with 3.5 GPA and 23 ACT, or 3.2 GPA and 25 ACT; all one year only. Presidential Scholarship: $1,250; 3.5 GPA and 25 ACT; renewable with 3.5 cumulative GPA. John Marshall Scholarship: tuition waiver plus $1,250 stipend; 3.5 GPA and 30 ACT; renewable yearly with 3.5 cumulative college GPA. Yeager scholarship: full tuition and fees, full room and board, book allowance, stipend, personal computer for use during program, and $4,000 toward study abroad; ACT 28/ SAT 1260 (exclusive of Writing). *Athletic:* 59 full-time freshmen received athletic scholarships; average amount $7,188.

Cumulative student debt: 62% of graduating class had student loans; average debt was $17,932.

FINANCIAL AID PROCEDURES

Forms required: FAFSA, state aid form.

Dates and Deadlines: Priority date 3/1; no closing date. Applicants notified on a rolling basis starting 5/1; must reply within 2 week(s) of notification.

Transfers: Priority date 1/1.

CONTACT

Nadine Hamrick, Director of Financial Aid
One John Marshall Drive, Huntington, WV 25755
(304) 696-3162

Mountain State University
Beckley, West Virginia
www.mountainstate.edu
Federal Code: 003807

4-year private university and health science college in large town.

Enrollment: 4,053 undergrads, 26% part-time. 294 full-time freshmen.

Selectivity: Open admission; but selective for some programs.

BASIC COSTS (2008-2009)

Tuition and fees: $8,400.

Room and board: $6,116.

Additional info: Certain programs require additional costs: health science and culinary/hospitality are $320 per credit hour.

FINANCIAL AID PICTURE (2006-2007)

Students with need: Out of 213 full-time freshmen who applied for aid, 184 were judged to have need. Of these, 184 received aid, and 26 had their full need met. Average financial aid package met 31% of need; average scholarship/grant was $3,377; average loan was $2,344. For part-time students, average financial aid package was $4,601.

Students without need: No-need awards available for academics, alumni affiliation, athletics, leadership, minority status.

Scholarships offered: 11 full-time freshmen received athletic scholarships; average amount $2,920.

Cumulative student debt: 83% of graduating class had student loans; average debt was $27,903.

FINANCIAL AID PROCEDURES

Forms required: FAFSA.

Dates and Deadlines: No deadline. Applicants notified on a rolling basis starting 4/1.

CONTACT

Michelle Sarrett, Vice President of Finance
609 South Kanawha Street, Beckley, WV 25802-9003
(304) 929-1517

Ohio Valley University
Vienna, West Virginia
www.ovu.edu
Federal Code: 003819

4-year private university and liberal arts college in small city, affiliated with Church of Christ.

Enrollment: 526 undergrads, 4% part-time. 107 full-time freshmen.

Selectivity: Admits 50 to 75% of applicants.

BASIC COSTS (2007-2008)

Tuition and fees: $15,120.

Per-credit charge: $435.

Room and board: $6,140.

FINANCIAL AID PICTURE (2007-2008)

Students with need: Average financial aid package met 66% of need; average scholarship/grant was $8,600; average loan was $3,401. For part-time students, average financial aid package was $10,000.

Students without need: No-need awards available for academics, alumni affiliation, athletics, job skills, leadership, music/drama.

Cumulative student debt: 80% of graduating class had student loans; average debt was $31,600.

FINANCIAL AID PROCEDURES

Forms required: FAFSA.

Dates and Deadlines: Priority date 2/15; no closing date. Applicants notified on a rolling basis starting 3/15; must reply within 4 week(s) of notification.

Transfers: No deadline. Applicants notified on a rolling basis starting 3/15; must reply within 4 week(s) of notification.

CONTACT

Dennis Cox, Director of Student Financial Services
One Campus View Drive, Vienna, WV 26105
(304) 865-6081

Potomac State College of West Virginia University

Keyser, West Virginia
www.potomacstatecollege.edu   Federal Code: 003829

2-year public branch campus and junior college in small town.

Enrollment: 1,198 undergrads.

Selectivity: Open admission.

BASIC COSTS (2007-2008)

Tuition and fees: $2,596; out-of-state residents $8,360.

Per-credit charge: $108; out-of-state residents $348.

Room and board: $6,494.

Additional info: Students residing in selected counties in bordering states receive reduced out-of-state tuition rates. Tuition/fee waivers available for adults.

FINANCIAL AID PICTURE

Students with need: Need-based aid available for full-time and part-time students. Work study available nights, weekends, and for part-time students.

Students without need: No-need awards available for academics, athletics, leadership.

FINANCIAL AID PROCEDURES

Forms required: FAFSA.

Dates and Deadlines: Priority date 3/1; no closing date. Applicants notified on a rolling basis starting 4/1; must reply within 2 week(s) of notification.

CONTACT

Beth Little, Director of Enrollment Services
One Grand Central Park, Suite 2090, Keyser, WV 26726
(304) 788-6820

Salem International University

Salem, West Virginia
www.salemu.edu   Federal Code: 003820

4-year for-profit university and liberal arts college in rural community.

Enrollment: 342 undergrads. 129 full-time freshmen.

BASIC COSTS (2007-2008)

Tuition and fees: $13,950.

Per-credit charge: $450.

Room and board: $5,420.

FINANCIAL AID PICTURE

Students with need: Need-based aid available for full-time and part-time students. Work study available nights, weekends, and for part-time students.

Students without need: No-need awards available for academics.

Scholarships offered: Scholarships: extensive amount awarded; based on high school GPA, standardized test scores. Breed-related awards: students in the equine career and industry management program. Awards for GED diploma recipients: based on academic excellence.

FINANCIAL AID PROCEDURES

Forms required: FAFSA.

Dates and Deadlines: Priority date 4/15; no closing date. Applicants notified on a rolling basis starting 2/15; must reply within 4 week(s) of notification.

Transfers: Priority date 3/1; closing date 4/15. Applicants notified on a rolling basis starting 3/1; must reply by 4/15.

CONTACT

Patricia Zinsmeister, VP for Financial Aid and Compliance
223 West Main Street, Salem, WV 26426
(304) 326-1303

Shepherd University

Shepherdstown, West Virginia
www.shepherd.edu   Federal Code: 003822

4-year public university in small town.

Enrollment: 3,548 undergrads, 12% part-time. 691 full-time freshmen.

Selectivity: Admits over 75% of applicants.

BASIC COSTS (2007-2008)

Tuition and fees: $4,564; out-of-state residents $12,036.

Per-credit charge: $186; out-of-state residents $497.

Room and board: $6,714.

Additional info: Tuition/fee waivers available for minority students.

FINANCIAL AID PICTURE (2007-2008)

Students with need: Out of 595 full-time freshmen who applied for aid, 361 were judged to have need. Of these, 344 received aid, and 66 had their full need met. Average financial aid package met 79% of need; average scholarship/grant was $4,205; average loan was $3,202. For part-time students, average financial aid package was $8,717.

Students without need: 163 full-time freshmen who did not demonstrate need for aid received scholarships/grants; average award was $7,238. No-need awards available for academics, art, athletics, job skills, leadership, minority status, music/drama, state/district residency.

Scholarships offered: *Merit:* Presidential: up to $5,000; requires 3.5 GPA, 26 ACT or 1200 SAT; renewable with 3.5 GPA. Academic: up to $1,500; requires 3.2 GPA, 21 ACT or 1000 SAT, renewable with 3.0 GPA. Leadership: up to $3,000; requires 3.0 GPA, 21 ACT, or 1000 SAT; nonrenewable.

Athletic: 38 full-time freshmen received athletic scholarships; average amount $5,527.

Cumulative student debt: 61% of graduating class had student loans; average debt was $18,994.

FINANCIAL AID PROCEDURES

Forms required: FAFSA, state aid form.

Dates and Deadlines: Priority date 3/1; no closing date. Applicants notified on a rolling basis starting 3/15; must reply within 3 week(s) of notification.

Transfers: No deadline. Applicants notified on a rolling basis starting 11/1; must reply within 3 week(s) of notification.

CONTACT

Sandra Oerly-Bennett, Director of Financial Aid
PO Box 3210, Shepherdstown, WV 25443-3210
(304) 876-5470

Southern West Virginia Community and Technical College

Mount Gay, West Virginia
www.southernwv.edu   Federal Code: 003816

2-year public community college in small town.

Enrollment: 2,516 undergrads.

Selectivity: Open admission; but selective for some programs.

BASIC COSTS (2007-2008)

Tuition and fees: $1,776; out-of-state residents $6,624.
Per-credit charge: $74; out-of-state residents $276.

FINANCIAL AID PICTURE

Students with need: Need-based aid available for full-time and part-time students.

FINANCIAL AID PROCEDURES

Forms required: FAFSA.
Dates and Deadlines: No deadline. Applicants notified on a rolling basis.

CONTACT

Cindy Whitlock, Financial Aid Director
PO Box 2900, Mount Gay, WV 25637
(304) 792-7098 ext. 256

University of Charleston

Charleston, West Virginia
www.ucwv.edu   Federal Code: 003818

4-year private university and liberal arts college in small city.
Enrollment: 1,134 undergrads, 4% part-time. 324 full-time freshmen.
Selectivity: Admits 50 to 75% of applicants.

BASIC COSTS (2008-2009)

Tuition and fees: $23,150.
Per-credit charge: $400.
Room and board: $8,325.
Additional info: Tuition for pharmacy students: $25,224.

FINANCIAL AID PICTURE (2007-2008)

Students with need: Average financial aid package met 80% of need; average scholarship/grant was $4,500; average loan was $6,900. For part-time students, average financial aid package was $4,150.
Students without need: No-need awards available for academics, alumni affiliation, athletics, leadership, music/drama, state/district residency.

FINANCIAL AID PROCEDURES

Forms required: FAFSA, state aid form, institutional form.
Dates and Deadlines: Priority date 3/1; closing date 8/30. Applicants notified on a rolling basis starting 4/1; must reply by 5/1 or within 4 week(s) of notification.
Transfers: Applicants notified on a rolling basis starting 4/1; must reply by 5/1 or within 4 week(s) of notification.

CONTACT

Janet Ruge, Director of Financial Aid
2300 MacCorkle Avenue, SE, Charleston, WV 25304
(304) 357-4759

Valley College of Technology

Martinsburg, West Virginia
www.vct.edu   Federal Code: G26094

2-year for-profit business and career college in small city.
Enrollment: 43 undergrads. 10 full-time freshmen.

BASIC COSTS (2008-2009)

Tuition and fees: $7,300.
Per-credit charge: $225.
Additional info: Tuition varies according to program.

FINANCIAL AID PICTURE (2006-2007)

Students with need: 59% of average financial aid package awarded as scholarships/grants, 41% awarded as loans/jobs. Need-based aid available for part-time students.

FINANCIAL AID PROCEDURES

Forms required: FAFSA, institutional form.
Dates and Deadlines: No deadline. Applicants notified on a rolling basis.
Transfers: No deadline. Applicants notified on a rolling basis.

CONTACT

Jessica Colon, Financial Aid Administrator
287 Aikens Center, Martinsburg, WV 25404
(304) 263-0979

West Liberty State College

West Liberty, West Virginia
www.westliberty.edu   Federal Code: 003823

4-year public liberal arts college in rural community.
Enrollment: 2,236 undergrads, 8% part-time. 500 full-time freshmen.
Selectivity: Admits over 75% of applicants.

BASIC COSTS (2007-2008)

Tuition and fees: $4,172; out-of-state residents $10,192.
Per-credit charge: $174; out-of-state residents $425.
Room and board: $5,984.

FINANCIAL AID PICTURE (2007-2008)

Students with need: 48% of average financial aid package awarded as scholarships/grants, 52% awarded as loans/jobs. Need-based aid available for part-time students. Work study available nights, weekends, and for part-time students.
Students without need: No-need awards available for academics, alumni affiliation, art, athletics, leadership, music/drama.
Additional info: Non-need based student employment available at food service, college union, bookstore, and tutoring office. Resident assistant and campus security jobs also available.

FINANCIAL AID PROCEDURES

Forms required: FAFSA.
Dates and Deadlines: Priority date 3/1; no closing date. Applicants notified on a rolling basis starting 2/15; must reply within 2 week(s) of notification.
Transfers: Financial aid transcript required from all previous colleges attended regardless of whether aid was received.

CONTACT

Scott Cook, Financial Aid Director
Box 295, West Liberty, WV 26074-0295
(304) 336-8016

West Virginia State Community and Technical College

Institute, West Virginia
www.wvsctc.edu   Federal Code: 040386

2-year public community and technical college in small town.
Enrollment: 1,639 undergrads, 37% part-time. 286 full-time freshmen.
Selectivity: Open admission; but selective for some programs.

BASIC COSTS (2007-2008)

Tuition and fees: $2,766; out-of-state residents $7,718.

FINANCIAL AID PICTURE

Students with need: Work study available nights, weekends, and for part-time students.
Students without need: No-need awards available for academics, state/district residency.
Additional info: All students, part-time or full-time may apply for tuition waivers.

FINANCIAL AID PROCEDURES

Dates and Deadlines: Closing date 6/15.

CONTACT

Mary Blizzard, Director, Office of Student Financial Assistance
PO Box 1000, Institute, WV 25112-1000
(304) 766-3131

West Virginia University

Morgantown, West Virginia
www.wvu.edu   Federal Code: 003827

4-year public university in small city.

Enrollment: 21,145 undergrads, 7% part-time. 4,678 full-time freshmen.

Selectivity: Admits over 75% of applicants.

BASIC COSTS (2007-2008)

Tuition and fees: $4,722; out-of-state residents $14,600.

Per-credit charge: $197; out-of-state residents $608.

Room and board: $7,046.

Additional info: Tuition/fee waivers available for minority students.

FINANCIAL AID PICTURE (2007-2008)

Students with need: Out of 2,099 full-time freshmen who applied for aid, 1,658 were judged to have need. Of these, 1,310 received aid, and 590 had their full need met. Average financial aid package met 75% of need; average scholarship/grant was $3,598; average loan was $4,413. For part-time students, average financial aid package was $4,461.

Students without need: 920 full-time freshmen who did not demonstrate need for aid received scholarships/grants; average award was $2,101. No-need awards available for academics, alumni affiliation, art, athletics, job skills, leadership, minority status, music/drama, state/district residency.

Scholarships offered: 51 full-time freshmen received athletic scholarships; average amount $9,876.

Additional info: February 1 closing date for freshman scholarships.

FINANCIAL AID PROCEDURES

Forms required: FAFSA, state aid form.

Dates and Deadlines: Closing date 3/1. Applicants notified on a rolling basis starting 3/15; must reply within 4 week(s) of notification.

CONTACT

Kaye Widney, Director of Financial Aid
Admissions and Records Office, Morgantown, WV 26506-6009
(800) 344-9881

West Virginia University at Parkersburg

Parkersburg, West Virginia
www.wvup.edu   Federal Code: 003828

4-year public branch campus and community college in large town.

Enrollment: 3,141 undergrads, 30% part-time. 540 full-time freshmen.

Selectivity: Open admission; but selective for some programs.

BASIC COSTS (2007-2008)

Tuition and fees: $1,824; out-of-state residents $6,460.

Per-credit charge: $76; out-of-state residents $269.

FINANCIAL AID PICTURE (2007-2008)

Students with need: Out of 460 full-time freshmen who applied for aid, 430 were judged to have need. Of these, 430 received aid, and 135 had their full need met. Average financial aid package met 77% of need; average scholarship/grant was $5,400; average loan was $3,000. For part-time students, average financial aid package was $3,900.

Students without need: 65 full-time freshmen who did not demonstrate need for aid received scholarships/grants; average award was $950. No-need awards available for academics, state/district residency.

Cumulative student debt: 79% of graduating class had student loans; average debt was $12,750.

FINANCIAL AID PROCEDURES

Forms required: FAFSA.

Dates and Deadlines: Priority date 3/1; no closing date. Applicants notified on a rolling basis; must reply within 2 week(s) of notification.

CONTACT

August Kafer, Director of Financial Aid
300 Campus Drive, Parkersburg, WV 26104-8647
(304) 424-8210

West Virginia Wesleyan College

Buckhannon, West Virginia
www.wvwc.edu   Federal Code: 003830

4-year private liberal arts college in small town, affiliated with United Methodist Church.

Enrollment: 1,210 undergrads, 1% part-time. 401 full-time freshmen.

Selectivity: Admits over 75% of applicants.

BASIC COSTS (2008-2009)

Tuition and fees: $22,880.

Room and board: $6,470.

FINANCIAL AID PICTURE (2007-2008)

Students with need: Out of 363 full-time freshmen who applied for aid, 318 were judged to have need. Of these, 318 received aid, and 82 had their full need met. Average financial aid package met 84.4% of need; average scholarship/grant was $17,627; average loan was $3,144. Need-based aid available for part-time students.

Students without need: 83 full-time freshmen who did not demonstrate need for aid received scholarships/grants; average award was $9,010. No-need awards available for academics, alumni affiliation, art, athletics, leadership, music/drama, religious affiliation.

Scholarships offered: 42 full-time freshmen received athletic scholarships; average amount $11,033.

Cumulative student debt: 72% of graduating class had student loans; average debt was $20,501.

FINANCIAL AID PROCEDURES

Forms required: FAFSA.

Dates and Deadlines: Priority date 2/15; no closing date. Applicants notified on a rolling basis starting 3/15; must reply within 4 week(s) of notification.

Transfers: No deadline. Applicants notified on a rolling basis starting 3/15; must reply within 4 week(s) of notification. Financial aid transcripts required from all institutions previously attended.

CONTACT

Deborah Bond, Director of Financial Aid
59 College Avenue, Buckhannon, WV 26201-2998
(304) 473-8080

Wheeling Jesuit University

Wheeling, West Virginia
www.wju.edu   Federal Code: 003831

4-year private university and liberal arts college in small city, affiliated with Roman Catholic Church.

Enrollment: 1,093 undergrads, 12% part-time. 240 full-time freshmen.

Selectivity: Admits 50 to 75% of applicants.

BASIC COSTS (2008-2009)
Tuition and fees: $24,390.
Room and board: $7,650.

FINANCIAL AID PICTURE (2007-2008)
Students with need: Out of 225 full-time freshmen who applied for aid, 207 were judged to have need. Of these, 207 received aid, and 72 had their full need met. Average financial aid package met 89% of need; average scholarship/grant was $6,236; average loan was $4,165. For part-time students, average financial aid package was $5,925.
Students without need: 33 full-time freshmen who did not demonstrate need for aid received scholarships/grants; average award was $11,111. No-need awards available for academics, alumni affiliation, athletics, leadership, music/drama.
Scholarships offered: 11 full-time freshmen received athletic scholarships; average amount $5,227.
Cumulative student debt: 90% of graduating class had student loans; average debt was $22,750.

FINANCIAL AID PROCEDURES
Forms required: FAFSA.
Dates and Deadlines: Priority date 2/15; no closing date. Applicants notified on a rolling basis starting 3/15; must reply within 2 week(s) of notification.
Transfers: No deadline. Applicants notified on a rolling basis starting 3/15; must reply within 2 week(s) of notification. Academic scholarships available to qualified transfer students.

CONTACT
Christie Tomczyk, Director of Financial Aid
316 Washington Avenue, Wheeling, WV 26003-6295
(800) 624-6992 ext. 2304

Wisconsin

Alverno College
Milwaukee, Wisconsin
www.alverno.edu   Federal Code: 003832

4-year private liberal arts college for women in very large city, affiliated with Roman Catholic Church.
Enrollment: 2,251 undergrads, 26% part-time. 271 full-time freshmen.
Selectivity: Admits over 75% of applicants.

BASIC COSTS (2008-2009)
Tuition and fees: $18,161.
Per-credit charge: $739.
Room and board: $6,336.
Additional info: Tuition and fees may vary by program.

FINANCIAL AID PICTURE (2007-2008)
Students with need: Out of 254 full-time freshmen who applied for aid, 232 were judged to have need. Of these, 232 received aid. For part-time students, average financial aid package was $8,583.
Students without need: 28 full-time freshmen who did not demonstrate need for aid received scholarships/grants; average award was $6,345. No-need awards available for academics, alumni affiliation, leadership.
Scholarships offered: Academic scholarships; $14,800 to $33,800. Alverno Scholars of Wisconsin; $10,000; one available for each Wisconsin county.
Cumulative student debt: 89% of graduating class had student loans; average debt was $23,948.

FINANCIAL AID PROCEDURES
Forms required: FAFSA, institutional form.
Dates and Deadlines: Priority date 2/15; no closing date. Applicants notified on a rolling basis starting 3/15; must reply within 2 week(s) of notification.

Transfers: No deadline. Applicants notified on a rolling basis; must reply within 2 week(s) of notification. Transfer students are eligible for academic scholarships.

CONTACT
Dan Goyette, Director of Financial Aid
3400 South 43rd Street, Milwaukee, WI 53234-3922
(414) 382-6046

Bellin College of Nursing
Green Bay, Wisconsin
www.bcon.edu   Federal Code: 006639

4-year private nursing college in small city.
Enrollment: 259 undergrads.
Selectivity: Admits less than 50% of applicants.

BASIC COSTS (2007-2008)
Tuition and fees: $16,839.
Per-credit charge: $772.

FINANCIAL AID PICTURE
Students with need: Need-based aid available for full-time and part-time students. Work study available nights, weekends, and for part-time students.
Students without need: No-need awards available for academics.
Scholarships offered: Academic Scholarship; $1,000-$2,500 renewable conditionally; based on high school GPA, ACT scores. Dr. Fergus Scholarship; approximately $2,500 renewable annually; awarded to Merit Scholarship recipient.
Additional info: Freshmen and sophomores receive aid through University of Wisconsin-Green Bay. Juniors and seniors receive aid through Bellin College of Nursing.

FINANCIAL AID PROCEDURES
Forms required: FAFSA.
Dates and Deadlines: Priority date 3/1; no closing date. Applicants notified on a rolling basis starting 4/1; must reply within 2 week(s) of notification.
Transfers: No deadline. Applicants notified on a rolling basis starting 4/1; must reply within 2 week(s) of notification. Students with 4-year degrees ineligible for all federal and state grant programs.

CONTACT
Lena Goodman, Director of Financial Aid
PO Box 23400, Green Bay, WI 54305-3400
(920) 433-5801

Beloit College
Beloit, Wisconsin
www.beloit.edu   Federal Code: 003835

4-year private liberal arts college in large town.
Enrollment: 1,286 undergrads. 325 full-time freshmen.
Selectivity: Admits 50 to 75% of applicants.

BASIC COSTS (2008-2009)
Tuition and fees: $31,540.
Per-credit charge: $985.
Room and board: $6,696.
Additional info: Tuition/fee waivers available for adults.

FINANCIAL AID PICTURE (2007-2008)
Students with need: Out of 262 full-time freshmen who applied for aid, 206 were judged to have need. Of these, 206 received aid, and 153 had their full need met. Average financial aid package met 97% of need; average scholarship/grant was $19,818; average loan was $3,312.

Students without need: 83 full-time freshmen who did not demonstrate need for aid received scholarships/grants; average award was $10,870. No-need awards available for academics, leadership, minority status, music/drama.

Scholarships offered: Presidential Scholarships: $13,000-$15,000 per year; campus interview required. Merit-based scholarship: $4,000-$15,000 per year; 6 awarded.

Cumulative student debt: 70% of graduating class had student loans; average debt was $23,314.

FINANCIAL AID PROCEDURES

Forms required: FAFSA, state aid form, institutional form.

Dates and Deadlines: Closing date 3/1. Applicants notified on a rolling basis starting 4/1; must reply by 5/1 or within 2 week(s) of notification.

Transfers: No deadline. Applicants notified on a rolling basis starting 4/1; must reply by 5/1 or within 2 week(s) of notification.

CONTACT

Jane Hessian, Director of Financial Aid
700 College Street, Beloit, WI 53511-5595
(608) 363-2663

Blackhawk Technical College

Janesville, Wisconsin
www.blackhawk.edu   Federal Code: 005390

2-year public technical college in small city.

Enrollment: 2,294 undergrads, 56% part-time. 349 full-time freshmen.

Selectivity: Open admission; but selective for some programs.

BASIC COSTS (2007-2008)

Tuition and fees: $2,958; out-of-state residents $17,313.

Per-credit charge: $92; out-of-state residents $571.

Additional info: Material fees vary by program; minimum $4 per course. $10 per credit fee for online courses.

FINANCIAL AID PICTURE (2006-2007)

Students with need: 54% of average financial aid package awarded as scholarships/grants, 46% awarded as loans/jobs. Need-based aid available for part-time students.

FINANCIAL AID PROCEDURES

Dates and Deadlines: Priority date 4/30; no closing date. Applicants notified on a rolling basis starting 3/15; must reply within 2 week(s) of notification.

CONTACT

Sue Ullrick, Financial Aid Officer
Box 5009, Janesville, WI 53547-5009
(608) 757-7664

Cardinal Stritch University

Milwaukee, Wisconsin
www.stritch.edu   Federal Code: 003837

4-year private university in very large city, affiliated with Roman Catholic Church.

Enrollment: 3,180 undergrads, 6% part-time. 254 full-time freshmen.

Selectivity: Admits over 75% of applicants.

BASIC COSTS (2007-2008)

Tuition and fees: $19,074.

Per-credit charge: $582.

Room and board: $5,750.

Additional info: Additional $55 per credit for the nursing program.

FINANCIAL AID PICTURE

Students with need: Need-based aid available for full-time and part-time students.

Students without need: No-need awards available for academics, art, athletics, music/drama.

FINANCIAL AID PROCEDURES

Forms required: FAFSA, institutional form.

Dates and Deadlines: Priority date 4/15; no closing date. Applicants notified on a rolling basis starting 3/1; must reply within 3 week(s) of notification.

CONTACT

Amy Hoss, Director of Financial Aid
6801 North Yates Road, Box 516, Milwaukee, WI 53217-7516
(414) 410-4048

Carroll College

Waukesha, Wisconsin
www.cc.edu   Federal Code: 003838

4-year private liberal arts college in small city, affiliated with Presbyterian Church (USA).

Enrollment: 2,925 undergrads, 15% part-time. 645 full-time freshmen.

Selectivity: Admits 50 to 75% of applicants.

BASIC COSTS (2008-2009)

Tuition and fees: $21,926.

Per-credit charge: $260.

Room and board: $6,694.

FINANCIAL AID PICTURE (2007-2008)

Students with need: Out of 587 full-time freshmen who applied for aid, 458 were judged to have need. Of these, 458 received aid, and 380 had their full need met. Average financial aid package met 100% of need; average scholarship/grant was $11,969; average loan was $2,453. Need-based aid available for part-time students.

Students without need: 160 full-time freshmen who did not demonstrate need for aid received scholarships/grants; average award was $8,225. No-need awards available for academics, alumni affiliation, art, leadership, music/drama, ROTC.

Scholarships offered: Trustee Scholarship; $11,000 per year. Voorhees Scholarship; $10,000 per year. Charles Caroll Scholarship; $8,500 per year.

Cumulative student debt: 73% of graduating class had student loans; average debt was $21,794.

FINANCIAL AID PROCEDURES

Forms required: FAFSA.

Dates and Deadlines: No deadline. Applicants notified on a rolling basis starting 2/15; must reply by 5/1 or within 2 week(s) of notification.

Transfers: No deadline. Applicants notified on a rolling basis.

CONTACT

Dawn Scott, Director of Student Financial Services
100 North East Avenue, Waukesha, WI 53186-9988
(262) 524-7296

Carthage College

Kenosha, Wisconsin
www.carthage.edu   Federal Code: 003839

4-year private liberal arts college in small city, affiliated with Evangelical Lutheran Church in America.

Enrollment: 2,372 undergrads, 6% part-time. 685 full-time freshmen.

Selectivity: Admits over 75% of applicants.

BASIC COSTS (2008-2009)

Tuition and fees: $26,500.

Per-credit charge: $380.

Room and board: $7,500.

Additional info: Tuition/fee waivers available for minority students.

FINANCIAL AID PICTURE (2007-2008)

Students with need: 67% of average financial aid package awarded as scholarships/grants, 33% awarded as loans/jobs. Need-based aid available for part-time students.

Students without need: No-need awards available for academics, alumni affiliation, art, leadership, minority status, music/drama, religious affiliation.

Scholarships offered: Lincoln Scholarship Program: range from 75% tuition to full tuition, room and board, renewable; separate scholarship application; 17 awarded. Math/Science Scholarship: three awarded; range from $17,000/year to full tuition, renewable; requires separate scholarship application, restricted to math and natural science majors. French/German Scholarship: four awarded; $17,000/year, renewable; requires separate scholarship application, restricted to French and German majors. Fine Arts Scholarships: $500-$10,000/year, renewable; requires separate audition/portfolio showing, open to majors and non majors in music and theater, and majors in studio art or graphic design. Tarble Scholarships: number awarded variable; up to $17,000 year, renewable; requires separate scholarship application, restricted to California residents.

FINANCIAL AID PROCEDURES

Forms required: FAFSA.

Dates and Deadlines: Priority date 2/15; no closing date. Applicants notified on a rolling basis starting 3/1.

Transfers: Priority date 3/1; no deadline. Applicants notified on a rolling basis starting 3/1.

CONTACT

Vatistas Vatistas, Director of Financial Aid
2001 Alford Park Drive, Kenosha, WI 53140-1994
(262) 551-6001

Chippewa Valley Technical College

Eau Claire, Wisconsin
www.cvtc.edu
Federal Code: 005304

2-year public technical college in small city.

Enrollment: 5,529 undergrads..

Selectivity: Open admission; but selective for some programs.

BASIC COSTS (2007-2008)

Tuition and fees: $2,936; out-of-state residents $17,291.

Per-credit charge: $92; out-of-state residents $571.

Additional info: Material fees vary by program; minimum $4 per course. $10 per credit fee for online courses.

FINANCIAL AID PICTURE

Students with need: Need-based aid available for full-time and part-time students. Work study available nights, weekends, and for part-time students.

Scholarships offered: TOP Grant: $250 per semester, up to $1,000 total; must be enrolled full-time in Wisconsin technical college within 3 years of graduating from a Wisconsin high school, maintain minimum semester 2.0 GPA, and enroll in occupational associate degree or one-two year technical diploma program.

FINANCIAL AID PROCEDURES

Forms required: FAFSA.

Dates and Deadlines: Priority date 3/15; no closing date. Applicants notified on a rolling basis starting 6/1; must reply within 2 week(s) of notification.

CONTACT

Mary Gorud, Financial Aid Officer
620 West Clairemont Avenue, Eau Claire, WI 54701-6162
(715) 833-6250

College of Menominee Nation

Keshena, Wisconsin
www.menominee.edu
Federal Code: 031251

2-year private community college in rural community.

Enrollment: 505 undergrads, 54% part-time. 56 full-time freshmen.

Selectivity: Open admission; but selective for some programs.

BASIC COSTS (2007-2008)

Tuition and fees: $6,100.

Per-credit charge: $200.

FINANCIAL AID PICTURE

Students with need: Need-based aid available for full-time and part-time students. Work study available nights.

Students without need: This college awards aid only to students with need.

FINANCIAL AID PROCEDURES

Forms required: FAFSA.

Dates and Deadlines: Applicants notified on a rolling basis.

Transfers: No deadline. Applicants notified on a rolling basis.

CONTACT

Kathleen Klaus, Financial Aid Director
N 172 State Highway 47/55, Keshena, WI 54135
(715) 799-5600 ext. 3039

Columbia College of Nursing

Milwaukee, Wisconsin
www.ccon.edu
Federal Code: 003838

4-year private nursing college in very large city.

Enrollment: 218 undergrads.

BASIC COSTS (2008-2009)

Tuition and fees: $19,397.

Per-credit charge: $590.

Room and board: $5,600.

FINANCIAL AID PICTURE

Students with need: Need-based aid available for full-time and part-time students. Work study available nights, weekends, and for part-time students.

Students without need: No-need awards available for academics.

Additional info: Students must apply to and meet financial aid requirements of Mount Mary College.

FINANCIAL AID PROCEDURES

Forms required: FAFSA.

Dates and Deadlines: No deadline. Applicants notified on a rolling basis starting 2/15; must reply by 5/1 or within 2 week(s) of notification.

CONTACT

Shereen Kressin, Associate Dean, Administration and Finance
Mount Mary College Enrollment Office, Milwaukee, WI 53222-4597

Concordia University Wisconsin

Mequon, Wisconsin
www.cuw.edu
Federal Code: 003842

4-year private university and liberal arts college in large town, affiliated with Lutheran Church - Missouri Synod.

Enrollment: 3,356 undergrads, 42% part-time. 435 full-time freshmen.

Selectivity: Admits 50 to 75% of applicants.

BASIC COSTS (2008-2009)

Tuition and fees: $19,990.

Per-credit charge: $830.

Room and board: $7,500.

FINANCIAL AID PICTURE (2007-2008)

Students with need: Out of 407 full-time freshmen who applied for aid, 340 were judged to have need. Of these, 335 received aid, and 127 had their full need met. Average financial aid package met 80% of need; average scholarship/grant was $10,802; average loan was $5,419. For part-time students, average financial aid package was $9,437.

Students without need: 82 full-time freshmen who did not demonstrate need for aid received scholarships/grants; average award was $9,532. No-need awards available for academics, religious affiliation.

Cumulative student debt: 78% of graduating class had student loans; average debt was $22,020.

FINANCIAL AID PROCEDURES

Forms required: FAFSA.

Dates and Deadlines: Priority date 4/1; no closing date. Applicants notified on a rolling basis starting 3/1; must reply within 3 week(s) of notification.

CONTACT

Steve Taylor, Director of Financial Aid

12800 North Lake Shore Drive, Mequon, WI 53097

(262) 243-4392

DeVry University: **Milwaukee**

Milwaukee, Wisconsin

www.devry.edu

4-year for-profit university in very large city.

Enrollment: 108 undergrads, 61% part-time. 10 full-time freshmen.

BASIC COSTS (2007-2008)

Tuition and fees: $13,020.

Per-credit charge: $490.

FINANCIAL AID PICTURE (2006-2007)

Students with need: Out of 7 full-time freshmen who applied for aid, 6 were judged to have need. Of these, 5 received aid. Average financial aid package met 32% of need; average scholarship/grant was $5,250; average loan was $4,225. For part-time students, average financial aid package was $7,480.

Students without need: 1 full-time freshmen who did not demonstrate need for aid received scholarships/grants; average award was $16,865. No-need awards available for academics.

FINANCIAL AID PROCEDURES

Forms required: FAFSA.

Dates and Deadlines: No deadline. Applicants notified on a rolling basis.

CONTACT

100 East Wisconsin Avenue, Suite 2550, Milwaukee, WI 53202

(414) 278-7677

Edgewood College

Madison, Wisconsin

www.edgewood.edu

Federal Code: 003848

4-year private liberal arts college in small city, affiliated with Roman Catholic Church.

Enrollment: 1,860 undergrads.

Selectivity: Admits over 75% of applicants.

BASIC COSTS (2008-2009)

Tuition and fees: $20,040.

Per-credit charge: $630.

Room and board: $6,570.

FINANCIAL AID PICTURE (2006-2007)

Students with need: 51% of average financial aid package awarded as scholarships/grants, 49% awarded as loans/jobs. Need-based aid available for part-time students. Work study available nights, weekends, and for part-time students.

Students without need: No-need awards available for academics, alumni affiliation, art, leadership, minority status, music/drama, religious affiliation.

Additional info: Auditions required for music scholarships, portfolios required for fine arts scholarships, essays required for a number of institutional scholarships, including AHANA Student Advancement Award, Alumni Association Scholarship, O'Connor Memorial Scholarship.

FINANCIAL AID PROCEDURES

Forms required: FAFSA, institutional form.

Dates and Deadlines: Priority date 3/1; no closing date. Applicants notified on a rolling basis starting 3/30; must reply within 2 week(s) of notification.

CONTACT

Kari Gribble, Director of Financial Aid

1000 Edgewood College Drive, Madison, WI 53711-1997

(608) 663-2206

Fox Valley Technical College

Appleton, Wisconsin

www.fvtc.edu

Federal Code: 009744

2-year public technical college in small city.

Enrollment: 5,694 undergrads, 57% part-time. 555 full-time freshmen.

Selectivity: Open admission; but selective for some programs.

BASIC COSTS (2007-2008)

Tuition and fees: $3,185; out-of-state residents $17,540.

Per-credit charge: $92; out-of-state residents $571.

Additional info: Material fees vary by program; minimum $4 per course. $10 per credit fee for online courses.

FINANCIAL AID PICTURE (2006-2007)

Students with need: 44% of average financial aid package awarded as scholarships/grants, 56% awarded as loans/jobs.

FINANCIAL AID PROCEDURES

Forms required: FAFSA.

Dates and Deadlines: Priority date 3/1; no closing date. Applicants notified on a rolling basis.

CONTACT

Mary Moede, Financial Aid Officer

1825 North Bluemound Drive, Appleton, WI 54912-2277

(920) 735-5645

Gateway Technical College

Kenosha, Wisconsin

www.gtc.edu

Federal Code: 005389

2-year public technical college in small city.

Enrollment: 5,442 undergrads.

Selectivity: Open admission; but selective for some programs.

BASIC COSTS (2007-2008)

Tuition and fees: $3,280; out-of-state residents $17,635.

Per-credit charge: $92; out-of-state residents $571.

Additional info: Materials fees vary by program; minimum $4 per course.

FINANCIAL AID PICTURE

Students with need: Need-based aid available for full-time and part-time students.

Students without need: No-need awards available for state/district residency.

FINANCIAL AID PROCEDURES

Forms required: FAFSA, institutional form.

Dates and Deadlines: Priority date 7/1; no closing date. Applicants notified on a rolling basis starting 5/1; must reply within 2 week(s) of notification.

CONTACT

Janice Riutta, Director of Student Financial Aid

3520 30th Avenue, Kenosha, WI 53144-1690

(262) 564-3072

Herzing College

Madison, Wisconsin

www.herzing.edu/madison   Federal Code: 009621

3-year for-profit business and technical college in small city.

Enrollment: 900 undergrads.

Selectivity: Open admission; but selective for some programs.

BASIC COSTS (2007-2008)

Additional info: Tuition is $335 per credit hour for most on-campus courses; $375 for on-line courses. Book use included in tuition.

FINANCIAL AID PICTURE

Students with need: Need-based aid available for full-time and part-time students.

FINANCIAL AID PROCEDURES

Forms required: FAFSA, institutional form.

Dates and Deadlines: No deadline. Applicants notified on a rolling basis.

CONTACT

Beverly Faga, Director of Student Services

5218 East Terrace Drive, Madison, WI 53718

(608) 249-6611

Lac Courte Oreilles Ojibwa Community College

Hayward, Wisconsin

www.lco.edu   Federal Code: 017199

2-year public community college in small town.

Enrollment: 576 undergrads, 41% part-time. 78 full-time freshmen.

Selectivity: Open admission.

BASIC COSTS (2008-2009)

Tuition and fees: $4,075.

Per-credit charge: $135.

FINANCIAL AID PICTURE

Students with need: Need-based aid available for full-time students.

FINANCIAL AID PROCEDURES

Forms required: FAFSA.

Dates and Deadlines: No deadline. Applicants notified on a rolling basis.

CONTACT

Raymond Burns, Financial Aid Officer

13466 West Trepania Road, Hayward, WI 54843

Lakeland College

Sheboygan, Wisconsin

www.lakeland.edu   Federal Code: 003854

4-year private liberal arts college in small city, affiliated with United Church of Christ.

Enrollment: 2,918 undergrads, 64% part-time. 181 full-time freshmen.

Selectivity: Admits 50 to 75% of applicants.

BASIC COSTS (2008-2009)

Tuition and fees: $18,435.

Per-credit charge: $615.

Room and board: $6,360.

Additional info: Tuition at time of enrollment locked for 4 years.

FINANCIAL AID PICTURE (2007-2008)

Students with need: Out of 181 full-time freshmen who applied for aid, 180 were judged to have need. Of these, 178 received aid, and 36 had their full need met. Average financial aid package met 75% of need; average scholarship/grant was $10,395; average loan was $3,527. For part-time students, average financial aid package was $5,131.

Students without need: 87 full-time freshmen who did not demonstrate need for aid received scholarships/grants; average award was $7,607. No-need awards available for academics.

Cumulative student debt: 88% of graduating class had student loans; average debt was $26,871.

FINANCIAL AID PROCEDURES

Forms required: FAFSA, institutional form.

Dates and Deadlines: Priority date 3/31; closing date 7/1. Applicants notified on a rolling basis starting 2/1; must reply within 2 week(s) of notification.

CONTACT

Patty Taylor, Director of Financial Aid

Box 359, Sheboygan, WI 53082-0359

(920) 565-1297

Lakeshore Technical College

Cleveland, Wisconsin

www.gotoltc.edu   Federal Code: 009194

2-year public technical college in rural community.

Enrollment: 2,121 undergrads, 67% part-time. 124 full-time freshmen.

Selectivity: Open admission.

BASIC COSTS (2007-2008)

Tuition and fees: $2,895; out-of-state residents $17,250.

Per-credit charge: $92; out-of-state residents $571.

Additional info: Materials fees vary by program; minimum $4 per course. $10 per credit fee for online courses.

FINANCIAL AID PICTURE

Students with need: Need-based aid available for full-time and part-time students. Work study available nights.

Students without need: This college awards aid only to students with need.

FINANCIAL AID PROCEDURES

Forms required: FAFSA, institutional form.

Dates and Deadlines: Priority date 6/1; no closing date. Applicants notified on a rolling basis starting 6/1; must reply within 3 week(s) of notification.

CONTACT

Corey Givens-Novak, Financial Aid Manager

1290 North Avenue, Cleveland, WI 53015-9761

(920) 693-1118

Lawrence University

Appleton, Wisconsin
www.lawrence.edu   Federal Code: 003856

4-year private music and liberal arts college in small city.

Enrollment: 1,400 undergrads, 2% part-time. 357 full-time freshmen.

Selectivity: Admits 50 to 75% of applicants. GED not accepted.

BASIC COSTS (2008-2009)

Tuition and fees: $33,264.

Room and board: $6,957.

FINANCIAL AID PICTURE (2007-2008)

Students with need: Out of 273 full-time freshmen who applied for aid, 211 were judged to have need. Of these, 211 received aid, and 161 had their full need met. Average financial aid package met 91% of need; average scholarship/grant was $18,100; average loan was $5,000. Need-based aid available for part-time students.

Students without need: 84 full-time freshmen who did not demonstrate need for aid received scholarships/grants; average award was $13,480. No-need awards available for academics, alumni affiliation, minority status, music/drama, state/district residency.

Scholarships offered: Warch Scholarships: $15,000 per year. Trustee Scholarships: $12,000 per year. Presidential Scholarships: $9,000 per year. Alumni Scholarships: $7,000 per year. Conservatory Scholarships: $2,000-$12,000 per year.

Cumulative student debt: 74% of graduating class had student loans; average debt was $25,374.

Additional info: The first $1,000 (aggregate) of independently-sponsored scholarships received by a needy student will reduce student's loan or work-study commitment. Half of scholarships in excess of $1,000 will offset loan or work-study and the other half will reduce institutional grant funding.

FINANCIAL AID PROCEDURES

Forms required: FAFSA, institutional form.

Dates and Deadlines: Priority date 3/15; no closing date. Applicants notified on a rolling basis starting 3/15; must reply by 5/1 or within 2 week(s) of notification.

Transfers: Priority date 4/1. Applicants notified on a rolling basis starting 5/23.

CONTACT

Steven Syverson, Vice President for Enrollment Management
Box 599, Appleton, WI 54912-0599
(920) 832-6583

Madison Area Technical College

Madison, Wisconsin
www.madison.tec.wi.us   Federal Code: 004007

2-year public community and technical college in small city.

Enrollment: 14,647 undergrads.

Selectivity: Open admission; but selective for some programs.

BASIC COSTS (2007-2008)

Tuition and fees: $2,921; out-of-state residents $17,366.

Per-credit charge: $92; out-of-state residents $571.

Additional info: Material fees vary by program; minimum $4 per course. $10 per credit fee for online courses.

FINANCIAL AID PICTURE (2006-2007)

Students with need: 55% of average financial aid package awarded as scholarships/grants, 45% awarded as loans/jobs.

FINANCIAL AID PROCEDURES

Forms required: FAFSA.

Dates and Deadlines: Priority date 4/15; no closing date. Applicants notified on a rolling basis starting 4/15.

CONTACT

Timothy Jacobson, Financial Aid Supervisor
3350 Anderson Street, Madison, WI 53704-2599

Maranatha Baptist Bible College

Watertown, Wisconsin
www.mbbc.edu   Federal Code: 016394

4-year private Bible college in large town, affiliated with Baptist faith.

Enrollment: 829 undergrads, 4% part-time. 218 full-time freshmen.

Selectivity: Admits 50 to 75% of applicants.

BASIC COSTS (2007-2008)

Tuition and fees: $9,486.

Per-credit charge: $268.

Room and board: $5,500.

FINANCIAL AID PICTURE (2006-2007)

Students with need: Out of 202 full-time freshmen who applied for aid, 172 were judged to have need. Of these, 172 received aid, and 14 had their full need met. Average financial aid package met 40% of need; average scholarship/grant was $3,396; average loan was $2,296. For part-time students, average financial aid package was $5,246.

Students without need: 5 full-time freshmen who did not demonstrate need for aid received scholarships/grants; average award was $688. No-need awards available for academics.

Cumulative student debt: 50% of graduating class had student loans; average debt was $15,043.

FINANCIAL AID PROCEDURES

Forms required: FAFSA.

Dates and Deadlines: Priority date 3/1; no closing date. Applicants notified on a rolling basis starting 2/1; must reply within 2 week(s) of notification.

Transfers: Financial aid transcript or equivalent required.

CONTACT

Randy Hibbs, Financial Aid Director
745 West Main Street, Watertown, WI 53094
(920) 206-2318

Marian College of Fond du Lac

Fond du Lac, Wisconsin
www.mariancollege.edu   Federal Code: 003861

4-year private liberal arts college in large town, affiliated with Roman Catholic Church.

Enrollment: 1,958 undergrads, 28% part-time. 267 full-time freshmen.

Selectivity: Admits over 75% of applicants.

BASIC COSTS (2007-2008)

Tuition and fees: $18,665.

Per-credit charge: $300.

Room and board: $5,220.

FINANCIAL AID PICTURE (2007-2008)

Students with need: Out of 253 full-time freshmen who applied for aid, 221 were judged to have need. Of these, 221 received aid, and 76 had their full need met. Average financial aid package met 87% of need; average scholarship/grant was $10,478; average loan was $4,491. For part-time students, average financial aid package was $9,372.

Students without need: 32 full-time freshmen who did not demonstrate need for aid received scholarships/grants; average award was $4,312. No-need awards available for academics, ROTC, state/district residency.

Scholarships offered: Academic Achievement Award: $7,500; based on 3.5 GPA, 25 ACT, top 15% of class; 7 awarded. Presidential Scholarship: $5,000; based on 3.1 GPA, top 20% of class. Naber Leadership Scholarship: $3,000; based on 2.5 GPA, top 50% of class.

Cumulative student debt: 90% of graduating class had student loans; average debt was $20,800.

FINANCIAL AID PROCEDURES

Forms required: FAFSA, institutional form.

Dates and Deadlines: Priority date 3/1; no closing date. Applicants notified on a rolling basis starting 3/1; must reply within 4 week(s) of notification.

CONTACT

Debra McKinney, Director of Financial Aid

45 South National Avenue, Fond du Lac, WI 54935-4699

(920) 923-7614

Marquette University

Milwaukee, Wisconsin

www.marquette.edu

Federal Code: 003863

4-year private university in very large city, affiliated with Roman Catholic Church.

Enrollment: 7,742 undergrads, 3% part-time. 1,811 full-time freshmen.

Selectivity: Admits 50 to 75% of applicants.

BASIC COSTS (2008-2009)

Tuition and fees: $28,128.

Per-credit charge: $810.

Room and board: $9,280.

Additional info: Required fees include cost of UPASS, which allows unlimited use of Milwaukee County Bus System.

FINANCIAL AID PICTURE (2007-2008)

Students with need: Out of 1,391 full-time freshmen who applied for aid, 1,050 were judged to have need. Of these, 1,049 received aid, and 703 had their full need met. Average financial aid package met 84% of need; average scholarship/grant was $14,214; average loan was $5,304. For part-time students, average financial aid package was $7,138.

Students without need: 364 full-time freshmen who did not demonstrate need for aid received scholarships/grants; average award was $8,474. No-need awards available for academics, athletics, leadership, music/drama, ROTC.

Scholarships offered: *Merit:* Ignatius Scholarships: $6,000-$11,000. College Scholarships: $5,000. Raynor Scholarships: full tuition; 3 awarded. National Merit Scholarships: $2,000. *Athletic:* 25 full-time freshmen received athletic scholarships; average amount $24,238.

Cumulative student debt: 88% of graduating class had student loans; average debt was $32,231.

FINANCIAL AID PROCEDURES

Forms required: FAFSA.

Dates and Deadlines: Priority date 2/1; no closing date. Applicants notified on a rolling basis starting 3/20; must reply by 5/1 or within 3 week(s) of notification.

Transfers: No deadline. Applicants notified on a rolling basis starting 3/15; must reply by 5/1 or within 3 week(s) of notification. Transfer scholarships available.

CONTACT

Susan Teerink, Director of Student Financial Aid

PO Box 1881, Milwaukee, WI 53201-1881

(414) 288-0200

Mid-State Technical College

Wisconsin Rapids, Wisconsin

www.mstc.edu

Federal Code: 005380

2-year public technical college in large town.

Enrollment: 2,960 undergrads.

Selectivity: Open admission; but selective for some programs.

BASIC COSTS (2007-2008)

Tuition and fees: $3,056; out-of-state residents $17,411.

Per-credit charge: $92; out-of-state residents $571.

Additional info: Material fees vary by program; minimum $4 per course.

FINANCIAL AID PICTURE

Students with need: Need-based aid available for full-time and part-time students. Work study available nights, weekends, and for part-time students.

Students without need: No-need awards available for academics, leadership.

FINANCIAL AID PROCEDURES

Forms required: FAFSA.

Dates and Deadlines: No deadline. Applicants notified on a rolling basis starting 5/30; must reply within 2 week(s) of notification.

CONTACT

MaryJo Green, Financial Aid Supervisor

500 32nd Street North, Wisconsin Rapids, WI 54494

(715) 422-5501

Milwaukee Area Technical College

Milwaukee, Wisconsin

www.matc.edu

Federal Code: 003866

2-year public junior and technical college in very large city.

Enrollment: 14,482 undergrads, 65% part-time. 1,007 full-time freshmen.

Selectivity: Open admission; but selective for some programs and for out-of-state students.

BASIC COSTS (2007-2008)

Tuition and fees: $2,954; out-of-state residents $17,399.

Per-credit charge: $92; out-of-state residents $571.

Additional info: Material fees vary by program; minimum $4 per course. $10 per credit fee for online courses. Tuition/fee waivers available for minority students.

FINANCIAL AID PICTURE

Students with need: Need-based aid available for full-time and part-time students.

Students without need: No-need awards available for academics.

FINANCIAL AID PROCEDURES

Forms required: FAFSA.

Dates and Deadlines: Priority date 3/15; no closing date. Applicants notified on a rolling basis starting 4/15.

Transfers: No deadline. Applicants notified on a rolling basis starting 4/15.

CONTACT

Al Pinckney, Director of Financial Aid

700 West State Street, Milwaukee, WI 53233-1443

(414) 297-6279

Milwaukee Institute of Art & Design

Milwaukee, Wisconsin
www.miad.edu   Federal Code: 014203

4-year private visual arts college in very large city.

Enrollment: 636 undergrads.

BASIC COSTS (2007-2008)

Tuition and fees: $24,900.
Per-credit charge: $805.
Room and board: $7,200.

FINANCIAL AID PICTURE

Students with need: Need-based aid available for full-time and part-time students. Work study available nights, weekends, and for part-time students.
Students without need: No-need awards available for academics, art, leadership.
Scholarships offered: One full admission scholarship; several half, 1/3 and 1/4 admission scholarships. All awards based on portfolio and grade point average.

FINANCIAL AID PROCEDURES

Forms required: FAFSA.
Dates and Deadlines: Priority date 3/1; no closing date. Applicants notified on a rolling basis starting 4/1; must reply by 5/1 or within 4 week(s) of notification.
Transfers: No deadline. Applicants notified on a rolling basis starting 4/1; must reply by 5/1 or within 2 week(s) of notification.

CONTACT

Lloyd Mueller, Executive Director of Financial Aid
273 East Erie Street, Milwaukee, WI 53202
(414) 291-3272

Milwaukee School of Engineering

Milwaukee, Wisconsin
www.msoe.edu   Federal Code: 003868

4-year private university in very large city.

Enrollment: 2,317 undergrads, 11% part-time. 541 full-time freshmen.
Selectivity: Admits 50 to 75% of applicants.

BASIC COSTS (2008-2009)

Tuition and fees: $27,300.
Per-credit charge: $475.
Room and board: $6,825.
Additional info: $1,140 technology package required for all full-time first-year students. Includes laptop computer, software, Internet, insurance and repairs, upgrade every two years, wireless access, training and support, and compatibility computing throughout campus.

FINANCIAL AID PICTURE (2006-2007)

Students with need: Out of 501 full-time freshmen who applied for aid, 429 were judged to have need. Of these, 429 received aid, and 74 had their full need met. Average financial aid package met 68% of need; average scholarship/grant was $14,289; average loan was $1,768. For part-time students, average financial aid package was $11,005.
Students without need: 112 full-time freshmen who did not demonstrate need for aid received scholarships/grants; average award was $12,507. No-need awards available for academics, ROTC.
Scholarships offered: President Scholarship; full tuition; awarded to students with high academic standing; 8 awarded each year to first-time, full-time students.
Cumulative student debt: 86% of graduating class had student loans; average debt was $35,875.

FINANCIAL AID PROCEDURES

Forms required: FAFSA.
Dates and Deadlines: Priority date 3/15; no closing date. Applicants notified on a rolling basis starting 3/1; must reply within 2 week(s) of notification.

CONTACT

Steven Midthun, Director, Financial Aid
1025 North Broadway, Milwaukee, WI 53202-3109
(414) 277-7223

Moraine Park Technical College

Fond du Lac, Wisconsin
www.morainepark.edu   Federal Code: 005303

2-year public technical college in large town.

Enrollment: 4,000 undergrads.
Selectivity: Open admission; but selective for some programs.

BASIC COSTS (2007-2008)

Tuition and fees: $2,803; out-of-state residents $17,248.
Per-credit charge: $92; out-of-state residents $571.
Additional info: Material fees vary by program; minimum $4 per course. $10 per credit fee for online courses.

FINANCIAL AID PICTURE

Students with need: Need-based aid available for full-time and part-time students. Work study available nights.
Students without need: No-need awards available for academics, job skills, leadership, minority status, state/district residency.

FINANCIAL AID PROCEDURES

Forms required: FAFSA, institutional form.
Dates and Deadlines: Priority date 5/1; no closing date. Applicants notified on a rolling basis starting 6/15; must reply within 2 week(s) of notification.

CONTACT

Karen Zuehlke, Student Financials Partner
235 North National Avenue, Fond du Lac, WI 54935-1940
(920) 924-6320

Mount Mary College

Milwaukee, Wisconsin
www.mtmary.edu   Federal Code: 003869

4-year private liberal arts college for women in very large city, affiliated with Roman Catholic Church.

Enrollment: 1,203 undergrads, 33% part-time. 119 full-time freshmen.
Selectivity: Admits 50 to 75% of applicants.

BASIC COSTS (2008-2009)

Tuition and fees: $20,350.
Per-credit charge: $575.
Room and board: $6,994.

FINANCIAL AID PICTURE (2007-2008)

Students with need: Average financial aid package met 58% of need; average scholarship/grant was $9,065; average loan was $3,885. For part-time students, average financial aid package was $13,264.
Students without need: No-need awards available for academics, alumni affiliation, art, leadership, music/drama.
Cumulative student debt: 84% of graduating class had student loans; average debt was $24,264.

FINANCIAL AID PROCEDURES

Forms required: FAFSA.
Dates and Deadlines: Priority date 3/11; no closing date. Applicants notified on a rolling basis starting 1/1; must reply within 2 week(s) of notification.

CONTACT
Debra Duff, Director of Financial Aid
2900 North Menomonee River Parkway, Milwaukee, WI 53222
(414) 256-1258

Nicolet Area Technical College
Rhinelander, Wisconsin
www.nicoletcollege.edu   Federal Code: 008919

2-year public community and technical college in small town.
Enrollment: 1,100 undergrads.
Selectivity: Open admission; but selective for some programs.

BASIC COSTS (2007-2008)
Tuition and fees: $2,873; out-of-state residents $17,228.
Per-credit charge: $92; out-of-state residents $571.
Additional info: Material fees vary by program; minimum $4 per course. $10 per credit fee for online courses.

FINANCIAL AID PICTURE
Students with need: Work study available nights, weekends, and for part-time students.

FINANCIAL AID PROCEDURES
Forms required: FAFSA, institutional form.
Dates and Deadlines: Priority date 4/15; no closing date. Applicants notified on a rolling basis starting 6/1; must reply within 2 week(s) of notification.

CONTACT
William Peshel, Director of Financial Aid
Box 518, Rhinelander, WI 54501
(715) 365-4423

Northcentral Technical College
Wausau, Wisconsin
www.ntc.edu   Federal Code: 005387

2-year public community and technical college in small city.
Enrollment: 2,634 undergrads, 55% part-time. 361 full-time freshmen.
Selectivity: Open admission; but selective for some programs.

BASIC COSTS (2007-2008)
Tuition and fees: $2,912; out-of-state residents $17,267.
Per-credit charge: $92; out-of-state residents $571.
Additional info: Materials fees vary by program; minimum $4 per course.

FINANCIAL AID PICTURE
Students with need: Need-based aid available for full-time and part-time students. Work study available nights.

FINANCIAL AID PROCEDURES
Forms required: FAFSA.
Dates and Deadlines: No deadline. Applicants notified on a rolling basis.
Transfers: No deadline.

CONTACT
Sue Berens, Director of Financial Aid
1000 West Campus Drive, Wausau, WI 54401
(715) 675-3331 ext. 4028

Northeast Wisconsin Technical College
Green Bay, Wisconsin
www.nwtc.edu   Federal Code: 005301

2-year public community and technical college in small city.
Enrollment: 5,853 undergrads, 57% part-time. 847 full-time freshmen.

Selectivity: Open admission; but selective for some programs.

BASIC COSTS (2007-2008)
Tuition and fees: $2,962; out-of-state residents $17,407.
Per-credit charge: $92; out-of-state residents $571.
Additional info: Material fees vary by program; minimum $4 per course.

FINANCIAL AID PICTURE (2006-2007)
Students with need: 57% of average financial aid package awarded as scholarships/grants, 43% awarded as loans/jobs. Need-based aid available for part-time students. Work study available nights.

FINANCIAL AID PROCEDURES
Forms required: FAFSA.
Dates and Deadlines: Priority date 4/1; no closing date. Applicants notified on a rolling basis starting 5/1; must reply within 2 week(s) of notification.

CONTACT
Heather Hill, Financial Aid Director
2740 West Mason Street, Green Bay, WI 54307-9042
(920) 498-5444

Northland College
Ashland, Wisconsin
www.northland.edu   Federal Code: 003875

4-year private liberal arts college in small town, affiliated with United Church of Christ.
Enrollment: 656 undergrads, 6% part-time. 150 full-time freshmen.
Selectivity: Admits 50 to 75% of applicants.

BASIC COSTS (2008-2009)
Tuition and fees: $23,101.
Per-credit charge: $410.
Room and board: $6,440.

FINANCIAL AID PICTURE (2007-2008)
Students with need: Out of 140 full-time freshmen who applied for aid, 128 were judged to have need. Of these, 128 received aid, and 17 had their full need met. Average financial aid package met 87% of need; average scholarship/grant was $15,049; average loan was $3,995. Need-based aid available for part-time students.
Students without need: 23 full-time freshmen who did not demonstrate need for aid received scholarships/grants; average award was $9,309. No-need awards available for academics, alumni affiliation, art, job skills, leadership, minority status, music/drama, religious affiliation, state/district residency.
Cumulative student debt: 79% of graduating class had student loans; average debt was $23,630.

FINANCIAL AID PROCEDURES
Forms required: FAFSA.
Dates and Deadlines: Priority date 4/15; no closing date. Applicants notified on a rolling basis starting 3/1; must reply by 5/1 or within 4 week(s) of notification.

CONTACT
Deb Milanowski, Director of Financial Aid
1411 Ellis Avenue, Ashland, WI 54806
(715) 682-1255

Ripon College
Ripon, Wisconsin
www.ripon.edu   Federal Code: 003884

4-year private liberal arts college in small town.
Enrollment: 977 undergrads, 1% part-time. 262 full-time freshmen.

Selectivity: Admits over 75% of applicants.

BASIC COSTS (2008-2009)

Tuition and fees: $24,245.

Per-credit charge: $890.

Room and board: $6,770.

FINANCIAL AID PICTURE (2007-2008)

Students with need: Out of 248 full-time freshmen who applied for aid, 215 were judged to have need. Of these, 215 received aid, and 112 had their full need met. Average financial aid package met 96% of need; average scholarship/grant was $16,333; average loan was $4,716. Need-based aid available for part-time students.

Students without need: 46 full-time freshmen who did not demonstrate need for aid received scholarships/grants; average award was $17,907. No-need awards available for academics, alumni affiliation, art, leadership, minority status, music/drama, religious affiliation, ROTC, state/district residency.

Scholarships offered: Pickard Scholarships: one full tuition and ten $60,000; both by invitation only. Presidential Scholarships: $48,000; minimum 3.8 GPA, top 5% of class, ACT 30, SAT 1340; by invitation only. Knop Scholars Program: $50,000; science major, 3.8 GPA, top 5% of class, interview, by invitation only; one awarded. Faculty Scholarships: $40,000; 3.76 GPA, ACT 29, SAT 1300. Dean's Scholarships: $34,000; 3.51 GPA, ACT 27, SAT 1220. Founder's Scholarships: $28,000; 3.36 GPA, ACT 25, SAT 1140. Honor Scholarships: $24,000; 3.2 GPA, ACT 24, SAT 1110. U.S. Army ROTC Scholarships: starting at $80,000. Diversity Scholarships: $20,000; application required. Forensics Scholarships: $20,000; interview. All SAT scores exclusive of Writing. Valedictorian Scholarships: $24,000. Art Scholarships: $20,000 maximum award; portfolio. Theatre Scholarships: $20,000 maximum; interview. Music Scholarships: $20,000; audition. Service Awards: $20,000; not available to academic scholarship recipients. Boy/Girl State Scholarships: $16,000 maximum award. Legacy Awards: $8,000. United Church of Christ Scholarships: $8,000; application required. National Latin Exam: $8,000.

Cumulative student debt: 87% of graduating class had student loans; average debt was $19,929.

FINANCIAL AID PROCEDURES

Forms required: FAFSA.

Dates and Deadlines: Priority date 3/1; no closing date. Applicants notified on a rolling basis starting 3/1; must reply within 2 week(s) of notification.

Transfers: Must reply within 2 week(s) of notification.

CONTACT

Steven Schuetz, Director of Financial Aid

300 Seward Street, Ripon, WI 54971-0248

(920) 748-8101

St. Norbert College

De Pere, Wisconsin

www.snc.edu   Federal Code: 003892

4-year private liberal arts college in large town, affiliated with Roman Catholic Church.

Enrollment: 2,045 undergrads, 1% part-time. 552 full-time freshmen.

Selectivity: Admits over 75% of applicants.

BASIC COSTS (2008-2009)

Tuition and fees: $25,926.

Per-credit charge: $798.

Room and board: $6,781.

FINANCIAL AID PICTURE (2006-2007)

Students with need: Out of 441 full-time freshmen who applied for aid, 340 were judged to have need. Of these, 340 received aid, and 109 had their full need met. Average financial aid package met 89% of need; average scholarship/grant was $13,493; average loan was $3,466. For part-time students, average financial aid package was $8,519.

Students without need: 156 full-time freshmen who did not demonstrate need for aid received scholarships/grants; average award was $7,472. No-need awards available for academics, art, leadership, minority status, music/drama, ROTC, state/district residency.

FINANCIAL AID PROCEDURES

Forms required: FAFSA.

Dates and Deadlines: Priority date 3/1; no closing date. Applicants notified on a rolling basis starting 3/15; must reply within 2 week(s) of notification.

CONTACT

Jeff Zahn, Director of Financial Aid

100 Grant Street, De Pere, WI 54115-2099

(920) 403-3071

Silver Lake College

Manitowoc, Wisconsin

www.sl.edu   Federal Code: 003850

4-year private business and liberal arts college in large town, affiliated with Roman Catholic Church.

Enrollment: 380 undergrads, 54% part-time. 38 full-time freshmen.

Selectivity: Admits 50 to 75% of applicants.

BASIC COSTS (2008-2009)

Tuition and fees: $19,194.

Per-credit charge: $595.

Room and board: $7,150.

FINANCIAL AID PICTURE (2007-2008)

Students with need: Out of 35 full-time freshmen who applied for aid, 34 were judged to have need. Of these, 34 received aid, and 8 had their full need met. Average financial aid package met 78% of need; average scholarship/grant was $10,737; average loan was $3,398. For part-time students, average financial aid package was $6,838.

Students without need: 1 full-time freshmen who did not demonstrate need for aid received scholarships/grants; average award was $10,000. No-need awards available for academics, art, athletics, leadership, music/drama, religious affiliation, state/district residency.

Scholarships offered: Presidential Scholarship: $8,000. Founder's Scholarship: $7,000. Dean's Scholarship: $6,000. Honors Scholarship: $5,000. All scholarships merit-based.

Cumulative student debt: 83% of graduating class had student loans; average debt was $24,029.

FINANCIAL AID PROCEDURES

Forms required: FAFSA.

Dates and Deadlines: Priority date 3/15; no closing date. Applicants notified on a rolling basis starting 3/15; must reply within 2 week(s) of notification.

Transfers: No deadline. Applicants notified on a rolling basis starting 3/15; must reply within 2 week(s) of notification. Transfer Merit Scholarships and Phi Theta Kappa Scholarships available, as well as other institutional scholarship and grant assistance.

CONTACT

Michelle Krajnik, Director of Student Financial Aid

2406 South Alverno Road, Manitowoc, WI 54220-9319

(920) 686-6122

Southwest Wisconsin Technical College

Fennimore, Wisconsin

www.swtc.edu   Federal Code: 007699

2-year public technical college in rural community.

Enrollment: 1,457 undergrads.

BASIC COSTS (2007-2008)

Tuition and fees: $2,872; out-of-state residents $17,227.

Per-credit charge: $92; out-of-state residents $571.

Additional info: Materials fees vary by program; minimum $4 per course. $10 per credit fee for online courses.

FINANCIAL AID PICTURE

Students with need: Work study available nights.

FINANCIAL AID PROCEDURES

Forms required: FAFSA, institutional form.

Dates and Deadlines: Priority date 4/15; no closing date. Applicants notified on a rolling basis starting 5/15; must reply within 4 week(s) of notification.

CONTACT

Joy Kite, Director of Financial Aid

1800 Bronson Boulevard, Fennimore, WI 53809

(608) 822-3262 ext. 2319

University of Wisconsin-Baraboo/Sauk County

Baraboo, Wisconsin

www.baraboo.uwc.edu

Federal Code: 003897

2-year public branch campus and liberal arts college in large town.

Enrollment: 520 undergrads.

BASIC COSTS (2007-2008)

Tuition and fees: $4,710; out-of-state residents $11,694.

Per-credit charge: $178; out-of-state residents $469.

Additional info: Minnesota reciprocity tuition: $164 per credit hour.

FINANCIAL AID PICTURE

Students with need: Need-based aid available for full-time and part-time students. Work study available nights.

Students without need: This college awards aid only to students with need.

Scholarships offered: Campus scholarships; $250 to full tuition.

FINANCIAL AID PROCEDURES

Forms required: FAFSA, institutional form.

Dates and Deadlines: Priority date 4/15; no closing date. Applicants notified on a rolling basis starting 4/15; must reply within 3 week(s) of notification.

Transfers: Must reply within 3 week(s) of notification.

CONTACT

Marilyn Krump, Director of Financial Aid

1006 Connie Road, Baraboo, WI 53913-1098

(608) 263-7727

University of Wisconsin-Eau Claire

Eau Claire, Wisconsin

www.uwec.edu

Federal Code: 003917

4-year public university in small city.

Enrollment: 9,947 undergrads, 5% part-time. 2,019 full-time freshmen.

Selectivity: Admits 50 to 75% of applicants.

BASIC COSTS (2007-2008)

Tuition and fees: $5,841; out-of-state residents $13,414.

Per-credit charge: $207; out-of-state residents $523.

Room and board: $5,150.

Additional info: Minnesota reciprocity tuition: $223 per credit hour.

FINANCIAL AID PICTURE (2006-2007)

Students with need: Out of 1,523 full-time freshmen who applied for aid, 834 were judged to have need. Of these, 825 received aid, and 635 had their full need met. Average financial aid package met 95% of need; average scholarship/grant was $4,444; average loan was $4,210. For part-time students, average financial aid package was $6,102.

Students without need: 356 full-time freshmen who did not demonstrate need for aid received scholarships/grants; average award was $1,666. No-need awards available for academics, art, leadership, minority status, music/drama, state/district residency.

Scholarships offered: Chancellor's Award; full in-state tuition for 1 year; 6 awards. Dean's Awards; $1,000; 20 awards. Wisconsin Academic Excellence Scholars; $2,250; for selected high school valedictorians; renewable. National Merit Scholarship finalists; full in-state fees; for top 25% of high school class with 25 ACT; some require 28-30 ACT.

Cumulative student debt: 65% of graduating class had student loans; average debt was $18,466.

FINANCIAL AID PROCEDURES

Forms required: FAFSA.

Dates and Deadlines: Priority date 4/15; no closing date. Applicants notified on a rolling basis starting 4/15.

CONTACT

Kathleen Sahlhoff, Director of Financial Aid

112 Schofield Hall, Eau Claire, WI 54701

(715) 836-3373

University of Wisconsin-Fond du Lac

Fond du Lac, Wisconsin

www.fdl.uwc.edu

Federal Code: 003897

2-year public junior college in large town.

Enrollment: 714 undergrads, 34% part-time. 181 full-time freshmen.

Selectivity: Admits over 75% of applicants.

BASIC COSTS (2007-2008)

Tuition and fees: $4,543; out-of-state residents $11,527.

Per-credit charge: $178; out-of-state residents $469.

Additional info: Minnesota reciprocity tuition: $164 per credit hour.

FINANCIAL AID PICTURE (2006-2007)

Students with need: 57% of average financial aid package awarded as scholarships/grants, 43% awarded as loans/jobs. Need-based aid available for part-time students.

Students without need: No-need awards available for academics, leadership, music/drama.

FINANCIAL AID PROCEDURES

Forms required: FAFSA.

Dates and Deadlines: Priority date 4/15; no closing date. Applicants notified on a rolling basis starting 6/1; must reply within 2 week(s) of notification.

CONTACT

Marilyn Krump, Director of Financial Aid

400 University Drive, Fond du Lac, WI 54935-2998

(920) 929-3600

University of Wisconsin-Fox Valley

Menasha, Wisconsin

www.uwfoxvalley.uwc.edu

Federal Code: 011459

2-year public liberal arts college in small city.

Enrollment: 1,747 undergrads.

BASIC COSTS (2007-2008)

Tuition and fees: $4,492; out-of-state residents $11,476.

Per-credit charge: $178; out-of-state residents $469.

Additional info: Minnesota reciprocity tuition: $164 per credit hour.

FINANCIAL AID PICTURE

Students with need: Need-based aid available for full-time and part-time students. Work study available nights, weekends, and for part-time students.

FINANCIAL AID PROCEDURES

Forms required: FAFSA.

Dates and Deadlines: Priority date 4/15; no closing date. Applicants notified on a rolling basis starting 6/1; must reply within 3 week(s) of notification.

CONTACT

Marilyn Krump, Director of Financial Aid

1478 Midway Road, Menasha, WI 54952-2850

University of Wisconsin-Green Bay

Green Bay, Wisconsin

www.uwgb.edu   Federal Code: 003899

4-year public university and liberal arts college in small city.

Enrollment: 5,546 undergrads, 17% part-time. 986 full-time freshmen.

Selectivity: Admits 50 to 75% of applicants.

BASIC COSTS (2007-2008)

Tuition and fees: $5,959; out-of-state residents $13,532.

Per-credit charge: $201; out-of-state residents $516.

Room and board: $5,200.

FINANCIAL AID PICTURE (2007-2008)

Students with need: Out of 848 full-time freshmen who applied for aid, 570 were judged to have need. Of these, 546 received aid, and 200 had their full need met. Average financial aid package met 77% of need; average scholarship/grant was $4,685; average loan was $3,526. For part-time students, average financial aid package was $8,737.

Students without need: 28 full-time freshmen who did not demonstrate need for aid received scholarships/grants; average award was $1,727. No-need awards available for academics, art, athletics, leadership, minority status, music/drama.

Scholarships offered: 23 full-time freshmen received athletic scholarships; average amount $8,051.

Cumulative student debt: 66% of graduating class had student loans; average debt was $16,114.

Additional info: Auditions required for music and theater scholarships. Tuition is waived for children of Wisconsin soldiers and policemen who were slain in the line of duty. Tuition is also waived for all veterans.

FINANCIAL AID PROCEDURES

Forms required: FAFSA.

Dates and Deadlines: Priority date 4/15; no closing date. Applicants notified on a rolling basis starting 11/1; must reply within 3 week(s) of notification.

CONTACT

Ron Ronnenberg, Director of Financial Aid and Student Employment

2420 Nicolet Drive, Green Bay, WI 54311-7001

(920) 465-2075

University of Wisconsin-La Crosse

La Crosse, Wisconsin

www.uwlax.edu   Federal Code: 003919

4-year public university in small city.

Enrollment: 8,358 undergrads, 4% part-time. 1,725 full-time freshmen.

Selectivity: Admits 50 to 75% of applicants.

BASIC COSTS (2007-2008)

Tuition and fees: $5,850; out-of-state residents $13,423.

Per-credit charge: $203; out-of-state residents $519.

Room and board: $5,130.

FINANCIAL AID PICTURE (2006-2007)

Students with need: Out of 1,333 full-time freshmen who applied for aid, 740 were judged to have need. Of these, 679 received aid, and 100 had their full need met. Average financial aid package met 70% of need; average scholarship/grant was $4,937; average loan was $2,753. For part-time students, average financial aid package was $6,130.

Students without need: 44 full-time freshmen who did not demonstrate need for aid received scholarships/grants; average award was $1,412. No-need awards available for academics, alumni affiliation, art, leadership, minority status, music/drama, ROTC.

Cumulative student debt: 62% of graduating class had student loans; average debt was $12,145.

FINANCIAL AID PROCEDURES

Forms required: FAFSA, institutional form.

Dates and Deadlines: Priority date 3/15; no closing date. Applicants notified on a rolling basis starting 3/10; must reply by 5/10 or within 3 week(s) of notification.

CONTACT

Louise Janke, Associate Director of Financial Aid

1725 State Street, Room 115 Main Hall, La Crosse, WI 54601

(608) 785-8604

University of Wisconsin-Madison

Madison, Wisconsin

www.wisc.edu   Federal Code: 003895

4-year public university in small city.

Enrollment: 28,999 undergrads, 5% part-time. 5,982 full-time freshmen.

Selectivity: Admits 50 to 75% of applicants.

BASIC COSTS (2007-2008)

Tuition and fees: $7,188; out-of-state residents $21,438.

Room and board: $7,390.

FINANCIAL AID PICTURE

Students with need: Need-based aid available for full-time and part-time students.

Students without need: No-need awards available for academics, alumni affiliation, art, athletics, job skills, leadership, minority status, music/drama, religious affiliation, ROTC, state/district residency.

FINANCIAL AID PROCEDURES

Forms required: FAFSA, institutional form.

Dates and Deadlines: No deadline. Applicants notified on a rolling basis starting 4/1; must reply within 9 week(s) of notification.

CONTACT

Susan Fischer, Director Student Financial Services

Armory & Gymnasium, Madison, WI 53706-1481

(608) 262-3060

University of Wisconsin-Manitowoc

Manitowoc, Wisconsin

www.manitowoc.uwc.edu   Federal Code: 003897

2-year public branch campus and liberal arts college in large town.

Enrollment: 530 undergrads, 26% part-time. 192 full-time freshmen.

BASIC COSTS (2007-2008)

Tuition and fees: $4,899; out-of-state residents $11,882.

FINANCIAL AID PICTURE

Students with need: Need-based aid available for full-time and part-time students. Work study available nights.

Students without need: This college awards aid only to students with need.

FINANCIAL AID PROCEDURES

Forms required: FAFSA, institutional form.

Dates and Deadlines: Priority date 3/1; no closing date. Applicants notified on a rolling basis starting 5/1; must reply within 2 week(s) of notification.

Transfers: Priority date 5/1; no deadline.

CONTACT

Christopher Lewis, Assistant Dean for Student Services

705 Viebahn Street, Manitowoc, WI 54220-6699

(920) 683-4707

University of Wisconsin-Marathon County

Wausau, Wisconsin

www.uwmc.uwc.edu   Federal Code: 003903

2-year public college in small city.

Enrollment: 1,380 undergrads.

BASIC COSTS (2007-2008)

Tuition and fees: $4,507; out-of-state residents $11,491.

Per-credit charge: $178; out-of-state residents $469.

Additional info: Minnesota reciprocity tuition: $164 per credit hour.

FINANCIAL AID PICTURE (2006-2007)

Students with need: Need-based aid available for full-time and part-time students. Work study available nights.

Students without need: This college awards aid only to students with need.

FINANCIAL AID PROCEDURES

Forms required: FAFSA, institutional form.

Dates and Deadlines: Priority date 4/15; no closing date. Applicants notified on a rolling basis starting 6/1; must reply within 3 week(s) of notification.

CONTACT

Marilyn Krump, Director of Financial Aid

518 South Seventh Avenue, Wausau, WI 54401-5396

(715) 261-6235

University of Wisconsin-Marinette

Marinette, Wisconsin

www.marinette.uwc.edu   Federal Code: 003897

2-year public branch campus and liberal arts college in large town.

Enrollment: 327 undergrads.

BASIC COSTS (2007-2008)

Tuition and fees: $4,490; out-of-state residents $11,474.

Per-credit charge: $178; out-of-state residents $469.

Additional info: Minnesota reciprocity tuition: $163.75 per credit hour.

FINANCIAL AID PICTURE

Students with need: Need-based aid available for full-time and part-time students. Work study available nights.

Students without need: This college awards aid only to students with need.

FINANCIAL AID PROCEDURES

Forms required: FAFSA.

Dates and Deadlines: Priority date 4/15; no closing date. Applicants notified on a rolling basis.

CONTACT

Cynthia Bailey, Assistant Campus Dean for Student Services

750 West Bay Shore Street, Marinette, WI 54143

(715) 735-4301

University of Wisconsin-Milwaukee

Milwaukee, Wisconsin

www.uwm.edu   Federal Code: 003896

4-year public university in very large city.

Enrollment: 22,937 undergrads, 13% part-time. 4,273 full-time freshmen.

Selectivity: Admits over 75% of applicants.

BASIC COSTS (2007-2008)

Tuition and fees: $6,958; out-of-state residents $16,686.

Per-credit charge: $258; out-of-state residents $663.

Room and board: $6,950.

FINANCIAL AID PICTURE (2007-2008)

Students with need: Out of 3,249 full-time freshmen who applied for aid, 2,503 were judged to have need. Of these, 2,415 received aid, and 574 had their full need met. Average financial aid package met 48% of need; average scholarship/grant was $5,479; average loan was $4,081. For part-time students, average financial aid package was $6,854.

Students without need: 32 full-time freshmen who did not demonstrate need for aid received scholarships/grants; average award was $2,421. No-need awards available for academics, art, athletics.

Scholarships offered: 3 full-time freshmen received athletic scholarships; average amount $933.

Cumulative student debt: 58% of graduating class had student loans; average debt was $12,639.

FINANCIAL AID PROCEDURES

Forms required: FAFSA.

Dates and Deadlines: Priority date 3/1; no closing date. Applicants notified on a rolling basis starting 3/1.

Transfers: No deadline. Applicants notified on a rolling basis starting 3/15; must reply within 2 week(s) of notification.

CONTACT

Jane Hojan-Clark, Executive Director of Financial Aid

Box 749, Milwaukee, WI 53201

(414) 229-6300

University of Wisconsin-Oshkosh

Oshkosh, Wisconsin

www.uwosh.edu   Federal Code: 003920

4-year public university in small city.

Enrollment: 9,844 undergrads, 12% part-time. 1,730 full-time freshmen.

Selectivity: Admits over 75% of applicants.

BASIC COSTS (2007-2008)

Tuition and fees: $5,689; out-of-state residents $13,262.

Per-credit charge: $205; out-of-state residents $521.

Room and board: $5,392.

Additional info: Minnesota reciprocity tuition: $223 per credit hour.

FINANCIAL AID PICTURE (2006-2007)

Students with need: Out of 1,125 full-time freshmen who applied for aid, 765 were judged to have need. Of these, 765 received aid. Average financial aid package met 40% of need; average scholarship/grant was $1,700; average loan was $3,000. For part-time students, average financial aid package was $2,500.

Students without need: 450 full-time freshmen who did not demonstrate need for aid received scholarships/grants; average award was $835. No-need awards available for academics, alumni affiliation, art, leadership, minority status, music/drama, state/district residency.

Cumulative student debt: 68% of graduating class had student loans; average debt was $18,000.

FINANCIAL AID PROCEDURES

Forms required: FAFSA.

Dates and Deadlines: Priority date 3/15; no closing date. Applicants notified on a rolling basis starting 4/15; must reply within 2 week(s) of notification.

Transfers: Must send financial aid transcript to university.

CONTACT

Beatrice Contreras, Director of Financial Aid
800 Algoma Boulevard, Oshkosh, WI 54901-8602
(920) 424-3377

University of Wisconsin-Parkside

Kenosha, Wisconsin
www.uwp.edu   Federal Code: 005015

4-year public university in small city.

Enrollment: 4,624 undergrads, 23% part-time. 831 full-time freshmen.

Selectivity: Admits over 75% of applicants.

BASIC COSTS (2007-2008)

Tuition and fees: $5,759; out-of-state residents $13,332.

Per-credit charge: $201; out-of-state residents $516.

Room and board: $5,890.

Additional info: Minnesota Reciprocity tuition and fees: $6,298 full-time; $223 per credit hour.

FINANCIAL AID PICTURE (2006-2007)

Students with need: 52% of average financial aid package awarded as scholarships/grants, 48% awarded as loans/jobs. Need-based aid available for part-time students. Work study available nights, weekends, and for part-time students.

Students without need: No-need awards available for academics, art, athletics, minority status, music/drama, state/district residency.

FINANCIAL AID PROCEDURES

Forms required: FAFSA.

Dates and Deadlines: Priority date 3/15; no closing date. Applicants notified on a rolling basis starting 4/1; must reply within 2 week(s) of notification.

CONTACT

Randall McCready, Director of Financial Aid
PO Box 2000, Kenosha, WI 53141-2000
(262) 595-2574

University of Wisconsin-Platteville

Platteville, Wisconsin
www.uwplatt.edu   Federal Code: 003921

4-year public university in large town.

Enrollment: 6,252 undergrads, 9% part-time. 1,462 full-time freshmen.

Selectivity: Admits over 75% of applicants.

BASIC COSTS (2007-2008)

Tuition and fees: $5,746; out-of-state residents $13,319.

Per-credit charge: $201; out-of-state residents $516.

Room and board: $5,420.

Additional info: Minnesota reciprocity tuition: $223 per credit hour.

FINANCIAL AID PICTURE

Students with need: Need-based aid available for full-time and part-time students. Work study available nights, weekends, and for part-time students.

Students without need: This college awards aid only to students with need.

FINANCIAL AID PROCEDURES

Forms required: FAFSA.

Dates and Deadlines: Priority date 3/15; no closing date. Applicants notified on a rolling basis starting 6/1; must reply within 2 week(s) of notification.

CONTACT

Liz Tucker, Director of Financial Aid
One University Plaza, Platteville, WI 53818
(608) 342-1836

University of Wisconsin-Richland

Richland Center, Wisconsin
www.richland.uwc.edu   Federal Code: 003897

2-year public liberal arts college in small town.

Enrollment: 452 undergrads.

BASIC COSTS (2007-2008)

Tuition and fees: $4,690; out-of-state residents $11,674.

Per-credit charge: $178; out-of-state residents $469.

Additional info: Minnesota reciprocity tuition: $164 per credit hour.

FINANCIAL AID PICTURE (2006-2007)

Students with need: 47% of average financial aid package awarded as scholarships/grants, 53% awarded as loans/jobs. Need-based aid available for part-time students. Work study available nights, weekends, and for part-time students.

Students without need: This college awards aid only to students with need.

Scholarships offered: Richland Campus Foundation Scholarships available for new, continuing and transfer students.

FINANCIAL AID PROCEDURES

Forms required: FAFSA.

Dates and Deadlines: Priority date 4/15; no closing date. Applicants notified on a rolling basis starting 5/15; must reply within 3 week(s) of notification.

CONTACT

John Poole, Assistant Campus Dean
1200 Highway 14 West, Richland Center, WI 53581
(608) 647-6186 ext. 3

University of Wisconsin-River Falls

River Falls, Wisconsin
www.uwrf.edu   Federal Code: 003923

4-year public university and liberal arts college in large town.

Enrollment: 6,007 undergrads. 1,287 full-time freshmen.

Selectivity: Admits over 75% of applicants.

BASIC COSTS (2007-2008)

Tuition and fees: $5,885; out-of-state residents $13,458.

Per-credit charge: $204; out-of-state residents $519.

Room and board: $4,964.

Additional info: Minnesota reciprocity tuition and fees: $6,660 full-time, $223 per credit hour.

FINANCIAL AID PICTURE

Students with need: Need-based aid available for full-time and part-time students. Work study available nights, weekends, and for part-time students.
Students without need: This college awards aid only to students with need.

FINANCIAL AID PROCEDURES

Forms required: FAFSA.
Dates and Deadlines: Priority date 3/15; no closing date. Applicants notified on a rolling basis starting 4/1; must reply within 4 week(s) of notification.
Transfers: No deadline. Applicants notified on a rolling basis starting 4/1.

CONTACT

Sandra Oftedahl, Director of Financial Aid
410 South 3rd Street, River Falls, WI 54022-5001
(715) 425-3141

University of Wisconsin-Rock County

Janesville, Wisconsin
www.rock.uwc.edu   Federal Code: 003897

2-year public branch campus and liberal arts college in small city.
Enrollment: 848 undergrads.
Selectivity: Admits over 75% of applicants.

BASIC COSTS (2007-2008)

Tuition and fees: $4,543; out-of-state residents $11,527.
Per-credit charge: $178; out-of-state residents $468.

FINANCIAL AID PICTURE

Students with need: Need-based aid available for full-time and part-time students. Work study available nights, weekends, and for part-time students.
Students without need: This college awards aid only to students with need.

FINANCIAL AID PROCEDURES

Forms required: FAFSA, institutional form.
Dates and Deadlines: Priority date 4/15; no closing date. Applicants notified on a rolling basis starting 6/1; must reply within 3 week(s) of notification.

CONTACT

Marilyn Krump, Director of Financial Aid
2909 Kellogg Avenue, Janesville, WI 53546-5699
(608) 758-6523

University of Wisconsin-Sheboygan

Sheboygan, Wisconsin
www.sheboygan.uwc.edu   Federal Code: 003897

2-year public community and junior college in small city.
Enrollment: 728 undergrads.

BASIC COSTS (2007-2008)

Tuition and fees: $4,535; out-of-state residents $11,519.
Per-credit charge: $178; out-of-state residents $469.

FINANCIAL AID PICTURE (2007-2008)

Students with need: 66% of average financial aid package awarded as scholarships/grants, 34% awarded as loans/jobs. Need-based aid available for part-time students.
Students without need: No-need awards available for academics, leadership, music/drama.
Additional info: Scholarship deadline 2/28.

FINANCIAL AID PROCEDURES

Forms required: FAFSA, institutional form.
Dates and Deadlines: Priority date 4/15; no closing date. Applicants notified on a rolling basis starting 6/1; must reply within 2 week(s) of notification.
Transfers: No deadline. Applicants notified on a rolling basis.

CONTACT

Marilyn Krump, Director of Financial Aid
One University Drive, Sheboygan, WI 53081
(920) 459-6633

University of Wisconsin-Stevens Point

Stevens Point, Wisconsin
www.uwsp.edu   Federal Code: 003924

4-year public university in large town.
Enrollment: 8,621 undergrads, 6% part-time. 1,632 full-time freshmen.
Selectivity: Admits 50 to 75% of applicants.

BASIC COSTS (2007-2008)

Tuition and fees: $5,834; out-of-state residents $13,407.
Per-credit charge: $201; out-of-state residents $516.
Room and board: $4,832.
Additional info: Minnesota reciprocity tuition and fees: $6,377 full-year or $223 per credit hour.

FINANCIAL AID PICTURE (2006-2007)

Students with need: Out of 1,390 full-time freshmen who applied for aid, 765 were judged to have need. Of these, 727 received aid, and 448 had their full need met. Average financial aid package met 96% of need; average scholarship/grant was $4,466; average loan was $3,215. For part-time students, average financial aid package was $5,596.
Students without need: 114 full-time freshmen who did not demonstrate need for aid received scholarships/grants; average award was $2,022. No-need awards available for academics, alumni affiliation, art, music/drama, ROTC.
Cumulative student debt: 71% of graduating class had student loans; average debt was $17,494.
Additional info: Tuition discounts offered to qualified residents from other states.

FINANCIAL AID PROCEDURES

Forms required: FAFSA.
Dates and Deadlines: Priority date 3/15; closing date 6/15. Applicants notified on a rolling basis starting 5/1; must reply within 4 week(s) of notification.
Transfers: No deadline.

CONTACT

Paul Watson, Director of Financial Aid
Student Services Center, Stevens Point, WI 54481
(715) 346-4771

University of Wisconsin-Stout

Menomonie, Wisconsin
www.uwstout.edu   Federal Code: 003915

4-year public university in large town.
Enrollment: 7,429 undergrads, 11% part-time. 1,476 full-time freshmen.
Selectivity: Admits over 75% of applicants.

BASIC COSTS (2007-2008)

Tuition and fees: $7,272; out-of-state residents $15,018.
Per-credit charge: $179; out-of-state residents $437.
Room and board: $4,994.
Additional info: Laptop computer included in the cost of tuition.

FINANCIAL AID PICTURE (2007-2008)

Students with need: Out of 1,175 full-time freshmen who applied for aid, 766 were judged to have need. Of these, 766 received aid, and 365 had their full need met. Average financial aid package met 86% of need; average scholarship/grant was $4,892; average loan was $4,169. For part-time students, average financial aid package was $7,372.

Students without need: 35 full-time freshmen who did not demonstrate need for aid received scholarships/grants; average award was $1,667. No-need awards available for academics.

Scholarships offered: Wisconsin Academic Excellence Scholarship: $2,250; selected by high school. National Merit Finalist Scholarship: $2,000; automatically awarded to NMSQT finalist. National Merit Semifinalist Scholarship: $1,000; automatically awarded to NMSQT semifinalist. Chancellor's Academic Honor Scholarship: $1,000; automatically awarded to top 5% of high school class with ACT of 25 who enroll by July 15th.

Cumulative student debt: 73% of graduating class had student loans; average debt was $23,825.

FINANCIAL AID PROCEDURES

Forms required: FAFSA.

Dates and Deadlines: Priority date 3/15; no closing date. Applicants notified on a rolling basis starting 4/1; must reply within 4 week(s) of notification.

CONTACT

Beth Boisen, Director of Financial Aid

1 Clocktower Plaza, Menomonie, WI 54751

(715) 232-1363

University of Wisconsin-Superior

Superior, Wisconsin

www.uwsuper.edu   Federal Code: 003925

4-year public university and liberal arts college in large town.

Enrollment: 2,450 undergrads, 17% part-time. 343 full-time freshmen.

Selectivity: Admits 50 to 75% of applicants.

BASIC COSTS (2007-2008)

Tuition and fees: $5,907; out-of-state residents $13,480.

Per-credit charge: $207; out-of-state residents $523.

Room and board: $4,720.

Additional info: Minnesota reciprocity tuition: $223 per credit hour.

FINANCIAL AID PICTURE (2007-2008)

Students with need: Out of 252 full-time freshmen who applied for aid, 199 were judged to have need. Of these, 194 received aid, and 64 had their full need met. For part-time students, average financial aid package was $7,135.

Students without need: 15 full-time freshmen who did not demonstrate need for aid received scholarships/grants; average award was $3,197. No-need awards available for academics, alumni affiliation, art, leadership, minority status, music/drama, ROTC, state/district residency.

Additional info: Tuition Assistance Program (TAP) available to non-resident students on limited basis.

FINANCIAL AID PROCEDURES

Forms required: FAFSA.

Dates and Deadlines: Priority date 4/1; no closing date. Applicants notified on a rolling basis starting 3/15; must reply by 5/1 or within 4 week(s) of notification.

Transfers: No deadline. Applicants notified on a rolling basis starting 3/15; must reply by 5/1 or within 4 week(s) of notification.

CONTACT

Anne Podgorak, Director of Financial Aid

Belknap and Catlin, PO Box 2000, Superior, WI 54880

(715) 394-8200

University of Wisconsin-Washington County

West Bend, Wisconsin

washington.uwc.edu   Federal Code: 003897

2-year public branch campus and liberal arts college in large town.

Enrollment: 917 undergrads, 30% part-time.

Selectivity: Open admission.

BASIC COSTS (2007-2008)

Tuition and fees: $4,528; out-of-state residents $11,512.

Per-credit charge: $178; out-of-state residents $469.

FINANCIAL AID PICTURE

Students with need: Need-based aid available for full-time and part-time students. Work study available weekends and for part-time students.

Students without need: No-need awards available for academics.

FINANCIAL AID PROCEDURES

Forms required: FAFSA.

Dates and Deadlines: Priority date 4/15; no closing date. Applicants notified on a rolling basis starting 4/30; must reply within 3 week(s) of notification.

Transfers: No deadline.

CONTACT

Marilyn Krump, Director of Financial Aid

400 University Drive, West Bend, WI 53095

(262) 335-5207

University of Wisconsin-Waukesha

Waukesha, Wisconsin

www.waukesha.uwc.edu   Federal Code: 003897

2-year public branch campus and junior college in small city.

Enrollment: 1,777 undergrads, 35% part-time. 840 full-time freshmen.

BASIC COSTS (2007-2008)

Tuition and fees: $4,507; out-of-state residents $11,491.

Per-credit charge: $178; out-of-state residents $469.

Additional info: Minnesota reciprocity tuition: $175 per credit hour.

FINANCIAL AID PICTURE

Students with need: Need-based aid available for full-time and part-time students. Work study available nights, weekends, and for part-time students.

Students without need: No-need awards available for academics, art, leadership, minority status, music/drama.

Scholarships offered: University of Wisconsin-Waukesha Scholarship Program; numerous scholarships; amounts vary.

FINANCIAL AID PROCEDURES

Forms required: FAFSA.

Dates and Deadlines: Priority date 4/15; no closing date. Applicants notified on a rolling basis starting 5/15; must reply within 3 week(s) of notification.

CONTACT

Judy Becker, Coordinator of Financial Aid

1500 University Drive, Waukesha, WI 53188

(262) 521-5210

University of Wisconsin-Whitewater

Whitewater, Wisconsin

www.uww.edu   Federal Code: 003926

4-year public university in large town.

Enrollment: 9,180 undergrads, 8% part-time. 2,007 full-time freshmen.

Selectivity: Admits over 75% of applicants.

BASIC COSTS (2007-2008)
Tuition and fees: $5,858; out-of-state residents $13,431.
Room and board: $4,474.

FINANCIAL AID PICTURE
Students with need: Need-based aid available for full-time and part-time students. Work study available nights, weekends, and for part-time students.
Students without need: No-need awards available for academics, alumni affiliation, art, leadership, minority status, music/drama, ROTC, state/district residency.

FINANCIAL AID PROCEDURES
Forms required: FAFSA.
Dates and Deadlines: Priority date 3/15; no closing date. Applicants notified on a rolling basis starting 4/1; must reply within 3 week(s) of notification.
Transfers: No deadline. Applicants notified on a rolling basis starting 4/1; must reply within 3 week(s) of notification.

CONTACT
Carol Miller, Director of Financial Aid
800 West Main Street, Whitewater, WI 53190-1790
(262) 472-1130

Viterbo University
La Crosse, Wisconsin
www.viterbo.edu
Federal Code: 003911

4-year private university and liberal arts college in small city, affiliated with Roman Catholic Church.
Enrollment: 1,922 undergrads, 22% part-time. 362 full-time freshmen.
Selectivity: Admits over 75% of applicants.

BASIC COSTS (2008-2009)
Tuition and fees: $19,490.
Per-credit charge: $560.
Room and board: $6,380.
Additional info: Additional fees for some art, dietetics, science courses, and nursing clinicals. Tuition/fee waivers available for minority students.

FINANCIAL AID PICTURE
Students with need: Need-based aid available for full-time and part-time students. Work study available nights, weekends, and for part-time students.
Students without need: No-need awards available for academics, alumni affiliation, art, athletics, leadership, minority status, music/drama, ROTC.
Scholarships offered: Fine arts scholarships: up to $10,000 per year; for incoming full-time freshmen and transfer students talented in areas of art, music or theater. Dr. Scholl Scholarship: full, 4-year tuition; must enroll full-time and maintain 3.5 GPA, 1 awarded. Viterbo University Scholarship: $1,000-$8,000 per year; based on academic history; incoming freshmen and transfers automatically considered; renewable.

FINANCIAL AID PROCEDURES
Forms required: FAFSA, institutional form.
Dates and Deadlines: Priority date 3/15; no closing date. Applicants notified on a rolling basis starting 4/1; must reply within 3 week(s) of notification.

CONTACT
Terry Norman, Director of Financial Aid
900 Viterbo Drive, La Crosse, WI 54601-8804
(608) 796-3900

Waukesha County Technical College
Pewaukee, Wisconsin
www.wctc.edu
Federal Code: 005294

2-year public technical college in large town.
Enrollment: 5,047 undergrads, 63% part-time. 468 full-time freshmen.
Selectivity: Open admission; but selective for some programs.

BASIC COSTS (2007-2008)
Tuition and fees: $3,047; out-of-state residents $17,402.
Per-credit charge: $92; out-of-state residents $571.
Additional info: Materials fees vary by program; minimum $4 per course. $10 per credit fee for online courses.

FINANCIAL AID PICTURE
Students with need: Need-based aid available for full-time students. Work study available nights.
Students without need: No-need awards available for academics.

FINANCIAL AID PROCEDURES
Forms required: FAFSA, institutional form.
Dates and Deadlines: Priority date 3/31; no closing date. Applicants notified on a rolling basis.

CONTACT
Ben Dobner, Manager/Financial Aid
800 Main Street, Pewaukee, WI 53072
(262) 691-5436

Western Technical College
La Crosse, Wisconsin
www.westerntc.edu
Federal Code: 003840

2-year public community and technical college in small city.
Enrollment: 4,564 undergrads.
Selectivity: Open admission; but selective for some programs.

BASIC COSTS (2007-2008)
Tuition and fees: $2,998; out-of-state residents $17,353.
Per-credit charge: $92; out-of-state residents $571.
Room and board: $3,820.
Additional info: Materials fees vary by program; minimum $4 per course. Tuition/fee waivers available for unemployed or children of unemployed.

FINANCIAL AID PICTURE
Students with need: Need-based aid available for full-time and part-time students. Work study available nights, weekends, and for part-time students.

FINANCIAL AID PROCEDURES
Forms required: FAFSA, institutional form.
Dates and Deadlines: Priority date 3/1; no closing date. Applicants notified on a rolling basis starting 4/1.

CONTACT
Judith Erickson, Student Financial Services Manager
PO Box 908, La Crosse, WI 54602-0908
(608) 785-9302

Wisconsin Indianhead Technical College
Shell Lake, Wisconsin
www.witc.edu
Federal Code: 011824

2-year public technical college in rural community.
Enrollment: 3,106 undergrads, 51% part-time. 438 full-time freshmen.
Selectivity: Open admission; but selective for some programs.

BASIC COSTS (2007-2008)

Tuition and fees: $3,037; out-of-state residents $17,392.

Per-credit charge: $92; out-of-state residents $571.

Additional info: Materials fees vary by program; minimum $4 per course. $10 per credit fee for online courses.

FINANCIAL AID PICTURE (2006-2007)

Students with need: 49% of average financial aid package awarded as scholarships/grants, 51% awarded as loans/jobs. Need-based aid available for part-time students. Work study available nights, weekends, and for part-time students.

Students without need: This college awards aid only to students with need.

FINANCIAL AID PROCEDURES

Forms required: FAFSA.

Dates and Deadlines: Priority date 4/1; no closing date. Applicants notified on a rolling basis starting 5/9; must reply by 9/1 or within 4 week(s) of notification.

CONTACT

Shane Evenson, Director of Financial Aid

505 Pine Ridge Drive, Shell Lake, WI 54871

(715) 468-2815 ext. 2246

Wisconsin Lutheran College

Milwaukee, Wisconsin

www.wlc.edu   Federal Code: 014658

4-year private liberal arts college in very large city, affiliated with Wisconsin Evangelical Lutheran Synod.

Enrollment: 692 undergrads.

BASIC COSTS (2007-2008)

Tuition and fees: $19,564.

Per-credit charge: $550.

Room and board: $6,910.

FINANCIAL AID PICTURE

Students with need: Need-based aid available for full-time and part-time students. Work study available nights, weekends, and for part-time students.

Students without need: No-need awards available for academics, art, leadership, minority status, music/drama, state/district residency.

Scholarships offered: Presidential Scholarship: $8,000 ($9,000 if ACT is 30 or greater); based on ACT score of 27 or higher plus top 10% of HS class or 3.7 GPA; no limit on number of awards. Academic Scholarship: $7,500; ACT score of 24 or higher and top 25% of high school class or 3.4 GPA. To qualify, students must be admitted in good standing by May 1.

FINANCIAL AID PROCEDURES

Forms required: FAFSA, institutional form.

Dates and Deadlines: Priority date 3/1; no closing date. Applicants notified on a rolling basis starting 3/15; must reply within 2 week(s) of notification.

Transfers: Transfer scholarship and transfer grant available for qualifying students.

CONTACT

Linda Loeffel, Director of Financial Aid

8800 West Bluemound Road, Milwaukee, WI 53226-4699

(414) 443-8856

Wyoming

Casper College

Casper, Wyoming

www.caspercollege.edu   Federal Code: 003928

2-year public community college in small city.

Enrollment: 2,875 undergrads, 36% part-time. 598 full-time freshmen.

Selectivity: Open admission; but selective for some programs and for out-of-state students.

BASIC COSTS (2007-2008)

Tuition and fees: $1,668; out-of-state residents $4,644.

Per-credit charge: $63; out-of-state residents $187.

Room and board: $3,830.

Additional info: Western Undergraduate Exchange students pay $93.50 per credit-hour and $2244 per year for full-time students.

FINANCIAL AID PICTURE

Students with need: Need-based aid available for full-time and part-time students. Work study available nights, weekends, and for part-time students.

Students without need: No-need awards available for academics, art, athletics, leadership, music/drama, state/district residency.

FINANCIAL AID PROCEDURES

Forms required: FAFSA.

Dates and Deadlines: Priority date 3/15; no closing date. Applicants notified on a rolling basis starting 4/1.

Transfers: No deadline. Applicants notified on a rolling basis starting 4/1.

CONTACT

Darry Voigt, Director of Financial Aid

125 College Drive, Casper, WY 82601

(307) 268-2510

Central Wyoming College

Riverton, Wyoming

www.cwc.edu   Federal Code: 005018

2-year public community college in large town.

Enrollment: 1,155 undergrads, 43% part-time. 229 full-time freshmen.

Selectivity: Open admission; but selective for some programs.

BASIC COSTS (2007-2008)

Tuition and fees: $1,992; out-of-state residents $4,968.

Per-credit charge: $62; out-of-state residents $186.

Room and board: $3,100.

Additional info: Western Undergraduate Exchange students pay $2,232 or $93 per credit hour.

FINANCIAL AID PICTURE (2007-2008)

Students with need: Out of 133 full-time freshmen who applied for aid, 101 were judged to have need. Of these, 101 received aid. Need-based aid available for part-time students.

Students without need: No-need awards available for academics, alumni affiliation, art, athletics, leadership, minority status, music/drama, state/district residency.

Scholarships offered: Honors Scholarships: in-state tuition and general fees plus $300 book stipend; for graduating high school seniors with minimum 3.5 GPA or 25 ACT. Seniors Scholarships: in-state tuition; for graduating high school seniors with 3.0-3.49 GPA or 22 ACT. Full academic scholarships: in-state tuition, general fees, room and board, books and supplies; for Wyoming National Merit finalists.

Cumulative student debt: 30% of graduating class had student loans; average debt was $6,625.

FINANCIAL AID PROCEDURES

Forms required: FAFSA, institutional form.
Dates and Deadlines: Priority date 4/15; no closing date. Applicants notified on a rolling basis starting 5/1; must reply within 2 week(s) of notification.

CONTACT

Jacque Burns, Director of Financial Aid
2660 Peck Avenue, Riverton, WY 82501
(307) 855-2150

Eastern Wyoming College

Torrington, Wyoming
ewc.wy.edu
Federal Code: 003929

2-year public community college in small town.
Enrollment: 618 undergrads, 30% part-time. 188 full-time freshmen.
Selectivity: Open admission.

BASIC COSTS (2007-2008)

Tuition and fees: $1,968; out-of-state residents $4,944.
Per-credit charge: $62; out-of-state residents $186.
Room and board: $3,594.
Additional info: Students from Western Undergraduate Exchange pay $2,232 tuition plus fees per year; $93 per credit hour.

FINANCIAL AID PICTURE

Students with need: Need-based aid available for full-time and part-time students. Work study available nights, weekends, and for part-time students.
Students without need: No-need awards available for academics, alumni affiliation, art, athletics, leadership, music/drama.
Additional info: Installment payment plan on room and board contracts offered.

FINANCIAL AID PROCEDURES

Forms required: FAFSA, institutional form.
Dates and Deadlines: Priority date 3/15; no closing date. Applicants notified on a rolling basis starting 1/1.

CONTACT

Pam Palermo, Financial Aid Director
3200 West C Street, Torrington, WY 82240
(800) 658-3195 ext. 8325

Laramie County Community College

Cheyenne, Wyoming
www.lccc.wy.edu
Federal Code: 009259

2-year public community college in small city.
Enrollment: 2,931 undergrads, 42% part-time. 286 full-time freshmen.
Selectivity: Open admission; but selective for some programs.

BASIC COSTS (2007-2008)

Tuition and fees: $2,088; out-of-state residents $5,064.
Per-credit charge: $62; out-of-state residents $186.
Room and board: $5,472.
Additional info: Students from Western Undergraduate Exchange schools and Nebraska residents pay $2,832 in tuition and fees per year; $118 per credit hour.

FINANCIAL AID PICTURE (2007-2008)

Students with need: Need-based aid available for part-time students.
Students without need: No-need awards available for academics, art, athletics, music/drama.

FINANCIAL AID PROCEDURES

Forms required: FAFSA, institutional form.
Dates and Deadlines: Priority date 4/1; no closing date. Applicants notified on a rolling basis starting 6/1; must reply within 2 week(s) of notification.

CONTACT

Dennis Schroeder, Director of Financial Aid
1400 East College Drive, Cheyenne, WY 82007-3299
(307) 778-1215

Northwest College

Powell, Wyoming
www.northwestcollege.edu
Federal Code: 003931

2-year public community college in small town.
Enrollment: 1,765 undergrads.
Selectivity: Open admission; but selective for some programs and for out-of-state students.

BASIC COSTS (2007-2008)

Tuition and fees: $2,022; out-of-state residents $4,998.
Per-credit charge: $62; out-of-state residents $186.
Room and board: $3,488.
Additional info: Students from Western Undergraduate Exchange schools pay $2,232 tuition; $93 per credit hour.

FINANCIAL AID PICTURE

Students with need: Work study available nights.
Students without need: No-need awards available for academics, athletics.
Additional info: Interview, essay recommended for scholarships.

FINANCIAL AID PROCEDURES

Forms required: FAFSA, institutional form.
Dates and Deadlines: Priority date 5/1; no closing date. Applicants notified on a rolling basis starting 5/1; must reply within 2 week(s) of notification.

CONTACT

Beverly Bell, Director of Financial Aid
231 West 6th Street, Powell, WY 82435
(307) 754-6104

Sheridan College

Sheridan, Wyoming
www.sheridan.edu
Federal Code: 003930

2-year public community college in large town.
Enrollment: 1,518 undergrads, 35% part-time. 300 full-time freshmen.
Selectivity: Open admission; but selective for some programs.

BASIC COSTS (2007-2008)

Tuition and fees: $2,016; out-of-state residents $4,992.
Per-credit charge: $62; out-of-state residents $186.
Room and board: $3,920.

FINANCIAL AID PICTURE (2006-2007)

Students with need: 64% of average financial aid package awarded as scholarships/grants, 36% awarded as loans/jobs. Need-based aid available for part-time students. Work study available nights, weekends, and for part-time students.
Students without need: No-need awards available for academics, art, athletics, leadership, music/drama, state/district residency.
Scholarships offered: Merit scholarships; in-state tuition and fees; must have 25 ACT or 1120 SAT (exclusive of Writing); renewable.

FINANCIAL AID PROCEDURES

Forms required: FAFSA, institutional form.

Dates and Deadlines: Priority date 3/1; no closing date. Applicants notified on a rolling basis; must reply within 3 week(s) of notification.

CONTACT

Randy Thompson, Director of Financial Aid
PO Box 1500, Sheridan, WY 82801-1500
(307) 674-6446 ext. 2100

University of Wyoming

Laramie, Wyoming
www.uwyo.edu   Federal Code: 003932

4-year public university in large town.
Enrollment: 9,140 undergrads, 15% part-time. 1,553 full-time freshmen.
Selectivity: Admits over 75% of applicants.

BASIC COSTS (2007-2008)

Tuition and fees: $3,554; out-of-state residents $10,394.
Per-credit charge: $94; out-of-state residents $322.
Room and board: $7,274.
Additional info: International students must pay an additional $35 fee per semester.

FINANCIAL AID PICTURE (2006-2007)

Students with need: Out of 1,233 full-time freshmen who applied for aid, 706 were judged to have need. Of these, 695 received aid, and 197 had their full need met. Average financial aid package met 66% of need; average scholarship/grant was $3,001; average loan was $2,810. For part-time students, average financial aid package was $5,899.
Students without need: 324 full-time freshmen who did not demonstrate need for aid received scholarships/grants; average award was $4,062. No-need awards available for alumni affiliation, art, athletics, leadership, music/drama, ROTC, state/district residency.
Scholarships offered: *Merit:* Western Heritage Scholarship: number awarded and packages vary. President's High School Honor Scholarship: covers undergraduate fees and tuition; number awarded varies. *Athletic:* 85 full-time freshmen received athletic scholarships; average amount $6,925.
Cumulative student debt: 49% of graduating class had student loans; average debt was $16,005.

FINANCIAL AID PROCEDURES

Forms required: FAFSA.
Dates and Deadlines: Priority date 3/1; no closing date. Applicants notified on a rolling basis starting 3/1.

CONTACT

David Gruen, Director of Student Financial Aid
1000 East University Avenue/Department 3435, Laramie, WY 82071
(307) 766-2116

Western Wyoming Community College

Rock Springs, Wyoming
www.wwcc.wy.edu   Federal Code: 003933

2-year public community college in large town.
Enrollment: 2,139 undergrads, 54% part-time. 231 full-time freshmen.
Selectivity: Open admission; but selective for some programs.

BASIC COSTS (2007-2008)

Tuition and fees: $1,828; out-of-state residents $4,804.
Per-credit charge: $59; out-of-state residents $178.
Room and board: $3,610.

FINANCIAL AID PICTURE (2007-2008)

Students with need: Need-based aid available for part-time students.

Students without need: No-need awards available for academics, art, athletics, music/drama, state/district residency.

FINANCIAL AID PROCEDURES

Forms required: FAFSA.
Dates and Deadlines: Priority date 4/1; no closing date. Applicants notified on a rolling basis starting 3/15; must reply within 2 week(s) of notification.

CONTACT

Stacee Hanson, Financial Aid Director
Box 428, Rock Springs, WY 82902-0428
(307) 382-1643

Part IV

Scholarship Lists

Academic scholarships

Alabama
Alabama State University
Amridge University
Athens State University
Auburn University at Montgomery
Bevill State Community College
Birmingham-Southern College
Bishop State Community College
Calhoun Community College
Central Alabama Community College
Chattahoochee Valley Community College
Faulkner University
Gadsden State Community College
George C. Wallace State Community College
    George C. Wallace Community College at
      Dothan
Huntingdon College
J. F. Drake State Technical College
Jacksonville State University
Jefferson Davis Community College
Jefferson State Community College
Judson College
Lurleen B. Wallace Community College
Marion Military Institute
Northeast Alabama Community College
Northwest-Shoals Community College
Oakwood University
Samford University
Snead State Community College
Southeastern Bible College
Spring Hill College
Stillman College
Troy University
Tuskegee University
University of Alabama
University of Alabama
    Birmingham
    Huntsville
University of Mobile
University of Montevallo
University of North Alabama
University of South Alabama
University of West Alabama

Alaska
Alaska Bible College
Alaska Pacific University
University of Alaska
    Anchorage
    Fairbanks
    Southeast

Arizona
Arizona State University
Arizona State University West
Arizona Western College
Cochise College
DeVry University
    Phoenix
Dine College
Eastern Arizona College
Embry-Riddle Aeronautical University: Prescott
    Campus
Grand Canyon University
Mesa Community College
Northern Arizona University
Northland Pioneer College
Pima Community College
Prescott College
Scottsdale Community College
South Mountain Community College
Southwestern College
University of Arizona
Yavapai College

Arkansas
Arkansas Northeastern College
Arkansas State University
Arkansas State University
    Beebe
    Mountain Home
Arkansas Tech University
Central Baptist College
Crowley's Ridge College
Ecclesia College
Harding University
Henderson State University
Hendrix College
John Brown University
Lyon College
Mid-South Community College
National Park Community College
North Arkansas College
Northwest Arkansas Community College
Ouachita Baptist University
Philander Smith College
Phillips Community College of the University of
    Arkansas
Rich Mountain Community College
Southeast Arkansas College
Southern Arkansas University
Southern Arkansas University Tech
University of Arkansas
University of Arkansas
    Community College at Hope
    Fort Smith
    Monticello
    Pine Bluff
University of Arkansas Community College at
    Morrilton
University of Central Arkansas
University of the Ozarks
Williams Baptist College

California
Academy of Art University
Alliant International University
American Academy of Dramatic Arts: West
American Jewish University
Art Institute
    of California: Los Angeles
    of California: Orange County
Azusa Pacific University
Bethany University
Bethesda Christian University
Biola University
Brooks College
California Baptist University
California College of the Arts
California Institute of Technology
California Institute of the Arts
California Lutheran University
California Maritime Academy
California Polytechnic State University: San Luis
    Obispo
California State Polytechnic University: Pomona
California State University
    Chico
    Dominguez Hills
    Fresno
    Fullerton
    Long Beach
    Monterey Bay
    Northridge
    San Marcos
    Stanislaus

Chaffey College
Chapman University
Claremont McKenna College
Cogswell Polytechnical College
College of the Canyons
College of the Siskiyous
Columbia College
Concordia University
Deep Springs College
    Fremont
    Long Beach
    Pomona
    Sherman Oaks
Dominican School of Philosophy and Theology
Dominican University of California
East Los Angeles College
El Camino College
Empire College
Fashion Institute of Design and Merchandising
    Los Angeles
    San Diego
    San Francisco
Fresno Pacific University
Glendale Community College
Golden Gate University
Golden West College
Harvey Mudd College
Holy Names University
Hope International University
Humboldt State University
Humphreys College
The King's College and Seminary
La Sierra University
Life Pacific College
Loyola Marymount University
Marymount College
The Master's College
Mendocino College
Menlo College
Merced College
Mills College
Mount St. Mary's College
Mount San Jacinto College
National Hispanic University
NewSchool of Architecture & Design
Notre Dame de Namur University
Occidental College
Ohlone College
Orange Coast College
Otis College of Art and Design
Pacific States University
Patten University
Pepperdine University
Pitzer College
Riverside Community College
St. Mary's College of California
Samuel Merritt University
San Diego Christian College
San Diego State University
San Francisco Art Institute
San Francisco State University
San Joaquin Delta College
San Jose State University
Santa Clara University
Santa Rosa Junior College
School of Urban Missions: Oakland
Scripps College
Simpson University
Soka University of America
Sonoma State University
Southern California Institute of Architecture
Taft College
University of California
    Berkeley
    Irvine
    Los Angeles
    Riverside
    San Diego
    Santa Barbara
    Santa Cruz
University of California: Merced
University of La Verne

University of Redlands
University of San Diego
University of San Francisco
University of Southern California
University of the Pacific
Vanguard University of Southern California
Westmont College
Westwood College of Technology
    Westwood College: Inland Empire
Whittier College
William Jessup University
Woodbury University
Yuba Community College District

Colorado
Adams State College
Arapahoe Community College
Colorado Christian University
Colorado College
Colorado Mountain College
Colorado Northwestern Community College
Colorado School of Mines
Colorado State University
Colorado State University
    Pueblo
Colorado Technical University
Community College of Denver
    Westminster
Fort Lewis College
Front Range Community College
Johnson & Wales University: Denver
Mesa State College
Metropolitan State College of Denver
Northeastern Junior College
Otero Junior College
Pueblo Community College
Regis University
Remington College
    Colorado Springs
Rocky Mountain College of Art & Design
Trinidad State Junior College
University of Colorado
    Boulder
    Colorado Springs
    Denver
University of Denver
University of Northern Colorado
Western State College of Colorado

Connecticut
Albertus Magnus College
Briarwood College
Central Connecticut State University
Clemens College
Eastern Connecticut State University
Fairfield University
Housatonic Community College
Lyme Academy College of Fine Arts
Mitchell College
Northwestern Connecticut Community College
Norwalk Community College
Quinnipiac University
Sacred Heart University
St. Joseph College
Southern Connecticut State University
Trinity College
Tunxis Community College
University of Bridgeport
University of Connecticut
University of Hartford
University of New Haven
Western Connecticut State University

Delaware
Delaware State University
Goldey-Beacom College
University of Delaware
Wesley College
Wilmington University

District of Columbia
American University
Catholic University of America

Corcoran College of Art and Design
Gallaudet University
George Washington University
Howard University
Southeastern University
Trinity Washington University

Florida
Art Institute of Fort Lauderdale
Baptist College of Florida
Barry University
Beacon College
Bethune-Cookman University
Brevard Community College
Broward Community College
Carlos Albizu University
Central Florida Community College
Chipola Junior College
Clearwater Christian College
    Miramar
    Orlando
Eckerd College
Embry-Riddle Aeronautical University
Embry-Riddle Aeronautical University:
    Worldwide Campus
Flagler College
Florida Agricultural and Mechanical University
Florida Atlantic University
Florida Christian College
Florida College
Florida Community College at Jacksonville
Florida Gulf Coast University
Florida Institute of Technology
Florida International University
Florida Keys Community College
Florida Southern College
Florida State University
Gulf Coast Community College
Hobe Sound Bible College
Hodges University
Indian River Community College
International Academy of Design and
    Technology: Tampa
Jacksonville University
Johnson & Wales University: North Miami
Jones College
Lake City Community College
Lake-Sumter Community College
Lynn University
Manatee Community College
Miami Dade College
New College of Florida
North Florida Community College
Northwood University
    Florida
Nova Southeastern University
Okaloosa-Walton College
Palm Beach Atlantic University
Palm Beach Community College
Pasco-Hernando Community College
Pensacola Junior College
Polk Community College
Ringling College of Art and Design
Rollins College
St. Leo University
St. Petersburg College
Saint Thomas University
Santa Fe Community College
Schiller International University
Seminole Community College
South Florida Community College
South University: West Palm Beach Campus
Southeastern University
Stetson University
Tallahassee Community College
Trinity College of Florida
University of Central Florida
University of Florida
University of Miami
University of North Florida
University of South Florida
University of Tampa

University of West Florida
Warner Southern College
Webber International University

Georgia
Agnes Scott College
Albany State University
Albany Technical College
Andrew College
Armstrong Atlantic State University
    of Atlanta
Athens Technical College
Augusta State University
Berry College
Brenau University
Brewton-Parker College
Clark Atlanta University
Clayton State University
Coastal Georgia Community College
Columbus State University
Covenant College
Dalton State College
Darton College
    Alpharetta
    Decatur
East Georgia College
Emmanuel College
Emory University
Fort Valley State University
Gainesville State College
Georgia College and State University
Georgia Highlands College
Georgia Institute of Technology
Georgia Southern University
Georgia Southwestern State University
Georgia State University
Gordon College
Herzing College
Kennesaw State University
LaGrange College
Macon State College
Medical College of Georgia
Mercer University
Middle Georgia College
Morehouse College
North Georgia College & State University
Oglethorpe University
Oxford College of Emory University
Paine College
Piedmont College
Reinhardt College
Savannah College of Art and Design
Savannah River College
Savannah State University
Savannah Technical College
Shorter College
South Georgia College
Southern Polytechnic State University
Spelman College
Thomas University
Toccoa Falls College
Truett-McConnell College
University of Georgia
University of West Georgia
Valdosta State University
Waycross College
Wesleyan College
Young Harris College

Hawaii
Brigham Young University-Hawaii
Chaminade University of Honolulu
Hawaii Pacific University
Hawaii Tokai International College
University of Hawaii
    Honolulu Community College
    Manoa
    West Oahu

Idaho
Boise Bible College
Boise State University

Brigham Young University-Idaho
College of Idaho
Eastern Idaho Technical College
Idaho State University
Lewis-Clark State College
North Idaho College
Northwest Nazarene University
University of Idaho

Illinois
Augustana College
Aurora University
Benedictine University
Black Hawk College
Blackburn College
Bradley University
Carl Sandburg College
Chicago State University
City Colleges of Chicago
    Kennedy-King College
    Malcolm X College
College of DuPage
College of Lake County
Columbia College Chicago
Concordia University
Danville Area Community College
DePaul University
    Addison
    Chicago
    Tinley Park
DeVry University: Online
Dominican University
East-West University
Eastern Illinois University
Elgin Community College
Elmhurst College
Eureka College
Governors State University
Greenville College
Harper College
Heartland Community College
Highland Community College
Illinois College
Illinois Eastern Community Colleges
    Frontier Community College
    Lincoln Trail College
    Olney Central College
    Wabash Valley College
Illinois Institute of Art: Schaumburg
Illinois Institute of Technology
Illinois State University
Illinois Wesleyan University
Joliet Junior College
Judson University
Kaskaskia College
Kishwaukee College
Knox College
Lake Forest College
Lake Land College
Lewis University
Lexington College
Lincoln Christian College and Seminary
Lincoln College
Lincoln Land Community College
Loyola University Chicago
MacCormac College
MacMurray College
McHenry County College
McKendree University
Millikin University
Monmouth College
Moody Bible Institute
Moraine Valley Community College
Morrison Institute of Technology
National-Louis University
North Central College
North Park University
Northeastern Illinois University
Northern Illinois University
Northwestern Business College
Oakton Community College
Olivet Nazarene University

Parkland College
Principia College
Quincy University
Rend Lake College
Richland Community College
Robert Morris College: Chicago
Rock Valley College
Rockford College
Roosevelt University
St. Francis Medical Center College of Nursing
St. Xavier University
Sauk Valley Community College
School of the Art Institute of Chicago
Shimer College
South Suburban College of Cook County
Southeastern Illinois College
Southern Illinois University Carbondale
Southern Illinois University Edwardsville
Spoon River College
Springfield College in Illinois
Trinity Christian College
Trinity International University
Triton College
University of Chicago
University of Illinois
    Chicago
    Springfield
    Urbana-Champaign
University of St. Francis
VanderCook College of Music
Waubonsee Community College
West Suburban College of Nursing
Western Illinois University
Western Illinois University: Quad Cities
Wheaton College

Indiana
Ancilla College
Anderson University
Ball State University
Bethel College
Butler University
Calumet College of St. Joseph
DePauw University
DeVry University: Indianapolis
Earlham College
Franklin College
Goshen College
Grace College
Hanover College
Holy Cross College
Huntington University
Indiana Institute of Technology
Indiana State University
Indiana University
    Bloomington
    East
    Kokomo
    Northwest
    South Bend
    Southeast
Indiana University-Purdue University Fort
    Wayne
Indiana University-Purdue University
    Indianapolis
Indiana Wesleyan University
Manchester College
Marian College
Oakland City University
Purdue University
Purdue University
    Calumet
    North Central
Rose-Hulman Institute of Technology
Saint Joseph's College
St. Mary-of-the-Woods College
Saint Mary's College
Taylor University
Taylor University Fort Wayne
Tri-State University
University of Evansville
University of Indianapolis

University of St. Francis
University of Southern Indiana
Valparaiso University
Vincennes University
Wabash College

Iowa
AIB College of Business
Allen College
Ashford University
Briar Cliff University
Buena Vista University
Central College
Clarke College
Coe College
Cornell College
Des Moines Area Community College
Dordt College
Drake University
Ellsworth Community College
Emmaus Bible College
Faith Baptist Bible College and Theological
  Seminary
Graceland University
Grand View College
Grinnell College
Hawkeye Community College
Iowa Central Community College
Iowa State University
Iowa Wesleyan College
Kaplan University
  Cedar Falls
  Cedar Rapids
  Davenport
  Mason City
Loras College
Luther College
Mercy College of Health Sciences
Morningside College
Mount Mercy College
North Iowa Area Community College
Northeast Iowa Community College
Northwestern College
St. Ambrose University
St. Luke's College
Simpson College
Southeastern Community College
  North Campus
Southwestern Community College
University of Dubuque
University of Iowa
University of Northern Iowa
Upper Iowa University
Waldorf College
Wartburg College
Western Iowa Tech Community College
William Penn University

Kansas
Allen County Community College
Baker University
Barclay College
Barton County Community College
Benedictine College
Bethany College
Bethel College
Butler County Community College
Central Christian College of Kansas
Coffeyville Community College
Colby Community College
Cowley County Community College
Dodge City Community College
Donnelly College
Emporia State University
Fort Hays State University
Friends University
Garden City Community College
Hesston College
Highland Community College
Hutchinson Community College
Independence Community College
Johnson County Community College

Kansas City Kansas Community College
Kansas State University
Kansas Wesleyan University
Labette Community College
Manhattan Area Technical College
Manhattan Christian College
McPherson College
MidAmerica Nazarene University
Neosho County Community College
Newman University
North Central Kansas Technical College
Ottawa University
Pittsburg State University
Pratt Community College
Seward County Community College
Southwestern College
Sterling College
Tabor College
University of Kansas
University of Kansas Medical Center
University of St. Mary
Washburn University
Wichita State University

Kentucky
Asbury College
Ashland Community and Technical College
Beckfield College
Bellarmine University
Bluegrass Community and Technical College
Brescia University
Centre College
Clear Creek Baptist Bible College
Eastern Kentucky University
Georgetown College
Hopkinsville Community College
Jefferson Community and Technical College
Kentucky Christian University
Kentucky Mountain Bible College
Kentucky State University
Kentucky Wesleyan College
Louisville Technical Institute
Maysville Community and Technical College
Mid-Continent University
Midway College
Morehead State University
Murray State University
National College
  Danville
  Florence
  Lexington
  Louisville
  Pikeville
  Richmond
Northern Kentucky University
Owensboro Community and Technical College
St. Catharine College
Somerset Community College
Southeast Kentucky Community and Technical
  College
Spencerian College: Lexington
Thomas More College
Transylvania University
Union College
University of Kentucky
University of Louisville
University of the Cumberlands
Western Kentucky University

Louisiana
Bossier Parish Community College
Centenary College of Louisiana
Delgado Community College
Dillard University
Grambling State University
Louisiana College
Louisiana State University
  Alexandria
Louisiana State University and Agricultural and
  Mechanical College
Louisiana State University Health Sciences
  Center

Louisiana Tech University
Loyola University New Orleans
McNeese State University
Nicholls State University
Northwestern State University
  Baton Rouge
St. Joseph Seminary College
School of Urban Missions: New Orleans
Southeastern Louisiana University
Southern University and Agricultural and
  Mechanical College
Tulane University
University of Louisiana at Lafayette
University of Louisiana at Monroe
University of New Orleans

Maine
Bowdoin College
College of the Atlantic
Eastern Maine Community College
Husson College
Maine College of Art
Maine Maritime Academy
New England School of Communications
St. Joseph's College
Southern Maine Community College
Thomas College
Unity College
University of Maine
University of Maine
  Augusta
  Farmington
  Fort Kent
  Machias
University of New England
University of Southern Maine
Washington County Community College
York County Community College

Maryland
Allegany College of Maryland
Baltimore Hebrew University
Baltimore International College
Bowie State University
Capitol College
Carroll Community College
Cecil College
Chesapeake College
College of Notre Dame of Maryland
College of Southern Maryland
Columbia Union College
Community College of Baltimore County
Coppin State University
DeVry University: Bethesda
Frederick Community College
Frostburg State University
Garrett College
Goucher College
Hood College
Johns Hopkins University
Johns Hopkins University: Peabody
  Conservatory of Music
Loyola College in Maryland
Maryland Institute College of Art
McDaniel College
Montgomery College
Mount St. Mary's University
Prince George's Community College
St. Mary's College of Maryland
Salisbury University
Towson University
University of Maryland
  Baltimore County
  College Park
  Eastern Shore
  University College
Villa Julie College
Washington Bible College
Washington College
Wor-Wic Community College

Massachusetts
American International College
Anna Maria College
Assumption College
Atlantic Union College
Babson College
Bard College at Simon's Rock
Bay Path College
Becker College
Benjamin Franklin Institute of Technology
Bentley College
Berklee College of Music
Boston Architectural College
Boston College
Boston University
Brandeis University
Bridgewater State College
Bristol Community College
Bunker Hill Community College
Cape Cod Community College
Caritas Laboure College
Clark University
College of the Holy Cross
Curry College
Dean College
Eastern Nazarene College
Elms College
Emerson College
Emmanuel College
Endicott College
Fisher College
Fitchburg State College
Framingham State College
Franklin W. Olin College of Engineering
Gordon College
Hampshire College
Hellenic College/Holy Cross
Holyoke Community College
Lasell College
Lesley University
Marian Court College
Massachusetts College of Art
Massachusetts College of Liberal Arts
Massachusetts College of Pharmacy and Health
  Sciences
Massachusetts Maritime Academy
Merrimack College
Mount Holyoke College
Mount Wachusett Community College
New England Conservatory of Music
New England Institute of Art
Newbury College
Nichols College
North Shore Community College
Northeastern University
Northern Essex Community College
Pine Manor College
Quinsigamond Community College
Regis College
Simmons College
Smith College
Stonehill College
Suffolk University
Tufts University
University of Massachusetts
  Amherst
  Boston
  Dartmouth
  Lowell
Wentworth Institute of Technology
Western New England College
Westfield State College
Wheaton College
Wheelock College
Worcester Polytechnic Institute

Michigan
Adrian College
Albion College
Alma College
Alpena Community College
Andrews University

Aquinas College
Baker College
  of Auburn Hills
  of Cadillac
  of Clinton Township
  of Flint
  of Jackson
  of Muskegon
  of Owosso
  of Port Huron
Bay de Noc Community College
Calvin College
Central Michigan University
Cleary University
College for Creative Studies
Concordia University
Cornerstone University
Davenport University
Delta College
Eastern Michigan University
Ferris State University
Finlandia University
Glen Oaks Community College
Gogebic Community College
Grace Bible College
Grand Rapids Community College
Grand Valley State University
Great Lakes Christian College
Hillsdale College
Hope College
Jackson Community College
Kalamazoo College
Kalamazoo Valley Community College
Kellogg Community College
Kendall College of Art and Design of Ferris
  State University
Kettering University
Kirtland Community College
Kuyper College
Lake Superior State University
Lansing Community College
Lawrence Technological University
Macomb Community College
Madonna University
Marygrove College
Michigan Jewish Institute
Michigan State University
Michigan Technological University
Mid Michigan Community College
Monroe County Community College
Montcalm Community College
Mott Community College
Northern Michigan University
Northwestern Michigan College
Northwood University: Michigan
Oakland Community College
Oakland University
Olivet College
Rochester College
Sacred Heart Major Seminary
Saginaw Valley State University
Schoolcraft College
Siena Heights University
Southwestern Michigan College
Spring Arbor University
University of Detroit Mercy
University of Michigan
University of Michigan
  Dearborn
  Flint
Walsh College of Accountancy and Business
  Administration
Washtenaw Community College
Wayne State University
Western Michigan University

Minnesota
Anoka Technical College
Augsburg College
Bemidji State University
Bethany Lutheran College
Bethel University

Brown College
Carleton College
College of St. Benedict
College of St. Catherine
College of St. Scholastica
College of Visual Arts
Concordia College: Moorhead
Concordia University: St. Paul
Crossroads College
Crown College
Dakota County Technical College
  Edina
Dunwoody College of Technology
Gustavus Adolphus College
Hamline University
Inver Hills Community College
Itasca Community College
Lake Superior College
Le Cordon Bleu College of Culinary Arts
Macalester College
Martin Luther College
Metropolitan State University
Minneapolis College of Art and Design
Minnesota School of Business: Shakopee
Minnesota State College - Southeast Technical
Minnesota State Community and Technical
  College: Fergus Falls
Minnesota State University
  Mankato
  Moorhead
Normandale Community College
North Central University
North Hennepin Community College
Northland Community & Technical College
Northwestern College
Oak Hills Christian College
Pine Technical College
Rainy River Community College
Rasmussen College
  Mankato
Saint Cloud State University
St. Cloud Technical College
St. John's University
St. Mary's University of Minnesota
St. Olaf College
Southwest Minnesota State University
University of Minnesota
  Crookston
  Duluth
  Morris
  Twin Cities
University of St. Thomas
Walden University
Winona State University

Mississippi
Alcorn State University
Belhaven College
Blue Mountain College
Coahoma Community College
Copiah-Lincoln Community College
Delta State University
East Central Community College
East Mississippi Community College
Hinds Community College
Holmes Community College
Itawamba Community College
Jackson State University
Magnolia Bible College
Meridian Community College
Millsaps College
Mississippi College
Mississippi Gulf Coast Community College
  Jefferson Davis Campus
Mississippi State University
Mississippi University for Women
Mississippi Valley State University
Pearl River Community College
Rust College
Tougaloo College
University of Mississippi
University of Mississippi Medical Center

Wesley College
William Carey University

Missouri
Avila University
Calvary Bible College and Theological Seminary
Central Methodist University
College of the Ozarks
Columbia College
Conception Seminary College
Cottey College
Crowder College
Culver-Stockton College
  Kansas City
Drury University
East Central College
Evangel University
Fontbonne University
Hannibal-LaGrange College
Harris-Stowe State University
Jefferson College
Kansas City Art Institute
Lincoln University
Lindenwood University
Maryville University of Saint Louis
Metropolitan Community College: Blue River
Metropolitan Community College: Longview
Metropolitan Community College: Maple
  Woods
Metropolitan Community College: Penn Valley
Missouri Baptist University
Missouri Southern State University
Missouri State University
Missouri State University: West Plains
Missouri Valley College
Missouri Western State University
Moberly Area Community College
North Central Missouri College
Northwest Missouri State University
Ozark Christian College
Park University
Research College of Nursing
Rockhurst University
St. Charles Community College
St. Louis Christian College
Saint Louis University
Southeast Missouri State University
Southwest Baptist University
State Fair Community College
Stephens College
Three Rivers Community College
Truman State University
University of Central Missouri
University of Missouri
  Columbia
  Kansas City
  Missouri University of Science and
    Technology
  St. Louis
Washington University in St. Louis
Webster University
Westminster College
William Jewell College
William Woods University

Montana
Carroll College
Dawson Community College
Flathead Valley Community College
Miles Community College
Montana State University
  Billings
  Bozeman
  Northern
Montana Tech of the University of Montana
Rocky Mountain College
Stone Child College
University of Great Falls
University of Montana: Missoula
University of Montana: Western

Nebraska
Bellevue University
Central Community College
Chadron State College
Clarkson College
College of Saint Mary
Concordia University
Creative Center
Creighton University
Dana College
Doane College
Grace University
Hastings College
Metropolitan Community College
Mid-Plains Community College Area
Midland Lutheran College
Nebraska Christian College
Nebraska Methodist College of Nursing and
  Allied Health
Nebraska Wesleyan University
Northeast Community College
Peru State College
Southeast Community College
Union College
University of Nebraska
  Kearney
  Lincoln
  Omaha
Wayne State College
Western Nebraska Community College
York College

Nevada
  of Las Vegas
DeVry University: Henderson
Sierra Nevada College
Truckee Meadows Community College
University of Nevada
  Las Vegas
  Reno
University of Southern Nevada
Western Nevada College

New Hampshire
Chester College of New England
Colby-Sawyer College
Daniel Webster College
Franklin Pierce University
Hesser College
Keene State College
New England College
Plymouth State University
Rivier College
St. Anselm College
Southern New Hampshire University
Thomas More College of Liberal Arts
University of New Hampshire
University of New Hampshire at Manchester

New Jersey
Berkeley College
Bloomfield College
Burlington County College
Caldwell College
Centenary College
The College of New Jersey
College of St. Elizabeth
Cumberland County College
DeVry University: North Brunswick
Drew University
Felician College
Georgian Court University
Kean University
Mercer County Community College
Monmouth University
Montclair State University
New Jersey Institute of Technology
Ocean County College
Passaic County Community College
Ramapo College of New Jersey
Raritan Valley Community College
Richard Stockton College of New Jersey

Rider University
Rowan University
Rutgers, The State University of New Jersey
    Camden Regional Campus
    New Brunswick/Piscataway Campus
    Newark Regional Campus
Saint Peter's College
Salem Community College
Seton Hall University
Somerset Christian College
Stevens Institute of Technology
Union County College
Warren County Community College
William Paterson University of New Jersey

New Mexico
Central New Mexico Community College
Clovis Community College
College of Santa Fe
College of the Southwest
Eastern New Mexico University
Institute of American Indian Arts
Mesalands Community College
New Mexico Highlands University
New Mexico Institute of Mining and Technology
New Mexico Junior College
New Mexico Military Institute
New Mexico State University
New Mexico State University
    Alamogordo
Northern New Mexico College
San Juan College
Santa Fe Community College
Southwestern Indian Polytechnic Institute
University of New Mexico
Western New Mexico University

New York
Adelphi University
Adirondack Community College
Albany College of Pharmacy
Alfred University
ASA Institute of Business and Computer
    Technology
Bard College
Berkeley College
Berkeley College of New York City
Briarcliffe College
Bryant & Stratton Business Institute
    Bryant & Stratton College: Albany
    Bryant & Stratton College: Syracuse
Canisius College
Cayuga County Community College
Cazenovia College
City University of New York
    Baruch College
    Brooklyn College
    City College
    College of Staten Island
    Hunter College
    John Jay College of Criminal Justice
    Lehman College
    Medgar Evers College
    Queens College
    York College
Clarkson University
College of Mount St. Vincent
College of New Rochelle
College of Saint Rose
College of Westchester
Columbia University
    School of General Studies
Columbia-Greene Community College
Concordia College
Cooper Union for the Advancement of Science
    and Art
Culinary Institute of America
Daemen College
DeVry Institute of Technology
    New York
Dominican College of Blauvelt
Dowling College

D'Youville College
Eastman School of Music of the University of
    Rochester
Elmira College
Eugene Lang College The New School for
    Liberal Arts
Fashion Institute of Technology
Finger Lakes Community College
Five Towns College
Fordham University
Fulton-Montgomery Community College
Globe Institute of Technology
Hamilton College
Hartwick College
Hilbert College
Hobart and William Smith Colleges
Hofstra University
Houghton College
Iona College
Ithaca College
Jamestown Business College
Jamestown Community College
Jefferson Community College
Jewish Theological Seminary of America
Keuka College
King's College
Laboratory Institute of Merchandising
Le Moyne College
Long Island Business Institute
Manhattan College
Manhattan School of Music
Manhattanville College
Mannes College The New School for Music
Marist College
Marymount Manhattan College
Medaille College
Metropolitan College of New York
Molloy College
Monroe College
Mount St. Mary College
Nassau Community College
Nazareth College of Rochester
New York Institute of Technology
New York University
Niagara County Community College
Niagara University
Nyack College
Onondaga Community College
Pace University
Parsons The New School for Design
Paul Smith's College
Polytechnic University
Pratt Institute
Rensselaer Polytechnic Institute
Roberts Wesleyan College
Rochester Institute of Technology
Russell Sage College
Sage College of Albany
Saint Bonaventure University
St. Francis College
St. John Fisher College
St. John's University
St. Joseph's College
St. Joseph's College: Suffolk Campus
St. Lawrence University
St. Thomas Aquinas College
Schenectady County Community College
Siena College
State University of New York
    Albany
    Binghamton
    Buffalo
    College at Brockport
    College at Buffalo
    College at Cortland
    College at Fredonia
    College at Geneseo
    College at Old Westbury
    College at Oneonta
    College at Plattsburgh
    College at Potsdam

    College of Agriculture and Technology at
        Cobleskill
    College of Agriculture and Technology at
        Morrisville
    College of Environmental Science and
        Forestry
    College of Technology at Alfred
    Farmingdale
    Institute of Technology at Utica/Rome
    Maritime College
    Oswego
    Purchase
    Stony Brook
Suffolk County Community College
Syracuse University
Tompkins-Cortland Community College
Trocaire College
Union College
University of Rochester
Utica College
Vaughn College of Aeronautics and Technology
Villa Maria College of Buffalo
Wagner College
Webb Institute
Wells College
Westchester Community College
Yeshiva Mikdash Melech

North Carolina
Alamance Community College
Appalachian State University
Asheville-Buncombe Technical Community
    College
Barton College
Beaufort County Community College
Belmont Abbey College
Blue Ridge Community College
Brevard College
Brunswick Community College
Campbell University
Carolinas College of Health Sciences
Carteret Community College
Catawba College
Catawba Valley Community College
Central Carolina Community College
Central Piedmont Community College
Chowan University
Coastal Carolina Community College
College of the Albemarle
Davidson College
Davidson County Community College
DeVry University: Charlotte
Duke University
Durham Technical Community College
East Carolina University
Elizabeth City State University
Elon University
Fayetteville State University
Forsyth Technical Community College
Gardner-Webb University
Gaston College
Greensboro College
Guilford College
Haywood Community College
High Point University
Isothermal Community College
James Sprunt Community College
Johnson & Wales University: Charlotte
Johnson C. Smith University
Johnston Community College
Lees-McRae College
Lenoir Community College
Lenoir-Rhyne College
Livingstone College
Mars Hill College
Martin Community College
McDowell Technical Community College
Meredith College
Methodist University
Montgomery Community College
Montreat College
Mount Olive College

Nash Community College
North Carolina Agricultural and Technical State
    University
North Carolina Central University
North Carolina School of the Arts
North Carolina State University
North Carolina Wesleyan College
Peace College
Pfeiffer University
Pitt Community College
Queens University of Charlotte
Randolph Community College
Richmond Community College
Roanoke Bible College
Roanoke-Chowan Community College
Rockingham Community College
Rowan-Cabarrus Community College
St. Andrews Presbyterian College
St. Augustine's College
Salem College
Sampson Community College
Sandhills Community College
Shaw University
Southeastern Community College
Stanly Community College
Surry Community College
University of North Carolina
    Asheville
    Chapel Hill
    Charlotte
    Greensboro
    Wilmington
Vance-Granville Community College
Wake Forest University
Wake Technical Community College
Warren Wilson College
Wayne Community College
Western Carolina University
Western Piedmont Community College
Wilkes Community College
Wilson Community College
Wingate University
Winston-Salem State University

North Dakota
Bismarck State College
Dickinson State University
Jamestown College
Lake Region State College
Mayville State University
Minot State University
Minot State University: Bottineau Campus
North Dakota State College of Science
North Dakota State University
Rasmussen College: Fargo
Trinity Bible College
University of Mary
University of North Dakota
Valley City State University
Williston State College

Ohio
AEC Southern Ohio College
    Brown Mackie College: Findlay
Art Academy of Cincinnati
Art Institute of Cincinnati
Ashland University
Baldwin-Wallace College
Bluffton University
Bowling Green State University
Bowling Green State University: Firelands
    College
Bryant & Stratton College
    Willoughby Hills
Bryant & Stratton College: Cleveland
Capital University
Case Western Reserve University
Cedarville University
Central Ohio Technical College
Central State University
Chatfield College

Cincinnati State Technical and Community
  College
Cleveland Institute of Art
Cleveland Institute of Music
Cleveland State University
College of Mount St. Joseph
College of Wooster
Columbus College of Art and Design
Cuyahoga Community College
  Metropolitan Campus
David N. Myers University
Defiance College
Denison University
  Columbus
Edison State Community College
Franciscan University of Steubenville
Heidelberg College
Hiram College
Hocking College
James A. Rhodes State College
Jefferson Community College
John Carroll University
Kent State University
Kent State University
  Ashtabula
  East Liverpool
  Salem
  Stark
  Trumbull
  Tuscarawas
Kent State University: Geauga
Kenyon College
Kettering College of Medical Arts
Lake Erie College
Lakeland Community College
Lorain County Community College
Lourdes College
Malone College
Marietta College
Marion Technical College
MedCentral College of Nursing
Mercy College of Northwest Ohio
Miami University
  Hamilton Campus
  Oxford Campus
Mount Union College
Mount Vernon Nazarene University
Muskingum College
Northwest State Community College
Notre Dame College
Oberlin College
Ohio Christian University
Ohio Dominican University
Ohio Northern University
Ohio State University
  Agricultural Technical Institute
  Columbus Campus
  Lima Campus
  Mansfield Campus
  Marion Campus
  Newark Campus
Ohio University
Ohio University
  Southern Campus at Ironton
Ohio Wesleyan University
Otterbein College
Owens Community College
  Toledo
Pontifical College Josephinum
School of Advertising Art
Shawnee State University
Sinclair Community College
Southern State Community College
Stark State College of Technology
Terra Community College
Tiffin University
Union Institute & University
University of Akron
University of Akron: Wayne College
University of Cincinnati
University of Cincinnati
  Clermont College

University of Dayton
University of Findlay
University of Northwestern Ohio
University of Rio Grande
University of Toledo
Urbana University
Ursuline College
Walsh University
Wilmington College
Wittenberg University
Wright State University
Wright State University: Lake Campus
Xavier University
Youngstown State University

Oklahoma
Cameron University
Carl Albert State College
Connors State College
DeVry University: Oklahoma City Center
East Central University
Langston University
Mid-America Christian University
Northeastern Oklahoma Agricultural and
  Mechanical College
Northeastern State University
Northwestern Oklahoma State University
Oklahoma Baptist University
Oklahoma Christian University
Oklahoma City Community College
Oklahoma City University
Oklahoma Panhandle State University
Oklahoma State University
Oklahoma State University
  Oklahoma City
Oklahoma Wesleyan University
Oral Roberts University
Redlands Community College
Rogers State University
Rose State College
St. Gregory's University
Seminole State College
Southeastern Oklahoma State University
Southern Nazarene University
Southwestern Christian University
Southwestern Oklahoma State University
Tulsa Community College
University of Central Oklahoma
University of Oklahoma
University of Science and Arts of Oklahoma
University of Tulsa
Western Oklahoma State College

Oregon
Cascade College
Central Oregon Community College
Chemeketa Community College
Clackamas Community College
Clatsop Community College
Concordia University
Corban College
DeVry University: Portland
Eastern Oregon University
Eugene Bible College
George Fox University
Lewis & Clark College
Linfield College
Linn-Benton Community College
Marylhurst University
Mt. Hood Community College
Multnomah Bible College
Northwest Christian College
Oregon Health & Science University
Oregon Institute of Technology
Oregon State University
Pacific Northwest College of Art
Pacific University
Portland State University
Southern Oregon University
Treasure Valley Community College
Umpqua Community College
University of Oregon

University of Portland
Warner Pacific College
Western Oregon University
Willamette University

Pennsylvania
Albright College
Allegheny College
Alvernia College
Arcadia University
Baptist Bible College of Pennsylvania
Bloomsburg University of Pennsylvania
Bryn Athyn College of the New Church
Bryn Mawr College
Bucknell University
Bucks County Community College
Business Institute of Pennsylvania
Butler County Community College
Cabrini College
California University of Pennsylvania
Cambria-Rowe Business College
Carlow University
Carnegie Mellon University
Cedar Crest College
Central Pennsylvania College
Chatham University
Chestnut Hill College
Cheyney University of Pennsylvania
Clarion University of Pennsylvania
Community College of Allegheny County
Community College of Beaver County
Delaware Valley College
DeSales University
  Fort Washington
Dickinson College
Drexel University
Duquesne University
East Stroudsburg University of Pennsylvania
Edinboro University of Pennsylvania
Elizabethtown College
Franklin & Marshall College
Gannon University
Geneva College
Gettysburg College
Grove City College
Gwynedd-Mercy College
Harcum College
Harrisburg Area Community College
Holy Family University
Immaculata University
Indiana University of Pennsylvania
Johnson College
Juniata College
Keystone College
King's College
Kutztown University of Pennsylvania
La Roche College
La Salle University
Lackawanna College
Lafayette College
Lancaster Bible College
Lebanon Valley College
Lehigh Carbon Community College
Lehigh University
Lincoln University
Lock Haven University of Pennsylvania
Lycoming College
Manor College
Mansfield University of Pennsylvania
Marywood University
Mercyhurst College
Messiah College
Millersville University of Pennsylvania
Misericordia University
Montgomery County Community College
Moore College of Art and Design
Moravian College
Mount Aloysius College
Muhlenberg College
Newport Business Institute: Lower Burrell
Northampton Community College
Peirce College

Penn State
  Abington
  Altoona
  Beaver
  Berks
  Brandywine
  Dubois
  Erie, The Behrend College
  Fayette, The Eberly Campus
  Greater Allegheny
  Harrisburg
  Hazleton
  Lehigh Valley
  Mont Alto
  New Kensington
  Schuylkill
  Shenango
  University Park
  Wilkes-Barre
  Worthington Scranton
  York
Pennsylvania College of Technology
Pennsylvania Highlands Community College
Pennsylvania Institute of Technology
Philadelphia Biblical University
Philadelphia University
Point Park University
Robert Morris University
Rosemont College
St. Francis University
Saint Joseph's University
St. Vincent College
Seton Hill University
Shippensburg University of Pennsylvania
Slippery Rock University of Pennsylvania
Susquehanna University
Swarthmore College
Temple University
Thiel College
Thomas Jefferson University: College of Health
  Professions
Triangle Tech
  DuBois
  Pittsburgh
University of Pittsburgh
University of Pittsburgh
  Bradford
  Greensburg
  Johnstown
  Titusville
University of Scranton
University of the Arts
University of the Sciences in Philadelphia
Ursinus College
Valley Forge Christian College
Valley Forge Military College
Vet Tech Institute
Villanova University
Washington & Jefferson College
Waynesburg University
Westminster College
Westmoreland County Community College
Widener University
Wilkes University
Wilson College
York College of Pennsylvania

Puerto Rico
Colegio Pentecostal Mizpa
Inter American University of Puerto Rico
  Aguadilla Campus
  Arecibo Campus
  Bayamon Campus
  San German Campus
Pontifical Catholic University of Puerto Rico
Turabo University
Universidad del Este
Universidad Metropolitana
Universidad Politecnica de Puerto Rico
University of Puerto Rico
  Bayamon University College
  Cayey University College

Humacao
Mayaguez
Utuado
University of the Sacred Heart

Rhode Island
Bryant University
Johnson & Wales University: Providence
New England Institute of Technology
Providence College
Rhode Island College
Roger Williams University
Salve Regina University
University of Rhode Island
Zion Bible College

South Carolina
Aiken Technical College
Allen University
Anderson University
Charleston Southern University
The Citadel
Clemson University
Coastal Carolina University
Coker College
College of Charleston
Columbia College
Columbia International University
Converse College
Erskine College
Florence-Darlington Technical College
Francis Marion University
Furman University
Greenville Technical College
Horry-Georgetown Technical College
Lander University
Limestone College
Morris College
Newberry College
North Greenville University
Piedmont Technical College
Presbyterian College
South Carolina State University
Southern Wesleyan University
Spartanburg Methodist College
Tri-County Technical College
University of South Carolina
University of South Carolina
    Beaufort
    Salkehatchie Regional Campus
    Sumter
    Union
    Upstate
Williamsburg Technical College
Winthrop University
Wofford College
York Technical College

South Dakota
Augustana College
Black Hills State University
Dakota State University
Dakota Wesleyan University
Kilian Community College
Mount Marty College
Northern State University
South Dakota School of Mines and Technology
South Dakota State University
Southeast Technical Institute
University of Sioux Falls
University of South Dakota

Tennessee
Aquinas College
Austin Peay State University
Belmont University
Bethel College
Bryan College
Carson-Newman College
Christian Brothers University
Columbia State Community College
Crichton College
Cumberland University

DeVry University: Memphis
Dyersburg State Community College
East Tennessee State University
Free Will Baptist Bible College
Freed-Hardeman University
Hiwassee College
Jackson State Community College
Johnson Bible College
King College
Lambuth University
Lane College
Lee University
LeMoyne-Owen College
Lincoln Memorial University
Lipscomb University
Martin Methodist College
Maryville College
Memphis College of Art
Middle Tennessee State University
Milligan College
Motlow State Community College
Nashville State Community College
    Nashville
National College of Business & Technology
    National College: Bristol
Northeast State Technical Community College
O'More College of Design
Pellissippi State Technical Community College
Rhodes College
Roane State Community College
Southern Adventist University
Southwest Tennessee Community College
Tennessee State University
Tennessee Technological University
Tennessee Temple University
Tennessee Wesleyan College
Trevecca Nazarene University
Tusculum College
Union University
University of Memphis
University of Tennessee
    Chattanooga
    Knoxville
    Martin
University of Tennessee Health Science Center
University of the South
Vanderbilt University
Volunteer State Community College
Walters State Community College

Texas
Abilene Christian University
Alvin Community College
Angelina College
Angelo State University
Austin College
Baylor University
Central Texas College
Clarendon College
Coastal Bend College
College of the Mainland
Collin County Community College District
Commonwealth Institute of Funeral Service
Concordia University at Austin
Dallas Baptist University
    Irving
DeVry University: Houston
East Texas Baptist University
El Paso Community College
Frank Phillips College
Galveston College
Hardin-Simmons University
Hill College
Houston Baptist University
Howard College
Howard Payne University
Huston-Tillotson University
Jacksonville College
Jarvis Christian College
Kilgore College
Lee College
LeTourneau University

Lon Morris College
Lone Star College System
Lubbock Christian University
McMurry University
Midland College
Midwestern State University
Mountain View College
North Central Texas College
North Lake College
Northeast Texas Community College
Northwest Vista College
Northwood University: Texas
Odessa College
Our Lady of the Lake University of San Antonio
Palo Alto College
Panola College
Prairie View A&M University
Rice University
St. Edward's University
St. Mary's University
Sam Houston State University
San Jacinto College
Schreiner University
South Plains College
South Texas College
Southern Methodist University
Southwestern Adventist University
Southwestern University
Stephen F. Austin State University
Sul Ross State University
Tarleton State University
Tarrant County College
Texarkana College
Texas A&M International University
Texas A&M University
Texas A&M University
    Baylor College of Dentistry
    Commerce
    Galveston
    Kingsville
    Texarkana
Texas Christian University
Texas Lutheran University
Texas Southern University
Texas State Technical College
    Sweetwater
    Waco
Texas State University: San Marcos
Texas Tech University
Texas Wesleyan University
Trinity University
Trinity Valley Community College
Tyler Junior College
University of Dallas
University of Houston
University of Houston
    Downtown
    Victoria
University of Mary Hardin-Baylor
University of North Texas
University of St. Thomas
University of Texas
    Austin
    Dallas
    El Paso
    Medical Branch at Galveston
    Pan American
    of the Permian Basin
    San Antonio
    Tyler
University of the Incarnate Word
Vernon College
Victoria College
Wayland Baptist University
West Texas A&M University
Western Technical College
Western Texas College
Wharton County Junior College

Utah
Brigham Young University
College of Eastern Utah

DeVry University: Sandy
Dixie State College of Utah
LDS Business College
Salt Lake Community College
Snow College
Southern Utah University
University of Utah
Utah State University
Utah Valley State College
Weber State University
Westminster College

Vermont
Bennington College
Castleton State College
Champlain College
College of St. Joseph in Vermont
Goddard College
Green Mountain College
Johnson State College
Landmark College
Lyndon State College
Marlboro College
New England Culinary Institute
Norwich University
St. Michael's College
Southern Vermont College
Sterling College
University of Vermont
Vermont Technical College

Virginia
Averett University
Blue Ridge Community College
Bluefield College
Bridgewater College
    Richmond
Central Virginia Community College
Christendom College
Christopher Newport University
College of William and Mary
    Arlington
Eastern Mennonite University
ECPI College of Technology: Virginia Beach
Emory & Henry College
Ferrum College
George Mason University
Germanna Community College
Hampden-Sydney College
Hampton University
Hollins University
J. Sargeant Reynolds Community College
James Madison University
Jefferson College of Health Sciences
John Tyler Community College
Liberty University
Longwood University
Lynchburg College
Mary Baldwin College
Marymount University
Mountain Empire Community College
    Bluefield
    Charlottesville
    Danville
    Harrisonburg
    Lynchburg
    Martinsville
Norfolk State University
Northern Virginia Community College
Old Dominion University
Piedmont Virginia Community College
Radford University
Randolph College
Randolph-Macon College
Regent University
Richard Bland College
Roanoke College
St. Paul's College
Shenandoah University
Southern Virginia University
Southside Virginia Community College
Southwest Virginia Community College

Sweet Briar College
University of Mary Washington
University of Richmond
University of Virginia
University of Virginia's College at Wise
Virginia Commonwealth University
Virginia Military Institute
Virginia State University
Virginia Union University
Virginia Wesleyan College
Virginia Western Community College
Washington and Lee University
Wytheville Community College

Washington
Art Institute of Seattle
Bastyr University
Bellevue Community College
Big Bend Community College
Central Washington University
Centralia College
City University of Seattle
Clark College
Columbia Basin College
Cornish College of the Arts
    Federal Way
Everett Community College
Evergreen State College
Gonzaga University
Grays Harbor College
Heritage University
Northwest College of Art
Northwest University
Olympic College
Pacific Lutheran University
Peninsula College
Saint Martin's University
Seattle Pacific University
Seattle University
South Puget Sound Community College
South Seattle Community College
Tacoma Community College
Trinity Lutheran College
University of Puget Sound
University of Washington
Walla Walla Community College
Walla Walla University
Washington State University
Wenatchee Valley College
Western Washington University
Whatcom Community College
Whitman College
Whitworth University
Yakima Valley Community College

West Virginia
Alderson-Broaddus College
Bethany College
Bluefield State College
Concord University
Davis and Elkins College
Fairmont State University
Glenville State College
Marshall University
Mountain State University
Ohio Valley University
Potomac State College of West Virginia
    University
Salem International University
Shepherd University
University of Charleston
West Liberty State College
West Virginia State Community and Technical
    College
West Virginia University
West Virginia University at Parkersburg
West Virginia Wesleyan College
Wheeling Jesuit University

Wisconsin
Alverno College
Bellin College of Nursing

Beloit College
Cardinal Stritch University
Carroll College
Carthage College
College of Menominee Nation
Columbia College of Nursing
Concordia University Wisconsin
DeVry University: Milwaukee
Edgewood College
Lakeland College
Lakeshore Technical College
Lawrence University
Maranatha Baptist Bible College
Marian College of Fond du Lac
Marquette University
Mid-State Technical College
Milwaukee Area Technical College
Milwaukee Institute of Art & Design
Milwaukee School of Engineering
Moraine Park Technical College
Mount Mary College
Northland College
Ripon College
St. Norbert College
Silver Lake College
University of Wisconsin
    Baraboo/Sauk County
    Eau Claire
    Fond du Lac
    Green Bay
    La Crosse
    Madison
    Milwaukee
    Oshkosh
    Parkside
    Richland
    River Falls
    Rock County
    Sheboygan
    Stevens Point
    Stout
    Superior
    Washington County
    Waukesha
    Whitewater
Viterbo University
Waukesha County Technical College
Wisconsin Lutheran College

Wyoming
Casper College
Central Wyoming College
Eastern Wyoming College
Laramie County Community College
Northwest College
Sheridan College
Western Wyoming Community College

Art scholarships

Alabama
Alabama State University
Athens State University
Auburn University at Montgomery
Birmingham-Southern College
Chattahoochee Valley Community College
Faulkner University
Gadsden State Community College
Huntingdon College
Jacksonville State University
Jefferson State Community College
Judson College
Lurleen B. Wallace Community College
Northeast Alabama Community College
Northwest-Shoals Community College
Snead State Community College
Troy University
University of Alabama
University of Alabama
    Birmingham
    Huntsville
University of Mobile
University of Montevallo
University of North Alabama
University of South Alabama

Alaska
University of Alaska
    Fairbanks

Arizona
Arizona State University
Eastern Arizona College
Northern Arizona University
Northland Pioneer College
Pima Community College
University of Arizona

Arkansas
Arkansas State University
Arkansas Tech University
Harding University
Henderson State University
Hendrix College
John Brown University
Lyon College
Southern Arkansas University
University of Arkansas
University of Arkansas
    Pine Bluff
University of Central Arkansas
University of the Ozarks
Williams Baptist College

California
Academy of Art University
Art Institute
    of California: Orange County
Biola University
California Baptist University
California College of the Arts
California Institute of the Arts
California Lutheran University
California Polytechnic State University: San Luis
    Obispo
California State University
    Chico
    Dominguez Hills
    Fresno
    Long Beach
    Stanislaus
Chapman University
College of the Canyons

College of the Siskiyous
Concordia University
El Camino College
Irvine Valley College
The Master's College
Mount St. Mary's College
Otis College of Art and Design
Pepperdine University
Riverside Community College
San Diego State University
San Francisco Art Institute
Santa Rosa Junior College
Sonoma State University
University of California
    Irvine
    Riverside
    San Diego
    Santa Cruz
University of La Verne
University of Redlands
University of Southern California
Westmont College
Whittier College

Colorado
Adams State College
Colorado State University
Colorado State University
    Pueblo
Fort Lewis College
Mesa State College
Metropolitan State College of Denver
Northeastern Junior College
Rocky Mountain College of Art & Design
University of Colorado
    Boulder
    Denver
University of Denver
Western State College of Colorado

Connecticut
Albertus Magnus College
Fairfield University
Lyme Academy College of Fine Arts
Northwestern Connecticut Community College
Sacred Heart University
University of Connecticut
University of Hartford

Delaware
University of Delaware

District of Columbia
Corcoran College of Art and Design
George Washington University
Howard University

Florida
Barry University
Chipola Junior College
Eckerd College
Flagler College
Florida Agricultural and Mechanical University
Florida Community College at Jacksonville
Florida International University
Florida Keys Community College
Florida Southern College
Jacksonville University
Lake-Sumter Community College
Manatee Community College
Miami Dade College
North Florida Community College
Okaloosa-Walton College
Ringling College of Art and Design

Rollins College
St. Petersburg College
Santa Fe Community College
Seminole Community College
Stetson University
Tallahassee Community College
University of Florida
University of South Florida
University of Tampa
University of West Florida
Warner Southern College

Georgia
Albany State University
Andrew College
Armstrong Atlantic State University
    of Atlanta
Augusta State University
Berry College
Brenau University
Clark Atlanta University
Columbus State University
Covenant College
Darton College
Emmanuel College
Emory University
Gainesville State College
Georgia College and State University
Georgia Highlands College
Georgia Southern University
Georgia State University
Kennesaw State University
LaGrange College
Mercer University
Middle Georgia College
Morehouse College
North Georgia College & State University
Piedmont College
Reinhardt College
Savannah College of Art and Design
Shorter College
University of West Georgia
Valdosta State University
Wesleyan College
Young Harris College

Hawaii
Brigham Young University-Hawaii
Chaminade University of Honolulu
University of Hawaii
    Manoa

Idaho
College of Idaho
Idaho State University
Lewis-Clark State College
North Idaho College
Northwest Nazarene University
University of Idaho

Illinois
Augustana College
Aurora University
Black Hawk College
Bradley University
Carl Sandburg College
College of DuPage
College of Lake County
Columbia College Chicago
DePaul University
Eastern Illinois University
Elgin Community College
Elmhurst College
Eureka College
Greenville College
Harper College
Illinois College
Illinois Institute of Art: Schaumburg
Illinois State University
Illinois Wesleyan University
Judson University
Knox College
Lake Forest College

Lewis University
Lincoln College
MacMurray College
McKendree University
Millikin University
Monmouth College
North Central College
North Park University
Northeastern Illinois University
Oakton Community College
Olivet Nazarene University
Parkland College
Quincy University
Rend Lake College
Robert Morris College: Chicago
Sauk Valley Community College
School of the Art Institute of Chicago
South Suburban College of Cook County
Southeastern Illinois College
Southern Illinois University Carbondale
Southern Illinois University Edwardsville
Springfield College in Illinois
Trinity Christian College
University of Illinois
    Chicago
    Springfield
    Urbana-Champaign
University of St. Francis
Waubonsee Community College
Western Illinois University
Wheaton College

Indiana
Bethel College
Goshen College
Grace College
Huntington University
Indiana State University
Indiana University
    Bloomington
    Southeast
Indiana Wesleyan University
Marian College
Oakland City University
St. Mary-of-the-Woods College
Saint Mary's College
Taylor University
University of Evansville
University of Indianapolis
University of St. Francis
University of Southern Indiana
Valparaiso University
Vincennes University
Wabash College

Iowa
Ashford University
Briar Cliff University
Buena Vista University
Central College
Clarke College
Coe College
Cornell College
Dordt College
Drake University
Ellsworth Community College
Graceland University
Grand View College
Iowa Central Community College
Iowa State University
Iowa Wesleyan College
Kirkwood Community College
Luther College
Morningside College
Mount Mercy College
North Iowa Area Community College
Northwestern College
St. Ambrose University
Simpson College
Southeastern Community College
    North Campus
University of Iowa

University of Northern Iowa

Kansas
Allen County Community College
Baker University
Benedictine College
Bethany College
Bethel College
Butler County Community College
Coffeyville Community College
Cowley County Community College
Emporia State University
Fort Hays State University
Friends University
Garden City Community College
Highland Community College
Kansas City Kansas Community College
Kansas State University
Kansas Wesleyan University
McPherson College
MidAmerica Nazarene University
Neosho County Community College
Newman University
Pittsburg State University
Pratt Community College
Sterling College
University of Kansas
University of St. Mary
Washburn University
Wichita State University

Kentucky
Bellarmine University
Brescia University
Eastern Kentucky University
Georgetown College
Jefferson Community and Technical College
Kentucky State University
Kentucky Wesleyan College
Louisville Technical Institute
Midway College
Morehead State University
Murray State University
Northern Kentucky University
Thomas More College
Transylvania University
University of Kentucky
University of Louisville
University of the Cumberlands
Western Kentucky University

Louisiana
Centenary College of Louisiana
Dillard University
Grambling State University
Louisiana College
Louisiana State University and Agricultural and
    Mechanical College
Louisiana Tech University
Loyola University New Orleans
McNeese State University
Northwestern State University
Southeastern Louisiana University
University of Louisiana at Monroe

Maine
Maine College of Art
University of Maine
University of Maine
    Machias
York County Community College

Maryland
Bowie State University
Carroll Community College
Chesapeake College
College of Notre Dame of Maryland
Goucher College
Maryland Institute College of Art
Montgomery College
Mount St. Mary's University
Salisbury University
University of Maryland

Baltimore County
College Park
Eastern Shore
Villa Julie College

Massachusetts
Boston Architectural College
Boston University
Bristol Community College
Cape Cod Community College
Endicott College
Holyoke Community College
Lesley University
Massachusetts College of Art
Massachusetts College of Liberal Arts
School of the Museum of Fine Arts
University of Massachusetts
    Amherst
    Lowell

Michigan
Adrian College
Albion College
Alma College
Alpena Community College
Aquinas College
Calvin College
Central Michigan University
College for Creative Studies
Concordia University
Eastern Michigan University
Ferris State University
Glen Oaks Community College
Gogebic Community College
Grand Rapids Community College
Grand Valley State University
Hillsdale College
Hope College
Jackson Community College
Kendall College of Art and Design of Ferris
    State University
Madonna University
Marygrove College
Michigan State University
Michigan Technological University
Monroe County Community College
Mott Community College
Northern Michigan University
Northwestern Michigan College
Oakland University
Olivet College
Saginaw Valley State University
Siena Heights University
Southwestern Michigan College
Spring Arbor University
University of Michigan
University of Michigan
    Flint
Wayne State University
Western Michigan University

Minnesota
Bemidji State University
Bethany Lutheran College
Bethel University
College of St. Benedict
College of Visual Arts
Concordia University: St. Paul
Gustavus Adolphus College
Hamline University
Minneapolis College of Art and Design
Minnesota State Community and Technical
    College: Fergus Falls
Minnesota State University
    Mankato
    Moorhead
North Hennepin Community College
Riverland Community College
Saint Cloud State University
St. John's University
St. Mary's University of Minnesota
Southwest Minnesota State University

University of Minnesota
    Twin Cities
Winona State University

Mississippi
Belhaven College
Copiah-Lincoln Community College
Delta State University
East Mississippi Community College
Hinds Community College
Itawamba Community College
Meridian Community College
Millsaps College
Mississippi College
Mississippi State University
University of Mississippi
William Carey University

Missouri
Avila University
College of the Ozarks
Columbia College
Cottey College
Crowder College
Culver-Stockton College
Drury University
East Central College
Evangel University
Fontbonne University
Hannibal-LaGrange College
Jefferson College
Kansas City Art Institute
Lincoln University
Lindenwood University
Maryville University of Saint Louis
Missouri Southern State University
Missouri State University
Missouri Western State University
Moberly Area Community College
Northwest Missouri State University
Park University
St. Charles Community College
Saint Louis University
Southeast Missouri State University
Southwest Baptist University
State Fair Community College
Truman State University
University of Central Missouri
University of Missouri
    Columbia
    Kansas City
    St. Louis
Webster University
William Jewell College
William Woods University

Montana
Dawson Community College
Montana State University
    Billings
    Bozeman
Rocky Mountain College
University of Great Falls
University of Montana: Missoula
University of Montana: Western

Nebraska
Central Community College
Chadron State College
Concordia University
Creative Center
Creighton University
Dana College
Doane College
Hastings College
Mid-Plains Community College Area
Midland Lutheran College
Nebraska Wesleyan University
Peru State College
University of Nebraska
    Kearney
    Lincoln
    Omaha

Wayne State College
Western Nebraska Community College

Nevada
Sierra Nevada College
Truckee Meadows Community College
University of Nevada
    Las Vegas
    Reno

New Hampshire
Chester College of New England
Colby-Sawyer College
Keene State College
New England College
University of New Hampshire

New Jersey
Caldwell College
Centenary College
College of St. Elizabeth
Drew University
Georgian Court University
Kean University
Monmouth University
Montclair State University
New Jersey Institute of Technology
Richard Stockton College of New Jersey
Rider University
Rowan University
Rutgers, The State University of New Jersey
    Camden Regional Campus
    New Brunswick/Piscataway Campus
    Newark Regional Campus
Union County College

New Mexico
College of Santa Fe
Eastern New Mexico University
Institute of American Indian Arts
New Mexico Junior College
University of New Mexico

New York
Adelphi University
Alfred University
Canisius College
City University of New York
    Brooklyn College
    College of Staten Island
College of New Rochelle
College of Saint Rose
Daemen College
Fashion Institute of Technology
Hobart and William Smith Colleges
Hofstra University
Houghton College
Jamestown Community College
Manhattanville College
Marymount Manhattan College
Molloy College
Nazareth College of Rochester
Nyack College
Parsons The New School for Design
Pratt Institute
Rensselaer Polytechnic Institute
Roberts Wesleyan College
Rochester Institute of Technology
Sage College of Albany
Saint Bonaventure University
St. John's University
School of Visual Arts
Siena College
State University of New York
    Binghamton
    College at Fredonia
    College at Geneseo
    College at Plattsburgh
    College at Potsdam
    Purchase
    Stony Brook
Suffolk County Community College
Syracuse University

Villa Maria College of Buffalo

North Carolina
Appalachian State University
Barton College
Brevard College
College of the Albemarle
Davidson College
Duke University
East Carolina University
Elon University
Greensboro College
High Point University
Mars Hill College
Meredith College
Mount Olive College
North Carolina School of the Arts
Queens University of Charlotte
Rockingham Community College
St. Augustine's College
Shaw University
University of North Carolina
    Asheville
    Chapel Hill
    Greensboro
Wake Forest University
Warren Wilson College
Western Carolina University
Wilkes Community College
Wingate University

North Dakota
Dickinson State University
Jamestown College
Minot State University
North Dakota State University
Trinity Bible College
University of North Dakota

Ohio
Art Academy of Cincinnati
Art Institute of Cincinnati
Ashland University
Bluffton University
Bowling Green State University
Bowling Green State University: Firelands
    College
Capital University
Case Western Reserve University
Central State University
Cleveland Institute of Art
Cleveland State University
College of Mount St. Joseph
Columbus College of Art and Design
Cuyahoga Community College
        Metropolitan Campus
Denison University
Hiram College
Kent State University
Kent State University
    Ashtabula
    East Liverpool
    Salem
    Stark
    Trumbull
    Tuscarawas
Kent State University: Geauga
Lake Erie College
Lakeland Community College
Lourdes College
Marietta College
Miami University
    Oxford Campus
Mount Union College
Muskingum College
Ohio Northern University
Ohio State University
    Agricultural Technical Institute
    Columbus Campus
    Lima Campus
    Mansfield Campus
    Marion Campus

Newark Campus
Ohio University
Ohio Wesleyan University
Otterbein College
Pontifical College Josephinum
School of Advertising Art
Southern State Community College
University of Akron
University of Akron: Wayne College
University of Cincinnati
University of Dayton
University of Toledo
Ursuline College
Wittenberg University
Wright State University
Xavier University

Oklahoma
Cameron University
Carl Albert State College
Northeastern Oklahoma Agricultural and
    Mechanical College
Northeastern State University
Northwestern Oklahoma State University
Oklahoma Baptist University
Oklahoma Christian University
Oklahoma City University
Oklahoma Panhandle State University
Oklahoma State University
Oral Roberts University
St. Gregory's University
Southeastern Oklahoma State University
Southwestern Oklahoma State University
Tulsa Community College
University of Central Oklahoma
University of Oklahoma
University of Science and Arts of Oklahoma
University of Tulsa
Western Oklahoma State College

Oregon
Art Institute of Portland
Clackamas Community College
Eastern Oregon University
George Fox University
Lane Community College
Linn-Benton Community College
Pacific Northwest College of Art
Pacific University
Portland State University
Southern Oregon University
Western Oregon University

Pennsylvania
Albright College
Arcadia University
Bloomsburg University of Pennsylvania
Bucknell University
California University of Pennsylvania
Carnegie Mellon University
Cedar Crest College
Clarion University of Pennsylvania
Drexel University
East Stroudsburg University of Pennsylvania
Edinboro University of Pennsylvania
Elizabethtown College
Franklin & Marshall College
Immaculata University
Indiana University of Pennsylvania
Juniata College
Keystone College
Kutztown University of Pennsylvania
Lehigh University
Lock Haven University of Pennsylvania
Lycoming College
Manor College
Mansfield University of Pennsylvania
Marywood University
Mercyhurst College
Messiah College
Moore College of Art and Design
Mount Aloysius College

Muhlenberg College
Northampton Community College
Oakbridge Academy of Arts
Point Park University
Rosemont College
Saint Joseph's University
Seton Hill University
Slippery Rock University of Pennsylvania
Temple University
University of the Arts
Ursinus College
York College of Pennsylvania

Puerto Rico
Humacao Community College
University of Puerto Rico
    Mayaguez

Rhode Island
Rhode Island College
University of Rhode Island

South Carolina
Anderson University
Clemson University
Coastal Carolina University
Coker College
College of Charleston
Columbia College
Converse College
Erskine College
Furman University
Lander University
Limestone College
University of South Carolina
Winthrop University

South Dakota
Augustana College
Dakota State University
Dakota Wesleyan University
Mount Marty College
Northern State University
South Dakota State University
University of Sioux Falls
University of South Dakota

Tennessee
Austin Peay State University
Belmont University
Bryan College
Carson-Newman College
Cumberland University
East Tennessee State University
Free Will Baptist Bible College
Freed-Hardeman University
Jackson State Community College
Lambuth University
Lipscomb University
Martin Methodist College
Maryville College
Memphis College of Art
Middle Tennessee State University
Milligan College
Motlow State Community College
Northeast State Technical Community College
Pellissippi State Technical Community College
Rhodes College
Roane State Community College
Southern Adventist University
Tennessee Technological University
Union University
University of Memphis
University of Tennessee
    Chattanooga
    Knoxville
    Martin
Volunteer State Community College

Texas
Abilene Christian University
Angelina College
Austin College
Baylor University

Clarendon College
College of the Mainland
Collin County Community College District
Galveston College
Hardin-Simmons University
Houston Baptist University
Howard College
Howard Payne University
Huston-Tillotson University
Kilgore College
Lee College
Lon Morris College
McMurry University
Midwestern State University
Northeast Texas Community College
Our Lady of the Lake University of San Antonio
Panola College
Rice University
Richland College
St. Edward's University
San Jacinto College
Schreiner University
Southern Methodist University
Southwestern University
Tarleton State University
Texas A&M University
Texas A&M University
    Commerce
Texas Christian University
Texas Lutheran University
Texas State University: San Marcos
Texas Tech University
Tyler Junior College
University of Dallas
University of Houston
University of Mary Hardin-Baylor
University of Texas
    Austin
    El Paso
    Pan American
    San Antonio
    Tyler
University of the Incarnate Word
Victoria College
Wayland Baptist University
West Texas A&M University
Western Technical College
Western Texas College

Utah
Brigham Young University
College of Eastern Utah
Dixie State College of Utah
Salt Lake Community College
Southern Utah University
University of Utah
Utah State University
Utah Valley State College
Weber State University
Westminster College

Vermont
Bennington College
Castleton State College
Goddard College
Green Mountain College
Landmark College
University of Vermont

Virginia
Averett University
Bluefield College
Christopher Newport University
Eastern Mennonite University
Emory & Henry College
Hollins University
James Madison University
Longwood University
Lynchburg College
Old Dominion University
Radford University
Randolph College

Southern Virginia University
Sweet Briar College
University of Mary Washington
University of Richmond
University of Virginia's College at Wise
Virginia Commonwealth University
Virginia Intermont College
Virginia Polytechnic Institute and State
    University
Virginia State University
Virginia Wesleyan College

Washington

Art Institute of Seattle
Big Bend Community College
Central Washington University
Centralia College
Clark College
Everett Community College
Evergreen State College
Grays Harbor College
Northwest College of Art
Northwest University
Pacific Lutheran University
Seattle Pacific University
Trinity Lutheran College
University of Puget Sound
University of Washington
Washington State University
Western Washington University
Whitman College
Whitworth University

West Virginia

Bethany College
Bluefield State College
Concord University
Davis and Elkins College
Fairmont State University
Marshall University
Shepherd University
West Liberty State College
West Virginia University
West Virginia Wesleyan College

Wisconsin

Cardinal Stritch University
Carroll College
Carthage College
Edgewood College
Milwaukee Institute of Art & Design
Mount Mary College
Northland College
Ripon College
St. Norbert College
Silver Lake College
University of Wisconsin
        Baraboo/Sauk County
        Eau Claire
        Green Bay
        La Crosse
        Madison
        Manitowoc
        Milwaukee
        Oshkosh
        Parkside
        Richland
        River Falls
        Stevens Point
        Superior
        Waukesha
        Whitewater
Viterbo University
Wisconsin Lutheran College

Wyoming

Casper College
Central Wyoming College
Eastern Wyoming College
Laramie County Community College
Sheridan College
University of Wyoming
Western Wyoming Community College

Athletic scholarships

Archery

Arizona
Dine College M,W

California
College of the Redwoods M

Texas
Texas A&M University W

Badminton

California
Fresno City College M,W

New Jersey
New Jersey Institute of Technology M

Texas
Texas Southmost College M,W

Wisconsin
Milwaukee Area Technical College M

Baseball

Alabama
Alabama Agricultural and Mechanical
    University M
Alabama State University M
Auburn University M
Auburn University at Montgomery M
Bevill State Community College M
Central Alabama Community College M
Chattahoochee Valley Community College M
Concordia College M
Faulkner State Community College M
Gadsden State Community College M
George C. Wallace State Community College
        George C. Wallace Community College at
        Dothan M
Jacksonville State University M
Jefferson Davis Community College M
Jefferson State Community College M
Lawson State Community College M
Lurleen B. Wallace Community College M
Miles College M
Northwest-Shoals Community College M
Samford University M
Shelton State Community College M
Snead State Community College M
Southern Union State Community College M
Spring Hill College M
Troy University M
Tuskegee University M
University of Alabama M
University of Alabama
        Birmingham M
        Huntsville M
University of Mobile M
University of Montevallo M
University of North Alabama M
University of South Alabama M
University of West Alabama M

Arizona
Arizona State University M
Arizona Western College M

Central Arizona College M
Chandler-Gilbert Community College
        Pecos M
Cochise College M
Eastern Arizona College M
Gateway Community College M
Glendale Community College M
Grand Canyon University M
Pima Community College M
Scottsdale Community College M
South Mountain Community College M
University of Arizona M
Yavapai College M

Arkansas
Arkansas State University M
Arkansas Tech University M
Ecclesia College M
Harding University M
Henderson State University M
Lyon College M
Ouachita Baptist University M
Southern Arkansas University M
University of Arkansas M
University of Arkansas
        Fort Smith M
        Little Rock M
University of Central Arkansas M
Williams Baptist College M

California
Azusa Pacific University M
Bethany University M
Biola University M
California Baptist University M
California Polytechnic State University: San Luis
    Obispo M
California State Polytechnic University: Pomona
    M
California State University
        Chico M
        Dominguez Hills M
        Fresno M
        Fullerton M
        Long Beach M
        Los Angeles M
        Northridge M
        Sacramento M
        San Bernardino M
        Stanislaus M
Concordia University M
Fresno City College M
Fresno Pacific University M
Grossmont College M
Loyola Marymount University M
The Master's College M
Patten University M
Pepperdine University M
Point Loma Nazarene University M
St. Mary's College of California M
San Diego State University M
San Jose State University M
Santa Clara University M
Sonoma State University M
Stanford University M
University of California
        Berkeley M
        Davis M
        Irvine M
        Los Angeles M
        Riverside M
        Santa Barbara M
University of San Diego M

University of San Francisco M
University of Southern California M
University of the Pacific M
Vanguard University of Southern California M
Westmont College M
William Jessup University M
Yuba Community College District M

Colorado
Colorado Christian University M
Colorado Northwestern Community College M
Colorado School of Mines M
Colorado State University
        Pueblo M
Lamar Community College M
Mesa State College M
Metropolitan State College of Denver M
Northeastern Junior College M
Otero Junior College M
Regis University M
Trinidad State Junior College M
University of Northern Colorado M

Connecticut
Central Connecticut State University M
Fairfield University M
Post University M
Quinnipiac University M
Southern Connecticut State University M
University of Bridgeport M
University of Connecticut M
University of Hartford M
University of New Haven M

Delaware
Delaware State University M
University of Delaware M
Wilmington University M

District of Columbia
George Washington University M
Georgetown University M
Howard University M

Florida
Barry University M
Bethune-Cookman University M
Brevard Community College M
Broward Community College M
Central Florida Community College M
Chipola Junior College M
Daytona Beach Community College M
Eckerd College M
Edward Waters College M
Embry-Riddle Aeronautical University M
Flagler College M
Florida Atlantic University M
Florida College M
Florida Community College at Jacksonville M
Florida Gulf Coast University M
Florida Institute of Technology M
Florida International University M
Florida Memorial University M
Florida Southern College M
Florida State University M
Gulf Coast Community College M
Hillsborough Community College M
Indian River Community College M
Jacksonville University M
Lake City Community College M
Lake-Sumter Community College M
Lynn University M
Manatee Community College M
Miami Dade College M
North Florida Community College M
Northwood University
        Florida M
Nova Southeastern University M
Okaloosa-Walton College M
Palm Beach Community College M
Pasco-Hernando Community College M
Pensacola Junior College M
Polk Community College M

Rollins College M
Saint Johns River Community College M
St. Leo University M
St. Petersburg College M
Saint Thomas University M
Santa Fe Community College M
South Florida Community College M
Stetson University M
Tallahassee Community College M
University of Central Florida M
University of Florida M
University of Miami M
University of North Florida M
University of South Florida M
University of Tampa M
University of West Florida M
Warner Southern College M
Webber International University M

Georgia
Abraham Baldwin Agricultural College M
Albany State University M
Andrew College M
Armstrong Atlantic State University M
Augusta State University M
Berry College M
Brewton-Parker College M
Clark Atlanta University M
Columbus State University M
Covenant College M
Darton College M
Emmanuel College M
Georgia College and State University M
Georgia Institute of Technology M
Georgia Perimeter College M
Georgia Southern University M
Georgia Southwestern State University M
Georgia State University M
Gordon College M
Kennesaw State University M
Mercer University M
Middle Georgia College M
Morehouse College M
Paine College M
Reinhardt College M
Savannah State University M
Shorter College M
Southern Polytechnic State University M
Thomas University M
Truett-McConnell College M
University of Georgia M
University of West Georgia M
Valdosta State University M
Young Harris College M

Hawaii
Hawaii Pacific University M
University of Hawaii
        Manoa M

Idaho
College of Idaho M
College of Southern Idaho M
Lewis-Clark State College M
Northwest Nazarene University M

Illinois
Black Hawk College M
Bradley University M
Carl Sandburg College M
Chicago State University M
College of Lake County M
Danville Area Community College M
Eastern Illinois University M
Elgin Community College M
Highland Community College M
Illinois Central College M
Illinois Eastern Community Colleges
        Lincoln Trail College M
        Olney Central College M
        Wabash Valley College M
Illinois Institute of Technology M
Illinois State University M

John A. Logan College M
Judson University M
Kankakee Community College M
Kaskaskia College M
Kishwaukee College M
Lake Land College M
Lewis and Clark Community College M
Lewis University M
Lincoln College M
McHenry County College M
McKendree University M
Moraine Valley Community College M
Morton College M
Northwestern University M
Olivet Nazarene University M
Parkland College M
Quincy University M
Rend Lake College M
Robert Morris College: Chicago M
St. Xavier University M
Sauk Valley Community College M
South Suburban College of Cook County M
Southeastern Illinois College M
Southern Illinois University Carbondale M
Southern Illinois University Edwardsville M
Spoon River College M
Springfield College in Illinois M
Trinity Christian College M
Trinity International University M
University of Illinois
    Chicago M
    Urbana-Champaign M
University of St. Francis M
Western Illinois University M

Indiana
Ancilla College M
Ball State University M
Bethel College M
Butler University M
Calumet College of St. Joseph M
Goshen College M
Grace College M
Huntington University M
Indiana Institute of Technology M
Indiana State University M
Indiana University
    Bloomington M
    Southeast M
Indiana University-Purdue University Fort
    Wayne M
Indiana Wesleyan University M
Marian College M
Oakland City University M
Purdue University M
Saint Joseph's College M
Taylor University M
University of Evansville M
University of Indianapolis M
University of Notre Dame M
University of St. Francis M
University of Southern Indiana M
Valparaiso University M
Vincennes University M

Iowa
Ashford University M
Briar Cliff University M
Clarke College M
Des Moines Area Community College M
Dordt College M
Ellsworth Community College M
Graceland University M
Grand View College M
Indian Hills Community College M
Iowa Central Community College M
Iowa Lakes Community College M
Iowa Wesleyan College M
Iowa Western Community College M
Kirkwood Community College M
Morningside College M
Muscatine Community College M

North Iowa Area Community College M
Northwestern College M
St. Ambrose University M
Southeastern Community College
    North Campus M
Southwestern Community College M
University of Iowa M
University of Northern Iowa M
Waldorf College M
William Penn University M

Kansas
Allen County Community College M
Baker University M
Barton County Community College M
Benedictine College M
Bethany College M
Brown Mackie College
    Salina M
Butler County Community College M
Central Christian College of Kansas M
Cloud County Community College M
Coffeyville Community College M
Colby Community College M
Cowley County Community College M
Dodge City Community College M
Emporia State University M
Fort Scott Community College M
Friends University M
Garden City Community College M
Hesston College M
Highland Community College M
Hutchinson Community College M
Independence Community College M
Johnson County Community College M
Kansas City Kansas Community College M
Kansas State University M
Kansas Wesleyan University M
Labette Community College M
MidAmerica Nazarene University M
Neosho County Community College M
Newman University M
Ottawa University M
Pittsburg State University M
Pratt Community College M
Seward County Community College M
Sterling College M
Tabor College M
University of Kansas M
University of St. Mary M
Washburn University M
Wichita State University M

Kentucky
Alice Lloyd College M
Asbury College M
Bellarmine University M
Brescia University M
Campbellsville University M
Eastern Kentucky University M
Georgetown College M
Kentucky State University M
Kentucky Wesleyan College M
Lindsey Wilson College M
Mid-Continent University M
Morehead State University M
Murray State University M
Northern Kentucky University M
Pikeville College M
St. Catharine College M
Union College M
University of Kentucky M
University of Louisville M
University of the Cumberlands M
Western Kentucky University M

Louisiana
Bossier Parish Community College M
Centenary College of Louisiana M
Delgado Community College M
Grambling State University M
Louisiana State University

Shreveport M
Louisiana State University and Agricultural and
    Mechanical College M
Louisiana Tech University M
McNeese State University M
Nicholls State University M
Northwestern State University M
Southeastern Louisiana University M
Southern University and Agricultural and
    Mechanical College M
Tulane University M
University of Louisiana at Lafayette M
University of Louisiana at Monroe M
University of New Orleans M

Maine
University of Maine M

Maryland
Anne Arundel Community College M
Chesapeake College M
College of Southern Maryland M
Columbia Union College M
Community College of Baltimore County M
Coppin State University M
Garrett College M
Hagerstown Community College M
Harford Community College M
Mount St. Mary's University M
Prince George's Community College M
Towson University M
University of Maryland
    Baltimore County M
    College Park M
    Eastern Shore M

Massachusetts
American International College M
Boston College M
Dean College M
Northeastern University M
Stonehill College M
University of Massachusetts
    Amherst M

Michigan
Aquinas College M
Central Michigan University M
Concordia University M
Eastern Michigan University M
Glen Oaks Community College M
Grand Rapids Community College M
Grand Valley State University M
Henry Ford Community College M
Hillsdale College M
Kalamazoo Valley Community College M
Kellogg Community College M
Lake Michigan College M
Macomb Community College M
Madonna University M
Michigan State University M
Mott Community College M
Muskegon Community College M
Northwood University: Michigan M
Oakland University M
Rochester College M
Saginaw Valley State University M
Siena Heights University M
Spring Arbor University M
University of Michigan M
Wayne State University M,W

Minnesota
Concordia University: St. Paul M
Minnesota State University
    Mankato M
Saint Cloud State University M
Southwest Minnesota State University M
University of Minnesota
    Crookston M
    Duluth M
    Twin Cities M
Winona State University M

Mississippi
Alcorn State University M
Belhaven College M
Copiah-Lincoln Community College M
Delta State University M
East Mississippi Community College M
Hinds Community College M
Holmes Community College M
Itawamba Community College M
Jackson State University M
Meridian Community College M
Mississippi Gulf Coast Community College
    Jefferson Davis Campus M
Mississippi State University M
Mississippi Valley State University M
Northwest Mississippi Community College M
Southwest Mississippi Community College M
University of Mississippi M
University of Southern Mississippi M
William Carey University M

Missouri
Avila University M
Central Methodist University M
College of the Ozarks M
Crowder College M
Culver-Stockton College M
Drury University M
Evangel University M
Hannibal-LaGrange College M
Harris-Stowe State University M
Jefferson College M
Lincoln University M
Metropolitan Community College: Longview M
Metropolitan Community College: Maple
    Woods M
Missouri Baptist University M
Missouri Southern State University M
Missouri State University M
Missouri Valley College M
Missouri Western State University M
North Central Missouri College M
Northwest Missouri State University M
Park University M
Research College of Nursing M
Rockhurst University M
St. Charles Community College M
Saint Louis University M
Southeast Missouri State University M
Southwest Baptist University M
Three Rivers Community College M
Truman State University M
University of Central Missouri M
University of Missouri
    Columbia M
    Missouri University of Science and
        Technology M
    St. Louis M
William Jewell College M
William Woods University M

Montana
Miles Community College M
Montana State University
    Billings M

Nebraska
Bellevue University M
Concordia University M
Creighton University M
Dana College M
Doane College M
Hastings College M
Mid-Plains Community College Area M
Midland Lutheran College M
Peru State College M
University of Nebraska
    Kearney M
    Lincoln M
    Omaha M
Wayne State College M
Western Nebraska Community College M

York College M

Nevada
College of Southern Nevada M
University of Nevada
    Las Vegas M
    Reno M

New Hampshire
Franklin Pierce University M
Hesser College M
Southern New Hampshire University M

New Jersey
Bloomfield College M
Brookdale Community College M
Burlington County College M
Caldwell College M
Fairleigh Dickinson University
    Metropolitan Campus M
Mercer County Community College M
Monmouth University M
New Jersey Institute of Technology M
Rider University M
Rutgers, The State University of New Jersey
    New Brunswick/Piscataway Campus M
Saint Peter's College M
Salem Community College M
Seton Hall University M
Sussex County Community College M

New Mexico
College of the Southwest M
Eastern New Mexico University M
New Mexico Highlands University M
New Mexico Junior College M
New Mexico Military Institute M
New Mexico State University M
University of New Mexico M

New York
Adelphi University M
Canisius College M
City University of New York
    Queens College M
College of Saint Rose M
Concordia College M
Dominican College of Blauvelt M
Dowling College M
Fordham University M
Globe Institute of Technology M
Hofstra University M
Iona College M
Le Moyne College M
Long Island University
    Brooklyn Campus M
    C. W. Post Campus M
Manhattan College M
Marist College M
Mercy College M
Molloy College M
Monroe College M
Monroe Community College M
New York Institute of Technology M
Niagara University M
Nyack College M
Pace University M
Saint Bonaventure University M
St. John's University M
St. Thomas Aquinas College M
Siena College M
State University of New York
    Albany M
    Binghamton M
    Buffalo M
    Stony Brook M
Wagner College M

North Carolina
Appalachian State University M
Barton College M
Belmont Abbey College M
Brevard College M

Campbell University M
Catawba College M
Davidson College M
Duke University M
East Carolina University M
Elon University M
Gardner-Webb University M
High Point University M
Lenoir Community College M
Lenoir-Rhyne College M
Louisburg College M
Mars Hill College M
Montreat College M
Mount Olive College M
North Carolina Agricultural and Technical State
    University M
North Carolina State University M
Pfeiffer University M
Pitt Community College M
St. Andrews Presbyterian College M
St. Augustine's College M
Shaw University M
Southeastern Community College M
University of North Carolina
    Asheville M
    Chapel Hill M
    Charlotte M
    Greensboro M
    Pembroke M
    Wilmington M
Wake Forest University M
Western Carolina University M
Wingate University M

North Dakota
Dickinson State University M
Jamestown College M
Mayville State University M
Minot State University M
Minot State University: Bottineau Campus M
North Dakota State University M
University of Mary M
University of North Dakota M
Valley City State University M
Williston State College M

Ohio
Ashland University M
Bowling Green State University M
Cedarville University M
Clark State Community College M
Cleveland State University M
Kent State University M
Lakeland Community College M
Malone College M
Miami University
    Oxford Campus M
Mount Vernon Nazarene University M
Notre Dame College M
Ohio Dominican University M
Ohio State University
    Columbus Campus M
Ohio University M
Shawnee State University M
Sinclair Community College M
University of Akron M
University of Cincinnati M
University of Dayton M
University of Findlay M
University of Rio Grande M
University of Toledo M
Urbana University M
Walsh University M
Wright State University M
Xavier University M
Youngstown State University M

Oklahoma
Bacone College M
Cameron University M
Carl Albert State College M
Connors State College M

East Central University M
Northeastern Oklahoma Agricultural and
    Mechanical College M
Northeastern State University M
Northwestern Oklahoma State University M
Oklahoma Baptist University M
Oklahoma City University M
Oklahoma Panhandle State University M
Oklahoma State University M
Oklahoma Wesleyan University M
Oral Roberts University M
Redlands Community College M
Rose State College M
St. Gregory's University M
Seminole State College M
Southeastern Oklahoma State University M
Southern Nazarene University M
Southwestern Oklahoma State University M
University of Central Oklahoma M
University of Oklahoma M
University of Science and Arts of Oklahoma M
Western Oklahoma State College M

Oregon
Blue Mountain Community College M
Chemeketa Community College M
Clackamas Community College M
Concordia University M
Corban College M
Eastern Oregon University M
Lane Community College M
Linn-Benton Community College M
Mt. Hood Community College M
Oregon Institute of Technology M
Oregon State University M
Portland State University M
Southwestern Oregon Community College M
Treasure Valley Community College M
University of Oregon M
University of Portland M

Pennsylvania
Bloomsburg University of Pennsylvania M
California University of Pennsylvania M
Chestnut Hill College M
Clarion University of Pennsylvania M
Duquesne University M
East Stroudsburg University of Pennsylvania M
Gannon University M
Indiana University of Pennsylvania M
Kutztown University of Pennsylvania M
La Salle University M
Lackawanna College M
Lehigh University M
Lock Haven University of Pennsylvania M
Mansfield University of Pennsylvania M
Mercyhurst College M
Millersville University of Pennsylvania M
Penn State
    University Park M
Philadelphia University M
Point Park University M
Saint Joseph's University M
Seton Hill University M
Shippensburg University of Pennsylvania M
Slippery Rock University of Pennsylvania M
Temple University M
University of Pittsburgh M
University of the Sciences in Philadelphia M
Villanova University M
West Chester University of Pennsylvania M

Puerto Rico
Inter American University of Puerto Rico
    Aguadilla Campus M
    Bayamon Campus M
    Metropolitan Campus M
    Ponce Campus M,W
    San German Campus M
Turabo University M
Universidad del Este M
Universidad Metropolitana M,W

Universidad Politecnica de Puerto Rico M
University of Puerto Rico
    Carolina Regional College M
    Cayey University College M
    Humacao M
    Mayaguez M
    Utuado M

Rhode Island
Bryant University M
Community College of Rhode Island M
University of Rhode Island M

South Carolina
Anderson University M
Charleston Southern University M
The Citadel M
Claflin University M
Clemson University M
Coastal Carolina University M
Coker College M
College of Charleston M
Erskine College M
Francis Marion University M
Furman University M
Lander University M
Limestone College M
Morris College M
Newberry College M
North Greenville University M
Presbyterian College M
Southern Wesleyan University M
Spartanburg Methodist College M
University of South Carolina M
University of South Carolina
    Aiken M
    Sumter M
    Upstate M
Voorhees College M
Winthrop University M
Wofford College M

South Dakota
Augustana College M
Dakota State University M
Dakota Wesleyan University M
Mount Marty College M
South Dakota State University M
University of Sioux Falls M

Tennessee
Austin Peay State University M
Belmont University M
Bethel College M
Bryan College M
Carson-Newman College M
Chattanooga State Technical Community
    College M
Christian Brothers University M
Cleveland State Community College M
Columbia State Community College M
Crichton College M
Cumberland University M
Dyersburg State Community College M
East Tennessee State University M
Freed-Hardeman University M
Hiwassee College M
Jackson State Community College M
King College M
Lambuth University M
Lee University M
LeMoyne-Owen College M
Lincoln Memorial University M
Lipscomb University M
Middle Tennessee State University M
Milligan College M
Motlow State Community College M
Roane State Community College M
Southwest Tennessee Community College M
Tennessee Technological University M
Tennessee Temple University M
Tennessee Wesleyan College M
Trevecca Nazarene University M

Tusculum College M
Union University M
University of Memphis M
University of Tennessee
    Knoxville M
    Martin M
Vanderbilt University M
Volunteer State Community College M
Walters State Community College M

Texas
Abilene Christian University M
Alvin Community College M
Angelina College M
Angelo State University M
Baylor University M
Blinn College M
Clarendon College M
Dallas Baptist University M
El Paso Community College M
Frank Phillips College M
Galveston College M
Grayson County College M
Hill College M
Houston Baptist University M
Howard College M
Jarvis Christian College M
Lamar University M
Laredo Community College M
Lon Morris College M
Lubbock Christian University M
McLennan Community College M
North Central Texas College M
Northwood University: Texas M
Odessa College M
Paris Junior College M
Prairie View A&M University M
Ranger College M
Rice University M
St. Edward's University M
St. Mary's University M
Sam Houston State University M
San Jacinto College M
Tarleton State University M
Texas A&M University M
Texas A&M University
    Kingsville M
Texas Christian University M
Texas Southern University M
Texas Southmost College M
Texas State University: San Marcos M
Texas Tech University M
University of Houston M
University of Texas
    Arlington M
    Austin M
    Pan American M
    San Antonio M
University of the Incarnate Word M
Vernon College M
Wayland Baptist University M
West Texas A&M University M
Western Texas College M
Wharton County Junior College M
Wiley College M

Utah
Brigham Young University M
College of Eastern Utah M
Dixie State College of Utah M
Salt Lake Community College M
Southern Utah University M
University of Utah M
Utah Valley State College M

Vermont
University of Vermont M

Virginia
Bluefield College M
College of William and Mary M
George Mason University M
James Madison University M

Liberty University M
Longwood University M
Norfolk State University M
Old Dominion University M
Radford University M
St. Paul's College M
University of Richmond M
University of Virginia M
University of Virginia's College at Wise M
Virginia Commonwealth University M
Virginia Intermont College M
Virginia Military Institute M
Virginia Polytechnic Institute and State
    University M
Virginia State University M

Washington
Big Bend Community College M
Central Washington University M
Centralia College M
Columbia Basin College M
Edmonds Community College M
Everett Community College M
Gonzaga University M
Grays Harbor College M
Green River Community College M
Lower Columbia College M
Olympic College M
Saint Martin's University M
Spokane Community College M
Tacoma Community College M
University of Washington M
Walla Walla Community College M
Washington State University M
Yakima Valley Community College M

West Virginia
Alderson-Broaddus College M
Bluefield State College M
Concord University M
Davis and Elkins College M
Marshall University M
Ohio Valley University M
Potomac State College of West Virginia
    University M
Salem International University M
Shepherd University M
University of Charleston M
West Liberty State College M
West Virginia University M
West Virginia Wesleyan College M
Wheeling Jesuit University M

Wisconsin
Cardinal Stritch University M
Milwaukee Area Technical College M,W
University of Wisconsin
    Milwaukee M
    Parkside M
Viterbo University M

Basketball

Alabama
Alabama Agricultural and Mechanical
    University M,W
Alabama State University M,W
Auburn University M,W
Auburn University at Montgomery M,W
Bevill State Community College M,W
Chattahoochee Valley Community College M,W
Concordia College M,W
Faulkner State Community College M,W
Faulkner University M
Gadsden State Community College M,W
Jacksonville State University M,W
Jefferson Davis Community College M
Judson College W
Lawson State Community College M,W
Lurleen B. Wallace Community College M,W
Marion Military Institute M

Miles College M,W
Northwest-Shoals Community College M,W
Samford University M,W
Shelton State Community College M,W
Snead State Community College M,W
Southern Union State Community College M,W
Spring Hill College M,W
Troy University M,W
Tuskegee University M,W
University of Alabama M,W
University of Alabama
    Birmingham M,W
    Huntsville M,W
University of Mobile M,W
University of Montevallo M,W
University of North Alabama M,W
University of South Alabama M,W
University of West Alabama M,W

Alaska
University of Alaska
    Anchorage M,W
    Fairbanks M,W

Arizona
Arizona State University M,W
Arizona Western College M,W
Central Arizona College M,W
Chandler-Gilbert Community College
    Pecos M,W
Cochise College M,W
Eastern Arizona College M,W
Glendale Community College M,W
Grand Canyon University M,W
Mesa Community College M,W
Northern Arizona University M,W
Pima Community College M,W
Scottsdale Community College M,W
South Mountain Community College M,W
University of Arizona M,W
Yavapai College M,W

Arkansas
Arkansas State University M,W
Arkansas Tech University M,W
Ecclesia College M,W
Harding University M,W
Henderson State University M,W
John Brown University M,W
Lyon College M,W
North Arkansas College M,W
Ouachita Baptist University M,W
Philander Smith College M,W
Southern Arkansas University M,W
University of Arkansas M,W
University of Arkansas
    Fort Smith M,W
    Little Rock M,W
    Monticello M,W
    Pine Bluff M,W
University of Central Arkansas M,W
Williams Baptist College M,W

California
Azusa Pacific University M,W
Bethany University M,W
Biola University M,W
California Baptist University M,W
California Polytechnic State University: San Luis
    Obispo M,W
California State Polytechnic University: Pomona
    M,W
California State University
    Bakersfield M
    Chico M,W
    Dominguez Hills M,W
    Fresno M,W
    Fullerton M,W
    Long Beach M,W
    Los Angeles M,W
    Northridge M,W
    Sacramento M,W
    San Bernardino M,W

Stanislaus M,W
Concordia University M,W
Dominican University of California M,W
Fresno City College M,W
Fresno Pacific University M,W
Grossmont College M,W
Holy Names University M,W
Hope International University M,W
Humboldt State University M,W
Loyola Marymount University M,W
The Master's College M,W
Notre Dame de Namur University M,W
Pepperdine University M,W
Point Loma Nazarene University M,W
St. Mary's College of California M,W
San Diego Christian College M,W
San Diego State University M,W
San Jose State University M,W
Santa Clara University M,W
Sonoma State University M,W
Stanford University M,W
University of California
    Berkeley M,W
    Davis M,W
    Irvine M,W
    Los Angeles M,W
    Riverside M,W
    Santa Barbara M,W
University of San Diego M,W
University of San Francisco M,W
University of Southern California M,W
University of the Pacific M,W
Vanguard University of Southern California
    M,W
Westmont College M,W
William Jessup University M,W
Yuba Community College District M,W

Colorado
Adams State College M,W
Colorado Christian University M,W
Colorado Northwestern Community College
    M,W
Colorado School of Mines M,W
Colorado State University M,W
Colorado State University
    Pueblo M,W
Fort Lewis College M,W
Lamar Community College M
Mesa State College M,W
Metropolitan State College of Denver M,W
Northeastern Junior College M,W
Otero Junior College M,W
Regis University M,W
Trinidad State Junior College M
University of Colorado
    Boulder M,W
    Colorado Springs M,W
University of Denver M,W
University of Northern Colorado M,W
Western State College of Colorado M,W

Connecticut
Central Connecticut State University M,W
Fairfield University M,W
Post University M,W
Quinnipiac University M,W
Sacred Heart University M,W
Southern Connecticut State University M,W
University of Bridgeport M,W
University of Connecticut M,W
University of Hartford M,W
University of New Haven M,W

Delaware
Delaware State University M,W
Goldey-Beacom College M,W
University of Delaware M,W
Wilmington University M,W

District of Columbia
American University M,W
George Washington University M,W

Georgetown University M,W
Howard University M,W
University of the District of Columbia M,W

Florida
Barry University M,W
Bethune-Cookman University M,W
Brevard Community College M,W
Broward Community College M,W
Central Florida Community College M,W
Chipola Junior College M,W
Daytona Beach Community College M,W
Eckerd College M,W
Edward Waters College M,W
Embry-Riddle Aeronautical University M
Flagler College M,W
Florida Agricultural and Mechanical University M
Florida Atlantic University M,W
Florida College M
Florida Community College at Jacksonville M,W
Florida Gulf Coast University M,W
Florida Institute of Technology M,W
Florida International University M,W
Florida Memorial University M,W
Florida Southern College M,W
Florida State University M,W
Gulf Coast Community College M,W
Hillsborough Community College M,W
Indian River Community College M,W
Jacksonville University M,W
Lynn University M,W
Manatee Community College M
Miami Dade College M,W
North Florida Community College W
Nova Southeastern University M,W
Okaloosa-Walton College M,W
Palm Beach Community College M,W
Pasco-Hernando Community College M
Pensacola Junior College M,W
Polk Community College M
Rollins College M,W
Saint Johns River Community College M
St. Leo University M,W
St. Petersburg College M,W
Santa Fe Community College M,W
Stetson University M,W
Tallahassee Community College M,W
University of Central Florida M,W
University of Florida M,W
University of Miami M,W
University of North Florida M,W
University of South Florida M,W
University of Tampa M,W
University of West Florida M,W
Warner Southern College M,W
Webber International University M,W

Georgia
Abraham Baldwin Agricultural College M
Albany State University M,W
Andrew College W
Armstrong Atlantic State University M,W
Augusta State University M,W
Berry College M,W
Brenau University W
Brewton-Parker College M,W
Clark Atlanta University M,W
Clayton State University M,W
Coastal Georgia Community College M
Columbus State University M,W
Covenant College M,W
Darton College W
Emmanuel College M,W
Fort Valley State University M,W
Georgia College and State University M,W
Georgia Institute of Technology M,W
Georgia Perimeter College M,W
Georgia Southern University M,W
Georgia Southwestern State University M,W
Georgia State University M,W
Kennesaw State University M,W

Mercer University M,W
Middle Georgia College M,W
Morehouse College M
North Georgia College & State University M,W
Paine College M,W
Reinhardt College M,W
Savannah State University M,W
Shorter College M,W
Southern Polytechnic State University M,W
Truett-McConnell College M,W
University of Georgia M,W
University of West Georgia M,W
Valdosta State University M,W

Hawaii
Brigham Young University-Hawaii M,W
Chaminade University of Honolulu M
Hawaii Pacific University M
University of Hawaii
　　Hilo M
　　Manoa M,W

Idaho
Boise State University M,W
College of Idaho M,W
College of Southern Idaho M,W
Idaho State University M,W
Lewis-Clark State College M,W
North Idaho College M,W
Northwest Nazarene University M,W
University of Idaho M,W

Illinois
Black Hawk College M,W
Black Hawk College: East Campus M,W
Bradley University M,W
Carl Sandburg College M,W
Chicago State University M,W
City Colleges of Chicago
　　Kennedy-King College M,W
　　Malcolm X College M,W
　　Wright College M,W
College of Lake County M,W
Danville Area Community College M,W
DePaul University M,W
Eastern Illinois University M,W
Elgin Community College M,W
Highland Community College M,W
Illinois Central College M,W
Illinois Eastern Community Colleges
　　Lincoln Trail College M,W
　　Olney Central College M,W
　　Wabash Valley College M,W
Illinois Institute of Technology M,W
Illinois State University M,W
John A. Logan College M,W
Judson University M,W
Kankakee Community College M,W
Kaskaskia College M,W
Kishwaukee College M,W
Lake Land College M,W
Lewis and Clark Community College M,W
Lewis University M,W
Lincoln College M,W
Lincoln Land Community College M,W
Loyola University Chicago M,W
McHenry County College M,W
McKendree University M,W
Moraine Valley Community College M,W
Morton College M,W
Northwestern University M,W
Olivet Nazarene University M,W
Parkland College M,W
Quincy University M,W
Rend Lake College M,W
Robert Morris College: Chicago M,W
St. Xavier University M
Sauk Valley Community College M,W
Shawnee Community College M,W
South Suburban College of Cook County M,W
Southeastern Illinois College M,W
Southern Illinois University Carbondale M,W

Southern Illinois University Edwardsville M,W
Spoon River College M,W
Trinity Christian College M,W
Trinity International University M,W
University of Illinois
　　Chicago M,W
　　Springfield M,W
　　Urbana-Champaign M,W
University of St. Francis M,W
Waubonsee Community College M,W
Western Illinois University M,W

Indiana
Ancilla College M,W
Ball State University M,W
Bethel College M,W
Butler University M,W
Calumet College of St. Joseph M,W
Goshen College M,W
Grace College M,W
Huntington University M,W
Indiana Institute of Technology M,W
Indiana State University M,W
Indiana University
　　Bloomington M,W
　　South Bend M,W
　　Southeast M,W
Indiana University-Purdue University Fort Wayne M,W
Indiana University-Purdue University Indianapolis M,W
Indiana Wesleyan University M,W
Marian College M,W
Oakland City University M,W
Purdue University M,W
Purdue University
　　Calumet M,W
Saint Joseph's College M,W
St. Mary-of-the-Woods College W
Taylor University M,W
Taylor University Fort Wayne M,W
University of Evansville M,W
University of Indianapolis M,W
University of Notre Dame M,W
University of St. Francis M,W
University of Southern Indiana M,W
Valparaiso University M,W
Vincennes University M,W

Iowa
AIB College of Business W
Ashford University M,W
Briar Cliff University M,W
Clarke College M,W
Clinton Community College M
Des Moines Area Community College M,W
Dordt College M,W
Drake University M,W
Ellsworth Community College M,W
Graceland University M,W
Grand View College M,W
Indian Hills Community College M
Iowa Central Community College M,W
Iowa Lakes Community College M,W
Iowa State University M,W
Iowa Wesleyan College M,W
Iowa Western Community College M,W
Kirkwood Community College M,W
Marshalltown Community College M,W
Morningside College M,W
North Iowa Area Community College M,W
Northwestern College M,W
St. Ambrose University M,W
Southeastern Community College
　　North Campus M
Southwestern Community College M,W
University of Iowa M,W
University of Northern Iowa M,W
Waldorf College M,W
William Penn University M,W

Kansas
Allen County Community College M,W
Baker University M,W
Barton County Community College M,W
Benedictine College M,W
Bethany College M,W
Bethel College M,W
Brown Mackie College
　　Salina M,W
Butler County Community College M,W
Central Christian College of Kansas M,W
Cloud County Community College M,W
Coffeyville Community College M,W
Colby Community College M,W
Cowley County Community College M,W
Dodge City Community College M,W
Emporia State University M,W
Fort Hays State University M,W
Fort Scott Community College M,W
Friends University M,W
Garden City Community College M,W
Hesston College M,W
Highland Community College M,W
Hutchinson Community College M,W
Independence Community College M,W
Johnson County Community College M,W
Kansas City Kansas Community College M,W
Kansas State University M,W
Kansas Wesleyan University M,W
Labette Community College M,W
McPherson College M,W
MidAmerica Nazarene University M,W
Neosho County Community College M,W
Newman University M,W
Ottawa University M,W
Pittsburg State University M,W
Pratt Community College M,W
Seward County Community College M,W
Southwestern College M,W
Sterling College M,W
Tabor College M,W
University of Kansas M,W
University of St. Mary M,W
Washburn University M,W
Wichita State University M,W

Kentucky
Alice Lloyd College M,W
Asbury College M,W
Bellarmine University M,W
Brescia University M,W
Campbellsville University M,W
Eastern Kentucky University M,W
Georgetown College M,W
Kentucky State University M,W
Kentucky Wesleyan College M,W
Lindsey Wilson College M,W
Midway College W
Morehead State University M,W
Murray State University M,W
Northern Kentucky University M,W
Pikeville College M,W
St. Catharine College M,W
Union College M,W
University of Kentucky M,W
University of Louisville M,W
University of the Cumberlands M,W
Western Kentucky University M,W

Louisiana
Bossier Parish Community College M
Centenary College of Louisiana M,W
Delgado Community College M
Dillard University M,W
Grambling State University M,W
Louisiana State University and Agricultural and Mechanical College M,W
Louisiana Tech University M,W
Loyola University New Orleans M,W
McNeese State University M,W
Nicholls State University M,W
Northwestern State University M,W

Southeastern Louisiana University M,W
Southern University
    New Orleans M,W
Southern University and Agricultural and
    Mechanical College M,W
Tulane University M,W
University of Louisiana at Lafayette M,W
University of Louisiana at Monroe M,W
University of New Orleans M,W
Xavier University of Louisiana M,W

Maine
University of Maine M,W
University of Maine
    Augusta M,W

Maryland
Allegany College of Maryland M,W
Anne Arundel Community College M,W
Bowie State University M,W
Chesapeake College M,W
College of Southern Maryland M,W
Columbia Union College M,W
Community College of Baltimore County M,W
Coppin State University M,W
Garrett College M,W
Hagerstown Community College M,W
Harford Community College M,W
Howard Community College M,W
Loyola College in Maryland M,W
Morgan State University M,W
Mount St. Mary's University M,W
Prince George's Community College M,W
Towson University M,W
University of Maryland
    Baltimore County M,W
    College Park M,W
    Eastern Shore M,W

Massachusetts
American International College M,W
Assumption College M,W
Bentley College M,W
Boston College M,W
Boston University M,W
College of the Holy Cross M,W
Dean College M,W
Merrimack College M,W
Mount Ida College M
Northeastern University M,W
Roxbury Community College M
Stonehill College M,W
University of Massachusetts
    Amherst M,W
    Lowell M,W

Michigan
Alpena Community College M,W
Aquinas College M,W
Central Michigan University M,W
Concordia University M,W
Cornerstone University M,W
Davenport University M,W
Delta College M,W
Eastern Michigan University M,W
Ferris State University M,W
Glen Oaks Community College M,W
Gogebic Community College M,W
Grand Rapids Community College M,W
Grand Valley State University M,W
Henry Ford Community College M,W
Hillsdale College M,W
Kalamazoo Valley Community College M,W
Kellogg Community College M,W
Kirtland Community College M,W
Lake Michigan College M,W
Lake Superior State University M,W
Lansing Community College M,W
Macomb Community College M,W
Madonna University M,W
Michigan State University M,W
Michigan Technological University M,W
Mott Community College M,W

Muskegon Community College M,W
Northern Michigan University M,W
Northwood University: Michigan M,W
Oakland Community College M,W
Oakland University M,W
Rochester College M,W
Saginaw Valley State University M,W
Siena Heights University M,W
Southwestern Michigan College M,W
Spring Arbor University M,W
University of Detroit Mercy M,W
University of Michigan M,W
University of Michigan
    Dearborn M,W
Wayne State University M,W
Western Michigan University M,W

Minnesota
Bemidji State University M,W
Concordia University: St. Paul M,W
Minnesota State University
    Mankato M,W
    Moorhead M,W
Saint Cloud State University M,W
Southwest Minnesota State University M,W
University of Minnesota
    Crookston M,W
    Duluth M,W
    Twin Cities M,W
Winona State University M,W

Mississippi
Alcorn State University M,W
Belhaven College M,W
Blue Mountain College M,W
Coahoma Community College M,W
Copiah-Lincoln Community College M,W
Delta State University M,W
East Central Community College M,W
East Mississippi Community College M,W
Hinds Community College M,W
Holmes Community College M,W
Itawamba Community College M,W
Jackson State University M,W
Meridian Community College M,W
Mississippi Gulf Coast Community College
    Jefferson Davis Campus M,W
Mississippi State University M,W
Mississippi Valley State University M,W
Northwest Mississippi Community College M,W
Southwest Mississippi Community College
    M,W
Tougaloo College M,W
University of Mississippi M,W
University of Southern Mississippi M,W
William Carey University M,W

Missouri
Avila University M,W
Central Methodist University M,W
College of the Ozarks M,W
Columbia College M,W
Cottey College W
Crowder College W
Culver-Stockton College M,W
Drury University M,W
Evangel University M,W
Hannibal-LaGrange College M,W
Harris-Stowe State University M,W
Jefferson College W
Lincoln University M,W
Metropolitan Community College: Penn Valley
    M
Missouri Baptist University M,W
Missouri Southern State University M,W
Missouri State University M,W
Missouri Valley College M,W
Missouri Western State University M,W
Moberly Area Community College M,W
North Central Missouri College M,W
Northwest Missouri State University M,W
Park University M,W

Research College of Nursing M,W
Rockhurst University M,W
Saint Louis University M,W
Southeast Missouri State University M,W
Southwest Baptist University M,W
St. Louis Community College
    Meramec M,W
State Fair Community College M,W
Stephens College W
Three Rivers Community College M,W
Truman State University M,W
University of Central Missouri M,W
University of Missouri
    Columbia M,W
    Kansas City M,W
    Missouri University of Science and
        Technology M,W
    St. Louis M,W
William Jewell College M,W
William Woods University M,W

Montana
Carroll College M,W
Dawson Community College M,W
Miles Community College M,W
Montana State University
    Billings M,W
    Bozeman M,W
    Northern M,W
Montana Tech of the University of Montana
    M,W
Rocky Mountain College M,W
University of Great Falls M,W
University of Montana: Missoula M,W
University of Montana: Western M,W

Nebraska
Bellevue University M
Central Community College M
Chadron State College M,W
College of Saint Mary W
Concordia University M,W
Creighton University M,W
Dana College M,W
Doane College M,W
Hastings College M,W
Kaplan University
    Lincoln M,W
Mid-Plains Community College Area M,W
Midland Lutheran College M,W
Nebraska College of Technical Agriculture M,W
Northeast Community College M,W
Peru State College M,W
University of Nebraska
    Kearney M,W
    Lincoln M,W
    Omaha M,W
Wayne State College M,W
Western Nebraska Community College M,W
York College M,W

Nevada
University of Nevada
    Las Vegas M,W
    Reno M,W

New Hampshire
Franklin Pierce University M,W
Hesser College M,W
St. Anselm College M,W
Southern New Hampshire University M,W
University of New Hampshire M,W

New Jersey
Bloomfield College M,W
Brookdale Community College M,W
Burlington County College M,W
Caldwell College M,W
Essex County College M,W
Fairleigh Dickinson University
    Metropolitan Campus M,W
Felician College M,W
Georgian Court University W

Mercer County Community College M,W
Monmouth University M,W
New Jersey Institute of Technology M,W
Rider University M,W
Rutgers, The State University of New Jersey
    New Brunswick/Piscataway Campus M,W
Saint Peter's College M,W
Salem Community College M,W
Seton Hall University M,W
Union County College W

New Mexico
College of the Southwest M
Eastern New Mexico University M,W
New Mexico Highlands University M,W
New Mexico Junior College M,W
New Mexico Military Institute M
New Mexico State University M,W
University of New Mexico M,W
Western New Mexico University M,W

New York
Adelphi University M,W
Canisius College M,W
City University of New York
    Queens College M,W
Colgate University M,W
College of Saint Rose M,W
Concordia College M,W
Daemen College M,W
Dominican College of Blauvelt M,W
Dowling College M,W
Fordham University M,W
Genesee Community College M,W
Globe Institute of Technology M,W
Hofstra University M,W
Houghton College M,W
Iona College M,W
Le Moyne College M,W
Long Island University
    Brooklyn Campus M,W
    C. W. Post Campus M,W
Manhattan College M,W
Marist College M,W
Mercy College M,W
Molloy College M,W
Monroe College M
Monroe Community College M
New York Institute of Technology M
Niagara County Community College M,W
Niagara University M,W
Nyack College M,W
Pace University M,W
Roberts Wesleyan College M,W
Saint Bonaventure University M,W
St. Francis College M,W
St. John's University M,W
St. Thomas Aquinas College M,W
Siena College M,W
State University of New York
    Albany M,W
    Binghamton M,W
    Buffalo M,W
    Stony Brook M,W
Syracuse University M,W
Wagner College M,W

North Carolina
Appalachian State University M,W
Barton College M,W
Belmont Abbey College M,W
Brevard College M,W
Campbell University M,W
Catawba College M,W
Davidson College M,W
Duke University M,W
East Carolina University M,W
Elizabeth City State University M,W
Elon University M,W
Fayetteville State University M,W
Gardner-Webb University M,W
High Point University M,W

Johnson C. Smith University M,W
Lees-McRae College M,W
Lenoir Community College M
Lenoir-Rhyne College M,W
Livingstone College M,W
Louisburg College M,W
Mars Hill College M,W
Montreat College M,W
Mount Olive College M,W
North Carolina Agricultural and Technical State
     University M,W
North Carolina Central University M,W
North Carolina State University M,W
Pfeiffer University M,W
Queens University of Charlotte M,W
St. Andrews Presbyterian College M,W
St. Augustine's College M,W
Shaw University M,W
University of North Carolina
     Asheville M,W
     Chapel Hill M,W
     Charlotte M,W
     Greensboro M,W
     Pembroke M,W
     Wilmington M,W
Wake Forest University M,W
Western Carolina University M,W
Wingate University M,W
Winston-Salem State University M,W

North Dakota
Bismarck State College M,W
Dickinson State University M,W
Jamestown College M,W
Lake Region State College M,W
Mayville State University M,W
Minot State University M,W
Minot State University: Bottineau Campus M,W
North Dakota State College of Science M,W
North Dakota State University M,W
University of Mary M,W
University of North Dakota M,W
Valley City State University M,W
Williston State College M,W

Ohio
Ashland University M,W
Bowling Green State University M,W
Cedarville University M,W
Central State University M,W
Cincinnati State Technical and Community
     College M,W
Clark State Community College M,W
Cleveland State University M,W
Columbus State Community College M,W
Edison State Community College M,W
Kent State University M,W
Lakeland Community College M,W
Malone College M,W
Miami University
     Oxford Campus M,W
Mount Vernon Nazarene University M,W
Notre Dame College M,W
Ohio Dominican University M,W
Ohio State University
     Columbus Campus M,W
Ohio University M,W
Owens Community College
     Toledo M,W
Shawnee State University M,W
Sinclair Community College M,W
Southern State Community College M,W
University of Akron M,W
University of Cincinnati M,W
University of Dayton M,W
University of Findlay M,W
University of Rio Grande M,W
University of Toledo M,W
Urbana University M,W
Ursuline College W
Walsh University M,W
Wright State University M,W

Xavier University M,W
Youngstown State University M,W

Oklahoma
Bacone College M,W
Cameron University M,W
Carl Albert State College M,W
Connors State College M,W
East Central University M,W
Langston University M,W
Northeastern Oklahoma Agricultural and
     Mechanical College M,W
Northeastern State University M,W
Northwestern Oklahoma State University M,W
Oklahoma Baptist University M,W
Oklahoma Christian University M,W
Oklahoma City University M,W
Oklahoma Panhandle State University M,W
Oklahoma State University M,W
Oklahoma Wesleyan University M,W
Oral Roberts University M,W
Redlands Community College M,W
Rogers State University M,W
St. Gregory's University M,W
Seminole State College M,W
Southeastern Oklahoma State University M,W
Southern Nazarene University M,W
Southwestern Oklahoma State University M,W
University of Central Oklahoma M,W
University of Oklahoma M,W
University of Science and Arts of Oklahoma
     M,W
University of Tulsa M,W
Western Oklahoma State College M,W

Oregon
Blue Mountain Community College M,W
Cascade College M,W
Chemeketa Community College M,W
Clackamas Community College M,W
Concordia University M,W
Corban College M,W
Eastern Oregon University M,W
Lane Community College M,W
Linn-Benton Community College M,W
Mt. Hood Community College M,W
Northwest Christian College M,W
Oregon Institute of Technology M,W
Oregon State University M,W
Portland Community College M,W
Portland State University M,W
Southern Oregon University M,W
Southwestern Oregon Community College M,W
Treasure Valley Community College M,W
University of Oregon M,W
University of Portland M,W
Warner Pacific College M,W

Pennsylvania
Bloomsburg University of Pennsylvania M,W
Bucknell University M,W
California University of Pennsylvania M,W
Carlow University W
Chestnut Hill College M,W
Cheyney University of Pennsylvania M,W
Clarion University of Pennsylvania M,W
Community College of Beaver County M
Drexel University M,W
Duquesne University M,W
East Stroudsburg University of Pennsylvania
     M,W
Edinboro University of Pennsylvania M,W
Gannon University M,W
Harcum College M,W
Holy Family University M,W
Indiana University of Pennsylvania M,W
Kutztown University of Pennsylvania M,W
La Salle University M,W
Lackawanna College M,W
Lehigh University M,W
Lock Haven University of Pennsylvania M,W
Mansfield University of Pennsylvania M,W

Mercyhurst College M,W
Millersville University of Pennsylvania M,W
Penn State
     University Park M,W
Philadelphia University M,W
Point Park University M,W
Robert Morris University M,W
St. Francis University M,W
Saint Joseph's University M,W
Seton Hill University M,W
Shippensburg University of Pennsylvania M,W
Slippery Rock University of Pennsylvania M,W
Temple University M,W
University of Pittsburgh M,W
University of Pittsburgh
     Johnstown M,W
     Titusville M,W
University of the Sciences in Philadelphia M,W
Valley Forge Military College M
Villanova University M,W
West Chester University of Pennsylvania M,W
Westminster College M,W

Puerto Rico
Bayamon Central University M,W
Inter American University of Puerto Rico
     Aguadilla Campus M,W
     Arecibo Campus M
     Bayamon Campus M,W
     Fajardo Campus M
     Guayama Campus M,W
     Metropolitan Campus M,W
     Ponce Campus M,W
     San German Campus M,W
Turabo University M,W
Universidad del Este M,W
Universidad Metropolitana M,W
University of Puerto Rico
     Bayamon University College M,W
     Carolina Regional College M,W
     Cayey University College M,W
     Humacao M,W
     Mayaguez M,W
     Ponce M,W
     Utuado M,W
University of the Sacred Heart M

Rhode Island
Bryant University M,W
Community College of Rhode Island M,W
Providence College M,W
University of Rhode Island M,W

South Carolina
Aiken Technical College M
Allen University M
Anderson University M,W
Charleston Southern University M,W
The Citadel M
Claflin University M,W
Clemson University M,W
Coastal Carolina University M,W
Coker College M,W
College of Charleston M,W
Columbia College W
Converse College W
Erskine College M,W
Francis Marion University M,W
Furman University M,W
Lander University M,W
Limestone College M,W
Morris College M,W
Newberry College M,W
North Greenville University M,W
Presbyterian College M,W
South Carolina State University M,W
Southern Wesleyan University M,W
Spartanburg Methodist College M,W
University of South Carolina M,W
University of South Carolina
     Aiken M,W
     Upstate M,W

Voorhees College M,W
Winthrop University M,W
Wofford College M,W

South Dakota
Augustana College M,W
Black Hills State University M,W
Dakota State University M,W
Dakota Wesleyan University M,W
Mount Marty College M,W
Northern State University M,W
South Dakota School of Mines and Technology
     M,W
South Dakota State University M,W
University of Sioux Falls M,W
University of South Dakota M,W

Tennessee
Austin Peay State University M,W
Belmont University M,W
Bethel College M,W
Bryan College M,W
Carson-Newman College M,W
Chattanooga State Technical Community
     College M,W
Christian Brothers University M,W
Cleveland State Community College M,W
Columbia State Community College M,W
Crichton College M
Cumberland University M,W
Dyersburg State Community College M,W
East Tennessee State University M,W
Freed-Hardeman University M,W
Hiwassee College M,W
Jackson State Community College M,W
King College M,W
Lambuth University M,W
Lane College M,W
Lee University M,W
LeMoyne-Owen College M,W
Lincoln Memorial University M,W
Lipscomb University M,W
Martin Methodist College M,W
Middle Tennessee State University M,W
Milligan College M,W
Motlow State Community College M,W
Roane State Community College M,W
Southwest Tennessee Community College M,W
Tennessee State University M,W
Tennessee Technological University M,W
Tennessee Temple University M,W
Tennessee Wesleyan College M,W
Trevecca Nazarene University M,W
Tusculum College M,W
Union University M,W
University of Memphis M,W
University of Tennessee
     Chattanooga M,W
     Knoxville M,W
     Martin M,W
Vanderbilt University M,W
Volunteer State Community College M,W
Walters State Community College M,W

Texas
Abilene Christian University M,W
Angelina College M,W
Angelo State University M,W
Baylor University M,W
Blinn College M,W
Clarendon College M,W
Collin County Community College District M,W
Frank Phillips College M,W
Grayson County College M,W
Hill College M,W
Houston Baptist University M,W
Howard College M,W
Jacksonville College M,W
Jarvis Christian College M,W
Kilgore College M,W
Lamar University M,W
Lee College M

Lon Morris College M,W
Lubbock Christian University M,W
McLennan Community College M,W
Midland College M,W
Midwestern State University M,W
Odessa College M,W
Panola College M,W
Paris Junior College M,W
Prairie View A&M University M,W
Ranger College M,W
Rice University M,W
St. Edward's University M,W
St. Mary's University M,W
Sam Houston State University M,W
San Jacinto College W
South Plains College M,W
Southern Methodist University M,W
Southwestern Assemblies of God University M,W
Stephen F. Austin State University M,W
Tarleton State University M,W
Temple College M,W
Texas A&M University M,W
Texas A&M University
        Commerce M,W
        Kingsville M,W
Texas Christian University M,W
Texas Southern University M,W
Texas State University: San Marcos M,W
Texas Tech University M,W
Texas Woman's University W
Trinity Valley Community College M,W
Tyler Junior College M,W
University of Houston M,W
University of North Texas M,W
University of Texas
        Arlington M,W
        Austin M,W
        Pan American M,W
        San Antonio M,W
University of the Incarnate Word M,W
Wayland Baptist University M,W
Weatherford College M,W
West Texas A&M University M,W
Wiley College M,W

Utah
Brigham Young University M,W
College of Eastern Utah M,W
Dixie State College of Utah M,W
Salt Lake Community College M,W
Snow College M,W
Southern Utah University M,W
University of Utah M,W
Utah State University M,W
Utah Valley State College M,W
Weber State University M,W
Westminster College M,W

Vermont
St. Michael's College M,W
University of Vermont M,W

Virginia
Bluefield College M,W
College of William and Mary M,W
George Mason University M,W
Hampton University M,W
James Madison University M,W
Liberty University M,W
Longwood University M,W
Norfolk State University M,W
Old Dominion University M,W
Radford University M,W
St. Paul's College M,W
University of Richmond M,W
University of Virginia M,W
University of Virginia's College at Wise M,W
Virginia Commonwealth University M,W
Virginia Intermont College M,W
Virginia Military Institute M

Virginia Polytechnic Institute and State University M,W
Virginia State University M,W
Virginia Union University M,W

Washington
Big Bend Community College M,W
Central Washington University M,W
Centralia College M,W
Clark College M,W
Columbia Basin College M,W
Edmonds Community College M,W
Everett Community College M,W
Evergreen State College M,W
Gonzaga University M,W
Grays Harbor College M,W
Green River Community College M,W
Highline Community College M,W
Lower Columbia College M,W
North Seattle Community College M,W
Northwest University M,W
Olympic College M,W
Peninsula College M,W
Saint Martin's University M,W
Seattle Pacific University M,W
Seattle University M,W
Spokane Community College M,W
Tacoma Community College M,W
University of Washington M,W
Walla Walla Community College M,W
Washington State University M,W
Western Washington University M,W
Whatcom Community College M,W
Yakima Valley Community College M,W

West Virginia
Alderson-Broaddus College M,W
Bluefield State College M,W
Concord University M,W
Davis and Elkins College M,W
Fairmont State University M,W
Glenville State College M,W
Marshall University M,W
Mountain State University M
Ohio Valley University M,W
Potomac State College of West Virginia University M,W
Salem International University M,W
Shepherd University M,W
University of Charleston M,W
West Liberty State College M,W
West Virginia University M,W
West Virginia Wesleyan College M,W
Wheeling Jesuit University M,W

Wisconsin
Cardinal Stritch University M,W
Marquette University M,W
Silver Lake College M,W
University of Wisconsin
        Green Bay M,W
        Milwaukee M,W
        Parkside M,W
Viterbo University M,W

Wyoming
Casper College M,W
Central Wyoming College M,W
Eastern Wyoming College M
Laramie County Community College M
Northwest College M,W
Sheridan College M,W
University of Wyoming M,W
Western Wyoming Community College M,W

Bowling

Arkansas
Arkansas State University W
University of Arkansas
        Pine Bluff W

Delaware
Delaware State University W

Florida
Bethune-Cookman University W

Illinois
McKendree University M,W
Robert Morris College: Chicago M,W

Indiana
Calumet College of St. Joseph M,W
Vincennes University M,W

Kansas
Newman University M,W
Wichita State University M,W

Kentucky
Pikeville College M,W

Louisiana
Southern University and Agricultural and
        Mechanical College W

Maryland
Bowie State University W
Coppin State University W
Morgan State University W
Prince George's Community College M,W

Michigan
Aquinas College M,W
Saginaw Valley State University M

Mississippi
Jackson State University M,W
Mississippi Valley State University M,W

Missouri
Missouri Baptist University M,W

Nebraska
University of Nebraska
        Lincoln W

New Jersey
Fairleigh Dickinson University
        Metropolitan Campus W

New York
Adelphi University W
Globe Institute of Technology M,W

North Carolina
Blue Ridge Community College M
Johnson C. Smith University W
Livingstone College M,W
North Carolina Central University M,W
St. Augustine's College W
Shaw University W

Pennsylvania
Cheyney University of Pennsylvania W

Texas
Prairie View A&M University W
Texas Southern University W

Virginia
Norfolk State University W

Cheerleading

Alabama
Bevill State Community College M,W
Chattahoochee Valley Community College M,W
Faulkner State Community College M,W
Gadsden State Community College W
Northwest-Shoals Community College M,W
Shelton State Community College M,W
Southern Union State Community College M,W

Troy University M,W
University of Alabama M,W
University of Alabama
        Huntsville M,W

Arizona
Glendale Community College M,W

Arkansas
University of Arkansas M,W
University of Arkansas
        Fort Smith M,W
        Monticello M,W
University of Central Arkansas M,W
Williams Baptist College M,W

California
California Baptist University M,W
Hope International University M,W

Delaware
University of Delaware M,W

Florida
Pensacola Junior College M,W
University of Central Florida M,W
Warner Southern College M,W
Webber International University M,W

Georgia
Albany State University W
Brewton-Parker College M,W
Mercer University M,W
Reinhardt College M,W
University of West Georgia M,W
Valdosta State University W

Hawaii
Hawaii Pacific University M,W
University of Hawaii
        Manoa M,W

Idaho
Boise State University M,W
North Idaho College M,W

Illinois
Kaskaskia College M,W
Lincoln College M,W
McKendree University M,W
Northwestern University M,W
Olivet Nazarene University M,W
Rend Lake College W
Southern Illinois University Carbondale M,W

Indiana
Ancilla College M,W
Grace College M,W
Indiana Institute of Technology M,W
Indiana Wesleyan University M,W
Marian College M,W
Oakland City University W
University of St. Francis M,W

Iowa
Iowa Western Community College M,W
Waldorf College W
William Penn University W

Kansas
Allen County Community College M,W
Baker University M,W
Barton County Community College M,W
Benedictine College M,W
Central Christian College of Kansas M,W
Coffeyville Community College M,W
Cowley County Community College M,W
Dodge City Community College M,W
Emporia State University M,W
Fort Scott Community College W
Garden City Community College M,W
Labette Community College M,W
McPherson College M,W
MidAmerica Nazarene University M,W

Neosho County Community College M,W
Ottawa University M,W
Pittsburg State University M,W
Pratt Community College M,W
Seward County Community College M,W
Southwestern College M,W
Tabor College M,W
Washburn University M,W
Wichita State University M,W

Kentucky
Bellarmine University M,W
Murray State University M,W
Union College M,W
University of Louisville M,W
University of the Cumberlands M,W

Louisiana
Bossier Parish Community College M,W
Delgado Community College W
McNeese State University M,W
Southeastern Louisiana University M,W
University of Louisiana at Lafayette M,W
University of Louisiana at Monroe M,W

Maryland
College of Southern Maryland M,W
Morgan State University W
University of Maryland
    College Park W

Michigan
Northwood University: Michigan M,W
University of Detroit Mercy M,W

Mississippi
Copiah-Lincoln Community College M,W
Itawamba Community College M,W
Mississippi Gulf Coast Community College
    Jefferson Davis Campus M,W
Northwest Mississippi Community College M,W
University of Mississippi M,W
William Carey University M,W

Missouri
Avila University W
Culver-Stockton College M,W
Drury University M,W
Evangel University M,W
Hannibal-LaGrange College M,W
Harris-Stowe State University M,W
Missouri Baptist University M,W
Missouri Southern State University M,W
Missouri Valley College M,W
Moberly Area Community College M,W
Northwest Missouri State University M,W
Southeast Missouri State University M,W
University of Missouri
    Kansas City M,W
William Jewell College M,W

Nebraska
Dana College M,W
Hastings College W

Nevada
University of Nevada
    Las Vegas M,W
    Reno M,W

New Mexico
New Mexico Junior College M,W

New York
Hofstra University M,W
Nyack College M,W

North Carolina
Brevard College M,W
Campbell University W
Elon University M,W
Gardner-Webb University M,W
Lenoir-Rhyne College M,W

Mars Hill College M,W
Methodist University M,W
University of North Carolina
    Wilmington M,W

Ohio
Ashland University W
Kent State University M,W
University of Rio Grande M,W
Urbana University W

Oklahoma
Cameron University M,W
Carl Albert State College W
Langston University M,W
Northeastern Oklahoma Agricultural and
    Mechanical College M,W
Northwestern Oklahoma State University M,W
Oklahoma Christian University W
Oklahoma City University M,W
Oklahoma Panhandle State University M,W
Oral Roberts University M,W
Southeastern Oklahoma State University W
Southern Nazarene University M,W
Southwestern Oklahoma State University M,W
University of Science and Arts of Oklahoma
    M,W
University of Tulsa M,W
Western Oklahoma State College M,W

Oregon
Southwestern Oregon Community College M,W
University of Oregon W

Pennsylvania
Kutztown University of Pennsylvania W
Lackawanna College W
Penn State
    University Park M,W
St. Francis University M,W
Seton Hill University M,W
Temple University M,W
West Chester University of Pennsylvania W

Puerto Rico
University of Puerto Rico
    Carolina Regional College M,W
    Humacao M,W

South Carolina
Anderson University W
Clemson University M,W
Limestone College M,W
Morris College M,W
Newberry College W
North Greenville University M,W
Spartanburg Methodist College M,W

South Dakota
Dakota Wesleyan University M,W

Tennessee
Bethel College M,W
Crichton College W
Cumberland University M,W
Freed-Hardeman University W
Hiwassee College M,W
King College M,W
Lambuth University M,W
Tennessee Technological University M,W
Tennessee Wesleyan College M,W
Tusculum College W
University of Memphis M,W
University of Tennessee
    Martin M,W

Texas
Angelina College M,W
Clarendon College M,W
East Texas Baptist University M,W
Houston Baptist University M,W
Howard College M,W
Jacksonville College M,W

Lon Morris College M,W
Lubbock Christian University M,W
Ranger College M,W
St. Edward's University M,W
San Jacinto College M,W
South Plains College M,W
Southern Methodist University M,W
Southwestern Assemblies of God University W
Tarleton State University M,W
Texas Southern University M,W
Tyler Junior College M,W
Western Texas College W

Utah
Brigham Young University M,W
Snow College M,W

Virginia
Liberty University M,W
Old Dominion University M,W
Virginia Intermont College W

Washington
University of Washington M,W
Walla Walla Community College W

West Virginia
Mountain State University M,W
University of Charleston M,W

Wyoming
University of Wyoming M,W
Western Wyoming Community College W

Cricket

California
College of the Redwoods M

Cross-country

Alabama
Alabama Agricultural and Mechanical
    University M,W
Alabama State University M,W
Auburn University M,W
Bevill State Community College W
Jacksonville State University M,W
Lurleen B. Wallace Community College M,W
Miles College M,W
Northwest-Shoals Community College M
Samford University M,W
Southern Union State Community College M,W
Spring Hill College M,W
Troy University M,W
University of Alabama M,W
University of Alabama
    Birmingham W
    Huntsville M,W
University of Mobile M,W
University of North Alabama M,W
University of South Alabama M,W
University of West Alabama M,W

Alaska
University of Alaska
    Anchorage M,W
    Fairbanks M,W

Arizona
Arizona State University M,W
Central Arizona College M,W
Dine College M,W
Gateway Community College M,W
Glendale Community College M,W
Mesa Community College M,W
Northern Arizona University M,W
Paradise Valley Community College M,W
Pima Community College M,W
Scottsdale Community College M,W

University of Arizona M,W
Yavapai College W

Arkansas
Arkansas State University M,W
Arkansas Tech University W
Harding University M,W
Henderson State University W
Lyon College M,W
Ouachita Baptist University W
Southern Arkansas University W
University of Arkansas M,W
University of Arkansas
    Little Rock M,W
    Monticello W
    Pine Bluff M,W
University of Central Arkansas M,W

California
Azusa Pacific University M,W
Biola University M,W
California Polytechnic State University: San Luis
    Obispo M,W
California State Polytechnic University: Pomona
    M,W
California State University
    Chico M,W
    Dominguez Hills W
    Fresno M,W
    Fullerton M,W
    Long Beach M,W
    Los Angeles M,W
    Northridge M,W
    Sacramento M,W
    Stanislaus M,W
Concordia University M,W
Fresno City College M,W
Fresno Pacific University M,W
Holy Names University M,W
Humboldt State University M,W
Loyola Marymount University M,W
The Master's College M,W
Notre Dame de Namur University M,W
Pepperdine University M,W
Point Loma Nazarene University M,W
St. Mary's College of California M,W
San Diego State University W
San Jose State University W
Santa Clara University M,W
Santiago Canyon College M,W
Stanford University M,W
University of California
    Berkeley M,W
    Davis M,W
    Irvine M,W
    Los Angeles M,W
    Riverside M,W
    Santa Barbara M,W
University of San Diego M,W
University of San Francisco M,W
University of Southern California M,W
University of the Pacific W
Vanguard University of Southern California
    M,W
Westmont College M,W
William Jessup University M,W
Yuba Community College District M,W

Colorado
Adams State College M,W
Colorado Christian University M,W
Colorado Northwestern Community College M
Colorado School of Mines M,W
Colorado State University M,W
Colorado State University
    Pueblo W
Fort Lewis College M,W
Mesa State College W
Regis University M,W
University of Colorado
    Boulder M,W
    Colorado Springs M,W

University of Northern Colorado W
Western State College of Colorado M,W

Connecticut
Central Connecticut State University M,W
Fairfield University M,W
Post University M
Quinnipiac University M,W
Sacred Heart University M,W
Southern Connecticut State University M,W
University of Connecticut M,W
University of Hartford M,W
University of New Haven M,W

Delaware
Delaware State University M,W
Goldey-Beacom College M
Wilmington University M,W

District of Columbia
American University M,W
George Washington University M,W
Georgetown University M,W
Howard University M,W

Florida
Bethune-Cookman University M,W
Embry-Riddle Aeronautical University M,W
Flagler College M,W
Florida Atlantic University M,W
Florida Institute of Technology M,W
Florida Southern College M,W
Florida State University M,W
Jacksonville University W
Nova Southeastern University W
St. Leo University M,W
Saint Thomas University M,W
Stetson University M,W
University of Central Florida M,W
University of Florida M,W
University of Miami M,W
University of North Florida M,W
University of South Florida M,W
University of Tampa M,W
University of West Florida M,W
Warner Southern College M,W
Webber International University M,W

Georgia
Albany State University M,W
Andrew College M,W
Augusta State University M,W
Berry College M,W
Brenau University W
Clark Atlanta University M,W
Clayton State University M,W
Columbus State University M,W
Covenant College M,W
Georgia College and State University M,W
Georgia Institute of Technology M,W
Georgia Southern University W
Georgia Southwestern State University W
Georgia State University M,W
Kennesaw State University M,W
Mercer University M,W
Middle Georgia College M,W
Morehouse College M
Paine College M,W
Reinhardt College M,W
Savannah State University M,W
Shorter College M,W
Truett-McConnell College M,W
University of Georgia M,W
University of West Georgia M,W
Young Harris College M,W

Hawaii
Brigham Young University-Hawaii M,W
Chaminade University of Honolulu M,W
Hawaii Pacific University M,W
University of Hawaii
　　Hilo M,W
　　Manoa W

Idaho
Boise State University M,W
College of Idaho M,W
Idaho State University M,W
Lewis-Clark State College M,W
Northwest Nazarene University M,W
University of Idaho M,W

Illinois
Bradley University M,W
Chicago State University M,W
College of Lake County M,W
Danville Area Community College M,W
DePaul University M,W
Eastern Illinois University M,W
Illinois Institute of Technology M,W
Illinois State University M,W
Judson University M,W
Lewis University M,W
Lincoln College M,W
Loyola University Chicago M,W
McKendree University M,W
Moraine Valley Community College M,W
Morton College M,W
Northwestern University W
Olivet Nazarene University M,W
Rend Lake College M,W
Robert Morris College: Chicago M,W
St. Xavier University M,W
Sauk Valley Community College M,W
Southern Illinois University Carbondale M,W
Southern Illinois University Edwardsville M,W
Trinity Christian College M,W
University of Illinois
　　Chicago M,W
　　Urbana-Champaign M,W
University of St. Francis M,W
Waubonsee Community College M,W
Western Illinois University M,W

Indiana
Ball State University M,W
Bethel College M,W
Butler University M,W
Calumet College of St. Joseph M,W
Goshen College M,W
Grace College M,W
Huntington University M,W
Indiana Institute of Technology M,W
Indiana State University M,W
Indiana University
　　Bloomington M,W
Indiana University-Purdue University Fort
　　Wayne M,W
Indiana University-Purdue University
　　Indianapolis M,W
Indiana Wesleyan University M,W
Marian College M,W
Oakland City University M,W
Purdue University M,W
Saint Joseph's College M,W
Taylor University M,W
University of Evansville M,W
University of Indianapolis M,W
University of Notre Dame M,W
University of St. Francis M,W
University of Southern Indiana M,W
Valparaiso University M,W
Vincennes University M,W

Iowa
Ashford University M,W
Briar Cliff University M,W
Clarke College M,W
Dordt College M,W
Drake University M,W
Ellsworth Community College M,W
Graceland University M,W
Grand View College M,W
Iowa State University M,W
Morningside College M,W
North Iowa Area Community College M,W

Northwestern College M,W
St. Ambrose University M,W
University of Iowa M,W
University of Northern Iowa M,W
William Penn University M,W

Kansas
Allen County Community College M,W
Baker University M,W
Barton County Community College M,W
Benedictine College M,W
Bethany College M,W
Bethel College M,W
Butler County Community College M,W
Central Christian College of Kansas M,W
Cloud County Community College M,W
Coffeyville Community College M,W
Colby Community College M,W
Cowley County Community College M,W
Dodge City Community College M,W
Emporia State University M,W
Fort Hays State University M,W
Fort Scott Community College M,W
Garden City Community College M,W
Highland Community College M,W
Hutchinson Community College M,W
Johnson County Community College M,W
Kansas City Kansas Community College M,W
Kansas State University M,W
Kansas Wesleyan University M,W
McPherson College M,W
MidAmerica Nazarene University M,W
Neosho County Community College M,W
Newman University M,W
Ottawa University M,W
Pittsburg State University M,W
Pratt Community College M,W
Southwestern College M,W
Sterling College M,W
Tabor College M,W
University of Kansas M,W
Wichita State University M,W

Kentucky
Asbury College M,W
Bellarmine University M,W
Campbellsville University M,W
Eastern Kentucky University M,W
Georgetown College M,W
Kentucky State University M,W
Lindsey Wilson College M,W
Midway College W
Morehead State University M,W
Murray State University M,W
Northern Kentucky University M,W
Pikeville College M,W
Union College M,W
University of Kentucky M,W
University of Louisville M,W
University of the Cumberlands M,W
Western Kentucky University M,W

Louisiana
Centenary College of Louisiana M,W
Dillard University M,W
Grambling State University M,W
Louisiana State University and Agricultural and
　　Mechanical College M,W
Louisiana Tech University M,W
McNeese State University M,W
Nicholls State University M,W
Northwestern State University M,W
Southeastern Louisiana University M,W
Southern University
　　New Orleans M,W
Southern University and Agricultural and
　　Mechanical College M,W
University of Louisiana at Lafayette M,W
University of Louisiana at Monroe M,W
Xavier University of Louisiana M,W

Maine
University of Maine M,W

Maryland
Bowie State University M,W
Columbia Union College M,W
Coppin State University M,W
Hagerstown Community College M,W
Loyola College in Maryland M,W
Morgan State University M,W
Mount St. Mary's University M,W
Towson University M,W
University of Maryland
　　Baltimore County M,W
　　Eastern Shore M,W

Massachusetts
American International College M,W
Boston College M,W
Boston University M,W
Merrimack College W
Northeastern University M,W
Stonehill College M,W
University of Massachusetts
　　Amherst M,W
　　Lowell M,W

Michigan
Aquinas College M,W
Central Michigan University M,W
Concordia University M,W
Cornerstone University M,W
Davenport University M,W
Delta College M
Eastern Michigan University M,W
Ferris State University M,W
Grand Rapids Community College M,W
Grand Valley State University M,W
Hillsdale College M,W
Kirtland Community College M,W
Lake Superior State University M,W
Lansing Community College M,W
Macomb Community College M,W
Madonna University M,W
Michigan State University M,W
Michigan Technological University W
Mott Community College M,W
Northern Michigan University W
Northwood University: Michigan M,W
Oakland Community College M,W
Oakland University M,W
Saginaw Valley State University M,W
Siena Heights University M,W
Spring Arbor University M,W
University of Detroit Mercy M,W
University of Michigan M,W
Wayne State University M,W
Western Michigan University M,W

Minnesota
Concordia University: St. Paul M,W
Minnesota State University
　　Mankato M,W
　　Moorhead M,W
Saint Cloud State University M,W
University of Minnesota
　　Duluth M,W
　　Twin Cities M,W
Winona State University W

Mississippi
Alcorn State University M,W
Belhaven College M,W
Blue Mountain College M,W
Delta State University W
Jackson State University M,W
Mississippi State University M,W
Mississippi Valley State University M,W
Tougaloo College M,W
University of Mississippi M,W
University of Southern Mississippi M,W

Missouri
Central Methodist University M,W
Drury University M,W

Evangel University M,W
Hannibal-LaGrange College M,W
Lincoln University W
Missouri Baptist University M,W
Missouri Southern State University M,W
Missouri State University M,W
Missouri Valley College M,W
Northwest Missouri State University M,W
Park University M,W
Research College of Nursing M,W
Saint Louis University M,W
Southeast Missouri State University M,W
Southwest Baptist University M,W
Truman State University M,W
University of Central Missouri M,W
University of Missouri
    Columbia M,W
    Kansas City M,W
    Missouri University of Science and
      Technology M,W
William Jewell College M,W
William Woods University M,W

Montana
Carroll College M,W
Flathead Valley Community College M,W
Montana State University
    Billings M,W
    Bozeman M,W
University of Great Falls M,W
University of Montana: Missoula M,W

Nebraska
College of Saint Mary W
Concordia University M,W
Creighton University M,W
Dana College M,W
Doane College M,W
Hastings College M,W
Midland Lutheran College M,W
University of Nebraska
    Kearney M,W
    Lincoln M,W
    Omaha W
Wayne State College M,W

Nevada
University of Nevada
    Las Vegas W
    Reno W

New Hampshire
Southern New Hampshire University M,W
University of New Hampshire M,W

New Jersey
Bloomfield College M,W
Caldwell College W
Fairleigh Dickinson University
    Metropolitan Campus M,W
Felician College M,W
Georgian Court University W
Monmouth University M,W
Rider University M,W
Rutgers, The State University of New Jersey
    New Brunswick/Piscataway Campus M,W
Saint Peter's College M,W
Seton Hall University M,W

New Mexico
College of the Southwest M,W
Eastern New Mexico University M,W
New Mexico Highlands University M,W
New Mexico Junior College M,W
New Mexico State University M,W
University of New Mexico M,W

New York
Adelphi University M,W
Canisius College M,W
City University of New York
    Queens College M,W
College of Saint Rose M,W

Daemen College M,W
Fordham University M,W
Globe Institute of Technology M,W
Hofstra University M,W
Houghton College M,W
Iona College M,W
Le Moyne College M,W
Long Island University
    Brooklyn Campus M,W
    C. W. Post Campus M,W
Manhattan College M,W
Marist College M,W
Mercy College M,W
Molloy College M,W
New York Institute of Technology M,W
Niagara University M,W
Nyack College M,W
Pace University M,W
Roberts Wesleyan College M,W
St. Francis College M,W
St. John's University W
St. Thomas Aquinas College M,W
Siena College M,W
State University of New York
    Albany M,W
    Binghamton M,W
    Buffalo M,W
    Stony Brook M,W
Syracuse University M,W
Wagner College M,W

North Carolina
Appalachian State University M,W
Barton College M,W
Belmont Abbey College M,W
Brevard College M,W
Campbell University M,W
Catawba College M,W
Davidson College M,W
East Carolina University M,W
Elon University M,W
Fayetteville State University M,W
Gardner-Webb University M,W
High Point University M,W
Johnson C. Smith University M,W
Lees-McRae College M,W
Lenoir-Rhyne College M,W
Livingstone College M,W
Mars Hill College M,W
Montreat College M,W
Mount Olive College M,W
North Carolina Agricultural and Technical State
    University M,W
North Carolina Central University M,W
North Carolina State University M,W
Pfeiffer University M,W
Queens University of Charlotte M,W
St. Andrews Presbyterian College M,W
St. Augustine's College M,W
Shaw University M,W
University of North Carolina
    Asheville M,W
    Chapel Hill M,W
    Charlotte M,W
    Greensboro M,W
    Pembroke M,W
    Wilmington M,W
Wake Forest University M,W
Western Carolina University M,W
Wingate University M,W
Winston-Salem State University M,W

North Dakota
Dickinson State University M,W
Jamestown College M,W
Minot State University M,W
North Dakota State University M,W
University of Mary M,W
University of North Dakota M,W

Ohio
Ashland University M,W
Bowling Green State University M,W
Cedarville University M,W
Central State University M,W
Cleveland State University W
Kent State University M,W
Malone College M,W
Miami University
    Oxford Campus M,W
Mount Vernon Nazarene University M,W
Notre Dame College M,W
Ohio Dominican University M,W
Ohio State University
    Columbus Campus M,W
Ohio University M,W
Shawnee State University M,W
University of Akron M,W
University of Dayton M,W
University of Findlay M,W
University of Rio Grande M,W
University of Toledo M,W
Ursuline College W
Walsh University M,W
Wright State University M,W
Xavier University M,W
Youngstown State University M,W

Oklahoma
Cameron University M
East Central University M,W
Langston University M,W
Oklahoma Baptist University M,W
Oklahoma Christian University M,W
Oklahoma Panhandle State University M,W
Oklahoma State University M,W
Oklahoma Wesleyan University M,W
Oral Roberts University M,W
St. Gregory's University M,W
Southeastern Oklahoma State University W
Southern Nazarene University M,W
Southwestern Oklahoma State University W
University of Central Oklahoma M,W
University of Oklahoma M,W
University of Tulsa M,W

Oregon
Cascade College M,W
Clackamas Community College M,W
Concordia University M,W
Corban College M,W
Eastern Oregon University M,W
Lane Community College M,W
Mt. Hood Community College M,W
Oregon Institute of Technology M,W
Portland State University M,W
Southern Oregon University M,W
Southwestern Oregon Community College M,W
University of Oregon M,W
University of Portland M,W
Warner Pacific College M,W

Pennsylvania
Bloomsburg University of Pennsylvania M,W
California University of Pennsylvania M,W
Chestnut Hill College M,W
Cheyney University of Pennsylvania M,W
Clarion University of Pennsylvania M,W
Duquesne University M,W
East Stroudsburg University of Pennsylvania
    M,W
Edinboro University of Pennsylvania M,W
Gannon University M,W
Holy Family University M,W
Indiana University of Pennsylvania M,W
Kutztown University of Pennsylvania M,W
La Salle University M,W
Lackawanna College M,W
Lehigh University M,W
Lock Haven University of Pennsylvania M,W
Mansfield University of Pennsylvania W
Mercyhurst College M,W

Millersville University of Pennsylvania M,W
Penn State
    University Park M,W
Philadelphia University M,W
Point Park University M,W
Robert Morris University M,W
St. Francis University M,W
Saint Joseph's University M,W
Seton Hill University M,W
Shippensburg University of Pennsylvania M,W
Slippery Rock University of Pennsylvania M,W
University of Pittsburgh M,W
University of the Sciences in Philadelphia M,W
Villanova University M,W
West Chester University of Pennsylvania M,W
Westminster College W

Puerto Rico
Bayamon Central University M,W
Inter American University of Puerto Rico
    Aguadilla Campus M,W
    Bayamon Campus M,W
    Guayama Campus M,W
    San German Campus M,W
Turabo University M,W
Universidad del Este M,W
Universidad Metropolitana M,W
Universidad Politecnica de Puerto Rico M
University of Puerto Rico
    Carolina Regional College M,W
    Cayey University College M,W
    Humacao M,W
    Mayaguez M,W
    Ponce M,W
    Utuado M,W
University of the Sacred Heart M,W

Rhode Island
Bryant University M,W
Providence College M,W
University of Rhode Island M,W

South Carolina
Anderson University M,W
Charleston Southern University M,W
The Citadel M,W
Claflin University M,W
Clemson University M,W
Coastal Carolina University M,W
Coker College M,W
College of Charleston M,W
Converse College W
Erskine College M,W
Francis Marion University M,W
Furman University M,W
Lander University W
Limestone College M,W
Morris College M,W
Newberry College M,W
North Greenville University M,W
Presbyterian College M,W
South Carolina State University M,W
Southern Wesleyan University M,W
Spartanburg Methodist College M,W
University of South Carolina W
University of South Carolina
    Aiken W
    Upstate M,W
Voorhees College M,W
Winthrop University M,W
Wofford College M,W

South Dakota
Augustana College M,W
Black Hills State University M,W
Dakota Wesleyan University M,W
Mount Marty College M,W
South Dakota School of Mines and Technology
    M,W
South Dakota State University M,W
University of Sioux Falls M,W
University of South Dakota M,W

Tennessee
Austin Peay State University M,W
Belmont University M,W
Bethel College M,W
Bryan College M,W
Carson-Newman College M,W
Christian Brothers University M,W
Crichton College M,W
Cumberland University M,W
East Tennessee State University M,W
Hiwassee College M,W
King College M,W
Lambuth University M,W
Lee University M,W
LeMoyne-Owen College M
Lincoln Memorial University M,W
Lipscomb University M,W
Middle Tennessee State University M,W
Milligan College M,W
Tennessee Technological University M,W
Tennessee Wesleyan College M,W
Tusculum College M,W
Union University M,W
University of Memphis M,W
University of Tennessee
    Chattanooga M,W
    Knoxville M,W
    Martin M,W
Vanderbilt University W

Texas
Abilene Christian University M,W
Angelo State University M,W
Baylor University M,W
Dallas Baptist University W
Lamar University M,W
Midwestern State University W
Northwood University: Texas M,W
Prairie View A&M University M,W
Rice University M,W
St. Edward's University M,W
Sam Houston State University M,W
South Plains College M,W
Southern Methodist University W
Stephen F. Austin State University M,W
Tarleton State University M,W
Texas A&M University M,W
Texas A&M University
    Commerce M,W
Texas Christian University M,W
Texas Southern University M,W
Texas State University: San Marcos M,W
Texas Tech University M,W
University of Houston M,W
University of North Texas M,W
University of Texas
    Arlington M,W
    Austin M,W
    Pan American M,W
    San Antonio M,W
University of the Incarnate Word M,W
Wayland Baptist University M,W
West Texas A&M University M,W
Western Texas College M,W

Utah
Brigham Young University M,W
Dixie State College of Utah M,W
University of Utah W
Utah State University M,W
Utah Valley State College M,W
Weber State University M,W

Vermont
University of Vermont M,W

Virginia
Bluefield College M,W
College of William and Mary M,W
George Mason University M,W
Hampton University M,W
James Madison University W

Liberty University M,W
Longwood University M,W
Norfolk State University M,W
Radford University M,W
St. Paul's College M,W
University of Richmond W
University of Virginia M,W
University of Virginia's College at Wise M,W
Virginia Military Institute M,W
Virginia Polytechnic Institute and State
    University M,W
Virginia State University M,W

Washington
Central Washington University M,W
Clark College M,W
Everett Community College M,W
Evergreen State College M,W
Gonzaga University M,W
Highline Community College M,W
Northwest University M,W
Saint Martin's University M,W
Seattle Pacific University M,W
Seattle University M,W
Spokane Community College M,W
University of Washington M,W
Washington State University M,W
Western Washington University M,W

West Virginia
Alderson-Broaddus College M,W
Bluefield State College M,W
Concord University M,W
Davis and Elkins College M,W
Glenville State College M,W
Marshall University M,W
Ohio Valley University M,W
University of Charleston M,W
West Liberty State College M,W
West Virginia University W
West Virginia Wesleyan College M,W
Wheeling Jesuit University M,W

Wisconsin
Cardinal Stritch University M,W
Marquette University M,W
Milwaukee Area Technical College M,W
Silver Lake College M,W
University of Wisconsin
    Green Bay M,W
    Milwaukee M,W
    Parkside M,W

Wyoming
University of Wyoming M,W

Diving

Alabama
Auburn University M,W
University of Alabama M,W

Arizona
Arizona State University M,W
Northern Arizona University W
University of Arizona M,W

Arkansas
Ouachita Baptist University M,W
University of Arkansas W

California
California Baptist University M,W
California Polytechnic State University: San Luis
    Obispo M,W
California State University
    Northridge M,W
College of the Redwoods M
San Diego State University W
San Jose State University W
Stanford University M,W

University of California
    Berkeley M,W
    Davis M,W
    Irvine M,W
University of San Diego W
University of Southern California M,W

Colorado
Colorado State University W
University of Denver M,W

Connecticut
Central Connecticut State University W
Fairfield University M,W
University of Connecticut M,W

District of Columbia
George Washington University M,W
Howard University M,W

Florida
Florida State University M,W
Indian River Community College M,W
University of Florida M,W
University of Miami M,W

Georgia
Georgia Institute of Technology M,W
Georgia Southern University W
University of Georgia M,W

Hawaii
University of Hawaii
    Manoa M,W

Illinois
Eastern Illinois University M,W
Illinois Institute of Technology M,W
Illinois State University W
Lincoln College M,W
Northwestern University M,W
Southern Illinois University Carbondale M,W
University of Illinois
    Chicago M,W
    Urbana-Champaign W
Western Illinois University M,W

Indiana
Ball State University M,W
Indiana University
    Bloomington M,W
Indiana University-Purdue University
    Indianapolis M,W
Purdue University M,W
University of Evansville M,W
University of Notre Dame M,W
Valparaiso University M,W

Iowa
University of Iowa M,W

Kentucky
Asbury College M,W
University of Kentucky M,W
University of Louisville M,W
Western Kentucky University M

Maine
University of Maine M,W

Maryland
Loyola College in Maryland M,W
Towson University M,W
University of Maryland
    Baltimore County M,W

Massachusetts
Boston College M,W
Boston University M,W
Northeastern University W
University of Massachusetts
    Amherst M,W

Michigan
Eastern Michigan University M,W
Grand Rapids Community College M,W
Grand Valley State University M,W
Hillsdale College W
Michigan State University M,W
Northern Michigan University W
Oakland University M,W
University of Michigan M,W
Wayne State University M,W

Minnesota
Minnesota State University
    Mankato M,W
    Moorhead M
Saint Cloud State University M,W
University of Minnesota
    Twin Cities M,W

Mississippi
Delta State University M,W

Missouri
Drury University M,W
Saint Louis University M,W
University of Missouri
    Columbia M,W

Nebraska
University of Nebraska
    Kearney W
    Lincoln W

Nevada
University of Nevada
    Las Vegas M
    Reno W

New Hampshire
University of New Hampshire W

New Jersey
Rider University M,W
Rutgers, The State University of New Jersey
    New Brunswick/Piscataway Campus M,W
Saint Peter's College M,W

New Mexico
University of New Mexico W

New York
Fordham University M,W
Iona College M,W
Marist College M,W
Niagara University M,W
Saint Bonaventure University M,W
St. Francis College M,W
Siena College W
State University of New York
    Binghamton M,W
    Stony Brook M,W
Syracuse University M,W

North Carolina
Davidson College M,W
East Carolina University M,W
University of North Carolina
    Chapel Hill M,W
    Wilmington M,W

North Dakota
University of North Dakota M,W

Ohio
Ashland University M,W
Bowling Green State University M,W
Cleveland State University M,W
Miami University
    Oxford Campus M,W
Notre Dame College W
Ohio State University
    Columbus Campus M,W
Ohio University M,W

University of Akron W
University of Findlay M,W
University of Toledo W
Wright State University M,W

Pennsylvania
Clarion University of Pennsylvania M,W
Drexel University M,W
Gannon University M,W
Indiana University of Pennsylvania M,W
La Salle University M,W
Lehigh University M,W
Penn State
     University Park M,W
St. Francis University W
Slippery Rock University of Pennsylvania M,W
University of Pittsburgh M,W
Villanova University W
West Chester University of Pennsylvania M,W

Rhode Island
University of Rhode Island M,W

South Carolina
Clemson University M,W
College of Charleston M,W
University of South Carolina M,W

South Dakota
University of South Dakota M,W

Tennessee
University of Tennessee
     Knoxville M,W

Texas
Southern Methodist University M,W
Texas A&M University M,W
Texas Christian University M,W
University of Houston W
University of North Texas W
University of Texas
     Austin M,W

Utah
Brigham Young University M,W
University of Utah M,W

Vermont
University of Vermont W

Virginia
George Mason University M,W
James Madison University W
Old Dominion University M,W
Radford University W
University of Richmond W
University of Virginia M,W
Virginia Military Institute M
Virginia Polytechnic Institute and State
     University M,W

West Virginia
West Virginia University M,W

Wisconsin
University of Wisconsin
     Green Bay M,W
     Milwaukee M,W

Wyoming
University of Wyoming M,W

Equestrian

California
California State University
     Fresno W

Delaware
Delaware State University W

Georgia
Berry College W
University of Georgia W

Idaho
College of Southern Idaho M,W

Indiana
St. Mary-of-the-Woods College W

Kansas
Kansas State University W

Kentucky
Midway College W
Murray State University M,W

Massachusetts
Mount Ida College W
Stonehill College W

Nebraska
Nebraska College of Technical Agriculture M,W

New York
Dowling College W
Vassar College M,W

North Carolina
St. Andrews Presbyterian College M,W

Oklahoma
Oklahoma Panhandle State University M,W
Oklahoma State University W

Oregon
Linn-Benton Community College M,W

Pennsylvania
Seton Hill University W

South Carolina
University of South Carolina W

South Dakota
South Dakota State University W

Tennessee
University of Tennessee
     Martin W

Texas
Baylor University W
Southern Methodist University W
Texas A&M University W
Texas Christian University W
West Texas A&M University W

Virginia
Virginia Intermont College M,W

Wyoming
Laramie County Community College M,W

Fencing

California
California State University
     Fullerton M,W
Stanford University M,W

Illinois
Northwestern University W

Indiana
University of Notre Dame M,W

Michigan
University of Detroit Mercy M,W
Wayne State University M,W

New Jersey
Fairleigh Dickinson University
     Metropolitan Campus W
New Jersey Institute of Technology M,W
Rutgers, The State University of New Jersey
     New Brunswick/Piscataway Campus M,W

New York
City University of New York
     Queens College W
St. John's University M,W

Ohio
Cleveland State University M,W
Ohio State University
     Columbus Campus M,W

Pennsylvania
Penn State
     University Park M,W
Temple University W

Field Hockey

California
Stanford University W
University of California
     Berkeley W
University of the Pacific W

Connecticut
Fairfield University W
Quinnipiac University W
Southern Connecticut State University W
University of Connecticut W

Delaware
University of Delaware W

District of Columbia
Georgetown University W

Illinois
Northwestern University W

Indiana
Ball State University W

Iowa
University of Iowa W

Kentucky
Bellarmine University W
University of Louisville W

Maine
University of Maine W

Maryland
Towson University W
University of Maryland
     College Park W

Massachusetts
American International College W
Boston College W
Boston University W
Northeastern University W
Stonehill College W
University of Massachusetts
     Amherst W

Michigan
Central Michigan University W
Michigan State University W
University of Michigan W

Missouri
Missouri State University W
Saint Louis University W

New Hampshire
Franklin Pierce University W
University of New Hampshire W

New Jersey
Monmouth University W
Rider University W
Rutgers, The State University of New Jersey
     New Brunswick/Piscataway Campus W

New York
Colgate University W
Hofstra University W
Houghton College W
Long Island University
     C. W. Post Campus W
Siena College W
State University of New York
     Albany W
Syracuse University W

North Carolina
Appalachian State University W
Catawba College W
Davidson College W
Duke University W
University of North Carolina
     Chapel Hill W
Wake Forest University W

Ohio
Kent State University W
Miami University
     Oxford Campus W
Notre Dame College W
Ohio State University
     Columbus Campus W
Ohio University W

Pennsylvania
Bloomsburg University of Pennsylvania W
Drexel University W
East Stroudsburg University of Pennsylvania W
Indiana University of Pennsylvania W
Kutztown University of Pennsylvania W
La Salle University W
Lehigh University W
Lock Haven University of Pennsylvania W
Mansfield University of Pennsylvania W
Mercyhurst College W
Millersville University of Pennsylvania W
Penn State
     University Park W
Philadelphia University W
Robert Morris University W
St. Francis University W
Saint Joseph's University W
Seton Hill University W
Shippensburg University of Pennsylvania W
Slippery Rock University of Pennsylvania W
Temple University W
Villanova University W
West Chester University of Pennsylvania W

Rhode Island
Bryant University W
Providence College W
University of Rhode Island W

Vermont
University of Vermont W

Virginia
College of William and Mary W
James Madison University W
Longwood University W
Old Dominion University W
Radford University W
University of Richmond W
University of Virginia W
Virginia Commonwealth University W

Football (non-tackle)

Illinois
Olivet Nazarene University M

Louisiana
Southern University and Agricultural and
Mechanical College M

Michigan
Southwestern Michigan College M

Football (tackle)

Alabama
Alabama Agricultural and Mechanical
University M
Alabama State University M
Auburn University M
Faulkner University M
Jacksonville State University M
Miles College M
Samford University M
Troy University M
Tuskegee University M
University of Alabama M
University of Alabama
Birmingham M
University of North Alabama M
University of West Alabama M

Arizona
Arizona State University M
Arizona Western College M
Eastern Arizona College M
Glendale Community College M
Mesa Community College M
Northern Arizona University M
Pima Community College M
Scottsdale Community College M
University of Arizona M

Arkansas
Arkansas State University M
Arkansas Tech University M
Harding University M
Henderson State University M
Ouachita Baptist University M
Southern Arkansas University M
University of Arkansas M
University of Arkansas
Monticello M
Pine Bluff M
University of Central Arkansas M

California
Azusa Pacific University M
California Polytechnic State University: San Luis
Obispo M
California State University
Fresno M
Sacramento M
Fresno City College M
Grossmont College M
Humboldt State University M
San Diego State University M
San Jose State University M
Stanford University M
University of California
Berkeley M
Davis M
Los Angeles M
University of Southern California M
Yuba Community College District M

Colorado
Adams State College M
Colorado School of Mines M

Colorado State University M
Fort Lewis College M
Mesa State College M
University of Colorado
Boulder M
University of Northern Colorado M
Western State College of Colorado M

Connecticut
Sacred Heart University M
Southern Connecticut State University M
University of Connecticut M

Delaware
Delaware State University M
University of Delaware M

District of Columbia
Georgetown University M
Howard University M

Florida
Bethune-Cookman University M
Florida Agricultural and Mechanical University
M
Florida Atlantic University M
Florida State University M
University of Central Florida M
University of Florida M
University of Miami M
University of South Florida M
Webber International University M

Georgia
Albany State University M
Clark Atlanta University M
Fort Valley State University M
Georgia Institute of Technology M
Georgia Military College M
Georgia Southern University M
Morehouse College M
Savannah State University M
Shorter College M
University of Georgia M
University of West Georgia M
Valdosta State University M

Hawaii
University of Hawaii
Manoa M

Idaho
Boise State University M
Idaho State University M
University of Idaho M

Illinois
Eastern Illinois University M
Illinois State University M
McKendree University M
Northwestern University M
Olivet Nazarene University M
Quincy University M
St. Xavier University M
Southern Illinois University Carbondale M
Trinity International University M
University of Illinois
Urbana-Champaign M
University of St. Francis M
Western Illinois University M

Indiana
Ball State University M
Indiana State University M
Indiana University
Bloomington M
Marian College M
Purdue University M
Saint Joseph's College M
Taylor University M
University of Indianapolis M
University of Notre Dame M
University of St. Francis M

Iowa
Briar Cliff University M
Dordt College M
Ellsworth Community College M
Graceland University M
Iowa Central Community College M
Iowa State University M
Iowa Wesleyan College M
Morningside College M
North Iowa Area Community College M
Northwestern College M
St. Ambrose University M
University of Iowa M
University of Northern Iowa M
Waldorf College M
William Penn University M

Kansas
Baker University M
Benedictine College M
Bethany College M
Bethel College M
Butler County Community College M
Coffeyville Community College M
Dodge City Community College M
Emporia State University M
Fort Hays State University M
Fort Scott Community College M
Friends University M
Garden City Community College M
Highland Community College M
Hutchinson Community College M
Independence Community College M
Kansas State University M
Kansas Wesleyan University M
McPherson College M
MidAmerica Nazarene University M
Ottawa University M
Pittsburg State University M
Southwestern College M
Sterling College M
Tabor College M
University of Kansas M
University of St. Mary M
Washburn University M

Kentucky
Campbellsville University M
Eastern Kentucky University M
Georgetown College M
Kentucky Christian University M
Kentucky State University M
Kentucky Wesleyan College M
Murray State University M
Pikeville College M
Union College M
University of Kentucky M
University of Louisville M
University of the Cumberlands M
Western Kentucky University M

Louisiana
Grambling State University M
Louisiana State University and Agricultural and
Mechanical College M
Louisiana Tech University M
McNeese State University M
Nicholls State University M
Northwestern State University M
Southeastern Louisiana University M
Southern University and Agricultural and
Mechanical College M
Tulane University M
University of Louisiana at Lafayette M
University of Louisiana at Monroe M

Maine
University of Maine M

Maryland
Bowie State University M
Morgan State University M

Towson University M
University of Maryland
College Park M

Massachusetts
American International College M
Boston College M
Dean College M
Northeastern University M
Stonehill College M
University of Massachusetts
Amherst M

Michigan
Central Michigan University M
Eastern Michigan University M
Ferris State University M
Grand Rapids Community College M
Grand Valley State University M
Hillsdale College M
Michigan State University M
Michigan Technological University M
Northern Michigan University M
Northwood University: Michigan M
Saginaw Valley State University M
University of Michigan M
Wayne State University M,W
Western Michigan University M

Minnesota
Bemidji State University M
Concordia University: St. Paul M
Minnesota State University
Mankato M
Moorhead M
Saint Cloud State University M
Southwest Minnesota State University M
University of Minnesota
Crookston M
Duluth M
Twin Cities M
Winona State University M

Mississippi
Alcorn State University M
Belhaven College M
Coahoma Community College M
Copiah-Lincoln Community College M
Delta State University M
East Central Community College M
East Mississippi Community College M
Hinds Community College M
Holmes Community College M
Itawamba Community College M
Jackson State University M
Mississippi Gulf Coast Community College
Jefferson Davis Campus M
Mississippi State University M
Mississippi Valley State University M
Northwest Mississippi Community College M
Southwest Mississippi Community College M
University of Mississippi M
University of Southern Mississippi M

Missouri
Avila University M
Central Methodist University M
Culver-Stockton College M
Evangel University M
Lincoln University M
Missouri Southern State University M
Missouri State University M
Missouri Valley College M
Missouri Western State University M
Northwest Missouri State University M
Southeast Missouri State University M
Southwest Baptist University M
Truman State University M
University of Central Missouri M
University of Missouri
Columbia M
Missouri University of Science and
Technology M

William Jewell College M

Montana
Carroll College M
Montana State University
    Bozeman M
    Northern M
Montana Tech of the University of Montana M
Rocky Mountain College M
University of Montana: Missoula M
University of Montana: Western M

Nebraska
Chadron State College M
Concordia University M
Dana College M
Doane College M
Hastings College M
Midland Lutheran College M
Peru State College M
University of Nebraska
    Kearney M
    Lincoln M
    Omaha M
Wayne State College M

Nevada
University of Nevada
    Las Vegas M
    Reno M

New Hampshire
University of New Hampshire M

New Jersey
Monmouth University M
Rutgers, The State University of New Jersey
    New Brunswick/Piscataway Campus M

New Mexico
Eastern New Mexico University M
New Mexico Highlands University M
New Mexico Military Institute M
New Mexico State University M
University of New Mexico M
Western New Mexico University M

New York
Hofstra University M
Long Island University
    C. W. Post Campus M
State University of New York
    Albany M
    Buffalo M
    Stony Brook M
Syracuse University M
Wagner College M

North Carolina
Appalachian State University M
Brevard College M
Catawba College M
Duke University M
East Carolina University M
Elizabeth City State University M
Elon University M
Fayetteville State University M
Gardner-Webb University M
Johnson C. Smith University M
Lenoir-Rhyne College M
Livingstone College M
Mars Hill College M
North Carolina Agricultural and Technical State
    University M
North Carolina Central University M
North Carolina State University M
St. Augustine's College M
Shaw University M
University of North Carolina
    Chapel Hill M
    Pembroke M
Wake Forest University M
Western Carolina University M

Wingate University M
Winston-Salem State University M

North Dakota
Dickinson State University M
Jamestown College M
Mayville State University M
Minot State University M
North Dakota State College of Science M
North Dakota State University M
University of Mary M
University of North Dakota M
Valley City State University M

Ohio
Ashland University M
Bowling Green State University M
Kent State University M
Malone College M
Miami University
    Oxford Campus M
Ohio Dominican University M
Ohio State University
    Columbus Campus M
Ohio University M
University of Akron M
University of Cincinnati M
University of Findlay M
University of Toledo M
Urbana University M
Walsh University M
Youngstown State University M

Oklahoma
East Central University M
Langston University M
Northeastern Oklahoma Agricultural and
    Mechanical College M
Northeastern State University M
Northwestern Oklahoma State University M
Oklahoma Panhandle State University M
Oklahoma State University M
Southeastern Oklahoma State University M
Southwestern Oklahoma State University M
University of Central Oklahoma M
University of Oklahoma M
University of Tulsa M

Oregon
Eastern Oregon University M
Oregon State University M
Portland State University M
Southern Oregon University M
University of Oregon M

Pennsylvania
Bloomsburg University of Pennsylvania M
California University of Pennsylvania M
Cheyney University of Pennsylvania M
Clarion University of Pennsylvania M
Duquesne University M
East Stroudsburg University of Pennsylvania M
Edinboro University of Pennsylvania M
Gannon University M
Indiana University of Pennsylvania M
Kutztown University of Pennsylvania M
Lackawanna College M
Lehigh University M
Lock Haven University of Pennsylvania M
Mansfield University of Pennsylvania M
Mercyhurst College M
Millersville University of Pennsylvania M
Penn State
    University Park M
Robert Morris University M
St. Francis University M
Seton Hill University M
Shippensburg University of Pennsylvania M
Slippery Rock University of Pennsylvania M
Temple University M
University of Pittsburgh M
Valley Forge Military College M
Villanova University M

West Chester University of Pennsylvania M
Westminster College M

Rhode Island
Bryant University M
University of Rhode Island M

South Carolina
Charleston Southern University M
The Citadel M
Clemson University M
Coastal Carolina University M
Furman University M
Newberry College M
North Greenville University M
Presbyterian College M
South Carolina State University M
University of South Carolina M
Wofford College M

South Dakota
Augustana College M
Black Hills State University M
Dakota State University M
Dakota Wesleyan University M
Northern State University M
South Dakota School of Mines and Technology
    M
South Dakota State University M
University of Sioux Falls M
University of South Dakota M

Tennessee
Austin Peay State University M
Bethel College M
Carson-Newman College M
Cumberland University M
Lambuth University M
Lane College M
Middle Tennessee State University M
Tennessee State University M
Tennessee Technological University M
Tusculum College M
University of Memphis M
University of Tennessee
    Chattanooga M
    Knoxville M
    Martin M
Vanderbilt University M

Texas
Abilene Christian University M
Angelo State University M
Baylor University M
Blinn College M
Kilgore College M
Midwestern State University M
Prairie View A&M University M
Rice University M
Sam Houston State University M
Southern Methodist University M
Southwestern Assemblies of God University M
Stephen F. Austin State University M
Tarleton State University M
Texas A&M University M
Texas A&M University
    Commerce M
    Kingsville M
Texas Christian University M
Texas Southern University M
Texas State University: San Marcos M
Texas Tech University M
Trinity Valley Community College M
Tyler Junior College M
University of Houston M
University of North Texas M
University of Texas
    Austin M
West Texas A&M University M

Utah
Brigham Young University M
Dixie State College of Utah M

Snow College M
Southern Utah University M
University of Utah M
Utah State University M
Weber State University M

Virginia
College of William and Mary M
Hampton University M
James Madison University M
Liberty University M
Norfolk State University M
University of Richmond M
University of Virginia M
University of Virginia's College at Wise M
Virginia Military Institute M
Virginia Polytechnic Institute and State
    University M
Virginia State University M
Virginia Union University M

Washington
Central Washington University M
University of Washington M
Washington State University M
Western Washington University M

West Virginia
Concord University M
Fairmont State University M
Glenville State College M
Marshall University M
Shepherd University M
University of Charleston M
West Liberty State College M
West Virginia University M
West Virginia Wesleyan College M

Wyoming
University of Wyoming M

Golf

Alabama
Alabama State University M,W
Auburn University M,W
Central Alabama Community College M
Faulkner State Community College M,W
Gadsden State Community College M
Jacksonville State University M,W
Northwest-Shoals Community College M
Samford University M,W
Spring Hill College M,W
Troy University M,W
University of Alabama M,W
University of Alabama
    Birmingham M,W
University of Mobile M,W
University of Montevallo M,W
University of North Alabama M
University of South Alabama M,W

Arizona
Arizona State University M,W
Chandler-Gilbert Community College
    Pecos M,W
Eastern Arizona College M
Gateway Community College M,W
Glendale Community College M
Grand Canyon University M
Mesa Community College M
Northern Arizona University W
Paradise Valley Community College M,W
Pima Community College M,W
Scottsdale Community College M
University of Arizona M,W

Arkansas
Arkansas State University M,W
Arkansas Tech University M
Harding University M,W

Henderson State University M,W
Lyon College M,W
Ouachita Baptist University M
University of Arkansas M,W
University of Arkansas
   Fort Smith M,W
   Little Rock M,W
   Monticello M,W
   Pine Bluff M,W
University of Central Arkansas M,W

California
California Baptist University M,W
California Polytechnic State University: San Luis
   Obispo M,W
California State University
   Bakersfield M
   Chico M,W
   Dominguez Hills M
   Fresno M,W
   Long Beach M,W
   Northridge M
   Sacramento M
   San Bernardino M
   Stanislaus M
Concordia University M,W
Fresno City College M,W
Holy Names University M
Loyola Marymount University M
The Master's College M
Notre Dame de Namur University M,W
Pepperdine University M,W
Point Loma Nazarene University M
St. Mary's College of California M,W
San Diego State University M,W
San Jose State University M,W
Santa Clara University M,W
Santiago Canyon College M,W
Sonoma State University M
Stanford University M,W
University of California
   Berkeley M,W
   Davis M,W
   Irvine M,W
   Los Angeles M,W
   Santa Barbara M
University of San Diego M
University of San Francisco M,W
University of Southern California M,W
University of the Pacific M
William Jessup University M

Colorado
Adams State College M,W
Colorado Christian University M,W
Colorado School of Mines M,W
Colorado State University M,W
Colorado State University
   Pueblo M,W
Fort Lewis College M
Mesa State College W
Regis University M,W
Trinidad State Junior College M,W
University of Colorado
   Boulder M,W
   Colorado Springs M
University of Denver M,W
University of Northern Colorado M,W

Connecticut
Central Connecticut State University M
Fairfield University M,W
Quinnipiac University M
Sacred Heart University M,W
University of Connecticut M
University of Hartford M,W
University of New Haven M

Delaware
Goldey-Beacom College M,W
Wilmington University M

District of Columbia
George Washington University M
Georgetown University M,W

Florida
Barry University M,W
Bethune-Cookman University M,W
Brevard Community College M
Daytona Beach Community College W
Eckerd College W
Embry-Riddle Aeronautical University M,W
Flagler College M,W
Florida Atlantic University M,W
Florida Gulf Coast University M,W
Florida Institute of Technology M,W
Florida International University W
Florida Southern College M,W
Florida State University M,W
Jacksonville University M,W
Lake City Community College W
Lynn University M,W
Northwood University
   Florida M,W
Nova Southeastern University M,W
Rollins College M,W
St. Leo University M,W
St. Petersburg College W
Saint Thomas University M
Stetson University M,W
University of Central Florida M,W
University of Florida M,W
University of Miami W
University of North Florida M
University of South Florida M,W
University of Tampa M
University of West Florida M,W
Warner Southern College M,W
Webber International University M,W

Georgia
Abraham Baldwin Agricultural College M
Andrew College M,W
Armstrong Atlantic State University M
Augusta State University M,W
Berry College M,W
Clayton State University M
Columbus State University M
Covenant College M
Darton College M,W
Georgia College and State University M
Georgia Institute of Technology M
Georgia Southern University M
Georgia Southwestern State University M,W
Georgia State University M,W
Kennesaw State University M
Mercer University M,W
Reinhardt College M
Shorter College W
Thomas University M,W
Truett-McConnell College M
University of Georgia M,W
Valdosta State University M
Young Harris College M,W

Hawaii
Chaminade University of Honolulu M,W
Hawaii Pacific University M
University of Hawaii
   Hilo M
   Manoa M,W

Idaho
Boise State University M,W
College of Idaho M,W
Idaho State University M,W
Lewis-Clark State College M,W
Northwest Nazarene University M
University of Idaho M,W

Illinois
Black Hawk College M
Bradley University M,W

Chicago State University M,W
College of Lake County M,W
Danville Area Community College M,W
DePaul University M
Eastern Illinois University M,W
Elgin Community College M
Highland Community College M
Illinois State University M,W
John A. Logan College M,W
Kaskaskia College M,W
Kishwaukee College M,W
Lewis and Clark Community College M
Lewis University M,W
Lincoln College M,W
Loyola University Chicago M,W
McKendree University M,W
Moraine Valley Community College M
Northwestern University M,W
Olivet Nazarene University M
Parkland College M
Quincy University M,W
Rend Lake College M,W
Robert Morris College: Chicago M,W
Sauk Valley Community College M
Southern Illinois University Carbondale M,W
Southern Illinois University Edwardsville M,W
Springfield College in Illinois M
University of Illinois
   Springfield M,W
   Urbana-Champaign M,W
University of St. Francis M,W
Waubonsee Community College M
Western Illinois University M,W

Indiana
Ancilla College M,W
Ball State University M
Bethel College M
Butler University M,W
Calumet College of St. Joseph M,W
Goshen College M
Grace College M
Huntington University M
Indiana Institute of Technology M,W
Indiana State University M
Indiana University
   Bloomington M,W
Indiana University-Purdue University Fort
   Wayne M,W
Indiana University-Purdue University
   Indianapolis M,W
Indiana Wesleyan University M
Marian College M,W
Oakland City University M,W
Purdue University M,W
Saint Joseph's College M,W
Taylor University M
University of Evansville M,W
University of Indianapolis M,W
University of Notre Dame M,W
University of St. Francis M,W
University of Southern Indiana M,W
Vincennes University M

Iowa
Ashford University M
Briar Cliff University M,W
Clarke College M,W
Dordt College M
Drake University M,W
Ellsworth Community College M,W
Graceland University M,W
Grand View College M,W
Indian Hills Community College M
Iowa Central Community College M,W
Iowa Lakes Community College M,W
Iowa State University M,W
Iowa Wesleyan College M,W
Kirkwood Community College M
Marshalltown Community College M,W
Morningside College M,W
North Iowa Area Community College M,W

Northwestern College M,W
St. Ambrose University M,W
Scott Community College M,W
Southeastern Community College
   North Campus M,W
Southwestern Community College M
University of Iowa M,W
University of Northern Iowa M,W
Waldorf College M,W
William Penn University M

Kansas
Allen County Community College M,W
Baker University M,W
Barton County Community College M,W
Benedictine College M,W
Bethany College M
Bethel College M,W
Central Christian College of Kansas M,W
Coffeyville Community College M,W
Colby Community College M,W
Dodge City Community College M,W
Friends University M
Hutchinson Community College M
Johnson County Community College M
Kansas City Kansas Community College M
Kansas State University M,W
Kansas Wesleyan University M,W
Newman University M,W
Ottawa University M
Pittsburg State University M
Pratt Community College M,W
Southwestern College M,W
University of Kansas M,W
Washburn University M
Wichita State University M,W

Kentucky
Bellarmine University M,W
Brescia University M,W
Campbellsville University M,W
Eastern Kentucky University M,W
Georgetown College M,W
Kentucky State University M
Kentucky Wesleyan College M,W
Lindsey Wilson College M,W
Morehead State University M
Murray State University M,W
Northern Kentucky University M,W
Pikeville College M,W
St. Catharine College M,W
Union College M,W
University of Kentucky M,W
University of Louisville M,W
University of the Cumberlands M,W
Western Kentucky University M,W

Louisiana
Centenary College of Louisiana M,W
Grambling State University M
Louisiana State University and Agricultural and
   Mechanical College M,W
Louisiana Tech University M
McNeese State University M,W
Nicholls State University M,W
Southeastern Louisiana University M
Southern University and Agricultural and
   Mechanical College M
University of Louisiana at Lafayette M
University of Louisiana at Monroe M
University of New Orleans M

Maryland
College of Southern Maryland M,W
Coppin State University W
Harford Community College M
Loyola College in Maryland M
Mount St. Mary's University M,W
Towson University M
University of Maryland
   College Park M,W

Massachusetts
Boston College M,W

Michigan
Aquinas College M,W
Concordia University M
Cornerstone University M
Davenport University M,W
Delta College M,W
Eastern Michigan University M,W
Ferris State University M,W
Grand Rapids Community College M
Grand Valley State University M,W
Kalamazoo Valley Community College M
Kirtland Community College M,W
Lake Michigan College M
Lansing Community College M
Madonna University M,W
Michigan State University M,W
Mott Community College M
Muskegon Community College M
Northern Michigan University M
Northwood University: Michigan M,W
Oakland Community College M
Oakland University M,W
Saginaw Valley State University M
Siena Heights University M
Spring Arbor University M
University of Detroit Mercy M,W
University of Michigan M,W
Wayne State University M
Western Michigan University W

Minnesota
Concordia University: St. Paul M,W
Minnesota State University
    Mankato M,W
    Moorhead W
Saint Cloud State University M,W
Southwest Minnesota State University W
University of Minnesota
    Crookston M,W
    Twin Cities M,W
Winona State University M,W

Mississippi
Alcorn State University M,W
Belhaven College M,W
Copiah-Lincoln Community College M
Delta State University M
East Mississippi Community College M,W
Itawamba Community College M
Jackson State University M,W
Meridian Community College M
Mississippi Gulf Coast Community College
    Jefferson Davis Campus M
Mississippi State University M,W
Mississippi Valley State University M,W
Northwest Mississippi Community College M,W
Southwest Mississippi Community College M
University of Mississippi M,W
University of Southern Mississippi M,W
William Carey University M,W

Missouri
Avila University W
Central Methodist University M,W
Culver-Stockton College M,W
Drury University M,W
Evangel University M,W
Hannibal-LaGrange College M
Lincoln University M
Metropolitan Community College: Penn Valley
    M
Missouri Baptist University M,W
Missouri Southern State University M
Missouri State University M,W
Missouri Valley College M,W
Missouri Western State University M
Northwest Missouri State University W
Park University M,W
Research College of Nursing M,W

Rockhurst University M,W
Saint Louis University M
Southwest Baptist University M
Truman State University M,W
University of Central Missouri M
University of Missouri
    Columbia M,W
    Kansas City M,W
    St. Louis M,W
William Jewell College M,W
William Woods University M,W

Montana
Carroll College W
Miles Community College M,W
Montana State University
    Billings M,W
    Bozeman W
    Northern W
Montana Tech of the University of Montana
    M,W
Rocky Mountain College M,W
University of Great Falls M,W
University of Montana: Missoula W
University of Montana: Western M,W

Nebraska
Chadron State College W
Concordia University M,W
Creighton University M,W
Dana College W
Doane College M,W
Hastings College M,W
Mid-Plains Community College Area M
Midland Lutheran College M,W
Nebraska College of Technical Agriculture M,W
Peru State College W
University of Nebraska
    Kearney M,W
    Lincoln M,W
Wayne State College M,W

Nevada
University of Nevada
    Las Vegas M
    Reno M,W

New Hampshire
Franklin Pierce University M

New Jersey
Brookdale Community College M
Caldwell College M
Fairleigh Dickinson University
    Metropolitan Campus M,W
Monmouth University M,W
Rider University M
Rutgers, The State University of New Jersey
    New Brunswick/Piscataway Campus M,W
Saint Peter's College M
Salem Community College M
Seton Hall University M

New Mexico
College of the Southwest M,W
New Mexico Junior College M
New Mexico Military Institute M
New Mexico State University M,W
University of New Mexico M,W
Western New Mexico University W

New York
Adelphi University M
Canisius College M
College of Saint Rose M
Daemen College M
Dominican College of Blauvelt M
Dowling College M
Hofstra University M,W
Iona College M
Le Moyne College M
Long Island University
    Brooklyn Campus M,W

Manhattan College M
Mercy College M
Niagara University M
Nyack College M
Pace University M,W
Saint Bonaventure University M
St. John's University M,W
St. Thomas Aquinas College M,W
Siena College M,W
State University of New York
    Albany W
    Binghamton M
Wagner College M,W

North Carolina
Appalachian State University M,W
Barton College M
Belmont Abbey College M
Brevard College M
Campbell University M,W
Catawba College M,W
Davidson College M
Duke University M,W
East Carolina University M,W
Elon University M,W
Fayetteville State University M
Gardner-Webb University M,W
High Point University M,W
Johnson C. Smith University M,W
Johnston Community College M
Lees-McRae College M
Lenoir-Rhyne College M,W
Louisburg College M,W
Mars Hill College M
Montreat College M,W
Mount Olive College M
North Carolina Central University M,W
North Carolina State University M,W
Pfeiffer University M,W
Pitt Community College M
Queens University of Charlotte M,W
St. Andrews Presbyterian College M
St. Augustine's College M
University of North Carolina
    Chapel Hill M,W
    Charlotte M
    Greensboro M,W
    Pembroke M
    Wilmington M,W
Wake Forest University M,W
Western Carolina University M,W
Wingate University M,W

North Dakota
Dickinson State University M,W
Jamestown College M,W
Minot State University M,W
North Dakota State University W
University of Mary M,W
University of North Dakota M,W

Ohio
Ashland University M,W
Bowling Green State University M,W
Cedarville University M
Central State University M,W
Cleveland State University M,W
Kent State University M,W
Lakeland Community College M,W
Malone College M,W
Miami University
    Oxford Campus M
Mount Vernon Nazarene University M
Notre Dame College M,W
Ohio Dominican University M,W
Ohio State University
    Columbus Campus M,W
Ohio University M
Shawnee State University M
Sinclair Community College M
University of Akron M
University of Dayton M,W

University of Findlay M,W
University of Toledo M,W
Urbana University M
Ursuline College W
Walsh University M,W
Wright State University M
Xavier University M,W
Youngstown State University M,W

Oklahoma
Cameron University M,W
East Central University M,W
Northeastern State University M,W
Northwestern Oklahoma State University M,W
Oklahoma Baptist University M,W
Oklahoma Christian University M
Oklahoma City University M,W
Oklahoma Panhandle State University M,W
Oklahoma State University M,W
Oklahoma Wesleyan University M
Oral Roberts University M,W
Redlands Community College W
St. Gregory's University M,W
Seminole State College M,W
Southern Nazarene University M,W
Southwestern Oklahoma State University M,W
University of Central Oklahoma M,W
University of Oklahoma M,W
University of Tulsa M,W

Oregon
Concordia University M,W
Corban College M
Oregon State University M,W
Portland State University M,W
Southwestern Oregon Community College M,W
University of Oregon M,W
University of Portland M,W

Pennsylvania
California University of Pennsylvania M,W
Chestnut Hill College M,W
Clarion University of Pennsylvania M
Drexel University M
Duquesne University M
Gannon University M,W
Holy Family University M
Indiana University of Pennsylvania M
Kutztown University of Pennsylvania W
La Salle University M,W
Lackawanna College M,W
Lehigh University M,W
Mercyhurst College M,W
Millersville University of Pennsylvania M
Penn State
    University Park M,W
Philadelphia University M
Robert Morris University M,W
St. Francis University M,W
Saint Joseph's University M
Seton Hill University M,W
Slippery Rock University of Pennsylvania M,W
Temple University M
University of Pittsburgh
    Titusville M
University of the Sciences in Philadelphia M,W
West Chester University of Pennsylvania M,W

Rhode Island
Bryant University M
University of Rhode Island M

South Carolina
Anderson University M,W
Charleston Southern University M,W
The Citadel W
Clemson University M
Coastal Carolina University M,W
Coker College M
College of Charleston M,W
Francis Marion University M
Furman University M,W
Lander University M

Limestone College M,W
Morris College M
Newberry College M,W
North Greenville University M
Presbyterian College M,W
South Carolina State University M
Southern Wesleyan University M
Spartanburg Methodist College M,W
University of South Carolina M,W
University of South Carolina
    Aiken M
Winthrop University M,W
Wofford College M,W

South Dakota
Augustana College M,W
Dakota Wesleyan University M,W
Northern State University W
South Dakota School of Mines and Technology
    M,W
South Dakota State University M,W
University of Sioux Falls M,W

Tennessee
Austin Peay State University M,W
Belmont University M,W
Bethel College M,W
Carson-Newman College M
Christian Brothers University M,W
Crichton College M,W
Cumberland University M,W
East Tennessee State University M,W
Hiwassee College M,W
King College M,W
Lambuth University M,W
Lee University M
LeMoyne-Owen College M,W
Lincoln Memorial University M,W
Lipscomb University M,W
Martin Methodist College M
Middle Tennessee State University M,W
Milligan College M
Tennessee Technological University M,W
Tennessee Wesleyan College M,W
Trevecca Nazarene University M,W
Tusculum College M,W
Union University M
University of Memphis M,W
University of Tennessee
    Chattanooga M,W
    Knoxville M,W
    Martin M
Vanderbilt University M,W
Walters State Community College M,W

Texas
Abilene Christian University M
Baylor University M,W
Dallas Baptist University W
Hill College M
Lamar University M,W
Lon Morris College M,W
Lubbock Christian University M,W
McLennan Community College M
Midland College M
Northwood University: Texas M,W
Odessa College M
Paris Junior College M
Prairie View A&M University M,W
Ranger College M,W
Rice University M
St. Edward's University M,W
St. Mary's University M
Sam Houston State University M,W
Southern Methodist University M,W
Stephen F. Austin State University M
Tarleton State University W
Texas A&M University M,W
Texas A&M University
    Commerce M
Texas Christian University M,W
Texas Southern University M,W

Texas State University: San Marcos M,W
Texas Tech University M,W
Texas Wesleyan University M
Tyler Junior College M,W
University of Houston M
University of North Texas M,W
University of Texas
    Arlington M
    Austin M,W
    Pan American M,W
    San Antonio M,W
University of the Incarnate Word M,W
Wayland Baptist University M
West Texas A&M University M,W

Utah
Brigham Young University M,W
Dixie State College of Utah M
Southern Utah University M
University of Utah M
Utah State University M
Utah Valley State College M,W
Weber State University M,W

Virginia
Bluefield College M
Hampton University M,W
James Madison University M,W
Liberty University M
Longwood University M,W
Old Dominion University M
Radford University M,W
St. Paul's College M
University of Richmond M,W
University of Virginia M,W
Virginia Commonwealth University M
Virginia Intermont College M
Virginia Military Institute M
Virginia Polytechnic Institute and State
    University M
Virginia State University M,W
Virginia Union University M,W

Washington
Centralia College W
Columbia Basin College M,W
Edmonds Community College M,W
Gonzaga University M,W
Grays Harbor College M,W
Green River Community College M
Olympic College M,W
Saint Martin's University M,W
Spokane Community College M,W
Tacoma Community College M,W
University of Washington M,W
Walla Walla Community College M,W
Washington State University M,W
Western Washington University M,W

West Virginia
Bluefield State College M
Concord University M
Davis and Elkins College M
Glenville State College M,W
Marshall University M,W
Ohio Valley University M,W
Salem International University M,W
University of Charleston M
West Liberty State College M,W
West Virginia Wesleyan College M,W
Wheeling Jesuit University M,W

Wisconsin
Marquette University M
Silver Lake College M,W
University of Wisconsin
    Green Bay M,W
    Parkside M

Wyoming
Eastern Wyoming College M
University of Wyoming M,W

Gymnastics

Alabama
Auburn University W
University of Alabama W

Alaska
University of Alaska
    Anchorage W

Arizona
Arizona State University W
University of Arizona W

Arkansas
University of Arkansas W

California
California State University
    Fullerton W
    Sacramento W
San Jose State University W
Stanford University M,W
University of California
    Berkeley M,W
    Davis W
    Los Angeles W
    Santa Barbara W

Colorado
University of Denver W

Connecticut
Southern Connecticut State University W
University of Bridgeport W

District of Columbia
George Washington University W
Howard University M,W

Florida
University of Florida W

Georgia
University of Georgia W

Idaho
Boise State University W

Illinois
Illinois State University W
University of Illinois
    Chicago M,W
    Urbana-Champaign M,W

Indiana
Ball State University W

Iowa
Iowa State University W
University of Iowa M,W

Kansas
Fort Hays State University M

Kentucky
University of Kentucky W

Louisiana
Centenary College of Louisiana W
Louisiana State University and Agricultural and
    Mechanical College W

Maryland
Columbia Union College M,W
Towson University W
University of Maryland
    College Park W

Michigan
Central Michigan University W
Eastern Michigan University W
Michigan State University W

University of Michigan M,W
Western Michigan University W

Minnesota
University of Minnesota
    Twin Cities M,W
Winona State University W

Missouri
Southeast Missouri State University W
University of Missouri
    Columbia W

Nebraska
University of Nebraska
    Lincoln M,W

New Hampshire
University of New Hampshire W

New Jersey
Rutgers, The State University of New Jersey
    New Brunswick/Piscataway Campus W

North Carolina
North Carolina State University W
University of North Carolina
    Chapel Hill W

Ohio
Bowling Green State University W
Kent State University W
Ohio State University
    Columbus Campus M,W

Oklahoma
University of Oklahoma M,W

Oregon
Oregon State University W

Pennsylvania
Penn State
    University Park M,W
Temple University M,W
University of Pittsburgh W
West Chester University of Pennsylvania W

Rhode Island
University of Rhode Island W

Tennessee
Southern Adventist University M,W

Texas
Texas Woman's University W

Utah
Brigham Young University W
Southern Utah University W
University of Utah W
Utah State University W

Virginia
College of William and Mary M,W

Washington
Seattle Pacific University W
University of Washington W

West Virginia
West Virginia University W

Ice hockey

Alabama
University of Alabama
    Huntsville M

Alaska
University of Alaska
    Anchorage M
    Fairbanks M

Colorado
Colorado College M
University of Denver M,W

Connecticut
Quinnipiac University M,W
Sacred Heart University M,W
University of Connecticut M,W

Illinois
McKendree University M,W

Indiana
University of Notre Dame M

Maine
University of Maine M,W

Massachusetts
American International College M
Bentley College M
Boston College M,W
Boston University W
Merrimack College M
Northeastern University M,W
University of Massachusetts
        Amherst M
        Lowell M

Michigan
Ferris State University M
Lake Superior State University M
Michigan State University M
Michigan Technological University M
Northern Michigan University M
University of Michigan M
University of Michigan
        Dearborn M
Wayne State University M,W
Western Michigan University M

Minnesota
Bemidji State University M
Minnesota State University
        Mankato M,W
Saint Cloud State University M,W
University of Minnesota
        Duluth M,W
        Twin Cities M,W

Nebraska
University of Nebraska
        Omaha M

New Hampshire
New England College M,W
University of New Hampshire M,W

New York
Canisius College M
Clarkson University M,W
Colgate University M,W
Monroe Community College M
Niagara University M,W
Rensselaer Polytechnic Institute M,W
St. Lawrence University M,W

North Dakota
Minot State University: Bottineau Campus M
University of North Dakota M,W

Ohio
Bowling Green State University M
Ohio State University
        Columbus Campus M,W

Pennsylvania
Mercyhurst College M,W
Robert Morris University M,W

Rhode Island
Providence College M,W

Vermont
University of Vermont M,W

Judo

Hawaii
Hawaii Tokai International College M,W

Kentucky
University of the Cumberlands M,W

New York
Roberts Wesleyan College M,W

Puerto Rico
Inter American University of Puerto Rico
        Aguadilla Campus M,W
Turabo University W
University of Puerto Rico
        Cayey University College W
        Humacao M,W

Lacrosse

California
Notre Dame de Namur University M
Stanford University W
University of California
        Davis W

Colorado
Regis University W
University of Denver M,W

Connecticut
Central Connecticut State University W
Fairfield University M,W
Quinnipiac University M,W
Sacred Heart University M,W
Southern Connecticut State University W
University of Hartford M
University of New Haven W

Delaware
University of Delaware M,W
Wilmington University W

District of Columbia
American University W
Georgetown University M,W

Florida
St. Leo University M

Illinois
Northwestern University W
Robert Morris College: Chicago W

Indiana
University of Notre Dame M,W

Kentucky
Bellarmine University M
University of Louisville W

Maryland
Anne Arundel Community College M,W
College of Southern Maryland W
Community College of Baltimore County M,W
Harford Community College M,W
Johns Hopkins University M,W
Loyola College in Maryland M,W
Mount St. Mary's University M,W
Towson University M,W
University of Maryland
        Baltimore County M,W
        College Park M,W

Massachusetts
American International College M,W
Boston College W
Boston University W
Dean College M,W
Mount Ida College M
Stonehill College W
University of Massachusetts
        Amherst M,W
        Lowell M

Michigan
Davenport University M,W

Minnesota
University of Minnesota
        Duluth M

New Hampshire
Franklin Pierce University M,W
Southern New Hampshire University M,W
University of New Hampshire W

New Jersey
Georgian Court University W
Monmouth University W
Rutgers, The State University of New Jersey
        New Brunswick/Piscataway Campus M,W

New York
Adelphi University M,W
Canisius College M,W
Colgate University M,W
Dominican College of Blauvelt M,W
Dowling College M
Globe Institute of Technology M
Hofstra University M,W
Iona College W
Le Moyne College M,W
Long Island University
        Brooklyn Campus W
        C. W. Post Campus M,W
Manhattan College M,W
Marist College M,W
Molloy College M,W
Monroe Community College M
New York Institute of Technology M
Niagara University W
Pace University M
St. John's University M
St. Thomas Aquinas College W
Siena College M,W
State University of New York
        Albany M,W
        Binghamton M,W
        Stony Brook M,W
Syracuse University M,W
Wagner College M,W

North Carolina
Catawba College M
Davidson College W
Duke University M
Lees-McRae College M,W
Lenoir-Rhyne College M
Mars Hill College M
Pfeiffer University M,W
Queens University of Charlotte M,W
St. Andrews Presbyterian College M
University of North Carolina
        Chapel Hill M,W
Wingate University M

Ohio
Notre Dame College W
Ohio State University
        Columbus Campus M,W

Oregon
University of Oregon W

Pennsylvania
Bloomsburg University of Pennsylvania W
Chestnut Hill College W
Drexel University M,W
Duquesne University W
East Stroudsburg University of Pennsylvania W
Gannon University W
Indiana University of Pennsylvania W
La Salle University W
Lehigh University M,W
Lock Haven University of Pennsylvania W
Mercyhurst College M,W
Millersville University of Pennsylvania W
Penn State
        University Park M,W
Philadelphia University W
Robert Morris University M,W
St. Francis University W
Saint Joseph's University M,W
Seton Hill University M,W
Shippensburg University of Pennsylvania W
Temple University W
West Chester University of Pennsylvania W

Rhode Island
Bryant University M,W

South Carolina
Limestone College M,W
Presbyterian College M,W

Tennessee
Tennessee Wesleyan College M
Vanderbilt University W

Vermont
University of Vermont M,W

Virginia
College of William and Mary W
James Madison University W
Longwood University W
Old Dominion University W
University of Richmond W
University of Virginia M,W
Virginia Military Institute M
Virginia Polytechnic Institute and State
        University W

West Virginia
Wheeling Jesuit University M

Rifle

Alabama
Jacksonville State University M,W

Alaska
University of Alaska
        Fairbanks M,W

California
University of San Francisco M,W

Georgia
Mercer University M
North Georgia College & State University M,W

Kentucky
Morehead State University M,W
Murray State University M,W
University of Kentucky M,W

Mississippi
University of Mississippi W

Nebraska
University of Nebraska
        Lincoln W

Nevada
University of Nevada
　Reno M,W

Ohio
University of Akron W

South Carolina
The Citadel M,W

Tennessee
Austin Peay State University W
Tennessee Technological University M,W
University of Memphis M,W
University of Tennessee
　Martin M,W

Texas
Texas Christian University W

Virginia
Virginia Military Institute M

West Virginia
West Virginia University M,W

Rodeo

Alabama
Troy University M,W
University of West Alabama M

Arizona
Central Arizona College M
Cochise College M
Dine College M,W

Arkansas
Southern Arkansas University M,W
University of Arkansas
　Monticello M,W

Colorado
Northeastern Junior College M,W

Idaho
Boise State University M,W
College of Southern Idaho M,W

Kansas
Coffeyville Community College M,W
Colby Community College M
Dodge City Community College M,W
Fort Hays State University M
Fort Scott Community College M,W
Garden City Community College M,W
Pratt Community College M,W

Kentucky
Murray State University M,W

Louisiana
McNeese State University M,W

Missouri
Missouri Valley College M,W
Northwest Missouri State University M,W

Montana
Dawson Community College M,W
Miles Community College M,W
Montana State University
　Bozeman M,W
　Northern M,W
University of Montana: Missoula M
University of Montana: Western M,W

Nebraska
Chadron State College M,W
Nebraska College of Technical Agriculture M,W

New Mexico
Eastern New Mexico University M,W
New Mexico Junior College M,W

North Dakota
Dickinson State University M

Oklahoma
Northeastern Oklahoma Agricultural and
　Mechanical College M,W
Northwestern Oklahoma State University M,W
Oklahoma Panhandle State University M,W
Rogers State University M,W
Southeastern Oklahoma State University M,W
Southwestern Oklahoma State University M,W

Oregon
Blue Mountain Community College M,W
Eastern Oregon University M,W

South Dakota
National American University
　Rapid City M,W

Tennessee
University of Tennessee
　Martin M,W

Texas
Clarendon College M,W
Howard College M,W
North Central Texas College M
Odessa College M,W
Panola College M,W
Ranger College M,W
Sam Houston State University M,W
South Plains College M,W
Tarleton State University M,W
Vernon College M,W
Weatherford College M
Western Texas College M,W
Wharton County Junior College M,W

Utah
Southern Utah University M,W

Washington
Walla Walla Community College M,W

Wyoming
Casper College M,W
Central Wyoming College M,W
Eastern Wyoming College M,W
Laramie County Community College M,W
Sheridan College M,W
University of Wyoming M,W

Rowing (crew)

Alabama
University of Alabama W

California
California State University
　Sacramento W
Humboldt State University W
Loyola Marymount University W
San Diego State University W
University of California
　Berkeley M,W
　Davis W
　Irvine M,W
University of Southern California W

Connecticut
Fairfield University W

Delaware
University of Delaware W

District of Columbia
George Washington University M,W
Georgetown University M,W

Florida
Barry University W
Florida Institute of Technology W
Jacksonville University M,W
Nova Southeastern University W
University of Central Florida W
University of Miami W
University of Tampa W

Indiana
Indiana University
　Bloomington W
University of Notre Dame W

Iowa
University of Iowa W

Kansas
Kansas State University W
University of Kansas W

Kentucky
Murray State University W
University of Louisville W

Massachusetts
Boston College W
Boston University M,W
Northeastern University M,W
University of Massachusetts
　Amherst W

Michigan
Eastern Michigan University W
Michigan State University W
University of Michigan W

Nebraska
Creighton University W

New Jersey
Rutgers, The State University of New Jersey
　New Brunswick/Piscataway Campus M,W

New York
Dowling College M,W
Fordham University W
Marist College W
State University of New York
　Buffalo W
Syracuse University M,W

North Carolina
Duke University W
University of North Carolina
　Chapel Hill W

Ohio
Ohio State University
　Columbus Campus W
University of Dayton W

Oklahoma
University of Tulsa W

Pennsylvania
Drexel University M,W
Duquesne University W
Lehigh University W
Mercyhurst College M,W
Philadelphia University M,W
Robert Morris University W
Saint Joseph's University M,W
Temple University M,W

South Carolina
Clemson University W

Tennessee
University of Tennessee
　Knoxville W

Texas
Southern Methodist University W
University of Texas
　Austin W

Virginia
University of Virginia W

Washington
Gonzaga University W
University of Washington M,W
Washington State University W
Western Washington University M,W

West Virginia
University of Charleston W
West Virginia University W

Rugby

California
University of California
　Berkeley M

Illinois
Eastern Illinois University W

Pennsylvania
West Chester University of Pennsylvania W

Skiing

Alaska
University of Alaska
　Anchorage M,W
　Fairbanks M,W

Colorado
Colorado Mountain College M,W
University of Colorado
　Boulder M,W
University of Denver M,W
Western State College of Colorado M,W

Idaho
Boise State University M
College of Idaho M,W

Massachusetts
University of Massachusetts
　Amherst M,W

Michigan
Michigan Technological University W
Northern Michigan University M,W

Minnesota
Saint Cloud State University W
University of Minnesota
　Twin Cities M,W

Montana
Montana State University
　Bozeman W
Rocky Mountain College M,W

Nevada
Sierra Nevada College M,W
University of Nevada
　Reno M,W

New Hampshire
University of New Hampshire M,W

New Mexico
University of New Mexico M,W

New York
Roberts Wesleyan College M,W

Tennessee
Carson-Newman College M,W

Utah
University of Utah M,W

Vermont
University of Vermont M,W

West Virginia
Davis and Elkins College M,W

Wisconsin
University of Wisconsin
    Green Bay M,W

Soccer

Alabama
Auburn University W
Auburn University at Montgomery M,W
Marion Military Institute M
Samford University W
Shelton State Community College W
Spring Hill College M,W
Troy University W
University of Alabama W
University of Alabama
    Birmingham M,W
    Huntsville M,W
University of Mobile M,W
University of Montevallo M,W
University of North Alabama W
University of South Alabama W

Arizona
Arizona State University W
Arizona Western College M
Chandler-Gilbert Community College
    Pecos M,W
Cochise College W
Embry-Riddle Aeronautical University: Prescott
    Campus M,W
Glendale Community College M,W
Grand Canyon University M,W
Mesa Community College M
Northern Arizona University W
Paradise Valley Community College M,W
Pima Community College M,W
Scottsdale Community College M
South Mountain Community College M
University of Arizona W
Yavapai College M

Arkansas
Arkansas State University W
Harding University M,W
John Brown University M,W
Lyon College M,W
Ouachita Baptist University M,W
University of Arkansas M,W
University of Arkansas
    Little Rock M,W
University of Central Arkansas M,W
Williams Baptist College M

California
Azusa Pacific University M,W
Bethany University M,W
Biola University M,W
California Baptist University M,W
California Polytechnic State University: San Luis
    Obispo M,W
California State Polytechnic University: Pomona
    M,W
California State University
    Bakersfield M,W
    Chico M,W

Dominguez Hills M,W
Fresno W
Fullerton M,W
Los Angeles M,W
Northridge M
Sacramento M,W
San Bernardino M,W
Stanislaus M,W
Concordia University M,W
Dominican University of California M,W
Fresno City College M,W
Fresno Pacific University M,W
Grossmont College W
Holy Names University M,W
Hope International University M,W
Humboldt State University M,W
Loyola Marymount University M,W
The Master's College M,W
Notre Dame de Namur University M,W
Pepperdine University W
Point Loma Nazarene University M,W
St. Mary's College of California M,W
San Diego Christian College M
San Diego State University M,W
San Jose State University M,W
Santa Clara University M,W
Santiago Canyon College M,W
Sonoma State University M,W
Stanford University M,W
University of California
    Berkeley M,W
    Davis M,W
    Irvine M,W
    Los Angeles M,W
    Santa Barbara M,W
University of San Diego M,W
University of San Francisco M,W
University of Southern California W
University of the Pacific W
Vanguard University of Southern California
    M,W
Westmont College M,W
William Jessup University M,W
Yuba Community College District M,W

Colorado
Adams State College W
Colorado Christian University M,W
Colorado College W
Colorado School of Mines M
Colorado State University
    Pueblo M,W
Fort Lewis College M,W
Mesa State College M,W
Metropolitan State College of Denver M,W
Regis University M,W
University of Colorado
    Boulder M,W
    Colorado Springs M
University of Denver M,W
University of Northern Colorado W

Connecticut
Central Connecticut State University M,W
Fairfield University M,W
Post University M,W
Quinnipiac University M,W
Sacred Heart University M,W
Southern Connecticut State University M,W
University of Bridgeport M,W
University of Connecticut M,W
University of Hartford M,W
University of New Haven M,W

Delaware
Delaware State University W
Goldey-Beacom College M,W
University of Delaware M,W
Wilmington University M,W

District of Columbia
American University M,W
George Washington University M,W

Georgetown University M,W
Howard University M

Florida
Barry University M,W
Eckerd College M,W
Embry-Riddle Aeronautical University M,W
Flagler College M,W
Florida Atlantic University M,W
Florida College M,W
Florida Institute of Technology M,W
Florida International University M,W
Florida Southern College M,W
Florida State University W
Jacksonville University M,W
Lynn University M,W
Northwood University
    Florida M,W
Nova Southeastern University M,W
Polk Community College W
Rollins College M,W
St. Leo University M,W
Saint Thomas University M,W
Stetson University M,W
University of Central Florida M,W
University of Florida W
University of Miami W
University of North Florida M,W
University of South Florida M,W
University of Tampa M,W
University of West Florida M,W
Warner Southern College M,W
Webber International University M,W

Georgia
Andrew College M,W
Berry College M,W
Brenau University W
Brewton-Parker College M,W
Clayton State University M,W
Columbus State University W
Covenant College M,W
Emmanuel College M,W
Georgia College and State University W
Georgia Military College M,W
Georgia Perimeter College M,W
Georgia Southern University M,W
Georgia Southwestern State University M,W
Georgia State University M,W
Gordon College M,W
Kennesaw State University W
Mercer University M,W
Middle Georgia College M,W
North Georgia College & State University M,W
Reinhardt College M,W
Shorter College M,W
Southern Polytechnic State University M
Thomas University M,W
Truett-McConnell College M,W
University of Georgia W
University of West Georgia W
Young Harris College M,W

Hawaii
Brigham Young University-Hawaii M,W
Hawaii Pacific University M,W
University of Hawaii
    Manoa W

Idaho
Boise State University W
College of Idaho M,W
Idaho State University W
Northwest Nazarene University W
University of Idaho W

Illinois
Bradley University M
College of Lake County M,W
DePaul University M,W
Eastern Illinois University M,W
Elgin Community College M,W
Illinois Institute of Technology M,W

Illinois State University W
Judson University M,W
Kankakee Community College M
Kishwaukee College M
Lewis and Clark Community College M,W
Lewis University M,W
Lincoln College M,W
Lincoln Land Community College M
Loyola University Chicago M,W
McHenry County College M
McKendree University M,W
Moraine Valley Community College M,W
Morton College M
Northwestern University M,W
Olivet Nazarene University M,W
Parkland College M,W
Quincy University M,W
Robert Morris College: Chicago M,W
St. Xavier University M,W
South Suburban College of Cook County M
Southern Illinois University Edwardsville M,W
Springfield College in Illinois M,W
Trinity Christian College M,W
Trinity International University M,W
University of Illinois
    Chicago M
    Springfield M
    Urbana-Champaign W
University of St. Francis M,W
Waubonsee Community College W
Western Illinois University M,W

Indiana
Ancilla College M
Bethel College M
Butler University M,W
Calumet College of St. Joseph M,W
Goshen College M,W
Grace College M,W
Huntington University M,W
Indiana Institute of Technology M,W
Indiana State University W
Indiana University
    Bloomington M,W
Indiana University-Purdue University Fort
    Wayne M,W
Indiana University-Purdue University
    Indianapolis M,W
Indiana Wesleyan University M,W
Marian College M,W
Oakland City University M,W
Purdue University W
Saint Joseph's College M,W
St. Mary-of-the-Woods College W
Taylor University M,W
Taylor University Fort Wayne M
University of Evansville M,W
University of Indianapolis M,W
University of Notre Dame M,W
University of St. Francis M,W
University of Southern Indiana M,W
Valparaiso University M,W

Iowa
Ashford University M,W
Briar Cliff University M,W
Clarke College M,W
Dordt College M,W
Drake University M,W
Graceland University M,W
Grand View College M,W
Iowa Central Community College M,W
Iowa State University W
Iowa Wesleyan College M,W
Kirkwood Community College M
Morningside College M,W
North Iowa Area Community College M,W
Northwestern College M,W
St. Ambrose University M,W
Scott Community College M,W
University of Iowa W
University of Northern Iowa W

Waldorf College M,W
William Penn University M,W

Kansas
Allen County Community College M,W
Baker University M,W
Barton County Community College M,W
Benedictine College M,W
Bethany College M,W
Bethel College M,W
Butler County Community College W
Central Christian College of Kansas M,W
Cloud County Community College M,W
Coffeyville Community College M,W
Emporia State University W
Friends University M,W
Garden City Community College M,W
Hesston College M
Hutchinson Community College W
Johnson County Community College M
Kansas City Kansas Community College M
Kansas Wesleyan University M,W
MidAmerica Nazarene University M,W
Neosho County Community College M,W
Newman University M,W
Ottawa University M,W
Southwestern College M,W
Sterling College M,W
Tabor College M,W
University of Kansas W
University of St. Mary M,W
Washburn University W

Kentucky
Asbury College M,W
Bellarmine University M,W
Brescia University M,W
Campbellsville University M,W
Georgetown College M,W
Kentucky Wesleyan College M,W
Lindsey Wilson College M,W
Mid-Continent University M
Midway College W
Morehead State University W
Murray State University W
Northern Kentucky University M,W
Pikeville College M,W
St. Catharine College M,W
Union College M,W
University of Kentucky M,W
University of Louisville M,W
University of the Cumberlands M,W
Western Kentucky University M

Louisiana
Bossier Parish Community College W
Centenary College of Louisiana M,W
Louisiana College M
Louisiana State University and Agricultural and
    Mechanical College W
McNeese State University W
Nicholls State University W
Northwestern State University W
Southeastern Louisiana University W
Southern University and Agricultural and
    Mechanical College W
University of Louisiana at Lafayette W
University of Louisiana at Monroe W

Maine
University of Maine M,W
University of Maine
    Augusta W

Maryland
Anne Arundel Community College M,W
Chesapeake College M,W
College of Southern Maryland M,W
Columbia Union College M,W
Community College of Baltimore County M,W
Hagerstown Community College M,W
Harford Community College M,W
Loyola College in Maryland M,W

Mount St. Mary's University M,W
Prince George's Community College W
Towson University M,W
University of Maryland
    Baltimore County M,W
    College Park M,W
    Eastern Shore M

Massachusetts
American International College W
Boston College M,W
Boston University M,W
Dean College M,W
Merrimack College W
Mount Ida College M,W
Northeastern University M,W
Stonehill College M,W
University of Massachusetts
    Amherst M,W
    Lowell M,W

Michigan
Aquinas College M,W
Central Michigan University W
Concordia University M,W
Cornerstone University M,W
Davenport University M,W
Delta College M
Eastern Michigan University W
Grand Rapids Community College W
Grand Valley State University W
Madonna University M,W
Michigan State University M,W
Northern Michigan University W
Northwood University: Michigan M,W
Oakland University M,W
Rochester College M,W
Saginaw Valley State University M,W
Siena Heights University M,W
Southwestern Michigan College M,W
Spring Arbor University M,W
University of Detroit Mercy M,W
University of Michigan M,W
Western Michigan University M,W

Minnesota
Bemidji State University W
Concordia University: St. Paul W
Minnesota State University
    Mankato W
    Moorhead W
Saint Cloud State University W
Southwest Minnesota State University W
University of Minnesota
    Crookston W
    Duluth W
    Twin Cities W
Winona State University W

Mississippi
Alcorn State University W
Belhaven College M,W
Delta State University M,W
East Mississippi Community College M
Hinds Community College M
Holmes Community College M
Meridian Community College M
Mississippi State University W
University of Mississippi W
University of Southern Mississippi W
William Carey University M,W

Missouri
Avila University M,W
Central Methodist University M,W
Columbia College M
Culver-Stockton College M,W
Drury University M,W
East Central College M
Hannibal-LaGrange College M,W
Harris-Stowe State University M,W
Jefferson College M
Missouri Baptist University M,W

Missouri Southern State University M,W
Missouri State University M,W
Missouri Valley College M,W
Northwest Missouri State University W
Park University M,W
Research College of Nursing M,W
Rockhurst University M,W
Saint Louis University M,W
Southeast Missouri State University W
Southwest Baptist University W
St. Louis Community College
    Meramec M,W
Truman State University M,W
University of Central Missouri W
University of Missouri
    Columbia W
    Kansas City M
    Missouri University of Science and
        Technology M,W
    St. Louis M,W
William Jewell College M,W
William Woods University M,W

Montana
Carroll College W
Flathead Valley Community College M
Montana State University
    Billings M,W
Rocky Mountain College W
University of Great Falls W
University of Montana: Missoula W

Nebraska
Bellevue University M,W
College of Saint Mary W
Concordia University M,W
Creighton University M,W
Dana College M,W
Doane College M,W
Hastings College M,W
Midland Lutheran College W
Wayne State College W
Western Nebraska Community College M,W
York College M,W

Nevada
University of Nevada
    Las Vegas M,W
    Reno W

New Hampshire
Franklin Pierce University M,W
Hesser College M,W
Southern New Hampshire University M,W
University of New Hampshire M,W

New Jersey
Bloomfield College M,W
Burlington County College M,W
Caldwell College M,W
Essex County College M
Fairleigh Dickinson University
    Metropolitan Campus M,W
Felician College M,W
Georgian Court University W
Mercer County Community College M,W
Monmouth University M,W
New Jersey Institute of Technology M,W
Rider University M,W
Rutgers, The State University of New Jersey
    New Brunswick/Piscataway Campus M,W
Saint Peter's College M,W
Salem Community College W
Seton Hall University M,W
Sussex County Community College W

New Mexico
College of the Southwest M,W
New Mexico Highlands University W
University of New Mexico M,W

New York
Adelphi University M,W
Bryant & Stratton Business Institute
    Bryant & Stratton College: Syracuse M,W
Canisius College M,W
City University of New York
    Queens College M,W
Colgate University M,W
College of Saint Rose M,W
Concordia College M,W
Daemen College M,W
Dominican College of Blauvelt M,W
Dowling College M,W
Fordham University M,W
Genesee Community College W
Globe Institute of Technology M,W
Hartwick College M
Hofstra University M,W
Houghton College M,W
Iona College M,W
Jamestown Community College M
Le Moyne College M,W
Long Island University
    Brooklyn Campus M,W
    C. W. Post Campus M,W
Manhattan College M,W
Marist College M,W
Mercy College M
Molloy College M,W
Monroe Community College M,W
New York Institute of Technology M,W
Niagara University M,W
Nyack College M,W
Pace University W
Roberts Wesleyan College M,W
Saint Bonaventure University M,W
St. Francis College M
St. John's University M,W
St. Thomas Aquinas College M,W
Siena College M,W
State University of New York
    Albany M,W
    Binghamton M,W
    Buffalo M,W
    College at Oneonta M
    Stony Brook M,W
Syracuse University W
Wagner College W

North Carolina
Appalachian State University M
Barton College M,W
Belmont Abbey College M,W
Brevard College M,W
Campbell University M,W
Catawba College M,W
Davidson College M,W
Duke University M,W
East Carolina University W
Elon University M,W
Gardner-Webb University M,W
High Point University M,W
Lees-McRae College M,W
Lenoir-Rhyne College M,W
Louisburg College M,W
Mars Hill College M,W
Montreat College M,W
Mount Olive College M,W
North Carolina State University M,W
Pfeiffer University M,W
Queens University of Charlotte M,W
St. Andrews Presbyterian College M,W
University of North Carolina
    Asheville M,W
    Chapel Hill M,W
    Charlotte M,W
    Greensboro M,W
    Pembroke M
    Wilmington M,W
Wake Forest University M,W
Western Carolina University W
Wingate University M,W

North Dakota
Jamestown College M,W
North Dakota State University W
University of Mary M,W
University of North Dakota W

Ohio
Ashland University M,W
Bowling Green State University M,W
Bryant & Stratton College
    Willoughby Hills M
Cedarville University M,W
Cincinnati State Technical and Community
    College M,W
Cleveland State University M,W
Kent State University W
Lakeland Community College M
Malone College M,W
Miami University
    Oxford Campus W
Mount Vernon Nazarene University M,W
Notre Dame College W
Ohio Dominican University M,W
Ohio State University
    Columbus Campus M,W
Shawnee State University M,W
Southern State Community College M
University of Akron M,W
University of Dayton M,W
University of Findlay M,W
University of Rio Grande M,W
University of Toledo W
Urbana University M,W
Ursuline College W
Walsh University M,W
Wright State University M
Xavier University M,W
Youngstown State University W

Oklahoma
East Central University W
Northeastern State University M,W
Northwestern Oklahoma State University W
Oklahoma Baptist University M,W
Oklahoma Christian University M,W
Oklahoma City University M,W
Oklahoma State University W
Oklahoma Wesleyan University M,W
Oral Roberts University M,W
Rogers State University M,W
St. Gregory's University M,W
Southern Nazarene University M,W
Southwestern Oklahoma State University M,W
University of Central Oklahoma W
University of Oklahoma W
University of Science and Arts of Oklahoma
    M,W
University of Tulsa M,W

Oregon
Cascade College M,W
Concordia University M,W
Corban College M,W
Eastern Oregon University M,W
Northwest Christian College M,W
Oregon Institute of Technology W
Oregon State University M,W
Portland State University W
Southern Oregon University W
Southwestern Oregon Community College M,W
University of Oregon W
University of Portland M,W
Warner Pacific College W

Pennsylvania
Bloomsburg University of Pennsylvania M,W
California University of Pennsylvania M,W
Carlow University W
Chestnut Hill College M,W
Clarion University of Pennsylvania W
Drexel University M,W
Duquesne University M,W

East Stroudsburg University of Pennsylvania
    M,W
Edinboro University of Pennsylvania W
Gannon University M,W
Holy Family University M,W
Indiana University of Pennsylvania W
Kutztown University of Pennsylvania M,W
La Salle University M,W
Lackawanna College W
Lehigh University M,W
Lock Haven University of Pennsylvania M,W
Mercyhurst College M,W
Millersville University of Pennsylvania M,W
Penn State
    University Park M,W
Philadelphia University M,W
Point Park University M,W
Robert Morris University M,W
St. Francis University M,W
Saint Joseph's University M,W
Seton Hill University M,W
Shippensburg University of Pennsylvania M,W
Slippery Rock University of Pennsylvania M,W
Temple University M,W
University of Pittsburgh M,W
Villanova University M,W
West Chester University of Pennsylvania M,W

Puerto Rico
Inter American University of Puerto Rico
    Aguadilla Campus M
    Bayamon Campus M
    Guayama Campus M
    San German Campus M
Turabo University M
University of Puerto Rico
    Carolina Regional College W
    Cayey University College M
    Mayaguez M

Rhode Island
Bryant University M,W
Community College of Rhode Island M,W
Providence College M,W
University of Rhode Island M,W

South Carolina
Anderson University M,W
Charleston Southern University M,W
The Citadel M,W
Clemson University M,W
Coastal Carolina University M,W
Coker College M,W
College of Charleston M,W
Columbia College W
Converse College W
Erskine College M,W
Francis Marion University M,W
Furman University M,W
Lander University M,W
Limestone College M,W
Newberry College M,W
North Greenville University M,W
Presbyterian College M,W
Southern Wesleyan University M,W
Spartanburg Methodist College M,W
University of South Carolina M,W
University of South Carolina
    Aiken M
    Upstate M,W
Winthrop University M,W
Wofford College M,W

South Dakota
Augustana College W
Dakota State University M,W
Dakota Wesleyan University M,W
Mount Marty College M,W
South Dakota State University W
University of Sioux Falls M,W
University of South Dakota W

Tennessee
Austin Peay State University W
Belmont University M,W
Bethel College M,W
Bryan College M,W
Carson-Newman College M,W
Christian Brothers University M,W
Crichton College M,W
Cumberland University M,W
East Tennessee State University M,W
Freed-Hardeman University M,W
Hiwassee College M,W
King College M,W
Lambuth University M,W
Lee University M,W
Lincoln Memorial University M,W
Lipscomb University M,W
Martin Methodist College M,W
Middle Tennessee State University W
Milligan College M,W
Tennessee Technological University W
Tennessee Temple University M
Tennessee Wesleyan College M,W
Trevecca Nazarene University M,W
Tusculum College M,W
Union University M,W
University of Memphis M,W
University of Tennessee
    Chattanooga W
    Knoxville W
    Martin W
Vanderbilt University W

Texas
Angelo State University W
Baylor University W
Cedar Valley College M
Dallas Baptist University W
Hill College W
Lon Morris College M,W
Midwestern State University M,W
Northwood University: Texas M,W
Prairie View A&M University W
Ranger College M
Rice University W
St. Edward's University M,W
St. Mary's University M,W
Sam Houston State University W
Southern Methodist University M,W
Stephen F. Austin State University W
Texas A&M University W
Texas A&M University
    Commerce W
Texas Christian University W
Texas Southern University W
Texas State University: San Marcos W
Texas Tech University W
Texas Woman's University W
Tyler Junior College M
University of Houston W
University of North Texas W
University of Texas
    Austin W
    San Antonio W
University of the Incarnate Word M,W
Wayland Baptist University W
West Texas A&M University M,W

Utah
Brigham Young University W
Dixie State College of Utah M,W
University of Utah W
Utah State University W
Utah Valley State College W
Westminster College M,W

Vermont
University of Vermont M,W

Virginia
Bluefield College M,W
College of William and Mary M,W

George Mason University M,W
James Madison University M,W
Liberty University M,W
Longwood University M,W
Old Dominion University M,W
Radford University M,W
University of Richmond M,W
University of Virginia M,W
Virginia Commonwealth University M,W
Virginia Military Institute M
Virginia Polytechnic Institute and State
    University M,W

Washington
Central Washington University W
Clark College M,W
Columbia Basin College M,W
Edmonds Community College M,W
Everett Community College M,W
Evergreen State College M,W
Gonzaga University M,W
Green River Community College M
Highline Community College M,W
Lower Columbia College W
Northwest University M,W
Olympic College M,W
Peninsula College M
Saint Martin's University M,W
Seattle Pacific University M
Seattle University M,W
Spokane Community College W
Tacoma Community College M,W
University of Washington M,W
Walla Walla Community College M,W
Washington State University W
Western Washington University M,W
Whatcom Community College M
Yakima Valley Community College W

West Virginia
Alderson-Broaddus College M
Concord University W
Davis and Elkins College M,W
Marshall University M,W
Mountain State University W
Ohio Valley University M,W
Salem International University M,W
Shepherd University M,W
University of Charleston M,W
West Virginia University M,W
West Virginia Wesleyan College M,W
Wheeling Jesuit University M,W

Wisconsin
Cardinal Stritch University M,W
Marquette University M,W
Milwaukee Area Technical College M,W
University of Wisconsin
    Green Bay M,W
    Milwaukee M,W
    Parkside M,W
Viterbo University M,W

Wyoming
Central Wyoming College M,W
Laramie County Community College M,W
University of Wyoming W
Western Wyoming Community College M,W

Softball

Alabama
Alabama State University W
Auburn University W
Bevill State Community College W
Central Alabama Community College W
Chattahoochee Valley Community College W
Concordia College W
Faulkner State Community College W
Faulkner University W
Gadsden State Community College W

George C. Wallace State Community College
  George C. Wallace Community College at
    Dothan M
Jacksonville State University W
Jefferson Davis Community College W
Jefferson State Community College W
Judson College W
Lurleen B. Wallace Community College M
Marion Military Institute W
Miles College W
Samford University W
Shelton State Community College W
Snead State Community College W
Southern Union State Community College W
Spring Hill College W
Troy University W
University of Alabama W
University of Alabama
  Birmingham W
  Huntsville W
University of Mobile W
University of North Alabama W
University of West Alabama W

Arizona
Arizona State University W
Arizona Western College W
Central Arizona College W
Chandler-Gilbert Community College
  Pecos W
Eastern Arizona College W
Gateway Community College W
Glendale Community College W
Mesa Community College W
Paradise Valley Community College W
Pima Community College W
Scottsdale Community College W
South Mountain Community College W
University of Arizona W

Arkansas
Henderson State University W
Lyon College W
Ouachita Baptist University W
Southern Arkansas University W
University of Arkansas W
University of Arkansas
  Monticello W
University of Central Arkansas W
Williams Baptist College W

California
Azusa Pacific University W
Bethany University W
Biola University W
California Baptist University W
California Polytechnic State University: San Luis
  Obispo W
California State University
  Bakersfield W
  Chico W
  Dominguez Hills W
  Fresno W
  Fullerton W
  Long Beach W
  Northridge W
  Sacramento W
  San Bernardino W
  Stanislaus W
Concordia University W
Dominican University of California W
Fresno City College W
Grossmont College W
Holy Names University W
Hope International University W
Humboldt State University W
Loyola Marymount University W
Notre Dame de Namur University W
Patten University W
Point Loma Nazarene University W
St. Mary's College of California W
San Diego State University W

San Jose State University W
Santa Clara University W
Sonoma State University W
Stanford University W
University of California
  Berkeley W
  Davis W
  Los Angeles W
  Riverside W
  Santa Barbara W
University of San Diego W
University of the Pacific W
Vanguard University of Southern California W
William Jessup University W
Yuba Community College District W

Colorado
Adams State College W
Colorado Northwestern Community College W
Colorado School of Mines W
Colorado State University W
Colorado State University
  Pueblo W
Fort Lewis College W
Mesa State College W
Otero Junior College W
Regis University W
Trinidad State Junior College W
University of Colorado
  Colorado Springs W
University of Northern Colorado W

Connecticut
Central Connecticut State University W
Fairfield University W
Post University W
Quinnipiac University W
Sacred Heart University W
Southern Connecticut State University W
University of Bridgeport W
University of Connecticut W
University of New Haven W

Delaware
Delaware State University W
Goldey-Beacom College W
University of Delaware W
Wilmington University W

Florida
Barry University W
Bethune-Cookman University W
Brevard Community College W
Broward Community College W
Central Florida Community College W
Chipola Junior College W
Daytona Beach Community College W
Eckerd College W
Edward Waters College W
Florida Atlantic University W
Florida Community College at Jacksonville W
Florida Gulf Coast University W
Florida Institute of Technology W
Florida Southern College W
Florida State University W
Gulf Coast Community College W
Hillsborough Community College W
Indian River Community College W
Jacksonville University W
Lake City Community College W
Lake-Sumter Community College W
Lynn University W
Manatee Community College W
Miami Dade College W
North Florida Community College W
Northwood University
  Florida W
Nova Southeastern University W
Okaloosa-Walton College W
Palm Beach Community College W
Pasco-Hernando Community College W
Pensacola Junior College W
Polk Community College W

Rollins College W
Saint Johns River Community College W
St. Leo University W
St. Petersburg College W
Saint Thomas University W
Santa Fe Community College W
South Florida Community College W
Stetson University W
Tallahassee Community College W
University of Central Florida W
University of Florida W
University of North Florida W
University of South Florida W
University of Tampa W
University of West Florida W
Warner Southern College W
Webber International University W

Georgia
Abraham Baldwin Agricultural College W
Albany State University W
Andrew College W
Armstrong Atlantic State University W
Augusta State University W
Brenau University W
Brewton-Parker College W
Clark Atlanta University W
Coastal Georgia Community College W
Columbus State University W
Covenant College W
Darton College W
Emmanuel College W
Georgia College and State University W
Georgia Institute of Technology W
Georgia Perimeter College W
Georgia Southern University W
Georgia Southwestern State University W
Georgia State University W
Gordon College W
Kennesaw State University W
Mercer University W
Middle Georgia College W
North Georgia College & State University W
Paine College W
Reinhardt College W
South Georgia College W
Thomas University W
Truett-McConnell College W
University of Georgia W
University of West Georgia W
Valdosta State University W
Young Harris College W

Hawaii
Brigham Young University-Hawaii W
Chaminade University of Honolulu W
Hawaii Pacific University W
University of Hawaii
  Hilo W
  Manoa W

Idaho
College of Idaho W
College of Southern Idaho M,W
North Idaho College W
Northwest Nazarene University W

Illinois
Black Hawk College W
Bradley University W
Carl Sandburg College W
College of Lake County W
Danville Area Community College W
DePaul University W
Eastern Illinois University W
Elgin Community College W
Highland Community College W
Illinois Central College W
Illinois Eastern Community Colleges
  Lincoln Trail College W
  Olney Central College W
  Wabash Valley College W
Illinois State University W

John A. Logan College W
Judson University W
Kankakee Community College W
Kaskaskia College W
Kishwaukee College W
Lake Land College W
Lewis University W
Lincoln College W
Lincoln Land Community College W
McHenry County College W
McKendree University W
Moraine Valley Community College W
Morton College W
Northwestern University W
Olivet Nazarene University W
Parkland College W
Quincy University W
Rend Lake College W
Robert Morris College: Chicago W
St. Xavier University W
Sauk Valley Community College W
Shawnee Community College W
South Suburban College of Cook County W
Southeastern Illinois College W
Southern Illinois University Carbondale W
Southern Illinois University Edwardsville W
Spoon River College W
Springfield College in Illinois W
Trinity Christian College W
Trinity International University W
University of Illinois
  Chicago W
  Springfield W
  Urbana-Champaign W
University of St. Francis W
Waubonsee Community College W
Western Illinois University W

Indiana
Ancilla College W
Ball State University W
Bethel College W
Butler University W
Calumet College of St. Joseph W
Goshen College W
Grace College W
Huntington University W
Indiana Institute of Technology W
Indiana State University W
Indiana University
  Bloomington W
Indiana University-Purdue University Fort
  Wayne W
Indiana University-Purdue University
  Indianapolis W
Indiana Wesleyan University W
Marian College W
Oakland City University W
Purdue University W
Saint Joseph's College W
St. Mary-of-the-Woods College W
Taylor University W
University of Evansville W
University of Indianapolis W
University of Notre Dame W
University of St. Francis W
University of Southern Indiana W
Valparaiso University W

Iowa
Ashford University W
Briar Cliff University W
Clarke College W
Dordt College W
Drake University W
Ellsworth Community College W
Graceland University W
Grand View College W
Indian Hills Community College W
Iowa Central Community College W
Iowa Lakes Community College W
Iowa State University W

Iowa Wesleyan College W
Iowa Western Community College W
Kirkwood Community College W
Marshalltown Community College W
Morningside College W
Muscatine Community College W
North Iowa Area Community College W
Northwestern College W
St. Ambrose University W
Southeastern Community College
    North Campus W
Southwestern Community College W
University of Iowa W
University of Northern Iowa W
Waldorf College W
William Penn University W

Kansas
Allen County Community College W
Baker University W
Barton County Community College W
Benedictine College W
Bethany College W
Brown Mackie College
    Salina W
Butler County Community College W
Central Christian College of Kansas W
Cloud County Community College W
Coffeyville Community College W
Colby Community College W
Cowley County Community College W
Dodge City Community College W
Emporia State University W
Fort Hays State University W
Fort Scott Community College W
Friends University W
Garden City Community College W
Highland Community College W
Hutchinson Community College W
Independence Community College W
Johnson County Community College W
Kansas City Kansas Community College W
Kansas Wesleyan University W
Labette Community College W
McPherson College W
MidAmerica Nazarene University W
Neosho County Community College W
Newman University W
Ottawa University W
Pittsburg State University W
Pratt Community College W
Seward County Community College W
Southwestern College W
Sterling College W
Tabor College W
University of Kansas W
University of St. Mary W
Washburn University W
Wichita State University W

Kentucky
Bellarmine University W
Brescia University W
Campbellsville University W
Eastern Kentucky University W
Georgetown College W
Kentucky State University W
Kentucky Wesleyan College W
Lindsey Wilson College W
Mid-Continent University W
Midway College W
Morehead State University W
Northern Kentucky University W
Pikeville College W
St. Catharine College W
Union College W
University of Kentucky W
University of Louisville M
University of the Cumberlands W
Western Kentucky University W

Louisiana
Bossier Parish Community College W
Centenary College of Louisiana W
Louisiana State University and Agricultural and
    Mechanical College W
Louisiana Tech University W
McNeese State University W
Nicholls State University W
Northwestern State University W
Southeastern Louisiana University W
Southern University and Agricultural and
    Mechanical College W
University of Louisiana at Lafayette W
University of Louisiana at Monroe W

Maine
University of Maine W

Maryland
Anne Arundel Community College W
Bowie State University W
Chesapeake College W
College of Southern Maryland W
Columbia Union College W
Community College of Baltimore County W
Coppin State University W
Hagerstown Community College W
Morgan State University W
Mount St. Mary's University W
Prince George's Community College W
Towson University W
University of Maryland
    Baltimore County W
    College Park W
    Eastern Shore W

Massachusetts
American International College W
Boston College W
Boston University W
Dean College W
Merrimack College W
Mount Ida College W
Stonehill College W
University of Massachusetts
    Amherst W

Michigan
Alpena Community College W
Aquinas College W
Central Michigan University W
Concordia University W
Cornerstone University W
Delta College W
Eastern Michigan University W
Ferris State University W
Glen Oaks Community College W
Grand Valley State University W
Henry Ford Community College W
Hillsdale College W
Kalamazoo Valley Community College W
Kellogg Community College W
Lake Michigan College W
Lake Superior State University W
Madonna University W
Michigan State University W
Mott Community College W
Muskegon Community College W
Northwood University: Michigan W
Oakland Community College W
Oakland University W
Rochester College W
Saginaw Valley State University W
Siena Heights University W
Spring Arbor University W
University of Detroit Mercy W
University of Michigan W
Wayne State University M,W
Western Michigan University W

Minnesota
Bemidji State University W
Concordia University: St. Paul W
Minnesota State University
    Mankato W
    Moorhead W
Saint Cloud State University W
Southwest Minnesota State University W
University of Minnesota
    Crookston W
    Duluth W
    Twin Cities W
Winona State University W

Mississippi
Alcorn State University W
Belhaven College W
Copiah-Lincoln Community College W
Delta State University W
East Central Community College W
East Mississippi Community College W
Hinds Community College W
Holmes Community College W
Itawamba Community College W
Jackson State University W
Meridian Community College W
Mississippi Gulf Coast Community College
    Jefferson Davis Campus W
Mississippi State University W
Mississippi Valley State University W
Northwest Mississippi Community College W
Southwest Mississippi Community College W
University of Mississippi W
University of Southern Mississippi W
William Carey University W

Missouri
Avila University W
Central Methodist University W
Columbia College W
Culver-Stockton College W
Drury University M,W
East Central College W
Evangel University W
Hannibal-LaGrange College W
Harris-Stowe State University W
Jefferson College W
Lincoln University W
Missouri Baptist University W
Missouri Southern State University W
Missouri State University W
Missouri Valley College W
Missouri Western State University W
North Central Missouri College W
Northwest Missouri State University W
Park University W
Research College of Nursing W
Rockhurst University W
St. Charles Community College W
Saint Louis University W
Southeast Missouri State University W
Southwest Baptist University W
St. Louis Community College
    Meramec W
Truman State University W
University of Central Missouri W
University of Missouri
    Columbia W
    Kansas City W
    Missouri University of Science and
        Technology W
    St. Louis W
William Jewell College W
William Woods University W

Montana
Montana State University
    Billings W
University of Great Falls W

Nebraska
Bellevue University W
College of Saint Mary W
Concordia University W
Creighton University W
Dana College W
Doane College W
Hastings College W
Mid-Plains Community College Area W
Midland Lutheran College W
Peru State College W
University of Nebraska
    Kearney W
    Lincoln W
    Omaha W
Wayne State College W
Western Nebraska Community College W
York College W

Nevada
College of Southern Nevada W
University of Nevada
    Las Vegas W
    Reno W

New Hampshire
Franklin Pierce University W
Hesser College W
Southern New Hampshire University M,W

New Jersey
Bloomfield College W
Brookdale Community College W
Burlington County College W
Caldwell College W
Fairleigh Dickinson University
    Metropolitan Campus W
Felician College W
Georgian Court University W
Mercer County Community College W
Monmouth University W
Rider University W
Rutgers, The State University of New Jersey
    New Brunswick/Piscataway Campus W
Saint Peter's College W
Salem Community College W
Seton Hall University W

New Mexico
College of the Southwest W
Eastern New Mexico University W
New Mexico Highlands University W
New Mexico State University W
University of New Mexico W
Western New Mexico University W

New York
Adelphi University W
Canisius College W
City University of New York
    Queens College W
Colgate University W
College of Saint Rose W
Concordia College W
Dominican College of Blauvelt W
Dowling College W
Fordham University W
Globe Institute of Technology W
Hofstra University W
Iona College W
Le Moyne College W
Long Island University
    Brooklyn Campus W
    C. W. Post Campus W
Manhattan College W
Marist College W
Mercy College W
Molloy College W
New York Institute of Technology W
Niagara University W
Nyack College W
Pace University W

Saint Bonaventure University W
St. John's University W
St. Thomas Aquinas College W
Siena College W
State University of New York
    Albany W
    Binghamton W
    Buffalo W
    Stony Brook W
Syracuse University W
Wagner College W

North Carolina
Barton College W
Belmont Abbey College W
Brevard College W
Campbell University W
Catawba College W
East Carolina University W
Elizabeth City State University W
Elon University W
Fayetteville State University W
Gardner-Webb University W
Johnson C. Smith University W
Lees-McRae College W
Lenoir-Rhyne College W
Louisburg College W
Mars Hill College W
Montreat College W
Mount Olive College W
North Carolina Central University W
North Carolina State University W
Pfeiffer University W
Pitt Community College W
Queens University of Charlotte W
St. Andrews Presbyterian College W
St. Augustine's College W
Shaw University W
University of North Carolina
    Chapel Hill W
    Charlotte W
    Greensboro W
    Pembroke W
    Wilmington W
Western Carolina University W
Wingate University W
Winston-Salem State University W

North Dakota
Dickinson State University W
Jamestown College W
Mayville State University W
Minot State University W
North Dakota State University W
University of Mary W
University of North Dakota W
Valley City State University W

Ohio
Ashland University W
Bowling Green State University W
Cedarville University W
Cleveland State University W
Kent State University W
Lakeland Community College W
Malone College W
Miami University
    Oxford Campus W
Mount Vernon Nazarene University W
Notre Dame College W
Ohio Dominican University W
Ohio State University
    Columbus Campus W
Ohio University W
Shawnee State University W
Southern State Community College W
University of Akron W
University of Dayton W
University of Findlay W
University of Rio Grande W
University of Toledo W
Urbana University W

Ursuline College W
Walsh University W
Wright State University W
Youngstown State University W

Oklahoma
Bacone College W
Cameron University W
Carl Albert State College W
Connors State College W
East Central University W
Northeastern Oklahoma Agricultural and
    Mechanical College W
Northeastern State University W
Northwestern Oklahoma State University W
Oklahoma Baptist University W
Oklahoma Christian University W
Oklahoma City University W
Oklahoma Panhandle State University M,W
Oklahoma State University W
Rogers State University M,W
Rose State College W
St. Gregory's University W
Seminole State College W
Southeastern Oklahoma State University W
Southern Nazarene University W
Southwestern Oklahoma State University W
University of Central Oklahoma W
University of Oklahoma W
University of Science and Arts of Oklahoma W
University of Tulsa W
Western Oklahoma State College W

Oregon
Blue Mountain Community College W
Clackamas Community College W
Concordia University W
Corban College W
Eastern Oregon University W
Northwest Christian College W
Oregon Institute of Technology W
Oregon State University W
Portland State University W
Southern Oregon University W
Southwestern Oregon Community College W
University of Oregon W

Pennsylvania
Bloomsburg University of Pennsylvania W
California University of Pennsylvania W
Carlow University W
Chestnut Hill College W
Clarion University of Pennsylvania W
Community College of Beaver County W
Drexel University W
East Stroudsburg University of Pennsylvania W
Edinboro University of Pennsylvania W
Gannon University W
Holy Family University W
Indiana University of Pennsylvania W
Kutztown University of Pennsylvania W
La Salle University W
Lackawanna College W
Lehigh University W
Lock Haven University of Pennsylvania W
Mansfield University of Pennsylvania W
Mercyhurst College W
Millersville University of Pennsylvania W
Penn State
    University Park W
Philadelphia University W
Point Park University W
Robert Morris University W
St. Francis University W
Saint Joseph's University W
Seton Hill University W
Shippensburg University of Pennsylvania W
Slippery Rock University of Pennsylvania W
Temple University W
University of Pittsburgh W
University of the Sciences in Philadelphia W
Villanova University W

West Chester University of Pennsylvania W
Westminster College W

Puerto Rico
Inter American University of Puerto Rico
    Aguadilla Campus M,W
    Bayamon Campus M,W
    Guayama Campus M,W
    Ponce Campus M,W
Universidad del Este M
Universidad Metropolitana M,W
University of Puerto Rico
    Carolina Regional College W
    Cayey University College M,W
    Humacao W
    Mayaguez W
    Ponce M,W
    Utuado M,W

Rhode Island
Bryant University W
Community College of Rhode Island W
Providence College W
University of Rhode Island W

South Carolina
Aiken Technical College W
Anderson University W
Charleston Southern University W
Claflin University W
Coastal Carolina University W
Coker College W
College of Charleston W
Erskine College W
Francis Marion University W
Furman University W
Lander University W
Limestone College W
Morris College W
Newberry College W
North Greenville University W
Presbyterian College W
South Carolina State University W
Southern Wesleyan University W
Spartanburg Methodist College W
University of South Carolina W
University of South Carolina
    Aiken W
    Upstate W
Voorhees College W
Winthrop University W

South Dakota
Augustana College W
Dakota State University W
Dakota Wesleyan University W
Mount Marty College W
Northern State University W
South Dakota State University W
University of Sioux Falls W
University of South Dakota W

Tennessee
Austin Peay State University W
Belmont University W
Bethel College W
Carson-Newman College W
Christian Brothers University W
Cleveland State Community College W
Crichton College M,W
Cumberland University W
Dyersburg State Community College W
East Tennessee State University W
Freed-Hardeman University W
Hiwassee College W
Jackson State Community College W
King College W
Lambuth University W
Lee University W
LeMoyne-Owen College W
Lincoln Memorial University W
Lipscomb University W
Martin Methodist College W

Middle Tennessee State University W
Milligan College W
Motlow State Community College W
Roane State Community College W
Southwest Tennessee Community College W
Tennessee Technological University W
Tennessee Wesleyan College W
Trevecca Nazarene University W
Tusculum College W
Union University W
University of Tennessee
    Chattanooga W
    Knoxville W
    Martin W
Volunteer State Community College W
Walters State Community College W

Texas
Abilene Christian University W
Alvin Community College W
Angelo State University W
Baylor University W
Blinn College M
Clarendon College W
Frank Phillips College W
Galveston College W
Grayson County College W
Hill College W
Houston Baptist University W
Howard College W
Lon Morris College W
Midland College W
Midwestern State University W
Northwood University: Texas W
Odessa College W
Paris Junior College W
Prairie View A&M University W
Ranger College W
St. Edward's University W
Sam Houston State University W
Stephen F. Austin State University W
Tarleton State University W
Temple College W
Texas A&M University W
Texas A&M University
    Kingsville W
Texas Southern University W
Texas State University: San Marcos W
Texas Tech University W
Texas Woman's University W
University of Houston W
University of North Texas W
University of Texas
    Arlington W
    Austin W
    San Antonio W
University of the Incarnate Word W
Vernon College W
Western Texas College W
Wiley College W

Utah
Brigham Young University W
Dixie State College of Utah W
Salt Lake Community College W
Snow College W
Southern Utah University W
University of Utah W
Utah State University W
Utah Valley State College W

Vermont
University of Vermont W

Virginia
Bluefield College W
Hampton University W
James Madison University W
Liberty University W
Longwood University W
Norfolk State University W
Radford University W
St. Paul's College W

University of Virginia W
University of Virginia's College at Wise W
Virginia Intermont College W
Virginia Polytechnic Institute and State
    University W
Virginia State University W
Virginia Union University W

Washington
Big Bend Community College W
Central Washington University W
Centralia College W
Columbia Basin College W
Edmonds Community College W
Everett Community College W
Grays Harbor College W
Green River Community College W
Highline Community College W
Lower Columbia College W
Olympic College W
Peninsula College W
Saint Martin's University W
Seattle University W
Spokane Community College W
University of Washington W
Walla Walla Community College W
Western Washington University W
Yakima Valley Community College W

West Virginia
Alderson-Broaddus College W
Bluefield State College W
Concord University W
Davis and Elkins College W
Glenville State College W
Marshall University W
Mountain State University W
Ohio Valley University W
Potomac State College of West Virginia
    University W
Salem International University W
Shepherd University W
University of Charleston W
West Liberty State College W
West Virginia Wesleyan College W
Wheeling Jesuit University W

Wisconsin
Cardinal Stritch University W
University of Wisconsin
    Green Bay W
    Parkside W
Viterbo University W

Squash

Nebraska
University of Nebraska
    Lincoln W

New York
Fordham University M

Swimming

Alabama
Auburn University M,W
University of Alabama M,W

Alaska
University of Alaska
    Fairbanks W

Arizona
Arizona State University M,W
Northern Arizona University M,W
University of Arizona M,W

Arkansas
Henderson State University M,W
John Brown University W
Ouachita Baptist University M,W
University of Arkansas W
University of Arkansas
    Little Rock M,W

California
Biola University M,W
California Baptist University M,W
California Polytechnic State University: San Luis
    Obispo M,W
California State University
    Bakersfield M,W
    Northridge M,W
    San Bernardino M,W
Concordia University M,W
Fresno Pacific University M,W
Grossmont College M,W
Loyola Marymount University W
Pepperdine University W
San Diego State University W
San Jose State University W
Stanford University M,W
University of California
    Berkeley M,W
    Davis M,W
    Irvine M,W
    Los Angeles W
    Santa Barbara M,W
University of San Diego W
University of Southern California M,W
University of the Pacific M,W

Colorado
Colorado School of Mines M,W
Colorado State University W
Metropolitan State College of Denver M,W
University of Denver M,W
University of Northern Colorado W

Connecticut
Central Connecticut State University W
Fairfield University M,W
Southern Connecticut State University M,W
University of Bridgeport W
University of Connecticut M,W

Delaware
University of Delaware W

District of Columbia
George Washington University M,W
Georgetown University M,W
Howard University M,W

Florida
Broward Community College M,W
Florida Atlantic University M,W
Florida Southern College M,W
Florida State University M,W
Indian River Community College M,W
St. Leo University M,W
University of Florida M,W
University of Miami W
University of North Florida W
University of Tampa M,W

Georgia
Brenau University W
Darton College M,W
Georgia Institute of Technology M,W
Georgia Southern University W
University of Georgia M,W

Hawaii
University of Hawaii
    Manoa M,W

Idaho
Boise State University W
College of Idaho M,W

Illinois
Eastern Illinois University M,W
Illinois Institute of Technology M,W
Illinois State University W
Lewis University M,W
Lincoln College M,W
Northwestern University M,W
Southern Illinois University Carbondale M,W
University of Illinois
    Chicago M,W
    Urbana-Champaign W
Western Illinois University M,W

Indiana
Ball State University M,W
Indiana University
    Bloomington M,W
Indiana University-Purdue University
    Indianapolis M,W
Purdue University M,W
University of Evansville M,W
University of Indianapolis M,W
University of Notre Dame M,W
Valparaiso University M,W
Vincennes University M,W

Iowa
Iowa Central Community College M,W
Iowa State University W
Morningside College M,W
University of Iowa M,W
University of Northern Iowa W

Kansas
University of Kansas W

Kentucky
Asbury College M,W
University of Kentucky M,W
University of Louisville M,W
University of the Cumberlands M,W
Western Kentucky University M,W

Louisiana
Centenary College of Louisiana M,W
Louisiana State University and Agricultural and
    Mechanical College M,W
Tulane University W
University of Louisiana at Monroe M,W
University of New Orleans W

Maine
University of Maine W

Maryland
Loyola College in Maryland M,W
Mount St. Mary's University W
Towson University M,W
University of Maryland
    Baltimore County M,W
    College Park M,W

Massachusetts
Boston College M,W
Boston University M,W
Northeastern University W
University of Massachusetts
    Amherst M,W
    Lowell M

Michigan
Eastern Michigan University M,W
Grand Rapids Community College M,W
Grand Valley State University M,W
Hillsdale College W
Michigan State University M,W
Northern Michigan University W
Oakland University M,W
University of Michigan M,W
Wayne State University M,W

Minnesota
Minnesota State University
    Mankato M,W
Saint Cloud State University M,W
University of Minnesota
    Twin Cities M,W

Mississippi
Delta State University M,W

Missouri
Drury University M,W
Missouri State University M,W
Saint Louis University M,W
Stephens College W
Truman State University M,W
University of Missouri
    Columbia M,W
    Missouri University of Science and
        Technology M

Nebraska
University of Nebraska
    Kearney W
    Lincoln W

Nevada
University of Nevada
    Las Vegas M,W
    Reno W

New Hampshire
University of New Hampshire W

New Jersey
New Jersey Institute of Technology M,W
Rider University M,W
Rutgers, The State University of New Jersey
    New Brunswick/Piscataway Campus M,W
Saint Peter's College M,W
Seton Hall University M,W

New Mexico
New Mexico State University W
University of New Mexico W

New York
Adelphi University M,W
Canisius College W
City University of New York
    Queens College M,W
College of Saint Rose M,W
Fordham University M,W
Iona College M,W
Long Island University
    C. W. Post Campus W
Manhattan College W
Marist College M,W
Monroe Community College M,W
Niagara University M,W
Saint Bonaventure University M,W
St. Francis College M,W
Siena College W
State University of New York
    Binghamton M,W
    Buffalo M,W
    Stony Brook M,W
Syracuse University M,W
Wagner College W

North Carolina
Campbell University W
Catawba College M,W
Davidson College M,W
East Carolina University M,W
Gardner-Webb University M,W
Lenoir-Rhyne College W
Mars Hill College M,W
North Carolina Agricultural and Technical State
    University W
North Carolina State University M,W
Pfeiffer University M,W
University of North Carolina

Chapel Hill M,W
Wilmington M,W
Wingate University M,W

North Dakota
University of North Dakota M,W

Ohio
Ashland University M,W
Bowling Green State University M,W
Cleveland State University M,W
Miami University
    Oxford Campus M,W
Notre Dame College W
Ohio State University
    Columbus Campus M,W
Ohio University W
University of Akron W
University of Findlay M,W
University of Toledo W
Wright State University M,W
Xavier University M,W
Youngstown State University W

Oregon
Oregon State University W

Pennsylvania
Bloomsburg University of Pennsylvania M,W
California University of Pennsylvania M,W
Clarion University of Pennsylvania M,W
Drexel University M,W
Duquesne University M,W
East Stroudsburg University of Pennsylvania W
Edinboro University of Pennsylvania W
Gannon University M,W
Indiana University of Pennsylvania M,W
Kutztown University of Pennsylvania M,W
La Salle University M,W
Lehigh University M,W
Lock Haven University of Pennsylvania W
Mansfield University of Pennsylvania W
Millersville University of Pennsylvania W
Penn State
    University Park M,W
St. Francis University W
Shippensburg University of Pennsylvania M,W
Slippery Rock University of Pennsylvania M,W
University of Pittsburgh M,W
Villanova University W
West Chester University of Pennsylvania M,W
Westminster College W

Puerto Rico
Bayamon Central University M,W
Inter American University of Puerto Rico
    Bayamon Campus M,W
Turabo University M,W
University of Puerto Rico
    Cayey University College M,W
    Humacao M,W
    Mayaguez M,W
University of the Sacred Heart M,W

Rhode Island
Bryant University M,W
University of Rhode Island M,W

South Carolina
Clemson University M,W
College of Charleston M,W
Limestone College M,W
University of South Carolina M,W

South Dakota
South Dakota State University M,W
University of South Dakota M,W

Tennessee
Lambuth University M,W
University of Tennessee
    Knoxville M,W

Texas
Rice University W
Southern Methodist University M,W
Texas A&M University M,W
Texas Christian University M,W
University of Houston W
University of North Texas W
University of Texas
    Austin M,W
University of the Incarnate Word M,W

Utah
Brigham Young University M,W
University of Utah M,W

Vermont
University of Vermont W

Virginia
George Mason University M,W
James Madison University W
Radford University W
University of Richmond W
University of Virginia M,W
Virginia Military Institute M
Virginia Polytechnic Institute and State
    University M,W

Washington
Seattle University M,W
University of Washington M,W
Washington State University W

West Virginia
Marshall University W
West Virginia University M,W
West Virginia Wesleyan College M,W
Wheeling Jesuit University M,W

Wisconsin
University of Wisconsin
    Green Bay M,W
    Milwaukee M,W

Wyoming
University of Wyoming M,W

Synchronized swimming

Alabama
University of Alabama
    Birmingham W

California
Stanford University W

New York
Canisius College W

Texas
University of the Incarnate Word W

Table tennis

Arizona
South Mountain Community College M,W

Puerto Rico
Inter American University of Puerto Rico
    Aguadilla Campus M,W
    Bayamon Campus M,W
    Metropolitan Campus M,W
    Ponce Campus M,W
Universidad Metropolitana M,W
University of Puerto Rico
    Carolina Regional College M,W
    Cayey University College M,W
    Mayaguez M,W

Ponce M,W

Tennis

Alabama
Alabama Agricultural and Mechanical
    University M,W
Alabama State University M,W
Auburn University M,W
Auburn University at Montgomery M,W
Central Alabama Community College M,W
Faulkner State Community College M,W
Gadsden State Community College M,W
Jacksonville State University M,W
Judson College W
Marion Military Institute W
Northwest-Shoals Community College W
Samford University M,W
Snead State Community College W
Spring Hill College M,W
Troy University M,W
University of Alabama M,W
University of Alabama
    Birmingham M,W
    Huntsville M,W
University of Mobile W
University of Montevallo W
University of North Alabama M,W
University of South Alabama M,W

Arizona
Arizona State University M,W
Eastern Arizona College W
Gateway Community College M,W
Glendale Community College M,W
Grand Canyon University W
Northern Arizona University M,W
Paradise Valley Community College M,W
Pima Community College M,W
Scottsdale Community College M,W
South Mountain Community College M,W
University of Arizona M,W

Arkansas
Arkansas State University W
Arkansas Tech University W
Harding University M,W
Henderson State University W
John Brown University M,W
Lyon College M,W
Ouachita Baptist University M,W
Southern Arkansas University W
University of Arkansas M,W
University of Arkansas
    Fort Smith M,W
    Little Rock M,W
University of Central Arkansas W

California
Azusa Pacific University M
Biola University M,W
California Baptist University M,W
California Polytechnic State University: San Luis
    Obispo M,W
California State Polytechnic University: Pomona
    M,W
California State University
    Bakersfield W
    Fresno M,W
    Fullerton W
    Long Beach W
    Los Angeles M,W
    Northridge W
    Sacramento M,W
Concordia University M,W
Dominican University of California M,W
Fresno City College M,W
Fresno Pacific University M,W
Grossmont College M,W
Hope International University M,W
Loyola Marymount University M,W

The Master's College W
Notre Dame de Namur University W
Pepperdine University M,W
Point Loma Nazarene University M,W
St. Mary's College of California M,W
San Diego State University M,W
San Jose State University W
Santa Clara University M,W
Sonoma State University M,W
Stanford University M,W
University of California
    Berkeley M,W
    Irvine M,W
    Los Angeles M,W
    Riverside M,W
    Santa Barbara M,W
University of San Diego M,W
University of San Francisco M,W
University of Southern California M,W
University of the Pacific M,W
Vanguard University of Southern California
    M,W
Westmont College M,W
Yuba Community College District M,W

Colorado
Colorado Christian University M,W
Colorado State University W
Colorado State University
    Pueblo M,W
Mesa State College M,W
Metropolitan State College of Denver M,W
University of Colorado
    Boulder W
University of Denver M,W
University of Northern Colorado M,W

Connecticut
Fairfield University M,W
Quinnipiac University M,W
Sacred Heart University M,W
University of Connecticut M,W
University of Hartford M,W
University of New Haven W

Delaware
Delaware State University M,W
Goldey-Beacom College M

District of Columbia
George Washington University M,W
Georgetown University M,W
Howard University M,W

Florida
Barry University M,W
Bethune-Cookman University M,W
Broward Community College M,W
Central Florida Community College W
Eckerd College M,W
Embry-Riddle Aeronautical University M,W
Flagler College M,W
Florida Atlantic University M,W
Florida Community College at Jacksonville W
Florida Gulf Coast University M,W
Florida Institute of Technology M,W
Florida International University W
Florida Southern College M,W
Florida State University M,W
Hillsborough Community College W
Jacksonville University M,W
Lynn University M,W
Northwood University.
    Florida M,W
Nova Southeastern University W
Pasco-Hernando Community College W
Rollins College M,W
St. Leo University M,W
Saint Thomas University M,W
Stetson University M,W
University of Central Florida M,W
University of Florida M,W
University of Miami M,W

University of North Florida M,W
University of South Florida M,W
University of Tampa W
University of West Florida M,W
Warner Southern College M,W
Webber International University M,W

Georgia
Abraham Baldwin Agricultural College M,W
Albany State University W
Armstrong Atlantic State University M,W
Augusta State University M,W
Berry College M,W
Brenau University W
Clark Atlanta University W
Clayton State University M,W
Columbus State University M,W
Darton College M,W
Emmanuel College M,W
Fort Valley State University M,W
Georgia College and State University M,W
Georgia Institute of Technology M,W
Georgia Perimeter College M,W
Georgia Southern University M,W
Georgia Southwestern State University M,W
Georgia State University M,W
Gordon College W
Kennesaw State University W
Mercer University M,W
Morehouse College M
North Georgia College & State University M,W
Reinhardt College M,W
Savannah State University W
Shorter College M,W
South Georgia College W
University of Georgia M,W
Young Harris College W

Hawaii
Brigham Young University-Hawaii M,W
Chaminade University of Honolulu M,W
Hawaii Pacific University M,W
University of Hawaii
    Hilo M,W
    Manoa M,W

Idaho
Boise State University M,W
College of Idaho W
Idaho State University M,W
Lewis-Clark State College M,W
University of Idaho M,W

Illinois
Bradley University M,W
Chicago State University M,W
College of Lake County M,W
DePaul University M,W
Eastern Illinois University M,W
Elgin Community College M,W
Illinois State University M,W
Judson University M,W
Lake Land College M,W
Lewis and Clark Community College M,W
Lewis University M,W
McHenry County College M,W
McKendree University M,W
Moraine Valley Community College M,W
Northwestern University M,W
Olivet Nazarene University M,W
Quincy University M,W
Rend Lake College W
Robert Morris College: Chicago W
Sauk Valley Community College M,W
Southern Illinois University Carbondale M,W
Southern Illinois University Edwardsville M,W
University of Illinois
    Chicago M,W
    Springfield M,W
    Urbana-Champaign M,W
University of St. Francis M,W
Waubonsee Community College M,W
Western Illinois University M,W

Indiana
Ball State University M,W
Bethel College M,W
Butler University M,W
Calumet College of St. Joseph M,W
Goshen College M,W
Grace College M,W
Huntington University M,W
Indiana Institute of Technology M,W
Indiana State University M,W
Indiana University
    Bloomington M,W
Indiana University-Purdue University Fort
    Wayne M,W
Indiana University-Purdue University
    Indianapolis M,W
Indiana Wesleyan University M,W
Marian College M,W
Oakland City University M,W
Purdue University M,W
Taylor University M,W
University of Evansville M,W
University of Indianapolis M,W
University of Notre Dame M,W
University of Southern Indiana M,W
Valparaiso University M,W
Vincennes University M

Iowa
Clarke College M,W
Dordt College M,W
Drake University M,W
Graceland University M,W
Iowa State University W
Morningside College M,W
St. Ambrose University M,W
University of Iowa M,W
University of Northern Iowa W

Kansas
Baker University M,W
Barton County Community College M,W
Benedictine College M,W
Bethany College M,W
Bethel College M,W
Central Christian College of Kansas M,W
Cowley County Community College M,W
Emporia State University M,W
Fort Hays State University W
Friends University M,W
Hutchinson Community College M,W
Independence Community College M,W
Johnson County Community College M,W
Kansas State University W
Kansas Wesleyan University M,W
Labette Community College W
Newman University M,W
Seward County Community College M,W
Southwestern College M,W
Tabor College M,W
University of Kansas W
Washburn University M,W
Wichita State University M,W

Kentucky
Asbury College M,W
Bellarmine University M,W
Brescia University W
Campbellsville University M,W
Eastern Kentucky University M,W
Georgetown College M,W
Kentucky Wesleyan College W
Lindsey Wilson College M,W
Midway College W
Morehead State University M,W
Murray State University M,W
Northern Kentucky University M,W
Pikeville College M,W
Union College M,W
University of Kentucky M,W
University of Louisville M,W

University of the Cumberlands M,W
Western Kentucky University M,W

Louisiana
Centenary College of Louisiana M,W
Dillard University M,W
Grambling State University M,W
Louisiana State University and Agricultural and
    Mechanical College M,W
Louisiana Tech University W
McNeese State University W
Nicholls State University M,W
Northwestern State University W
Southeastern Louisiana University M,W
Southern University and Agricultural and
    Mechanical College M,W
University of Louisiana at Lafayette M,W
Xavier University of Louisiana M,W

Maryland
College of Southern Maryland M,W
Coppin State University M,W
Loyola College in Maryland M,W
Morgan State University M,W
Mount St. Mary's University M,W
Towson University M,W
University of Maryland
    Baltimore County M,W
    College Park W
    Eastern Shore M,W

Massachusetts
Boston College M,W
Boston University W
Merrimack College W
Stonehill College M,W
University of Massachusetts
    Amherst W
    Lowell M,W

Michigan
Aquinas College M,W
Eastern Michigan University W
Ferris State University M,W
Glen Oaks Community College W
Grand Rapids Community College M,W
Grand Valley State University M,W
Henry Ford Community College M,W
Lake Superior State University M,W
Michigan State University M,W
Michigan Technological University W
Muskegon Community College W
Northwood University: Michigan M,W
Oakland Community College W
Oakland University W
Saginaw Valley State University W
Spring Arbor University M,W
University of Detroit Mercy W
University of Michigan M,W
Wayne State University M,W
Western Michigan University M,W

Minnesota
Bemidji State University W
Minnesota State University
    Mankato M,W
    Moorhead W
Saint Cloud State University M,W
Southwest Minnesota State University W
University of Minnesota
    Crookston W
    Duluth W
    Twin Cities M,W
Winona State University M,W

Mississippi
Alcorn State University M,W
Belhaven College M,W
Copiah-Lincoln Community College M,W
Delta State University M,W
Hinds Community College M,W
Holmes Community College M,W
Meridian Community College M,W

Mississippi Gulf Coast Community College
    Jefferson Davis Campus M,W
Mississippi State University M,W
Mississippi Valley State University M,W
Northwest Mississippi Community College M,W
Southwest Mississippi Community College
    M,W
Tougaloo College M,W
University of Mississippi M,W
University of Southern Mississippi M,W

Missouri
Drury University M,W
Evangel University M,W
Lincoln University W
Missouri Baptist University W
Missouri Southern State University W
Missouri Valley College M,W
Missouri Western State University W
Northwest Missouri State University M,W
Research College of Nursing M,W
Rockhurst University M,W
Saint Louis University M,W
Southeast Missouri State University W
Southwest Baptist University M,W
Stephens College W
Truman State University M,W
University of Missouri
    Columbia W
    Kansas City M,W
    St. Louis M,W
William Jewell College M,W

Montana
Montana State University
    Billings M,W
    Bozeman M,W
University of Montana: Missoula M,W

Nebraska
Concordia University M,W
Creighton University M,W
Hastings College M,W
Midland Lutheran College M,W
University of Nebraska
    Kearney M,W
    Lincoln M,W

Nevada
University of Nevada
    Las Vegas M,W
    Reno M,W

New Hampshire
Franklin Pierce University M,W
Southern New Hampshire University M,W

New Jersey
Bloomfield College M
Caldwell College M
Fairleigh Dickinson University
    Metropolitan Campus M,W
Georgian Court University M
Monmouth University M,W
New Jersey Institute of Technology M,W
Rider University M,W
Rutgers, The State University of New Jersey
    New Brunswick/Piscataway Campus M,W
Saint Peter's College M,W
Seton Hall University W

New Mexico
Eastern New Mexico University W
New Mexico Military Institute M
New Mexico State University M,W
University of New Mexico M,W
Western New Mexico University M,W

New York
Adelphi University M,W
City University of New York
    Queens College M,W
College of Saint Rose W

Concordia College M,W
Dowling College M,W
Fordham University M,W
Hofstra University M,W
Le Moyne College M,W
Long Island University
    Brooklyn Campus W
    C. W. Post Campus W
Manhattan College M,W
Marist College M,W
Mercy College M
Molloy College W
Niagara University M,W
Pace University M,W
Saint Bonaventure University M,W
St. Francis College M,W
St. John's University M,W
Siena College M,W
State University of New York
    Albany W
    Binghamton M,W
    Buffalo M,W
    Stony Brook M,W
Syracuse University W
Wagner College M,W

North Carolina
Appalachian State University M,W
Barton College M,W
Brevard College M,W
Campbell University M,W
Catawba College M,W
Davidson College M,W
Duke University M,W
East Carolina University M,W
Elon University M,W
Fayetteville State University W
Gardner-Webb University M,W
High Point University M,W
Johnson C. Smith University M,W
Lees-McRae College M,W
Lenoir-Rhyne College M,W
Mars Hill College M,W
Mount Olive College M,W
North Carolina Agricultural and Technical State
    University W
North Carolina Central University M,W
North Carolina State University M,W
Pfeiffer University M,W
Queens University of Charlotte M,W
St. Andrews Presbyterian College W
St. Augustine's College M,W
Shaw University M,W
University of North Carolina
    Asheville M,W
    Chapel Hill M,W
    Charlotte M,W
    Greensboro M,W
    Wilmington M,W
Wake Forest University M,W
Western Carolina University W
Wingate University M,W
Winston-Salem State University M,W

North Dakota
University of Mary M,W
University of North Dakota W

Ohio
Bowling Green State University M,W
Cedarville University M,W
Central State University M,W
Cleveland State University M,W
Malone College M,W
Miami University
    Oxford Campus W
Notre Dame College M
Ohio Dominican University M,W
Ohio State University
    Columbus Campus M,W
Shawnee State University W
Sinclair Community College M,W

University of Akron W
University of Dayton M,W
University of Findlay M,W
University of Toledo M,W
Ursuline College W
Walsh University M,W
Wright State University M,W
Xavier University M,W
Youngstown State University M,W

Oklahoma
Cameron University M,W
East Central University M,W
Northeastern State University W
Oklahoma Baptist University M,W
Oklahoma Christian University M,W
Oklahoma State University M,W
Oklahoma Wesleyan University M,W
Oral Roberts University M,W
Seminole State College M,W
Southeastern Oklahoma State University M,W
Southern Nazarene University M,W
University of Central Oklahoma M,W
University of Oklahoma M,W
University of Tulsa M,W

Oregon
Portland State University W
Southern Oregon University W
University of Oregon M,W
University of Portland M,W

Pennsylvania
Bloomsburg University of Pennsylvania M,W
California University of Pennsylvania W
Carlow University W
Chestnut Hill College M,W
Clarion University of Pennsylvania W
Drexel University M,W
Duquesne University M,W
East Stroudsburg University of Pennsylvania
    M,W
Edinboro University of Pennsylvania M,W
Holy Family University W
Indiana University of Pennsylvania W
Kutztown University of Pennsylvania M,W
La Salle University M,W
Lehigh University M,W
Mercyhurst College M,W
Millersville University of Pennsylvania M,W
Penn State
    University Park M,W
Philadelphia University M,W
Robert Morris University M,W
St. Francis University M,W
Saint Joseph's University M,W
Seton Hill University M,W
Shippensburg University of Pennsylvania W
Slippery Rock University of Pennsylvania W
Temple University M,W
University of Pittsburgh W
University of the Sciences in Philadelphia M,W
West Chester University of Pennsylvania M,W
Westminster College W

Puerto Rico
Inter American University of Puerto Rico
    Aguadilla Campus M,W
    Bayamon Campus M,W
    San German Campus M,W
Turabo University M,W
University of Puerto Rico
    Bayamon University College M,W
    Carolina Regional College M,W
    Cayey University College M,W
    Humacao W
    Mayaguez M,W
    Ponce M,W
    Utuado M,W
University of the Sacred Heart M

Rhode Island
Bryant University M,W
University of Rhode Island M,W

South Carolina
Anderson University M,W
Charleston Southern University M,W
The Citadel M
Claflin University M,W
Clemson University M,W
Coastal Carolina University M,W
Coker College M,W
College of Charleston M,W
Columbia College W
Converse College W
Erskine College M,W
Francis Marion University M,W
Furman University M,W
Lander University M,W
Limestone College M,W
Morris College M,W
Newberry College M,W
North Greenville University M,W
Presbyterian College M,W
South Carolina State University M,W
Spartanburg Methodist College M,W
University of South Carolina M,W
University of South Carolina
    Aiken M
    Upstate M,W
Winthrop University M,W
Wofford College M,W

South Dakota
Dakota State University M,W
Northern State University W
South Dakota State University M,W
University of Sioux Falls M,W

Tennessee
Austin Peay State University M,W
Belmont University M,W
Bethel College M,W
Carson-Newman College M,W
Christian Brothers University M,W
Cumberland University M,W
East Tennessee State University M,W
King College M,W
Lambuth University M,W
Lee University M,W
LeMoyne-Owen College M,W
Lincoln Memorial University M,W
Lipscomb University M,W
Martin Methodist College M,W
Middle Tennessee State University M,W
Milligan College M,W
Tennessee Technological University M,W
Tennessee Wesleyan College M,W
Tusculum College M,W
Union University M,W
University of Memphis M,W
University of Tennessee
    Chattanooga M,W
    Knoxville M,W
    Martin M,W
Vanderbilt University M,W

Texas
Abilene Christian University M,W
Baylor University M,W
Collin County Community College District M,W
Dallas Baptist University W
Lamar University M,W
Laredo Community College M,W
Lee College W
McLennan Community College W
Midwestern State University M,W
North Central Texas College W
Prairie View A&M University M,W
Rice University M,W
St. Edward's University M,W
St. Mary's University M,W

Sam Houston State University M,W
Southern Methodist University M,W
Stephen F. Austin State University W
Tarleton State University W
Temple College M,W
Texas A&M University M,W
Texas A&M University
    Kingsville M,W
Texas Christian University M,W
Texas Southern University M,W
Texas State University: San Marcos W
Texas Tech University M,W
Tyler Junior College M,W
University of Houston W
University of Texas
    Austin M,W
    Pan American M,W
    San Antonio M,W
University of the Incarnate Word M,W
Weatherford College W

Utah
Brigham Young University M,W
Dixie State College of Utah W
Southern Utah University W
University of Utah M,W
Utah State University M,W
Weber State University M,W

Virginia
Bluefield College M,W
College of William and Mary M,W
George Mason University M,W
Hampton University M,W
James Madison University M,W
Liberty University M,W
Longwood University M,W
Norfolk State University M,W
Old Dominion University M,W
Radford University M,W
St. Paul's College M,W
University of Richmond M,W
University of Virginia M,W
University of Virginia's College at Wise M,W
Virginia Commonwealth University M,W
Virginia Military Institute M
Virginia Polytechnic Institute and State
    University M,W
Virginia State University M,W
Virginia Union University M,W

Washington
Gonzaga University M,W
Green River Community College M,W
Spokane Community College M,W
University of Washington M,W
Washington State University W

West Virginia
Bluefield State College M,W
Concord University M,W
Marshall University W
Salem International University M
Shepherd University M,W
University of Charleston M,W
West Liberty State College M,W
West Virginia University W
West Virginia Wesleyan College M,W

Wisconsin
Marquette University M,W
University of Wisconsin
    Green Bay M,W
    Milwaukee W

Wyoming
University of Wyoming W

Track and field

Alabama
Alabama Agricultural and Mechanical
University M,W
Alabama State University M,W
Auburn University M,W
Lawson State Community College M
Miles College M,W
Samford University M,W
Troy University M,W
University of Alabama M,W
University of Alabama
Birmingham W
Huntsville M,W
University of South Alabama M,W

Arizona
Arizona State University M,W
Central Arizona College M,W
Gateway Community College M,W
Glendale Community College M,W
Mesa Community College M,W
Northern Arizona University M,W
Paradise Valley Community College M,W
Pima Community College M,W
Scottsdale Community College M,W
University of Arizona M,W

Arkansas
Arkansas State University M,W
Ecclesia College M,W
Harding University M,W
University of Arkansas M,W
University of Arkansas
Little Rock M,W
Pine Bluff M,W
University of Central Arkansas M,W

California
Azusa Pacific University M,W
Biola University M,W
California Polytechnic State University: San Luis
Obispo M,W
California State Polytechnic University: Pomona
M,W
California State University
Bakersfield M,W
Chico M,W
Dominguez Hills W
Fresno M,W
Fullerton M,W
Long Beach M,W
Los Angeles M,W
Northridge M,W
Sacramento M,W
Stanislaus M,W
Concordia University M,W
Fresno City College M,W
Fresno Pacific University M,W
Humboldt State University M,W
Pepperdine University W
Point Loma Nazarene University M,W
San Diego State University W
Santa Clara University M,W
Santiago Canyon College M,W
Sonoma State University W
Stanford University M,W
University of California
Berkeley M,W
Irvine M,W
Los Angeles M,W
Riverside M,W
Santa Barbara M,W
University of Southern California M,W
Vanguard University of Southern California
M,W
Westmont College M,W
William Jessup University M,W
Yuba Community College District M,W

Colorado
Adams State College M,W
Colorado School of Mines M,W
Colorado State University M,W
Mesa State College W
University of Colorado
Boulder M,W
Colorado Springs M,W
University of Northern Colorado M,W
Western State College of Colorado M,W

Connecticut
Central Connecticut State University M,W
Quinnipiac University M,W
Sacred Heart University M,W
Southern Connecticut State University W
University of Connecticut M,W
University of New Haven M,W

Delaware
Delaware State University M,W
Goldey-Beacom College M,W
University of Delaware W

District of Columbia
American University M,W
Georgetown University M,W
Howard University M,W

Florida
Bethune-Cookman University M,W
Edward Waters College M
Embry-Riddle Aeronautical University M,W
Florida Agricultural and Mechanical University
M,W
Florida Atlantic University W
Florida International University M,W
Florida Memorial University M
Florida State University M,W
Jacksonville University W
University of Central Florida W
University of Florida M,W
University of Miami M,W
University of North Florida M,W
University of South Florida M,W
Warner Southern College M,W
Webber International University M,W

Georgia
Albany State University M,W
Berry College M,W
Clark Atlanta University M,W
Fort Valley State University M,W
Georgia Institute of Technology M,W
Georgia Southern University W
Georgia State University M,W
Kennesaw State University M,W
Morehouse College M
Paine College M,W
Savannah State University M,W
Shorter College M,W
University of Georgia M,W

Hawaii
University of Hawaii
Manoa W

Idaho
Boise State University M,W
College of Idaho M,W
Idaho State University M,W
Lewis-Clark State College W
Northwest Nazarene University M,W
University of Idaho M,W

Illinois
Bradley University W
Chicago State University M,W
Danville Area Community College M,W
DePaul University M,W
Eastern Illinois University M,W
Illinois State University M,W
Lewis University M,W

Loyola University Chicago M,W
McKendree University M,W
Olivet Nazarene University M,W
Rend Lake College M,W
Robert Morris College: Chicago W
Southern Illinois University Carbondale M,W
Southern Illinois University Edwardsville M,W
Trinity Christian College M,W
University of Illinois
Chicago M,W
Urbana-Champaign M,W
University of St. Francis M,W
Western Illinois University M,W

Indiana
Ball State University M,W
Goshen College M,W
Grace College M,W
Huntington University M,W
Indiana Institute of Technology M,W
Indiana State University M,W
Indiana University
Bloomington M,W
Indiana University-Purdue University Fort
Wayne W
Indiana Wesleyan University M,W
Marian College M,W
Purdue University M,W
Saint Joseph's College M,W
Taylor University M,W
University of Indianapolis M,W
University of Notre Dame M,W
University of St. Francis M,W
Valparaiso University M,W
Vincennes University M,W

Iowa
Ashford University M,W
Briar Cliff University M,W
Clarke College M,W
Dordt College M,W
Drake University M,W
Graceland University M,W
Iowa Lakes Community College M,W
Iowa State University M,W
Iowa Wesleyan College M,W
Morningside College M,W
North Iowa Area Community College M,W
Northwestern College M,W
St. Ambrose University M,W
University of Iowa M,W
University of Northern Iowa M,W
William Penn University M,W

Kansas
Allen County Community College M,W
Baker University M,W
Barton County Community College M,W
Benedictine College M,W
Bethany College M,W
Bethel College M,W
Butler County Community College M,W
Cloud County Community College M,W
Coffeyville Community College M,W
Colby Community College M,W
Cowley County Community College M,W
Emporia State University M,W
Fort Hays State University M,W
Friends University M,W
Garden City Community College M,W
Highland Community College M,W
Hutchinson Community College M,W
Independence Community College M,W
Johnson County Community College M,W
Kansas City Kansas Community College M,W
Kansas State University M,W
Kansas Wesleyan University M,W
McPherson College M,W
MidAmerica Nazarene University M,W
Neosho County Community College M,W
Ottawa University M,W
Pittsburg State University M,W

Pratt Community College M,W
Southwestern College M,W
Sterling College M,W
Tabor College M,W
University of Kansas M,W
Wichita State University M,W

Kentucky
Bellarmine University M,W
Campbellsville University M,W
Eastern Kentucky University M,W
Kentucky State University M,W
Lindsey Wilson College M,W
Morehead State University M,W
Murray State University W
Pikeville College M,W
University of Kentucky M,W
University of Louisville M,W
University of the Cumberlands M,W
Western Kentucky University M,W

Louisiana
Grambling State University M,W
Louisiana State University and Agricultural and
Mechanical College M,W
Louisiana Tech University M,W
McNeese State University M,W
Nicholls State University W
Northwestern State University M,W
Southeastern Louisiana University M,W
Southern University and Agricultural and
Mechanical College M,W
University of Louisiana at Lafayette M,W
University of Louisiana at Monroe M,W

Maine
University of Maine M,W

Maryland
Bowie State University M,W
Columbia Union College M,W
Coppin State University M,W
Hagerstown Community College M,W
Morgan State University M,W
Mount St. Mary's University M,W
Towson University M,W
University of Maryland
Baltimore County M,W
College Park M,W
Eastern Shore M,W

Massachusetts
American International College M,W
Boston College M,W
Boston University M,W
Northeastern University M,W
Stonehill College M,W
University of Massachusetts
Amherst M,W
Lowell M,W

Michigan
Aquinas College M,W
Central Michigan University M,W
Cornerstone University M,W
Davenport University M,W
Eastern Michigan University M,W
Ferris State University M,W
Grand Rapids Community College M,W
Grand Valley State University M,W
Hillsdale College M,W
Lake Superior State University M,W
Macomb Community College M,W
Michigan State University M,W
Michigan Technological University W
Northern Michigan University M,W
Northwood University: Michigan M,W
Oakland Community College M,W
Saginaw Valley State University M,W
Siena Heights University M,W
University of Detroit Mercy M,W
University of Michigan M,W
Western Michigan University M,W

Minnesota
Bemidji State University M,W
Concordia University: St. Paul M,W
Minnesota State University
    Mankato M,W
    Moorhead M,W
Saint Cloud State University M,W
University of Minnesota
    Duluth M,W
    Twin Cities M,W
Winona State University W

Mississippi
Alcorn State University M,W
Hinds Community College M
Holmes Community College M
Jackson State University M,W
Mississippi State University M,W
Mississippi Valley State University M,W
University of Mississippi M,W
University of Southern Mississippi M,W

Missouri
Central Methodist University M,W
Evangel University M,W
Hannibal-LaGrange College M,W
Lincoln University M,W
Missouri Baptist University W
Missouri Southern State University M,W
Missouri State University M,W
Missouri Valley College M,W
Northwest Missouri State University M,W
Park University M,W
Saint Louis University M,W
Southeast Missouri State University M,W
Southwest Baptist University M,W
Truman State University M,W
University of Central Missouri M,W
University of Missouri
    Columbia M,W
    Kansas City M,W
    Missouri University of Science and
      Technology M,W
William Jewell College M,W

Montana
Montana State University
    Bozeman M,W
University of Montana: Missoula M,W

Nebraska
Chadron State College M,W
Concordia University M,W
Dana College M,W
Doane College M,W
Hastings College M,W
Midland Lutheran College M,W
University of Nebraska
    Kearney M,W
    Lincoln M,W
Wayne State College M,W

Nevada
University of Nevada
    Las Vegas W
    Reno W

New Hampshire
University of New Hampshire M,W

New Jersey
Essex County College M,W
Fairleigh Dickinson University
    Metropolitan Campus M,W
Felician College M,W
Monmouth University M,W
Rider University M,W
Rutgers, The State University of New Jersey
    New Brunswick/Piscataway Campus M,W
Saint Peter's College M,W
Seton Hall University M,W

New Mexico
College of the Southwest M,W
Eastern New Mexico University M,W
New Mexico Highlands University W
New Mexico Military Institute M
New Mexico State University W
University of New Mexico M,W

New York
Adelphi University M,W
City University of New York
    Queens College M,W
Fordham University M,W
Globe Institute of Technology M,W
Houghton College M,W
Iona College M,W
Long Island University
    Brooklyn Campus M,W
Manhattan College M,W
Marist College M,W
New York Institute of Technology M,W
Pace University M,W
Roberts Wesleyan College M,W
St. Francis College M,W
St. John's University W
St. Thomas Aquinas College M,W
State University of New York
    Albany M,W
    Binghamton M,W
    Buffalo M,W
    Stony Brook M,W
Syracuse University M,W
Wagner College M,W

North Carolina
Appalachian State University M,W
Brevard College M,W
Campbell University M,W
Davidson College M,W
East Carolina University M,W
Elon University W
Fayetteville State University W
Gardner-Webb University M,W
High Point University M,W
Johnson C. Smith University M,W
Lees-McRae College M,W
Lenoir-Rhyne College M,W
Livingstone College M,W
Mars Hill College M,W
Montreat College M,W
North Carolina Agricultural and Technical State
    University M,W
North Carolina Central University M,W
North Carolina State University M,W
Queens University of Charlotte M,W
St. Augustine's College M,W
Shaw University M,W
University of North Carolina
    Asheville M,W
    Chapel Hill M,W
    Charlotte M,W
    Pembroke M
    Wilmington M,W
Wake Forest University M,W
Western Carolina University M,W
Winston-Salem State University M,W

North Dakota
Dickinson State University M,W
Jamestown College M,W
Minot State University M,W
North Dakota State University M,W
University of Mary M,W
University of North Dakota M,W

Ohio
Ashland University M,W
Bowling Green State University M,W
Cedarville University M,W
Central State University M,W
Kent State University M,W
Malone College M,W

Miami University
    Oxford Campus M,W
Notre Dame College M,W
Ohio State University
    Columbus Campus M,W
Ohio University W
University of Akron M,W
University of Dayton W
University of Findlay M,W
University of Rio Grande M,W
University of Toledo W
Ursuline College W
Walsh University M,W
Wright State University W
Xavier University M,W
Youngstown State University M,W

Oklahoma
Langston University M,W
Oklahoma Baptist University M,W
Oklahoma Christian University M,W
Oklahoma State University M,W
Oklahoma Wesleyan University M,W
Oral Roberts University M,W
Southern Nazarene University M,W
University of Central Oklahoma M,W
University of Oklahoma M,W
University of Tulsa M,W

Oregon
Cascade College M,W
Clackamas Community College M,W
Concordia University M,W
Eastern Oregon University M,W
Lane Community College M,W
Mt. Hood Community College M,W
Oregon Institute of Technology M,W
Portland State University M,W
Southern Oregon University M,W
Southwestern Oregon Community College M,W
University of Oregon M,W
University of Portland M,W
Warner Pacific College M,W

Pennsylvania
Bloomsburg University of Pennsylvania M,W
California University of Pennsylvania M,W
Cheyney University of Pennsylvania M,W
Clarion University of Pennsylvania M,W
Duquesne University M,W
East Stroudsburg University of Pennsylvania
    M,W
Edinboro University of Pennsylvania M,W
Holy Family University M,W
Indiana University of Pennsylvania M,W
Kutztown University of Pennsylvania M,W
La Salle University M,W
Lehigh University M,W
Lock Haven University of Pennsylvania M,W
Millersville University of Pennsylvania M,W
Penn State
    University Park M,W
Robert Morris University M,W
St. Francis University M,W
Saint Joseph's University M,W
Seton Hill University M,W
Shippensburg University of Pennsylvania M,W
Slippery Rock University of Pennsylvania M,W
Temple University M,W
University of Pittsburgh M,W
Villanova University M,W
West Chester University of Pennsylvania M,W

Puerto Rico
Bayamon Central University M,W
Inter American University of Puerto Rico
    Aguadilla Campus M,W
    Bayamon Campus M,W
    Fajardo Campus M,W
    Guayama Campus M,W
    Metropolitan Campus M,W
    Ponce Campus M,W
    San German Campus M,W

Turabo University M,W
Universidad del Este M,W
Universidad Metropolitana M,W
University of Puerto Rico
    Bayamon University College M,W
    Carolina Regional College M,W
    Cayey University College M,W
    Humacao M,W
    Mayaguez M,W
    Ponce M,W
    Utuado M,W
University of the Sacred Heart M,W

Rhode Island
Bryant University M,W
Providence College M,W
University of Rhode Island M,W

South Carolina
Anderson University M,W
Charleston Southern University M,W
The Citadel M,W
Claflin University M,W
Clemson University M,W
Coastal Carolina University M,W
Furman University M,W
Limestone College M,W
Morris College M,W
South Carolina State University M,W
University of South Carolina M,W
Voorhees College M,W
Winthrop University M,W
Wofford College M,W

South Dakota
Augustana College M,W
Black Hills State University M,W
Dakota State University M,W
Dakota Wesleyan University M,W
Mount Marty College M,W
Northern State University M,W
South Dakota School of Mines and Technology
    M,W
South Dakota State University M,W
University of Sioux Falls M,W
University of South Dakota M,W

Tennessee
Austin Peay State University W
Belmont University M,W
Bethel College M,W
Crichton College M,W
East Tennessee State University M,W
King College M,W
Lipscomb University M,W
Martin Methodist College M,W
Middle Tennessee State University M,W
Milligan College M,W
Tennessee Technological University W
University of Memphis M,W
University of Tennessee
    Chattanooga M,W
    Knoxville M,W
Vanderbilt University W

Texas
Abilene Christian University M,W
Angelo State University M,W
Baylor University M,W
Dallas Baptist University W
Lamar University M,W
Northwood University: Texas M,W
Prairie View A&M University M,W
Rice University M,W
Sam Houston State University M,W
South Plains College M,W
Stephen F. Austin State University M,W
Tarleton State University M,W
Texas A&M University M,W
Texas A&M University
    Commerce M,W
Texas Christian University M,W
Texas Southern University M,W

Texas State University: San Marcos M,W
Texas Tech University M,W
University of Houston M,W
University of North Texas M,W
University of Texas
    Austin M,W
    Pan American M,W
    San Antonio M,W
University of the Incarnate Word M,W
Wayland Baptist University M,W
Wiley College M,W

Utah
Brigham Young University M,W
Southern Utah University M,W
University of Utah W
Utah State University M,W
Utah Valley State College M,W
Weber State University M,W

Vermont
University of Vermont M,W

Virginia
College of William and Mary M,W
George Mason University M,W
Hampton University M,W
James Madison University W
Liberty University M,W
Norfolk State University M,W
Radford University M,W
St. Paul's College M,W
University of Richmond W
University of Virginia M,W
Virginia Commonwealth University M,W
Virginia Military Institute M,W
Virginia Polytechnic Institute and State
    University M,W
Virginia State University M,W
Virginia Union University M,W

Washington
Central Washington University M,W
Clark College M,W
Evergreen State College M,W
Highline Community College M,W
Northwest University M,W
Saint Martin's University M,W
Seattle Pacific University M,W
Seattle University M,W
Spokane Community College M,W
University of Washington M,W
Washington State University M,W
Western Washington University M,W

West Virginia
Alderson-Broaddus College M,W
Glenville State College M,W
Marshall University M,W
University of Charleston W
West Liberty State College M,W
West Virginia University W
West Virginia Wesleyan College M,W
Wheeling Jesuit University M,W

Wisconsin
Marquette University M,W
Milwaukee Area Technical College M,W
University of Wisconsin
    Milwaukee M,W
    Parkside M,W

Wyoming
University of Wyoming M,W

Volleyball

Alabama
Alabama Agricultural and Mechanical
    University W
Alabama State University W

Auburn University W
Bevill State Community College W
Central Alabama Community College W
Faulkner State Community College M,W
Gadsden State Community College W
Jacksonville State University W
Jefferson Davis Community College W
Judson College W
Lawson State Community College W
Miles College W
Northwest-Shoals Community College W
Samford University W
Southern Union State Community College W
Spring Hill College W
Troy University W
Tuskegee University W
University of Alabama W
University of Alabama
    Birmingham W
    Huntsville W
University of Montevallo W
University of North Alabama W
University of South Alabama W
University of West Alabama W

Alaska
University of Alaska
    Anchorage W
    Fairbanks W

Arizona
Arizona State University W
Arizona Western College W
Chandler-Gilbert Community College
    Pecos W
Eastern Arizona College W
Embry-Riddle Aeronautical University: Prescott
    Campus W
Glendale Community College W
Grand Canyon University W
Northern Arizona University W
Pima Community College W
Scottsdale Community College W
University of Arizona W
Yavapai College W

Arkansas
Arkansas State University W
Arkansas Tech University W
Harding University W
Henderson State University W
John Brown University W
Lyon College W
Ouachita Baptist University W
Southern Arkansas University W
University of Arkansas W
University of Arkansas
    Fort Smith W
    Little Rock W
    Pine Bluff W
University of Central Arkansas W
Williams Baptist College W

California
Azusa Pacific University W
Bethany University W
Biola University W
California Baptist University M,W
California Polytechnic State University: San Luis
    Obispo W
California State Polytechnic University: Pomona
    W
California State University
    Bakersfield W
    Chico W
    Dominguez Hills W
    Fresno W
    Fullerton W
    Long Beach M,W
    Los Angeles W
    Northridge M,W
    Sacramento W
    San Bernardino W

Stanislaus W
Concordia University W
Dominican University of California W
Fresno City College W
Fresno Pacific University W
Grossmont College M,W
Holy Names University M,W
Hope International University M,W
Humboldt State University W
Loyola Marymount University W
The Master's College W
Notre Dame de Namur University W
Pepperdine University M,W
Point Loma Nazarene University W
St. Mary's College of California W
San Diego Christian College W
San Diego State University W
San Jose State University W
Santa Clara University W
Sonoma State University W
Stanford University M,W
University of California
    Berkeley W
    Davis M,W
    Irvine M,W
    Los Angeles M,W
    Riverside W
    Santa Barbara M,W
University of San Diego W
University of San Francisco W
University of Southern California M,W
University of the Pacific M,W
Vanguard University of Southern California W
Westmont College W
William Jessup University W
Yuba Community College District W

Colorado
Adams State College W
Colorado Christian University W
Colorado Northwestern Community College W
Colorado School of Mines W
Colorado State University W
Colorado State University
    Pueblo W
Fort Lewis College W
Lamar Community College W
Mesa State College W
Metropolitan State College of Denver W
Northeastern Junior College W
Otero Junior College W
Regis University W
Trinidad State Junior College W
University of Colorado
    Boulder W
    Colorado Springs W
University of Denver W
University of Northern Colorado W
Western State College of Colorado W

Connecticut
Central Connecticut State University W
Fairfield University W
Post University W
Quinnipiac University W
Sacred Heart University M,W
Southern Connecticut State University W
University of Bridgeport W
University of Connecticut W
University of Hartford W
University of New Haven W

Delaware
Delaware State University W
University of Delaware W
Wilmington University W

District of Columbia
American University W
George Washington University W
Georgetown University W
Howard University W

Florida
Barry University M,W
Bethune-Cookman University W
Brevard Community College W
Broward Community College W
Eckerd College M,W
Embry-Riddle Aeronautical University W
Flagler College W
Florida Agricultural and Mechanical University
    W
Florida Atlantic University W
Florida College W
Florida Community College at Jacksonville W
Florida Gulf Coast University W
Florida Institute of Technology W
Florida International University W
Florida Memorial University W
Florida Southern College W
Florida State University W
Hillsborough Community College W
Indian River Community College W
Jacksonville University W
Lake-Sumter Community College W
Lynn University W
Manatee Community College W
Miami Dade College W
Northwood University
    Florida W
Nova Southeastern University W
Palm Beach Community College W
Pasco-Hernando Community College W
Pensacola Junior College W
Polk Community College W
Rollins College W
St. Leo University W
St. Petersburg College W
Saint Thomas University W
South Florida Community College W
Stetson University W
University of Central Florida W
University of Florida W
University of Miami W
University of North Florida W
University of South Florida W
University of Tampa W
University of West Florida W
Warner Southern College M,W
Webber International University W

Georgia
Abraham Baldwin Agricultural College W
Albany State University W
Armstrong Atlantic State University W
Augusta State University W
Berry College W
Brenau University W
Brewton-Parker College W
Clark Atlanta University W
Covenant College W
Fort Valley State University W
Georgia Institute of Technology W
Georgia Southern University W
Georgia State University M,W
Mercer University W
Paine College W
Savannah State University W
University of Georgia W
University of West Georgia W

Hawaii
Brigham Young University-Hawaii W
Chaminade University of Honolulu W
Hawaii Pacific University W
University of Hawaii
    Hilo W
    Manoa M,W

Idaho
Boise State University W
College of Idaho W
College of Southern Idaho W
Idaho State University W

Lewis-Clark State College W
North Idaho College W
Northwest Nazarene University W
University of Idaho W

Illinois
Black Hawk College W
Bradley University W
Carl Sandburg College W
Chicago State University W
College of Lake County W
Danville Area Community College W
DePaul University W
Eastern Illinois University W
Elgin Community College W
Highland Community College W
Illinois Central College W
Illinois Institute of Technology W
Illinois State University W
John A. Logan College W
Judson University W
Kankakee Community College W
Kaskaskia College W
Kishwaukee College W
Lake Land College W
Lewis and Clark Community College W
Lewis University M,W
Lincoln College W
Loyola University Chicago M,W
McHenry County College W
McKendree University W
Moraine Valley Community College W
Morton College W
Northwestern University W
Olivet Nazarene University W
Parkland College W
Quincy University M,W
Rend Lake College W
Robert Morris College: Chicago W
St. Xavier University W
Sauk Valley Community College W
Shawnee Community College W
South Suburban College of Cook County W
Southern Illinois University Carbondale W
Southern Illinois University Edwardsville W
Springfield College in Illinois W
Trinity Christian College W
Trinity International University W
University of Illinois
    Chicago W
    Springfield W
    Urbana-Champaign W
University of St. Francis W
Waubonsee Community College W
Western Illinois University W

Indiana
Ancilla College W
Ball State University M,W
Bethel College W
Butler University W
Calumet College of St. Joseph M,W
Goshen College W
Grace College W
Huntington University W
Indiana Institute of Technology W
Indiana State University W
Indiana University
    Bloomington W
    Southeast W
Indiana University-Purdue University Fort
    Wayne M,W
Indiana University-Purdue University
    Indianapolis W
Indiana Wesleyan University W
Marian College W
Oakland City University W
Purdue University W
Saint Joseph's College W
Taylor University W
Taylor University Fort Wayne W
University of Evansville W

University of Indianapolis W
University of Notre Dame W
University of St. Francis W
University of Southern Indiana W
Valparaiso University W
Vincennes University W

Iowa
Ashford University W
Briar Cliff University W
Clarke College M,W
Clinton Community College W
Des Moines Area Community College W
Dordt College W
Drake University W
Ellsworth Community College W
Graceland University M,W
Grand View College W
Indian Hills Community College W
Iowa Central Community College W
Iowa Lakes Community College W
Iowa State University W
Iowa Wesleyan College W
Iowa Western Community College W
Kirkwood Community College W
Morningside College W
North Iowa Area Community College W
Northwestern College W
St. Ambrose University M,W
Southeastern Community College
    North Campus W
Southwestern Community College W
University of Iowa W
University of Northern Iowa W
Waldorf College W
William Penn University W

Kansas
Allen County Community College W
Baker University W
Barton County Community College W
Benedictine College W
Bethany College W
Bethel College W
Butler County Community College W
Central Christian College of Kansas W
Cloud County Community College W
Coffeyville Community College W
Colby Community College W
Cowley County Community College W
Dodge City Community College W
Emporia State University W
Fort Hays State University W
Fort Scott Community College W
Friends University W
Garden City Community College W
Hesston College W
Highland Community College W
Hutchinson Community College W
Independence Community College W
Johnson County Community College W
Kansas City Kansas Community College W
Kansas State University W
Kansas Wesleyan University W
Labette Community College W
McPherson College W
MidAmerica Nazarene University W
Neosho County Community College W
Newman University W
Ottawa University W
Pittsburg State University W
Pratt Community College W
Seward County Community College W
Southwestern College W
Sterling College W
Tabor College W
University of Kansas W
University of St. Mary W
Washburn University W
Wichita State University W

Kentucky
Asbury College W
Bellarmine University W
Brescia University W
Campbellsville University W
Eastern Kentucky University W
Georgetown College W
Kentucky State University W
Kentucky Wesleyan College W
Lindsey Wilson College W
Midway College W
Morehead State University W
Murray State University W
Northern Kentucky University W
Pikeville College W
Union College W
University of Kentucky W
University of Louisville W
University of the Cumberlands W
Western Kentucky University W

Louisiana
Centenary College of Louisiana W
Dillard University W
Louisiana State University and Agricultural and
    Mechanical College W
Louisiana Tech University W
McNeese State University W
Nicholls State University W
Northwestern State University W
Southeastern Louisiana University W
Southern University and Agricultural and
    Mechanical College W
University of Louisiana at Lafayette W
University of Louisiana at Monroe W
University of New Orleans W
Xavier University of Louisiana W

Maine
University of Maine W

Maryland
Bowie State University W
College of Southern Maryland W
Community College of Baltimore County W
Coppin State University W
Garrett College W
Hagerstown Community College W
Harford Community College W
Loyola College in Maryland W
Morgan State University W
Prince George's Community College W
Towson University W
University of Maryland
    Baltimore County W
    College Park W
    Eastern Shore W

Massachusetts
American International College W
Boston College W
Dean College W
Elms College M,W
Merrimack College W
Mount Ida College M
Northeastern University W
Stonehill College W
University of Massachusetts
    Lowell W

Michigan
Alpena Community College W
Aquinas College W
Central Michigan University W
Concordia University W
Cornerstone University W
Davenport University M,W
Delta College W
Eastern Michigan University W
Ferris State University W
Glen Oaks Community College W
Grand Rapids Community College W

Grand Valley State University W
Hillsdale College W
Kalamazoo Valley Community College W
Kellogg Community College W
Lake Michigan College W
Lake Superior State University W
Lansing Community College W
Macomb Community College W
Madonna University W
Michigan State University W
Michigan Technological University W
Mott Community College W
Muskegon Community College W
Northern Michigan University W
Northwood University: Michigan W
Oakland Community College W
Oakland University W
Rochester College W
Saginaw Valley State University W
Siena Heights University W
Spring Arbor University W
University of Michigan W
University of Michigan
    Dearborn W
Wayne State University M,W
Western Michigan University W

Minnesota
Bemidji State University W
Concordia University: St. Paul W
Minnesota State University
    Mankato W
    Moorhead W
Saint Cloud State University W
Southwest Minnesota State University W
University of Minnesota
    Crookston W
    Duluth W
    Twin Cities W
Winona State University W

Mississippi
Alcorn State University W
Belhaven College W
Jackson State University W
Mississippi State University W
Mississippi Valley State University W
University of Mississippi W
University of Southern Mississippi W

Missouri
Avila University W
Central Methodist University W
College of the Ozarks W
Columbia College W
Cottey College W
Culver-Stockton College W
Drury University W
East Central College W
Evangel University W
Hannibal-LaGrange College W
Harris-Stowe State University W
Jefferson College W
Metropolitan Community College: Longview W
Missouri Baptist University M,W
Missouri Southern State University W
Missouri State University W
Missouri Valley College M,W
Missouri Western State University W
Northwest Missouri State University W
Park University M,W
Research College of Nursing W
Rockhurst University W
Saint Louis University W
Southeast Missouri State University W
Southwest Baptist University W
State Fair Community College W
Stephens College W
Three Rivers Community College W
Truman State University W
University of Central Missouri W
University of Missouri

Columbia W
Kansas City W
St. Louis W
William Jewell College W
William Woods University M,W

Montana
Carroll College W
Miles Community College W
Montana State University
  Billings W
  Bozeman W
  Northern W
Montana Tech of the University of Montana W
Rocky Mountain College W
University of Great Falls W
University of Montana: Missoula W
University of Montana: Western W

Nebraska
Bellevue University W
Central Community College W
Chadron State College W
College of Saint Mary W
Concordia University W
Creighton University W
Dana College W
Doane College W
Hastings College W
Mid-Plains Community College Area W
Midland Lutheran College W
Nebraska College of Technical Agriculture M,W
Peru State College W
University of Nebraska
  Kearney W
  Lincoln W
  Omaha W
Wayne State College W
Western Nebraska Community College W
York College W

Nevada
University of Nevada
  Las Vegas W
  Reno W

New Hampshire
Franklin Pierce University W
Hesser College M,W
University of New Hampshire W

New Jersey
Bloomfield College W
Fairleigh Dickinson University
  Metropolitan Campus W
Georgian Court University W
New Jersey Institute of Technology M,W
Rider University W
Rutgers, The State University of New Jersey
  New Brunswick/Piscataway Campus W
  Newark Regional Campus M
Saint Peter's College W
Seton Hall University W

New Mexico
College of the Southwest W
Eastern New Mexico University W
New Mexico Highlands University W
New Mexico State University W
University of New Mexico W
Western New Mexico University W

New York
Adelphi University W
Canisius College W
City University of New York
  Queens College W
Colgate University W
College of Saint Rose W
Concordia College M,W
Daemen College W
Dominican College of Blauvelt W
Dowling College W

Fordham University W
Genesee Community College W
Globe Institute of Technology W
Hofstra University W
Houghton College W
Iona College W
Le Moyne College W
Long Island University
  Brooklyn Campus W
  C. W. Post Campus W
Manhattan College W
Marist College W
Mercy College W
Molloy College W
New York Institute of Technology W
Niagara University W
Nyack College W
Pace University W
Roberts Wesleyan College M,W
Saint Bonaventure University W
St. Francis College W
St. John's University W
Siena College W
State University of New York
  Albany W
  Binghamton W
  Buffalo W
  Stony Brook W
Syracuse University W
Wagner College W

North Carolina
Appalachian State University W
Barton College W
Brevard College W
Campbell University W
Catawba College W
Davidson College W
Duke University W
East Carolina University M,W
Elizabeth City State University W
Elon University W
Fayetteville State University W
Gardner-Webb University W
High Point University W
Johnson C. Smith University W
Lees-McRae College M,W
Lenoir Community College W
Lenoir-Rhyne College W
Livingstone College W
Louisburg College W
Mars Hill College W
Montreat College W
Mount Olive College W
North Carolina Agricultural and Technical State
  University W
North Carolina Central University W
North Carolina State University W
Pfeiffer University W
Pitt Community College W
Queens University of Charlotte W
St. Andrews Presbyterian College W
St. Augustine's College W
Shaw University W
Southeastern Community College W
University of North Carolina
  Asheville W
  Chapel Hill W
  Charlotte W
  Greensboro W
  Pembroke W
  Wilmington W
Wake Forest University W
Western Carolina University W
Wingate University W
Winston-Salem State University W

North Dakota
Bismarck State College W
Dickinson State University W
Jamestown College W
Mayville State University W

Minot State University W
Minot State University: Bottineau Campus W
North Dakota State College of Science W
North Dakota State University W
University of Mary W
University of North Dakota W
Valley City State University W
Williston State College W

Ohio
Ashland University W
Bowling Green State University W
Cedarville University W
Central State University W
Clark State Community College W
Cleveland State University W
Kent State University W
Lakeland Community College W
Malone College W
Miami University
  Oxford Campus W
Mount Vernon Nazarene University W
Notre Dame College W
Ohio Dominican University W
Ohio State University
  Columbus Campus M,W
Ohio University W
Shawnee State University W
Sinclair Community College W
Southern State Community College W
University of Akron W
University of Dayton W
University of Findlay W
University of Rio Grande W
University of Toledo W
Urbana University W
Ursuline College W
Walsh University W
Wright State University W
Xavier University W
Youngstown State University W

Oklahoma
Cameron University W
East Central University W
Langston University W
Northeastern Oklahoma Agricultural and
  Mechanical College W
Oklahoma Panhandle State University W
Oklahoma Wesleyan University W
Oral Roberts University W
Redlands Community College W
St. Gregory's University W
Seminole State College M,W
Southeastern Oklahoma State University W
Southern Nazarene University W
University of Central Oklahoma W
University of Oklahoma W
University of Tulsa W

Oregon
Blue Mountain Community College W
Cascade College W
Chemeketa Community College W
Clackamas Community College W
Concordia University W
Corban College W
Eastern Oregon University W
Lane Community College W
Linn-Benton Community College W
Mt. Hood Community College W
Northwest Christian College W
Oregon Institute of Technology W
Oregon State University W
Portland State University W
Southern Oregon University W
Southwestern Oregon Community College W
Treasure Valley Community College W
University of Oregon W
University of Portland W
Warner Pacific College W

Pennsylvania
California University of Pennsylvania W
Carlow University W
Chestnut Hill College W
Cheyney University of Pennsylvania W
Community College of Beaver County W
Duquesne University W
East Stroudsburg University of Pennsylvania W
Edinboro University of Pennsylvania W
Gannon University W
Harcum College W
Holy Family University W
Indiana University of Pennsylvania W
Kutztown University of Pennsylvania W
La Salle University W
Lackawanna College W
Lehigh University W
Lock Haven University of Pennsylvania W
Mercyhurst College M,W
Millersville University of Pennsylvania W
Penn State
  University Park M,W
Philadelphia University W
Point Park University W
Robert Morris University W
St. Francis University M,W
Seton Hill University W
Shippensburg University of Pennsylvania W
Slippery Rock University of Pennsylvania W
Temple University W
University of Pittsburgh W
University of Pittsburgh
  Titusville W
University of the Sciences in Philadelphia W
Villanova University W
West Chester University of Pennsylvania W
Westminster College W

Puerto Rico
Bayamon Central University M,W
Inter American University of Puerto Rico
  Aguadilla Campus M,W
  Bayamon Campus M,W
  Metropolitan Campus M,W
  Ponce Campus M,W
  San German Campus M,W
Turabo University M,W
Universidad del Este M,W
Universidad Metropolitana M,W
University of Puerto Rico
  Bayamon University College M,W
  Carolina Regional College M,W
  Cayey University College M,W
  Humacao M,W
  Mayaguez M,W
  Ponce M,W
  Utuado M,W
University of the Sacred Heart M,W

Rhode Island
Bryant University W
Community College of Rhode Island W
University of Rhode Island W

South Carolina
Anderson University W
Charleston Southern University W
The Citadel W
Claflin University W
Clemson University W
Coastal Carolina University W
Coker College W
College of Charleston W
Columbia College W
Converse College W
Francis Marion University W
Furman University W
Lander University W
Limestone College W
Morris College W
Newberry College W
North Greenville University W

Presbyterian College W
South Carolina State University W
Southern Wesleyan University W
Spartanburg Methodist College W
University of South Carolina W
University of South Carolina
    Aiken W
    Upstate W
Voorhees College W
Winthrop University W
Wofford College W

South Dakota
Augustana College W
Black Hills State University W
Dakota State University W
Dakota Wesleyan University W
Mount Marty College W
National American University
    Rapid City W
South Dakota School of Mines and Technology
    W
South Dakota State University W
University of Sioux Falls W

Tennessee
Austin Peay State University W
Belmont University W
Bethel College W
Bryan College W
Carson-Newman College W
Christian Brothers University W
Crichton College W
Cumberland University W
East Tennessee State University W
Freed-Hardeman University W
Hiwassee College W
King College W
Lambuth University W
Lane College W
Lee University W
LeMoyne-Owen College W
Lincoln Memorial University W
Lipscomb University W
Martin Methodist College W
Middle Tennessee State University W
Milligan College W
Tennessee Technological University W
Tennessee Temple University W
Tennessee Wesleyan College W
Trevecca Nazarene University W
Tusculum College W
Union University W
University of Memphis W
University of Tennessee
    Chattanooga W
    Knoxville W
    Martin W

Texas
Abilene Christian University W
Alvin Community College W
Angelo State University W
Baylor University W
Blinn College W
Clarendon College W
Dallas Baptist University W
Frank Phillips College W
Galveston College W
Hill College W
Houston Baptist University W
Jarvis Christian College W
Lamar University W
Laredo Community College W
Lee College W
Lubbock Christian University W
Midwestern State University W
North Central Texas College W
Panola College W
Paris Junior College W
Prairie View A&M University W
Ranger College W

Rice University W
St. Edward's University W
St. Mary's University W
Sam Houston State University W
Southern Methodist University W
Southwestern Assemblies of God University W
Stephen F. Austin State University W
Tarleton State University W
Temple College W
Texas A&M University W
Texas A&M University
    Commerce W
    Kingsville W
Texas Christian University W
Texas Southern University W
Texas Southmost College W
Texas State University: San Marcos W
Texas Tech University W
Texas Woman's University W
Tyler Junior College W
University of Houston W
University of North Texas W
University of St. Thomas W
University of Texas
    Arlington W
    Austin W
    Pan American W
    San Antonio W
University of the Incarnate Word W
Vernon College W
Wayland Baptist University W
West Texas A&M University W
Western Texas College W
Wharton County Junior College W
Wiley College W

Utah
Brigham Young University M,W
College of Eastern Utah W
Dixie State College of Utah W
Salt Lake Community College W
Snow College W
University of Utah W
Utah State University W
Utah Valley State College W
Weber State University W
Westminster College W

Virginia
Bluefield College W
College of William and Mary W
George Mason University M,W
Hampton University W
James Madison University W
Liberty University W
Norfolk State University W
Radford University W
St. Paul's College W
University of Virginia W
University of Virginia's College at Wise W
Virginia Commonwealth University W
Virginia Intermont College W
Virginia Polytechnic Institute and State
    University W
Virginia State University W
Virginia Union University W

Washington
Big Bend Community College W
Central Washington University W
Centralia College W
Clark College W
Columbia Basin College W
Edmonds Community College W
Everett Community College W
Evergreen State College W
Gonzaga University W
Grays Harbor College W
Green River Community College W
Highline Community College W
Lower Columbia College W
Northwest University W

Olympic College W
Saint Martin's University W
Seattle Pacific University W
Seattle University W
Spokane Community College W
Tacoma Community College W
University of Washington W
Walla Walla Community College W
Washington State University W
Western Washington University W
Whatcom Community College W
Yakima Valley Community College W

West Virginia
Alderson-Broaddus College W
Bluefield State College W
Concord University W
Davis and Elkins College W
Glenville State College W
Marshall University W
Mountain State University W
Ohio Valley University W
Salem International University W
Shepherd University W
University of Charleston W
West Liberty State College W
West Virginia University W
West Virginia Wesleyan College W
Wheeling Jesuit University W

Wisconsin
Cardinal Stritch University M,W
Marquette University W
Milwaukee Area Technical College W
University of Wisconsin
    Green Bay W
    Milwaukee M,W
    Parkside W
Viterbo University W

Wyoming
Casper College W
Central Wyoming College W
Eastern Wyoming College W
Laramie County Community College W
Northwest College W
Sheridan College W
University of Wyoming W
Western Wyoming Community College W

Water polo

Arizona
Arizona State University W

California
California Baptist University M,W
California State University
    Bakersfield W
    Long Beach M,W
Concordia University M
Fresno Pacific University M,W
Grossmont College M,W
Loyola Marymount University M,W
Pepperdine University M
San Diego State University W
San Jose State University W
Santa Clara University M,W
Sonoma State University W
Stanford University M,W
University of California
    Berkeley M,W
    Davis M,W
    Irvine M,W
    Los Angeles M,W
University of Southern California M,W
University of the Pacific M,W

District of Columbia
George Washington University M

Florida
Broward Community College W
Florida Atlantic University W

Hawaii
Chaminade University of Honolulu M
University of Hawaii
    Manōa W

Indiana
Indiana University
    Bloomington W

Michigan
University of Michigan W

New York
City University of New York
    Queens College M,W
Fordham University M
Hartwick College W
Iona College W
Marist College W
St. Francis College M,W
Siena College W
Wagner College W

Pennsylvania
Gannon University M,W
Mercyhurst College M,W
Slippery Rock University of Pennsylvania M,W

Puerto Rico
University of Puerto Rico
    Mayaguez M

Weight lifting

Puerto Rico
Inter American University of Puerto Rico
    Aguadilla Campus M,W
    Ponce Campus M,W
    San German Campus M,W
Turabo University M,W
Universidad del Este M,W
Universidad Metropolitana M
University of Puerto Rico
    Carolina Regional College M,W
    Cayey University College M,W
    Humacao M,W
    Utuado M,W

Washington
Olympic College M,W

Wrestling

Arizona
Arizona State University M
Embry-Riddle Aeronautical University: Prescott
    Campus M
Grand Canyon University M

California
California Polytechnic State University: San Luis
    Obispo M
California State University
    Bakersfield M
    Fresno M
    Fullerton M
Fresno City College M
Stanford University M
University of California
    Davis M

Colorado
Adams State College M
Colorado School of Mines M
Mesa State College M
University of Northern Colorado M

Western State College of Colorado M

Connecticut
Sacred Heart University M

Delaware
Delaware State University M

District of Columbia
American University M
Howard University M

Idaho
Boise State University M
North Idaho College M

Illinois
City Colleges of Chicago
        Wright College M,W
Lincoln College M
McKendree University M
Northwestern University M
Rend Lake College M
Southern Illinois University Edwardsville M
University of Illinois
        Urbana-Champaign M

Indiana
Indiana University
        Bloomington M
Purdue University M
University of Indianapolis M

Iowa
Briar Cliff University M
Ellsworth Community College M
Iowa Central Community College M
Iowa State University M
North Iowa Area Community College M
Northwestern College M
University of Iowa M
University of Northern Iowa M
Waldorf College M
William Penn University M

Kansas
Colby Community College M
Fort Hays State University M
Labette Community College M
Neosho County Community College M
Newman University M
Pratt Community College M

Kentucky
Campbellsville University M
University of the Cumberlands M,W

Maryland
University of Maryland
        College Park M

Massachusetts
American International College M
Boston University M

Michigan
Central Michigan University M
Eastern Michigan University M
Grand Rapids Community College M
Michigan State University M
Muskegon Community College M
University of Michigan M

Minnesota
Minnesota State University
        Mankato M
        Moorhead M
Saint Cloud State University M
Southwest Minnesota State University M
University of Minnesota
        Twin Cities M

Missouri
Hannibal-LaGrange College M
Missouri Baptist University M
Missouri Valley College M,W
St. Louis Community College
        Meramec M
Truman State University M
University of Central Missouri M
University of Missouri
        Columbia M

Montana
Montana State University
        Northern M
University of Great Falls M

Nebraska
Chadron State College M
Dana College M
Hastings College M
University of Nebraska
        Kearney M
        Lincoln M
        Omaha M
York College M

New Jersey
Rider University M
Rutgers, The State University of New Jersey
        New Brunswick/Piscataway Campus M

New York
Hofstra University M
Niagara County Community College M
State University of New York
        Binghamton M
        Buffalo M
Wagner College M

North Carolina
Appalachian State University M
Campbell University M
Davidson College M
Duke University M
Gardner-Webb University M
North Carolina Agricultural and Technical State
        University M
North Carolina State University M
University of North Carolina
        Chapel Hill M
        Greensboro M
        Pembroke M

North Dakota
Dickinson State University M
Jamestown College M
North Dakota State University M
University of Mary M

Ohio
Ashland University M
Cleveland State University M
Kent State University M
Notre Dame College M
Ohio State University
        Columbus Campus M
Ohio University M
University of Findlay M

Oklahoma
Oklahoma State University M
University of Central Oklahoma M
University of Oklahoma M

Oregon
Clackamas Community College M
Oregon State University M
Portland State University M
Southern Oregon University M
Southwestern Oregon Community College M
University of Oregon M

Pennsylvania
Bloomsburg University of Pennsylvania M
Clarion University of Pennsylvania M
Drexel University M
Duquesne University M
East Stroudsburg University of Pennsylvania M
Edinboro University of Pennsylvania M
Gannon University M
Kutztown University of Pennsylvania M
Lehigh University M
Lock Haven University of Pennsylvania M
Mercyhurst College M
Millersville University of Pennsylvania M
Penn State
        University Park M
Seton Hill University M
Shippensburg University of Pennsylvania M
Slippery Rock University of Pennsylvania M
University of Pittsburgh M
University of Pittsburgh
        Johnstown M

Puerto Rico
Inter American University of Puerto Rico
        Bayamon Campus M
University of Puerto Rico
        Bayamon University College M
        Cayey University College M
        Humacao M
        Mayaguez M
University of the Sacred Heart M

Rhode Island
Bryant University M

South Carolina
Anderson University M
The Citadel M
Limestone College M
Newberry College M
Spartanburg Methodist College M

South Dakota
Augustana College M
Dakota Wesleyan University M
Northern State University M
South Dakota State University M

Tennessee
Carson-Newman College M
Cumberland University M
King College M
University of Tennessee
        Chattanooga M

Utah
Utah Valley State College M

Virginia
Old Dominion University M
University of Virginia M
Virginia Military Institute M
Virginia Polytechnic Institute and State
        University M

Washington
Highline Community College M
Yakima Valley Community College M

West Virginia
West Liberty State College M
West Virginia University M

Wisconsin
University of Wisconsin
        Parkside M

Wyoming
Northwest College M
University of Wyoming M
Western Wyoming Community College M

Music/drama scholarships

Alabama
Alabama State University
Auburn University at Montgomery
Bevill State Community College
Birmingham-Southern College
Chattahoochee Valley Community College
Faulkner University
Gadsden State Community College
Huntingdon College
Jacksonville State University
Jefferson State Community College
Judson College
Lurleen B. Wallace Community College
Marion Military Institute
Northeast Alabama Community College
Northwest-Shoals Community College
Samford University
Snead State Community College
Southeastern Bible College
Troy University
University of Alabama
University of Alabama
   Birmingham
   Huntsville
University of Mobile
University of Montevallo
University of North Alabama
University of South Alabama
University of West Alabama

Alaska
University of Alaska
   Fairbanks

Arizona
Arizona State University
Eastern Arizona College
Northern Arizona University
Northland Pioneer College
Pima Community College
South Mountain Community College
Southwestern College

Arkansas
Arkansas Northeastern College
Arkansas State University
Arkansas State University
   Beebe
Arkansas Tech University
Crowley's Ridge College
Ecclesia College
Harding University
Henderson State University
Hendrix College
John Brown University
Lyon College
National Park Community College
Northwest Arkansas Community College
Ouachita Baptist University
Phillips Community College of the University of
   Arkansas
Southern Arkansas University
University of Arkansas
University of Arkansas
   Fort Smith
   Monticello
   Pine Bluff
University of Central Arkansas
University of the Ozarks
Williams Baptist College

California
American Academy of Dramatic Arts: West
Azusa Pacific University
Bethany University
Bethesda Christian University
Biola University
California Baptist University
California Institute of the Arts
California Lutheran University
California Polytechnic State University: San Luis
   Obispo
California State University
   Chico
   Dominguez Hills
   Fresno
   Long Beach
   Stanislaus
Chapman University
College of the Canyons
College of the Siskiyous
Concordia University
Dominican University of California
El Camino College
Fresno Pacific University
Holy Names University
Hope International University
Irvine Valley College
La Sierra University
Loyola Marymount University
The Master's College
Mills College
Mount St. Mary's College
Mount San Jacinto College
Notre Dame de Namur University
Pepperdine University
Riverside Community College
San Diego Christian College
San Diego State University
San Francisco Conservatory of Music
Santa Clara University
Santa Rosa Junior College
Simpson University
Sonoma State University
University of California
   Irvine
   Riverside
   San Diego
   Santa Cruz
University of La Verne
University of Redlands
University of San Diego
University of Southern California
University of the Pacific
Vanguard University of Southern California
Westmont College
William Jessup University
Yuba Community College District

Colorado
Adams State College
Colorado Christian University
Colorado School of Mines
Colorado State University
Colorado State University
   Pueblo
Fort Lewis College
Mesa State College
Metropolitan State College of Denver
Northeastern Junior College
University of Colorado
   Boulder
   Denver
University of Denver

University of Northern Colorado
Western State College of Colorado

Connecticut
Albertus Magnus College
Fairfield University
Sacred Heart University
University of Connecticut
University of Hartford

Delaware
Delaware State University
University of Delaware

District of Columbia
American University
Catholic University of America
George Washington University
Howard University

Florida
Baptist College of Florida
Barry University
Bethune-Cookman University
Central Florida Community College
Chipola Junior College
Clearwater Christian College
Daytona Beach Community College
Eckerd College
Flagler College
Florida Atlantic University
Florida Christian College
Florida College
Florida Community College at Jacksonville
Florida Gulf Coast University
Florida International University
Florida Southern College
Gulf Coast Community College
Indian River Community College
Jacksonville University
Lake-Sumter Community College
Lynn University
Manatee Community College
Miami Dade College
North Florida Community College
Nova Southeastern University
Okaloosa-Walton College
Palm Beach Atlantic University
Rollins College
St. Leo University
St. Petersburg College
Saint Thomas University
Santa Fe Community College
Seminole Community College
South Florida Community College
Southeastern University
Stetson University
Tallahassee Community College
University of Florida
University of Miami
University of North Florida
University of South Florida
University of Tampa
University of West Florida
Warner Southern College

Georgia
Agnes Scott College
Albany State University
Andrew College
Armstrong Atlantic State University
Augusta State University
Berry College
Brenau University
Brewton-Parker College
Clark Atlanta University
Columbus State University
Covenant College
Darton College
Emmanuel College
Emory University
Gainesville State College
Georgia College and State University

Georgia Southern University
Georgia State University
Gordon College
Kennesaw State University
LaGrange College
Mercer University
Middle Georgia College
Morehouse College
North Georgia College & State University
Oglethorpe University
Paine College
Piedmont College
Savannah College of Art and Design
Savannah State University
Shorter College
Spelman College
Toccoa Falls College
Truett-McConnell College
University of West Georgia
Valdosta State University
Wesleyan College
Young Harris College

Hawaii
Brigham Young University-Hawaii
Hawaii Pacific University
University of Hawaii
   Manoa

Idaho
Boise Bible College
Boise State University
College of Idaho
Idaho State University
Lewis-Clark State College
North Idaho College
Northwest Nazarene University
University of Idaho

Illinois
Augustana College
Aurora University
Benedictine University
Black Hawk College
Bradley University
College of DuPage
College of Lake County
Columbia College Chicago
Concordia University
DePaul University
Eastern Illinois University
Elgin Community College
Elmhurst College
Eureka College
Greenville College
Harper College
Illinois College
Illinois State University
Illinois Wesleyan University
Judson University
Kishwaukee College
Knox College
Lake Forest College
Lewis University
Lincoln College
Loyola University Chicago
MacMurray College
McHenry County College
McKendree University
Millikin University
Monmouth College
Moody Bible Institute
North Central College
North Park University
Northeastern Illinois University
Northwestern University
Oakton Community College
Olivet Nazarene University
Parkland College
Quincy University
Rend Lake College
Rockford College

Roosevelt University
St. Xavier University
Shimer College
South Suburban College of Cook County
Southeastern Illinois College
Southern Illinois University Carbondale
Southern Illinois University Edwardsville
Trinity Christian College
Trinity International University
University of Illinois
    Chicago
    Springfield
    Urbana-Champaign
University of St. Francis
VanderCook College of Music
Waubonsee Community College
Western Illinois University
Wheaton College

Indiana
Anderson University
Ball State University
Bethel College
Butler University
DePauw University
Goshen College
Grace College
Hanover College
Huntington University
Indiana Institute of Technology
Indiana State University
Indiana University
    Bloomington
    Southeast
Indiana Wesleyan University
Manchester College
Marian College
Oakland City University
Purdue University
Saint Joseph's College
St. Mary-of-the-Woods College
Taylor University
Taylor University Fort Wayne
Tri-State University
University of Evansville
University of Indianapolis
University of St. Francis
University of Southern Indiana
Valparaiso University
Vincennes University
Wabash College

Iowa
Ashford University
Briar Cliff University
Buena Vista University
Central College
Clarke College
Coe College
Cornell College
Dordt College
Drake University
Ellsworth Community College
Emmaus Bible College
Faith Baptist Bible College and Theological
    Seminary
Graceland University
Grand View College
Iowa Central Community College
Iowa State University
Iowa Wesleyan College
Iowa Western Community College
Kirkwood Community College
Loras College
Luther College
Morningside College
Mount Mercy College
North Iowa Area Community College
Northwestern College
St. Ambrose University
Simpson College
Southwestern Community College

University of Dubuque
University of Iowa
University of Northern Iowa
Waldorf College
Wartburg College
Western Iowa Tech Community College
William Penn University

Kansas
Allen County Community College
Baker University
Barclay College
Benedictine College
Bethany College
Bethel College
Butler County Community College
Central Christian College of Kansas
Coffeyville Community College
Colby Community College
Cowley County Community College
Dodge City Community College
Emporia State University
Fort Hays State University
Friends University
Garden City Community College
Hesston College
Highland Community College
Kansas City Kansas Community College
Kansas State University
Kansas Wesleyan University
McPherson College
MidAmerica Nazarene University
Neosho County Community College
Newman University
Ottawa University
Pittsburg State University
Pratt Community College
Southwestern College
Sterling College
Tabor College
University of Kansas
University of St. Mary
Washburn University
Wichita State University

Kentucky
Asbury College
Ashland Community and Technical College
Bellarmine University
Brescia University
Centre College
Eastern Kentucky University
Georgetown College
Kentucky Christian University
Kentucky Mountain Bible College
Kentucky State University
Kentucky Wesleyan College
Morehead State University
Murray State University
Northern Kentucky University
Thomas More College
Transylvania University
Union College
University of Kentucky
University of Louisville
University of the Cumberlands
Western Kentucky University

Louisiana
Bossier Parish Community College
Centenary College of Louisiana
Delgado Community College
Dillard University
Grambling State University
Louisiana College
Louisiana State University and Agricultural and
    Mechanical College
Louisiana Tech University
McNeese State University
Northwestern State University
Southeastern Louisiana University
University of Louisiana at Lafayette

University of Louisiana at Monroe

Maine
University of Maine
University of Maine
    Augusta
    Machias
University of Southern Maine

Maryland
Bowie State University
College of Notre Dame of Maryland
Columbia Union College
Goucher College
Hood College
Johns Hopkins University: Peabody
    Conservatory of Music
Montgomery College
Mount St. Mary's University
Salisbury University
Towson University
University of Maryland
    Baltimore County
    College Park
    Eastern Shore
Villa Julie College
Washington Bible College

Massachusetts
Anna Maria College
Atlantic Union College
Berklee College of Music
Boston Conservatory
Boston University
Bristol Community College
Cape Cod Community College
Dean College
Eastern Nazarene College
Emerson College
Gordon College
Holyoke Community College
Massachusetts College of Liberal Arts
Massachusetts Maritime Academy
New England Conservatory of Music
North Shore Community College
University of Massachusetts
    Amherst
Western New England College

Michigan
Adrian College
Albion College
Alma College
Alpena Community College
Andrews University
Aquinas College
Calvin College
Central Michigan University
Concordia University
Cornerstone University
Eastern Michigan University
Ferris State University
Glen Oaks Community College
Gogebic Community College
Grace Bible College
Grand Rapids Community College
Grand Valley State University
Great Lakes Christian College
Hillsdale College
Hope College
Jackson Community College
Macomb Community College
Madonna University
Marygrove College
Michigan State University
Monroe County Community College
Mott Community College
Northern Michigan University
Northwestern Michigan College
Oakland University
Olivet College
Rochester College
Saginaw Valley State University

Schoolcraft College
Siena Heights University
Southwestern Michigan College
Spring Arbor University
University of Detroit Mercy
University of Michigan
University of Michigan
    Flint
Wayne State University
Western Michigan University

Minnesota
Augsburg College
Bemidji State University
Bethany Lutheran College
Bethel University
College of St. Benedict
Concordia University: St. Paul
Crossroads College
Crown College
Gustavus Adolphus College
Hamline University
Itasca Community College
Martin Luther College
Minnesota State Community and Technical
    College: Fergus Falls
Minnesota State University
    Mankato
    Moorhead
Normandale Community College
North Central University
Northwestern College
Riverland Community College
Saint Cloud State University
St. John's University
St. Mary's University of Minnesota
St. Olaf College
Southwest Minnesota State University
University of Minnesota
    Morris
    Twin Cities
University of St. Thomas
Winona State University

Mississippi
Belhaven College
Copiah-Lincoln Community College
Delta State University
East Mississippi Community College
Hinds Community College
Itawamba Community College
Jackson State University
Meridian Community College
Millsaps College
Mississippi College
Mississippi Gulf Coast Community College
    Jefferson Davis Campus
Mississippi State University
Mississippi University for Women
Pearl River Community College
Rust College
University of Mississippi
William Carey University

Missouri
Avila University
Calvary Bible College and Theological Seminary
Central Methodist University
College of the Ozarks
Columbia College
Cottey College
Crowder College
Culver-Stockton College
Drury University
East Central College
Evangel University
Fontbonne University
Hannibal-LaGrange College
Harris-Stowe State University
Jefferson College
Lincoln University
Lindenwood University

Missouri Baptist University
Missouri Southern State University
Missouri State University
Missouri Western State University
Moberly Area Community College
North Central Missouri College
Northwest Missouri State University
Park University
Rockhurst University
St. Charles Community College
St. Louis Christian College
Saint Louis University
Southeast Missouri State University
Southwest Baptist University
State Fair Community College
Truman State University
University of Central Missouri
University of Missouri
    Columbia
    Kansas City
    Missouri University of Science and
      Technology
    St. Louis
Webster University
Westminster College
William Jewell College
William Woods University

Montana
Carroll College
Dawson Community College
Montana State University
    Billings
    Bozeman
Rocky Mountain College
University of Great Falls
University of Montana: Missoula

Nebraska
Central Community College
Chadron State College
College of Saint Mary
Concordia University
Creighton University
Dana College
Doane College
Grace University
Hastings College
Mid-Plains Community College Area
Midland Lutheran College
Nebraska Wesleyan University
Northeast Community College
Peru State College
University of Nebraska
    Kearney
    Lincoln
    Omaha
Wayne State College
Western Nebraska Community College
York College

Nevada
Truckee Meadows Community College
University of Nevada
    Las Vegas
    Reno

New Hampshire
Colby-Sawyer College
Franklin Pierce University
Keene State College
New England College
Plymouth State University
University of New Hampshire

New Jersey
Caldwell College
Drew University
Georgian Court University
Kean University
Montclair State University
New Jersey Institute of Technology
Richard Stockton College of New Jersey

Rider University
Rowan University
Rutgers, The State University of New Jersey
    Camden Regional Campus
    New Brunswick/Piscataway Campus
    Newark Regional Campus
Stevens Institute of Technology
William Paterson University of New Jersey

New Mexico
College of Santa Fe
College of the Southwest
Eastern New Mexico University
Mesalands Community College
New Mexico Highlands University
New Mexico Junior College
University of New Mexico

New York
Adelphi University
Alfred University
Canisius College
City University of New York
    Brooklyn College
    College of Staten Island
    Queens College
College of Saint Rose
Concordia College
Eastman School of Music of the University of
    Rochester
Eugene Lang College The New School for
    Liberal Arts
Five Towns College
Hobart and William Smith Colleges
Hofstra University
Houghton College
Ithaca College
Jamestown Community College
Juilliard School
Manhattan School of Music
Manhattanville College
Mannes College The New School for Music
Marist College
Marymount Manhattan College
Molloy College
Nazareth College of Rochester
Niagara University
Nyack College
Rensselaer Polytechnic Institute
Roberts Wesleyan College
Russell Sage College
Saint Bonaventure University
St. John's University
Skidmore College
State University of New York
    Binghamton
    Buffalo
    College at Fredonia
    College at Geneseo
    College at Plattsburgh
    College at Potsdam
    Purchase
    Stony Brook
Suffolk County Community College
Syracuse University
University of Rochester
Villa Maria College of Buffalo
Wagner College

North Carolina
Appalachian State University
Barton College
Brevard College
Campbell University
Catawba College
Catawba Valley Community College
Chowan University
College of the Albemarle
Davidson College
Elon University
Fayetteville State University
Gardner-Webb University

Greensboro College
High Point University
Isothermal Community College
Lees-McRae College
Lenoir-Rhyne College
Livingstone College
Meredith College
Methodist University
Montreat College
Mount Olive College
North Carolina Agricultural and Technical State
    University
North Carolina Central University
North Carolina School of the Arts
Pfeiffer University
Queens University of Charlotte
Roanoke Bible College
St. Andrews Presbyterian College
St. Augustine's College
Salem College
Shaw University
Southeastern Community College
University of North Carolina
    Asheville
    Chapel Hill
    Charlotte
    Greensboro
    Wilmington
Wake Forest University
Western Carolina University
Wilkes Community College
Wingate University

North Dakota
Dickinson State University
Jamestown University
Lake Region State College
Mayville State University
Minot State University
Minot State University: Bottineau Campus
North Dakota State College of Science
North Dakota State University
Trinity Bible College
University of Mary
University of North Dakota
Valley City State University

Ohio
Ashland University
Baldwin-Wallace College
Bluffton University
Bowling Green State University
Bowling Green State University: Firelands
    College
Capital University
Case Western Reserve University
Cedarville University
Central State University
Cleveland Institute of Music
Cleveland State University
College of Mount St. Joseph
College of Wooster
Cuyahoga Community College
    Metropolitan Campus
Denison University
Heidelberg College
Hiram College
Kent State University
Kent State University
    Ashtabula
    East Liverpool
    Salem
    Stark
    Trumbull
    Tuscarawas
Kent State University: Geauga
Lake Erie College
Lakeland Community College
Malone College
Marietta College
Miami University
    Oxford Campus

Mount Union College
Mount Vernon Nazarene University
Muskingum College
Oberlin College
Ohio Northern University
Ohio State University
    Agricultural Technical Institute
    Columbus Campus
    Lima Campus
    Mansfield Campus
    Marion Campus
    Newark Campus
Ohio University
Ohio Wesleyan University
Otterbein College
Pontifical College Josephinum
Southern State Community College
Tiffin University
University of Akron
University of Akron: Wayne College
University of Cincinnati
University of Dayton
University of Findlay
University of Rio Grande
University of Toledo
Urbana University
Walsh University
Wittenberg University
Wright State University
Xavier University

Oklahoma
Cameron University
Carl Albert State College
Mid-America Christian University
Northeastern Oklahoma Agricultural and
    Mechanical College
Northeastern State University
Northwestern Oklahoma State University
Oklahoma Baptist University
Oklahoma Christian University
Oklahoma City University
Oklahoma Panhandle State University
Oklahoma State University
Oklahoma Wesleyan University
Oral Roberts University
Rogers State University
St. Gregory's University
Southeastern Oklahoma State University
Southwestern Christian University
Southwestern Oklahoma State University
Tulsa Community College
University of Central Oklahoma
University of Oklahoma
University of Science and Arts of Oklahoma
University of Tulsa
Western Oklahoma State College

Oregon
Blue Mountain Community College
Cascade College
Clackamas Community College
Concordia University
Corban College
Eastern Oregon University
Eugene Bible College
George Fox University
Lane Community College
Lewis & Clark College
Linfield College
Linn-Benton Community College
Northwest Christian College
Pacific University
Portland State University
Southern Oregon University
Treasure Valley Community College
University of Oregon
University of Portland
Warner Pacific College
Western Oregon University
Willamette University

Pennsylvania
Albright College
Arcadia University
Baptist Bible College of Pennsylvania
Bloomsburg University of Pennsylvania
Bucknell University
California University of Pennsylvania
Carnegie Mellon University
Cedar Crest College
Chatham University
Clarion University of Pennsylvania
Delaware Valley College
DeSales University
Drexel University
Duquesne University
East Stroudsburg University of Pennsylvania
Edinboro University of Pennsylvania
Elizabethtown College
Franklin & Marshall College
Gannon University
Geneva College
Gettysburg College
Immaculata University
Indiana University of Pennsylvania
Kutztown University of Pennsylvania
Lancaster Bible College
Lebanon Valley College
Lehigh University
Lincoln University
Lock Haven University of Pennsylvania
Lycoming College
Mansfield University of Pennsylvania
Marywood University
Mercyhurst College
Messiah College
Moravian College
Mount Aloysius College
Muhlenberg College
Northampton Community College
Point Park University
St. Francis University
Saint Joseph's University
St. Vincent College
Seton Hill University
Slippery Rock University of Pennsylvania
Susquehanna University
Temple University
Thiel College
University of the Arts
Ursinus College
Valley Forge Christian College
Valley Forge Military College
Widener University
Wilkes University
York College of Pennsylvania

Puerto Rico
Humacao Community College
Universidad Politecnica de Puerto Rico
University of Puerto Rico
   Aguadilla
   Humacao
   Mayaguez

Rhode Island
Rhode Island College
University of Rhode Island

South Carolina
Allen University
Anderson University
The Citadel
Clemson University
Coastal Carolina University
Coker College
College of Charleston
Columbia College
Converse College
Erskine College
Francis Marion University
Furman University
Lander University

Limestone College
Newberry College
Presbyterian College
Southern Wesleyan University
Spartanburg Methodist College
University of South Carolina
Winthrop University
Wofford College

South Dakota
Augustana College
Dakota State University
Dakota Wesleyan University
Mount Marty College
Northern State University
South Dakota State University
University of Sioux Falls
University of South Dakota

Tennessee
Austin Peay State University
Belmont University
Bethel College
Bryan College
Carson-Newman College
Christian Brothers University
Crichton College
Cumberland University
Dyersburg State Community College
East Tennessee State University
Free Will Baptist Bible College
Freed-Hardeman University
Hiwassee College
Jackson State Community College
Johnson Bible College
King College
Lambuth University
Lee University
LeMoyne-Owen College
Lincoln Memorial University
Lipscomb University
Martin Methodist College
Maryville College
Middle Tennessee State University
Milligan College
Northeast State Technical Community College
Pellissippi State Technical Community College
Rhodes College
Roane State Community College
Southern Adventist University
Tennessee Technological University
Tennessee Temple University
Tennessee Wesleyan College
Trevecca Nazarene University
Union University
University of Memphis
University of Tennessee
   Chattanooga
   Knoxville
   Martin
Vanderbilt University
Volunteer State Community College
Walters State Community College

Texas
Abilene Christian University
Angelina College
Angelo State University
Austin College
Baylor University
Clarendon College
College of the Mainland
Collin County Community College District
Concordia University at Austin
Dallas Baptist University
East Texas Baptist University
Frank Phillips College
Galveston College
Hardin-Simmons University
Hill College
Houston Baptist University
Howard College

Howard Payne University
Huston-Tillotson University
Jacksonville College
Kilgore College
Lee College
Lon Morris College
Lubbock Christian University
McMurry University
Midland College
Midwestern State University
Northeast Texas Community College
Odessa College
Our Lady of the Lake University of San Antonio
Panola College
Paris Junior College
Rice University
Richland College
St. Edward's University
St. Mary's University
San Jacinto College
Schreiner University
Southern Methodist University
Southwestern Adventist University
Southwestern University
Stephen F. Austin State University
Tarleton State University
Texas A&M University
Texas A&M University
   Commerce
Texas Christian University
Texas Lutheran University
Texas State University: San Marcos
Texas Tech University
Texas Wesleyan University
Trinity University
Tyler Junior College
University of Dallas
University of Houston
University of Mary Hardin-Baylor
University of Texas
   Austin
   El Paso
   Pan American
   San Antonio
   Tyler
University of the Incarnate Word
Vernon College
Victoria College
Wayland Baptist University
West Texas A&M University
Western Technical College
Western Texas College
Wharton County Junior College

Utah
Brigham Young University
College of Eastern Utah
Dixie State College of Utah
Salt Lake Community College
Snow College
Southern Utah University
University of Utah
Utah State University
Utah Valley State College
Weber State University
Westminster College

Vermont
Bennington College
Castleton State College
Goddard College
Green Mountain College
Landmark College
Norwich University

Virginia
Averett University
Bluefield College
Bridgewater College
Christopher Newport University
Emory & Henry College
George Mason University

Hampton University
Hollins University
James Madison University
Liberty University
Longwood University
Lynchburg College
Norfolk State University
Old Dominion University
Radford University
Randolph College
Roanoke College
Shenandoah University
Southern Virginia University
Sweet Briar College
University of Mary Washington
University of Richmond
University of Virginia
University of Virginia's College at Wise
Virginia Commonwealth University
Virginia Intermont College
Virginia Military Institute
Virginia State University
Virginia Wesleyan College

Washington
Big Bend Community College
Central Washington University
Centralia College
Clark College
Everett Community College
Gonzaga University
Grays Harbor College
Northwest University
Pacific Lutheran University
Saint Martin's University
Seattle Pacific University
Seattle University
Trinity Lutheran College
University of Puget Sound
University of Washington
Walla Walla Community College
Walla Walla University
Washington State University
Western Washington University
Whitman College
Whitworth University

West Virginia
Alderson-Broaddus College
Bethany College
Bluefield State College
Concord University
Davis and Elkins College
Fairmont State University
Glenville State College
Marshall University
Ohio Valley University
Shepherd University
University of Charleston
West Liberty State College
West Virginia University
West Virginia Wesleyan College
Wheeling Jesuit University

Wisconsin
Beloit College
Cardinal Stritch University
Carroll College
Carthage College
Edgewood College
Lawrence University
Marquette University
Mount Mary College
Northland College
Ripon College
St. Norbert College
Silver Lake College
University of Wisconsin
   Baraboo/Sauk County
   Eau Claire
   Fond du Lac
   Green Bay

La Crosse
Madison
Manitowoc
Oshkosh
Parkside
Richland
River Falls
Rock County
Sheboygan
Stevens Point
Superior
Waukesha
Whitewater
Viterbo University
Wisconsin Lutheran College

Wyoming
Casper College
Central Wyoming College
Eastern Wyoming College
Laramie County Community College
Sheridan College
University of Wyoming
Western Wyoming Community College

ROTC scholarships

Air Force ROTC

Alabama
Alabama State University
Auburn University
Auburn University at Montgomery
Birmingham-Southern College
Bishop State Community College
Faulkner University
Huntingdon College
Jefferson State Community College
Marion Military Institute
Miles College
Samford University
Shelton State Community College
Spring Hill College
Stillman College
Troy University
Tuskegee University
University of Alabama
University of Alabama
    Birmingham
University of Mobile
University of Montevallo
University of South Alabama
University of West Alabama

Alaska
Alaska Pacific University
University of Alaska
    Anchorage

Arizona
Arizona State University
Coconino County Community College
DeVry University
    Phoenix
Embry-Riddle Aeronautical University: Prescott
    Campus
Estrella Mountain Community College
Gateway Community College
Mesa Community College
Northern Arizona University
Phoenix College
Pima Community College
Southwestern College
University of Arizona
Yavapai College

Arkansas
John Brown University
Northwest Arkansas Community College
University of Arkansas
University of Arkansas
    Fort Smith

California
Antelope Valley College
Biola University
California Baptist University
California Institute of Technology
California Lutheran University
California State University
    Dominguez Hills
    Fresno
    Los Angeles
    Northridge
    Sacramento
    San Bernardino
    San Marcos
Chabot College
Chapman University
Claremont McKenna College
College of San Mateo
College of the Sequoias
Cuyamaca College
De Anza College
Foothill College
Fresno City College
Harvey Mudd College
Holy Names University
Irvine Valley College
The King's College and Seminary
Los Angeles City College
Los Angeles Mission College
Loyola Marymount University
MiraCosta College
Mission College
Mount San Antonio College
Mount San Jacinto College
National University
Occidental College
Ohlone College
Pepperdine University
Pitzer College
Point Loma Nazarene University
Pomona College
Riverside Community College
Sacramento City College
St. Mary's College of California
Samuel Merritt College
San Diego Christian College
San Diego City College
San Diego State University
San Francisco State University
San Jose State University
Santa Clara University
Scripps College
Solano Community College
Sonoma State University
Stanford University
University of California
    Berkeley
    Davis
    Irvine
    Los Angeles
    Riverside
    Santa Cruz
University of Redlands
University of San Diego
University of San Francisco
University of Southern California
University of the Pacific
Vanguard University of Southern California
Ventura College
West Valley College
Westmont College
Whittier College

Colorado
Aims Community College
Arapahoe Community College
Colorado Christian University
Colorado School of Mines
Colorado State University
Front Range Community College
Metropolitan State College of Denver
Regis University
University of Colorado
    Boulder
    Denver
University of Denver
University of Northern Colorado

Connecticut
Capital Community College
Central Connecticut State University
Eastern Connecticut State University
Fairfield University
Quinnipiac University
Southern Connecticut State University
Tunxis Community College
University of Connecticut
University of Hartford
Wesleyan University
Western Connecticut State University
Yale University

Delaware
Delaware State University
University of Delaware
Wilmington University

District of Columbia
American University
Catholic University of America
George Washington University
Georgetown University
Howard University
University of the District of Columbia

Florida
Barry University
Bethune-Cookman University
Brevard Community College
Broward Community College
Clearwater Christian College
Daytona Beach Community College
Eckerd College
Embry-Riddle Aeronautical University
Florida Agricultural and Mechanical University
Florida College
Florida International University
Florida Southern College
Florida State University
Hillsborough Community College
Lynn University
Miami Dade College
St. Leo University
Santa Fe Community College
Tallahassee Community College
University of Central Florida
University of Miami
University of South Florida
University of Tampa
University of West Florida

Georgia
Agnes Scott College
Clark Atlanta University
Clayton State University
Emory University
Georgia Institute of Technology
Georgia State University
Kennesaw State University
Morehouse College
Southern Polytechnic State University
Spelman College
University of Georgia
Valdosta State University

Hawaii
Brigham Young University-Hawaii
Chaminade University of Honolulu
Hawaii Pacific University
University of Hawaii
    Honolulu Community College
    Manoa
    West Oahu

Idaho
Lewis-Clark State College
Northwest Nazarene University
University of Idaho

Illinois
Elmhurst College
Governors State University
Illinois Institute of Technology
John A. Logan College
Judson University
Lewis University
Lincoln Land Community College
Loyola University Chicago
McKendree University
North Central College
North Park University
Northeastern Illinois University
Northwestern University
Parkland College
St. Xavier University
Shawnee Community College
Southern Illinois University Carbondale
Southern Illinois University Edwardsville
University of Chicago
University of Illinois
    Chicago
    Urbana-Champaign
Wheaton College

Indiana
Bethel College
Butler University
DePauw University
Holy Cross College
Indiana State University
Indiana University
    Bloomington
    South Bend
    Southeast
Indiana University-Purdue University
    Indianapolis
Purdue University
Rose-Hulman Institute of Technology
St. Mary-of-the-Woods College
Saint Mary's College
Tri-State University
University of Notre Dame
Valparaiso University
Vincennes University

Iowa
Coe College
Grand View College
Hawkeye Community College
Iowa State University
Iowa Western Community College
University of Iowa

Kansas
Baker University
Haskell Indian Nations University
Kansas State University
Manhattan Christian College
MidAmerica Nazarene University
University of Kansas
University of St. Mary
Washburn University

Kentucky
Asbury College
Bellarmine University
Centre College
Georgetown College
Kentucky State University
Northern Kentucky University
Thomas More College
Transylvania University
University of Kentucky
University of Louisville
Western Kentucky University

Louisiana
Delgado Community College
Dillard University
Louisiana State University and Agricultural and
    Mechanical College

Loyola University New Orleans
Northwestern State University
Our Lady of the Lake College
Southern University
    New Orleans
Southern University and Agricultural and
    Mechanical College
Tulane University
University of Louisiana at Monroe
University of New Orleans
Xavier University of Louisiana

Maine
University of Maine
    Augusta
University of Southern Maine

Maryland
Bowie State University
Johns Hopkins University
Loyola College in Maryland
Prince George's Community College
Towson University
University of Maryland
    College Park

Massachusetts
American International College
Amherst College
Anna Maria College
Assumption College
Babson College
Bay Path College
Becker College
Bentley College
Boston College
Boston University
Brandeis University
Bridgewater State College
Clark University
College of the Holy Cross
Curry College
Eastern Nazarene College
Elms College
Endicott College
Gordon College
Harvard College
Holyoke Community College
Massachusetts Institute of Technology
Massachusetts Maritime Academy
Merrimack College
Middlesex Community College
Mount Holyoke College
Northeastern University
Pine Manor College
Quinsigamond Community College
Salem State College
Smith College
Springfield College
Tufts University
University of Massachusetts
    Amherst
    Lowell
Wellesley College
Western New England College
Westfield State College
Williams College
Worcester Polytechnic Institute
Worcester State College

Michigan
Concordia University
Eastern Michigan University
Finlandia University
Lansing Community College
Lawrence Technological University
Michigan State University
Michigan Technological University
Oakland University
Spring Arbor University
University of Michigan
University of Michigan
    Dearborn

Wayne State University

Minnesota
Anoka-Ramsey Community College
Augsburg College
Century Community and Technical College
College of St. Catherine
College of St. Scholastica
Concordia College: Moorhead
Concordia University: St. Paul
Hamline University
Inver Hills Community College
Macalester College
Minnesota State University
    Moorhead
Normandale Community College
North Central University
Northwestern College
University of Minnesota
    Crookston
    Duluth
    Twin Cities
University of St. Thomas

Mississippi
Belhaven College
Mississippi State University
Mississippi University for Women
Northwest Mississippi Community College
University of Mississippi
University of Southern Mississippi
William Carey University

Missouri
Central Bible College
Central Methodist University
Columbia College
Fontbonne University
Harris-Stowe State University
Lincoln University
Saint Louis University
Southeast Missouri State University
St. Louis Community College
    Meramec
Stephens College
University of Central Missouri
University of Missouri
    Columbia
    Missouri University of Science and
        Technology
    St. Louis
Washington University in St. Louis
Webster University
Westminster College
William Woods University

Montana
Montana State University
    Bozeman

Nebraska
Bellevue University
Clarkson College
College of Saint Mary
Concordia University
Creighton University
Dana College
Doane College
Grace University
Nebraska Wesleyan University
University of Nebraska
    Lincoln
    Medical Center
    Omaha
York College

New Hampshire
Colby-Sawyer College
Daniel Webster College
Franklin Pierce University
Keene State College
New England College
Plymouth State University

Rivier College
St. Anselm College
Southern New Hampshire University
University of New Hampshire
University of New Hampshire at Manchester

New Jersey
Brookdale Community College
The College of New Jersey
Fairleigh Dickinson University
    College at Florham
    Metropolitan Campus
Kean University
Monmouth University
Montclair State University
New Jersey Institute of Technology
Princeton University
Ramapo College of New Jersey
Raritan Valley Community College
Rutgers, The State University of New Jersey
    Camden Regional Campus
    New Brunswick/Piscataway Campus
    Newark Regional Campus
Saint Peter's College
Stevens Institute of Technology
Union County College
William Paterson University of New Jersey

New Mexico
Central New Mexico Community College
Dona Ana Branch Community College of New
    Mexico State University
National American University: Rio Rancho
New Mexico State University
New Mexico State University
    Alamogordo
University of New Mexico

New York
Adelphi University
Albany College of Pharmacy
Cazenovia College
Clarkson University
College of Mount St. Vincent
College of Saint Rose
Columbia University
Columbia University
    School of General Studies
Cornell University
Dowling College
Elmira College
Fordham University
Globe Institute of Technology
Hamilton College
Hudson Valley Community College
Iona College
Ithaca College
Jewish Theological Seminary of America
Le Moyne College
Manhattan College
Maria College
Molloy College
Monroe Community College
Nazareth College of Rochester
New York Institute of Technology
Onondaga Community College
Rensselaer Polytechnic Institute
Roberts Wesleyan College
Rochester Institute of Technology
Russell Sage College
Sage College of Albany
St. Francis College
St. John Fisher College
St. Joseph's College: Suffolk Campus
St. Lawrence University
St. Thomas Aquinas College
Schenectady County Community College
Siena College
Skidmore College
State University of New York
    Albany
    Binghamton

College at Brockport
College at Cortland
College at Geneseo
College at Old Westbury
College at Potsdam
College of Environmental Science and
    Forestry
College of Technology at Canton
Stony Brook
Syracuse University
Union College
University of Rochester
Utica College
Vaughn College of Aeronautics and Technology
Wells College

North Carolina
Belmont Abbey College
Bennett College
Davidson College
Duke University
East Carolina University
Elon University
Fayetteville State University
Gardner-Webb University
Greensboro College
Guilford College
Guilford Technical Community College
High Point University
Johnson C. Smith University
Meredith College
Methodist University
North Carolina Agricultural and Technical State
    University
North Carolina Central University
North Carolina State University
Peace College
Queens University of Charlotte
St. Augustine's College
Shaw University
University of North Carolina
    Chapel Hill
    Charlotte
    Greensboro
    Pembroke
Wingate University

North Dakota
Mayville State University
North Dakota State University
University of North Dakota

Ohio
Ashland University
Baldwin-Wallace College
Bowling Green State University
Capital University
Case Western Reserve University
Cedarville University
Central State University
Cleveland Institute of Art
College of Mount St. Joseph
Columbus State Community College
Cuyahoga Community College
    Metropolitan Campus
Heidelberg College
Hocking College
Kent State University
Kent State University
    Ashtabula
    East Liverpool
    Salem
    Stark
    Trumbull
    Tuscarawas
Lourdes College
Malone College
Miami University
    Hamilton Campus
    Middletown Campus
    Oxford Campus
Mount Union College

Ohio Northern University
Ohio State University
   Columbus Campus
   Lima Campus
   Mansfield Campus
   Marion Campus
   Newark Campus
Ohio University
Ohio University
   Lancaster Campus
Ohio Wesleyan University
Otterbein College
Owens Community College
   Toledo
Sinclair Community College
University of Akron
University of Akron: Wayne College
University of Cincinnati
University of Dayton
University of Findlay
University of Toledo
Wilberforce University
Wittenberg University
Wright State University
Xavier University
Youngstown State University

Oklahoma
Langston University
Northeastern Oklahoma Agricultural and
   Mechanical College
Oklahoma Baptist University
Oklahoma Christian University
Oklahoma City University
Oklahoma State University
Oral Roberts University
Rogers State University
Rose State College
St. Gregory's University
Southern Nazarene University
University of Oklahoma
University of Tulsa

Oregon
Clackamas Community College
Concordia University
Corban College
George Fox University
Linfield College
Linn-Benton Community College
Oregon State University
Pacific University
Portland State University
University of Portland
Warner Pacific College
Western Oregon University

Pennsylvania
Bloomsburg University of Pennsylvania
Bryn Mawr College
Cabrini College
California University of Pennsylvania
Carlow University
Carnegie Mellon University
Chatham University
Drexel University
Duquesne University
East Stroudsburg University of Pennsylvania
Eastern University
Keystone College
King's College
La Roche College
La Salle University
Lackawanna College
Luzerne County Community College
Marywood University
Misericordia University
Penn State
   Abington
   Altoona
   Brandywine
   Hazleton

   University Park
   Wilkes-Barre
   Worthington Scranton
Philadelphia Biblical University
Point Park University
Robert Morris University
Rosemont College
Saint Joseph's University
St. Vincent College
Seton Hill University
Swarthmore College
Temple University
Thomas Jefferson University: College of Health
   Professions
University of Pennsylvania
University of Pittsburgh
University of Pittsburgh
   Greensburg
University of Scranton
University of the Sciences in Philadelphia
Valley Forge Military College
Villanova University
Washington & Jefferson College
West Chester University of Pennsylvania
Widener University
Wilkes University

Puerto Rico
Bayamon Central University
Inter American University of Puerto Rico
   Aguadilla Campus
   Bayamon Campus
   Fajardo Campus
   Metropolitan Campus
   San German Campus
Pontifical Catholic University of Puerto Rico
Universidad Metropolitana
Universidad Politecnica de Puerto Rico
University of Puerto Rico
   Carolina Regional College
   Mayaguez
   Rio Piedras

South Carolina
Anderson University
Benedict College
Charleston Southern University
The Citadel
Clemson University
College of Charleston
Midlands Technical College
South Carolina State University
Southern Wesleyan University
Tri-County Technical College
University of South Carolina
University of South Carolina
   Salkehatchie Regional Campus

South Dakota
Dakota State University
South Dakota State University

Tennessee
Austin Peay State University
Carson-Newman College
Christian Brothers University
Free Will Baptist Bible College
LeMoyne-Owen College
Lipscomb University
Rhodes College
Roane State Community College
Southwest Tennessee Community College
Tennessee State University
Tennessee Technological University
University of Memphis
University of Tennessee
   Knoxville
Vanderbilt University

Texas
Angelo State University
Austin Community College
Baylor University

Concordia University at Austin
Dallas Baptist University
Houston Community College System
Huston-Tillotson University
Lon Morris College
McLennan Community College
Midwestern State University
North Central Texas College
Our Lady of the Lake University of San Antonio
Rice University
St. Edward's University
St. Mary's University
San Antonio College
Southern Methodist University
Tarrant County College
Texas A&M University
Texas Christian University
Texas Lutheran University
Texas State University: San Marcos
Texas Tech University
Texas Wesleyan University
Texas Woman's University
Trinity University
University of Dallas
University of Houston
University of Mary Hardin-Baylor
University of North Texas
University of St. Thomas
University of Texas
   Arlington
   Austin
   Dallas
   El Paso
   San Antonio
Wayland Baptist University
Weatherford College

Utah
Brigham Young University
LDS Business College
Salt Lake Community College
University of Utah
Utah State University
Utah Valley State College
Weber State University
Westminster College

Vermont
Lyndon State College
Norwich University
St. Michael's College

Virginia
George Mason University
James Madison University
Liberty University
Mary Baldwin College
Piedmont Virginia Community College
University of Virginia
Virginia Military Institute
Virginia Polytechnic Institute and State
   University

Washington
Central Washington University
Clark College
Highline Community College
Saint Martin's University
Seattle Pacific University
Seattle University
South Puget Sound Community College
Spokane Community College
University of Washington
Washington State University

West Virginia
Fairmont State University
Shepherd University
West Virginia University

Wisconsin
Alverno College
Carroll College

Carthage College
Maranatha Baptist Bible College
Marquette University
Milwaukee School of Engineering
University of Wisconsin
   Madison
   Milwaukee
   Superior
   Whitewater
Wisconsin Lutheran College

Wyoming
Laramie County Community College
University of Wyoming

Army ROTC

Alabama
Alabama Agricultural and Mechanical
   University
Alabama State University
Auburn University
Auburn University at Montgomery
Birmingham-Southern College
Bishop State Community College
Chattahoochee Valley Community College
Faulkner University
Gadsden State Community College
Huntingdon College
Jacksonville State University
Jefferson State Community College
Judson College
Marion Military Institute
Miles College
Northwest-Shoals Community College
Samford University
Shelton State Community College
Spring Hill College
Stillman College
Troy University
Tuskegee University
University of Alabama
University of Alabama
   Birmingham
   Huntsville
University of Mobile
University of Montevallo
University of North Alabama
University of South Alabama

Alaska
University of Alaska
   Fairbanks

Arizona
Arizona State University
Coconino County Community College
Embry-Riddle Aeronautical University: Prescott
   Campus
Gateway Community College
Grand Canyon University
Mesa Community College
Northern Arizona University
Paradise Valley Community College
Phoenix College
Pima Community College
University of Arizona
Yavapai College

Arkansas
Arkansas State University
Arkansas Tech University
Central Baptist College
Harding University
Henderson State University
Hendrix College
John Brown University
Northwest Arkansas Community College
Ouachita Baptist University
Ouachita Technical College
Philander Smith College

University of Arkansas
University of Arkansas
  Fort Smith
  Little Rock
  Monticello
  Pine Bluff
University of Central Arkansas
Williams Baptist College

California
Azusa Pacific University
Biola University
California Baptist University
California Institute of Technology
California Lutheran University
California Polytechnic State University: San Luis
  Obispo
California State Polytechnic University: Pomona
California State University
  Dominguez Hills
  Fresno
  Fullerton
  Long Beach
  Los Angeles
  Northridge
  Sacramento
  San Bernardino
  San Marcos
Chabot College
Chapman University
City College of San Francisco
Claremont McKenna College
College of San Mateo
Cuyamaca College
De Anza College
Diablo Valley College
El Camino College
Foothill College
Fresno City College
Harvey Mudd College
Holy Names University
The King's College and Seminary
Los Angeles City College
Los Angeles Mission College
Loyola Marymount University
Menlo College
MiraCosta College
Mount San Jacinto College
National Hispanic University
National University
Occidental College
Pepperdine University
Pitzer College
Point Loma Nazarene University
Pomona College
Riverside Community College
Sacramento City College
St. Mary's College of California
Samuel Merritt College
San Diego Christian College
San Diego City College
San Diego State University
San Francisco State University
Santa Clara University
Scripps College
Sonoma State University
Stanford University
University of California
  Berkeley
  Davis
  Irvine
  Los Angeles
  Riverside
  Santa Barbara
  Santa Cruz
University of La Verne
University of Redlands
University of San Diego
University of San Francisco
University of Southern California
Vanguard University of Southern California
West Valley College

Westmont College
Whittier College

Colorado
Arapahoe Community College
Colorado Christian University
Colorado College
Colorado School of Mines
Colorado State University
Colorado State University
  Pueblo
Colorado Technical University
Community College of Denver
Front Range Community College
Metropolitan State College of Denver
Red Rocks Community College
Regis University
University of Colorado
  Boulder
  Colorado Springs
  Denver
University of Denver
University of Northern Colorado

Connecticut
Capital Community College
Central Connecticut State University
Eastern Connecticut State University
Fairfield University
Quinnipiac University
Sacred Heart University
Southern Connecticut State University
Trinity College
Tunxis Community College
University of Bridgeport
University of Connecticut
University of Hartford
Western Connecticut State University
Yale University

Delaware
Delaware State University
University of Delaware
Wesley College
Wilmington University

District of Columbia
American University
Catholic University of America
George Washington University
Georgetown University
Howard University
Trinity Washington University
University of the District of Columbia

Florida
Barry University
Bethune-Cookman University
Brevard Community College
Broward Community College
Clearwater Christian College
Daytona Beach Community College
Eckerd College
Embry-Riddle Aeronautical University
Florida Agricultural and Mechanical University
Florida Atlantic University
Florida College
Florida Institute of Technology
Florida International University
Florida Memorial University
Florida Southern College
Florida State University
Hillsborough Community College
Miami Dade College
Okaloosa-Walton College
Pasco-Hernando Community College
Pensacola Junior College
Polk Community College
St. Leo University
Santa Fe Community College
South Florida Community College
Southeastern University
Stetson University

Tallahassee Community College
University of Central Florida
University of Miami
University of South Florida
University of Tampa
University of West Florida
Valencia Community College

Georgia
Agnes Scott College
Albany State University
Armstrong Atlantic State University
Augusta State University
Clark Atlanta University
Clayton State University
Columbus State University
Darton College
Emory University
Fort Valley State University
Georgia College and State University
Georgia Institute of Technology
Georgia Military College
Georgia Southern University
Georgia State University
Kennesaw State University
Mercer University
Morehouse College
North Georgia College & State University
Paine College
Savannah College of Art and Design
Savannah State University
Southern Polytechnic State University
Spelman College
University of Georgia
University of West Georgia

Hawaii
Brigham Young University-Hawaii
Chaminade University of Honolulu
Hawaii Pacific University
University of Hawaii
  Honolulu Community College
  Manoa
  West Oahu
  Windward Community College

Idaho
Boise State University
Brigham Young University-Idaho
College of Idaho
Idaho State University
Lewis-Clark State College
Northwest Nazarene University
University of Idaho

Illinois
Aurora University
Benedictine University
Bradley University
Carl Sandburg College
Chicago State University
DePaul University
Eastern Illinois University
Elmhurst College
Governors State University
Illinois Institute of Technology
Illinois State University
Illinois Wesleyan University
John A. Logan College
Judson University
Kankakee Community College
Kishwaukee College
Lewis and Clark Community College
Lewis University
Lincoln Land Community College
Loyola University Chicago
McKendree University
Monmouth College
North Central College
Northeastern Illinois University
Northern Illinois University
Northwestern University
Olivet Nazarene University

Parkland College
Robert Morris College: Chicago
Shawnee Community College
Southern Illinois University Carbondale
Southern Illinois University Edwardsville
Spoon River College
University of Chicago
University of Illinois
  Chicago
  Urbana-Champaign
Waubonsee Community College
Western Illinois University
Wheaton College

Indiana
Ball State University
Bethel College
Butler University
DePauw University
Franklin College
Holy Cross College
Indiana State University
Indiana University
  Bloomington
  Kokomo
  Northwest
  South Bend
  Southeast
Indiana University-Purdue University
  Indianapolis
Indiana Wesleyan University
Marian College
Purdue University
Purdue University
  Calumet
Rose-Hulman Institute of Technology
St. Mary-of-the-Woods College
Saint Mary's College
University of Indianapolis
University of Notre Dame
University of Southern Indiana
Valparaiso University
Vincennes University

Iowa
Allen College
Clarke College
Coe College
Drake University
Grand View College
Hawkeye Community College
Iowa State University
Iowa Western Community College
Loras College
University of Dubuque
University of Iowa
University of Northern Iowa

Kansas
Baker University
Benedictine College
Kansas State University
Manhattan Christian College
MidAmerica Nazarene University
Pittsburg State University
University of Kansas
University of St. Mary
Washburn University

Kentucky
Asbury College
Bellarmine University
Campbellsville University
Centre College
Eastern Kentucky University
Georgetown College
Jefferson Community and Technical College
Kentucky Christian University
Kentucky State University
Kentucky Wesleyan College
Midway College
Morehead State University
Murray State University

Northern Kentucky University
Thomas More College
Transylvania University
Union College
University of Kentucky
University of Louisville
University of the Cumberlands
Western Kentucky University

Louisiana
Delgado Community College
Dillard University
Grambling State University
Louisiana College
Louisiana State University
    Alexandria
    Shreveport
Louisiana State University and Agricultural and
    Mechanical College
Louisiana Tech University
Loyola University New Orleans
Northwestern State University
Southeastern Louisiana University
Southern University
    New Orleans
Southern University and Agricultural and
    Mechanical College
Tulane University
University of Louisiana at Lafayette
University of Louisiana at Monroe
University of New Orleans
Xavier University of Louisiana

Maine
Colby College
Husson College
Maine Maritime Academy
New England School of Communications
St. Joseph's College
Unity College
University of Maine
University of Maine
    Augusta
University of New England
University of Southern Maine

Maryland
Allegany College of Maryland
Bowie State University
Capitol College
College of Notre Dame of Maryland
Coppin State University
Goucher College
Hood College
Johns Hopkins University
Loyola College in Maryland
Maryland Institute College of Art
McDaniel College
Morgan State University
Mount St. Mary's University
Prince George's Community College
Salisbury University
Towson University
University of Baltimore
University of Maryland
    Baltimore County
    College Park
Villa Julie College

Massachusetts
American International College
Assumption College
Babson College
Bay Path College
Becker College
Bentley College
Boston College
Boston University
Brandeis University
Bridgewater State College
Clark University
College of the Holy Cross
Curry College

Eastern Nazarene College
Elms College
Emmanuel College
Endicott College
Fitchburg State College
Framingham State College
Gordon College
Hampshire College
Harvard College
Holyoke Community College
Massachusetts Institute of Technology
Massachusetts Maritime Academy
Mount Holyoke College
Nichols College
Northeastern University
Pine Manor College
Quinsigamond Community College
Roxbury Community College
Salem State College
Simmons College
Smith College
Springfield College
Stonehill College
Suffolk University
Tufts University
University of Massachusetts
    Amherst
    Dartmouth
Wellesley College
Wentworth Institute of Technology
Western New England College
Westfield State College
Wheaton College
Worcester Polytechnic Institute
Worcester State College

Michigan
Alma College
Calvin College
Central Michigan University
Concordia University
Eastern Michigan University
Ferris State University
Finlandia University
Grace Bible College
Kalamazoo College
Lansing Community College
Lawrence Technological University
Michigan State University
Michigan Technological University
Northern Michigan University
Spring Arbor University
University of Michigan
University of Michigan
    Dearborn
Washtenaw Community College
Western Michigan University

Minnesota
Anoka-Ramsey Community College
Augsburg College
Bethany Lutheran College
College of St. Benedict
College of St. Catherine
Concordia College: Moorhead
Concordia University: St. Paul
Gustavus Adolphus College
Lake Superior College
Minnesota State University
    Mankato
    Moorhead
Normandale Community College
North Central University
Northwestern College
Saint Cloud State University
St. John's University
St. Mary's University of Minnesota
University of Minnesota
    Twin Cities
University of St. Thomas
Winona State University

Mississippi
Alcorn State University
Belhaven College
Hinds Community College
Jackson State University
Millsaps College
Mississippi College
Mississippi State University
Mississippi University for Women
Mississippi Valley State University
Tougaloo College
University of Mississippi
University of Southern Mississippi
William Carey University

Missouri
Avila University
Calvary Bible College and Theological Seminary
Central Bible College
Central Methodist University
College of the Ozarks
Columbia College
Drury University
Evangel University
Fontbonne University
Harris-Stowe State University
Lincoln University
Lindenwood University
Maryville University of Saint Louis
Missouri Baptist University
Missouri State University
Missouri Valley College
Missouri Western State University
Northwest Missouri State University
Park University
Research College of Nursing
Rockhurst University
Saint Louis University
Southwest Baptist University
St. Louis Community College
    Florissant Valley
    Meramec
State Fair Community College
Stephens College
Truman State University
University of Central Missouri
University of Missouri
    Columbia
    Kansas City
    Missouri University of Science and
    Technology
    St. Louis
Washington University in St. Louis
Webster University
Wentworth Military Junior College
Westminster College
William Woods University

Montana
Carroll College
Montana State University
    Bozeman
Montana Tech of the University of Montana
University of Montana: Missoula

Nebraska
Bellevue University
Chadron State College
Clarkson College
College of Saint Mary
Concordia University
Creighton University
Dana College
Doane College
Grace University
Nebraska Methodist College of Nursing and
    Allied Health
Nebraska Wesleyan University
University of Nebraska
    Lincoln
    Medical Center
    Omaha

Wayne State College
York College

Nevada
College of Southern Nevada
Sierra Nevada College
Truckee Meadows Community College
University of Nevada
    Las Vegas
    Reno

New Hampshire
Colby-Sawyer College
Daniel Webster College
Dartmouth College
Franklin Pierce University
Granite State College
New England College
Plymouth State University
Rivier College
St. Anselm College
Southern New Hampshire University
University of New Hampshire
University of New Hampshire at Manchester

New Jersey
Bloomfield College
Brookdale Community College
Caldwell College
The College of New Jersey
Fairleigh Dickinson University
    College at Florham
    Metropolitan Campus
Kean University
Montclair State University
New Jersey Institute of Technology
Princeton University
Raritan Valley Community College
Rider University
Rowan University
Rutgers, The State University of New Jersey
    Camden Regional Campus
    New Brunswick/Piscataway Campus
    Newark Regional Campus
Saint Peter's College
Seton Hall University
Stevens Institute of Technology

New Mexico
Central New Mexico Community College
Dona Ana Branch Community College of New
    Mexico State University
New Mexico Military Institute
New Mexico State University
University of New Mexico

New York
Adelphi University
Albany College of Pharmacy
Alfred University
Canisius College
Cazenovia College
City University of New York
    Baruch College
    Lehman College
    Queens College
Clarkson University
Colgate University
College of New Rochelle
College of Saint Rose
Columbia University
Columbia University
    School of General Studies
Cornell University
Daemen College
D'Youville College
Elmira College
Erie Community College
    City Campus
    North Campus
    South Campus
Finger Lakes Community College
Fordham University

Globe Institute of Technology
Hamilton College
Herkimer County Community College
Hilbert College
Hofstra University
Houghton College
Hudson Valley Community College
Iona College
Ithaca College
Jewish Theological Seminary of America
Le Moyne College
Long Island University
 Brooklyn Campus
 C. W. Post Campus
Manhattan College
Maria College
Marist College
Medaille College
Mohawk Valley Community College
Molloy College
Monroe College
Monroe Community College
Nassau Community College
Nazareth College of Rochester
New York Institute of Technology
New York University
Niagara County Community College
Niagara University
Onondaga Community College
Orange County Community College
Pace University
Polytechnic University
Rensselaer Polytechnic Institute
Roberts Wesleyan College
Rochester Institute of Technology
Russell Sage College
Sage College of Albany
Saint Bonaventure University
St. Francis College
St. John Fisher College
St. John's University
St. Joseph's College: Suffolk Campus
St. Lawrence University
Siena College
Skidmore College
State University of New York
 Albany
 Binghamton
 Buffalo
 College at Brockport
 College at Buffalo
 College at Cortland
 College at Geneseo
 College at Old Westbury
 College at Potsdam
 College of Agriculture and Technology at
  Morrisville
 College of Environmental Science and
  Forestry
 College of Technology at Alfred
 College of Technology at Canton
 Institute of Technology at Utica/Rome
 Maritime College
 Oswego
 Stony Brook
Syracuse University
Union College
University of Rochester
Utica College
Vaughn College of Aeronautics and Technology
Wagner College

North Carolina
Appalachian State University
Belmont Abbey College
Bennett College
Campbell University
Catawba College
College of the Albemarle
Davidson College
Duke University
East Carolina University

Elizabeth City State University
Elon University
Fayetteville State University
Gardner-Webb University
Greensboro College
Guilford College
Guilford Technical Community College
High Point University
Johnson C. Smith University
Lenoir-Rhyne College
Livingstone College
Meredith College
Methodist University
North Carolina Agricultural and Technical State
 University
North Carolina Central University
North Carolina State University
Peace College
Pfeiffer University
Pitt Community College
Queens University of Charlotte
St. Augustine's College
Shaw University
University of North Carolina
 Chapel Hill
 Charlotte
 Greensboro
 Pembroke
Wake Forest University
Wingate University
Winston-Salem State University

North Dakota
Mayville State University
North Dakota State University
University of North Dakota

Ohio
Baldwin-Wallace College
Bowling Green State University
Capital University
Case Western Reserve University
Cedarville University
Central State University
Cincinnati State Technical and Community
 College
Cleveland Institute of Art
Cleveland State University
College of Mount St. Joseph
Columbus State Community College
Denison University
DeVry University
 Columbus
Franciscan University of Steubenville
Heidelberg College
Hocking College
John Carroll University
Kent State University
Kent State University
 Ashtabula
 East Liverpool
 Salem
 Stark
 Trumbull
 Tuscarawas
Lourdes College
Malone College
Miami University
 Oxford Campus
Mount Union College
Notre Dame College
Ohio Dominican University
Ohio Northern University
Ohio State University
 Columbus Campus
 Lima Campus
 Mansfield Campus
 Marion Campus
 Newark Campus
Ohio University
Ohio University
 Lancaster Campus

Ohio Wesleyan University
Otterbein College
Owens Community College
 Toledo
Sinclair Community College
Tiffin University
University of Akron
University of Akron: Wayne College
University of Cincinnati
University of Cincinnati
 Clermont College
University of Dayton
University of Findlay
University of Rio Grande
University of Toledo
Ursuline College
Wilberforce University
Wittenberg University
Wright State University
Xavier University
Youngstown State University

Oklahoma
Cameron University
Langston University
Northeastern State University
Oklahoma Christian University
Oklahoma City University
Oklahoma State University
Rose State College
Southern Nazarene University
University of Central Oklahoma
University of Oklahoma

Oregon
Central Oregon Community College
Corban College
Eastern Oregon University
Linn-Benton Community College
Northwest Christian College
Oregon Institute of Technology
Oregon State University
Pacific University
Portland State University
University of Oregon
University of Portland
Warner Pacific College
Western Oregon University

Pennsylvania
Alvernia College
Arcadia University
Bloomsburg University of Pennsylvania
Bucknell University
Cabrini College
California University of Pennsylvania
Carlow University
Carnegie Mellon University
Cedar Crest College
Chatham University
Cheyney University of Pennsylvania
Clarion University of Pennsylvania
Community College of Philadelphia
DeSales University
Dickinson College
Drexel University
Duquesne University
East Stroudsburg University of Pennsylvania
Eastern University
Edinboro University of Pennsylvania
Gannon University
Geneva College
Gettysburg College
Harrisburg Area Community College
Indiana University of Pennsylvania
Keystone College
King's College
Kutztown University of Pennsylvania
La Roche College
La Salle University
Lackawanna College
Lafayette College

Lehigh Carbon Community College
Lehigh University
Lincoln University
Lock Haven University of Pennsylvania
Lycoming College
Marywood University
Mercyhurst College
Millersville University of Pennsylvania
Misericordia University
Moravian College
Muhlenberg College
Neumann College
Penn State
 Abington
 Altoona
 Berks
 Brandywine
 Erie, The Behrend College
 Harrisburg
 Hazleton
 Lehigh Valley
 Mont Alto
 University Park
 Wilkes-Barre
 Worthington Scranton
Pennsylvania College of Technology
Point Park University
Robert Morris University
Rosemont College
St. Francis University
Saint Joseph's University
Seton Hill University
Shippensburg University of Pennsylvania
Slippery Rock University of Pennsylvania
Susquehanna University
Swarthmore College
Temple University
University of Pennsylvania
University of Pittsburgh
University of Pittsburgh
 Bradford
 Greensburg
University of Scranton
University of the Sciences in Philadelphia
Valley Forge Military College
Villanova University
Washington & Jefferson College
Waynesburg University
West Chester University of Pennsylvania
Westminster College
Widener University
Wilkes University
Wilson College
York College of Pennsylvania

Puerto Rico
American University of Puerto Rico
Bayamon Central University
Caribbean University
Inter American University of Puerto Rico
 Aguadilla Campus
 Arecibo Campus
 Bayamon Campus
 Guayama Campus
 Metropolitan Campus
 San German Campus
Pontifical Catholic University of Puerto Rico
Turabo University
Universidad del Este
Universidad Metropolitana
Universidad Politecnica de Puerto Rico
University of Puerto Rico
 Aguadilla
 Arecibo
 Bayamon University College
 Carolina Regional College
 Cayey University College
 Humacao
 Mayaguez
 Ponce
 Rio Piedras
 Utuado

Rhode Island
Brown University
Bryant University
Community College of Rhode Island
Johnson & Wales University: Providence
Providence College
Rhode Island College
Roger Williams University
Salve Regina University
University of Rhode Island
Zion Bible College

South Carolina
Allen University
Anderson University
Benedict College
The Citadel
Claflin University
Clemson University
Columbia College
Converse College
Denmark Technical College
Furman University
Lander University
Limestone College
Midlands Technical College
Morris College
Newberry College
North Greenville University
Orangeburg-Calhoun Technical College
Presbyterian College
South Carolina State University
Southern Wesleyan University
Spartanburg Methodist College
Tri-County Technical College
University of South Carolina
University of South Carolina
    Lancaster
    Salkehatchie Regional Campus
    Sumter
    Upstate
Voorhees College
Winthrop University
Wofford College

South Dakota
Black Hills State University
Dakota State University
Mount Marty College
National American University
    Rapid City
South Dakota School of Mines and Technology
South Dakota State University
University of South Dakota

Tennessee
Austin Peay State University
Belmont University
Carson-Newman College
Christian Brothers University
Cumberland University
East Tennessee State University
Free Will Baptist Bible College
Jackson State Community College
LeMoyne-Owen College
Lipscomb University
Middle Tennessee State University
Milligan College
Pellissippi State Technical Community College
Rhodes College
Roane State Community College
Southwest Tennessee Community College
Tennessee Technological University
Trevecca Nazarene University
University of Memphis
University of Tennessee
    Chattanooga
    Knoxville
    Martin
Vanderbilt University
Walters State Community College

Texas
Angelina College
Austin Community College
Central Texas College
Collin County Community College District
Concordia University at Austin
Dallas Baptist University
Del Mar College
El Centro College
El Paso Community College
Houston Baptist University
Houston Community College System
Huston-Tillotson University
Laredo Community College
Lon Morris College
Lubbock Christian University
Mountain View College
Our Lady of the Lake University of San Antonio
Prairie View A&M University
Rice University
St. Edward's University
St. Mary's University
St. Philip's College
Sam Houston State University
San Antonio College
Southern Methodist University
Southwestern Assemblies of God University
Stephen F. Austin State University
Tarleton State University
Tarrant County College
Texas A&M University
Texas A&M University
    Kingsville
Texas Christian University
Texas Lutheran University
Texas Southern University
Texas State University: San Marcos
Texas Tech University
Texas Wesleyan University
Texas Woman's University
University of Dallas
University of Houston
University of Houston
    Downtown
University of North Texas
University of St. Thomas
University of Texas
    Arlington
    Austin
    Dallas
    El Paso
    Pan American
    San Antonio
University of the Incarnate Word
Wayland Baptist University

Utah
Brigham Young University
Dixie State College of Utah
LDS Business College
Salt Lake Community College
Southern Utah University
University of Utah
Utah State University
Utah Valley State College
Weber State University
Westminster College

Vermont
Castleton State College
Champlain College
Johnson State College
Middlebury College
Norwich University
St. Michael's College
University of Vermont
Vermont Technical College

Virginia
Christopher Newport University
College of William and Mary
George Mason University

Hampden-Sydney College
Hampton University
J. Sargeant Reynolds Community College
James Madison University
John Tyler Community College
Liberty University
Longwood University
Mary Baldwin College
Marymount University
Norfolk State University
Old Dominion University
Piedmont Virginia Community College
Radford University
Randolph-Macon College
Richard Bland College
St. Paul's College
Southern Virginia University
Southside Virginia Community College
Thomas Nelson Community College
University of Richmond
University of Virginia
Virginia Commonwealth University
Virginia Military Institute
Virginia Polytechnic Institute and State
    University
Virginia State University
Virginia Union University
Virginia Wesleyan College
Washington and Lee University

Washington
Central Washington University
Clark College
    Federal Way
Gonzaga University
Highline Community College
Northwest University
Pacific Lutheran University
Saint Martin's University
Seattle Pacific University
Seattle University
Spokane Community College
Spokane Falls Community College
University of Puget Sound
University of Washington
Washington State University
Whitworth University

West Virginia
Fairmont State University
Marshall University
University of Charleston
West Virginia University

Wisconsin
Alverno College
Bellin College of Nursing
Carroll College
Carthage College
Maranatha Baptist Bible College
Marian College of Fond du Lac
Marquette University
Milwaukee School of Engineering
Mount Mary College
Ripon College
St. Norbert College
University of Wisconsin
    Eau Claire
    Green Bay
    La Crosse
    Madison
    Milwaukee
    Oshkosh
    Parkside
    Platteville
    River Falls
    Stevens Point
    Whitewater
Viterbo University
Wisconsin Lutheran College

Wyoming
University of Wyoming

Naval ROTC

Alabama
Auburn University
Stillman College

Arizona
Gateway Community College
Mesa Community College
Pima Community College
Southwestern College
University of Arizona

California
California Maritime Academy
California State University
    San Marcos
Contra Costa College
Diablo Valley College
Foothill College
Fullerton College
The King's College and Seminary
Los Angeles City College
Loyola Marymount University
Mission College
National Hispanic University
National University
Point Loma Nazarene University
Riverside Community College
Sacramento City College
Samuel Merritt College
San Diego State University
San Francisco State University
Sonoma State University
Stanford University
University of California
    Berkeley
    Davis
    Los Angeles
    Santa Cruz
University of Redlands
University of San Diego
University of Southern California

Colorado
Regis University
University of Colorado
    Boulder

Connecticut
Capital Community College
Tunxis Community College

District of Columbia
Catholic University of America
George Washington University
Georgetown University
University of the District of Columbia

Florida
Clearwater Christian College
Embry-Riddle Aeronautical University
Florida Agricultural and Mechanical University
Florida Community College at Jacksonville
Florida State University
Jacksonville University
Pasco-Hernando Community College
Santa Fe Community College
Tallahassee Community College
University of North Florida
University of South Florida
University of Tampa

Georgia
Armstrong Atlantic State University
Clark Atlanta University
Clayton State University
Emory University
Georgia Institute of Technology
Georgia State University
Morehouse College
Savannah State University

Southern Polytechnic State University
Spelman College

Hawaii
University of Hawaii
    Hawaii Community College

Idaho
Lewis-Clark State College
University of Idaho

Illinois
Illinois Institute of Technology
Judson University
Lincoln Land Community College
Loyola University Chicago
Northwestern University
Parkland College
Shawnee Community College
University of Illinois
    Chicago
    Urbana-Champaign

Indiana
Bethel College
Indiana University
    South Bend
Indiana University-Purdue University
    Indianapolis
Purdue University
Saint Mary's College
University of Notre Dame

Iowa
Hawkeye Community College
Iowa State University

Kansas
University of Kansas
Washburn University

Louisiana
Dillard University
Louisiana State University and Agricultural and
    Mechanical College
Louisiana Tech University
Loyola University New Orleans
Southern University
    New Orleans
Southern University and Agricultural and
    Mechanical College
Tulane University
University of New Orleans
Xavier University of Louisiana

Maine
Husson College
Maine Maritime Academy
University of Maine
University of Maine
    Augusta

Maryland
University of Maryland
    College Park

Massachusetts
Babson College
Becker College
Boston College
Boston University
Clark University
College of the Holy Cross
Harvard College
Massachusetts Institute of Technology
Massachusetts Maritime Academy
Northeastern University
Tufts University
Worcester Polytechnic Institute
Worcester State College

Michigan
Eastern Michigan University
Finlandia University
Lawrence Technological University
University of Michigan
University of Michigan
    Dearborn

Minnesota
Anoka-Ramsey Community College
Augsburg College
Concordia University: St. Paul
Lake Superior College
Macalester College
Normandale Community College
University of Minnesota
    Twin Cities
University of St. Thomas

Mississippi
East Mississippi Community College
Tougaloo College
University of Mississippi

Missouri
Columbia College
Lincoln University
Stephens College
University of Missouri
    Columbia
    Missouri University of Science and
        Technology
William Woods University

Nebraska
University of Nebraska
    Lincoln
York College

New Hampshire
Rivier College

New Jersey
Montclair State University

New Mexico
Central New Mexico Community College
National American University: Río Rancho
University of New Mexico

New York
Albany College of Pharmacy
City University of New York
    Queens College
College of New Rochelle
College of Saint Rose
Columbia University
Cornell University
Eastman School of Music of the University of
    Rochester
Fordham University
Globe Institute of Technology
Jewish Theological Seminary of America
Maria College
Molloy College
Monroe Community College
New York University
Rensselaer Polytechnic Institute
Rochester Institute of Technology
Russell Sage College
State University of New York
    College at Brockport
    Maritime College
Union College
University of Rochester

North Carolina
Belmont Abbey College
Duke University
Guilford College
Guilford Technical Community College
Lenoir-Rhyne College
North Carolina State University

Peace College
University of North Carolina
    Chapel Hill

Ohio
Cleveland Institute of Art
Cleveland State University
Cuyahoga Community College
    Metropolitan Campus
Miami University
    Hamilton Campus
    Middletown Campus
    Oxford Campus
Ohio State University
    Columbus Campus
    Lima Campus
    Mansfield Campus
    Marion Campus
    Newark Campus
Ohio University
    Lancaster Campus

Oklahoma
University of Oklahoma

Oregon
Oregon State University
Warner Pacific College
Western Oregon University

Pennsylvania
Carlow University
Carnegie Mellon University
Chatham University
Drexel University
Duquesne University
Penn State
    University Park
Saint Joseph's University
Swarthmore College
Temple University
Thomas Jefferson University: College of Health
    Professions
University of Pennsylvania
University of Pittsburgh
Villanova University
Widener University

Puerto Rico
Inter American University of Puerto Rico
    Bayamon Campus
    Ponce Campus
Universidad Metropolitana

South Carolina
The Citadel
Midlands Technical College
University of South Carolina
University of South Carolina
    Salkehatchie Regional Campus

Tennessee
Belmont University
Christian Brothers University
University of Memphis
Vanderbilt University

Texas
Houston Baptist University
Huston-Tillotson University
Lon Morris College
Prairie View A&M University
Rice University
Texas A&M University
Texas A&M University
    Galveston
University of Houston
University of Texas
    Austin

Utah
University of Utah
Weber State University

Westminster College

Vermont
Norwich University

Virginia
Hampton University
Mary Baldwin College
New River Community College
Norfolk State University
Old Dominion University
University of Virginia
Virginia Military Institute
Virginia Polytechnic Institute and State
    University

Washington
Seattle Pacific University
Seattle University
Spokane Community College
University of Washington
Washington State University

Wisconsin
Marquette University
Milwaukee School of Engineering
Mount Mary College
University of Wisconsin
    Madison
Wisconsin Lutheran College

Glossary

Academic Competitiveness Grant. A federal financial aid award to students in their first two years of undergraduate study who are eligible for a Pell Grant and have successfully completed a rigorous high school academic program, as determined by their state or local education agency. The maximum award is $750 for the first year of undergraduate study and $1,300 for the second year, both of which are in addition to the Pell Grant award.

Accelerated program. A college program of study completed in less time than is usually required, most often by attending classes in summer or by taking extra courses during the regular academic terms.

Accreditation. A process that ensures that a college meets acceptable standards in its programs, facilities, and services. Only colleges that are accredited by an agency recognized by the U.S. Department of Education may distribute federal financial aid to their students. Every college described in this book is accredited by such an agency.

Advanced placement. Admission or assignment of a first-year college student to an advanced course in a certain subject on the basis of evidence that he or she has already completed the equivalent of the college's course in that subject.

Advanced Placement Program® (AP®). A program of the College Board that provides high schools with course descriptions of college subjects and AP® Examinations in those subjects. The AP Program offers 38 exams in 22 subject areas. High schools offer the courses and administer the examinations to interested students. Most colleges and universities in the United States accept qualifying AP Exam grades for credit, advanced placement, or both.

AmeriCorps. A national network of community service programs for which people volunteer and from which they earn an education award that can used to pay for college or pay back student loans.

Articulation agreement. A formal agreement between two higher-education institutions, stating specific policies relating to transfer of credits and recognition of academic achievement in order to facilitate the successful transfer of students without duplication of course work.

Associate degree. A degree granted by a college or university upon completion of a two-year, full-time program of study or its part-time equivalent. In general, the associate of arts (A.A.) or associate of science (A.S.) program is similar to the first two years of a four-year college curriculum. The associate in applied science (A.A.S.) is awarded by many colleges on completion of technological or vocational programs of study.

Award letter. A means of notifying admitted students of the financial aid being offered by the college or university. The award letter provides information on the types and amounts of aid offered, as well as the students' responsibilities, and the conditions governing the awards. Usually the award letter gives students the opportunity to accept or decline the aid offered, and a deadline by which to respond.

Bachelor's degree. A degree received upon completion of a four- or five-year full-time program of study (or its part-time equivalent) at a college or university. The bachelor of arts (B.A.), bachelor of science (B.S.), and bachelor of fine arts (B.F.A.) are the most common such degrees. College catalogs describe the types of degrees awarded in each major.

Bursar. The college official responsible for handling billing and payments for tuition, fees, housing, etc.

Business college. A college that primarily prepares students to work in an office or entrepreneurial setting. The curriculum may focus on management, clerical positions, or both.

Campus-based programs. Federal financial aid programs that are administered directly by the college's financial aid office, which awards these funds to students using federal guidelines. Includes the Federal Supplemental Educational Opportunity Grant Program, Federal Perkins Loan Program, and the Federal Work-Study Program.

Candidates' reply date. The date by which admitted students must accept or decline an offer of admission and (if any) the college's offer of financial aid. Most colleges and universities follow the College Board-sponsored Candidates' Reply Date Agreement (CRDA), under which they agree to not require a decision from applicants for admission in the fall semester before May 1. The purpose of this agreement is to give applicants time to hear from all the colleges to which they have applied before having to make a commitment to any of them.

Certificate. An award for completing a particular program or course of study, sometimes given by two-year colleges or vocational or technical schools.

CLEP®. See *College-Level Examination Program®*.

College-Level Examination Program (CLEP). A series of examinations in undergraduate courses that provides students of any age the opportunity to demonstrate college-level achievement, thereby reducing costs and time to degree completion. The examinations, which are sponsored by the College Board, are administered at colleges year round. All CLEP® exams are delivered on computer, providing test-takers instant score results.

College Scholarship Service® (CSS®). See *CSS/Financial Aid PROFILE®*.

Community/junior college. A college offering two-year programs leading to an associate degree. Community colleges are public institutions, while junior colleges are privately operated on a not-for-profit basis. Most two-year colleges offer both vocational programs (also called "career" or "terminal" programs), as well as the first two years of a four-year program ("academic" or "transfer" programs). Students in the vocational program usually go directly into a career after graduation, while students in the academic program usually intend to transfer to a four-year institution or an upper-division college.

Comprehensive fee. If the college combines tuition, fees, room, and board expenses, that single figure is called a comprehensive fee.

Consortium. A group of colleges and universities that share a common geographic location. Consortiums of colleges in the same town often allow students at one institution to take classes at neighboring consortium colleges and use facilities such as libraries at the member colleges. Larger consortiums, at the state or regional level, may offer in-state tuition to out-of-state students.

Cooperative education (co-op). A program in which students alternate class attendance and employment in business, industry, or government. Co-op students are typically paid for their work and may receive academic credit for their participation in the program. Under a cooperative plan, five years are normally required for completion of a bachelor's degree, but graduates have the advantage of about a year's practical work experience in addition to their studies.

Core curriculum. A group of courses, usually in the liberal arts, designated by a college as one of the requirements for a degree. Some colleges have both core-curriculum requirements and general-education requirements.

Cost of attendance. A number of expenses, among them tuition and fees (including loan fees), books and supplies, and the student's living expenses while attending school. The cost of attendance is estimated by the school, within guidelines established by federal regulation. The cost of attendance is compared with the student's expected family contribution to determine the student's need for financial aid.

Coverdell Education Savings Account (ESA). A federal income-tax provision (formerly referred to as the Education IRA) that enables taxpayers to establish a college savings plan. A maximum of $2,000 may be contributed annually to the account, which earns interest and/or dividends on a tax-free basis.

Credit by examination. Academic credit granted by a college to entering students who have demonstrated proficiency in college-level studies through examinations such as those sponsored by the College Board's Advanced Placement Program and College-Level Examination Program. It is a means of cutting college costs by reducing the number of courses needed to earn a degree.

Credit Hour. The standard unit of measurement for a college course. Each credit hour requires one classroom hour per week. Most college courses are offered in one to five credit-hour increments. For financial aid purposes, students taking at least 12 credit hours of classes in a semester are considered to be attending the college full-time, and students taking at least six credit hours are considered half-time.

CSS code. A four-digit College Board number that students use to designate colleges or scholarship programs to receive their CSS/Financial Aid PROFILE information. If a college requires financial aid applicants to submit the PROFILE, its CSS code will appear in its description in Part III of this book. A complete list of all CSS codes can also be downloaded from the CSS/Financial Aid PROFILE Web site.

CSS/Financial Aid PROFILE®. A Web-based application service offered by the College Board and used by some colleges, universities, and private scholarship programs to award their private financial aid funds. Students complete the online application and supplements, if required. CSS processes and reports the application data to institutions. CSS/Financial Aid PROFILE is not a federal form and may not be used to apply for federal student aid.

Deferred admission. Postponing enrollment, usually for one year, after being accepted for admission by a college.

Dependent student. For financial aid purposes, such students are either under the age of 24, attend an undergraduate program, are not married, do not have children of their own, are not orphans or wards of the court, or veterans of the active-duty armed services. The term is used to define eligibility for certain financial aid programs, regardless of whether or not the student lives with a parent, receives financial support from a parent, or is claimed on a parent's tax return. If a student is defined as dependent, parental financial information must be supplied on the Free Application for Federal Student Aid, (FAFSA), and institutional aid applications.

Direct Loan Program. See *Federal Direct Loan Program*.

District. See *In-district tuition*.

Dual enrollment. The practice in which a student enrolls in college courses while still in high school, earning both high school and college credit for his or her work.

Early Action. A nonbinding early-decision program in which a student can receive an admission decision from one or more colleges and universities earlier than the standard response date but is not required to accept the admission offer or to make a deposit before May 1. Compare to *Early Decision*, which is a binding program.

Early action single choice. An early-action program in which the student may only apply early action to one college or university.

Early Decision. A binding program where students can receive an admission decision from one college or university before applications are due for regular admission. Participating students commit to enroll at the college if admitted and offered a satisfactory financial aid package.

Elective. A course, not required for one's chosen major or the college's core curriculum, that is selected to fulfill credit hours required for graduation.

Employer tuition assistance. Money that employers offer to employees or their dependents for use in paying education costs. Tuition assistance is considered an outside resource when colleges award financial aid.

Expected family contribution (EFC). The total amount students and their families are expected to pay toward college costs from their income and assets for one academic year. The amount is derived from a need analysis of the family's overall financial circumstances. The *federal methodology* is used to determine a student's eligibility for federal and state student aid. Colleges and private aid programs may use a different methodology to determine eligibility for nonfederal financial aid. Frequently, these private institutions use the *institutional methodology*.

FAFSA. See *Free Application for Federal Student Aid*.

FAFSA on the Web. An electronic option for completing the Free Application for Federal Student Aid (www.fafsa.ed.gov).

Family Educational Rights and Privacy Act (FERPA). A federal law that protects the privacy of student education records. The law applies to all schools that receive funds under an applicable program of the U.S. Department of Education. FERPA gives parents certain rights with respect to their children's education records. These rights transfer to the student when he or she reaches the age of 18 or attends a school beyond the high school level.

Federal code number. A six-digit number that identifies a specific college to which students want their FAFSA information submitted. Each college's federal code appears in its profile in Part III of this book. Formerly known as the Title IV code.

Federal Direct Loan Program. A program that allows participating schools to administer subsidized and unsubsidized Stafford and PLUS loans directly to student and parent borrowers. Direct loans have mostly the same terms and conditions as FFELP loans. Funds for these programs are provided by the federal government.

Federal Family Education Loan Program (FFELP). The subsidized and unsubsidized Federal Stafford Loan, PLUS Loan, and Loan Consolidation programs. Funds for these programs are provided by lenders, and the loans are guaranteed by the federal government.

Federal methodology (FM). A need-analysis formula used by colleges and universities to determine students' financial need for the purpose of awarding federal financial aid. Most colleges also use this methodology to determine need for the purpose of awarding their own institutional funds, but some colleges use the *institutional methodology* for that. The federal methodology uses information submitted by students on the FAFSA to assess their ability to pay for college and calculate their expected family contribution.

Federal Parents' Loan for Undergraduate Students (PLUS). A program that permits parents of undergraduate students to borrow up to the full cost of education, less any other financial aid the student may have received.

Federal Pell Grant Program. A federally sponsored and administered program that provides need-based grants to undergraduate students. Congress annually sets the dollar range. As of July 1, 2008, a Pell Grant cannot exceed $4,731 per year. Eligibility for Pell Grants is based on a student's expected family contribution, the total cost of attendance at the college, and whether the student is attending the college full-time or part-time.

Federal Perkins Loan Program. A federally funded campus-based program that provides low-interest student loans. The maximum amount of loan funds available to an individual for undergraduate and graduate education is $40,000. Repayment need not begin until completion of the student's education, and it may be deferred for limited periods of service in the military, Peace Corps, or approved comparable organizations. The total debt may be forgiven by the federal government if the recipient enters a career of service as a public health nurse, law enforcement officer, public school teacher, or social worker.

Federal Stafford Loan. A program that allows students to borrow money for educational expenses from banks and other lending institutions (and sometimes from the colleges themselves). Subsidized Stafford loans are offered by colleges based on need. The federal government pays the interest on subsidized loans while the borrower is in college, and repayment does not begin until completion of the student's education. Unsubsidized Stafford loans are non-need-based; anyone may apply for one regardless of their ability to pay for college. The interest on unsubsidized loans begins accumulating immediately. For both programs, the amounts that may be borrowed depend on the student's year in school.

Federal student aid. A number of programs sponsored by the federal government that award students loans, grants, or work-study jobs for the purpose of meeting their financial need. To receive any federal student aid, a student must demonstrate financial need by filing the Free Application for Federal Student Aid and meet certain other eligibility requirements.

Federal Supplemental Educational Opportunity Grant Program (SEOG). A federal campus-based program that provides need-based grants of up to $4,000 a year for undergraduate study. Each college is given a certain total amount of SEOG money each year to distribute among their financial aid applicants and determines the amount to which the student is entitled.

Federal Work-Study Program. A campus-based financial aid program that allows students to meet some of their financial need by working on- or off-campus while attending school. The wages earned are used to help pay the student's educational costs for the academic year. Job opportunities vary from campus to campus. The time commitment for a work-study job is usually between 10 and 15 hours each week.

Fee waiver. The waiver that significantly reduces the amount a student must pay for an application for admission, application for institutional financial aid, standardized tests, or other college-related expenses. Fee waivers are most commonly awarded to low-income students, but are sometimes also awarded to students who are senior citizens or in the military. See also *Tuition and fee waiver.*

Financial aid. Money awarded to students to help them pay for college. Financial aid comes in the form of gifts (scholarships and grants) and self-help aid (loans and work-study opportunities). Most aid is awarded on the basis of financial need, but some awards are non-need-based. Both need-based and non-need-based aid may or may not be offered on the additional basis of merit.

Financial aid application form. A form that collects information on the student, his or her income and assets, and (for dependent students) his or her parents' income and assets.

Financial aid award letter. See *Award letter.*

Financial aid package. The total financial aid offered to a student by a college, including all loans, grants, scholarships, and work-study opportunities.

Financial aid PROFILE. See *CSS/Financial Aid PROFILE.*

Financial need. The difference between the total cost of attending a college and a student's expected family contribution (EFC). Financial aid grants, loans, and work-study will be offered by each college to fill all or a portion of the student's need.

529 Plan. See *Section 529 Plan.*

Fixed interest rate. An interest rate on a loan that is fixed for the lifetime of the loan. Compare to *Variable interest rate.*

For-profit college/university. A higher-education institution not supported by taxes and operated as a for-profit business, either as a publicly traded corporation or as a privately held company. Sometimes referred to as a "proprietary" college.

Free Application for Federal Student Aid (FAFSA). A form completed by all applicants for federal student aid. The FAFSA is also available on the Web, at www.fafsa.ed.gov. In many states, completion of the FAFSA is also sufficient to establish eligibility for state-sponsored aid programs. There is no charge for completing the FAFSA, and you can file it anytime after January 1 of the year for which you are seeking aid (e.g., after January 1, 2008, for the academic year 2008–2009).

Full need. A student's entire financial need at a college. A college that offers a financial aid package covering the complete difference between the cost of attendance and the expected family contribution is "meeting full need." See also *Gapping.*

Full-time status. Enrollment at a college or university for 12 or more credit hours per semester. Students must be enrolled full-time to qualify for the maximum award available to them from federal grant programs.

Gapping. A practice by which a college does not meet the full financial need of an admitted student, leaving a gap that must be filled by the student's own financial resources, in addition to the student's expected family contribution.

General education requirements. Courses that give undergraduates a background in all major academic disciplines: natural sciences, social sciences, mathematics, literature, language, and fine arts. Most colleges have general education requirements that students complete in their first and second years, giving students a chance to sample a wide range of courses before selecting a major. At some colleges, general education courses are referred to as the core curriculum; at others, a few courses within the general education requirements are core courses that all students must take.

Gift aid. Financial aid in the form of scholarships or grants that do not have to be repaid.

Grant. A financial aid award given to a student that does not have to be paid back. The terms "grant" and "scholarship" are often used interchangeably to refer to gift aid, but grants tend to be awarded solely on the basis of financial need, while scholarships may require the student to demonstrate merit.

Half-time status. Enrollment at a college or university for at least 6 credit hours per semester, but fewer than the 12 credit hours required to qualify as full-time. Students must be enrolled at least half-time to qualify for federal student aid loan programs.

Health sciences college. An institution of higher education that primarily prepares students to enter work in a clinic, hospital, or private medical practice. For a complete description of health-related fields of study, see the *College Board Book of Majors*.

HOPE Education Tax Credit. A federal income tax credit of as much as $1,650 per dependent student annually. It is available to eligible taxpayers based on out-of-pocket tuition and fee expenditures for the first two years of undergraduate study, according to income eligibility guidelines. See also *Lifetime Learning Tax Credit*.

Independent student. For financial aid purposes, a student who is either 24 years old or older, married, a veteran, an orphan, or has legal dependents. Independent students do not need to provide parental information to be considered for federal financial aid programs. However, private institutions may require independent students to provide parental information on their institutional forms in order to be considered for nonfederal sources of funding.

In-district tuition. The tuition charged by a community college or state university to residents of the district from which it draws tax support. Districts are usually individual counties or cities, but sometimes are larger.

Individual Retirement Account (IRA). A retirement account that earns income tax-free. Money withdrawn for college expenses is not charged the penalty that normally would be incurred for withdrawing IRA money before age 59½, but is taxed as regular income.

In-state tuition. The tuition that a public institution charges residents of its state. Some community colleges and state universities charge this rate to students who are not residents of their district, but who are residents of their state.

Institutional form. A financial aid application form custom-made by a particular college or university. Some institutional forms are designed to collect additional information on a family's finances beyond what is collected on the FAFSA, and are required of all financial aid applicants. Others serve specific purposes and are only required from certain students, for example early-decision applicants or student athletes.

Institutional methodology (IM). A need-analysis formula used by some colleges and universities to determine students' financial need and award their own institutional funds. Compared to the *federal methodology*, the IM takes into account a broader and deeper picture of family assets to determine a student's expected family contribution. Most colleges that use the IM collect this additional information through the CSS/Financial Aid PROFILE form, but some collect it using their own customized institutional forms.

International Baccalaureate (IB). A comprehensive and rigorous two-year curriculum (usually taken in the final two years of high school) that is similar to the final year of secondary school in Europe. Some colleges award credit or advanced placement to students who have completed an IB program.

Internship. Any short-term, supervised work, usually related to a student's major, for which academic credit is earned. The work can be full- or part-time, on or off campus, paid or unpaid. Some majors require the student to complete an internship.

Junior college. See *Community/junior college*.

Lender. An organization authorized to make educational loans to students.

Liberal arts. The study of the humanities (literature, the arts, and philosophy), history, foreign languages, social sciences, mathematics, and natural sciences. Liberal arts study guides students in developing general knowledge and reasoning ability rather than specific skills.

Liberal arts college. A college that emphasizes the liberal arts in its core curriculum and academic offerings and does not offer vocation or professional programs.

Lifetime Learning Tax Credit. A federal income tax credit of as much as $2,000 per household annually; available to eligible taxpayers based on "out-of-pocket" tuition and fee expenditures, according to income eligibility guidelines. Unlike the HOPE Education Tax Credit, it can be used for any year of postsecondary study.

Major. The subject area in which students concentrate during their undergraduate study. At most colleges, students take a third to half of their courses in the major; the rest of their course work is devoted to core requirements and electives.

Maritime college/institute/academy. An institution of higher education that prepares students to operate commercial shipping or fishing vessels. Upon graduation, students of most maritime academies are commissioned as officers in the United States Merchant Marine, and simultaneously commissioned as officers in the U.S. Navy Reserve.

Master Promissory Note (MPN). A special type of promissory note used to obtain a Federal Stafford loan. The MPN is designated for use as both a single-year and a multi-year note (for four-year and graduate/professional schools). Borrowers can sign a MPN once, the time they first borrow, and then receive additional loans during the same year or in subsequent years without signing an additional note.

Merit aid. Financial aid awarded on the basis of academic qualifications, artistic or athletic talent, leadership qualities, or similar qualities. Most merit aid comes in the form of scholarships. Merit aid may be non-need-based, or the merit criteria may be in addition to a requirement that the student demonstrate financial need.

National Science and Mathematics Access to Retain Talent (SMART) Grant. A federal grant program for Pell Grant recipients who are in their third or fourth year of undergraduate study, have declared a major in the sciences, mathematics, engineering, technology, or certain foreign languages, and have maintained a GPA of at least 3.0 in that major. The maximum annual award is $4,000, in addition to the student's Pell Grant.

Need analysis. The process of analyzing the student's household and financial information to calculate an EFC and financial need. See also *Federal Methodology, Institutional Methodology.*

Need-analysis form. See *Financial aid application form.*

Need-based aid. Financial aid (scholarships, grants, loans, or work-study opportunities) given to students who have demonstrated financial need, calculated by subtracting the student's expected family contribution from a college's total cost of attendance. The largest source of need-based aid is the federal government, but colleges, states, and private foundations also award need-based aid to eligible students.

Need-blind admissions. The policy of determining whether a student should be admitted to a college without regard to his or her financial need.

Non-need-based aid. Financial aid awarded without regard to the student's demonstrated ability to pay for college. Unsubsidized loans and scholarships awarded solely on the basis of merit are both non-need-based. Some financial aid sponsors also offer non-need-based grants tied not to merit, but to other qualities, such as state of residence or participation in ROTC.

Nursing college. An institution of higher education that primarily prepares students to become registered nurses (RNs) or licensed practical nurses (LPNs).

Open admission. The college admissions policy of admitting high school graduates and other adults generally without regard to conventional academic qualifications, such as high school subjects, high school grades, and admissions test scores. Virtually all applicants with high school diplomas or their equivalent are accepted, although some programs of study may have additional requirements.

Origination fee. A fee charged to a borrower to cover the costs of processing a loan. The origination fee is usually a percentage of the total amount being borrowed. The origination fee for any loan will be disclosed in the promissory note for that loan.

Out-of-state tuition. The tuition a public college or university charges residents of other states.

Outside resources. Student financial aid granted by a source other than the college that the college must take into account when assembling an aid package. Examples of common outside resources include scholarships from private foundations, employer tuition assistance, and veterans' educational benefits.

Parents' contribution. The amount a student's parents are expected to pay toward college costs from their income and assets. It is derived from need analysis of the parents' overall financial situation. The parents' contribution and the student's contribution together constitute the total expected family contribution (EFC).

Parents' Loan for Undergraduate Students. See *Federal Parents' Loan for Undergraduate Students*.

Part-time status. Enrollment at a college or university for 11 or fewer credit hours per semester.

Pell Grant. See *Federal Pell Grant Program*.

Perkins Loan. See *Federal Perkins Loan Program*.

PLUS loan. See *Federal Parents' Loan for Undergraduate Students*.

Prepaid tuition plan. See *Section 529 Plans*.

Priority date. The date by which applications for financial aid must be received to be given the strongest possible consideration. The college will consider the financial need of applicants who make the priority date before any other applicants. Qualified applicants who do not make the priority date are considered on a first-come, first-served basis, and are only offered financial aid if (and to the extent to which) the college still has sufficient money left over after all the offers it has made. Can also refer to the priority date for admissions applications, where, again, the college will make offers to the priority applicants first, and then consider subsequent applicants on a first-come, first-served basis, making offers only if there is still room in the incoming class.

Private college/university. An educational institution of higher education not supported by public taxes and operated on a not-for-profit basis. May be independent or affiliated with a religious denomination.

PROFILE. See *CSS/Financial Aid PROFILE*.

Promissory note. A binding legal document that a borrower signs to get a loan. By signing this note, a borrower promises to repay the loan, with interest, in specified installments. The promissory note also includes any information about origination fees, grace periods, deferment or cancellation provisions, and the borrower's rights and responsibilities with respect to that loan.

Proprietary college/university. See *For-profit college/university*.

PSAT/NMSQT® (Preliminary SAT/National Merit Scholarship Qualifying Test). A preparatory tool for the SAT that is administered by high schools to sophomores and juniors each year in October. The PSAT/NMSQT® serves as the qualifying test for scholarships awarded by the National Merit Scholarship Corporation.

Public college/university. An institution of higher education supported by public taxes.

Quarter. An academic calendar period of about 12 weeks. Four quarters make up an academic year, but at colleges using the quarter system, students make normal academic progress by attending three quarters each year. In some colleges, students can accelerate their progress by attending all four quarters in one or more years.

Regular admission. At colleges with early-action or early-decision plans, "regular" admission is the round of admissions conducted in January or February, after the early-admission rounds.

Renewal FAFSA. A simplified reapplication form for federal student aid. The Renewal FAFSA allows continuing students to update the prior year's FAFSA, rather than completing the entire FAFSA for each award year.

Reserve Officers Training Corps (ROTC). Programs conducted by certain colleges in cooperation with the United States Air Force, Army, and Navy reserves. Participating students may receive a merit scholarship while they are in college, and will enter the reserves of their service branch as an officer upon graduation. Naval ROTC includes the Marine Corps. (The Coast Guard and Merchant Marine do not sponsor ROTC programs.) Local recruiting offices of the services themselves can supply detailed information about these programs, as can participating colleges.

Residency requirements. The minimum number of terms that a student must spend taking courses on campus (as opposed to independent study, transfer credits from other colleges, or credit-by-examination) to be eligible for graduation. Can also refer to the minimum amount of time a student is required to have lived in-state in order to qualify for the in-state tuition rate at a public college or university.

Rolling admission. An admission procedure by which the college considers each student's application as soon as all the required credentials, such as school record and test scores, have been received. The college usually notifies an applicant of its decision without delay. At many colleges, rolling admission allows for early notification and works much like nonbinding early-action programs.

SAR. See *Student Aid Report.*

Satisfactory academic progress. Standards set by a college or university to determine whether a student is meeting sufficient academic standards. The student must achieve these standards to continue to receive financial aid.

SAT®. The College Board's test of critical reading, writing, and mathematical reasoning abilities, given on specified dates throughout the year at test centers in the United States and other countries. The SAT® is required by many colleges and sponsors of financial aid programs, and many colleges use scores on the SAT as criteria for the awarding of merit scholarships.

SAT Subject Tests™. College Board tests in specific subjects, given at test centers in the United States and other countries on specified dates throughout the year. Used by colleges not only to help with decisions about admission, but also in course placement.

Scholarship. A type of financial aid that doesn't have to be repaid. Grants are often based on financial need. Scholarships may be based on need, on need combined with merit, or solely on the basis of merit or some other qualification, such as minority status.

School. In this book, used generically to refer interchangeably to colleges, universities, and other institutions of higher education. At some universities, a "school" is a subdivision of the university—for example, the administrative unit that offers nursing courses may be called the "college of nursing" at one institution, and the "school of nursing" at another.

Section 529 Plans. State-sponsored college savings programs commonly referred to as "529 Plans" after the

section of the Internal Revenue Code that provides the plan's tax breaks. There are two kinds: Section 529 college savings plans and Section 529 prepaid tuition plans.

Section 529 Prepaid Tuition Plan. State-sponsored plans through which parents can pay in advance for tuition at public institutions in their state of residence.

Self-help aid. Student financial aid, such as loans and work-study jobs, that requires repayment or employment.

Semester. A period of about 16 weeks. Colleges on a semester system offer two semesters of instruction a year; there may also be an additional summer session.

SEOG. See *Federal Supplemental Educational Opportunity Grant.*

Simplified needs test. In Federal Methodology need analysis, the simplified needs test excludes assets from the Expected Family Contribution calculation for low- to moderate-income families who file simplified tax returns (1040A, 1040EZ).

SMART Grant. See *National Science and Mathematics Access to Retain Talent Grant.*

Stafford Loan. See *Federal Stafford Loan Program.*

Student Aid Report (SAR). A report produced by the U.S. Department of Education and sent to students in response to their having filed the Free Application for Federal Student Aid (FAFSA). The SAR contains information the student provided on the FAFSA as well as the federally calculated expected family contribution.

Student expense budget. A calculation of the annual cost of attending college that is used to determine your financial need. Student expense budgets usually include tuition and fees, books and supplies, room and board, personal expenses, and transportation. Sometimes additional expenses are included for students with special education needs, students who have a disability, or students who are married or have children.

Student's contribution. The amount you are expected to pay toward college costs from your income and assets. The amount is derived from a need analysis of your resources. Your contribution and your parents' contribution together compose the total expected family contribution.

Subsidized loan. A loan awarded to a student on the basis of financial need. The federal government or the state awarding the loan pays the borrower's interest while they are in college at least half-time, thereby subsidizing the loan.

Supplemental Educational Opportunity Grant. See *Federal Supplemental Educational Opportunity Grant*.

Taxable income. Income earned from wages, salaries, tips, as well as interest income, dividends, alimony, estates or trust income, business or farm profits, and rental or property income. Some scholarship awards must be reported as taxable income.

Teacher's college. A college that specializes in preparing students to teach in elementary or secondary schools. Most teacher's colleges offer a curriculum that combines a study of the liberal arts with the study of pedagogy.

Terminal program. An education program designed to prepare students for immediate employment. These programs usually can be completed in fewer than four years beyond high school and are available in most community colleges and trade schools.

Title IV code. See *Federal code number*.

Transfer program. An academic program in a community or junior college primarily for students who plan to continue their studies in a four-year college or university.

Transfer student. A student who has attended another college for any period, which may be defined by various colleges as any time from a single term up to three years. A transfer student may receive credit for all or some of the courses successfully completed before the transfer.

Trimester. An academic calendar period of about 15 weeks. Three trimesters make up one year. Students normally progress by attending two of the trimesters each year and in some colleges can accelerate their progress by attending all three trimesters in one or more years.

Tuition and fee waiver. Some colleges reduce the tuition and/or fees for some categories of students, such as adults, senior citizens, or children of alumni.

Two-year college. A college that offers only two years of undergraduate study. See *Community/junior college*; see also *Upper-division college*.

Undergraduate. A student in the freshman, sophomore, junior, or senior year of study, as opposed to a graduate student who has earned an undergraduate degree and is pursuing a master's, doctoral, or professional degree.

Unmet need. The difference between a specific student's total available resources and the total cost for the student's attendance at a specific institution.

Unsubsidized loan. An education loan that is non-need-based and therefore not subsidized by the federal government; the borrower is responsible for accrued interest throughout the life of the loan.

Upper-division college. A college that offers only the junior and senior years of study. Students must complete their freshman and sophomore years at other institutions before entering the upper-division institution to earn their bachelor's degree.

Variable interest rate. An interest rate that changes on an annual basis to better reflect market rates.

Virtual college/university. A degree-granting, accredited institution wherein all courses are delivered by distance learning, with no physical campus.

William D. Ford Federal Direct Loan Program. See *Federal Direct Loan Program*.

Work-study. An arrangement by which a student combines employment and college study. The employment may be an integral part of the academic program (as in cooperative education and internships) or simply a means of paying for college (as in the need-based *Federal Work-Study Program*).

Alphabetical Index of Colleges

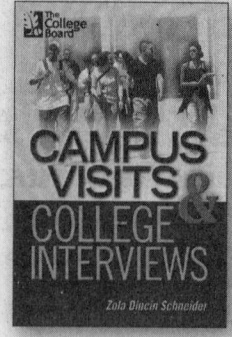